Archbold

International

Criminal

Courts

AUSTRALIA
Law Book Co.
Sydney

CANADA and USA
Carswell
Toronto

HONG KONG
Sweet & Maxwell Asia

NEW ZEALAND
Brookers
Wellington

SINGAPORE and MALAYSIA
Sweet & Maxwell
Singapore and Kuala Lumpur

**A CIP Catalogue record for this book is available
from the British Library**

ISBN 0 421 906200

9 780421 906204

Archbold

International Criminal Courts
Practice,
Procedure and Evidence

LONDON
SWEET & MAXWELL

Published by
Sweet & Maxwell Limited,
100 Avenue Road, London NW3 3PF
www.thomson.com
Typeset by LBJ Typesetting Ltd of Kingsclere
Printed and bound in Great Britain by
CPI Bath

EDITORS

KARIM A.A. KHAN
of Lincoln's Inn, Barrister

RODNEY DIXON
of Inner Temple, Barrister

JUDGE SIR ADRIAN FULFORD Q.C.
Judge of the International Criminal Court

FOREWORD

The primary responsibility for punishing crimes of international concern such as genocide, crimes against humanity and war crimes belongs to national criminal jurisdictions. This may seem an odd proposition with which to begin a foreword to a book on international criminal courts. However, it is important to understand that international criminal courts such as the ad hoc tribunals for the Former Yugoslavia (ICTY) and Rwanda (ICTR) and the International Criminal Court (ICC) are only needed where national courts either cannot or will not act. In the case of the ICC, this underlying rationale is embodied in the fundamental principle of complementarity; the ICC will act only where States are unwilling or unable genuinely to investigate or prosecute genocide, crimes against humanity and war crimes.

Viewed in this light, international criminal courts can be seen to have two roles. First, an international court may act as a court of last resort, ensuring that perpetrators of the most serious international crimes are not granted impunity if national courts cannot or will not act. Second, the development of international criminal courts has encouraged States to exercise their responsibility to prosecute and punish international crimes by strengthening their relevant domestic mechanisms. For example, many States have recently reviewed, adopted or amended their legislation governing the domestic prosecution and punishment of genocide, crimes against humanity and war crimes. This includes laws creating specialized domestic courts such as those in Kosovo and Bosnia and Herzegovina which are included in this edition of *Archbold: International Criminal Courts*, as well as legislation pertaining to regular domestic civilian and military courts. These national courts will be the primary actors in putting an end to impunity for serious international crimes.

International criminal courts will only be able to try a limited number of cases at any time. One cannot and should not expect these courts immediately to put an end to serious international crimes or to substitute for the efforts of national courts. International criminal justice in the broad sense is a collective responsibility. National and international institutions must work together in accordance with their respective mandates as part of an interdependent system of criminal justice. Recent years have seen an expansion of the number and kind of institutions which play a part in this system.For example, hybrid domestic-international tribunals have recently been set up to try alleged perpetrators of international crimes in places including Sierra Leone and East Timor.

These different courts rely on, learn from and cooperate with each other in many different ways. The ICC itself was established to overcome the limitations of relying on *ad hoc* tribunals such as the ICTY and ICTR, by creating a standing court which is immediately available with broad geographical jurisdiction. The experiences—both positive and negative—of the *ad hoc* tribunals also served to guide the drafters of the Rome Statute in designing many of the features of the ICC. In its early stages, the ICC took into account the practice of the *ad hoc* tribunals in preparing the Regulations of the Court and other documents. The jurisprudence of the *ad hoc* tribunals and national courts has already been referred to in pleadings before the ICC. Meanwhile, national and international courts have begun to refer to the Rome Statute in their jurisprudence.

International criminal justice also involves much broader cooperation between courts and States, international organizations and civil society. For example, the Rome Statute obligates States Parties and other States accepting the jurisdiction of the ICC to fully cooperate in the investigation and prosecution of crimes before the Court. Cooperation of States will be particularly important to obtaining the necessary arrest and surrender of persons to the ICC. The ICC will also need cooperation from all relevant parties in obtaining evidence, in providing logistical support in relation to investigations and the protection of victims and witnesses and in enforcing sentences of convicted persons. The ICC in turn may cooperate with and provide assistance to States in relation to national investigations or trials. Obtaining State cooperation has also been an issue faced by the ICTY and ICTR, and will be an issue for any international tribunal.

The second edition of *Archbold: International Criminal Courts* comes at an opportune time. The ICC has just begun its judicial activities. Within two years of the judges and the Prosecutor taking office, three States Parties had referred situations on their territory to the Prosecutor, and the Security Council had referred a situation occurring on the territory of a non-State Party. Investigations are ongoing in three of these situations—the Democratic Republic of Congo; Uganda and Darfur, Sudan—and the first arrest warrants have been issued in the situation in Uganda. This edition incorporates the pertinent developments since the entry into force of the Rome Statute, including most notably the Regulations of the Court adopted by the judges on May 26, 2004 and subsequently accepted by the States Parties. As such, this edition will serve as a useful resource for practitioners in the first cases before the ICC.

This edition will undoubtedly also be of great assistance to practitioners before other courts, including both national and international courts, as well as others interested in the law and practice of these courts. Chapters on the establishment, structure and powers of international criminal courts provide the context in which these courts operate. In addition to addressing the specific procedural issues confronted by the ICC, ad hoc tribunals and Special Courts, the book details the substantive international criminal law; as well as issues such as defences, sentencing, compensation and reparations; which may also apply before national courts. Moreover, by bringing the different international courts and other related developments together in one text, *Archbold: International Criminal Courts* reflects and may contribute to the interdependent nature of the relationship that exists among different national and international courts in the areas of genocide, crimes against humanity and war crimes.

I therefore recommend this book both to those interested in the law and practice of specific international criminal courts and to those interested more generally in the emerging system of international criminal justice.

Philippe Kirsch
November 2005

PREFACE

The second edition of *Archbold: International Criminal Courts: Practice, Procedure, and Evidence* is long overdue. The law, practice and procedure have evolved considerably since the inaugural edition in 2002. The jurisprudence of international criminal courts continues to break new ground in the quest for an all-embracing and coherent system of international criminal justice.

In 2004 the international community lost one of its most eminent Judges, Sir Richard May, who was the Consulting Editor on the first edition of *Archbold International*. His passing away has left an immense void. For so long, Sir Richard had been the face of the ICTY, as he tirelessly and with steadfast authority and intuition presided over important and historic international trials. He provided us with invaluable advice and inspiration for *Archbold International*, which we will always miss and always remember.

We dedicate this new edition to Sir Richard May and his enduring contribution to international criminal justice.

We are deeply honoured that Sir Adrian Fulford, Judge of the ICC, has agreed to be the Consulting Editor of the book. Sir Adrian is currently centrally involved in the foundational work of the ICC as the ground for the first cases is primed. We are most grateful for his insightful comments on the ICC Regulations, which have been included, and for all the assistance he has provided with this edition. Sir Adrian has added to and embellished Chapter 1, the Introduction, which was written by Sir Richard May for the first edition. We look forward to working together in the invigorating years ahead for *Archbold International*.

In the tradition of *Archbold*, we have not altered the structure of the original book. The new work incorporates the latest developments and up to date jurisprudence before the ad hoc International Tribunals for the former Yugoslavia (ICTY) and Rwanda (ICTR), the Special Court for Sierra Leone, and the Special Panels for Serious Crimes in East Timor (the mandate of which ended on May 20, 2005). In particular, the chapters on trial procedure and evidence have been substantially supplemented, as the courts have continued to fuse common law, civil law and other traditions to fashion a fair and workable system.

The ICC awaits its first cases with investigations underway in various countries. The next edition will surely include the first jurisprudence from the ICC. As with the first edition, however, we have included all the relevant documents from the ICC, and in addition, references to the ICC Regulations recently adopted by the Judges.

Judge Philippe Kirsch, the President of the ICC, has written the Foreword for this edition, providing his thoughts on the future of the ICC, for which we owe him many thanks. He deserves the highest praise for his vision and efforts in steering the ICC in these critical formative years.

Two new courts to try international crimes have emerged: the Extraordinary Chambers in the Courts of Cambodia for the Prosecution of Crimes committed during the period of the Democratic Kampuchea and the Iraqi Special Tribunal (IST). We have incorporated the legislation of these courts and references to them throughout the chapters. Furthermore, references to the relevant documents for the specialised courts in Kosovo, Bosnia and Herzegovina, and the *Lockerbie* case appear in this edition. In this way, we hope that the book will serve as a resource for those involved with the full spectrum of courts dealing with international crimes and that useful comparisons may be drawn.

In the same vein, the chapter dealing in brief with the international crimes of terrorism and related crimes and extradition procedures remains for completeness, even though some have indicated it may be out of place in a book on international criminal courts. The relationship between these areas of international criminal law and the mandates of international criminal courts should be a subject of interest and of study for those working in these fields and with practices often extending across them. Increasingly, jurisprudence and procedure from one field is cited or becomes relevant in another.

The Appendices, however, have been amended and scaled down, leaving only certain documents printed in full, with the balance cited with the exact web addresses where the full document can be located for ease of reference for the reader. Due to space limitations we have only been able to include the most essential documents from the ICC and the ad hoc Tribunals, but not the special courts (although websites are included for these courts and the relevant provisions are cited in full in the chapters and referenced in the tables). The modern trend is increasingly to use the web as the basis for research where the most up-to-date versions of documents can always be obtained. Textbooks will not in the future include lengthy documents (which often become outdated after going to print) if they are readily available on the internet. *Archbold International* is hopefully setting a worthy example in this respect.

Following requests from many practitioners, we have, in reorganising the Appendices, included the web references for the international treaties most cited before international courts so that these documents are easily accessible. We trust that the right balance has now been struck between substantive commentary and reference documents.

We are indebted to so many people for the new edition:

We wish to thank Sebastian van de Vliet, Head of the Office of Legal Aid and Detention Matters at the ICTY, and the staff of his office, in particular Sam Shoamanesh, for contributing the final chapter, Chapter 20, to the book on legal aid and defence counsel matters. It will provide priceless guidance to the defence side before all courts. The chapter is packed with the "inside" details of how the system functions in practise. We are immensely grateful for this outstanding contribution. It must be noted that the views expressed in the chapter are those of the author alone and do not necessarily reflect the views of the ICTY or the United Nations in general.

Our gratitude is also expressed to Norman Farrell, Legal Co-ordinator, Office of the Prosecutor, ICTY, and former Chief, Appeals Section, Office of the Prosecutor, ICTY and ICTR, and to Vladimir Tochilovsky, Legal Adviser and Trial Attorney, Office of the Prosecutor, ICTY, for their views and most helpful input in respect to certain sections of the book.

There are many to whom we have turned for advice, new ideas and encouragement and who have consistently supported us: Judge Richard Goldstone, Mohamed Othman, Geoffrey Nice Q.C., Joanna Korner

Q.C., David Tolbert, Professor Guy Goodwin-Gill, Steven Kay Q.C., Fahrudin Ibrisimovic, and Michael Mansfield Q.C.

We have been extremely fortunate to have a number of excellent research and editorial assistants as part of our team: Caroline Buisman and Susan Park have dedicated so much of their time to the production and polishing of this edition; it would not be of the high standard without their relentless efforts. We also wish to thank for their first-rate work: Christopher Black, Michelle Butler, Alex Demirdjian, and Maxim Kogen. The unflagging dedication of all of the assistants has been hugely appreciated and has directly contributed to the success of the book. It is hoped that they will continue to work with us on developing *Archbold International*.

Our publishers, Sweet & Maxwell, deserve the biggest thanks. They have kept the entire project on track and provided never-ending assistance. The second edition aims to consolidate the profile and use of the book in international criminal law circles, largely due to the enterprise and loyalty of our publishers.

We will continue to review and update the work as the law and procedure alters and expands with a view to further editions in the future. It is essential that Judges, practitioners, governments, academics and all those affected by international criminal law are kept abreast of the current state of the law in a field which is certainly a growth industry.

International criminal courts have assumed a permanent and distinguished position on the international stage and within national jurisdictions to try serious international crimes. It can no longer be lamented that such crimes will go unpunished, even though the court system is in its infancy when compared with our domestic traditions. It can be claimed with some justification that due respect is being given to the international rule of law.

The law is stated as at October 1, 2005.

Rodney Dixon   Karim Khan
London

October 2005

CONTENTS

CONTENTS

APPENDICES

APPENDIX A

INTERNATIONAL TREATIES

APPENDIX B

ICC

CONTENTS

CONTENTS

APPENDIX D

ICTR

CONTENTS

APPENDIX E

BOSNIA AND HERZEGOVINA

APPENDIX F

CAMBODIA

APPENDIX G

EAST TIMOR

APPENDIX H

IRAQ

APPENDIX I

KOSOVO

Contents

APPENDIX J

SIERRA LEONE

APPENDIX K

TERRORISM AND RELATED OFFENCES

APPENDIX L

EXTRADITION AND MUTUAL ASSISTANCE

APPENDIX M

THE LOCKERBIE CASES

APPENDIX N

SAMPLE INDICTMENTS AND CHARGES

For Appendices E to N inclusive, please view online at:
www.sweetandmaxwell.co.uk/archboldinternational

TABLE OF CASES

TABLE OF CASES

TABLE OF CASES

TABLE OF CASES

TABLE OF CASES

TABLE OF CASES

TABLE OF STATUTES

CHAPTER 1

INTRODUCTION

The late Sir Richard May, whose untimely death has robbed the world **1–1**
equally of a judge and an academic of the first rank, noted in the first edition of
this work that the original Archbold was an early nineteenth-century English
barrister and author of legal textbooks. His writings were on various subjects
and most have disappeared without trace; however one, *Criminal Pleading,
Evidence and Practice*, was destined to become the bible of generations of
criminal practitioners in England and Wales. It is still performing that role,
now in its 57th edition, and is relied upon as the essential guide for the English
criminal courts in all matters of law, practice and procedure. On the
international stage, the growing number of courts and tribunals, each with its
own statute, rules of procedure and evidence, and regulations (or similar
provisions), and each promulgating its own unique jurisprudence, has made
this a particularly complex area for the practitioner and the aim of the editors
of this work, now in its second edition, is to set out in one volume and in a way
that provides for ease of understanding and comparison all aspects of the
relevant law and procedure for the international criminal courts together with
an accompanying commentary. A principal aim of this work therefore is to
provide a comprehensive practical guide covering all areas of international
criminal law in a form which is readily accessible to practitioners and which
makes it readily possible to track comparative developments.

The necessary parts of the relevant statutes, rules and regulations governing
the structures of the various international courts and tribunals are reproduced
so that readers may easily compare the differing texts. Beside the Statutes of
the ICC, ICTY and ICTR, the relevant parts of the Statute of and the Rules
and Regulations for the Special Panel for East Timor and the Special Court for
Sierra Leone have been included. Thus the key provisions of all of the
institutions currently operating in this field are available in this volume. Of
particular note are the powers to obtain co-operation from States and the
powers of coercion. These latter powers have proved to be important in the
case of the ad hoc Tribunals: some instances of a lack of State co-operation
continues to provide a problem and the Tribunals have had to resort to powers
relating to the production of documents and execution of search warrants in
order to obtain it. The resulting law is thoroughly discussed in Chapter 4,
below.

It is encouraging to observe that academics continue to write prolifically on
the jurisprudence and substantive law of the international courts, thereby
demonstrating the importance and the dynamic nature of the work that is
being undertaken by these courts. The days are long gone when it could be said
that international criminal law was solely a topic of academic and historical
interest. This has occurred, not least, because the International Criminal
Tribunals for the former Yugoslavia (ICTY) and Rwanda (ICTR) continue to
have a burgeoning caseload; the International Criminal Court (ICC) is
investigating and preparing for its first cases arising out of events in the Sudan,
Uganda and the Democratic Republic of the Congo; the Special Court for
Sierra Leone has returned its first decisions; judges have now been appointed

to the War Crimes Court in Sarajevo; and the Special Court for Cambodia and the Special Tribunal for Iraq should begin their work in the foreseeable future.

Creating the procedures and systems that enable this ever-expanding work of the international criminal courts to take place has involved a blending or fusion of important parts of the common-law and civil-law systems, as has been well-demonstrated in case of the ICC. Whilst the suggested differences between the two systems have been perhaps somewhat overstated, a sustained attempt has nonetheless been made at the ICC to take the best from both so that, in the result, a form of adversarial, rather than inquisitorial trial will take place which will be subject to a high degree of case-management at the pre-trial, trial and appeal stages. This work puts the particular and unique trial processes of each of the courts and tribunals into their true international context, whilst at the at the same time highlighting the variations that exist between them. Self-evidently, creating international courts and tribunals is far from being simply a matter of creating new procedures and structures. An international court can only operate according to international law. Thus, this work also identifies the sources of the relevant law and discusses the principles of interpretation of that law, including the Vienna Convention on the Law of Treaties, the Rome Statute of the ICC and the extensive jurisprudence of the ICTY and ICTR on the topic.

1–2   The substantive law is fully covered in clear statements of the law resorting to genocide, crimes against humanity, war crimes and individual responsibility. The ad hoc Tribunals have continued to develop the law significantly in the field of individual criminal responsibility, in particular developing the concepts of common purpose and joint criminal responsibility, which are of special importance when trying cases of mass crime during a time of war. These matters are discussed in this work and the developments are brought up-to-date, including that relating to the important topic of command responsibility where the jurisprudence has continued to be dynamic. This volume includes the relevant statutory provisions for both the Special Court for Cambodia and the Special Tribunal for Iraq.

There is an extensive account of the history, definition and development of the law relating to war crimes and to the establishment of the character of an armed conflict which has been much addressed in the ICTY. There is, similarly, a full account of recent developments in the law relating to crimes against humanity, including those at the Diplomatic Conference in Rome for the establishment of the ICC where the essential features of such crimes were clarified. The work deals with the ICTY/ICTR jurisprudence on the subject and that of domestic courts, together with academic work and that of the International Law Commission. Likewise, the history and law of genocide are fully covered, together with the developments in the ICTY and ICTR, the developments in the latter being of particular significance. The work also covers the crime of aggression which, as is pointed out below, will be prosecuted by the ICC for the first time since Nuremberg, although a definition of this offence has yet to be agreed.

1–3   As discussed below, the corpus of international criminal law has rapidly expanded, particularly in the fields of terrorism, hi-jacking, drug-trafficking and money-laundering crimes which, by their nature, involve a cross-border dimension. States have sought to combat these crimes by means of treaties and agreements, co-operation and the establishment of international organs. These crimes do not, as yet, form part of the subject-matter jurisdiction of any international criminal court and are tried in domestic courts. However, this part of international criminal law forms another component of the subject, of growing importance with the heightened international concern about terrorism. The various conventions dealing with terrorism, hi-jacking, money-laundering and other such matters, are produced in this work, together with relevant commentary.

One chapter deals with the defences open to an accused before international criminal courts, and it is to be noted that little reliance has been placed on specific defences such as diminished responsibility, insanity or intoxication in the ad hoc Tribunals. (Instead, the accused have tended to put everything in issue.) Nonetheless, these defences are all considered, together with self-defence, duress, superior orders and other defences, with reference to the case law (including the important Nuremberg case law) and the relevant statutes and rules, in particular the Rome Statute of the ICC. Similarly, the relevant provisions for the special courts in East Timor, Sierra Leone and Cambodia are set out.

This discussion includes consideration of the important maxims *ne bis in idem* (or rule against double jeopardy, *i.e.* the principle that a person should not be tried twice for the same offence) and *nullum crimen sine lege* (*i.e.* the principle that a person should not be convicted for something which was not a criminal offence at the time when it was committed). Both principles are reflected in the law of international courts and the relevant statutory provisions are set out and discussed.

Turning next to matters of procedure, the statutory provisions and rules in **1-4** relation to pre-trial proceedings are all reproduced, including those in relation to investigations and arrest warrants, and those in relation to "preliminary proceedings", *i.e.* proceedings after the arrest or surrender of an accused, including initial appearance, pleas of guilty and provisional release (a developing area of jurisprudence in the ICTY) and pre-trial preparation. This latter topic has proved to be of great importance in the ICTY. As a result, the practice has developed over the years and the rules have been amended with provisions for the appointment of a pre-trial judge and for active pre-trial management by the Trial Chamber in order to clarify the issues in the trial and shorten them by means of the imposition of deadlines and putting limits on the number of witnesses. Similar, though by no means identical, arrangements have been put in place for the ICC; detailed, court-driven case management is seen as a critical factor in reducing the daunting length that can be achieved by trials of this kind.

There continue to be many challenges in the ICTY/ICTR to the form of indictments; so much so, that they remain standard. The statutory provisions relating to indictments are reproduced and the case law on the form and amendments of indictments is discussed and summarised; in particular the requirements in drafting indictments for specificity and a concise statement of the material facts and crimes charged (but not the evidence relied on).

The various differences between the tribunals as regards evidence and **1-5** procedure are demonstrated in the separate chapters on this subject that set out and compare the relevant rules of the ICC, ICTY, ICTR and East Timor.

The ICTY has pointed out that it must possess, as an international court, the inherent power to deal with conduct which interferes with its administration of justice. Accordingly, the powers of international courts to deal with contempts and offences against the administration of justice are all considered in this work. This is a matter dealt with in the Statute of the ICC and the Rules of the ICTY and ICTR and has given rise to a surprising amount of litigation for the latter Tribunals, leading to amendments to the rules and clarification of the procedures. These developments are fully covered, together with all the relevant cases and the provisions for the ICC in the Rome Statute as well as the courts in East Timor and Sierra Leone.

Little of a comprehensive nature has been written about the practice of international courts in relation to sentencing. It is, therefore, of particular importance that this work contains a wide-ranging account, including discussion of the aims of sentencing and the factors in determining individual sentences. The account, likewise, fully covers matters which have been considered as mitigation. The elaborate provisions in the ICC for compensation and restitution reflect the enhanced role for victims in the procedures of that institution: these are reproduced and discussed, as are the provisions for review and commutation of sentence in the various courts.

A chapter is devoted to the practice in relation to appeals and review of decisions of international criminal courts. Since the decision of the Nuremberg tribunals were without appeal, the practice referred to is necessarily that of the ad hoc Tribunals. That developing practice is covered, together with the ICC Statute and Rules.

The final chapter sets out some of the complex arrangements that exist in these various judicial bodies for legal aid and defence counsel matters. It is to be noted that there are some notable differences between the courts and tribunals in this respect: for instance the Special Court for Sierra Leone has created an Office of the Principal Defender which oversees the individual defence teams, and it is particularly designed to provide advice and substantive assistance to all teams in the preparation of their cases. One interesting issue that may arise with the passing of time is whether the dictates of cost and efficiency will lead to attempts to establish within these courts either a public defender system or hybrid arrangements, with defence teams comprising lawyers who are (permanently) court-based as well as advocates selected from the ranks of independent counsel.

CHAPTER 2

ESTABLISHMENT AND JURISDICTION OF THE COURTS, AND SOURCES OF LAW

I. HISTORICAL BACKGROUND

International criminal courts are a recent phenomenon. Their origins **2–1** lie in the Tribunals that tried members of the Axis Powers after the Second World War on the basis that crimes of such seriousness and magnitude could not be left unpunished by the international community. These prosecutions emanated from the *Agreement for the Prosecution and Punishment of the Major War Criminals of the European Axis Powers and the Charter of the International Military Tribunal*, August 8, 1945, 82 U.N.T.S. 279.

Some fifty years later, ad hoc International Criminal Tribunals for the former Yugoslavia (ICTY) and Rwanda (ICTR) were set up. They are the first of their kind—international courts established by the Security Council under Chapter VII of the Charter of the United Nations as a measure for the restoration of peace and security in strife-torn regions of the world. The Tribunals were created by UN Security Council Resolution 827 of May 25, 1993 in the case of the ICTY, and Resolution 955 of November 8, 1994 for the ICTR. The ICTY is based in the Hague, the Netherlands, while the Office of the Prosecutor for the ICTR is located in Kigali, Rwanda, with the Court in Arusha,

Tanzania. The ICTR's Statute provides for a common Prosecutor and Appeals Chamber with the ICTY. Separate Prosecutor's offices have been established with different Deputy Prosecutors.

2–2   Subsequently, in July 1998 a draft statute for a permanent international criminal court (ICC) was adopted by an assembly of States. It is known as the Rome Statute of the International Criminal Court (UN Doc. A/Conf. 183/9, July 17, 1998). The statute requires that a minimum of 60 States must ratify the treaty incorporating the statute before the court can be established. The required number of State ratifications was reached in April 2002, and in accordance with the statute of the ICC, the jurisdiction of the ICC commenced on July 1, 2002. The ICC will only have jurisdiction over offences committed after this date. The seat of the ICC is in the Hague.

Since the Rome conference, another kind of international criminal court has emerged: courts with jurisdiction to try international crimes under United Nations transitional arrangements as occurred in 1999 with the establishment of the United Nations Transitional Administration for East Timor (UNTAET), and with the creation of a Special Court for Sierra Leone. A similar proposal was considered by the UN for Cambodia, and an agreement has now been reached with the Cambodian government to establish a special court. Most recently a Special Tribunal has been established for Iraq. The establishing legislation and documentation for these courts have been included in the appendices.

2–3   The work of the ad hoc Tribunals and the special courts will lay the foundation for the ICC. Judge Louise Arbour, the former Chief Prosecutor of the ICTY and ICTR highlighted this historic mission in the following terms: "[M]y greatest aspiration is to be part of laying the foundation for a permanent international criminal court; to show these tribunals can produce the kind of quality we expect from a model domestic system." (Cited in K. Makin, "From Bench to Bosnia", *Canadian Lawyer*, September 1996).

Previous international criminal courts have not been particularly helpful in offering guidance to the Tribunals, special courts and the ICC. The Nuremberg and Tokyo Trials were exceptional, "one off" proceedings before military tribunals. The factual circumstances and the nature of the evidence were different. The prosecutions were largely document-based. The evidentiary rules also encouraged prosecutions that relied more on documentary evidence than on witnesses.

2–4   The Commission of Experts for the former Yugoslavia (which was established by the Security Council prior to the ICTY to investigate the formation of the ICTY) recognised in formulating guidelines to undertake its tasks that:

> "The approach to evidentiary and procedural issues taken at Nuremberg, where there was an extremely high degree of reliance on documentary evidence and relatively little emphasis placed on the accused's right to full answer and defence, would not be acceptable today because of post-World War II developments in international human rights law" (W. Fenrick (Member of Commission of Experts), "In the Field with UNCOE: Investigating Atrocities in the Territory of the former Yugoslavia", 34 *Military Law and Law of War Review*, 1995, 36). Also see *Prosecutor v. Tadić*, Decision on the Prosecutor's Motion requesting Protective Measures for Victims and Witnesses, August 10, 1995, paras 19–21.

In addition, contemporary international and regional courts, such as the International Court of Justice and the European Court of Human Rights, do not have any jurisdiction to prosecute individuals for criminal offences. They focus in the main on the responsibilities of States and State-like entities, and have, thus, adopted approaches that facilitate factual inquiries and entail levels of proof concordant with assigning such responsibility to States.

The ICC, Tribunals and special courts are, therefore, embarking upon a maiden voyage in trying international crimes for the purposes of establishing individual criminal responsibility. They have had to function on an on-going basis as international criminal courts for a variety of cases involving the prosecution of individuals.

II. APPLICABLE LAW

2–5 The law applicable before the ICC, the ad hoc Tribunals, and the special courts is international law. It is important to identify the sources of international law. Practitioners have to rely upon these sources to determine and define the applicable law before international criminal courts.

A. SOURCES: TREATY AND CUSTOM

2–6 International law comprises two main bodies of law: conventional (treaty) law and customary law. The Statute of the International Court of Justice defines the recognised sources of international law in Article 38:

"(a) international conventions, whether general or particular . . .;
(b) international custom, as evidence of a general practice accepted as law;
(c) the general principles of law recognised by civilised nations;
(d) . . . judicial decisions and the teachings of the most highly qualified publicists of various nations, as subsidiary means of the determination of rules of law."

Unlike in national systems, there is no central legislative body for the international community that enacts international law. Only law that is accepted by States as binding upon them whether in treaty form or as a matter of custom, forms part of the corpus of international law. General principles of law, and judicial decisions are other, less relied upon, sources of international law.

(1) Treaty law

2–7 There is no strict hierarchy of the sources of international law, other than judicial decisions and the teachings of publicists being a subsidiary source. Treaty law is an especially strong source of law as treaties embody the mutual promises of signatory States. Article 2(1)(a) of the *Vienna Convention on the Law of Treaties* 1969 defines a treaty as "an international agreement concluded between States in written form and governed by international law". One of the most basic principles of international law is the principle of *pacta sunt servanda*—nations are bound to keep the promises they make between themselves.

The Statute of the ICC is treaty based. There are numerous treaties widely ratified by States, which form the basis of international human- itarian and criminal law, including the *1907 Hague Conventions*, the four *1949 Geneva Conventions*, the two *1977 Geneva Protocols* additional thereto, the *1948 Convention on the Prevention and Punishment of the Crime of Genocide*, and the *1984 Convention against Torture and other Cruel Inhuman or Degrading Treatment or Punishment*.

(2) Customary law

2–8   Customary law consists of unwritten rules that are "evidence of a general practice accepted as law" (ICJ Statute, Art. 38(1)(b). Unlike treaty law which is applicable only to the signatory States, customary law is universal; all States are bound by established customary law. There are strict criteria for the determination of whether a customary rule exists.

Elements of custom

2–9   The classic formulation of customary law is set by the International Law Commission working paper, 1950, UN Doc. A/CN.4/16, March 3, 1950, at 5:

> "The emergence of a principle or rule of customary international law would seem to require presence of the following elements:
> (i) concordant practice by a number of States with reference to a type of situation falling within the domain of international relations;
> (ii) continuation or repetition of the practice over a considerable period of time;
> (iii) conception that the practice is required by, or consistent with prevailing international law; and
> (iv) general acquiescence in the practice by other States.
> Of course the presence of each of these elements is to be established as a fact by a competent international authority."

2–10   A contemporary definition of the International Law Association (London Conference, Report of 63rd Conference, 936)—having recog- nised that there are "inherent serious difficulties" (p. 3) in setting out the rules on the subject, the definition was formulated as:

> "A rule of customary international law is one which is created and sustained by the constant and uniform practice of States and other subjects of international law in or impinging upon their international legal relations, in circumstances which give rise to a legitimate expectation of

similar conduct in the future . . . If a sufficiently extensive and representative number of States participate in such a practice in a consistent manner, the resulting rule is one of 'general customary international law' . . . such a rule is binding on all States." (p. 8)

The ICJ has on several occasions outlined the requirements of **2–11** customary law: *S.S. Lotus* case [1927] P.C.I.J., ser. A, No. 10 and *North Sea Continental Shelf* cases 1969 I.C.J. 3: "Not only must the acts concerned amount to settled practice, but they must also be such, or be carried out in such a way, as to be evidence of a belief that this practice is rendered obligatory by the existence of a rule requiring it . . . The States concerned must therefore feel that they are conforming to what amounts to a legal obligation. The frequency, or even habitual character of the acts is not in itself enough." (p. 44)

The required density of the acts was also clarified in the *North Sea* case:

"Although the passage of only a short period of time is not necessarily, or itself a bar to the formation of a new rule of customary international law on the basis of what was originally a purely conventional rule, an indispensable requirement would be that within the period in question, short though it might be, State practice, including that of States whose interests are specially effected, should have been both extensive and virtually uniform in the sense of the provision invoked." (p. 43)

It is also necessary to consider whether there are divergent views and **2–12** conduct in State practice—the inquiry must not be limited to those States that support the rule of customary law: see, *Advisory Opinion on the Legality of the Threat or Use of Nuclear Weapons*, I.C.J. Rep. 1996, p. 226 at 254–5 in which the ICJ noted the UN General Assembly resolutions asserting the illegality of the threat or use of nuclear weapons, but in light of the opposition of certain States to these resolutions was unable to hold that they represented binding customary law.

The most recent pronouncement on customary law was in *Democratic Republic of Congo v. Belgium*, 2000 I.C.J. No. 121. The ICJ examined State practice to determine whether under customary law there was any exception to the rule according immunity from criminal jurisdiction to an incumbent Minister of Foreign Affairs where he was suspected of committing war crimes and crimes against humanity, and found they it was unable to deduce such a rule in customary law. The ICJ noted that it had "carefully examined State practice" and specifically reviewed "national legislation" and "those few decisions of national higher courts" (para. 58).

Custom before international criminal courts

The Secretary-General's Report for the ICTY Statute notes: **2–13**

"34. In the view of the Secretary-General, the application of the principle nullum crimen sine lege requires that the international tribunal should apply rules of international humanitarian law which are beyond any doubt part of customary law so that the problem of adherence of some but not all

States to specific conventions does not arise. This would appear to be particularly important in the context of an international tribunal prosecuting persons responsible for serious violations of international humanitarian law.

35. The part of conventional international humanitarian law which has beyond doubt become part of international customary law is the law applicable in armed conflict as embodied in: the Geneva Conventions of August 12, 1949 for the Protection of War Victims; the Hague Convention (IV) Respecting the Laws and Customs of War on Land and the Regulations annexed thereto of October 18, 1907; the Convention on the Prevention and Punishment of the Crime of Genocide 1948; and the Charter of the International Military Tribunal of August 8, 1945."

2–14   A Bench of the Appeals Chamber held in *Delalic*, Decision on Application for Leave to Appeal (Form of the Indictment), October 15, 1996:

"26. . . . the Tribunal's Statute does not create new offences but rather serves to give the Tribunal jurisdiction over offences which are already part of customary law. As the Secretary-General comments in his Report on the Tribunal's Statute (S/25704): '. . . the international tribunal should apply rules of international humanitarian law which are beyond any doubt part of customary law so that the problem of adherence of some but not all States to specific conventions does not arise' (para. 34).

27. . . . the Report of the Secretary-General to the Security Council of 1993 on the Statute of this Tribunal in his exposition of Articles 2,3,4 and 5 of the Statute clearly referred the crimes enumerated in them to their sources of international humanitarian law, for example, the Geneva Conventions of 1949, the Hague Convention (IV) of 1907, the Nuremberg Charter of 1945 and the Genocide Convention of 1948. The Bench takes the view, therefore, that Articles 2,3,4 and 5 of the Statute are shorthand for the corresponding norms of international humanitarian law . . . ."

By comparison, the Secretary-General's Report on the ICTR Statute (S/1995/134, February 13, 1995), states:

"12. . . . the Security Council has elected to take a more expansive approach to the choice of the applicable law than the one underlying the statute of the Yugoslav Tribunal, and included within the subject-matter jurisdiction of the Rwanda Tribunal international instruments regardless of whether they were considered part of customary international law or whether they have customarily entailed the individual criminal responsibility of the perpetrator of the crime. Article 4 of the statute, accordingly, includes violations of Additional Protocol II, which, as a whole, has not yet been universally recognized as part of customary international law, and for the first time criminalizes common Article 3 of the four Geneva Conventions."

For decisions of the ICTY and ICTR that have discussed the applicability of customary international law see, for example, *Prosecutor v. Tadić*, Decision on the Defence Motion for Interlocutory Appeal on Jurisdiction, October 2, 1995, paras 86–137; *Prosecutor v. Delalic et al.*, Judgment, February 20, 2001, paras 64–72; *Prosecutor v. Milošević*, Decision on Preliminary Motions, November 8, 2001; *Prosecutor v. Strugar et al.*, Decision on Defence Preliminary Motion Challenging Jurisdiction, June 7, 2002; and, *Prosecutor v. Kayishema*, Judgment, May 21, 1999, paras 87–190.

Statute of the International Criminal Court, Art. 21

Applicable law

21.—1. The Court shall apply:　　　　　　　　　　　　　　　　　　**2–15**
  (a) In the first place, this Statute, Elements of Crimes and its Rules of Procedure and Evidence;
  (b) In the second place, where appropriate, applicable treaties and the principles and rules of international law, including the established principles of the international law of armed conflict;
  (c) Failing that, general principles of law derived by the Court from national laws of legal systems of the world including, as appropriate, the national laws of States that would normally exercise jurisdiction over the crime, provided that those principles are not inconsistent with this statute and with international law and internationally recognized norms and standards.

2. The Court may apply principles and rules of law as interpreted in its previous decisions.

3. The application and interpretation of law pursuant to this article must be consistent with internationally recognized human rights, and be without any adverse distinction founded on grounds such as gender as defined in article 7, paragraph 3, age, race, colour, language, religion or belief, political or other opinion, national, ethnic or social origin, wealth, birth or other status.

(3) General principles of law

One of the main reasons for the inclusion of paragraph (c) in Article　**2–16**
38(1) of the ICJ Statute was to avoid a situation of *non liquet* whereby the Permanent Court of International Justice would be hamstrung by the absence of applicable legal rules. The same reasoning supports the applicability of Article 38(1)(c) of the ICJ Statute in the context of international criminal courts.

It is clear that a court is not obliged to review the practices of every "civilised nation" in order to discern a general principle. It suffices that the court reviews the main legal systems of the world: see *Prosecutor v. Erdemović*, Judgment, Separate and Dissenting opinion of Judge Stephen, October 7, 1997, p. 12, para. 25.

The ICTY and ICTR have held that in discerning general principle, the court will review the jurisprudence of such jurisdictions as are accessible to it in an effort to discern a general trend, policy or principle underlying the express rule of a particular jurisdiction which comports with the object and purpose of the International Tribunal. (*Ibid.* See also, *Prosecutor v. Erdemović*, Judgment, Separate and Dissenting opinion of Judge Stephen, October 7, 1997, para. 63, 65: "reference may be had by an international tribunal such as ours to principles of legal reasoning and the analogous treatment of similar crimes in domestic contexts where they are of assistance in promoting 'a viable and mature international jurisprudence'").

(4) Judicial decisions

Article 38(1)(d) of the ICJ Statute refers to "judicial decisions and　**2–17**
the teachings of the most highly qualified publicists of the various nations". They do not constitute "sources" of law. Rather, such

decisions and teachings may be referred to in order to confirm or elaborate the content, application or interpretation of international conventions, international customary law or general principles of law. This is borne out by the language of paragraph (d), which does not seek to create a free-standing source of law, but rather identifies a "subsidiary means for the interpretation of rules".

The persuasive effect and practical utility of judicial decisions from different judicial bodies depends upon a number of factors including the type of court making a determination, its constitution and composition, the circumstances surrounding a case and the problem actually being addressed. Care is required when considering the weight to be accorded to different decisions or judgments and the extent to which they should contribute to the findings and jurisprudence of international criminal courts. As was stated in *Prosecutor v. Tadić*, Decision on the Prosecutor's Motion Requesting Protective Measures for Victims and Witnesses, August 10, 1995, para. 18:

> "Although the Report of the Secretary-General states that many of the provisions in the Statute are formulations based upon provisions found in existing international instruments, it does not indicate the relevance of the interpretation given to these provisions by other international judicial bodies. This lack of guidance is particularly troubling because of the unique character of the International Tribunal."

In the absence of such explicit guidance, the judges of the ad hoc Tribunals have had cause to consider the value of different decisions and case law from international, regional and national courts and tribunals.

Nuremberg and other post Second World War tribunals

2–18   In the *Erdemović* Judgment, one judge of the Appeals Chamber referred to the decisions of Military Tribunals as a "source of law" after finding that no general principles of law could be discerned on a particular question. The learned judge held that the jurisprudence of the Nuremberg Trial "should be mentioned in the first place" as a most persuasive source of law. (See *Prosecutor v. Erdemović*, Judgment, Separate and Dissenting opinion of Judge Li, October 7, 1997, para. 4.) On the other hand, the remaining judges all found it possible after reviewing and evaluating relevant post Second World War cases, to discern a *general principle of law* applicable to the problem at hand, and did not regard the Nuremberg Judgment as a "source". (See *Prosecutor v. Erdemović*, Judgment, Joint and Separate opinion of Judge McDonald and Judge Vohrah, October 7, 1997, para. 66, 72; Separate and Dissenting opinion of Judge Stephen, paras 25–26; Separate and Dissenting Opinion of Judge Cassesse, para. 12.)

Notwithstanding this distinction, it is arguable that the Nuremberg Judgment is a source of law by dint of its principles being unanimously adopted by the UN General Assembly: see, *Nuremberg Principles: Principles of International Law recognized in the Charter of the Nuremberg Tribunal and in the Judgment of the Tribunal* (1950), UNGAOR, 5th session, Supp No. 12, UN Doc A/1316 (1950).

A distinction must be drawn between the Nuremberg Judgment's substantive and procedural law contributions. What may have acquired the status of international customary law are its findings on substantive law issues; for example, its definition and application of crimes against humanity. What did not were its administrative or procedural rules: see, *Prosecutor v. Tadić*, Decision on the Prosecutor's Motion Requesting Protective Measures for Victims and Witnesses, August 10, 1995, paras 19–21.

As to the status accorded to the post Second World War military tribunals constituted under Control Council Law No. 10 (December 20, 1945), there is uncertainty as to the authority to be accorded to their pronouncements. Our view is that such tribunals were applying international law (see, *Trial of Frederick Flick and Five others ("Flick case")*, *Trials of War Criminals*, Vol. VI, p. 188). Other tribunals, drawing their authority from the same source (Control Council Law No. 10) viewed their status differently: see, *Trial of Erhard Milch ("Milch case")*, *Trials of War Criminals*, Vol. III, p. 778, where the Tribunal stated "[i]t must be constantly borne in mind that this is an American Court of Justice, applying the ancient and fundamental concepts of Anglo-Saxon jurisprudence". The division of opinion has been acknowledged by the ICTY:

> "In relation to the post-World War Two Military Tribunals constituted under the London Charter or Control Council Law No. 10, doubt remains as to whether any of these military Tribunals were truly 'international in character'. . . . to the extent that [these Tribunals] were held to be international, this was merely with regard to their constitution, character and competence." (*Prosecutor v. Erdemović*, Judgment, Joint and Separate Opinion of Judge McDonald and Judge Vohrah, October 7, 1996, para. 54)

Accordingly, rather than applying a single hard and fast rule as to the weight to be given the jurisprudence emanating from the post Second World War military tribunals, it will be necessary to review the constitution of a particular tribunal, the questions raised in the case, and the extent to which a given tribunal viewed itself shackled (in theory or in practice) to its own national legislation or case law. There may be instances where the law applied by a post Second World War tribunal can be considered purely international (and declaratory of principles of international law), whilst other issues may have been treated in a manner which necessitate their being considered no more persuasive than that of a judgment rendered by a domestic court.

Regional courts and other international bodies

The ad hoc Tribunals have repeatedly relied upon the jurisprudence **2–19** of regional human rights courts such as the European Court of Human Rights and the Inter-American Court of Human Rights. (See, for example, *Prosecutor v. Kovacevic*, Decision stating reasons for Appeals Chamber's Order of May 29, 1998, July 2, 1998, para. 32.)

They have similarly referred to the findings of international bodies such as UN Special Rapporteurs, or the findings of the Human Rights

Committee. (See, for example, *Prosecutor v. Furundžija*, Judgment, December 10, 1998, p. 55.)

The Statutes of the ICC, ICTY, ICTR, and the special courts reflect the provisions and practices contained in the leading international human rights instruments concerning the rights of accused persons and victims. (See, *Prosecutor v. Tadić*, Decision on the Prosecutor's Motion Requesting Protective Measures for Victims and Witnesses, August 10, 1995, para. 25; and, *Prosecutor v. Barayagwiza*, Decision (Prosecutor's Request for Review or Reconsideration), Declaration of Judge Nieto Navio, March 31, 2000, para. 15: "this Tribunal's fundamental aim is to vindicate the highest standards of international criminal justice, in providing an impartial and equitable system of justice.")

The extent to which war crimes' prosecutions require different standards due to their unique character is a source of some debate: *Prosecutor v. Tadić*, Decision on the Prosecutor's Motion Requesting Protective Measures for Victims and Witnesses, August 10, 1995, paras 28–30: "The interpretations of Article 6 of the ECHR by the European Court of Human Rights are meant to apply to ordinary criminal and, for Article 6(1), civil adjudication's. By contrast, the International Tribunal is adjudicating crimes which are considered so horrific as to warrant universal jurisdiction. The International Tribunal is . . . comparable to a military tribunal, which often has limited rights of due process and more lenient rules of evidence"; and, *X v. Federal Republic of Germany*, Application/Requete No. 6946/75, 76 at pp. 115–6, cited in *Prosecutor v. Kovacevic*, Decision Stating Reasons for Appeals Chamber's order of May 29, 1998, Separate Opinion of Judge Shahabuddeen, July 2, 1998, p. 4: "[T]he exceptional character of criminal proceedings involving war crimes committed during World War II renders . . . inapplicable the principles developed in the case law of the Commission and the Court of Human Rights in cases involving other criminal offences."

A pronouncement from the Appeals Chamber: "As a matter of juristic logic, any flexibility in applying the requirements concerning time [for delay in bringing an accused before a competent Tribunal] to the case of war crimes has to find its justification not in the nature of the crimes themselves, but in the difficulties of investigating, preparing and presenting cases relating to them. Consequently, that flexibility is not a licence for disregarding the requirements where they can be complied with. It is only 'the austerity of tabulated legalism', an idea not much favoured where, as here, a generous interpretation is called for, which could lead to the view that, once a crime is categorised as a war crime, that suffices to justify the conclusion that the requirements concerning time may be safely put aside. In this case, it is not easy to see what difficulty beset the authorities in bringing the appellant from the Tribunal's detention unit to the Trial Chamber. That scarcely inter-galactic passage involved no more than a fifteen minute drive by motor car on a macadamised road. To plead the nature of the crimes in justification of the manifest breach of an applicable requirement which was both of overriding importance and capable of being respected with the same ease as in the ordinary case is to transform an important legal principle into a statement of affectionate aspiration." (*Prosecutor v. Barayagwiza*, Decision (Prosecutor's Request for Review or Reconsideration), Separate Opinion of Judge Shahabuddeen, March 31, 2000, paras 36–37).

National courts

As with the jurisprudence emanating from regional human rights' **2–20**
treaty bodies, regard must be had to the issues encountered in the
domestic context and the constitutive instrument of the national court
in order to accurately evaluate the relevance of a decision or practice of
a national court. As was held in *Prosecutor v. Furundžija*, Judgment,
December 10, 1998, para. 194:

> For a correct appraisal of this [international or national] case law, it is
> important to bear in mind, with each of the cases to be examined, the
> forum in which the case was heard, as well as the law applied, as these
> factors determine its authoritative value. In addition, one should be
> constantly mindful of the need for great caution in using national case law
> for the purpose of determining whether customary rules of international
> criminal law have evolved in a particular matter.

See also, *Prosecutor v. Blaškić*, Judgment on the Request of the
Republic of Croatia for Review of the Decision of Trial Chamber II of
July 18, 1997, October 29, 1997, para. 23; *Prosecutor v. Barayagwiza*,
Decision (Prosecutor's Request for Review or Reconsideration), Sepa-
rate Opinion of Judge Shahabuddeen, March 31, 2000, para. 44:

> "It is possible to argue that [given the nascent state of international
> criminal law] . . . a measure of liberality in using domestic law ideas is
> both natural and permissible . . . . But it is not necessary to pursue the
> argument further. The reason is that, altogether apart from the question
> of whether a particular line of municipal decisions is part of the law of the
> Tribunal, no statutory authority needs be cited to enable a court to benefit
> from the scientific value of the thinking of other jurists, provided that the
> court remains the master of its own house. Thus, nothing prevents a judge
> from consulting the reasoning of judges in other jurisdictions in order to
> work out his own solution to an issue before him; the navigation lights
> offered by the reflections of the former can be welcome without being
> obtrusive."

(5) Precedent or *stare decisis*

The judicial decisions and practices of other international, regional, **2–21**
and national courts and tribunals can assist an international criminal
court in a number of ways: they may provide evidence of established or
developing international custom, or they may be surveyed in order to
discern a general principle of law, or may be considered in order to
inform a court's approach to an issue.

It is clear, however, that such decisions and jurisprudence do not bind
the ad hoc International Tribunals in the formal sense. As was held by
an ICTY trial Chamber, "[i]t might thus seem that decisions from the
Appeals Chamber of the Tribunal on the provisions of the Statute
ought to be binding on Trial Chambers, this being the fundamental
basis of the appellate process. However, decisions from the same or
other jurisdictions which have not construed the same provisions in
their decisions as the case being considered are of merely 'persuasive'

value." (*Prosecutor v. Delalic et al.* (Judgment) November 16, 1998, para. 167).

It is a generally accepted rule of international law that the principle of precedent or *stare decisis* does not apply between international courts. In the case of the ICJ this is expressly stated: "The decision of the Court has no binding force except between the parties and in respect of a particular case." (ICJ Statute, Article 159). There is no formal doctrine of precedent binding the Chambers of the European Court of Human Rights.

In respect of the binding effect of the decisions of the Appeals Chamber and Trial Chambers of the ICTY and ICTR on each other, see the decision of the Appeals Chamber in *Prosecutor v. Aleksovski*, Judgment, March 24, 2000, pp. 39–49. After acknowledging that there was no provision in the ICTY Statute dealing with the applicability of precedent to the Tribunal's determinations, the Appeals Chamber referred to Article 25 of the Statute (governing the right of parties to appeal an issue) and held that the Tribunal could best discharge its mandate of prosecuting persons responsible for serious violations of international humanitarian law by adopting "an approach which, while recognising the need for certainty, stability, and predictability in criminal law, also recognises that there may be instances in which a strict absolute application of a principle may lead to an injustice." It concluded "that a proper construction of the Statute, taking due account of its text and purpose, yields to the conclusion that . . . the Appeals Chamber should follow its previous decisions, but should be free to depart from them for cogent reasons in the interests of justice." (paras 101 and 107; instances where the interests of justice would be served by departing from an authority included: where the earlier decision had been decided on the wrong legal principle, or made *per incuriam* (para. 108)).

Turning to the effect of a previous decision of the Appeals Chamber on a Trial Chamber, the Appeals Chamber held that the *ratio decidendi* of such decisions were binding. Three reasons were given for this conclusion: (i) it was based upon the hierarchical structure of the Statute conferring upon the Appeals Chamber the responsibility to definitively settle certain questions of law and fact; (ii) it was necessitated by the requirements of certainty and predictability in the applicability of the law; and, (iii) such a conclusion was held to be consistent with the right to a fair trial, which would not be achieved if like cases were not treated alike. It could not be achieved, if every Chamber could state the law as they saw fit:

> "In such a system, it would be possible to have four statements of the law . . . on a single legal issue—one from the Appeals Chamber and one from each of the three Trial Chambers. This would be inconsistent with the intention of the Security Council, which, . . . envisaged a tribunal comprising three trial chambers and one appeals chamber, applying a single, unified, coherent and rational corpus of law." (para. 113)

Whilst Trial Chambers are not bound by the decisions of other Trial Chambers, they are free to refer and follow a decision of another Trial Chamber if they find it persuasive (see, para. 114).

(6) Works of leading publicists and international legal texts

The utility of academic works lies in their evidential uses. They are **2–22** widely used in order to establish the content or scope of international law at a material time.

In respect of collective international academic effort, the work of the International Law Commission (ILC) has merited special consideration by the ICTY and ICTR by virtue of the eminence of its members and the invariably high standard of its Reports. The ILC's work could thus constitute evidence of customary law; or shed light on customary rules that are of uncertain content or are in the process of formation; or be indicative of the legal views of eminently qualified publicists representing the legal systems of the world.

Similarly, greater reference will be made to the Statute of the ICC before other international criminal courts. Though the ICC Statute does not bind the ad hoc Tribunals and does not purport to encapsulate contemporary international law (see, Article 10 of the ICC Statute), it is indicative of the current legal views of various states and may provide evidence of *opinio juris* of a large number of States:

> "Resort may be had *cum grano salis* to these provisions [of the Rome Statute] to help elucidate customary international law. Depending upon the matter at issue, the Rome Statute may be taken to restate, reflect or clarify customary rules or crystallise them, whereas in some areas it creates new law or modifies existing law" (*Prosecutor v. Furundžija*, Judgment, December 10, 1998, para. 227).

See also *Prosecutor v. Kordić and Čerkez*, Decision on the Joint Defence Motion to Dismiss the amended indictment for lack of Jurisdiction based on the limited jurisdictional reach of Articles 2 and 3, March 2, 1999, paras 23–25.

B. INTERNATIONAL HUMANITARIAN LAW

International humanitarian law is a branch of international law, with **2–23** a treaty or customary basis, which can be applied before international criminal courts.

(1) Jus in bello

The term "international humanitarian law" incorporates the rules **2–24** governing the actual conduct of armed conflict (*jus in bello*) and not the rules governing the lawfulness of the resort to armed conflict (*jus ad bellum*). The cardinal principle being that the *jus in bello* applies irrespective of whether the conflict was lawful or not under the *jus ad bellum*. The rules applicable to the lawfulness of armed conflict are covered in Chapter 14 on "Crimes of Aggression".

International humanitarian law (IHL) is the modern term for the "laws of war". It consists of those rules that place limitations on the conduct of the belligerent parties during armed conflict, and aims to mitigate the human suffering caused by such conflict. IHL spans the law applicable both to persons not involved in hostilities (including civilians, captured soldiers, and the wounded and sick) and to the actual conduct of hostilities.

(2) Laws of war

2–25   The term "laws of war" is a well-recognised term of art. Although the term "war" has been superseded by "armed conflict", the "laws of war" is still widely used. There is a long history behind the development of the laws of war, which first existed as customary practices in warfare. The need to clarify these customs led States to negotiate and accept binding instruments—treaties, conventions and protocols. The treaty-making process dates back to the 1860s when two significant treaties were concluded: in Geneva in 1864, a convention on the rules in respect of wounded soldiers, and in St Petersburg in 1868, a convention prohibiting the use of explosive rifle bullets. Herein lie the beginnings of the two main branches of the laws of war: the Geneva law covering the victims of war who have fallen into enemy hands, and the Hague law, regulating the conduct of waging war and the lawful means and methods of warfare.

Geneva law

2–26   Following the 1864 treaty, a treaty was concluded in 1899 extending the rules of the 1864 treaty to the wounded, sick and shipwrecked. The next major development occurred in 1929, following the First World War, when the International Committee of the Red Cross (ICRC) convened a diplomatic conference in Geneva. It produced an improved treaty on the treatment of the wounded and sick, and, most importantly, a separate Convention on the treatment of prisoners of war.

The events of the Spanish Civil War and Second World War provided the basis for further developments in the Geneva law. A diplomatic conference was held in 1949 under the auspices of the ICRC in Geneva. The existing Geneva conventions were revised, and four conventions were agreed to, including a new convention on the protection of civilians in time of war (*Geneva Convention IV*). The other three 1949 Geneva Conventions were: *Geneva Convention I for the Amelioration of the Condition of the Wounded and Sick in Armed Forces in the Field*; *Geneva Convention II for the Amelioration of the Condition of Wounded, Sick and Shipwrecked Members of Armed Forces at Sea*; *Geneva Convention III Relative to the Treatment of Prisoners of War*.

2–27   The two main innovations of the four 1949 Geneva Conventions were (i) the grave breach provisions, and (ii) the introduction of a common Article 3 to all four Conventions.

Each Convention identified certain grave breaches for which the Contracting Parties were obliged "to search for persons alleged to have committed, or to have ordered to be committed, such grave breaches" and to "bring such persons, regardless of their nationality, before its own courts" (see, *e.g.*, Article 146 of Geneva Convention IV). The notion of individual criminal responsibility for serious breaches of the Geneva law was thus embodied in the Conventions.

Common Article 3 to the four Conventions provided that the parties were bound by a list of fundamental rules "applicable in the case of armed conflict not of an international character". This Article signified the first codification of a basic set of rules applicable in internal armed conflict.

The provisions and application of the Geneva Conventions are discussed in Chapter 11 on "War Crimes".

Hague law

The first enactment of "the Hague" branch of international human- **2–28**
itarian law occurred in 1863 when during the course of the American civil war, the President of the United States of America promulgated the *Instructions for the Government of Armies of the United States in the Field* (known as the *Lieber Code*). The Code covered a wide spectrum of rules applicable to land warfare, including the conduct of war. The Code was the precursor of the first international treaty on the conduct of hostilities, the 1868 *St Petersburg Declaration Renouncing the Use*, in *Time of War, of Explosive Projectiles Under 400 Grammes Weight*.

Thereafter, the first Hague Peace Conference was held in 1899 where it was agreed to codify the "laws and customs of war on land". The Conference adopted a *Convention with Respect to the Laws and Customs of War on Land*, with annexed *Regulations on Land Warfare*. The Convention was slightly revised at the second Hague Peace Conference in 1907. The development of this body of law was halted by the outbreak of the First World War.

Only in 1925 were States again able to agree on a new treaty in the aftermath of the First World War, the *Protocol for the Prohibition of the Use in War of Asphyxiating, Poisonous or Other Gases, and of Bacteriological Methods of Warfare*. The post Second World War period did not generate any significant interest in the Hague law, the one exception being the 1954 *Hague Convention for the Protection of Cultural Property in the Event of Armed Conflict*.

The application of the Hague law is discussed in Chapter 11 on "War Crimes".

Customary law

During the codification processes it was recognised that much of the **2–29**
law continued to exist in the form of unwritten customary principles. This position was confirmed by the provisions of what has become known as the Martens Clause, first included in the Preamble to the 1899 Hague Convention II:

> "Until a more complete code of laws of war is issued, the high contracting
> Parties think it right to declare that in cases not included in the

Regulations adopted by them, the populations and belligerents remain under the protection and empire of the principles of international law, as they result from the usages established between civilised nations, from the laws of humanity and the requirements of the public conscience."

A common Article in each of the 1949 Geneva Conventions draws on the terminology of the Martens Clause, and reaffirms that even if a party denounces the Convention, it will "in no way impair the obligations which the Parties to the conflict shall remain bound to fulfil by virtue of the principles of the law of nations, as they result from the usage established among civilized peoples, from the laws of humanity and the dictates of the public conscience" (see GC I, Art. 63; GC II, Art. 62; GC III, Art. 142; and GC IV, Art. 158).

2–30   It is widely recognised that the most fundamental customary principles, upon which the main humanitarian treaties are founded, are that the right of belligerents to adopt means and methods of destroying the enemy are not without limits, and that the concepts of proportionality and discrimination must provide the yardstick. The principle of proportionality aims to place limitations on the use of force and the means of military action. Discrimination is about the appropriate selection of targets and weaponry. Three customary principles flow from the principles of proportionality and discrimination: (i) the principle of military necessity (only the lawful force required for the submission of the enemy with a minimum expenditure of time, life and resources may be applied); (ii) the principle of humanity (the use of force not required for this purpose is prohibited); and (iii) the principle of chivalry (dishonourable means of conduct during armed conflict are prohibited).

Additional Protocols

2–31   The two main branches of international humanitarian law, the Geneva and the Hague law, were evaluated and brought together by the Diplomatic Conference in Geneva in four yearly sessions from 1974–7, culminating in the adoption of the 1977 *Protocols Additional to the Geneva Conventions*. Protocol I is designed for the protection of victims in international conflict, whereas Protocol II applies to non-international conflicts. The provisions of the Protocols span both the protections to be afforded in the conduct of armed hostilities and to persons captured by the adversary.

(3) Second World War precedents

2–32   The decisions of international judicial bodies have played an important role in the development and interpretation of international humanitarian law, in particular the International Military Tribunals, which sat in Nuremberg and Tokyo following the Second World War. The judgments of these Tribunals established the fundamental principles for holding the perpetrators of international crimes, including those in official positions, criminally responsible for their unlawful acts (see, 1946 *Nuremberg Judgment*; and, International Military Tribunal for the Far East, *Judgment*, 1948).

The majority of post Second World War trials were conducted in national and military courts established by the occupying States. These are reported in two series, the *Trials of War Criminals before the Nürnberg Military Tribunals* (US Government Printing Office, Washington DC, 1950), a compilation of the decisions of cases tried by the US authorities under Control Council No. 10 in occupied territories; and, the *Law Reports of the Trials of War Criminals* (UN War Crimes Commission, His Majesty's Stationery Office, 1949), a compilation of cases from various national jurisdictions which held trials after the Second World War in occupied territories and in their own national courts.

C. International Criminal Law

(1) Definition

The term "international criminal law" refers to a relatively new legal discipline that governs the enforcement of the international humanitarian law and other substantive bodies of criminal law with an international dimension. The discipline, thus, encompasses all international crimes, including war crimes, crimes against humanity, genocide, terrorism, hi-jacking and related offences, drug offences, money laundering, corruption, crimes against the environment, and fraud and tax offences.   **2–33**

Each of these crimes are discussed in detail in chapters that follow: "War Crimes"—Chapter 11; "Crimes against Humanity"—Chapter 12; "Genocide"—Chapter 13; and, "Other crimes under international criminal law"—Chapter 15.

(2) Vertical and horizontal enforcement

The enforcement of international criminal law consists of a vertical and a horizontal dimension. The horizontal component derives from the different forms of international co-operation between States in criminal matters. The primary means being various extradition and mutual assistance treaties and arrangements that exist between States to assist each other in the application of their domestic criminal laws.   **2–34**

International criminal courts represent the vertical component of international criminal law in that they embody a supranational approach and procedure to the prosecution of certain international crimes, namely war crimes, crimes against humanity and genocide. No international criminal courts as yet have jurisdiction in respect of other crimes under international criminal law, such as terrorism or drug offences. Even though States may have signed up to international treaties in respect of these offences, the agreements have been limited to arrangements of mutual co-operation in the implementation of their national laws.

III. AD HOC INTERNATIONAL CRIMINAL TRIBUNALS

A. ESTABLISHMENT BY SECURITY COUNCIL

2–35   The ad hoc International Criminal Tribunals for the former Yugoslavia and Rwanda were established under Chapter VII of the United Nations' Charter by the Security Council as a measure to restore international peace and security.

As the Tribunals were enacted by the Security Council under Chapter VII of the UN Charter, all member States are obliged "to accept and carry out the decisions of the Security Council" (Article 25). Also see, Articles 24, 41, 48, and 49 of the UN Charter. Accordingly, Articles 29 and 28 of the ICTY and ICTR Statutes, respectively, require States to "co-operate with the International Tribunal in the investigation and prosecution" of serious violations, and to "comply without undue delay with any request for assistance or an order issued by a Trial Chamber". Moreover, Article 103 of the UN Charter provides: "In the event of a conflict between the obligations of the Members of the United Nations under the present Charter and their obligations under any other international agreement, their obligations under the present Charter shall prevail".

The Appeals Chamber of the Tribunals has confirmed that the Tribunals were established lawfully under the UN charter: see, *Prosecutor v. Tadić*, Decision on the Defence Motion for Interlocutory Appeal on Jurisdiction, October 2, 1995, paras 9–48; *Prosecutor v. Kanyabashi*, Decision on the Defence Motion on Jurisdiction, June 18, 1997. For the powers of the Tribunals see Chapter 4, "Powers of the Courts".

B. JURISDICTION

(1) ICTY Statute, Arts 1, 2, 3, 4, 5, 6, 8, 9, 10

Competence of the International Tribunal

2–36   **1.** The International Tribunal shall have the power to prosecute persons responsible for serious violations of international humanitarian law committed in the territory of the former Yugoslavia since 1991 in accordance with the provisions of the present Statute.

Grave breaches of the Geneva Conventions of 1949

2–37   **2.** The International Tribunal shall have the power to prosecute persons committing or ordering to be committed grave breaches of the Geneva Conventions of August 12, 1949, namely the following acts against persons or property protected under the provisions of the relevant Geneva Convention:

    (a) wilful killing;
    (b) torture or inhuman treatment, including biological experiments;
    (c) wilfully causing great suffering or serious injury to body or health;
    (d) extensive destruction and appropriation of property, not justified by military necessity and carried out unlawfully and wantonly;

(e) compelling a prisoner of war or a civilian to serve in the forces of a hostile power;
(f) wilfully depriving a prisoner of war or a civilian of the rights of fair and regular trial;
(g) unlawful deportation or transfer or unlawful confinement of a civilian;
(h) taking civilians as hostages.

Violations of the laws or customs of war

3. The International Tribunal shall have the power to prosecute persons violating the laws or customs of war. Such violations shall include, but not be limited to:

2–38

(a) employment of poisonous weapons or other weapons calculated to cause unnecessary suffering;
(b) wanton destruction of cities, towns or villages, or devastation not justified by military necessity;
(c) attack, or bombardment, by whatever means, of undefended towns, villages, dwellings, or buildings;
(d) seizure of, destruction or wilful damage done to institutions dedicated to religion, charity and education, the arts and sciences, historic monuments and works of art and science;
(e) plunder of public or private property.

Genocide

4.—1. The International Tribunal shall have the power to prosecute persons committing genocide as defined in paragraph 2 of this article or of committing any of the other acts enumerated in paragraph 3 of this article.

2–39

2. Genocide means any of the following acts committed with intent to destroy, in whole or in part, a national, ethnical, racial or religious group, as such:
(a) killing members of the group;
(b) causing serious bodily or mental harm to members of the group;
(c) deliberately inflicting on the group conditions of life calculated to bring about its physical destruction in whole or in part;
(d) imposing measures intended to prevent births within the group;
(e) forcibly transferring children of the group to another group.
3. The following acts shall be punishable:
(a) genocide;
(b) conspiracy to commit genocide;
(c) direct and public incitement to commit genocide;
(d) attempt to commit genocide;
(e) complicity in genocide.

Crimes against humanity

5. The International Tribunal shall have the power to prosecute persons responsible for the following crimes when committed in armed conflict, whether international or internal in character, and directed against any civilian population:

2–40

(a) murder;
(b) extermination;
(c) enslavement;
(d) deportation;
(e) imprisonment;
(f) torture;
(g) rape;
(h) persecutions on political, racial and religious grounds;
(i) other inhumane acts.

Personal jurisdiction

2–41   **6.** The International Tribunal shall have jurisdiction over natural persons pursuant to the provisions of the present Statute.

Territorial and temporal jurisdiction

2–42   **8.** The territorial jurisdiction of the International Tribunal shall extend to the territory of the former Socialist Federal Republic of Yugoslavia, including its land surface, airspace and territorial waters. The temporal jurisdiction of the International Tribunal shall extend to a period beginning on January 1, 1991.

Concurrent jurisdiction

2–43   **9.—1.** The International Tribunal and national courts shall have concurrent jurisdiction to prosecute persons for serious violations of international humanitarian law committed in the territory of the former Yugoslavia since January 1, 1991.

2. The International Tribunal shall have primacy over national courts. At any stage of the procedure, the International Tribunal may formally request national courts to defer to the competence of the International Tribunal in accordance with the present Statute and the Rules of Procedure and Evidence of the International Tribunal.

Non-bis-in-idem

2–44   **10.—1.** No person shall be tried before a national court for acts constituting serious violations of international humanitarian law under the present Statute, for which he or she has already been tried by the International Tribunal.

2. A person who has been tried by a national court for acts constituting serious violations of international humanitarian law may be subsequently tried by the International Tribunal only if:

(a) the act for which he or she was tried was characterized as an ordinary crime; or

(b) the national court proceedings were not impartial or independent, were designed to shield the accused from international criminal responsibility, or the case was not diligently prosecuted.

3. In considering the penalty to be imposed on a person convicted of a crime under the present Statute, the International Tribunal shall take into account the extent to which any penalty imposed by a national court on the same person for the same act has already been served.

(2) ICTR Statute, Arts 1, 2, 3, 4, 5, 7, 8, 9

Competence of the International Tribunal for Rwanda

2–45   **1.** The International Tribunal for Rwanda shall have the power to prosecute persons responsible for serious violations of international humanitarian law committed in the territory of Rwanda and Rwandan citizens responsible for such violations committed in the territory of neighbouring States between January 1, 1994 and December 31, 1994, in accordance with the provisions of the present Statute.

Genocide

2–46   **2.—1.** The International Tribunal for Rwanda shall have the power to prosecute persons committing genocide as defined in paragraph 2 of this article or of committing any of the other acts enumerated in paragraph 3 of this article.

2. Genocide means any of the following acts committed with intent to destroy, in whole or in part, a national, ethnical, racial or religious group, as such:

    (a) Killing members of the group;
    (b) Causing serious bodily or mental harm to members of the group;
    (c) Deliberately inflicting on the group conditions of life calculated to bring about its physical destruction in whole or in part;
    (d) Imposing measures intended to prevent births within the group;
    (e) Forcibly transferring children of the group to another group.

3. The following acts shall be punishable:

    (a) Genocide;
    (b) Conspiracy to commit genocide;
    (c) Direct and public incitement to commit genocide;
    (d) Attempt to commit genocide;
    (e) Complicity in genocide.

Crimes against Humanity

3. The International Tribunal for Rwanda shall have the power to prosecute persons responsible for the following crimes when committed as part of a widespread or systematic attack against any civilian population on national, political, ethnic, racial or religious grounds: **2–47**

    (a) Murder;
    (b) Extermination;
    (c) Enslavement;
    (d) Deportation;
    (e) Imprisonment;
    (f) Torture;
    (g) Rape;
    (h) Persecutions on political, racial and religious grounds;
    (i) Other inhumane acts.

Violations of Article 3 common to the Geneva Conventions and of Additional Protocol II

4. The International Tribunal for Rwanda shall have the power to prosecute persons committing or ordering to be committed serious violations of Article 3 common to the Geneva Conventions of August 12, 1949 for the Protection of War Victims, and of Additional Protocol II thereto of June 8, 1977. These violations shall include, but shall not be limited to: **2–48**

    (a) Violence to life, health and physical or mental well-being of persons, in particular murder as well as cruel treatment such as torture, mutilation or any form of corporal punishment;
    (b) Collective punishments;
    (c) Taking of hostages;
    (d) Acts of terrorism;
    (e) Outrages upon personal dignity, in particular humiliating and degrading treatment, rape, enforced prostitution and any form of indecent assault;
    (f) Pillage;
    (g) The passing of sentences and the carrying out of executions without previous judgment pronounced by a regularly constituted court, affording all the judicial guarantees which are recognised as indispensable by civilised peoples;
    (h) Threats to commit any of the foregoing acts.

Personal jurisdiction

2–49   **5.** The International Tribunal for Rwanda shall have jurisdiction over natural persons pursuant to the provisions of the present Statute.

Territorial and temporal jurisdiction

2–50   **7.** The territorial jurisdiction of the International Tribunal for Rwanda shall extend to the territory of Rwanda including its land surface and airspace as well as to the territory of neighbouring States in respect of serious violations of international humanitarian law committed by Rwandan citizens. The temporal jurisdiction of the International Tribunal for Rwanda shall extend to a period beginning on January 1, 1994 and ending on December 31, 1994.

Concurrent jurisdiction

2–51   **8.**—1. The International Tribunal for Rwanda and national courts shall have concurrent jurisdiction to prosecute persons for serious violations of international humanitarian law committed in the territory of Rwanda and Rwandan citizens for such violations committed in the territory of the neighbouring States, between January 1, 1994 and December 31, 1994.

2. The International Tribunal for Rwanda shall have the primacy over the national courts of all States. At any stage of the procedure, the International Tribunal for Rwanda may formally request national courts to defer to its competence in accordance with the present Statute and the Rules of Procedure and Evidence of the International Tribunal for Rwanda.

Non bis in idem

2–52   **9.**—1. No person shall be tried before a national court for acts constituting serious violations of international humanitarian law under the present Statute, for which he or she has already been tried by the International Tribunal for Rwanda.

2. A person who has been tried before a national court for acts constituting serious violations of international humanitarian law may be subsequently tried by the International Tribunal for Rwanda only if:

    (a) The act for which he or she was tried was characterised as an ordinary crime; or

    (b) The national court proceedings were not impartial or independent, were designed to shield the accused from international criminal responsibility, or the case was not diligently prosecuted.

3. In considering the penalty to be imposed on a person convicted of a crime under the present Statute, the International Tribunal for Rwanda shall take into account the extent to which any penalty imposed by a national court on the same person for the same act has already been served.

(3) Defining features of offences

2–53   The experience of the ICTY and ICTR has been that the proper investigation and prosecution of international crimes requires an appreciation of the distinct legal characteristics of these crimes. They are not typical national crimes. Instead, they include, in the context of intensive armed conflicts, the mass killing, torture, rape, and inhumane treatment of hundreds and thousands of civilians, and the widespread destruction of dwellings and property. The factual allegations are usually that entire cities and towns have been devastated, their populations murdered, imprisoned, or forcibly removed. The sheer scale and severity of these factual circumstances are never encountered in national prosecutions. The aim before international criminal courts is not to try 10,000 murder cases, but to conduct crimes against humanity and war crimes' trials.

It is the international components of the crimes under the Tribunals' jurisdiction that are the defining features of its unique mandate, but which also present the most legal and factual difficulties. Thus, although the familiar domestic elements of offences, like the *mens rea*, *actus reus*, and causation, are clearly relevant, they assume a new character in an international setting, while separate international elements are also frequently relevant.

For all the offences, except genocide, it is necessary to prove that an **2–54** armed conflict existed, and establish a relationship between the offence and the conflict. For the grave breach provisions of Article 2 of the ICTY Statute to be applicable, the conflict must be of an international nature. See, *The Prosecutor v. Tadić*, Decision on the Defence Motion for Interlocutory Appeal on Jurisdiction, October 2, 1995, paras 79–84. The issue of characterising conflicts has been before other international courts and bodies, including the International Court of Justice in the *Nicaragua* case (1986, I.C.J. Reports, 14). Although these cases are not binding on the Tribunals, they may be taken into account together with other relevant authorities on the classification question (see, Decision on the Defence Motion for Interlocutory Appeal on Jurisdiction, October 2, 1995, pp. 44–48).

On the other hand, the conflict has to be internal to render certain provisions of Article 4 of the ICTR Statute applicable. In terms of the Appeals Chamber's decision, the provisions of common Article 3 of the Geneva Conventions apply during all conflicts, irrespective of whether the conflict is international or internal. Additional Protocol II, however, only applies during internal armed conflicts.

There is a distinction between offences relating to the conduct of **2–55** hostilities, which are prohibited by the 1907 Hague Conventions, the 1977 Additional Protocols, and international customary rules (in other words, the body of international humanitarian law that regulates the means and methods of warfare used by the parties to conduct armed conflicts, which outlaws, for example, military attacks on civilians and civilian objects), and the offences committed against persons captured by their adversary, which can be charged both under the grave breach provisions, common Article 3, and other provisions of the Geneva Conventions, and as crimes against humanity if they occur on a widespread or systematic scale. The elements of these separate offences are very different, and thus generate divergent evidentiary priorities. In particular, the complexities of charging for illegal conduct in the course of waging armed hostilities, and specifically balancing military necessity with the object of protecting civilians from the excesses of armed conflicts, require special evidentiary considerations.

The mass component of crimes against humanity, namely, the **2–56** widespread or systematic elements, and their relation to the perpetrator's alleged acts, are unique to international law. The ways in which a massive attack on a civilian population can be proven to be systematic differ vastly from proving individual or isolated incidents. Similarly, the offence of genocide has distinct elements. In particular, genocide has a heightened form of intention—the specific intent to destroy a national, racial, ethnic, or religious group in whole or in part.

(See, Chapters 11, 12 and 13 on "War Crimes", "Crimes against Humanity", and "Genocide", respectively, for the jurisdictional requirements and elements of these offences.)

(4) Primacy of Tribunals

2–57   Articles 9 and 8 of the ICTY and ICTR Statutes respectively permit the Tribunals to have cases and investigations before national courts deferred to the Tribunals. As a result of recent rule changes the Tribunal may now refer cases indicted by the Tribunals back to national courts irrespective of whether the accused is in the custody of the Tribunals. (See Rule 11*bis* of each of the ICTY and ICTR Rules, and the Security Council Presidential Statement of July 23, 2002, included at Appendix C5.)

C. INDIVIDUAL CRIMINAL RESPONSIBILITY

(1) ICTY Statute, Art. 7

Individual criminal responsibility

2–58   **7.**—1. A person who planned, instigated, ordered, committed or otherwise aided and abetted in the planning, preparation or execution of a crime referred to in articles 2 to 5 of the present Statute, shall be individually responsible for the crime.

2. The official position of any accused person, whether as Head of State or Government or as a responsible Government official, shall not relieve such person of criminal responsibility nor mitigate punishment.

3. The fact that any of the acts referred to in articles 2 to 5 of the present Statute was committed by a subordinate does not relieve his superior of criminal responsibility if he knew or had reason to know that the subordinate was about to commit such acts or had done so and the superior failed to take the necessary and reasonable measures to prevent such acts or to punish the perpetrators thereof.

4. The fact that an accused person acted pursuant to an order of a Government or of a superior shall not relieve him of criminal responsibility, but may be considered in mitigation of punishment if the International Tribunal determines that justice so requires.

The ICTR Statute contains the same provisions on individual criminal responsibility in Article 6.

For the application of the provisions on individual criminal responsibility see Chapter 10.

(2) General Considerations

2–59   When the Statutes for the ICTY and ICTR were adopted it was beyond doubt that those who plan, order, or commit serious violations of international humanitarian law, or who otherwise participate in the

28

commission of such offences, may be held individually responsible for such violations.

The principle of holding perpetrators individually liable is rooted in the Judgment of the Trial of the Major War Criminals sitting at Nuremberg, which found that individual criminal responsibility has "long been recognised [. . .] individuals can be punished for violations of International Law. Crimes against International Law are committed by men not abstract entities, and only by punishing individuals who commit such crimes can be the provisions of International Law be enforced" (Proceedings of the International Military Tribunal sitting at Nuremberg, Germany, H.M. Attorney General by H.M.'s Stationery Office, London, 1950, Part 22, 447).

Individual criminal responsibility under the ICTY and ICTR Statutes **2–60** extends to serving heads of State, government officials and persons acting in an official capacity. There is no head of State immunity or defence for acting in an official capacity, nor can it be relied upon to mitigate punishment. These provisions also draw upon the precedents following the Second World War. This position was confirmed in *Prosecutor v. Milošević*, Decision on Preliminary Motions, November 8, 2001, paras 26–34.

Acting upon an order of a State or Government cannot relieve the perpetrator of the offence of criminal liability. Obedience to superior orders may be considered to be a mitigating factor in sentence.

The doctrine of superior responsibility was incorporated into the Statutes of the ICTY and ICTR. No preceding international criminal court had included this form of individual criminal responsibility. The provision is unique in that it does not create strict liability for superiors, whether military or political, who fail to prevent or punish their subordinates from committing serious violations, but does permit a superior to be held criminally liable for the same underlying offence committed by his or her subordinate, in certain circumstances.

Articles 6(3) and 7(3) require that the superior "knew or had reason to know" that the subordinate was about to commit the offence or had done so, and that the superior failed to take the "necessary and reasonable measures" to prevent the offence or punish the perpetrator, in order that the superior be held responsible for the commission of the offence. (See, Chapter 10 on "Forms of Participation in Offences".)

IV. ICC

A. ICC STATUTE

(1) Jurisdiction

Statute of the International Criminal Court, Arts 1, 5, 11, 12, 13, 14, 16, 17, 18, 19, 20

The Court

1. An International Criminal Court ("the Court") is hereby established. It **2–61** shall be a permanent institution and shall have the power to exercise its jurisdiction over persons for the most serious crimes of international concern, as referred to in this Statute, and shall be complementary to national criminal jurisdictions. The jurisdiction and functioning of the Court shall be governed by the provisions of this Statute.

Crimes within the jurisdiction of the Court

2–62   5.—1. The jurisdiction of the Court shall be limited to the most serious crimes of concern to the international community as a whole. The Court has jurisdiction in accordance with this Statute with respect to the following crimes:

    (a) The crime of genocide;
    (b) Crimes against humanity;
    (c) War crimes;
    (d) The crime of aggression.

2. The Court shall exercise jurisdiction over the crime of aggression once a provision is adopted in accordance with articles 121 and 123 defining the crime and setting out the conditions under which the Court shall exercise jurisdiction with respect to this crime. Such a provision shall be consistent with the relevant provisions of the Charter of the United Nations.

Jurisdiction ratione temporis

2–63   11.—1. The Court has jurisdiction only with respect to crimes committed after the entry into force of this Statute.

2. If a State becomes a Party to this Statute after its entry into force, the Court may exercise its jurisdiction only with respect to crimes committed after the entry into force of this Statute for that State, unless that State has made a declaration under article 12, paragraph 3.

Preconditions to the exercise of jurisdiction

2–64   12.—1. A State which becomes a Party to this Statute thereby accepts the jurisdiction of the Court with respect to the crimes referred to in article 5.

2. In the case of article 13, paragraph (a) or (c), the Court may exercise its jurisdiction if one or more of the following States are Parties to this Statute or have accepted the jurisdiction of the Court in accordance with paragraph 3:

    (a) The State on the territory of which the conduct in question occurred or, if the crime was committed on board a vessel or aircraft, the State of registration of that vessel or aircraft;
    (b) The State of which the person accused of the crime is a national.

3. If the acceptance of a State which is not a Party to this Statute is required under paragraph 2, that State may, by declaration lodged with the Registrar, accept the exercise of jurisdiction by the Court with respect to the crime in question. The accepting State shall co-operate with the Court without any delay or exception in accordance with Part 9.

Exercise of jurisdiction

2–65   13. The Court may exercise its jurisdiction with respect to a crime referred to in article 5 in accordance with the provisions of this Statute if:

    (a) A situation in which one or more of such crimes appears to have been committed is referred to the Prosecutor by a State Party in accordance with article 14;
    (b) A situation in which one or more of such crimes appears to have been committed is referred to the Prosecutor by the Security Council acting under Chapter VII of the Charter of the United Nations; or
    (c) The Prosecutor has initiated an investigation in respect of such a crime in accordance with article 15.

Referral of a situation by a State Party

14.—1. A State Party may refer to the Prosecutor a situation in which one or **2–66**
more crimes within the jurisdiction of the Court appear to have been
committed requesting the Prosecutor to investigate the situation for the
purpose of determining whether one or more specific persons should be
charged with the commission of such crimes.

2. As far as possible, a referral shall specify the relevant circumstances and
be accompanied by such supporting documentation as is available to the State
referring the situation.

Deferral of investigation or prosecution

16. No investigation or prosecution may be commenced or proceeded with **2–67**
under this Statute for a period of 12 months after the Security Council, in a
resolution adopted under Chapter VII of the Charter of the United Nations,
has requested the Court to that effect; that request may be renewed by the
Council under the same conditions.

Issues of admissibility

17.—1. Having regard to paragraph 10 of the Preamble and article 1, the **2–68**
Court shall determine that a case is inadmissible where:
   (a) The case is being investigated or prosecuted by a State which has
      jurisdiction over it, unless the State is unwilling or unable genuinely
      to carry out the investigation or prosecution;
   (b) The case has been investigated by a State which has jurisdiction over
      it and the State has decided not to prosecute the person concerned,
      unless the decision resulted from the unwillingness or inability of the
      State genuinely to prosecute;
   (c) The person concerned has already been tried for conduct which is the
      subject of the complaint, and a trial by the Court is not permitted
      under article 20, paragraph 3;
   (d) The case is not of sufficient gravity to justify further action by the
      Court.

2. In order to determine unwillingness in a particular case, the Court shall
consider, having regard to the principles of due process recognised by international law, whether one or more of the following exist, as applicable:
   (a) The proceedings were or are being undertaken or the national
      decision was made for the purpose of shielding the person concerned
      from criminal responsibility for crimes within the jurisdiction of the
      Court referred to in article 5;
   (b) There has been an unjustified delay in the proceedings which in the
      circumstances is inconsistent with an intent to bring the person
      concerned to justice;
   (c) The proceedings were not or are not being conducted independently
      or impartially, and they were or are being conducted in a manner
      which, in the circumstances, is inconsistent with an intent to bring the
      person concerned to justice.

3. In order to determine inability in a particular case, the Court shall
consider whether, due to a total or substantial collapse or unavailability of its
national judicial system, the State is unable to obtain the accused or the
necessary evidence and testimony or otherwise unable to carry out its
proceedings.

Preliminary rulings regarding admissibility

18.—1. When a situation has been referred to the Court pursuant to article **2–69**
13 (a) and the Prosecutor has determined that there would be a reasonable
basis to commence an investigation, or the Prosecutor initiates an investigation

31

pursuant to articles 13 (c) and 15, the Prosecutor shall notify all States Parties and those States which, taking into account the information available, would normally exercise jurisdiction over the crimes concerned. The Prosecutor may notify such States on a confidential basis and, where the Prosecutor believes it necessary to protect persons, prevent destruction of evidence or prevent the absconding of persons, may limit the scope of the information provided to States.

2. Within one month of receipt of that notification, a State may inform the Court that it is investigating or has investigated its nationals or others within its jurisdiction with respect to criminal acts which may constitute crimes referred to in article 5 and which relate to the information provided in the notification to States. At the request of that State, the Prosecutor shall defer to the State's investigation of those persons unless the Pre-Trial Chamber, on the application of the Prosecutor, decides to authorize the investigation.

3. The Prosecutor's deferral to a State's investigation shall be open to review by the Prosecutor six months after the date of deferral or at any time when there has been a significant change of circumstances based on the State's unwillingness or inability genuinely to carry out the investigation.

4. The State concerned or the Prosecutor may appeal to the Appeals Chamber against a ruling of the Pre-Trial Chamber, in accordance with article 82. The appeal may be heard on an expedited basis.

5. When the Prosecutor has deferred an investigation in accordance with paragraph 2, the Prosecutor may request that the State concerned periodically inform the Prosecutor of the progress of its investigations and any subsequent prosecutions. States Parties shall respond to such requests without undue delay.

6. Pending a ruling by the Pre-Trial Chamber, or at any time when the Prosecutor has deferred an investigation under this article, the Prosecutor may, on an exceptional basis, seek authority from the Pre-Trial Chamber to pursue necessary investigative steps for the purpose of preserving evidence where there is a unique opportunity to obtain important evidence or there is a significant risk that such evidence may not be subsequently available.

7. A State which has challenged a ruling of the Pre-Trial Chamber under this article may challenge the admissibility of a case under article 19 on the grounds of additional significant facts or significant change of circumstances.

Challenges to the jurisdiction of the Court or the admissibility of a case

2–70   **19.**—1. The Court shall satisfy itself that it has jurisdiction in any case brought before it. The Court may, on its own motion, determine the admissibility of a case in accordance with article 17.

2. Challenges to the admissibility of a case on the grounds referred to in article 17 or challenges to the jurisdiction of the Court may be made by:

> (a) An accused or a person for whom a warrant of arrest or a summons to appear has been issued under article 58;
>
> (b) A State which has jurisdiction over a case, on the ground that it is investigating or prosecuting the case or has investigated or prosecuted; or
>
> (c) A State from which acceptance of jurisdiction is required under article 12.

3. The Prosecutor may seek a ruling from the Court regarding a question of jurisdiction or admissibility. In proceedings with respect to jurisdiction or admissibility, those who have referred the situation under article 13, as well as victims, may also submit observations to the Court.

4. The admissibility of a case or the jurisdiction of the Court may be challenged only once by any person or State referred to in paragraph 2. The challenge shall take place prior to or at the commencement of the trial. In exceptional circumstances, the Court may grant leave for a challenge to be

brought more than once or at a time later than the commencement of the trial. Challenges to the admissibility of a case, at the commencement of a trial, or subsequently with the leave of the Court, may be based only on article 17, paragraph 1 (c).

5. A State referred to in paragraph 2 (b) and (c) shall make a challenge at the earliest opportunity.

6. Prior to the confirmation of the charges, challenges to the admissibility of a case or challenges to the jurisdiction of the Court shall be referred to the Pre-Trial Chamber. After confirmation of the charges, they shall be referred to the Trial Chamber. Decisions with respect to jurisdiction or admissibility may be appealed to the Appeals Chamber in accordance with article 82.

7. If a challenge is made by a State referred to in paragraph 2 (b) or (c), the Prosecutor shall suspend the investigation until such time as the Court makes a determination in accordance with article 17.

8. Pending a ruling by the Court, the Prosecutor may seek authority from the Court:
   (a) To pursue necessary investigative steps of the kind referred to in article 18, paragraph 6;
   (b) To take a statement or testimony from a witness or complete the collection and examination of evidence which had begun prior to the making of the challenge; and
   (c) In co-operation with the relevant States, to prevent the absconding of persons in respect of whom the Prosecutor has already requested a warrant of arrest under article 58.

9. The making of a challenge shall not affect the validity of any act performed by the Prosecutor or any order or warrant issued by the Court prior to the making of the challenge.

10. If the Court has decided that a case is inadmissible under article 17, the Prosecutor may submit a request for a review of the decision when he or she is fully satisfied that new facts have arisen which negate the basis on which the case had previously been found inadmissible under article 17.

11. If the Prosecutor, having regard to the matters referred to in article 17, defers an investigation, the Prosecutor may request that the relevant State make available to the Prosecutor information on the proceedings. That information shall, at the request of the State concerned, be confidential. If the Prosecutor thereafter decides to proceed with an investigation, he or she shall notify the State to which deferral of the proceedings has taken place.

Ne bis in idem

20.—1. Except as provided in this Statute, no person shall be tried before the Court with respect to conduct which formed the basis of crimes for which the person has been convicted or acquitted by the Court.   **2–71**

2. No person shall be tried by another court for a crime referred to in article 5 for which that person has already been convicted or acquitted by the Court.

3. No person who has been tried by another court for conduct also proscribed under article 6, 7 or 8 shall be tried by the Court with respect to the same conduct unless the proceedings in the other court:
   (a) Were for the purpose of shielding the person concerned from criminal responsibility for crimes within the jurisdiction of the Court; or
   (b) Otherwise were not conducted independently or impartially in accordance with the norms of due process recognized by international law and were conducted in a manner which, in the circumstances, was inconsistent with an intent to bring the person concerned to justice.

(2) Relationship with States

The regime of cooperation between the ICC and States is different from the ICTY and ICTR as the ICC is not imbued with coercive powers (except, arguably, if the ICC receives a referral by the Security   **2–72**

Council under Chapter VII, although no specific provision is made to this effect in the ICC Statute). Article 86 reads as follows: "States Parties shall, in accordance with the provisions of this Statute, cooperate fully with the Court in its investigation and prosecution of crimes within the jurisdiction of the Court", and Article 87(1)(a) provides: "The Court shall have the authority to make requests to States Parties for cooperation. The requests shall be transmitted through the diplomatic channel or any other appropriate channel as may be designated by each State Party upon ratification, acceptance, approval or accession." Article 87(5) states: "The Court may invite any State not party to this Statute to provide assistance under this Part on the basis of an ad hoc arrangement, an agreement with such State or any other appropriate basis."

The remedy for non-compliance is set out in Article 87(7):

"Where a State Party fails to comply with a request to co-operate by the Court contrary to the provisions of this Statute, thereby preventing the Court from exercising its functions and powers under this Statute, the Court may make a finding to that effect and refer the matter to the Assembly of States Parties or, where the Security Council referred the matter to the Court, to the Security Council."

2–73   Article 72 of the ICC Statute provides a State with a right to intervene where it considers that its national security interests will be prejudiced, and establishes a detailed procedure that operates in the event of such intervention. Article 72 imposes the obligation on the State to take all reasonable steps to cooperate with the Court, and suggests measures the Court may take to avoid a confrontation between the Court and the State on this sensitive question. Where no such cooperative resolution can be achieved, Article 72 establishes a two-pronged procedure: where the Court has the information within its control or can obtain it other than by a request for cooperation, the Court may order disclosure, but if the information lies within the exclusive control of the State claiming a national security exception, the Court cannot order a State to hand over the information. (See Chapter 4 on "Powers of the Courts" for a detailed examination of the disclosure of national security information.)

On the other hand, the position before the ICTY and ICTR is as set out in the Appeals Chambers in *Prosecutor v. Blaškić*, Judgment on the Request of the Republic of Croatia for Review of the Decision of Trial Chamber II of July 18, 1997, October 29, 1997. It held that States can be ordered by the Tribunals to produce information or evidence in their possession, and that they are obliged to fulfil such orders, failing which they may be reported to the Security Council by the Tribunal. The Chamber concerned is thus empowered to make a determination as to whether the State is in compliance or not. The Chamber may also decide to adjudicate whether any State information is subject to exclusion due to national security interests. Such interests if asserted by a State cannot automatically exclude that information. The information requested must refer to specific categories of documentation. The Appeals Chamber also held that State officials cannot be directly ordered to provide information or evidence. The Tribunals are required to direct their orders in this respect to the State concerned. Private individuals and State officials acting in their private capacity may be ordered in person to appear before the Tribunals and hand over documents, failing which they may be held in contempt, and fined or imprisoned. (See Chapter 4 on "Powers of the Courts".)

(3) The ICC Regulations

Introduction

The ICC's Regulations have been created in a particular context.   **2–74**
Unlike the ad hoc tribunals, the court was not created as a reaction to a particular set of dire events that called for a rapid and effective judicial response. To the contrary, given the court only has jurisdiction over offences committed since July 2002 and any alleged atrocities perpetrated after that date are likely to take some time to be translated into arrests, charges and prosecutions, the court has been extended the unparalleled advantage of being able to reflect on the experience of other courts and tribunals, and generally to take time over the formulation of the Regulations of the Court, which are likely to be a key element in determining the shape and nature of the cases it will determine.

Indeed, it would be difficult to overstate the debt that the ICC owes to the ad hoc tribunals in this regard; although only time will reveal if the Regulations have succeeded in helping to provide an effective response to the vicissitudes occasioned by cases of this kind—not least their complexity, the dangers they pose to victims and witnesses and, on occasion, their length—the court has been provided with a unique opportunity to put in place the mechanisms by which fair, effective and speedy trials can take place. The ICC has drawn heavily on the experience of the ICTY and the ICTR in particular, and has sought to avoid at least some of the problems with which those tribunals have had to contend.

The Regulations are, in the main, currently untried and untested; accordingly, this Chapter can do no more than highlight what at present appear to be some key and interesting features. One objective running through them is revealed in the steps that have been taken to resolve the enduring, though perhaps sometimes overstated tension that exists between the adversarial and inquisitorial systems. Although no generalisation will (at this stage) adequately encapsulate either the spirit that lies behind the Regulations or the likely application of them in practice, what appears clear is that whilst the parties will be left with responsibility for presenting their respective cases, solid foundations have been laid down that will enable the court to take strong, proactive case-management decisions to ensure that trials are dealt with as speedily as justice will allow.

The Regulations are included in the appendices for the ICC. A brief commentary on key selected regulations follows.

Regulation 12

This Regulation is an attempt to ameliorate the apparently uncom-   **2–75**
promising terms of both Article 39 (1) which states that the Appeals Division "shall be composed of the President and four other judges",

and Article 39 (4) which provides that "Judges assigned to the Appeals Division shall serve only in that division". What happens in the event of illness or the disqualification of one of the Appeal Division Judges? Given the apparent absence of a means of seconding a temporary judge to this Division in such circumstances, the Regulations have provided a solution. This problem does not exist for either the Trial or the Pre-Trial Divisions because Article 39 (4) provides explicitly for the temporary transfer of judges between those Divisions. The operation of this provision is likely to lead to challenge on the basis that the Regulations cannot "legislate" in this manner and that, laudable though the motive may be, the solution lies in an amendment of the Statute.

Regulation 26

2–76   The expectation is that this will be, in the main, a "paperless" court. A substantial amount of time (and not inconsiderable sums of money) have been expended in ensuring that the systems are in place for all documents to be filed and dealt with by the court electronically. Whilst allowance will be made for those who do not have access to computers, the parties will be expected to deal with every stage of the court process via the court's electronic system.

Regulation 28

2–77   This is the first of a number of Regulations that spell out the likely approach of the court to case-management. Although this Regulation is almost undoubtedly no more than a statement of the court's inherent powers, it sends out a clear indication to the parties that the court will be seeking, where necessary, both clarification of the issues in play at each stage of the judicial process and full particularity of those issues.

Regulation 30

2–78   Status conferences are likely to comprise a key tool in the deployment of the court's interventionist approach. Not only will these conferences occur during both the pre-trial and trial stage of proceedings, but they can be held, within the court's discretion, in a variety of different ways: conventional court hearings, via audio or video link or by way of written submissions. Given the international nature of these cases, it is to be hoped that substantial time and costs can be saved by modern methods of communication—audio and video digital technology is now so impressive that they often provide a more than satisfactory replacement for face-to-face hearings in many instances.

Regulation 43

2–79   This regulation makes it clear that although the parties retain responsibility for the presentation of their respective cases, the court is likely to exercise a tight degree of control over both the evidence to be introduced and the method of its introduction, so as to avoid delays, repetition, and irrelevant material.

Regulation 44

It is to be observed with this provision that the court will not only keep a list of (approved) experts, but perhaps more significantly it can order the parties to instruct one or more joint experts. Furthermore, the court can instruct an expert of its own volition. This provision, properly utilised, could lead to a reduction in trial costs and it should provide the court with a means of narrowing down the true issues that need to be raised during a trial.

2–80

Regulation 48

Particularly in the early stages of the court's work, this may prove to be a contentious regulation, depending on the extent to which the Pre-Trial Division adopts a proactive stance and whether the prosecutor perceives court interventions at an early stage of an investigation as unwelcome. In the event, the prosecutor may particularly resist serving detailed documentation at early stages of the proceedings, and the court will need to establish a modus vivendi for the Prosecutor and the Pre-Trial Division, particularly given that although the court has certain clear and important obligations from the earliest stages of a case, nonetheless it is not acting as a true inquisitorial tribunal: the responsibility for the investigation and prosecution of cases rests with the Office of the Prosecutor.

2–81

Regulation 52

The approach and style adopted for charging is likely to be a cardinal issue: the length, detail and scope of the documents containing the charges, together with the ability to amend them, will have an undoubted and profound impact on the likely length of cases. The experience of the ICTY and ICTR has been, in the view of some commentators, not the happiest in the sense that the indictments have sometimes become very substantial documents in their own right, containing so many particulars that the prosecution in seeking to prove them has ended up creating self-imposed obligations that have undoubtedly (and perhaps unnecessarily) prolonged the length of cases. A generous reading of Regulation 55 (the authority of the Chamber to modify the legal characterisation of facts) may render it unnecessary for the prosecution to attempt to cover every possible eventuality when drafting the charges a defendant faces.

2–82

Regulation 54

The ability to make orders of the kind contained in this regulation may in due course prove to be one of the strongest tools available to the court as regards case-management. If utilised properly, the court should

2–83

be able to identify the true issues in a case, along with the evidence strictly relevant to those issues, whilst concurrently closing off subsidiary, peripheral or irrelevant matters. It is likely that attempts will be made—particularly on behalf of defendants—to challenge the court's right to force the parties to reveal in advance the issues that they may wish to raise and the evidence on which they may seek to rely, as well as the court's authority to limit the length and scope of the evidence to be called. The length of trials before the ICC may depend to a signicant extent on how those arguments are resolved.

Regulation 55

2–84   An issue that will undoubtedly arise is the extent to which the Trial Chamber, following the confirmation of charges by the Pre-Trial Chamber (Article 61 (11)—and particularly after the trial has commenced—can modify the charges. Without rehearsing the competing arguments that are likely to arise in this regard, the greater the degree of flexibility the Trial Chamber has as regards amendment or modification of the legal characterisation of facts, the shorter in the first instance it is likely the charges will need to be. If the prosecution realise they do not have to provide for every possible eventuality that may arise during the case (because there is scope for amendment or modification), there will be no need for what may otherwise be perceived as over-charging.

Regulations 67 and 68

2–85   The combined effect of these Regulations is that although "lead" counsel will need to have a minimum experience of 10 years, they may be assisted in the presentation of a case by counsel who merely satisfies the criteria laid down in the Regulations of the Registry. This is to ensure that overall responsibility for a case rests with appropriately qualified counsel, whilst permitting support by those of lesser experience.

Regulation 76

2–86   It will be interesting to see how the court interprets the exact ambit of this Regulation, and whether it entitles the court to "impose" counsel on a defendant who declines to be represented. Much will turn on the meaning in this context of, and the circumstances covered by the words "in the interests of justice". The trial of Slobodan Milošević before the ICTY has demonstrated how difficult an issue this can prove to be.

Regulation 77

2–87   This is a Regulation that may prove to be of significance. Particularly during the early stages of a case an accused may well not have access to local lawyers, and the roster of duty counsel may not provide, at short notice, someone who is suitably qualified to deal with the particular relevant countries or the issues with which the court is concerned. An experienced, court-based lawyer may well provide the best representation in these circumstances. Moreover, many defence counsel selected by defendants may have no knowledge of the laws or the procedures with which they will have to contend. Recourse to public defence counsel may prove to be a very significant benefit, and, moreover, defence counsel may instruct the Office of Public Counsel for the defence to handle defined areas of a case on their behalf. If this system, which is somewhat limited at present, works successfully it may provide the basis for a hybrid defence system which includes a significant public-defender element. Whilst upholding the overall right of an accused to counsel of his choice, this regulation could ensure that each defence team will be able to draw on the substantial body of experience that ought rapidly to be gained by the Office of Public Counsel for the defence.

Regulation 78

Given that defence counsel must obtain the leave of the court before withdrawing from a case, can the court refuse to give leave, and if so, what are the criteria to be applied? The circumstances in which a lawyer may seek to depart from proceedings are endlessly various, and, depending on how it is interpreted, this regulation may not sit particularly comfortably alongside the right of defendants to counsel of their choice. Similar issues exist for Regulation 82 (withdrawal of legal representatives of victims).

2–88

B. PRINCIPLE OF COMPLEMENTARITY

The existing international criminal courts are a precursor to the ICC, yet they show that the ICC will not be the only means of trying international crimes. The increased readiness of the international community to prosecute international crimes has both generated the momentum to launch the ICC, and resulted in a mushrooming of other international courts. Ad hoc International Tribunals, and trials in neutral countries (see, below) are all mechanisms that could be invoked despite the ICC's jurisdiction. The ICC's mandate will not be retrospective (Article 11), and hence any offences committed before its establishment will have to be dealt with by other courts.

2–89

Special courts may also enjoy wide support as they are based on the consent of the State concerned, and are spearheaded by the national system, with an injection of international assistance. An international tribunal is thus not imposed or instituted to replace the domestic system. Such arrangements appear to accord with a fundamental principle underlying the ICC, that of "complementarity" with national courts, which permits the ICC only to have jurisdiction if the State(s) that could exercise jurisdiction is "unwilling or unable genuinely to carry out the investigation or prosecution" (Article 17). In this way, the

ICC aims to serve as a mechanism to encourage national courts to investigate and prosecute international crimes, rather than an institution that erodes the authority of domestic judiciaries.

2–90   Article 17 of the ICC Statute is founded on the principle of "complementarity" as laid down in the Preamble and Article 1, which states that the ICC "shall be complementary to national criminal jurisdictions". Article 17(1) and (2) set out criteria by which "unwillingness" and "inability" may be determined. Arguably, the Security Council acting under Chapter VII of the UN Charter (as it did when the ICTY and the ICTR were established) could refer a matter to the ICC irrespective of the complementarity requirements of the ICC Statute.

The range of courts now functioning shows the adaptability of international justice to differing post conflict circumstances. Some countries have chosen Truth Commissions as a means of addressing the crimes committed during their conflicts. However, it is uncertain whether Truth Commission options, which result in amnesties being granted, would suffice to exclude the ICC's jurisdiction. Much could depend upon the manner in which a commission is established, its guiding principles and practices, and the basis upon which amnesties are approved. Criteria will have to be developed to adjudicate these matters.

2–91   The decision in *Pinochet No. 3* (*R v. Bow Street Metropolitan Stipendiary Magistrate, ex p. Pinochet Ugarte (No. 3)* [2000] 1 A.C. 147 H.L.(E.)) demonstrates that an amnesty against prosecution granted by one country (Chile) does not necessarily bind another (the United Kingdom) in the application of its law.

V. UN SPECIAL COURTS

2–92   Another type of international criminal courts are those created with jurisdiction to try international crimes under United Nations transitional arrangements. To date, such courts have been established in East Timor under the United Nations Transitional Administration for East Timor (UNTAET), and in Sierra Leone by agreement between the UN and the Government of Sierra Leone to create a Special Court to prosecute serious international crimes and crimes under the law of Sierra Leone.

Article 33 of Chapter VI of the UN Charter provides:

"(1) The parties to any dispute, the continuance of which is likely to endanger the maintenance of international peace and security, shall, first of all, seek a solution by negotiation, enquiry, mediation, conciliation, arbitration, judicial settlement, resort to regional agencies or arrangements, or other peaceful means of their own choice.

(2) The Security Council shall, when it deems necessary, call upon the parties to settle their dispute by such means".

Under this Chapter, unlike Chapter VII, the Security Council may only make recommendations to the parties, which they are not obligated to implement (see, Art. 36(1) and Art. 38).

A. EAST TIMOR

In East Timor, the Panels for Serious Criminal Offences were established by regulation under the UN Transitional Administration for East Timor (UNTAET) that assumed authority in East Timor in the wake of the mass violence that engulfed the region in the second half of 1999 (see UNTAET Regulation Nos 1999/1, 2000/11, 2000/15, 2000/16, 2000/25 and 2000/30). The jurisdiction of the Panels for Serious Criminal Offences is limited to the period of the recent conflicts in 1999, namely January 1, 1999–October 25, 1999. The background to these conflicts, which spans the past two decades, is thus excluded from the court's ambit.   **2–93**

The Panels were established within the District Court in Dili with exclusive jurisdiction to deal with serious criminal offences, and called the Special Panels for Serious Crimes. In particular, the Panels were assigned jurisdiction over the international crimes of genocide, crimes against humanity and war crimes committed on the territory of East Timor (see, Sections 1 and 2 of UNTAET Regulation No. 2000/15).

The Panels consist of a mixture of national and international judges, with an internationally appointed prosecutor (known as the General Prosecutor of the United Nations Transitional Administration for East Timor), supported by prosecutors from East Timor and other countries an East Timorese deputy. The Panels are an innovative variation on the ad hoc International Tribunals, which have blended both international and national components. An advantage of the East Timor model is that it ensures a healthy degree of national participation in the administration of justice.

The mandate of this court ended on May 20, 2005 and no further cases will be tried.   **2–94**

B. SIERRA LEONE

The Special Court in Sierra Leone was established following a Security Council Resolution (1315 of August 14, 2000) in which the Secretary-General was requested to negotiate an agreement with the Government of Sierra Leone to create an independent special court. An agreement was concluded to establish the court on January 16, 2002, with the Statute of the Special Court annexed thereto. The agreement was adopted into the law of Sierra Leone by the passing of the *Special Court Agreement Ratification Act* 2002. As the Court was not established under Chapter VII of the UN Charter, the provisions of this Chapter cannot be relied upon as a response to a challenge to the legality of the establishment of the Special Court.   **2–95**

The Special Court has adopted the Rules of Proccedure and Evidence of the ICTR, with any necessary changes to be made by the Judges of the court when they first meet in early 2003. The Prosecutor has been appointed and the first indictments are expected in the first quarter of 2003.

The Court will have jurisdiction over "persons who bear the greatest responsibility" for serious violations of international humanitarian law, crimes against humanity, and crimes under Sierra Leonean law relating to sexual violence against children and malicious damage to property, committed in the territory of Sierra Leone after November 30, 1996 (see, Articles 1–5 of the Statute). In accordance with Article 10 of the Statute, "an amnesty granted to any person falling within the jurisdiction of the Special Court shall not be a bar to prosecution".

The budget of the Court is funded by contributing States (not the UN), numbering 29, who have pledged to provide the necessary financial backing for the Court for a period of three years.

VI. LOCKERBIE PRECEDENT

2–96   The *Lockerbie* case provides an example of another means by which the international community can act to enable crimes of international significance to be prosecuted.

The explosion of PanAm flight 103 on December 21, 1988 over the town of Lockerbie created international attention and concern, and heightened major international political sensitivities. With the United Nations unable to intervene directly in Libya to arrest and try the suspects, the Security Council imposed economic sanctions on Libya. Given the international profile and ramifications of the trial of the Libyan suspects, a compromise had to be reached with the Security Council and between the parties as to the nature and venue of the proceedings.

Even though it was agreed that the case would be tried under Scottish law, the trial took place on neutral territory—Camp Zeist in the Netherlands. The case is reported as *Her Majesty's Advocate v. Abdelbaset Ali Mohmed Al Megrahi and Al Amin Khalifa Fahima*, Camp Zeist, The Netherlands.

A precedent has thereby been set for trying international crimes outside of the domestic setting. When a domestic jurisdiction is not acceptable to the parties, whether for want of appearance of impartiality or for other substantive reasons, the *Lockerbie* case provides a model for trying such cases.

In the trial, the verdict was delivered on January 31, 2001. One accused, Al-Megrahi, was convicted and jailed for life for his part in the bombing. His co-accused, Fahima was found not guilty of the same charges and was released. Al-Megrahi filed his appeal on June 11, 2001. The appeal against conviction, also heard at Camp Zeist, was dismissed with the judges finding in their opinion of March 14, 2002, that none of the grounds of appeal were well-founded. He has been transferred to a prison in Scotland to serve his sentence of life imprisonment.

CHAPTER 3

STRUCTURE OF THE COURTS

I. ICC

A. BASIC STRUCTURE

Statute of the International Criminal Court, Arts 2–4, 35–50, 52

Organs of the Court
34. The Court shall be composed of the following organs: **3–1**
    (a) The Presidency;
    (b) An Appeals Division, a Trial Division and a Pre-Trial Division;
    (c) The Office of the Prosecutor;
    (d) The Registry.

B. STATUTORY PROVISIONS AND RULES

(1) ICC Statute

Statute of the International Criminal Court, Arts 2, 3, 4, 38, 39, 42, 43, 52, 35, 36, 37, 40, 41, 44, 45, 46, 47, 48, 49, 50

Relationship of the Court with the United Nations

3–2   **2.** The Court shall be brought into relationship with the United Nations through an agreement to be approved by the Assembly of States Parties to this Statute and thereafter concluded by the President of the Court on its behalf.

Seat of the Court

3–3   **3.**—1. The seat of the Court shall be established at The Hague in the Netherlands ("the host State").

2. The Court shall enter into a headquarters agreement with the host State, to be approved by the Assembly of States Parties and thereafter concluded by the President of the Court on its behalf.

3. The Court may sit elsewhere, whenever it considers it desirable, as provided in this Statute.

Legal status and powers of the Court

3–4   **4.**—1. The Court shall have international legal personality. It shall also have such legal capacity as may be necessary for the exercise of its functions and the fulfilment of its purposes.

2. The Court may exercise its functions and powers, as provided in this Statute, on the territory of any State Party and, by special agreement, on the territory of any other State.

The Presidency

3–5   **38.**—1. The President and the First and Second Vice-Presidents shall be elected by an absolute majority of the judges. They shall each serve for a term of three years or until the end of their respective terms of office as judges, whichever expires earlier. They shall be eligible for re-election once.

2. The First Vice-President shall act in place of the President in the event that the President is unavailable or disqualified. The Second Vice-President shall act in place of the President in the event that both the President and the First Vice-President are unavailable or disqualified.

3. The President, together with the First and Second Vice-Presidents, shall constitute the Presidency, which shall be responsible for:

    (a) The proper administration of the Court, with the exception of the Office of the Prosecutor; and

    (b) The other functions conferred upon it in accordance with this Statute.

4. In discharging its responsibility under paragraph 3 (a), the Presidency shall coordinate with and seek the concurrence of the Prosecutor on all matters of mutual concern.

Chambers

3–6   **39.**—1. As soon as possible after the election of the judges, the Court shall organize itself into the divisions specified in article 34, paragraph (b). The Appeals Division shall be composed of the President and four other judges, the

Trial Division of not less than six judges and the Pre-Trial Division of not less than six judges. The assignment of judges to divisions shall be based on the nature of the functions to be performed by each division and the qualifications and experience of the judges elected to the Court, in such a way that each division shall contain an appropriate combination of expertise in criminal law and procedure and in international law. The Trial and Pre-Trial Divisions shall be composed predominantly of judges with criminal trial experience.

    2. (a) The judicial functions of the Court shall be carried out in each division by Chambers.

      (b) (i) The Appeals Chamber shall be composed of all the judges of the Appeals Division;

        (ii) The functions of the Trial Chamber shall be carried out by three judges of the Trial Division;

      (iii) The functions of the Pre-Trial Chamber shall be carried out either by three judges of the Pre-Trial Division or by a single judge of that division in accordance with this Statute and the Rules of Procedure and Evidence;

      (c) Nothing in this paragraph shall preclude the simultaneous constitution of more than one Trial Chamber or Pre-Trial Chamber when the efficient management of the Court's workload so requires.

    3. (a) Judges assigned to the Trial and Pre-Trial Divisions shall serve in those divisions for a period of three years, and thereafter until the completion of any case the hearing of which has already commenced in the division concerned.

      (b) Judges assigned to the Appeals Division shall serve in that division for their entire term of office.

    4. Judges assigned to the Appeals Division shall serve only in that division. Nothing in this article shall, however, preclude the temporary attachment of judges from the Trial Division to the Pre-Trial Division or vice versa, if the Presidency considers that the efficient management of the Court's workload so requires, provided that under no circumstances shall a judge who has participated in the pre-trial phase of a case be eligible to sit on the Trial Chamber hearing that case.

The Office of the Prosecutor

42.—1. The Office of the Prosecutor shall act independently as a separate **3–7** organ of the Court. It shall be responsible for receiving referrals and any substantiated information on crimes within the jurisdiction of the Court, for examining them and for conducting investigations and prosecutions before the Court. A member of the Office shall not seek or act on instructions from any external source.

    2. The Office shall be headed by the Prosecutor. The Prosecutor shall have full authority over the management and administration of the Office, including the staff, facilities and other resources thereof. The Prosecutor shall be assisted by one or more Deputy Prosecutors, who shall be entitled to carry out any of the acts required of the Prosecutor under this Statute. The Prosecutor and the Deputy Prosecutors shall be of different nationalities. They shall serve on a full-time basis.

    3. The Prosecutor and the Deputy Prosecutors shall be persons of high moral character, be highly competent in and have extensive practical experience in the prosecution or trial of criminal cases. They shall have an excellent knowledge of and be fluent in at least one of the working languages of the Court.

    4. The Prosecutor shall be elected by secret ballot by an absolute majority of the members of the Assembly of States Parties. The Deputy Prosecutors shall be elected in the same way from a list of candidates provided by the Prosecutor. The Prosecutor shall nominate three candidates for each position of Deputy

Prosecutor to be filled. Unless a shorter term is decided upon at the time of their election, the Prosecutor and the Deputy Prosecutors shall hold office for a term of nine years and shall not be eligible for re-election.

5. Neither the Prosecutor nor a Deputy Prosecutor shall engage in any activity which is likely to interfere with his or her prosecutorial functions or to affect confidence in his or her independence. They shall not engage in any other occupation of a professional nature.

6. The Presidency may excuse the Prosecutor or a Deputy Prosecutor, at his or her request, from acting in a particular case.

7. Neither the Prosecutor nor a Deputy Prosecutor shall participate in any matter in which their impartiality might reasonably be doubted on any ground. They shall be disqualified from a case in accordance with this paragraph if, *inter alia*, they have previously been involved in any capacity in that case before the Court or in a related criminal case at the national level involving the person being investigated or prosecuted.

8. Any question as to the disqualification of the Prosecutor or a Deputy Prosecutor shall be decided by the Appeals Chamber.

   (a) The person being investigated or prosecuted may at any time request the disqualification of the Prosecutor or a Deputy Prosecutor on the grounds set out in this article;

   (b) The Prosecutor or the Deputy Prosecutor, as appropriate, shall be entitled to present his or her comments on the matter;

9. The Prosecutor shall appoint advisers with legal expertise on specific issues, including, but not limited to, sexual and gender violence and violence against children.

The Registry

3–8   **43.**—1. The Registry shall be responsible for the non-judicial aspects of the administration and servicing of the Court, without prejudice to the functions and powers of the Prosecutor in accordance with article 42.

2. The Registry shall be headed by the Registrar, who shall be the principal administrative officer of the Court. The Registrar shall exercise his or her functions under the authority of the President of the Court.

3. The Registrar and the Deputy Registrar shall be persons of high moral character, be highly competent and have an excellent knowledge of and be fluent in at least one of the working languages of the Court.

4. The judges shall elect the Registrar by an absolute majority by secret ballot, taking into account any recommendation by the Assembly of States Parties. If the need arises and upon the recommendation of the Registrar, the judges shall elect, in the same manner, a Deputy Registrar.

5. The Registrar shall hold office for a term of five years, shall be eligible for re-election once and shall serve on a full-time basis. The Deputy Registrar shall hold office for a term of five years or such shorter term as may be decided upon by an absolute majority of the judges, and may be elected on the basis that the Deputy Registrar shall be called upon to serve as required.

6. The Registrar shall set up a Victims and Witnesses Unit within the Registry. This Unit shall provide, in consultation with the Office of the Prosecutor, protective measures and security arrangements, counselling and other appropriate assistance for witnesses, victims who appear before the Court, and others who are at risk on account of testimony given by such witnesses. The Unit shall include staff with expertise in trauma, including trauma related to crimes of sexual violence.

Regulations of the Court

3–9   **52.**—1. The judges shall, in accordance with this Statute and the Rules of Procedure and Evidence, adopt, by an absolute majority, the Regulations of the Court necessary for its routine functioning.

2. The Prosecutor and the Registrar shall be consulted in the elaboration of the Regulations and any amendments thereto.

3. The Regulations and any amendments thereto shall take effect upon adoption unless otherwise decided by the judges. Immediately upon adoption, they shall be circulated to States Parties for comments. If within six months there are no objections from a majority of States Parties, they shall remain in force.

Service of judges

35.—1. All judges shall be elected as full-time members of the Court and shall be available to serve on that basis from the commencement of their terms of office.

3–10

2. The judges composing the Presidency shall serve on a full-time basis as soon as they are elected.

3. The Presidency may, on the basis of the workload of the Court and in consultation with its members, decide from time to time to what extent the remaining judges shall be required to serve on a full-time basis. Any such arrangement shall be without prejudice to the provisions of article 40.

4. The financial arrangements for judges not required to serve on a full-time basis shall be made in accordance with article 49.

Qualifications, nomination and election of judges

36.—1. Subject to the provisions of paragraph 2, there shall be 18 judges of the Court.

3–11

2. (a) The Presidency, acting on behalf of the Court, may propose an increase in the number of judges specified in paragraph 1, indicating the reasons why this is considered necessary and appropriate. The Registrar shall promptly circulate any such proposal to all States Parties.

(b) Any such proposal shall then be considered at a meeting of the Assembly of States Parties to be convened in accordance with article 112. The proposal shall be considered adopted if approved at the meeting by a vote of two thirds of the members of the Assembly of States Parties and shall enter into force at such time as decided by the Assembly of States Parties.

(c) (i) Once a proposal for an increase in the number of judges has been adopted under subparagraph (b), the election of the additional judges shall take place at the next session of the Assembly of States Parties in accordance with paragraphs 3 to 8, and article 37, paragraph 2;

(ii) Once a proposal for an increase in the number of judges has been adopted and brought into effect under subparagraphs (b) and (c)(i), it shall be open to the Presidency at any time thereafter, if the workload of the Court justifies it, to propose a reduction in the number of judges, provided that the number of judges shall not be reduced below that specified in paragraph 1. The proposal shall be dealt with in accordance with the procedure laid down in subparagraphs (a) and (b). In the event that the proposal is adopted, the number of judges shall be progressively decreased as the terms of office of serving judges expire, until the necessary number has been reached.

3. (a) The judges shall be chosen from among persons of high moral character, impartiality and integrity who possess the qualifications required in their respective States for appointment to the highest judicial offices.

(b) Every candidate for election to the Court shall:

       (i) Have established competence in criminal law and procedure, and the necessary relevant experience, whether as judge, prosecutor, advocate or in other similar capacity, in criminal proceedings; or

      (ii) Have established competence in relevant areas of international law such as international humanitarian law and the law of human rights, and extensive experience in a professional legal capacity which is of relevance to the judicial work of the Court;

   (c) Every candidate for election to the Court shall have an excellent knowledge of and be fluent in at least one of the working languages of the Court.

4. (a) Nominations of candidates for election to the Court may be made by any State Party to this Statute, and shall be made either:

       (i) By the procedure for the nomination of candidates for appointment to the highest judicial offices in the State in question; or

      (ii) By the procedure provided for the nomination of candidates for the International Court of Justice in the Statute of that Court.

Nominations shall be accompanied by a statement in the necessary detail specifying how the candidate fulfils the requirements of paragraph 3.

   (b) Each State Party may put forward one candidate for any given election who need not necessarily be a national of that State Party but shall in any case be a national of a State Party.

   (c) The Assembly of States Parties may decide to establish, if appropriate, an Advisory Committee on nominations. In that event, the Committee's composition and mandate shall be established by the Assembly of States Parties.

5. For the purposes of the election, there shall be two lists of candidates:

List A containing the names of candidates with the qualifications specified in paragraph 3(b)(i); and

List B containing the names of candidates with the qualifications specified in paragraph 3(b)(ii).

A candidate with sufficient qualifications for both lists may choose on which list to appear. At the first election to the Court, at least nine judges shall be elected from list A and at least five judges from list B. Subsequent elections shall be so organized as to maintain the equivalent proportion on the Court of judges qualified on the two lists.

6. (a) The judges shall be elected by secret ballot at a meeting of the Assembly of States Parties convened for that purpose under article 112. Subject to paragraph 7, the persons elected to the Court shall be the 18 candidates who obtain the highest number of votes and a two-thirds majority of the States Parties present and voting.

   (b) In the event that a sufficient number of judges is not elected on the first ballot, successive ballots shall be held in accordance with the procedures laid down in subparagraph (a) until the remaining places have been filled.

7. No two judges may be nationals of the same State. A person who, for the purposes of membership of the Court, could be regarded as a national of more than one State shall be deemed to be a national of the State in which that person ordinarily exercises civil and political rights.

8. (a) The States Parties shall, in the selection of judges, take into account the need, within the membership of the Court, for:

       (i) The representation of the principal legal systems of the world;

      (ii) Equitable geographical representation; and

     (iii) A fair representation of female and male judges.

   (b) States Parties shall also take into account the need to include judges with legal expertise on specific issues, including, but not limited to, violence against women or children.

9. (a) Subject to subparagraph (b), judges shall hold office for a term of nine years and, subject to subparagraph (c) and to article 37, paragraph 2, shall not be eligible for re-election.

   (b) At the first election, one third of the judges elected shall be selected by lot to serve for a term of three years; one third of the judges elected shall be selected by lot to serve for a term of six years; and the remainder shall serve for a term of nine years.

   (c) A judge who is selected to serve for a term of three years under subparagraph (b) shall be eligible for re-election for a full term.

10. Notwithstanding paragraph 9, a judge assigned to a Trial or Appeals Chamber in accordance with article 39 shall continue in office to complete any trial or appeal the hearing of which has already commenced before that Chamber.

Judicial vacancies

37.—1. In the event of a vacancy, an election shall be held in accordance **3–12** with article 36 to fill the vacancy.

2. A judge elected to fill a vacancy shall serve for the remainder of the predecessor's term and, if that period is three years or less, shall be eligible for re-election for a full term under article 36.

Independence of the judges

40.—1. The judges shall be independent in the performance of their **3–13** functions.

2. Judges shall not engage in any activity which is likely to interfere with their judicial functions or to affect confidence in their independence.

3. Judges required to serve on a full-time basis at the seat of the Court shall not engage in any other occupation of a professional nature.

4. Any question regarding the application of paragraphs 2 and 3 shall be decided by an absolute majority of the judges. Where any such question concerns an individual judge, that judge shall not take part in the decision.

Excusing and disqualification of judges

41.—1. The Presidency may, at the request of a judge, excuse that judge **3–14** from the exercise of a function under this Statute, in accordance with the Rules of Procedure and Evidence.

2. (a) A judge shall not participate in any case in which his or her impartiality might reasonably be doubted on any ground. A judge shall be disqualified from a case in accordance with this paragraph if, *inter alia*, that judge has previously been involved in any capacity in that case before the Court or in a related criminal case at the national level involving the person being investigated or prosecuted. A judge shall also be disqualified on such other grounds as may be provided for in the Rules of Procedure and Evidence.

   (b) The Prosecutor or the person being investigated or prosecuted may request the disqualification of a judge under this paragraph.

   (c) Any question as to the disqualification of a judge shall be decided by an absolute majority of the judges. The challenged judge shall be entitled to present his or her comments on the matter, but shall not take part in the decision.

Staff

44.—1. The Prosecutor and the Registrar shall appoint such qualified staff **3–15** as may be required to their respective offices. In the case of the Prosecutor, this shall include the appointment of investigators.

2. In the employment of staff, the Prosecutor and the Registrar shall ensure the highest standards of efficiency, competency and integrity, and shall have regard, *mutatis mutandis*, to the criteria set forth in article 36, paragraph 8.

3. The Registrar, with the agreement of the Presidency and the Prosecutor, shall propose Staff Regulations which include the terms and conditions upon which the staff of the Court shall be appointed, remunerated and dismissed. The Staff Regulations shall be approved by the Assembly of States Parties.

4. The Court may, in exceptional circumstances, employ the expertise of gratis personnel offered by States Parties, intergovernmental organizations or non-governmental organizations to assist with the work of any of the organs of the Court. The Prosecutor may accept any such offer on behalf of the Office of the Prosecutor. Such gratis personnel shall be employed in accordance with guidelines to be established by the Assembly of States Parties.

Solemn undertaking

3–16 45. Before taking up their respective duties under this Statute, the judges, the Prosecutor, the Deputy Prosecutors, the Registrar and the Deputy Registrar shall each make a solemn undertaking in open court to exercise his or her respective functions impartially and conscientiously.

Removal from office

3–17 46.—1. A judge, the Prosecutor, a Deputy Prosecutor, the Registrar or the Deputy Registrar shall be removed from office if a decision to this effect is made in accordance with paragraph 2, in cases where that person:

    (a) Is found to have committed serious misconduct or a serious breach of his or her duties under this Statute, as provided for in the Rules of Procedure and Evidence; or

    (b) Is unable to exercise the functions required by this Statute.

2. A decision as to the removal from office of a judge, the Prosecutor or a Deputy Prosecutor under paragraph 1 shall be made by the Assembly of States Parties, by secret ballot:

    (a) In the case of a judge, by a two-thirds majority of the States Parties upon a recommendation adopted by a two-thirds majority of the other judges;

    (b) In the case of the Prosecutor, by an absolute majority of the States Parties;

    (c) In the case of a Deputy Prosecutor, by an absolute majority of the States Parties upon the recommendation of the Prosecutor.

3. A decision as to the removal from office of the Registrar or Deputy Registrar shall be made by an absolute majority of the judges.

4. A judge, Prosecutor, Deputy Prosecutor, Registrar or Deputy Registrar whose conduct or ability to exercise the functions of the office as required by this Statute is challenged under this article shall have full opportunity to present and receive evidence and to make submissions in accordance with the Rules of Procedure and Evidence. The person in question shall not otherwise participate in the consideration of the matter.

Disciplinary measures

3–18 47. A judge, Prosecutor, Deputy Prosecutor, Registrar or Deputy Registrar who has committed misconduct of a less serious nature than that set out in article 46, paragraph 1, shall be subject to disciplinary measures, in accordance with the Rules of Procedure and Evidence.

Privileges and immunities

3–19 48.—1. The Court shall enjoy in the territory of each State Party such privileges and immunities as are necessary for the fulfilment of its purposes.

2. The judges, the Prosecutor, the Deputy Prosecutors and the Registrar shall, when engaged on or with respect to the business of the Court, enjoy the same privileges and immunities as are accorded to heads of diplomatic missions and shall, after the expiry of their terms of office, continue to be accorded immunity from legal process of every kind in respect of words spoken or written and acts performed by them in their official capacity.

3. The Deputy Registrar, the staff of the Office of the Prosecutor and the staff of the Registry shall enjoy the privileges and immunities and facilities necessary for the performance of their functions, in accordance with the agreement on the privileges and immunities of the Court.

4. Counsel, experts, witnesses or any other person required to be present at the seat of the Court shall be accorded such treatment as is necessary for the proper functioning of the Court, in accordance with the agreement on the privileges and immunities of the Court.

5. The privileges and immunities of:
   (a) A judge or the Prosecutor may be waived by an absolute majority of the judges;
   (b) The Registrar may be waived by the Presidency;
   (c) The Deputy Prosecutors and staff of the Office of the Prosecutor may be waived by the Prosecutor;
   (d) The Deputy Registrar and staff of the Registry may be waived by the Registrar.

Salaries, allowances and expenses

49. The judges, the Prosecutor, the Deputy Prosecutors, the Registrar and the Deputy Registrar shall receive such salaries, allowances and expenses as may be decided upon by the Assembly of States Parties. These salaries and allowances shall not be reduced during their terms of office.   **3–20**

Official and working languages

50.—1. The official languages of the Court shall be Arabic, Chinese, English, French, Russian and Spanish. The judgements of the Court, as well as other decisions resolving fundamental issues before the Court, shall be published in the official languages. The Presidency shall, in accordance with the criteria established by the Rules of Procedure and Evidence, determine which decisions may be considered as resolving fundamental issues for the purposes of this paragraph.   **3–21**

2. The working languages of the Court shall be English and French. The Rules of Procedure and Evidence shall determine the cases in which other official languages may be used as working languages.

3. At the request of any party to a proceeding or a State allowed to intervene in a proceeding, the Court shall authorize a language other than English or French to be used by such a party or State, provided that the Court considers such authorization to be adequately justified.

(2) ICC Rules of Procedure and Evidence

Section II

The Office of the Prosecutor

ICC Rules of Procedure and Evidence, rr. 9–21

Operation of the Office of the Prosecutor

9. In discharging his or her responsibility for the management and administration of the Office of the Prosecutor, the Prosecutor shall put in place regulations to govern the operation of the Office. In preparing or amending   **3–22**

these regulations, the Prosecutor shall consult with the Registrar on any matters that may affect the operation of the Registry.

Retention of information and evidence

3–23   **10.** The Prosecutor shall be responsible for the retention, storage and security of information and physical evidence obtained in the course of the investigations by his or her Office.

Delegation of the Prosecutor's functions

3–24   **11.** Except for the inherent powers of the Prosecutor set forth in the Statute, *inter alia*, those described in articles 15 and 53, the Prosecutor or a Deputy Prosecutor may authorize staff members of the Office of the Prosecutor, other than those referred to in article 44, paragraph 4, to represent him or her in the exercise of his or her functions.

SECTION III

THE REGISTRY

SUBSECTION 1

GENERAL PROVISIONS RELATING TO THE REGISTRY

Qualifications and election of the Registrar and the Deputy Registrar

3–25   **12.**—1. As soon as it is elected, the Presidency shall establish a list of candidates who satisfy the criteria laid down in article 43, paragraph 3, and shall transmit the list to the Assembly of States Parties with a request for any recommendations.

2. Upon receipt of any recommendations from the Assembly of States Parties, the President shall, without delay, transmit the list together with the recommendations to the plenary session.

3. As provided for in article 43, paragraph 4, the Court, meeting in plenary session, shall, as soon as possible, elect the Registrar by an absolute majority, taking into account any recommendations by the Assembly of States Parties. In the event that no candidate obtains an absolute majority on the first ballot, successive ballots shall be held until one candidate obtains an absolute majority.

4. If the need for a Deputy Registrar arises, the Registrar may make a recommendation to the President to that effect. The President shall convene a plenary session to decide on the matter. If the Court, meeting in plenary session, decides by an absolute majority that a Deputy Registrar is to be elected, the Registrar shall submit a list of candidates to the Court.

The Deputy Registrar shall be elected by the Court, meeting in plenary session, in the same manner as the Registrar.

Functions of the Registrar

3–26   **13.**—1. Without prejudice to the authority of the Office of the Prosecutor under the Statute to receive, obtain and provide information and to establish channels of communication for this purpose, the Registrar shall serve as the channel of communication of the Court.

2. The Registrar shall also be responsible for the internal security of the Court in consultation with the Presidency and the Prosecutor, as well as the host State.

Operation of the Registry

14.—1. In discharging his or her responsibility for the organization and management of the Registry, the Registrar shall put in place regulations to govern the operation of the Registry. In preparing or amending these regulations, the Registrar shall consult with the Prosecutor on any matters which may affect the operation of the Office of the Prosecutor. The regulations shall be approved by the Presidency.   **3–27**

2. The regulations shall provide for defence counsel to have access to appropriate and reasonable administrative assistance from the Registry.

Records

15.—1. The Registrar shall keep a database containing all the particulars of each case brought before the Court, subject to any order of a judge or Chamber providing for the non-disclosure of any document or information, and to the protection of sensitive personal data. Information on the database shall be available to the public in the working languages of the Court.   **3–28**

2. The Registrar shall also maintain the other records of the Court.

SUBSECTION 2

VICTIMS AND WITNESSES UNIT

Responsibilities of the Registrar relating to victims and witnesses

16.—1. In relation to victims, the Registrar shall be responsible for the performance of the following functions in accordance with the Statute and these Rules: **3–29**

(a) Providing notice or notification to victims or their legal representatives;

(b) Assisting them in obtaining legal advice and organizing their legal representation, and providing their legal representatives with adequate support, assistance and information, including such facilities as may be necessary for the direct performance of their duty, for the purpose of protecting their rights during all stages of the proceedings in accordance with rules 89 to 91;

(c) Assisting them in participating in the different phases of the proceedings in accordance with rules 89 to 91;

(d) Taking gender-sensitive measures to facilitate the participation of victims of sexual violence at all stages of the proceedings.

2. In relation to victims, witnesses and others who are at risk on account of testimony given by such witnesses, the Registrar shall be responsible for the performance of the following functions in accordance with the Statute and these Rules:

(a) Informing them of their rights under the Statute and the Rules, and of the existence, functions and availability of the Victims and Witnesses Unit;

(b) Ensuring that they are aware, in a timely manner, of the relevant decisions of the Court that may have an impact on their interests, subject to provisions on confidentiality.

3. For the fulfilment of his or her functions, the Registrar may keep a special register for victims who have expressed their intention to participate in relation to a specific case.

4. Agreements on relocation and provision of support services on the territory of a State of traumatized or threatened victims, witnesses and others who are at risk on account of testimony given by such witnesses may be negotiated with the States by the Registrar on behalf of the Court. Such agreements may remain confidential.

Functions of the Unit

3–30　　17.—1. The Victims and Witnesses Unit shall exercise its functions in accordance with article 43, paragraph 6.

2. The Victims and Witnesses Unit shall, *inter alia*, perform the following functions, in accordance with the Statute and the Rules, and in consultation with the Chamber, the Prosecutor and the defence, as appropriate:
  (a) With respect to all witnesses, victims who appear before the Court, and others who are at risk on account of testimony given by such witnesses, in accordance with their particular needs and circumstances:
    (i) Providing them with adequate protective and security measures and formulating long-and short-term plans for their protection;
    (ii) Recommending to the organs of the Court the adoption of protection measures and also advising relevant States of such measures;
    (iii) Assisting them in obtaining medical, psychological and other appropriate assistance;
    (iv) Making available to the Court and the parties training in issues of trauma, sexual violence, security and confidentiality;
    (v) Recommending, in consultation with the Office of the Prosecutor, the elaboration of a code of conduct, emphasizing the vital nature of security and confidentiality for investigators of the Court and of the defence and all intergovernmental and non-governmental organizations acting at the request of the Court, as appropriate;
    (vi) Cooperating with States, where necessary, in providing any of the measures stipulated in this rule;
  (b) With respect to witnesses:
    (i) Advising them where to obtain legal advice for the purpose of protecting their rights, in particular in relation to their testimony;
    (ii) Assisting them when they are called to testify before the Court;
    (iii) Taking gender-sensitive measures to facilitate the testimony of victims of sexual violence at all stages of the proceedings.

3. In performing its functions, the Unit shall give due regard to the particular needs of children, elderly persons and persons with disabilities. In order to facilitate the participation and protection of children as witnesses, the Unit may assign, as appropriate, and with the agreement of the parents or the legal guardian, a child-support person to assist a child through all stages of the proceedings.

Responsibilities of the Unit

3–31　　18. For the efficient and effective performance of its work, the Victims and Witnesses Unit shall:
  (a) Ensure that the staff in the Unit maintain confidentiality at all times;
  (b) While recognizing the specific interests of the Office of the Prosecutor, the defence and the witnesses, respect the interests of the

witness, including, where necessary, by maintaining an appropriate separation of the services provided to the prosecution and defence witnesses, and act impartially when cooperating with all parties and in accordance with the rulings and decisions of the Chambers;

(c) Have administrative and technical assistance available for witnesses, victims who appear before the Court, and others who are at risk on account of testimony given by such witnesses, during all stages of the proceedings and thereafter, as reasonably appropriate;

(d) Ensure training of its staff with respect to victims' and witnesses' security, integrity and dignity, including matters related to gender and cultural sensitivity;

(e) Where appropriate, cooperate with intergovernmental and non-governmental organizations.

Expertise in the Unit

19. In addition to the staff mentioned in article 43, paragraph 6, and subject **3–32** to article 44, the Victims and Witnesses Unit may include, as appropriate, persons with expertise, *inter alia*, in the following areas:

(a) Witness protection and security;
(b) Legal and administrative matters, including areas of humanitarian and criminal law;
(c) Logistics administration;
(d) Psychology in criminal proceedings;
(e) Gender and cultural diversity;
(f) Children, in particular traumatized children;
(g) Elderly persons, in particular in connection with armed conflict and exile trauma;
(h) Persons with disabilities;
(i) Social work and counselling;
(j) Health care;
(k) Interpretation and translation.

SUBSECTION 3

COUNSEL FOR THE DEFENCE

Responsibilities of the Registrar relating to the rights of the defence

20.—1. In accordance with article 43, paragraph 1, the Registrar shall **3–33** organize the staff of the Registry in a manner that promotes the rights of the defence, consistent with the principle of fair trial as defined in the Statute. For that purpose, the Registrar shall, *inter alia*:

(a) Facilitate the protection of confidentiality, as defined in article 67, paragraph 1(b);
(b) Provide support, assistance, and information to all defence counsel appearing before the Court and, as appropriate, support for professional investigators necessary for the efficient and effective conduct of the defence;
(c) Assist arrested persons, persons to whom article 55, paragraph 2, applies and the accused in obtaining legal advice and the assistance of legal counsel;
(d) Advise the Prosecutor and the Chambers, as necessary, on relevant defence-related issues;
(e) Provide the defence with such facilities as may be necessary for the direct performance of the duty of the defence;

(f) Facilitate the dissemination of information and case law of the Court to defence counsel and, as appropriate, cooperate with national defence and bar associations or any independent representative body of counsel and legal associations referred to in sub-rule 3 to promote the specialization and training of lawyers in the law of the Statute and the Rules.

2. The Registrar shall carry out the functions stipulated in sub-rule 1, including the financial administration of the Registry, in such a manner as to ensure the professional independence of defence counsel.

3. For purposes such as the management of legal assistance in accordance with rule 21 and the development of a Code of Professional Conduct in accordance with rule 8, the Registrar shall consult, as appropriate, with any independent representative body of counsel or legal associations, including any such body the establishment of which may be facilitated by the Assembly of States Parties.

Assignment of legal assistance

3–34   **21.**—1. Subject to article 55, paragraph 2 (c), and article 67, paragraph 1 (d), criteria and procedures for assignment of legal assistance shall be established in the Regulations, based on a proposal by the Registrar, following consultations with any independent representative body of counsel or legal associations, as referred to in rule 20, sub-rule 3.

2. The Registrar shall create and maintain a list of counsel who meet the criteria set forth in rule 22 and the Regulations. The person shall freely choose his or her counsel from this list or other counsel who meets the required criteria and is willing to be included in the list.

3. A person may seek from the Presidency a review of a decision to refuse a request for assignment of counsel. The decision of the Presidency shall be final. If a request is refused, a further request may be made by a person to the Registrar, upon showing a change in circumstances.

4. A person choosing to represent himself or herself shall so notify the Registrar in writing at the first opportunity.

5. Where a person claims to have insufficient means to pay for legal assistance and this is subsequently found not to be so, the Chamber dealing with the case at that time may make an order of contribution to recover the cost of providing counsel.

C. AMENDMENT OF PROVISIONS

PART 11

ASSEMBLY OF STATES PARTIES

Statute of the International Criminal Court, Arts 51–52, 112, 121–125

Assembly of States Parties

3–35   **112.**—1. An Assembly of States Parties to this Statute is hereby established. Each State Party shall have one representative in the Assembly who may be accompanied by alternates and advisers. Other States which have signed this Statute or the Final Act may be observers in the Assembly.

2. The Assembly shall:

(a) Consider and adopt, as appropriate, recommendations of the Preparatory Commission;

(b) Provide management oversight to the Presidency, the Prosecutor and the Registrar regarding the administration of the Court;

(c) Consider the reports and activities of the Bureau established under paragraph 3 and take appropriate action in regard thereto;

(d) Consider and decide the budget for the Court;

(e) Decide whether to alter, in accordance with article 36, the number of judges;

(f) Consider pursuant to article 87, paragraphs 5 and 7, any question relating to non-cooperation;

(g) Perform any other function consistent with this Statute or the Rules of Procedure and Evidence.

3. (a) The Assembly shall have a Bureau consisting of a President, two Vice-Presidents and 18 members elected by the Assembly for three-year terms.

(b) The Bureau shall have a representative character, taking into account, in particular, equitable geographical distribution and the adequate representation of the principal legal systems of the world.

(c) The Bureau shall meet as often as necessary, but at least once a year. It shall assist the Assembly in the discharge of its responsibilities.

4. The Assembly may establish such subsidiary bodies as may be necessary, including an independent oversight mechanism for inspection, evaluation and investigation of the Court, in order to enhance its efficiency and economy.

5. The President of the Court, the Prosecutor and the Registrar or their representatives may participate, as appropriate, in meetings of the Assembly and of the Bureau.

6. The Assembly shall meet at the seat of the Court or at the Headquarters of the United Nations once a year and, when circumstances so require, hold special sessions. Except as otherwise specified in this Statute, special sessions shall be convened by the Bureau on its own initiative or at the request of one third of the States Parties.

7. Each State Party shall have one vote. Every effort shall be made to reach decisions by consensus in the Assembly and in the Bureau. If consensus cannot be reached, except as otherwise provided in the Statute:

(a) Decisions on matters of substance must be approved by a two-thirds majority of those present and voting provided that an absolute majority of States Parties constitutes the quorum for voting;

(b) Decisions on matters of procedure shall be taken by a simple majority of States Parties present and voting.

8. A State Party which is in arrears in the payment of its financial contributions towards the costs of the Court shall have no vote in the Assembly and in the Bureau if the amount of its arrears equals or exceeds the amount of the contributions due from it for the preceding two full years. The Assembly may, nevertheless, permit such a State Party to vote in the Assembly and in the Bureau if it is satisfied that the failure to pay is due to conditions beyond the control of the State Party.

9. The Assembly shall adopt its own rules of procedure.

10. The official and working languages of the Assembly shall be those of the General Assembly of the United Nations.

Amendments

121.—1. After the expiry of seven years from the entry into force of this **3–36** Statute, any State Party may propose amendments thereto. The text of any proposed amendment shall be submitted to the Secretary-General of the United Nations, who shall promptly circulate it to all States Parties.

2. No sooner than three months from the date of notification, the Assembly of States Parties, at its next meeting, shall, by a majority of those present and

voting, decide whether to take up the proposal. The Assembly may deal with the proposal directly or convene a Review Conference if the issue involved so warrants.

3. The adoption of an amendment at a meeting of the Assembly of States Parties or at a Review Conference on which consensus cannot be reached shall require a two-thirds majority of States Parties.

4. Except as provided in paragraph 5, an amendment shall enter into force for all States Parties one year after instruments of ratification or acceptance have been deposited with the Secretary-General of the United Nations by seven-eighths of them.

5. Any amendment to articles 5, 6, 7 and 8 of this Statute shall enter into force for those States Parties which have accepted the amendment one year after the deposit of their instruments of ratification or acceptance. In respect of a State Party which has not accepted the amendment, the Court shall not exercise its jurisdiction regarding a crime covered by the amendment when committed by that State Party's nationals or on its territory.

6. If an amendment has been accepted by seven-eighths of States Parties in accordance with paragraph 4, any State Party which has not accepted the amendment may withdraw from this Statute with immediate effect, notwithstanding article 127, paragraph 1, but subject to article 127, paragraph 2, by giving notice no later than one year after the entry into force of such amendment.

7. The Secretary-General of the United Nations shall circulate to all States Parties any amendment adopted at a meeting of the Assembly of States Parties or at a Review Conference.

Amendments to provisions of an institutional nature

3–37　　**122.**—1. Amendments to provisions of this Statute which are of an exclusively institutional nature, namely, article 35, article 36, paragraphs 8 and 9, article 37, article 38, article 39, paragraphs 1 (first two sentences), 2 and 4, article 42, paragraphs 4 to 9, article 43, paragraphs 2 and 3, and articles 44, 46, 47 and 49, may be proposed at any time, notwithstanding article 121, paragraph 1, by any State Party. The text of any proposed amendment shall be submitted to the Secretary-General of the United Nations or such other person designated by the Assembly of States Parties who shall promptly circulate it to all States Parties and to others participating in the Assembly.

2. Amendments under this article on which consensus cannot be reached shall be adopted by the Assembly of States Parties or by a Review Conference, by a two-thirds majority of States Parties. Such amendments shall enter into force for all States Parties six months after their adoption by the Assembly or, as the case may be, by the Conference.

Review of the Statute

3–38　　**123.**—1. Seven years after the entry into force of this Statute the Secretary-General of the United Nations shall convene a Review Conference to consider any amendments to this Statute. Such review may include, but is not limited to, the list of crimes contained in article 5. The Conference shall be open to those participating in the Assembly of States Parties and on the same conditions.

2. At any time thereafter, at the request of a State Party and for the purposes set out in paragraph 1, the Secretary-General of the United Nations shall, upon approval by a majority of States Parties, convene a Review Conference.

3. The provisions of article 121, paragraphs 3 to 7, shall apply to the adoption and entry into force of any amendment to the Statute considered at a Review Conference.

Transitional Provision

124. Notwithstanding article 12, paragraphs 1 and 2, a State, on becoming a **3–39** party to this Statute, may declare that, for a period of seven years after the entry into force of this Statute for the State concerned, it does not accept the jurisdiction of the Court with respect to the category of crimes referred to in article 8 when a crime is alleged to have been committed by its nationals or on its territory. A declaration under this article may be withdrawn at any time. The provisions of this article shall be reviewed at the Review Conference convened in accordance with article 123, paragraph 1.

Signature, ratification, acceptance, approval or accession

125.—1. This Statute shall be open for signature by all States in Rome, at **3–40** the headquarters of the Food and Agriculture Organization of the United Nations, on 17 July 1998. Thereafter, it shall remain open for signature in Rome at the Ministry of Foreign Affairs of Italy until 17 October 1998. After that date, the Statute shall remain open for signature in New York, at United Nations Headquarters, until 31 December 2000.

2. This Statute is subject to ratification, acceptance or approval by signatory States. Instruments of ratification, acceptance or approval shall be deposited with the Secretary-General of the United Nations.

3. This Statute shall be open to accession by all States. Instruments of accession shall be deposited with the Secretary-General of the United Nations.

Rules of Procedure and Evidence

51.—1. The Rules of Procedure and Evidence shall enter into force upon **3–41** adoption by a two-thirds majority of the members of the Assembly of States Parties.

2. Amendments to the Rules of Procedure and Evidence may be proposed by:
    (a) Any State Party;
    (b) The judges acting by an absolute majority; or
    (c) The Prosecutor.
Such amendments shall enter into force upon adoption by a two-thirds majority of the members of the Assembly of States Parties.

3. After the adoption of the Rules of Procedure and Evidence, in urgent cases where the Rules do not provide for a specific situation before the Court, the judges may, by a two-thirds majority, draw up provisional Rules to be applied until adopted, amended or rejected at the next ordinary or special session of the Assembly of States Parties.

4. The Rules of Procedure and Evidence, amendments thereto and any provisional Rule shall be consistent with this Statute. Amendments to the Rules of Procedure and Evidence as well as provisional Rules shall not be applied retroactively to the detriment of the person who is being investigated or prosecuted or who has been convicted.

5. In the event of conflict between the Statute and the Rules of Procedure and Evidence, the Statute shall prevail.

Regulations of the Court

52.—1. The judges shall, in accordance with this Statute and the Rules of **3–42** Procedure and Evidence, adopt, by an absolute majority, the Regulations of the Court necessary for its routine functioning.

2. The Prosecutor and the Registrar shall be consulted in the elaboration of the Regulations and any amendments thereto.

3. The Regulations and any amendments thereto shall take effect upon adoption unless otherwise decided by the judges. Immediately upon adoption,

they shall be circulated to States Parties for comments. If within six months there are no objections from a majority of States Parties, they shall remain in force.

D. FUNDING

PART 12

FINANCING

Statute of the International Criminal Court, Arts 113–118

Financial Regulations

3–43   **113.** Except as otherwise specifically provided, all financial matters related to the Court and the meetings of the Assembly of States Parties, including its Bureau and subsidiary bodies, shall be governed by this Statute and the Financial Regulations and Rules adopted by the Assembly of States Parties.

Payment of expenses

3–44   **114.** Expenses of the Court and the Assembly of States Parties, including its Bureau and subsidiary bodies, shall be paid from the funds of the Court.

Funds of the Court and of the Assembly of States Parties

3–45   **115.** The expenses of the Court and the Assembly of States Parties, including its Bureau and subsidiary bodies, as provided for in the budget decided by the Assembly of States Parties, shall be provided by the following sources:

    (a) Assessed contributions made by States Parties;
    (b) Funds provided by the United Nations, subject to the approval of the General Assembly, in particular in relation to the expenses incurred due to referrals by the Security Council.

Voluntary contributions

3–46   **116.** Without prejudice to article 115, the Court may receive and utilize, as additional funds, voluntary contributions from Governments, international organizations, individuals, corporations and other entities, in accordance with relevant criteria adopted by the Assembly of States Parties.

Assessment of contributions

3–47   **117.** The contributions of States Parties shall be assessed in accordance with an agreed scale of assessment, based on the scale adopted by the United Nations for its regular budget and adjusted in accordance with the principles on which that scale is based.

Annual audit

3–48   **118.**—The records, books and accounts of the Court, including its annual financial statements, shall be audited annually by an independent auditor.

II. ICTY AND ICTR

A. Basic Structure

Statute of the ICTY, Art. 11

Organization of the International Tribunal

11. The International Tribunal shall consist of the following organs: **3–49**
  (a) the Chambers, comprising three Trial Chambers and an Appeals
      Chamber;
  (b) the Prosecutor; and
  (c) a Registry, servicing both the Chambers and the Prosecutor.

Statute of the ICTR, Art. 10

Organisation of the International Tribunal for Rwanda

10. The International Tribunal for Rwanda shall consist of the following   **3–50**
organs:
  (a) The Chambers, comprising three Trial Chambers and an Appeals
      Chamber;
  (b) The Prosecutor;
  (c) A Registry.

The seat of the ICTY is at the Hague, the ICTR at Arusha, Tanzania.
The working languages of the Tribunals are English and French.

B. Registry

(1) ICTY

Statute of the ICTY, Art. 17

The Registry

17.—1. The Registry shall be responsible for the administration and servic-   **3–51**
ing of the International Tribunal.
  2. The Registry shall consist of a Registrar and such other staff as may be
required.
  3. The Registrar shall be appointed by the Secretary-General after consultation with the President of the International Tribunal. He or she shall serve for
a four-year term and be eligible for reappointment. The terms and conditions
of service of the Registrar shall be those of an Assistant Secretary-General of
the United Nations.
  4. The staff of the Registry shall be appointed by the Secretary-General on
the recommendation of the Registrar.

(2) ICTR

Statute of the ICTR, Art. 16

The Registry

16.—1. The Registry shall be responsible for the administration and servic-   **3–52**
ing of the International Tribunal for Rwanda.

2. The Registry shall consist of a Registrar and such other staff as may be required.

3. The Registrar shall be appointed by the Secretary-General after consultation with the President of the International Tribunal for Rwanda. He or she shall serve for a four-year term and be eligible for re-appointment. The terms and conditions of service of the Registrar shall be those of an Assistant Secretary-General of the United Nations.

4. The Staff of the Registry shall be appointed by the Secretary-General on the recommendation of the Registrar.

Also see, Rules 30–36 of the ICTY and ICTR Rules, which pertain to the Registry.

C. JUDGES AND THE PRESIDENT

(1) ICTY

Statute of the ICTY, Arts 12, 13, 13*bis*, 13*ter*, 13*quater*, 14, 30

Composition of the Chambers

3–53   **12.**—1. The Chambers shall be composed of sixteen permanent independent judges, no two of whom may be nationals of the same State, and a maximum at any one time of nine *ad litem* independent judges appointed in accordance with article 13*ter*, paragraph 2, of the Statute, no two of whom may be nationals of the same State.

2. Three permanent judges and a maximum at any one time of six *ad litem* judges shall be members of each Trial Chamber. Each Trial Chamber to which *ad litem* judges are assigned may be divided into sections of three judges each, composed of both permanent and *ad litem* judges. A section of a Trial Chamber shall have the same powers and responsibilities as a Trial Chamber under the Statute and shall render judgement in accordance with the same rules.

3. Seven of the permanent judges shall be members of the Appeals Chamber. The Appeals Chamber shall, for each appeal, be composed of five of its members.

4. A person who for the purposes of membership of the Chambers of the International Tribunal could be regarded as a national of more than one State shall be deemed to be a national of the State in which that person ordinarily exercises civil and political rights.

Qualifications of judges

3–54   **13.** The permanent and *ad litem* judges shall be persons of high moral character, impartiality and integrity who possess the qualifications required in their respective countries for appointment to the highest judicial offices. In the overall composition of the Chambers and sections of the Trial Chambers, due account shall be taken of the experience of the judges in criminal law, international law, including international humanitarian law and human rights law.

Election of permanent judges

3–55   **13*bis*.**—1. Fourteen of the permanent judges of the International Tribunal shall be elected by the General Assembly from a list submitted by the Security Council, in the following manner:

(a) The Secretary-General shall invite nominations for judges of the International Tribunal from States Members of the United Nations and non-member States maintaining permanent observer missions at United Nations Headquarters;

(b) Within sixty days of the date of the invitation of the Secretary-General, each State may nominate up to two candidates meeting the qualifications set out in article 13 of the Statute, no two of whom shall be of the same nationality and neither of whom shall be of the same nationality as any judge who is a member of the Appeals Chamber and who was elected or appointed a permanent judge of the International Criminal Tribunal for the Prosecution of Persons Responsible for Genocide and Other Serious Violations of International Humanitarian Law Committed in the Territory of Rwanda and Rwandan Citizens Responsible for Genocide and Other Such Violations Committed in the Territory of Neighbouring States, between 1 January 1994 and 31 December 1994 (hereinafter referred to as "The International Tribunal for Rwanda") in accordance with article 12*bis* of the Statute of that Tribunal;

(c) The Secretary-General shall forward the nominations received to the Security Council. From the nominations received the Security Council shall establish a list of not less than twenty-eight and not more than forty-two candidates, taking due account of the adequate representation of the principal legal systems of the world;

(d) The President of the Security Council shall transmit the list of candidates to the President of the General Assembly. From that list the General Assembly shall elect fourteen permanent judges of the International Tribunal. The candidates who receive an absolute majority of the votes of the States Members of the United Nations and of the non-member States maintaining permanent observer missions at United Nations Headquarters, shall be declared elected. Should two candidates of the same nationality obtain the required majority vote, the one who received the higher number of votes shall be considered elected.

2. In the event of a vacancy in the Chambers amongst the permanent judges elected or appointed in accordance with this article, after consultation with the Presidents of the Security Council and of the General Assembly, the Secretary-General shall appoint a person meeting the qualifications of article 13 of the Statute, for the remainder of the term of office concerned.

3. The permanent judges elected in accordance with this article shall be elected for a term of four years. The terms and conditions of service shall be those of the judges of the International Court of Justice. They shall be eligible for re-election.

Election and appointment of ad litem *judges*

13ter.—1. The *ad litem* judges of the International Tribunal shall be elected **3–56** by the General Assembly from a list submitted by the Security Council, in the following manner:

(a) The Secretary-General shall invite nominations for *ad litem* judges of the International Tribunal from States Members of the United Nations and non-member States maintaining permanent observer missions at United Nations Headquarters.

(b) Within sixty days of the date of the invitation of the Secretary-General, each State may nominate up to four candidates meeting the qualifications set out in article 13 of the Statute, taking into account the importance of a fair representation of female and male candidates.

(c) The Secretary-General shall forward the nominations received to the Security Council. From the nominations received the Security Council shall establish a list of not less than fifty-four candidates, taking due account of the adequate representation of the principal legal systems of the world and bearing in mind the importance of equitable geographical distribution.

(d) The President of the Security Council shall transmit the list of candidates to the President of the General Assembly. From that list the General Assembly shall elect the twenty-seven *ad litem* judges of the International Tribunal. The candidates who receive an absolute majority of the votes of the States Members of the United Nations and of the non-member States maintaining permanent observer missions at United Nations Headquarters shall be declared elected.

(e) The *ad litem* judges shall be elected for a term of four years. They shall not be eligible for re-election.

2. During their term, *ad litem* judges will be appointed by the Secretary-General, upon request of the President of the International Tribunal, to serve in the Trial Chambers for one or more trials, for a cumulative period of up to, but not including, three years. When requesting the appointment of any particular *ad litem* judge, the President of the International Tribunal shall bear in mind the criteria set out in article 13 of the Statute regarding the composition of the Chambers and sections of the Trial Chambers, the considerations set out in paragraphs 1 (b) and (c) above and the number of votes the *ad litem* judge received in the General Assembly.

Status of ad litem *judges*

3–57   **13quater.**—1. During the period in which they are appointed to serve in the International Tribunal, *ad litem* judges shall:

(a) Benefit from the same terms and conditions of service mutatis mutandis as the permanent judges of the International Tribunal;

(b) Enjoy, subject to paragraph 2 below, the same powers as the permanent judges of the International Tribunal;

(c) Enjoy the privileges and immunities, exemptions and facilities of a judge of the International Tribunal;

(d) Enjoy the power to adjudicate in pre-trial proceedings in cases other than those that they have been appointed to try.

2. During the period in which they are appointed to serve in the International Tribunal, *ad litem* judges shall not:

(a) Be eligible for election as, or to vote in the election of, the President of the Tribunal or the Presiding Judge of a Trial Chamber pursuant to article 14 of the Statute;

(b) Have power:

(i) To adopt rules of procedure and evidence pursuant to article 15 of the Statute. They shall, however, be consulted before the adoption of those rules;

(ii) To review an indictment pursuant to article 19 of the Statute;

(iii) To consult with the President in relation to the assignment of judges pursuant to article 14 of the Statute or in relation to a pardon or commutation of sentence pursuant to article 28 of the Statute.

Officers and members of the Chambers

3–58   **14.**—1. The permanent judges of the International Tribunal shall elect a President from amongst their number.

2. The President of the International Tribunal shall be a member of the Appeals Chamber and shall preside over its proceedings.

3. After consultation with the permanent judges of the International Tribunal, the President shall assign four of the permanent judges elected or

appointed in accordance with Article 13*bis* of the Statute to the Appeals Chamber and nine to the Trial Chambers.

4. Two of the permanent judges of the International Tribunal for Rwanda elected or appointed in accordance with article 12*bis* of the Statute of that Tribunal shall be assigned by the President of that Tribunal, in consultation with the President of the International Tribunal, to be members of the Appeals Chamber and permanent judges of the International Tribunal.

5. After consultation with the permanent judges of the International Tribunal, the President shall assign such *ad litem* judges as may from time to time be appointed to serve in the International Tribunal to the Trial Chambers.

6. A judge shall serve only in the Chamber to which he or she was assigned.

7. The permanent judges of each Trial Chamber shall elect a Presiding Judge from amongst their number, who shall oversee the work of the Trial Chamber as a whole.

The status, privileges and immunities of the International Tribunal

30.—1. The Convention on the Privileges and Immunities of the United Nations of 13 February 1946 shall apply to the International Tribunal, the judges, the Prosecutor and his staff, and the Registrar and his staff.   **3–59**

2. The judges, the Prosecutor and the Registrar shall enjoy the privileges and immunities, exemptions and facilities accorded to diplomatic envoys, in accordance with international law.

3. The staff of the Prosecutor and of the Registrar shall enjoy the privileges and immunities accorded to officials of the United Nations under articles V and VII of the Convention referred to in paragraph 1 of this article.

4. Other persons, including the accused, required at the seat of the International Tribunal shall be accorded such treatment as is necessary for the proper functioning of the International Tribunal.

(2) ICTR

Statute of the ICTR, Arts 11–13

Provisions for the appointment of *ad litem* judges for the ICTR were also included in the ICTR Statute by Security Council Resolution 1431 (2002).   **3–60**

Composition of the Chambers

11.—1. The Chambers shall be composed of sixteen permanent independent judges, no two of whom may be nationals of the same State, and a maximum at any one time of nine *ad litem* independent judges appointed in accordance with article 12*ter*, paragraph 2, of the present Statute, no two of whom may be nationals of the same State.   **3–61**

2. Three permanent judges and a maximum at any one time of six *ad litem* judges shall be members of each Trial Chamber. Each Trial Chamber to which *ad litem* judges are assigned may be divided into sections of three judges each, composed of both permanent and *ad litem* judges. A section of a Trial Chamber shall have the same powers and responsibilities as a Trial Chamber under the present Statute and shall render judgement in accordance with the same rules.

3. Seven of the permanent judges shall be members of the Appeals Chamber. The Appeals Chamber shall, for each appeal, be composed of five of its members.

4. A person who for the purposes of membership of the Chambers of the International Tribunal for Rwanda could be regarded as a national of more

than one State shall be deemed to be a national of the State in which that person ordinarily exercises civil and political rights.

Qualification and Election of Judges

3–62   **12.** The permanent and *ad litem* judges shall be persons of high moral character, impartiality and integrity who possess the qualifications required in their respective countries for appointment to the highest judicial offices. In the overall composition of the Chambers and sections of the Trial Chambers, due account shall be taken of the experience of the judges in criminal law, international law, including international humanitarian law and human rights law.

Election of permanent judges

3–63   **12*bis*.**—1. Eleven of the permanent judges of the International Tribunal for Rwanda shall be elected by the General Assembly from a list submitted by the Security Council, in the following manner:

  (a) The Secretary-General shall invite nominations for permanent judges of the International Tribunal for Rwanda from States Members of the United Nations and non-member States maintaining permanent observer missions at United Nations Headquarters;

  (b) Within sixty days of the date of the invitation of the Secretary-General, each State may nominate up to two candidates meeting the qualifications set out in article 12 of the present Statute, no two of whom shall be of the same nationality and neither of whom shall be of the same nationality as any judge who is a member of the Appeals Chamber and who was elected or appointed a permanent judge of the International Tribunal for the Prosecution of Persons Responsible for Serious Violations of International Humanitarian Law Committed in the Territory of the former Yugoslavia since 1991 (hereinafter referred to as 'the International Tribunal for the Former Yugoslavia') in accordance with article 13*bis* of the Statute of that Tribunal;

  (c) The Secretary-General shall forward the nominations received to the Security Council. From the nominations received the Security Council shall establish a list of not less than twenty-two and not more than thirty-three candidates, taking due account of the adequate representation on the International Tribunal for Rwanda of the principal legal systems of the world;

  (d) The President of the Security Council shall transmit the list of candidates to the President of the General Assembly. From that list the General Assembly shall elect eleven permanent judges of the International Tribunal for Rwanda. The candidates who receive an absolute majority of the votes of the States Members of the United Nations and of the non-member States maintaining permanent observer missions at United Nations Headquarters, shall be declared elected. Should two candidates of the same nationality obtain the required majority vote, the one who received the higher number of votes shall be considered elected.

  2.—In the event of a vacancy in the Chambers amongst the permanent judges elected or appointed in accordance with this article, after consultation with the Presidents of the Security Council and of the General Assembly, the Secretary-General shall appoint a person meeting the qualifications of article 12 of the present Statute, for the remainder of the term of office concerned.

  3.—The permanent judges elected in accordance with this article shall be elected for a term of four years. The terms and conditions of service shall be those of the permanent judges of the International Tribunal for the Former Yugoslavia. They shall be eligible for re-election.

Election and Appointment of ad litem *judges*

12ter.—1. The *ad litem* judges of the International Tribunal for Rwanda shall **3–64**
be elected by the General Assembly from a list submitted by the Security
Council, in the following manner:

(a) The Secretary-General shall invite nominations for *ad litem* judges of
the International Tribunal for Rwanda from States Members of the
United Nations and non-member States maintaining permanent
observer missions at United Nations Headquarters;

(b) Within sixty days of the date of the invitation of the Secretary-
General, each State may nominate up to four candidates meeting the
qualifications set out in article 12 of the present Statute, taking into
account the importance of a fair representation of female and male
candidates;

(c) The Secretary-General shall forward the nominations received to the
Security Council. From the nominations received the Security Council
shall establish a list of not less than thirty-six candidates, taking due
account of the adequate representation of the principal legal systems
of the world and bearing in mind the importance of equitable
geographical distribution;

(d) The President of the Security Council shall transmit the list of
candidates to the President of the General Assembly. From that list
the General Assembly shall elect the eighteen *ad litem* judges of the
International Tribunal for Rwanda. The candidates who receive an
absolute majority of the votes of the States Members of the United
Nations and of the non-member States maintaining permanent
observer missions at United Nations Headquarters shall be declared
elected;

(e) The *ad litem* judges shall be elected for a term of four years. They shall
not be eligible for re-election.

2. During their term, *ad litem* judges will be appointed by the Secretary-
General, upon request of the President of the International Tribunal for
Rwanda, to serve in the Trial Chambers for one or more trials, for a
cumulative period of up to, but not including, three years. When requesting the
appointment of any particular *ad litem* judge, the President of the International
Tribunal for Rwanda shall bear in mind the criteria set out in article 12 of the
present Statute regarding the composition of the Chambers and sections of the
Trial Chambers, the considerations set out in paragraphs 1(b) and (c) above
and the number of votes the *ad litem* judge received in the General Assembly.

Status of Ad Litem *Judges*

12quater.—1. During the period in which they are appointed to serve in the **3–65**
International Tribunal for Rwanda, *ad litem* judges shall:

(a) Benefit from the same terms and conditions of service *mutatis mutandis*
as the permanent judges of the International Tribunal for Rwanda;

(b) Enjoy, subject to paragraph 2 below, the same powers as the permanent judges of the International Tribunal for Rwanda;

(c) Enjoy the privileges and immunities, exemptions and facilities of a
judge of the International Tribunal for Rwanda;

(d) Enjoy the power to adjudicate in pre-trial proceedings in cases other
than those that they have been appointed to try.

2. During the period in which they are appointed to serve in the International Tribunal for Rwanda, *ad litem* judges shall not:

(a) Be eligible for election as, or to vote in the election of, the President
of the International Tribunal for Rwanda or the Presiding Judge of a
Trial Chamber pursuant to article 13 of the present Statute;

(b) Have power:

(i) To adopt rules of procedure and evidence pursuant to article 14
of the present Statute. They shall, however, be consulted before
the adoption of those rules;

(ii) To review an indictment pursuant to article 18 of the present Statute;

(iii) To consult with the President of the International Tribunal for Rwanda in relation to the assignment of judges pursuant to article 13 of the present Statute or in relation to a pardon or commutation of sentence pursuant to article 27 of the present Statute.

Officers and Members of the Chambers

3–66   **13.**—1. The permanent judges of the International Tribunal for Rwanda shall elect a President from amongst their number.

2. The President of the International Tribunal for Rwanda shall be a member of one of its Trial Chambers.

3. After consultation with the permanent judges of the International Tribunal for Rwanda, the President shall assign two of the permanent judges elected or appointed in accordance with article 12*bis* of the present Statute to be members of the Appeals Chamber of the International Tribunal for the Former Yugoslavia and eight of the Trial Chambers of the International Tribunal for Rwanda.

4. The members of the Appeals Chamber of the International Tribunal for the Former Yugoslavia shall also serve as the members of the Appeals Chamber of the International Tribunal for Rwanda.

5. After consultation with the permanent judges of the International Tribunal for Rwanda, the President shall assign such *ad litem* judges as may from time to time be appointed to serve in the International Tribunal for Rwanda to the Trial Chambers.

6. A judge shall serve only in the Chamber to which he or she was assigned.

7. The permanent judges of each Trial Chamber shall elect a Presiding Judge from amongst their number, who shall oversee the work of that Trial Chamber as a whole.

Also see, Rules 14–29 of both the Rules of the ICTY and ICTR, which pertain to Chambers, including the internal functioning of the Chambers.

D. OFFICE OF THE PROSECUTOR

(1) ICTY Statute

Statute of the ICTY, Art. 16

The Prosecutor

3–67   **16.**—1. The Prosecutor shall be responsible for the investigation and prosecution of persons responsible for serious violations of international humanitarian law committed in the territory of the former Yugoslavia since 1 January 1991.

2. The Prosecutor shall act independently as a separate organ of the International Tribunal. He or she shall not seek or receive instructions from any Government or from any other source.

3. The Office of the Prosecutor shall be composed of a Prosecutor and such other qualified staff as may be required.

4. The Prosecutor shall be appointed by the Security Council on nomination by the Secretary-General. He or she shall be of high moral character and

possess the highest level of competence and experience in the conduct of investigations and prosecutions of criminal cases. The Prosecutor shall serve for a four-year term and be eligible for reappointment. The terms and conditions of service of the Prosecutor shall be those of an Under-Secretary-General of the United Nations.

5. The staff of the Office of the Prosecutor shall be appointed by the Secretary-General on the recommendation of the Prosecutor.

(2) ICTR Statute

Statute of the ICTR, Art. 15

The Prosecutor

15.—1. The Prosecutor shall be responsible for the investigation and **3–68** prosecution of persons responsible for serious violations of international humanitarian law committed in the territory of Rwanda and Rwandan citizens responsible for such violations committed in the territory of neighbouring States, between 1 January 1994 and 31 December 1994.

2. The Prosecutor shall act independently as a separate organ of the International Tribunal for Rwanda. He or she shall not seek or receive instructions from any government or from any other source.

3. The Office of the Prosecutor shall be composed of a Prosecutor and such other qualified staff as may be required.

4. The Prosecutor shall be appointed by the Security Council on nomination by the Secretary-General. He or she shall be of high moral character and possess the highest level of competence and experience in the conduct of investigations and prosecutions of criminal cases. The Prosecutor shall serve for a four-year term and be eligible for reappointment. The terms and conditions of service of the Prosecutor shall be those of an Under-Secretary-General of the United Nations.

5. The staff of the Office of the Prosecutor shall be appointed by the Secretary-General on the recommendation of the Prosecutor.

Also see, Rules 37 and 38 of both the Rules of the ICTY and ICTR.

E. DEFENCE

ICTY Rules of Procedure and Evidence, rr. 44, 45, 45*bis*, 46

Appointment, Qualifications and Duties of Counsel

44.—(A) Counsel engaged by a suspect or an accused shall file a power of **3–69** attorney with the Registrar at the earliest opportunity. Subject to any determination by a Chamber pursuant to Rule 46 or 77, a counsel shall be considered qualified to represent a suspect or accused if the counsel satisfies the Registrar that he or she:

(i) is admitted to the practice of law in a State, or is a university professor of law;

(ii) has written and oral proficiency in one of the two working languages of the Tribunal, unless the Registrar deems it in the interests of justice to waive this requirement, as provided for in paragraph (B);

(iii) is a member in good standing of an association of counsel practicing at the Tribunal recognised by the Registrar;

    (iv) has not been found guilty or otherwise disciplined in relevant disciplinary proceedings against him in a national or international forum, including proceedings pursuant to the Code of Professional Conduct for Defence Counsel Appearing Before the International Tribunal, unless the Registrar deems that, in the circumstances, it would be disproportionate to exclude such counsel;

    (v) has not been found guilty in relevant criminal proceedings;

    (vi) has not engaged in conduct whether in pursuit of his or her profession or otherwise which is dishonest or otherwise discreditable to a counsel, prejudicial to the administration of justice, or likely to diminish public confidence in the International Tribunal or the administration of justice, or otherwise bring the International Tribunal into disrepute; and

    (vii) has not provided false or misleading information in relation to his or her qualifications and fitness to practice or failed to provide relevant information.

(B) At the request of the suspect or accused and where the interests of justice so demand, the Registrar may admit a counsel who does not speak either of the two working languages of the Tribunal but who speaks the native language of the suspect or accused. The Registrar may impose such conditions as deemed appropriate, including the requirement that the counsel or accused undertake to meet all translations and interpretation costs not usually met by the Tribunal, and counsel undertakes not to request any extensions of time as a result of the fact that he does not speak one of the working languages. A suspect or accused may seek the President's review of the Registrar's decision.

(C) In the performance of their duties counsel shall be subject to the relevant provisions of the Statute, the Rules, the Rules of Detention and any other rules or regulations adopted by the Tribunal, the Host Country Agreement, the Code of Professional Conduct for Defence Counsel Appearing Before the International Tribunal and the codes of practice and ethics governing their profession and, if applicable, the Directive on the Assignment of Defence Counsel adopted by the Registrar and approved by the permanent Judges.

(D) An Advisory Panel shall be established to assist the President and the Registrar in all matters relating to defence counsel. The Panel members shall be selected from representatives of professional associations and from counsel who have appeared before the Tribunal. They shall have recognised professional legal experience. The composition of the Advisory Panel shall be representative of the different legal systems. A Directive of the Registrar shall set out the structure and areas of responsibility of the Advisory Panel.

Assignment of Counsel

3–69.1   **45.**—(A) Whenever the interests of justice so demand, counsel shall be assigned to suspects or accused who lack the means to remunerate such counsel. Such assignments shall be treated in accordance with the procedure established in a Directive set out by the Registrar and approved by the permanent Judges.

(B) For this purpose, the Registrar shall maintain a list of counsel who:

    (i) fulfil all the requirements of Rule 44, although the language requirement of Rule 44 (A)(ii) may be waived by the Registrar as provided for in the Directive;

    (ii) possess established competence in criminal law and/or international criminal law/international humanitarian law/international human rights law;

    (iii) possess at least seven years of relevant experience, whether as a judge, prosecutor, attorney or in some other capacity, in criminal proceedings; and

    (iv) have indicated their availability and willingness to be assigned by the Tribunal to any person detained under the authority of the Tribunal

lacking the means to remunerate counsel, under the terms set out in
the Directive.

(C) The Registrar shall maintain a separate list of counsel who, in addition
to fulfilling the qualification requirements set out in paragraph (B), are readily
available as "duty counsel" for assignment to an accused for the purposes of
the initial appearance, in accordance with Rule 62.

(D) The Registrar shall, in consultation with the permanent Judges, establish the criteria for the payment of fees to assigned counsel.

(E) Where a person is assigned counsel and is subsequently found not to be
lacking the means to remunerate counsel, the Chamber may, on application by
the Registrar, make an order of contribution to recover the cost of providing
counsel.

(F) A suspect or an accused electing to conduct his or her own defence shall
so notify the Registrar in writing at the first opportunity.

Detained Persons

45bis. Rules 44 and 45 shall apply to any person detained under the **3–69.2**
authority of the Tribunal.

Misconduct of Counsel

46.—(A) If a Judge or a Chamber finds that the conduct of a counsel is **3–69.3**
offensive, abusive or otherwise obstructs the proper conduct of the proceedings,
or that a counsel is negligent or otherwise fails to meet the standard of
professional competence and ethics in the performance of his duties, the
Chamber may, after giving counsel due warning:

    (i) refuse audience to that counsel; and/or

    (ii) determine, after giving counsel an opportunity to be heard, that
        counsel is no longer eligible to represent a suspect or an accused
        before the Tribunal pursuant to Rule 44 and 45.

(B) A Judge or a Chamber may also, with the approval of the President,
communicate any misconduct of counsel to the professional body regulating the
conduct of counsel in the counsel's State of admission or, if a university
professor of law and not otherwise admitted to the profession, to the governing
body of that counsel's University.

(C) Under the supervision of the President, the Registrar shall publish and
oversee the implementation of a Code of Professional Conduct for defence
counsel.

ICTR Rules of Procedure and Evidence, rr. 44, 44bis, 45, 45bis, 45ter, 45quater, 46

Appointment and Qualifications of Counsel

44.—(A) Counsel engaged by a suspect or an accused shall file his power of **3–70**
attorney with the Registrar at the earliest opportunity. Subject to verification
by the Registrar, a counsel shall be considered qualified to represent a suspect
or accused, provided that he is admitted to the practice of law in a State, or is a
University professor of law.

(B) In the performance of their duties counsel shall be subject to the
relevant provisions of the Statute, the Rules, the Rules of Detention and any
other rules or regulations adopted by the Tribunal, the Host Country Agreement, the Code of Conduct and the codes of practice and ethics governing their
profession and, if applicable, the Directive on the Assignment of Defence
Counsel.

Duty Counsel

44bis.—(A) A list of duty counsel who speak one or both working languages **3–71**
of the Tribunal and have indicated their willingness to be assigned pursuant to
this Rule shall be kept by the Registrar.

(B) Duty counsel shall fulfill the requirements of Rule 44, and shall be situated within reasonable proximity to the Detention Facility and the Seat of the Tribunal.

(C) The Registrar shall at all times ensure that duty counsel will be available to attend the Detention Facility in the event of being summoned.

(D) If an accused, or suspect transferred under Rule 40 *bis*, is unrepresented at any time after being transferred to the Tribunal, the Registrar shall as soon as practicable summon duty counsel to represent the accused or suspect until counsel is engaged by the accused or suspect, or assigned under Rule 45.

(E) In providing initial legal advice and assistance to a suspect transferred under Rule 40 *bis*, duty counsel shall advise the suspect of his or her rights including the rights referred to in Rule 55 (A).

Assignment of Counsel

3–72   **45.**—(A) A list of counsel who speak one or both of the working languages of the Tribunal, meet the requirements of Rule 44, have at least 10 years' relevant experience, and have indicated their willingness to be assigned by the Tribunal to indigent suspects or accused, shall be kept by the Registrar.

(B) The criteria for determination of indigence shall be established by the Registrar and approved by the Judges.

(C) In assigning counsel to an indigent suspect or accused, the following procedure shall be observed:

  (i) A request for assignment of counsel shall be made to the Registrar;

  (ii) The Registrar shall enquire into the financial means of the suspect or accused and determine whether the criteria of indigence are met;

  (iii) If he decides that the criteria are met, he shall assign counsel from the list; if he decides to the contrary, he shall inform the suspect or accused that the request is refused.

(D) If a request is refused, a further reasoned request may be made by the suspect or the accused to the Registrar upon showing a change in circumstances.

(E) The Registrar shall, in consultation with the Judges, establish the criteria for the payment of fees to assigned counsel.

(F) If a suspect or an accused elects to conduct his own defence, he shall so notify the Registrar in writing at the first opportunity.

(G) Where an alleged indigent person is subsequently found not to be indigent, the Chamber may make an order of contribution to recover the cost of providing counsel.

(H) Under exceptional circumstances, at the request of the suspect or accused or his counsel, the Chamber may instruct the Registrar to replace an assigned counsel, upon good cause being shown and after having been satisfied that the request is not designed to delay the proceedings.

(I) It is understood that Counsel will represent the accused and conduct the case to finality. Failure to do so, absent just cause approved by the Chamber, may result in forfeiture of fees in whole or in part. In such circumstances the Chamber may make an order accordingly. Counsel shall only be permitted to withdraw from the case to which he has been assigned in the most exceptional circumstances.

Detained Persons

3–73   **45bis.** Rules 44 and 45 shall apply to any person detained under the authority of the Tribunal.

Availability of Counsel

3–73.1   **Rule 45ter.** (A) Counsel and Co-Counsel, whether assigned by the Registrar or appointed by the client for the purposes of proceedings before the Tribunal, shall furnish the Registrar, upon date of such assignment or appointment, a written undertaking that he will appear before the Tribunal within a reasonable time as specified by the Registrar.

(B) Failure by Counsel or Co-Counsel to appear before the Tribunal, as undertaken, shall be a ground for withdrawal by the Registrar of the assignment of such Counsel or Co- Counsel or the refusal of audience by the Tribunal or the imposition of any other sanctions by the Chamber concerned.

Assignment of Counsel in the Interests of Justice

Rule 45*quater*. The Trial Chamber may, if it decides that it is in the interests of justice, instruct the Registrar to assign a counsel to represent the interests of the accused.   **3–73.2**

Misconduct of Counsel

46.—(A) A Chamber may, after a warning, impose sanctions against a counsel if, in its opinion, his conduct remains offensive or abusive, obstructs the proceedings, or is otherwise contrary to the interests of justice. This provision is applicable *mutatis mutandis* to Counsel for the Prosecution.   **3–73.3**

(B) A Judge or a Chamber may also, with the approval of the President, communicate any misconduct of counsel to the professional body regulating the conduct of counsel in his State of admission or, if a professor and not otherwise admitted to the profession, to the governing body of his University.

(C) If a counsel assigned pursuant to Rule 45 is sanctioned in accordance with Sub-Rule A) by being refused audience, the Chamber shall instruct the Registrar to replace the counsel.

(D) The Registrar may set up a Code of Professional Conduct enunciating the principles of professional ethics to be observed by counsel appearing before the Tribunal, subject to adoption by the Plenary Meeting. Amendments to the Code shall be made in consultation with representatives of the Prosecutor and Defence counsel, and subject to adoption by the Plenary Meeting. If the Registrar has strong grounds for believing that Counsel has committed a serious violation of the Code of Professional Conduct so adopted, he may report the matter to the President or the Bureau for appropriate action under this rule.

F. PRISON SERVICES

(1) ICTY Statute

Statute of the ICTY, Art. 27

Enforcement of sentences

27. Imprisonment shall be served in a State designated by the International Tribunal from a list of States which have indicated to the Security Council their willingness to accept convicted persons. Such imprisonment shall be in accordance with the applicable law of the State concerned, subject to the supervision of the International Tribunal.   **3–74**

(2) ICTR Statute

Statute of the ICTR, Art. 26

Enforcement of Sentences

26. Imprisonment shall be served in Rwanda or any of the States on a list of States which have indicated to the Security Council their willingness to accept convicted persons, as designated by the International Tribunal for Rwanda.   **3–75**

Such imprisonment shall be in accordance with the applicable law of the State concerned, subject to the supervision of the International Tribunal for Rwanda.

Each Tribunal has its own detention unit under the authority of the Registries for accused awaiting trial and during proceedings before the Tribunals (see the Rules governing the detention of persons for each Tribunal in Appendix C and D respectively).

G. FUNDING

(1) ICTY Statute

Statute of the ICTY, Art. 32

Expenses of the International Tribunal

3–76   **32.** The expenses of the International Tribunal shall be borne by the regular budget of the United Nations in accordance with Article 17 of the Charter of the United Nations.

(2) ICTR Statute

Statute of the ICTR, Art. 30

Expenses of the International Tribunal for Rwanda

3–77   **30.** The expenses of the International Tribunal for Rwanda shall be expenses of the Organisation in accordance with Article 17 of the Charter of the United Nations.

III. SPECIAL COURTS

A. EAST TIMOR

Regulation No. 2000/11 on the Organization of Courts in East Timor (as amended by reg. 2001/25), ss.1, 2, 2A, 2B, 2C, 3–6, 6A, 7, 10–24, 27–36, 38

Judicial Authority

3–78   **1.** Judicial authority in East Timor shall be exclusively vested in courts that are established by law and composed of both East Timorese and international judges who are appointed to these courts in accordance with UNTAET Regulation No. 1999/3.

Independence of the Judiciary

3–79   **2.**—2.1 Judges shall perform their duties independently and impartially, and in accordance with applicable laws in East Timor and the oath or solemn declaration given by them to the Transitional Administrator pursuant to UNTAET Regulation No. 1999/3.

2.2 Judges shall decide matters before them without prejudice and in accordance with their impartial assessment of the facts and their understanding of the law, without improper influence, direct or indirect, from any source.

2.3 Judges, notwithstanding their rank or grade within the hierarchy of courts have to respect all decisions made by the Court of Appeal. Such decisions are binding and the independence of the individual judge is not affected.

Reassignment of Judges

2A.—2A.1 Notwithstanding the appointment of judges to particular District **3–80** Courts, the President of the Court of Appeal may, as appropriate, reassign any judge to another District Court.

2A.2 he Transitional Administrator, upon recommendation of the Transitional Judicial Service Commission and at the request of the judge concerned, may authorize a judge to take up another assignment where, in the opinion of the Transitional Judicial Service Commission, the other assignment is in accordance with the criteria provided in Section

2A.3 In deciding whether to recommend to the Transitional Administrator that a judge be authorized to take up another assignment, the Transitional Judicial Service Commission must be satisfied of all of the following:

   (a) that the other assignment will not undermine, or be reasonably perceived to undermine, the judicial independence or impartiality of the judge concerned;
   (b) that the judge concerned will not engage in work as a legal practitioner or as an employee of or consultant to a legal practice;
   (c) that the judge concerned will not accept a directorship for any organization whose primary purpose is profit-related, whether or not profit is actually realized;
   (d) that the judge concerned will not take part in any political activity or accept public office; and
   (e) that the judge concerned will not accept any financial gain or reward, other than royalties earned as an author.

2A.4 During any period of reassignment pursuant to Section 2A.2, the judicial authority of the judge concerned shall be suspended; however, he or she shall continue to receive judicial compensation as though the reassignment had not occurred.

Incompatibility

2B.—1 The position of a judge is incompatible with any other professional **3–81** activity, paid or unpaid, except the publication of articles and books.

2B.2 The position of a judge is incompatible with the membership in the directorate of any governmental or non-governmental organization or company.

2B.3 The position of a judge is incompatible with any political activity such as an office in a political party or in a public office.

Leave

2C. The Transitional Administrator may grant at the request of a judge and **3–82** upon recommendation of the Transitional Judicial Service Commission a paid leave for a limited period of time up to six months. Any eventual professional activity during such a leave needs a formal explicit permission by the Transitional Administrator in accordance with Section 2A.2 of the present Regulation.

Refusal of Justice

3. No judge may refuse to hear, try or decide a case that is brought before **3–83** the court in accordance with the relevant procedural provisions.

Courts in East Timor

3–84   **4.** The judiciary in East Timor shall be composed of District Courts, as determined by the present regulation, and one Court of Appeal.

Applicable Law

3–85   **5.**—5.1 In exercising their jurisdiction, the courts in East Timor shall apply the law of East Timor as promulgated by Section 3 of UNTAET Regulation No. 1999/1.

5.2 Courts shall have jurisdiction in respect of crimes committed in East Timor prior to 25 October 1999 only insofar as the law on which the offence is based is consistent with Section 3.1 of UNTAET Regulation No. 1999/1 or any other UNTAET regulation.

5.3 Courts shall have jurisdiction in respect of civil claims, which arose in East Timor prior to 25 October 1999 only insofar as the law on which the claim is based is consistent with Section 3.1 of UNTAET Regulation No. 1999/1 or any other UNTAET regulation.

I DISTRICT COURTS

Composition of the District Courts

3–86   **6.**—6.1 Each District Court shall be composed of both international and East Timorese judges who are appointed to the respective court by the Transitional Administrator in accordance with Regulation No. 1999/3.

6.2 The judges may sit individually or in panels of three judges in accordance with the provisions of the present Regulation.

6.3 The number of judges at each District Court shall be determined by the President of the Court of Appeal based on the caseload of each court.

Judge Administrator

3–87   **6A.**—6A.1 There shall be a Judge in each District Court who is appointed Judge Administrators by the President of the Court of Appeal to serve for a renewable period of one year.

6A.2 The Judge Administrator for each District Court shall be responsible to the President of the Court of Appeal for all administrative matters of that court and shall submit periodic reports to the President of the Court of Appeal.

6A.3 In carrying out his or her functions each Judge Administrator shall report to the President of the Court of Appeal and shall be subject to his or her direction and control.

Territorial Jurisdictions of the District Courts

7.—7.1 Until such time as additional District Courts are established in East Timor, District Courts shall be established in the following locations:

    (a) Baucau, with jurisdiction for the districts of Baucau, Lautem, Viqueque and Manatuto;

    (b) Suai, with jurisdiction for Suai, Cova Lima, Bobonaro, Ainaro and Manufahi;

    (c) Oecussi, with jurisdiction for Oecussi;

    (d) Dili, with jurisdiction for the districts of Dili, Liquica, Ermera and Aileu.

Until such time as conditions are met for the establishment of additional District Courts, the territorial jurisdiction of existing District Courts may be re-defined by UNTAET directive.

7.2 Each District Court shall exercise its functions and powers, as provided by law, on the territory of its area of jurisdiction. In the event that a District Court lacks jurisdiction over a case, which comes before it, that District Court shall refer the case to the competent District Court of jurisdiction. The Court of Appeal shall settle any dispute between two or more courts regarding the jurisdiction over a case.

7.3 For a transitional period and until otherwise determined by the Transitional Administrator, the judges appointed to the District Court in Dili shall have jurisdiction throughout the entire territory of East Timor.

Legal Cooperation

10.—10.1 Any District Court in East Timor shall cooperate with the request **3–88** of another District Court to

  (a) interrogate witnesses who are registered or permanently accommodated in the area of the requested court's jurisdiction;
  (b) carry out at-the-scene examinations or re-enactment of crimes in the area of the requested court's jurisdiction;
  (c) serve summonses of the requesting court on witnesses in the requested court's jurisdiction;
  (d) serve decisions of the requesting court on individuals in the requested court's jurisdiction;
  (e) execute the decisions of the requesting court if the subject of dispute is
  (f) located in the requested court's jurisdiction;
  (g) access files of the requested court for information purposes or decision.

10.2 The request may not be rejected except in the case of lack of jurisdiction of the requested court.

Single Judges

11. Unless otherwise expressly provided in this or in another UNTAET **3–89** Regulation, a single judge shall hear and conduct the trial of any criminal or civil case.

Panel of judges

12.—12.1 Any criminal matter that carries a penalty of imprisonment **3–90** exceeding five years shall be heard by a panel of three judges if the public prosecutor in the indictment or the accused person or his or her legal representative in the response, makes a request for trial by a panel.

12.2 In any civil matter in which the claim exceeds $US 1000, either party may at any stage prior to the commencement of the trial request by application to the Court for the matter to be heard by a panel of three judges.

12.3 The trials of all serious crimes named in Section 9 of the present Regulation shall be conducted by a panel of judges.

12.4 Relatives up to second degree as well as spouses and partners shall not sit as judges in the same panel.

Investigating Judge

13. In criminal matters, there shall be at least one judge assigned as **3–91** investigating judge at every District Court in East Timor.

II COURT OF APPEAL

Jurisdiction of the Court of Appeal

14.—14.1 There shall be established a Court of Appeal for East Timor. The **3–92** Court shall have its seat in Dili.

14.2 The Court of Appeal shall have jurisdiction to hear appeals of final judgements rendered by any District Court in East Timor, and such other matters as are provided for in the present or any other UNTAET regulation.

Composition of the Court of Appeal

3–93 **15.**—15.1 The Court of Appeal shall be composed of judges appointed by the Transitional Administrator to the Court of Appeal in accordance with UNTAET Regulation No. 1999/3.

15.2 The judges shall sit in panels of three judges. The panel shall take its decisions by majority vote. The vote of each judge shall have equal weight.

15.3 Relatives up to second degree as well as spouses or partners shall not sit as judges on the same panel.

15.4 In the event of an appeal on a matter provided in Section 9 of the present regulation, the Transitional Administrator, after consultation with the President of the Court of Appeal, shall establish a panel with the expertise to hear and decide such appeals. Such panels shall be composed of both East Timorese and international judges, appointed to the Court in accordance with UNTAET Regulation No. 1999/3.

IV ORGANS OF THE COURTS AND THEIR COMPETENCIES

President of the Court of Appeal

3–93.1 **16.**—16.1 There shall be a President of the Court of Appeal.

16.2 The criteria and means of appointment of the President of the Court of Appeal will be set out in a Directive promulgated by the Transitional Administrator. Until the mentioned criteria and means of appointment shall have been so promulgated, the President shall continue to be appointed under the prior procedure and the mandate of the office shall include all the competencies given by the present Regulation.

16.3 Upon appointment of the President of the Court of Appeal, the Transitional Administrator shall designate one member of the Court of Appeal to carry out the functions of the President of the Court of Appeal in the event that the President of the Court of Appeal is unavailable or otherwise unable to exercise his or her functions.

Competencies of the President of the Court of Appeal

3–93.2 **17.**—17.1 The President of the Court of Appeal shall be responsible for the overall administration of the courts in East Timor. In particular, he or she shall have the competency to supervise the work of District Courts, submit to the Transitional Administrator an annual report on its activities as well as on the activities of all the other courts in East Timor.

17.2 For the purpose mentioned in Section 17.1, the President of the Court of Appeal shall have the power to issue Administrative instructions to all the courts in East Timor.

17.3 In every new calendar year, the President of the Court of Appeal shall prepare a precise plan outlining the general system of distribution of incoming cases to the judges of the court and the District Courts for that year. The plan shall be published in the Official Gazette of East Timor.

17.4 Except where provided otherwise in the present regulation, the President of the Court of Appeal shall have the responsibility of ensuring law and order within the court building and its premises.

17.5 Where a matter of administrative practice arises that has not been regulated by the present Regulation, the matter shall be decided by the President of the Court of Appeal.

Presiding Judges of District Court Panels

18.—18.1 There shall be a Presiding Judge on each panel who will be the judge to whom the case was initially distributed.   **3–93.3**

18.2 Each Presiding Judge shall conduct the proceedings of the panel.

18.3 The Presiding Judge shall not give directions to the other judges of the panel on substantive matters of law, their assessment of the evidence, or their findings in a case.

18.4 The Presiding Judge or, where applicable, the individual judge shall ensure order in the courtroom.

Additional Judges for District Court Panels

19.—19.1 In cases of special importance or gravity, or of an expected duration of more than three consecutive trial days, the Judge Administrator may decide to assign an additional judge from a different panel of the same court to attend the trial sessions of a relevant panel.   **3–93.4**

19.2 The additional judge shall not have a vote and shall not participate in the proceedings, unless one of the three regular judges of the panel is unable to attend one or more of the trial sessions, due to illness, death or any other serious reason that prevents the regular judge from attending the trial sessions in this period.

19.3 Final decision shall be taken in accordance with Section 30.1 of UNTAET Regulation 2000/30. The same procedure shall apply also for non criminal cases.

Disqualification of Judges

20.—20.1 The President of the Court of Appeal on the level of the Court of Appeal, or the Judge Administrator on the level of the District Court may, at the request of a judge of the respective court or a party to a proceeding, excuse that judge from the exercise of a function in any case in which impartiality of the judge might reasonably be doubted on any ground.   **3–93.5**

20.2 Except as provided in Section 10 of UNTAET Regulation 2000/30, a judge shall be disqualified from a case in accordance with the present section if that judge has previously been involved in any capacity in that case before the court.

20.3 A judge of the Court of Appeal shall be obliged to request the President of the Court of Appeal, and a judge of any District Court shall be obliged to request the Judge Administrator, to be excused from the exercise of any function in any case in which a party to the proceedings is a spouse, partner or a relative of second degree of that judge.

20.4 Any question as to the disqualification of a judge shall be decided on the level of the Court of Appeal by the President of the Court of Appeal, on the level of a District Court by the Judge Administrator of the respective District Court.

20.5. In case of any suggestion of disqualification of a Judge Administrator, matters shall be decided by the President of the Court of Appeal.

Court Registry

21.—21.1 There shall be a Registry at every court in East Timor.   **3–93.6**

21.2 The Registry shall have responsibility for the receipt of documents to be filed in the court, for organizing court documents and ensuring security of court documents, and for such other functions as are permitted by an UNTAET regulation or directive. The staff of the registry shall exercise these responsibilities under the direction of the Judge Administrator or the President of the Court of Appeal.

21.3 The staff of the Registry shall have legal and administrative skills, and shall be appointed by the Public Service Commission, pursuant to UNTAET Regulation No. 2000/3.

Court Staff

3–93.7   **22.**—22.1 Each court in East Timor shall have such qualified staff as may be required for the proper functioning of the court and the discharge of the responsibilities of its judges. The court staff shall exercise these responsibilities under the direction of the Judge Administrator or the President of the Court of Appeal.

22.2 Each individual judge or panel of judges shall be assisted dur ing proceedings by such court staff as may be necessary.

22.3 The court staff shall be selected by the Public Service Commission, pursuant to UNTAET Regulation No. 2000/3.

22.4 The President of the Court of Appeal shall have the powers to assign and reassign court staff to any court or office as deemed necessary for an equitable distribution of human resources and for work expediency.

Translation Service

3–93.8   **23.** Courts shall provide translation and interpretation services in every case where a party to the proceedings, or a judge, or a witness, or expert witness does not sufficiently speak or understand the language spoken in that court.

Prosecution Service

3–93.9   **24.** A Prosecution Service shall be established within the jurisdiction of every District Court in East Timor in accordance with applicable law.

Legal Representation at Hearings

3–93.10   **27.**—27.1 A party to a proceeding before a court in East Timor has the right to a legal representative of its own choosing.

27.2 UNTAET shall ensure that efficient procedures and responsive mechanisms for effective and equal access to lawyers are provided for all persons within the territory of East Timor, in observance of UNTAET Regulation 2001/24, without any discrimination based on sex, race, color, language, religion, political or other opinion, national, ethnic or social origin, association with a national minority, property, birth or any other status.

VI RIGHTS AND DUTIES OF JUDGES

Tenure

3–93.11   **28.**—28.1 After an initial period of no less than two but no more than three years, judges shall be appointed for life.

28.2 During the initial period referred to in Subsection 28.1, the performance of duties of every judge shall be monitored by an experienced judge, as nominated by the President of the Court of Appeal, who shall have the duty to give guidance and supervise judges in their initial period. The experienced judge shall only monitor the professional conduct of the judge, including the judge's integrity and dedication, attendance, ability to cope with the workload, independence and impartiality shown in dealing with the cases, without interference, or influence upon, the substantive decisions of the judge. The experienced judge shall submit periodic reports to the Transitional Judicial

Service Commission every six months in order to evaluate the performance of the judge on the aforementioned criteria. Prior to submission of a report to the Commission, the judge concerned must be accorded an opportunity to comment on the report.

28.3 At the end of the initial period, or at any given time before, the Transitional Judicial Service Commission, in accordance with UNTAET Regulation No. 1999/3, may recommend that the judge be appointed for life, unless the performance of the duties of that judge, as specified in Section 28.2 of the present regulation, was unsatisfactory, in which case the judge shall be dismissed from judicial service.

Rights, Duties and Prohibitions

29.—29.1 Upon appointment for life, every judge shall enjoy the following guarantees: **3–93.12**

    (a) A judge shall be removed only in the cases provided for in Section 13.3 of UNTAET Regulation No. 1999/3 or Section 28.3 of the present regulation upon recommendation of the Transitional Judicial Service Commission;

    (b) A judge may be re-assigned or appointed to another court in East Timor, where the interests of justice so require, by the President of the Court of Appeal in accordance with Section 2A.1 of the present Regulation;

    (c) A judge shall be remunerated in accordance with the salary scheme determined by an UNTAET directive for the East Timor Administration; the remuneration shall not be subject to any reduction other than due to general taxes and levies imposed equally on all citizens;

    (d) A judge shall be appointed for life, with compulsory retirement at the age of 65; the conditions of service shall not be altered to their disadvantage during their term of office, except as part of a uniform public economic measure, after consultations with representatives of members of the judiciary.

29.2 All judges shall comply with the provisions of the Code of Ethics, as prepared by the Transitional Judicial Service Commission, pursuant to Section 15 of UNTAET Regulation No.1999/3.

Disclosure of Information

30. Judges shall not disclose any information or personal data related to or obtained in the discharge of their functions, except where authorized by the President of the Court of Appeal for public information or research purposes.   **3–93.13**

Privileges and Immunities

31.—31.1 Judges shall enjoy such privileges and immunities as are provided by law.   **3–93.14**

31.2 In particular, judges shall not be liable or otherwise responsible for any adverse effects or any damage caused by any of their acts or omissions committed in the course of the discharge of their functions, except where such effects or damage are caused by intentional and wrongful conduct.

Disciplinary Measures

32. A Judge who has committed misconduct in office shall be subject to disciplinary measures, as defined in UNTAET Regulation No. 1999/3.   **3–93.15**

Remuneration of Non-Judicial Staff

33. Registrars and court clerks shall receive remuneration in accordance with the salary scheme determined by an UNTAET directive for the East Timor Administration.   **3–93.16**

VII Administrative Matters

Financial and Technical Support

3–93.17   **34.** During the transitional period, UNTAET shall provide the necessary financial and technical support to the courts in East Timor.

Working Languages

3–93.18   **35.** The working languages of the courts in East Timor, during the transitional period, shall be, as appropriate, Tetum, Portuguese, Bahasa Indonesia and English.

Seal

3–93.19   **36.** Each court shall have a seal, bearing the court's insignia, for sealing writs and other
official documents of the respective court, as determined by an UNTAET Directive.

Official Insignia

3–93.20   **38.** No court in East Timor shall bear any political insignia other than the insignia of the United Nations and UNTAET. Political manifestations within the court building are not permitted.

Also see, sections 22 and 23 of Regulation No. 2000/15 for the composition of the Panels and qualifications of the judges. For provisions on the powers of the Public Prosecutor and the Investigating Judge, replacement of the Public Prosecutor, and participation by Investigating Judges as Trial Judges, see sections 7–10 of Regulation No. 2000/30 as amended by Regulation No. 2001/25. For the regulations governing the appointment, remuneration, promotion, and the codes of ethics of judges and prosecutors, as well as the organization of the Public Prosecution Service in East Timor, including the General Prosecutor, see Regulation 2000/16 as amended by Regulation 2001/26.

B. Sierra Leone

Statute of the Special Court for Sierra Leone, Arts 11–16

Competence of the Special Court

3–94   **1.**—1. The Special Court shall, except as provided in subparagraph (2), have the power to prosecute persons who bear the greatest responsibility for serious violations of international humanitarian law and Sierra Leonean law committed in the territory of Sierra Leone since 30 November 1996, including those leaders who, in committing such crimes, have threatened the establishment of and implementation of the peace process in Sierra Leone.

2. Any transgressions by peacekeepers and related personnel present in Sierra Leone pursuant to the Status of Mission Agreement in force between the United Nations and the Government of Sierra Leone or agreements between Sierra Leone and other Governments or regional organizations, or, in the absence of such agreement, provided that the peacekeeping operations were undertaken with the consent of the Government of Sierra Leone, shall be within the primary jurisdiction of the sending State.

3. In the event the sending State is unwilling or unable genuinely to carry out an investigation or prosecution, the Court may, if authorized by the Security Council on the proposal of any State, exercise jurisdiction over such persons.

Concurrent jurisdiction

8.—1. The Special Court and the national courts of Sierra Leone shall have concurrent jurisdiction.   **3–94.1**

2. The Special Court shall have primacy over the national courts of Sierra Leone. At any stage of the procedure, the Special Court may formally request a national court to defer to its competence in accordance with the present Statute and the Rules of Procedure and Evidence.

Organization of the Special Court

11. The Special Court shall consist of the following organs: **3–94.2**
   a The Chambers, comprising one or more Trial Chambers and an Appeals Chamber;
   b The Prosecutor; and
   c The Registry.

Composition of the Chambers

12.—1. The Chambers shall be composed of not less than eight (8) or more   **3–95**
than eleven (11) independent judges, who shall serve as follows:
   a. Three judges shall serve in the Trial Chamber, of whom one shall be a judge appointed by the Government of Sierra Leone, and two judges appointed by the Secretary-General of the United Nations (hereinafter "the Secretary-General").
   b. Five judges shall serve in the Appeals Chamber, of whom two shall be judges appointed by the Government of Sierra Leone, and three judges appointed by the Secretary-General.

2. Each judge shall serve only in the Chamber to which he or she has been appointed.

3. The judges of the Appeals Chamber and the judges of the Trial Chamber, respectively, shall elect a presiding judge who shall conduct the proceedings in the Chamber to which he or she was elected. The presiding judge of the Appeals Chamber shall be the President of the Special Court.

4. If, at the request of the President of the Special Court, an alternate judge or judges have been appointed by the Government of Sierra Leone or the Secretary-General, the presiding judge of a Trial Chamber or the Appeals Chamber shall designate such an alternate judge to be present at each stage of the trial and to replace a judge if that judge is unable to continue sitting.

Qualification and appointment of judges

13.—1. The judges shall be persons of high moral character, impartiality   **3–96**
and integrity who possess the qualifications required in their respective countries for appointment to the highest judicial offices. They shall be independent in the performance of their functions, and shall not accept or seek instructions from any Government or any other source.

2. In the overall composition of the Chambers, due account shall be taken of the experience of the judges in international law, including international humanitarian law and human rights law, criminal law and juvenile justice.

3. The judges shall be appointed for a three-year period and shall be eligible for reappointment.

Rules of Procedure and Evidence

3–97   **14.**—1. The Rules of Procedure and Evidence of the International Criminal Tribunal for Rwanda obtaining at the time of the establishment of the Special Court shall be applicable *mutatis mutandis* to the conduct of the legal proceedings before the Special Court.

2. The judges of the Special Court as a whole may amend the Rules of Procedure and Evidence or adopt additional rules where the applicable Rules do not, or do not adequately, provide for a specific situation. In so doing, they may be guided, as appropriate, by the Criminal Procedure Act, 1965, of Sierra Leone.

The Prosecutor

3–98   **15.**—1. The Prosecutor shall be responsible for the investigation and prosecution of persons who bear the greatest responsibility for serious violations of international humanitarian law and crimes under Sierra Leonean law committed in the territory of Sierra Leone since 30 November 1996. The Prosecutor shall act independently as a separate organ of the Special Court. He or she shall not seek or receive instructions from any Government or from any other source.

2. The Office of the Prosecutor shall have the power to question suspects, victims and witnesses, to collect evidence and to conduct on-site investigations. In carrying out these tasks, the Prosecutor shall, as appropriate, be assisted by the Sierra Leonean authorities concerned.

3. The Prosecutor shall be appointed by the Secretary-General for a three-year term and shall be eligible for re-appointment. He or she shall be of high moral character and possess the highest level of professional competence, and have extensive experience in the conduct of investigations and prosecutions of criminal cases.

4. The Prosecutor shall be assisted by a Sierra Leonean Deputy Prosecutor, and by such other Sierra Leonean and international staff as may be required to perform the functions assigned to him or her effectively and efficiently. Given the nature of the crimes committed and the particular sensitivities of girls, young women and children victims of rape, sexual assault, abduction and slavery of all kinds, due consideration should be given in the appointment of staff to the employment of prosecutors and investigators experienced in gender-related crimes and juvenile justice.

5. In the prosecution of juvenile offenders, the Prosecutor shall ensure that the child-rehabilitation programme is not placed at risk and that, where appropriate, resort should be had to alternative truth and reconciliation mechanisms, to the extent of their availability.

The Registry

3–99   **16.**—1. The Registry shall be responsible for the administration and servicing of the Special Court.

2. The Registry shall consist of a Registrar and such other staff as may be required.

3. The Registrar shall be appointed by the Secretary-General after consultation with the President of the Special Court and shall be a staff member of the United Nations. He or she shall serve for a three-year term and be eligible for re-appointment.

4. The Registrar shall set up a Victims and Witnesses Unit within the Registry. This Unit shall provide, in consultation with the Office of the Prosecutor, protective measures and security arrangements, counselling and other appropriate assistance for witnesses, victims who appear before the Court and others who are at risk on account of testimony given by such witnesses. The Unit personnel shall include experts in trauma, including trauma related to crimes of sexual violence and violence against children.

Working language
24. The working language of the Special Court shall be English.   **3–99.1**

C. Cambodia

Law on the Establishment of the Extraordinary Chambers in the Courts of Cambodia for the Prosecution of Crimes Committed during the Period of Democratic Kampuchea, Arts 2, 9–15, 16–28, 30–32, 38–39, 41–47

Competence
2. Extraordinary Chambers shall be established in the existing court struc-   **3–100**
ture, namely the trial court and the supreme court to bring to trial senior
leaders of Democratic Kampuchea and those who were most responsible for
the crimes and serious violations of Cambodian laws related to crimes,
international humanitarian law and custom, and international conventions
recognized by Cambodia, that were committed during the period from 17 April
1975 to 6 January 1979
   Senior leaders of Democratic Kampuchea and those who were most responsible for the above acts are hereinafter designated as "Suspects".

Composition of the Extraordinary Chambers
9. The Trial Chamber shall be an Extraordinary Chamber composed of five   **3–101**
professional judges, of whom three are Cambodian judges with one as
president, and two foreign judges; and before which the Co-Prosecutors shall
present their cases. The president shall appoint one or more clerks of the court
to participate.
   The Supreme Court Chamber, which shall serve as both appellate chamber
and final instance, shall be an Extraordinary Chamber composed of seven
judges, of whom four are Cambodian judges with one as president, and three
foreign judges; and before which the Co-Prosecutors shall present their cases.
The president shall appoint one or more clerks of the court to participate.

Appointment of judges
10. The judges of the Extraordinary Chambers shall be appointed from   **3–102**
among the currently practising judges or are additionally appointed in accordance with the existing procedures for appointment of judges; all of whom shall
have high moral character, a spirit of impartiality and integrity, and experience, particularly in criminal law or international law, including international
humanitarian law and human rights law.
   Judges shall be independent in the performance of their functions, and shall
not accept or seek any instructions from any government or any other source.
   11. The Supreme Council of the Magistracy shall appoint at least seven
Cambodian judges to act as judges of the Extraordinary Chambers, and shall
appoint reserve judges as needed, and shall also appoint the President of each
of the Extraordinary Chambers from the above Cambodian judges so
appointed, in accordance with the existing procedures for appointment of
judges.
   The reserve Cambodian judges shall replace the appointed Cambodian
judges in case of their absence. These reserve judges may continue to perform
their regular duties in their respective courts.

The Supreme Council of the Magistracy shall appoint at least five individuals of foreign nationality to act as foreign judges of the Extraordinary Chambers upon nomination by the Secretary-General of the United Nations.

The Secretary-General of the United Nations shall submit a list of not less than seven candidates for foreign judges to the Royal Government of Cambodia, from which the Supreme Council of the Magistracy shall appoint five sitting judges and at least two reserve judges. In addition to the foreign judges sitting in the Extraordinary Chambers and present at every stage of the proceedings, the President of each Chamber may, on a case-by-case basis, designate one or more reserve foreign judges already appointed by the Supreme Council of the Magistracy to be present at each stage of the trial, and to replace a foreign judge if that judge is unable to continue sitting.

12. All judges under this law shall enjoy equal status and conditions of service according to each level of the Extraordinary Chambers.

Each judge under this law shall be appointed for the period of these proceedings.

13. Judges shall be assisted by Cambodian and international staff as needed in their offices.

In choosing staff to serve as assistants and law clerks, the Director of the Office of Administration shall interview if necessary and, with the approval of the Cambodian judges by majority vote, hire staff who shall be appointed by the Royal Government of Cambodia. The Deputy Director of the Office of Administration shall be responsible for the recruitment and administration of all international staff. The number of assistants and law clerks shall be chosen in proportion to the Cambodian judges and foreign judges.

Cambodian staff shall be selected from Cambodian civil servants or other qualified nationals of Cambodia, if necessary.

Decisions of the Extraordinary Chambers

3–103   **14.**—1. The judges shall attempt to achieve unanimity in their decisions. If this is not possible, the following shall apply:

    a. a decision by the Extraordinary Chamber of the trial court shall require the affirmative vote of at least four judges;

    b. a decision by the Extraordinary Chamber of the appeals court shall require the affirmative vote of at least five judges.

2. When there is no unanimity, the decision of the Extraordinary Chambers shall contain the opinions of the majority and the minority.

Co-Prosecutors

3–104   **16.** All indictments in the Trial Chamber shall be the responsibility of two prosecutors, one Cambodian and another foreign, hereinafter referred to as Co-Prosecutors, who shall work together to prepare indictments against the Suspects in the Extraordinary Chambers.

17. The Co-Prosecutors in the trial court shall have the right to appeal the verdict of the Extraordinary Chamber of the trial court.

The Co-Prosecutors in the appeals court shall have the right to appeal the decision of the Extraordinary Chamber of the appeals court.

18. The Supreme Council of the Magistracy shall appoint Cambodian prosecutors and Cambodian reserve prosecutors as necessary from among the Cambodian professional judges.

The reserve prosecutors shall replace the appointed prosecutors in case of their absence. These reserve prosecutors may continue to perform their regular duties in their respective courts.

One foreign prosecutor with the competence to appear in both Extraordinary Chambers shall be appointed by the Supreme Council of the Magistracy upon nomination by the Secretary-General of the United Nations.

The Secretary-General of the United Nations shall submit a list of at least two candidates for foreign Co-Prosecutor to the Royal Government of Cambodia, from which the Supreme Council of the Magistracy shall appoint one prosecutor and one reserve prosecutor.

19. The Co-Prosecutors shall be appointed from among those individuals who are appointed in accordance with the existing procedures for selection of prosecutors who have high moral character and integrity and who are experienced in the conduct of investigations and prosecutions of criminal cases.

The Co-Prosecutors shall be independent in the performance of their functions and shall not accept or seek instructions from any government or any other source.

20. The Co-Prosecutors shall prosecute in accordance with existing procedures in force. If these existing procedures do not deal with a particular matter, or if there is uncertainty regarding their interpretation or application or if there is a question regarding their consistency with international standards, the Co-Prosecutors may seek guidance in procedural rules established at the international level.

In the event of disagreement between the Co-Prosecutors the following shall apply:

The prosecution shall proceed unless the Co-Prosecutors or one of them requests within thirty days that the difference shall be settled in accordance with the following provisions;

The Co-Prosecutors shall submit written statements of facts and the reasons for their different positions to the Director of the Office of Administration.

The difference shall be settled forthwith by a Pre-Trial Chamber of five judges, three Cambodian judges appointed by the Supreme Council of the Magistracy, one of whom shall be President, and two foreign judges appointed by the Supreme Council of the Magistracy upon nomination by the Secretary-General of the United Nations. The appointment of the above judges shall follow the provisions of Article 10 of this Law.

Upon receipt of the statements referred to in the third paragraph, the Director of the Office of Administration shall immediately convene the Pre-Trial Chamber and communicate the statements to its members.

A decision of the Pre-Trial Chamber, against which there is no appeal, requires the affirmative vote of at least four judges. The decision shall be communicated to the Director of the Office of Administration, who shall publish it and communicate it to the Co-Prosecutors. They shall immediately proceed in accordance with the decision of the Chamber. If there is no majority as required for a decision, the prosecution shall proceed.

In carrying out the prosecution, the Co-Prosecutors may seek the assistance of the Royal Government of Cambodia if such assistance would be useful to the prosecution, and such assistance shall be provided.

21. The Co-Prosecutors under this law shall enjoy equal status and conditions of service according to each level of the Extraordinary Chambers.

Each Co-Prosecutor shall be appointed for the period of these proceedings.

In the event of the absence of the foreign Co-Prosecutor, he or she shall be replaced by the reserve foreign Co-Prosecutor.

22. Each Co-Prosecutor shall have the right to choose one or more deputy prosecutors to assist him or her with prosecution before the chambers. Deputy foreign prosecutors shall be appointed by the foreign Co-Prosecutor from a list provided by the Secretary-General.

The Co-prosecutors shall be assisted by Cambodian and international staff as needed in their offices. In choosing staff to serve as assistants, the Director of the Office of Administration shall interview, if necessary, and with the approval of the Cambodian Co-Prosecutor, hire staff who shall be appointed by the Royal Government of Cambodia. The Deputy Director of the Office of Administration shall be responsible for the recruitment and administration of all foreign staff. The number of assistants shall be chosen in proportion to the Cambodian prosecutors and foreign prosecutors.

Cambodian staff shall be selected from Cambodian civil servants and, if necessary, other qualified nationals of Cambodia.

Investigations

3–105　　**23.** All investigations shall be the joint responsibility of two investigating judges, one Cambodian and another foreign, hereinafter referred to as Co-Investigating Judges, and shall follow existing procedures in force. If these existing procedures do not deal with a particular matter, or if there is uncertainty regarding their interpretation or application or if there is a question regarding their consistency with international standards, the Co-Investigating Judges may seek guidance in procedural rules established at the international level.

In the event of disagreement between the Co-Investigating Judges the following shall apply:

The investigation shall proceed unless the Co-Investigating Judges or one of them requests within thirty days that the difference shall be settled in accordance with the following provisions.

The Co-Investigating Judges shall submit written statements of facts and the reasons for their different positions to the Director of the Office of Administration.

The difference shall be settled forthwith by the Pre-Trial Chamber referred to in Article 20.

Upon receipt of the statements referred to in the third paragraph, the Director of the Office of Administration shall immediately convene the Pre-Trial Chamber and communicate the statements to its members.

A decision of the Pre-Trial Chamber, against which there is no appeal, requires the affirmative vote of at least four judges. The decision shall be communicated to the Director of the Office of Administration, who shall publish it and communicate it to the Co-Investigating Judges. They shall immediately proceed in accordance with the decision of the Pre-Trial Chamber. If there is no majority as required for a decision, the investigation shall proceed.

The Co-Investigating Judges shall conduct investigations on the basis of information obtained from any institution, including the Government, United Nations organs, or non-governmental organizations.

The Co-Investigating Judges shall have the power to question suspects and victims, to hear witnesses, and to collect evidence, in accordance with existing procedures in force. In the event the Co-Investigating Judges consider it necessary to do so, they may issue an order requesting the Co-Prosecutors also to interrogate the witnesses.

In carrying out the investigations, the Co-Investigating Judges may seek the assistance of the Royal Government of Cambodia, if such assistance would be useful to the investigation, and such assistance shall be provided.

24. During the investigation, Suspects shall be unconditionally entitled to assistance of counsel of their own choosing, and to have legal assistance assigned to them free of charge if they cannot afford it, as well as the right to interpretation, as necessary, into and from a language they speak and understand.

25. The Co-Investigating Judges shall be appointed from among the currently practising judges or who are additionally appointed in accordance with the existing procedures for appointment of judges; all of whom shall have high moral character, a spirit of impartiality and integrity, and experience. They shall be independent in the performance of their functions and shall not accept or seek instructions from any government or any other source.

26. The Cambodian Co-Investigating Judge and the reserve Investigating Judges shall be appointed by the Supreme Council of the Magistracy from among the Cambodian professional judges.

The reserve Investigating Judges shall replace the appointed Investigating Judges in case of their absence. The reserve Investigating Judges may continue to perform their regular duties in their respective courts.

The Supreme Council of the Magistracy shall appoint the foreign Co-Investigating Judge for the period of the investigation, upon nomination by the Secretary-General of the United Nations.

The Secretary-General of the United Nations shall submit a list of at least two candidates for foreign Co-Investigating Judge to the Royal Government of Cambodia, from which the Supreme Council of the Magistracy shall appoint one Investigating Judge and one reserve Investigating Judge.

27. All Investigating Judges under this law shall enjoy equal status and conditions of service.

Each Investigating Judge shall be appointed for the period of the investigation.

In the event of the absence of the foreign Co-Investigating Judge, he or she shall be replaced by the reserve Co-Investigating Judge.

28. The Co-Investigating Judges shall be assisted by Cambodian and international staff as needed in their offices.

In choosing staff to serve as assistants, the Co-Investigating Judges shall comply with the spirit of the provisions set forth in Article 13 of this law.

Office of Administration

30. The staff of the judges, the investigating judges and prosecutors of the **3–106** Extraordinary Chambers shall be supervised by an Office of Administration.

This Office shall have a Cambodian Director, a foreign Deputy Director and such other staff as necessary.

31. The Director of the Office of Administration shall be appointed by the Royal Government of Cambodia for a two-year term and shall be eligible for reappointment.

The Director of the Office of Administration shall be responsible for the overall management of the Office of Administration, except in matters that are subject to United Nations rules and procedures.

The Director of the Office of Administration shall be appointed from those with significant experience in court administration and fluency in one of the foreign languages used in the Extraordinary Chambers, and shall be a person of high moral character and integrity.

The foreign Deputy Director shall be appointed by the Secretary-General of the United Nations and assigned by the Royal Government of Cambodia, and shall be responsible for the recruitment and administration of all international staff, as required by the foreign components of the Extraordinary Chambers, the Co-Investigating Judges, the Co-Prosecutors' Office, and the Office of Administration. The Deputy Director shall administer the resources provided through the United Nations Trust Fund.

The Office of Administration shall be assisted by Cambodian and international staff as necessary. All Cambodian staff of the Office of Administration shall be appointed by the Royal Government of Cambodia at the request of the Director. Foreign staff shall be appointed by the Deputy Director.

Cambodian staff shall be selected from Cambodian civil servants and, if necessary, other qualified nationals of Cambodia.

32. All staff assigned to the judges, Co-Investigating Judges, Co-Prosecutors, and Office of Administration shall enjoy the same working conditions according to each level of the Extraordinary Chambers.

Status, Rights, Privileges and Immunities

41. The foreign judges, the foreign Co-Investigating Judge, the foreign Co-**3–107** Prosecutor and the Deputy Director of the Office of Administration, together with their families forming part of their household, shall enjoy all of the privileges and immunities, exemptions and facilities accorded to diplomatic agents in accordance with the 1961 Vienna Convention on Diplomatic Relations. Such officials shall enjoy exemption from taxation in Cambodia on their salaries, emoluments and allowances.

42.—1. Cambodian judges, the Co-Investigating Judge, the Co-Prosecutor, the Director of the Office of Administration and personnel shall be accorded immunity from legal process in respect of words spoken or written and all acts performed by them in their official capacity. Such immunity shall continue to be accorded after termination of employment with the Extraordinary Chambers, the Pre-Trial Chamber and the Office of Administration.

2. International personnel shall be accorded in addition:
   a. immunity from legal process in respect of words spoken or written and all acts performed by them in their official capacity. Such immunity shall continue to be accorded after termination of employment with the co-investigating judges, the co-prosecutors, the Extraordinary Chambers, the Pre-Trial Chamber and the Office of Administration;
   b. immunity from taxation on salaries, allowances and emoluments paid to them by the United Nations;
   c. immunity from immigration restriction;
   d. the right to import free of duties and taxes, except for payment for services, their furniture and effects at the time of first taking up their official duties in Cambodia.

3. The counsel of a suspect or an accused who has been admitted as such by the Extraordinary Chambers shall not be subjected by the Government to any measure that may affect the free and independent exercise of his or her functions under the Law on the Establishment of the Extraordinary Chambers.
   In particular, the counsel shall be accorded:
   a. immunity from personal arrest or detention and from seizure of personal baggage relating to his or her functions in the proceedings;
   b. inviolability of all documents relating to the exercise of his or her functions as a counsel of a suspect or accused;
   c. immunity from criminal or civil jurisdiction in respect of words spoken or written and acts performed in his or her capacity as counsel. Such immunity shall continue to be accorded after termination of their function as counsel of a suspect or accused.

4. The archives of the co-investigating judges, the co-prosecutors, the Extraordinary Chambers, the Pre -Trial Chamber and the Office of Administration and in general all documents and materials made available to, belonging to, or used by it them, wherever located in the Kingdom of Cambodia and by whomsoever held, shall be inviolable for the duration of the proceedings.

Expenses

3–108   **44.** The expenses and salaries of the Extraordinary Chambers shall be as follows:
   1. The expenses and salaries of the Cambodian administrative officials and staff, the Cambodian judges and reserve judges, investigating judges and reserve investigating judges, and prosecutors and reserve prosecutors shall be borne by the Cambodian national budget;
   2. The expenses of the foreign administrative officials and staff, the foreign judges, Co-investigating judge and Co-prosecutor sent by the Secretary-General of the United Nations shall be borne by the United Nations;
   3. The defence counsel may receive fees for mounting the defence;
   4. The Extraordinary Chambers may receive additional assistance for their expenses from other voluntary funds contributed by foreign governments, international institutions, non-governmental organizations, and other persons wishing to assist the proceedings.

Absence of foreign judges, investigating judges or prosecutors

46. In order to ensure timely and smooth implementation of this law, in the **3–109** event any foreign judges or foreign investigating judges or foreign prosecutors fail or refuse to participate in the Extraordinary Chambers, the Supreme Council of the Magistracy shall appoint other judges or investigating judges or prosecutors to fill any vacancies from the lists of foreign candidates provided for in Article 11, Article 18, and Article 26. In the event those lists are exhausted, and the Secretary-General of the United Nations does not supplement the lists with new candidates, or in the event that the United Nations withdraws its support from the Extraordinary Chambers, any such vacancies shall be filled by the Supreme Council of the Magistracy from candidates recommended by the Governments of Member States of the United Nations or from among other foreign legal personalities.

If, following such procedures, there are still no foreign judges or foreign investigating judges or foreign prosecutors participating in the work of the Extraordinary Chambers and no foreign candidates have been identified to occupy the vacant positions, then the Supreme Council of the Magistracy may choose replacement Cambodian judges, investigating judges or prosecutors.

Penalties

38. All penalties shall be limited to imprisonment.   **3–110**

39. Those who have committed any crime as provided in Articles 3 new, 4, 5, 6, 7 and 8 shall be sentenced to a prison term from five years to life imprisonment.

In addition to imprisonment, the Extraordinary Chamber of the trial court may order the confiscation of personal property, money, and real property acquired unlawfully or by criminal conduct.

The confiscated property shall be returned to the State.

Location of the Extraordinary Chambers

43. The Extraordinary Chambers established in the trial court and the **3–111** Supreme Court shall be located in Phnom Penh.

Working Languages

                                                                                3–111.1

45. The official working language of the Extraordinary Chambers shall be Khmer, with translations into English, French and Russian.

Existence of the Court

                                                                                3–111.2

47. The Extraordinary Chambers in the courts of Cambodia shall automatically dissolve following the definitive conclusion of these proceedings.

Agreement between the United Nations and the Royal Government of Cambodia concerning the Prosecution under Cambodian Law of Crimes Committed during the Period of Democratic Kampuchea, Arts 2–10, 14–28

The Law on the Establishment of Extraordinary Chambers

2. The present Agreement recognizes that the Extraordinary Chambers **3–112** have subject matter jurisdiction consistent with that set forth in "the Law on the Establishment of the Extraordinary Chambers in the Courts of Cambodia for the Prosecution of Crimes Committed During the Period of Democratic Kampuchea" (hereinafter: "the Law on the Establishment of the Extraordinary Chambers"), as adopted and amended by the Cambodian Legislature under the Constitution of Cambodia. The present Agreement further recognizes that the Extraordinary Chambers have personal jurisdiction over senior leaders of Democratic Kampuchea and those who were most responsible for the crimes referred to in Article 1 of the Agreement.

2. The present Agreement shall be implemented in Cambodia through the Law on the Establishment of the Extraordinary Chambers as adopted and amended. The Vienna Convention on the Law of Treaties, and in particular its Articles 26 and 27, applies to the Agreement.

3. In case amendments to the Law on the Establishment of the Extraordinary Chambers are deemed necessary, such amendments shall always be preceded by consultations between the parties.

Judges

3–113   **3.**—1. Cambodian judges, on the one hand, and judges appointed by the Supreme Council of the Magistracy upon nomination by the Secretary-General of the United Nations (hereinafter: "international judges"), on the other hand, shall serve in each of the two Extraordinary Chambers.

2. The composition of the Chambers shall be as follows:
   a. The Trial Chamber: three Cambodian judges and two international judges;
   b. The Supreme Court Chamber, which shall serve as both appellate chamber and final instance: four Cambodian judges and three international judges.

3. The judges shall be persons of high moral character, impartiality and integrity who possess the qualifications required in their respective countries for appointment to judicial offices. They shall be independent in the performance of their functions and shall not accept or seek instructions from any Government or any other source.

4. In the overall composition of the Chambers due account should be taken of the experience of the judges in criminal law, international law, including international humanitarian law and human rights law.

5. The Secretary-General of the United Nations undertakes to forward a list of not less than seven nominees for international judges from which the Supreme Council of the Magistracy shall appoint five to serve as judges in the two Chambers. Appointment of international judges by the Supreme Council of the Magistracy shall be made only from the list submitted by the Secretary-General.

6. In the event of a vacancy of an international judge, the Supreme Council of the Magistracy shall appoint another international judge from the same list.

7. The judges shall be appointed for the duration of the proceedings.

8. In addition to the international judges sitting in the Chambers and present at every stage of the proceedings, the President of a Chamber may, on a case-by-case basis, designate from the list of nominees submitted by the Secretary-General, one or more alternate judges to be present at each stage of the proceedings, and to replace an international judge if that judge is unable to continue sitting.

Decision-making

3–114   **4.**—1. The judges shall attempt to achieve unanimity in their decisions. If this is not possible, the following shall apply:
   a. A decision by the Trial Chamber shall require the affirmative vote of at least four judges;
   b. A decision by the Supreme Court Chamber shall require the affirmative vote of at least five judges.

2. When there is no unanimity, the decision of the Chamber shall contain the views of the majority and the minority.

Investigating judges

5.—1. There shall be one Cambodian and one international investigating **3–115** judge serving as co-investigating judges. They shall be responsible for the conduct of investigations.

2. The co-investigating judges shall be persons of high moral character, impartiality and integrity who possess the qualifications required in their respective countries for appointment to such a judicial office.

3. The co-investigating judges shall be independent in the performance of their functions and shall not accept or seek instructions from any Government or any other source. It is understood, however, that the scope of the investigation is limited to senior leaders of Democratic Kampuchea and those who were most responsible for the crimes and serious violations of Cambodian penal law, international humanitarian law and custom, and international conventions recognized by Cambodia, that were committed during the period from 17 April 1975 to 6 January 1979.

4. The co-investigating judges shall cooperate with a view to arriving at a common approach to the investigation. In case the co-investigating judges are unable to agree whether to proceed with an investigation, the investigation shall proceed unless the judges or one of them requests within thirty days that the difference shall be settled in accordance with Article 7.

5. In addition to the list of nominees provided for in Article 3, paragraph 5, the Secretary-General shall submit a list of two nominees from which the Supreme Council of the Magistracy shall appoint one to serve as an international co-investigating judge, and one as a reserve international co-investigating judge.

6. In case there is a vacancy or a need to fill the post of the international co-investigating judge, the person appointed to fill this post must be the reserve international co-investigating judge.

7. The co-investigating judges shall be appointed for the duration of the proceedings.

Prosecutors

6.—1. There shall be one Cambodian prosecutor and one international **3–116** prosecutor competent to appear in both Chambers, serving as co-prosecutors. They shall be responsible for the conduct of the prosecutions.

2. The co-prosecutors shall be of high moral character, and possess a high level of professional competence and extensive experience in the conduct of investigations and prosecutions of criminal cases.

3. The co-prosecutors shall be independent in the performance of their functions and shall not accept or seek instructions from any Government or any other source. It is understood, however, that the scope of the prosecution is limited to senior leaders of Democratic Kampuchea and those who were most responsible for the crimes and serious violations of Cambodian penal law, international humanitarian law and custom, and international conventions recognized by Cambodia, that were committed during the period from 17 April 1975 to 6 January 1979.

4. The co-prosecutors shall cooperate with a view to arriving at a common approach to the prosecution. In case the prosecutors are unable to agree whether to proceed with a prosecution, the prosecution shall proceed unless the prosecutors or one of them requests within thirty days that the difference shall be settled in accordance with Article 7.

5. The Secretary-General undertakes to forward a list of two nominees from which the Supreme Council of the Magistracy shall select one international co-prosecutor and one reserve international co-prosecutor.

6. In case there is a vacancy or a need to fill the post of the international co-prosecutor, the person appointed to fill this post must be the reserve international co-prosecutor.

7. The co-prosecutors shall be appointed for the duration of the proceedings.

8. Each co-prosecutor shall have one or more deputy prosecutors to assist him or her with prosecutions before the Chambers. Deputy international prosecutors shall be appointed by the international co-prosecutor from a list provided by the Secretary-General.

Settlement of differences between the co-investigating judges or the co-prosecutors

3–117   **7.**—1. In case the co-investigating judges or the co-prosecutors have made a request in accordance with Article 5, paragraph 4, or Article 6, paragraph 4, as the case may be, they shall submit written statements of facts and the reasons for their different positions to the Director of the Office of Administration.

2. The difference shall be settled forthwith by a Pre-Trial Chamber of five judges, three appointed by the Supreme Council of the Magistracy, with one as President, and two appointed by the Supreme Council of the Magistracy upon nomination by the Secretary-General. Article 3, paragraph 3, shall apply to the judges.

3. Upon receipt of the statements referred to in paragraph 1, the Director of the Office of Administration shall immediately convene the Pre-Trial Chamber and communicate the statements to its members.

4. A decision of the Pre-Trial Chamber, against which there is no appeal, requires the affirmative vote of at least four judges. The decision shall be communicated to the Director of the Office of Administration, who shall publish it and communicate it to the co-investigating judges or the co-prosecutors. They shall immediately proceed in accordance with the decision of the Chamber. If there is no majority, as required for a decision, the investigation or prosecution shall proceed.

Office of Administration

3–118   **8.**—1. There shall be an Office of Administration to service the Extraordinary Chambers, the Pre-Trial Chamber, the co-investigating judges and the Prosecutors' Office.

2. There shall be a Cambodian Director of this Office, who shall be appointed by the Royal Government of Cambodia. The Director shall be responsible for the overall management of the Office of Administration, except in matters that are subject to United Nations rules and procedures.

3. There shall be an international Deputy Director of the Office of Administration, who shall be appointed by the Secretary-General. The Deputy Director shall be responsible for the recruitment of all international staff and all administration of the international components of the Extraordinary Chambers, the Pre-Trial Chamber, the co-investigating judges, the Prosecutors' Office and the Office of Administration. The United Nations and the Royal Government of Cambodia agree that, when an international Deputy Director has been appointed by the Secretary-General, the assignment of that person to that position by the Royal Government of Cambodia shall take place forthwith.

4. The Director and the Deputy Director shall cooperate in order to ensure an effective and efficient functioning of the administration.

Crimes falling within the jurisdiction of the Extraordinary Chambers

3–119   **9.** The subject-matter jurisdiction of the Extraordinary Chambers shall be the crime of genocide as defined in the 1948 Convention on the Prevention and Punishment of the Crime of Genocide, crimes against humanity as defined in the 1998 Rome Statute of the International Criminal Court and grave breaches of the 1949 Geneva Conventions and such other crimes as defined in Chapter II of the Law on the Establishment of the Extraordinary Chambers as promulgated on 10 August 2001.

Penalties

10. The maximum penalty for conviction for crimes falling within the jurisdiction of the Extraordinary Chambers shall be life imprisonment.

3–120

Premises

14.—The Royal Government of Cambodia shall provide at its expense the premises for the co-investigating judges, the Prosecutors' Office, the Extraordinary Chambers, the Pre-Trial Chamber and the Office of Administration. It shall also provide for such utilities, facilities and other services necessary for their operation that may be mutually agreed upon by separate agreement between the United Nations and the Government.

3–121

Cambodian personnel

15. Salaries and emoluments of Cambodian judges and other Cambodian personnel shall be defrayed by the Royal Government of Cambodia.

3–122

International personnel

16. Salaries and emoluments of international judges, the international co-investigating judge, the international co-prosecutor and other personnel recruited by the United Nations shall be defrayed by the United Nations.

3–123

Financial and other assistance of the United Nations

17. The United Nations shall be responsible for the following:
   a. remuneration of the international judges, the international co-investigating judge, the international co-prosecutor, the Deputy Director of the Office of Administration and other international personnel;
   b. costs for utilities and services as agreed separately between the United Nations and the Royal Government of Cambodia;
   c. remuneration of defence counsel;
   d. witnesses' travel from within Cambodia and from abroad;
   e. safety and security arrangements as agreed separately between the United Nations and the Government;
   f. such other limited assistance as may be necessary to ensure the smooth functioning of the investigation, the prosecution and the Extraordinary Chambers.

3–124

Inviolability of archives and documents

18. The archives of the co-investigating judges, the co-prosecutors, the Extraordinary Chambers, the Pre-Trial Chamber and the Office of Administration, and in general all documents and materials made available, belonging to or used by them, wherever located in Cambodia and by whomsoever held, shall be inviolable for the duration of the proceedings.

3–125

Privileges and immunities of international judges, the international co-investigating judge, the international co-prosecutor and the Deputy Director of the Office of Administration

19.—1. The international judges, the international co-investigating judge, the international co-prosecutor and the Deputy Director of the Office of Administration, together with their families forming part of their household,

3–126

shall enjoy the privileges and immunities, exemptions and facilities accorded to diplomatic agents in accordance with the 1961 Vienna Convention on Diplomatic Relations. They shall, in particular, enjoy:

    a. personal inviolability, including immunity from arrest or detention;
    b. immunity from criminal, civil and administrative jurisdiction in conformity with the Vienna Convention;
    c. inviolability for all papers and documents;
    d. exemption from immigration restrictions and alien registration;
    e. the same immunities and facilities in respect of their personal baggage as are accorded to diplomatic agents.

2. The international judges, the international co-investigating judge, the international co-prosecutor and the Deputy Director of the Office of Administration shall enjoy exemption from taxation in Cambodia on their salaries, emoluments and allowances.

Privileges and immunities of Cambodian and international personnel

3–127   **20.**—1. Cambodian judges, the Cambodian co-investigating judge, the Cambodian co-prosecutor and other Cambodian personnel shall be accorded immunity from legal process in respect of words spoken or written and all acts performed by them in their official capacity under the present Agreement. Such immunity shall continue to be accorded after termination of employment with the co-investigating judges, the co-prosecutors, the Extraordinary Chambers, the Pre-Trial Chamber and the Office of Administration.

2. International personnel shall be accorded:

    a. immunity from legal process in respect of words spoken or written and all acts performed by them in their official capacity under the present Agreement. Such immunity shall continue to be accorded after termination of employment with the co-investigating judges, the co-prosecutors, the Extraordinary Chambers, the Pre-Trial Chamber and the Office of Administration;
    b. immunity from taxation on salaries, allowances and emoluments paid to them by the United Nations;
    c. immunity from immigration restrictions;
    d. the right to import free of duties and taxes, except for payment for services, their furniture and effects at the time of first taking up their official duties in Cambodia.

3. The United Nations and the Royal Government of Cambodia agree that the immunity granted by the Law on the Establishment of the Extraordinary Chambers in respect of words spoken or written and all acts performed by them in their official capacity under the present Agreement will apply also after the persons have left the service of the co-investigating judges, the co-prosecutors, the Extraordinary Chambers, the Pre-Trial Chamber and the Office of Administration.

Counsel

3–128   **21.**—1. The counsel of a suspect or an accused who has been admitted as such by the Extraordinary Chambers shall not be subjected by the Royal Government of Cambodia to any measure which may affect the free and independent exercise of his or her functions under the present Agreement.

2. In particular, the counsel shall be accorded:

    a. immunity from personal arrest or detention and from seizure of personal baggage;
    b. inviolability of all documents relating to the exercise of his or her functions as a counsel of a suspect or accused;
    c. immunity from criminal or civil jurisdiction in respect of words spoken or written and acts performed by them in their official capacity

as counsel. Such immunity shall continue to be accorded to them after termination of their functions as a counsel of a suspect or accused.

3. Any counsel, whether of Cambodian or non-Cambodian nationality, engaged by or assigned to a suspect or an accused shall, in the defence of his or her client, act in accordance with the present Agreement, the Cambodian Law on the Statutes of the Bar and recognized standards and ethics of the legal profession.

Witnesses and experts

22. Witnesses and experts appearing on a summons or a request of the judges, the co-investigating judges, or the co-prosecutors shall not be prosecuted, detained or subjected to any other restriction on their liberty by the Cambodian authorities. They shall not be subjected by the authorities to any measure which may affect the free and independent exercise of their functions. **3–129**

Protection of victims and witnesses

23. The co-investigating judges, the co-prosecutors and the Extraordinary Chambers shall provide for the protection of victims and witnesses. Such protection measures shall include, but shall not be limited to, the conduct of *in camera* proceedings and the protection of the identity of a victim or witness. **3–130**

Security, safety and protection of persons referred to in the present Agreement

24. The Royal Government of Cambodia shall take all effective and adequate actions which may be required to ensure the security, safety and protection of persons referred to in the present Agreement. The United Nations and the Government agree that the Government is responsible for the security of all accused, irrespective of whether they appear voluntarily before the Extraordinary Chambers or whether they are under arrest. **3–131**

Obligation to assist the co-investigating judges, the co-prosecutors and the Extraordinary Chambers

25. The Royal Government of Cambodia shall comply without undue delay with any request for assistance by the co-investigating judges, the co-prosecutors and the Extraordinary Chambers or an order issued by any of them, including, but not limited to: **3–132**
  a. identification and location of persons;
  b. service of documents;
  c. arrest or detention of persons;
  d. transfer of an indictee to the Extraordinary Chambers.

Languages

26.—1. The official language of the Extraordinary Chambers and the Pre-Trial Chamber is Khmer. **3–133**

2. The official working languages of the Extraordinary Chambers and the Pre-Trial Chamber shall be Khmer, English and French.

3. Translations of public documents and interpretation at public hearings into Russian may be provided by the Royal Government of Cambodia at its discretion and expense on condition that such services do not hinder the proceedings before the Extraordinary Chambers.

Practical arrangements

27.—1. With a view to achieving efficiency and cost-effectiveness in the operation of the Extraordinary Chambers, a phased-in approach shall be adopted for their establishment in accordance with the chronological order of the legal process. **3–134**

2. In the first phase of the operation of the Extraordinary Chambers, the judges, the coinvestigating judges and the co-prosecutors will be appointed along with investigative and prosecutorial staff, and the process of investigations and prosecutions shall be initiated.

3. The trial process of those already in custody shall proceed simultaneously with the investigation of other persons responsible for crimes falling within the jurisdiction of the Extraordinary Chambers.

4. With the completion of the investigation of persons suspected of having committed the crimes falling within the jurisdiction of the Extraordinary Chambers, arrest warrants shall be issued and submitted to the Royal Government of Cambodia to effectuate the arrest.

5. With the arrest by the Royal Government of Cambodia of indicted persons situated in its territory, the Extraordinary Chambers shall be fully operational, provided that the judges of the Supreme Court Chamber shall serve when seized with a matter. The judges of the Pre-Trial Chamber shall serve only if and when their services are needed.

Withdrawal of cooperation

3–135　　28. Should the Royal Government of Cambodia change the structure or organization of the Extraordinary Chambers or otherwise cause them to function in a manner that does not conform with the terms of the present Agreement, the United Nations reserves the right to cease to provide assistance, financial or otherwise, pursuant to the present Agreement.

D. IRAQ

Statute of the Iraqi Special Tribunal, Arts 1–10, 16, 28–29, 31, 33–35

Establishment and Competence of the Tribunal

3–136　　1.—a) A Tribunal is hereby established and shall be known as The Iraqi Special Tribunal (the "Tribunal"). The jurisdiction and functioning of the Tribunal and its associated bodies as defined in Article 3 below shall be governed by the provisions of this Statute. The Tribunal shall be an independent entity and not associated with any Iraqi government departments.

b) The Tribunal shall have jurisdiction over any Iraqi national or resident of Iraq accused of the crimes listed in Articles 11 to 14 below, committed since July 17, 1968 and up until and including May 1, 2003, in the territory of the Republic of Iraq or elsewhere, including crimes committed in connection with Iraq's wars against the Islamic Republic of Iran and the State of Kuwait. This includes jurisdiction over crimes listed in Articles 12 and 13 committed against the people of Iraq (including its Arabs, Kurds, Turcomans, Assyrians and other ethnic groups, and its Shi'ites and Sunnis) whether or not committed in armed conflict.

c) The Tribunal shall only have jurisdiction over natural persons.

Organization of the Tribunal

3–137　　3.—a) The Tribunal's judiciary shall consist of the following:
　　　　1. one or more Trial Chambers;
　　　　2. an Appeals Chamber, which shall have the power to review the decisions of the Trial Chambers referred to above; and

3. the Tribunal Investigative Judges.

b) The Tribunal will also have a Prosecutions Department.

c) The Tribunal will also have an Administration Department., which shall provide administrative services to the Tribunal's judiciary and the Prosecutions Department.

28. The judges, investigative judges, prosecutors and the Director of the Administration Department shall be Iraqi nationals, except as provided for in Article 4(d).

29.—a) The Tribunal and the national courts of Iraq shall have concurrent jurisdiction to prosecute persons for those offences prescribed in Article 14 that fall within the jurisdiction of the Tribunal.

b) The Tribunal shall have primacy over all other Iraqi courts with respect to the crimes stipulated in Articles 11 to 13.

c) At any stage of the procedure, the Tribunal may demand of any other Iraqi court to transfer any case being tried by it involving any crimes stipulated in Articles 11 to 14 to the Tribunal, and such court shall be required to transfer such case.

33. No officer, prosecutor, investigative judge, judge or other personnel of the Tribunal shall have been a member of the Ba'ath Party.

The Trial Chambers and the Appeals Chamber

4.—a) The Chambers shall be composed of permanent independent judges, **3–138** and independent reserve judges.

b) Each Trial Chamber shall consist of five permanent judges.

c) (i) The Appeals Chamber shall be composed of nine members. Once appointed the Appeals Chamber shall select one of its members to fill the position of President of the Appeals Chamber. No member of any Trial Chamber can simultaneously be a member of the Appeals Chamber or a Tribunal Investigative Judge.

(ii) The President of the Appeals Chamber shall also be the President of the Tribunal and will overview the administrative and financial aspects of the Tribunal.

d) The Governing Council or the Successor Government, if it deems necessary, can appoint non-Iraqi judges who have experience in the crimes encompassed in this statute, and who shall be persons of high moral character, impartiality and integrity.

Qualification and Selection of the Judges

5.—a) The permanent and reserve judges shall be persons of high moral **3–139** character, impartiality and integrity who possess the qualifications required for appointment to the highest judicial offices. In the overall composition of the Chambers, due account shall be taken of the experience of the judges in criminal law and trial procedures.

b) Iraqi candidates for permanent and reserve judges in the Trial Chambers need not be serving judges, and could be lawyers and jurists (who should also have the necessary experience and qualifications). Judges in the Appeals Chamber must be serving or former judges.

c) Judges are to be nominated and appointed by the Governing Council or the Successor Government, after consultation with the Judicial Council.

d) The permanent judges of each Trial Chamber shall elect a Presiding Judge from amongst their number, who shall oversee the work of the Trial Chamber as a whole.

e) The permanent and reserve judges shall be appointed for a term of five years. The terms and conditions of service shall be those of the judges of the Iraqi judicial system as set out in the Law Number 160 of 1979 (Judicial Organization Law), save that matters of compensation shall be set by the Governing Council or the Successor Government in light of the increased risks associated with the position.

    f) (1) A judge shall be disqualified for any of the following reasons:

        i. He or she has a criminal record including a felony unless the felony is a political or false charge made by the Ba'ath Party regime;

        ii. He or she has made a material misrepresentation; or

        iii. He or she fails to carry out his or her duties without good reason.

      (2) The decision to disqualify a judge shall be taken by the majority of permanent judges of the Tribunal after conducting appropriate investigations.

      (3) The decision to disqualify the President shall be taken by the Governing Council or the Successor Government.

The Presidency of the Tribunal

3–140   **6.**—a) The President shall:

      (1) chair the proceedings of the Appeals Chamber.

      (2) assign the judges to particular Trial Chambers;

      (3) assign, from time to time, any reserve judges to a Trial Chamber; and

      (4) have overall responsibility for the administration of the Tribunal.

    b) The President of the Tribunal shall be required to appoint non-Iraqi nationals to act in advisory capacities or as observers to the Trial Chambers and to the Appeals Chamber. The role of the non-Iraqi nationals shall be to provide assistance to the judges with respect to international law and the experience of similar tribunals (whether international or otherwise), and to monitor the protection by the Tribunal of general due process of law standards. In appointing such non-Iraqi experts, the President of the Tribunal shall be entitled to request assistance from the international community, including the United Nations.

    c) The non-Iraqi advisors and observers referred to in the above paragraph shall also be persons of high moral character, impartiality and integrity. In this regard, it would be preferable that such non-Iraqi advisor or observer shall have the following experience: (i) such person shall have acted in either a judicial or prosecutorial capacity in his or her respective country, or (ii) such person shall have experience in international war crimes trials or tribunals.

Tribunal Investigative Judges

3–141   **7.**—a) The Tribunal Investigative Judges shall be appointed in order to investigate individuals for the commission of crimes stipulated in Articles 11 to 14.

    b) Tribunal Investigative Judges are to be nominated and appointed by the Governing Council or the Successor Government, after consultation with the Judicial Council.

    c) There shall be up to twenty permanent Tribunal Investigative Judges, and up to ten reserve investigative judges.

    d) The permanent and reserve investigative judges shall be persons of high moral character, impartiality and integrity who possess the qualifications required for appointment to the highest judicial offices. In the selection of investigative judges, due account shall be taken of the experience of the judges in criminal law and trial procedures.

e) The Tribunal Investigative Judges shall be headed by a Chief Tribunal Investigative Judge, who shall be chosen by the Tribunal Investigative Judges from among them.

f) The Chief Tribunal Investigative Judge shall assign cases to individual tribunal investigative judges.

g) Each Office of the Tribunal Investigative Judge shall be composed of the Tribunal Investigative Judge and such other qualified staff as may be required.

h) In accordance with Iraqi criminal procedure, each Tribunal Investigative Judge shall have the power to issue subpoenas, arrest warrants and indictments with respect to individuals that they are investigating.

i) Each Tribunal Investigative Judge may gather evidence from whatever source he considers suitable.

j) Each Tribunal Investigative Judge shall act independently as a separate organ of the Tribunal. He or she shall not seek or receive instructions from any Governmental Department, or from any other source, including the Governing Council or the Successor Government.

k) The decisions or orders of the Tribunal Investigative Judge can be appealed to the Appeals Chamber within fifteen days of the notification or deemed notification of the decision.

l) Each Tribunal Investigative Judge shall be appointed for a term of three years. The terms and conditions of service shall be those of the investigative judges of the Iraqi judicial system as set out in Law Number 160 of 1979 (Judicial Organization Law), save that matters of compensation shall be set by the Governing Council or the Successor Government in light of the increased risks associated with the position.

m) (1) Any Tribunal Investigative Judge shall be disqualified for any of the following reasons:

    i) He or she has a criminal record including a felony unless the felony is a political or false charge made by the Ba'ath Party regime;

    ii) He or she has made a material misrepresentation; or

    iii) He or she fails to carry out his or her duties without good reason.

  (2) The decision to disqualify a Tribunal Investigative Judge shall be taken by the majority of permanent judges of the Tribunal, after conducting appropriate investigations.

n) The Chief Tribunal Investigative Judge shall be required to appoint non-Iraqi nationals to act in advisory capacities or as observers to the Tribunal Investigative Judges. The role of the non-Iraqi nationals and observers shall be to provide assistance to the Tribunal Investigative Judges with respect to the investigations and prosecution of cases covered by the this Statute (whether in an international context or otherwise), and to monitor the protection by the Tribunal Investigative Judges of general due process of law standards. In appointing such advisors, the Chief Tribunal Investigative Judge shall be entitled to request assistance from the international community, including the United Nations.

o) The non-Iraqi advisors and observers referred to in this Article shall also be persons of high moral character, impartiality and integrity. In this regard, it would be preferable that such non-Iraqi advisor or observer shall have the following experience: (i) such person shall have acted in either a judicial or prosecutorial capacity in his or her respective country, or (ii) such person shall have experience in international war crimes trials or tribunals.

The Prosecutions Department

3–142 8.—a) The Prosecutions Department shall be responsible for the prosecution of persons responsible for crimes within the jurisdiction of the Tribunal.

b) Each Prosecutor shall act independently. He or she shall not seek or receive instructions from any Governmental Department or from any other source, including the Governing Council or the Successor Government.

c) The Prosecutions Department shall consist of up to twenty Prosecutors.

d) Prosecutors are to be nominated and appointed by the Governing Council or the Successor Government after consultation with the Judicial Council.

e) The Prosecution Department shall be headed by a Chief Prosecutor, who shall be selected from among the Prosecutors.

f) (1) A prosecutor shall be disqualified for any of the following reasons:
   i) He or she has a criminal record including a felony unless the felony is a political or false charge made by the Ba'ath Party regime;
   ii) He or she has made a material misrepresentation; or
   iii) He or she fails to carry out his or her duties without good reason.

(2) The decision to disqualify a Prosecutor shall be taken by the Chief Prosecutor, after conducting appropriate investigations.

g) Each Office of the Prosecutor shall be composed of a Prosecutor and such other qualified staff as may be required.

h) The Chief Prosecutor shall assign individual cases to a Prosecutor. Such Prosecutor shall have the right to be involved in the investigative stages of a case and shall be the individual who prosecutes such case, consistent with the powers granted to prosecutors pursuant to Law Number 23 of 1971 (Iraqi Criminal Procedure Law).

i) Each Prosecutor shall be appointed for a term of three years. The terms and conditions of service shall be those of prosecutors of the Iraqi judicial system as set out in Law Number 159 of 1979 (The Law of Prosecutors), save that matters of compensation shall be set by the Governing Council or the Successor Government.

j) The Chief Prosecutor shall be required to appoint non-Iraqi nationals to act in advisory capacities or as observers to the prosecutors. The role of the non-Iraqi nationals and observers shall be to provide assistance to the prosecutors of the Tribunal with respect to the investigations and prosecution of cases covered by this Statute (whether in an international context or otherwise), and to monitor the performance of the Prosecutor. In appointing such advisors, the Chief Prosecutor shall be entitled to request assistance from the international community, including the United Nations.

k) The non-Iraqi advisors and observers referred to in this Article shall also be persons of high moral character, impartiality and integrity. In this regard, it would be preferable that such non-Iraqi advisor or observer shall have the following experience: (i) such person shall have acted in a prosecutorial capacity in his or her respective country, or (ii) such person shall have experience in international war crimes trials or tribunals.

The Administration Department

3–143 9.—a) The Administration Department shall consist of a Director of the Administration Department and such other staff as may be required.

   b) The Administration Department shall be responsible for the administration and servicing of the Tribunal and the Prosecutions Department.

   c) The Director of the Administration Department shall initially be appointed by the Governing Council or the Successor Government. He or she shall serve for a three year term and be eligible for reappointment. The terms and conditions of service of the Director of the Administration Department shall be those of a General Director in an Iraqi government department.

   d) The staff of the Administration Department shall be appointed by the Director of the Administration Department.

   e) The Director of the Administration Department shall appoint a public relations expert to the position of spokesman of the Tribunal. Such spokesman shall give regular briefings to the press and the public at large with respect to the developments relating to the Tribunal.

Jurisdiction

10. The Tribunal shall have jurisdiction over any Iraqi national or resident   **3–144** of Iraq accused of the crimes listed in Articles 11–14, committed since July 17, 1968 and up and until May 1, 2003, in the territory of Iraq or elsewhere, namely:

   a) The crime of genocide;

   b) Crimes against humanity;

   c) War crimes; or

   d) Violations of certain Iraqi laws listed in Article 14 below.

Rules of Procedure and Evidence

16. The President of the Tribunal shall draft rules of procedure and   **3–145** evidence for the conduct of the pre-trial phase of the proceedings, trials and appeals, the admission of evidence, the protection of victims and witnesses and other appropriate matters (including regulations with respect to the disqualification of judges or prosecutors), where the applicable law, including this Statute does not, or does not adequately provide for a specific situation. He shall be guided by the Iraqi Criminal Procedure Law. Such rules shall be adopted by a majority of the permanent judges of the Tribunal.

Privileges and Immunities

31.—a) The Tribunal, the judges, the Tribunal Investigative Judges, the   **3–146** Prosecutors, the Director of the Administration Department and their staffs shall have immunity from civil suits for their official acts.

   b) Other persons, including the accused, required at the seat of the Tribunal shall be accorded such treatment as is necessary for the proper functioning of the Tribunal.

Seat of the Court

2. The Tribunal shall have its seat in the City of Baghdad, or, following a   **3–147** written proposal made by the President of the Tribunal, in any other Governorate in Iraq as determined by the Governing Council or the Successor Government.

Language

34. Arabic shall be the official language of the Tribunal.   **3–148**

Expenses

3–149   **35.** The expenses of the Tribunal shall be borne by the regular budget of the Government of Iraq.

POWERS OF THE COURTS

I. POWERS OF COERCION UNDER CHAPTER VII OF THE UN CHARTER

A. ICTY AND ICTR STATUTORY PROVISIONS

ICTR Statute, Art. 17, ICTY Statute, Art. 18

Investigation and preparation of indictment

1. The Prosecutor shall initiate investigations *ex-officio* or on the basis of **4–1** information obtained from any source, particularly from Governments, United Nations organs, intergovernmental and non-governmental organisations. The Prosecutor shall assess the information received or obtained and decide whether there is sufficient basis to proceed.

2. The Prosecutor shall have the power to question suspects, victims and witnesses, to collect evidence and to conduct on-site investigations. In carrying out these tasks, the Prosecutor may, as appropriate, seek the assistance of the State authorities concerned.

3. If questioned, the suspect shall be entitled to be assisted by counsel of his own choice, including the right to have legal assistance assigned to him without

payment by him in any such case if he does not have sufficient means to pay for it, as well as to necessary translation into and from a language he speaks and understands.

4. Upon a determination that a *prima facie* case exists, the Prosecutor shall prepare an indictment containing a concise statement of the facts and the crime or crimes with which the accused is charged under the Statute. The indictment shall be transmitted to a judge of the Trial Chamber.

ICTR Statute, Art. 18, ICTY Statute, Art. 19

Review of the indictment

4–2   1. The judge of the Trial Chamber to whom the indictment has been transmitted shall review it. If satisfied that a *prima facie* case has been established by the Prosecutor, he shall confirm the indictment. If not so satisfied, the indictment shall be dismissed.

2. Upon confirmation of an indictment, the judge may, at the request of the Prosecutor, issue such orders and warrants for the arrest, detention, surrender or transfer of persons, and any other orders as may be required for the conduct of the trial.

ICTR Statute, Art. 28, ICTY Statute, Art. 29

Cooperation and judicial assistance

4–3   1. States shall cooperate with the International Tribunal in the investigation and prosecution of persons accused of committing serious violations of international humanitarian law.

2. States shall comply without undue delay with any request for assistance or an order issued by a Trial Chamber, including, but not limited to:
(a) the identification and location of persons;
(b) the taking of testimony and the production of evidence;
(c) the service of documents;
(d) the arrest or detention of persons;
(e) the surrender or the transfer of the accused to the International Tribunal.

B. ICTY AND ICTR RULES OF PROCEDURE

ICTY and ICTR Rules of Procedure and Evidence, rr. 7*bis*, 11*bis*, 54, 54*bis*, 55, 56, 58, 59, 59*bis*, 61, 77

ICTY

Primacy of the Tribunal

4–4   **7*bis*.**—(A) In addition to cases to which Rule 11, Rule 13, Rule 59 or Rule 61 applies, where a Trial Chamber or a permanent Judge is satisfied that a State has failed to comply with an obligation under Article 29 of the Statute which relates to any proceedings before that Chamber or Judge, the Chamber or Judge may advise the President, who shall report the matter to the Security Council.

(B) If the Prosecutor satisfies the President that a State has failed to comply with an obligation under Article 29 of the Statute in respect of a request by the Prosecutor under Rule 8, Rule 39 or Rule 40, the President shall notify the Security Council thereof.

ICTR

Primacy of the Tribunal

7bis.—(A) Except in cases to which Rules 11, 13, 59 or 61 applies, where a Trial Chamber or a Judge is satisfied that a State has failed to comply with an obligation under Article 28 of the Statute relating to any proceedings before that Chamber or Judge, the Chamber or Judge may request the President to report the matter to the Security Council.

(B) If the Prosecutor satisfies the President that a State has failed to comply with an obligation under Article 28 of the Statute in respect of a request by the Prosecutor under Rules 8 or 40, the President shall notify the Security Council thereof.

ICTY

Referral of the Indictment to Another Court

11bis.—(A) After an indictment has been confirmed and prior to the **4–5** commencement of trial, irrespective of whether or not the accused is in the custody of the Tribunal, the President may appoint a bench of three Permanent Judges selected from the Trial Chambers (hereinafter referred to as the "Referral Bench"), which solely and exclusively shall determine whether the case should be referred to the authorities of a State:

    (i) in whose territory the crime was committed; or

    (ii) in which the accused was arrested; or

    (iii) having jurisdiction and being willing and adequately prepared to accept such a case,

so that those authorities should forthwith refer the case to the appropriate court for trial within that State.

(B) The Referral Bench may order such referral proprio motu or at the request of the Prosecutor, after having given to the Prosecutor and, where applicable, the accused, the opportunity to be heard and after being satisfied that the accused will receive a fair trial and that the death penalty will not be imposed or carried out.

(C) In determining whether to refer the case in accordance with paragraph (A), the Referral Bench shall, in accordance with Security Council resolution 1534 (2004) , consider the gravity of the crimes charged and the level of responsibility of the accused.

(D) Where an order is issued pursuant to this Rule:

    (i) the accused, if in the custody of the Tribunal, shall be handed over to the authorities of the State concerned;

    (ii) the Referral Bench may order that protective measures for certain witnesses or victims remain in force;

    (iii) the Prosecutor shall provide to the authorities of the State concerned all of the information relating to the case which the Prosecutor considers appropriate and, in particular, the material supporting the indictment;

    (iv) the Prosecutor may send observers to monitor the proceedings in the national courts on her behalf.

(E) The Referral Bench may issue a warrant for the arrest of the accused, which shall specify the State to which he is to be transferred to trial.

(F) At any time after an order has been issued pursuant to this Rule and before the accused is found guilty or acquitted by a national court, the Referral Bench may, at the request of the Prosecutor and upon having given to the State authorities concerned the opportunity to be heard, revoke the order and make a formal request for deferral within the terms of Rule 10.

(G) Where an order issued pursuant to this Rule is revoked by the Referral Bench, it may make a formal request to the State concerned to transfer the accused to the seat of the Tribunal and the State shall accede to such a request without delay in keeping with Article 29 of the Statute. The Referral Bench or a Judge may also issue a warrant for the arrest of the accused.

(H) A Referral Bench shall have the powers of, and insofar as applicable shall follow the procedures laid down for, a Trial Chamber under the Rules.

(I) An appeal by the accused or the Prosecutor shall lie as of right from a decision of the Referral Bench whether or not to refer a case. Notice of appeal shall be filed within fifteen days of the decision unless the accused was not present or represented when the decision was pronounced, in which case the time-limit shall run from the date on which the accused is notified of the decision.

ICTR

Referral of the Indictment to Another Court

11*bis*.—(A) If an indictment has been confirmed, whether or not the accused is in the custody of the Tribunal, the President may designate a Trial Chamber which shall determine whether the case should be referred to the authorities of a State:

(i) in whose territory the crime was committed; or

(ii) in which the accused was arrested; or

(iii) having jurisdiction and being willing and adequately prepared to accept such a case,

so that those authorities should forthwith refer the case to the appropriate court for trial within that State.

(B) The Trial Chamber may order such referral *proprio motu* or at the request of the Prosecutor, after having given to the Prosecutor and, where the accused is in the custody of the Tribunal, the accused, the opportunity to be heard.

(C) In determining whether to refer the case in accordance with paragraph (A), the Trial Chamber shall satisfy itself that the accused will receive a fair trial in the courts of the State concerned and that the death penalty will not be imposed or carried out.

(D) Where an order is issued pursuant to this Rule:

(i) the accused, if in the custody of the Tribunal, shall be handed over to the authorities of the State concerned;

(ii) the Trial Chamber may order that protective measures for certain witnesses or victims remain in force;

(iii) the Prosecutor shall provide to the authorities of the State concerned all of the information relating to the case which the Prosecutor considers appropriate and, in particular, the material supporting the indictment;

(iv) the Prosecutor may send observers to monitor the proceedings in the courts of the State concerned on his behalf.

(E) The Trial Chamber may issue a warrant for the arrest of the accused, which shall specify the State to which he is to be transferred for trial.

(F) At any time after an order has been issued pursuant to this Rule and before the accused is found guilty or acquitted by a court in the State concerned, the Trial Chamber may, at the request of the Prosecutor and upon having given to the authorities of the State concerned the opportunity to be heard, revoke the order and make a formal request for deferral within the terms of Rule 10.

(G) Where an order issued pursuant to this Rule is revoked by the Trial Chamber, it may make a formal request to the State concerned to transfer the accused to the seat of the Tribunal, and the State shall accede to such a request without delay in keeping with Article 28 of the Statute. The Trial Chamber or a Judge may also issue a warrant for the arrest of the accused.

(H) An appeal by the accused or the Prosecutor shall lie as of right from a decision of the Trial Chamber whether or not to refer a case. Notice of appeal shall be filed within fifteen days of the decision unless the accused was not present or represented when the decision was pronounced, in which case the time- limit shall run from the date on which the accused is notified of the decision.

ICTY and ICTR

General Rule

54. At the request of either party or *proprio motu*, a Judge or a Trial Chamber may issue such orders, summonses, subpoenas, warrants and transfer orders as may be necessary for the purposes of an investigation or for the preparation or conduct of the trial.

4–6

ICTY

Orders Directed to States for the Production of Documents

54bis.—(A) A party requesting an order under Rule 54 that a State produce documents or information shall apply in writing to the relevant Judge or Trial Chamber and shall:

4–7

    (i) identify as far as possible the documents or information to which the application relates;

    (ii) indicate how they are relevant to any matter in issue before the Judge or Trial Chamber and necessary for a fair determination of that matter; and

    (iii) explain the steps that have been taken by the applicant to secure the State's assistance.

(B) The Judge or Trial Chamber may reject an application under paragraph (A) in limine if satisfied that:

    (i) the documents or information are not relevant to any matter in issue in the proceedings before them or are not necessary for a fair determination of any such matter; or

    (ii) no reasonable steps have been taken by the applicant to obtain the documents or information from the State.

(C) (i) A decision by a Judge or a Trial Chamber under paragraph (B) or (E) shall be subject to:

        (a) review under Rule 108 bis; or

        (b) appeal.

    (ii) An appeal under paragraph (i) shall be filed within seven days of filing of the impugned decision. Where such decision is rendered orally, this time-limit shall run from the date of the oral decision, unless

(a) the party challenging the decision was not present or represented when the decision was pronounced, in which case the time-limit shall run from the date on which the challenging party is notified of the oral decision; or

(b) the Trial Chamber has indicated that a written decision will follow, in which case the time-limit shall run from filing of the written decision.

(D) (i) Except in cases where a decision has been taken pursuant to paragraph (B) or paragraph (E), the State concerned shall be given notice of the application, and not less than fifteen days' notice of the hearing of the application, at which the State shall have an opportunity to be heard.

(ii) Except in cases where the Judge or Trial Chamber determines otherwise, only the party making the application and the State concerned shall have the right to be heard.

(E) If, having regard to all circumstances, the Judge or Trial Chamber has good reasons for so doing, the Judge or Trial Chamber may make an order to which this Rule applies without giving the State concerned notice or the opportunity to be heard under paragraph (D), and the following provisions shall apply to such an order:

(i) the order shall be served on the State concerned;

(ii) subject to paragraph (iv), the order shall not have effect until fifteen days after such service;

(iii) a State may, within fifteen days of service of the order, apply by notice to the Judge or Trial Chamber to have the order set aside, on the grounds that disclosure would prejudice national security interests. Paragraph (F) shall apply to such a notice as it does to a notice of objection;

(iv) where notice is given under paragraph (iii), the order shall thereupon be stayed until the decision on the application;

(v) paragraphs (F) and (G) shall apply to the determination of an application made pursuant to paragraph (iii) as they do to the determination of an application of which notice is given pursuant to paragraph (D);

(vi) the State and the party who applied for the order shall, subject to any special measures made pursuant to a request under paragraphs (F) or (G), have an opportunity to be heard at the hearing of an application made pursuant to paragraph (E)(iii) of this Rule.

(F) The State, if it raises an objection pursuant to paragraph (D), on the grounds that disclosure would prejudice its national security interests, shall file a notice of objection not less than five days before the date fixed for the hearing, specifying the grounds of objection. In its notice of objection the State:

(i) shall identify, as far as possible, the basis upon which it claims that its national security interests will be prejudiced; and

(ii) may request the Judge or Trial Chamber to direct that appropriate protective measures be made for the hearing of the objection, including in particular:

(a) hearing the objection in camera and ex parte;

(b) allowing documents to be submitted in redacted form, accompanied by an affidavit signed by a senior State official explaining the reasons for the redaction;

(c) ordering that no transcripts be made of the hearing and that documents not further required by the Tribunal be returned directly to the State without being filed with the Registry or otherwise retained.

(G) With regard to the procedure under paragraph (F) above, the Judge or Trial Chamber may order the following protective measures for the hearing of the objection:

(i) the designation of a single Judge from a Chamber to examine the documents or hear submissions; and/or

(ii) that the State be allowed to provide its own interpreters for the hearing and its own translations of sensitive documents.

(H) Rejection of an application made under this Rule shall not preclude a subsequent application by the requesting party in respect of the same documents or information if new circumstances arise.

(I) An order under this Rule may provide for the documents or information in question to be produced by the State under appropriate arrangements to protect its interests, which may include those arrangements specified in paragraphs (F)(ii) or (G).

ICTR

Rule 54*bis* has not been incorporated within the ICTR Rules and Procedure and Evidence.

ICTY

Execution of Arrest Warrants

55.—(A) A warrant of arrest shall be signed by a permanent Judge. It shall include an order for the prompt transfer of the accused to the Tribunal upon the arrest of the accused.

4–8

(B) The original warrant shall be retained by the Registrar, who shall prepare certified copies bearing the seal of the Tribunal.

(C) Each certified copy shall be accompanied by a copy of the indictment certified in accordance with Rule 47(G) and a statement of the rights of the accused set forth in Article 21 of the Statute, and in Rules 42 and 43 *mutatis mutandis*. If the accused does not understand either of the official languages of the Tribunal and if the language understood by the accused is known to the Registrar, each certified copy of the warrant of arrest shall also be accompanied by a translation of the statement of the rights of the accused in that language.

(D) Subject to any order of a Judge or Chamber, the Registrar may transmit a certified copy of a warrant of arrest to the person or authorities to which it is addressed, including the national authorities of a State in whose territory or under whose jurisdiction the accused resides, or was last known to be, or is believed by the Registrar to be likely to be found.

(E) The Registrar shall instruct the person or authorities to which a warrant is transmitted that at the time of arrest the indictment and the statement of the rights of the accused be read to the accused in a language that he or she understands and that the accused be cautioned in that language that the accused has the right to remain silent, and that any statement he or she makes shall be recorded and may be used in evidence.

(F) Notwithstanding paragraph (E), if at the time of arrest the accused is served with, or with a translation of, the indictment and the statement of rights of the accused in a language that the accused understands and is able to read, these need not be read to the accused at the time of arrest.

(G) When an arrest warrant issued by the Tribunal is executed by the authorities of a State, or an appropriate authority or international body, a member of the Office of the Prosecutor may be present as from the time of the arrest.

ICTR

Execution of Arrest Warrants

55.—(A) A warrant of arrest shall be signed by a Judge and shall bear the seal of the Tribunal. It shall be accompanied by a copy of the indictment, and a statement of the rights of the accused. These rights include those set forth in Article 20 of the Statute, and in Rules 42 and 43 *mutatis mutandis*, together with the right of the accused to remain silent, and to be cautioned that any statement he makes shall be recorded and may be used in evidence.

(B) The Registrar shall transmit to the national authorities of the State in whose territory or under whose jurisdiction or control the accused resides, or was last known to be, three sets of certified copies of:

    (i) The warrant for arrest of the accused and an order for his surrender to theTribunal;

    (ii) The confirmed indictment;

    (iii) A statement of the rights of the accused; and if necessary a translation thereof in a language understood by the accused.

(C) The Registrar shall instruct the said authorities to:

    (i) Cause the arrest of the accused and his transfer to the Tribunal;

    (ii) Serve a set of the aforementioned documents upon the accused;

    (iii) Cause the documents to be read to the accused in a language understood by him and to caution him as to his rights in that language; and

    (iv) Return one set of the documents together with proof of service, to the Tribunal.

(D) When an arrest warrant issued by the Tribunal is executed, a member of the Prosecutor's Office may be present as from the time of arrest.

ICTY and ICTR

Cooperation of States

4–9   **56.** The State to which a warrant of arrest or a transfer order for a witness is transmitted shall act promptly and with all due diligence to ensure proper and effective execution thereof, in accordance with Article 29 of the Statute.

ICTY and ICTR

National Extradition Provisions

4–10   **58.** The obligations laid down in Article 29 of the Statute shall prevail over any legal impediment to the surrender or transfer of the accused or of a witness to the Tribunal which may exist under the national law or extradition treaties of the State concerned.

ICTY and ICTR

Failure to Execute a Warrant or Transfer Order

4–11   **59.**—(A) Where the State to which a warrant of arrest or transfer order has been transmitted has been unable to execute the warrant, it shall report forthwith its inability to the Registrar, and the reasons therefor.

(B) If, within a reasonable time after the warrant of arrest or transfer order has been transmitted to the State, no report is made on action taken, this shall be deemed a failure to execute the warrant of arrest or transfer order and the Tribunal, through the President, may notify the Security Council accordingly.

ICTY

Transmission of Arrest Warrants

4–12   **59bis.**—(A) Notwithstanding Rules 55 to 59, on the order of a permanent Judge, the Registrar shall transmit to an appropriate authority or international body or the Prosecutor a copy of a warrant for the arrest of an accused, on such terms as the Judge may determine, together with an order for the prompt transfer of the accused to the Tribunal in the event that the accused be taken into custody by that authority or international body or the Prosecutor.

(B) At the time of being taken into custody an accused shall be informed immediately, in a language the accused understands, of the charges against him or her and of the fact that he or she is being transferred to the Tribunal. Upon such transfer, the indictment and a statement of the rights of the accused shall be read to the accused and the accused shall be cautioned in such a language.

(C) Notwithstanding paragraph (B), the indictment and statement of rights of the accused need not be read to the accused if the accused is served with these, or with a translation of these, in a language the accused understands and is able to read.

ICTR

Rule 59*bis* has not been incorporated within the ICTR Rules of Procedure and Evidence.

ICTY and ICTR

Procedure in Case of Failure to Execute a Warrant

61.—(A) If, within a reasonable time, a warrant of arrest has not been executed, and personal service of the indictment has consequently not been effected, the Judge who confirmed the indictment shall invite the Prosecutor to report on the measures taken. When the Judge is satisfied that:

4–13

> (i) the Registrar and the Prosecutor have taken all reasonable steps to secure the arrest of the accused, including recourse to the appropriate authorities of the State in whose territory or under whose jurisdiction and control the person to be served resides or was last known to them to be; and
>
> (ii) if the whereabouts of the accused are unknown, the Prosecutor and the Registrar have taken all reasonable steps to ascertain those whereabouts, including by seeking publication of advertisements pursuant to Rule 60, the Judge shall order that the indictment be submitted by the Prosecutor to the Trial Chamber of which the Judge is a member.

(B) Upon obtaining such an order the Prosecutor shall submit the indictment to the Trial Chamber in open court, together with all the evidence that was before the Judge who initially confirmed the indictment. The Prosecutor may also call before the Trial Chamber and examine any witness whose statement has been submitted to the confirming Judge. In addition, the Trial Chamber may request the Prosecutor to call any other witness whose statement has been submitted to the confirming Judge.

(C) If the Trial Chamber is satisfied on that evidence, together with such additional evidence as the Prosecutor may tender, that there are reasonable grounds for believing that the accused has committed all or any of the crimes charged in the indictment, it shall so determine. The Trial Chamber shall have the relevant parts of the indictment read out by the Prosecutor together with an account of the efforts to effect service referred to in Sub-rule (A) above.

(D) The Trial Chamber shall also issue an international arrest warrant in respect of the accused which shall be transmitted to all States. Upon request by the Prosecutor or *proprio motu*, after having heard the Prosecutor, the Trial Chamber may order a State or States to adopt provisional measures to freeze the assets of the accused, without prejudice to the rights of third parties.

(E) If the Prosecutor satisfies the Trial Chamber that the failure to effect personal service was due in whole or in part to a failure or refusal of a State to cooperate with the Tribunal in accordance with Article 29 of the Statute, the Trial Chamber shall so certify. After consulting the Presiding Judges of the Chambers, the President shall notify the Security Council thereof in such manner as the President thinks fit.

ICTY and ICTR

Procedure in Case of Contempt of Court

4–14   **77.**—(A) The Tribunal in the exercise of its inherent power may hold in contempt those who knowingly and wilfully interfere with its administration of justice, including any person who

    (i) being a witness before a Chamber, contumaciously refuses or fails to answer a question;

    (ii) discloses information relating to those proceedings in knowing violation of an order of a Chamber;

    (iii) without just excuse fails to comply with an order to attend before or produce documents before a Chamber;

    (iv) threatens, intimidates, causes any injury or offers a bribe to, or otherwise interferes with, a witness who is giving, has given, or is about to give evidence in proceedings before a Chamber, or a potential witness; or

    (v) threatens, intimidates, offers a bribe to, or otherwise seeks to coerce any other person, with the intention of preventing that other person from complying with an obligation under an order of a Judge or Chamber.

(B) Any incitement or attempt to commit any of the acts punishable under paragraph (A) is punishable as contempt of the Tribunal with the same penalties. (Amended 4 Dec 1998, amended 13 Dec 2001)

(C) When a Chamber has reason to believe that a person may be in contempt of the Tribunal, it may:

    (i) direct the Prosecutor to investigate the matter with a view to the preparation and submission of an indictment for contempt;

    (ii) where the Prosecutor, in the view of the Chamber, has a conflict of interest with respect to the relevant conduct, direct the Registrar to appoint an amicus curiae to investigate the matter and report back to the Chamber as to whether there are sufficient grounds for instigating contempt proceedings; or

    (iii) initiate proceedings itself.

(D) If the Chamber considers that there are sufficient grounds to proceed against a person for contempt, the Chamber may:

    (i) in circumstances described in paragraph (C)(i), direct the Prosecutor to prosecute the matter; or

    (ii) in circumstances described in paragraph (C)(ii) or (iii), issue an order in lieu of an indictment and either direct amicus curiae to prosecute the matter or prosecute the matter itself.

(E) The rules of procedure and evidence in Parts Four to Eight shall apply mutatis mutandis to proceedings under this Rule. (Amended 13 Dec 2001)

(F) Any person indicted for or charged with contempt shall, if that person satisfies the criteria for determination of indigence established by the Registrar, be assigned counsel in accordance with Rule 45. (Revised 12 Nov 1997, amended 13 Dec 2001)

(G) The maximum penalty that may be imposed on a person found to be in contempt of the Tribunal shall be a term of imprisonment not exceeding seven years, or a fine not exceeding 100,000 Euros, or both. (Amended 4 Dec 1998, amended 1 Dec 2000 and 13 Dec 2000, amended 13 Dec 2001)

(H) Payment of a fine shall be made to the Registrar to be held in a separate account.

(I) If a counsel is found guilty of contempt of the Tribunal pursuant to this Rule, the Chamber making such finding may also determine that counsel is no longer eligible to represent a suspect or accused before the Tribunal or that such conduct amounts to misconduct of counsel pursuant to Rule 46, or both. (Amended 13 Dec 2001)

(J) Any decision rendered by a Trial Chamber under this Rule shall be subject to appeal. Notice of appeal shall be filed within fifteen days of filing of the impugned decision. Where such decision is rendered orally, the notice shall be filed within fifteen days of the oral decision, unless

    (i) the party challenging the decision was not present or represented when the decision was pronounced, in which case the time-limit shall run from the date on which the challenging party is notified of the oral decision; or

    (ii) the Trial Chamber has indicated that a written decision will follow, in which case the time-limit shall run from filing of the written decision.

(K) In the case of decisions under this Rule by the Appeals Chamber sitting as a Chamber of first instance, an appeal may be submitted in writing to the President within fifteen days of the filing of the impugned decision. Such appeal shall be decided by five different Judges as assigned by the President. Where the impugned decision is rendered orally, the appeal shall be filed within fifteen days of the oral decision, unless

    (i) the party challenging the decision was not present or represented when the decision was pronounced, in which case the time-limit shall run from the date on which the challenging party is notified of the oral decision; or

    (ii) the Appeals Chamber has indicated that a written decision will follow, in which case the time-limit shall run from filing of the written decision.

The ICTR Rules are the same, except Rules 54*bis* and 59*bis* have not been adopted by the ICTR. A Rule 55*bis* is included in the ICTR Rules, providing for a warrant of arrest to be issued to all States. It is also to be noted that the procedure in case of contempt of court leads to different consequences before the ICTY and ICTR. Whereas the rule enunciated above is the one found within the ICTY rules—which can lead to seven years imprisonment and a maximum of a €100,000 fine— Rule 77 of the ICTR may lead to a five year imprisonment with a maximum fine of US$10,000.

C. INVESTIGATIONS

Articles 18 and 17 of the ICTY and ICTR Statutes, respectively, empower the Prosecutor to initiate investigations *ex-officio* or to do so on the basis of information received from other sources such as governments, inter-governmental and non-governmental organisations. In particular, the Articles entrench the Prosecutor's powers to question suspects, witnesses and victims. They also empower the Prosecutor to collect evidence and conduct on-site investigations. **4–15**

For all of these different forms of investigation, the Prosecutor may seek the assistance of States, which are obliged to cooperate and comply with any requests or orders issued by the Trial Chambers, pursuant to

Articles 29 and 28 of the ICTY and ICTR Statutes, respectively. The position was affirmed in *Prosecutor v. Tihomir Blaškić*, Judgment on Request of Republic of Croatia for Review of Decision of Trial Chamber II, October 29, 1997, para. 63 (hereinafter *Blaškić Subpoena Appeal*), in which the Appeals Chamber held that "a plain reading of Article 29 of the Statute makes it clear that it does not envisage any exception to the obligation of States to comply with requests and orders of a Trial Chamber". The assistance of international organisations may be sought by the Prosecutor; although the obligation of international organisations to cooperate is not explicitly expressed in the Statute, it is provided for in a limited fashion within the Rules of Procedure and Evidence. This obligation is also inherent to their nature; this will be developed under paragraphs 4–35 and 4–37.

(1) Obligations of States

4–16   The bases of the obligation to comply with any orders of the Tribunals are the Security Council Resolutions 827 of 1993 and 955 of 1994, establishing the ICTY and the ICTR, respectively. These resolutions were passed in accordance with the Chapter VII powers conferred on the Security Council in the UN Charter. In terms of Article 25 of the Charter, all UN member States are required to carry out the decisions of the Security Council. In fact, the Security Council decided, by way of the enumerated Resolutions, that all States shall cooperate *fully* with the International Tribunal and its organs. Stemming from this obligation is the consequential responsibility for States to adopt any measures necessary under their domestic law to implement the provisions of the Resolution and the Statute, *including* the obligation of States to comply with requests for assistance or orders issued by a Trial Chamber. The Statute of International ad hoc Tribunals only mentions that States shall fully cooperate, whereas the Statute of the International Criminal Court adds, at Article 88, that States Parties shall ensure that there are procedures available under their national law for all of the forms of cooperation. Yet it may be observed that, if a State omits to adopt the necessary amendments to its legislation and that it offers the necessary cooperation to the International Tribunals, its failure to cooperate will remain theoretical.

4–17   In *Prosecutor v. Dusko Tadić*, Decision on the Defence Motion for Interlocutory Appeal on Jurisdiction, October 2, 1995, para. 31, the Appeals Chamber examined the nature of the Security Council's Chapter VII powers, stating "these powers are **coercive** *vis-à-vis* the culprit State or entity. But they are also **mandatory** *vis-à-vis the other Member States, who are under an obligation to cooperate with the Organization (Article 2, paragraph 5, Articles 25, 48) and with one another (Articles 49), in the implementation of the action or measures decided by the Security Council"*.

4–18   The obligation of States to cooperate with the Tribunals in the investigation and prosecution of cases is fundamental to the work of the Tribunals because unlike national courts, the International Tribunals do not have any enforcement agents at their disposal to perform these functions. The Tribunals, therefore, rely on States for all forms of cooperation enumerated in the Statute (*Blaškić Subpoena Appeal*, para.

26). The first President of the ICTY had stated in the Tribunal's 1994 report that, in contrast with the Nuremberg and Tokyo tribunals where the Allied Powers had full authority over the territory of Germany and Japan respectively, the ICTY is not endowed with direct enforcement powers as it has no law enforcement agents at its disposal entitled to carry out investigations, subpoena witnesses, or serve arrest warrants in the territories of States Members of the United Nations (ICTY First Annual Report, UN Doc A/49/342–S/1994/1007 (1994), para. 84).

Rule 58 and irrelevance of national legislation concerns

The Rules reinforce this unqualified obligation of States to cooperate with the Tribunals. Rule 58 of the ICTY provides that "the obligations laid down in Article 29 of the Statute shall prevail over any legal impediment to the surrender or transfer of the accused or of a witness to the Tribunal which may exist under the national law or extradition treaties of the State concerned". This provision pre-empts any suggestion by national authorities that they are unable to comply with their Article 29 obligations to surrender or transfer an accused as a result of their national laws or extradition treaties. Rule 58 follows the general principle of international law, embodied in international jurisprudence and found at Article 27 of the Vienna Convention on the Law of Treaties, that a State may not invoke its internal law as a justification for its failure to perform an international obligation. This principle is also crystallised in the Articles on State Responsibility developed by the International Law Commission (see Article 32, Irrelevance of internal law in Report of the International Law Commission on the work of its Fifty-third session, *Official Records of the General Assembly, Fifty-sixth session, Supplement No. 10* (A/56/10), chp.IV.E.1). **4–19**

In *Prosecutor v. Milošević*, Decision on Preliminary Motions, November 8, 2001, para. 45, the Trial Chamber, stated as follows: "the purpose of Rule 58 is to ensure that domestic procedures relating to the surrender and transfer of a person, from a State in respect of whom a request for arrest and transfer has been made, are not used as a basis for not complying with the request". By and large States have not raised their national law as a basis for refusing to cooperate with the Tribunal (see ICTY Third Annual Report (1995-1996), UN Doc A/51/292 S/1996/665 (1996) and Sixth Annual Report (1998–1999), UN Doc A/54/187 S/1998/846 (1999)). Nevertheless, it must be noted that the national legislation of certain States has been an obstacle in the transfer of an accused in at least two cases. In *The Prosecutor v. Dusko Tadić* before the ICTY, the International Tribunal had requested the transfer of the accused by German authorities that held him in custody in November 1994; it is only after modifying its internal legislation that Germany was enabled to fulfil the request in April 1995, some six months after the initial request. In *The Prosecutor v. Elizaphan Ntakirutmana* before the ICTR, the US District Court for the Southern District of Texas refused to grant the transfer of the accused since no treaty existed between the United States of America and the International Tribunal allowing it (In the Matter of Surrender of Elizaphan Ntakirutimana, U.S. Dist. Ct. Southern Dist. of TX, Laredo Div., Misc. No. L–96–5 (17 Dec. 1997)). **4–20**

Lengthy proceedings and appeals made it that, although he was originally arrested in September 1996, it is only in March 2000 that the Ntakirutimana was handed over to the ICTR.

(2) On-site investigations

4–21   Although Articles 19(2) and 18(2) of the ICTY and ICTR Statutes, respectively, recognise that in carrying out investigations the Prosecutor may seek the assistance of the States concerned, the Prosecutor is not obliged to do so. Thus the Prosecutor may conduct investigations directly on the territory of the State concerned (see *Prosecutor v. Dario Kordic and Mario Cerkez*, Decision Stating Reasons for Trial Chamber's Ruling of June 1 1999 Rejecting Defence Motion to Suppress Evidence, June 25, 1999).

The Statutes expressly acknowledge the power of the Prosecutor to conduct on-site investigations without the consent of the State concerned. The provision may be contentious as it impinges upon the sovereignty of the State on whose territory the on-site investigation is conducted. In inter-State mutual assistance relations, on-site investigations generally require the consent of the State on whose territory the investigation takes place. The opposition of certain States to permitting on-site investigations was evident in the FRY's (Federal Republic of Yugoslavia) refusal, despite its statutory obligations, to allow the ICTY's Prosecutor access to Kosovo in 1999 to conduct on-site investigations.

(3) Defence investigations

4–22   Although no mention is made of the powers of the defence to conduct such on-site investigations, the Trial Chambers could order a State to provide access for this purpose on the basis of the Trial Chambers' plenary powers under Articles 19 and 18 of the ICTY and ICTR Statutes, respectively, and Rule 54. This power of the court was used in the *Prosecutor v. Krstić* (Case No.IT-98–33-A, Decision on Application for Subpoenas, July 1, 2003) when the defence was seeking to hold meetings with two potential witnesses that held positions within their respective government (see paragraph 4–36 concerning State officials).

This power is also inherited by the cornerstone Article 21 of the Statute on the rights of the accused, most specifically the right of the accused to have adequate time and facilities for the preparation of his defence. In a decision in the case *Prosecutor v. Hadžihasanović and Kubura*, the ICTY also recognised that Defence access to archives of an international organisation was necessary to guarantee a fair trial to the accused (see Case No. IT-01–47-T, Decision on Defence Motion for Access to EUMM Archives, December 15, 2003, p.3). The Defence counsel in this case had previous access to the archives of the UNPROFOR and that of the British Battalion of the UNPROFOR, which demonstrates that the Defence needs to conduct its on investigation. It must be understood that the procedure of the ad hoc tribunals is mainly influenced by common law procedure despite the obvious presence of the continental regime. In this adversarial environment, each party needs to conduct its own investigation, as the Prosecution does not have the obligation to investigate for both parties. The situation is different for the Prosecution at the ICC, which will have the additional role to search evidence against the accused and exculpatory material.

D. ARREST AND DETENTION

Articles 19(2) and 18(2) of the Statutes of the ICTY and ICTR, respectively, authorise a judge to issue a warrant of arrest or an order of detention after confirmation of an indictment. Articles 20(2) and 19(2), of the ICTY and ICTR, respectively, require a person against whom an arrest warrant or a detention order has been issued to be taken into custody. In accordance with their general obligation to cooperate with the Tribunals (as set out in Articles 29 and 28) in the investigation and prosecution of cases, States are required to comply with such orders and warrants for arrest and transfer of accused to the respective Tribunals. Rule 56 of the ICTY and ICTR obligates States to give effect to such arrest warrants by arresting and promptly transferring accused persons to the Tribunals.   **4–23**

In addition, in more urgent situations, Rule 40 and Rule 40*bis* of the ICTY and ICTR gives the Tribunals the power to request a State to provisionally arrest a suspect or accused person or take "all necessary measures to prevent the escape" of such a person. This power of provisional arrest was utilised by the Prosecutor in the *Barayagwiza* case (ICTR) to effect Barayagwiza's arrest in the Cameroon in 1996.

(1) Definition of arrest

Rule 2 of the ICTY and ICTR provides that an arrest is an "act of taking a suspect into custody pursuant to a warrant of arrest or under Rule 40". In *Prosecutor v. Dokmanovic*, Decision on the Motion for Release by the Accused Slavko Dokmanovic, October 22, 1997, para. 28, the Trial Chamber regarded a restraint on a person's freedom of movement imposed by law enforcement officials as a "necessary component of arrest". On the facts of the case, the Trial Chamber found Dokmanovic to have been "arrested" only when he entered the UNTAES compound in Croatian territory. The Trial Chamber reasoned that prior to this, he had freely consented to being carried to the compound in the UNTAES vehicle from the Federal Republic of Yugoslavia, and thus had not been arrested until reaching the compound.   **4–24**

(2) The manner in which arrests are effected

In accordance with Rule 55 of the ICTY and ICTR, warrants of arrest are sent to the appropriate authorities in States or entities in which the accused person is believed to be residing. Since the signing of the   **4–25**

Dayton Peace Agreement, all previously issued arrest warrants and any further arrest warrants issued by the ICTY have been and are transmitted to IFOR, and its successor SFOR. Rule 56 of the ICTY and ICTR requires the States receiving such a request or order for arrest and transfer to act with due diligence in executing the request or order.

Although cooperation is the primary method for arrest and transfer, it is not the only means to bring persons before the Tribunal. An additional mechanism for arrest and transfer has been provided for in Rule 59*bis* of the ICTY (see *Prosecutor v. Dokmanovic*, Decision on the Motion for Release by the Accused Slavko Dokmanovic, October 22, 1997, paras 35 and 41). It allows for a copy of an arrest warrant to be transmitted to an appropriate authority, international body or the Prosecutor requiring that body or authority to take the accused into custody and transfer him to the Tribunal (*Prosecutor v. Dokmanovic*, Decision on the Motion for Release by the Accused Slavko Dokmanovic, October 22, 1997, para. 36). The Rule is consistent with Articles 19(2) and 20(2) of the ICTY Statute, which do not require that an arrest warrant be directed to a State only or that only States can arrest and transfer accused persons to the Tribunal (*Prosecutor v. Dokmanovic*, Decision on the Motion for Release by the Accused Slavko Dokmanovic, October 22, 1997, paras 37–38).

Rule 55(C) of the ICTY and ICTR requires that when the Registrar is aware of the language spoken by an accused, and the fact that the accused is not familiar with the official languages of the Tribunal, that the certified copy of the warrant of arrest be accompanied by a translation of the statement of the rights of the accused. When an accused is arrested and transferred to the Tribunal in terms of Rule 59*bis*, he must be informed of the charges against him and the fact that he is being transferred to the Tribunal in a language that he under-stands (Rule 59*bis*(B)). The accused is not however entitled to receive a copy of his arrest warrant in a language that he understands.

(3) Lawfulness of arrests, transfers and surrenders

4–26   In *Prosecutor v. Dokmanovic*, Decision on the Motion for Release by the Accused Slavko Dokmanovic, October 22, 1997, para. 56, the Tribunal found that a ruse to lure an accused into a situation so that he or she may be arrested does not amount to forcible abduction or kidnapping. In that case Dokmanovic entered an UNTAES vehicle in the Federal Republic of Yugoslavia (FRY) in the belief that he was being taken into the UNTAES—controlled territory of Eastern Slavonia in Croatia to make arrangements regarding his property situated there. The Trial Chamber at paras 27–32 found him to have entered the vehicle voluntarily.

Given that the Tribunal found Dokmanovic's arrest and transfer to be lawful, the question did not arise whether the Tribunal had the authority to exercise its jurisdiction over an accused person who had been unlawfully transferred to the Tribunal. However, this question did arise before the ICTY in the *Todorovic case* on account of his allegations that in 1998, whilst living in the FRY he was abducted by agents of the ICTY and taken against his will to Bosnia and Herzegovina, where he was handed over to SFOR at an Air Base in Tuzla, Bosnia and Herzegovina. At that point he was arrested and transferred to the custody of the ICTY (see *Prosecutor v. Todorovic*, Decision Stating Reasons for the Trial Chamber's Order of March 4, 1999 on Defence Motion for Evidentiary Hearing on the Arrest of the Accused Todorovic, March 25, 1999).

In *Todorovic's* case the Appeals Chamber affirmed the Trial Chamber's earlier ruling denying Todorovic's motion for an evidentiary hearing on his arrest. The basis of the refusal was that there was insufficient factual and legal material regarding the circumstances of Todorovic's arrest to justify such a hearing and that the accused bore the onus of establishing the unlawfulness of his arrest. (*Prosecutor v. Todorovic*, Decision on Appeal by Stevan Todorovic against the Oral Decision of March 4, 1999 and the written decision of March 25, 1999 of Trial Chamber III, October 13, 1999.)

In *Prosecutor v. Nikolic*, Decision on Defence Motion Challenging the Exercise of Jurisdiction by the Tribunal, October 9, 2002, the Trial Chamber denied the accused's motion to dismiss the indictment on the basis that he had been arrested and brought before the Tribunal illegally. Even though the Chamber accepted that the accused had been allegedly illegally arrested in the FRY and transferred to the territory of Bosnia and Herzegovina by some unknown individuals, his arrest by SFOR in Bosnia and transfer to the ICTY was lawful as it could not be concluded that SFOR or the Prosecutor were involved in the alleged illegal arrest in the FRY. Moreover, assessing the level of violence used against the Accused, the Trial Chamber observed that the assumed facts did not at all show that the treatment of the Accused by the unknown individuals was of such an egregious nature.

Writ of habeas corpus

The Statutes and Rules do not make provision for a writ of habeus **4–27** corpus. The accused Todorovic filed a petition for a writ of habeus corpus on November 15, 1999. The Trial Chamber granted the accused an evidentiary hearing on the matter. Thereafter, the accused pleaded guilty to certain of the charges and as the case did not proceed, the petition was not heard (see, *Prosecutor v. Todorovic*, Decision on Prosecution Motion to Withdraw Counts of the Indictment and Defence Motion to Withdraw Pending Motions, February 26, 2001).

In *Barayagwiza v. Prosecutor*, November 3, 1999, the Appeals Chamber found the conduct of the case to be egregious because of "the combination of delays that seemed to occur at virtually every stage of the Appellant's case. The failure to hear the *writ of habeas corpus*, the delay in hearing the Extremely Urgent Motion, the prolonged detention of the Appellant without an indictment" (para. 109). The cumulative effect of these violations left the Chamber "with no acceptable option but to order the dismissal of the charges with prejudice and the Appellant's immediate release from custody". In finding an abuse of process (see, para. 101), the Appeals Chamber regarded release to be the only appropriate remedy because "to proceed with the Appellant's trial when such violations have been committed, would cause irreparable damage to the integrity of the judicial process" (para. 108). The

Appeals Chamber also found release to be "the only effective remedy for the cumulative breaches of the accused's rights" and that this disposition might "deter the commission of such serious violations in the future".

The Appeals Chamber revised this judgment on March 31, 2000 holding that new facts presented to it by the Prosecutor diminished the gravity of the infringements of the accused's rights. The accused's claim to be released was dismissed. The Appeals Chamber held that the infringements of the accused's rights should be taken into account in sentence, if he was convicted; if acquitted, he should receive financial compensation. (See, *Barayagwiza v. Prosecutor*, Decision (Prosecutor's Request for Review or Reconsideration), March 31, 2000.)

4–28   In *Prosecutor v. Slobodan Milošević*, Decision on Preliminary Motions, November 8, 2001, the Trial Chamber dismissed the accused's allegation that his surrender to the Tribunal had been unlawful and thus that the Tribunal lacked jurisdiction. The Chamber rejected the accused's allegation that the Serbian government had no power to arrest and transfer Milošević, given that the arrest warrants were sent to the FRY (paras 45–46). It found that in light of the important purpose behind Rule 58, "notwithstanding the fact that the surrender was made by the government of the Republic of Serbia, rather than the Federal Republic of Yugoslavia to whom the request was made, the provisions of Rule 58 apply and, consequently, the transfer was effected in accordance with the provisions of the Statute". In response to the accused's contention that Article 18 of the Federal Constitution of the FRY does not provide for the extradition or transfer of Yugoslav citizens, the Trial Chamber reiterated Article 27 of the Vienna Convention on the Law of Treaties, which denies parties the right to invoke their internal laws as justification for failure to perform a treaty obligation. The Chamber held that if the FRY is unable to rely on its internal laws then, *a fortiori*, neither may the accused (para. 47).

In response to the accused's allegation that these grounds of unlawfulness cumulatively raise the doctrine of abuse of process, the Tribunal stated that the circumstances of Milošević's arrest did not constitute an egregious violation of his rights. It distinguished *Barayagwiza's* case from *Milošević's* case on the basis that Barayagwiza had been detained for eleven months without being notified of the charges against him (see *Prosecutor v. Slobodan Milošević*, Decision on Preliminary Motions, November 8, 2001, paras 48–51).

It remains to be seen whether an illegal abduction will be regarded as an abuse of process, and if so, what remedy will follow. Arguably the only effective remedy in the face of an illegal abduction is dismissal with prejudice like in *Barayagwiza's* case.

In *Prosecutor v. Brdanin*, Decision on Petition for a Writ of Habeas Corpus on Behalf of Radislav Brdanin, December 8, 1999, paras 4–5, the Chamber found that "this Tribunal has no power to issue writs in the name of any Sovereign or other head of State, and it is not a court of civil jurisdiction which can hear the proceedings commenced by such a writ. But the Tribunal certainly does have both the power and the procedure to resolve a challenge to the lawfulness of a detainee's detention". The power emanates from Rule 72, when an application for habeas corpus amounts to a challenge to jurisdiction in a wide sense, or Rule 73 in other cases (*Prosecutor v. Brdanin*, Decision on Petition for a

Writ of Habeas Corpus on Behalf of Radislav Brdanin, December 8, 1999, para. 6. Also see *Prosecutor v. Slobodan Milošević*, Decision on Preliminary Motions, November 8, 2001, para. 38, in which the Trial Chamber recognised a right to challenge the lawfulness of an arrest or detention under the Statute based on the existence of such a right as a matter of customary international law).

(4) Failure by States to execute arrest warrants

In order to monitor compliance with a State's obligations under Article 29, Rule 59(A) of the ICTY and ICTR requires a State to report its inability to execute an arrest warrant. Rule 59(B) creates a presumption that a State which does not report on whether an arrest warrant has been executed, has failed to execute the warrant, and authorises the Tribunal to inform the Security Council of the non-compliance.   **4–29**

Rule 61 of the ICTY and ICTR prescribes the steps to be taken when a warrant of arrest is not executed. It provides that if the Prosecutor is able to satisfy the Tribunal that "there are reasonable grounds for believing that the accused has committed all or any of the crimes charged in the indictment" it shall issue an international arrest warrant in respect of the accused, which shall be transmitted to all States. If the Prosecutor is able to satisfy the Tribunal that the failure to execute the arrest warrant is "due in whole or in part to a failure or a refusal of a State to cooperate with the Tribunal in accordance with Article 29 of the Statute", the President of the Tribunal is obligated to report this finding to the Security Council. Pursuant to Rule 61 hearings, the refusal of Republika Srpska, the FRY and Croatia to cooperate with the Tribunal in the surrender of the accused Nikolic, Karadzic, Mladic and Rajic was reported to the Security Council on various occasions in 1995 and 1996 (see, ICTY Third Annual Report (1995–1996), UN Doc A/51/292S/1996/665 (1996)).

Upon receiving such a report, the Security Council may react to the failure of the State to cooperate in accordance with its powers under the UN Charter. See, for example, SC Resolution 1207 of November 17, 1998, dealing with the FRY's failure to cooperate in the arrest and surrender of the "Vukovar Three".

Rule 61 proceedings were relied upon in the early years of the ICTY when no accused were arrested, to lead evidence before the Tribunal and increase the pressure on States to arrest indictees. This rule is now seldom invoked before the ICTY.

E. Search and Seizure

Articles 19(2) and 18(2) of the ICTY and ICTR Statutes, respectively empower the Chambers to issue orders or warrants as are necessary for the conduct of a trial upon request by the Prosecutor, and once an indictment has been confirmed. Articles 18(2) and 17(2) of the ICTY and ICTR Statutes respectively, authorise the Prosecutor to collect   **4–30** evidence. Thus, the Prosecutor may obtain search warrants from the Chambers for its investigations. One of the means for the execution of such warrants is set out in Article 18(2) of the Statute, which provides that in carrying out his or her investigations, the Prosecutor may request the assistance of the State authorities concerned. It is not the only means for the execution of warrants, as evidenced in the Trial Chamber's decision in *Prosecutor v. Dario Kordic and Mario Cerkez*, Decision Stating Reasons for Trial Chamber's Ruling of June 1, 1999 Rejecting Defence Motion to Suppress Evidence, June 25, 1999.

Kordic's motion sought to suppress information obtained in a search at the Defence Office of Vitez Municipality on September 23, 1998. The search had been conducted pursuant to a search warrant issued by a Tribunal Judge on September 18, 1998. Kordic sought the exclusion of the evidence on the basis of the manner in which the warrant had been executed. He alleged that it had violated the sovereignty of Bosnia-Herzegovina on account of the direct enforcement action of the Prosecutor within the boundaries of a sovereign State.

The Trial Chamber upheld the lawfulness of the Prosecutor's investigations on the territory of a State without obtaining the assistance of that State. It held that Article 18(2) gives the Prosecutor a discretion to seek the assistance of any State in collecting evidence or in carrying out an investigation. The Prosecutor is not, however, obliged to seek such cooperation. The Chamber rejected the allegation that the search had violated the sovereignty of Bosnia. It drew attention to the obligation of all States to cooperate with the Tribunal and comply with any orders issued by a Trial Chamber, as well as the qualified nature of the prohibition on the interference in the domestic jurisdiction of a State under Article 2(7) of the UN Charter. This article expressly recognises that the non-intervention rule "shall not prejudice the application of enforcement measures under Chapter VII". Thus, the Chamber confirmed the power of the Prosecutor to act directly within the jurisdiction of a State.

F. WITNESS SUMMONSES, PRODUCTION ORDERS AND SUBPOENAS

4–31   The power of the Tribunals to issue "orders, and warrants for the arrest, detention, surrender or transfer of persons, and any other orders as may be required for the conduct of the trial" at the request of the Prosecutor and upon confirmation of an indictment is enshrined in Articles 19(2) and 18(2) of the ICTY and ICTR Statutes, respectively.

The right to request Chambers to issue such orders or warrants is extended in Rule 54 of the ICTY and ICTR, which provides that "at the request of either party or *proprio motu*, a Judge or a Trial Chamber may issue such orders, summonses, subpoenas, warrants and transfer orders as may be necessary for the purposes of an investigation or for the preparation or conduct of the trial" (see, *Prosecutor v. Simić, et al.*, Decision on Application for Leave to Appeal Against Trial Chamber Decision of March 7, 2000, May 3, 2000, in which the Appeals Chamber rejected an application for leave to appeal, holding that a Trial Chamber is clearly empowered, under Rule 54, to issue orders *proprio motu*. This practice was affirmed in *Prosecutor v. Blaškić*, Order for the Production of Documents Used to prepare for Testimony, April 22, 1999, in which the Trial Chamber, *proprio motu*, ordered the production of the war diary relied upon by Blaškić in the preparation of his testimony). Pursuant to Rule 54, the defence can request orders from the Trial Chamber for the purposes of the investigation, preparation and conduct of the case.

The wording of Rule 54 is non-restrictive. It is applicable to the issue of orders and warrants even prior to the confirmation of an indictment. Given that States are obliged to comply with all requests or orders issued by a Trial Chamber in terms of Article 29(2) and 28(2), which may pertain to the identification and location of persons as well as the taking of testimony, the Chambers must be able to issue orders or summonses prior to the confirmation of an indictment.

(1) The definition of "necessary" in Rule 54

In the *Prosecutor v. Delalic et al.*, Decision of the President on the   **4–32** Prosecutor's Motion for the Production of Notes Exchanged between Zejnil Delalic and Zdravcko Mucic, November 11, 1996, para. 39, the Trial Chamber examined the meaning of "necessary for the purposes of an investigation or for the preparation or conduct of a trial" under Rule 54. President Cassese stated that the test was twofold. The order had to be necessary for the Prosecutor to obtain the material and the material had to be relevant to an investigation being conducted by the Prosecutor. He continued that "as with any search or seizure warrant, the Prosecutor cannot simply conduct a "fishing expedition" (see also, *Prosecutor v. Delalic et al.*, Decision on the Motion by the Accused Zejnil Delalic for the Disclosure of Evidence, September 26, 1996 and *Prosecutor v. Delalic et al.*, Decision on the Motion ex parte by the Defence of Zdravko Mucic concerning the issue of Subpoena to an Interpreter, July 8, 1997, para. 13).

(2) Orders

The Tribunals are empowered to issue orders to the Prosecutor, the Defence or a sovereign State. Accordingly, the Tribunal has ordered the Prosecutor to provide it with information on the status of negotiations pertaining to obtaining custody of an accused (*Prosecutor v. Gagovic* Order Pursuant to Rule 54 in Gagovic, May 13, 1997); as well as witness statements, and the number of witnesses and other documentary material it might seek to introduce at trial (known as scheduling orders) pursuant to Rule 65*ter*(E). In *Prosecutor v. Simić et al.*, Order on Defence Requests for Judicial Assistance for the Production of Information, March 7, 2000, the Trial Chamber ordered the Prosecution to disclose documents and information pertaining to the alleged illegal abduction of Todorovic, which were required for a future evidentiary hearing. Pursuant to Rule 54, the Defence are obliged to respond to an indictment and the Prosecution's pre-trial brief (see, *Prosecutor v. Kovacevic*, Kovacevic Scheduling Order, March 5, 1998).

Binding orders to States

4–33   The *Blaškic Subpoena Appeal*, at para. 26, confirmed the existence of a power to issue binding orders to States. The Tribunal held that it could issue binding orders to Croatia for the production of documents, which Croatia was obliged to comply with in terms of Article 29 of the Statute. The power to issue such orders, included orders for the production of documents which implicated the national security concerns or other sensitive evidentiary material of a State (*Blaškic Subpoena Appeal*, para. 64. On the content and specificity of such orders, see paragraph 4–34 below).

Although recognising the power of the Tribunal to compel States to disclose material, the Appeals Chamber regarded cooperation rather than coercion as the preferred means of interaction between the Tribunal and States (see, para. 31). The Chamber endorsed the Prosecutor's contention that "as a matter of policy and in order to foster good relations with States, . . . co-operative processes should wherever possible be used, . . . they should be used first, and . . . resort to mandatory compliance powers expressly given by Article 29(2) should be reserved for cases in which they are really necessary".

Conditions for the issuance of orders

The reasonable efforts test

4–34   One of the conditions for granting a request under Article 29 (ICTY) or Article 28 (ICTR) is a showing that reasonable efforts have been made to secure assistance of the State (enshrined in Rule 54*bis*(A)(iii)) and that those efforts have been unsuccessful (see *Prosecutor v. Bagosora et al.*, Case No. ICTR-98–41-T, Request to the Government of Rwanda for Cooperation and Assistance Pursuant to Article 28 of the Statute (TC), March 10, 2004, para. 4; recently confirmed in *Bagosora et al.*, Decision on Request for Assistance Pursuant to Article 28 of the Statute (TC), 27 May 2005, para. 2).

Rule 54*bis* was adopted by the ICTY on November 17, 1999 and seems to be the crystallisation of paragraph 32 of the *Blaškić Subpoena Appeal* decision. The Appeals Chamber upheld that any request for an order for production of documents issued under Article 29, paragraph 2, of the Statute, whether before or after the commencement of a trial, must (1) identify specific documents and not broad categories; (2) set out succinctly the reasons why such documents are deemed relevant to the trial; (3) not be unduly onerous and (4) give the requested State sufficient time for compliance. The first two criterias are now sub-paragraph (i) and (ii) of Rule 54*bis*(A) and sub-paragraph (iii) represents the reasonable efforts test.

In a recent decision, the Trial Chamber in the *Milutinovic* case ordered the Applicant (the Defence in this matter) to reformulate its request as it did not indicate how the documents sought were relevant to the issues in the case and that parts of its request contains "a description that is vague and obscure" thus failing to identify the documents sought (see *Prosecutor v. Milutinovic et al.*, Trial Chamber, Case No. IT-99–37-PT, Decision on Application of Dragoljub Ojdanic for Binding Orders Pursuant to Rule 54*bis*, 23 March 2005, p. 5 and 6).

International and humanitarian organizations

Although the ICTY recognised that the issue in the case concerning the International Committee of the Red Cross (ICRC) was not whether it had jurisdiction or could compel the ICRC to produce information, the Chamber's ruling is relevant to whether information obtained by an employee during the course of their employment with the ICRC can be disclosed in testimony before the Tribunal. In *Prosecutor v. Simić et al.*, ex parte Confidential, Decision on the Prosecution Motion under Rule 73 for a Ruling Concerning the Testimony of a Witness, July 27, 1999, para. 73, the Trial Chamber found that the parties to the Geneva Conventions and Protocols have assumed "a conventional obligation to ensure non-disclosure in judicial proceedings of information relating to the work of the ICRC in the possession of an ICRC employee, and that conversely the ICRC has a right to insist on such non-disclosure by parties to the Geneva Conventions and the Protocols". The Trial Chamber held that the right to non-disclosure in respect of the ICRC exists under customary international law. The finding recognises the indispensable character of non-disclosure to the effective discharge of the ICRC's mandate to guarantee the observance of minimum humanitarian standards. Thus, the Chamber afforded the ICRC an unqualified right to non-disclosure of information obtained by employees whilst in the employ of the ICRC in judicial proceedings.

4–35

Note the Separate Opinion of Judge David Hunt, in which he argued that in every case the Tribunal would have to weigh the competing interests. The correct test was "whether the evidence to be given by the witness in breach of the obligations of confidentiality owed to the ICRC is so essential to the case of the relevant party (here the Prosecution) as to outweigh the risk of serious consequences of the breach of confidence in the particular case" (see *Prosecutor v. Simić et al.*, Separate Opinion of Judge David Hunt on Prosecutor's Motion for a Ruling Concerning the Testimony of a Witness, July 27, 1999, para. 35. See also, *Prosecutor v. Simić et al.*, Decision Denying Request for Assistance in Securing Documents and Witnesses from the International Committee of the Red Cross, June 7, 2000, in which the Trial Chamber denied Todorovic's motion for an order requesting assistance in securing documents from the ICRC finding the law in the earlier ICRC decision dispositive of the issue in the absence of Todorovic showing otherwise. Judge Hunt again appended a separate opinion reiterating his earlier view).

In the case of other international organisations, such a confidentiality interest might not weigh as heavily as that of the ICRC. Such is the case of the European Union Monitoring Mission (EUMM) which was called to assist Defence counsel of the accused in *Prosecutor v. Hadžihasanović and Kubura* (Decision on Defence Motion for Access to EUMM Archives, December 15, 2003, Trial Chamber II). The Trial Chamber's approach was non-confrontational—a similar approach is adopted by the ICC in its Statute (see Article 119, ICC Statute, on dispute resolution) as it did not deem necessary to have recourse to Rule 54*bis* since Rule 54 was sufficient for the purposes of the decision, refused to issue binding orders and instead invited the EUMM to grant access to the Defence to its archives. It has to be noted that the EUMM had argued that Rule 54*bis* did not apply; the Trial Chamber noted that the rule was entitled "Orders Directed to States for the Production of Documents" but that member States of the EUMM are under an obligation to cooperate with the Tribunal pursuant to Article 29 of the Statute. This decision is of interest since in this case, the concerned international organisation had the capacity to gather information and maintain archives, in comparison to the NATO decision in the *Milutinovic* case illustrated in section 4–30 where the information was gathered by States individually and not by the organisation itself. The Trial Chamber took a practical approach, one designed to assist the requesting party in its quest for material that may assist in the course of the trial while maintaining a non-aggressive method towards an international organisation.

Nevertheless, an earlier decision seems to contradict the EUMM's position that Rule 54*bis* isn't applicable to the organisation. In the *Kordić and Čerkez* case, the Trial Chamber ordered—pursuant to "Article 29 of the Statute of the International Tribunal and Rules 54, 54*bis* and 81 of the Rules"—the Member States of the European Community at the time of entry into force of the Memorandum (creating the EUMM, previously ECMM) to disclose to the Defence the documents and material requested (see *Prosecutor v. Dario Kordic and Mario Cerkez*, Case No. IT–95–14–2, Order for the Production of Documents by the European Community Monitoring Mission and its Member States, August 4, 2000).

State officials

4–36   The Appeals Chamber in the *Blaškić Subpoena Appeal* stated that the Tribunals are not empowered to issue binding orders to specific State officials (see para. 43). The Appeals Chamber found that it may address orders to States, but that as a matter of customary international law it is for the State concerned to determine which officials or organs should be responsible for implementing the Tribunal's orders. This ruling was however distinguished in the *Krstic* case, as the Appeals Chamber noted that the *Blaškić Subpoena Appeal* decision did not have to "determine the issue of whether a subpoena could be issued to a person to give evidence of what he saw or heard at a time when he was a State official or in the course of exercising his official functions" (see *Prosecutor v. Radislav Krstic*, Case No. IT–98–33–A, Decision on Application for Subpoenas, July 1, 2003, para. 24, hereinafter " *Krstic Subpoena Appeal*"). In fact, the *Blaškić Subpoena Appeal* was concerned with the production of documents. The ruling that a subpoena could not be addressed to State officials acting in their official capacity was justified by that such officials are "mere instruments of a State and their official action can only be attributed to the State" (*Blaškić Subpoena Appeal* decision, para. 38 and 44).

The *Blaškić Subpoena Appeal* decision rules that a State official enjoys a functional immunity. The Appeals Chamber issued this ruling in the limited scenario of a State official acting as the custodian of official documents and it "did not say that the functional immunity enjoyed by the State officials includes an immunity against being compelled to give evidence of what the official saw or heard in the course of exercising his official functions" (see *Krstic Subpoena Appeal*, para. 27). For this reason, the Appeals Chamber ordered that subpoenas be issued to two State officials in the *Krstic* case.

NATO and NATO countries

The early workings of the ICTY demonstrate that the obligations of international organization are not a novelty. On December 24, 1995, Judge Claude Jorda issued an Order to the IFOR to arrest all individuals indicted by the International Tribunal, to inform them of charges laid against them and to transfer them at the earliest opportunity (see *All Cases*, Ordonnance Rendue le Decembre 24, 1995 par le Juge Claude Jorda).   **4–37**

In *Prosecutor v. Simić et al.*, Decision on the Motion for Judicial Assistance to be provided by SFOR and others, October 18, 2000, the Trial Chamber ordered SFOR, its responsible authority, NATO, and each of the States participating in SFOR to disclose to the Defence copies of documentation and information regarding the arrest of the accused Todorovic, who was challenging the lawfulness of his arrest. The Chamber based its decision on the provisions of Article 29 of the ICTY Statute. Application was made by NATO and the NATO countries to review this decision before the Appeals Chamber. However, the accused pleaded guilty shortly thereafter and the Appeals Chamber vacated the Trials Chamber's decision and held that the point concerning disclosure was moot. (See, *Prosecutor v. Todorovic*, Order on Request for Review Pursuant to Rule 108*bis* of Decision on Motion for Judicial Assistance to be Provided by SFOR and Others, March 27, 2001.)

The question has risen in another case before the ICTY—*Prosecutor v. Milutinovic et al.*, Case No. IT-99–37–PT, raised by co-accused Dragoljub Ojdanic—and the matter has not been concluded as it stands. A decision of the Trial Chamber on March 23, 2005 requested the applicant to reformulate its request in a precise manner, indicating the documents sought, as well as their relevancy and necessity to the case. Should it follow the Tribunal's jurisprudence, Trial Chamber I will opt for the production of documents to the Defence counsel of the accused, whether it be with or without a binding order. Detailed motions have been filed regarding this issue. Ultimately, it seems that the NATO organisation suggests future requests to be addressed to the member States as NATO itself "had no independent intelligence gathering capacity. Any such capacity is possessed by individual member States" (see Letter dated December 2, 2004 in the same case, reference number CJ(2004)0959). Member States cannot hide behind the creation of international organisations and it is shown in this case that matters often go back to States themselves. This may not be the case for organizations that have intelligence or information-gathering capacity as it was shown earlier in the case of the EUMM.

Types of orders

4–38   The Tribunal may be required to issue other orders pursuant to Rule 54 pertaining to: the safe conduct of witnesses (*Prosecutor v. Tadić*, Decision on the Defence Motion to Summon and Protect Defence Witnesses, and on the Giving of Evidence by Video-link, June 25, 1996, para. 12, and *Prosecutor v. Dokmanovic*, Order on Defence Motion for Safe Conduct, June 12, 1998, para. 26, as well as *Prosecutor v. Delalic et al.*, Order Granting Safe Conduct to Defence Witness, June 25, 1998); orders allowing video-link testimony (*Prosecutor v. Tadić*, Decision on the Defence Motion to Summon and Protect Defence Witnesses, and on the Giving of Evidence by Video-link, June 25, 1996, para. 19); anonymity of witnesses when the strict conditions for such orders are met (*Prosecutor v. Tadić*, Decision on the Prosecutor's Motion for Protective Measures for Victims and Witnesses, August 10, 1995, para. 66; it should, however, be noted that this example has never been followed and it is therefore highly questionable whether Chambers would still accept such practice); and, orders intended to avoid out-of-court communications between the parties and their witnesses during recess, so that no new evidence is brought to trial that had not been previously disclosed (*Kupreškić et al.*, Decision on Communication between the Parties and their Witnesses, September 21, 1998).

ICTY and ICTR Rule 69 allows for orders for non-disclosure of the identity of a victim or witness in exceptional circumstances when they may be in danger or at risk, until they are brought under the protection of the Tribunal. Thus, in *Prosecutor v. Tadić*, Decision on the Defence Motion to Summon and Protect Defence Witnesses, and on the Giving of Evidence by Video-link, June 25, 1996, para. 27, the Trial Chamber ordered that the identity of the witnesses be concealed pursuant to Rule 69.

Rule 71 empowers a Trial Chamber, at the request of either party or *proprio motu*, to order that a deposition be taken for use at trial (see *Prosecutor v. Aleksovski*, Joint Motion by Prosecution and Defence for Deposition Evidence, September 25, 1997 see also *Prosecutor v. Kvočka et al.*, Decision to Proceed by Way of Deposition pursuant to Rule 71, November 15, 1999, and *Prosecutor v. Kupreškić et al.*, Decision on Appeal by Dragan Papic Against Ruling to Proceed by Deposition, July 15, 1999).

(3) Summonses

4–39   ICTY Rule 54 authorises the Tribunal to issue summonses for persons to appear before the Tribunals to give testimony (see *Prosecutor v. Tadić*, Decision on the Defence Motion to Summon and Protect Defence Witnesses, and on the Giving of Evidence by Video-link, June 25, 1996, paras 5–6). The Defence sought summonses for 14 witnesses to appear before the Tribunal, and others at another location to provide testimony by video-link. The decision set out the requirements of the summons, such as the time and place for appearance and penalty for non-compliance).

In *Prosecutor v. Blaškić*, Decision of Trial Chamber I on the Appearance of Colonel Robert Stewart, March 25, 1999, the Trial

Chamber called a witness pursuant to Rule 98 of the ICTY, which permits the Chamber to *"proprio motu* summon witnesses and order their attendance" (see also, *Prosecutor v. Kupreškić et al.*, Witness Summons by the Chamber pursuant to Rule 98 of the Rules of Procedure and Evidence, September 30, 1998).

(4) Subpoenas

In the *Blaškić Subpoena Appeal*, para. 25, the Appeals Chamber held   **4–40**
that the Tribunal cannot issue "subpoenas" (orders under penalty) to States as the Tribunal does not possess any powers of enforcement. Any penalty imposed upon a State failing to comply with a subpoena issued by the Tribunal would not be penal in nature. The Appeals Chamber went on to hold that the Tribunal may not subpoena State officials, as they are merely instruments of a State and subject to functional immunity (see, para. 38).

The Appeals Chamber did, however, determine that the Tribunal is empowered to subpoena individuals acting in their private capacity (para. 47; see also *Prosecutor v. Delalic et al.*, Order on the Motion of the Defence for Hazim Delić for the issuance of Subpoenas, June 25, 1998).

The Tribunals have, *inter alia*, subpoenaed an expert witness (see   **4–41**
Prosecutor v. Kovacevic, Decision on Defence Request to Cross-Examine the Prosecutor's Expert Witness, July 3, 1998); as well as a former force Commander of the United Nations Assistance Mission in Rwanda, Major-General Romeo Dallaire (see *Prosecutor v. Akayesu*, Decision on the Defence Motion to Subpoena a Witness November 19, 1997). In the latter case, the Defence sought to subpoena other accused persons as witnesses or experts, but these motions were rejected to protect the rights of those accused enshrined in Article 20(4)(g) of the ICTR Statute (see *Prosecutor v. Akayesu*, Decision on the Defence Motion for Summons and Protection of Witnesses Called by the Defence, February 23, 1998 and *Prosecutor v. Akayesu*, Decision on the Defence Motion for the Appearance of an Accused as an Expert Witness, March 9, 1998).

The ICTY has found that it has no authority to issue a subpoena to the Organisation for Security and Cooperation in Europe, because it is an international organisation (see *Prosecutor v. Kovacevic*, Decision Refusing Defence Motion for Subpoena, June 23, 1998).

(5) Contempt Proceedings

The Tribunal needs to ensure the good conduct of proceedings and   **4–42**
the cooperation of all parties in order to accomplish its work. For this reason, a Trial Chamber, pursuant to Rule 77, may hold in contempt those who knowingly and wilfully interfere with its administration of justice.

A number of contempt proceedings have taken place before the International Tribunal, including cases of witness refusal to answer questions and intimidating witnesses.

In a recent case, a Trial Chamber re-affirmed that the Tribunal has the inherent power to punish a conduct which tends to obstruct, prejudice or abuse its administration of justice, despite the fact that the offence of contempt is not in the Statute but rather in the Rules of Procedure and Evidece (*Prosecutor v. Limaj*, Judgment in the Case of Beqa Beqaj, May 5, 2005). In this case, it was found that an individual, relative of one of the accused in the *Limaj* case, had interfered with the administration of justice by inciting a witness to withdraw his statement in the case. The Chamber found Mr Beqaj guilty under one count and sentenced him to four months of imprisonment.

The Milošević case has given rise to contempt proceedings, the latest case being the fourth. Following the completion of the examination in chief of witness Kosta Bulatović by the accused Slobodan Milošević, the latter became ill and was not allowed by the medical unit to step back in the courtroom until recovery. The next day, as cross-examination was to begin, Mr Bulatović refused to answer the questions of the Prosecution in the absence of the witness, despite being ordered to do so by the Trial Chamber. The Tribunal found Mr Bulatovic guilty of contempt as he had knowingly refused to answer the questions in cross-examination. The Trial Chamber was of the opinion that the test of "knowingly and wilfully" interfering with the Tribunal's administration of justice by "contumaciously" refusing to answer questions was satisfied when the witness deliberately refused to comply with an order of the Trial Chamber to answer questions and persisted in that refusal when fully advised of the position and given a further opportunity to respond (*Prosecutor v. Slobodan Milošević*, Case No. IT-02-54-R77-4, Decision on Contempt of the Tribunal, May 13, 2005, para.16). This interpretation is more restrictive than the one previously adopted by the Trial Chamber in the matter of witness K12 which refused to testify, fearing that his identity would be leaked by the accused. In that case, the Trial Chamber had read "contumacious" in the sense of "perverse" (see Transcript of Hearing, November 18, 2002, T. 12975 in *Prosecutor v. Slobodan Milošević*). Judge Kwon dissented in the matter of witness K12 (see Trial Chamber Finding in the Matter of Witness K12, November 21, 2002) and believed that all that is required to be established is that a witness before a Chamber must refuse to answer a question despite the request made by the Chamber to that effect. It seems that this is the approach adopted in the Bulatovic contempt procedure.

G. REFERRAL OF AN INDICTMENT TO ANOTHER COURT

General rule

4-43   Rule 11*bis* provides that after an indictment has been confirmed and prior to the commencement of trial, the Tribunal may determine whether the case should be referred to the authorities of a State. The rule allows to transfer cases to a State in whose territory the crime was committed or in which the accused was arrested; the State must also have jurisdiction and be willing and adequately prepared to accept such a case.

The initiative for such referrals belongs to the Trial Chamber and to the Prosecution; the accused may not make such request, although he will have the opportunity to be heard in such proceedings. The Chamber may order such referral *proprio motu*. Before doing so, the Chamber must be satisfied that the accused will receive a fair trial and that the death penalty will not be imposed, as it is not a penalty provided for by the Statute. However, it must be noted that the disposition related to death penalty only appears in the Rules of Procedure and Evidence of the ICTY, not in the Rules of the ICTR. Nevertheless, the riding principle remains that in the Statute, the only penalty provided for are imprisonment and return of any property and proceeds acquired by criminal conduct (Article 23). The ICTY has been relatively active in relation to the referral procedure. One accused, Radovan Stankovic, has been referred to the War Crimes Chamber of the Bosnia and Herzegovina State Court in Sarajevo in September 2005. Two other accused should shortly be handed over to Croatia following the same procedure. As far as the ICTR is concerned, in June 2004 the defendants at the ICTR went on strike after negotiations occurred between the President of the ICTR and Rwandan delegates. The defendants interrupted their strike only after they received a letter from the President of the ICTR guaranteeing them that no decisions had been made yet on the matter but if cases were to be referred to Rwanda, such would only be done with guarantees that fair trial principles would be respected.

The referral bench must consider the gravity of the crimes charged and the level of responsibility of the accused, before making the final determination.

4–44 Adopted on November 12, 1997, Rule 11*bis* has been used only very recently, with the the opening of the War Crimes Chamber of the State Court of Bosnia and Herzegovina in Sarajevo. The rule was revised on September 30, 2002 in order to give effect to the broad strategy endorsed by the Security Council for the completion of all Tribunal trial activities at first instance by 2008 (see S/PRST/2002/21; S/RES/1329 (2000). The rule was created with the idea of transferring mid- to low-level cases to national courts, in order to alleviate the docket of the International tribunals. The recent address of the President of the Tribunal clearly refers to 11*bis* as a factor affecting the work load of the ICTY and the achievement of the completion strategy (see TM /MOW/976e, Statement by Judge Theodor Meron, President, International Criminal Tribunal for the Former Yugoslavia, to the Security Council June 13, 2005; also see Assessments and report of Judge Theodor Meron, President of the International Criminal Tribunal for the Former Yugoslavia, provided to the Security Council pursuant to paragraph 6 of Security Council resolution 1534 (2004), S/2005/343, paras 12–16, hereinafter "*President's Assessments 2005*").

4–45 The Office of the Prosecutor has filed ten rule 11*bis* motions as of May 25, 2005; these were all filed between September 2, 2004 and February 8, 2005 (see *President's Assessments 2005*, Enclosure V). On May 17, 2005, the ICTY issued its first decision on a Prosecutor's motion to refer a case to the domestic authorities of a State in the case of *Prosecutor v. Stankovic* (Case No. IT-96–23/2-PT). Considering the level of responsibility of the accused and the gravity of the crimes alleged in the indictment, this referral to the national authorities of Bosnia and Herzegovina was deemed appropriate. The motion for referral was granted after the Referral bench considered the question of the compatibility of the laws of Bosnia and Herzegovina with the Tribunal's Statute, reviewed the laws applicable to the events in 1992 in Bosnia and Herzegovina, reviewed the prospects for the accused to receive a fair trial before the War Crimes Chamber of the State Court of Bosnia and Herzegovina, satisfied itself that adequate measures were in place for the protection of witnesses and satisfied itself that the death penalty would not be imposed. It must be noted that the Prosecutor must monitor and report the proceedings of this case before the State Court of Bosnia and Herzegovina (see *Prosecutor v. Stanković*, Case No. IT-96–23/2-PT, Decision on Referral of Case Under Rule 11*Bis*, May 17, 2005).

II. POWERS OF COOPERATION UNDER THE ICC STATUTE

A. Cooperative Nature of ICC–State Relations

(1) Introduction

4–46   As with the ICTY and the ICTR, the ICC will be dependent on States and their enforcement agents for all forms of cooperation necessary for the investigation and prosecution of serious violations of international humanitarian law. Justice Louise Arbour, the former Prosecutor of the International Tribunals, endorsed the fact that "a treaty-based International Criminal Court will depend, in practical terms, on effective State cooperation for its proper functioning, just as much as the ad hoc Tribunals for the former Yugoslavia and Rwanda do" (unpublished Statement of Justice Louise Arbour to the Preparatory Committee on the Establishment of an International Criminal Court, December 8, 1997, p. 3). It is probably for this reason that the drafters of the ICC Statute dedicated an entire chapter comprised of 17 articles to international cooperation and judicial assistance. Having witnessed the difficulties of the ad hoc tribunals in, *inter alia*, getting access to evidence and arresting suspects, it was necessary to prepare the ICC for various situations related to cooperation and endowing the Court with the necessary tools to respond to these situations.

(2) Provisions of ICC Statute

Statute of the International Criminal Court, Art. 86

General obligation to cooperate
4–47   86. States Parties shall, in accordance with the provisions of this Statute, cooperate with the Court in its investigation and prosecution of crimes within the jurisdiction of the Court.

4–48   An important distinction between the Tribunals and the ICC is that by virtue of the formers' establishment as an enforcement measure of the Security Council under Chapter VII of the UN Charter, all member

States of the UN are bound to implement its requests and orders, whereas under the ICC Statute, only those States that ratify the treaty, thereby becoming States parties to the treaty, will be obliged to cooperate. The possibility of other States that have not ratified the treaty being obliged to cooperate with the ICC exists when the Security Council acting under Chapter VII refers a case to the ICC. (See, Article 25 of the Charter regarding the obligation of member States to carry out the decisions of the Security Council.) The power of referral is recognised in Article 13(b) of the ICC Statute.

Even in the absence of a Security Council referral, a non-party State may accept an ad hoc obligation to cooperate with the ICC in terms of Article 87(5)(a) of the Statute, which provides as follows:

> "The Court may invite any State not party to this Statute to provide assistance under this Part on the basis of an ad hoc arrangement, an agreement with such State or any other appropriate basis."

Article 87(1) identifies the channels through which requests for assistance from the ICC must be made to States. They may be transmitted through the diplomatic channel or other appropriate channels designated by a State upon ratification as well as through INTERPOL.

For the Prosecution's powers with respect to investigations see Article 53 and 54 of the ICC Statute, cited in Chapter 6.

Availability of procedures under national law

Statute of the International Criminal Court, Article 88

88. States Parties shall ensure that there are procedures available under their national law for all of the forms of cooperation which are specified under this Part.   **4–49**

Arrest and surrender

Statute of the International Criminal Court, Arts 89, 90

Surrender of persons to the Court

89.—1. The Court may transmit a request for the arrest and surrender of a person, together with the material supporting the request outlined in article 91, to any State on the territory of which that person may be found and shall request the cooperation of that State in the arrest and surrender of such a person. States Parties shall, in accordance with the provisions of this Part and the procedure under their national law, comply with requests for arrest and surrender.   **4–50**

Competing requests

90.—1. A State Party which receives a request from the Court for the surrender of a person under article 89 shall, if it also receives a request from any other State for the extradition of the same person for the same conduct   **4–51**

which forms the basis of the crime for which the Court seeks the person's surrender, notify the Court and the requesting State of that fact.

2. Where the requesting State is a State Party, the requested State shall give priority to the request from the Court if:

(a) The Court has, pursuant to article 18 or 19, made a determination that the case in respect of which surrender is sought is admissible and that determination takes into account the investigation or prosecution conducted by the requesting State in respect of its request for extradition; or

(b) The Court makes the determination described in subparagraph (a) pursuant to the requested State's notification under paragraph 1.

3. Where a determination under paragraph 2 (a) has not been made, the requested State may, at its discretion, pending the determination of the Court under paragraph 2 (b), proceed to deal with the request for extradition from the requesting State but shall not extradite the person until the Court has determined that the case is inadmissible. The Court's determination shall be made on an expedited basis.

4. If the requesting State is a State not Party to this Statute the requested State, if it is not under an international obligation to extradite the person to the requesting State, shall give priority to the request for surrender from the Court, if the Court has determined that the case is admissible.

5. Where a case under paragraph 4 has not been determined to be admissible by the Court, the requested State may, at its discretion, proceed to deal with the request for extradition from the requesting State.

6. In cases where paragraph 4 applies except that the requested State is under an existing international obligation to extradite the person to the requesting State not Party to this Statute, the requested State shall determine whether to surrender the person to the Court or extradite the person to the requesting State. In making its decision, the requested State shall consider all the relevant factors, including but not limited to:

(a) The respective dates of the requests;

(b) The interests of the requesting State including, where relevant, whether the crime was committed in its territory and the nationality of the victims and of the person sought; and

(c) The possibility of subsequent surrender between the Court and the requesting State.

4–52   7. Where a State Party which receives a request from the Court for the surrender of a person also receives a request from any State for the extradition of the same person for conduct other than that which constitutes the crime for which the Court seeks the person's surrender:

(a) The requested State shall, if it is not under an existing international obligation to extradite the person to the requesting State, give priority to the request from the Court;

(b) The requested State shall, if it is under an existing international obligation to extradite the person to the requesting State, determine whether to surrender the person to the Court or to extradite the person to the requesting State. In making its decision, the requested State shall consider all the relevant factors, including but not limited to those set out in paragraph 6, but shall give special consideration to the relative nature and gravity of the conduct in question.

8. Where pursuant to a notification under this article, the Court has determined a case to be inadmissible, and subsequently extradition to the requesting State is refused, the requested State shall notify the Court of this decision.

4–53   Although the terminology of Article 89(1) is mandatory ("shall [. . .] comply with requests for arrest and surrender"), a number of other Articles leave States with a discretion as to whether or not to comply with a request for arrest and surrender by the ICC, effectively allowing for refusals of requests.

For example, under Article 90(6) on competing requests, a State party may receive a request for surrender from the ICC and an extradition request from another State not party to the treaty to which it owes an international extradition obligation. In these circumstances, and when the case has been ruled admissible, the Statute permits the requested State to determine whether to surrender the person to the ICC or extradite the person to the other requesting State. Article 90(6) sets out a number of factors for consideration by the requested State in making the determination, but the decision remains discretionary. The ICC may not order the requested State to surrender the accused to the ICC, instead of extraditing to the non-party State. See also, Article 90(7) and Article 98 on cooperation with respect to waiver of immunity and consent to surrender.

4–54   Despite the reluctance of States that refuse to extradite their nationals in inter-State relations, the parties at Rome eliminated this ground of refusal from the Statute. Accordingly States will not be permitted to refuse a surrender request which involves one of their nationals. In this regard, Article 102 of the ICC Statute provides as follows:

Use of terms

4–55   **102.** For the purposes of this Statute:
    (a) "surrender" means the delivering up of a person by a State to the Court, pursuant to this Statute.
    (b) "extradition" means the delivering up of a person by one State to another as provided by treaty, convention or national legislation.

By confirming the distinction between surrender to the ICC and extradition between two sovereign States, many of the concerns of States that underpin the non-extradition of nationals were eliminated. This distinction had been developed in doctrine as vertical and horizontal cooperation. Requests of assistance during the early years of the ad hoc tribunals shows a confusion for State administrations which often fell back on the procedure applied to extradition in their dealing with the international tribunals. The *Blaškić Subpoena Appeal* made it clear that this wasn't the case and that States, when dealing with international criminal jurisdiction, had to put aside inter-State practice in order to fully comply with their international obligations towards the international community as a whole.

The hearing of witnesses

4–56   Consistent with the cooperative nature of Part 9 of the Statute, the Statute does not oblige States to secure the presence of witnesses before the ICC. Instead, Article 93 provides:

Other forms of cooperation

4–57   **93.**—1. States Parties shall, in accordance with the provisions of this Part and under procedures of national law, comply with requests by the Court to provide the following assistance in relation to investigations or prosecutions:

. . .

    (e) Facilitating the voluntary appearance of persons as witnesses or experts before the Court;

    (f) The temporary transfer of persons as provided in paragraph 7;

. . .

5. Before denying a request for assistance under paragraph 1 (l), the requested State shall consider whether the assistance can be provided subject to specified conditions, or whether the assistance can be provided at a later date or in an alternative manner, provided that if the Court or the Prosecutor accepts the assistance subject to conditions, the Court or the Prosecutor shall abide by them.

6. If a request for assistance is denied, the requested State Party shall promptly inform the Court or the Prosecutor of the reasons for such denial.

7.   (a) The Court may request the temporary transfer of a person in custody for purposes of identification or for obtaining testimony or other assistance. The person may be transferred if the following conditions are fulfilled:

      (i) The person freely gives his or her informed consent to the transfer; and

      (ii) The requested State agrees to the transfer, subject to such conditions as that State and the Court may agree.

  (b) The person being transferred shall remain in custody. When the purposes of the transfer have been fulfilled, the Court shall return the person without delay to the requested State.

4–58   Article 93(1)(e) requires States parties to comply with the ICC's requests with regard to facilitating the witness or expert volunteers to appear before the ICC.

Similarly, Article 93(1)(f) read with Article 93(7) allows persons in custody to be transferred to the ICC for the purposes of identification or giving testimony only when they consent to such a transfer. Even when the person in custody agrees to such a transfer, in the absence of consent from the custodial State, the ICC will not be able to obtain their transfer for the purposes laid down in the Article. The voluntary nature of this cooperation is underscored by the fact that a witnesses' or expert's failure to respond to a summons is not an offence against the Administration of Justice in Article 70 of the Statute.

The ICC may thus have to resort to video-link testimony as permitted under Article 69(2) or to depositions.

4–59   Interestingly, Article 93(5) and (6) provide a mechanism where a State considers denying a request for assistance. The striking measures adopted by the Court to avoid judge-made law once again resurface in this provision which demands from States to consider whether assistance can be provided subject to specific conditions or considering alternative manners. Consequently, States will have to demonstrate much goodwill and refrain from steadily denying requests of assistance, which could cost repetitive dispute settlement proceedings.

Disclosure of national security information

4–60   The case for an obligation to disclose national security information is succinctly put by the Appeals Chamber in the *Blaškić Subpoena Appeal*, para. 65:

"To admit that a State holding such documents may unilaterally assert national security claims and refuse to surrender those documents could lead to the stultification of international criminal proceedings: those documents might prove crucial for deciding whether the accused is innocent or guilty. The very *raison d'etre* of the International Tribunal would then be undermined".

Unlike the ICTY and ICTR Statutes, the ICC Statute does not oblige States to disclose documents that implicate their national security concerns when the provisions in Article 72 of the ICC Statute have been exhausted. Article 93(4) of the ICC Statute provides:

"In accordance with article 72, a State Party may deny a request for assistance, in whole or in part, only if the request concerns the production of any documents or disclosure of evidence which relates to its national security."

Statute of the International Criminal Court, Art. 72

Protection of national security information

72.—1. This article applies in any case where the disclosure of the information or documents of a State would, in the opinion of that State, prejudice its national security interests. Such cases include those falling within the scope of article 56, paragraphs 2 and 3, article 61, paragraph 3, article 64, paragraph 3, article 67, paragraph 2, article 68, paragraph 6, article 87, paragraph 6 and article 93, as well as cases arising at any other stage of the proceedings where such disclosure may be at issue.   **4–61**

2. This article shall also apply when a person who has been requested to give information or evidence has refused to do so or has referred the matter to the State on the ground that disclosure would prejudice the national security interests of a State and the State concerned confirms that it is of the opinion that disclosure would prejudice its national security interests.

3. Nothing in this article shall prejudice the requirements of confidentiality applicable under article 54, paragraph 3(e) and (f), or the application of article 73.

4. If a State learns that information or documents of the State are being, or are likely to be, disclosed at any stage of the proceedings, and it is of the opinion that disclosure would prejudice its national security interests, that State shall have the right to intervene in order to obtain resolution of the issue in accordance with this article.

5. If, in the opinion of a State, disclosure of information would prejudice its national security interests, all reasonable steps will be taken by the State, acting in conjunction with the Prosecutor, the defence or the Pre-Trial Chamber or Trial Chamber, as the case may be, to seek to resolve the matter by co-operative means. Such steps may include: **4–62**

(a) Modification or clarification of the request;

(b) A determination by the Court regarding the relevance of the information or evidence sought, or a determination as to whether the evidence, though relevant, could be or has been obtained from a source other than the requested State;

(c) Obtaining the information or evidence from a different source or in a different form; or

(d) Agreement on conditions under which the assistance could be provided including, among other things, providing summaries or redactions, limitations on disclosure, use of in camera or ex parte proceedings, or other protective measures permissible under the Statute and the Rules of Procedure and Evidence.

6. Once all reasonable steps have been taken to resolve the matter through co-operative means, and if the State considers that there are no means or conditions under which the information or documents could be provided or disclosed without prejudice to its national security interests, it shall so notify the Prosecutor or the Court of the specific reasons for its decision, unless a specific description of the reasons would itself necessarily result in such prejudice to the State's national security interests.

4–63   7. Thereafter, if the Court determines that the evidence is relevant and necessary for the establishment of the guilt or innocence of the accused, the Court may undertake the following actions:

(a) Where disclosure of the information or document is sought pursuant to a request for cooperation under Part 9 or the circumstances described in paragraph 2, and the State has invoked the ground for refusal referred to in article 93, paragraph 4:

   (i) The Court may, before making any conclusion referred to in subparagraph 7 (a) (ii), request further consultations for the purpose of considering the State's representations, which may include, as appropriate, hearings in camera and ex parte;

   (ii) If the Court concludes that, by invoking the ground for refusal under article 93, paragraph 4, in the circumstances of the case, the requested State is not acting in accordance with its obligations under this Statute, the Court may refer the matter in accordance with article 87, paragraph 7, specifying the reasons for its conclusion; and

   (iii) The Court may make such inference in the trial of the accused as to the existence or non-existence of a fact, as may be appropriate in the circumstances; or

(b) In all other circumstances:

   (i) Order disclosure; or

   (ii) To the extent it does not order disclosure, make such inference in the trial of the accused as to the existence or non-existence of a fact, as may be appropriate in the circumstances.

4–64   Article 72 establishes a detailed procedure to be followed by States asserting that the disclosure of information would prejudice their national security interests, incorporating many of the procedural suggestions for dealing with sensitive national security information suggested by the *Blaškić* Appeals Chamber.

One of the more contentious debates on national security information in the Rome negotiations on the ICC Statute concerned who would arbitrate a State's national security claims. Those States seeking a strong cooperation regime based on compliance favoured the Court as the final arbiter. Other States argued that consideration of the matter by the Court could in itself compromise a State's national security interests.

The resulting provision allows the State concerned to determine its own national security concerns but obliges it to undertake all reasonable steps to seek to resolve the matter by co-operative means. These means are set out in Article 72(5). Thus, the Court might modify or clarify a request, obtain the information from a different source or agree on the conditions under which the assistance might be provided. Such conditions may include redactions and use of *in camera* or *ex parte* proceedings.

4–65   Article 72(7) governs the situation when a State and the Prosecutor or Defence are unable to come to an acceptable agreement in relation to the information sought. The procedure followed depends on who has control of the sensitive information. When the information is controlled by the State from whom the Prosecutor or Defence has sought cooperation, the ICC may not order disclosure. It may only, after further consultations, and after coming to the conclusion that the State's failure to disclose the disputed evidence is not a legitimate invocation of that State's national security concerns, refer the matter to the Assembly of States Parties or the Security Council depending upon the origin of the referral (see Article 72(7)(a)(ii)). The Assembly of States Parties is established pursuant to Article 112, to perform a variety of functions, including dealing with any question of non-cooperation under Articles 87(5) or 87(7). When the Article 72 procedure fails to obtain the desired result, the Court may draw an inference as to the existence or otherwise of a fact at the trial of the accused (see Article 72(7)(a)(iii)).

When the sensitive national security information is not in the control of the State from whom cooperation has been sought, the ICC may order its disclosure when it is relevant and necessary for the establishment of an accused's guilt or innocence (see Article 72(7)(b)). When it does not order disclosure, it may make the same inference set out in Article 72(7)(a)(ii)).

B. ICC RULES OF PROCEDURE AND EVIDENCE

Rules of Procedure and Evidence, rr. 176, 177, 184, 192, 195

Organs of the Court responsible for the transmission and receipt of any communications relating to international cooperation and judicial assistance

4–66

176.—1. Upon and subsequent to the establishment of the Court, the Registrar shall obtain from the Secretary-General of the United Nations any communication made by States pursuant to article 87, paragraphs 1(a) and 2.

2. The Registrar shall transmit the requests for cooperation made by the Chambers and shall receive the responses, information and documents from requested States. The Office of the Prosecutor shall transmit the requests for cooperation made by the Prosecutor and shall receive the responses, information and documents from requested States.

3. The Registrar shall be the recipient of any communication from States concerning subsequent changes in the designation of the national channels charged with receiving requests for cooperation, as well as of any change in the language in which requests for cooperation should be made, and shall, upon request, make such information available to States Parties as may be appropriate.

4. The provisions of sub-rule 2 are applicable *mutatis mutandis* where the Court requests information, documents or other forms of cooperation and assistance from an intergovernmental organization.

5. The Registrar shall transmit any communications referred to in sub-rules 1 and 3 and rule 177, sub-rule 2, as appropriate, to the Presidency or the Office of the Prosecutor, or both.

Channels of communication

4–67

177.—1. Communications concerning the national authority charged with receiving requests for cooperation made upon ratification, acceptance, approval or accession shall provide all relevant information about such authorities.

2. When an intergovernmental organization is asked to assist the Court under article 87, paragraph 6, the Registrar shall, when necessary, ascertain its designated channel of communication and obtain all relevant information relating thereto.

Arrangements for surrender

4–68   184.—1. The requested State shall immediately inform the Registrar when the person sought by the Court is available for surrender.

2. The person shall be surrendered to the Court by the date and in the manner agreed upon between the authorities of the requested State and the Registrar.

3. If circumstances prevent the surrender of the person by the date agreed, the authorities of the requested State and the Registrar shall agree upon a new date and manner by which the person shall be surrendered.

4. The Registrar shall maintain contact with the authorities of the host State in relation to the arrangements for the surrender of the person to the Court.

Transfer of a person in custody

4–69   192.—1. Transfer of a person in custody to the Court in accordance with article 93, paragraph 7, shall be arranged by the national authorities concerned in liaison with the Registrar and the authorities of the host State.

2. The Registrar shall ensure the proper conduct of the transfer, including the supervision of the person while in the custody of the Court.

3. The person in custody before the Court shall have the right to raise matters concerning the conditions of his or her detention with the relevant Chamber.

4. In accordance with article 93, paragraph 7(b), when the purposes of the transfer have been fulfilled, the Registrar shall arrange for the return of the person in custody to the requested State.

Provision of information

4–70   195.—1. When a requested State notifies the Court that a request for surrender or assistance raises a problem of execution in respect of article 98, the requested State shall provide any information relevant to assist the Court in the application of article 98. Any concerned third State or sending State may provide additional information to assist the Court.

2. The Court may not proceed with a request for the surrender of a person without the consent of a sending State if, under article 98, paragraph 2, such a request would be inconsistent with obligations under an international agreement pursuant to which the consent of a sending State is required prior to the surrender of a person of that State to the Court.

C. REGULATIONS OF THE ICC

Regulations 107, 108, 109, 110, 111, 112

Arrangements and agreements on cooperation

4–71   107.—1. All agreements with any State not party to the Statute or any intergovernmental organization, setting out a general framework for cooperation on matters within the competency of more than one organ of the Court, shall be negotiated under the authority of the President who shall seek recommendations from the Advisory Committee on Legal Texts. Such agreements shall be concluded by the President on behalf of the Court. The existence of an agreement concluded in accordance with this sub-regulation does not preclude the Prosecutor from entering into those agreements referred to in article 54, paragraph 3 (d).

2. Each organ of the Court shall inform the Presidency of any arrangement or agreement on cooperation, not being one setting out a general framework for cooperation as referred to in sub-regulation 1, that the organ intends to negotiate, unless such information is inappropriate for reasons of confidentiality. Subject to article 54, paragraph 3 (d), and to reasons of confidentiality, such arrangements and agreements shall be concluded by the President or by delegation by the relevant organ under whose authority the arrangement or agreement has been negotiated.

Ruling regarding the legality of a request for cooperation

108.—1. In case of a dispute regarding the legality of a request for cooperation under article 93, a requested State may apply for a ruling from the competent Chamber.   **4–72**

2. A ruling under sub-regulation 1 may be sought only after a declaration has been made by the requesting body that consultations have been exhausted and within 15 days following such declaration. In case of requests under article 99, paragraph 4, and should no further consultations be possible, the requested State may seek a ruling within 15 days from the day on which the requested State is informed of or became aware of the direct execution.

3. An application under sub-regulation 1 shall not of itself have suspensive effect, unless the Chamber so orders.

4. The Chamber may hear from participants to the proceedings on the matter.

5. If the Chamber rejects the application referred to in sub-regulation 1, the Chamber may grant the requested State additional time within which it shall execute the request or the Chamber shall lift any suspension of direct execution.

Failure to comply with a request for cooperation

109.—1. An application for a finding under article 87, paragraph 7, may be made to the competent Chamber by the requesting body either where no application has been made under regulation 108, following the lapse of the time limit referred to in sub-regulation 2 of that provision, or where an application has been made, following a ruling by the Chamber under sub-regulation 5 of that provision and, if applicable, following the lapse of the time limit referred to therein.   **4–73**

2. When a Chamber ha s made a request for cooperation, proceedings under article 87, paragraph 7, may be initiated by that Chamber. Sub-regulation 1 shall apply *mutatis mutandis.*

3. Before making a finding in accordance with article 87, paragraph 7, the Chamber shall hear from the requested State.

4. Where a finding under article 87, paragraph 7, has been made, the President shall refer the matter to the Assembly or the Security Council in accordance with that provision and, as regards the Security Council, in accordance with the agreement to be concluded under article 2.

Cooperation for the purposes of notification by way of personal service

110.—For the purposes of notification by way of personal service as described in regulation 31, sub-regulation 4, the requesting body shall, where necessary, make a request for cooperation to the relevant State under articles 93, paragraph 1 (d), and 99, paragraph 1.   **4–74**

Information about admissibility ruling

4–75   **111.**—When transmitting a request for the arrest and surrender of a person in accordance with article 89, paragraph 1, the Registrar shall enclose a copy of any relevant admissibility ruling of the Court.

Views of the surrendering State in or after admissibility proceedings

4–76   **112.**—At any time before making a decision on a challenge to admissibility based on the grounds set out in article 17, paragraph 1 (a), the Chamber shall hear from the State which originally surrendered the person as to whether that State objects to the transfer of the person to the State which brought the challenge to admissibility.

4–77   The newly adopted Regulations of the Court were approved by the Judges of the Court on 26 May 2005 pursuant to Article 52 of the Statute. The Statute does not precisde nor define the role such regulations will play, yet a quick glance allows one to define them as practice directives. They are made of nine chapters, including Chapter 7 related to Cooperation and Enforcement.

Content of the Regulations related to Cooperation

4–78   Regulation 107 concerns agreements the Court establishes with States not party to the Statute or international organisations. The ad hoc tribunals experience in this regard include the agreement both the ICTY and ICTR had with Switzerland which at the time was not a member of the United Nations. Switzerland had then adopted a detailed Federal Order on December 21, 1995 covering several issues including voluntary transmission of information and evidence, deferral by Swiss courts, transfer of persons being prosecuted, procedural action and other requests of international tribunals and enforcement of custodial sentences pronounced by the international tribunals. It is interesting to note that such an agreement would not preclude the Prosecution to enter into agreements necessary to facilitate the cooperation of a State, intergovernmental organisation or person pursuant to Article 54(3)(d) of the Statute.

4–79   Regulation 108 concerns the "other forms of cooperation" envisaged by Article 93 of the Rome Statute. Indeed, where Articles 86 and 87 are general provisions and where Article 88 to 92 concern the arrest and surrender of a suspect, Article 93 imposes on State Parties to comply with requests of the Court to provide assistance on a myriad of topics including identification and whereabouts of persons or the location of items; taking of evidence, including testimony under oath, and the production of evidence; questioning of any person being investigated or prosecuted; service of documents, including judicial documents; facilitating the voluntary appearance of persons as witnesses or experts before the Court; examination of places or sites, including the exhumation and examination of grave sites; execution of searches and seizures; etc. Evidently, variations from one State to another with respect to judicial procedure will raise numerous questions. For this reason, paragraph 3 of Article 93 demands from States to consult with the Court when a particular measure is prohibited in a State on the basis of an existing fundamental legal principle of general application.

Having this possibility of conflicting laws in mind, Regulation 108 has been developed to allow States to apply for a ruling from the Court. Such a ruling may be saught if consultations have been exhausted.

Regulation 109 applies for Article 87(7) of the Statute relating to the **4–80** power of the Court to make a finding of non-compliance of a State. The proceedings may be inititated by the competent Chamber. It is also provided that the Chamber must hear the requested State before making a finding. Paragraph 3 of Regulation 109 is equivalent to Rule 7*bis* of the ICTY and ICTR Rules of Procedure and Evidence as it allows the President of the Court to refer the matter, once a finding has been made, to the Assembly or to the Security Council if the Security Council referred the case to the Court.

Regulation 110 must be read in conjunction with Regulation 31 and **4–81** concerns the procedure of notification. Regulation 31 sets a procedure by which each party to a case must be notified of any document registered by the Registry (unless the submitting party requests otherwise). Regulation 110 provides that for the purposes of notification by way of personal service as described in regulation 31, sub-regulation 4, the requesting body shall, where necessary, make a request for cooperation to the relevant State under Articles 93, paragraph 1 (d) and 99, paragraph 1.

D. UK INTERNATIONAL CRIMINAL LAW ACT

Production or disclosure prejudicial to national security

39.—(1) Nothing in any of the provisions of this Part, or any corresponding **4–82** provision of an Act of the Scottish Parliament, requires or authorises the production of documents, or the disclosure of information, which would be prejudicial to the security of the United Kingdom.

(2) For the purposes of any such provision a certificate signed by or on behalf of the Secretary of State to the effect that it would be prejudicial to the security of the United Kingdom for specified documents to be produced, or for specified information to be disclosed, is conclusive evidence of that fact.

The United Kindgom signed the Rome Statute on November 30, **4–83** 1998 and adopted the implementing law in 2001, depositing its instrument of ratification on October 4, 2001. It is thus one of 99 members of the Assembly of State Parties of the International Criminal Court.

The *International Criminal Law Act* (2001, Chapter 17) contains detailed dispositions on the procedure to be applied when cooperating with the ICC. Part 2, 3 and 4 of the Law cover all issues related to the arrest and delivery of persons, the various forms of assistance and the enforcement of sentences.

The content of Article 39 of the Law is interesting as it deals with national security concerns, a ground of refusal which should be avoided by the reading of Article 72 of the Rome Statute. Indeed, the mechanism in place at the ICC should allow the resolution of possible national security concerns, via procedures such as *in camera* or *ex parte* proceedings.

It remains to be seen how these dispositions will come into play once requests for assistance are issued by the ICC. The United Kingdom has generally cooperated with the ad hoc tribunals and cooperation issues should not be problematic.

III. UN SPECIAL COURTS

A. STATUTORY PROVISIONS OF EAST TIMOR AND SIERRA LEONE

(1) East Timor

UNTAET Regulation No. 2000/11, March 6, 2000, s.10 (as amended by reg. 2001/25)

Legal Cooperation

4–84   **10.**—10.1 Any District Court in East Timor shall cooperate with the request of another District Court to
  (a) interrogate witnesses who are registered or permanently accommodated in the area of the requested court's jurisdiction;
  (b) carry out at-the-scene examinations or re-enactment of crimes in the area of the requested court's jurisdiction;
  (c) serve summonses of the requesting court on witnesses in the requested court's jurisdiction;
  (d) serve decisions of the requesting court on individuals in the requested court's jurisdiction;
  (e) execute the decisions of the requesting court if the subject of dispute is located in the requested court's jurisdiction;
  (f) access files of the requested court for information purposes or decision.

10.2 The request may not be rejected except in the case of lack of jurisdiction of the requested court.

Transitional Rules of Criminal Procedure, UNTAET/REG/2000/30; September 25, 2000, amended by 2001/25; September 14, 2001

Powers of the Investigating Judge

4–85   9.1 In accordance with Section 13 of UNTAET Regulation No. 2000/11, there shall be at least one Investigating Judge at every District Court in East Timor empowered to ensure that the rights of every person subject to a criminal investigation and the rights of any alleged victims of the suspected crime under investigation are respected.

9.2 As provided by law or UNTAET regulations, the Investigating Judge shall issue warrants or other orders lawfully requested by the public prosecutor whenever, in the course of a criminal investigation, there are reasonable grounds to do so as provided in the present regulation.

9.3 Except as otherwise provided in the present regulation, a warrant or order from an Investigating Judge shall be obtained for the following measures:
  (a) arrest of a suspect;
  (b) detention or continued detention of a suspect;
  (c) exhumation;
  (d) forensic examination;
  (e) search of locations and buildings;

(f) seizure of goods or items, including seizure or opening of mail;

(g) intrusive body search;

(h) physical examination, including the taking and examination of blood, DNA, samples, and other bodily specimens;

(i) interception of telecommunication and electronic data transfer;

(j) other warrants involving measures of a coercive character in accordance with the applicable law.

9.4 All warrants shall be issued in duplicate. The original shall be kept by the prosecutor and added to the file of the case; a copy will be furnished to the suspect or person concerned, except when to do so would endanger the results of the investigations.

9.5 In order to safeguard the rights of a suspect, as listed in Section 6 of the present regulation, the Investigating Judge shall prohibit any actions of the investigating authorities that are in violation of the rights of the suspect.

9.6 The Investigating Judge shall not interfere with the responsibilities of the public prosecutor in directing the criminal investigations, as defined in Section 7 of the present regulation.

9.7 Notwithstanding any other provision of law, any warrant or measure ordered by the Investigating Judge at the seat of the public prosecutor assigned to the case is valid and may be executed anywhere in East Timor without any further formal request to other judicial authorities.

9.8 A warrant or order issued by the Investigating Judge pursuant to Section 9.2 of the present regulation shall identify by name or official capacity the persons who are authorized to execute the warrant or order. Unless otherwise specified in the warrant or order, the following provisions shal l apply:

(a) A warrant or order for arrest of a suspect may be executed by any law enforcementofficer anywhere in East Timor;

(b) A warrant or order for detention or continued detention of a suspect may be executed by the warden of any official detention facility in East Timor;

(c) A warrant for exhumation may be executed under the supervision and control of any official qualified as provided in Section 18.5 of the present regulation;

(d) A warrant or order for forensic examination may be executed by any official qualified as provided in Section 18.5 of the present regulation;

(e) A warrant or order for search of locations and buildings may be executed by any law enforcement officer in East Timor who is duly authorized by UNTAET regulations;

(f) A warrant or order for seizure of goods or items may be executed by any law enforcement officer in East Timor who is duly authorized by UNTAET regulations;

(g) A warrant or order for an intrusive body search may be executed by any person with appropriate medical qualifications as provided in Section 16.3 of the present regulation;

(h) A warrant or order for physical examination, including the taking and examination of blood, DNA samples, and other bodily specimens may be executed by any person as provided in Section 16.5 of the present regulation;

(i) A warrant for interception of telecommunication and electronic data transfer may be executed by the requesting prosecutor.

Habeas Corpus

47.1 A person is entitled to be immediately released from any unlawful **4–86** arrest or detention by means of the *habeas corpus* proceeding defined in the present Section. The proceeding defined in the present Section is available to a petitioner at any time, independent of any criminal proceeding.

47.2 In the present regulation, 'unla wful arrest or detention' means any arrest or detention made in violation of this or other UNTAET Regulations.

47.3 The Dili District Court has jurisdiction to decide any petition filed pursuant to the present Section. Any person acting on behalf of the arrested person or detainee and, if necessary, assisted by a legal representative, may file a petition for *habeas corpus* before any court in East Timor. If the petition is filed in any court other than the Dili District Court, the petition shall be immediately transferred to the Dili District Court from the court in which it was filed. The petition shall contain the following information; provided, however, that a petition submitted without the assistance of a legally trained representative shall not be rejected because of formal defects:

(a) an identification of the arrested person or detainee;
(b) a summary of the case;
(c) a statement of the grounds for the request;
(e) a statement of the specific rules violated; and
(f) a statement of the authority under which the arrest or detention was made.

47.4 Upon receipt of the petition, the Registry of the court shall forward the petition to the Registry of the court for assignment of the matter to an individual Judge as provided in the plan for distribution of incoming cases, and to the public prosecutor. The Judge shall conduct a hearing of the case within 24 hours of assignment of the case, after notice to the petitioner and to the person whose release is being sought. The case shall be assigned to a judge who has had no prior participation in regard to the matter.

47.5 After hearing the petitioner and the public prosecutor, the court shall decide the matter in the same session.

47.6 The decision of the court shall contain the following information:

(a) an identification of the arrested person or detainee;
(b) a summary of case;
(c) a statement of the legal grounds for the admission or rejection of the petition; and
(d) the appropriate orders.

47.7 If the court orders the release of the arrested person or detainee, the order shall be executed immediately, and the public prosecutor shall order an investigation of the matter.

Also see, UNTAET Regulation 2000/30 (as amended by 2001/25) s.15 (searches of premises and seizure), s.16 (search of persons), s.19A (arrest warrant), and s.47 (habeus corpus).

(2) Sierra Leone

Agreement Between the United Nations and the Government of Sierra Leone on the Establishment of a Special Court for Sierra Leone, Art. 16

Cooperation with the Special Court, Art. 17

4–87   **17.**—1. The Government shall cooperate with all organs of the Special Court at all stages of the proceedings. It shall, in particular, facilitate access to the Prosecutor to sites, persons and relevant documents required for the investigation.

2. The Government shall comply without undue delay with any request for assistance by the Special Court or an order issued by the Chambers, including, but not limited to:

(a) Identification and location of persons;
(b) Service of documents;
(c) Arrest or detention of persons;
(d) Transfer of an indictee to the Court.

B. Powers of Special Courts

As the special courts are established under the auspices of the UN's **4–88** transitional arrangements or with the agreement of the States concerned, the powers of the courts are regulated by such arrangements or agreements. It is evident that the States concerned have undertaken to fully cooperate with the UN special courts. The special courts thus possess the same powers as the national courts in respect of conducting investigations, executing arrest warrants, and the production of evidence during trial proceedings within the borders of the States over which they have jurisdiction. The existing procedures for cooperation in criminal proceedings with other States may be invoked if necessary. For example, if an accused before the court for Sierra Leone is in another country and needs to be extradited back to Sierra Leone for trial.

The Special Panels for Serious Crimes completed its work on May 20, 2005 with 84 defendants convicted and three acquitted.

C. Search and Seizure

East Timor

The Transitional Rules of Criminal Procedure (TRCP) provide **4–89** specific regulations for search and seizure of premises and persons. Section 15 of the TRCP states that a warrant from the investigative judge is required in order to enter and conduct a search of premises, except in cases of urgency where permission cannot be previously obtained. Such a warrant will be granted if there are reasonable grounds to believe that such search would produce evidence necessary for the investigation or would lead to the arrest of a suspect whose arrest warrant has previously been issued. As in most national and international legislations, a warrant will not be required when the police has reasonable grounds to believe that evidence of a crime is located in the premises and that it may be tampered, removed or destroyed, it is necessary to preserve the scene of the crime, the police are in pursuit of a suspect, there is immediate danger to the safety and security of persons.

In relation to the search of persons, Section 16 provides that an **4–90** Investigative Judge may issue a warrant when the search of the body of a person is intrusive. A warrant is also requested to collect any body specimen of the suspect. Exception is made for cases where the public prosecutor or the police require a blood sample or any other body specimen and that a warrant cannot be obtained within reasonable time for the purposes of preserving the evidence necessary for the investigation.

A warrant will also be required to search, intercept or seize any **4–91** written or electronic mail, monitor or record telephonic or other electronic communication. This is provided by Section 17 of the TRCP.

CHAPTER 5

PRINCIPLES OF INTERPRETATION

I. STATUTORY PROVISIONS

A. THE VIENNA CONVENTION ON THE LAW OF TREATIES 1969

The Vienna Convention on the Law of Treaties 1969, Arts 31–33

General Rule of interpretation

31.—1. A treaty shall be interpreted in good faith in accordance with the **5–1** ordinary meaning to be given to the terms of the treaty in their context and in the light of its object and purpose.

2. The context for the purpose of the interpretation of a treaty shall comprise in addition to the text, including its preamble and annexes:

  (a) any agreement relating to the treaty which was made between all the parties in connexion with the conclusion of the treaty;

  (b) any instrument which was made by one or more parties in connexion with the conclusion of the treaty and accepted by the other parties as an instrument related to the treaty.

3. There shall be taken into account, together with the context:

  (a) any subsequent agreement between the parties regarding the interpretation of the treaty or the application of its provisions;

  (b) any subsequent practice in the application of the treaty which establishes the agreement of the parties regarding its interpretation;

  (c) any relevant rules of international law applicable in the relations between the parties.

(4) A special meaning shall be given to a term if it is established that the parties so intended.

Supplementary means of interpretation

5–2   **32.** Recourse may be had to supplementary means of interpretation including the preparatory work of the treaty and the circumstances of its conclusion, in order to confirm the meaning resulting from the application of Article 31, or to determine the meaning when the interpretation according to Article 31:
    (a) leaves the meaning ambiguous or obscure; or
    (b) leads to a result which is manifestly absurd or unreasonable.

Interpretation of Treaties authenticated in two or more languages

5–3   **33.**—1. When a treaty has been authenticated in two or more languages, the text is equally authoritative in each language, unless the treaty provides or the parties agree that, in case of divergence, a particular text shall prevail.
    2. A version of the treaty in a language other than one of those which was authenticated shall be considered an authentic text only if the treaty so provides or the parties so agree.
    3. The terms of the treaty are presumed to have the same meaning in each authentic text.
    4. Except where a particular text prevails in accordance with paragraph 1, when a comparison of the authentic texts discloses a difference of meaning which the application of Article 31 and 32 does not remove, the meaning which best reconciles the texts, having regard to the object and purpose of the treaty, shall be adopted.

B. ICC

1. ICC Statute

Statute of the International Criminal Court, Arts 9, 10, 21, 128

Elements of Crimes

5–4   **9.**—1. Elements of Crimes shall assist the Court in the interpretation and application of articles 6, 7 and 8. They shall be adopted by a two-thirds majority of the members of the Assembly of States Parties.
    2. [. . .]
    3. The Elements of Crimes and amendments thereto shall be consistent with this Statute.

5–5   **10.** Nothing in this Part shall be interpreted as limiting or prejudicing in any way existing or developing rules of international law for purposes other than this Statute.

Applicable law

5–6   **21.**1. The Court shall apply:
    (a) In the first place, this Statute, Elements of Crimes and its Rules of Procedure and Evidence;
    (b) In the second place, where appropriate, applicable treaties and the principles and rules of international law, including the established principles of the international law of armed conflict;

(c) Failing that, general principles of law derived by the Court from national laws of legal systems of the world including, as appropriate, the national laws of States that would normally exercise jurisdiction over the crime, provided that those principles are not inconsistent with this Statute and with international law and internationally recognized norms and standards.

2. The Court may apply principles and rules of law as interpreted in its previous decisions.

3. The application and interpretation of law pursuant to this article must be consistent with internationally recognized human rights, and be without any adverse distinction founded on grounds such as gender as defined in article 7, paragraph 3, age, race, colour, language, religion or belief, political or other opinion, national, ethnic or social origin, wealth, birth or other status.

Authentic texts

128. The original of this Statute, of which the Arabic, Chinese, English, French, Russian and Spanish texts are equally authentic, shall be deposited with the Secretary-General of the United Nations, who shall send certified copies thereof to all States.

5–7

2. ICC—Elements of Crimes

General introduction

1. Pursuant to article 9, the following Elements of Crimes shall assist the Court in the interpretation and application of articles 6, 7 and 8, consistent with the Statute. The provisions of the Statute, including article 21 and the general principles set out in Part 3, are applicable to the Elements of Crimes.

10. The use of short titles for the crimes has no legal effect.

5–8

C. ICTY

ICTY Rules of Procedure and Evidence, r. 7

Authentic Texts

7. The English and French texts of the Rules shall be equally authentic. In case of discrepancy, the version which is more consonant with the spirit of the Statute and the Rules shall prevail.

5–9

D. ICTR

ICTR Rules of Procedure and Evidence, r. 7

Authentic Texts

7. The English and French texts of the Rules shall be equally authentic. In case of discrepancy, the version which is more consonant with the spirit of the Statute and the Rules shall prevail.

5–10

E. East Timor

Regulation No 1999/1, s.2, s.3, s.5

Observance of internationally recognized standards

5–11　　**2.** In exercising their functions, all persons undertaking public duties or holding public office in East Timor shall observe internationally recognized human rights standards, as reflected, in particular, in:

- The Universal Declaration on Human Rights of December 10, 1948;
- The International Covenant on Civil and Political Rights of December 16, 1966 and its Protocols;
- The International Covenant on Economic, Social and Cultural Rights of December 16, 1966;
- The Convention on the Elimination of All Forms of Racial Discrimination of December 21, 1965;
- The Convention on the Elimination of All Forms of Discrimination Against Women of December 17, 1979;
- The Convention Against Torture and other Cruel, Inhumane or Degrading Treatment or Punishment of December 17, 1984;
- The International Convention on the Rights of the Child of November 20, 1989.

They shall not discriminate against any person on any ground such as sex, race, colour, language, religion, political or other opinion, national, ethnic or social origin, association with a national community, property, birth or all other status.

Applicable law in East Timor

5–12　　**3.**—3.1 Until replaced by UNTAET regulations or subsequent legislation of democratically established institutions of East Timor, the laws applied in East Timor prior to October 25, 1999 shall apply in East Timor insofar as they do not conflict with the standards referred to in section 2, the fulfillment of the mandate given to UNTAET under United Nations Security Council resolution 1272 (1999), or the present or any other regulation and directive issued by the Transitional Administrator.

3.2 Without prejudice to the review of other legislation, the following laws, which do not comply with the standards referred to in section 2 and 3 of the present regulation, as well as any subsequent amendments to these laws and their administrative regulations, shall no longer be applied in East Timor:

- Law on Anti-Subversion;
- Law on Social Organizations;
- Law on National Security;
- Law on National Protection and Defense;
- Law on Mobilization and Demobilization;
- Law on Defense and Security.

3.3 Capital punishment is abolished.

Entry into force and promulgation of regulations issued by UNTAET

5–13　　**5.**—5.1 [. . .]

5.2 UNTAET regulations shall be issued in English, Portuguese and Bahasa Indonesian. Translations in Tetun shall be made available as required. In case of divergence, the English text shall prevail. The regulations shall be published in a manner that ensures their wide dissemination by public announcement and publication.

II. PRINCIPLES OF INTERPRETATION

A. INTRODUCTION

The ad hoc Tribunals for the Former Yugoslavia and Rwanda **5–14** exercise international criminal jurisdiction based upon a Statute which is largely silent as to the elements of the offences or the degree of responsibility capable of attracting international penal law. The ICC approach is very different. Resolution F of Annex I of the Final Act of the Rome Conference (a/Conf.183/C.1/L.76/Add.14, p. 19), established a Preparatory Commission of the ICC to prepare draft texts on the Rules of Procedure and Evidence and on the Elements of the Crimes (Resolution F, paras 5(a)-(b)). Finalised draft texts of the Rules of Procedure and Evidence ((PCNICC/2000/1/Add.1), November 2, 2000) and of the Elements of the Crimes ((PCNICC/2000/1/Add.2), November 2, 2000) have been prepared, and once adopted by the State parties, these will be applied by the ICC.

As with other international (and domestic) legal instruments, a **5–15** varying degree of flexibility is available to judges when interpreting different Articles of the Statute or applicable provision of the Rules of Procedure and Evidence, depending upon the nature of the Article or rule, its drafting, and the problem encountered in a particular case. Such judicial discretion was acknowledged in *Prosecutor v. Delalic et al.*, Judgment, November 16, 1998, para. 158:

> "The Trial Chamber is aware that the meaning of the word 'interpretation' in the context of statutes, including the Statute of the Tribunal, may be explained both in a broad and in a narrow sense. In its broad sense, it involves the creative activities of the judge in extending, restricting or modifying a rule of law contained in its statutory form. In its narrow sense, it could be taken to denote the role of a judge in explaining the meaning of words or phrases used in the statute. Within the context of the provisions of the Rules, the meaning of 'interpretation' assumes a special complexity. This is because of the approach adopted in the formulation of these provisions, which accommodate principles of law from the main legal systems of the world."

Article 21 of the ICC Statute sets out a hierarchy of the applicable **5–16** law to be applied by that court. Whilst there is no comparable provision in the Statutes of the ICTY and the ICTR, broadly the same hierarchy has been identified by the judges in the case law which has developed. For example, in *Prosecutor v. Erdemović*, Judgment, Joint Separate Opinion of Judge McDonald and Judge Vohrah, October 7, 1997, paras 3–5, it was explained that:

> "The first step in the proper construction of the Statute and Rules must **5–17** always involve an examination of the provisions of the Statute and Rules themselves. The terms used in these instruments must be construed according to their plain and ordinary meaning consistently with Article 32 of the Vienna Convention on the Law of Treaties. Regard may also be had to the preparatory work relating to the formulation of the Statute and the

Rules, consistently with Article 32 of that Treaty. The second step involves a consideration of international law authorities which may offer further elucidation of the meaning of terms employed in the Statute and the Rules. However, no credence may be given to such international authorities if they are inconsistent with the spirit, object and purpose of the Statute and Rules as discerned from the plain meaning of the terms used therein. The third step, in the event that international authority is entirely lacking or is insufficient, is that recourse may then be had to national law to assist in the interpretation of terms or concepts used in the Statute and Rules. Again, no credence may be given to such national law authorities if they do not comport with the spirit, object and purpose of the Statute and Rules."

B. VIENNA CONVENTION ON THE INTERPRETATION OF TREATIES

(1) Summary

5–18   The Statutes of the ICTY and the ICTR are not treaties but are *sui generis* legal instruments which resemble treaties in certain important respects. Accordingly, it is by now well settled that the Tribunals may have recourse to the Vienna Convention on the Law of Treaties, May 23, 1969, 1155 UNTS 331, when interpreting their Statutes (see, for example, *Prosecutor v. Tadić*, Decision on the Prosecutor's motion requesting protective measures for victims and witnesses, August 10, 1995, para. 18; *Prosecutor v. Bagasora*, Decision on the admissibility of the Prosecutor's appeal from the decision of a confirming judge dismissing an indictment against Theoneste Bagasora and 28 others, June 8, 1998, paras 28-29; *Prosecutor v. Delalic et al.*, Judgment, November 16, 1998, para. 1161).

Such a conclusion is warranted both by the nature of the Statutes and by the Vienna Convention itself. The principles enunciated in the Vienna Convention are generally regarded as reflecting customary international law (see, for example, *Maritime Delimitation and Territorial Questions case (Qatar v. Bahrain)*, ICJ Reports 1995, p. 6, at para. 18). The Vienna Convention principles of interpretation are applicable to the ICC, the ad hoc Tribunals and the Special Courts for East Timor and Sierra Leone in the interpretation of international provisions.

(2) Interpreting the Rules of Procedure and Evidence

5–19   Recourse may be had to the Vienna Convention on the Law of Treaties when interpreting the provisions of the Rules of Procedure and Evidence of the ICC, ICTY and ICTR. This is because the principles of the Vienna Convention "reflect customary principles of interpretation" (see *Prosecutor v. Joseph Kanyabashi*, Joint Separate and Concurring Opinion of Judge Wang Tieya and Judge Rafael Nieto-Navia, June 3, 1999, para. 11. See also, *Prosecutor v. Momcilo Krajisnik & Biljana Plavsic*, Decision on Momcilo Krajisnik's motion for provisional release, Dissenting Opinion of Judge Patrick Robinson, October 8, 2001, paras 10, 15).

The Rules of Procedure and Evidence of both ad hoc Tribunals and the ICC are meant to give effect to their Statutes. The Statutes have primacy, however, as the constitutive instruments establishing the Tribunals and the ICC. The Rules of Procedure and Evidence are meant to facilitate the achievement of the Statutes objectives. Rules of Procedure and Evidence cannot, however, extend the powers of a Tribunal or court beyond those envisaged by the Statute (see *Prosecutor v. Mrkšić et al.*, Decision on the Motion for Release by the Accused Slavko Dorkmanovic, October 22, 1997, para. 40; *Prosecutor v. Tadić*, Decision on the Defence Motion for interlocutory appeal on jurisdiction, October 2, 1995, para. 4).

It has been explained that "the relation of rules of practice to the work of justice is intended to be that of a handmaid rather than mistress, and the Court ought not to be so far bound and tied by rules, which are after all only rules of general procedure, as to be compelled to do what will cause injustice in the particular case." *In re Coles and Ravenshear* ([1907] 1 KB 1, at 4, referred to and approved of in *Prosecutor v. Barayagwiza*, Decision (Prosecutor's Request for Review or Reconsideration), Separate Opinion of Judge Shahabuddeen, March 31, 2000, para. 53). Whilst *Coles and Ravenshear* concerned rules of civil procedure, Judge Shahabuddeen argued that "with proper caution, the idea inspiring it applies generally to all rules of procedure to temper the tendency to rely too confidently, or too simplistically, on the maxim *dura lex, sed lex*". He concluded that such an approach would not "necessarily collide . . . with the general principle regulating the interpretation of penal provisions and believe that it represents the view broadly taken in all jurisdictions". **5–20**

C. Object and Purpose

The first principle encapsulated in Article 31(1) of the Vienna Convention is that a treaty be interpreted in good faith in accordance with the ordinary meaning to be given to the terms of a treaty in their context and in light of their object and purpose. **5–21**

(1) Object

The primary aims of the ICTY and the ICTR were to punish serious violations of international humanitarian law committed on those territories, thereby contributing to national reconciliation and the restoration and maintenance of peace (see S/Res/955 (1994), November 8, 1994; also see *Prosecutor v. Tadić*, Decision on the Prosecutor's Motion Requesting Protective Measures for Victims and Witnesses, August 10, 1995, para. 18). The Trial Chamber in *Delalic et al.*, Judgment, November 16, 1998, para. 170 explained **5–22**

"The interpretations of the provisions must, therefore, take into consideration the objects of the Statute and the social and political considerations which gave rise to their creation. The kinds of grave violations of international humanitarian law which were the motivating factors for the establishment of the Tribunal continue to occur in many other parts of the world, and continue to exhibit new forms and permutations. The international community can only come to terms with the hydra-headed elusiveness of human conduct through a reasonable as well as purposive interpretation of the existing provisions of international customary law."

(2) Purpose

5–23   The purposive or teleological approach to interpretation is widely used in Human Rights Treaties and national constitutions. In the context of the European Court of Human Rights, for example, see *Soering v. UK* (1989) 11 EHRR 439; *Handyside v. United Kingdom* (1976) 1 EHRR 737. In *Prosecutor v. Delalic et al.*, Judgment, November 16, 1998, para. 266 the Trial Chamber approved of Theodor Meron's approach (in *Classification of armed conflict in the Former Yugoslavia: Nicaragua's Fallout*, 92 AJIL (1998) 236 at 239) which stated that when "interpreting the law, our goal should be to avoid paralyzing the legal process as much as possible and, in the case of humanitarian conventions, to enable them to serve their protective goals".

In *Delalic*, the Trial Chamber further explained that

> "The Commentary to the Fourth Geneva Convention charges us not to forget that 'the Geneva Conventions have been drawn up first and foremost to protect individuals, and not to serve State interests' and thus it is the view of the Trial Chamber that their protections should be applied to as broad a category of persons as possible." (para. 263, footnote omitted).

Consistent with the language of the Vienna Convention on the Law of Treaties, a proper application of the Statutes and Rules of Procedure and Evidence of the ICC, ICTY, ICTR and the special courts for East Timor and Sierra Leone requires that purposive and contextual (rather than literal or rigid) principles of interpretation be applied.

D. Context

5–24   Article 31(1) of the Vienna Convention refers to the "context" of a treaty. Article 31(2) provides guidance as to what that term includes. The main body of Article 31(2) expressly provides that the "preambles and annexes" of a treaty are part of its context.

Article 31(2)(a) states that agreements made by all the parties in connexion with the conclusion of the treaty form part of the treaty's context and can be taken into account in interpreting that treaty. Article 31(2)(b) provides that any instrument made by one or more parties in connexion with the conclusion of the treaty and accepted by the other parties as such may also form part of the context and be taken into account in interpreting the treaty.

The fact that the ICC, the ad hoc Tribunals and Special Courts for Sierra Leone and East Timor must interpret there own constitutive documents in light of their own legal context means that they may not be able to automatically rely upon interpretations made by other judicial bodies in different circumstances. In *Prosecutor v. Tadić*, Decision on the Prosecutor's Motion Requesting Protective Measures for Victims and Witnesses, August 10, 1996, paras 28–30, this was explained in relation to the jurisprudence of the European Court of Human Rights:

> "The interpretations of Article 6 of the ECHR are meant to apply to the common criminal and, for Article 6(1), civil adjudications. By contrast, the International Tribunal is adjudicating crimes considered so horrific as to warrant universal jurisdiction. The International Tribunal is, in certain respects, comparable to a military tribunal, which often has limited rights of due process and more lenient rules of evidence. ... While the jurisprudence of other international judicial bodies is relevant when examining the meaning of concepts such as "fair trial" whether or not the correct balance is struck depends on the context of the legal system in which the concepts are being applied."

Also see, *Prosecutor v. Kovacevic*, Decision Stating Reasons for Appeals **5–25** Chamber's Order of May 29, 1998, Separate Opinion of Judge Shahabuddeen, July 2, 1998, p. 4 which recalled the words of the European Commission of Human Rights that:

> "'[T]he exceptional character of criminal proceedings involving war crimes committed during World War II renders ... inapplicable the principles developed in the case-law of the Commission and the Court of Human Rights in connection with cases involving other criminal offences.' The principles are not irrelevant, but their application has to take account of the peculiarities and difficulties of proceedings before the Tribunal. The resulting need for reasonable judicial flexibility is apparent."

E. RECOURSE TO SUPPLEMENTARY MEANS OF INTERPRETATION

Article 32 of the Vienna Convention permits recourse to supplemen- **5–26** tary means of interpretation including the preparatory works of a treaty and the circumstances of its conclusion in order to confirm an interpretation arrived at via Article 31. Reference to such preparatory works and circumstances is also permitted where the application of Article 31 still leaves the meaning of a provision "ambiguous or obscure" or where an Article 31 interpretation "leads to a result which is manifestly absurd or unreasonable".

(1) Reports of the Secretary-General

The Statutes of both ad hoc Tribunals contain no annexes, but were **5–27** themselves annexed to other documents. The draft Statute of the ICTY was annexed to the *Report of the Secretary-General pursuant to Paragraph 2 of Security Council Resolution 808 (1993)* (S/25704 and Add. 1), (presented May 3, 1993). The Security Council "approved" this Report in *Resolution 827 (1993)*, May 25, 1993 which established the ICTY. The Statute of the ICTR was annexed to Security Council Resolution *955 (1994)*, November 8, 1994. It was *followed* rather than *preceded* by a Report from the Secretary-General (*The Report of the Secretary-General pursuant to paragraph 5 of Security Council Resolution 955 (1994) (November 8, 1994)* UN Doc S/1995/134, February 13, 1995 at para. 7).

Both the *Secretary-General's Report*, in the case of the ICTY, and *Security Council Resolution 955*, in the case of the ICTR, may be appropriately considered part of the context of those Statutes (see, *Prosecutor v. Tadić*, Decision on the Prosecutor's Motion Requesting Protective Measures for Victims and Witnesses, August 10, 1995, para. 18: "The context of the [ICTY] Statute is indicated by the Report of the Secretary-General of May 3, 1993 . . . which contained a draft Statute adopted by the Security Council without amendment"). It is clear that the Secretary-General's Report of May 3, 1993 is "an important part of the legislative history of the Tribunal" to which recourse may appropriately be had (see *Prosecutor v. Kordić and Čerkez*, Decision on the Joint Defence Motion to strike Paragraphs 20 and 22 and all references to 7(3) as providing a separate or alternative basis for imputing criminal responsibility, March 2, 1999, para. 5).

5–28   It will not normally be necessary for the ICTY or the ICTR to have recourse to Articles 31(2)(a)–(b) and 31(3) of the Vienna Convention. Those Articles focus their attention on any preceding or subsequent agreements or practice by the parties to a treaty concluded in the traditional manner. There are no parties, in the strict sense, to the ICTY or the ICTR Statutes. They were passed by the Security Council in the exercise of its Chapter VII powers and are hence are binding upon all member States of the United Nations. Article 25 of the UN Charter States: "The Members of the United Nations agree to accept and carry out the decisions of the Security Council in accordance with the present Charter".

It may, however, be argued that Articles 31(2)(a)–(b) and 31(3) are relevant by analogy. For example, that some of the documents and statements made by various members of the Security Council prior to the vote establishing the ad hoc Tribunals, or the interpretative declarations made after it, are akin to either "agreements relating to the treaty which was made between all the parties in connexion with the conclusion of the treaty" (Vienna Convention of the Law of Treaties, Art. 31(2)(a)), or "subsequent agreement[s] . . . regarding the interpretation of the treaty or the application of its provisions" (Vienna Convention of the Law of Treaties, Art. 31(3)(a)). Such arguments are redundant, however, as such statements are clearly legitimate aids to statutory construction under Article 32 of the Vienna Convention.

(2) Commission of Experts Reports

5–29   A "Commission of Experts" preceded each ad hoc Tribunal (see S/Res 780 (1992), 6 Oct 1992, para. 2 in the case of the ICTY and S/Res 953 (1994), July 1, 1994 in the case of the ICTR). Each Commission produced Interim and Final Reports that were laid before the Security Council. (In the case of the Former Yugoslavia see: Letter from the Secretary-General to the President of the Security Council, Feb 9, 1993,

UN Doc. S/1993/25274 (1993) transmitting the *Interim Report of the Commission of Experts Established pursuant to Security Council Resolution 780 (1992)*; Letter from the Secretary-General to the President of the Security Council, 4 Oct, 1993, UN Doc. S/26545 (1993) transmitting the *Second Interim Report of the Commission of Experts Established pursuant to Security Council Resolution 780 (1992)*; Letter from the Secretary-General to the President of the Security Council, May 24, 1994, UN Doc. S/1994/674 (1994) transmitting the *Final Report of the Commission of Experts Established pursuant to Security Council Resolution 780 (1992))*.

In the case of Rwanda see: Letter from the Secretary-General to the President of the Security Council, October 1, 1994, UN Doc S/1994/1125 (1994) transmitting *Preliminary Report of the Independent Commission of Experts Established in Accordance with Security Council Resolution 935 (1994)* and Letter from the Secretary-General to the President of the Security Council, December 9, 1994, UN Doc S/1994/1405 (1994) transmitting the *Final Report of the Independent Commission of Experts Established in Accordance with Security Council Resolution 935 (1994)*.

The *Interim Report of the Commission of Experts Established pursuant to Security Council Resolution 780 (1992)* was expressly referred to in Security Council Resolution 808 which agreed to establish the ICTY, whilst the *Preliminary Report of the Independent Commission of Experts Established in Accordance with Security Council Resolution 935 (1994)* was referred to in Security Council Resolution 955 which established the ICTR and adopted its Statute.

As far as Article 32 is concerned, a distinction must be drawn **5–30** between the Reports which were prepared and submitted *prior* to the establishment of each ad hoc Tribunal, and Reports submitted after that time. Reports not submitted to the Security Council when a Tribunal was established (and particularly its Statute adopted) cannot be said to have influenced either the Security Council, or amount to "preparatory work". Similarly, such reports cannot be said to be a relevant "circumstance" in a Statutes adoption. Whether such reports could provide *evidence* as to the circumstances existing at the time of the particular Statutes conclusion (rather than itself comprising part of those circumstances) is a separate matter. Whilst it would be a matter of evidence, it seems that reference to a report for such a purpose would not be impermissible.

Accordingly, only the *Interim Report of the Commission of Experts Established pursuant to Security Council Resolution 780 (1992)* in the case of the ICTY and the *Preliminary Report of the Independent Commission of Experts Established in Accordance with Security Council Resolution 935 (1994)* in the case of the ICTR would be preparatory material relevant for consideration under Article 32. The remaining reports, however, could be relevant to various issues as they qualify as the writings of "the most highly qualified publicists" under Article 38(1)(d) of the ICJ Statute.

(3) Interpretative statements

After the Security Council established the ICTY by Resolutions 808 **5–31** and 827, and the ICTR by Resolution 955, various members of the Security Council made statements. After the adoption of Security

Council Resolution 827, Madeleine Albright, then the United States Permanent Representative to the United Nations, stated: ". . . the members of the Council have recognised that the Statute raises several technical issues that can be addressed through interpretative statements. In particular, we understand that other members of the Council share our view regarding the following clarifications related to the Statute: . . ." See *Provisional verbatim record of the Three Thousand Two Hundred and Seventeenth Meeting* [of the Security Council], S/PV.3217, May 25, 1993, p. 15.

Statements made in the Security Council following the debates and votes establishing the two ad hoc Tribunals "can be regarded as providing an authoritative interpretation of the Statute" (see *Prosecutor v. Tadić*, Decision on the Defence Motion for interlocutory appeal on jurisdiction, October 2, 1995, para. 88. See also *Prosecutor v. Kordić and Čerkez*, Decision on the Joint Defence Motion to dismiss the amended indictment for lack of jurisdiction based on the limited jurisdictional reach of Articles 2 and 3, March 2, 1999, para. 29).

(4) Drafting history and origins of a rule

5–32   Article 14 of the ICTR Statute and Article 15 of the ICTY Statute mandate the judges to adopt rules of procedure and evidence for the conduct of the pre-trial phase of the proceedings, trials and appeals, the admission of evidence, the protection of victims and witnesses and other appropriate matters. The Judges were initially assisted in the drafting process by the submission of various draft rules and recommendations by various national and international organisations. In *Prosecutor v. Erdemović*, Judgment, Joint and separate opinion of Judge McDonald and Judge Vohrah, October 7, 1997, p. 5, para. 6, the Appeals Chamber explicitly referred to the assistance provided them by the Government of the United States of America stating that ". . . an examination of the preparatory work relating to the drafting of the Rules reveals the parentage of the expression 'plea of guilty or not guilty' in Rule 62 . . . [and] that reflects substantially Rule 15 of the *Suggestions Made by the Government of the United States of America* . . . Accordingly, we can see no impropriety in turning to the common law for guidance as to the proper meaning to be given to the guilty plea . . .".

5–33   The ICTY and the ICTR Rules of Procedure and Evidence are adopted or amended in plenary (see Rules 6 of the ICTY/R RPE). The discussions in plenary are confidential and are not reported. It may be difficult, therefore, for the parties to construct arguments regarding a rules origin or the preferred manner of interpretation if they are unaware of what national tradition or purpose inspired a particular rules adoption or amendment. If a domestic tradition is to inform the interpretation of a provision, the parties may, in many cases, have to rely upon the judges notifying them as to a rules origin.

This problem was removed by the approach taken in the ICC. Not only have the Rules of Procedure and Evidence and the Elements of the Crimes been drafted (PCNICC/2000/1/Add1–2, November 2, 2000), statements of the State Parties in adopting them are publicly available (see *Summary of Statement made in plenary in connection with the adoption of the report of the Working Group on the Rules of Procedure and Evidence and the report of the Working Group on Elements of Crime*, PCNICC/2000/INF/4, July 13, 2000).

(5) National Rules of Interpretation

In *Prosecutor v. Delalic et al.*, Judgment, November 16, 1998, para. 159 **5–34** the Trial Chamber noted that

> "The Tribunal's Statute and Rules consist of a fusion and synthesis of two dominant legal traditions, these being the common law system . . . and the civil law system, . . . It has thus become necessary, and not merely expedient, for the interpretation of their provisions, to have regard to the different approaches of these legal traditions. It is conceded that a particular legal system's approach to statutory interpretation is shaped essentially by the particular history and traditions of that jurisdiction. However, since the essence of interpretation is to discover the true purpose and intent of the statute in question, invariably, the search of the judge interpreting a provision under whichever system, is necessarily the same."

In effect, the Trial Chamber found that regardless of the system involved, or the technical rules being applied, a general and underlying aim of statutory interpretation is to allow the true intent and purpose of a statute to be given effect. (Also see, *Prosecutor v. Tadić*, Decision on the Defence Motion for Interlocutory Appeal on Jurisdiction, October 2, 1995, paras 71–87 which considered that "literal" "teleological" and "logical and systematic" principles of interpretation.) Notwithstanding the utility that may be drawn from various rules of interpretation, it is suggested that recourse to national principles of interpretation will largely be unnecessary in light of the applicability of the Vienna Convention, which sets out the appropriate principles of interpretation to be followed.

(6) National case law as an aid to construction

The origins of a particular provision may be relevant to interpreta- **5–35** tion in the international context. The operation of a provision in civil or common law systems, may provide evidence as to the role it should play on the international plane. In *Prosecutor v. Erdemović*, Judgment, Joint and separate opinion of Judge McDonald and Judge Vohrah, October 7, 1997, paras 3–7:

> "There is no stricture in international law which prevents the Tribunal from making reference to national law for guidance as to the true meaning of concepts and terms used in the Statute and the Rules. When treaties use technical legal terms derived from the laws of member States, the Court naturally looks at the laws of those member States to see what the terms mean."

However it is impermissible to simply import a national definition of a word or concept "lock, stock and barrel" to the international setting.

In *Prosecutor v. Blaškić*, Judgment on the Request of the Republic of Croatia for Review of the Decision of Trial Chamber II of July 18, 1997, October 29, 1997, para. 23 it is stated:

> "The Appeals Chamber holds that domestic judicial views or approaches should be handled with the greatest caution at the international level, lest one should fail to make due allowance for the unique characteristics of international criminal proceedings."

Also, *Prosecutor v. Delalic et al.*, Judgment, November 16, 1998, para. 431: "In any national legal system, terms are utilised in a specific legal context and are attributed their own specific connotations by the jurisprudence of that system. Such connotations may not necessarily be relevant when these terms are applied in an international jurisdiction." *Cf. Prosecutor v. Delalic et al.*, Decision on Motion to Preserve and Provide Evidence, Separate Opinion of Judge Hunt, April 22, 1999, paras 5–6 (footnotes omitted) "common sense must be permitted to prevail in relation to practice matters arising in international criminal litigation, and it cannot be disregarded simply because it also prevails in relation to practice matters in some national law systems".

5–36   In *Prosecutor v. Erdemović*, Judgment, Separate and Dissenting Opinion of Judge Cassese, October 7, 1997, para. 6, the correct approach was explained in the following terms:

> "[a]ny time international provisions include notions and terms of art originating in national criminal law, the interpreter must first determine whether these notions or terms are given a *totally autonomous* meaning in the international context, ie, whether, once transposed onto the international level, they have acquired a new lease of life, absolutely independent of their original meaning. If the result to this enquiry is negative, the international judge must satisfy himself whether the transplant . . . entails for the notion or term an *adaptation* or *adjustment* to the characteristic features of international proceedings. This exploration should be undertaken by examining whether the general context of international proceedings and the object of the provisions regulating them delineate with sufficient precision the scope and purpose of the notion and its role in the international setting. Only if this enquiry leads to negative conclusions is one warranted to draw upon national legislation and case law and apply the national legal construct or terms as they are conceived and interpreted in the national context. As a rule of thumb it can be said that normally neither the first nor the third hypothetical situation arises; it is more plausible and in keeping with the purpose and spirit of international proceedings that the second will prevail."

These "propositions" will only apply if *notwithstanding* the review of a particular notion or term of art in accordance with its ordinary meaning and in light of its object and purpose (Vienna Convention, Article 31(1)) the notion or term remains unclear as to scope or application (see *Prosecutor v. Erdemović*, Judgment, Separate and Dissenting Opinion of Judge Cassese, October 7, 1997, para. 2).

F. Approach to Construction

(1) Like cases treated alike

5–37   Like cases should be treated alike and "possibly by the same reasoning" (see, *Barcelona Traction, Light and Power Company Ltd*, Preliminary Objection, Judgment, ICJ Reports 1964, p. 6, at 65, Judge

Tanaka, Separate Opinion). The primary concern, however, is to do justice in a particular case (see *Prosecutor v. Barayagwiza*, Decision (Prosecutor's Request for Review or Reconsideration), Declaration of Judge Nieto Navio, March 31, 2000, para. 15).

(2) Declarations/Advisory opinions not given

It is not the practice of the tribunal to inform the parties in advance how it will interpret certain provisions of the Rules. In principle, the Tribunal interprets the Rules in its written and oral decisions on concrete matters raised before it" (see *Prosecutor v. Laurent Semanza*, Decision on the defence motion for the interpretation of Rules 89(A), (B), (C), (D) & 90(F) & (G) of the Rules of Procedure and Evidence and the recall of a witness, December 1, 2000, para. 3). **5–38**

(3) In *dubio pro reo*

The ICC, ad hoc Tribunals and Special Courts conduct criminal trials. As such, an accused may expect that a statute or provision be read restrictively, consistent with the principle *in dubio pro reo*. **5–39**

The *in dubio pro reo* principle is accepted as a general principle of law and operates in criminal matters so that where a statute or rule may be fairly interpreted in two or more ways, the version favourable to the accused should be selected. (*Prosecutor v. Akayesu*, Judgment, September 2, 1998, para. 319. See also, *Prosecutor v. Tadić*, Decision on Appellant's Motion for the Extension of the Time-Limit and Admission of Additional Evidence, October 15, 1998, para. 73.)

In practice, *in dubio pro reo*, has been invoked by the judges in several cases before both ad hoc Tribunals and held to be a relevant consideration when interpreting the Statute and Rules of Procedure and Evidence. In the ICTR context, for example, it was invoked in order to decide the meaning of Article 2(2)(a) of the ICTR Statute (which reproduces the corresponding provision of the Genocide Convention of 1948). Article 2(2)(a) uses the words "killing" in its English version and "meurtre" in the French version. "Killing" could include both intentional and unintentional homicide, whilst "meurtre" is a more precise term capable of only including intentional homicide. Invoking the *in dubio pro reo* principle, the *Akayesu* Trial Chamber adopted the latter interpretation (see *Prosecutor v. Akayesu*, Judgment, September 2, 1998, para. 501).

(4) Policy considerations as an aid to interpretation

In his separate and dissenting opinion in *Prosecutor v. Erdemović*, October 7, 1997, p. 13, para. 11(ii), Judge Cassese forcefully rejected the appropriateness of policy considerations as an aid to interpretation stating that: **5–40**

"[T]he majority of the Appeals Chamber has embarked upon a detailed investigation of 'practical policy considerations' and has concluded by upholding 'policy considerations' substantially based on English law. I submit that this examination is *extraneous to the task of our Tribunal*. This International Tribunal is called upon to apply international law, in particular our Statute and principles and rules of international humanitarian law and international criminal law. ... [A] policy-orientated approach in the area of criminal law runs contrary to the fundamental customary principle of *nullum crimen sine lege*. ... An international court must apply *lex lata*, that is to say. The existing rules of international law as they are created through the sources of the international legal system. If it has instead recourse to policy considerations or moral principles, it acts *ultra vires*."

5–41   An alternative view, however, has been explained by (then Professor) Judge Rosalyn Higgins (in *Problems and Process: International Law and How we use it* (Clarendon Press, Oxford) (1994), pp. 5–7):

"Reference to the 'correct legal view' or 'rules' can never avoid the element of choice (though it can seek to disguise it), nor can it provide guidance to the preferable decision. In making this choice one must inevitably have consideration for the humanitarian, moral, and social purposes of the laws ... Where there is ambiguity or uncertainty, the policy-directed choice can properly be made."

(Also see, *Prosecutor v. Erdemović*, Judgment, Joint and separate opinion of Judge McDonald and Judge Vohrah, October 7, 1997, paras 73–78.)

The purposive approach allows the interpreter to look to the purpose of a provision in order to apply it. Such an approach commends itself under Article 31(1) of the Vienna Convention. Policy considerations may include the *raison d'etre* of a provision, consideration of the mischief against which it is aimed, and the consequences upon the values which it seeks to protect of a contrary ruling. If this is so, it appears that, apart from terminology, there may be little difference of substance (or result) between a judge taking a "purposive approach" to interpretation, or seeking to interpret it having regard to "practical policy considerations".

(5) Conflict in two or more official texts

5–42   Article 128 of the ICC Statute provides that the Arabic, English, Chinese, French, Russian and Spanish texts are all equally authentic. Article 33 of the Vienna Convention establishes that where there is an apparent divergence between two or more equally authentic texts, then unless the treaty provides that a particular text shall prevail, the version which best reconciles the texts in view of their object and purpose be followed. Like the rest of the Vienna Convention this provision is considered as reflecting customary international law (see *Maritime Delimitation and Territorial Questions case (Qatar v. Bahrain)*, ICJ Reports 1995, p. 6, at para. 18), and will, therefore, apply to any case where there is an apparent divergence between two or more equally authentic texts.

Even though they may not have been necessary in light of Article 33 of the Vienna Convention, Rules 7 of the ICTY and ICTR Rules of Procedure and Evidence specifically provide that where a discrepancy appears between two versions of the Rules then "the version which is more consonant with the spirit of the Statute and the Rules shall prevail".

(6) Principle of "effectiveness"

It would be contrary to the principle of effectiveness (*principe de l'effet utile*) to interpret a word so as to make it redundant (see *Prosecutor v. Blaškić*, Judgment on the Request of the Republic of Croatia for Review of the Decision of Trial Chamber II of 18 July 1997, 29 October 1997, para. 13). Similarly, "[I]t is axiomatic that a rule cannot be rendered meaningless by a restrictive interpretation of other provisions of the same instrument" (*Prosecutor v. Mrkšić et al.*, Decision on the Motion for Release by the Accused Slavko Dokmanovic, October 22, 1997, para. 41). **5–43**

(7) Presumption against lacunae

If it appears that there is a gap in international customary law or treaty law when interpreting a Statute, international courts may draw upon general principles of criminal law as they derive from the convergence of principal penal systems of the world. Where necessary such principles will be used to fill any *lacunae* in the Statutes and in customary law. "However, it is always necessary to bear in mind the dangers of wholesale incorporation of principles of national law into the unique system of international criminal law as applied by the International Tribunal" (*Prosecutor v. Kupreškić et al.*, Judgment, January 14, 2000, para. 677). **5–44**

It is not permissible, however, to read words into a Statute or provision that may appear to have been deliberately omitted by the legislating authority. Judges do, however have discretion to read words into a statute where the missing words appear to have been occasioned by a simple drafting error or legislative oversight (see, for example, *Prosecutor v. Delalic et al.*, Judgment, November 16, 1998, paras 408–413):

> "The accepted view is that if the legislature has not used words sufficiently comprehensive to include within its prohibition all the cases which should naturally fall within the mischief intended to be prevented, the interpreter is not competent to extend them. . . . It has always been the practice of courts not to fill omissions in legislation when this can be said to have been deliberate. It would seem, however, where the omission was accidental, it is usual to supply the missing words to give the legislation the meaning intended."

(8) *Ejusdem generis*

Article 5(i) of the ICTY Statute deals with "other inhumane acts" as crimes against humanity. In *Prosecutor v. Kupreškić et al.*, Judgment, January 14, 2000, paras 562–564, the Trial Chamber accepted that the **5–45** term "other inhuman acts" was drawn from Article 6(c) of the London Agreement and Article II(I)(c) of Control Council Law No. 10 and that the *ejusdem generis* rule had been relied upon by various post Second World War courts with regards to the London Agreement. However "this interpretative rule lacks precision and is too general to provide a safe yardstick for the work of the Tribunal".

Applying the *ejusdem generis* rule, the expression "other inhumane acts" would cover actions similar to those specifically provided for in Article 5. The rule was held to be inapplicable in the absence of clear parameters as to what the term "other inhuman acts" should include. Without these, the term "other inhuman acts" was held to be so wide that it would violate the principle of specificity required in criminal law. "Once the legal parameters for determining the content of the category of 'inhumane acts' are identified, resort to the *ejusdem generis* rule for the purpose of comparing and assessing the gravity of the prohibited act may be warranted" (*Prosecutor v. Kupreškić et al.*, Judgment, 14 January 2000, para. 566).

(9) *Expressio unius est exclusio alterius*

5–46   In *Prosecutor v. Kupreškić et al.*, Judgment, January 14, 2000, para. 623, the Trial Chamber declined to identify which rights constitute fundamental rights for the purpose of persecution under Article 5 of the ICTY Statute. It held that "the interests of justice would not be served by so doing, as the explicit inclusion of particular fundamental rights could be interpreted as the implicit exclusion of other rights (*expressio unius est exclusio alterius*)." The Trial Chamber noted that this was not the approach taken to crimes against humanity in customary international law, where the category "other inhuman acts" allows the court flexibility to determine the cases before them.

(10) *Lex specialis derogat generali*

5–47   The maxim *lex specialis derogat generali* is also know as the principle of speciality. If an action is regulated by both a general provision and a specific one, "the latter prevails as most appropriate being more specifically directed towards that action". The principle of speciality "reflects a principle laid down in general international law and in many national criminal systems" (see *Prosecutor v. Kupreškić et al.*, Judgment, January 14, 2000, paras 683–684. Also see *Prosecutor v. Blaškić*, Decision of Trial Chamber I on the Defence Motion to Dismiss, September 3, 1998; *Prosecutor v. Tadić*, Decision on Appellant's Motion for the Exclusion of Time-Limit and Admission of Additional Evidence, October 15, 1998, para. 44).

(11) *Iura novit curia*

5–48   This principle states that it is for a court of law to determine what relevant legal provisions are applicable and how facts should be legally challenged. In other words, that it is for a court to establish the law, whilst the parties must prove the facts. The *iura novit curia principle* is normally applied in international judicial proceedings (see, *e.g. Lotus* case, *PCIJ*, Judgment No. 9, September 7, 1927, Series A, No. 10, p. 31; *Military and Paramilitary Activities against Nicaragua* ,27 June 1986, ICJ Reports 1986, pp. 24–26, para. 29). However, the principle should not be followed in proceedings before international criminal courts, where the rights of the individual accused are at stake. It would also violate Article 21(4)(a) of the ICTY Statute, which provides that an accused shall be informed "promptly and in detail", of the "nature and cause of the charge against him" (see *Prosecutor v. Kupreškić et al.*, Judgment, January 14, 2000, para. 740.

(12) Mandatory or Directory construction

The "language of a statute, however mandatory in form, may be **5–49** deemed directory whenever legislative purpose can be best carried out by [adopting a directory] construction" (82 *Corpus Juris Secundum* (Brooklyn 1990), pp. 871–872, stating also, at p. 969 that "a statute may be mandatory in some respects, and directory in others", also see *Craies in Statute Law*, 7th ed. (London, 1971), pp. 62, 249–250, and 260–271).

(13) Effect of Rome Statute on the ad hoc Tribunals and Special Courts

Article 10 of the ICC Statute provides that nothing in it shall be **5–50** interpreted as limiting or prejudicing in any way existing or developing rules of international law other than for the ICC Statute itself. Article 10 was included to emphasise that the ICC regime was not intended to hinder the development of customary international law. That the ICC Statute, including the Finalised Draft Elements of the Crimes and the Finalised Draft Rules of Procedure and Evidence will inform the jurisprudence of the ad hoc Tribunals and the Special Courts for Sierra Leone and East Timor to a considerable extent, can hardly be denied. Nor is this impermissible. In *Prosecutor v. Furundžija*, Judgment, December 10, 1998, para. 227, the Trial Chamber observed that

> "[t]he Rome Statute of the International Criminal Court may, in many areas, be regarded as indicative of the legal views, *i.e. opinio juris* of a great number of States. Resort may be had *cum grano salis* to these provisions to help elucidate customary international law. Depending upon the matter at issue, the Rome Statute may be taken to restate, reflect, or clarify customary rules or crystallise them, whereas in some areas it creates new law or modifies existing law."

CHAPTER 6

INDICTMENTS

I. STATUTORY PROVISIONS

A. ICC

(1) ICC STATUTE

ROME STATUTE OF THE INTERNATIONAL CRIMINAL COURT, ARTS 53, 54, 61

INITIATION OF AN INVESTIGATION

53.—1. The Prosecutor shall, having evaluated the information made available to him or her, initiate an investigation unless he or she determines that there is no reasonable basis to proceed under this Statute. In deciding whether to initiate an investigation, the Prosecutor shall consider whether:
  (a) The information available to the Prosecutor provides a reasonable basis to believe that a crime within the jurisdiction of the Court has been or is being committed;

6–1

   (b) The case is or would be admissible under article 17; and

   (c) Taking into account the gravity of the crime and the interests of victims, there are nonetheless substantial reasons to believe that an investigation would not serve the interests of justice.

If the Prosecutor determines that there is no reasonable basis to proceed and his or her determination is based solely on subparagraph (c) above, he or she shall inform the Pre-Trial Chamber.

2. If, upon investigation, the Prosecutor concludes that there is not a sufficient basis for a prosecution because:

   (a) There is not a sufficient legal or factual basis to seek a warrant or summons under article 58;

   (b) The case is inadmissible under article 17; or

   (c) A prosecution is not in the interests of justice, taking into account all the circumstances, including the gravity of the crime, the interests of victims and the age or infirmity of the alleged perpetrator, and his or her role in the alleged crime;

the Prosecutor shall inform the Pre-Trial Chamber and the State making a referral under article 14 or the Security Council in a case under article 13, paragraph (b), of his or her conclusion and the reasons for the conclusion.

3. (a) At the request of the State making a referral under article 14 or the Security Council under article 13, paragraph (b), the Pre-Trial Chamber may review a decision of the Prosecutor under paragraph 1 or 2 not to proceed and may request the Prosecutor to reconsider that decision.

   (b) In addition, the Pre-Trial Chamber may, on its own initiative, review a decision of the Prosecutor not to proceed if it is based solely on paragraph 1(c) or 2.

   (c) In such a case, the decision of the Prosecutor shall be effective only if confirmed by the Pre-Trial Chamber.

4. The Prosecutor may, at any time, reconsider a decision whether to initiate an investigation or prosecution based on new facts or information.

Duties and powers of the Prosecutor with respect to investigations

6–2   **54.**—1. The Prosecutor shall:

   (a) In order to establish the truth, extend the investigation to cover all facts and evidence relevant to an assessment of whether there is criminal responsibility under this Statute, and, in doing so, investigate incriminating and exonerating circumstances equally;

   (b) Take appropriate measures to ensure the effective investigation and prosecution of crimes within the jurisdiction of the Court, and in doing so, respect the interests and personal circumstances of victims and witnesses, including age, gender as defined in article 7, paragraph 3, and health, and take into account the nature of the crime, in particular where it involves sexual violence, gender violence or violence against children; and

   (c) Fully respect the rights of persons arising under this Statute.

2. The Prosecutor may conduct investigations on the territory of a State:

   (a) In accordance with the provisions of Part 9; or

   (b) As authorized by the Pre-Trial Chamber under article 57, paragraph 3(d).

3. The Prosecutor may:

   (a) Collect and examine evidence;

   (b) Request the presence of and question persons being investigated, victims and witnesses;

   (c) Seek the cooperation of any State or intergovernmental organization or arrangement in accordance with its respective competence and/or mandate;

(d) Enter into such arrangements or agreements, not inconsistent with this Statute, as may be necessary to facilitate the cooperation of a State, intergovernmental organization or person;

(e) Agree not to disclose, at any stage of the proceedings, documents or information that the Prosecutor obtains on the condition of confidentiality and solely for the purpose of generating new evidence, unless the provider of the information consents; and

(f) Take necessary measures, or request that necessary measures be taken, to ensure the confidentiality of information, the protection of any person or the preservation of evidence.

Confirmation of the charges before trial

61.—1. Subject to the provisions of paragraph 2, within a reasonable time **6–3** after the person's surrender or voluntary appearance before the Court, the Pre-Trial Chamber shall hold a hearing to confirm the charges on which the Prosecutor intends to seek trial. The hearing shall be held in the presence of the Prosecutor and the person charged, as well as his or her counsel.

2. The Pre-Trial Chamber may, upon request of the Prosecutor or on its own motion, hold a hearing in the absence of the person charged to confirm the charges on which the Prosecutor intends to seek trial when the person has:

(a) Waived his or her right to be present; or

(b) Fled or cannot be found and all reasonable steps have been taken to secure his or her appearance before the Court and to inform the person of the charges and that a hearing to confirm those charges will be held.

In that case, the person shall be represented by counsel where the Pre-Trial Chamber determines that it is in the interests of justice.

3. Within a reasonable time before the hearing, the person shall:

(a) Be provided with a copy of the document containing the charges on which the Prosecutor intends to bring the person to trial; and

(b) Be informed of the evidence on which the Prosecutor intends to rely at the hearing.

The Pre-Trial Chamber may issue orders regarding the disclosure of information for the purposes of the hearing.

4. Before the hearing, the Prosecutor may continue the investigation and may amend or withdraw any charges. The person shall be given reasonable notice before the hearing of any amendment to or withdrawal of charges. In case of a withdrawal of charges, the Prosecutor shall notify the Pre-Trial Chamber of the reasons for the withdrawal.

5. At the hearing, the Prosecutor shall support each charge with sufficient evidence to establish substantial grounds to believe that the person committed the crime charged. The Prosecutor may rely on documentary or summary evidence and need not call the witnesses expected to testify at the trial.

6. At the hearing, the person may:

(a) Object to the charges;

(b) Challenge the evidence presented by the Prosecutor; and

(c) Present evidence.

7. The Pre-Trial Chamber shall, on the basis of the hearing, determine whether there is sufficient evidence to establish substantial grounds to believe that the person committed each of the crimes charged. Based on its determination, the Pre-Trial Chamber shall:

(a) Confirm those charges in relation to which it has determined that there is sufficient evidence, and commit the person to a Trial Chamber for trial on the charges as confirmed;

(b) Decline to confirm those charges in relation to which it has determined that there is insufficient evidence;

(c) Adjourn the hearing and request the Prosecutor to consider:

        (i) Providing further evidence or conducting further investigation with respect to a particular charge; or

        (ii) Amending a charge because the evidence submitted appears to establish a different crime within the jurisdiction of the Court.

8. Where the Pre-Trial Chamber declines to confirm a charge, the Prosecutor shall not be precluded from subsequently requesting its confirmation if the request is supported by additional evidence.

9. After the charges are confirmed and before the trial has begun, the Prosecutor may, with the permission of the Pre-Trial Chamber and after notice to the accused, amend the charges. If the Prosecutor seeks to add additional charges or to substitute more serious charges, a hearing under this article to confirm those charges must be held. After commencement of the trial, the Prosecutor may, with the permission of the Trial Chamber, withdraw the charges.

10. Any warrant previously issued shall cease to have effect with respect to any charges which have not been confirmed by the Pre-Trial Chamber or which have been withdrawn by the Prosecutor.

11. Once the charges have been confirmed in accordance with this article, the Presidency shall constitute a Trial Chamber which, subject to paragraph 9 and to article 64, paragraph 4, shall be responsible for the conduct of subsequent proceedings and may exercise any function of the Pre-Trial Chamber that is relevant and capable of application in those proceedings.

(2) ICC Rules

Rules of Procedure and Evidence, rr. 104, 105, 106, 107, 108, 109, 110, 121, 122, 128, 129, 130

Evaluation of information by the Prosecutor

6–4   **104.**—1. In acting pursuant to article 53, paragraph 1, the Prosecutor shall, in evaluating the information made available to him or her, analyse the seriousness of the information received.

2. For the purposes of sub-rule 1, the Prosecutor may seek additional information from States, organs of the United Nations, intergovernmental and non-governmental organizations, or other reliable sources that he or she deems appropriate, and may receive written or oral testimony at the seat of the Court. The procedure set out in rule 47 shall apply to the receiving of such testimony.

Notification of a decision by the Prosecutor not to initiate an investigation

6–5   **105.**—1. When the Prosecutor decides not to initiate an investigation under article 53, paragraph 1, he or she shall promptly inform in writing the State or States that referred a situation under article 14, or the Security Council in respect of a situation covered by article 13, paragraph (b).

2. When the Prosecutor decides not to submit to the Pre-Trial Chamber a request for authorization of an investigation, rule 49 shall apply.

3. The notification referred to in sub-rule 1 shall contain the conclusion of the Prosecutor and, having regard to article 68, paragraph 1, the reasons for the conclusion.

4. In case the Prosecutor decides not to investigate solely on the basis of article 53, paragraph 1(c), he or she shall inform in writing the Pre-Trial Chamber promptly after making that decision.

5. The notification shall contain the conclusion of the Prosecutor and the reasons for the conclusion.

Notification of a decision by the Prosecutor not to prosecute

106.—1. When the Prosecutor decides that there is not a sufficient basis for prosecution under article 53, paragraph 2, he or she shall promptly inform in writing the Pre-Trial Chamber, together with the State or States that referred a situation under article 14, or the Security Council in respect of a situation covered by article 13, paragraph (b).   **6–6**

2. The notifications referred to in sub-rule 1 shall contain the conclusion of the Prosecutor and, having regard to article 68, paragraph 1, the reasons for the conclusion.

Request for review under article 53, paragraph 3(a)

107.—1. A request under article 53, paragraph 3, for a review of a decision by the Prosecutor not to initiate an investigation or not to prosecute shall be made in writing, and be supported with reasons, within 90 days following the notification given under rule 105 or 106.   **6–7**

2. The Pre-Trial Chamber may request the Prosecutor to transmit the information or documents in his or her possession, or summaries thereof, that the Chamber considers necessary for the conduct of the review.

3. The Pre-Trial Chamber shall take such measures as are necessary under articles 54, 72 and 93 to protect the information and documents referred to in sub-rule 2 and, under article 68, paragraph 5, to protect the safety of witnesses and victims and members of their families.

4. When a State or the Security Council makes a request referred to in sub-rule 1, the Pre-Trial Chamber may seek further observations from them.

5. Where an issue of jurisdiction or admissibility of the case is raised, rule 59 shall apply.

Decision of the Pre-Trial Chamber under article 53, paragraph 3(a)

108.—1. A decision of the Pre-Trial Chamber under article 53, paragraph 3(a), must be concurred in by a majority of its judges and shall contain reasons. It shall be communicated to all those who participated in the review.   **6–8**

2. Where the Pre-Trial Chamber requests the Prosecutor to review, in whole or in part, his or her decision not to initiate an investigation or not to prosecute, the Prosecutor shall reconsider that decision as soon as possible.

3. Once the Prosecutor has taken a final decision, he or she shall notify the Pre-Trial Chamber in writing. This notification shall contain the conclusion of the Prosecutor and the reasons for the conclusion. It shall be communicated to all those who participated in the review.

Review by the Pre-Trial Chamber under article 53, paragraph 3(b)

109.—1. Within 180 days following a notification given under rule 105 or 106, the Pre-Trial Chamber may on its own initiative decide to review a decision of the Prosecutor taken solely under article 53, paragraph 1(c) or 2(c). The Pre-Trial Chamber shall inform the Prosecutor of its intention to review his or her decision and shall establish a time limit within which the Prosecutor may submit observations and other material.   **6–9**

2. In cases where a request has been submitted to the Pre-Trial Chamber by a State or by the Security Council, they shall also be informed and may submit observations in accordance with rule 107.

Decision by the Pre-Trial Chamber under article 53, paragraph 3(b)

110.—1. A decision by the Pre-Trial Chamber to confirm or not to confirm a decision taken by the Prosecutor solely under article 53, paragraph 1(c) or 2(c), must be concurred in by a majority of its judges and shall contain reasons. It shall be communicated to all those who participated in the review.   **6–10**

2. When the Pre-Trial Chamber does not confirm the decision by the Prosecutor referred to in sub-rule 1, he or she shall proceed with the investigation or prosecution.

Proceedings before the confirmation hearing

6–11   **121.**—1. A person subject to a warrant of arrest or a summons to appear under article 58 shall appear before the Pre-Trial Chamber, in the presence of the Prosecutor, promptly upon arriving at the Court. Subject to the provisions of articles 60 and 61, the person shall enjoy the rights set forth in article 67. At this first appearance, the Pre-Trial Chamber shall set the date on which it intends to hold a hearing to confirm the charges. It shall ensure that this date, and any postponements under sub-rule 7, are made public.

2. In accordance with article 61, paragraph 3, the Pre-Trial Chamber shall take the necessary decisions regarding disclosure between the Prosecutor and the person in respect of whom a warrant of arrest or a summons to appear has been issued. During disclosure:

    (a) The person concerned may be assisted or represented by the counsel of his or her choice or by a counsel assigned to him or her;

    (b) The Pre-Trial Chamber shall hold status conferences to ensure that disclosure takes place under satisfactory conditions. For each case, a judge of the Pre-Trial Chamber shall be appointed to organize such status conferences, on his or her own motion, or at the request of the Prosecutor or the person;

    (c) All evidence disclosed between the Prosecutor and the person for the purposes of the confirmation hearing shall be communicated to the Pre-Trial Chamber.

3. The Prosecutor shall provide to the Pre-Trial Chamber and the person, no later than 30 days before the date of the confirmation hearing, a detailed description of the charges together with a list of the evidence which he or she intends to present at the hearing.

4. Where the Prosecutor intends to amend the charges pursuant to article 61, paragraph 4, he or she shall notify the Pre-Trial Chamber and the person no later than 15 days before the date of the hearing of the amended charges together with a list of evidence that the Prosecutor intends to bring in support of those charges at the hearing.

5. Where the Prosecutor intends to present new evidence at the hearing, he or she shall provide the Pre-Trial Chamber and the person with a list of that evidence no later than 15 days before the date of the hearing.

6. If the person intends to present evidence under article 61, paragraph 6, he or she shall provide a list of that evidence to the Pre-Trial Chamber no later than 15 days before the date of the hearing. The Pre-Trial Chamber shall transmit the list to the Prosecutor without delay. The person shall provide a list of evidence that he or she intends to present in response to any amended charges or a new list of evidence provided by the Prosecutor.

7. The Prosecutor or the person may ask the Pre-Trial Chamber to postpone the date of the confirmation hearing. The Pre-Trial Chamber may also, on its own motion, decide to postpone the hearing.

8. The Pre-Trial Chamber shall not take into consideration charges and evidence presented after the time limit, or any extension thereof, has expired.

9. The Prosecutor and the person may lodge written submissions with the Pre-Trial Chamber, on points of fact and on law, including grounds for excluding criminal responsibility set forth in article 31, paragraph 1, no later than three days before the date of the hearing. A copy of these submissions shall be transmitted immediately to the Prosecutor or the person, as the case may be.

10. The Registry shall create and maintain a full and accurate record of all proceedings before the Pre-Trial Chamber, including all documents transmit-

ted to the Chamber pursuant to this rule. Subject to any restrictions concerning confidentiality and the protection of national security information, the record may be consulted by the Prosecutor, the person and victims or their legal representatives participating in the proceedings pursuant to rules 89 to 91.

Proceedings at the confirmation hearing in the presence of the person charged

122.—1. The Presiding Judge of the Pre-Trial Chamber shall ask the officer **6–12** of the Registry assisting the Chamber to read out the charges as presented by the Prosecutor. The Presiding Judge shall determine how the hearing is to be conducted and, in particular, may establish the order and the conditions under which he or she intends the evidence contained in the record of the proceedings to be presented.

2. If a question or challenge concerning jurisdiction or admissibility arises, rule 58 applies.

3. Before hearing the matter on the merits, the Presiding Judge of the Pre-Trial Chamber shall ask the Prosecutor and the person whether they intend to raise objections or make observations concerning an issue related to the proper conduct of the proceedings prior to the confirmation hearing.

4. At no subsequent point may the objections and observations made under sub-rule 3 be raised or made again in the confirmation or trial proceedings.

5. If objections or observations referred to in sub-rule 3 are presented, the Presiding Judge of the Pre-Trial Chamber shall invite those referred to in sub-rule 3 to present their arguments, in the order which he or she shall establish. The person shall have the right to reply.

6. If the objections raised or observations made are those referred to in sub-rule 3, the Pre-Trial Chamber shall decide whether to join the issue raised with the examination of the charges and the evidence, or to separate them, in which case it shall adjourn the confirmation hearing and render a decision on the issues raised.

7. During the hearing on the merits, the Prosecutor and the person shall present their arguments in accordance with article 61, paragraphs 5 and 6.

8. The Pre-Trial Chamber shall permit the Prosecutor and the person, in that order, to make final observations.

9. Subject to the provisions of article 61, article 69 shall apply *mutatis mutandis* at the confirmation hearing.

Amendment of the charges

128.—1. If the Prosecutor seeks to amend charges already confirmed before **6–13** the trial has begun, in accordance with article 61, the Prosecutor shall make a written request to the Pre-Trial Chamber, and that Chamber shall so notify the accused.

2. Before deciding whether to authorize the amendment, the Pre-Trial Chamber may request the accused and the Prosecutor to submit written observations on certain issues of fact or law.

3. If the Pre-Trial Chamber determines that the amendments proposed by the Prosecutor constitute additional or more serious charges, it shall proceed, as appropriate, in accordance with rules 121 and 122 or rules 123 to 126.

Notification of the decision on the confirmation of charges

129. The decision of the Pre-Trial Chamber on the confirmation of charges **6–14** and the committal of the accused to the Trial Chamber shall be notified, if possible, to the Prosecutor, the person concerned and his or her counsel. Such decision and the record of the proceedings of the Pre-Trial Chamber shall be transmitted to the Presidency.

Constitution of the Trial Chamber

6–15   **130.** When the Presidency constitutes a Trial Chamber and refers the case to it, the Presidency shall transmit the decision of the Pre-Trial Chamber and the record of the proceedings to the Trial Chamber. The Presidency may also refer the case to a previously constituted Trial Chamber.

B. ICTY

(1) ICTY STATUTE

STATUTE OF THE ICTY, ARTS 18, 19

INVESTIGATION AND PREPARATION OF INDICTMENT

6–16   **18.**—1. The Prosecutor shall initiate investigations *ex-officio* or on the basis of information obtained from any source, particularly from Governments, United Nations organs, intergovernmental and non-governmental organisations. The Prosecutor shall assess the information received or obtained and decide whether there is sufficient basis to proceed.

2. The Prosecutor shall have the power to question suspects, victims and witnesses, to collect evidence and to conduct on-site investigations. In carrying out these tasks, the Prosecutor may, as appropriate, seek the assistance of the State authorities concerned.

3 [. . .]

4. Upon a determination that a *prima facie* case exists, the Prosecutor shall prepare an indictment containing a concise statement of the facts and the crime or crimes with which the accused is charged under the Statute. The indictment shall be transmitted to a judge of the Trial Chamber.

Review of the indictment

6–17   **19.**—1. The judge of the Trial Chamber to whom the indictment has been transmitted shall review it. If satisfied that a *prima facie* case has been established by the Prosecutor, he shall confirm the indictment. If not so satisfied, the indictment shall be dismissed.

(2) ICTY Rules

Rules of Procedure and Evidence, rr. 47, 50, 51, 52, 53, 53*bis*

Submission of Indictment by the Prosecutor

6–18   **47.**—(A) An indictment, submitted in accordance with the following procedure, shall be reviewed by a Judge designated in accordance with Rule 28 for this purpose.

(B) The Prosecutor, if satisfied in the course of an investigation that there is sufficient evidence to provide reasonable grounds for believing that a suspect has committed a crime within the jurisdiction of the Tribunal, shall prepare and forward to the Registrar an indictment for confirmation by a Judge, together with supporting material.

(C) The indictment shall set forth the name and particulars of the suspect, and a concise statement of the facts of the case and of the crime with which the suspect is charged.

(D) The Registrar shall forward the indictment and accompanying material to the designated Judge, who will inform the Prosecutor of the date fixed for review of the indictment.

(E) The reviewing Judge shall examine each of the counts in the indictment, and any supporting materials the Prosecutor may provide, to determine, applying the standard set forth in Article 19, paragraph 1, of the Statute, whether a case exists against the suspect.

(F) The reviewing Judge may:
    (i) request the Prosecutor to present additional material in support of any or all counts;
    (ii) confirm each count;
    (iii) dismiss each count; or
    (iv) adjourn the review so as to give the Prosecutor the opportunity to modify the indictment.

(G) The indictment as confirmed by the Judge shall be retained by the Registrar, who shall prepare certified copies bearing the seal of the Tribunal. If the accused does not understand either of the official languages of the Tribunal and if the language understood is known to the Registrar, a translation of the indictment in that language shall also be prepared, and shall be included as part of each certified copy of the indictment.

(H) Upon confirmation of any or all counts in the indictment,
    (i) the Judge may issue an arrest warrant, in accordance with Rule 55 (A), and any orders as provided in Article 19 of the Statute, and
    (ii) the suspect shall have the status of an accused.

(I) The dismissal of a count in an indictment shall not preclude the Prosecutor from subsequently bringing an amended indictment based on the acts underlying that count if supported by additional evidence.

Amendment of Indictment

50.—(A) (i) The Prosecutor may amend an indictment: **6–19**
        (a) at any time before its confirmation, without leave;
        (b) between its confirmation and the assignment of the case to a Trial Chamber, with the leave of the Judge who confirmed the indictment, or a Judge assigned by the President; and
        (c) after the assignment of the case to a Trial Chamber, with the leave of that Trial Chamber or a Judge of that Chamber, after having heard the parties.
    (ii) Independently of any other factors relevant to the exercise of the discretion, leave to amend an indictment shall not be granted unless the Trial Chamber or Judge is satisfied there is evidence which satisfies the standard set forth in Article 19, paragraph 1, of the Statute to support the proposed amendment.
    (iii) Further confirmation is not required where an indictment is amended by leave.
    (iv) Rule 47 (G) and Rule 53*bis* apply *mutatis mutandis* to the amended indictment.

(B) If the amended indictment includes new charges and the accused has already appeared before a Trial Chamber in accordance with Rule 62, a further appearance shall be held as soon as practicable to enable the accused to enter a plea on the new charges.

(C) The accused shall have a further period of thirty days in which to file preliminary motions pursuant to Rule 72 in respect of the new charges and, where necessary, the date for trial may be postponed to ensure adequate time for the preparation of the defence.

Withdrawal of Indictment

51.—(A) The Prosecutor may withdraw an indictment: **6–20**

      (i) at any time before its confirmation, without leave;

      (ii) between its confirmation and the assignment of the case to a Trial Chamber, with the leave of the Judge who confirmed the indictment, or a Judge assigned by the President; and

      (iii) after the assignment of the case to a Trial Chamber, by motion before that Trial Chamber pursuant to Rule 73.

(B) The withdrawal of the indictment shall be promptly notified to the suspect or the accused and to the counsel of the suspect or accused.

Public Character of Indictment

6–21   **52.** Subject to Rule 53, upon confirmation by a Judge of a Trial Chamber, the indictment shall be made public.

Non-disclosure

6–22   **53.**—(A) In exceptional circumstances, a Judge or a Trial Chamber may, in the interests of justice, order the non-disclosure to the public of any documents or information until further order.

(B) When confirming an indictment the Judge may, in consultation with the Prosecutor, order that there be no public disclosure of the indictment until it is served on the accused, or, in the case of joint accused, on all the accused.

(C) A Judge or Trial Chamber may, in consultation with the Prosecutor, also order that there be no disclosure of an indictment, or part thereof, or of all or any part of any particular document or information, if satisfied that the making of such an order is required to give effect to a provision of the Rules, to protect confidential information obtained by the Prosecutor, or is otherwise in the interests of justice.

(D) Notwithstanding paragraphs (A), (B) and (C), the Prosecutor may disclose an indictment or part thereof to the authorities of a State or an appropriate authority or international body where the Prosecutor deems it necessary to prevent an opportunity for securing the possible arrest of an accused from being lost.

Service of Indictment

6–23   **53bis.**—(A) Service of the indictment shall be effected personally on the accused at the time the accused is taken into custody or as soon as reasonably practicable thereafter.

(B) Personal service of an indictment on the accused is effected by giving the accused a copy of the indictment certified in accordance with Rule 47 (G).

C. ICTR

(1) ICTR Statute

Statute of the ICTR, Arts 17, 18

Investigation and preparation of indictment

6–24   **17.**—1. The Prosecutor shall initiate investigations ex officio or on the basis of information obtained from any source, particularly from Governments, United Nations organs, intergovernmental and non-governmental organisations. The Prosecutor shall assess the information received or obtained and decide whether there is sufficient basis to proceed.

2. The Prosecutor shall have the power to question suspects, victims and witnesses, to collect evidence and to conduct on-site investigations. In carrying out these tasks, the Prosecutor may, as appropriate, seek the assistance of the State authorities concerned.

3. If questioned, the suspect shall be entitled to be assisted by counsel of his or her own choice, including the right to have legal assistance assigned to the suspect without payment by him or her in any such case if he or she does not have sufficient means to pay for it, as well as necessary translation into and from a language he or she speaks and understands.

4. Upon a determination that a *prima facie* case exists, the Prosecutor shall prepare an indictment containing a concise statement of the facts and the crime or crimes with which the accused is charged under the Statute. The indictment shall be transmitted to a judge of the Trial Chamber.

Review of the Indictment

18.—1. The judge of the Trial Chamber to whom the indictment has been   **6–25**
transmitted shall review it. If satisfied that a *prima facie* case has been established by the Prosecutor, he or she shall confirm the indictment. If not so satisfied, the indictment shall be dismissed.

2. Upon confirmation of an indictment, the judge may, at the request of the Prosecutor, issue such orders and warrants for the arrest, detention, surrender or transfer of persons, and any other orders as may be required for the conduct of the trial.

(2) ICTR Rules

Rules of Procedure and Evidence, rr. 47, 50, 51, 52, 53, 53*bis*

Submission of Indictment by the Prosecutor

47.—(A) An indictment, submitted in accordance with the following pro-   **6–26**
cedure, shall be reviewed by a Judge designated in accordance with Rule 28 for this purpose.

(B) The Prosecutor, if satisfied in the course of an investigation that there is sufficient evidence to provide reasonable grounds for believing that a suspect has committed a crime within the jurisdiction of the Tribunal, shall prepare and forward to the Registrar an indictment for confirmation by a Judge, together with supporting material.

(C) The indictment shall set forth the name and particulars of the suspect, and a concise statement of the facts of the case and of the crime with which the suspect is charged.

(D) The Registrar shall forward the indictment and accompanying material to the designated Judge, who will inform the Prosecutor of the scheduled date for review of the indictment.

(E) The reviewing Judge shall examine each of the counts in the indictment, and any supporting materials the Prosecutor may provide, to determine, applying the standard set forth in Article 18 of the Statute, whether a case exists against the suspect.

(F) The reviewing Judge may:
(i) Request the Prosecutor to present additional material in support of any or all counts, or to take any further measures which appear appropriate;
(ii) Confirm each count;

    (iii) Dismiss each count; or

    (iv) Adjourn the review so as to give the Prosecutor the opportunity to modify the indictment.

(G) The indictment as confirmed by the Judge shall be retained by the Registrar, who shall prepare certified copies bearing the seal of the Tribunal. If the accused does not understand either of the official languages of the Tribunal and if the language understood is known to the Registrar, a translation of the indictment in that language shall also be prepared, and a copy of the translation attached to each certified copy of the indictment.

(H) Upon confirmation of any or all counts in the indictment:

    (i) The Judge may issue an arrest warrant, in accordance with Sub-Rule 55 (A), and any orders as provided in Article 19 of the Statute; and

    (ii) The suspect shall have the status of an accused.

(I) The dismissal of a count in an indictment shall not preclude the Prosecutor from subsequently bringing an amended indictment based on the acts underlying that count if supported by additional evidence.

Amendment of Indictment

6–27   **50.**—(A) (i) The Prosecutor may amend an indictment, without prior leave, at any time before its confirmation, but thereafter, until the initial appearance of the accused before a Trial Chamber pursuant to Rule 62, only with leave of the Judge who confirmed it but, in exceptional circumstances, by leave of a Judge assigned by the President. At or after such initial appearance, an amendment of an indictment may only be made by leave granted by that Trial Chamber pursuant to Rule 73. If leave to amend is granted, Rule 47 (G) and Rule 53*bis* apply *mutatis mutandis* to the amended indictment.

    (ii) In deciding whether to grant leave to amend the indictment, the Trial Chamber or, where applicable, a Judge shall, *mutatis mutandis*, follow the procedures and apply the standards set out in Sub-Rules 47(E) and (F) in addition to considering any other relevant factors.

(B) If the amended indictment includes new charges and the accused has already appeared before a Trial Chamber in accordance with Rule 62, a further appearance shall be held as soon as practicable to enable the accused to enter a plea on the new charges.

(C) The accused shall have a further period of thirty days in which to file preliminary motions pursuant to Rule 72 in respect of the new charges and, where necessary, the date for trial may be postponed to ensure adequate time for the preparation of the defence.

Withdrawal of Indictment

6–28   **51.**—(A) The Prosecutor may withdraw an indictment, without prior leave, at any time before its confirmation, but thereafter, until the initial appearance of the accused before a Trial Chamber pursuant to Rule 62, only with leave of the Judge who confirmed it but, in exceptional circumstances, by leave of a Judge assigned by the President. At or after such initial appearance an indictment may only be withdrawn by leave granted by a Trial Chamber pursuant to Rule 73.

(B) The withdrawal of the indictment shall be promptly notified to the suspect or the accused and to the counsel of the suspect or accused.

Public Character of Indictment

6–29   **52.**—Subject to Rule 53, upon confirmation by a Judge of a Trial Chamber, the indictment shall be made public.

Non-disclosure

53.—(A) In exceptional circumstances, a Judge or a Trial Chamber may, in   **6–30**
the interests of justice, order the non-disclosure to the public of any documents
or information until further order.

(B) When confirming an indictment the Judge may, in consultation with the
Prosecutor, order that there be no public disclosure of the indictment until it is
served on the accused, or, in the case of joint accused, on all the accused.

(C) A Judge or Trial Chamber may, in consultation with the Prosecutor, also
order that there be no disclosure of an indictment, or part thereof, or of all or
any part of any particular document or information, if satisfied that the making
of such an order is required to give effect to a provision of the Rules, to protect
confidential information obtained by the Prosecutor, or is otherwise in the
interests of justice.

(D) Notwithstanding sub-rules (A), (B) and (C), the Prosecutor may disclose
an indictment or part thereof to the authorities of a State or an appropriate
authority or international body where the Prosecutor deems it necessary to
secure the possible arrest of an accused.

Service of Indictment

53bis.—(A) Service of the indictment shall be effected personally on the   **6–31**
accused at the time the accused is taken into the custody of the Tribunal or as
soon as possible thereafter.

(B) Personal service of an indictment on the accused is effected by giving
the accused a copy of the indictment certified in accordance with Rule 47 (G).

D. East Timor

Regulation 2000/30, ss.9, 24, 26 (as amended by reg. 2001/25)

Powers of the Investigating Judge

9.—9.1 In accordance with Section 13 of UNTAET Regulation No. 2000/11,   **6–32**
there shall be at least one Investigating Judge at every District Court in East
Timor empowered to ensure that the rights of every person subject to a
criminal investigation and the rights of any alleged victims of the suspected
crime under investigation are respected.

9.2 As provided by law or UNTAET regulations, the Investigating Judge
shall issue warrants or other orders lawfully requested by the public prosecutor
whenever, in the course of a criminal investigation, there are reasonable
grounds to do so as provided in the present regulation.

9.3 Except as otherwise provided in the present regulation, a warrant or
order from an Investigating Judge shall be obtained for the following measures:
   (a) arrest of a suspect;
   (b) detention or continued detention of a suspect;
   (c) exhumation;
   (d) forensic examination;
   (e) search of locations and buildings;
   (f) seizure of goods or items, including seizure or opening of mail;
   (g) intrusive body search;
   (h) physical examination, including the taking and examination of blood,
        DNA, samples, and other bodily specimens;
   (i) interception of telecommunication and electronic data transfer;
   (j) other warrants involving measures of a coercive character in accorda
        ce with the applicable law.

9.4 All warrants shall be issued in duplicate. The original shall be kept by the prosecutor and added to the file of the case; a copy will be furnished to the suspect or person concerned, except when to do so would endanger the results of the investigations.

9.5 In order to safeguard the rights of a suspect, as listed in Section 6 of the present regulation, the Investigating Judge shall prohibit any actions of the investigating authorities that are in violation of the rights of the suspect.

9.6 The Investigating Judge shall not interfere with the responsibilities of the public prosecutor in directing the criminal investigations, as defined in Section 7 of the present regulation.

9.7 Notwithstanding any other provision of law, any warrant or measure ordered by the Investigating Judge at the seat of the public prosecutor assigned to the case is valid and may be executed anywhere in East Timor without any further formal request to other judicial authorities.

9.8 A warrant or order issued by the Investigating Judge pursuant to Section 9.2 of the present regulation shall identify by name or official capacity the persons who are authorized to execute the warrant or order. Unless otherwise specified in the warrant or order, the following provisions shall apply:

(a) A warrant or order for arrest of a suspect may be executed by any law enforcement officer anywhere in East Timor;

(b) A warrant or order for detention or continued detention of a suspect may be executed by the warden of any official detention facility in East Timor;

(c) A warrant for exhumation may be executed under the supervision and control of any official qualified as provided in Section 18.5 of the present regulation;

(d) A warrant or order for forensic examination may be executed by any official qualified as provided in Section 18.5 of the present regulation;

(e) A warrant or order for search of locations and buildings may be executed by any law enforcement officer in East Timor who is duly authorized by UNTAET regulations;

(f) A warrant or order for seizure of goods or items may be executed by any law enforcement officer in East Timor who is duly authorized by UNTAET regulations;

(g) A warrant or order for an intrusive body search may be executed by any person with appropriate medical qualifications as provided in Section 16.3 of the present regulation;

(h) A warrant or order for physical examination, including the taking and examination of blood, DNA samples, and other bodily specimens may be executed by any person as provided in Section 16.5 of the present regulation;

(i) A warrant for interception of telecommunication and electronic data transfer may be executed by the requesting prosecutor.

Presentation of Indictment

6–33 24.—24.1 Upon completion of the investigation, if the result so warrants, the Public Prosecutor shall present a written indictment of the suspect to the competent District Court. The indictment shall include:

(a) the name and particulars of the accused;

(b) a complete and accurate description of the crime imputed to the accused;

(c) a concise statement of the facts upon which the accusation is made;

(d) a statement identifying the provisions of law alleged to have been violated by the accused;

(e) the identification of the victims, unless measures to protect the identity of the victims are being sought; and

(f) a request for the trial of the accused.

24.2 Together with the indictment, the public prosecutor shall present to the court a list describing the evidence that supports the indictment.

24.3 When the indictment is presented to the court, the powers of the Investigating Judge terminate, except the powers of the Investigating Judge described in Section 9.3(c) through (j) of the present regulation.

24.4 Upon presentation of the indictment to the court, the following must be made available by the prosecutor to the accused and his or her legal representative:

(a) Copies of all documentary evidence intended to be offered by the prosecution at trial;

(b) All statements in the possession of the prosecution of any witness whose testimony is intended to be offered by the prosecution at trial;

(c) All information in any form in the possession of the prosecution which tends to negate the guilt of the accused or to mitigate the gravity of the offenses charged in the indictment;

24.5 Meaningful access to physical evidence in the possession of the prosecution shall be provided to the accused, his or her legal representatives and expert witnesses. Procedures for providing such access shall be as agreed between the parties or as ordered by the court.

24.6 If the Court finds that full compliance with Section 24.4 of the present regulation will likely lead to serious endangerment of the security of a witness or his or her family, the Court may permit disclosure of redacted or summarized descriptions of the affected material.

24.7 The duty of the prosecutor pursuant to Section 24.4 of the present regulation is a continuing duty, so that qualifying material coming later into possession of the prosecutor must immediately be made available to the accused and his or her legal representative.

Receipt and Notification of the Indictment

26.—26.1 Upon receipt of the indictment by the Court, the case file shall be registered by the Registry of the Court. In accordance with Section 17.1 and 35 of UNTAET Regulation No. 2000/11, the case file shall be forwarded by the Registry to the Panel of Judges or to an individual judge, according to UNTAET regulations and the plan of distribution of incoming cases.

6–34

26.2 The Registrar shall ensure that a notification is promptly served upon the accused and his or her legal representative. The notification shall include a copy of the indictment and the date upon which it was received by the Court, and shall inform the accused and legal representative that the defence has the right to submit a response to the indictment within forty five days of receipt of the indictment by the Court.

26.3 The response, if any, shall be filed at the Court and may include legal and factual observations of the accused with respect to the indictment, any preliminary motions the accused wishes to raise and a list of the evidence and witnesses to be presented by the defence during the trial.

E. SIERRA LEONE

Statute of the Special Court for Sierra Leone, Art. 15

The Prosecutor

15.—1. The Prosecutor shall be responsible for the investigation and prosecution of persons most responsible for serious violations of international humanitarian law and crimes under Sierra Leonean law committed in the

6–35

territory of Sierra Leone since 30 November 1996. The Prosecutor shall act independently as a separate organ of the Special Court. He or she shall not seek or receive instructions from any Government or from any other source.

2. The Office of the Prosecutor shall have the power to question suspects, victims and witnesses, to collect evidence and to conduct on-site investigations. In carrying out these tasks, the Prosecutor shall, as appropriate, be assisted by the Sierra Leonean authorities concerned.

3. The Prosecutor shall be appointed by the Secretary-General for a four-year term and shall be eligible for reappointment. He or she shall be of high moral character and possess the highest level of professional competence and have extensive experience in the conduct of investigations and prosecution of criminal cases.

4. The Prosecutor shall be assisted by a Sierra Leonean Deputy Prosecutor, and by such other Sierra Leonean and international staff as may be required to perform the functions assigned to him or her effectively and efficiently. Given the nature of the crimes committed and the particular sensitivities of girls, young women and children victims of rape, sexual assault, abduction and slavery of all kinds, due consideration should be given in the appointment of staff to the employment of prosecutors and investigators experienced in gender-related crimes and juvenile justice.

5. In the prosecution of juvenile offenders, the Prosecutor shall ensure that the child-rehabilitation programme is not placed at risk and that, where appropriate, resort should be had to alternative truth and reconciliation mechanisms, to the extent of their availability. The Rules of ICTR on the confirmation of indictments will thus apply to the Special Court.

Rules of Procedure and Evidence of the Special Court for Sierra Leone, rr. 47, 50, 51, 52, 53

Review of Indictment

6–36　　**47.**—(A) An indictment submitted in accordance with the following procedure shall be approved by the Designated Judge.

(B) The Prosecutor, if satisfied in the course of an investigation that a suspect has committed a crime or crimes within the jurisdiction of the Special Court, shall prepare and submit to the Registrar an indictment for approval by the aforementioned Judge.

(C) The indictment shall contain, and be sufficient if it contains, the name and particulars of the suspect, a statement of each specific offence of which the named suspect is charged and a short description of the particulars of the offence. It shall be accompanied by a Prosecutor's case summary briefly setting out the allegations he proposes to prove in making his case.

(D) The Registrar shall submit the indictment and accompanying material to the Designated Judge for review.

(E) The designated Judge shall review the indictment and the accompanying material to determine whether the indictment should be approved. The Judge shall approve the indictment if he is satisfied that:

　　i. the indictment charges the suspect with a crime or crimes within the jurisdiction of the Special Court; and

　　ii. that the allegations in the Prosecution's case summary would, if proven, amount to the crime or crimes as particularised in the indictment.

(F) The Designated Judge may approve or dismiss each count.

(G) If at least one count is approved, the indictment shall go forward. If no count is approved, the indictment shall be returned to the Prosecutor.

(H) Upon approval of the indictment:

　　i. The Judge may, at the request of the Prosecutor, issue such orders and warrants for the arrest, detention, surrender or transfer of persons, and any other orders as may be required for the proceedings in accordance with these Rules.; and

    ii. The suspect shall have the status of an accused.

(I) The dismissal of a count in an indictment shall not preclude the Prosecutor from subsequently submitting an amended indictment including that count.

Amendment of Indictment

50.—(A) The Prosecutor may amend an indictment, without prior leave, at any time before its approval, but thereafter, until the initial appearance of the accused pursuant to Rule 61, only with leave of the Designated Judge who reviewed it but, in exceptional circumstances, by leave of another Judge. At or after such initial appearance, an amendment of an indictment may only be made by leave granted by a Trial Chamber pursuant to Rule 73. If leave to amend is granted, Rule 47(G) and Rule 52 apply to the amended indictment.   **6–37**

(B) If the amended indictment includes new charges and the accused has already made his initial appearance in accordance with Rule 61:

    i. A further appearance shall be held as soon as practicable to enable the accused to enter a plea on the new charges;

    ii. Within seven days from such appearance, the Prosecutor shall disclose all materials envisaged in Rule 66(A)(i) pertaining to the new charges;

    iii. The accused shall have a further period of ten days from the date of such disclosure by the Prosecutor in which to file preliminary motions pursuant to Rule 72 and relating to the new charges.

Withdrawal of Indictment

51.—(A) The Prosecutor may withdraw an indictment at any time before its approval pursuant to Rule 47.   **6–38**

(B) After the approval of an indictment pursuant to Rule 47, but prior to the commencement of the trial, the Prosecutor may withdraw an indictment upon providing to the Trial Chamber in open court a statement of the reasons for the withdrawal.

(C) Once the trial of an accused has commenced, the Prosecutor may withdraw an indictment only by leave granted by the Trial Chamber.

(D) The withdrawal of the indictment shall be promptly notified to the accused and to counsel for the accused.

Service of Indictment

52.—(A) Service of the indictment shall be effected personally on the accused at the time the accused is taken into the custody of the Special Court or as soon as possible thereafter.   **6–39**

(B) Personal service of an indictment on the accused is effected by giving the accused a copy of the indictment approved in accordance with Rule 47.

(C) An indictment that has been permitted to proceed by the Designated Judge shall be retained by the Registrar, who shall prepare certified copies bearing the seal of the Special Court. If the accused does not understand English and if the language understood is a written language known to the Registrar, a translation of the indictment in that language shall also be prepared. In the case that the accused is illiterate or his language is an oral language, the Registrar will ensure that the indictment is read to the accused by an interpreter, and that he is served with a recording of the interpretation.

(D) Subject to Rule 53, upon approval by the Designated Judge the indictment shall be made public.

Non-disclosure

53.—(A) In exceptional circumstances, the Designated Judge may, in the interests of justice, order the non-disclosure to the public of any documents or information until further order.   **6–40**

(B) When approving an indictment the Designated Judge may, on the application of the Prosecutor, order that there be no public disclosure of the indictment until it is served on the accused, or, in the case of joint accused, on all the accused.

(C) The Designated Judge or the Trial Chamber may, on the application of the Prosecutor, also order that there be no disclosure of an indictment, or part thereof, or of all or any part of any particular document or information, if satisfied that the making of such an order is required to give effect to a provision of the Rules, to protect confidential information obtained by the Prosecutor, or is otherwise in the interests of justice.

II. CONFIRMATION OF INDICTMENTS

A. PREPARATION OF INDICTMENTS

6–41   To prepare an indictment, the Prosecutor must conduct investigations by questioning suspects, conducting on-site investigations, and collecting evidence (see Articles 18(2) ICTY Statute; 17(2) ICTR Statute; and 15(2) SCSL Statute). For further details regarding the Prosecutor's investigative powers see Rules 39–43 of the Rules of Procedure and Evidence of the ICTY, ICTR and SCSL, describing the Prosecutor's powers to summon witnesses, victims and suspects, and to conduct on-site investigations.

At the ICC, the investigation conducted by the Prosecutor is subject to control of the Pre-Trial Chamber in that the Pre-Trial Chamber authorises the commencement of the investigations by the Prosecutor (Article 15 ICC Statute) and issues a warrant of arrest upon the application of the Prosecutor (Article 58 ICC Statute). Other than those restrictions the Prosecutor has similar investigative powers as the ICTY and ICTR Prosecutors (54(3) ICC Statute).

(1) Powers of investigation

6–42   The Prosecutor of the ICTY and ICTR may initiate investigations *ex officio* or on the basis of information obtained from any source, including governments, intergovernmental/non-governmental organisations and UN organs, after having determined that this information provides a sufficient basis to proceed with an investigation (see Articles 18(1) ICTY Statute; and 17(1) ICTR Statute; and 15(1) SCSL Statute).

When such investigations lead the Prosecutor to conclude that a *prima facie* case exists, he or she is required to prepare an indictment containing a concise statement of the facts and the crimes with which the accused is charged (see Articles 18(4) ICTY Statute; 17(4) ICTR Statute; and 47(B) SCSL Rules). At the ICTY and the ICTR the Prosecutor is required to submit an indictment to the Trial Chamber, while at the SCSL the Prosecutor is required to submit an indictment to the Registrar for approval by the Designated Judge.

6–43   The Prosecutor of the ICC is given the power, *proprio motu*, to initiate an investigation (see Article 15 of the ICC Statute). Pursuant to Article 15, prior to the commencement of an investigation, the Prosecutor must conduct a preliminary examination of any information received. If after the preliminary examination the Prosecutor concludes that the information provided constitutes a reasonable basis to proceed with an investigation, he or she must submit to the Pre-Trial Chamber a request for authorisation of an investigation together with the supporting material collected (see Article 15(2)). The Pre-Trial Chamber is required to authorise the *proprio motu* investigation when it considers, on the basis of the material presented, that there is a reasonable basis to proceed with an investigation and the case appears to fall within the jurisdiction of the Court (see Article 14(4)). There is nothing preventing the Prosecutor returning to the Pre-Trial Chamber with further evidence once the Chamber has refused to authorise an investigation (see Article 15(5)).

In addition, the Prosecutor may receive information regarding alleged crimes within the jurisdiction of the Court from States' parties and initiate an investigation in accordance with Article 14 in order to determine whether any persons should be charged (see Article 13(a)).

Another means to trigger the Prosecutor's powers of investigation is when the Security Council, acting under Chapter VII of the UN Charter, refers a situation in which one or more of the crimes within the Court's jurisdiction appears to have been committed (see Article 13(b)).

Upon finalisation of an investigation, the Prosecutor shall submit the documents containing charges on which the Prosecutor intends to bring the person to trial to the Pre-Trial Chamber. The Pre-Trial Chamber then evaluates whether the evidence collected by the Prosecutor is sufficient to issue the indictment (Article 61 ICC Statute).

(Articles 13–17 of the ICC Statute are cited in Chapter 2.)

(2) Admissibility considerations

Article 53 of the ICC Statute is the guiding provision. In cases when the Prosecutor has had information made available to him, he or she shall assess it and initiate an investigation unless he or she determines that there is no reasonable basis to proceed. Unlike the Prosecutor for the ICTY, ICTR and SCSL, the ICC Prosecutor has to assess whether the case will be admissible before the ICC under Article 17. The Prosecutor is obliged to consider admissibility in light of the ICC's complementary jurisdiction with national courts, which gives national courts priority in the investigation and prosecution of crimes falling within the subject matter jurisdiction of the ICC, and allows the ICC to exercise jurisdiction only when the requisites of Articles 17 are met.

6–44

Once the Prosecutor has determined that the case might be admissible and there are reasonable grounds to believe that a crime within the ICC's jurisdiction has been committed, the Prosecutor is justified in initiating an investigation. Like the Prosecutor for the ICTY, ICTR and SCSL, the ICC Prosecutor is empowered to, *inter alia*, question suspects, victims and witnesses (Article 54(3)(b)); collect and examine evidence (Article 54(3)(a)); seek the cooperation of any State or intergovernmental organisation (Article 54(3)(c)) as well as conduct investigations on the territory of a State in accordance with the Statute (Article 54(2)).

Unlike the ICTY, ICTR or SCSL Statutes, the ICC Statute provides for review of a decision by a Prosecutor not to proceed with an investigation, when a State or the Security Council so requests or when the Pre-Trial Chamber, on its own initiative, decides to conduct such a review (see Article 53(3)).

B. CONFIRMATION PROCEDURE

6–45   According to Rule 47(B) of the ICTY and SCSL, if the Prosecutor is satisfied during the course of an investigation that there is "sufficient evidence to provide reasonable grounds for believing that a suspect has committed a crime within the jurisdiction of the Tribunal", the Prosecutor shall prepare an indictment for confirmation by a Judge, together with supporting material. The indictment must be transmitted to a Judge of the Trial Chamber (Articles 19(1) and 18(1) of the ICTY and ICTR Statutes respectively) who is required to confirm the indictment upon finding that the Prosecutor has established a *prima facie* case. As aforementioned the Prosecutor at the SCSL has to submit the indictment to the Registrar for approval by the Designated Judge. See further, Rules 47(E) of ICTY, ICTR and SCSL Tribunals Rules of Procedure and Evidence, which affirm the *prima facie* standard for confirmation by the Judge.

(1) Prima facie case

6–46   If the Trial Chamber Judge is not satisfied that a *prima facie* case has been established the indictment should be dismissed (see Article 19(1) of the ICTY Statue; Article 18(1) of the ICTR Statute, as well as 47(E) and (F) SCSL Rules). On the relationship between the tests set out in Article 19(1) and Rule 47(B) of the ICTY of the (see *Prosecutor v. Rajic*, Review of Indictment, August 29, 1995). Judge Sidhwa stated that the expression "reasonable grounds for believing" in Rule 47(B) neither raises nor lowers the standard of proof required by the expression "*prima facie*" case. Thus, the review standard for both the Prosecutor and the Judge or Trial Chamber are the same. Judge Sidhwa stated that "reasonable grounds for believing" implied that a reasonable man would believe that the suspect had committed the offence in question. Also see *Prosecutor v. Kovavevic*, Decision on Defence Motion for Provisional Release, January 20, 1998, para. 20, in which the Trial Chamber confirmed Judge Sidhwa's findings, by holding that the "confirmation of indictment is not trial on the merits". In that case, the Defence's contention that the Prosecutor had to prove the mens rea to secure confirmation of the indictment was dismissed.

     A leading case on the test to be applied in determining whether a *prima facie* case has been established is Judge McDonald's ruling in *Prosecutor v. Kordic*, Decision on Review of Indictment, November 10, 1995: "a *prima facie* case for this purpose is understood to be a credible case which would (if not contradicted by the Defence) be a sufficient basis to convict the accused on the charge" (pp. 2-3). This test was followed in *Prosecutor v. Milošević*, Decision on Review of Indictment, November 22, 2001, paras 11–14. Also see *Prosecutor v. Milošević*, Decision on Application to Amend Indictment and on Confirmation of Amended Indictment, June 29, 2001 in which Judge Hunt adopted a test akin to determining a judgment of acquittal under Rule 98*bis*, although he stated that the substance of the test was the same as Judge McDonald's test.

The test under the ICC Statute for establishing whether an indict-   **6–47**
ment should be confirmed is set out in Article 61(5) and (9). It requires
the Prosecutor to establish each charge with sufficient evidence to
establish substantial grounds to believe that the person committed the
crimes charged. Either documentary or summary evidence may be
presented to meet the standard established in Article 61(5). There is no
need to call any of the witnesses expected to testify at trial. The
"substantial grounds to believe" standard contrasts with the wording in
the ICTY and ICTR Statutes, which require the Prosecutor to show a
prima facie case.

Other than confirming or dismissing counts, the Judge of the Trial
Chamber (ICTY/ICTR) may request the Prosecutor to present addi-
tional material in support of any or all of the counts or to take any
further measures which appear appropriate, or adjourn the review so as
to give the Prosecutor the opportunity to modify the indictment (see
ICTY/ICTR Rule 47(F)). Once an indictment has been confirmed the
Judge is able to issue such orders and warrants for the arrest and
detention of persons as may be required (see Articles 19 and 18 of the
ICTY and ICTR Statutes, read with Rule 47(H) as well as 47(H) of the
SCSL Rules). As for issuing warrants at the UNTAET see Section 9.2 of
the Regulations.

If the Judge dismisses a count in an indictment because the Prosecutor has failed to establish a *prima facie* case, the Prosecutor is not
precluded from bringing an amended indictment based on acts underlying that count when evidence supports the count (see Rule 47(I) for all
three Tribunals).

(2) Review of confirmation

In general, a decision to confirm an indictment pursuant to Rule 47 is   **6–48**
not reviewable by a Trial Chamber, as it is a matter that falls within
the Judge or Trial Chamber's discretion. However, exceptional circumstances may warrant review (see *Prosecutor v. Nahimana*, Decision on the
Preliminary Motion filed by the Defence based on Defects in the Form
of the Indictment, November 24, 1997, para. 8, finding that review
might be permissible where a confirming decision was flagrantly in
violation of the Rules or the Statute or was inconsistent with principles
of fairness. Also see, *Prosecutor v. Ntagerura*, November 28, 1997, para. 32
and *Prosecutor v. Kovacevic*, Decision on Defence Motion to Strike
Confirmed Amended Indictment, July 3, 1998).

(3) ICC confirmation procedure

The ICC Statute contains a two-stage procedure. The "preliminary"   **6–49**
charges will be drawn up by the Prosecutor when he or she applies for
the issuance of a warrant of arrest or a summons to appear for the
accused. Pursuant to Article 58, the application of the Prosecutor shall,
in particular, contain: a specific reference to the crimes which the
person is alleged to have committed; a concise statement of the facts

which are alleged to constitute those crimes; a summary of the evidence and any other information which establish reasonable grounds to believe that the person committed those crimes. After the "preliminary" charges and before confirmation of the "final charges", the Prosecutor may continue the investigation and may amend or withdraw any charges (Article 61(4)). The "final" charges have to be submitted to the Pre-Trial Chamber for confirmation.

Article 61(1) of the ICC Statute provides that a confirmation hearing must take place within a reasonable time of a person's surrender or voluntary appearance before the Court. The confirmation hearing takes place before the three Judges who comprise the Pre-Trial Chamber. Article 57(2)(a) requires rulings on whether there are substantial grounds to believe that the accused committed the crimes charged, to be confirmed by a majority of Judges of the Pre-Trial Chamber. Other rulings merely require a single Judge of the Pre-Trial Chamber to exercise the functions required (see Article 57(2)(b)).

The confirmation hearing to confirm the charges on which the Prosecutor intends to seek trial is usually in the presence of the Prosecutor, the person charged and his or her counsel (Article 61(1)). See Article 61(2) regarding the circumstances in which the Pre-Trial Chamber may hold a hearing in the absence of the person charged. Article 61(3) requires that the accused be provided with the indictment and be informed of the evidence on which the Prosecutor intends to rely at the hearing within a reasonable amount of time before the hearing.

6–50 A further feature of the ICC Statute confirmation procedure is that the Defence can challenge the Prosecutor's evidence and present evidence (see Article 61(6)). The Defence is given the benefit of notice of the evidence to be relied upon by the Prosecutor at trial and the benefit of testing the strength of that evidence. The Statute does not provide guidance on the effect of the Defence presenting evidence that raises doubts regarding the Prosecution's case. The Pre-Trial Chamber will have to determine the effect of the presentation of such evidence on confirmation of the charges.

6–51 The options available to the Pre-Trial Chamber when considering whether there are substantial grounds for believing that the person concerned committed the crimes charged are similar to those in the ICTY and ICTR Statutes. The Pre-Trial Chamber may confirm those charges which meet the "substantial grounds to believe" test, decline to confirm those charges which do not meet this test, or adjourn the hearing to provide the Prosecutor with an opportunity to provide further evidence or to amend the charge to fit the crimes supported by the evidence (see Article 61(7)).

Like the ICTY and ICTR Statutes, Article 61(8) of the ICC Statute recognises that the Prosecutor may seek confirmation of a charge previously presented which failed to be confirmed when it is supported by additional evidence.

Once the charges have been confirmed by the Pre-Trial Chamber, the Presidency shall constitute a Trial Chamber responsible for the conduct of all subsequent proceedings (Article 61(11)).

III. FORM OF INDICTMENTS

A. Basic Rule

The indictment must contain a concise statement of the facts and the crime or crimes with which the accused is charged (see Article 18(4) of the ICTY Statute, Article 17(4) of the ICTR Statute and Rule 47(C) of the SCSL Rules). Articles 21(4)(a) and 20(4)(a) of the ICTY and ICTR Statutes respectively set out the requirements of the form of the indictment. They provide that the accused is entitled to be informed of the nature and cause of the charge against him. Rule 47(C) of the ICTY/ICTR and SCSL expands on the requirements of these Articles. The Rule provides that the "indictment set forth the name and particulars of the suspect and a concise statement of the facts of the case and of the crime with which the suspect is charged".

6–52

The Prosecutor is also required to prepare supporting material to forward with the indictment to the Confirming Judge (see Rule 47(B)). Rule 47(E) directs that along with each count of the indictment, the supporting material should be examined to determine whether a *prima facie* case exists against an accused. The indictment must identify the facts that underpin the charges against the accused, and the supporting material must contain the evidence that supports the charges. The Indictment is "the only accusatory instrument": *Prosecutor v. Andráe Ntagerura, Emmanuel Bagambiki, and Samuel Imanishimwe*, February 25, 2004, *Judgment and Sentence*, para. 29. Thus, the supporting material may not be used to fill in any gaps which may exist in the material facts pleaded in the indictment: see *Prosecutor v. Brdanin*, Decision on Motion to Dismiss Indictment, October 5, 1999, para. 13.

The SCSL adopted similar principles to those of the ICTY and the ICTR. In *Prosecutor v. Sesay*, the Court held:

> "The fundamental requirement of an indictment in international law as a basis for criminal responsibility underscores its importance and nexus with the principle of *nullum crimen sine lege* as a *sine qua non* of international criminal responsibility. Therefore, as the foundation instrument of criminal adjudication, the requirements of due process demand adherence, within limits of reasonable practicability, to the regime of rules governing the framing of indictments." (*Prosecutor v. Sesay*, Decision and Order on Defence Preliminary Motion for Defects in the Form of the Indictment, October 13, 2003, para. 5; as referred to by *Prosecutor v. Kanu*, Decision and Order on Defence Preliminary Motion for Defects in the Form of the Indictment, November 19, 2003, para. 5).

(1) Concise statement facts and crimes charged

The required form of an indictment has been developed by the Tribunals in their decisions on challenges to indictments brought by the Defence. Pursuant to Rule 72(A) of ICTY/ICTR and 72(B) of SCSL, the Defence is entitled to file preliminary motions challenging the form of the indictment.

6–53

An indictment is of a "summary nature" and functions to "succinctly demonstrate that the accused allegedly committed the crime" (see *Prosecutor v. Delalic*, Decision on Motion by the Accused Delić based on Defects in the Form of the Indictment, October 2, 1996).

In examining the position of indictments in national law and the degree of specificity required, the Trial Chamber in *Prosecutor v. Kvočka*, Decision on Defence Preliminary Motions on the Form of the Indictment, April 12, 1999, paras 14–18, recognised that although a minimum amount of information must be provided in an indictment for it to be valid in form, the "degree of particularity required in indictments before the International Tribunal is different from, and perhaps not as high as, the particularity required in domestic criminal law jurisdictions". The Trial Chamber at para. 17, stipulated that this difference is partly due to the massive scale of the crimes falling within the Tribunal's jurisdiction, which might make it impossible to identify all the victims, the perpetrators and the means employed to carry out the crimes. Unlike national crimes, international crimes often involve numerous perpetrators acting in concert with one another, such as, in the operation of detention camps (see further: *Prosecutor v. Sesay*, Decision and Order on Defence Preliminary Motion for Defects in the Form of the Indictment, October 13, 2003, paras 9 and 12).

6–54   The basic rule embodied in Articles 18(4) ICTY Statute, 17(4) ICTR Statute and 17(4) SCSL Statute, and Rule 47(C) of each of them, is that the indictment must contain a concise statement of the facts and the crime or crimes with which the accused is charged (see *Prosecutor v. Tadić*, Decision on the Defence Motion on the Form of the Indictment, November 14, 1995; *Prosecutor v. Delalic*, Decision on Motion by the Accused Zejnil Delalic based on Defects in the Form of the Indictment, October 2, 1996; *Prosecutor v. Kovacevic*, Decision on Defence Motion for Provisional Release, January 20, 1998, *Prosecutor v. Kupreškić et al.*, Decision on Defence Challenges to Form of the Indictment, May 15, 1998; *Prosecutor v. Krnojelac*, Decision on Defence Preliminary Motion on the Form of the Indictment, February 24, 1999, and same case decision of February 11, 2000; *Prosecutor v. Krnojelac*, Decision on Form of Second Amended Indictment, May 11, 2000; *Prosecutor v. Kunarac*, Decision on Defence Preliminary Motion on the form of the Indictment, October 23, 1998; *Prosecutor v. Kordić and Čerkez*, Decision on Defence Application for Bill of Particulars, March 2, 1999; *Prosecutor v. Kvočka et al.*, Decision on Defence Preliminary Motions on the form of the Indictment, April 12, 1999; *Prosecutor v. Sesay*, Decision and Order on Defence Preliminary Motion for Defects in the Form of the Indictment, October 13, 2003, para. 5).

The indictment must be "sufficiently clear to enable the accused to understand the nature and cause of the charges brought against him" (see *Prosecutor v. Kanyabashi*, Decision on Defence Preliminary Motion for Defects in the Form of the Indictment, May 31, 2000, para. 5.1).

6–55   In *Prosecutor v. Krnojelac*, Decision on Defence Preliminary Motion on the Form of the Indictment, February 24, 1999, para. 12, the Trial Chamber stated that "the extent of the Prosecutor's obligation to give particulars in an indictment is to ensure that the accused has a 'concise statement of the facts' upon which reliance is placed to establish the offences charged, but only to the extent that such statement enables the accused to be informed of 'the nature and cause of the charge against him' and in 'adequate time [. . .] for the preparation of his defence". In other words, the accused is entitled to particulars "necessary in order for the accused to prepare his defence and to avoid prejudicial surprise" (see *Prosecutor v. Delalic*, Decision on the Accused Mucic's Motion for Particulars, June 26, 1996, para. 9). The Sesay decision confirmed the principle that the Accused is entitled to be informed promptly and in detail of the nature of the charges against him, as embodied in Article 17 of the SCSL Statute (*Prosecutor v. Sesay*, Decision and Order on Defence Preliminary Motion for Defects in the Form of the Indictment, October 13, 2003, para. 5). The cumulative effect of this principle combined with the requirement pursuant to Rule 47(C) that the crimes in the indictment need to be charged with sufficient detail "is to ensure the integrity of the proceedings against an Accused person and to guarantee that there are no undue procedural constrains or burdens on his ability to adequately and effectively prepare his defence" (*Prosecutor v. Sesay*, Decision and Order on Defence Preliminary Motion for Defects in the Form of the Indictment, October 13, 2003, para. 6; see also *Prosecutor v. Kanu*, Decision and Order on Defence Preliminary Motion on Defects in the Form of the Indictment, April 1, 2004, para. 33).

(2) Evidence and elements of the offences

There is a difference between the facts of the case and the evidence required to prove those facts. "The facts must be pleaded whilst the evidence is adduced at trial. It is then for the Trial Chamber to determine at the end of the trial whether there is enough evidence to support the charges pleaded in the indictment. It follows that 'disputes as to issues of fact are for determination at trial' and not via motions relating to the form of the indictment" (see *Prosecutor v. Krajisnik*, Decision Concerning Preliminary Motion on the Form of the Indictment, August 1, 2000, para. 8; *Prosecutor v. Brdanin*, Decision on Motion to Dismiss Indictment, October 5, 1999, para. 15; and *Prosecutor v. Kvočka*, Decision on Defence Preliminary Motions on the Form of the Indictment, April 12, 1999, para. 40). Accordingly, challenges to the facts in an indictment, such as whether or not the actions of an accused can be regarded as part of a widespread or systematic attack against a civilian population, are to be resolved at trial, and cannot be the basis of a challenge to an indictment (see *Prosecutor v. Kunarac*, Decision on the Form of the Indictment, November 4, 1999, para. 13).

6–56

It is unnecessary to set out the precise legal elements of the crimes charged for the purpose of notifying the accused of the nature of the charges he or she is facing. It is sufficient for the indictment to contain the statutory provisions which support the crimes charged (see *Prosecutor v. Delalic*, Decision on Motion by the Accused Delić based on Defects in the Form of the Indictment, November 15, 1996, para. 21; *Prosecutor v. Karemera et al.*, Decision on the Preliminary Defence Motion to Dismiss the Amended Indictment for Defects in Form, April 7, 2004, para. 10).

6–57

In *Prosecutor v. Kvočka*, Decision on Defence Preliminary Motions on the form of the Indictment, April 12, 1999, para. 36, the Trial Chamber confirmed that there is no requirement that the indictment alleges the elements of the particular crimes, and a failure to do so did not render the indictment defective. The Chamber noted that reference in the indictment to the specific Article that had been violated, incorporated the elements set out in that Article.

Similarly, in *Prosecutor v. Kordić and Čerkez*, Decision on Defence Application for Bill of Particulars, March 2, 1999, paras 6–8, the Trial Chamber rejected a suggestion by the Defence that the Prosecutor identify the facts which support each element of an offence charged. The Chamber held that all that is required under Article 18(4) and Rule 47(C) is a concise statement of the facts and the crimes the accused is alleged to have committed.

6–58   The indictment does not need to provide evidence by which an accused's particular responsibility will be established, it need only identify the material facts: see *Prosecutor v. Krnojelac*, Decision on Defence Preliminary Motion on the Form of the Indictment, February 24, 1999, para. 7. In *Prosecutor v. Krnojelac*, Decision on Defence Preliminary Motion on the Form of the Indictment, February 11, 2000, the Trial Chamber stated that the material facts depend on the nature of the case the Prosecutor is seeking to establish. The Chamber held at para. 18, that "the materiality of such things as the identity of the victim, the place and date of the events for which the accused is alleged to be responsible, and the description of the events themselves, necessarily depends upon the alleged proximity of the accused to those events". See further SCSL cases: *Prosecutor v. Sesay*, Decision and Order on Defence Preliminary Motion for Defects in the Form of the Indictment, October 13, 2003, para. 7 principle v; *Prosecutor v. Meakic et al*, Decision on Dusan Fustar's Preliminary Motion on the Form of the Indictment, April 4, 2003.

(3) Facts beyond scope of offences charged

6–59   The Prosecutor may allege facts of its case which go beyond the limited scope of the crimes charged in an indictment: see *Prosecutor v. Kabiligi and Ntabakuze*, Decision on the Defence Motions Objecting to a Lack of Jurisdiction and Seeking to Declare the Indictment Void Ab Initio, April 13, 2000, para. 33. The Prosecutor can include "allegations of facts or circumstances that relate to the Prosecution's entire theory of a case that paint a more full picture of the events of a given case for other purposes, including *inter alia* providing context, showing relationships, and demonstrating the large-scale nature of the crimes. The Prosecution legitimately also may seek to prove elements of the crimes by inference to acts dating before 1994." The Trial Chamber rejected the submission by the defence that the indictment's concise statement of the facts is limited strictly to the crimes charged.

The additional facts, including detailed historical background, serve to place in their context the material facts which are alleged in the indictment when dealing with each count or group of counts. It is in relation to those material facts, rather than the background facts of a general nature only, that the accused is entitled to proper particularity: see *Prosecutor v. Kunarac*, Decision on Defence Preliminary Motion on the

Form of the Amended Indictment, October 21, 1998, p. 1; *Prosecutor v. Krnolejac*, Decision on the Defence Preliminary Motion on the Form of the Indictment, February 24, 1999, para. 24; *Prosecutor v. Kunarac*, Decision on the Form of the Indictment, November 4, 1999, para. 8. To the extent that the material allegations in the specifically charged crimes depend on the factual background allegations, the latter needs to be proven at trial: see *Prosecutor v. Strugar et al.*, Decision on Defence Preliminary Motion Concerning the Form of the Indictment, June 28, 2002, para. 10; *Prosecutor v. Kunarac*, Decision on the Form of the Indictment, November 4, 1999, para. 8.

(4) Defective indictments

If an indictment fails to provide an accused with a specific statement **6–60** of the facts and the crimes the accused is alleged to have committed it will be held to be defective (see *Prosecutor v. Tadić*, Decision on Defence Motion on the Form of the Indictment, November 14, 1995, para. 12). In that case the indictment had not set out the accused's specific conduct or the nature and extent of his participation in the several courses of conduct which were alleged over the months concerned in relation to one count in the indictment. See further *Prosecutor v. Kvočka*, Decision on Defence Preliminary Motions on the Form of the Indictment, April 12, 1999, requiring the Prosecutor to set out the "specific acts alleged to have been committed by the accused" as this information was a part of the "concise statement of facts" required by Article 18(4) of the ICTY Statute.

Citing the July 9, 2004 Appeal Judgment in *Niyitegeka v. The Prosecutor*, the Trial Chamber in *Prosecutor v. Protais Zigiranyirazo*, "Decision on the Defence Preliminary Motion Objecting to the Form of the Amended Indictment", July 15, 2004, at p. 5, emphasised that "a defective indictment may cause the Appeals Chamber to reverse a conviction. It is therefore of the utmost importance that any formal defects of an indictment be cured before proceeding to trial."

In *Prosecutor v. Karemera*, Decision on the Defence Motion, pursuant to Rule 72 of Rules of Procedure and Evidence, pertaining to, *inter alia*, lack of jurisdiction and defects in the form of the Indictment, April 25, 2001, para. 16, the Trial Chamber stated as follows:

> "The Chamber notes that allegations within an indictment are defective in their form if they are not sufficiently clear and precise, in the way they are spelt out and with respect to their factual and legal constituent elements, so as to enable the Accused to fully understand the nature and the cause of the charges brought against him."

The Chamber referred to *Prosecutor v. Nsengiyumva*, Decision on the Defence Motion Raising Objections on Defects in the Form of the Indictment and to Personal Jurisdiction on the Amended Indictment, May 12, 2000, para. 1, which held that "for an indictment to be sustainable, facts alleging an offence must demonstrate the specific conduct of the accused constituting the offence" (also see, *Prosecutor v. Kanyabashi*, Decision on Defence Preliminary Motion for Defects in the Form of the Indictment, May 31, 2000, para. 5.1 ("an Indictment must be sufficiently clear to enable the Accused to fully understand the nature and cause of the charges brought against him")).

For a case in which an indictment was dismissed before the Special Panel for East Timor see *Prosecutor v. Pedro*, May 23, 1999.

B. SPECIFICITY

(1) Basic rule

6–61   In *Prosecutor v. Protais Zigiranyirazo*, "Decision on the Defence Preliminary Motion Objecting to the Form of the Amended Indictment", July 15, 2004, at page 5 the Trial Chamber emphasised the importance of pleading the charges in the indictment with sufficient specificity. The Trial Chamber noted: "As a preliminary matter, the Chamber observes that any lack of precision or specificity in an indictment interferes with judicial economy. Not only does a clear and unambiguous indictment lie in the interest of the Accused as a matter of right; but the Prosecutor also benefits from a clear and unambiguous indictment since it enables him to focus his case and hence allocate his limited resources reasonably. During the trial, a precise and specific indictment ensures an efficient use of valuable court time. The Chamber emphasizes thus the importance of a specific, precise, clear and unambiguous indictment as an essential prerequisite for a fair and expeditious trial."

In the SCSL case *Prosecutor v. Sesay*, the Trial Chamber held:

> "in framing an indictment, the degree of specificity required must necessarily depend upon such variables as (i) the nature of the allegations; (ii) the nature of the specific crimes charged, (iii) the scale or magnitude on which the acts or events allegedly took place (iv) the circumstances under which the crimes were allegedly committed, (v) the duration of time over which the said acts or events constituting the crimes occurred, (vi) the time span between the occurrence of the events and the filing of the indictment, (vii) the totality of the circumstances surrounding the commission of the alleged crimes" (*Prosecutor v. Sesay*, Decision and Order on Defence Preliminary Motion for Defects in the Form of the Indictment, October 13, 2003, para. 8; quoted in *Prosecutor v. Kanu*, Decision and Order on Defence Preliminary Motion for Defects in the Form of the Indicted, November 19, 2003, para. 19).

The indictment should "articulate each charge specifically and separately, and identify the particular acts in a satisfactory manner in order to inform the accused of the charges against which he has to defend himself" (see *Prosecutor v. Delalic*, Decision on Motion by the Accused Delalic based on Defects in the Form of the Indictment, November 15, 1996, para. 14).

In *Prosecutor v. Nsengiyumva*, Decision on the Defence Motion Raising Objections on Defects in the Form of the Indictment and to the Personal Jurisdiction on the Amended Indictment, May 12, 2000, the Trial Chamber stated: "It is a general principle of criminal law that all the facts of a given offence attributed to an accused person are to be set out in the indictment against him or her. Therefore, for an indictment to be sustainable, facts alleging an offence must demonstrate the specific conduct of the accused constituting the offence. Rule 47(C) of the Rules of Evidence and Procedure of the Tribunal (the 'Rules') reflects this principle when it prescribes that 'The indictment shall set forth the name and particulars of the suspect, and a concise statement of the facts of the case and of the crime with which the suspect is charged'."

The determination of whether an indictment is pleaded with sufficient particularity depends on whether "it sets out the material facts of the Prosecution case with enough detail to inform a defendant clearly of the charges against him so that he may prepare his defence" (*Prosecutor v. Kupreškić et al.*, Appeal Judgment, October 23, 2001, para. 88).

The materiality of a particular fact needs to be viewed in the context of the Prosecutor's case. "A decisive factor in determining the degree of specificity with which the Prosecution is required to particularise the facts of its case in the indictment is the nature of the alleged criminal conduct charged to the accused. For example, in a case where the Prosecution alleges that an accused personally committed the criminal acts, the material facts, such as the identity of the victim, the time and place of the events and the means by which the acts were committed, have to be pleaded in detail." (*Kupreškić et al.*, Appeal Judgment, October 23, 2001, para. 89; also see *Krnojelac*, Decision on preliminary motion on form of amended indictment, February 11, 2000, para. 18; and *Brdanin*, Decision of February 20, 2001, para. 22).

On the other hand, there may be circumstances where the sheer scale of the alleged offences "makes it impracticable to require a high degree of specificity in such matters as the identity of the victims and the dates for the commission of the crimes" (*Kvočka*, Decision of April 12, 1999, para. 17; also see Brdanin, Decision of June 26, 2001, para. 61; and *Prosecutor v. Erdemović*, Indictment, May 22, 1996, para. 12). "The materiality of such details as the identity of the victim, the place and date of the events for which an accused is alleged to be responsible, and the description of the event themselves necessarily depends upon the alleged proximity of that accused to those events" (*Ljubicic*, Decision on the defence motion on the form of the indictment, March 15, 2002, p. 4).

It may be the case that the Prosecution does not have all the information given the massive scale of the alleged offences. This is, however, not readily accepted as justification for lack of greater detail. "Where the Prosecution cannot provide greater detail, then the indictment must clearly indicate that it provides the best information available to the Prosecutor" (*Prosecutor v. Ntagerura et al.*, Judgment and Sentence, 25 February 2004, para. 32). This is, however, not necessarily a remedy for lack of detail. In *The Prosecutor v. Mrkšić*, Decision on Form of the Indictment, June 19, 2003, para. 13, the Trial Chamber held: "In the situation where an indictment does not plead the material facts with the requisite degree of specificity because the necessary information is not in the Prosecution's possession, doubt must arise as to whether it is fair to the accused for the trial to proceed."

The Appeals Chamber in *Kupreškić* emphasised that "the Prosecution is expected to know its case before it goes to trial. It is not acceptable for the Prosecution to omit the material aspects of its main allegations in the indictment with the aim of moulding the case against the accused in the course of the trial depending on how the evidence unfolds. There are, of course, instances in criminal trials where the evidence turns out differently than expected. Such a situation may require the indictment to be amended, an adjournment to be granted, or certain evidence to be excluded as not being within the scope of the indictment" (para. 92).

The Appeals Chamber found that it was impermissible to charge the accused in a general way and when the Prosecution "could, and should, have been more specific in setting out the allegations in the Amended Indictment" (paras 95–97). The Prosecution must allege the material facts of the alleged criminal conduct of the accused that go to the accused's role in the alleged offence (see para. 98).

It is not acceptable that "the supporting material given during the discovery process can be used by the prosecution to fill any gaps in the material facts pleaded in the indictment [. . .] Where the discovered material does not cure the imprecision in the indictment, the dangers of an imprecise indictment remain—such as in relation to subsequent pleas of *autrefois acquit and autrefois convict*" (*Krnojelac*, Decision on the Defence Preliminary Motion on the Form of the Indictment, February 24, 1999, paras 14–15).

It is not sufficient that an accused is made aware of the case to be established upon only one of the alternative bases pleaded. The accused must be able to prepare his defence on either or both alternatives (see *Krnojelac*, Decision on Defence Preliminary Motion on the Form of the Indictment, February 24, 1999, para. 13 and page 7, note 21).

If the indictment is not specific enough the Trial Chamber may order the Prosecution to file additional particulars. The interests of justice demand that the particulars be included in the indictment itself. Obviously the Prosecutor cannot include particulars containing new allegations for which no leave for amendment was granted (*Prosecutor v. Bikindi*, Decision on the Amended Indictment and the Taking of a Plea based on the Said Indictment, May 11, 2005, paras 7–8).

(2) Location, date, identity and means

6–62 In most cases, the massive scale of the alleged crimes may prevent the Prosecution from identifying many of the victims with precision. The Prosecutor cannot be expected to "to do the impossible" (*Prosecutor v. Brdanin and Tadić*, Decision on Objections by Momir Tadić to the Form of the Amended Indictment, February 20, 2001, para. 22; *Prosecutor v. Kanu*, Decision and Order on Defence Preliminary Motion for Defects in the Form of the Indicted, November 19, 2003, para. 21).

However, if the Prosecution is in a position to provide more details, it should (*Prosecutor v. Kupreškić et al.*, Appeal Judgment, October 23, 2001, paras 89–90; *Prosecutor v. Kvočka et al.*, Decision on Defence Preliminary Motions on the Form of the Indictment, April 12, 1999, para. 23). The Prosecution must provide some identification of the victims at least by reference to their category or position as a group (*Prosecutor v. Ntagerura et al.*, Judgment and Sentence, February 25, 2004, para. 32; *Prosecutor v. Brdanin and Talić*, Decision on Objections by Momir Talić to the Form of the Amended Indictment, February 20, 2001, para. 22; *Prosecutor v.*

Krnojelac, Decision on Form of Second Amended Indictment, May 11, 2000, para. 18; *Prosecutor v. Krnojelac*, Decision on the Defence Preliminary Motion on the Form of the Indictment, February 24, 1999, para. 58).

If a precise date cannot be specified, a reasonable range of dates should be provided (*Prosecutor v. Ntagerura et al.*, Judgment and Sentence, Febuary 25, 2004, para. 32; *Prosecutor v. Brđanin and Taliác*, Decision on Objections by Momir Talic to the Form of the Amended Indictment, February 20, 2001, para. 22).

Such details as the exact address of the property destroyed, or the name of its owner, are not necessary to be provided in an indictment which covers a small area with the vase number of property allegedly destroyed in that area. It is sufficient to indicate the name of the villages, hamlets or areas where the houses or barns concerned were located (*Prosecutor v. Ademi*, Decision on the Second Defence Motion on the Form of the Indictment, January 21, 2002, p. 4).

Where the Prosecution is in a position to provide details as to the means by which the crime is perpetrated, it should identify the method of commission of the crime, or the manner in which it was committed (*Prosecutor v. Kvočka et al.*, Decision on Defence Preliminary Motions on the Form of the Indictment, April 12, 1999, para. 24).

Although the SCSL applies the principles on the framing of indictments developed by the ICTY and the ICTR (*Prosecutor v. Sesay*, Decision and Order on Defence Preliminary Motion for Defects in the Form of the Indictment, October 13, 2003, para. 7), the SCSL seems to be the most lenient court with regards to specificity in the indictment acknowledging that "specificity in cases of such extraordinary crimes, as alleged, is not absolute" (*Prosecutor v. Kanu*, Decision and Order on Defence Preliminary Motion for Defects in the Form of the Indicted, November 19, 2003, para. 24). The Court held that "[a]t the end of the day, in the Chamber's view, *"having regard to the cardinal principle of the criminal law that the Prosecution must prove the case against an accused beyond reasonable doubt, the onus is on the Prosecution to adduce evidence at the trial to support the charges, however formulated"*. In effect, the Prosecution must stand or fall by their own charges (original emphasis). *"However, the Chamber wishes to emphasize that it remains true [. . .] that, in the ultimate analysis, the crux of the matter is whether the Prosecution have proved their case beyond a reasonable doubt predicated upon the charges as formulated"* (original emphasis) (*Prosecutor v. Kanu*, Decision and Order on Defence Preliminary Motion for Defects in the Form of the Indicted, November 19, 2003, para. 21 see further para. 25; *Prosecutor v. Sesay*, Decision and Order on Defence Preliminary Motion for Defects in the Form of the Indictment, October 13, 2003, para. 23).

(3) Vague phrases

6–63

Phrases such as "including but not limited to" as well as other ambiguous phrases such as "among others" are to be avoided in order to ensure that the indictment is specific and not too vague for the purposes of identifying the crimes against which the accused must defend himself of herself (see *Prosecutor v. Blaškić*, Decision on the

Defence Motion to Dismiss the Indictment based Upon Defects in the Form thereof, April 4, 1997, paras 22–24; *Prosecutor v. Kanu*, Decision and Order on Defence Preliminary Motion for Defect in the Form of the Indictment, November 19, 2003, para. 17; *Prosecutor v. Sesay*, Decision and Order on Defence Preliminary Motion for Defects in the Form of the Indictment, October 13, 2003, para. 5). The Trial Chamber stated that such phrases were "vague and subject to interpretation and they do not belong in the indictment when it is issued against the accused" *Prosecutor v. Blaškić* (para. 22).

Also note: "As to the objection by the *Radic* Defence to the use of the term 'including' in the Amended Indictment, there will be certain situations in which its use is acceptable and others in which it will not be. The Prosecution is directed, in respect of those parts of the Amended Indictment where the term is used to signify some of the victims of a crime, to list, to the extent possible, additional names of victims. The *Radic* Defence also objects to the use of the term 'and/or' in the Amended Indictment. The Trial Chamber finds that this is essentially an evidentiary matter and that it is best left to be determined at trial, on the basis of the evidence presented" (*Kvočka et al.*, Decision on Defence Preliminary Motions on the Form of the Indictment, April 12, 1999, para. 26).

See further the SCSL case *Prosecutor v. Kanu* where phrases such as "included but not limited to" in some paragraphs were so inextricably linked with other key elements of the alleged crimes that they were acceptable, while in other paragraphs they were not (*Prosecutor v. Kanu*, Decision and Order on Defence Preliminary Motion for Defect in the Form of the Indictment, November 19, 2003, para. 17). The use of such phrases is "clearly permissible in situations where the alleged criminality was of what seems to be cataclysmic dimensions" (*Prosecutor v. Sesay*, Decision and Order on Defence Preliminary Motion for Defects in the Form of the Indictment, October 13, 2003, para. 23), and where statistical data collection can hardly be more accurate than that (*Prosecutor v. Kanu*, Decision and Order on Defence Preliminary Motion for Defect in the Form of the Indictment, November 19, 2003, para. 19).

C. FORMS OF PARTICIPATION

(1) Charges alleging both command responsibility and direct participation

6–64 When an accused is charged with individual criminal responsibility under Article 7(1) of the ICTY Statute, Article 6(1) of the ICTR Statute and Article 6(1) of the SCSL Statute, as well as command responsibility under Article 7(3) of the ICTY Statute, Article 6(3) of the ICTR Statute and Article 6(3) of the SCSL Statute, the indictment must clearly separate the acts relied upon for each of these charges (see *Prosecutor v. Delalic*, Decision on Motion by the Accused Delić based on Defects in the Form of the Indictment, November 15, 1996, para. 18; *Prosecutor v. Nahimana*, November 17, 1998; *Prosecutor v. Blaškić*, Decision on the Defence Motion to Dismiss the Indictment based Upon Defects in the Form thereof, April 4, 1997, para. 32; and *Krnojelac*, Decision on Preliminary Motion on Form of Amended Indictment, February 11, 2000. But see *Prosecutor v. Kanyabashi*, Decision on Defence Preliminary Motion for Defects in the Form of the Indictment, May 31, 2000, paras 5.8–5.11).

However, in Sesay the SCSL held that individual criminal responsibility and superior criminal responsibility are not mutually exclusive and can be properly charged both cumulatively and alternatively based on the same set of facts (*Prosecutor v. Sesay*, Decision and Order on Defence Preliminary Motion for Defects in the Form of the Indictment, October 13, 2003, para. 7, principle XII).

The form of participation of "the accused in a crime is a material averment which should be clearly laid out in the indictment in order to clarify it and make plain the prosecution case" (*Prosecutor v. Dosen*, Decision on Preliminary Motions, February 10, 2000, para. 12).

In order for an indictment not to be defective it must, when taken as a whole, set out the nature of the responsibility alleged against the accused (*Prosecutor v. Krnojelac*, Decision on Defence Preliminary Motion on the Form of the Indictment, February 24, 1999, para. 7). The indictment charging an accused with one of the different forms of participation should clearly articulate which form and whether the Prosecutor is relying upon command or direct responsibility or both (see *Dosun and Kolundzija*, Decision on Preliminary Motions, February 10, 2000, para. 18 and see *Tadić*, Decision on the Defence Motion on the Form of Indictment, November 14, 1995, para. 12).

(2) Charges under multiple forms of individual criminal responsibility

The above principle was re-emphasised in *Prosecutor v. Ntagerura et al.*, **6–65**
Judgment and Sentence, February 25, 2004. It was also made clear that the indictment has to indicate the mode of participation under Article 6(1) of the ICTR Statute with which the Accused is charged (paras 36 and 37):

> "36. Although no rule specifies the content of the 'count', it is evident from the context of Rule 47 that this term refers to the legal characterisation or qualification of the crime alleged in the concise statement of facts of the crime. This legal qualification must include both the crime alleged and the mode of the accused's alleged participation. Thus, a 'count' defines the *nature of the charge* referred to in Article 20(4)(a) of the Statute.
> 37. Accordingly, each count in the indictment should indicate the precise legal qualification of the crime charged which should be based on the material facts alleged in the indictment. The count must also clearly identify the mode of the accused's alleged participation in the crime; mere reference to Article 6(1) of the Statute, which lists multiple forms of individual criminal responsibility, is insufficient."

Lack of such specifics regarding the modes of participation renders an indictment defective. In *The Prosecutor v. Zigiranyirazo*, Decision on the Defence Preliminary Motion Objecting to the Form of the Amended Indictment, Rule 72 (A) (ii) of the Rules of Procedure and Evidence, July 15, 2004, p. 8 the Prosecutor was ordered to modify the Amended Indictment to include such specifics. The Chamber held at p. 8:

> i. With respect to all Counts, the Prosecutor should only plead the types of personal responsibility pursuant to Article 6(1) of the Statute that he intends to rely upon.
> ii. With respect to all Counts, the Prosecutor should clearly indicate upon which factual allegations he bases his pleadings of personal responsibility pursuant to Article 6(1) of the Statute.

The same position was taken by the Appeals Chamber in *Krnojelac*, which held: "Since Article [6(1)] allows for several forms of direct criminal responsibility, a failure to specify in the indictment which form or forms of liability the Prosecution is pleading gives rise to ambiguity. The Appeals Chamber considers that such ambiguity should be avoided and holds therefore that, where it arises, the Prosecution must identify the form or forms the liability alleged for each count as soon as possible and, in any event, before the start of the Trial." (*Prosecutor v. Krnojelac*, Appeal Judgment, September 17, 2003, para. 138; also see *Prosecutor v Muvunyi*, Decision on the Prosecutor's Motion for Leave to Amend the Indictment, February 23, 2005, para. 52)

(3) Joint criminal enterprise

6–66   An indictment charging joint criminal enterprise is required to include the nature of the enterprise, the time periods and persons involved, and the nature of the accused's participation in the criminal enterprise (*Krnojelac*, Decision on Form of Amended Indictment, May 11, 2000). An indictment charging joint criminal enterprise must clearly articulate the meaning of "committed" if it is not alleged that the accused personally committed the crimes in question (see Decision on Form of Further Amended Indictment and Prosecution Application to Amend, *Prosecutor v. Brdjanin and Talic*, June 26, 2001 and Decision Varying Decision on Form of Further Amended Indictment, July 2, 2001, para. 5). To clearly delineate the meaning of "committed" in charging an accused, the indictment should contain a statement which dispels any suggestion that "committed" refers to the accused physically perpetrating any of the crimes personally. In the absence of such a statement, the word "committed" would have to be struck from any indictments alleging joint criminal enterprise in which the accused did not personally perpetrate the crime in question. See both the indictments for Bosnia and Croatia, at para. 5, against Slobodan Milošević (see Appendix N), in which the word "committed" is used in the sense of Slobodan Milošević's participation in a joint criminal enterprise consistent with the Decision on Form of Further Amended Indictment and Prosecution Application to Amend, June 26, 2001 (see further Chapter 10 on Forms of Participation in Offences, Part VI on charging the different forms of participation).

In *Kanu* the Chamber found that the Prosecutor has no obligation to charge an Accused either with the basic Joint Criminal Enterprise concept of liability or extended concept of liability (*Prosecutor v. Kanu*, Decision and Order on Defence Preliminary Motion for Defect in the Form of the Indictment, November 19, 2003, para. 14).

(4) Charges for superior responsibility

In order to comply with the requisite that all material facts be set out **6–67** in an indictment, an indictment charging superior responsibility under Article 7(3) of the ICTY Statute (Article 6(3) for ICTR and SCSL) must include the relationship between the accused and the perpetrators, which is most material, as well as "the conduct of the accused by which he may be found (a) to have known or had reason to know that the acts were about to be done, or had been done, by those others, and (b) to have failed to take necessary and reasonable measures to prevent such acts or to punish the persons who did them" (see *Prosecutor v. Krnojelac*, Decision on Defence Preliminary Motion on the Form of the Indictment, February 11, 2000, para. 18; *Prosecutor v. Krajisnik*, Decision Concerning Preliminary Motion on the Form of the Indictment, August 1, 2000, para. 9; *Prosecutor v. Ntagerura et al.*, Judgment and Sentence, February 25, 2004, para. 33).

The SCSL was even more specific than that. In *Sesay* the court accepted that the minimum material facts to be pleaded in the indictments in relation to charges of superior responsibility are:

(a) (i)   that the accused held a superior postion;
    (ii) in relation to subordinates, sufficiently identified;
    (iii) that the accused had effective control over the said subordinates;
    (iv) that he allegedly bears responsibility for their criminal acts;
(b) (i)   that the accused knew or had reason to know that the crimes were about to be committed by his subordinates;
    (ii) the related conduct of those subordinates for whom he is alleged to be responsible;
    (iii) the accused failed to take the necessary and reasonable means to prevent such crimes or to punish the persons who committed them. (*Prosecutor v. Sesay*, Decision and Order on Defence Preliminary Motion for Defects in the Form of the Indictment, October 13, 2003, para. 13).

The specificity required of the identity of the victims, the time and place of the events, and the manner in which the offences were allegedly committed is not as high where the accused is charged with superior responsibility rather than individual responsibility. However, "the accused must be informed not only of his own alleged conduct giving rise to criminal responsibility but also of the acts and crimes of his alleged subordinates or accomplices. Thus, pleading accomplice or superior responsibility does not obviate the Prosecution's obligation to particularise the underlying criminal events for which it seeks to hold the accused responsible, particularly where the accused was allegedly in close proximity to the events" (*Prosecutor v. Ntagerura et al.*, Judgment and Sentence, February 25, 2004, para. 35).

(5) Aiding and abetting

When an accused is alleged to incur individual criminal responsibility **6–68** for aiding and abetting, the material facts relate to the "conduct of the accused by which he may be found to have planned, instigated, ordered, committed or otherwise aided and abetted in the planning, preparation or execution of those acts" (see *Prosecutor v. Krnojelac*, Decision on Defence Preliminary Motion on the Form of the Indictment, February 11, 2000, para. 18).

When an accused is alleged to have personally committed the crime charged the material facts require the greatest precision and must therefore "so far as it is possible to do so, include the identity of the victim, the place and approximate date of those acts and the means by which the offence was committed" (see *Prosecutor v. Krnojelac*, Decision on Defence Preliminary Motion on the Form of the Indictment, February 11, 2000, para. 18).

D. CUMULATIVE CHARGING

(1) Basic rule

6–69   The Chambers of the ICTY/ ICTR and SCSL have accepted the Prosecution's practice of charging an accused with more than one offence within the subject-matter jurisdiction of the Tribunals for the same conduct (see for example *Prosecutor v. Akayesu*, September 2, 1998, para. 461; *Prosecutor v. Krnojelac*, Decision on the Defence Preliminary Motion on the Form of the Indictment, February 24, 1999 and *Prosecutor v. Kvočka*, Decision on Defence Motions on the Form of the Indictment, April 12, 1999, para. 47 and *Prosecutor v. Kordic*, Decision on Defence Motion to Dismiss or Alternatively to Order the prosecutor to Elect between Counts, March 1, 1999). The practice of charging an accused with more than one offence for the same conduct is referred to as cumulative charging. The Appeals Chamber in the *Prosecutor v. Delalic et al.*, Judgment, February 20, 2001, confirmed that: "Cumulative charging is to be allowed in light of the fact that, prior to the presentation of all of the evidence, it is not possible to determine to a certainty which of the charges brought against an accused will be proven." The Trial Chamber is better poised, after the parties' presentation of the evidence, to evaluate which of the charges may be retained based upon the sufficiency of the evidence (para. 400).

The International Military Tribunal at Nuremberg convicted many of its defendants of both war crimes and crimes against humanity arising from the same conduct.

See *Prosecutor v. Tadić*, Decision on Defence Motion on Form of the Indictment, November 14, 1995, in which the Chamber left the issue of cumulative charging for consideration at the penalty stage of proceedings, stating that "what can, however, be stated with certainty is that penalty cannot be made to depend upon whether offences arising from the same conduct are alleged cumulatively or in the alternative. What is to be punished by penalty is proven criminal conduct and that will not depend upon technicalities of pleading." Also see, *Prosecutor v. Delalic*, Decision on Motion by the Accused Zejnil Delalic based on Defects in the Form of the Indictment, October 2, 1996, in which the Trial Chamber followed the Tadić Trial Chamber's reasoning.

(2) Conditions for cumulative charging

In *Prosecutor v. Kupreškić*, Decision on Defence Challenges to Form of **6–70** the Indictment, May 15, 1998, the Chamber examined the propriety of cumulative charging and held that it was permissible as long as the crimes charged in respect of the same conduct protect different values for society or contain different elements. The Chamber held that "the Prosecutor may be justified in bringing cumulative charges when the Articles of the Statute referred to are designed to protect different values and when each Article requires proof of a legal element not required by the others". In *Prosecutor v. Delalic*, Appeals Chamber Judgment, February 20, 2001, para. 412, the Appeals Chamber held that "reasons of fairness to the accused and the consideration that only distinct crimes may justify multiple convictions, lead to the conclusion that multiple criminal convictions entered under different statutory provisions but based on the same conduct are permissible only if each statutory provision involved has a materially distinct element not contained in the other. An element is materially distinct from another if it requires proof of a fact not required by the other."

The test for permitting cumulative charges to be included in an indictment in the ICTY jurisprudence differs slightly from that followed by the ICTR in *Prosecutor v. Akayesu*, September 2, 1998, paras 461 onwards. In that decision, the ICTR stated that such charging would, in addition to the circumstances recognised by the ICTY in *Kupreškić*, be permissible where it is "necessary to record a conviction for both offences in order fully to describe what the accused did". The ICTR Chamber held, unlike the ICTY Chamber in the *Kupreškić* decision, that if *any* of these conditions were met the Prosecutor might charge an accused cumulatively. In other words, the ICTR did not find that all three conditions had to be met conjunctively before the indictment could contain cumulative charges.

The *Akayesu Trial Chamber* stated, para. 468, as follows: "On the basis **6–71** of national and international law and jurisprudence, the Chamber concludes that it is acceptable to convict the accused of two offences in relation to the same set of facts in the following circumstances: (1) where the offences have different elements; or (2) where the provisions creating the offences protect different interests; or (3) where it is necessary to record a conviction for both offences in order fully to describe what the accused did. However, the Chamber finds that it is not justifiable to convict an accused of two offences in relation to the same set of facts where (a) one offence is a lesser included offence of the other, for example, murder and grievous bodily harm, robbery and theft, or rape and indecent assault; or (b) where one offence charges accomplice liability and the other offence charges liability as a principal, e.g. genocide and complicity in genocide." Note that in the subsequent decision of *Prosecutor v. Kayishema and Ruzindana*, May 21, 1999, para. 625 onwards, the ICTR did not follow the *Akayesu Trial Chamber* in accepting three alternative situations in which cumulative charging would be permissible. It relied only on the two conditions recognised in the ICTY jurisprudence, but like the *Akayesu Trial Chamber* recognised that these conditions could be disjunctive. See Judge Khan's Dissenting Opinion, para. 23, in which he held that "the line of international jurisprudence has evolved to hold that where the prosecution has charged such different crimes based upon the same facts, the matter falls for consideration once an accused is ultimately found guilty. And, the consequence of cumulative charging charges can suitably be dealt with at the stage of sentencing rather than at verdict." *See Prosecutor v. Rutuganda*, December 6, 1999 and *Prosecutor v. Musema*, January 27, 2000, in which the majority in both Chambers followed the approach set out above by Judge Khan in his dissenting opinion in *Prosecutor v. Kayishema and Ruzindana*, May 21, 1999.

6–72 In *Prosecutor v. Kupreškić*, January 14, 2000, para. 668 onwards, the ICTY Trial Chamber undertook a detailed inquiry into cumulative charging, examining both substantive and procedural questions. As regards charging murder under Article 3 on war crimes and Article 5(a) on crimes against humanity the Chamber stated that:

"Following the principles set out above, the relevant question here is whether murder as a war crime requires proof of facts which murder as a crime against humanity does not require, and *vice versa* (the *Blockburger* test). Another relevant question is whether the prohibition of murder as a war crime protects different values from those safeguarded by the prohibition of murder as a crime against humanity.

With regard to the former question, while murder as a crime against humanity requires proof of elements that murder as a war crime does not require (the offence must be part of a systematic or widespread attack on the civilian population), this is not reciprocated. As a result, the *Blockburger* test is not fulfilled, or in other words the two offences are not in a relationship of reciprocal speciality. The prohibition of murder as a crime against humanity is *lex specialis* in relation to the prohibition of murder as a war crime.

In addressing the latter question, it can generally be said that the substantive provisions of the Statute pursue the same general objective (deterring serious breaches of humanitarian law and, if these breaches are committed, punishing those responsible for them). In addition, they protect the same general values in that they are designed to ensure respect for human dignity. Admittedly, within this common general framework, Articles 3 and 5 may pursue some specific aims and protect certain specific values. Thus, for instance, the prohibition of war crimes aims at ensuring a minimum of humanitarian concern between belligerents as well as maintaining a distinction between combatants' behaviour toward enemy combatants and persons not participating in hostilities. The prohibition of crimes against humanity, on the other hand, is more focused on discouraging attacks on the civilian population and the persecution of identifiable groups of civilians.

However, as under Article 5 of the Statute crimes against humanity fall within the Tribunal's jurisdiction only when committed in armed conflict, the difference between the values protected by Article 3 and Article 5 would seem to be inconsequential.

As explained above, the validity of the criterion based on the difference in values protected is disputable if it is not also supported by reciprocal speciality between the two offences. It follows that, given also the marginal difference in values protected, the Trial Chamber may convict the Accused of violating the prohibition of murder as a crime against humanity only if it finds that the requirements of murder under both Article 3 and under Article 5 are proved.

See paras 713–719 regarding the implications of cumulative charging on sentencing by the Chambers (holding that an accused convicted on cumulative charges will serve the sentences concurrently, but that the

Chambers may aggravate the sentence for the more serious offence if it "considers that the less serious offence committed by the same conduct significantly adds to the heinous nature of the prevailing offence, for instance because the less serious offence is characterised by distinct, highly reprehensible elements of its own."

The Trial Chamber concluded that when the Prosecutor believes that **6–73** the facts simultaneously violate more than one provision in the Statute, the Prosecutor should set out charges under both (or more) provisions.

Trial Chambers have emphasised that the issue of cumulative charging must be resolved bearing in mind two considerations. The rights of the accused person must be safeguarded and the Prosecutor must be given all the powers the Statute permits, to enable him or her to fulfil his or her role efficiently and to serve the interests of justice. Consideration should therefore be given to the accused's right to be informed promptly and in detail of the nature and cause of the charges against him (Article 21(4)(a)) of the ICTY Statute, Article 20(4)(a) of the ICTR Statute and Article 17(4)(a) in the case of SCSL). In other instances when the facts appear to violate more than one provision, the Prosecutor should charge in the alternative rather than cumulatively. The Chamber advised that in cases of doubt the Prosecutor should suggest that conduct falls under a stricter and more serious provision of the Statute, adding however that in the event that proof thereof is unconvincing, the act falls under a less serious provision.

For arguments based on the idea that cumulative charging breaches the double jeopardy rule see *Prosecutor v. Krnojelac*, Decision on Defence Preliminary Motion on the Form of the Indictment, February 24, 1999, para. 5; and see *Prosecutor v. Akayesu*, September 2, 1998, para. 461.

E. OTHER CHALLENGES TO INDICTMENTS

In *Prosecutor v. Kordic*, Decision on the Joint Defence Motion to Strike **6–74** Counts 37 and 40 for Failure to Plead all the Required Elements under Article 2(D), March 2, 1999, para. 4, the Trial Chamber held that the "failure to allege specifically in the Amended Indictment that the destroyed property was protected under the Geneva Conventions does not render the Amended Indictment invalid, as the accused is charged with a 'grave breach as recognised by Article 2(d) . . . of the Statute', and the provisions of that Article, which include the element of protection of property, are therefore incorporated by reference in Counts 37 and 40".

In *Prosecutor v. Kunarac*, Decision on the Form of the Indictment, November 4, 1999, paras 16 and 17, one of the bases for challenging the form of the indictment related to the imprecision/vagueness of the alleged time periods. The Trial Chamber found that: "The time period in paragraph 11.5 of the Amended Indictment—'[o]n one occasion, during their detention [. . .]'—is too vague. For example, it is unclear whether the forced naked dancing took place before witness FWS-75 and victim A.B. were taken to the Hotel Zelengora around November 20, 1992 or on or after 'the night when FWS-75 and the other women' were brought back to the Brena apartment. Similarly, '[o]n the night when FWS-75 and the other women were brought back to the apartment', as well as '[i]n December 1992', when FWS-75 was allegedly handed over to Janko Janjic, are too vague."

In the same decision, para. 18, the Defence challenged the failure to identify two women victims in the indictment. The Trial Chamber upheld this challenge to the form of the indictment, finding that "the identity of the two women is necessary because it is a material fact to be proved at Trial". Further, the Defence asserted that "pursuant to the provisions of Rule 96(ii), the Prosecutor must state in the Amended Indictment 'in what manner were the victims exposed to violence, force, confinement and physical duress, threats' and, failing that, 'an important element of the criminal act is missing'" (para. 25). The Trial Chamber at para. 25, upheld the Defence's challenge, stating that "as the Prosecutor does rely upon the circumstances mentioned in Rule 96(ii), those circumstances, amongst others, constitute material allegations, particulars of which the accused is entitled to know in order to properly prepare his defence. The Amended Indictment as it stands, lacks such particulars."

If the Defence disagrees with the facts alleged in the indictment this is not a legitimate basis to object to the form of the indictment (see *Kvočka Trial Chamber*, Decision on Defence Preliminary Motions on the Form of the Indictment, April 12, 1999, para. 40; *Prosecutor v. Krnojelac*, Decision on Defence Preliminary Motion on the Form of the Indictment, February 24, 1999, para. 20, as well as *Prosecutor v. Delalic et al.*, Decision on Motion by the Accused Zejnil Delalic based on Defects in the Form of the Indictment, October 2, 1996, para. 10).

IV. AMENDMENT OF INDICTMENTS

A. GUIDING PRINCIPLES

ICCPR Requirements: Right to be informed of charges

6–75   The ad hoc Tribunals have had to balance the Prosecution's obligation to prosecute the most serious international crimes, which might require accommodating changes in prosecutorial strategy as well as amendments to indictments as a result of discovering new evidence, with guaranteeing the fairness of trial proceedings and upholding the rights of the accused. Whether a proposed amendment will impact on the accused's right to a fair trial is dependent on the stage in the proceedings at which an amendment is sought as well as the substance of the amendment. Other concerns might relate to the impact of amending an indictment on future cases. An amendment might require the application of Rule 50(C) of ICTY and ICTR for a trial date to be postponed to allow the Defence adequate time to prepare. Such a delay could affect upcoming trials. No such provision has been adopted at the SCSL.

In *Prosecutor v. Kovacevic*, Decision on Motion to Amend Indictment, March 5, 1998, para. 12, the Trial Chamber had to decide upon an application to amend the indictment which would have had serious consequences for the accused. The initial indictment contained a single count of complicity in genocide. The Prosecutor sought to amend the indictment to include 14 new counts for crimes under Articles 2, 3 and 5 of the Statute. The Trial Chamber rejected the application for leave to amend because it found that the amendments were so substantial that they would amount to a new indictment, and their inclusion would lead to delay in the proceedings. The Chamber held that to allow the amendments would prejudice the right of the accused to a fair and expeditious trial. The Appeals Chamber however allowed the Prosecution's appeal against this decision. In *Prosecutor v. Kovacevic*, Decision Stating Reasons for Appeals Chamber Order of May 29, 1998, July 2, 1998, paras 20–37, the Appeals Chamber stated that "no doubt, size can be taken into account in considering whether any injustice would be caused to the accused; but, provided other relevant requirements are met, a court would be slow to deny the prosecution a right to amend on that ground only. The Trial Chamber did not consider whether any possible injustice arising from size could be remedied by disallowing only some of the amendments, in which case, the prosecution could have been asked to indicate its preferences: it rejected the whole." The Appeals Chamber did not find the size of the amendments objectionable, and rejected the other contentions for denying leave to amend, in relation to delay in the proceedings (paras 26–33) and the infringement of the right to have charges disclosed promptly (paras 34-36). (Also see, *Prosecutor v. Kabiligi and Ntabakuze*, Decision on the Prosecutor's Motion to Amend the Indictment, October 8, 1999, para. 52, following the ruling in Kovacevic on the issue of the increased size of an indictment).

6–76

The Appeals Chamber in *Kovacevic*, para. 36, stated: "Whatever the true meaning of 'any' in Article 9(2) of the ICCPR, a point addressed by defence counsel, the Chamber does not accept that the requirement to inform an arrested person of any charges against him was breached in this case. Article 20, sub-paragraph 2 of the Statute of the International Tribunal is analogous to Article 9(2) of the ICCPR, requiring, however, that the person be 'immediately informed of the charges against him'. The Report of the Secretary-General submitting the draft Statute to the Security Council, referring to that Article, states that '[a] person against whom an indictment has been confirmed would . . . be informed of the contents of the indictment and taken into custody'. That is consistent with the view that what was visualised was that an arrested person would be promptly told of the charges contained in the indictment on the basis of which he was arrested. That was done in this case." Also see, *Separate Opinion of Judge Shahabuddeen* in which he differs with the majority on the point of whether there had been a failure to disclose the charges promptly. He interpreted the requirement that an accused be informed of any charges against him in Article 9(2) of the ICCPR to mean all charges and not some charges.

Unfair Prejudice

It appears from several decisions that the fundamental issue in deciding whether to grant leave to amend an indictment is whether the amendment is, taking all circumstances into account, unfairly prejudi-

6–77

cial to the accused. In assessing unfair prejudice the Chambers consider, *inter alia*, (1) the potential of the amended indictment to improve clarity and precision of the case to be met; (2) the diligence of the prosecution in amending the indictment; and (3) any undue delay or prejudice imposed on the defence by adopting the amendment indictment: *Prosecutor v. Karemera*, Decision on Severance of Andre Rwamakuba and for Leave to File Amended Indictment, February 14, 2005, para. 35; *Prosecutor v. Mpambara*, March 4, 2005, para. 8. In the process of considering these factors, the Chambers follow the procedures and apply the standards set out in Rules 47(E) and (F). In addition to the factors, set out above, these Rules require consideration of the establishment of a *prima facie* case (*Prosecutor v. Zigiranyirazo*, Decision on the Prosecution Conditional Motion for Leave to Amend the Indictment and on the Defence Counter-Motion Objecting to the Form of the Recast Indictment, March 2, 2005, para. 12).

In *Prosecutor v. Ndindliyimana et al.*, Decision on Prosecutor's Motion Under Rule 50 for Leave to Amend the Indictment Issued on January 20, 2000 and Confirmed on January 28, 2000, March 26, 2004, para. 42, the Trial Chamber sets out in detail the relevant circumstances to consider when balancing the prosecution's right to seek an amendment of the indictment, pursuant to Rule 50, with the possible adverse effect on the accused's right to a fair trial. The Trial Chamber mentioned as non-exhaustive examples of relevant circumstances: (i) the effect of the proposed amended indictment on the right to an expeditious trial, to prompt notices of the charges against them, and to adequate time and facilities in order to prepare their defence; (ii) whether any additional time can be granted to the accused for the preparation of their defence; (iii) reasonableness of resulting delays in the scheduled start day of trial, and the length of the trial itself; (iv) effect on the time spent by the Accused in pre-trial detention; (v) nature and scope of the proposed amendment; (vi) whether the accused and Trial Chamber had prior notice of the Prosecutor's intention to seek leave to amend the indictment, the nature of the notice, and any improper tactical advantage gained by the prosecution as a result of the proposed amended Indictment; (vii) the evidentiary basis of the new charges, if any, and the timing of their discovery; (viii) judicial economy; and (ix) whether the proposed amended indictment, through more specificity and accuracy, allows the accused to better respond and prepare for trial, or shortens the length of the trial proceedings, thus protecting rather than prejudicing the accused persons' rights to a fair trial.

The Prosecution may offer substantial amendments and is thereby not required to show that it cannot proceed on the existing indictment (*Prosecutor v. Karemera et al.*, Decision on Prosecutor's Interlocutory Appeal Against Trial Chamber III Decision of October 8, 2003 Denying Leave to File an Amended Indictment, December 19, 2003, paras 11–12). As clearly established above, the Chambers are led by the principle of fairness to the accused in deciding whether to grant leave to amend an indictment. Any adverse impact on fairness to the accused may be remedied by giving him adequate time to prepare his defence of the amended case and investigate the new facts (*Prosecutor v. Zigiranyerazo*, Decision on Prosecutor's Request for Leave to Amend the Indictment and on Defence Urgent Motion for an Order to Disclose Supporting Material in Respect of the Prosecutor's Motion for Leave to Amend the

Indictment, October 15, 2003, para. 19; *Prosecutor v. Ndindliyimana et al.*, Decision on Prosecutor's Motion Under Rule 50 for Leave to Amend the Indictment Issued on January 20, 2000 and Confirmed on January 28, 2000, March 26, 2004, para. 55).

Where amendments sharpen and clarify the indictment, thereby increasing fairness and efficiency, they should be granted and, generally speaking, even encouraged (*Prosecutor v. Karemera et al.*, Decision on the Prosecutor's Motion for Leave to Amend the Indictment, February 13, 2004, para. 46. Also see *Prosecutor v. Muhimana*, Decision on Motion to Amend Indictment, January 21, 2004, where leave to amend was granted because the proposed indictment provided a more detailed and comprehensive account of the criminal acts alleged and the Prosecution theory of criminal liability, and accordingly, the amendment improved the fairness of the trial). However, the question is when such is the case. In *Prosecutor v. Bizimungu et al.*, Decision on Prosecutor's Interlocutory Appeal Against Trial Chamber II Decision of October 6, 2003 Denying Leave to File Amended Indictment, February 12, 2004, leave to amend the indictment was denied because the amended indictment aimed to expand the theory of the accused's liability from the originally confirmed indictment, which risks to be prejudicial.

Undue Delay

In *Prosecutor v. Karemera et al.*, Decision on Prosecutor's Interlocutory **6–78** Appeal Against Trial Chamber III Decision of October 8, 2003 Denying Leave to File an Amended Indictment, December 19, 2003, the Appeals Chamber, while confirming the Trial Chamber's decision to grant leave to the prosecution to amend the indictment, set out the general principle that the right of an accused to be tried without delay is one of the factors to be taken into consideration, but that this factor has to be assessed in context of the effect on the overall proceedings. An unjustifiable loss of time certainly negates the granting of leave to amend the indictment (*Prosecutor v. Karemera et al.*, Decision on the Prosecutor's Motion for Leave to Amend the Indictment, February 13, 2004, para. 41). However, in situations where the amended indictment will streamline the case, while causing the initial delay, the Trial Chamber should grant leave to amend the indictment.

Lack of Due Diligence

The lack of diligence of the Prosecution in amending an indictment is **6–79** an important factor to be considered in whether to grant leave to amend. The Prosecution should not attempt to include new allegations in an amended indictment where the allegations are, in fact, not new but, with due diligence, could have been found and charged in the confirmed indictment (*Prosecutor v. Karemera et al.*, Decision on the Prosecutor's Motion for Leave to Amend the Indictment, February 13, 2004, para. 25. Also see: *Prosecutor v. Muvunyi*, Decision on the Prosecutor's Motion for Leave to Amend the Indictment, February 24, 2005, paras 46–47, where the Trial Chamber held that the Prosecution lacked due diligence in failing to seek amendment earlier, a failure which was unjustifiable). Moreover, the Prosecution cannot gain a strategic advantage by holding an amendment in abeyance while the defence spends time and resources preparing for allegations the Prosecution no longer intend to pursue. "Strategic efforts to undermine the conduct of proceedings cannot be tolerated, especially if designed to disadvantage the ability of the defence to respond to the Prosecution's case." *Prosecutor v. Karemera et al.*, Decision on Prosecutor's Interlocutory Appeal Against Trial Chamber III Decision of October 8, 2003 Denying Leave to File an Amended Indictment, December 19, 2003, para 20. Also see *Prosecutor v. Mpambara*, Decision on the Prosecution's Request for Leave to File an Amended Indictment, March 4, 2005, para. 15, where it was held that strategic advantage cannot be a reason for the Prosecution to delay giving notice of their intention to amend the indictment. Lack of due diligence will, however, not result in rejection of leave to amend the indictment where the amendment would enhance the overall fairness of the trial by providing more particulars (*Prosecutor v. Mpambara*, March 4, 2005, para. 8).

The stage of the proceedings is influential in determining whether an amendment of the indictment is acceptable. In *Prosecutor v. Bikindi*, Decision on the Defence Motion Challenging the Temporal Jurisdiction of the Tribunal and Objecting to the Form of the Indictment and the Prosecutor's Motion Seeking Leave to File an Amended Indictment, September 22, 2003, para. 29, the Trial Chamber held that the mere adding of an alternative charge of complicity and three paragraphs of new facts does not unduly prejudice the accused where the case is not yet scheduled for trial. In *Prosecutor v. Muvunyi*, Decision on the Prosecutor's Motion for Leave to Amend the Indictment, February 24, 2005, para. 48, the Trial Chamber held that amending the indictment on the eve of trial would cause substantial prejudice to the accused and his right to prepare his defence, and would likely prolong his pre-trial detention.

Discovery of Further Crimes

6–80   An indictment might require amendment because an investigation is not static and could lead to the uncovering of further crimes that have to be included in the indictment (which was regarded as an acceptable ground to amend the indictment in *Prosecutor v. Renzaho*, Decision Sur La Requête du Procureur Demandant L'Autorisation de Déposer un Acte d'Accusation Modifié, March 18, 2005), or lead to the withdrawal of other charges although there is no need for an amendment of the indictment in case of the latter. The Prosecution can simply announce in its opening statement that it does not intend to present evidence on those charges: *Prosecutor v. Muvunyi*, Decision on the Prosecutor's Motion for Leave to Amend the Indictment, February 23, 2005, para. 31.

In *Prosecutor v. Niyitegeka*, Decision on Prosecutor's Request for Leave to File an Amended Indictment, June 21, 2000, the Trial Chamber stated at para. 33, that "in general, an amendment to a confirmed existing Indictment is sought for the following reasons: to add new charges to a confirmed Indictment, to expand and elaborate upon factual allegations adduced in support of existing confirmed counts, or to make minor changes to the indictment". (Also see, *Prosecutor v. Kajelijeli*, Decision on Prosecutor's Motion to Correct the Indictment dated December 22, 2000 and Motion for Leave to File an Amended Indictment; Warning to the Prosecutor's Counsels pursuant to Rule 46(a), January 25, 2001, para. 24).

For the general principles governing the amendment of indictments before the East Timor Special Panel for Serious Crimes see *Lino de Carvalho v. Prosecutor*, Judgment, Court of Appeal of East Timor, October 29, 2001.

B. PRE-TRIAL PROCEDURE

The decision to apply to amend an indictment lies within the **6–81** Prosecutor's discretion. A Trial Chamber may only "express its belief and invite the Prosecutor to amend should he share such belief" (see *Prosecutor v. Nikolic*, Decision of Trial Chamber I, Review of Indictment Pursuant to Rule 61, October 20, 1995, para. 32. Also see, *Prosecutor v. Akayesu*, Motion for Leave to Amend the Indictment, October 3, 1997). In that decision, the ICTR stated that the Prosecutor has no obligation to transmit to the Defence the request to amend the indictment during the pre-trial stage. In practice applications to amend indictments before trial are heard *ex parte*. The ruling suggests that the application is *ex parte*.

Prior to the amendment of Rule 50 of the ICTR Rules, which was adopted on April 24, 2004, the standard of proof, law and jurisprudence of the ICTR and ICTY differed on the application of the amendment procedure.

Pursuant to Rule 50 of the ICTY Rules, leave to amend an indictment shall not be granted unless the Trial Chamber or Judge is satisfied there is evidence which satisfies the standard set forth in Article 19, paragraph 1, of the Statute to support the proposed amendment. A Trial Chamber may want to verify, with the assistance of the witnesses' statements pointed out by the Prosecution, that there is evidence to support the amendment which would satisfy the standard set forth in Article 19. For this reason, the Prosecution may be directed to provide the statements to the Trial Chamber (*Prosecutor v. Mrkšić et al.*, Decision on Form of Second Modified Consolidated Amended Indictment, October 29, 2004, para. 25.) Leave to amend an indictment would not ordinarily be granted unless there is *prima facie* evidence available to support the additional matter or charge. In such cases, the test for granting leave to amend is the same as for confirmation of an indictment (*Prosecutor v. Mejakić et al.*, Order on Prosecution's Motion to Amend Consolidated Indictment Schedules A through F, The Rule 65*ter* Witness Summaries, and the Pre-Trial Brief Incident Summaries, October 26, 2004, p. 2; *Prosecutor v. Milošević et al.*, Decision on Application to Amend Indictment and on Confirmation of Amended Indictment, Confirming Judge, June 29, 2001, para. 3).

Before its amendment was incorporated, Rule 50 of the ICTR Rules did not lay down any specific standard of proof for the amendment of an indictment. A Trial Chamber did not need to be satisfied that a *prima facie* case existed against the accused for the new charges. However the Prosecutor needed to demonstrate that there were sufficient grounds both in fact and law to allow the amendments (Rule 50 of the ICTR *Prosecutor v. Kabiligi and Ntabakuze*, Decision on the Prosecutor's Motion to Amend the Indictment, October 8, 1999, paras. 42–43). A Trial Chamber seized with a motion requesting leave to amend an indictment, pursuant to Rule 50, against an accused who had already been indicted, had no cause to inquire into a *prima facie* basis for the proposed amendments to the indictment.

In considering the Prosecutor's request for leave to file an amended indictment pursuant to Rule 50, it used to be sufficient for the Prosecutor to establish the factual basis and the legal motivation in support of the motion (*Prosecutor v. Niyitegeka*, Decision on Prosecutor's Request for Leave to File an Amended Indictment, T. Ch. II, June 21, 2000, paras. 43–45; *Prosecutor v. Barayagwiza*, Decision on the Prosecutor's Request for Leave to File an Amended Indictment, April 11, 2000, p. 3).

Since the adoption of the amendment to ICTR Rule 50 on April 24, 2004, this Rule is now similar to ICTY Rule 50 and asks for consideration of a *prima facie* case. Since this amendment, the Trial Chambers at the ICTR indeed assess whether the Prosecutor established a *prima facie* case in relation to the proposed amendments (for example, *Prosecutor v. Zigiranyirazo*, Decision on the Prosecution Conditional Motion for Leave to Amend the Indictment and on the Defence Counter-Motion Objecting to the Form of the Recast Indictment, March 2, 2005, para. 12; *Prosecutor v. Karemera*, Decision on Prosecution Motion for Leave to File Amended Indictment and Filing of Further Supporting Material, Rule 47(E), 47(F) and 50(A) of the Rules of Procedure and Evidence, February 18, 2005).

Moreover, the Prosecutor has the burden to establish that a proposed amendment of the indictment is in the interest of justice. The interest of justice is evaluated on the basis of factors, such as, the rights of the accused to be fully informed of the charges against him, have adequate time and resources for the preparation of his defence, and to be tried without undue delay: *Prosecutor v. Muvunyi*, Decision on the Prosecutor's Motion for Leave to Amend the Indictment, February 24, 2005, paras 26–27.

Similiar principles apply at the SCSL.

(1) Before confirmation

6–82   The ICTY, ICTR and SCSL Rules provide that before an indictment has been confirmed by the confirming Judge the indictment may be amended by the Prosecutor at any time without leave: see Rule 50(A)(i)(a), Rule 50(A) and 50(A), respectively.

(2) After confirmation

6–83   Once the indictment has been confirmed, but before the case has been assigned to a Trial Chamber, Rule 50(A)(i)(b) of the ICTY permits amendment with leave of the confirming Judge or another

Judge assigned by the President. As for the ICTR and SCSL, Rule 50(A) provides that after confirmation, until the initial appearance of the accused before the Trial Chamber in terms of Rule 62, leave to amend may only be granted by the confirming Judge or another Judge assigned by the President, but only in exceptional circumstances. At or after such initial appearance, an amendment of an indictment may only be made by leave granted by a Trial Chamber.

Once an indictment has been confirmed, a Prosecutor may not amend the indictment without prior judicial approval (see *Prosecutor v. Kajelijeli*, Decision on Prosecutor's Motion to Correct the Indictment dated December 22, 2000 and Motion For Leave to File an Amended Indictment; Warning to the Prosecutor's Counsels Pursuant to Rule 46(a), January 25, 2001, para. 18). The Trial Chamber also warned that once leave to correct or amend is given, the correction or amendment may not go beyond what was permitted or directed by the Trial Chamber; also see *Prosecutor v. Krnojelac*, Decision on Prosecutor's Response to Decision of February 24, 1999, May 20, 1999, para. 9.

C. PROCEDURE AT TRIAL STAGE

6–84 Once a case has been assigned to a Chamber, an indictment may only be amended with leave of the Trial Chamber or Judge of that Trial Chamber once the parties have been heard (ICTY Rule 50(A)(i)(c)). For the ICTR and SCSL, Rule 50(A) requires that the Trial Chamber grant leave to amend after the initial appearance of the accused. Once a case has been assigned to a Trial Chamber, the amended indictment does not need to be confirmed (ICTY Rule 50(A)(ii)).

The parties have an opportunity to be heard when amendment is sought under ICTY Rule 50(A)(i)(c) as it could affect the accused's case and preparation of his defence. Rule 50(B) of the ICTY, ICTR and SCSL also provides that the accused plead to any new charges before the Trial Chamber. Under Rule 50(C) of the ICTY and ICTR, the accused has 30 days in which to file preliminary motions under Rule 72, for example, motions alleging defects in the form of the new indictment. Where necessary, the trial date may be postponed to allow the accused to prepare his defence on the new charges (see Rule 50(C)). While, under Rule 50(C) of the SCSL Rules, the accused only has ten days in which to file preliminary motions; no provisions are made for the postponement.

V. WITHDRAWAL OF INDICTMENTS

6–85 Under Rule 51(A) of the ICTY and ICTR and Rule 50 of the SCSL Rules, leave can be granted to withdraw an indictment, depending on the stage when leave is sought. The Rule provides that the Prosecutor may withdraw an indictment without prior leave at any time before confirmation of an indictment.

(1) Withdrawal after confirmation

6–86   Rule 51(A) of the ICTY and ICTR requires that once the indictment
has been confirmed and until the initial appearance of the accused
before the Trial Chamber pursuant to Rule 62, it may only be
withdrawn with leave of the confirming Judge. Rule 51(A) of the ICTR
stipulates that in exceptional circumstances another Judge appointed
by the President may grant such leave. Rule 51(B) of the SCSL Rules
governs such withdrawals. It allows the Prosecutor to withdraw an
indictment upon providing to the Trial Chamber in open court a
statement of the reasons for the withdrawal.

Applications for leave to withdraw indictments prior to the initial
appearance have been made in the following cases: *Prosecutor v. Alilovic*,
Decision on Motion by the Prosecutor for Withdrawal of Indictment
Against Stipo Alilovic, December 23, 1997 (on the basis of the death of
the accused—granted) and Order Granting Leave for Withdrawal of
Charges against Govedarica, Gruban, Janjic, Kostic, Paspalj, Popovic,
Predojevic, Savic, Babic, and Saponja, May 8, 1998 and Order Granting
leave for Withdrawal of Charges against Janic, Kondic, Lajic, Saponja
and Timarac, May 5, 1998 (on the basis of the death of Janic and on the
grounds of the appropriateness of prosecution of other accused in a
national court rather than before the ICTY as part of a revision of
Prosecution strategy when faced with a large increase in the number of
arrests and voluntary surrenders, and considering the Tribunals'
resources).

In *Prosecutor v. Strugar et al.*, Order Authorising the Withdrawal of the
Charges Against Milan Zec Without Prejudice, July 26, 2001, the Judge,
assigned by the President, authorised the Prosecutor to withdraw all
charges in the Indictment against Milan Zec "without future prejudice". The Prosecutor in her motion had indicated that "additional
evidence obtained during investigations conducted after the indictment
was confirmed to have revealed that the Prosecution's evidence is, at
this stage, insufficient to sustain the charges against the accused".

In *Prosecutor v. Ntuyahaga*, Decision on the Prosecutor's Motion to
Withdraw the Indictment, March 18, 1999, the Trial Chamber granted
the Prosecutor's request to withdraw the indictment against the
accused Ntuyahaga despite the fact that the Defence opposed such
withdrawal on the ground that they wished for the Trial Chamber to
make a determination on the innocence of the accused. The Belgium
government had shown an interest to initiate criminal proceedings
against Ntuyahaga and appeared as an *Amicus Curiae* in the hearing of
March 16, 1999 on the Prosecutor's request for withdrawal of the
indictment. The Trial Chamber rejected the Prosecutor's submissions
that the request should be granted on the ground that this would
promote the exercise of concurrent jurisdiction by Belgium; on the
contrary, the Trial Chamber emphasised the Tribunal's primacy. Nevertheless, the Trial Chamber granted the motion acknowledging the
Prosecutor's sole responsibility to decide whether or not to initiate and
proceed with criminal investigations. Consequently, the immediate
release of the accused from the Tribunal's Detention Facilities was
ordered. On its own initiative the Registrar provided the Government
of Tanzania with a document titled "Safe Conduct" requesting "Mem-

ber States of the United Nations, other States, International Organizations and all other persons to whom it may concern, to accord safe conduct to Bernard Ntuyahaga and extend to him any necessary cooperation to enable him to move freely in or transit through, without let or hindrance, any country to his final destination, in accordance with the relevant provisions of International Law". The Prosecutor filed a motion requesting the Chamber to rescind this "Safe Conduct" document on the ground that the Registrar had no authority to issue such a document. The Trial Chamber agreed that the Registrar went beyond its vested powers in issuing the said document, and was anxious that this Registrar's initiative would not set a precedent. The Chamber nonetheless held that the Prosecutor had no standing in bringing her motion because the case was closed before the Tribunal and the authorities of Tanzania had refrained from acting on the Registrar's request and had arrested the released accused (Declaration on a Point of Law by Judge Laíty Kama, President of the Tribunal, Judge Lennard Aspegren and Judge Navanethem Pillay, April 22, 1999).

In *Prosecutor v. Rusatira*, Decision on the Prosecutor's *Ex Parte* Application for Leave to Withdraw the Indictment, August 14, 2002, the Trial Chamber granted the Prosecutor's request to withdraw the indictment against the accused Rusatira because there was insufficient evidence against him but left open to the Prosecutor the possibility to seek "the confirmation of another indictment against him, based on new or additional evidence".

(2) Withdrawal after initial appearance

At or after the initial appearance of the accused before the Trial Chamber, an indictment may only be withdrawn when leave is granted by the Trial Chamber pursuant to Rule 73 on motions for other relief. At the SCSL according to Rule 51(C), the indictment could be withdrawn only by leave granted by the Trial Chamber. In *Prosecutor v. Dukic*, Decision Rejecting the Application to Withdraw the Indictment and Order for Provisional Release, April 24, 1996, the proceedings were held to be at the trial stage because the accused had made an initial appearance before the Trial Chamber. This decision followed an earlier decision in which an application for leave to withdraw had been made to the confirming Judge, Judge Karibi-Whyte, who had declined jurisdiction because the matter was at trial.

6–87

Although the Prosecutor has a discretion to decide when to apply for leave to withdraw an indictment, it is not unfettered. As a *prima facie* case has to be established against an accused before confirmation of an indictment, the confirming Judge or Trial Chamber would have to determine whether there are legitimate reasons for granting leave to withdraw an indictment.

Applications for leave to withdraw indictments have been made in the following cases: *Prosecutor v. Dukic*, Decision Rejecting the Application to Withdraw the Indictment and Order for Provisional Release, April 24, 1996 (on the grounds of the ill-health of the accused, but rejected by the Chamber as a basis for withdrawal); *Prosecutor v. Alilovic*, Decision on Motion by the Prosecutor for Withdrawal of Indictment

Against Stipo Alilovic, December 23, 1997 (on the basis of the death of the accused—granted); *Prosecutor's Motion under Rule 51 for leave to withdraw the Indictment against the accused Marinko Katava*, December 18, 1997; *Prosecutor's Motion under Rule 51 for Leave to Withdraw the indictment against the Accused Ivan Santic*, December 18, 1997;*Prosecutor's Motion under Rule 51 for leave to Withdraw the Indictment against the accused Pero Skopljak*, December 18, 1997 (on the basis of insufficient evidence to justify criminal proceedings against an accused—all granted). A withdrawal of an indictment can also be applied for as a result of a plea agreement, as occurred in *Prosecutor v. Todorovic*, Decision on Prosecution Motion to Withdraw Counts of the Indictment and Defence Motion to Withdraw Pending Motions, February 26, 2001. In *Prosecutor v. Nenad Banović*, Decision on Motion by the Prosecutor for Withdrawal of Indictment against Nenad Banović, April 10, 2002, the Trial Chamber granted the Prosecution's application to withdraw the indictment on the grounds that there was insufficient evidence to proceed to trial against the accused on the significant changes in the indictment. In relation to the withdrawal of charges when an impartial investigation shows the charges to be unfounded, see Article 14 of the Guidelines on the Role of Prosecutors adopted by the Eighth United Nations Congress on the Prevention of Crime and Treatment of Offenders in 1990, UN Doc A/CONF.144/28, ch. 1 (1990).

CHAPTER 7

PRE-TRIAL PROCEDURE

I. INVESTIGATIONS

The starting point of any proceedings before international criminal courts is the investigation stage. The Prosecutor is primarily responsible for investigating and conducting investigations.

A. DUTIES AND POWERS OF THE PROSECUTOR

(1) Statutory provisions and rules

ICC

Statute of the ICC, Arts 15, 53, 54

The Prosecutor

15.—1. The prosecutor may initiate investigations *proprio motu* on the basis of information on crimes within the jurisdiction of the Court.   **7–1**

221

2. The Prosecutor shall analyse the seriousness of the information received. For this purpose, he or she may seek additional information from States, organs of the United Nations, intergovernmental and non-governmental organizations, or other reliable sources that he or she deems appropriate, and may receive written or oral testimony at the seat of the Court.

3. If the Prosecutor concludes that there is reasonable basis to proceed with an investigation, he or she shall submit to the Pre-Trial Chamber a request for authorization of an investigation, together with any supporting material collected. Victims may make representations to the Pre-Trial Chamber, in accordance with the Rules of Procedure and Evidence.

4. If the Pre-Trial Chamber, upon examination of the request and the supporting material, considers that there is reasonable basis to proceed with an investigation, and that the case appears to fall within the jurisdiction of the Court, it shall authorize the commencement of the investigation, without prejudice to subsequent determination by the Court with regard to jurisdiction and admissibility of a case.

5. The refusal of Pre-Trial Chamber to authorise the investigation shall not preclude the presentation of a subsequent request by the Prosecutor based on new facts of evidence regarding the same situation.

6. If, after the preliminary examination referred in paragraph 1 and 2, the Prosecutor concludes that the information provided does not constitute a reasonable basis for an investigation, he or she shall inform those who provided the information. This shall not preclude the Prosecutor from considering further information submitted to him or her regarding the same situation in the light of new facts or evidence.

Initiation of an investigation

7–2   **53.**—1. The Prosecutor shall, having evaluated the information made available to him or her, initiate an investigation unless he or she determines that there is no reasonable basis to proceed under this Statute. In deciding whether to initiate an investigation, the Prosecutor shall consider whether:

    (a) The information available to the Prosecutor provides a reasonable basis to believe that a crime within the jurisdiction of the Court has been or is being committed;

    (b) The case is or would be admissible under article 17;

    (c) Taking into account the gravity of the crime and the interests of the victims, there are nonetheless substantial reasons to believe that an investigation would not serve the interests of justice.

7–3   2. If, upon investigation, the Prosecutor concludes that there is not a sufficient basis for a prosecution because:

    (a) There is no sufficient legal or factual basis to seek warrant or summons under article 58;

    (b) The case is inadmissible under article 17;

    (c) A prosecution is not in the interest of justice, taking into account all the circumstances, including the gravity of the crime, the interest of victims and the age or infirmity of the alleged perpetrator, and his role in the alleged crime; under article 14 or the Security Council in a case under article 13, paragraph (b), of his or her conclusion and the reasons for the conclusion.

    (d) At the request of the State making a referral under article 14 or the Security Council under article 13, paragraph (b) the Pre-Trial Chamber may review a decision of the Prosecutor under paragraph 1 or 2 not to proceed and may request the Prosecutor to reconsider that decision.

3. In addition, the Pre-Trial Chamber may, on its own initiative, review a decision of the Prosecutor not to proceed if it is based solely on paragraph 1 (c) or 2 (c). In such a case, the decision of the Prosecutor shall be effective only if confirmed by the Pre-Trial Chamber.

4. The Prosecutor may, at any time, reconsider a decision whether to initiate an investigation or prosecution based on new facts or information.

Duties and powers of the Prosecutor with respect to investigations
54.—1. The Prosecutor shall: **7–4**
   (a) In order to establish the truth, extend the investigation to cover all facts and evidence relevant to an assessment of whether there is criminal responsibility under this Statute, and, in doing so, investigate incriminating and exonerating circumstances equally;
   (b) Take appropriate measures to ensure the effective investigation and prosecution of crimes within the jurisdiction of the Court, and in doing so, respect the interests and personal circumstances of victims and witnesses, including age, gender as defined in article 7, paragraph 3, and health, and take into account the nature of the crime, in particular where it involves sexual violence, gender violence or violence against children; and
   (c) Fully respect the rights of persons arising under this Statute.
2. The Prosecutor may conduct investigations on the territory of a State:
   (a) In accordance with the provisions of Part 9; or
   (b) As authorized by the Pre-Trial Chamber under article 57, paragraph 3 (d).
3. The Prosecutor may:
   (a) Collect and examine evidence;
   (b) Request the presence of and question persons being investigated, victims and witnesses;
   (c) Seek the cooperation of any State or intergovernmental organization or arrangement in accordance with its respective competence and/or mandate;
   (d) Enter into such arrangements or agreements, not inconsistent with this Statute, as may be necessary to facilitate the cooperation of a State, intergovernmental organization or person;
   (e) Agree not to disclose, at any stage of the proceedings, documents or information that the Prosecutor obtains on the condition of confidentiality and solely for the purpose of generating new evidence, unless the provider of the information consents; and
   (f) Take necessary measures, or request that necessary measures be taken, to ensure the confidentiality of information, the protection of any person or the preservation of evidence.

ICC Rules of Procedure and Evidence, rr. 46, 47, 48, 62, 104, 105

Information provided to the Prosecutor under Article 15, paragraphs 1 and 2
46. Where information is submitted under article 15, paragraph 1, or where   **7–5**
oral or written testimony is received pursuant to article 15, paragraph 2, at the seat of the Court, the Prosecutor shall protect the confidentiality of such information and testimony or take any other necessary measures, pursuant to his/her duties under the Statute.

Testimony under Article 15, paragraph 2
47.—1. The provisions of rules 111 and 112 shall apply, *mutatis mutandis*, to   **7–6**
testimony received by the Prosecutor pursuant to article 15, paragraph 2.
2. When the Prosecutor considers that there is a serious risk that it might not be possible for the testimony to be taken subsequently, he/she may request the Pre-Trial Chamber to take such measures as may be necessary to ensure

the efficiency and integrity of the proceedings and, in particular, to appoint a counsel or a judge from the Pre-Trial Chamber to be present during the taking of the testimony in order to protect the rights of the defence. If the Testimony is subsequently presented in the proceedings, its admissibility shall be governed by article 69, and given such weight as determined by the relevant Chamber.

Determination of reasonable basis to proceed with an investigation under Article 15, paragraph 3

7–7   **48.** In determining whether there is reasonable basis to proceed with an investigation under article 15, paragraph 3, the Prosecutor shall consider the factors set out in article 53, paragraph 1 (a) to (c).

Proceedings under Article 19, paragraph 10

7–8   **62.**—1. If the Prosecutor makes a request under article 19, paragraph 10, he/she shall make the request to the Chamber that made the latest ruling on admissibility. The provisions of rules 58, 59 and 61 shall be applicable.

2. The State or States whose challenge to admissibility under article 19, paragraph 2, provoked the decision of inadmissibility provided for in article 19, paragraph 10, shall be notified of the request of the Prosecutor and shall be given a time-limit within which to make representations.

Evaluation of information by the Prosecutor

7–9   **104.**—1. In acting pursuant to article 53, paragraph 1, the Prosecutor shall, in evaluating the information made available to him/her, analyse the seriousness of the information received.

2. For the purposes of sub-rule 1, the Prosecutor may seek additional information from States, organs of the United Nations, intergovernmental and non-governmental organisations, or other reliable sources that he/she deems appropriate, and may receive written or oral testimony at the seat of the Court. The procedure set out in rule 47 shall apply to the receiving of such testimony.

Notification of a decision by the Prosecutor not to initiate an investigation

7–10   **105.**—1. When the Prosecutor decides not to initiate an investigation under article 53, paragraph 1, he/she shall promptly inform in writing the State or States that referred a situation under article 14, or the Security Council in respect of the situation covered by article 13, paragraph (b).

2. When the Prosecutor decides not to submit to the Pre-Trial Chamber a request for authorization of an investigation, rule 49 shall apply.

3. The notification referred to in sub-rule 1 shall contain the conclusion of the Prosecution and, having regard to article 68, paragraph 1, the reasons for the conclusion.

4. After the first appearance, a request for interim release must be made in writing. The Prosecutor shall be given notice of such a request. The Pre-Trial Chamber shall decide after having received observations in writing of the Prosecutor and the detained person. The Pre-Trial Chamber may decide to hold a hearing, at the request of the Prosecutor or the detained person or on its own initiative. A hearing must be held at least once every year.

ICTY

Statute of the ICTY, Arts 16, 18

The Prosecutor

7–11   **16.**—1. The Prosecutor shall be responsible for the investigation and the prosecution of persons responsible for serious violations of international humanitarian law committed in the territory of the former Yugoslavia since January 1991.

2. The Prosecutor shall act independently as a separate organ of the International Tribunal. He or she shall not seek or receive instruction from any Government or from any other source.

3. The office of the Prosecutor shall be composed of a Prosecutor and such other qualified stuff as may be required.

4. The Prosecutor shall be appointed by the Security Council on nomination by the Secretary-General. He or she shall be of a high moral character and posses the highest level of competence and experience in the conduct of investigation and prosecutions of criminal cases. The Prosecutor shall serve a four-year term and be eligible for re-appointment. The terms and conditions of service of the Prosecutor shall be those of an Under-Secretary-General of the United Nations.

5. The staff of the Office of the Prosecutor shall be appointed by the Secretary-General on the recommendation of the Prosecutor.

Investigation and preparation of indictment

18.—1. The prosecutor shall initiate investigations ex-officio or on the basis of information obtained from any source, particularly from Governments, United Nations organs, intergovernmental and non-governmental organisations. The Prosecutor shall assess the information received or obtained and decide whether there is sufficient basis to proceed.   **7–12**

2. The Prosecutor shall have the power to question suspects, victims and witnesses, to collect evidence and to conduct on-site investigations. In carrying out these tasks, the Prosecutor may, as appropriate, seek the assistance of the State authorities concerned.

3. If questioned, the suspect shall be entitled to be assisted by counsel of his own choice, including the right to have legal assistance assigned to him without payment by him in any case if he does not have sufficient means to pay for it, as well as to necessary translation into and from a language he speaks and understands.

4. Upon a determination that a *prima facie* case exists, the Prosecutor shall prepare and indictment containing a concise statement of the facts and the crime or crimes with which the accused is charged under the Statute. The Indictment shall be transmitted to a judge of the Trial Chamber.

ICTY Rules of Evidence and Procedure, rr. 8, 9, 39, 40, 41, 47

Request for information

8. Where it appears to the Prosecutor that a crime within the jurisdiction of the Tribunal is or has been the subject of investigations or criminal proceedings instituted in the courts of any State, the Prosecutor may request the State to forward all relevant information in that respect, and the State shall transmit such information to the Prosecutor forthwith in accordance with article 29 of the Statute.   **7–13**

Prosecutor's request for deferral

9. Where it appears to the Prosecutor that in any such investigations or criminal proceedings instituted in the courts of any State: **7–14**

   (i) The act being investigated or which is the subject of those proceedings is characterized as an ordinary crime;

  (ii) There is a lack of impartiality or independence, or the investigations or proceedings are designed to shield the accused from international criminal responsibility, or the case is not diligently prosecuted; or

 (iii) What is issued is closely related to, or otherwise involves, significant factual or legal questions which may have implications for investigations or prosecutions before the Tribunal;

The Prosecutor may propose to the Trial Chamber designated by the President that a formal request be made that such court defer to the competence of the Tribunal.

Conduct of investigations

7–15   **39.** In the conduct of an investigation, the Prosecutor may:
  (i) Summon and question suspects, victims and witnesses and record their statements, collect evidence and conduct on-site investigations;
  (ii) Undertake such other matters as may appear necessary for completing the investigation and the preparation and the conduct of the prosecution at the trial, including the taking of special measures to provide for the safety of potential witnesses and informants;
  (iii) Seek, to that end, the assistance of any State authority concerned, as well as of any relevant international body including the International Criminal Police Organization (INTERPOL); and
  (iv) Request such orders as may be necessary from the Trial Chamber or a Judge.

Provisional measures

7–16   **40.** In case of urgency, the Prosecutor may request any State:
  (i) To arrest a suspect or an accused provisionally;
  (ii) To seize physical evidence;
  (iii) To take all necessary measures to prevent the escape of a suspect or an accused, injury to or intimidation of a victim or witness, or the destruction of evidence.

The State concerned shall comply forthwith, in accordance with article 29 of the Statute.

Retention of Information

7–17   **41.** Subject to Rule 81, the Prosecutor shall be responsible for the retention, storage and security of information and physical material obtained in the course of the Prosecutor's investigations until formally tendered into evidence.

Submission of Indictment by the Prosecutor

7–18   **47.**—(A) An indictment, submitted in accordance with the following procedure, shall be reviewed by a Judge designated in accordance with Rule 28 for this purpose.

(B) The Prosecutor, if satisfied in the course of an investigation that there is sufficient evidence to provide reasonable grounds for believing that a suspect has committed a crime within the jurisdiction of the Tribunal, shall prepare and forward to the Registrar an indictment for confirmation by a Judge, together with supporting material.

(C) The indictment shall set forth the name and particulars of the suspect, and a concise statement of the facts of the case and of the crime with which the suspect is charged.

(D) The Registrar shall forward the indictment and accompanying material to the designated Judge, who will inform the Prosecutor of the date fixed for review of the indictment.

(E) The reviewing Judge shall examine each of the counts in the indictment, and any supporting materials the Prosecutor may provide, to determine, applying the standard set forth in Article 19, paragraph 1, of the Statute, whether a case exists against the suspect.

(F) The reviewing Judge may:

(i) request the Prosecutor to present additional material in support of any or all counts;

(ii) confirm each count;

(iii) dismiss each count; or

(iv) adjourn the review so as to give the Prosecutor the opportunity to modify the indictment.

(G) The indictment as confirmed by the Judge shall be retained by the Registrar, who shall prepare certified copies bearing the seal of the Tribunal. If the accused does not understand either of the official languages of the Tribunal and if the language understood is known to the Registrar, a translation of the indictment in that language shall also be prepared, and shall be included as part of each certified copy of the indictment.

(H) Upon confirmation of any or all counts in the indictment,

(i) the Judge may issue an arrest warrant, in accordance with Rule 55 (A), and any orders as provided in Article 19 of the Statute, and

(ii) the suspect shall have the status of an accused.

(I) The dismissal of a count in an indictment shall not preclude the Prosecutor from subsequently bringing an amended indictment based on the acts underlying that count if supported by additional evidence.

ICTR

Statute of the International Tribunal for Rwanda, Art. 17

Investigation and preparation of indictment

7–19

17.—1. The Prosecutor shall initiate investigations ex officio or on the basis of information obtained from any source, particularly from Governments, United Nations organs, intergovernmental and non-governmental organizations. The Prosecutor shall assess the information received or obtained and decide whether there is sufficient basis to proceed.

2. The Prosecutor shall have the power to question suspects, victims and witnesses, to collect evidence and to conduct on-site investigations. In carrying out these tasks, the Prosecutor may, as appropriate, seek the assistance of the State authorities concerned.

3. If questioned, the suspect shall be entitled to be assisted by counsel of his or her own choice, including the right to have legal assistance assigned to the suspect without payment by him or her in any such case if he or she does not have sufficient means to pay for it, as well as to necessary translation into and from a language he or she speaks and understands.

4. Upon a determination that a *prima facie* case exists, the Prosecutor shall prepare an indictment containing a concise statement of the facts and the crime or crimes with which the accused is charged under the Statute. The indictment shall be transmitted to a judge of the Trial Chamber.

ICTR Rules of Procedure and Evidence, rr. 8, 9, 39, 40, 41, 47

Request for Information

7–20

8. Where it appears to the Prosecutor that a crime within the jurisdiction of the Tribunal is or has been the subject of investigations or criminal proceedings instituted in the courts of any State, he may request the State to forward to him all relevant information in that respect, and the State shall transmit to him such information forthwith in accordance with Article 28 of the Statute.

Prosecutor's Application for Deferral

7–21   **9.** Where it appears to the Prosecutor that crimes which are the subject of investigations or criminal proceedings instituted in the courts of any State:
- (i) Are the subject of an investigation by the Prosecutor;
- (ii) Should be the subject of an investigation by the Prosecutor considering, *inter alia*:
  - (a) The seriousness of the offences;
  - (b) The status of the accused at the time of the alleged offences;
  - (c) The general importance of the legal questions involved in the case;
- (iii) Are the subject of an indictment in the Tribunal,

the Prosecutor may apply to the Trial Chamber designated by the President to issue a formal request that such court defer to the competence of the Tribunal.

Conduct of Investigations

7–22   **39.** In the conduct of an investigation, the Prosecutor may:
- (i) summon and question suspects, victims and witnesses and record their statements, collect evidence and conduct on-site investigations;
- (ii) undertake such other matters as may appear necessary for completing the investigation and the preparation and conduct of the prosecution at the trial, including the taking of special measures to provide for the safety of potential witnesses and informants;
- (iii) seek, to that end, the assistance of any State authority concerned, as well as of any relevant international body including the International Criminal Police Organization (INTERPOL); and
- (iv) request such orders as may be necessary from a Trial Chamber or a Judge.

Provisional Measures

7–23   **40.**—(A) In case of urgency, the Prosecutor may request any State:
- (i) To arrest a suspect and place him in custody;
- (ii) To seize all physical evidence;
- (iii) To take all necessary measures to prevent the escape of a suspect or an accused, injury to or intimidation of a victim or witness, or the destruction of evidence.

The State concerned shall comply forthwith, in accordance with Article 28 of the Statute.

(B) Upon showing that a major impediment does not allow the State to keep the suspect in custody or to take all necessary measures to prevent his escape, the Prosecutor may apply to a Judge designated by the President for an order to transfer the suspect to the seat of the Tribunal or to such other place as the Bureau may decide, and to detain him provisionally. After consultation with the Prosecutor and the Registrar, the transfer shall be arranged between the State authorities concerned, the authorities of the host Country of the Tribunal and the Registrar.

(C) In the cases referred to in paragraph B, the suspect shall, from the moment of his transfer, enjoy all the rights provided for in Rule 42, and may apply for review to a Trial Chamber of the Tribunal. The Chamber, after hearing the Prosecutor, shall rule upon the application.

(D) The suspect shall be released if (i) the Chamber so rules; or (ii) the Prosecutor fails to issue an indictment within twenty days of the transfer.

Preservation of Information

7–24   **41.**—(A) The Prosecutor shall be responsible for the preservation, storage and security of information and physical evidence obtained in the course of his investigations.

(B) The Prosecutor shall draw up an inventory of all materials seized from the accused, including documents, books, papers, and other objects, and shall serve a copy thereof on the accused. Materials that are of no evidentiary value shall be returned without delay to the accused.

Submission of Indictment by the Prosecutor

47.—(A) An indictment, submitted in accordance with the following pro- **7–25**
cedure, shall be reviewed by a Judge designated in accordance with Rule 28 for this purpose.

(B) The Prosecutor, if satisfied in the course of an investigation that there is sufficient evidence to provide reasonable grounds for believing that a suspect has committed a crime within the jurisdiction of the Tribunal, shall prepare and forward to the Registrar an indictment for confirmation by a Judge, together with supporting material.

(C) The indictment shall set forth the name and particulars of the suspect, and a concise statement of the facts of the case and of the crime with which the suspect is charged.

(D) The Registrar shall forward the indictment and accompanying material to the designated Judge, who will inform the Prosecutor of the scheduled date for review of the indictment.

(E) The reviewing Judge shall examine each of the counts in the indictment, and any supporting materials the Prosecutor may provide, to determine, applying the standard set forth in Article 18 of the Statute, whether a case exists against the suspect.

(F) The reviewing Judge may:
  (i) Request the Prosecutor to present additional material in support of any or all counts, or to take any further measures which appear appropriate;
  (ii) Confirm each count;
  (iii) Dismiss each count; or
  (iv) Adjourn the review so as to give the Prosecutor the opportunity to modify the indictment.

(G) The indictment as confirmed by the Judge shall be retained by the Registrar, who shall prepare certified copies bearing the seal of the Tribunal. If the accused does not understand either of the official languages of the Tribunal and if the language understood is known to the Registrar, a translation of the indictment in that language shall also be prepared, and a copy of the translation attached to each certified copy of the indictment.

(H) Upon confirmation of any or all counts in the indictment:
  (i) The Judge may issue an arrest warrant, in accordance with Sub-Rule 55 (A), and any orders as provided in Article 19 of the Statute; and
  (ii) The suspect shall have the status of an accused.

(I) The dismissal of a count in an indictment shall not preclude the Prosecutor from subsequently bringing an amended indictment based on the acts underlying that count if supported by additional evidence.

East Timor

Regulation 2000/30, ss.7, 9, 10, 13, 14 (as amended by Regulation 2001/25)

Powers of the Public Prosecutor

7.—7.1 The exclusive competence to conduct criminal investigations is **7–26**
vested in the Public Prosecution Service as provided for in UNTAET Regulation No. 2000/16. The competent Public Prosecutor is the only authority

empowered to issue an indictment, except as provided in Section 44.2 of the present regulation.

7.2 The Public Prosecutor shall direct criminal investigations in order to establish the truth of the facts under investigation. In doing so, the public prosecutor shall investigate incriminating and exonerating circumstances equally.

7.3 The Public Prosecutor shall have all appropriate means to ensure the effective investigation and prosecution of crimes. In doing so, the public prosecutor shall respect the interests and personal circumstances of victims and witnesses.

7.4 In particular, the public prosecutor may:
   (a) collect and examine evidence;
   (b) request the presence of and question persons being investigated, victims and witnesses; and
   (c) seek the cooperation of any authority in accordance with its respective competence.

7.5 In accordance with UNTAET Regulation No. 2000/16, the police and any other competent body shall act under the direction and supervision of the public prosecutor.

7.6 The public prosecutor shall, at all times, fully respect the rights of persons as provided under the present and any other UNTAET regulation.

7.7 The public prosecutor shall be the authority empowered to keep the files of the case during the investigations.

Powers of the Investigating Judge

7–27 9.—9.1 In accordance with Section 13 of UNTAET Regulation No. 2000/11, there shall be at least one Investigating Judge at every District Court in East Timor empowered to ensure that the rights of every person subject to a criminal investigation and the rights of any alleged victims of the suspected crime under investigation are respected.

9.2 As provided by law or UNTAET regulations, the Investigating Judge shall issue warrants or other orders lawfully requested by the public prosecutor whenever, in the course of a criminal investigation, there are reasonable grounds to do so as provided in the present regulation.

9.3 Except as otherwise provided in the present regulation, a warrant or order from an Investigating Judge shall be obtained for the following measures:
   (a) arrest of a suspect;
   (b) detention or continued detention of a suspect;
   (c) exhumation;
   (d) forensic examination;
   (e) search of locations and buildings;
   (f) seizure of goods or items, including seizure or opening of mail;
   (g) intrusive body search;
   (h) physical examination, including the taking and examination of blood, DNA, samples, and other bodily specimens;
   (i) interception of telecommunication and electronic data transfer;
   (j) other warrants involving measures of a coercive character in accorda nce with the applicable law.

9.4 All warrants shall be issued in duplicate. The original shall be kept by the prosecutor and added to the file of the case; a copy will be furnished to the suspect or person concerned, except when to do so would endanger the results of the investigations.

9.5 In order to safeguard the rights of a suspect, as listed in Section 6 of the present regulation, the Investigating Judge shall prohibit any actions of the investigating authorities that are in violation of the rights of the suspect.

9.6 The Investigating Judge shall not interfere with the responsibilities of the public prosecutor in directing the criminal investigations, as defined in Section 7 of the present regulation.

9.7 Notwithstanding any other provision of law, any warrant or measure ordered by the Investigating Judge at the seat of the public prosecutor assigned to the case is valid and may be executed anywhere in East Timor without any further formal request to other judicial authorities.

9.8 A warrant or order issued by the Investigating Judge pursuant to Section 9.2 of the present regulation shall identify by name or official capacity the persons who are authorized to execute the warrant or order. Unless otherwise specified in the warrant or order, the following provisions shall apply:

(a) A warrant or order for arrest of a suspect may be executed by any law enforcement officer anywhere in East Timor;

(b) A warrant or order for detention or continued detention of a suspect may be executed by the warden of any official detention facility in East Timor;

(c) A warrant for exhumation may be executed under the supervision and control of any official qualified as provided in Section 18.5 of the present regulation;

(d) A warrant or order for forensic examination may be executed by any official qualified as provided in Section 18.5 of the present regulation;

(e) A warrant or order for search of locations and buildings may be executed by any law enforcement officer in East Timor who is duly authorized by UNTAET regulations;

(f) A warrant or order for seizure of goods or items may be executed by any law enforcement officer in East Timor who is duly authorized by UNTAET regulations;

(g) A warrant or order for an intrusive body search may be executed by any person with appropriate medical qualifications as provided in Section 16.3 of the present regulation;

(h) A warrant or order for physical examination, including the taking and examination of blood, DNA samples, and other bodily specimens may be executed by any person as provided in Section 16.5 of the present regulation;

(i) A warrant for interception of telecommunication and electronic data transfer may be executed by the requesting prosecutor.

Participation by Investigating Judge as Trial Judge

10. Participation in a case as an Investigating Judge does not disqualify a judge from sitting as a trial judge at later stages of proceedings in the same matter. All questions of judicial disqualification shall be addressed as provided in UNTAET Regulation 2000/11.

7–28

Reporting of a Crime

13.—13.1 Any person may report orally or in writing to the Public Prosecutor or the police the commission of an act of a criminal nature. The reporting of such events is mandatory for public officers, insofar as they do not belong to the categories of individuals defined in Section 35.3(b) and (c) and obtained the information in the delivery of their services.

7–29

13.2 Whenever a crime is reported the relevant officer or Public Prosecutor shall make a record of the reported facts. After that statement is read to the reporting person, in a language that he or she understands, that person shall sign the record. If the person who reported the facts cannot read or write a thumb print shall suffice.

13.3 Following the report, the Public Prosecutor may, as appropriate, initiate an investigation and may for that purpose order the police to carry out the necessary measures.

13.4 Where the commission of a crime has been reported to the police, the relevant officer shall immediately submit a copy of the record to the competent

Public Prosecutor. If the investigation is urgent in nature, the police may take immediate measures to obtain more information about the suspected crime and to ensure that evidence is not destroyed, falsified, lost or tainted prior to reporting the crime to the Public Prosecutor.

General Rules for Collection of Evidence

7–30   **14.**—14.1 The Public Prosecutor and the police shall strive to collect the most direct evidence.

14.2 The origin of any physical and documentary evidence to be presented at the trial shall be established for the record 14.3 In any interview of a victim of a crime under investigation:

(a) the relevant officer shall advise the victim of the right to be notified of proceedings at which the victim has a right to be heard pursuant to the present regulation.

(b) the relevant officer shall record the identity and contact information for any victim who indicates a desire to be so notified.

(c) the proceedings shall be conducted by a female officer in cases of a female victim of a sexual assault, unless the victim does not object to a different procedure.

SCSL

Statute of the SCSL, Art. 15(1)

The Prosecutor

7–31   **15.**—1. The Prosecutor shall be responsible for the investigation and prosecution of persons who bear the greatest responsibility for serious violations of international humanitarian law and crimes under Sierra Leonean law committed in the territory of Sierra Leone since 30 November 1996. The Prosecutor shall act independently as a separate organ of the Special Court. He or she shall not seek or receive instructions from any Government or from any other source.

Rules of Procedure and Evidence of the SCSL, rr. 8, 9, 39, 40, 41, 47

Requests and Orders

7–32   **8.**(A) The Government of Sierra Leone shall cooperate with all organs of the Special Court at all stages of the proceedings. Requests by any organ of the Special Court shall be complied with in accordance with Article 17 of the Agreement. An order issued by a Chamber or by a Judge shall have the same force or effect as if issued by a Judge, Magistrate or Justice of the Peace of a Sierra Leone court.

(B) Except in cases to which Rule 11, 13, 59 or 60 applies, where a Chamber or a Judge is satisfied that the Government of Sierra Leone has failed to comply with a request made in relation to any proceedings before that Chamber or Judge, the Chamber or Judge may refer the matter to the President to take appropriate action.

(C) The Special Court may invite third States not party to the Agreement to provide assistance on the basis of an ad hoc arrangement, an agreement with such State or any other appropriate basis.

(D) Where a third State, which has entered into an ad hoc arrangement or an agreement with the Special Court, fails to cooperate with requests pursuant to any such arrangement or agreement, the President may take appropriate action.

(E) Where it appears to the Prosecutor that a crime within the jurisdiction of the Special Court is or has been the subject of investigations or criminal proceedings instituted in the courts of any State, he may request the State to forward to him all relevant information in that respect. The Government of Sierra Leone shall transmit to him such information forthwith in accordance with Article 17 of the Agreement.

Application for Deferral

9. Where it appears that crimes which are the subject of investigations or proceedings instituted in the courts of a State: **7–33**
    (i) Are the subject of an investigation by the Prosecutor;
    (ii) Should be the subject of an investigation by the Prosecutor considering, amongst others:
        (a) The seriousness of the offences;
        (b) The status of the accused at the time of the alleged offences;
        (c) The general importance of the legal questions involved in the case;
    (iii) Are the subject of an indictment in the Special Court,
    (iv) Fall within Rule 72(B),
The Prosecutor may apply for an order or request for deferral under Rule 10.

Conduct of Investigations

39. In the conduct of an investigation, the Prosecutor may: **7–34**
    (i) Summon and question suspects, interview victims and witnesses and record their statements, collect evidence and conduct on-site investigations;
    (ii) Take all measures deemed necessary for the purpose of the investigation, including the taking of any special measures to provide for the safety, the support and the assistance of potential witnesses and sources;
    (iii) Seek, to that end, the assistance of any State authority concerned, as well as of any relevant international body including the International Criminal Police Organization (INTERPOL); and
    (iv) Request such orders as may be necessary from a Trial Chamber or a Judge.

Provisional Measures

40.(A) In case of urgency, the Prosecutor may request any State: **7–35**
    (i) To arrest a suspect and place him in custody in accordance with the laws of that State;
    (ii) To seize all physical evidence;
    (iii) To take all necessary measures to prevent the escape of a suspect or an accused, injury to or intimidation of a victim or witness, or the destruction of evidence.

(B) Within 10 days from any arrest under Sub-Rule (A) above, the Prosecutor shall apply to the Designated Judge for an order pursuant to Rule 40*bis* to transfer the suspect to the Detention Facility or to such other place as the President may decide, with the advice of the Registrar, and to detain him provisionally. After consultation with the Prosecutor and the Registrar, the transfer shall be arranged between the authorities concerned, and the Registrar.

(C) The suspect shall be released if:
    (i) the Chamber so rules; or

(ii) the Prosecutor fails to apply for an order under rule 40*bis* within ten
days of the arrest.

Preservation of Information

7-36   **41.**(A) The Prosecutor shall be responsible for the preservation, storage and
security of information and physical evidence obtained in the course of his
investigations.

(B) The Prosecutor shall draw up an inventory of all materials seized from
the accused, including documents, books, papers, and other objects, and shall
serve a copy thereof on the accused. Materials that are of no evidentiary value
shall be returned without delay to the accused.

Review of Indictment

7-37   **47.**(A) An indictment submitted in accordance with the following procedure
shall be approved by the Designated Judge.

(B) The Prosecutor, if satisfied in the course of an investigation that a
suspect has committed a crime or crimes within the jurisdiction of the Special
Court, shall prepare and submit to the Registrar an indictment for approval by
the aforementioned Judge.

(C) The indictment shall contain, and be sufficient if it contains, the name
and particulars of the suspect, a statement of each specific offence of which the
named suspect is charged and a short description of the particulars of the
offence. It shall be accompanied by a Prosecutor's case summary briefly setting
out the allegations he proposes to prove in making his case.

(D) The Registrar shall submit the indictment and accompanying material
to the Designated Judge for review.

(E) The designated Judge shall review the indictment and the accompanying
material to determine whether the indictment should be approved. The Judge
shall approve the indictment if he is satisfied that:

(i) the indictment charges the suspect with a crime or crimes within the
jurisdiction of the Special Court; and

(ii) that the allegations in the Prosecution's case summary would, if
proven, amount to the crime or crimes as particularised in the
indictment.

(F) The Designated Judge may approve or dismiss each count.

(G) If at least one count is approved, the indictment shall go forward. If no
count is approved, the indictment shall be returned to the Prosecutor.

(H) Upon approval of the indictment:

(i) The Judge may, at the request of the Prosecutor, issue such orders
and warrants for the arrest, detention, surrender or transfer of
persons, and any other orders as may be required for the proceedings
in accordance with these Rules.; and

(ii) The suspect shall have the status of an accused.

(I) The dismissal of a count in an indictment shall not preclude the
Prosecutor from subsequently submitting an amended indictment including
that count.

B. SUSPECTS

(1) Statutory provisions and rules

ICC

ICC Statute, Art. 55

Rights of persons during an investigation

7-38   **55.**—1. In respect of an investigation under this Statute, a person:

(a) Shall not be compelled to incriminate himself or herself or to confess
    guilt;
(b) Shall not be subjected to any form of coercion, duress or threat, to
    torture or to any other form of cruel, inhuman or degrading treat-
    ment or punishment;
(c) Shall, if questioned in a language other than a language the person
    fully understands and speaks, have, free of any cost, the assistance of
    a competent interpreter and such translations as are necessary to
    meet the requirements of fairness; and
(d) Shall not be subjected to arbitrary arrest or detention, and shall not
    be deprived of his or her liberty except on such grounds and in
    accordance with such procedures as are established in this Statute.
2. Where there are grounds to believe that a person has committed a crime
within the jurisdiction of the Court and that person is about to be questioned
either by the Prosecutor, or by national authorities pursuant to a request made
under Part 9, that person shall also have the following rights of which he or she
shall be informed prior to being questioned:
(a) To be informed, prior to being questioned, that there are grounds to
    believe that he or she has committed a crime within the jurisdiction of
    the Court;
(b) To remain silent, without such silence being a consideration in the
    determination of guilt or innocence;
(c) To have legal assistance of the person's choosing, or, if the person
    does not have legal assistance, to have legal assistance assigned to
    him or her, in any case where the interests of justice so require, and
    without payment by the person in any such case if the person does not
    have sufficient means to pay for it; and
(d) To be questioned in the presence of counsel unless the person has
    voluntarily waived his or her right to counsel.

ICC Rules of Procedure and Evidence, r. 111, 112.

Rule 111: Record of questioning in general

1. A record shall be made of formal statements made by any person who is
questioned in connection with an investigation or with proceedings. The record
shall be signed by the person who records and conducts the questioning and by
the person who is questioned and his or her counsel, if present, and, where
applicable, the Prosecutor or the judge who is present. The record shall note
the date, time and place of, and all persons present during the questioning. It
shall also be noted when someone has not signed the record as well as the
reasons therefor.

2. When the Prosecutor or national authorities question a person, due
regard shall be given to article 55. When a person is informed of his or her
rights under article 55, paragraph 2, the fact that this information has been
provided shall be noted in the record.

7–39

Rule 112: Recording of questioning in particular cases

1. Whenever the Prosecutor questions a person to whom article 55, paragraph 2, applies, or for whom a warrant of arrest or a summons to appear has
been issued under article 58, paragraph 7, the questioning shall be audio- or
video-recorded, in accordance with the following procedure:
(a) The person questioned shall be informed, in a language he or she fully
    understands and speaks, that the questioning is to be audio- or video-
    recorded, and that the person concerned may object if he or she so
    wishes. The fact that this information has been provided and the

7–40

response given by the person concerned shall be noted in the record. The person may, before replying, speak in private with his or her counsel, if present. If the person questioned refuses to be audio- or videorecorded, the procedure in rule 111 shall be followed;

(b) A waiver of the right to be questioned in the presence of counsel shall be recorded in writing and, if possible, be audio- or video-recorded;

(c) In the event of an interruption in the course of questioning, the fact and the time of the interruption shall be recorded before the audio- or video-recording ends as well as the time of resumption of the questioning;

(d) At the conclusion of the questioning, the person questioned shall be offered the opportunity to clarify anything he or she has said and to add anything he or she may wish. The time of conclusion of the questioning shall be noted;

(e) The tape shall be transcribed as soon as practicable after the conclusion of the questioning and a copy of the transcript supplied to the person questioned together with a copy of the recorded tape or, if multiple recording apparatus was used, one of the original recorded tapes;

(f) The original tape or one of the original tapes shall be sealed in the presence of the person questioned and his or her counsel, if present, under the signature of the Prosecutor and the person questioned and the counsel, if present.

2. The Prosecutor shall make every reasonable effort to record the questioning in accordance with sub-rule 1. As an exception, a person may be questioned without the questioning being audio- or video-recorded where the circumstances prevent such recording taking place. In this case, the reasons for not recording the questioning shall be stated in writing and the procedure in rule 111 shall be followed.

3. When, pursuant to sub-rule 1 (a) or 2, the questioning is not audio- or videorecorded, the person questioned shall be provided with a copy of his or her statement.

4. The Prosecutor may choose to follow the procedure in this rule when questioning other persons than those mentioned in sub-rule 1, in particular where the use of such procedures could assist in reducing any subsequent traumatization of a victim of sexual or gender violence, a child or a person with disabilities in providing their evidence. The Prosecutor may make an application to the relevant Chamber.

5. The Pre-Trial Chamber may, in pursuance of article 56, paragraph 2, order that the procedure in this rule be applied to the questioning of any person.

ICTY

Statute of the ICTY, Art. 20

Commencement and conduct of trial proceedings

7–41   **20.** The Trial Chambers shall ensure that a trial is fair and expeditious and that proceedings are conducted in accordance with the rules of procedure and evidence, with full respect for the rights of the accused and due regard for the protection of victims and witnesses.

ICTY Rules of Procedure and Evidence, rr. 40*bis*, 42, 43

Transfer and Provisional Detention of Suspects

7–42   **40***bis.*—(A) In the conduct of an investigation, the Prosecutor may transmit to the Registrar, for an order by a Judge assigned pursuant to Rule 28, a request for the transfer to and provisional detention of a suspect in the premises of the detention unit of the Tribunal. This request shall indicate the grounds upon which the request is made and, unless the Prosecutor wishes only to question the suspect, shall include a provisional charge and a summary of the material upon which the Prosecutor relies.

(B) The Judge shall order the transfer and provisional detention of the suspect if the following conditions are met:

    (i) the Prosecutor has requested a State to arrest the suspect provisionally, in accordance with Rule 40, or the suspect is otherwise detained by State authorities;

    (ii) after hearing the Prosecutor, the Judge considers that there is a reliable and consistent body of material which tends to show that the suspect may have committed a crime over which the Tribunal has jurisdiction; and

    (iii) the Judge considers provisional detention to be a necessary measure to prevent the escape of the suspect, injury to or intimidation of a victim or witness or the destruction of evidence, or to be otherwise necessary for the conduct of the investigation.

(C) The order for the transfer and provisional detention of the suspect shall be signed by the Judge and bear the seal of the Tribunal. The order shall set forth the basis of the application made by the Prosecutor under paragraph (A), including the provisional charge, and shall state the Judge's grounds for making the order, having regard to paragraph (B). The order shall also specify the initial time-limit for the provisional detention of the suspect, and be accompanied by a statement of the rights of a suspect, as specified in this Rule and in Rules 42 and 43.

(D) the provisional detention of a suspect shall be ordered for a period not exceeding thirty days from the date of the transfer of the suspect to the seat of the Tribunal. At the end of that period, at the Prosecutor's request, the Judge who made the order, or another permanent Judge of the same Trial Chamber, may decide, subsequent to an inter partes hearing of the Prosecutor and the suspect assisted by counsel, to extend the detention for a period not exceeding thirty days, if warranted by the needs of the investigation. At the end of that extension, at the Prosecutor's request, the Judge who made the order, or another permanent Judge of the same Trial Chamber, may decide, subsequent to an inter partes hearing of the Prosecutor and the suspect assisted by counsel, to extend the detention for a further period not exceeding thirty days, if warranted by special circumstances. The total period of detention shall in no case exceed ninety days, at the end of which, in the event the indictment has not been confirmed and an arrest warrant signed, the suspect shall be released or, if appropriate, be delivered to the authorities of the requested State.

(E) The provisions in rules 55(B) to 59*bis* shall apply *mutatis mutandis* to the execution of the transfer order and the provisional detention order relative to a suspect.

(F) After being transferred to the seat of the Tribunal, the suspect, assisted by counsel, shall be brought, without delay, before the Judge who made the order, or another permanent Judge of the same Trial Chamber, who shall ensure that the rights of the suspect are respected.

(G) During detention, the Prosecutor and the suspect or the suspect's counsel may submit to the Trial Chamber of which the Judge who made the order is a member, all applications relative to the propriety of provisional detention or to the suspect's release.

(H) Without prejudice to paragraph (D), the Rules relating to the detention on remand of accused persons shall apply *mutatis mutandis* to the provisional detention of persons under this Rule.

Rights of suspects during investigation

42.—(A) A suspect who is to be questioned by the Prosecutor shall have the following rights, of which the Prosecutor shall inform the suspect prior to questioning, in a language the suspect speaks and understands:

7–43

   (i) The right to be assisted by counsel of the suspect's choice or to be assigned legal assistance without payment if the suspect does not have sufficient means to pay for it;

  (ii) The right to have the free assistance of an interpreter if the suspect cannot understand or speak the language used in the questioning; and

 (iii) The right to remain silent, and to be cautioned that any statement the suspect makes shall be recorded and may be used in evidence.

(B) Questioning of a suspect shall not proceed without the presence of counsel unless the suspect has voluntarily waived the right to counsel. In case of waiver, if the suspect subsequently expresses a desire to have counsel, questioning shall thereupon cease, and shall only resume when the suspect has obtained or has been assigned counsel.

Recording Questioning of Suspects

7–44   **43.** Whenever the Prosecutor questions a suspect, the questioning shall be audio-recorded or video-recorded, in accordance with the following procedure:

   (i) the suspect shall be informed in a language the suspect understands that the questioning is being audio-recorded or video-recorded;

  (ii) in the event of a break in the course of the questioning, the fact and the time of the break shall be recorded before audio-recording or video-recording ends and the time of resumption of the questioning shall also be recorded;

 (iii) at the conclusion of the questioning the suspect shall be offered the opportunity to clarify anything the suspect has said, and to add anything the suspect may wish, and the time of conclusion shall be recorded;

 (iv) a copy of the recorded tape will be supplied to the suspect or, if multiple recording apparatus was used, one of the original recorded tapes;

  (v) after a copy has been made, if necessary, of the recorded tape, the original recorded tape or one of the original tapes shall be sealed in the presence of the suspect under the signature of the Prosecutor and the suspect; and

 (vi) the tape shall be transcribed if the suspect becomes an accused.

ICTR

Statute of the ICTR, Art. 19

Commencement and conduct of trial proceedings

7–45   **20.**1. The Trial Chambers shall ensure that a trial is fair and expeditious and that proceedings are conducted in accordance with the Rules of Procedure and Evidence, with full respect for the rights of the accused and due regard for the protection of victims and witnesses.

2. A person against whom an indictment has been confirmed shall, pursuant to an order or an arrest warrant of the International Tribunal for Rwanda, be taken into custody, immediately informed of the charges against him or her and transferred to the International Tribunal for Rwanda.

3. The Trial Chamber shall read the indictment, satisfy itself that the rights of the accused are respected, confirm that the accused understands the indictment, and instruct the accused to enter a plea. The Trial Chamber shall then set the date for trial.

4. The hearings shall be public unless the Trial Chamber decides to close the proceedings in accordance with its Rules of Procedure and Evidence.

ICTR Rules of Procedure and Evidence, rr. 40*bis*, 42, 43

Transfer and Provisional Detention of Suspects

40*bis*.—(A) In the conduct of an investigation, the Prosecutor may transmit
to the Registrar, for an order by a Judge assigned pursuant to Rule 28, a
request for the transfer to and provisional detention of a suspect in the
premises of the detention unit of the Tribunal. This request shall indicate the
grounds upon which the request is made and, unless the Prosecutor wishes only
to question the suspect, shall include a provisional charge and a summary of
the material upon which the Prosecutor relies.

7–46

(B) The Judge shall order the transfer and provisional detention of the
suspect if the following conditions are met:

   (i) The Prosecutor has requested a State to arrest the suspect and to
      place him in custody, in accordance with Rule 40, or the suspect is
      otherwise detained by a State;

   (ii) After hearing the Prosecutor, the Judge considers that there is a
      reliable and consistent body of material which tends to show that the
      suspect may have committed a crime over which the Tribunal has
      jurisdiction; and

   (iii) The Judge considers provisional detention to be a necessary measure
      to prevent the escape of the suspect, physical or mental injury to or
      intimidation of a victim or witness or the destruction of evidence, or
      to be otherwise necessary for the conduct of the investigation.

(C) The provisional detention of the suspect may be ordered for a period not
exceeding 30 days from the day after the transfer of the suspect to the
detention unit of the Tribunal.

(D) The order for the transfer and provisional detention of the suspect shall
be signed by the Judge and bear the seal of the Tribunal. The order shall set
forth the basis of the request made by the Prosecutor under Sub-Rule (A),
including the provisional charge, and shall state the Judge's grounds for
making the order, having regard to Sub-Rule (B). The order shall also specify
the initial time limit for the provisional detention of the suspect, and be
accompanied by a statement of the rights of a suspect, as specified in this Rule
and in Rules 42 and 43.

(E) As soon as possible, copies of the order and of the request by the
Prosecutor are served upon the suspect and his counsel by the Registrar.

(F) At the Prosecutor's request indicating the grounds upon which it is made
and if warranted by the needs of the investigation, the Judge who made the
initial order, or another Judge of the same Trial Chamber, may decide,
subsequent to an inter partes hearing and before the end of the period of
detention, to extend the provisional detention for a period not exceeding 30
days.

(G) At the Prosecutors request indicating the grounds upon which it is made
and if warranted by special circumstances, the Judge who made the initial
order, or another Judge of the same Trial Chamber, may decide, subsequent to
an inter partes hearing and before the end of the period of detention, to extend
the detention for a further period not exceeding 30 days.

(H) The total period of provisional detention shall in no case exceed 90 days
after the day of transfer of the suspect to the Tribunal, at the end of which, in
the event the indictment has not been confirmed and an arrest warrant signed,
the suspect shall be released or, if appropriate, be delivered to the authorities
of the State to which the request was initially made.

(I) The provisions in Rules 55(B) to 59 shall apply *mutatis mutandis* to the
execution of the order for the transfer and provisional detention of the suspect.

(J) After his transfer to the seat of the Tribunal, the suspect, assisted by his
counsel, shall be brought, without delay, before the Judge who made the initial
order, or another Judge of the same Trial Chamber, who shall ensure that his
rights are respected.

(K) During detention, the Prosecutor, the suspect or his counsel may submit to the Trial Chamber of which the Judge who made the initial order is a member, all applications relative to the propriety of provisional detention or to the suspect's release.

(L) Without prejudice to Sub-Rules (C) to (H), the Rules relating to the detention on remand of accused persons shall apply *mutatis mutandis* to the provisional detention of persons under this Rule.

Rights of suspects during investigation

7–47   **42.**—(A) A suspect who is to be questioned by the Prosecutor shall have the following rights, of which he shall be informed by the Prosecutor prior to questioning, in a language he speaks and understands:

      (i) The right to be assisted by counsel of his choice or to have legal assistance assigned to him without payment if he does not have sufficient means to pay for it;

     (ii) The right to have the free assistance of an interpreter if he cannot understand or speak the language to be used for questioning; and

    (iii) The right to remain silent, and to be cautioned that any statement he makes shall be recorded and may be used in evidence.

(B) Questioning of a suspect shall not proceed without the presence of counsel unless the suspect has voluntarily waived his right to counsel. In case of waiver, if the suspect subsequently expresses a desire to have counsel, questioning shall thereupon cease, and shall only resume when the suspect has obtained or has been assigned counsel.

Recording Questioning of Suspects

7–48   **43.** Whenever the Prosecutor questions a suspect, the questioning shall be audio-recorded or video-recorded, in accordance with the following procedure:

      (i) The suspect shall be informed in a language he understands that the questioning is being audio-recorded or video-recorded;

     (ii) In the event of a break in the course of the questioning, the fact and the time of the break shall be recorded before audio-recording or video-recording ends and the time of resumption of the questioning shall also be recorded;

    (iii) At the conclusion of the questioning the suspect shall be offered the opportunity to clarify anything he has said, and to add anything he may wish, and the time of conclusion shall be recorded;

    (iv) The content of the recording shall then be transcribed as soon as practicable after the conclusion of questioning and a copy of the transcript supplied to the suspect, together with a copy of the recording or, if multiple recording apparatus was used, one of the original recorded tapes; and

     (v) After a copy has been made, if necessary, of the recorded tape for purposes of transcription, the original recorded tape or one of the original tapes shall be sealed in the presence of the suspect under the signature of the Prosecutor and the suspect.

Also see Chapter 4 on Powers of the Court for more detail on the extent of the powers available to the Prosecutor to conduct investigations.

East Timor

Regulation 2000/30, s.6 (as amended by Regulation 2001/25)

Rights of the Suspect and Accused

6.—6.1 All persons accused of a crime shall be presumed innocent until **7–49** proven guilty in accordance with the law, the provisions of this and other UNTAET regulations.

6.2 Immediately upon arrest, the suspect shall be informed by the arresting police officers of the reasons for his or her arrest and any charges against him or her, and shall also be informed that he or she has the following rights:

(a) the right to remain silent and not to admit guilt, and that silence will not be interpreted as an admission;

(b) the right to contact a relative or close friend and be visited by such person;

(c) the right to contact a legal representative and communicate with him or her confidentially;

(d) the right that a legal representative will be appointed if the suspect is unable to pay for a lawyer;

(e) the right to be brought before an Investigating Judge within 72 hours upon arrest;

(f) the right to be questioned in the presence of a legal representative, unless the right is waived; and

(g) if the suspect is a foreign national, the right to contact diplomatic or consular officials of his or her country.

6.3 At every stage of the proceedings, the suspect and the accused shall be informed by the public prosecutor that he or she has the following rights:

(a) the right to be assisted by and to communicate freely and without supervision with a legal representative of his or her own choosing and to have such legal representation provided to him or her without cost where the suspect does not have sufficient means to pay for it;

(b) the right to be informed in detail, and in a language which he or she understands, of the nature and cause of the charges against him or her;

(c) the right to have the free assistance of an interpreter if he or she cannot understand or speak one of the official languages of the court;

(d) the right to have adequate time and facilities for the preparation of his or her defense;

(e) the right to request the Public Prosecutor or Investigating Judge to order or conduct specific investigations in order to establish his or her innocence;

(f) the right to be tried without undue delay;

(g) the right to examine, or have examined, the witnesses against him or her and to obtain the attendance and examination of witnesses on his or her behalf under the same conditions as adverse witnesses;

(h) the right not to be compelled to testify against himself or herself or to admit guilt, and that if he or she chooses not to speak in the proceeding, such silence will not be held against him or her in the determination of innocence or guilt;

(i) the right to be free from any form of coercion, duress or threat, torture, or any other form of cruel, inhuman or degrading treatment or punishment;

(j) the right to be in contact with close relatives and be visited by such persons.

(k) the right, if under detention, to have, upon request, the grounds of his or her detention reviewed by a competent judge or panel of judges at regular intervals.

Also see, s.19A of Reg. 2000/30 on arrests of suspects set out at paragraph 7–72.

SCSL

7–50   See Article 15(2) of the Statute of the Special Court set out at paragraph 7–31. As per Article 14 of the Statute (paragraph 7–75) the Rules of the ICTR are also applicable.

SCSL Rules of Procedure and Evidence, rr. 40*bis*, 42, 43

Transfer and Provisional Detention of Suspects

7–51   **40***bis.* (A) In the conduct of an investigation, the Prosecutor may transmit to the Registrar, for an order by the Designated Judge, a request for the transfer and/or provisional detention of a suspect in the premises of the Detention Facility. This request shall indicate the grounds upon which the request is made and, unless the Prosecutor wishes only to question the suspect, shall include a provisional charge and a brief summary of the material upon which the Prosecutor relies.

(B) The Designated Judge shall order the transfer and provisional detention of the suspect if the following conditions are met:

     (i) The Prosecutor has requested a State to arrest the suspect and to place him in custody, in accordance with Rule 40, or the suspect is otherwise detained by a State;

     (ii) Where there are provisional charges, and where there is reason to believe that the suspect may have committed a crime or crimes specified in those provisional charges over which the Special Court has jurisdiction; and

     (iii) The Designated Judge considers provisional detention to be a necessary measure to prevent the escape of the suspect, physical or mental injury to or intimidation of a victim or witness or the destruction of evidence, or to be otherwise necessary for the conduct of the investigation.

(C) The provisional detention of the suspect may be ordered for a period not exceeding 30 days from the day after the transfer of the suspect to the Detention Facility.

(D) The order for the transfer and provisional detention of the suspect shall be signed by the Designated Judge and bear the seal of the Special Court. The order shall set forth the basis of the request made by the Prosecutor under Sub-Rule (A), including the provisional charge, and shall state the Designated Judge's grounds for making the order, having regard to Sub-Rule (B). The order, shall also specify the initial time limit for the provisional detention of the suspect and when served on the suspect be accompanied by a statement of his rights, as specified in this Rule and in Rules 42 and 43.

(E) As soon as possible, copies of the order and of the request by the Prosecutor shall be served upon the suspect and his counsel by the Registrar.

(F) At the Prosecutor's request indicating the grounds upon which it is made and if warranted by the needs of the investigation, the Designated Judge who made the initial order, or another Designated Judge, may decide, subsequent to an inter partes hearing and before the end of the period of detention, to extend the provisional detention for a period not exceeding 30 days.

(G) At the Prosecutor's request indicating the grounds upon which it is made and if warranted by special circumstances, the Designated Judge who made the initial order, or another Designated Judge, may decide, subsequent to an inter partes hearing and before the end of the period of detention, to extend the detention for a further period not exceeding 30 days.

(H) The total period of provisional detention shall in no case exceed 90 days after the day of transfer of the suspect to the Special Court, at the end of which, in the event the indictment has not been approved and an arrest warrant signed, the suspect shall be released or, if appropriate, be delivered to the authorities of the State to which the request was initially made.

(I) The provisions in Rules 55(B) to 59 shall apply to the execution of the order for the transfer and provisional detention of the suspect.

(J) After his transfer to the seat of the Special Court, the suspect, assisted by his counsel, shall be brought, without delay, before the Designated Judge who made the initial order, or another Designated Judge, who shall ensure that his rights are respected.

(K) During detention, the Prosecutor, the suspect or his counsel may submit to the Trial Chamber all applications relative to the propriety of provisional detention or to the suspect's release.

(L) Without prejudice to Sub-Rules (C) to (H), the Rules of Detention shall apply to the provisional detention of persons under this Rule.

Rights of Suspects during Investigation

42. (A) A suspect who is to be questioned by the Prosecutor shall have the following rights, of which he shall be informed by the Prosecutor prior to questioning, in a language he speaks and understands: **7–52**
  (i) The right to legal assistance of his own choosing, including the right to have legal assistance provided by the Defence Office where the interests of justice so require and where the suspect does not have sufficient means to pay for it;
  (ii) The right to have the free assistance of an interpreter if he cannot understand or speak the language to be used for questioning; and
  (iii) The right to remain silent, and to be cautioned that any statement he makes shall be recorded and may be used in evidence.

(B) Questioning of a suspect shall not proceed without the presence of counsel unless the suspect has voluntarily waived his right to counsel. In case of waiver, if the suspect subsequently expresses a desire to have counsel, questioning shall thereupon cease, and shall only resume when the suspect has obtained or has been assigned counsel.

Recording Questioning of Suspects

43. Whenever the Prosecutor questions a suspect, the questioning, including any waiver of the right to counsel, shall be audio-recorded or video-recorded, in accordance with the following procedure: **7–53**
  (i) The suspect shall be informed in a language he speaks and understands that the questioning is being audio-recorded or video-recorded;
  (ii) In the event of a break in the course of the questioning, the fact and the time of the break shall be recorded before audio-recording or video-recording ends and the time of resumption of the questioning shall also be recorded;
  (iii) At the conclusion of the questioning the suspect shall be offered the opportunity to clarify anything he has said, and to add anything he may wish, and the time of conclusion shall be recorded;
  (iv) The content of the recording shall then be transcribed as soon as practicable after the conclusion of questioning and a copy of the transcript supplied to the suspect, together with a copy of the recording or, if multiple recording apparatus was used, one of the original recorded tapes; and

(v) After a copy has been made, if necessary, of the recorded tape for purposes of transcription, the original recorded tape or one of the original tapes shall be sealed in the presence of the suspect under the signature of the Prosecutor and the suspect.

II. ORDERS AND WARRANTS

A. General Rule

The same rule applies before the ICTY and ICTR, and in both Tribunals is frequently relied upon as a general provision to seek orders for the preparation and conduct of proceedings.

General Rule

7–54   54. At the request of either party or *proprio motu*, a Judge or a Trial Chamber may issue such orders, summonses, subpoenas, warrants and transfer orders as may be necessary for the purposes of an investigation or for the preparation or conduct of the trial.

B. Arrest Warrants

(1) Statutory provisions and rules

ICC

Statute of the ICC, Arts 57(3), 58, 91, 92

Functions and powers of the Pre-Trial Chamber

7–55   57(3).—

    i. At the request of the Prosecutor, issue such orders and warrants as may be required for the purposes of an investigation;

    ii. Upon the request of a person who has been arrested or has appeared pursuant, issue such orders, including measures such as those described in article 56, or seek such cooperation pursuant to Part 9 as may be necessary to assist the person in the preparation of his or her defence.

    iii. Where a warrant of arrest or a summons has been issued under article 58, and having due regard to the strength of the evidence and the rights of the parties concerned, as provided for in this Statute and the Rules of Procedure and Evidence, seek the cooperation of States pursuant to article 93, paragraph 1(j), to take protective measures for the purpose of forfeiture, in particular for the ultimate benefit of victims.

Issuance by the Pre-Trial Chamber of a warrant of arrest or a summons to appear

7–56   58.—1. At any time after the initiation of an investigation, the Pre-Trial Chamber shall, on the application of the Prosecutor, issue a warrant of arrest of a person if, having examined the application and the evidence or other information submitted by the Prosecutor, it is satisfied that:

(a) There are reasonable grounds to believe that the person has committed a crime within the jurisdiction of the Court; and
(b) The arrest of the person appears necessary;
  (i) To ensure the person's appearance at trial;
  (ii) To ensure that person does not obstruct or endanger the investigation or the court proceedings, or
  (iii) Where applicable, to prevent the person from continuing with the
  commission of that crime or a related crime which is within the
  jurisdiction of the Court and which arises out of the same
  circumstances.
2. The application of the Prosecutor shall contain: **7–57**
(a) The name of the person and any other relevant identifying
information;
(b) A specific reference to the crimes within the jurisdiction of the Court
which the person is alleged to have committed;
(c) A concise statement of the facts which are alleged to constitute those
crimes;
(d) A summary of the evidence and any other information which establish
reasonable grounds to believe that the person committed those
crimes; and
(e) The reason why the Prosecutor believes that the arrest of the person
is necessary.
3. The warrant of arrest shall contain:
(a) The name of the person and any other relevant identifying
information;
(b) A specific reference to the crimes within the jurisdiction of the Court
for which the person's arrest is sought; and
(c) A concise statement of the facts which are alleged to constitute those
crimes.
4. The warrant of arrest shall remain in effect until otherwise ordered by
the Court.
5. On the basis of the warrant of arrest, the Court may request the
provisional arrest or the arrest and surrender of the person under Part 9.
6. The Prosecutor may request the Pre-Trial Chamber to amend the **7–58**
warrant of arrest by modifying or adding to the crimes specified therein. The
Pre-Trial Chamber shall so amend the warrant if it is satisfied that there are
reasonable grounds to believe that the person committed the modified or
additional crimes.
7. As an alternative to seeking a warrant of arrest, the Prosecutor may
submit an application requesting that the Pre-Trial Chamber issue a summons
for the person to appear. If the Pre-Trial Chamber is satisfied that there are
reasonable grounds to believe that the person committed the crime alleged and
that a summons is sufficient to ensure the person's appearance, it shall issue
the summons, with or without conditions restricting liberty (other than
detention) if provided by national law, for the person to appear. The summons
shall contain:
(a) The name of the person and any other relevant identifying
information;
(b) The specified date on which the person is to appear;
(c) A specified reference to the crimes within the jurisdiction of the Court
which the person is alleged to have committed; and
(d) A concise statement of the facts which are alleged to constitute the
crime. The summons shall be served on the person.

Contents of request for arrest and surrender

91.—1. A request for arrest and surrender shall be made in writing. In **7–59**
urgent cases, a request may be made by a medium capable of delivering a
written record, provided that a request shall be confirmed through the channel
provided for in article 87, paragraph 1(a).

2. In the case of a request for the arrest and surrender of a person for whom a warrant of arrest has been issued by the Pre-Trial Chamber under article 58, the request shall contain or be supported by:

    (a) Information describing the person sought, sufficient to identify the person, and information as to that person's probable location;

    (b) A copy of the warrant of arrest; and

    (c) Such documents, statements or information as may be necessary to meet the requirements for the surrender process in the requested State, except that those requirements should not be more burdensome than those applicable to requests for extradition pursuant to treaties or arrangements between the requested State and other States and should, if possible, be less burdensome, taking into account the distinct nature of the Court.

3. In the case of a request for the arrest and surrender of a person already convicted, the request shall contain or be supported by:

    (a) A copy of any warrant of arrest for that person;

    (b) A copy of the judgment of conviction;

    (c) Information to demonstrate that the person sought is the one referred to in the judgment of conviction; and

    (d) If the person sought has been sentenced, a copy of the sentence imposed and, in the case of a sentence for imprisonment, a statement of any time already served and the time remaining to be served.

4. Upon the request of the Court, a State Party shall consult with the Court, either generally or with respect to a specific matter, regarding any requirements under its national law that may apply under paragraph 2(c). During the consultations, the State Party shall advise the Court of the specific requirements of its national law.

Provisional Arrest

7–60   **92.**—1. In urgent cases, the Court may request the provisional arrest of the person sought, pending presentation of the request of surrender and the documents supporting the request as specified in article 91.

2. The request for provisional arrest shall be made by any medium capable of delivering a written record and shall contain:

    (a) Information describing the person sought, sufficient to identify the person, and information as to that person's probable location;

    (b) A concise statement of the crimes for which the person's arrest is sought and of the facts which are alleged to constitute those crimes, including, where possible, the date and location of the crime;

    (c) A statement of the existence of a warrant of arrest or a judgment of conviction against the person sought; and

    (d) A statement that a request for surrender of the person sought will follow.

3. A person who is provisionally arrested may be released from custody if the requested State has not received the request for surrender and the documents supporting the request as specified in article 91 within the time limits specified in the Rules of Procedure and Evidence. However, the person may consent to surrender before the expiration of this period if permitted by the law of the requested State. In such a case, the requested State shall proceed to surrender the person to the Court as soon as possible.

4. The fact that the person sought has been released from custody pursuant to paragraph 3 shall not prejudice the subsequent arrest and surrender of that person if the request for surrender and the documents supporting the request are delivered at a later date.

ICC Rules of Procedure and Evidence, rr.117, 123

Rule 117: Detention in the custodial State

1. The Court shall take measures to ensure that it is informed of the arrest **7–61** of a person in response to a request made by the Court under article 89 or 92. Once so informed, the Court shall ensure that the person receives a copy of the arrest warrant issued by the Pre-Trial Chamber under article 58 and any relevant provisions of the Statute. The documents shall be made available in a language that the person fully understands and speaks.

2. At any time after arrest, the person may make a request to the Pre-Trial Chamber for the appointment of counsel to assist with proceedings before the Court and the Pre-Trial Chamber shall take a decision on such request.

3. A challenge as to whether the warrant of arrest was properly issued in accordance with article 58, paragraph 1 (a) and (b), shall be made in writing to the Pre-Trial Chamber. The application shall set out the basis for the challenge. After having obtained the views of the Prosecutor, the Pre-Trial Chamber shall decide on the application without delay.

4. When the competent authority of the custodial State notifies the Pre-Trial Chamber that a request for release has been made by the person arrested, in accordance with article 59, paragraph 5, the Pre-Trial Chamber shall provide its recommendations within any time limit set by the custodial State.

5. When the Pre-Trial Chamber is informed that the person has been granted interim release by the competent authority of the custodial State, the Pre-Trial Chamber shall inform the custodial State how and when it would like to receive periodic reports on the status of the interim release.

Rule 123: Measures to ensure the presence of the person concerned at the confirmation hearing

1. When a warrant of arrest or summons to appear in accordance with **7–62** article 58, paragraph 7, has been issued for a person by the Pre-Trial Chamber and the person is arrested or served with the summons, the Pre-Trial Chamber shall ensure that the person is notified of the provisions of article 61, paragraph 2.

2. The Pre-Trial Chamber may hold consultations with the Prosecutor, at the request of the latter or on its own initiative, in order to determine whether there is cause to hold a hearing on confirmation of charges under the conditions set forth in article 61, paragraph 2 (b). When the person concerned has a counsel known to the Court, the consultations shall be held in the presence of the counsel unless the Pre-Trial Chamber decides otherwise.

3. The Pre-Trial Chamber shall ensure that a warrant of arrest for the person concerned has been issued and, if the warrant of arrest has not been executed within a reasonable period of time after the issuance of the warrant, that all reasonable measures have been taken to locate and arrest the person.

ICTY

Statute of the ICTY, Arts 19, 20

Review of the indictment

19.—1. The judge of the Trial Chamber to whom the indictment has been **7–63** transmitted shall review it. If satisfied that a *prima facie* case has been established by the Prosecutor, he shall confirm the indictment. If not so satisfied, the indictment shall be dismissed.

2. Upon confirmation of an indictment, the judge may, at the request of the Prosecutor, issue such orders and warrants for the arrest, detention, surrender or transfer of persons, and any other orders as may be required for the conduct of the trial.

Commencement and conduct of trial proceedings

7–64   **20.**—1. A person against whom an indictment has been confirmed shall, pursuant to an order or an arrest warrant of the International Tribunal, be taken into custody, immediately informed of the charges against him and transferred to the International Tribunal.

2. The Trial Chamber shall read the indictment, satisfy itself that the rights of the accused are respected, confirm that the accused understands the indictment, and instruct the accused to enter a plea. The Trial Chamber shall then set the date for trial.

3. The hearing shall be public unless the Trial Chamber decides to close the proceedings in accordance with rules of procedure and evidence.

The same provisions are contained in Articles 18 and 19 of the ICTR Statute.

ICTY Rules of Procedure and Evidence, rr. 55, 59, 59*bis*, 61

Execution of arrest warrants

7–65   **55.**—(A) A warrant shall be signed by a Judge. It shall include an order for the prompt transfer of the accused to the Tribunal upon the arrest of the accused.

(B) The original warrant shall be retained by the Registrar, that shall prepare certified copies bearing the seal of the Tribunal.

(C) Each certified copy shall be accompanied by a copy of the indictment certified in accordance with Rule 47(G) and a statement of the rights of the accused set forth in article 21 of the Statute, and in Rules 43 *mutatis mutandis*. If the accused does not understand either of the official languages of the Tribunal and if the language understood by the accused is known to the Registrar, each certified copy of the warrant of arrest shall also be accompanied by a translation of the statement of the rights of the accused in that language.

(D) Subject to any order of a Judge or Chamber, The Registrar may transmit a certified copy of a warrant of arrest to the person or authorities to which it is addressed, including the national authorities of a State in whose territory or under whose jurisdiction the accused resides, or was last known to be, or is believed by the Registrar to be likely to be found.

(E) The Registrar shall instruct the person or authorities to which a warrant is transmitted that at the time of arrest the indictment and the statement of the rights of the accused be read to the accused in a language that he or she understands and that the accused is cautioned in that language that accused has the right to remain silent, and that any statement he/she makes shall be recorded and may be used as evidence.

(F) Notwithstanding Sub-rule (E), if at the time of arrest the accused is served with, or with a translation of, the indictment and the statement of rights of the accused in a language that the accused understands and is able to read, these not be read to the accused at the time of the arrest.

(G) When an arrest warrant issued by the Tribunal is executed by the authorities of a State, or an appropriate authority or international body, a member of the Office of the Prosecutor may be present as from the time of the arrest.

Failure to Execute a Warrant or Transfer Order

7–66   **59.**—(A) Where the State to which a warrant of arrest or transfer order has been transmitted has been unable to execute the warrant, it shall report forthwith its inability to the Registrar, and the reasons therefor.

(B) If, within a reasonable time after the warrant of arrest or transfer order has been transmitted to the State, no report is made on action taken, this shall be deemed a failure to execute the warrant of arrest or transfer order and the Tribunal, through the President, may notify the Security Council accordingly.

Transmission of arrest warrants

59bis.—(A) Notwithstanding Rules 55 to 59, on the order of a Judge, the Registrar shall transmit to an appropriate authority or international body or the Prosecutor a copy of a warrant for the arrest of an accused, on such terms as the Judge may determine, together with an order for the prompt transfer of the accused to the Tribunal in the event that the accused be taken into custody by the authority or international body or the Prosecutor.

7–67

(B) At the time of being taken into custody an accused shall be informed immediately, an a language the accused understands, of the charges against him/her and of the fact that he/she is being transferred to the Tribunal. Upon such transfer, the indictment and a statement of rights of the accused shall be read to the accused and the accused shall be cautioned in such a language.

(C) Notwithstanding Sub-rule (B), the indictment and the statement of rights of the accused need not be read to the accused if the accused is served with these, or with a translation of these, in a language the accused understands and is able to read.

Procedure in Case of Failure to Execute a Warrant

61.—(A) If, within a reasonable time, a warrant of arrest has not been executed, and personal service of the indictment has consequently not been effected, the Judge who confirmed the indictment shall invite the Prosecutor to report on the measures taken. When the Judge is satisfied that:

7–68

  (i) the Registrar and the Prosecutor have taken all reasonable steps to secure the arrest of the accused, including recourse to the appropriate authorities of the State in whose territory or under whose jurisdiction and control the person to be served resides or was last known to them to be; and

  (ii) if the whereabouts of the accused are unknown, the Prosecutor and the Registrar have taken all reasonable steps to ascertain those whereabouts, including by seeking publication of advertisements pursuant to Rule 60,

the Judge shall order that the indictment be submitted by the Prosecutor to the Trial Chamber of which the Judge is a member.

(B) Upon obtaining such an order the Prosecutor shall submit the indictment to the Trial Chamber in open court, together with all the evidence that was before the Judge who initially confirmed the indictment. The Prosecutor may also call before the Trial Chamber and examine any witness whose statement has been submitted to the confirming Judge. In addition, the Trial Chamber may request the Prosecutor to call any other witness whose statement has been submitted to the confirming Judge.

(C) If the Trial Chamber is satisfied on that evidence, together with such additional evidence as the Prosecutor may tender, that there are reasonable grounds for believing that the accused has committed all or any of the crimes charged in the indictment, it shall so determine. The Trial Chamber shall have the relevant parts of the indictment read out by the Prosecutor together with an account of the efforts to effect service referred to in Sub-rule (A) above.

(D) The Trial Chamber shall also issue an international arrest warrant in respect of the accused which shall be transmitted to all States. Upon request by the Prosecutor or *proprio motu*, after having heard the Prosecutor, the Trial Chamber may order a State or States to adopt provisional measures to freeze the assets of the accused, without prejudice to the rights of third parties.

(E) If the Prosecutor satisfies the Trial Chamber that the failure to effect personal service was due in whole or in part to a failure or refusal of a State to cooperate with the Tribunal in accordance with Article 29 of the Statute, the Trial Chamber shall so certify. After consulting the Presiding Judge of the Chambers, the President shall notify the Security Council thereof in such a manner as the President thinks fit.

ICTR

ICTR Rules of Procedure and Evidence, rr. 55, 59, 61

Execution of Arrest Warrants

7–69   **55.**—(A) A warrant of arrest shall be signed by a Judge and shall bear the seal of the Tribunal. It shall be accompanied by a copy of the indictment, and a statement of the rights of the accused. These rights include those set forth in Article 20 of the Statute, and in Rules 42 and 43 *mutatis mutandis*, together with the right of the accused to remain silent, and to be cautioned that any statement he makes shall be recorded and may be used in evidence.

(B) The Registrar shall transmit to the national authorities of the State in whose territory or under whose jurisdiction or control the accused resides, or was last known to be, three sets of certified copies of:

    (i) The warrant for arrest of the accused and an order for his surrender to the Tribunal;

    (ii) The confirmed indictment;

    (iii) A statement of the rights of the accused; and if necessary a translation thereof in a language understood by the accused.

(C) The Registrar shall instruct the said authorities to:

    (i) Cause the arrest of the accused and his transfer to the Tribunal;

    (ii) Serve a set of the aforementioned documents upon the accused;

    (iii) Cause the documents to be read to the accused in a language understood by him and to caution him as to his rights in that language; and

    (iv) Return one set of the documents together with proof of service, to the Tribunal.

(D) When an arrest warrant issued by the Tribunal is executed, a member of the Prosecutor's Office may be present as from the time of arrest.

Failure to Execute a Warrant of Arrest or Transfer Order

7–70   **59.**—(A) Where the State to which a warrant of arrest or transfer order has been transmitted has been unable to execute the warrant of arrest or transfer order, it shall report forthwith its inability to the Registrar, and the reasons therefore.

(B) If, within a reasonable time after the warrant of arrest or transfer order has been transmitted to the State, no report is made on action taken, this shall be deemed a failure to execute the warrant of arrest or transfer order and the Tribunal, through the President, may notify the Security Council accordingly.

Procedure in Case of Failure to Execute a Warrant of Arrest

7–71   **61.**—(A) If, within a reasonable time, a warrant of arrest has not been executed, and personal service of the indictment has consequently not been effected, the Judge who confirmed the indictment shall invite the Prosecutor to report on the measures taken. When the Judge is satisfied that:

    (i) The Registrar and the Prosecutor have taken all reasonable steps to secure the arrest of the accused, including recourse to the appropriate authorities of the State in whose territory or under whose jurisdiction and control the accused to be served resides or was last known to be; and

    (ii) If the whereabouts of the accused are unknown, the Prosecutor and the Registrar have taken all reasonable steps to ascertain those whereabouts, including by seeking publication of advertisement pursuant to Rule 60,

the Judge shall order that the indictment be submitted by the Prosecutor to his Trial Chamber.

(B) Upon obtaining such an order the Prosecutor shall submit the indictment to the Trial Chamber in open court, together with all the evidence that was before the Judge who initially confirmed the indictment and any other evidence submitted to him after confirmation of the indictment. The Prosecutor may also call before the Trial Chamber and examine any witness whose statement has been submitted to the confirming Judge.

(C) If the Trial Chamber is satisfied on that evidence, together with such additional evidence as the Prosecutor may tender, that there are reasonable grounds for believing that the accused has committed all or any of the crimes charged in the indictment, it shall so determine. The Trial Chamber shall have the relevant parts of the indictment read out by the Prosecutor together with an account of the efforts to effect service referred to in Sub-Rule (A) above.

(D) The Trial Chamber shall also issue an international arrest warrant in respect of the accused which shall be transmitted to all States. Upon request by the Prosecutor or *proprio motu*, after having heard the Prosecutor, the Trial Chamber may order a State or States to adopt provisional measures to freeze the assets of the accused, without prejudice to the rights of third parties.

(E) If, during the hearing, the Prosecutor satisfies the Trial Chamber that the failure to effect personal service of the indictment was due in whole or in part to a failure or refusal of a State to co-operate with the Tribunal in accordance with Article 28 of the Statute, the Trial Chamber shall so certify. After consulting the Presiding Judges of the Chambers, the President shall notify the Security Council thereof in such manner as he thinks fit.

East Timor

Regulation 2000/30, ss.19A, 20, 21 (as amended by Regulation 2001/25) Arrest Warrant

19A.—19A.1 If there are reasonable grounds to believe that a person has **7–72** committed a crime, the public prosecutor may request the Investigating Judge to issue a warrant for the arrest of that person in accordance with the rules established in the present section.

19A.2 The arrest warrant shall contain the following:

    (a) the name of the suspect and any other identifying information;

    (b) identity of the alleged victims;

    (c) a summary of the facts which are alleged to constitute a crime and a specific reference to the crime for which the arrest of the suspect is sought, including a reference to the relevant legal provisions at issue; and

    (d) the name and signature of the Investigating Judge.

19A.3 Upon arrest, the suspect shall be informed of his or her rights, in accordance with Section 6 of the present regulation, and shall be given a copy of the warrant.

19A.4 The police may arrest a suspect without a warrant when, in the course of ordinary law enforcement activities,

    (a) the suspect is found in the act of committing a crime; or

    (b) there are reasonable grounds to believe that the suspect has committed a crime and that there is an immediate likelihood that before a warrant could be obtained the suspect will flee or destroy, falsify or taint evidence, or endanger public safety or the integrity of the victims or witnesses; or

    (c) the police are in hot pursuit of a suspect immediately after commission of a crime and evidence of the suspect's participation in the crime is found in the suspect's possession.

19A.5 In cases defined in Section 19A.4 of the present regulation, the police shall immediately inform the public prosecutor of all circumstances and the restrictive measures applied, and shall submit the report to the public prosecutor without undue delay.

19A.6 Upon receipt of the report pursuant to Section 19A.5 of the present regulation, the public prosecutor may:

    (a) request the issuance of the corresponding warrants from the Investigating Judge, in accordance with the rules provided in the present regulation; or

    (b) continue the investigation, but order the suspect to be released from custody; or

    (c) dismiss the case and order the suspect to be released from custody.

19A.7 Where a suspect is arrested and detained after a warrant has been issued, the public prosecutor may dismiss the case and request the Investigating Judge to order the release of the suspect in the following circumstances:

    (a) there is insufficient evidence that a crime has been committed;

    (b) the acts under investigation are found to be of non-criminal nature;

    (c) the period to investigate the crime (statute of limitation) has elapsed;

    (d) the suspect has already been tried by a court for the same offences and has been finally convicted or acquitted; or

    (e) there is sufficient evidence that a crime has been committed, but the evidence against the suspect is not sufficient and there is no reasonable possibility to bring additional evidence into the case.

19A.8 Where the case has been dismissed pursuant to Section 19A.6 or 19A.7 of the present regulation, the public prosecutor shall immediately notify the alleged victim of the dismissal of the case, in a manner meeting the requirements of Section 12.4 of the present regulation and that prevents undue danger to the safety, well-being and privacy of those who provided information to the prosecutor, so that the victim may exercise the rights defined in Section 25 of the present regulation.

19A.9 As soon as practicable after the time a suspect is placed in detention, the police shall notify the family of the suspect.

Review Hearing

7–73   **20.**—20.1 Within 72 hours of arrest, the Investigating Judge shall hold a hearing to review the lawfulness of the arrest and detention of the suspect. At this hearing the suspect must be present, along with his or her legal representative, if such a legal representative has been retained or appointed.

20.2 The review hearing shall be closed to the public, unless requested otherwise by the suspect and ordered by the Investigating Judge.

20.3 Pursuant to Section 6 of the present regulation, the Investigating Judge shall inform the suspect of the rights to which he or she is entitled during the investigations, including the right to legal representation.

20.4 The suspect may raise objections before the Investigating Judge concerning any allegation of ill treatment or violations of his or her human rights by police officers or other authorities, or the unlawfulness of his or her detention.

20.5 If the suspect makes a statement, the Investigating Judge, the public prosecutor and the legal representative of the suspect may ask pertinent questions to the suspect with respect to his or her statement. If the suspect makes a statement which includes an admission of guilt, the Investigating Judge shall proceed as provided in Section 29A of the present regulation 20.6 At the conclusion of the hearing the Investigating Judge may:

    (a) confirm the arrest and order the detention of the suspect;

    (b) order substitute restrictive measures instead of detention, as provided in Section 21 of the present regulation; or

    (c) order the release of the suspect.

20.7 The Investigating Judge may confirm the arrest and order the detention of the suspect when:

    (a) there are reasons to believe that a crime has been committed; and

    (b) there is sufficie nt evidence to support a reasonable belief that the suspect was the perpetrator; and

    (c) there are reasonable grounds to believe that such detention is necessary.

20.8 Reasonable grounds for detention exist when:

    (a) there are reasons to believe that the suspect will flee to avoid criminal proceedings; or

    (b) there is the risk that evidence may be tainted, lost, destroyed or falsified; or

    (c) there are reasons to believe that witnesses or victims may be pressured, manipulated or their safety endangered; or

    (d) there are reasons to believe that the suspect will continue to commit offences or poses a danger to public safety or security.

20.9 The Investigating Judge shall review the detention of a suspect every thirty days and issue orders for the further detention, substitute restrictive measures or for the release of the suspect.

20.10 Unless otherwise provided in UNTAET regulations, a suspect may be kept in pretrial detention for a period of no more than six months from the date of arrest.

20.11 Taking into consideration the prevailing circumstances in East Timor, in the case of a crime carrying imprisonment for more than five years under the law, the Investigating Judge or the Judge to whom the matter has been referred upon the filing of the indictment may, at the request of the public prosecutor, and if the interest of justice so requires, based on compelling grounds, extend the maximum period of pretrial detention by an additional three months.

20.12 On exceptional grounds, and taking into account the prevailing circumstances in East Timor, for particularly complex cases of crimes carrying imprisonment of ten years or more under the law, the Investigating Judge or the Judge to whom the matter has been referred upon the filing of the indictment may, at the request of the public prosecutor, order the continued detention of a suspect, if the interest of justice so requires, and as long as the length of pretrial detention is reasonable in the circumstances, and having due regard to international standards of fair trial.

20.13 Pursuant to United Nations Security Council Resolutions 1264 (1999) and 1272 (1999), and taking into consideration the prevailing circumstances in East Timor, all warrants for detention issued by the Investigating Judge or public prosecutor prior to the coming into force of the present regulation shall be deemed valid and in accord with the present regulation.

Substitute Restrictive Measures

21.—21.1 As an alternative to an order for detention, the Investigating Judge may order one or more of the following substitute restrictive measures, if he or she believes it is necessary to ensure the integrity of evidence related to

7–74

the alleged crime or the safety or security of the victims, witnesses and other persons related to the proceedings:

　　(a) house detention of the suspect, alone or under the custody of another person;

　　(b) the submission of the suspect to the care or supervision of a person or an institution;

　　(c) a regime of periodical visits of the suspect to an agency or authority designated by the Investigating Judge;

　　(d) the prohibition of the suspect from leaving an area designated by the Investigating Judge;

　　(e) the prohibition of the suspect from appearing at identified places or meeting a named individual; or

　　(f) the prohibition of the suspect from staying in the family home, if the alleged crime is related to domestic violence.

21.2 The Investigating Judge may order that a monetary bond or other surety be posted to guarantee the appearance of the suspect or accused at subsequent proceedings, in an amount that the Investigating Judge determines, in addition to any substitute restrictive measures listed in Section 21.1 of the present regulation.

21.3 A monetary bond or other surety posted as provided in Section 21.2 of the present regulation shall be deposited with the Court and shall be forfeited if the Court finds that the conditions of the bond or surety have been violated. Any bond or surety not forfeited shall be refunded or returned if the Court finds that all conditions of the bond or surety have been met. Any forfeited bond or surety shall accrue to the consolidated budget of East Timor.

SCSL

Statute of the SCSL, Art. 14

Rules of Procedure and Evidence

7–75　　14.—1. The Rules of Procedure and Evidence of the International Criminal Tribunal for Rwanda obtaining at the time of the establishment of the Special Court shall be applicable *mutatis mutandis* to the conduct of the legal proceedings before the Special Court.

2. The judges of the Special Court as a whole may amend the Rules of Procedure and Evidence or adopt additional rules where the applicable Rules do not, or do not adequately, provide for a specific situation. In so doing, they may be guided, as appropriate, by the Criminal Procedure Act, 1965, of Sierra Leone.

SCSL Rules of Procedure and Evidence, rr. 55, 59

Execution of Arrest Warrants

7–76　　55.—(A) A warrant of arrest shall be signed by the Designated Judge and shall bear the seal of the Special Court. It shall be accompanied by a copy of the indictment, and a statement of the rights of the accused.

(B) The Registrar shall transmit to the relevant authorities of Sierra Leone in whose territory or under whose jurisdiction or control the accused resides, or was last known to be, three sets of certified copies of:

　　(i) The warrant for arrest of the accused and an order for his transfer to the Special Court;

(ii) The approved indictment;

(iii) A statement of the rights of the accused; and if necessary a translation thereof in a language understood by the accused.

(C) The Registrar shall request the said authorities to:

(i) Cause the arrest of the accused and his transfer to the Special Court;

(ii) Serve a set of the aforementioned documents upon the accused;

(iii) Cause the documents to be read to the accused in a language understood by him and to caution him as to his rights in that language; and

(iv) Return one set of the documents together with proof of service, to the Special Court.

(D) When an arrest warrant issued by the Special Court is executed, a member of the Prosecutor's Office may be present as from the time of arrest.

Failure to Execute a Warrant of Arrest or Transfer Order

59.—(A) Where the Sierra Leone authorities, to whom a warrant of arrest   **7–77**
or transfer order has been transmitted, are unable to execute the warrant of arrest or transfer order, they shall report forthwith their inability to the Registrar, and the reasons therefore.

(B) If, within a reasonable time after the warrant of arrest or transfer order has been transmitted to the Sierra Leone authorities, no report is made on action taken, this shall be deemed a failure to execute the warrant of arrest or transfer order and the Registrar may refer to the President to take appropriate action.

(2) Form of Arrest Warrants

For the correct form of arrest warrants see, for example, *Prosecutor v.*   **7–78**
J. Nzirorera, Decision on the Defence motion challenging the legality of the arrest and detention of the accused, September 7, 2000.

For legality of arrests of suspects see, for example, *Prosecutor v. Karemera*, Decision of December 10, 1999, para. 4.3.1; *Prosecutor v. Ngirumpatse*, Decision of December 10, 1999, para. 56; and *Prosecutor v. Kajelijeli*, Decision of May 8, 2000, paras 34 and 35. Trial Chambers lack jurisdiction to review the legality of the arrest of a suspect in so far as the arrest has been pursuant to the laws of the arresting State.

For the legality of arrests see Chapter 4 on Powers of the Court.

III. PRELIMINARY PROCEEDINGS

A. INITIAL APPEARANCE

(1) Statutory provisions and rules

ICC

Statute of the ICC, Art. 60

Initial Proceedings before the Court

60.—1. Upon the surrender of the person to the Court, or the person's   **7–79**
appearance before the Court voluntarily or pursuant to the summons, the Pre-Trial Chamber shall satisfy itself that the person has been informed of the

crimes which he or she is alleged to have committed, and of his or her rights under this Statute, including the right to apply for interim release pending trial.

2. A person subject to a warrant of arrest may apply for interim release pending trial. If the Pre-Trial Chamber is satisfied that the conditions set forth in article 58, paragraph 1, are met, the person shall continue to be detained. If it is not so satisfied, the Pre-Trial Chamber shall release the person, with or without conditions.

3. The Pre-Trial Chamber shall periodically review its ruling an the release or detention of the person, and may do so at any time on the request of the Prosecutor or the person. Upon such review, it may modify its ruling as to detention, release or conditions of release, if it is satisfied that the changed circumstances so require.

4. The Pre-Trial Chamber shall ensure that a person is not detained for an unreasonable period prior to trial due to inexcusable delay by the Prosecutor. If such delay occurs, the Court shall consider releasing the person, with or without conditions.

5. If necessary, the Pre-Trial Chamber may issue a warrant of arrest to secure the presence of a person who has been released.

ICC Rules of Procedure and Evidence, rr.118, 119 (see paragraphs 7–112 and 7–113 below)

ICTY

7–80   Unlike the ICC, the initial appearance before the ICTY, ICTR and SCSL takes place before a Trial Chamber.

ICTY Rules of Procedure and Evidence, r. 62

Initial appearance of accused

7–81   **62.**—(A) Upon transfer of an accused to the seat of the Tribunal, the President shall forthwith assign the case to a Trial Chamber. The accused shall be brought before that Trial Chamber or a Judge thereof without delay, and shall be formally charged. The Trial Chamber or the Judge shall:

    (i) satisfy itself, himself or herself that the right of the accused to counsel is respected;

    (ii) read or have the indictment read to the accused in a language the accused understands, and satisfy itself, himself or herself that the accused understands the indictment;

    (iii) inform the accused that, within thirty days of the initial appearance, he or she will be called upon to enter a plea of guilty or not guilty on each count but that, should the accused so request, he or she may immediately enter a plea of guilty or not guilty on one or more count;

    (iv) if the accused fails to enter a plea at the initial or any further appearance, enter a plea of not guilty on the accused's behalf;

    (v) in case of a plea of not guilty, instruct the Registrar to set a date for trial;

    (vi) in case of a plea of guilty:

        (a) if before the Trial Chamber, act in accordance with Rule 62*bis*, or

        (b) if before a Judge, refer the plea to the Trial Chamber so that it may act in accordance with Rule 62*bis*;

(vii) instruct the Registrar to set such other dates as appropriate.

(B) Where the interests of justice so require, the Registrar may assign a duty counsel as within Rule 45 (C) to represent the accused at the initial appearance. Such assignments shall be treated in accordance with the relevant provisions of the Directive referred to in Rule 45 (A).

ICTR

ICTR Rules of Procedure and Evidence, r. 62

Initial Appearance of Accused and Plea

62.—(A) Upon his transfer to the Tribunal, the accused shall be brought before a Trial Chamber or a Judge thereof without delay, and shall be formally charged. The Trial Chamber or the Judge shall: **7–82**

   (i) Satisfy itself or himself that the right of the accused to counsel is respected;

  (ii) Read or have the indictment read to the accused in a language he understands, and satisfy itself or himself that the accused understands the indictment;

 (iii) Call upon the accused to enter a plea of guilty or not guilty on each count; should the accused fail to do so, enter a plea of not guilty on his behalf;

 (iv) In case of a plea of not guilty, instruct the Registrar to set a date for trial;

  (v) In case of a plea of guilty:

    (a) if before a Judge, refer the plea to the Trial Chamber so that it may act in accordance with Rule 62 (B); or

    (b) if before a Trial Chamber, act in accordance with Rule 62 (B).

(B) If an accused pleads guilty in accordance with Rule 62 (A)(v), or requests to change his plea to guilty, the Trial Chamber shall satisfy itself that the guilty plea:

   (i) is made freely and voluntarily;

  (ii) is an informed plea;

 (iii) is unequivocal; and

 (iv) is based on sufficient facts for the crime and accused's participation in it, either on the basis of objective indicia or of lack of any material disagreement between the parties about the facts of the case.

Thereafter the Trial Chamber may enter a finding of guilt and instruct the Registrar to set a date for the sentencing hearing.

East Timor

Regulation 2000/30, s.20 (as amended by Regulation 2001/25)

Review Hearing

20.—20.1 Within 72 hours of arrest, the Investigating Judge shall hold a hearing to review the lawfulness of the arrest and detention of the suspect. At this hearing the suspect must be present, along with his or her legal representative, if such a legal representative has been retained or appointed.   **7–83**

20.2 The review hearing shall be closed to the public, unless requested otherwise by the suspect and ordered by the Investigating Judge.

20.3 Pursuant to Section 6 of the present regulation, the Investigating Judge shall inform the suspect of the rights to which he or she is entitled during the investigations, including the right to legal representation.

20.4 The suspect may raise objections before the Investigating Judge concerning any allegation of ill treatment or violations of his or her human rights by police officers or other authorities, or the unlawfulness of his or her detention.

20.5 If the suspect makes a statement, the Investigating Judge, the public prosecutor and the legal representative of the suspect may ask pertinent questions to the suspect with respect to his or her statement. If the suspect makes a statement which includes an admission of guilt, the Investigating Judge shall proceed as provided in Section 29A of the present regulation 20.6 At the conclusion of the hearing the Investigating Judge may:

(a) confirm the arrest and order the detention of the suspect;
(b) order substitute restrictive measures instead of detention, as provided in Section 21 of the present regulation; or
(c) order the release of the suspect.

20.7 The Investigating Judge may confirm the arrest and order the detention of the suspect when:

(a) there are reasons to believe that a crime has been committed; and
(b) there is sufficie nt evidence to support a reasonable belief that the suspect was the perpetrator; and
(c) there are reasonable grounds to believe that such detention is necessary.

20.8 Reasonable grounds for detention exist when:

(a) there are reasons to believe that the suspect will flee to avoid criminal proceedings; or
(b) there is the risk that evidence may be tainted, lost, destroyed or falsified; or
(c) there are reasons to believe that witnesses or victims may be pressured, manipulated or their safety endangered; or
(d) there are reasons to believe that the suspect will continue to commit offences or poses a danger to public safety or security.

20.9 The Investigating Judge shall review the detention of a suspect every thirty days and issue orders for the further detention, substitute restrictive measures or for the release of the suspect.

20.10 Unless otherwise provided in UNTAET regulations, a suspect may be kept in pretrial detention for a period of no more than six months from the date of arrest.

20.11 Taking into consideration the prevailing circumstances in East Timor, in the case of a crime carrying imprisonment for more than five years under the law, the Investigating Judge or the Judge to whom the matter has been referred upon the filing of the indictment may, at the request of the public prosecutor, and if the interest of justice so requires, based on compelling grounds, extend the maximum period of pretrial detention by an additional three months.

20.12 On exceptional grounds, and taking into account the prevailing circumstances in East Timor, for particularly complex cases of crimes carrying imprisonment of ten years or more under the law, the Investigating Judge or the Judge to whom the matter has been referred upon the filing of the indictment may, at the request of the public prosecutor, order the continued detention of a suspect, if the interest of justice so requires, and as long as the length of pretrial detention is reasonable in the circumstances, and having due regard to international standards of fair trial.

20.13 Pursuant to United Nations Security Council Resolutions 1264 (1999) and 1272 (1999), and taking into consideration the prevailing circumstances in East Timor, all warrants for detention issued by the Investigating Judge or public prosecutor prior to the coming into force of the present regulation shall be deemed valid and in accord with the present regulation.

SCSL

SCSL Rules of Procedure and Evidence, r. 61

Initial Appearance of Accused and Plea

61. Upon his transfer to the Special Court, the accused shall be brought   **7–84**
before the Designated Judge as soon as practicable, and shall be formally
charged. The Designated Judge shall:
  (i) Satisfy himself that the right of the accused to counsel is respected,
      and in so doing, shall question the accused with regard to his means
      and instruct the Registrar to provide legal assistance to the accused as
      necessary, unless the accused elects to act as his own counsel or
      refuses representation;
 (ii) Read or have the indictment read to the accused in a language he
      speaks and understands, and satisfy himself that the accused under-
      stands the indictment;
(iii) Call upon the accused to enter a plea of guilty or not guilty on each
      count; should the accused fail to do so, enter a plea of not guilty on his
      behalf;
 (iv) In case of a plea of not guilty, instruct the Registrar to set a date for
      trial;
  (v) In case of a plea of guilty, shall refer the plea to the Trial Chamber so
      that it may act in accordance with Rule 62.

B. GUILTY PLEAS

(1) Statutory provisions and rules

ICC

Statute of the ICC, Art. 65

Proceedings on an admission of guilt

65.—1. Where the accused makes an admission of guilt pursuant to article   **7–85**
64, paragraph 8(a), the Trial Chamber shall determine whether:
  (a) The accused understands the nature and consequences of the
      admission of guilt;
  (b) The admission is voluntarily made by the accused after sufficient
      consultation with defence counsel; and
  (c) The admission of guilt is supported by the facts of the case that are
      contained in:
       (i) The charges brought by the Prosecutor and admitted by the
           accused;
      (ii) Any materials presented by the Prosecutor which supplements
           the charges and which the accused accepts; and
     (iii) Any other evidence, such as the testimony of witnesses, presented
           by the Prosecutor or the accused.
 2. Where the Trial Chamber is satisfied that the matters referred to in
paragraph 1 are established, it shall consider the admission of guilt, together

with any additional evidence presented, as establishing all the essential facts that are required to prove the crime to which the admission of guilt relates, and may convict the accused of that crime.

3. Where the Trial Chamber is not satisfied that the matters referred to in paragraph 1 are established, it shall consider the admission of guilt as not having been made, in which case it shall order that the trial be continued under the ordinary trial procedures provided by this Statute and may remit the case to another Trial Chamber.

4. Where the Trial Chamber is of the opinion that a more complete presentation of the facts of the case is required in the interest of justice, in particular in the interest of victims, the Trial Chamber may:

(a) Request the Prosecutor to present additional evidence, including the testimony of witnesses; or

(b) Order that the trial be continued under the ordinary trial procedures provided by this Statute, in which case it shall consider the admission of guilt as not having been made and may remit the case to another Trial Chamber.

5. Any discussions between the Prosecutor and the defence regarding modification of the charges, the admission of guilt or the penalty to be imposed shall not be binding on the Court.

ICC Rules of Procedure and Evidence, r. 139

Decision on admission of guilt

7–86   **139.**—1. After having proceeded in accordance with article 65, paragraph 1, the Trial Chamber, in order to decide whether to proceed in accordance with article 65, paragraph 4, may invite the views of the Prosecutor and the defence.

2. The Trial Chamber shall then make its decision on the admission of guilt and shall give reasons for this decision, which shall be placed on record.

ICTY

ICTY Rules of Procedure and Evidence, rr. 62*bis*, 62*ter*

Guilty pleas

7–87   **62bis.** If an accused pleads guilty in accordance with Rule 62 (vi), or requests to change his or her plea to guilty and the Trial Chamber is satisfied that:

(i) the guilty plea has been made voluntarily;

(ii) the guilty plea is informed;

(iii) the guilty plea is not equivocal; and

(iv) there is a sufficient factual basis for the crime and the accused's participation in it, either on the basis of independent indicia or on lack of any material disagreement between the parties about the facts of the case,

the Trial Chamber may enter a finding of guilt and instruct the Registrar to set a date for the sentencing hearing.

Plea agreement procedure

7–88   **62ter.**—(A) The Prosecutor and the defence may agree that, upon the accused entering a plea of guilty to the indictment or to one or more counts of the indictment, the Prosecutor shall do one or more of the following before the Trial Chamber:

    (i) apply to amend the indictment accordingly;
    (ii) submit that a specific sentence or sentencing range is appropriate;
    (iii) not oppose a request by the accused for a particular sentence or sentencing range.
  (B) The Trial Chamber shall not be bound by any agreement specified in paragraph (A).
  (C) If a plea agreement has been reached by the parties, the Trial Chamber shall require the disclosure if the agreement in open session or, on a showing of good cause, in closed session, at the time the accused pleads guilty in accordance with Rule 62 (vi), or requests to change his or her plea to guilty.

ICTR

ICTR Rules of Procedure and Evidence, rr. 62, 62*bis*

Initial Appearance of Accused and Plea

62.—(A) Upon his transfer to the Tribunal, the accused shall be brought   **7–89**
before a Trial Chamber or a Judge thereof without delay, and shall be formally charged. The Trial Chamber or the Judge shall:
    (i) Satisfy itself or himself that the right of the accused to counsel is respected;
    (ii) Read or have the indictment read to the accused in a language he speaks and understands, and satisfy itself or himself that the accused understands the indictment;
    (iii) Call upon the accused to enter a plea of guilty or not guilty on each count; should the accused fail to do so, enter a plea of not guilty on his behalf;
    (iv) In case of a plea of not guilty, instruct the Registrar to set a date for trial;
    (v) In case of a plea of guilty:
        (a) if before a Judge, refer the plea to the Trial Chamber so that it may act in accordance with Rule 62 (B); or
        (b) if before a Trial Chamber, act in accordance with Rule 62 (B).
  (B) If an accused pleads guilty in accordance with Rule 62 (A)(v), or requests to change his plea to guilty, the Trial Chamber shall satisfy itself that the guilty plea:
    (i) is made freely and voluntarily;
    (ii) is an informed plea;
    (iii) is unequivocal; and
    (iv) is based on sufficient facts for the crime and accused's participation in it, either on the basis of objective indicia or of lack of any material disagreement between the parties about the facts of the case.
  Thereafter the Trial Chamber may enter a finding of guilt and instruct the Registrar to set a date for the sentencing hearing.

Plea Agreement Procedure

62*bis*.—(A) The Prosecutor and the Defence may agree that, upon the   **7–90**
accused entering a plea of guilty to the indictment or to one or more counts of the indictment, the Prosecutor shall do one or more of the following before the Trial Chamber:
    (i) apply to amend the indictment accordingly;
    (ii) submit that a specific sentence or sentencing range is appropriate;
    (iii) not oppose a request by the accused for a particular sentence or sentencing range.

(B) The Trial Chamber shall not be bound by any agreement specified in paragraph (A).

(C) If a plea agreement has been reached by the parties, the Trial Chamber shall require the disclosure of the agreement in open session or, on a showing of good cause, in closed session, at the time the accused pleads guilty in accordance with Rule 62 (A) (v), or requests to change his or her plea to guilty.

East Timor

Regulation 2000/30, s.29A (as amended by Regulation 2001/25)

Proceedings on an Admission of Guilt

7–91   **29A.1.** Where the accused makes an admission of guilt in any proceedings before the Investigating Judge, or before a different judge or panel at any time before a final decision in the case, the court or judge before whom the admission is made shall determine whether:

(a) The accused understands the nature and consequences of the admission of guilt;

(b) The admission is voluntarily made by the accused after sufficient consultation with defense counsel; and

(c) The admission of guilt is supported by the facts of the case that are contained in:

  (i) The charges as alleged in the indictment and admitted by the accused;

  (ii) Any materials presented by the prosecutor which support the indictment and which the accused accepts; and

  (iii) Any other evidence, such as the testimony of witnesses, presented by the prosecutor or the accused.

29A.2. Where the court is satisfied that the matters referred to in Section 29A.1 of the present regulation are established, it shall consider the admission of guilt, together with any additional evidence presented, as establishing all the essential facts that are required to prove the crime to which the admission of guilt relates, and may convict the accused of that crime.

29A.3. Where the court is not satisfied that the matters referred to in Section 29A.1 are established, it shall consider the admission of guilt as not having been made, in which event it shall order that the trial be continued under the ordinary trial procedures provided in this Regulation.

29A.4. Where the Court is of the opinion that a more complete presentation of the facts of the case is required in the interests of justice, taking into account the interests of the victims, the court may:

(a) Request the prosecutor to present additional evidence, including the testimony of witnesses; or

(b) Order that the trial be continued under the ordinary trial procedures provided in this Regulation, in which event it shall consider the admission of guilt as not having been made.

29A.5. Any discussions between the prosecutor and the defense regarding modification of the charges, the admission of guilt or the penalty to be imposed shall not be binding on the court.

SCSL

SCSL Rules of Procedure and Evidence, rr. 61, 62

Initial Appearance of Accused and Plea

7–92   **61.** Upon his transfer to the Special Court, the accused shall be brought before the Designated Judge as soon as practicable, and shall be formally charged. The Designated Judge shall:

  (i) Satisfy himself that the right of the accused to counsel is respected, and in so doing, shall question the accused with regard to his means and instruct the Registrar to provide legal assistance to the accused as necessary, unless the accused elects to act as his own counsel or refuses representation;

  (ii) Read or have the indictment read to the accused in a language he speaks and understands, and satisfy himself that the accused understands the indictment;

  (iii) Call upon the accused to enter a plea of guilty or not guilty on each count; should the accused fail to do so, enter a plea of not guilty on his behalf;

  (iv) In case of a plea of not guilty, instruct the Registrar to set a date for trial;

  (v) In case of a plea of guilty, shall refer the plea to the Trial Chamber so that it may act in accordance with Rule 62.

Procedure upon Guilty Plea

62.—(A) If an accused pleads guilty in accordance with Rule 61(v), or requests to change his plea to guilty, the Trial Chamber shall satisfy itself that the guilty plea: **7–93**

  (i) s made freely and voluntarily;

  (ii) is an informed plea;

  (iii) is unequivocal;

  (iv) is based on sufficient facts for the crime and accused's participation in it, either on the basis of independent indicia or of lack of any material disagreement between the parties about the facts of the case.

(B) Thereafter the Trial Chamber may enter a finding of guilt and instruct the Registrar to set a date for the sentencing hearing.

(2) Procedure for entering guilty pleas

Guilty pleas have been entered in various cases before the ICTY and ICTR: see, for example, *Prosecutor v. Erdemović*, Judgment, Appeals Chamber, October 7, 1997; *Prosecutor v. Kambanda*, Judgment and Sentence, September 4, 1998; and *Prosecutor v. Ruggiu*, Judgment and Sentence, June 1, 2000. In each case, the Trial Chamber has had to satisfy itself all of the requirements of ICTY Rule 62*bis* and ICTR/SCSL Rule 62(B) have been met. According to these Rules, the Chamber needs to be satisfied that: (i) the plea has been made voluntarily; (ii) the Accused is informed about the consequences of pleading guilty, as well as, waiving some of his fundamental rights (the right to plead not guilty and require the Prosecution to prove the charges in the Indictment beyond a reasonable doubt at a public trial; the right to prepare and put forward a defence to the charges at such public trial; the right to be tried without undue delay; the right to be tried in his presence, and to defend himself in person at trial or through legal assistance of his own choosing at trial; the right to examine at his trial, or have examined, the witnesses against him and to obtain the attendance and examination of witnesses on his behalf at a trial under the same conditions as witnesses against him; and the right not to be compelled to testify against himself (*Prosecutor v. Deronjic*, Plea Agreement, September 29, 2003, para. 13)); (iii) the guilty plea is not equivocal; and (iv) there is a sufficient factual basis for the crime and the Accused's   **7–94** participation in it, either on the basis of independent indicia or on lack of any material disagreement between the parties about the facts of the case.

Accused have pleaded guilty before the East Timor Special Panel for Serious Crimes: see, for example, *Prosecutor v. Fernandes*, Judgment, January 25, 2001 (the court having verified at paragraph 6 that the accused understood the nature and consequences of the admission of guilt; his guilty plea was made voluntarily; and was unequivocal); *Prosecutor v. dos Santos*, Judgment, May 14, 2002; and *Prosecutor v. Bere*, Judgment, May 15, 2001, in which the accused admitted his involvement in the offence, but did not plead guilty as he sought to rely on the defence of duress, which resulted in the continuation of the full trial.

See further Chapter 18.

C. QUESTIONING OF SUSPECTS AND ACCUSED

(1) Statutory provisions and rules

ICC Rules of Procedure and Evidence, rr. 111, 112

Record of questioning in general

7–95   **111.**—1. A record shall be made of formal statements made by any person who is questioned in connection with an investigation or with proceedings. The record shall be signed by the person who records and conducts the questioning and by the person who is questioned and his or her counsel, if present, and, where applicable, the Prosecutor or the judge who is present. The record shall note the date, time and place of, and all persons present during the questioning. It shall also be noted when someone has not signed the record as well as the reasons therefor.

2. When the Prosecutor or national authorities question a person, due regard shall be given to article 55. When a person is informed of his or her rights under article 55, paragraph 2, the fact that this information has been provided shall be noted in the record.

Recording of questioning in particular cases

7–96   **112.**—1. Whenever the Prosecutor questions a person to whom article 55, paragraph 2, applies, or for whom a warrant of arrest or a summons to appear has been issued under article 58, paragraph 7, the questioning shall be audio-or video-recorded, in accordance with the following procedure:

  (a) The person questioned shall be informed, in a language he or she fully understands and speaks, that the questioning is to be audio- or video-recorded, and that the person concerned may object if he or she so wishes. The fact that this information has been provided and the response given by the person concerned shall be noted in the record. The person may, before replying, speak in private with his or her counsel, if present. If the person questioned refuses to be audio-or video-recorded, the procedure in rule 111 shall be followed;

  (b) A waiver of the right to be questioned in the presence of counsel shall be recorded in writing and, if possible, be audio-or video-recorded;

(c) In the event of an interruption in the course of questioning, the fact and the time of the interruption shall be recorded before the audio-or video-recording ends as well as the time of resumption of the questioning;

(d) At the conclusion of the questioning, the person questioned shall be offered the opportunity to clarify anything he or she has said and to add anything he or she may wish. The time of conclusion of the questioning shall be noted;

(e) The tape shall be transcribed as soon as practicable after the conclusion of the questioning and a copy of the transcript supplied to the person questioned together with a copy of the recorded tape or, if multiple recording apparatus was used, one of the original recorded tapes;

(f) The original tape or one of the original tapes shall be sealed in the presence of the person questioned and his or her counsel, if present, under the signature of the Prosecutor and the person questioned and the counsel, if present.

2. The Prosecutor shall make every reasonable effort to record the questioning in accordance with sub-rule 1. As an exception, a person may be questioned without the questioning being audio-or video-recorded where the circumstances prevent such recording taking place. In this case, the reasons for not recording the questioning shall be stated in writing and the procedure in rule 111 shall be followed.

3. When, pursuant to sub-rule 1(a) or 2, the questioning is not audio-or video-recorded, the person questioned shall be provided with a copy of his or her statement.

4. The Prosecutor may choose to follow the procedure in this rule when questioning other persons than those mentioned in sub-rule 1, in particular where the use of such procedures could assist in reducing any subsequent traumatization of a victim of sexual or gender violence, a child or a person with disabilities in providing their evidence. The Prosecutor may make an application to the relevant Chamber.

5. The Pre-Trial Chamber may, in pursuance of article 56, paragraph 2, order that the procedure in this rule be applied to the questioning of any person.

ICTY

ICTY Rules of Procedure and Evidence, rr. 42, 43, 63

Rights of suspects during investigation
See Rule 42 set out at paragraph 7–43.   **7–97**

Recording questioning of suspects
43. Whenever the Prosecutor questions a suspect, the questioning shall be   **7–98**
audio-recorded or video-recorded, in accordance with the following procedure:

(i) the suspect shall be informed in a language the suspect speaks and understands that the questioning is being audio-recorded or video-recorded;

(ii) in the event of a break in the course of the questioning, the fact and the time of the break shall be recorded before audio-recording or video-recording ends and the time of resumption of the questioning shall also be recorded;

(iii) at the conclusion of the questioning the suspect shall be offered the opportunity to clarify anything the suspect has said, and to add anything the suspect may wish, and the time of conclusion shall be recorded;

(iv) a copy of the recorded tape will be supplied to the suspect or, if multiple recording apparatus was used, one of the original recorded tapes;

(v) after a copy has been made, if necessary, of the recorded tape, the original recorded tape or one of the original tapes shall be sealed in the presence of the suspect under the signature of the Prosecutor and the suspect; and

(vi) the tape shall be transcribed if the suspect becomes an accused.

Questioning of accused

7–99   **63.**—(A) Questioning by the Prosecutor of an accused, including after the initial appearance, shall not proceed without the presence of counsel unless the accused has voluntarily and expressly agreed to proceed without counsel present. If the accused subsequently expresses a desire to have counsel, questioning shall thereupon cease, and shall only resume when the accused's counsel is present.

(B) The questioning, including any waiver of he right to counsel, shall be audio-recorded or video-recorded in accordance with the procedure provided for in Rule 43. the Prosecutor shall at the beginning of the questioning caution the accused in accordance with Rule 42(A)(iii).

ICTR Rules of Procedure and Evidence, rr. 42, 43, 63

7–100   The ICTR Rules 42 and 63 are identical.

Recording questioning of suspects

7–101   **43.**— Whenever the Prosecutor questions a suspect, the questioning shall be audio-recorded or video-recorded, in accordance with the following procedure:

(i) The suspect shall be informed in a language he speaks and understands that the questioning is being audio-recorded or video-recorded;

(ii) In the event of a break in the course of the questioning, the fact and the time of the break shall be recorded before audio-recording or video-recording ends and the time of resumption of the questioning shall also be recorded;

(iii) At the conclusion of the questioning the suspect shall be offered the opportunity to clarify anything he has said, and to add anything he may wish, and the time of conclusion shall be recorded;

(iv) The content of the recording shall then be transcribed as soon as practicable after the conclusion of questioning and a copy of the transcript supplied to the suspect, together with a copy of the recording or, if multiple recording apparatus was used, one of the original recorded tapes; and

(v) After a copy has been made, if necessary, of the recorded tape for purposes of transcription, the original recorded tape or one of the original tapes shall be sealed in the presence of the suspect under the signature of the Prosecutor and the suspect.

East Timor

Transitional Rules of Criminal Justice, UNTAET Regulation 2000/30 (September 25, 2000) as amended by 2001/25 (September 14, 2001)

Review Hearing

20.—20.1 Within 72 hours of arrest, the Investigating Judge shall hold a hearing to review the lawfulness of the arrest and detention of the suspect. At this hearing the suspect must be present, along with his or her legal representative, if such a legal representative has been retained or appointed. **7–102**

20.2 The review hearing shall be closed to the public, unless requested otherwise by the suspect and ordered by the Investigating Judge.

20.3 Pursuant to Section 6 of the present regulation, the Investigating Judge shall inform the suspect of the rights to which he or she is entitled during the investigations, including the right to legal representation.

20.4 The suspect may raise objections before the Investigating Judge concerning any allegation of ill treatment or violations of his or her human rights by police officers or other authorities, or the unlawfulness of his or her detention.

20.5 If the suspect makes a statement, the Investigating Judge, the public prosecutor and the legal representative of the suspect may ask pertinent questions to the suspect with respect to his or her statement. If the suspect makes a statement which includes an admission of guilt, the Investigating Judge shall proceed as provided in Section 29A of the present regulation.

Also see, Reg. 2000/30 ss.6–7.

SCSL

SCSL Rules of Procedure and Evidence, rr. 42, 43, 63

Rights of Suspects during Investigation

42.—(A) A suspect who is to be questioned by the Prosecutor shall have the following rights, of which he shall be informed by the Prosecutor prior to questioning, in a language he speaks and understands: **7–103**

    (i) The right to legal assistance of his own choosing, including the right to have legal assistance provided by the Defence Office where the interests of justice so require and where the suspect does not have sufficient means to pay for it;

   (ii) The right to have the free assistance of an interpreter if he cannot understand or speak the language to be used for questioning; and

  (iii) The right to remain silent, and to be cautioned that any statement he makes shall be recorded and may be used in evidence.

(B) Questioning of a suspect shall not proceed without the presence of counsel unless the suspect has voluntarily waived his right to counsel. In case of waiver, if the suspect subsequently expresses a desire to have counsel, questioning shall thereupon cease, and shall only resume when the suspect has obtained or has been assigned counsel.

Recording Questioning of Suspects

43. Whenever the Prosecutor questions a suspect, the questioning, including any waiver of the right to counsel, shall be audio-recorded or video-recorded, in accordance with the following procedure: **7–104**

(i) The suspect shall be informed in a language he speaks and understands that the questioning is being audio-recorded or video-recorded;
(ii) In the event of a break in the course of the questioning, the fact and the time of the break shall be recorded before audio-recording or video-recording ends and the time of resumption of the questioning shall also be recorded;
(iii) At the conclusion of the questioning the suspect shall be offered the opportunity to clarify anything he has said, and to add anything he may wish, and the time of conclusion shall be recorded;
(iv) The content of the recording shall then be transcribed as soon as practicable after the conclusion of questioning and a copy of the transcript supplied to the suspect, together with a copy of the recording or, if multiple recording apparatus was used, one of the original recorded tapes; and
(v) After a copy has been made, if necessary, of the recorded tape for purposes of transcription, the original recorded tape or one of the original tapes shall be sealed in the presence of the suspect under the signature of the Prosecutor and the suspect.

Questioning of the Accused

7–105   **63.**—(A) Questioning by the Prosecutor of an accused, including after the initial appearance, shall not proceed without the presence of counsel unless the accused has voluntarily and expressly agreed to proceed without counsel present. If the accused subsequently expresses a desire to have counsel, questioning shall thereupon cease, and shall only resume when the accused's counsel is present.

(B) The questioning, including any waiver of the right to counsel, shall be audio-recorded and, if possible, video-recorded in accordance with the procedure provided for in Rule 43. The Prosecutor shall at the beginning of the questioning caution the accused in accordance with Rule 42(A)(iii).

(2) Rules applicable to questioning the suspect or accused

Right to remain silent

7–106   The accused is not obliged to answer any questions during an interview by the Prosecution. Should he choose not to be interviewed, his failure to answer any questions cannot be used against him during the proceedings. See, *Prosecutor v. Delalic et al.*, Decision on Zdravko Mucic's Motion for the Exclusion of Evidence, September 2, 1997, in which the Trial Chamber considered (i) the admissibility of an interview conducted by national authorities; and, (ii) whether an interview conducted by the Prosecution had been oppressive.

Right to counsel

7–107   Recent jurisprudence has emphasised the importance of the right to legal representation of suspects and accused persons when being questioned. In *Bagosora et al.*, where one of the accused, General Kabiligi, challenged the admission of the transcripts of his interview which had been conducted in absence of counsel, the Chamber emphasised that, along with the right to silence, the right to *immediate* assistance of counsel "is rooted in the concern that an individual, when detained by officials for interrogation, is often fearful, ignorant and vulnerable; that fear and ignorance can lead to false confessions by the innocent; and that vulnerability can lead to abuse of the innocent and guilty alike, particularly when a suspect is held incommunicado and in isolation" (*Prosecutor v. Bagosora et al.*, Decision on the Prosecutor's Motion for the Admission of Certain Materials Under Rule 89(C), October 14, 2004, para. 16). The Trial Chamber also explained that legal representation during preliminary questioning is important to have explanation from counsel about other rights at the preliminary stage, such as the right to silence, the privilege against self-incrimination and the right to be cautioned that any statement made may be used as evidence against the accused (at para. 21).

The essential question is whether a suspect or accused voluntarily waived his right to counsel. The Prosecutor has the burden to prove "convincingly and beyond reasonable doubt" that a suspect or accused voluntarily waived his right to be represented (*Prosecutor v. Delalic et al.*, Decision on Zdravko Mucic's Motion For the Exclusion of Evidence, September 2, 1997, para. 42). This standard of proof was initially brought in connection with allegations of oppressive conduct during a suspect's or accused's questioning (Delalic, see above), but was recently held to apply to the voluntary waiver of the right to representation: *Prosecutor v. Bagosora et al.*, Decision on the Prosecutor's Motion for the Admission of Certain Materials Under Rule 89(C), October 14, 2004, paras 17 and 18. Paragraph 17 states: "National courts in which the right to counsel is recognized have elaborated that *a waiver cannot be voluntary unless a detainee knows of the right to which he is entitled.* To be so informed, the suspect must be informed that the right includes the right to the *prompt* assistance of counsel, prior to and during any questioning. *Any implication that the right is conditional, or that the presence of counsel may be delayed until after the questioning, renders any waiver defective.*" (Footnotes omitted.)

Paragraph 18 makes it clear that the waiver must be express and unequivocal: "Once the detainee has been fully apprised of his right to the assistance of counsel, he or she is in a position to voluntarily waive the right. *The waiver must be shown "convincingly and beyond reasonable doubt". It must be express and unequivocal, and must clearly relate to the interview in which the statement in question is taken.*

On this basis, the Chamber excluded the interview of the accused Gratien Kabiligi even though he had volunteered to be interviewed in absence of counsel. The Trial Chamber was of the opinion that Kabiligi's voluntariness was based on "a misperception that his right to counsel was conditional upon being informed of the case against him" (which he had not been yet) (para. 19) and related to a preliminary interview only (para. 20). In the ICTY the interview of the Accused Haradin Bala was excluded on similar grounds, although based on Rule 63 rather than on Rule 42 of ICTY Rules of Procedure and Evidence. In *Limaj et al.*, the Trial Chamber held that "given the materiality of the role of the Accused in the case, the failure to comply with Rule 63, and the significance of Rule 63 to the integrity of the proceedings in this Tribunal, and their fairness, the Chamber is persuaded, in the exercise of its discretion, that the challenged evidence should be excluded"

(*Prosecutor v. Limaj et al.*, Confidential Decision on Defence Motion to Exclude Statements Made by Haradin Bala in Interview of February 17, 2003, para. 14).

The accused is not entitled to be given the opportunity to be interviewed under the application of a polygraph: see *Prosecutor v. Naletilic*, Decision on the Request of the Accused to be given the Opportunity to be Interrogated under Application of a Polygraph, November 27, 2000.

See further discussion on Rule 95 ICTY/ICTR, Chapter 9 of this work.

D. PROVISIONAL RELEASE

(1) Statutory provisions and rules

ICC

Statute of the ICC, Arts 58, 59, 60

Issuance by the Pre-Trial Chamber of a warrant of arrest or a summons to appear

7–108 **58.**—1. At any time after the initiation of an investigation, the Pre-Trial Chamber shall, on the application of the Prosecutor, issue a warrant of arrest of a person if, having examined the application and the evidence or other information submitted by the Prosecutor, it is satisfied that:

(a) There are reasonable grounds to believe that the person has committed a crime within the jurisdiction of the Court; and
(b) The arrest of the person appears necessary:
  (i) To ensure the person's appearance at trial,
  (ii) To ensure that the person does not obstruct or endanger the investigation or the court proceedings, or
  (iii) Where applicable, to prevent the person from continuing with the commission of that crime or a related crime which is within the jurisdiction of the Court and which arises out of the same circumstances.

Arrest proceedings in the custodial State

7–109 **59.**—1. A State Party which has received a request for provisional arrest or for arrest and surrender shall immediately take steps to arrest the person in question in accordance with its laws and the provisions of Part 9.

2. A person arrested shall be brought promptly before the competent judicial authority in the custodial State which shall determine, in accordance with the law of that State, that:

(a) The warrant applies to that person;
(b) The person has been arrested in accordance with the proper process; and
(c) The person's rights have been respected.

3. The person arrested shall have the right to apply to the competent authority in the custodial State for interim release pending surrender.

4. In reaching a decision on any such application, the competent authority in the custodial State shall consider whether, given the gravity of the alleged crimes, there are urgent and exceptional circumstances to justify interim release and whether necessary safeguards exist to ensure that the custodial State can fulfil its duty to surrender the person to the Court. It shall not be open to the competent authority of the custodial State to consider whether the warrant of arrest was properly issued in accordance with article 58, paragraph 1(a) and (b).

5. The Pre-Trial Chamber shall be notified of any request for interim release and shall make recommendations to the competent authority in the custodial State. The competent authority in the custodial State shall give full consideration to such recommendations, including any recommendations on measures to prevent the escape of the person, before rendering its decision.

6. If the person is granted interim release, the Pre-Trial Chamber may request periodic reports on the status of the interim release.

7. Once ordered to be surrendered by the custodial State, the person shall be delivered to the Court as soon as possible.

Initial proceedings before the Court

60.—1. Upon the surrender of the person to the Court, or the person's appearance before the Court voluntarily or pursuant to a summons, the Pre-Trial Chamber shall satisfy itself that the person has been informed of the crimes which he or she is alleged to have committed, and of his or her rights under this Statute, including the right to apply for interim release pending trial.

7–110

2. A person subject to a warrant of arrest may apply for interim release pending trial. If the Pre-Trial Chamber is satisfied that the conditions set forth in article 58, paragraph 1, are met, the person shall continue to be detained. If it is not so satisfied, the Pre-Trial Chamber shall release the person, with or without conditions.

3. The Pre-Trial Chamber shall periodically review its ruling on the release or detention of the person, and may do so at any time on the request of the Prosecutor or the person. Upon such review, it may modify its ruling as to detention, release or conditions of release, if it is satisfied that changed circumstances so require.

4. The Pre-Trial Chamber shall ensure that a person is not detained for an unreasonable period prior to trial due to inexcusable delay by the Prosecutor. If such delay occurs, the Court shall consider releasing the person, with or without conditions.

5. If necessary, the Pre-Trial Chamber may issue a warrant of arrest to secure the presence of a person who has been released.

ICC Rules of Procedure and Evidence, rr. 117, 118, 119

Detention in the custodial State

117.—1. The Court shall take measures to ensure that it is informed of the arrest of a person in response to a request made by the Court under article 89 or 92. Once so informed, the Court shall ensure that the person receives a copy of the arrest warrant issued by the Pre-Trial Chamber under article 58 and any relevant provisions of the Statute. The documents shall be made available in a language that the person fully understands and speaks.

7–111

2. At any time after arrest, the person may make a request to the Pre-Trial Chamber for the appointment of counsel to assist with proceedings before the Court and the Pre-Trial Chamber shall take a decision on such request.

3. A challenge as to whether the warrant of arrest was properly issued in accordance with article 58, paragraph 1(a) and (b), shall be made in writing to

the Pre-Trial Chamber. The application shall set out the basis for the challenge. After having obtained the views of the Prosecutor, the Pre-Trial Chamber shall decide on the application without delay.

4. When the competent authority of the custodial State notifies the Pre-Trial Chamber that a request for release has been made by the person arrested, in accordance with article 59, paragraph 5, the Pre-Trial Chamber shall provide its recommendations within any time limit set by the custodial State.

5. When the Pre-Trial Chamber is informed that the person has been granted interim release by the competent authority of the custodial State, the Pre-Trial Chamber shall inform the custodial State how and when it would like to receive periodic reports on the status of the interim release.

Pre-trial detention at the seat of the Court

7–112   **118.**—1. If the person surrendered to the Court makes an initial request for interim release pending trial, either upon first appearance in accordance with rule 121 or subsequently, the Pre-Trial Chamber shall decide upon the request without delay, after seeking the views of the Prosecutor.

2. The Pre-Trial Chamber shall review its ruling on the release or detention of a person in accordance with article 60, paragraph 3, at least every 120 days and may do so at any time on the request of the person or the Prosecutor.

3. After the first appearance, a request for interim release must be made in writing. The Prosecutor shall be given notice of such a request. The Pre-Trial Chamber shall decide after having received observations in writing of the Prosecutor and the detained person. The Pre-Trial Chamber may decide to hold a hearing, at the request of the Prosecutor or the detained person or on its own initiative. A hearing must be held at least once every year.

Conditional release

7–113   **119.**—1. The Pre-Trial Chamber may set one or more conditions restricting liberty, including the following:
  (a) The person must not travel beyond territorial limits set by the Pre-Trial Chamber without the explicit agreement of the Chamber;
  (b) The person must not go to certain places or associate with certain persons as specified by the Pre-Trial Chamber;
  (c) The person must not contact directly or indirectly victims or witnesses;
  (d) The person must not engage in certain professional activities;
  (e) The person must reside at a particular address as specified by the Pre-Trial Chamber;
  (f) The person must respond when summoned by an authority or qualified person designated by the Pre-Trial Chamber;
  (g) The person must post bond or provide real or personal security or surety, for which the amount and the schedule and mode of payment shall be determined by the Pre-Trial Chamber;
  (h) The person must supply the Registrar with all identity documents, particularly his or her passport.

2. At the request of the person concerned or the Prosecutor or on its own initiative, the Pre-Trial Chamber may at any time decide to amend the conditions set pursuant to sub-rule 1.

3. Before imposing or amending any conditions restricting liberty, the Pre-Trial Chamber shall seek the views of the Prosecutor, the person concerned, any relevant State and victims that have communicated with the Court in that case and whom the Chamber considers could be at risk as a result of a release or conditions imposed.

4. If the Pre-Trial Chamber is convinced that the person concerned has failed to comply with one or more of the obligations imposed, it may, on such

basis, at the request of the Prosecutor or on its own initiative, issue a warrant of arrest in respect of the person.

5. When the Pre-Trial Chamber issues a summons to appear pursuant to article 58, paragraph 7, and intends to set conditions restricting liberty, it shall ascertain the relevant provisions of the national law of the State receiving the summons. In a manner that is in keeping with the national law of the State receiving the summons, the Pre-Trial Chamber shall proceed in accordance with sub-rules 1, 2 and 3. If the Pre-Trial Chamber receives information that the person concerned has failed to comply with conditions imposed, it shall proceed in accordance with sub-rule 4.

ICTY

ICTY Rules of Procedure and Evidence, rr. 64, 65

Detention on Remand

64. Upon being transferred to the seat of the Tribunal, the accused shall be detained in facilities provided by the host country, or by another country. In exceptional circumstances, the accused may be held in facilities outside of the host country. The President may, on the application of a party, request modification of the conditions of detention of an accused.   **7–114**

Provisional release

65.—(A) Once detained, an accused may not be released except upon an order of a Chamber.   **7–115**

(B) Release may be ordered by a Trial Chamber only after giving the host country and the State to which the accused seeks to be released the opportunity to be heard and only if it is satisfied that the accused will appear for trial and, if released, will not pose a danger to any victim, witness or other person.

(C) The Trial Chamber may impose such conditions upon the release of the accused as it may determine appropriate, including the execution of a bail bond and the observance of such conditions as are necessary to ensure the presence of the accused for trial and the protection of others.

(D) Any decision rendered under this Rule by a Trial Chamber shall be subject to appeal. Subject to paragraph (F) below, an appeal shall be filed within seven days of filing of the impugned decision. Where such decision is rendered orally, the application shall be filed within seven days of the oral decision, unless

  (i) the party challenging the decision was not present or represented when the decision was pronounced, in which case the time-limit shall run from the date on which the challenging party is notified of the oral decision; or

  (ii) the Trial Chamber has indicated that a written decision will follow, in which case, the time-limit shall run from filing of the written decision. (Amended July 21, 2005)

(E) The Prosecutor may apply for a stay of a decision by the Trial Chamber to release an accused on the basis that the Prosecutor intends to appeal the decision, and shall make such an application at the time of filing his or her response to the initial application for provisional release by the accused.

(F) Where the Trial Chamber grants a stay of its decision to release an accused, the Prosecutor shall file his or her appeal not later than one day from the rendering of that decision. (Amended 17 Nov 1999)

(G) Where the Trial Chamber orders a stay of its decision to release the accused pending an appeal by the Prosecutor, the accused shall not be released until either:

    (i) the time-limit for the filing of an appeal by the Prosecutor has expired, and no such appeal is filed;

    (ii) the Appeals Chamber dismisses the appeal; or

    (iii) the Appeals Chamber otherwise orders. (Amended July 21, 2005)

(H) If necessary, the Trial Chamber may issue a warrant of arrest to secure the presence of an accused who has been released or is for any other reason at liberty. The provisions of Section 2 of Part Five shall apply *mutatis mutandis.*

(I) Without prejudice to the provisions of Rule 107, the Appeals Chamber may grant provisional release to convicted persons pending an appeal or for a fixed period if it is satisfied that:

    (i) the appellant, if released, will either appear at the hearing of the appeal or will surrender into detention at the conclusion of the fixed period, as the case may be;

    (ii) the appellant, if released, will not pose a danger to any victim, witness or other person, and

    (iii) special circumstances exist warranting such release.

The provisions of paragraphs (C) and (H) shall apply *mutatis mutandis.*

ICTR

ICTR Rules of Procedure and Evidence, rr. 64, 65

Detention on Remand

7–116   **64.** Upon his transfer to the Tribunal, the accused shall be detained in facilities provided by the host country or by another country. The President may, on the application of a party, request modification of the conditions of detention of an accused.

Provisional Release

7–117   **65.**—(A) Once detained, an accused may not be provisionally released except upon an order of a Trial Chamber.

(B) Provisional release may be ordered by a Trial Chamber only after giving the host country and the country to which the accused seeks to be released the opportunity to be heard, and only if it is satisfied that the accused will appear for trial and, if released, will not pose a danger to any victim, witness or other person.

(C) The Trial Chamber may impose such conditions upon the provisional release of the accused as it may determine appropriate, including the execution of a bail bond and the observance of such conditions as are necessary to ensure the presence of the accused at trial and the protection of others.

(D) Any decision rendered under this Rule shall be subject to appeal in cases where leave is granted by a bench of three Judges of the Appeals Chamber, upon good cause being shown. Subject to paragraph (F) below, applications for leave to appeal shall be filed within seven days of filing of the impugned decision. Where such decision is rendered orally, the application shall be filed within seven days of the oral decision unless:

    (i) the party challenging the decision was not present or represented when the decision was pronounced, in which case the time-limit shall run from the date on which the challenging party is notified of the oral decision; or

    (ii) the Trial Chamber has indicated that a written decision will follow, in which case, the time-limit shall run from filing of the written decision.

(E) The Prosecutor may apply for a stay of a decision by the Trial Chamber to release an accused on the basis that the Prosecutor intends to appeal the decision, and shall make such an application at the time of filing his or her response to the initial application for provisional release by the accused.

(F) Where the Trial Chamber grants a stay of its decision to release an accused, the Prosecutor shall file his or her appeal not later than one day from the rendering of that decision.

(G) Where the Trial Chamber orders a stay of its decision to release the accused pending an appeal by the Prosecutor, the accused shall not be released until either:

(i) the time-limit for the filing of an application for leave to appeal by the Prosecutor has expired, and no such application is filed;

(ii) a bench of three Judges of the Appeals Chamber rejects the application for leave to appeal;

(iii) the Appeals Chamber dismisses the appeal; or

(iv) a bench of three Judges of the Appeals Chamber or the Appeals Chamber otherwise orders.

(H) If necessary, the Trial Chamber may issue a warrant of arrest to secure the presence of an accused who has been provisionally released or is for any other reason at large. The provisions of Section 2 of Part Five shall apply mutatis mutandis.

(I) Without prejudice to the provisions of Rule 107, the Appeals Chamber may grant provisional release to convicted persons pending an appeal or for a fixed period if it is satisfied that:

(i) the appellant, if released, will either appear at the hearing of the appeal or will surrender into detention at the conclusion of the fixed period, as the case may be;

(ii) the appellant, if released, will not pose a danger to any victim, witness or other person, and

(iii) special circumstances exist warranting such release.

The provisions of paragraphs (C) and (H) shall apply mutatis mutandis.

East Timor

Regulation 2000/30, s.20 (as amended by Regulation 2001/25)

Review Hearing

20.—20.1 Within 72 hours of arrest, the Investigating Judge shall hold a **7-118** hearing to review the lawfulness of the arrest and detention of the suspect. At this hearing the suspect must be present, along with his or her legal representative, if such a legal representative has been retained or appointed.

20.2 The review hearing shall be closed to the public, unless requested otherwise by the suspect and ordered by the Investigating Judge.

20.3 Pursuant to Section 6 of the present regulation, the Investigating Judge shall inform the suspect of the rights to which he or she is entitled during the investigations, including the right to legal representation.

20.4 The suspect may raise objections before the Investigating Judge concerning any allegation of ill treatment or violations of his or her human rights by police officers or other authorities, or the unlawfulness of his or her detention.

20.5 If the suspect makes a statement, the Investigating Judge, the public prosecutor and the legal representative of the suspect may ask pertinent questions to the suspect with respect to his or her statement. If the suspect makes a statement which includes an admission of guilt, the Investigating Judge shall proceed as provided in Section 29A of the present regulation 20.6 At the conclusion of the hearing the Investigating Judge may:

  (a) confirm the arrest and order the detention of the suspect;

  (b) order substitute restrictive measures instead of detention, as provided in Section 21 of the present regulation; or

  (c) order the release of the suspect.

20.7 The Investigating Judge may confirm the arrest and order the detention of the suspect when:

  (a) there are reasons to believe that a crime has been committed; and

  (b) there is sufficient evidence to support a reasonable belief that the suspect was the perpetrator; and

  (c) there are reasonable grounds to believe that such detention is necessary.

20.8 Reasonable grounds for detention exist when:

  (a) there are reasons to believe that the suspect will flee to avoid criminal proceedings; or

  (b) there is the risk that evidence may be tainted, lost, destroyed or falsified; or

  (c) there are reasons to believe that witnesses or victims may be pressured, manipulated or their safety endangered; or

  (d) there are reasons to believe that the suspect will continue to commit offences or poses a danger to public safety or security.

20.9 The Investigating Judge shall review the detention of a suspect every thirty days and issue orders for the further detention, substitute restrictive measures or for the release of the suspect.

20.10 Unless otherwise provided in UNTAET regulations, a suspect may be kept in pretrial detention for a period of no more than six months from the date of arrest.

20.11 Taking into consideration the prevailing circumstances in East Timor, in the case of a crime carrying imprisonment for more than five years under the law, the Investigating Judge or the Judge to whom the matter has been referred upon the filing of the indictment may, at the request of the public prosecutor, and if the interest of justice so requires, based on compelling grounds, extend the maximum period of pretrial detention by an additional three months.

20.12 On exceptional grounds, and taking into account the prevailing circumstances in East Timor, for particularly complex cases of crimes carrying imprisonment of ten years or more under the law, the Investigating Judge or the Judge to whom the matter has been referred upon the filing of the indictment may, at the request of the public prosecutor, order the continued detention of a suspect, if the interest of justice so requires, and as long as the length of pretrial detention is reasonable in the circumstances, and having due regard to international standards of fair trial.

20.13 Pursuant to United Nations Security Council Resolutions 1264 (1999) and 1272 (1999), and taking into consideration the prevailing circumstances in East Timor, all warrants for detention issued by the Investigating Judge or public prosecutor prior to the coming into force of the present regulation shall be deemed valid and in accord with the present regulation.

SCSL

SCSL Rules of Procedure and Evidence, rr. 64, 65

Detention on Remand

7–119   **64.** Upon his transfer to the Special Court, the accused shall be detained in the Detention Facility, or facilities otherwise made available pursuant to Rule 8(C). The Registrar, in a case where he considers it necessary, may order special measures of detention of an accused outside the Detention Facility. The order of the Registrar shall be put before the President for endorsement within 48 hours of the order being issued.

Bail

65.—(A) Once detained, an accused shall not be granted bail except upon an order of a Judge or Trial Chamber.   **7–120**

(B) Bail may be ordered by a Judge or a Trial Chamber after hearing the State to which the accused seeks to be released and only if it is satisfied that the accused will appear for trial and, if released, will not pose a danger to any victim, witness or other person.

(C) An accused may only make one application for bail to the Judge or Trial Chamber unless there has been a material change in circumstances.

(D) The Judge or Trial Chamber may impose such conditions upon the granting of bail to the accused as it may determine appropriate, including the execution of a bail bond and the observance of such conditions as are necessary to ensure the presence of the accused at trial and the protection of others.

(E) Any decision rendered under this Rule shall be subject to appeal in cases where leave is granted by a Single Judge of the Appeals Chamber, upon good cause being shown. Applications for leave to appeal shall be filed within seven days of the impugned decision.

(F) If necessary, the Trial Chamber may issue a warrant of arrest to secure the presence of an accused who has been granted bail or is for any other reason at large. The provisions of Section 2 of Part V shall apply.

(G) The Prosecutor may appeal a decision to grant bail. In the event of such an appeal, the accused shall remain in custody until the appeal is heard and determined.

(H) Appeals from bail decisions shall be heard by a bench of at least three Appeals Chamber Judges.

(2) Conditions of provisional release

ICTY

(a) General principles

ICTY Rule 65 was amended in plenary on November 30, 1999 to exclude any showing of "exceptional circumstances" by the accused in order to be provisionally released. Under the present rule the Chamber, after hearing from the host country, need only be satisfied that (i) the accused will appear for trial: and if released, (ii) will not pose a danger to any victim, witness or other person. The burden of proof that these conditions are met is on the Accused (See *Prosecutor v. Haradinaj*, Decision on Ramush Haradinaj's Motion on Provisional Release, June 6, 2005, para. 21). The Trial Chamber must render a reasoned opinion on the application (*Prosecutor v. Sainovic and Ojdanac*, [Appeals Chamber] Decision on Provisional Release, October 30, 2002, para. 6).   **7–121**

Since Rule 65 was amended to remove the requirement of showing "exceptional circumstances", detention should be the exception and not the rule (*Prosecutor v. Hadžihasanović et al.*, Decision Granting Provisional Release, December 19, 2001), although the Trial Chamber held in Jokic that the removal of the exceptional circumstances "has neither made detention the exception and release the rule, nor resulted in the situation that despite amendment, detention remains the rule and release the exception" (*Prosecutor v. Jokic*, Order on Miodrag Jokic for Provisional Release, February 20, 2002, para. 17; *Prosecutor v. Limaj et al*, Decision on Provisional Release of Fatmir Limaj, September 12, 2003, p. 8).

Under the present and former rule the Trial Chamber is not obliged to provisionally release an Accused even if satisfied about these two conditions. These two conditions are minimum requirements for granting provisional release but it remains a matter for the exercise of the Trial Chamber's discretion, which "must be exercised in light of all the circumstances of the case. It is necessary for an Accused to satisfy the Chamber that release is appropriate in a particular case. While it is accepted that detention is the most severe measure that can be imposed on an Accused and is to be used only when no other measures can achieve the effect of detention, it is recognised that this does not preclude the use of detention in an appropriate case" (*Prosecutor v. Seselj*, Decision on Defence Motion for Provisional Release, July 23, 2004, para. 6; *Prosecutor v. Sermak and Markac*, Decision on Ivan Sermak's and Mladen Markac's Motions for Provisional Release, April 29, 2004). Thus, the Trial Chamber must balance the public interest requirements with the presumption of innocence and the respect for the right of liberty of the Accused (*Prosecutor v. Jokic*, Order on Miodrag Jokic for Provisional Relase, February 20, 2002, para. 18; *Prosecutor v. Limaj et al*, Decision on Provisional Release of Fatmir Limaj, September 12, 2003, p. 8).

7–122   Although the emphasis is different under the current Rule 65, the Trial Chamber looks at similar criteria considered relevant prior to the rule change. In assessing the likelihood that someone will reappear for trial, (i) the guarantees of the government in the residing region of the Accused are most essential (*Prosecutor v. Haradinaj*, Decision on Ramush Haradinaj's Motion on Provisional Release, June 6, 2005, para. 21; *Prosecutor v. Sainovic and Ojdanac*, Decision on Application of Nikola Sainovic and Dragoljub Ojdanac for Provisional Release, June 26, 2002, para. 16; *Prosecutor v. Delić*, Decision on Defence Request for Provisional Release, May 6, 2005, p. 4; *Prosecutor v. Milutinovic*, Decision on Second Application for Provisional Release, April 14, 2005, paras 8 *et seq.*).

In assessing whether the Accused poses a danger to any victim, witness or other person, (ii) the situation cannot be looked at *in abstracto*; a concrete danger needs to be identified (*Prosecutor v. Haradinaj*, Decision on Ramush Haradinaj's Motion on Provisional Release, June 6, 2005, para. 22; *Prosecutor v. Prlić et al.*, Decision on Motions for Reconsideration, Clarification, Request for Release and Applications for Leave to Appeal, September 8, 2004, para. 28).

ICTY Rule 65 was amended on July 21, 2005 with the result that any Decision of a Trial Chamber on a provisional release application is now subject to appeal without the need for a bench of three judges of the Appeals Chamber to grant leave upon good cause being shown. As of September 2005, ICTR Rule 65 remains unchanged.

(b) Balancing factors

Additional factors which are relevant for the determination whether **7–123** to grant provisional release were set out by the Appeals Chamber (*Prosecutor v. Sainovic and Ojdanac*, [Appeals Chamber] Decision on Provisional Release, October 30, 2002, para. 6), namely the following:

(i) the seriousness of the criminal offences with which the Accused is charged;

(ii) the length of the prison term the Accused is likely to face if convicted;

(iii) the circumstances of the Accused's surrender;

(iv) the degree of cooperation given by the authorities of the State to which the Accused seeks to be released;

(v) the guarantees offered by those authorities and any personal guarantees offered by the Accused;

(vi) the likelihood that, in case of breach of the conditions of provisional release, the relevant authorities will re-arrest the Accused if he declines to surrender;

(vii) the Accused's degree of cooperation with the Prosecution.

Since all accused before the ICTY are alleged to have committed serious crimes for which they potentially face a severe punishment, the first two factors are not necessarily decisive for the Trial Chamber in deciding upon a request for provisional release. It nonetheless remains a relevant consideration (*Prosecutor v. Haradinaj et al.*, Decision on Ramush Haradinaj's Motion on Provisional Release, June 6, 2005, para. 24; Prosecutor v. Prlić et al, Decision on Motions for Reconsideration, Clarification, Request for Release and Applications for Leave to Appeal, September 8, 2004, para. 29).

An accused who has been in pre-trial detention already for a lengthy period prior to his request for provisional release may stand a better chance in his application. However, in *Seselj* a pre-trial detention of 15 months was considered not to be unreasonable "in light of the legal and factual complexity of the case, and in particular the number of witness statements and evidence that has to be disclosed to the Accused and the relevant procedural actions". Thus this ground did not constitute a ground per se for allowing the request (*Prosecutor v. Seselj*, Decision on Defence Motion for Provisional Release, July 23, 2004, paras 9, 11).

With regard to the government guarantees the Appeals Chamber found that the weight given such guarantees "may depend a great deal on the personal circumstances of the applicant, notably because of the position that he held prior to his arrest" (*Prosecutor v. Sainovic and Ojdanac*, [Appeals Chamber] Decision on Provisional Release, October 30, 2002, para. 7). The Appeals Chamber also held that these circumstances must not only be evaluated at the time of the decision on provisional release but also, as far as foreseeable, at the time when the case is due for trial and the Accused is expected to return to The Hague (*ibid.*, para. 7).

(c) Hearing on application for provisional release

The applicant for provisional release is not entitled to be heard orally **7–124** as of right. Rather, an oral hearing will not necessarily be held without a showing of good cause. In *Krnojelac* the Trial Chamber held: "The general practice of the International Tribunal is not to hear oral argument on such motions prior to the trial unless good reason is shown for its need in the particular case. That general practice is soundly based upon the peculiar circumstances in which the International Tribunal operates, in that counsel appearing for accused persons before it invariably have to travel long distances from where they ordinarily practice in order to appear for such oral argument; counsel appearing for the prosecution are often appearing in other trials currently being heard; and the judges comprising the Trial Chamber in question are usually engaged in other trials at the time when the motion has to be determined" (*Prosecutor v. Krnojelac*, Decision on the Defence Preliminary Motion on the Form of the Indictment, February 24, 1999, para. 65). Counsel has to identify the particular reasons upon which he wishes to put oral arguments (*ibid.*, para. 66).

(d) Conditions for provisional release

7–125   In performing the balancing exercise in determining whether provisional release should be granted in a particular case, a Trial Chamber may consider whether conditions attached to any such order would be sufficient to overcome any objections to provisional release as might exist. Various conditions have been imposed in cases before the ICTY to this end. For example, in *Prosecutor v. Sainovic et al.*, Decision on applications for provisional release, June 26, 2002, the following conditions were imposed:

(a) to remain within the confines of the municipality of Belgrade;

(b) to surrender his passport to the Ministry of Justice;

(c) to report each day to the police at a police station designated by the Ministry of Justice;

(d) to provide the address at which he will be staying to the Ministry of Justice and to the Registrar of the International Tribunal before leaving the United Nations Detention Unit;

(e) to consent to having the Ministry of Justice check with the local police about his presence and to the making of occasional, unannounced visits upon the Accused by the Ministry of Justice or by a person designated by the Registrar of the International Tribunal;

(f) to make himself available for interview with the Prosecution when requested;

(g) not to have any contact with any other co-accused in the case;

(h) not to have any contact whatsoever or in any way interfere with any victim or potential witness or otherwise interfere in any way with the proceedings or the administration of justice;

(i) not to discuss his case with anyone, including the media, other than his own counsel;

(j) to continue to co-operate with the International Tribunal;

(k) to comply strictly with any requirements of the authorities of the FRY and the Republic of Serbia necessary to enable them to comply with their obligations under this Order and their guarantees;

(l) to return to the International Tribunal at such time and on such date as the Trial Chamber may order;

(m) to comply strictly with any further order of the Trial Chamber varying the terms of, or terminating, his provisional release.

(e) Concrete examples

Guarantees from the authorities in power in the receiving state   **7–126** (usually State officials acting in an official capacity) are, in practice, considered a pre-requisite to the granting of provisional release in cases before the ICTY. In the context of Kosovo, where UNMIK is the authority charged with overall administration, the "guarantees" of the elected Prime Minister of Kosovo, or the provisional institutions were considered "without significant value" by the Prosecution as it was UNMIK, not the provisional institutions that had the resources and competence to enforce the necessary "guarantees". (See *Prosecution v. Limaj*, Prosecution's Response to Application for Provisional Release filed by the Accused Fatmir Limaj, July 8, 2003, para.15) The source of the "guarantee" was critical in the granting of provisional release in the case of Ramush Haradinaj and, apparently, in denying that of Fatmir Limaj. Both Haradinaj and Limaj were from Kosovo. Both were political figures (Haradinaj was the serving Prime Minister at the time of his indictment and surrender. Limaj was parliamentary head of the PDK political party at the time his indictment was made public). Both had been members of the KLA. Notwithstanding the broad similarity, Haradinaj's request for provisional release was granted and Limaj's was not.

In the later case of *Haradinaj*, the Trial Chamber took into consideration: the exemplary circumstances of the surrender of Mr Haradinaj, references of the Special Representative of the Secretary General (SRSG) in Kosovo, the former commander of Kosovo Force "KFOR" and the President of Kosovo about the Accused's character, the Accused's own undertaking to comply fully with any order made by the Trial Chamber, the guarantees provided by UNMIK to ensure that the Accused will not flee or disturb potential witnesses against him. Unlike the earler Kosovan KLA case of *Limaj*; where UNMIK refused to give any guarantees for Limaj's return to The Hague, in *Haradinaj*, UNMIK made it clear that it was positively able and willing to provide any guarantees that may be required for a provisional release of that Accused. The Trial Chamber further observed that there was no reason to believe that Haradinaj's provisional release would have any impact on the safety of witnesses or induce perpetrators from the previous incidents to threaten these witnesses. The Trial Chamber held that "since it has not been shown that the Accused could pose a concrete danger to anyone, including victims and witnesses, the Trial Chamber is not satisfied that a negative impact on the public perception of the safety of potential witnesses suffices as a ground for denying provisional release" (*Prosecutor v. Haradinaj et al.*, Decision on Ramush Haradinaj's Motion on Provisional Release, June 6, 2005, paras 33–48).

It has to be noted that, the essential difference in the *Limaj* case was that the Trial Chamber did not accept the Defence argument that Limaj was in the process of voluntarily surrendering, which was based upon: (i) a radio interview the Accused gave to a journalist while he was on a skiing holiday in Slovenia stating he had just heard of the indictment and would return to Kosovo and voluntarily surrender to the ICTY; (ii) the Accused's almost immediate telephone contact with the Prime Minister of Kosovo thereafter, requesting that arrangements be made for his voluntary surrender to the ICTR; (iii) evidence from the Prime Minister of Kosovo testifying that he had a meeting the same day the indictment was made public with the Special Representative of Secretary General (SRSG) in Kosovo; and (iv) the Prime Minister informed the SRSG of Limaj's whereabouts and requested that arrangements be made for his immediate return to Kosovo and transmission on to The Hague. (*Prosecutor v. Limaj et al.*, Decision on Provisional Release of Fatmir Limaj, September 12, 2003, p. 9).

In *Halilovic* the Trial Chamber denied the application by the Defence for provisional release during trial despite the fact that the Prosecution had not opposed the Defence application. The Defence argued that whilst provisional release of an accused "in the middle of trial" may cause practical difficulties, "exceptional circumstances" justified the Application being granted. The Defence submitted that Mr. Halilovic had fully complied with the conditions imposed on him in connection with his pre-trial provisional release over two years, and argued that this past record was a reliable indicator that he would continue to comply with any conditions the Trial Chamber were minded to impose. Despite no requirement for a showing of "exceptional circumstances" in the Rules, the Defence argued that such circumstances existed which merited the accused's provisional release *during* trial. These "exceptional circumstances" included: (i) the serious death threats that were made against the son of the accused; (ii) the real risk that the family of the accused would otherwise be ejected from their apartment in Sarajevo; and (iii) the fact that, due to his indigence, the accused would not be able to pay for his family to travel to The Hague, so he would not see them until after the end of the trial. The Trial Chamber rejected these arguments because the Defence had relied on old guarantees from the Government of Bosnia and had not obtained guarantees from the Government that the accused would re-appear in The Hague when ordered and would not contact any Prosecution witnesses during the requested provisional release. Given the advanced stage of the Prosecution case, the Trial Chamber held that the Defence had failed to show that exceptional circumstances existed justifying the granting of the Defence application. (*Prosecutor v. Halilovic*, Decision on Motion for Provisional Release, April 21, 2005).

(f) Temporary release to attend funerals

7–127   In *Mrkšić* the Trial Chamber granted Mrkšić's request to attend his mother's funeral on compassionate grounds, subject to certain conditions and guarantees, namely the following: Mrkšić was allowed to leave to go to Belgrade and back for three days in total; he would be transported back and forth from the UN Detention Unit to the airport in the Netherlands by the Dutch authorities and be delivered into the custody of and accompanied throughout the trip by a designated official of the government of Serbia and Montenegro; he was prohibited from having any contact, or in any way interfering with victims or potential witnesses, or with the proceedings, or the administration of justice; he was further prohibited from discussing his case with anyone (including the media), other than Counsel; he was not to seek access to documents and archives; he was to comply with any further requirements imposed by the authorities of Serbia and Montenegro in fulfilling their duties, as well as the Trial Chamber, including the potential variation of the terms or the termination of his provisional release; the transport expenses were to be covered by Mr Mrkšić or the government of Serbia and Montenegro, who would also assume responsibility for the personal security and safety of Mr Mrkšić while on provisional release (*Prosecutor v. Mrkšić*, Decision Pursuant to Rule 65 granting Mrkšić's request to attend his mother's funeral, January 30, 2004).

On similar grounds and conditions Haradinaj was allowed provisional release to attend his brother's funeral (*Prosecutor v. Haradinaj et al.*, Decision on Urgent Defence Motion on Behalf of Ramush Haradinaj for Provisional Release, April 16, 2005).

Thus, it appears that Trial Chambers are reasonably compassionate in cases where the Accused requests provisional release on grounds of attending funerals. However, in *Radic* the Trial Chamber reiterated its discretion not to grant provisional release even if the requirements of Rule 65(B) are met and denied a request for provisional release for a period of five days to attend a memorial service (*Prosecutor v. Radic*, Decision on Request by the Accused Radic for Provisional Release, May 20, 2004).

ICTR

In contrast to the ICTY, the Judges at the ICTR originally declined to amend Rule 65 to delete the requirement of a showing of "exceptional circumstances". Defence arguments that "exceptional circumstances" should be read-out of the rules were also rejected. (See *Prosecutor v. Ndayambaje*, Decision on the Defence Motion for the Provisional Release of the Accused, October 21, 2001, para. 20; *Prosecutor v. Sagahutu*, Decision on Leave to Appeal Against the Refusal to Grant Provisional Release, March 26, 2003.) In *Prosecutor v. Bicamumpaka*, Decision on Motion for Provisional Release, July 25, 2001, the Trial Chamber confirmed that provisional release may only be ordered in exceptional circumstances, after hearing from the host country if it is satisfied that the accused will appear for trial and, if released, will not pose a danger to any victim, witness or other person. The Chamber considered whether the following factors amounted to exceptional circumstances within the meaning of Rule 65(B): length of detention resulting in undue delay; the alleged lack of conclusive evidence; and serious illness. It took into consideration:

1. the gravity and factual and legal complexity of the charges against the accused;
2. the gravity of the sentence he might be facing, should he be found guilty;
3. the complexity of the joint proceedings which adds to their overall length; and
4. the necessity to deliberate and render decisions on the pre-trial Motions filed by the Parties, and the Accused's right to be tried

7–128

without undue delay envisioned under Article 20(c) of the ICTR Statute.

7–129 The Chamber found that the length of detention of the accused does not constitute "exceptional circumstances" within the meaning of Rule 65(B) of the Rules, nor does serious illness, relying on *Prosecutor v. Rutaganda*, Decision on the request filed by the Defence for the provisional release of G. Rutaganda, February 7, 1997, which held that: "serious illness does not itself justify the provisional release of an accused as long as adequate medical treatment can be administered to him by the Tribunal". A number of detainees were detained five to six years prior to trial and another few years during trial (see for example, Bagosora, the leading accused at the ICTR who was arrested in 1996, who waited in pre-trial detention until Sept. 2002 for the trial to commence which is still ongoing).

On May 26–27, 2003, the ICTR Judges finally amended Rule 65, deleting the requirement of "exceptional circumstances". The amendment entered into force with immediate effect since the amendment was beneficial to the rights of the Accused (*Prosecutor v. Ngirumpatse*, Decision on the Motion by Ngirumpatse's Defence to Find the Accused's Detention Unlawful or, in the Alternative, to Order his Provisional Release, August 18, 2003, para. 24). In reality this amendment has not made a significant difference because most applications fail on one of the two conditions still applicable to provisional release applications, namely that the accused will appear for trial and, if released, will not pose a danger to any victim, witness or other person (*Prosecutor v. Rukundo*, Decision On Defence Motion to Fix a Date for the Commencement of the Trial of Father Emmanuel Rukundo or, in the Alternative, to Request His Provisional Release Rule 65, Rule 65*bis* and Rule 73*bis* of the Rules of Procedure and Evidence, August 18, 2003, para. 21; *Prosecutor v. Ngirumpatse*, Decision on the Motion by Ngirumpatse's Defence to Find the Accused's Detention Unlawful or, in the Alternative, to Order his Provisional Release, August 18, 2003, para. 26; *Prosecutor v. Rukundo*, Decision on the Motion for Provisional Release of Father Emmanuel Rukundo (Rule 65(B) of the Rules of Procedure and Evidence, July 15, 2004, para. 16). As the Trial Chamber held in Rukundo, "[f]ailure to satisfy a single prong of the Rule 65(B) is fatal to an application for provisional release" (*Prosecutor v. Rukundo*, Decision On Defence Motion to Fix a Date for the Commencement of the Trial of Father Emmanuel Rukundo or, in the Alternative, to Request His Provisional Release Rule 65, Rule 65*bis* and Rule 73*bis* of the Rules of Procedure and Evidence, August 18, 2003).

Unlike at the SCSL (see below) but similar to the ICTY, the ICTR requires applications for provisional release to be dealt with by a Trial Chamber, not by a single judge. Failure to abide by this requirement constitutes a successful ground of appeal (*Prosecutor v. Rukundo*, Decision on Appeal from the Decision of Trial Chamber III of August 18, 2003 denying Application for Provisional Release, March 8, 2004).

The Accused is entitled to file renewed applications for provisional release, provided that there is a change of circumstances or otherwise new grounds falling for consideration (*Prosecutor v. Rukundo*, Decision on the Motion for Provisional Release of Father Emmanuel Rukundo (Rule 65(B) of the Rules of Procedure and Evidence, July 15, 2004, para. 13).

Provisional release has never been granted at the ICTR, either before, or after the amendment of Rule 65.

East Timor

For a case before the Special Panel in East Timor in which the **7–130**
accused was conditionally released see *Prosecutor v. Leki*, Decision,
February 21, 2001. In *Prosecutor v. Sarmento et al.*, Decision on the
Request for the release of the accused Benjamin Sarmento, Romerio
Tilman and Joao Sarmento, March 22, 2002, none of the accused was
provisionally released.

SCSL

(a) General principles

Judges at the SCSL have constructed their own set of criteria **7–131**
applicable to provisional release or, as frequently referred to at the
SCSL, "bail", which is comparable to the ICTY set of criteria (*Prosecutor
v. Norman et al.*, Fofana—Decision on Application for Bail Pursuant to
Rule 65, August 5, 2004, para. 61):
  i. The granting of bail is a matter [. . .] entirely within either the
     discretion of the Judge or that of the Trial Chamber so seized
     of the Application.
  ii. The Judge or the Trial Chamber will grant bail only after
      hearing the State to which the Accused seeks to be released.
  iii. The Judge or the Trial Chamber in the exercise of that
       discretion in favour of the Accused, has to do so only if he is
       satisfied that the Accused will appear for trial. This requires
       that the Applicant furnishes legal, moral or material guaran-
       tees to assure the Judge or the Chamber that he will not escape
       if released on bail.
  iv. The Judge or the Trial Chamber, before ordering the release
      on bail, should also be satisfied that the Accused, if released,
      will not pose a danger to any victim or witness or other person.
In exercising their discretion the Judge or the Trial Chamber needs
to balance "the public interest and the presumption of innocence of the
Accused as enshrined in the provisions of Article 17(3) of the Statute"
(*ibid*, para. 63). "[T]his two-pronged test, and consequently the right of
the Accused to be released on bail, has to be ultimately based on an
assessment of whether the public interest requirements related to the
appearance of the Accused at trial and the safety of victims and
witnesses outweigh the need to ensure the Accused's right to liberty"
(*Prosecutor v. Sesay*, Sesay—Decision on Appeal Against Refusal of Bail,
December 14, 2004, para. 45).

(b) Balancing factors

The Special Court has not granted provisional release in any of the **7–132**
cases it has currently heard. The Judges usually refer to the particular
circumstances applicable to the SCSL as the main reason to reject a

bail application. The judges have, however, confirmed that the fundamental principle is that each individual case must be decided on its merits (*Prosecutor v. Sesay*, Sesay—Decision on Appeal Against Refusal of Bail, December 14, 2004, para. 37).

In *Sesay* the Judge stated: "I would suggest that it could be argued that the particular situation of the Special Court and its direct presence in the territory of Sierra Leone and more specifically in Freetown, the capital of this Country, makes it an even more important, difficult and sensitive situation than that of the ICTR which sits in Tanzania, a neighbouring country to Rwanda." The Appeals Chamber in the same trial, while confirming the Trial Chamber's Decision, stated on this matter that "[i]n the particular situation of Sierra Leone, public interest factors such as the ability of the authorities to uphold conditions may take on a greater relevance. While in principle a Judge could be satisfied that a particular accused would appear for trial notwithstanding any lack of police enforcement capability, at the same time conditions and guarantees need to be meaningful" (*Prosecutor v. Sesay*, Sesay—Decision on Appeal Against Refusal of Bail, December 14, 2004, paras 35–36; referring to *Prosecutor v. Sesay*, Decision on Application of Issa Sesay for Provisional Relase, March 31, 2004, para. 55).

Another reason for the SCSL reluctance is that "[g]ranting bail to an Accused before the Special Court entails that he will be released in the country where he is alleged to have committed the crimes for which he has been indicted" (*Prosecutor v. Sesay et al.*, Decision on the Motion by Morris Kallon for Bail, February 23, 2004, para. 38). Given that the Accused knows the potential evidence against him after the documents upon which the indictment was issued were disclosed to him, the judges fear that the Accused might be able to identify the Prosecution witnesses, despite the applicable orders for protective measures (*Prosecutor v. Sesay*, Sesay—Decision on Appeal Against Refusal of Bail, December 14, 2004, para. 54).

The overall security situation and the lack of local police facilities to enforce or monitor conditions of the bail makes the granting of provisional release difficult in the context of the Sierra Leone. (*Prosecutor v. Sesay et al*, Sesay—Decision On appeal Against Refusal of Bail, December 14, 2004, paras 28 and 36–37; see also *Prosecutor v. Norman et al.*, Fofana—Appeal Against Decision Refusing Bail, March 11, 2005, para. 31). Relevant also in this regard is "the inability of the Special Court to directly perform any arrest on the territory of Sierra Leone and the current diminished capability of the national authorities to promptly and efficiently provide any police supervision or intervention in case of flight of the Accused" (*Prosecutor v. Sesay*, Sesay—Decision on Appeal Against Refusal of Bail, December 14, 2004, para. 49).

Acknowledging that Rule 65 does not specifically refer to any criteria other than that the Accused should reappear for trial and meanwhile not pose any danger to any person, "a release on bail is and should also inextricably be conditioned by factors which are germane to the gravity of the offence for which the applicant is indicted, and the sentence that is likely to be meted out to him if convicted" (*Prosecutor v. Norman et al.*, Fofana—Decision on Application for Bail Pursuant to Rule 65, August 5, 2004, para. 72). This is a consideration not only for the protection of victims and potential witnesses but also for the Accused himself because release within the local community of Sierra Leone where the crimes were allegedly committed, "could well undermine his own safety and, indeed, his appearance for trial" (*Prosecutor v. Sesay et al.*, Decision on the Motion by Morris Kallon for Bail, February 23, 2004, para. 44).

An argument that "the Accused participated in the peace process that followed the end of the hostilities", while certainly mitigating, should the Accused be convicted, does not provide evidence that the Accused "will appear for trial" (*Prosecutor v. Sesay*, Sesay—Decision on Appeal Against Refusal of Bail, December 14, 2004, para. 51).

(c) Burden of Proof on Applications for Bail

"[I]n matters relating to bail, the burden of establishing that the Applicant has fulfilled the conditions laid down in Rule 65(B), lies on him as the person seeking to benefit from the exercise of the Court's discretion in favour of granting those measures in his favour. I am also however, of the opinion and do so hold in this matter, as I did in Brima Bail Application, that the prosecution has an equally formidable burden of negating the facts advanced by the Defence and to demonstrate that the requisite conditions have neither been met nor would they be fulfilled by the Applicant" (*Prosecutor v. Norman et al.*, Fofana—Decision on Application for Bail Pursuant to Rule 65, August 5, 2004, para. 61). "I am therefore unable to rule out the possibility that the Judge may have erred in holding that the burden of establishing that the conditions laid down in Rule 65(B) have been fulfilled rests on the Accused (*Prosecutor v. Norman et al.*, Fofana—Decision on Application for Leave to Appeal Bail Decision, November 5, 2004, para. 19). The Appeals Chamber, however, ruled that: "Rule 65(B) (note the force of "only") confirms that the burden lies squarely on the applicant" (*Prosecutor v. Norman et al.*, Fofana—Appeal Against Decision Refusing Bail, March 11, 2005, para. 33). "Bail applications should not be decided by mechanistic application of the burden of proof: the court must feel fully satisfied that the Rule 65(B) conditions will be met and that there are effective means of recalling the applicant if they are not" (*Prosecutor v. Norman et al.*, Fofana—Appeal Against Decision Refusing Bail, March 11, 2005, para. 34). **7–133**

It should be emphasised that the burden of proof applied at the trial level has no bearing on bail applications, neither has the behaviour of a person being granted bail any bearing on the question of guilt or innocence based on the evidence presented at trial. In *Norman et al.*, the Trial Chamber held that "[w]hether a defendant will turn up for trial or intimidate witnesses cannot logically be affected by the burden or standard of proof that will prevail at his trial, nor by presuming him innocent or guilty of the offences charged (since innocent defendants may nevertheless try to avoid a lengthy trial or to threaten those who have made statements against them)" (*Prosecutor v. Norman et al.*, Fofana—Appeal Against Decision Refusing Bail, March 11, 2005, para. 37).

ICC

Conditions similar to those developed by the jurisprudence of the ICTY context have been incorporated in Rule 119 of the ICC Rules of Procedure and Evidence. Importantly, Rule 119(4) details the standard **7–134** required before the provisional release granted to an Accused is revoked: the Pre-Trial Chamber must be "convinced" that the person concerned *has* failed to comply with one or more of the conditions imposed. It seems that "convinced" equates to proof beyond reasonable doubt, rather than a lesser standard of substantial grounds to believe that conditions have been breached, or may be breached.

E. PRE-TRIAL JUDGE

(1) Statutory provisions and rules

ICC

ICC Statute, Arts 56, 57, 61

Role of the Pre-Trial Chamber in relation to a unique investigative opportunity

7–135   56.—1.

(a) Where the Prosecutor considers an investigation to present a unique opportunity to take testimony or a statement from a witness or to examine, collect or test evidence, which may not be available subsequently for the purposes of a trial, the Prosecutor shall so inform the Pre-Trial Chamber.

(b) In that case, the Pre-Trial Chamber may, upon request of the Prosecutor, take such measures as may be necessary to ensure the efficiency and integrity of the proceedings and, in particular, to protect the rights of the defence.

(c) Unless the Pre-Trial Chamber orders otherwise, the Prosecutor shall provide the relevant information to the person who has been arrested or appeared in response to a summons in connection with the investigation referred to in subparagraph (a), in order that he or she may be heard on the matter.

2. The measures referred to in paragraph 1(b) may include:

(a) Making recommendations or orders regarding procedures to be followed;

(b) Directing that a record be made of the proceedings;

(c) Appointing an expert to assist;

(d) Authorizing counsel for a person who has been arrested, or appeared before the Court in response to a summons, to participate, or where there has not yet been such an arrest or appearance or counsel has not been designated, appointing another counsel to attend and represent the interests of the defence;

(e) Naming one of its members or, if necessary, another available judge of the Pre-Trial or Trial Division to observe and make recommendations or orders regarding the collection and preservation of evidence and the questioning of persons;

(f) Taking such other action as may be necessary to collect or preserve evidence.

3.

(a) Where the Prosecutor has not sought measures pursuant to this article but the Pre-Trial Chamber considers that such measures are required to preserve evidence that it deems would be essential for the defence at trial, it shall consult with the Prosecutor as to whether there is good reason for the Prosecutor's failure to request the measures. If upon consultation, the Pre-Trial Chamber concludes that the Prosecutor's failure to request such measures is unjustified, the Pre-Trial Chamber may take such measures on its own initiative.

(b) A decision of the Pre-Trial Chamber to act on its own initiative under this paragraph may be appealed by the Prosecutor. The appeal shall be heard on an expedited basis.

4. The admissibility of evidence preserved or collected for trial pursuant to this article, or the record thereof, shall be governed at trial by article 69, and given such weight as determined by the Trial Chamber.

Functions and powers of the Pre-Trial Chamber

7–136

57.—1. Unless otherwise provided in this Statute, the Pre-Trial Chamber shall exercise its functions in accordance with the provisions of this article.

2. (a) Orders or rulings of the Pre-Trial Chamber issued under articles 15, 18, 19, 54, paragraph 2, 61, paragraph 7, and 72 must be concurred in by a majority of its judges.

(b) In all other cases, a single judge of the Pre-Trial Chamber may exercise the functions provided for in this Statute, unless otherwise provided for in the Rules of Procedure and Evidence or by a majority of the Pre-Trial Chamber.

3. In addition to its other functions under this Statute, the Pre-Trial Chamber may:

(a) At the request of the Prosecutor, issue such orders and warrants as may be required for the purposes of an investigation;

(b) Upon the request of a person who has been arrested or has appeared pursuant to a summons under article 58, issue such orders, including measures such as those described in article 56, or seek such cooperation pursuant to Part 9 as may be necessary to assist the person in the preparation of his or her defence;

(c) Where necessary, provide for the protection and privacy of victims and witnesses, the preservation of evidence, the protection of persons who have been arrested or appeared in response to a summons, and the protection of national security information;

(d) Authorize the Prosecutor to take specific investigative steps within the territory of a State Party without having secured the cooperation of that State under Part 9 if, whenever possible having regard to the views of the State concerned, the Pre-Trial Chamber has determined in that case that the State is clearly unable to execute a request for cooperation due to the unavailability of any authority or any component of its judicial system competent to execute the request for cooperation under Part 9.

(e) Where a warrant of arrest or a summons has been issued under article 58, and having due regard to the strength of the evidence and the rights of the parties concerned, as provided for in this Statute and the Rules of Procedure and Evidence, seek the cooperation of States pursuant to article 93, paragraph 1 (k), to take protective measures for the purpose of forfeiture, in particular for the ultimate benefit of victims.

Confirmation of the charges before trial

7–137

61.—1. Subject to the provisions of paragraph 2, within a reasonable time after the person's surrender or voluntary appearance before the Court, the Pre-Trial Chamber shall hold a hearing to confirm the charges on which the Prosecutor intends to seek trial. The hearing shall be held in the presence of the Prosecutor and the person charged, as well as his or her counsel.

2. The Pre-Trial Chamber may, upon request of the Prosecutor or on its own motion, hold a hearing in the absence of the person charged to confirm the charges on which the Prosecutor intends to seek trial when the person has:

(a) Waived his or her right to be present; or

(b) Fled or cannot be found and all reasonable steps have been taken to secure his or her appearance before the Court and to inform the person of the charges and that a hearing to confirm those charges will be held.

In that case, the person shall be represented by counsel where the Pre-Trial Chamber determines that it is in the interests of justice.

3. Within a reasonable time before the hearing, the person shall:

(a) Be provided with a copy of the document containing the charges on which the Prosecutor intends to bring the person to trial; and

(b) Be informed of the evidence on which the Prosecutor intends to rely at the hearing.

The Pre-Trial Chamber may issue orders regarding the disclosure of information for the purposes of the hearing.

4. Before the hearing, the Prosecutor may continue the investigation and may amend or withdraw any charges. The person shall be given reasonable notice before the hearing of any amendment to or withdrawal of charges. In case of a withdrawal of charges, the Prosecutor shall notify the Pre-Trial Chamber of the reasons for the withdrawal.

5. At the hearing, the Prosecutor shall support each charge with sufficient evidence to establish substantial grounds to believe that the person committed the crime charged. The Prosecutor may rely on documentary or summary evidence and need not call the witnesses expected to testify at the trial.

6. At the hearing, the person may:

(a) Object to the charges;

(b) Challenge the evidence presented by the Prosecutor; and

(c) Present evidence.

7. The Pre-Trial Chamber shall, on the basis of the hearing, determine whether there is sufficient evidence to establish substantial grounds to believe that the person committed each of the crimes charged. Based on its determination, the Pre-Trial Chamber shall:

(a) Confirm those charges in relation to which it has determined that there is sufficient evidence, and commit the person to a Trial Chamber for trial on the charges as confirmed;

(b) Decline to confirm those charges in relation to which it has determined that there is insufficient evidence;

(c) Adjourn the hearing and request the Prosecutor to consider:

(i) Providing further evidence or conducting further investigation with respect to a particular charge; or

(ii) Amending a charge because the evidence submitted appears to establish a different crime within the jurisdiction of the Court.

8. Where the Pre-Trial Chamber declines to confirm a charge, the Prosecutor shall not be precluded from subsequently requesting its confirmation if the request is supported by additional evidence.

9. After the charges are confirmed and before the trial has begun, the Prosecutor may, with the permission of the Pre-Trial Chamber and after notice to the accused, amend the charges. If the Prosecutor seeks to add additional charges or to substitute more serious charges, a hearing under this article to confirm those charges must be held. After commencement of the trial, the Prosecutor may, with the permission of the Trial Chamber, withdraw the charges.

10. Any warrant previously issued shall cease to have effect with respect to any charges which have not been confirmed by the Pre-Trial Chamber or which have been withdrawn by the Prosecutor.

11. Once the charges have been confirmed in accordance with this article, the Presidency shall constitute a Trial Chamber which, subject to paragraph 9

and to article 64, paragraph 4, shall be responsible for the conduct of subsequent proceedings and may exercise any function of the Pre-Trial Chamber that is relevant and capable of application in those proceedings.

ICC Rules of Procedure and Evidence, rr. 114, 115,116, 122

Rule 114: Unique investigative opportunity under article 56

1. Upon being advised by the Prosecutor in accordance with article 56, paragraph 1 (a), the Pre-Trial Chamber shall hold consultations without delay with the Prosecutor and, subject to the provisions of article 56, paragraph 1 (c), with the person who has been arrested or who has appeared before the Court pursuant to summons and his or her counsel, in order to determine the measures to be taken and the modalities of their implementation, which may include measures to ensure that the right to communicate under article 67, paragraph 1 (b), is protected.   **7–138**

2. A decision of the Pre-Trial Chamber to take measures pursuant to article 56, paragraph 3, must be concurred in by a majority of its judges after consultations with the Prosecutor. During the consultations, the Prosecutor may advise the Pre-Trial Chamber that intended measures could jeopardize the proper conduct of the investigation.

Rule 115: Collection of evidence in the territory of a State Party under article 57, paragraph 3 (d)

1. Where the Prosecutor considers that article 57, paragraph 3 (d), applies, the Prosecutor may submit a written request to the Pre-Trial Chamber for authorization to take certain measures in the territory of the State Party in question. After a submission of such a request, the Pre-Trial Chamber shall, whenever possible, inform and invite views from the State Party concerned.   **7–139**

2. In arriving at its determination as to whether the request is well founded, the Pre-Trial Chamber shall take into account any views expressed by the State Party concerned. The Pre-Trial Chamber may, on its own initiative or at the request of the Prosecutor or the State Party concerned, decide to hold a hearing.

3. An authorization under article 57, paragraph 3 (d), shall be issued in the form of an order and shall state the reasons, based on the criteria set forth in that paragraph. The order may specify procedures to be followed in carrying out such collection of evidence.

Rule 116: Collection of evidence at the request of the defence under article 57, paragraph 3 (b)

1. The Pre-Trial Chamber shall issue an order or seek cooperation under article 57, paragraph 3 (b), where it is satisfied: **7–140**
   (a) That such an order would facilitate the collection of evidence that may be material to the proper determination of the issues being adjudicated, or to the proper preparation of the person.s defence; and
   (b) In a case of cooperation under Part 9, that sufficient information to comply with article 96, paragraph 2, has been provided.

2. Before taking a decision whether to issue an order or seek cooperation under article 57, paragraph 3 (b), the Pre-Trial Chamber may seek the views of the Prosecutor.

Rule 122: Proceedings at the confirmation hearing in the presence of the person charged

1. The Presiding Judge of the Pre-Trial Chamber shall ask the officer of the Registry assisting the Chamber to read out the charges as presented by the Prosecutor. The Presiding Judge shall determine how the hearing is to be   **7–141**

conducted and, in particular, may establish the order and the conditions under which he or she intends the evidence contained in the record of the proceedings to be presented.

2. If a question or challenge concerning jurisdiction or admissibility arises, rule 58 applies.

3. Before hearing the matter on the merits, the Presiding Judge of the Pre-Trial Chamber shall ask the Prosecutor and the person whether they intend to raise objections or make observations concerning an issue related to the proper conduct of the proceedings prior to the confirmation hearing.

4. At no subsequent point may the objections and observations made under sub-rule 3 be raised or made again in the confirmation or trial proceedings.

5. If objections or observations referred to in sub-rule 3 are presented, the Presiding Judge of the Pre-Trial Chamber shall invite those referred to in sub-rule 3 to present their arguments, in the order which he or she shall establish. The person shall have the right to reply.

6. If the objections raised or observations made are those referred to in sub-rule 3, the Pre-Trial Chamber shall decide whether to join the issue raised with the examination of the charges and the evidence, or to separate them, in which case it shall adjourn the confirmation hearing and render a decision on the issues raised.

7. During the hearing on the merits, the Prosecutor and the person shall present their arguments in accordance with article 61, paragraphs 5 and 6.

8. The Pre-Trial Chamber shall permit the Prosecutor and the person, in that order, to make final observations.

9. Subject to the provisions of article 61, article 69 shall apply *mutatis mutandis* at the confirmation hearing.

ICTY

ICTY Rules of Procedure and Evidence, r. 65*ter*

Pre-Trial Judge

7–142   **65*ter*.**—(A) The Presiding Judge of the Trial Chamber shall, no later than seven days after the initial appearance of the accused, designate from among its members a Judge responsible for the pre-trial proceedings (hereinafter "pre-trial Judge").

(B) The pre-trial Judge shall, under the authority and supervision of the Trial Chamber seised of the case, coordinate communication between the parties during the pre-trial phase. The pre-trial Judge shall ensure that the proceedings are not unduly delayed and shall take any measure necessary to prepare the case for a fair and expeditious trial.

(C) The pre-trial Judge shall be entrusted with all of the pre-trial functions set forth in Rule 66, Rule 67, Rule 73*bis* and Rule 73*ter*, and with all or part of the functions set forth in Rule 73.

(D)
  (i) The pre-trial Judge may be assisted in the performance of his or her duties by one of the Senior Legal Officers assigned to Chambers.
  (ii) The pre-trial Judge shall establish a work plan indicating, in general terms, the obligations that the parties are required to meet pursuant to this Rule and the dates by which these obligations must be fulfilled.
  (iii) Acting under the supervision of the pre-trial Judge, the Senior Legal Officer shall oversee the implementation of the work plan and shall keep the pre-trial Judge informed of the progress of the discussions between and with the parties and, in particular, of any potential difficulty. He or she shall present the pre-trial Judge with reports as

appropriate and shall communicate to the parties, without delay, any observations and decisions made by the pre-trial Judge.

(iv) The pre-trial Judge shall order the parties to meet to discuss issues related to the preparation of the case, in particular, so that the Prosecutor can meet his or her obligations pursuant to paragraphs (E) (i) to (iii) of this Rule and for the defence to meet its obligations pursuant to paragraph (G) of this Rule and of Rule 73*ter*.

(v) Such meetings are held *inter partes* or, at his or her request, with the Senior Legal Officer and one or more of the parties. The Senior Legal Officer ensures that the obligations set out in paragraphs (E) (i) to (iii) of this Rule and, at the appropriate time, that the obligations in paragraph (G) and Rule 73*ter*, are satisfied in accordance with the work plan set by the pre-trial Judge.

(vi) The presence of the accused is not necessary for meetings convened by the Senior Legal Officer.

(vii) The Senior Legal Officer may be assisted by a representative of the Registry in the performance of his or her duties pursuant to this Rule and may require a transcript to be made.

(E) Once any existing preliminary motions filed within the time-limit provided by Rule 72 are disposed of, the pre-trial Judge shall order the Prosecutor, upon the report of the Senior Legal Officer, and within a time-limit set by the pre-trial Judge and not less than six weeks before the Pre-Trial Conference required by Rule 73*bis*, to file the following:

(i) the final version of the Prosecutor's pre-trial brief including, for each count, a summary of the evidence which the Prosecutor intends to bring regarding the commission of the alleged crime and the form of responsibility incurred by the accused; this brief shall include any admissions by the parties and a statement of matters which are not in dispute; as well as a statement of contested matters of fact and law;

(ii) the list of witnesses the Prosecutor intends to call with:

    (a) the name or pseudonym of each witness;

    (b) a summary of the facts on which each witness will testify;

    (c) the points in the indictment as to which each witness will testify, including specific references to counts and relevant paragraphs in the indictment;

    (d) the total number of witnesses and the number of witnesses who will testify against each accused and on each count;

    (e) an indication of whether the witness will testify in person or pursuant to Rule 92*bis* by way of written statement or use of a transcript of testimony from other proceedings before the Tribunal; and

    (f) the estimated length of time required for each witness and the total time estimated for presentation of the Prosecutor's case.

(iii) the list of exhibits the Prosecutor intends to offer stating where possible whether the defence has any objection as to authenticity. The Prosecutor shall serve on the defence copies of the exhibits so listed.

(F) After the submission by the Prosecutor of the items mentioned in paragraph (E), the pre-trial Judge shall order the defence, within a time-limit set by the pre-trial Judge, and not later than three weeks before the Pre-Trial Conference, to file a pre-trial brief addressing the factual and legal issues, and including a written statement setting out:

(i) in general terms, the nature of the accused's defence;

(ii) the matters with which the accused takes issue in the Prosecutor's pre-trial brief; and

(iii) in the case of each such matter, the reason why the accused takes issue with it.

(G) After the close of the Prosecutor's case and before the commencement of the defence case, the pre-trial Judge shall order the defence to file the following:

  (i) a list of witnesses the defence intends to call with:
    (a) the name or pseudonym of each witness;
    (b) a summary of the facts on which each witness will testify;
    (c) the points in the indictment as to which each witness will testify;
    (d) the total number of witnesses and the number of witnesses who will testify for each accused and on each count;
    (e) an indication of whether the witness will testify in person or pursuant to Rule 92*bis* by way of written statement or use of a transcript of testimony from other proceedings before the Tribunal; and
    (f) the estimated length of time required for each witness and the total time estimated for presentation of the defence case; and
  (ii) a list of exhibits the defence intends to offer in its case, stating where possible whether the Prosecutor has any objection as to authenticity. The defence shall serve on the Prosecutor copies of the exhibits so listed.

(H) The pre-trial Judge shall record the points of agreement and disagreement on matters of law and fact. In this connection, he or she may order the parties to file written submissions with either the pre-trial Judge or the Trial Chamber.

(I) In order to perform his or her functions, the pre-trial Judge may *proprio motu*, where appropriate, hear the parties without the accused being present. The pre-trial Judge may hear the parties in his or her private room, in which case minutes of the meeting shall be taken by a representative of the Registry.

(J) The pre-trial Judge shall keep the Trial Chamber regularly informed, particularly where issues are in dispute and may refer such disputes to the Trial Chamber.

(K) The pre-trial Judge may set a time for the making of pre-trial motions and, if required, any hearing thereon. A motion made before trial shall be determined before trial unless the Judge, for good cause, orders that it be deferred for determination at trial. Failure by a party to raise objections or to make requests which can be made prior to trial at the time set by the Judge shall constitute waiver thereof, but the Judge for cause may grant relief from the waiver.

(L)
  (i) After the filings by the Prosecutor pursuant to paragraph (E), the pre-trial Judge shall submit to the Trial Chamber a complete file consisting of all the filings of the parties, transcripts of status conferences and minutes of meetings held in the performance of his or her functions pursuant to this Rule.
  (ii) The pre-trial Judge shall submit a second file to the Trial Chamber after the defence filings pursuant to paragraph (G).

(M) The Trial Chamber may *proprio motu* exercise any of the functions of the pre-trial Judge.

(N) Upon a report of the pre-trial Judge, the Trial Chamber shall decide, should the case arise, on sanctions to be imposed on a party which fails to perform its obligations pursuant to the present Rule. Such sanctions may include the exclusion of testimonial or documentary evidence.

The ICTR and SCSL Rules do not contain any provision for a Pre-Trial Judge. The pre-trial proceedings are conducted by the Trial Chamber.

East Timor

7–143   See Reg. 2000/30, s.9 paragraph 7–26 and Reg. 2000/30, s.20 paragraph 7–114.

F. PRELIMINARY MOTIONS

(1) Statutory provisions and rules

ICC

ICC Rules of Procedure and Evidence, rr. 58, 133, 134

Proceedings under Article 19

58.—1. A request or application made under article 19 shall be in writing   **7–144**
and contain the basis for it.

2. When a Chamber receives a request or application raising a challenge or question concerning its jurisdiction or the admissibility of a case in accordance with article 19, paragraph 2 or 3, or is acting on its own motion as provided for in article 19, paragraph 1, it shall decide on the procedure to be followed and may take appropriate measures for the proper conduct of the proceedings. It may hold a hearing. It may join the challenge or question to a confirmation or a trial proceeding as long as this does not cause undue delay, and in this circumstance shall hear and decide on the challenge or question first.

3. The Court shall transmit a request or application received under sub-rule 2 to the Prosecutor and to the person referred to in article 19, paragraph 2, who has been surrendered to the Court or who has appeared voluntarily or pursuant to a summons, and shall allow them to submit written observations to the request or application within a period of time determined by the Chamber.

4. The Court shall rule on any challenge or question of jurisdiction first and then on any challenge or question of admissibility.

Motions challenging admissibility or jurisdiction

133. Challenges to the jurisdiction of the Court or the admissibility of the   **7–145**
case at the commencement of the trial, or subsequently with the leave of the
Court, shall be dealt with by the Presiding Judge and the Trial Chamber in
accordance with rule 58.

Motions relating to the trial proceedings

134.—1. Prior to the commencement of the trial, the Trial Chamber on its   **7–146**
own motion, or at the request of the Prosecutor or the defence, may rule on any issue concerning the conduct of the proceedings. Any request from the Prosecutor or the defence shall be in writing and, unless the request is for an ex parte procedure, served on the other party. For all requests other than those submitted for an ex parte procedure, the other party shall have the opportunity to file a response.

2. At the commencement of the trial, the Trial Chamber shall ask the Prosecutor and the defence whether they have any objections or observations concerning the conduct of the proceedings which have arisen since the confirmation hearings. Such objections or observations may not be raised or made again on a subsequent occasion in the trial proceedings, without leave of the Trial Chamber in this proceeding.

3. After the commencement of the trial, the Trial Chamber, on its own motion, or at the request of the Prosecutor or the defence, may rule on issues that arise during the course of the trial.

ICTY

ICTY Rules of Procedure and Evidence, rr. 72, 73

Preliminary motions (amended July 21, 2005)

7–147   **72.**—(A) Preliminary motions, being motions which:
  (i) challenge jurisdiction;
  (ii) allege defects in the form of the indictment;
  (iii) seek the severance of counts joined in one indictment under Rule 49 or seek separate trials under Rule 82(B); or
  (iv) raise objections based on the refusal of a request for assignment of counsel made under Rule 45(C)
shall be in writing and be brought not later than thirty days after disclosure by the Prosecutor to the defence of all material and statements referred to in Rule 66(A)(i) and shall be disposed of not later than sixty days after they were filed and before the commencement of the opening statements provided for in Rule 84.

(B) Decisions on preliminary motions are without interlocutory appeal save:
  (i) in the case of motions challenging jurisdiction;
  (ii) in other cases where certification has been granted by the Trial Chamber, which may grant such certification if the decision involves an issue that would significantly affect the fair and expeditious conduct of the proceedings or the outcome of the trial, and for which, in the opinion of the Trial Chamber, an immediate resolution by the Appeals Chamber may materially advance the proceedings.

7–148   (C) Appeals under paragraph (B)(i) shall be filed within fifteen days and requests for certification under paragraph (B)(ii) shall be filed within seven days of filing of the impugned decision. Where such decision is rendered orally, this time-limit shall run from the date of the oral decision, unless:
  (i) the party challenging the decision was not present or represented when the decision was pronounced, in which case the time-limit shall run from the date on which the challenging party is notified of the oral decision; or
  (ii) the Trial Chamber has indicated that a written decision will follow, in which case, the time-limit shall run from filing of the written decision.
If certification is given, a party shall appeal to the Appeals Chamber within seven days of the filing of the decision to certify.

(D) For the purpose of paragraphs (A)(i) and (B)(i), a motion challenging jurisdiction refers exclusively to a motion which challenges an indictment on the ground that it does not relate to:
  (i) any of the persons indicated in Articles 1, 6, 7 and 9 of the Statute;
  (ii) the territories indicated in Articles 1, 8 and 9 of the Statute;
  (iii) the period indicated in Articles 1, 8 and 9 of the Statute;
  (iv) any of the violations indicated in Articles 2, 3, 4, 5 and 7 of the Statute.

Other Motions

7–149   **73.**—(A) After a case is assigned to a Trial Chamber, either party may at any time move before the Chamber by way of motion, not being a preliminary motion, for appropriate ruling or relief. Such motions may be written or oral, at the discretion of the Trial Chamber.

(B) Decisions on all motions are without interlocutory appeal save with certification by the Trial Chamber, which may grant such certification if the decision involves an issue that would significantly affect the fair and expeditious conduct of the proceedings or the outcome of the trial, and for which, in the opinion of the Trial Chamber, an immediate resolution by the Appeals Chamber may materially advance the proceedings.

(C) Requests for certification shall be filed within seven days of the filing of the impugned decision. Where such decision is rendered orally, this time-limit shall run from the date of the oral decision, unless:

    (i) the party challenging the decision was not present or represented when the decision was pronounced, in which case the time-limit shall run from the date on which the challenging party is notified of the oral decision; or

    (ii) the Trial Chamber has indicated that a written decision will follow, in which case the time-limit shall run from filing of the written decision.

If certification is given, a party shall appeal to the Appeals Chamber within seven days of the filing of the decision to certify.

(D) Irrespective of any sanctions which may be imposed under Rule 46 (A), when a Chamber finds that a motion is frivolous or is an abuse of process, the Registrar shall withhold payment of fees associated with the production of that motion and/ or costs thereof.

ICTR

ICTR Rules of Procedure and Evidence, rr. 72, 73

Preliminary Motions

72.—(A) Preliminary motions, being motions which: **7–150**

    (i) challenge jurisdiction;

    (ii) allege defects in the form of the indictment;

    (iii) seek the severance of counts joined in one indictment under Rule 49 or seek separate trials under Rule 82 (B); or

    (iv) raise objections based on the refusal of a request for assignment of counsel made under Rule 45 (C) shall be in writing and be brought not later than thirty days after disclosure by the Prosecutor to the Defence of all material and statements referred to in Rule 66 (A) (i) and shall be disposed of not later than sixty days after they were filed and before the commencement of the opening statements provided for in Rule 84. The Trial Chamber may rule on such motions based solely on the briefs of the parties, unless it is decided to hear the motion in open Court.

(B) Decisions on preliminary motions are without interlocutory appeal, save:

    (i) in the case of motions challenging jurisdiction, where an appeal by either party lies as of right;

    (ii) in other cases where certification has been granted by the Trial Chamber, which may grant such certification if the decision involves an issue that would significantly affect the fair and expeditious conduct of the proceedings or the outcome of the trial, and for which, in the opinion of the Trial Chamber, an immediate resolution by the Appeals Chamber may materially advance the proceedings.

(C) Appeals under paragraph (B)(i) shall be filed within fifteen days and requests for certification under paragraph (B)(ii) shall be filed within seven days of filing of the impugned decision. Where such decision is rendered orally, this time-limit shall run from the date of the oral decision, unless

    (i) the party challenging the decision was not present or represented when the decision was pronounced, in which case the time-limit shall run from the date on which the challenging party is notified of the oral decision; or

    (ii) the Trial Chamber has indicated that a written decision will follow, in which case, the time-limit shall run from filing of the written decision.

If certification is given, a party shall appeal to the Appeals Chamber within seven days of the filing of the decision to certify.

(D) For purposes of paragraphs (A)(i) and (B)(i), a motion challenging jurisdiction refers exclusively to a motion which challenges an indictment on the ground that it does not relate to:

(i) any of the persons indicated in Articles 1, 5, 6 and 8 of the Statute;

(ii) the territories indicated in Articles 1, 7 and 8 of the Statute;

(iii) the period indicated in Articles 1, 7, and 8 of the Statute; or

(iv) any of the violations indicated in Articles 2, 3, 4 and 6 of the Statute.

(E) An appeal brought under paragraph (B)(i) may not be proceeded with if a bench of three Judges of the Appeals Chamber, assigned by the presiding Judge of the Appeals Chamber, decides that the appeal is not capable of satisfying the requirements of paragraph (D), in which case the appeal shall be dismissed.

(F) Objections to the form of the indictment, including an amended indictment, shall be raised by a party in one motion only, unless otherwise allowed by a Trial Chamber.

(G) Failure to comply with the time limits prescribed in this Rule shall constitute a waiver of the rights. The Trial Chamber may, however, grant relief from the waiver upon showing good cause.

Motions

7–151　　**73.**—(A) Subject to Rule 72, either party may move before a Trial Chamber for appropriate ruling or relief after the initial appearance of the accused. The Trial Chamber, or a Judge designated by the Chamber from among its members, may rule on such motions based solely on the briefs of the parties, unless it is decided to hear the motion in open Court.

(B) Decisions rendered on such motions are without interlocutory appeal save with certification by the Trial Chamber, which may grant such certification if the decision involves an issue that would significantly affect the fair and expeditious conduct of the proceedings or the outcome of the trial, and for which, in the opinion of the Trial Chamber, an immediate resolution by the Appeals Chamber may materially advance the proceedings.

(C) Requests for certification shall be filed within seven days of the filing of the impugned decision. Where such decision is rendered orally, this time-limit shall run from the date of the oral decision, unless

(i) the party challenging the decision was not present or represented when the decision was pronounced, in which case the time-limit shall run from the date on which the challenging party is notified of the oral decision; or

(ii) the Trial Chamber has indicated that a written decision will follow, in which case the time-limit shall run from filing of the written decision.

If certification is granted, a party shall appeal to the Appeals Chamber within seven days of the filing of the decision to certify.

(D) Where a date has been set for the hearing of a motion, including a preliminary motion, any additional motions to be heard on that date and any supporting material to the motions must be filed at least ten days before the hearing of the motion. Failure to observe this Rule will mean that the later motion will not be considered on the hearing date, nor will any adjournment of the original motion be granted on the basis of subsequent motions filed, save in exceptional circumstances.

(E) A responding party shall, thereafter, file any reply within five days from the date on which Counsel received the motion.

(F) In addition to the sanctions envisaged by Rule 46, a Chamber may impose sanctions against Counsel if Counsel brings a motion, including a preliminary motion, that, in the opinion of the Chamber, is frivolous or is an abuse of process. Such sanctions may include non-payment, in whole or in part, of fees associated with the motion and/or costs thereof.

(G) Notwithstanding the time limits in Rule 72(A), the time limit in the present Rule applies.

East Timor

Regulation 2000/30, ss.26, 27 (as amended by Regulation 2001/25)

Receipt and Notification of the Indictment

26.—26.1 Upon receipt of the indictment by the Court, the case file shall be registered by the Registry of the Court. In accordance with Section 17.1 and 35 of UNTAET Regulation No. 2000/11, the case file shall be forwarded by the Registry to the Panel of Judges or to an individual judge, according to UNTAET regulations and the plan of distribution of incoming cases. **7–152**

26.2 The Registrar shall ensure that a notification is promptly served upon the accused and his or her legal representative. The notification shall include a copy of the indictment and the date upon which it was received by the Court, and shall inform the accused and legal representative that the defence has the right to submit a response to the indictment within forty five days of receipt of the indictment by the Court.

26.3 The response, if any, shall be filed at the Court and may include legal and factual observations of the accused with respect to the indictment, any preliminary motions the accused wishes to raise and a list of the evidence and witnesses to be presented by the defence during the trial.

Motions

27.—27.1 Preliminary motions may be raised prior to the commencement of the trial. Such motions are those which: **7–153**
  (a) allege defects in the form of the indictment;
  (b) seek severance of counts joined in one indictment or separate trials in cases of coaccused; or
  (c) raise objections based upon refusal of a request for assignment of counsel

27.2 After the case is assigned to a panel or judge, any party may at any time lodge a motion with the court, other than a preliminary motion as described in the preceding subsection, for appropriate relief. Motions for appropriate relief may be oral or written at the discretion of the Court.

27.3 Decisions on motions, except as provided in Sections 23 and 27.4 of the present regulation, are not subject to interlocutory appeal. The granting of a motion to dismiss the case for any reason shall be deemed a final decision in the case and shall be subject to appeal as provided in Part VII of the present regulation.

27.4 The Court of Appeal may grant leave to immediately appeal from a decision on a motion where:
  (a) the decision from which appeal is sought would cause such prejudice to the case of the party seeking leave to appeal as could not be cured by the final decision of the trial;
  (b) the issue on which appeal is sought is of general importance to proceedings before the courts of East Timor; or,
  (c) upon other good cause being shown by the party seeking leave to appeal.

SCSL

SCSL Rules of Procedure and Evidence, rr. 72, 73

Preliminary Motions

7–154　　72.—(A) Preliminary motions by either party shall be brought within 21 days following disclosure by the Prosecutor to the Defence of all the material envisaged by Rule 66(A)(i).

(B) Preliminary motions by the accused are:
  (i) Objections based on lack of jurisdiction;
  (ii) Objections based on defects in the form of the indictment;
  (iii) Applications for severance of crimes joined in one indictment under Rule 49, or for separate trials under Rule 82(B);
  (iv) Objections based on the denial of request for assignment of counsel; or
  (v) Objections based on abuse of process.

(C) Objections based on lack of jurisdiction or to the form of the indictment, including an amended indictment, shall be raised by a party in one motion only, unless otherwise allowed by the Trial Chamber.

(D) The Trial Chamber shall, except as provided by Sub-Rules (E) and (F) below, dispose of preliminary motions before the trial, and its decisions thereon shall not be subject to interlocutory appeal.

(E) Preliminary motions made in the Trial Chamber prior to the Prosecutor's opening statement which raise a serious issue relating to jurisdiction shall be referred to a bench of at least three Appeals Chamber Judges, where they will proceed to a determination as soon as practicable.

(F) Preliminary motions made in the Trial Chamber prior to the Prosecutor's opening statement which, in the opinion of the Trial Chamber, raise an issue that would significantly affect the fair and expeditious conduct of the proceedings or the outcome of a trial shall be referred to a bench of at least three Appeals Chamber Judges, where they will proceed to a determination as soon as practicable.

(G) Where the Trial Chamber refers a motion to the Appeals Chamber pursuant to Sub-Rules (E) or (F) above, any party wishing to file additional written submissions must seek leave from the Appeals Chamber which will impose time limits for further submissions, responses and replies if leave is granted.

(H) References by the Trial Chamber pursuant to Sub-Rules (E) and (F) above shall not operate as a stay of proceedings. Such references shall not operate as a stay of the trial itself unless the Trial or Appeal Chamber so orders.

(I) This Rule shall be deemed to have entered into force on the 7th of March, 2003.

Motions

7–155　　73.—(A) Subject to Rule 72, either party may move before the Designated Judge or a Trial Chamber for appropriate ruling or relief after the initial appearance of the accused. The Designated Judge or the Trial Chamber, or a Judge designated by the Trial Chamber from among its members, shall rule on such motions based solely on the written submissions of the parties, unless it is decided to hear the parties in open Court.

(B) Decisions rendered on such motions are without interlocutory appeal. However, in exceptional circumstances and to avoid irreparable prejudice to a party, the Trial Chamber may give leave to appeal. Such leave should be sought within 3 days of the decision and shall not operate as a stay of proceedings unless the Trial Chamber so orders.

(C) Whenever the Trial Chamber and the Appeals Chamber of the Court are seized of the same Motion raising the same or similar issue or issues, the Trial Chamber shall stay proceedings on the said Motion before it until a final determination of the said Motion by the Appeals Chamber.

(D) Irrespective of any sanctions which may be imposed under Rule 46(A), when a Chamber finds that a motion is frivolous or is an abuse of process, the Registrar shall withhold payment of all or part of the fees associated with the production of that motion and/or costs thereof.

Numerous pre-trial motions have been brought before the ICTY and ICTR: see Chapter 2 on Jurisdiction; Chapter 6 on Indictments (challenges made before trial) and Chapter 19 (standard of interlocutory appeal Rule 73).

G. PRE-TRIAL CONFERENCES

(1) Statutory provisions and rules

ICC

ICC Rules of Procedure and Evidence, r. 132

132.—1. Promptly after it is constituted, the Trial Chamber shall hold a status conference in order to set the date of the trial. The Trial Chamber, on its own motion, or at the request of the Prosecutor or the defence, may postpone the date of the trial. The Trial Chamber shall ensure that this date and any postponements are made public.

2. In order to facilitate the affair and expeditious conduct of the proceedings, the Trial Chamber may confer with the parties by holding status conferences as necessary.

7–156

ICTY

ICTY Rules of Procedure and Evidence, rr. 65*bis*, 73*bis*, 73*ter*

Status Conferences

65*bis*.—(A) A Trial Chamber or a Trial Chamber Judge shall convene a status conference within one hundred and twenty days of the initial appearance of the accused and thereafter within one hundred and twenty days after the last status conference:

  (i) to organize exchanges between the parties so as to ensure expeditious preparation for trial;
  (ii) to review the status of his or her case and to allow the accused the opportunity to raise issues in relation thereto, including the mental and physical condition of the accused.

(B) The Appeals Chamber or an Appeals Chamber Judge shall convene a status conference, within one hundred and twenty days of the filing of a notice

7–157

of appeal and thereafter within one hundred and twenty days after the last status conference, to allow any person in custody pending appeal the opportunity to raise issues in relation thereto, including the mental and physical condition of that person.

(C) With the written consent of the accused, given after receiving advice from his counsel, a status conference under this Rule may be conducted

    (i) in his presence, but with his counsel participating either via teleconference or video-conference; or

    (ii) in Chambers in his absence, but with his participation via teleconference if he so wishes and/or participation of his counsel via teleconference or video-conference.

Pre-Trial Conference

7–158   **73*bis*.**—(A) Prior to the commencement of the trial, the Trial Chamber shall hold a Pre-Trial Conference.

(B) In the light of the file submitted to the Trial Chamber by the pre-trial Judge pursuant to Rule 65*ter* (L)(i), the Trial Chamber may call upon the Prosecutor to shorten the estimated length of the examination-in-chief for some witnesses.

(C) In the light of the file submitted to the Trial Chamber by the pre-trial Judge pursuant to Rule 65*ter* (L)(i), the Trial Chamber, after having heard the Prosecutor, shall determine

    (i) the number of witnesses the Prosecutor may call; and

    (ii) the time available to the Prosecutor for presenting evidence.

(D) After having heard the Prosecutor, the Trial Chamber may fix a number of crime sites or incidents comprised in one or more of the charges in respect of which evidence may be presented by the Prosecutor which, having regard to all the relevant circumstances, including the crimes charged in the indictment, their classification and nature, the places where they are alleged to have been committed, their scale and the victims of the crimes, are reasonably representative of the crimes charged.

(E) After commencement of the trial, the Prosecutor may file a motion to vary the decision as to the number of crime sites or incidents in respect of which evidence may be presented or the number of witnesses that are to be called or for additional time to present evidence and the Trial Chamber may grant the Prosecutor's request if satisfied that this is in the interests of justice.

Pre-Defence Conference

7–159   **73*ter*.**—(A) Prior to the commencement by the defence of its case the Trial Chamber may hold a Conference.

(B) In the light of the file submitted to the Trial Chamber by the pre-trial Judge pursuant to Rule 65*ter*(L)(ii), the Trial Chamber may call upon the defence to shorten the estimated length of the examination-in-chief for some witnesses.

(C) In the light of the file submitted to the Trial Chamber by the pre-trial Judge pursuant to Rule 65*ter*(L)(ii), the Trial Chamber, after having heard the defence, shall set the number of witnesses the defence may call.

(D) After commencement of the defence case, the defence may, if it considers it to be in the interests of justice, file a motion to reinstate the list of witnesses or to vary the decision as to which witnesses are to be called.

(E) After having heard the defence, the Trial Chamber shall determine the time available to the defence for presenting evidence.

(F) During a trial, the Trial Chamber may grant a defence request for additional time to present evidence if this is in the interests of justice.

ICTR

ICTR Rules of Procedure and Evidence, rr. 65*bis*, 73*bis*, 73*ter*

Status Conferences

65*bis*.—(A) A status conference may be convened by a Trial Chamber or a **7–160**
Judge thereof. Its purpose is to organise exchanges between the parties so as to
ensure expeditious trial proceedings.

(B) The Appeals Chamber or an Appeals Chamber Judge may convene a
status conference.

(C) A status conference held pursuant to paragraph (B) of this Rule may be
conducted with the participation of counsel via tele-conference or video-
conference.

Pre-Trial Conference

73*bis*.—(A) The Trial Chamber shall hold a Pre-Trial Conference prior to **7–161**
the commencement of the trial.

(B) At the Pre-Trial Conference the Trial Chamber or a Judge, designated
from among its members, may order the Prosecutor, within a time limit set by
the Trial Chamber or the said Judge, and before the date set for trial, to file
the following:

    (i) A pre-trial brief addressing the factual and legal issues;

    (ii) Admissions by the parties and a statement of other matters not in
        dispute;

    (iii) A statement of contested matters of fact and law;

    (iv) A list of witnesses the Prosecutor intends to call with:

        (a) The name or pseudonym of each witness;

        (b) A summary of the facts on which each witness will testify;

        (c) The points in the indictment on which each witness will testify;
            and

        (d) The estimated length of time required for each witness;

    (v) A list of exhibits the Prosecutor intends to offer stating, where
        possible, whether or not the Defence has any objection as to
        authenticity.

The Trial Chamber or the Judge may order the Prosecutor to provide the
Trial Chamber with copies of written statements of each witness whom the
Prosecutor intends to call to testify.

(C) The Trial Chamber or the designated Judge may order the Prosecutor
to shorten the examination-in-chief of some witnesses.

(D) The Trial Chamber or the designated Judge may order the Prosecutor
to reduce the number of witnesses, if it considers that an excessive number of
witnesses are being called to prove the same facts.

(E) After commencement of Trial, the Prosecutor, if he considers it to be in
the interests of justice, may move the Trial Chamber for leave to reinstate the
list of witnesses or to vary his decision as to which witnesses are to be called.

(F) At the Pre-Trial Conference, the Trial Chamber or the designated Judge
may order the Defence to file a statement of admitted facts and law and a pre-
trial brief addressing the factual and legal issues, not later than seven days
prior to the date set for trial.

Pre-Defence Conference

73*ter*.—(A) The Trial Chamber may hold a Conference prior to the **7–162**
commencement by the Defence of its case.

(B) At that Conference, the Trial Chamber or a Judge, designated from among its members, may order that the Defence, before the commencement of its case but after the close of the case for the prosecution, file the following:
- (i) Admissions by the parties and a statement of other matters which are not in dispute;
- (ii) A statement of contested matters of fact and law;
- (iii) A list of witnesses the Defence intends to call with:
  - (a) The name or pseudonym of each witness;
  - (b) A summary of the facts on which each witness will testify;
  - (c) The points in the indictment as to which each witness will testify; and
  - (d) The estimated length of time required for each witness;
- (iv) A list of exhibits the Defence intends to offer in its case, stating where possible whether or not the Prosecutor has any objection as to authenticity.

The Trial Chamber or the Judge may order the Defence to provide the Trial Chamber and the Prosecutor with copies of the written statements of each witness whom the Defence intends to call to testify.

(C) The Trial Chamber or the designated Judge may order the Defence to shorten the estimated length of the examination-in-chief for some witnesses.

(D)
The Trial Chamber or the designated Judge may order the Defence to reduce the number of witnesses, if it considers that an excessive number of witnesses are being called to prove the same facts.

(E) After commencement of the Defence case, the Defence, if it considers it to be in the interests of justice, may move the Trial Chamber for leave to reinstate the list of witnesses or to vary its decision as to which witnesses are to be called.

East Timor

Regulation 2000/30, ss.26, 29 (as amended by Regulation 2000/25)

Receipt and Notification of the Indictment

7–163   **26.**—26.1 Upon receipt of the indictment by the Court, the case file shall be registered by the Registry of the Court. In accordance with Section 17.1 and 35 of UNTAET Regulation No. 2000/11, the case file shall be forwarded by the Registry to the Panel of Judges or to an individual judge, according to UNTAET regulations and the plan of distribution of incoming cases.

26.2 The Registrar shall ensure that a notification is promptly served upon the accused and his or her legal representative. The notification shall include a copy of the indictment and the date upon which it was received by the Court, and shall inform the accused and legal representative that the defence has the right to submit a response to the indictment within forty five days of receipt of the indictment by the Court.

26.3 The response, if any, shall be filed at the Court and may include legal and factual observations of the accused with respect to the indictment, any preliminary motions the accused wishes to raise and a list of the evidence and witnesses to be presented by the defence during the trial.

Preliminary Hearing

7–164   **29.**—29.1 Upon receipt of the response of the defence provided in Section 26.3 of the present regulation, or upon the expiration of the term defined in Section 26.2 of the present regulation, the court shall summon the parties to a preliminary hearing to be held within twenty days thereafter.

29.2 At the hearing described in Section 29.1 or 44.5 of the present regulation, the court shall:
  (a) satisfy itself that the accused has read or has had the indictment read to him or her and understands the nature of the charges against him or her;
  (b) ensure that the right of the accused to counsel has been respected;
  (c) rule on any motions or requests for evidence or additional investigation, or if the accused has failed to file any motions or requests, ensure that the accused understood his or her rights in that regard;
  (d) afford the accused the opportunity to make a statement concerning the charges, which may include a plea of not guilty or an admission of guilt as to all or any portion of the charges; and,
  (e) determine what evidence and witnesses the defence would intend to present to the court.
29.3 Upon reviewing the requests for evidence presented by the parties, the panel of judges or the judge shall issue any necessary rulings and, after consultation with the parties, set a date for trial.
29.4 The accused or his or her legal representative may request the court for an extension of time to prepare the case and, if necessary for the defence, to present additional evidence.
29.5 At their own motion or at the request of the accused or his or her legal representative, the panel of judges or the competent judge, shall assess the necessity of the detention of the accused in accordance with Section 20 of the present regulation and may order any measure consistent with Section 20.6 of the present regulation.

SCSL

SCSL Rules of Procedure and Evidence, rr. 65*bis*, 73*bis*, 73*ter*

Status Conferences

65*bis*. A status conference may be convened by the Designated Judge or by **7–165** the Trial Chamber. The status conference shall:
  i. organize exchanges between the parties so as to ensure expeditious trial proceedings;
  ii. review the status of his case and to allow the accused the opportunity to raise issues in relation thereto.

Pre-Trial Conference

73*bis*.—(A) The Trial Chamber or a Judge designated from among its **7–166** members shall hold a Pre Trial Conference prior to the commencement of the trial.
(B) At the Pre Trial Conference the Trial Chamber or a Judge designated from among its members may order the Prosecutor, within a time limit set by the Trial Chamber or the said Judge, and before the date set for trial, to file the following:
  (i) A pre trial brief addressing the factual and legal issues;
  (ii) Admissions by the parties and a statement of other matters not in dispute;
  (iii) A statement of contested matters of fact and law;
  (iv) A list of witnesses the Prosecutor intends to call with:
    (a) The name or pseudonym of each witness;
    (b) A summary of the facts on which each witness will testify;

(c) The points in the indictment on which each witness will testify; and

(d) The estimated length of time required for each witness;

(v) A list of exhibits the Prosecutor intends to offer stating, where possible, whether or not the defence has any objection as to authenticity.

The Trial Chamber or the said Judge may order the Prosecutor to provide the Trial Chamber with copies of written statements of each witness whom the Prosecutor intends to call to testify.

(C) The Trial Chamber or a Judge designated from among its members may order the Prosecutor to shorten the examination in chief of some witnesses.

(D) The Trial Chamber or a Judge designated from among its members may order the Prosecutor to reduce the number of witnesses, if it considers that an excessive number of witnesses are being called to prove the same facts.

(E) After the commencement of the Trial, the Prosecutor may, if he considers it to be in the interests of justice, move the Trial Chamber for leave to reinstate the list of witnesses or to vary his decision as to which witnesses are to be called.

(F) At the Pre-Trial Conference, the Trial Chamber or a Judge designated from among its members may order the defence to file a statement of admitted facts and law and a pre-trial brief addressing the factual and legal issues, not later than seven days prior to the date set for trial.

Pre-Defence Conference

7–167   **73ter.**—(A) The Trial Chamber or a Judge designated from among its members may hold a Conference prior to the commencement by the defence of its case.

(B) At that Conference, the Trial Chamber or a Judge designated from among its members may order that the defence, before the commencement of its case but after the close of the case for the prosecution, file the following:

Admissions by the parties and a statement of other matters which are not in dispute;

(i) A statement of contested matters of fact and law;

(ii) A list of witnesses the defence intends to call with:

(iii) The name or pseudonym of each witness;

(a) A summary of the facts on which each witness will testify;

(b) The points in the indictment as to which each witness will testify; and

(c) The estimated length of time required for each witness;

(iv) A list of exhibits the defence intends to offer in its case, stating where possible whether or not the Prosecutor has any objection as to authenticity.

The Trial Chamber or the said Judge may order the Defence to provide the Trial Chamber and the Prosecutor with copies of the written statements of each witness whom the Defence intends to call to testify.

(C) The Trial Chamber or a Judge designated from among its members may order the defence to shorten the estimated length of the examination in chief for some witnesses.

(D) The Trial Chamber or a Judge designated from among its members may order the defence to reduce the number of witnesses, if it considers that an excessive number of witnesses are being called to prove the same facts.

(E) After the commencement of the defence case, the defence may, if it considers it to be in the interests of justice, move the Trial Chamber for leave to reinstate the list of witnesses or to vary its decision as to which witnesses are to be called.

(2) Case Management

The aforementioned Rules on pre-trial procedures and conferences have **7–168** been enacted to shorten the length of trials, and ensure that the proceedings focus on the genuine issues in dispute.

The overriding objective in implementing these rules is to guarantee fair and expeditious proceedings and equality between the parties in the preparation of the case (see, *Prosecutor v. Krajisnik*, Decision on Prosecution Motion for Clarification in respect of Application of Rules 65*ter*, 66(B) and 67(C), August 1, 2001). Accordingly, the Trial Chamber interpreted the requirement in Rule 65*ter*(E)(iii) for the Prosecution to file a list of exhibits to mean that the exhibits themselves should be filed and disclosed, even though the Prosecution is not strictly required to disclose its exhibits under Rule 66, unless the Defence triggers reciprocal disclosure (please note that the ICTY rule on reciprocal disclosure has been removed. See further section 7 IV C (paragraphs 7–206 *et seq.*)). To do otherwise "would . . . allow a narrow interpretation of the Rules to override elementary notions of a fair trial".

The Prosecution may be permitted to modify her list of exhibits (see, *Prosecutor v. Ndayambaje et al.*, Decision on Prosecutor's Motion to Modify her List of Exhibits, December 14, 2002). Additional witnesses can be added to the list of Prosecution witnesses if it is in the interests of justice to do so, as provided for in ICTY/ICTR Rule 73*bis* (E): see, *Prosecutor v. Milošević*, Decision on Prosecution Motion for Leave to Call Additional Witnesses, August 30, 2002. Similar rules apply to the Defence. (73*ter*(D) ICTY and 73*ter*(E) ICTR/SCSL. See further paragraph 8–72.

Rule 73*ter*(iv) ICTR Rules permits the Trial Chamber to order the Defence **7–168.1** to disclose the written statements of each witness whom the Defence intends to call to testify. This is a discretionary matter and the judges, although allowed, are not obliged to issue such an order. In *Bagosora et al.*, three of the four Accused were ordered to disclose the written statements of the witnesses they intended to call to testify. The fourth Accused, Gratien Kabiligi, was granted delay to file a pre-defence brief, a list of witnesses and summaries of their anticipated testimonies and to present his defence (Decision on Postponement of Defence of Accused Kabiligi, April 21, 2005).

On October 17, 2005, during the testimony of a witness called by another Accused, the Prosecution requested the Trial Chamber by oral application to order the Kabiligi Defence to disclose a written statement they had obtained from that witness in the course of their own investigations. Relying on Rule 73*ter,* the Prosecution claimed that they had the right to receive that statement, which they needed to properly cross-examine that witness. The Defence opposed the application, arguing that no such disclosure obligation existed in the Rules and that Rule 73*ter* did not apply before the Kabiligi Defence had made a final determination on the witnesses they intended to call in their defence.

On October 18, 2005 the Trial Chamber in *Bagosora et al.* rendered an oral Decision dismissing the Prosecutor's request for disclosure and emphasized, not only that Rule 73*ter* did not apply at this stage, but also that Rule 73*ter* did not oblige judges to order the Defence to disclose statements of their listed witnesses at any stage (*Bagasora*, Registry Transcript, October 18, 2005).

In the ICTY, no equivalent of Rule 73*ter*(iv) exists. Pursuant to Rule 73*ter* of the ICTY Rules the Trial Chamber may order the Defence to disclose the names and identifying information of their witnesses, as well as sufficiently detailed *summaries* of their anticipated testimonies. Also see *Prosecutor v. Blaškić*, Decision on the Prosecutor's Motion for seven days advance disclosure of defence witnesses and defence witness statements, September 3, 1998, where the Trial Chamber refused the Prosecution application to order the Defence to disclose prior statements made by the defence witnesses.

IV. DISCLOSURE

A. Prosecutor's Duties

(1) Statutory provisions and rules

ICC

ICC Statute, Arts 61, 64

Confirmation of the charges before trial

7–169   **61.**—1. Subject to the provisions of paragraph 2, within a reasonable time after the person's surrender or voluntary appearance before the Court, the Pre-Trial Chamber shall hold a hearing to confirm the charges on which the Prosecutor intends to seek trial. The hearing shall be held in the presence of the Prosecutor and the person charged, as well as his or her counsel.

2. The Pre-Trial Chamber may, upon request of the Prosecutor or on its own motion, hold a hearing in the absence of the person charged to confirm the charges on which the Prosecutor intends to seek trial when the person has:

     (a) Waived his or her right to be present; or

     (b) Fled or cannot be found and all reasonable steps have been taken to secure his or her appearance before the Court and to inform the person of the charges and that a hearing to confirm those charges will be held.

In that case, the person shall be represented by counsel where the Pre-Trial Chamber determines that it is in the interests of justice.

3. Within a reasonable time before the hearing, the person shall:

     (a) Be provided with a copy of the document containing the charges on which the Prosecutor intends to bring the person to trial; and

     (b) Be informed of the evidence on which the Prosecutor intends to rely at the hearing.

The Pre-Trial Chamber may issue orders regarding the disclosure of information for the purposes of the hearing.

Functions and powers of the Trial Chamber

7–170   **64.**—3. Upon assignment of a case for trial in accordance with this Statute, the Trial Chamber assigned to deal with the case shall:

     (a) Confer with the parties and adopt such procedures as are necessary to facilitate the fair and expeditious conduct of the proceedings;

     (b) Determine the language or languages to be used at trial; and

     (c) Subject to any other relevant provisions of this Statute, provide for disclosure of documents or information not previously disclosed, sufficiently in advance of the commencement of the trial to enable adequate preparation for trial.

ICC Rules of Procedure and Evidence, rr. 76, 77, 81, 82, 84

Pre-trial disclosure relating to prosecution witnesses

7–171   **76.**—1. The Prosecutor shall provide the defence with the names of witnesses whom the Prosecutor intends to call to testify and copies of any prior statements made by those witnesses. This shall be done sufficiently in advance to enable the adequate preparation of the defence.

2. The Prosecutor shall subsequently advise the defence of the names of any additional prosecution witnesses and provide copies of their statements when the decision is made to call those witnesses.

3. The statements of prosecution witnesses shall be made available in original and in a language which the accused fully understands and speaks.

4. This rule is subject to the protection and privacy of victims and witnesses and the protection of confidential information as provided for in the Statute and rules 81 and 82.

Inspection of material in possession or control of the Prosecutor

77. The Prosecutor shall, subject to the restrictions on disclosure as provided for in the Statute and in rules 81 and 82, permit the defence to inspect any books, documents, photographs and other tangible objects in the possession or control of the Prosecutor, which are material to the preparation of the defence or are intended for use by the Prosecutor as evidence for the purposes of the confirmation hearing or at trial, as the case may be, or were obtained from or belonged to the person.

7–172

Restrictions on disclosure

81.—1. Reports, memoranda and other internal documents prepared by a party, its assistants or representatives in connection with the investigation or preparation of the case are not subject to disclosure.

7–173

2. Where material or information is in the possession or control of the Prosecutor which must be disclosed in accordance with the Statute, but disclosure may prejudice further or ongoing investigations, the Prosecutor may apply to the Chamber dealing with the matter for a ruling as to whether the material or information must be disclosed to the defence. The matter shall be heard on ex parte basis by the Chamber. However, the Prosecutor may not introduce such material or information into evidence during the confirmation hearing or the trial without adequate prior disclosure to the accused.

3. Where steps have been taken to ensure the confidentiality of information, in accordance with articles 54, 57, 64, 72 and 93, and, in accordance with article 68, to protect the safety of witnesses and victims and members of their families, such information shall not be disclose, except in accordance with those articles. When the disclosure of such information may create a risk to safety of the witness, the Court shall take measures to inform the witness in advance.

4. The Chamber dealing the matter shall, on its own motion or at the request of the Prosecutor, the accused or any State, take the necessary steps to ensure the confidentiality of information, in accordance with articles 54, 72 and 93, and, in accordance with article 68, to protect the safety of witnesses and victims and members of their families, including by authorizing the non-disclosure of their identity prior to the commencement of the trial.

7–174

5. Where material or information is in the possession or control of the Prosecutor which is withheld under article 68, paragraph 5, such material and information may not be subsequently introduced into evidence during the confirmation hearing or the trial without adequate prior disclosure to the accused.

6. Where material or information is in the possession or control of the defence which is subject to disclosure, it may be withheld in circumstances similar to those which would allow the Prosecutor to rely on article 68, paragraph 5, and a summary thereof submitted instead. Such material and information may not be subsequently introduced into evidence during the confirmation hearing or the trial without adequate prior disclosure to the Prosecutor.

Restrictions on disclosure of material and information protected under article 54, paragraph 3(e)

7–175   **82.**—1. Where material or information is in the possession or control of the Prosecutor which is protected under article 54, paragraph 3 (e), the Prosecutor may not subsequently introduce such material or information into evidence without the prior consent of the provider of the material or information and adequate prior disclosure to the accused.

2. If the Prosecutor introduces material or information protected under article 54, paragraph 3(e), into evidence, a Chamber may not order the production of additional evidence received from the provider of the initial material or information, nor may a Chamber for the purpose of obtaining such additional evidence itself summon the provider or a representative of the provider as a witness or order their attendance.

3. If the Prosecutor calls a witness to introduce in evidence any material or information that has been protected under article 54, paragraph 3(e), a Chamber may not compel that witness to answer any question relating to the material or information or its origin, if the witness declines to answer on grounds of confidentiality.

4. The right of the accused to challenge evidence which has been protected under article 54, paragraph 3(e), shall remain unaffected subject only to limitations contained in sub-rules 2 and 3.

5. A Chamber dealing with the matter may order, upon application by the defence, that, in the interest of justice, material or information in the possession of the accused, which has been provided to the accused under the same conditions as set forth in article 54, paragraph 3(e), and which is to be introduced into evidence, shall be subject to mutatis mutandis to sub-rules 1, 2 and 3.

Disclosure and additional evidence for trial

7–176   **84.** In order to enable the parties to prepare for trial and to facilitate the fair and expeditious conduct of the proceedings, the Trial Chamber shall, in accordance with article 64, paragraphs 3 (c) and 6 (b), and article 67, paragraph (2), and subject to article 68, paragraph 5, make any necessary orders for disclosure of documents or information not previously disclosed and for the production of additional evidence. To avoid delay and to ensure that the trial commences on a set date, any such orders shall include strict time limits which shall be kept under review by the Trial Chamber.

ICTY

ICTY Rules of Procedure and Evidence, rr. 66, 70

Disclosure by the Prosecutor

7–177   **66.**—(A) Subject to the provisions of Rules 53 and 69, the Prosecutor shall make available to the defence in a language which the accused understands

    (i) within thirty days of the initial appearance of the accused, copies of the supporting material which accompanied the indictment when confirmation was sought as well as all prior statements obtained by the Prosecutor from the accused; and

    (ii) within the time-limit prescribed by the Trial Chamber or by the pre-trial Judge appointed pursuant to Rule 65*ter*, copies of the statements of all witnesses whom the Prosecutor intends to call to testify at trial, and copies of all written statements taken in accordance with Rule

92*bis*; copies of the statements of additional prosecution witnesses shall be made available to the defence when a decision is made to call those witnesses.

(B) The Prosecutor shall, on request, permit the defence to inspect any books, documents, photographs and tangible objects in the Prosecutor's custody or control, which are material to the preparation of the defence, or are intended for use by the Prosecutor as evidence at trial or were obtained from or belonged to the accused.

(C) Where information is in the possession of the Prosecutor, the disclosure of which may prejudice further or ongoing investigations, or for any other reasons may be contrary to the public interest or affect the security interests of any State, the Prosecutor may apply to the Trial Chamber sitting in camera to be relieved from an obligation under the Rules to disclose that information. When making such application the Prosecutor shall provide the Trial Chamber (but only the Trial Chamber) with the information that is sought to be kept confidential.

Matters not subject to disclosure

70.—(A) Notwithstanding the provisions of Rules 66 and 67, reports, memoranda, or other internal documents prepared by a party, its assistants or representatives in connection with the investigation or preparation of the case, are not subject to disclosure or notification under those Rules.   **7–178**

(B) If the Prosecutor is in possession of information which has been provided to the Prosecutor on a confidential basis and which has been used solely for the purpose of generating new evidence, that initial information and its origin shall not be disclosed by the Prosecutor without the consent of the person or entity providing the initial information and shall in any event not be given in evidence without prior disclosure to the accused.

(C) If, after obtaining the consent of the person or entity providing information under this Rule, the Prosecutor elects to present as evidence any testimony, document or other material so provided, the Trial Chamber, notwithstanding Rule 98, may not order either party to produce additional evidence received from the person or entity providing the initial information, nor may the Trial Chamber for the purpose of obtaining such additional evidence itself summon that person or a representative of that entity as a witness or order their attendance. A Trial Chamber may not use its power to order the attendance of witnesses or to require production of documents in order to compel the production of such additional evidence.

(D) If the Prosecutor calls a witness to introduce in evidence any information provided under this Rule, the Trial Chamber may not compel that witness to answer any question relating to the information or its origin, if the witness declines to answer on grounds of confidentiality.

(E) The right of the accused to challenge the evidence presented by the Prosecution shall remain unaffected subject only to the limitations contained in paragraphs (C) and (D).

(F) The Trial Chamber may order upon an application by the accused or defence counsel that, in the interests of justice, the provisions of this Rule shall apply *mutatis mutandis* to specific information in the possession of the accused.

(G) Nothing in paragraph (C) or (D) above shall affect a Trial Chamber's power under Rule 89 (D) to exclude evidence if its probative value is substantially outweighed by the need to ensure a fair trial.

ICTR

ICTR Rules of Procedure and Evidence, rr. 66, 70

Disclosure of materials by the Prosecutor

66. Subject to the provisions of Rules 53 and 69;   **7–179**

(A) The Prosecutor shall disclose to the Defence:
  (i) Within 30 days of the initial appearance of the accused copies of the supporting material which accompanied the indictment when confirmation was sought as well as all prior statements obtained by the Prosecutor from the accused, and
  (ii) No later than 60 days before the date set for trial, copies of the statements of all witnesses whom the Prosecutor intends to call to testify at trial; upon good cause shown a Trial Chamber may order that copies of the statements of additional prosecution witnesses be made available to the Defence within a prescribed time.

(B) At the request of the Defence, the Prosecutor shall, subject to Sub-Rule (C), permit the Defence to inspect any books, documents, photographs and tangible objects in his custody or control, which are material to the preparation of the defence, or are intended for use by the Prosecutor as evidence at trial or were obtained from or belonged to the accused.

(C) Where information or materials are in the possession of the Prosecutor, the disclosure of which may prejudice further or ongoing investigations, or for any other reasons may be contrary to the public interest or affect the security interests of any State, the Prosecutor may apply to the Trial Chamber sitting in camera to be relieved from the obligation to disclose pursuant to Sub-Rules (A) and (B). When making such an application the Prosecutor shall provide the Trial Chamber, and only the Trial Chamber, with the information or materials that are sought to be kept confidential.

Matters not Subject to Disclosure

7-180   **70.**—(A) Notwithstanding the provisions of Rules 66 and 67, reports, memoranda, or other internal documents prepared by a party, its assistants or representatives in connection with the investigation or preparation of the case, are not subject to disclosure or notification under the aforementioned provisions.

(B) If the Prosecutor is in possession of information which has been provided to him on a confidential basis and which has been used solely for the purpose of generating new evidence, that initial information and its origin shall not be disclosed by the Prosecutor without the consent of the person or entity providing the initial information and shall in any event not be given in evidence without prior disclosure to the accused.

(C) If, after obtaining the consent of the person or entity providing information under this Rule, the Prosecutor elects to present as evidence any testimony, document or other material so provided, the Trial Chamber, notwithstanding Rule 98, may not order either party to produce additional evidence received from the person or entity providing the initial information, nor may the Trial Chamber for the purpose of obtaining such additional evidence itself summon that person or a representative of that entity as a witness or order their attendance.

(D) If the Prosecutor calls as a witness the person providing or a representative of the entity providing information under this Rule, the Trial Chamber may not compel the witness to answer any question the witness declines to answer on grounds of confidentiality.

(E) The right of the accused to challenge the evidence presented by the Prosecution shall remain unaffected subject only to limitations contained in Sub-Rules (C) and (D).

(F) Nothing in Sub-Rule (C) or (D) above shall affect a Trial Chamber's power under Rule 89 (C) to exclude evidence if its probative value is substantially outweighed by the need to ensure a fair trial.

East Timor

Regulation 2000/30, s.24 (as amended by Regulation 2000/25)

Presentation of Indictment

24.—24.1 Upon completion of the investigation, if the result so warrants, **7–181**
the Public Prosecutor shall present a written indictment of the suspect to the
competent District Court. The indictment shall include:
    (a) the name and particulars of the accused;
    (b) a complete and accurate description of the crime imputed to the
        accused;
    (c) a concise statement of the facts upon which the accusation is made;
    (d) a statement identifying the provisions of law alleged to have been
        violated by the accused;
    (e) the identification of the victims, unless measures to protect the
        identity of the victims are being sought; and
    (f) a request for the trial of the accused.
24.2 Together with the indictment, the public prosecutor shall present to
the court a list describing the evidence that supports the indictment.
24.3 When the indictment is presented to the court, the powers of the
Investigating Judge terminate, except the powers of the Investigating Judge
described in Section 9.3 (c) through
    (j) of the present regulation.
24.4 Upon presentation of the indictment to the court, the following must be
made available by the prosecutor to the accused and his or her legal
representative:
    (a) Copies of all documentary evidence intended to be offered by the
        prosecution at trial;
    (b) All statements in the possession of the prosecution of any witness
        whose testimony is intended to be offered by the prosecution at trial;
    (c) All information in any form in the possession of the prosecution which
        tends to negate the guilt of the accused or to mitigate the gravity of
        the offenses charged in the indictment;
24.5 Meaningful access to physical evidence in the possession of the
prosecution shall be provided to the accused, his or her legal representatives
and expert witnesses. Procedures for providing such access shall be as agreed
between the parties or as ordered by the court.
24.6 If the Court finds that full compliance with Section 24.4 of the present
regulation will likely lead to serious endangerment of the security of a witness
or his or her family, the Court may permit disclosure of redacted or
summarized descriptions of the affected material.
24.7 The duty of the prosecutor pursuant to Section 24.4 of the present
regulation is a continuing duty, so that qualifying material coming later into
possession of the prosecutor must immediately be made available to the
accused and his or her legal representative.

SCSL

SCSL Rules of Procedure and Evidence, rr. 66, 70

Disclosure of materials by the Prosecutor

66. (A) Subject to the provisions of Rules 50, 53, 69 and 75, the Prosecutor **7–182**
shall:

    (i) Within 30 days of the initial appearance of an accused, disclose to the Defence copies of the statements of all witnesses whom the Prosecutor intends to call to testify and all evidence to be presented pursuant to Rule 92*bis* at trial.

    (ii) Continuously disclose to the Defence copies of the statements of all additional prosecution witnesses whom the Prosecutor intends to call to testify, but not later than 60 days before the date for trial, or as otherwise ordered by a Judge of the Trial Chamber either before or after the commencement of the trial, upon good clause being shown by the Prosecution. Upon good cause being shown by the Defence, a Judge of the Trial Chamber may order that copies of the statements of additional prosecution witnesses that the Prosecutor does not intend to call be made available to the defence within a prescribed time.

    (iii) At the request of the defence, subject to Sub-Rule (B), permit the defence to inspect any books, documents, photographs and tangible objects in his custody or control, which are material to the preparation of the defence, upon a showing by the defence of categories of, or specific, books, documents, photographs and tangible objects which the defence considers to be material to the preparation of a defence, or to inspect any books, documents, photographs and tangible objects in his custody or control which are intended for use by the Prosecutor as evidence at trial or were obtained from or belonged to the accused.

(B) Where information or materials are in the possession of the Prosecutor, the disclosure of which may prejudice further or ongoing investigations, or for any other reasons may be contrary to the public interest or affect the security interests of any State, the Prosecutor may apply to a Judge designated by the President sitting ex parte and in camera, but with notice to the Defence, to be relieved from the obligation to disclose pursuant to Sub-Rule (A). When making such an application the Prosecutor shall provide, only to such Judge, the information or materials that are sought to be kept confidential.

Matters not Subject to Disclosure

7–183   **70.**—(A) Notwithstanding the provisions of Rules 66 and 67, reports, memoranda, or other internal documents prepared by a party, its assistants or representatives in connection with the investigation or preparation of the case, are not subject to disclosure or notification under the aforementioned provisions.

(B) If the Prosecutor is in possession of information which has been provided to him on a confidential basis and which has been used solely for the purpose of generating new evidence, that initial information and its origin shall not be disclosed by the Prosecutor without the consent of the person or entity providing the initial information and shall in any event not be given in evidence without prior disclosure to the accused.

(C) If, after obtaining the consent of the person or entity providing information under this Rule, the Prosecutor elects to present as evidence any testimony, document or other material so provided, the Trial Chamber may not order either party to produce additional evidence received from the person or entity providing the initial information, nor may the Trial Chamber for the purpose of obtaining such additional evidence itself summon that person or a representative of that entity as a witness or order their attendance. The consent shall be in writing.

(D) If the Prosecutor calls as a witness the person providing or a representative of the entity providing information under this Rule, the Trial Chamber may not compel the witness to answer any question the witness declines to answer on grounds of confidentiality.

(E) The right of the accused to challenge the evidence presented by the Prosecution shall remain unaffected subject only to limitations contained in Sub-Rules (C) and (D).

(F) Nothing in Sub-Rule (C) or (D) above shall affect a Trial Chamber's power to exclude evidence under Rule 95.

(2) Nature of disclosure duties

The expression "prior statements obtained by the Prosecutor from the accused", within the meaning of Sub-rule 66(A)(i) of the ICTY/ICTR Rules (the SCSL does not refer to it), whether the prior statements were obtained by the Prosecution or whether they originate from any other source must be understood to refer to all statements made by the accused during questioning in any type of judicial proceeding which may be in the possession of the Prosecutor, but only such statements. Utterances of a different kind, for example, speeches to the media or orders written by the accused, do not constitute "statements" for the purposes of Rule 66 (A)(i) (see *Prosecutor v. Blaškić*, Decision on the Defence Motion for Sanctions for the Prosecutor's Failure to Comply with Sub-rule 66(A) of the Rules and the Decision of January 27, 1997 Compelling the Production of All Statements of the Accused, July 15, 1998, p. 3; see *Prosecutor v. Kordić and Čerkez*, Order on Motion to Compel Compliance by the Prosecutor with Rules 66(A) and 68, February 26, 1999, p. 3).

7–184

Witness statements under Rule 66(A)(ii) refer to "all previous statements of all Prosecution witnesses, in whatever form" (*Prosecutor v. Casimir Bizimungu et al.*, Decision on Prosper Mugiraneza's Motion to Require Strict Compliance with Rule 66(A)(ii), May 5, 2004, para. 7). However, the Trial Chamber held that "only when the Witness is to testify on the same subject matter as his previous testimony that this previous testimony shall constitute a witness statement within the meaning of Rule 66(A)(ii) and is therefore subject to disclosure" (*ibid.*, para. 8).

Rule 66 mandates disclosure of all witness statements in the possession of all the Prosecution, irrespective of their form or source. The SCSL defined a witness statement under Rule 66(A)(i) as "any statement or declaration made by a witness in relation to an event he or she witnessed and recorded in any form by an official in the course of an investigation" (*Prosecutor v. Norman et al.*, Decision on Disclosure of Witness Statements and Cross-Examination, July 16, 2004, para. 10; *Prosecutor v. Brima et al.*, Decision on Joint Defence Motion on Disclosure of all Original Witness Statements, Interview Notes and Investigators' Notes Pursuant to Rules 66 and/or 68, May 4, 2005, para. 16). The parties are expected to act *bona fides* at all times in carrying out their disclosure obligations. Given this premise, "any allegation by the Defence as to a violation of disclosure rules by the Prosecution should be substantiated by *prima facie* proof of such a violation" (*Prosecutor v. Brima et al.*, Decision on Joint Defence Motion on Disclosure of all Original Witness Statements, Interview Notes and Investigators' Notes Pursuant to Rules 66 and/or 68, May 4, 2005, para. 16; *Prosecutor v. Sesay*, Decision on Defence Motion for Disclosure Pursuant to Rules 66 and 68 of the Rules, July 9, 2004, para. 27; *Prosecutor v. Norman*, Oral Decision July 16, 2004, p. 2005).

(3) Disclosure hearings

7–185   Rule 66(C) does not require *ex parte* hearings to decide applications for non-disclosure of sensitive material (see *Prosecutor v. Brdjanin et al.*, Decision on Prosecution Application for oral hearing of Rule 66(C) Motion, June 1, 2001 which held that Rule 66(C) refers to the application for non-disclosure being made to "the Trial Chamber sitting *in camera*", and it requires the Prosecution to provide the information which is sought to be kept confidential "only to the Trial Chamber"). The provisions of the rule mean no more than a hearing in the absence of the public, as provided for in Rule 79 ("Closed Sessions"). The distinction drawn in Rule 66(C) between the application (which would normally have to be made on notice to the defence) and the material in question (which must be provided only to the Trial Chamber, and not to the defence) contemplates that such an application need not necessarily be an *ex parte* one.

     See also, *Prosecutor v. Nyiramasuhuko et al.*, Decision on the Prosecutor's ex parte motion pursuant to Rule 66(C) to be relieved of obligation to disclose certain documents, May 31, 2002.

(4) Application of Rule 70 of ICTY, ICTR and SCSL

(a) Rule 70(A): Reports, memoranda and internal documents not subject to disclosure

7–186   The Prosecution is not obliged to disclose documents it has received pursuant to Rule 70(A), and information referred to in Rule 66(C).

     On the basis of Rule 70(A) "any reports, memoranda, or other internal documents prepared by a party, its assistants or representatives in connection with the investigation or preparation of the case, are not subject to disclosure or notification" (see the SCSL case of *Prosecutor v. Brima et al.*, Decision on Joint Defence Motion on Disclosure of all Original Witness Statements, Interview Notes and Investigators' Notes Pursuant to Rules 66 and/or 68, May 4, 2005, para. 16).

     In *Prosecutor v. Blaškić*, Decision on the production of discovery materials, January 27, 1997, para. 40, the Trial Chamber held that "notes of the investigator [. . .] must fall within the scope of Sub-rule 70(A) and not be subject to disclosure or notification". The decision was followed in the ICTR case of *Prosecutor v. Ndayambaje* and the SCSL case of *Prosecutor v. Brima et al.* However, investigator's notes are disclosable to the extent that they refer to statements made by a witness (*Prosecutor v. Norman et al.*, Decision on Disclosure of Witness Statements and Cross-Examination, July 16, 2004, paras 7 and 16; *Prosecutor v. Brima et al*, Decision on Joint Defence Motion on Disclosure of all Original Witness Statements, Interview Notes and Investigators' Notes Pursuant to Rules 66 and/or 68, May 4, 2005, para. 16).

     In *Ndayambaje* the Trial Chamber ruled that the questionnaires of the Prosecutor containing questions asked to prosecution witnesses during their interviews are covered by Rule 70(A) and thus not subject to the disclosure duties set out in the Rules (*Prosecutor v. Ndayambaje*, Decision on Defence Motion for Disclosure, Rule 66, 70(A), and 73 of the Rules, September 25, 2001, paras. 13–16). The Appeals Chamber in *Niyitegeka* overturned this ruling, stating that questionnaires put to witnesses constitute witness statements pursuant to Rule 66(A)(ii) and should be distinguished from internal documents prepared by the party under Rule 70(A) (*Prosecutor v. Niyitegeka*, Appeals Chamber Judgment, July 9, 2004, paras 33–34).

(b) Rule 70(B): evidence disclosed "confidentially" and "solely for the purpose of generating new evidence"

Rule 70(B) embodies safeguards designed to encourage States and **7–187** Organisations to cooperate and disclose sensitive evidence to the Tribunal without having to fear that the Accused and, or the public will be able to review that material. Rule 70(B) "creates an incentive for such cooperation by permitting the sharing of information on a confidential basis and by guaranteeing information providers that the confidentiality of the information they offer and of the information's sources will be protected (*Prosecutor v. Milošević*, Public Version of Confidential Decision on the Interpretation and Application of Rule 70, (Appeals Chamber) October 23, 2002, paras. 18ii and 19). Indeed, the Appeals Chamber noted that Rule 70 provides the basis for cooperation between the Prosecution and governments and other bodies in the possession of sensitive information that may be useful to the investigations conducted by the OTP (*ibid.*, para. 9).

In *Blaškić* it was held that "the exceptions to disclosure in Sub-Rules 70(B) to (E) were introduced into the rules to permit the use, as and when appropriate, of certain information which, in the absence of explicit provisions, would either not have been provided to the Prosecutor or have been unusable on account of its confidential nature or its origin" (*Prosecutor v. Blaškić*, Decision on Trial Chamber I on the Prosecutor's Motion for Video Deposition and Protective Measures, November 13, 1997; as referred to in *Prosecutor v. Milošević*, Public Version of Confidential Decision on the Interpretation and Application of Rule 70 [Appeals Chamber], October 23, 2002, para. 19). These guarantees of confidentiality are necessary for this Tribunal, of which the Prosecution is an integral organ, to be able to fulfil its functions (*Prosecutor v. Brdanin and Tadić*, Public Version of the Confidential Decision on the Alleged Illegality of Rule 70, May 6, 2002, para. 18).

The limitations inherent to Rule 70(B) are not based on the intent of the provider of the information (*Prosecutor v. Milošević*, Public Version of Confidential Decision on the Interpretation and Application of Rule 70 [Appeals Chamber], October 23, 2002, para. 21).

The Trial Chamber in *Milošević* considered that Rule 70(B) applications depended on whether (i) the evidence is the provision of the witness (testimony) rather than information; (ii) the Prosecution could have found the witness anyway, and (iii) the testimony corroborated other evidence already in the possession of the Prosecutor (*Prosecutor v. Milošević*, Decision on Prosecution's Motion to Grant Specific Protection Pursuant to Rule 70, July 25, 2002, para. 10). The Appeals Chamber ruled that none of these factors was relevant in determining whether the information attracted Rule 70(B) protection. The Appeals Chamber held that testimony is capable of being information under Rule 70(B): "when a person possessing important knowledge is made available to the Prosecutor on a confidential basis, not only the informant's identity and the general subject of his knowledge constitute the 'information' shielded by Rule 70, but also the substance of the information shared by the person—often, as in this case, presented in summary form in a witness statement". (*Prosecutor v. Milošević*, Public Version of Confidential Decision on the Interpretation and Application of Rule 70 [Appeals Chamber], October 23, 2002, paras 22–23). Moreover, the Appeals Chamber did not agree with the Trial Chamber's conclusion that the fact that an informant may have been identified by the Prosecutor on their own suggests that the informant's knowledge was not "provided [. .] on a confidential basis" or it was "used solely for the purpose of generating new evidence" (*ibid.*, para. 24).

The Appeals Chamber also held that Trial Chambers possess limited discretion to "police the application of Rule 70 in order to prevent its misapplication" (*ibid.*, para. 26). Trial Chambers are merely allowed to examine whether the information was indeed provided on a confidential basis, applying an objective test. Trial Chambers may be satisfied of the confidential basis by (i) considering the information itself, (ii) accepting the assertion on the Rule 70(B) nature of information by the Prosecutor, (iii) confirmation from the information provider or (iv) any indication from the face of the document itself that it was provided on the confidential basis (*ibid.*, para. 29).

(c) ICTY Rule 70(F): applications by the Defence

7–188 Rule 70(F) in the ICTY Rules of Procedure and Evidence finds no equivalent in the Rules of the ICTR or Special Court for Sierra Leone. Pursuant to Rule 70(F) of the ICTY Rules of Procedure and Evidence, the Defence may make an application for Rule 70 protection to be afforded to specific information in the possession of the Accused. This may be granted by the Trial Chamber if in the "interests of justice". In *Oric*, the Trial Chamber rejected a Defence application under Rule 70(F) holding that the request was premature as the information it sought to protect under the rule, was information which was not yet in the possession of the Defence. However, it was not in the possession of the Defence because the provider of the information was only willing to disclose the information if guaranteed confidentiality. The Appeals Chamber overruled the reasoning of the Trial Chamber. The Appeals Chamber held that as the Prosecutor is able to guarantee a provider of information confidentiality by dint of Rule 70(B), Rule 70(F) was clearly intended to put the Defence in a similar position. This was clear from the explicit wording of Rule 70(F) which was to apply "*mutatis mutandis* to specific information in the possession of the accused".

Moreover, the Appeals Chamber held that "[t]he purpose of Rule 70(F) is to encourage third parties to provide confidential information to the Defence in the same way as Rule 70(B) encourages parties to do the same for the Prosecution, regardless of any further disclosure of that confidential information. [. . .] Read within the context of the Rule therefore, and with its purpose in mind, the reference of Rule 70(F) to 'specific information in the possession of the Accused' is not a condition of the making of an order that the rule applies; it is a reference to what the rule will apply to after the making of an order that it is to apply. The circumstance that the Accused is not now in possession of such information is therefore pertinent" (*Prosecutor v. Oric*, Public Redacted Version of "Decision on Interlocutory Appeal Concerning Rule 70" issued on March 24, 2004, March 26, 2004, paras 6–7).

(d) ICTY Rule 70(G); ICTR/SCSL Rule 70(F)

Rule 70(G) of the ICTY Rules of Procedure are identical to Rule 70(F) of the ICTR and SCSL Rules of Procedure and Evidence. This Rule grants power to Trial Chambers "under Rule 89(D) to exclude evidence if its probative value is substantially outweighed by the need to ensure a fair trial". ICTR Rule 70(F) refers to Rule 89(C) and SCSL Rule 70(F) refers to Rule 95 because neither system has incorporated a provision similar to Rule 89(D). As the Appeals Chamber held, "[d]esigned to ensure that the restrictions in paragraphs (C) and (D) do not undermine the bedrock requirement of fair trial when the Rule is properly invoked, paragraph (G) also gives Trial Chambers a tool to protect that requirement if the Rule has been misused" (*Prosecutor v. Milošević*, Public Version of Confidential Decision on the Interpretation and Application of Rule 70 [Appeals Chamber], October 23, 2002, para. 26).

7–189

B. EXCULPATORY EVIDENCE

(1) Statutory provisions and rules

ICC

ICC Statute, Arts 54(1)(a), 67(2)

Duties and powers of the Prosecutor with respect to investigations
54.—1. The Prosecutor shall:
  (a) In order to establish the truth, extend the investigation to cover all facts and evidence relevant to an assessment of whether there is criminal responsibility under this Statute, and, in doing so, investigate incriminating and exonerating circumstances equally;

7–190

Rights of the accused
67.—2. In addition to any other disclosure provided for in this Statute, the Prosecutor shall, as soon as practicable, disclose to the defence evidence in the Prosecutor's possession or control which he or she believes shows or tends to show the innocence of the accused, or to mitigate the guilt of the accused, or which may affect the credibility of prosecution evidence. In case of doubt as to the application of this paragraph, the Court shall decide.

7–191

ICC Rules of Procedure and Evidence, r. 83

Ruling on exculpatory evidence under article 67, paragraph 2

7–192   **83.** The Prosecutor may request as soon as practicable a hearing on an ex parte basis before the Chamber dealing with the matter for the purpose of obtaining a ruling under article 67, paragraph 2.

ICTY

ICTY Rules of Procedure and Evidence, r. 68

Disclosure of Exculpatory and Other Relevant Material

7–193   **68.** Subject to the provisions of Rule 70.

   (i) the Prosecutor shall, as soon as practicable, disclose to the Defence any material which in the actual knowledge of the Prosecutor may suggest the innocence or mitigate the guilt of the accused or affect the credibility of Prosecution evidence;

   (ii) without prejudice to paragraph (i), the Prosecutor shall make available to the defence, in electronic form, collections of relevant material held by the Prosecutor, together with appropriate computer software with which the defence can search such collections electronically;

   (iii) the Prosecutor shall take reasonable steps, if confidential information is provided to the Prosecutor by a person or entity under Rule 70 (B) and contains material referred to in paragraph (i) above, to obtain the consent of the provider to disclosure of that material, or the fact of its existence, to the accused;

   (iv) the Prosecutor shall apply to the Chamber sitting in camera to be relieved from an obligation under paragraph (i) to disclose information in the possession of the Prosecutor, if its disclosure may prejudice further or ongoing investigations, or for any other reason may be contrary to the public interest or affect the security interests of any State, and when making such application, the Prosecutor shall provide the Trial Chamber (but only the Trial Chamber) with the information that is sought to be kept confidential;

   (v) notwithstanding the completion of the trial and any subsequent appeal, the Prosecutor shall disclose to the other party any material referred to in paragraph (i) above.

ICTR

ICTR Rules of Procedure and Evidence, r. 68

Disclosure of Exculpatory and Other Relevant Material

7–194   **68.**—(A) The Prosecutor shall, as soon as practicable, disclose to the Defence any material, which in the actual knowledge of the Prosecutor may suggest the innocence or mitigate the guilt of the accused or affect the credibility of Prosecution evidence.

   (B) Where possible, and with the agreement of the Defence, and without prejudice to paragraph (A), the Prosecutor shall make available to the Defence, in electronic form, collections of relevant material held by the Prosecutor, together with appropriate computer software with which the defence can search such collections electronically.

(C) The Prosecutor shall take reasonable steps, if confidential information is provided to the Prosecutor by a person or entity under Rule 70(B) and contains material referred to in paragraph (A) above, to obtain the consent of the provider to disclosure of that material, or the fact of its existence, to the accused.

(D) The Prosecutor shall apply to the Chamber sitting in camera to be relieved from an obligation under the Rules to disclose information in the possession of the Prosecutor, if its disclosure may prejudice further or ongoing investigations, or for any other reason may be contrary to the public interest or affect the security interests of any State, and when making such application, the Prosecutor shall provide the Trial Chamber (but only the Trial Chamber) with the information that is sought to be kept confidential.

(E) Notwithstanding the completion of the trial and any subsequent appeal, the Prosecutor shall disclose to the other party any material referred to in paragraph (A) above.

SCSL

SCSL Rules of Procedure and Evidence, r. 68

Disclosure of Exculpatory Evidence

7–195

68.—(A) The Prosecutor shall, within 14 days of receipt of the Defence Case Statement, make a statement under this Rule disclosing to the defence the existence of evidence known to the Prosecutor which may be relevant to issues raised in the Defence Case Statement.

(B) The Prosecutor shall, within 30 days of the initial appearance of the accused, make a statement under this Rule disclosing to the defence the existence of evidence known to the Prosecutor which in any way tends to suggest the innocence or mitigate the guilt of the accused or may affect the credibility of prosecution evidence. The Prosecutor shall be under a continuing obligation to disclose any such exculpatory material.

(2) Requirements of Rule 68

ICC

7–196

The Prosecutor of the ICC has a duty to search for incriminating and exonerating evidence equally (Art. 54(1)(a)). This is a very real difference in function from investigations conducted by the Prosecutor of the ad hoc Tribunals or other hybrid courts. The responsibility on the Defence to identify with precision those materials that are exculpatory should be somewhat reduced by dint of the positive obligation placed on the Prosecutor to investigate obtain and disclose such information, material or evidence.

ICTY

(a) General principles

7–197

As acknowledged by some Trial Chambers, "Rule 68 performs an important function [. . .] i[t] forms part of the [P]rosecution's duty as ministers of justice assisting in the administration of justice [. . .] The

[P]rosecution's obligation under Rule 68 is not a secondary one [. .] it is as important as the obligation to prosecute" (*Prosecutor v. Kordić and Čerkez*, Decision on Motions to Extend for Filing Appelant's Briefs, May 11, 2001, para. 14; *Prosecutor v. Blaškić*, Decision on Production of Discovery Materials, January 27, 1997, para. 50.1; as referred by *Prosecutor v. Blaškić*, Appeals Chamber Judgment, July 29, 2004, para. 264)

Disclosure of exculpatory material is fundamental to the fairness of proceedings before the Tribunals (*Prosecutor v. Krstic*, Appeals Chamber Judgment, April 19, 2004, para. 180).

The Appeals Chamber in *Blaškić* affirmed that the OTP "has the duty to establish procedures designed to ensure that, particularly in instances where the same witnesses testify in different cases, the evidence provided by such witnesses is re-examined in light of Rule 68 to determine whether any material has to be disclosed" (*Prosecutor v. Blaškić*, Appeals Chamber Judgment, July 29, 2004, para. 302).

(b) Definition: "exculpatory"; "evidence" and "known"

7–198   Exculpatory evidence is "material which is known to the Prosecutor and which is favourable to the accused in the sense that it tends to suggest the innocence or mitigate the guilt of the accused or may affect the credibility of the prosecution evidence" (*Prosecutor v. Delalic et al.*, Decision on the Request of the Accused Pursuant to Rule 68 for Exculpatory Information, June 24, 1997, para. 12; affirmed in *Prosecutor v. Krstic*, Appeals Judgment, April 19, 2004, para. 178).

The expression "evidence" is intended to include any material which may put the accused on notice that material exists which may assist him in his defence, and it is not limited to material which is itself admissible in evidence (see *Prosecutor v. Krnojelac*, Record of Rulings Made in Status Conference, September 14, 1999, p. 2; affirmed in *Prosecutor v. Krstic*, Appeals Judgment, April 19, 2004, para. 178).

The Chamber established the meaning of the term "known". The disclosure obligation under Rule 68 before its amendment related to "the existence of evidence known" to the Prosecutor. By amendment, this phrase has been replaced by "material [. . .] in the actual knowledge of the Prosecutor". The Chamber reasoned that a literal interpretation might suggest that mere knowledge of exculpatory evidence in the hands of a third party would suffice to engage the responsibility of the Prosecutor under this provision. However, to adopt such a meaning, would, in the extreme, allow countless motions to be filed with the sole intention of engaging the Prosecutor into investigations and disclosure of issues which the moving party considered were "known" to the Prosecutor. This would not be in conformity with Article 15 of the Statute. Under that provision, the Prosecutor is responsible for investigations. He shall act independently and not receive instructions from any source.

The Chamber equated "known" to "custody and control" or "possession" with the result that the obligation on the Prosecutor to disclose possible exculpatory evidence would be effective only when the Prosecutor is in actual custody, possession, or control of the evidence (*Prosecutor v. Blaškić*, Decision on the Production of Discovery Materials, January 27, 1997, paras 47 and 50).

(c) Amendments to Rule 68: Requirement of "actual knowledge" and electronic disclosure

Rule 68 of the ICTY Rules of Procedure and Evidence was amended **7–199** on December 12, 2003. The revised Rule 68(i) requires the Prosecution to disclose to the Defence "any material which in the *actual* knowledge of the Prosecutor may suggest the innocence or mitigate the guilt of the accused or affect the credibility of Prosecution evidence". Despite requiring what is apparently the higher level of "actual knowledge", the change in Rule 68(i) has not changed the disclosure obligations of the Prosecution in practice given that the rule change seems to have only given form to the way the Rule was being interpreted by Trial Chambers prior to the Rule change.

Another significant amendment to Rule 68 was the addition of the Prosecution's obligation to make available to the Defence, without prejudice to their principal duty to disclose exculpatory material, as soon as practicable pursuant to Rule 68(i), in electronic form, "collections of relevant material held by the Prosecutor, together with appropriate computer software with which the Defence can search such collections electronically" (68(ii)).

As a result of this amendment, electronic search systems have been made available to the Defence, which enables the Defence to find their own exculpatory materials from the general database of information provided by the Prosecution (but limited to that). The downside for Defence is that, once "relevant" documents have been placed on the Electronic Database System (EDS) the Prosecution has fulfilled their Rule 68 disclosure duty without having to identify, out of the thousands of documents placed on the EDS, which materials are exculpatory (*Prosecutor v. Krstic*, Appeals Chamber Judgment, April 19, 2004, para. 190). Another factor to be considered is that not all evidence in the possession of the Prosecution is placed on the EDS database. Vast quantities of information and evidence are retained by the Prosecution in its own electronic storage and retrieval (SDB) system to which the Defence have no access.

As the Appeals Chamber in *Blaškić* held, the Defence must exercise due diligence in identifying the exculpatory material among reasonably accessible material (*Prosecutor v. Blaškić*, Appeals Chamber's Judgment, July 29, 2004, para. 296).

However, although the Prosecutor has no *prima facie* obligation to identify exculpatory material, "as a matter of practice and in order to secure a fair and expeditious trial, the Prosecution should normally indicate which material it is disclosing under the Rule and it is no answer to say that the Defence are in a better position to identify it" (*Prosecutor v. Krajisnik and Plavsic*, Decision on Motion from Momcilo Krajisnik to Compel Disclosure of Exculpatory Evidence Pursuant to Rule 68, July 19, 2001, p.2).

Moreover, in *Limaj et al.*, the Prosecution was ordered to undertake a search on the disclosure system to ensure that the Defence had received all necessary disclosures and, given the large amount of documents on the EDS system coupled to the various deficiences of that system (not least a retrieval rate of only about 70 per cent), to ensure that the required disclosures were sufficiently and clearly identified to the Defence. (*Prosecutor v. Limaj et al.*, Oral Decision, June 1, 2005, pp. 6814–6818.)

(d) Rule 68 disclosure duty at the post-trial stage

7–200   In *Prosecutor v. Blaškić*, Decision on the Appellant's Motions for the Production of Material, Suspension or Extension of the Briefing Schedule, and Additional Filings, September 26, 2000, the Appeals Chamber identified the duty of the Prosecution to disclose exculpatory evidence at the post-trial stage as of "great importance". The Appeals Chamber concluded that "the duty of the Prosecution to disclose the Defence the existence of such evidence pursuant to Rule 68 continues at least until the date when the Trial Chamber delivers its judgment" (para. 31). Moreover, the application of Rule 68 is not confined to the trial process and continues in proceedings before the Appeals Chamber (para. 32).

The Appeals Chamber held that under Rule 68, "the initial decision as to whether evidence is exculpatory has to be made by the Prosecutor. Without further proof that the Prosecution abused its judgment, the Appeals Chamber is not inclined to intervene in the exercise of its discretion by the Prosecution. It is for the Appellant to seek out the transcript of the testimony of the several witnesses referred to in the Production Motion to show the Appeals Chamber that the evidence is exculpatory" (para. 39). The obligation lies with the Defence to establish to the satisfaction of the Trial Chamber that there are other materials within the scope of Rule 68 in the possession of the Prosecution if the Prosecution asserts it is in compliance with Rule 68 (see *Prosecutor v. Delalic et al.*, Decision on the application of the accused Zejnil Delalic for Disclosure of Evidence, September 26, 1996; and *Prosecutor v. Blaškić*, Decision on the Defence Motion for Sanctions for Prosecution repeated violations of Rule 68, April 29, 1998; *Prosecutor v. Sikirica et al.*, Decision on Kolundzija defence request to compel disclosure of exculpatory evidence, August 31, 2001).

ICTR

(a) Scope of Rule 68 disclosure duty

7–201   The ICTY definition of exculpatory evidence and the application thereof has been influential at the ICTR. As to the requirements of Rule 68, see, for example, *Prosecutor v. Bagilishema*, Decision on the Request of the Defence for an Order for Disclosure by the Prosecutor of the Admissions of Guilt of Witnesses Y, Z and AA, June 8, 2000. The Trial Chamber held that Rule 68 requires two main elements. First, the evidence must be known to the Prosecutor, and, second, it must in some way be exculpatory.

In *Casimir Bizimungu et al.*, the Trial Chamber held that the Defence has to show good cause that there is exculpatory evidence available to the Prosecutor (*Prosecutor v. Casimir Bizimungu et al.*, Decision on Prosper Mugiraneza's Motion to Compel Disclosure of Exculpatory Evidence Pursuant to Rule 68, December 10, 2003, para. 20).

The duty upon the Prosecution to disclose pursuant to Rule 68 does not imply that the "Prosecution should be forced to hunt for materials that it has no knowledge of. It does mean however that where the Defence has specific knowledge of a document covered by the Rule not currently within the possession or control of the Prosecution, and requests that document in specific terms, the Prosecution should attempt to bring such documents within its control or possession where the circumstances suggest that the Prosecution is in a better position than the Defence to do so, and, once this is successfully done, should be disclosed to the Defence; provided it is shown that the Defence had made prior efforts to obtain such document by its own means. This obligation stems from the Prosecution's inherent duty to fully investigate a case before this court, and applies particularly in relation to obtaining previous statements made by Prosecution witnesses before the Rwandan Authorities, where, as a practical reality, the Prosecution enjoys greater leverage than the Defence" (*Prosecutor v. Casimir Bizimungu et al.*, Decision on Motion of Accused Bicamumpaka for Disclosure of Exculpatory Evidence, April 23, 2004, para. 9; *Prosecutor v. Casimir Bizimungu et al.*, Decision on Prosper Mugiraneza's Motion Pursuant to Rule 68 for Exculpatory Evidence, May 25, 2004, para. 9 and Decision on Prosper Mugiraneza's Motion Pursuant to Rule 68 for Exculpatory Evidence Related to Witness GKI, September 14, 2004, para 10).

Thus, "Rule 68(A) does not impose an obligation on the Prosecutor to search for materials which he does not admit having knowledge of nor does it entitle the Defence to embark on a fishing expedition to obtain exculpatory material" (*Prosecutor v. Casimir Bizimungu et al.*, Decision on Prosper Mugiraneza's Motion Pursuant to Rule 68 for Exculpatory Evidence Related to Witness GKI, September 14, 2004, para 10; *rosecutor v. Casimir Bizimungu et al.*, Decision on Bicamumpaka's Motion for Disclosure of Exculpatory Evidence (MDR Files), November 17, 2004, para. 14).

(b) Amendents to Rule 68

On April 24, 2004, ICTR Rule 68 incorporated similar amendments made by the ICTY to Rule 68. The new amendment by the ICTR judges to Rule 68(B) is not as stringent as that to the ICTY Rule 68(ii). Amended Rules 68(B) provides: Where possible, and with the agreement of the Defence, and without prejudice to paragraph (A), the Prosecutor shall make available to the Defence, ... Thus, Rule 68(B) creates no new disclosure obligation per se on the Prosecutor. The wording of Rule 68(B) suggests that such obligation exists only where possible, in agreement with the defence and without prejudice to Rule 68(A). The amendment to Rule 68(B) led the Defence in *Casimir Bizimungu* to file a motion to have access to "specific collections of relevant material held by the Prosecution, together with the appropriate computer software to search such collections" (*Prosecutor v. Casimir Bizimungu et al.*, Decision on the Motion of Bicamumpaka and Mugenzi for Disclosure of Relevant Material, December 1, 2004, para. 1). The Chamber rejected the Defence's submission that Rule 68(B) widened the scope of the Prosecutor's disclosure duty in that not only exculpatory, but also relevant material needed to be disclosed. The Trial Chamber stated that "[t]he Trial Chamber is of the view that Rule 68(B) creates no new disclosure obligation on the Prosecution, as suggested by the Defence. The Rule merely permits the Prosecution to use modern technology to discharge its disclosure obligations under Rule 68(A) and any other Rule such as Rule 66. The use of the expression "relevant material" in Rule 68 (B) and the change in the title of the Rule can only refer to material which the Prosecutor is under an obligation to disclose under the Rules. The provision does not give the Defence the right to conduct an unrestricted search of the electronic databases of the Prosecution for material which the Prosecution is under no obligation to disclose under the Rules. Material which the Prosecutor is under no obligation to disclose cannot be "relevant" to the Defence" (*ibid.*, para. 9).

SCSL

7–202 The SCSL Trial Chamber in *Norman et al.*, defined the legal obligation to disclose "as soon as practicable" exculpatory evidence as: "(a) exculpatory evidence that in any way tends to suggest the innocence of the Accused, (b) exculpatory evidence that in any way tends to mitigate the guilt of the Accused, and (c) exculpatory evidence that may effect the credibility of prosecution evidence" (*Prosecutor v. Norman et al.*, Decision on Motion to Compel the Production of Exculpatory Witness Statements, Witness Summaries and Materials Pursuant to Rule 68, July 8, 2004, para. 22).

The Defence has the burden to make a *prima facie* showing of the exculpatory character of the evidence sought from the Prosecution (*ibid.*, para. 24, referring to *Prosecutor v. Delalic et al.*, Decision on the Request of the Accused Hazim Delić Pursuant to Rule 68 for Exculpatory Information, June 24, 1997, para. 13; *Prosecutor v. Blaškić*, Decision on the Production of Discovery Materials, January 27, 1997, para. 50).

Also, the Defence needs to specify what the information is about, what it is requested for and to what extent it is exculpatory (*ibid.*, para. 26). In short, the procedure adopted is broadly identical to those pertaining before the ICTY and ICTR

(3) Remedies pursuant to Rule 68*bis*

7–203 In *Prosecutor v. Krnojelac*, Decision on Motion by Prosecution to modify Order of Compliance with Rule 68, November 1, 1999, it was held that in order to ensure the Prosecutor's compliance with its obligation to disclose exculpatory material to the accused in accordance with Rule 68, it may be appropriate to require a signed report from a representative of the Prosecution team certifying from his personal knowledge that a full search for the existence of Rule 68 material has been conducted of all the materials in the possession of the Prosecution or otherwise within its knowledge. The member of the team who signs the report is to identify in the report his knowledge of that material which enables him to certify. A failure to comply with Rule 68 may lead to a trial being reopened: see *Prosecutor v. Furundžija*, Decision, July 16, 1998. In *Blaškić*, Decision on Defence Motion for Sanctions for the Prosecution Continuing Violation of Rule 68, September 28, 1998, the Chamber took the view that a "sanctions approach" to non-compliance was not appropriate as the issue is whether the defence has been prejudiced and what remedy is required.

On December 13, 2001, Rule 68*bis* was adopted by the ICTY enabling the Pre-Trial Judge and, or Trial Chamber to impose sanctions on a party failing to abide by its disclosure obligations. Neither the ICTR nor the SCSL have introduced a similar rule. This does not preclude them from exercising their inherent powers to impose sanctions where the party seeking sanctions against the other party has demonstrated that it suffered prejudice and where this party acted diligently (*Prosecutor v. Casimir Bizimungu et al.*, Decision on Prosper Mugiraneza's Motion for Appropriate Relief for Violation of Rule 66, February 4, 2005, para. 10)

Rule 68*bis* provides the Trial Chambers "with the broad discretionary power to impose sanctions to on a defaulting party, *proprio motu* if necessary" (*Prosecutor v. Krstic*, Appeal Judgment, para. 212).

The ground rule is that "possible violations of Rule 68 are governed less by a system of sanctions than by the judge's definitive evaluation of the evidence presented by either of the parties and the possibility which the opposing party will have had to contest it" (*Prosecutor v. Blaškić*; Decision on Defence Motion for Sanctions for the Prosecutor's Continuing Violation of Rule 68, September 28, 1998, p.3)

The Chamber has affirmed that it will impose sanctions on the Prosecution where it finds that (1) the Prosecution is in breach of their Rule 68 obligation to disclose and (2) the Defence case has been prejudiced by the non-compliance (*Prosecutor v. Krstic*, Appeals Chamber Judgment, April 19, 2004, para. 153).

In *Prosecutor v. Krstic* the Appeals Chamber found that the Prosecution had breached its disclosure obligations to the Defence, and concluded that "the implementation of a systematic disclosure methodology [. . .] must be revised so as to ensure future compliance with the obligations incumbent upon the Office of the Prosecutor" (*Prosecutor v. Krstic*, Appeals Chamber Judgment, April 19, 2004, para. 214).

(4) Relationship between Rule 68 and obligation of confidentiality

Rule 70 confidentiality does not preclude the disclosure of material pursuant to Rule 68 disclosure obligations (*Prosecutor v. Brdjanin*, Decision on Motion to Relief from Rule 68 Violations by the Prosecutor and for Sanctions to be Imposed Pursuant to Rule 68*bis* and Motion for Adjournment While Matters Affecting Justice and a Fair Trial Can be Resolved, October 30, 2002, para. 29).

7–204

With respect to the open session testimony of Blaškić, the Appeals Chamber noted that such testimony given in other trials is generally encompassed by the Prosecution's disclosure obligation pursuant to Rule 68 of the Rules. Consequently, the Prosecution explained that it "did conduct its normal searches through the open and closed session material in related cases"(Prosecution's Reply to Defence "Response to Prosecution's Notice of Completion of Pending Rule 68 Reviews and Disclosure", March 14, 2003, paras 13–14, Prosecution Response, para. 14.). However, the Appeals Chamber recalled that "the Prosecution may still be relieved of the obligations under Rule 68, if the existence of the relevant exculpatory evidence is known and the evidence is accessible to the appellant, as the appellant would not be prejudiced materially by this violation" (*Prosecutor v. Blaškić*, Decision on the Appellant's Motions for the Production of Material, Suspension or Extension of the Briefing Schedule, and Additional Filings, September 26, 2000, para. 38.). (Also see *Prosecutor v. Kordic*, Decision on Appellant's Notice and Supplement Notice of Prosecution's Non-Compliance with its Disclosure Obligation under Rule 68 of the Rules, February 11, 2004, para. 20.)

East Timor

7–205   See Section 24.4(c) of Regulation 2000/30 (cited above).

C. RECIPROCAL DISCLOSURE

(1) Statutory provisions and rules

ICC

ICC Rules of Procedure and Evidence, rr. 78, 79, 80

Inspection of material in possession or control of the defence

7–206   **78.** The defence shall permit the Prosecutor to inspect any books, documents, photographs and other tangible objects in the possession or control of the defence, which are intended for use by the defence as evidence for the purposes of the confirmation hearing or at trial.

Disclosure by the defence

7–207   **79.**—1. The defence shall notify the Prosecutor of its intent to:
     (a) Raise the existence of an alibi, in which case the notification shall specify the place or places at which the accused claims to have been present at the time of the alleged crime and the names of witnesses and any other evidence upon which the accused intends to rely to establish the alibi; or
     (b) Raise a ground for excluding criminal responsibility provided for in article 31, paragraph 1, in which case the notification shall specify the names of witnesses and any other evidence upon which the accused intends to rely to establish the ground.
     2. With due regard to time limits set forth in other rules, notification under sub-rule 1 shall be given sufficiently in advance to enable the Prosecutor to

prepare adequately and to respond. The Chamber dealing with the matter may grant the Prosecutor an adjournment to address the issue raised by the defence.

3. Failure of the defence to provide notice under this rule shall not limit its right to raise matters dealt with in sub-rule 1 and to present evidence.

4. This rule does not prevent a Chamber from ordering disclosure of any other evidence.

Procedures for raising a ground for excluding criminal responsibility under article 31, paragraph 3

80.—1. The defence shall give notice to both the Trial Chamber and the **7–208** Prosecutor if it intends to raise a ground for excluding criminal responsibility under article 31, paragraph 3. This shall be done sufficiently in advance of the commencement of the trial to enable the Prosecutor to prepare adequately for trial.

2. Following notice given under sub-rule 1, the Trial Chamber shall hear both the Prosecutor and the defence before deciding whether the defence can raise a ground for excluding criminal responsibility.

3. If the defence is permitted to raise the ground, the Trial Chamber may grant the Prosecutor an adjournment to address that ground.

ICTY

ICTY Rules of Procedure and Evidence, r. 67

Additional Disclosure

67—(A) Within the time-limit prescribed by the Trial Chamber or by the **7–209** pre-trial Judge appointed pursuant to Rule 65*ter*:

  (i) the defence shall notify the Prosecutor of its intent to offer:

   (a) the defence of alibi; in which case the notification shall specify the place or places at which the accused claims to have been present at the time of the alleged crime and the names and addresses of witnesses and any other evidence upon which the accused intends to rely to establish the alibi;

   (b) any special defence, including that of diminished or lack of mental responsibility; in which case the notification shall specify the names and addresses of witnesses and any other evidence upon which the accused intends to rely to establish the special defence; and

  (ii) the Prosecutor shall notify the defence of the names of the witnesses that the Prosecutor intends to call in rebuttal of any defence plea of which the Prosecutor has received notice in accordance with paragraph (i) above.

(B) Failure of the defence to provide notice under this Rule shall not limit the right of the accused to testify on the above defences.

(C) If either party discovers additional evidence or material which should have been disclosed earlier pursuant to the Rules, that party shall immediately disclose that evidence or material to the other party and the Trial Chamber.

ICTR

ICTR Rules of Procedure and Evidence, r. 67

Reciprocal Disclosure of Evidence

67. Subject to the provisions of Rules 53 and 69:   **7–210**

(A) As early as reasonably practicable and in any event prior to the commencement of the trial:
  (i) The Prosecutor shall notify the defence of the names of the witnesses that he intends to call to establish the guilt of the accused and in rebuttal of any defence plea of which the Prosecutor has received notice in accordance with Sub-Rule (ii) below;
  (ii) The defence shall notify the Prosecutor of its intent to enter:
    (a) The defence of alibi; in which case the notification shall specify the place or places at which the accused claims to have been present at the time of the alleged crime and the names and addresses of witnesses and any other evidence upon which the accused intends to rely to establish the alibi;
    (b) Any special defence, including that of diminished or lack of mental responsibility; in which case the notification shall specify the names and addresses of witnesses and any other evidence upon which the accused intends to rely to establish the special defence.
(B) Failure of the defence to provide such notice under this Rule shall not limit the right of the accused to rely on the above defences.
(C) If the defence makes a request pursuant to Rule 66(B), the Prosecutor shall in turn be entitled to inspect any books, documents, photographs and tangible objects, which are within the custody or control of the defence and which it intends to use as evidence at the trial.
(D) If either party discovers additional evidence or information or materials which should have been produced earlier pursuant to the Rules, that party shall promptly notify the other party and the Trial Chamber of the existence of the additional evidence or information or materials.

East Timor

Receipt and Notification of the Indictment

7–211   26.—26.1 Upon receipt of the indictment by the Court, the case file shall be registered by the Registry of the Court. In accordance with Section 17.1 and 35 of UNTAET Regulation No. 2000/11, the case file shall be forwarded by the Registry to the Panel of Judges or to an individual judge, according to UNTAET regulations and the plan of distribution of incoming cases.

26.2 The Registrar shall ensure that a notification is promptly served upon the accused and his or her legal representative. The notification shall include a copy of the indictment and the date upon which it was received by the Court, and shall inform the accused and legal representative that the defence has the right to submit a response to the indictment within forty five days of receipt of the indictment by the Court.

26.3 The response, if any, shall be filed at the Court and may include legal and factual observations of the accused with respect to the indictment, any preliminary motions the accused wishes to raise and a list of the evidence and witnesses to be presented by the defence during the trial.

SCSL

SCSL Rules of Procedure and Evidence, r. 67

Reciprocal Disclosure of Evidence

7–212   67. Subject to the provisions of Rules 53 and 69:

(A) As early as reasonably practicable and in any event prior to the commencement of the trial:

    (i) The Prosecutor shall notify the defence of the names of the witnesses that he intends to call to establish the guilt of the accused and in rebuttal of any defence plea of which the Prosecutor has received notice in accordance with Sub-Rule (ii) below, or any defence pleaded in the Defence Case Statement served under Sub-Rule (C);

    (ii) The defence shall notify the Prosecutor of its intent to enter:

        (a) The defence of alibi; in which case the notification shall specify the place or places at which the accused claims to have been present at the time of the alleged crime and the names and addresses of witnesses and any other evidence upon which the accused intends to rely to establish the alibi;

        (b) Any special defence, including that of diminished or lack of mental responsibility; in which case the notification shall specify the names and addresses of witnesses and any other evidence upon which the accused intends to rely to establish the special defence.

(B) Failure of the defence to provide such notice under this Rule shall not limit the right of the accused to rely on the above defences.

(C) To assist the Prosecutor with its disclosure obligations pursuant to Rule 68, the defence may prior to trial provide the Prosecutor with a Defence Case Statement. The Defence Case Statement shall:

    (i) set out in general terms the nature of the accused's defence;

    (ii) indicate the matters on which he takes issue with the prosecution; and

    (iii) set out, in the case of each such matter, the reason why he takes issue with the prosecution.

(D) If either party discovers additional evidence or information or materials which should have been produced earlier pursuant to the Rules, that party shall promptly notify the other party and the Trial Chamber of the existence of the additional evidence or information or materials.

(2) Alibi notices

In *Prosecutor v. Kvočka et al.*, Decision on the defence of alibi for the accused Zoran Zigic, July 21, 2000, the Trial Chamber permitted the accused to file his alibi notice after the commencement of the trial. The Chamber based its decision on Rule 127(A) which authorises the Chamber to enlarge time-limits on good cause shown (in this case being that alibi was the accused's only defence, and the trial would not be delayed as the Prosecution indicated it would not suffer any prejudice or require additional time to respond to the defence).

7–213

Also see *Prosecutor v. Delalic et al.*, Order disposing of Motions filed by the Defence, January 27, 1997, para. 3.

The accused may still raise the defence of alibi in his testimony if he does not file an alibi notice. The evidence of his alibi witnesses are however liable to be excluded (see *Prosecutor v. Kupreškić et al.*, Decision, January 11, 1999).

(3) Amendment of Reciprocal Disclosure

In amendments effected on December 12, 2003, ICTY Rule 67, formerly entitled "Reciprocal Disclosure", was renamed "Additional Disclosure" and provision 67(C) was deleted in its entirety. Under the

7–214

old Rule 67(C), reciprocal disclosure was triggered by the Defence in the event they made a request pursuant to Rule 66(B) to inspect any books, documents, photographs or tangible objects within the Prosecution's control which are material to the preparation of the defence case and which are intended to be used by the Prosecution as evidence at trial. With the deletion of Rule 67(C), the Defence is now no longer obligated to make a reciprocal disclosure of such materials to the Prosecution. No similar amendment has been made to the ICTR RPE so the Rule 67(C) duty to reciprocally disclose remains unchanged at the ICTR.

At the SCSL the Rule is entitled "Reciprocal Disclosure", but does not include the principle similar to that under Rule 67(C) ICTR Rules. The ICC Rules, on the other hand, broaden Defence's disclosure duties even further. Rule 78 namely dictates that the Defence " shall permit the Prosecutor to inspect any books, documents, photographs and other tangible objects in the possession or control of the Defence, which are intended for use by the Defence as evidence for the purposes of the confirmation hearing or at Trial" (Rule 78). This Rule appears to suggest that even in absence of a Defence's request for inspection of the Prosecution's materials such as books, documents, photographs and other tangible objects, the Prosecutor has the right to inspect such materials in the possession of the Defence.

SCSL Rule 67(C) does not exist in any of the other systems. Pursuant to Rule 67(C) SCSL Rules, the Defence may provide the Prosecution with a Defence Case Statement prior to Trial, indicating in general terms the Accused's defence and the issues he takes with the Prosecution and why. This sub-rule aims to facilitate the disclosure of the exculpatory material by the Prosecution. Although the Defence is under no obligation to provide such Defence Case Statement, in doing so, the Defence triggers an additional disclosure duty upon the Prosecution to "make a statement under this Rule disclosing to the Defence the existence of evidence known to the Prosecutor which may be relevant to issues raised in the Defence Case Statement" (Rule 68(A)).

(4) Timely Disclosure

Rule 67(C) ICTY Rules and Rule 67(D) ICTR/SCSL Rules

7–215   Rule 67(C) of the ICTY Rules and Rules 67(D) of those in the ICTR and SCSL oblige either party to promptly notify the other and the Trial Chamber of the existence of additional materials discovered by them that should have been disclosed earlier under the rules. The prompt notification of such additional materials does not mean that the Trial Chamber will allow the use of the documents in trial, even if the requirements of Rule 89(C) are met. However, failing to abide by Rule 67(C) of the ICTY Rules (Rule 67(D) of the ICTR / SCSL RPE) may well result in the Trial Chamber refusing to accept the relevant document into evidence.

Rule 67(C) of the ICTY and Rule 67(D) of the ICTR and SCSL Rules of Procedure and Evidence refer to "additional evidence or materials", which indicates that the rule does not provide a disclosure basis for evidence or material separate to those detailed in Rules 67(A) and 67(B) of the respective Rules of Procedure and Evidence. There is a difference, however, in the terms of Rule 67(C) of the ICTY Rules which requires the party discovering the additional material falling for disclosure to "immediately disclose" that material to the other party. Rule 67(D) of the ICTY and SCSL Rules of Procedure, however, only requires such a party to "promptly notify" the other party of the "existence" of such evidence. It seems that the ICTY Rule places a duty to act with greater speed and greater openness than the corresponding Rule 67(D) of the ICTR and SCSL Rules of Procedure and Evidence. This is because the wording of Rule 67(C) of the ICTY Rules of Procedure and Evidence is clearly intended, as far as possible, to place the party who has suffered the non-disclosure in the same position that party would have been in had the disclosure been made "in time". No additional order is required. Once the material is identified it is to be disclosed. A literal construction of the ICTR / SCSL rule would allow the party who had failed to disclose that which should have been disclosed under the Rules, the ability to further delay matters by simply "notify[ing]" the party as to the "existence" of the information, thereby perhaps requiring motions, argument or court orders to actually obtain the evidence or material.

The Special Court of Sierra Leone has affirmed the principle that where evidence is disclosed so late "as to prejudice the fairness of the Trial, the Trial Chamber will apply appropriate remedies, which may include the exclusion of such evidence" (*Prosecutor v. Brima et al.*, Decision on Joint Defence Motion on Disclosure of all Original Witness Statements, Interview Notes and Investigators' Notes Pursuant to Rules 66 and/or 68, May 4, 2005, para. 16; *Prosecutor v. Sesay*, Ruling on Oral Application for the Exclusion of Statements of Witness TFL-141 Dated Respectively October 9, 2004, October 19, 2004 and October 20, 2004, and January 10, 2005, February 3, 2005, para. 20(F); *Prosecutor v. Brima*, Kanu Decision on Motions for Exclusion of Prosecution Witness Statements and Stay on Filling Prosecution Statements, July 30, 2004, para. 20; *Prosecutor v. Sesay et al.*, Ruling on the Oral of the Exclusion of Part of the Testimony of Witness TF1-199, July 26, 2004, para. 7; *Prosecutor v. Sesay et al.*, Ruling on Oral Application for the Exclusion of "Additional Witness Statements" for Witness TF1-060, July 23, 2004, para. 10; *Prosecutor v. Brima et al.*, Brima Decision on Motion for Exclusion of Prosecution Witness Statements and Stay of Filling of Prosecution Statements, August 2, 2004, para. 20; *Prosecutor v. Norman et al.*, Oral Decision on July 16, 2004, p. 5).

Late disclosure by the prosecution in the defence case.

If the Prosecution intends to present a document during the defence case, which is not in evidence, they must disclose it to the Defence, and inform them of their intention to use the document in question at least 24 hours before a Defence witness appears, "unless the Defence has provided the Prosecution with the information they need to prepare their cross-examination a little too late" (*Prosecutor v. Hadžihasanović*, Oral Decision of November 29, 2004, p. 12527).

7–216

Although the Trial Chamber in *Rutaganda* did not give such a specific disclosure deadline, it allowed the Accused one day extra to familiarise himself with the newly disclosed materials which were intended to be used by the Prosecutor in cross-examination of the Accused. Given that the documents in question had been raised by the Accused during examination-in-chief, the Appeals Chamber found that the Trial Chamber had not erred in exercising its discretion to admit the said documents during cross-examination of the Accused (*Prosecutor v. Rutaganda*, Appeals Chamber Judgment, May 26, 2003, paras 282–284). Likewise, the Trial Chamber in the ICTY case of *Limaj et al* allowed the Accused Limaj an extra day to review a book which had not been previously disclosed and which the Prosecution intended to use in their cross-examination of the Accused (*Prosecutor v. Limaj et al.*, Oral Decision of May 23, 2005, Transcript, p. 6116).

Notwithstanding this principle, it was held in *Milošević* that documents which were not disclosed could be used in cross-examination but should only be accepted as exhibits if they contain material that is already in evidence. (*Prosecutor v. Milošević*, Decision on Prosecution Motion for Reconsideration Regarding Evidence of Defence Witnesses Mitar Balevic, Vladislav Jovanovic, Vukasin Andric, and Dobre Aleksovski and Decision *proprio motu* Reconsidering Admission of Exhibits 837 and 838 Regarding Evidence of Defence Witness Barry Lituchy, May 17, 2005, para. 11.)

Also see Chapter 8.

Heavy work-load or administrative difficulties within the OTP

7–217   A heavy workload is no excuse for failure to disclose evidence in a timely and proper manner. (*Prosecutor v. Brdjanin*, Decision on Motion to Relief from Rule 68 Violations by the Prosecutor and for Sanctions to be Imposed Pursuant to Rule 68*bis* and Motion for Adjournment While Matters Affecting Justice and a Fair Trial Can be Resolved, October 30, 2002, para. 29). Neither are internal hindrances within the OTP: In *Ndindiliyimana et al.*, the Trial Chamber refused to excuse "a state of affairs in which the Prosecution Section of the Office of the Prosecutor (OTP) and the Investigation Section of the same office are so disconnected as to permit a seven-month delay purportedly between the taking of a statement and its being brought to the attention of Prosecuting Counsel. The OTP is one office and the Chamber refuses to condone apportionment of blames between or among the different section is of the OTP. There is a collective responsibility for the OTP. Nor does the Chamber accept as excusable the cryptic reference to the departure of two investigators as explaining the failing here. The lapse simple should not have been allowed to occur" (*Prosecutor v. Ndindiliyimana et al.*, Decision on Prosecution Motion to Vary its List of Witnesses: Rule 73*bis*(E) of the Rules, February 11, 2005, para. 24). Also see paragraph 8–49 (Evidence for the Prosecution) After the Prosecution made a series of late disclosures in *Halilovic* the Trial Chamber ordered the Prosecution to file leave with the pre-trial Judge in the event of any additional disclosure after the set completion date with a detailed explanation of why that material was not previously disclosed, or else the Prosecution would be precluded from making the late disclosure (*Prosecutor v. Halilovic*, Decision on Defence Objection to Prosecution Continued Disclosure, May 7, 2004, page 2).

Proofing of witnesses

At the ICTY and especially at the ICTR, various Defence teams have   **7–218**
raised concerns about the lengthy proofing sessions conducted by the
Prosecution with their witnesses which often result in new evidence
being obtained for the first time during the trial process, and often only
a day or so before the witness is due to testify. Such new evidence is
then sometimes disclosed in the form of an unsigned "supplementary
information sheet" (ICTY) or a "will-say statement" (ICTR).

ICTY

In *Limaj et al.*, the Trial Chamber denied the Defence request that
proofing sessions conducted by the Prosecution during the trial phase of
proceedings be video-taped or otherwise transcribed and disclosed to
the Defence. The Trial Chamber also denied the Defence request that
the Prosecution be ordered to disclose signed supplementary statements from such witnesses, as opposed to unsigned supplementary
information sheets. The Trial Chamber found that "[l]ate notice is an
issue which may require measures to overcome resulting difficulties to
the Defence. That will depend on the circumstances. Any examples
raised will be considered on its merits. Except perhaps where the
subject of a notice of a new item of evidence, or a change of evidence is
extensive, there is not any sufficient reason to require a signed
statement" (*Prosecutor v. Limaj et al.*, Decision on Defence Motion on
Prosecution Practice of "Proofing" Witnesses, December 10, 2004, p. 3).
In a subsequent decision, the same Trial Chamber stated the following:
"[w]hile it would be preferable if this could be achieved at an earlier
time, there are practical considerations that often lead to this occurring
when the witness arrives in The Hague shortly before giving evidence.
Should a supplementary information sheet present a particular difficulty for the Defence, this can often be met by the deferral of the
evidence of the witness, or of cross-examination, to allow time to the
Defence to deal with the difficulty. In this case it appears that some of
the supplementary sheets listed in the schedule were not even delivered
to the Defence before the commencement of the witness's evidence, due
to the failure of the Prosecution to deal promptly with the production of
a supplementary information sheet and to serve it. This clearly
increases the risk that the evidence or cross-examination of the witness
will need to be delayed. There can also be cases where a matter
disclosed for the first time in a supplementary information sheet is of
very considerable significance such that some more drastic disruption to
the trial may be required in the interests of justice. That is not a
feature of this present case" (*Prosecutor v. Limaj et al.*, Decision on Joint
Defence Motion on Prosecution's Late and Incomplete Disclosure, June
7, 2005, para. 26). Disputes may arise as to whether the information is
indeed new. It is often a matter of interpretation of paragraphs in the
indictment. If such dispute arises between the parties, the Trial
Chamber has to consider whether the information is alluded to in the
indictment with sufficient specificity.

ICTR

In *Bagosora et al.*, the Trial Chamber held that anticipated testimony
of a Prosecution witness which was disclosed to the Defence through

the unsigned "will-say" statement at the most a few days prior to the witness's appearance in court is admissible where the Defence is provided with sufficient time to prepare adequate cross-examination (*Prosecutor v. Bagosora et al.*, Decision on Admissibility of Evidence of Witness DBQ, November 18, 2003).

In order to determine the admissibility of "will-say" statements, the Trial Chamber has to consider three distinct matters: 1) the relevance of the evidence to the charges in the indictment, which would be undermined if the evidence constitutes entirely new charges; 2) whether the will-say statement provides any additional details to the witness's original statement or other material disclosed to the Defence, 3) assuming that the information indeed constitutes new evidence, whether the new evidence should be admitted and under what conditions (*Prosecutor v. Bagosora et al.*, Decision on Admissibility of Evidence of Witness DBQ, November 18, 2003, para. 14).

In order to determine whether evidence is new the Trial Chamber may consider the witness's own prior statement, any indication in the indictment or pre-trial brief of the events in question in combination with the length of time that the Defence has been put on notice that a particular witness will testify to that event, and the level of change the evidence brings in comparison with the charges as known to the Defence (*Prosecutor v. Bagosora et al.*, Decision on Admissibility of Evidence of Witness DP, November 18, 2003, para.6).

The amount of additional time needed for the Defence to prepare the cross-examination in relation to the new evidence depends on whether it is necessary for the Defence to conduct investigations. In some cases a two-day notice period may be sufficient (*Prosecutor v. Bagosora et al.*, Decision on Admissibility of Evidence of Witness DP, November 18, 2003, para.8).

Where the Defence is tardy in making proper use of the extra time given, the Trial Chamber will not give any additional time if the investigations have not actually been carried out. In such situation the Defence would fail to meet the onus of demonstrating that further postponement of the evidence of the witness in question is necessary to comply with the fair trial principles, particularly to "have adequate time and facilities for the preparation of his or her defence" as set out in article 20(b) of the ICTR Statute (*Prosecution v. Bagosora et al*, Written Reasons for Oral Decision of February 18, 2004 on Motions for Further Postponements of Testimony of Witness DBQ, March 1, 2004, paras 8–10).

The Trial Chamber in *Bagosora et al.* expressed its concern on numerous occasions that "there is no systematic practice of interviewing witnesses well in advance of their testimony, particularly where it may be evident from the date of their witness statements or other factors that new evidence is likely to be forthcoming" (*Prosecutor v. Bagosora et al.*, Decision on Admissibility of Evidence of Witness DP, November 18, 2003, para.9).

In *Nahimana et al.*, the Chamber ruled that entirely new evidence, disclosed two days prior to testimony, would be disregarded because the Defence was taken by surprise and was therefore prejudiced. The new material did not supplement details that already appeared and could therefore not be disclosed pursuant to Rule 67(D), despite the fact that the Trial Chamber accepted that evidence was new to the Prosecution as well. The procedure suggested was to take a fresh, signed witness statement (Oral Ruling of March 1, 2001, pp. 9564–9562).

In *Casimir Bizimungu*, new evidence, which was not disclosed in any "will-say" statement was excluded because of its prejudicial effect (Oral Decision of December 3, 2003). Decisions on this matter will be taken on a case-by-case basis.

TRIAL PROCEDURE

I. CASE PRESENTATION

A. JOINT AND SEPARATE TRIALS

(1) Statutory provisions and rules

ICC Rules of Procedure and Evidence, r. 136

Joint and separate trials

136.—1. Persons accused jointly shall be tried together unless the Trial **8–1** Chamber, on its own motion or at the request of the Prosecutor or the defence, orders that separate trials are necessary, in order to avoid serious prejudice to the accused, to protect the interests of justice or because a person jointly accused has made an admission of guilt and can be proceeded against in accordance with article 65, paragraph 2.

2. In joint trials, each accused shall be accorded the same rights as if such accused were being tried separately.

ICTY/ICTR

ICTY and ICTR Rules of Procedure and Evidence

Joinder of Accused

8–2   **48.** Persons accused of the same or different crimes committed in the course of the same transaction may be jointly charged and tried.

Joinder of Trials (only a rule before ICTR, not ICTY)

8–3   **48*bis*.** Persons who are separately indicted, accused of the same or different crimes committed in the course of the same transaction, may be tried together, with leave granted by a Trial Chamber pursuant to Rule 73.

Joinder of Crimes

8–4   **49.** Two or more crimes may be joined in one indictment if the series of acts committed together form the same transaction, and the said crimes were committed by the same accused.

Joint and Separate Trials

8–5   **82.**—(A) In joint trials, each accused shall be accorded the same rights as if such accused were being tried separately.

(B) The Trial Chamber may order that persons accused jointly under Rule 48 be tried separately if it considers it necessary in order to avoid a conflict of interests that might cause serious prejudice to an accused, or to protect the interests of justice.

East Timor

8–6   There is no provision on joint and separate trials in the Rules of Procedure for the Special Courts for East Timor.

Sierra Leone

SCSL Rules of Procedure, rr. 48, 49, 82

Joinder of Accused or Trials

8–7   **48.**—(A) Persons accused of the same or different crimes committed in the course of the same transaction may be jointly indicted and tried.

(B) Persons who are separately indicted, accused of the same or different crimes committed in the course of the same transaction, may be tried together, with leave granted by a Trial Chamber pursuant to Rule 73.

(C) A Trial Chamber may order the concurrent hearing of evidence common to the trials of persons separately indicted or joined in separate trials and who are accused of the same or different crimes committed in the course of the same transaction. Such a hearing may be granted with leave of a Trial Chamber pursuant to Rule 73.

Joinder of Crimes

49.— Two or more crimes may be joined in one indictment if the series of acts committed together form the same transaction, and the said crimes were committed by the same accused.   **8–8**

Joint and Separate Trials

82.—(A) In joint trials, each accused shall be accorded the same rights as if he were being tried separately.   **8–9**

(B) The Trial Chamber may order that persons accused jointly under Rule 48 be tried separately if it considers it necessary in order to avoid a conflict of interests that might cause serious prejudice to an accused, or to protect the interests of justice.

(2) Legal criteria for joinder of accused

The decision to grant the joinder of accused lies within the discretion   **8–10**
of the Trial Chamber weighing the overall interests of justice and the rights of the accused. *Prosecutor v. Milošević*, Reasons for Decision on Prosecution Interlocutory Appeal from Refusal to Order Joinder, April 18, 2002, paras 3–6 and 22–32). The SCSL Trial Chamber in *Brima et al.* explained the discretion pursuant to Rule 48 in the following terms:

"it is trite law that where a discretion is vested in an authority or a body, such discretion is to be exercised reasonably and judiciously, and, we should add, in the case of an application of such dimension and complexity, 'with great circumspection' due to the extraordinary nature of the procedure which is the subject-matter of the application whilst at the same time keeping an open judicial mind to the issue [. . .] Furthermore, it is the Chamber's view that the primary focus of the exercise of a discretion under Rule 48(C) should be on how the extraordinary procedure applied for would impact upon the rights of the Accused in question, and not how it would or would not enhance the Prosecution's capability in presenting its case in an efficient manner. It is important for the Court to preserve such a focus especially where it has ordered separate joint trials for each category of accused persons. Unless the Court is satisfied that the Prosecution has established that the exceptional procedure sought would not impact adversely, or be prejudicial to, the right of the accused to be tried fairly and expeditiously, and that the integrity of the proceedings would not be compromised, the presumption should be against granting the Order" (*Prosecutor v. Brima et al.*, Decision on the Prosecution Motion for Concurrent Hearing of Evidence Common to Cases SCSL–2004–15–PT and SCSL–2004–16–PT, May 11, 2004, paras 30–31).

In essence, "if the allegations contained in the indictment support the existence of a common transaction amongst accused, and if no material prejudice arises to the accused as a result of joinder, joinder may be granted", even if the accused were not charged together

(*Prosecutor v. Bagosora et al.*, Decision on the Prosecutor's motion for joinder, ICTR Trial Chamber, June 29, 2000, para. 108; also see, *Prosecutor v. Ntagerura et al.*, Decision on the Prosecutor's Motion for Joinder, October 11, 1999; and, *Prosecutor v. Nyiramasuhuko et al.*, Decision on the Prosecutor's Motion for Joinder of Trials, October 5, 1999; *Prosecutor v. Brima et al.*, Decision on the Prosecution Motion for Concurrent Hearing of Evidence Common to Cases SCSL-2004–15-PT and SCSL-2004–16-PT, May 11, 2004, para. 29).

Involvement in the same transaction must be shown by connections "to specific material elements which demonstrate on the one hand the existence of an offence, of a criminal act which is objectively punishable and specifically determined in time and space, and on the other hand prove the existence of a common scheme, strategy or plan, and that the accused therefore acted together and in concert" (*Prosecutor v. Kayishema, Ntakirutimana and Ruzindana*, Decision on the Motion of the Prosecutor to Sever, to Join in a Superseding Indictment, and to Amend the Superseding Indictment, March 27, 1997, p. 3).

The acts or omissions of the accused which are alleged to form the same transaction need not be criminal or illegal in themselves. "However, the acts of the accused should satisfy the following:

(1) Be connected to material elements of a criminal act. For example the acts of the accused may be non-criminal/legal acts in furtherance of future criminal acts;

(2) The criminal acts which the acts of the accused are connected to must be capable of specific determination in time and space, and;

(3) The criminal acts which the acts of the accused are connected to must illustrate the existence of a common scheme, strategy or plan (*The Prosecutor v. Kabiligi and Ntabakuze*, Decision on the Defence Motion Requesting an Order for Separate Trials, September 30, 1998, p. 2).

8–11 The factors that must be taken into consideration when assessing whether the interests of justice will be served by joinder include:

"There are reasons of undoubted public interest why joint offences should be tried jointly. Savings in expense and time are a factor of importance. It is also desirable, and in the interests of transparent justice, that the same verdict and the same treatment should be returned against all the persons jointly tried with respect to the offences committed in the same transaction. It is also to avoid the discrepancies and inconsistencies inevitable from the separate trial of joint offenders. Hence, the principles of administration of criminal justice have always accepted the practice of trying joint offenders irrespective of the attendant inevitable minimum prejudices" (*Prosecutor v. Delalic et al.*, Decision on the Motion by Defendant Delalic Requesting Procedures for Final Determination of the Charges Against Him, July 1, 1998, para. 35).

In addition to these considerations, joinder may allow for a more consistent and detailed presentation of the evidence; for better protection of the victim's and witnesses' physical and mental safety by eliminating the need for them to make several journeys and to repeat their testimony; and joinder may reduce the risks of contradictions in the decision rendered when related and indivisible facts are examined. (See *Prosecutor v. Kayishema*, Decision on the Joinder of the Accused and Setting the Date for Trial, November 6, 1996, p. 3.)

These considerations must be balanced against the rights of the accused to a trial without undue delay and any other prejudice to the accused that may be caused by joinder (see, *Prosecutor v. Bagosora et al.*, Decision on the Prosecutor's motion for joinder, ICTR Trial Chamber, June 29, 2000, paras 145–156).

For the purposes of joinder, the Trial Chamber shall act on the Prosecutor's factual allegations contained in the indictment, in the absence of evidence to the contrary. A joinder application is not to be treated as a trial. (See, *Prosecutor v. Bagosora et al.*, Decision on the Prosecutor's motion for joinder, ICTR Trial Chamber, June 29, 2000, paras 119–122).

(3) Definition of same transaction

The Appeals Chamber in the *Prosecutor v. Milošević*, Decision on   **8–12**
Prosecution interlocutory appeal from refusal to order joinder, February 1, 2002, held that the interpretation of the expression "the same transaction" in Rule 49 is a question of law. The Chamber found that upon the correct interpretation of Rule 49, the acts alleged in the Croatia, Bosnia, and Kosovo Indictments against the accused form part of the same transaction, and that the three indictments should therefore be joined and tried together. The Appeals Chamber held that the Trial Chamber had erred in its interpretation of Rule 49 as requiring the acts to be "committed together". Although the English version of Rule 49 refers to "series of acts committed together", the French version does not state that the acts need to be committed together but, rather, that the acts need to be committed as part of the same transaction (. . . si les actes incriminés ont été commis à l'occasion de la même operation. . .). Also Rule 48 has omitted the requirement of "committed together" while there is no reason why the test for the joinder of offences (Rule 49) and the joinder of defendants (Rule 48) should be different. The English version of Rule 49, if the text were to be read literally, is also at odds with the definition of "transaction" as spelled out in Rule 2. In order to avoid the discrepancy between the French and English version of Rule 49 and the dichotomy between the different Rules, the Appeals Chamber held that Rule 49 should not be read in isolation and does not require the offences to be "committed together" (*Prosecutor v. Milošević*, Reasons for Decision on Prosecution Interlocutory Appeal from Refusal to Order Joinder, 18 April 2002, paras. 13–18). What it *does* require is that, in accordance with the definition of "transaction" in Rule 2, the acts are part of a common scheme, strategy or plan.

In the present case, the Appeals Chamber held that the allegations in the three distinct indictments relating to Kosovo, Croatia and Bosnia formed part of the same transaction. This, despite the time lapse between the events in Croatia and Bosnia on the one hand and the events in Kosovo on the other, that the joint criminal enterprise pleaded in the Kosovo indictment was stated to have come into existence "no later than October 1998", and that Kosovo, unlike Croatia and Bosnia, was a province of Serbia at the time the events occurred. The Appeals Chamber's reasoning was as follows:

"A common scheme, strategy or plan may include the achievement of a long term aim. Here, that long term aim is alleged to have been to establish or to maintain control by the Serb authorities over particular areas which were or were once part of the former Yugoslavia. Each of the stages of the conflict in the Balkans has been marked by conflict breaking out in different places at different times, either as a result of or as requiring action by the Serb authorities (so the prosecution would have it) to ensure domination of those areas. A joint criminal enterprise to remove forcibly the majority of the non-Serb population from areas which the Serb authorities wished to establish or to maintain as Serbian controlled areas by the commission of the crimes charged remains the same transaction notwithstanding the fact that it is put into effect from time to time and over a long period of time as required. Despite the misleading allegation in the Kosovo indictment, therefore, the Appeals Chamber is satisfied that the events alleged in all three indictments do form part of the same transaction." (*Prosecutor v. Milošević*, Reasons for Decision on Prosecution Interlocutory Appeal from Refusal to Order Joinder, April 18, 2002, para. 21, and more generally, paras 19–21).

For other case law, see *Prosecutor v. Ntakirutimana et al.*, Decision on the Prosecutor's Motion to Join the Indictments ICTR 96–10-I and ICTR 96–17-T, February 22, 2001 (holding, *inter alia*, that the acts of the accused may form part of the same transaction notwithstanding that they were carried out in different areas and over different periods, providing that there is a sufficient nexus between the acts committed in the two areas).

(4) Severance

(a) General Principles

8–13   The fact that accused are charged together does not necessarily mean that it would be proper to try them together. Rule 82 of the ICTY, ICTR and SCSL Rules of Procedure and Evidence provide for accused persons to be tried separately if there is a conflict of interests that might cause serious prejudice to one or more accused or if such severance is otherwise considered necessary to protect the interests of justice.

The Decision on severance is a matter within the discretion of the Trial Chamber, after considering: (i) the nature of the possible prejudice to an accused; (ii) the advantages of a joint trial (uniform presentation and consistent treatment of evidence and procedure, avoiding unnecessary repetitive calling of witnesses in several trials *Prosecutor v. Bagosora et al.*, Decision on Motions By Ntabakuze for Severance and to Establish a Reasonable Schedule for the Presentation of Prosecution Witnesses, September 9, 2003, para. 22); and (iii) the mechanisms for mitigating the claimed prejudice by means other than severance (*Prosecutor v. Bagosora et al.*, Appeals Chamber Decision, October 28, 2003 p. 5; *Prosecutor v. Ntahobali*, Decision on Ntahobali's Motion for Separate Trial, February 2, 2005, para. 32; *Prosecutor v. Brdanin and Talic*, Appeals Chamber Decision on Request to Appeal, May 16, 2000; and *Prosecutor v. Ntahobali*, Decision on Ntahobali's Motion for Separate Trial, February 2, 2005, para. 39). The Trial Chamber in *Bagosora et al.* summarised the above considerations as follows:

"The preference for joint trials of individuals accused of acting in concert in the commission of a crime is not based merely on administrative efficiency. A joint trial relieves the hardship that would otherwise be imposed on witnesses, whose repeated attendance might not be secured; enhances fairness as between the accused by ensuring a uniform presentation of evidence and procedure against all; and minimizes the possibility of inconsistencies in treatment of evidence, sentencing or other matters, that could arise from separate trials"

(*Prosecutor v. Bagosora et al.*, Decision on Motions By Ntabakuze for Severance and to Establish a Reasonable Schedule for the Presentation of Prosecution Witnesses, September 9, 2003, para. 22; further see *Prosecutor v. Delalic et al.*, Decision on Motions for Separate Trial Filed by the Accused Zejnil Delalic and the Accused Zdravko Mucic, September 25, 1996, para. 7; *Prosecutor v. Brdanin and Talic*, Decision on Motions By Momir Talic for a Separate Trial and for Leave to File a Reply, March 9, 2000, para. 31; *Prosecutor v. Simić et al.*, Decision on Defence Motion to Sever Defendants and Counts, March 15, 1999, para. 13).

(b) Conflict of Interests

The existence, or not, of a conflict of interests between different **8–14** Accused in the same trial will be determined on a case-by-case basis. (*Prosecutor v. Ndayambaje*, Decision on defence motion for separate trial, April 25, 2001). The same case surveyed other instances where conflict of interests were alleged: concurrent presentation of the evidence pertaining to one Accused with evidence pertaining to the another does not *per se* constitute a conflict. Nor does calling a co-Accused to testify during a joint trial constitute a conflict of interests between the Accused. See *Prosecutor v. Ndayambaje*, Decision on defence motion for separate trial, April 25, 2001); Also see, *Prosecutor v. Kovacevic*, Decision on the motion for joinder of accused and concurrent presentation of evidence, May 14, 1998 (conflict could arise due to one of the accused being charged with a different crime requiring the introduction of different evidence); *Prosecutor v. Delalic et al.*, Decision on motions for separate trials filed by accused Zejnil Delalic and accused Zdravko Mucic, September 25, 1996 (there is no basis for separate trial of distinct issues arising in one indictment; *Simić et al.*, Decision on Defence Motion to Sever Defendants and Counts, March 15, 1999 (prejudice arising from testimony, or refusal to testify, of Co-Accused which would not arise in single trials could be mitigated by the regular rules of admissibility); *Prosecutor v. Bagosora et al.*, Decision on Motions by Ntabakuze for Severance and to Establish a Reasonable Schedule for the Presentation of Prosecution Witnesses, September 9, 2003, para. 23 (testimony of an accused cannot be compelled by a co-accused in a joint trial; nor can an accused, at least prior to his own conviction, be compelled to testify at a separate trial of the co-accused); and *Prosecutor v. Bagosora et al.*, Decision on Request for Severance by Accused Kabiligi, March 24, 2005 (the fact that former Lead Counsel of the Accused

Kabiligi was removed and replaced by former co-Counsel of co-Accused, who initially acted as *interim* Lead Counsel, did not constitute a conflict of interests; nor did the submission that the Accused Kabiligi's right to adequate time and facilities for the preparation of his defence required a delay; while, in order to preserve the right to a speedy trial of his co-Accused, the trial should continue without undue delay). The fact that there is evidence which may, in law, be admissible against one accused and not the others, is not necessarily a ground for severance in an international tribunal where trial is by judges without a jury, since it is generally assumed that judges can rise above such risk of prejudice and apply their professional judicial minds to the assessment of evidence (*Prosecutor v. Barayagwiza*, Decision on the Request of the Defence for Severance and Separate Trial, September 26, 2000).

(c) Interests of Justice

8–15   For cases concerning protecting the interests of justice see *Prosecutor v. Ngirumpatse et al.*, Decision on Prosecutor's motion for joinder of accused and on the Prosecutor's motion for severance of the accused, July 29, 2000, paras 31–40; and, *Prosecutor v. Dokmanovic*, December 2, 1997, in which the Chamber ordered that the accused be tried separately from his co-accused who were not in custody as yet to protect his right to be tried without undue delay. However, the mere fact that an accused's trial would be speedier if he or she were tried alone is not of itself a reason for severance (*Prosecutor v. Ndayambaje*, Decision on defence motion for separate trial, April 25, 2001).

Severance can apply to individual accused or to a separate group of accused from other accused (see, *Prosecutor v. Ngirumpatse et al.*, Decision on Prosecutor's motion for joinder of accused and on the Prosecutor's motion for severance of the accused, July 29, 2000, paras 22–24, which cites the *Blaškić et al.* case in which the accused Kordić and Čerkez were separated as a unit and tried together).

In *Karemera et al.*, of the accused Rwamakuba was severed from the main trial on the grounds that the charges and the supporting facts in the proposed amended indictment were unique and relevant to Rwamakuba only, and the amended indictment narrowed the allegations of joint criminal enterprise. Severance in this case was considered to simplify and shorten the trials of each Accused and was therefore in the interests of justice. (*Prosecutor v. Karemera et al.*, Decision on Severance of Andre Rwamakuba and for Leave to File Amended Indictment *Articles 6, 11, 12 quater, 18 and 20 of the Statute; Rules 47, 50 and 82(B) of the Rules of Procedure and Evidence*, February 14, 2005, paras 29–32).

(d) ICC

8–16   ICC Rule 136 is similar to the ICTY and ICTR Rules save that there is a presumption in favour of joinder. Separate trials will only be ordered where separation is considered necessary in order to avoid serious prejudice to the accused, to protect the interests of justice or because an accused has pleaded guilty.

B. PRESENCE OF ACCUSED FOR TRIAL

(1) Statutory provisions and rules

ICC Statute, Art. 63

Trial in the presence of the accused

63.—1. The accused shall be present during the trial.   **8–17**

2. If the accused, being present before the Court, continues to disrupt the trial, the Trial Chamber may remove the accused and shall make provisions for him or her to observe that trial and instruct counsel from outside the courtroom, through the use of communications technology, if required. Such measures shall be taken only in exceptional circumstances after other reasonable alternatives have proved inadequate and only for such duration as is strictly required.

ICC Rules of Procedure and Evidence, Rule 124

Rule 124: Waiver of the right to be present at the confirmation hearing

1. If the person concerned is available to the Court but wishes to waive the   **8–18**
right to be present at the hearing on confirmation of charges, he or she shall submit a written request to the Pre-Trial Chamber, which may then hold consultations with the Prosecutor and the person concerned, assisted or represented by his or her counsel.

2. A confirmation hearing pursuant to article 61, paragraph 2 (a), shall only be held when the Pre-Trial Chamber is satisfied that the person concerned understands the right to be present at the hearing and the consequences of waiving this right.

3. The Pre-Trial Chamber may authorize and make provision for the person to observe the hearing from outside the courtroom through the use of communications technology, if required.

4. The waiving of the right to be present at the hearing does not prevent the Pre-Trial Chamber from receiving written observations on issues before the Chamber from the person concerned.

ICTY

Statute of the ICTY, Art. 21(4)(d)

Rights of the accused

21.—   **8–19**

[. . .]

    (d) to be tried in his presence, and to defend himself in person or through legal assistance of his own choosing; to be informed, if he does not have legal assistance, of this right; and to have legal assistance assigned to him, in any case where the interests of justice so require, and without payment by him in any such case if he does not have sufficient means to pay for it;

        [. . .]

Rules of Procedure and Evidence of the ICTY, r. 80(B)

Control of Proceedings

8–20　　80.—(B) The Trial Chamber may order the removal of an accused from the courtroom and continue the proceedings in the absence of the accused if the accused has persisted in disruptive conduct following a warning that such conduct may warrant the removal of the accused from the courtroom.

ICTR

Statute of the ICTR, Art. 20(4)(d)

Rights of the Accused

8–21　　20.—

　　　　[. . .]

　　　　(d) To be tried in his or her presence, and to defend himself or herself in person or through legal assistance of his or her own choosing; to be informed, if he or she does not have legal assistance, of this right; and to have legal assistance assigned to him or her, in any case where the interest of justice so require, and without payment by him or her in any such case if he or she does not have sufficient means to pay for it;

　　　　　　[. . .]

Rules of Procedure and Evidence of the ICTR, r. 80(B)

Control of Proceedings

8–22　　80.—(B) The Trial Chamber may order the removal of an accused from the proceedings and continue the proceedings in his absence if he has persisted in disruptive conduct following a warning that he may be removed.

Rules of Procedure and Evidence of the ICTR, r. 82*bis*

Trial in the Absence of Accused

8–23　　82*bis*. If an accused refuses to appear before the Trial Chamber for trial, the Chamber may order that the trial proceed in the absence of the accused for so long as his refusal persists, provided that the Trial Chamber is satisfied that:
　　　　(i) the accused has made his initial appearance under Rule 62;
　　　　(ii) the Registrar has duly notified the accused that he is required to be present for trial;
　　　　(iii) the interests of the accused are represented by counsel.

East Timor

Regulation 2000/30, s.5 (as amended by Regulation 2001/25)

Trial in the Presence of the Accused

8–24　　5.—5.1 No trial of a person shall be held *in absentia*, except in the circumstances defined in the present regulation. The accused must be present at the hearing conducted pursuant to Section 29 of the present regulation, unless the accused is removed from the court under the provisions of Section 49.2 of the present regulation.

5.2 If at any stage following the hearing provided in Section 29 of the present regulation the accused flees or is otherwise voluntarily absent, the proceedings may continue until their conclusion.

5.3 If at any stage the accused is removed from the court under the provisions of Section 49.2 of the present regulation, the proceedings may continue until their conclusion unless the court finds for good cause shown that the provisions of Section 49.2 of the present regulation no longer apply.

SCSL

Statute of the SCSL, Art. 17(4)(d)

Rights of the Accused

17.—   **8–25**

[. . .]

(d) To be tried in his or her presence, and to defend himself or herself in person or through legal assistance of his or her own choosing; to be informed, if he or she does not have legal assistance, of this right; and to have legal assistance assigned to him or her, in any case where the interest of justice so require, and without payment by him or her in any such case if he or she does not have sufficient means to pay for it;

[. . .]

Rules of Procedure and Evidence of the SCSL, r. 80(B)

Control of Proceedings

80.—(B) The Trial Chamber may order the removal of an accused from the   **8–26** proceedings and continue the proceedings in his absence if he has persisted in disruptive conduct following a warning that he may be removed. In the event of removal, where possible, provision should be made for the accused to follow the proceedings by video link.

(2) Trial *in absentia*

The principle is that the trial should take place in the presence of the   **8–27** Accused. There are, nevertheless, recognised exceptions.

Based on Rule 80(B) of the ICTY/ICTR/SCSL Rules, Article 63 of the ICC Statute and Regulation 5 of East-Timor Regulations, a persistently disruptive accused may, following a warning (although Article 63 ICC does not mention a warning), be removed from the courtroom while the trial against him continues in his absence. SCSL Rule 80(B) states that, where possible, a removed accused should be allowed to follow the proceedings by video link.

Moreover, an accused can waive the right to be present during the trial proceedings, where a person is duly informed of his ongoing trial and chooses not to be present (*Prosecutor v. Barayagwiza*, Decision on Defence Counsel Motion to Withdraw, November 2, 2000, paras 5–7).

At the time of this decision the ICTR Rules did not yet include a provision allowing trials *in absentia* other than Rule 80(B). On May 27, 2003, the ICTR has introduced a legal basis for trials *in absentia* in certain conditions (Rule 82*bis*).

Rule 82*bis* is not incorporated in the SCSL Rules. It is, however, recognised that trial *in absentia* is allowed in limited circumstances. As the Trial Chamber in *Sesay* put it:

> "The Chamber, accordingly, emphasizes that it is settled law, nationally and internationally, that while an accused person has the right to be tried in his presence, there are circumstance under which a trial in the absence of the accused can be permitted. While due consideration must be given to ensure that all rights to a fair trial are respected, an Accused person charged with serious crimes who refuses to appear in court should not be permitted to obstruct the judicial machinery by preventing the commencement or a continuation of trials by deliberately being absent, after his initial appearance, or by refusing to appear in court after he has been afforded the right to do so, and particularly in circumstances as in this case, where no just cause, such as illness, has been advanced to justify absence."

(*Prosecutor v. Sesay*, Ruling on the Issue of the Refusal of the Accused Sesay and Kallon to Appear for their Trial, January 19, 2005, para. 15; see also *Prosecutor v. Gbao*, Ruling on the Issue of the Refusal of the Third Accused, Augustine Gbao, to Attend Hearing of the Special Court for Sierra Leone on July 7, 2004 and Succeeding Days, July 13, 2004, para. 8).

In *Milošević*, the Appeals Chamber went a step further than that, despite the fact that the ICTY Rules do not embody any legal basis for trials *in absentia* other than Rule 80(B). The Appeals Chamber confirmed the Trial Chamber's position that, in case of illness, a ground wholly outside the responsibility of the accused, the trial may continue in absence of the accused, even if the accused is eager to be present. Milošević's poor health was the principal reason to impose Defence Counsel on him so that the trial could continue with Defence Counsel representing Milošević's interests when he would be absent due to his illness. As the Appeals Chamber held: "If Milošević's health problems resurface with sufficient gravity, however, the presence of Assigned Counsel will enable the trial to continue even if Milošević is temporarily unable to participate" (*Prosecutor v. Milošević*, Decision on Interlocutory on Appeal of the Trial Chamber's Decision on the Assignment of Defence Counsel, November 1, 2004, para. 20).

It has also been held that the right of an accused to be tried in his or her presence does not of itself prevent witness evidence from being taken by deposition (*Prosecutor v. Naletilic and Martinovic*, Decision on Prosecutor's Motion to Take Depositions for Use at Trial (Rule 71), ICTY Trial Chamber, November 10, 2000).

The East Timor Regulation and the ICC Statute also explicitly allow for trials in absence of the accused where certain conditions are met. (See, for example UNTAET Reg. 2000/30, section 5).

The Iraqi Special Tribunal also allows for trials *in absentia*. Rule 56 of the Rules of Procedure and Evidence provides for trials *in absentia* pursuant to Iraqi law. The law states that both defendants who have not yet been arrested and those who were taken into custody but then escaped could be tried *in absentia* (see Iraqi Criminal Proceedings Law with amendments, No. 23 of 1971, para. 135).

Under the ICC Statute, it seems that significant importance is placed on the presence of the Accused during trial. This is apparent from the express language of Article 63 of the Statute which provides that "the accused *shall* be present during the trial". The only express exception to this is where the accused proves disruptive (Article 63(2)). Under the ICC Rules of Procedure, however, the regime allows an accused who is otherwise available to the court, but who wishes to absent himself from the confirmation hearing, to do so provided such waiver is submitted in writing and that it is an informed waiver. In the event that the Court accedes to the request and does not require the attendance of the accused, there is provision (similar to the facilities detailed in Article 63(2) of the Statute) for the use of communication technology to enable such an accused to still observe the proceedings from outside the courtroom.

C. ONUS AND BURDEN OF PROOF

(1) Statutory provisions and rules

ICC

ICC Statute, Art. 66

Presumption of innocence

66.—1. Everyone shall be presumed innocent until proved guilty before the Court in accordance with the applicable law.　　　　　　　　　　　　**8–28**

2. The onus is on the Prosecutor to prove the guilt of the accused.

3. In order to convict the accused, the Court must be convinced of the guilt of the accused beyond reasonable doubt.

ICTY

Rules of Procedure and Evidence, r. 87(A)

Deliberations

87.—(A) When both parties have completed their presentation of the case, the Presiding Judge shall declare the hearing closed, and the Trial Chamber shall deliberate in private. A finding of guilt may be reached only when a majority of the Trial Chamber is satisfied that guilt has been proved beyond reasonable doubt.　　　　　　　　　　　　**8–29**

ICTR/SCSL

Rules of Procedure and Evidence, r. 87(A)

Deliberations

87.—(A) After presentation of closing arguments, the Presiding Judge shall declare the hearing closed, and the Trial Chamber shall deliberate in private. A finding of guilty may be reached only when a majority of the Trial Chamber is satisfied that guilt has been proved beyond reasonable doubt.　　　**8–30**

East Timor

Regulation 2000/30, s.6 (as amended by Regulation 2001/25)

Rights of the Suspect and Accused

8–31   **6.**—6.1 All persons accused of a crime shall be presumed innocent until proven guilty in accordance with the law, the provisions of this and other UNTAET regulations.

[. . .]

6.3 At every stage of the proceedings, the suspect and the accused shall be informed by the public prosecutor that he or she has the following rights:

[. . .]

(e) the right to request the Public Prosecutor or Investigating Judge to order or conduct specific investigations in order to establish his or her innocence

(2) Burden on the Prosecution

8–32   The general principle is that the Prosecution bears the burden of proving the allegations contained in the indictment.

> "It is a fundamental requirement of any judicial system that the person who has invoked its jurisdiction and desires the tribunal or court to take action on his behalf must prove his case to its satisfaction. As a matter of common sense, therefore, the legal burden of proving all facts essential to their claims normally rests upon the plaintiff in a civil suit or the prosecutor in criminal proceedings" (*Delalic et al.*, Judgment, ICTY Trial Chamber, November 16, 1998, para. 599).

The standard of proof that the Prosecution is required to meet to discharge the burden is "to prove the case alleged against the accused beyond a reasonable doubt. At the conclusion of the case the accused is entitled to the benefit of the doubt as to whether the offence has been proved" (*Delalic et al.*, Judgment, ICTY Trial Chamber, November 16, 1998, para. 601).

For an example of a case in which it was alleged on appeal that the "beyond reasonable doubt" standard was not correctly applied by the Trial Chamber, see *Prosecutor v. Akayesu*, Judgment, ICTR Appeals Chamber, June 1, 2001, paras 171 *et seq.*

It is noteworthy, that the newly created Iraqi Special Tribunal does not expressly provide for guilt to be proven "beyond a reasonable doubt". The Rules of Procedure and Evidence existing in Iraqi law, and applicable before the Special Tribunal only require that a court or Tribunal be "satisfied" of guilt by the evidence presented (Law On Criminal Proceedings with Amendments, No. 23 of 1971, para. 213(A)).

(3) Burden on the Defence

8–33   When the accused is bound by law to prove a fact, for example that he is not of a sound mind, the legal burden of proving such a fact rests with the defence. However, "the accused is required to prove any issues which he might raise on the balance of probabilities" (*Delalic et al.*, Judgment, ICTY Trial Chamber, November 16, 1998, para. 603).

As to the accused's response to the charges laid against him, "the accused is only required to lead such evidence as would, if believed and uncontradicted, induce a reasonable doubt as to whether his version might not be true, rather than that of the Prosecution. Thus the evidence which he brings should be enough to suggest a reasonable possibility" (*Delalic et al.*, Judgment, ICTY Trial Chamber, November 16, 1998, para. 603).

In cases where the Defence relies on an alibi, the Defence is not required to prove the existence of the facts but is merely required to disclose evidence in support of the alibi. Contrary to the Defence submission in *Kayishema and Ruzindana*, this in no way shifts the burden of proof. Consistent with the principle of presumption of innocence, the Prosecution retains the burden to prove the case beyond a reasonable doubt. The Appeals Chamber in *Foca* emphasised that "the Prosecution bore the onus of establishing the facts alleged in the Indictment. Having raised the issue of alibi, the accused bore no onus in establishing that alibi. It was for the Prosecution to establish that, despite the evidence of the alibi, the facts alleged in the Indictment were nevertheless true" (*Prosecutor v. Kunarac*, Judgment, February 22, 2001, para. 625; see also *Prosecutor v. Kayishema and Ruzindana*, Appeals Chamber Judgment, June 1, 2001, paras 107, 110).

In sentencing, while aggravating circumstances must be proved beyond a reasonable doubt, mitigating circumstances need only be established on the balance of probabilities (*Delalic et al.*, Judgment, ICTY Appeals Chamber, February 20, 2001, para. 590; *Prosecutor v. Kunarac et al.*, Judgment, ICTY Trial Chamber, February 22, 2001, para. 847; *Prosecutor v. Sikirica et al.*, Sentencing Judgment, ICTY Trial Chamber, November 13, 2001, para. 110).

(4) Other burdens

In the ICTY, it has been held that in an application for provisional release, the applicable burden of proof is discharged on the balance of probabilities and not on the higher standard of proof beyond reasonable doubt. (See, *Prosecutor v. Krajisnik and Plavsic*, Decision on Momcilo Krajisnik's Notice of Motion for Provisional Release, October 8, 2001, para. 30.) (*cf.* ICC Rule 119(4).)

8–34

Other evidentiary burdens have also been articulated, and others may continue to develop in the case law. For instance, in one case it was held that for a document to be admissible as evidence, the party relying on it must establish that it has "sufficient *indicia* of reliability" (see *Musema v. Prosecutor*, Judgment, ICTR Appeals Chamber, November 6, 2001, paras 43–48).

Article 66 of the ICC Statute incorporates similar principles to those detailed above. Section 6.1 UNTAET Regulation incorporates the principle of the presumption of innocence until proven guilty. There is, however, no affirmative, express, duty on the Judges of the Special Panel for Serious Crimes in East Timor to acquit any person of whom the guilt has not been established beyond a reasonable doubt. It is noteworthy, in this regard, that Section 6.3(e) embodies as one of the fundamental rights of an accused "the right to request the Public Prosecutor or Investigating Judge to order or conduct specific investigations in order to establish his or her innocence".

D. OPENING STATEMENTS

(1) Statutory provisions and rules

ICC

Statute, Art. 64(8)

Functions and Powers of the Trial Chamber

8–35 64.—8.
  (a) At the commencement of the trial, the Trial Chamber shall have read to the accused the charges previously confirmed by the Pre-Trial Chamber. The Trial Chamber shall satisfy itself that the accused understands the nature of the charges. It shall afford him or her the opportunity to make an admission of guilt in accordance with article 65 or to plead not guilty.

Rules and Procedure of Evidence, r. 140(1)

Directions for the Conduct of the Proceedings and Testimony

8–36 140.—1. If the Presiding Judge does not give directions under article 64, paragraph 8, the Prosecutor and the defence shall agree on the order and manner in which the evidence shall be submitted to the Trial Chamber. If no agreement can be reached, the Presiding Judge shall issue directions.

ICTY Rules of Procedure and Evidence, rr. 84, 84*bis*

Opening Statements

8–37 84. Before presentation of evidence by the Prosecutor, each party may make an opening statement. The defence may, however, elect to make its statement after the conclusion of the Prosecutor's presentation of evidence and before the presentation of evidence for the defence.

Statement of the Accused

8–38 84*bis*.—(A) After the opening statements of the parties or, if the defence elects to defer its opening statement pursuant to Rule 84, after the opening statement of the Prosecutor, if any, the accused may, if he or she so wishes, and the Trial Chamber so decides, make a statement under the control of the Trial Chamber. The accused shall not be compelled to make a solemn declaration and shall not be examined about the content of the statement.

(B) The Trial Chamber shall decide on the probative value, if any, of the statement.

ICTR Rules of Procedure and Evidence, r. 84

Opening Statements

84. Before presentation of evidence by the Prosecutor, each party may make an opening statement. The defence may, however, elect to make its statement after the conclusion of the Prosecutor's presentation of evidence and before the presentation of evidence for the defence.

8–39

East Timor

Regulation 2000/30, s. 30 (as amended by Regulation 2001/25)

Trial Proceedings

30.—30.1 All judges who are required to participate in the final decision of the case must be present at all sessions of the trial.

30.2 On the date and time determined in accordance with Section 29.3 of the present regulation, the competent judge shall call upon the parties, shall verify their identities; shall enter such information into the record and shall declare the trial open.

30.3 Where the hearing is before a panel of judges, in accordance with Section 18.2 of UNTAET Regulation No. 2000/11, the Presiding judge shall identify one judge of the panel as the judge rapporteur. The judge rapporteur shall have primary responsibility for preparation of the final written decision in the case.

30.4 The Court shall confirm that the accused has read or has had the indictment read to him or her and understands the nature of the charges, that the right of the accused to counsel has been respected, shall remind the accused of his or her right to remain silent, and shall determine what statements or admissions, if any, the accused will make regarding the crimes alleged. If the accused makes an admission of guilt, the Court shall proceed as provided in Section 29A of the present regulation.

30.5 Where the accused decides to make a statement, the Court may question him or her about the statement. The Court may then invite the Public Prosecutor and legal representative of the accused for additional questions.

30.6 The Public Prosecutor and the legal representative of the accused may object to any question posed by each other on grounds of relevancy or if the question is designed to embarrass or harass the witness. The Court shall decide on such objections as they are raised.

30.7 The accused shall be given the opportunity to address the Court regarding any issue raised during the hearing, provided that such issue is relevant to the proceedings.

30.8 The accused shall sit beside his or her legal representative and may consult with him or her throughout the hearing without any restriction.

8–40

SCSL Rules of Procedure and Evidence, r. 84

Opening Statements

84.—At the opening of his case, each party may make an opening statement confined to the evidence he intends to present in support of his case. The Trial Chamber may limit the length of those statements in the interests of justice.

8–41

E. PRESENTATION OF EVIDENCE

(1) Statutory provisions and rules

ICC

Statute, Art. 64(8)

Functions and Powers of the Trial Chamber

8–42   **64.—**8.
>   (a) At the commencement of the trial, the Trial Chamber shall have read to the accused the charges previously confirmed by the Pre-Trial Chamber. The Trial Chamber shall satisfy itself that the accused understands the nature of the charges. It shall afford him or her the opportunity to make an admission of guilt in accordance with article 65 or to plead not guilty.

Rules of Procedure and Evidence, rr. 140, 141

Directions for the conduct of the proceedings and testimony

8–43   **140.—**1. If the Presiding Judge does not give directions under article 64, paragraph 8, the Prosecutor and the defence shall agree on the order and manner in which the evidence shall be submitted to the Trial Chamber. If no agreement can be reached, the Presiding Judge shall issue directions.
2. In all cases, subject to article 64, paragraphs 8(b) and 9, article 69, paragraph 4, and rule 88, sub-rule 5, a witness may be questioned as follows:
>   (a) A party that submits evidence in accordance with article 69, paragraph 3, by way of a witness, has the right to question that witness;
>   (b) The prosecution and the defence have the right to question that witness about relevant matters related to the witness's testimony and its reliability, the credibility of the witness and other relevant matters;
>   (c) The Trial Chamber has the right to question a witness before or after a witness is questioned by a participant referred to in sub-rules 2(a) or (b);
>   (d) The defence shall have the right to be the last to examine a witness.
3. Unless otherwise ordered by the Trial Chamber, a witness other than an expert, or an investigator if he or she has not yet testified, shall not be present when the testimony of another witness is given. However, a witness who has heard the testimony of another witness shall not for that reason alone be disqualified from testifying. When a witness testifies after hearing the testimony of others, this fact shall be noted in the record and considered by the Trial Chamber when evaluating the evidence.

Closure of evidence and closing statements

8–44   **141.—**1. The Presiding Judge shall declare when the submission of evidence is closed.
2. The Presiding Judge shall invite the Prosecutor and the defence to make their closing statements. The defence shall always have the opportunity to speak last.

ICTY/ICTR Rules of Procedure and Evidence, r. 85

Presentation of Evidence

8–45   **85.—**(A) Each party is entitled to call witnesses and present evidence. Unless otherwise directed by the Trial Chamber in the interests of justice, evidence at the trial shall be presented in the following sequence:

  (i) evidence for the prosecution;
 (ii) evidence for the defence;
(iii) prosecution evidence in rebuttal;
(iv) defence evidence in rejoinder;
 (v) evidence ordered by the Trial Chamber pursuant to Rule 98; and
(vi) any relevant information that may assist the Trial Chamber in
     determining an appropriate sentence if the accused is found guilty on
     one or more of the charges in the indictment.
(B) Examination-in-chief, cross-examination and re-examination shall be
allowed in each case. It shall be for the party calling a witness to examine such
witness in chief, but a Judge may at any stage put any question to the witness.
(C) If the accused so desires, the accused may appear as a witness in his or
her own defence.

East Timor

Regulation 2000/30, s. 33 (as amended by Regulation 2001/25)

Presentation of Evidence

33.—33.1 Each party is entitled to call witnesses and present evidence. The   **8–46**
presentation of evidence shall be directed by the Individual Judge or Presiding
Judge. Unless otherwise ordered, evidence at trial shall be presented in the
following sequence:
  (a) the statement of the accused, if he or she chooses to make a
      statement;
  (b) evidence of the prosecution;
  (c) evidence of the defence;
33.2 After the defence has presented its case the prosecution shall be given
the opportunity to respond to the defence evidence. The defence will then be
allowed to reply to the prosecution. The court shall call any additional
witnesses it wishes to hear or evidence that it wishes to be presented after the
parties have completed their submissions.
33.3 Evidence shall be presented in the most direct manner possible, subject
to the other sections of the present regulation.
33.4 A statement or confession made by the accused before an Investigating
Judge may be admitted as evidence, if the Court finds that any admission of
guilt contained in such a statement was made in compliance with the
provisions of Section 29A.

SCSL Rules of Procedure and Evidence, r. 85

Presentation of Evidence

85.—(A) Each party is entitled to call witnesses and present evidence.   **8–47**
Unless otherwise directed by the Trial Chamber in the interests of justice,
evidence at the trial shall be presented in the following sequence:
  i. Evidence for the prosecution;
 ii. Evidence for the defence;
iii. Prosecution evidence in rebuttal, with leave of the Trial Chamber;
iv. Evidence ordered by the Trial Chamber.
(B) Examination-in-chief, cross-examination and re-examination shall be
allowed in each case. It shall be for the party calling a witness to examine him
in chief, but a Judge may at any stage put any question to the witness.

(C) The accused may, if he so desires, appear as a witness in his own defence. If he chooses to do so, he shall give his evidence under oath or affirmation and, as the case may be, thereafter call his witnesses.

(D) Evidence may be given directly in court, or via such communications media, including video, closed-circuit television, as the Trial Chamber may order.

(2) Presentation of the Evidence Pursuant to Rule 85(A)

(a) General

8–48   The order in which the evidence shall be presented is set out in Rule 85. Unless otherwise directed by the Trial Chamber in the interests of justice, this order will be followed.

Rule 85(A) does not provide a right to the parties to produce any further evidence after the close of their case. Rule 85(A) merely deals with the order in which evidence is to be presented "where entitlement to lead such evidence exists" (*Prosecutor v. Kunarac et al.*, Decision of Defence Motions for Rejoinder, October 31, 2000, para. 14).

(b) Evidence for the Prosecution

8–49   In principle the Prosecution has to present all of its evidence in the Prosecution's case, unless the evidence qualifies as rebuttal evidence or fresh evidence. (*Prosecutor v. Delalic et al.*, Appeals Chamber Judgment, February 20, 2001, para. 275; *Prosecutor v. Krstic*, Decision on the Defence Motions to Exclude Exhibits in Rebuttal and Motion for Continuance, May 4, 2001, para. 9; *Prosecutor v. Kunarač, Kovac and Vukovič*, Decision on Defence Motion for Rejoinder, October 31, 2000, para. 14; and *Prosecutor v. Milošević*, Decision on Prosecution Motion for Reconsideration Regarding Evidence of Defence Witnesses Mitar Balevic, Vladislav Jovanovic, Vukasin Andric, and Dobre Aleksovski and Decision *Proprio Motu* Reconsidering Admission of Exhibits 837 and 838 Regarding Evidence of Defence Witness Barry Lituchy, May 17, 2005, para. 17).

The reason that the Trial Chamber is fairly strict on the application of this principle was clearly spelled out in *Milošević* (*ibid.*, para. 14):

> "It would plainly undermine the Chamber's control of the trial through careful allocation of time to the Prosecution and Defence to present their cases, if the Prosecution were permitted to lead its own evidence during the Defence case in order to respond to the particular points raised by Defence witnesses who are simply answering the case or charges made against the Accused that emerged in the course of the prosecution evidence. It is, therefore, distinctly possible the evidence of a defence witness may be left "in the air" without any specific contradictory evidence. In such circumstances it will be for the Trial Chamber to evaluate the evidence against the background of all other relevant evidence in the case. At the end of the day, it remains open to the Trial Chamber, should it be faced with a particular problem arising out of the way in which evidence was presented, to order the production of further

evidence, or ex proprio motu summon witness pursuant to Rule 98 of the Rules."

However, in limited circumstances, evidence may be introduced after the Prosecution closed their case even where it does not qualify as rebuttal or fresh evidence. This may be the case where the evidence is used to test the credibility of a defence witness in cross-examination or to refresh the witness's memory, regardless of whether the Prosecution had the evidence in their possession before the closing of their case. Admission of documents during the defence case will only be allowed for these purposes and such documents "can only be admitted in a limited manner and can only be used to establish the credibility of the oral testimony of the witness or to refresh the witness's memory" (*Prosecutor v. Hadžihasanović*, Oral Decision of November 29, 2004, pp. 12523–12527 at p.12527).

In other circumstances, the Prosecution "may present new documents only if it wants to reinforce evidence that it has presented already or if it wants to introduce new elements that concern the criminal responsibility of the accused" *Prosecutor v. Hadžihasanović*, Oral Decision of November 29, 2004, pp. 12524–12525; also see *Prosecutor v. Milošević*, Decision on Prosecution Motion for Reconsideration Regarding Evidence of Defence Witnesses Mitar Balevic, Vladislav Jovanovic, Vukasin Andric, and Dobre Aleksovski and Decision *Proprio Motu* Reconsidering Admission of Exhibits 837 and 838 Regarding Evidence of Defence Witness Barry Lituchy, May 17, 2005, para. 11).

Material for which no basis of admission has been made out cannot be tendered into evidence. Thus, if a witness is confronted with a document upon which the witness cannot comment in any useful sense, this document should not be admitted (*ibid.*, paras 9 and 10, confirming *Hadžihasanović* above).

(c) Rebuttal Evidence

The Appeals Chamber in *Celebici* held that evidence will be admitted **8–50** as rebuttal evidence only where it relates to "a significant issue arising directly out of defence evidence which could not reasonably have been anticipated" and "where it is reasonably foreseeable by the Prosecution that some gap in the proof of guilt needs to be filled by the evidence called by it, it is inappropriate to admit it in rebuttal, and the Prosecution 'cannot call additional evidence merely because its case has been met by certain evidence to contradict it' [. . .] Where such evidence could not have been brought as part of the Prosecution case–in-chief because it was not in the hands of the Prosecution at the time, this does not render it admissible as rebuttal evidence. The fact that 'evidence is newly obtained', if that evidence does not meet the standard for admission of rebuttal evidence, will not render it admissible as rebuttal evidence. It merely puts it into the category of evidence, to which a different basis of admissibility applies" (*Prosecutor v. Delalic et al.*, Appeals Chamber Judgment, February 20, 2001, paras 273, 275 and 276; see also: *Prosecutor v. Krstic*, Decision on the Defence Motions to Exclude Exhibits in Rebuttal and Motion for Continuance, May 4, 2001, para. 8; *Prosecutor v. Blagojević and Jokic*, Decision on Prosecution's

Motion to Admit Evidence in Rebuttal and Incorporated Motion to
Admit Evidence Under Rule 92*bis* in its Case on Rebuttal and to Re-
open its Case for a Limited Purpose, September 13, 2004, paras 5–6).

The Trial Chamber in *Kordic* held that rebuttal evidence should be
limited "strictly to matters which were not already covered in the
Prosecution case" and "only highly probative evidence on a significant
issue in response to Defence evidence and not merely reinforcing the
Prosecution case in chief will be permitted" (*Prosecutor v. Kordić and
Čerkez*, Oral Decision of October 18, 2000, T. 26646–47). Evidence of
low probative value or concerned with a fundamental part of the
Prosecution case-in-chief is thus clearly precluded from being admitted.
(*Prosecutor v. Krstic*, Decision on the Defence Motions to Exclude
Exhibits in Rebuttal and Motion for Continuance, May 4, 2001, para.
11).

The Special Court of Sierra Leone has held that if a new matter
arises in the defence case and arises out of Defence examination-in-
chief (not cross examination by the Prosecutor) the Prosecutor can
produce the evidence in rebuttal unless the new matter is collateral,
that is, not relevant to matters which need to be proved as part of the
Prosecutor's accusations against the Accused (see *Prosecutor v. Norman et
al.*, Ruling on Defence Oral Application to Call OTP Investigators Who
Took Down in Writing Statements of Prosecution Witness TF2–021,
December 7, 2004, paras 20–23).

(d) Rejoinder Evidence

8–51   The test of admissibility of evidence in rejoinder is the same test as
for rebuttal. Hence, the Defence is only entitled to lead evidence in
rejoinder, if the Prosecution raises new issues during their case in
rebuttal (*Prosecutor v. Kunarac et al.*, Decision of Defence Motions for
Rejoinder, October 31, 2000). The same principles apply equally to the
admissibility of exhibits in rejoinder (*Prosecutor v. Naletelic and Martinovic*,
Decision on the Admission of Exhibits Tendered During the Rejoinder
Case, October 23, 2002). The proposed evidence in rejoinder must
directly arise out of rebuttal evidence and "could not be expected to
have been addressed during the Defence case" (*Prosecutor v. Galić*,
Decision on Rejoinder Evidence, April 2, 2003). The new issue must
have been raised by the Prosecution, not by the Defence during cross-
examination (*Prosecutor v. Kunarac et al.*, Decision of Defence Motions for
Rejoinder, October 31, 2000, para. 13; Also see *Prosecutor v. Kunarac et
al.*, Oral Decision, TT.6075–6076).

(e) Fresh Evidence

8–52   If fresh evidence is available, the Prosecution can apply to re-open its
case. The Appeals Chamber in *Celebici* determined that the Prosecution
could re-open its case if the Prosecution had obtained fresh evidence,
which was not available during its case-in-chief, if two conditions were
met: (i) the Prosecution has to demonstrate that the evidence would
not have been found with the exercise of reasonable diligence before

the close of the case; (ii) the probative value of the new evidence outweighs the prejudice against the accused because of its late admission (*Prosecutor v. Delalic et al.*, Appeals Chamber Judgment, February 20, 2001, para. 283; *Prosecutor v. Krstic*, Decision on the Defence Motions to Exclude Exhibits in Rebuttal and Motion for Continuance, May 4, 2001, para. 12; *Prosecutor v. Blagojević and Jokic*, Decision on Prosecution's Motion to Admit Evidence in Rebuttal and Incorporated Motion to Admit Evidence Under Rule 92*bis* in its Case on Rebuttal and to Re-open its Case for a Limited Purpose, September 13, 2004, para. 8).

(3) Judicial Control Pursuant Rule 85(B)

In situations where Judges pose questions to a witness on the stand, **8–53** their questions should be lead by the principle of impartiality and their truth-finding objective. As the jurisprudence has established, "Judge[s] should [. . .] be subjectively free from bias, [and . . .] there should be nothing in the surrounding circumstance which objectively gives rise to an appearance of bias; that impartiality must be assessed with regard to the perception of a hypothetical fair-minded observer with sufficient knowledge of the actual circumstance to make a reasonable judgement; that this hypothetical fair-minded observer is in a position different to that of the parties" (*Prosecutor v. Hadizhasanovic*, Decision on Defence Motion Seeking Clarification of the Trial Chamber's Objective in its Questions Addressed to Witnesses, February 4, 2005; *Prosecutor v. Furundžija*, Appeals Judgment, July 21, 2000, para. 189; *Prosecutor v. Brdjanin and Talic*, Decision on Application by Momir Talic for the Disqualification and Withdrawal of a Judge, May 18, 2000, para 15; *Prosecutor v. Krajisnic*, Decision on the Defence Application for Withdrawal of a Judge from the Trial, January 22, 2003, para. 14; *Prosecutor v. Rutaganda*, Appeals Judgment, May 26, 2003, paras 36–125; and *Prosecutor v. Bagilishema*, Grounds for the Appeals Judgment, July 3, 2002, para. 100).

In order to achieve these objectives and safeguard the Judges' reputation as independent arbiters, it may be necessary to allow the parties to ask additional questions to a witness after a Judge has asked questions, or to intervene during the Judge's questioning (*Prosecutor v. Hadizhasanovic*, Decision on Defence Motion Seeking Clarification of the Trial Chamber's Objective in its Questions Addressed to Witnesses, February 4, 2005).

See also paragraph 8–73 below on Cross-Examination Pursuant to Rule 90.

F. CONTROL OF PROCEEDINGS

(1) Statutory provisions and rules

ICC

ICC Statute, Arts 64(8)(b), 69

Functions and powers of the Trial Chamber
   64.—(8) **8–54**

(b) At the trial, the presiding judge may give directions for the conduct of proceedings, including to ensure that they are conducted in a fair and impartial manner. Subject to any directions of the presiding judge, the parties may submit evidence in accordance with the provisions of this Statute.

Evidence

8–55   **69.**—3. The parties may submit evidence relevant to the case, in accordance with article 64. The Court shall have the authority to request the submission of all evidence that it considers necessary for the determination of the truth.

ICC Rules of Procedure and Evidence, rr. 101, 140

Time limits

8–56   **101.**—1. In making any order setting time limits regarding the conduct of any proceedings, the Court shall have regard to the need to facilitate fair and expeditious proceedings, bearing in mind in particular the rights of the defence and the victims.

2. Taking into account the rights of the accused, in particular under article 67, paragraph (1)(c), all those participating in the proceedings to whom any order is directed shall endeavour to act as expeditiously as possible, within the time limit ordered by the Court.

Directions for the conduct of the proceedings and testimony

8–57   **140.**—1. If the Presiding Judge does not give directions under article 64, paragraph 8, the Prosecutor and the defence shall agree on the order and manner in which the evidence shall be submitted to the Trial Chamber. If no agreement can be reached, the Presiding Judge shall issue directions.

PRE-TRIAL CONFERENCE

ICC Regulations of the Court, rr. 28, 43

Questions by a Chamber

8–58   **28.**—1. A Chamber may order the participants to clarify or to provide additional details on any document within a time limit specified by the Chamber.

2. A Chamber may order the participants to address specific issues in their written or oral submissions within a time limit specified by the Chamber.

3. The provisions are without prejudice to the inherent powers of the Chamber.

Testimony of witnesses

8–59   **43.**—Subject to the Statute and the Rules, the Presiding Judge, in consultation with the other members of the Chamber, shall determine the mode and order of questioning witnesses and presenting evidence so as to:

(a) Make the questioning of witnesses and the presentation of evidence fair and effective for the determination of the truth;

(b) Avoid delays and ensure the effective use of time.

ICC Code of Judicial Ethics, a. 8

Conduct during proceedings

8.—1. In conducting judicial proceedings, judges shall maintain order, act in **8–60** accordance with commonly accepted decorum, remain patient and courteous towards all participants and members of the public present and require them to act likewise.

2. Judges shall exercise vigilance in controlling the manner of questioning of witnesses or victims in accordance with the Rules and give special attention to the right of participants to the proceedings to equal protection and benefit of the law.

3. Judges shall avoid conduct or comments which are racist, sexist or otherwise degrading and, to the extent possible, ensure that any person participating in the proceedings refrains from such comments or conduct.

ICTY

ICTY Rules of Procedure and Evidence, rr. 65*ter*(L), 73*bis*, 73*ter*, 90(F–H)

Pre-Trial Judge

65*ter*.—(L)　　　　　　　　　　　　　　　　　　　　　　　　　　　　**8–61**
　　(i) After the filings by the Prosecutor pursuant to paragraph (E), the pre-
　　　　trial Judge shall submit to the Trial Chamber a complete file
　　　　consisting of all the filings of the parties, transcripts of status
　　　　conferences and minutes of meetings held in the performance of his
　　　　or her functions pursuant to this Rule.
　　(ii) The pre-trial Judge shall submit a second file to the Trial Chamber
　　　　after the defence filings pursuant to paragraph (G).

Pre-Trial Conference

73*bis*.—(A) Prior to the commencement of the trial, the Trial Chamber **8–62** shall hold a Pre-Trial Conference.

(B) In the light of the file submitted to the Trial Chamber by the pre-trial Judge pursuant to Rule 65*ter* (L)(i), the Trial Chamber may call upon the Prosecutor to shorten the estimated length of the examination-in-chief for some witnesses.

(C) In the light of the file submitted to the Trial Chamber by the pre-trial Judge pursuant to Rule 65*ter* (L)(i), the Trial Chamber, after having heard the Prosecutor, shall determine
　　(i) the number of witnesses the Prosecutor may call; and
　　(ii) the time available to the Prosecutor for presenting evidence.

(D) After having heard the Prosecutor, the Trial Chamber may fix a number of crime sites or incidents comprised in one or more of the charges in respect of which evidence may be presented by the Prosecutor which, having regard to all the relevant circumstances, including the crimes charged in the indictment, their classification and nature, the places where they are alleged to have been committed, their scale and the victims of the crimes, are reasonably representative of the crimes charged.

(E) After commencement of the trial, the Prosecutor may file a motion to vary the decision as to the number of crime sites or incidents in respect of which evidence may be presented or the number of witnesses that are to be called or for additional time to present evidence and the Trial Chamber may grant the Prosecutor's request if satisfied that this is in the interests of justice.

Pre-Defence Conference

8–63   **73*ter*.**—(A) Prior to the commencement by the defence of its case the Trial Chamber may hold a Conference.

(B) In the light of the file submitted to the Trial Chamber by the pre-trial Judge pursuant to Rule 65*ter*(L)(ii), the Trial Chamber may call upon the defence to shorten the estimated length of the examination-in-chief for some witnesses.

(C) In the light of the file submitted to the Trial Chamber by the pre-trial Judge pursuant to Rule 65*ter*(L)(ii), the Trial Chamber, after having heard the defence, shall set the number of witnesses the defence may call.

(D) After commencement of the defence case, the defence may, if it considers it to be in the interests of justice, file a motion to reinstate the list of witnesses or to vary the decision as to which witnesses are to be called.

(E) After having heard the defence, the Trial Chamber shall determine the time available to the defence for presenting evidence.

(F) During a trial, the Trial Chamber may grant a defence request for additional time to present evidence if this is in the interests of justice.

Testimony of Witnesses

8–64   **90.**—(F) The Trial Chamber shall exercise control over the mode and order of interrogating witnesses and presenting evidence so as to:

      (i) Make the interrogation and presentation effective for the ascertainment of the truth; and

      (ii) Avoid needless consumption of time.

(G) The Trial Chamber may refuse to hear a witness whose name does not appear on the list of witnesses compiled pursuant to Rules 73*bis* (C) and 73*ter* (C).

    (H)(i) Cross-examination shall be limited to the subject-matter of the evidence-in-chief and matters affecting the credibility of the witness and, where the witness is able to give evidence relevant to the case for the cross-examining party, to the subject-matter of that case.

      (ii) In the cross-examination of a witness who is able to give evidence relevant to the case for the cross-examination party, counsel shall put to that witness the nature of the case of the party for whom that counsel appears which is in contradiction of the evidence given by the witness.

      (iii) The Trial Chamber may, in the exercise of its discretion, permit enquiry into additional matters.

ICTR

ICTR Rules of Procedure and Evidence, rr. 73*bis*, 73*ter*, 90(F–G)

Pre-Trial Conference

8–65   **73*bis*.**—(A) Prior to the commencement of the trial, the Trial Chamber shall hold a Pre-Trial Conference.

(B) In the light of the file submitted to the Trial Chamber by the pre-trial Judge pursuant to Rule 65*ter*(L)(i), the Trial Chamber may call upon the

Prosecutor to shorten the estimated length of the examination-in-chief for some witnesses.

In the light of the file submitted to the Trial Chamber by the pre-trial Judge pursuant to Rule 65*ter*(L)(i), the Trial Chamber, after having heard the Prosecutor, shall set the number of witnesses the Prosecutor may call.

(D) After commencement of the trial, the Prosecutor may, if he or she considers it to be in the interests of justice, file a motion to reinstate the list of witnesses or to vary the decision as to which witnesses are to be called.

(E) After having heard the Prosecutor, the Trial Chamber shall determine the time available to the Prosecutor for presenting evidence.

(F) During a trial, the Trial Chamber may grant the Prosecutor's request for additional time to present evidence if this is in the interests of justice.

Pre-Defence Conference

73ter.—(A) The Trial Chamber may hold a Conference prior to the commencement by the Defence of its case.   **8–66**

(C) At that Conference, the Trial Chamber or a Judge, designated from among its members, may order that the Defence, before the commencement of its case but after the close of the case for the prosecution, file the following:

  (i) Admissions by the parties and a statement of other matters which are not in dispute;
  (ii) A statement of contested matters of fact and law;
  (iii) A list of witnesses the Defence intends to call with:
    (a) The name or pseudonym of each witness;
    (b) A summary of the facts on which each witness will testify;
    (c) The points in the indictment as to which each witness will testify; and
    (d) The estimated length of time required for each witness;
  (iv) A list of exhibits the Defence intends to offer in its case, stating where possible whether or not the Prosecutor has any objection as to authenticity.

The Trial Chamber or the Judge may order the Defence to provide the Trial Chamber and the Prosecutor with copies of the written statements of each witness whom the Defence intends to call to testify.

(C) The Trial Chamber or the designated Judge may order the Defence to shorten the estimated length of the examination- in-chief for some witnesses.

(D) The Trial Chamber or the designated Judge may order the Defence to reduce the number of witnesses, if it considers that an excessive number of witnesses are being called to prove the same facts.

(E) After commencement of the Defence case, the Defence, if it considers it to be in the interests of justice, may move the Trial Chamber for leave to reinstate the list of witnesses or to vary its decision as to whic h witnesses are to be called.

Testimony of Witness

90.—(F) The Trial Chamber shall exercise control over the mode and order of interrogating witnesses and presenting evidence so as to: **8–67**

  (i) Make the interrogation and presentation effective for the ascertainment of the truth; and
  (ii) Avoid needless consumption of time.
  (G)(i) Cross-examination shall be limited to the subject-matter of the evidence-in-chief and matters affecting the credibility of the witness and, where the witness is able to give evidence relevant to the case for the cross-examining party, to the subject-matter of the case.
  (ii) In the cross-examination of a witness who is able to give evidence relevant to the case for the cross-examining party, counsel shall put to

that witness the nature of the case of the party for whom that counsel appears which is in contradiction of the evidence given by the witness.

(iii) The Trial Chamber may, in the exercise of its discretion, permit enquiry into additional matters.

East Timor

Regulation 2000/30, s.36.6 (as amended by Regulation 2001/25)

Witness Testimony

8–68   **36.**—36.6 Unless otherwise determined by the court, witnesses shall be examined first by the court, then by the party calling the witness, then the opposing party. The Presiding Judge shall allow other judges of the panel to pose additional questions to the witness.

36.7 The Presiding Judge shall exercise control over the mode and order of questioning witnesses, so as to make the presentation of evidence effective for the ascertainment of the truth, avoid needless consumption of time and to ensure that experts and witnesses are questioned without pressure and without violation of their personal dignity.

SCSL

SCSL Rules of Procedure and Evidence, rr. 73*bis*, 73*ter*, 90(F)

Pre Trial Conference

8–69   **73***bis***.**—(A) The Trial Chamber or a Judge designated from among its members shall hold a Pre Trial Conference prior to the commencement of the trial.

(B) At the Pre Trial Conference the Trial Chamber or a Judge designated from among its members may order the Prosecutor, within a time limit set by the Trial Chamber or the said Judge, and before the date set for trial, to file the following:

   i. A pre trial brief addressing the factual and legal issues;

   ii. Admissions by the parties and a statement of other matters not in dispute;

   iii. A statement of contested matters of fact and law;

   iv. A list of witnesses the Prosecutor intends to call with:

      a. The name or pseudonym of each witness;

      b. A summary of the facts on which each witness will testify;

      c. The points in the indictment on which each witness will testify; and

      d. The estimated length of time required for each witness;

   v. A list of exhibits the Prosecutor intends to offer stating, where possible, whether or not the defence has any objection as to authenticity.

      The Trial Chamber or the said Judge may order the Prosecutor to provide the Trial Chamber with copies of written statements of each witness whom the Prosecutor intends to call to testify.

(C) The Trial Chamber or a Judge designated from among its members may order the Prosecutor to shorten the examination in chief of some witnesses.

(D) The Trial Chamber or a Judge designated from among its members may order the Prosecutor to reduce the number of witnesses, if it considers that an excessive number of witnesses are being called to prove the same facts.

(E) After the commencement of the Trial, the Prosecutor may, if he considers it to be in the interests of justice, move the Trial Chamber for leave to reinstate the list of witnesses or to vary his decision as to which witnesses are to be called.

(F) At the Pre-Trial Conference, the Trial Chamber or a Judge designated from among its members may order the defence to file a statement of admitted facts and law and a pre-trial brief addressing the factual and legal issues, not later than seven days prior to the date set for trial.

Pre Defence Conference

73ter—(A) The Trial Chamber or a Judge designated from among its   **8–70** members may hold a Conference prior to the commencement by the defence of its case.

(B) At that Conference, the Trial Chamber or a Judge designated from among its members may order that the defence, before the commencement of its case but after the close of the case for the prosecution, file the following:

- i. Admissions by the parties and a statement of other matters which are not in dispute;
- ii. A statement of contested matters of fact and law;
- iii. A list of witnesses the defence intends to call with:
  - a. The name or pseudonym of each witness;
  - b. A summary of the facts on which each witness will testify;
  - c. The points in the indictment as to which each witness will testify; and
  - d. The estimated length of time required for each witness;
- iv. A list of exhibits the defence intends to offer in its case, stating where possible whether or not the Prosecutor has any objection as to authenticity.

The Trial Chamber or the said Judge may order the Defence to provide the Trial Chamber and the Prosecutor with copies of the written statements of each witness whom the Defence intends to call to testify.

(C) The Trial Chamber or a Judge designated from among its members may order the defence to shorten the estimated length of the examination in chief for some witnesses.

(D) The Trial Chamber or a Judge designated from among its members may order the defence to reduce the number of witnesses, if it considers that an excessive number of witnesses are being called to prove the same facts.

(E) After the commencement of the defence case, the defence may, if it considers it to be in the interests of justice, move the Trial Chamber for leave to reinstate the list of witnesses or to vary its decision as to which witnesses are to be called.

Testimony of Witness

90.—(F) The Trial Chamber shall exercise control over the mode and order   **8–71** of interrogating witnesses and presenting evidence so as to:

- i. Make the interrogation and presentation effective for the ascertainment of the truth; and
- ii. Avoid the wasting of time.

(2) Variation of the Prosecution Witness List

It has been a priority of the Trial Chambers to shorten the time it   **8–72** has taken for trials to be completed. To this end, Chambers have restricted the time allowed for the presentation of the Prosecution and Defence cases.

Rule 73*bis*(E) of the ICTY and SCSL Rules of Procedure and Evidence (broadly similar to Rule 73*bis*(D) of the ICTR Rules of Procedure and Evidence) provides the Chamber with a discretionary power to restrict the presentation of evidence in the Prosecution's case.

A bench of three Judges of the Appeals Chamber in the *Prosecutor v. Milošević*, Reasons for refusal of leave to appeal from decision to impose time limit, May 16, 2002, noted that the Chamber's power to control proceedings during the course of the trial is an inherent power and not only based on Rule 73*bis*(E) (see para.10). In this decision the bench found that the 14-month restriction imposed by the Trial Chamber on the presentation of the Prosecution case for the Kosovo indictment, should not be interfered with, and in particular that the Chamber had not invaded the independence of the Prosecutor to conduct its own case (see paras 11–13).

Where the Prosecution wishes to rely on witnesses not on their witness list, they have to file an application for leave to amend pursuant to Rule 73*bis*(E). In *Prosecutor v. Casimir Bizimungu et al.*, Decision on the Motions for Variation of the Prosecutor's Initial Witness List, May 19, 2004, para. 2, the Trial Chamber at the ICTR made it clear that, if the Prosecution intends to file a request to vary the witness list pursuant to Rule 73*bis*(E), the Prosecution should clarify why, and "the Trial Chamber expects diligence and rigour from the Prosecutor in his filings of such witness lists and motions".

In *Malilovic* the Tribunal accepted the inclusion of 34 new exhibits and two new witnesses without any difficulty because they were the results of "recent analysis and interviews" (*Prosecutor v. Malilovic*, Decision on Prosecution's Motions for Leave to Add Exhibits and Witnesses to its Exhibit and Witness List Pursuant to Rule 65*ter* (E), October 17, 2003).

Late disclosure, as well as the probative value of the proposed testimony may lead the Trial Chamber to reject a request to vary the witness list (*Prosecutor v. Bagasora et al.*, Decision on Prosecution Motion for Addition of Witnesses Pursuant to Rule 73*bis*(E), June 26, 2003, para. 14; also see the SCSL case: *Prosecutor v. Norman et al.*, Decision on Prosecution Request for Leave to Call Additional Expert Witness Dr. William Haglund, October 1, 2004, para. 14).

The fact that the delay is caused by internal communication difficulties within the OTP is not necessarily a ground for refusal to add a particular witness to the witness list; this will depend on whether sufficient time is given to the Defence to prepare for the cross-examination of the anticipated witness in order to avoid an element of surprise detrimental to the Defence (*Prosecutor v. Norman et al.*, Decision on Prosecution Request for Leave to Call Additional Witnesses, July 29, 2004, para. 18), or whether the Defence suffers prejudice in any other way (*Prosecutor v. Norman et al.*, Decision on Prosecution Request for Leave to Call Additional Expert Witness Dr. William Haglund, October 1, 2004, paras 17, 20 and 21; *Prosecutor v. Norman et al.*, Decision on Prosecution Request for Leave to Call Additional Witnesses, July 29, 2004, paras 24 and 28).

Whether or not a variation of the witness list is in interest of justice is a discretionary matter for the Trial Chamber to decide and a flexible approach should be adopted. (See *Prosecutor v. Ntagerura et al.*, Decision on Defence for Ntagerura's Motion to Amend its witness List Pursuant to Rule 73*ter*(E), June 4, 2002, para. 10; *Prosecutor v. Ndindiliyimana et al.*, Decision on Prosecution Motion to Vary its List of Witnesses: Rule 73*bis*(E) of the Rules, February 11, 2005, para. 21; *Prosecutor v. Casimir Bizimungu*, Decision on Prosecutor's Very Urgent Motion Pursuant to Rule 73*bis*(E) to Vary the Prosecutor's List of Witnesses Filed on May 25, 2004, September 3, 2004, para. 17). In exercising its discretion the Trial Chamber should consider factors such as the materiality of the testimony, complexity of the case, prejudice to the defence, including elements of surprise, on-going investigations, replacements and collaboration of evidence (Bagosora; *Prosecutor v. Casimir Bizimungu*, Decision on Prosecutor's Very Urgent Motion Pursuant to Rule 73*bis*(E) to Vary the Prosecutor's List of Witnesses Filed on May 25, 2004, September 3, 2004, para. 16; *Prosecutor v. Ndindiliyimana et al.*, Decision on Prosecution Motion to Vary its List of Witnesses: Rule 73*bis*(E) of the Rules, February 11, 2005, para. 20).

> "The Prosecution's duty under the Statute to present the best available evidence to prove its case has to be balanced against the right of the Accused to have adequate time and facilities to prepare his Defence and his right to be tried without undue delay" (See *Prosecutor v. Nahimana et al.*, Decision on Prosecutor's Oral Motion for Leave to Amend the List of Selected Witnesses, June 26, 2001, para. 20; *Prosecutor v. Norman et al.*, Decision on Prosecution Request for Leave to Call Additional Witnesses, July 29, 2004, para. 16).

In another decision in *Nahimana et al.*, the Trial Chamber explained that relevant considerations in assessing whether the "interests of justice" and "good cause" requirements were made out included "the seriousness of the charges, non-compellability of witness testimony and the need for protection of witnesses which it has balanced with dictates of due process and fundamental fairness" (*Prosecutor v. Nahimana et al.*, Decision on Oral Application by Defence Counsel Concerning Witness X, January 19, 2002, para. 20; *Prosecutor v. Norman et al.*, Decision on Prosecution Request for Leave to Call Additional Expert Witness Dr. William Haglund, October 1, 2004, para. 13).

The credibility of the witness to be added to the witness list is not a consideration because that can be challenged in cross-examination. The addition of a witness cannot be used to substantially modify the charges against the Accused (*Prosecutor v. Casimir Bizimungu*, Decision on Prosecutor's Very Urgent Motion Pursuant to Rule 73*bis*(E) to Vary the Prosecutor's List of Witnesses Filed on May 25, 2004, September 3, 2004, paras 21–22).

In the SCSL case of *Norman et al.*, the Trial Chamber held that it must "draw a balance between the Statutory rights of the accused persons, [. . .], to a fair and expeditious trial and equally important and very challenging right of the Prosecution for access to evidence and all material that will contribute not only to discharging the onerous legal burden that it bears to proof the guilt of the accused beyond all reasonable doubt, but also to furnish the Court with evidence that would contribute to fulfilling its mission of ensuring that justice is done to all parties", and that exclusion of the proposed expert evidence "would unduly hinder the expeditiousness of the proceedings, [. . .], are still very far from being concluded, would contravene the principle of equality of arms and defeat the course of justice that this Expert's evidence is intended to serve" (*Prosecutor v. Norman et al.*, Decision on Prosecution Request for Leave to Call Additional Expert Witness Dr. William Haglund, October 1, 2004, paras 22 and 23).

(3) Cross-Examination Pursuant to Rule 90

8–73   In principle, an accused is entitled to make "full answer and defence" to the Prosecutor's case against him. One of the tools to achieve that goal is cross-examination, which is unlimited save in the extent circumscribed under Rules,90(F) and (H) of the ICTY Rules, Rules 90(F) and (G) of the ICTR Rules, and Rule 90(F) SCSL Rules. Rule 90(F) allows the Chamber to intervene, *inter alia* to avoid needless consumption of time. Rule 90(G) of ICTR and 90(H) of ICTY Rules of Procedure and Evidence is used to limit the scope of cross-examination of witnesses (as confirmed in: *Prosecutor v. Kajelijeli*, Decision on Kajelijeli's Motion to Limit the Scope of Cross-Examination of Witness JN, November 12, 2002). Rule 90(F) and (H) ICTY; Rules 90(F) and (G) ICTR, and Rule 90(F) SCSL are, however, not designed to limit cross-examination unnecessarily; only when the questions are not relevant should the Chamber intervene. The Appeals Chamber in *Akayesu* said the following:

"It is clear to the Appeals Chamber that the Presiding Judge of the Trial Chamber had actually sought to underscore the vital distinction to be made, during cross-examination, between matters germane to the case and other extraneous comments of a general nature. In other words, when Judge Kama directed the parties to ask questions that are directly related to the facts as described in the Indictment, and not general questions, he was reminding them, properly so, that cross-examination should not be impeded by matters that where immaterial and/or not relevant to the case [. . .].

Such clarification was in no way intended to restrict or limit cross-examination. It was solely meant to guide the proceedings to ensure that there were no undue departure from the case at bar. Accordingly, the Appeals Chamber finds that in so doing the Presiding Judge was merely performing his duty to exercise control over the process of examination and cross-examination of witnesses appearing before the Chamber as has since been enacted under the Rules. Consequently, the Appeals Chamber finds that Judge Kama's remarks imposed no undue limitation on the scope of cross-examination nor did they unfairly deprive Akayesu of his right to cross-examine Prosecution witnesses" (*Prosecutor v. Akayesu*, Appeals Chamber Judgment, June 1, 2001, para. 318).

Pursuant to Rule 90(G) ICTR and Rule 90(H) ICTY the cross-examining party is entitled to test the credibility of the witness. This is the foundation of the requirement for the the Prosecution (in combination with their duty of disclosure under Rule 66(A)(ii) and Rule 66(B)) to obtain for the defence prior statements, judicial records and any other documents or statements relevant to judicial proceedings of the witness elsewhere, as these documents may prove relevant to test the credibility of the witness pursuant Rule 90(G) ICTR and Rule 90(H) ICTY. For the same reason, an order may be made to re-call the witness for further cross-examination once the said documents have been received (*Prosecutor v. Kajelijeli*, Decision on Juvenal Kajelijeli's Motion Requesting the Recalling of Prosecution Witness GAO, November 2, 2001; *Prosecutor v. Nyiramasuhuko et al.*, Decision on the Defence Motion for Disclosure of the Declarations of the Prosecutor's Witnesses Detained in Rwanda, and All Other Documents or Information Pertaining to the Judicial Proceedings in Their Respect, September 18, 2001; *Prosecutor v. Nahimana, Ngeze and Barayagwiza*, Oral Ruling on September 4, 2001).

Prior versions of Rule 90(G) ICTR and Rule 90(H) of the ICTY Rules of Procedure and Evidence which governed cross-examination of witnesses, were somewhat general in nature. Cross examination, as of right, was limited to points raised in examination-in-chief or other matters affecting the credibility of the witness. By way of amendment of the Rules in plenary dated November 17, 1999 in the case of the ICTY and May 27, 2003 in the case of the ICTR, the parties have a right (as of law) to cross-examine a witness on (1) the subject-matter of the evidence-in-chief; (2) matters affecting the credibility of the witness; (3) the subject-matter of the case (if and where the witness is able to give evidence relevant to the case for the cross-examining party); (4) other matters with the permission of the Chamber. The fundamental difference with old Rule 90(G)of the ICTR Rules and Rule 90(H) ICTY Rules is that there is now an additional ground for cross-examination as of right. Leave is not required in order to cross-examine a witness on the subject-matter of the case, even if not addressed in examination-in-chief, where the witness is able to give relevant evidence. The current rule applies equally to the Prosecution and Defence.

In *Hadžihasanović*, the ICTY Trial Chamber affirmed that the scope of cross-examination is limited to Rule 90(H)(i) of the Rules of Procedure and Evidence (see also *Prosecutor v. Milošević*, Decision on Prosecution Motion for Reconsideration Regarding Evidence of Defence Witnesses Mitar Balevic, Vladislav Jovanovic, Vukasin Andric, and Dobre Aleksovski and Decision *Proprio Motu* Reconsidering Admission of Exhibits 837 and 838 Regarding Evidence of Defence Witness Barry Lituchy, May 17, 2005, para. 9).

In the course of cross-examination, pursuant to ICTY Rule 90(H)(ii), the Prosecution may confront the witness with any disclosed documents. Since the Defence is under no disclosure obligation, the Defence may also confront a prosecution witness with any document considered appropriate. This is so whether or not the relevant document has previously been exhibited, tendered or marked for identification.

Notwithstanding that the Prosecution is required to present its evidence during its case-in-chief, the Prosecution is entitled to confront a defence witness with a document which has not yet been tendered, and may request that it be admitted into evidence, in the course of cross-examination, but only in limited circumstances (*Prosecutor v. Hadžihasanović*, Oral Decision of November 29, 2004, pp. 12525–12527).

The East Timor Regulation and the SCSL Rules have not adopted the amendments to Rule 90(G)-(H). Thus, there is no guideline other than that the Trial Chamber shall exercise control over the mode and order of interrogating witnesses and presenting evidence. In order for the interrogation and presentation to be effective for ascertainment of the truth and avoid wasting time (Rule 90(F) SCSL). Section 36.7 UNTAET Regulation is the same with the addition that the Presiding

Judge shall ensure that the questioning shall take place without pressure and violation of the personal dignity of experts and witnesses.

The ICC regime deserves special attention. ICC Rule 140 is entitled "directions for the conduct of the proceedings and testimony". It is Rule 140, therefore which governs the examination and cross-examination of witnesses. Article 64(8)(b) of the ICC Statute entrusts the Presiding Judge with authority to give such directions as are necessary to ensure the fair and impartial conduct of the trial. Under Rule 140(1), if the Presiding Judge does not otherwise give directions, the parties can decide amongst themselves the order and manner in which evidence is submitted. However, if agreement is not possible between the parties, the Presiding Judge "shall" issue directions. Importantly, Rule 140(2)(d) provides that: "The defence shall have the right to be last to examine a witness." It appears that this is so whether the witness falling for questioning is a Defence witness or not.

There is no rule in the ICTY and ICTR regarding when a witness should testify. In some common-law systems like England and Wales, if an accused decides to give evidence, he shall give evidence first, before any other evidence for the defence is called. This is not a requirement in the ICTY or ICTR. Rule 140(3) of the ICC Rules of Procedure and Evidence provides that a witness other than an expert, or an investigator, shall not be present when the testimony of another witness is given. However, a witness who has heard the testimony of another witness will not, for that reason alone, be disqualified from testifying. However, when a witness testifies who has heard the testimony of others, that fact will be "noted in the record and considered by the Trial Chamber when considering evidence". Given the weight a Trial Chamber may give evidence could be affected by whether a witness has heard other testimony relating to the case (particularly, it would appear, other testimony from a witness belonging to the party that calls him) this may prove an incentive for accused persons who wish to give evidence, to give evidence first before other defence witnesses are heard. It will be interesting to see how this rule impacts upon the work of the ICC, because proceedings are likely to be public, open, and widely reported and disseminated, particularly in the geographical areas related to the crime where one would expect most of the witnesses to come from. Even if witnesses are not "present" when the testimony of other witnesses are given, it seems that many will be aware of the evidence given through television, internet, radio and print media as long as trials are public and freely reported.

See also Section E above on Presentation of the Evidence

G. TRIAL MOTIONS

(1) Statutory provisions and rules

ICC Rules of Procedure and Evidence, r. 134

Motions relating to the trial proceedings

8–74   **134.**—1. Prior to the commencement of the trial, the Trial Chamber on its own motion, or at the request of the Prosecutor or the defence, may rule on any issue concerning the conduct of the proceedings. Any request from the

Prosecutor or the defence shall be in writing and, unless the request is for an ex parte procedure, served on the other party. For all requests other than those submitted for an *ex parte* procedure, the other party shall have the opportunity to file a response.

2. At the commencement of the trial, the Trial Chamber shall ask the Prosecutor and the defence whether they have any objections or observations concerning the conduct of the proceedings which have arisen since the confirmation hearings. Such objections or observations may not be raised or made again on a subsequent occasion in the trial proceedings, without leave of the Trial Chamber in this proceeding.

3. After the commencement of the trial, the Trial Chamber, on its own motion, or at the request of the Prosecutor or the defence, may rule on issues that arise during the course of the trial.

ICTY

ICTY Rules of Procedure and Evidence, rr. 72, 73

Preliminary Motions

72.—(A) Preliminary motions, being motions which   **8–75**
    (i) challenge jurisdiction;
    (ii) allege defects in the form of the indictment;
    (iii) seek the severance of counts joined in one indictment under Rule 49 or seek separate trials under Rule 82 (B); or
    (iv) raise objections based on the refusal of a request for assignment of counsel made under Rule 45 (C) shall be in writing and be brought not later than thirty days after disclosure by the Prosecutor to the defence of all material and statements referred to in Rule 66 (A)(i) and shall be disposed of not later than sixty days after they were filed and before the commencement of the opening statements provided for in Rule 84.

(B) Decisions on preliminary motions are without interlocutory appeal save
    (i) in the case of motions challenging jurisdiction;
    (ii) in other cases where certification has been granted by the Trial Chamber, which may grant such certification if the decision involves an issue that would significantly affect the fair and expeditious conduct of the proceedings or the outcome of the trial, and for which, in the opinion of the Trial Chamber, an immediate resolution by the Appeals Chamber may materially advance the proceedings.

(C) Appeals under paragraph (B)(i) shall be filed within fifteen days and requests for certification under paragraph (B)(ii) shall be filed within seven days of filing of the impugned decision. Where such decision is rendered orally, this time-limit shall run from the date of the oral decision, unless
    (i) the party challenging the decision was not present or represented when the decision was pronounced, in which case the time-limit shall run from the date on which the challenging party is notified of the oral decision; or
    (ii) the Trial Chamber has indicated that a written decision will follow, in which case, the time-limit shall run from filing of the written decision.

If certification is given, a party shall appeal to the Appeals Chamber within seven days of the filing of the decision to certify.

(D) For the purpose of paragraphs (A)(i) and (B)(i), a motion challenging jurisdiction refers exclusively to a motion which challenges an indictment on the ground that it does not relate to:

    (i) any of the persons indicated in Articles 1, 6, 7 and 9 of the Statute;
    (ii) the territories indicated in Articles 1, 8 and 9 of the Statute;
    (iii) the period indicated in Articles 1, 8 and 9 of the Statute;
    (iv) any of the violations indicated in Articles 2, 3, 4, 5 and 7 of the Statute.

(E) An appeal brought under paragraph (B)(i) may not be proceeded with if a bench of three Judges of the Appeals Chamber, assigned by the President, decides that the appeal is not capable of satisfying the requirement of paragraph (D), in which case the appeal shall be dismissed.(Amended 1 Dec 2000 and 13 Dec 2000, amended 12 Dec 2002)

Other Motions

8–76   **73.**—(A) After a case is assigned to a Trial Chamber, either party may at any time move before the Chamber by way of motion, not being a preliminary motion, for appropriate ruling or relief. Such motions may be written or oral, at the discretion of the Trial Chamber.

(B) Decisions on all motions are without interlocutory appeal save with certification by the Trial Chamber, which may grant such certification if the decision involves an issue that would significantly affect the fair and expeditious conduct of the proceedings or the outcome of the trial, and for which, in the opinion of the Trial Chamber, an immediate resolution by the Appeals Chamber may materially advance the proceedings.

(C) Requests for certification shall be filed within seven days of the filing of the impugned decision. Where such decision is rendered orally, this time-limit shall run from the date of the oral decision, unless

    (i) the party challenging the decision was not present or represented when the decision was pronounced, in which case the time-limit shall run from the date on which the challenging party is notified of the oral decision; or
    (ii) the Trial Chamber has indicated that a written decision will follow, in which case the time-limit shall run from filing of the written decision.

If certification is given, a party shall appeal to the Appeals Chamber within seven days of the filing of the decision to certify.

(D) Irrespective of any sanctions which may be imposed under Rule 46 (A), when a Chamber finds that a motion is frivolous or is an abuse of process, the Registrar shall withhold payment of fees associated with the production of that motion and/ or costs thereof.

ICTR

ICTR Rules of Procedure and Evidence, rr. 72, 73

Preliminary Motions

8–77   **72.**—(A) Preliminary motions, being motions which:
    (i) challenge jurisdiction;
    (ii) allege defects in the form of the indictment;
    (iii) seek the severance of counts joined in one indictment under Rule 49 or seek separate trials under Rule 82 (B); or
    (iv) raise objections based on the refusal of a request for assignment of counsel made under Rule 45 (C) shall be in writing and be brought not later than thirty days after disclosure by the Prosecutor to the Defence of all material and statements referred to in Rule 66 (A) (i) and shall be disposed of not later than sixty days after they were filed

and before the commencement of the opening statements provided for in Rule 84. The Trial Chamber may rule on such motions based solely on the briefs of the parties, unless it is decided to hear the motion in open Court.

(B) Decisions on preliminary motions are without interlocutory appeal, save:

(i) in the case of motions challenging jurisdiction, where an appeal by either party lies as of right;

(ii) in other cases where certification has been granted by the Trial Chamber, which may grant such certification if the decision involves an issue that would significantly affect the fair and expeditious conduct of the proceedings or the outcome of the trial, and for which, in the opinion of the Trial Chamber, an immediate resolution by the Appeals Chamber may materially advance the proceedings.

(C) Appeals under paragraph (B)(i) shall be filed within fifteen days and requests for certification under paragraph (B)(ii) shall be filed within seven days of filing of the impugned decision. Where such decision is rendered orally, this time-limit shall run from the date of the oral decision, unless

(i) the party challenging the decision was not present or represented when the decision was pronounced, in which case the time- limit shall run from the date on which the challenging party is notified of the oral decision; or

(ii) the Trial Chamber has indicated that a written decision will follow, in which case, the time-limit shall run from filing of the written decision.

If certification is given, a party shall appeal to the Appeals Chamber within seven days of the filing of the decision to certify.

(D) For purposes of paragraphs (A)(i) and (B)(i), a motion challenging jurisdiction refers exclusively to a motion which challenges an indictment on the ground that it does not relate to:

(i) any of the persons indicated in Articles 1, 5, 6 and 8 of the Statute;

(ii) the territories indicated in Articles 1, 7 and 8 of the Statute;

(iii) the period indicated in Articles 1, 7, and 8 of the Statute; or

(iv) any of the violations indicated in Articles 2, 3, 4 and 6 of the Statute.

(E) An appeal brought under paragraph (B)(i) may not be proceeded with if a bench of three Judges of the Appeals Chamber, assigned by the presiding Judge of the Appeals Chamber, decides that the appeal is not capable of satisfying the requirements of paragraph (D), in which case the appeal shall be dismissed.

(F) Objections to the form of the indictment, including an amended indictment, shall be raised by a party in one motion only, unless otherwise allowed by a Trial Chamber.

(G) Failure to comply with the time limits prescribed in this Rule shall constitute a waiver of the rights. The Trial Chamber may, however, grant relief from the waiver upon showing good cause.

Other Motions

73.—(A) After a case is assigned to a Trial Chamber, either party may at any time move before the Chamber by way of motion, not being a preliminary motion, for appropriate ruling or relief. Such motions may be written or oral, at the discretion of the Trial Chamber.

(B) Decisions on all motions are without interlocutory appeal save with certification by the Trial Chamber, which may grant such certification if the decision involves an issue that would significantly affect the fair and expeditious conduct of the proceedings or the outcome of the trial, and for which, in the opinion of the Trial Chamber, an immediate resolution by the Appeals Chamber may materially advance the proceedings.

(C) Requests for certification shall be filed within seven days of the filing of the impugned decision. Where such decision is rendered orally, this time-limit shall run from the date of the oral decision, unless

> (i) the party challenging the decision was not present or represented when the decision was pronounced, in which case the time-limit shall run from the date on which the challenging party is notified of the oral decision; or
>
> (ii) the Trial Chamber has indicated that a written decision will follow, in which case the time-limit shall run from filing of the written decision.

If certification is given, a party shall appeal to the Appeals Chamber within seven days of the filing of the decision to certify.

(D) Irrespective of any sanctions which may be imposed under Rule 46 (A), when a Chamber finds that a motion is frivolous or is an abuse of process, the Registrar shall withhold payment of fees associated with the production of that motion and/ or costs thereof.

East Timor

Regulation 2000/30, s. 27 (as amended by Regulation 2001/25)

Motions

8–78   27.—27.1 Preliminary motions may be raised prior to the commencement of the trial. Such motions are those which:

> (a) allege defects in the form of the indictment;
> (b) seek severance of counts joined in one indictment or separate trials in cases of co-accused; or
> (c) raise objections based upon refusal of a request for assignment of counsel.

27.2 After the case is assigned to a panel or judge, any party may at any time lodge a motion with the court, other than a preliminary motion as described in the preceding subsection, for appropriate relief. Motions for appropriate relief may be oral or written at the discretion of the Court

27.3 Decisions on motions, except as provided in Sections 23 and 27.4 of the present regulation, are not subject to interlocutory appeal. The granting of a motion to dismiss the case for any reason shall be deemed a final decision in the case and shall be subject to appeal as provided in Part VII of the present regulation.

27.4 The Court of Appeal may grant leave to immediately appeal from a decision on a motion where:

> (a) the decision from which appeal is sought would cause such prejudice to the case of the party seeking leave to appeal as could not be cured by the final decision of the trial;
> (b) the issue on which appeal is sought is of general importance to proceedings before the courts of East Timor; or,
> (c) upon other good cause being shown by the party seeking leave to appeal.

SCSL

SCSL Rules of Procedure and Evidence, rr. 72, 73

Preliminary Motions

72.—(A) Preliminary motions by either party shall be brought within 21 **8–79** days following disclosure by the Prosecutor to the Defence of all the material envisaged by Rule 66(A)(i).

(B) Preliminary motions by the accused are:

    i. Objections based on lack of jurisdiction;

    ii. Objections based on defects in the form of the indictment;

    iii. Applications for severance of crimes joined in one indictment under Rule 49, or for separate trials under Rule 82(B);

    iv. Objections based on the denial of request for assignment of counsel; or

    v. Objections based on abuse of process.

(C) Objections based on lack of jurisdiction or to the form of the indictment, including an amended indictment, shall be raised by a party in one motion only, unless otherwise allowed by the Trial Chamber.

(D) The Trial Chamber shall, except as provided by Sub-Rules (E) and (F) below, dispose of preliminary motions before the trial, and its decisions thereon shall not be subject to interlocutory appeal.

(E) Preliminary motions made in the Trial Chamber prior to the Prosecutor's opening statement which raise a serious issue relating to jurisdiction shall be referred to a bench of at least three Appeals Chamber Judges, where they will proceed to a determination as soon as practicable.

(F) Preliminary motions made in the Trial Chamber prior to the Prosecutor's opening statement which, in the opinion of the Trial Chamber, raise an issue that would significantly affect the fair and expeditious conduct of the proceedings or the outcome of a trial shall be referred to a bench of at least three Appeals Chamber Judges, where they will proceed to a determination as soon as practicable.

(G) Where the Trial Chamber refers a motion to the Appeals Chamber pursuant to Sub-Rules (E) or (F) above, any party wishing to file additional written submissions must seek leave from the Appeals Chamber which will impose time limits for further submissions, responses and replies if leave is granted.

(H) References by the Trial Chamber pursuant to Sub-Rules (E) and (F) above shall not operate as a stay of proceedings. Such references shall not operate as a stay of the trial itself unless the Trial or Appeal Chamber so orders.

(I) This Rule shall be deemed to have entered into force on the 7th of March, 2003.

See Chapter 19 for discussion on Interlocutory Appeal.

Motions

73.—(A) Subject to Rule 72, either party may move before the Designated Judge or a Trial Chamber for appropriate ruling or relief after the initial appearance of the accused. The Designated Judge or the Trial Chamber, or a Judge designated by the Trial Chamber from among its members, shall rule on such motions based solely on the written submissions of the parties, unless it is decided to hear the parties in open Court.

(B) Decisions rendered on such motions are without interlocutory appeal. However, in exceptional circumstances and to avoid irreparable prejudice to a party, the Trial Chamber may give leave to appeal. Such leave should be sought within 3 days of the decision and shall not operate as a stay of proceedings unless the Trial Chamber so orders.

(C) Whenever the Trial Chamber and the Appeals Chamber of the Court are seized of the same Motion raising the same or similar issue or issues, the Trial Chamber shall stay proceedings on the said Motion before it until a final determination of the said Motion by the Appeals Chamber.

(D) Irrespective of any sanctions which may be imposed under Rule 46(A), when a Chamber finds that a motion is frivolous or is an abuse of process, the Registrar shall withhold payment of all or part of the fees associated with the production of that motion and/ or costs thereof.

H. SUBMISSION OF NO CASE TO ANSWER

(1) Statutory provisions and rules

ICC

8–80 There is no specific provision for a "no case to answer" submission in trial proceedings before the ICC. The general provision on motions in trial proceedings could be relied upon to bring such an application:

ICC Rules of Procedure and Evidence, r. 134(3)

Motions Relating to the Trial Proceedings
8–81 134.—3. After the commencement of the trial, the Trial Chamber, on its own motion, or at the request of the Prosecutor or the defence, may rule on issues that arise during the course of the trial.

ICTY

8–82 Until December 8, 2004 ICTY Rule 98*bis* was equivalent to ICTR Rule 98*bis*. By amendment of December 8, 2004 Rule 98*bis* was amended into:

ICTY Rules of Procedure and Evidence, r. 98*bis*

8–83 98*bis*—At the close of the Prosecutor's case, the Trial Chamber shall, by oral decision and after hearing the oral submissions of the parties, enter a judgment of acquittal on any count if there is no evidence capable of supporting a conviction.

ICTR

ICTR Rules of Procedure and Evidence, r. 98*bis*

Motion for Judgment of Acquittal

98*bis***.**—(A) An accused may file a motion for the entry of judgement of acquittal on one or more offences charged in the indictment within seven days after the close of the Prosecutor's case and, in any event, prior to the presentation of evidence by the defence pursuant to Rule 85 (A)(ii).   **8–84**

(B) The Trial Chamber shall order the entry of judgement of acquittal on motion of an accused or *proprio motu* if it finds that the evidence is insufficient to sustain a conviction on that or those charges.

East Timor

There is no specific provision for a "half-time" submission before the special courts for East Timor; however, such an application could arguably be made under the following general provision: **8–85**

Regulation 2000/30, s.30 (as amended by Regulation 2001/25)

Trial Proceedings

30.—30.8 The accused shall sit beside his or her legal representative and may consult with him or her throughout the hearing without any restriction.   **8–86**

SCSL

SCSL Rules of Procedure and Evidence, r. 98

Motion for Judgment of Acquittal

98.—If, after the close of the case for the prosecution, there is no evidence capable of supporting a conviction on one or more counts of the indictment, the Trial Chamber shall enter a judgment of acquittal on those counts.   **8–87**

(2) Test to be applied

Rule 98*bis* gives effect to the presumption of innocence and the principle that the Prosecutor has the burden to prove every element of the counts charged beyond a reasonable doubt (Rule 87(A)): *The Prosecutor v. Delalic et al.*, Judgment of November 16, 1998, paras 599 and 601. See also: *Prosecutor v. André Ntagerura, Emmanuel Bagambiki, Samuel Imanishimwe*, Separate and Concurring Opinion (sic) of Judge Williams on Imanishimwe's Defence Motion for Judgment of Acquittal on Count of Conspiracy to Commit Genocide Pursuant to Rule 98*bis*, March 13, 2002, para.4).   **8–88**

The ICTY Appeals Chamber in *Prosecutor v. Jelisic* held in its decision of July 5, 2001 that:

> "The capacity of the prosecution evidence (if accepted) to sustain a conviction beyond reasonable doubt by a reasonable trier of fact is the key concept; thus the test is not whether the trier would in fact arrive at a conviction beyond reasonable doubt on the prosecution evidence (if accepted) but whether it could. At the close of the case for the prosecution, the Chamber may find that the prosecution evidence is sufficient to sustain a conviction beyond reasonable doubt and yet, even if no defence evidence is subsequently adduced, proceed to acquit at the end of the trial, if in its own view of the evidence, the prosecution has not in fact proved guilt beyond reasonable doubt" (para. 37).

This decision followed the Appeals Chamber's earlier decision in *Prosecutor v. Delalic et al.*, February 20, 2001, para. 434. Also see, *Prosecutor v. Kunarac*, Decision on motion for acquittal, July 3, 2000, pp. 3–6; and, *Prosecutor v. Kvočka*, Decision on defence motions for acquittal, December 15, 2000, para. 12.

The Trial Chamber in *Semanza* emphasised that on the basis of this standard "all that is required of the Prosecution is to establish a *prima facie* case against the Accused": *The Prosecutor v. Semanza*, Decision on the Defence Motion for a Judgment of Acquittal in Respect of Laurent Semanza after Quashing the Counts contained in the Third Amended Indictment (Article 98*bis* of the Rules of Procedure and Evidence) and Decision on the Prosetuor's Urgent Motion for Suspension of Time-Limit for Response to the Defence Motion for a Judgment of Acquittal, September 27, 2001, para 15.

The evidence must be such that a reasonable trier of fact *could* convict, not that it *would* or *should* convict (*Prosecutor v. Jelisic*, Appeals Chamber Judgment, para.37; *Prosecutor v. Kordić and Čerkez*, Decision on Defence Motions for Judgment of Acquittal, April 6, 2000, para. 26; *Prosecutor v. Milošević*, Decision on Motion for Judgment of Acquittal, June 16, 2004, para.13(6)), and on which a reasonable Chamber could be satisfied beyond reasonable doubt that the Accused is guilty (*Milošević*, para. 13(7)). This standard "is not met by any evidence; there must be some evidence which could properly lead to a conviction" (*Prosecutor v. Kordić and Čerkez*, Decision on Defence Motions for Judgment of Acquittal, April 6, 2000, para. 26). In determining whether there is such evidence the Trial Chamber must assess whether the Prosecution evidence is actually probative of the elements of crimes charged in the indictment (*Prosecutor v. Bagosora et al.*, Decision on Motions on Judgment of Acquittal, February 2, 2005, para. 10).

A 98*bis* Motion may succeed where the Prosecutor did not present sufficient evidence to support all essential ingredients of a count: "if on the basis of evidence adduced by the Prosecution, an ingredient required as a matter of law to constitute the crime is missing, that evidence would also be insufficient to sustain a conviction" (*Prosecutor v. Nahimana, Barayagwiza, Ngeze*, Reasons for Oral Decision of September 17, 2002 on the Motions for Acquittal, Rule 98*bis* of the Rules of Procedure and Evidence, September 25, 2002, para. 19. See also: Jelisic Appeals Chamber Judgment, paras 59–61, and: *Prosecutor v. Sikirica, Dozen, and Kolundzija*, Judgment on Defence Motions to Acquit, September 3, 2001, para. 9). At the submission of no case to answer stage of proceedings (sometime called "half time"), Trial Chambers are not concerned with "the respective credit of witnesses, or [..] the strengths and weaknesses of contradictory or different evidence, whether oral or documentary" (*Prosecutor v. Strugar*, Decision on Defence Motion Requesting Judgment of Acquittal Pursuant to Rule 98*bis*, June 21, 2004) unless the Prosecution's case has completely broken down, "either on its own presentation, or as a result of such fundamental questions being raised through cross-examination as to the reliability and credibility of witnesses that the Prosecution is left without a case" (*Prosecutor v. Kordić and Čerkez*, Decision on Defence Motions for Judgment of Acquittal, April 6, 2000, para. 28. See also : *Prosecutor v. Brdjanin*, Concerning Allegations Against Milka Maglov, Decision on Motion for Acquittal Pursuant to Rule 98*bis*, March 19, 2004; *Prosecutor v. Naletilic and Martinovic*, Decision on Motions for Acquittal, February 28, 2002, para. 20). The Trial Chamber in *The Prosecutor v. Milošević*, Decision on Motion for Judgment of Acquittal, June 16, 2004, para. 31(2) held: "Where there is some evidence, but it is such that, taken at its highest, a Trial Chamber could not convict on it, the Motion is to be allowed. This will be the case even if the weakness in the evidence derives from the weight to be attached to it, for example, the credibility of a witness. This is in accordance with the exception to the general principle in common law jurisdictions that issues of credibility and reliability must be left to the jury as the tribunal of fact.

There is a clear development both at the ICTY and the ICTR to limit Rule 98*bis* applications. While the ICTY presently only allows oral applications, recent case law at the ICTR suggests that Trial Chambers are also becoming increasingly determined in seeking to discourage defence teams from going "overboard" with 98*bis* Motions. It does seem that a practice had emerged in which the procedural safeguard of such submissions was being abused, with every count on the indictment sometimes being challenged, despite the known lower threshold applicable at the stage of no case to answer. In other cases such as in *Bagosora et al.*, the Trial Chamber dismissed all grounds and submissions contained in the Defence submission of no case to answer. The Trial Chamber noted that the written submission itself extended to more than 600 pages. (*Prosecutor v. Bagosora et al.*, Decision on Motions on Judgment of Acquittal, February 2, 2005, paras 8–9).

The first oral 98*bis* application under the new ICTY Rule was rendered in *Oric* on June 8, 2005. The Trial Chamber affirmed that "the last amendment to Rule 98*bis* does not in any way change the standard of review applied by the Trial Chamber in its Rule 98*bis* exercise which therefore remains as set out and repeatedly applied by these Trial Chambers, set out in the *Jelisic* Appeals Judgment (*Prosecutor v. Oric, Oral 98*bis *Ruling, June 8, 2005, T.*8983). In that case, two counts on the indictment were dismissed. (*ibid.*, tt. 9032–9034).

There is currently, no equivalent of Rule 98(*bis*) in the ICC Rules of Procedure and Evidence. It appears open, however, to the Defence to make any appropriate submission of no case to answer at the close of the Prosecution case. Indeed, Rule 134(3) of the ICC Rule would entitle the Trial Chamber to dismiss any counts or counts which had not been proved to the requisite standard *proprio moto*. Rule 134(3) provides that "[a]fter the commencement of the trial, the Trial Chamber, on its own motion, or at the request of the Prosecutor or the defence, may rule on issues that arise during the course of trial."

I. Closing Arguments

(1) Statutory provisions and rules

ICC Rules of Procedure and Evidence, r. 141

Closure of evidence and closing statements

8–89   **141.**—1. The Presiding Judge shall declare when the submission of evidence is closed.

2. The Presiding Judge shall invite the Prosecutor and the defence to make their closing statements. The defence shall always have the opportunity to speak last.

ICTY Rules of Procedure and Evidence, r. 86

Closing Arguments

8–90   **86.**—(A) After the presentation of all the evidence, the Prosecutor may present a closing argument; whether or not the Prosecutor does so, the defence may make a closing argument. The Prosecutor may present a rebuttal argument to which the defence may present a rejoinder.

(B) Not later than five days prior to presenting a closing argument, a party shall file a final trial brief.

(C) The parties shall also address matters of sentencing in closing arguments.

ICTR Rules of Procedure and Evidence, r. 86

Closing Arguments

8–91   **86.**—(A) After the presentation of all the evidence, the Prosecutor may present a closing argument. Whether or not the Prosecutor does so, the Defence may make a closing argument. The Prosecutor may present a rebuttal argument to which the Defence may present a rejoinder.

(B) A party shall file a final trial brief with the Trial Chamber not later tha n five days prior to the day set for the presentation of that party's closing argument.

(C) The parties shall also address matters of sentencing in closing arguments.

East Timor

Regulation 2000/30, s.38 (as amended by Regulation 2001/25)

Final Statements

8–92   **38.** After all evidence has been presented and considered, the Court shall close the presentation and hearing of evidence and shall request the Public Prosecutor to make his or her closing statement. Thereafter, the accused or his or her legal representative shall be allowed to make a closing statement.

SCSL Rules of Procedure and Evidence, r. 86

Closing Arguments

86.—(A) After the presentation of all the evidence, the Prosecutor shall and **8–93**
the defence may present a closing argument.

(B) A party shall file a final trial brief with the Trial Chamber not later than
five days prior to the day set for the presentation of that party's closing
argument.

(C) The parties shall inform the Trial Chamber of the anticipated length of
closing arguments; the Trial Chamber may limit the length of those arguments
in the interests of justice.

J. Amicus Curiae

(1) Statutory provisions and rules

ICC Rules of Procedure and Evidence, r. 103

Amicus curiae and other forms of submission

103.—1. At any stage of the proceedings, a Chamber may, if it considers it **8–94**
desirable for the proper determination of the case, invite or grant leave to a
State, organization or person to submit, in writing or orally, any observation on
any issue that the Chamber deems appropriate.

2. The Prosecutor and the defence shall have the opportunity to respond to
the observations submitted under sub-rule 1.

3. A written observation submitted under sub-rule 1 shall be filed with the
Registrar, who shall provide copies to the Prosecutor and the defence. The
Chamber shall determine what time limits shall apply to the filing of such
observations.

ICTY/ICTR/SCSL

ICTY Rules of Procedure and Evidence, r. 74

Amicus Curiae

74. A Chamber may, if it considers it desirable for the proper determination **8–95**
of the case, invite or grant leave to a State, organization or person to appear
before it and make submissions on any issue specified by the Chamber.

East Timor

Regulation 2000/30, s.37.2 (as amended by Regulation 2001/25)

Other Evidence

37.—37.2 The court, on its own motion or on request by a party, may order **8–96**
the re-enactment of the crime scheme. In that case, the court and the parties
shall be present at the location of the crime.

An *amicus curiae* can be appointed to assist the Trial Chamber in the following ways:
- (a) making any submissions properly open to the accused by way of preliminary or other pre-trial motion;
- (b) making any submissions or objections to evidence properly open to the accused during the trial proceedings and cross-examining witnesses as appropriate;
- (c) drawing to the attention of the Trial Chamber any exculpatory or mitigating evidence; and
- (d) acting in any other way which designated counsel considers appropriate in order to secure a fair trial.

(*Prosecutor v. Milošević*, Order Inviting Designation of *Amicus Curiae*, August 30, 2001; October 30, 2001; November 23, 2001)

In a later Decision the Trial Chamber added the following areas where the *amicus curiae* should assist:
- (1) drawing the attention of the Trial Chamber to any defences, for example, self-defence, which may properly be open to the accused to raise on the evidence; and
- (2) making submissions as to the relevance, if any, in this trial of the NATO air campaign in Kosovo;
- (3) identifying witnesses whom the Trial Chamber may itself wish to call pursuant to Rule 98 of the Rules;
- (4) in any other way the Trial Chamber considers appropriate.

(*Prosecutor v. Milošević*, Order Concerning Amici Curiae, January 11, 2002)

An *amicus curiae* must be impartial and a reasonable perception of bias on the part of an *amicus curiae* may trigger the Trial Chamber to revoke the person's appointment as *amicus curiae*. In its Decision Concerning an Amicus Curiae of October 10, 2002, the Trial Chamber in *Milosevic* put it as follows:

"Implicit in the concept of an amicus curiae is the trust that the court reposes in "the friend" to act fairly in the performance of his duties. In the circumstances, the Chamber cannot be confident that the amicus curiae will discharge his duties (which include bringing to its attention any defences open to the accused) with the required impartiality."

II. RIGHTS OF THE ACCUSED

A. FAIR TRIAL GUARANTEES

(1) Statutory provisions and rules

ICC Statute, Art. 64, 66, 67

Functions and powers of the Trial Chamber

8–97   64.—2. The Trial Chamber shall ensure that a trial is fair and expeditious and is conducted with full respect for the rights of the accused and due regard for the protection of victims and witnesses.

Presumption of innocence

66.—1. Everyone shall be presumed innocent until proved guilty before the   **8–98**
Court in accordance with the applicable law.

2. The onus is on the Prosecutor to prove the guilt of the accused.

3. In order to convict the accused, the Court must be convinced of the guilt
of the accused beyond reasonable doubt.

Rights of the accused

67.—1. In the determination of any charge, the accused shall be entitled to   **8–99**
a public hearing, having regard to the provisions of this Statute, to a fair
hearing conducted impartially, and to the following minimum guarantees, in
full equality:

(a) To be informed promptly and in detail of the nature, cause and
content of the charge, in a language which the accused fully understands and speaks;

(b) To have adequate time and facilities for the preparation of the
defence and to communicate freely with counsel of the accused's
choosing in confidence;

(c) To be tried without undue delay;

(d) Subject to article 63, paragraph 2, to be present at the trial, to
conduct the defence in person or through legal assistance of the
accused's choosing, to be informed, if the accused does not have legal
assistance, of this right and to have legal assistance assigned by the
Court in any case where the interests of justice so require, and
without payment if the accused lacks sufficient means to pay for it;

(e) To examine, or have examined, the witnesses against him or her and
to obtain the attendance and examination of witnesses on his or her
behalf under the same conditions as witnesses against him or her. The
accused shall also be entitled to raise defences and to present other
evidence admissible under this Statute;

(f) To have, free of any cost, the assistance of a competent interpreter
and such translations as are necessary to meet the requirements of
fairness, if any of the proceedings of or documents presented to the
Court are not in a language which the accused fully understands and
speaks;

(g) Not to be compelled to testify or to confess guilt and to remain silent,
without such silence being a consideration in the determination of
guilt or innocence;

(h) To make an unsworn oral or written statement in his or her defence;
and

(i) Not to have imposed on him or her any reversal of the burden of proof
or any onus of rebuttal.

2. In addition to any other disclosure provided for in this Statute, the
Prosecutor shall, as soon as practicable, disclose to the defence evidence in the
Prosecutor's possession or control which he or she believes shows or tends to
show the innocence of the accused, or to mitigate the guilt of the accused, or
which may affect the credibility of prosecution evidence. In case of doubt as to
the application of this paragraph, the Court shall decide.

ICTY

ICTY Statute, Art. 21

Rights of the accused

21.—1. All persons shall be equal before the International Tribunal.   **8–100**

2. In the determination of charges against him, the accused shall be entitled to a fair and public hearing, subject to article 22 of the Statute.

3. The accused shall be presumed innocent until proved guilty according to the provisions of the present Statute.

4. In the determination of any charge against the accused pursuant to the present Statute, the accused shall be entitled to the following minimum guarantees, in full equality:

    (a) to be informed promptly and in detail in a language which he understands of the nature and cause of the charge against him;

    (b) to have adequate time and facilities for the preparation of his defence and to communicate with counsel of his own choosing;

    (c) to be tried without undue delay;

    (d) to be tried in his presence, and to defend himself in person or through legal assistance of his own choosing; to be informed, if he does not have legal assistance, of this right; and to have legal assistance assigned to him, in any case where the interests of justice so require, and without payment by him in any such case if he does not have sufficient means to pay for it;

    (e) to examine, or have examined, the witnesses against him and to obtain the attendance and examination of witnesses on his behalf under the same conditions as witnesses against him;

    (f) to have the free assistance of an interpreter if he cannot understand or speak the language used in the International Tribunal;

    (g) not to be compelled to testify against himself or to confess guilt.

ICTR

ICTR Statute, Art. 20

Rights of the Accused

8–101   **20.**—1. All persons shall be equal before the International Tribunal for Rwanda.

2. In the determination of charges against him or her, the accused shall be entitled to a fair and public hearing, subject to article 21 of the Statute.

3. The accused shall be presumed innocent until proven guilty according to the provisions of the present Statute.

4. In determination of any charge against the accused pursuant to the present Statute, the accused shall be entitled to the following minimum guarantees, in full equality:

    (a) To be informed promptly and in detail in a language which he or she understands of the nature and cause of the charge against him or her;

    (b) To have adequate time and facilities for the preparation of his or her defence and to communicate with counsel of his or her own choosing;

    (c) To be tried without undue delay;

    (d) To be tried in his or her presence, and to defend himself or herself in person or through legal assistance of his or her own choosing; to be informed, if he or she does not have legal assistance, of this right; and to have legal assistance assigned to him or her, in any case where the interest of justice so require, and without payment by him or her in any such case if he or she does not have sufficient means to pay for it;

    (e) To examine, or have examined, the witnesses against him or her and to obtain the attendance and examination of witnesses on his or her behalf under the same conditions as witnesses against him or her;

    (f) To have the free assistance of an interpreter if her or she cannot understand or speak the language used in the International Tribunal for Rwanda;

    (g) Not to be compelled to testify against himself or herself or to confess guilt.

East Timor

Regulation 2000/30, ss.2, 6 (as amended by Regulation 2001/15)

Fair Trial and Due Process

2.—2.1 All persons shall be equal before the courts of law. In the determina- **8–102** tion of any criminal charge against a person or of the rights and obligations of a person in a suit of law, that person shall be entitled to a fair and public hearing by a competent court established in accordance with UNTAET Regulations No. 2000/11, No. 2000/14 and No. 2000/15.

2.2 Criminal justice shall be administered by the Courts according to the law. No person may be subjected to any kind of punishment except under the provisions prescribed by the law.

2.3 No person shall be subjected to arbitrary arrest or detention. No person shall be deprived of his or her liberty except on such grounds and in accordance with such procedures as prescribed in the present regulation and other applicable UNTAET Regulations.

Rights of the Suspect and Accused

6.—6.1 All persons accused of a crime shall be presumed innocent until **8–103** proven guilty in accordance with the law, the provisions of this and other UNTAET regulations.

6.2 Immediately upon arrest, the suspect shall be informed by the arresting police officers of the reasons for his or her arrest and any charges against him or her, and shall also be informed that he or she has the following rights:

    (a) the right to remain silent and not to admit guilt, and that silence will not be interpreted as an admission;

    (b) the right to contact a relative or close friend and be visited by such person;

    (c) the right to contact a legal representative and communicate with him or her confidentially;

    (d) the right that a legal representative will be appointed if the suspect is unable to pay for a lawyer;

    (e) the right to be brought before an Investigating Judge within 72 hours upon arrest;

    (f) the right to be questioned in the presence of a legal representative, unless the right is waived; and

    (g) if the suspect is a foreign national, the right to contact diplomatic or consular officials of his or her country.

6.3 At every stage of the proceedings, the suspect and the accused shall be informed by the public prosecutor that he or she has the following rights:

    (a) the right to be assisted by and to communicate freely and without supervision with a legal representative of his or her own choosing and to have such legal representation provided to him or her without cost where the suspect does not have sufficient means to pay for it;

    (b) the right to be informed in detail, and in a language which he or she understands, of the nature and cause of the charges against him or her;

    (c) the right to have the free assistance of an interpreter if he or she cannot understand or speak one of the official languages of the court;

   (d) the right to have adequate time and facilities for the preparation of his or her defense;

   (e) the right to request the Public Prosecutor or Investigating Judge to order or conduct specific investigations in order to establish his or her innocence;

   (f) the right to be tried without undue delay;

   (g) the right to examine, or have examined, the witnesses against him or her and to obtain the attendance and examination of witnesses on his or her behalf under the same conditions as adverse witnesses;

   (h) the right not to be compelled to testify against himself or herself or to admit guilt, and that if he or she chooses not to speak in the proceeding, such silence will not be held against him or her in the determination of innocence or guilt;

   (i) the right to be free from any form of coercion, duress or threat, torture, or any other form of cruel, inhuman or degrading treatment or punishment;

   (j) the right to be in contact with close relatives and be visited by such persons.

   (k) the right, if under detention, to have, upon request, the grounds of his or her detention reviewed by a competent judge or panel of judges at regular intervals.

SCSL

SCSL Statute, Art. 17

Rights of the accused

8–104   **17.**—1. All accused shall be equal before the Special Court.

2. The accused shall be entitled to a fair and public hearing, subject to measures ordered by the Special Court for the protection of victims and witnesses.

3. The accused shall be presumed innocent until proved guilty according to the provisions of the present Statute.

4. In the determination of any charge against the accused pursuant to the present Statute, he or she shall be entitled to the following minimum guarantees, in full equality:

   a. To be informed promptly and in detail in a language which he or she understands of the nature and cause of the charge against him or her;

   b. To have adequate time and facilities for the preparation of his or her defence and to communicate with counsel of his or her own choosing;

   c. To be tried without undue delay;

   d. To be tried in his or her presence, and to defend himself or herself in person or through legal assistance of his or her own choosing; to be informed, if he or she does not have legal assistance, of this right; and to have legal assistance assigned to him or her, in any case where the interests of justice so require, and without payment by him or her in any such case if he or she does not have sufficient means to pay for it;

   e. To examine, or have examined, the witnesses against him or her and to obtain the attendance and examination of witnesses on his or her behalf under the same conditions as witnesses against him or her;

   f. To have the free assistance of an interpreter if he or she cannot understand or speak the language used in the Special Court;

   g. Not to be compelled to testify against himself or herself or to confess guilt.

(2) General principles

The concept of a fair trial is the cornerstone of the work of the ad **8–105**
hoc International Tribunals and the ICC. The overriding consideration
in all proceedings before international criminal courts is the fairness of
the proceedings, as provided for in Articles 20(1) and 19(1) of the ICTY
and ICTR Statutes respectively, and similarly to the mixed Tribunals
and the ICC: "The Trial Chambers shall ensure that a trial is fair." As
was held in *Prosecutor v. Tadić*, Judgment, ICTY Appeals Chamber, July
15, 1999, para. 43: "This provision mirrors the corresponding guarantee
provided for in international and regional human rights instruments:
the International Covenant on Civil and Political Rights (1966)
(ICCPR), the European Convention on Human Rights (1950), and the
American Convention on Human Rights (1969). The right to a fair trial
is central to the rule of law: it upholds the due process of law."

The Trial Chamber in the Delalic case found the ICCPR and the
ECHR to be "authoritative and helpful" in interpreting the ICTY
Statute and Rules (*Prosecutor v. Delalic*, Judgment, Trial Chamber,
November 16, 1998, para. 27).

The principle of legality must be respected for proceedings to be fair.
As held in *Prosecutor v. Aleksovski*, Judgment, Appeals Chamber, March
24, 2000, para. 126, "a person may only be found guilty of a crime in
respect of acts which constituted a violation of the law at the time of
their commission." Also see, *Prosecutor v. Kordic*, Judgment, Trial Chambers, February 26, 2001, paras 192–194.

A fair trial demands that certain minimum requirements are met to
protect the rights of the accused, as set out in Article 20 of the ICTR
Statute and 21 of the ICTY Statute.

The rights of victims must also be taken into consideration, but "the
Tribunal's Statute makes the rights of the accused the first consideration, and the need to protect victims and witnesses the secondary
consideration" (*Prosecutor v. Brdanin*, Decision on third motion by
Prosecution for protective measures, November 8, 2000, para. 13; also
see, *Prosecutor v. Tadić*, Decision on the Prosecution's motion requesting
protective measures for witness R, July 31, 1996 at 4).

The principle of a fair trial must not result in there being an **8–106**
excessive infringement on the rights of the Prosecution, for example, to
conduct effective cross-examination of the Defence witnesses (see,
Prosecutor v. Blaškić, Decision on the defence motion for protective
measures for witnesses D/H and D/I, September 25, 1998). This and
other considerations, such as the expediency of the trial, requires a
balancing exercise between the principle of judicial economy and the
right of the Accused to a fair trial. It has to be noted that "judicial
economy should never outweigh the right of the Accused to a fair trial"
(*Prosecutor v. Krajisnik*, Decision on Prosecution's Motion for Judicial
Notice of Adjudicated Facts and Admission of Written Statements of
Witnesses Pursuant to Rule 92*bis*, February 28, 2003, para. 20). In *Brima
et al.* (SCSL), the Judge held in this respect that "a tribunal's reputation
and credibility must be measured not in terms of judicial economy but
its capability to deliver superior quality justice fairly and dispassionately, and with reasonable expedition" (*Prosecutor v. Brima et al.*,
Decision on the Prosecution Motion for Concurrent Hearing of Evi-

dence Common to Cases SCSL-2004–15-PT and SCSL-2004–16-PT, May 11, 2004, para. 35).

The Trial Chamber in *Brima et al.* further held that "as a sovereign entity within its jurisdictional competence, a court must not recoil from its supreme responsibility of maintaining the integrity of its proceedings both in the interests of the Prosecution and the Defence, and more so in protecting the procedural and substantive due process rights of persons accused of crime until proven guilty. To sacrifice those rights in favour of political or economic expediency is tantamount to abdicating its sovereign attributes of independence. Hence, it must be emphasised that the limited judicial life-span of a Court cannot provide justification in law for abridging or curtailing the rights of an accused person to a fair trial" (*Prosecutor v. Brima et al.*, Decision on the Prosecution Motion for Concurrent Hearing of Evidence Common to Cases SCSL-2004–15-PT and SCSL-2004–16-PT, May 11, 2004, para. 47).

The failure to hear a party against whom the Trial Chamber is provisionally inclined is not consistent with the requirement of a fair trial. The Statute and Rules must be read to include the rights of parties to be heard in accordance with the judicial character of the Trial Chambers. See, *Prosecutor v. Jelisic*, Judgment, Appeals Chamber, July 5, 2001, para. 27.

(3) To be informed promptly of the charge

8–107   The right to be informed of the charge against the accused finds practical effect in the form of the indictment and the disclosure obligations that the Prosecution must fulfil.

A delay of 11 months before being informed of the general nature of the charges from the time of the accused's detention was held to be a violation of the accused's right to be promptly informed of the charges against him (see, *Prosecutor v. Jean-Bosco Barayagwiza*, Decision, November 2, 1999, paras 78–86). In *Prosecutor v. Talic*, Decision on motion for release, December 10, 1999 it was held that amendments to the indictment previously notified to the accused, do not permit the accused to argue that he has not been informed of the charges against him.

The indictment has to provide sufficient details of the charges against the accused. The reason for that is to abide by the fair trial principles, set out in Article 20 and Rule 47, and "to ensure that the accused has a 'concise statement of the facts' upon which reliance is placed to establish the offences charged, but only to the extent that such statement enables the accused to be informed of 'the nature and cause of the charge against him' and in 'adequate time [. . .] for the preparation of his defence'", (*Prosecutor v. Krnojelac*, Decision on Defence Preliminary Motion on the Form of the Indictment, February 24, 1999, para. 12.) and "to avoid prejudicial surprise" (*Prosecutor v. Delalic*, Decision on the Accused Mucic's Motion for Particulars, June 26, 1996, para. 9).

This applies to all charges including those of a more general nature. As held by the Appeals Chamber in *Kupreškić* regarding the crime of persecution: "the fact that the offence of persecution is a so-called "umbrella" crime does not mean that an indictment need not specifically plead the material aspects of the Prosecution case with the same details as other crimes. Persecution cannot, because of its nebulous character, be used as a catch-all-charge. Pursuant to elementary principles of criminal pleading, it is not sufficient for an indictment to charge a crime in generic terms" (*Prosecutor v. Kupreškić et al.*, Appeals Chamber's Judgment, October 23, 2001, para. 98). The same could be said about conspiracy to commit genocide. See futher chapter 6 (Indictments).

The accused is not entitled under Article 21(4)(a) of the ICTY Statute to a translation of all documents in the case in a language he understands, "but only to evidence, which forms the basis of the determination by the Chamber of the charges against the accused; and that this right is ensured, inter alia, by the fact that all evidence admitted at trial is provided in a language the accused understands" (*Prosecutor v. Naletilic and Martinovic*, Decision on defence's motion concerning translation of all documents, October 18, 2001; also see, *Prosecutor v. Delalic et al.*, Decision on defence application for forwarding documents in the language of the accused, September 25, 1996; and, *Prosecutor v. Muhimana*, Décision relative à la requête de la défense aux fins de traduction des documents de l'accusation et des actes de procédure en kinyarwanda, langue de l'accusé, et en français, langue de son conseil, November 6, 2001).

The accused is not entitled to be informed of the legal ingredients of the crimes with which he is charged (see, *Prosecutor v. Kordic*, Decision on joint defence motion to dismiss for lack of jurisdiction portions of the amended indictment alleging "failure to punish" liability, March 2, 1999; also see, *Prosecutor v. Kayishema and Ruzindana*, Decision on the joint defence motion requesting the interpretation of Rule 67 of the Rules, June 15, 1998.)

(4) Preparation of defence

The accused is entitled to an equality of arms in the preparation and presentation of his defence, which at minimum means that the accused must have adequate time and facilities for his defence (see, *Prosecutor v. Tadić*, Judgment, ICTY Appeals Chamber, July 15, 1999, para. 47.)

8–108

However, the principle of equality of arms must be interpreted in light of the powers and resources of the International Tribunal (see *Tadić* Appeal Judgment):

> 52. . . . the Appeals Chamber is of the view that under the Statute of the International Tribunal the principle of equality of arms must be given a more liberal interpretation than that normally upheld with regard to proceedings before domestic courts. This principle means that the Prosecution and the Defence must be equal before the Trial Chamber. It follows that the Chamber shall provide every practicable facility it is capable of granting under the Rules and Statute when faced with a request by a party for assistance in presenting its case. The Trial Chambers are mindful of the difficulties encountered by the parties in tracing and gaining access to evidence in the territory of the former Yugoslavia where some States have not been forthcoming in complying with their legal obligation to co-operate with the Tribunal. Provisions under the Statute and the Rules exist to alleviate the difficulties faced by

the parties so that each side may have equal access to witnesses. The Chambers are empowered to issue such orders, summonses, subpoenas, warrants and transfer orders as may be necessary for the purposes of an investigation or for the preparation or conduct of the trial. This includes the power to:

(1) adopt witness protection measures, ranging from partial to full protection;

(2) take evidence by video-link or by way of deposition;

(3) summon witnesses and order their attendance;

(4) issue binding orders to States for, *inter alia*, the taking and production of evidence; and

(5) issue binding orders to States to assist a party or to summon a witness and order his or her attendance under the Rules.

A further important measure available in such circumstances is:

(6) for the President of the Tribunal to send, at the instance of the Trial Chamber, a request to the State authorities in question for their assistance in securing the attendance of a witness.

In addition, whenever the aforementioned measures have proved to be to no avail, a Chamber may, upon the request of a party or *proprio motu*:

(7) order that proceedings be adjourned or, if the circumstances so require, that they be stayed. 53. Relying on the principle of equality of arms, the Defence is submitting that the Appellant did not receive a fair trial because relevant and admissible evidence was not presented due to lack of cooperation of the authorities in the *Republika Srpska* in securing the attendance of certain witnesses. The Defence is not complaining that the Trial Chamber was negligent in responding to a request for assistance. The Appeals Chamber finds that the Defence has not substantiated its claim that the Appellant was not given a reasonable opportunity to present his case. There is no evidence to show that the Trial Chamber failed to assist him when seised of a request to do so.

(5) Tried without undue delay

8–109   All accused have a right to a trial without undue delay. Trials should not be postponed if it would result in a delaying domino effect on other awaiting trials. The rights of the accused to a trial without undue delay has to be assessed in light of the same right of other accused. Joinder of an accused should not be permitted when it would cause undue delay to the trials of the other accused to whom joinder was sought. See, *Prosecutor v. Kunarac*, Decision on joinder of trials, February 9, 2000, paras 10–11. Also see, *Prosecutor v. Kvočka et al.*, Decision on Prosecution motion to join trials, April 14, 2000.

The unavailability of a Judge of the Trial Chamber should not prejudice the right of the accused to be tried without undue delay (see, *Prosecutor v. Kordic*, Decision on Prosecution request to proceed by deposition, November 3, 1999).

(6) Right to defence counsel

(a) Right to choose defence counsel

8–110   The accused is entitled to defence counsel of his choice, although this right is not unlimited, particularly for indigent accused, and subject to the Registrar's discretion. The choice is limited to those counsel who fulfil the criteria of Rules 44 and 45 of ICTY/ICTR/SCSL and the Directives on Assignment of Defence Counsel. There is a broad discretion on the Registrar not only to determine who is qualified under the Tribunals' criteria, but also to look beyond those criteria if the interests of justice so require (*Prosecutor v. Akayesu*, Appeals Chamber Judgment, June 1, 2001, para. 62). Fairness to the accused requires nonetheless that, in exercising his discretion, the Registrar should respect the choice of all accused "unless there exist well-founded reasons not to assign Counsel of choice" (*Prosecutor v. Martic*, Decision on Appeal Against Decision of Registry, August 2, 2002, p. 4).

(b) Right to self-representation

In principle, the accused can decide to represent himself. In *Milošević*, **8–111** the Trial Chamber nonetheless ruled *proprio motu* and against the wishes of the Accused, that the right to fair trial required it to appoint *amicus curiae* "not to represent the accused, but to assist in proper determination of the case" (*Prosecutor v. Milošević*, Order inviting designation of *amicus curiae*, August 30, 2001; October 30, 2001; November 23, 2001; January 11, 2002).

In August 2004, the Trial Chamber in *Milošević* went one step further and imposed defence counsel on the Accused. In an oral decision on September 2, 2004, (for the main part, upheld by the Appeals Chamber) the Trial Chamber justified the imposition of counsel by referring to the excessive delays caused by the accused's ill health. In its written reasons in support of the oral decision, the Trial Chamber held that "the right of an accused person to represent himself is not unfettered, and in the circumstances of this case, it is both competent to assign counsel to the accused and in the interests of justice to do so" (*Prosecutor v. Milošević*, Reasons for Decision on Assignment of Defence Counsel, September 22, 2004, para. 1; see also paras 33–34). While upholding the Trial Chamber's decision, the Appeals Chamber ordered the Trial Chamber to amend the Order on Modalities giving greater priority to the Accused's right to conduct his own defence (*Prosecutor v. Milošević*, Decision on Interlocutory Appeal of the Trial Chamber's Decision on the Assignment of Defence Counsel, November 1, 2004, para. 17).

Already in 2000, Counsel was imposed on Barayagwiza, an accused before the ICTR. Moreover, in 2002 the ICTR Rules introduced Rule 45 *quarter*, allowing the Registrar to appoint Counsel even if the Accused wishes to conduct a case without representation.

In conclusion, the right to self-representation has been restricted by the Tribunals.

(c) Breakdown of trust

Withdrawal of Defence Counsel and replacement by another is **8–112** possible only where the Accused is able to demonstrate that there are exceptional circumstances justifying his request for replacement of counsel and the request is with good cause (*Prosecutor v. Delalic et al.*, Order on the Motion to withdraw as Counsel due to Conflict of Interest,

June 24, 1999). For this to be the case, the accused's reasons underlying his request must be genuine and the request not be made "for frivolous reasons or in a desire to pervert the course of justice, e.g., by causing additional delay" (*Prosecutor v. Delalic et al.*, Decision on Request by Accused Mucic for Assignment of new counsel, June 24, 1996, para. 3). A complete breakdown of trust or a potential conflict of interest constitute grounds fulfilling these criteria. A complete breakdown of communication "could adversely affect the rights of the accused", which would render the trial unfair if the Accused and assigned Counsel were to be required to continue their professional relationship (*ibid.*, para. 4).

In *Prosecutor v. Blagojević*, the Registrar (by Decision of May 23, 2003) assigned independent legal counsel to advise the accused on his rights in relation to assignment of counsel because there was a complete breakdown of trust between counsel and accused. On the independent legal counsel's advice, the client filed a Motion to have his Lead Counsel withdrawn. By Decision on Independent Counsel for Vidoje Blagojević's Motion to Instruct the Registrar to Appoint New Lead and Co-Counsel, July 3, 2003, the Trial Chamber rejected client's request for withdrawal of his Lead Counsel. The Trial Chamber held that "as a matter of policy, this Trial Chamber does not want to encourage a course of action by which accused appearing before this Tribunal can unilaterally destroy their relationship with assigned counsel and then be granted new lead counsel—and co-counsel—of their choosing. This course of action, particularly in the advanced stages of these complex proceedings, could lead to a long delay of proceedings before the Tribunal" (para. 113). The Trial Chamber further held: "In this case, the Trial Chamber recognises that friction exists between the Accused and his Counsel. Friction is not, however, equal to a fundamental lack of trust due to misconduct or manifest negligence. Choosing to cease communications with counsel is not equivalent to counsel breaching their obligation to communicate and consult with their client. A lack of trust in counsel based on disagreements in approach to ones defence, including the criteria upon which to determine the appropriate candidate for co-counsel, is distinguishable from a lack of trust due to a breach by counsel in fulfilling his professional and ethical responsibilities in the course of representation." (para. 120.)

(d) Conflict of Interest

8–113   For a decision on the potential conflict of interest arising between client and counsel due to the possibility of counsel being called as a witness see, *Prosecutor v. Simić et al.*, Decision on the Prosecution motion to resolve conflict of interest regarding attorney Borislav Pisarevic, March 25, 1999). In this decision, the notion of conflict of interest was defined as follows:

> "A conflict of interest between an attorney and a client arises in any situation where, by reason of certain circumstances, representation by such an attorney prejudices, or could prejudice, the interests of the client and the wider interests of justice.
> [. . .]

[S]uch a conflict affects the essential fairness of the trial, and in respect of the Tribunal, implicates, first, the responsibility of the Trial Chamber under Article 20, paragraph 1, to 'ensure that a trial is fair [. . .] with full respect for the rights of the accused' [. . .] and secondly, 'the right of the accused under Article 21, paragraph 2, of the Statute to a fair trial.' (at p. 4)

In *Mejakic et al.*, the Appeals Chamber overturned the Trial Chamber's ruling that there was not yet a potential conflict of interest in a situation where a defence counsel represented two accused who were charged with similar crimes in separate trials, but where the Prosecutor had not yet made the final determination as to whether to call one accused against the other and was, in any event, not in a position to subpoena him. The Appeals Chamber held that the fact that defence counsel could potentially influence the decision of the one accused whether or not to testify against the other sufficed to establish a potential conflict of interest (*Prosecutor v. Mejakic et al.*, Decision on Appeal by the Prosecution to Resolve Conflict of Interest Regarding Attorney Jovan Simić, October 6, 2004, para. 13, (overturning: Decision on Prosecution's Second Motion to Resolve Conflict of Interest Regarding Attorney Jovan Simić, June 17, 2004)).

(7) Attendance of witnesses

The accused has the right to examine all witnesses against him and to obtain the attendance of witnesses on his behalf. The accused can make use of the Chamber's powers to order the attendance of witnesses required for the defence case. The accused can also seek protective measures for defence witnesses under Rule 75. **8–114**

The primary consideration in determining whether witnesses should be available for cross-examination by the accused is the overriding obligation of the Chamber to ensure a fair trial under Articles 20 and 21 of the Statute (see, *Prosecutor v. Sikirica et al.*, Decision on Prosecution's application to admit transcripts under Rule 92*bis*, May 23, 2001. Also see, *Prosecutor v. Kordic*, ICTY Appeals Chamber, Decision on appeal regarding statement of a deceased witness, July 21, 2000.)

(8) Self-incrimination

The accused has a right not to testify against himself. It is his right to choose whether to testify in his own case (see, Rule 85(C)). The Statute and Rules of the ICC, ICTY, ICTR and SCSL do not provide that an adverse inference, or any other inference, can be drawn from an accused's failure to testify (see, *Delalic et al.* decision cited below). Also see, *Prosecutor v. Kvočka et al.*, Decision on the defence of alibi for the accused Zoran Zigic, July 21, 2000, in which it was confirmed that the notice required under Rule 67(A) of the use of the defence of alibi should not be read as limiting the right of the accused to testify in his own defence. **8–115**

It does not infringe the rights of the accused to order the production of documents which by his own assertion were relied upon by him to prepare for his testimony (see, *Prosecutor v. Blaškić*, Order for the production of documents used to prepare testimony, April 22, 1999).

However, an accused cannot be compelled to provide a handwriting sample; see, *Prosecutor v. Delalic et al.*, Decision on the Prosecution's oral requests for the admission of Exhibit 155 into evidence and for an order to compel the accused, Zdravko Mucic, to provide a handwriting sample, January 19, 1998, paras 47–50, including:

> 47. The Trial Chamber is not satisfied that a handwriting sample *per se* can be regarded as forming material proof against an accused. We hold that where the material factor absent in the incriminating elements is the handwriting sample of the accused, the Trial Chamber cannot compel the accused to supply the missing element. To do so will be to infringe the provisions of Article 21 sub-paragraph 4(g) which protects the accused from self-incrimination. It is different where the accused voluntarily complies on demand without coercion.
>
> 48. It has been argued that in the instant case the Order for a handwriting sample bears no relevance to the case before the Trial Chamber. The Trial Chamber rejects this contention. The reason for requiring the handwriting sample is admittedly to ascertain conclusively the authorship of Exhibit 155. If authenticated, the letter will act as a sufficient admission of its contents in respect of certain counts in the indictment against the author. The obvious implication is that the accused would have been compelled by an Order of the Trial Chamber to assist the Prosecution in its investigation, and probably provide the evidence to incriminate himself. The fact that the handwriting sample *per se* is neutral evidence is not the issue. If the handwriting sample taken together with other evidence will constitute material evidence to prove the charge against the accused, then the Order of the Trial Chamber would have compelled the production of self-incriminating evidence.
>
> 49. There is no duty in law or morals for the accused to fill a vacuum created by the investigative procedural gap of the Prosecution. Self-preservation is the first principle of life. It is an elementary principle of proof, that he who alleges must prove the subject matter of his allegation. Since the Prosecution alleges the authorship of Exhibit 155, it has to discharge the burden of proof unaided by the Defence.

B. COMPENSATION

ICC

ICC Rules of Procedure and Evidence, r. 173

Request for compensation

8–116   173.—1. Anyone seeking compensation on any of the grounds indicated in article 85 shall submit a request, in writing, to the Presidency, which shall designate a Chamber composed of three judges to consider the request. These judges shall not have participated in any earlier judgement of the Court regarding the person making the request.

2. The request for compensation shall be submitted not later than six months from the date the person making the request was notified of the decision of the Court concerning:

(a) The unlawfulness of the arrest or detention under article 85, paragraph 1;
(b) The reversal of the conviction under article 85, paragraph 2;
(c) The existence of a grave and manifest miscarriage of justice under article 85, paragraph 3.

3. The request shall contain the grounds and the amount of compensation requested.

4. The person requesting compensation shall be entitled to legal assistance.

Procedure for seeking compensation

174.—1. A request for compensation and any other written observation by the person filing the request shall be transmitted to the Prosecutor, who shall have an opportunity to respond in writing. Any observations by the Prosecutor shall be notified to the person filing the request.

2. The Chamber designated under rule 173, sub-rule 1, may either hold a hearing or determine the matter on the basis of the request and any written observations by the Prosecutor and the person filing the request. A hearing shall be held if the Prosecutor or the person seeking compensation so requests.

3. The decision shall be taken by the majority of the judges. The decision shall be notified to the Prosecutor and to the person filing the request.

Amount of compensation

175. In establishing the amount of any compensation in conformity with article 85, paragraph 3, the Chamber designated under rule 173, sub-rule 1, shall take into consideration the consequences of the grave and manifest miscarriage of justice on the personal, family, social and professional situation of the person filing the request.

East Timor

Regulation 2000/30, s.51 (as amended by Regulation 2001/25)

Variation of Time Limits

51.—51.1 Any of the time limits referred to in this regulation, may, upon good cause being shown, be enlarged or reduced by the competent court.

8–117

51.2 For good cause shown, the competent court may recognize as validly done any act done after the expiration of a time prescribed by this regulation or prescribed by an order of the same or an inferior court, on such terms as are just.

Compensation for Miscarriage of Justice

52.—52.1 Where a conviction is reversed on the basis of newly discovered evidence, which shows a miscarriage of justice, and where the evidence was not concealed by the convict, the convict may be compensated in accordance with a separate UNTAET directive.

8–118

52.2 Any person who is subjected to unlawful arrest or detention shall be entitled to compensation in an amount and from a source of public funds which are allocated to the administration of justice, to be determined by the competent court. An award of compensation pursuant to the present section may be made as a part of the final disposition of a criminal case involving the claimant, or by means of a separate civil action.

The East Timor Regulation and the ICC Rules provide scope for compensation. In the ICTY, ICTR and SCSL Rules on the other hand, there are no specific provisions for compensation to be granted to accused persons. However, in the Appeals Chamber's decision in *Prosecutor v. Barayagwiza*, March 31, 2000, the Chamber confirmed that financial compensation could be granted to the accused should he be found not guilty, given that the Chamber found that his rights had been infringed during the pre-trial stage. In *Prosecutor v. Nahimana*, Judgment, December 3, 2003, Barayagwiza was, however, found guilty and instead of providing any financial compensation, the Trial Chamber reduced his sentence from life to 35 years.

III. PROTECTION OF WITNESSES AND VICTIMS

A. STATUTORY PROVISIONS AND RULES

ICC

ICC Statute, Art. 68

Protection of the victims and witnesses and their participation in the proceedings

8–119 **68.**—1. The Court shall take appropriate measures to protect the safety, physical and psychological well-being, dignity and privacy of victims and witnesses. In so doing, the Court shall have regard to all relevant factors, including age, gender as defined in article 7, paragraph 3, and health, and the nature of the crime, in particular, but not limited to, where the crime involves sexual or gender violence or violence against children. The Prosecutor shall take such measures particularly during the investigation and prosecution of such crimes. These measures shall not be prejudicial to or inconsistent with the rights of the accused and a fair and impartial trial.

2. As an exception to the principle of public hearings provided for in article 67, the Chambers of the Court may, to protect victims and witnesses or an accused, conduct any part of the proceedings *in camera* or allow the presentation of evidence by electronic or other special means. In particular, such measures shall be implemented in the case of a victim of sexual violence or a child who is a victim or a witness, unless otherwise ordered by the Court, having regard to all the circumstances, particularly the views of the victim or witness.

3. Where the personal interests of the victims are affected, the Court shall permit their views and concerns to be presented and considered at stages of the proceedings determined to be appropriate by the Court and in a manner which is not prejudicial to or inconsistent with the rights of the accused and a fair and impartial trial. Such views and concerns may be presented by the legal representatives of the victims where the Court considers it appropriate, in accordance with the Rules of Procedure and Evidence.

4. The Victims and Witnesses Unit may advise the Prosecutor and the Court on appropriate protective measures, security arrangements, counselling and assistance as referred to in article 43, paragraph 6.

5. Where the disclosure of evidence or information pursuant to this Statute may lead to the grave endangerment of the security of a witness or his or her family, the Prosecutor may, for the purposes of any proceedings conducted prior to the commencement of the trial, withhold such evidence or information and instead submit a summary thereof. Such measures shall be exercised in a manner which is not prejudicial to or inconsistent with the rights of the accused and a fair and impartial trial.

6. A State may make an application for necessary measures to be taken in respect of the protection of its servants or agents and the protection of confidential or sensitive information.

ICC Rules of Evidence and Procedure, rr. 85, 86, 87, 88

Definition of victims

85. For the purposes of the Statute and the Rules of Procedure and **8–120** Evidence:
  (a) "Victims" means natural persons who have suffered harm as a result of the commission of any crime within the jurisdiction of the Court;
  (b) Victims may include organizations or institutions that have sustained direct harm to any of their property which is dedicated to religion, education, art or science or charitable purposes, and to their historic monuments, hospitals and other places and objects for humanitarian purposes.

General principle

86. A Chamber in making any direction or order, and other organs of the Court in performing their functions under the Statute or the Rules, shall take into account the needs of all victims and witnesses in accordance with Article 68, in particular, children, elderly persons, persons with disabilities and victims of sexual or gender violence.

Protective measures

87.—1. Upon the motion of the Prosecutor or the Defence or upon the **8–121** request of a witness or a victim or his or her legal representative, if any, or on its own motion, and after having consulted with the Victims and Witnesses Unit, as appropriate, a Chamber may order measures to protect a victim, a witness or another person at risk on account of testimony given by a witness pursuant to article 68, paragraphs 1 and 2. The Chamber shall seek to obtain, whenever possible, the consent of the person in respect of whom the protective measure is sought prior to ordering the protective measure.

2. A motion or request under sub-rule 1 shall be governed by rule 134, provided that:
  (a) Such a motion or request shall not be submitted ex parte;
  (b) A request by a witness or by a victim or his or her legal representative, if any, shall be served on both the Prosecutor and the defence, each of whom shall have the opportunity to respond;
  (c) A motion or request affecting a particular witness or a particular victim shall be served on that witness or victim or his or her legal representative, if any, in addition to the other party, each of whom shall have the opportunity to respond;
  (d) When the Chamber proceeds on its own motion, notice and opportunity to respond shall be given to the Prosecutor and the defence, and to any witness or any victim or his or her legal representative, if any, who would be affected by such protective measure; and
  (e) A motion or request may be filed under seal, and, if so filed, shall remain sealed until otherwise ordered by a Chamber. Responses to motions or requests filed under seal shall also be filed under seal.

3. A Chamber may, on a motion or request under sub-rule 1, hold a hearing, **8–122** which shall be conducted in camera, to determine whether to order measures to prevent the release to the public or press and information agencies, of the identity or the location of a victim, a witness or other person at risk on account of testimony given by a witness by ordering, *inter alia*:

(a) That the name of the victim, witness or other person at risk on account of testimony given by a witness or any information which could lead to his or her identification, be expunged from the public records of the Chamber;

(b) That the Prosecutor, the defence or any other participant in the proceedings be prohibited from disclosing such information to a third party;

(c) That testimony be presented by electronic or other special means, including the use of technical means enabling the alteration of pictures or voice, the use of audio-visual technology, in particular videoconferencing and closed-circuit television, and the exclusive use of the sound media;

(d) That a pseudonym be used for a victim, a witness or other person at risk on account of testimony given by a witness; or

(e) That a Chamber conduct part of its proceedings in camera.

Special measures

8–123   88.—1. Upon the motion of the Prosecutor or the defence, or upon the request of a witness or a victim or his or her legal representative, if any, or on its own motion, and after having consulted with the Victims and Witnesses Unit, as appropriate, a Chamber may, taking into account the views of the victim or witness, order special measures such as, but not limited to, measures to facilitate the testimony of a traumatized victim or witness, a child, an elderly person or a victim of sexual violence, pursuant to article 68, paragraphs 1 and 2. The Chamber shall seek to obtain, whenever possible, the consent of the person in respect of whom the special measure is sought prior to ordering that measure.

2. A Chamber may hold a hearing on a motion or a request under sub-rule 1, if necessary in camera or ex parte, to determine whether to order any such special measure, including but not limited to an order that a counsel, a legal representative, a psychologist or a family member be permitted to attend during the testimony of the victim or the witness.

3. For *inter partes* motions or requests filed under this rule, the provisions of rule 87, sub-rules 2(b) to (d), shall apply *mutatis mutandis*.

4. A motion or request filed under this rule may be filed under seal, and if so filed shall remain sealed until otherwise ordered by a Chamber. Any responses to *inter partes* motions or requests filed under seal shall also be filed under seal.

5. Taking into consideration that violations of the privacy of a witness or victim may create risk to his or her security, a Chamber shall be vigilant in controlling the manner of questioning a witness or victim so as to avoid any harassment or intimidation, paying particular attention to attacks on victims of crimes of sexual violence

ICTY

Statute of ICTY, Art. 20; 22

Commencement and conduct of trial proceedings

8–124   20.—1. The Trial Chambers shall ensure that a trial is fair and expeditious and that proceedings are conducted in accordance with the rules of procedure and evidence, with full respect for the rights of the accused and due regard for the protection of victims and witnesses.

Protection of victims and witnesses

8–125   22. The International Tribunal shall provide in its rules of procedure and evidence for the protection of victims and witnesses. Such protection measures shall include, but shall not be limited to, the conduct of in camera proceedings and the protection of the victim's identity.

ICTY Rules of Procedure and Evidence, rr. 69, 75, 79

Protection of Victims and Witnesses

69.—(A) In exceptional circumstances, the Prosecutor may apply to a Judge or Trial Chamber to order the non-disclosure of the identity of a victim or witness who may be in danger or at risk until such person is brought under the protection of the Tribunal.

(B) In the determination of protective measures for victims and witnesses, the Judge or Trial Chamber may consult the Victims and Witnesses Section.

(C) Subject to Rule 75, the identity of the victim or witness shall be disclosed in sufficient time prior to the trial to allow adequate time for preparation of the defence.

8–126

Measures for the Protection of Victims and Witnesses

75.—(A) A Judge or a Chamber may, *proprio motu* or at the request of either party, or of the victim or witness concerned, or of the Victims and Witnesses Section, order appropriate measures for the privacy and protection of victims and witnesses, provided that the measures are consistent with the rights of the accused.

(B) A Chamber may hold an in camera proceeding to determine whether to order:

    (i) measures to prevent disclosure to the public or the media of the identity or whereabouts of a victim or a witness, or of persons related to or associated with a victim or witness by such means as:

        (a) expunging names and identifying information from the Tribunal's public records;

        (b) non-disclosure to the public of any records identifying the victim;

        (c) giving of testimony through image- or voice- altering devices or closed circuit television; and

        (d) assignment of a pseudonym;

    (ii) closed sessions, in accordance with Rule 79;

    (iii) appropriate measures to facilitate the testimony of vulnerable victims and witnesses, such as one-way closed circuit television.

(C) The Victims and Witnesses Section shall ensure that the witness has been informed before giving evidence that his or her testimony and his or her identity may be disclosed at a later date in another case, pursuant to Rule 75 (F).

(D) A Chamber shall, whenever necessary, control the manner of questioning to avoid any harassment or intimidation.

(E) When making an order under paragraph (A) above, a Judge or Chamber shall wherever appropriate state in the order whether the transcript of those proceedings relating to the evidence of the witness to whom the measures relate shall be made available for use in other proceedings before the Tribunal.

(F) Once protective measures have been ordered in respect of a victim or witness in any proceedings before the Tribunal (the "first proceedings"), such protective measures:

    (i) shall continue to have effect *mutatis mutandis* in any other proceedings before the Tribunal (the "second proceedings") unless and until they are rescinded, varied or augmented in accordance with the procedure set out in this Rule; but

    (ii) shall not prevent the Prosecutor from discharging any disclosure obligation under the Rules in the second proceedings, provided that the Prosecutor notifies the Defence to whom the disclosure is being made of the nature of the protective measures ordered in the first proceedings.

(G) A party to the second proceedings seeking to rescind, vary or augment protective measures ordered in the first proceedings must apply:

8–127

    (i) to any Chamber, however constituted, remaining seised of the first proceedings; or

    (ii) if no Chamber remains seised of the first proceedings, to the Chamber seised of the second proceedings.

(H) Before determining an application under paragraph (G)(ii) above, the Chamber seised of the second proceedings shall obtain all relevant information from the first proceedings, and shall consult with any Judge who ordered the protective measures in the first proceedings, if that Judge remains a Judge of the Tribunal.

(I) An application to a Chamber to rescind, vary or augment protective measures in respect of a victim or witness may be dealt with either by the Chamber or by a Judge of that Chamber, and any reference in this Rule to "a Chamber" shall include a reference to "a Judge of that Chamber".

Closed Sessions

8–128　　**79.**—(A) The Trial Chamber may order that the press and the public be excluded from all or part of the proceedings for reasons of:

    (i) public order or morality;

    (ii) safety, security or non-disclosure of the identity of a victim or witness as provided in Rule 75; or

    (iii) the protection of the interests of justice.

(B) The Trial Chamber shall make public the reasons for its order.

ICTR

ICTR Statute, Art. 19(1); 21

Commencement and conduct of trial proceedings

8–129　　**19.**—1. The Trial Chambers shall ensure that a trial is fair and expeditious and that proceedings are conducted in accordance with the Rules of Procedure and Evidence, with full respect for the rights of the accused and due regard for the protection of victims and witnesses.

Protection of victims and witnesses

8–130　　**21.** The International Tribunal for Rwanda shall provide in its rules of procedure and evidence for the protection of victims and witnesses. Such protection measures shall include, but shall not be limited to, the conduct of in camera proceedings and the protection of the victims identity.

ICTR Rules of Procedure and Evidence, rr. 69, 75, 79

Protection of Victims and Witnesses

8–131　　**69.**—(A) In exceptional circumstances, either of the parties may apply to a Trial Chamber to order the non-disclosure of the identity of a victim or witness who may be in danger or at risk, until the Chamber decides otherwise.

(B) In the determination of protective measures for victims and witnesses, the Trial Chamber may consult the Victims and Witness Support Unit.

(C) Subject to Rule 75, the identity of the victim or witness shall be disclosed within such time as determined by Trial Chamber to allow adequate time for preparation of the Prosecution and the Defence.

Measures for the Protection of Victims and Witnesses

75.—(A) A Judge or a Chamber may, proprio motu or at the request of either party, or of the victim or witness concerned, or of the Victims and Witnesses Support Unit, order appropriate measures to safeguard the privacy and security of victims and witnesses, provided that the measures are consistent with the rights of the accused.

(B) A Chamber may hold an in camera proceeding to determine whether to order notably:

   (i) Measures to prevent disclosure to the public or the media of the identity or whereabouts of a victim or a witness, or of persons related to or associated with him by such means as:

      (a) Expunging names and identifying information from the Tribunal's public records;

      (b) Non-disclosure to the public of any records identifying the victim;

      (c) Giving of testimony through image- or voice- altering devices or closed circuit television; and

      (d) Assignment of a pseudonym;

   (ii) Closed sessions, in accordance with Rule 79;

   (iii) Appropriate measures to facilitate the testimony of vulnerable victims and witnesses, such as one-way closed circuit television.

(C) The Victims and Witnesses Section shall ensure that the witness has been informed before giving evidence by the party calling that witness that his testimony and his identity may be disclosed at a later date in another case, pursuant to Rule 75 (F).

(D) A Chamber shall control the manner of questioning to avoid any harassment or intimidation.

(E) When making an order under paragraph (A) above, a Judge or a Chamber shall wherever appropriate state in the order whether the transcript of those proceedings relating to the evidence of the witness to whom the measures relate shall be made available for use in other proceedings before the Tribunal.

(F) Once protective measures have been ordered in respect of a victim or witness in any proceedings before the Tribunal (the "first proceedings"), such protective measures:

   (i) shall continue to have effect mutatis mutandis in any other proceedings before the Tribunal (the "second proceedings") unless and until they are rescinded, varied or augmented in accordance with the procedure set out in this Rule; but

   (ii) shall not prevent the Prosecutor from discharging any disclosure obligation under the Rules in the second proceedings, provided that the Prosecutor notifies the Defence to whom the disclosure is being made of the nature of the protective measures ordered in the first proceedings.

(G) A party to the second proceedings seeking to rescind, vary or augment protective measures ordered in the first proceedings must apply:

   (i) to any Chamber, however constituted, remaining seised of the first proceedings; or

   (ii) if no Chamber remains seised of the first proceedings, to the Chamber seised of the second proceedings.

(H) Before determining an application under paragraph (G)(ii) above, the Chamber seised of the second proceedings shall obtain all relevant information from the first proceedings, and shall consult with any Judge who ordered the protective measures in the first proceedings, if that Judge remains a Judge of the Tribunal.

(I) An application to a Chamber to rescind, vary or augment protective measures in respect of a victim or witness may be dealt with either by the Chamber or by a Judge of that Chamber, and any reference in this Rule to "a Chamber" shall include a reference to "a Judge of that Chamber".

Closed Sessions

8–132   79.—(A) The Trial Chamber may order that the press and the public be excluded from all or part of the proceedings for reasons of:
(i)   public order or morality;
(ii) safety, security or non-disclosure of the identity of a victim or witness as provided in Rule 75; or
(iii) the protection of the interests of justice.
(B) The Trial Chamber shall make public the reasons for its order.

East Timor

UNTAET Regulation 2000/15, s.24

Witness Protection

8–133   24.—24.1 The panels shall take appropriate measures to protect the safety, physical and psychological well-being, dignity and privacy of victims and witnesses. In so doing, the panels shall have regard to all relevant factors, including age, gender, health and the nature of the crime, in particular, but not limited to, where the crime involves sexual or gender violence or violence against children.
24.2 Procedures regarding the protection of witnesses shall be elaborated in an UNTAET directive.

UNTAET Regulation 2000/30, ss.35, 36.8 (as amended by Regulation 2001/25)

Witnesses

8–134   35.—35.1 All persons summoned to testify in a criminal case are required to do so. Witnesses shall be notified as provided in Section 2.4 of the present regulation. The court shall consider measures for the protection of witnesses where necessary. Such measures may include, but shall not be limited to, the conduct of *in camera* proceedings and the protection of a victim's identity.

Witness Testimony

8–135   36.—36.8 The Court shall take appropriate measures to protect the safety, physical and psychological well-being, dignity and privacy of victims and witnesses. In doing so, the Court shall have regard to all relevant factors, including age, gender, health, religion, and the nature of the crime, in particular, but not limited to, whether the crime involves sexual or gender violence or violence against children.

SCSL

SCSL Statute, Art. 16(4)

The Registry

8–136   16.—4. The Registrar shall set up a Victims and Witnesses Unit within the Registry. This Unit shall provide, in consultation with the Office of the Prosecutor, protective measures and security arrangements, counselling and other appropriate assistance for witnesses, victims who appear before the Court and others who are at risk on account of testimony given by such witnesses. The Unit personnel shall include experts in trauma, including trauma related to crimes of sexual violence and violence against children.

SCSL Rules of Procedure and Evidence, rr. 69, 75, 79

Protection of Victims and Witnesses

69.—(A) In exceptional circumstances, either of the parties may apply to a   **8–137**
Judge of the Trial Chamber or the Trial Chamber to order the non-disclosure of the identity of a victim or witness who may be in danger or at risk, until the Judge or Chamber decides otherwise.

(B) In the determination of protective measures for victims and witnesses, the Judge or Trial Chamber may consult the Witnesses and Victims Section.

(C) Subject to Rule 75, the identity of the victim or witness shall be disclosed in sufficient time before a witness is to be called to allow adequate time for preparation of the prosecution and the defence.

Measures for the Protection of Victims and Witnesses

75.—(A) A Judge or a Chamber may, on its own motion, or at the request of   **8–138**
either party, or of the victim or witness concerned, or of the Witnesses and Victims Section, order appropriate measures to safeguard the privacy and security of victims and witnesses, provided that the measures are consistent with the rights of the accused.

(B) A Judge or a Chamber may hold an in camera proceeding to determine whether to order:
  - i. Measures to prevent disclosure to the public or the media of the identity or whereabouts of a victim or a witness, or of persons related to or associated with him by such means as:
    - a. Expunging names and identifying information from the Special Court's public records;
    - b. Non-disclosure to the public of any records identifying the victim or witness;
    - c. Giving of testimony through image- or voice- altering devices or closed circuit television, video link or other similar technologies; and
    - d. Assignment of a pseudonym;
  - ii. Closed sessions, in accordance with Rule 79;
  - iii. Appropriate measures to facilitate the testimony of vulnerable victims and witnesses, such as one-way closed circuit television.

(C) A Judge or a Chamber shall control the manner of questioning to avoid any harassment or intimidation.

(D) The Witnesses and Victims Section shall ensure that the witness has been informed before giving evidence that his or her testimony and his or her identity may be disclosed at a later date in another case, pursuant to Rule 75(F).

(E) When making an order under Sub-Rule (A) above, a Judge or Chamber shall wherever appropriate state in the order whether the transcript of those proceedings relating to the evidence of the witness to whom the measures relate shall be made available for use in other proceedings before the Special Court.

(F) Once protective measures have been ordered in respect of a witness or victim in any proceedings before the Special Court (the "first proceedings"), such protective measures:
  - i. shall continue to have effect *mutatis mutandis* in any other proceedings before the Special Court (the "second proceedings") unless and until

they are rescinded, varied or augmented in accordance with the procedure set out in this Rule; but;

ii. shall not prevent the Prosecutor from discharging any disclosure obligation under the Rules in the second proceedings, provided that the Prosecutor notifies the Defence to whom the disclosure is being made of the nature of the protective measures ordered in the first proceedings.

(G) A party to the second proceedings seeking to rescind, vary or augment protective measures ordered in the first proceedings shall apply to the Chamber seized of the second proceedings.

(H) Before determining an application under Sub-Rule (G) above, if the effect of the change serves to decrease the protective measures granted to the victim or witness by the Chamber in the first proceedings, the Chamber seized of the second proceedings shall obtain relevant information from the first proceedings, and may consult with any Judge who ordered the protective measures in the first proceedings, or the relevant Chamber.

(I) An application to a Chamber to rescind, vary or augment protective measures in respect of a victim or witness may be dealt with either by the Chamber or by a Judge of that Chamber, and any reference in this Rule to "a Chamber" shall include a reference to "a Judge of that Chamber".

Closed Sessions

8–139　　79.—(A) The Trial Chamber may order that the press and the public be excluded from all or part of the proceedings for reasons of:

i. national security; or

ii. protecting the privacy, security or non-disclosure of the identity of a victim or witness as provided in Rule 75; or

iii. protecting the interest of justice.

(B) The Trial Chamber shall make public the reasons for its order.

(C) In the event that it is necessary to exclude the public, the Trial Chamber should if appropriate permit representatives of the press and/or monitoring agencies to remain. Such representatives should, if appropriate, have access to the transcripts of closed sessions.

B. MEASURES OF PROTECTION

8–140　　The protection of victims and witnesses in the ICTY, ICTR and SCSL is divided into two stages: pre-trial and during trial. Rule 69 of the ICTY, ICTR and SCSL Rules of Procedure and Evidence provides that potential witnesses and victims can be granted protective measures in the pre-trial and trial phases of the case. Once the matter comes to trial, the parties have to apply under Rule 75 of the ICTY, ICTR and SCSL Rules of Procedure and Evidence for such victims and witnesses to have specific protective measures extended during the trial phase.

Protection can be granted to witnesses under these Rules in respect of both the public, and the accused and his or her defence team.

(1) Protection before trial

8–141　　It is not permissible for the Prosecution to redact the names and identifying features of witnesses before the supporting material of an indictment is disclosed to the accused under Rule 66(A)(i) without the

Trial Chamber's authority to do so. The Prosecution is required to apply to the Trial Chamber under Rule 69 if it wishes to withhold the identity of witnesses to the defence. As with all measures that may be imposed to protect the victims and witnesses, full consideration should be given to the rights of the accused.

As is clear from the language of Article 20(1) ICTY Statute and 19(1) ICTR Statute, emphasising the "full respect for rights of the accused and due regard for the protection of victims and witnesses" are emphasised, the rights of the accused must prevail over the protection of witnesses. As Judge Dolenc reasoned in his Separate and Dissenting Opinion in *Bagasora et al:* "The minimal guarantees under Article 21(4) are 'non-negotiable' and cannot be balanced against other interests. The use of the word 'minimum' demonstrates that these enumerated rights are an essential component of every trial" (*Prosecutor v. Bagosora et al.*, Separate and Dissenting Opinion of Judge Pavel Dolenc on the Decision and Scheduling Order on the Prosecution Motion for Harmonisation and Modification of Protective Measures for Witnesses, December 5, 2001, paras 11 and 14; also see *Prosecutor v. Brdanin and Talic*, Decision on Motion by Prosecution for Protected Measures, July 3, 2000, para. 31, where the Trial Chamber acknowledged that "the need to carry any balancing exercise which limits the rights of the accused necessarily results in a less than perfect trial").

Not all Trial Chambers, however, have rejected a balancing exercise. In the recent ICTY case of *Haradinaj et al.*, the Trial Chamber referred to its duty "to strike a fair balance between the right of the Accused to a fair trial on the one side, and the protection of victims and witnesses and the right of the public to access of information on the other side, the right of the Accused encompassing, in particular, the right to be allowed adequate time for the preparation of a defence, and to cross-examine witnesses testifying against the Accused" (*Prosecutor v. Haradinaj et al.*, Decision on Prosecution's Application for Pre-Trial Protective Measures for Witnesses, May 20, 2005, p. 4). In any event, it is clear from the case law that the rights of the Accused should be duly considered when decisions are made regarding the protection of victims and witnesses.

Absent specific evidence of the risk that particular witnesses will be interfered with, the extraordinary measures provided by Rule 69 cannot be justified. The assessment of risk and danger must be done on a witness by witness basis, and the Prosecution bears the onus of establishing "exceptional circumstances" (see, *Prosecutor v. Brdanin*, Decision on Motion by Prosecution for Protective Measures, July 3, 2000, paras 13, 16–18, and 22–28).

Where the likelihood that a particular victim or witness may be in danger or at risk has in fact been established, the Trial Chamber will limit the rights of the accused to the extent that the identity of the victim or witness will not be disclosed to the defence until such time required to provide adequate time for the defence to prepare before trial (See, *Brdanin* decision, paras 31–32; and, *Prosecutor v. Tadić*, Decision on the Prosecutor's Motion Requesting Protective Measures for Victims and Witnesses, August 10, 1995, para. 72). As Rule 69(C) has now been amended at the ICTR, disclosure of identifying details can be done on a rolling basis during trial, provided that adequate time is given to the Defence to prepare cross-examination. SCSL Rule 69(C) is even more specific, stating that the identity of the victim or witness shall be disclosed "in sufficient time before a witness is to be called".

Exceptional circumstances

8–142   The prevailing circumstances in the former Yugoslavia cannot by themselves amount to exceptional circumstances. As was held in the *Brdanin* decision:

> "This Tribunal has always been concerned solely with the former Yugoslavia, and Rule 69(A) was adopted by the judges against a background of ethnic and political enmities which existed in the former Yugoslavia at that time. The Tribunal was able to frame its Rules to fit the task at hand; the judges who framed them feared even at that time that many victims and witnesses of atrocities would be deterred from testifying about those crimes or would be concerned about the possible negative consequences which their testimony could have for themselves or their relatives. Accordingly, the use by those judges of the adjective 'exceptional' in Rule 69(A) was not an accidental one. To be exceptional, the circumstances must therefore go beyond what has been, since before the Tribunal was established, the rule—or the prevailing (or normal) circumstances—in the former Yugoslavia" (para. 11).

Also see, *Prosecutor v. Tadić*, Decision on the Prosecutor's Motion Requesting Protective Measures for Victims and Witnesses, August 10, 1995, para. 23; and, *Prosecutor v. Blaškić*, Decision on the Application of the Prosecutor dated October 17, 1996 requesting protective measures for victims and witnesses, November 5, 1996, para. 24.

Protection of witnesses in one case cannot be justified by the fear that the prosecution may have difficulties in finding witnesses who are willing to testify in future cases (*Brdanin* decision, para. 30).

The test

8–143   The Prosecution must show that the disclosure to the accused and his defence team of the identity of a witness at this stage, despite the obligation imposed upon the accused and his defence team not to disclose it to the public, may put the witness in danger or at risk. There must be some objective foundation for the fear that the witness may be in danger or at risk. The fears of a potential witness are not in themselves sufficient to establish a real likelihood that the witness may be in danger, and something more than that must be demonstrated before an interference with the right of the accused to know the witness's identity is warranted. (See *Prosecutor v. Brdanin and Talic*, First Decision on Motion by Prosecution for Protected Measures, July 21, 2000, para. 26; Second Decision, October 27, 2000, para. 19; Third Decision, November 8, 2000, paras 13 and 16; and *Prosecutor v. Milošević*, Order to the Accused on Protected Measures for Defence Witnesses, May 27, 2004; *Prosecutor v. Bagosora et al.*, Decision on Bagosora Motion for Protection of Witnesses, September 1, 2003).

The risk to witnesses testifying before the Tribunal is assessed according to the specific circumstances of a particular witness (*Prosecutor v. Brdanin and Talic*, Second Decision on Motion by Prosecution for Protected Measures, October 27, 2000, para. 21).

Ex parte hearings

The general principle is that "applications by either party for protective measures are determined on an *ex parte* basis where the persons to be protected would otherwise be identified" (*Prosecutor v. Simić*, Decision on (1) Application by Todorovic to re-open the decision of July 27, 1999, (2) Motion by ICRC to re-open scheduling order of November 18, 1999, and (3) Conditions for access to material, February 28, 2000, para. 40; *Prosecutor v. Haradinaj et al.*, Decision on Prosecution's Application for Pre-Trial Protective Measures for Witnesses, May 20, 2005, pp. 4–5).

8–144

However, *ex parte* hearings are only justified where disclosure to the other party of the information in the application or the fact of the application itself would be likely to prejudice unfairly the party making the application or some person related to the application. The party seeking the relief on an *ex parte* basis must identify with some care why unfair prejudice would be caused by revealing the detail of the application, or the application itself, to the other party. (See, *Simić* Decision, paras 41–43; *Prosecutor v. Brdjanin*, Decision on second motion by Prosecution for protective measures, October 27, 2000, para. 11; and *Prosecutor v. Kordić and Čerkez*, Order to Prosecution to Refile its *ex parte* Filing in Response to Motion by Kordic for Disclosure in Relation to Witness "AT", March 31, 2003, para. 4).

In addition to filing an application on an *ex parte* basis, the party must file *inter partes* but confidentially, its justification for non-disclosure of the identity of the witness, which as far as possible discloses to the other party the basis for the application without revealing the identity of the particular witness for whom protection is sought. The other party must be given sufficient information to enable them to determine whether to oppose the relief sought. (See, *Prosecutor v. Brdanin*, Decision on third motion by Prosecution for protective measures, November 8, 2000, paras 6–11.)

"Reasonable time before trial" for disclosure of identity

What constitutes a "reasonable time before trial" will depend on the circumstances of each witness for which protection has been granted under Rule 69. Witnesses who directly implicate the accused are more important to the accused in the preparation of his defence than those who prove the underlying offences (*Brdanin* decision, para. 34).

8–145

The number of witnesses to be investigated by the defence and under what circumstances the investigations will take place are also relevant considerations (*Brdanin* decision, para. 38).

A general guideline should be that unless a very few witnesses have been the subject of protection orders, a period somewhat longer than 30 days before trial is likely to be required to permit the accused to prepare properly (*Brdanin* decision, para. 38). In *Prosecutor v. Kordic*, Order for measures to protect victims and witnesses, January 15, 1999, the Chamber ordered a 21-day and 30-day limit in the following terms:

> "2. all material that has been disclosed to the Kordic Defence and Cerkez Defence in redacted form pursuant to the Order for the Disclosure of Documents and Extension of Protective Measures issued by this Trial Chamber on November 27, 1998 shall be disclosed to the Kordic Defence and Cerkez Defence in full, without redaction, not less than twenty-one days prior to the date set for commencement of the trial;
> 3. the Prosecutor may, with the approval of the Trial Chamber, make limited redactions to any written statement or testimony which was not part of the material supporting the original Indictment or the Amended Indictment concerning the identity and whereabouts of the person making or providing such written statement or testimony;
> 4. if the person making or providing any such written statement or testimony is a current or former citizen, national or subject of the former Yugoslavia or any of its parts, the written statements and testimony of such person, as redacted, shall be disclosed to the Kordic Defence and Cerkez Defence immediately and shall be disclosed to the Kordic Defence and Cerkez Defence in full, without redaction, not less than twenty-one days prior to the date set for commencement of the trial;
> 5. if the person making or providing any such written statement or testimony is not a current or former citizen, national or subject of the former Yugoslavia or any of its part, the written statements and testimony of such person, as redacted, shall be disclosed to the Kordic Defence and Cerkez Defence immediately and shall be disclosed to the Kordic Defence and Cerkez Defence in full, without redaction, not less than thirty days prior to the date set for commencement of the trial"

Disclosure to the defence of the identity and statements of a limited number of witnesses has been delayed until 10 days before the witness is due to testify (see, *Prosecutor v. Kordic*, Order for delayed disclosure of statements and protective measures, March 19, 1999.)

Until July 6, 2002, Rule 69(C) at the ICTR provided: "Subject to Rule 75, the identity of the victim or witness shall be disclosed in sufficient time prior to trial". Already before this amendment the phrase "time prior to trial" was interpreted to mean "prior to the witness's testimony" (*Prosecutor v. Niyitegeka*, Decision on Prosecutor's Motion for Protective Measures for Witnesses, July 12, 2000, paras 15 and 16).

This Rule was amended on July 6, 2002. Rule 69(C) now provides that: "Subject to Rule 75, the identity of the victim or witness shall be disclosed within such time as determined by the Trial Chamber to allow adequate time for preparation of the prosecution and the defence." The amendment was to enable the Prosecutor to disclose identifying information on a rolling basis as the trial goes along.

The meaning of the word "adequate" in Rule 69(C) "must be assessed in light of the rights of the accused set out in Article 19 and 20 of the Statute", which is determined on a case-by-case assessment (*Prosecutor v. Bagosora et al.*, Decision on Defence Motion for Reconsideration of the Trial Chamber's Decision and Scheduling Order of December 5, 2001, July 18, 2003, paras 13 and 15). Given that SCSL Rule 69(C) is similar to ICTR Rule 69(C) and the interpretation thereof, it seems a logical conclusion that Rule 69(C) SCSL Rules is interpreted as above.

Non-disclosure to the public

Aside from non-disclosure to the accused, victims and witnesses can **8–146** have their identities protected from the public in the pre-trial phase. In many cases, Trial Chambers have granted similar protective measures from the public, with similar definitions, in the following terms:

(1) The Defence shall not divulge to the media any non-public documents provided by the Prosecutor, including the witness statements or any other materials disclosed to the Defence pursuant to Rules 66 and 68;

(2) Unless directly necessary in order to prepare and present its case, the Defence shall not disclose to the public:

    (i) any name or information enabling witnesses to be identified, or the whereabouts of the confirmed or potential witnesses disclosed by the Prosecutor;

    (ii) any documentary evidence, physical or otherwise, or any written statement of a confirmed or potential witness or the contents, in whole or in part, of any non-public evidence, statement or prior testimony;

(3) If the Defence deems it necessary to disclose such information in order to prepare and present its case, it shall inform each recipient of any non-public information that he or she is forbidden to copy, reproduce or publicise them, in whole or in part, or to disclose or show them to any other person; and a person who has been provided with such information shall be required to return it to the Defence as soon as it is no longer needed for preparing and presenting the case;

(4) The Defence shall keep a log of the name, address and function of any person or entity receiving the information alluded to under (4) as well as the date of disclosure;

(5) If a member of the Defence team withdraws from the case, any confidential material in his or her possession shall be returned to the lead Defence counsel and, upon the conclusion of the case or upon lead Defence counsel ceasing to represent the accused, the Defence shall return to the Registry of the Tribunal all disclosed materials and copies thereof which are not included in the public record;

(6) (i) The accused, his Defence counsel, and their representatives who are acting pursuant to their instructions or requests, shall contact Prosecutor witnesses or potential witnesses, or any person identified in material disclosed to the accused, his Defence counsel, and their representatives acting pursuant to their instructions or requests only on reasonable prior written notice to the Prosecution; if a witness so requests, the Prosecution may be present at any meetings between that witness and the Defence; and

    (ii) The Prosecution shall contact a witness or a potential witness identified to it by the Defence, or a person identified in material disclosed by the accused, his Defence counsel, and their representatives acting pursuant to their instructions or requests only on reasonable prior written notice to the Defence; if a witness so requests, the Defence

411

may be present at any meetings between that witness and the Prosecution.

See, *inter alia*, *Prosecutor v. Hadžihasanović et al.*, Order on Protective Measures, February 1, 2002.

Disclosure to Defence in other cases

8–147 A practice has developed before the Tribunals that permits the accused in one case getting access to protected material, including witness testimony or statements, in other cases in certain circumstances (see, Chapter 7 on pre-trial procedure for rules relating to disclosure). The protected measures in question could relate either to protections granted pre-trial under Rule 69, or specific protections granted for the purposes of trial (see Rule 75(D)).

When such disclosure is ordered by the Chamber that originally granted the protective measures, the party obtaining access is ordered to abide by similar protective measures and can be ordered to comply with additional measures. For example:

(1) For the purposes of this disposition:
   (a) the "Prosecution" means the Prosecutor of the Tribunal and her staff;
   (b) the "Moving Parties", means and includes only the accused Enver Hadžihasanović, Mehmed Alagic and Amir Kubura (the "Accused") and such counsel and their immediate legal assistants, and others specifically assigned by the Tribunal to the Accused's trial defence teams and specifically identified in a list to be maintained by each lead counsel and filed with the *Hadžihasanović* Chamber *ex parte* and under seal within ten days of the entry of this order. Any and all additions and deletions to the initial list in respect of any of the above categories of persons who are necessarily identified and properly involved in the preparation of the defence shall be notified to that Trial Chamber in similar fashion within seven days of such additions or deletions;
   (c) the "public" means all persons, governments, organisations, entities, clients, associations and groups, other than the judges of the Tribunal and the staff of the Registry (assigned to either Chambers or the Registry), the Prosecution and the Moving Parties, as defined above. The "public" specifically includes, without limitation, family, friends and associates of all of the Accused, the accused in other cases or proceedings before the Tribunal and defence counsel in other cases or proceedings before the Tribunal;
   (d) the "media" means all video, audio and print media personnel, including journalists, authors, television and radio personnel, their agents and representatives;

(2) The Prosecution shall provide the Registry with the material relevant to the Witness, redacted as requested by the Prosecution, for disclosure to the Moving Parties;

(3) Rule 70 material, if any, shall not be disclosed unless prior authorization is obtained by the Prosecution from the relevant

authorities; the Prosecution shall be responsible for informing the Registry as appropriate;

(4) The Moving Parties shall not disclose to the media any confidential or non-public materials provided by the Prosecution;

(5) Save as is directly and specifically necessary for the preparation and presentation of their case and only on leave being first granted by the *Hadžihasanović* Chamber, the Moving Parties shall not disclose to the public:

(a) the names, identifying information or whereabouts of any witness or potential witness identified to them by the Prosecution; or

(b) any evidence (including documentary, physical or other evidence) or any written statement of a witness or potential witness, or the substance, in whole or in part, of any such non-public evidence, statement or prior testimony disclosed to them;

(6) If the Moving Parties find it directly and specifically necessary to disclose such information for the preparation and presentation of their case and having obtained leave from the *Hadžihasanović* Chamber to do so, they shall inform each person among the public to whom non-public material or information (such as witness statements, prior testimony, or videos, or the contents thereof), is shown or disclosed, that such a person is not to copy, reproduce or publicise such statement or evidence, and is not to show or disclose it to any other person. If provided with the original or any copy or duplicate of such material, such person shall return it to the Moving Parties when such material is no longer necessary for the preparation and presentation of their case;

(7) If a member of the defence teams concerned withdraws from the case, all material in his or her possession shall be returned to their lead defence counsel;

(3) Protection during trial

Before the commencement of the trial, the parties may apply to the **8–148** Trial Chamber requesting protective measures for witnesses when they testify during the trial under Rules 75 and 79. Any protective measures that particular witnesses may have enjoyed in the pre-trial phase under Rule 69 may continue to apply during the trial, depending on the nature of the Chamber's initial order (some orders are to apply throughout the proceedings, others operate until a specified time before trial when additional measures under Rule 75 may have to be applied for).

Any of the protective measures set out in Rules 75 and 79 can be ordered. The protective measures during trial can thus range from non-disclosure of the witness's identity to the accused and giving testimony from behind screens so that the witness's anonymity is protected from the accused, to protecting the witness's identity from the public or media in various ways, including testifying in closed session or in open session but with facial or audio distortions so that the witness's identity could be protected.

It has to be noted that the application of Rule 75 must be in compliance with the rights of the accused (Rule 75(A)).

8–149   The only case in which the identity of a witness has been concealed from the accused (but with the Judges knowing the identity) was in the *Prosecutor v. Tadić*, Decision on the Prosecutor's Motion requesting protective measures for victims and witnesses, August 10, 1995 (Judge Stephen dissenting, supported by *Prosecutor v. Blaškić*, Decision on the Application of the Prosecutor dated October 17, 1996 requesting protective measures for victims and witnesses, November 5, 1996). Also see, *Prosecutor v. Tadić*, Decision on the Prosecutor's motion requesting protective measures for witness L, November 14, 1995.

In many cases that followed, protective measures as outlined in Rule 75 and 79 have been granted to conceal the witness's identity in various forms from the public and media. For example, see *Prosecutor v. Krnojelac*, Order on Protective Measures for Witnesses at Trial, October 26, 2000, in which 26 witnesses were permitted to testify in public by using pseudonyms, and with the use of screening from the public and facial distortion; and, *Prosecutor v. Semanza*, ICTR, Decision on the Prosecution Motion for the Protection of Witnesses, December 10, 1998.

In the *Prosecutor v. Kordic*, the ICTY Trial Chamber heard the Prosecution's applications for protective measures on a witness by witness basis before each was called during the trial.

The applications are usually heard *in camera* in terms of Rule 75 given that the subject matter of the application concerns the witness's particular circumstances which the Chamber has to decide warrant the non-disclosure to the public of the witness's testimony.

The Defence are entitled to apply for the same protective measures under Rules 75 and 79. For example, see *Prosecutor v. Kajelijeli*, ICTR, Decision on Juvenal Kajelijeli's Motion for Protective Measures for Defence Witnesses, April 3, 2001; *Prosecutor v. Bagambiki et al.*, ICTR, Decision on the Motion by Emmanuel Bagambiki's Defence seeking orders for Protective Measures for its Witnesses, September 7, 2000.

The test under Rules 75 and 79

8–150   The granting of protective measures depends on the particular circumstances and merits of each case. (See, *Prosecutor v. Furundžija*, Decision on Prosecutor's Motion requesting protective measures for witnesses 'A' and 'B' at trial, June 11, 1998.)

As a guiding principle, parties are required to demonstrate that the measures sought are consistent with the rights of the accused, in particular the right to a public hearing, balanced against the particular circumstances faced by the witness or victim.

The considerations will substantially differ depending on whether the application is for anonymity from the accused or only from the public and media. In the latter category, protective measures are often granted providing that a legitimate fear of a security threat or danger has been identified that requires protective measures, the effect of which on the public nature of proceedings would be justified in the circumstances. (For example, see *Prosecutor v. Milošević*, Decision granting protective measures for individual witnesses, February 19, 2002; and, *Prosecutor v. Krnojelac*, Order on Protective Measures for Witnesses at Trial, October 26, 2000.)

An application in the former category has only arisen in one case, as cited above. For the guidelines for witness anonymity from the accused see *Prosecutor v. Tadić*, Decision on the Prosecutor's Motion requesting protective measures for victims and witnesses, August 10, 1995, paras 62–76.

Answering questions

Protective measures may also be granted in respect of the questions a witness may be required to answer. However, the witness may not invoke Rule 70 when answering questions, as this rule deals with information provided to the Prosecution on a confidential basis and used solely to generate new evidence (see, *Prosecutor v. Blaškić*, Decision of Trial Chamber I on protective measures for General Philippe Morillon, witness of the Trial Chamber, May 12, 1999). The Trial Chamber did order that the witness should not be asked about any of the sources of his information insofar as they directly affect the safety of UN peace-keeping forces or the State of which the witness is a national, and the witness was permitted to indicate to the Chamber if any of the requested information was confidential.

8–151

C. PARTICIPATION IN PROCEEDINGS

ICC Rules of Procedure and Evidence, rr. 89, 90

Application for participation of victims in the proceedings

89.—1. In order to present their views and concerns, victims shall make written application to the Registrar, who shall transmit the application to the relevant Chamber. Subject to the provisions of the Statute, in particular article 68, paragraph 1, the Registrar shall provide a copy of the application to the Prosecutor and the defence, who shall be entitled to reply within a time limit to be set by the Chamber. Subject to the provisions of sub-rule 2, the Chamber shall then specify the proceedings and manner in which participation is considered appropriate, which may include making opening and closing statements.

8–152

2. The Chamber, on its own initiative or on the application of the Prosecutor or the defence, may reject the application if it considers that the person is not a victim or that the criteria set forth in article 68, paragraph 3, are not otherwise fulfilled. A victim whose application has been rejected may file a new application later in the proceedings.

3. An application referred to in this rule may also be made by a person acting with the consent of the victim, or a person acting on behalf of a victim, in the case of a victim who is a child or, when necessary, a victim who is disabled.

4. Where there are a number of applications, the Chamber may consider the applications in such a manner as to ensure the effectiveness of the proceedings and may issue one decision.

Legal representatives of victims

8–153   **90.**—1. A victim shall be free to choose a legal representative.

2. Where there are a number of victims, the Chamber may, for the purposes of ensuring the effectiveness of the proceedings, request the victims or particular groups of victims, if necessary with the assistance of the Registry, to choose a common legal representative or representatives. In facilitating the coordination of victim representation, the Registry may provide assistance, *inter alia*, by referring the victims to a list of counsel, maintained by the Registry, or suggesting one or more common legal representatives.

3. If the victims are unable to choose a common legal representative or representatives within a time limit that the Chamber may decide, the Chamber may request the Registrar to choose one or more common legal representatives.

4. The Chamber and the Registry shall take all reasonable steps to ensure that in the selection of common legal representatives, the distinct interests of the victims, particularly as provided in article 68, paragraph 1, are represented and that any conflict of interest is avoided.

5. A victim or group of victims who lack the necessary means to pay for a common legal representative chosen by the Court may receive assistance from the Registry, including, as appropriate, financial assistance.

6. A legal representative of a victim or victims shall have the qualifications set forth in rule 22, sub-rule 1.

ICC Rules of Procedure and Evidence, rr. 92, 93

Notification to victims and their legal representatives

8–154   **92.**—1. This rule on notification to victims and their legal representatives shall apply to all proceedings before the Court, except in proceedings provided for in Part 2.

2. In order to allow victims to apply for participation in the proceedings in accordance with rule 89, the Court shall notify victims concerning the decision of the Prosecutor not to initiate an investigation or not to prosecute pursuant to article 53. Such a notification shall be given to victims or their legal representatives who have already participated in the proceedings or, as far as possible, to those who have communicated with the Court in respect of the situation or case in question. The Chamber may order the measures outlined in sub-rule 8 if it considers it appropriate in the particular circumstances.

3. In order to allow victims to apply for participation in the proceedings in accordance with rule 89, the Court shall notify victims regarding its decision to hold a hearing to confirm charges pursuant to article 61. Such a notification shall be given to victims or their legal representatives who have already participated in the proceedings or, as far as possible, to those who have communicated with the Court in respect of the case in question.

4. When a notification for participation as provided for in sub-rules 2 and 3 has been given, any subsequent notification as referred to in sub-rules 5 and 6 shall only be provided to victims or their legal representatives who may participate in the proceedings in accordance with a ruling of the Chamber pursuant to rule 89 and any modification thereof.

5. In a manner consistent with the ruling made under rules 89 to 91, victims or their legal representatives participating in proceedings shall, in respect of those proceedings, be notified by the Registrar in a timely manner of:

    (a) Proceedings before the Court, including the date of hearings and any postponements thereof, and the date of delivery of the decision;

    (b) Requests, submissions, motions and other documents relating to such requests, submissions or motions.

  6. Where victims or their legal representatives have participated in a certain stage of the proceedings, the Registrar shall notify them as soon as possible of the decisions of the Court in those proceedings.

  7. Notifications as referred to in sub-rules 5 and 6 shall be in writing or, where written notification is not possible, in any other form as appropriate. The Registry shall keep a record of all notifications. Where necessary, the Registrar may seek the co-operation of States Parties in accordance with article 93, paragraph 1(d) and (l).

  8. For notification as referred to in sub-rule 3 and otherwise at the request of a Chamber, the Registrar shall take necessary measures to give adequate publicity to the proceedings. In doing so, the Registrar may seek, in accordance with Part 9, the co-operation of relevant States Parties, and seek the assistance of intergovernmental organizations.

Views of victims or their legal representatives

  93. A Chamber may seek the views of victims or their legal representatives participating pursuant to rules 89 to 91 on any issue, *inter alia*, in relation to issues referred to in rules 107, 109, 125, 128, 136, 139 and 191. In addition, a Chamber may seek the views of other victims, as appropriate.

                       8–155

ICC Regulations of the Court, r. 86

Participation of victims in the proceedings under rule 89

  86.—1. For the purposes of rule 89 and subject to rule 102 a victim shall make a written application to the Registrar who shall develop standard forms for that purpose which shall be approved in accordance with regulation 23, subregulation 2. These standard forms shall, to the extent possible, be made available to victims, groups of victims, or intergovernmental and nongovernmental organizations, which may assist in their dissemination, as widely as possible. These standard forms shall, to the extent possible, be used by victims.

                       8–156

  2. The standard forms or other applications described in sub-regulation 1 shall contain, to the extent possible, the following information:

    (a) The identity and address of the victim, or the address to which the victim requests all communications to be sent; in case the application is presented by someone other than the victim in accordance with rule 89, subrule 3, the identity and address of that person, or the address to which that person requests all communications to be sent;

    (b) If the application is presented in accordance with rule 89, subrule 3, evidence of the consent of the victim or evidence on the situation of the victim, being a child or a disabled person, shall be presented together with the application, either in writing or in accordance with rule 102;

    (c) A description of the harm suffered resulting from the commission of any crime within the jurisdiction of the Court, or, in case of a victim being an organization or institution, a description of any direct harm as described in rule 85 (b);

    (d) A description of the incident, including its location and date and, to the extent possible, the identity of the person or persons the victim believes to be responsible for the harm as described in rule 85;

    (e) Any relevant supporting documentation, including names and addresses of witnesses;

(f) Information as to why the personal interests of the victim are affected;

(g) Information on the stage of the proceedings in which the victim wishes to participate, and, if applicable, on the relief sought;

(h) Information on the extent of legal representation, if any, which is envisaged by the victim, including the names and addresses of potential legal representatives, and information on the victim's or victims' financial means to pay for a legal representative.

3. Victims applying for participation in the trial and/or appeal proceedings shall, to the extent possible, make their application to the Registrar before the start of the stage of the proceedings in which they want to participate.

4. The Registrar may request further information from victims or those presenting an application in accordance with rule 89, sub-rule 3, in order to ensure that such application contains, to the extent possible, the information referred to in sub-regulation 2, before transmission to a Chamber. The Registrar may also seek additional information from States, the Prosecutor and intergovernmental or non-governmental organizations.

5. The Registrar shall present all applications described in this regulation to the Chamber together with a report thereon. The Registrar shall endeavour to present one report for a group of victims, taking into consideration the distinct interests of the victims.

6. Subject to any order of the Chamber, the Registrar may also submit one report on a number of applications received in accordance with sub-regulation 1 to the Chamber seized of the case or situation in order to assist that Chamber in issuing only one decision on a number of applications in accordance with rule 89, sub-rule 4. Reports covering all applications received in a certain time period may be presented on a periodic basis.

7. Before deciding on an application, the Chamber may request, if necessary with the assistance of the Registrar, additional information from, *inter alia*, States, the Prosecutor, the victims or those acting on their behalf or with their consent. If information is received from States or the Prosecutor, the Chamber shall provide the relevant victim or victims with an opportunity to respond.

8. A decision taken by a Chamber under rule 89 shall apply throughout the proceedings in the same case, subject to the powers of the relevant Chamber in accordance with rule 91, sub-rule 1.

9. There shall be a specialised unit dealing with victims' participation and reparations under the authority of the Registrar. This unit shall be responsible for assisting victims and groups of victims.

ICTY/ICTR/SCSL

8–157 There is no provision for the participation of victims in proceedings either at the pre-trial or trial stage in the ICTY, ICTR or the SCSL. The Prosecution does, however, present evidence of the impact of offences on victims during trial.

East Timor

Regulation 2000/30, ss.12, 25 (as amended by Regulation 2001/25)

The Victim

8–158 12.—12.1 A victim shall be accorded those rights provided in the present regulation, in addition to any other rights provided by law or other UNTAET regulations.

12.2 The status of a person, organization or institution as a victim is not related to whether the perpetrator is identified, apprehended, prosecuted or convicted, and is independent of any familial relationship with the perpetrator.

12.3 Any victim has the right to be heard at a review hearing before the Investigating Judge, and at any hearing on an application for conditional release pursuant to Section 43 of the present regulation. In the exercise of this right, the victim may be represented in court by a legal representative. An individual victim has the right to be notified by the prosecutor, or by the police in proceedings pursuant to Section 44 of the present regulation, in advance of the time and place of review hearings referred to in Sections 20, 29.5 and 43 of the present regulation, provided that the victim has previously indicated in a reasonable manner to the court, prosecutor or investigating officer a desire to be so notified.

12.4 It is not required that the notification of a victim be written or that it be in strict accord with Section 2.4 of the present regulation; provided, however, that the notice is of a nature which is reasonable under the circumstances and is likely to convey actual notice of the proceedings in sufficient time to permit the exercise of the victim's rights. Defects in the notification of a victim at any stage shall not deprive the Court of jurisdiction to proceed.

12.5 A victim may request to the court to be heard at stages of the criminal proceedings other than review hearings.

12.6 The victim has the right to request the Public Prosecutor to conduct specific investigations or to take specific measures in order to prove the guilt of the suspect. The Public Prosecutor may accept or reject the request.

12.7 The Investigating Judge or a court may direct that several victims will be represented in the same case through a single representative.

12.8 The Public Prosecutor shall take reasonable steps to keep the victims informed of the progress of the case.

Trust Fund

25.—25.1 A Trust Fund may be established by decision of the Transitional Administrator in consultation with the National Consultative Council for the benefit of victims of crimes within the jurisdiction of the panels, and of the families of such victims.   **8–159**

25.2 The panels may order money and other property collected through fines, forfeiture, foreign donors or other means to be transferred to the Trust Fund.

25.3 The Trust Fund shall be managed according to criteria to be determined by an UNTAET directive.

IV. JUDGMENT

A. Deliberations

(1) Statutory provisions and rules

ICC Rules of Procedure and Evidence, r. 142

Deliberations

142.—1. After the closing statements, the Trial Chamber shall retire to deliberate, in camera. The Trial Chamber shall inform all those who participated in the proceedings of the date on which the Trial Chamber will pronounce   **8–160**

its decision. The pronouncement shall be made within a reasonable period of time after the Trial Chamber has retired to deliberate.

2. When there is more than one charge, the Trial Chamber shall decide separately on each charge. When there is more than one accused, the Trial Chamber shall decide separately on the charges against each accused.

Additional hearings on matters related to sentence or reparations

8–161   **143.** Pursuant to article 76, paragraphs 2 and 3, for the purpose of holding a further hearing on matters related to sentence and, if applicable, reparations, the Presiding Judge shall set the date of the further hearing. This hearing can be postponed, in exceptional circumstances, by the Trial Chamber, on its own motion or at the request of the Prosecutor, the defence or the legal representatives of the victims participating in the proceedings pursuant to rules 89 to 91 and, in respect of reparations hearings, those victims who have made a request under rule 94.

ICTY/ICTR Rules of Procedure and Evidence, r. 87

Deliberations

8–162   **87.**—(A) When both parties have completed their presentation of the case, the Presiding Judge shall declare the hearing closed, and the Trial Chamber shall deliberate in private. A finding of guilt may be reached only when a majority of the Trial Chamber is satisfied that guilt has been proved beyond reasonable doubt.

(B) The Trial Chamber shall vote separately on each charge contained in the indictment. If two or more accused are tried together under Rule 48, separate findings shall be made as to each accused.

(C) If the Trial Chamber finds the accused guilty on one or more of the charges contained in the indictment, it shall at the same time determine the penalty to be imposed in respect of each finding of guilt.

East Timor

Regulation 2000/30, s.39.1 (as amended by Regulation 2001/25)

Decision

8–163   **39.**—39.1 After the hearing is completed, the Court shall begin deliberations in private. The Court shall decide in accordance with Section 6.2 of UNTAET Regulation No. 2000/11. The Court shall pronounce on the guilt or innocence of the accused. If the accused is found guilty, the Court shall state the qualification of the crime and its penalty.

39.2 If the accused is found guilty, the Court in its discretion may receive additional evidence from the parties before determining the appropriate penalty.

SCSL Rules of Procedure and Evidence, r. 87

Deliberations

8–164   **87.**—(A) After presentation of closing arguments, the Presiding Judge shall declare the hearing closed, and the Trial Chamber shall deliberate in private. A finding of guilty may be reached only when a majority of the Trial Chamber is satisfied that guilt has been proved beyond reasonable doubt.

(B) The Trial Chamber shall vote separately on each count contained in the indictment. If two or more accused are tried together under Rule 48, separate findings shall be made as to each accused.

(C) If the Trial Chamber finds the accused guilty on one or more of the counts contained in the indictment, it shall also determine the penalty to be imposed in respect of each of the counts.

B. Delivering Judgment

(1) Statutory provisions and rules

ICC Rules of Procedure and Evidence, r. 144

Delivery of the decisions of the Trial Chamber

144.—1. Decisions of the Trial Chamber concerning admissibility of a case, the jurisdiction of the Court, criminal responsibility of the accused, sentence and reparations shall be pronounced in public and, wherever possible, in the presence of the accused, the Prosecutor, the victims or the legal representatives of the victims participating in the proceedings pursuant to rules 89 to 91, and the representatives of the States which have participated in the proceedings.   **8–165**

2. Copies of all the above-mentioned decisions shall be provided as soon as possible to:
   (a) All those who participated in the proceedings, in a working language of the Court;
   (b) The accused, in a language he or she fully understands or speaks, if necessary to meet the requirements of fairness under article 67, paragraph 1(f).

ICTY

ICTY Statute, Art. 23

Judgment

23.—1. The Trial Chambers shall pronounce judgments and impose sentences and penalties on persons convicted of serious violations of international humanitarian law.   **8–166**

2. The judgment shall be rendered by a majority of the judges of the Trial Chamber, and shall be delivered by the Trial Chamber in public. It shall be accompanied by a reasoned opinion in writing, to which separate or dissenting opinions may be appended.

ICTY Rules of Procedure and Evidence, r. 98*ter*

Judgment

98*ter*.—(A) The judgment shall be pronounced in public, on a date of which notice shall have been given to the parties and counsel and at which they shall be entitled to be present, subject to the provisions of Sub-rule 102 (B).   **8–167**

(B) If the Trial Chamber finds the accused guilty of a crime and concludes from the evidence that unlawful taking of property by the accused was associated with it, it shall make a specific finding to that effect in its judgment. The Trial Chamber may order restitution as provided in Rule 105.

(C) The judgment shall be rendered by a majority of the Judges. It shall be accompanied or followed as soon as possible by a reasoned opinion in writing, to which separate or dissenting opinions may be appended.

(D) A copy of the judgment and of the Judges' opinions in a language which the accused understands shall as soon as possible be served on the accused if in custody. Copies thereof in that language and in the language in which they were delivered shall also as soon as possible be provided to counsel for the accused.

ICTR

ICTR Statute, Art. 22

Judgment

8–168   22.—1. The Trial Chambers shall pronounce judgments and impose sentences and penalties on persons convicted of serious violations of international humanitarian law.

2. The judgment shall be rendered by a majority of the judges of the Trial Chamber, and shall be delivered by the Trial Chamber in public. It shall be accompanied by a reasoned opinion in writing, to which separate or dissenting opinions may be appended.

ICTR Rules of Procedure and Evidence, r. 88

Judgment

8–169   88.—(A) The judgment shall be pronounced in public, on a date of which notice shall have been given to the parties and counsel and at which they shall be entitled to be present.

(B) If the Trial Chamber finds the accused guilty of a crime and concludes from the evidence that unlawful taking of property by the accused was associated with it, it shall make a specific finding to that effect in its judgment. The Trial Chamber may order restitution as provided in Rule 105.

(C) The judgment shall be rendered by a majority of the Judges. It shall be accompanied or followed as soon as possible by a reasoned opinion in writing. Separate or dissenting opinions may be appended.

East Timor

Regulation 2000/30, s. 39 (as amended by 2001/15)

Decision

8–170   39.—39.3 The Court shall prepare a final written decision. The final written decision shall be registered by the Registrar as an official entry into the court file. The written decision shall contain the following elements:

    (a) the identification of the Court, the identity of the judges and the identification of the parties;
    (b) an account of the events and circumstances of the case tried by the Court;
    (c) an account of the facts that the court considered proved and facts that were not proved;
    (d) an account of the factual and legal grounds of those considerations;
    (e) a finding in relation to the innocence or guilt of the accused identifying the section applied of the penal legislation;
    (f) an order relating to the penalty if the accused is found guilty;
    (g) an order relating to the costs of the trial;
    (h) an order relating to the disposal of physical evidence seized during the investigations;
    (i) an order pursuant to Section 50.2, if applicable;
    (j) an order pursuant to Section 52.2, if applicable; and
    (k) the signatures of all judges.

39.4 The court may release its written decision upon the end of deliberations in the same session or schedule a separate session for the release of its written decision, within a maximum of 20 days. Each party shall be given a copy of the written decision.

SCSL

SCSL Statute, Art. 18

Judgment

8–171

18. The Judgment shall be rendered by a majority of judges of the Trial Chamber or the Appeals Chamber, and shall be delivered in public. It shall be accompanied by a reasoned opinion in writing, to which separate or dissenting opinions may be appended.

SCSL Rules of Procedure and Evidence, r. 88

Judgment

8–172

88.—(A) The judgement shall be pronounced in public.
(B) If the Trial Chamber finds the accused guilty of a crime, the Trial Chamber may order the forfeiture of the property, proceeds and any assets acquired unlawfully or by criminal conduct as provided in Rule 104.
(C) The judgement shall be rendered by a majority of the Judges. It shall be accompanied by a reasoned opinion in writing. Separate or dissenting opinions may be appended.

(2) The effect of Rule 98*ter*

8–173

Before Chambers render their judgments the parties are informed of the date on which the judgment will be delivered.
In the *Jelisic* Judgment, in which the Trial Chamber dismissed the case at the close of the Prosecution's case, the Chamber rejected the Prosecution's argument that "the effect of Rule 98*ter* could not deprive the Prosecution of its right to submit a closing argument on the law and

facts" (*Jelisic* Judgment, ICTY Trial Chamber, December 14, 1999, para. 16—on appeal, the Appeals Chamber ruled that the Prosecution should have had an opportunity to be heard on the question of whether the evidence was sufficient to sustain a conviction, see *Jelisic* Judgment, ICTY Appeals Chamber, July 5, 2001, paras 22–29).

C. ACQUITTED PERSONS

(1) Statutory provisions and rules

ICC

Statute, Art. 81 (3) (c)

Appeal Against Decision of Acquittal or Conviction or Against Sentence
8–174   81.—(3)
   (c) In case of an acquittal, the accused shall be released immediately, subject to the following:
      (i) Under exceptional circumstances, and having regard, *inter alia*, to the concrete risk of flight, the seriousness of the offence charged and the probability of success on appeal, the Trial Chamber, at the request of the Prosecutor, may maintain the detention of the person pending appeal;
      (ii) A decision by the Trial Chamber under subparagraph (c)(i) may be appealed in accordance with the Rules of Procedure and Evidence.

ICTY

ICTY Rules of Procedure and Evidence, r. 99

Status of the acquitted person
8–175   99.—(A) Subject to Sub-rule (B), in the case of an acquittal or the upholding of a challenge to jurisdiction, the accused shall be released immediately.
   (B) If, at the time the judgement is pronounced, the Prosecutor advises the Trial Chamber in open court of the Prosecutor's intention to file notice of appeal pursuant to Rule 108, the Trial Chamber may, on application in that behalf by the Prosecutor and upon hearing the parties, in its discretion, issue an order for the continued detention of the accused, pending the determination of the appeal.

ICTR

ICTR Rules of Procedure and Evidence, r. 99

Status of the acquitted person
8–176   99.—(A) In case of acquittal, the accused shall be released immediately.

(B) If, at the time the judgement is pronounced, the Prosecutor advises the Trial Chamber in open court of his intention to file notice of appeal pursuant to Rule 108, the Trial Chamber may, at the request of the Prosecutor, issue a warrant for the arrest and further detention of the accused to take effect immediately.

East Timor

Regulation 2000/30, s.42.1 (as amended by Regulation 2001/25)

Court Orders and Sentences

42.—42.1 Any order or decision of a court shall be executed by the **8–177** competent authorities immediately upon the release of the written decision of the court. It is the responsibility of the public prosecutor to notify other competent authorities of their duties pursuant to this Section.

42.2 A decision declaring the acquittal of an accused shall result in his or her immediate release or in the cancellation of any restrictive measure.

SCSL

SCSL Rules of Procedure and Evidence, r. 99

Status of the acquitted person

99.—(A) In case of acquittal, the Special Court shall, subject to Sub-Rule **8–178** (B) below, order the release of the accused.

(B) If, at the time the acquittal is pronounced, the Prosecutor advises the Trial Chamber in open court of his intention to file notice of appeal pursuant to Rule 108, the Trial Chamber may, on application of the Prosecutor and upon hearing the parties, in its discretion, issue an order for the continued detention of the accused, pending the determination of the appeal.

(2) Application

In addition to the circumstances in which an accused is acquitted or a **8–179** challenge to jurisdiction is upheld, a Trial Chamber may order the immediate release of the accused at the time of judgment if the sentence imposed in the judgment is less than time already spent in pre-trial detention (*Prosecutor v. Aleksovski*, Order for the Immediate Release of Zlatko Aleksovski, ICTY Trial Chamber, May 7, 1999).

Rule 99 was invoked for the first time when the accused Zejnil Delalic was acquitted, and although the Prosecution did appeal his acquittal, he was released from custody as no application was made by the Prosecution under Rule 99(B) (see, *Prosecutor v. Delalic et al.*, Judgment, ICTY Trial Chamber, November 16, 1998, para. 1291).

CHAPTER 9

RULES OF EVIDENCE

I. GENERAL RULES

A. INTRODUCTION

The rules of evidence of international criminal courts are by nature **9–1** skeletal. They are not set out in precise detail as often occurs in domestic systems.

Judges and lawyers from a wide variety of national systems (common law, civil law, and others) participate before international courts, requiring the rules to combine the legal traditions of many countries. Most importantly, the rules of evidence are guided by the general adversarial nature of international criminal courts and by the types of cases that are tried before the courts.

More flexible rules of evidence are needed to control the presentation **9–2** and admission of evidence in cases involving complex factual scenarios, with potentially hundreds of witnesses and thousands of exhibits. The rules also have to be designed to take account of the adversarial features of the courts. There is no "investigating judge" in the international system, responsible for investigating and trying the case, although the ICC has included the Pre-Trial Chamber with limited control powers during the investigation. The judges are reliant on the Prosecution and Defence to litigate the case before them, and hence the need for clearly defined rules to govern such proceedings.

As no international jury system has been adopted, the judges are the triers of fact and law. As a result, the rules of evidence do not have to be fashioned to protect a jury from lay prejudices. Greater latitude for the introduction of evidence can be afforded professional judges in the exercise of their fact-finding duties. As the SCSL Trial Chamber held in *Brima et al.*, reasoning adopted by many Trial Chambers of all Tribunals, "[i]ssues before the Special Court are conducted before professional judges, who by virtue of their education and experience are able to ponder independently without prejudice to each and every case which will be brought before them" (*Prosecutor v. Brima et al.*, Decision on the Prosecution Motion for Concurrent Hearing of Evidence Common to Cases SCSL-2004–15-PT and SCSL-2004–16-PT, May 11, 2004, para. 38; *Prosecutor v. Gbao*, Order on the Urgent Request for Direction on the Time to Respond and/or an Extension of Time for the Filling of a Response to the Prosecution Motions, May 15, 2003, p. 2; *Prosecutor v. Delalic*, Decision on the Motion of the Prosecution for the Admissibility of Evidence, January 19, 1998, para. 20; and *Prosecutor v. Ntakirutimana et al.*, Decision on the Prosecutor's Motion to Join the Indictments ICTR 96–10-I and ICTR 96–17-T, February 22, 2001, para. 26).

9–3 The ICTY and ICTR are by and large adversarial criminal courts. The Prosecution is responsible for independently investigating and indicting alleged perpetrators, and presenting the evidence to support the cases during trial (see, ICTY, ICTR and SCSL Rule 85). The Defence, on the other hand, has the opportunity to challenge the Prosecution case, and call its own evidence, although the burden of proving the innocence of the accused does not rest on the Defence. Instead, the burden of proving the guilt of the accused rests on the Prosecution, the standard being proof beyond a reasonable doubt (see, ICTY, ICTR and SCSL Rule 87).

9–4 The same system will essentially characterise the ICC. The Prosecution will bear responsibility for investigating and indicting cases, and proving them beyond reasonable doubt at trial if the accused is to be convicted (see, Article 66 of the ICC Statute). The existence and functions of the Pre-trial Chamber in the ICC (which does not exist in the ICTY and ICTR) will facilitate greater judicial management of the investigation and pre-trial phases (see, Article 56 of the ICC Statute).

The East Timor Special Panel for Serious Crimes operates on a similar basis. The Public Prosecutor is responsible for investigations and is the only authority empowered to issue an indictment (see, Section 7 of Regulation 2000/30). The investigating judge, on the other hand, has the authority to issue warrants and other orders necessary for the criminal investigation (see, Section 9 of Regulation 2000/30).

The newly created Iraqi Special Tribunal does not expressly provide for guilt to be proven "beyond a reasonable doubt". The Rules of Procedure and Evidence existing in Iraqi law, and applicable before the Special Tribunal only require that a court or Tribunal be "satisfied" of guilt by the evidence presented (Law On Criminal Proceedings with Amendments, No. 23 of 1971, para. 213(A)).

B. Applicability of National Rules

The ICTY, ICTR and SCSL Rules specifically provide that the Tribunals shall not be bound by national rules of evidence: see Rule 89(A) for each Tribunal. The ICC Rules contain a similar provision in Rule 63(5).   **9–5**

Moreover, Article 69(8) of the ICC Statute provides that "When deciding on the relevance or admissibility of evidence collected by a State, the Court shall not rule on the application of the State's national law." The Court will be bound by its own Statute, Rules and case law in determining issues of admissibility and not those of a particular State. The same position was adopted by the ICTY Trial Chamber in the *Prosecutor v. Delalic et al.*, Decision on Zdravko Mucic's Motion for the Exclusion of Evidence, September 2, 1997, paras 47–55.

National rules may nevertheless be drawn upon in support of general principles of law that can be cited before international criminal courts. Article 21(1) of the ICC Statute provides: **9–6**

> The Court shall apply:
> (a) In the first place, this Statute, Elements of Crimes and its Rules of Procedure and Evidence;
> (b) In the second place, where appropriate, applicable treaties and the principles and rules of international law, including the established principles of the international law of armed conflict;
> (c) Failing that, general principles of law derived by the Court from national laws of legal systems of the world including, as appropriate, the national laws of States that would normally exercise jurisdiction over the crime, provided that those principles are not inconsistent with this Statute and with international law and internationally recognized norms and standards.

Rule 89(B) of the ICTY, ICTR and SCSL contains a similar provision:

> In cases not otherwise provided for in this Section, a Chamber shall apply rules of evidence which will best favour a fair determination of the matter before it and are consonant with the spirit of the Statute and the general principles of law.

By contrast, the applicable rules of procedure of the Special Panels for East Timor are based largely on the national rules of East Timor, as the special panels are part of the national system of criminal justice established under the United Nations Transitional Administration in East Timor. Aspects of the rules applicable before the ad hoc International Tribunals have been incorporated into the national rules adopted by the Transitional Administration, for example see Section 34 of Regulation 2000/30 on the Rules of Evidence and Section 36 on Witnesses, which were clearly influenced by the similar rules applicable before the ICTY and ICTR.   **9–7**

The Special Court for Sierra Leone, on the other hand, is bound to apply the Rules of Procedure and Evidence in force before the ICTR (see, Article 14 of the Statute of the Special Court). However, Article 114 provides that the Judges of the Special Court may amend the Rules and adopt additional rules. No specific national rules or variations of the ICTR Rules were enacted to apply before the Sierra Leone court. On March 7, 2003, the SCSL has adopted their own set of Rules of Procedure and Evidence which was largely based on the ICTR Rules. Since their enactment, the SCSL Rules have been amended five times.

II. RULES OF ADMISSIBILITY

(1) Statutory Provisions and Rules

ICC

ICC Statute, Arts 64(9), 69(1)-(4)

Functions and powers of the Trial Chamber

9–8   **64.**—9. The Trial Chamber shall have, *inter alia*, the power on application of a party or on its own motion to:
    (a) Rule on the admissibility or relevance of evidence; and
    (b) Take all necessary steps to maintain order in the course of a hearing.

Evidence

9–9   **69.**—1. Before testifying, each witness shall, in accordance with the Rules of Procedure and Evidence, give an undertaking as to the truthfulness of the evidence to be given by that witness.

    2. The testimony of a witness at trial shall be given in person, except to the extent provided by the measures set forth in article 68 or in the Rules of Procedure and Evidence. The Court may also permit the giving of *viva voce* (oral) or recorded testimony of a witness by means of video or audio technology, as well as the introduction of documents or written transcripts, subject to this Statute and in accordance with the Rules of Procedure and Evidence. These measures shall not be prejudicial to or inconsistent with the rights of the accused.

    3. The parties may submit evidence relevant to the case, in accordance with article 64. The Court shall have the authority to request the submission of all evidence that it considers necessary for the determination of the truth.

    4. The Court may rule on the relevance or admissibility of any evidence, taking into account, *inter alia*, the probative value of the evidence and any prejudice that such evidence may cause to a fair trial or to a fair evaluation of the testimony of a witness, in accordance with the Rules of Procedure and Evidence.

    5. The Court shall respect and observe privileges on confidentiality as provided for in the Rules of Procedure and Evidence.

ICC Rules of Procedure and Evidence, rr. 63, 64, 65, 66, 67, 68

General provisions relating to evidence

9–10   **63.**—1. The rules of evidence set forth in this chapter, together with article 69, shall apply in proceedings before all Chambers.

2. A Chamber shall have the authority, in accordance with the discretion described in article 64, paragraph 9, to assess freely all evidence submitted in order to determine its relevance or admissibility in accordance with article 69.

3. A Chamber shall rule on an application of a party or on its own motion, made under article 64, subparagraph 9(a), concerning admissibility when it is based on the grounds set out in article 69, paragraph 7.

4. Without prejudice to article 66, paragraph 3, a Chamber shall not impose a legal requirement that corroboration is required in order to prove any crime within the jurisdiction of the Court, in particular, crimes of sexual violence.

5. The Chambers shall not apply national laws governing evidence, other than in accordance with article 21.

Procedure relating to the relevance or admissibility of evidence

64.—1. An issue relating to relevance or admissibility must be raised at the time when the evidence is submitted to a Chamber. Exceptionally, when those issues were not known at the time when the evidence was submitted, it may be raised immediately after the issue has become known. The Chamber may request that the issue be raised in writing. The written motion shall be communicated by the Court to all those who participate in the proceedings, unless otherwise decided by the Court.

9–11

2. A Chamber shall give reasons for any rulings it makes on evidentiary matters. These reasons shall be placed in the record of the proceedings if they have not already been incorporated into the record during the course of the proceedings in accordance with article 64, paragraph 10, and rule 137, sub-rule 1.

3. Evidence ruled irrelevant or inadmissible shall not be considered by the Chamber.Compellability of witnesses

65.—1. A witness who appears before the Court is compellable by the Court to provide testimony, unless otherwise provided for in the Statute and the Rules, in particular rules 73, 74 and 75.

2. Rule 171 applies to a witness appearing before the Court who is compellable to provide testimony under sub-rule 1.

Solemn undertaking

66.—1. Except as described in sub-rule 2, every witness shall, in accordance with article 69, paragraph 1, make the following solemn undertaking before testifying:

9–12

> "I solemnly declare that I will speak the truth, the whole truth and nothing but the truth."

2. A person under the age of 18 or a person whose judgement has been impaired and who, in the opinion of the Chamber, does not understand the nature of a solemn undertaking may be allowed to testify without this solemn undertaking if the Chamber considers that the person is able to describe matters of which he or she has knowledge and that the person understands the meaning of the duty to speak the truth.

3. Before testifying, the witness shall be informed of the offence defined in article 70, paragraph 1(a).

Live testimony by means of audio or video-link technology

67.—1. In accordance with article 69, paragraph 2, a Chamber may allow a witness to give *viva voce* (oral) testimony before the Chamber by means of audio or video technology, provided that such technology permits the witness to be

9–13

431

examined by the Prosecutor, the defence, and by the Chamber itself, at the time that the witness so testifies.

2. The examination of a witness under this rule shall be conducted in accordance with the relevant rules of this chapter.

3. The Chamber, with the assistance of the Registry, shall ensure that the venue chosen for the conduct of the audio or video-link testimony is conducive to the giving of truthful and open testimony and to the safety, physical and psychological well-being, dignity and privacy of the witness.

Prior recorded testimony

9–14   **68.**— When the Pre-Trial Chamber has not taken measures under article 56, the Trial Chamber may, in accordance with article 69, paragraph 2, allow the introduction of previously recorded audio or video testimony of a witness, or the transcript or other documented evidence of such testimony, provided that:

    (a) If the witness who gave the previously recorded testimony is not present before the Trial Chamber, both the Prosecutor and the defence had the opportunity to examine the witness during the recording; or

    (b) If the witness who gave the previously recorded testimony is present before the Trial Chamber, he or she does not object to the submission of the previously recorded testimony and the Prosecutor, the defence and the Chamber have the opportunity to examine the witness during the proceedings.

ICTY

ICTY Rules of Procedure and Evidence, rr. 89, 90, 92*bis*

General Provisions

9–15   **89.**—(A) A Chamber shall apply the rules of evidence set forth in this Section, and shall not be bound by national rules of evidence.

(B) In cases not otherwise provided for in this Section, a Chamber shall apply rules of evidence which will best favour a fair determination of the matter before it and are consonant with the spirit of the Statute and the general principles of law.

(C) A Chamber may admit any relevant evidence which it deems to have probative value.

(D) A Chamber may exclude evidence if its probative value is substantially outweighed by the need to ensure a fair trial.

(E) A Chamber may request verification of the authenticity of evidence obtained out of court.

(F) A Chamber may receive the evidence of a witness orally or, where the interests of justice allow, in written form.

Testimony of Witnesses

9–16   **90.**—(A) Every witness shall, before giving evidence, make the following solemn declaration: "I solemnly declare that I will speak the truth, the whole truth and nothing but the truth."

(B) A child who, in the opinion of the Chamber, does not understand the nature of a solemn declaration, may be permitted to testify without that formality, if the Chamber is of the opinion that the child is sufficiently mature to be able to report the facts of which the child had knowledge and understands the duty to tell the truth. A judgment, however, cannot be based on such testimony alone.

(C) A witness, other than an expert, who has not yet testified shall not be present when the testimony of another witness is given. However, a witness who has heard the testimony of another witness shall not for that reason alone be disqualified from testifying.

(D) Notwithstanding paragraph (C), upon order of the Chamber, an investigator in charge of a party's investigation shall not be precluded from being called as a witness on the ground that he or she has been present in the courtroom during the proceedings.

(E) A witness may object to making any statement which might tend to incriminate the witness. The Chamber may, however, compel the witness to answer the question. Testimony compelled in this way shall not be used as evidence in a subsequent prosecution against the witness for any offence other than false testimony.

(F) The Trial Chamber shall exercise control over the mode and order of interrogating witnesses and presenting evidence so as to
   (i) make the interrogation and presentation effective for the ascertainment of the truth; and
   (ii) avoid needless consumption of time.

(G) The Trial Chamber may refuse to hear a witness whose name does not appear on the list of witnesses compiled pursuant to Rules 73*bis*(C) and 73*ter*(C).

  (H) (i) Cross-examination shall be limited to the subject-matter of the evidence-in-chief and matters affecting the credibility of the witness and, where the witness is able to give evidence relevant to the case for the cross-examining party, to the subject-matter of that case.

    (ii) In the cross-examination of a witness who is able to give evidence relevant to the case for the cross-examining party, counsel shall put to that witness the nature of the case of the party for whom that counsel appears which is in contradiction of the evidence given by the witness.

    (iii) The Trial Chamber may, in the exercise of its discretion, permit enquiry into additional matters.

Proof of Facts other than by Oral Evidence

92*bis*.—(A) A Trial Chamber may admit, in whole or in part, the evidence of a witness in the form of a written statement in lieu of oral testimony which goes to proof of a matter other than the acts and conduct of the accused as charged in the indictment. **9–17**

   (i) Factors in favour of admitting evidence in the form of a written statement include but are not limited to circumstances in which the evidence in question:
     (a) is of a cumulative nature, in that other witnesses will give or have given oral testimony of similar facts;
     (b) relates to relevant historical, political or military background;
     (c) consists of a general or statistical analysis of the ethnic composition of the population in the places to which the indictment relates;
     (d) concerns the impact of crimes upon victims;
     (e) relates to issues of the character of the accused; or
     (f) relates to factors to be taken into account in determining sentence.

   (ii) Factors against admitting evidence in the form of a written statement include whether:
     (a) there is an overriding public interest in the evidence in question being presented orally;

     (b) a party objecting can demonstrate that its nature and source renders it unreliable, or that its prejudicial effect outweighs its probative value; or

     (c) there are any other factors which make it appropriate for the witness to attend for cross-examination.

(B) A written statement under this Rule shall be admissible if it attaches a declaration by the person making the written statement that the contents of the statement are true and correct to the best of that person's knowledge and belief and

    (i) the declaration is witnessed by:

      (a) a person authorised to witness such a declaration in accordance with the law and procedure of a State; or

      (b) a Presiding Officer appointed by the Registrar of the Tribunal for that purpose; and

    (ii) the person witnessing the declaration verifies in writing:

      (a) that the person making the statement is the person identified in the said statement;

      (b) that the person making the statement stated that the contents of the written statement are, to the best of that person's knowledge and belief, true and correct;

      (c) that the person making the statement was informed that if the content of the written statement is not true then he or she may be subject to proceedings for giving false testimony; and

      (d) the date and place of the declaration.

The declaration shall be attached to the written statement presented to the Trial Chamber.

(C) A written statement not in the form prescribed by paragraph (B) may nevertheless be admissible if made by a person who has subsequently died, or by a person who can no longer with reasonable diligence be traced, or by a person who is by reason of bodily or mental condition unable to testify orally, if the Trial Chamber:

    (i) is so satisfied on a balance of probabilities; and

    (ii) finds from the circumstances in which the statement was made and recorded that there are satisfactory *indicia* of its reliability.

(D) A Chamber may admit a transcript of evidence given by a witness in proceedings before the Tribunal which goes to proof of a matter other than the acts and conduct of the accused.

(E) Subject to Rule 127 or any order to the contrary, a party seeking to adduce a written statement or transcript shall give fourteen days notice to the opposing party, who may within seven days object. The Trial Chamber shall decide, after hearing the parties, whether to admit the statement or transcript in whole or in part and whether to require the witness to appear for cross-examination.

ICTR

ICTR Rules of Procedure and Evidence, rr. 89, 90, 92*bis*

General Provisions

9–18   **89.**—(A) The rules of evidence set forth in this Section shall govern the proceedings before the Chambers. The Chambers shall not be bound by national rules of evidence.

(B) In cases not otherwise provided for in this Section, a Chamber shall apply rules of evidence which will best favour a fair determination of the matter before it and are consonant with the spirit of the Statute and the general principles of law.

(C) A Chamber may admit any relevant evidence which it deems to have probative value.

(D) A Chamber may request verification of the authenticity of evidence obtained out of court.

Testimony of Witnesses

90.—(A) Witnesses shall, in principle, be heard directly by the Chambers unless a Chamber has ordered that the witness be heard by means of a deposition as provided for in Rule 71.

9–19

(B) Every witness shall, before giving evidence, make the following solemn declaration:

> "I solemnly declare that I will speak the truth, the whole truth and nothing but the truth."

(C) A child who, in the opinion of the Chamber, does not understand the nature of a solemn declaration, may be permitted to testify without that formality, if the Chamber is of the opinion that the child is sufficiently mature to be able to report the facts of which the child had knowledge and understands the duty to tell the truth. A judgement, however, cannot be based on such testimony alone.

(D) A witness, other than an expert, who has not yet testified shall not be present when the testimony of another witness is given. However, a witness who has heard the testimony of another witness shall not for that reason alone be disqualified from testifying.

(E) A witness may refuse to make any statement which might tend to incriminate him. The Chamber may, however, compel the witness to answer the question. Testimony compelled in this way shall not be used as evidence in a subsequent prosecution against the witness for any offence other than perjury.

(F) The Trial Chamber shall exercise control over the mode and order of interrogating witnesses and presenting evidence so as to:
  (i) Make the interrogation and presentation effective for the ascertainment of the truth; and
  (ii) Avoid needless consumption of time.
(G) (i) Cross-examination shall be limited to the subject-matter of the evidence-in-chief and matters affecting the credibility of the witness and, where the witness is able to give evidence relevant to the case for the cross-examining party, to the subject-matter of the case.
  (ii) In the cross-examination of a witness who is able to give evidence relevant to the case for the cross-examining party, counsel shall put to that witness the nature of the case of the party for whom that counsel appears which is in contradiction of the evidence given by the witness.
  (iii) The Trial Chamber may, in the exercise of its discretion, permit enquiry into additional matters.

Proof of Facts other than by Oral Evidence

The ICTR Rules were amended at the Plenary Session of July 5–6, 2002 to include the same provisions in ICTR Rule 92*bis*.

9–20

East Timor

Regulation 2000/30, ss.34.1, 36, 37.1 (as amended by 2001/25)

Rules of Evidence

34.—34.1 The Court may admit and consider any evidence that it deems is relevant and has probative value with regard to issues in dispute.

9–21

34.2 The Court may exclude any evidence if its probative value is substantially outweighed by its prejudicial effect, or is unnecessarily cumulative with other evidence. No evidence shall be admitted if obtained by methods that cast substantial doubt on its reliability or if its admission is antithetical to, and would seriously damage, the integrity of the proceedings, including without limitation evidence obtained through torture, coercion or threats to moral or physical integrity.

Witness Testimony

9–22   **36.**—36.1 Witnesses shall be heard directly by the Court, unless for good cause the Court determines that a different procedure may be used. Any procedure for the presentation of witness testimony must take account of the rights of all parties to a fair hearing.

36.2 Prior to testifying, a witness shall take the following oath or affirmation: "I solemnly swear or affirm that the testimony I shall give to this court in this trial, shall be the truth, the whole truth and nothing but the truth." A witness may use the sacred texts of his or her faith to take the oath.

36.3 On exceptional grounds, the Court may allow the statement of a witness or expert witness to be admitted in evidence or may allow the presentation of the evidence of a witness by deposition, video-link testimony, or any other method it deems appropriate, in the following circumstances:

     (a) the witness or expert witness has died or is otherwise permanently incapable of testifying in court due to his or her physical condition or health; or

     (b) the prosecutor and accused and legal representative agree with such proceeding; or

     (c) the direct interrogation of the witness or expert witness can not be expected due to the inaccessibility of that person or due to the distance of the domicile of that person or place of current residence from the place of the hearing and taking into consideration the importance of the statement of that person for the trial; or

     (d) it is provided in the present regulation.

36.4 Prior statements of a witness may be used to refresh the recollection of the witness who made them. If the recollection of the witness cannot be refreshed, the prior statements may be used as substantive evidence.

36.5 A witness who has not yet testified shall not be present in the court room. A witness shall not be permitted to discuss his or her testimony with another witness or with other interested persons before testifying. A witness who has heard the testimony of another witness shall not automatically be disqualified from testifying.

Other Evidence

9–23   **37.**—37.1 Physical or documentary evidence collected during the investigations may be presented to a witness during his or her testimony so that the witness can identify such evidence and testify as to its relevance. The court may decide whether documentary evidence shall be read out in court either partially or entirely.

SCSL

SCSL Rules of Procedure and Evidence, rr. 89, 90, 92*bis*

General Provisions

9–24   **89.**—(A) The rules of evidence set forth in this Section shall govern the proceedings before the Chambers. The Chambers shall not be bound by national rules of evidence.

(B) In cases not otherwise provided for in this Section, a Chamber shall apply rules of evidence which will best favour a fair determination of the matter before it and are consonant with the spirit of the Statute and the general principles of law.

(C) A Chamber may admit any relevant evidence.

Testimony of Witnesses

90.—(A) Witnesses may give evidence directly, or as described in Rules 71 and 85 (D).

9–25

(B) Every adult witness shall, before giving evidence, make one of the following solemn declarations:

> "I solemnly declare that I will speak the truth, the whole truth and nothing but the truth."
> Or
> "I solemnly swear on the [insert holy book] that I will speak the truth, the whole truth and nothing but the truth."

(C) A child shall, be permitted to testify if the Chamber is of the opinion that he is sufficiently mature to be able to report the facts of which he had knowledge, that he understands the duty to tell the truth, and is not subject to undue influence. However, he shall not be compelled to testify by solemn declaration.

(D) A witness, other than an expert, who has not yet testified may not be present without leave of the Trial Chamber when the testimony of another witness is given. However, a witness who has heard the testimony of another witness shall not for that reason alone be disqualified from testifying.

(E) A witness may refuse to make any statement which might tend to incriminate him. The Chamber may, however, compel the witness to answer the question. Testimony compelled in this way shall not be used as evidence in a subsequent prosecution against the witness for any offence other than false testimony under solemn declaration.

(F) The Trial Chamber shall exercise control over the mode and order of interrogating witnesses and presenting evidence so as to:
 i. Make the interrogation and presentation effective for the ascertainment of the truth; and
 ii. Avoid the wasting of time.

Alternative Proof of Fact

92bis.—(A) A Chamber may admit as evidence, in whole or in part, information in lieu of oral testimony.

9–26

(B) The information submitted may be received in evidence if, in the view of the Trial Chamber, it is relevant to the purpose for which it is submitted and if its reliability is susceptible of confirmation.

(C) A party wishing to submit information as evidence shall give 10 days notice to the opposing party. Objections, if any, must be submitted within 5 days.

A. Guidelines of Admissibility

(1) Discretion to Admit or Exclude Evidence

Rule 89(C) of the ICTY, ICTR and SCSL Rules; Article 69(4) of the ICC Statute and Section 34(1) of the UNTAET Regulation are the essential rules governing the admission of evidence. All evidence must

9–27

pass the admissibility test, meeting the standards of relevancy, probative value and reliability. The rules on the admissibility of evidence have been clarified in various cases before the ICTY and ICTR. The overriding principle is that the purpose of the rules on evidence is "to promote a fair and expeditious trial and the Trial Chambers must have the flexibility to achieve this goal" (*Prosecutor v. Aleksovski*, Decision on Prosecutor's Appeal on Admissibility of Evidence, February 16, 1999, para. 19). The general trend is thus one of admitting any relevant evidence with probative value, leaving the Trial Chamber with the discretion to determine the weight to be accorded such evidence in the context of all the evidence admitted when considering its verdict (see, *Prosecutor v. Blaškić*, Judgment, Trial Chamber, March 3, 2000, para. 34; and, *Prosecutor v. Musema*, Judgment, Trial Chamber, January 27, 2000, para. 41).

The determination of the admissibility of any evidence under Rule 89(C) of the ICTY and ICTR (similar to 89(C) of the SCSL Rules, Article 69(4) of the ICC Statute and Section 34(1) of the UNTAET Regulation) is a discretionary matter, which implies that the Trial Chamber has the power not only to admit but also to exclude evidence under Rule 89(C). This is so, even where the evidence is relevant and probative, since "Rule 89(C) does not command, but merely permits, admission of the evidence" (*Prosecutor v. Bagosora et al.*, Decision on Admissibility of Proposed Testimony of Witness DBY, September 18, 2003, para. 4; confirmed on appeal in: Decision on Prosecutor's Interlocutory Appeals Regarding Exclusion of Evidence, December 19, 2003; *Prosecutor v. Rutaganda*, Appeals Judgment, May 26, 2003, paras 265 and 275). As the Trial Chamber asserted in *Bagosora et al.*, "[w]hile a Chamber is always free to disregard information which is unreliable or irrelevant, the purpose of rules of admissibility, including Rule 92*bis*, is to provide a preliminary threshold for the exclusion of irrelevant, unreliable or otherwise improper information" (*Prosecutor v. Bagosora et al.*, Decision on Admission of Statements of Deceased Witnesses, January 19, 2005, para. 17). Along the same line, the Trial Chamber has "an obligation to refuse evidence which is not relevant, or does not have probative value. Evidence whose reliability cannot adequately be tested by the Defence cannot have probative value" (*Prosecutor v. Bagosora et al.*, Decision on Admissibility of Evidence of Witness DBQ, November 18, 2003, para. 8).

Furthermore, it has to be noted that the broad discretion under rule 89(C) is limited by the requirement under Rule 89(B) "that the rules of evidence applied by a Chamber must be those which best favour a fair determination of the matter before the Chamber and which are consonant with the Tribunal's Statute and the general principles of law; the exercise of discretion under Rule 89(C) ought therefore to be in harmony with the Statute and the other Rules to the greatest extent possible" (*Prosecutor v. Milošević*, Decision on Admissibility of Prosecution Investigator's Evidence, September 30, 2002, para. 18).

The SCSL fully endorses the principles set out by the ICTY and ICTR, but emphasised in one case the significant difference that evidence only needs to be relevant pursuant to 89(C) SCSL, while Rule 89(C) ICTY and ICTR requires evidence to be relevant and probative (*Prosecutor v. Brima et al.*, Decision on Joint Defence Motion to Exclude all Evidence from Witness TF1–277 pursuant to Rule 89(C) and/or Rule

95; May 24, 2005, para. 13). The Appeals Chamber in *Norman et al.* defined the purpose of 89(C) SCSL as follows: "Rule 89(C) ensures that the administration of justice will not be brought into disrepute by artificial or technical rules, often devised for jury trial, which prevent judges from having access to information which is relevant. Judges sitting alone can be trusted to give second hand evidence appropriate weight, in the context of the evidence as a whole and according to well-understood forensic standards. The Rule is designed to avoid sterile legal debate over admissibility so the Court can concentrate on the pragmatic issue" (*Prosecutor v. Norman et al.*, Fofana-Appeals Against Decision Refusing Bail, March 11, 2005, para. 26; also see *Prosecutor v. Brima et al.*, Decision on Joint Defence Motion to Exclude all Evidence from Witness TF1–277 pursuant to Rule 89(C) and/or Rule 95; May 24, 2005, para. 14).

(2) Relevance and Probative Value

The dominant concepts are "relevancy" and "probative value." As a starting point, evidence must be relevant to an allegation or issue in the trial. There must be a nexus between it and the subject matter (see, *Prosecutor v. Tadić*, Decision on Defence Motion on Hearsay, August 5, 1996, para. 18; *Prosecutor v. Kupreškić et al.*, Decision on Evidence of the Good Character of the Accused and the Defence of Tu Quoque, February 17, 1999; and, *Prosecutor v. Musema*, Judgment, Trial Chamber, January 27, 2000, para. 39). The probative value of evidence relates to whether it tends to prove an issue, which is relevant to the proceedings (*Prosecutor v. Delalic et al.*, Decision on the Prosecutor's Oral Requests for the Admission of Exhibit 155 into Evidence and for an Order to Compel the Accused, Zdravko Mucic, to provide a handwriting sample, January 19, 1998, para. 29). **9–28**

In *Bagosora et al.* the Trial Chamber held that "[r]elevance, probative value and even prejudice are all relational concepts. The content of the putative facts must be defined and then evaluated in relation to their possible value as proof of the existence of a crime as described in the indictment. The nature of this evaluation explains the discretion conferred on the Trial Chamber by Rule 89(C)" (*Prosecutor v. Bagosora et al.*, Decision on Admissibility of Proposed Testimony of Witness DBY, September 18, 2003, para. 18).

(3) Probative value versus prejudice

Under Rule 89(D) of the ICTY Rules (similar to Article 69(4) ICC and Section 34.2 UNTAET Regulation), evidence may be excluded at any stage of the proceedings (even after it has been admitted) if its probative value is substantially outweighed by the need to ensure a fair trial (see, *Prosecutor v. Tadić*, Decision on Defence Motion on Hearsay, August 5, 1996, para. 18). At the ICTR and the SCSL, no equivalent of Rule 89(D) exists. Jurisprudence has, however, demonstrated that the Rwanda Tribunal attaches great importance to fair trial principles in its determination of admissibility. In *Prosecutor v. Akayesu*, Judgment, **9–29**

September 2, 1998, para. 136, the Trial Chamber held that it "can freely assess the probative value of all relevant evidence. The Chamber had thus determined that in accordance with Rule 89, any relevant evidence having probative value may be admitted into evidence, provided that it is being in accordance with the requisites of a fair trial" (see also para. 133). Also Rule 70(F) suggests that the Trial Chamber should exercise its discretion pursuant to Rule 89(C) in compliance with the principle of fairness. Rule 70(F) provides: Nothing in Sub-Rule (C) or (D) above shall affect a Trial Chamber's power under Rule 89 (C) to exclude evidence if its probative value is substantially outweighed by the need to ensure a fair trial. The same reasoning may apply to the SCSL, being heavily influenced by the ICTR and the body of Rules being similar although Rule 70(F) SCSL refers to Rule 95, not Rule 89(C), which suggests that the Trial Chamber should exercise its discretion to exclude only if the evidence is obtained in violation of Rule 95, which requires a greater violation than Rule 89(C).

Relevant and probative evidence may therefore be excluded on the ground of prejudice. Judge Shahabuddeen held in his separate opinion in *Prosecutor v. Nahimana et al.*: "it being recognised that all relevant Prosecution evidence is prejudicial to the Accused and the more probative the more prejudicial, still it is possible in some cases to say that the probative value of the particular evidence is outweighed by its prejudicial effects; in such a case the evidence is to be excluded" (*Prosecutor v. Nahimana et al.*, Decision on the Interlocutory Appeals, Separate Opinion of Judge Shahabuddeen, September 15, 2003, para. 90).

Similarly, the Appeals Chamber has affirmed that "the Trial Chamber has a broad discretion to direct the course of the proceedings in accordance with its fundamental duty to ensure a fair and expeditious trial pursuant to Article 19(1) of the Statute. In pursuit of these goals, the Trial Chamber may choose to exclude otherwise relevant and probative evidence where its prejudicial effect will adversely affect the fairness or expeditiousness of the proceedings. The Prosecutor has not shown that the Trial Chamber erred in law in doing so in this case." (*Prosecutor v. Bagosora et al.*, Decision on Prosecutor's Interlocutory Appeals regarding Exclusion of Evidence, December 19, 2003, para 16.)

ICC Article 69(4) refers to prejudice as one of the factors to be taken into consideration in assessing the admissibility of evidence. There is no firm duty to exclude evidence which is prejudicial to the defendant; rather, this is a factor for the Trial Chamber to consider in exercising its discretionary power to admit or exclude evidence. UNTAET Section 34.2, on the other hand, reads similar to ICTY Rule 89(D).

(4) Reliability

9–30   Evidence can only be relevant and probative if it is reliable. In other words: "The reliability of evidence does not constitute a separate condition of admissibility; rather it provides the basis for the findings of relevance and probative value required under Rule 89(C) for evidence to be admitted. As a general principle, the Chamber attaches probative value to evidence according to its credibility and relevance to the allegations at issue" (*Prosecutor v. Musema*, Judgment, Trial Chamber, January 27, 2000, paras 38–39. Also see: *Prosecutor v. Brdanin & Talic*, Order on the Standards governing the admission of evidence, February 15, 2002, para. 24; *Prosecutor v. Delalic et al.*, Decision on the Prosecution's Oral Requests for the Admission of Exhibit 155 into Evidence and for an Order to Compel the Accused, Zdravko Muci, to Provide a Handwriting Sample, January 21, 1998, para. 32).

Reliability has to be assessed in the context of the facts of each particular case, and requires a consideration of the circumstances under which the evidence arose, the content of the evidence, whether and how the evidence is corroborated, as well as the truthfulness, voluntariness, and trustworthiness of the evidence (see, *Prosecutor v. Musema*, Judgment, Trial Chamber, January 27, 2000, para. 42; *Prosecutor v. Tadić*, Decision on Defence Motion on Hearsay, August 5, 1996, para. 19; *Prosecutor v. Kajelijeli*, Decision on Motion to Limit the Admissibility of Evidence, June 2, 2001; and, before the East Timor Special Panel, *Prosecutor v. Marques et al.*, Judgment, December 11, 2001, paras 673–676).

The Appeals Chamber in the SCSL case of *Norman et al.*, held: "Evidence is admissible once it is shown to be relevant: the question of its reliability is determined thereafter, and is not a condition for its admission (*Prosecutor v. Norman et al.*, Fofana-Appeals Against Decision Refusing Bail, March 11, 2005, para. 24; also see *Prosecutor v. Brima et al.*, Decision on Joint Defence Motion to Exclude all Evidence from Witness TF1–277 pursuant to Rule 89(C) and/or Rule 95, May 24, 2005, para. 15).

(5) Evidence of Facts not in the Indictment

A Trial Chamber may exclude evidence which deals with matters that are not addressed in the indictment with sufficient specificity. The Trial Chamber may exclude such evidence, on the grounds that it lacks relevance or probative value, or, most probably, where the principles of fairness so require due to lack of notice, or uncertainty of what the charges are. This was emphasised by the Appeals Chamber in *Prosecutor v. Bagosora et al.*, Decision on Prosecutor's Interlocutory Appeals Regarding Exclusion of Evidence, December 19, 2003, para. 16: **9–31**

> "[T]he Trial Chamber has a broad discretion to direct the course of the proceedings in accordance with its fundamental duty to ensure a fair and expeditious trial pursuant to Article 19(1) of the Statute. In pursuit of these goals, the Trial Chamber may choose to exclude otherwise relevant and probative evidence where its prejudicial effect will adversely affect the fairness or expeditiousness of the proceedings" (see also *Prosecutor v. Ntagerura, Imanishimwe and Bagambiki*, Oral Decision, February 14, 2001, French Transcripts, p. 161, line 24 and further).

In *Bizimungu* the Appeals Chamber confirmed the Trial Chamber's decision to exclude evidence in relation to facts not pleaded in the indictment with sufficient specificity, based on the following reasoning:

> "The Trial Chamber found that to permit the Prosecutor to lead the evidence excluded would cause prejudice to Bizimungu's defence as he had

not been given sufficient notice of the allegations as guaranteed by Article 20 of the Statute because Ruhengeri *préfecture* had not been specifically identified in contrast to other geographical regions. The fact that the evidence may have been admissible pursuant to Rule 89 does not show any error on the part of the Trial Chamber in concluding that in the interests of ensuring the fairness of the trial it should be excluded" (*Prosecutor v. Bizimungu*, Decision on Prosecution's Interlocutory Appeals against Decision of the Trial Chamber on Exclusion of Evidence, June 25, 2004, para. 18; see also *Kupreškić et al.*, where the Appeals Chamber held that in a situation where the evidence turned out differently than anticipated in the indictment may require "certain evidence to be excluded as not being within the scope of the indictment: (*Prosecutor v. Kupreškić et al.*, Appeals Chamber Judgment, October 23, 2001, para. 92).

These decisions suggest that the core question is, whether the evidence would prejudice the accused if it would be admitted. The answer to this question will depend, *inter alia*, on the degree of difference between the proposed evidence and the charges in the indictment. Citing *Rutaganda*, the Trial Chamber in *Hadžihasanović & Kubura* held that, "before a Chamber holds that an alleged fact is not material or that differences between the wording of the indictment and the evidence adduced are minor, it must generally ensure that such a finding is not prejudicial to the accused and that the issue will be to determine whether an accused could reasonably identify the crime and conduct specified in each paragraph of the indictment" (*Prosecutor v. Hadžihasanović & Kubura*, Decision on Motion of the Accused Hadžihasanović Regarding the Prosecution's Examination of Witnesses on Alleged Violations not Covered by the Indictment, March 16, 2004, p. 5). This holding indicates that when making a determination whether evidence not directly linked to the indictment may be admitted, the Court will take into account the possible prejudicial effect on the accused. In addition, exclusion of evidence that does not directly relate to facts charged in the indictment is not the only remedy available. The Prosecutor may also apply to amend the indictment.

(6) Evidence concerning Matters Outside of Temporal Jurisdiction

9–32   As for evidence falling outside the scope of the temporal jurisdiction of the Tribunal (ICTY from 1991 onwards; ICTR 1994 only; SCSL from November 30, 1996 onwards; UNTAET prior to October 25, 1999; ICC from July 1, 2002 onwards; Iraqi Special Tribunal, from July 17, 1968 up until and including May 1, 2003,), the relevance and probative value to the charges against the accused are questionable. In *Bagosora et al.*, the Trial Chamber determined that evidence relating to facts outside the scope of temporal jurisdiction would only be admissible if: 1) relevant to the offence continuing to the mandate year, or 2) it explains the context or background, or 3) as similar fact evidence (*Prosecutor v. Bagosora et al.*, Decision on Admissibility of Proposed Testimony of Witness DBY, September 18, 2003, see further discussion on Rule 93, ss. 9–38).

In principle, the Trial Chamber will only deal with requests to exclude if objection to its admission was made at the time of testimony.

However a Trial Chamber may decide to deal with such matters even after the testimony in question has finished where the interests of justice so require (*Prosecutor v. Bizimungu et al.*, Decision on Motion from Casimir Bizimungu opposing to the Admissibility of the Testimony of Witnesses GKB, GAP, GKC, GKD and GFA, January 23, 2004, para. 18).

B. ORAL AND WRITTEN TESTIMONY

ICTY Rule 89(F) provides that a chamber may receive witness testimony orally or where the interests of justice allow, in written form. This provision modifies the former Rule 90(A) which provided that witnesses shall, in principle, be heard directly by the chamber (which has been deleted).

9–33

The general principle at the ICTY is that proposed written evidence which has probative value, relevance and reliability in accordance with Rule 89(C) may be admitted in the interest of justice within the meaning of Rule 89(F). The determination of the "interests of justice" under Rule 89(F) must be made on a case-by-case evaluation, taking into consideration the surrounding circumstances, as well as the proposed evidence of the witness. In its evaluation, a Trial Chamber may consider factors, such as the lack of opportunity to assess the credibility of the witness, the lack of cross-examination and the curtailment of a right to a fair and public hearing, although these factors could also play a role in the determination of the weight that should be attached to the evidence in question (*Prosecutor v. Milošević*, Decision on Interlocutory Appeal on the Admissibility of Evidence-in-Chief in the Form of Written Statements, September 30, 2003, paras 20–21).

The Appeals Chamber in *Milošević* found, as a matter of law, the following type of situation to be within the scope of Rule 89(F): "the witness (a) is present in court, (b) is available for cross-examination and any questioning by the judges, and (c) attests that the statement accurately reflects his or her declaration and what he or she would say if examined" (*Prosecutor v. Milošević*, Decision on Interlocutory Appeal on the Admissibility of Evidence-in-Chief in the Form of Written Statements, September 30, 2003, disposition).

Rule 92*bis*, being the *lex specialis* of the *lex generalis* Rule 89(C), limits the application of Rule 89(F). Written statements given by prospective witnesses to OTP investigators or others for the purposes of legal proceedings (statements falling within the scope of Rule 92*bis*) can only be admitted on the basis of Rule 89(F) if their admission does not violate Rule 92*bis* unless "(i) [. . .] there has been no objection taken to it, or (ii) [. . .] it has otherwise become admissible—where, for example, the written statement is asserted to contain a prior statement inconsistent with the witness's evidence" (*Prosecutor v. Milošević*, Appeals Chamber, Decision on Admissibility of Prosecution Investigator's Evidence, September 30, 2002, para. 18).

The ICTR Rules have not included Rule 89(F). Instead, the ICTR practice of admission of written evidence has been guided by the general principle that "[w]itnesses shall, in principle, be heard directly by the Chambers unless a Chamber has ordered that the witnesses be heard by means of a deposition as provided by Rule 71" as set out in Rule 90(A). This principle clearly gives preference to oral testimony and does not at all provide the same leeway to admit written testimony as Rule 89(F) of the ICTY Rules.

Attempts have been made by the ICTR Prosecution to apply Rule 89(F) of the ICTY Rules by analogy to the ICTR practice. They sought to rely on 89(C) independently of the only ground for admission of written evidence, namely, Rule 92*bis*. These attempts have been unsuccessful because there is no counterpart of Rule 89(F) in the ICTR Rules and "[t]he principle of legality would be violated by the admission of the witness's statement in the absence of an express change of the Rules" (*Prosecutor v. Bagosora et al.*, Oral Decision of November 20, 2003, as confirmed in: Decision on Certification of Appeal concerning Admission of Written Statement of Witness XXO, December 11, 2003, para. 2).

Moreover, the Chamber has made clear that Rule 92*bis* in conjunction with the general requirement of oral testimony set out in Rule 90(A) indicates that written testimony can only be admitted on the basis of Rule 92*bis* (*Prosecutor v. Bagosora et al.*, Decision on Admission of Statements of Deceased witnesses, January 19, 2005, para. 15; *Prosecutor v. Muhimana*, Decision on Prosecution Motion for Admission of Witness Statements (Rule 89(C) and 92*bis*), May 20, 2004, paras 23–28; *Prosecutor v. Nyiramasuhuko et al.*, Decision on Prosecutor's Motion to Remove from Her Witness List Five Diseased Witnesses, and to Admit into Evidence the Witness Statements of Four of the Said Witnesses, January 22, 2003, para. 20).

As stated in *Nyiramasuhuko et al.* the later decision, "the general requirements under Rule 89 that admissible evidence be relevant and probative applies in addition to, and not in lieu of, the more specific provisions of Rule 92*bis*". Hence, in seeking to admit written evidence before the ICTR, the parties cannot bypass the requirements under Rule 92*bis*. Rule 89(C) can only be used as a basis for tendering exhibits, not witness statements that fall within the scope of Rule 92*bis*.

The SCSL Rule 90(A) is similar to the ICTR Rule 90(A) in that it sets out the principle that evidence should be heard orally, although not in any stringent terms. There is no equivalent of ICTY Rule 89(F) within the SCSL body of rules. The language used in Section 36.1 of UNTAET Regulation is more compelling, in that it states that witnesses shall be heard directly by the Court (unless good cause makes the Court determine that a different procedure may be used). This language is more stringent than either Rule 90(A) ICTR or Rule 90(A) SCSL. Article 69(2) ICC also states that witness testimony shall be given in person. The same provision, however, allows the introduction of documents or written transcripts, subject to the Statute and the Rules.

C. Proof of Facts other than by Oral Evidence

(1) Documentary Evidence

There is no rule or statutory provision governing the admissibility of **9–34**
documentary evidence before the ICTY, ICTR and SCSL. Section 37.1
of the UNTAET Regulation, on the other hand, deals with documentary
evidence (documentary and physical evidence may be presented to a
witness). Also, Article 69(2) of the ICC Statute refers to introduction of
documents. The general scheme for the admissibility of evidence has
been applied by the ICTY and ICTR to regulate the introduction of
documentary evidence.

In *The Prosecutor v. Brdanin & Talic*, Order on the Standards governing
the admission of evidence, February 15, 2002, para. 18, the Trial
Chamber held that "the threshold standard for the admission of
evidence [. . .] should not be set excessively high, as often documents
are sought to be admitted into evidence, not as ultimate proof of guilt
or innocence, but to provide a context and complete the picture
presented by the evidence in general". (See also *The Prosecutor v. Tadić*,
Judgment on Allegations of Contempt against Prior Counsel, Milan
Vujin, Appeals Chamber, January 31, 2000, para. 94, where the Appeals
Chamber held that a document may be admitted, not so much to prove
the guilt of the accused, but to "demonstrate a particular course of
conduct or to explain the events in issue which took place within that
period".)

The party seeking admission of a document needs to demonstrate on
a balance of probabilities that there are *indicia* of relevance, probative
value and reliability under Rule 89(C) (*Prosecutor v. Musema*, Judgment,
January 27, 2000, para. 56; see also: *Prosecutor v. Brdanin & Talic*, Order
on the Standards governing the admission of evidence, February 15,
2002, para. 18, principle 3; *Prosecutor v. Bagosora et al.*, Decision on
Admission of Tab 19 of Binder Produced in Connection with the
Appearance of Witness Maxwell and Nkole, September 13, 2004, para.
7). The threshold to establish *indicia* of reliability is low; only where the
evidence is "so lacking in terms of the *indicia* of reliability as to be
devoid of any probative value", would documents be excluded on that
basis (*Prosecutor v. Rutaganda*, Appeals Chamber Judgment, May 26,
2004, para. 216). Reliability and credibility are not synonymous. The
Judges are not concerned with the credibility of documentary evidence
when determining its admissibility (*Prosecutor v. Musema*, Judgment,
January 27, 2000, para. 57. See also: *Prosecutor v. Delalic et al.*, Decision
on the Motion of the Prosecution for the Admissibility of Evidence, June
21, 1998).

In order to assess whether the required *indicia* of reliability are
sufficiently established for the admission of a document, the Trial
Chamber will consider factors, such as: (1) the place where the
document was seized; (2) the chain of custody after seizure of the
document; (3) corroboration of the contents of the document with other
evidence; (4) the nature of the document itself such as signature,
stamps, handwriting (*Prosecutor v. Bagosora et al.*, Decision on Admission
of Tab 19 of Binder Produced in Connection with the Appearance of

Witness Maxwell and Nkole, September 13, 2004, para. 8; *Prosecutor v. Delalic et al.*, Appeals Chamber Decision on Application of Defendant Zejnil Delalic for Leave to Appeal Against the Decision of the Trial Chamber of January 19, 1998 for the Admissibility of Evidence, March 4, 1998, para. 18; *Prosecutor v. Kordić and Čerkez*, Decision on Prosecutor's Submissions Concerning "Zagreb Exhibits" and Presidential Transcripts, December 1, 2000, paras 43–44; *Prosecutor v. Brdanin and Talic*, Order on the Standards Governing the Admission of Evidence, February 15, 2002, para. 20).

The ICTY, ICTR and SCSL Rules, as well as the UNTAET Regulation and ICC Rules do not require a witness to produce documentary exhibits in order to be admissible. The Prosecution or Defence may introduce documents directly under Rule 89, providing they display sufficient indication of reliability (see, *Prosecutor v. Delalic et al.*, Decision on Motion for the Admissibility of Evidence, January 19, 1998, para. 22; *The Prosecutor v. Brdanin & Talic*, Order on the Standards governing the admission of evidence, February 15, 2002, para. 18). Their admission does not necessarily mean that the statements contained in them present an accurate portrayal of the facts (*Prosecutor v. Delalic et. al*, Decision on the Motion of the Prosecution for the Admissibility of Evidence, June 21, 1998 para. 20; *Prosecutor v. Naletelic and Martinovic*, Decision on the Admission of Exhibits Tendered During the Rejoinder Case, October 23, 2002; Also see, *Prosecutor v. Delalic et al.*, Decision on the Tendering of Prosecution Exhibits 104–108, February 9, 1998; *Prosecutor v. Blaškić*, Judgment, March 3, 2000, para. 35; *Prosecutor v. Kordic*, Decision on Prosecutor's Submissions Concerning "Zagreb Exhibits" and Presidential Transcripts, December 1, 2000; and *The Prosecutor v. Brdanin & Talic*, Order on the Standards governing the admission of evidence, February 15, 2002).

As set out below, statements and documents can be admitted under Rule 92*bis* without the presence of the author or witness, or under Rule 94(B), but the standards under Rule 89(C) must still be met.

Authenticity and proof of authorship are matters for weight, not so much for admissibility (*Prosecutor v. Brdanin & Talic*, Order on the Standards governing the admission of evidence, February 15, 2002, paras 18 and 19).

The moving party nonetheless needs to provide an explanation of what the document is and indications about the authenticity of the document, "that is, that the document is actually that the moving party purports it to be" (*Prosecutor v. Bagosora et al.*, Decision on Admission of Tab 19 of Binder Produced in Connection with the Appearance of Witness Maxwell and Nkole, September 13, 2004, para. 8). The Trial Chamber in *Bagosora et al.*, held: "Authenticity and reliability are overlapping concepts: the fact that the document is what it purports to be enhances the likely truth of the contents thereof" (*ibid.*, para. 8).

In *Bagosora et al.*, the Trial Chamber excluded 22 handwritten documents, attached to an FBI report. Neither the FBI official who had photocopied the documents, nor anyone else was in a position to say where the documents came from and who wrote them. The Trial Chamber held that "[a]lthough the prosecution attempted to correlate the contents of the documents with other evidence in the case, it did not do so with sufficient particularity to suggest that the documents are, indeed, authentic and reliable" (*Prosecutor v. Bagosora et al.*, Decision on Admission of Tab 19 of Binder Produced in Connection with the Appearance of Witness Maxwell and Nkole, September 13, 2004, para. 10).

(2) Admissibility of witness statements pursuant to Rule 92*bis*

(a) General Principles

Under Rule 92*bis* of the ICTY, ICTR and SCSL Rules of Procedure and Evidence, the Chambers have discretion to admit evidence of a witness in written form in whole or in part. Factors to be taken into consideration when exercising this discretion include:

    (1) whether the statement or transcript sought to be admitted satisfies Rule 89(C), in that it is relevant and has probative value;

    (2) whether it goes to proof of a matter other than the acts and conduct of the accused as charged in the Indictment;

    (3) whether the formal requirements of Rule 92*bis*(B) have been met;

    (4) whether to admit the statement in the exercise of the Trial Chamber's discretion. (*Prosecutor v Bagosora et al.*, Decision on Prosecutor's Motion for the Admission of Written Witness Statements Under Rule 92*bis* (March 9, 2004) at para. 16.

9–35

This resembles the Appeals Chamber's reasoning that "the general propositions which are implicit in Rule 89(C)—that evidence is admissible only if it is relevant and that it is relevant only if it has probative value—remain applicable to Rule 92*bis*" (*Prosecutor v. Milošević*, Decision on Admissibility of Prosecution Investigator's Evidence, September 30, 2002, para. 18; *Prosecutor v. Galić*, June 7, 2002, Decision on Interlocutory Appeal Concerning Rule 92*bis* (C), Para. 31).

The Tribunals have established various rules and guidelines regarding the use of Rule 92*bis*. In *Prosecutor v. Brdjanin and Talic*, Decision on 'Objection and/or Consent to Rule 92*bis* Admission of Witness Statements Number One', January 30, 2002, paras 4–5, the main principles were set out as follows: (i) evidence which goes directly to the acts or conduct of the accused cannot be admitted regardless how repetitive it is (see, para. 30); (ii) the cumulative nature of the evidence is relevant for evidence that does not go directly to the acts or conduct of the accused (see, para. 30); (iii) in superior responsibility cases, the Chamber will exercise extreme caution before admitting written statements relevant to the acts and conduct of subordinates for which the accused was allegedly responsible (see, paras 17–18); and, (iv) the applicant is expected to give some general information about which other witnesses will give similar evidence and the nature of the overlap, and the parties should assist the Chamber by adequately addressing the relevant considerations set out in the Rule (see, para. 30). (Also see, *Prosecutor v. Naletilic and Martinovic*, Decision regarding Prosecutor's Notice of Intent to Offer Transcripts under Rule 92*bis*(D), July 9, 2001.)

9–36

If parts of a written statement are inadmissible based on these criteria, these parts should be edited out in order to make the statement admissible under Rule 92*bis*. Contrary to what the Prosecution in *Bagosora et al.* suggested, the Trial Chamber has no discretion to admit statements which include inadmissible parts "subject to an "understanding" that inadmissible portions will be ignored." The Trial Chamber held that:

> While a Chamber is always free to disregard information which is unreliable or irrelevant, the purpose of rules of admissibility, including Rule 92*bis* is to provide a preliminary threshold for the exclusion of irrelevant, unreliable or otherwise improper information. Conditional admission would, in effect, destroy the preliminary threshold, leaving all parties in doubt as to which portions of the statements were properly before the Chamber as evidence, and which portions were not (*Prosecutor v. Bagosora et al.*, Decision on Admission of Statements of Deceased witnesses, January 19, 2005, para. 17).

(b) Acts and Conduct of the Accused

9–37　　　　In the case of *Prosecutor v. Milošević*, Decision on Prosecution's Request to have Written Statements Admitted under Rule 92*bis*, March 21, 2002; the Chamber held that the phrase "acts and conduct of the accused" in Rule 92*bis* should be given its ordinary meaning: "deeds and behaviour of the accused. It should not be extended by fanciful interpretation. No mention is made of acts and conduct by alleged co-perpetrators, subordinates, or indeed, of anybody else. Had the rule been intended to extend to acts and conduct of alleged co-perpetrators or subordinates it would have said so" (see, para. 22).

However, if the conduct is that of co-perpetrators or subordinates it is "relevant to whether cross-examination should be allowed and not to whether a statement should be admitted" (see, para. 22).

This approach appears to have changed. In *Prosecutor v. Galić*, June 7, 2002, Decision on Interlocutory Appeal Concerning Rule 92*bis*(C), Para. 10, the Appeals Chamber defined the categories of written statements that would be excluded under Rule 92*bis* (A) as going to proof of acts or conduct of the accused as those:

> "upon which the prosecution relies to establish:
> [. . .]
> (b) that he planned, instigated or ordered the crimes charged, or
> (d) that he was a superior to those who actually did commit the crimes, or
> (e) that he knew or had reason to know that those crimes were about to be or had been committed by his subordinates, or
> [. . .]
> (g) that he had participated in [a] joint criminal enterprise, or
> (h) that he shared with the person who actually did commit the crimes charged the requisite intent for those crimes."

The Appeals Chamber further noted that "[t]he "conduct" of an accused person may also in the appropriate case include his omission to act"(para. 11). In the same decision, the Appeals Chamber indicated that:

> "Rule 92*bis* was primarily intended to be used to establish what has now become known as "crime-base" evidence, rather than the acts and conduct

of what may be described as the accused's immediately proximate subordinates – that is, subordinates of the accused of whose conduct it would be easy to infer that he knew or had reason to know" (para. 16).

In *Prosecutor v. Blagojević and Jokic*, June 12, 2003, First Decision on Prosecutor's Motion for Admission of Witness Statements and Prior Testimony Pursuant to Rule 92*bis*, Para.17, "indirect references to the acts and conduct of [the] Accused through other means including, for example, references to the acts and conduct of persons who held the positions which [the] Accused are alleged to have held", were held to be inadmissible in 92*bis* statements as going to proof of acts and conduct of the accused.In *Prosecutor v. Galić*, June 7, 2002, Decision on Interlocutory Appeal Concerning Rule 92*bis* (C), paras 13–15, the Appeals Chamber held:

"[P]roximity would also be relevant to the exercise of the Trial Chamber's discretion in deciding whether the evidence should be admitted in written form at all. Where the evidence is so pivotal to the prosecution case, and where the person whose acts and conduct the written statement describes is so proximate to the accused, the Trial Chamber may decide that it would not be fair to the accused to permit the evidence to be given in written form. [References deleted]
The exercise of the discretion as to whether the evidence should be admitted in written form at all becomes more difficult in the special and sensitive situation posed by a charge of command responsibility. That is because, as the jurisprudence demonstrates in cases where the crimes charged involve widespread criminal conduct by the subordinates of the accused (or those alleged to be his subordinates), there is often but a short step from a finding that the acts constituting the crimes charged were committed by such subordinates to a finding that the accused knew or had reason to know that those crimes were about to be or had been committed by them. Where the criminal conduct of those subordinates was widespread, the inference is often drawn that, for example, "there is no way that the accused could not have known or heard about it".
In such cases, it may well be that the subordinates of the accused (or those alleged to be his subordinates) are so proximate to the accused that (a) the evidence of their acts and conduct which the prosecution seeks to prove by a Rule 92*bis* statement becomes sufficiently pivotal to the prosecution case that it would not be fair to the accused to permit the evidence to be given in written form or (b) the absence of the opportunity to cross-examine the maker of the statement would in fairness preclude the use of the statement in any event. It must be emphasized, however, that the rejection of the written statement in any of these situations is not based upon any identification of that person's acts or conduct with the acts or conduct of the accused.

(c) Cross-Examination

The Chamber needs to strike a balance between ensuring that the trial is both fair and expeditious. Exercising its discretion under Rule 92*bis*, the Chamber may decide to exclude the proposed 92*bis* evidence in its totality because of the proximity to the guilt of the accused. This will be the case, for example, when the evidence concerns the acts of

9–38

subordinates of the accused. Alternatively, it may decide to admit the proposed evidence, thereby saving substantial time in examination in chief, but on the condition that the witnesses attend cross-examination (see *Prosecutor v. Milošević*, Decision on Prosecution's Request to have Written Statements Admitted under Rule 92*bis*, March 21, 2002, para. 26; *Prosecutor v. Bagosora et al.*, Decision on Prosecutor's Motion for the Admission of Written Witness Statements Under Rule 92*bis*, March 9, 2004).

In *Prosecutor v. Milošević*, Decision on Prosecution's Request to have Written Statements Admitted under Rule 92*bis*, March 21, 2002, paras 18–20, the documents proposed as 92*bis* statements related to the deportations and killings that had allegedly occurred in various munici- palities in Kosovo, which the Prosecution alleged were the result of concerted Serb actions to expel Kosovo Albanians, and that the accused had participated in this criminal enterprise as a co-perpetrator (without suggesting that he had committed any of these crimes personally in a physical sense). The accused, on the other hand, maintained that the deportations and killings were, in summary, the result of actions of the Kosovo Liberation Army (KLA) and NATO.

The Chamber held that although the statements that the Prosecu- tion sought to admit did not go to the "acts and conduct of the accused" (and could thus be admitted), they did relate to a "'critical element of the Prosecution's case' or put another way, to a live and important issue between the parties, as opposed to a peripheral or marginally relevant issue" (see, para. 24). The requirements of a fair trial, in the Cham- ber's view, demanded that the accused be given the right to cross- examine the witnesses.

In *Prosecutor v. Sikirica*, Decision on Prosecution's Application to Admit Transcripts Under Rule 92*bis*, May 23, 2001, the Trial Chamber stated that the principal criterion for determining whether a witness should appear for cross-examination is the overriding obligation of a Chamber to ensure a fair trial; among the matters for consideration are whether the transcript goes to the proof of a critical element of the Prosecution's case against the accused (see, paras 3–4). Even if the evidence of a witness does not relate to the conduct of an accused, it can have such a significant and direct bearing on the case against the accused that the accused should have the opportunity to cross-examine the witness (see, para. 35).

(d) Cumulative Nature

9–39   On the cumulative nature of the evidence, the Chamber stated that this was a factor in favour of admission. The Chamber possesses a discretion under Rule 92*bis* to employ the Tribunal's limited resources in a judicious and efficient manner (see *Prosecutor v. Milošević*, Decision on Prosecution's Request to have Written Statements Admitted under Rule 92bis, March 21, 2002, para. 23).

In *Prosecutor v. Blagojević and Jokic*, June 12, 2003, First Decision on Prosecutor's Motion for Admission of Witness Statements and Prior Testimony Pursuant to Rule 92*bis*. para. 20, the Trial Chamber stated that:

> "[W]hile Rule 92*bis* permits for the admission of cumulative evidence on matters other than the acts and conduct of the accused through written

statements, this Rule should not be interpreted by the parties to the proceedings as an invitation to tender unnecessarily cumulative or repetitive evidence . . . One criteria used to establish whether a trial is fair is if an accused is tried without undue delay. The admission of unnecessarily cumulative or repetitive evidence may affect the expeditious nature of the proceedings, and therefore will not be admitted[footnotes omitted]."

(e) Admission of Statements of Deceased Witnesses

Rule 92*bis*(C) allows for the admission of statements of deceased **9–40** witnesses, provided that the Chamber is satisfied on the balance of probabilities that the witness is dead or has disappeared, and that the statement has "satisfactory *indicia* of reliability (*Prosecutor v. Bagasora et al.*, Decision on Admission of Statements of Deceased Witnesses, January 19, 2005, para. 15; *Prosecutor v. Galić*, Decision on Interlocutory Appeal Concerning Rule 92*bis*(C) June 7, 2002, para. 24 ("Both in form and in substance, Rule 92*bis* (C) merely excuses the necessary absence of the declaration required by Rule 92*bis* (B) for written statements to become admissible under Rule 92*bis* (A)"); *Prosecutor v. Muhimana*, Decision on the Prosecution Motion for Admission of Witness Statements (Rule 89 (C) and 92*bis*), May 20, 2004, para. 26; *Prosecutor v. Nyiramasuhuko et al.*, Decision on the Prosecutor's Motion to Remove From Her Witness List Five Deceased Witnesses and to Admit Into Evidence the Witness Statements of Four of the Said Witnesses, January 22, 2003, para. 21)).

In *Prosecutor v. Kordic*, Decision on Appeal regarding Statement of a deceased Witness, July 21, 2000 it was held that the Rules express a preference for live testimony, and if the statements of witnesses deceased are to be admissible at all, it would be so under the residual power of the Trial Chamber to admit "any relevant evidence which it deems to have probative value" (Rule 89(C).

(f) Procedural requirements under 92*bis*(B)

Where a statement comes within the scope of Rule 92*bis* based on the **9–41** subject matter of its content, it needs to be determined whether the procedural requirements laid out in Rule 92*bis*(B) have been met. Only where both the substantive and the procedural requirements have been met, a written statement is admissible under Rule 92*bis*. A question remains when a statement meets the requirements of Rule 92*bis*(B), particularly, whether the statement was taken by an OTP investigator or someone else for the purposes of legal proceedings, and if so, whether that means that the statement can be admitted under a rule, other than Rule 92*bis* (*e.g.* Rule 89(C) or 89(F)). On this matter the Appeals Chamber held:

"A party cannot be permitted to tender a written statement given by a prospective witness to an investigator of the OTP under Rule 89(C) in order to avoid the stringency of Rule 92*bis*", but "Rule 92*bis* has no effect upon hearsay material which was not prepared for the purposes of legal proceedings". The Trial Chamber found that the reference by the Appeals

Chamber to material "prepared for the purposes of legal proceedings" was intended to relate to material prepared for the purposes of legal proceedings before this Tribunal, such as a witness statement taken by a Prosecution investigator in answer to the content of statements given by witnesses for the purposes of this case. The preparation of a statement in the terms discussed above clearly leads to the conclusion that any such statement is prepared for the purposes of these proceedings. Such a statement would only, therefore, be admissible under the terms of Rules 89(F) or 92*bis* of the Rules.

(*Prosecutor v. Milošević*, Decision on Prosecution Motion for Reconsideration Regarding Evidence of Defence Witnesses Mitar Balevic, Vladislav Jovanovic, Vukasin Andric, and Dobre Aleksovski and Decision *Proprio Motu* Reconsidering Admission of Exhibits 837 and 838 Regarding Evidence of Defence Witness Barry Lituchy, May 17, 2005, para. 12; citing with approval: *Prosecutor v. Galić*, Decision on Interlocutory Appeal Concerning Rule 92*bis*(C), June 7, 2002, para. 31; also see *Prosecutor v. Milošević*, Decision on Interlocutory Appeal on the Admissibility of Evidence-in-Chief in the Form of Written Statements, September 30, 2003, paras 12–13).

This, however, does not preclude the admission of written witness statements taken by OTP investigators or others for the purposes of legal proceedings: (i) where there has been no objection to its admission, or (ii) where it has become admissible in another way, for example, "the written statement is asserted to contain the prior statement inconsistent with the witness's evidence" (*Prosecutor v. Milošević*, Decision on Admissibility of Prosecution Investigator's Evidence, September 30, 2002, para. 18; *Prosecutor v. Milošević*, Decision on Interlocutory Appeal on the Admissibility of Evidence-in-Chief in the Form of Written Statements, September 30, 2003, para. 13).

Moreover, the mere fact that a written statement has been prepared for the purposes of legal proceedings does not on its own suffice to conclude that the statement can only be admitted pursuant to Rule 92*bis*. For that to be the case, the statement must have been taken with the intention to use it *in lieu* of oral testimony (*Prosecutor v. Milošević*, Decision on Interlocutory Appeal on the Admissibility of Evidence-in-Chief in the Form of Written Statements, September 30, 2003, para. 18).

On the same reasoning, Rule 92*bis* is not applicable to a written witness statement of a witness who is available to appear before the Tribunal, not only for cross-examination pursuant to Rule 92*bis*(E), but also to testify to the accuracy of the written prior statement, no matter how brief (*Prosecutor v. Milošević*, Decision on Interlocutory Appeal on the Admissibility of Evidence-in-Chief in the Form of Written Statements, September 30, 2003, paras 16–17).

D. Hearsay

9–42   There is no rule governing the admissibility of hearsay evidence before the ICTY, ICTR, and SCSL. The Trial Chambers of the ICTY, ICTR and SCSL have refrained from adopting a practice to exclude all hearsay evidence. There is in effect no rule declaring hearsay evidence *per se* inadmissible.

The general scheme for the admissibility of evidence as set out in Rule 89 for the ICTY, the ICTR and SCSL has guided the Chambers in their deliberations about hearsay evidence.

The Appeals Chamber in *Galić* defined the scope of admissibility of hearsay evidence pursuant to Rule 89(C), in that, Rule 89(C) "permits the admission of hearsay evidence (that is, evidence of statements made out of court), in order to prove the truth of such statements rather than merely the fact that they were made. Hearsay evidence may be oral, as where a witness relates what someone else had told him out of court, or written, as when (for example) an official report written by someone who is not called as a witness is tendered in evidence. Rule 89(C) clearly encompasses both these forms of hearsay evidence" (*Prosecutor v. Galić*, Decision on Interlocutory Appeal Concerning Rule 92*bis*(C) June 7, 2002, para. 27).

In *Prosecutor v. Tadić*, Decision on Defence Motion on Hearsay, August 5, 1996, para. 7, the Trial Chamber held that "out-of-court statements that are relevant and found to have probative value are admissible". The same position was taken by the Trial Chamber in *Prosecutor v. Blaškić*, Decision on Standing Objection of the Defence to the Admission of Hearsay with no Inquiry as to its Reliability, January 21, 1998.

Hearsay evidence can thus be admitted to prove the truth of its contents, and the fact that it is hearsay does not necessarily deprive the evidence of its probative value. The Chamber must be satisfied of its reliability given the context and character of the evidence for it to be admitted. In addition, the absence of the opportunity to cross-examine the witness is a factor to be taken into account when assessing the probative value of the evidence, and if it is admitted, the weight to be assigned to such evidence. (See, *Prosecutor v. Aleksovski*, Decision on Prosecutor's Appeal on Admissibility of Evidence, February 16, 1999, para. 15; and, *Prosecutor v. Semanza*, Decision on the Defence Motion For Exclusion of Evidence on the Basis of Violations of the Rules of Evidence, Res Gestae, Hearsay and Violations of the Statute and Rules of the Tribunal, August 23, 2000. Also, see cases cited above in relation to Rule 92*bis;* also see *Prosecutor v. Milošević*, Decision on Testimony of Defence Witness Dragan Jasovic, April 15, 2005, p. 5, where the Trial Chamber held that hearsay evidence may be admitted if sufficient *indicia* of reliability is established; *Prosecutor v. Galić*, Decision on Interlocutory Appeal Concerning Rule 92*bis*(C) June 7, 2002, para. 27.)

The Appeals Chamber in *Prosecutor v. Milošević*, Decision on Admissibility of Prosecution Investigator's Evidence, September 30, 2002, para. 18, confirmed that "although it depends upon infinitely variable circumstances of the particular case, the weight or probative value to be afforded to hearsay evidence will usually be less than that given to the testimony of a witness who has given it under a form of oath and who has been cross-examined".

The Chamber in *Blaškić* nonetheless indicated that the right to cross-examination, incorporated as part of the fair trial provisions of Article 21(4)(e) Statute and Article 20(4)(e) ICTR Statute, applies to "the witness testifying before the Trial Chamber and not to the initial declarant whose statement has been transmitted to this Trial Chamber by the witness" (see *Prosecutor v. Blaškić*, Decision on Standing Objection of the Defence to the Admission of Hearsay with no Inquiry as to its Reliability, January 21,1998, para. 29).

Moroever, in *Limaj et al.*, the Presiding Judge took the position that "whether any weight, and if so, what weight will attach to [hearsay opinion] will depend to what extent the question of hearsay is clarified by other evidence and it is shown to be reliable [. . .] Let it be clear that we, in receiving this evidence, will treat it as merely, in a sense, an introductory summary and it will be of no weight in our view unless later witnesses substantiate the basis for it [. . .] [W]e will not ourselves attach any weight to what is said about these facts if that does not prove to be substantiated by other evidence" (*Prosecutor v. Limaj et al.*, Oral Ruling of November 18, 2004, pp. 447–449).

In *Bagosora et al.* the Trial Chamber held that hearsay evidence "has limited probative value standing alone. The reliability of the testimony and its probative value are likely to depend primarily on corroborative or contradictory evidence to be presented later by the Defence or Prosecution" (*Prosecutor v. Bagosora et al.*, Decision on Admissibility of Evidence of Witness DP, November 18, 2003, para. 8). The Trial Chamber of the ICTY, stated: "It will be important, however, to evaluate with care the reliability of any hearsay evidence which has been admitted before reliance is placed on it for the purpose of establishing guilt" (*Prosecutor v. Limaj et al.*, Decision on the Prosecution's Motions to Admit Prior Statements as Substantive Evidence, April 25, 2005, para. 27).

In the SCSL case of *Brima et al.*, the Trial Chamber held that "[i]t is well settled in the practice of international tribunals that hearsay evidence is admissible" (*Prosecutor v. Brima et al.*, Decision on Joint Defence Evidence to Exclude All Evidence from Witness TF1–277 Pursuant to Rule 89(C) and/or Rule 95, May 24, 2005, para. 12). Rule 89(C), which is not restrictive in its provisions, allows the Trial Chamber a broad discretion to admit hearsay evidence (*Prosecutor v. Norman et al.*, Fofana-Appeal Against Decision Refusing Bail, March 11, 2005, para. 22). The *Brima* decision is a clear indicator that the SCSL favours a system of admission rather than exclusion. As the Trial Chamber held, "[t]he probative value of hearsay evidence is something to be considered by the Trial Chamber at the end of the trial when weighing and evaluating the evidence as whole, in light of the context and nature of the evidence itself, including the credibility and reliability of the relevant witness" (*ibid.*, para. 15).

In *Prosecutor v. Marques et al.*, Judgment, December 11, 2001, para. 677, before the Special Panel for Serious Crimes of the East Timor court, it was held that hearsay evidence from witnesses who had heard from other witnesses that the accused was involved in the crime, should be assigned little weight, and did not result in any certainty about the conduct of the accused.

E. PRIOR INCONSISTENT STATEMENTS

(1) ICTY

9–43   In two oral Decisions (Trial Transcript of April 2, 2003, p. 17931; Trial Transcript of April 15, 2003, p. 16480), the Trial Chamber in *Simić et al.* held that the Prosecution was not allowed to put prior inconsistent statements to the witness, either to impeach the witness or to refresh his memory. In its Certification Decision relating to the first ruling, the Trial Chamber relied on the finding in *Milošević* that the inclusion of Rule 92*bis* was to limit the admissibility of this "very special type of hearsay evidence" (*Prosecutor v. Milošević*, Decision on Admissibility of Prosecutors Investigator's Evidence, September 30, 2002, p. 11). The Trial Chamber stated that "Rule 92*bis* allows the Trial Chamber to admit, in whole or in part, the written evidence of a witness and that portions of the witness statement that are struck out by the Trial Chamber for non-compliance with Rule 92*bis* may not be resurrected by parties for the purpose of cross-examination of the credibility of the witness, and may not be treated as a prior representation for cross-examination purposes as they exist only for the purpose of the Rule 92*bis* procedure and do not stand alone" (*Prosecutor v. Simić et al.*, Decision on Prosecutors Motion for Trial Chambers Redetermination of its Decision of April 2, 2003 Relating to Cross-Examination of Defence Rule 92*bis* Witnesses or Alternatively Certification under Rule 73(B) of the Rules of Procedure and Evidence, April 28, 2003, pp. 2–3).

The Appeals Chamber found that the Trial Chamber erred in holding that a witness cannot be cross-examined on alleged inconsistencies between his prior statements, which had not been admitted under Rule 92*bis*, and his in-court testimony. They also found that the Trial Chamber erred in holding that such statement cannot be used for the purpose of refreshing the witness's memory during cross-examination (*Prosecutor v. Simić et al.*, Decision on Prosecution Interlocutory Appeals on the Use of Statements not Admitted into Evidence Pursuant to Rule 92*bis* as a Basis to Challenge Credibility and to Refresh Memory, May 23, 2003, paras 19–20).

In *Limaj et al.*, the Trial Chamber went a step further in holding for the first time that prior inconsistent statements can be admitted as substantive evidence. The Trial Chamber held that prior inconsistent statements of witnesses on the stand cannot be admitted as substantive evidence under Rule 89(F) or 92*bis*, but may be admitted under Rule 89(C) if relevant and probative (*Prosecutor v. Limaj et al.*, Decision on the Prosecution's Motions to Admit Prior Statements as Substantive Evidence, April 25, 2005, paras 16 and 17). Applying this reasoning, the Trial Chamber admitted, as substantive evidence, as evidence of the truth of their contents, pursuant to Rule 89(C), video-recorded statements of two witnesses who had been declared hostile because in their oral testimony they were found to have departed from their previous statements given to the investigator (*ibid.*, para 34). The principal reason for the admission into evidence, was that both statements were on video, which were shown and discussed at length at trial. Accordingly, the Trial Chamber considered that the statements were sufficiently reliable to be considered as probative and therefore admissible under Rule 89(C). The Trial Chamber held that, it would consider all the evidence at the deliberation stage of proceedings and then determine what weight, if any, to attach to the prior statements (*ibid.*, paras 17, 22, 23, 25, 33).

(2) ICTR and SCSL

The ICTR and SCSL have acknowledged that prior inconsistent **9–44** statements "are generally admissible in international criminal trials as a means to impeach the credibility of a witness" (*Prosecutor v. Norman et* *al.*, Oral Decision of July 16, 2004, pp. 8–9; *Prosecutor v. Niyitegeka;* Appeals Chamber Judgment, July 9, 2004, para. 33; *Prosecutor v. Akayesu*, Appeals Chamber Judgment, June 1, 2001, paras 124–147).

The witness may be asked to confirm that he or she made a statement and may be cross-examined on the contents thereof in general terms without being shown the statement. Where the prior statement is in writing, the witness should be shown the statement before questions concerning alleged inconsistencies can be asked to the witness, "and if the statement is proved the statement is admitted into the records as evidence" (*Prosecutor v. Norman et al.*, Oral Decision of July 16, 2004, pp. 7–8).

In *Norman et al.*, the Trial Chamber set out the following principles as regards prior inconsistent statements:

"(1) A Witness may be cross-examined as to previous statements made by him or her in writing or reduced into writing or recorded on audio tape or video tape or otherwise, relative to the subject matter of the case in circumstances where an inconsistency has emerged during the course of *viva voce* testimony between a prior statement and the testimony.

(2) In conducting cross-examination and inconsistencies between *viva voce* testimony and a previous statement, the witness should first be asked whether or not he or she has made the statement being referred to. The circumstances of making the statement, sufficient to designate the situation, must be put to the witness when asking this question.

(3) Should the witness disclaim making the statement, evidence may be provided in support of the allegation that he or she did in fact make it.

(4) That a witness may be cross-examined as to previous statements made by him or her relative to the subject matter of the case without the statement being shown to him or her. However, where it is intended to contradict such witness with a statement, his or her attention must, before the contradictory proof can be given, be directed to those parts of the statement alleged to be contradictory.

(5) That the Trial Chamber may direct that the portion of the witness statement that is the subject of cross-examination and alleged contradiction with a *viva voce* testimony be admitted into a court record and marked as an exhibit."

(*Prosecutor v. Norman et al.*, Oral Decision of July 16, 2004, pp. 8–9).

In these circumstances, prior inconsistent statements can be admitted at the SCSL pursuant to Rule 89(C). Trial Chambers at the ICTR have adopted similar approaches and generally held that prior inconsistent statements can be exhibited pursuant to Rule 89(C), the weight to be determined at a later stage. However, the Appeals Chamber in *Akayesu* confirmed the Trial Chamber's finding that "[i]n the circumstances, the probative value attached to the [prior] statements is, in the Chamber's view, considerably less than direct sworn testimony before the Chamber" (*Prosecutor v. Akayesu*, Appeals Chamber Judgment, June 1, 2001, para. 133; confirming *Prosecutor v. Akayesu*, Judgment, September 2, 1998, para. 137). The Trial Chamber in *Kayishema and Ruzindana* adopted a similar reasoning, stating that "inconsistencies may raise doubts in relation to the particular piece of evidence in question or, where such inconsistencies are found to be material, to the witnesses' evidence as a whole" (*Prosecutor v. Kayishema and Ruzindana*, Judgment, May 21, 1999, para. 77).

(3) East Timor

Unlike the ICTY, ICTR and SCSL where there is no provision which   **9–45**
deals specifically with admissibility of prior statements, the UNTAET
Regulation has incorporated a provision stating that prior-statements
may be used to refresh a witness's memory. If the witness's memory
cannot be refreshed, the prior statement can be admitted as substantive
evidence (Reg. 36.4).

(4) ICC

The ICC Rules also include a provision enabling the parties to use   **9–46**
prior recorded statements in two distinct situations: (i) where a witness
does not testify in court, and both parties had the opportunity to
examine the witness during the recording of the prior statement; (ii)
where the witness testifies in court, and the witness consents to the use
of the prior recorded statement and the parties and the Chamber had
the opportunity to examine the witness during the proceedings.

F. INVESTIGATOR'S REPORTS

In *Kordic*, the Prosecution applied for witness statements, transcripts   **9–47**
of prior witness testimony and documents, together with an investigator's report about these materials, to be admitted in the form of a
"dossier" of evidence concerning a particular attack on a village in
central Bosnia. The Trial Chamber decided that the dossier could not
be admitted "wholesale".

The Chamber considered the evidence category by category. With
respect to the investigator's report, the Chamber held that although
"[t]he International Tribunal is not bound to reject hearsay evidence
the position with regard to the Report is somewhat different. The
Investigator is not reporting as a contemporary witness of fact, he has
only recently collated statements and other materials for the purpose of
this Application. He could, in reality, only give evidence that material
was or was not in the Dossier. The Report therefore is of little or no
probative value and will not be admitted into evidence" (see, *Prosecutor
v. Kordic*, Decision on the Prosecution Application to admit the Tulica
Report and Dossier into Evidence, July 29, 1999, paras 19–20).

In relation to the witness statements, the Chamber held: "It is
proposed that the witness statements should be produced by the
Investigator, and would not be subject to cross-examination by the
accused unless the Defence could justify the need to do so. The Trial
Chamber is of the view that whilst it could admit the witness
statements under Rule 89(C), this is not an appropriate case for the
exercise of its discretion under that provision, as it would amount to the
wholesale admission of hearsay untested by cross-examination, namely
the attack on Tulica, and would be of no probative value. The Trial
Chamber therefore declines to admit the witness statements into

evidence, however, draws attention to Rule 94*ter* of the Rules" (see, para. 23, Rule 94*ter*, which has now been deleted, allowed for the admission of affidavits).

The transcripts were admitted on the grounds that there were significant and relevant matters not covered by cross-examination in the other cases which ought to be raised in the present case (see, paras 26–28). The judges left open the possibility for the Defence to make an application for cross-examination of the witness. This finding was based on the Appeals Chamber's decision in the *Aleksovski* case (see, *Prosecutor v. Zlatko Aleksovski*, Decision on Prosecutor's Appeal on Admissibility of Evidence, February 16, 1999, paras 27–28). The documentary evidence was introduced under Rule 89(C) as it was deemed to have probative value (Decision, paras 32–36; Also see, *Prosecutor v. Kordic*, Decision on Appeal regarding the Admission into Evidence of Seven Affadavits and One Formal Statement, September 18, 2000).

In *Milošević*, the Trial Chamber excluded evidence from a Prosecution investigator because the evidence consisted of a summary compiled by him of numerous written statements of potential witnesses. The Trial Chamber considered that the investigator's conclusions amounted to hearsay evidence of little or no probative value and it was the Trial Chamber's function to determine the weight of the evidence on which the conclusions were based. Being prepared with the specific purpose of proving the guilt of the Accused in the present case, the OTP investigator's conclusions on the testimony of anticipated witnesses may not appear to the public as an independent evaluation of the evidence. (English transcript of Milošević's Trial of February 20, 2002, pp. 672–673 and May 30, 2002 pp. 5931–5933, 5936, 5940–5944). The Trial Chamber's position that there was no need for the investigator's assistance was confirmed by the Appeal's Chamber stating that "[w]hatever expertise the OTP investigator may claim to have in relation to such a task, the Trial Chamber was entitled to decline his assistance in the very task which it had to perform for itself" (*Prosecutor v. Milošević*, Decision on Admissibility of Prosecution Investigator's Evidence, September 30, 2002, para. 17).

Another important consideration adopted by the Trial Chamber and confirmed by the Appeals Chamber was that the deprivation of the right to cross-examine the makers of the statement would not be compensated by allowing the Defence to cross-examine the employee of the OTP who summarised the witness statements. As the Appeals Chamber pointed out "[i]t would of course be quite wrong for the Trial Chamber, in determining the issues in the trial, to refer to material which may be available to it but which is not in evidence, and it was entitled to take the view that, in the circumstances of this case, it was inappropriate for the Trial Chamber itself to cross-examine upon such material when that material was not in evidence" (*Prosecutor v. Milošević*, Decision on Admissibility of Prosecution Investigator's Evidence, September 30, 2002, paras 22–24; English transcript of Milošević's Trial of May 30, 2002 p. 5933).

In *Bizimungu et al.*, the OTP sought to introduce a report of a factual witness, who, as a Rwandan employee of the OTP, was asked to prepare a report on anti-Tutsi propaganda in the Rwandan media before and during the genocide. The OTP insisted that the report was not an expert report and thus, its admission was subject to the requirements of

Rule 89(C) only. The Trial Chamber excluded the report because the broadcasts and print media on which the report had been based had not been fully disclosed to the Defence, thereby making an effective cross-examination almost impossible and hindering the Court's ability to determine the credibility of the report and its author. The Trial Chamber did not exclude the report simply because it constituted a non-expert opinion. Instead, it held that reports based on non-expert opinion are admissible in limited circumstances only, stating that, "while a non-expert, like consultant or investigator, may prepare a report which contains opinion evidence on matters of a non-technical nature for the consideration of the Chamber, such a report should be based on the factual circumstances the witness observed or heard" (*Prosecutor v. Bizimungu et al.*, pp.29–31; Also see, *Prosecutor v. Kordic*, Oral Decision of October 6, 2000, tt. 26093–26100).

G. HOSTILE WITNESSES

The issue of hostile witnesses has not been dealt with in the law of the **9–48** Tribunals and has only arisen at the ICTY. In Prosecutor *Limaj et al.*, the Trial Chamber was seized of a Prosecution application to declare a witness "adverse" or "hostile". The Chamber's response to the application was that in order for such an application to be evaluated there need be "some clear indication of materially different answers on this occasion from the past" (*Prosecutor v. Limaj et al.*, T.2104.). On the second occassion the Chamber was confronted with a similar application; it emphasised that "materially" refers to material to the case of the party calling the witness, (*ibid.*, T.2740).

In deciding upon the application, the Trial Chamber first noted that a hostile witness should be considered "a witness who's not prepared to answer truthfully and willingly" (*ibid.*, t.2141). To qualify as such, the witness should be "refusing to answer questions, giving false testimony or withholding relevant information" (*ibid.*, t.2143).

If, however, there exist sufficient uncertainty on the evidence to "leave it at the moment unclear whether the difference is due to some reasonably simple explanation or is a change of position absolutely on the part of the witness", the Chamber held that "it is left without a view that [such] is motivated by a hostility in the relevant sense" (*ibid.*, t.2144).

In response to a second Prosecution application to declare another of its witnesses hostile, the Chamber in *Limaj et al.*, deemed it appropriate to seek guidance on the issue of hostility from various common-law jurisdictions. The issue was, of necessity, largely confined to a survey of common law systems, because the concept of hostility is unknown in civil law procedures (*ibid.*, tt.2735–2736). The Chamber recalled the general (common-law) position that a party calling a witness may not discredit that witness unless the witness is unwilling and not just unfavourable to the party calling him or her (*ibid.*, t.2736). In order to declare a witness adverse or hostile "the determinative consideration is whether it appears to the Chamber that the witness is not prepared to tell the truth at the instance of the party calling the witness" (*ibid.*, t.2738). The Trial Chamber further held:

"To assess whether a witness is adverse or hostile [. . .], the Court will have regard to the witness' demeanour, the terms of any inconsistent statement, and the circumstances in which it was made. There is no distinction in principle in this respect between a witness who gives evidence inconsistent with a witness statement, one who is reluctant to say anything, or one who professes to have forgotten what happened" (*ibid.*, t.2737)

On a third occasion, the Chamber upheld its earlier oral rulings in the *Limaj* case and added that "it appears settled, at least in common-law jurisdictions, that it is not objectionable for the prosecution to call a witness, even if the witness has indicated that he is likely to be hostile" (*ibid.*, t.3164). It further stated that leading questions by the investigator in connection with the witness' prior statement do not invalidate the use of that statement for the purpose of having a witness be declared adverse or hostile (*ibid.*, t.3163).

H. CONFESSIONS

(1) Statutory provisions and rules

ICC

9–49   The ICC Rules do not have a specific provision on confessions. Article 55(1) provides that in respect of an investigation, a person "shall not be compelled to incriminate himself or herself or to confess guilt". Article 67(1) provides that an accused will not be compelled "to confess guilt." Also see Article 65 on admissions of guilt (paragrap 7–85).

ICTY

ICTY Rules of Procedure and Evidence, r. 92

Confessions

9–50   92. A confession by the accused given during questioning by the Prosecutor shall, provided the requirements of Rule 63 were strictly complied with, be presumed to have been free and voluntary unless the contrary is proved.

ICTR

ICTR Rules of Procedure and Evidence, r. 92

Confessions

9–51   92. A confession by the accused given during questioning by the Prosecutor shall, provided the requirements of Rule 63 were strictly complied with, be presumed to have been free and voluntary unless the contrary is proved.

East Timor

Regulation 2000/30, s.33.4 (as amended by Regulation 2001/25)

Presentation of Evidence

33.—33.4 A statement or confession made by the accused before an Investigating Judge may be admitted as evidence, if the Court finds that any admission of guilt contained in such a statement was made in compliance with the provisions of Section 29A.

9–52

SCSL

SCSL Rules of Procedure and Evidence, r. 92

Confessions

A confession by the suspect or the accused given during questioning by the Prosecutor shall, provided the requirements of Rule 43 and Rule 63 were complied with, be presumed to have been free and voluntary.

9–53

(2) General Provisions

See Chapter 7 and Chapter 18 in respect of the procedure to be followed for guilty pleas. For a case before the East Timor Court concerning a confession see, *Prosecutor v. Fernandes*, Court of Appeal, June 29, 2001.

9–54

I. EVIDENCE OF CONSISTENT PATTERN

(1) Statutory provisions and rules

ICC

There exists no provision on evidence of consistent pattern at the ICC.

9–55

ICTY

ICTY Rules of Procedure and Evidence, r. 93

Evidence of Consistent Pattern of Conduct

93.—(A) Evidence of a consistent pattern of conduct relevant to serious violations of international humanitarian law under the Statute may be admissible in the interests of justice.

9–56

(B) Acts tending to show such a pattern of conduct shall be disclosed by the Prosecutor to the defence pursuant to Rule 66.

ICTR

ICTR Rules of Procedure and Evidence, r. 93

Evidence of Consistent Pattern of Conduct

9–57 93.—(A) Evidence of a consistent pattern of conduct relevant to serious violations of international humanitarian law under the Statute may be admissible in the interests of justice.

(B) Acts tending to show such a pattern of conduct shall be disclosed by the Prosecutor to the defence pursuant to Rule 66.

East-Timor

9–58 There is no specific provision on the admissibility of evidence of a consistent pattern in the Transitional Rules of Criminal Procedure. In practice, such evidence could be considered by the court under the general scheme of admissible evidence provided for in Section 34 of the Rules.

SCSL

SCSL Rules of Procedure and Evidence, r. 93

Evidence of Consistent Pattern of Conduct

9–59 93.—(A) Evidence of a consistent pattern of conduct relevant to serious violations of international humanitarian law under the Statute may be admissible in the interests of justice.

(B) Acts tending to show such a pattern of conduct shall be disclosed by the Prosecutor to the defence pursuant to Rule 66.

(2) Evidence of consistent pattern

9–60 For evidence to be admissible under Rule 93 ICTY, ICTR, or SCSL it has to be relevant, probative and reliable pursuant to Rule 89(C) and its admission must be in the interests of justice. As confirmed by the Appeals Chamber, "Rule 93 must be read in conjunction with Rule 89(C), which permits a Trial Chamber to admit any relevant evidence which it deems to have probative value. Even where pattern evidence is relevant and deemed probative, the Trial Chamber may still decide to exclude the evidence in the interests of justice when its admission could lead to unfairness in the trial proceedings, such as when the probative value of the proposed evidence is outweighed by its prejudicial effect, pursuant to the Chamber's duty to ensure a fair and expeditious trial as

required by Article 19(1) of the Statute of the International Tribunal."
(*Prosecutor v. Bagosora et al.*, Decision on Prosecutor's Interlocutory
Appeals regarding Exclusion of Evidence, December 19, 2003, para 13).

Rule 93 is not an open invitation to introduce evidence that blackens
the character of the accused. Although not explicitly excluded, the
jurisprudence of the Tribunals suggests that bad character evidence *per
se* is not admissible. A general principle of criminal law rooted in
common-law jurisdictions and adopted by the ICTY, ICTR and SCSL is
that "evidence as to the character of an accused is generally inadmissible to show the accused's propensity to act in conformity therewith"
(*Prosecutor v. Kupreškić*, Decision on Evidence of Good Character of the
Accused and the Defence of *Tu Quoque*, February 17, 1999, para. 31;
Prosecutor v. Bagasora et al., Decision on Admissibility of Proposed
Testimony of Witness DBY, September 18, 2003, para. 12). This implies
that evidence of prior criminal behaviour of the accused even where the
behaviour concerns identical wrongdoing to the charges in the indictment, is "not admissible if the only purpose for their introduction is to
establish that the accused was capable of committing the offence, is
inclined to commit the offence, or on some prior occasion actually did
have the intent to commit the criminal offence" (*ibid.*, para. 12). The
reasons for excluding such evidence is that it "so severely blacken[s]
the reputation of the accused as to make acquittal virtually impossible,
even though the direct evidence of the commission of the offence is
weak. Further, dealing with evidence of past conduct may be unduly
distracting and time consuming, leading to an unfocused trial that
undermines the truth-finding function" (*ibid.*, para. 12).

Only where "the evidence of the other offence or offences goes
beyond showing the mere disposition to commit crime or a particular
kind of crime and points in some other way to the commission of the
offence in question", the evidence may be admissible if, and only if,
compliant with Rule 89(C) and its probative value outweighs its
prejudicial effect (*Prosecutor v. Nahimana et al.*, Decision on the Interlocutory Appeals, Separate Opinion of Judge Shahabuddeen, September 5,
2000, para. 20). Based on this reasoning evidence may be admissible "to
prove intent, or disprove accident or mistake, to prove identity or
disprove innocent associations" or "prove a pattern, design or systematic course of conduct by the accused where his explanation on the basis
of coincidence would be an affront to common sense" (*ibid.*, para. 20).

The Appeals Chamber confirmed these various interpretations of
Rule 93, stating:

> "Rule 93 does not create an exception to Rule 89(C), but rather is
> illustrative of a specific type of evidence which may be admitted by a Trial
> Chamber. Rule 93 must be read in conjunction with Rule 89(C), which
> permits a Trial Chamber to admit any relevant evidence which it deems to
> have probative value. Even where pattern evidence is relevant and deemed
> probative, the Trial Chamber may still decide to exclude the evidence in
> the interests of justice when its admission could lead to unfairness in the
> trial proceedings, such as when the probative value of the proposed
> evidence is outweighed by its prejudicial effect, pursuant to the Chamber's
> duty to ensure a fair and expeditious trial as required by Article 19(1) of
> the Statute of the International Tribunal."

(*Prosecutor v Bagosora et al.*, Decision on Prosecutor's Interlocutory
Appeals Regarding Exclusion of Evidence, December 19, 2003, para.
13).

There are, however, purposes for which the parties are entitled to introduce bad character or similar evidence to undermine the credibility of the accused as a witness. It may be taken into account in relation to his guilt or innocence if "it bears on the questions as to whether the conduct alleged [. . .] was deliberate or accidental, and whether it is likely that a person of good character would have acted in the way alleged" (*Prosecutor v. Tadić*, Case, Judgment on Allegations of Contempt against Prior Counsel, Milan Vujin, January 31, 2000, paras 128 and 130).

The determination of whether the admission of evidence within the scope of Rule 93 is in the interests of justice is made on a case by case basis. In *Prosecutor v. Krnojelac*, Judgment, March 15, 2002, para. 4, the Trial Chamber interpreted "[e]vidence of a consistent pattern of conduct relevant to serious violations of international humanitarian law under the Statute" under Rule 93 to be circumstantial evidence. In the particular circumstances it held that admission of the proposed evidence was in the interests of justice.

Rule 93 was applied by the Trial Chamber in *Prosecutor v. Kvočka et al.*, Judgment, Trial Chamber, November 2, 2001, para. 663. The Chamber held that credible testimony could be used as corroborating evidence of a consistent pattern of conduct.

The Appeals Chamber in *Prosecutor v. Kupreškić et al.*, Appeal Judgment, October 23, 2001, para. 323, emphasised the Prosecutor's obligation under Rule 93(B) in conjunction with Rule 66(A) to disclose to the Defence any evidence of a consistent pattern of conduct in due time prior to its introduction. Pursuant to Rule 65*ter* such evidence must already be specified in the Prosecutor's Pre-Trial Brief.

J. JUDICIAL NOTICE

(1) Statutory provisions and rules

ICC

ICC Statute, Art. 69

Evidence

9–61   **69.**—6. The Court shall not require proof of facts of common knowledge but may take judicial notice of them.

ICC Rules of Procedure and Evidence, Art. 69

Agreements as to evidence

9–62   **69.** The Prosecutor and the defence may agree that an alleged fact, which is contained in the charges, the contents of a document, the expected testimony of a witness or other evidence is not contested and, accordingly, a Chamber may consider such alleged fact as being proven, unless the Chamber is of the opinion that a more complete presentation of the alleged facts is required in the interests of justice, in particular the interests of the victims.

ICTY

ICTY Rules of Procedure and Evidence, r. 94

Judicial Notice

94.—(A) A Trial Chamber shall not require proof of facts of common knowledge but shall take judicial notice thereof.

(B) At the request of a party or *proprio motu*, a Trial Chamber, after hearing the parties, may decide to take judicial notice of adjudicated facts or documentary evidence from other proceedings of the Tribunal relating to matters at issue in the current proceedings.

9–63

ICTR

ICTR Rules of Procedure and Evidence, r. 94

Judicial Notice

94.—(A) A Trial Chamber shall not require proof of facts of common knowledge but shall take judicial notice thereof.

(B) At the request of a party or *proprio motu*, a Trial Chamber, after hearing the parties, may decide to take judicial notice of adjudicated facts or documentary evidence from other proceedings of the Tribunal relating to the matter at issue in the current proceedings.

9–64

East Timor

There is no specific provision on judicial notice in the Transitional Rules of Criminal Procedure. In practice, judicial notice of facts could be taken by the court under the general scheme of admissible evidence provided for in Section 34 of the Rules.

9–65

SCSL

SCSL Rules of Procedure and Evidence, r. 94

Judicial Notice

94.—(A) A Chamber shall not require proof of facts of common knowledge but shall take judicial notice thereof.

(B) At the request of a party or of its own motion, a Chamber, after hearing the parties, may decide to take judicial notice of adjudicated facts or documentary evidence from other proceedings of the Special Court relating to the matter at issue in the current proceedings.

9–66

(2) Facts that can be judicially noticed

(a) Common Knowledge under Rule 94(A)

9–67   Pursuant to Rule 94(A) the Chamber is mandated to take judicial notice of acts of common knowledge. In *Prosecutor v Casimir Bizimungu et al.*, Decision on the Prosecution's Motion for Judicial Notice Pursuant to Rules 73,89, and 94, December 2, 2003, para. 23, the Trial Chamber defined facts of common knowledge under Rule 94(A) as "facts of such notoriety, so well known and acknowledged that no reasonable individual with relevant concern can possibly dispute them". Thus, the threshold of admissibility under Rule 94 is fairly high.

     In *Bagosora et al.*, matters of common knowledge were described as "facts which are not subject to dispute among reasonable persons, including common or universally known facts such as historical facts, generally known geographical facts and the laws of nature, or facts that are generally known within the area of the Tribunal's territorial jurisdiction", as well as "facts which are readily verifiable by reference to a reliable and authoritative source" (*Prosecutor v. Bagosora et al.*, Decision on the Prosecutor's Motion for Judicial Notice Pursuant to Rules 73, 89, and 94, April 11, 2003, para. 44). Matters of common knowledge must also be reasonably indisputable in order to come within the scope of Rule 94(A). Judicial economy is not to be achieved by exercising unfair prejudice upon the accused, neither should it relieve the Prosecutor of their burden to prove beyond the reasonable doubt the highly controversial core elements of the crimes charged in the indictment (*ibid.*, para. 50).

(b) Adjudicated Facts pursuant to Rule 94(B)

9–68   Where facts are not of common knowledge, the Trial Chamber still has a discretion under Rule 94(B) to take judicial notice of "adjudicated facts or documentary evidence from other proceedings of the Tribunal relating to matters at issue in the current proceedings" (*Prosecutor v Bizimungu et al.*, Decision on the Prosecution's Motion for Judicial Notice Pursuant to Rules 73, 89, and 94, December 2, 2003, para. 34; *Prosecutor v. Bagosora et al.*, Decision on the Prosecutor's Motion for Judicial Notice Pursuant to Rules 73, 89, and 94, April 11, 2003, para. 59). The Trial Chamber may also exercise that discretion "to refuse judicial notice of adjudicated facts if the interests of justice, including the right of the Accused to a fair, public and expeditious trial, so require" (*Prosecutor v. Hadžihasanović et al.*, Decision on Judicial Notice of Adjudicated Facts Following the Motion Submitted by Counsel for the Accused Hadžihasanović and Kubura on January 20, 2005, April 14, 2005; *Prosecutor v. Krajisnik*, Decision on Third and Fourth Prosecution Motions for Judicial Notice of Adjudicated Facts, March 24, 2005).

     In *Hadžihasanović*, citing with approval the *Krajisnik* decision (*Prosecutor v. Krajisnik*, Decision on Prosecution Motion for Judicial Notice of Adjudicated Facts and for Admission of Written Statements Pursuant to Rule 92*bis*, February 28, 2003, para. 15, approved by the Appeals

Chamber in *Prosecutor v. Milošević*, Appeals Chamber Decision on Prosecution's Interlocutory Appeal Against the Trial Chamber's April 10, 2003 Decision on Prosecution Motion for Judicial Notice of Adjudicated Facts, October 28, 2003), the Trial Chamber held that, if the following conditions are cumulatively met, Trial Chambers are invited to exercise their discretion pursuant to Rule 94(B) to allow judicial notice of facts which: (i) are distinct, concrete and identifiable; (ii) are restricted to factual findings and do not include legal characterisations; (iii) are contested at trial and form part of a judgment which has either not been appealed or has been finally settled on appeal or the facts were contested at trial and now form part of a judgment which is under appeal, but falls within issues which are not in dispute on appeal; (iv) do not have any direct bearing on the criminal responsibility of the accused; (v) are not the subject of (reasonable) dispute between the parties in the present case; (vi) are not based on plea agreements in previous cases; and (vii) do not negatively affect the right of the accused to a fair trial (*Prosecutor v. Hadžihasanović*, Final Decision on Judicial Notice of Adjudicated Facts, April 20, 2004, further see *Prosecutor v. Mejakic*, Decision on Prosecution Motion for Judicial Notice Pursuant to Rule 94(B), April 1, 2004).

Similar conclusions were drawn in ICTR cases. The Trial Chambers in *Bagosora* and *Ntakirutimana*, for example, held that, a fact cannot be qualified as an "adjudicated" fact if it derives from proceedings of legal institutions, other than the Tribunal, or where appeal is still an option (*Prosecutor v. Bagosora et al.*, Decision on the Prosecutor's Motion for Judicial Notice Pursuant to Rules 73, 89, and 94, April 11, 2003, para. 59; *Prosecutor v. Ntakirutimana*, Decision on the Prosecutor's Motion for Judicial Notice of Adjudicated Facts, November 22, 2001, para. 26).

An adjudicated fact or document does not need to be unchallenged or unchallengeable as long as it was admitted into evidence by a Chamber of this Tribunal only, which in this case is the ICTR (*Prosecutor v. Bizimungu et al.*, Decision on the Prosecution's Motion for Judicial Notice Pursuant to Rules 73, 89, and 94, December 2, 2003, para. 35; *Prosecutor v. Bizimungu et al.*, Decision on Jerome Clement Bicamumpaka's Motion for Judicial Notice of a Rwandan Judgment of December 8, 2000 and in the Alternative for an Order to Disclose Exculpatory Evidence, December 15, 2004, para. 19).

Adjudicated facts do not include facts contained in judgments based on guilty pleas, or admissions voluntarily made by the parties; neither do they include facts in the introductory part, historical background or legal conclusions of a judgment. Moreover, the adjudicated facts must be relevant and advance judicial economy (*Prosecutor v. Bizimungu et al.*, Decision on the Prosecutor's Motion and Notice of Adjudicated Facts, December 10, 2004, paras 11,14, 15, 16; *Prosecutor v. Bizimungu et al.*, Decision on Prosper Mugiraneza's First Motion for Judicial Notice Pursuant to Rule 94(B), December 10, 2004; *Prosecutor v. Bagosora et al.*, Decision on the Prosecutor's Motion for Judicial Notice Pursuant to Rules 73, 89, and 94, April 11, 2003, para. 64).

The Trial Chambers in *Bizimungu* and *Bagosora* emphasised that judicial notice should not be taken of "facts which would have a bearing upon the guilt or innocence of the accused or which are central to the prosecution case" (*Prosecutor v. Bizimungu et al.*, Decision on the Prosecutor's Motion and Notice of Adjudicated Facts, December 10, 2004, para.

21; *Prosecutor v. Bagosora et al.*, Decision on the Prosecutor's Motion for Judicial Notice Pursuant to Rules 73, 89, and 94, April 11, 2003, para. 61).

In order to file a potentially successful motion pursuant to Rule 94(B) it is important to indicate with precision the facts of which the taking of judicial notice is requested. It is not sufficient to refer to entire documents or parts thereof (*Prosecutor v. Bizimungu et al.*, Decision on the Prosecutor's Motion and Notice of Adjudicated Facts, December 10, 2004, para. 19; *Prosecutor v. Bizimungu et al.*, Decision on the Prosecution's Motion for Judicial Notice Pursuant to Rules 73, 89, and 94, December 2, 2003, para. 38).

(c) Examples

9–69   Judicial notice has been taken of statements and documents emanating from the United Nations, and agreements between government representatives: see, *Prosecutor v. Delalic et al.*, Judgment, November 16, 1998, para. 90.

The Trial Chamber in *Prosecutor v. Simić et al.*, Decision on the Pre-trial Motion by the Prosecution Requesting the Trial Chamber to Take Judicial Notice of the International Character of the Conflict in Bosnia-Herzegovina, March 25, 1999, refused the Prosecutor's application to take judicial notice of the international nature of the conflict, either as a fact of common knowledge, or as an adjudicated fact under Rule 94(B) based on the findings of the *Tadić* and *Celebici* judgements. The Prosecution sought the ruling in order to render Article 2 of the ICTY Statute applicable, which requires the existence of an international armed conflict. The Trial Chamber held that judicial notice may only be taken of factual findings, but not of a legal characterisation. The court cannot take judicial notice of matters over which there is a reasonable dispute between the parties. The Chamber did take judicial notice of certain undisputed facts, such as, the proclamation of independence of Bosnia and Herzegovina. (Also see, *Prosecutor v. Kvočka et al.*, Decision on Judicial Notice, June 8, 2000.)

9–70   In *Prosecutor v. Semanza*, Decision on the Prosecutor's Further Motion for Judicial Notice Pursuant to Rules 94 and 54, March 15, 2001, the ICTR Trial Chamber refused the Prosecution's application to take judicial notice under Rule 94(B) that Tutsis were killed in Rwanda with intent to destroy their ethnic group. The Chamber held that Rule 94(B) could not be applied to such a complex matter as intent as it may prejudice the rights of the accused. A balance had to be struck between conserving judicial time and the rights of the accused. (Also see, *Prosecutor v. Semanza*, Decision on the Prosecutor's Motion for Judicial Notice and Presumptions of Facts pursuant to Rules 94 and 54, November 3, 2000; and *Prosecutor v. Nyiramasuhuko et al.*, Decision on the Prosecutor's Motion for Judicial Notice and Admission of Evidence, May 15, 2002).

There must have been a final determination by a Trial Chamber, where there is no appeal, or in the event of an appeal, by the Appeals Chamber, for another Chamber to consider taking judicial notice of adjudicated facts or documentary evidence from those proceedings under Rule 94(B): (see, *Prosecutor v. Aleksovski*, Dissenting Opinion of Judge Patrick Robinson on the Decision on Prosecutor's Appeal on Admissibility of Evidence, February 16, 1999, paras 13–15; see also *Prosecutor v. Bizimungu et al.*, Decision on Bicamumpaka's Motion for Judicial Notice, February 11, 2004; *Prosecutor v. Bizimungu et al.*, Decision on the Prosecutor's Motion and Notice of Adjudicated Facts, December 10, 2004, para. 24).

In *Prosecutor v. Bizimungu et al.*, Decision on the Prosecutor's Motion and Notice of Adjudicated Facts, December 10, 2004, the Trial Chamber declined to take judicial notice of any of the proposed facts other than the fact that Rwanda was a member of the Genocide Convention and the protocols of the Geneva Conventions.

In *Prosecutor v. Karemera et al.*, Decision Relative a Requête du Procureur aux Fins de Constat Judiciare, April 30, 2004, the Trial Chamber took judicial notice of a number of official documents dealing with the structure of the Rwandan government and the Arusha Accords, but refused to take judicial notice of other documents such as the Encyclopedia Brittanica, reports of human rights organisations, and other documents related to the events in 1994.

In *Nyiramasuhuko*, while acknowledging the previous judgments have made conclusions about the nature of the conflict in Rwanda and the crimes committed therein, the Trial Chamber preferred "in the circumstances of the present case to hear evidence and arguments on the issue, rather than to take judicial notice" of the legal conclusions proposed for judicial notice (*Prosecutor v. Nyiramasuhuko*, Decision the Prosecutor's Motion for Judicial Notice and Admission of Evidence, May 15, 2002, paras 121–127).

In *Kajelijeli*, the Trial Chamber declined to take judicial notice of certain facts amounting to legal conclusions and including propositions disputing that only Tutsis were attacked, and that there were widespread and systematic attacks which were organised and planned (*Prosecutor v. Kajelijeli*, Decision on Prosecutor's Motion for Judicial Notice Pursuant to Rule 94 of the Rules, April 16, 2002, para. 19).

(d) SCSL

In *Norman et al.*, the Trial Chamber held that the rationale behind the   **9–71**
doctrine of judicial notice is twofold: "(i) to expedite the trial by dispensing with the need to submit formally proof on issues that are patently indisputable, and (ii) to foster consistency and uniformity of decision on factual issues where diversity in factual findings would be unfair" (*Prosecutor v. Norman et al.*, Decision of Prosecution's Motion for Judicial Notice and Admission of Evidence, June 2, 2004, para. 24; influenced by: *Prosecutor v. Semanza*, Decision on Prosecutor's Motion for Judicial Notice and Presumptions of Facts Pursuant to Rule 94 and 54, November 3, 2000, para. 4; *Prosecutor v. Simić*, Decision on Pre-Trial Motion by the Prosecution Requesting the Trial Chamber to Take Judicial Notice of the International Character of the Conflict in Bosnia and Herzegovina, March 25, 1999, p. 3).

Similar to the interpretation given to Rule 94 by the ICTY and the ICTR, the SCSL Trial Chamber in *Norman et al.* interpreted Rule 94, on its plain and literal construction, to authorise the taking of judicial notice of the following three distinct categories of facts: "(i) facts of common knowledge, (ii) adjudicated facts from other proceedings before the Court, and (iii) documentary evidence from other proceedings before the Court" (*ibid.*, para. 24).

Generally, Trial Chambers at the SCSL rely on the ICTY and ICTR jurisprudence on matters, such as the threshold level of "common knowledge". The Trial Chamber in *Norman et al.* observed that "despite the exacting requirements that facts must rise to a level of "common knowledge" to be judicially noticed, yet there is authority for the proposition that "a proposition need not to be universally accepted in order to qualify as common knowledge, implying that courts may take judicial notice of facts that are not scientifically provable or beyond all dispute under Rule 94(A) of the Rules" (*Prosecutor v. Norman et al.*, Decision of Prosecution's Motion for Judicial Notice and Admission of Evidence, June 2, 2004, para. 27; citing: *Prosecutor v. Semanza*, Decision on Prosecutor's Motion for Judicial Notice and Presumptions of Facts Pursuant to Rule 94 and 54, November 3, 2000, para. 31).

Inaccurate facts cannot be judicially noticed, regardless whether they amount to facts of "common knowledge". Hence, once a Court makes a preliminary determination that a fact is one of common knowledge within a court's jurisdiction, it must then proceed to a judicial evaluation of whether the fact merits the characterisation of one that is "reasonably indisputable" (*Prosecutor v. Norman et al.*, Decision of Prosecution's Motion for Judicial Notice and Admission of Evidence, June 2, 2004, para. 29; citing: *Prosecutor v. Semanza*, Decision on Prosecutor's Motion for Judicial Notice and Presumptions of Facts Pursuant to Rule 94 and 54, November 3, 2000).

(e) ICC

9–72   Unique to the ICC is that it included the provision allowing the parties to agree among themselves that the fact is undisputed, although the Trial Chamber can nevertheless decide that it wishes to hear evidence on the matter.

K. DEPOSITIONS

(1) Statutory provisions and rules

ICC

9–73   There is no Rule on deposition at the ICC. The procedure described in Rule 68 of ICC Rules (Prior Recorded Testimony, see above) comes closest to a deposition without, however, the requirement of the presence of a Presiding Officer, appointed by the Trial Chamber and the other requirements inherent to the taking of deposition evidence.

ICTY

ICTY Rules of Procedure and Evidence, r. 71

Depositions

71.—(A) Where it is in the interests of justice to do so, a Trial Chamber **9–74**
may order, *proprio motu* or at the request of a party, that a deposition be taken
for use at trial, whether or not the person whose deposition is sought is able
physically to appear before the Tribunal to give evidence. The Trial Chamber
shall appoint a Presiding Officer for that purpose.

(B) The motion for the taking of a deposition shall indicate the name and
whereabouts of the person whose deposition is sought, the date and place at
which the deposition is to be taken, a statement of the matters on which the
person is to be examined, and of the circumstances justifying the taking of the
deposition.

(C) If the motion is granted, the party at whose request the deposition is to
be taken shall give reasonable notice to the other party, who shall have the
right to attend the taking of the deposition and cross-examine the person
whose deposition is being taken.

(D) Deposition evidence may be taken either at or away from the seat of the
Tribunal, and it may also be given by means of a video-conference.

(E) The Presiding Officer shall ensure that the deposition is taken in
accordance with the Rules and that a record is made of the deposition,
including cross-examination and objections raised by either party for decision
by the Trial Chamber. The Presiding Officer shall transmit the record to the
Trial Chamber.

ICTR

ICTR Rules of Procedure and Evidence, r. 71

Depositions

71.—(A) At the request of either party, a Trial Chamber may, in excep- **9–75**
tional circumstances and in the interests of justice, order that a deposition be
taken for use at trial, and appoint, for that purpose, a Presiding Officer.

(B) The motion for the taking of a deposition shall be in writing and shall
indicate the name and whereabouts of the witness whose deposition is sought,
the date and place at which the deposition is to be taken, a statement of the
matters on which the person is to be examined, and of the exceptional
circumstances justifying the taking of the deposition.

(C) If the motion is granted, the party at whose request the deposition is to
be taken shall give reasonable notice to the other party, who shall have the
right to attend the taking of the deposition and cross-examine the witness.

(D) The deposition may also be given by means of a video-conference.

(E) The Presiding Officer shall ensure that the deposition is taken in
accordance with the Rules and that a record is made of the deposition,
including cross-examination and objections raised by either party for decision
by the Trial Chamber. He shall transmit the record to the Trial Chamber.

East Timor

Regulation 2000/30, s.36.3 (as amended by Regulation 2001/25)

Witness Testimony

9–76 **36.**—36.3 On exceptional grounds, the Court may allow the statement of a witness or expert witness to be admitted in evidence or may allow the presentation of the evidence of a witness by deposition, video-link testimony, or any other method it deems appropriate, in the following circumstances:

 (a) the witness or expert witness has died or is otherwise permanently incapable of testifying in court due to his or her physical condition or health; or

 (b) the prosecutor and accused and legal representative agree with such proceeding; or

 (c) the direct interrogation of the witness or expert witness can not be expected due to the inaccessibility of that person or due to the distance of the domicile of that person or place of current residence from the place of the hearing and taking into consideration the importance of the statement of that person for the trial; or

 (d) it is provided in the present regulation.

SCSL

SCSL Rules of Procedure and Evidence, r. 71

Depositions

9–77 **71.**—(A) At the request of either party, a Trial Chamber may, in exceptional circumstances and in the interests of justice, order that a deposition be taken for use at trial and appoint for that purpose a Legal Officer.

(B) The motion for the taking of a deposition shall be in writing and shall indicate the name and whereabouts of the witness whose deposition is sought, the date and place at which the deposition is to be taken, a statement of the matters on which the person is to be examined, and of the interests of justice justifying the taking of the deposition.

(C) If the motion is granted, the party at whose request the deposition is to be taken shall give reasonable notice to the other party, who shall have the right to attend the taking of the deposition and cross-examine the witness.

(D) The deposition may also be given by means of a video-conference.

(E) The Legal Officer shall ensure that the deposition is taken in accordance with the Rules and that a record is made of the deposition, including cross-examination and objections raised by either party for decision by the Trial Chamber. He shall transmit the record to the Trial Chamber.

(2) Deposition evidence

(a) Exceptional Circumstances

9–78 In its original form, deposition evidence pursuant to Rule 71 of the ICTY, ICTR and SCSL Rules of Procedure and Evidence, could only be taken if the party requesting it, had established the existence of exceptional circumstances and that the taking of deposition evidence was in the interests of justice. Gradually the Trial Chambers became more ready to find exceptional circumstances within the meaning of Rule 71. Even the unavailability of a Judge was found to be an exceptional circumstance (*Prosecutor v. Kordić & Čerkez*, Decision on the Prosecutor's Request to Proceed by Deposition, April 13, 1999; *Prosecutor v. Kupreškić et al.*, Decision on Prosecutor's Request to Proceed by Deposition, February 25, 1999). In *Prosecutor v. Kupreškić et al.*, Decision on Appeal by Dragan Papic against Ruling to Proceed by Deposition, Appeals Chamber, July 15, 1999, the Appeals Chamber limited the interpretation of Rule 71 to its original meaning, which was that the application thereof should be an exception to the general rule that the Trial Chamber should hear direct evidence.

ICTY Rule 71 was amended and incorporated in the Rules on July 10, 1998. The term "exceptional circumstances" has now been removed. The taking of a deposition of evidence still needs to be in the interests of justice, which depends on the importance and the disputable nature of the evidence. In reality the amendment to the ICTY Rule has not significantly changed the deposition practice since most requests are founded on "interests of justice" arguments, rather than arguments focusing on the existence of exceptional circumstances.

Rule 71 of the ICTR Rules of Procedure and Evidence, however, still requires a finding of "exceptional circumstances" to justify the taking of a deposition. The Trial Chamber must also be satisfied that the taking of such a deposition is in the interests of justice.

Factors which determine whether there are exceptional circumstances justifying a deposition of evidence are, *inter alia*, the witness's age, frailty, poor mental or physical conditions (*Prosecutor v. Bagosora et al.*, Decision on Prosecutor's Motion for Deposition of Witness OW, December 5, 2001, para. 12; *Prosecutor v. Muvunyi*, Decision on Prosecutor's Extremely Urgent Motion for the Deposition of Witness QX, November 11, 2003). However, where the witness's psychiatric state is such that it could jeopardize his or her mental health, deposition will not be taken (*Prosecutor v. Bagosora et al.*, Decision on Prosecutor's Motion to Allow Witness DBO to Give Testimony by Means of Deposition, August 25, 2004). Moreover, the mere fact that a witness enjoys the status of a protected witness, is poor or fearful does not amount to an exceptional circumstance within the meaning of Rule 71. These are matters which can be addressed by the Tribunal's Witness and Victim Support Section (*Prosecutor v. Semanza*, Decision on Semanza's Motion for Subpoenas, Depositions, and Disclosure, October 20, 2000, para. 27).

The refusal of the authorities of the residing country of the witness to allow the witness's transfer to the Tribunal may amount to an exceptional circumstance where the party seeking deposition has made all efforts to secure the attendance of the witness (*Prosecutor v. Niyitegeka*, Decision on the Prosecutor's Amended Extremely Urgent Motion for the Deposition of a Detained Witness pursuant to Rule 71, October 4, 2002, para. 5).

The Trial Chamber is more lenient on the exceptional circumstances where both parties agree (*Prosecutor v. Kvočka and Others*, Decision to Proceed by Way of Deposition Pursuant to Rule 71, November 15, 1999).

(b) Interests of Justice

9–79   Chambers are more reluctant to accept that the deposition is in the interests of justice. The following criteria were established to determine whether deposition is in the interests of justice: (1) the testimony of the witness must be sufficiently important to make it unfair to proceed without it; (2) the witness is unwilling or unavailable to give *viva voce* testimony; (3) the right of the Accused to confront the witness will not be prejudiced by taking a deposition; and (4) "the practical considerations (including logistical difficulty, expense, and security risks) of holding a deposition in the proposed location [should] not outweigh the potential benefits to be gained by doing so" (*Prosecutor v. Bagosora et al.*, Decision on Prosecutor's Motion to Allow Witness DBO to Give Testimony by Means of Deposition, August 25, 2004; *Prosecutor v. Bagosora et al.*, Decision on Prosecutor's Motion for Deposition of Witness OW, December 5, 2001, paras 13–15).

    Another factor favouring deposition is the fact that "the witness proposed for deposition will not present eyewitness evidence directly implicating the accused in the crimes charged, or alternatively, their evidence will be of a repetitive nature in the sense that many witnesses will give evidence of similar facts" (*Prosecutor v. Naletilic et al.*, Decision on Prosecutor's Motion to Take Depositions for Use at Trial (Rule 71), November 10, 2000, para. 4; see also: *Prosecutor v. Niyitegeka*, Decision on the Prosecutor's Amended Extremely Urgent Motion for the Deposition of a Detained Witness pursuant to Rule 71, October 4, 2002, para. 3).

    If there are other means available to meet the concerns which form the basis of the request for deposition, namely, the use of video-link testimony; the interests of justice requirement would require the use of such methods in order to allow the Trial Chamber to directly assess a witness's credibility. (*Prosecutor v. Simba*, Decision on the Defence Request for Taking the Evidence of Witness FMP1 by Deposition, February 9, 2005, para. 4; *Prosecutor v. Bagosora et al.*, Decision on Prosecution Request for Deposition of Witness BT, October 4, 2004.)

    If a deposition does take place, the accused has the right to attend (*Prosecutor v. Muvunyi*, Decision on the Request of the Accused for Certification to Appeal Against the Decision Authorising the Deposition of Prosecution Witness QX, November 27, 2003, para. 7).

L. Sexual Assault Cases

(1) Statutory provisions and rules

ICC

ICC Rules of Procedure and Evidence, rr. 70, 71, 72

Principles of evidence in cases of sexual violence

9–80   **70.** In cases of sexual violence, the Court shall be guided by and, where appropriate, apply the following principles:

(a) Consent cannot be inferred by reason of any words or conduct of a victim where force, threat of force, coercion or taking advantage of a coercive environment undermined the victim's ability to give voluntary and genuine consent;

(b) Consent cannot be inferred by reason of any words or conduct of a victim where the victim is incapable of giving genuine consent;

(c) Consent cannot be inferred by reason of the silence of, or lack of resistance by, a victim to the alleged sexual violence;

(d) Credibility, character or predisposition to sexual availability of a victim or witness cannot be inferred by reason of the sexual nature of the prior or subsequent conduct of a victim or witness.

Evidence of other sexual conduct

71. In the light of the definition and nature of the crimes within the jurisdiction of the Court, and subject to article 69, paragraph 4, a Chamber shall not admit evidence of the prior or subsequent sexual conduct of a victim or witness.   **9–81**

In camera procedure to consider relevance or admissibility of evidence

72.—1. Where there is an intention to introduce or elicit, including by means of the questioning of a victim or witness, evidence that the victim consented to an alleged crime of sexual violence, or evidence of the words, conduct, silence or lack of resistance of a victim or witness as referred to in principles (a) through (d) of rule 70, notification shall be provided to the Court which shall describe the substance of the evidence intended to be introduced or elicited and the relevance of the evidence to the issues in the case.   **9–82**

2. In deciding whether the evidence referred to in sub-rule 1 is relevant or admissible, a Chamber shall hear in camera the views of the Prosecutor, the defence, the witness and the victim or his or her legal representative, if any, and shall take into account whether that evidence has a sufficient degree of probative value to an issue in the case and the prejudice that such evidence may cause, in accordance with article 69, paragraph 4. For this purpose, the Chamber shall have regard to article 21, paragraph 3, and articles 67 and 68, and shall be guided by principles (a) to (d) of rule 70, especially with respect to the proposed questioning of a victim.

3. Where the Chamber determines that the evidence referred to in sub-rule 2 is admissible in the proceedings, the Chamber shall state on the record the specific purpose for which the evidence is admissible. In evaluating the evidence during the proceedings, the Chamber shall apply principles (a) to (d) of rule 70.

ICTY

ICTY Rules of Procedure and Evidence, r. 96

Evidence in Cases of Sexual Assault

96. In cases of sexual assault: **9–83**

(i) no corroboration of the victim's testimony shall be required;

(ii) consent shall not be allowed as a defence if the victim

(a) has been subjected to or threatened with or has had reason to fear violence, duress, detention or psychological oppression, or

(b) reasonably believed that if the victim did not submit, another might be so subjected, threatened or put in fear;

      (iii) before evidence of the victim's consent is admitted, the accused shall satisfy the Trial Chamber in camera that the evidence is relevant and credible;

      (iv) prior sexual conduct of the victim shall not be admitted in evidence.

ICTR

ICTR Rules of Procedure and Evidence, r. 96

Rules of Evidence in Cases of Sexual Assault

9–84   **96.** In cases of sexual assault:

      (i) Notwithstanding Rule 90 (C), no corroboration of the victim's testimony shall be required;

      (ii) Consent shall not be allowed as a defence if the victim:

          (a) Has been subjected to or threatened with or has had reason to fear violence, duress, detention or psychological oppression; or

          (b) Reasonably believed that if the victim did not submit, another might be so subjected, threatened or put in fear.

      (iii) Before evidence of the victim's consent is admitted, the accused shall satisfy the Trial Chamber *in camera* that the evidence is relevant and credible;

      (iv) Prior sexual conduct of the victim shall not be admitted in evidence or as defence.

East Timor

Regulation 2000/30, s.34.3 (as amended by 2001/25)

Rules of Evidence

9–85   **34.**—34.3 In cases of sexual assault:

      (a) no corroboration of the victim's testimony shall be required;

      (b) consent shall not be allowed as a defence if the victim:

          (1) has been subjected to or threatened with or has had reason to fear violence, duress, detention or psychological oppression, or

          (2) reasonably believed that if the victim did not submit, another person might be so subjected, threatened or put in fear;

      (c) before evidence of the victim's consent is admitted, the accused shall satisfy the court, *in camera*, that the evidence is relevant and credible;

      (d) prior sexual conduct of the victim shall not be admitted as evidence.

SCSL

SCSL Rules of Procedure and Evidence, r. 96

Rules of Evidence in Cases of Sexual Assaults

9–86   **96.** In cases of sexual violence, the Court shall be guided by and, where appropriate, apply the following principles:

i. Consent cannot be inferred by reason of any words or conduct of a victim where force, threat of force, coercion or taking advantage of a coercive environment undermined the victim's ability to give voluntary and genuine consent;

ii. Consent cannot be inferred by reason of any words or conduct of a victim where the victim is incapable of giving genuine consent;

iii. Consent cannot be inferred by reason of the silence of, or lack of resistance by, a victim to the alleged sexual violence;

iv. Credibility, character or predisposition to sexual availability of a victim or witness cannot be inferred by reason of sexual nature of the prior or subsequent conduct of a victim or witness.

(2) Admissibility in sexual assault cases

Several ICTY cases have attempted to explain the reasons underlying Rule 96 (*Prosecutor v. Tadić*, Decision on the Prosecutor's Motion Requesting Measures for Victims and Witnesses, August 10, 1995, para. 49, refers in this perspective to the "consideration of the unique concerns of victims of sexual assault"). Specific reference has been made to "the nature of the conflict during which the crimes over which the International Tribunal has jurisdiction were committed and where appalling allegations have been made of the systematic and mass rape of women". (*Prosecutor v. Delalic et al.*, Decision on the Prosecution's motion for redaction of the public record, June 5, 1997, para. 44.) **9–87**

Indeed, when crimes of a sexual violence nature are committed, under force, coercion or coercive circumstances, as part of genocide, crimes against humanity or war crimes, issues as consent or evidence of prior or subsequent sexual conduct do not seem relevant.

In addition, because of "fear of reprisals, retraumatization and feelings of shame" witnesses are generally reluctant to appear as witnesses before the Tribunal, which formed another good reason for having a special evidentiary rule on sexual violence (Rule 96(i) RPE ICTY/R has been commented on by several ICTY/R Chambers, *inter alia*, *Prosecutor v. Tadić*, Opinion and Judgment, May 7, 1997, para. 536; *Prosecutor v. Akayesu*, Judgment, September 2, 1998, para. 135; *Prosecutor v. FurundÀija*, Judgment, December 10, 1998, para. 116; *Prosecutor v. Kayishema and Ruzindana*, Judgment and Sentence, May 21, 1999, para. 70; *Prosecutor v. Musema*, Judgment and Sentence, January 27, 2000, para. 45; *Prosecutor v. Aleksovski*, Appeals Chamber, March 24, 2000, para. 62; *Prosecutor v. Kunarac et al.*, Judgment, February 22, 2001, para. 566).

The purpose of Rule 96(i) was to accord "the testimony of a sexual assault victim the same presumption of reliability as the testimony of victims of other crimes" (*Prosecutor v. Tadić*, Judgment, May 7, 1997, para. 536). The general principles for the admissibility of evidence before the Tribunals are, thus, applicable in the same way to sexual assault cases. (Also see, *Prosecutor v. Akayesu*, Judgment, September 2, 1998, paras 133–136.)

In *Prosecutor v. Furundžija*, Judgment, December 10, 1998, para. 271, the Trial Chamber noted that "consent" is vitiated by captivity, and that it was these coercive contexts which Rule 96 sought to take into account.

The prior sexual conduct of a victim shall not be admissible in terms of Rule 96(iv). The nature of the crimes laid down in the Statute do not justify challenging the victim's prior or subsequent sexual conduct. To admit such evidence would "lead to a confusion of the issues" essentially trying "to call the reputation of the victim into question" and would only bring "further distress and emotional damage to the witness.": see, *Prosecutor v. Delalic et al.*, Decision on the Prosecutor's Motion for the Redaction of the Public Record, June 5, 1997, para. 48; *Prosecutor v. Delalic et al.*, Judgment, November 16, 1998, para. 70).

M. Self-Incrimination

(1) Statutory provisions and rules

ICC

ICC Statute, Art. 69(5)

Evidence

9–88   **69.**—5. The Court shall respect and observe privileges on confidentiality as provided for in the Rules of Procedure and Evidence.

ICC Rules of Procedure and Evidence, rr. 73, 74, 75

Privileged communications and information

9–89   **73.**—1. Without prejudice to article 67, paragraph 1(b), communications made in the context of the professional relationship between a person and his or her legal counsel shall be regarded as privileged, and consequently not subject to disclosure, unless:

    (a) The person consents in writing to such disclosure; or

    (b) The person voluntarily disclosed the content of the communication to a third party, and that third party then gives evidence of that disclosure.

2. Having regard to rule 63, sub-rule 5, communications made in the context of a class of professional or other confidential relationships shall be regarded as privileged, and consequently not subject to disclosure, under the same terms as in sub-rules 1(a) and 1(b) if a Chamber decides in respect of that class that:

    (a) Communications occurring within that class of relationship are made in the course of a confidential relationship producing a reasonable expectation of privacy and non-disclosure;

    (b) Confidentiality is essential to the nature and type of relationship between the person and the confidant; and

    (c) Recognition of the privilege would further the objectives of the Statute and the Rules.

3. In making a decision under sub-rule 2, the Court shall give particular regard to recognizing as privileged those communications made in the context of the professional relationship between a person and his or her medical doctor, psychiatrist, psychologist or counsellor, in particular those related to or involving victims, or between a person and a member of a religious clergy; and in the latter case, the Court shall recognize as privileged those communications made in the context of a sacred confession where it is an integral part of the practice of that religion.

4. The Court shall regard as privileged, and consequently not subject to disclosure, including by way of testimony of any present or past official or employee of the International Committee of the Red Cross (ICRC), any information, documents or other evidence which it came into the possession of in the course, or as a consequence, of the performance by ICRC of its functions under the Statutes of the International Red Cross and Red Crescent Movement, unless:

    (a) After consultations undertaken pursuant to sub-rule 6, ICRC does not object in writing to such disclosure, or otherwise has waived this privilege; or

    (b) Such information, documents or other evidence is contained in public statements and documents of ICRC.

5. Nothing in sub-rule 4 shall affect the admissibility of the same evidence obtained from a source other than ICRC and its officials or employees when such evidence has also been acquired by this source independently of ICRC and its officials or employees.

6. If the Court determines that ICRC information, documents or other evidence are of great importance for a particular case, consultations shall be held between the Court and ICRC in order to seek to resolve the matter by cooperative means, bearing in mind the circumstances of the case, the relevance of the evidence sought, whether the evidence could be obtained from a source other than ICRC, the interests of justice and of victims, and the performance of the Court's and ICRC's functions.

Self-incrimination by a witness

9–90

74.—1. Unless a witness has been notified pursuant to rule 190, the Chamber shall notify a witness of the provisions of this rule before his or her testimony.

2. Where the Court determines that an assurance with respect to self-incrimination should be provided to a particular witness, it shall provide the assurances under sub-rule 3, paragraph (c), before the witness attends, directly or pursuant to a request under article 93, paragraph (1)(e).

3. (a) A witness may object to making any statement that might tend to incriminate him or her.

    (b) Where the witness has attended after receiving an assurance under sub-rule 2, the Court may require the witness to answer the question or questions.

    (c) In the case of other witnesses, the Chamber may require the witness to answer the question or questions, after assuring the witness that the evidence provided in response to the questions:

        (i) Will be kept confidential and will not be disclosed to the public or any State; and

        (ii) Will not be used either directly or indirectly against that person in any subsequent prosecution by the Court, except under articles 70 and 71.

4. Before giving such an assurance, the Chamber shall seek the views of the Prosecutor, ex parte, to determine if the assurance should be given to this particular witness.

5. In determining whether to require the witness to answer, the Chamber shall consider:

    (a) The importance of the anticipated evidence;

    (b) Whether the witness would be providing unique evidence;

    (c) The nature of the possible incrimination, if known; and

    (d) The sufficiency of the protections for the witness, in the particular circumstances.

6. If the Chamber determines that it would not be appropriate to provide an assurance to this witness, it shall not require the witness to answer the

question. If the Chamber determines not to require the witness to answer, it may still continue the questioning of the witness on other matters.

7. In order to give effect to the assurance, the Chamber shall:

    (a) Order that the evidence of the witness be given in camera;

    (b) Order that the identity of the witness and the content of the evidence given shall not be disclosed, in any manner, and provide that the breach of any such order will be subject to sanction under article 71;

    (c) Specifically advise the Prosecutor, the accused, the defence counsel, the legal representative of the victim and any Court staff present of the consequences of a breach of the order under subparagraph (b);

    (d) Order the sealing of any record of the proceedings; and

    (e) Use protective measures with respect to any decision of the Court to ensure that the identity of the witness and the content of the evidence given are not disclosed.

8. Where the Prosecutor is aware that the testimony of any witness may raise issues with respect to self-incrimination, he or she shall request an in camera hearing and advise the Chamber of this, in advance of the testimony of the witness. The Chamber may impose the measures outlined in sub-rule 7 for all or a part of the testimony of that witness.

9. The accused, the defence counsel or the witness may advise the Prosecutor or the Chamber that the testimony of a witness will raise issues of self-incrimination before the witness testifies and the Chamber may take the measures outlined in sub-rule 7.

10. If an issue of self-incrimination arises in the course of the proceedings, the Chamber shall suspend the taking of the testimony and provide the witness with an opportunity to obtain legal advice if he or she so requests for the purpose of the application of the rule.

Incrimination by family members

9–91   **75.**—1. A witness appearing before the Court, who is a spouse, child or parent of an accused person, shall not be required by a Chamber to make any statement that might tend to incriminate that accused person. However, the witness may choose to make such a statement.

2. In evaluating the testimony of a witness, a Chamber may take into account that the witness, referred to in sub-rule 1, objected to reply to a question which was intended to contradict a previous statement made by the witness, or the witness was selective in choosing which questions to answer.

Also see, Articles 55(1) and 67(1) of the ICC Statute.

ICTY

ICTY Statute of the ICTY, Art. 21(4)(g)

Rights of the accused

9–92   **21.**—4.

    (g) not to be compelled to testify against himself or to confess guilt.

ICTY Rules of Procedure and Evidence, rr. 90(E), 97

Testimony of Witnesses

9–93   **90.**—(E) A witness may object to making any statement which might tend to incriminate the witness. The Chamber may, however, compel the witness to answer the question. Testimony compelled in this way shall not be used as evidence in a subsequent prosecution against the witness for any offence other than false testimony.

Lawyer-Client Privilege

97.—All communications between lawyer and client shall be regarded as privileged, and consequently not subject to disclosure at trial, unless:

    (i) the client consents to such disclosure; or

    (ii) the client has voluntarily disclosed the content of the communication to a third party, and that third party then gives evidence of that disclosure.

9–94

ICTR

ICTR Statute of the ICTR, Art. 20(4)(g)

Rights of the Accused

20.—4.

    (g) Not to be compelled to testify against himself or herself or to confess guilt.

9–95

ICTR Rules of Procedure and Evidence, r. 90(E), 97

Testimony of Witnesses

90.—A witness may refuse to make any statement which might tend to incriminate him. The Chamber may, however, compel the witness to answer the question. Testimony compelled in this way shall not be used as evidence in a subsequent prosecution against the witness for any offence other than perjury.

9–96

Lawyer-Client Privilege

97.—(A) All communications between lawyer and client shall be regarded as privileged, and consequently disclosure cannot be ordered, unless:

    (i) The client consents to such disclosure; or

    (ii) The client has voluntarily disclosed the content of the communication to a third party, and that third party then gives evidence of that disclosure.

(B) Nothing in this rule shall be interpreted as permitting the use of confidentiality between Counsel and Client to conceal the participation of Counsel in illegal practices such as fee-splitting with client.

9–97

East Timor

Regulation 2000/30, s.35.(2, 3, 4, 5) (as amended by Regulation 2001/25)

Witnesses

35.—35.2 The following persons are not required to testify: The spouse or partner, the parents, children or relatives of the accused within the second degree.

9–98

481

35.3 The following categories of persons are able to testify only with the consent of the accused:

    (a) A duly ordained priest or monk when summoned to testify in relation to information revealed by the accused during the course of religious duties rendered by that priest or monk to the accused;

    (b) A lawyer when summoned to testify in relation to information provided by the accused as his or her client; and

    (c) A medical professional when summoned to testify in relation to information obtained from the accused in the delivery of his or her services to the accused. For purposes of the present section, the term "medical professional" includes, without limitation, medical doctors, psychiatrists, psychologists, counsellors, and their professional assistants.

35.4 No witness may be compelled to incriminate himself or herself. If it appears to the Presiding Judge that a question asked of a witness is likely to elicit a response that might incriminate the witness, the Judge shall advise the witness of his or her right not to answer the question.

35.5 No witness may be compelled to incriminate the witness' spouse or partner, parents, children, or relatives within the second degree.

35.7 The provisions of subsection 35.3 of the present regulation apply at all stages of investigative, trial and post-trial proceedings, and apply also to the benefit of victims and all other persons. For purposes of the present subsection, anyone who is questioned at any stage of proceedings by any party or investigator, by the representative of any party or investigator, or by a judge shall be deemed to be a witness. No witness whose testimony pertaining to the accused would require the consent of the accused under subsection 35.3 of the present regulation may be questioned concerning the same categories of information pertaining to any other person except with the consent of the person to whom the information pertains. No disclosure of information protected under the present subsection or subsection 35.3 of the present regulation may be compelled in any form.

SCSL

SCSL Statute of the SCSL, Art. 17(4)(g)

Rights of the Accused

9–99   17.—4.

    (g) Not to be compelled to testify against himself or herself or to confess guilt.

SCSL Rules of Procedure and Evidence, r. 90(E), 97

Testimony of Witnesses

9–100   90. [. . .]

    (E) A witness may refuse to make any statement which might tend to incriminate him. The Chamber may, however, compel the witness to answer the question. Testimony compelled in this way shall not be used as evidence in a subsequent prosecution against the witness for any offence other than false testimony under solemn declaration.

Lawyer-Client Privilege

9–101   97. All communications between lawyer and client shall be regarded as privileged, and consequently disclosure cannot be ordered, unless:

i. The client consents to such disclosure; or
ii. The client has voluntarily disclosed the content of the communication to a third party, and that third party then gives evidence of that disclosure.
iii. The client has alleged ineffective assistance of counsel, in which case the privilege is waived as to all communications relevant to the claim of ineffective assistance.

(2) Self-Incrimination

The defence does not have standing to invite the Trial Chamber to appoint counsel for a prosecution witness where such witness risks making a self-incriminatory statement. (*Prosecutor v. Bagosora et al.*, Decision on Defence Motion to Preclude Portions of the Anticipated Testimony of Prosecution Witness DCH, for the Postponement of DCH's Testimony, and for the Appointment of Defence Counsel for DCH, March 29, 2004, para. 10)   **9–102**

(3) Right to silence

The Tribunal may not draw an adverse inference from an accused's silence when not answering questions in interview and when not testifying at trial. (See, *Prosecutor v. Delalic et al.*, Decision on the Prosecution's Oral Requests for the Admission of Exhibit 155 into Evidence and for an Order to Compel the Accused, Zdrauko Mucic, to provide a Handwriting Sample, January 19, 1998).   **9–103**

(4) Privilege

The ICTY and ICTR do not have a rule similar to ICC Rule 73(4)–(6) regarding the ICRC. See, *Prosecutor v. Simić et al., ex p.* Confidential Decision on the Prosecution Motion under Rule 73 for a Ruling Concerning the Testimony of a Witness, July 27, 1999, which concerned an IRCR witness who was not ordered to attend court to testify.   **9–104**

By amendment of the ICTR Rules of May 27, 2003, Rule 97(B) was introduced. Pursuant to this Rule, Counsel-Client confidentiality cannot be extended to conceal illegal practices, including fee-splitting arrangements. The drafters of the Code of Conduct for Counsel before the ICC have included an even more robust proposal, namely, to oblige Counsel to inform the Registrar not only of any fee-splitting arrangement that may exist between his or her supporting staff and the client or any other such arrangement between any client and any Counsel, but also "of any request of such arrangements by a client after having advised the client of the prohibition of such practice" (Draft Code of Conduct for Counsel before the ICC, Rule 19(2)(c)).

III. EXCLUSION OF EVIDENCE

A. GROUNDS FOR EXCLUSION

(1) Statutory provisions and rules

ICC

ICC Statute, Art. 69(7)

Evidence

9–105   69.—7. Evidence obtained by means of a violation of this Statute or internationally recognized human rights shall not be admissible if:

    (a) The violation casts substantial doubt on the reliability of the evidence; or

    (b) The admission of the evidence would be antithetical to and would seriously damage the integrity of the proceedings.

ICTY

ICTY Rules of Procedure and Evidence, r. 95

Exclusion of Certain Evidence

9–106   95. No evidence shall be admissible if obtained by methods which cast substantial doubt on its reliability or if its admission is antithetical to, and would seriously damage, the integrity of the proceedings.

ICTR

ICTR Rules of Procedure and Evidence, r. 95

Exclusion of Evidence on the Grounds of the Means by which it was Obtained

9–107   95. No evidence shall be admissible if obtained by methods which cast substantial doubt on its reliability or if its admission is antithetical to, and would seriously damage, the integrity of the proceedings.

East Timor

Regulation 2000/30, s.34(2) (as amended by Regulation 2001/25)

Rules of Evidence

9–108   34.—34.2 The Court may exclude any evidence if its probative value is substantially outweighed by its prejudicial effect, or is unnecessarily cumulative with other evidence. No evidence shall be admitted if obtained by methods that cast substantial doubt on its reliability or if its admission is antithetical to, and would seriously damage, the integrity of the proceedings, including without limitation evidence obtained through torture, coercion or threats to moral or physical integrity.

SCSL

SCSL Rules of Procedure and Evidence, r. 95

Exclusion of Evidence
95. No evidence shall be admitted if its admission would bring the admin-   **9–109**
istration of justice into serious disrepute.

(2) Grounds for excluding evidence

Rule 95 is the "residual exclusionary provision"; it is "a summary of   **9–110**
the provisions in the Rules which enable exclusion of evidence" (see, *Prosecutor v. Delalic et al.*, Decision on Zdravko Mucic's Motion for the Exclusion of Evidence, September 2, 1997, paras 43–44). In this decision, the Trial Chamber confirmed that the source of the evidence is fundamental to its reliability (paras 41–42). Furthermore, as internationally accepted fair trial rights are incorporated into the Tribunals' Statutes and Rules, violations of these rights in the obtaining of evidence would affect the integrity of the proceedings, and could lead to the exclusion of the evidence (paras 43–45).

This Rule has been invoked in a number of cases, including, *Prosecutor v. Kordic*, Decision Stating Reasons for the Trial Chamber's Ruling of June 1, 1999 Rejecting Defence Motion to Suppress Evidence, June 25, 1999, concerning the admissibility of material seized in a search. Also see, *Prosecutor v. Nyiramasuhuko*, Decision on the Defence Motion for Exclusion of Evidence and Restitution of Property Seized, October 12, 2000.

The source of the evidence is important in the assessment of the reliability of the evidence. In *Delalic*, the Trial Chamber held: "For evidence to be reliable, it must be [. . .] obtained under circumstances which cast no doubt on its nature and character" (*Prosecutor v. Delalic et al.*, Decision on Zdravko Mucic's Motion for the Exclusion of Evidence, September 2, 1997, para. 41).

The scope of Rule 95 is wide; evidence obtained in an armed search (*Prosecutor v. Kordić and Čerkez*, Decision Stating Reasons for Trial Chamber's Ruling of June 1, 1999 Rejecting Defence Motion to Suppress Evidence, June 25, 1999, at pp. 3–5); in irregular investigation procedures (*Prosecutor v. Delalic et al.*, Decision on Zdravko Mucic's Motion for the Exclusion of Evidence, September 2, 1997, para. 45); or by a breach of the Rules of Procedure and Evidence may be found inadmissible (*Prosecutor v. Delalic et al.*, Decision on Zdravko Mucic's Motion for the Exclusion of Evidence, September 2, 1997, para. 41).

Improper procedure, regardless whether the quality of evidence has been affected and whether the procedure was conducted by investigators of the Tribunal, may trigger the Trial Chamber's exclusionary discretion pursuant to Rule 95.

Interviews conducted in violation of the safeguards enshrined in the statutes and rules may be excluded, particularly where they were taken in absence of counsel without the explicit and informed waiver of the suspect or accused. If there is any doubt about the voluntariness of the interview the OTP has the burden to prove "beyond reasonable doubt and convincingly" that the interview was conducted voluntarily (*Prosecutor v. Delalic et al.*, Decision on Zdravko Mucic's Motion For the Exclusion of Evidence, September 2, 1997, para. 42; *Prosecutor v. Bagosora et al.*, Decision on the Prosecutor's Motion for the Admission of Certain Materials Under Rule 89(C), October 14, 2004, para. 16). The Trial Chamber in *Bagosora et al.* also explained that legal representation during preliminary questioning is important to have explanation from counsel about other rights at the preliminary stage, such as the right to silence, the privilege against self-incrimination and the right to be cautioned that any statement made may be used as evidence against the Accused (at para. 21).

The essential question is whether a suspect or accused voluntarily waived his right to counsel. The Prosecutor has the burden to prove "convincingly and beyond reasonable doubt" that a suspect or accused voluntarily waived his right to be represented (*Prosecutor v. Delalic et al.*, Decision on Zdravko Mucic's Motion For the Exclusion of Evidence, September 2, 1997, para. 42). This standard of proof was initially brought in connection with allegations of oppressive conduct during a suspect's or accused's questioning (*Delalic*, see above), but was recently held to apply to the voluntary waiver of the right to representation: *Prosecutor v. Bagosora et al.*, Decision on the Prosecutor's Motion for the Admission of Certain Materials Under Rule 89(C), October 14, 2004, paras 17 and 18: "National courts in which the right to counsel is recognized have elaborated that a waiver cannot be voluntary unless a detainee knows of the right to which he is entitled. To be so informed, the suspect must be informed that the right includes the right to the prompt assistance of counsel, prior to and during any questioning. Any implication that the right is conditional, or that the presence of counsel may be delayed until after the questioning, renders any waiver defective [. . .] Once the detainee has been fully apprised of his right to the assistance of counsel, he or she is in a position to voluntarily waive the right. The waiver must be shown 'convincingly and beyond reasonable doubt.' It must be express and unequivocal, and must clearly relate to the interview in which the statement in question is taken."

At the SCSL the threshold for the application of Rule 95 seems to be higher than at the ICTY and ICTR, given their clear preference for admission rather than exclusion of evidence. In *Brima et al.*, the Trial Chamber found that "the Defence has not made out a case for the exclusion of evidence, let alone for the exclusion of the Witness's evidence in its entirety. Nor has anything been put before us which would justify the conclusion that the admission of the evidence would bring the administration of justice into serious disrepute pursuant to Rule 95. On the contrary, the evidence in our view is so clearly relevant that the judicial process would be brought into disrepute by excluding it" (*Prosecutor v. Brima et al.*, Decision on Joint Defence Motion to Exclude Al Evidence From Witness TF1–277 Pursuant to Rule 89(C) and/or Rule 95, May 24, 2005, para. 24).

See Further Rules 42, 43, 63, Chapter 7.

IV. POWERS OF TRIAL CHAMBERS

(1) Statutory provisions and rules

ICC

ICC Statute, Arts 64(6)(b), 69(3)

Functions and powers of the Trial Chamber

69.—6. In performing its functions prior to trial or during the course of a trial, the Trial Chamber may, as necessary: **9–111**
    (a) Exercise any functions of the Pre-Trial Chamber referred to in article 61, paragraph 11;
    (b) Require the attendance and testimony of witnesses and production of documents and other evidence by obtaining, if necessary, the assistance of States as provided in this Statute;

Evidence

69.—3. The parties may submit evidence relevant to the case, in accordance with article 64. The Court shall have the authority to request the submission of all evidence that it considers necessary for the determination of the truth.   **9–112**

ICTY

ICTY Rules of Procedure and Evidence, r. 98

Power of Chambers to Order Production of Additional Evidence

98. A Trial Chamber may order either party to produce additional evidence. It may *proprio motu* summon witnesses and order their attendance.   **9–113**

ICTR

ICTR Rules of Procedure and Evidence, r. 98

Power of Chambers to Order Production of Additional Evidence

98. A Trial Chamber may *proprio motu* order either party to produce additional evidence. It may itself summon witnesses and order their attendance.   **9–114**

East Timor

Regulation 2000/30, ss.33.2, 36.6 (as amended by Regulation 2001/25)

Presentation of Evidence

33.—33.2 After the defence has presented its case the prosecution shall be given the opportunity to respond to the defence evidence. The defence will then be allowed to reply to the prosecution. The court shall call any additional   **9–115**

witnesses it wishes to hear or evidence that it wishes to be presented after the parties have completed their submissions.

Witness Testimony

9–116   36.—36.6 Unless otherwise determined by the court, witnesses shall be examined first by the court, then by the party calling the witness, then the opposing party. The Presiding Judge shall allow other judges of the panel to pose additional questions to the witness.

(2) The calling of witnesses by the Trial Chamber

9–117   In *Prosecutor v. Blaškić*, Decisions, March 25, 1999, the Trial Chamber ordered various witnesses who had not been called by the Prosecution or Defence to appear before the Chamber pursuant to Rule 98. They were ordered to appear before the Prosecution and Defence closing addresses, with all parties permitted to examine them.

In the SCSL case of *Norman et al.*, upon Defence's request, the Trial Chamber ordered the Prosecutor to call as a witness the OTP investigators who took down in writing statements of a prosecution witness, which were allegedly inconsistent with the witness's oral testimony. The Defence asserted that the appearance of the investigators who took down the statements in question was important to enable the Chamber to adequately and effectively: "(i) test the credibility of the said witness, (ii) assess the veracity of the statements given by the said witness to the OTP investigators, and (iii) determine what weight to attach to the witness's testimony" (*Prosecutor v. Norman et al.*, Ruling on Defence Oral Application to Call OTP Investigators Who Took Down in Writing Statements of Prosecution Witness TF2–021, December 7, 2004, para. 3). In granting the Defence's request and denying the Prosecutor's submission that investigators' records are for internal use only and therefore not subject to judicial inquiry, the Trial Chamber took account of the presumption of regularity of the criminal proceedings which cannot legitimately apply to the specific and contentious, factual and legal issues in question (*ibid.*, paras 14–17).

V. EXPERT TESTIMONY

(1) Statutory provisions and rules

ICC

ICC Regulations of the Court, r. 44

Experts

9–118   44.—1. The Registrar shall create and maintain a list of experts accessible at all times to all organs of the Court and to all participants. Experts shall be included on such a list following an appropriate indication of expertise in the relevant field. A person may seek review by the Presidency of a negative decision of the Registrar.

2. The Chamber may direct the joint instruction of an expert by the participants.

3. On receipt of the report prepared by an expert jointly instructed, a participant may apply to the Chamber for leave to instruct a further expert.

4. The Chamber may *proprio motu* instruct an expert.

5. The Chamber may issue any order as to the subject of an expert report, the number of experts to be instructed, the mode of their instruction, the manner in which their evidence is to be presented and the time limits for the preparation and notification of their report.

ICTY

ICTY Rules of Procedure and Evidence, r. 94*bis*

Testimony of Expert Witnesses

94*bis*.—(A) The full statement of any expert witness to be called by a party shall be disclosed within the time-limit prescribed by the Trial Chamber or by the pre-trial Judge.

9–119

(B) Within thirty days of disclosure of the statement of the expert witness, or such other time prescribed by the Trial Chamber or pre-trial Judge, the opposing party shall file a notice indicating whether:

    (i) it accepts the expert witness statement; or

    (ii) it wishes to cross-examine the expert witness; and

    (iii) it challenges the qualifications of the witness as an expert or the relevance of all or parts of the report and, if so, which parts

(C) If the opposing party accepts the statement of the expert witness, the statement may be admitted into evidence by the Trial Chamber without calling the witness to testify in person.

ICTR

ICTR Rules of Procedure and Evidence, r. 94*bis*

Testimony of Expert Witnesses

94*bis*.—(A) Notwithstanding the provisions of Rule 66 (A) (ii), Rule 73*bis* (B) (iv) (b) and Rule 73*ter* (B) (iii) (b) of the present Rules, the full statement of any expert witness called by a party shall be disclosed to the opposing party as early as possible and shall be filed with the Trial Chamber not less than twenty-one days prior to the date on which the expert is expected to testify.

9–120

(B) Within fourteen days of filing of the statement of the expert witness, the opposing party shall file a notice to the Trial Chamber indicating whether:

    (i) It accepts or does not accept the witness's qualification as an expert;

    (ii) It accepts the expert witness statement; or

    (iii) It wishes to cross-examine the expert witness.

(C) If the opposing party accepts the statement of the expert witness, the statement may be admitted into evidence by the Trial Chamber without calling the witness to testify in person.

East Timor

There is no section dealing specifically with qualification requirements for expert witnesses. This deletion does not seem to preclude expert witness from testifying as indicated by the high number of

9–121

references to expert witnesses in the UNTAET Regulation. Sections 36.3, 36.7, 36.9, 18.5, 24.5 and 31 give guidance to participation of expert witnesses in the court proceedings.

SCSL

SCSL Rules of Procedure and Evidence, r. 94*bis*

Testimony of Expert Witnesses
  94*bis*.—(A) Notwithstanding the provisions of Rule 66(A), Rule 73*bis* (B)(iv)(b) and Rule 73*ter* (B)(iii)(b) of the present Rules, the full statement of any expert witness called by a party shall be disclosed to the opposing party as early as possible and shall be filed with the Trial Chamber not less than twenty one days prior to the date on which the expert is expected to testify.
  (B) Within fourteen days of filing of the statement of the expert witness, the opposing party shall file a notice to the Trial Chamber indicating whether:
     i. It accepts the expert witness statement; or
     ii. It wishes to cross examine the expert witness.
  (C) If the opposing party accepts the statement of the expert witness, the statement may be admitted into evidence by the Trial Chamber without calling the witness to testify in person.

(2) Scope of expert testimony

(a) Requirements to qualify as an expert

9–122   Expert witnesses have testified in most cases before the ICTY, ICTR and SCSL. The nature of the offences charged often require experts in the military, political and constitutional fields to assist the Chamber on specialised subjects, such as the command structures of armed forces. The standard for admission of expert testimony is whether the specialised knowledge possessed by the expert, applied to the evidence which is the foundation of the opinion, may assist the Chamber in understanding the evidence. As the Trial Chamber put it in *Akayesu*, expert testimony is admissible if it is "intended to enlighten the Judges on specific issues of a technical nature, requiring special knowledge in a specific field" (*Prosecutor v. Akayesu*, Decision on a Defence Motion for the appearance of an Accused as an expert Witness, March 9, 1998. This definition was repeated in *Prosecutor v. Nahimana et al.*, Decision on the Expert Witnesses for the Defence, January 24, 2003, para. 2). The expert evidence needs to be relevant and of assistance to the Chamber in its deliberations (*Prosecutor v. Nahimana et al.*, Decision on the Expert Witnesses for the Defence, January 24, 2003, paras 6 and 11).
  In *Bagosora et al.*, the Trial Chamber held that: "[i]t is widely accepted and the parties in this case do not dispute that the role of an expert is to provide opinions or inferences to assist the finders of fact in understanding factual issues. In addition, there is no dispute that before being permitted to submit opinion testimony, the Chamber must find that the expert is competent in her proposed field or fields of

expertise. The expert must possess some specialised knowledge acquired through education, experience, or training in a field that may assist the fact finders to understand the evidence or to assess a fact at issue" (*Prosecutor v. Bagosora et al.*, Oral Decisions on Defence Objections and Motions to Exclude the Testimony and Report of the Prosecution's proposed Expert Witness, Dr. Alison DesForges, or to Postpone her Testimony at Trial, September 4, 2002, para. 5; See also *Prosecutor v. Nahimana et al.*, Oral Decision, May 20, 2002, pp. 122–126).

In *Bizimungu et al.*, the Trial Chamber declined to qualify a proposed expert witness on Rwanda Constitutional Law because his claim to be a Constitutional Law Expert rested primarily on his membership of the court and *conseil d'état*. As the witness himself acknowledged, such membership did not suffice to establish his expertise in Constitutional Law. As he was vague on other matters that would support his claim to be an expert in Constitutional Law, he was not qualified to testify as an expert witness (*Prosecutor v. Bizimungu et al.*, Oral Decision on Qualification of Prosecution Expert Jean Rubaduka, March 24, 2005, p. 15).

The party seeking to rely on an expert has the burden of "demonstrating the qualifications of an expert witness, and the expert witness' relevance and probative value" (*Prosecutor v. Bizimungu et al.*, Oral Decision on Qualification of Prosecution Witness Jean Rubaduka, March 24, 2005).

(b) Subject Matter

In the *Celebici* case (*Prosecutor v. Delalic et al.*), an expert on the **9–123** nationality of the victims testified in order to determine whether they enjoyed protection under Geneva Convention IV as being of a different nationality to the perpetrators.

In *Kordić and Čerkez*, a phonetic expert was not qualified to testify as an expert witness on the reaction of the Accused to the UN Peacekeeping officers' information that a mosque was being shelled as "he would be trespassing on the Trial Chamber's province" (*Prosecutor v. Kordić and Čerkez*, T. October 6, 2000, pp. 26093–26100).

At the ICTR, expert witnesses have been authorized to testify on such matters as the role of military forces in Rwanda in 1994; the socio-economic and political situation leading up to 1994; the role of the media in Rwandan society; the perpetration of human rights violations in 1994; and the organisation of civil defence (*Prosecutor v. Bagosora et al.*, Decision on Motion for Exclusion of Expert Witness Statement of Filip Reyntjens, September 28, 2004, para. 8).

Expert witnesses are generally not permitted to testify about matters that are properly for the Chamber to adjudicate. For example, a military expert cannot testify about whether an accused exercised sufficient control in the circumstances of a case to render him criminally liable under the doctrine of command responsibility. In addition, experts cannot testify about legal issues which are properly for the Chamber to determine. For example, an expert witness on the legal meaning of the specific intent requirement of the offence of genocide would not be permitted (*Prosecutor v. Nahimana et al.*, Decision on the Expert Witnesses for the Defence, January 24, 2003, paras 16 and 22. See also *Prosecutor v. Nahimana et al.*, Decision to reconsider the Trial

Chamber's Decision of January 24, 2003 on the Defence Expert Witnesses, February 25, 2003, p. 4).

The Trial Chamber in the ICTY held that expert reports can only be used to prove general events, not for the determination of the guilt of a specific alleged perpetrator (*Prosecutor v. Kovacevic*, Official Transcript, July 6, 1998, p. 71; *Prosecutor v. Kordić and Čerkez*, Official Transcript, January 28, 2000, pp. 13268–13306). The expert report of Madame DesForges was accepted despite the fact that she discussed the culpability of the four persons accused in great detail (*Prosecutor v. Bagosora et al.*, Oral Decisions on Defence Objections and Motions to Exclude the Testimony and Report of the Prosecution's proposed Expert Witness, Dr. Alison DesForges, or to Postpone her Testimony at Trial, September 4, 2002). On similar grounds Ms Nowrojee's testimony was, however, limited to her investigations of sexual crimes in Rwanda, based on her interviews and investigations in the field; she was not entitled to address the legal conclusions she had drawn therefrom (*Prosecutor v. Bagosora et al.*, T. July 12, 2004, pp. 72–73)

(c) Hearsay

9–124   In *Kovacevic*, the Trial Chamber admitted an expert report of a judge who, in his report, had summarised, analysed and collated information from 400 witnesses, with the note that, "there is no question of this defendant being convicted on any count on the basis of this evidence. And we shall require other evidence before we consider taking any such course" (*Prosecutor v. Kovacevic*, Official Transcript, July 6, 1998, pp. 69–71 and 75).

In *Kordić and Čerkez*, the Trial Chamber excluded a book, proposed for admission as the work of an expert, because it did not assist the Trial Chamber much, as it was "littered [. . .] with examples of conclusions, drawing inferences, drawing conclusions, which it is the duty of this Trial Chamber to consider and to draw if appropriate or to reject" (*Prosecutor v. Kordić and Čerkez*, Official Transcript, January 28, 2000, pp. 13305–07).

In *Bagilishema*, the Chamber discounted the expert witness, Mr Ndengejeho's testimony, as it was based on information which derived from "unidentified sources"—hearsay—and "lack[ed] sufficient details to be reliable." (*Prosecutor v. Bagilishema*, Judgment, June 7, 2001, para. 139).

In *Bizimungu et al.*, the Trial Chamber excluded a proposed report of a factual witness, resembling an expert report. The Trial Chamber held, while agreeing that it had a wide discretion to admit relevant evidence, "it has serious doubts as to how helpful and useful this report would be to the Trial Chamber when it is required to assess its value. The unavailability [. . .] to the Trial Chamber of all materials which the witness used in compiling the report will make its task extremely difficult, if not impossible. The Trial Chamber cannot take for granted, or accept without question, the authenticity and reliability of the limited experts which the witness and the prosecutor have provided for the guidance of the Trial Chamber in assessing the probative value of the report" (*Prosecutor v. Bizimungu*, Oral Decision, October 8, 2004, p. 31).

In *Prosecutor v. Aleksovski*, Decision on Prosecutor's Appeal on Admissibility of Evidence, February 16, 1999, the Appeals Chamber held that testimony in the *Blaškić* case, including expert evidence, could be admitted as hearsay evidence, pursuant to sub-note 89(C) in the *Aleksovski* case. Judge Robinson dissented, and in relation to the expert evidence, noted that it violated Rule 94*bis* to admit this testimony as according to the rule expert testimony had to be given in person unless the opposing party accepted the admission of the expert report.

(d) Disclosure of report and other materials

Disclosure of the full statements of the expert witnesses should be **9–125** made, as a matter of principle, as early as possible (*Prosecutor v. Bagosora et al.*, Decision on Motion for Exclusion of Expert Witness Statement of Filip Reyntjens, September 28, 2004, para. 17).

The Court ordered the disclosure of the report of Alison DesForges, a leading expert at the ICTR, more than two months before her anticipated testimony. The Prosecution's indication that her report would be similar to previous reports filed in six other cases did not satisfy the disclosure obligations pursuant to Rule 94*bis* (A), and resulted in postponement of the trial (*Prosecutor v. Bizimungu et al.*, Decision on Mugenzi's Confidential Motion for the Filing, Service, or Disclosure of Expert Reports and/or Statements, November 10, 2004, para. 21).

In *Bagosora et al.*, the Prosecutor's failure to timely disclose Alison Des Forges' report resulted in a delay of the commencement of trial for a period of five months. In another case, however, the Trial Chamber declined to order the Prosecutor to have expert witness reports prepared more than 21 days before the testimony of the expert at trial (*Prosecutor v. Karemera et al.*, Décision Relative à la Requête de L'Accusé Nzirorera aux fins de la Communication des Rapports des Témoins Experts du Procureur, April 2, 2004).

CHAPTER 10

FORMS OF PARTICIPATION IN OFFENCES

I. STATUTORY PROVISIONS

A. ICC

Statute, Arts 25, 27, 28, 30

Individual criminal responsibility

25.—1. The Court shall have jurisdiction over natural persons pursuant to **10–1**
this Statute.

2. A person who commits a crime within the jurisdiction of the Court shall
be individually responsible and liable for punishment in accordance with this
Statute.

3. In accordance with this Statute, a person shall be criminally responsible
and liable for punishment for a crime within the jurisdiction of the Court if
that person:

(a) Commits such a crime, whether as an individual, jointly with another
    or through another person, regardless of whether that other person is
    criminally responsible;

(b) Orders, solicits or induces the commission of such a crime which in fact occurs or is attempted;

(c) For the purpose of facilitating the commission of such a crime, aids, abets or otherwise assists in its commission or its attempted commission, including providing the means for its commission;

(d) In any other way contributes to the commission or attempted commission of such a crime by a group of persons acting with a common purpose. Such contribution shall be intentional and shall either:

    (i) Be made with the aim of furthering the criminal activity or criminal purpose of the group, where such activity or purpose involves the commission of a crime within the jurisdiction of the Court; or

    (ii) Be made in the knowledge of the intention of the group to commit the crime;

(e) In respect of the crime of genocide, directly and publicly incites others to commit genocide;

(f) Attempts to commit such a crime by taking action that commences its execution by means of a substantial step, but the crime does not occur because of circumstances independent of the person's intentions. However, a person who abandons the effort to commit the crime or otherwise prevents the completion of the crime shall not be liable for punishment under this Statute for the attempt to commit that crime if that person completely and voluntarily gave up the criminal purpose.

4. No provision in this Statute relating to individual criminal responsibility shall affect the responsibility of States under international law.

Irrelevance of official capacity

10–2 **27.**—1. This Statute shall apply equally to all persons without any distinction based on official capacity. In particular, official capacity as a Head of State or Government, a member of a Government or parliament, an elected representative or a government official shall in no case exempt a person from criminal responsibility under this Statute, nor shall it, in and of itself, constitute a ground for reduction of sentence.

2. Immunities or special procedural rules which may attach to the official capacity of a person, whether under national or international law, shall not bar the Court from exercising its jurisdiction over such a person.

Responsibility of commanders and other superiors

10–3 **28.** In addition to other grounds of criminal responsibility under this Statute for crimes within the jurisdiction of the Court:

(a) A military commander or person effectively acting as a military commander shall be criminally responsible for crimes within the jurisdiction of the Court committed by forces under his or her effective command and control, or effective authority and control as the case may be, as a result of his or her failure to exercise control properly over such forces, where:

    (i) That military commander or person either knew or, owing to the circumstances at the time, should have known that the forces were committing or about to commit such crimes; and

    (ii) That military commander or person failed to take all necessary and reasonable measures within his or her power to prevent or repress their commission or to submit the matter to the competent authorities for investigation and prosecution.

(b) With respect to superior and subordinate relationships not described in paragraph (a), a superior shall be criminally responsible for crimes within the jurisdiction of the Court committed by subordinates under his or her effective authority and control, as a result of his or her failure to exercise control properly over such subordinates, where:

(i) The superior either knew, or consciously disregarded information which clearly indicated, that the subordinates were committing or about to commit such crimes;

(ii) The crimes concerned activities that were within the effective responsibility and control of the superior; and

(iii) The superior failed to take all necessary and reasonable measures within his or her power to prevent or repress their commission or to submit the matter to the competent authorities for investigation and prosecution.

Mental element

30.—1. Unless otherwise provided, a person shall be criminally responsible and liable for punishment for a crime within the jurisdiction of the Court only if the material elements are committed with intent and knowledge.

2. For the purposes of this article, a person has intent where:

(a) In relation to conduct, that person means to engage in the conduct;

(b) In relation to a consequence, that person means to cause that consequence or is aware that it will occur in the ordinary course of events.

3. For the purposes of this article, "knowledge" means awareness that a circumstance exists or a consequence will occur in the ordinary course of events. "Know" and "knowingly" shall be construed accordingly.

10–4

B. ICTY

Statute for the International Tribunal, Art. 7

Individual criminal responsibility

7.—1. A person who planned, instigated, ordered, committed or otherwise aided and abetted in the planning, preparation or execution of a crime referred to in articles 2 to 5 of the present Statute, shall be individually responsible for the crime.

2. The official position of any accused person, whether as Head of State or Government or as a responsible Government official, shall not relieve such person of criminal responsibility nor mitigate punishment.

3. The fact that any of the acts referred to in articles 2 to 5 of the present Statute was committed by a subordinate does not relieve his superior of criminal responsibility if he knew or had reason to know that the subordinate was about to commit such acts or had done so and the superior failed to take the necessary and reasonable measures to prevent such acts or to punish the perpetrators thereof.

4. The fact that an accused person acted pursuant to an order of a Government or of a superior shall not relieve him of criminal responsibility, but may be considered in mitigation of punishment if the International Tribunal determines that justice so requires.

10–5

C. ICTR

Statute for the International Tribunal for Rwanda, Art. 6

Individual Criminal Responsibility

10–6   **6.**—1. A person who planned, instigated, ordered, committed or otherwise aided and abetted in the planning, preparation or execution of a crime referred to in Articles 2 to 4 of the present Statute, shall be individually responsible for the crime.

2. The official position of any accused person, whether as Head of state or government or as a responsible government official, shall not relieve such person of criminal responsibility nor mitigate punishment.

3. The fact that any of the acts referred to in Articles 2 to 4 of the present Statute was committed by a subordinate does not relieve his or her superior of criminal responsibility if he or she knew or had reason to know that the subordinate was about to commit such acts or had done so and the superior failed to take the necessary and reasonable measures to prevent such acts or to punish the perpetrators thereof.

4. The fact that an accused person acted pursuant to an order of a government or of a superior shall not relieve him or her of criminal responsibility, but may be considered in mitigation of punishment if the International Tribunal for Rwanda determines that justice so requires.

D. East Timor

UNTAET Regulation 2000/15, June 6, 2000, ss 14, 15, 16, 18

On the Establishment of Panels with Exclusive Jurisdiction over Serious Criminal Offences

Individual criminal responsibility

10–7   **14.**—14.1. The panels shall have jurisdiction over natural persons pursuant to the present regulation.

14.2. A person who commits a crime within the jurisdiction of the panels shall be individually responsible and liable for punishment in accordance with the present regulation.

14.3. In accordance with the present regulation, a person shall be criminally responsible and liable for punishment for a crime within the jurisdiction of the panels if that person:

    (a) commits such a crime, whether as an individual, jointly with another or through another person, regardless of whether that other person is criminally responsible;

    (b) orders, solicits or induces the commission of such a crime which in fact occurs or is attempted;

    (c) for the purpose of facilitating the commission of such a crime, aids, abets or otherwise assists in its commission or its attempted commission, including providing the means for its commission;

    (d) in any other way contributes to the commission or attempted commission of such a crime by a group of persons acting with a common purpose. Such contribution shall be intentional and shall either:

        (i) be made with the aim of furthering the criminal activity or criminal purpose of the group, where such activity or purpose

> involves the commission of a crime within the jurisdiction of the panels; or
>
> (ii) be made in the knowledge of the intention of the group to commit the crime;
>
> (e) in respect of the crime of genocide, directly and publicly incites others to commit genocide;
>
> (f) attempts to commit such a crime by taking action that commences its execution by means of a substantial step, but the crime does not occur because of circumstances independent of the person's intentions. However, a person who abandons the effort to commit the crime or otherwise prevents the completion of the crime shall not be liable for punishment under the present regulation for the attempt to commit that crime if that person completely and voluntarily gave up the criminal purpose.

Irrelevance of official capacity

15.—15.1. The present regulation shall apply equally to all persons without any distinction based on official capacity. In particular, official capacity as a Head of State or Government, a member of a Government or parliament, an elected representative or a government official shall in no case exempt a person from criminal responsibility under the present regulation, nor shall it, in and of itself, constitute a ground for reduction of sentence.   **10–8**

15.2. Immunities or special procedural rules which may attach to the official capacity of a person, whether under national or international law, shall not bar the panels from exercising its jurisdiction over such a person.

Responsibility of commanders and other superiors

16. In addition to other grounds of criminal responsibility under the present regulation for serious criminal offences referred to in Sections 4 to 7 of the present regulation, the fact that any of the acts referred to in the said Sections 4 to 7 was committed by a subordinate does not relieve his superior of criminal responsibility if he knew or had reason to know that the subordinate was about to commit such acts or had done so and the superior failed to take the necessary and reasonable measures to prevent such acts or to punish the perpetrators thereof.   **10–9**

Mental element

18.—18.1. A person shall be criminally responsible and liable for punishment for a crime within the jurisdiction of the panels only if the material elements are committed with intent and knowledge.   **10–10**

18.2. For the purposes of the present Section, a person has "intent" where:
  (a) In relation to conduct, that person means to engage in the conduct;
  (b) In relation to a consequence, that person means to cause that consequence or is aware that it will occur in the ordinary course of events.

18.3. For the purposes of the present Section, "knowledge" means awareness that a circumstance exists or a consequence will occur in the ordinary course of events. "Know" and "knowingly" shall be construed accordingly.

E. Sierra Leone

Statute of Special Court for Sierra Leone, Art. 6

Individual criminal responsibility

6.—1. A person who planned, instigated, ordered, committed or otherwise aided and abetted in the planning, preparation or execution of a crime referred to in articles 2 to 4 of the present Statute shall be individually responsible for the crime.   **10–11**

2. The official position of any accused persons, whether as Head of State or Government or as a responsible government official, shall not relieve such person of criminal responsibility nor mitigate punishment.

3. The fact that any of the acts referred to in articles 2 to 4 of the present Statute was committed by a subordinate does not relieve his or her superior of criminal responsibility if he or she knew or had reason to know that the subordinate was about to commit such acts or had done so and the superior had failed to take the necessary and reasonable measures to prevent such acts or to punish the perpetrators thereof.

4. The fact that an accused person acted pursuant to an order of a Government or of a superior shall not relieve him or her of criminal responsibility, but may be considered in mitigation of punishment if the Special Court determines that justice so requires.

5. Individual criminal responsibility for the crimes referred to in article 5 shall be determined in accordance with the respective laws of Sierra Leone.

F. CAMBODIA

Law on the Establishment of Extraordinary Chambers in the Courts of Cambodia for the Prosecution of Crimes Committed during the Period of Democratic Kampuchea, as amended, Art. 29

Individual Responsibility

10–12   29. Any Suspect who planned, instigated, ordered, aided and abetted, or committed the crimes referred to in article 3 new, 4, 5, 6, 7 and 8 of this law shall be individually responsible for the crime.

The position or rank of any Suspect shall not relieve such person of criminal responsibility or mitigate punishment.

The fact that any of the acts referred to in Articles 3 new, 4, 5, 6, 7 and 8 of this law were committed by a subordinate does not relieve the superior of personal criminal responsibility if the superior had effective command and control or authority and control over the subordinate, and the superior knew or had reason to know that the subordinate was about to commit such acts or had done so and the superior failed to take the necessary and reasonable measures to prevent such acts or to punish the perpetrators.

The fact that a Suspect acted pursuant to an order of the Government of Democratic Kampuchea or of a superior shall not relieve the Suspect of individual criminal responsibility.

G. IRAQ

Statute of Iraqi Special Tribunal, Art. 15

Individual Criminal Responsibility

10–13   15.—a) A person who commits a crime within the jurisdiction of this Tribunal shall be individually responsible and liable for punishment in accordance with this Statute.

b) In accordance with this Statute, and the provisions of Iraqi criminal law, a person shall be criminally responsible and liable for punishment for a crime within the jurisdiction of the Tribunal if that person:

1. Commits such a crime, whether as an individual, jointly with another or through another person, regardless of whether that other person is criminally responsible;
2. Orders, solicits or induces the commission of such a crime which in fact occurs or is attempted;
3. For the purpose of facilitating the commission of such a crime, aids, abets or otherwise assists in its commission or its attempted commission, including providing the means for its commission;
4. In any other way contributes to the commission or attempted commission of such a crime by a group of persons acting with a common purpose. Such contribution shall be intentional and shall either:
   i. Be made with the aim of furthering the criminal activity or criminal purpose of the group, where such activity or purpose involves the commission of a crime within the jurisdiction of the Tribunal; or
   ii. Be made in the knowledge of the intention of the group to commit the crime;
5. In respect of the crime of genocide, directly and publicly incites others to commit genocide;
6. Attempts to commit such a crime by taking action that commences its execution by means of a substantial step, but the crime does not occur because of circumstances independent of the person's intentions. However, a person who abandons the effort to commit the crime or otherwise prevents the completion of the crime shall not be liable for punishment under this Statute for the attempt to commit that crime if that person completely and voluntarily gave up the criminal purpose.

c) The official position of any accused person, whether as president, prime minister, member of the cabinet, chairman or a member of the Revolutionary Command Council, a member of the Arab Socialist Ba'ath Party Regional Command or Government (or an instrumentality of either) or as a responsible Iraqi Government official or member of the Ba'ath Party or in any other capacity, shall not relieve such person of criminal responsibility nor mitigate punishment. No person is entitled to any immunity with respect to any of the crimes stipulated in Articles 11 to 14.

d) The fact that any of the acts referred to in Articles 11 to 14 of the present Statute was committed by a subordinate does not relieve his superior of criminal responsibility if he knew or had reason to know that the subordinate was about to commit such acts or had done so and the superior failed to take the necessary and reasonable measures to prevent such acts or to submit the matter to the competent authorities for investigation and prosecution.

e) The fact that an accused person acted pursuant to an order of a Government or of a superior shall not relieve him of criminal responsibility, but may be considered in mitigation of punishment if the Tribunal determines that justice so requires.

II. DIRECT FORMS OF PARTICIPATION

After the First World War, the Commission on the Responsibility of **10–14** the Authors of the War and on Enforcement of Penalties recommended that "all persons belonging to enemy countries, however high their position may have been, without distinction of rank, including chiefs of States, who have been guilty of offences against the laws and customs of war or the laws of humanity, are liable to criminal prosecution." This position was confirmed by several countries in the 1919 Paris Peace Treaty. See, Commission on the Responsibility of the Authors of the

War and on Enforcement of Penalties—Report Presented to the Preliminary Peace Conference, Versailles, March 29, 1919, reprinted in (1920) 14 AJIL 95, 121.

Article 6 of the 1945 Nuremberg Charter called for individual responsibility for crimes against peace, violations of the laws or customs of war, and crimes against humanity. The Military Tribunals in occupied Germany enforced the Charter's principles under the terms of Article II, paragraph 2, of Control Council Law No. 10, which stated:

> "Any person without regard to nationality or the capacity in which he acted, is deemed to have committed a crime as defined in paragraph 1 of this Article, if he was (a) a principal or (b) was [sic] an accessory to the commission of any such crime or ordered or abetted the same or (c) took a consenting part therein or (d) was connected with plans or enterprises involving its commission or (e) was a member of any organization or group connected with the commission of any such crime . . .".

It is, therefore, settled law that "[t]he principle of individual responsibility and punishment for crimes under international law recognized at Nürnberg is the cornerstone of international criminal law. This principle is the enduring legacy of the Nürnberg Charter and Judgment which gives meaning to the prohibition of crimes under international law by ensuring that the individuals who commit such crimes incur responsibility and are liable to punishment" (Commentary to I.L.C. Draft Code of Crimes Against the Peace and Security of Mankind, art. 2, 1996, p. 19). The ICRC has also determined that the rule "Individuals are criminally responsible for war crimes they commit" has achieved the status of customary international law and is applicable in both international and non-international conflicts (ICRC, *Customary International Humanitarian Law*, 2005, p. 551).

Similarly, the concept of direct individual criminal responsibility for assisting, aiding and abetting, or participating in (as opposed to actually committing) an international crime is based in customary international law. See, *e.g.*, ICRC, *Customary International Humanitarian Law*, 2005, p. 554 (stating that individual criminal responsibility for committing, attempting to commit, assisting in, facilitating, or aiding or abetting the commission of a war crime, is "a norm of customary international law applicable in both international and non-international armed conflicts"); Article 4(1) of the Convention Against Torture and Other Cruel, Inhuman or Degrading Treatment or Punishment, U.N.G.A. resolution 39/46 (December 10, 1984) (using the phrase "complicity or participation in torture"); Article III of the International Convention on the Suppression and Punishment of the Crime of Apartheid (citing as criminally culpable those who "participate in, directly incite, or conspire in[, or] . . . [d]irectly abet, encourage or co-operate in the commission of the crime of apartheid."

The principles of individual criminal responsibility articulated in Articles 7(1) and 6(1) of the ICTY and ICTR Statutes are based on the notion that those who do not physically commit the crime in question are still liable for other forms of participation. In *Prosecutor v. Delalic et al.*, the Trial Chamber stated:

> "The principles of individual criminal responsibility enshrined in Article 7, paragraph 1, of the Statute reflect the basic understanding that individual

criminal responsibility for the offences under the jurisdiction of the International Tribunal is not limited to persons who directly commit the crimes in question. Instead, as stated in the Report of the Secretary-General: 'all persons who participate in the planning, preparation or execution of serious violations of international humanitarian law in the former Yugoslavia contribute to the commission of the violation and are, therefore, individually responsible'." *Prosecutor v. Delalic et al.*, Judgment, Trial Chamber, November 16, 1998, para. 319 (footnote omitted).

In *Prosecutor v. Akayesu*, an ICTR Trial Chamber elaborated upon the scope of Article 6(1) of the ICTR Statute, stating:

"[I]n addition to responsibility as principal perpetrator, the Accused can be held responsible for the criminal acts of others where he plans with them, instigates them, orders them or aids and abets them to commit those acts. . . . Article 6(1) covers various stages of the commission of a crime, ranging from its initial planning to its execution, through its organization" (*Prosecutor v. Delalic et al.*, Judgment, Trial Chamber, paras 472–73).

All these forms of participation in offences will render a person liable to prosecution when the acts or omissions (*actus reus*) are accompanied by the requisite intention (*mens rea*) for the particular offence. The required conduct and the contribution played by such conduct vary in accordance with the different modes of participation, as does the *mens rea* (see, *Prosecutor v. Kayishema and Ruzindana*, Judgment, ICTR Trial Chamber, May 21, 1999, paras 199 and 207).

A. Planning, Instigating, Ordering

Even though an individual may not physically commit a crime under the Statute, he or she will still be liable when he participates directly in **planning** a crime. Planning implies "that one or several persons contemplate designing the commission of a crime at both the preparatory and execution phases" (*Prosecutor v. Akayesu*, Judgment, ICTR Trial Chamber, September 2, 1998, para. 480). In *Semanza*, the ICTR Trial Chamber stated, "The level of participation in the planning must be substantial such as actually formulating the criminal plan or endorsing a plan proposed by another" (*Prosecutor v. Semanza*, Judgment, ICTR Trial Chamber, May 15, 2003, para. 380).

10–15

By **instigating** or "urging, encouraging, or prompting" another person to commit a crime, an individual incurs responsibility for the actual commission of that crime (*Prosecutor v. Semanza*, Judgment, ICTR Trial Chamber, May 15, 2003, para. 381; *Prosecutor v. Akayesu*, Judgment, ICTR Trial Chamber, September 2, 1998, para. 482). However, a causal relationship between the instigation and commission of the crime must be proved before an instigator will be deemed criminally responsible (see, *Prosecutor v. Bagilishema*, Judgment, ICTR Trial Chamber, June 7, 2001, para. 30 and *Prosecutor v. Blaškić*, Judgment, Trial Chamber, March 3, 2000, para. 278). The *Blaškić* Trial Judgment stated that this accords with "[t]he ordinary meaning of instigating, namely, 'bring about'" (*Prosecutor v. Blaškić*, Judgment, Trial Chamber, March 3, 2000, para. 280).

In respect of instigating genocide, Article 6(1) does not require the direct and public characteristics of incitement to genocide found in Article 2(3)(c) of the ICTR Statute (*Prosecutor v. Akayesu*, Judgment, ICTR Trial Chamber, September 2, 1998, paras 478–482) Instigation under Article 6 (1) "involves prompting another to commit an offence; but this is different from incitement in that it is punishable only where it leads to the actual commission of an offence desired by the instigator" (*Prosecutor v. Akayesu*, Judgment, ICTR Trial Chamber, September 2, 1998, para. 482).

A person may incur responsibility for **ordering** the commission of one of the crimes proscribed in the Statutes. "Ordering implies a superior-subordinate relationship between the person giving the order and the one executing it. In other words, the person in a position of authority uses it to convince another to commit an offence" (*Prosecutor v. Akayesu*, Judgment, ICTR Trial Chamber, September 2, 1998, para. 483). However, a formal superior-subordinate relationship is not required (*Prosecutor v. Kordić and Čerkez*, Judgment, Appeals Chamber, December 17, 2004, para. 28).

Direct intent regarding the accused's own planning, instigating, or ordering will establish the requisite *mens rea* for these modes of responsibility (*Prosecutor v. Kordić and Čerkez*, Judgment, Appeals Chamber, December 17, 2004, para. 29). Furthermore, for ordering under Article 7(1) of the ICTY Statute, "a standard of *mens rea* that is lower than direct intent may apply [. . .] a person who orders an act or omission with the awareness of the substantial likelihood that a crime will be committed in the execution of that order, has the requisite *mens rea* for establishing responsibility [. . .] pursuant to ordering. Ordering with such awareness has to be regarded as accepting that crime" (*Prosecutor v. Kordić and Čerkez*, Judgment, Appeals Chamber, December 17, 2004, para. 30, citing *Prosecutor v. Blaškić*, Judgment, Appeals Chamber, July 29, 2004, para. 42). The requisite *mens rea* for planning is "the awareness of the substantial likelihood that a crime will be committed in the execution of that plan," which indicates acceptance of that crime (*Prosecutor v. Kordić and Čerkez*, Judgment, Appeals Chamber, December 17, 2004, para. 31). Instigating requires "the awareness of the substantial likelihood that a crime will be committed in the execution of that instigation," which indicates acceptance of that crime (*Prosecutor v. Kordić and Čerkez*, Judgment, Appeals Chamber, December 17, 2004, para. 32).

B. Committing

10–16 Committing a crime "covers physically perpetrating a crime or engendering a culpable omission in violation of criminal law" (*Prosecutor v. Krstic*, Judgment, Trial Chamber, August 2, 2001, para. 601, citing *Prosecutor v. Tadić*, Judgment, Appeals Chamber, July 15, 1999, para. 188, and *Prosecutor v. Kunarac*, Judgment, Trial Chamber, February 22, 2001, para. 390). The Appeals Chamber of the ICTY has defined committing as "first and foremost the physical perpetration of a crime by the offender himself" (*Prosecutor v. Tadić*, Judgment, Appeals Chamber, July

15, 1999, para. 188, quoted in *Prosecutor v. Krnojelac*, Judgment, Trial Chamber, March 15, 2002, para. 73).

C. AIDING AND ABETTING

In *Vasiljevic*, the Appeals Chamber considered that "[a]iding and abetting the commission of a crime is usually considered to incur a lesser degree of individual criminal responsibility than committing a crime" (*Prosecutor v. Vasiljevic*, Judgment, Appeals Chamber, February 25, 2004, para. 102). In *Akayesu*, the ICTR Trial Chamber noted, "Aiding and abetting, which may appear to be synonymous, are indeed different. Aiding means giving assistance to someone. Abetting, on the other hand, would involve facilitating the commission of an act by being sympathetic thereto" (*Prosecutor v. Akayesu*, Judgment, ICTR Trial Chamber, September 2, 1998, para. 484; also see, *Prosecutor v. Semanza*, Judgment, ICTR Trial Chamber, May 15, 2003, para. 384). It further noted that individual criminal responsibility under Article 6(1) can be incurred where there was either aiding or abetting; both are not required at the same time. "In both instances, it is not necessary for the person aiding or abetting another to commit the offence to be present during the commission of the crime" (*Prosecutor v. Akayesu*, Judgment, September 2, 1998, para. 484).

In *Prosecutor v. Krnojelac*, Judgment, March 15, 2002, an ICTY Trial Chamber reviewed the existing Tribunal case law and determined that aiding and abetting requires the following:

(i) "It must be demonstrated that the aider and abettor carried out an act which consisted of practical assistance, encouragement or moral support to a principal offender" (para. 88, footnote omitted);

(ii) "The act of assistance need not have caused the act of the principal offender, but it must have had a substantial effect on the commission of the crime by the principal offender. The act of assistance may be either an act or omission, and it may occur before, during or after the act of the principal offender" (para. 88, footnotes omitted);

(iii) "Presence alone at the scene of a crime is not conclusive of aiding and abetting unless it is demonstrated to have a significant or legitimising or encouraging effect on the principal offender" (para. 89, footnote omitted);

(iv) "The *mens rea* . . . requires that the aider and abettor knew (in the sense that he was aware) that his own acts assisted in the commission of the specific crime in question by the principal offender (para. 90, footnote omitted);

(v) "The aider and abettor must be aware of the essential elements of the crime committed by the principal offender, including the principal offender's *mens rea*" (para. 90);

(vi) "However, the aider and abettor need not share the *mens rea* of the principal offender" (para. 90, footnote omitted).

(1) Actus Reus

Definition

10–18   In *Prosecutor v. Vasiljevic*, the Appeals Chamber defined the *actus reus* of aiding and abetting as follows: "The aider and abettor carries out acts specifically directed to assist, encourage or lend moral support to the perpetration of a certain specific crime (murder, extermination, rape, torture, wanton destruction of civilian property, etc.), and this support has a substantial effect upon the perpetration of the crime" (*Prosecutor v. Vasiljevic*, Judgment, Appeals Chamber, February 25, 2004, para. 102, quoted with approval in *Prosecutor v. Blaškić*, Judgment, Appeals Chamber, July 29, 2004, para. 45). In *Prosecutor v. Furundžija*, the Trial Chamber held that the *actus reus* of aiding and abetting "consists of practical assistance, encouragement, or moral support which has a substantial effect on the perpetration of the crime" (*Prosecutor v. Furundžija*, Judgment, Trial Chamber, December 10, 1998, para. 249, quoted with approval in *Prosecutor v. Blaškić*, Judgment, Appeals Chamber, July 29, 2004, para. 46).

Tangible v. intangible assistance

10–19   In considering the nature of the assistance required to satisfy the *actus reus* for the offence of aiding and abetting, the Trial Chamber in *Prosecutor v. Furundžija* distinguished between tangible and intangible assistance. The assistance need not be tangible; moral support or encouragement of a principal is sufficient (*Prosecutor v. Furundžija*, Judgment, Trial Chamber, December 10, 1998, para. 199). The Trial Chamber in *Furundžija* noted, "Article 25 of the Rome Statute [. . .] also clearly contemplates assistance in either physical form or in the form of moral support" (*Prosecutor v. Furundžija*, Judgment, Trial Chamber, December 10, 1998, para. 231).

10–20   In *Furundžija*, the Trial Chamber examined customary international law in giving content to both the *actus reus* (*Prosecutor v. Furundžija*, Judgment, Trial Chamber, December 10, 1998, paras 200–234) and the *mens rea* (paras 236–244) required for the offence of aiding and abetting. It referred to the British case *Trial of Franz Schonfeld and Nine Others*, LRWC Vol. XI, 64–73, in which the Advocate General gave examples of the manner in which a person may participate without providing tangible assistance: "[I]f he watched for his companions in order to prevent surprise, or remained at a convenient distance in order to favour their escape, if necessary, or was in such a situation as to be able readily to come to their assistance, the knowledge of which was calculated to give additional confidence to his companions, he was, in contemplation of law, present, aiding and abetting" (*Trial of Franz Schonfeld and Nine Others*, Essen, June 11–26, 1946, LRWC Vol. XI, p. 70).

Presence and authority as a form of assistance (omissions)

10–21   The post-World War II jurisprudence highlights the fact that the presence of a person with the requisite level of authority can constitute assistance in the form of moral support, and, with the accompanying *mens rea*, can render a person liable as an aider and abettor (*Prosecutor v. Furundžija*, Judgment, December 10, 1998, Trial Chamber, paras 205–209, citing the *Synagogue* and *Pig-cart Parade* cases from the German Supreme Court in the British Occupied Zone). This position was also taken by the *Akayesu* Trial Chamber, which considered that the Accused's position as Mayor (*bourgmestre*) was highly significant in finding him criminally liable for aiding and abetting (*Prosecutor v. Akayesu*, Judgment, ICTR Trial Chamber, September 2, 1998, para. 693). The ICTR Trial Chamber found "that the Accused, having had reason to know that sexual violence was occurring, aided and abetted the following acts of sexual violence, by allowing them to take place on or near the premises of the bureau communal and by facilitating the commission of such sexual violence through his words of encouragement in other acts of sexual violence which, by virtue of his authority, sent a clear signal of official tolerance for sexual violence, without which these acts would not have taken place" (para. 694, quoted in *Prosecutor v. Furundžija*, Judgment, Trial Chamber, December 10, 1998, para. 209).

In *Prosecutor v. Blaškić*, the Trial Chamber held "that the *actus reus* of aiding and abetting may be perpetrated through an omission, provided this failure to act had a decisive effect on the commission of the crime and that it was coupled with the requisite *mens rea*. In this respect, the mere presence at the crime scene of a person with superior authority, such as a military commander, is a probative indication for determining whether that person encouraged or supported the perpetrators of the crime" (*Prosecutor v. Blaškić*, Judgment, Trial Chamber, May 3, 2000, para. 284 (footnotes omitted)). On appeal, the Appeals Chamber left "open the possibility that in the circumstances of a given case, an omission may constitute the *actus reus* of aiding and abetting" (*Prosecutor v. Blaškić*, Judgment, Appeals Chamber, July 29, 2004, para. 47).

To aid and abet by omission, the failure to act must have a significant, "decisive" (*Prosecutor v. Blaškić*, Judgment, Trial Chamber, May 3, 2000, para. 284), or "substantial" (*Prosecutor v. Blaškić*, Judgment, Appeals Chamber, July 29, 2004, para. 48) effect on the commission of the crime. (Also see, *Prosecutor v. Akayesu*, Judgment, ICTR Trial Chamber, September 2, 1998, para. 705; *Prosecutor v. Aleksovski*, Judgment, Trial Chamber, June 25, 1999, para. 64; *Prosecutor v. Delalic et al.*, Judgment, Trial Chamber, November 16, 1998, para. 842; *Prosecutor v. Tadić*, Judgment, Trial Chamber, May 7, 1997, para. 686.)

Thus presence alone is insufficient to prove aiding and abetting unless it can be shown that such presence lent legitimacy or encouragement to the acts of the principal (*Prosecutor v. Kunarac*, Judgment, Trial Chamber, February 22, 2001, para. 393 ("Presence alone at the scene of the crime is not conclusive of aiding and abetting unless it is shown to have a significant legitimising or encouraging effect on the principal."), citing *Prosecutor v. Tadić*, Judgment, Trial Chamber, May 7, 1997, para. 689, and *Prosecutor v. Furundžija*, Judgment, Trial Chamber, December 10, 1998, para. 232). Also see, *Prosecutor v. Kvočka et al.*, Judgment, Trial Chamber, November 2, 2001, para. 257. An individual's presence will likely have the requisite legitimising or encouraging effect when the person present has sufficient status and authority to have such an effect on the actions of the principal (see, *Prosecutor v. Aleksovski*, Judgment, Trial Chamber, June 25, 1999, para. 65).

10–22   In *Prosecutor v. Aleksovski*, Judgment, June 25, 1999, para. 87, the Trial Chamber found:

> "By being present during the mistreatment, and yet not objecting to it notwithstanding its systematic nature and the authority he had over its perpetrators, the accused was necessarily aware that such tacit approval would be construed as a sign of his support and encouragement. He thus contributed substantially to the mistreatment. Accordingly, the accused must be held responsible for aiding and abetting under Article 7(1) in the physical and mental abuse which detainees were subjected to during the body searches on 15 and 16 April 1993."

Causal relationship between the assistance and commission of the crime

10–23   There is no need for any assistance rendered to bear a causal relationship to the commission of the offence by the principal. Customary international law recognises an accomplice's liability as long as the assistance has a substantial effect on the commission of the crime. See, *Prosecutor v. Furundžija*, Judgment, Trial Chamber, December 10, 1998, paras 209 ("[A]ssistance need not constitute an indispensable element, that is, a *conditio sine qua non* for the acts of the principal.") and 234 ("The position under customary international law seems therefore to be best reflected in the proposition that the assistance must have a substantial effect on the commission of the crime."). Also see, *Trial of Otto Ohlendorf and Others (Einsatzgruppen)*, in *Trials of War Criminals Before the Nuremberg Military Tribunals under Control Council Law No. 10*, Vol. IV, discussed in *Prosecutor v. Furundžija*, Judgment, Trial Chamber, December 10, 1998, para. 217; *Prosecutor v. Bagilishema*, Judgment, ICTR Trial Chamber, para. 33; *Prosecutor v. Blaškić*, Judgment, Trial Chamber, May 3, 2000, para. 285.

In *Blaškić* the Appeals Chamber considered "that proof of a cause-effect relationship between the conduct of the aider and abettor and the commission of the crime, or proof that such conduct served as a condition precedent to the commission of the crime, is not required. [Furthermore,] the *actus reus* of aiding and abetting a crime may occur before, during, or after the principal crime has been perpetrated, and that the location at which the *actus reus* takes place may be removed from the location of the principal crime" (*Prosecutor v. Blaškić*, Judgment, Appeals Chamber, July 29, 2004, para. 48).

(2) *Mens rea*

10–24   An aider or abetter need not share the *mens rea* of the principal, in the sense of an intention to commit the crime in question. Rather, the accomplice must have knowledge that his actions will assist the principal in the perpetration of the crime (*Prosecutor v. Furundžija*, Judgment, Trial Chamber, December 10, 1998, paras 245, 249). In *Tadić*, the Trial Chamber stated that the intent requirement "involves awareness of the act of participation coupled with a conscious decision to participate by planning, instigating, ordering, committing, or otherwise aiding and abetting in the commission of a crime" (*Prosecutor v. Tadić*, Judgment, Trial Chamber, May 7 1997, para. 674, quoted in *Prosecutor v. Delalic et al*, Judgment, Trial Chamber, November 16, 1998, para. 326, and *Prosecutor v. Aleksovski*, Judgment, Trial Chamber, June 25, 1999, para. 61). In *Vasiljevic*, the Appeals Chamber stated: "In the case of aiding and abetting, the requisite mental element is knowledge that the acts performed by the aider and abettor assist the commission of the specific crime of the principal" (*Prosecutor v. Vasiljevic*, Judgment, Appeals Chamber, February 25, 2004, para. 102).

An aider or abetter does not need to know the exact crime that was intended or committed. "If he is aware that one of a number of crimes will probably be committed, and one of those crimes is in fact committed, he has intended to facilitate the commission of that crime, and is guilty as an aider and abettor" (*Prosecutor v. Furundžija*, Judgment, Trial Chamber, December 10, 1998, para. 246, quoted with approval in *Prosecutor v. Blaškić*, Judgment, Appeals Chamber, July 29, 2004, para. 50). The Appeals Chamber in *Blaškić* overturned the Trial Chamber's holding that "in addition to knowledge that his acts assist the commission of the crime, the aider and abettor needs to have intended to provide assistance, or as a minimum, accepted that such assistance would be a possible and foreseeable consequence of his conduct" (*Prosecutor v. Blaškić*, Judgment, Appeals Chamber, July 29, 2004, para. 49, quoting *Prosecutor v. Blaškić*, Judgment, Trial Chamber, May 3, 2000, para. 286).

For the specific intent crimes of genocide and persecution, the ICTY Appeals Chamber has held "that an individual who aids and abets a specific intent offense may be held responsible if he assists the commission of the crime knowing the intent behind the crime" (*Prosecutor v. Krstic*, Judgment, Appeals Chamber, April 19, 2004, para. 140 (footnote omitted)). In *Krstic*, the Appeals Chamber held that a conviction for aiding and abetting genocide does not require proof of shared intent. Rather, a conviction for aiding and abetting genocide follows "upon proof that the defendant knew about the principal perpetrator's genocidal intent" (*Prosecutor v. Krstic*, Judgment, Appeals Chamber, April 19, 2004, para. 140). In *Krnojelac*, the Appeals Chamber considered "that the aider and abettor in persecution, an offence with a specific intent, must be aware not only of the crime whose perpetration he is facilitating but also of the discriminatory intent of the perpetrators of that crime. He need not share the intent but he must be aware of the discriminatory context in which the crime is to be committed and know that his support or encouragement has a substantial effect on its perpetration" (*Prosecutor v. Krnojelac*, Judgment, Appeals Chamber, September 17, 2003, para. 52). Also see, *Prosecutor v. Vasiljevic*, Judgment, Appeals Chamber, February 25, 2004, para. 142 ("In order to convict him [the Appellant] for aiding and abetting the crime of persecution, the Appeals Chamber must establish that the Appellant had knowledge that the principal perpetrators of the joint criminal enterprise intended to commit the underlying crimes, and by their acts they intended to discriminate against the Muslim population, and that, with that knowledge, the Appellant made a substantial contribution to the commission of the discriminatory acts by the principal perpetrators" (footnote omitted)).

The ICTR jurisprudence has been inconsistent on whether the requisite *mens rea* for aiding and abetting genocide under Article 6(1) is shared specific intent or knowledge of the principal perpetrator's genocidal intent. The trial judgments in *Akayesu* and *Ntakirutimana*, for example, required the shared specific intent of the perpetrator, whereas the trial judgments in *Kayishema and Ruzindana*, *Musema*, and *Semanza* required only knowledge of the principal's genocidal intent. See, *Prosecutor v. Akayesu*, Judgment, ICTR Trial Chamber, September 2, 1998, para. 485; *Prosecutor v. E. Ntakirutimana and G. Ntakirutimana*, Judgment, ICTR Trial Chamber, February 1, 2003, para. 787; *Prosecutor v. Kayishema and Ruzindana*, Judgment, ICTR Trial Chamber, May 21, 1999, paras 203–207; *Prosecutor v. Musema*, Judgment, ICTR Trial Chamber, January 27, 2000, para. 181; *Prosecutor v. Semanza*, Judgment, ICTR Trial Chamber, May 15, 2003, paras 387–395.

D. Common Purpose and Joint Criminal Enterprise

(1) Common purpose or design or joint criminal enterprise

10–25   This mode of liability is referred to as, inter alia, common purpose, common plan, common design, and joint criminal enterprise. In *Prosecutor v. Brdjanin and Talic*, Decision on Form of Further Amended Indictment and Prosecution Application to Amend, June 26, 2001, para. 24, the Trial Chamber preferred the use of the label "joint criminal enterprise" to the terms "common purpose" or "design". The Rome Statute, Article 25, paragraph 3(d), uses the term "common purpose" (see discussion in *Prosecutor v. Tadić*, Judgment, Appeals Chamber, July 15, 1999, para. 222).

In *Prosecutor v. Tadić*, the ICTY Appeals Chamber considered that "the commission of one of the crimes envisaged in Articles 2, 3, 4, or 5 of the Statute might also occur through participation in the realisation of a common design or purpose" (para. 188) in part because "[a]n interpretation of the Statute based on its object and purpose leads to the conclusion that the Statute intends to extend the jurisdiction of the International Tribunal to *all* those 'responsible for serious violations of international humanitarian law' committed in the former Yugoslavia (Article 1)" (*Prosecutor v. Tadić*, Judgment, Appeals Chamber, July 15, 1999, para. 189). It explained:

> "It [the Statute] does not exclude those modes of participating in the commission of crimes which occur where several persons having a common purpose embark on criminal activity that is then carried out either jointly or by some members of this plurality of persons. Whoever contributes to the commission of crimes by the group of persons or some members of the group, in execution of a common criminal purpose, may be held to be criminally liable, subject to certain conditions" (para. 190).

The wording of Article 7(1), as well as the provisions setting out the substantive crimes, particularly Article 2 and Article 4(3), which prohibits conspiracy, incitement, attempt, and complicity to commit genocide, indicates that "responsibility for serious violations of international humanitarian law is not limited merely to those who actually carry out the *actus reus* of the enumerated crimes but appears to extend also to other offenders" (*Prosecutor v. Tadić*, Judgment, Appeals Chamber, July 15, 1999, para. 189). This reasoning also applies to Article 6(1) of the ICTR Statute.

As a matter of policy, "to hold criminally liable as a perpetrator only the person who materially performs the criminal act would disregard the role as co-perpetrators of all those who in some way made it possible for the perpetrator to carry out that criminal act. At the same time, depending upon the circumstances, to hold the latter liable only as aiders and abettors might understate the degree of their criminal responsibility" (*Prosecutor v. Tadić*, Judgment, Appeals Chamber, July 15, 1999, para. 192). It held "that the notion of common design as a form of accomplice liability is firmly established in customary international law and in addition is upheld, albeit implicitly, in the Statute of the International Tribunal" (*Prosecutor v. Tadić*, Judgment, Appeals Chamber, July 15, 1999, para. 220). In his Separate Opinion to the Decision on Dragoljub Ojdanic's Motion Challenging Jurisdiction—Joint Criminal Enterprise, Judge Shahabuddeen clarifies this statement of the Appeals Chamber by noting that the Appeals Chamber was not saying that a participant in a JCE is merely an aider and abettor. In his opinion, "[i]t would seem that what was meant was that the participants in a joint criminal enterprise were themselves accomplices—accomplices of each other—and that they therefore engaged 'a form of accomplice liability'" (*Prosecutor v. Milutinovic et al.*, Decision on Dragoljub Ojdanic's Motion Challenging Jurisdiction—Joint Criminal Enterprise, Appeals Chamber, May 31, 2003, Separate Opinion of Judge Shahabuddeen, para. 7).

Recognition of the implicit inclusion of this mode of liability in the Statute also takes account of the nature of international crimes, which are commonly committed during wartime. These crimes are mostly committed by groups of persons acting in pursuance of a common criminal purpose or design (see *Prosecutor v. Tadić*, Judgment, Appeals Chamber, July 15, 1999, para. 191). Although only some of these persons may actually physically perpetrate the crime in question, the participation of other persons is often crucial to facilitating the offence (see *Prosecutor v. Tadić*, Judgment, Appeals Chamber, July 15, 1999, para. 191).

(2) The three categories of joint criminal enterprise

After reviewing post-World War II case law, the Appeals Chamber in *Tadić* determined that there are "three distinct categories" of joint criminal enterprise (JCE) (*Prosecutor v. Tadić*, Judgment, Appeals Chamber, July 15, 1999, para. 195). **10–26**

JCE 1

The first category of JCE includes cases of "co-perpetratorship" (*Prosecutor v. Tadić*, Judgment, Appeals Chamber, July 15, 1999, para. 198), in which "all co-defendants, acting pursuant to a common design, **10–27** possess the same criminal intention" (*Prosecutor v. Tadić*, Judgment, Appeals Chamber, July 15, 1999, para. 196). The *actus reus* and *mens rea* requirements for a participant in a joint criminal enterprise, to kill for example, who did not or cannot be proven to have committed the crime are as follows: "(i) the accused must voluntarily participate in one aspect of the common design (for instance, by inflicting non-fatal violence upon the victim, or by providing material assistance to or facilitating the activities of his co-perpetrators); and (ii) the accused, even if not personally effecting the killing, must nevertheless intend this result" (*Prosecutor v. Tadić*, Judgment, Appeals Chamber, July 15, 1999, para. 196).

10–28   An example of JCE 1 would be a situation in which a group of individuals formulates a plan to kill, and each individual possesses the intention to kill regardless of his or her specific role in the plan. Each individual will be liable for his or her part played in the killing as long as he or she voluntarily participates in the common design, regardless of the form that participation takes. An individual will only be liable when he or she intends the result, that is, the killing (see *Prosecutor v. Tadić*, Judgment, Appeals Chamber, July 15, 1999, para. 196). Each individual must share the same intent (see *Prosecutor v. Tadic*, Judgment, Appeals Chamber, July 15, 1999, para. 228).

JCE 2: Concentration camp cases

10–29   The second category is seen as "a variant of the first category" (*Prosecutor v. Tadić*, Judgment, Appeals Chamber, July 15, 1999, para. 203) and has been referred to as the "systemic" form of JCE (*Prosecutor v. Kvočka et al.*, Judgment, Appeals Chamber, February 28, 2005, para. 82). It "is characterized by the existence of an organized criminal system, in particular in the case of concentration or detention camps" (*Prosecutor v. Kvočka et al.*, Judgment, Appeals Chamber, February 28, 2005, para. 82 (footnote omitted)). In *Tadić*, the Appeals Chamber considered that, in the post-World War II "concentration camp" cases, "common purpose was applied to instances where the offences charged were alleged to have been committed by members of military or administrative units such as those running concentration camps; i.e., by groups of persons acting pursuant to a concerted plan" (*Prosecutor v. Tadić*, Judgment, Appeals Chamber, July 15, 1999, para. 202). In general, the accused held an "objective 'position of authority'" (*Prosecutor v. Tadić*, Judgment, Appeals Chamber, July 15, 1999, para. 203). The Appeals Chamber determined that the objective and subjective elements required in these cases were the following:

> "[T]he required *actus reus* was the active participation in the enforcement of a system of repression, as it could be inferred from the position of authority and the specific functions held by each accused. The *mens rea* element comprised: (i) knowledge of the nature of the system and (ii) the intent to further the common concerted design to ill-treat inmates. It is important to note that, in these cases, the requisite intent could also be inferred from the position of authority held by the camp personnel" (*Prosecutor v. Tadić*, Judgment, Appeals Chamber, July 15, 1999, para. 203).

Despite the relevance of an accused's position of authority, "[j]oint criminal enterprise responsibility does not require any showing of superior responsibility" (*Prosecutor v. Kvočka et al.*, Judgment, Appeals Chamber, February 28, 2005, para. 104). Furthermore, "participation in a joint criminal enterprise pursuant to Article 7(1) of the Statute and superior responsibility pursuant to Article 7(3) of the Statute are distinct categories of individual criminal responsibility, each with specific legal requirements" (*Prosecutor v. Kvočka et al.*, Judgment, Appeals Chamber, February 28, 2005, para. 104, citing *Prosecutor v. Blaškić*, Judgment, Appeals Chamber, July 29, 2004, para. 91).

JCE 3: Natural and foreseeable consequences

In the *Brdjanin and Talic* Decision, the Trial Chamber considered JCE 3 "an *extended* form of joint criminal enterprise" (*Prosecutor v. Brdjanin and Talic*, Decision on Form of Further Amended Indictment and Prosecution Application to Amend, June 26, 2001, para. 27; also see, *Prosecutor v. Kvočka et al.*, Judgment, Appeals Chamber, February 28, 2005, para. 83). The third category of JCE includes "cases involving a common design to pursue one course of conduct where one of the perpetrators commits an act which, while outside the common design, was nevertheless a natural and foreseeable consequence of the effecting of that common purpose" (*Prosecutor v. Tadić*, Judgment, Appeals Chamber, July 15, 1999, para. 204). The *mens rea* of JCE 3 can be summarised as follows: "(i) the intention to take part in a joint criminal enterprise and to further— individually or jointly—the criminal purposes of that enterprise; and (ii) the foreseeability of the possible commission by other members of the group of offences that do not constitute the object of the common criminal purpose" (*Prosecutor v. Tadić*, Judgment, Appeals Chamber, July 15, 1999, para. 220). **10–30**

JCE 3 requires "a criminal intention to participate in a common criminal design and the foreseeability that criminal acts other than those envisaged in the common criminal design are likely to be committed by other participants in the common design" (*Prosecutor v. Tadić*, Judgment, Appeals Chamber, July 15, 1999, para. 206). A conviction under JCE 3 requires that the crime not included in the joint criminal enterprise was "a predictable consequence of the execution of the common design and the accused was either reckless or indifferent to that risk" (*Prosecutor v. Tadić*, Judgment, Appeals Chamber, July 15, 1999, para. 204). The Appeals Chamber pointed out that "more than negligence is required. What is required is a state of mind in which a person, although he did not intend to bring about a certain result, was aware that the actions of the group were most likely to lead to that result but nevertheless willingly took that risk. In other words, the so-called *dolus eventualis* is required (also called 'advertent recklessness' in some national legal systems)" (*Prosecutor v. Tadić*, Judgment, Appeals Chamber, July 15, 1999, para. 220; also see, *Prosecutor v. Brdjanin & Talic*, Decision on Form of Further Amended Indictment and Prosecution Application to Amend, June 26, 2001, paras 28–31).

In *Tadić*, the Appeals Chamber gave the example of a common purpose to remove forcibly members of one ethnicity from an area in order to effect ethnic cleansing, with the consequence that some of **10–31** those members are killed. Although the common purpose or design might not specifically include murder, the possibility that some of these people might be killed during the forcible removal at gunpoint would be foreseeable (*Prosecutor v. Tadić*, Judgment, Appeals Chamber, July 15, 1999, para. 204).

(3) *Actus reus*

10–32   Regarding the three categories of JCE, the Appeals Chamber in *Tadić* summarised the objective elements as follows:

i. "A plurality of persons. They need not be organised in a military, political or administrative structure" (*Prosecutor v. Tadić*, Judgment, Appeals Chamber, July 15, 1999, para. 227);

ii. "The existence of a common plan, design or purpose which amounts to or involves the commission of a crime provided for in the Statute" but which need not be "previously arranged or formulated. The common plan or purpose may materialise extemporaneously and be inferred from the fact that a plurality of persons acts in unison to put into effect a joint criminal enterprise" (para. 227);

iii. "Participation of the accused in the common design involving the perpetration of one of the crimes provided for in the Statute," which "need not involve commission of a specific crime under one of those provisions (for example, murder, extermination, torture, rape, etc.), but may take the form of assistance in, or contribution to, the execution of the common plan or purpose" (para. 227).

Also see, *Prosecutor v. Vasiljevic*, Judgment, Appeals Chamber, February 25, 2004, para. 100; *Prosecutor v. Kvočka et al.*, Judgment, Appeals Chamber, February 28, 2005, para. 96.

It need not be shown that the accused made "a substantial contribution to the joint criminal enterprise" (*Prosecutor v. Kvočka et al.*, Judgment, Appeals Chamber, February 28, 2005, para. 97). Nevertheless, "[i]n practice, the significance of the accused's contribution will be relevant to demonstrating that the accused shared the intent to pursue the common purpose" (*Prosecutor v. Kvočka et al.*, Judgment, Appeals Chamber, February 28, 2005, para. 97).

In *Prosecutor v. Brdjanin*, the Trial Chamber dismissed JCE as a mode of individual criminal responsibility for the Accused, citing "the extra-ordinarily broad nature of this case" (*Prosecutor v. Brdjanin*, Judgment, Trial Chamber, September 1, 2004, paras 355–356). It found that there was "no direct evidence to establish [. . .] an understanding or agreement between the Accused and the Relevant Physical Perpetrators" (*Prosecutor v. Brdjanin*, Judgment, Trial Chamber, September 1, 2004, para. 353). Furthermore, it found that no such agreement could be "the only reasonable inference available from the evidence" (*Prosecutor v. Brdjanin*, Judgment, Trial Chamber, September 1, 2004, para. 353–354). The Trial Chamber emphasised:

> "[F]or the purposes of establishing individual criminal responsibility pursuant to the theory of JCE it is not sufficient to prove an understanding or an agreement to commit a crime between the Accused and a person in

charge or in control of a military or paramilitary unit committing a crime. The Accused can only be held criminally responsible under the mode of liability of JCE if the Prosecution establishes beyond reasonable doubt that he had an understanding or entered into an agreement with the Relevant Physical Perpetrators to commit the particular crime eventually perpetrated or if the crime perpetrated by the Relevant Physical Perpetrators is a natural and foreseeable consequence of the crime agreed upon by the Accused and the Relevant Physical Perpetrators" (*Prosecutor v. Brdjanin*, Judgment, Trial Chamber, September 1, 2004, para. 347 (footnote omitted)).

The *Brdjanin* Trial Judgment is currently under appeal.

(4) *Mens rea*

The different forms of *mens rea* required to complement the acts forming a part of a common purpose or design distinguish the first two categories with the last. The *Tadić* Appeals Judgment states:

10–33

"With regard to the first category, what is required is the intent to perpetrate a certain crime (this being the shared intent on the part of all co-perpetrators). With regard to the second category [. . .], personal knowledge of the system of ill-treatment is required (whether proved by express testimony or a matter of reasonable inference from the accused's position of authority), as well as the intent to further this common concerted system of ill-treatment. With regard to the third category, what is required is the intention to participate in and further the criminal activity or the criminal purpose of a group and to contribute to the joint criminal enterprise or in any event to the commission of a crime by the group. In addition, responsibility for a crime other than the one agreed upon in the common plan arises only if, under the circumstances of the case, (i) it was foreseeable that such a crime might be perpetrated by one or other members of the group and (ii) the accused willingly took that risk" (*Prosecutor v. Tadić*, Judgment, Appeals Chamber, July 15, 1999, para. 228; also see, para. 220).

On the issue of JCE 3 and genocide, a specific intent crime, see *Prosecutor v. Rwamakuba*, Decision on Interlocutory Appeal Regarding Application of Joint Criminal Enterprise to the Crime of Genocide, ICTR Appeals Chamber, October 22, 2004.

(5) Joint criminal enterprise v. aiding and abetting

The case law of the ICTY uses the term "accomplice" to refer to both co-perpetrator and aider and abettor, depending on the context (*Prosecutor v. Krnojelac*, Judgment, Appeals Chamber, September 17, 2003, para. 70 (footnote omitted)). However, joint criminal enterprise and aiding and abetting are distinct modes of criminal liability and must be distinguished from one another, "both to accurately describe the crime and to fix an appropriate sentence. Aiding and abetting generally involves a lesser degree of individual criminal responsibility than co-perpetration in a joint criminal enterprise" (*Prosecutor v. Kvočka et al.*,

10–34

Judgment, Appeals Chamber, February 28, 2005, para. 92 (footnote omitted)). The Appeals Chamber in *Tadić* outlined the following distinctions:

    (i) "The aider and abettor is always an accessory to a crime perpetrated by another person, the principal.

   (ii) In the case of aiding and abetting no proof is required of the existence of a common concerted plan, let alone of the pre-existence of such a plan. No plan or agreement is required: indeed, the principal may not even know about the accomplice's contribution.

  (iii) The aider and abettor carries out acts specifically directed to assist, encourage or lend moral support to the perpetration of a certain specific crime (murder, extermination, rape, torture, wanton destruction of civilian property, etc.), and this support has a substantial effect upon the perpetration of the crime. By contrast, in the case of acting in pursuance of a common purpose or design, it is sufficient for the participant to perform acts that in some way are directed to the furthering of the common plan or purpose.

  (iv) In the case of aiding and abetting, the requisite mental element is knowledge that the acts performed by the aider and abettor assist the commission of a specific crime by the principal. By contrast, in the case of common purpose or design more is required (i.e., either intent to perpetrate the crime or intent to pursue the common criminal design plus foresight that those crimes outside the criminal common purpose were likely to be committed), as stated above" (para. 229).

Also see, *Prosecutor v. Krnojelac*, Judgment, Appeals Chamber, September 17, 2003, para. 33; *Prosecutor v. Vasiljevic*, Judgment, Appeals Chamber, February 25, 2004, para. 102; *Prosecutor v. Kvočka et al.*, Judgment, Appeals Chamber, February 28, 2005, para. 89.

The distinction between aiding and abetting a crime and participation in a common purpose or design is reflected in the ICC Statute. Article 25 distinguishes between a person who "for the purpose of facilitating the commission of such a crime, aids, abets or otherwise assists in its commission or its attempted commission, including providing the means for its commission" (Rome Statute Art. 25(3)(c)) and a person who "contributes to the commission or attempted commission of such a crime by a group of persons acting with a common purpose" (Art. 25(3)(d)). (See discussion in *Prosecutor v. Furundžija*, Judgment, Trial Chamber, December 10, 1998, para. 216 (not challenged on appeal).)

In *Prosecutor v. Kvočka et al.*, Judgment, November 2, 2001, para. 273, the Trial Chamber found that aiding and abetting in its traditional form may exist in relation to a joint criminal enterprise, and that in the case of such an aider and abettor, knowledge combined with substantial contribution to the enterprise, is sufficient to maintain liability (also see, *Prosecutor v. Kvočka et al.*, Judgment, Appeals Chamber, February 28, 2005, para. 188). However, over a period of time, an aider and abettor who assists in the criminal enterprise as an accomplice, may become a co-perpetrator, when his "participation lasts for an extensive period or he becomes more directly involved in maintaining the functioning of the enterprise. By sharing the intent of the joint criminal enterprise, the aider or abettor becomes a co-perpetrator" (*Prosecutor v. Kvočka et al.*, Judgment, Trial Chamber, November 2, 2001, para. 284). It is as a result of this length of time or further involvement that his intent to carry out the joint criminal enterprise may be inferred and his status graduated to that of a co-perpetrator. See, *Prosecutor v. Kvočka et al.*, Judgment, Appeals Chamber, February 28, 2005, para. 88.

On appeal, "[t]he Appeals Chamber emphasize[d] that joint criminal enterprise is simply a means of committing a crime; it is not a crime in itself. Therefore, it would be inaccurate to refer to aiding and abetting a joint criminal enterprise. The aider and abettor assists the principal perpetrator or perpetrators in committing the crime" (*Prosecutor v. Kvočka et al.*, Judgment, Appeals Chamber, February 28, 2005, para. 91). On the issue of responsibility for aiding and abetting a single perpetrator, as opposed to aiding and abetting a group engaged in a joint criminal enterprise, the Appeals Chamber considered:

> "[W]hether an aider and abettor is held responsible for assisting an individual crime committed by a single perpetrator or for assisting in all the crimes committed by the plurality of persons involved in a joint criminal enterprise depends on the effect of the assistance and on the knowledge of the accused. The requirement that an aider and abettor must make a substantial contribution to the crime in order to be held responsible applies whether the accused is assisting in a crime committed by an individual or in crimes committed by a plurality of persons. Furthermore, the requisite mental element applies equally to aiding and abetting a crime committed by an individual or a plurality of persons. Where the aider and abettor only knows that his assistance is helping a single person to commit a single crime, he is only liable for aiding and abetting that crime. This is so even if the principal perpetrator is part of a joint criminal enterprise involving the commission of further crimes. Where, however, the accused knows that his assistance is supporting the crimes of a group of persons involved in a joint criminal enterprise and shares that intent, then he may be found criminally responsible for the crimes committed in furtherance of that common purpose as a co-perpetrator" (*Prosecutor v. Kvočka et al.*, Judgment, Appeals Chamber, February 28, 2005, para. 90, also see, para. 188).

On the level of participation required for criminal liability as either an aider or abettor or co-perpetrator in respect of offences committed in such camps or detention facilities, the Trial Chamber held, "when a detention facility is operated in a manner which makes the discriminatory and persecutory intent of the operation patently clear, anyone who knowingly participates in any significant way in the operation of the facility or assists or facilitates its activity, incurs individual criminal responsibility for participation in the criminal enterprise" (*Prosecutor v. Kvočka et al.*, Judgment, Trial Chamber, November 2, 2001, para. 306). Whether the responsibility is that of a co-perpetrator or aider and abettor depends upon his position in the organisational hierarchy and the degree of participation (*Prosecutor v. Kvočka et al.*, Judgment, Trial Chamber, November 2, 2001, para. 306).

10–35

The Trial Chamber emphasised that not all persons working in such detention camps would be individually criminally responsible. Only those whose participation was significant, in other words, those whose acts or omissions made the detention facility run smoothly or efficiently would be liable (*Prosecutor v. Kvočka et al.*, Judgment, Trial Chamber, November 2, 2001, para. 309). This holding was overturned on appeal (*Prosecutor v. Kvočka et al.*, Judgment, Appeals Chamber, February 28, 2005, paras 97, 187). The Appeals Chamber noted "there is no specific legal requirement that the accused make a substantial contribution to the joint criminal enterprise" (*Prosecutor v. Kvočka*, Judgment, Appeals Chamber, February 28, 2005, para. 97). It considered that an accused need only contribute to the common purpose and need not contribute substantially or significantly. However, "the significance and scope of the material participation of an individual in a joint criminal enterprise may be relevant in determining whether that individual had the requisite *mens rea*" of shared intent (*Prosecutor v. Kvočka et al.*, Judgment, Appeals Chamber, February 28, 2005, para. 188, also see para. 97). It need not be proven that the crimes could or would not have occurred without the accused's participation; therefore, the Appeals Chamber rejected "the argument that an accused did not participate in the joint criminal enterprise because he was easily replaceable" (*Prosecutor v. Kvočka et al.*, Judgment, Appeals Chamber, February 28, 2005, para. 98, also see, para. 193).

III. SUPERIOR RESPONSIBILITY

10–36   In *Prosecutor v. Delalic et al.*, the Trial Chamber stated: "The doctrine of command responsibility is ultimately predicated upon the power of the superior to control the acts of his subordinates. A duty is placed upon the superior to exercise this power so as to prevent and repress the crimes committed by his subordinates, and a failure by him to do so in a diligent manner is sanctioned by the imposition of individual criminal responsibility in accordance with the doctrine. It follows that there is a threshold at which persons cease to possess the necessary powers of control over the actual perpetrators of offences and, accordingly, cannot properly be considered their "superiors" within the meaning of Article 7(3) of the Statute" (*Prosecutor v. Delalic et al.*, Judgment, Trial Chamber, November 16, 1998, para. 377).

According to the ICRC, the rule that "[c]ommanders and other superiors are criminally responsible for war crimes pursuant to their orders [. . .] is a norm of customary international law applicable in both international and non-international armed conflicts" (ICRC, *Customary International Law*, 2005, p. 556).

Three elements must be proved before a person may incur command responsibility for the actions of his subordinates: (1) The existence of a superior-subordinate relationship between the accused and the perpetrator of the crimes; (2) knowledge of the superior that his subordinate is about to commit or has committed a crime and (3) failure of the superior to prevent or punish the commission of the crime (see *Prosecutor v. Kordić and Čerkez*, Judgment, Trial Chamber, February 26, 2001, para. 401). These elements are reflected in Article 28 of the ICC Statute and have achieved the status of customary international law to be applied in both international and non-international armed conflicts (ICRC, *Customary International Law*, 2005, p. 558).

A. Superior–Subordinate Relationship

10–37   The threshold for determining command responsibility is whether the superior exercises effective control over the subordinate, regardless of the nature of that authority (see, *Prosecutor v. Delalic et al.*, Judgment,

Appeals Chamber, February 20, 2001, para. 256 and Article 28 of the
ICC Statute). Accordingly, substantial influence as a form of control
that in any sense falls short of the possession of effective control over a
subordinate would be insufficient for the application of command
responsibility (see *Prosecutor v. Delalic et al.*, Judgment, Appeals Chamber, paras 258–266; also see, *Prosecutor v. Kordic*, Judgment, Trial
Chamber, February 26, 2001, para. 415).

(1) Effective control

Effective control is the material ability to prevent and punish the   **10–38**
commission of offences (*Prosecutor v. Delalic et al.*, Judgment, Appeals
Chamber, February 20, 2001, para. 197, quoting and endorsing the
finding on this issue in *Prosecutor v. Delalic et al.*, Judgment, Trial
Chamber, November 16, 1998, paras 377–378 and 395. Also see,
Prosecutor v. Blaškić, Judgment, Trial Chamber, May 3, 2000, para. 301;
Prosecutor v. Kordić and Čerkez, Judgment, Appeals Chamber, December
17, 2004, para. 840). A commander does not have to have any legal
authority to prevent or punish the acts of his subordinate. He may set
in motion proceedings against a subordinate by submitting a report to
the appropriate authorities (see *Prosecutor v. Blaškić*, Judgment, Trial
Chamber, May 3, 2000, para. 302, affirmed *Prosecutor v. Blaškić*, Judgment, Appeals Chamber, July 29, 2004, paras 68–69). This would be
sufficient for the purposes of establishing effective control of the
commander over his subordinate.
Given that the test for command responsibility rests on "effective
control", more than one superior may be held liable for the same crime
committed by a subordinate (see *Prosecutor v. Aleksovski*, Judgment, Trial
Chamber, June 25, 1999, para. 106).
See *Prosecutor v. Kordić and Čerkez*, Judgment, Trial Chamber, February
26, 2001, paras 418–424 on the elements for determining superior
authority. In the *Blaškić* Appeal, the Appellant argued "that to establish
that effective control existed at the time of the commission of subordinates' crimes, proof is required that the accused was not only able to
issue orders but that the orders were actually followed. The Appeals
Chamber consider[ed] that this provides another example of effective
control exercised by the commander" (*Prosecutor v. Blaškić*, Appeals
Chamber, July 29, 2004, para. 69).

(2) De facto v. de jure superiors

A superior may be liable for the acts of subordinates based on his *de*   **10–39**
facto or *de jure* authority as long as he exercises effective control over the
actions of his subordinates (see *Prosecutor v. Delalic et al.*, Judgment, Trial
Chamber, February 20, 2001, paras 188–195). Thus "formal designation
as a commander should not be considered to be a necessary prerequisite for command responsibility to attach" (*Prosecutor v. Delalic et al.*,
Judgment, Trial Chamber, November 16, 1998, para. 370 (see also
generally paras 364–378)). This takes account of the fact that in many
contemporary conflicts, *de facto* command structures exist, in which the

commanders have no formal commission or appointment. These commanders would escape liability if a formal letter of authority were a prerequisite to enforcing humanitarian law (see, *Prosecutor v. Delalic et al.*, Judgment, Appeals Chamber, para. 193). The *de facto* commander must exercise substantially similar powers of control over subordinates for criminal liability to attach (*Prosecutor v. Delalic et al.*, Judgment, Appeals Chamber, February 20, 2001, para. 197). Also see, *Prosecutor v. Bagilishema*, Judgment, Appeals Chamber, July 3, 2002, para. 50.

(3) Civilian v. military superiors

10–40   Civilian and political leaders that exercise effective control over subordinates may also be superiors for the purposes of command responsibility (see, *Prosecutor v. Delalic et al.*, Judgment, Appeals Chamber, February 20, 2001, paras 195 and 196; also see, *Prosecutor v. Aleksovski*, Judgment, Appeals Chamber, March 24, 2000, para. 76 and *Prosecutor v. Kayishema and Ruzindana*, Judgment, ICTR Trial Chamber, May 21, 1999, para. 213, as well as *Prosecutor v. Musema*, Judgment, ICTR Trial Chamber, January 27, 2000, para. 148). The use of the generic term "superior" coupled with its juxtaposition to the individual criminal responsibility of "Heads of State or Government" or "responsible Government officials" reflects the intention of the drafters to make Articles 6(3) and 7(3) applicable to "political leaders and other civilian superiors in positions of authority" (see, *Prosecutor v. Delalic et al.*, Judgment, Trial Chamber, November 16, 1998, para. 356 and *Prosecutor v. Kayishema and Ruzindana*, Judgment, ICTR Trial Chamber, May 21, 1999, para. 214). This is consistent with customary international law.

Such civilian superiors must, however, exercise powers of effective control over their subordinates before they will be held responsible for their subordinates (*Prosecutor v. Musema*, Judgment, ICTR Trial Chamber, January 27, 2000, para. 141; also see, *Prosecutor v. Bagilishema*, Judgment, ICTR Trial Chamber, June 7, 2001, paras 42–43; ICC Statute, Article 28).

It should be observed that Article 28 of the ICC Statute adopts a different mental standard for superiors other than military commanders or persons effectively acting as military commanders, declaring them to be criminally liable only if they "knew, or consciously disregarded information which clearly indicated, that the subordinates were committing or about to commit crimes" within the jurisdiction of the Court.

(4) Direct v. indirect subordination

10–41   In *Prosecutor v. Delalic et al.*, Judgment, February 20, 2001, paras 254–255, the Appeals Chamber endorsed the Trial Chamber's finding (*Prosecutor v. Delalic et al.*, Judgment, Trial Chamber, November 16, 1998, para. 354) that a commander may be responsible for the actions of his or her subordinates, even when there is not a direct relationship, "so long as the fundamental requirement of an effective power to control the subordinate, in the sense of preventing or punishing criminal conduct is satisfied". In *Kordić and Čerkez*, the Appeals Chamber stated that, as a matter of law, command responsibility is not limited geographically or to direct subordinates (*Prosecutor v. Kordić and Čerkez*, Judgment, Appeals Chamber, December 17, 2004, para. 828).

The extended legal duty of commanders is found in Article 87(1) of Additional Protocol I of the Geneva Conventions. This Article extends a commander's duties to "other persons under their control". Article 87 states:

> 1. The High Contracting Parties and the Parties to the conflict shall require military commanders, with respect to members of the armed forces under their command and other persons under their control, to prevent and, where necessary, to suppress and to report to competent authorities breaches of the Conventions and of this Protocol.
> 2. In order to prevent and suppress breaches, High Contracting Parties and Parties to the conflict shall require that, commensurate with their level of responsibility, commanders ensure that members of the armed forces under their command are aware of their obligations under the Conventions and this Protocol.
> 3. The High Contracting Parties and Parties to the conflict shall require any commander who is aware that subordinates or other persons under his control are going to commit or have committed a breach of the Conventions or of this Protocol, to initiate such steps as are necessary to prevent such violations of the Conventions or this Protocol, and, where appropriate, to initiate disciplinary or penal action against violators thereof.

The ICRC Commentary on Article 87 gives an example of such other persons—being local persons in a situation when a hostile army has occupied a territory (also see, *Prosecutor v. Kordić and Čerkez*, Judgment, Trial Chamber, February 26, 2001, para. 415).

In *Prosecutor v. Kunarac*, Judgment, February 22, 2001, para. 399, the Trial Chamber recognised that a superior would be criminally liable for the actions of those that are temporarily (or on an ad hoc basis) under his effective control.

B. MENS REA

10–42 Command responsibility only arises in situations when a superior actually knows that a subordinate is about to commit a crime or has committed a crime, or when a superior "has reason to know" that a subordinate is about to commit a crime or has committed a crime.

(1) Knew that the subordinate was about to commit acts or had done so

10–43 Actual knowledge may be established through direct or circumstantial evidence, but may not be presumed (see *Prosecutor v. Blaškić*, Judgment, Trial Chamber, May 3, 2000, para. 307). The Final Report of the United Nations Commission of Experts (para. 58) enumerates the indicia pointing to a superior's knowledge, which include the number, type and scope of illegal acts; the number and nature of the troops involved; the geographical location of the acts; the widespread nature of the acts; the *modus operandi* of similar illegal acts and location of the superior at the appropriate times. Also see, *Prosecutor v. Blaškić*, Judgment, Appeals Chamber, July 29, 2004, para. 57; *Prosecutor v. Delalic et al.*, Judgment, Trial Chamber, November 16, 1998, para. 386; *Prosecutor v. Bagilishema*, Judgment, June 7, 2001, para. 46.

In *Blaškić*, the Appeals Chamber considered that "[t]he indicators of effective control are more a matter of evidence than of substantive law, and those indicators are limited to showing that the accused had the power to prevent, punish, or initiate measures leading to proceedings against the alleged perpetrators where appropriate. The appeal in this regard is therefore rejected" (*Prosecutor v. Blaškić*, Appeals Chamber, July 29, 2004, para. 69 (footnotes omitted)).

(2) Had reason to know that the subordinate was about to commit acts or had done so

10–44   In the absence of actual knowledge, a superior will be criminally liable only if he had reason to know that a subordinate was about to commit acts or had done so. A superior is not under a duty to know (*Prosecutor v. Delalic et al.*, Judgment, Appeals Chamber, February 20, 2001, para. 226: "Neglect of a duty to acquire such knowledge, however, does not feature in the provision as a separate offence, and a superior is not therefore liable under the provision for such failures but only for failing to take necessary and reasonable measures to prevent or to punish", quoted in *Prosecutor v. Blaškić*, Judgment, Appeals Chamber, July 29, 2004, para. 62). Customary international law recognises that superiors are only liable when they "had information which should have enabled them to conclude in the circumstances at the time, that he was committing or was going to commit such a breach and if they did not take feasible measures within their power to prevent or repress the breach" (Art. 86(2) Additional Protocol I). See, Article 86(2) of 1977 Geneva Protocol I Additional to the Geneva Conventions of 1949 which provides that:

> [1] [. . .]
> [2] The fact that a breach of the Conventions or of this Protocol was committed by a subordinate does not absolve his superiors from penal or disciplinary responsibility, as the case may be, if they knew, or had information which should have enabled them to conclude in the circumstances existing at the time, that he was committing or was going to commit such a breach and if they did not take all feasible measures within their powers to prevent or repress the breach.

In *Prosecutor v. Delalic et al.*, February 20, 2001, para. 235, the Appeals Chamber concluded that the consistency in language in Article 86(2) and the ILC Draft Code and Report evidences a consensus on the standard of *mens rea* for command responsibility. Thus "had reason to know" in the ICTY Statute is interpreted as "had information enabling them to conclude" as set out in Article 86(1). As an element of knowledge has to be proved, a superior will not be responsible on a strict liability basis (see *Prosecutor v. Delalic et al.*, Judgment, Appeals Chamber, February 20, 2001, para. 239).

In the end, each case should be examined individually to determine the requisite *mens rea*, taking account of the superior's situation at the appropriate time (*Prosecutor v. Delalic et al.*, Judgment, Appeals Chamber, February 20, 2001, para. 239).

It is not necessary that a superior receive information about actual unlawful acts for command responsibility to attach. In *Blaškić*, the Appeals Chamber accepted the *Delalic et al.* Appeal Judgment as having "settled the issue of the interpretation of the standard of 'had reason to know'" (*Prosecutor v. Blaškić*, Judgment, Appeals Chamber, July 29, 2004, para. 62). In particular, the *Blaškić* Appeal Judgment endorsed the statement from the *Delalic et al.* Appeal that "a superior will be criminally responsible through the principles of superior responsibility only if information was available to him which would have put him on notice of offences committed by subordinates" (*Prosecutor v. Delalic et al.*, Judgment, Appeals Chamber, February 20, 2001, para. 241 (footnote omitted), quoted in *Prosecutor v. Blaškić*, Judgment, Appeals Chamber, July 29, 2004, para. 62). The ICRC Commentary (para. 3545) on Additional Protocol I refers to different types of information which a superior might have that might put him on notice of such unlawful acts. Through being put on notice, the superior would be required to undertake further investigations and act accordingly. His failure to do so would render him criminally liable (see, *Prosecutor v. Kordic*, Judgment, Trial Chamber, February 26, 2001, para. 437). It is in this sense that a superior may be held to have "had reason to know" for the purposes of command responsibility.

10–45

The types of information which might put a superior on notice would include the tactical situation; the level of training of the officers and troops; as well as their character traits (see *Prosecutor v. Delalic et al.*, Judgment, Appeals Chamber, February 20, 2001, para. 238). The information may be oral or written and the superior need not have acquainted himself with it, as long as it is in his possession (*Prosecutor v. Delalic et al.*, Judgment, Appeals Chamber, February 20, 2001, para. 239).

In *Prosecutor v. Delalic et al.*, Judgment, November 16, 1998, para. 393, the Trial Chamber emphasised that it made no finding on the present state of customary international law on the subject of command responsibility and noted the provisions in Article 28 of the ICC Statute which provides that a commander may be held responsible for the actions of his subordinates where he knew or should have known of the offences committed or about to be committed by forces under his effective command or control.

The Appeals Chambers of the ICTY and ICTR have rejected criminal negligence as a basis of liability for command responsibility (*Prosecutor v. Bagilishema*, Judgment, ICTR Appeals Chamber, December 13, 2002, para. 34; *Prosecutor v. Blaškić*, Judgment, Appeals Chamber, July 29, 2004, para. 63). The *Bagilishema* Appeal Judgment states: "References to 'negligence' in the context of superior responsibility are likely to lead to confusion of thought [. . .] The law imposes upon a superior a duty to prevent crimes which he knows or has reason to know were about to be committed, and to punish crimes which he knows or has reason to know had been committed, by subordinates over whom he has effective control. A military commander, or a civilian superior, may therefore be held responsible if he fails to discharge his duties as a superior either by deliberately failing to perform them or by culpably or wilfully disregarding them" (*Prosecutor v. Bagilishema*, Judgment, ICTR Appeals Chamber, December 13, 2002, para. 35, endorsed by *Prosecutor v. Blaškić*, Judgment, Appeals Chamber, July 29, 2004, para. 63).

C. Failure to Take Necessary and Reasonable Measures to Prevent or Punish

10–46   A superior is under a duty to prevent or punish crimes after they are committed by taking necessary and reasonable measures. As the ICRC Commentary on Article 87(3) of Additional Protocol I explains, this duty is recognised because of the fact that commanders more than any other persons are able to prevent breaches through a number of different methods as a result of their being "on the spot and able to exercise control over the troops and the weapons that they use" (ICRC Commentary on Additional Protocol I, para. 3560). In *Blaškić*, the Appeals Chamber considered that "the Trial Chamber did not err in finding to the effect that the responsibility of a commander for his failure to punish was recognised in customary law prior to the commission of crimes relevant to the Indictment" (*Prosecutor v. Blaškić*, Judgment, Appeals Chamber, July 29, 2004, para. 85; also see, ICRC, *Customary International Humanitarian Law*, 2005, p. 558).

Articles 6(3) and 7(3) of the ICTR and ICTY Statutes provide that a superior is expected to take "necessary and reasonable measures" to prevent or punish crimes under the Statute. "Necessary measures" are those measures required to discharge the obligation to prevent or punish and "reasonable measures" are those measures which a superior was able to take in the particular circumstances (see *Prosecutor v. Blaškić*, Judgment, Trial Chamber, May 3, 2000, para. 333 and *Prosecutor v. Bagilishema*, Judgment, Trial Chamber, June 7, 2001, para. 47). Accordingly, the type of action required of the superior depends on the particular circumstances and is not dependent upon his legal powers. This was endorsed by the Trial Chamber in *Prosecutor v. Delalic et al.*, Judgment, November 16, 1998, para. 395, which stated that a superior should be held "responsible for failing to take measures that are within his material possibility" (quoted with approval in *Prosecutor v. Blaškić*, Judgment, Appeals Chamber, July 29, 2004, para. 417; also see, *Prosecutor v. Kordic*, Judgment, Trial Chamber, February 26, 2001, para. 445). This approach is consistent with the superior-subordinate relationship in which actual ability to exercise control is paramount rather than the formal status of the superior (see *Prosecutor v. Kordic*, Judgment, Trial Chamber, February 26, 2001, para. 443).

In *Prosecutor v. Blaškić*, Judgment, May 3, 2000, para. 336, the Trial Chamber ruled that the obligation to "prevent or punish" does not provide an accused the opportunity to choose between these two measures (also see, *Prosecutor v. Bagilishema*, Judgment, ICTR Trial Chamber, June 7, 2001, para. 49). Thus when a superior knows of an accused's future criminal acts and fails to prevent them he will not have the option of punishing them in lieu of having acted. The Appeals Chamber noted, "The failure to punish and failure to prevent involve different crimes committed at different times: the failure to punish concerns past crimes committed by subordinates, whereas the failure to prevent concerns future crimes of subordinates" (*Prosecutor v. Blaškić*, Judgment, Appeals Chamber, July 29, 2004, para. 83).

There is no requirement that there be a causal link between a superior's failure to act and the commission of the crime for command responsibility to attach (*Prosecutor v. Blaškic*, Judgment, Appeals Chamber, July 29, 2004, para. 77: "The Appeals Chamber is therefore not persuaded by the Appellant's submission that the existence of causality between a commander's failure to prevent subordinates' crimes and the occurrence of these crimes, is an element of command responsibility that requires proof by the Prosecution in all circumstances of a case. Once again, it is more a question of fact to be established on a case by case basis, than a question of law in general.") Also see, *Prosecutor v. Kordić and Čerkez*, Judgment, Appeals Chamber, December 17, 2004, para. 832; *Prosecutor v. Delalic et al.*, Judgment, Trial Chamber, November 16, 1998, para. 398; *Prosecutor v. Kordić and Čerkez*, Judgment, Trial Chamber, February 26, 2001, para. 447).

IV. CHARGING DIFFERENT FORMS OF PARTICIPATION

In order to ensure that the Prosecution's case against the accused is clear, the indictment charging an accused with one of the different forms of participation should clearly lay out the form of participation of an accused (*e.g.* planning, instigating, ordering). It should set out whether the Prosecution is relying upon command or a direct form of responsibility or both (*Prosecutor v. Dosun and Kolundzija*, Decision on Preliminary Motions, February 10, 2000, para. 18; also see, *Prosecutor v. Tadić*, Decision on the Defence Motion on the Form of Indictment, November 14, 1995, para. 12). Thus the Prosecution's form of pleading should specify precisely and expressly the nature of the responsibility alleged in relation to each individual count against an accused and should not be a general pleading regarding the different types of responsibility the accused may bear (*Prosecutor v. Krnojelac*, Decision on Preliminary Motion on Form of Amended Indictment, February 11, 2000).

10–47

(1) Charging joint criminal enterprise

In *Prosecutor v. Kvočka et al.*, Judgment, November 2, 2001, paras 246–248, the Trial Chamber dismissed the complaints of the defence regarding the introduction of joint criminal enterprise into the Prosecution's pre-trial brief, which it alleged expanded the responsibility of the accused. The basis of such dismissal rested on the Trial Chamber's endorsement of the finding in *Prosecutor v. Tadić*, Judgment, Appeals Chamber, July 15, 1999, that participation in a joint criminal enterprise falls within the scope of Article 7(1) of the ICTY Statute. The Trial

10–48

Chamber also rejected the idea that in the absence of joint criminal enterprise being expressly pleaded, the Trial Chamber would not be able to apply it (also see, *Prosecutor v. Krstic*, Judgment, Trial Chamber, August 2, 2001, para. 602). In *Prosecutor v. Kvočka et al.*, Judgment, November 2, 2001, para. 247, the Trial Chamber emphasised that charges relating to "instigated, committed or otherwise aided and abetted" included responsibility for participating in a joint criminal enterprise.

10–49   In order that an accused is able to comprehend the case against him, the Prosecution is required to include in the indictment the nature of the joint criminal enterprise; the time period involved; the persons involved, and the nature of the accused's participation in the joint criminal enterprise (see *Prosecutor v. Krnojelac*, Decision on Form of Amended Indictment, May 11, 2000).

When an accused is alleged to have been a part of a joint criminal enterprise but the evidence does not support his having personally "committed" the crime charged, the indictment should clarify this point so that he knows the case he has to meet. This should be done in a statement which dispels any suggestion that "committed" refers to the accused physically perpetrating any of the crimes charged personally (see *Prosecutor v. Brdjanin and Talic*, Decision on Form of Further Amended Indictment and Prosecution Application to Amend, June 26, 2001 and *Prosecutor v. Brdjanin and Talic*, Decision Varying Decision on Form of Further Amended Indictment, July 2, 2001). In the absence of such a statement, the word "committed" would have to be struck from any indictments alleging joint criminal enterprise in which the accused did not personally perpetrate the crime in question.

In both the "Bosnia" and "Croatia" indictments (para. 5 in both indictments) against Slobodan Milošević, the word "committed" is used in the sense of Slobodan Milošević's participation in a joint criminal enterprise and thus accords with *Prosecutor v. Brdjanin and Talic*, Decision on Form of Further Amended Indictment and Prosecution Application to Amend.

(2) Cumulative charges and convictions for direct responsibility and superior responsibility for the same conduct

10–50   A finding of responsibility under Article 6(1) (or 7(1) in the case of the ICTY Statute) does not prevent a chamber from finding responsibility additionally under Article 6(3) for the same conduct of an accused person (or 7(3) in the case of the ICTY Statute) (see *Prosecutor v. Kayishema and Ruzindana*, Judgment, ICTR Trial Chamber, May 21, 1999, para. 210).

Thus, in *Kayishema and Ruzindana* the ICTR Trial Chamber held:

"For the reasons stated above, pursuant to Article 6(1) of the Statute, Kayishema is individually responsible for instigating, ordering, committing or otherwise aiding and abetting in the planning, preparation and execution of genocide by the killing and causing of serious bodily harm to the Tutsis at the Complex on April 17, 1994.

Additionally, under Article 6(3) of the Statute, Kayishema is responsible, for genocide, as superior, for the mass killing and injuring of the

Tutsi at the Complex on April 17, 1994, undertaken by his subordinates. The assailants at the Complex including gendarmes, members of the *Interahamwe*, local officials, including prison wardens, *conseillers* and *bour-gmestres*. The Trial Chamber finds that Kayishema had *de jure* control over most of the assailants and *de facto* control over all the attackers. The evidence proves that Kayishema was leading and directing the massacre. As stated in the Legal Findings on Criminal Responsibility, because Kayishema himself participated in the massacres, it is self-evident that he knew that his subordinates were about to attack and failed to take reasonable and necessary measures to prevent them, when he had the material ability to do so" (*Prosecutor v. Kayishema and Ruzindana*, Judgment, ICTR Trial Chamber, May 21, 1999, paras 554–555).

In giving an example of liability arising from the same conduct under both articles 7(1) and 7(3) of the ICTY Statute, the Trial Chamber in *Prosecutor v. Delalic et al.*, Judgment, November 16, 1998, para. 1222, stated:

> "[I]n practice there are factual situations rendering the charging and convicting of the same person under both Articles 7(1) and 7(3) perfectly appropriate. For instance, consider the situation where the commander or person exercising superior authority personally gives orders to his subordinates to beat the victim to death, and joins them in beating the victim to death. There is here criminal liability under Article 7(1) as a participant in the perpetration of the offence, and under Article 7(3) as a superior. Liability in this case is not mutually exclusive, since the exercise of superior authority in this case is not only the result of an omission to prevent the commission of the crime. It is a positive act of knowledge of the crime and participation in its commission."

In *Prosecutor v. Delalic et al.*, Judgment, November 16, 1998, para. 1223, the Trial Chamber stated that in such a scenario the superior should be liable as both a superior and a direct participant, but, in order to avoid imposing double sentencing for the same conduct, "it should be sufficient to regard his conduct as an aggravating circumstance attracting enhanced punishment". The Appeals Chamber in this case stated:

10–51

> "Where criminal responsibility for an offence is alleged under one count pursuant to both Article 7(1) and Article 7(3), and where the Trial Chamber finds that both direct responsibility and responsibility as a superior are proved, even though only one conviction is entered, the Trial Chamber must take into account the fact that both types of responsibility were proved in its consideration of sentence. This may most appropriately be considered in terms of imposing punishment on the accused for two separate offences encompassed in the one count. Alternatively, it may be considered in terms of the direct participation aggravating the Article 7(3) responsibility (as discussed above) or the accused's seniority or position of authority aggravating his direct responsibility under Article 7(1)" (*Prosecutor v. Delalic et al.*, Judgment, Appeals Chamber, February 20, 2001, para. 745, quoted in *Prosecutor v. Kordić and Čerkez*, Judgment, Appeals Chamber, December 17, 2004, para. 33).

In *Prosecutor v. Kordic* Judgment, February 26, 2001, para. 371, the Trial Chamber was of the view that, where the evidence demonstrates that a superior knew of the crimes of his subordinates but also instigated or planned or aided and abetted in these crimes, the type of responsibility incurred may "be better characterized by Article 7(1)" (also see, *Prosecutor v. Karadzic and Mladic*, Review of Indictments Pursuant to Rule 61 of the Rules of Procedure and Evidence, July 16, 1996, para. 83). This view was echoed in *Prosecutor v. Krstic*, Judgment, August 2, 2001, para. 605: "The Trial Chamber adheres to the belief that where a commander participates in the commission of a crime through his subordinates, by "planning", "instigating" or "ordering" the commission of the crime, any responsibility under Article 7(3) is subsumed under Article 7(1).").

Where individual criminal responsibility can be found pursuant to both Article 7(1) and 7(3), the Appeals Chamber states:

"The provisions of Article 7(1) and Article 7(3) of the Statute connote distinct categories of criminal responsibility. However, the Appeals Chamber considers that, in relation to a particular count, it is not appropriate to convict under both Article 7(1) and Article 7(3) of the Statute. Where both Article 7(1) and Article 7(3) responsibility are alleged under the same count, and where the legal requirements pertaining to both of these heads of responsibility are met, a Trial Chamber should enter a conviction on the basis of Article 7(1) only, and consider the accused's superior position as an aggravating factor in sentencing" (*Prosecutor v. Kordić and Čerkez*, Judgment, Appeals Chamber, December 17, 2004, para. 34; also see, *Prosecutor v. Blaškić*, Judgment, Appeals Chamber, July 29, 2004, para. 91).

The Appeals Chamber in both *Blaškić* and *Kordić and Čerkez* overturned "the concurrent conviction pursuant to Article 7(1) and Article 7(3) of the Statute in relation to the same counts based on the same facts" (*Prosecutor v. Blaškić*, Judgment, Appeals Chamber, July 29, 2004, para. 92; *Prosecutor v. Kordić and Čerkez*, Judgment, Appeals Chamber, December 17, 2004, para. 35).

The Trial Chamber in *Prosecutor v. Blaškić*, Judgment, May 3, 2000, para. 337, considered that a superior's liability under Article 7(3) through his failure to prevent or punish *past* crimes, may encourage the commission of further crimes under Article 7(1), and thus lead to the superior's responsibility under Article 7(1). Also see, *Prosecutor v. Kordic*, Judgment, Trial Chamber, February 26, 2001, para. 371.

CHAPTER 11

WAR CRIMES

I. STATUTORY PROVISIONS

A. ICC

Statute, Art. 8

11–1   8.—1. The Court shall have jurisdiction in respect of war crimes in particular when committed as a part of a plan or policy or as part of a large-scale commission of such crimes.

2. For the purpose of this Statute, "war crimes" means:

(a) Grave breaches of the Geneva Conventions of August 12, 1949, namely, any of the following acts against persons or property protected under the provisions of the relevant Geneva Convention: . . . [The same breaches in Art. 2 of the ICTY Statute are then listed; however, the Rome Statute, art. 8(2)(a)(v) of reads "or other protected person" whereas the ICTY Statute, Art. 2(e) reads "or a civilian." Art. 8(2)(a)(vi) of the Rome Statute and Art. 2(f) of the ICTY Statute also read "or other protected person" and "or a civilian" respectively. Art. 8(2)(a)(vii) of the Rome Statute lack "of a civilian" contained in Art. 2(g) of the ICTY Statute. Art. 8(2)(a)(viii) of the Rome Statute reads "Taking of hostages." Art. 2(h) of the ICTY Statute reads "taking civilians as hostages."]

(b) Other serious violations of the laws and customs applicable in international armed conflict, within the established framework of international law, namely, any of the following acts:

   (i) Intentionally directing attacks against the civilian population as such or against individual civilians not taking direct part in hostilities;

   (ii) Intentionally directing attacks against civilian objects, that is, objects which are not military objectives;

   (iii) Intentionally directing attacks against personnel, installations, material, units or vehicles involved in a humanitarian assistance or peacekeeping mission in accordance with the Charter of the United Nations, as long as they are entitled to the protection given to civilians or civilian objects under the international law of armed conflict;

   (iv) Intentionally launching an attack in the knowledge that such attack will cause incidental loss of life or injury to civilians or damage to civilian objects or widespread, long-term and severe damage to the natural environment which would be clearly excessive in relation to the concrete and direct overall military advantage anticipated;

   (v) Attacking or bombarding, by whatever means, towns, villages, dwellings or buildings which are undefended and which are not military objectives;

   (vi) Killing or wounding a combatant who, having laid down his arms or having no longer means of defence, has surrendered at discretion;

   (vii) Making improper use of a flag of truce, of the flag or of the military insignia and uniform of the enemy or of the United Nations, as well as of the distinctive emblems of the Geneva Conventions, resulting in death or serious personal injury;

   (viii) The transfer, directly or indirectly, by the Occupying Power of parts of its own civilian population into the territory it occupies, or the deportation or transfer of all or parts of the population of the occupied territory within or outside this territory;

(ix) Intentionally directing attacks against buildings dedicated to religion, education, art, science or charitable purposes, historic monuments, hospitals and places where the sick and wounded are collected, provided they are not military objectives;

(x) Subjecting persons who are in the power of an adverse party to physical mutilation or to medical or scientific experiments of any kind which are neither justified by the medical, dental or hospital treatment of the person concerned nor carried out in his or her interest, and which cause death to or seriously endanger the health of such person or persons;

(xi) Killing or wounding treacherously individuals belonging to the hostile nation or army;

(xii) Declaring that no quarter will be given;

(xiii) Destroying or seizing the enemy's property unless such destruction or seizure be imperatively demanded by the necessities of war;

(xiv) Declaring abolished, suspended or inadmissible in a court of law the rights and actions of the nationals of the hostile party;

(xv) Compelling the nationals of the hostile party to take part in the operations of war directed against their own country, even if they were in the belligerent's service before the commencement of the war;

(xvi) Pillaging a town or place, even when taken by assault;

(xvii) Employing poison or poisoned weapons;

(xviii) Employing asphyxiating, poisonous or other gases, and all analogous liquids, materials or devices;

(xix) Employing bullets which expand or flatten easily in the human body, such as bullets with a hard envelope which does not entirely cover the core or is pierced with incisions;

(xx) Employing weapons, projectiles and material and methods of warfare which are of a nature to cause superfluous injury or unnecessary suffering or which are inherently indiscriminate in violation of the international law of armed conflict, provided that such weapons, projectiles and material and methods of warfare are the subject of a comprehensive prohibition and are included in an annex to this Statute, by an amendment in accordance with the relevant provisions set forth in articles 121 and 123;

(xxi) Committing outrages upon personal dignity, in particular humiliating and degrading treatment;

(xxii) Committing rape, sexual slavery, enforced prostitution, forced pregnancy, as defined in article 7, paragraph 2 (f), enforced sterilization, or any other form of sexual violence also constituting a grave breach of the Geneva Conventions;

(xxiii) Utilizing the presence of a civilian or other protected person to render certain points, areas or military forces immune from military operations;

(xxiv) Intentionally directing attacks against buildings, material, medical units and transport, and personnel using the distinctive emblems of the Geneva Conventions in conformity with international law;

(xxv) Intentionally using starvation of civilians as a method of warfare by depriving them of objects indispensable to their survival, including wilfully impeding relief supplies as provided for under the Geneva Conventions;

(xxvi) Conscripting or enlisting children under the age of fifteen years into the national armed forces or using them to participate actively in hostilities.

(c) In the case of an armed conflict not of an international character, serious violations of article 3 common to the four Geneva Conventions of August 12, 1949, namely, any of the following acts committed

11–2

531

against persons taking no active part in the hostilities, including members of armed forces who have laid down their arms and those placed hors de combat by sickness, wounds, detention or any other cause:

    (i) Violence to life and person, in particular murder of all kinds, mutilation, cruel treatment and torture;

    (ii) Committing outrages upon personal dignity, in particular humiliating and degrading treatment;

    (iii) Taking of hostages;

    (iv) The passing of sentences and the carrying out of executions without previous judgement pronounced by a regularly constituted court, affording all judicial guarantees which are generally recognized as indispensable.

(d) Paragraph 2(c) applies to armed conflicts not of an international character and thus does not apply to situations of internal disturbances and tensions, such as riots, isolated and sporadic acts of violence or other acts of a similar nature.

(e) Other serious violations of the laws and customs applicable in armed conflicts not of an international character, within the established framework of international law, namely, any of the following acts:

    (i) Intentionally directing attacks against the civilian population as such or against individual civilians not taking direct part in hostilities;

    (ii) Intentionally directing attacks against buildings, material, medical units and transport, and personnel using the distinctive emblems of the Geneva Conventions in conformity with international law;

    (iii) Intentionally directing attacks against personnel, installations, material, units or vehicles involved in a humanitarian assistance or peacekeeping mission in accordance with the Charter of the United Nations, as long as they are entitled to the protection given to civilians or civilian objects under the international law of armed conflict;

    (iv) Intentionally directing attacks against buildings dedicated to religion, education, art, science or charitable purposes, historic monuments, hospitals and places where the sick and wounded are collected, provided they are not military objectives;

    (v) Pillaging a town or place, even when taken by assault;

    (vi) Committing rape, sexual slavery, enforced prostitution, forced pregnancy, as defined in article 7, paragraph 2 (f), enforced sterilization, and any other form of sexual violence also constituting a serious violation of article 3 common to the four Geneva Conventions;

    (vii) Conscripting or enlisting children under the age of fifteen years into armed forces or groups or using them to participate actively in hostilities;

    (viii) Ordering the displacement of the civilian population for reasons related to the conflict, unless the security of the civilians involved or imperative military reasons so demand;

    (ix) Killing or wounding treacherously a combatant adversary;

    (x) Declaring that no quarter will be given;

    (xi) Subjecting persons who are in the power of another party to the conflict to physical mutilation or to medical or scientific experiments of any kind which are neither justified by the medical, dental or hospital treatment of the person concerned nor carried out in his or her interest, and which cause death to or seriously endanger the health of such person or persons;

    (xii) Destroying or seizing the property of an adversary unless such destruction or seizure be imperatively demanded by the necessities of the conflict;

(f) Paragraph 2(e) applies to armed conflicts not of an international character and thus does not apply to situations of internal disturbances and tensions, such as riots, isolated and sporadic acts of violence or other acts of a similar nature. It applies to armed conflicts that take place in the territory of a State when there is protracted armed conflict between governmental authorities and organized armed groups or between such groups.

3. Nothing in para. 2 (c) and (e) shall affect the responsibility of a Government to maintain or re-establish law and order in the State or to defend the unity and territorial integrity of the State, by all legitimate means.

B. ICTY

Statute of the International Tribunal, Arts 2, 3

Grave breaches of the Geneva Conventions of 1949

2. The International Tribunal shall have the power to prosecute persons committing or ordering to be committed grave breaches of the Geneva Conventions of August 12, 1949, namely the following acts against persons or property protected under the provisions of the relevant Geneva Convention: **11–3**

   (a) wilful killing;
   (b) torture or inhuman treatment, including biological experiments;
   (c) wilfully causing great suffering or serious injury to body or health;
   (d) extensive destruction and appropriation of property, not justified by military necessity and carried out unlawfully and wantonly;
   (e) compelling a prisoner of war or a civilian to serve in the forces of a hostile power;
   (f) wilfully depriving a prisoner of war or a civilian of the rights of a fair and regular trial;
   (g) unlawful deportation or transfer or unlawful confinement of a civilian;
   (h) taking civilians as hostages.

Violations of the laws or customs of war

3. The International Tribunal shall have the power to prosecute persons violating the laws or customs of war. Such violations shall include, but not be limited to: **11–4**

   (a) employment of poisonous weapons or other weapons calculated to cause unnecessary suffering;
   (b) wanton destruction of cities, towns or villages, or devastation not justified by military necessity;
   (c) attack, or bombardment, by whatever means, of undefended towns, villages, dwellings, or buildings;
   (d) seizure of, destruction or wilful damage done to institutions dedicated to religion, charity and education, the arts and sciences, historic monuments and works of art and science;
   (e) plunder of public or private property.

C. ICTR

Statute of the International Tribunal for Rwanda, Art. 4

Violations of Article 3 Common to the Geneva Conventions and of Additional Protocol II

The International Tribunal for Rwanda shall have the power to prosecute persons committing or ordering to be committed serious violations of Article 3 common to the Geneva Conventions of August 12, 1949 for the Protection of **11–5**

War Victims, and of Additional Protocol II thereto of June 8, 1977. These violations shall include, but shall not be limited to:

- (a) Violence to life, health and physical or mental well-being of persons, in particular murder as well as cruel treatment such as torture, mutilation or any form of corporal punishment;
- (b) Collective punishments;
- (c) Taking of hostages;
- (d) Acts of terrorism;
- (e) Outrages upon personal dignity, in particular humiliating and degrading treatment, rape, enforced prostitution and any form of indecent assault;
- (f) Pillage;
- (g) The passing of sentences and carrying out of executions without previous judgement pronounced by a regularly constituted court, affording all the judicial guarantees which are recognised as indispensable by civilised peoples;
- (h) Threats to commit any of the foregoing acts.

D. EAST TIMOR

Regulation 2000/15, ss.6, 7

War crimes

11–6   **6.**—6.1. For the purposes of the present regulation, "war crimes" means:

- (a) Grave breaches of the Geneva Conventions of 12 August 1949, namely, any of the following acts against persons or property protected under the provisions of the relevant Geneva Convention:
  - (i) Wilful killing;
  - (ii) Torture or inhuman treatment, including biological experiments;
  - (iii) Wilfully causing great suffering, or serious injury to body or health;
  - (iv) Extensive destruction and appropriation of property, not justified by military necessity and carried out unlawfully and wantonly;
  - (v) Compelling a prisoner of war or other protected person to serve in the forces of a hostile Power;
  - (vi) Wilfully depriving a prisoner of war or other protected person of the rights of fair and regular trial;
  - (vii) Unlawful deportation or transfer or unlawful confinement;
  - (viii) Taking of hostages.
- (b) Other serious violations of the laws and customs applicable in international armed conflict, within the established framework of international law, namely, any of the following acts:
  - (i) Intentionally directing attacks against the civilian population as such or against individual civilians not taking direct part in hostilities;
  - (ii) Intentionally directing attacks against civilian objects, that is, objects which are not military objectives;
  - (iii) Intentionally directing attacks against personnel, installations, material, units or vehicles involved in a humanitarian assistance or peacekeeping mission in accordance with the Charter of the United Nations, as long as they are entitled to the protection given to civilians or civilian objects under the international law of armed conflict;
  - (iv) Intentionally launching an attack in the knowledge that such attack will cause incidental loss of life or injury to civilians or

damage to civilian objects or widespread, long-term and severe damage to the natural environment which would be clearly excessive in relation to the concrete and direct overall military advantage anticipated;

(v) Attacking or bombarding, by whatever means, towns, villages, dwellings or buildings which are undefended and which are not military objectives;

(vi) Killing or wounding a combatant who, having laid down his arms or having no longer means of defence, has surrendered at discretion;

(vii) Making improper use of a flag of truce, of the flag or of the military insignia and uniform of the enemy or of the United Nations, as well as of the distinctive emblems of the Geneva Conventions, resulting in death or serious personal injury;

(viii) The transfer, directly or indirectly, by the Occupying Power of parts of its own civilian population into the territory it occupies, or the deportation or transfer of all or parts of the population of the occupied territory within or outside this territory;

(ix) Intentionally directing attacks against buildings dedicated to religion, education, art, science or charitable purposes, historic monuments, hospitals and places where the sick and wounded are collected, provided they are not military objectives;

(x) Subjecting persons who are in the power of an adverse party to physical mutilation or to medical or scientific experiments of any kind which are neither justified by the medical, dental or hospital treatment of the person concerned nor carried out in his or her interest, and which cause death to or seriously endanger the health of such person or persons;

(xi) Killing or wounding treacherously individuals belonging to the hostile nation or army;

(xii) Declaring that no quarter will be given;

(xiii) Destroying or seizing the enemy's property unless such destruction or seizure be imperatively demanded by the necessities of war;

(xiv) Declaring abolished, suspended or inadmissible in a court of law the rights and actions of the nationals of the hostile party;

(xv) Compelling the nationals of the hostile party to take part in the operations of war directed against their own country, even if they were in the belligerent's service before the commencement of the war;

(xvi) Pillaging a town or place, even when taken by assault;

(xvii) Employing poison or poisoned weapons;

(xviii) Employing asphyxiating, poisonous or other gases, and all analogous liquids, materials or devices;

(xix) Employing bullets which expand or flatten easily in the human body, such as bullets with a hard envelope which does not entirely cover the core or is pierced with incisions;

(xx) Employing weapons, projectiles and material and methods of warfare which are of a nature to cause superfluous injury or unnecessary suffering or which are inherently indiscriminate in violation of the international law of armed conflict;

(xxi) Committing outrages upon personal dignity, in particular humiliating and degrading treatment;

(xxii) Committing rape, sexual slavery, enforced prostitution, forced pregnancy, as defined in Section 5.2(e) of the present regulation, enforced sterilization, or any other form of sexual violence also constituting a grave breach of the Geneva Conventions;

(xxiii) Utilizing the presence of a civilian or other protected person to render certain points, areas of military forces immune from military operations;

(xxiv) Intentionally directing attacks against buildings, material, medical units and transport, and personnel using the distinctive emblems of the Geneva Conventions in conformity with international law;

(xxv) Intentionally using starvation of civilians as a method of warfare by depriving them of objects indispensable to their survival, including wilfully impeding relief supplies as provided for under the Geneva Conventions;

(xxvi) Conscripting or enlisting children under the age of fifteen years into the national armed forces or using them to participate actively in hostilities.

(c) In the case of an armed conflict not of an international character, serious violations of Article 3 common to the four Geneva Conventions of 12 August 1949, namely, any of the following acts committed against persons taking no active part in the hostilities, including members of armed forces who have laid down their arms and those placed *hors de combat* by sickness, wounds, detention or any other cause:

(i) Violence to life and person, in particular murder of all kinds, mutilation, cruel treatment and torture;

(ii) Committing outrages upon personal dignity, in particular humiliating and degrading treatment;

(iii) Taking of hostages;

(iv) The passing of sentences and the carrying out of executions without previous judgement pronounced by a regularly constituted court, affording all judicial guarantees which are generally recognized as indispensable.

(d) Section 6.1(c) of the present regulation applies to armed conflicts not of an international character and thus does not apply to situations of internal disturbances and tensions, such as riots, isolated and sporadic acts of violence or other acts of a similar nature.

(e) Other serious violations of the laws and customs applicable in armed conflicts not of an international character, within the established framework of international law, namely, any of the following acts:

(i) Intentionally directing attacks against the civilian population as such or against individual civilians not taking part in hostilities;

(ii) Intentionally directing attacks against buildings, material, medical units and transport, and personnel using the distinctive emblems of the Geneva Conventions in conformity with international law;

(iii) Intentionally directing attacks against personnel, installations, material, units or vehicles involved in a humanitarian assistance or peacekeeping mission in accordance with the Charter of the United Nations, as long as they are entitled to the protection given to civilians or civilian objects under the international law of armed conflict;

(iv) Intentionally directing attacks against buildings dedicated to religion, education, art, science or charitable purposes, historic monuments, hospitals and places where the sick and wounded are collected, provided they are not military objectives;

(v) Pillaging a town or place, even when taken by assault;

(vi) Committing rape, sexual slavery, enforced prostitution, forced pregnancy, as defined in Section 5.2(e) of the present regulation, enforced sterilization, and any other form of sexual violence also constituting a serious violation of Article 3 common to the four Geneva Conventions;

(vii) Conscripting or enlisting children under the age of fifteen years into armed forces or groups or using them to participate actively in hostilities;

(viii) Ordering the displacement of the civilian population for reasons related to the conflict, unless the security of the civilians involved or imperative military reasons so demand;

(ix) Killing or wounding treacherously a combatant adversary;
(x) Declaring that no quarter will be given;
(xi) Subjecting persons who are in the power of another party to the conflict to physical mutilation or to medical or scientific experiments of any kind which are neither justified by the medical, dental or hospital treatment of the person concerned nor carried out in his or her interest, and which cause death to or seriously endanger the health of such person or persons;
(xii) Destroying or seizing the property of an adversary unless such destruction or seizure be imperatively demanded by the necessities of the conflict;
(f) Section 6.1(e) of the present regulation applies to armed conflicts not of an international character and thus does not apply to situations of internal disturbances and tensions, such as riots, isolated and sporadic acts of violence or other acts of a similar nature. It applies to armed conflicts that take place in the territory of a State when there is protracted armed conflict between governmental authorities and organized armed groups or between such groups.

6.2. Nothing in Section 6.1(c) and (e) of the present regulation shall affect the responsibility of a Government to maintain or re-establish law and order in the State or to defend the unity and territorial integrity of the State, by all legitimate means.

Torture

7.—7.1. For the purposes of the present regulation, torture means any act by   **11–7**
which severe pain or suffering, whether physical or mental, is intentionally inflicted on a person for such purposes as obtaining from him/her or a third person information or a confession, punishing him/her for an act he/she or a third person has committed or is suspected of having committed, or humiliating, intimidating or coercing him/her or a third person, or for any reason based on discrimination of any kind. It does not include pain or suffering arising only from, inherent in or incidental to lawful sanctions.

7.2. This Section is without prejudice to any international instrument or national legislation which does or may contain provisions of wider application.

7.3. No exceptional circumstances whatsoever, whether a state of war or a threat of war, internal political instability or any other public emergency, may be invoked as a justification of torture.

E. Sierra Leone

Statute of the Special Court for Sierra Leone, Arts 3, 4

Violations of Article 3 common to the Geneva Conventions and of Additional Protocol II

3. The Special Court shall have the power to prosecute persons who   **11–8**
committed or ordered the commission of serious violations of article 3 common to the Geneva Conventions of 12 August 1949 for the Protection of War Victims, and of Additional Protocol II thereto of 8 June 1977. These violations shall include:
a. Violence to life, health and physical or mental well-being of persons, in particular murder as well as cruel treatment such as torture, mutilation or any form of corporal punishment;
b. Collective punishments;

    c. Taking of hostages;
    d. Acts of terrorism;
    e. Outrages upon personal dignity, in particular humiliating and degrading treatment, rape, enforced prostitution and any form of indecent assault;
    f. Pillage;
    g. The passing of sentences and the carrying out of executions without previous judgement pronounced by a regularly constituted court, affording all the judicial guarantees which are recognized as indispensable by civilized peoples;
    h. Threats to commit any of the foregoing acts.

Other Serious Violations of International Humanitarian Law

11–9   4. The Special Court shall have the power to prosecute persons who committed the following serious violations of international humanitarian law:
    a. Intentionally directing attacks against the civilian population as such or against individual civilians not taking direct part in hostilities;
    b. Intentionally directing attacks against personnel, installations, material, units or vehicles involved in a humanitarian assistance or peacekeeping mission in accordance with the Charter of the United Nations, as long as they are entitled to the protection given to civilians or civilian objects under the international law of armed conflict;
    c. Conscripting or enlisting children under the age of 15 years into armed forces or groups or using them to participate actively in hostilities.

F. CAMBODIA

Agreement Between the United Nations and the Royal Government of Cambodia Concerning the Prosecution Under Cambodian Law of Crimes Committed During the Period of Democratic Kampuchea, Art. 9

Crimes falling within the jurisdiction of the Extraordinary Chambers

11–10   9. The subject-matter jurisdiction of the Extraordinary Chambers shall be the crime of genocide as defined in the 1948 Convention on the Prevention and Punishment of the Crime of Genocide, crimes against humanity as defined in the 1998 Rome Statute of the International Criminal Court and grave breaches of the 1949 Geneva Conventions and such other crimes as defined in Chapter II of the Law on the Establishment of the Extraordinary Chambers as promulgated on 10 August 2001.

Law on the Establishment of Extraordinary Chambers in the Courts of Cambodia for the Prosecution of Crimes Committed During the Period of Democratic Kampuchea, as amended, Articles 6, 7

Article 6

11–11   6. The Extraordinary Chambers shall have the power to bring to trial all Suspects who committed or ordered the commission of grave breaches of the Geneva Conventions of 12 August 1949, such as the following acts against

persons or property protected under provisions of these Conventions, and which were committed during the period 17 April 1975 to 6 January 1979:
— wilful killing;
— torture or inhumane treatment;
— wilfully causing great suffering or serious injury to body or health;
— destruction and serious damage to property, not justified by military necessity and carried out unlawfully and wantonly;
— compelling a prisoner of war or a civilian to serve in the forces of a hostile power;
— wilfully depriving a prisoner of war or civilian the rights of fair and regular trial;
— unlawful deportation or transfer or unlawful confinement of a civilian;
— taking civilians as hostages.

Article 7
7. The Extraordinary Chambers shall have the power to bring to trial all Suspects most responsible for the destruction of cultural property during armed conflict pursuant to the 1954 Hague Convention for Protection of Cultural Property in the Event of Armed Conflict, and which were committed during the period from 17 April 1975 to 6 January 1979.

G. IRAQ

The Statute of the Iraqi Special Tribunal, Art. 13

War Crimes
13. For the purposes of this Statute, "war crimes" means: **11–12**
a) Grave breaches of the Geneva Conventions of 12 August 1949, namely, any of the following acts against persons or property protected under the provisions of the relevant Geneva Convention:
1. Willful killing;
2. Torture or inhuman treatment, including biological experiments;
3. Willfully causing great suffering, or serious injury to body or health;
4. Extensive destruction and appropriation of property, not justified by military necessity and carried out unlawfully and wantonly;
5. Willfully denying the right of a fair trial to a prisoner of war or other protected person;
6. Compelling a prisoner of war or other protected person to serve in the forces of a hostile power;
7. Unlawful confinement;
8. Unlawful deportation or transfer; and
9. Taking of hostages.
b) Other serious violations of the laws and customs applicable in international armed conflict, within the established framework of international law, namely, any of the following acts:
1. Intentionally directing attacks against the civilian population as such or against individual civilians not taking direct part in hostilities;
2. Intentionally directing attacks against civilians objects, that is, objects which are not military objectives;
3. Intentionally directing attacks against personnel, installations, material, units or vehicles involved in a peacekeeping mission in

accordance with the Charter of the United Nations or in a humanitarian assistance mission, as long as they are entitled to the protection given to civilians or civilian objects under the international law of armed conflict;

4. Intentionally launching an attack in the knowledge that such attack will cause incidental loss of life or injury to civilians or damage to civilian objects which would be clearly excessive in relation to the concrete and direct overall military advantage anticipated;

5. Intentionally launching an attack in the knowledge that such attack will cause widespread, long-term and severe damage to the natural environment which would be clearly excessive in relation to the concrete and direct overall military advantage anticipated;

6. Attacking or bombarding, by whatever means, towns, villages, dwellings or buildings which are undefended and which are not military objectives;

7. Killing or wounding a combatant who, having laid down his arms or having no longer means of defense, has surrendered at discretion;

8. Making improper use of a flag of truce, of the flag or of the military insignia and uniform of the enemy or of the United Nations, as well as of the distinctive emblems of the Geneva Conventions, resulting in death or serious personal injury;

9. The transfer, directly or indirectly, by the Government of Iraq or any of its instrumentalities (including by an instrumentality of the Arab Socialist Ba'ath Party), of parts of its own civilian population into any territory it occupies, or the deportation or transfer of all or parts of the population of the occupied territory within or outside this territory;

10. Intentionally directing attacks against buildings that are dedicated to religion, education, art, science or charitable purposes, historic monuments, hospitals and places where the sick and wounded are collected, provided they are not military objectives;

11. Subjecting persons of another nation to physical mutilation or to medical or scientific experiments of any kind that are neither justified by the medical, dental or hospital treatment of the person concerned nor carried out in his or her interest, and which cause death to or seriously endanger the health of such person or persons;

12. Killing or wounding treacherously individuals belonging to the hostile nation or army;

13. Declaring that no quarter will be given;

14. Destroying or seizing the property of an adverse party unless such destruction or seizure be imperatively demanded by the necessities of war;

15. Declaring abolished, suspended or inadmissible in a court of law, or otherwise depriving, the rights and actions of the nationals of the adverse party;

16. Compelling the nationals of the hostile party to take part in the operations of war directed against their own country, even if they were in the belligerent's service before the commencement of the war;

17. Pillaging a town or place, even when taken by assault;

18. Employing poison or poisoned weapons;

19. Employing asphyxiating, poisonous or other gases, and all analogous liquids, materials or devices;

20. Employing bullets which expand or flatten easily in the human body, such as bullets with a hard envelope which does not entirely cover the core or is pierced with incisions;

21. Committing outrages upon personal dignity, in particular humiliating and degrading treatment;
22. Committing rape, sexual slavery, enforced prostitution, forced pregnancy, or any other form of sexual violence of comparable gravity;
23. Utilizing the presence of a civilian or other protected person to render certain points, areas or military forces immune from military operations;
24. Intentionally directing attacks against buildings, material, medical units and transport, and personnel using the distinctive emblems of the Geneva Conventions in conformity with international law;
25. Intentionally using starvation of civilians as a method of warfare by depriving them of objects indispensable to their survival, including willfully impeding relief supplies as provided for under international law; and
26. Conscripting or enlisting children under the age of fifteen years into the national armed forces or using them to participate actively in hostilities.

c) In the case of an armed conflict, any of the following acts committed against persons taking no active part in the hostilities, including members of armed forces who have laid down their arms and those placed *hors de combat* by sickness, wounds, detention or any other cause:
　　1. Violence to life and person, in particular murder of all kinds, mutilation, cruel treatment and torture;
　　2. Committing outrages upon personal dignity, in particular humiliating and degrading treatment;
　　3. Taking of hostages; and
　　4. The passing of sentences and the carrying out of executions without previous judgment pronounced by a regularly constituted court, affording all judicial guarantees which are generally recognized as indispensable.

d) Serious violations of the laws and customs of war applicable in armed conflict not of an international character, within the established framework of international law, namely, any of the following acts:
　　1. Intentionally directing attacks against the civilian population as such or against individual civilians not taking direct part in hostilities;
　　2. Intentionally directing attacks against buildings, material, medical units and transport, and personnel using the distinctive emblems of the Geneva Conventions in conformity with international law;
　　3. Intentionally directing attacks against personnel, installations, material, units, or vehicles involved in a peacekeeping mission in accordance with the Charter of the United Nations or in a humanitarian assistance mission, as long as they are entitled to the protection given to civilians or civilian objects under the international law of armed conflict;
　　4. Intentionally directing attacks against buildings that are dedicated to religion, education, art, science, or charitable purposes, historic monuments, hospitals and places where the sick and wounded are collected, provided they are not military objectives;
　　5. Pillaging a town or place, even when taken by assault;
　　6. Committing rape, sexual slavery, enforced prostitution, forced pregnancy, or any other form of sexual violence of comparable gravity;
　　7. Conscripting or enlisting children under the age of fifteen years into armed forces or groups or using them to participate actively in hostilities;

8. Ordering the displacement of the civilian population for reasons related to the conflict, unless the security of the civilians involved or imperative military reasons so demand;
9. Killing or wounding treacherously a combatant adversary;
10. Declaring that no quarter will be given;
11. Subjecting persons who are in the power of another party to the conflict to physical mutilation or to medical or scientific experiments of any kind that are neither justified by the medical, dental or hospital treatment of the person concerned nor carried out in his or her interest, and which cause death to or seriously endanger the health of such person or persons; and
12. Destroying or seizing the property of an adversary, unless such destruction or seizure be imperatively demanded by the necessities of the conflict.

II. DEFINITION OF WAR CRIMES

A. HISTORY

11–13   The term "war crimes" covers a broad range of offences that have been prohibited in conventional and customary international law over many decades. From the earliest attempts at codification of the laws of war in the 1860s, the underlying principle had been to limit the excessive horrors of war by outlawing those acts which were unnecessary in achieving war's purpose: that of sufficiently weakening the enemy. Historically, this large group of crimes has been structured along two general axes: on the one hand, the law is divided between the "Law of The Hague" ("Hague Law") and the "Law of Geneva" ("Geneva Law") and, on the other, between the law applicable in international armed conflicts and that applicable in internal armed conflicts. While developments since at least the adoption of the 1977 Protocols Additional to the Geneva Conventions of 1949 have tended to blur these categories, especially in the case of the former distinction, they continue to be of more than merely historical interest.

Hague Law concerns the means and methods of conducting warfare and contains general rules concerning the conduct of hostilities. It is so-named as the principal foundations of this branch of the law are the Conventions agreed to at peace conferences held in The Hague. Principal among these were the 1899 Convention (II) with Respect to the Laws and Customs of War on Land and the 1907 Hague Convention (IV) Respecting the Laws and Customs of War on Land and the Regulations annexed thereto. The core principle of this body of law is the restriction expressed in Article 22 of the Regulations of 1899 and 1907: "The right of belligerents to adopt means of injuring the enemy is not unlimited."

11–14   Geneva Law, on the other hand, focuses on the victims of war: those combatants who have fallen *hors de combat* for whatever reason, civilians who have fallen into the hands of the opposing side, and those in occupied territory. Its principal developments have taken place via conventions agreed to in Geneva. While this body of law initially concerned itself exclusively with the condition of wounded and ill combatants (at first on land and later at sea), its reach has gradually been extended and the 1949 Geneva Conventions included civilians. The two bodies of law were for the first time codified in one convention in 1977 with the Protocols Additional to the Geneva Conventions.

"War crimes" for a long time constituted the entire body of acts which concerned International Humanitarian Law (IHL), or the law of war as it was known. The law before the Second World War consisted of the various Hague and Geneva Conventions in force, as well as the customary rules which had never been codified. Apart from the inclusion of a "new" category of crimes, "crimes against humanity" in the Nuremberg Charter, the greatest innovation in contemporary IHL was the inclusion in the four 1949 Geneva Conventions of a compliance mechanism, coupled with a list of specified offences, which together came to be known as the "grave breaches" provisions. When defining the law covering war crimes, it is usual to state that it includes the grave breaches of the 1949 Geneva Conventions as well as other violations of the laws and customs of war. The Statute of the ICTY deals with war crimes in this way.

11–15

B. ROME CONFERENCE

The Statute of the International Criminal Court (ICC), adopted at the Diplomatic Conference organised for the purpose in July 1998 in Rome, contains the most recent pronouncement by the international community on the definition of "war crimes". The ICC Statute, in particular Article 8 thereof, together with the jurisprudence of the ICTY and ICTR, constitutes the current state of international law relating to war crimes.

11–16

Article 8(1) of the ICC Statute states, "The Court shall have jurisdiction in respect of war crimes in particular when committed as a part of a plan or policy or as part of a large scale commission of such crimes." Prior to the adoption of the ICC Statute, there was disagreement as to the inclusion of a threshold clause limiting to some extent the Court's jurisdiction over war crimes. An alternative formulation would have granted jurisdiction to the Court over war crimes *only* "when committed as part of a plan or policy or as part of a large-scale commission of such crimes" (see *Report of the Preparatory Committee on the Establishment of an International Criminal Court*, A/CONF.183/2/Add.1, April 14, 1998, p. 25). The final version grants the Court broader jurisdiction but ensures that emphasis will be placed on the planned, organised or large-scale, and often thus the most serious, commission of these crimes.

The ICC Statute divides the crimes prohibited into the following categories: grave breaches of the 1949 Geneva Conventions; other serious violations of the laws and customs applicable in international armed conflict; serious violations of Article 3 common to the four 1949 Geneva Conventions in the case of an armed conflict not of an international character; and, other serious violations of the laws and customs applicable in armed conflicts not of an international character. In contrast to the Statute of the ICTY, therefore, the Statute of the

11–17

ICC maintains a much clearer distinction between international and internal armed conflicts.

The Statute of the ICC continues the trend started by the 1977 Additional Protocols in not distinguishing between Hague law and Geneva law. While Articles 8(2)(a) and 8(2)(c) (grave breaches and common Article 3 respectively) still fit into the category of Geneva law, the catch-all provisions of Articles 8(2)(b) and (e) make no distinction whatsoever between the two bodies of law.

III. ICC ELEMENTS

Elements of Crimes

War crimes

Introduction

11–18   8. The elements for war crimes under article 8, paragraph 2(c) and (e), are subject to the limitations addressed in article 8, paragraph 2(d) and (f), which are not elements of crimes.

The elements for war crimes under article 8, paragraph 2, of the Statute shall be interpreted within the established framework of the international law of armed conflict including, as appropriate, the international law of armed conflict applicable to armed conflict at sea.

With respect to the last two elements listed for each crime:
- There is no requirement for a legal evaluation by the perpetrator as to the existence of an armed conflict or its character as international or non-international;
- In that context there is no requirement for awareness by the perpetrator of the facts that established the character of the conflict as international or non-international;
- There is only a requirement for the awareness of the factual circumstances that established the existence of an armed conflict that is implicit in the terms "took place in the context of and was associated with".

Article 8(2)(a)

Article 8(2)(a)(i)

War crime of wilful killing

Elements

11–19   1. The perpetrator killed one or more persons. (The term "killed" is interchangeable with the term "caused death". This footnote applies to all elements which use either of these concepts.)

2. Such person or persons were protected under one or more of the Geneva Conventions of 1949.

3. The perpetrator was aware of the factual circumstances that established that protected status. (This mental element recognizes the interplay between

articles 30 and 32. This footnote also applies to the corresponding element in each crime under article 8(2)(a), and to the element in other crimes in article 8(2) concerning the awareness of factual circumstances that establish the status of persons or property protected under the relevant international law of armed conflict. With respect to nationality, it is understood that the perpetrator needs only to know that the victim belonged to an adverse party to the conflict. This footnote also applies to the corresponding element in each crime under article 8(2)(a).)

4. The conduct took place in the context of and was associated with an international armed conflict. (The term "international armed conflict" includes military occupation. This footnote also applies to the corresponding element in each crime under article 8(2)(a).)

5. The perpetrator was aware of factual circumstances that established the existence of an armed conflict.

Article 8(2)(a)(ii)–1

War crime of torture

Elements. (As element 3 requires that all victims must be "protected persons" under one or more of the Geneva Conventions of 1949, these elements do not include the custody or control requirement found in the elements of article 7(1)(e).)

1. The perpetrator inflicted severe physical or mental pain or suffering upon one or more persons.

11–20

2. The perpetrator inflicted the pain or suffering for such purposes as: obtaining information or a confession, punishment, intimidation or coercion or for any reason based on discrimination of any kind.

3. Such person or persons were protected under one or more of the Geneva Conventions of 1949.

4. The perpetrator was aware of the factual circumstances that established that protected status.

5. The conduct took place in the context of and was associated with an international armed conflict.

6. The perpetrator was aware of factual circumstances that established the existence of an armed conflict.

Article 8(2)(a)(ii)–2

War crime of inhuman treatment

Elements

1. The perpetrator inflicted severe physical or mental pain or suffering upon one or more persons.

11–21

2. Such person or persons were protected under one or more of the Geneva Conventions of 1949.

3. The perpetrator was aware of the factual circumstances that established that protected status.

4. The conduct took place in the context of and was associated with an international armed conflict.

5. The perpetrator was aware of factual circumstances that established the existence of an armed conflict.

Article 8(2)(a)(ii)–3

War crime of biological experiments

Elements

11–22
1. The perpetrator subjected one or more persons to a particular biological experiment.
2. The experiment seriously endangered the physical or mental health or integrity of such person or persons.
3. The intent of the experiment was non-therapeutic and it was neither justified by medical reasons nor carried out in such person's or persons' interest.
4. Such person or persons were protected under one or more of the Geneva Conventions of 1949.
5. The perpetrator was aware of the factual circumstances that established that protected status.
6. The conduct took place in the context of and was associated with an international armed conflict.
7. The perpetrator was aware of factual circumstances that established the existence of an armed conflict.

Article 8(2)(a)(iii)

War crime of wilfully causing great suffering

Elements

11–23
1. The perpetrator caused great physical or mental pain or suffering to, or serious injury to body or health of, one or more persons.
2. Such person or persons were protected under one or more of the Geneva Conventions of 1949.
3. The perpetrator was aware of the factual circumstances that established that protected status.
4. The conduct took place in the context of and was associated with an international armed conflict.
5. The perpetrator was aware of factual circumstances that established the existence of an armed conflict.

Article 8(2)(a)(iv)

War crime of destruction and appropriation of property

Elements

11–24
1. The perpetrator destroyed or appropriated certain property.
2. The destruction or appropriation was not justified by military necessity.
3. The destruction or appropriation was extensive and carried out wantonly.
4. Such property was protected under one or more of the Geneva Conventions of 1949.
5. The perpetrator was aware of the factual circumstances that established that protected status.

6. The conduct took place in the context of and was associated with an international armed conflict.

7. The perpetrator was aware of factual circumstances that established the existence of an armed conflict.

Article 8(2)(a)(v)

War crime of compelling service in hostile forces

Elements

1. The perpetrator coerced one or more persons, by act or threat, to take part in military operations against that person's own country or forces or otherwise serve in the forces of a hostile power.   **11–25**

2. Such person or persons were protected under one or more of the Geneva Conventions of 1949.

3. The perpetrator was aware of the factual circumstances that established that protected status.

4. The conduct took place in the context of and was associated with an international armed conflict.

5. The perpetrator was aware of factual circumstances that established the existence of an armed conflict.

Article 8(2)(a)(vi)

War crime of denying a fair trial

Elements

1. The perpetrator deprived one or more persons of a fair and regular trial by denying judicial guarantees as defined, in particular, in the third and the fourth Geneva Conventions of 1949.   **11–26**

2. Such person or persons were protected under one or more of the Geneva Conventions of 1949.

3. The perpetrator was aware of the factual circumstances that established that protected status.

4. The conduct took place in the context of and was associated with an international armed conflict.

5. The perpetrator was aware of factual circumstances that established the existence of an armed conflict.

Article 8(2)(a)(vii)–1

War crime of unlawful deportation and transfer

Elements

1. The perpetrator deported or transferred one or more persons to another State or to another location.   **11–27**

2. Such person or persons were protected under one or more of the Geneva Conventions of 1949.

3. The perpetrator was aware of the factual circumstances that established that protected status.

4. The conduct took place in the context of and was associated with an international armed conflict.

5. The perpetrator was aware of factual circumstances that established the existence of an armed conflict.

Article 8(2)(a)(vii)–2

War crime of unlawful confinement

Elements

11–28   1. The perpetrator confined or continued to confine one or more persons to a certain location.

2. Such person or persons were protected under one or more of the Geneva Conventions of 1949.

3. The perpetrator was aware of the factual circumstances that established that protected status.

4. The conduct took place in the context of and was associated with an international armed conflict.

5. The perpetrator was aware of factual circumstances that established the existence of an armed conflict.

Article 8(2)(a)(viii)

War crime of taking hostages

Elements

11–29   1. The perpetrator seized, detained or otherwise held hostage one or more persons.

2. The perpetrator threatened to kill, injure or continue to detain such person or persons.

3. The perpetrator intended to compel a State, an international organization, a natural or legal person or a group of persons to act or refrain from acting as an explicit or implicit condition for the safety or the release of such person or persons.

4. Such person or persons were protected under one or more of the Geneva Conventions of 1949.

5. The perpetrator was aware of the factual circumstances that established that protected status.

6. The conduct took place in the context of and was associated with an international armed conflict.

7. The perpetrator was aware of factual circumstances that established the existence of an armed conflict.

Article 8(2)(b)

Article 8(2)(b)(i)

War crime of attacking civilians

Elements

11–30   1. The perpetrator directed an attack.

2. The object of the attack was a civilian population as such or individual civilians not taking direct part in hostilities.

3. The perpetrator intended the civilian population as such or individual civilians not taking direct part in hostilities to be the object of the attack.

4. The conduct took place in the context of and was associated with an international armed conflict.

5. The perpetrator was aware of factual circumstances that established the existence of an armed conflict.

Article 8(2)(b)(ii)

War crime of attacking civilian objects

Elements

1. The perpetrator directed an attack.   **11–31**

2. The object of the attack was civilian objects, that is, objects which are not military objectives.

3. The perpetrator intended such civilian objects to be the object of the attack.

4. The conduct took place in the context of and was associated with an international armed conflict.

5. The perpetrator was aware of factual circumstances that established the existence of an armed conflict.

Article 8(2)(b)(iii)

War crime of attacking personnel or objects involved in a humanitarian assistance or peacekeeping mission

Elements

1. The perpetrator directed an attack.   **11–32**

2. The object of the attack was personnel, installations, material, units or vehicles involved in a humanitarian assistance or peacekeeping mission in accordance with the Charter of the United Nations.

3. The perpetrator intended such personnel, installations, material, units or vehicles so involved to be the object of the attack.

4. Such personnel, installations, material, units or vehicles were entitled to that protection given to civilians or civilian objects under the international law of armed conflict.

5. The perpetrator was aware of the factual circumstances that established that protection.

6. The conduct took place in the context of and was associated with an international armed conflict.

7. The perpetrator was aware of factual circumstances that established the existence of an armed conflict.

Article 8(2)(b)(iv)

War crime of excessive incidental death, injury, or damage

Elements

1. The perpetrator launched an attack.   **11–33**

2. The attack was such that it would cause incidental death or injury to civilians or damage to civilian objects or widespread, long-term and severe damage to the natural environment and that such death, injury or damage would be of such an extent as to be clearly excessive in relation to the concrete and direct overall military advantage anticipated. (The expression "concrete and direct overall military advantage" refers to a military advantage that is foreseeable by the perpetrator at the relevant time. Such advantage may or may not be temporally or geographically related to the object of the attack. The fact that this crime admits the possibility of lawful incidental injury and collateral damage does not in any way justify any violation of the law applicable in armed conflict. It does not address justifications for war or other rules related to *jus ad bellum*. It reflects the proportionality requirement inherent in determining the legality of any military activity undertaken in the context of an armed conflict.)

3. The perpetrator knew that the attack would cause incidental death or injury to civilians or damage to civilian objects or widespread, long-term and severe damage to the natural environment and that such death, injury or damage would be of such an extent as to be clearly excessive in relation to the concrete and direct overall military advantage anticipated. (As opposed to the general rule set forth in paragraph 4 of the General Introduction, this knowledge element requires that the perpetrator make the value judgement as described therein. An evaluation of that value judgement must be based on the requisite information available to the perpetrator at the time.)

4. The conduct took place in the context of and was associated with an international armed conflict.

5. The perpetrator was aware of factual circumstances that established the existence of an armed conflict.

Article 8(2)(b)(v)

War crime of attacking undefended places. (The presence in the locality of persons specially protected under the Geneva Conventions of 1949 or of police forces retained for the sole purpose of maintaining law and order does not by itself render the locality a military objective.)

Elements

11–34 1. The perpetrator attacked one or more towns, villages, dwellings or buildings.

2. Such towns, villages, dwellings or buildings were open for unresisted occupation.

3. Such towns, villages, dwellings or buildings did not constitute military objectives.

4. The conduct took place in the context of and was associated with an international armed conflict.

5. The perpetrator was aware of factual circumstances that established the existence of an armed conflict.

Article 8(2)(b)(vi)

War crime of killing or wounding a person hors de combat

Elements

11–35 1. The perpetrator killed or injured one or more persons.

2. Such person or persons were *hors de combat*.

3. The perpetrator was aware of the factual circumstances that established this status.

4. The conduct took place in the context of and was associated with an international armed conflict.

5. The perpetrator was aware of factual circumstances that established the existence of an armed conflict.

Article 8(2)(b)(vii)–1

War crime of improper use of a flag of truce

Elements

1. The perpetrator used a flag of truce.   **11–36**

2. The perpetrator made such use in order to feign an intention to negotiate when there was no such intention on the part of the perpetrator.

3. The perpetrator knew or should have known of the prohibited nature of such use. (This mental element recognizes the interplay between article 30 and article 32. The term "prohibited nature" denotes illegality.)

4. The conduct resulted in death or serious personal injury.

5. The perpetrator knew that the conduct could result in death or serious personal injury.

6. The conduct took place in the context of and was associated with an international armed conflict.

7. The perpetrator was aware of factual circumstances that established the existence of an armed conflict.

Article 8(2)(b)(vii)–2

War crime of improper use of a flag, insignia or uniform of the hostile party

Elements

1. The perpetrator used a flag, insignia or uniform of the hostile party.   **11–37**

2. The perpetrator made such use in a manner prohibited under the international law of armed conflict while engaged in an attack.

3. The perpetrator knew or should have known of the prohibited nature of such use. (This mental element recognizes the interplay between article 30 and article 32. The term "prohibited nature" denotes illegality.)

4. The conduct resulted in death or serious personal injury.

5. The perpetrator knew that the conduct could result in death or serious personal injury.

6. The conduct took place in the context of and was associated with an international armed conflict.

7. The perpetrator was aware of factual circumstances that established the existence of an armed conflict.

Article 8(2)(b)(vii)–3

War crime of improper use of a flag, insignia or uniform of the United Nations

Elements

1. The perpetrator used a flag, insignia or uniform of the United Nations.   **11–38**

2. The perpetrator made such use in a manner prohibited under the international law of armed conflict.

3. The perpetrator knew of the prohibited nature of such use. (This mental element recognizes the interplay between article 30 and article 32. The "should have known" test required in the other offences found in article 8(2)(b)(vii) is not applicable here because of the variable and regulatory nature of the relevant prohibitions.)

4. The conduct resulted in death or serious personal injury.

5. The perpetrator knew that the conduct could result in death or serious personal injury.

6. The conduct took place in the context of and was associated with an international armed conflict.

7. The perpetrator was aware of factual circumstances that established the existence of an armed conflict.

Article 8(2)(b)(vii)–4

War crime of improper use of the distinctive emblems of the Geneva Conventions

Elements

11–39
1. The perpetrator used the distinctive emblems of the Geneva Conventions.

2. The perpetrator made such use for combatant purposes ("Combatant purposes" in these circumstances means purposes directly related to hostilities and not including medical, religious or similar activities.) in a manner prohibited under the international law of armed conflict.

3. The perpetrator knew or should have known of the prohibited nature of such use. (This mental element recognizes the interplay between article 30 and article 32. The term "prohibited nature" denotes illegality.)

4. The conduct resulted in death or serious personal injury.

5. The perpetrator knew that the conduct could result in death or serious personal injury.

6. The conduct took place in the context of and was associated with an international armed conflict.

7. The perpetrator was aware of factual circumstances that established the existence of an armed conflict.

Article 8(2)(b)(viii)

The transfer, directly or indirectly, by the Occupying Power of parts of its own civilian population into the territory it occupies, or the deportation or transfer of all or parts of the population of the occupied territory within or outside this territory

Elements

11–40
1. The perpetrator:
   (a) Transferred (The term "transfer" needs to be interpreted in accordance with the relevant provisions of international humanitarian law.) directly or indirectly, parts of its own population into the territory it occupies; or
   (b) Deported or transferred all or parts of the population of the occupied territory within or outside this territory.

2. The conduct took place in the context of and was associated with an international armed conflict.

3. The perpetrator was aware of factual circumstances that established the existence of an armed conflict.

Article 8(2)(b)(ix)

War crime of attacking protected objects. (The presence in the locality of persons specially protected under the Geneva Conventions of 1949 or of police forces retained for the sole purpose of maintaining law and order does not by itself render the locality a military objective.)

Elements

1. The perpetrator directed an attack.   **11–41**

2. The object of the attack was one or more buildings dedicated to religion, education, art, science or charitable purposes, historic monuments, hospitals or places where the sick and wounded are collected, which were not military objectives.

3. The perpetrator intended such building or buildings dedicated to religion, education, art, science or charitable purposes, historic monuments, hospitals or places where the sick and wounded are collected, which were not military objectives, to be the object of the attack.

4. The conduct took place in the context of and was associated with an international armed conflict.

5. The perpetrator was aware of factual circumstances that established the existence of an armed conflict.

Article 8(2)(b)(x)–1

War crime of mutilation

Elements

1. The perpetrator subjected one or more persons to mutilation, in particular   **11–42**
by permanently disfiguring the person or persons, or by permanently disabling or removing an organ or appendage.

2. The conduct caused death or seriously endangered the physical or mental health of such person or persons.

3. The conduct was neither justified by the medical, dental or hospital treatment of the person or persons concerned nor carried out in such person's or persons' interest. (Consent is not a defence to this crime. The crime prohibits any medical procedure which is not indicated by the state of health of the person concerned and which is not consistent with generally accepted medical standards which would be applied under similar medical circumstances to persons who are nationals of the party conducting the procedure and who are in no way deprived of liberty. This footnote also applies to the same element for article 8(2)(b)(x)–2.)

4. Such person or persons were in the power of an adverse party.

5. The conduct took place in the context of and was associated with an international armed conflict.

6. The perpetrator was aware of factual circumstances that established the existence of an armed conflict.

Article 8(2)(b)(x)–2

War crime of medical or scientific experiments

Elements

11–43
1. The perpetrator subjected one or more persons to a medical or scientific experiment.
2. The experiment caused death or seriously endangered the physical or mental health or integrity of such person or persons.
3. The conduct was neither justified by the medical, dental or hospital treatment of such person or persons concerned nor carried out in such person's or persons' interest.
4. Such person or persons were in the power of an adverse party.
5. The conduct took place in the context of and was associated with an international armed conflict.
6. The perpetrator was aware of factual circumstances that established the existence of an armed conflict.

Article 8(2)(b)(xi)

War crime of treacherously killing or wounding

Elements

11–44
1. The perpetrator invited the confidence or belief of one or more persons that they were entitled to, or were obliged to accord, protection under rules of international law applicable in armed conflict.
2. The perpetrator intended to betray that confidence or belief.
3. The perpetrator killed or injured such person or persons.
4. The perpetrator made use of that confidence or belief in killing or injuring such person or persons.
5. Such person or persons belonged to an adverse party.
6. The conduct took place in the context of and was associated with an international armed conflict.
7. The perpetrator was aware of factual circumstances that established the existence of an armed conflict.

Article 8(2)(b)(xii)

War crime of denying quarter

Elements

11–45
1. The perpetrator declared or ordered that there shall be no survivors.
2. Such declaration or order was given in order to threaten an adversary or to conduct hostilities on the basis that there shall be no survivors.
3. The perpetrator was in a position of effective command or control over the subordinate forces to which the declaration or order was directed.
4. The conduct took place in the context of and was associated with an international armed conflict.
5. The perpetrator was aware of factual circumstances that established the existence of an armed conflict.

Article 8(2)(b)(xiii)

War crime of destroying or seizing the enemy's property

Elements

1. The perpetrator destroyed or seized certain property.
2. Such property was property of a hostile party.
3. Such property was protected from that destruction or seizure under the international law of armed conflict.
4. The perpetrator was aware of the factual circumstances that established the status of the property.
5. The destruction or seizure was not justified by military necessity.
6. The conduct took place in the context of and was associated with an international armed conflict.
7. The perpetrator was aware of factual circumstances that established the existence of an armed conflict.

11–46

Article 8(2)(b)(xiv)

War crime of depriving the nationals of the hostile power of rights or actions

Elements

1. The perpetrator effected the abolition, suspension or termination of admissibility in a court of law of certain rights or actions.
2. The abolition, suspension or termination was directed at the nationals of a hostile party.
3. The perpetrator intended the abolition, suspension or termination to be directed at the nationals of a hostile party.
4. The conduct took place in the context of and was associated with an international armed conflict.
5. The perpetrator was aware of factual circumstances that established the existence of an armed conflict.

11–47

Article 8(2)(b)(xv)

War crime of compelling participation in military operations

Elements

1. The perpetrator coerced one or more persons by act or threat to take part in military operations against that person's own country or forces.
2. Such person or persons were nationals of a hostile party.
3. The conduct took place in the context of and was associated with an international armed conflict.
4. The perpetrator was aware of factual circumstances that established the existence of an armed conflict.

11–48

Article 8(2)(b)(xvi)

War crime of pillaging

Elements

1. The perpetrator appropriated certain property.

11–49

2. The perpetrator intended to deprive the owner of the property and to appropriate it for private or personal use. (As indicated by the use of the term "private or personal use", appropriations justified by military necessity cannot constitute the crime of pillaging.)

3. The appropriation was without the consent of the owner.

4. The conduct took place in the context of and was associated with an international armed conflict.

5. The perpetrator was aware of factual circumstances that established the existence of an armed conflict.

Article 8(2)(b)(xvii)

War crime of employing poison or poisoned weapons

Elements

11–50   1. The perpetrator employed a substance or a weapon that releases a substance as a result of its employment.

2. The substance was such that it causes death or serious damage to health in the ordinary course of events, through its toxic properties.

3. The conduct took place in the context of and was associated with an international armed conflict.

4. The perpetrator was aware of factual circumstances that established the existence of an armed conflict.

Article 8(2)(b)(xviii)

War crime of employing prohibited gases, liquids, materials, or devices

Elements

11–51   1. The perpetrator employed a gas or other analogous substance or device.

2. The gas, substance or device was such that it causes death or serious damage to health in the ordinary course of events, through its asphyxiating or toxic properties. (Nothing in this element shall be interpreted as limiting or prejudicing in any way existing or developing rules of international law with respect to the development, production, stockpiling and use of chemical weapons.)

3. The conduct took place in the context of and was associated with an international armed conflict.

4. The perpetrator was aware of factual circumstances that established the existence of an armed conflict.

Article 8(2)(b)(xix)

War crime of employing prohibited bullets

Elements

11–52   1. The perpetrator employed certain bullets.

2. The bullets were such that their use violates the international law of armed conflict because they expand or flatten easily in the human body.

3. The perpetrator was aware that the nature of the bullets was such that their employment would uselessly aggravate suffering or the wounding effect.

4. The conduct took place in the context of and was associated with an international armed conflict.

5. The perpetrator was aware of factual circumstances that established the existence of an armed conflict.

Article 8(2)(b)(xx)

War crime of employing weapons, projectiles or materials or methods of warfare listed in the Annex to the Statute

Elements

[*Elements will have to be drafted once weapons, projectiles or material or methods of warfare have been included in an annex to the Statute.*]   **11–53**

Article 8(2)(b)(xxi)

War crime of outrages upon personal dignity

Elements

1. The perpetrator humiliated, degraded or otherwise violated the dignity of   **11–54**
one or more persons. (For this crime, "persons" can include dead persons. It is understood that the victim need not personally be aware of the existence of the humiliation or degradation or other violation. This element takes into account relevant aspects of the cultural background of the victim.)

2. The severity of the humiliation, degradation or other violation was of such degree as to be generally recognized as an outrage upon personal dignity.

3. The conduct took place in the context of and was associated with an international armed conflict.

4. The perpetrator was aware of factual circumstances that established the existence of an armed conflict.

Article 8(2)(b)(xxii)–1

War crime of rape

Elements

1. The perpetrator invaded (The concept of "invasion" is intended to be   **11–55**
broad enough to be gender-neutral.) the body of a person by conduct resulting in penetration, however slight, of any part of the body of the victim or of the perpetrator with a sexual organ, or of the anal or genital opening of the victim with any object or any other part of the body.

2. The invasion was committed by force, or by threat of force or coercion, such as that caused by fear of violence, duress, detention, psychological oppression or abuse of power, against such person or another person, or by taking advantage of a coercive environment, or the invasion was committed against a person incapable of giving genuine consent. (It is understood that a

person may be incapable of giving genuine consent if affected by natural, induced or age-related incapacity. This footnote also applies to the corresponding elements of article 8(2)(b)(xxii)–3, 5 and 6.)

3. The conduct took place in the context of and was associated with an international armed conflict.

4. The perpetrator was aware of factual circumstances that established the existence of an armed conflict.

Article 8(2)(b)(xxii)–2

War crime of sexual slavery (Given the complex nature of this crime, it is recognized that its commission could involve more than one perpetrator as a part of a common criminal purpose.)

Elements

11–56 1. The perpetrator exercised any or all of the powers attaching to the right of ownership over one or more persons, such as by purchasing, selling, lending or bartering such a person or persons, or by imposing on them a similar deprivation of liberty. (It is understood that such deprivation of liberty may, in some circumstances, include exacting forced labour or otherwise reducing a person to servile status as defined in the Supplementary Convention on the Abolition of Slavery, the Slave Trade, and Institutions and Practices Similar to Slavery of 1956. It is also understood that the conduct described in this element includes trafficking in persons, in particular women and children.)

2. The perpetrator caused such person or persons to engage in one or more acts of a sexual nature.

3. The conduct took place in the context of and was associated with an international armed conflict.

4. The perpetrator was aware of factual circumstances that established the existence of an armed conflict.

Article 8(2)(b)(xxii)–3

War crime of enforced prostitution

Elements

11–57 1. The perpetrator caused one or more persons to engage in one or more acts of a sexual nature by force, or by threat of force or coercion, such as that caused by fear of violence, duress, detention, psychological oppression or abuse of power, against such person or persons or another person, or by taking advantage of a coercive environment or such person's or persons' incapacity to give genuine consent.

2. The perpetrator or another person obtained or expected to obtain pecuniary or other advantage in exchange for or in connection with the acts of a sexual nature.

3. The conduct took place in the context of and was associated with an international armed conflict.

4. The perpetrator was aware of factual circumstances that established the existence of an armed conflict.

Article 8(2)(b)(xxii)–4

War crime of forced pregnancy

Elements

1. The perpetrator confined one or more women forcibly made pregnant, **11–58**
with the intent of affecting the ethnic composition of any population or
carrying out other grave violations of international law.

2. The conduct took place in the context of and was associated with an
international armed conflict.

3. The perpetrator was aware of factual circumstances that established the
existence of an armed conflict.

Article 8(2)(b)(xxii)–5

War crime of enforced sterilization

Elements

1. The perpetrator deprived one or more persons of biological reproductive **11–59**
capacity. (The deprivation is not intended to include birth-control measures
which have a non-permanent effect in practice.)

2. The conduct was neither justified by the medical or hospital treatment of
the person or persons concerned nor carried out with their genuine consent. (It
is understood that "genuine consent" does not include consent obtained
through deception.)

3. The conduct took place in the context of and was associated with an
international armed conflict.

4. The perpetrator was aware of factual circumstances that established the
existence of an armed conflict.

Article 8(2)(b)(xxii)–6

War crime of sexual violence

Elements

1. The perpetrator committed an act of a sexual nature against one or more **11–60**
persons or caused such person or persons to engage in an act of a sexual nature
by force, or by threat of force or coercion, such as that caused by fear of
violence, duress, detention, psychological oppression or abuse of power, against
such person or persons or another person, or by taking advantage of a coercive
environment or such person's or persons' incapacity to give genuine consent.

2. The conduct was of a gravity comparable to that of a grave breach of the
Geneva Conventions.

3. The perpetrator was aware of the factual circumstances that established
the gravity of the conduct.

4. The conduct took place in the context of and was associated with an
international armed conflict.

5. The perpetrator was aware of factual circumstances that established the
existence of an armed conflict.

Article 8(2)(b)(xxiii)

War crime of using protected persons as shields

Elements

11–61   1. The perpetrator moved or otherwise took advantage of the location of one or more civilians or other persons protected under the international law of armed conflict.

2. The perpetrator intended to shield a military objective from attack or shield, favour or impede military operations.

3. The conduct took place in the context of and was associated with an international armed conflict.

4. The perpetrator was aware of factual circumstances that established the existence of an armed conflict.

Article 8(2)(b)(xxiv)

War crime of attacking objects or persons using the distinctive emblems of the Geneva Conventions

Elements

11–62   1. The perpetrator attacked one or more persons, buildings, medical units or transports or other objects using, in conformity with international law, a distinctive emblem or other method of identification indicating protection under the Geneva Conventions.

2. The perpetrator intended such persons, buildings, units or transports or other objects so using such identification to be the object of the attack.

3. The conduct took place in the context of and was associated with an international armed conflict.

4. The perpetrator was aware of factual circumstances that established the existence of an armed conflict.

Article 8(2)(b)(xxv)

War crime of starvation as a method of warfare

Elements

11–63   1. The perpetrator deprived civilians of objects indispensable to their survival.

2. The perpetrator intended to starve civilians as a method of warfare.

3. The conduct took place in the context of and was associated with an international armed conflict.

4. The perpetrator was aware of factual circumstances that established the existence of an armed conflict.

Article 8(2)(b)(xxvi)

War crime of using, conscripting or enlisting children

Elements

11–64   1. The perpetrator conscripted or enlisted one or more persons into the national armed forces or used one or more persons to participate actively in hostilities.

2. Such person or persons were under the age of 15 years.

3. The perpetrator knew or should have known that such person or persons were under the age of 15 years.

4. The conduct took place in the context of and was associated with an international armed conflict.

5. The perpetrator was aware of factual circumstances that established the existence of an armed conflict.

Article 8(2)(c)

Article 8(2)(c)(i)–1

War crime of murder

Elements

1. The perpetrator killed one or more persons.

11–65

2. Such person or persons were either *hors de combat*, or were civilians, medical personnel, or religious personnel (The term "religious personnel" includes those non-confessional non-combatant military personnel carrying out a similar function.) taking no active part in the hostilities.

3. The perpetrator was aware of the factual circumstances that established this status.

4. The conduct took place in the context of and was associated with an armed conflict not of an international character.

5. The perpetrator was aware of factual circumstances that established the existence of an armed conflict.

Article 8(2)(c)(i)–2

War crime of mutilation

Elements

1. The perpetrator subjected one or more persons to mutilation, in particular by permanently disfiguring the person or persons, or by permanently disabling or removing an organ or appendage.

11–66

2. The conduct was neither justified by the medical, dental or hospital treatment of the person or persons concerned nor carried out in such person's or persons' interests.

3. Such person or persons were either *hors de combat*, or were civilians, medical personnel or religious personnel taking no active part in the hostilities.

4. The perpetrator was aware of the factual circumstances that established this status.

5. The conduct took place in the context of and was associated with an armed conflict not of an international character.

6. The perpetrator was aware of factual circumstances that established the existence of an armed conflict.

Article 8(2)(c)(i)–3

War crime of cruel treatment

Elements

1. The perpetrator inflicted severe physical or mental pain or suffering upon one or more persons.

11–67

2. Such person or persons were either *hors de combat*, or were civilians, medical personnel, or religious personnel taking no active part in the hostilities.

3. The perpetrator was aware of the factual circumstances that established this status.

4. The conduct took place in the context of and was associated with an armed conflict not of an international character.

5. The perpetrator was aware of factual circumstances that established the existence of an armed conflict.

Article 8(2)(c)(i)–4

War crime of torture

Elements

11–68   1. The perpetrator inflicted severe physical or mental pain or suffering upon one or more persons.

2. The perpetrator inflicted the pain or suffering for such purposes as: obtaining information or a confession, punishment, intimidation or coercion or for any reason based on discrimination of any kind.

3. Such person or persons were either *hors de combat*, or were civilians, medical personnel or religious personnel taking no active part in the hostilities.

4. The perpetrator was aware of the factual circumstances that established this status.

5. The conduct took place in the context of and was associated with an armed conflict not of an international character.

6. The perpetrator was aware of factual circumstances that established the existence of an armed conflict.

Article 8(2)(c)(ii)

War crime of outrages upon personal dignity

Elements

11–69   1. The perpetrator humiliated, degraded or otherwise violated the dignity of one or more persons. (For this crime, "persons" can include dead persons. It is understood that the victim need not personally be aware of the existence of the humiliation or degradation or other violation. This element takes into account relevant aspects of the cultural background of the victim.)

2. The severity of the humiliation, degradation or other violation was of such degree as to be generally recognized as an outrage upon personal dignity.

3. Such person or persons were either *hors de combat*, or were civilians, medical personnel or religious personnel taking no active part in the hostilities.

4. The perpetrator was aware of the factual circumstances that established this status.

5. The conduct took place in the context of and was associated with an armed conflict not of an international character.

6. The perpetrator was aware of factual circumstances that established the existence of an armed conflict.

Article 8(2)(c)(iii)

War crime of taking hostages

Elements

11–70   1. The perpetrator seized, detained or otherwise held hostage one or more persons.

2. The perpetrator threatened to kill, injure or continue to detain such person or persons.

3. The perpetrator intended to compel a State, an international organization, a natural or legal person or a group of persons to act or refrain from acting as an explicit or implicit condition for the safety or the release of such person or persons.

4. Such person or persons were either *hors de combat*, or were civilians, medical personnel or religious personnel taking no active part in the hostilities.

5. The perpetrator was aware of the factual circumstances that established this status.

6. The conduct took place in the context of and was associated with an armed conflict not of an international character.

7. The perpetrator was aware of factual circumstances that established the existence of an armed conflict.

Article 8(2)(c)(iv)

War crime of sentencing or execution without due process

Elements

1. The perpetrator passed sentence or executed one or more persons. (The   **11–71** elements laid down in these documents do not address the different forms of individual criminal responsibility, as enunciated in articles 25 and 28 of the Statute.)

2. Such person or persons were either *hors de combat*, or were civilians, medical personnel or religious personnel taking no active part in the hostilities.

3. The perpetrator was aware of the factual circumstances that established this status.

4. There was no previous judgment pronounced by a court, or the court that rendered judgment was not "regularly constituted", that is, it did not afford the essential guarantees of independence and impartiality, or the court that rendered judgment did not afford all other judicial guarantees generally recognized as indispensable under international law. (With respect to elements 4 and 5, the Court should consider whether, in the light of all relevant circumstances, the cumulative effect of factors with respect to guarantees deprived the person or persons of a fair trial.)

5. The perpetrator was aware of the absence of a previous judgement or of the denial of relevant guarantees and the fact that they are essential or indispensable to a fair trial.

6. The conduct took place in the context of and was associated with an armed conflict not of an international character.

7. The perpetrator was aware of factual circumstances that established the existence of an armed conflict.

Article 8(2)(e)

Article 8(2)(e)(i)

War crime of attacking civilians

Elements

1. The perpetrator directed an attack.   **11–72**

2. The object of the attack was a civilian population as such or individual civilians not taking direct part in hostilities.

3. The perpetrator intended the civilian population as such or individual civilians not taking direct part in hostilities to be the object of the attack.

4. The conduct took place in the context of and was associated with an armed conflict not of an international character.

5. The perpetrator was aware of factual circumstances that established the existence of an armed conflict.

Article 8(2)(e)(ii)

War crime of attacking objects or persons using the distinctive emblems of the Geneva Conventions

Elements

11–73 1. The perpetrator attacked one or more persons, buildings, medical units or transports or other objects using, in conformity with international law, a distinctive emblem or other method of identification indicating protection under the Geneva Conventions.

2. The perpetrator intended such persons, buildings, units or transports or other objects so using such identification to be the object of the attack.

3. The conduct took place in the context of and was associated with an armed conflict not of an international character.

4. The perpetrator was aware of factual circumstances that established the existence of an armed conflict.

Article 8(2)(e)(iii)

War crime of attacking personnel or objects involved in a humanitarian assistance or peacekeeping mission

Elements

11–74 1. The perpetrator directed an attack.

2. The object of the attack was personnel, installations, material, units or vehicles involved in a humanitarian assistance or peacekeeping mission in accordance with the Charter of the United Nations.

3. The perpetrator intended such personnel, installations, material, units or vehicles so involved to be the object of the attack.

4. Such personnel, installations, material, units or vehicles were entitled to that protection given to civilians or civilian objects under the international law of armed conflict.

5. The perpetrator was aware of the factual circumstances that established that protection.

6. The conduct took place in the context of and was associated with an armed conflict not of an international character.

7. The perpetrator was aware of factual circumstances that established the existence of an armed conflict.

Article 8(2)(e)(iv)

War crime of attacking protected objects. (The presence in the locality of persons specially protected under the Geneva Conventions of 1949 or of police forces retained for the sole purpose of maintaining law and order does not by itself render the locality a military objective.)

Elements

1. The perpetrator directed an attack.   **11–75**
2. The object of the attack was one or more buildings dedicated to religion, education, art, science or charitable purposes, historic monuments, hospitals or places where the sick and wounded are collected, which were not military objectives.
3. The perpetrator intended such building or buildings dedicated to religion, education, art, science or charitable purposes, historic monuments, hospitals or places where the sick and wounded are collected, which were not military objectives, to be the object of the attack.
4. The conduct took place in the context of and was associated with an armed conflict not of an international character.
5. The perpetrator was aware of factual circumstances that established the existence of an armed conflict.

Article 8(2)(e)(v)

War crime of pillaging

Elements

1. The perpetrator appropriated certain property.   **11–76**
2. The perpetrator intended to deprive the owner of the property and to appropriate it for private or personal use. (As indicated by the use of the term "private or personal use", appropriations justified by military necessity cannot constitute the crime of pillaging.)
3. The appropriation was without the consent of the owner.
4. The conduct took place in the context of and was associated with an armed conflict not of an international character.
5. The perpetrator was aware of factual circumstances that established the existence of an armed conflict.

Article 8(2)(e)(vi)–1

War crime of rape

Elements

1. The perpetrator invaded (The concept of "invasion" is intended to be   **11–77**
broad enough to be gender-neutral.) the body of a person by conduct resulting in penetration, however slight, of any part of the body of the victim or of the perpetrator with a sexual organ, or of the anal or genital opening of the victim with any object or any other part of the body.

2. The invasion was committed by force, or by threat of force or coercion, such as that caused by fear of violence, duress, detention, psychological oppression or abuse of power, against such person or another person, or by taking advantage of a coercive environment, or the invasion was committed against a person incapable of giving genuine consent. (It is understood that a person may be incapable of giving genuine consent if affected by natural, induced or age-related incapacity. This footnote also applies to the corresponding elements in article 8(2)(e) (vi)–3, 5 and 6.)

3. The conduct took place in the context of and was associated with an armed conflict not of an international character.

4. The perpetrator was aware of factual circumstances that established the existence of an armed conflict.

Article 8(2)(e)(vi)–2

War crime of sexual slavery. (Given the complex nature of this crime, it is recognized that its commission could involve more than one perpetrator as a part of a common criminal purpose.)

Elements

11–78   1. The perpetrator exercised any or all of the powers attaching to the right of ownership over one or more persons, such as by purchasing, selling, lending or bartering such a person or persons, or by imposing on them a similar deprivation of liberty. (It is understood that such deprivation of liberty may, in some circumstances, include exacting forced labour or otherwise reducing a person to servile status as defined in the Supplementary Convention on the Abolition of Slavery, the Slave Trade, and Institutions and Practices Similar to Slavery of 1956. It is also understood that the conduct described in this element includes trafficking in persons, in particular women and children.)

2. The perpetrator caused such person or persons to engage in one or more acts of a sexual nature.

3. The conduct took place in the context of and was associated with an armed conflict not of an international character.

4. The perpetrator was aware of factual circumstances that established the existence of an armed conflict.

Article 8(2)(e)(vi)–3

War crime of enforced prostitution

Elements

11–79   1. The perpetrator caused one or more persons to engage in one or more acts of a sexual nature by force, or by threat of force or coercion, such as that caused by fear of violence, duress, detention, psychological oppression or abuse of power, against such person or persons or another person, or by taking advantage of a coercive environment or such person's or persons' incapacity to give genuine consent.

2. The perpetrator or another person obtained or expected to obtain pecuniary or other advantage in exchange for or in connection with the acts of a sexual nature.

3. The conduct took place in the context of and was associated with an armed conflict not of an international character.

4. The perpetrator was aware of factual circumstances that established the existence of an armed conflict.

Article 8(2)(e)(vi)–4

War crime of forced pregnancy

Elements

1. The perpetrator confined one or more women forcibly made pregnant, **11–80** with the intent of affecting the ethnic composition of any population or carrying out other grave violations of international law.

2. The conduct took place in the context of and was associated with an armed conflict not of an international character.

3. The perpetrator was aware of factual circumstances that established the existence of an armed conflict.

Article 8(2)(e)(vi)–5

War crime of enforced sterilization

Elements

1. The perpetrator deprived one or more persons of biological reproductive **11–81** capacity. (The deprivation is not intended to include birth-control measures which have a non-permanent effect in practice.)

2. The conduct was neither justified by the medical or hospital treatment of the person or persons concerned nor carried out with their genuine consent. (It is understood that "genuine consent" does not include consent obtained through deception.)

3. The conduct took place in the context of and was associated with an armed conflict not of an international character.

4. The perpetrator was aware of factual circumstances that established the existence of an armed conflict.

Article 8(2)(e)(vi)–6

War crime of sexual violence

Elements

1. The perpetrator committed an act of a sexual nature against one or more **11–82** persons or caused such person or persons to engage in an act of a sexual nature by force, or by threat of force or coercion, such as that caused by fear of violence, duress, detention, psychological oppression or abuse of power, against such person or persons or another person, or by taking advantage of a coercive environment or such person's or persons' incapacity to give genuine consent.

2. The conduct was of a gravity comparable to that of a serious violation of article 3 common to the four Geneva Conventions.

3. The perpetrator was aware of the factual circumstances that established the gravity of the conduct.

4. The conduct took place in the context of and was associated with an armed conflict not of an international character.

5. The perpetrator was aware of factual circumstances that established the existence of an armed conflict.

Article 8(2)(e)(vii)

War crime of using, conscripting and enlisting children

Elements

11–83   1. The perpetrator conscripted or enlisted one or more persons into an armed force or group or used one or more persons to participate actively in hostilities.

2. Such person or persons were under the age of 15 years.

3. The perpetrator knew or should have known that such person or persons were under the age of 15 years.

4. The conduct took place in the context of and was associated with an armed conflict not of an international character.

5. The perpetrator was aware of factual circumstances that established the existence of an armed conflict.

Article 8(2)(e)(viii)

War crime of displacing civilians

Elements

11–84   1. The perpetrator ordered a displacement of a civilian population.

2. Such order was not justified by the security of the civilians involved or by military necessity.

3. The perpetrator was in a position to effect such displacement by giving such order.

4. The conduct took place in the context of and was associated with an armed conflict not of an international character.

5. The perpetrator was aware of factual circumstances that established the existence of an armed conflict.

Article 8(2)(e)(ix)

War crime of treacherously killing or wounding

Elements

11–85   1. The perpetrator invited the confidence or belief of one or more combatant adversaries that they were entitled to, or were obliged to accord, protection under rules of international law applicable in armed conflict.

2. The perpetrator intended to betray that confidence or belief.

3. The perpetrator killed or injured such person or persons.

4. The perpetrator made use of that confidence or belief in killing or injuring such person or persons.

5. Such person or persons belonged to an adverse party.

6. The conduct took place in the context of and was associated with an armed conflict not of an international character.

7. The perpetrator was aware of factual circumstances that established the existence of an armed conflict.

Article 8(2)(e)(x)

War crime of denying quarter

Elements

1. The perpetrator declared or ordered that there shall be no survivors.   **11–86**

2. Such declaration or order was given in order to threaten an adversary or to conduct hostilities on the basis that there shall be no survivors.

3. The perpetrator was in a position of effective command or control over the subordinate forces to which the declaration or order was directed.

4. The conduct took place in the context of and was associated with an armed conflict not of an international character.

5. The perpetrator was aware of factual circumstances that established the existence of an armed conflict.

Article 8(2)(e)(xi)–1

War crime of mutilation

Elements

1. The perpetrator subjected one or more persons to mutilation, in particular   **11–87** by permanently disfiguring the person or persons, or by permanently disabling or removing an organ or appendage.

2. The conduct caused death or seriously endangered the physical or mental health of such person or persons.

3. The conduct was neither justified by the medical, dental or hospital treatment of the person or persons concerned nor carried out in such person's or persons' interest. (Consent is not a defence to this crime. The crime prohibits any medical procedure which is not indicated by the state of health of the person concerned and which is not consistent with generally accepted medical standards which would be applied under similar medical circumstances to persons who are nationals of the party conducting the procedure and who are in no way deprived of liberty. This footnote also applies to the similar element in article 8(2)(e)(xi)–2.)

4. Such person or persons were in the power of another party to the conflict.

5. The conduct took place in the context of and was associated with an armed conflict not of an international character.

6. The perpetrator was aware of factual circumstances that established the existence of an armed conflict.

Article 8(2)(e)(xi)–2

War crime of medical or scientific experiments

Elements

1. The perpetrator subjected one or more persons to a medical or scientific   **11–88** experiment.

2. The experiment caused the death or seriously endangered the physical or mental health or integrity of such person or persons.

3. The conduct was neither justified by the medical, dental or hospital treatment of such person or persons concerned nor carried out in such person's or persons' interest.

4. Such person or persons were in the power of another party to the conflict.

5. The conduct took place in the context of and was associated with an armed conflict not of an international character.

6. The perpetrator was aware of factual circumstances that established the existence of an armed conflict.

Article 8(2)(e)(xii)

War crime of destroying or seizing the enemy's property

Elements

11–89   1. The perpetrator destroyed or seized certain property.

2. Such property was property of an adversary.

3. Such property was protected from that destruction or seizure under the international law of armed conflict.

4. The perpetrator was aware of the factual circumstances that established the status of the property.

5. The destruction or seizure was not required by military necessity.

6. The conduct took place in the context of and was associated with an armed conflict not of an international character.

7. The perpetrator was aware of factual circumstances that established the existence of an armed conflict.

IV. JURISDICTIONAL PREREQUISITES

A. ARMED CONFLICT

11–90   War crimes must be committed in the course of, or in connection with, an armed conflict. The Appeals Chamber of the International Tribunals stated in this regard:

> "International humanitarian law governs the conduct of both internal and international armed conflicts. Appellant correctly points out that for there to be a violation of this body of law, there must be an armed conflict" (*The Prosecutor v. Tadić*, Decision on the Defence Motion for Interlocutory Appeal on Jurisdiction Appeals Chamber, October 2, 1995, para. 67.)

The defendants before the International Military Tribunal ("IMT") sitting in Nuremberg in 1946 raised the defence that there was no war when the crimes alleged were committed. They had argued that Germany was no longer bound by the rules of land warfare in many of the occupied territories by virtue of the fact that "Germany had completely subjugated those territories and incorporated them into the German Reich, a fact which gave Germany the authority to deal with the occupied countries as though they were part of Germany" (Judgment of the IMT, p. 84). The IMT held:

"The doctrine [of subjugation] was never considered to be applicable so long as there was an army in the field attempting to restore the occupied countries to their true owners, and in this case, therefore, the doctrine could not apply to any territories occupied after September 1, 1939" (Judgment of the IMT, p. 84).

The IMT, therefore, applied the laws of war to the crimes allegedly committed by the defendants on the basis that the presence of armies "in the field" provided the necessary condition for the continued existence of war.

The Appeals Chamber in the *Tadić* Jurisdiction Decision next elaborated on the definition of an armed conflict and the nexus required to the commission of the prohibited acts, the accused and the victim in the following terms:

11–91

"The geographical and temporal frame of reference [. . .] is broad. This conception is reflected in the fact that beneficiaries of common Article 3 of the Geneva Conventions are those taking no active part (or no longer taking active part) in the hostilities. This indicates that the rules contained in [common] article 3 [. . .] apply outside the narrow geographical context of the actual theatre of combat operations [. . .] The nexus required is only a relationship between the conflict and the [acts], not that the [acts] occurred in the midst of battle . . .
[W]e find that an armed conflict exists whenever there is a resort to armed force between States or protracted armed violence between governmental authorities and organised armed groups or between such groups within a State. International humanitarian law applies from the initiation of such armed conflicts and extends beyond the cessation of hostilities until a general conclusion of peace is reached; or in the case of internal conflicts, peaceful settlement is achieved. Until that moment, international humanitarian law continues to apply in the whole territory of the warring States or, in the case of internal conflicts, the whole territory under the control of a party, whether or not actual combat takes place there" (*Prosecutor v. Tadić*, Decision on the Defence Motion for Interlocutory Appeal on Jurisdiction, Appeals Chamber, October 2, 1995, paras 69–70).

It is evident that an internal disturbance must rise to the level of "protracted armed violence" to render international humanitarian law applicable (*Prosecutor v. Akayesu*, Judgment, Trial Chamber, September 2, 1998, para. 603, holding that the ascertainment of the intensity of a non-international conflict does not depend on the subjective judgment of the parties to the conflict). The *Delalic et al.* Trial Judgment held: "[I]n the latter situation (*i.e.* non-international armed conflicts), in order to distinguish from cases of civil unrest or terrorist activities, the emphasis is on the protracted extent of the armed violence and the extent of organisation of the parties involved" (*Prosecutor v. Delalic et al.*, Judgment, Trial Chamber, November 16, 1998, para. 182).

It is not a requirement that the perpetrator of alleged war crimes be a "public agent or government representative" and act in such a capacity to support or fulfil the war effort (*Prosecutor v. Akayesu*, Judgment, Appeals Chamber, June 1, 2001, paras 444–445).

In order to distinguish between genuine armed conflicts and "mere acts or banditry" or "short lived rebellions", the ICTR Trial Chamber in *Akayesu* referred to the alternative reference criteria outlined in the ICRC commentary to common article 3 (*Prosecutor v. Akayesu*, Judgment, Trial Chamber, September 12, 1998, para. 619). This commentary resulted from the various amendments discussed but not adopted during the 1949 Diplomatic Conference in Geneva. The criteria referenced were:

> "1. That the Party in revolt against the de jure Government possesses an organised military force, an authority responsible for its acts, acting within a determinate territory and having the means of respecting and ensuring the respect for the Convention.
> 2. That the legal Government is obliged to have recourse to the regular military forces against insurgents organised as military in possession of a part of the national territory.
> 3.   (a) That the de jure Government has recognised the insurgents as belligerents; or
>   (b) That is has claimed for itself the rights of a belligerent; or
>   (c) That is has accorded the insurgents recognition as belligerents for the purposes only of the present Convention; or
>   (d) That the dispute has been admitted to the agenda of the Security Council or the General Assembly of the United Nations as being a threat to international peace, a breach of peace, or an act of aggression."

Due to the different thresholds of application for common article 3 of the Geneva Conventions and Additional Protocol II to the Geneva Conventions, it is also useful to consider the criteria for the application of Additional Protocol II for some guidance on what is considered to be an internal armed conflict. The ICRC Commentary to the Protocol states:

> "a non-international armed conflict is distinct from an international armed conflict because of the legal status of the parties opposing each other; the parties to the conflict are not sovereign States, but the government of a single State in conflict with one or more armed factions within its territory.
> It is therefore appropriate to raise the question whether all forms of violent opposition to a government, from simple localized rioting to a general confrontation with all the characteristics of a war, can be considered as non-international armed conflicts.
> The expression "armed conflict" gives an important indication in this respect since it introduces a material criterion: the existence of open hostilities between armed forces which are organized to a greater or lesser degree. Internal disturbances, characterized by isolated or sporadic acts of violence, do not therefore constitute armed conflict in a legal sense, even if the government is forced to resort to police forces or even to armed units for the purpose of restoring law and order. Within these limits, non-international armed conflict seems to be a situation in which hostilities break out between armed forces or organized armed groups within the territory of a single State. Insurgents fighting against the established order would normally seek to overthrow the government in power or alternatively to bring about a secession so as to set up a new State" (Jean Pictet (ed.), General Introduction to the Commentary on Protocol II, ICRC, Geneva, pp. 1319–1320).

From this commentary, it would appear that the key indication of an armed conflict, rather than an internal disturbance, is the collective character of the confrontation between forces. A degree of organisation is required from the armed forces which is greater than the actions of isolated individuals without any overarching co-ordination.

To shed further light on the intentions of the drafters of Additional Protocol II, the recommendations of the preparatory commission set up to facilitate its drafting should be examined. In 1971, a Sub-Group of the Working Group at the Conference of Government Experts was established to consider the drafting of the new instruments to supplement the Geneva Conventions. It adopted three criteria that had to be met on the side of the insurgents for the recognition of the existence of an internal armed Conflict, and which were indeed incorporated into the text of article 1 of Protocol II.

(i) *a responsible command*
        According to the ICRC Commentary:

> "The existence of a responsible command implies some degree of organization of the insurgent armed group or dissident armed forces, but this does not necessarily mean that there is a hierarchical system of military organization similar to that of regular armed forces. It means an organization capable, on the one hand of planning and carrying out sustained and concerted military operations, and on the other, of imposing discipline in the name of a de facto authority." (Commentary to Protocol Additional to the Geneva Conventions of 12 August 1949, and relating to the Protection of Victims of Non-International Armed Conflicts (Protocol II), June 8, 1977, para. 4463).

(ii) *such control over part of the territory as to enable them to carry out sustained and concerted military operations and*

> "In many conflicts there is considerable movement in the theatre of hostilities; it often happens that territorial control changes hands rapidly. Sometimes domination of a territory will be relative, for example, when urban centres remain in government hands while rural areas escape their authority. In practical terms, if the insurgent armed groups are organized in accordance with the requirements of the Protocol, the extent of the territory they can claim to control will be that which escapes the control of the government armed forces. However, there must be some degree of stability in the control of even a modest area of land for them to be capable of effectively applying the rules of the Protocol" (Commentary to Protocol Additional to the Geneva Conventions of 12 August 1949, and relating to the Protection of Victims of Non-International Armed Conflicts (Protocol II), June 8, 1977, para. 4467).

Likewise, "sustained" means that the operations are kept going or kept up continuously. The emphasis is therefore on continuity and persistence. "Concerted" means agreed upon, planned and contrived, done in agreement according to a plan *i.e.* They refer to military operations conceived and planned by organized armed groups. (Commentary to Protocol Additional to the Geneva Conventions of 12 August 1949, and relating to the Protection of Victims of Non-International Armed Conflicts (Protocol II), June 8, 1977, paras 4468—4469).

(iii) the ability to implement the Protocol.
According to the ICRC Commentary,

> "This is the fundamental criterion which justifies the other elements of the definition: being under responsible command and in control of a part of the territory concerned, the insurgents must be in a position to implement the Protocol. The threshold for application therefore seems fairly high. Yet apart from the fact that it reflects the desire of the Diplomatic Conference, it must be admitted that this threshold has a degree of realism. The conditions laid down in this para. 1, as analysed above, correspond with actual circumstances in which the parties may reasonably be expected to apply the rules developed in the Protocol, since they have the minimum infrastructure required therefor" (Commentary to Protocol Additional to the Geneva Conventions of 12 August 1949, and relating to the Protection of Victims of Non-International Armed Conflicts (Protocol II), June 8, 1977, para. 4470).

These criteria would appear to restrict the applicability of Additional Protocol II to conflicts of a certain degree of intensity. Thus, not all cases of non-international armed conflict are covered, as is the case with common article 3.

Geographic scope of the armed conflict

11–92   The Geneva Conventions do not specify the geographic scope of a non-international armed conflict. However, in *Tadić* the ICTY held:

> "[T]he fact that beneficiaries of common article 3 of the Geneva Conventions are those taking no active part (or no longer taking active part) in the hostilities [. . .] indicates that the rules contained in article 3 also apply outside the narrow geographical context of the actual theatre of combat operations. Similarly, certain language in Protocol II to the Geneva Conventions also suggests a broad scope" (*Prosecution v. Tadić*, Decision on the Defence Motion for Interlocutory Appeal on Jurisdiction, Appeals Chamber, October 2, 1995, para. 60).

It concluded that: "until [a peaceful settlement is achieved], international humanitarian law continues to apply . . . in the whole territory under the control of a party, whether or not actual combat takes place there" (*Prosecution v. Tadić*, Decision on the Defence Motion for Interlocutory Appeal on Jurisdiction, Appeals Chamber, October 2, 1995, para. 70).

This Appeals Chamber test was later applied by the Trial Chamber in its judgment to find that an armed conflict did exist in the geographic area under consideration. It stated:

> "In considering the conflict relating to the events in Opstina Prijedor, the Trial Chamber is not . . . bound to confine its attention to the immediate area of that Opstina or to the time of the alleged offence but may consider the ongoing conflict between the Government of the Republic of Bosnia and Herzegovina and the Bosnian Serb forces in its entirety" (*Prosecutor v. Tadić*, Judgment, Trial Chamber, May 7, 1997, para. 566).

This approach is confirmed in *Blaškić*, which stated "it is not necessary to establish the existence of an armed conflict within each municipality concerned. It suffices to establish the existence of a conflict within the whole region of which the municipalities are a part" (*Prosecutor v. Blaškić*, Judgment, Trial Chamber, March 3, 2000, para. 64).

B. INTERNATIONAL ARMED CONFLICT AND PROTECTED PERSONS' STATUS

(1) Requirements of the grave breaches provisions

The early Conventions were clearly adopted in the context of wars **11–93** waged between States. It became apparent over the course of the twentieth century, however, that if International Humanitarian Law was to retain its full effectiveness, its protection would have to be extended to armed conflicts not having an international character, or internal conflicts. The ICTY Appeals Chamber described the process whereby State practice came to accept the applicability of certain basic rules to internal armed conflict (*Prosecutor v. Tadic*, Decision on the Defence Motion for Interlocutory Appeal on Jurisdiction, Appeals Chamber, October 2, 1995, paras 96—102). The 1949 Geneva Conventions recognised this development by the inclusion of common Article 3, which is applicable to such conflicts.

While the 1949 Geneva Conventions explicitly extended the ambit of certain basic rules to internal conflicts, they also reinforced the distinction between the two bodies of law by making the grave breaches regime applicable only in the context of international armed conflicts (see common Article 2 of the Geneva Conventions). The "universal mandatory criminal jurisdiction among contracting States" (*Tadić* Jurisdiction Decision, para. 79) created by the grave breaches provisions of the 1949 Geneva Conventions concerns only those who commit the specified offences in the course of an international armed conflict and only when committed against persons or property "protected" by the four Conventions. "Protected" status refers to the fact that to enjoy the protection offered by the mandatory punishment mechanism contained in the grave breaches provisions, the requirements prescribed under each Convention must be met. A civilian victim of the conflict must be "in the hands of a Party to the conflict or Occupying Power of which they are not nationals" (Fourth Geneva Convention 1949, Article 4). Each of the four 1949 Conventions lists those who are "protected" under each Convention.

The "protected person" element is thus interlinked with the inter- **11–94** nationality requirement. Aside from the grave breaches provisions, there are other offences that are only prohibited in international armed conflict, although few of them have been charged before the ICTY. The "conduct of hostilities" offences, unlawful attacks on civilians and civilian objects, are prohibited in both conflicts, and the classification of the conflict does not arise.

Establishing the character of the Yugoslav conflict has been a thorny issue. Its classification was essential to determining which body of international humanitarian law was applicable: the body of law for international conflicts or that for internal conflicts. This issue never arose in the Rwandan context as the conflict was considered entirely internal. The ICTR Statute contains no offences for international armed conflict.

(2) Jurisprudence

11–95   Following a drawn out process, commencing in 1995, and spanning some five cases and nearly the same number of years, the Appeals Chamber settled the internationality and protected persons issues in its *Tadić* judgment of July 15, 1999, at para. 80. The Trial Chamber had acquitted the Accused/Appellant in *Tadić* on all grave breach charges under Article 2 of the ICTY Statute on the basis that the victims referred to in those counts had not been proved to be "protected persons".

In determining the applicability of Article 2, and thus of the grave breaches regime, in the case before it, the Trial Chamber in *Tadić* reached its conclusion by examining whether the victims of the alleged crimes were in the hands of a party to the conflict of which they were not nationals. The Chamber relied upon the ICJ's formulation in the *Nicaragua Case* of "effective control" in order to determine whether one State, the Federal Republic of Yugoslavia (Serbia and Montenegro) ("FRY") and its army, the VJ, were in control of the army of Republika Srpska, the VRS. If this were found to be the case, the victims of the actions of the VRS would effectively be in the hands of the FRY, a State of which they were not nationals, and thus "protected persons". The Chamber concluded (Judge McDonald dissenting) that, although the FRY provided the VRS with logistical support, *matériel* and even officers, the necessary "effective control" had not been proved.

11–96   The Appeals Chamber reversed this decision holding that the concept of "protected person" implicitly refers to a test of control; the only question was the form and extent such control should take. Finding that the test adopted by the ICJ was not consonant with the logic of the law of State responsibility and was not supported by judicial and State practice, it adopted instead the less stringent test of "overall control":

> "In order to attribute the acts of a military or paramilitary group to a State, it must be proved that the State wields overall control over the group, not only by equipping and financing the group, but also by coordinating or helping in the general planning of its military activity. Only then can the State be held internationally accountable for any misconduct of the group. However, it is not necessary that, in addition, the State should also issue, either to the head or to members of the group, instructions for the commission of specific acts contrary to international law" (*Prosecutor v. Tadić*, Judgment, Appeals Chamber, July 15, 1999, para. 131).

Using this legal finding, and on the basis of the factual evidence that the Trial Chamber had accepted as having been proved, the Appeals Chamber concluded that the Prosecution had succeeded in establishing that the Yugoslav Army (VJ) was in overall control of Bosnian Serb forces (VRS):

> "Such control manifested itself not only in financial, logistical and other assistance and support, but also, and more importantly, in terms of

participation in the general direction, coordination and supervision of the activities and operations of the VRS. This sort of control is sufficient for the purposes of the legal criteria required by international law" (*Prosecutor v. Tadić*, Judgment, Appeals Chamber, July 15, 1999, , para. 156).

The Trial Chamber in the subsequent *Blaškić* decision (*Prosecutor v. Blaškić*, Judgment, March 3, 2000, para. 75), followed this test for establishing whether or not a particular conflict is international or internal. The Appeals Chamber again confirmed the reasoning of the *Tadić* Appeal Judgment in *Prosecutor v. Delalic et al.*, Judgment, February 20, 2001, para. 26. Also see, *Prosecutor v. Blaškić*, Judgment, Appeals Chamber, July 29, 2004, para. 170. ("In order for the International Tribunal to prosecute an individual for grave breaches of the Geneva Conventions under Article 2 of the Statute, the offence must be committed, *inter alia*: (i) in the context of an international armed conflict; and (ii) against persons or property defined as 'protected' under the Geneva Conventions.") **11–97**

(3) Nationality

In the *Delalic et al.* case, the Trial Chamber considered in some detail the position of civilians in the context of violent State succession in which the dictates of domestic nationality legislation were not clear. The Trial Chamber held that it would not rely solely on a formal requirement of nationality: **11–98**

"The provisions of domestic legislation on citizenship in a situation of violent State succession cannot be determinative of the protected status of persons caught up in conflicts which ensue from such events. The Commentary to the Fourth Geneva Convention charges us not to forget that 'the Conventions have been drawn up first and foremost to protect individuals, and not to serve State interests' and thus it is the view of this Trial Chamber that their protections should be applied to as broad a category of persons as possible. It would, indeed, be contrary to the intention of the Security Council, which was concerned with effectively addressing a situation that it had determined to be a threat to international peace and security, and with ending the suffering of all those caught up in the conflict, for the International Tribunal to deny the application of the Fourth Geneva Convention to any particular group of persons solely on the basis of their citizenship status under domestic law" (*Prosecutor v. Delalic et al.*, Judgment, Trial Chamber, November 16, 1998, para. 263, footnotes omitted).

The case concerned Bosnian Serb civilians (the Trial Chamber determined that the internees did not qualify for prisoner-of-war status) who had been captured and interned by armed forces of the Bosnian Government. The captives had the same nationality (Bosnian) as their captors and could, strictly speaking, not qualify as "protected persons". The broader interpretation of nationality, however, precipitated its finding that the Bosnian Serb victims were protected persons, thereby setting a precedent to be followed in other cases. **11–99**

The Appeals Chamber in *Delalic et al.*, building on the statement in the *Tadić* Appeal Judgment (para. 165) that "already in 1949 the legal bond of nationality was not regarded as crucial and allowance was made for special cases", confirmed the reasoning of the Trial Chamber. It held that the nationality requirement of the Fourth Geneva Convention should "be interpreted within the framework of humanitarian law" (*Prosecutor v. Delalic et al.*, Judgment, Appeals Chamber, February 20, 2001, para. 75) and that the dictates of national law on the issue were merely facts which assisted the Tribunal in coming to a decision based on international law (paras 76–77). Also see, paras 82–83, 98; *Tadić* Appeal Judgment, para. 166.

11–100   On the Croatian side of the conflict in Bosnia the same questions were clarified in the decisions in the *Prosecutor v. Blaškić*, Judgment, Trial Chamber, March 3, 2000, and *Prosecutor v. Kordić and Čerkez*, Judgment, Trial Chamber, February 26, 2001. Also see, *Prosecutor v. Blaškić*, Judgment, Appeal Chamber, July 29, 2004, paras 170–182; *Prosecutor v. Kordić and Čerkez*, Judgment, Appeals Chamber, December 17, 2004, paras 322–323, 328–331.

Both cases involved the activities of the armed forces of the Bosnian Croats, the Croatian Defence Council ("HVO"), in the Lasva Valley of central Bosnia. The Chambers presiding over these cases had to determine whether the conflicts between the Bosnian Croats and Bosnian Muslims, in which the alleged crimes were committed, had been internal or international.

(4) Definition of internationality

11–101   The *Blaškić* Trial Chamber took as its starting point the dictum in the *Tadić* Appeal Judgment that an internal conflict on the territory of a State could become international if "(i) another State intervenes in that conflict through its troops, or alternatively if (ii) some of the participants in the internal armed conflict act on behalf of that other State" (*Tadić* Appeal Judgment, para. 84). It examined both means of demonstrating the internationality of a conflict.

The Trial Chamber found ample evidence of Croatia's direct intervention in Bosnia-Herzegovina, relying in the process on the testimony of several witnesses who had seen either units or officers of the Croatian Army ("HV") on active service in the accused's zone of command. The Trial Chamber also cited contemporaneous correspondence from Bosnian officials to the UN and other bodies complaining of the presence and activities of Croatian troops in Bosnia as evidence of the international nature of the conflict. UN Security Council resolutions also confirmed the presence of Croatian troops in Bosnia in the Trial Chamber's view. Finally, there was evidence of the existence of orders to members of the HV in the accused's zone of command that they should remove their HV insignia so that observers would not detect their presence in Bosnia-Herzegovina.

11–102   The Trial Chamber then considered the second leg of the internationality test. As evidence of Croatia's overall control over the HVO and, hence, of the indirect intervention of Croatia in Bosnia-Herzegovina, the Trial Chamber accepted evidence of a number of factors.

First, the direct intervention discussed above as evidence of "overall control".

Secondly, the Trial Chamber analysed the territorial ambitions which Croatia had harboured for some time over the territory of Bosnia-Herzegovina and, connected thereto, the fact that the HVO shared this goal of a greater Croatia which would include large swathes of Bosnian territory. While the Trial Chamber accepted in principle the notion that the personal ambition of a leader, in this case President Tudjman of Croatia, should be separated from the official position of the State, it held that in an authoritarian regime like Croatia at the time, this distinction could not apply.

Thirdly, the Trial Chamber noted that the shared goals mentioned had consequences on the "decision-making mechanism of the Croatian Community of Herceg-Bosna (hereinafter the 'HZHB')" (para. 110). By this it meant that Croatia was able to control the Bosnian Croats either through officers in the region or via the Bosnian Croats who shared its goals.

Fourthly, the Trial Chamber accepted that the HDZ ruling party in Croatia had overall control of its local counterpart in Bosnia-Herzegovina. The Trial Chamber also found established a high degree of political co-ordination between the respective leaders of Croatia and of the Bosnian Croats and noted that Bosnian Croat leaders who did not share Croatia's (or Tudjman's) aims were replaced by loyal leaders.

Lastly, the Trial Chamber placed considerable reliance on military aspects of Croatia's overall control. It accepted that the HVO shared personnel, at all levels, with the HV. Further, Croatia provided the Bosnian Croats with financial and logistical support as well as large quantities of arms and material. HVO troops were trained in Croatia.

Together these factors were sufficient to establish Croatia's overall control over the Bosnian Croats and confirm the internationality of the conflict.

On appeal, the Appellant did "not challenge the Trial Chamber's findings regarding the international character of the conflict" (*Blaškić* Appeal Judgment, para. 171).

In the *Kordić and Čerkez* case, the Prosecution presented the Trial **11–103** Chamber with similar evidence of Croatia's direct and indirect involvement in the conflict. While the Trial Chamber did not accept that Croatian troops had been sighted in central Bosnia, it nevertheless found that Croatia's direct involvement had been established. Importantly, it held that such direct involvement could be established not only by placing Croatia's troops in the immediate area of the conflict (the accused's zone of command), but also by placing them in adjacent areas where their presence played a strategic role. The Trial Chamber accepted that this element had been proved by showing, for instance, that Croatian troops had been deployed in adjacent areas to fight the Bosnian Serbs which had the effect of freeing up Bosnian Croats (the HVO) to intensify their combat with the Bosnian Muslims.

In respect of Croatia's indirect intervention in the conflict between the Bosnian Croats and Muslims, the Trial Chamber divided the *Tadić* Appeals Chamber's test into two parts: the provision of assistance; and, the participation by Croatia in the organisation, co-ordination and planning of the HVO's military operations (para. 115). Relying on the Prosecution's evidence which was essentially the same as the evidence led in the *Blaškić* case, the Trial Chamber found the conflict to have been internationalised by Croatia's overall control of the HVO (para. 146).

The Appeals Chamber upheld the overall control test (*Prosecutor v. Kordić and Čerkez*, Judgment, Appeals Chamber, December 17, 2004, paras 306–307). However, it considered the evidence insufficient to prove "that Croatia directly intervened in the armed conflict in Central Bosnia" (para. 355) and "that Croatian troops were indeed sent to Central Bosnia" (para. 360). Regarding the Trial Chamber's two-part test for indirect intervention, the Appeals Chamber ruled that the criteria were satisfied (para. 361) and "that Croatia exercised overall control over the HVO at the relevant time" (para. 369). The Appeals Chamber also considered "that Croatia provided logistical support to the forces of both the HVO and the ABiH" but in "two different armed conflicts, i.e. the one of the HVO and the ABiH against the Serbs, and the one between the HVO and the ABiH" (para. 372). Despite the provision of assistance to two parties, the Appeals Chamber found it did "not affect the question of whether Croatia participated in the organisation, coordination or planning of military operations by the HVO" and that Croatia could have supported both parties logistically while only controlling the HVO (para. 372). Lastly, the Appeals Chamber considered that the fact that Croatia and Bosnia-Herzegovina denied the existence of a state of war between them could not "rule out the characterisation of the conflict as being international" (para. 373). The Appeals Chamber thus upheld "the Trial Chamber's finding that the armed conflict between the HVO and the ABiH was international in character" (para. 374).

(5) Prisoners of war

11–104   Article 4(A) of Geneva Convention III sets out the requirements for the achievement of prisoner of war status:

"Prisoners of war, in the sense of the present Convention, are persons belonging to one of the following categories, who have fallen into the power of the enemy:
(1) Members of the armed forces of a Party to the conflict, as well as members of militias or volunteer corps forming part of such armed forces.
(2) Members of other militias and members of other volunteer corps, including those of organized resistance movements, belonging to a Party to the conflict and operating in or outside their own territory, even if this territory is occupied, provided that such militias or volunteer corps, including such organised resistance movements, fulfil the following conditions:
   (a) that of being commanded by a person responsible for his subordinates;
   (b) that of having a fixed distinctive sign recognizable at a distance;
   (c) that of carrying arms openly;
   (d) that of conducting their operations in accordance with the laws and customs of war.
(3) Members of regular armed forces who profess allegiance to a government or an authority not recognized by the Detaining Power.
(4) Persons who accompany the armed forces without actually being members thereof, such as civilian members of military aircraft crews, war correspondents, supply contractors, members of labour

units or of services responsible for the welfare of the armed forces,
provided that they have received authorization, from the armed
forces which they accompany, who shall provide them for that
purpose with an identity card similar to the annexed model.

(5) Members of crews, including masters, pilots and apprentices, of the
merchant marine and crews of civil aircraft of the Parties to the
conflict, who do not benefit by more favourable treatment under any
other provisions of international law.

(6) Inhabitants of a non-occupied territory, who on the approach of the
enemy spontaneously take up arms to resist the invading forces,
without having had time to form themselves into regular armed
units, provided they carry arms openly and respect the laws and
customs of war."

Persons who meet the criteria of any of these categories are
protected by Geneva Convention III as prisoners of war. Unlike for
civilians, the nationality of the victim is not relevant in determining
"protected person" status.

These provisions are supplemented and modified by Articles 43
("Armed forces") and 44 ("Combatants and prisoners or war") of
Additional Protocol I. In particular, Article 44(3) of Additional Protocol
I states:

"In order to promote the protection of the civilian population from the
effects of hostilities, combatants are obliged to distinguish themselves
from the civilian population while they are engaged in an attack or in a
military operation preparatory to an attack. Recognizing, however, that
there are situations in armed conflicts where, owing to the nature of the
hostilities an armed combatant cannot so distinguish himself, he shall
retain his status as a combatant, provided that, in such situations, he
carries his arms openly:
(a) during each military engagement, and
(b) during such time as he is visible to the adversary while he is
engaged in a military deployment preceding the launching of an
attack in which he is to participate."

Furthermore, Article 44(4) provides protection even if these require-   **11–105**
ments are not fulfilled:

"A combatant who falls into the power of an adverse Party while failing to
meet the requirements set forth in the second sentence of para. 3 shall
forfeit his right to be a prisoner of war, but he shall, nevertheless, be given
protections equivalent in all respects to those accorded to prisoners of war
by the Third Convention and by this Protocol. This protection includes
protections equivalent to those accorded to prisoners of war by the Third
Convention in the case where such a person is tried and punished for any
offences he has committed."

There is no "prisoner of war" status in internal conflict, and
Additional Protocol II does not contain any provisions on the subject.

In the judgment in the *Delalic et al.* case, the Trial Chamber
considered whether any of the victims qualified as prisoners of war,
holding that it is "difficult, on the evidence presented to it, to conclude
that any of the victims [. . .] satisfied these requirements. While it is
apparent that some of the persons detained [. . .] had been in possession of weapons and may be considered to have participated to some
degree in 'hostilities', this is not sufficient to render them entitled to

prisoner of war status" (para. 269). In addition, the Trial Chamber was "not convinced that the [. . .] detainees constituted a *levée en masse*. This concept refers to a situation where territory has not yet been occupied, but is being invaded by an external force, and the local inhabitants of areas in the line of this invasion take up arms to resist and defend their homes [. . .] Article 4(A)(6) undoubtedly places a somewhat high burden on local populations to behave as if they were professional soldiers" (para. 270; also, see *Kordić and Čerkez*, Appeal Judgment, paras 48–51).

The Chamber noted that in international armed conflict there is no gap "between the Third and Fourth Geneva Conventions. If an individual is not entitled to the protections of the Third Convention as a prisoner of war [. . .] he or she necessarily falls within the ambit of Convention IV, provided that its article 4 requirements are satisfied" (para. 271). Also see, Article 50 of Additional Protocol I; Article 5 of Geneva Convention IV; and Article 5 of Geneva Convention III, which requires that where there is any doubt whether a person belongs to any of the recognised prisoner of war categories, he must be granted the protection of the Convention until his status is determined by a competent tribunal.

C. Offences Prohibited in all Conflicts

11–106   As mentioned above, the laws prohibiting war crimes have traditionally been divided between those applicable to international (inter-State) and to internal (domestic) armed conflicts. Most notably, the scheme of the 1949 Geneva Conventions distinguishes between breaches punishable during international conflict and the more limited set of rules that apply during non-international conflict as provided for in Article 3 common to all four of the Geneva Conventions. The 1977 Protocols additional to the Geneva Conventions re-enforce this classification: Additional Protocol I applies to international armed conflicts, whereas Additional Protocol II applies to internal armed conflicts.

The separation between the laws applicable to international and internal conflicts has, however, increasingly been viewed as blurred. Under the Geneva Conventions and Additional Protocols, many of the same war crimes are prohibited in both kinds of conflicts. For example, crimes during internal conflict are also crimes during international conflict; the lesser is thus included in the greater.

11–107   More significantly, it is now accepted that certain rules apply irrespective of the nature of the conflict. The ICTY Appeals Chamber's *Tadić* Jurisdiction Decision established that while Article 2 of the ICTY Statute undoubtedly applies only to international armed conflicts (para. 84), this does not mean that Article 3 of the Statute therefore applies only to internal conflicts. Article 3 incorporates all serious violations of international humanitarian law other than the offences specifically mentioned under the Statute's other heads of jurisdiction *ratione materiae* (see *Tadić* Jurisdiction Decision, paras 89–93). The Appeals Chamber found that Article 3 of the Statute included common Article 3 to the Geneva Conventions and that the prohibitions contained in common Article 3 are applicable under customary international law to all conflicts, whether international or internal: "with respect to the minimum rules in common Article 3, the character of the conflict is irrelevant" (*Tadić* Jurisdiction Decision, para. 102). Violations of these rules may be charged under Article 3 of the ICTY Statute for any armed conflict, irrespective of its character. The Prosecutor is, therefore, only required to prove that an armed conflict existed and that the alleged violations were related to such a conflict. It is not necessary for the Prosecutor to prove specifically that the conflict was either international or internal.

Not all rules governing international armed conflict have been extended to apply to internal conflict. When the extension has occurred, it "has not taken place in the form of a full and mechanical transplant [. . .] rather, the general essence of those rules, and not the detailed regulation they may contain, has become applicable to internal conflicts" (*Tadić* Jurisdiction Decision, para. 126). Article 3 of the Statute thus includes both violations that apply to all conflicts (such as common Article 3) and those that apply only in international armed conflict. The other offences which can be charged under Article 3 of the Statute irrespective of the nature of the conflict are unlawful attacks on civilians and civilian objects, including cultural property, "as well as prohibition of means of warfare proscribed in international armed conflicts and ban of certain methods of conducting hostilities" (see *Tadić* Jurisdiction Decision, para. 127).

V. GRAVE BREACHES OF THE GENEVA CONVENTIONS

A. WILFUL KILLING

The elements of the grave breach of wilful killing were set out in the *Celebici* case (*Prosecutor v. Delalic et al.*, Judgment, Trial Chamber, November 16, 1998). The accused were charged with both "wilful killing" under Article 2 and with "murder" under Article 3, a common practice followed in numerous other cases (see, *Delalic et al.* Appeal Judgment, para. 400, on the rationale for cumulative charging). The Trial Chamber first determined that there is no qualitative distinction between the two concepts; they differ only in the jurisdictional requirements. The rationale the Trial Chamber followed was that "the primary purpose of common article 3 [. . .] was to extend 'the elementary considerations of humanity' to internal armed conflicts" (para. 423). Therefore, just "as it is prohibited to kill protected persons in international armed conflict, so it is prohibited to kill those taking no active part in hostilities which constitute an internal armed conflict. In this spirit of equality of protection, there can be no reason to attach meaning to the difference of terminology utilised in common article 3 and the articles referring to 'grave breaches' of the Conventions" (para. 423).

As for the elements of the grave breach of "wilful killing", the Trial Chamber held in respect of the physical act required that the death of

11–108

the victim constitutes the *actus reus*, the substantial cause of which is the act or omission of the accused (para. 424). In respect of the *mens rea* the Trial Chamber concluded as follows:

> "the Trial Chamber is in no doubt that the necessary intent, meaning *mens rea*, required to establish the crimes of wilful killing and murder, as recognised in the Geneva Conventions, is present where there is demonstrated an intention on the part of the accused to kill, or inflict serious injury in reckless disregard of human life" (para. 439).

It is important to note, as the Trial Judgment in *Delalic et al.* demonstrated that there are numerous ways of describing the elements of "wilful killing" (or "murder"). The specific usages of national jurisdictions can also complicate the matter. For instance, while the Trial Chamber in the *Blaškić* Judgment accepted the analysis of the *Delalic et al.* Judgment, it described the elements a little differently:

> "For the material element of the offence, it must be proved that the death of the victim was the result of the actions of the accused as a commander. The intent, or *mens rea*, needed to establish the offence of wilful killing exists once it has been demonstrated that the accused intended to cause death or serious bodily injury which, as it is reasonable to assume, he had to understand was likely to lead to death" (*Prosecutor v. Blaškić*, Judgment, Trial Chamber, March 3, 2000, para. 153).

The Appeals Chamber in *Delalic et al.* considered cumulative convictions under both Articles 2 and 3 of the ICTY Statute for crimes arising out of the same acts. The Appeals Chamber held:

> "reasons of fairness to the accused and the consideration that only distinct crimes may justify multiple convictions, lead to the conclusion that multiple criminal convictions entered under different statutory provisions but based on the same conduct are permissible only if each statutory provision involved has a materially distinct element not contained in the other. An element is materially distinct from another if it requires proof of a fact not required by the other" (para. 412).

The Appeals Chamber defined the grave breach of wilful killing as consisting of the following elements:

> "a. death of the victim as the result of the action(s) of the accused,
> b. who intended to cause death or serious bodily injury which, as it is reasonable to assume, he had to understand was likely to lead to death,
> c. and which he committed against a protected person" (para. 422, footnote omitted).

As such, "[t]he definition of wilful killing under Article 2 contains a materially distinct element not present in the definition of murder under Article 3: the requirement that the victim be a protected person. This requirement necessitates proof of a fact not required by the elements of murder [under Article 3], because the definition of a protected person includes, yet goes beyond what is meant by an individual taking no active part in the hostilities" (para. 423).

For the element of murder applicable before the Special Panel for Serious Crimes for East Timor see *Prosecutor v. Fernandez*, Judgment, February 27, 2001; and *Prosecutor v. Carmona*, Judgment, April 19, 2001.

B. TORTURE OR INHUMAN TREATMENT

The offence of torture as a grave breach has been included in **11–109** numerous indictments before the ICTY but the judgments rendered by the different Trial Chambers have not always been consistent. The *Delalic et al.* Trial Judgment states that the "torture of persons not taking an active part in hostilities is absolutely prohibited by the Geneva Conventions, both in internal and international armed conflicts" (para. 446). It added that torture is prohibited by both conventional and customary international law, and supported this conclusion by an extensive analysis of international conventions and the jurisprudence of international and regional human rights courts and bodies (paras 452–454). It further stated that the prohibition of torture is a norm of *jus cogens* (para. 454; also see, *Furundžija* Trial Judgment, paras 144, 153–157). The Trial Chamber accepted that the definition of torture provided by the Convention against Torture and Other Cruel, Inhuman or Degrading Treatment or Punishment, 1984 ("the Torture Convention"), had achieved the status of customary international law (para. 459).

The requisite elements for a finding of torture were set out as **11–110** follows:

"In view of the above discussion, the Trial Chamber therefore finds that the elements of torture, for the purposes of applying Articles 2 and 3 of the Statute, may be enumerated as follows:
(i) There must be an act or omission that causes severe pain or suffering, whether mental or physical,
(ii) which is inflicted intentionally,
(iii) and for such purposes as obtaining information or a confession from the victim, or a third person, punishing the victim for an act he or she or a third person has committed or is suspected of having committed, intimidating or coercing the victim or a third person, or for any reason based on discrimination of any kind,
(iv) and such act or omission being committed by, or at the instigation of, or with the consent or acquiescence of, an official or other person acting in an official capacity" (*Prosecutor v. Delalic et al.*, Judgment, Trial Chamber, November 16, 1998, para. 494).

The Trial Chamber rejected the contention by the Defence that the **11–111** motive for torture be restricted to the obtaining of confessions or information from the victim and accepted the broader category of purposes mentioned in part (iii). In addition, it accepted that as long as it complied with the requirements set out in the definition, rape would constitute torture, and could be charged as such (*Prosecutor v. Delalic et al.*, Judgment, Trial Chamber, November 16, 1998, para. 496; also see, paras 475–493). Finally, the Trial Chamber accepted that the requirement of the torture being committed by a State official could be interpreted as including officials of non-State parties (para. 473). This was to ensure protection for potential victims of torture in internal armed conflicts (if charged under Article 3 common to the Geneva Conventions and Article 3 of the ICTY Statute).

The Trial Chamber in the *Foca* case (*Prosecutor v. Kunarac et al.*, **11–112** Judgment, February 22, 2001) did not agree completely with the approach adopted by the *Celebici* Trial Chamber in *Delalic et al.* in one respect. Although the charges of torture in this case were brought under Articles 3 and 5 of the Statute, the discussion of the definition of torture is equally relevant to the grave breaches. While the Trial Chamber accepted that the definition of torture provided in the Torture Convention did indeed reflect customary international law, it held that it did so for purposes of the Convention and the protection of human rights only, and that International Humanitarian Law, containing penal elements, was not necessarily restricted to applying the same standards. The element the Trial Chamber queried was the requirement that the perpetrator of the torture had to be a State official or someone acting in an official capacity:

"The Trial Chamber concludes that the definition of torture under international humanitarian law does not comprise the same elements as the definition of torture generally applied under human rights law. In particular, the Trial Chamber is of the view that the presence of a state official or of any other authority-wielding person in the torture process is not necessary for the offence to be regarded as torture under international humanitarian law.

On the basis of what has been said, the Trial Chamber holds that, in the field of international humanitarian law, the elements of the offence of torture, under customary international law are as follows:

(i) The infliction, by act or omission, of severe pain or suffering, whether physical or mental.
(ii) The act or omission must be intentional.
(iii) The act or omission must aim at obtaining information or a confession, or at punishing, intimidating or coercing the victim or a third person, or at discriminating, on any ground, against the victim or a third person" (*Prosecutor v. Kunarac et al.*, Judgment, Trial Chamber, February 22, 2001, paras 496–497, footnotes omitted).

The Trial Chamber in *Furundžija* added that "from the specific viewpoint of international criminal law relating to armed conflicts," the torture "must be linked to an armed conflict" as a fourth element of the definition and "at least one of the persons involved in the torture process must be a public official or must at any rate act in a non-private capacity, *e.g.* as a de facto organ of a State or any other authority-wielding entity" as a fifth element (*Prosecutor v. Furundžija*, Judgment, Trial Chamber, December 10, 1998, para. 162, *affirmed Prosecutor v. Furundžija*, Judgment, Appeals Chamber, July 21, 2000, para. 111).

11–113 The judgment of the Appeals Chamber in the *Foca* case has clarified the issue to some extent (*Prosecutor v. Kunarac et al.*, Judgment, Appeals Chamber, June 12, 2002, paras 142–148). The Appeals Chamber distinguished the statement by the Appeals Chamber in its earlier decision in the *Furundžija* Appeal Judgment to the effect that at least one of the persons involved in the torture must be a public official or at least act in a non-private capacity. It did so on the basis that, while this statement was unobjectionable in the realm of human rights law and State responsibility, it did not "wholly reflect [. . .] customary international law regarding the meaning of the crime of torture generally" (para. 147). The Appeals Chamber noted:

"The Trial Chamber in the present case was therefore right in taking the position that the public official requirement is not a requirement under customary international law in relation to the criminal responsibility of an individual for torture outside of the framework of the Torture Convention. However, the Appeals Chamber notes that the Appellants in the present case did not raise the issue as to whether a person acting in a private capacity could be found guilty of the crime of torture; nor did the Trial Chamber have the benefit of argument on the issue of whether that question was the subject of previous consideration by the Appeals Chamber" (*Prosecutor v. Kunarac et al.*, Appeals Judgment, para. 148).

Regarding the difference between torture under Article 2 and under Article 3, the Appeals Chamber in *Delalic et al.* held, "Because the term itself is identical under both provisions, the sole distinguishing element stems from the protected person requirement under Article 2. As a result, torture under Article 2 contains an element requiring proof of a fact not required by torture under Article 3, but the reverse is not the case" (*Prosecutor v. Delalic et al.*, Judgment, Appeals Chamber, February 20, 2001, para. 425).

The closely related grave breach of "inhuman treatment" was also considered in the *Delalic et al.* Trial Judgment. The Trial Chamber noted that inhuman treatment, like torture, is forbidden by both conventional and customary international law. The same instruments that outlaw torture also prohibit inhuman treatment. The Trial Chamber accepted the basic premise that inhuman treatment is treatment which is not humane and agreed with the Commentary to the Fourth Geneva Convention (Ed. Jean S. Pictet, ICRC, 1958, at p. 204, "ICRC Commentary on GC IV") that "treatment"   **11–114**

"'must be understood here in its most general sense as applying to all aspect's of a man's life . . . The purpose of this Convention is simply to define the correct way to behave towards a human being, who himself wishes to receive humane treatment and who may, therefore, also give it to his fellow human beings'" (para. 524, quoting ICRC Commentary on GC IV, at p. 204).

After an extensive review of the jurisprudence of the European Court of Human Rights and the Human Rights Committee, the Trial Chamber stated: **11–115**

"inhuman treatment is an intentional act or omission, that is an act which, judged objectively, is deliberate and not accidental, which causes serious mental or physical suffering or injury or constitutes a serious attack on human dignity" (para. 543).

Furthermore, Article 2 (grave breaches) requires that inhuman treatment be committed against a protected person (*Delalic et al.* Appeal Judgment, para. 426, *quoted in Blaškić* Appeal Judgment, para. 665; also see, *Kordić and Čerkez* Appeal Judgment, para. 39).

The Trial Chamber in the *Blaškić* Trial Judgment has also accepted this definition (para. 154), including that "inhuman treatment" can encompass acts which also form parts of other offences, such as torture and violations of the principle of humane treatment (para. 155; also see, *Delalic et al.* Trial Judgment, para. 544). The Trial Chamber in *Blaškić* agreed that whether a particular act constitutes inhuman treatment is a factual question to be decided on the basis of all the circumstances in a particular case (para. 155; also see, *Delalic et al.* Trial

Judgment, para. 544). It is evident that while torture can constitute inhuman treatment, and such treatment can amount to torture, these offences are also qualitatively different. Torture requires a "prohibited purpose" (such as the extraction of information), whereas this is not a prerequisite for an act to constitute inhuman treatment (see, *Delalic et al.* Trial Judgment, para. 542).

In *Blaškić*, the Appeals Chamber affirmed the Appellant's conviction for inhuman treatment by using detainees as human shields on the basis of an omission by the Appellant. The Appeals Chamber found:

> "in the absence of proof that he positively ordered the use of human shields, the Appellant's criminal responsibility is properly expressed as an omission . . . The Appeals Chamber accordingly finds that the elements constituting the crime of inhuman treatment have been met: there was an omission to care for protected persons which was deliberate and not accidental, caused serious mental harm, and constituted a serious attack on human dignity" (para. 670).

Upon affirming the conviction for inhuman treatment under Article 2, the Appeals Chamber dismissed the conviction under Article 3 because "[a] conviction for cruel treatment under Article 3 does not require proof of a fact not required by Article 2" (para. 671). The Appeals Chamber "considered the sole distinguishing element between Article 2 (inhuman treatment) and Article 3 (cruel treatment): that the former contains the protected person status of the victim as an element not present in the latter" (*Blaškić* Appeal Judgment, para. 671, footnotes omitted). It noted that the "protected person" definition under Article 4 of Geneva Convention IV "has been extended to [. . .] apply to bonds of ethnicity" (para. 671, footnote omitted).

C. WILFULLY CAUSING GREAT SUFFERING OR SERIOUS INJURY TO BODY OR HEALTH

11–116　　　The ICRC Commentary on Geneva Convention IV, at p. 599, explains that this grave breach "refers to suffering inflicted without the ends in view for which torture is inflicted or biological experiments carried out". Several cases before the ICTY have dealt with this offence. In the *Celebici* case, the Trial Chamber, rejecting the prosecution's submission that this provision of the Statute encompassed two, separate offences, decided that it was, in fact, one offence, the elements of which are framed in the alternative (*Delalic et al.*, Judgment, Trial Chamber, November 16, 1998, para. 506). The Trial Chamber referred to the ICRC Commentary and confirmed that the distinguishing feature of torture was the prohibited purpose of the offence (para. 508). It also held that the suffering incurred can be mental or physical (para. 509).

The Trial Chamber held that the offence constitutes:

> "an act or omission that is intentional, being an act which, judged objectively, is deliberate and not accidental, which causes serious mental or physical suffering or injury. It covers those acts that do not meet the

purposive requirements for the offence of torture, although clearly all acts constituting torture could also fall within the ambit of this offence" (*Delalic et al.*, Trial Judgment, para. 511).

As with the other grave breaches, wilfully causing great suffering or serious injury to body or health must be committed against a protected person (*Delalic et al.* Appeal Judgment, para. 424). This requirement distinguishes this offence from that of cruel treatment under Article 3, which requires that it be "committed against a person taking no active part in the hostilities" (*Delalic et al.* Appeal Judgment, para. 424).

The Trial Chamber in *Blaškić* accepted the Trial Chamber's pronouncements in *Delalic et al.* (*Blaškić*, Trial Judgment, para. 156). In the *Kordić and Čerkez* Trial Judgment, the Trial Chamber adopted essentially the same definition of the offence, but distinguished it from inhuman treatment:

> "This crime is distinguished from that of inhuman treatment in that it requires a showing of serious mental or physical injury. Thus, acts where the resultant harm relates solely to an individual's human dignity are not included within this offence" (*Prosecutor v. Kordić and Čerkez*, Judgment, Trial Chamber, February 26, 2001, para. 245).

D. EXTENSIVE DESTRUCTION AND APPROPRIATION OF PROPERTY, NOT JUSTIFIED BY MILITARY NECESSITY AND CARRIED OUT UNLAWFULLY AND WANTONLY

11–117

This grave breach was extensively considered in the *Blaškić and Kordić and Čerkez* Judgments. Both cases concerned the conflict between Bosnian Croats and Bosnian Muslims in Central Bosnia during the period 1992 to 1994. The conflict was characterised by alleged attacks on small villages by the HVO and the targeting of Muslim civilians and civilian property. Blaškić had been charged as the commander of the HVO forces in Central Bosnia, whereas Kordic had been charged predominantly in his role as a powerful political figure in the region. The crime base in the two cases was similar.

The accused in *Blaškić* was charged *inter alia* under Articles 2(d), 7(1) and 7(3) of the Statute with having "planned, instigated, ordered or otherwise aided and abetted in the planning, preparation or execution of the wanton and extensive destruction, devastation and plunder of Bosnian Muslim dwellings, buildings, businesses, civilian personal property and livestock" (*Prosecutor v. Blaškić*, Second Amended Indictment, April 25, 1997, para. 10) in a number of towns and villages. The Trial Chamber confirmed that "[t]o constitute a grave breach, the destruction unjustified by military necessity must be extensive, unlawful and wanton" (*Blaškić* Trial Judgment, para. 157).

11–118

The Trial Chamber found, on the basis of the evidence, that the attacks had been planned at a high level of the military hierarchy. Troops had been brought into the area well in advance of the attacks, and warnings had been issued to some witnesses by their Croatian neighbours of an impending attack on the Muslims. Other evidence of the planned nature of the attacks was the fact that Croat inhabitants of some of the villages had been warned and left before the attacks started. The attacks were found to have been carried out with substantial military resources and in a manner that military experts agreed evidenced a high level of planning. The Trial Chamber rejected all evidence by the Defence that the attacks were justified by military imperatives. It held that most of the villages attacked, including Ahmici, which suffered the brunt of the devastation, had little or no strategic importance, hosted no military targets, and were not defended.

11–119   On the other hand, the Trial Chamber accepted that a village like Ahmici held significant cultural importance for the Muslims of the area due to its mosque and the number of religious leaders who came from the area. This was an important factor in the targeting of the village by the HVO and demonstrated the discriminatory nature of the attack. In conclusion, the Trial Chamber held that:

> "The methods of attack and the scale of the crimes committed against the Muslim population or the edifices symbolising their culture sufficed to establish beyond reasonable doubt that the attack was aimed at the Muslim civilian population" (*Blaškić* Judgment, para. 425).

11–120   The evidence relied upon by the Trial Chamber as evidence of the accused's responsibility consisted of orders he had given before the attack which he sought to justify as "defence" orders, *i.e.* orders readying his forces to defend themselves against aggression. The Trial Chamber, however, interpreted them as orders of aggression which launched the attacks on the various villages and towns. The nature of the attacks was also found by the Trial Chamber to support the conclusion that they were committed under orders:

> "Lastly, the idea that these crimes could have been committed by uncontrolled elements is impossible to reconcile with the scale and uniformity of the crimes committed on 16 April in the municipality of Vitez . . . The planned nature and, in particular, the fact that all these units acted in a perfectly co-ordinated manner presupposes in fact that those troops were responding to a single command, which accordingly could only be superior to the commander of each of those units" (*Blaškić* Judgment, para. 467).

The convictions for the destruction and plunder in the Ahmici area (counts 11–13 of the Second Amended Indictment) were overturned on appeal (*Prosecutor v. Blaškić*, Judgment, Appeals Chamber, July 29, 2004). Regarding Blaškić's responsibility under Article 7(1) of the ICTY Statute, the Appeals Chamber considered that the trial evidence and new evidence admitted on appeal pursuant to Rule 115 of the ICTY Rules of Procedure and Evidence did not prove beyond a reasonable doubt that Blaškić had planned and ordered the commission of the crimes (paras 324–348). Regarding his responsibility under Article 7(3) of the ICTY Statute, the Appeals Chamber again considered relevant trial evidence and additional evidence admitted on appeal. It concluded that Blaškić "lacked effective control over the military units responsible for the commission of crimes in the Ahmici area on April 16, 1993, in the sense of a material ability to prevent or punish criminal conduct, and therefore the constituent elements of command responsibility [were] not satisfied" (para. 421).

In the *Kordić and Čerkez* case, the Trial Chamber dealt in more detail with the elements of the crime. This was necessary as the Defence had argued that, save for certain specified property and property in occupied territory, the Geneva Conventions do not provide general protection of property in enemy territory (*Kordić and Čerkez* Trial Judgment, para. 333). There is no definition of the term "occupied territory" in the Geneva Conventions. The Trial Chamber accepted the definition provided in Article 42 of the 1907 Regulations annexed to the Hague Convention IV, which has achieved customary status (paras 338–339):

> "Territory is considered occupied when it is actually placed under the authority of the hostile army. The occupation extends only to the territory where such authority has been established and can be exercised."

The Trial Chamber held that the question whether a particular territory is occupied is one of fact to be decided on a case by case basis. The Trial Chamber set out the following definition of the elements of the grave breach of extensive destruction of property:

11–121

> "(i) Where the property destroyed is of a type accorded general protection under the Geneva Conventions of 1949, regardless of whether or not it is situated in occupied territory; and the perpetrator acted with the intent to destroy the property in question or in reckless disregard of the likelihood of its destruction; or
> (ii) Where the property destroyed is accorded protection under the Geneva Conventions, on account of its location in occupied territory; and the destruction occurs on a large scale; and
> (iii) the destruction is not justified by military necessity; and the perpetrator acted with the intent to destroy the property in question or in reckless disregard of the likelihood of its destruction" (*Kordić and Čerkez* Judgment, para. 341).

The Appeals Chamber noted the Trial Chamber's description of the crime of extensive destruction of property, under the above conditions listed by the Trial Judgment (para. 341), as "constitut[ing] a grave breach of the Geneva Conventions and a crime *qua custom*" (*Prosecutor v. Kordić and Čerkez*, Judgment, Appeals Chamber, December 17, 2004, para. 75). In addition, the Appeals Chamber concluded that the wanton destruction of cities, towns or villages, or devastation not justified by military necessity, in violation of Article 3(b) of the ICTY Statute, was also part of customary international law at the time it was allegedly committed in this case (paras 75–76).

An example of a provision according property general protection as provided for in (i) above is Article 18 of Geneva Convention IV which states, "Civilian hospitals organized to give care to the wounded and sick, infirm and maternity cases, may in no circumstances be the object of an attack but shall at all times be respected and protected by the Parties to the conflict". On the other hand, Article 53 of Geneva Convention IV sets forth the prohibition on the destruction of property in occupied territory, as provided for in (ii) above.

E. COMPELLING A PRISONER OF WAR OR A CIVILIAN TO SERVE IN THE FORCES
OF A HOSTILE POWER

11–122   This grave breach has not as yet been included in any indictment issued by the Prosecutor of the ICTY. The ICRC Commentaries explain that this is an offence *sui generis* and that its historical precedent was Article 23 of the Regulations to the Fourth Hague Convention of 1907, which "forbids a belligerent to compel the nationals of the hostile party to take part in the operations of war directed against their own country, even if they were in the belligerent's service before the commencement of the war" (ICRC Commentary to GC IV at p. 600).

Civilians and prisoners of war (POWs) can be compelled legitimately to undertake certain work. The labour of POWs is regulated by Article 50 of Geneva Convention III:

"Besides work connected with camp administration, installation or main-tenance, prisoners of war may be compelled to do only such work as is included in the following classes:
(a) Agriculture;
(b) Industries connected with the production or extraction of raw materials, and manufacturing industries, with the exception of metallurgical, machinery and chemical industries; public works and building operations which have no military character or purpose;
(c) Transport and handling of stores which are not military in character or purpose;
(d) Commercial business, and arts and crafts;
(e) Domestic service;
(f) Public utility services having no military character or purpose. . ."

11–123   The status of civilian protected persons is regulated according to whether the civilian is an alien in the territory of a party to the conflict or is in occupied territory. The first category of civilian is protected by Article 40 of Geneva Convention IV:

"Protected persons may be compelled to work only to the same extent as nationals of the Party to the conflict in whose territory they are.
If protected persons are of enemy nationality, they may only be compelled to do work which is normally necessary to ensure the feeding, sheltering, clothing, transport and health of human beings and which is not directly related to the conduct of military operations . . ."

11–124   While the Article is based on Article 23 of the Regulations of the Fourth Hague Convention of 1907, Article 40 advances that earlier provision in that it prohibits not only forced participation in the operations of war, but also compulsory enlistment more broadly conceived, *i.e.* forced participation in any work that assists the enemy by feeding and supplying the armed forces (ICRC Commentary to GC IV, at p. 254).

Civilians in occupied territory are covered by Article 51 of Convention IV, which directly prohibits the compulsion to serve in the occupying power's armed forces and regulates the kinds of work permissible:

"The Occupying Power may not compel protected persons to serve in its armed or auxiliary forces. No pressure or propaganda which aims at securing voluntary enlistment is permitted.

The Occupying Power may not compel protected persons to work unless they are over eighteen years of age, and then only on work which is necessary either for the needs of the army of occupation, or for the public utility services, or for the feeding, sheltering, clothing, transportation or health of the population of the occupied country. Protected persons may not be compelled to undertake any work which would involve them in the obligation of taking part in military operations. The Occupying Power may not compel protected persons to employ forcible means to ensure the security of the installations where they are performing compulsory labour.
[. . .]
In no case shall requisition of labour lead to a mobilization of workers in an organization of a military or semi-military character."

In *Blaškić*, the Appeals Chamber noted, "Violations of Article 51 of Geneva Convention IV would ordinarily fall within the ambit of Article 3 of the Statute, and more specifically within the category—as defined by the Appeals Chamber—constituted by infringements of the Geneva Conventions other than those classified as grave breaches" (para. 594). However, the Appeals Chamber did not have to decide upon such violations in that case because "the Appellant was not indicted for violations of these provisions, but only for inhuman treatment (recognised by Article 2 of the Statute) and cruel treatment of detainees as a violation of the laws or customs of war (recognised by Article 3 of the Statute and common Article 3(1)(a) (cruel treatment) of the Geneva Conventions)" (para. 594).

F. Wilfully Depriving a Prisoner of War or Civilian of the Rights of a Fair and Regular Trial

This grave breach has not yet been included in any ICTY indictment. **11–125** In relation to POWs, Chapter III, "Penal and Disciplinary Sanctions" of Part III of Geneva Convention III prescribes how POWs are to be disciplined and what procedural safeguards must be in place. Article 84 sets out the basic position:

"A prisoner of war shall be tried only by a military court, unless the existing laws of the Detaining Power expressly permit the civil courts to try a member of the armed forces of the Detaining Power in respect of the particular offence alleged to have been committed by the prisoner of war.
In no circumstances whatever shall a prisoner of war be tried by a court of any kind which does not offer the essential guarantees of independence and impartiality as generally recognized, and, in particular, the procedure of which does not afford the accused the rights and means of defence provided for in Article 105."

Article 105 details the procedural rights to which a POW is entitled. The essence of the provision is that the POW is entitled to present his or her defence with the assistance of a qualified advocate or counsel of his or her own choice, to call defence witnesses, to be aided by an interpreter and to be informed of the particulars of the charges against him or her in a language he or she understands and in sufficient time before trial to enable him or her and his or her counsel to prepare. The

advocate or counsel must also be provided with a period of at least two
weeks and the necessary facilities to enable him to prepare a proper
defence. He or she shall be able to confer with the accused in private.
The Protecting Power also has a role to play and, in particular, is
entitled to have its representatives attend the trial of the accused.
Article 86 provides: "No prisoner of war may be punished more than
once for the same act or on the same charge".

11–126   The rights of civilians in occupied territory in respect of fair and
regular trials are contained in a number of Articles (64–78) in Section
III, "Occupied Territories" of Part III of Geneva Convention IV. The
penal laws of the occupied territory shall, to the extent possible, remain
in force, and the courts of such territories shall continue to function
and implement the penal law of the territories. The occupying power
shall, however, have the right to subject civilians to penal provisions in
order to enable it to fulfil its obligations under the Convention and to
maintain its security (Article 64). These new penal provisions should
not have retroactive effect (Article 65). Articles 71 and 72 contain the
most important procedural rights for the trials of civilians and these
correlate closely with those enjoyed by POWs. Civilians are entitled to a
regular trial after being made aware of the charges against them in a
language which they understand (Article 71). They can present their
defence with the assistance of qualified counsel of their choice and they
are entitled to call any witnesses in their defence. They are to be aided
by an interpreter where necessary (Article 72) and they have the right
to appeal against a conviction (Article 73). The Protecting Power again
has a role to play and its representatives can attend the trial of a
civilian (Article 74).

This grave breach "can be split into a number of different offences,
for example: making a [prisoner of war/protected person] appear before
an exceptional court, without notifying the Protecting Power, without
defending counsel, etc." (ICRC Commentaries to GC III and GC IV,
pp. 628 and 600, respectively). Therefore, the grave breach is committed when any of the constituent elements relating to the concept of
a fair and regular trial are missing.

G. Unlawful Deportation or Transfer or Unlawful Confinement of a Civilian

11–127   Despite the grouping of these breaches under one heading in the
ICTY's Statute, the ICRC Commentary to the Fourth Geneva Convention (at p. 599) clarifies that they refer to different offences: the first
two phrases refer to breaches of Articles 45 and 49 of that Convention,
which deal with, respectively, the transfer of protected persons to a
Power not party to the Convention, and the transfer of protected
persons from occupied territory.

"Unlawful confinement" represents the codification under international law of what the Commentary accepts is already criminal under
most national legal systems. In the *Delalic et al.* case, three of the
accused were charged with this offence. The Trial Chamber concluded:

"[. . .] the confinement of civilians during armed conflict may be permissible in limited cases, but has in any event to be in compliance with the

provisions of articles 42 and 43 of Geneva Convention IV. The security of the State concerned might require the internment of civilians and, furthermore, the decision of whether a civilian constitutes a threat to the security of the State is largely left to its discretion. However, it must be borne in mind that the measure of internment for reasons of security is an exceptional one and can never be taken on a collective basis. An initially lawful internment clearly becomes unlawful if the detaining party does not respect the basic procedural rights of the detained persons and does not establish an appropriate court or administrative board as prescribed in article 43 of Geneva Convention IV" (para.583).

On the evidence the Trial Chamber found that the confinement of at **11–128** least some of the detainees (those who had no arms when captured and who had not participated in armed conflict) was unlawful as:

"[. . .] there existed no serious and legitimate reason to conclude that they seriously prejudiced the security of the detaining power. To the contrary, it appears that the confinement of civilians in the Celebici prison-camp was a collective measure aimed at a specific group of persons, based mainly on their ethnic background, and not a legitimate security measure. As stated above, the mere fact that a person is a national of, or aligned with, an enemy party, cannot be considered as threatening the security of the opposing party where he is living, and is not, therefore, a valid reason for interning him" (para. 1134).

The Trial Chamber accepted that States retain a great deal of discretion in determining whether particular civilians constitute a threat to their security and, consequently, what security measures they may take to combat the threat. Where, however, the illegality of the confinement was clear, or where procedural safeguards have not been implemented, the Trial Chamber recorded findings against the accused (see, para. 583).

On appeal, the Appeals Chamber agreed with the Trial Chamber that the confinement of civilians would be unlawful if such confinement did not comply with Articles 42 and 43 of the Fourth Geneva Convention; that is, the security of the detaining power makes it absolutely necessary, and the confinement has been judicially or administratively tested and periodically reviewed (para. 322). The Defence raised the argument that once the detainees have been found to be "protected persons" (and therefore in the hands of a party to the conflict of which they are not nationals), their loyalty could be questioned and they became *ipso facto* security risks (para. 326). The Appeals Chamber found there was no contradiction between a finding that the detainees belonged to the opposing party in the conflict and the finding that some of them could not reasonably be considered threats to the security of the detaining power. The Defence submission was rejected on the basis that it would undo the Convention in that whole populations would then suddenly become amenable to internment merely by virtue of belonging to the opposing party. Each civilian detained must be assessed individually to determine whether he or she poses a particular risk to the detaining power (para. 327).

The Prosecution's appeal concerned the finding by the Trial Cham- **11–129** ber that the Prosecution had not proved that two of the accused had been in a position to affect the continued detention of civilians. The Prosecution argued that this standard in effect imported the requirement of superior authority into the test for ordinary responsibility (*i.e.* Article 7(1)) responsibility), and, more generally, that the Trial Chamber erred in requiring proof of such a requirement at all (paras 336–337). The Prosecution contended that the requirements for a conviction on this charge under Article 7(1) were (i) the unlawful confinement of civilians, (ii) knowledge of such unlawful confinement, and (iii) participation in the confinement of those persons. The third element of the offence would be satisfied if the duties of prison guards, for instance, included the maintenance of an illegal system (para. 341). The Appeals Chamber decided that the language used by the Trial Chamber did not mean that it was importing the test for superior responsibility into Article 7(1). It held that something more than mere knowing "participation" in a generally illegal scheme must be proved to sustain a conviction for "committing" (as opposed to accomplice liability) the grave breach of unlawful confinement (para. 342). The Appeals Chamber did not attempt an exhaustive delineation of the kinds of acts that would render an accused liable under this provision, but held that primary responsibility should be reserved for those liable in a more direct or complete sense for the unlawful confinement of civilians (para. 343). Regarding the Prosecution's contention that mere knowing participation in a system of unlawful confinement of civilians should be sufficient to sustain a conviction, the Appeals Chamber adopted the following line of reasoning:

> "This, however, poses the question of what such a guard is expected to do under such circumstances. The implication from the Prosecution submissions is that such a guard must release the prisoners. The Appeals Chamber, however, does not accept that a guard's omission to take unauthorised steps to release prisoners will suffice to constitute the commission of the crime of unlawful confinement. The Appeals Chamber also finds it difficult to accept that such a guard must cease to supervise those detained in the camp to avoid such liability, particularly in light of the fact that among the detainees there may be persons who are lawfully confined because they genuinely do pose a threat to the security of the State" (*Prosecutor v. Delalic et al.*, Judgment, February 20, 2001, para. 342).

The Trial Chamber's judgment in the *Kordić and Čerkez* case, which was rendered a week after the Appeals Chamber's decision in *Delalic et al.*, is consonant with, and relies for support on, the Trial Chamber's decision in *Delalic et al.* insofar as the grave breach of unlawful confinement of civilians is concerned. Also see, *Kordić and Čerkez* Appeal Judgment, paras 69–73. The Appeals Chamber in *Kordić and Čerkez* cites the *Delalic et al.* Appeal Judgment in holding that:

> "[T]he detention or confinement of civilians will be unlawful in the following two circumstances:
> (i) when a civilian or civilians have been detained in contravention of Article 42 of Geneva Convention IV, i.e., they are detained without reasonable grounds to believe that the security of the Detaining Power makes it absolutely necessary ; and
> (ii) where the procedural safeguards required by Article 43 of Geneva Convention IV are not complied with in respect of detained civilians, even where their initial detention may have been justified" (*Kordić and Čerkez* Appeal Judgment, para. 73, *citing Delalic et al.* Appeal Judgment, para. 322).

For the element of the offences of unlawful deportation or transfer of civilians charged as a crime against humanity under Article 5(d) and (i) respectively, see *Prosecutor v. Krstic*, Judgment, Trial Chamber, August 2, 2001, paras 519–532. The Chamber held, "Both deportation and forcible transfer relate to the involuntary and unlawful evacuation of individuals from the territory in which they reside" without grounds permitted by international law (para. 521). However, they "are not synonymous in customary international law. Deportation presumes transfer beyond State borders, whereas forcible transfer relates to displacements within a State" (para. 521). Also see, *Prosecutor v. Krnojelac*, Judgment, Trial Chamber, March 15, 2002, para. 474, *quoted in Prosecutor v. Stakic*, Judgment, Trial Chamber, July 31, 2003, para. 672.

Articles 49 and 147 of Geneva Convention IV, and Article 85(4)(a) of Additional Protocol I all condemn deportation or forcible transfer of protected persons. Article 17 of Protocol II, applicable to internal conflicts, likewise prohibits the "displacement" of civilians. Evacuation of the population is permitted "if the security of the population or imperative military reasons so demand" (Article 49 of GC IV and Article 17 of Protocol II). Article 49 requires that persons evacuated be transferred back to their homes "as soon as hostilities in the area in question have ceased".

The Trial Chamber in *Naletilic and Martinovic* was the first to consider the unlawful transfer of a civilian was charged as a grave breach of the Geneva Conventions under Article 2(g) of the ICTY Statute. The same acts were also charged as crimes against humanity (persecution) under Article 5(h) of the ICTY Statute (*Prosecutor v. Naletilic and Martinovic*, Second Amended Indictment, October 16, 2001, paras 25–34, 53–54; also see, *Prosecutor v. Naletilic and Martinovic*, Judgment, Trial Chamber, March 31, 2003, paras 512–513, 669).

The Trial Chamber considered that "[f]orcible transfer is the movement of individuals under duress from where they reside to a place that is not of their choosing" (*Naletilic and Martinovic* Trial Judgment, para. 519). To prove unlawful transfer and deportation as a grave breach, it articulated the following test:

"i) the general requirements of Article 2 of the Statute are fulfilled;
ii) the occurrence of an act or omission, not motivated by the security of the population or imperative military reasons, leading to the transfer of a person from occupied territory or within occupied territory;
iii) the intent of the perpetrator to transfer a person" (para. 521).

The requisite intent is "to have the person (or persons) removed, which implies the aim that the person is not returning" (para. 520). In this way, deportation and forcible transfer differ from evacuation, which "is a provisional measure" and may be carried out using force (Commentary to Geneva Convention IV, at pp. 220, 280). The Trial Judgment also noted, "Transfers motivated by an individual's own genuine wish to leave, are lawful" (para. 519). To determine whether an individual consented, the Chamber considered Article 31 of Geneva Convention IV, which prohibits physical and moral coercion of protected persons (para. 519).

Both Naletilic and Martinovic were convicted of the unlawful transfer of a civilian as a grave breach of the Geneva Conventions (paras. 569–571). As of June 2005, the appeal is pending.

In *Prosecutor v. Stakic*, the Trial Chamber eliminated the requirement that the crime of deportation must involve transfers across internationally recognised borders. It considered that the prohibition of deportation serves to protect "the right and expectation of individuals to be able to remain in their homes and communities without interference by an aggressor, whether from the same or another State" (para. 677). Therefore, "the actus reus of forcibly removing, essentially uprooting, individuals from the territory and the environment in which they have been lawfully present [. . .] is the rationale for imposing criminal responsibility and not the destination resulting from such a removal" (para. 677). As such, for the purpose of this case, the Trial Chamber found:

> "that Article 5(d) of the Statute must be read to encompass forced population displacements both across internationally recognised borders and de facto boundaries, such as constantly changing frontlines, which are not internationally recognised. The crime of deportation in this context is therefore to be defined as the forced displacement of persons by expulsion or other coercive acts for reasons not permitted under international law from an area in which they are lawfully present to an area under the control of another party" (para. 679).

As defined in *Stakic*, the crime of deportation requires that it involve "forced" or "forcible" displacement, which "refer[s] not only to acts of physical violence but also to other forms of coercion" (para. 682, *citing Krnojelac* Trial Judgment, para. 475; *Krstic* Trial Judgment, para. 529; *Kunarac et al.* Trial Judgment, para. 542). With regards to the ICTY Statute, "the question of whether a border was internationally recognised or merely de facto is immaterial" (para. 684). Furthermore, criminal responsibility for the crime of deportation does not require "a minimum number of individuals must have been forcibly transferred" (para. 685). Displacement by a party to a conflict is not rendered lawful by the assistance of humanitarian agencies (para. 683).

The *Stakic* Trial Chamber agreed with the *Naletilic and Martinovic* Trial Judgment that the requisite mens rea is that the perpetrator must intend "that the victim is 'removed, which implies the aim that the person is not returning.' If a victim were to return, this would consequently not have an impact on the criminal responsibility of the perpetrator who removed the victim" (*Stakic* Trial Judgment, para. 687, quoting *Naletilic and Martinovic* Trial Judgment, para. 520 and footnote 1362).

As of June 2005, the *Stakic* appeal is pending.

H. TAKING CIVILIANS AS HOSTAGES

11–130   In the *Blaškić* Judgment, the Trial Chamber held that "civilian hostages are persons unlawfully deprived of their freedom, often arbitrarily and sometimes under threat of death" (*Blaškić* Trial Judgment, para. 158). The Prosecution would have to establish, furthermore, "that, at the time of the supposed detention, the allegedly censurable act was perpetrated in order to obtain a concession or gain an advantage" (para. 158). The evidence led by the Prosecution was that, over a period of a few days in April 1993, over 2200 Muslims, all of whom the Trial Chamber accepted had been placed *hors de combat*, were detained in various localities, all within the accused's zone of command. At this time, the 3rd Corps of the Bosnian Army was allegedly apparently advancing on the Bosnian Croat position. In order to forestall this eventuality, a prominent Bosnian detainee was instructed to telephone various military and political Bosnian leaders and tell them that, if the advance continued, the detainees would all be killed. He was also forced to make a speech on television to the effect that all Muslims should hand over their weapons. Additional advantage was gained from the detention of the hostages by forcing the prominent Bosnian detainee to sign a peace agreement that was put before him. The Trial Chamber accepted this evidence and concluded that the offence of taking civilians hostage had been proved.

In the *Kordic and Cerkez* case, the Trial Chamber discussed the **11–131** definitions of hostage-taking that had been used by the United States Military Tribunal in Nuremburg in the *Hostages Trial: Wilhelm List and Others*. The Trial Chamber also discussed the definition provided by the International Convention Against the Taking of Hostages, which does not apply during armed conflicts; Article 147 of Geneva Convention IV and the ICRC Commentary thereto, which applies in international armed conflicts; and common Article 3(1)(b) of the Geneva Conventions, which applies in internal armed conflicts. It also noted with approval the *Blaškić* analysis of the offence and came to the following conclusion:

> "Consequently, the Chamber finds that an individual commits the offence of taking civilians as hostages when he threatens to subject civilians, who are unlawfully detained, to inhuman treatment or death as a means of achieving the fulfilment of a condition" (para. 314).

Kordic was acquitted at trial of the counts involving hostages (*Kordić and Čerkez*, Trial Judgment, para. 802). Cerkez's convictions for hostage-taking were overturned on appeal (*Kordić and Čerkez*, Appeal Judgment, para. 939).

Although the Appeals Chamber in *Blaškić* overturned the convictions for hostage-taking (para. 646), its discussion of the issue is instructive. The *Blaškić* Appeals Judgment quotes the *Kordić and Čerkez* Trial Judgment, which states:

> "It would, thus, appear that the crime of taking civilians as hostages consists of the unlawful deprivation of liberty, including the crime of unlawful confinement [. . .]
>
> The additional element [. . .] is the issuance of a conditional threat in respect of the physical and mental well-being of civilians who are unlawfully detained. The ICRC Commentary identifies this additional element as a 'threat either to prolong the hostage's detention or to put him to death'. In the Chamber's view, such a threat must be intended as a coercive measure to achieve the fulfilment of a condition" (*Blaškić* Appeal Judgment, para. 638, *quoting Kordić and Čerkez*, Trial Judgment, paras 312–313).

The Appeals Chamber determined in *Blaškić* that "the essential element in the crime of hostage-taking is the use of a threat concerning detainees so as to obtain a concession or gain an advantage; a situation of hostage-taking exists when a person seizes or detains and threatens to kill, injure or continue to detain another person in order to compel a third party to do or to abstain from doing something as a condition for the release of that person" (para. 639). It noted: "The crime of hostage-taking is prohibited by Common Article 3 of the Geneva Conventions, Articles 34 and 147 of Geneva Convention IV, and Article 75(2)(c) of Additional Protocol I" (para. 639). Although Article 34 of Geneva Convention IV states only: "The taking of hostages is prohibited", the ICRC Commentary states: "In accordance with the spirit of the Convention, the word 'hostages' must be understood in the widest possible sense" (ICRC Commentary, p. 230, *quoted* in *Blaškić* Appeal Judgment, fn. 1333).

VI. VIOLATIONS OF THE LAWS AND CUSTOMS OF WAR

A. DEFINITION

11–132   In his Report on the Statute, the Secretary-General of the United Nations stated that Article 3 of the ICTY Statute was based on the 1907 Hague Convention (IV) Respecting the Laws and Customs of War on Land and on the Regulations annexed to the Convention, which have acquired the status of customary international law (Report of the Secretary-General pursuant to para. 2 of Security Council Resolution 808 (1993), S/25704, May 3, 1993, paras 41, 44).

Confirming that the list of prohibitions in Article 3 of the ICTY Statute is "merely illustrative, not exhaustive" (*Tadić* Jurisdiction Decision, para. 87), the Appeals Chamber defined the scope of the provision. Referring to the Secretary-General's comments on the nature of the Hague Convention (IV), the Appeals Chamber stated that the "comments suggest that Article 3 is intended to cover both Geneva and Hague rules law (sic)" (para. 87). After considering the list of violations in Article 3, the Appeals Chamber concluded that "this list may be construed to include other infringements of international humanitarian law" (para. 87) and that "Article 3 functions as a residual clause designed to ensure that no serious violation of international humanitarian law is taken away from the jurisdiction of the International Tribunal. Article 3 aims to make such jurisdiction watertight and inescapable" (*Tadić* Jurisdiction Decision, para. 91).

Article 3 incorporates all serious violations of international humanitarian law other than the grave breaches of the Geneva Conventions, crimes against humanity, and genocide:

"[. . .] Article 3 is a general clause covering all violations of humanitarian law not falling under Article 2 or covered by Articles 4 or 5, more specifically: (i) violations of the Hague law on international conflicts; (ii) infringements of provisions of the Geneva Conventions other than those classified as "grave breaches" by those Conventions; (iii) violations of common Article 3 and other customary rules on internal conflicts; (iv) violations of agreements binding upon the parties to the conflict, considered *qua* treaty law, *i.e.*, agreements which have not turned into customary international law" (*Tadić* Jurisdiction Decision, para. 89).

The Appeals Chamber specified the conditions which must be satisfied for an offence to be subject to prosecution under Article 3 of the Statute: **11–133**

"(i) the violation must constitute an infringement of a rule of international humanitarian law; (ii) the rule must be customary in nature or, if it belongs to treaty law, the required conditions must be met . . . ; (iii) the violation must be 'serious' . . . ; (iv) the violation of the rule must entail, under customary or conventional law, the individual criminal responsibility of the person breaching the rule" (*Tadić* Jurisdiction Decision, para. 94).

(Also see, *Prosecutor v. Kunarac et al.*, Judgment, Appeals Chamber, June 12, 2002, paras 55–70; *Prosecutor v. Galić*, Judgment, Trial Chamber, December 5, 2003, paras 11–32; *Prosecutor v. Strugar*, Judgment, Trial Chamber, January 31, 2005, paras 218–233.)

In the *Tadić* Jurisdiction Decision, the Appeals Chamber held that the Tribunal is not restricted to applying only customary law under Article 3. The Tribunal is entitled to apply conventional international law binding upon the parties to the conflict. The Appeals Chamber explained the rationale as follows:

"It should be emphasised [. . .] that the only reason behind the stated purpose of the drafters that the International Tribunal should apply customary international law was to avoid violating the principle of *nullum crimen sine lege* in the event that a party to the conflict did not adhere to a specific treaty. (Report of the Secretary-General, at para. 34). It follows that the International Tribunal is authorised to apply, in addition to customary international law, any treaty which: (i) was unquestionably binding on the parties at the time of the alleged offence; and (ii) was not in conflict with or derogating from peremptory norms of international law, as are most customary rules of international humanitarian law [. . .] representatives of the United States, the United Kingdom and France all agreed that Article 3 of the Statute did not exclude application of international agreements binding on the parties. (Provisional Verbatim Record, of the U.N.SCOR, 3217th Meeting., at 11, 15, 19, U.N. Doc. S/PV.3217 (May 25, 1993).)

We conclude that, in general, such agreements fall within our jurisdiction under Article 3 of the Statute" (*Tadić* Jurisdiction Decision, paras 143–144).

The Appeals Chamber held that Article 3 vested the Tribunal with subject matter jurisdiction in respect of the violations of common Article 3, even though the Statute does not expressly refer to common Article 3. It held that violations of common Article 3 may be prosecuted under Article 3 of the Statute as long as they fulfil the conditions, cited above, for an offence to be subject to prosecution under Article 3 of the Statute (*Tadić* Jurisdiction Decision, paras 89 and 94). **11–134**

In support of this contention, the Appeals Chamber noted that the record of proceedings before the Security Council demonstrated that the Security Council intended to include common Article 3 within Article 3 of the Tribunal's Statute (*Tadić* Jurisdiction Decision, para. 88, *quoting* the interpretative statements by the Permanent Representatives **11–135** of France, the United States, the United Kingdom and the Representative of Hungary, *Provisional Verbatim Record of the 3217th Meeting*, at 11, 15, 19 and 20, UN Doc S/PV.3217, May 25, 1993).

As part of its finding that breaches of the rules on internal conflict do give rise to individual criminal responsibility, the Appeals Chamber held that criminal liability may be incurred for breaches of common Article 3: "customary international law imposes criminal liability for serious violations of common Article 3" (*Tadić* Jurisdiction Decision, para. 134; also see paras 127–130, and 133–137).

The ICTR Statute expressly includes the provisions of common Article 3, and provides that the Tribunal has jurisdiction to prosecute serious violations of Additional Protocol II (Article 4 of the ICTR Statute). For the ICTY, it has been confirmed that provisions in Additional Protocols I and II are prosecutable under Article 3; see *Prosecutor v. Strugar et al.*, Trial Chamber, Decision on Defence Preliminary Motion Challenging Jurisdiction, June 7, 2002, paras 11–24.

B. THE CONDUCT OF HOSTILITIES

(1) Basic rules

11–136   Prior to the cases brought before the ICTY, no prosecutions had occurred for violations of the laws governing the conduct of hostilities. The main charges laid by the ICTY Prosecutor have been for unlawful attacks on civilians and civilian objects as violations of the laws or customs of war, recognised by Article 3 of the Statute; customary law (on account of the *Tadić* Jurisdiction Decision, para. 127); Article 51(2) of Additional Protocol I and Article 13(2) of Additional Protocol II (for unlawful attacks on civilians); and Article 52(1) of Additional Protocol I (for unlawful attacks on civilian objects). The *Tadić* Jurisdiction Decision confirmed that violations of the Additional Protocols may be charged under Article 3 of the Statute, see paras 91–93. (Also see *Prosecutor v. Strugar et al.*, Decision on Defence Preliminary Motion Challenging Jurisdiction, June 7, 2002, paras 11–24; *Prosecutor v. Strugar*, Judgment, Trial Chamber, January 31, 2005, paras 215–233.)

Indictments have also been issued for destruction as a grave breach under Article 2(d) ("extensive destruction and appropriation of property, not justified by military necessity and carried out unlawfully and wantonly") and under Article 3(b) ("wanton destruction of cities, towns or villages, or devastation not justified by military necessity"); for plunder of property, as recognised by Article 3(e) ("plunder of public or private property"); and for destruction of institutions dedicated to religion or education, as recognised by Article 3(d) ("seizure of, destruction or wilful damage done to institutions dedicated to religion, charity and education, the arts and sciences, historic monuments and works of art and science"). The basic rule for the general protection of civilians against the effects of hostilities is set out in Article 48 of Additional Protocol I: "In order to ensure respect for and protection of the civilian population and civilian objects, the Parties to the conflict shall at all times distinguish between the civilian population and combatants and between civilian objects and military objectives and accordingly shall direct their operations only against military objectives".

The ICTY's jurisprudence has clarified that prohibited attacks are: **11–137**

"[P]rohibited attacks are those launched deliberately against civilians or civilian objects in the course of an armed conflict and are not justified by military necessity. They must have caused deaths and/or serious bodily injuries within the civilian population or extensive damage to civilian objects" (*Prosecutor v. Kordić and Čerkez*, Trial Judgment, February 26, 2001, para. 328, *citing Prosecutor v. Blaškić*, Trial Judgment, March 3, 2000, para. 180. Also see, *Prosecutor v. Strugar*, Judgment, Trial Chamber, January 31, 2005, para. 280).

The Appeals Chamber corrected the *Blaškić* Trial Judgment by emphasising "that there is an absolute prohibition on the targeting of civilians in customary international law" (*Blaškić* Appeal Judgment, para. 109).

In *Kordić and Čerkez*, the Appeals Chamber held that the Trial Chamber's approach was correct in "consider[ing] that Article 3 of the Statute covers not only violations which are based in customary international law but also those based on treaties" (*Kordić and Čerkez* Appeals Judgment, paras 41–42). The Appeals Chamber also considered the Trial Chamber correct in finding "that Additional Protocol I constituted applicable treaty law in the present case, and [. . .] that 'whether [Additional Protocol I] reflected customary law at the relevant time in this case is beside the point'" (para. 41, *quoting Kordić and Čerkez* Trial Judgment, para. 167). The Appeals Chamber stressed the finding made in the *Tadić* Jurisdiction Decision:

"the only reason behind the stated purpose of the drafters [of the Statute] that the International Tribunal should apply customary international law was to avoid violating the principle of *nullum crimen sine lege* in the event that a party to the conflict did not adhere to a specific treaty'" (*Kordić and Čerkez* Appeal Judgment, para. 46, *quoting Tadić* Appeal Decision on Jurisdiction, para. 143).

Although other decisions have applied customary international law to abide by the principle of legality, in the *Kordić and Čerkez* case, the Appeals Chamber referred "to applicable treaty law that established a crime at the time of its commission, provided that this crime is encompassed in the Statute" (para. 46).

The case law has recited the relevant provision from the Additional Protocols:

"Civilians and civilian objects are protected by, *inter alia*, Geneva Convention IV [. . .] The protection of civilians and civilian objects is augmented by Additional Protocol I [. . .] Article 51(2) of Additional Protocol I provides that

The civilian population as such, as well as individual civilians, shall not be the object of attack.

However, civilians will no longer enjoy the protection afforded by Additional Protocol I if 'they take a direct part in hostilities' [Additional Protocol I, Article 51(3)].

Article 52(1) of Additional Protocol I defines civilian objects as 'all objects which are not military objectives'. Military objectives are defined in para. 2 as 'those objects which by their nature, location, purpose or use make an effective contribution to military action and whose total or partial destruction, capture, neutralization, in the circumstances ruling at the time, offers a definite military advantage.' Article 52(2) further states that '[a]ttacks shall be limited strictly to military objectives'" (*Kordić and Čerkez* Trial Judgment, paras 326–327).

In *Kordić and Čerkez*, the Appeals Chamber laid out elements of the crime of unlawful attack against civilians and civilian objects under treaty law, in particular Additional Protocol I (paras 47–68). Citing the definition of the term attack in Article 49 of Additional Protocol I ("acts of violence against the adversary, whether in offence or in defence"), the Appeals Chamber concluded that, "in determining whether an unlawful attack on civilians occurred, the issue of who first made use of force is irrelevant" (para. 47). Furthermore, as stipulated in Article 51(2) and (3) of Additional Protocol I, it is a "fundamental principle of international customary law" that a "civilian population as such shall not be the object of attack" (para. 48). In determining individual criminal responsibility, "the burden of proof as to whether a person is a civilian rests on the Prosecution" (para. 48, *citing Blaškić* Appeal Judgment, para. 111). Despite the precautions required to protect civilians and civilian objects, "international law recognises that this does not imply that collateral [civilian] damage is unlawful *per se*" (para. 52). The Appeals Chamber considered "that criminal responsibility for unlawful attack on civilians or civilian objects" requires that the attack "caused death, serious injury, or any other criminal act listed in Article 3 of the Statute, or any consequence being of the same gravity, to civilians" (paras 67–68; also see, the reasoning in paras 58–66).

Article 13(2) of Additional Protocol II, relating to the protection of victims in internal armed conflicts, states:

> "The civilian population as such, as well as individual civilians, shall not be the object of attack. Acts or threats of violence the primary purpose of which is to spread terror among the civilian population are prohibited."

The Appeals Chamber in *Blaškić* stated: "The protection of civilians reflects a principle of customary international law that is applicable in internal and international armed conflicts, and the prohibition of an attack on civilians, outlined in [Article 51(2) of Additional Protocol I and Article 13(2) of Additional Protocol II], reflects the current status of customary international law" (para. 157, footnotes omitted). For a discussion of the test of applicability of common Article 3 and Additional Protocol II, see, *e.g. Prosecutor v. Kayishema and Ruzindana*, Judgment, ICTR Trial Chamber, May 21, 1999, paras 169–190, which found both accused not guilty of violations of common Article 3 and Additional Protocol II (see, paras 590–624).

(2) Military necessity

11–138   Although the *Blaškić* and *Kordić* trial judgments stated that attacks carried out as a result of military necessity are not unlawful, the *Blaškić* Appeal Judgment makes clear "that there is an absolute prohibition on the targeting of civilians in customary international law" (para. 109). The concept of military necessity has not been explicitly defined by the ICTY. The Trial Chamber in *Blaškić* did mention the absence of military objectives as a reason for a finding that the attacks on the various villages targeted the civilian population (paras 402–409), concluding that: "The Trial Chamber is therefore convinced beyond any reasonable doubt that no military objective justified these attacks." (para. 410). In *Kordić and Čerkez* the Trial Chamber did not attempt to define military necessity, but it did review the evidence relating to the village attacks to assess the validity of the military objectives raised by the Defence. The Trial Chamber found that:

> "[T]he overwhelming evidence points to a well-organised and planned HVO attack upon Ahmici with the aim of killing or driving out the Muslim population, resulting in a massacre. The assertion that this attack was justified strategically, defensively, or in any other way, is wholly without foundation: such defenders as were available were taken completely by surprise and any defence put up thereafter was rudimentary, as the results of the day show." (para. 642).

The Appeals Chamber in *Kordić and Čerkez* referred to the definition of military necessity in Article 14 of the Lieber Code of 1863 as "the necessity of those measures which are indispensable for securing the ends of the war, and which are lawful according to the modern law and usages of war" (*Kordić and Čerkez* Appeal Judgment, para. 686; also see, *Strugar* Trial Judgment, footnote 939). The Appeals Chamber reasoned, "It follows that the unnecessary or wanton application of force is prohibited and that 'a belligerent may apply only that amount and kind of force necessary to defeat the enemy'" (*Kordić and Čerkez* Appeal Judgment, para. 686, *quoting* Christopher Greenwood in Fleck (ed.), *The Handbook of Humanitarian Law in Armed Conflicts*, para. 130).

In the *Strugar* Judgment (para. 295), the Trial Chamber defined the concept of military necessity by referring to the definition of military objectives in Article 52(2) of Additional Protocol I, which states:

> "Attacks shall be limited strictly to military objectives. In so far as objects are concerned, military objectives are limited to those objects which by their nature, location, purpose or use make an effective contribution to military action and whose total or partial destruction, capture or neutralization, in the circumstances ruling at the time, offers a definite military advantage."

Also see, *Strugar* Trial Judgment, footnote 939; *Prosecutor v. Galić*, Judgment, Trial Chamber, December 5, 2003, para. 51.

It is also unlawful for an attack on a military objective to incur collateral civilian deaths or destruction of civilian property, which is disproportionate to the military objectives attained. The concept of "proportionality" has not been explored before the Tribunal in any great detail. In an effort to explain the high civilian casualties in the attack on the village of Ahmici, the Defence in *Blaškić* argued that the type of operation, fighting in built up areas, inevitably led to the high civilian casualties, which it termed "collateral casualties". The Trial Chamber rejected this argument on the basis that there had been no legitimate military objectives in the first place (para. 406). The Trial

Chamber did not therefore weigh the military objectives against the civilian casualties.

Further jurisprudence on "military necessity" and "proportionality" resulted in the case *Prosecutor v. Galić*, which concerned the siege of Sarajevo. The *Galić* Trial Judgment broadly defined military necessity as "'doing what is necessary to achieve a war aim'" (*Galić* Trial Judgment, footnote 76, quoting Pietro Vierri, *Dictionary of the international law of armed conflict* (ICRC, 1992) p. 75; also see, *Strugar* Trial Judgment, footnote 939). The *Galić* Trial Judgment noted:

> "The principle of military necessity acknowledges the potential for unavoidable civilian death and injury ancillary to the conduct of legitimate military operations. However, this principle requires that destroying a particular military objective will provide some type of advantage in weakening the enemy military forces. Under no circumstance are civilians to be considered legitimate military targets. Consequently, attacking civilians or the civilian population as such cannot be justified by invoking military necessity" (*Galić* Trial Judgment, footnote 76).

Citing Article 52(3) of Additional Protocol I, the Trial Chamber stated: "In case of doubt as to whether an object which is normally dedicated to civilian purposes is being used to make an effective contribution to military action, it shall be presumed not to be so used" (*Galić* Trial Judgment, para. 51).

The *Strugar* Trial Judgment cited the *Galić* Trial Judgment in holding:

> "Whether a military advantage can be achieved must be decided [. . .] from the perspective of the 'person contemplating the attack, including the information available to the latter, that the object is being used to make an effective contribution to military action.' In other words, each case must be determined on its facts" (*Strugar* Trial Judgment, para. 295, *quoting Galić* Trial Judgment, para. 51).

In *Galić* the indictment charged two accused, Galić and Milošević, successive Corps Commanders of the Sarajevo Romanija Corps, with a range of offences committed during the siege. It was alleged that this Corps controlled all Bosnian Serb territory around Sarajevo by September 1992. The charges were grouped into three main components: the infliction of terror upon the civilian population of Sarajevo, sniping and shelling. The Trial Judgment states that these headings were "evidently descriptive categorizations of the counts, to which the Majority attaches no particular legal significance" (para. 65). The Majority further considered "that 'Infliction of terror' is not an appropriate designation of the offence considered here because actual infliction of terror is not a required element of the offence" (para. 65). Instead, the Majority referred to "the offence charged in Count 1 as 'the crime of terror against the civilian population', or simply 'the crime of terror', a purported violation of the laws or customs of war" (para. 65).

The infliction of terror charge is encapsulated in a single Article 3 count for each accused: the unlawful infliction of terror set out in the second part of Article 51(2) of Additional Protocol I: "Acts or threats of violence the primary purpose of which is to spread terror among the civilian population are prohibited." The same prohibition is contained in Article 13(2) of Additional Protocol II. The infliction of terror was allegedly caused by the continuous sniping and shelling of civilians in the city over a period of approximately 44 months. The sniping and shelling counts are contained in one count each under Article 3 of the Statute: an attack on civilians (as set out in Article 51 of AP I and in Article 13 of AP II) in each case. (Also see, *Prosecutor v. Galić*, Decision on the Motion for the Entry of Acquittal for Accused Stanislav Galić, October 3, 2002, in which the Trial Chamber dismissed in large part the accused's challenge to the sufficiency of evidence presented at the end of the Prosecution's case under Rule 98*bis*.)

Noting that this judgment was the first by an international tribunal to pronounce on the charge of terror against the civilian population (*Galić* Trial Judgment, para. 66), the Majority considered

> "whether the Tribunal has jurisdiction over the crime of terror against the civilian population, but only to the extent relevant to the charge in this case. That is to say, the Majority is not required to decide whether an offence of terror in a general sense falls within the jurisdiction of the Tribunal, but only whether a specific offence of killing and wounding civilians in time of armed conflict with the intention to inflict terror on the civilian population, as alleged in the Indictment, is an offence over which it has jurisdiction" (para. 87).

It limited its analysis to "the legal regime of the Geneva Conventions and the Additional Protocols and not in international efforts directed against 'political' varieties of terrorism" and noted "that 'terrorism' has never been singly defined under international law" (footnote 150). However, it observed that Geneva Convention IV and the Additional Protocols prohibit "terror against the civilian population in times of war" (footnote 150).

The majority found that the four Tadić conditions (see paragraph 11–133) were satisfied and "that serious violations of the second part of Article 51(2), and specifically the violations alleged in this case causing death or injury, entailed individual criminal responsibility in 1992" (para. 130). Based on the facts of the case, the Majority concluded that it was "not required to pronounce on a crime of terror consisting only of threats" or "allegations of harm other than the causing of death or serious injury to civilians" (para. 132). It found "that the offence [. . .] was criminalized in a precise and accessible manner by 1992, and that this was known or should have been known to the Accused. Therefore there is no affront to the principle of nullum crimen sine lege" (para. 132).

The majority concluded that "the crime of terror against the civilian population in the form charged in the Indictment is constituted of the elements common to offences falling under Article 3 of the Statute, as well as of the following specific elements:

> 1. Acts of violence directed against the civilian population or individual civilians not taking direct part in hostilities causing death or serious injury to body or health within the civilian population.
> 2. The offender wilfully made the civilian population or individual civilians not taking direct part in hostilities the object of those acts of violence.
> 3. The above offence was committed with the primary purpose of spreading terror among the civilian population" (para. 133).

The majority held that the actual infliction of terror is not an element of the crime of terror; thus, it is not required "to prove a causal connection between the unlawful acts of violence and the production of terror" (para. 134). Furthermore, the "acts of violence", include only unlawful attacks against civilians and not legitimate attacks against combatants (para. 135). The Majority accepted the Prosecution's description of "terror" as "extreme fear" (para. 137).

According to the majority, the *mens rea* of the crime of terror is signified by "primary purpose" (para. 136). It excludes "dolus eventualis or recklessness from the intentional state specific to terror. Thus the Prosecution is required to prove not only that the Accused accepted the likelihood that terror would result from the illegal acts—or, in other words, that he was aware of the possibility that terror would result—but that that was the result which he specifically intended. The crime of terror is a specific-intent crime" (para. 136).

The majority concluded:

> "an offence constituted of acts of violence wilfully directed against the civilian population or individual civilians causing death or serious injury to body or health within the civilian population with the primary purpose of spreading terror among the civilian population – namely the crime of terror as a violation of the laws or customs of war – formed part of the law to which the Accused and his subordinates were subject to during the Indictment period. The Accused knew or should have known that this was so. Terror as a crime within international humanitarian law was made effective in this case by treaty law. The Tribunal has jurisdiction ratione materiae by way of Article 3 of the Statute. Whether the crime of terror also has a foundation in customary law is not a question which the Majority is required to answer" (para. 138).

(3) Reprisals

11–139   Reprisals have been referred to as:

> "an act illegal in itself but permissible in reasonable proportion and with proper safeguards as a response to illegal acts already committed by the enemy and as a deterrent to their recurrence." (Best, *War & Law since 1945*, p. 192)

However, Additional Protocol I prohibits reprisals against protected persons and objects generally (Article 20) and, in particular, prohibits reprisals against the civilian population or civilians and civilian objects (Article 51(6) and Article 52(1)) and making the following the object of reprisals: cultural objects and places of worship (Article 53(c)); objects indispensable to the survival of the civilian population (Article 54(4)); the natural environment (Article 55(2)); works or installations containing dangerous forces (Article 56(4)). There are no similar provisions contained in Additional Protocol II for internal conflict. Article 4(4) of the 1954 Hague Convention requires States Parties to refrain "from any act directed by way of reprisals against cultural property" (see, *Strugar* Trial Judgment, para. 305). In *Galić*, the Trial Chamber noted that "the language of Article 51(6) of Additional Protocol I implies that the prohibition against reprisals cannot be waived on the grounds of military necessity" (footnote 77).

Reprisals are another of the offences not enumerated but covered by Article 3 of the ICTY Statute. The offence was first considered in a Rule 61 hearing. The Trial Chamber in its decision of March 8, 1996 in *Prosecutor v. Martic*, Review of Indictment Pursuant to Rule 61, noted:

"The prohibition against attacking the civilian population as such as well as individual civilians must be respected in all circumstances regardless of the behaviour of the other party. The opinion of the great majority of legal authorities permits the Trial Chamber to assert that no circumstances would legitimise an attack against civilians even if it were a response proportionate to a similar violation perpetrated by the other party. The exclusion of the application of the principle of reprisals in the case of such fundamental humanitarian norms is confirmed by Article 1 Common to all Geneva Conventions. Under this provision, the High Contracting Parties undertake to respect and to ensure respect for the Conventions in all circumstances, even when the behaviour of the other party might be considered wrongful. The International Court of Justice considered that this obligation does not derive only from the Geneva Conventions themselves but also from the general principles of humanitarian law (*Case concerning Military and Paramilitary Activities in and against Nicaragua*, Nicaragua v. United States of America, merits, I.C.J. Reports 1986, para. 220)" (para. 15).

The Trial Chamber found that reprisals against civilians and civilian objects were prohibited in internal armed conflict (para. 16) and in all circumstances and armed conflicts as a matter of customary law (para. 17).

In *Prosecutor v. Kupreškić et al.*, the Trial Chamber stated that the protection of civilians and civilian objects may be reduced and suspended, "at least according to some authorities, when civilians may legitimately be the object of reprisals" (para. 522). However, it clearly rebutted two arguments the Trial Chamber felt the Defence presented explicitly or implicitly to justify the attacks against the Muslim population in the Lasva Valley. The first argument was "the Defence's allegation [that] similar attacks were allegedly being perpetrated by the Muslims against the Croat population" (para. 511). In response the Trial Chamber stressed "the irrelevance of reciprocity, particularly in relation to obligations found within international humanitarian law which have an absolute and non-derogable character. It thus follows that the *tu quoque* defence has no place in contemporary international humanitarian law" (para. 511).

The second argument was "to challenge the civilian character of the Muslim population of Ahmici by alleging that the village of Ahmici was not an undefended village" (para. 512). Before considering the military or civilian character of the population in Ahmici, the Trial Chamber emphasised that, regardless, "at a minimum, large numbers of civilian casualties would have been interspersed among the combatants" (para. 513). The Trial Chamber stressed that the key point is:

"the sacrosanct character of the duty to protect civilians, which entails, amongst other things, the absolute character of the prohibition of reprisals against civilian populations. Even if it can be proved that the Muslim population of Ahmici was not entirely civilian but comprised some armed elements, still no justification would exist for widespread and indiscriminate attacks against civilians. Indeed, even in a situation of full-scale armed conflict, certain fundamental norms still serve to unambiguously outlaw such conduct, such as rules pertaining to proportionality" (para. 513).

The Trial Chamber stated that reprisals are prohibited under customary international law when civilians are in the hands of the adversary and that Article 51(6) of Additional Protocol I prohibits reprisals against civilians in combat zones while Article 52(1) prohibits reprisals against civilian objects (para. 527). It then went on to discuss whether these provisions had become customary international law or general rules of international law (paras 527–536). It noted that "that while reprisals could have had a modicum of justification in the past, when they constituted practically the only effective means of compelling the enemy to abandon unlawful acts of warfare and to comply in future with international law, at present they can no longer be justified in this manner" (para. 530).

It concluded that: "the demands of humanity and the dictates of public conscience, as manifested in *opinio necessitatis*, have by now brought about the formation of a customary rule also binding upon those few States that at some stage did not intend to exclude the abstract legal possibility of resorting to the reprisals under discussion" (para. 533). Furthermore, in this case, the parties were bound by treaty provisions prohibiting reprisals (para. 536). It concluded that, "in international law there is no justification for attacks on civilians carried out either by virtue of the *tu quoque* principle (i.e. the argument whereby the fact that the adversary is committing similar crimes offers a valid defence to a belligerent's crimes) or on the strength of the principle of reprisals. Hence the accused cannot rely on the fact that allegedly there were also atrocities committed by Muslims against Croatian civilians" (para. 765).

Even in cases of lawful reprisals, the Trial Chamber emphasised that their use is restricted by the following:

> (a) the principle whereby they must be a last resort in attempts to impose compliance by the adversary with legal standards (which entails, amongst other things, that they may be exercised only after a prior warning has been given which has failed to bring about the discontinuance of the adversary's crimes); (b) the obligation to take special precautions before implementing them (they may be taken only after a decision to this effect has been made at the highest political or military level; in other words they may not be decided by local commanders); (c) the principle of proportionality (which entails not only that the reprisals must not be excessive compared to the precedent unlawful act of warfare, but also that they must stop as soon as that unlawful act has been discontinued) and; (d) 'elementary considerations of humanity'" (para. 535).

For a discussion of "reprisal quotas", see *Kordic and Cerkez* Appeal Judgment, para. 686 *et seq.*

C. OTHER VIOLATIONS IN INTERNATIONAL AND INTERNAL ARMED CONFLICT

11–140 Another convenient distinction used in International Humanitarian Law is between the grave breaches of the Geneva Conventions of 1949 and other violations of the laws and customs of war. The grave breaches do not, however, occupy a privileged position in contemporary humanitarian law. In fact, violations of the grave breach provisions are charged less frequently in indictments issued by the ICTY due to the extra burden of proving an international armed conflict and establishing the status of the victims as protected persons. (See, for example, *Prosecutor v. Hadžihasanović et al.*, Amended Indictment, January 11, 2002, in which the original Article 2 charges were withdrawn by the Prosecution for reasons of "judicial economy".)

Article 3 of the ICTY Statute contains many of the same offences prosecutable irrespective of the nature of the conflict, many of which are the same offences included as the grave breaches.

Article 3 enumerates the traditional Hague law offences, which are taken directly from the 1907 Regulations to the Hague Convention (IV).

(1) Enumerated offences under Article 3

Employment of poisonous weapons or other weapons calculated to cause unnecessary suffering, Art. 3(a)

The ICTY has not had occasion to charge this offence. The *Tadić* Jurisdiction Decision, however, has confirmed that the use of such weapons attracts the same illegality now as it did when first singled out for proscription in some of the earliest codifications: the 1868 St. Petersburg Declaration and the 1874 Final Project of an International Declaration Concerning the Laws and Customs of War (Article 13). In its review of the development of rules governing the conduct of warfare in internal conflicts, the Appeals Chamber highlighted particularly the use of chemical weapons by Iraq against the Kurds as a case in point. The use of these weapons was condemned by many nations as a violation of international law and, specifically, of the 1925 Geneva Protocol for the Prohibition of the Use in War of Asphyxiating Poisonous or Other Gases, and of Bacteriological Methods of Warfare. On this basis, the Appeals Chamber found that a general consensus had been reached that the use of such weapons was outlawed even in internal conflicts (*Tadić* Jurisdiction Decision, paras 119–124).

11–141

Wanton destruction of cities, towns or villages, or devastation not justified by military necessity, Art. 3(b)

The Trial Chamber in *Prosecutor v. Kordić and Čerkez* held that:

11–142

> "the elements for the crime of wanton destruction not justified by military necessity charged under Article 3(b) of the Statute are satisfied where:
> (i) the destruction of property occurs on a large scale;
> (ii) the destruction is not justified by military necessity; and
> (iii) the perpetrator acted with the intent to destroy the property in question or in reckless disregard of the likelihood of its destruction."
> (*Kordić and Čerkez* Trial Judgment, para. 346; also see, *Kordić and Čerkez* Appeal Judgment, para. 74).

The Trial Chamber went on to add that:

"while property situated on enemy territory is not protected under the Geneva Conventions, and is therefore not included in the crime of extensive destruction of property listed as a grave breach of the Geneva Conventions, the destruction of such property is criminalised under Article 3 of the Statute" (*Kordic and Cerkez* Trial Judgment, para. 347; also see, *Kordić and Čerkez* Appeal Judgment, para. 74).

The Appeals Chamber found "that the crime envisaged by Article 3(b) of the Statute was part of international customary law at the time it was allegedly committed" (*Kordić and Čerkez* Appeal Judgment, para. 76).

The Trial Chamber found both accused guilty of the offence of wanton destruction not justified by military necessity on the basis of evidence indicating the massive and widespread nature of the destruction caused. A particularly helpful aid to the Trial Chamber in this regard was a video produced by the Prosecution of the area covered by the indictment which was taken from a helicopter that indicated the extent and intensity of the damage caused to the relevant villages.

In *Prosecutor v. Strugar*, the Trial Chamber explained that "Article 3(b) codifies two crimes: 'wanton destruction of cities, towns or villages, or devastation not justified by military necessity'" (para. 291). In this case, the Accused was charged "with devastation not justified by military necessity, punishable as a violation of the laws or customs of war under Article 3(b) of the Statute" (para. 290). The Trial Chamber considered, "From a linguistic point of view, the meaning of the two terms, "devastation" and "destruction," is largely identical" and that "the two offences have been treated together by a number of instruments of international humanitarian law" (para. 291). In this case, the Trial Chamber decided "to equate the two crimes, while recognising that in other contexts, *e.g.* laying waste to crops or forests, the crime of devastation may have a wider application" (para. 291).

The Trial Chamber noted that the only jurisprudence dealing with the crime of "devastation not justified by military necessity" are the *Blaškić* Trial and Appeal Judgments and the *Brdjanin* Trial Judgment (footnote 935). However, it pointed out that the *Kordić and Čerkez* Trial Judgment identified the above elements of the crime of "wanton destruction not justified by military necessity", which the Appeals Chamber endorsed in that case (para. 292; also see, *Prosecutor v. Naletilic and Martinovic*, Judgment, Trial Chamber, March 31, 2003, para. 579 (under appeal)). In *Strugar*, the Trial Chamber adapted this definition of "wanton destruction" and applied it to "devastation not justified by military necessity" for that case (para. 293).

The *Strugar* Trial Chamber held that the first element "requires a showing that a considerable number of objects were damaged or destroyed [but] does not require destruction in its entirety of a city, town or village" (para. 294). Regarding the second requirement, the Trial Chamber defined military necessity by referring to the definition of military objectives in Article 52 of Additional Protocol I (para. 295). The requisite *mens rea* for a crime under Article 3(b) is satisfied "when the perpetrator acted with either direct or indirect intent, the latter requiring knowledge that devastation was a probable consequence of his acts" (*Strugar* Trial Judgment, para. 296, *citing Kordić and Čerkez* Trial Judgment, para. 346, and *Brdjanin* Trial Judgment, para. 593).

The Trial Chamber summarized the elements of the crime of "devastation not justified by military necessity" in the *Strugar* case as the following: "(a) destruction or damage of property on a large scale; (b) the destruction or damage was not justified by military necessity; and (c) the perpetrator acted with the intent to destroy or damage the property or in the knowledge that such destruction or damage was a probable consequence of his acts" (para. 297).

Attack, or bombardment, by whatever means, of undefended towns, villages, dwellings or buildings, Art. 3(c)

This offence is the equivalent of unlawful attacks on civilians and   **11–143** civilian objects as proscribed in Additional Protocols I and II. (See section on "Conduct of hostilities" in this Chapter for the elements of these offences; also see, Articles 25 and 27 of the 1907 Hague Convention IV.)

Seizure of, destruction or wilful damage done to institutions dedicated to religion, charity and education, the arts and sciences, historic monuments and works of art and science, Art. 3(d)

In the Judgment in *Blaškić*, the Trial Chamber defined this offence as   **11–144** follows:

> "The damage or destruction must have been committed intentionally to institutions which may clearly be identified as dedicated to religion or education and which were not being used for military purposes at the time of the acts. In addition, the institutions must not have been in the immediate vicinity of military objectives" (para. 185).

During the attacks that formed the subject of the indictment, a number of mosques and other religious institutions were destroyed or damaged. The question was whether this destruction was intentional or whether the buildings destroyed were collateral damage of legitimate military attacks. Whereas the Defence asserted that the mosques became locations of fighting, the Prosecution argued that they had been deliberately mined. Relying on the testimony of military personnel that mosques were destroyed by placing explosives around them, and that mosques would have made a very poor refuge for soldiers, the Trial Chamber concluded that the destruction had been deliberate (see paras 419–423).

On appeal, the Appeals Chamber reversed and vacated the convictions under Count 14 of the indictment, Destruction of Institutions Dedicated to Religion or Education.

The Trial Chamber in the Judgment in *Kordic and Cerkez* accepted the definition of the offence adopted in the *Blaškić* Judgment, noting that, in relation to the more general prohibition on attacks against civilian objects, this offence is a form of *lex specialis* for acts against cultural heritage (para. 361, *cited in Strugar* Trial Judgment, para. 302). While the Trial Chamber also pointed out that the specific count in the indictment was narrower than the offence set out in the Statute in that no charges were laid for the seizure of, or destruction or damage done to, institutions of charity, the arts and sciences, works of art and science, or historic monuments (para. 358), the Chamber noted that the elements described above are applicable *mutatis mutandis* to these other offences (para. 361).

On Appeal, the Appeals Chamber noted that, under conventional law, two forms of protection exist for cultural historical and religious monuments. The first is the general protection pursuant to, *inter alia*, Article 52 of Additional Protocol I, which applies to civilian objects. It prohibits destruction of a building or monument "unless it has turned into a military object by offering the attacking side 'a definite military advantage' at the time of attack" (*Kordić and Čerkez* Appeal Judgment, para. 89). The second is the special protection afforded to certain objects pursuant to Article 53 of Additional Protocol I, which applies to three types of objects: "historic monuments, works of art, and places of worship, provided they constitute the cultural or spiritual heritage of peoples (para. 90, footnote omitted). The Appeals Chamber held that although educational institutions are listed in Article 3(d) of the Statute and Article 52 of Additional Protocol I, not all educational buildings fulfil the criteria for protection as cultural property (para 92).

In *Naletilic and Martinovic*, the Trial Chamber rejected the *Blaškić* holding "that protected institutions 'must not have been in the vicinity of military objectives'" (*Naletilic and Martinovic* Trial Judgment, para. 604, quoting *Blaškić* Trial Judgment, para. 185). It laid out the following elements for a crime under Article 3(d) of the ICTY:

"i) the general requirements of Article 3 of the Statute are fulfilled;
  ii) the destruction regards an institution dedicated to religion;
  iii) the property was not used for military purposes;
  iv) the perpetrator acted with the intent to destroy the property"
(*Naletilic and Martinovic* Trial Judgment, para. 605).

In *Prosecutor v. Strugar*, the Accused was charged "with destruction or wilful damage done to institutions dedicated to religion, charity and education, the arts and sciences, historic monuments and works of art and science, punishable under Article 3(d) of the Statute (*Strugar* Trial Judgment, para. 298). According to the *Strugar* Trial Chamber, treaty and customary international law relevant to this crime include Article 27 of the Hague Regulations of 1907, the Hague Convention of 1954, Article 53 of Additional Protocol I and Article 16 of Additional Protocol II (para. 303). Referring to the ICRC Commentary to the Additional Protocols, the *Kordić and Čerkez* Appeals Judgment considered the basic idea underlying Article 1 of the 1954 Hague Convention and Article 53 of Additional Protocol I to be the same even though they use different terminology (para. 91; also see, *Strugar* Trial Judgment, para. 307). Although the 1954 Hague Convention and the Additional Protocols prohibit acts of hostility "directed" against cultural property, the *Strugar* Trial Judgment held that, under Article 3(d) of the ICTY Statute, "a requisite element of the crime charged in the Indictment is actual damage or destruction occurring as a result of an act directed against this property" (para. 308).

In *Strugar*, the Trial Chamber found that no military necessity arose in this case to justify the shelling of the Old Town in Dubrovnik; thus, it did not consider what was required for a waiver of the protections in the 1907 Hague Regulations, the 1954 Hague Convention, or the Additional Protocols (para. 309). It held that "the protection accorded to cultural property is lost where such property is used for military purposes" (*Strugar* Trial Judgment, para. 310). Furthermore, it concluded "it is the use of cultural property and not its location that determines whether and when the cultural property would lose its protection. Therefore, [. . .] the special protection awarded to cultural property itself may not be lost simply because of military activities or military installations in the immediate vicinity of the cultural property" (para. 310). It acknowledged that "the practical result may be that it cannot be established that the acts which caused destruction of or damage to cultural property were 'directed against' that cultural property, rather than the military installation or use in its immediate vicinity" (para. 310). The requisite mens rea of this crime is "that a perpetrator must act with a direct intent to damage or destroy the property in question" (*Strugar* Trial Judgment para. 311).

In *Strugar*, the Trial Chamber held:

> "For the purposes of this case, an act will fulfil the elements of the crime of destruction or wilful damage of cultural property, within the meaning of Article 3(d) of the Statute and in so far as that provision relates to cultural property, if: (i) it has caused damage or destruction to property which constitutes the cultural or spiritual heritage of peoples; (ii) the damaged or destroyed property was not used for military purposes at the time when the acts of hostility directed against these objects took place; and (iii) the act was carried out with the intent to damage or destroy the property in question" (para. 312).

It considered that the definition in the ICTY's jurisprudence reflects customary international law (para. 312).

Plunder of public or private property, Art. 3(e)

In the Judgment in *Delalic et al.*, the Trial Chamber held in respect of the offence of "plunder":   **11–145**

> "[I]t is to be observed that the prohibition against the unjustified appropriation of public and private enemy property is general in scope, and extends both to acts of looting committed by individual soldiers for their private gain, and to the organized seizure of property undertaken within the framework of a systematic economic exploitation of occupied territory. Contrary to the submissions of the Defence, the fact that it was acts of the latter category which were made the subject of prosecutions before the International Military Tribunal at Nürnberg and in the subsequent proceedings before the Nürnberg Military Tribunals does not demonstrate the absence of individual criminal liability under international law for individual acts of pillage committed by perpetrators motivated by personal greed. In contrast, when seen in a historical perspective, it is clear that the prohibition against pillage was directed precisely against violations of the latter kind. Consistent with this view, isolated instances of theft of personal property of modest value were

treated as war crimes in a number of trials before French Military Tribunals following the Second World War. Commenting upon this fact, the United Nations War Crimes Commission correctly described such offences as 'war crimes of the more traditional type'" (para. 590, footnotes omitted).

The Trial Chamber stated that it was not necessary to decide whether or not the terms "plunder" and "pillage" were synonymous under international law, but that it was clear that "plunder", as used in the ICTY's Statute.

"should be understood to embrace all forms of unlawful appropriation of property in armed conflict for which individual criminal responsibility attaches under international law, including those acts traditionally described as 'pillage'" (para. 591).

On the evidence before it, the Trial Chamber dismissed the charge of plunder. The evidence was to the effect that watches, other jewellery and money were taken from detainees in the Celebici detention camp. While the Trial Chamber agreed that the prohibition against plunder in international law protected important values, it was not convinced that the monetary value of the possessions taken was such as to entail grave consequences for the victims (para. 1154).

In *Blaškić*, the Appeals Chamber confirmed this view of the offence of plunder (para. 147; also see, *Kordić and Čerkez* Appeal Judgment, para. 79; *Blaškić* Trial Judgment, para. 184; *Kordić and Čerkez* Trial Judgment, paras 352–353). The *Blaškić* Appeals Judgment states: "The prohibition against pillage may therefore be considered to be part of customary international law" (para. 148). The Appeals Chamber overturned the convictions under Count 13 for destruction and plunder of property. At trial, the Trial Chamber convicted the accused on the basis that he was responsible for the actions of his subordinates who had looted the villages during the attacks. The plunder included taking money and other valuables from individuals, as well as the wholesale looting of houses not totally destroyed in the attacks (para. 424).

In *Kordić and Čerkez*, the Appeals Chamber listed norms of international humanitarian law prohibiting plunder, including pillage (*Kordić and Čerkez* Appeal Judgment, para. 77). It held that "[t]he prohibition of plunder is general in its application and not limited to occupied territories" (para. 78), and it noted "that in accordance with Geneva Convention IV, the Statute itself does not draw a difference between public or private property" (para. 79, footnote omitted).

The Appeals Chamber clarified that, pursuant to Article 3 and Article 1 of the Statute, only serious violations fall within the jurisdiction of the Tribunal. According to the *Tadić* Jurisdiction Decision, "serious" entails "a breach of a rule protecting important values *and* a breach that involves grave consequences for the victim" (*Kordić and Čerkez* Appeal Judgment, para. 80, citing *Tadić* Jurisdiction Decision, para. 94). It found: "The prohibition of unjustified appropriation of private or public property is without a doubt a rule that protects important values" (para. 81). Regarding the requirement of grave consequences for the victim, it agreed with the holding of the *Delalic et al.* Trial Judgment and the *Tadić* Jurisdiction Decision "that there is a consequential link between the monetary value of the appropriated property and the gravity of the consequences for the victim" (*Kordić and Čerkez* Appeal Judgment, para. 82, *citing Delalic et al.* Trial Judgment, para. 1154). However, the Appeals Chamber stressed that the threshold level of value must be determined on a case-by-case basis (para. 82). Furthermore, the Appeals Chamber considered "that a serious violation could be assumed in circumstances where appropriations take place vis-à-vis a large number of people, even though there are no grave consequences for each individual. In this case it would be the overall effect on the civilian population and the multitude of offences committed that would make the violation serious" (para. 83).

In general, the elements of the crime of plunder are the intentional and unlawful appropriation of private or public property and the fulfilment of the requisite seriousness of the crime pursuant to Article 3 of the Statute in conjunction with Article 1 (para. 84).

(2) Common Article 3 elements

The provisions of common Article 3 are: **11–146**

"In the case of armed conflict not of an international character occurring in the territory of one of the High Contracting Parties, each Party to the conflict shall be bound to apply, as a minimum, the following provisions:

(1) Persons taking no active part in the hostilities, including members of the armed forces who have laid down their arms and those placed hors de combat by sickness, wounds, detention, or any other cause, shall in all circumstances be treated humanely, without any adverse distinction founded on race, colour, religion or faith, sex, birth or wealth, or any other similar criteria. To this end the following acts are and shall remain prohibited at any time and in any place whatsoever with respect to the above-mentioned persons:

    a. violence to life and person, in particular murder of all kinds, mutilation, cruel treatment and torture;

    b. taking of hostages;

    c. outrages upon personal dignity, in particular humiliating and degrading treatment;

    d. the passing of sentences and the carrying out of executions without previous judgment pronounced by a regularly constituted court, affording all the judicial guarantees which are recognised as indispensable by civilized peoples.

(2) The wounded and the sick shall be collected and cared for. An impartial humanitarian body, such as the International Committee of the Red Cross, may offer its services to the Parties to the conflict.

The Parties to the conflict should further endeavour to bring into force, by means of special agreements, all or part of the other provisions of the present Convention.

The application of the preceding provisions shall not affect the legal status of the Parties to the conflict."

Article 3 of the ICTY Statute encompasses *any* violation of the laws and customs of war not already covered by Articles 2, 4 and 5. The most frequently charged violations not listed in Article 3 are those contained in Article 3 common to the 1949 Geneva Conventions.

Violence to life and person, in particular murder of all kinds, mutilation, cruel treatment and torture

11–147   The elements of murder are the same as the grave breach of wilful killing except for the requisite status of the victim. In the *Kordic and Cerkez* case, the Trial Chamber concluded as follows:

"Following the findings of the *Celebici* and *Blaškić* Trial Chambers, the Trial Chamber finds that the elements of the offence of 'murder' under Article 3 of the Statute are similar to those which define a 'wilful killing' under Article 2 of the Statute, with the exception that under Article 3 of the Statute the offence need not have been directed against a 'protected person' but against a person 'taking no active part in the hostilities'" (para. 233, footnotes omitted; also see, *Kordić and Čerkez* Appeal Judgment, paras 36–37; *Delalic et al.* Appeals Judgment, paras 422–423).

The Trial Chamber had set out the elements of wilful killing:

"Accordingly, the Chamber finds that, in relation to the crime of wilful killing, the *actus reus*—the physical act necessary for the offence—is the death of the victim as a result of the actions or omissions of the accused. In this regard, the Chamber observes that the conduct of the accused must be a substantial cause of the death of the victim, who must have been a 'protected person'. To satisfy the *mens rea* for wilful killing, it must be established that the accused had the intent to kill, or to inflict serious bodily injury in reckless disregard of human life" (para. 229, footnotes omitted).

In relation to the offence of cruel treatment, the Appeals Chamber in the *Celebici* case held:

Cruel treatment as a violation of the laws or customs of war is
   a. an intentional act or omission [. . .] which causes serious mental or physical suffering or injury or constitutes a serious attack on human dignity,
   b. committed against a person taking no active part in the hostilities.
The offence of wilfully causing great suffering under Article 2 contains an element not present in the offence of cruel treatment under Article 3: the protected person status of the victim (*Delalic et al.* Appeal Judgment, para. 424, footnote omitted, *quoted in Blaškić* Appeal Judgment, para. 595).

Although the Appeals Chamber in *Blaškić* "noted that the use of forced labour is not always unlawful", it found that trench-digging, under certain circumstances, can amount to cruel treatment in violation of Article 3 of the ICTY Statute and common Article 3(1)(a) of the Geneva Conventions:

"Any order to compel protected persons to dig trenches or to prepare other forms of military installations, in particular when such persons are ordered to do so against their own forces in an armed conflict, constitutes cruel treatment" (*Blaškić* Appeal Judgment, para. 597).

In general, "the treatment of non-combatant detainees may be considered cruel where, together with the other requisite elements, that treatment causes serious mental or physical suffering or injury or constitutes a serious attack on human dignity" (*Blaškić* Appeal Judgment, para. 597).

For the offence of torture under common Article 3, apart from the jurisdictional requirements of the Article 2 offences, the elements are the same as those of the grave breach of torture. In the second of the *Foca* cases, *Prosecutor v. Krnojelac*, the Trial Chamber held: "The definition of the offence of torture is the same regardless of the Article of the Statute under which the acts of the Accused have been charged" (*Prosecutor v. Krnojelac* Judgment, Trial Chamber, March 15, 2002, para. 178, *citing Delalic et al.* Trial Judgment, paras 468–469; *Furundžija* Trial Judgment, paras 139, 153–154; *Kunarac* Trial Judgment, para. 497; *Prosecutor v. Kvočka et al.*, Judgment, Trial Chamber, November 2, 2001, para. 158). However, the Appeals Chamber in *Delalic et al.* pointed out that protected person requirement of Article 2 distinguishes it from Article 3 (para. 425). The offence has regularly been charged together with the grave breach of torture. (See Trial Chamber's Judgment in the *Celebici* case, paras 913–924).

As with the grave breach of torture, rape can constitute torture when charged under Article 3 (see, *e.g.*, *Delalic et al.* Trial Judgment, paras 941–943, *affirmed Delalic et al.* Appeal Judgment, paras 488–499). In the Judgment in *Prosecutor v. Furundžija*, December 10, 1998, the Trial Chamber stated "that among the possible purposes of torture one must also include that of humiliating the victim" (para. 162).

Taking of hostages

The Trial Chamber in the Judgment in the *Blaškić* case, when discussing the elements of the comparable grave breach, stated: "The elements of the offence are similar to those of Article 3(b) of the Geneva Conventions covered under Article 3 of the Statute" (para. 158). When considering the offence as charged under Article 3 (common Article 3(b)), it held as follows:

11–148

> "Consonant with the spirit of the Fourth Convention, the Commentary sets out that the term 'hostage' must be understood in the broadest sense. The definition of hostages must be understood as being similar to that of civilians taken as hostages within the meaning of grave breaches under Article 2 of the Statute, that is—persons unlawfully deprived of their freedom, often wantonly and sometimes under threat of death. The parties did not contest that to be characterised as hostages the detainees must have been used to obtain some advantage or to ensure that a belligerent, other person or other group of persons enter into some undertaking" (para. 187, footnote omitted).

The Trial Chamber in their Judgment in the *Kordić and Čerkez* case concurred with this analysis (paras 319–320), and held "that, in the context of an international armed conflict, the elements of the offence of taking of hostages under Article 3 of the Statute are essentially the same as those of the offence of taking civilians as hostage as described by Article 2(h)" (para. 320).

Outrages upon personal dignity, in particular humiliating and degrading treatment

The Trial Chamber in the Judgment in the first *Foca* case (*Prosecutor v. Kunarac et al.*, February 22, 2001) held that "this Trial Chamber understands an outrage upon personal dignity to be any act or omission

11–149

which would be generally considered to cause serious humiliation, degradation or otherwise be a serious attack on human dignity" (para. 507). The Trial Chamber did not accept the requirement stated in *Prosecutor v. Aleksovski*, Judgment, Trial Chamber, June 25, 1999, para. 56, that the suffering would have to be "lasting". It held that, as long as the humiliation or degradation is real or serious, it would not also have to be lasting. Such a requirement would mean that the offence could never be proved if any victim was in the process of recovering or had recovered from the experience. There is no "minimum temporal requirement of the effects of an outrage upon personal dignity" (para. 501). The humiliation of the victim must be so serious as to satisfy an objective standard, that is whether a reasonable person would be outraged (*Aleksovski* Trial Judgment, para. 54, *quoted in Kunarac et al.* Trial Judgment, para. 504; also see, *Kunarac et al.* Appeal Judgment, paras 162–163). The Trial Chamber considered "a purely subjective assessment would be unfair to the accused because the accused's culpability would be made to depend not on the gravity of the act but on the sensitivity of the victim" (*Aleksovski* Trial Judgment, para. 54, *quoted in Kunarac et al.* Trial Judgment, para. 504; also see, *Prosecutor v. Aleksovski*, Judgment, Appeals Chamber, May 30, 2001, para. 37).

On the *mens rea* required, the Trial Chamber stated:

> "The Trial Chamber is of the view that the requirement of an intent to commit the specific act or omission which gives rise to criminal liability in this context involves a requirement that the perpetrator be aware of the objective character of the relevant act or omission. It is a necessary aspect of a true intention to undertake a particular action that there is an awareness of the nature of that act. As the relevant act or omission for an outrage upon personal dignity is an act or omission which would be generally considered to cause serious humiliation, degradation or other-wise be a serious attack on human dignity, an accused must know that his act or omission is of that character—ie, that it could cause serious humiliation, degradation or affront to human dignity. This is not the same as requiring that the accused knew of the *actual* consequences of the act" (*Kunarac et al.* Trial Judgment, para. 512).

On Appeal, the Appeals Chamber held that "the Trial Chamber properly demonstrated that the crime of outrages upon personal dignity requires only a knowledge of the "possible" consequences of the charged act or omission" (*Kunarac et al.* Appeal Judgment, para. 165). In *Aleksovski*, the Appeals Chamber held that it was not a specific intent crime (*Aleksovski* Appeal Judgment, para. 27).

Accordingly, the elements required to be proved for a conviction of this offence are:

> "(i) that the accused intentionally committed or participated in an act or omission which would be generally considered to cause serious humilia-tion, degradation or otherwise be a serious attack on human dignity, and
> (ii) that he knew that the act or omission could have that effect."
> (*Kunarac et al.* Trial Judgment, para 514).

The Appeals Chamber in *Aleksovski* found "that it is not an element of offences under Article 3 of the Statute, nor of the offence of outrages upon personal dignity, that the perpetrator had a discriminatory intent or motive" (*Aleksovski* Appeal Judgment, para. 28).

The evidence led in the *Kunarac et al.* case was that the victims, a number of women, had been enslaved as the personal property of the accused for a period of six months, continuously raped during that period, and been forced to do all the household chores. While this evidence was sufficient to convict the accused on charges of rape and enslavement, the Trial Chamber held that there was "no evidence upon which it would be appropriate to convict the accused for outrages upon personal dignity that is not already covered by other convictions" (para. 743). By contrast, where another accused kept three young women as slaves in his apartment for a period, during which time they were raped, beaten, threatened, kept in continual fear, made to perform all household chores and to dance naked on a table, and eventually sold, the Trial Chamber held that, apart from being sufficient to sustain rape and enslavement convictions, this evidence was also sufficient for a finding of guilt in respect of the charge of outrages upon personal dignity (paras 780–782).

On appeal, the Trial Chamber's findings were upheld (see *Prosecutor v. Kunarac et al.*, Judgment, Appeals Chamber, June 12, 2002, paras 162–166; *Aleksovski* Appeal Judgment, paras 28, 37–38. Also see *Prosecutor v. Kvočka*, Judgment, Trial Chamber, November 2, 2001, paras 166–168).

The passing of sentences and the carrying out of executions without previous judgment pronounced by a regularly constituted court, affording all the judicial guarantees which are recognised as indispensable by civilised peoples

As with the similar Article 2 offence ("wilfully depriving a prisoner of war or a civilian of the rights of fair and regular trial"), this offence has not been charged before the ICTY. The ICRC Commentaries provide some guidance as to the application of this provision. While the Commentary to GC IV makes it clear that this provision does nothing to limit the State's right to prosecute, sentence and punish criminal activity according to the law, it also stipulates that it will have to be undertaken according to acceptable standards (see ICRC Commentary to GC IV, pp. 39–40). **11–150**

CHAPTER 12

CRIMES AGAINST HUMANITY

I. STATUTORY PROVISIONS

A. ICC

Statute, Art. 7

Crimes against humanity

12–1 **7.**—(1) For the purpose of this Statute, "crime against humanity" means any of the following acts when committed as part of a widespread or systematic attack directed against any civilian population, with knowledge of the attack:
  (a) Murder;
  (b) Extermination;
  (c) Enslavement;
  (d) Deportation or forcible transfer of population;
  (e) Imprisonment or other severe deprivation of physical liberty in violation of fundamental rules of international law;
  (f) Torture;
  (g) Rape, sexual slavery, enforced prostitution, forced pregnancy, enforced sterilization, or any other form of sexual violence of comparable gravity;
  (h) Persecution against any identifiable group or collectivity on political, racial, national, ethnic, cultural, religious, gender as defined in paragraph 3, or other grounds that are universally recognized as impermissible under international law, in connection with any act referred to in this paragraph or any crime within the jurisdiction of the Court;
  (i) Enforced disappearance of persons;
  (j) The crime of apartheid;
  (k) Other inhumane acts of a similar character intentionally causing great suffering, or serious injury to body or to mental or physical health.

12–2 (2) For the purpose of paragraph 1:
  (a) "Attack directed against any civilian population" means a course of conduct involving the multiple commission of acts referred to in paragraph 1 against any civilian population, pursuant to or in furtherance of a State or organizational policy to commit such attack;
  (b) "Extermination" includes the intentional infliction of conditions of life, *inter alia* the deprivation of access to food and medicine, calculated to bring about the destruction of part of a population;
  (c) "Enslavement" means the exercise of any or all of the powers attaching to the right of ownership over a person and includes the exercise of such power in the course of trafficking in persons, in particular women and children;
  (d) "Deportation or forcible transfer of population" means forced displacement of the persons concerned by expulsion of other coercive acts from the area in which they are lawfully present, without grounds permitted under international law;
  (e) "Torture" means the intentional infliction of severe pain or suffering, whether physical or mental, upon a person in the custody or under the control of the accused; except that torture shall not include pain or suffering arising only from, inherent in or incidental to, lawful sanctions;
  (f) "Forced pregnancy" means the unlawful confinement of a woman forcibly made pregnant, with the intent of affecting the ethnic

composition of any population or carrying out other grave violations of international law. This definition shall not in any way be interpreted as affecting national laws relating to pregnancy;

(g) "Persecution" means the intentional and severe deprivation of fundamental rights contrary to international law by reason of the identity of the group or collectivity;

(h) "The crime of apartheid" means inhumane acts of a character similar to those referred to in paragraph 1, committed in the context of an institutionalized regime of systematic oppression and domination by one racial group over any other racial group or groups and committed with the intention of maintaining that regime;

(i) "Enforced disappearance of persons" means the arrest, detention or abduction of persons by, or with the authorization, support or acquiescence of, a State or a political organization, followed by a refusal to acknowledge that deprivation of freedom or to give information on the fate or whereabouts of those persons, with the intention of removing them from the protection of the law for a prolonged period of time.

(3) For the purpose of this Statute, it is understood that the term "gender" refers to the two sexes, male and female, within the context of society. The term "gender" does not indicate any meaning different from the above.

B. ICTY

Statute of the ICTY, Art. 5

Crimes against humanity

5. The International Tribunal shall have the power to prosecute persons responsible for the following crimes when committed in armed conflict, whether international or internal in character, and directed against any civilian population:

12–3

    (a) murder;
    (b) extermination;
    (c) enslavement;
    (d) deportation;
    (e) imprisonment;
    (f) torture;
    (g) rape;
    (h) persecutions on political, racial and religious grounds;
    (i) other inhumane acts.

C. ICTR

Statute of the ICTR, Art. 3

Crimes against Humanity

3. The International Tribunal for Rwanda shall have the power to prosecute persons responsible for the following crimes when committed as part of a widespread or systematic attack against any civilian population on national, political, ethnic, racial or religious grounds:

12–4

    (a) Murder;
    (b) Extermination;
    (c) Enslavement;
    (d) Deportation;
    (e) Imprisonment;
    (f) Torture;
    (g) Rape;
    (h) Persecutions on political, racial and religious grounds;
    (i) Other inhumane acts.

D. EAST TIMOR

Regulation No. 2000/15, s.5

Crimes Against Humanity

12–5   **5.**—5.1. For the purposes of the present regulation, "crimes against humanity" means any of the following acts when committed as part of a widespread or systematic attack and directed against any civilian population, with knowledge of the attack:
    (a) Murder;
    (b) Extermination;
    (c) Enslavement;
    (d) Deportation or forcible transfer of population;
    (e) Imprisonment or other severe deprivation of physical liberty in violation of fundamental rules of international law;
    (f) Torture;
    (g) Rape, sexual slavery, enforced prostitution, forced pregnancy, enforced sterilization, or any other form of sexual violence of comparable gravity;
    (h) Persecution against any identifiable group or collectivity on political, racial, national, ethnic, cultural, religious, gender as defined in Section 5.3 of the present regulation, or other grounds that are universally recognized as impermissible under international law, in connection with any act referred to in this paragraph or any crime within the jurisdiction of the panels;
    (i) Enforced disappearance of persons;
    (j) The crime of apartheid;
    (k) Other inhumane acts of a similar character intentionally causing great suffering, or serious injury to body or to mental or physical health.
    5.2. For the purposes of Section 5.1 of the present regulation:
    (a) "Extermination" includes the intentional infliction of conditions of life, *inter alia* the deprivation of access to food and medicine, calculated to bring about the destruction of part of a population;
    (b) "Enslavement" means the exercise of any or all of the powers attaching to the right of ownership over a person and includes the exercise of such power in the course of trafficking in persons, in particular women and children;
    (c) "Deportation or forcible transfer of population" means forced displacement of the persons concerned by expulsion or other coercive acts from the area in which they are lawfully present, without grounds permitted under international law;
    (d) "Torture" means the intentional infliction of severe pain or suffering, whether physical or mental, upon a person in the custody or under the control of the accused; except that torture shall not include pain or

suffering arising only from, inherent in or incidental to, lawful sanctions;

(e) "Forced pregnancy" means the unlawful confinement of a woman forcibly made pregnant, with the intent of affecting the ethnic composition of any population or carrying out other grave violations of international law. This definition shall not in any way be interpreted as affecting national laws relating to pregnancy;

(f) "Persecution" means the intentional and severe deprivation of fundamental rights contrary to international law by reason of the identity of the group or collectivity;

(g) "The crime of apartheid" means inhumane acts of a character similar to those referred to in Section 5.1, committed in the context of an institutionalised regime of systematic oppression and domination by one racial group over any other racial group or groups and committed with the intention of maintaining that regime;

(h) "Enforced disappearance of persons" means the arrest, detention or abduction of persons by, or with the authorization, support or acquiescence of, a State or a political organization, followed by a refusal to acknowledge that deprivation of freedom or to give information on the fate or whereabouts of those persons, with the intention of removing them from the protection of the law for a prolonged period of time.

5.3. For the purpose of the present regulation, the term "gender" refers to the two sexes, male and female, within the context of society. The term "gender" does not indicate any meaning different from the above.

E. Sierra Leone

Statute of the Special Court for Sierra Leone, Art. 2

Crimes against humanity

2. The Special Court shall have the power to prosecute persons who committed the following crimes as part of a widespread or systematic attack against any civilian population:

12–6

(a) Murder;
(b) Extermination;
(c) Enslavement;
(d) Deportation;
(e) Imprisonment;
(f) Torture;
(g) Rape, sexual slavery, enforced prostitution, forced pregnancy and any other form of sexual violence;
(h) Persecution on political, racial, ethnic or religious grounds;
(i) Other inhumane acts.

F. Cambodia

Law on the Establishment of Extraordinary Chambers in the Courts of Cambodia for the Prosecution of Crimes Committed During the Period of Democratic Kampuchea, as amended, Art. 5

Crimes against humanity

5. The Extraordinary Chambers shall have the power to bring to trial all Suspects who committed crimes against humanity during the period 17 April 1975 to 6 January 1979.

12–7

Crimes against humanity, which have no statute of limitations, are any acts committed as part of a widespread or systematic attack directed against any civilian population, on national, political, ethnical, racial or religious grounds, such as:

— murder;
— extermination;
— enslavement;
— deportation;
— imprisonment;
— torture;
— rape;
— persecutions on political, racial, and religious grounds;
— other inhumane acts.

G. IRAQ

The Statute of the Iraqi Special Tribunal, Art. 12

Crimes Against Humanity

12–8   12. a) For the purposes of this Statute, "crimes against humanity" means any of the following acts when committed as part of a widespread or systematic attack directed against any civilian population, with knowledge of the attack:

1. Murder;
2. Extermination;
3. Enslavement;
4. Deportation or forcible transfer of population;
5. Imprisonment or other severe deprivation of physical liberty in violation of fundamental norms of international law;
6. Torture;
7. Rape, sexual slavery, enforced prostitution, forced pregnancy, or any other form of sexual violence of comparable gravity;
8. Persecution against any identifiable group or collectivity on political, racial, national, ethnic, cultural, religious, gender or other grounds that are universally recognized as impermissible under international law, in connection with any act referred to in this paragraph or any crime within the jurisdiction of the Tribunal;
9. Enforced disappearance of persons; and
10. Other inhumane acts of a similar character intentionally causing great suffering, or serious injury to body or to mental or physical health.

b) For the purposes of paragraph a):

1. "Attack directed against any civilian population" means a course of conduct involving the multiple commission of acts referred to in the above paragraph against any civilian population, pursuant to or in furtherance of a state or organizational policy to commit such attack;
2. "Extermination" includes the intentional infliction of conditions of life, such as the deprivation of access to food and medicine, calculated to bring about the destruction of part of a population;
3. "Enslavement" means the exercise of any or all of the powers attaching to the right of ownership over a person and includes the exercise of such power in the course of trafficking in persons, in particular women and children;
4. "Deportation or forcible transfer of population" means forced displacement of the persons concerned by expulsion or other coercive acts from the area in which they are lawfully present, without grounds permitted under international law;

5. "Torture" means the intentional infliction of severe pain or suffering, whether physical or mental, upon a person in the custody or under the control of the accused; except that torture shall not include pain or suffering arising only from, inherent in, or incidental to lawful sanctions;

6. "Persecution" means the intentional and severe deprivation of fundamental rights contrary to international law by reason of the identity of the group or collectivity; and

7. "Enforced disappearance of persons" means the arrest, detention or abduction of persons by, or with the authorization, support or acquiescence of, the State or a political organization, followed by a refusal to acknowledge that deprivation of freedom or to give information on the fate or whereabouts of those persons, with the intention of removing them from the protection of the law for a prolonged period of time.

II. DEFINITION

A. HISTORY

The definition of crimes against humanity has evolved since this concept first received international legal recognition in the *St. Petersburg Declaration of 1868*, which limited the use of explosive or incendiary projectiles as "contrary to the laws of humanity". The First Hague Peace Conference in 1899 unanimously adopted the Martens Clause as part of the Preamble to the *Hague Convention respecting the laws and customs of war on land*, which provides: "Until a more complete code of the laws of war is issued, the High Contracting Parties think it right to declare that, in cases not included in the Regulations adopted by them, populations and belligerents remain under the protection and empire of the principles of international law, as they result from the usages established between civilized nations, from the laws of humanity and the requirements of the public conscience." This Clause has been incorporated in most subsequent humanitarian law treaties.

The first indication of the crimes which would be included in the definition of crimes against humanity was given in the *Declaration of France, Great Britain and Russia* on May 24, 1915 denouncing the massacres by the Ottoman Empire of Armenians in Turkey as "crimes against humanity and civilization for which all the members of the Turkish Government will be held responsible together with its agents implicated in the massacres". The 1919 Versailles Peace Conference Commission made it clear that these crimes included murders and massacres, systematic terrorism, putting hostages to death, torture of civilians, deliberate starvation of civilians, rape, abduction of girls and women for the purposes of enforced prostitution, deportation of civilians, internment of civilians under inhuman conditions, forced labour of civilians in connection with the military operations of the enemy, imposition of collective penalties and deliberate bombardment of undefended places and hospitals. The 1946 Nuremberg Charter embodied the first definition of crimes against humanity for the purposes of assigning individual criminal responsibility for these crimes before the International Military Tribunal at Nuremberg.

12–9

B. ROME CONFERENCE

12–10   The most recent pronouncement by States on the definition of crimes against humanity occurred in Rome in August 1998 at the Diplomatic Conference for the establishment of a permanent International Criminal Court (ICC). The conclusions of the Rome Conference, together with the jurisprudence of the ICTY and the ICTR, provide the basis for the current elements of crimes against humanity.

The *chapeau* of Article 7 of the ICC Statute reflects the general definition of crimes against humanity under international law: "For the purposes of this Statute, 'crime against humanity' means any of the following acts [which are listed thereafter] when committed as part of a widespread or systematic attack directed against any civilian population, with knowledge of the attack". This provision captures the essence of such crimes, namely that they are acts that occur during a widespread or systematic attack on any civilian population in either times of war or peace.

12–11   The drafting history of this provision reveals that little consensus existed in respect of most of these elements before the Diplomatic Conference in Rome. There was no fundamental disagreement over the prerequisite that the acts must be committed as part of an attack on any civilian population. However, it was unresolved whether these acts needed to take place during armed conflict, and if they had to occur on discriminatory grounds (see, *Report of the Ad Hoc Committee on the Establishment of an International Criminal Court* (G.A., 50th Sess., Supp. No. 22, A/50/22, 1995), paras 77–80; *Report of the Preparatory Committee on the Establishment of an International Criminal Court*, Volume 1, Proceedings of the Preparatory Committee During March–April and August 1996 (G.A., 51st Sess., Supp. No. 22, A/51/22, 1996), paras 82–90; *Decisions Taken by the Preparatory Committee at its Session Held 11 to February 21, 1997*, (A/AC.249/1997/L.5, 1997), pp. 4–6; *Report of the Preparatory Committee on the Establishment of an International Criminal Court, Draft Statute & Draft Final Act*, (A/Conf.183/2/Add.1, 1998), pp. 30–33).

It is evident from the *chapeau* that the State delegates finally decided not to include either of these requirements with the exception of persecution, which in accordance with paragraph 1(h) of Article 7 requires that the acts be committed on certain discriminatory grounds.

12–12   Another point of divergence arose over whether the attack had to be both widespread *and* systematic, or only one or the other. The matter was resolved in favour of the alternative formulation. A concern had been to exclude isolated and random acts, and ordinary crimes under national law, from the ambit of crimes against humanity. This has been achieved through the requirement of the acts being *either* widespread *or* systematic. Either of these conditions will ensure that single, isolated, dispersed or random acts, which do not rise to the level of crimes against humanity, cannot be prosecuted. In *Prosecutor v. Tadic*, the ICTY Trial Chamber held: "It is therefore the desire to exclude isolated or random acts from the notion of crimes against humanity that led to the inclusion of the requirement that the acts must be directed against a civilian 'population', and either a finding of widespreadness [. . .] or systematicity" (*Prosecutor v. Tadic*, Judgment, Trial Chamber, May 7,

1997, para. 648). Similarly, in *Prosecutor v. Akayesu*, an ICTR Trial Chamber held: "The Chamber considers that it is a prerequisite that the act must be committed as part of a widespread or systematic attack and not just a random act of violence. The act can be part of a widespread or systematic attack and need not be part of both" (*Prosecutor v. Akayesu*, Judgment, Trial Chamber, September 2, 1998, para. 579).

Crimes against humanity are thus crimes "which either by their magnitude and savagery or by their large number or by the fact that a similar pattern was applied [. . .] endangered the international community or shocked the conscience of mankind" (see, *History of the United Nations War Crimes Commission and the Development of the Laws of War*, 1943, p. 179).

III. ELEMENTS OF THE OFFENCE

A. ICC ELEMENTS

Elements of Crimes

Article 7

Crimes against humanity

Introduction

1. Since article 7 pertains to international criminal law, its provisions, consistent with article 22, must be strictly construed, taking into account that crimes against humanity as defined in article 7 are among the most serious crimes of concern to the international community as a whole, warrant and entail individual criminal responsibility, and require conduct which is impermissible under generally applicable international law, as recognized by the principal legal systems of the world.

2. The last two elements for each crime against humanity describe the context in which the conduct must take place. These elements clarify the requisite participation in and knowledge of a widespread or systematic attack against a civilian population. However, the last element should not be interpreted as requiring proof that the perpetrator had knowledge of all characteristics of the attack or the precise details of the plan or policy of the State or organization. In the case of an emerging widespread or systematic attack against a civilian population, the intent clause of the last element indicates that this mental element is satisfied if the perpetrator intended to further such an attack.

3. "Attack directed against a civilian population" in these context elements is understood to mean a course of conduct involving the multiple commission of acts referred to in article 7, paragraph 1, of the Statute against any civilian population, pursuant to or in furtherance of a State or organizational policy to commit such attack. The acts need not constitute a military attack. It is understood that "policy to commit such attack" requires that the State or organization actively promote or encourage such an attack against a civilian population. (A policy which has a civilian population as the object of the attack

12–13

would be implemented by State or organizational action. Such a policy may, in exceptional circumstances, be implemented by a deliberate failure to take action, which is consciously aimed at encouraging such attack. The existence of such a policy cannot be inferred solely from the absence of governmental or organizational action.)

Article 7(1)(a)

Crime against humanity of murder

Elements

12–14   1. The perpetrator killed (The term "killed" is interchangeable with the term "caused death". This footnote applies to all elements which use either of these concepts.) one or more persons.

2. The conduct was committed as part of a widespread or systematic attack directed against a civilian population.

3. The perpetrator knew that the conduct was part of or intended the conduct to be part of a widespread or systematic attack against a civilian population.

Article 7(1)(b)

Crime against humanity of extermination

Elements

12–15   1. The perpetrator killed (The conduct could be committed by different methods of killing, either directly or indirectly.) one or more persons, including by inflicting conditions of life calculated to bring about the destruction of part of a population. (The infliction of such conditions could include the deprivation of access to food and medicine.)

2. The conduct constituted, or took place as part of, (The term "as part of" would include the initial conduct in a mass killing.) a mass killing of members of a civilian population.

3. The conduct was committed as part of a widespread or systematic attack directed against a civilian population.

4. The perpetrator knew that the conduct was part of or intended the conduct to be part of a widespread or systematic attack directed against a civilian population.

Article 7(1)(c)

Crime against humanity of enslavement

Elements

12–16   1. The perpetrator exercised any or all of the powers attaching to the right of ownership over one or more persons, such as by purchasing, selling, lending or bartering such a person or persons, or by imposing on them a similar deprivation of liberty. (It is understood that such deprivation of liberty may, in some circumstances, include exacting forced labour or otherwise reducing a person to a servile status as defined in the Supplementary Convention on the Abolition of Slavery, the Slave Trade, and Institutions and Practices Similar to Slavery of 1956. It is also understood that the conduct described in this element includes trafficking in persons, in particular women and children.)

2. The conduct was committed as part of a widespread or systematic attack directed against a civilian population.

3. The perpetrator knew that the conduct was part of or intended the conduct to be part of a widespread or systematic attack directed against a civilian population.

Article 7(1)(d)

Crime against humanity of deportation or forcible transfer of population

Elements

1. The perpetrator deported or forcibly (The term "forcibly" is not restricted to physical force, but may include threat of force or coercion, such as that caused by fear of violence, duress, detention, psychological oppression or abuse of power against such person or persons or another person, or by taking advantage of a coercive environment.) transferred ("Deported or forcibly transferred" is interchangeable with "forcibly displaced".), without grounds permitted under international law, one or more persons to another State or location, by expulsion or other coercive acts.

2. Such person or persons were lawfully present in the area from which they were so deported or transferred.

3. The perpetrator was aware of the factual circumstances that established the lawfulness of such presence.

4. The conduct was committed as part of a widespread or systematic attack directed against a civilian population.

5. The perpetrator knew that the conduct was part of or intended the conduct to be part of a widespread or systematic attack directed against a civilian population.

12–17

Article 7(1)(e)

Crime against humanity of imprisonment or other severe deprivation of physical liberty

Elements

1. The perpetrator imprisoned one or more persons or otherwise severely deprived one or more persons of physical liberty.

2. The gravity of the conduct was such that it was in violation of fundamental rules of international law.

3. The perpetrator was aware of the factual circumstances that established the gravity of the conduct.

4. The conduct was committed as part of a widespread or systematic attack directed against a civilian population.

5. The perpetrator knew that the conduct was part of or intended the conduct to be part of a widespread or systematic attack directed against a civilian population.

12–18

Article 7(1)(f)

Crime against humanity of torture (It is understood that no specific purpose need be proved for this crime.)

Elements

12–19   1. The perpetrator inflicted severe physical or mental pain or suffering upon one or more persons.

2. Such person or persons were in the custody or under the control of the perpetrator.

3. Such pain or suffering did not arise only from, and was not inherent in or incidental to, lawful sanctions.

4. The conduct was committed as part of a widespread or systematic attack directed against a civilian population.

5. The perpetrator knew that the conduct was part of or intended the conduct to be part of a widespread or systematic attack directed against a civilian population.

Article 7(1)(g)–1

Crime against humanity of rape

Elements

12–20   1. The perpetrator invaded (The concept of "invasion" is intended to be broad enough to be gender-neutral.) the body of a person by conduct resulting in penetration, however slight, of any part of the body of the victim or of the perpetrator with a sexual organ, or of the anal or genital opening of the victim with any object or any other part of the body.

2. The invasion was committed by force, or by threat of force or coercion, such as that caused by fear of violence, duress, detention, psychological oppression or abuse of power, against such person or another person, or by taking advantage of a coercive environment, or the invasion was committed against a person incapable of giving genuine consent. (It is understood that a person may be incapable of giving genuine consent if affected by natural, induced or age-related incapacity. This footnote also applies to the corresponding elements of article 7(1)(g)–3, 5 and 6.)

3. The conduct was committed as part of a widespread or systematic attack directed against a civilian population.

4. The perpetrator knew that the conduct was part of or intended the conduct to be part of a widespread or systematic attack directed against a civilian population.

Article 7(1)(g)–2

Crime against humanity of sexual slavery (Given the complex nature of this crime, it is recognized that its commission could involve more than one perpetrator as a part of a common criminal purpose.)

Elements

12–21   1. The perpetrator exercised any or all of the powers attaching to the right of ownership over one or more persons, such as by purchasing, selling, lending or bartering such a person or persons, or by imposing on them a similar deprivation of liberty. (It is understood that such deprivation of liberty may, in some circumstances, include exacting forced labour or otherwise reducing a person to a servile status as defined in the Supplementary Convention on the Abolition of Slavery, the Slave Trade, and Institutions and Practices Similar to Slavery of 1956. It is also understood that the conduct described in this element includes trafficking in persons, in particular women and children.)

2. The perpetrator caused such person or persons to engage in one or more acts of a sexual nature.

3. The conduct was committed as part of a widespread or systematic attack directed against a civilian population.

4. The perpetrator knew that the conduct was part of or intended the conduct to be part of a widespread or systematic attack directed against a civilian population.

Article 7(1)(g)–3

Crime against humanity of enforced prostitution

Elements

1. The perpetrator caused one or more persons to engage in one or more acts of a sexual nature by force, or by threat of force or coercion, such as that caused by fear of violence, duress, detention, psychological oppression or abuse of power, against such person or persons or another person, or by taking advantage of a coercive environment or such person's or persons' incapacity to give genuine consent.

2. The perpetrator or another person obtained or expected to obtain pecuniary or other advantage in exchange for or in connection with the acts of a sexual nature.

3. The conduct was committed as part of a widespread or systematic attack directed against a civilian population.

4. The perpetrator knew that the conduct was part of or intended the conduct to be part of a widespread or systematic attack directed against a civilian population.

12–22

Article 7(1)(g)–4

Crime against humanity of forced pregnancy

Elements

1. The perpetrator confined one or more women forcibly made pregnant, with the intent of affecting the ethnic composition of any population or carrying out other grave violations of international law.

2. The conduct was committed as part of a widespread or systematic attack directed against a civilian population.

3. The perpetrator knew that the conduct was part of or intended the conduct to be part of a widespread or systematic attack directed against a civilian population.

12–23

Article 7(1)(g)–5

Crime against humanity of enforced sterilization

Elements

1. The perpetrator deprived one or more persons of biological reproductive capacity. (The deprivation is not intended to include birth-control measures which have a non-permanent effect in practice.)

12–24

2. The conduct was neither justified by the medical or hospital treatment of the person or persons concerned nor carried out with their genuine consent. (It is understood that "genuine consent" does not include consent obtained through deception.)

3. The conduct was committed as part of a widespread or systematic attack directed against a civilian population.

4. The perpetrator knew that the conduct was part of or intended the conduct to be part of a widespread or systematic attack directed against a civilian population.

Article 7(1)(g)–6

Crime against humanity of sexual violence

Elements

12–25 1. The perpetrator committed an act of a sexual nature against one or more persons or caused such person or persons to engage in an act of a sexual nature by force, or by threat of force or coercion, such as that caused by fear of violence, duress, detention, psychological oppression or abuse of power, against such person or persons or another person, or by taking advantage of a coercive environment or such person's or persons' incapacity to give genuine consent.

2. Such conduct was of a gravity comparable to the other offences in article 7, paragraph 1(g), of the Statute.

3. The perpetrator was aware of the factual circumstances that established the gravity of the conduct.

4. The conduct was committed as part of a widespread or systematic attack directed against a civilian population.

5. The perpetrator knew that the conduct was part of or intended the conduct to be part of a widespread or systematic attack directed against a civilian population.

Article 7(1)(h)

Crime against humanity of persecution

Elements

12–26 1. The perpetrator severely deprived, contrary to international law (This requirement is without prejudice to paragraph 6 of the General Introduction to the Elements of Crimes.), one or more persons of fundamental rights.

2. The perpetrator targeted such person or persons by reason of the identity of a group or collectivity or targeted the group or collectivity as such.

3. Such targeting was based on political, racial, national, ethnic, cultural, religious, gender as defined in article 7, paragraph 3, of the Statute, or other grounds that are universally recognized as impermissible under international law.

4. The conduct was committed in connection with any act referred to in article 7, paragraph 1, of the Statute or any crime within the jurisdiction of the Court. (It is understood that no additional mental element is necessary for this element other than that inherent in element 6.)

5. The conduct was committed as part of a widespread or systematic attack directed against a civilian population.

6. The perpetrator knew that the conduct was part of or intended the conduct to be part of a widespread or systematic attack directed against a civilian population.

Article 7(1)(i)

Crime against humanity of enforced disappearance of persons (Given the complex nature of this crime, it is recognized that its commission will normally involve more than one perpetrator as a part of a common criminal purpose. This crime falls under the jurisdiction of the Court only if the attack referred to in elements 7 and 8 occurs after the entry into force of the Statute.)

Elements

1. The perpetrator: **12–27**
   (a) Arrested, detained (The word "detained" would include a perpetrator who maintained an existing detention. It is understood that under certain circumstances an arrest or detention may have been lawful.) or abducted one or more persons; or
   (b) Refused to acknowledge the arrest, detention or abduction, or to give information on the fate or whereabouts of such person or persons.
2. (a) Such arrest, detention or abduction was followed or accompanied by a refusal to acknowledge that deprivation of freedom or to give information on the fate or whereabouts of such person or persons; or
   (b) Such refusal was preceded or accompanied by that deprivation of freedom.
3. The perpetrator was aware that (This element, inserted because of the complexity of this crime, is without prejudice to the General Introduction to the Elements of Crimes.):
   (a) Such arrest, detention or abduction would be followed in the ordinary course of events by a refusal to acknowledge that deprivation of freedom or to give information on the fate or whereabouts of such person or persons (It is understood that, in the case of a perpetrator who maintained an existing detention, this element would be satisfied if the perpetrator was aware that such a refusal had already taken place.); or
   (b) Such refusal was preceded or accompanied by that deprivation of freedom.
4. Such arrest, detention or abduction was carried out by, or with the authorization, support or acquiescence of, a State or a political organization.
5. Such refusal to acknowledge that deprivation of freedom or to give information on the fate or whereabouts of such person or persons was carried out by, or with the authorization or support of, such State or political organization.
6. The perpetrator intended to remove such person or persons from the protection of the law for a prolonged period of time.
7. The conduct was committed as part of a widespread or systematic attack directed against a civilian population.
8. The perpetrator knew that the conduct was part of or intended the conduct to be part of a widespread or systematic attack directed against a civilian population.

Article 7(1)(j)

Crime against humanity of apartheid

Elements

1. The perpetrator committed an inhumane act against one or more persons.   **12–28**

2. Such act was an act referred to in article 7, paragraph 1, of the Statute, or was an act of a character similar to any of those acts. (It is understood that "character" refers to the nature and gravity of the act.)

3. The perpetrator was aware of the factual circumstances that established the character of the act.

4. The conduct was committed in the context of an institutionalized regime of systematic oppression and domination by one racial group over any other racial group or groups.

5. The perpetrator intended to maintain such regime by that conduct.

6. The conduct was committed as part of a widespread or systematic attack directed against a civilian population.

7. The perpetrator knew that the conduct was part of or intended the conduct to be part of a widespread or systematic attack directed against a civilian population.

Article 7(1)(k)

Crime against humanity of other inhumane acts

Elements

12–29   1. The perpetrator inflicted great suffering, or serious injury to body or to mental or physical health, by means of an inhumane act.

2. Such act was of a character similar to any other act referred to in article 7, paragraph 1, of the Statute. (It is understood that "character" refers to the nature and gravity of the act.)

3. The perpetrator was aware of the factual circumstances that established the character of the act.

4. The conduct was committed as part of a widespread or systematic attack directed against a civilian population.

5. The perpetrator knew that the conduct was part of or intended the conduct to be part of a widespread or systematic attack directed against a civilian population.

B. NEXUS WITH ARMED CONFLICT

12–30   Crimes against humanity need not be linked to armed hostilities or an armed conflict. This requirement was contained in the Nuremberg and Tokyo Tribunal Charters, which provided in Articles 6(c) and 5(c) respectively, that the acts must be carried out "in execution of or in connection with any crime within the jurisdiction of the Tribunal", namely "crimes against peace" and "war crimes", which are premised on the existence of armed conflict. It is interesting to note that Allied Control Council Law No. 10 of December 20, 1945 in Article 11(1)(c) eliminated this nexus for the national trials that followed the Nuremberg Trial.

The ICTY Statute provides that the acts must be "committed in armed conflict", whereas the Statute for the ICTR has not included this requirement.

Most significantly, Article 7 of the ICC Statute does not require any nexus with armed conflict. This position accords with the definition of crimes against humanity under international criminal law. In *Prosecutor v. Tadic*, the ICTY Appeals Chamber found, "It is by now a settled rule of customary international law that crimes against humanity do not require a connection to international armed conflict" (*Prosecutor v. Tadic*, Decision on the Defence Motion for Interlocutory Appeal on Jurisdiction, Appeals Chamber, October 2, 1995, para. 141).

C. Attack on the Civilian Population

Any of the enumerated acts listed in paragraph 1 of Article 7 of the **12–31** ICC Statute, and the ICTY, ICTR, East Timor, Sierra Leone, Cambodia and Iraq provisions, alone can constitute crimes against humanity. There is no requirement that more than one of the enumerated acts be committed (for example, murder *and* torture), or a combination thereof. In the *Akayesu* Trial Judgment the accused was, *inter alia*, convicted of crimes against humanity for torture by itself (*Prosecutor v. Akayesu*, Judgment, Trial Chamber, September 2, 1998, paras 676—684).

The acts must, however, occur as part of an attack. The acts could constitute the attack itself. For example, the mass murder of civilians may suffice as an attack against the civilian population. There is no requirement that a separate attack against the same civilians, within which the murders were committed, should be proven (see, *Akayesu* Trial Judgment, para. 581).

(1) Definition of attack

The definition of "attack" which can either be "widespread or **12–32** systematic" is elaborated upon in paragraph 2(a) of Article 7 of the ICC Statute. The meaning of "attack" does not necessarily equate with "military attack" as defined by international humanitarian law. Article 49(1) of Additional Protocol I defines "attacks" within the military context as "acts of violence against the adversary, whether in offence or in defence". (Also see, *Report of the Preparatory Committee on the Establishment of an International Criminal Court*, Volume 1, Proceedings of the Preparatory Committee During March–April and August 1996 (G.A., 51st Sess., Supp. No. 22, A/51/22, 1996), para. 86.)

Instead, "attack" refers more generally to a campaign or operation conducted against the civilian population—a "course of conduct" is the terminology used in paragraph 2(a) of the ICC Statute. As stated in *Prosecutor v. Tadić*, Judgment, Appeals Chamber, July 15, 1999, para. 251, the concepts of "attack" and "armed conflict" are not identical. In the context of a crime against humanity, the attack on a civilian population could encompass any mistreatment of civilians. Under the ICTY's Statute the attack must be committed in armed conflict, which is not a requirement under the ICC, ICTR, East Timor, Sierra Leone, Cambodia and Iraq Statutes. (Also see, *Prosecutor v. Kunarac et al.*, Judgment, Appeals Chamber, June 12, 2002, para. 86.) The attack need not even involve military forces or armed hostilities, or any violent force at all. In *Prosecutor v. Akayesu*, the ICTR Trial Chamber held: "An attack may also be non violent in nature, like imposing a system of apartheid, which is declared a crime against humanity in Article 1 of the Apartheid Convention of 1973, or exerting pressure on the population to act in a particular manner, may come under the purview of an attack, if orchestrated on a massive scale or in a systematic manner" (*Prosecutor v. Akayesu*, Judgment, Trial Chamber, September 2, 1998, para. 581).

(2) Nexus between attack and individual acts

12–33   It is necessary to determine when an individual accused's acts can be regarded as being part of an attack against the civilian population. There must be a sufficient nexus between the unlawful acts of the accused and the attack (see, *Akayesu* Trial Judgment, para. 579; *Report of I.L.C. Special Rapporteur D. Thiam*, Ybk I.L.C. 1986, Vol. II, I.L.C. A/CN.4/466, para. 93).

The ICC Statute does not make clear the precise degree of nexus that is required. However, the relationship can be revealed in a variety of ways, which will depend on the factual circumstances of each case. Reliable indicia would include: the similarities between the accused's acts and the acts occurring within the attack; the nature of the events and circumstances surrounding the accused's acts; the temporal and geographical proximity of the accused's acts with the attack; and the nature and extent of the accused's knowledge of the attack when the accused commits the acts, as discussed below. Of particular significance, will be the manner in which the accused's acts are associated with or further the policy underlying the attack (see, *Report of I.L.C. Special Rapporteur D. Thiam*, Ybk I.L.C. 1986, Vol. II, I.L.C. A/CN.4/466, para. 93: "what counted was not the mass aspect, but the link between the act and the cruel and barbarous political system").

In particular, the accused's acts need not be perpetrated during the actual commission of the entire or any part of the widespread or systematic attack (see, *Prosecutor v. Tadic*, Judgment, Trial Chamber, May 7, 1997, para. 632). It is also not essential that the accused's acts precisely resemble any of the particular acts that characterise the attack, for example, if an accused commits torture when the general pattern of the conduct involves widespread killings of civilians. The fundamental requirement is that the acts must not be *unrelated* to the attack, capable of being characterised as the isolated and random conduct of an individual acting alone (see, *Tadić* Trial Judgment, para. 644, which emphasises that crimes against humanity are "collective" in "nature" and "exclude single or isolated acts which [. . .] do not rise to the level of crimes against humanity").

(3) Civilian population

12–34   The acts must be directed at a "civilian 'population'" to constitute a crime against humanity. This requirement does not mean that the entire population of a State, entity, or territory must be subjected to the attack (see, *Prosecutor v. Tadic*, Judgment, Trial Chamber, May 7, 1997, para. 644).

The use of the term "population" implies the collective nature of the crimes to the exclusion of single acts. In *Tadic*, the ICTY Trial Chamber concluded that "the emphasis is not on the individual victim but rather on the collective" (*Prosecutor v. Tadic*, Judgment, Trial Chamber, May 7, 1997, para. 644). The "civilian population" includes persons of any Nationality". Crimes against humanity can be committed against civilians of the same nationality as the perpetrator, against stateless persons, and against civilians of a different nationality (*Prosecutor v. Tadic*, Judgment, Trial Chamber, May 7, 1997, para. 635).

As stated in *Prosecutor v. Kunarac et al.*, Judgment, Appeals Chamber, June 12, 2002, para. 91: "In order to determine whether the attack [is directed against the population], the Trial Chamber will consider, *inter alia*, the means and method used in the course of the attack, the status of the victims, their number, the discriminatory nature of the attack, the nature of the crimes committed in its course, the resistance to the assailants at the time and the extent to which the attacking force may be said to have complied or attempted to comply with the precautionary requirements of the laws of war."

The term "civilian" includes all persons who have taken no active part in hostilities, or are no longer doing so, including members of armed forces who laid down their arms and persons placed *hors de combat* by sickness, wounds, detention or any other reason. This definition is based upon the categories of persons protected by common Article 3 of the Geneva Conventions. Both the *Tadic* and *Akayesu* Trial Judgments adopted this definition (*Prosecutor v. Tadic*, Judgment, Trial Chamber, May 7, 1997, paras 637—638; *Prosecutor v. Akayesu*, Judgment, Trial Chamber, September 2, 1998, para. 582).

A population does not necessarily lose its civilian character when individuals within the population do not fall within the definition of civilians (see, Additional Protocol I, Article 50. Also see, *Tadić* Trial Judgment, para. 638; *Akayesu* Trial Judgment, para. 582). Noting the ICRC Commentary to Additional Protocol I, the Appeals Chamber stated "in order to determine whether the presence of soldiers within a civilian population deprives the population of its civilian character, the number of soldiers, as well as whether they are on leave, must be examined" (*Prosecutor v. Blaškić*, Judgment, Appeals Chamber, July 29, 2004, para. 115).

Combatants

Although it is clear that a civilian population must be targeted, **12–35** determining which particular individual qualifies as a civilian for the purposes of crimes against humanity is more difficult. All non-combatants and persons who have laid down their arms, including prisoners of war under the Geneva Conventions, can be victims of crimes against humanity. It has been held that persons actively involved in resistance movements can be victims of crimes against humanity. (In this regard, see *Prosecutor v. Mrkšić et al.* ("Vukovar Hospital Decision"), Review of the Indictment Pursuant to Rule 61 of the Rules of Procedure and Evidence, April 3, 1996, paras 29 and 32; *Tadić* Trial Judgment, para. 643; *Fédération Nationale des Déportés et Internes Résistants et Patriotes v. Barbie*, (1985) I.L.R., pp. 139–140. Also see, the broad definition given to civilians for the purposes of the Geneva Conventions in *Prosecutor v. Delalic et al.*, Judgment, November 16, 1998, paras 244–277.) However, the *Blaškić* Appeal Judgment clearly states:

> "Read together, Article 50 of Additional Protocol I and Article 4A of the Third Geneva Convention establish that members of the armed forces, and members of militias or volunteer corps forming part of such armed forces, cannot claim civilian status. Neither can members of organized resistance groups, provided that they are commanded by a person responsible for his subordinates, that they have a fixed distinctive sign recognizable at a distance, that they carry arms openly, and that they conduct their operations in accordance with the laws and customs of war. However, the Appeals Chamber considers that the presence within a population of members of resistance groups, or former combatants, who have laid down their arms, does not alter its civilian characteristic. The Trial Chamber was correct in this regard.
>
> However, the Trial Chamber's view that the specific situation of the victim at the time the crimes were committed must be taken into account in determining his standing as a civilian may be misleading. The ICRC Commentary is instructive on this point and states:
>
>> 'All members of the armed forces are combatants, and only members of the armed forces are combatants. This should therefore dispense with the concept of quasi-combatants, which has sometimes been used on the basis of activities related more or less directly with the war effort. Similarly, any concept of a part-time status, a semi-civilian, semi-military status, soldier by night and peaceful citizen by day, also disappears. A civilian who is incorporated in an armed organization such as that mentioned in paragraph 1, becomes a member of the military and a combatant throughout the duration of the hostilities (or in any case, until he is permanently demobilized by the responsible command referred to in paragraph 1), whether or not he is in combat, or for the time being armed. If he is wounded, sick or shipwrecked, he is entitled to the protection of the First and Second Conventions (Article 44, paragraph 8), and, if he is captured, he is entitled to the protection of the Third Convention (Article 44, paragraph 1).'
>
> As a result, the specific situation of the victim at the time the crimes are committed may not be determinative of his civilian or non-civilian status. If he is indeed a member of an armed organization, the fact that he is not armed or in combat at the time of the commission of crimes, does not accord him civilian status." (*Prosecutor v. Blaskic*, Judgment, Appeals Chamber, July 29, 2004, paras 113—114, footnotes omitted).

In addition to not requiring a nexus to armed conflict, it is unnecessary for crimes against humanity to demonstrate that the victims are linked to any particular side in the attack against the civilian population, even if this occurs during armed conflict. War crimes, on the other hand, can only be committed by perpetrators on one side of an armed conflict against persons linked to the adversary (see, *Prosecutor v. Delalic* Judgment Trial Chamber, November 16, 1998, paras 193–198).

The Special Panel for Serious Crimes in East Timor has followed the jurisprudence of the ad hoc International Tribunals regarding the definition of "any population" in section 5 of Reg. 2000/15, see *Prosecutor v. Marques et al.*, ("*Los Palos*" case) Judgment, December 11, 2001, para. 638.

D. WIDESPREAD AND SYSTEMATIC REQUIREMENTS

It is not required that each act which occurs within the attack be widespread or systematic, provided that the acts form part of an attack with these characteristics (see, *Prosecutor v. Mrkšić et al.* ("Vukovar Hospital Decision"), Review of the Indictment Pursuant to Rule 61 of the Rules of Procedure and Evidence, April 3, 1996, para. 30; *Prosecutor v. Tadić*, Judgment, Trial Chamber, May 7, 1997, para. 649; *Prosecutor v. Kunarac et al.*, Judgment, Appeals Chamber, June 12, 2002, para. 96; and *Prosecutor v. Blaškić* Judgment Appeals Chamber, July 29, 2004, para. 101). **12–36**

In other words, if some murders, some rapes, and some beatings take place, each form of conduct need not be widespread or systematic, if together the acts satisfy either of these conditions. The individual's actions themselves need not be widespread or systematic, provided that they form part of such an attack. The commission of a single act, such as one murder, in the context of a broader campaign against the civilian population, can constitute a crime against humanity (see, *Tadić Judgment*, para. 649: "Clearly, a single act by a perpetrator taken within the context of a widespread or systematic attack against a civilian population entails individual criminal responsibility and an individual perpetrator need not commit numerous offences to be held liable". The *Blaškić Appeal Judgment*, para. 101, emphasised "that the acts of the accused need only be a part of this attack, and all other conditions being met, a single or limited number of acts on his or her part would qualify as a crime against humanity, unless those acts may be said to be isolated or random" (footnote omitted). Also see, *Vukovar Hospital Decision*, para. 30.

(1) Definitions of requirements

The ICC Statute clearly envisages that the attack can be widespread *or* systematic in nature. This position is in accordance with the definition of crimes against humanity under customary international law. In *Prosecutor v. Tadic*, for example, the ICTY Trial Chamber found: "While this issue has been the subject of considerable debate, it is now well established that [. . .] the acts [. . .] can [. . .] occur on either a widespread basis or in a systematic manner. Either one of these is sufficient to exclude isolated or random acts" (*Prosecutor v. Tadic*, Judgment, Trial Chamber, May 7, 1997, para. 646). Also see, *Tadic* Trial Judgment, para. 648; *Prosecutor v. Blaskic*, Judgment, Appeals Chamber, July 29, 2004, para. 98; *Prosecutor v. Kordic and Cerkez*, Judgment, Appeals Chamber, December 17, 2004, para. 93; Vukovar Hospital Decision, para. 30; I.L.C. Draft Code of Crimes Against the Peace and Security of Mankind, *Report of the International Law Commission on the Work of its Forty-eighth Session*, 6 May—26 July 1996, G.A.O.R., 51st Sess., Supp. No. 10, 30, U.N. Doc. A/51/10, pp. 94—95, in which the Draft Code provides that the acts must be "committed in a systematic manner or on a large scale"). **12–37**

The "widespread or systematic" requirement is fundamental in distinguishing crimes against humanity from common crimes, which do not rise to the level of crimes against humanity (see, *Tadić* Trial Judgment, paras 646 and 648). The ICTY has determined that "the phrase 'widespread' refers to the large-scale nature of the attack and the number of targeted persons, while the phrase 'systematic' refers to the organised nature of the acts of violence and the improbability of their random occurrence" (see, *Prosecutor v. Kordić and Cerkez*, Judgment, Appeals Chamber, December 17, 2004, para. 94, footnote omitted).

Widespread

12–38   The term "widespread" refers "to the number of victims" (*Prosecutor v. Tadić* Judgment Trial Chamber, May 7, 1997, para. 648).

The concept includes "massive, frequent, large scale action, carried out collectively with considerable seriousness and directed against a multiplicity of victims" (see, *Prosecutor v. Akayesu* Judgment Trial Chamber, September 2, 1998, para. 580).

Also see, *Prosecutor v. Marques*, Judgment, Special Panel for Serious Crimes, East Timor, December 11, 2001, paras 636–637.

Systematic

12–39   The term "systematic" indicates "a pattern or methodical plan" (*Prosecutor v. Tadić*, Judgment Trial Chamber, May 7, 1997, para. 648), which is "thoroughly organised and following a regular pattern on the basis of a common policy involving substantial public or private resources" (*Prosecutor v. Akayesu*, Judgment Trial Chamber, September 2, 1998, para. 580). In *Prosecutor v. Blaškić*, Judgment, Trial Chamber, March 3, 2000, para. 203, the Trial Chamber held that the "systematic" requirement refers to the following four elements: (1) "the existence of a political objective, a plan pursuant to which the attack is perpetual or an ideology, in the broad sense of the word, that is, to destroy, persecute or weaken a community"; (2) "the perpetration of a criminal act on a very large scale against a group of civilians or the repeated and continuous commission of inhumane acts linked to one another"; (3) "the perpetration and use of significant public or private resources, whether military or other"; (4) "the implication of high-level political and/or military authorities in the definition and establishment of the methodical plan" (footnotes omitted). In this way, the full spectrum of sufficiently serious attacks can qualify as crimes against humanity to the exclusion of isolated and random incidents.

The determination of what factual scenarios constitute a widespread or systematic attack depend on the merits of each case. Some practical guidance has already been provided in the case law that arose from the Second World War and, more recently, before the ad hoc International Tribunals. The *Tadić* Trial Judgment held that the commission of inhumane acts against the population in one municipality, Prijedor, which included three detention camps and mass expulsions from the area, were sufficiently widespread and systematic (*Prosecutor v. Tadić*, Judgment Trial Chamber, May 7, 1997, paras 660, 714). The *Blaškić*

Appeal Judgment considered, "Patterns of crimes, in the sense of the non-accidental repetition of similar criminal conduct on a regular basis, are a common expression of such systematic occurrence" (*Prosecutor v. Blaškić* Judgment, Appeals Chamber, July 29, 2004, para. 101, footnote omitted).

The *Kunarac* Appeal Judgment, para. 98, considered that "proof that the attack was directed against a civilian population and that it was widespread or systematic, are legal elements of the crime. But to prove these elements, it is not necessary to show that they were the result of the existence of a policy or plan. It may be useful in establishing that the attack was directed against a civilian population and that it was widespread or systematic (especially the latter) to show that there was in fact a policy or plan, but it may be possible to prove these things by reference to other matters. Thus, the existence of a plan or policy may be evidentially relevant, but is not a legal element of the crime" (*Prosecutor v. Kunarac et al.*, Judgment, Appeals Chamber, June 12, 2002, para. 98). Also see, *Prosecutor v. Blaškić* Judgment, Appeals Chamber, July 29, 2004, para. 100.

(2) Multiple acts

The delegates at the Rome Conference decided to include a particular definition of "attack directed against any civilian population" by providing in Article 7(2)(a) that it "means a course of conduct involving the multiple commission of acts referred to in paragraph 1 against any civilian population, pursuant to or in furtherance of a State or organisational policy to commit such attack". The attack, which according to the *chapeau* can be either widespread *or* systematic, has to at least involve *multiple acts* and emanate from or contribute to a State or organizational *policy*.   **12–40**

By "multiple acts" is meant more than a single, isolated act. Even a systematic attack has to involve more than a few incidents. Similarly, a widespread attack should, and by its very nature is likely to, be based upon or carry forward a policy. A widespread attack need not, however, be systematic and *vice versa*. As described above, each term has distinct and different qualities, which if satisfied render the offences a crime against humanity.

(3) State or organisational policy

The requirement of a "State or organisational policy" is another component of the "widespread or systematic" attack on the civilian population. It constitutes a basis for ensuring that random or isolated acts are excluded from the scope of crimes against humanity (see, *Prosecutor v. Tadić*, Judgment, Trial Chamber, May 7, 1997, para. 653).   **12–41**

As such, the attack must be committed pursuant to (*i.e.* following, complying with, or continuing from) or in furtherance of (*i.e.* promoting, supporting, aiding, or enhancing) this policy, irrespective of whether the attack is widespread or systematic. This policy need not be formalised, and can be deduced from the manner and circumstances in which the acts occur. In *Prosecutor v. Tadic*, the ICTY Trial Chamber stated, "a policy need not be formalized and can be deduced from the way in which the acts occur. Notably, if the acts occur on a widespread or systematic basis that demonstrates a policy to commit those acts, whether formalized or not" (*Prosecutor v. Tadic*, Judgment, Trial Chamber, May 7, 1997, para. 653). In *Prosecutor v. Akayesu*, the Trial Chamber held, "There is no requirement that this policy must be adopted formally as the policy of a state. There must however be some kind of preconceived plan or policy" (*Prosecutor v. Akayesu*, Judgment, Trial Chamber, September 2, 1998, para. 580). The Trial Chamber in *Prosecutor v. Kupreskic et al.* held that, "although the concept of crimes against humanity necessarily implies a policy element, there is some doubt as to whether it is strictly a requirement, as such, for crimes against humanity" (*Prosecutor v. Kupreskic et al.*, Judgment, Trial Chamber, January 14, 2000, para. 551). The Trial Judgment in *Prosecutor v. Kordic and Cerkez* supports this view: "[T]he existence of a plan or policy should better be regarded as indicative of the systematic character of offences charged as crimes against humanity" (*Prosecutor v. Kordic and Cerkez*, Judgment, Trial Chamber, February 26, 2001, para. 182).

12–42   In essence, the policy element only requires that the acts of individuals alone, which are isolated, un-coordinated, and haphazard, be excluded (see, I.L.C. Draft Code of Crimes Against the Peace and Security of Mankind, *Report of the International Law Commission on the Work of its Forty-eighth Session*, 6 May–July 26, 1996, G.A.O.R., 51st Sess., Supp. No. 10, 30, U.N. Doc. A/51/10, p. 94: "This alternative is intended to exclude the situation in which an individual commits an inhumane act while acting on his own initiative pursuant to his own criminal plan [. . .] This type of isolated criminal conduct on the part of a single individual would not constitute a crime against humanity". Also see, *Prosecutor v. Dragan Nikolic*, Review of Indictment Pursuant to Rule 61 of the Rules of Procedure and Evidence, October 20, 1995, para. 26).

The policy need not be one of a State. It can also be an *organisational* policy. Non-State actors, or private individuals, who exercise *de facto* power can constitute the entity behind the policy (see, *Report of the International Law Commission on the Work of its Forty-third Session* (1991) G.A.O.R., 46st Sess., Supp. No. 10, U.N. Doc. A/46/10, p. 266; I.L.C. Draft Code of Crimes Against the Peace and Security of Mankind, *Report of the International Law Commission on the Work of its Forty-eighth Session*, 6 May–July 26, 1996, G.A.O.R., 51st Sess., Supp. No. 10, 30, U.N. Doc. A/51/10, p. 94; In *Prosecutor v. Tadic*, the Trial Chamber found, "the law in relation to crimes against humanity has developed to take into account forces which, although not those of the legitimate government, have de facto control over, or are able to move freely within, defined territory" (*Prosecutor v. Tadic*, Judgment, Trial Chamber, May 7, 1997, para. 654). This view is supported by *Prosecutor v. Bagilishema*, Judgment, Trial Chamber, June 7, 2001, para. 78, and *Prosecutor v. Kayishema and Ruzindana*, Judgment, Trial Chamber, para. 126. Also see, *Kadic v. Karadzic*, 70 F.3d 232 (2nd Cir. 1995), holding that non-State actors could be held liable for the commission of genocide, war crimes, and crimes against humanity, cert. denied, 518 U.S. 1005 (1996).

E. MENS REA

The accused must commit the acts with knowledge of the broader **12–43** widespread or systematic attack on the civilian population (see, *Prosecutor v. Tadic*, Judgment, Trial Chamber, May 7, 1997, para. 656; *Prosecutor v. Tadic*, Judgment, Appeals Chamber, July 15, 1999, paras 250, 271; and *R v. Finta* (1994) 1 R.C.S. 701).

This requirement does not entail knowledge of the entire attack in all of its detail (see, *Prosecutor v. Kunarac et al.*, Judgment, Trial Chamber, February 22, 2001, para. 419; affirmed on appeal, *Prosecutor v. Kunarac et al.*, Judgment, Appeals Chamber, June 12, 2002, paras 102, 104; followed in *Prosecutor v. Marques et al.*, Special Panel for Serious Crimes, East Timor, Judgment, December 11, 2001, paras 640–641. Also see, Vol. I Entscheidungen des Öbersten Gerichtshofes Für Die Britische Zone in Strafsachen, case 2, pp. 6–10; case 4, pp. 19–25; case 16, pp. 60–62; case 23, pp. 91–95; case 25, pp. 105–110; case 31, pp. 122–126; and, case 34, pp. 141–143). It is irrelevant whether the accused intended his act to be directed against the targeted population or merely against his victim. "It is the attack, not the acts of the accused, which must be directed at the target population and the accused need only know that his acts are part thereof" (*Prosecutor v. Kunarac et al.*, Judgment, Appeals Chamber, June 12, 2002, para. 103). The perpetrator does not need to know about a plan or policy to commit such an attack (*ibid.* para. 104).

Furthermore, the knowledge can be actual or constructive. In *Prosecutor v. Tadic*, the Trial Chamber held, "While knowledge is thus required, it is examined on an objective level and factually can be implied from the circumstances" (*Prosecutor v. Tadic*, Judgment, Trial Chamber, May 7, 1997, para. 657; also see, *R v. Finta* (1994) 1 R.C.S. 701). In particular, it is not necessary to demonstrate that the perpetrator knew that his actions were inhumane, or rose to the level of crimes against humanity.

It must, of course, be demonstrated that the accused had the intent to commit the underlying offence or offences with which he is charged. The acts need not be committed with a discriminatory intent on any particular ground, except for persecution (see, *Affirmation of the Principles of International Law recognized by the Charter of the Nuremberg Tribunal*, G.A. Resolution 95(I)). Although the *Tadić* Trial Judgment held otherwise, it did so on the basis that the *Secretary-General's Report* stipulated a requirement of discriminatory intent for all crimes against humanity (*Prosecutor v. Tadić*, Judgment, Trial Chamber, May 7, 1997, paras 650–652). The Appeals Chamber overruled this finding, holding that a showing of discriminatory intent is only required for persecution and no other crime against humanity (*Prosecutor v. Tadić*, Judgment, Appeals Chamber, July 15, 1999, paras 281–305).

The motive of the perpetrator is irrelevant, provided that it can be shown that the person acted with the required knowledge of the attack, and in the case of persecution harboured a discriminatory intent (see, *Prosecutor v. Tadić*, Judgment, Appeals Chamber, July 15, 1999, para. 255 ("crimes against humanity can be committed for purely personal reasons"); *Attorney General v. Eichmann*, 36 I.L.C., pp. 243–244; and, *R. v. Finta*, (1994) 1 R.C.S. 70, p. 819). "[T]he accused need not share the purpose or goal behind the attack" (*Prosecutor v. Kunarac et al.*, Judgment, Appeals Chamber, June 12, 2002, para. 103).

IV. ENUMERATED OFFENCES

A. PERSECUTION

(1) Introduction

12–44　　　Persecution is a particular crime against humanity that has occupied the centre stage of the ad hoc International Tribunals. Before the ICTY it has been relied upon to charge and prosecute the campaigns of ethnic cleansing that occurred in many parts of Bosnia.

In the *Tadić* Judgment, the Trial Chamber defined the crime of persecution under Article 5(h) of the ICTY Statute as follows: "The elements of the crime of persecution are the occurrence of a persecutory act or omission and a discriminatory basis for that act or omission on one of the listed grounds, specifically race, religion or politics. As discussed above, the persecutory act must be intended to cause, and result in, an infringement on an individual's enjoyment of a basic or fundamental right. The notion of persecutory act provides broad coverage, including acts mentioned elsewhere in the Statute as well as acts which, although not in and of themselves inhumane, are considered inhumane because of the discriminatory grounds on which they are taken" (*Prosecutor v. Tadic*, Judgment, Trial Chamber, May 7, 1997, para. 715; also see, *Prosecutor v. Krnojelac*, Judgment, Appeals Chamber, September 17, 2003, para. 185; *Prosecutor v. Vasiljevic*, Judgment, Appeals Chamber, February 24, 2004, para. 113; *Prosecutor v. Blaskic*, Judgment, Appeals Chamber, July 29, 2004, paras 131, 135).

(2) Persecutory acts

12–45　　　The Trial Chamber in *Prosecutor v. Kordić and Čerkez*, Judgment, February 26, 2001, para. 192 recognised that persecution had not been comprehensively defined under international law or in the case law. The term "persecutory act" can include acts enumerated elsewhere in the ICTY Statute as well as acts not specifically listed therein. The *Tadić* Trial Judgment supported the decisions of the Tribunals established under the Nuremberg Charter, Tokyo Charter and Control Council Law No. 10.

The case law from these Tribunals held that a variety of acts can constitute persecution (see, International Military Tribunal, *Trial of the Major War Criminals*, pp. 491–492, "a series of discriminatory laws were passed, which limited the offices and professions . . . restrictions were placed on their family life and their rights of citizenship"; at pp. 180–181, "a boycott of Jewish enterprises was approved by the Nazi Reich Cabinet", and at pp. 339–340, "an ordinance withdrawing Jews from the protection of the laws"; the *Ministries Case*, Trials of War Criminals

Before the Nuremberg Military Tribunals Under Control Council No. 10, Vol. XIV, pp. 610–611, "depriving them of the opportunity inherent in all human beings to study, to practise professions . . . subject to senseless degradations, humiliations, and insults"; and the *Einsatzgruppen Trial*, Trials of War Criminals Before the Nuremberg Military Tribunals Under Control Council No. 10, Vol. IV, p. 435, "inciting of the population to abuse, maltreat, and slay their fellow citizens . . . to stir up passion, hate, violence, and destruction among the people themselves, aims at breaking the moral backbone").

Many of these acts were not punishable as separate crimes under the jurisdiction of these Tribunals. The requirement included in these Charters that crimes against humanity be committed "in connection with any crimes within the jurisdiction of the Tribunal" did not limit the persecutory acts to crimes otherwise punishable under the Tribunals' Charters.

With respect to acts specifically enumerated in other Articles of the ICTY Statute, the Trial Chamber in *Tadić* held that "crimes enumerated in Articles 2 and 3 of the Statute which also fulfil the elements of persecution, including the common elements of crimes against humanity, can be encompassed in a finding of persecution under Article 5(h) of the Statute" (*Prosecutor v. Tadic*, Judgment, Trial Chamber, May 7, 1997, para. 700).

With respect to acts not specifically mentioned in the Statute, the Trial Chamber in *Tadić* held that "the crime of persecution encompasses a variety of acts, including, *inter alia*, those of a physical, economic or judicial nature, that violate an individual's right to the equal enjoyment of his basic rights" (*Prosecutor v. Tadic*, Judgment, Trial Chamber, May 7, 1997, para. 710). Also see, *Prosecutor v. Kupreškić et al.*, Judgment, Trial Chamber, January 14, 2000, para. 581.

As examples, the Trial Chamber in *Tadić* cited the following acts: incitement to murder and extermination, economic deprivation/discrimination of a personal (as opposed to industrial) nature, plunder of property, discriminatory judicial and legal practice, restrictions placed on family life, exclusion from certain professions, restrictions placed on rights to citizenship, and the creation of ghettos (*Prosecutor v. Tadic*, Judgment, Trial Chamber, May 7, 1997, paras 704–710). As further noted by the Trial Chamber, "persecution can take numerous forms, so long as the common element of discrimination in regard to the enjoyment of a basic or fundamental right is present, and persecution does not necessarily require a physical element" (*Prosecutor v. Tadic*, Judgment, Trial Chamber, May 7, 1997, para. 707).

Consequently, the Trial Chamber found the accused guilty of persecution for his role in the following acts: attacks on a civilian population; seizure, collection, segregation, and forced transfer of civilians to camps; the calling-out of civilians; and beatings and killings of civilians (*Prosecutor v. Tadic*, Judgment, Trial Chamber, May 7, 1997, para. 717). In *Prosecutor v. Kupreškić*, Judgment, Trial Chamber, January 14, 2000, para. 621, a four-part test was set out for the *actus reus* of persecution. The act must be constituted by (1) "the gross or blatant denial," (2) "on discriminatory grounds," (3) "of a fundamental right, laid down in international customary or treaty law," (4) "reaching the same level of gravity as the other" crimes against humanity enumerated in Article 5 of the Statute. In *Prosecutor v. Kordić and Čerkez*,

Judgment, Trial Chamber, February 26, 2001, paras 194–196, the Trial Chamber emphasised that the acts must reach a similar level of gravity as other offences listed in Article 5, to the exclusion of some acts from the realm of criminal persecution. Also see, *Kordić and Čerkez* Appeal Judgment, para. 102.

(3) Discriminatory grounds

12–46   The ICTY and ICTR's jurisprudence indicates that the crime of persecution must be committed on discriminatory grounds, specifically race, religion or politics (see, *Prosecutor v. Tadic*, Judgment, Trial Chamber, May 7, 1997, , para. 715). No other crimes against humanity have this requirement (see, *Prosecutor v. Tadić*, Judgment, Appeals Chamber, July 15, 1999, paras 281–305).

Article 6(c) of the *Charter of the International Military Tribunal* at Nuremberg recognised two separate categories of crimes against humanity, namely "murder, extermination, enslavement, deportation, and other inhumane acts committed against any civilian population, *or* persecutions on political, racial or religious grounds" (emphasis added). In its formulation of the principles of law recognised by the Charter and in the judgment of the Nuremberg Tribunal, the International Law Commission maintained this distinction (see, *Report of the International Law Commission to the General Assembly*, G.A.O.R., Fifth Sess., Supp. No. 12, UN Doc. A/1316, in Yearbook of the International Law Commission (1950), vol. II, p. 377, para. 120).

Accordingly, criminal liability attaches to the inhumane acts, and there is an additional element of culpability when such acts are committed on discriminatory grounds, namely persecution. Thus an accused can be held responsible for the crime of persecution and the separate acts that constitute this offence. This interpretation is consistent with post-Second World War case law (see, *Trial of the Major War Criminals before the International Military Tribunal* (1947) pp. 247–253; and the *Eichmann* case which held that all of the acts which the accused "did with the object of exterminating the Jewish people also amounts *ipso facto* to persecution of Jews on national, racial, religious, and political grounds" (*Attorney General of Israel v. Eichmann*, International Law Reports (1968) Vol. 36, p. 239)).

It is necessary for the accused to share the aim of the discriminatory policy and not merely to know of the policy (see, *Prosecutor v. Kordić and Čerkez*, Judgment, Trial Chamber, February 26, 2001, paras 211–220; *Prosecutor v. Kordić and Čerkez*, Judgment, Appeals Chamber, December 17, 2004, paras 110–112). Also see, *Prosecutor v. Blaškić*, Judgment, Trial Chamber, March 3, 2000, paras 235, 244 and 260; *Prosecutor v. Blaškić*, Judgment, Appeals Chamber, July 29, 2004, paras 164–166.

B. MURDER

12–47   The ICTR Trial Chamber in *Prosecutor v. Akayesu*, Judgment, Trial Chamber, September 2, 1998, para. 589, defined the elements of murder as follows: "1. the victim is dead; 2. the death resulted from an unlawful act or omission of the accused or a subordinate; 3. at the time of the killing the accused or a subordinate had the intention to kill or inflict grievous bodily harm on the deceased having known that such bodily harm is likely to cause the victim's death, and is reckless whether death ensues or not".

In addition, when murder is charged as a crime against humanity, it must be committed as part of a widespread or systematic attack against a civilian population and the victim must be a member of the civilian population (*Prosecutor v. Akayesu* Judgment, Trial Chamber, September 2,1998, para. 590). These requirements apply equally to all of the enumerated crimes against humanity set out below.

Also see, *Prosecutor v. Krstic*, Judgment, Trial Chamber, August 2, 2001, para. 485.

For the definition of murder, as charged under national law before the Special Panel for Serious Crimes, East Timor; see *Prosecutor v. Leki*, Judgment, June 11, 2001; and, *Prosecutor v. Tavares*, Judgment, October 28, 2001. Crimes against humanity have now been charged in numerous cases before the East Timor court, see, for example, *Prosecutor v. Marques et al.*, Judgment, December 11, 2001; *Prosecutor v. da Silva et al.*, Judgment, December 5, 2002; *Prosecutor v. Lopes et al.*, ("*Passabe* case"), Judgment, December 12, 2004; *Prosecutor v. Kuswandi et al.*, ("*Liquisa church massacre* case"), Judgment, November 29, 2002; and, *Prosecutor v. Guterres et al.*, ("*Dili Rally* case"), case No. 2/2002.

C. EXTERMINATION

The ICTR Trial Chamber defined extermination as "a crime which **12–48** by its very nature is directed against a group of individuals. Extermination differs from murder in that it requires an element of mass destruction which is not required for murder" (*Prosecutor v. Akayesu*, Judgment, Trial Chamber, para. 591; also see, *Prosecutor v. Kayishema*, Judgment, Trial Chamber, May 21, 1999, paras 141—147, and *Prosecutor v. Rutaganda*, Judgment, Trial Chamber, December 6, 1999, paras 82—84).

It must be shown that the accused or his subordinate participated in the killing of certain named or described persons (see, *Prosecutor v. Akayesu*, Judgment, Trial Chamber, September 2, 1998, para. 592). There is no requirement that the named or described persons be part of an ethnic, racial, national, or religious group or that a specific intent exist to destroy the named or described persons. Extermination differs from genocide to this extent. The extermination must form part of an attack against the civilian population on discriminatory grounds: national, political, ethnic, racial or religious (see, *Akayesu* Trial Judgment, para. 592).

Extermination was defined by the ICTY for the first time in *Prosecutor* **12–49** *v. Krstic*, Judgment, Trial Chamber, August 2, 2001. The Trial Chamber held that murder and extermination have similar elements, but extermination has further requirements, namely, "there must be evidence that a particular population was targeted and that its members were killed or otherwise subjected to conditions of life calculated to bring about the destruction of a numerically significant part of the population" (*Krstic* Trial Judgment, para. 503).

Extermination can be distinguished from genocide in that it "may be retained when the crime is directed against an entire group of individuals even though no discriminatory intent nor intention to destroy the group as such on national, ethnical, racial or religious grounds has been demonstrated; or where the targeted population does not share any common national, ethnical, racial or religious characteristics" (*Prosecutor v. Krstic*, Judgment, Trial Chamber, August 2, 2001, para. 500; also see, *Prosecutor v. Krstic*, Judgment, Appeals Chamber, April 19, 2004, paras 220, 223; *Prosecutor v. Musema*, Judgment, Appeals Chamber, November 16, 2001, para. 366).

D. ENSLAVEMENT

12–50   This crime against humanity has seldom been charged. The accused in the *Kunarac et al.* case were indicted for enslavement and convicted. On appeal, the Appeals Chamber reviewed the elements of enslavement and stated that the defining characteristic of the crime is the destruction of the juridical personality of a victim "as a result of the exercise of any or all the powers attaching to the right of ownership" (*Prosecutor v. Kunarac et al.*, Judgment, Appeals Chamber, June 12, 2002, para. 117).

The Appeals Chamber held:

"The Appeals Chamber accepts the chief thesis of the Trial Chamber that the traditional concept of slavery, as defined in the 1926 Slavery Convention and often referred to as 'chattel slavery', has evolved to encompass various contemporary forms of slavery which are also based on the exercise of any or all of the powers attaching to the right of ownership. In the case of these various contemporary forms of slavery, the victim is not subject to the exercise of the more extreme rights of ownership associated with 'chattel slavery', but in all cases, as a result of the exercise of any or all of the powers attaching to the right of ownership, there is some destruction of the juridical personality, the destruction is greater in the case of 'chattel slavery' but the difference is one of degree. The Appeals Chamber considers that, at the time relevant to the alleged crimes, these contemporary forms of slavery formed part of enslavement as a crime against humanity under customary international law.

The Appeals Chamber will however observe that the law does not know of a 'right of ownership over a person'. Article 1(1) of the 1926 Slavery Convention speaks more guardedly 'of a person over whom any or all of the powers attaching to the right of ownership are exercised'. That language is to be preferred.

The Appeals Chamber considers that the question whether a particular phenomenon is a form of enslavement will depend on the operation of the factors or indicia of enslavement identified by the Trial Chamber. These factors include the 'control of someone's movement, control of physical environment, psychological control, measures taken to prevent or deter escape, force, threat of force or coercion, duration, assertion of exclusivity, subjection to cruel treatment and abuse, control of sexuality and forced labour'. Consequently, it is not possible exhaustively to enumerate all of the contemporary forms of slavery which are comprehended in the expansion of the original idea; this Judgment is limited to the case in hand. In this respect, the Appeals Chamber would also like to refer to the finding of the Trial Chamber in paragraph 543 of the Trial Judgment stating:

> 'The Prosecutor also submitted that the mere ability to buy, sell, trade or inherit a person or his or her labours or services could be a relevant factor. The Trial Chamber considers that the *mere ability* to do so is insufficient, such actions actually occurring could be a relevant factor.'

However, this particular aspect of the Trial Chamber's Judgment not having been the subject of argument, the Appeals Chamber does not consider it necessary to determine the point involved." (*Prosecutor v. Kunarac et al.* Judgment, Appeals Chamber, June 12, 2002, paras 117–119).

The Appeals Chamber confirmed that the lack of consent is not an element of the offence, but consent may provide evidence of the exercise of the rights of ownership over the victim (*Prosecutor v. Kunarac et al.*, Judgment, Appeals Chamber, June 12, 2002, para. 120).

E. TORTURE

12–51 In the *Prosecutor v. Kunarac et al.*, Judgment, February 22, 2001, the Trial Chamber defined torture as follows: "(i) The infliction, by act or omission, of severe pain or suffering, whether physical or mental. (ii) The act or omission must be intentional. (iii) The act of omission must aim at obtaining information or a confession, or at punishing, intimidating or coercing the victim or a third person, or at discriminating, on any ground, against the victim or a third person" (para. 497, footnotes omitted).

12–52 The Appeals Judgment in this case confirmed the definition as being reflective of customary international law (*Prosecutor v. Kunarac et al.*, Judgment, Appeals Chamber, June 12, 2002, paras 146–148). In particular, the intent required is that the accused intended to cause severe pain or suffering, whether physical or mental, to the victim in pursuance of one of the prohibited purposes of the crime of torture (*Prosecutor v. Kunarac et al.* Appeals Judgment, para. 153). The fact that the accused's conduct, which fulfilled one of the prohibited purposes, also was intended to achieve another non-listed purpose, such as a sexual desire, is immaterial (*Prosecutor v. Kunarac et al.* Appeals Judgment, para. 155).

12–53 In addition, the Appeals Chamber stated that it was not a requirement under customary international law that the perpetrator was a public official or acting in an official capacity for purposes of assigning individual criminal responsibility for torture outside of the framework of the Torture Convention (*Prosecutor v. Kunarac et al.* Appeals Judgment, para. 148). The Torture Convention has a "public official" requirement. However, for prosecutions before the ad hoc International Tribunals, torture perpetrated in a private capacity is sufficient. The Geneva Conventions and Additional Protocols do not provide that torture must be committed in an official context. This position was followed in *Prosecutor v. Marques et al.*, Special Panel for Serious Crimes, East Timor,

Judgment, December 11, 2001, paras 656–661. Earlier decisions had insisted on the public official requirement, but are no longer applicable; see for example, *Prosecutor v. Delalic et al.*, Judgment, Trial Chamber, November 16, 1998, paras 473–474; *Prosecutor v. Furundžija*, Judgment, Trial Chamber, December 10, 1998, paras 162–163 and 253; and, *Prosecutor v. Akayesu*, Judgment, Trial Chamber, September 2, 1998, para. 594.

The Appeals Chamber stated that as sexual violence necessarily gives rise to severe pain and suffering, whether physical or mental, it can be characterised as an act of torture (*Prosecutor v. Kunarac et al*, Judgment, Appeals Chamber, June 12, 2002, para. 150).

F. RAPE

12–54   In the *Kunarac et al.* Judgment, February 22, 2001, the Trial Chamber defined rape in the following terms: "the actus reus of the crime of rape in international law is constituted by: the sexual penetration, however slight: (a) of the vagina or anus of the victim by the penis of the perpetrator or any other object used by the perpetrator; or (b) the mouth of the victim by the penis of the perpetrator; where such sexual penetration occurs without the consent of the victim. Consent for this purpose must be consent given voluntarily, as a result of the victim's free will, assessed in the context of the surrounding circumstances. The *mens rea* is the intention to effect this sexual penetration, and the knowledge that it occurs without the consent of the victim" (para. 460).

The Appeals Chamber confirmed the Trial Chamber's definition (*Prosecutor v. Kunarac et al*, Judgment, Appeals Chamber, June 12, 2002, para. 128). In addition, the Appeals Chamber held that the threat or use of force or resistance is not an element of the offence. It may provide evidence of non-consent, but coercive circumstances without the threat or use of force may be sufficient to demonstrate the absence of consent (*Kunarac et al.*, Appeals Judgment, paras 128–130).

For a definition of rape from the Special Panel for Serious Crimes, East Timor, see *Prosecutor v. Soaeres*, Judgment, September 12, 2002, paras 56–58. In this case the accused was convicted of a single rape charged under the penal code applicable in East Timor. The offence was not charged as a crime against humanity. See, the Partly Dissenting Opinion of Judge Ramos on whether the applicable national law on rape comports with internationally recognised human rights standards as foreseen by section 3 of Reg. 1/1999. The provisions of the domestic law only prohibit rape out of marriage.

G. DEPORTATION

12–55   "Both deportation and forcible transfer relate to the involuntary and unlawful evacuation of individuals from the territory in which they reside [. . .] Deportation presumes transfer beyond State borders, whereas forcible transfer relates to displacements within a State"

(*Prosecutor v. Krstic*, Judgment, Trial Chamber, August 2, 2001, para. 521). "However, the distinction has no bearing on the condemnation of such practices in international humanitarian law" (*Krstic* Trial Judgment, para. 522).

In *Prosecutor v. Kupreškić et al.*, Judgment, Trial Chamber, January 14, 2000, it was held that forcible displacement within or between national borders is included as an inhumane act under Article 5(i) of the ICTY Statute defining crimes against humanity (para. 566).

H. IMPRISONMENT

For the purposes of charging imprisonment as a crime against humanity, the term "should be understood as arbitrary imprisonment, that is to say, the deprivation of liberty of the individual without due process of law, as part of a widespread or systematic attack directed against a civilian population" (*Prosecutor v. Kordić and Čerkez*, Judgment, Trial Chamber, February 26, 2001, para. 302; affirmed *Prosecutor v. Kordić and Čerkez*, Judgment, Appeals Chamber, December 17, 2004, para. 116).

12–56

A distinction must be drawn between lawful and unlawful imprisonment. The imprisonment of civilians is unlawful when civilians are detained in contravention of Article 42 of Geneva Convention IV (*i.e.* they are detained without reasonable grounds to believe that the security of the Detaining Power makes it absolutely necessary); or where the procedural safeguards required by Article 43 of Geneva Convention IV are not complied with in respect of detained civilians, even where the initial detention may have been lawful and justified (*Prosecutor v. Kordić and Čerkez*, Judgment, Trial Chamber, February 26, 2001, para. 303).

The Appeals Chamber found "that not all of these elements necessarily have to be met in order to establish liability for unlawful confinement pursuant to Article 5(e) of the Statute: the existence of an international armed conflict, an element of Articles 42 and 43 of Geneva Convention IV, is not required for imprisonment as a crime against humanity" (*Prosecutor v. Kordić and Čerkez*, Judgment, Appeals Chamber, December 17, 2004, para. 115).

It would seem that imprisonment could not be charged as a crime against humanity for non-civilian victims, although this issue has not as yet been litigated.

I. OTHER INHUMANE ACTS

The crime of "other inhumane acts" is "a residual category, which encompasses acts not specifically enumerated" (*Prosecutor v. Kordić and Čerkez*, Judgment, Trial Chamber, February 26, 2001, para. 269; affirmed *Prosecutor v. Kordić and Čerkez*, Judgment, Appeals Chamber, December 17, 2004, para. 117; also see, *Prosecutor v. Kupreškić et al.*, Judgment, Trial Chamber, January 14, 2000, para. 563).

12–57

In *Tadic*, the ICTY Trial Chamber held that the threshold to be reached by other acts to be incorporated in this category are that the acts must be "similar in gravity to those listed in the preceding sub-paragraphs" (*Prosecutor v. Tadic*, Judgment, Trial Chamber, May 7, 1997, para. 729). In *Kupreskic et al.*, the Trial Chamber elaborated that they must be "carried out in a systematic manner and on a large scale. In other words, they must be as serious as the other classes of crimes provided for in the other provisions of Article 5" (*Prosecutor v. Kupreskic et al.*, Judgment, Trial Chamber, January 14, 2000, para. 566).

12–58   The acts "must in fact cause injury to a human being in terms of physical or mental integrity, health or human dignity" (*Prosecutor v. Tadic*, Judgment, Trial Chamber, May 7, 1997, para. 729; also see, *Prosecutor v. Blaskic*, Judgment, Trial Chamber, March 3, 2000, para. 243). Acts such as mutilation and other types of severe bodily harm, beatings and other acts of violence, and serious physical and mental injury have been found to constitute inhumane acts (see, *Tadić* Trial Judgment, para. 730, and *Blaškić*, Trial Judgment, para. 239). The *Kupreškić et al.* Judgment has taken a broader view of the acts that may be characterised as "inhumane acts", and included the forcible transfer of groups of civilians, enforced prostitution, and enforced disappearances (*Prosecutor v. Kupresic*, Judgment, Trial Chamber, January 14, 2000, para. 566).

The Appeals Chamber in *Kordić and Čerkez* considered, "Inhumane acts as a crime against humanity is comprised of acts which fulfill the following conditions: the victim must have suffered serious bodily or mental harm; the degree of severity must be assessed on a case-by-case basis with due regard for the individual circumstances; the suffering must be the result of an act or omission of the accused or his subordinate; and when the offence was committed, the accused or his subordinate must have been motivated by the intent to inflict serious bodily or mental harm upon the victim" (*Prosecutor v. Kordic and Cerkez*, Judgment, Appeals Chamber, December 17, 2004, para. 117).

V. SENTENCE

12–59   It is not settled whether crimes against humanity are inherently more serious than war crimes to justify a heavier penalty. See, *e.g.* *Prosecutor v. Erdemović*, Judgment, Appeals Chamber, Joint Separate Opinion of Judge McDonald and Judge Vohrah, October 7, 1997, paras 20–26, explaining that "*all things being equal*, a punishable offence, if charged and proven as a crime against humanity, is more serious and should ordinarily entail a heavier penalty than if it were proceeded upon on the basis that it were a war crime". Also see, *Prosecutor v. Tadić*, Sentencing Judgment, Trial Chamber, November 11, 1999, para. 28; *Prosecutor v. Tadić*, Sentencing Judgment, Trial Chamber, July 14, 1997, paras 73–74, in which the accused was consistently sentenced to an extra year in respect of punishable acts when they were characterised as crimes against humanity as opposed to when they were charged as war crimes. However, see *Prosecutor v. Tadić*, Judgment in Sentencing Appeals, Appeals Chamber, January 26, 2000, para. 69, which held "there is in law no distinction between the seriousness of a crime against humanity and that of a war crime [. . .] the authorized penalties are also the same"; and, the Separate and Dissenting Opinion of Judge Li in *Prosecutor v. Erdemović*, Judgment, Appeals Chamber, October 7, 1997, para. 20, which stated that "it is groundless to assert that a crime against humanity is necessarily more serious than a war crime". In this regard, see also, *Prosecutor v. Erdemović*, Sentencing Judgment, March 5, 1998, Separate Opinion of Judge Shahabuddeen, p. 8; and, *Prosecutor v. Akayesu*, Judgment, Trial Chamber, September 2, 1998, para. 470.

In any event, it must be recognised that crimes against humanity by definition must be regarded as one of the gravest categories of crimes for the purposes of punishment (see, *Prosecutor v. Kambanda*, Judgment and Sentence, Trial Chamber, September 4, 1998, para. 43).

VI. CHARGING CRIMES AGAINST HUMANITY

The same acts can be charged as different crimes against humanity (for example, a massacre as "persecution" and "murder"), and as war crimes (for example, as a violation of the grave breach provisions of the 1949 Geneva Conventions).   **12–60**

(1) Cumulative charges

The Tribunals' jurisprudence clearly affirms that indictments may   **12–61** include charges under different Articles for the same underlying conduct: "the Prosecutor may be justified in bringing cumulative charges when the Articles of the Statute referred to are designed to protect different values and when each Article requires proof of a legal element not required by the others" (*Prosecutor v. Kupreskic et al.*, Decision on Defence Challenges to Form of the Indictment, May 15, 1998; see also, *Prosecutor v. Delalic et al.*, Judgment, Appeals Chamber, February 20, 2001, para. 400; *Prosecutor v. Delalic et al.*, Decision on Application for Leave by Hazim Delic (Defects in the Form of the Indictment), Bench of the Appeals Chamber, December 6, 1996, para. 35; *Prosecutor v. Delalic et al.*, Decision on Motion by the Accused Zejnil Delalic based on Defects in the Form of the Indictment, Trial Chamber, October 2, 1996, para. 24).

Trial Chambers have convicted accused under two or more Articles   **12–62** arising from the same proven acts: "(1) where the offences have different elements; or (2) where the provisions creating the offences protect different interests; or (3) where it is necessary to record a conviction for both offences in order to fully describe what the accused did" (*Prosecutor v. Akayesu*, Judgment, Trial Chamber, September 2, 1998 para. 468). In *Akayesu*, the accused was convicted at trial of genocide and crimes against humanity for the same underlying acts.

The *Tadić* Trial Judgment also regarded the Article 2, 3, and 5 charges in that case as separate substantive offences when adjudicating the underlying facts of each of these charges. The accused was convicted of both Article 3 and 5 charges (see, *Prosecutor v. Tadić*, Judgment, Trial Chamber, May 7, 1997, pp. 286–300).

12–63   The Trial Chambers have held that the penalties and sentences for each cumulative conviction need not be served *consecutively*, and in all cases to date the Trial Chambers have imposed *concurrent* sentences (see, *Prosecutor v. Delalic et al.* Judgment, Trial Chamber, November 16, 1998, para. 1286; *Prosecutor v. Furundžija*, Judgment, Trial Chamber, December 10, 1998, paras 294–296).

In justifying cumulative charging, the Trial Chambers have endorsed the reasoning of the *Tadić* Trial Chamber that this "is a matter that will only be relevant insofar as it might affect penalty, it can best be dealt with if and when matters of penalty fall for consideration. What can, however, be said with certainty is that penalty cannot be made to depend upon whether offences arising from the same conduct are alleged cumulatively or in the alternative. What is to be punished by penalty is proven criminal conduct and that will not depend upon technicalities of pleading" (*Prosecutor v. Tadić*, Decision on Motion on Form of the Indictment, November 14, 1995, p. 10).

12–64   The Trial Chamber in the *Akayesu* case held: "the offences under the Statute [. . .] crimes against humanity, and violations of article 3 common to the Geneva Conventions [. . .] have different elements and, moreover, are intended to protect different interests [. . .] These crimes have different purposes and are, therefore, never co-extensive. Thus it is legitimate to charge these crimes in relation to the same set of facts" (*Prosecutor v. Akayesu*, Judgment, Trial Chamber, September 2, 1998, para. 469). The view expressed is that the accused suffers no prejudice or unfairness as a result of the cumulative charging of these offences.

Since this finding, the Appeals Chamber has considered the issue and held:

> "[M]ultiple criminal convictions entered under different statutory provisions but based on the same conduct are permissible only if each statutory provision involved has a materially distinct element not contained in the other. An element is materially distinct from another if it requires proof of a fact not required by the other.
>
> Where this test is not met, the Chamber must decide in relation to which offence it will enter a conviction. This should be done on the basis of the principle that the conviction under the more specific provision should be upheld. Thus if a set of facts is regulated by two provisions, one of which contains an additional materially distinct element, then a conviction should be entered only under that provision" (*Prosecutor v. Delalic et al.*, Judgment, Appeals Chamber, February 20, 2001, paras 412–413).

Also see, *Prosecutor v. Jelisic*, Judgment, Appeals Chamber, July 5, 2001, para. 82, which found cumulative convictions under Articles 3 and 5 to be permissible, based on the test set out in the *Delalic* Judgment on Appeal; and, *Prosecutor v. Kupreškić et al.*, Judgment, Appeals Chamber, October 23, 2001, paras 387–388).

There may be some overlap in the elements of each offence, and accordingly, evidence to prove an element of one offence may be sufficient to prove the same element in another offence. However, the different elements of each offence have to be satisfied separately.

See Chapter 5 on form of the indictment.

(2) Charging persecution

Acts charged as persecution can be re-charged as other crimes **12–65**
against humanity as they consist of different elements and protect
different interests. In particular, the crime of persecution consists of
various acts which infringe upon the basic rights of individuals in
discriminatory ways and can include discriminatory legislation and
practices; intimidation, harassment, and terrorising; inhuman treatment; torture; confinement; deportation; and killing (see, *Prosecutor v.
Tadić*, Judgment, Trial Chamber, May 7, 1997, paras 703–710). The
prohibition against all of these forms of widespread or systematic
discrimination serves to protect civilian populations from persecutory
behaviour.

Other crimes against humanity, such as murder, torture, and rape,
may only be charged if these particular crimes are committed as part of
a widespread or systematic attack on the civilian population. They serve
to protect the population from only a specific form of unlawful
behaviour. The *Tadić* Trial Chamber permitted the accused to be
charged with both persecution and other crimes against humanity for
the same acts (see, *Prosecutor v. Tadić*, Decision on Motion on Form of
the Indictment, November 14, 1995, p. 10).

The Trial Chambers in other cases have also permitted the same
practice (see, *Prosecutor v. Kupreškić et al.*, Decision on Defence Challenges to Form of the Indictment, May 15, 1998).

VII. CONSIDERATIONS OF PROOF

A critical issue to be addressed during each case is what evidence will **12–66**
be sufficient to prove the widespread or systematic attack on the
civilian population. Such attacks by their very nature involve infinite
acts and complex and multi-layered forms of organisation and conduct
(see, *Pohl* case, Trials of War Criminals Before the Nuremberg Military
Tribunals Under Control Council Law No. 10, Vol. II, p. 49, which
stated that in "an elaborate and complex operation", the execution
thereof occurs "far removed from the original planners. As may be
expected, we find the various participants in the programme tossing the
shuttlecock of responsibility from one to the other").

It is not possible to lead evidence concerning every aspect of each
attack. Trials would become too lengthy and cumbersome if witnesses
were called to testify about every alleged incident in campaigns
allegedly waged against the civilian population. One approach which
may be pursued is to focus on the planning, preparation and execution
of the overall campaign against the civilian population, in question, at
the highest levels of organisation, and use particular incidents to
illustrate the various components of the campaign. In this way individual perpetrators could be fitted into the overall criminal scheme.

One practical method for presenting the evidence to establish **12–67**
widespread or systematic attacks on the civilian population arose in the
Kordic and Cerkez case. The Prosecution suggested that an investigator
could be called to provide a summary of the incidents that occurred in

each area. It was submitted that the Defence could cross-examine the investigator and identify any of the witnesses referred to by the investigator whom it may wish to cross-examine on issues genuinely in dispute. The Prosecutor stated that the primary purpose of this proposal was to identify procedures that permit as much evidence to be received in the shortest time. These procedures could ensure that important evidence is not excluded in the interests of conducting expeditious proceedings.

The "dossier"

12–68   It was proposed that the investigator's testimony could be provided from a "dossier" (or summary) of relevant witness statements, prior testimony, and documents, which had been prepared by the investigator. The dossier could be read and admitted by the Trial Chamber without having to hear all of the witnesses unless the Defence could demonstrate to the Chamber that it was essential to cross-examine a witness on matters that were properly in dispute. In this way, time need not be wasted on hearing evidence that is unchallenged (see, *Prosecutor v. Kordić and Čerkez*, Prosecutor's Skeleton Argument for Procedural Possibilities, June 3, 1999).

12–69   The Nuremberg and Second World War Trials permitted witness statements to be admitted without the witness's presence before the court. Statements were relied upon by the court in reaching their decision. Article VII of Ordinance 7 that governed trials subsequent to the International Military Tribunal at Nuremberg (and which was similar to the Nuremberg provisions) stated that:

> "The tribunals shall not be bound by technical rules of evidence. They shall adopt and apply to the greatest possible extent expeditious and non-technical procedure, and shall admit any evidence which they deem to have probative value. Without limiting the foregoing general rules, the following shall be deemed admissible if they appear to the tribunal to contain information of probative value relating to the charges: affidavits, depositions, interrogations, and other statements . . . The tribunal shall afford the opposing party such opportunity to question the authenticity or probative value of such evidence as in the opinion of the tribunal the ends of justice require."

The Uniform Rules of Procedure for the Tribunals provided in Rule 21 that "statements of witnesses made 'in lieu of an oath' may be admitted in evidence if otherwise competent and admissible and containing statements having probative value".

12–70   The *Kordić and Čerkez* Trial Chamber decided that the dossier could not be admitted "wholesale". The Chamber considered the evidence category by category. With respect to the investigator's report, the Chamber held that although "The International Tribunal is not bound to reject hearsay evidence . . . the position with regard to the Report is somewhat different. The Investigator is not reporting as a contemporary witness of fact, he has only recently collated statements and other materials for the purpose of this Application. He could, in reality, only give evidence that material was or was not in the Dossier. The Report therefore is of little or no probative value and will not be admitted into evidence" (*Prosecutor v. Kordić and Čerkez*, Decision on the Prosecution Application to Admit the Tulica Report and Dossier into Evidence, July 29, 1999, paras 19–20).

In relation to the witness statements, the Trial Chamber held: "It is proposed that the witness statements should be produced by the Investigator, and would not be subject to cross-examination by the accused unless the Defence could justify the need to do so. The Trial Chamber is of the view that whilst it could admit the witness statements under Rule 89(C), this is not an appropriate case for the exercise of its discretion under that provision, as it would amount to the wholesale admission of hearsay untested by cross-examination, namely the attack on Tulica, and would be of no probative value. The Trial Chamber therefore declines to admit the witness statements into evidence, however, draws attention to Rule 94*ter* of the Rules" (*Prosecutor v. Kordic and Cerkez*, Decision on the Prosecution Application to Admit the Tulica Report and Dossier into Evidence, July 29, 1999, para. 23).

The transcripts of prior testimony were admitted without precluding **12–71** the Defence from applying to cross-examine the witnesses on the grounds that there were significant and relevant matters not covered by cross-examination in the other cases which ought to be raised in the present case (*Prosecutor v. Kordic and Cerkez*, Decision on the Prosecution Application to Admit the Tulica Report and Dossier into Evidence, July 29, 1999, paras 26–28). This finding was based on the Appeals Chamber's decision in the *Aleksovski* case (see, *Prosecutor v. Aleksovski*, Decision on Prosecutor's Appeal on Admissibility of Evidence, February 16, 1999, paras 27–28). Finally, the documentary evidence was introduced under Rule 89(C) as it was deemed to have probative value (*Prosecutor v. Kordić and Čerkez*, Decision on the Prosecution Application to Admit the Tulica Report and Dossier into Evidence, July 29, 1999, paras 32–36).

See Chapter 9 on the admissibility of evidence.

CHAPTER 13

GENOCIDE

I. STATUTORY PROVISIONS

A. ICC

Statute, Art. 6

Genocide

6. For the purpose of this Statute "genocide" means any of the following **13–1** acts committed with the intent to destroy, in whole or in part, a national, ethnical, racial or religious group, as such:

(a) Killing members of the group;
(b) Causing serious bodily or mental harm to members of the group;
(c) Deliberately inflicting on the group conditions of life calculated to bring about its physical destruction in whole or in part;
(d) Imposing measures intended to prevent births within the group;
(e) Forcibly transferring children of the group to another group.

B. ICTY

Statute of the ICTY, Art. 4

13–2   **4.**—(1) The International tribunal shall have the power to prosecute persons committing genocide as defined in paragraph 2 of this article or for committing any of the other acts enumerated in paragraph 3 of this article.

(2) Genocide means any of the following acts committed with intent to destroy, in whole or in part, a national, ethnical, racial or religious group, as such:
(a) Killing members of the group;
(b) Causing serious bodily or mental harm to members of the group;
(c) Deliberately inflicting on the group conditions of life calculated to bring about its physical destruction in whole or in part;
(d) Imposing measures intended to prevent births within the group;
(e) Forcibly transferring children of the group to another group.
(3) The following acts shall be punishable:
(a) Genocide;
(b) Conspiracy to commit genocide;
(c) Direct and public incitement to commit genocide;
(d) Attempt to commit genocide;
(e) Complicity in genocide.

C. ICTR

Statute of the ICTR, Art. 2

Genocide

13–3   **2.**—(1) The International Tribunal for Rwanda shall have the power to prosecute persons committing genocide as defined in paragraph 2 of this article or of committing any of the other acts enumerated in paragraph 3 of this article

(2) Genocide means any of the following acts committed with intent to destroy, in whole or in part, a national, ethnical, racial or religious group, as such:
(a) Killing members of the group;
(b) Causing serious bodily or mental harm to members of the group;
(c) Deliberately inflicting on the group conditions of life calculated to bring about its physical destruction in whole or in part;
(d) Imposing measures intended to prevent births within the group;
(e) Forcibly transferring children of the group to another group.
(3) The following acts shall be punishable:
(a) Genocide;
(b) Conspiracy to commit genocide;

  (c) Direct and public incitement to commit genocide;
  (d) Attempt to commit genocide;
  (e) Complicity in genocide.

D. East Timor

Regulation 2000/15, s.4 (as amended by Regulation 2001/30)

Genocide

4. For the purposes of the present regulation, "genocide" means any of the **13–4**
following acts committed with intent to destroy, in whole or in part, a national,
ethnical, racial or religious group, as such:
  (a) Killing members of the group;
  (b) Causing serious bodily or mental harm to members of the group;
  (c) Deliberately inflicting on the group conditions of life calculated to
      bring about its physical destruction in whole or in part;
  (d) Imposing measures intended to prevent births within the group;
  (e) Forcibly transferring children of the group to another group.

E. Sierra Leone

Genocide has not been included within the crimes falling within the **13–5**
jurisdiction of the court. The Report of the Secretary-General on the
establishment of the court for Sierra Leone notes that genocide was not
included because "of the lack of evidence that the massive, large-scale
killing in Sierra Leone was at any time perpetrated against an
identified national, ethnic, racial or religious group with an intent to
annihilate the group as such" (para. 13). (See Appendix J.)

F. Cambodia

Law on the Establishment of the Extraordinary Chambers in the Courts of Cambodia for the Prosecution of Crimes Committed during the Period of Democratic Kampuchea (January 2, 2001)

Article 4

The Extraordinary Chambers shall have the power to bring to trial **13–6**
all Suspects who committed the crimes of genocide as defined in the
Convention on the Prevention and Punishment of the Crime of
Genocide of 1948, and which were committed during the period from 17
April 1975 to 6 January 1979.

The acts of genocide, which have no statute of limitations, mean any
acts committed with the intent to destroy, in whole or in part, a
national, ethnical, racial or religious group as such:
  – killing members of the group;

665

- causing serious bodily or mental harm to members of the group;
- deliberately inflicting on the group conditions of life calculated to bring about its physical destruction in whole or in part;
- imposing measures intended to prevent births within the group;
- forcibly transferring children from one group to another group.

The following acts shall be punishable under this Article:

- attempts to commit acts of genocide;
- conspiracy to commit acts of genocide;
- participation in acts of acts of genocide.

G. IRAQ

The Statute of the Iraqi Special Tribunal, Articles 10–11

Article 10

13–7   The Tribunal shall have jurisdiction over any Iraqi national or resident of Iraq accused of the crimes listed in Articles 11–14, committed since July 17, 1968 and up and until May 1, 2003, in the territory of Iraq or elsewhere, namely:

a) The crime of genocide . . .;

Article 11

a) For the purposes of this Statute and in accordance with the Convention on the Prevention and Punishment of the Crime of Genocide, dated December 9, 1948, as ratified by Iraq on January 20, 1959, "genocide" means any of the following acts committed with intent to destroy, in whole or in part, a national, ethnical, racial or religious group, as such:

1. killing members of the group;
2. causing serious bodily or mental harm to members of the group;
3. deliberately inflicting on the group conditions of life calculated to bring about its physical destruction in whole or in part;
4. imposing measures intended to prevent births within the group; and
5. forcibly transferring children of the group to another group.

b) The following acts shall be punishable:

1. genocide;
2. conspiracy to commit genocide;
3. direct and public incitement to commit genocide;
4. attempt to commit genocide; and
5. complicity in genocide.

II. BACKGROUND

13–8   The term "genocide" was first used by the jurist Rafael Lemkin in 1944 to characterise the deliberate plan of the Nazis to exterminate the Jews and Gypsies (R. Lemkin, *Axis Rule in Occupied Europe*, 1944).

A few years later, the term came to describe a crime in the *Convention on the Prevention and Punishment of the Crime of Genocide* signed in Paris on December 9, 1948. The Convention is now considered part of international customary law (see *Advisory Opinion on Reservations to the Convention on the Prevention and Punishment of the Crime of Genocide*, ICJ Rep. 1951). The provisions of the Genocide Convention have been included verbatim in the statutes of *inter alia* the ICC, ICTY, and ICTR.

Since the Second World War no other international crime has received more prominence. Numerous victims and observers have claimed that genocide has been committed in modern armed conflicts around the world. The use of the term "genocide" has become synonymous with the most egregious violations of human rights. It has been crowned the most contemptible of all crimes, and assumed a position at the apex of the hierarchy of international crime. The Secretary-General's Report for the ICTR labels genocide the most notorious of all crimes. Before the advent of the International Tribunals, genocide had never been prosecuted as a crime by an international or national court. In the *Eichmann Trial* before the Israeli national courts, genocidal conduct was prosecuted under national laws which echoed the provisions of the 1948 Genocide Convention, but the offences were not charged as "genocide".

Genocide has been charged in most cases before the ICTR, and in a select few before the ICTY. No genocide charges have yet been brought before the Special Panel for serious crimes in East Timor.

III. ELEMENTS OF THE OFFENCE

A. ICC ELEMENTS

Finalized Text of Elements of Crimes

Genocide

6. Notwithstanding the normal requirement for a mental element provided **13–9** for in Article 30, and recognising that knowledge of the circumstances will usually be addressed in proving genocidal intent, the appropriate requirement, if any, for the mental element will need to be decided by the Court on a case-by-case basis.

Genocide by killing

6(a).—(1) The perpetrator killed one or more persons—the term "killed" is **13–10** interchangeable with the term "causing death".

(2) Such person or persons belonged to a particular national, ethnical, racial or religious group.

(3) The perpetrator intended to destroy, in whole or in part, that national, ethnical, racial or religious group, as such.

(4) The conduct took place in the context of a manifest pattern of similar conduct directed against that group or was conduct that could itself effect such destruction-the term "in the context of" would include acts in an emerging pattern. The term "manifest" is an objective qualification.

Genocide by causing serious bodily or mental harm

13-11   **6(b).**—(1) The perpetrator caused serious bodily or mental harm to one or more persons-this conduct may include, but is not necessarily restricted to acts of torture, rape, sexual violence or inhumane or degrading treatment.

(2) Such person or persons belonged to a particular national, ethnical, racial or religious group.

(3) The perpetrator intended to destroy, in whole or in part, that national, ethnical, racial or religious group, as such.

(4) The conduct took place in the context of a manifest pattern of similar conduct directed against that group or was conduct that could itself effect such destruction.

Genocide by inflicting conditions of life calculated to bring about physical destruction

13-12   **6(c).**—(1) The perpetrator inflicted certain conditions of life upon one or more persons.

(2) Such person or persons belonged to a particular national, ethnical, racial or religious group.

(3) The perpetrator intended to destroy, in whole or in part, that national, ethnical, racial or religious group, as such.

(4) The conditions of life were calculated to bring about the physical destruction, in whole or in part, of that particular national, ethnical, racial or religious group, as such—the term "conditions of life" may include, but is not restricted to, deliberate deprivation of resources indispensable for survival such as food and medical services, or systematic expulsion from homes.

(5) The conduct took place in the context of a manifest pattern of similar conduct directed against that group or was conduct that could itself effect such destruction.

Genocide by imposing measures to prevent births

13-13   **6(d).**—(1) The perpetrator imposed certain measures upon one or more persons.

(2) This person or persons belonged to a particular national, ethnical, racial or religious group.

(3) The perpetrator intended to destroy, in whole or in part, that national, ethnical, racial or religious group, as such.

(4) The conduct took place in the context of a manifest pattern of similar conduct directed against that group or was conduct that could itself effect such destruction.

Genocide by forcibly transferring children

13-14   **6(e).**—(1) The perpetrator forcibly transferred one or more persons. The term "forcibly" is not restricted to physical force, but may include threat of force or coercion, such as that caused by fear of violence, duress, detention, psychological oppression or abuse of power, against such person or persons or another persons, or by taking advantage of coercive environment.

(2) The person or persons were under the age of 18.

(3) The perpetrator knew or should have known that the persons were under the age of 18.

B. INTENT TO DESTROY THE GROUP

13-15   As was held in the *Rutaganda* Trial Judgment (paras 59–60):

"59. Genocide is distinct from other crimes because it requires *dolus specialis*, a special intent. Special intent of a crime is the specific intention which, as an element of the crime, requires that the perpetrator clearly intended the result charged. The *dolus specialis* of the crime of genocide lies in "the intent to destroy, in whole or in part, a national, ethnical, racial or religious group, as such" . . .

60. In concrete terms, for any of the acts charged to constitute genocide, the said acts must have been committed against one or more persons because such person or persons were members of a specific group, and specifically, because of their membership in this group. Thus, the victim is singled out not by reason of his individual identity, but rather on account of his being a member of a national, ethnical, racial or religious group. The victim of the act is, therefore, a member of a given group selected as such, which, ultimately, means the victim of the crime of genocide is the group itself and not the individual alone. The perpetration of the act charged, therefore, extends beyond its actual commission, for example, the murder of a particular person, to encompass the realization of the ulterior purpose to destroy, in whole or in part, the group of which the person is only a member."

[The next paragraph is 13–19]

The intent of the crime of genocide has three fundamental components: **13–19**
   1. Intention to destroy a group;
   2. The intention to destroy that group in whole or in part;
   3. Intention to destroy a group that is identifiable by:
      (a) nationality;
      (b) race;
      (c) ethnicity; or
      (d) religion.
Three of the five acts capable of constituting genocide require proof of a result: killing members of the group; causing serious bodily or mental harm to members of the group; and forcibly transferring children of the group to another group.

The other two acts do not demand such proof, but require an intent of deliberately inflicting on the group conditions of life calculated to bring about its physical destruction in whole or in part or imposing measures intended to prevent births within the group.

Proof of a crime of result also requires evidence that the act itself is a   **13–20**
"substantial cause" of the outcome (see *Delalic et al.* Trial Judgment, para. 424).

The *actus reus* of an offence may be either an act of commission or an act of omission. The principle applies to all of the acts of genocide enumerated in the Genocide Convention.

The defining feature of genocide is that it must be proven that the   **13–21**
alleged direct perpetrator possessed the "specific intent" or *dolus specialis* to destroy the group in whole or in part. Where this intent is not established, the act of the direct perpetrator remains punishable, but not as genocide. It may be classified as a crime against humanity. (See the discussion below on other forms of liability for genocide, where the *dolus specialis* is not required.)

A "specific intent" offence requires performance of the *actus reus* but in association with an intent or purpose that goes beyond the mere performance of the act (see the *Akayesu* Trial Judgment, para. 498).

As to the meaning of the requisite specific intent, see the *Krstic* Trial Judgment, para. 571 (footnotes omitted):

"571. The preparatory work of the Genocide Convention clearly shows that the drafters envisaged genocide as an enterprise whose goal, or objective, was to destroy a human group, in whole or in part. United Nations General Assembly resolution 96(I) defined genocide as "the *denial* of the right of existence of entire human groups". The draft Convention prepared by the Secretary-General presented genocide as a criminal act which aims to destroy a group, in whole or in part, and specified that this definition excluded certain acts, which may result in the total or partial destruction of a group, but are committed in the absence of an intent to destroy the group. The International Law Commission upheld this interpretation and indicated that "a general intent to commit one of the enumerated acts combined with a general awareness of the probable consequences of such an act with respect to the immediate victim or victims is not sufficient for the crime of genocide. The definition of this crime *requires a particular state of mind or a specific intent* with respect to the overall consequence of the prohibited act". The International Court of Justice insisted, in its Opinion on the *Legality of the Threat or Use of Nuclear Weapons*, that specific intent to destroy was required and indicated that "the prohibition of genocide would be pertinent in this case if the recourse to nuclear weapons did indeed entail the element of intent, towards a group as such, required by the provision quoted above". The ICTR adopted the same interpretation. In the *Prosecutor v. Jean Kambanda*, the Trial Chamber stated: "the crime of genocide is unique because of its element of *dolus specialis* (special intent) which requires that the crime be committed with the intent 'to destroy in whole or in part, a national, ethnic, racial or religious group as such'". In *Kayishem and Ruzindana*, the Trial Chamber also emphasised that "genocide requires the aforementioned specific intent to exterminate a protected group (in whole or in part)". Moreover, the Chamber notes that the domestic law of some States distinguishes genocide by the existence of a plan to destroy a group. Some legal commentators further contend that genocide embraces those acts whose foreseeable or probable consequence is the total or partial destruction of the group without any necessity of showing that destruction was the goal of the act. Whether this interpretation can be viewed as reflecting the status of customary international law at the time of the acts involved here is not clear. For the purpose of this case, the Chamber will therefore adhere to the characterisation of genocide which encompass only acts committed with the goal of destroying all or part of the group."

The existence of a plan or policy is not a legal ingredient of a crime, but may facilitate the proof of the requisite specific intent (*Jelisic* Appeal Judgment, para. 48).

13–22 If an accused knowingly aided and abetted another in the commission of genocide while being unaware that the principal offender had the special genocidal intent, the accused could be prosecuted for complicity in murder but not for complicity in genocide. On the other hand, if the accused knowingly assists in the commission of an underlying crime such as murder and "knew or had reason to know that the principal offender was acting with genocidal intent, the accused would be an aider and abettor to genocide even though he did not share the murderer's intent to destroy the group" (*Akayesu* Trial Judgment, para. 451) (See the discussion in para. 13–28 below on Complicity).

If the accused accompanied or preceded the act with some form of genocidal declaration or speech, its content may assist in establishing the special intent. Alternatively, the Prosecution can rely on the context of the crime, its massive scale, and elements of its perpetration that indicated hatred of the group and a desire for its destruction. In the

Akayesu Trial Judgment, the Trial Chamber said that genocidal intent could be inferred from the facts, and in particular their massive and/or systematic nature, or their atrocity (para. 478; see also the *Kayishema and Ruzindana* Judgment and Sentence para. 93). Furthermore:

> "[t]his is why, in the absence of a confession from the accused, his intent can be inferred from a certain number of presumptions of fact. The Chamber considers that it is possible to deduce the genocidal intent inherent in a particular act charged from the general context of the perpetration of other culpable acts systematically directed against that same group, whether these acts were committed by the same offender or by others. Other factors, such as the scale of atrocities committed, their general nature, in a region or a country or the fact of deliberately and systematically targeting victims on account of their membership of a particular group, while excluding the members of other groups, can enable the Chamber to infer the genocidal intent of a particular act" (*Akayesu* Trial Judgment, para. 523).

Although the Genocide Convention does not recognise cultural gen-   **13–23**
ocide as a criminal act falling within its scope, proof of attacks directed against cultural monuments or institutions, committed in association with killing, may be relied upon to infer genocidal rather than a homicidal intent. (See the *Krstic* Trial Judgment, para.580.)

Genocidal intent need not be clearly expressed, but it may be implied by factors including the general political doctrine giving rise to the criminal acts or the repetition of destructive and discriminatory acts (see *Karadzic and Mladic* Decision of Review under Rule 61).

The specific nature of some means used to achieve the objective of "ethnic cleansing" is indicative of the fact that the perpetration of the acts is designed to reach the very foundations of the group. For example, the systematic rape of women is in some cases intended to transmit a new ethnic identity to the child; and the destruction of mosques or Catholic churches is designed to extinguish the centuries-long presence of a group (*Karadzic and Mladic* Decision of Review under Rule 61, para. 94).

The offence of genocide "does not require proof that the perpetrator chose the most efficient method to accomplish his objective of destroying the targeted part. Even where the method selected will not implement the perpetrator's intent to the fullest, leaving that destruction incomplete, this ineffectiveness alone does not preclude a finding of genocidal intent." *Krstic* Appeal Judgment, para. 32.

The motive of the accused is irrelevant; provided that the specific intent is clear, the accused can be held liable for the commission of genocide (*Tadić* Appeal Judgment, paras. 268, 269. *See also* the *Kayishema and Ruzindana* Appeal Judgment, para. 161). (See below, paragraph 13–24.)

C. DESTRUCTION OF THE GROUP

The offender must intend "to destroy" a protected group. "Custom-   **13–24**
ary international law limits the definition of genocide to those acts seeking the physical or biological destruction of all or part of the

group" (see, *Krstic* trial judgment, para. 580). The meaning of "as such" is that the intention must be to destroy the group as "'a separate and distinct entity, and not merely some individuals because of their membership in a particular group' [. . .] Genocide therefore differs from the crime of persecution in which the perpetrator chooses his victims because they belong to a specific community but does not necessarily seek to destroy the community as such" (*Jelisic* Trial Judgment, para. 79).

Forcible transfer of a population can lead to the "material destruction" of a group (*Krstic* Appeal Judgment, para. 31), although forcible transfer does not in and of itself constitute a genocidal act (*Krstic* Appeal Judgment, para. 33).

Destruction of the group does not include the "mere dissolution of a group" (*Stakic* Trial Judgment, para. 519).

Intent to destroy a group "may, in principle, be established if the destruction is related to a significant section of the group, such as its leadership" (*Stakic* Trial Judgment, para. 525).

The systematic elimination of the male members of a part of a group may have detrimental consequences for the physical survival of that group as a whole, and so may support a finding that the perpetrators intended to destroy part of the group (*Krstic* Appeal Judgment, para. 28).

The words "as such", constitute an important element of genocide, and serve to reconcile the two diverging approaches for and against the inclusion of a motivational component as an additional element of the crime (*Niyitegeka* Appeal Judgment, para. 53):

> "The term 'as such' has the *effet utile* of drawing a clear distinction between mass murder and crimes in which the perpetrator targets a specific group because of its nationality, race, ethnicity or religion. In other words, the term 'as such' clarifies the specific intent requirement. It does not prohibit a conviction for genocide in a case in which the perpetrator was also driven by other motivations that are legally irrelevant in this context. Thus the Trial Chamber was correct in interpreting 'as such' to mean that the proscribed acts were committed against the victims *because of* their membership in the protected group, but not *solely* because of such membership."

D. IN WHOLE OR IN PART

13–25   Acts of genocide must be committed with the intent to destroy a protected group "in whole or in part".

The International Law Commission considered in 1996 that: "It is not necessary to intend to achieve the complete annihilation of a group from every corner of the globe. None the less the crime of genocide by its very nature requires the intention to destroy at least a substantial part of a particular group [. . .] The main characteristic of genocide is its object: the act must be directed toward the destruction of a *group*. Groups consist of individuals, and therefore, destructive action must, in the last analysis, be taken against individuals. However, these individuals are important not *per se* but only as members of the group to which they belong" (UN doc., A/51/10 (1996) Suppl. No. 10, p. 89).

The act may be committed against an individual or individuals, but it is a requirement that "the victim is chosen not because of individual identity, but rather on account of his membership of a national, ethnical, racial or religious group" (*Akayesu* Trial Judgment, para. 521).

Genocide must involve the intent to destroy a "substantial" part, although not necessarily a "very important part" (*Jelisic* Trial Judgment, paras 81–82). There is no numeric threshold of victims necessary to establish genocide (*Semanza* Trial Judgment, para. 316, *Gacumbitsi* Trial Judgment, 17 June 2004, para. 253; *Stakic* Trial Judgment, para. 522), but the numeric size of the targeted part of the group in relation to the size of the group itself is a factor in determining whether the group is a substantial part (*Krstic* Appeal Judgment, paras 12, 14; *Brdanin* Trial Judgment, para. 702).   **13–26**

"[I]n part requires the intention to destroy a considerable number of individuals who are part of the group" (*Kayishema and Ruzindana* Judgment and Sentence, para. 97. See also the *Bagilishema* Trial Judgment, para. 64.) Genocide could target a limited geographic zone (*Jelisic* Trial Judgment, para. 83), which is a finding affirmed by the *Krstic* Appeal Judgment (paras 15–18) by implication.

The intent to destroy a group "even if only in part, means seeking to destroy a distinct part of the group as opposed to an accumulation of isolated individuals within it. Although the perpetrators of genocide need not seek to destroy the entire group protected by the Convention, they must view the part of the group they wish to destroy as a distinct entity which must be eliminated as such" (*Krstic* Trial Judgment, para. 590). Based on this view the Trial Chamber in *Krstic* found that "the intent to kill all the Bosnian Muslim men of military age in Srebrenica constitutes an intent to destroy in part the Bosnian Muslim group within the meaning of Article 4 and therefore must be qualified as genocide" (*Krstic* Trial Judgment, para 598). This proposition was followed with some hesitation in the *Stakic* Trial Judgment (para. 523) but was affirmed in the *Krstic* Appeal Judgment (paras 19, 22; see also *Brdanin* Trial Judgment, paras 703, 736, 967, where the Trial Chamber found that the Bosnian Muslims and Bosnian Croats of the Autonomous Region of Krajina constituted parts of the protected groups.)

The requirement that the intended destruction contemplate the group "in whole or in part" should not be confused with the scale of the participation by an individual offender.

E. RACIAL, NATIONAL, ETHNIC OR RELIGIOUS GROUPS

The definition of the crime of genocide does not require that the intent to destroy a group be based solely on one of the enumerated grounds of nationality, ethnicity, race, or religion (*Ntakirutimana* Appeal Judgment, para. 363)   **13–27**

It is unclear whether, for the purposes of genocide, a group can be defined in terms of the negative, such as "non-Serbs". The *Jelesic* Trial Judgment advocated the "negative approach" and held that all excluded individuals would make up a distinct group (para. 71). The Trial Chamber in *Stakic* disagreed (as did the Trial Chamber in

Brdanin, para. 685, concurring with *Stakic*), holding that "the elements of genocide must be considered in relation to each group separately" (*Stakic* para. 512, *Brdanin* para. 686).

(1) National groups

13–28 The term "national group" refers to a "collection of people who are perceived to share a legal bond based on common citizenship, coupled with the reciprocity of rights and duties" (*Akayesu* Trial Judgment, para. 512, citing as authority for this statement the judgment of the International Court of Justice in the *Nottebohm* Case (1955 ICJ Rep. p. 24)).

The concept of a national group, and the other groups included in the definition of genocide, "must be assessed in the light of a particular political, social, and cultural context. Moreover, for the purposes of applying the Genocide Convention, membership of a group is, in essence, a subjective rather than an objective concept. The victim is perceived by the perpetrator of genocide as belonging to a group slated for destruction" (*Musema* Trial Judgment, para. 161). The determination of the relevant group (racial, ethnical etc.) has to be made on a case-by-case basis (*Blagojević & Jokic* Trial Judgment, para. 667).

However, certain groups are excluded from the protected groups, namely political and economic groups because "from a reading of the *travaux preparatoires* of the Genocide Convention . . . they are considered to be 'non-stable' or 'mobile' groups which one joins through individual, voluntary commitment" (*Musema* Trial Judgment, para. 162).

Auto-genocide, or mass killing of members of the group to which the perpetrators themselves belong, has been presented under the list of national groups. It is argued that, since this constitutes the intentional destruction of part of a national group, it satisfies the definition of the Convention.

(2) Racial groups

13–29 It has been held that "the conventional definition of racial group is based on the hereditary physical traits often identified with a geographical region, irrespective of linguistic, cultural, national or religious factors (*Akayesu* Trial Judgment, para. 514; *Kayishema and Ruzindana* Judgment and Sentence, para. 98).

The International Convention for the Elimination of All Forms of Racial Discrimination uses the term "racial group" in Articles 1(4), 2(2) and 7, and in Article 1(1) defines "racial discrimination" as: "[a]ny distinction, exclusion, restriction or preference based on race, colour, descent, or national or ethnic origin". The term "racial group" itself is not defined in the Genocide Convention.

(3) Ethnic groups

13–30 The International Law Commission, in its Code of Crimes against the Peace and Security of Mankind of 1996, changed the word "ethnical" in the definition of genocide to "ethnic" but in the Rome Statute's definition of genocide, the Diplomatic Conference returned to "ethnical" although the word "ethnic" appears elsewhere in the instrument. The word "ethnical" was used recently by the International Court of Justice (*Application of the Convention on the Prevention and Punishment of the Crime of Genocide (Bosnia and Herzegovina v. Yugoslavia), Further request for the indication of Provisional Measures*, September 13, 1993, ICJ Rep. 325 at pp. 342–343), and it also appears in Article 7 of the *International Convention for the Elimination of All Forms of Racial Discrimination*.

"Ethnic origin" is not a prohibited ground of discrimination listed in the *Universal Declaration of Human Rights* or the *International Covenant on Civil and Political Rights* (pursuant to Articles 2(1) and 26, implying it must be covered by other terms such as race, colour and nationality. Article 27 of the ICCPR, however, protects "ethnic, religious or linguistic minorities").

The *International Covenant on the Elimination of All Forms of Racial Discrimination*, in Article 1(1) mentions "race, colour, descent, or national or ethnic origin".

The preparatory work on the Genocide Convention reflects that the term "ethnical" was added at a later stage in order to better define the types of groups protected by the Convention and ensure that the term "national" would not be understood as encompassing purely political groups (UN Doc. A/C.6/SR.73). (See also the. *Krstic* Trial Judgment, paras 555–557.)

The International Law Commission in the draft Code of Crimes Against the Peace and Security of Mankind, concluded that it was necessary to maintain both the "ethnic" and "racial" references (UN Doc.A/CN.4.398, para. 58).

In the *Akayesu* Trial Judgment (para. 513), the Chamber stated: "An ethic group is generally defined as a group whose members share a common language or culture". The Trial Chamber found that:

> 701. Hence the question to be addressed is against which group the genocide was allegedly committed. Although the Prosecutor did not specifically state so in the Indictment, it is obvious, in the light of the context in which the alleged acts were committed, the testimonies presented and the Prosecutor's closing statement, that the genocide was committed against the Tutsi group. Article 2(2) of the Statute, like the Genocide Convention, provides that genocide may be committed against a national, ethnical, racial or religious group. [. . .]
>
> 702. In the light of the facts brought to its attention during the trial, the Chamber is of the opinion that, in Rwanda in 1994, the Tutsi constituted a group referred to as "ethnic" in official classifications. Thus, the identity cards at the time included a reference to "*ubwoko*" in Kinyarwanda or "*ethnie*" (ethnic group) in French which, depending on the case, referred to the designation Hutu or Tutsi, for example. The Chamber further noted that all the Rwandan witnesses who appeared before it invariably answered spontaneously and without hesitation the questions of the Prosecutor regarding their ethnic identity. Accordingly, the Chamber finds that, in any case, at the time of the alleged events, the Tutsi did indeed constitute a stable and permanent group and were identified as such by all.

The *Akayesu* Trial Judgment had also found that it was the intention of the drafters of the Genocide Convention to protect any stable and permanent group, not only the four groups specified in the Convention.

This finding was abandoned in favour of a subjective definition of the group, to be determined casuistically by reference to the objective particulars of a given social or historical context, and by the subjective perceptions of the perpetrators (*See Kayishema & Ruzindana* Judgment and Sentence, para. 98; *Rutaganda* Trial Judgment, paras 56–58; *Bagilishema* Trial Judgment para. 65; *Musema* Trial Judgment paras 160–163).

In the *Kayishema* Judgment and Sentence the Chamber held: "An ethnical group is one whose members share a common language and culture; or a group which distinguishes itself, as such (self identification); or a group identified as such by others, including perpetrators of the crimes (identification by others)" (para. 98).

More recently, determination of a protected group has been made on a case-by-case basis, consulting both objective and subjective criteria (see *Semanza* Trial Judgment, para. 316; *Kajelijeli* Trial Judgment, para. 813; *Gacumbitsi* Trial Judgment, paras 254–255).

(4) Religious Groups

13–31   In the *Kayishema and Ruzindana* Judgment and Sentence (para. 98) the Trial Chamber concluded that: "[a] religious group includes denomination or mode of worship or a group sharing common beliefs". The *Akayesu* Trial Judgment defined a religious group as "one whose members share the same religion, denomination or mode of worship" (para. 515).

The Human Rights Committee has stated that "religion" should not be limited to "traditional religions or to religions and beliefs with institutional character analogous to those of traditional religions" (UN Doc.CCPR/C/21/Rev.1/Add.4, para. 2 (1993)).

IV. ACTS OF GENOCIDE

A. KILLING

13–32   In the *Semanza* Trial Judgment (para. 319) it was held that criminal liability for genocide by killing members of a group requires, in addition to showing that an accused possessed an intent to destroy the group as such, in whole or in part, the following:

1. the perpetrator intentionally killed one or more members of the group, without the necessity of premeditation; and
2. such victim or victims belonged to the targeted ethnical, racial, national, or religious group.

(See also *Akayesu* Trial Judgment, para. 588, where the two material elements of killing were identified as (1) The victim is dead; and (2) the death resulted from an unlawful act or omission of the accused or a subordinate.)

The reference to "members of the group" as victims of a genocidal act in paragraph (a) of Article 2 of the Genocide Convention means that the act itself must involve the killing of at least two members of the group.

Premeditated killing is not required; intention suffices (*Kayishema and Ruzindana* Appeal Judgment, para. 151)

B. Causing Serious Bodily or Mental Harm

Causing serious bodily or mental harm to members of the group does not necessarily mean that the harm must be permanent and irremediable (*Gacumbitsi* Trial Judgment, para. 291); but it must be harm that results in a grave and long-term disadvantage to a person's ability to lead a normal and constructive life (*Blagojević & Jokic Trial* Judgment, para. 645).

13–33

The Preparatory Committee of the ICC in a draft provision on genocide said that the "reference to 'mental harm' is understood to mean more than the minor or temporary impairment of mental faculties" (Draft Statute of the ICC Part 2, Jurisdiction, Admissibility and Applicable Law, UN Doc.A/AC.249/1998/CRP.8, p. 2). (See *Ntagerura et al* Trial Judgment, para. 664)

The Prosecution need not demonstrate a causal relationship between acts of violence and the destruction of the group. The Prosecution must prove that one or more victims actually suffered physical or mental harm, and if this act is perpetrated with the requisite mental element, the crime has been committed.

Serious bodily or mental harm includes acts of bodily or mental torture, inhumane or degrading treatment, rape, sexual violence, and persecution (*Rutaganda* Trial Judgment, para. 51).

Trial Chambers at the ICTR have held, with reference to the International Law Commission, that causing serious bodily or mental harm to members of the group covers two types of harm that may be inflicted on an individual: bodily harm involving some type of physical injury, and mental harm involving some type of impairment of mental faculties (*Gacumbitsi* Trial Judgment, para. 291).

C. Deliberately Inflicting Conditions of Life Calculated to Destroy the Group

The means of inflicting conditions of life calculated to destroy the group include: subjecting a group of people to a subsistence diet; systematic expulsion from homes; the reduction of essential medical services below minimum requirements; creating circumstances which will lead to a slow death, such as lack of proper housing, clothing, hygiene and medical care or excessive work or physical exertion; rape; starving a group of people, and withholding sufficient living accommodation for a reasonable period (*Brdanin Trial* Judgment, para. 691; *Kayishema and Ruzindana* Judgment and Sentence, paras 115–116). Methods of destruction do not necessarily need to lead immediately to the deaths of members of the group.

13–34

By such methods the perpetrator must ultimately seek the physical destruction of members of the group, even though the methods do not immediately kill, or lead immediately to the death of, members of the group (see *Brdanin* Trial Judgment, para. 691; *Kayishema and Ruzindana* Judgment and Sentence, para.116).

Customary international law limits the definition of genocide to those acts seeking the physical destruction of all or part of the group. "An enterprise attacking only the cultural or sociological characteristics of a human group in order to annihilate those elements which give to that group its own identity distinct from the rest of the community would not fall under the definition of genocide" (*Krstic* Trial Judgment, para. 580, affirmed in the *Krstic* Appeal Judgment, paras 25–26).

D. IMPOSING CONDITIONS INTENDED TO PREVENT BIRTHS

13–35   The *actus reus* of this offence consists of the imposition of the conditions or measures; it need not be proven that they have actually succeeded.

The Trial Chamber in the *Karadzic and Mladic* Decision on Review of the Indictment under Rule 61 concluded that the systematic rape of women is in some cases intended to transmit a new ethnic identity to the child, and could constitute genocide (para. 94).

The Trial Chambers in *Akayesu* (para. 507) and in *Kayishema and Ruzindana* (Judgment and Sentence para. 117) held that rape could be subsumed within "imposing conditions intended to prevent births". The Trial Chamber in *Akayesu* held that the measures intended to prevent births within the group should be construed as:

1. sexual mutilation;
2. the practice of sterilization;
3. forced birth control;
4. separation of the sexes; and
5. prohibition of marriages (para. 508).

Measures intended to prevent births within the group can be physical as well as mental. Rape can be a measure intended to prevent births when the person raped refuses subsequently to procreate, in the same way that members of a group can be led through threats or trauma, not to procreate (*Akayesu* Appeal Judgment, para. 508). (See also *Rutaganda* Trial Judgment, para. 53; *Musema* Trial Judgment, para. 158.)

E. FORCIBLY TRANSFERRING CHILDREN

13–36   The objective of this prohibition is to prevent the direct act of forcibly transferring children, and also to sanction threats or intimidation which would lead to the forcible transfer of children from one group to the next (see *Akayesu* Trial Judgment, para. 509).

V. PUNISHABLE FORMS OF PARTICIPATION

A. CONSPIRACY TO COMMIT GENOCIDE

Genocide is the only international crime over which the ICC, ICTY **13–37**
and ICTR (and now the IST) have jurisdiction for which conspiracy to
commit the offence may be charged. Conspiracy to commit genocide
only requires proof of an actual or implied agreement to commit
genocide. As with all charges of conspiracy, the Prosecution does not
have to prove that the commission of the offence, namely a genocide,
did in fact occur.

The principles applicable to this offence were clearly set out in the
Musema Trial Judgment, (which finding was undisturbed on appeal), at
paras 184–198 (footnotes omitted):

"184. Article 2(3)(b) of the Statute provides that the Tribunal shall have
the power to prosecute persons charged with the crime of conspiracy to
commit genocide. The Prosecutor has charged the Accused with such a
crime under Count 3 of the Indictment.

185. The Chamber notes that the crime of conspiracy to commit
genocide covered in the Statute is taken from the Genocide Convention.
The '*Travaux Préparatoires*' of the Genocide Convention suggest that the
rationale for including such an offence was to ensure, in view of the
serious nature of the crime of genocide, that the mere agreement to
commit genocide should be punishable even if no preparatory act has
taken place. Indeed, during the debate preceding the adoption of the
Convention, the Secretariat advised that, in order to comply with General
Assembly resolution 96(I), the Convention would have to take into
account the imperatives of the prevention of the crime of genocide:

'This prevention may involve making certain acts punishable which do
not themselves constitute genocide, for example, certain material acts
preparatory to genocide, an agreement or a conspiracy with a view to
committing genocide, or systematic propaganda inciting to hatred and
thus likely to lead to genocide.'

186. The Chamber notes that Common Law systems tend to view
'*entente*' or conspiracy as a specific form of criminal participation, punishable in itself. Under Civil Law, conspiracy or '*complot*' derogates from the
principle that a person cannot be punished for mere criminal intent
('*résolution criminelle*') or for preparatory acts committed. In Civil Law
systems, conspiracy (*complot*) is punishable only where its purpose is to
commit certain crimes considered as extremely serious, such as undermin-
ing the security of the State.

187. With respect to the constituent elements of the crime of conspiracy
to commit genocide, the Chamber notes that, according to the '*Travaux
Préparatoires*' of the Genocide Convention, the concept of conspiracy relied
upon the Anglo-Saxon doctrine of conspiracy. [. . .]

188. For its part, the United Nations War Crimes Commission defined
conspiracy as follows:

"The doctrine of conspiracy is one under which it is a criminal offence
to conspire or to take part in an allegiance to achieve an unlawful
object, or to achieve a lawful object by unlawful means.'

189. Civil Law distinguishes two types of *actus reus*, qualifying two '*levels*'
of '*complot*' or conspiracy. Following an increasing level of gravity, the first
level concerns (*le complot* simple) simple conspiracy, and the second level (*le*

complot suivi d'actes matériels) conspiracy followed by material acts. Simple conspiracy is usually defined as a concerted agreement to act, decided upon by two or more persons (*résolution d'agir concertée et arrêtée entre deux ou plusieurs personnes*) while the conspiracy followed by preparatory acts is an aggravated form of conspiracy where the concerted agreement to act is followed by preparatory acts. Both forms of '*complot*' require that the following three common elements of the offence be met: (1) an agreement to act [*la résolution d'agir*]; (2) concerted wills [*le concert de volontés*]; and (3) the common goal to achieve the substantive offence [*l'objectif commun de commettre l'infraction principale*].

190. Under Common Law, the crime of conspiracy is constituted when two or more persons agree to a common objective, the objective being criminal.

191. The Chamber notes that the constitutive elements of conspiracy, as defined under both systems, are very similar. Based on these elements, the Chamber holds that conspiracy to commit genocide is to be defined as an agreement between two or more persons to commit the crime of genocide.

192. With respect to the *mens rea* of the crime of conspiracy to commit genocide, the Chamber notes that it rests on the concerted intent to commit genocide, that is to destroy, in whole or in part, a national, ethnic, racial or religious group, as such. Thus, it is the view of the Chamber that the requisite intent for the crime of conspiracy to commit genocide is, *ipso facto*, the intent required for the crime of genocide, that is the *dolus specialis* of genocide.

193. It emerges from this definition that, as far as the crime of conspiracy to commit genocide is concerned, it is, indeed, the act of conspiracy itself, in other words, the process ('*procédé*') of conspiracy, which is punishable and not its result. The Chamber notes, in this regard, that under both Civil and Common Law systems, conspiracy is an inchoate offence ('*infraction formelle*') which is punishable by virtue of the criminal act as such and not as consequence of the result of that act.

194. The Chamber is of the view that the crime of conspiracy to commit genocide is punishable even if it fails to produce a result, that is to say, even if the substantive offence, in this case genocide, has not actually been perpetrated. [This particular finding was affirmed by the respective Trial Chambers in the following cases: *Niyitegeka* (para. 423); *Nahimana et al.* (para. 1044); *Kajelijeli* (para. 788).]

195. Moreover, the Chamber raised the question as to whether an accused could be convicted of both genocide and conspiracy to commit genocide.

196. Under Civil Law systems, if the conspiracy is successful and the substantive offence is consummated, the accused will only be convicted of the substantive offence and not of the conspiracy. Further, once the substantive crime has been accomplished and the criminal conduct of the accused is established, there is no reason to punish the accused for his mere *résolution criminelle* (criminal intent), or even for the preparatory acts committed in furtherance of the substantive offence. Therefore an accused can only be convicted of conspiracy if the substantive offence has not been realized or if the Accused was part of a conspiracy which has been perpetrated by his co-conspirators, without his direct participation.

197. Under Common Law, an accused can, in principle, be convicted of both conspiracy and a substantive offence, in particular, where the objective of the conspiracy extends beyond the offences actually committed. However, this position has incurred much criticism. Thus, for example, according to Don Stuart:

"The true issue is not whether evidence has been used twice to achieve convictions but rather whether the fundamental nature of the conspiracy offence is best seen [. . .] as purely preventive, incomplete offence, auxiliary offence to the principal offence and having no true independent rationale to exist on its own alongside the full offence. On this view it inexorably follows that once the completed offence has been committed there is no justification for also punishing the incomplete offence."

198. In the instant case, the Chamber has adopted the definition of conspiracy most favourable to [the accused], whereby an accused cannot be convicted of both genocide and conspiracy to commit genocide on the basis of the same acts. Such a definition is in keeping with the intention of the Genocide Convention. Indeed, the *'Travaux Préparatoires'* show that the crime of conspiracy was included to punish acts which, in and of themselves, did not constitute genocide. The converse implication of this is that no purpose would be served in convicting an accused, who has already been found guilty of genocide, for conspiracy to commit genocide, on the basis of the same acts.

The Trial Chamber in *Nahimana et al.* (para.1048) supplemented this statement with the following:

"The Chamber [. . .] considers that conspiracy to commit genocide can be comprised of individuals acting in an institutional capacity as well as or even independently of their personal links with each other. Institutional coordination can form the basis of a conspiracy among those individuals who control the institutions that are engaged in coordinated action. The Chamber considers the act of coordination to be the central element that distinguishes conspiracy from 'conscious parallelism', the concept put forward by the Defence to explain the evidence in this case."

B. Direct and Public Incitement to Commit Genocide

The act consists of "directly provoking the perpetrator(s) to commit **13–38** genocide, whether through speeches, shouting or threats uttered in public places or at public gatherings, or through the sale or dissemination, offer for sale or display of written material or printed matter in public places or at public gatherings, or through the public display of placards or posters, or through any other means of audiovisual communication" (*Akayesu* Trial Judgment, para. 559).

Whether incitement is "public" is evaluated on the basis of two factors: (1) the place where the incitement occurred; and (2) whether or not assistance was selective or limited. "According to the International Law Commission, public incitement is characterized by a call for criminal action to a number of individuals in a public place or to members of the general public at large by such means as the mass media, for example, radio or television." (*Niyitegeka* Trial Judgment, para. 431.)

The *mens rea* for the offence "lies in the intent to directly prompt or provoke another to commit genocide. It implies a desire on the part of the perpetrator to create by his actions a particular state of mind necessary to commit such a crime in the minds of the person(s) he is so engaging" (*Akayesu* Trial Judgment, para. 560). The person who is so inciting must have the specific intent to commit genocide, namely to destroy the protected group in whole or in part.

However, it is not necessary to prove that the incitement was successful, or that it produced the result expected by the perpetrator (*Akayesu* Trial Judgment, para. 562); incitement is a crime regardless of whether it has the effect it intends to have (*Nahimana et al.*, para. 1029).

The Trial Chamber in *Nahimana et al.* had the occasion to pronounce upon the specific role of the media (editors and publishers) in crimes of incitement (paras 1001 *et seq.*).

"The nature of media is such that causation of killing and other acts of genocide will necessarily be effected by an immediately proximate cause in addition to the communication itself. [T]his does not diminish the causation to be attributed to the media, or the criminal accountability of those responsible for the communication" (paras 952–953).

The crime of direct and public incitement to commit genocide is an inchoate offence that continues in time until the contemplated acts are completed (*Nahimana et al.* Trial Judgment, para. 1017).

C. ATTEMPT

13–39   Attempt to commit genocide is another inchoate offence that applies only to genocide before international criminal courts. There is no jurisdiction to try persons for attempts to commit war crimes or crimes against humanity.

It would be a matter of degree to determine if a partly fulfilled genocide should be charged as an attempt or whether it could qualify as a genocide itself on the basis that a substantial part of a protected group had already been destroyed.

There has to date not been any decision rendered on a charge of attempt to commit genocide.

D. COMPLICITY

13–40   [See also paragraph 13–37 above.]

In addition to being charged for genocide as the principal perpetrator, it is permissible to charge those who are accomplices in the commission of genocide. It must first be proven that the predicate offence of genocide has been committed for an accused to be found guilty of complicity in genocide (*Blagojević & Jokić* Trial Judgment, para. 638). It is not necessary for the perpetrator of the principal offence to have been tried (*Akayesu* Trial Judgment, paras 529–531. See also *Stakic* Trial Judgment, para. 533, *Brdanin Trial* Judgment, para. 728, and *Krstic* Appeal Judgment, para. 35). Neither is it necessary for the perpetrator(s) of the principal offence to be identified (*Krstic* Appeal Judgment, para. 143).

An act that an accused has been charged with cannot be characterised as both an act of genocide, and as an act of complicity in genocide. An individual cannot be both a principal perpetrator and the accomplice thereto in respect of a particular act (*Akayesu* Trial Judgment, para. 532; *Brdanin Trial* Judgment, para. 728).

Various forms of participation can constitute complicity including complicity by procuring means (such as weapons), complicity by knowingly aiding and abetting; and complicity by instigation (*Akayesu* Trial Judgment, para. 537; *Brdanin Trial* Judgment, para. 729).

The Appeals Chamber of the ICTY in *Krstic* considered an appeal against the appellant's conviction as a participant in a joint criminal enterprise to commit genocide, *i.e.* as a perpetrator. The Trial Chamber had found that the appellant had genocidal intent, and the Appeals Chamber overturned this finding, concluding instead that it could only be proven that the appellant had knowledge of the genocidal intent of others, and that he did nothing to prevent the use of resources under his control from being used in the killings (para. 134). The Appeal Chamber accordingly held that the appellant's liability was "more properly expressed" as that of an aider and abettor to genocide (para. 137). A conviction for aiding and abetting genocide, upon proof that the defendant knew about the principal perpetrator's genocidal intent, is therefore permissible (*Krstic* Appeal Judgment, para. 139).

The construction of the respective statutes of the two ad hoc Tribunals resulted in the inclusion of '*complicity*' as a punishable act of genocide, and '*aiding and abetting*' as a mode of liability. It has since been established that complicity in genocide encompasses aiding and abetting (*Krstic* Appeal Judgment, paras 138–140, *Ntakirutimana* Appeal Judgment, para. 371). In general, complicity in genocide requires the accomplice to have the specific intent. However, where complicity takes the form of aiding and abetting genocide, specific intent is not required; what is required is for the accused to know of the specific intent of the principal perpetrators (*Ntakirutimana* Appeal Judgment, paras 371, 500; *Semanza* Appeal Judgment, para. 316).

VI. CHARGING GENOCIDE

It is permissible to charge an accused for participating in the commission of genocide in more than one form, for example as a direct participant and as an accomplice, providing that each form of alleged criminal responsibility relates to different underlying acts (*Akayesu* Trial Judgment, para. 532; *Kambanda* Trial Judgment, para. 40(4)). **13–41**

In cases before the ICTY and ICTR, accused have been charged pursuant to both under Articles 7(1) and 7(3), and Articles 6(1) and 6(3) respectively, (Articles 7(3) and 6(3) relating to superior responsibility).

Due to the specific intent requirement of the offence of genocide, the question has arisen whether an accused can be charged under the doctrine of superior responsibility merely for failing to prevent or punish the offence of genocide. The ICTR has answered this question in the affirmative (*Ntagerura et al.* Trial Judgment, para. 694). In *Ntagerura et al.*, one of the accused was found responsible for genocide under Article 6(3), but note that the accused was a civilian and was found to have had superior responsibility for certain radio broadcasts. The case was on appeal at the time of writing.)

The question as to whether a superior must himself possess the necessary genocidal intent, or rather must only know or have reason to know that his subordinates have a genocidal state of mind, remains somewhat open. The bulk of authority supports the position that a superior need not have the specific intent, but need only know or have reason to know that his subordinates have a genocidal state of mind (*Krstic* Trial Judgment paras 647–652; *Brdanin Trial* Judgment, para. 719; *Blagojević & Jokic* Trial Judgment, para. 686). The Trial Chamber in *Ntagerura et al.*, for example, stated comprehensively that:

"A superior will be found to have possessed or will be imputed with the requisite mens rea sufficient to incur criminal responsibility provided that: (i) the superior had actual knowledge, established through direct or circumstantial evidence, that his subordinates were about to commit, were committing, or had committed, a crime under the statute; or (ii) the superior possessed information providing notice of the risk of such offences by indicating the need for additional investigations in order to ascertain whether such offences were about to be committed, were being committed, or had been committed by subordinates (para. 629)."

Note, however, that the Trial Chamber in the *Stakic* Rule 98*bis* Decision followed the alternative approach and held that "[i]t follows from Article 4 and the unique nature of genocide that the *dolus specialis* is required for responsibility under Article 7(3) as well" (para. 92).

(The Appeal Chamber of the ICTY is yet to issue a judgment on this question, but both the Stakic and Brdanin judgments were on appeal at the time of writing.)

13–42   Ethnic cleansing campaigns can be charged as genocide when it can be shown that the intent of the campaign was the destruction of the group. The crime base for alleged war crimes and crimes against humanity could overlap with the unlawful acts that constitute genocide, however, the distinctive elements of genocide have to be established for an accused to be found guilty of this offence. An accused can be convicted of war crimes, crimes against humanity, and genocide for the same underlying acts, although the sentence imposed must reflect the overall conduct (*Delalic et al.* Appeal Judgment, paras 412–413; *Krstic* Appeal Judgment, paras 216–233).

Rape and sexual violence can be charged as genocide, and should not be viewed any differently from other genocidal acts, provided that they were committed with the specific intent to destroy the group in whole or in part (see, *Akayesu* Trial Judgment, paras 731–732, in which it was held that sexual violence was an integral part of the process of destruction, specifically targeting Tutsi women).

13–42   The Appeals Chamber of the ICTY has established that, as regards joint criminal enterprise as a mode of liability for genocide, "criminal liability can attach to an accused for any crime that falls outside of an agreed upon joint criminal enterprise", including genocide (*Brdanin* Decision on Interlocutory Appeal, para. 9).

"The elements of a crime are those facts which the Prosecution must prove to establish that the conduct of the perpetrator constituted the crime alleged. However, participants other than the direct perpetrator of the criminal act may also incur liability for a crime, and in many cases different *mens rea* standards may apply to direct perpetrators and other persons. The third category of joint criminal enterprise liability is, as with other forms of criminal liability, such as command responsibility or aiding and abetting, not an element of a particular crime. It is a mode of liability through which an accused may be individually criminally responsible despite not being the direct perpetrator of the offence. An accused convicted of a crime under the third category of joint criminal enterprise need not be shown to have intended to commit the crime or even to have known with certainty that the crime was to be committed. Rather, it is sufficient that that accused entered into a joint criminal enterprise to commit a different crime with the awareness that the commission of that agreed upon crime made it reasonably foreseeable to him that the crime charged would be committed by other members of the joint criminal enterprise, and it was committed." (*Prosecutor v. Brdanin*, Decision on Interlocutory Appeal, Appeal Chamber, March 19, 2004, para. 5 (footnotes omitted))

CHAPTER 14

CRIMES OF AGGRESSION

I. STATUTORY PROVISIONS

A. ICC

Statute, Arts 5, 121, 123

Crimes within the jurisdiction of the Court

5.—1. The jurisdiction of the Court shall be limited to the most serious **14–1**
crimes of concern to the international community as a whole. The Court has
jurisdiction in accordance with this Statute with respect to the following
crimes:

(. . .]
(d) The crime of aggression.

2. The Court shall exercise jurisdiction over the crime of aggression once a
provision is adopted in accordance with articles 121 and 123 defining the crime
and setting out the conditions under which the Court shall exercise jurisdiction
with respect to this crime. Such a provision shall be consistent with the
relevant provisions of the Charter of the United Nations.

Amendments

121.—1. After the expiry of seven years from the entry into force of this **14–2**
Statute, any State Party may propose amendments thereto. The text of any
proposed amendment shall be submitted to the Secretary-General of the
United Nations, who shall promptly circulate it to all States Parties.

2. No sooner than three months from the date of notification, the next
Assembly of States Parties shall, by a majority of those present and voting,
decide whether to take up the proposal. The Assembly may deal with the
proposal directly or convene a Review Conference if the issue involved so
warrants.

3. The adoption of an amendment at a meeting of the Assembly of States
Parties or at a Review Conference on which consensus cannot be reached shall
require a two-thirds majority of States Parties.

4. Except as provided in paragraph 5, an amendment shall enter into force for all States Parties one year after instruments of ratification or acceptance have been deposited with the Secretary-General of the United Nations by seven-eighths of them.

5. Any amendment to article 5 of this Statute shall enter into force for those States Parties which have accepted the amendment one year after the deposit of their instruments of ratification or acceptance. In respect of a State Party which has not accepted the amendment, the Court shall not exercise its jurisdiction regarding a crime covered by the amendment when committed by that State Party's nationals or on its territory.

6. If an amendment has been accepted by seven-eighths of States Parties in accordance with paragraph 4, any State Party which has not accepted the amendment may withdraw from the Statute with immediate effect, notwithstanding paragraph 1 of article 127, but subject to paragraph 2 of article 127, by giving notice no later than one year after the entry into force of such amendment.

7. The Secretary-General of the United Nations shall circulate to all States Parties any amendment adopted at a meeting of the Assembly of States Parties or at a Review Conference.

Review of the Statute

14–3   **123.**—1. Seven years after the entry into force of this Statute the Secretary-General of the United Nations shall convene a Review Conference to consider any amendments to this Statute. Such review may include, but is not limited to, the list of crimes contained in article 5. The Conference shall be open to those participating in the Assembly of States Parties and on the same conditions.

2. At any time thereafter, at the request of a State Party and for the purposes set out in paragraph 1, the Secretary-General of the United Nations shall, upon approval by a majority of States Parties, convene a Review Conference.

3. The provisions of article 121, paragraphs 3 to 7, shall apply to the adoption and entry into force of any amendment to the Statute considered at a Review Conference.

B. OTHER COURTS

14–4   None of the other international criminal courts have jurisdiction over crimes against aggression. The ICC will be the first international court since the Nuremberg Tribunal to prosecute crimes against aggression.

II. UN DEFINITION

UN Charter, Arts 39–42, 51

14–5   **39.** The Security Council shall determine the existence of any threat to the peace, breach of the peace, or act of aggression and shall make recommendations, or decide what measures shall be taken in accordance with Articles 41 and 42, to maintain or restore international peace and security.

40. In order to prevent an aggravation of the situation, the Security Council may, before making the recommendations or deciding upon the measures provided for in Article 39, call upon the parties concerned to comply with such provisional measures as it deems necessary or desirable. Such provisional measures shall be without prejudice to the rights, claims, or position of the parties concerned. The Security Council shall duly take account of failure to comply with such provisional measures.

41. The Security Council may decide what measures not involving the use of armed force are to be employed to give effect to its decisions, and it may call upon the Members of the United Nations to apply such measures. These may include complete or partial interruption of economic relations and of rail, sea, air, postal, telegraphic, radio, and other means of communication, and the severance of diplomatic relations.

42. Should the Security Council consider that measures provided for in Article 41 would be inadequate or have proved to be inadequate, it may take such action by air, sea, or land forces as may be necessary to maintain or restore international peace and security. Such action may include demonstrations, blockade, and other operations by air, sea, or land forces of Members of the United Nations.

51. Nothing in the present Charter shall impair the inherent right of individual or collective self-defence if an armed attack occurs against a Member of the United Nations, until the Security Council has taken measures necessary to maintain international peace and security. Measures taken by Members in the exercise of this right of self-defence shall be immediately reported to the Security Council and shall not in any way affect the authority and responsibility of the Security Council under the present Charter to take at any time such action as it deems necessary in order to maintain or restore international peace and security.

As the prevention of aggression is one of the main aims of the United **14–6** Nations, a project to define the crime of aggression was initiated in the aftermath of the Second World War. It proved extremely difficult to reach a consensus on defining the scope and elements of the crime of aggression. In 1974 the General Assembly of the UN completed the project to define aggression and passed United Nations General Assembly Resolution 3314 (XXIX):

3. Any of the following acts, regardless of a declaration of war, shall, subject to and in accordance with the provisions of article 2, qualify as an act of aggression:
(a) The invasion or attack by the armed forces of a State of the territory of another State, or any military occupation, however temporary, resulting from such invasion or attack, or any annexation by the use of force of the territory of another State or part thereof,
(b) Bombardment by the armed forces of a State against the territory of another State or the use of any weapons by a State against the territory of another State;
(c) The blockade of the ports or coasts of a State by the armed forces of another State;
(d) An attack by the armed forces of a State on the land, sea or air forces, or marine and air fleets of another State;
(e) The use of armed forces of one State which are within the territory of another State with the agreement of the receiving State, in contravention of the conditions provided for in the agreement or any extension of their presence in such territory beyond the termination of the agreement;
(f) The action of a State in allowing its territory, which it has placed at the disposal of another State, to be used by that other State for perpetrating an act of aggression against a third State;

(g) The sending by or on behalf of a State of armed bands, groups, irregulars or mercenaries, which carry out acts of armed force against another State of such gravity as to amount to the acts listed above, or its substantial involvement therein.

III. NUREMBERG DEFINITION

14–7   The Nuremberg Tribunal provides the main authority for the prosecution of crimes of aggression before international criminal courts. (See Judgment of the Nuremberg International Military Tribunal, 1946, 41 AJIL 172; (1947) British Command Paper, cmd 6469, p.36. Also see Judgment of the Trial before the Tokyo International Military Tribunal, LRTWC, Vol XIV, 136 and also Judgments in I.G Farben, LRTWC, Vol X, pp. 30–40; Krupp, LRTWC, Vol X, pp. 102–130; High Command, LRTWC, Vol XII, pp. 65–71; Greiser, Vol XIII, pp. 108–10 and Takashi Sakai, LRTWC, Vol XIV, pp. 1–7.)

Article 6(a) of the 1945 Charter of the International Military Tribunal (IMT) at Nuremberg defined crimes against peace as "planning, preparation, initiation or waging of a war of aggression, or a war in violation of international treaties, agreements or assurances, or participation in a common plan or conspiracy [to commit these acts]". (U.K.T.S 4(1945) cmd. 6671; S.U.N.T.S 251.) Also see Article 5(A) of the Charter of the International Military Tribunal for the Far East, Tokyo. War, as a crime of aggression, had not been the subject of a criminal trial before the establishment of the IMT. The Kellogg-Briand Pact of 1928 prohibited the use of aggression by States. It did not provide for individual criminal responsibility for killing on behalf of an aggressor State.

Crimes against peace were charged before the IMT. The charge was criticised on the grounds that it was based on *ex post facto* law. Such a view was rejected in the Judgment of the International Military Tribunal at Nuremberg, The Law of the Charter, Cmd 6469, p.36, where the Hague Convention of 1907, Draft League of Nations Treaty of Mutual Assistance, 1923, Declaration of the Assembly of the League of Nations, September 24, 1927 and Sixth (Havana) Pan-American Conference Resolution of February 18, 1928 were all considered by the Tribunal in holding "that resort to a war of aggression is not merely illegal but criminal".

The final judgment therefore concluded that the IMT charter was the expression of existing international law, and not *ex post facto* legislation. The IMT found that aggression is the "supreme international crime differing only from other war crimes in that it contains within itself the accumulated evil of the whole". (See Trial of the Major War Criminals Before the International Criminal Tribunal, Nuremberg, 1947, Vol 1, at 186.)

14–8   In the High Command Trial responsibility for the crime of aggression was explained in the following terms:

"[. . .] as in ordinary criminal cases, so in the crime denominated aggressive war, the same elements must all be present to constitute criminality. There first must be actual knowledge that an aggressive war is intended and that if launched it will be an aggressive war. But mere knowledge is not sufficient to make participation even by high ranking officers in the war criminal. It requires in addition that the possessor of such knowledge, after he acquires it shall be in a position to shape or influence the policy that brings about its initiation or its continuance after initiation, either by furthering or hindering or preventing it. If he does the former, he becomes criminally responsible. If he does the latter to the extent of his ability, then the action shows the lack of criminal intent with respect to such a policy." (LRTWC, Vol XII, pp. 68, 69.)

IV. ELEMENTS OF THE OFFENCE

The crime of aggression was left undefined in the ICC Statute. It was **14–9** not possible to include in the Statute a definition of aggression acceptable to all parties. The Court may not exercise jurisdiction over the crime of aggression until an agreement is reached at a Review Conference. Under Articles 5, 121 and 123, the Statute may only be amended to include a definition of aggression no sooner than seven years after the entry into force of the Statute.

In light of the limited precedent on the subject, United Nations General Assembly Resolution 3314 will be the likely starting point for defining the elements of the crime. (For a summary of various proposals currently under discussion see, Proceedings of the Preparatory Commission at its eighth session, September 24 to October 5, 2001, Annex III, PCNICC/2001/L3/Rev/1 and more recently PCNICC/2001/L3/Rev/1 and PCNICC/2002/2/Add.2. Also see PCNICC/2002/WGCA/L.1 and Add.1.) The political sensitivities of agreeing on the parameters of the offence are likely to hamper the investigation and charging of crimes of aggression before the ICC for some time.

Under Article 39 of the UN Charter, the Security Council has competence to determine whether an act of aggression has been committed. The first finding by the Security Council that "aggression" had occurred was made in 1976 when South Africa was condemned for its aggression in Angola (SC Res 387, (1976), SCOR, 20th Year, Resolutions and Decisions, p.11). The ICC will have to address the effect of such a determination if the ICC were also seized of the matter, should such a situation arise in the future.

CHAPTER 15

OTHER OFFENCES UNDER INTERNATIONAL CRIMINAL LAW

I. INTRODUCTION

The corpus of international criminal law has rapidly expanded in the **15–1** past few decades. A vast body of substantive law has emerged particularly in the fields of terrorism, hijacking, drug trafficking and money laundering as States have realised the need for defining and prohibiting common offences and crimes that by their nature possess a cross-border dimension. Inter-State treaties and agreements are the means by which States have agreed to prohibit and punish unlawful conduct in their territories, co-operate to ensure judicial action, and establish international organs to assist and monitor national proceedings.

Most significantly, in the field of inter-State judicial co-operation and assistance, many new agreements have been signed in recent years. The international scheme of extradition and mutual assistance arrangements is now more advanced and sophisticated. In an effort to combat cross-border crime and minimise the use of sovereign borders as a means of evading justice, States have sought innovative ways of co-operating and sharing resources.

The international crimes and procedures outlined in this chapter do **15–2** not form part of the subject-matter jurisdiction of any of the international criminal courts as yet. It is anticipated that certain of the international crimes may be included in the ambit of the ICC in the

693

future, or that specialised international courts could be established with jurisdiction over particular international crimes not covered by an existing international criminal court.

This chapter focuses on the international crimes that are still only investigated and tried through domestic systems, and the procedures that States employ to judicially assist one another in these proceedings. This body of international criminal law stands alongside the supranational component of the discipline, the international criminal courts. Increasingly, these two main strands will each have to be interpreted and applied in the context of developments in the other.

II. OFFENCES

A. Terrorism and Related Offences

(1) Main international treaties, agreements and documents

15–3
(a) Convention on the Prevention and Punishment of Crimes against Internationally Protected Persons, including Diplomatic Agents (1973)
(b) International Convention against the Taking of Hostages (1979)
(c) Vienna Convention on the Physical Protection of Nuclear Material (1980)
(d) Montreal Convention on the Marking of Plastic Explosives for the Purpose of Detection (1991)
(e) International Convention for the Suppression of Terrorist Bombings (1997)
(f) International Convention for the Suppression of the Financing of Terrorism (1999)

(2) Overview

15–4
A heightened focus by the international community on international terrorism and global security has again placed the offence of terrorism and related offences under the spotlight. The offence has for decades lacked an internationally accepted definition, and comprehensive treaty to suppress terrorism. There has been a continuing resort by governments over the years to the international treaty-making process, particularly under the auspices of the UN, to curb transnational terrorism.

The treaties discussed below are evidence of the trend to reach consensus, albeit on narrowly defined aspects of the offence and related matters. Despite these successes, diplomatic efforts to reach a general and complete internationally recognised arrangement for the punishment of terrorism have failed. The prominent political dimensions of the offence continue to make it difficult to reach a workable definition of the offence and mechanisms to thwart the commission of the offence.

It is most likely for these reasons that the offence was not included in the ICC Statute at this stage. It will be possible, nevertheless, to charge acts of terrorism under the offences within the jurisdiction of the ICC where the elements of the offences can be made out.

(3) Summary of relevant substantive provisions

Convention on the Prevention and Punishment of Crimes against Internationally Protected Persons, including Diplomatic Agents 1973

This Convention was adopted by the General Assembly of the United Nations on December 14, 1973.   **15–5**

The Convention provides that Heads of State (or deputies or substitutes thereof), Heads of Government and Ministers of Foreign Affairs including members of their families as well as representatives or officials of other States, are "internationally protected persons".

The Convention prohibits various offences against internationally protected persons, including: (a) murder, kidnapping or other attacks upon the person or liberty of such protected persons; (b) violent attacks on official premises, means of transport; and (c) threats or attempts to commit such acts.

The Convention requires States to make these offences punishable by "appropriate penalties" and also to take all appropriate measures to prevent such attacks. It provides for the "extradition or prosecution" mechanism of alleged offenders, as well as for the exchange of information and co-ordination of joint measures.

International Convention against the Taking of Hostages 1979

This Convention was adopted by the General Assembly of the United Nations on December 17, 1979.   **15–6**

The Convention defines the offence of "taking of hostages" as any act by which a "person seizes or detains and threatens to kill, to injure or to continue to detain another person in order to compel a State, an international intergovernmental organisation, a natural or juridical person or a group of persons, to do or abstain from doing any act as an explicit or implicit condition for the release of the hostage".

It provides for the "extradition or prosecution" mechanism of alleged offenders, as well as for the exchange of information and co-ordination of joint measures. However, extradition is not to be granted if the requested State has reasons to believe that the request has been made for the purpose of prosecuting the alleged offender on account of his race, religion, nationality, ethnic origin or political opinion.

International Convention for the Suppression of Terrorist Bombings 1997

This Convention was adopted by the General Assembly of the United Nations on December 15, 1997.   **15–7**

The Convention defines the offence of "terrorist bombing" as any act by which a person "unlawfully and intentionally delivers, places, discharges or detonates an explosive or other lethal device in, into or against a place of public use, a State or government facility, a public transportation system or an infrastructure facility", "with the intent to cause death or serious bodily injury" or "extensive destruction" resulting in major economic loss.

It provides for the "extradition or prosecution" mechanism of alleged offenders, as well as for the exchange of information and co-ordination of joint measures. However, extradition is not to be granted if the requested State has reasons to believe that the request has been made for the purpose of prosecuting the alleged offender on account of his race, religion, nationality, ethnic origin or political opinion.

International Convention for the Suppression of the Financing of Terrorism 1999

15–8   This Convention was adopted by the General Assembly of the United Nations on December 9, 1999.

The Convention defines the offence of "financing terrorism" as any act by which a person "by any means, directly or indirectly, unlawfully and wilfully, provides or collects funds with the intention that they should be used or in the knowledge that they are to be used, in full or in part, in order to carry out [. . .] any act intended to cause death or serious bodily injury to persons not taking active part in a conflict" or any act which has been defined in one of the treaties listed in its annex, namely:

(i) Convention for the Suppression of Unlawful Seizure of Aircraft, done at The Hague on December 16, 1970;

(ii) Convention for the Suppression of Unlawful Acts against the Safety of Civil Aviation, done at Montreal on September 23, 1971;

(iii) Convention on the Prevention and Punishment of Crimes against Internationally Protected Persons, including Diplomatic Agents, adopted by the General Assembly of the United Nations on December 14, 1973;

(iv) International Convention against the Taking of Hostages, adopted by the General Assembly of the United Nations on December 17, 1979;

(v) Convention on the Physical Protection of Nuclear Material, adopted at Vienna on March 3, 1980;

(vi) Protocol for the Suppression of Unlawful Acts of Violence at Airports Serving International Civil Aviation, supplementary to the Convention for the Suppression of Unlawful Acts against the Safety of Civil Aviation, done at Montreal on February 24, 1988;

(vii) Convention for the Suppression of Unlawful Acts against the Safety of Maritime Navigation, done at Rome on March 10, 1988;

(viii) Protocol for the Suppression of Unlawful Acts against the Safety of Fixed Platforms located on the Continental Shelf, done at Rome on March 10, 1988; and,

(ix) International Convention for the Suppression of Terrorist Bombings, adopted by the General Assembly of the United Nations on December 15, 1997.

The Convention provides for the freezing or seizure of funds. Funds **15–9** derived from forfeitures may be used for compensation to victims. It also provides for the "extradition or prosecution" mechanism of alleged offenders, as well as for the exchange of information and co-ordination of joint measures. The Convention provides that mutual legal assistance may not be denied on the the grounds of bank secrecy. Also, extradition may not be denied on the grounds of the offence being a fiscal offence or a politically connected offence.

The Convention also requires the State parties to adopt legislation to prevent and counter in their territories the preparation of offences falling within the scope of the Convention and the annexed treaties.

Vienna Convention on the Physical Protection of Nuclear Material 1980

The Convention defines "nuclear material", "enriched uranium" and **15–10** "international nuclear transport" (namely, carriage of a consignment of nuclear material by any means of transportation), and applies to (a) all transport of nuclear material for peaceful purposes; and (b) to nuclear material storage and transport, even in domestic use.

The Convention stipulates that assurances must be given by State parties that the nuclear material is protected at the levels required by Annex 1 to the Convention if transportation of nuclear material, including importation or exportation, is to be permitted.

The only criterion of internationality with respect to the carriage of nuclear materials is that it must be transported beyond the territory of the State where the shipment originates.

Unlawful receipt, possession, use, transfer, alteration, disposal or **15–11** dispersal of nuclear material are prohibited if liable to cause harm, as well as theft, embezzlement or threat to use nuclear material. State parties must provide for the punishment of these offences in their national legislation. Under the Convention, such offences are extraditable and also subject to the "extradite or prosecute" principle. The Convention provides for the exchange of information and mutual assistance between States parties.

Montreal Convention on the Marking of Plastic Explosives for the Purpose of Detection 1991

The Convention seeks to prohibit and prevent the manufacture of **15–12** unregistered explosives. It requires the States parties to prohibit in their territory the transit of unmarked explosives and to strictly control the possession and transfer of unmarked explosives (held before the entry into force of the Convention) with a view to their destruction.

The Convention creates the International Explosive Technical Commission to make recommendations to the States parties and evaluate technical developments relating to the manufacture, marking and detection of explosives. The Convention further provides for the provision of technical assistance and the exchange of information among its parties.

B. HI-JACKING AND OFFENCES AGAINST MARITIME AND AVIATION SECURITY

(1) Main international treaties, agreements and documents

15–13   (a) Tokyo Convention on Offences and Certain Other Acts Committed on Board Aircraft (1963);
   (b) Hague Convention for the Suppression of Unlawful Seizure of Aircraft (1970);
   (c) Montreal Convention for the Suppression of Unlawful Acts against the Safety of Civil Aviation (1971);
   (d) Vienna Convention on the Physical Protection of Nuclear Material (1980).
   (e) Protocol on the Suppression of Unlawful Acts of Violence at Airports Serving International Civil Aviation, supplementary to the Convention for the Suppression of Unlawful Acts against the Safety of Civil Aviation (1988);
   (f) Convention for the Suppression of Unlawful Acts against the Safety of Maritime Navigation (1988) and its Protocol;
   (g) Protocol for the Suppression of Unlawful Acts against the Safety of Fixed Platforms Located on the Continental Shelf (1988);

(2) Overview

15–14   The most significant Convention on offences against transport safety is the Montreal Convention of 1971. Although previous efforts (Tokyo, 1963, and the Hague, 1970) were important in laying the necessary foundation, the Montreal Convention provided the first clear working definitions and rules (for instance, with respect to the "extradite or prosecute" principle).

The Convention on the Safety of Maritime Navigation was influenced by the Montreal Convention and largely structured along the same lines.

Most of the conventions in this area provide for the "extradite or prosecute" mechanism for alleged offenders, and also make provision for mutual assistance and the exchange of information between State parties.

(3) Summary of relevant substantive provisions

Tokyo Convention on Offences and Certain Other Acts Committed on Board Aircraft 1963

15–15   All acts are prohibited which "may or do jeopardize the safety of the aircraft or of persons or property therein, or which jeopardize good order and discipline" on board aircraft while in flight, on the surface of the high seas or in the territory of any country not party to the Convention. The Convention does not set out and define particular offences. Jurisdiction is to be exercised by the State of registration of the aircraft. The Convention excludes offences committed entirely within the jurisdiction of the State of registration.

The Convention grants the aircraft commander powers to impose all reasonable measures on any person who has committed or is about to commit any act which may jeopardise flight safety. While offences are considered to have taken place in the territory of the State of registration, there is no obligation on the parties to extradite offenders to this State.

Hague Convention for the Suppression of Unlawful Seizure of Aircraft 1970

This Convention defines the offence of "unlawful seizure of aircraft"   **15–16**
as the act of any person who "unlawfully, by force or threat thereof, or by any other form of intimidation, seizes, or exercises control of, that aircraft, or attempts to perform any such act". Like the Tokyo Convention, it provides definitions for the moment when the aircraft is considered to be in flight (namely, when all external doors are closed following embarkation), and the moment when the aircraft is deemed to have finished its flight (namely, when all external doors are opened for disembarkation, or in the case of a forced landing, the moment competent authorities take over responsibility for the aircraft and property on board). The Convention requires the State parties to punish hijackers.

The criterion for application of the Convention is not whether the flight is domestic or international, but only if the place of take-off or actual landing is located outside the territory of the State of registration.

State parties are expected to introduce measures enabling them to assert jurisdiction in certain cases, for example, when the offence is committed on board an aircraft registered in their State.

Montreal Convention for the Suppression of Unlawful Acts against the Safety of Civil Aviation 1971

This Convention contains a more comprehensive list of offences.   **15–17**
These include: performing an act of violence against a person on board an aircraft in flight if such act is likely to endanger flight safety; causing damage to an aircraft; placing any device or substance which is likely to destroy or cause damage to the aircraft; and, communicating false information which may endanger the safety of the aircraft in flight.

The Montreal Convention mirrors the Hague Convention on the definition of the time an aircraft is considered to be in flight, and includes the definition of aircraft in service (namely, from the beginning of the pre-flight preparation of the aircraft by ground personnel until 24 hours after landing). It also follows the Hague Convention in that the type of flight is irrelevant as long as the place of landing or take-off are situated outside the territory of the State of registration. The Convention requires State parties to impose "severe penalties" for such acts.

State parties are obliged to immediately make preliminary inquiries into the facts of all alleged violations, and the Convention provides for the "extradite-or-prosecute" mechanism, as well as for mutual assistance in trying offences under the Convention.

Protocol on the Suppression of Unlawful Acts of Violence at Airports Serving International Civil Aviation, supplementary to the Montreal Convention for the Suppression of Unlawful Acts against the Safety of Civil Aviation 1988

15–18   The Protocol extends the offences to any acts liable to endanger the safety of airports serving civil aviation.

Convention for the Suppression of Unlawful Acts against the Safety of Maritime Navigation 1988

15–19   The Convention defines a "ship" as any vessel not permanently affixed to the seabed. The terms of the Convention follow the provisions of the Montreal Convention, with the necessary adaptations to maritime navigation, in relation to the offences which are prohibited, the cases and circumstances when jurisdiction may be exercised, extradition, communications and mutual assistance, and the authority of the ship's master to deliver offenders.

The Convention applies to ships navigating through, from or into, limits of territorial seas. State parties must provide for "appropriate penalties". It also requires the State parties to "extradite or deliver" the offenders. Disputes between the State parties are to be settled by the ICJ.

Protocol for the Suppression of Unlawful Acts against the Safety of Fixed Platforms Located on the Continental Shelf 1988

15–20   The Protocol extends the offences defined in the Convention to similar acts committed with respect to "fixed platforms", defined as artificial islands, installations or structures permanently attached to the seabed for economic purposes.

C. DRUG OFFENCES

(1) Main international treaties, agreements and documents

15–21   (a) UN Single Convention on Narcotic Drugs (1961).

(b) UN Convention on Psychotropic Substances (1971).
(c) UN Convention against the Illicit Traffic in Narcotic Drugs and
     Psychotropic Substances (1988).

(2) Overview

The three main international drug control treaties are designed to be   **15–22**
mutually supportive and complementary. The first two treaties of 1961
and 1971 codify internationally applicable control measures to ensure
the availability of narcotic drugs and psychotropic substances for
medical and scientific purposes, but to prevent their diversion into illicit
channels and for illegal uses. These treaties also incorporate general
provisions on illicit trafficking and drug abuse. The 1988 Convention
specifically focuses on combating illicit drug trafficking.

The 1961 Single Convention permits each State to develop a programme of action suited to its own circumstances, while still adhering
to the general requirements of the Convention. Activities such as
"cultivation and production, manufacture, extraction, preparation, possession, offering, offering for sale, distribution, purchase, sale, delivery
on any terms whatsoever, brokerage, dispatch, dispatch in transit,
transport, importation and exportation of the substances listed under
the Convention" are prohibited and State parties required to penalise
them.

(3) Summary of relevant substantive provisions

UN Single Convention on Narcotic Drugs, 1961

This Convention aims to combat drug abuse by coordinated inter-   **15–23**
national action. Two forms of intervention and control were created to
work in tandem. First, the Convention seeks to limit the possession,
use, trade in, distribution, import, export, manufacture and production
of drugs exclusively to medical and scientific purposes. Secondly, the
Convention targets drug trafficking through international co-operation
to deter and discourage drug traffickers.

The Convention defines a range of controlled substances (for example, opium, coca leaves and cannabis and derivatives thereof) and
requires State parties to undertake various control and reporting
measures, thereby setting a minimum standard, as parties are not
precluded from adopting and implementing stricter regulations than
those in the Convention.

The Convention provides for the prosecution or extradition of   **15–24**
offenders, as well as the seizure and confiscation of drugs and related
substances and equipment. It also requires State parties to "take all
practicable measures for the prevention of abuse of drugs and for the
early identification, treatment, education, after-care, rehabilitation and
social reintegration of the persons involved and [to] co-ordinate their
efforts to these ends" and to "promote [as far as possible] the training
of personnel in the treatment, after-care, rehabilitation and social
reintegration of abusers of drugs".

Convention on Psychotropic Substances, 1971

15–25   The 1971 Convention establishes an international control system for psychotropic substances. It constitutes a response to the diversification of the spectrum of abusive drugs. The Convention introduced controls over numerous synthetic drugs taking into account their potential for abuse, balanced against their therapeutic value.

States parties are required to take measures with respect to:

(a) licences, applicable to the manufacture of controlled substances;

(b) records, applicable to exempt preparations;

(c) prohibition of, and restrictions on, export and import;

(d) inspection, applicable to the manufacture of substances;

(e) preparation and delivery of reports to the International Narcotics Control Board established by the Single Convention on Narcotic Drugs, 1961; and,

(f) penal provisions, to the extent necessary for the repression of acts contrary to laws or regulations adopted pursuant to the Convention.

15–26   With respect to prevention, the parties must "take all practicable measures for the prevention of abuse of psychotropic substances and for the early identification, treatment, education, after-care, rehabilitation and social reintegration of the persons involved and [to] co-ordinate their efforts to these ends" and to "promote [as far as possible] the training of personnel in the treatment, after-care, rehabilitation and social reintegration of abusers of psychotropic substances".

15–27   In relation to illegal traffic of controlled substances, States parties are obliged to: (a) make arrangements at the national level for the co-ordination of preventive and repressive action against illicit traffic; (b) assist each other in the campaign against the illicit traffic in psychotropic substances; (c) co-operate closely with each other and with the competent international organisations of which they are members with a view to maintaining a co-ordinated campaign against the illicit traffic; (d) ensure that international co-operation between the appropriate agencies be conducted in an expeditious manner; and (e) ensure that, where legal papers are transmitted internationally for the purpose of judicial proceedings, the transmittal be effected in an expeditious manner to the bodies designated by the parties.

The Convention provides for the prosecution or extradition of offenders, as well as seizure and confiscation of psychotropic substances and related equipment.

Convention against the Illicit Traffic in Narcotic Drugs and Psychotropic Substances, 1988

15–28   This Convention introduced comprehensive measures against drug trafficking, including provisions against money laundering and the diversion of precursor chemicals. In particular, the Convention provides for international co-operation through the extradition of drug traffickers, controlled deliveries and transfer of proceeds.

The Convention obliges the State parties to penalise offenders with measures appropriate to the nature of the drug offences, such as imprisonment or other forms of deprivation of liberty, pecuniary sanctions and confiscation, and if appropriate, that "the offender shall undergo measures such as treatment, education, aftercare, rehabilitation or social reintegration". The prohibited offences are as follows:

(a) the production, manufacture, extraction, preparation, offering, offering for sale, distribution, sale, delivery on any terms whatsoever, brokerage, dispatch, dispatch in transit, transport, importation or exportation of any narcotic drug or any psychotropic substance contrary to the provisions of the 1961 Convention, the 1961 Convention as amended and the 1971 Convention;

15–29

(b) the cultivation of opium poppy, coca bush or cannabis plant for the purpose of the production of narcotic drugs contrary to the provisions of the 1961 Convention and the 1961 Convention as amended;

(c) the possession or purchase of any narcotic drug or psychotropic substance for the purpose of any of the activities enumerated in (a) above;

(d) the manufacture, transport or distribution of equipment, materials or of substances listed in Table I and Table II, knowing that they are to be used in or for the illicit cultivation, production or manufacture or narcotic drugs or psychotropic substances;

(e) the organization, management or financing of any of the offences enumerated in (a), (b), (c) or (d) above;

(f) the conversion or transfer of property, in the knowledge that such property is derived from any offence or offences established in the Convention, or from an act of participation in such offence or offences, for the purpose of concealing or disguising the illicit origin of the property or of assisting any person who is involved in the commission of such an offence or offences to evade the legal consequences of his actions;

(g) the concealment or disguise of the true nature, source, location, disposition, movement, rights with respect to, or ownership of property, knowing that such property is derived from an offence or offences established in accordance with the Convention, or from an act of participation in such an offence or offences;

(h) the acquisition, possession or use of property, knowing, at the time of receipt, that such property was derived from an offence or offences established in accordance with the Convention or from an act of participation in such offence or offences;

15–30

(i) the possession of equipment or materials or substances listed in Schedules to the Convention, knowing that they are being or are to be used in or for the illicit cultivation, production or manufacture of narcotic drugs or psychotropic substances;

(j) publicly inciting or inducing others, by any means, to commit any of the offences established in accordance with this article or to use narcotic drugs or psychotropic substances illicitly;

(k) participation in, association or conspiracy to commit, attempts to commit and aiding, abetting, facilitating and counselling the commission of any of the offences established in accordance with the Convention;

(l) when committed intentionally, the possession, purchase or cultivation of narcotic drugs or psychotropic substances for personal consumption contrary to the provisions of the 1961 Convention, the 1961 Convention as amended or the 1971 Convention.

15–31   The Convention provides that the seriousness of the offences may be determined by taking into consideration additional factors such as:

(a) The involvement in the offence of an organised criminal group to which the offender belongs;

(b) The involvement of the offender in other international organised criminal activities;

(c) The involvement of the offender in other illegal activities facilitated by the commission of the offence;

(d) The use of violence or arms by the offender;

(e) The fact that the offender holds a public office and that the offence is connected with the office in question;

(f) The victimisation or use of minors;

(g) The fact that the offence is committed in a penal institution or in an educational institution or social service facility or in their immediate vicinity or in other places to which school children and students resort for educational, sports and social activities; and,

(h) Prior conviction, particularly for similar offences, whether foreign or domestic, to the extent permitted under the domestic law of a party.

15–32   Parties are also required to establish under their domestic laws a lengthy statute of limitations period in which to commence proceedings.

This Convention provides for the prosecution or extradition of offenders, as well as for seizure and confiscation of controlled substances; and for mutual assistance, co-operation and cross-training of enforcement personnel. The Convention also allows the controlled delivery of illegal substances with the purpose of identifying and bringing to justice the main perpetrators of the illegal trade.

D. MONEY LAUNDERING

(1) Summary of relevant provisions of international treaties and agreements

European Convention on Laundering, Search, Seizure and Confiscation of the Proceeds from Crime 1990

15–33   The Convention aims to facilitate transnational co-operation and mutual assistance in the investigation of crimes, as well as the tracking down, seizure and confiscation of the proceeds of crimes.

State parties to the Convention must: (a) criminalise the laundering of the proceeds of crimes; and (b) confiscate instrumentalities and proceeds (or property, the value of which corresponds to such proceeds).

The Convention provides for investigative assistance, for instance, in securing evidence, transferring information to another State without a request, adoption of common investigative techniques, and lifting of bank secrecy. With respect to provisional measures, the Convention provides for freezing of bank accounts and seizure of property to prevent its removal from the jurisdiction. Lastly, with respect to measures to confiscate the proceeds of crime, the Convention provides for enforcement by the requested State of a confiscation order made abroad, as well as for the institution of domestic proceedings leading to confiscation at the request of another State.

E. Corruption

(1) Main international treaties, agreements and documents

(a) The US Foreign Corrupt Practices Act (FCPA) (1977);   **15–34**
(b) OECD Convention on Combating Bribery of Foreign Public Officials in International Business Transactions (1997);
(c) Interamerican Convention Against Corruption (1996);
(d) European Conventions on the Fight against Corruption involving officials of the European Communities or officials of Member States of the European Union:
  (i) Civil Law Convention (November 4, 1999);
  (ii) Criminal Law Convention (January 27, 1999);
(e) Convention on the Protection of the European Communities Financial Interests and its Protocols (July 26, 1995).

(2) Overview

All international conventions on corruption require State parties to   **15–35**
criminalise corruption by incorporating provisions in their national legislation to make corruption a criminal offence. One of the main problems associated with this offence is the lack of enforcement of anti-corruption laws. Accordingly, most conventions and treaties provide for extradition arrangements, or alternatively, prosecution under local laws when the requested State does not extradite the accused.

The type of corruption regulated by these Conventions is both general and targeted at international business transactions, and includes bribery of public officers. In the case of the FCPA, political parties and candidates to public positions are also included.

Most Conventions are based on the following common elements:
  (i) corruption may be active (with respect to the offeror) or passive (with respect to the offeree); and,
  (ii) corruption involves (with respect to the active offender): offering, giving, promising to give or authorising the giving of anything of value in order to obtain or retain business (in the case of corruption in international business), or in order for public officials to act or refrain from acting in their public capacities.

The Civil Law Convention on the Fight Against Corruption involving EU Officials provides for compensation of damages suffered by victims of corrupt practices. The June 19, 1997 Protocol to the Convention on the Protection of the European Communities Financial Interests and its Protocols of 1995 extended corruption to include money laundering of proceeds from corrupt activities.

(3) Summary of relevant substantive provisions

US Foreign Corrupt Practices Act, 1977

15–36   The US Foreign Corrupt Practices Act (FCPA) is one of the oldest legislative measures against corruption in international business. It was enacted in 1977 (amended in 1998) and makes it a criminal offence for a US firm or citizen (expanded to include the same acts committed by foreigners in the US) to "give, promise to give, offer or authorize" anything of value to foreign government officials, political parties, party officials and candidates for public offices in order to obtain or retain business.

The Act establishes substantial monetary (to a maximum of US$ 2 million) and custodial (imprisonment terms of up to five years) sanctions. Its provisions have served as model for many bilateral and multilateral treaties on corruption, notably the OECD and the Inter-American Conventions.

Offences under the FCPA are extraditable according to US extradition treaties and conventions, which usually provide for extradition of all offences punishable with imprisonment of at least one year (or in older treaties, subject to lists of extraditable offences).

Organisation for Economic Cooperation and Development (OECD) Convention on Combating Bribery of Foreign Public Officials in International Business Transactions, 1997

15–37   The OECD Convention was adopted in November 1997 by the 30 OECD member States plus Argentina, Brazil, Bulgaria, and Chile, in Paris, and largely follows the FCPA provisions.

The Convention requires the State parties to criminalise the bribery of foreign public officials in all branches of government, whether appointed or elected; any person exercising a public function, including functions in a public agency or public enterprise; and any official or agent of a public international organisation. However, unlike the FCPA, the Convention does not directly cover political parties or candidates. The Convention includes complicity, incitement and authorisation in the commission of the offences, and also provides for liability against legal persons.

State parties are obligated to introduce in their laws "effective, proportionate and dissuasive criminal penalties" including imprisonment terms long enough to allow for extradition and included under lists of extraditable offences. The Convention also requires parties to provide for the seizure and confiscation of assets and the application of other sanctions. State parties must enter into consultations in the event more than one of them asserts jurisdiction.

In addition, States parties must prohibit "off the books" accounts and similar practices used to bribe foreign public officials or to hide such bribery. The Convention also provides for State parties to afford each other mutual legal assistance and extradition in the implementation of their obligations.

Inter-American Convention Against Corruption, 1996

The Inter-American Convention was adopted to address a wide range **15–38** of measures to prevent or to punish bribery and other forms of corruption involving the public sector. Article VIII stipulates that State parties must adopt laws to address transnational bribery, similar in content to the FCPA.

European Union Conventions on the fight against Corruption involving officials of the European Communities or officials of Member States of the European Union

(i) Civil Law Convention (November 4, 1999)   **15–39**
The Convention provides for compensation to victims of corruption, which is defined as "requesting, offering, giving or accepting, directly or indirectly, a bribe or any other undue advantage or prospect thereof, which distorts the proper performance of any duty or behaviour required of the recipient of the bribe, the undue advantage or the prospect thereof".

The Convention contains provisions to allow victims of corruption to claim compensation from the relevant State when it was responsible for the offence and also to render unlawful all clauses providing for corruption in contracts concluded under the laws of State parties.

It requires the Parties to "cooperate effectively in matters relating to civil proceedings in cases of corruption, especially concerning the service of documents, obtaining evidence abroad, jurisdiction, recognition and enforcement of foreign judgments and litigation costs, in accordance with the provisions of relevant international instruments on international co-operation in civil and commercial matters to which they are Party, as well as with their internal law".

(ii) Criminal Law Convention (January 27, 1999)
The Convention incorporates definitions of active and passive bribery **15–40** of domestic and foreign public and private sector officials and members, international organisations, international parliamentary assemblies, judges and officials of international courts, as well as provisions against trading in influences, money laundering of proceeds from corruption practices, and directs States to adopt accounting offences in their legislation.

Furthermore, the Convention provides for corporate criminal liability, and that States must ensure appropriate punishment in their legislation against these crimes, including extraditable imprisonment terms.

Under the Convention specialised task forces have been created and State parties are obliged to provide international co-operation and mutual assistance in judicial matters in the fulfilment of their obliga-tions. The Convention's primary enforcement mechanism is the pro-vision for extradition, or alternatively, prosecution when persons are requested for extradition by another State party.

Convention on the Protection of the European Communities Financial Interests and its Protocols, July 26, 1995

15–41   The Convention provides that it is illegal to use and present false, incorrect or incomplete documents and statements related to (a) expenditures resulting in misappropriation or wrongful retention of funds of the budget of the European Communities; and (b) revenues resulting in illegal diminution of the budget of the European Communities.

There are three Protocols to this Convention:

- (a) September 27, 1996: outlines definitions of passive and active corruption and sets out the obligations of countries to provide for adequate punishment with appropriate means including provision for extradition;
- (b) November 29, 1996: extends jurisdiction to the European Court of Justice (ECJ) for the interpretation of the Convention; and,
- (c) June 19, 1997: extends criminal responsibility to money laun-dering and provides for the liability of legal persons with respect to money laundering and active and passive corruption. Sanctions against legal persons include: (i) exclusion from entitlement to financial benefits or aid; (ii) temporal or perma-nent disqualification from commercial activities; (iii) placing under supervision; (iv) being subject to a judicial winding-up order; (v) seizure and confiscation of assets. In addition, this Protocol provides for the protection of data exchanged in respect of crimes under the Convention and its Protocols.

F. CRIMES AGAINST THE ENVIRONMENT

(1) Main international treaties, agreements and documents

15–42   (a) Convention on International Trade in Endangered Species of Wild Fauna and Flora (1973);
- (b) London Convention on the Prevention of Marine Pollution by Dumping of Wastes and Other Matter (1972) and its Protocol (1996).
- (c) Council of Europe Draft Convention for the Protection of the Environment through Criminal Law (1996).

(2) Overview

15–43   The subject of environmental crime spans a varied range of unlawful conduct. In general, the regulation of environmental crime at the international level can be divided into two main categories: waste dumping, and trade in endangered species.

The London Convention on Dumping is the main international instrument in this field. It has enjoyed widespread support with 78 parties signed up to the Convention.

The Washington Convention on International Trade in Endangered Species of Wild Fauna and Flora (CITES) has been a major success. It has 158 signatories. Despite the lack of severe punishments for the commission of violations of its provisions, no species listed in the Convention's appendices has become extinct since CITES entered into force.

(3) Summary of relevant substantive provisions

Convention on International Trade in Endangered Species of Wild Fauna and Flora, 1973

The Washington Convention on International Trade in Endangered Species of Wild Fauna and Flora (CITES) aims to ensure that international trade in specimens of wild animals and plants does not threaten their survival.

CITES contains several definitions for local approval mechanisms for all trade purposes of endangered species; sets out lists of endangered species; and regulates the circumstances where trade in those species is permitted.

It also requires the parties to prohibit trade in violation of CITES and penalise the trade and possession of endangered specimens.

The lists of endangered species can be reviewed and modified by the State parties by two-thirds of the votes of the Conference of the Parties to be held at least every two years.

15–44

London Convention on the Prevention of Marine Pollution by Dumping of Wastes and Other Matter, 1972 and its Protocol, 1996

The Convention requires the State parties to prohibit and regulate dumping (defined as the intentional disposal at sea of wastes or other matter) and establishes a system of prior approvals for dumping of certain materials, while others are black-listed or wholly prohibited (for example, cadmium, mercury, radioactive materials, crude oil and others).

The Convention further stipulates that State parties must take "appropriate measures to prevent and punish" activities in contravention of the Convention, and provides for the "development of procedures for [its] effective application".

The 1996 Protocol is intended to replace the Convention. It introduces a "precautionary approach", which requires that "appropriate preventative measures are taken when there is reason to believe that wastes or other matter introduced into the marine environment are likely to cause harm even when there is no conclusive evidence to prove a causal relation between inputs and their effects". The Protocol further provides that "The polluter should, in principle, bear the cost of

15–45

pollution" and the parties "should ensure that the Protocol should not simply result in pollution being transferred from one part of the environment to another".

G. FRAUD AND TAX OFFENCES

(1) Main international treaties, agreements and documents

15–46
    (a) Convention on the Protection of the European Communities' Financial Interests (1995);
    (b) Council Regulation No. 2988/95 of December 18, 1995 on the Protection of the European Communities' Financial Interests (1995);
    (c) Convention on Insider Trading (1989);
    (d) Protocol to the Convention on Insider Trading (1989).

(2) Overview

15–47
    The importance of regulation in this field was again underscored recently with the collapse of the Enron company in the USA, and the criminal proceedings instituted against its directors. The Convention on Insider Trading (1989) as amended by the 1989 Protocol, was adopted by the member states of the Council of Europe to set up machinery to co-ordinate their endeavours at an international level to address unlawful practices in ever increasing internationalised markets. Article 1 of the Convention defines "insider trading" as follows:

1. For the purposes of this Convention an irregular operation of insider trading means an irregular operation carried out by a person:
    a. who is the president or chairman, or a member of a board of directors or other administrative or supervisory organ, or is the authorised agent or in the employment of an issuer of securities, and has effected or caused to be effected an operation on an organised stock market knowingly using information not yet disclosed to the public, the possession of which he obtained by reason of his occupation and the disclosure of which was likely to have a significant influence on the stock market, with a view to securing an advantage for himself or a third party;
    b. who has entered into the transactions described above knowingly using not yet disclosed information which he obtained in the performance of his duties or in the course of his occupation;
    c. who has entered into the transactions described above knowingly using not yet disclosed information communicated to him by one of the persons mentioned in a or b above.

H. Organised Crime

(1) Overview

The UN Convention Against Transnational Organised Crime **15–48**
(adopted by the United Nations General Assembly on November 15,
2000) requires State parties to criminalise a wide range of activities,
including corruption and money laundering. It is novel in that it obliges
parties to consider the provision of assistance to victims of transnational crimes.

(2) Summary of relevant provisions of international treaties and agreements

United Nations Convention against Transnational Organised Crime, 2000

The Convention aims to promote co-operation to prevent and combat **15–49**
transnational crime. It provides several definitions of such offences. The
"transnationality" criteria are multiple, namely: (a) if an offence is
committed in more than one State; (b) if an offence is committed in
one State, but a substantial part of its preparation, planning, direction
or control take place in another State; (c) if an offence is committed in
one State but involves an organised criminal group that engages in
criminal activities in more than one State; or (d) if an offence is
committed in one State but has substantial effects in another State.

The Convention requires State parties to penalise, amongst others, **15–50**
the following activities:

(a) agreeing with one or more other persons to commit a serious
    crime for a purpose relating directly or indirectly to the
    obtaining of a financial or other material benefit and, where
    required by domestic law, involving an act undertaken by one of
    the participants in furtherance of the agreement or involving
    an organised criminal group;

(b) any conduct by a person who, with knowledge of either the aim
    and general criminal activity of an organised criminal group or
    its intention to commit the crimes in question, takes an active
    part in criminal activities of the organised criminal group or
    other activities of the organised criminal group in the
    knowledge that his or her participation will contribute to the
    achievement of the above-described criminal aim;

(c) organising, directing, aiding, abetting, facilitating or counsell-
    ing the commission of serious crime involving an organised
    criminal group;

(d) the conversion or transfer of property, in the knowledge that
    such property comes from the commission of crimes, for the
    purpose of concealing or disguising the illicit origin of the
    property;

(e) the concealment or disguise of the true nature, source, location,
    disposition, movement or ownership of or rights with respect to

property, knowing that such property is the proceeds of a crime;

(f) corruption, consisting of the promise, offering or giving to a public official, directly or indirectly, of an undue advantage, for the official himself or herself or another person or entity, in order that the official act or refrain from acting in the exercise of his or her official duties, or the solicitation or acceptance by a public official, directly or indirectly, of an undue advantage, for the official himself or herself or another person or entity, in order that the official act or refrain from acting in the exercise of his or her official duties; and,

(g) the use of physical force, threats or intimidation or the promose, offering or giving of an undue advantage to induce false testimony or to interfere in the giving of testimony to interfere with the exercise of official duties by a justice or law enforcement official.

15–51   The Convention requires the parties to ensure that all legal persons can be charged with offences under this Convention. Notably, the Convention also provides for assistance and protection for victims, as well as for the exchange of assistance and records between national law enforcement agencies.

The Convention obliges parties to institute regulatory supervisory regimes for financial and non-financial institutions in order to detect money laundering operations.

15–52   The Convention provides for the identification, tracing, freezing, confiscation and seizure of any items related to offences under the Convention as well as for international co-operation and mutual assistance. The Convention requires delivery of offenders for extradition purposes or alternatively prosecution. In addition, extradition may not be denied on the grounds that the crimes for which extradition is sought involve fiscal matters.

Finally, the Convention requires the parties to consider the conclusion of bilateral or multilateral agreements for the conduct of joint investigations of crimes.

III. PROCEDURE

A. EXTRADITION ARRANGEMENTS

(1) Main international treaties, agreements and documents

15–53
(a) UN Model Treaty on Extradition (1990);
(b) European Convention on Extradition (1957);
(c) Additional Protocol to European Convention on Extradition (1975);
(d) Second Additional Protocol to European Convention on Extradition (1978);
(e) Commonwealth Scheme for the Rendition of Fugitive Offenders (1966);

(f) Convention on Simplified Extradition Procedure between Member States of the European Union;

(g) Convention relating to Extradition between Member States of the European Union (1996).

(2) Overview

Extradition is the legal process by which persons charged with or convicted of a crime in a sovereign State, but arrested in a foreign State are returned by this State, the Requested State, to the State where the crime was charged, or the conviction was recorded, the Requesting State. Extradition is not applicable to persons suspected of having committed offences, but who have not been charged with any offence, or to persons whose presence is required as a witness, or to civil proceedings. It is distinguishable from deportation or expulsion.   **15–54**

Extradition is enforced between States on the basis of treaties entered into by States, such as the European Convention on Extradition. In the absence of a treaty, a State is under no legal obligation under international law to extradite fugitives. States may under their national law extradite to foreign States without an extradition agreement with those States.

Most States have entered into extradition treaties with foreign States. Such treaties usually provide for reciprocal surrender of persons arrested within the respective States' jurisdictions; the crimes covered by the extradition arrangement; the exceptions to extraditions; whether an evidentiary showing is required; the doctrine of specialty (the principle that the accused cannot be tried or punished for any offence other than that for which extradition is granted); and, the position in respect of requests for the surrender of the States' own nationals. Depending on the national law of the State concerned, the judicial branch may be empowered to render a decision against the extradition of the requested person. The final decision always rests with the national government of the State.   **15–55**

See, Articles 89–90 of the ICC Statute dealing with the relationship between extradition arrangements and requests emanating from the ICC, and Chapter 2 on Powers of the Courts.

B. MUTUAL ASSISTANCE

(1) Main international treaties, agreements and documents

(a) UN Model Treaty on Mutual Assistance (1990);   **15–56**

(b) Optional Protocol to the UN Model Treaty on Mutual Assistance in Criminal Matters concerning the Proceeds of Crime (1990);

(c) European Convention on Mutual Assistance in Criminal Matters (1959);

(d) Additional Protocol to European Convention on Mutual Assistance in Criminal Matters (1978);

  (e) Second Additional Protocol to European Convention on Mutual Assistance in Criminal Matters (2001);
  (f) Scheme Relating to Mutual Assistance in Criminal Matters within the Commonwealth (1986), and 1990 amendments;
  (g) UN Model Treaty on the Transfer of Proceedings in Criminal Matters (1990);
  (h) UN Model Treaty on the Transfer of Foreign Prisoners (1985);
  (i) Constitution of Interpol (1956);
  (j) Europol Convention (1995).

(2) Overview

15–57   Mutual assistance in criminal matters encompasses the laws governing the manner in which a State may assist foreign States in the investigation and prosecution of criminal offences committed in those States. These laws are embodied in treaties between States and the national laws of each State on mutual assistance matters.

Mutual assistance applies not only between States. States are also obliged to offer assistance to the ICC, and the ICTY and ICTR, in the investigation and prosecution of crimes within the jurisdiction of these international criminal courts (see, Chapter 4 on Powers of the Courts).

CHAPTER 16

CONTEMPT, OFFENCES AGAINST THE ADMINISTRATION OF
JUSTICE & REMOVAL FROM OFFICE

I. STATUTORY PROVISIONS

A. ICC

(1) ICC Statute, Arts 46, 47, 70, 71

Removal from office

46.—1. A judge, the Prosecutor, a Deputy Prosecutor, the Registrar or the   **16–1**
Deputy Registrar shall be removed from office if a decision to this effect is
made in accordance with paragraph 2, in cases where that person:
   (a) Is found to have committed serious misconduct or a serious breach of
       his or her duties under this Statute, as provided for in the Rules of
       Procedure and Evidence; or
   (b) Is unable to exercise the functions required by this Statute.
   2. A decision as to the removal from office of a judge, the Prosecutor or a
Deputy Prosecutor under paragraph 1 shall be made by the Assembly of States
Parties, by secret ballot:
   (a) In the case of a judge, by a two-thirds majority of the States Parties
       upon a recommendation adopted by a two-thirds majority of the other
       judges;

    (b) In the case of the Prosecutor, by an absolute majority of the States Parties;

    (c) In the case of a Deputy Prosecutor, by an absolute majority of the States Parties upon the recommendation of the Prosecutor.

3. A decision as to the removal from office of the Registrar or Deputy Registrar shall be made by an absolute majority of the judges.

4. A judge, Prosecutor, Deputy Prosecutor, Registrar or Deputy Registrar whose conduct or ability to exercise the functions of the office as required by this Statute is challenged under this article shall have full opportunity to present and receive evidence and to make submissions in accordance with the Rules of Procedure and Evidence. The person in question shall not otherwise participate in the consideration of the matter.

Disciplinary measures

16–2   **47.** A judge, Prosecutor, Deputy Prosecutor, Registrar or Deputy Registrar who has committed misconduct of a less serious nature than that set out in article 46, paragraph 1, shall be subject to disciplinary measures, in accordance with the Rules of Procedure and Evidence.

Offences against the administration of justice

16–3   **70.**—1. The Court shall have jurisdiction over the following offences against its administration of justice when committed intentionally:

    (a) Giving false testimony when under an obligation pursuant to article 69, paragraph 1, to tell the truth;

    (b) Presenting evidence that the party knows is false or forged;

    (c) Corruptly influencing a witness, obstructing or interfering with the attendance or testimony of a witness, retaliating against a witness for giving testimony or destroying, tampering with or interfering with the collection of evidence;

    (d) Impeding, intimidating or corruptly influencing an official of the Court for the purpose of forcing or persuading the official not to perform, or to perform improperly, his or her duties;

    (e) Retaliating against an official of the Court on account of duties performed by that or another official;

    (f) Soliciting or accepting a bribe as an official of the Court in connection with his or her official duties.

2. The principles and procedures governing the Court's exercise of jurisdiction over offences under this article shall be those provided for in the Rules of Procedure and Evidence. The conditions for providing international cooperation to the Court with respect to its proceedings under this article shall be governed by the domestic laws of the requested State.

3. In the event of conviction, the Court may impose a term of imprisonment not exceeding five years, or a fine in accordance with the Rules of Procedure and Evidence, or both.

4(a) Each State Party shall extend its criminal laws penalizing offences against the integrity of its own investigative or judicial process to offences against the administration of justice referred to in this article, committed on its territory, or by one of its nationals;

    (b) Upon request by the Court, whenever it deems it proper, the State Party shall submit the case to its competent authorities for the purpose of prosecution. Those authorities shall treat such cases with diligence and devote sufficient resources to enable them to be conducted effectively.

Sanctions for misconduct before the Court

16–4   **71.**—1. The Court may sanction persons present before it who commit misconduct, including disruption of its proceedings or deliberate refusal to comply with its directions, by administrative measures other than imprisonment, such as temporary or permanent removal from the courtroom, a fine or other similar measures provided for in the Rules of Procedure and Evidence.

2. The procedures governing the imposition of the measures set forth in paragraph 1 shall be those provided for in the Rules of Procedure and Evidence.

(2) ICC Rules of Procedure and Evidence

CHAPTER 2

COMPOSITION AND ADMINISTRATION OF THE COURT

SECTION IV

SITUATIONS THAT MAY AFFECT THE FUNCTIONING OF THE COURT

SUBSECTION 1

REMOVAL FROM OFFICE AND DISCIPLINARY MEASURES

General principle

23. A judge, the Prosecutor, a Deputy Prosecutor, the Registrar and a Deputy Registrar shall be removed from office or shall be subject to disciplinary measures in such cases and with such guarantees as are established in the Statute and the Rules.

16–5

Definition of serious misconduct and serious breach of duty

24.—1. For the purposes of article 46, paragraph 1 (a), "serious misconduct" shall be constituted by conduct that:

16–6

    (a) If it occurs in the course of official duties, is incompatible with official functions, and causes or is likely to cause serious harm to the proper administration of justice before the Court or the proper internal functioning of the Court, such as:

        (i) Disclosing facts or information that he or she has acquired in the course of his or her duties or on a matter which is *sub judice*, where such disclosure is seriously prejudicial to the judicial proceedings or to any person;

        (ii) Concealing information or circumstances of a nature sufficiently serious to have precluded him or her from holding office;

        (iii) Abuse of judicial office in order to obtain unwarranted favourable treatment from any authorities, officials or professionals; or

    (b) If it occurs outside the course of official duties, is of a grave nature that causes or is likely to cause serious harm to the standing of the Court.

2. For the purposes of article 46, paragraph 1 (a), a "serious breach of duty" occurs where a person has been grossly negligent in the performance of his or her duties or has knowingly acted in contravention of those duties. This may include, *inter alia*, situations where the person:

    (a) Fails to comply with the duty to request to be excused, knowing that there are grounds for doing so;

(b) Repeatedly causes unwarranted delay in the initiation, prosecution or trial of cases, or in the exercise of judicial powers.

Definition of misconduct of a less serious nature

16–7   **25.**—1. For the purposes of article 47, "misconduct of a less serious nature" shall be constituted by conduct that:

(a) If it occurs in the course of official duties, causes or is likely to cause harm to the proper administration of justice before the Court or the proper internal functioning of the Court, such as:
  (i) Interfering in the exercise of the functions of a person referred to in article 47;
  (ii) Repeatedly failing to comply with or ignoring requests made by the Presiding Judge or by the Presidency in the exercise of their lawful authority;
  (iii) Failing to enforce the disciplinary measures to which the Registrar or a Deputy Registrar and other officers of the Court are subject when a judge knows or should know of a serious breach of duty on their part; or
(b) If it occurs outside the course of official duties, causes or is likely to cause harm to the standing of the Court.

2. Nothing in this rule precludes the possibility of the conduct set out in sub-rule 1(a) constituting "serious misconduct" or "serious breach of duty" for the purposes of article 46, paragraph 1 (a).

Receipt of complaints

16–8   **26.**—1. For the purposes of article 46, paragraph 1, and article 47, any complaint concerning any conduct defined under rules 24 and 25 shall include the grounds on which it is based, the identity of the complainant and, if available, any relevant evidence. The complaint shall remain confidential.

2. All complaints shall be transmitted to the Presidency, which may also initiate proceedings on its own motion, and which shall, pursuant to the Regulations, set aside anonymous or manifestly unfounded complaints and transmit the other complaints to the competent organ. The Presidency shall be assisted in this task by one or more judges, appointed on the basis of automatic rotation, in accordance with the Regulations.

Common provisions on the rights of the defence

16–9   **27.**—1. In any case in which removal from office under article 46 or disciplinary measures under article 47 is under consideration, the person concerned shall be so informed in a written statement.

2. The person concerned shall be afforded full opportunity to present and receive evidence, to make written submissions and to supply answers to any questions put to him or her.

3. The person may be represented by counsel during the process established under this rule.

Suspension from duty

16–10   **28.** Where an allegation against a person who is the subject of a complaint is of a sufficiently serious nature, the person may be suspended from duty pending the final decision of the competent organ.

Procedure in the event of a request for removal from Office

16–11   **29.**—1. In the case of a judge, the Registrar or a Deputy Registrar, the question of removal from office shall be put to a vote at a plenary session.

2. The Presidency shall advise the President of the Bureau of the Assembly of States Parties in writing of any recommendation adopted in the case of a judge, and any decision adopted in the case of the Registrar or a Deputy Registrar.

3. The Prosecutor shall advise the President of the Bureau of the Assembly of States Parties in writing of any recommendation he or she makes in the case of a Deputy Prosecutor.

4. Where the conduct is found not to amount to serious misconduct or a serious breach of duty, it may be decided in accordance with article 47 that the person concerned has engaged in misconduct of a less serious nature and a disciplinary measure imposed.

Procedure in the event of a request for disciplinary measures

30.—1. In the case of a judge, the Registrar or a Deputy Registrar, any decision to impose a disciplinary measure shall be taken by the Presidency.

2. In the case of the Prosecutor, any decision to impose a disciplinary measure shall be taken by an absolute majority of the Bureau of the Assembly of States Parties.

3. In the case of a Deputy Prosecutor:
    (a) Any decision to give a reprimand shall be taken by the Prosecutor;
    (b) Any decision to impose a pecuniary sanction shall be taken by an absolute majority of the Bureau of the Assembly of States Parties upon the recommendation of the Prosecutor.

4. Reprimands shall be recorded in writing and shall be transmitted to the President of the Bureau of the Assembly of States Parties.

16–12

Removal from office

31. Once removal from office has been pronounced, it shall take effect immediately. The person concerned shall cease to form part of the Court, including for unfinished cases in which he or she was taking part.

16–13

Disciplinary measures

32. The disciplinary measures that may be imposed are:
    (a) A reprimand; or
    (b) A pecuniary sanction that may not exceed six months of the salary paid by the Court to the person concerned.

16–14

CHAPTER 9

OFFENCES AND MISCONDUCT AGAINST THE COURT

SECTION I

OFFENCES AGAINST THE ADMINISTRATION OF JUSTICE UNDER ARTICLE 70

Exercise of jurisdiction

162.—1. Before deciding whether to exercise jurisdiction, the Court may consult with States Parties that may have jurisdiction over the offence.

2. In making a decision whether or not to exercise jurisdiction, the Court may consider, in particular:

16–15

(a) The availability and effectiveness of prosecution in a State Party;
(b) The seriousness of an offence;
(c) The possible joinder of charges under article 70 with charges under articles 5 to 8;
(d) The need to expedite proceedings;
(e) Links with an ongoing investigation or a trial before the Court; and
(f) Evidentiary considerations.

3. The Court shall give favourable consideration to a request from the host State for a waiver of the power of the Court to exercise jurisdiction in cases where the host State considers such a waiver to be of particular importance.

4. If the Court decides not to exercise its jurisdiction, it may request a State Party to exercise jurisdiction pursuant to article 70, paragraph 4.

Application of the Statute and the Rules

16–16   **163.**—1. Unless otherwise provided in sub-rules 2 and 3, rule 162 and rules 164 to 169, the Statute and the Rules shall apply *mutatis mutandis* to the Court's investigation, prosecution and punishment of offences defined in article 70.

2. The provisions of Part 2, and any rules thereunder, shall not apply, with the exception of article 21.

3. The provisions of Part 10, and any rules thereunder, shall not apply, with the exception of articles 103, 107, 109 and 111.

Periods of limitation

16–17   **164.**—1. If the Court exercises jurisdiction in accordance with rule 162, it shall apply the periods of limitation set forth in this rule.

2. Offences defined in article 70 shall be subject to a period of limitation of five years from the date on which the offence was committed, provided that during this period no investigation or prosecution has been initiated. The period of limitation shall be interrupted if an investigation or prosecution has been initiated during this period, either before the Court or by a State Party with jurisdiction over the case pursuant to article 70, paragraph 4 (a).

3. Enforcement of sanctions imposed with respect to offences defined in article 70 shall be subject to a period of limitation of 10 years from the date on which the sanction has become final. The period of limitation shall be interrupted with the detention of the convicted person or while the person concerned is outside the territory of the States Parties.

Investigation, prosecution and trial

16–18   **165.**—1. The Prosecutor may initiate and conduct investigations with respect to the offences defined in article 70 on his or her own initiative, on the basis of information communicated by a Chamber or any reliable source.

2. Articles 53 and 59, and any rules thereunder, shall not apply.

3. For purposes of article 61, the Pre-Trial Chamber may make any of the determinations set forth in that article on the basis of written submissions, without a hearing, unless the interests of justice otherwise require.

4. A Trial Chamber may, as appropriate and taking into account the rights of the defence, direct that there be joinder of charges under article 70 with charges under articles 5 to 8.

Sanctions under article 70

16–19   **166.**—1. If the Court imposes sanctions with respect to article 70, this rule shall apply.

2. Article 77, and any rules thereunder, shall not apply, with the exception of an order of forfeiture under article 77, paragraph 2 (b), which may be ordered in addition to imprisonment or a fine or both.

3. Each offence may be separately fined and those fines may be cumulative. Under no circumstances may the total amount exceed 50 per cent of the value of the convicted person's identifiable assets, liquid or realizable, and property, after deduction of an appropriate amount that would satisfy the financial needs of the convicted person and his or her dependants.

4. In imposing a fine the Court shall allow the convicted person a reasonable period in which to pay the fine. The Court may provide for payment of a lump sum or by way of instalments during that period.

5. If the convicted person does not pay a fine imposed in accordance with the conditions set forth in sub-rule 4, appropriate measures may be taken by the Court pursuant to rules 217 to 222 and in accordance with article 109. Where, in cases of continued wilful non-payment, the Court, on its own motion or at the request of the Prosecutor, is satisfied that all available enforcement measures have been exhausted, it may as a last resort impose a term of imprisonment in accordance with article 70, paragraph 3. In the determination of such term of imprisonment, the Court shall take into account the amount of fine paid.

SECTION II

MISCONDUCT BEFORE THE COURT UNDER ARTICLE 71

Disruption of proceedings

170. Having regard to article 63, paragraph 2, the Presiding Judge of the Chamber dealing with the matter may, after giving a warning: **16–20**
- (a) Order a person disrupting the proceedings of the Court to leave or be removed from the courtroom; or,
- (b) In case of repeated misconduct, order the interdiction of that person from attending the proceedings.

Refusal to comply with a direction by the Court

171.—1. When the misconduct consists of deliberate refusal to comply with **16–21** an oral or written direction by the Court, not covered by rule 170, and that direction is accompanied by a warning of sanctions in case of breach, the Presiding Judge of the Chamber dealing with the matter may order the interdiction of that person from the proceedings for a period not exceeding 30 days or, if the misconduct is of a more serious nature, impose a fine.

2. If the person committing misconduct as described in sub-rule 1 is an official of the Court, or a defence counsel, or a legal representative of victims, the Presiding Judge of the Chamber dealing with the matter may also order the interdiction of that person from exercising his or her functions before the Court for a period not exceeding 30 days.

3. If the Presiding Judge in cases under sub-rules 1 and 2 considers that a longer period of interdiction is appropriate, the Presiding Judge shall refer the matter to the Presidency, which may hold a hearing to determine whether to order a longer or permanent period of interdiction.

4. A fine imposed under sub-rule 1 shall not exceed 2,000 euros, or the equivalent amount in any currency, provided that in cases of continuing misconduct, a new fine may be imposed on each day that the misconduct continues, and such fines shall be cumulative.

5. The person concerned shall be given an opportunity to be heard before a sanction for misconduct, as described in this rule, is imposed.

Conduct covered by both Articles 70 and 71

172. If conduct covered by article 71 also constitutes one of the offences **16–22** defined in article 70, the Court shall proceed in accordance with article 70 and rules 162 to 169.

(3) ICC Regulations of the Court

29. Non-compliance with these Regulations and with orders of a Chamber
1. In the event of non-compliance by a participant with the provisions of any regulation, or with an order of a Chamber made thereunder, the Chamber may issue any order that is deemed necessary in the interests of justice.
2. This provision is without prejudice to the inherent powers of the Chamber.

119. Receipt and administration of complaints
1. All complaints against a judge, the Prosecutor, a Deputy Prosecutor, the Registrar or the Deputy Registrar concerning conduct defined under rules 24 and 25 shall be submitted directly to the Presidency, which shall notify the person against whom the complaint has been directed of that complaint.
2. The Presidency shall make all necessary arrangements for administrative assistance when dealing with a complaint.

120. Procedure under rule 26, sub-rule 2
1. The Presidency shall be assisted by three judges, appointed on the basis of automatic rotation following the English alphabet of the surnames of all judges not comprising the Presidency or the judge being complained against, in order to determine whether a complaint is anonymous or manifestly unfounded.
2. The judges appointed in accordance with sub-regulation 1 shall, where necessary, seek additional comments from either the person being complained against or the complainant and shall make a recommendation to the Presidency on whether such complaint is admissible or should be set aside in accordance with rule 26, sub-rule 2. The appointed judges shall also make a recommendation as to whether the complaint against a judge, the Registrar or Deputy Registrar relates to conduct which falls manifestly outside the scope of rule 24.
3. The Presidency shall decide whether to accept any recommendation described in sub-regulation 2.
4. If a complaint relates to a member of the Presidency, he or she shall not carry out any function as a member of the Presidency with regard to the complaint and his or her functions in that respect shall be exercised by the next available judge having precedence in accordance with regulation 10.

121. Decision under rule 26, sub-rule 2, and transmission of complaint to the competent organ
1. In case the Presidency decides that a complaint against a judge, the Registrar or Deputy Registrar is not anonymous or manifestly unfounded, it shall transmit the complaint to a plenary session, unless the Presidency determines that the conduct complained of falls manifestly outside the scope of rule 24, in which case the matter shall be considered by the Presidency in accordance with article 47, rule 30, sub-rule 1 and regulation 122.
2. In case the Presidency decides that a complaint against the Prosecutor or a Deputy Prosecutor is not anonymous or manifestly unfounded, it shall:
   (a) With regard to the Prosecutor, transmit the complaint to the Bureau of the Assembly;
   (b) With regard to the Deputy Prosecutor, transmit the complaint to the Prosecutor.

122. Procedure before the Presidency on disciplinary measures for a judge, the Registrar or the Deputy Registrar
1. When it is determined in accordance with regulation 121, sub-regulation 1, that a complaint should be considered by the Presidency, that complaint shall be dealt with in accordance with rule 27.

2. If the Presidency decides to impose disciplinary measures, the judge, Registrar or Deputy Registrar concerned may file an appeal against that decision to a plenary session within 30 days of notification of the decision.

123. Procedure for removal from office of a judge, the Registrar or the Deputy Registrar

1. The judges appointed under regulation 120, sub-regulation 1, shall conduct the proceedings under article 46, paragraph 4, and rule 27 and shall report thereon to a plenary session.

2. The procedure to be followed prior to the adoption of any recommendation concerning a judge under article 46, paragraph 2, and rule 29, sub-rule 1, is without prejudice to any additional procedure to be followed by the Assembly under article 46, paragraph 4, and rule 27.

124. Suspension from duty

1. For the purposes of rule 28, a judge, the Prosecutor, a Deputy Prosecutor, the Registrar or the Deputy Registrar may be suspended from duty following the decision of the Presidency under rule 26, sub-rule 2, by the organ competent to make a decision under article 46, paragraphs 2 and 3.

2. Suspension from duty shall not affect salary and allowances.

125. Initiation of proceedings by the Presidency

In cases where the Presidency initiates proceedings on its own motion, the preliminary assessment of whether complaints are anonymous or manifestly unfounded under rule 26, sub-rule 2, shall not be required and regulations 121 to 124 shall apply mutatis mutandis.

B. ICTY

ICTY Rules of Procedure and Evidence, rr. 77, 77*bis*, 91

Contempt of the Tribunal

77.—(A) The Tribunal in the exercise of its inherent power may hold in contempt those who knowingly and wilfully interfere with its administration of justice, including any person who

16–24

(i) being a witness before a Chamber, contumaciously refuses or fails to answer a question;

(ii) discloses information relating to those proceedings in knowing violation of an order of a Chamber;

(iii) without just excuse fails to comply with an order to attend before or produce documents before a Chamber;

(iv) threatens, intimidates, causes any injury or offers a bribe to, or otherwise interferes with, a witness who is giving, has given, or is about to give evidence in proceedings before a Chamber, or a potential witness; or

(v) threatens, intimidates, offers a bribe to, or otherwise seeks to coerce any other person, with the intention of preventing that other person from complying with an obligation under an order of a Judge or Chamber.

(B) Any incitement or attempt to commit any of the acts punishable under paragraph (A) is punishable as contempt of the Tribunal with the same penalties.

(C) When a Chamber has reason to believe that a person may be in contempt of the Tribunal, it may:

(i) direct the Prosecutor to investigate the matter with a view to the preparation and submission of an indictment for contempt;

(ii) where the Prosecutor, in the view of the Chamber, has a conflict of interest with respect to the relevant conduct, direct the Registrar to appoint an amicus curiae to investigate the matter and report back to the Chamber as to whether there are sufficient grounds for instigating contempt proceedings; or

(iii) initiate proceedings itself.

(D) If the Chamber considers that there are sufficient grounds to proceed against a person for contempt, the Chamber may:

(i) in circumstances described in paragraph (C) (i), direct the Prosecutor to prosecute the matter; or

(ii) in circumstances described in paragraph (C) (ii) or (iii), issue an order in lieu of an indictment and either direct *amicus curiae* to prosecute the matter or prosecute the matter itself.

(E) The rules of procedure and evidence in Parts Four to Eight shall apply *mutatis mutandis* to proceedings under this Rule.

16–25 (F) Any person indicted for or charged with contempt shall, if that person satisfies the criteria for determination of indigence established by the Registrar, be assigned counsel in accordance with Rule 45.

(G) The maximum penalty that may be imposed on a person found to be in contempt of the Tribunal shall be a term of imprisonment not exceeding seven years, or a fine not exceeding €100,000, or both.

(H) Payment of a fine shall be made to the Registrar to be held in a separate account.

(I) If a counsel is found guilty of contempt of the Tribunal pursuant to this Rule, the Chamber making such finding may also determine that counsel is no longer eligible to represent a suspect or accused before the Tribunal or that such conduct amounts to misconduct of counsel pursuant to Rule 46, or both.

(J) Any decision rendered by a Trial Chamber under this Rule shall be subject to appeal. Notice of appeal shall be filed within fifteen days of filing of the impugned decision. Where such decision is rendered orally, the notice shall be filed within fifteen days of the oral decision, unless

(i) the party challenging the decision was not present or represented when the decision was pronounced, in which case the time-limit shall run from the date on which the challenging party is notified of the oral decision; or

(ii) the Trial Chamber has indicated that a written decision will follow, in which case the time-limit shall run from filing of the written decision.

(K) In the case of decisions under this Rule by the Appeals Chamber sitting as a Chamber of first instance, an appeal may be submitted in writing to the President within fifteen days of the filing of the impugned decision. Such appeal shall be decided by five different Judges as assigned by the President. Where the impugned decision is rendered orally, the appeal shall be filed within fifteen days of the oral decision, unless

(i) the party challenging the decision was not present or represented when the decision was pronounced, in which case the time-limit shall run from the date on which the challenging party is notified of the oral decision; or

(ii) the Appeals Chamber has indicated that a written decision will follow, in which case the time-limit shall run from filing of the written decision.

Payment of fines

16–26 **77bis.**—(A) In imposing a fine under Rule 77 or Rule 91, a Chamber shall specify the time for its payment.

(B) Where a fine imposed under Rule 77 or Rule 91 is not paid within the time specified, the Chamber imposing the fine may issue an order requiring the person on whom the fine is imposed to appear before, or to respond in writing to, the Tribunal to explain why the fine has not been paid.

(C) After affording the person on whom the fine is imposed an opportunity to be heard, the Chamber may make a decision that appropriate measures be taken, including:

  (i) extending the time for payment of the fine;

  (ii) requiring the payment of the fine to be made in instalments;

  (iii) in consultation with the Registrar, requiring that the moneys owed be deducted from any outstanding fees owing to the person by the Tribunal where the person is a counsel retained by the Tribunal pursuant to the Directive on the Assignment of Defence Counsel;

  (iv) converting the whole or part of the fine to a term of imprisonment not exceeding twelve months.

(D) In addition to a decision under paragraph (C), the Chamber may find the person in contempt of the Tribunal and impose a new penalty applying Rule 77(G), if that person was able to pay the fine within the specified time and has wilfully failed to do so. This penalty for contempt of the Tribunal shall be additional to the original fine imposed.

(E) The Chamber may, if necessary, issue an arrest warrant to secure the person's presence where he or she fails to appear before or respond in writing pursuant to an order under paragraph (B). A State or authority to whom such a warrant is addressed, in accordance with Article 29 of the Statute, shall act promptly and with all due diligence to ensure proper and effective execution thereof. Where an arrest warrant is issued under this Sub-rule, the provisions of Rules 45, 57, 58, 59, 59*bis*, and 60 shall apply *mutatis mutandis*. Following the transfer of the person concerned to the Tribunal, the provisions of Rules 64, 65 and 99 shall apply *mutatis mutandis*.

(F) Where under this Rule a penalty of imprisonment is imposed, or a fine is converted to a term of imprisonment, the provisions of Rules 102, 103 and 104 and Part Nine shall apply *mutatis mutandis*.

(G) Any finding of contempt or penalty imposed under this Rule shall be subject to appeal as allowed for in Rule 77 (J).

False Testimony under Solemn Declaration

91.—(A) A Chamber, *proprio motu* or at the request of a party, may warn a witness of the duty to tell the truth and the consequences that may result from a failure to do so.   **16–27**

(B) If a Chamber has strong grounds for believing that a witness has knowingly and wilfully given false testimony, it may:

  (i) direct the Prosecutor to investigate the matter with a view to the preparation and submission of an indictment for false testimony; or

  (ii) where the Prosecutor, in the view of the Chamber, has a conflict of interest with respect to the relevant conduct, direct the Registrar to appoint an *amicus curiae* to investigate the matter and report back to the Chamber as to whether there are sufficient grounds for instigating proceedings for false testimony.

(C) If the Chamber considers that there are sufficient grounds to proceed against a person for giving false testimony, the Chamber may:

  (i) in circumstances described in paragraph (B) (i), direct the Prosecutor to prosecute the matter; or

  (ii) in circumstances described in paragraph (B) (ii), issue an order in lieu of an indictment and direct amicus curiae to prosecute the matter.

(D) The rules of procedure and evidence in Parts Four to Eight shall apply   **16–28**
mutatis mutandis to proceedings under this Rule.

(E) Any person indicted for or charged with false testimony shall, if that person satisfies the criteria for determination of indigence established by the Registrar, be assigned counsel in accordance with Rule 45.

(F) No Judge who sat as a member of the Trial Chamber before which the witness appeared shall sit for the trial of the witness for false testimony.

(G) The maximum penalty for false testimony under solemn declaration shall be a fine of €100,000 or a term of imprisonment of seven years, or both. The payment of any fine imposed shall be paid to the Registrar to be held in the account referred to in Rule 77 (H).

(H) Paragraphs (B) to (G) apply mutatis mutandis to a person who knowingly and willingly makes a false statement in a written statement taken in accordance with Rule 92*bis* which the person knows or has reason to know may be used as evidence in proceedings before the Tribunal.

(I) Any decision rendered by a Trial Chamber under this Rule shall be subject to appeal. Notice of appeal shall be filed within fifteen days of filing of the impugned decision. Where such decision is rendered orally, the notice shall be filed within fifteen days of the oral decision, unless

(i) the party challenging the decision was not present or represented when the decision was pronounced, in which case the time-limit shall run from the date on which the challenging party is notified of the oral decision; or

(ii) the Trial Chamber has indicated that a written decision will follow, in which case the time-limit shall run from filing of the written decision.

C. ICTR

ICTR Rules of Procedure and Evidence, rr. 77, 91

Misconduct of Counsel

16–29   **46.**—(A) A Chamber may, after a warning, impose sanctions against a counsel if, in its opinion, his conduct remains offensive or abusive, obstructs the proceedings, or is otherwise contrary to the interests of justice. This provision is applicable mutatis mutandis to Counsel for the prosecution.

(B) A Judge or a Chamber may also, with the approval of the President, communicate any misconduct of counsel to the professional body regulating the conduct of counsel in his State of admission or, if a professor and not otherwise admitted to the profession, to the governing body of his University.

(C) If a counsel assigned pursuant to Rule 45 is sanctioned in accordance with Sub-Rule A) by being refused audience, the Chamber shall instruct the Registrar to replace the counsel.

(D) The Registrar may set up a Code of Professional Conduct enunciating the principles of professional ethics to be observed by counsel appearing before the Tribunal, subject to adoption by the Plenary Meeting. Amendments to the Code shall be made in consultation with representatives of the Prosecutor and Defence counsel, and subject to adoption by the Plenary Meeting. If the Registrar has strong grounds for believing that Counsel has committed a serious violation of the Code of Professional Conduct so adopted, he may report the matter to the President or the Bureau for appropriate action under this rule.

Contempt of the Tribunal

16–30   **77.**—(A) The Tribunal in the exercise of its inherent power may hold in contempt those who knowingly and wilfully interfere with its administration of justice, including any person who (i) being a witness before a Chamber, contumaciously refuses or fails to answer a question;

(ii) discloses information relating to those proceedings in knowing violation of an order of a Chamber;

(iii) without just excuse fails to comply with an order to attend before or produce documents before a Chamber;

    (iv) threatens, intimidates, causes any injury or offers a bribe to, or otherwise interferes with, a witness who is giving, has given, or is about to give evidence in proceedings before a Chamber, or a potential witness; or

    (v) threatens, intimidates, offers a bribe to, or otherwise seeks to coerce any other person, with the intention of preventing that other person from complying with an obligation under an order of a Judge or Chamber.

(B) Any incitement or attempt to commit any of the acts punishable under paragraph (A) is punishable as contempt of the Tribunal with the same penalties.

(C) When a Chamber has reason to believe that a person may be in contempt of the Tribunal, it may:

    (i) direct the Prosecutor to investigate the matter with a view to the preparation and submission of an indictment for contempt;

    (ii) where the Prosecutor, in the view of the Chamber, has a conflict of interest with respect to the relevant conduct, direct the Registrar to appoint an amicus curiae to investigate the matter and report back to the Chamber as to whether there are sufficient grounds for instigating contempt proceedings; or

    (iii) initiate proceedings itself.

(D) If the Chamber considers that there are sufficient grounds to proceed against a person for contempt, the Chamber may:

    (i) in circumstances described in paragraph (C) (i), direct the Prosecutor to prosecute the matter; or

    (ii) in circumstances described in paragraph (C) (ii) or (iii), issue an order in lieu of an indictment and either direct amicus curiae to prosecute the matter or prosecute the matter itself.

(E) The Rules of Procedure and Evidence in Parts Four to Eight shall apply mutatis mutandis to proceedings under this Rule.

(F) Any person indicted for or charged with contempt shall, if that person satisfies the criteria for determination of indigence established by the Registrar, be assigned counsel in accordance with Rule 45.

(G) The maximum penalty that may be imposed on a person found to be in contempt of the Tribunal shall be a term of imprisonment not exceeding five years, or a fine not exceeding USD10,000, or both.

(H) Payment of a fine shall be made to the Registrar to be held in a separate account.

(I) If a counsel is found guilty of contempt of the Tribunal pursuant to this Rule, the Chamber making such finding may also determine that counsel is no longer eligible to represent a suspect or accused before the Tribunal or that such conduct amounts to misconduct of counsel pursuant to Rule 46, or both.

(J) Any decision rendered by a Trial Chamber under this Rule shall be subject to appeal. Notice of appeal shall be filed within fifteen days of filing of the impugned decision. Where such decision is rendered orally, the notice shall be filed within fifteen days of the oral decision, unless:

    (i) the party challenging the decision was not present or represented when the decision was pronounced, in which case the time- limit shall run from the date on which the challenging party is notified of the oral decision; or

    (ii) the Trial Chamber has indicated that a written decision will follow, in which case the time- limit shall run from filing of the written decision.

(K) In the case of decisions under this Rule by the Appeals Chamber sitting as a Chamber of first instance, an appeal may be submitted in writing to the President within fifteen days of the filing of the impugned decision. Such appeal shall be decided by five different Judges as assigned by the President. Where the impugned decision is rendered orally, the appeal shall be filed within fifteen days of the oral decision, unless:

    (i) the party challenging the decision was not present or represented when the decision was pronounced, in which case the time- limit shall run from the date on which the challenging party is notified of the oral decision; or

(ii) the Appeals Chamber has indicated that a written decision will follow, in which case the time-limit shall run from filing of the written decision.

False Testimony under Solemn Declaration

16–31   **91.**—(A) A Chamber, proprio motu or at the request of a party, may warn a witness of the duty to tell the truth and the consequences that may result from a failure to do so.

(B) If a Chamber has strong grounds for believing that a witness has knowingly and wilfully given false testimony, it may:

(i) direct the Prosecutor to investigate the matter with a view to the preparation and submission of an indictment for false testimony; or

(ii) where the Prosecutor, in the view of the Chamber, has a conflict of interest with respect to the relevant conduct, direct the Registrar to appoint an amicus curiae to investigate the matter and report back to the Chamber as to whether there are sufficient grounds for instigating proceedings for false testimony.

(C) If the Chamber considers that there are sufficient grounds to proceed against a person for giving false testimony, the Chamber may:

(i) in circumstances described in paragraph (B) (i), direct the Prosecutor to prosecute the matter; or

(ii) in circumstances described in paragraph (B) (ii), issue an order in lieu of an indictment and direct amicus curiae to prosecute the matter.

(D) The Rules of Procedure and Evidence in Parts Four to Eight shall apply mutatis mutandis to proceedings under this Rule.

(E) Any person indicted for or charged with false testimony shall, if that person satisfies the criteria for determination of indigence established by the Registrar, be assigned counsel in accordance with Rule 45.

(F) No Judge who sat as a member of the Trial Chamber before which the witness appeared shall sit for the trial of the witness for false testimony.

(G) The maximum penalty for false testimony under solemn declaration shall be a fine of USD10, 000 or a term of imprisonment of five years, or both. The payment of any fine imposed shall be paid to the Registrar to be held in the account referred to in Rule 77 (H).

(H) Paragraphs (B) to (G) apply mutatis mutandis to a person who knowingly and willingly makes a false statement in a written statement taken in accordance with Rule 92 bis which the person knows or has reason to know may be used as evidence in proceedings before the Tribunal.

(I) Any decision rendered by a Trial Chamber under this Rule shall be subject to appeal. Notice of appeal shall be filed within fifteen days of filing of the impugned decision. Where such decision is rendered orally, the notice shall be filed within fifteen days of the oral decision, unless:

(i) the party challenging the decision was not present or represented when the decision was pronounced, in which case the time- limit shall run from the date on which the challenging party is notified of the oral decision; or

(ii) the Trial Chamber has indicated that a written decision will follow, in which case the time-limit shall run from filing of the written decision.

D. East Timor

Regulation No. 2000/30, s.49, as amended by Regulation 2001/25, Sept 14, 2001

On Transitional Rules of Criminal Procedure

Control of Proceedings

49.—49.1 [. . .]   **16–32**

49.2 [. . .]

49.3 Any person who:

    (a) being a witness before the court, wilfully refuses or fails to answer a question after being ordered by the court to do so;

    (b) discloses information relating to proceedings in knowing violation of an order of the court;

    (c) without excuse fails to comply with a summons or order to appear or produce documents or other evidence before the court;

    (d) threatens, intimidates, coerces, injures, offers a bribe to, or in any way interferes with a witness in proceedings before a court, an official of the court, or any other person with the intention of perverting that other person from complying with an obligation under an order of the court; or,

    (e) in any manner knowingly and wilfully interferes with the administration of justice by the court,

is guilty of contempt and shall be punished as hereinafter provided, according to the principles of due process.

49.4 The maximum penalty that may be imposed on a person found in contempt under the present section is a term of imprisonment not to exceed 1 year, a fine not to exceed US$1,000, or both.

49.5 If it appears to the Court that proceedings pursuant to the present Section are warranted, the Court shall notify the person against whom the proceedings may be taken of the nature and facts of the occurrence, and shall order such a person to show cause why such proceedings should not be taken and a penalty imposed. The Court shall promptly receive any submission offered by the person before determining the disposition of the matter. If the court imposes a penalty, the person may take an appeal under the procedures of Part VII of the present Regulation. In such an appeal, the judge who imposed the penalty shall be deemed the respondent.

E. Sierra Leone

(1) SCSL Statute, Articles 37–42

Obstructing Justice

37.—(1) Any person who wilfully obstructs, perverts or defeats the course of   **16–33**
justice in relation to the Special Court commits an offence and shall be liable, on conviction to a fine not exceeding two million leones or a term of imprisonment not exceeding two years or to both such fine and imprisonment.

(2) Without prejudice to the generality of subsection (1), a person is deemed wilfully to obstruct, pervert or defeat the course of justice who, in any existing or proposed proceeding of the Special Court—

    (a) dissuades or attempts to dissuade a person by threats, bribes or other corrupt means from giving evidence; or

    (b) accepts, obtains, agrees to accept or attempts to obtain a bribe or other corrupt consideration to abstain from giving evidence.

Obstructing Officials

16–34   **38.** Any person who resists or wilfully obstructs—

    (a) An official of the Special Court in the execution of his duty, or any person lawfully acting in aid of such an official; or

    (b) Any person executing an order of the Special Court,

Commits an offence and shall be liable on conviction, to a fine not exceeding two million leones or to a term of imprisonment not exceeding two years or to both fine and imprisonment.

Bribery of Judges and Officials

16–35   **39.** Subject to articles 12 and 13 of the Agreement, any person who—

    (a) being a judge or an official of the Special Court, corruptly accepts, obtains, agrees to accept or attempts to obtain for himself or any other person any money, valuable consideration, office, place or employment—

        (i) in respect of anything done or omitted or to be done in his official capacity; or

        (ii) with intent to interfere in any other way with the administration of justice of the Special Court; or

    (b) gives or offers, corruptly, to a judge or an official of the Special Court any money, valuable consideration, office, place or employment—

        (i) in respect of anything done or omitted or to be done in his or her official capacity; or

        (ii) with intent to interfere in any other way with the administration of justice of the Special Court;

commits an offence and shall be liable on conviction to a fine not exceeding thirty million leones or to a term of imprisonment not exceeding ten years or to both such fine and imprisonment.

Intimidation of officials and witnesses

16–36   **40.** Any person who, wrongfully or without lawful authority, for the purpose of compelling another person to abstain from doing anything that he has a lawful right to do, or to do anything that he has a lawful right to abstain from doing, in relation to a proceeding of the Special Court, causes the other person reasonably, in all the circumstances, to fear for his safety or the safety of any other person commits an offence and shall be liable on conviction to a fine not exceeding two million leones or to a term of imprisonment not exceeding two years or two both such fine and imprisonment.

Fabricating Evidence

16–37   **41.** Any person who, with intent to mislead the Special Court in an existing or proposed proceeding, by any means other than perjury or incitement to perjury—

    (a) fabricates anything with intent that it be used as evidence before the Special Court; or

    (b) knowingly makes use of fabricated evidence;

commits an offence and shall be liable on conviction to a fine not exceeding two million leones or to a term of imprisonment not exceeding two years or to both such fine and imprisonment.

Offences outside Sierra Leone

42. Any person who commits outside Sierra Leone any act or omission in relation to the Special Court that, if committed in Sierra Leone, would be an offence under this Act, may be tried as if he had committed that act or omission in Sierra Leone.

16–38

(2) SCSL Rules of Procedure and Evidence, May 29, 2004

Misconduct of counsel

46.—(A) A Chamber may, after a warning, impose sanctions against or refuse audience to a counsel, if, in its opinion, his conduct remains offensive or abusive, obstructs the proceedings, or is otherwise contrary to the interests of justice. This provision is applicable to counsel for the prosecution.

16–39

(B) A Chamber may determine that counsel is no longer eligible to represent a suspect or accused before the Special Court, pursuant to Rule 45. If declared ineligible, removed counsel shall transmit to replacement counsel all materials relevant to the representation.

(C) Counsel who bring motions, or conduct other activities, that in the opinion of a Chamber are either frivolous or constitute abuse of process may be sanctioned for those actions as the Chamber may direct. Sanctions may include fines upon counsel; non-payment, in whole or in part, of fees associated with the motion or its costs, or such other sanctions as the Chamber may direct.

(D) A Judge or a Chamber may also, with the approval of the President, communicate any misconduct of counsel to the professional body regulating the conduct of counsel in his State of admission.

(E) If a counsel assigned pursuant to Rule 45 is sanctioned by being refused audience, the Chamber shall instruct the Registrar to replace the counsel.

(F) This Rule is applicable to counsel for the prosecution as well as counsel appearing for the Defence and to any counsel appearing as amicus curiae.

(G) The Registrar may set up a Code of Professional Conduct enunciating the principles of professional ethics to be observed by counsel having right of audience before the Special Court, subject to adoption by the Plenary Meeting. Amendments to the Code shall be made in consultation with representatives of the Prosecutor and Defence counsel, and subject to adoption by the Plenary Meeting. If the Registrar has strong grounds for believing that counsel has committed a serious violation of the Code of Professional Conduct so adopted, he may report the matter to the President for appropriate action under this rule.

(H) Decisions made by a Trial Chamber under Sub-Rules (A) to (C) above may be appealed with leave from that Chamber. Where such leave is refused, the Party may apply to a bench of at least three Appeals Chamber Judges for leave.

False Testimony under Solemn Declaration

91.—(A) A Chamber, on its own initiative or at the request of a party, may warn a witness of the duty to tell the truth and the consequences that may result from a failure to do so.

16–40

(B) If a Chamber has strong grounds for believing that a witness may have knowingly and wilfully given false testimony, the Chamber may follow the procedure, as applicable, in Rule 77.

(C) The maximum penalty for false testimony under solemn declaration shall be a fine of 2 million Leones or a term of imprisonment of 2 years, or both. The payment of any fine imposed shall be made to the Registrar to be held in the separate account referred to in Rule 77(H).

(D) Sub-Rules (A) to (C) shall apply to a person who knowingly and wilfully makes a false statement in a written statement which the person knows, or has reason to know, may be used in evidence in proceedings before the Special Court.

Contempt of the Special Court

16–41   77.—(A) The Special Court, in the exercise of its inherent power, may punish for contempt any person who knowingly and willfully interferes with its administration of justice, including any person who:

    i. being a witness before a Chamber, subject to Rule 90(E) refuses or fails to answer a question;

    ii. discloses information relating to proceedings in knowing violation of an order of a Chamber;

    iii. without just excuse fails to comply with an order to attend before or produce documents before a Chamber;

    iv. threatens, intimidates, causes any injury or offers a bribe to, or otherwise interferes with, a witness who is giving, has given, or is about to give evidence in proceedings before a Chamber, or a potential witness;

    v. threatens, intimidates, offers a bribe to, or otherwise seeks to coerce any other person, with the intention of preventing that other person from complying with an obligation under an order of a Judge or Chamber; or

    vi. knowingly assists an accused person to evade the jurisdiction of the Special Court.

(B) Any incitement or attempt to commit any of the acts punishable under Sub-Rule (A) is punishable as contempt of the Special Court with the same penalties.

(C) When a Judge or Trial Chamber has reason to believe that a person may be in contempt of the Special Court, it may:

    i. deal with the matter summarily itself;

    ii. refer the matter to the appropriate authorities of Sierra Leone; or

    iii. direct the Registrar to appoint an experienced independent counsel to investigate the matter and report back to the Chamber as to whether there are sufficient grounds for instigating contempt proceedings. If the Chamber considers that there are sufficient grounds to proceed against a person for contempt, the Chamber may issue an order in lieu of an indictment and direct the independent counsel to prosecute the matter.

(D) Proceedings under Sub-Rule (C)(iii) above may be assigned to be heard by a single judge of the Trial Chamber or a Trial Chamber.

(E) The rules of procedure and evidence in Parts IV to VIII shall apply, as appropriate, to proceedings under this Rule.

(F) Any person indicted for or charged with contempt shall, if that person satisfies the criteria for determination of indigence established by the Registrar, be entitled to legal assistance in accordance with Rule 45.

(G) The maximum penalty that may be imposed on a person found to be in contempt of the Special Court pursuant to Sub-Rule (C)(i) shall be a term of imprisonment not exceeding six months, or a fine not exceeding 2 million Leones, or both; and the maximum penalty pursuant to Sub-Rule (C)(iii) shall be a term of imprisonment for seven years or a fine not exceeding 2 million leones, or both.

(H) Payment of a fine shall be made to the Registrar to be held in a separate account.

(I) If a counsel is found guilty of contempt of the Special Court pursuant to this Rule, the Chamber making such finding may also determine that counsel is no longer eligible to appear before the Special Court or that such conduct amounts to misconduct of counsel pursuant to Rule 46, or both.

(J) Any decision rendered by a Single Judge or Trial Chamber under this Rule shall be subject to appeal.

(K) Appeals pursuant to this Rule shall be heard by a bench of at least three Judges of the Appeals Chamber. In accordance with Rule 117 such appeals may be determined entirely on the basis of written submissions.

(L) In the event of contempt occurring during proceedings before the Appeals Chamber or a Judge of the Appeals Chamber, the matter may be dealt with summarily from which there shall be no right of appeal or referred to a Trial Chamber for proceedings in accordance with Sub-Rules (C) to (I) above.

II. DEFINITION

There are no provisions detailing contempt or offences against the administration of justice in the Statutes of the ICTY or ICTR. Rather contempt is provided for in Rules 77 of the ICTY and ICTR Rules of Procedure and Evidence. Rule 91 of the ICTY and ICTR Rules deals with false testimony under oath. In relation to both Rules 77 and 91, the ICTY Rules of Procedure are considerably more detailed than the corresponding Rules of the ICTR. Article 70 of the ICC Statute specifically provides for offences against the administration of justice. Rather than provide a definition for contempt, or offences against the administration of justice, the ICC Statute and ICTY and ICTR Rules instead identify various types of conduct prohibited as offences within the jurisdiction of the court.

16–42

In East Timor, contempt is dealt with briefly in Rule 49 of the Transitional Rules of Procedure. The Special Court for Sierra Leone adopts the detailed approach to contempt of the ICTY and provides for a slightly broadened definition of this model in rule 77 of the Rules of Procedure and Evidence. Likewise, it emulates the ICC Statute in its treatment of offences against the administration of justice. This scheme is laid down in Part VII of the *Special Court Agreement Ratification Act 2002*.

Contempt has been judicially considered as being "conduct which obstructs, prejudices or abuses the Tribunal's administration of justice" (see *Prosecutor v. Tadić*, Judgment on Allegations of Contempt Against Prior Counsel, Milan Vujin, January 31, 2000, para. 18. Approved of in *Prosecutor v. Aleksovski*, Judgment on Appeal by Anto Nobilo Against Finding of Contempt, May 30, 2001, paras 30, 36). In *Prosecutor v. Brdanin (Concerning Allegations against Milka Maglov)*, the Trial Chamber similarly described contempt of court as "an act or an omission intended to interfere with the due administration of justice" (*Prosecutor v. Brdanin (Concerning Allegations against Milka Maglov)*, Decision on Motion for Acquittal pursuant to Rule 98bis, ICTY Trial Chamber, March 19, 2004, para. 15).

16–43

In a recent case before the ICTY, an indictment for contempt took a new turn, charging the accused in the alternative with contempt, attempt to commit contempt and incitement to contempt. In the summary judgment against Beqa Beqaj, the Trial Chamber held that its inherent power to punish conduct which tends to obstruct, prejudice or abuse its administration of justice was sufficient to deal with the various modes of contempt charged (*Prosecutor v. Beqaj*, Summary Judgment, May 5, 2005).

Examples of conduct alleged to be contemptuous include: putting forward a case knowing it to be false and manipulating witnesses (*Prosecutor v. Tadić*, Judgment on Allegations of Contempt Against Prior Counsel, Milan Vujin, January 31, 2000 paras 134, 138, 150, 160); disclosure by two accused persons of the identity of a witness who was the subject of a witness protection order (*Prosecutor v. Elizaphan Ntakirutimana and Gerard Ntakirutimana*, Decision on Prosecution Motion for Contempt of Court and on two Defence Motions for Disclosure, July 16, 2001); counsel falsely presenting themselves as investigators from the Tribunal, intimidating witnesses and trying to tamper with evidence (*Prosecutor v. Nyiramasuhuko et al.*, Decision on the Prosecutor's allegations of contempt, the harmonisation of the witness protection measures and warning to the Prosecutor's counsel, July 10, 2001); harassment, intimidation and bribery of a potential defence witness by defence counsel and an accused in an attempt to make the witness testify on behalf of the accused (*Prosecutor v. Simić et al.*, Judgment in the Matter of Contempt Allegations Against an Accused and his Counsel, June 30, 2000); disclosing information (name of protected witness) in violation of an order prohibiting such disclosure (*Prosecutor v. Aleksovski*, Judgment on Appeal by Anto Nobilo Against Finding of Contempt, May 30, 2001; *Prosecutor v. Blaškić*, Order for the Immediate Cessation of Violations of Protective Measures for Witnesses, ICTY Duty Judge, December 2, 2004); and, requesting a prosecution witness to repudiate their earlier statement (*Prosecutor v. Beqaj*, Summary Judgment, May 5, 2005).

III. JURISDICTION

16–44   There is no express power in the ICTY and ICTR Statutes dealing with contempt or offences against the administration of justice. Notwithstanding this, the Tribunal has an inherent power, deriving from its judicial function to "ensure that its exercise of the jurisdiction which is expressly given to it by that Statute is not frustrated and that its basic judicial functions are safeguarded. As an international criminal court, the Tribunal must therefore possess the inherent power to deal with conduct which interferes with its administration of justice" (see *Prosecutor v. Tadić*, Judgment on Allegations of Contempt Against Prior Counsel, Milan Vujin, January 31, 2000, paras 13 and 18 (referring, *inter alia*, to *Nuclear Test Case*, ICJ Reports 1974, pp. 259–260, para. 23, followed by *Prosecutor v. Blaškić*, Judgment on the Request of the Republic of Croatia for Review of the Decision of Trial Chamber II of July 18, 1997, October 29, 1997, fn. 27, para. 25). Also see *Prosecutor v. Delalic*, Decision of the President on the Prosecution's Motion for the Production of Notes Exchanged between Zejnil Delalic and Zdravko Mucic, November 11, 1996; *obiter dictum* in *Blaškić*, Judgment on the Request of the Republic of Croatia for Review of the Decision of Trial Chamber II of July 18, 1997, October 29, 1997, para. 59, and followed by *Prosecutor v. Brdanin (Concerning Allegations against Milka Maglov)*, Decision on Motion for Acquittal pursuant to Rule 98bis, ICTY Trial Chamber, March 19, 2004, para. 15).

The Tribunal's inherent jurisdiction to deal with contempt has existed ever since its creation, and the extent of that power has not altered by reason of the various amendments made to the Tribunal's Rules of Procedure and Evidence, or by reason of its decisions interpreting or clarifying that power (*Prosecutor v. Aleksovski*, Judgment on Appeal by Anto Nobilo Against Finding of Contempt, May 30, 2001, para. 38). Because of this, jurisdiction for contempt would exist even absent a provision dealing with contempt in the Rules of Procedure and Evidence. The fact that amendments to the Rules are alleged to widen conduct regarded as contemptuous was, therefore, irrelevant to a Chamber's consideration of a charge of contempt (see *Prosecutor v. Tadić*, Judgment on Allegations of Contempt Against Prior Counsel, Milan Vujin, January 31, 2000), paras 27–28).

For a detailed review of the development of Rule 77 of the ICTY Rules of Procedure and Evidence (see *Prosecutor v. Tadić*, Judgment on Allegations of Contempt Against Prior Counsel, Milan Vujin, January 31, 2000, paras 19–23).

Scope of the law

Whilst the Tribunals have an inherent jurisdiction to deal with contempt, the *content* of that inherent power must be discerned by reference to "the usual sources of international law" (*Prosecutor v. Tadić*, Judgment on Allegations of Contempt Against Prior Counsel, Milan Vujin, January 31, 2000, para. 13); and not by reference to the wording of the Rule (*Prosecutor v. Aleksovski*, Judgment on Appeal by Anto Nobilo against finding of Contempt, May 30, 2001, para. 30).

16–45

In determining the content of the inherent power to deal with contempt the Appeals Chamber reviewed Article 18(c) of the Charter of the International Military Tribunal annexed to the 1945 London agreement, three contempt cases heard under Allied Control Council Law No. 10 (December 20, 1945) and various national approaches to contempt (*Prosecutor v. Tadić*, Judgment on Allegations of Contempt Against Prior Counsel, Milan Vujin, Janaury 31, 2000, paras 14–17), citing Trials of War Criminals Before the Nuremberg Military Tribunals under Control Council Law No 10: *US v. Karl Brandt*, June 27, 1947, pp. 968–970 (where a prosecution witness assaulted one of the accused in court); *US v. Jospeh Altstoetter*, July 17,1947, pp. 974–975, 978, 992 (where defence counsel and a private individual attempted improperly to influence an expert medical witness by making false representations, and mutilated an expert report in an attempt to influence the signatories of the report to join in altering it; and *US v. Alfried Krupp von Bohlen und Halbach*, January 21, 1948, pp. 1003, 1005–1006, 1088, 1011 (where defence counsel staged a walk out, and failed to appear, in protest of a ruling against their clients, but which conduct was ultimately dealt with on a disciplinary basis).

IV. PROCEEDINGS

The Prosecutor or the Defence may bring allegations of contempt to the attention of the Chamber or the Chamber may act *proprio motu* (see *Prosecutor v. Delalic et al.*, Decision of the President on the Prosecution's

16–46

Motion for the Production of Notes Exchanged between Zejnil Delalic and Zdravko Mucic, November 11, 1996).

Standard of evidence required to initiate proceedings

16–47   There must be *prima facie* evidence of contempt before a Trial Chamber makes orders relating to contempt investigations or proceedings (see *Prosecutor v. Nyiramasuhuko et al.*, Decision on the Prosecutor's allegations of contempt, the harmonisation of the witness protection measures and warning to the Prosecutor's counsel, July 10, 2001, para. 7 and *Prosecutor v. Simić et al.*, Scheduling Order in the Matter of Allegations against Milan Simić and his Counsel, July 7, 1999).

In *Prosecutor v. Nyiramasuhuko et al.*, Decision on the Prosecutor's Allegations of Contempt, the Harmonisation of the Witness Protection Measures and Warning to the Prosecutor's Counsel, July 10, 2001, para. 9, the imprecision of allegations in terms of who was intimidated by whom, the reliance on double-hearsay evidence and the Prosecutor's own recognition of error in singling out one of the persons on contempt charges led the Chamber to hold that it "is not satisfied that the contemptuous conduct alleged may have taken place, and/or may be attributed to the Defence teams concerned, so as to justify an order for investigations".

Similarly, in *Prosecutor v Seselj*, the Trial Chamber found the "unsubstantiated allegations of the Accused" given without "so much as a scintilla of evidence to support his very grave allegations" can not satisfy the threshold standard set out in rule 77(c)(i) and therefore "there is absolutely no basis upon which to proceed". Indeed, the Trial Chamber further found that the Accused's behaviour amounted to a "serious abuse of the opportunity afforded to him to have access to a public forum at this Tribunal" and that any future unsubstantiated accusation "is more likely to meet with sanctions" (*Prosecutor v Seselj*, Decision on Certain Allegations Made in Motion Number 23, ICTY Trial Chamber, November 18, 2003).

Standard of evidence required for conviction

16–48   A conviction on the basis of a charge of contempt requires proof beyond reasonable doubt (*Prosecutor v. Simić et al.*, Judgment in the Matter of Contempt Allegations Against an Accused and his Counsel, June 30, 2000, paras 99–100. Also see *Prosecutor v. Aleksovski*, Judgment on Appeal by Anto Nobilo against finding of Contempt, May 30, 2001, para. 47: "mere disbelief in a witness's denial of a particular fact does not by itself permit a tribunal of fact to accept beyond reasonable doubt the truth which he denied".)

Making the allegation

16–49   Given the gravity of allegations of contempt, any allegations should be brought on the basis of "properly prepared and substantiated submissions" (see *Prosecutor v. Nyiramasuhuko et al.*, Decision on the

Prosecutor's allegations of contempt, the harmonisation of the witness protection measures and warning to the Prosecutor's counsel, July 10, 2001, para. 12). The crucial matter, however, was that the respondent was made aware at all times of the case he had to meet (*Prosecutor v. Tadić*, Judgment on Allegations of Contempt Against Prior Counsel, Milan Vujin, January 31, 2000, para. 5).

The desirability of "properly prepared and substantiated submissions" is particularly important in light of the ICTY and ICTR Rules of Procedure and Evidence, which recognise a Chamber's right, *proprio motu*, to initiate proceedings for contempt. When Chambers initiate proceedings there is the danger of their acting as both Prosecutor and Judge in relation to contempt charges. It is therefore preferable that contempt proceedings proceed by way of an indictment with the Prosecutor bearing the burden of proof. In any event, where a Chamber does initiate contempt proceedings itself, it is essential that any charge of contempt be formulated with the precision of an indictment to protect the rights of the accused person (see *Prosecutor v. Aleksovski*, Judgment on Appeal by Anto Nobilo against finding of Contempt, May 30, 2001, para. 56).

AMICI APPOINTED TO PROSECUTE CONTEMPT

An attempt to avoid the danger of the Trial Chamber acting as both **16–50** Prosecutor and Judge in contempt proceedings was made in the concerning allegations against Milka Maglov, co-counsel for Radoslav Brdanin. In these proceedings, the Trial Chamber appointed an amicus Prosecutor, Brenda Hollis, to formulate and pursue the indictment (*Prosecutor v. Brdanin*, Ordering Instigating Proceedings Against Milka Maglov, ICTY Trial Chamber, May 8, 2003). Regardless, an application by Ms Maglov to the ICTY Bureau for the disqualification and withdrawal of the Brdanin Trial Chamber judges from determining the contempt proceedings against her was dismissed. In dismissing Ms Maglov's application, Judge Theodor Meron noted that "the applicant has failed to establish that a fair-minded observer, with sufficient knowledge of the circumstances of this case to make a reasonable judgement, would conclude that the Trial Chamber might not bring an impartial and unprejudiced mind to the issues arising in this case". (*Prosecutor v. Brdanin*, Decision on Application for Disqualification, ICTY Bureau, June 11, 2004, para. 35).

It should be noted at this juncture that Judge Meron also ruled that the contempt proceedings arising in *Prosecutor v. Milošević* should be returned to the Trial Chamber in charge of the case where the contempt occurred (*Prosecutor v. Jovanovic*, Order Determining Competent Trial Chamber in a Case of Contempt, ICTY President, December 1, 2003).

REFUSAL TO ANSWER QUESTIONS AS CONTEMPT OF COURT

A similar issue arose in *Prosecutor v. Milošević, Contempt Proceedings* **16–51** *against Kosta Bulatovic* (Decision on contempt of the Tribunal, Trial Chamber, May 13, 2005, para. 7). In this case, the witness, Bulatovic, refused to answer any questions without the presence of Slobodan Milošević. A motion to move the charges to another Chamber "as the key issue was whether the Chamber's order that the Trial should proceed in the absence of the accused was valid" was refused. In doing so, the Trial Chamber ruled that "it was not appropriate [. . .] to review that decision in the context of the proceedings for contempt". Likewise an application to challenge jurisdiction on the basis of the nullity of the original decision to proceed was deemed "incompetent" by the Chamber, as it did not fall within the definition of a preliminary motion challenging jurisdiction under rule 72(D) *Prosecutor v. Milošević, Contempt Proceedings against Kosta Bulatovic*, Decision on contempt of the Tribunal, Trial Chamber, May 13, 2005, para 8; See also *Prosecutor v. Milošević, Contempt Proceedings against Kosta Bulatovic*, Separate opinion of Judge Bonomy, Trial Chamber, May 13, 2005, paras 4–11).

More information as to the procedural safeguards considered in the Brdanin proceedings can be found in: *Prosecutor v. Brdanin* (Concerning Allegations against Milka Maglov), Decision confirming vacation of prior orders and termination of proceedings, ICTY Trial Chamber, December 17, 2004; *Prosecutor v. Brdanin* (Concerning Allegations against Milka Maglov), Clarification of notice by Amicus Curiae Prosecutor of intent to provide the Office of the Prosecutor with legal arguments, conclusions of law and authority contained in confidential filings, ICTY Trial Chamber, July 21, 2004; *Prosecutor v. Brdanin* (Concerning Allegations Against Milka Maglov), Decision on request to Trial Chamber Under Rule 73 to Certify Permission to appeal decision on motion for acquittal under Rule 98bis dated March 19, 2004, ICTY Trial Chamber, April 20, 2004; *Prosecutor v. Brdanin* (Concerning Allegations Against Milka Maglov), Decision on Motion for Acquittal Pursuant to Rule 98bis, ICTY Trial Chamber, March 19, 2004; *Prosecutor v. Brdanin* (Concerning Allegations against Milka Maglov), Decision on Motion by Amicus Curiae Prosecutor to amend allegations of contempt of the Tribunal, ICTY Trial Chamber, February 6, 2004. These proceedings against Milka Maglov were subsequently not pursued by the ICTY Office of the Prosecutor.

16–52   Rule 91 of the ICTY, ICTR and Sierra Leone Rules of Procedure and Evidence specifically acknowledge a Chambers right, *proprio motu*, or at the request of any party, to warn a witness to tell the truth and to warn the witnesses of the consequences which may result from a failure to do so. If the Chamber has "strong grounds" for believing that a witness has "knowingly and wilfully" given false evidence, the Chamber may direct the Prosecutor to investigate the matter with a view to preferring an indictment for false testimony (see *Prosecutor v. Tadić*, Order for the Prosecution to investigate the false testimony of Dragan Opacic, December 5, 1996, p. 2). Rule 91, therefore, goes some way towards safeguarding the role of the judges as impartial arbiters of fact and law.

Seriousness

16–53   Before contempt proceedings are initiated, the alleged contempt should attain a sufficient level of seriousness. Contempt proceedings, particularly against counsel, should not be lightly undertaken. No court can function efficiently without a relationship of trust between counsel and the judges. "Counsel is an officer of the court, and in judicial proceedings quite often the court must act on counsel's word, which given as an officer of the court, is accepted as trust, unless there is good reason to doubt his *bona fides*" (see *Prosecutor v. Aleksovski*, Judgment on Appeal by Anto Nobilo against finding of Contempt, Separate Opinion of Judge Patrick Robinson, May 30, 2001, para. 2).

16–54

In *Prosecutor v. Elizaphan Ntakirutimana and Gerard Ntakirutimana*, Decision on Prosecution Motion for Contempt of Court and on two Defence Motions for Disclosure, July 16, 2001, paras 10–12, the Trial Chamber found that the disclosure in violation of the witness protection order was not sufficiently serious to be tantamount to contempt. The statement of the protected witness fell to be disclosed by the Prosecutor under the Rule 68 obligations as it amounted to exculpatory material. The Prosecutor had sought to vary the witness protection measures in order to comply with her disclosure obligations. Accordingly, the context of the alleged breach of the Chamber's protection order did not justify a finding of contempt.

In *Prosecutor v. Furundžija*, The Trial Chamber's Formal Complaint to the Prosecutor concerning the conduct of the Prosecution, June 5, 1998, para. 11, the Trial Chamber ruled that the consistent pattern of non-compliance by the Prosecutor with the Tribunal's orders was not covered by Rule 77. The Trial Chamber held that Rule 77 only covered the most extreme cases of interference with the course and administration of justice. The Prosecutor's conduct fell short of knowing and wilful interference, and accordingly fell outside the inherent powers of contempt recognised in Rule 77. Staff members or witnesses of the Office of the Prosecutor, however, have no immunity under Rule 77 or Rule 91, however, and can be held accountable, for example, if they fail contumaciously to answer a question, or attempt to interfere with a witness (see *Prosecutor v. Delalic et al.*, Decision of the President on the Prosecution's Motion for the Production of Notes Exchanged between Zejnil Delalic and Zdravko Mucic, November 11, 1996).

In *Prosecutor v Jovanovic*, the Trial Chamber confirmed the withdrawal of an indictment and termination of proceedings against Dusko Jovanovic for his alleged contempt of the Tribunal. This decision followed a Prosecution Motion to Withdraw which annexed a statement by Mr Jovanovic acknowledging full personal and professional responsibility for publishing the details of a protected witness, in violation of protective measures Orders of the Tribunal. The accused, Mr Jovanovic had arranged that this statement was published in a Serbian daily newspaper, and had expressed regret concerning any harm his actions may have caused the protected witness and the administration of justice (*Prosecutor v Jovanovic*, Decision Confirming Withdrawal of Indictment and Termination of Proceedings, ICTY Trial Chamber, April 19, 2004). Initially, the Trial Chamber had found that a "prima facie case for contempt pursuant to Rule 77(A)(ii) of the Rules" had been established, and it was on this basis that the indictment against Dusko Jovanovic was confirmed (*Prosecutor v. Jovanovic*, Decision on Review of Indictment and Order for non-disclosure of supporting material, ICTY Trial Chamber, April 7, 2003).

Likewise, in *Prosecutor v. Brdanin (Concerning Allegations against Milka Maglov)*, one count of the three count indictment against Milka Maglov was dismissed on 98bis application, as the act concerned did not violate both the spirit and the letter of the Trial Chamber's order. The act charged was disclosing the whereabouts of a protected witness to a member of the public, who, along with many other people in the community, already knew the whereabouts of the protected witness *Prosecutor v. Brdanin (Conerning Allegations against Milka Maglov)*, Decision on Motion for Acquittal Pursuant to Rule 98bis, ICTY Trial Chamber, March 19, 2004, para 10.

Further, in *Prosecutor v. Milošević*, a provisional finding of contempt on the part of a witness, was later overturned on the basis of a threat assessment by the Victims and Witnesses Section which stated that the reason for the witness' refusal to give evidence was perhaps driven by his fear of retribution to his family. This finding would appear to uphold the additional requirements of "knowingly" and "wilfully" interfering with the administration of justice (*Prosecutor v. Milošević*, Trial Chamber finding in the matter of witness K12, ICTY Trial Chamber, November 21, 2002.

In assessing the alleged contempt it should be emphasised that the law of contempt is "not designed to buttress the dignity of the judges or to punish mere affronts or insults to a court or tribunal; rather it is justice itself which is flouted by a contempt of court, not the individual court or judge who is attempting to administer justice" (*Prosecutor v. Aleksovski*, Judgment on Appeal by Anto Nobilo against finding of Contempt, May 30, 2001, para. 36; *Prosecutor v. Tadić*, Judgment on Allegations of Contempt Against Prior Counsel, Milan Vujin, January 31, 2000, para. 16).

Mere negligence will never amount to contempt. Such conduct, could be dealt with by way of disciplinary action, but could never justify imprisonment or a substantial fine even were the unintended consequences of such negligence to interfere with the Tribunal's administration of justice (*Prosecutor v. Aleksovski*, Judgment on Appeal by Anto Nobilo against finding of Contempt, May 30, 2001, para. 45; *Prosecutor v. Brdanin (Concerning Allegations against Milka Maglov)*, Decision on Motion for Acquittal pursuant to Rule 98bis, ICTY Trial Chamber, March 19, 2004, para. 40).

Further contempt proceedings will no doubt clarify this area of the law in the recent indictments for contempt against Stjepan Seselj and Domagoj Margetic; and Ivica Marijacic and Markica Rebic which deal with violations of protective measures orders through publication of protected information in newspapers.

Knowledge

16–55   In *Prosecutor v. Aleksovski*, Judgment on Appeal by Anto Nobilo against finding of Contempt, May 30, 2001, para. 43, the Appeals Chamber considered the meaning of a "knowing violation" of an order of a Chamber under Rule 77(A)(iii) (now rule 77(A)(ii)) of the ICTY Rules of Procedure and Evidence. The Appeals Chamber held that actual knowledge of an order was not required before it could be violated knowingly. It was sufficient that the person charged with contempt acted in wilful blindness, meaning that the defendant "suspected that the fact existed (or was aware that its existence was highly probable) but refrained from finding out whether it did exist because he wanted be able to deny knowledge of it (or he just did not want to find out that it did exist)" (Approved in *Prosecutor v Brdanin (Concerning Allegations against Milka Maglov)*, Decision on Motion for Acquittal pursuant to Rule 98bis, ICTY Trial Chamber, March 19, 2004, para 38).

The Appeals Chamber also found that in relation to a knowing violation of an order of the Tribunal it was not necessary to establish that a person charged with contempt intended to violate the order. It was sufficient if the person charged "acted with reckless indifference as to whether his act was in violation of the order" (para. 54).

In *Prosecutor v. Brdanin (Concerning Allegations Against Milka Maglov)*, the Trial Chamber found that "intimidation of a witness as contempt of court requires proof that: a) the accused engaged in conduct that is likely to intimidate a witness; and b) the accused acted knowingly and wilfully". In terms of this "knowledge" requirement, the Trial Chamber went on to clarify that "for each form of criminal contempt, the Prosecution must establish that the accused acted with specific intent to interfere with the Tribunal's due administration of justice" (*Prosecutor v. Brdanin (Concerning Allegations against Milka Maglov)*, Decision on Motion for Acquittal pursuant to Rule 98bis, ICTY Trial Chamber, March 19, 2004, para. 16, see also paras 22, 24, 29, 41).

Applying a similar line of reasoning, the Trial Chamber in *Prosecutor v. Milošević* determined that for conduct to be "contumacious" it had to be "perverse" (*Prosecutor v. Milošević*, Contempt Proceedings against witness K12, November 18, 2002, T33). However, it must be noted that Judge Kwon dissented on this point stating that "contumacious" did not require an additional element to "knowingly and willingly", but merely proof of an obstinate refusal to answer questions "without a reasonable excuse" (*Prosecutor v. Milošević*, Trial Chamber finding in the matter of witness K12, Dissenting Opinion of Judge Kwon, November 21, 2002).

The "knowledge" requirement in the Bulatovic proceedings was construed narrowly, and did not include matters of subjective intention as to the purpose of refusal. Instead, the Trial Chamber determined that the "knowledge" requirement was satisfied where it can be shown that an order to comply was communicated to the Respondent and the Respondent subsequently refused to comply. The Chamber stated "he thus defied the authority of the court and created the risk that the [. . .] administration of justice would be brought into disrepute" (*Prosecutor v. Milošević*, Contempt Proceedings against Kosta Bulatovic (Decision on contempt of the Tribunal), Trial Chamber, May 13, 2005, para. 16–17).

In absentia proceedings

In *Prosecutor v. Blaškić*, Subpoena Decision, October 29, 1997, para. 59, the Appeals Chamber held that "in absentia proceedings may be exceptionally warranted in cases involving contempt of the International Tribunal, where the person charged fails to appear in court, thus obstructing the administration of justice".   **16–56**

Domestic proceedings

16–57   In *Prosecutor v. Milošević*, the Government of Serbia and Montenegro responded to a request from the ICTY to investigate the circumstances surrounding the publication in a newspaper of the identity of a protected witness. The authorities of Serbia and Montenegro discovered the identity of the journalist but notified the Tribunal that they would take no further steps as the journalist's actions were not a crime under domestic legislation at the time. The ICTY Trial Chamber, despite not having a specific provision in its Statute for the institution of domestic contempt proceedings on its behalf, "reminded" the authorities of Serbia and Montenegro that "whatever is provided for in their domestic legislation, article 29 of the International Tribunal's Statute imposes upon all States the obligation to comply with any request for assistance or order of a Trial Chamber" (*Prosecutor v. Milošević*, Order Concerning the Response of the Government of Serbia and Montenegro to the Trial Chamber's request for an investigation into violation of its order for protective measures, ICTY Trial Chamber, April 10, 2003). It is arguably for this reason that the ICC Statute specifically provides for domestic assistance in contempt matters.

In contrast to the Tribunals, Article 70(4)(b) of the ICC Statute recognises the possibility of contempt proceedings being instituted and prosecuted in the national courts of States Parties. The judicial economy in using national courts to prosecute these offences, as well as the far greater range of penalties available at national level, mean that, in many cases, it may be preferable to deal with offences against the administration of justice at the national level, rather than before the ICC. Considerations which the ICC might take into account in deciding whether to exercise jurisdiction include "the availability and effectiveness of prosecution in a State Party" and "the seriousness of an offence". See Rule 162 of the ICC Rules of Procedure and Evidence.

To give effect to this possible course of action, Article 70(4)(a) of the Rome Statute requires that each State party to the Rome Statute, pass implementing legislation to enable it to conduct proceedings in the event that offences against the administration of justice are committed by its nationals or on its territory. When national authorities prosecute offences against the administration of justice, they are required to "treat such cases with diligence and devote sufficient resources to enable them to be conducted effectively" (see ICC Statute Article 70(4)(b)).

V. PENALTIES

A. ICC

16–58   The ICC Statute proscribes a maximum penalty of five years in addition to a fine upon conviction of an offence against the administration of justice (see article 70(3)). Rule 172 of the ICC Rules provides that if conduct which amounts to misconduct under Article 71 of the

ICC Statute also constitutes an offence against the administration of justice under Article 70, the Court must proceed in accordance with Article 70 and prosecute as contempt. Rule 166(3) of the ICC Rules of Procedure and Evidence provides that fines may be issued in respect of each separate offence and may be cumulative. Under no circumstances may the total amount exceed fifty per cent of the value of the convicted person's identifiable assets after deduction of an appropriate amount that would satisfy the financial needs of the convicted person and his or her dependants. See Rule 166(5) regarding the action the Court may take if a person fails to pay such a fine.

Rule 164(2) of the ICC Rules provides for a period of limitation of five years from the date of commission of the offence provided that no investigation or prosecution is initiated during that period. Enforcement of sanctions with respect to Article 70 of the ICC statute are subject to a limitation period of 10 years from the date the sanction becomes final. Time stops running with the detection of the convicted person, or whilst the person is outside the territory of the States Parties (Rule 164(3)).

B. ICTY

Rules 77(G) and 91(G) of the ICTY Rules of Procedure and Evidence **16–59** provide for a maximum term of seven years imprisonment and a fine not exceeding €100,000 in the event of a conviction for contempt or giving false testimony under oath.

Contempt by counsel is viewed as a particularly serious offence. See *Prosecutor v. Tadić*, Judgment on allegations of contempt against prior counsel, Milan Vujin, January 31, 2000, paras 166–168:

> "Courts and tribunals necessarily rely very substantially upon the honesty and propriety of counsel in the conduct of litigation. Counsel are permitted important privileges by the law which are justified only upon the basis that they can be trusted not to abuse them. Where counsel's conduct was intended to assist his client "that was bad enough" but where counsel had acted against the interests of his client, particularly where his client was in custody, and fully reliant on his Counsel for assistance, "that was worse" and the contempt required punishment, which served not only as retribution but also as deterrence."

The Tribunal imposed a fine of Dfl 15,000 against Milan Vujin, but gave no reasons why, in spite of the seriousness of the case and the abuse of trust entailed by the contempt, it was inappropriate to sentence Vujin to a term of imprisonment (*Prosecutor v. Tadić*, Judgment on Allegations of Contempt Against Prior Counsel, Milan Vujin, January 31, 2000, para. 173).

In addition to the fine, the Appeals Chamber (paras 168–172) **16–60** considered Vujin to be guilty of professional misconduct under the *Code of Professional Conduct for Defence Counsel Appearing before the International Tribunal*. Although the provisions of the rule on refusing audience to Counsel under rule 46 and the provisions on Article 20 of the Directive on the Assignment of Defence Counsel were not directly applicable to

Vujin's case, the Chamber considered his conduct to be substantially worse than that which permits the Registrar to strike counsel off the list pursuant to the Article 20 Directive. The Chamber, therefore, directed the Registrar to consider striking Vujin off the list of assigned counsel and to notify his misconduct to the professional body he belonged to (see *Prosecutor v. Tadić*, Judgment on Allegations of Contempt Against Prior Counsel, Milan Vujin, January 31, 2000, para. 172. See also *Prosecutor v. Tadić*, Appeal Judgment on Allegations of Contempt Against Prior Counsel, Milan Vujin, February 27, 2001, in which the Appeals Chamber hearing the appeal from a differently constituted Appeals Chamber (in relation to its first instance finding of contempt) endorsed the finding that original Counsel can expect either to be suspended or stuck off the assigned counsel list in the event of a finding of contempt under Rule 77).

Contempt committed by the witness Bulatovic in refusing to answer questions was considered by the Trial Chamber to be a serious contempt of the Tribunal in *Prosecutor v. Milošević*. In this case, the Chamber took into account the serious health problems of the Respondent in order to avoid the imposition of a custodial sentence which would usually be given in a case of this nature (*Prosecutor v. Milošević, Contempt Proceedings against Kosta Bulatovic* (Decision on contempt of the Tribunal), Trial Chamber, May 13, 2005, para. 18).

C. ICTR

16–61   The ICTR rules appear far more lenient than the equivalent provisions of the ICTY or the ICC by providing for maximum sentences of imprisonment of no more than six months or a fine not exceeding six months in the case of contempt under Rule 77(a), and twelve months and a fine not exceeding ten thousand US dollars in the case of false testimony under oath under Rule 91(D).

D. EAST TIMOR

16–62   Section 49.4 of UNTAET Regulation 2000/30 as amended by Regulation 2001/25 provides that the maximum penalty for contempt is a term of imprisonment not to exceed one year and a fine not to exceed US$1,000.

E. SIERRA LEONE

16–63   The Sierra Leone rules distinguish between contempt dealt with summarily by a Judge or a Trial Chamber and contempt dealt with by the appointment of an independent investigating counsel and indictment for contempt. In relation to the former, rule 77 provides for a maximum penalty of no more than 6 months imprisonment or a fine not exceeding 2 million leones. On the other hand, in relation to the latter, the maximum penalty is set at seven years imprisonment, or a fine of not exceeding 2 million leones, or both. If the person committing the contempt is a counsel before the Special Court, the Chamber may find that the conduct amounts to misconduct and may also determine that the counsel is no longer eligible to appear before the Special Court.

VI. APPEAL

The Rules of both ad hoc Tribunals recognise a right of Appeal, **16–64** within fifteen days of the handing down of the finding of contempt (see Rule 77(J) in the case of the ICTY and Rule 77(D) of the ICTR Rules). Rule 91(I) of the ICTY Rules and rule 91(F) of the ICTR Rules of Procedure and Evidence provides for a right of appeal against a finding of giving false testimony under oath within fifteen days of the filing of the impugned decision.

Where a penalty is imposed for contempt under section 49.3 of UNTAET Regulation No. 2000/30, a right of appeal to the Court of Appeal in Dili is provided for by section 49.5. The notice of appeal, against the finding of contempt, shall be filed no more than ten working days after the impugned decision is released (section 40.2). Section 49.5 provides that the judge who imposed the penalty for contempt be deemed the respondent.

The Special Court for Sierra Leone, in rule 77(J–L) of its Rules of Procedure and Evidence, allows for appeal of a finding of contempt by a single judge or a Trial Chamber. Appeals are to be heard by a panel of three Appeals Chamber judges and can be dealt with exclusively by written submission.

The decision in *Prosecutor v. Tadić*, Judgment on allegations of **16–65** contempt against prior counsel, Milan Vujin, January 31, 2000 was unique in the sense that the initial hearing on the contempt allegations and ruling arose from an Appeals Chamber decision. The respondent filed an appeal, despite the absence of a provision in Rule 77 of the Rules of Procedure and Evidence providing for a right to appeal a decision of the Appeals Chamber. At the full Appeal hearing the Appeals Chamber found that the "preferred course in this case would have been for the contempt trial to have been initially referred to a Trial Chamber, thereby providing for the possibility of appeal, rather than being heard by the Appeals Chamber, ruling in the first instance". It recognised a right of appeal because the Rules and Statute must be interpreted so as to respect the internationally recognised standards regarding the rights of an accused including Article 14 of the International Covenant on Civil and Political Rights which recognises a right of review by a higher tribunal (*Prosecutor v. Tadić*, Appeal Judgment on Allegations of Contempt Against Prior Counsel, Milan Vujin, February 27, 2001 and see Separate Opinion of Judge Wald Dissenting from the finding of Jurisdiction, Prosecutor v. Tadić, Appeal Judgment on Allegations of Contempt Against Prior Counsel, Milan Vujin, February 27, 2001).

VII. MISCONDUCT BY HIGH OFFICIALS OF THE COURT

16–66   The ICTY and ICTR Statutes do not provide for the removal of any of the high officials of those Tribunals (Judges, Prosecutor, Registrar) in the event of misconduct. Article 46 of the Rome Statute, however, provides a mechanism for the removal of a judge, the Prosecutor, Deputy Prosecutor, Registrar and Deputy Registrar in the event that such a person is found to have committed serious misconduct or a serious breach of their duties. (Article 84(1)(c) provides that grounds for revision of a person's conviction or sentence may lie in the case of serious misconduct or serious breach of duty by a judge of sufficient seriousness to justify that judges removal from office.)

It does not appear that Article 46 is *lex specialis* Article 70 to the extent that a High Official of the Court will be immune from prosecution under Article 70, but can only be removed from office. Rather it provides a means for that person's removal from office and a prosecution may follow if the requirements of Article 70 are made out.

A judge, the Prosecutor, and Deputy Prosecutor may only be removed by a secret vote by the Assembly of State Parties. In the event of a judge, removal requires both a recommendation of two-thirds of the other judges as well as a two-thirds majority of the State Parties (Article 46(2)(a)). These onerous requirements are to preserve judicial independence.

The Prosecutor can be removed from office by an absolute majority of votes by the States Parties (Article 46(2)(b)). The Deputy Prosecutor can be removed by an absolute majority of States Parties upon a recommendation of the Prosecutor. The Registrar and Deputy Registrar can be dismissed by an absolute majority of votes by the judges (Article 46(2)(c)).

The person whose conduct is impugned has the right to present and receive evidence and make submissions in accordance with the Rules of Procedure and Evidence (Article 46(4)).

The threshold of the impugned conduct being "serious" must be made out. It includes either misconduct or inability that causes that official to be unable to carry out their official functions (Article 46(4)). Rule 24 of the ICC Rules of Procedure and Evidence defines "serious misconduct" which occurs in the course of a persons duties as conduct that "causes or is likely to cause serious harm to the proper administration of justice before the court or proper internal functioning of the court". Examples given include disclosing confidential facts or information acquired in the course of that persons duties, or *sub judice*, "where such disclosure is seriously prejudicial to the judicial proceedings or any person" (Rule 24(1)(a)(i)). Another would be improperly concealing information of a sufficiently serious nature to have precluded that person from holding office (Rule 24(1)(a)(ii)) or abuse of office to obtain "unwarranted favourable treatment" (Rule 24(1)(a)(iii)).

16–67   Misconduct not arising from a persons official duties may also warrant removal if it "is of a grave nature that causes or is likely to cause serious harm to the standing of the court" (Rule 24(1)(b)).

A "serious breach of duties" is also defined as having occurred for the purpose of Article 46 where a person has been "grossly negligent in the performance of his or her duties or has knowingly acted in contravention of those duties" (Rule 24(2)). Examples may include when a person fails to comply with a duty to excuse himself from a case knowing that there were ground for so doing (Rule 24(2)(a)) and repeatedly causing unwarranted delay in the initiation, prosecution or trial of cases or in the exercise of judicial powers.

"Misconduct of a less serious nature" is defined in Rule 25. Complaints against any of the high officials included within Article 46 can be made and will be transmitted to the Presidency (Rule 26(1)). Anonymous or manifestly unfounded complaints will be set aside. The Presidency has the power to initiate proceedings of its own motion (Rule 26(2)). **16–68**

Disciplinary measures for the purposes of Article 48 include a formal reprimand or a pecuniary sanction amounting to not more that six months of the salary paid to the official by the court (Rule 32).

Lesser officials of the court, of course, will be subject to the usual disciplinary requirements of their contracts. In the event that such an official commits an offence against the administration of justice within the meaning of Article 70, there is nothing that would prevent their prosecution before the ICC. **16–69**

Rule 8 provides for the adoption of a code of conduct for counsel. Breach of this code could lead to non-payment of fees by the Registrar, removal from the list of counsel, reporting the alleged misconduct to counsel's Bar or professional association, or prosecution under Article 70 (see also *Code of Professional Conduct for Defence Counsel Appearing before the International Tribunal* (IT/125), Rule 46). Also see ICTR Rule 73(E) (withholding counsel's fees and/or imposing costs in the case of frivolous motions or motions amounting to an abuse of process) and Rule 108*bis* (G) (entitling the Appeals Chamber to impose "appropriate sanctions on a party which fails to perform its obligations pursuant [to that] section of the Rules").

The Special Court for Sierra Leone adopts a less detailed approach to misconduct, regulating against bribery of judges and officials (section 39 Special Court Ratification Act) and misconduct by counsel (article 46 Rules of Evidence and Procedure). Judges and officials found to be breaching the provision against bribery are, on conviction, liable to a fine not exceeding thirty million leones or a term of imprisonment not exceeding ten years, or both. In relation to counsel, if a Chamber forms the view that conduct of a counsel is offensive, abusive, obstructive, otherwise contrary to the interests of justice, or if a counsel brings motions or conducts other activities that are frivolous or constitute an abuse of process, they may be sanctioned by the Chamber. Sanctions may include fines, non-payment of fees or such other sanctions as the Chamber directs. A Chamber may also determine that a counsel is no longer eligible to represent a suspect and may communicate any misconduct to the professional body regulating conduct in the counsel's home state. For the purposes of this rule, "counsel" includes prosecution, defence and *amicus curiae* counsel.

CHAPTER 17

DEFENCES AND PROCEDURAL BARS TO JURISDICTION

I. STATUTORY PROVISIONS

A. ICC

Non bis in idem

20.—1. Except as provided in this Statute, no person shall be tried before **17–1**
the Court with respect to conduct which formed the basis of crimes for which
the person has been convicted or acquitted by the Court.

749

2. No person shall be tried by another court for a crime referred to in article 5 for which that person has already been convicted or acquitted by the Court.

3. No person who has been tried by another court for conduct also proscribed under article 6, 7 or 8 shall be tried by the Court with respect to the same conduct unless the proceedings in the other court:

(a) Were for the purpose of shielding the person concerned from criminal responsibility for crimes within the jurisdiction of the Court; or

(b) Otherwise were not conducted independently or impartially in accordance with the norms of due process recognized by international law and were conducted in a manner which, in the circumstances, was inconsistent with an intent to bring the person concerned to justice.

Nullum crimen sine lege

17-2   **22.**—1. A person shall not be criminally responsible under this Statute unless the conduct in question constitutes, at the time it takes place, a crime within the jurisdiction of the Court.

2. The definition of a crime shall be strictly construed and shall not be extended by analogy. In case of ambiguity, the definition shall be interpreted in favour of the person being investigated, prosecuted or convicted.

3. This article shall not affect the characterization of any conduct as criminal under international law independently of this Statute.

Nulla poena sine lege

17-3   **23.** A person convicted by the Court may be punished only in accordance with this Statute.

Exclusion of jurisdiction over persons under eighteen

17-4   **26.** The Court shall have no jurisdiction over any person who was under the age of 18 at the time of the alleged commission of a crime.

Irrelevance of official capacity

17-5   **27.**—1. This Statute shall apply equally to all persons without any distinction based on official capacity. In particular, official capacity as a Head of State or Government, a member of a Government or parliament, an elected representative or a government official shall in no case exempt a person from criminal responsibility under this Statute, nor shall it, in and of itself, constitute a ground for reduction of sentence.

2. Immunities or special procedural rules which may attach to the official capacity of a person, whether under national or international law, shall not bar the Court from exercising its jurisdiction over such a person.

Non-applicability of statute of limitations

17-6   **29.** The crimes within the jurisdiction of the Court shall not be subject to any statute of limitations.

Grounds for excluding criminal responsibility

17-7   **31.**—1. In addition to other grounds for excluding criminal responsibility provided for in this Statute, a person shall not be criminally responsible if, at the time of that person's conduct:

(a) The person suffers from a mental disease or defect that destroys that person's capacity to appreciate the unlawfulness or nature of his or

her conduct, or capacity to control his or her conduct to conform to
the requirements of law;
(b) The person is in a state of intoxication that destroys that person's
capacity to appreciate the unlawfulness or nature of his or her
conduct, or capacity to control his or her conduct to conform to the
requirements of law, unless the person has become voluntarily
intoxicated under such circumstances that the person knew, or
disregarded the risk, that, as a result of the intoxication, he or she
was likely to engage in conduct constituting a crime within the
jurisdiction of the Court;
(c) The person acts reasonably to defend himself or herself or another
person or, in the case of war crimes, property which is essential for
the survival of the person or another person or property which is
essential for accomplishing a military mission, against an imminent
and unlawful use of force in a manner proportionate to the degree of
danger to the person or the other person or property protected. The
fact that the person was involved in a defensive operation conducted
by forces shall not in itself constitute a ground for excluding criminal
responsibility under this subparagraph;
(d) The conduct which is alleged to constitute a crime within the
jurisdiction of the Court has been caused by duress resulting from a
threat of imminent death or of continuing or imminent serious bodily
harm against that person or another person, and the person acts
necessarily and reasonably to avoid this threat, provided that the
person does not intend to cause a greater harm than the one sought to
be avoided. Such a threat may either be:
   (i) Made by other persons; or
   (ii) Constituted by other circumstances beyond that person's control.
2. The Court shall determine the applicability of the grounds for excluding
criminal responsibility provided for in this Statute to the case before it.
3. At trial, the Court may consider a ground for excluding criminal
responsibility other than those referred to in paragraph 1 where such a ground
is derived from applicable law as set forth in article 21. The procedures
relating to the consideration of such a ground shall be provided for in the Rules
of Procedure and Evidence.

Mistake of fact or mistake of law

32.—1. A mistake of fact shall be a ground for excluding criminal respon-   **17–8**
sibility only if it negates the mental element required by the crime.
2. A mistake of law as to whether a particular type of conduct is a crime
within the jurisdiction of the Court shall not be a ground for excluding
criminal responsibility. A mistake of law may, however, be a ground for
excluding criminal responsibility if it negates the mental element required by
such a crime, or as provided for in article 33.

Superior orders and prescription of law

33.—1. The fact that a crime within the jurisdiction of the Court has been   **17–9**
committed by a person pursuant to an order of a Government or of a superior,
whether military or civilian, shall not relieve that person of criminal responsibility unless:
(a) The person was under a legal obligation to obey orders of the
Government or the superior in question;
(b) The person did not know that the order was unlawful; and
(c) The order was not manifestly unlawful.
2. For the purposes of this article, orders to commit genocide or crimes
against humanity are manifestly unlawful.

B. ICTY

Individual criminal responsibility

17–10   **7.**—1. [. . .]

2. The official position of any accused person, whether as Head of State or Government or as a responsible Government official, shall not relieve such person of criminal responsibility nor mitigate punishment.

3. [. . .]

4. The fact that an accused person acted pursuant to an order of a Government or of a superior shall not relieve him of criminal responsibility, but may be considered in mitigation of punishment if the International Tribunal determines that justice so requires.

Non bis in idem

17–11   **10.**—1. No person shall be tried before a national court for acts constituting serious violations of international humanitarian law under the present Statute, for which he or she has already been tried by the International Tribunal.

2. A person who has been tried by a national court for acts constituting serious violations of international humanitarian law may be subsequently tried by the International Tribunal only if:

    (a) the act for which he or she was tried was characterized as an ordinary crime; or

    (b) the national court proceedings were not impartial or independent, were designed to shield the accused from international criminal responsibility, or the case was not diligently prosecuted.

3. In considering the penalty to be imposed on a person convicted of a crime under the present Statute, the International Tribunal shall take into account the extent to which any penalty imposed by a national court on the same person for the same act has already been served.

Rules of Procedure and Evidence, r. 13

Non bis in idem

17–12   **13.** When the President receives reliable information to show that criminal proceedings have been instituted against a person before a court of any State for a crime for which that person has already been tried by the Tribunal, a Trial Chamber shall, following *mutatis mutandis* the procedure provided in Rule 10, issue a reasoned order requesting that court permanently to discontinue its proceedings. If that court fails to do so, the President may report the matter to the Security Council.

Reciprocal Disclosure

17–13   **67.**—(A) Within the time-limit prescribed by the Trial Chamber or by the pre-trial Judge appointed pursuant to Rule 65 ter:

    (i) the defence shall notify the Prosecutor of its intent to offer:

        (a) the defence of alibi; in which case the notification shall specify the place or places at which the accused claims to have been present at the time of the alleged crime and the names and addresses of witnesses and any other evidence upon which the accused intends to rely to establish the alibi;

        (b) any special defence, including that of diminished or lack of mental responsibility; in which case the notification shall specify the names and addresses of witnesses and any other evidence upon which the accused intends to rely to establish the special defence; and

(ii) the Prosecutor shall notify the defence of the names of the witnesses that the Prosecutor intends to call in rebuttal of any defence plea of which the Prosecutor has received notice in accordance with paragraph (i) above.

(B) Failure of the defence to provide notice under this Rule shall not limit the right of the accused to testify on the above defences.

(C) If either party discovers additional evidence or material which should have been disclosed earlier pursuant to the Rules, that party shall immediately disclose that evidence or material to the other party and the Trial Chamber.

C. ICTR

Statute of the International Tribunal for Rwanda, Art. 6

Individual Criminal Responsibility

6.—1. [. . .]   **17–14**

2. The official position of any accused person, whether as Head of State or Government or as a responsible Government official, shall not relieve such person of criminal responsibility nor mitigate punishment.

3. [. . .]

4.The fact that an accused person acted pursuant to an order of a Government or of a superior shall not relieve him or her of criminal responsibility, but may be considered in mitigation of punishment if the International Tribunal for Rwanda determines that justice so requires.

Non bis in idem

9.—1. No person shall be tried before a national court for acts constituting   **17–15**
serious violations of international humanitarian law under the present Statute, for which he or she has already been tried by the International Tribunal for Rwanda.

2. A person who has been tried before a national court for acts constituting serious violations of international humanitarian law may be subsequently tried by the International Tribunal for Rwanda only if:

(a) The act for which he or she was tried was characterised as an ordinary crime; or

(b) The national court proceedings were not impartial or independent, were designed to shield the accused from international criminal responsibility, or the case was not diligently prosecuted.

3. In considering the penalty to be imposed on a person convicted of a crime under the present Statute, the International Tribunal for Rwanda shall take into account the extent to which any penalty imposed by a national court on the same person for the same act has already been served.

Rules of Procedure and Evidence

Non bis in idem

13. When the President receives reliable information to show that criminal   **17–16**
proceedings have been instituted against a person before a court of any State for acts constituting serious violations of international humanitarian law under

the Statute for which that person has already been tried by the Tribunal, a Trial Chamber shall, following *mutatis mutandis* the procedure provided in Rule 10, issue a reasoned order requesting that court permanently to discontinue its proceedings. If that court fails to do so, the President may report the matter to the Security Council.

Reciprocal Disclosure of Evidence

17–17   **67.** Subject to the provisions of Rules 53 and 69:

(A) As early as reasonably practicable and in any event prior to the commencement of the trial:

    (i) The Prosecutor shall notify the defence of the names of the witnesses that he intends to call to establish the guilt of the accused and in rebuttal of any defence plea of which the Prosecutor has received notice in accordance with Sub-Rule (ii) below;

    (ii) The defence shall notify the Prosecutor of its intent to enter:

        (a) The defence of alibi; in which case the notification shall specify the place or places at which the accused claims to have been present at the time of the alleged crime and the names and addresses of witnesses and any other evidence upon which the accused intends to rely to establish the alibi;

        (b) Any special defence, including that of diminished or lack of mental responsibility; in which case the notification shall specify the names and addresses of witnesses and any other evidence upon which the accused intends to rely to establish the special defence.

(B) Failure of the defence to provide such notice under this Rule shall not limit the right of the accused to rely on the above defences.

(C) If the defence makes a request pursuant to Rule 66(B), the Prosecutor shall in turn be entitled to inspect any books, documents, photographs and tangible objects, which are within the custody or control of the defence and which it intends to use as evidence at the trial.

(D) If either party discovers additional evidence or information or materials which should have been produced earlier pursuant to the Rules, that party shall promptly notify the other party and the Trial Chamber of the existence of the additional evidence or information or materials.

D. East Timor

UNTAET Regulation 2000/15, June 6, 2000

On the Establishment of Panels with Exclusive Jurisdiction over Serious Criminal Offences

Nullum crimen sine lege

17–18   **12.**—12.1 A person shall not be criminally responsible under the present regulation unless the conduct in question constitutes, at the time it takes place, a crime under international law or the laws of East Timor.

12.2 The definition of a crime shall be strictly construed and shall not be extended by analogy. In case of ambiguity, the definition shall be interpreted in favour of the person being investigated, prosecuted or convicted.

12.3 The present Section shall not affect the characterization of any conduct as criminal under principles and rules of international law independently of the present regulation.

Nulla poena sine lege

13. A person convicted by a panel may be punished only in accordance with the present regulation.   **17–19**

Grounds for excluding criminal responsibility

19.—19.1 A person shall not be criminally responsible if, at the time of that person's conduct: **17–20**

  (a) the person suffers from a mental disease or defect that destroys that person's capacity to appreciate the unlawfulness or nature of his or her conduct, or capacity to control his or her conduct to conform to the requirements of law;

  (b) the person is in a state of intoxication that destroys that person's capacity to appreciate the unlawfulness or nature of his or her conduct, or capacity to control his or her conduct to conform to the requirements of law, unless the person has become voluntarily intoxicated under such circumstances that the person knew, or disregarded the risk, that, as a result of the intoxication, he or she was likely to engage in conduct constituting a crime within the jurisdiction of the panels;

  (c) the person acts reasonably to defend himself or herself or another person or, in the case of war crimes, property which is essential for the survival of the person or another person or property which is essential for accomplishing a military mission, against an imminent and unlawful use of force in a manner proportionate to the degree of danger to the person or the other person or property protected. The fact that the person was involved in a defensive operation conducted by forces shall not in itself constitute a ground for excluding criminal responsibility under this subparagraph;

  (d) the conduct which is alleged to constitute a crime within the jurisdiction of the panels has been caused by duress resulting from a threat of imminent death or of continuing or imminent serious bodily harm against that person or another person, and the person acts necessarily and reasonably to avoid this threat, provided that the person does not intend to cause a greater harm than the one sought to be avoided. Such a threat may either be:

    (i) made by other persons; or

    (ii) constituted by other circumstances beyond that person's control.

19.2 The panel shall determine the applicability of the grounds for excluding criminal responsibility provided for in the present regulation to the case before it.

19.3 At trial, the panel may consider a ground for excluding criminal responsibility other than those referred to in Section 19.1 of the present regulation where such a ground is derived from applicable law. The procedures relating to the consideration of such a ground shall be provided for in an UNTAET directive.

Mistake of fact or mistake of law

20.—1. A mistake of fact shall be a ground for excluding criminal responsibility only if it negates the mental element required by the crime.   **17–21**

2. A mistake of law as to whether a particular type of conduct is a crime within the jurisdiction of the panels shall not be a ground for excluding criminal responsibility. A mistake of law may, however, be a ground for excluding criminal responsibility if it negates the mental element required by such a crime, or as provided for in Section 21 of the present regulation.

Superior orders and prescription of law

17–22   **21.** The fact that an accused person acted pursuant to an order of a Government or of a superior shall not relieve him of criminal responsibility, but may be considered in mitigation of punishment if a panel determines that justice so requires.

E. SIERRA LEONE

Statute for the Special Court of Sierra Leone

Individual criminal responsibility

17–23   **6.**—(1) [. . .]

(2) The official position of any accused persons, whether as Head of State or Government or as a responsible government official, shall not relieve such person of criminal responsibility nor mitigate punishment.

(3) [. . .]

(4) The fact that an accused person acted pursuant to an order of a Government or of a superior shall not relieve him or her of criminal responsibility, but may be considered in mitigation of punishment if the Special Court determines that justice so requires.

Jurisdiction over persons of 15 years of age

17–24   **7.**—(1) The Special Court shall have no jurisdiction over any person who was under the age of 15 at the time of the alleged commission of the crime. Should any person who was at the time of the alleged commission of the crime between 15 and 18 years of age come before the Court, he or she shall be treated with dignity and a sense of worth, taking into account his or her young age and the desirability of promoting his or her rehabilitation, reintegration into and assumption of a constructive role in society, and in accordance with international human rights standards, in particular the rights of the child.

(2) In the disposition of a case against a juvenile offender, the Special Court shall order any of the following: care guidance and supervision orders, community service orders, counselling, foster care, correctional, educational and vocational training programmes, approved schools and, as appropriate, any programmes of disarmament, demobilization and reintegration or programmes of child protection agencies.

Non bis in idem

17–25   **9.**—1. No person shall be tried before a national court of Sierra Leone for acts for which he or she has already been tried by the Special Court.

2. A person who has been tried by a national court for the acts referred to in articles 2 and 4 of the present Statute may be subsequently tried by the Special Court if:

(a) The act for which he or she was tried was characterized as an ordinary crime; or

(b) The national court proceedings were not impartial or independent, were designed to shield the accused from international criminal responsibility or the case was not diligently prosecuted.

3. In considering the penalty to be imposed on a person convicted of a crime under the present Statute, the Special Court shall take into account the extent to which any penalty imposed by a national court on the same person for the same act has already been served.

Amnesty

10. An amnesty granted to any person falling within the jurisdiction of the Special Court in respect of the crimes referred to in articles 2 to 4 of the present Statute shall not be a bar to prosecution.

17–26

Special Court Agreement 2002, Ratification Act 2002 (Supplement to the Sierra Leone Gazette Vol. CXXX No. 11 dated March 7, 2002

Official position of the accused no bar to arrest etc

29. The existence of an immunity or special procedural rule attaching to the official capacity of any person shall not be a bar to the arrest and delivery of that person into the custody of the Special Court.

17–27

Rules of Procedure and Evidence, May 29, 2004

Double Jeopardy

13. When the President receives reliable information to show that criminal proceedings have been instituted against a person before a court of any State for acts for which that person has already been tried by the Special Court, he shall issue a reasoned order or request to such court seeking permanent discontinuance of its proceedings. If that court fails to do so, the President may take appropriate action.

17–28

Reciprocal Disclosure of Evidence

67. Subject to the provisions of Rules 53 and 69:

17–29

(A) As early as reasonably practicable and in any event prior to the commencement of the trial:

    i. The Prosecutor shall notify the defence of the names of the witnesses that he intends to call to establish the guilt of the accused and in rebuttal of any defence plea of which the Prosecutor has received notice in accordance with Sub-Rule (ii) below, or any defence pleaded in the Defence Case Statement served under Sub-Rule (C);

    ii. The defence shall notify the Prosecutor of its intent to enter:

        a. The defence of alibi; in which case the notification shall specify the place or places at which the accused claims to have been present at the time of the alleged crime and the names and addresses of witnesses and any other evidence upon which the accused intends to rely to establish the alibi;

        b. Any special defence, including that of diminished or lack of mental responsibility; in which case the notification shall specify the names and addresses of witnesses and any other evidence upon which the accused intends to rely to establish the special defence.

(B) Failure of the defence to provide such notice under this Rule shall not limit the right of the accused to rely on the above defences.

(C) To assist the Prosecutor with its disclosure obligations pursuant to Rule 68, the defence may prior to trial provide the Prosecutor with a Defence Case Statement. The Defence Case Statement shall:

    i. set out in general terms the nature of the accused's defence;

    ii. indicate the matters on which he takes issue with the prosecution; and

    iii. set out, in the case of each such matter, the reason why he takes issue with the prosecution.

(D) If either party discovers additional evidence or information or materials which should have been produced earlier pursuant to the Rules, that party shall promptly notify the other party and the Trial Chamber of the existence of the additional evidence or information or materials

F. Cambodia

Agreement Between the United Nations and the Royal Government of Cambodia Concerning the Prosecution Under Cambodian Law of Crimes Committed During the Period of Democratic Kampuchea, June 6, 2003

Amnesty

17-30   **11.**—(1) The Royal Government of Cambodia shall not request an amnesty or pardon for any persons who may be investigated for or convicted of crimes referred to in the present Agreement.

(2) This provision is based upon a declaration by the Royal Government of Cambodia that until now, with regard to matters covered in the law, there has been only one case, dated September 14, 1996, when a pardon was granted to only one person with regard to a 1979 conviction on the charge of genocide. The United Nations and the Royal Government of Cambodia agree that the scope of this pardon is a matter to be decided by the Extraordinary Chambers.

Law On The Establishment Of Extraordinary Chambers In The Courts Of Cambodia For The Prosecution Of Crimes Committed During The Period Of Democratic Kampuchea

Non-applicability of statute of limitations

17-31   **3.** The Extraordinary Chambers shall have the power to bring to trial all Suspects who committed any of these crimes set forth in the 1956 Penal Code of Cambodia, and which were committed during the period from April 17, 1975 to January 6, 1979:

— Homicide (Article 501, 503, 504, 505, 506, 507 and 508)
— Torture (Article 500)
— Religious Persecution (Articles 209 and 210)

The statute of limitations set forth in the 1956 Penal Code shall be extended for an additional 20 years for the crimes enumerated above, which are within the jurisdiction of the Extraordinary Chambers.

4. The acts of genocide, which have no statute of limitations [. . .]

5. Crimes against humanity, which have no statute of limitations [. . .]

Irrelevance of official capacity/Superior orders

17-32   **29.** The position or rank of any Suspect shall not relieve such person of criminal responsibility or mitigate punishment. [. . .]

The fact that a Suspect acted pursuant to an order of the Government of Democratic Kampuchea or of a superior shall not relieve the Suspect of individual criminal responsibility.

Amnesty or Pardon

17-33   **40.** The Royal Government of Cambodia shall not request an amnesty or pardon for any persons who may be investigated for or convicted of crimes referred to in Articles 3, 4, 5, 6, 7 and 8 of this law.

II. PROCEDURAL BARS TO JURISDICTION

A. Non Bis in Idem

In common law jurisdictions this maxim is referred to as double **17–34**
jeopardy. It seeks to ensure that an accused person is not tried twice for
the same crime and forms a part of most national legal systems. It
usually only applies to judgments within a State and does not apply
between different national legal systems (see *AP v. Italy, UN Committee
for Human Rights*, B 204/1986, ss.7.3).

Non bis in idem is enshrined in international and regional instruments.
Article 14(7) of the International Covenant on Civil and Political
Rights 1966 provides that "No one shall be liable to be tried or
punished again for an offence for which he has already been finally
convicted or acquitted in accordance with the law and penal procedure
of each country." See also Article 4 of the Seventh Additional Protocol
of the European Convention on Human Rights.

Under the Statutes of the ICTY and ICTR the International Tribunals have primacy over national courts. In this context, the principle
of *non bis in idem* would preclude further prosecution in a national court
when there has been a prosecution before one of the Tribunals (see rule
13 of the ICTY Rules of Procedure and Evidence which sets out the
reporting procedure to the Security-Council in the case that a State
fails to heed the order of a Trial Chamber requesting the State to
permanently discontinue domestic proceedings). When national courts
have prosecuted a case the *non bis in idem* principle should not "preclude
a subsequent trial before the International Tribunal in the following
two circumstances: (a) the act for which the person was tried was
characterised as an ordinary crime; or (b) the national court proceedings were not impartial or independent, were designed to shield the
accused from international criminal responsibility, or the case was not
diligently prosecuted. See specifically article 10 of the ICTY and article
9 of the ICTR Statutes, which enshrine the principle of *non bis in idem*.
In the two circumstances (a) and (b) described above, the *non bis in idem*
principle would not apply so as to prevent the Tribunals from prosecuting the accused again. See *Report of the International Tribunal for the
Prosecution of Persons Responsible for Serious Violations of International
Humanitarian Law committed in the Territory of the Former Yugoslavia since
1991*, UN Doc IT/68 First Annual Report (1994).

In *Prosecutor v. Tadić*, Decision on the Defence Motion on the Principle   **17–35**
of Non-Bis-In-Idem, November 14, 1995, the defence tried to raise *non
bis in idem* in light of the trial which had commenced in Germany. The
Trial Chamber dismissed the defence's contention, stating that, "there
can be no violation of *non-bis-in-idem*, under any known formulation of
that principle, unless the accused has already been tried. Since the
accused has not yet been the subject of a judgment on the merits on
any of the charges for which he has been indicted, he has not yet been
tried for those charges. As a result, the principle of *non-bis-in-idem* does
not bar his trial before this Tribunal".

Article 20 of the ICC Statute enshrines the principle of *non bis in
idem*. Under the principle of complementarity, the ICC's authority to

exercise jurisdiction in a case which has already been prosecuted before a national court is strictly limited. The ICC might only exercise jurisdiction when the requirements of Article 20(3) are met (referring to sham national trials or partial investigations and prosecutions in national courts). The Article 20 of the ICC Statute also addresses the situation of a conviction or acquittal by the ICC. No other court must try a person that has already been convicted or acquitted by the ICC for a crime set out in Article 5. In light of the fact that the Statute binds States parties only, the Court will have no power over other States which are not party to the Statute and which decide to prosecute someone acquitted or convicted by the ICC.

The Special Court for Sierra Leone provides in a similar manner to the ICTR and the ICTY, upholding the principle of *non bis in idem* in article 9 of its Statute.

B. NULLUM CRIMEN SINE LEGE

17–36   The maxim *nullum crimen sine lege* is translated "no crime without law", and originated in national law. Its entry into international law in an unequivocal form was seen in its recognition in the judgment of the Nuremberg Tribunal as well as a number of post Second World War instruments such as Article 11(2) of the Universal Declaration of Human Rights and Article 15(1) of the International Covenant on Civil and Political Rights (ICCPR).

Article 15 of the ICCPR and Article 7 of the European Convention on Human Rights (ECHR) enshrine the principle of *nullum crimen sine lege* in substantially the same terms:

> "**15.**—1. No one shall be held guilty of any criminal offence on account of any act or omission which did not constitute a criminal offence, under national or international law, at the time when it was committed. Nor shall a heavier penalty be imposed than the one that was applicable at the time when the criminal offence was committed. If, subsequent to the commission of the offence, provision is made by law for the imposition of the lighter penalty, the offender shall benefit thereby.
>
> 2. Nothing in this article shall prejudice the trial and punishment of any person for any act or omission which, at the time when it was committed, was criminal according to the general principles of law recognized by the community of nations."

The meaning and scope of the principle of *nullum crimen sine lege* has been elucidated in the jurisprudence of the ECHR. The essence of the European Court of Human Rights finding regarding this principle is that it should be "construed and applied . . . in such a way as to provide effective safeguards against arbitrary prosecution, conviction and punishment" (see *S.W. v. United Kingdom and C.R. v. United Kingdom* judgments of November 22, 1995 (Series A nos 335–B and 335–C, pp. 41–42, §§ 34–36, and pp. 68 and 69, §§ 32–34, respectively)).

17–37   In *Case of Streleyz, Kessler and Krenz v. Germany* (Applications nos 34044/96, 35532/97 and 44801/March 98, 22, 2001, para. 50) the European Court of Human Rights examined the contours of the principles in Article 7(1) by reaffirming the principles set out in *S.W. v. United Kingdom and C.R. v. United Kingdom* where it was stated that:

> "as the Court held in its *Kokkinakis v. Greece* judgment of May 25, 1993 (Series A no. 260–A, p. 22, Á 52), Article 7 is not confined to prohibiting the retrospective application of the criminal law to an accused's disadvantage: it also embodies, more generally, the principle that only the law can define a crime and prescribe a penalty (*nullum crimen, nulla poena sine lege*) and the principle that the criminal law must not be extensively construed to an accused's detriment, for instance by analogy. From these principles it follows that an offence must be clearly defined in the law. In its aforementioned judgment the Court added that this requirement is satisfied where the individual can know from the wording of the relevant provision and, if need be, with the assistance of the courts' interpretation of it, what acts and omissions will make him criminally liable."

The contours of *nullum crimen sine lege*, also prohibit judges legislating new substantive law (subject to the recognition that "[h]owever clearly drafted a legal provision may be, in any system of law, including criminal law, there is an inevitable element of judicial interpretation. There will always be a need for elucidation of doubtful points and for adaptation to changing circumstances [. . .] Article 7 of the Convention cannot be read as outlawing the gradual clarification of the rules of criminal liability through judicial interpretation from case to case, provided that the resultant development is consistent with the essence of the offence and could reasonably be foreseen": *S.W. v. United Kingdom and C.R. v. United Kingdom* quoted in *Case of Streleyz, Kessler and Krenz v. Germany* (Applications nos. 34044/96, 35532/97 and 44801/98, March 22, 2001, para. 50) which would contravene the doctrine of separation of powers (the constitutional aspect of the principle of *nullum crimen sine lege*); require the law-makers to draft clearly defined offences (the legislative aspect of this principle); and require judicial restraint on the part of judges in interpreting the definitions of crimes (the interpretative aspect of the principle). This is subject to the recognition that "However clearly drafted a legal provision may be, in any system of law, including criminal law, there is an inevitable element of judicial interpretation. There will always be a need for elucidation of doubtful points and for adaptation to changing circumstances [. . .] Article 7 of the Convention cannot be read as outlawing the gradual clarification of the rules of criminal liability through judicial interpretation from case to case, provided that the resultant development is consistent with the essence of the offence and could reasonably be foreseen" (*S.W. v. United Kingdom and C.R. v. United Kingdom* quoted in *Case of Streleyz, Kessler and Krenz v. Germany* (Applications nos 34044/96, 35532/97 and 44801/March 98, 22, 2001, para. 50)).

Article 22(2) of the ICC Statute elaborates on the *nullum crimen sine lege* principle in its interpretative aspect. It requires judicial restraint in defining a crime within the Court's jurisdiction, by requiring that the definition of these crimes be strictly construed and not extended by analogy. A bar to an extension by analogy of the crimes within the Court's jurisdiction seeks to ensure that substantially new crimes are not created. As part of the strict construction of the Statute, any ambiguity in a definition must be interpreted to the advantage of an accused person.

17–38

The fact that no Court exists with jurisdiction to adjudicate crimes proscribed by international law at the time the offences were committed is not a bar to prosecution and not a violation of the principle of *nullum crimen sine lege*. In the *High Command Trial* the Tribunal stated, "Even after the crime is charged to have been committed we know of no principle of justice that would give the defendant a vested right to a trial only in an existing forum. In the exercise of its sovereignty the State has the right to set up a Tribunal at any time it sees fit and confer jurisdiction on it to try violators of its criminal laws."

The fact that a Tribunal reserves its position as to the definition or interpretation of a defence (such as diminished responsibility) does not offend the principle of *nullum crimen sine lege* (see *Prosecutor v. Delalic et al.*, Judgment, Appeals Chamber, February 20, 2001, para. 576).

On the international plane the principle of *nullum crimen sine lege* functions to ensure that the law is sufficiently certain that States might know what their obligations are to an international Tribunal. The complementarity provisions of the ICC Statute mean that States have the right to prosecute offenders in the first instance and only when the strict conditions of Article 17 read with Article 20 are met, that jurisdiction might be deferred to the Court. States will thus require certainty regarding the nature of the crimes within the Court's jurisdiction, as a pre-requisite to their exercising their primary right to prosecute (see further Bruce Broomhall, Nullum Crimen Sine Lege, 447 at 451, in Otto Triffterer, *Commentary on the Rome Statute of the International Criminal Court: Observers' Notes, Article by Article*).

17–39   The controversy in the Nuremberg Tribunal's treatment of the *nullum crimen sine lege* principle, when faced with the argument that waging an aggressive war was not a crime in 1939, had a cautionary impact on the legislator's acceptance of the subject-matter jurisdiction of the ad hoc Tribunal. In his report, the Secretary-General stated that the ICTY would "apply rules [. . .] which are beyond any doubt part of customary law". See *Report of the Secretary-General pursuant to paragraph 2 of Security Council Resolution 808* (1993), May 3, 1993, UN Doc 5/25704 at 9. In the *Prosecutor v. Delalic et al.*, Judgment, February 20, 2001, para. 170, the Appeals Chamber endorsed an interpretation of the Secretary-General's statement that violations of common Article 3 of the Geneva Conventions had been criminalised for the first time with the establishment of the ICTR, as referring to the fact that "provisions for international jurisdiction over such violations were *expressly* made for the first time" rather than that the Security-Council was making new law: "This is so because the Security Council when it established the ICTR was not creating new law but was *inter alia* codifying existing customary rules for the purposes of the jurisdiction of the ICTR." See also *Prosecutor v. Erdemović*, Appeals Chamber, Joint Separate Opinion of Judge McDonald and Judge Vohrah, para. 78, and compare with Judge Cassese's (Separate and Dissenting Opinion of Judge Cassese, para. 11) rejection of a policy-oriented approach to criminal law as running foul of the principle of *nullum crimen sine lege*.)

C. NULLA POENA SINE LEGE

17–40   International instruments recognise the *nulla poena sine lege* principle which prohibits retroactive penalties. These instruments prohibit punishment being imposed which is more severe than would have been permissible at the time of the commission of the offence in question (see Universal Declaration of Human Rights, article 11(2); European Convention on Human Rights, article 7(1)). International Covenant on Civil and Political Rights, article 15(1) provides:

> "1. No one shall be held guilty of any criminal offence on account of any act or omission. Which did not constitute a criminal offence, under national or international law, at the time when it was committed. Nor shall a heavier penalty be imposed than the one that was applicable at the time when the criminal offence was committed. If subsequent to the commission of the offence, provision is made by law for the imposition of a light penalty, the offender shall benefit thereby.
> 2. Nothing in this Article shall prejudice the trial and punishment of any person for any act or omission which, at the time when it was committed, was criminal according to the general principles of law recognised by the community of nations."

The European Court of Human Rights has interpreted this principle (along with *nullum crimen sine lege*) to require that the law be "accessible" as well as "foreseeable" (see *SW v. United Kingdom*, 335–B European Court of Human Rights (Series A) at paras 35–36 (1995)).

This principle is enshrined in Article 23 of the ICC Statute. It "serves as a limit on the discretionary powers of the Court, which cannot impose punishment that is not set out in the Statute, or provided in accordance with its delegated legislation, and specifically the Rules of Procedure and Evidence" (see William A. Schabas, Nullum Poena Sine Lege, 463 at 466 in Otto Triffterer, *Commentary on the Rome Statute of the International Criminal Court: Observers' Notes, Article by Article*).

D. NON-APPLICABILITY OF STATUTE OF LIMITATIONS

The need to address national statutes of limitations applicable even **17–41** to the gravest crimes such as those within the jurisdiction of the ad hoc Tribunals and the ICC, led to international and regional responses through Resolutions and the signing of treaties. The need to sign such treaties arose from the fact that national statutes of limitations had the effect of barring prosecution and punishment of these serious crimes. Accordingly, on November 11, 1970, a little after the tenth instrument of ratification was deposited with the UN Secretary-General, the 1968 Convention on the Non-Applicability of Statutory Limitations to War Crimes and Crimes Against Humanity ("the 1968 Convention") came into force (754 UNTS 73). The movement to eliminate statutory limitations was taken up by the Council of Europe, in the signing of the European Convention on the Non Applicability of Statutory Limitation to Crimes Against Humanity and War Crimes of January 25, 1974 (ETS 82).

The 1968 Convention noted that none of the instruments, conventions or declarations relating to the prosecution of either war crimes or crimes against humanity provided for a period of limitations. It also noted that these crimes are amongst the gravest in international law. In order to ensure that national laws allowing for statutes of limitations to prevent punishment in respect of ordinary crimes do not apply to the international crimes (war crimes or crimes against humanity) the treaty requires States parties to adopt specific legislative or other measures to this effect (see article IV). In addition, these legislative or other measures must make possible the extradition of persons for these crimes in accordance with international law (see article III).

17–42   Although the low ratification status of the UN treaty has left its status as a customary rule contentious, Article 29 of the ICC Statute has provided clarification in its progressive development of this issue. It provides that the crimes falling within the subject-matter jurisdiction shall not be subject to any statute of limitations. No comparable provision can be found in the ICTY, ICTR or Special Court for Sierra Leone Statutes, with the implicit recognition that no such limitations would be applicable. This was confirmed by the ICTY Trial Chamber in *Mrda* which stated: "As for the issue of the lapse of time between the commission of the crime and the trial, the Trial Chamber recalls that the crimes against humanity and war crimes over which the Tribunal exercises jurisdiction belong to the most serious category of crimes. The importance of international prosecution of the perpetrators of such serious crimes diminishes only slightly over the years, if at all. On this point it is important to recall Article 1 of the *Convention on the Non-Applicability of Statutory Limitations to War Crimes and Crimes Against Humanity* (ratified by the former Yugoslavia on June 9, 1970 and currently in force in Bosnia and Herzegovina), which stipulates that such crimes are not subject to statutory limitation. For crimes of a seriousness justifying their exclusion from statutory limitation, the Trial Chamber considers that a lapse of time of almost twelve years between the commission of the crimes and sentencing proceedings is not so long as to be considered a factor for mitigation" (*Prosecutor v. Mrda*, Sentencing Judgment, ICTY Trial Chamber, March 31, 2004, at paras 103–104). The delegates at ICC could have adopted a similar approach to the issue of statutes of limitations as the ICTY, ICTR and Special Court for Sierra Leone, but in light of the complementarity of jurisdiction between the Court and national courts, it chose an explicit approach. An express provision ensures that when the Court seeks to exercise jurisdiction in accordance with Article 17 of the Statute, national authorities do not raise national statutes of limitation applicable to extradition to bar surrender to the Court.

On the possibility that Article 29 imposes substantive obligations on national authorities prohibiting statutes of limitations for these crimes, see William A. Schabas, "Non-Applicability of Statute of Limitations", 523 at 526, in Otto Triffterer, *Commentary on the Rome Statute of the International Criminal Court: Observers' Notes, Article by Article*.

Like the ICC, the Cambodian Extraordinary Chambers have opted for an express approach to the issue of statutes of limitation. Article 3 of the law proclaimed by the Cambodian government setting out the Extraordinary Chambers' jurisdiction extends the national statute of limitations for a further 20 years for homicide, torture and religious persecution. Further, acts of genocide (Article 4) and crimes against humanity (article 5) are specifically deemed to have no statute of limitations.

E. AMNESTIES AND TRUTH & RECONCILIATION COMMISSIONS

Amnesties enacted by national governments may come into conflict **17–43** with the jurisdiction of the ad hoc Tribunals and the ICC. Given the increasing use of amnesties during contemporary periods of national transition, this is an important issue in international criminal practice. Countries which have recently used an amnesty include: South Africa (Promotion of National Unity and Reconciliation Act 34 of 1995), Democratic Republic of the Congo (Lusaka Ceasefire Agreement 1999), Sudan (Sudan Peace Agreement April 21, 1997), Russian Federation (Chechnya Conflict July 1, 2003), Haiti (Governors Island Agreement July 1993), Argentina (Full Stop Law 1986), Brazil (Constitution 1988), El Salvador (1993), Chile (1978), Bulgaria, Hungary, Uganda, Cambodia, Uruguay, Guatemala, Honduras, Nicaragua, Namibia, Suriname and Columbia (proposed).

Given the ICTY, ICTR and ICC Statutes' silence on amnesties, a key question which the ICC is likely to face in the near future is whether, and to what extent, the ICC should defer to national transition to peace programmes involving legislative amnesties. The ICC, on the basis of the principle of complementarity, might consider the State unwilling or unable (Article 17) to prosecute the crimes that fall within its jurisdiction and enact for arrest and surrender of the persons to whom amnesty has been granted. Other circumstances in which the ICC deals with amnesties could be: by the prosecutor exercising his discretion to investigate (Article 15); in admissibility proceedings (Articles 18–19); or in deciding whether there have been genuine national proceedings against an accused (Article 20). Striking the appropriate balance between preventing impunity and respecting the rights of the subject State to exercise its national criminal jurisdiction will be no easy feat. Should the ICC choose to override a domestic amnesty, this could be a significant in-road into a State's sovereignty, and a fundamental erosion of the complementarity principle.

Some commentators suggest that the general international law climate which informed the development of the ICC Statute is important in determining how the Court should treat amnesties. Regarding the crimes of genocide, acts of torture and "grave breaches" of the Geneva Conventions of 1949, there is, in their respective treaties, duties to investigate, and/or criminalise, and/or prosecute. For example:

- Article 1 *Convention on the Prevention and Punishment of the Crime of Genocide*: "obligation to punish". Note also—*Reservations to the Convention on Genocide Advisory Opinion*, ICJ Reports, 1951, p. 15: "amnesty internationally unlawful".
- Article 4 *UN Convention Against Torture and Other Cruel, Inhuman and Degrading Treatment or Punishment*: "ensure that all acts of torture are offences under its criminal law [. . .] make these offences punishable by appropriate penalties which take into account their grave nature".
- Articles 49, 50, 129, 146 common to the four *Geneva Conventions of 1949* provide: "The High Contracting Parties undertake to enact any legislation necessary to provide effective penal sanctions for persons committing, or ordering to be committed, any of the grave breaches of the present Convention [. . .] Each

High Contracting Party shall be under the obligation to search for persons alleged to have committed, or to have ordered to be committed, such grave breaches, and shall bring such persons, regardless of their nationality, before its own courts".

These obligations now appear to be recognised as part of customary law. For example, in *Prosecutor v. Furundžija*, Trial Chamber Judgment, December 10, 1998, *obiter* para. 155, the Chamber stated: "it would be senseless to argue, on the one hand, that on account of the jus cogens value of the prohibition against torture, treaties or customary rules providing for torture would be null and void ab initio, and then be unmindful of a State say, taking national measures authorising or condoning torture or absolving its perpetrators through an amnesty law". Likewise, in *Priebke*, Military Court of Rome, July 22, 1997 para. 1.1.14(d), the Court noted that "the principle of imprescriptibility of war crimes and crimes against humanity enjoys the objective character of 'jus cogens'". For an alternative view of the position with respect to war crimes and crimes against humanity see *Barbie*, French Cour de Cassation, Chambre Criminelle, Judgment, January 26, 1984, 78 ILR 125.

However, with respect to other international crimes, while there may be a clear legal trend in state practice towards the inapplicability of domestic amnesties, there is no consistency of state practice. For state practice in favour of the incompatibility of amnesties with international crimes see:

- *UN Principles of International Cooperation for the Detection, Arrest, Extradition and Sentence of Persons that Commit War Crimes or Crimes Against Humanity*, adopted by UN Resolution 3074, December 3, 1973: These principles provide that states will not pass any law which may jeopardise their obligations related to the detection, arrest, extradition and sentencing of a person that has committed war crimes or crimes against humanity.

- Article 18 of the *Declaration on the Protection of All Persons from Enforced Disappearance* states that persons responsible for acts of enforced disappearance "shall not benefit from any special amnesty law or similar measure that might have the effect of exempting them from any criminal proceeding or sanction" (GA Resolution 47/133 of December 18, 1992).

- More persuasively, the Sierra Court for Sierra Leone has issued several decisions dismissing challenges to the Court's jurisdiction based on the amnesty contained within the Lome Peace Accord of 1999. These include: *Prosecutor v. Kallon and Kamara*, Decision on Challenge to Jurisdiction: Lome Accord Amnesty, March 13, 2004, Appeals Chamber, SCSL-2004–15 & 16-AR72(E); *Prosecutor v. Moinina Fofana*, Decision on Preliminary Motion on Lack of Jurisdiction: Illegal Delegation of Jurisdiction by Sierra Leone, SCSL-2004–14-AR72(E), May 25, 2004, Appeals Chamber; *Prosecutor v. Allieu Kondewa*, Decision on Lack of Jurisdiction/Abuse of Process: Amnesty provided by Lome Accord, SCSL-2004–14-AR72(E), May 25, 2004, Appeals Chamber; *Prosecutor v. Augustine Gbao*, Decision on Preliminary Motion on the Invalidity of the Agreement between the United Nations and the Government of Sierra Leone on the Establishment of the Special Court, SCSL-2004–15-AR72(E), May 25, 2004.

These decisions have essentially held that any national amnesty granted by Sierra Leone cannot operate to exclude liability for crimes under international law which are the subject of universal jurisdiction; nor can it deprive international courts, such as the Sierra Leone hybrid tribunal, of jurisdiction. The decisions are premised on article 10 of the Special Court's statute.

- Likewise, the national law implementing the Cambodia Extraordinary Chamber provides in Article 40 that the "Royal Government of Cambodia shall not request an amnesty or pardon for any persons who may be investigated for or convicted of crimes" within the jurisdiction of the Chambers. This reflects the position taken in article 11 of the UN Agreement with the Government of Cambodia which clarifies that the scope of one pardon granted by the Cambodian Government in 1996 is subject to review by the Extraordinary Chambers.

State practice which may be taken to support the compatibility of amnesties with international crimes includes:

- *AZAPO & Others v. President of the Republic of South Africa*, 1996, 17/96, SA 671, CC, SA Const Ct. In this case, the South African Constitutional Court upheld the legality of the amnesty law associated with the South African Truth and Reconciliation Commission, as neither violating the South African Constitution nor international law. As far as international law was concerned, the Court distinguished the circumstances, and attendant obligations of international conflicts from those occurring within a sovereign state. With the latter, it was argued, it is the state itself that is best equipped to determine measures to facilitate reconciliation and reconstruction.

While a specific prohibition of amnesties for international crimes is, as yet, lex ferenda, the position is somewhat stronger for the incompatibility of amnesties with international human rights law. For example, on several occasions, the various international and regional Human Rights Committees have made clear that the application of amnesty laws to serious human rights abuses is inconsistent with these international obligations:

- The UN Human Rights Commission has reported on the illegality of amnesty laws in Uruguay and Argentina: *Report of June 21, 1985*, UN Doc. E/CN.4/Sub.2/1985/16/Rev.1; *Rodriguez v. Uruguay*, July 19, 1994, 118 ILR 163; *Comentarios al informe Argentino*, April 5, 1995, UN Doc. CCPR/C/79/Add 46.
- The UN Human Rights Committee, in its General Comment No. 20 stated "amnesties are generally incompatible with the duty of Statues to investigate [acts of torture]".
- The UN Sub-Commission on the Prevention of Discrimination and Protection of Minorities has opposed the application of amnesties to serious violations of human rights: *Compilation of General Comments and General Recommendations Adopted by Human Rights Treaty Bodies*, 1994, UN Doc HRI\GEN\I\Rev.1 at 30.
- Amnesties have also been rejected by the Inter-American Court of Human Rights in *Garay Hermosilla et al. v. Chile* (Case 10.843, Report 36/96, October 15, 1996), *Chumbivilcas v. Peru* (Case 10.559, Report 1/96, March 1, 1996) and in the *Barrios Altos Case* (*Chumbipuma Aguirre et al. v. Peru*, Judgment of March 14, 2001, Inter-Am Ct HR, Ser C, No. 75, 2001 at paras 41–44).

A purposive approach to amnesties may well be adopted by the ICC until the law is clarified with respect to each particular type of international crime. As such, any state asserting amnesties for international crimes based on customary international law may be acting contrary to *jus cogens*. Further, for treaty crimes which are subject to a conventional obligation of *aut dedere aut judicare* (the obligation to submit the matter to the relevant authorities for prosecution in the same manner as national crimes), State parties adopting blanket amnesties or politically inspired amnesty legislation, may be in breach of their international obligations. On the other hand, where the international crime has no associated duty to submit for prosecution, state parties will not be in breach of international law in enacting an amnesty law.

Although the ICC Statute does not expressly conclude the issue and the general international law position is unsettled, some guidance can be inferred by interpreting the other provisions of the Rome Statute. It is not clear whether the "unwilling or unable" component of article 17(1)(b) of the ICC Statute would apply where there has been no specific investigation but an amnesty law has been passed. Presumably a decision by a national jurisdiction not to prosecute, following an investigation conducted under the guise of an effectively functioning Truth and Reconciliation Commission ("TRC"), would satisfy article 17(1)(b) on the basis of the complementarity principle. However, the imposition of an amnesty by legislation, could be construed as inconsistent with an intention to bring someone to justice under article 17(2)(c).

It should be noted here that an effective TRC is widely heralded as mirroring the South African model in which:

- Participants were required to give a full confession leading to public humiliation (by the broadcasting of testimony on national television);
- A lifetime ban on the participant holding a future position of public authority was imposed; and
- The payment of compensation by the participant to his or her victim/s was ordered.

It is perhaps conceivable that an amnesty targeted at national reconciliation, for low key perpetrators (reinforced by non-prosecutorial alternatives, such as a TRC), accompanying investigation and prosecution for those bearing greatest responsibility for the alleged crimes, could, of itself, provide the essential purpose of the "enforcement of international justice" (ICC Preamble). Whether this is an interpretation that the ICC will recognise is another matter. It is possible that the ICC could allow an amnesty for those bearing greatest responsibility to stand, on the basis that overriding a democratically adopted, alternative programme for accountability, seemingly not engineered in bad faith, would not be in the interests of justice. But, regardless of which approach the ICC adopts on limited and purposive amnesty laws, it seems clear that despite the absence of express authority in the ICC Statute, a blanket amnesty would appear to be inconsistent with the object and purpose of the Court (Article 31 *Vienna Convention on the Law of Treaties*).

Devising a pragmatic strategy for amnesties will require the ICC to assess the political and military context of any amnesty within the subject State. Issues such as whether intense military pressure not to prosecute falls within the category of "inability"; or whether a reluctance to jeopardise a democratic transition constitutes "unwillingness" within the terms of the Statute, will inevitably fall to the Court for resolution. It is arguable that an international judicial body is not the most competent, or appropriate, institution to assess the threat of the military in a particular state; or the likely effect of prosecutions on the stability of the State's political system. On the other hand, the strength of the ICC is that it can operate in a purely legal context, with none of the internal constraints that impose upon the domestic situation. An international court can take a stance that a domestic legal system operating under a precarious governmental mandate feels unable to take. Further, the ICC is sufficiently removed, and with such an authority that it can do so, potentially without triggering widespread instability.

As a final point, it must be noted that despite the international legal trend disparaging amnesties, the reality is that many are in fact externally brokered with the assistance of international organisations, such as the United Nations. Such amnesties may be very difficult for the Court to overturn, as they have in effect been sanctioned by the one organisation heralded as epitomising the interests of the international community.

For further information regarding the inter-relationship between international tribunals and truth and reconciliation decisions see: *Prosecutor v. Sam Hinga Norman*, Decision on Appeal by Truth and Reconciliation Commission for Sierra Leone and Chief Samuel Hinga Norman JP against the decision of his Lordship, Mr Justice Bankole Thompson delivered on October 30, 2003 to deny the TRC's request to hold a public hearing with Chief Samuel Hinga Norman JP, Appeals Chamber, SCSL-2003–08-PT, November 28, 2003. In this decision, the Appeals Chamber prohibited an indictee, Sam Hinga Norman, from participating in a public hearing before the TRC, but allowed him to voluntarily give testimony before the TRC by means of an affidavit. On this point, see also *Prosecutor v. Augustine Gbao*, Decision on Appeal by the Truth and Reconciliation Commission for Sierra Leone Against the Decision of Judge Bankole Thompson delivered on October 30, 2003 to deny the TRC's request to hold a public hearing with Augustine Gbao, Appeals Chamber, SCSL-2004–15-PT, May 7, 2004. See also: John Dugard, "Possible Conflicts of Jurisdiction with Truth Commissions", in Cassese, Gaeta, Jones (eds), *The Rome Statute and the International Criminal Court: a Commentary* (Oxford, 2002); Sadat, *Universal Jurisdiction, National Amnesties and Truth Commissions: Reconciling the Irreconcilable* (University of Pennsylvania Press, Pennsylvania, 2003); Robinson, "Serving the Interests of Justice: Amnesties, Truth Commissions and the International Criminal Court" (2003) 14(3) *European Journal of International Law* 481.

For more information regarding amnesties see: Burke-White, "Reframing Impunity: Applying Liberal International Law Theory to an Analysis of Amnesty Legislation" (2001) 42 *Harvard International Law Journal* 467; Naqvi, "Amnesty for War Crimes: Defining the Limits of International Recognition" (2003) 85(1) *International Review of the Red Cross*, 583 at 587; Slye, "The Legitimacy of Amnesties Under International Law and General Principles of Anglo-American Law: Is a Legitimate Amnesty Possible?" (2002) *Virginia Journal of International*

Law, 173; Scharf, "Swapping Amnesty for Peace: Was there a Duty to Prosecute International Crimes in Haiti?" (1996) 31 *Texas International Law Journal* 1; Gavron, "Amnesties in the Light of Developments in International Law and the Establishment of the International Criminal Court" (2002) 51 *International and Comparative Law Quarterly* 91; Scharf, "The Amnesty Exception to the Jurisdiction of the International Criminal Court" (1999) 32 *Cornell International Law Journal*, 509.

For further guidance regarding the operation and basis of truth and reconciliation commissions see: Hayner, "Fifteen Truth Commissions— 1974 to 1994: A Comparative Study" (1994) *Human Rights Quarterly* 27; Dugard, "Reconciliation and Justice: The South African Experience" (1998) 8 *Transnational Law and Contemporary Problems* 286; Schwartz, "South Africa's Truth and Reconciliation Commission: A Functional Equivalent to Prosecution" (1997) 3 *DePaul Digest of International Law* 3.

F. IMMUNITIES AND IRRELEVANCE OF OFFICIAL CAPACITY

(1) Immunities

17–44   The Report of the International Law Commission (ILC Report) on the Work of its Forty-Eighth Session (May 6,–July 26, 1996, UN Doc A/51/10), commentary (1) to article 7, summarised the rationale for holding heads of State and government responsible. Their positions of authority mean that they have the "the power to use or to authorise the use of the essential means of destruction and to mobilize the personnel required for carrying out these crimes" by abusing the "authority and power entrusted to" them. Commentary (1) and (6) to Article 7 of the ILC Report went on to state that

> "it would be paradoxical to allow the individuals who are, in some respects, the most responsible for the crimes covered by the Code [Code of Crimes against the Peace and Security of Mankind] to invoke the sovereignty of the State and to hide behind the immunity that is conferred on them by virtue of their positions particularly since these heinous crimes shock the conscience of mankind, violate some of the most fundamental rules international law and threaten international peace and security".

At the conclusion of the First World War, the Versailles Treaty provided for the prosecution of the German Head of State, Wilhelm II. From that time onwards inroads have been made on the absolute immunity from prosecution of heads of State and government, even when they were acting in an official capacity.

However, in many national laws and under general international law, the serving head of State or government enjoys "personal" or "absolute" immunity (*ratione personae*). It must be noted that this is distinct from the "state" or "functional" immunity attaching to the actions of a State (discussed below) which is sometimes known as *ratione materiae*. Immunity *ratione personae* applies to all acts performed during the tenure of the head of State's appointment, regardless of whether performed within the scope or purported scope of the person's official functions. Likewise, lesser officials (of a head of State) and former heads of State hold the benefit of *ratione materiae* only.

This notion was contradicted with respect to immunities before national courts in *Democratic Republic of Congo v. Belgium*, Case Concerning the Arrest Warrant of April 11, 2000, Judgment, ICJ, February 14, 2002 in which the Court, adopting a purposive approach, held that foreign ministers have immunity from national jurisdiction (as opposed to immunity from prosecution in international criminal courts) whilst in office, without distinction between acts performed in an official or private capacity. In its judgment, the ICJ (at para. 78) decided that the issuance and international circulation of the Belgian arrest warrant "failed to respect the immunity from criminal jurisdiction and inviolability which the incumbent Minister for Foreign Affairs of the Democratic Republic of the Congo enjoyed under international law".

Turning to the position of immunities before international courts, a foreign minister, or a head of State outside their period of office will enjoy immunity attaching only to acts performed in an official capacity (*ratione materiae*). See *Democratic Republic of Congo v. Belgium*, Case Concerning the Arrest Warrant of April 11, 2000, Judgment, ICJ, February 14, 2002 where the ICJ held that a foreign minister may be prosecuted after leaving office only if such crimes can be regarded as being committed in their "private capacity".

There is developing law to show that there are crimes under international law (*i.e.* crimes regulated by treaties ratified by the States in question which expressly purport to facilitate the prosecution of public officials for the crimes stipulated therein) to which immunity *ratione materiae* is not applicable: *Pinochet*, Judgment, House of Lords, March 24, 1999. Thus, former heads of State have recently been held as being subject to criminal jurisdiction for official acts falling within this specific category. For example, in the case involving Senator (formerly General) Pinochet, the UK House of Lords held that Senator Pinochet, as a former head of State, did not enjoy immunity from prosecution for the international crime of torture (see *Pinochet*, Judgment, House of Lords, March 24, 1999. Following the August 26, 2004 decision by the Chilean Supreme Court stripping Senator Pinochet of his former head of state immunity from prosecution, he may now be held accountable for the kidnapping, torture and disappearance of 19 political dissidents for which charges had been previously brought. The 9 to 8 ruling by the Court does not necessarily set a precedent for other cases against Pinochet as additional decisions on immunity will have to be made in other cases.

Another interesting case to watch on this issue is *Certain Criminal Proceedings in France (Democratic Republic of the Congo v. France)* which is currently before the International Court of Justice. In this case, the ICJ has so far rejected the DRC's application for provisional measures. In its application, the DRC had sought an order to annul French judicial proceedings involving allegations of crimes against humanity and torture by the President and various serving Ministers of the DRC against citizens of the DRC.

In light of the ICC's complementary jurisdiction, the ICC Statute has sought to regulate the situation in which the ICC might seek a State's co-operation over persons and yet respect that State's treaties and laws upholding immunities (see further article 98(1) governing co-operation with respect to waiver of immunity). It does this in Article 27 by confirming that no officials are excluded from criminal responsibility for the crimes within the ICC's subject-matter jurisdiction. Additionally, "as a compromise to avoid prejudicing principles and immunities applicable within the national criminal justice systems, it was clarified by article 27 that not withstanding 'immunities or special procedural rules' individual criminal responsibility for crimes under international law exists for everybody, including all persons acting in an official capacity whatsoever, paragraph 1, and that such 'immunities or special procedural rules . . . shall not bar the Court from exercising its jurisdiction over such a person', paragraph 2" (see Otto Triffterer, Commentary on Article 27, 501, in *Commentary on the Rome Statute of the International Criminal Court: Observers' Notes, Article by Article*). For those States that seek to exercise their primary right to prosecute, national laws on immunities might require amendment, in order to exclude such immunities.

The clear reference to immunities under either national or international law in article 27(2) of the ICC Statute ensures that once the ICC has custody, the overriding norm of individual responsibility without distinction based on official capacity (see below) is not frustrated by claims of immunity *ratione personae* or *ratione materiae*.

The ICC's explicit manner of dealing with immunities from prosecution can be contrasted with the ICTY, ICTR, Sierra Leone and Cambodia, which have dealt with head of state and other immunities from prosecution using the irrelevance of official capacity doctrine (see below for further discussion). Note: article 29 of the Sierra Leone Special Court Agreement Ratification Act 2002, states that an immunity attaching to the official capacity of any person shall not bar their arrest and delivery to the Special Court. While this is an explicit provision dealing with immunities, it relates to a person's immunity from arrest, not their immunity from prosecution.

(2) Irrelevance of official capacity

17–45   Irrelevance of official capacity featured in Article VII of the Nuremberg Charter, Article VI of the Tokyo Tribunal Charter, Article 4 of Control Council Law No. 10 as well as in Articles 7 and 6 of the ICTY and ICTR Statutes respectively. It is now enshrined in Article 27 of the Rome Statute for the ICC.

The Nuremberg Tribunal expressly affirmed individual criminal responsibility for State officials pursuant to Article VII of the Nuremberg Charter (see *In Re Goering*, Annual Digest, 13 (1946, No. 92)).

The irrelevance of official capacity whether as head of State, former head of State or government representative immunity is evidenced by the proceedings brought before the two ad hoc Tribunals against State officials. The ICTR has seen indictments issued against Jean Kambanda, (Prime Minister of the Interim Government of Rwanda, with *de jure* authority and *de facto* control over members of his government, who was found guilty after pleading guilty to genocide and crimes against humanity) as well as a catalogue of government ministers (amongst others, Jerome Bicamumpaka, Minister of Foreign Affairs, Casimir Bizimungu, Minister of Health and Eliezer Niyitegeka, Minister of Information) in which proceedings are at varying stages. As for the

ICTY, the indictment and trial of Slobodan Milošević, the former President and Head of State of the Federal Republic of Yugoslavia has left no Head of State or government official unaware of the irrelevance of official capacity for the commission of crimes under international law. Indeed, the ICTY Trial Chamber expressly dismissed a challenge to its jurisdiction based on Mr Milošević's official position in *Prosecution v. Milošević*, Decision on Preliminary Motion, November 8, 2001. Indictments against several prominent African leaders, including Samuel Hinga Norman, the current Minister of the Interior for Sierra Leone and Charles Taylor, the former Liberian President, have also been issued by the Special Court for Sierra Leone.

Like the other international Tribunals, the ICC Statute rules out the possibility of a reduction of sentence on the basis of official capacity. It provides that "nor shall it, in and of itself, constitute a ground for reduction of sentence". The ad hoc Tribunals explicitly rejected the official position of an accused as a ground for mitigating punishment (see article 7 ICTY Statute, article 6 ICTR Statute, article 6(2) Sierra Leone Statute, and article 29 Cambodian Law). In practice, an official position of an accused tends to play an aggravating role in determining sentence (*Prosecutor v. Momir Nikolic*, Sentencing Judgment, ICTY Trial Chamber, December 2, 2003, para. 125; *Prosecutor v. Stakic*, Judgment, ICTY Trial Chamber, July 31, 2003, para. 913; *Prosecutor v. Deronjic*, Sentencing Judgment, ICTY Trial Chamber, March 30, 2004, para. 194).

G. AGE

The age at which criminal prosecution should occur attracted considerable debate in the case of the Special Court of Sierra Leone. The special context of the conflict, characterised by the use of child combatants, meant that the Statute of the Special Court would have to take sufficient account of the age of the perpetrators. The nature of the crimes committed meant that there was support in some circles for "juvenile offenders" (as they are referred to in Article 7(2)), being prosecuted. Article 7(1) provides that the Special Court shall have jurisdiction over persons who were fifteen years of age at the time of the commission of the offence. Although recognising the Special Court's jurisdiction over juvenile offenders, the Statute takes cognisance of internationally recognised standards of juvenile justice. The Statute does this in a number of ways. It requires the Prosecution to ensure that the child-rehabilitation programme is not compromised by the prosecution of juvenile offenders and that when appropriate resort be had to alternative truth and reconciliation mechanisms (see article 15(5)). In addition, it requires that the overall composition of the judges of the Special Court should reflect experience in a variety of fields including juvenile justice (see article 13(1)). The requirement of juvenile justice experience is mirrored in the Office of the Prosecutor (see article 15(4)). The Secretary-General's Report summarised the other juvenile justice standards implicit in the Statute. He stated, para. 37, "In a trial of a juvenile offender, the Special Court should, to the

17–46

extent possible, order the immediate release of the accused, constitute a 'Juvenile Chamber', order the separation of the trial of a juvenile from that of an adult, and provide all legal and other assistance and order protective measures to ensure the privacy of the juvenile. The penalty of imprisonment is excluded in the case of a juvenile offender, and a number of alternative options of correctional or educational nature are provided instead." (For the alternatives in lieu of imprisonment see article 7(3)(f).)

Article 26 of the ICC Statute, provides that the ICC shall not have jurisdiction over persons under the age of eighteen at the time of the alleged commission of the offence. The exclusion of the ICC's jurisdiction stems from the disparate practices of different States in settling the age at which criminal responsibility attaches to the actions of a person. Consistent with the principle of complementarity in the ICC Statute, these persons under the age of eighteen are however still liable to prosecution before national courts in accordance with national laws identifying the age at which criminal responsibility attaches. Those juvenile offenders under the age of fifteen years who are unlawfully conscripted into the armed forces of a State so as to fall within the purview of Article 8(2)(b)(xxvi) or 8(2)(e)(vii) of the Statute should not be prosecuted before national courts in light of their status as victims of crimes violating international law.

It must also be noted that advanced age is considered a mitigating factor when determining sentence according to the jurisprudence of the international tribunals (*Prosecutor v. Plavsic*, Sentencing Judgment, ICTY Trial Chamber, February 27, 2003, para. 106; *Prosecutor v. Blaškić*, Judgment, ICTY Appeals Chamber, July 29, 2004, para. 696; *Prosecutor v. Strugar*, Judgment, ICTY Trial Chamber, January 31, 2005, para. 469; *Prosecutor v. Ntakirutimana and Ntakirutimana*, Judgment and Sentence, ICTR Trial Chamber, February 21, 2003, para. 898; *Prosecutor v. Ntakirutimana and Ntakirutimana*, Judgment, ICTR Appeals Chamber, December 13, 2004, para. 569).

III. SPECIFIC DEFENCES

17–47   The jurisprudence of the ad hoc Tribunals reveals defendants have:

- tended to deny any involvement in the crimes allegedly committed, rather than rely upon specific defences. For example see: *Prosecutor v. Akayesu*, Judgment, paras 29–32 (where it was contended that "the accused did not commit, order of participate in any of the killings, beatings or acts of sexual violence alleged in the Indictment"). See also *Prosecutor v. Kordic*, Judgment, Trial Chamber, February 26, 2001, para. 11, ("The defence case for both accused amounts to a complete denial of the prosecution case, putting virtually everything in dispute . . ." "Accordingly, there is a dispute as to whether the crimes underlying the charges against these accused were committed or not"); *Prosecutor v. Furundžija*, Trial Chamber, December 10, 1998, para. 48 ("As to the specific allegations in the Amended Indictment, the Defence contended that the accused is not guilty of the crimes alleged. It was asserted that the accused was not present for any sexual assault on Witness A . . .");
- Accused have challenged the interpretation of principles of international law, such as the international character of a conflict:

Prosecutor v. Aleksovski, Judgment, Trial Chamber, June 25, 1999, para. 32 ("The Defence, however, denies the involvement of the HV in that conflict. It, therefore, disagrees with the contention that the conflict correctly may be characterised as international in nature and that the victims of the alleged acts may be considered as protected persons under the Geneva Conventions of 1949"), as well as the illegality of the internment of large numbers of Muslim men in prison camps: ("It, however, is argued that the internment of these men was permissible under international law . . ."), para. 33; and

- challenged individual criminal responsibility based upon command responsibility on the basis of not having effective control over the prison guards: (*Prosecutor v. Aleksovski*, Judgment, Trial Chamber, June 25, 1999, para. 34, ("Regarding the alleged responsibility as a superior to the perpetrators of such acts, the Defence, as previously mentioned, does not contest that the accused was the commander of Kaonik prison during the time relevant to the indictment. However, it is submitted that the accused in this capacity was responsible only for the administrative aspects of running the prison and that he, as a civilian, did not have any authority or control over the prison guards, who were either HVO soldiers or members of the Military Police"). For further challenges to command responsibility, see *e.g. Prosecutor v. Kordic*, Judgment, Trial Chamber, February 26, 2001, para. 14 (Kordic stating that he was not part of a military chain of command and thus that he gave no orders to military organisations); *Prosecutor v. Kvočka*, Judgment, Trial Chamber, November 2, 2001, para. 330 (defendant Miroslav Kvočka alleging that he held no position of authority in the camp other than an ordinary guard)).

In *Prosecutor v. Aleksovski*, Judgment, Appeals Chamber, March 24, 2000, para. 51, the Appeals Chamber held that accused persons must raise all possible defences, where necessary in the alternative, during a trial and perhaps before a trial where the Rules of Procedure and Evidence so require. It stated that in general an accused person may not raise a defence for the first time on appeal.

A. INSANITY

In contrast, to the section below on diminished responsibility, the **17–48** Appeals Chamber confirmed that a plea challenging the presumption of sanity, by a plea of insanity (lack of mental capacity) if successful, would be a complete defence to a charge and lead to acquittal (see *Prosecutor v. Delalic et al.*, Appeals Chamber, February 20, 2001, para. 582). The Chamber commented upon the nature of that defence stating: "That is a defence in the true sense, in that the defendant bears the onus of establishing it—that, more probably than not, at the time of the offence he was labouring under such a defect of reason, from disease of the mind, as not to know the nature and quality of his act or, if he did know it, that he did not know that what he was doing was wrong."

Article 31(1)(a) of the ICC Statute recognises that a person will not be criminally responsible for his or her actions when he or she suffers from a mental disease or a defect which *destroys* his or her capacity to appreciate the lawfulness of his or her conduct or "capacity to control his or her conduct to conform to the requirements of law" at the time of that person's conduct. This defence has been held to be different from diminished mental responsibility. In *Prosecutor v. Delalic et al.*, Appeals Chamber, February 20, 2001, para. 587, the Appeals Chamber highlighted the fact that the ICC defence requires the *"destruction of* the defendant's capacity (and not merely the *impairment to*), and leads to an acquittal. It is akin to the defence of insanity".

Article 31(1)(a) of the ICC Statute sets out the requirements of the M'Naghten Rules followed in common law jurisdictions for establishing the defence of insanity.

It seems that a mental disease or defect may constitute a defence where it negates the special intent of a special intent crime. However, it has been held that there is no *per se* inconsistency between an immature, narcissistic and disturbed personality and the ability to form an intent to destroy a particular protected group (for the purposes of the crime of genocide): indeed, it is the borderline unbalanced personality who is more likely to be drawn to extreme racial and ethnical hatred than the more balanced modulated individual without personality defects (see *Prosecutor v. Jelisic*, Judgment, ICTY Appeals Chamber, July 5, 2001, para. 70).

B. ALIBI

17–49   In *Prosecutor v. Delalic et al.*, Judgment, February 20, 2001, para. 581, the Appeals Chamber referred to the term "defence of alibi" in Rule 67(A)(ii) by explaining: "It is a common misuse of the word to describe an alibi as a 'defence'. If a defendant raises an alibi, he is merely denying that he was in a position to commit the crime with which he is charged. That is not a *defence* in its true sense at all. By raising that issue, the defendant does no more than require the Prosecution to eliminate the reasonable possibility that the alibi is true."

The burden of proof rests upon the Prosecution to prove a case beyond reasonable doubt "notwithstanding that the Defence raised alibi" (*Prosecutor v. Kayishema and Ruzindana*, Judgment, Trial Chamber, May 21, 1999, para. 234; upheld on appeal in *Prosecutor v. Kayishema and Ruzindana*, Judgment (Reasons), ICTR Appeals Chamber, June 1, 2001, paras 98–134; and *Prosecutor v. Musema*, Judgment, Trial Chamber, January 27, 2000, para. 108 where it was held that: "[i]n establishing its case, when an alibi defence is introduced, the Prosecution must prove, beyond any reasonable doubt, that the accused was present and committed the crimes for which he is charged and thereby discredit the alibi defence. The alibi defence does not carry a separate burden of proof. If the defence is reasonably possibly true, it must be successful."

The Trial Chamber in *Kajelijeli* quoted *Musema* approvingly and stated that "the failure of the Defence to submit credible and reliable evidence of the Accused's alibi must not be construed as an indication of his guilt" (*Prosecutor v. Kajelijeli*, Judgment and Sentence, ICTR Trial Chamber, December 1, 2003, paras 165–167). Likewise, the Trial Chamber in *Niyitegeka* found that "where the alibi is rejected, a finding of guilt does not automatically follow; the evidence must be assessed and a conviction entered only if the allegation has been proved beyond reasonable doubt" (*Prosecutor v. Niyitegeka*, Judgment and Sentence, ICTR Trial Chamber, May 16, 2003, para. 52).

This approach to the appropriate onus of proof for an assertion of alibi was also followed in *Prosecution v. Vasiljevic*, Judgment, ICTY Trial Chamber, November 29, 2002, paras 14–15. In that case, the Chamber acknowledged that the lapse of ten years between the crime and giving of evidence necessarily led to discrepancies in witness testimonies and, hence, a much more difficult task for the prosecution (at para. 21). The Chamber clarified the position by stating (at para. 15):

> "it is not sufficient for the Prosecution merely to establish beyond reasonable doubt that the alibi is false in order to conclude that his guilt has been established beyond reasonable doubt. Acceptance by the Trial Chamber of the falsity of an alibi cannot establish the opposite to what it asserts. The Prosecution must also establish that the facts alleged in the Indictment are true beyond a reasonable doubt before a finding of guilt can be made against the accused."

See also *Prosecutor v. Kamuhanda*, Judgment and Sentence, ICTR Trial Chamber, January 22, 2004, paras 83–84; *Prosecutor v. Niyitegeka*, Judgment, ICTR Appeals Chamber, July 9, 2004, para 89; *Prosecutor v. Nahimana, Barayagwiza and Ngeze*, Judgment and Sentence, ICTR Trial Chamber, December 3, 2003, para 99; and *Prosecutor v. Ndindabahizi*, Judgment and Sentence, ICTR Trial Chamber, July 15, 2004, para 25.

The appropriate weight to be given to alibi evidence was considered in the *Ntakirutimana* Appeals Chamber decision. In this Judgment, the Chamber held that "when an accused testifies in support of his or her alibi after having heard other alibi evidence, a Trial Chamber is obligated to take this into account when assessing the weight to be given to such testimony" (*Prosecutor v. Ntakirutimana and Ntakirutimana*, Judgment, ICTR Appeals Chamber, December 13, 2004, para 393). See also *Prosecutor v. Ntakirutimana and Ntakirutimana*, Judgment and Sentence, ICTR Trial Chamber, February 21, 2003, paras 294, 463–468, 529–530).

It should also be noted that the raising of an alibi defence has, in the rarest instances, been characterised as an aggravating factor in sentencing (see *Prosecutor v. Kayishema & Ruzindana*, Sentencing Judgment, ICTR Trial Chamber, May 21, 1999; and on appeal *Prosecutor v. Kayishema & Ruzindana*, Judgment (Reasons), ICTR Appeals Chamber, June 1, 2001, paras 360, 362–363). At first instance, the Trial Chamber found the assertion of an alibi and the continual protests of innocence, in light of the gravity of the crimes charged, to be an aggravating factor. In coming to this conclusion, the Chamber relied upon the *Tadić* Sentencing Judgment, in which it was held that a denial of guilt did not entitle the accused to mitigation. On appeal, while noting that in *Tadić* the denial of guilt was not an aggravating factor, the Chamber did not find it necessary to pronounce on whether the assertion of an alibi and constant denials of guilt constitute aggravating circumstances. The Chamber instead found that such an error, if this is what the Trial Chamber's view was, would not amount to an abuse of discretion, such that it could be reviewed by the Appeals Chamber. In the author's view, the characterisation of the raising of an alibi as an aggravating factor in sentencing is something of an aberration in the jurisprudence.

17–50   Rule 67 of the Rules of Procedure and Evidence of the ICTY and ICTR require that the Defence notify the Prosecutor of its intent to enter a defence of alibi or any other special defence as early as reasonably practicable and prior to the commencement of trial. Although Rule 67(B) makes it clear that failure of the defence to provide notice of its intent to rely on any of the defences in Rule 67(A)(ii) does not preclude reliance on these defences, the Trial Chamber in *Kayishema and Ruzindana*, Trial Chamber, stated that "where good cause is not shown, for the application of Rule 67(B), the Trial Chamber is entitled to take into account this failure when weighing the credibility of the defence alibi and/or any special defences presented" (*Prosecutor v. Kayishema and Ruzindana*, Decision on the Prosecution Motion for a Ruling on the Defence continued non-compliance with Rule 67(A)(ii) and with the written and oral orders of the Trial Chamber, September 3, 1998 as well as *Prosecutor v. Musema*, Judgment, Trial Chamber, January 27, 2000, para. 107 (endorsing the approach to rule 67(B) taken in *Kayishema and Ruzindana*).This approach was applied in *Semanza*, in which the Trial Chamber stated that "where, as in this case, the Defence fails to show good cause for its failure to act in accordance with Rule 67(A)(ii)(a), the Chamber may take into account this failure when weighing the credibility of the alibi defence". In the case at hand, the Chamber found that such actions suggested that the Accused's alibi was "an afterthought" (*Prosecutor v. Semanza*, Judgment and Sentence, ICTR Trial Chamber, May 15, 2003, paras 81, 147). See also *Prosecutor v. Ntagerura*, Decision on Prosecutor's Motion for Ntagerura's defence to fulfil its obligations in respect of the reciprocal disclosure of evidence pursuant to rule 67(A)(ii) and 67(C), July 10, 2000, in which the Trial Chamber noted that failure to comply with the disclosure obligation regarding relying on a defence of alibi does not preclude relying on that defence).

The notification given to the Prosecutor pursuant to Rule 67(A)(ii) must specify the place or places the accused claims to have been present at the time of the alleged crime and the names and addresses of the witnesses as well as any other evidence which the accused intends to rely upon.

C. Intoxication

17–51   Article 31(1)(b) of the ICC Statute sets out intoxication as a ground for excluding criminal responsibility. Article 31(1)(b) is a *via media* between not recognising intoxication at all as a defence and recognising it as an unconditional defence, see further Albin Eser, Grounds for excluding Criminal Responsibility, 527 at 546 in Otto Triffterer, *Commentary on the Rome Statute of the International Criminal Court: Observers' Notes, Article by Article*:

> "The person is in a state of intoxication that destroys that person's capacity to appreciate the unlawfulness or nature of his or her conduct, or capacity to control his or her conduct to conform to the requirements of law, unless the person has become voluntarily intoxicated under such circumstances that the person knew, or disregarded the risk, that, as a

result of the intoxication, he or she was likely to engage in conduct constituting a crime within the jurisdiction of the Court."

For intoxication to exclude criminal responsibility the person has to be in a "state of intoxication", which State must stem from the consumption of exogenic substances acting as intoxicants rather than from any endogenic causes (see Albin Eser, Grounds for excluding Criminal Responsibility, 527 at 547 in Otto Triffterer, *Commentary on the Rome Statute of the International Criminal Court: Observers' Notes, Article by Article*).

The person's state of intoxication must destroy that "person's capacity to appreciate the unlawfulness or nature of his or her conduct, or capacity to control his or her conduct to conform to the requirements of law". Diminished capacity will not be sufficient for the purposes of excluding responsibility on this ground, the intoxicant must destroy a person's capacity to appreciate the unlawfulness of his or her conduct or to control it according to the requisites of the law.

Intoxication will not preclude responsibility when a person has voluntarily become intoxicated, knowing or aware of the risk that the intoxication will result in him or her engaging in a crime within the jurisdiction of the Statute. For an example of a case where intoxication was pleaded as a defence (and rejected) see UNTAET case of *Prosecutor v. Carlos Soares Carmona*, Judgment, April 19, 2001. Intoxication was also pleaded and rejected in *Prosecutor v. Simić*. In this case, the Trial Chamber found that "voluntary intoxication is not a mitigating factor to the crimes committed by Milan Simić" (*Prosecutor v. Simić*, Sentencing Judgment, ICTY Trial Chamber, October 17, 2002, para. 74).

D. Self-Defence, Defence of Another Person or Property

Article 31(1)(c) of the ICC Statute excludes criminal responsibility for an accused whose actions might otherwise constitute a crime in order to defend himself or another, and in limited circumstances when he acts to defend property. It provides that criminal responsibility is excluded if at the time of the person's conduct: **17–52**

> "The person acts reasonably to defend himself or herself or another person or, in the case of war crimes, property which is essential for the survival of the person or another person or property which is essential for accomplishing a military mission, against an imminent and unlawful use of force in a manner proportionate to the degree of danger to the person or the other person or property protected. The fact that the person was involved in a defensive operation conducted by forces shall not in itself constitute a ground for excluding criminal responsibility under this subparagraph."

In order for a person to successfully raise this ground for excluding criminal responsibility they would have to establish the existence of an "imminent and unlawful use of force". This does not require actual physical force it could include psychological threats which have an immediate coercive effect (see Albin Eser, Grounds for excluding

Criminal Responsibility, 527 at 549 in Otto Triffterer, *Commentary on the Rome Statute of the International Criminal Court: Observers' Notes, Article by Article*). The force must be unlawful, that is, contrary to any law or order. The person may act in self-defence or defence of another not only to protect his life or their life, but also his bodily harm or theirs as well as his or their liberty.

17–53   In order to invoke this ground to exclude criminal responsibility, the person will have to act "reasonably" and in a manner "proportionate to the degree of danger". Reasonableness implies a necessary and efficacious response, that is, the defence must "neither be excessive by causing more harm to the aggressor than is needed for diverting the attack or a danger not inapt by implying inefficient or otherwise futile means" (Albin Eser, Grounds for excluding Criminal Responsibility, 527 at 549 in Otto Triffterer, *Commentary on the Rome Statute of the International Criminal Court: Observers' Notes, Article by Article*). The only descriptive criterion for determining proportionality is use of the phrase "proportionate to the degree of danger to that person or other person or property protected". This means that when the degree of danger rises to the level of a threat to life or extreme bodily harm, defensive actions calculated to kill would be permissible.

Article 31(1)(c) recognises defence of property for the specific purposes of survival of that person or another, or for accomplishing a military mission. Such defence is limited by the requirements that there be an imminent and unlawful use of force, and that the defence of the property is done in a proportionate manner to the degree of danger to the property protected.

In the situations described in Article 31(1)(c), the existence of the use of force and the danger to that person or another or property essential for accomplishing a military mission must objectively exist and cannot only be the subjective belief of the defendant for criminal responsibility to be excluded (see Albin Eser, Grounds for excluding Criminal Responsibility, 527 at 549 in Otto Triffterer, *Commentary on the Rome Statute of the International Criminal Court: Observers' Notes, Article by Article*). When a defendant is not objectively faced with imminent use of force or danger he might rely on mistake of fact in Article 32 of the Statute.

In *Prosecutor v. Kordic*, Judgment, February 26, 2001, para. 449, the Trial Chamber recognised that self-defence is not provided for in the ICTY Statute as a ground for excluding criminal responsibility but that "defences" form a part of general principles of criminal law which the ICTY is obliged to consider in its decisions. In responding to the Defence claim that the Bosnian Croats were acting in self-defence, the Chamber, para. 452, referred to Article 31(1)(c) of the ICC Statute. Article 31(1)(c) provides that the involvement of a person in a defensive operation does not of itself constitute a ground for excluding criminal responsibility. The *Kordic* Trial Chamber emphasised that any arguments raising self-defence must accordingly be assessed on their own facts and circumstances, which will form the basis for a Trial Chamber's decision regarding whether self-defence applies to any of the charges. On Appeal, the *Kordić and Čerkez* Appeals Chamber rejected the argument that the Prosecutor was obliged to negate the Accused's assertion of self-defence. It stated that "the existence or the scope of self-defence under international law and the Statute is an issue the

Accused must demonstrate. Its absence is not an element of a crime that the Prosecution must prove beyond reasonable doubt" (*Prosecutor v. Kordić and Čerkez*, Judgment, Appeals Chamber, December 17, 2004, paras 835–838).

In *Prosecutor v. Stakic*, the Trial Chamber recognised that "as a matter of principle" soldiers have a "right to self-defence". However, the Chamber stressed that any armed response must be "proportionate to" and "temporally connected with" "the initial attack". The Defence was unable to establish these elements in relation to the actions under consideration, which the Trial Chamber held were "disproportionate" and "illegal" (*Prosecutor v. Stakic*, Judgment, ICTY Trial Chamber, July 31, 2003, paras 153–154).

E. SUPERIOR ORDERS

Members of the armed forces are expected to unquestioningly obey lawful orders of their superiors. However, "the obedience of a soldier is not the obedience of an automaton" (see *In re Ohlendorf (Einsatzgruppen Trial)*, United States Military Tribunal at Nuremberg, April 10, 1948, 15 ILR 656 (1948)).

17–54

If defendants were permitted to rely upon superior orders to avoid criminal responsibility an absurdity would result, because each person in the chain of command could claim that they followed superior orders of their government or superior so that only the dictator as the possessor of law making powers and supreme authority is liable (see *In re Von Leeb*, United States Military Tribunal at Nuremberg, Germany, October 28, 1948, 15 ILR 376 (1949)).

The absence of a defence of superior orders was recognised in Article 8 of the International Military Charter and is recognised in Article 7(4) of the ICTY Statute and Article 6(4) of the ICTR Statute. These instruments all recognise that acting pursuant to government or superior orders might be considered in mitigation of punishment (see, *e.g.*, the trial of *Gozawa Sadaichi*, British Military Court at Singapore, February 4, 1946 in which the Court took into account Chiba Masami and Tanno Shozo's status as subordinates in sentence. Also see the *Trial of Willem von Leeb et al.* (the High Command Trial), LRWC Vol. XII, pp. 74–75 for the application of the superior order plea to a commanding officer who knows that the men under his command are violating international law in pursuance of orders of his superiors passed to the men independently of the commander, ("by doing nothing he cannot wash his hands of international responsibility") and the Tribunal's reference to mitigating circumstances in accordance with Control Council Law No. 10).

Article 33(1) of the ICC Statute affirms the general principle that the fact that a subordinate commits a crime within the jurisdiction of the Statute pursuant to an order of a government or superior, whether civilian or military, will not relieve him of criminal responsibility. However, Article 33(1) determines the particular circumstances in which a subordinate shall be relieved of criminal responsibility. Thus unlike the ad hoc Tribunals, the ICC Statute recognises that a person

17–55

who satisfies the cumulative conditions of Article 33(1) shall be relieved of criminal responsibility, and will not only possibly have his sentence mitigated. Relief from such criminal responsibility will only be in circumstances when that person does not know that the order followed was unlawful which will only be in circumstances when the order is not manifestly unlawful.

The first leg of the three-fold test set out in Article 33(1) of the ICC Statute, to support a finding of absence of criminal responsibility, requires the subordinate to be under a legal obligation to obey the order of a government or superior (whether military or civilian) before he or she may be relieved of responsibility. Thus the crime committed by the subordinate must be committed pursuant to the order of the superior. If not, Article 33(1) will be inapplicable.

Orders of a *de facto* or *de jure* government may be issued by any of its branches by persons representing that government.

It is important that the order stems from a superior, whether civilian or military. The superior-subordinate relationship requires a superior to exercise effective control over subordinates committing the crimes within the Statute. It is not necessary that the order be given directly to the individual conducting it, as long as there is a superior–subordinate relationship between the person giving the order and the person executing it (*Prosecutor v. Naletilic and Martinovic*, Judgment, ICTY Trial Chamber, March 31, 2003, para. 61). In relation to civilian superiors, they should exercise substantially similar powers of control over subordinates as military superiors (see *Prosecutor v. Delalic et al.*, para. 378). The United States Military Tribunal at Nuremberg recognised control as determinative of the superior-subordinate relationship for the purposes of raising the defence of superior orders. (In *re Ohlendorf (Einsatzgruppen Trial)*, United States Military Tribunal at Nuremberg, April 10, 1948, 15 ILR 656 (1948)), the latter Tribunal held that superior means "superior in capacity and power to force a certain act. It does not mean superiority only in rank".

When the subordinate is under the mistaken belief that he is under an obligation to obey the orders of the superior, Article 32 of the ICC Statute on errors of fact or law would apply. In situations in which the subordinate is under a legal obligation to obey orders, and the subordinate acts out of malice of his or her own, rather than in pursuit of the order, he or she will not be able to plead superior orders (see *In re Ohlendorf & Others (Einsatzgruppen Trial)*, United States Military Tribunal at Nuremberg, April 10, 1948, 15 ILR 656 (1948)). In the *Einsatzgruppen Trial*, the Tribunal confirmed that the plea of superior orders would not avail an accused that is in accord with the principles and ideology of the superior. It stated "the doer may not plead innocence to a criminal act ordered by his superiors if he is in accord with the principle and intent of the superior . . . In order successfully to plead the defence of Superior Orders the opposition of the doer must be constant. It is not enough that he mentally rebel at the time the order is received. If at any time after receiving the order he acquiesces in its illegal character, the defence of superior orders is closed to him".

17–56   The second leg of the test for excluding criminal responsibility requires that the subordinate did not know that the order was unlawful. The inclusion of this leg of the test is to take account of genuine error on the part of a subordinate. For the subordinate to enjoy the benefits of this leg of the test, he or she would have to be unaware that the order was not lawful. The third leg of the test for excluding criminal responsibility considerably narrows the effect of the second leg of the test by disallowing the subordinate to be relieved of criminal responsibility when the order given is manifestly unlawful. Article 33(2) of the ICC Statute defines manifestly unlawful for the purposes of Article 33(1)(c) to refer to orders to commit genocide or crimes against humanity.

The notion of manifestly unlawful orders was recognised in the First World War Leipzig Trials. In the *Llandovery Castle* case, the German Supreme Court rejected the defence of obedience to superior orders. It stated: "It is certainly to be urged in favor of the military subordinates, that they are under no obligation to question the order of their superior officer, and they can count upon its legality. But no such confidence can be held to exist, if such an order is universally known to everybody, including also the accused, to be without any doubt whatever against the law". In that case the defendants had machine-gunned and shelled the survivors in the lifeboats of the Llandovery Castle (see also *High Command* Case in which the Tribunal used the phrase "illegal on its face").

When the order is manifestly unlawful or the defendant knew that the order was unlawful so as to exclude the possibility of raising Article 33(1) to avert criminal responsibility the defendant might still be able to raise his status as a subordinate in mitigation of punishment in accordance with Article 78 of the Statute. Unlike the express recognition of the mitigating effects of superior orders on punishment in the ad hoc tribunals, Article 33 makes no such provision. However, Article 78 allows the Court to take into account such factors as the gravity of the crime and individual circumstances of the convicted person in sentencing that person. In the *Llandovery Castle* case, the German Supreme Court, acknowledged that the defence of superior orders was a factor in mitigation of punishment.

A different factual matrix might graduate the defence of superior orders to a defence of duress. A factual matrix involving an immediate threat to the accused, which serves as the impulse for the accused to commit the international crime in question, might lead to a plea of duress on the part of the accused.

The difference between these two pleas might be subtle and a defence might be argued in which these pleas overlap. The *Einsatzgruppen Trial* distinguished the two pleas, applying different tests for each. For superior orders, the plea would require the accused to "show an excusable ignorance of their [orders'] illegality", whereas for duress the accused must establish a threat which is "imminent, real and inevitable". Duress and superior orders were unsuccessfully raised as overlapping defences in *Cesic*. In this case, the Trial Chamber ruled that a statement by one Prosecution witness, that the accused would not have committed a particular crime without an order to do so, was insufficient to establish a mitigating circumstance of superior orders. Likewise, the Chamber found that a reference by the accused to the danger of being killed if he did not obey orders, did not, on the balance of probabilities amount to a defence of duress (*Prosecutor v. Cesic*, Sentencing Judgment, ICTY Trial Chamber, March 11, 2004, pp. 30–31). The necessity of an ignorance of illegality on the part of the accused was underscored in

Mrda, in which the Trial Chamber rejected an assertion of superior orders in mitigation of punishment, stating "the orders were so manifestly unlawful that Darko Mrda must have been well aware that they violated the most elementary laws of war and basic dictates of humanity. The fact that he obeyed such orders, as opposed to acting on his own initiative, does not merit mitigation" (*Prosecutor v. Mrda*, Sentencing Judgment, ICTY Trial Chamber, March 31, 2004, para. 67).

It appears that under certain circumstances, superior orders may constitute duress (*cf. Prosecutor v. Erdemović*, Judgment, ICTY Appeals Chamber, October 7, 1997, Separate Opinion of Judge Stephen, paras 13–16).

F. Duress and Necessity

17–57   There may be situations in which the order given by a superior is manifestly unlawful, but the defendant is faced with no moral choice in light of his being under a threat or being coerced. This threat might stem from natural causes which endanger the defendant or pressure brought to bear by someone else. This threatened harm might lead the defendant to commit a crime in violation of international law in order to avoid a greater harm or an equal personal harm. The moral choice a defendant must be able to make is the choice between right and wrong action in the absence of suffering any immediate or imminent violence. If the defendant is not able to make such a choice, and the other grounds for raising this defence are successfully raised, the defendant should not be held criminally responsible (see, for example *I G Farben Trial* (Trial of Carl Kravch *et al.*) in which the Second World War Tribunal held that a plea of duress "is a complete defence where it is given under such circumstances as to afford the one receiving it no other moral choice than to comply therewith". See also *Krupp Trial*, LRWC, Vol. X, pp. 147, 149).

The elements for successfully pleading the defence of duress in the early jurisprudence of the Second World War appear to be as follows: the act was carried out in order to avoid an immediate danger which is extremely serious to the accused or someone else and is unavoidable (see *High Command Trial* (Von Leeb *et al.*) LRWC, Vol. X, "such immediate physical peril" and *Einsatzgruppen Trial* (Trial of Otto Ohlendorf *et al.*) "the threat, however, must be imminent, real and inevitable"); the honest belief of the accused of the existence of an impending threat of serious harm (see *Krupp Trial*: "the question is to be determined from the standpoint of the honest belief of the particular accused in question [. . .] The effect of the alleged compulsion is to be determined not by objective but by subjective standards"); the accused's actions in response to the threat are proportionate to the harm threatened (see *Krupp Trial*: "Necessity is a defence when it is shown that the act charged was done to avoid an evil severe and irreparable; that there was no other adequate means of escape; and that the remedy was not disproportioned [*sic*] to the evil"). When an accused goes beyond that which is required to avoid the harm, the defence will not be upheld (see *Flick Trial*, in which two of the industrialists defendants went beyond what was required of them by the German State in their employment of State-sponsored forced labour). In the event that an accused's will coincides with those from whom the threat stems, he will be precluded from successfully raising this defence (see *Krupp Trial*, in which the Tribunal held that "if, in the execution of the illegal act, the will of the accused be not thereby over-powered but instead coincides with the will of those from whom the alleged compulsion emanates, there is no necessity justifying the illegal conduct").

The plea of duress was raised in the *High Command Trial* (*in re Von Leeb*, United States Military Tribunal at Nuremberg, Germany, October 28, 1948, 15 ILR 376 (1949)). The Military Tribunal stated as follows: "The defendants in this case who received obviously criminal orders were placed in a difficult position, but servile compliance with orders clearly criminal for fear of some disadvantage or punishment not immediately threatened cannot be recognized as a defence. To establish the defence of coercion or necessity in the face of danger there must be a showing of circumstances such that a reasonable man would apprehend that he was in such imminent physical peril as to deprive him of freedom to choose the right and refrain from the wrong." **17–58**

In *Prosecutor v. Erdemović*, Appeals Chamber, October 7, 1997, para. 19, the ICTY Appeals Chamber was faced with the question whether duress is a defence to charges of crimes within its subject-matter jurisdiction. The majority of the Appeals Chamber of the ICTY found that duress does not afford a complete defence to a soldier charged with a crime against humanity or a war crime involving the taking of innocent lives. The question whether it might constitute a defence in relation to other types of crimes was not expressly addressed.

The Appeals Chamber, Joint Separate Opinion of Judge McDonald and Vohrah, para. 50, found no consistent practice accepted as law on the issue of duress as a defence to killing innocent human beings. These findings were echoed in respect of its audit of national laws in examining general principles of law recognised by civilised nations (*Prosecutor v. Erdemović*, Joint Separate Opinion of Judge McDonald and Vohrah, Appeals Chamber, October 7, 1997, para. 72). **17–59**

In coming to the conclusion that duress is factor to be considered in mitigation of punishment only and not a defence to crimes within the ICTY's jurisdiction, the Appeals Chamber, Joint Separate Opinion of Judge McDonald and Vohrah, para. 72, relied on the specific context in which the ICTY was established, as well as the nature of the crimes over which it exercises its mandate, being the "most serious violations of international humanitarian law". The Majority, paras 75–81 rejected an approach which would involve a balancing of harms for and against killing in favour of the application of a rule "that duress does not justify or excuse the killing of an innocent person". On this approach it is irrelevant whether the victims would have been killed anyway, and that the accused would be sacrificing his life for no reason. The difficulties in weighing whether duress affords a complete defence in different scenarios are avoided when the Court is asked to consider the accused's circumstances in the "flexible but effective facility provided by mitigation of punishment" (see Joint Separate Opinion of Judge McDonald and Vohrah, para. 81).

Cassese and Stephen JJ. found the majority position untenable for similar reasons. In their separate and dissenting opinions they found that duress may be raised as a defence to the killing of innocent persons. Cassese J. argued in short that:

"(1) under international criminal law duress may be generally urged as a defence, provided certain strict requirements are met; when it cannot be admitted as a defence, duress may nevertheless be acted upon as a mitigating circumstance; (2) with regard to war crimes or crimes against humanity whose underlying offence is murder or more generally the taking of human life, no special rule of customary international law has evolved on the matter; consequently, even with respect to these offences the *general rule on duress* applies; it follows that duress may amount to a defence provided that its stringent requirements are met. For offences involving killing, it is true, however, that one of the requirements (discussed at paragraph 42 below)—proportionality—would usually not be fulfilled. Nevertheless, in exceptional circumstances this requirement might be met, for example, when the killing would be *in any case* perpetrated by persons other than the one acting under duress (since then it is not a question of saving your own life by killing another person, but of simply saving your own life when the other person will inevitably die, which may not be 'disproportionate' as a remedy)." [footnote omitted].

For Stephen J. the Anglo-American authorities rationale for an exception to the defence of duress in respect of killing of innocent persons was inapplicable to Erdemović's situation. He reasoned that when there was no balancing of one life against another, the stated rationale behind excluding killing from the ambit of duress as a defence fell away, and duress could operate as a defence. The situations when this balancing would not take place would be when an accused person was helpless to save others from being killed, because they were going to be killed in any event.

As regards the relationship between superior orders and duress, the Appeals Chamber found that obedience to superior orders is not a defence *per se* but that such obedience is a factual element which can be taken into account in addition to other considerations in assessing whether the defence of duress or mistake of fact are made out (*Prosecutor v. Erdemović*, Joint Separate Opinion of Judge McDonald and Vohrah, Appeals Chamber, October 7, 1997, para. 34).

17–60   The majority in the *Erdemović* case established an approach in which duress would not be a ground for exclusion of criminal responsibility but might be a ground for mitigating a sentence. In the earlier jurisprudence of the Second World War Tribunals, in which duress was recognised as a defence which might exclude criminal responsibility, an accused's failure to successfully raise duress still warranted the possibility of a reduction in punishment (see, for example, the arguments for reduction of sentence from the death penalty to life imprisonment in the case of doubt regarding the accused's actions not being the result of duress in *Trial of Gustav Alfred Jepsen*). This approach was confirmed by the ICTY Trial Chamber in *Prosecutor v. Mrda*, where the Chamber stated "from a legal standpoint [. . .] superior orders may be pleaded in mitigation independently of duress, and vice versa". In any event, the lack of corroborating evidence for the accused's statements relating to duress meant that the Chamber was unable to accept it as a mitigating circumstance (*Prosecutor v. Mrda*, Sentencing Judgment, ICTY Trial Chamber, March 31, 2004, paras 65–66). An argument of duress was also dismissed as being without merit in *Kamuhanda*, where the ICTR Trial Chamber emphasised that the claimed duress had to occur prior to the acts for which the Accused was charged in order to make a valid argument (*Prosecutor v. Kamuhanda*, Judgment and Sentence, ICTR Trial Chamber, January 22, 2004, paras 78–79). Unlike the ICTY, the ICC Statute of the ICC recognises that duress will constitute a complete defence (that is, exclude criminal responsibility) when the pre-requisites of Article 31(1)(d) are satisfied by an accused person.

Article 31(1)(d) of the ICC Statute provides for duress to be a ground for excluding responsibility of an accused person when the conditions set out in that article are met. Article 31(1)(d) provides that a person shall not be criminally responsible under the ICC Statute if at the time of that person's conduct:

> "The conduct which is alleged to constitute a crime within the jurisdiction of the Court has been caused by duress resulting from a threat of imminent death or of continuing or imminent serious bodily harm against that person or another person, and the person acts necessarily and reasonably to avoid this threat, provided that the person does not intend to cause a greater harm than the one sought to be avoided. Such a threat may either be:
> (i) Made by other persons; or
> (ii) Constituted by other circumstances beyond that person's control."

Thus the threat to that person or another must stem from someone else or a particular circumstance beyond that person's control such as from natural forces. The threat must be of "imminent death" or serious bodily harm with the result that that person is under duress, in the sense that he or she feels that they are unable to "withstand the threat and, thus, is driven to the relevant criminal conduct" (Albin Eser, Grounds for excluding Criminal Responsibility, 527 at 551 in Otto Triffterer, *Commentary on the Rome Statute of the International Criminal Court: Observers' Notes, Article by Article*).

Article 31(1)(d) regulates the nature of the response which that person under duress may take and which would not render him criminally responsible. He or she must take action that is necessary and reasonable to avoid the threat, and this action must not result in greater harm than the harm that person is seeking to avoid. For the action to be necessary there must be no other means available, for the action to be reasonable it must be effective. The subjective nature of the proportionality requirement means that even if that person's actions do not avoid the greater harm, criminal responsibility may still be precluded when he or she intends to avoid the greater harm.

In the case of necessity the threat emanates from some kind of natural circumstance rather than that of persons.

In *Prosecutor v. Aleksovski*, Appeals Chamber, March 24, 2000, para. 55, **17–61** the Appeals Chamber declined to consider whether necessity constitutes a defence under international law, whether it is the same as the defence of duress or whether the principle *iura novit curia* should be applied to the case at hand.

Military necessity might, depending on the facts, exculpate an accused person. In the *High Command Trial*, the Tribunal emphasised that the defendants were "in many instances in retreat under arduous conditions wherein their commands were in serious danger of being cut-off. Under such circumstances, a commander must necessarily make quick decisions to meet the particular situation of his command. A great deal of latitude must be accorded to him under such circumstances. What constitutes devastation beyond military necessity in these situations requires detailed proof of an operational and tactical nature". In the *Hostages Trial*, the Tribunal recognised that the Hague Regulations are "superior to military necessities of the most urgent nature except where the Regulations themselves specifically provide the contrary" and alluded to Article 23(g) of the Regulations which prohibited the "destruction of enemy property except in cases when this destruction or seizure is urgently required by the necessities of war".

Both Tribunals recognised that military necessity might also justify (within the ambit of Article 23(g) of the Regulations) the destruction by a retreating army of public and private property which might give assistance and comfort to the enemy army.

However, the successful pleading of military necessity is the exception rather than the norm. In the *Milch Trial* and the *Krupp Trial* the Tribunals rejected the notion that the dictates of modern wars had suspended in several areas, previous international law.

Duress has been raised, so far unsuccessfully, in many cases, before the Special Panels for Serious Crimes in East Timor. See for example, *Prosecutor v. Julio Fernandes*, Judgment, Criminal Appeal No 7 of 2001, paras 9–15, May 15, 2001; *Prosecutor v. Carlos Soares Carmona*, Judgment, April 19, 2001; *Prosecutor v. Joseph Leki*, Judgment, June 11, 2001 and *Prosecutor v. Manuel Gonsalves Leto*, Judgment, May 15, 2001.

G. Consent

17–62   Rule 96 of both the ICTY and ICTR Rules provides the following in relation to evidence in cases of sexual assault:

"(ii) consent shall not be allowed as a defence if the victim
  (a) has been subjected to or threatened with or has had reason to fear violence, duress, detention or psychological oppression, or
  (b) reasonably believed that if the victim did not submit, another might be so subjected, threatened or put in fear;
(iii) before evidence of the victim's consent is admitted, the accused shall satisfy the Trial Chamber in camera that the evidence is relevant and credible".

Rule 96(ii) thus provides that consent shall not be allowed as a defence in sexual assault cases when a victim has been "subjected to or threatened with or has had reason to fear violence, duress, detention or psychological oppression" or when a victim reasonably believed that if they did not submit, another would be subjected to the assault.

In *Prosecutor v. Kunarac*, Trial Chamber, February 22, 2001, para. 464, the ICTY Tribunal had occasion to consider the meaning of consent as a "defence" in Rule 96 and interpreted it to refer to a defence in the non-technical sense. The Tribunal stated that "It understands the reference to consent as a 'defence' in Rule 96 as an indication of the understanding of the judges who adopted the rule of those matters which would be considered to negate apparent consent". It is not the technical shifting of the burden of proof to the defence.

In an earlier judgment, *Prosecutor v. Furundžija*, Trial Chamber, December 10, 1998, para. 271, Furundžija did not raise consent as a defence to charges on violations of the laws and customs of war under Article 3 of the Statute. However, the fact that one of the victims (Victim A) in that case was kept in captivity was considered to negate any consent. The Trial Chamber stated: "Further, it is the position of the Trial Chamber that any form of captivity vitiates consent."

Rule 72 of the ICC Rules of Procedure and Evidence provides that where there is an intention to introduce or elicit, including by means of the questioning of a victim or witness, evidence that the victim consented to an alleged crime of sexual violence, or evidence of the words, conduct, silence or lack of resistance of a victim or witness, notification shall be provided to the Court which shall describe the substance of the evidence intended to be introduced or elicited and the relevance of the evidence to the issues in the case. In deciding whether the evidence is relevant or admissible, a Chamber shall hear in camera the views of the Prosecutor, the defence, the witness and the victim or his or her legal representative, if any, and shall take into account whether that evidence has a sufficient degree of probative value to an issue in the case and the prejudice that such evidence may cause. Where the Chamber determines that the evidence is admissible in the proceedings, the Chamber shall state on the record the specific purpose for which the evidence is admissible.

In accordance with Rule 70 of the ICC Rules of Procedure and Evidence, in cases of sexual violence, the Court shall be guided by and, where appropriate, apply the following principles:

(a) Consent cannot be inferred by reason of any words or conduct of a victim where force, threat of force, coercion or taking an advantage of a coercive environment undermined the victim's ability to give voluntary and genuine consent;

(b) Consent cannot be inferred by reason of any words or conduct of a victim where the victim is incapable of giving genuine consent;

(c) Consent cannot be inferred by reason of the silence of, or lack of resistance by, a victim to the alleged sexual violence.

H. MISTAKE OF LAW OR FACT

(1) Mistake of Fact

Article 32(1) of the ICC Statute and section 20.1 of UNTAET **17–63** Regulation 2000/15 provide expressly for the limited circumstances in which mistake of fact constitutes a defence. In contrast, the Statutes of the ad hoc Tribunals contain no reference to any such defence, although suggestions can be found in their case law that it exists (see *Prosecutor v. Erdemović*, Judgment, ICTY Appeals Chamber, October 7, 1997, Separate and Dissenting Opinion of Judge Cassese, paras 10 and 37 and Separate Opinion of Judge McDonald and Judge Vohrah, para. 34).

Article 32(1) of the ICC Statute reiterates the general principle that a person will only be criminally responsible when they are found to have the necessary *mens rea*. Excluding criminal responsibility flows from the fact that Article 30(1) of the ICC Statute requires that "the material elements [of the offence] are committed with intent and knowledge". When there is an error of fact regarding these material elements the accused will not possess the required *mens rea* of that offence and thus liability will be excluded and the accused acquitted.

An example of a mistake of fact which would exclude the mental element required for the particular offence and thus exclude the criminal responsibility of the accused person would be a situation in which the accused does not realise that the building targeted is a hospital. In this instance the accused will not be aware that the building is protected under international humanitarian law and thus would not have the *mens rea* required for this crime in international law as set out in Article 8(2)(b)(ix) of the ICC Statute.

When criminal responsibility is not excluded, in other words, in cases when the error of fact does not pertain to a material element and thus negate the mental element of the crime, such an error might still be taken into account in sentencing.

The mistake of fact might be regarded by the ICC to be of such a nature that it should be regarded in mitigation of punishment (Otto Triffterer, Mistake of Fact or Mistake of Law, 555 at 567, in Otto Triffterer, *Commentary on the Rome Statute of the International Criminal Court: Observers' Notes, Article by Article*). The mandate for the Court to take a mistake of fact into account in mitigation of punishment stems from Article 78(1), which provides that the Court "in determining sentence . . . shall take into account such factors as the gravity of the crime and the individual circumstances of the convicted person". These mistakes might be taken into account as individual circumstances of the accused. In addition these mistakes might "even impinge on the judgment of 'the gravity of the crime' because not only does this consist of the harm but also of the (amount of) guilt in the sense of personal blame for committing the crime" (Otto Triffterer Mistake of fact or Mistake of Law, 555 at 567, in Otto Triffterer, *Commentary on the Rome Statute of the International Criminal Court: Observers' Notes, Article by Article*).

(2) Mistake of law

17–64   Examples of errors of law would include any of the following: an accused that is aware of a law but believes that it is inapplicable to him; an accused that mistakenly believes that the law is neither fundamental nor international in nature, and thus national; or mistaken belief on that which is impermissible under international law.

The rationale for allowing for error of law to perhaps (in accordance with the permissive use of "may" in Article 32(2)) exclude criminal responsibility follows from the fact that an accused that is unaware of the existence of a rule prohibiting the conduct in question is unaware of a legal element and is unable to decide between right and wrong. In these instances the accused's responsibility rests upon whether he could have avoided making the mistake (avoidability) (see Otto Triffterer

Mistake of fact or Mistake of Law, 555 at 564, in Otto Triffterer, *Commentary on the Rome Statute of the International Criminal Court: Observers' Notes, Article by Article*).

Article 32(2) stipulates that an accused person's mistaken belief that certain conduct does not fall within the jurisdiction of the Court will not shield him from criminal responsibility. An accused will be criminally responsible when his error does not relate to his perception of his conduct, but relates to his perception of whether that conduct falls within the particular type of conduct falling within the Court's jurisdiction. The use of mandatory language "shall" in Article 32(2) indicates that the Court may not *but* find an accused criminally responsible.

Other errors of law might not lead to a finding of criminal responsibility (see article 32(2)). The instances in which errors of law might be regarded as a ground for excluding criminal responsibility will be those in which because of an absence of knowledge of a prohibitive rule, the accused is unaware of the facts (the basis upon which the legal element is built upon), and cannot be held to be aware of the fact that his behaviour violates the prohibitive rule (see Otto Triffterer Mistake of Fact or Mistake of Law, 555 at 569, in Otto Triffterer, *Commentary on the Rome Statute of the International Criminal Court: Observers' Notes, Article by Article*). For instance a person can be liable for improper use of a flag, insignia or uniform of the hostile party only if he knew or should have known of the prohibited nature of such use: see ICC *Elements of Crimes*, Article 8(2)(b)(vii)–2.

17–65

In contrast to a mistake relating to the "prerequisite constitutive facts for the legal element" (Otto Triffterer Mistake of fact or Mistake of Law, 555 at 569, in Otto Triffterer, *Commentary on the Rome Statute of the International Criminal Court: Observers' Notes, Article by Article*) an accused might be mistaken in his evaluation of a legal situation. Thus for example he might be aware of all the underlying facts and circumstances but believe that a prohibitive rule is inapplicable to his conduct. In such an instance the accused would be criminally responsible because he is undertaking a legal evaluation which is not necessary and which is irrelevant to his responsibility.

The Court might judge that a legal error negates the mental element of the offence and excludes the accused's responsibility because of the unavoidable nature of the error. Although unavoidableness is not mentioned in Article 32, it is implicit as it is accepted as part of general principles of law (see Otto Triffterer Mistake of fact or Mistake of Law, 555 at 570, in Otto Triffterer, *Commentary on the Rome Statute of the International Criminal Court: Observers' Notes, Article by Article*).

17–66

When the Court finds an error of law for which an accused is still criminally responsible, Article 78(1) of the ICC Statute might still lead the Court to mitigate his punishment.

Note that in Article 33(1) of the ICC Statute a person that acts in pursuit of a superior order which they do not know to be unlawful and which is not manifestly unlawful will not be criminally responsible. Article 33(1) is accordingly an exception to the rule that an error of law will generally not exclude responsibility as set out in Article 32(2) of the ICC Statute.

IV. REJECTED DEFENCES

A. Necessity

17–67   It is not firmly established in the case law whether defences other than those expressly provided for in the statutes of international tribunals may be available on the basis that they are recognised under customary international law. The Appeals Chamber of the ICTY has on one occasion declined to determine whether "necessity" constitutes a defence under international law, or whether it is the same as the defence of duress (*Prosecutor v. Aleksovski*, Judgment, ICTY Appeals Chamber, March 24, 2000, paras 51–55).

B. Tu Quoque

17–68   It has been held that in humanitarian law, there is no defence based on any principle of *tu quoque* (*i.e.*, the argument whereby the fact that the adversary has also committed similar crimes offers a valid defence to the individuals accused), since the bulk of international humanitarian law lays down absolute obligations, namely obligations that are unconditional or in other words not based on reciprocity (*Prosecutor v. Kupreškić et al.*, Judgment, ICTY Trial Chamber, January 14, 2000, paras 515–520; see also *Prosecutor v. Kupreškić et al.*, Appeal Judgment, ICTY Appeal Chamber, October 23, 2001, para. 25; *Prosecutor v. Kupreškić et al.*, Decision on Defence Motion to Summon Witness, ICTY Trial Chamber, February 8, 1999, para. 15; *Prosecutor v. Kupreškić et al.*, Decision on Evidence of the Good Character of the Accused and the Defence of Tu Quoque, ICTY Trial Chamber, February 17, 1999). In recent proceedings before the Tribunals, the inapplicability of *tu quoque* has been acknowledged raised by parties, and it has not been not relied upon as a substantive defence (*Prosecutor v. Hadžihasanović & Kubura*, Decision on Defence Motion for Clarification of the Oral Decision of December 17, 2003 regarding the scope of cross-examination pursuant to rule 90(H) of the Rules, ICTY Trial Chamber, January 28, 2004, page 3; *Prosecutor v. Limaj et al.*, Pre-trial Brief of Fatmir Limaj and Pre-trial Brief of Isak Musliu, May 31, 2004, para. 9).

C. Diminished Responsibility

17–69   The issue of diminished mental responsibility as a defence was addressed in the ICTY Appeals Chamber in *Prosecutor v. Delalic et al.*, Judgment, February 20, 2001, para. 590. The Chamber has found that *diminished* responsibility is not a complete defence in international law, in the sense of excluding an accused person's criminal responsibility, but might be a ground for mitigation of sentence.

The Appeals Chamber stated (para. 583) that the mere "description of diminished mental responsibility as a 'special defence' in Rule 67(A)(ii) is insufficient to constitute it as such". For it to exist as a "special defence" in international law it would have to be found in the usual sources of international law. The *Delalic* Appeals Chamber went on to state that in the absence of customary or conventional international law, the defence would have to be found in the general principles of law recognised by civilised nations. The general principles of law recognised by civilised nations hold "diminished mental responsibility is relevant to the sentence to be imposed and is not a defence leading to an acquittal in the true sense. This is the appropriate general legal principle representing the international law to be applied by the Tribunal". See *Prosecutor v. Delalic et al.*, Appeals Chamber, February 20, 2001, para. 590).

This approach was followed by the ICTY Trial Chamber in *Vasiljevic*, in which it was clarified that the accused bears the onus of establishing a defence of diminished responsibility on the balance of probabilities. However, the Chamber noted that such a defence would not lead to acquittal, but merely to mitigation of sentence: *Prosecutor v. Vasiljevic*, Judgment, ICTY Trial Chamber, November 29, 2002, para. 282. The Chamber understood diminished mental responsibility in *Vasiljevic* to mean an "impairment to his capacity to appreciate the unlawfulness of or the nature of his conduct or to control his conduct so as to conform to the requirements of the law" (at para. 283). In the event, the partial defence of diminished mental capacity, related to the chronic alcoholism and exhaustion of the accused, coupled with his reaction to the death of his cousin, was rejected (at paras 284–295). In coming to this conclusion, the Chamber was guided by evidence relating to criminal accountability standards in the former Yugoslavia, which would have found the accused to be fully accountable in law under these same conditions (at paras 293–295).

In *Prosecutor v. Delalic et al.*, Judgment, February 20, 2002, para. 590 the Appeals Chamber explained that Rule 67(A)(ii)(b) (requiring the defence to notify the Prosecutor of its intent to offer the special defence of diminished mental responsibility) must be interpreted as referring to diminished mental responsibility where it is to be raised in mitigation of sentence. (See also *Prosecutor v. Sikirica et al.*, Sentencing Judgment, ICTY Trial Chamber, December 13, 2001, para. 197). It would appear that the fact that the accused may at the relevant time have been suffering from post-traumatic stress disorder does not necessarily mean that the accused had a condition which would give rise to mitigation of sentence (*Prosecutor v. Todorovic*, Sentencing Judgment, ICTY Trial Chamber, July 31, 2001, paras 93–95). Furthermore, personality disorders (such as "borderline, narcissistic and anti-social characteristics") are not relevant factors, although significant mental handicap can constitute a mitigating circumstance; and good character, "keen sense for the soldiering profession", or "poor family background" in combination with youth and an "immature and fragile" personality are also elements that may constitute mitigating circumstances (*Prosecutor v. Krstic*, Judgment, ICTY Trial Chamber, August 2, 2001, para. 714).

The *Delalic* Appeals Chamber, para. 587, found that there was no equivalent provision to diminished responsibility in the ICC Statute. It stated: "There is no express provision in the ICC Statute which is concerned with the consequences of an impairment to such a capacity."

CHAPTER 18

SENTENCING, COMPENSATION, RESTITUTION & IMPRISONMENT

I. SENTENCING: STATUTORY PROVISIONS

A. ICC

(1) ICC Statute

Statute, Arts 76, 77, 78, 80

Sentencing

18–1   **76.**—1. In the event of a conviction, the Trial Chamber shall consider the appropriate sentence to be imposed and shall take into account the evidence presented and submissions made during the trial that are relevant to the sentence.

2. Except where article 65 applies and before the completion of the trial, the Trial Chamber may on its own motion and shall, at the request of the Prosecutor or the accused, hold a further hearing to hear any additional evidence or submissions relevant to the sentence, in accordance with the Rules of Procedure and Evidence.

3. Where paragraph 2 applies, any representations under article 75 shall be heard during the further hearing referred to in paragraph 2 and, if necessary, during any additional hearing.

4. The sentence shall be pronounced in public and, wherever possible, in the presence of the accused.

Applicable penalties

18–2   **77.**—1. Subject to article 110, the Court may impose one of the following penalties on a person convicted of a crime referred to in article 5 of this Statute:

    (a) Imprisonment for a specified number of years, which may not exceed a maximum of 30 years; or

    (b) A term of life imprisonment when justified by the extreme gravity of the crime and the individual circumstances of the convicted person.

2. In addition to imprisonment, the Court may order:

    (a) A fine under the criteria provided for in the Rules of Procedure and Evidence;

    (b) A forfeiture of proceeds, property and assets derived directly or indirectly from that crime, without prejudice to the rights of bona fide third parties.

Determination of the sentence

18–3   **78.**—1. In determining the sentence, the Court shall, in accordance with the Rules of Procedure and Evidence, take into account such factors as the gravity of the crime and the individual circumstances of the convicted person.

2. In imposing a sentence of imprisonment, the Court shall deduct the time, if any, previously spent in detention in accordance with an order of the Court. The Court may deduct any time otherwise spent in detention in connection with conduct underlying the crime.

3. When a person has been convicted of more than one crime, the Court shall pronounce a sentence for each crime and a joint sentence specifying the total period of imprisonment. This period shall be no less than the highest individual sentence pronounced and shall not exceed 30 years imprisonment or a sentence of life imprisonment in conformity with article 77, paragraph 1(b).

Non-prejudice to national application of penalties and national laws

80. Nothing in this Part affects the application by States of penalties **18–4** prescribed by their national law, nor the law of States which do not provide for penalties prescribed in this Part.

(2) ICC Rules of Procedure and Evidence

Rules of Procedure and Evidence, rr. 143, 145, 146

Additional hearings on matters related to sentence or reparations

143. Pursuant to article 76, paragraphs 2 and 3, for the purpose of holding a **18–5** further hearing on matters related to sentence and, if applicable, reparations, the Presiding Judge shall set the date of the further hearing. This hearing can be postponed, in exceptional circumstances, by the Trial Chamber, on its own motion or at the request of the Prosecutor, the defence or the legal representatives of the victims participating in the proceedings pursuant to rules 89 to 91 and, in respect of reparations hearings, those victims who have made a request under rule 94.

Determination of sentence

145.—1. In its determination of the sentence pursuant to article 78, **18–6** paragraph 1, the Court shall:
- (a) Bear in mind that the totality of any sentence of imprisonment and fine, as the case may be, imposed under article 77 must reflect the culpability of the convicted person;
- (b) Balance all the relevant factors, including any mitigating and aggravating factors and consider the circumstances both of the convicted person and of the crime;
- (c) In addition to the factors mentioned in article 78, paragraph 1, give consideration, *inter alia*, to the extent of the damage caused, in particular the harm caused to the victims and their families, the nature of the unlawful behaviour and the means employed to execute the crime; the degree of participation of the convicted person; the degree of intent; the circumstances of manner, time and location; and the age, education, social and economic condition of the convicted person.

2. In addition to the factors mentioned above, the Court shall take into account, as appropriate:
- (a) Mitigating circumstances such as:
    - (i) The circumstances falling short of constituting grounds for exclusion of criminal responsibility, such as substantially diminished mental capacity or duress;
    - (ii) The convicted person's conduct after the act, including any efforts by the person to compensate the victims and any cooperation with the Court;

(b) As aggravating circumstances:
 (i) Any relevant prior criminal convictions for crimes under the jurisdiction of the Court or of a similar nature;
 (ii) Abuse of power or official capacity;
 (iii) Commission of the crime where the victim is particularly defenceless;
 (iv) Commission of the crime with particular cruelty or where there were multiple victims;
 (v) Commission of the crime for any motive involving discrimination on any of the grounds referred to in article 21, paragraph 3;
 (vi) Other circumstances which, although not enumerated above, by virtue of their nature are similar to those mentioned.

3. Life imprisonment may be imposed when justified by the extreme gravity of the crime and the individual circumstances of the convicted person, as evidenced by the existence of one or more aggravating circumstances.

Imposition of fines under article 77

18–7   **146.**—1. In determining whether to order a fine under article 77, paragraph 2 (a), and in fixing the amount of the fine, the Court shall determine whether imprisonment is a sufficient penalty. The Court shall give due consideration to the financial capacity of the convicted person, including any orders for forfeiture in accordance with article 77, paragraph 2 (b), and, as appropriate, any orders for reparation in accordance with article 75. The Court shall take into account, in addition to the factors referred to in rule 145, whether and to what degree the crime was motivated by personal financial gain.

2. A fine imposed under article 77, paragraph 2 (a), shall be set at an appropriate level. To this end, the Court shall, in addition to the factors referred to above, in particular take into consideration the damage and injuries caused as well as the proportionate gains derived from the crime by the perpetrator. Under no circumstances may the total amount exceed 75 per cent of the value of the convicted person's identifiable assets, liquid or realizable, and property, after deduction of an appropriate amount that would satisfy the financial needs of the convicted person and his or her dependants.

3. In imposing a fine, the Court shall allow the convicted person a reasonable period in which to pay the fine. The Court may provide for payment of a lump sum or by way of instalments during that period.

4. In imposing a fine, the Court may, as an option, calculate it according to a system of daily fines. In such cases, the minimum duration shall be 30 days and the maximum duration five years. The Court shall decide the total amount in accordance with sub-rules 1 and 2. It shall determine the amount of daily payment in the light of the individual circumstances of the convicted person, including the financial needs of his or her dependants.

5. If the convicted person does not pay the fine imposed in accordance with the conditions set above, appropriate measures may be taken by the Court pursuant to rules 217 to 222 and in accordance with article 109. Where, in cases of continued wilful non-payment, the Presidency, on its own motion or at the request of the Prosecutor, is satisfied that all available enforcement measures have been exhausted, it may as a last resort extend the term of imprisonment for a period not to exceed a quarter of such term or five years, whichever is less. In the determination of such period of extension, the Presidency shall take into account the amount of the fine, imposed and paid. Any such extension shall not apply in the case of life imprisonment. The extension may not lead to a total period of imprisonment in excess of 30 years.

6. In order to determine whether to order an extension and the period involved, the Presidency shall sit in camera for the purpose of obtaining the views of the sentenced person and the Prosecutor. The sentenced person shall have the right to be assisted by counsel.

7. In imposing a fine, the Court shall warn the convicted person that failure to pay the fine in accordance with the conditions set out above may result in an extension of the period of imprisonment as described in this rule.

(3) ICC Regulations of the Court, Adopted May 26, 2004

Regulations 116, 117, 118

Enforcement of fines, forfeiture orders and reparation orders

116.—1. For the purposes of enforcement of fines, forfeiture orders and **18–8** reparation orders, the Presidency, with the assistance of the Registry as appropriate, shallmake the arrangements necessary in order to, *inter alia*:
  (a) Receive payment of fines as described in article 77, paragraph 2 (a);
  (b) Receive, as described in article 109, paragraph 3, property or the proceeds of the sale of real property or, where appropriate, the sale of other property;
  (c) Account for interest gained on money received under (a) and (b) above;
  (d) Ensure the transfer of money to the Trust Fund or to victims, as appropriate.
  2. Following the transfer to or deposit in the Trust Fund of property or assets realized through enforcement of an order of the Court, the Presidency shall, subject to article 75, paragraph 2, and rule 98, decide on their disposition or allocation in accordance with rule 221.

Ongoing monitoring of financial situation of the sentenced person

117.—The Presidency shall, if necessary, and with the assistance of the **18–9** Registrar as appropriate, monitor the financial situation of the sentenced person on an ongoing basis, even following completion of a sentence of imprisonment, in order to enforce fines, forfeiture orders or reparation orders, and may, *inter alia*:
  (a) Request relevant information, expert opinions or reports, where necessary by way of a request for cooperation, and, if appropriate, on a periodic basis; Regulations of the Court ICC-BD/01–01–04 70
  (b) Contact, where appropriate in the manner described in rule 211, paragraph 1 (c), the sentenced person and his or her counsel in order to inquire into the financial situation of the sentenced person; (c) Ask for observations from the Prosecutor, victims and legal representatives of victims.

Procedure under rule 146, sub-rule 5

118.—1. In making its decision on the extension of the term of imprison- **18–10** ment in accordance with rule 146, sub-rules 5 and 6, the Presidency may ask for observations from States in which attempts to enforce fines did not succeed and shall ask for observations from the State in which the sentence of imprisonment is being served.
  2. Where the term of imprisonment has been extended under rule 146, subrule 5, and the sentenced person subsequently pays the fine or a portion thereof, the Presidency shall revoke or in case of partial payment reduce the extension previously ordered.

B. ICTY

(1) ICTY Statute

Statute of the International Tribunal, Arts 23, 24

Judgment

18–11   **23.**—1. The Trial Chambers shall pronounce judgments and impose sentences and penalties on persons convicted of serious violations of international humanitarian law.

Penalties

18–12   **24.**—1. The penalty imposed by the Trial Chamber shall be limited to imprisonment. In determining the terms of imprisonment, the Trial Chambers shall have recourse to the general practice regarding prison sentences in the courts of the former Yugoslavia.

2. In imposing the sentences, the Trial Chambers should take into account such factors as the gravity of the offence and the individual circumstances of the convicted person.

3. In addition to imprisonment, the Trial Chambers may order the return of any property and proceeds acquired by criminal conduct, including by means of duress, to their rightful owners.

(2) ICTY Rules of Procedure and Evidence

Rules of Procedure and Evidence, rr. 100, 101, 102

Sentencing Procedure on a Guilty Plea

18–13   **100.**—(A) If the Trial Chamber convicts the accused on a guilty plea, the Prosecutor and the defence may submit any relevant information that may assist the Trial Chamber in determining an appropriate sentence.

(B) The sentence shall be pronounced in a judgment in public and in the presence of the convicted person, subject to Rule 102(B)

Penalties

18–14   **101.**—(A) A convicted person may be sentenced to imprisonment for a term up to and including the remainder of the convicted person's life.

(B) In determining the sentence, the Trial Chamber shall take into account the factors mentioned in Article 24(2) of the Statute, as well as such factors as:

   (i) any aggravating circumstances;
   (ii) any mitigating circumstances including the substantial cooperation with the Prosecutor by the convicted person before or after conviction;
   (iii) the general practice regarding prison sentences in the courts of the former Yugoslavia;
   (iv) the extent to which any penalty imposed by a court of any State on the convicted person for the same act has already been served, as referred to in Article 10(3) of the Statute.

(C) Credit shall be given to the convicted person for the period, if any, during which the convicted person was detained in custody pending his surrender to the Tribunal or pending trial or appeal.

Status of the Convicted Person

102.—(A) The sentence shall begin to run from the day it is pronounced. However, as soon as notice of appeal is given, the enforcement of the judgment shall thereupon be stayed until the decision on the appeal has been delivered, the convicted person meanwhile remaining in detention, as provided in Rule 64.   **18–15**

(B) If, by a previous decision of the Trial Chamber, the convicted person has been released, or is for any other reason at liberty, and is not present when the judgment is pronounced, the Trial Chamber shall issue a warrant for the convicted person's arrest. On arrest, the convicted person shall be notified of the conviction and sentence, and the procedure provided in Rule 103 shall be followed.

C. ICTR

(1) ICTR Statute

Statute of the International Tribunal, Arts 22, 23

22. The Trial Chamber shall pronounce judgments and impose sentences and penalties on persons convicted of serious violations of international humanitarian law.   **18–16**

Penalties

23.—1. The penalty imposed by the Trial Chamber shall be limited to imprisonment. In determining the terms of imprisonment, the Trial Chamber shall have recourse to the general practice regarding prison sentences in the courts of Rwanda.   **18–17**

2. In imposing the sentences, the Trial Chamber should take into account such factors as the gravity of the offence and the individual circumstances of the convicted person.

3. In addition to imprisonment, the Trial Chamber may order the return of any property and proceeds acquired by criminal conduct, including by means of duress, to their rightful owners.

(2) ICTR Rules of Procedure and Evidence

Rules of Procedure and Evidence, rr. 100, 102

Sentencing Procedure on a Guilty Plea

100.—(A) If the Trial Chamber convicts the accused on a guilty plea, the Prosecutor and the Defence may submit any relevant information that may assist the Trial Chamber in determining an appropriate sentence.   **18–18**

(B) The sentence shall be pronounced in a judgment in public and in the presence of the convicted person, subject to Sub-Rule 102(B).

Penalties

101.—(A) A person convicted by the Tribunal may be sentenced to imprisonment for a fixed term or the remainder of his life.

(B) In determining the sentence, the Trial Chamber shall take into account the factors mentioned in Article 23 (2) of the Statute, as well as such factors as
   (i) any aggravating circumstances;
   (ii) any mitigating circumstances including the substantial co-operation with the Prosecutor by the convicted person before or after conviction;
   (iii) the general practice regarding prison sentences in the courts of Rwanda;
   (v) the extent to which any penalty imposed by a court of any State on the convicted person for the same act has already been served, as referred to in Article 9 (3) of the Statute.
(C) The Trial Chamber shall indicate whether multiple sentences shall be served consecutively or concurrently.
(D) Credit shall be given to the convicted person for the period, if any, during which the convicted person was detained in custody pending his surrender to the Tribunal or pending trial or appeal.

Status of the convicted person

18–19   **102.**—(A) Subject to the Trial Chamber's directions in terms of Rule 101, the sentence shall begin to run from the day it is pronounced under Rule 100(B). However, as soon as notice of appeal is given, the enforcement of the judgment shall thereupon be stayed until the decision on the appeal has been delivered, the convicted person meanwhile remaining in detention, as provided for in Rule 64.
(B) If, by a previous decision of the Trial Chamber, the convicted person has been provisionally released, or is for any reason at liberty, and he is not present when the judgment is pronounced, the Trial Chamber shall issue a warrant for his arrest. On arrest, he shall be notified of the conviction and sentence, and the procedure provided in Rule 103 shall be followed.

D. East Timor

Regulation No. 2000/15, s.10

18–20   On the establishment of panels with exclusive jurisdiction over serious criminal offences, June 6, 2000

Penalties

18–21   **10.**—10.1 A panel may impose one of the following penalties on a person convicted of a crime specified under Sections 4 to 7 of the present regulation:
   (a) Imprisonment for a specified term of years, which may not exceed a maximum of 25 years. In determining the terms of imprisonment for the crimes referred to in Sections 4 to 7 of the present regulation, the panel shall have recourse to the general practice regarding prison sentences in the courts of East Timor and under international tribunals for the crimes referred to in sections 8 and 9 of the present regulation, the penalties prescribed in the respective provisions of the applicable Penal Code in east Timor, shall apply.
   (b) A fine up to a maximum of US$500,000
   (c) A forfeiture of proceeds, property and assets derived directly from the crime, without prejudice to the rights of *bona fide* third parties.
10.2 In imposing the sentences, the panel shall take into account such factors as the gravity of the offence and the individual circumstances of the convicted person.

10.3 In imposing a sentence of imprisonment, the panel shall deduct the time, if any, previously spent in detention due to an order of the panel or any other court in East Timor (for the same criminal conduct). The panel may deduct any time otherwise spent in detention in connection with the conduct (underlying the crime).

Regulation No. 2000/30, ss.19, 42

UNTAET Regulation 2000/30, September 25, 2000, as amended by **18–22** UNTAET Regulation 2001/25, September 14, 2001.

Crediting pre-trial Detention

19.—Any period spent in pre-trial detention in relation to an alleged crime, **18–23** shall be credited against service of any subsequent sentence ordered in the same case.

Court Orders and Sentences

42.—42.1 Any order or decision of a court shall be executed by the **18–24** competent authorities immediately upon the release of the written decision of the court. It is the responsibility of the public prosecutor to notify other competent authorities of their duties pursuant to this section.

42.2 A decision declaring the acquittal of an accused shall result in his or her immediate release or the cancellation of any restrictive measure.

42.3 Upon final disposition of the case, including any appeal, the competent court shall determine whether any objects seized during the proceedings will be returned to the person who owns or possessed the objects, or whether they will be confiscated. If confiscation is ordered, the Court shall determine whether the objects will be destroyed or auctioned. Revenues from auction shall accrue to the consolidated budget of East Timor.

42.4 Where an accused is convicted and the penalty established is a term of imprisonment, the court shall inform the convict the content of the penalty, its duration and the place where the convict will be imprisoned. The convict shall also be informed of the rights and legal benefits to which he or she is entitled according to law.

42.5 The Court shall discount from the term of imprisonment the time the convict spent under pre-trial detention n respect of the crime for which the convict has been convicted. Prison sentences shall be supervised and executed by a District Court in accordance with Section 48 of the present Regulation. The convict may present any claim to the court in relation to the violation of his or her rights.

42.6 Where the penalty established is a term of imprisonment, the convict shall be imprisoned immediately, unless otherwise ordered. The court shall remand the convict to the custody of the competent authorities for transfer to the place where the convict shall be imprisoned. A file including the sentence shall be forwarded to the correctional authorities.

42.7 Correctional authorities shall administer the rules and conditions of confinement in accordance with international human rights standards and UNTAET Regulations.

42.8 Where an accused is convicted and the penalty established is a fine, such fine shall be payable to the Court at the date to be pronounced by the court. The court shall take into account the financial condition of the accused and shall establish an appropriate term and method for the payment of the fine. Revenues from the payment of fines or forfeiture of property shall accrue to the consolidated budget of East Timor.

42.9 Penalties in the form of fines and imprisonment are mutually independent. A fine shall not be converted into a penalty of imprisonment, and a penalty of imprisonment shall not be converted into a fine. A penalty in the form of fine may be executed on any property of the convict wherever situated.

42.10 Any party may, within five (5) working days of the date of release of the written decision claim miscalculations or typographical errors in the period of imprisonment or in the amount of the fine, or in any other provision of the decision. Where the Court finds that there has been such an error, it shall order immediate corrections.

E. Sierra Leone

(1) SCSL Statute

Statute of the Special Court of Sierra Leone, Arts 7, 19

Jurisdiction over persons of 15 years of age

18–25   7.—1. The Special Court shall have no jurisdiction over any person who was under the age of 15 at the time of the alleged commission of the crime. Should any person who was at the time of the alleged commission of the crime between 15 and 18 years of age come before the Court, he or she shall be treated with dignity and a sense of worth, taking into account his or her young age and the desirability of promoting his or her rehabilitation, reintegration into and assumption of a constructive role in society, and in accordance with international human rights standards, in particular the rights of the child.

2. In the disposition of a case against a juvenile offender, the Special Court shall order any of the following: care guidance and supervision orders, community service orders, counselling, foster care, correctional, educational and vocational training programmes, approved schools and, as appropriate, any programmes of disarmament, demobilization and reintegration or programmes of child protection agencies.

Penalties

18–26   19.—1. The Trial Chamber shall impose upon a convicted person, other than a juvenile offender, imprisonment for a specified number of years. In determining the terms of imprisonment, the Trial Chamber shall, as appropriate, have recourse to the practice regarding prison sentences in the International Criminal Tribunal for Rwanda and the national courts of Sierra Leone.

2. In imposing the sentences, the Trial Chamber should take into account such factors as the gravity of the offence and the individual circumstances of the convicted person.

3. In addition to imprisonment, the Trial Chamber may order the forfeiture of the property proceeds and any assets acquired unlawfully or by criminal conduct, and their return to their rightful owner or to the State of Sierra Leone.

(2) SCSL Rules of Procedure and Evidence

Rules of Procedure and Evidence, rr. 99, 100, 101, 102, 119

Status of the Acquitted Person

18–27   99.—(A) In case of acquittal, the Special Court shall, subject to Sub-Rule (B) below, order the release of the accused.

804

(B) If, at the time the acquittal is pronounced, the Prosecutor advises the Trial Chamber in open court of his intention to file notice of appeal pursuant to Rule 108, the Trial Chamber may, on application of the Prosecutor and upon hearing the parties, in its discretion, issue an order for the continued detention of the accused, pending the determination of the appeal.

Sentencing Procedure

100.—(A) If the Trial Chamber convicts the accused or the accused enters a guilty plea, the Prosecutor shall submit any relevant information that may assist the Trial Chamber in determining an appropriate sentence no more than 14 days after such conviction or guilty plea. The defendant shall thereafter, but no more that 21 days after the Prosecutor's filing submit any relevant information that may assist the Trial Chamber in determining an appropriate sentence.
    18–28

(B) Where the accused has entered a guilty plea, the Trial Chamber shall hear submissions of the parties at a sentencing hearing. Where the accused has been convicted by a Trial Chamber, the Trial Chamber may hear submissions of the parties at a sentencing hearing.

(C) The sentence may be pronounced in a judgment in public and in the presence of the convicted person, subject to Rule 102 (B).

Penalties

101.—(A) A person convicted by the Special Court, other than a juvenile offender, may be sentenced to imprisonment for a specific number of years.
    18–29

(B) In determining the sentence, the Trial Chamber shall take into account the factors mentioned in Article 19 (2) of the Statute, as well as such factors as:

    i. Any aggravating circumstances;
    ii. Any mitigating circumstances including the substantial cooperation with the Prosecutor by the convicted person before or after conviction;
    iii. The extent to which any penalty imposed by a court of any State on the convicted person for the same act has already been served, as referred to in Article 9 (3) of the Statute.

(C) The Trial Chamber shall indicate whether multiple sentences shall be served consecutively or concurrently.

(D) Any period during which the convicted person was detained in custody pending his transfer to the Special Court or pending trial or appeal, shall be taken into consideration on sentencing.

Status of the Convicted Person

102.—(A) Subject to the Trial Chamber's directions in terms of Rule 101, the sentence shall begin to run from the day it is pronounced under Rule 100(B). However, as soon as notice of appeal is given, the enforcement of the judgment shall thereupon be stayed until the decision on the appeal has been delivered, the convicted person meanwhile remaining in detention, as provided in Rule 64.
    18–30

(B) If, by a previous decision of the Trial Chamber, the convicted person has been provisionally released, or is for any other reason at liberty, and he is not present when the judgment is pronounced, the Trial Chamber shall issue a warrant for his arrest. On arrest, he shall be notified of the conviction and sentence, and the procedure provided in Rule 103 shall be followed.

Status of the Accused Following Judgment on Appeal

119.—(A) A sentence pronounced by the Appeals Chamber shall be enforced immediately.
    18–31

(B) Where the accused is not present when the Appeal judgment is due to be delivered, it may, unless it pronounces his acquittal, order his arrest or transfer to the Special Court.

II. AVAILABLE PENALTIES

18–32   The death penalty is not available at the ICC, ICTY, ICTR, the Special Panel for Serious Crimes in East Timor and the Special Court in Sierra Leone. Whilst the death penalty is provided for in the domestic laws of many States, many others are committed to its abolition or progressive abolition (see, *e.g.* ECHR, Protocol 6, Article 1; ICCPR, Second Optional Protocol). Accordingly, many States would have been unable to support international courts that provided for the death penalty. The Permanent Representative of New Zealand, for example, reminded the Security Council at the time the establishment of the ICTR was being debated, that "for over three decades the United Nations has been trying progressively to eliminate the death penalty. It would be entirely unacceptable—and a dreadful step backwards—to introduce it here" (UN Doc S/PV.3453, p. 16).

Article 77(1)(a) of the Rome Statute provides that a determinate sentence may be imposed on a convicted person for a term not exceeding 30 years. Article 77(1)(b) provides that in cases of "extreme gravity" and where the "individual circumstances of the convicted person" so warrant, a maximum sentence of life imprisonment may be imposed.

Article 77(2) of the Rome Statutes enables the ICC to impose fines *along with* sentences of imprisonment. A fine cannot be imposed as an alternative to a sentence of imprisonment. In deciding whether the imposition of a fine is required, the ICC shall first determine "whether imprisonment is a sufficient penalty" (ICC RPE, Rule 146(1)). To this end, the court shall take into account damage and injury caused and the proportionate gain made from the crime by the convicted person (ICC RPE, Rule 146(2)). Failure to pay the fine may, after a hearing (ICC RPE, Rule 146(6)) and as a last resort, result in an extension of imprisonment of up to one quarter of the convicted person's term or an extension of five years, whichever is the lesser (ICC RPE, Rule 146(5)).

18–33   Other than for contempt and false evidence under solemn declaration (see Chapter 15) fines are not available under the sentencing regime of the ICTY or ICTR. Article 23 of the ICTR, and Article 24 of the ICTY Statutes limit the available penalties to terms of imprisonment. Rules 101(a) of the Rules of Procedure and Evidence of the ICTY and ICTR provide that the maximum available sentence is life imprisonment. Life imprisonment is not defined in the respective Statutes, but may be given its ordinary meaning in light of the object and purpose of those provisions (see *Prosecutor v. Kayishema & Ruzindana*, Sentence, May 21, 1999, para. 31).

Article 19 of the Statute establishing the Special Court for Sierra Leone states that imprisonment shall be for a "specified number of years"; unless the accused is a juvenile (defined in Article 7 as an accused between 15 and 18 years of age at the time the alleged offence was committed). In the case of a juvenile, Article 7(2) limits the available penalties to ordering "care guidance and supervision orders, community service orders, counselling, foster care, correctional, educational and vocational training programmes, approved schools and, as appropriate, any programmes of disarmament, demobilization and reintegration programmes of child protection agencies" (Also see discussion of this issue in the Secretary-General's Report: *Individual criminal responsibility at 15 years of age*). As Article 19 requires the Special Court of Sierra Leone to have recourse to the practice regarding prison sentences of the ICTR, it is likely that, in the case of adults, the maximum penalty will be effectively amount to life imprisonment, even if expressed as a specified number of years.

The Special Panels for Serious Crimes in East Timor are not permitted to impose indeterminate sentences. Section 10.1(a) of UNTAET Regulation 2000/15, June 6, 2000, on the establishment of panels with exclusive jurisdiction over serious criminal offences, provides that a sentence of imprisonment must be "for a specified number of years, which may not exceed a maximum of 25 years". **18–34**

Section 10.1(b) of Regulation 2000/15 permits a convicted person to be fined up to a maximum of US$500,000. Section 10.1 suggests that sentences of imprisonment, a fine or forfeiture are alternative penalties. This seems to flow from the plain language of that section which states "[a] panel may impose *one* of the following penalties on a person convicted under sections 4 to 7 of the present regulation" (emphasis added). However, in *Prosecutor v. Joni Marques et al.*, Judgment, December 11, 2001, para. 1120, the Trial Chamber for Serious Crimes in Dili, East Timor sentenced the defendants to terms of imprisonment and declined to impose fines or make forfeiture orders only because of the "economic condition of the Defendants".

Suspended sentences

It seems that suspended sentences can also be imposed by international tribunals. For example in the ICTY case of *Prosecutor v. Bulatovic*, Judgment, May 13, 2005, para. 19, the Trial Chamber sentenced the accused convicted for serious contempt of court, and imposed "a sentence of four months imprisonment, but [. . .] suspend[ed] the operation of that sentence for a period of two years, so that the sentence shall not take effect unless during that period the Respondent commits another offence anywhere that is punishable with imprisonment, including contempt of court." (See also Chapter 16). **18–35**

PROCEDURE

Sentences are imposed after hearing representations from the parties. Article 76(2) on the ICC Statute provides that after a trial, the Chamber may, on its own motion, or at the request of either party, hold a further hearing where additional evidence or submissions relevant to sentence may be presented. The further evidence could include evidence from character witnesses or the presentation of psychological or psychiatric evidence. **18–36**

In cases where the guilty plea has been entered and accepted by the Trial Chamber pursuant to Rule 100 of ICTY and ICTR RPE and Rule 100(B) of SCSL RPE, the Trial Chamber is required to hear submissions by the Prosecutor and the Defence on any relevant information that may assist the Trial Chamber in determining an appropriate sentence. Under Rule 143 of ICC RPE this hearing can be postponed in "exceptional circumstances". Examples may include uncertainties arising out of the health of a convicted person, or postponement until after a co-accused's trial has been completed, or until promised cooperation of a sufficiently important nature has been given. Postponement of sentence is, however, not to be considered the norm. The reasons for the postponement must amount to an "exceptional" circumstance.

Article 78(2) of the Rome Statute, Rule 101(E) of the ICTY and ICTR and Rule 101(D) of SCSL Rules of Procedure and Evidence, Section 10.3 of UNTAET Regulation 2000/15 all provide that convicted persons shall be given credit for time served in custody in connection with the crime for which they have been convicted.

For place of imprisonment and review and commutation of sentence see Part XII below.

III. THE AIMS OF SENTENCING

18–37   Neither the ICC, ICTY, ICTR nor SCSL Statutes, or their respective Rules of Procedure and Evidence, detail the object and purpose of sentencing international crimes within their jurisdiction. In discerning the aims of sentencing, the ad hoc Tribunals have looked at the statements made by member States of the Security Council at the time of their establishment, and at the jurisprudence of the Tribunals (for example, see *Prosecutor v. Erdemović*, Sentencing Judgment, November 19, 1996, para. 57).

The sentencing aims of the Tribunals have been stated to be deterrence, protection of society, reprobation, retribution and reconciliation. These objectives are consonant with the Security Council's general aim of restoring and maintaining peace and security in the Former Yugoslavia and Rwanda (see *Prosecutor v. Erdemović*, Judgment, November 19, 1996, para. 58; *Prosecutor v. Tadić*, Judgment, November 11, 1999, para. 7 and *Prosecutor v. Kambanda*, Judgment and Sentence, September 4, 1998, para. 19; Also see *Prosecutor v. Joni Marques et al.* (*Los Palos* case) Judgment, December 11, 2001, para. 979 in which the Trial Panel for Serious Crimes in East Timor held that the penalties imposed by the panel were intended as retribution and as deterrence "namely to dissuade for ever, others who may be tempted in the future to perpetrate such atrocities by showing them that the international community shall not tolerate such serious violations of law and human rights").

Judge Mumba noted in her Separate Opinion in *Deronjic*, that "[i]nternational justice in cases similar to these, in this Tribunal, is not about unfair retribution; if that were the case, humanity should forget about reconciliation and its off-shoot, peace. It is my humble view that this Tribunal is not about vengeance, using the pen as the firearm, much as the victims' plight has been acknowledged; that would be erroneous, such a practice would amount to accepting the erroneous view that you can conquer hatred with hatred. This, in my view, does not work. Vengeance may be manifested in terms of a harsh sentence for an accused person who has pleaded guilty. In my humble opinion, rehabilitation, after turmoil, may serve to reduce the incidence of political instability and conflict" (*Prosecutor v. Deronjic*, Separate Opinion of Judge Mumba in Judgment, March 30, 2004, para. 3).

Deterrence and Retribution

Deterrence seeks to prevent future criminal behaviour—either in preventing the individual from committing a crime again (specific deterrence), or by sending a signal to would-be criminals that a sanction can be imposed (general deterrence). Retribution emphasises that punishment should be proportionate to the crime committed. Its focus is not on a societal value in punishing the individual, but on issuing a sanction because the offence merits penalty (*Prosecutor v. Todorovic*, Judgment, July 31, 2001, para. 30; *Prosecutor v. Aleksovski*, Appeal Judgment, March 24, 2000, para. 185; *Prosecutor v. Mucic et al.*, Appeal Judgment, April 8, 2003, para. 806; *Prosecutor v. Tadić*, Appeal Judgment, January 26, 2000, para. 48). **18–38**

In *Prosecutor v. Erdemović*, Judgment, November 29, 1996, para. 5, the Trial Chamber had referred to what it regarded as (at that time) the only precedents in international criminal law, namely the sentencing practice from the Nuremberg and Tokyo Tribunals. After reviewing these, the Trial Chamber concluded that the declarations and judgments of those International Tribunals indicate that sentencing is directed towards retribution and deterrence. These are to be regarded as the primary purposes of sentencing. (See *Prosecutor v. Tadić*, Judgment, November 11, 1999, para. 9; Also see *Prosecutor v. Delalic et al.*, Judgment, November 16, 1998, paras 1231 and 1234 where the Trial Chamber concluded that "retributive punishment by itself does not bring justice" and that "deterrence is probably the most important factor in the assessment of the appropriate sentences for violations of international humanitarian law.")

The Trial Chamber in *Prosecutor v. Furundžija*, Judgment, December 10, 1998, para. 288, stated: "it is the mandate and the duty of the International Tribunal, in contributing to reconciliation, to deter such crimes and combat impunity. It is only right that *punitur quia peccatur* (the individual must be punished because he broke the law) but also *punitur ne peccatur* (he must be punished so that he and others will not break the law). The Trial Chamber accepts that two important functions of punishment are retribution and deterrence". (In the case of East Timor also see *Prosecutor v. Joni Marques et al.* (*Los Palos* case), Judgment, December 11, 2001, para. 979 and *P v. Manve Bere*, Judgment, May 15, 2001, p. 14).

In *Prosecutor v. Aleksovski*, Judgment, June 25, 1999, para. 185, the Appeal Chamber cautioned that retribution should not be "understood as fulfilling a desire for revenge, but as truly expressing the outrage of the international community at these crimes" (also see *Prosecutor v. Furundžija*, Judgment, December 10, 1998, para. 288).

In *Prosecutor v. Kambanda*, Judgment and Sentence, September 4, 1998, para. 28, the Trial Chamber stated that "it is clear that the penalties imposed on accused persons found guilty by the Tribunal must be directed, on the one hand, at retribution of the said accused, who must see their crimes punished, and over and above that, on other hand, at deterrence, namely dissuading for good those who will attempt in future to perpetrate such atrocities by showing them that the international community was not ready to tolerate the serious violations of international humanitarian law and human rights" (also see *Prosecutor v. Akayesu*, Judgment, October 2, 1998, para. 19 and *Prosecutor v. Kayishema and Ruzindana*, Sentence, May 21, 1999, para. 2).

In *Prosecutor v. Stakic*, Judgment, July 31, 2003, para. 902, the Trial Chamber held "[i]n the context of combating international crimes, deterrence refers to the attempt to integrate or to reintegrate those persons who believe themselves to be beyond the reach of international criminal law. Such persons must be warned that they have to respect the fundamental global norms of substantive criminal law or face not only prosecution but also sanctions imposed by international tribunals. In modern criminal law this approach to general deterrence is more accurately described as deterrence aiming at reintegrating potential perpetrators into the global society".

In *Prosecutor v. Krnojelac*, Judgment, March 15, 2002, para. 508, the Trial Chamber stated that retribution was to be interpreted as "punishment of an offender for his specific criminal conduct" and general deterrence as "the general sentencing factors which form the backdrop" against which an accused should be sentenced.

Whilst the principle of public deterrence is relevant in determining the appropriate sentence, care should be taken not to accord it "undue prominence" (see *Prosecutor v. Krnojelac*, Judgment, March 15, 2002, para. 505, n. 1517 and *Prosecutor v. Tadić*, Sentencing Appeal Judgment, January 26, 2000, para. 48; *Prosecutor v. Todorovic*, Judgment, July 31, 2001, para. 30). The punishment should always fit the crime (*Prosecutor v. Krnojelac*, Judgment, March 15, 2002, para. 507).

In *Prosecutor v. Nikolic*, Judgment, December 23, 2003, para. 140, the Trial Chamber stated "retribution incorporates a principle of restraint; retribution requires the imposition of a just and appropriate punishment, and nothing more".

In *Prosecutor v. Sufa*, UNTAET Judgment, November 25, 2004, para. 36, the Trial Chamber stated "[i]n East Timor there is an additional requirement to deterrence because just across hard-guarded-border live hundreds of recalcitrant ex-militia men with the capability of once again destabilizing the country by means of murder".

Rehabilitation

18–39   In *Prosecutor v. Delalic et al.*, Judgment, February 20, 2001, para. 806, the Appeals Chamber of the ICTY held that, unlike in most national courts and some international and regional human rights instruments, which provide that rehabilitation should be one of the primary concerns for a court, this was not the case in the ICTY context. Rather, "The Appeals Chamber has consistently pointed out that the main purposes of sentencing of crimes within its jurisdiction are deterrence and retribution," and rehabilitation should not be given "undue weight". Also see *Prosecutor v. Erdemović*, Judgment, November 19, 1996, para. 66, where the rehabilitative goal of punishment, was held to be subservient to an "attempt to stigmatise the most serious violations of international humanitarian law and in particular to preclude their reoccurrence".

In *Prosecutor v. Krnojelac*, Judgment, March 15, 2002, para. 505, the Trial Chamber held that incapacitation of the dangerous and rehabilitation were of little significance in the context of the ICTY (see *Prosecutor v. Krnojelac*, Judgment, March 15, 2002, para. 505). However, in *Prosecutor v. Erdemović*, Judgment, March 5, 1998, the Trial Chamber held that the accused (then 26 years old) who had been 23 years old at the time he committed the offences, was no longer a threat to the public and "that he is reformable and should be given a second chance to start his life afresh upon release, whilst still young enough to do so" (also see *Prosecutor v. Kayishema and Ruzindana, Sentence*, May 21, 1999, para. 26 where the "relatively young age and the goal of rehabilitation" were considered relevant sentencing considerations).

In *Prosecutor v. Obrenovic*, Judgment, December 10, 2003, para. 53, the ICTY Trial Chamber held that "punishment must strive to attain a further goal: rehabilitation. The Trial Chamber observes that the concept of rehabilitation can be thought of broadly and can encompass all stages of the criminal proceedings, and not simply the post-conviction stage. Particularly in cases where the crime was committed on a discriminatory basis, like this case, the process of coming face-to-face with the statements of victims, if not the victims themselves, can inspire—if not reawaken—tolerance and understanding of "the other", thereby making it less likely that if given an opportunity to act in a discriminatory manner again, an accused would do so. Criminal proceedings are only the starting point; the process continues upon the return of a convicted person to society and makes an active contribution towards reconciliation".

Reconciliation

In *Prosecutor v. Consta Nunes*, UNTAET Judgment, December 10, 2003, para. 85, the Panel stated "the objective of punishing the perpetrators of the serious crimes committed in East Timor in 1999 is to avoid impunity and thereby to promote national reconciliation and the restoration of peace" (also see *Prosecutor v. Cloe*, UNTAET Judgment, November 16, 2004, para. 22).   **18–40**

IV. FACTORS IN DETERMINING SENTENCE

In determining the appropriate term of imprisonment the ad hoc   **18–41**
Tribunals shall have recourse to the sentencing practice of the Courts of Rwanda and the former Yugoslavia (see Article 23(1) of the ICTR Statute and 24(1) ICTY Statutes). The Statutes expressly make reference to the gravity of an offence and the individual circumstance of an

accused as factors to consider in imposing sentence (see Articles 23(2) and 24(2) respectively). The same is the case in the East Timor context (see Section 10.2 of Regulation 2000/15 of June 6, 2000). Article 19 of the Statute establishing the Special Court for Sierra Leone requires the court to have recourse to the sentencing practice of the ICTR and the national practice of the courts of Sierra Leone.

18–42   The ICC Statute and ICC Rules of Procedure and Evidence do not require that recourse be had to the sentencing practice of the territory where the crime was committed, though the ICC will not be prevented from considering such laws under Article 76(1) if relevant to the imposition of an "appropriate" sentence.

Article 78(1) of the ICC Statute requires the Court to take into account the gravity of the crime and the individual circumstances of the convicted person. The ICC Rules of Procedure and Evidence further provide that the sentence imposed "must reflect the culpability of the convicted person" (Rule 145(1)(a)) and "balance all the relevant factors including any mitigating and aggravating factors and consider the circumstances of both the convicted person and the crime" (Rule 145(1)(b)). Rule 145(1)(c) details additional factors relevant in the assessment of the appropriate sentence.

The Rules of Procedure and Evidence of the ICTY and ICTR refer to aggravating circumstances and mitigating circumstances, including substantial cooperation with the Prosecutor, as additional factors for consideration in sentencing (see Rules 101(B) of ICTY, ICTR and SCSL Rules of Procedure and Evidence).

In *Prosecutor v. Jelisic*, Judgment, July 5, 2001, para. 100, the Appeals Chamber held that a Trial Chamber has a "broad discretion as to which factors it may consider in sentencing and the weight to attribute to them." Similarly, in *Prosecutor v. Kambanda*, September 4, 1998, para. 30, the Trial Chamber held that

> "as far as the individualization of penalties is concerned, the judges of the Chamber cannot limit themselves to the factors mentioned in the Statute and the Rules . . . their unfettered discretion to evaluate the facts and attendant circumstances should enable them to take into account any other factor that they deem pertinent."

The overriding sentencing obligation must, however, be to "individualise a penalty to fit the individual circumstances of the accused and the gravity of the crime" (*Prosecutor v. Delalic et al.*, Judgment, October 9, 2001, para. Æ717. Also see *Prosecutor v. Krnojelac*, Judgment, March 15, 2002, para. 507).

It does not preclude the Trial Chamber from imposing the maximum sentence of life imprisonment, as the Appeal Chamber stated in *Prosecutor v. Musema*, Judgment, November 16, 2001, para. 396, "[i]f a Trial Chamber finds that mitigating circumstances exist, it is not precluded from imposing a sentence of life imprisonment, where the gravity of the offence requires the imposition of the maximum sentence provided for".

In determining sentence, the court will take into account the time already served by the accused in custody. For example see: ICC Statute, Art. 78(2); ICTY RPE, Rule 101(B(iv)) (credit for time served in another state) and Rule 101(C) (credit for time served while in the custody of the Tribunal); ICTR RPE, Rule 101(B(v)) (credit for time served in another state) Rule 101(D) (credit for time served while in the custody of the Tribunal); SCSL RPE, Rule 101(B(iii)) credit for time served in another state) Rule 101(D) (credit for time served while in the custody of the Tribunal) and UNTAET Regulation 2000/15, s.10.3 and UNTAET Regulation 2000/30, s.42.5 in the case of the Special Panels for Serious Crimes in East Timor.

A. RECOURSE TO NATIONAL SENTENCING PRACTICE

The ICTY (Article 24(1)), ICTR (Article 23(1)), Panels for Serious Crimes in East Timor (Regulation 2000/15, Section 10(1)(a)) and the Special Court for Sierra Leone (Article 19(1)) are required to have recourse to the sentencing practice of the State where most of the crimes within their jurisdiction were committed, when assessing sentence. **18–43**

The law that addresses violations of international humanitarian law in Yugoslavia is incorporated in Chapter 16 of the Criminal Code of the Former Yugoslavia (SFRY). In *Prosecutor v. Delalic et al.*, Judgment, February 20, 2001, para. 813, the Appeals Chamber held that whilst a Trial Chamber should "have recourse to" and should "take into account" the general practice regarding prison sentences in the courts of the former Yugoslavia, Trial Chambers were not obliged to "conform to that practice." There was "no jurisprudential or juridical basis for the assertion that the International Tribunal is bound by decisions of the courts of the former Yugoslavia" (*Prosecutor v. Tadić*, Judgment in Sentencing Appeal, January 26, 2000, para. 21).

What is required, however, "must go beyond merely reciting the relevant criminal code provisions of the former Yugoslavia; the general sentencing practice of the former Yugoslavia must also be considered" (*Prosecutor v. Krnojelac*, Judgment, March 15, 2002, para. 505).

Accordingly, the Trial Chamber could legitimately apply a sentence greater than that provided for under the laws of the Former Yugoslavia (see *Prosecutor v. Delalic et al.*, Judgment, November 16, 1998, para. 1212). Even though recourse to the sentencing practice of the Former Yugoslavia disclosed that the maximum penalty was death with an alternative of 20 years imprisonment, the Appeals Chamber has held that a life sentence of imprisonment would not violate the principle of legality—*nulla poena sine lege* (see *Prosecutor v. Delalic et al.*, Judgment, February 20, 2001, para. 817).

For a detailed review of the sentencing practice of the courts of the former Yugoslavia also see see *Prosecutor v. Aleksovski*, Appeal Judgment, March 24, 2000, paras 186–190.

Rwanda's national laws proscribing and punishing crimes against humanity and genocide, named the Rwandan Organic Law (on the Organization of Prosecutions for Offences constituting the Crime of Genocide or Crimes against Humanity, committed since October 1, 1990), sets out penalties for the commission of the crimes set out therein. The Organic Law divides accused persons into four categories, according to their acts and criminal participation. The first concerns **18–44** the "masterminds of the crimes (planners, organisers), persons in positions of authority, from persons who have exhibited excessive cruelty to perpetrators of sexual violence. All these people are punishable by a death penalty. The second category concerns perpetrators, conspirators or accomplices in criminal acts, who incur life imprisonment. The third category deals with persons who, in addition to committing a main crime, are guilty of other serious assaults against the person. Their sentence is short. The fourth and last category concerns persons who have committed offences against property" (see *Prosecutor v. Serushago*, Sentence, February 5, 1999, para. 17).

The Rwandan Penal Code provides for fixed-term sentences of up to a maximum of twenty years' imprisonment or, exceptionally, up to thirty years' imprisonment in cases of concurrent offences. The most serious crimes, such as murder, may be punished by life imprisonment or death. Rape is generally punishable by a sentence of five to ten years, which may be doubled for certain prescribed aggravating elements such as the young age of the victim, the position of authority of the accused, or the severity of the physical harm. The Code specifically provides that accomplices may be subjected to the same penalties as the principal authors of the crime. The Rwandan Organic Law indicates that, even for genocide and crimes against humanity, the ordinary Penal Code sentences shall apply with certain modifications, which include heightened penalties of death and life imprisonment, respectively, for Categories 1 and 2 perpetrators (*Prosecutor v. Semanza*, Judgment, May 15, 2003, para. 561).

The Organic law and other national laws are not binding on the ICTR, but, like the ICTY, the Tribunal is required to have recourse to them in determining a sentence (the statement of the ICTY Trial Chamber in *Prosecutor v. Erdemović*, Sentencing Judgment, November 29, 1996, para. 39 that "the reference to this practice can be used for guidance, but is not binding" has been endorsed by the ICTR in *Prosecutor v. Kambanda*, Judgment and Sentence, September 4, 1998, para. 23; *Prosecutor v. Akayesu*, Sentence, October 2, 1998, para. 14 and *Prosecutor v. Serushago*, Sentence, February 5, 1999, para. 18).

18–45   The ICTR has stipulated that although it will refer as much as practicable to Rwanda's general sentencing practice in relation to prison terms, a Chamber will prefer to "lean more on its unfettered discretion each time that it has to pass sentence on persons found guilty of crimes falling within its jurisdiction, taking into account the circumstances of the case and the standing of the accused persons" (see *Prosecutor v. Kambanda*, Judgment and Sentence, September 4, 1998, para. 25).

In *Prosecutor v. Krnojelac*, Judgment, March 15, 2002, para. 526, consistency in sentencing was described by the ICTY Trial Chamber as "one of the fundamental elements in any rational and fair system of criminal justice". Whilst a range or pattern of sentencing will emerge from the sentencing practice of the ad hoc Tribunals over time, the Trial Chamber would have regard to those sentences which have been imposed "in generally similar circumstances as to both offences and offenders". Whilst the Chamber could refer to such developing practice, it would do so "with considerable caution".

Whilst the aims of sentencing within national criminal systems may be considered by the Tribunals, a degree of caution is required. This is warranted by the fact that the *"ratione materiae* jurisdiction of the International Tribunal differs fundamentally from that of a national court" and means that national criminal justice systems punish "all sorts of offences, usually ordinary crimes" (*Prosecutor v. Erdemović*, Judgment, November 29, 1996, para. 62).

Section 10.1 (a) of UNTAET Regulation 2000/15 requires the Panel to have recourse to the general practice regarding prison sentences in the courts of East Timor and under international tribunals (see also UNTAET case of *Prosecutor v. Fernandez*, Judgment, February 27, 2001, para. G2).

B. GRAVITY OF THE CRIME

18–46 All the international courts require that the gravity of the crime shall be taken into account when determining sentence (see ICC Statute, Art. 78(1); ICTR State, Art. 23; ICTY Statute, Art. 24; UNTAET Regulation 2000/15, s.10.2, Statute establishing the Special Court in Sierra Leone, Art. 19).

In *Prosecutor v. Delalic et al.*, Judgment, February 20, 2002, para. 731, the Appeals Chamber reaffirmed "the principle that the gravity of the offence is the primary consideration in imposing sentence" (also see *Prosecutor v. Aleksovski*, Judgment, Appeals Chamber, March 24, 2000, para. 182, and *Prosecutor v. Todorovic*, Sentencing Judgment, July 31, 2001, para. 31). Similarly, in *Prosecutor v. Krnojelac*, Judgment, March 15, 2002, para. 522, it was held that "the sentence to be imposed must reflect the inherent gravity of the criminal conduct of the accused, and the determination of that issue requires consideration of the particular circumstances of the case, as well as the form and degree of the participation of the accused in the crime. The nature of the actions of others for which the accused is found to be responsible is therefore relevant, but those actions are considered principally by reference to the nature of the accused's responsibility for them".

A hierarchy of crimes?

18–47 In *Prosecutor v. Erdemović*, Judgment, October 7, 1997, the Appeals Chamber remitted the case to a Trial Chamber on the basis that the accused had pleaded guilty at first instance to a count charging him with a crime against humanity and had not been informed that that crime was more serious than a war crime, with which he had been alternatively charged. It held that "*all things being equal*, a punishable offence, if charged and proven as a crime against humanity is more serious and should ordinarily entail a heavier penalty than if it were proceeded upon as a war crime." This approach was justified in that crimes against humanity are distinguished by the systematic targeting of civilians and their additional contribution to a "broader scheme of violence" (see *Prosecutor v. Erdemović*, Judgment, Joint and Separate Opinion of Judge McDonald and Judge Vohrah, October 7, 1997, paras 20, 22).

18–48   The ICTR seems to also have fashioned a hierarchy of crimes. ICTR Trial Chambers have held that genocide is the "crime of crimes" and that common Article 3 and Additional Protocol II of the Geneva Conventions are "lesser crimes to Genocide and Crimes against humanity" (see *Prosecutor v. Kambanda*, Judgment and Sentence, September 4, 1998, para. 14; *Prosecutor v. Akayesu*, Sentence, October 2, 1998, paras 6–10; *Prosecutor v. Serushago*, Sentence, February 5, 1999, para. 15, and *Prosecutor v. Kayishema and Ruzindana*, Sentence, May 21, 1999, para. 9).

In *Prosecutor v. Erdemović*, Separate and Dissenting Opinion of Judge Li, October 7, 1997, the learned judge rejected the finding of the majority of the Appeals Chamber that crimes against humanity were intrinsically more serious than war crimes stating "with respect to these arguments, I submit, in the first place, that the gravity of a criminal act, and consequently the seriousness of its punishment, are determined by the intrinsic nature of the act itself and not by its classification under one category or another" (also see *Prosecutor v. Erdemović*, Sentencing Judgment, Separate Opinion of Judge Shahabudden, March 5, 1998, p. 9).

It seems that the reasoning of Judge Li and Judge Shahabudden, as detailed in their separate opinions in *Erdemović*, have been accepted as correctly stating the law. In *Prosecutor v. Tadić*, Judgment, January 26, 2000, para. 69, the Appeals Chamber reviewed its previous jurisprudence and rejected the argument that there is a distinction in seriousness between crimes against humanity and war crimes. It found "no basis for such a distinction in the Statute or the Rules of the International Tribunal construed in accordance with customary international law; the authorized penalties are also the same, the level in any particular case being fixed by reference to the circumstances of the case".

This finding has been subsequently followed by the Appeals Chamber in *Prosecutor v Aleksovski*, Judgment, March 24, 2000, para. 183 and in *Prosecutor v. Furundžija*, Judgment, July 21, 2000, paras 243, 247, and by Trial Chambers in *Prosecutor v. Kunarac*, Judgment, February 22, 2001, para. 851 and *Prosecutor v. Krnojelac*, Judgment, March 15, 2002, para. 511 and must now be regarded as representing the settled law of the Tribunal.

C. Aggravating circumstances

18–49   Pursuant to Rule 145(1)(b) of the ICC RPE, Rules 101(B)(i) of the ICTY, ICTR and SCSL RPE, and s.10.2 of UNTAET Regulation 2000/15, Trial Chambers are required to take into account any aggravating circumstances when determining the appropriate sentence.

A number of factors are deemed to aggravate the crime. These include: the nature of the crime, including how it was committed and its effects on the victims; the degree of an accused's responsibility (such as whether an accused is a commander or a direct participant) as well as premeditation.

Criminal acts not proved beyond a reasonable doubt cannot be taken into account as aggravating circumstances. See *Prosecutor v. Delalic et al.*,

Judgment, February 20, 2001, para. 763, "[t]he Appeals Chamber agrees that only those matters which are proved beyond reasonable doubt against an accused may be the subject of an accused's sentence or taken into account in aggravation of that sentence." Moreover, the "Trial Chamber cannot be expected to make findings in respect of matters which had not been specifically put before it, whether in the Indictment or during the trial".

This holding correlates with the opinion of the Trial Chamber in *Prosecutor v. Kunarac*, Judgment, February 22, 2001, para. 850 and *Prosecutor v. Semanza*, Judgment, May 15, 2003, para. 570, which held that it is improper for the Prosecutor to rely on allegations not included in the indictment in order to establish aggravating factors said to be relevant to sentence: "[e]ither the Prosecutor should charge such conduct as an offence, or, where it is not directly related to another charged offence, she should desist from citing such conduct as an aggravating factor. The Trial Chamber understands that the multiplicity of humanitarian law violations committed during an armed conflict as part of a common criminal scheme often cannot be succinctly captured in an indictment. Considerations of fairness to the accused and judicial economy, however, outweigh the wish to have each and every crime committed during a war brought to light and adjudged in whatever way—that is something which this International Tribunal simply cannot do" and "[i]t would circumvent the proper course of justice to rely on allegations of further uncharged criminality to increase the sentence of the accused. Where the Prosecutor has reliable evidence of criminal activity falling within the jurisdiction of the Tribunal, then she may choose to include those matters in the indictment against the accused".

(i) Cruelty

Rule 145(2)(b)(iv) of the ICC RPE specifically details cruelty as an aggravating factor to be considered when determining sentence. In *Prosecutor v. Blaškić*, Judgment, March 3, 1998, para. 783, the ICTY Trial Chamber declared that the "extreme cruelty of the beatings, the sadism with which they were inflicted and the especial humiliation which ensued" were significant considerations in determining sentence. Likewise, the Trial Chamber in *Prosecutor v. Todorovic*, Judgment, July 31, 2001, para. 65, considered "the particular cruelty shown in connection with these beatings, and their lengthy duration, to be an aggravating factor" to be considered in sentencing.

18–50

In the *Prosecutor v. Delić*, Judgment, November 16, 1998, para. 1268, the Trial Chamber noted "that the manner in which these crimes were committed are indicative of a sadistic individual who, at times, displayed a total disregard for the sanctity of human life and dignity" and considered it to be a significant aggravating factor for the purposes of sentencing.

In *Prosecutor v. Niyitegeka*, Judgment, May 16, 2003, para. 499(iv), the Trial Chamber took in aggravation the fact that "the Accused joined in the jubilation over the killing, decapitation and castration of Kabanda, and the piercing of his skull through the ears with a spike".

(ii) Scale of the crime

18–51   Rule 145(1)(c) of the ICC RPE states that the court shall give consideration to the extent of the damage caused by the convicted person when considering the appropriate sentence. In the context of the ad hoc Tribunals, the same applies. The greater the scale of the crime, the greater the number of victims the more weight will be attached to the aggravating features found (see, *Prosecutor v. Erdemović*, Judgment, March 5, 1998, para. 15. Also see *Prosecutor v. Tadić*, Judgment in Sentencing Appeals, January 26, 2000, paras 11–55 and *Prosecutor v. Kambanda*, Judgment and Sentence, September 4, 1998, para. 42; *Prosecutor v. Blagojević*, Judgment, January 17, 2005, para. 845).

(iii) Motive

18–52   Rule 145(2)(b)(v) of the ICC RPE specifically states that motive involving discrimination on grounds of gender, age, race, colour, language, religion, or belief, political or other opinion, national, ethnic or social origin, wealth, birth or other status shall be taken into account as aggravating factors when assessing sentence (in the ICTY context, see *Prosecutor v. Blaškić*, Judgment, March 3, 2000, para. 785, where the Trial Chamber noted the ethnic and religious discrimination that the victims suffered, amounted to persecution, and demanded a more severe penalty).

(iv) Status of the victim/vulnerability

18–53   The status of the victims as civilians, women and children may constitute an aggravating factor (see ICC RPE, Rule 145(2)(b)(iii). Also see, *Prosecutor v. Furundžija*, Judgment, December 10, 1998, para. 283; *Prosecutor v. Tadić*, Sentencing Judgment, November 11, 1999, para. 56 and *Prosecutor v. Blaškić*, Judgment, March 3, 2000, para. 783 and *Prosecutor v. Kunurac*, Judgment, February 22, 2001, para. 879, where the Trial Chamber considered the young age of the victim to be an aggravating factor).

18–54   The Trial Chambers of the ICTY and ICTR have consistently taken evidence regarding the accused's conduct during trial into account in determining sentence. In *Prosecutor v. Delalic et al.*, Judgment, February 20, 2001, paras 785–788, the Appeals Chamber held that the Trial Chamber had not erred in considering the conduct at trial of the accused *Mucic* to be an aggravating circumstance (the Trial Chamber described the appellant's behaviour as suggesting he regarded the trial as "a farce and an expensive joke"). The Appeals Chamber held that conduct during trial "is relevant to a Trial Chamber's determination of, for example, remorse for the acts committed, or the contrary, total lack of compassion" (at para. 788). The "extensive, detailed, lengthy and searching" cross-examination of victims by an accused cannot be considered evidence to counter an expression of remorse. This flows both from the presumption of innocence, and from defence counsel's obligation to his client (see *Prosecutor v. Simić*, Judgment, October 17, 2002, para. 93).

In *Prosecutor v. Deronjic*, Judgment, March 30, 2004, para. 198, the Trial Chamber held that the Accussed's approval of disarming the population of Glogova, which left them "at the disposal of the armed forces in the attack of May 9, 1992", constitutes an aggravating factor to the crime.

In UNTAET case *Prosecutor v. Soares*, Judgment, October 2, 2002, para. 66, the Trial Chamber, rather astonishingly, found the actions of the accused, who raped "a helpless woman, knowing that the victim already had a boyfriend", to be aggravating.

(v) Effect of crime on the victim

The physical and mental consequences of crime upon victims con-   **18–55**
stitute aggravating circumstances (see ICC RPE Rule 145(1)(c). In the ICTY context see *Prosecutor v. Delalic et al.*, Judgment, February 20, 2001, paras 1226, 1260, 1273). In *Prosecutor v. Krnojelac*, Judgment, March 15, 2002, para. 512, the Trial Chamber held that the consequences of the crime upon the victim who is *directly* injured are "always" a relevant consideration in assessing sentence.

However, where such consequences on the victim are part of the definition of the offence, "they may not be considered as an aggravating circumstance in imposing sentence, but the extent of the long-term physical, psychological and emotional suffering of the immediate victims is relevant to the gravity of the offences" (*Prosecutor v. Krnojelac*, Judgment, March 15, 2002, para. 512; see also *Prosecutor v. Blagojević*, Judgment, January 17, 2005, para. 845).

(vi) Effect of crime on the relatives of victims

In *Prosecutor v. Krnojelac*, Judgment, March 15, 2002, para. 512, the   **18–56**
Prosecution submitted that an *"in personam* evaluation" of the gravity of the crime should include consideration of the effect a crime had on the relatives of the immediate victims of the crime. The Trial Chamber, however, considered that "such effects are irrelevant to the culpability of the offender, and that it would be unfair to consider such effects in determining sentence." (*cf.* ICC RPE, Rule 145(1)(c) provides that in determining sentence consideration be given, *inter alia*, to the harm caused "to the victims *and their families*" (emphasis added)).

(vii) Willing participation

Willing participation in offences within the jurisdiction of inter-   **18–57**
national courts constitutes an aggravating feature to be considered in sentence (see ICC RPE, Rule 145(1)(c). See also ICTY cases of

Prosecutor v. Tadić, Judgment, July 14, 1997, para. 57; *Prosecutor v. Jelisic*, Judgment, December 14, 1999, paras 129–134; ICTR case of *Prosecutor v. Kayishema and Ruzindana*, Sentence, May 21, 1999, para. 13 and ICTR case of *Prosecutor v. Gacumbitsi*, Judgment, June 17, 2004, para. 345).

(viii) Superior responsibility

18–58   The accused's role as a commander or superior may constitute an aggravating consideration when determining sentence (for example, see, Trial Chamber decisions in: *Prosecutor v. Naletilic*, Judgment, March 31, 2003, para. 751; *Prosecutor v. Kupreškić*, Judgment, January 14, 2000, para. 862; *Prosecutor v. Furundžija*, Judgment, December 10, 1998, para. 283; *Prosecutor v. Delalic et al.*, Judgment, November 16, 1998, paras 1240–1243; decisions of the Appeals Chamber in: *Prosecutor v. Delalic et al.*, Judgment, February 20, 2001, paras 736–742; *Prosecutor v. Aleksovski*, Judgment, March 24, 2000, para. 187. Also see ICTR cases of *Prosecutor v. Kambanda*, Judgment and Sentence, September 4, 1998, paras 44, 61–62; *Prosecutor v. Akayesu*, Sentence, October 2, 1998, para. 26 and *Prosecutor v. Serushago*, Sentence, February 5, 1999, para. 29).

In *Prosecutor v. Blaškić*, Judgment, May 3, 2000, para. 789, the Trial Chamber stated that "when a commander fails in his duty to prevent the crime or to punish the perpetrator thereof he should receive a heavier sentence than the subordinates who committed the crime insofar as the failing conveys some tolerance or even approval on the part of the commander towards the commission of crimes by his subordinates and thus contributes to encouraging the commission of new crimes. It would not in fact be consistent to punish a simple perpetrator with a sentence equal or greater to that of the commander".

In *Prosecutor v. Kordić and Čerkez*, Judgment, February 26, 2001, para. 853, the Trial Chamber recognised superior responsibility, whether military or civilian, as an aggravating circumstance in sentencing. The fact that Kordic "was a politician makes no difference: he played his part as surely as the men who fired the guns. Indeed, the fact that he was a leader aggravates the offences".

In *Prosecutor v. Krnojelac*, Judgment, March 15, 2002, para. 514, the Trial Chamber noted that "the accused chose to bury his head in the sand and to ignore his responsibilities and the power which he had as warden of the [prison camp] to improve the situation of the non-Serb detainees. The sentence in this case must make it clear to others who (like the accused) seek to avoid the responsibilities of command which accompany the position which they have accepted that their failure to carry out those responsibilities will be punished".

In *Prosecutor v. Obrenovic*, Judgment, December 10, 2003, para. 100, the Trial Chamber recalled:

> "When a commander fails to ensure compliance with the principles of international humanitarian law such that he fails to prevent or punish his subordinates for the commission of crimes that he knew or had reason to know about, he will be held liable pursuant to Article 7(3). When a commander orders his subordinates to commit a crime within the jurisdic-

tion of the Tribunal, he will be held liable pursuant to Article 7(1) of the Statue. When commanders, through their own actions or inactions, fail in the duty, which stems from their position, training, and leadership skills, to set an example for their troops that would promote the principles underlying the laws and customs of war and thereby—either tacitly or implicitly—promote or encourage the commission of crimes, this may be seen as an aggravating circumstance."

The correct position seems to be that, all things being equal, a conviction under a Article 6(3) or 7(3) theory of liability under the respective Statutes of the ICTR and ICTY (superior responsibility) will attract a greater sentence than a conviction of their subordinates under Articles 6(1) or 7(1) (direct participation) of those Statutes because of the breach of trust and abdication of the responsibilities of command that are integral to a finding of superior responsibility. As a matter of law, however, it cannot be accurately said that a finding of superior responsibility is an "aggravating feature" because such a finding is an essential component for a conviction under that theory of liability.

(ix) Personal Authority where direct participation is alleged

The jurisprudence of the ICTY holds that a high-ranking position of **18–59** leadership held by a person criminally responsible under Article 7(1) of the Statute is an aggravating factor (for example see, Trial Chamber decisions in: *Prosecutor v. Kristic*, Judgment, August 2, 2001, para. 709; *Prosecutor v. Mrdja*, Judgment, March 31, 2004, para. 52). Similarly, in *Prosecutor v. Kupreškić et al.*, Appeal Judgment, para. 451, the Appeals Chamber ruled "[. . .]a Trial Chamber has the discretion to find that direct responsibility, under Article 7(1) of the Statute, is aggravated by a perpetrator's position of authority".

In *Prosecutor v. Babic*, Judgment, June 29, 2004, para. 61, the ICTY Trial Chamber considered Babic's leadership position as an aggravating circumstance because "as a regional leader he enlisted the resources of the SAO Kraijna to further the joint criminal enterprise and by his speeches and media exposure prepared the ground for the Serb population to accept that their goals could be achieved through acts of persecutions", and "by allowing the campaign of persecutions to continue he amplified its consequences".

In the ICTY case of *Prosecutor v. Stakic*, Judgment, July 31, 2003, para. 913, the Trial Chamber expressed "the commission of offences by a person in such a prominent position aggravates the sentence substantially": (Also see *Prosecutor v. Dragan Nikolic*, Judgment, December 18, 2003, March 24, 2000, para. 183; *Prosecutor v. Celebici*, Appeal Judgment, para. 745; *Prosecutor v. Aleksovski*, Appeal Judgment para. 183, "[. . .] the Accused's seniority or position of authority [may be considered as] aggravating his direct responsibility under Article 7(1)" and *Prosecutor v. Deronjic*, Judgment, March 30, 2004, para. 194).

In the ICTR case of *Prosecutor v. Kamuhanda*, Judgment, January 22, 2004, para. 764, the Trial Chamber held that:

"The high position [. . .] as a civil servant can be considered as an aggravating factor. Kamuhanda was a respected man, influential, and considered to be an intellectual. He was in the position to know and to appreciate the dignity and value of life, and also the value and importance of a peaceful coexistence between communities. He was in the position to promote the value of tolerance. Instead of doing so, he blamed people who were living peacefully for not taking part in the campaign of violence. He instigated and led an attack to kill people who had taken shelter in a place universally recognized to be a sanctuary, the Compound of the Gikomero Parish Church."

(x) Abuse of trust

18–60   Abuse of trust or official capacity constitutes an aggravating circumstance (see ICC Rule 145(2)(b)(ii)). In the ICTY case of *Prosecutor v. Todorovic*, Judgment, July 31, 2001, para. 61, the accused was Chief of Police in the area where the crimes were committed. This was viewed as an aggravating factor to be considered in sentence. As Chief of Police, Todorovic had a responsibility "to protect and defend all citizens of the municipality". Instead he "directly took part in offences which he should have been working to prevent or punish". Todorovic's "direct participation in the crimes, as well as his abuse of his position of authority and of people's trust in the institution, clearly constitute an aggravating factor".

In *Prosecutor v. Sikirica et al.*, Judgment, November 13, 2001, paras 139–140, the Trial Chamber considered that Sikirica's position as commander of security at Keraterm camp required him to prevent "outsiders from coming into the camp to mistreat the detainees". His failure to do so was an aggravating factor (also see *Sikirica et al.*, paras 172 and 210 in relation to his co-accused *Dosen and Kolundzija*).

(xi) Direct participation

18–61   The active and direct participation of an accused might be considered an aggravating factor (see ICC RPE Rule 145(1)(c) and also ICTY cases of *Prosecutor v. Furundžija*, Judgment, December 10, 1998, paras 281–282; *Prosecutor v. Erdemović*, Judgment, March 5, 1998, para. 15, where the accused's role as part of an execution squad murdering hundreds of Muslim civilians was regarded as an aggravating circumstance, "given the magnitude of the crime and the scale of the accused's role". Also see ICTR cases of *Prosecutor v. Kambanda*, Judgment and Sentence, September 4, 1998, para. 61(B)(vi); *Prosecutor v. Serushago*, Sentence, February 5, 1999, para. 30 and *Prosecutor v. Kayishema and Ruzindana*, Sentence, May 21, 1999, para. 13, which all recognise that the knowing and/or voluntary participation in offences within the jurisdiction of the Tribunals constitutes an aggravating circumstance relevant to sentence).

(xii) Individual Circumstances of the Accused

18–62   Rule 145(1)(c) of the ICC RPE requires the Court to look at "the circumstances of manner, time and location" as well as the "age, education, social and economic condition" of the convicted person when assessing sentence. These factors may aggravate or mitigate penalty as the case may be.

In *Prosecutor v. Tadić*, Judgment, July 14, 1997, para. 59, the defence had raised Tadić's upbringing "in a spirit of ethnic and religious tolerance" and his character as "capable of compassion towards and sensitivity for his fellows" as a mitigating factor in sentence. The Trial Chamber, however, found that "this, if anything, aggravates more than it mitigates: for such a man to have committed these crimes requires an even greater evil will on his part than that for lesser men".

(xiii) Double counting not permissible

Where a Trial Chamber has taken into account facts such as the vulnerability of a victim, or the length of time over which crimes were committed when considering the gravity of an offence "it would be impermissible double counting to take these matters into account again as matters of aggravation as well" (*Prosecutor v. Krnojelac*, Judgment, March 15, 2002, para. 517; *Prosecutor v. Jokic*, Judgment, March 18, 2004, para. 65).

18–63

In *Prosecutor v. Babic*, Judgment, June 29, 2004, para. 58, the Trial Chamber held that "the same element should not be assessed once as a constitutive element of the crime and a second time as an aggravating circumstance" (*Prosecutor v. Babic*, Judgment, June 29, 2004, para. 58).

D. Mitigating circumstances

Sub-rule 101(B)(ii) of the ICTY, ICTR and SCSL Rules of Procedure and Evidence and s. 10.2 of UNTAET Regulation 2000/15, require a Trial Chamber to take into account "any mitigating circumstances including the substantial cooperation with the Prosecutor by the convicted person before or after conviction" (also see ICC RPE, Rule 145(1)(b)).

18–64

The finding of mitigating circumstances "relates to assessment of sentence and in no way derogates from the gravity of the crime. It mitigates punishment, not the crime" (see *Prosecutor v. Kambanda*, Judgment and Sentence, September 4, 1998, paras 56–57 and its reference to *Prosecutor v. Erdemović*, Judgment, November 29, 1996, para. 46 in which the Trial Chamber quoted the US military tribunal's *obiter dictum* in the *Hostage Case* (*USA v. Wilhelm List*, Volume XI, Trials of War Criminals, p. 757) with approval that mitigation "of punishment does not in any sense of the word reduce the degree of the crime. It is more a matter of grace than of defence". Thus the "degree and magnitude of the crime is still an essential criterion for evaluation of sentence"). In *Prosecutor v. Niyitegeka*, Appeal Judgment, July 9, 2004, para. 267, the Trial Chamber stated "[p]roof of mitigating circumstances does not automatically entitle the Appellant to a 'credit' in the determination of the sentence; rather, it simply requires the Trial Chamber to consider such mitigating circumstances in its final determination". In *Prosecutor v. Erdemović*, Judgment, November 29, 1996, para. 86, the Trial Chamber examined mitigating circumstances under two headings. Firstly, those circumstances contemporary with the perpetration of the crime, such as mental incapacity, urgent necessity and low rank. Secondly, the accused's attitude after the commission of a crime. These mitigating circumstances would include: remorse, willingness to surrender to the Tribunal as well as cooperation with the Prosecutor.

(1) Circumstances Contemporaneous with the crime

(i) *Duress and Superior Orders*

18–65   Circumstances contemporary with the perpetration of the crime include duress. In *Prosecutor v. Erdemović*, Judgment, October 7, 1997, para. 19, the Appeals Chamber confirmed that duress does not afford a complete defence, but may be considered in mitigation of sentence (also see *Prosecutor v. Blaškić*, Judgment, March 3, 2000, para. 769. *Cf.* Rome Statute, Article 31(d), which provides that duress may be a defence to crimes within the ICC's jurisdiction). Rule 145(2)(a)(i) of the ICC RPE provides that where duress falls short of a complete defence under Article 31(d), it may nonetheless play some part in the convicted persons participation in the crime, and may be considered in mitigation of penalty. Superior orders are not a defence, but may mitigate penalty. Articles (4) and 7(4) of the ICTY and ICTR Statutes as well as UNTAET Regulation 2000/15, s. 21, respectively provide that "the facts that an accused person acted pursuant to an order of a Government or a superior shall not relieve him of criminal responsibility, but may be considered in mitigation of punishment if the International Tribunal determines that justice so requires". Superior orders were taken into account by the Trial Chamber in *Prosecutor v. Erdemović*, Sentencing Judgment, November 29, 1996, para. 46 (also see UNTAET case of *Prosecutor v. Joseph Leki*, Judgment, June 11, 2001, p. 10).

(ii) *Diminished Responsibility*

18–66   Diminished responsibility at the time an offence is committed will be a mitigating factor to be considered in sentence (see ICC RPE, Rule 145(2)(a)(i)). In *Prosecutor v. Delalic et al.*, Judgment, February 20, 2001, para. 590, the Appeals Chamber accepted that:

> "[. . .] the relevant general principle of law upon which, in effect, both the common law and the civil law systems have acted is that the defendant's diminished mental responsibility is relevant to the sentence to be imposed and is not a defence leading to an acquittal in the true sense. This is the appropriate general legal principle representing the international law to be applied in the Tribunal. Rule 67(A)(ii)(b) must therefore be interpreted as referring to diminished mental responsibility where it is to be raised by the defendant as a matter in mitigation of sentence."

(iii) *Vulnerability/low IQ*

18–67   In *Prosecutor v. Banović*, Judgment, October 28, 2003, paras 77–80, the Trial Chamber rejected the Defence's assertion that the below-average intelligence of the accused made him vulnerable to the war propaganda which spread collective hatred and rumours about the enemy's brutality and explained "the Accused's [lack of understanding of [. . .] the criminality of his behaviour". Moreover, "The Trial Chamber does not consider it appropriate in the present case to mitigate the sentence of the Accused on the basis of his immature and impulsive personality or below average intelligence. Nor does the Trial Chamber accept the argument that the the Accused did not have the strength of character to resist the war propaganda." (para. 81.)

The Special Panel for Serious Crimes in East Timor in *Prosecutor v. Cloe*, Judgment, November 16, 2004, para. 20, noted that the accused "were illiterate farmers who must be considered as victims of circumstance themselves, as they would not have committed the crimes without the despicable system of the Indonesian Armed Forces (TNI) to pit one part of the local population against aganother, and the campaign of militia violence unleashed by TNI after the Popular Consultation had turned out to be unfavourable to them" and considered it a mitigating factor. (Also see *Prosecutor v. Sufa*, UNTAET Judgment, November 25, 2004, para. 34.)

In *Prosecutor v. Soares*, Judgment, December 9, 2003, para. 229, the Special Panel for Serious Crimes in East Timor took as mitigation the fact that "[t]he accused person Salvador Soares, prior to the commission of the crime, for which he has been convicted, was living in a very coercive environment". Similarly in an earlier case, *Prosecutor v. Santos*, Judgment, May 14, 2002, para. 60(d), the Trial Chamber further noted that "[t]here were pressure from militia and ceremonies organized for young men to join criminal activities. [. . .] the coercive environment has been a factor for the accused in committing the crime, although [. . .] there are some who refused to join criminal activities. The fact that some joined while others were able to resist, does not mean that there was no coercive environment."

In the ICTR case of *Prosecutor v. Elizaphan and Ntakirutimana*, Judgment, February 21, 2003, para. 897, the Trial Chamber found that the accused "did not play a leading role in the attacks. He did not personally participate in these killings, nor was he found to have fired on refugees or even to have carried a weapon" and took this as a factor in mitigation.

(iv) *Acting to ameliorate the conditions of detainees*

If persons convicted by international courts nonetheless demonstrate that they took steps to ameliorate the condition of detainees or other prisoners under their control or influence, such conduct may be considered as a mitigating factor (see *Prosecutor v. Sikirica et al.*, Sentencing Judgment, November 13, 2001, para. 242; *Prosecutor v. Serushago*, Sentence, February 5, 1999, para. 38 and *Prosecutor v. Ntakirutimana*, Judgment, December 9, 2003, para 909).

18–68

Similarly, in *Prosecutor v. Akayesu*, Sentence, October 2, 1998, para. 35 the Trial Chamber considered Akayesu's efforts to prevent massacres for a period of time and found that but for that intervention, the killings would have started earlier. It considered his actions as a mitigating circumstance.

(2) Circumstances after commission of the crime

(i) *Remorse*

18–69   In order for remorse to constitute a mitigating factor in sentence, the remorse must be sincere. Sincerity might be gleaned from the statements and conduct of an accused as well as any medical or expert reports (*Prosecutor v. Todorovic*, Sentencing Judgment, July 31, 2001, para. 89). After considering statements made by the accused and various expert reports, the Trial Chamber in *Prosecutor v. Erdemović*, Sentencing Judgment, March 5, 1998, para. 16, found the accused to have expressed feelings of sorrow and remorse which "were genuine and real" (also see *Prosecutor v. Serushago*, Sentence, February 5, 1999, paras 40–41 and *Prosecutor v. Sikirica et al.*, Sentencing Judgment, November 13, 2001, para. 152; *Prosecutor v. Strugar*, Judgment, January 31, 2005, para. 471).

In *Prosecutor v. Jelisic*, Judgment, December 14, 1999, para. 127, mitigation afforded by the accused's guilty plea was reduced by the fact that he showed no real remorse (also see *Prosecutor v. Blaškić*, Judgment, March 3, 2000, para. 775, where the accused's expression of remorse was not accepted as genuine).

In *Prosecutor v. Kambanda*, Judgment and Sentence, September 4, 1998, para. 52, the Trial Chamber recognised that although remorse is not the only inference to be drawn from a guilty plea, most "national jurisdictions consider admissions of guilt as matters properly to be considered in mitigation of punishment."

(ii) *Substantial Cooperation*

18–70   Substantial cooperation is the only example given of a mitigating circumstance in Rule 101(B)(ii) of the ICTY and ICTR Rules of Procedure and Evidence. Where cooperation given to the office of the Prosecutor is full, substantial and unconditional, it may be accorded considerable significance in mitigating the penalty for the crime in question (see, for example, *Prosecutor v. Erdemović*, Sentencing Judgment, November 29, 1996, paras 99–101 and *Prosecutor v. Serushago*, Sentence, September 4, 1998, para. 31; *Prosecutor v. Blagojević*, Judgment, January 17, 2005, para. 857). Assistance can include providing the Prosecution with information regarding other massacres, the names and identities of persons involved and testimony against other accused persons. (See also UNTAET case of *Prosecutor v. Joao Fernandez*, Judgment, January 25, 2001, para. 20(a)). It seems that cooperation may be given by an accused, who nonetheless maintains a not guilty plea, or changes plea at a later stage (see *Prosecutor v. Ruggiu*, Judgment and Sentence, June 1, 2000, para. 58).

The threshold of "substantial cooperation" must, however, be met. Nonetheless, cooperation may be given which does not reach this threshold (see the Trial Chamber decision in *Prosecutor v. Tadić*, Sentencing Judgment, November 11, 1999, para. 22; also see the Appeals Chamber decision in *Prosecutor v. Tadić*, Judgment in Sentencing

Appeals, January 26, 2000, paras 63–64). In *Prosecutor v. Cesic*, Judgment, March 11, 2004, para. 62, the Trial Chamber ruled that "[t]he extent and quality of the information provided to the Prosecution are factors to take into account when determining whether the co-operation has been substantial." Cooperation also mitigates the sentence under Rule 145(2)(a)(ii) of the ICC RPE. Under this Rule, there is no requirement that the cooperation be "substantial," rather, the ICC when assessing sentence may take "any cooperation with the Court" into account.

Even absent genuine remorse, substantial cooperation with the Prosecutor will mitigate penalty and will do so irrespective of the motives for the cooperation. Even if the substantial cooperation is occasioned out of self-interest, it should be considered as a mitigating factor in determining sentence. In *Prosecutor v. Todorovic*, Sentencing Judgment, July 31, 2001, para. 86, the Trial Chamber held "that the fact that an accused has gained or may gain something pursuant to an agreement with the Prosecution does not preclude the Trial Chamber from considering his substantial cooperation as a mitigating circumstance in sentencing".

In more recent ICTY judgments it appears that the requirement of "substantial cooperation" has been gradually diminished. In *Prosecutor v. Banović*, Judgment, October 28, 2003, para. 61 the Trial Chamber stated "[t]he fact that he did agree to be interviewed may in itself, in some cases, be a sign of cooperation, however modest" and considers such cooperation in mitigation.

The commitment to cooperate further with the Prosecution in the future is an essential feature of plea agreements entered jointly by the accused and the OTP. It is a factor that the Trial Chamber takes into account in mitigation of the sentence. (See *Prosecutor v. Banović*, Judgment; October 28, 2003, para. 61; *Prosecutor v. Obrenovic*, Judgment, December 10, 2003, para. 128.)

(iii) *Guilty Plea*

A guilty plea may be evidence of remorse and contrition. A defendant **18–71** who enters a guilty plea should expect to be "treated accordingly". See UNTAET case of *P v. Augusto Dos Santos*, Judgment, May 14, 2002, para. 60. In the ICTY case of *Prosecutor v. Todorovic*, Sentencing Judgment, July 31, 2001, para. 80, the Trial Chamber held that guilty pleas should in principle give rise to a reduction in sentence. Also see ICTR cases of *Prosecutor v. Serushago*, Sentence, February 5, 1999, para. 35 and *Prosecutor v. Georges Ruggiu*, Judgment and Sentence, June 1, 2000, para. 55 and UNTAET case of *Prosecutor v. Joao Fernandez*, Judgment, January 25, 2001. The rationale for recognising a guilty plea in mitigation of sentence relates to the benefits that flow from the plea to the Tribunals both in terms of time and resources, and impact on the victims.

In *Prosecutor v. Sikirica et al.*, Sentencing Judgment, November 13, 2001, para. 149, the Trial Chamber explained the benefits of a guilty plea: "A guilty plea facilitates the work of the International Tribunal in two ways. First, by entering a plea of guilt before the commencement of his trial, an accused will save the International Tribunal the time and effort of a lengthy investigation and trial. Secondly, notwithstanding the timing of the guilty plea, a benefit accrues to the Trial Chamber, because a guilty plea contributes directly to one of the fundamental objectives of the International Tribunal: namely, its truth-finding function" (also see *Prosecutor v. Simić*, Judgment, October 17, 2002, para. 84, and ICTR case of *Prosecutor v. Kambanda*, Judgment and Sentence, September 4, 1998, para. 54; *Prosecutor v. Babic*, Judgment, June 29, 2004; para. 68). Thirdly, the guilty plea may obviate the need for victims and witnesses to give evidence, thus relieving the victims and witnesses from the stress of testifying at the Tribunal and giving evidence (see *Prosecutor v. Todorovic*, Judgment, July 31, 2001, para. 80–81; *Prosecutor v. Plavsic*; Judgment, February 27, 2003, para. 66; *Prosecutor v. Nikolic*, Judgment, para. 150). A guilty plea might also be an indication of remorse (*Prosecutor. Plavsic*, Judgment, February 27, 2003, para. 70). Repentance is another reason for entering a guilty plea (*Prosecutor v. Ruggiu*, Judgment, June 1, 2000, para. 55; *Prosecutor v. Jelisic*, Judgment, December 14, 1999, para. 127).

Mitigation and sentence reduction following a guilty plea is also an incentive to accused persons to enter such pleas if guilty of the crimes charged (*Prosecutor v. Erdemović*, Judgment 1998, para. 16). The effect of a guilty plea on sentence has been studied in the case of the ICTY: "Those who plead guilty are sentenced to an average of 101 months behind bars, while those who do not are sentenced to an average of 213 month in prison, or more than double those who do reach accommodation" (Meernik and Kink, "The Sentencing Determinants of the International Criminal Tribunal for the Former Yugoslavia: An Empirical and Doctrinal Analysis", 16 2003 *Leiden Journal of International Law* 745). Such sentence reduction is more discernable in cases before the ICTY than the ICTR. This may help explain, in part at least, why seventeen guilty pleas have so far been entered at the ICTY as opposed to only three before the ICTR. Also central to such consideration, however, is the fact that all the indictments before the ICTR contain counts alleging genocide. In the ICTR in *Prosecutor v. Kambanda*, Judgment, October 19, 2000, paras 2, 126, the accused who had been the Prime Minsiter of Rwanda, pleaded guilty to six counts of genocide, conspiracy to commit genocide, and crimes against humanity (extermination), and was sentenced to imprisonment for life, providing little or no incentive to others to accept responsibility for their actions.

In *Prosecutor v. Deronjic*, Judgment, March 30, 2004, Dissenting Opinion of Judge Schomburg, para. 14, the learned judge explained the effect of guilty pleas in the following terms:

"a) An analysis of various national legal systems shows that a guilty plea is generally accepted as a mitigating factor leading to a reduction of the sentence. Reasons justifying such mitigation include the willingness of an offender to co-operate in the administration of justice, the showing of remorse, acknowledgment of responsibility, sparing the victims from testifying and being cross-examined, the stage of proceedings at which the offender pleads guilty, and the circumstances in which the plea is tendered.

b) It becomes evident from the analysis, however, that in the majority of the countries under survey a guilty plea is given only little—if any—weight in relation to serious crimes. In Australia, Canada, China, England, and Germany, first degree murder attracts a mandatory sentence of life imprisonment that can not be altered by the acceptance of the guilty plea or confession of the accused. In Poland, a plea bargain is only possible in relation to misdemeanours, but not crimes. Similar provisions on guilty pleas or plea bargaining exist in other countries, *e.g.* Argentina, Brazil, and Chile.

　　c) In light of this analysis, and taking into consideration that a guilty plea can not derogate from the gravity of a crime, I believe that the guilty plea of Miroslav Deronjic only warrants little weight in sentencing."

A guilty plea will attract most credit when it is offered at the first available opportunity. However, the Tribunal has recognised a guilty plea will constitute mitigation even where it is entered after a trial's commencement (see *Prosecutor v. Sikirica et al.*, Judgment, November 13, 2001, paras 150–151; *Prosecutor v. Simić*, Judgment, para. 87 "some credit" was given for the guilty plea despite its lateness; Also see *Prosecutor v. Sufa*, Judgment, November, 25, 2004, para. 33 before the Special Panels for Serious Crimes in East Timor). Kolundzija's plea was entered after the trial had started and only prior to the commencement of the defence's case. The Trial Chamber considered "the additional savings to the International Tribunal on account of his [. . .] guilty plea" and held that he should receive close to full credit for his guilty plea (also see *Prosecutor v. Ruggiu*, ICTY Trial Chamber, June 1, 2000, para. 58). However, the Trial Chamber in *Prosecutor v. Momir Nikolic*, Judgment, December 2, 2003, para. 151, was critical of such assessment (see the discussion below in the Plea Agreement section), and stated " [. . .] the Trial Chamber takes note of the fact that other accused have been given credit for pleading guilty before the start of trial or at an early stage of the trial because of the savings of Tribunal resources. Both parties have made submissions that this aspect of a guilty plea should be considered as a mitigating factor. For the reasons stated above, the Trial Chamber will allocate little weight to this aspect of the benefits of a guilty plea."

18–72

In *Prosecutor v. Atolan*, Judgment, June 9, 2003, p. 7, the Special Panel for Serious Crimes in East Timor explained that "this Court has usually considered [the guilty plea], to represent an advantage for the accused, the reduction of the term which would be otherwise imposed at the end of the full trial, must be a material one, cutting around half of the term. A less drastic approach proved to be useless: after the first decision of the Special Panel, in the *Joao Fernandes* case, where the Court took a less lenient decision, more than one year elapsed before a second guilty plea was submitted."

In *Prosecutor v. Sikirica, Dosen and Kolundzija*, Judgment, November 13, 2001, para. 24, the Prosecution affirmed that it would not have accepted a plea of the nature ultimately accepted prior to the commencement of the case or while the charges of genocide were still pending against the Accused, Dusko Sikirica. Notwithstanding this, the Trial Chamber declined to give full credit for the subsequent guilty plea based upon a clarified understanding of the facts. Rather it explained that "while an accused who pleads guilty to the charges against him prior to the commencement of his trial will usually receive full credit for that plea, one who enters a plea of guilt any time thereafter will still stand to receive some credit, though not as much as he would have, had the plea been made prior to the commencement of the trial. Therefore, the Chamber holds that, despite the lateness of his guilty plea, Dusko Sikirica should receive some credit." (*ibid.*, para. 150–151).

(iv) *Conduct at trial*

18–73   In *Prosecutor v. Krnojelac*, Judgment, March 15, 2002, para. 520, the
Trial Chamber gave credit to the accused for the extent to which his
Counsel co-operated with it and the Prosecution. The Trial Chamber
noted that counsel for the defence had not compromised their obligations to the accused, but the restriction of issues to those actually in
dispute "enabled the Trial Chamber to complete the trial in much less
time than it would otherwise have taken." (Also see paragraph 18–54
above)

Conduct at the ICTY's UNDU has often been taken into account as a
mitigating factor (*Prosecutor v. Simić*, Judgment, October 17, 2002 para.
112; *Prosecutor v. Krnojelac*, Judgment, para. 520; *Prosecutor v. Krstic*,
Judgment, August 2, 2001, para. 715), however, in *Prosecutor v. Mimir
Nikolic*, Judgment, December 2, 2003, para. 168, the Trial Chamber
stated: "all accused are expected to comport themselves appropriately
while at the UNDU; failure to do so may constitute an aggravating
factor. Accordingly, this Trial Chamber will not accord significant
weight to this factor" (also see *Prosecutor v. Cesic*, Judgment, March 11,
2004, para. 86).

(v) *Surrender to the Tribunals*

18–74   The voluntary surrender of accused persons to the jurisdiction of
international courts will constitute a mitigating circumstance relevant
to sentence (see the Appeals Chamber's finding in *Prosecutor v. Kupreškić
et al.*, Judgment, January 14, 2000, para. 853; *Prosecutor v. Strugar*,
Judgment, January 31, 2005, para. 472). Also see *Prosecutor v. Kunarac*,
Judgment, February 27, 2001, para. 868 and *Prosecutor v. Simić*, Judgment, October 17, 2002, para. 107 (where the Trial Chamber noted
that, the accused's voluntary surrender may have had an impact on the
manner in which the ICTY was viewed in Republika Srpska, and noted
that the voluntary surrender obviated the need for and risk to potentially dangerous arrest operations). In the ICTR context see *Prosecutor v.
Serushago*, Sentence, February 5, 1999. In *Prosecution v. Simić*, Judgment,
October 17, 2003, para. 1097, the Chamber noted that "[a]lthough
Miroslav Tadić surrendered on February 14, 1998, and thus arguably, a
significant period of time after becoming aware of the existence of an
Indictment against him, the Trial Chamber finds this to constitute a
mitigating circumstance" (see also *Prosecutor v. Blagojević*, Judgment,
January 17, 2005, para. 857). In *Prosecution v. Obrenovic*, Judgment,
December 10, 2003, para. 136, the Trial Chamber noted that "Dragan
Obrenovic was arrested even though he had offered to surrender
voluntarily knowing of his status as a suspect". The Trial Chamber
found his offer to voluntarily surrender, to be a factor in mitigation of
sentence. However, since it would have to speculate whether or not
Dragan Obrenovic *would*, in fact, have voluntarily surrendered if given
the opportunity, the Trial Chamber, on the facts of that case, attached
little weight to this factor.

(vi) *Individual circumstances of an accused*

Age, family background as well as character may be relevant in mitigation of sentence (see, *e.g.*, ICC RPE, Rule 145(1)(c); *Prosecutor v. Consta Nunes*, UNTAET Judgment, December 10, 2003, para. 78). In *Prosecutor v. Erdemović*, Sentencing Judgment, Trial Chamber, March 5, 1998, para. 16, Erdemović's youth (twenty-three years of age) at the time he committed the crimes in question, combined with his character, were considered as mitigating factors. These circumstances showed that he was abe to reform and should be given a chance to start his life again upon release whilst he is still young enough to do so. **18–75**

In *Prosecutor v. Krnojelac*, Judgment, March 15, 2002, paras 515–516, it was accepted that the conformist personality of an accused whereby he felt unable to confront authority, may in certain circumstances, be a factor in mitigation. Similarly, the age of the accused (62 years) was considered as a matter to be taken into account in sentencing (para. 533). In *Prosecutor v. Kordic et al.*, Judgment, February 26, 2001, para. 848, the ICTY Trial Chamber considered that an accused's poor health could also be a factor in mitigation in certain cases. Also see *Prosecutor v. Krstic*, Judgment, August 2, 2001, para. 723. In *Prosecutor v. Simić*, Judgment, October 17, 2002, paras 95–101, the Trial Chamber considered that "issues concerning the ill health of a convicted person should normally be a matter for consideration in the execution of the sentence which is carried out [. . .] it is only in exceptional circumstances or 'rare' cases where ill health should be considered in mitigation". Noting that Milan Simić was a wheelchair-bound paraplegic requiring full-time medical attention, the Trial Chamber composed a "lesser sentence than Milan Simić would otherwise have received" (at para. 116).

In *Prosecutor v. Kunarac*, Appeal Judgment, June 12, 2002, paras 362 and 408, the Appeal Chamber held that "the factor that the Appellant is the father of three young children" is a mitigating factor (also see *Prosecutor v. Eremovic*, Judgment, March 5, 1998, para. 16; *Prosecutor v. Banović*, Judgment, October 28, 2003, para. 82; *Prosecutor v. Blagojević*, Judgment, January 17, 2005, para. 855). In *Prosecutor v. Tadić*, Judgment, November 11, 1999, para. 26, the married status of the accused was considered under personal circumstances separately from mitigating factors.

In *Prosecutor v. Atolan*, UNTAET Judgment, June 9, 2003, p. 8, the Special Panal for Serious Crimes in East Timor stated "the family condition of the accused is a generic element: the victim, as well, was a father of nine and his sons and his daughters, not to mention his wife, were present and were crying when he was abducted. But this was not enough to stop the accused"; thus, the medical condition of the accused's father was not considered relevant in mitigation.

The well-being of a dependent can be taken into consideration. In *Prosecutor v. Strugar*, Judgment, January 31, 2005, para. 469, the ICTY Trial Chamber was of the view "that the absence of the Accused while serving his sentence will be a particular hardship for his wife" who is in poor health and warrants some mitigation.

Individual health circumstances of the accused are also taken in mitigation of the sentence. In *Prosecutor v. Bulatovic* Judgment, May 13, 2005, para. 18, it was held that "the Respondent currently suffers from serious health problems which would make the service of a sentence of imprisonment more burdensome in his case than in that of the average person".

(vii) *Previous character*

18–76   In *Prosecutor v. Blaškić*, Judgment, March 3, 2000, para. 280, the Trial Chamber stated that character is examined in order to determine whether an accused can be rehabilitated. The fact that an accused has no prior criminal record should be considered in mitigation, as should an accused's family situation. Thus in *Prosecutor v. Jelisic*, Judgment, December 14, 1999, para. 124, the Trial Chamber considered the fact that Jelisic was the father of a child in mitigation of sentence. Also see *Prosecutor v. Krnojelac*, Judgment, March 15, 2002, para. 519, in which the accused's previous good character, his trouble-free return to work as a teacher *after* the alleged crimes were committed and his good conduct at the Detention facility were all considered in mitigation. However, in the UNTAET case of *Prosecutor v. Joao Fernandez*, Judgment, January 25, 2001, para. 20(c), the Trial Chamber took into consideration the accused's previous good record but found "this may be said of many accused persons and cannot be given any significant weight in the case of this gravity". It is clear, however, that previous convictions may aggravate penalty (for example, see ICC RPE, Rule 145(2)(b)(i)).

The absence of previous convictions is often taken in mitigation (see *Prosecutor v. Consta Nunes*, UNTAET Judgment, December 10, 2003, para. 78), however it must be noted that in *Kupreškić*, the the Trial Chamber stated:

> "[. . .] generally speaking, evidence of the accused's character prior to the events for which he is indicted before the International Tribunal is not a relevant issue inasmuch as (a) by their nature as crimes committed in the context of widespread violence and during a national or international emergency, war crimes and crimes against humanity may be committed by persons with no prior convictions or history of violence, and that consequently evidence of prior good, or bad, conduct on the part of the accused before the armed conflict began is rarely of any probative value before the International Tribunal, and (b) as a general principle of criminal law, evidence as to the character of an accused is generally indadmissible to show the accused's propensity to act in conformity therewith [. . .]" (Decision on Evidence of the Good Character of the Accused and the Defence of *Tu Quoque* of February 17, 1999 in *Prosecutor v. Kupreškić et al.*; see also *Prosecutor v. Blagojević*, Judgment, January 17, 2005, para. 853).

In *Prosecutor v. Ndindabahizi*, Judgment, para. 506, the ICTR Trial Chamber found "[i]n mitigation of the Accused's sentence, the Chamber has considered evidence that, before his participation in the Interim Government, the Accused was a member of the PSD, which was a moderate political party."

(viii) *Behaviour after the commission of the crimes*

18–77   Active engagement in the work aimed at bringing the communities back to the path of peaceful co-existence may be relevant in mitigation of the sentence:

"Vidoje Blagojević has been actively engaged in planning, managing and organizing a system of de-mining in the army of the Republika Srpska [. . .] [Jokic] personally took part in de-mining to ensure that it proceeded according to plan. All this took place in villages, hamlets, to which mostly Muslims were to return [. . .] The Trial Chamber considers the activities of Videoje Blagojević and Dragan Jokic in the work of de-mining a mitigating circumstance" (*Prosecutor v. Blagojevoc*, Judgment, January 17, 2005, paras 858–860).

In *Prosecutor v. Obrenovic*, Judgment, December 10, 2003, para. 144, the Trial Chamber found that "Dragan Obrenovic has, under the propulsion of his own conscience, begun the process toward rehabilitation", indicating that steps taken towards rehabilitation are a factor in mitigation of the sentence (*ibid.*, para. 146).

In *Prosecutor v. Jokic*, Judgment, March 18, 2004, paras 89–91, the Trial Chamber noted that "the day of the shelling of the Old Town of Dubrovnik [. . .] Jokic demonstrated in the radiogram to Minister Rudolf his regret for the events", acknowledging that "Jokic was instrumental in ensuring that a comprehensive ceasefire was agreed upon and implemented", and "after the war, Miodrag Jokic, participated in political activities programmatically aimed at promoting a peaceful solution to the conflicts in the region", and therefore accorded weight to these actions in mitigation (also see *Prosecutor v. Plavsic*, Judgment, February 27, 2003, para. 94).

(ix) *Double jeopardy*

Where a sentence is successfully appealed by the Prosecutor, the **18–78** revised sentence will be reduced from that which should properly have been imposed by a Trial Chamber at first instance. This reduction is to take account of the element of double jeopardy involved in a prosecution appeal (see *Prosecutor v. Aleksovski*, Judgment on Appeal, May 30, 2001 para. 190; *Prosecutor v. Krnojelac*, Judgment, March 15, 2002, para. 528).

E. Other considerations

In *Prosecutor v. Erdemović*, Sentencing Judgment, March 5, 1998, para. **18–79** 21, the Trial Chamber noted that:

"The International Tribunal, in addition to its mandate to investigate, prosecute and punish serious violations of international humanitarian law, has a duty, through its judicial functions, to contribute to the settlement of the wider issues of accountability, reconciliation and establishing the truth behind the evils perpetrated in the former Yugoslavia. Discovering the truth is a cornerstone of the rule of law and a fundamental step on the way to reconciliation: for it is the truth that cleanses the ethnic and religious hatreds and begins the healing process. The International Tribunal must demonstrate that those who have the honesty to confess are treated fairly as part of a process underpinned by principles of justice, fair trial and protection of the fundamental rights of the individual. On the other hand, the International Tribunal is a vehicle through which the international community expresses its outrage at the atrocities committed in the former Yugoslavia. Upholding values of international human rights means that whilst protecting the rights of the accused, the International Tribunal must not lose sight of the tragedy of the victims and the sufferings of their families."

V. PLEA AGREEMENTS

A. ICC

(1) ICC Statute, Art. 65

Proceedings on an admission of guilt

18–80   **65.**—1. Where the accused makes an admission of guilt pursuant to article 64, paragraph 8 (a), the Trial Chamber shall determine whether:
   (a) The accused understands the nature and consequences of the admission of guilt;
   (b) The admission is voluntarily made by the accused after sufficient consultation with defence counsel; and
   (c) The admission of guilt is supported by the facts of the case that are contained in:
      (i) The charges brought by the Prosecutor and admitted by the accused;
      (ii) Any materials presented by the Prosecutor which supplement the charges and which the accused accepts; and
      (iii) Any other evidence, such as the testimony of witnesses, presented by the Prosecutor or the accused.
   2. Where the Trial Chamber is satisfied that the matters referred to in paragraph 1 are established, it shall consider the admission of guilt, together with any additional evidence presented, as establishing all the essential facts that are required to prove the crime to which the admission of guilt relates, and may convict the accused of that crime.
   3. Where the Trial Chamber is not satisfied that the matters referred to in paragraph 1 are established, it shall consider the admission of guilt as not having been made, in which case it shall order that the trial be continued under the ordinary trial procedures provided by this Statute and may remit the case to another Trial Chamber.
   4. Where the Trial Chamber is of the opinion that a more complete presentation of the facts of the case is required in the interests of justice, in particular the interests of the victims, the Trial Chamber may:
   (a) Request the Prosecutor to present additional evidence, including the testimony of witnesses; or
   (b) Order that the trial be continued under the ordinary trial procedures provided by this Statute, in which case it shall consider the admission of guilt as not having been made and may remit the case to another Trial Chamber.
   5. Any discussions between the Prosecutor and the defence regarding modification of the charges, the admission of guilt or the penalty to be imposed shall not be binding on the Court.

(2) ICC Rules of Procedure and Evidence

Rules of Procedures and Evidence, r. 139

Decision on admission of guilt

139.—1. After having proceeded in accordance with article 65, paragraph 1, **18–81** the Trial Chamber, in order to decide whether to proceed in accordance with article 65, paragraph 4, may invite the views of the Prosecutor and the defence.

2. The Trial Chamber shall then make its decision on the admission of guilt and shall give reasons for this decision, which shall be placed on the record.

B. ICTY

ICTY Rules of Procedures and Evicedence, rr. 62*bis*, 62*ter*

Guilty Pleas

62*bis*.—If an accused pleads guilty in accordance with Rule 62 (vi), or **18–82** requests to change his or her plea to guilty and the Trial Chamber is satisfied that:

    (i) the guilty plea has been made voluntarily;

    (ii) the guilty plea is informed;

    (iii) the guilty plea is not equivocal; and

    (iv) there is a sufficient factual basis for the crime and the accused's participation in it, either on the basis of independent indicia or on lack of any material disagreement between the parties about the facts of the case,

the Trial Chamber may enter a finding of guilt and instruct the Registrar to set a date for the sentencing

Plea Agreement Procedure

62*ter*.—(A) The Prosecutor and the defence may agree that, upon the **18–83** accused entering a plea of guilty to the indictment or to one or more counts of the indictment, the Prosecutor shall do one or more of the following before the Trial Chamber:

    (i) apply to amend the indictment accordingly;

    (ii) submit that a specific sentence or sentencing range is appropriate;

    (iii) not oppose a request by the accused for a particular sentence or sentencing range.

(B) The Trial Chamber shall not be bound by any agreement specified in paragraph (A).

(C) If a plea agreement has been reached by the parties, the Trial Chamber shall require the disclosure if the agreement in open session or, on a showing of good cause, in closed session, at the time the accused pleads guilty in accordance with Rule 62 (vi), or requests to change his or her plea to guilty.

C. ICTR

ICTR Rules of Procedures and Evidence, rr. 62, 62*bis*

Initial Appearance of Accused and Plea

62.—(A) Upon his transfer to the Tribunal, the accused shall be brought **18–84** before a Trial Chamber or a Judge thereof without delay, and shall be formally charged. The Trial Chamber or the Judge shall:

      (i) Satisfy itself or himself that the right of the accused to counsel is respected;

     (ii) Read or have the indictment read to the accused in a language he speaks and understands, and satisfy itself or himself that the accused understands the indictment;

    (iii) Call upon the accused to enter a plea of guilty or not guilty on each count; should the accused fail to do so, enter a plea of not guilty on his behalf;

    (iv) In case of a plea of not guilty, instruct the Registrar to set a date for trial;

     (v) In case of a plea of guilty:

        (a) if before a Judge, refer the plea to the Trial Chamber so that it may act in accordance with Rule 62 (B); or

        (b) if before a Trial Chamber, act in accordance with Rule 62 (B).

  (B) If an accused pleads guilty in accordance with Rule 62 (A)(v), or requests to change his plea to guilty, the Trial Chamber shall satisfy itself that the guilty plea:

      (i) is made freely and voluntarily;

     (ii) is an informed plea;

    (iii) is unequivocal; and

    (iv) is based on sufficient facts for the crime and accused's participation in it, either on the basis of objective indicia or of lack of any material disagreement between the parties about the facts of the case.

Thereafter the Trial Chamber may enter a finding of guilt and instruct the Registrar to set a date for the sentencing hearing.

Plea Agreement Procedure

18–85   **62bis.**—(A) The Prosecutor and the Defence may agree that, upon the accused entering a plea of guilty to the indictment or to one or more counts of the indictment, the Prosecutor shall do one or more of the following before the Trial Chamber:

      (i) apply to amend the indictment accordingly;

     (ii) submit that a specific sentence or sentencing range is appropriate;

    (iii) not oppose a request by the accused for a particular sentence or sentencing range.

  (B) The Trial Chamber shall not be bound by any agreement specified in paragraph (A).

  (C) If a plea agreement has been reached by the parties, the Trial Chamber shall require the disclosure of the agreement in open session or, on a showing of good cause, in closed session, at the time the accused pleads guilty in accordance with Rule 62 (A) (v), or requests to change his or her plea to guilty.

D. EAST TIMOR

Regulation 2000/30, s.29A

18–86   UNTAET Regulation 2000/30, September 25, 2000, as amended by UNTAET Regulation 2001/25, September 14, 2001

Proceedings on an Admission of Guilt

18–87   **29A.**—29A.1 Where the accused makes an admission of guilt in any proceedings before the Investigating Judge, or before a different judge or panel at any time before a final decision in the case, the court or judge before whom the admission is made shall determine whether:

(a) The accused understands the nature and consequences of the admission of guilt;

(b) The admission is voluntarily made by the accused after sufficient consultation with defense counsel; and

(c) The admission of guilt is supported by the facts of the case that are contained in:

    (i) The charges as alleged in the indictment and admitted by the accused;

    (ii) Any materials presented by the prosecutor which support the indictment and which the accused accepts; and

    (iii) Any other evidence, such as the testimony of witnesses, presented by the prosecutor or the accused.

29A.2 Where the court is satisfied that the matters referred to in Section 29A.1 of the present regulation are established, it shall consider the admission of guilt, together with any additional evidence presented, as establishing all the essential facts that are required to prove the crime to which the admission of guilt relates, and may convict the accused of that crime.

29A.3 Where the court is not satisfied that the matters referred to in Section 29A.1 are established, it shall consider the admission of guilt as not having been made, in which event it shall order that the trial be continued under the ordinary trial procedures provided in this Regulation.

29A.4 Where the Court is of the opinion that a more complete presentation of the facts of the case is required in the interests of justice, taking into account the interests of the victims, the court may:

(a) Request the prosecutor to present additional evidence, including the testimony of witnesses; or

(b) Order that the trial be continued under the ordinary trial procedures provided in this Regulation, in which event it shall consider the admission of guilt as not having been made.

29A.5 Any discussions between the prosecutor and the defense regarding modification of the charges, the admission of guilt or the penalty to be imposed shall not be binding on the court.

E. SCSL

SCSL Rules of Procedures and Evidence, rr. 61, 62

Initial Appearance of Accused and Plea

61.—Upon his transfer to the Special Court, the accused shall be brought **18–88** before the Designated Judge as soon as practicable, and shall be formally charged. The Designated Judge shall:

    i. Satisfy himself that the right of the accused to counsel is respected, and in so doing, shall question the accused with regard to his means and instruct the Registrar to provide legal assistance to the accused as necessary, unless the accused elects to act as his own counsel or refuses representation;

    ii. Read or have the indictment read to the accused in a language he speaks and understands, and satisfy himself that the accused understands the indictment;

    iii. Call upon the accused to enter a plea of guilty or not guilty on each count; should the accused fail to do so, enter a plea of not guilty on his behalf;

    iv. In case of a plea of not guilty, instruct the Registrar to set a date for trial;

    v. In case of a plea of guilty, shall refer the plea to the Trial Chamber so that it may act in accordance with Rule 62.

Procedure upon Guilty Plea

18–89   **62.**—(A) If an accused pleads guilty in accordance with Rule 61(v), or requests to change his plea to guilty, the Trial Chamber shall satisfy itself that the guilty plea:

    i. is made freely and voluntarily;

    ii. is an informed plea;

    iii. is unequivocal;

    iv. is based on sufficient facts for the crime and accused's participation in it, either on the basis of independent indicia or of lack of any material disagreement between the parties about the facts of the case.

(B) Thereafter the Trial Chamber may enter a finding of guilt and instruct the Registrar to set a date for the sentencing hearing.

18–90   Originally the Statues of the ICTY and the ICTR did not provide mechanisms for pleading guilty. Nevertheless, there were six "plea agreements" reached on an ad-hoc basis between the OTP and the Defence until Rule 62*ter* was introduced in the Rules of Procedures and Evidence at the ICTY and Rule 62*bis* at the ICTR.

In *Prosecutor v. Momir Nikolic*, Judgment, December 2, 2003, paras 46–56 it was explained that:

> "46. [. . .] The Rule was proposed by the Prosecution to establish a formal procedure for a practice which was already somewhat established. It was thought that by having a procedure in the Rules for plea agreements, it would give guidance to all parties and the accused, who often come from systems where plea agreements are not common or not used at all.
> 47. Plea agreements are more frequently used in adversarial common law jurisdictions than in the more inquisitorial civil law jurisdictions, due to the role that judges, prosecutors and defence counsel play in the respective systems. Even in criminal justice systems where the use of plea agreements is common, the Trial Chamber notes that its use is less frequent in cases of serious felonies or in the most notorious cases.
> 48. In conferring on these agreements, the parties meet without the presence of any member of the trial chamber and effectively 'negotiate' the terms of an agreement, the result of which is an accused pleading guilty to one or more of the counts of the indictment. The 'negotiations' can result in the Prosecution agreeing to amend the indictment to withdraw certain charges or drop certain factual allegations. As part of the agreement, the accused agrees to waive many of the rights guaranteed to him or her under the Statute and recognised as fundamental rights in human rights law [see also *Prosecutor v. Babic*, Annex A to Plea Agreement, January 22, 2004, Para. 16; *Prosecutor v. Banović*, Plea Agreement, June 2, 2003, para. 7.]
> 49. Once an agreement has been reached, it is subject to review by the Trial Chamber. A trial chamber may inquire into the terms of the agreement to ensure that neither party was unfairly treated and particularly that the rights of the accused are respected. As indicated above, once the plea agreement has been accepted, a trial chamber will continue in its role as guarantor of the fairness of the proceedings and protector of the rights of the accused by inquiring into the nature of the guilty plea, pursuant to Rule 62*bis* of the Rules. Thus, while the parties have the autonomy to enter into plea agreements, the trial chambers retain the ultimate authority over both the process and the proceedings.
> 50. It is important to recall that under the Statute of the Tribunal and the Rules, the Prosecutor has the sole power to investigate alleged crimes which fall within the jurisdiction of the Tribunal and to prepare an indictment. This power extends to the sole competence to determine the

crime or crimes with which an accused is charged. Once the Prosecutor determines that a *prima facie* case exists and has prepared an indictment, the indictment must be confirmed by a judge. This process requires that the judge make a finding that a *prima facie* case exists, based on supporting material provided by the Prosecutor. In the event that the Prosecution seeks to amend the indictment after its confirmation and the assignment of the case to a trial chamber, it must seek leave of the trial chamber pursuant to Rule 50. Such leave is necessary also in cases where the Prosecution seeks to withdraw certain charges following a plea agreement. After hearing the parties, the trial chamber will determine whether to grant the Prosecution's request. In cases of plea agreements where the Prosecution has expressed its intention not to proceed to trial on certain charges, such motions are generally granted; a trial chamber may seek to satisfy itself that the remaining charges reflect the totality of the criminal conduct of the accused [also see: *Prosecutor v. Sikirica*, Judgment, November 13, 2001, para. 48].

    51. [. . .]

    52. In determining whether the conditions under Rule 62*bis* have been satisfied, the Trial Chamber will enquire into the circumstances of the guilty plea. In determining if the guilty plea was made voluntarily, a trial chamber may inquire into the reasons for the change of plea and, if the guilty plea is a result of a plea agreement, the conditions under which the agreement was reached. In deciding if the guilty plea is informed, a trial chamber may inquire into the accused's understanding of the elements of the crime or crimes to which he has pled guilty to ensure that his understanding of the requirements of the crime reflects his actual conduct and participation as well as his state of mind or intent when he committed the crime. In determining if a plea is equivocal, a trial chamber may question the defence as to its intention to raise any defences. In determining whether a sufficient factual basis for the crime exists, a trial chamber may find it necessary to ask the Prosecution to adduce additional or supporting evidence, or may ask the accused specific questions to clarify his particular conduct or involvement in the commission of the crime to which he has pled guilty. In questioning about the factual basis, a trial chamber may seek to ensure that the totality of the accused's criminal conduct is reflected and that an accurate historical record exists, as well as ensure that the accused is pleading guilty to no more than that for which he is, in fact, guilty.

    53. A trial chamber may also enquire into the terms of the plea agreement. [. . .]

    54. The Trial Chamber recalls the language of Rule 62*bis*: after satisfying itself that the four pre-requisites for accepting a guilty plea have been met, a trial chamber 'may' enter a finding of guilt. Thus, a trial chamber has discretion whether to accept a guilty plea. While the reason for not accepting a guilty plea may be that a trial chamber is not satisfied with the terms of the plea agreement or has concerns that the rights of the accused have not been adequately protected, a trial chamber may also reject a particular guilty plea based on a plea agreement because it does not consider that the plea agreement is in the interests of justice.

    55. An additional point of 'negotiation' in reaching a plea agreement might include Prosecution's agreement to recommend a particular sentence or sentencing range. Additional consideration for this recommendation on the part of the accused may include agreement to testify for the Prosecution in other cases before the Tribunal. As stated in Rule 62*ter* (B), a Trial Chamber is not bound by the recommendations of the parties."

The Trial Chamber further noted that:

"67. [. . .] the savings of time and resources due to a guilty plea has often been considered as a valuable and justifiable reason for the promotion of guilty pleas. This Trial Chamber cannot fully endorse this argument. While it appreciates this saving of Tribunal resources, the Trial Chamber finds that in cases of this magnitude, where the Tribunal has been entrusted by the United Nations Security Council—and by extension, the international community as a whole—to bring justice to the former Yugoslavia through criminal proceedings that are fair, in accordance with international human rights standards, and accord due regard to the rights of the accused and the interests of victims, the saving of resources cannot be given undue consideration or importance. The *quality* of the justice and the fulfillment of the mandate of the Tribunal, including the establishment of a complete and accurate record of the crimes committed in the former Yugoslavia, must not be compromised. Unlike national criminal justice systems, which often must turn to plea agreements as a means to cope with heavy and seemingly endless caseloads, the Tribunal has a fixed mandate. Its very *raison d'être* is to have criminal proceedings, such that the persons most responsible for serious violations of international humanitarian law are held accountable for their criminal conduct—not simply a portion thereof. Thus, while savings of time and resources may be a *result* of guilty pleas, this consideration should not be the main *reason* for promoting guilty pleas through plea agreements. If the Prosecutor makes a plea agreement such that the totality of an individuals criminal conduct is not reflected or the remaining charges do not sufficiently reflect the gravity of the offences committed by the accused, questions may arise as to whether justice is in fact being done. Article 21(1) of the Statute of the Tribunal: 'All persons shall be equal before the International Tribunal.' *See, e.g., Erdemović* Appeal Judgment, Joint Separate Opinion of Judge McDonald and Judge Vohrah, para. 2. *See also, Banović* Sentencing Judgment, para. 68; *Plavšic* Sentencing Judgment, para. 73. In relation to the status of victims, the Trial Chamber notes that while certain of those victims who were to have been called to testify may benefit from the guilty plea, other victims may find that the use of plea agreements is not preferable to a full, public trial. *See, Prosecutor v. Slobodan Milošević*, Case No. IT–02–54–A73.4, Dissenting Opinion of Judge David Hunt on Admissibility of Evidence in Chief in the Form of Written Statements, October 21, 2003, paras 21–22.

69. The Tribunal was established to prosecute and punish persons responsible for serious violations of international humanitarian law. Persons who plead guilty are convicted upon the acceptance of the guilty plea. Upon conviction, a Trial Chamber will determine an appropriate sentence and will take as its principal consideration, as will be discussed below, the gravity of the offence—and not the guilty plea—in determining an appropriate sentence. Thus, a guilty plea leads directly to the fulfilment of a fundamental purpose of this Tribunal.

70. Because a conviction is based on the accused's acceptance of responsibility and acknowledgement of the crime he committed, there can be no question about the actual guilt of that accused. Denial of the commission of the crime may no longer be an option for those who have convinced themselves that the Tribunal is biased or that its judgments are based on weak or even false evidence. As the guilty plea must be based on a sufficient factual basis, which often will include a statement of facts by the accused person and may be supplemented upon the request of the trial chamber, the underlying facts for each crime will be established. Thus, a purpose of the Tribunal is fulfilled.

71. As is often highlighted by the Prosecution, guilty pleas can substantially assist in its investigations and presentation of evidence at trials of other accused, including high ranking accused. The Trial Chamber recognises and appreciates the assistance that can be given and the knowledge that can be gained by *all* organs of the Tribunal from having persons who may have 'inside' information testify in other proceedings.

72. In relation to the Tribunal's mission to assist in restoring peace and bring reconciliation to the territory of the former Yugoslavia, guilty pleas can certainly contribute significantly. Through the acknowledgment of the crimes committed and the recognition of ones own role in the suffering of others, a guilty plea may be more meaningful and significant than a finding of guilt by a trial chamber to the victims and survivors. Without seeking to lessen the impact of a public pronouncement by the Tribunal of guilt following a trial, the Trial Chamber recognises that an admission of guilt from a person perceived as 'the enemy' may serve as an opening for dialogue and reconciliation between different groups. When an admission of guilt is coupled with a sincere expression of remorse, a significant opportunity for reconciliation may be created.

73. The Trial Chamber finds that, on balance, guilty pleas pursuant to plea agreements, may further the work—and the mandate—of the Tribunal. The Trial Chamber further finds, however, that based on the duties incumbent on the Prosecutor and the Trial Chambers pursuant to the Statute of the Tribunal, the use of plea agreements should proceed with caution and such agreements should be used only when doing so would satisfy the interests of justice."

This opinion is endorsed by the *Prosecutor v. Dragan Nikolic*, Judgment, December 18, 2003, para. 122. The judges stated:

"[A]s opposed to a pure guilty plea (Rule 62*bis* of the Rules), a plea agreement (Rule 62*ter* of the Rules), while having its own merits as an incentive to plead guilty, has two negative side effects. First, the admitted facts are limited to those in the agreement, which might not always reflect the entire available factual and legal basis. Second, it may be thought that an accused is confessing only because of the principle '*do ut des*' (give and take). Therefore, the reason why an accused entered a plea of guilt need to be analysed: were charges withdrawn, or was a sentence recommendation given? In any event, a plea agreement pursuant to Rule 62*ter* and 62*bis* of the Rules does not allow the Trial Chamber to depart from the mandate of this Tribunal, which is to bring the truth to light and justice to the people of the former Yugoslavia. Neither the public, nor the judges themselves come closer to know the truth beyond what is accepted in the plea agreement. This might create an unfortunate gap in the public and historical record of the concrete case, although, when coupled with an accused's substantial co-operation with the prosecution, an agreement grants more insights into previously undiscovered areas. However, while treating plea agreements with appropriate caution, it should be recalled that this Tribunal is not the final arbiter of historical facts. That is for historians. For the judiciary focusing on core issues of a criminal case before this International Tribunal, it is important that justice be done and be seen to be done."

In his dissenting opinion, Judge Schomburg was critical of the plea agreement negotiation process and dissatisfied with the its outcome: *Prosecutor v. Deronjic*, Dissenting Opinion of Judge Schomburg in Judgment, March 30, 2004, paras 11 and 19:

"11. I accept that, in order to break up a circle of silence among perpetrators, some promises can be made by the Prosecutor *vis-à-vis* credible and reliable perpetrators. However, these promises shall, *proprio motu*, be disclosed to the bench by the Prosecutor.
     a) Promises, furthermore, can not result in *de facto* granting partial amnesty/impunity by the Prosecutor, particularly not in an institution established to avoid impunity.

b) Amnesty can only be granted after an appropriate sentence has been determined.

c) A limited amnesty or early release, if at all, can only be granted by those to whom this power is or will be vested, based on a sentenced person's entire post-crime conduct, or in order to restore peace.

19. The crime before us, limited as it is described, has, however, all of the ingredients of one of the most heinous crimes against humanity. Therefore, the appropriate sentence can only be found in twenty years of imprisonment or higher, thereby adequately acknowledging the fate of the victims and their relatives. Everything else could be seen as an incentive for politicians, who might in future find themselves in a similar situation as Miroslav Deronjic was as of December 1991, to act in the same manner. Even if this person were brought before criminal court he/she would believe that he/she could buy him/herself more or less free by admitting some guilt and giving some information to the then competent prosecutor."

VI. APPELLATE REVIEW OF THE SENTENCING DECISIONS OF TRIAL CHAMBERS

18–91   (See generally, Chapter 19.)

Some Accused at the ICTY and ICTR have been successful on appeal in arguing for a reduction in their sentences (see further ICTY cases: *Prosecutor v. Dragan Nikolic*, Appeals Judgment, February 4, 2005; *Prosecutor v. Blaškić*, Appeals Judgment, July 29, 2004; *Prosecutor v. Cerkez*, Appeals Judgment, December 17, 2004; *Prosecutor v. Josipovic*, Appeals Judgment, October 23, 2001; *Prosecutor v. Erdemović*, Appeals Judgment, March 5, 1998; *Prosecutor v. Vasiljevic*, Appeals Judgment, February 25, 2004; and ICTR case: *Prosecutor v. Kajelijeli*, Appeals Judgment, May 23, 2005). Others have either been unsuccessful or had their sentences increased (see *Prosecutor v. Aleksovski*, Appeal Judgment, March 24, 2000, para. 183; *Prosecutor v. Semanza*, Appeals Judgment, May 20, 2005; *Prosecutor v. Krnojelac*, Appeals Judgment, September 17, 2003; *Prosecutor v. Krstic*, Appeals Judgment, April 19, 2004). In *Aleksovski*, the Appeal Chamber held that the Trial Chamber had failed to pay sufficient regard to the gravity of the accused's conduct and that his offences were not trivial. The Appeals Chamber held that the Trial Chamber had failed to properly take into account the accused's position as a superior. The Appeals Chamber noted that the accused's position as the warden of Kaonik Detention Facility, was a factor that "seriously aggravated" the accused's offences. "Instead of preventing violence against those he should have been protecting, Aleksovski allowed the detainees to be subjected to psychological terror and to be used for forced labour. Permitting detainees to be used for forced labour, such as trench-digging, and as human shields, had resulted in a sentence that was 'manifestly inadequate'. (Also see *Krnojelac* Appeal Judgment: the Appeal Chamber doubled the accused's seven-and-a-half year sentence to 15 years, based on the finding that the accused had wrongly been acquitted of "superior responsibility" charges.) In *Prosecutor v. Kupreškić*, Appeal Judgment, October 25, 2001, para. 408 the Appeals Chamber emphasised that:

"The most important point to recall is the fact that 'the appeal process [. . .] is not designed for the purpose of allowing parties to remedy their own failings or oversights during trial or sentencing.' Appellate proceedings do not constitute a trial *de novo* and are, rather, of a 'corrective nature.' The standard to be applied in this appeal will therefore be the following:

> [A]s a general rule, the Appeals Chamber will not substitute its sentence for that of a Trial Chamber unless 'it believes that the Trial Chamber has committed an error in exercising its discretion, or has failed to follow applicable law.' The Appeals Chamber will only intervene if it finds that the error was 'discernible.' As long as a Trial Chamber does not venture outside its 'discretionary framework' in imposing sentence, the Appeals Chamber will not intervene. It therefore falls on each appellant . . .to demonstrate how the Trial Chamber ventured outside its discretionary framework in imposing the sentence it did."

In cases where it is demonstrated that the Trial Chamber made a "discernible error" in the exercise of its sentencing discretion or failed to follow applicable law, some substitution in the sentence is possible. Although a "margin of deference" is given to a Trial Chamber's factual findings pursuant to Article 25 of the Statute, the Appeals Chamber has the power to reverse, revise, or affirm a particular sentence on appeal. In *Prosecutor v. Tadić*, Appeal Judgment, the Appeals Chamber reduced the 25 year sentence to 20 years. In *Prosecutor v. D. Nikolic*, Appeal Judgment, paras 96–97; the Appeals Chamber held that the Trial Chamber should not factor in the possibility of the early release when determining the appropriate sentence. The Appeals Chamber noted that:

> "The Trial Chamber, by imposing a sentence of 23 years, clearly—although not expressly—entered into a calculation to reflect the practice of the International Tribunal of granting early release after the convicted person has served two-thirds of his sentence: the term of 15 years clearly amounts to two-thirds of the sentence it effectively rendered. The Appeals Chamber considers that the Trial Chamber mechanically—not to say mathematically—gave effect to the possibility of an early release. By doing so, it attached too much weight to the possibility of an early release. As a consequence, the Appeals Chamber (Judge Shahabuddeen dissenting) finds that a reduction of sentence shall be granted."

Post conviction co-operation with the Prosecution

Post conviction cooperation by an accused with the Prosecutor is capable of amounting to a relevant factor when considering a reduction of sentence. In *Prosecutor v. Kupreškić*, Appeal Judgment, October 25, 2001, para. 463 the Appeals Chamber explained that: **18–92**

> "There is no provision in the Statute or the Rules that specifically permits the Appeals Chamber to take into account post-conviction substantial co-operation with the Prosecution. It is noted that there is precedent to suggest that post-conviction behaviour is not relevant to assessment of sentence on appeal. In a pre-appeal hearing decision in the case of Jelisic, the Appeals Chamber accepted that a report from the detention unit as to the appellant's post-sentencing behaviour was unavailable at the time of the trial but that "the Defendant's post-sentence behaviour could be

neither relevant to any issue before the Trial Chamber nor capable of being considered by it and therefore cannot show that the Trial Chamber committed any error in the exercise of its discretion.' On this basis, the evidence was rejected. See Prosecutor v Jelisic, Case No.: IT-95-10-A, Decision on Request to Admit Additional Evidence, November 15, 2000. What is clear, however, is that appellate proceedings are not intended to permit a *de novo* review of sentence, with Article 25 clearly limiting appeals to allegations of errors of law or fact invalidating the decision or occasioning a miscarriage of justice respectively. The instant case clearly does not fall within either category, as it is not alleged that the Trial Chamber erred in any way. However, the Appeals Chamber notes that Rule 101(B)(ii) requires the Trial Chamber to take into account 'any mitigating circumstances including the substantial co-operation with the Prosecution by the convicted person before or after conviction.' In light of the Rule, the Appeals Chamber considers that, in appropriate cases, co-operation between conviction and appeal could be a factor that the Appeals Chamber too may consider in order to reduce sentence. This will of course depend on the circumstances of each case and the degree of co-operation rendered[. . .]."

In *Prosecutor v. Kunarac*, Appeal Judgment, June 12, 2002, para. 141, the Appeals Chamber held that "in the specific context of a sentencing judgment following a plea agreement, the Appeals Chamber emphasises that Trial Chambers shall give due consideration to the recommendation of the parties and, should the sentence diverge substantially from that recommendation, give reasons for the departure. Those reasons, combined with the Trial Chamber's obligation pursuant to Article 23(2) of the Statute to render a Judgment 'accompanied by a reasoned opinion in writing,' will facilitate a meaningful exercise of the convicted person's right to appeal and allow the Appeals Chamber 'to understand and review the findings of the Trial Chamber.'"

VII. COMPENSATION AND RESTITUTION: STATUTORY PROVISIONS

A. ICC

(1) ICC Statute

Statute, Art. 75

Reparations to victims

18–93   **75.**—1. The Court shall establish principles relating to reparations to, or in respect of, victims, including restitution, compensation and rehabilitation. On this basis, in its decision the Court may, either upon request or on its own motion in exceptional circumstances, determine the scope and extent of any damage, loss and injury to, or in respect of, victims and will state the principles on which it is acting.

2. The Court may make an order directly against a convicted person specifying appropriate reparations to, or in respect of, victims, including restitution, compensation and rehabilitation.

Where appropriate, the Court may order that the award for reparations be made through the Trust Fund provided for in article 79.

3. Before making an order under this article, the Court may invite and shall take account of representations from or on behalf of the convicted person, victims, other interested persons or interested States.

4. In exercising its power under this article, the Court may, after a person is convicted of a crime within the jurisdiction of the Court, determine whether, in order to give effect to an order which it may make under this article, it is necessary to seek measures under article 93, paragraph 1.

5. A State Party shall give effect to a decision under this article as if the provisions of article 109 were applicable to this article.

6. Nothing in this article shall be interpreted as prejudicing the rights of victims under national or international law.

Applicable penalties

77.—1. [. . .]

2. In addition to imprisonment, the Court may order:

    (a) [. . .]

    (b) A forfeiture of proceeds, property and assets derived directly or indirectly from that crime, without prejudice to the rights of bona fide third parties.

18–94

Trust Fund

79.—1. A Trust Fund shall be established by decision of the Assembly of States Parties for the benefit of victims of crimes within the jurisdiction of the Court, and of the families of such victims.

2. The Court may order money and other property collected through fines or forfeiture to be transferred, by order of the Court, to the Trust Fund.

3. The Trust Fund shall be managed according to criteria to be determined by the Assembly of States Parties.

18–95

(2) ICC Rules of Procedure and Evidence

CHAPTER 7

Penalties

SUBSECTION 4

Reparations to victims

Rules of Procedure and Evidence, rr. 94–99, 147, 148

Procedure upon request

94.—1. A victim's request for reparations under article 75 shall be made in writing and filed with the Registrar. It shall contain the following particulars:

    (a) The identity and address of the claimant;

18–96

    (b) A description of the injury, loss or harm;
    (c) The location and date of the incident and, to the extent possible, the identity of the person or persons the victim believes to be responsible for the injury, loss or harm;
    (d) Where restitution of assets, property or other tangible items is sought, a description of them;
    (e) Claims for compensation;
    (f) Claims for rehabilitation and other forms of remedy;
    (g) To the extent possible, any relevant supporting documentation, including names and addresses of witnesses.

    2. At commencement of the trial and subject to any protective measures, the Court shall ask the Registrar to provide notification of the request to the person or persons named in the request or identified in the charges and, to the extent possible, to any interested persons or any interested States. Those notified shall file with the Registry any representation made under article 75, paragraph 3.

Procedure on the motion of the Court

18–97   **95.**—1. In cases where the Court intends to proceed on its own motion pursuant to article 75, paragraph 1, it shall ask the Registrar to provide notification of its intention to the person or persons against whom the Court is considering making a determination, and, to the extent possible, to victims, interested persons and interested States. Those notified shall file with the Registry any representation made under article 75, paragraph 3.
    2. If, as a result of notification under sub-rule 1:
    (a) A victim makes a request for reparations, that request will be determined as if it had been brought under rule 94;
    (b) A victim requests that the Court does not make an order for reparations, the Court shall not proceed to make an individual order in respect of that victim.

Publication of reparation proceedings

18–98   **96.**—1. Without prejudice to any other rules on notification of proceedings, the Registrar shall, insofar as practicable, notify the victims or their legal representatives and the person or persons concerned. The Registrar shall also, having regard to any information provided by the Prosecutor, take all the necessary measures to give adequate publicity of the reparation proceedings before the Court, to the extent possible, to other victims, interested persons and interested States.
    2. In taking the measures described in sub-rule 1, the Court may seek, in accordance with Part 9, the cooperation of relevant States Parties, and seek the assistance of intergovernmental organizations in order to give publicity, as widely as possible and by all possible means, to the reparation proceedings before the Court.

Assessment of reparations

18–99   **97.**—1. Taking into account the scope and extent of any damage, loss or injury, the Court may award reparations on an individualized basis or, where it deems it appropriate, on a collective basis or both.
    2. At the request of victims or their legal representatives, or at the request of the convicted person, or on its own motion, the Court may appoint appropriate experts to assist it in determining the scope, extent of any damage, loss and injury to, or in respect of victims and to suggest various options concerning the appropriate types and modalities of reparations. The Court shall invite, as appropriate, victims or their legal representatives, the convicted person as well

as interested persons and interested States to make observations on the reports of the experts.

3. In all cases, the Court shall respect the rights of victims and the convicted person.

Trust Fund

98.—1. Individual awards for reparations shall be made directly against a convicted person.

2. The Court may order that an award for reparations against a convicted person be deposited with the Trust Fund where at the time of making the order it is impossible or impracticable to make individual awards directly to each victim. The award for reparations thus deposited in the Trust Fund shall be separated from other resources of the Trust Fund and shall be forwarded to each victim as soon as possible.

3. The Court may order that an award for reparations against a convicted person be made through the Trust Fund where the number of the victims and the scope, forms and modalities of reparations makes a collective award more appropriate.

4. Following consultations with interested States and the Trust Fund, the Court may order that an award for reparations be made through the Trust Fund to an intergovernmental, international or national organization approved by the Trust Fund.

5. Other resources of the Trust Fund may be used for the benefit of victims subject to the provisions of article 79.

18–100

Cooperation and protective measures for the purpose of forfeiture under articles 57, paragraph 3 (e), and 75, paragraph 4

99.—1. The Pre-Trial Chamber, pursuant to article 57, paragraph 3 (e), or the Trial Chamber, pursuant to article 75, paragraph 4, may, on its own motion or on the application of the Prosecutor or at the request of the victims or their legal representatives who have made a request for reparations or who have given a written undertaking to do so, determine whether measures should be requested.

2. Notice is not required unless the Court determines, in the particular circumstances of the case, that notification could not jeopardize the effectiveness of the measures requested. In the latter case, the Registrar shall provide notification of the proceedings to the person against whom a request is made and so far as is possible to any interested persons or interested States.

3. If an order is made without prior notification, the relevant Chamber shall request the Registrar, as soon as is consistent with the effectiveness of the measures requested, to notify those against whom a request is made and, to the extent possible, to any interested persons or any interested States and invite them to make observations as to whether the order should be revoked or otherwise modified.

4. The Court may make orders as to the timing and conduct of any proceedings necessary to determine these issues.

18–101

Orders of forfeiture

147.—1. In accordance with article 76, paragraphs 2 and 3, and rules 63, sub-rule 1, and 143, at any hearing to consider an order of forfeiture, Chamber shall hear evidence as to the identification and location of specific proceeds, property or assets which have been derived directly or indirectly from the crime.

2. If before or during the hearing, a Chamber becomes aware of any bona fide third party who appears to have an interest in relevant proceeds, property or assets, it shall give notice to that third party.

18–102

3. The Prosecutor, the convicted person and any bona fide third party with an interest in the relevant proceeds, property or assets may submit evidence relevant to the issue.

4. After considering any evidence submitted, a Chamber may issue an order of forfeiture in relation to specific proceeds, property or assets if it is satisfied that these have been derived directly or indirectly from the crime.

Orders to transfer fines or forfeitures to the Trust Fund

18–103   **148.** Before making an order pursuant to article 79, paragraph 2, a Chamber may request the representatives of the Fund to submit written or oral observations to it.

(3) ICC Regulations of the Court, Adopted May 26, 2004, reg. 116

Enforcement of fines, forfeiture orders and reparation orders

18–104   **148.—1.** For the purposes of enforcement of fines, forfeiture orders and reparation orders, the Presidency, with the assistance of the Registry as appropriate, shall make the arrangements necessary in order to, *inter alia*:
(a)–(c) [. . .];
  (d) Ensure the transfer of money to the Trust Fund or to victims, as appropriate.

2. Following the transfer to or deposit in the Trust Fund of property or assets realized through enforcement of an order of the Court, the Presidency shall, subject to article 75, paragraph 2, and rule 98, decide on their disposition or allocation in accordance with rule 221.

B. ICTY

ICTY Statute, Art. 24

Penalties

18–105   **24.—1.** [. . .]
2. [. . .]
3. In addition to imprisonment, the Trial Chambers may order the return of any property and proceeds acquired by criminal conduct, including by means of duress, to their rightful owners.

C. ICTR

ICTR Statute, Art. 23

Penalties

18–106   **23.—1.** [. . .]
2. [. . .]
3. In addition to imprisonment, the Trial Chamber may order the return of any property and proceeds acquired by criminal conduct, including by means of duress, to their rightful owners.

D. East timor

Regulation No. 2000/30, ss.42, 49

VIII Execution of Orders and Decisions

Court Orders and Sentences

42.—42.11 [. . .]

42.12 [. . .]

42.13 Upon final disposition of the case, including any appeal, the competent court shall determine whether any objects seized during the proceedings will be returned to the person who owns or possessed the objects, or whether they will be confiscated. If confiscation is ordered, the Court shall determine whether the objects will be destroyed or auctioned. Revenues from auction shall accrue to the consolidated budget of East Timor.

42.14–42.15 [. . .]

18–107

Claim for Compensation by the Alleged Victim

49.—49.1 Independent from the commencement or completion of a criminal proceeding, an alleged victim may claim compensation for damages or losses suffered or inflicted by a suspected crime by filing a civil action before a competent court.

49.2 As a part of its disposition of a criminal case in which the accused is convicted of an offense as to which there are victims, and notwithstanding any separate civil action which goes forward pursuant to section 49.1 of the present regulation, the court may include in its disposition an order that requires the accused to pay compensation or reparations to the victim in an amount to be determined by the court. Any payment made by an accused to a victim in compliance with such an order shall be credited toward satisfaction of any civil judgment also rendered in the matter.

49.3 The procedure to be followed and the evidence to be heard in making the Court's determination concerning compensation or reparations to victims pursuant to section 49.2 of the present regulation may be regulated by a separate UNTAET directive.

18–108

E. Sierra Leone

(1) Statute of the Special Court of Sierra Leone, Art. 19

Penalties

19.—1. [. . .]

2. [. . .]

3. In addition to imprisonment, the Trial Chamber may order the forfeiture of the property proceeds and any assets acquired unlawfully or by criminal conduct, and their return to their rightful owner or to the State of Sierra Leone.

18–109

(2) SCSL Rules of Procedures and Evidence, rr. 104, 105

Forfeiture of Property

104.—(A) After a judgment of conviction containing a specific finding as provided in Rule 88 (B) the Trial Chamber, at the request of the Prosecutor or at its own initiative, may hold a special hearing to determine the matter of

18–110

property forfeiture, including the proceeds thereof, and may in the meantime order such provisional measures for the preservation and protection of the property or proceeds as it considers appropriate.

(B) The determination may extend to such property or proceeds, even in the hands of third parties not otherwise connected with the crime, for which the convicted person has been found guilty. Such third parties shall be entitled to appear at the hearing.

(C) The Trial Chamber may order the forfeiture of any property, proceeds and any assets it finds has been acquired unlawfully or by criminal conduct, and order its return to the rightful owner, or its transfer to the State of Sierra Leone, as circumstances may require.

Compensation to Victims

18–111   105.—(A) The Registrar shall transmit to the competent authorities of the States concerned the judgment finding the accused guilty of a crime which has caused injury to a victim.

(B) Pursuant to the relevant national legislation, a victim or persons claiming through him may bring an action in a national court or other competent body to obtain compensation.

(C) For the purposes of a claim made under Sub-Rule (B) the judgment of the Special Court shall be final and binding as to the criminal responsibility of the convicted person for such injury.

VIII. SUMMARY: COMPENSATION AND RESTITUTION

18–112   Article 75 of the Rome Statute and Rules 94–95 of the ICC RPE provide a mechanism whereby reparations can be made to victims of crime within the jurisdiction of the ICC. The reparations may take the form of restitution, compensation, and rehabilitation. However, reparations may take other forms (Article 75(1)).

Article 75(1) may be engaged upon the Trial Chamber receiving a request for reparations or, in exceptional circumstances, by a Trial Chamber triggering the Article 75 process of its own motion. Before reparations are ordered, the court shall take into account any representations received by the convicted person, victims, interested persons or interested States (Article 75(3)).

18–113   Rule 94 of the ICC RPE details the procedure to be followed when a request for reparations is received. Rule 94(1) requires that a request for reparations is made in writing and that it contains the name and address of the claimant, a description of the injury, loss or harm suffered and the place and date of the occurrence. Documentary evidence should be submitted to the Registrar, if available, as should the name of any witnesses (Rule 94(1)(g)). The victim should clearly state the reparation (restitution of assets, compensation or other remedy) sought (Rule 94(d)–(f)). It is clearly contemplated that protective measures will be available to the claimant should they be required (Rule 94(2)).

Rule 95 details the procedure to be followed where a court triggers the Article 75 procedure of its own motion. In this case, the court will give notification of its intention to proceed of its own motion to the parties, victims and interested persons and interested States. If the notification given by the Court results in a victim making a request for reparation, the Court will revert to the Rule 94 procedure (Rule 94(2)(a)). If a victim responds to the notification by requesting that reparations are not ordered, the court is not entitled to proceed and make an order in relation to that victim (Rule 95(2)(b)).

Rule 96 provides that the reparation proceedings are properly publicised and open to the public. Rule 98 requires that the reparations be made directly against convicted persons (Rule 98(1)). They may be paid either directly to the victim, or where this is not possible at the time the order is made, to the Trust Fund, established by Article 79 of the Rome Statute. Where there are a number of victims, the Court may order that the reparations are paid by the Trust fund to national and international organisations approved by the Trust fund (Rule 98(4)). Rule 99 provides for the freezing of assets either before or after trial, in order to safeguard the rights of the victims who may be entitled to reparations under Article 75.

Whilst Article 23(3) of the ICTR Statute and Article 24(3) of the ICTY Statute provide for the return of property and proceeds acquired by criminal conduct, it has not been used and it has not been considered necessary for the judges to adopt any Rules of Procedure and Evidence to detail a mechanism for restitution of property. Whilst property may be returned to the victims of crime, under the ICTY and ICTR Statutes, there is no express provision in the Statutes, or Rules that allows for compensation or other forms of reparations. **18–114**

Section 49.2 of UNTAET Regulation 2000/30 details the right of victims to claim compensation either in the civil court (section 49.1) or for it to be awarded by a criminal court at the end of the trial (section 49.2). The procedure to be adopted "may be regulated by a separate UNTAET directive" (section 49.3).

IX. COMPENSATION TO AN ARRESTED OR CONVICTED PERSON: STATUTORY PROVISIONS

A. ICC

(1) ICC Statute Art. 85

Compensation to an arrested or convicted person

85.—1. Anyone who has been the victim of unlawful arrest or detention shall have an enforceable right to compensation. **18–115**

2. When a person has by a final decision been convicted of a criminal offence, and when subsequently his or her conviction has been reversed on the ground that a new or newly discovered fact shows conclusively that there has been a miscarriage of justice, the person who has suffered punishment as a result of such conviction shall be compensated according to law, unless it is proved that the non-disclosure of the unknown fact in time is wholly or partly attributable to him or her.

3. In exceptional circumstances, where the Court finds conclusive facts showing that there has been a grave and manifest miscarriage of justice, it may in its discretion award compensation, according to the criteria provided in the Rules of Procedure and Evidence, to a person who has been released from

detention following a final decision of acquittal or a termination of the proceedings for that reason.

(2) ICC Rules of Procedure and Evidence

CHAPTER 10

Compensation to an arrested or convicted person

Rules of Procedure and Evidence, r. 173

Request for compensation

18–116   **173.**—1. Anyone seeking compensation on any of the grounds indicated in article 85 shall submit a request, in writing, to the Presidency, which shall designate a Chamber composed of three judges to consider the request. These judges shall not have participated in any earlier judgment of the Court regarding the person making the request.

2. The request for compensation shall be submitted not later than six months from the date the person making the request was notified of the decision of the Court concerning:

    (a) The unlawfulness of the arrest or detention under article 85, paragraph 1;

    (b) The reversal of the conviction under article 85, paragraph 2;

    (c) The existence of a grave and manifest miscarriage of justice under article 85, paragraph 3.

3. The request shall contain the grounds and the amount of compensation requested.

4. The person requesting compensation shall be entitled to legal assistance.

Procedure for seeking compensation

18–117   **174.**—1. A request for compensation and any other written observation by the person filing the request shall be transmitted to the Prosecutor, who shall have an opportunity to respond in writing. Any observations by the Prosecutor shall be notified to the person filing the request.

2. The Chamber designated under rule 173, sub-rule 1, may either hold a hearing or determine the matter on the basis of the request and any written observations by the Prosecutor and the person filing the request. A hearing shall be held if the Prosecutor or the person seeking compensation so requests.

3. The decision shall be taken by the majority of the judges. The decision shall be notified to the Prosecutor and to the person filing the request.

Amount of compensation

18–118   **175.** In establishing the amount of any compensation in conformity with article 85, paragraph 3, the Chamber designated under rule 173, sub-rule 1, shall take into consideration the consequences of the grave and manifest miscarriage of justice on the personal, family, social and professional situation of the person filing the request.

B. ICTY AND ICTR

18–119   Neither the ICTR nor the ICTR Statute or the Rules of Procedures and Evidence provide a mechanism for compensating the accused, whose rights have demonstrably been violated. In the Appeals Chamber

Decision in *Prosecutor v. Semanza*, Decision, May 31, 2000, disposition 6, the Chamber decided:

"that for the violation of his rights, the Appellant is entitled to a remedy which shall be given when judgment is rendered by the Trial Chamber, as follows:
(a) If he is found not guilty, the Appellant shall be entitled to financial compensation;
(b) If he is found guilty, the Appelant's sentence shall be reduced to take into account the violation of his rights, pursuant to Article 23 of the Statute."

In the Judgment following this Decision, *Prosecutor v. Semanza*, May 15, 2003, para. 580, the Chamber stated: "[c]onsidering the importance of these fundamental rights, the Chamber finds that it is appropriate to reduce the Accused's sentence by a period of six months".

In *Prosecutor v. Barayagwiza*, Judgment, December 3, 2003, paras 1106–1107, the Trial Chamber was of the view that the accused's conduct merited a sentence of life imprisonment but reduced the sentence to 35 years' imprisonment because the accused's rights had been violated at the pre-trial stage (this had, in fact, led an earlier Appeals Chamber to dismiss the indictment against the accused with prejudice to the Prosecutor and order the immediate release of the accused and his transfer back to Cameroon. See *Prosecutor v. Barayagwiza*, Decision, November 3, 1999, para. 113). The Trial Chamber's sentence reduction from life imprisonment to a term of 35 years was the direct result of the Appeals Chamber subsequent "Decision on the Prosecutor's Request for Review or Reconsideration", March 31, 2000, which set aside the original order of the Appeals Chamber and order that "[i]f the Appellant is found guilty, his sentence shall be reduced to take account of the violation of his rights" (Decision, March 31, 2000, para. 75(3)(b)).

The President of the ICTY received two requests for compensation from the brothers Zoran and Mirjan Kupreškić on December 21, 2001 and February 7, 2002 respectively. Upon learning of the Appeals Chamber decision of October 23, 2001 acquitting both of them on all counts, the brothers had claimed a right of compensation for their wrongful conviction and imprisonment. In letters dated May 22, 2002, the President of the ICTY recalled that neither the Statute nor Rules of Procedure and Evidence granted the right of compensation to persons wrongly prosecuted and convicted and that, without any specific provision in the Tribunal's founding texts, it was not possible for the judges of the Tribunal to rule on the matter. In correspondence dated September 19, 2000, the President referred the issue to the Secretary-General and on, March 6, 2002, sought the opinion of the President of the Security Council on the matter. (See ICTY Yearbook, A/57/379-S/2002/985, para. 28)

C. EAST TIMOR

Regulation 2000/30, September 25, 2000, as amended by Regulation 2001/25, September 14, 2001, s.52

Compensation for Miscarriages of Justice

18–120   52.—51.1 Where a conviction is reversed on the basis of newly discovered evidence which shows a miscarriage of justice, and where the evidence was not concealed by the convict, the convict may be compensated in accordance with a separate UNTAET directive.

52.2 Any person who is subjected to unlawful arrest or detention shall be entitled to compensation in an amount and from a source of public funds which are allocated to the administration of justice, to be determined by the competent court. An award of compensation pursuant to the present section may be made as part of a final disposition of a criminal case involving the claimant, or by means of a separate civil action.

X. SUMMARY: COMPENSATION TO AN ARRESTED OR CONVICTED PERSON

18–121   Article 85 of the Rome Statute entitled anyone who has been the victim of unlawful arrest or detention to have an enforceable right to compensation. Article 85(1) reproduces verbatim Article 9(5) of the International Convention of Civil and Political Rights 1966. There will be an unlawful arrest or detention when the provisions of Article 55 are violated or when other fundamental rights of the arrested or convicted person are breached. If an accused is held in custody on remand in accordance with the Rome Statute, and the ICC RPE, but subsequently acquitted for want of evidence or a "technicality" it will be very unlikely that compensation would be awarded unless Article 85(3) applied.

Article 85(2) provides a right to compensation where a person has been convicted of a criminal offence, but where it subsequently comes to light that there has been a miscarriage of justice. For a right of compensation to accrue under Article 85(2) the non-disclosure at trial of the newly discovered fact or evidence must not be wholly or partly attributable to the appellant.

Article 85(3) provides that in "exceptional circumstances", where there has been a "grave and manifest miscarriage of justice" a court *may* award compensation to a person who has been released from detention following a final decision of acquittal or a termination of the proceedings for that reason.

18–122   Rule 173 of the ICC RPE details how a request for compensation should be made. It provides that the request be made in writing and addressed to the Presidency, which shall designate a new trial chamber to determine the request. Rule 173(2) provides a six-month time limit from the date the claimant is notified of the decision concerning the unlawfulness of the arrest or detention, reversal of conviction, or the existence of a "grave and manifest miscarriage of justice". Rule 173(3) requires that the request contain the grounds relied upon and the quantum requested. Rule 173(4) safeguards the right to legal assistance in making the request. Rule 174 concerns the procedure for seeking compensation and provides, *inter alia*, for the request to be determined on the papers or with a hearing. Regardless of which option is chosen, both the person filing the request, as well as the Prosecutor, are entitled to participate.

Rule 175 states that the Chamber shall, in assessing quantum, consider the consequences of the "grave and manifest miscarriage of justice" on the "personal, family, social and professional situation of the person filing the request".

Rule 51 of UNTAET Regulation 2000/30 also provides for the right of compensation where there has been a miscarriage of justice. It is materially identical to the provisions of Article 85 of the Rome Statute.

XI. IMPRISONMENT, REVIEW AND COMMUTATION OF SENTENCE

A. ICC

(1) ICC Statute

PART 10

ENFORCEMENT

Statute, Arts 103–110

Role of States in enforcement of sentences of imprisonment
103.—1.   **18–123**

   (a) A sentence of imprisonment shall be served in a State designated by the Court from a list of States which have indicated to the Court their willingness to accept sentenced persons.

   (b) At the time of declaring its willingness to accept sentenced persons, a State may attach conditions to its acceptance as agreed by the Court and in accordance with this Part.

   (c) A State designated in a particular case shall promptly inform the Court whether it accepts the Court's designation.

2. (a) The State of enforcement shall notify the Court of any circumstances, including the exercise of any conditions agreed under paragraph 1, which could materially affect the terms or extent of the imprisonment. The Court shall be given at least 45 days' notice of any such known or foreseeable circumstances. During this period, the State of enforcement shall take no action that might prejudice its obligations under article 110.

   (b) Where the Court cannot agree to the circumstances referred to in subparagraph (a), it shall notify the State of enforcement and proceed in accordance with article 104, paragraph 1.

3. In exercising its discretion to make a designation under paragraph 1, the Court shall take into account the following:

(a) The principle that States Parties should share the responsibility for enforcing sentences of imprisonment, in accordance with principles of equitable distribution, as provided in the Rules of Procedure and Evidence;
(b) The application of widely accepted international treaty standards governing the treatment of prisoners;
(c) The views of the sentenced person;
(d) The nationality of the sentenced person;
(e) Such other factors regarding the circumstances of the crime or the person sentenced, or the effective enforcement of the sentence, as may be appropriate in designating the State of enforcement.

4. If no State is designated under paragraph 1, the sentence of imprisonment shall be served in a prison facility made available by the host State, in accordance with the conditions set out in the headquarters agreement referred to in article 3, paragraph 2. In such a case, the costs arising out of the enforcement of a sentence of imprisonment shall be borne by the Court.

Change in designation of State of enforcement

18–124
104.—1. The Court may, at any time, decide to transfer a sentenced person to a prison of another State.

2. A sentenced person may, at any time, apply to the Court to be transferred from the State of enforcement.

Enforcement of the sentence

18–125
105.—1. Subject to conditions which a State may have specified in accordance with article 103, paragraph 1 (b), the sentence of imprisonment shall be binding on the States Parties, which shall in no case modify it.

2. The Court alone shall have the right to decide any application for appeal and revision. The State of enforcement shall not impede the making of any such application by a sentenced person.

Supervision of enforcement of sentences and conditions of imprisonment

18–126
106.—1. The enforcement of a sentence of imprisonment shall be subject to the supervision of the Court and shall be consistent with widely accepted international treaty standards governing treatment of prisoners.

2. The conditions of imprisonment shall be governed by the law of the State of enforcement and shall be consistent with widely accepted international treaty standards governing treatment of prisoners; in no case shall such conditions be more or less favourable than those available to prisoners convicted of similar offences in the State of enforcement.

3. Communications between a sentenced person and the Court shall be unimpeded and confidential.

Transfer of the person upon completion of sentence

18–127
107.—1. Following completion of the sentence, a person who is not a national of the State of enforcement may, in accordance with the law of the State of enforcement, be transferred to a State which is obliged to receive him or her, or to another State which agrees to receive him or her, taking into account any wishes of the person to be transferred to that State, unless the State of enforcement authorizes the person to remain in its territory.

2. If no State bears the costs arising out of transferring the person to another State pursuant to paragraph 1, such costs shall be borne by the Court.

3. Subject to the provisions of article 108, the State of enforcement may also, in accordance with its national law, extradite or otherwise surrender the person

to a State which has requested the extradition or surrender of the person for purposes of trial or enforcement of a sentence.

Limitation on the prosecution or punishment of other offences

108.—1. A sentenced person in the custody of the State of enforcement shall not be subject to prosecution or punishment or to extradition to a third State for any conduct engaged in prior to that person's delivery to the State of enforcement, unless such prosecution, punishment or extradition has been approved by the Court at the request of the State of enforcement.

2. The Court shall decide the matter after having heard the views of the sentenced person.

3. Paragraph 1 shall cease to apply if the sentenced person remains voluntarily for more than 30 days in the territory of the State of enforcement after having served the full sentence imposed by the Court, or returns to the territory of that State after having left it.

18–128

Enforcement of fines and forfeiture measures

109.—1. States Parties shall give effect to fines or forfeitures ordered by the Court under Part 7, without prejudice to the rights of bona fide third parties, and in accordance with the procedure of their national law.

2. If a State Party is unable to give effect to an order for forfeiture, it shall take measures to recover the value of the proceeds, property or assets ordered by the Court to be forfeited, without prejudice to the rights of bona fide third parties.

3. Property, or the proceeds of the sale of real property or, where appropriate, the sale of other property, which is obtained by a State Party as a result of its enforcement of a judgment of the Court shall be transferred to the Court.

18–129

Review by the Court concerning reduction of sentence

110.—1. The State of enforcement shall not release the person before expiry of the sentence pronounced by the Court.

2. The Court alone shall have the right to decide any reduction of sentence, and shall rule on the matter after having heard the person.

3. When the person has served two thirds of the sentence, or 25 years in the case of life imprisonment, the Court shall review the sentence to determine whether it should be reduced. Such a review shall not be conducted before that time.

4. In its review under paragraph 3, the Court may reduce the sentence if it finds that one or more of the following factors are present:

    (a) The early and continuing willingness of the person to cooperate with the Court in its investigations and prosecutions;

    (b) The voluntary assistance of the person in enabling the enforcement of the judgments and orders of the Court in other cases, and in particular providing assistance in locating assets subject to orders of fine, forfeiture or reparation which may be used for the benefit of victims; or

    (c) Other factors establishing a clear and significant change of circumstances sufficient to justify the reduction of sentence, as provided in the Rules of Procedure and Evidence.

5. If the Court determines in its initial review under paragraph 3 that it is not appropriate to reduce the sentence, it shall thereafter review the question of reduction of sentence at such intervals and applying such criteria as provided for in the Rules of Procedure and Evidence.

18–130

(2) ICC Rules of Procedure, rr. 198, 199, 200, 201, 202, 203, 223, 224

Communications between the Court and States

18–131 198.—Unless the context otherwise requires, article 87 and rules 176 to 180 shall apply, as appropriate, to communications between the Court and a State on mattersrelating to enforcement of sentences.

Organ responsible under Part 10

18–132 199.—Unless provided otherwise in the Rules, the functions of the Court under Part 10 shall be exercised by the Presidency.

List of States of enforcement

18–133 200.—1. A list of States that have indicated their willingness to accept sentenced persons shall be established and maintained by the Registrar.

2. The Presidency shall not include a State on the list provided for in article 103, paragraph 1 (a), if it does not agree with the conditions that such a State attaches to its acceptance. The Presidency may request any additional information from that State prior to taking a decision.

3. A State that has attached conditions of acceptance may at any time withdraw such conditions. Any amendments or additions to such conditions shall be subject to confirmation by the Presidency.

4. A State may at any time inform the Registrar of its withdrawal from the list. Such withdrawal shall not affect the enforcement of the sentences in respect of persons that the State has already accepted.

5. The Court may enter bilateral arrangements with States with a view to establishing a framework for the acceptance of prisoners sentenced by the Court. Such arrangements shall be consistent with the Statute.

Principles of equitable distribution

18–134 201.—Principles of equitable distribution for purposes of article 103, paragraph 3, shall include:
(a) The principle of equitable geographical distribution;
(b) The need to afford each State on the list an opportunity to receive sentenced persons;
(c) The number of sentenced persons already received by that State and other States of enforcement;
(d) Any other relevant factors.

Timing of delivery of the sentenced person to the State of enforcement

18–135 202.—The delivery of a sentenced person from the Court to the designated State of enforcement shall not take place unless the decision on the conviction and the decision on the sentence have become final.

Views of the sentenced person

18–136 203.—1. The Presidency shall give notice in writing to the sentenced person that it is addressing the designation of a State of enforcement. The sentenced person shall, within such time limit as the Presidency shall prescribe, submit in writing his or her views on the question to the Presidency.

2. The Presidency may allow the sentenced person to make oral presentations.

3. The Presidency shall allow the sentenced person:
   (a) To be assisted, as appropriate, by a competent interpreter and to benefit from any translation necessary for the presentation of his or her views;
   (b) To be granted adequate time and facilities necessary to prepare for the presentation of his or her views.

Also see generally Rules 204–222 and Rule 225 of the ICC RPE.

Criteria for review concerning reduction of sentence

223.—In reviewing the question of reduction of sentence pursuant to article 110, paragraphs 3 and 5, the three judges of the Appeals Chamber shall take into account the criteria listed in article 110, paragraph 4 (a) and (b), and the following criteria:

   (a) The conduct of the sentenced person while in detention, which shows a genuine dissociation from his or her crime;
   (b) The prospect of the resocialization and successful resettlement of the sentenced person;
   (c) Whether the early release of the sentenced person would give rise to significant social instability;
   (d) Any significant action taken by the sentenced person for the benefit of the victims as well as any impact on the victims and their families as a result of the early release;
   (e) Individual circumstances of the sentenced person, including a worsening state of physical or mental health or advanced age.

18–137

Procedure for review concerning reduction of sentence

224.—1. For the application of article 110, paragraph 3, three judges of the Appeals Chamber appointed by that Chamber shall conduct a hearing, unless they decide otherwise in a particular case, for exceptional reasons. The hearing shall be conducted with the sentenced person, who may be assisted by his or her counsel, with interpretation, as may be required. Those three judges shall invite the Prosecutor, the State of enforcement of any penalty under article 77 or any reparation order pursuant to article 75 and, to the extent possible, the victims or their legal representatives who participated in the proceedings, to participate in the hearing or to submit written observations. Under exceptional circumstances, this hearing may be conducted by way of a videoconference or in the State of enforcement by a judge delegated by the Appeals Chamber.

2. The same three judges shall communicate the decision and the reasons for it to all those who participated in the review proceedings as soon as possible.

3. For the application of article 110, paragraph 5, three judges of the Appeals Chamber appointed by that Chamber shall review the question of reduction of sentence every three years, unless it establishes a shorter interval in its decision taken pursuant to article 110, paragraph 3. In case of a significant change in circumstances, those three judges may permit the sentenced person to apply for a review within the three-year period or such shorter period as may have been set by the three judges.

4. For any review under article 110, paragraph 5, three judges of the Appeals Chamber appointed by that Chamber shall invite written representations from the sentenced person or his or her counsel, the Prosecutor, the State of enforcement of any penalty under article 77 and any reparation order pursuant to article 75 and, to the extent possible, the victims or their legal representatives who participated in the proceedings. The three judges may also decide to hold a hearing.

5. The decision and the reasons for it shall be communicated to all those who participated in the review proceedings as soon as possible.

18–138

(3) ICC Regulations adopted May 26, 2004, regs 113, 114, 115

Enforcement unit within the Presidency

18–139   113.—1. The Presidency shall establish an enforcement unit within the Presidencyto assist it in the exercise of its functions under Part 10 of the Statute, in particular:
   (a) The supervision of enforcement of sentences and conditions of imprisonment; and
   (b) The enforcement of fines, forfeiture orders and reparation orders.
   2. The record for each sentenced person shall be maintained by the Registrar in accordance with rule 15.

Bilateral arrangements under rule 200, sub-rule 5

18–140   114.—Bilateral arrangements as described in rule 200, sub-rule 5, shall be negotiated under the authority of the Presidency and thereafter concluded with the relevant State by the President.

Exercise of functions under rule 214, sub-rule 4

18–141   115.—In the exercise of its functions under rule 214, sub-rule 4, the Presidency shall have due regard to the principles of international law on re-extradition.

B. ICTY

(1) ICTY Statute, Arts 27, 28

Enforcement of sentences

18–142   27. Imprisonment shall be served in a State designated by the International Tribunal from a list of States which have indicated to the Security Council their willingness to accept convicted persons. Such imprisonment shall be in accordance with the applicable law of the State concerned, subject to the supervision of the International Tribunal.

Pardon or commutation of sentences

18–143   28. If, pursuant to the applicable law of the State in which the convicted person is imprisoned, he or she is eligible for pardon or commutation of sentence, the State concerned shall notify the International Tribunal accordingly. The President of the International Tribunal, in consultation with the judges, shall decide the matter on the basis of the interests of justice and the general principles of law.

(2) ICTY Rules of Procedure and Evidence, rr. 103, 104, 123–125

Place of imprisonment

18–144   103.—(A) Imprisonment shall be served in a State designated by the Tribunal from a list of States which have indicated their willingness to accept convicted persons.

(B) Transfer of the convicted person to the State shall be effected as soon as possible after the time-limit for appeal has elapsed.

Supervision of imprisonment

104. All sentences of imprisonment shall be supervised by the Tribunal or a body designated by it.

18–145

Notification by States

123. If, according to the law of the State of imprisonment, a convicted person is eligible for pardon or commutation of sentence, the State shall, in accordance with Article 28 of the Statute, notify the Tribunal of such eligibility.

18–146

Determination by the President

124. The President shall, upon such notice, determine, in consultation with the members of the Bureau and any permanent Judges of the sentencing Chamber who remain Judges of the Tribunal, whether pardon or commutation is appropriate.

18–147

General Standards for Granting Pardon or Commutation

125. In determining whether pardon or commutation is appropriate, the President shall take into account, *inter alia*, the gravity of the crime or crimes for which the prisoner was convicted, the treatment of similarly-situated prisoners, the prisoner's demonstration of rehabilitation, as well as any substantial cooperation of the prisoner with the Prosecutor.

18–148

C. ICTR

(1) ICTR Statute, Arts 26, 27

Enforcement of sentences

26. Imprisonment shall be served in Rwanda or any of the States on a list of States which have indicated to the Security Council their willingness to accept convicted person. Such imprisonment shall be in accordance with the applicable law of the State concerned, subject to the supervision of the Tribunal.

18–149

Pardon or commutation of sentences

27. If, pursuant to the applicable law of the State in which the convicted person is imprisoned, he or she is eligible for pardon or commutation of sentence, the State concerned shall notify the International Tribunal for Rwanda accordingly. There shall only be pardon or commutation of sentence if the President of the International Tribunal for Rwanda, in consultation with the judges, so decides on the basis of the interests of justice and the general principles of law.

18–150

(2) ICTR Rules of Procedure and Evidence, rr. 104, 124–126

Supervision of imprisonment

104. All sentences of imprisonment shall be served under the supervision of the Tribunal or a body designated by it.

18–151

Notification by States

18–152 **124.** If, according to the law of a State in which a convicted person is imprisoned, he is eligible for pardon or commutation of sentence, the State shall, in accordance with Article 27 of the Statute, notify the Tribunal of such eligibility.

Determination by the President

18–153 **125.** The President shall, upon such notice, determine, in consultation with the members of the Bureau and any permanent Judges of the sentencing Chamber who remain Judges of the Tribunal, and after notification to the Government of Rwanda, whether pardon or commutation is appropriate.

General Standards for Granting Pardon or Commutation

18–154 **126.** In determining whether pardon or commutation is appropriate, the President shall take into account, *inter alia*, the gravity of the crime or crimes for which the prisoner was convicted, the treatment of similarly-situated prisoners, the prisoner's demonstration of rehabilitation, as well as any substantial cooperation of the prisoner with the Prosecutor.

D. EAST TIMOR

Regulation No. 2000/30, ss.43, 48

UNTAET Regulation 2000/30, September 25, 2000, as amended by UNTAET Regulation 2001/25, September 14, 2001

VIII EXECUTION OF ORDERS AND DECISIONS

Conditional Release After Trial

18–155 **43.**—43.1 Upon request by the convict or his or her legal representative, and after a hearing, a court may order the condition release of a convict who has been sentenced to a term of imprisonment where:
  (a) two thirds of the term of imprisonment has been completed;
  (b) a favourable report on the conduct of the convict has been presented to the court by correctional authorities; and
  (c) the convict poses no danger to public security or safety.

XII FINAL PROVISIONS

Supervision of the Execution of Prison Sentences

18–156 **48.**—48.1 All matters relating to the supervision and execution of a prison sentence shall be decided by the presiding judge of the panel or the individual judge who pronounced the sentence. In the event that such judge is no longer available or otherwise unable to exercise his or her functions, the Judge Administrator will designate a judge to deal with such matters.
  48.2. Prisoners may file complaints or request relating to the execution of their prison sentence, in writing, with the judge who pronounced the sentence

or, in the even that such judge is no longer available or otherwise unable to exercise his or her functions, with such other judge as may be designated by the President of the Court to deal with such matters.

E. SIERRA LEONE

(1) Statute of the Special Court of Sierra Leone, Arts 22, 23

Enforcement of sentences

22.—(1) Imprisonment shall be served in Sierra Leone. If circumstances so require, imprisonment may also be served in any of the States which have concluded with the International Criminal Tribunal for Rwanda or the International Criminal Tribunal for the former Yugoslavia an agreement for the enforcement of sentences, and which have indicated to the Registrar of the Special Court their willingness to accept convicted persons. The Special Court may conclude similar agreements for the enforcement of sentences with other States.

18–157

(2) Conditions of imprisonment, whether in Sierra Leone or in a third State, shall be governed by the law of the State of enforcement subject to the supervision of the Special Court. The State of enforcement shall be bound by the duration of the sentence, subject to article 23 of the present Statute.

Pardon or commutation of sentences

23. If, pursuant to the applicable law of the State in which the convicted person is imprisoned, he or she is eligible for pardon or commutation of sentence, the State concerned shall notify the Special Court accordingly. There shall only be a pardon or commutation of sentence if the President of the Special Court, in consultation with the judges, so decides on the basis of the interests of justice and the general principles of law.

18–158

(2) SCSL Rules of Procedures and Evidence, rr. 103, 123, 124

Place of Imprisonment

103.—(A) Imprisonment shall be served in Sierra Leone, unless circumstances require otherwise. The Special Court may conclude agreements with other countries willing to accept and imprison convicted persons.

18–159

(B) The place of imprisonment for each convicted person shall be designated by the President.

(C) Transfer of the convicted person to the place of imprisonment shall be effected as soon as possible after the time limit for appeal has lapsed.

PART IX—PARDON AND COMMUTATION OF SENTENCE

Notification by States

123.—If, pursuant to the applicable law of the State in which the convicted person is imprisoned, he is eligible for pardon or commutation of sentence, the State concerned shall, in accordance with Article 23 of the Statute, notify the Registrar.

18–160

Determination by the President

18–161   **124.**—There shall only be pardon or commutation of sentence if the President of the Special Court, in consultation with the judges, so decides on the basis of the interests of justice and the general principles of law.

XII. SUMMARY: IMPRISONMENT, REVIEW AND COMMUTATION OF SENTENCE

18–162   The provisions dealing with imprisonment, review and sentence are self-explanatory. Whilst prisoners detained by the ICC, ICTY, ICTR and SCSL pending or during trial or appeal, will be remanded at ICC Detention Facility for the ICC and UN Detention Facilities for ICTY, ICTR and SCSL, sentences after conviction will be served from a list of States who have expressed a willingness to accept such prisoners. The primary obligation is that the sentences be served in facilities that meet international minimum standards.

In deciding which country a convicted person should be sent to, the Court may take into account such matters as the views of the prisoner (ICC Statute Article 103(3)(c), ICC Rule 203) and his nationality (ICC Statute Article 103(3)(d)). Article 22 of the Statute of the Special Court for Sierra Leone provides that sentences shall be served in Sierra Leone, but that if required, sentences can also be served with States which have entered into agreements with the ICTR or ICTY regarding the enforcement of sentences.

As individuals will be held in different States, operating under different schemes regarding parole, pardon or commutation of sentence, consistency is required. This is achieved in the ICTY, ICTR and SCSL context by requiring the President of the Tribunal to be notified that a prisoner is eligible for pardon or commutation of sentence under the national regime of the host State. The President, in consultation with the judges of the Tribunal will then decide whether the prisoner will be pardoned or have his sentence commuted "on the basis of the interests of justice and the general principle of law" (ICTY Statute, Art. 28; ICTR Statute, Art. 27; SCSL Statue, Art. 23). Pardon and Commutation of sentence is dealt with in Rules 123, 124 and 125 of the ICTY RPE and Rules 124, 125 and 126 of the ICTR RPE. In the case of the ICTY, the procedure to be adopted has been set out in the *Practice Direction on the Procedure for the Determination of Applications for Pardon, Commutation of Sentence and Early release of Persons Convicted by the International Tribunal* (IT/46), April 7, 1999. (See Appendix C24 of this work). There have been at least nine cases in which the President of the ICTY has ordered the early release of the accused from the custody of the ICTY (Simić was released on October 27, 2003; Zaric on January 1, 2004; Blaškić on June 24, 2004; Dosen on February 28, 2003; Mucic on July 7, 2003; Aleksovski on November 14, 2001). Also see, *Prosecutor v. Sikirica et al.*, Order of the President on the Early Release of Dragan Kolundzia, December 5, 2001 and *Prosecutor v. Kvočka et al.*, Order of the President for the early Release of Milojica Kos. In *Kos*, the President noted that the *Practice Direction* does not lay down a procedure to be followed when a person has served enough of his sentence at the United Nations Detention Unit to be able to apply for early release under the law of "all the countries signatory to the agreement on the enforcement of sentences". There is no provision, however, in the Statute or Rules which precludes the Tribunal from ruling on a convicted person's application for early release in accordance with its implied powers. Accordingly, the application for early release could be considered by the ICTY, rather than being submitted to a country signatory to the enforcement of sentences. There have been at least two cases in which the President has denied requests for early release. On December 13, 2002, President Jorda denied the request for the early release of Miroslav Kvočka. (See ICTY Yearbook 2003, A/58/297-S/2003/829, para 19.) On June 24, 2004, President Meron denied the request for the early release of Miroslav Tadić. (See ICTY Yearbook 2004, A/59/215-S/2004/627, para 20.)

Article 110 of the Rome Statute provides that the State of enforce- **18–163** ment shall not release the prisoner before the expiry of the sentence pronounced by the ICC. The Court alone has the right to reduce or commute the sentence (Article 110(2)). The Court will conduct a mandatory review when the convicted person has served two-thirds of his sentence or 25 years in the case of life imprisonment (Article 110(3)). If the Court finds that the convicted person has willingly cooperated with the court in one of the ways detailed in Articles 110(4)(a)–(c) then the Court may reduce the sentence. If it is not considered appropriate, the Court will thereafter review the sentence at such intervals as provided for in the Rules of Procedure and Evidence. Rules 223 of the ICC RPE requires that the three judges of the Appeals Chamber that conduct the review to take into account specified criteria when considering whether to reduce the sentence being served. These include whether the sentenced person has genuinely disassociated him or herself from the crime (Rule 223(a)); the prospect of resocialiasation and resettlement of the convicted person (Rule 223(b)); whether early release *would* (not may) give rise to "significant" social instability (Rule 223(c)); any significant attempts made by the sentenced person for the benefit of the victims and any impact on the victims and their families that would be occasioned by an order of early release being granted (Rule 223(d)); and the individual circumstances of the accused specifically including (but not limited to), the sentenced person's "worsening physical or mental health or advanced age" (Rule 223(e)).

If the three judges of the ICC Appeals Chamber decide, pursuant to Article 110(5) of the Statute, that it is not appropriate to reduce the sentence, they are required to review the question of early release at regular intervals. Rule 224(3) of the ICC RPE requires the Appeals Chamber to review the issue of early release not later than every three years. The sentenced person, however, is permitted to reapply to the ICC within those three years (or such shorter interval at the Court may decide) if there is a significant change of circumstances.

CHAPTER 19

APPEALS AND REVIEWS

I. STATUTORY PROVISIONS

A. ICC

(1) ICC Statute

Statute of the ICC, Arts 81–84

Appeal against decision of acquittal or conviction or against sentence

81.—1. A decision under article 74 may be appealed in accordance with the **19–1**
Rules of Procedure and Evidence as follows:

    (a) The Prosecutor may make an appeal on any of the following grounds:
        (i) Procedural error,
        (ii) Error of fact, or
        (iii) Error of law;
    (b) The convicted person, or the Prosecutor on that person's behalf, may
        make an appeal on any of the following grounds:

    (i) Procedural error,
    (ii) Error of fact,
    (iii) Error of law, or
    (iv) Any other ground that affects the fairness or reliability of the proceedings or decision.

2. (a) A sentence may be appealed, in accordance with the Rules of Procedure and Evidence, by the Prosecutor or the convicted person on the ground of disproportion between the crime and the sentence;

   (b) If on an appeal against sentence the Court considers that there are grounds on which the conviction might be set aside, wholly or in part, it may invite the Prosecutor and the convicted person to submit grounds under article 81, paragraph 1 (a) or (b), and may render a decision on conviction in accordance with article 83;

   (c) The same procedure applies when the Court, on an appeal against conviction only, considers that there are grounds to reduce the sentence under paragraph 2 (a).

3. (a) Unless the Trial Chamber orders otherwise, a convicted person shall remain in custody pending an appeal;

   (b) When a convicted person's time in custody exceeds the sentence of imprisonment imposed, that person shall be released, except that if the Prosecutor is also appealing, the release may be subject to the conditions under subparagraph (c) below;

   (c) In case of an acquittal, the accused shall be released immediately, subject to the following:
     (i) Under exceptional circumstances, and having regard, *inter alia*, to the concrete risk of flight, the seriousness of the offence charged and the probability of success on appeal, the Trial Chamber, at the request of the Prosecutor, may maintain the detention of the person pending appeal;
     (ii) A decision by the Trial Chamber under subparagraph (c) (i) may be appealed in accordance with the Rules of Procedure and Evidence.

4. Subject to the provisions of paragraph 3 (a) and (b), execution of the decision or sentence shall be suspended during the period allowed for appeal and for the duration of the appeal proceedings.

Appeal against other decisions

19–2   **82.**—1. Either party may appeal any of the following decisions in accordance with the Rules of Procedure and Evidence:

   (a) A decision with respect to jurisdiction or admissibility;
   (b) A decision granting or denying release of the person being investigated or prosecuted;
   (c) A decision of the Pre-Trial Chamber to act on its own initiative under article 56, paragraph 3;
   (d) A decision that involves an issue that would significantly affect the fair and expeditious conduct of the proceedings or the outcome of the trial, and for which, in the opinion of the Pre-Trial or Trial Chamber, an immediate resolution by the Appeals Chamber may materially advance the proceedings.

2. A decision of the Pre-Trial Chamber under article 57, paragraph 3 (d), may be appealed against by the State concerned or by the Prosecutor, with the leave of the Pre-Trial Chamber. The appeal shall be heard on an expedited basis.

3. An appeal shall not of itself have suspensive effect unless the Appeals Chamber so orders, upon request, in accordance with the Rules of Procedure and Evidence.

4. A legal representative of the victims, the convicted person or a bona fide owner of property adversely affected by an order under article 75 may appeal

against the order for reparations, as provided in the Rules of Procedure and Evidence.

Proceedings on appeal

83.—1. For the purposes of proceedings under article 81 and this article, the Appeals Chamber shall have all the powers of the Trial Chamber.

2. If the Appeals Chamber finds that the proceedings appealed from were unfair in a way that affected the reliability of the decision or sentence, or that the decision or sentence appealed from was materially affected by error of fact or law or procedural error, it may:

(a) Reverse or amend the decision or sentence; or

(b) Order a new trial before a different Trial Chamber.

For these purposes, the Appeals Chamber may remand a factual issue to the original Trial Chamber for it to determine the issue and to report back accordingly, or may itself call evidence to determine the issue. When the decision or sentence has been appealed only by the person convicted, or the Prosecutor on that person's behalf, it cannot be amended to his or her detriment.

3. If in an appeal against sentence the Appeals Chamber finds that the sentence is disproportionate to the crime, it may vary the sentence in accordance with Part 7.

4. The judgment of the Appeals Chamber shall be taken by a majority of the judges and shall be delivered in open court. The judgment shall state the reasons on which it is based. When there is no unanimity, the judgment of the Appeals Chamber shall contain the views of the majority and the minority, but a judge may deliver a separate or dissenting opinion on a question of law.

5. The Appeals Chamber may deliver its judgment in the absence of the person acquitted or convicted.

Revision of conviction or sentence

84.—1. The convicted person or, after death, spouses, children, parents or one person alive at the time of the accused's death who has been given express written instructions from the accused to bring such a claim, or the Prosecutor on the person's behalf, may apply to the Appeals Chamber to revise the final judgment of conviction or sentence on the grounds that:

(a) New evidence has been discovered that:

    (i) Was not available at the time of trial, and such unavailability was not wholly or partially attributable to the party making application; and

    (ii) Is sufficiently important that had it been proved at trial it would have been likely to have resulted in a different verdict;

(b) It has been newly discovered that decisive evidence, taken into account at trial and upon which the conviction depends, was false, forged or falsified;

(c) One or more of the judges who participated in conviction or confirmation of the charges has committed, in that case, an act of serious misconduct or serious breach of duty of sufficient gravity to justify the removal of that judge or those judges from office under article 46.

2. The Appeals Chamber shall reject the application if it considers it to be unfounded. If it determines that the application is meritorious, it may, as appropriate:

(a) Reconvene the original Trial Chamber;

(b) Constitute a new Trial Chamber; or

(c) Retain jurisdiction over the matter,

with a view to, after hearing the parties in the manner set forth in the Rules of Procedure and Evidence, arriving at a determination on whether the judgment should be revised.

(2) ICC Rules

CHAPTER 8

Appeal and revision

SECTION I

General provisions

ICC Rules of Procedure and Evidence, rr. 149–161

Rules governing proceedings in the Appeals Chamber

19–5   **149.** Parts 5 and 6 and rules governing proceedings and the submission of evidence in the Pre-Trial and Trial Chambers shall apply *mutatis mutandis* to proceedings in the Appeals Chamber.

SECTION II

Appeals against convictions, acquittals, sentences and reparation orders

Appeal

19–6   **150.**—1. Subject to sub-rule 2, an appeal against a decision of conviction or acquittal under article 74, a sentence under article 76 or a reparation order under article 75 may be filed not later than 30 days from the date on which the party filing the appeal is notified of the decision, the sentence or the reparation order.

2. The Appeals Chamber may extend the time limit set out in sub-rule 1, for good cause, upon the application of the party seeking to file the appeal.

3. The appeal shall be filed with the Registrar.

4. If an appeal is not filed as set out in sub-rules 1 to 3, the decision, the sentence or the reparation order of the Trial Chamber shall become final.

Procedure for the appeal

19–7   **151.**—1. Upon the filing of an appeal under rule 150, the Registrar shall transmit the trial record to the Appeals Chamber.

2. The Registrar shall notify all parties who participated in the proceedings before the Trial Chamber that an appeal has been filed.

Discontinuance of the appeal

19–8   **152.**—1. Any party who has filed an appeal may discontinue the appeal at any time before judgment has been delivered. In such case, the party shall file with the Registrar a written notice of discontinuance of appeal. The Registrar shall inform the other parties that such a notice has been filed.

2. If the Prosecutor has filed an appeal on behalf of a convicted person in accordance with article 81, paragraph 1 (b), before filing any notice of discontinuance, the Prosecutor shall inform the convicted person that he or she intends to discontinue the appeal in order to give him or her the opportunity to continue the appeal proceedings.

Judgment on appeals against reparation orders

153.—1. The Appeals Chamber may confirm, reverse or amend a reparation order made under article 75.   **19–9**

2. The judgment of the Appeals Chamber shall be delivered in accordance with article 83, paragraphs 4 and 5.

SECTION III

Appeals against other decisions

Appeals that do not require the leave of the Court

154.—1. An appeal may be filed under article 81, paragraph 3 (c) (ii), or   **19–10**
article 82, paragraph 1 (a) or (b), not later than five days from the date upon which the party filing the appeal is notified of the decision.

2. An appeal may be filed under article 82, paragraph 1 (c), not later than two days from the date upon which the party filing the appeal is notified of the decision.

3. Rule 150, sub-rules 3 and 4, shall apply to appeals filed under sub-rules 1 and 2 of this rule.

Appeals that require leave of the Court

155.—1. When a party wishes to appeal a decision under article 82,   **19–11**
paragraph 1 (d), or article 82, paragraph 2, that party shall, within five days of being notified of that decision, make a written application to the Chamber that gave the decision, setting out the reasons for the request for leave to appeal.

2. The Chamber shall render a decision and shall notify all parties who participated in the proceedings that gave rise to the decision referred to in sub-rule 1.

Procedure for the appeal

156.—1. As soon as an appeal has been filed under rule 154 or as soon as   **19–12**
leave to appeal has been granted under rule 155, the Registrar shall transmit to the Appeals Chamber the record of the proceedings of the Chamber that made the decision that is the subject of the appeal.

2. The Registrar shall give notice of the appeal to all parties who participated in the proceedings before the Chamber that gave the decision that is the subject of the appeal, unless they have already been notified by the Chamber under rule 155, sub-rule 2.

3. The appeal proceedings shall be in writing unless the Appeals Chamber decides to convene a hearing.

4. The appeal shall be heard as expeditiously as possible.

5. When filing the appeal, the party appealing may request that the appeal have suspensive effect in accordance with article 82, paragraph 3.

Discontinuance of the appeal

157. Any party who has filed an appeal under rule 154 or who has obtained   **19–13**
the leave of a Chamber to appeal a decision under rule 155 may discontinue the appeal at any time before judgment has been delivered. In such case, the

party shall file with the Registrar a written notice of discontinuance of appeal. The Registrar shall inform the other parties that such a notice has been filed.

Judgment on the appeal

19–14   **158.**—1. An Appeals Chamber which considers an appeal referred to in this section may confirm, reverse or amend the decision appealed.

2. The judgment of the Appeals Chamber shall be delivered in accordance with article 83, paragraph 4.

SECTION IV

Revision of conviction or sentence

Application for revision

19–15   **159.**—1. An application for revision provided for in article 84, paragraph 1, shall be in writing and shall set out the grounds on which the revision is sought. It shall as far as possible be accompanied by supporting material.

2. The determination on whether the application is meritorious shall be taken by a majority of the judges of the Appeals Chamber and shall be supported by reasons in writing.

3. Notification of the decision shall be sent to the applicant and, as far as possible, to all the parties who participated in the proceedings related to the initial decision.

Transfer for the purpose of revision

19–16   **160.**—1. For the conduct of the hearing provided for in rule 161, the relevant Chamber shall issue its order sufficiently in advance to enable the transfer of the sentenced person to the seat of the Court, as appropriate.

2. The determination of the Court shall be communicated without delay to the State of enforcement.

3. The provisions of rule 206, sub-rule 3, shall be applicable.

Determination on revision

19–17   **161.**—1. On a date which it shall determine and shall communicate to the applicant and to all those having received notification under rule 159, sub-rule 3, the relevant Chamber shall hold a hearing to determine whether the conviction or sentence should be revised.

2. For the conduct of the hearing, the relevant Chamber shall exercise, *mutatis mutandis*, all the powers of the Trial Chamber pursuant to Part 6 and the rules governing proceedings and the submission of evidence in the Pre-Trial and Trial Chambers.

3. The determination on revision shall be governed by the applicable provisions of article 83, paragraph 4.

(3) ICC Regulations of the Court

Appeals and Revision

SECTION 4

APPEAL AND REVISION

REGULATIONS OF THE COURT ICC-BD/01–01–04 33

SUBSECTION 1

Appeal

Regulation 57

Appeal

For the purposes of rule 150, the appellant shall file a notice of appeal which **19–18**
shall state:
  (a) The name and number of the case;
  (b) The date of the decision of conviction or acquittal, sentence or
       reparation order appealed against;
  (c) Whether the appeal is directed against the whole decision or part
       thereof;
  (d) The relief sought.

Regulation 58

Document in support of the appeal

1. Having filed an appeal in accordance with regulation 57, the appellant **19–19**
shall file a document in support of the appeal within 90 days of notification of
the relevant decision.

2. The document in support of the appeal shall contain the grounds of
appeal. Each ground of appeal shall be divided into two parts:
  (a) The ground of appeal;
  (b) The legal and/or factual reasons in support of the ground of appeal.

3. The legal and/or factual reasons referred to in sub-regulation 2 (b) shall
be set out in separate paragraphs. Reference shall be made to the relevant part
of the record or any other document or source of information as regards any
factual issue. Each legal reason shall be set out together with reference to any
relevant article, rule, regulation or other applicable law, and any authority
cited in support thereof. Where applicable, the finding or ruling challenged in
the decision shall be identified, with specific reference to the page and
paragraph number.

4. Grounds of appeal may be advanced cumulatively or in the alternative.

5. The document in support of the appeal shall not exceed 100 pages.

Regulation 59

Response

19–20   1. A participant may file a response within 60 days of notification of the document in support of the appeal described in regulation 58 as follows:

(a) Each ground of appeal shall be answered separately, stating whether it is opposed, in whole or in part, together with the grounds put forward in support thereof; it shall also be stated whether the relief sought is opposed, in whole or in part, together with the grounds of opposition in support thereto;

(b) When facts are relied on that are not already set out in the appeal or the document in support of the appeal, reference shall be made to the relevant part of the record or any other document or source of information;

(c) Each legal reason relied on in support of the response shall be set out together with reference to any relevant article, rule, regulation or other applicable law, and any authority cited in support thereof.

2. The response shall not exceed 100 pages. To the extent possible, it shall be set out and numbered in the same order as in the document described in regulation 58.

Regulation 60

Reply

19–21   1. Whenever the Appeals Chamber considers it necessary in the interests of justice, it may order the appellant to file a reply within such time as it may specify in its order.

2. Any reply filed in accordance with sub-regulation 1 shall not exceed 50 pages. To the extent possible, it shall be set out and numbered in the same order as in the documents described in regulations 58 and 59.

Regulation 61

Variation of grounds of appeal presented before the Appeals Chamber

19–22   1. An application for variation of grounds of appeal shall state the name and number of the case and shall specify the variation sought and the reasons in support thereof.

2. The application for variation shall be filed as soon as the reasons warranting it become known.

3. Participants may file a response within seven days of notification of the application for variation.

4. The response shall state the name and number of the case and shall specify the legal or factual reasons advanced by way of opposition.

5. If the variation is granted, the Appeals Chamber shall specify both the time limit within which the appellant shall file the document setting out the grounds of appeal as varied and the page limit for that document. Regulation 58, sub-regulations 2 and 3, shall apply *mutatis mutandis*.

6. Any response to the document described in sub-regulation 5 shall be filed within the time limit specified by the Appeals Chamber. The Appeals Chamber may also fix a page limit for the response and otherwise regulation 59 shall apply *mutatis mutandis*.

7. Regulation 60 shall apply *mutatis mutandis* with regard to any reply to the response filed in accordance with sub-regulation 6.

Regulation 62

Additional evidence presented before the Appeals Chamber

1. A participant seeking to present additional evidence shall file an appli-   **19–23**
cation setting out:
  (a) The evidence to be presented;
  (b) The ground of appeal to which the evidence relates and the reasons, if
      relevant, why the evidence was not adduced before the Trial
      Chamber.

2. The Appeals Chamber may:
  (a) Decide to first rule on the admissibility of the additional evidence, in
      which case it shall direct the participant affected by the application
      filed under sub-regulation 1 to address the issue of admissibility of the
      evidence in his or her response, and to adduce any evidence in
      response only after a decision on the admissibility of that evidence has
      been issued by the Appeals Chamber; or
  (b) Decide to rule on the admissibility of the additional evidence jointly
      with the other issues raised in the appeal, in which case it shall direct
      the participant affected by the application filed under sub-regulation 1
      to both file a response setting out arguments on that application and
      to adduce any evidence in response.

3. The responses described in sub-regulation 2 shall be filed within a time
limit specified by the Appeals Chamber and shall be set out and numbered, to
the extent possible, in the same order as in the application to present evidence.

4. If several defendants are participants in the appeal, the evidence admitted
on behalf of any of them shall, where relevant, be considered in respect of all of
them.

Regulation 63

Consolidated appeals under rule 150

1. Unless otherwise ordered by the Appeals Chamber, in a case of more than   **19–24**
one appeal under rule 150:
  (a) When the Prosecutor appeals, he or she shall file one consolidated
      document in support of all appeals in accordance with regulation 58;
  (b) When more than one convicted person files a document in support of
      the appeal, the Prosecutor shall file a consolidated response in
      accordance with regulation 59.

2. Regulation 60 shall apply *mutatis mutandis* and any reply filed by the
Prosecutor shall be by way of a consolidated reply.

3. For a consolidated document in support of more than one appeal and a
consolidated response, as described in sub-regulation 1, the page limit shall be
100 pages plus a further 40 pages for each additional convicted or acquitted
person. The page limit for any consolidated reply as described in subregulation
2 shall be 50 pages plus a further 20 pages for each additional convicted or
acquitted person.

4. The time limit for filing a consolidated response by the Prosecutor shall
run from notification of the last document filed in support of the appeal by a
convicted person in a given case.

Regulation 64

Appeals under rule 154

1. An appeal filed under rule 154 shall state: **19–25**

    (a) The name and number of the case or situation;
    (b) The title and date of the decision being appealed;
    (c) The specific provision of the Statute pursuant to which the appeal is filed;
    (d) The relief sought.

2. Subject to sub-regulations 5 and 6, the appellant shall file a document in support of the appeal, with reference to the appeal, within 21 days of notification of the relevant decision. The document in support of the appeal shall set out the grounds of appeal and shall contain the legal and/or factual reasons in support of each ground of appeal. Each reason shall be set out in separate paragraphs. Reference shall be made to the relevant part of the record or any other document or source of information as regards any factual issue. Each legal reason shall be set out together with reference to any relevant article, rule, regulation or other applicable law, and any authority cited in support thereof. The document in support of the appeal shall, where applicable, identify the finding or ruling challenged in the decision, with specific reference to the page and paragraph number.

3. Grounds of appeal may be advanced cumulatively or in the alternative.

4. Subject to sub-regulations 5 and 6, a participant may file a response within 21 days of notification of the document in support of the appeal as follows:
    (a) Each ground of appeal shall be answered separately, stating whether it is opposed, in whole or in part, together with the grounds put forward in support thereof; it shall also be stated whether the relief sought is opposed, in whole or in part, together with the grounds of opposition in support thereto;
    (b) The legal and/or factual reasons in support.

5. For appeals filed under article 82, paragraph 1 (b), the document in support of the appeal shall be filed by the appellant within seven days of notification of the relevant decision. The response shall be filed within five days of notification of the document in support of the appeal.

6. For appeals filed under article 82, paragraph 1 (c), the document in support of the appeal shall be filed by the appellant within four days of notification of the relevant decision. The response shall be filed within two days of notification of the document in support of the appeal.

Regulation 65

Appeals under rule 155

19–26   1. An application for leave to appeal under rule 155 shall state the name and number of the case or situation and shall specify the legal and/or factual reasons in support thereof. If the facts relied upon in support are not apparent from the record of the proceedings, they shall, as far as possible, be substantiated by a solemn affirmation by a person having knowledge of the facts stated therein.

2. An application for leave to appeal under article 82, paragraph 1 (d), shall specify the reasons warranting immediate resolution by the Appeals Chamber of the matter at issue.

3. Participants may file a response within three days of notification of the application described in sub-regulation 1, unless the Pre-Trial or Trial Chamber concerned orders an immediate hearing of the application. In the latter case, the participants shall be afforded an opportunity to be heard orally.

4. When leave to appeal is granted, the appellant shall file, within ten days of notification of the decision granting leave to appeal, a document in support of the appeal in accordance with regulation 64, sub-regulation 2. Such document shall also contain the precise title and date of filing of the decision granting leave to appeal.

5. Participants may file a response within ten days of notification of the document in support of the appeal. Regulation 64, sub-regulation 4, shall apply *mutatis mutandis*.

SUBSECTION 2

Revision

Regulation 66

Procedure leading to the determination on revision

1. An application for revision under article 84, paragraph 1, and rule 159 **19–27** shall state the name and number of the original case. An application under article 84, paragraph 1 (a), shall set out the new facts or evidence, unknown or unavailable at the time of trial, and shall indicate the effect that the production of such facts or evidence at the trial might have had upon the decision of the Court. Other applications shall set out the reasons in accordance with article 84, paragraph 1 (b) or (c). The facts relied upon in any application for revision shall, as far as possible, be supported by a solemn affirmation by a person having knowledge of the facts. The application shall not exceed 100 pages.

2. As far as possible, the application for revision shall be notified to the participants in the original proceedings and to any other person having a direct interest in the revision proceedings. Such participants and persons may file a response within 40 days of notification of that application.

3. The response described in sub-regulation 2 shall contain the name and number of the case and shall set out the legal and/or factual reasons advanced in support thereof. Facts tending to deny or contradict the existence of the facts upon which the application is founded shall be outlined in the response and shall be supported by a solemn affirmation by a person having knowledge of such facts. The response shall not exceed 100 pages.

4. Whenever the Appeals Chamber considers it necessary in the interests of justice, it may order the appellant to file a reply within such time as it may specify in its order.

B. ICTY

(1) ICTY Statute and Rules

Statute of the ICTY, Arts 25, 26

Appellate proceedings

25.—1. The Appeals Chamber shall hear appeals from persons convicted by **19–28** the Trial Chambers or from the Prosecutor on the following grounds:
    (a) an error on a question of law invalidating the decision; or
    (b) an error of fact which has occasioned a miscarriage of justice.

2. The Appeals Chamber may affirm, reverse or revise the decisions taken by the Trial Chambers.

Review proceedings

19–29   **26.** Where a new fact has been discovered which was not known at the time of the proceedings before the Trial Chambers or the Appeals Chamber and which could have been a decisive factor in reaching the decision, the convicted person or the Prosecutor may submit to the International Tribunal an application for review of the judgment.

ICTY Rules of Procedure and Evidence, rr. 65, 72, 73, 108, 109, 111–115, 117–122

Provisional Release

19–30   **65.**—(A) Once detained, an accused may not be released except upon an order of a Chamber.

(B) Release may be ordered by a Trial Chamber only after giving the host country and the State to which the accused seeks to be released the opportunity to be heard and only if it is satisfied that the accused will appear for trial and, if released, will not pose a danger to any victim, witness or other person.

(C) The Trial Chamber may impose such conditions upon the release of the accused as it may determine appropriate, including the execution of a bail bond and the observance of such conditions as are necessary to ensure the presence of the accused for trial and the protection of others.

(D) Any decision rendered under this Rule by a Trial Chamber shall be subject to appeal. Subject to paragraph (F) below, an appeal shall be filed within seven days of filing of the impugned decision. Where such decision is rendered orally, the appeal shall be filed within seven days of the oral decision, unless

    (i) the party challenging the decision was not present or represented when the decision was pronounced, in which case the time-limit shall run from the date on which the challenging party is notified of the oral decision; or

    (ii) the Trial Chamber has indicated that a written decision will follow, in which case, the time-limit shall run from filing of the written decision.

19–31   (E) The Prosecutor may apply for a stay of a decision by the Trial Chamber to release an accused on the basis that the Prosecutor intends to appeal the decision, and shall make such an application at the time of filing his or her response to the initial application for provisional release by the accused.

(F) Where the Trial Chamber grants a stay of its decision to release an accused, the Prosecutor shall file his or her appeal not later than one day from the rendering of that decision.

(G) Where the Trial Chamber orders a stay of its decision to release the accused pending an appeal by the Prosecutor, the accused shall not be released until either:

    (i) the time-limit for the filing of an appeal by the Prosecutor has expired, and no such is filed;

    (ii) the Appeals Chamber dismisses the appeal; or

    (iii) the Appeals Chamber otherwise orders.

(H) If necessary, the Trial Chamber may issue a warrant of arrest to secure the presence of an accused who has been released or is for any other reason at liberty. The provisions of Section 2 of Part Five shall apply *mutatis mutandis.*

(I) Without prejudice to the provisions of Rule 107, the Appeals Chamber may grant provisional release to convicted persons pending an appeal or for a fixed period if it is satisfied that:

    (i) the appellant, if released, will either appear at the hearing of the appeal or will surrender into detention at the conclusion of the fixed period, as the case may be;

    (ii) the appellant, if released, will not pose a danger to any victim, witness or other person, and

(iii) special circumstances exist warranting such release.

The provisions of paragraphs (C) and (H) shall apply *mutatis mutandis*.

Preliminary Motions

72.—(A) Preliminary motions, being motions which   **19–32**
  (i) challenge jurisdiction;
  (ii) allege defects in the form of the indictment;
  (iii) seek the severance of counts joined in one indictment under Rule 49 or seek separate trials under Rule 82 (B); or
  (iv) raise objections based on the refusal of a request for assignment of counsel made under Rule 45 (C) shall be in writing and be brought not later than thirty days after disclosure by the Prosecutor to the defence of all material and statements referred to in Rule 66(A)(i) and shall be disposed of not later than sixty days after they were filed and before the commencement of the opening statements provided for in Rule 84.

(B) Decisions on preliminary motions are without interlocutory appeal save
  (i) in the case of motions challenging jurisdiction; ;
  (ii) in other cases where certification has been granted by the Trial Chamber, which may grant such certification if the decision involves an issue that would significantly affect the fair and expeditious conduct of the proceedings or the outcome of the trial, and for which, in the opinion of the Trial Chamber, an immediate resolution by the Appeals Chamber may materially advance the proceedings.

(C) Appeals under paragraph (B)(i) shall be filed within fifteen days and requests for certification under paragraph (B)(ii) shall be filed within seven days of filing of the impugned decision. Where such decision is rendered orally, this time-limit shall run from the date of the oral decision, unless
  (i) the party challenging the decision was not present or represented when the decision was pronounced, in which case the time-limit shall run from the date on which the challenging party is notified of the oral decision; or
  (ii) the Trial Chamber has indicated that a written decision will follow, in which case, the time-limit shall run from filing of the written decision.
If certification is given, a party shall appeal to the Appeals Chamber within seven days of the filing of the decision to certify.

(D) For the purpose of paragraphs (A)(i) and (B)(i), a motion challenging   **19–33**
jurisdiction refers exclusively to a motion which challenges an indictment on the ground that it does not relate to:
  (i) any of the persons indicated in Articles 1, 6, 7 and 9 of the Statute;
  (ii) the territories indicated in Articles 1, 8 and 9 of the Statute;
  (iii) the period indicated in Articles 1, 8 and 9 of the Statute;
  (iv) any of the violations indicated in Articles 2, 3, 4, 5 and 7 of the Statute.

Other Motions

73.—(A) After a case is assigned to a Trial Chamber, either party may at   **19–34**
any time move before the Chamber by way of motion, not being a preliminary motion, for appropriate ruling or relief. Such motions may be written or oral, at the discretion of the Trial Chamber.

(B) Decisions on all motions are without interlocutory appeal save with certification by the Trial Chamber, which may grant such certification if the decision involves an issue that would significantly affect the fair and expeditious conduct of the proceedings or the outcome of the trial, and for which, in the opinion of the Trial Chamber, an immediate resolution by the Appeals Chamber may materially advance the proceedings.

(C) Requests for certification shall be filed within seven days of the filing of the impugned decision. Where such decision is rendered orally, this time-limit shall run from the date of the oral decision, unless

    (i) the party challenging the decision was not present or represented when the decision was pronounced, in which case the time-limit shall run from the date on which the challenging party is notified of the oral decision; or

    (ii) the Trial Chamber has indicated that a written decision will follow, in which case the time-limit shall run from filing of the written decision.

If certification is given, a party shall appeal to the Appeals Chamber within seven days of the filing of the decision to certify.

(D) Irrespective of any sanctions which may be imposed under Rule 46(A), when a Chamber finds that a motion is frivolous or is an abuse of process, the Registrar shall withhold payment of fees associated with the production of that motion and/ or costs thereof.

Notice of Appeal

19–35   **108.** A party seeking to appeal a judgment shall, not more than thirty days from the date on which the judgment was pronounced, file a notice of appeal, setting forth the grounds. The Appellant should also identify the order, decision or ruling challenged with specific reference to the date of its filing, and/or the transcript page, and indicate the substance of the alleged errors and the relief sought. The Appeals Chamber may, on good cause being shown by motion, authorise a variation of the grounds of appeal.

Record on Appeal

19–36   **109.** The record on appeal shall consist of the trial record, as certified by the Registrar.

Appellant's Brief

19–37   **111.** An Appellant's brief setting out all the arguments and authorities shall be filed within seventy-five days of filing of the notice of appeal pursuant to Rule 108.

Respondent's Brief

19–38   **112.** A Respondent's brief of argument and authorities shall be filed within forty days of the filing of the Appellant's brief.

Brief in Reply

19–39   **113.** An Appellant may file a brief in reply within fifteen days after the filing of the Respondent's brief.

Date of Hearing

19–40   **114.** After the expiry of the time-limits for filing the briefs provided for in Rules 111, 112 and 113, the Appeals Chamber shall set the date for the hearing and the Registrar shall notify the parties.

Additional Evidence

19–41   **115—(A)** A party may apply by motion to present additional evidence before the Appeals Chamber. Such motion shall clearly identify with precision the specific finding of fact made by the Trial Chamber to which the additional evidence is directed, and must be served on the other party and filed with the Registrar not later than seventy-five days from the date of the judgement, unless good cause is shown for further delay. Rebuttal material may be presented by any party affected by the motion. (Amended 30 Sept 2002)

(B) If the Appeals Chamber finds that the additional evidence was not available at trial and is relevant and credible, it will determine if it could have been a decisive factor in reaching the decision at trial. If it could have been such a factor, the Appeals Chamber will consider the additional evidence and any rebuttal material along with that already on the record to arrive at a final judgement in accordance with Rule 117.

(C) The Appeals Chamber may decide the motion prior to the appeal, or at the time of the hearing on appeal. It may decide the motion with or without an oral hearing.

(D) If several defendants are parties to the appeal, the additional evidence admitted on behalf of any one of them will be considered with respect to all of them, where relevant.

Expedited Appeals Procedure

116bis.—(A) An appeal under Rule 72 or Rule 73 or appeal from a decision rendered under Rule 54bis, Rule 65, Rule 77 or Rule 91 shall be heard expeditiously on the basis of the original record of the Trial Chamber. Appeals may be determined entirely on the basis of written briefs.

(B) Rules 109 to 114 shall not apply to such appeals.

(C) The Presiding Judge, after consulting the members of the Appeals Chamber, may decide not to apply Rule 117 (D)

19–42

Judgment on Appeal

117.—(A) The Appeals Chamber shall pronounce judgment on the basis of the record on appeal together with such additional evidence as has been presented to it.

(B) The judgment shall be rendered by a majority of the Judges. It shall be accompanied or followed as soon as possible by a reasoned opinion in writing, to which separate or dissenting opinions may be appended.

(C) In appropriate circumstances the Appeals Chamber may order that the accused be retried according to law.

(D) The judgment shall be pronounced in public, on a date of which notice shall have been given to the parties and counsel and at which they shall be entitled to be present.

19–43

Status of the Accused following Appeal

118.—(A) A sentence pronounced by the Appeals Chamber shall be enforced immediately.

(B) Where the accused is not present when the judgment is due to be delivered, either as having been acquitted on all charges or as a result of an order issued pursuant to Rule 65, or for any other reason, the Appeals Chamber may deliver its judgment in the absence of the accused and shall, unless it pronounces an acquittal, order the arrest or surrender of the accused to the Tribunal.

19–44

Request for Review

119.—(A) Where a new fact has been discovered which was not known to the moving party at the time of the proceedings before a Trial Chamber or the Appeals Chamber, and could not have been discovered through the exercise of

19–45

due diligence, the defence or, within one year after the final judgment has been pronounced, the Prosecutor, may make a motion to that Chamber for review of the judgment. If, at the time of the request for review, any of the Judges who constituted the original Chamber are no longer Judges of the Tribunal, the President shall appoint a Judge or Judges in their place.

(B) Any brief in response to a request for review shall be filed within forty days of the filing of a request.

(C) Any brief in reply shall be filed within fifteen days after filing of the response.

Preliminary Examination

19–46 **120.** If a majority of Judges of the Chamber constituted pursuant to Rule 119 agree that the new fact, if proved, could have been a decisive factor in reaching a decision, the Chamber shall review the judgment, and pronounce a further judgment after hearing the parties.

Appeals

19–47 **121.** The judgment of a Trial Chamber on review may be appealed in accordance with the provisions of Part Seven.

Return of Case to Trial Chamber

19–48 **122.** If the judgment to be reviewed is under appeal at the time the motion for review is filed, the Appeals Chamber may return the case to the Trial Chamber for disposition of the motion.

C. ICTR

(1) ICTR Statute and Rules

Statute of the ICTR, Arts 24, 25

Appellate Proceedings

19–49 **24.**—1. The Appeals Chamber shall hear appeals from persons convicted by the Trial Chambers or from the Prosecutor on the following grounds:

(a) An error on a question of law invalidating the decision; or

(b) An error of fact which has occasioned a miscarriage of justice.

2. The Appeals Chamber may affirm, reverse or revise the decisions taken by the Trial Chambers.

Review Proceedings

19–50 **25.** Where a new fact has been discovered which was not known at the time of the proceedings before the Trial Chambers or the Appeals Chamber and which could have been a decisive factor in reaching the decision, the convicted person or the Prosecutor may submit to the International Tribunal for Rwanda an application for review of the judgment.

ICTR Rules of Procedure and Evidence, rr. 65, 72, 73, 107, 107*bis*, 108, 108*bis*, 109–117, 117*bis*, 117*ter*, 118–123

Provisional Release

19–51 **65.**—(A) Once detained, an accused may not be released except upon an order of a Chamber.

(B) Release may be ordered by a Trial Chamber only after giving the host country and the State to which the accused seeks to be released the opportunity to be heard and only if it is satisfied that the accused will appear for trial and, if released, will not pose a danger to any victim, witness or other person.

(C) The Trial Chamber may impose such conditions upon the release of the accused as it may determine appropriate, including the execution of a bail bond and the observance of such conditions as are necessary to ensure the presence of the accused for trial and the protection of others.

(D) Any decision rendered under this Rule by a Trial Chamber shall be subject to appeal in cases where leave is granted by a bench of three Judges of the Appeals Chamber, upon good cause being shown. Subject to paragraph (F) below, applications for leave to appeal shall be filed within seven days of filing of the impugned decision. Where such decision is rendered orally, the application shall be filed within seven days of the oral decision, unless

    (i) the party challenging the decision was not present or represented when the decision was pronounced, in which case the time-limit shall run from the date on which the challenging party is notified of the oral decision; or

    (ii) the Trial Chamber has indicated that a written decision will follow, in which case, the time-limit shall run from filing of the written decision.

(E) The Prosecutor may apply for a stay of a decision by the Trial Chamber to release an accused on the basis that the Prosecutor intends to appeal the decision, and shall make such an application at the time of filing his or her response to the initial application for provisional release by the accused.

(F) Where the Trial Chamber grants a stay of its decision to release an accused, the Prosecutor shall file his or her appeal not later than one day from the rendering of that decision.

(G) Where the Trial Chamber orders a stay of its decision to release the accused pending an appeal by the Prosecutor, the accused shall not be released until either:

    (i) the time-limit for the filing of an application for leave to appeal by the Prosecutor has expired, and no such application is filed;

    (ii) a bench of three Judges of the Appeals Chamber rejects the application for leave to appeal;

    (iii) the Appeals Chamber dismisses the appeal; or

    (iv) a bench of three Judges of the Appeals Chamber or the Appeals Chamber otherwise orders.

(H) If necessary, the Trial Chamber may issue a warrant of arrest to secure the presence of an accused who has been released or is for any other reason at liberty. The provisions of Section 2 of Part Five shall apply *mutatis mutandis.*

(I) Without prejudice to the provisions of Rule 107, the Appeals Chamber may grant provisional release to convicted persons pending an appeal or for a fixed period if it is satisfied that:

    (i) the appellant, if released, will either appear at the hearing of the appeal or will surrender into detention at the conclusion of the fixed period, as the case may be;

    (ii) the appellant, if released, will not pose a danger to any victim, witness or other person, and

    (iii) special circumstances exist warranting such release.

The provisions of paragraphs (C) and (H) shall apply *mutatis mutandis.*

Preliminary Motions

72.—(A) Preliminary motions, being motions which: **19–52**

    (i) challenge jurisdiction;

    (ii) allege defects in the form of the indictment;

    (iii) seek the severance of counts joined in one indictment under Rule 49 or seek separate trials under Rule 82 (B); or

    (iv) raise objections based on the refusal of a request for assignment of
counsel made under Rule 45 (C) shall be in writing and be brought
not later than thirty days after disclosure by the Prosecutor to the
Defence of all material and statements referred to in Rule 66 (A) (i)
and shall be disposed of not later than sixty days after they were filed
and before the commencement of the opening statements provided for
in Rule 84. The Trial Chamber may rule on such motions based solely
on the briefs of the parties, unless it is decided to hear the motion in
open Court.

(B) Decisions on preliminary motions are without interlocutory appeal, save:
    (i) in the case of motions challenging jurisdiction, where an appeal by
either party lies as of right;
    (ii) in other cases where certification has been granted by the Trial
Chamber, which may grant such certification if the decision involves
an issue that would significantly affect the fair and expeditious
conduct of the proceedings or the outcome of the trial, and for which,
in the opinion of the Trial Chamber, an immediate resolution by the
Appeals Chamber may materially advance the proceedings.

(C) Appeals under paragraph (B)(i) shall be filed within fifteen days and
requests for certification under paragraph (B)(ii) shall be filed within seven
days of filing of the impugned decision. Where such decision is rendered orally,
this time-limit shall run from the date of the oral decision, unless
    (i) the party challenging the decision was not present or represented
when the decision was pronounced, in which case the time-limit shall
run from the date on which the challenging party is notified of the
oral decision; or
    (ii) the Trial Chamber has indicated that a written decision will follow, in
which case, the time-limit shall run from filing of the written decision.
If certification is given, a party shall appeal to the Appeals Chamber within
seven days of the filing of the decision to certify.

(D) For purposes of paragraphs (A)(i) and (B)(i), a motion challenging
jurisdiction refers exclusively to a motion which challenges an indictment on
the ground that it does not relate to:
    (i) any of the persons indicated in Articles 1, 5, 6 and 8 of the Statute;
    (ii) the territories indicated in Articles 1, 7 and 8 of the Statute;
    (iii) the period indicated in Articles 1, 7, and 8 of the Statute; or
    (iv) any of the violations indicated in Articles 2, 3, 4 and 6 of the Statute.

(E) An appeal brought under paragraph (B)(i) may not be proceeded with if
a bench of three Judges of the Appeals Chamber, assigned by the presiding
Judge of the Appeals Chamber, decides that the appeal is not capable of
satisfying the requirements of paragraph (D), in which case the appeal shall be
dismissed.

(F) Objections to the form of the indictment, including an amended
indictment, shall be raised by a party in one motion only, unless otherwise
allowed by a Trial Chamber.

(G) Failure to comply with the time limits prescribed in this Rule shall
constitute a waiver of the rights. The Trial Chamber may, however, grant relief
from the waiver upon showing good cause.

Motions

19–53   **73.**—(A) Subject to Rule 72, either party may move before a Trial Chamber
for appropriate ruling or relief after the initial appearance of the accused. The
Trial Chamber, or a Judge designated by the Chamber from among its
members, may rule on such motions based solely on the briefs of the parties,
unless it is decided to hear the motion in open Court.

(B) Decisions rendered on such motions are without interlocutory appeal
save with certification by the Trial Chamber, which may grant such certifica-

tion if the decision involves an issue that would significantly affect the fair and expeditious conduct of the proceedings or the outcome of the trial, and for which, in the opinion of the Trial Chamber, an immediate resolution by the Appeals Chamber may materially advance the proceedings.

(C) Requests for certification shall be filed within seven days of the filing of the impugned decision. Where such decision is rendered orally, this time-limit shall run from the date of the oral decision, unless

    (i) the party challenging the decision was not present or represented when the decision was pronounced, in which case the time-limit shall run from the date on which the challenging party is notified of the oral decision; or

    (ii) the Trial Chamber has indicated that a written decision will follow, in which case the time-limit shall run from filing of the written decision.

If certification is granted, a party shall appeal to the Appeals Chamber within seven days of the filing of the decision to certify.

(D) Where a date has been set for the hearing of a motion, including a preliminary motion, any additional motions to be heard on that date and any supporting material to the motions must be filed at least ten days before the hearing of the motion. Failure to observe this Rule will mean that the later motion will not be considered on the hearing date, nor will any adjournment of the original motion be granted on the basis of subsequent motions filed, save in exceptional circumstances.

(E) A responding party shall, thereafter, file any reply within five days from the date on which Counsel received the motion.

(F) In addition to the sanctions envisaged by Rule 46, a Chamber may impose sanctions against Counsel if Counsel brings a motion, including a preliminary motion, that, in the opinion of the Chamber, is frivolous or is an abuse of process. Such sanctions may include non-payment, in whole or in part, of fees associated with the motion and/or costs thereof.

(G) Notwithstanding the time limits in Rule 72(A), the time limit in the present Rule applies.

General Provision

107. The rules of procedure and evidence that govern proceedings in the Trial Chambers shall apply *mutatis mutandis* to proceedings in the Appeals Chamber.

19–54

Practice Directions for the Appeals Chamber

107bis. The Presiding Judge of the Appeals Chamber may issue Practice Directions, in consultation with the President of the Tribunal, addressing detailed aspects of the conduct of proceedings before the Appeals Chamber.

19–55

Notice of Appeal

108. A party seeking to appeal a judgement shall, not more than thirty days from the date on which the judgement was pronounced, file a notice of appeal, setting forth the grounds. The Appellant should also identify the order, decision or ruling challenged with specific reference to the date of its filing, and/or the transcript page, and indicate the substance of the alleged errors and the relief sought. The Appeals Chamber may, on good cause being shown by motion, authorise a variation of the grounds of appeal.

19–56

Pre-Hearing Judge

108bis.—(A) The Presiding Judge of the Appeals Chamber may designate from among its members a Judge responsible for the pre-hearing proceedings (the "Pre-Hearing Judge").

19–57

(B) The Pre-Hearing Judge shall ensure that the proceedings are not unduly delayed and shall take any measures related to procedural matters, including the issuing of decisions, orders and directions with a view to preparing the case for a fair and expeditious hearing.

(C) The Pre-Hearing Judge shall record the points of agreement and disagreement between the parties on matters of law and fact. In this connection, he or she may order the parties to file further written submissions with the Pre-Hearing Judge or the Appeals Chamber.

(D) In order to perform his or her functions, the Pre-Appeal Judge may *proprio motu*, where appropriate, hear the parties without the convicted or acquitted person being present. The Pre-Appeal Judge may hear the parties in his or her office, in which case minutes of the meeting shall be taken by a representative of the Registry.

(E) A motion made in the course of the proceedings shall be determined before the hearing unless the Pre-Appeal Judge, for good cause, orders that it be deferred for determination by the Appeals Chamber. Failure by a party to raise objections or to make requests which can be made prior to the hearing shall constitute waiver thereof, but the Pre-Appeal Judge for good cause may grant relief from the waiver.

(F) The Pre-Appeal Judge shall keep the Appeals Chamber regularly informed, particularly where issues are in dispute and may refer such disputes to the Appeals Chamber.

(G) Upon a report of the Pre-Appeal Judge, the Appeals Chamber shall decide, should the case arise, on appropriate sanctions to be imposed on a party which fails to perform its obligations pursuant to the present Section of the Rules.

(H) The Appeals Chamber may *proprio motu* exercise any of the functions of the Pre-Appeal Judge.

Record on Appeal

19–58   109.—(A) The record on appeal shall consist of the trial record, as certified by the Registrar.

(B) A certified true copy of the record on appeal shall be promptly transmitted to the Appeals Unit of the Appeals Chamber of the International Criminal Tribunal for Rwanda, located in The Hague.

List of Certified Copies to the Parties

19–59   110. The Registrar shall make available to the parties the list of documents constituting the record on appeal as certified by him and shall provide them with any of these documents on demand.

Appellant's Brief

19–60   111. An Appellant's brief setting out all the arguments and authorities shall be filed within seventy-five days of filing of the notice of appeal pursuant to Rule 108.

Respondent's Brief

19–61   112. A Respondent's brief of argument and authorities shall be filed within forty days of the filing of the Appellant's brief.

Brief in Reply

19–62   113. An Appellant may file a brief in reply within fifteen days after the filing of the Respondent's brief.

Date of Hearing

114. After the expiry of the time-limits for filing the briefs provided for in Rules 111, 112 and 113, the Appeals Chamber shall set the date for the hearing and the Registrar shall notify the parties.

19–63

Additional Evidence

115.—(A) A party may apply by motion to present additional evidence before the Appeals Chamber. Such motion shall clearly identify with precision the specific finding of fact made by the Trial Chamber to which the additional evidence is directed, and must be served on the other party and filed with the Registrar not later than seventy-five days from the date of the judgement, unless good cause is shown for further delay. Rebuttal material may be presented by any party affected by the motion.

(B) If the Appeals Chamber finds that the additional evidence was not available at trial and is relevant and credible, it will determine if it could have been a decisive factor in reaching the decision at trial. If it could have been such a factor, the Appeals Chamber will consider the additional evidence and any rebuttal material along with that already on the record to arrive at a final judgement in accordance with Rule 118.

(C) The Appeals Chamber may decide the motion prior to the appeal, or at the time of the hearing on appeal. It may decide the motion with or without an oral hearing.

(D) If several defendants are parties to the appeal, the additional evidence admitted on behalf of any one of them will be considered with respect to all of them, where relevant.

19–64

Extension of Time Limits

116.—(A) The Appeals Chamber may grant a motion to extend a time limit upon a showing of good cause.

(B) Where the ability of the accused to make full answer and defence depends on the availability of a decision in an official language other than that in which it was originally issued, that circumstances shall be taken into account as good cause under the present Rule.

19–65

Expedited Appeals Procedure

117.—(A) An appeal under Rule 65, 72(D), 77 or 91 shall be heard expeditiously and may be determined entirely on the basis of the original record of the Trial Chamber. Appeals may be determined entirely on the basis of written briefs.

(B) Rules 109 to 114 shall not apply to such appeals.

(C) The Presiding Judge, after consulting the members of the Appeals Chamber, may decide not to apply Rule 118(D).

19–66

Parties' Books

117bis.—(A) In every appeal before the Appeals Chamber, the Appellant and the Respondent shall each prepare and file an Appeal Book respectively to be entitled "APPELLANT'S APPEAL BOOK" and "RESPONDENT'S APPEAL BOOK", in consecutively numbered pages or tabs arranged in the following order:

(i) a table of contents describing each document, including each exhibit, by its nature, date, and where applicable, number, with an indication of the page or tab where the document will be found in the Appeal Book, and

19–67

(ii) a legible copy of the pages of or excerpts from every document in the case to which the party actually refers in the party's briefs or intends to refer in the party's oral arguments.

(B) In every appeal before the Appeals Chamber, the Appellant and the Respondent shall each prepare and file a Book of Authorities respectively to be entitled "APPELLANT'S BOOK OF AUTHORITIES" and "RESPONDENT'S BOOK OF AUTHORITIES", in consecutively numbered pages or tabs arranged in the following order:

(i) a table of contents describing each document, including each exhibit, by its nature, date, and where applicable, number, with an indication of the page or tab where the document will be found in the Appeal Book, and

(ii) a legible copy of the pages of or excerpts from every reference material, including case law, statutory and regulatory provisions, from international and national sources, to which the party actually refers in the party's briefs or intends to refer in the party's oral arguments.

(C) Unless otherwise ordered in any particular case by the Appeals Chamber *proprio motu* or upon a motion by a party, each party shall file eight copies of his or her Appeal Book, and eight copies of his or her Book of Authorities, at the Registry two weeks before the date set for hearing.

(D) Failure to file the books prescribed above shall not bar the Appeals Chamber from rendering a judgment, a decision or an order as it sees fit in the appeal.

Filing of the Appeal Documents

19–68   **117ter.** The notice of Appeal under Rule 108 and, where necessary, the briefs earmarked under Rules 111, 112, 113, 115 and 117 shall be filed, by the parties, either with the Registry or with an officer of the Registry specifically designated by the Registrar at the Appeals Unit of the Appeals Chamber of the International Criminal Tribunal for Rwanda, located in The Hague. Two similar records shall be kept: one at the Registry of the Tribunal and the other in The Hague. Depending on the place of filing, each record shall consist of the original documents or certified true copies thereof.

Judgment on Appeal

19–69   **118.**—(A) The Appeals Chamber shall pronounce judgment on the basis of the record on appeal and on any additional evidence as has been presented to it.

(B) The judgment shall be rendered by a majority of the Judges. It shall be accompanied or followed as soon as possible by a reasoned opinion in writing, to which separate or dissenting opinions may be appended.

(C) In appropriate circumstances the Appeals Chamber may order that the accused be retried before the Trial Chamber.

(D) The judgment shall be pronounced in public, on a date of which notice shall have been given to the parties and counsel and at which they shall be entitled to be present.

(E) The written judgment shall be filed and registered with the Registry or with an officer of the Registry specifically designated by the Registrar at the Appeals Unit of the Appeals Chamber of the International Criminal Tribunal for Rwanda, located in The Hague.

Status of the Accused Following Judgment on Appeal

19–70   **119.**—(A) A sentence pronounced by the Appeals Chamber shall be enforced immediately.

(B) Where the accused is not present when the judgment is due to be delivered, either as having been acquitted on all charges or as a result of an order issued pursuant to Rule 65, or for any other reason, the Appeals Chamber may deliver its judgment in the absence of the accused and shall, unless it pronounces his acquittal, order his arrest or surrender to the Tribunal.

Request for Review

120.—(A) Where a new fact has been discovered which was not known to the moving party at the time of the proceedings before a Trial Chamber or the Appeals Chamber and could not have been discovered through the exercise of due diligence, the Defence or, within one year after the final judgement has been pronounced, the Prosecutor, may make a motion to that Chamber for review of the judgement. If, at the time of the request for review, any of the Judges who constituted the original Chamber are no longer Judges of the Tribunal, the President shall appoint a Judge or Judges in their place.

(B) Any brief in response to a request for review shall be filed within forty days of the filing of the request.

(C) Any brief in reply shall be filed within fifteen days after the filing of the response.

19–71

Preliminary Examination

121.1. If the Chamber which ruled on the matter decides that the new fact, if it had been proven, could have been a decisive factor in reaching a decision, the Chamber shall review the judgment, and pronounce a further judgment after hearing the parties.

19–72

Appeals

122. The judgment of a Trial Chamber on review may be appealed in accordance with the provisions of Part Seven.

19–73

Return of the Case to the Trial Chamber

123. If the judgment to be reviewed is under appeal at the time the motion for review is filed, the Appeals Chamber may return the case to the Trial Chamber for disposition of the motion.

19–74

D. East Timor

(1) Regulation 2000/11 on the Organisation of Courts in East Timor, ss.14, 15 (as amended by Regulation 2001/25, September 14, 2001)

II. Court of Appeal

Jurisdiction of the Court of Appeal

14.—14.1 There shall be established a Court of Appeal for East Timor. The Court shall have its seat in Dili.

14.2 The Court of Appeal shall have jurisdiction to hear appeals of final judgments rendered by any District Court in East Timor, and such other matters as are provided for in the present or any other UNTAET regulation.

19–75

Composition of the Court of Appeal

19–76 **15.**—15.1 The Court of Appeal shall be composed of judges appointed by the Transitional Administrator to the Court of Appeal in accordance with UNTAET Regulation No. 1999/3.

15.2 The judges shall sit in panels of three judges. The panel shall take its decisions by majority vote. The vote of each judge shall have equal weight.

15.3 Relatives up to second degree as well as spouses or partners shall not sit as judges on the same panel.

15.4 In the event of an appeal on a matter provided in Section 9 of the present regulation, the Transitional Administrator, after consultation with the President of the Court of Appeal, shall establish a panel with the expertise to hear and decide such appeals. Such panels shall be composed of both East Timorese and international judges, appointed to the Court in accordance with UNTAET Regulation No. 1999/3.

(2) UNTAET Regulation 2000/30 on the Transitional Rules of Criminal Procedure, ss.23, 27, 40, 41

Interlocutory Appeal

19–77 **23.**—23.1 A decision of the Investigating Judge pursuant to Section 20.6 of the present regulation may be appealed to the Court of Appeal by any of the parties, according to procedure set forth in this Section.

23.2 In an appeal pursuant to Section 23.1 of the present regulation, the petitioner shall present a written petition to the Court of Appeal within ten days of the decision and shall immediately serve a copy upon the respondent. The Court shall summon the parties to a hearing within ten days of the receipt of the petition. The respondent may file a written statement with the Court at any time prior to the hearing and shall immediately serve a copy upon the petitioner. Service of the respective written statements and the summons shall be as provided in Section 2.4 of the present regulation.

23.3 Any evidence relevant to an appeal pursuant to Section 23.1 of the present regulation may be proposed by the parties in their respective written statements.

23.4 The hearing shall be open to the public unless otherwise decided by the Court of Appeal. The parties shall be given the opportunity to present their arguments orally. Evidence, if any, shall be presented following, where appropriate, the rules established in Section 33 of the present regulation.

23.5 At the end of the hearing, the Court of Appeal shall decide and shall issue its decision in writing to the parties. The Court may confirm, reject or modify the decision from which appeal was taken.

23.6 If the ruling of the Investigating Judge is confirmed, the proceedings shall continue in accordance with the rules of the present regulation, as though the appeal had not been taken.

23.7 If the ruling of the Investigating Judge is rejected or modified, the Court of Appeal may:

(a) order the release of the suspect unless indicted before the expiration of the term established in Section 20.10 of the present regulation, in cases pursuant to Section 20.11 of the present regulation;

(b) order the release of the suspect or establish a date by which the indictment of the suspect must be presented, in cases pursuant to Section 20.12 of the present regulation;

(c) order or modify substitute restrictive measures as provided in Section 21 of the present regulation.

23.8 Upon the decision, the Court of Appeal shall remand the case to the competent District Court. All decisions defined in Section 23.7 of the present regulation shall be executed by the District Court, except that an order for the release of the suspect or for modification of substitute restrictive measures shall be executed immediately upon its issuance by the Court of Appeal.

23.9 Appeal proceedings under the present Section shall not interrupt the course of the investigations.

Motions

27.—27.1 Preliminary motions may be raised prior to the commencement of   **19–78**
the trial. Such motions are those which:

(a) allege defects in the form of the indictment;

(b) seek severance of counts joined in one indictment or separate trials in cases of coaccused; or

(c) raise objections based upon refusal of a request for assignment of counsel

27.2 After the case is assigned to a panel or judge, any party may at any time lodge a motion with the court, other than a preliminary motion as described in the preceding subsection, for appropriate relief. Motions for appropriate relief may be oral or written at the discretion of the Court.

27.3 Decisions on motions, except as provided in Sections 23 and 27.4 of the present regulation, are not subject to interlocutory appeal. The granting of a motion to dismiss the case for any reason shall be deemed a final decision in the case and shall be subject to appeal as provided in Part VII of the present regulation.

27.4 The Court of Appeal may grant leave to immediately appeal from a decision on a motion where:

(a) the decision from which appeal is sought would cause such prejudice to the case of the party seeking leave to appeal as could not be cured by the final decision of the trial;

(b) the issue on which appeal is sought is of general importance to proceedings before the courts of East Timor; or

(c) upon other good cause being shown by the party seeking leave to appeal.

VII. APPEALS

Appeal from Final Decisions

40.—40.1 A party may appeal to the Court of Appeal a final decision of a   **19–79**
District Court rendered pursuant to Section 39.4 of the present regulation, or any other order of an inferior court which constitutes the final disposition of a case to which the present regulation applies, or any order whose appeal under this Section is provided by any UNTAET regulation, on one or more of the following grounds:

(a) a violation of the rules of the criminal procedure;

(b) a violation of the procedural or substantive rights of the accused;

(c) inconsistency within grounds of the decision;

(d) material error of law or fact.

40.2 A party shall commence an appeal by filing a Notice of Appeal with the court of first instance. The Notice of Appeal shall be filed no more than ten (10) days after the appealed decision is released. If no Notice of Appeal is filed within this period, the party is deemed to have waived his or her right to appeal and the decision of first instance shall be final. The assertion of a cross-appeal pursuant to Section 40.4 of the present regulation does not require filing of a Notice of Appeal.

40.3 A party who has filed a Notice of Appeal shall file a written appeal statement with the court of first instance within thirty days after the filing of its Notice of Appeal. If no written appeal is filed within this period, the party concerned is deemed to have withdrawn the appeal, and the decision of first instance shall be final.

19–80   40.4 After a written appeal is filed, the Registrar of the court of first instance shall establish an appeal file and shall notify the respondent. The respondent has thirty (30) days from the receipt of the notification to file a response to the appeal. The response may include a crossappeal and shall be filed in the same manner as the written appeal statement. If the response includes a cross-appeal, the Registrar shall notify the appellant, who shall have fifteen (15) days to file a response to the cross-appeal.

40.5 The appeal or cross-appeal statement shall include the following, any or all of which may also be included in a response:

  (a) the identities of the parties;
  (b) a summary of the case, including a copy of the order from which appeal is taken;
  (c) the grounds for the appeal;
  (d) the evidence to be presented, if any;
  (e) the remedy sought; and
  (f) a designation of those portions of the record which are suggested by the submitting party for review by the Court of Appeal.

40.6 The notifications provided in Section 40.4 of the present regulation shall follow the procedure established in Section 2.4 of the present regulation.

40.7 After receipt of the response to the appeal and cross-appeal, if any, or after the periods allowed for such responses have expired, the Registrar of the court of first instance shall prepare the designated portions of the record and shall forward the case file and designated portions of the record to the Court of Appeal.

40.8 The cost of preparation of the designated portions of the record shall be deemed a cost of the appeal.

40.9 Upon receipt of the case file by the Court of Appeal, the Court of Appeal is competent with regard to all matters concerning the detention of the accused, until final disposition of the appeal. Upon final disposition of the appeal, the case may be remanded to the court of first instance for such further proceedings as may be ordered. After remand, if the accused continues under detention, the court of first instance is competent with regard to such matters.

Proceedings in the Court of Appeal

19–81   **41.**—41.1 The Court of Appeal shall set a date for a hearing of the appeal and shall notify the parties following the procedure established in Section 2.4 of the present regulation.

41.2 If there is no complaint in relation to evidence, the appeal may proceed on the record of evidence produced in the District Court. If new evidence has arisen that was not known to the moving party at the time of the prior proceedings and could not have been discovered through the exercise of due diligence, the Court of Appeal may, upon motion of the party, allow the presentation of such evidence or examination of witnesses at the appeal hearing. The costs of evidentiary proceedings shall be deemed costs of appeal and shall be calculated in the same manner as in first instance proceedings.

41.3 If witness testimony is ordered by the Court of Appeal, witnesses offered by the appellant shall be examined first, followed by the examination of witnesses offered by the respondent. A witness shall be questioned first by the Court, then by the party calling the witness, followed by the other party and then any further questions by the Court.

41.4 The decision of the Court of Appeal shall confirm, overrule or modify the decision of the District Court, giving regard to the provisions of Section 55 of the present regulation, and shall determine responsibility for the costs of appeal. If the decision of the court of first instance is not confirmed, the Court of Appeal may alter or amend the decision of the court of first instance or, in appropriate cases, order the initiation of new proceedings by the court of first instance.

41.5 A decision of the Court of Appeal shall contain the same elements as defined in Section 39.3 of the present regulation and shall address each issue raised by the appellant; provided, however, that the Court of Appeal may summarily dismiss any appeal, issue or claim for relief it finds to be patently frivolous or without merit. The Court of Appeal shall also assign responsibility for the costs of appeal; provided, however, that no portion of the costs may be assessed against an accused unless the Court finds that the assessed portion relates only to issues raised by the accused which are patently frivolous.

41.6 Where the appeal of the accused is dismissed, the Court of Appeal shall not modify the decision of the court of first instance such as to impose a greater penalty upon the accused.

41.7 The public prosecutor may withdraw an appeal by presenting a written statement to the Court of Appeal. The legal representative of the accused shall not withdraw an appeal without the written consent of the accused. In cases of joint accused, the withdrawal of one appellant does not affect other appellants.

E. SIERRA LEONE

Statute of the Special Court of Sierra Leone, Arts 20, 21

Appellate proceedings

20.—1. The Appeals Chamber shall hear appeals from persons convicted by a Trial Chamber or from the Prosecutor on the following grounds: **19–82**
    (a) A procedural error;
    (b) An error on a question of law invalidating the decision;
    (c) An error of fact which has occasioned a miscarriage of justice.

2. The Appeals Chamber may affirm, reverse or revise the decisions taken by the Trial Chamber.

3. The judges of the Appeals Chamber of the Special Court shall be guided by the decisions of the Appeals Chamber of the International Tribunals for the Former Yugoslavia and for Rwanda. In the interpretation and application of the laws of Sierra Leone, they shall be guided by the decisions of the Supreme Court of Sierra Leone.

Review proceedings

21.—1. Where a new fact has been discovered which was not known at the time of the proceedings before the Trial Chamber or the Appeals Chamber and which could have been a decisive factor in reaching the decision, the convicted person or the Prosecutor may submit an application for review of the judgment. **19–83**

2. An application for review shall be submitted to the Appeals Chamber. The Appeals Chamber may reject the application if it considers it to be unfounded. If it determines that the application is meritorious, it may, as appropriate:
    (a) Reconvene the Trial Chamber;
    (b) Retain jurisdiction over the matter.

SCSL Rules of Procedure and Evidence

Bail

65.—(A) Once detained, an accused shall not be granted bail except upon an order of a Judge or Trial Chamber. **19–84**

(B) Bail may be ordered by a Judge or a Trial Chamber after hearing the State to which the accused seeks to be released and only if it is satisfied that the accused will appear for trial and, if released, will not pose a danger to any victim, witness or other person.

(C) An accused may only make one application for bail to the Judge or Trial Chamber unless there has been a material change in circumstances.

(D) The Judge or Trial Chamber may impose such conditions upon the granting of bail to the accused as it may determine appropriate, including the execution of a bail bond and the observance of such conditions as are necessary to ensure the presence of the accused at trial and the protection of others.

(E) Any decision rendered under this Rule shall be subject to appeal in cases where leave is granted by a Single Judge of the Appeals Chamber, upon good cause being shown. Applications for leave to appeal shall be filed within seven days of the impugned decision.

(F) If necessary, the Trial Chamber may issue a warrant of arrest to secure the presence of an accused who has been granted bail or is for any other reason at large. The provisions of Section 2 of Part V shall apply.

(G) The Prosecutor may appeal a decision to grant bail. In the event of such an appeal, the accused shall remain in custody until the appeal is heard and determined.

(H) Appeals from bail decisions shall be heard by a bench of at least three Appeals Chamber Judges.

Preliminary Motions

19–85   72.—(A) Preliminary motions by either party shall be brought within 21 days following disclosure by the Prosecutor to the Defence of all the material envisaged by Rule 66(A)(i).

(B) Preliminary motions by the accused are:
    i. Objections based on lack of jurisdiction;
    ii. Objections based on defects in the form of the indictment;
    iii. Applications for severance of crimes joined in one indictment under Rule 49, or for separate trials under Rule 82(B);
    iv. Objections based on the denial of request for assignment of counsel; or
    v. Objections based on abuse of process.

(C) Objections based on lack of jurisdiction or to the form of the indictment, including an amended indictment, shall be raised by a party in one motion only, unless otherwise allowed by the Trial Chamber.

(D) The Trial Chamber shall, except as provided by Sub-Rules (E) and (F) below, dispose of preliminary motions before the trial, and its decisions thereon shall not be subject to interlocutory appeal.

(E) Preliminary motions made in the Trial Chamber prior to the Prosecutor's opening statement which raise a serious issue relating to jurisdiction shall be referred to a bench of at least three Appeals Chamber Judges, where they will proceed to a determination as soon as practicable.

(F) Preliminary motions made in the Trial Chamber prior to the Prosecutor's opening statement which, in the opinion of the Trial Chamber, raise an issue that would significantly affect the fair and expeditious conduct of the proceedings or the outcome of a trial shall be referred to a bench of at least three Appeals Chamber Judges, where they will proceed to a determination as soon as practicable.

(G) Where the Trial Chamber refers a motion to the Appeals Chamber pursuant to Sub-Rules (E) or (F) above, any party wishing to file additional written submissions must seek leave from the Appeals Chamber which will impose time limits for further submissions, responses and replies if leave is granted.

(H) References by the Trial Chamber pursuant to Sub-Rules (E) and (F) above shall not operate as a stay of proceedings. Such references shall not operate as a stay of the trial itself unless the Trial or Appeal Chamber so orders.

(I) This Rule shall be deemed to have entered into force on the 7th of March, 2003.

Motions

73.—(A) Subject to Rule 72, either party may move before the Designated Judge or a Trial Chamber for appropriate ruling or relief after the initial appearance of the accused. The Designated Judge or the Trial Chamber, or a Judge designated by the Trial Chamber from among its members, shall rule on such motions based solely on the written submissions of the parties, unless it is decided to hear the parties in open Court.

19–86

(B) Decisions rendered on such motions are without interlocutory appeal. However, in exceptional circumstances and to avoid irreparable prejudice to a party, the Trial Chamber may give leave to appeal. Such leave should be sought within 3 days of the decision and shall not operate as a stay of proceedings unless the Trial Chamber so orders.

(C) Whenever the Trial Chamber and the Appeals Chamber of the Court are seized of the same Motion raising the same or similar issue or issues, the Trial Chamber shall stay proceedings on the said Motion before it until a final determination of the said Motion by the Appeals Chamber.

General Provisions

106.—(A) Pursuant to Article 20 of the Statute, the Appeals Chamber shall hear appeals from persons convicted by the Trial Chamber or from the Prosecutor on the following grounds:

19–87

    a. A procedural error;

    b. An error on a question on law invalidating the decision;

    c. An error of fact which has occasioned a miscarriage of justice.

(B) The Appeals Chamber may affirm, reverse or revise the decisions taken by the Trial Chamber.

(C) The rules of procedure and evidence that govern proceedings in the Trial Chambers shall apply as appropriate to proceedings in the Appeals Chamber. Rule 107: Practice Directions for the Appeals Chamber (amended March 7, 2003)

The President may issue Practice Directions, in consultation with the Vice-President, addressing detailed aspects of the conduct of proceedings before the Appeals Chamber.

Notice of Appeal

108.—(A) Subject to Sub-Rule (B), a party seeking to appeal a judgement or sentence shall, not more than 14 days from the receipt of the full judgement and sentence, file with the Registrar and serve upon the other parties a written notice of appeal, setting forth the grounds.

19–88

(B) In appeals pursuant to Rules 77 and 91, the notice and grounds of appeal shall be filed within seven days of the receipt of the decision.

(C) In appeals pursuant to Rules 46, 65 and 73(B), the notice and grounds of appeal shall be filed within 7 days of the receipt of the decision to grant leave.

Pre-Hearing Judge

109.—(A) The Presiding Judge of the Appeals Chamber may designate from among its members a Pre-Hearing Judge.

19–89

(B) The Pre-Hearing Judge shall ensure that the proceedings are not unduly delayed and shall take any measures related to procedural matters, including the issuing of decisions, orders and directions with a view to preparing the case for a fair and expeditious hearing.

(C) The Pre-Hearing Judge shall record the points of agreement and disagreement between the parties on matters of law and fact. In this connection, he or she may order the parties to file further written submissions with the Pre-Hearing Judge or the Appeals Chamber.

(D) The Appeals Chamber may of its own initiative exercise any of the functions of the Pre-Hearing Judge.

Record on Appeal

19–90 110. The record on appeal shall consist of the parts of the trial record as designated by the Pre-Hearing Judge, as certified by the Registrar.

Appellant's Submissions

19–91 111. An Appellant's submissions shall be served on the other party or parties and filed with the Registrar within twenty one days of the notice of appeal pursuant to Rule 108.

Respondent's Submissions

19–92 112. A Respondent's submissions shall be served on the other party or parties and filed with the Registrar within fourteen days of the filing of the Appellant's submissions.

Submissions in Reply

19–93 113.—(A) An Appellant may file submissions in reply within five days after the filing of the Respondent's submissions.

(B) No further submissions may be filed except with leave of the Appeals Chamber.

Date of Hearing

19–94 114. After the expiration of the time-limits for filing the submissions provided for in Rules 111, 112 and 113, the Appeals Chamber shall set the date for the hearing in open court, unless it decides to rule on such appeals based solely on the submissions of the parties. The Registrar shall notify the parties accordingly.

Additional Evidence

19–95 115.—(A) A party may apply by motion to present before the Appeals Chamber additional evidence which was not available to it at the trial. Such motion must be served on the other party and filed with the Registrar not less than fifteen days before the date of the hearing.

(B) The Appeals Chamber shall authorize the presentation of such evidence if it considers that the interests of justice so require.

Judgment on Appeal

19–96 118.—(A) The Appeals Chamber shall pronounce judgement on the basis of the record on appeal and on any additional evidence as has been presented to it.

(B) The judgement shall be rendered by a majority of the Judges. It shall be accompanied or followed as soon as possible by a reasoned opinion in writing, to which separate or dissenting opinions may be appended.

(C) In appropriate circumstances the Appeals Chamber may order that the accused be retried before the Trial Chamber.

(D) If the Appeals Chamber reverses an acquittal of an accused by the Trial Chamber on any count, the Appeals Chamber shall proceed to sentence the accused in respect of that offence.

(E) The judgement shall be pronounced in public, on a date of which notice shall have been given to the parties and counsel and at which they shall be entitled to be present.

(F) The written judgement shall be filed and registered with the Registry.

Status of the Accused Following Judgment on Appeal

119.—(A) A sentence pronounced by the Appeals Chamber shall be enforced immediately.   **19–97**

(B) Where the accused is not present when the Appeal judgement is due to be delivered, it may, unless it pronounces his acquittal, order his arrest or transfer to the Special Court.

Review Proceedings

Request for Review

120. Where a new fact has been discovered which was not known at the time of the proceedings before the Trial Chamber or Appeals Chamber and which could have been a decisive factor in reaching the decision, the convicted person or the Prosecutor may submit an application for a review of the judgement.   **19–98**

Preliminary Examination

121. An application for review shall be submitted to the Appeals Chamber. The Appeals Chamber may reject the application if it considers it to be unfounded. If it determines that the application is meritorious, it may, as appropriate: **19–99**
    i. Reconvene the Trial Chamber;
    ii. Retain jurisdiction over the matter.

Appeals

122. The judgement of a Trial Chamber on review may be appealed in accordance with the provisions of Part VII.   **19–100**

II. INTERLOCUTORY APPEALS

A. PRELIMINARY MOTIONS

(1) Definition of preliminary motions

The ICC Rules, and the ICTY and ICTR Rules set out different procedures applicable to interlocutory appeals, based on whether leave is required (or certification is granted by the Trial Chamber) or leave of the court is not required to appeal (see ICC Rules 154–156; ICTY and   **19–101**

ICTR Rules 65, 72, 72). Article 82 of the ICC Statute is headed "Appeal against other decisions" and identifies decisions capable of being subject to interlocutory appeal. Though no definition of preliminary motions is found in the ICC Rules, Rule 72 in the Rules of Procedure and Evidence of the ICTY and ICTR define the motions which will be considered as preliminary motions. They are motions that challenge the jurisdiction of the Tribunals; allege defects in the form of the indictments; seek severance of counts or separate trials and raise objections based on the refusal of a request for the assignment of counsel. Rule 72 of the Rules of Procedure and Evidence of the Special Court for Sierra Leone (SCSL) define preliminary motions as the same as those listed in the ICTY and ICTR Rules, but adds that "objections based on abuse of process" are also the subject of preliminary motions. See also section 27 of UNTAET Regulation 2000/30.

(2) When may an interlocutory appeal be brought

19–102   Rule 154 of the ICC Rules of Procedure and Evidence details appeals which may be brought as of right, without the leave of the court (appeal against continued detention or release of an accused in the case of an acquittal under Article 81(3)(c)(ii), or against a decision with respect to jurisdiction or admissibility or granting or refusing provisional release under Article 82(1)(a)–(b)). Rule 155 details the appeals which require the leave of the court (appeals involving an issue that significantly affects the fair and expeditious conduct of proceedings, or the outcome of the trial and the resolution of which would materially advance the proceedings under Article 82(1)(d), or an appeal under Article 82(2) of the ICC Statute against a decision of the Pre-Trial Chamber to authorise the prosecutor to take specific investigative steps within the territory of a State Party, without its consent).

Rule 72(B) of both the ICTY and ICTR Rules provide that decisions on preliminary motions are without interlocutory appeal, except when the appeal relates to a challenge to jurisdiction or in other cases where certification has been granted by the Trial Chamber. In the ICTR, (though there is a right to appeal a decision on jurisdiction, an appeal cannot proceed unless a Bench of three Appeals Chamber Judges decides that the appeal is capable of satisfying the requirement for jurisdiction of Rule 72(D) of the ICTR Rules. There is no longer such a requirement in the ICTY. For certification by the Trial Chamber, the requirements of Rule 72(B) (ii) must be met.

In the SCSL, Rule 72(D) provides that decisions on preliminary matters are not subject to interlocutory appeal except in two circumstances: where the motion raises a serious issue relating to jurisdiction; or where, in the opinion of the Trial Chamber, it raises an issue that would significantly affect the fair and expeditous conduct of the proceedings or the outcome of trial. Where a motion meets either of these requirements, the matter is referred by the Trial Chamber to a Bench of three Appeals Chamber Judges for determination.

Section 27.3 of UNTAET Regulation 2000/30 states that except as provided for in section 23 (decision of the investigating judge) and section 27.4 (decisions with leave on the grounds that the decision sought to be impugned would cause such prejudice to the party seeking leave as would be incapable of being cured by the final decision of the trial, or that the issue on which appeal is being sought would be of general importance to the proceedings before the courts of East Timor or upon other good cause being shown), decisions on preliminary motions are not subject to interlocutory appeal. The granting of a motion to dismiss a case, however, is to be considered a final decision and does attract a right of appeal.

(3) Time limits for filing appeals

In relation to appeals that may be brought as of right, Rule 154(1) of **19–103** the ICC Rules of Procedure and Evidence states that appeals under Article 81(3)(c)(ii) or Article 82(1)(a)–(b) of the ICC Statute must be filed not later than five days from the date of notification of the impugned decision. Rule 154(2) requires that appeals under Article 82(1)(c) must be brought not later than two days from the date of notification of the impugned decision. In relation to appeals that require leave, Rule 155(1) states that appeals under Article 82(1)(d) or Article 82(2) shall be brought by way of written application within five days from the date of notification of the impugned decision. Regulation 64 and Regulation 65 of the ICC Regulations of the Court set out the procedural requirements and time limits for filing appeals under Rules 154 and 155.

In the case of the ICTY and ICTR Rule 72(A) of the ICTY and ICTR requires that preliminary motion be brought within 30 days of the Prosecutor disclosing to the defence all material and statements under Rule 66(A)(i). The Trial Chamber is also obliged by Rule 72(A) of both the ICTY and ICTR to dispose of all preliminary motions not later than 60 days after the motions were filed and before the commencement of opening statements.

Rule 72(C) of both the ICTY and ICTR Rules provide that appeals (ICTY) and applications for leave to appeal (ICTR) against decisions of the Trial Chambers on motions challenging jurisdiction must be filed within 15 days from the date of the filing of the impugned decision. Requests for certification must be filed within seven days of the filing of the impugned decision (see Rule 72(C)(i) and (ii) on when the time limits run from in the case of an oral decision of a Trial Chamber).

Where motions before a Trial Chamber of the SCSL raise matters of jurisdiction or issues affecting the fair and expeditious conduct of proceedings or outcome of a trial such motions are referred to a Bench of three Appeals Chamber Judges. As such, there are no time limits applicable.

Section 23.2 of UNTAET Regulation 2000/30 requires that the petitioner present the written petition against the decision of the investigating judge to the Court of Appeal within 10 days of the date of the impugned decision. The Court will then summon the parties within 10 days from receipt of the petition for a hearing of the appeal.

(4) Authority to file interlocutory appeals

In the case of the ICC see Rules 154–155 of ICC Rules of Procedure **19–104** and Evidence. In the case of the SCSL, see Rules 72 and 73. For authority within the ICTY, see the discussion below, and Rules 72 and

73. In relation to the ICTR, see Rules 72 and 73. In the case of the Special Panels for Serious Crimes in East Timor, see section 23 of UNTAET Regulation 2000/30.

Other than Articles 25 and 24 of the ICTY and ICTR Statutes, respectively, providing for appeals from convictions by a Trial Chamber, no mention is made in the Statutes of a basis for filing interlocutory appeals. In the *Prosecutor v. Tadić*, Decision on the Defence Motion for Interlocutory Appeal on Jurisdiction, October 2, 1995, paras 4–6, the Appeals Chamber stated that the Security Council had expected that the Statute, which was general in nature, would be supplemented by rules adopted by the Judges. A rule providing for interlocutory appeal was recognised as necessary for the sake of fairness, especially to the accused, and because "such a fundamental matter as the jurisdiction of the International Tribunal should not be kept for decision at the end of a potentially lengthy, emotional and expensive trial". The Appeals Chamber held, at para. 6, that, "the jurisdiction of this Chamber to hear and dispose of Appellant's interlocutory appeal [. . .] [is] [. . .] indisputable".

The contentious issue in the case of automatic interlocutory appeals based upon jurisdiction is whether the appeal is in fact a challenge to jurisdiction as defined in Rule 72(D) of the ICTY and ICTR Rules.

19–105   Rule 72(D) sets out the bases upon which an indictment may be challenged under the rubric of an interlocutory appeal against jurisdiction. The bases of challenge are defined negatively. The indictment may be challenged because it does not relate to: any of the persons in the Statute over which the Tribunal has jurisdiction; the territory of the former Yugoslavia; the temporal jurisdiction of the Tribunal; or, the subject-matter jurisdiction of the Tribunal.

In the *Prosecutor v. Tadić*, Decision on the Defence Motion for Interlocutory Appeal on Jurisdiction, October 2, 1995, para. 6, the Appeals Chamber examined the nature of jurisdictional challenges and found that: "All the grounds of contestation relied upon by Appellant result, in final analysis, in an assessment of the legal capability of the International Tribunal to try his case. What is this, if not in the end a question of jurisdiction?" These grounds pertained to the lawfulness of the establishment of the Tribunal, the Tribunal's primacy over national courts and subject-matter jurisdiction.

19–106   Subsequent to the *Tadić* Appeals Chamber decision some cases sought to classify the interlocutory appeals before the ICTY as jurisdictional in nature, but were rejected by the Appeals Chambers (see, for example, *Prosecutor v. Brdanin and Talic*, Decision on Interlocutory Appeal from Decision on Motion to Dismiss Indictment filed under Rule 72, November 16, 1999, *Prosecutor v. Delalic*, Decision on Application for Leave to Appeal by Hazim Delić, December 6, 1996 (defects in indictment form), *Prosecutor v. Simić*, Decision and Scheduling Order, May 18, 1999 (request for evidentiary hearing and for Prosecutor to make available documents relating to circumstances of Todorovic's arrest) and *Prosecutor v. Simić*, Decision on Interlocutory Appeal Filed by Prosecutor on October 26, 2000 from Trial Chamber Decision dated October 18, 2000, December 4, 2000.

The following cases pertain to interlocutory appeals filed before the ICTR challenging "jurisdiction" in accordance with the criteria set out in Rule 72(D) (previously Rule 72(H)) which were almost all rejected as falling outside the scope of these criteria: *Barayagwiza v. Prosecutor*, September 12, 2000 (challenging the existence of the indictment and the temporal jurisdiction of the ICTR); *Barayagwiza v. Prosecutor*, September 14, 2000 (indictment challenged on the basis that it includes charges lying outside the temporal jurisdiction of the ICTR); *Semanza v. Prosecutor*, December 4, 2000 (challenging the right to be heard, the impugned decision's basis on extraneous facts, the alleged amendments to the indictments); *Rwamakuba v. Prosecutor*, June 11, 2001 (challenging the legality of his arrest and detention in Namibia).

A Bench of the Appeals Chambers of the ICTY and ICTR have permitted interlocutory appeals, recognising that certain matters raise questions of jurisdiction: *Prosecutor v. Rwamakuba*, Decisionon Interlocutory Appeal Regarding Application of Joint Criminal Enterprise to the Crime of Genocide, 22 Ocotber 2004; *Prosecutor v. Milutinovic et al.*, Decision on Dragoljub Ojdanic's Motion Challenging Jurisdiction—Joint Criminal Enterprise, May 21, 2003; *Prosecutor v. Hadžihasanović et al.*, Decision on Interlocutory Appeal Challenging Jurisdiction in relation to Command Responsibility, July 16, 2003.

(5) Threshold for granting leave or certification to appeal from other preliminary motions

Article 82(1)(d) of the ICC Statute states that an appeal may lie   **19–107** against a decision that involves an issue that would "significantly affect the fair and expeditious conduct of the proceedings or the outcome of the trial", and for which "in the opinion of the Pre-Trial or Trial Chamber, an immediate resolution by the Appeals Chamber may materially advance the proceedings (see also Decision on the Prosecutor's Application for Leave to Appeal, Situation in the Democratic Republic of Congo, Pre-Trial Chamber I, ICC, March 14, 2005). This is the threshold that must be met for leave to be granted under Rule 155 of the ICC Rules of Procedure and Evidence. In the case of East Timor also see section 27.4, UNTAET Regulation 2000/30.

In the case of the ICTY, for all other preliminary motions, Rule 72(B)(ii) requires that certification must be granted by the Trial Chamber before an interlocutory appeal may be brought from decisions on other preliminary motions.

A Trial Chamber may grant certification if two criteria are present: first, if the decision involves an issue that would significantly affect the fair and expeditious conduct of the proceedings or the outcome of the trial; and second, the Trial Chamber finds that an immediate resolution by the Appeals Chamber may materially advance the proceedings.

Rule 72 was amended and came into force on May 8, 2002 (see *Amendment of Rules of Procedure and Evidence*, IT/203.) Prior to this amendment, interlocutory appeals from other preliminary motions required leave to appeal by a bench of three judges of the Appeals Chamber upon good cause being shown. By this amendment, the requirement of "good cause" being shown by an applicant has been replaced by a determination of whether the decision would significantly affect the fair and expeditious conduct of proceedings or outcome of trial, the resolution of which may materially advance the proceedings.

19–108   The jurisprudence of "good cause" as found in the former Rule 72 may be of guidance in determining whether certification should be granted. The test of good cause in the former Rule 72(B)(ii) originates from an amendment to the Rules of Procedure and Evidence at the Fourteenth plenary session in October and November 1997. Before 1997, the test for granting leave to appeal in respect of other preliminary motions was upon "serious cause" being shown (see *Prosecutor v. Delalic et al.*, Decision on Application for Leave to Appeal, October 14, 1996). The Appeals Chamber, para. 20, interpreted "serious cause" either to require an applicant to show "a grave error which would cause substantial prejudice to the accused or is detrimental to the interests of justice, or raises issues which are not only of general importance but are also directly material to the future development of trial proceedings, in that the decision by the Appeals Chamber would seriously impact upon further proceedings before the Trial Chamber". (For a list of further decisions under this rule when the test was still "serious cause" see J. Hocking, Interlocutory Appeals before the ICTY, in *Essays in Honour of Judge Gabrielle Kirk McDonald*, p. 459 at 466, note 35.)

In the case of the Special Court for Sierra Leone, Rule 73 deals with other motions not listed in Rule 72. Decisions rendered on such motions are without interlocutory appeal except that in exceptional circumstances and to avoid irreparable harm, a Trial Chamber may grant leave to appeal.

B. OTHER PRE-TRIAL AND TRIAL MOTIONS

(1) Applications for provisional release

19–109   Article 82(1)(b) of the ICC Statute provides for a right of appeal against a decision granting or denying the release of a person being investigated or prosecuted. Rule 154(1) further provides that such an appeal may be made as of right, without the leave of the court. Rule 65(D) of both the ICTY and ICTR Rules provide that any decisions on provisional release shall be subject to appeal where leave is granted by a Bench of three Appeal Chamber Judges, upon good cause being shown. Rule 65(E) of the SCSL provides that leave must be granted by a single Judge of the Appeals Chamber, upon good cause being shown.

Time limits for filing applications for leave to appeal

19–110   Rule 154(1) of the ICC Rules of Procedure and Evidence states that an appeal against the decision granting or denying release shall be made not later than five days from the date upon which the party filing is notified of the decision. Regulation 64 of the ICC Regulations of the Court sets out the filing requirements and time limits within which to file documents on appeal.

Rule 65(D) of the ICTY and ICTR Rules of Procedure and Evidence provides that applications for leave to appeal from a Trial Chamber's decision on provisional release shall be filed within seven days of the filing of the impugned decision. See Rule 65(D)(i) and (ii) of the ICTY and ICTR Rules regarding the time limits in cases of oral decisions by a Trial Chamber.

Rule 65(E) of the SCSL provides that applications for leave to appeal shall be filed within seven days of the impugned decision.

Threshold for granting leave to appeal

Leave to appeal is no longer required under the ICTY Rules. In relation to the ICTR Rules, the test of "good cause" is set out in Rule 65(D) and in Rule 65(E) of the SCSL. The test for leave to appeal under Rule 65(D) of the ICTR Rules was revised from "serious cause" to "good cause" in an amendment to the rules at the Thirteenth Plenary Session in July 1997.   **19–111**

The "good cause" test for an application for leave to appeal a decision on provisional release has required the applicant to demonstrate that the Trial Chamber may have erred in reaching the impugned decision (see *Prosecutor v. Stanisic*, Decision on Prosecution's Application for Leave to Appeal on Provisional Release, September 30, 2004). While a party is required to show the possibility of error on the part of the Trial Chamber, for good cause to be established, the possibility of error must be clearly established (see *Prosecutor v. Prlić et al.*, Decision on Motions for Re-Consideration, Clarification, Request for Release and Applications for Leave to Appeal, September 8, 2004). Good cause can be satisfied by demonstrating that the Trial Chamber's decision under review is inconsistent with other decisions of the Tribunal on the same issue (see *Prosecutor v. Cermak and Markac*, Decision on Joint Motion for Leave to Appeal Decision on Provisional Release, October 13, 2004).

In *Prosecutor v. Kunarac et al.*, the Appeals Chamber rejected Kunarac's application for leave to appeal from the Trial Chamber II's rejection of his application for provisional release. The Chamber held that "the Appellant has not shown good cause in the Defence Application, in that he has failed to state precisely why the Decision erred under applicable legal principles in the evaluation of the reasons for the Request" (see *Prosecutor v. Kunarac and Kovac*, Order Rejecting Application for Leave to Appeal, November 25, 1999; *Prosecutor v. Krajisnik and Plavsic*, Decision on Application for Leave to Appeal, December 14, 2001). In *Prosecutor v. Prlić et al.*, (Decision on Motions for Re-Consideration, Clarification, Request for Release and Applications for Leave to Appeal, September 8, 2004), the Chamber was not satisfied that the Prosecution, in relation to all seven alleged errors, demonstrated that the Trial Chamber may have erred in granting provisional release.

In *Prosecutor v. Blagojević, Obrenovic and Jokic*, Decision on Application by Dragan Jokic for Provisional Release, May 28, 2002, the Appeals Chamber concluded that the Trial Chamber had erred in determining that a guarantee from the relevant Bosnian governmental body was a prerequisite for provisional release. In the particular facts of that case the Chamber held that a guarantee from the Republika Srpska was sufficient, though it would not necessarily be sufficient in every case. The Appeals Chamber concluded that the Trial Chamber had erred in   **19–112** law in refusing the application for provisional release and ordered the accused released on certain conditions.

The ICTR has also interpreted "good cause" in Rule 65(D) on provisional release to require an applicant to show that a Trial Chamber erred in its assessment of the conditions for ordering release (see for example, *Kanyabashi v. Prosecutor*, Appeals Chamber, June 13, 2001).

(2) Other Motions

19–113   Rule 73(A) of both the ICTY and ICTR Statutes govern motions other than preliminary motions, and allows the Prosecutor or the Defence to seek relief by way of motion, whether oral or written. The ICC does not distinguish between preliminary and other motions. The Rules of the SCSL distinguishes between preliminary motions and motions, setting out different requirements for both.

Some examples of other motions in the ICTY include: motions challenging rulings to admit into evidence multiple hearsay statements contained in an anonymous document (*Prosecutor v. Kordić and Čerkez*, Decision on Application for Leave to Appeal, September 22, 2000); motions challenging decisions allowing the Prosecution to revise a witness list (*Prosecutor v. Kvočka*, Decision on Application for leave to Appeal, October 10, 2000); motions challenging the unfairness of giving the defence insufficient time to prepare the final trial brief and closing arguments (*Prosecutor v. Kordić and Čerkez*, Decision on Application for Leave to Appeal, December 5, 2000); motions challenging use of depositions at trial *inter alia* on the basis that depositions should only be taken in the presence of the accused (*Prosecutor v. Naletilic and Martinovic*, Decision on Application for leave to Appeal by the Accused Mladen Naletilic and notice of Joinder in that Application by the Accused Vinko Martinovic against the decision of Trial Chamber I of November 10, 2000, January 31, 2001).

Time limits for requesting certification for interlocutory appeal

19–114   Other motions may be filed at any time before an ICTY or ICTR Chamber. See Rule 73(A) of both the ICTY and ICTR Rules, respectively. Rule 73(C) of the ICTY and ICTR Rules requires that requests for certification for interlocutory appeal must be filed within seven days of the issuing of the impugned decision. In *Prosecutor v. Naletilic and Martinovic*, Decision on Application for leave to Appeal by the Accused Mladen Naletilic and Notice of Joinder in that Application by the Accused Vinko Martinovic against the decision of Trial Chamber I of November 27, 2000, February 2, 2001, an application was filed under the previous Rule 73, within nine days of filing of the impugned decision. It was thus filed out of time and application for leave to appeal was dismissed, with the Appeals Chamber confirming that the time period for filing begins to run from the date of the filing of the impugned decision (see ICTY and ICTR Rule 73(C)(i) and 73(C)(ii) regarding the time limits in respect of oral decisions).

If certification is given, a party shall appeal to the Appeals Chamber within seven days of the filing of the decision to certify.

Threshold for granting certification for interlocutory appeal

Rule 73(B) of the ICTY and ICTR Rules of Procedure and Evidence **19–115** establishes the criteria upon which a Trial Chamber will certify that an interlocutory appeal is warranted. Rule 73(B) sets out the presumption that all decisions on other motions that are brought under Rule 73(A) are without interlocutory appeal. The only exception is when certification is granted by the Trial Chamber. Before certification is given, the Trial Chamber must be satisfied that the decision involves an issue that would significantly affect the fair and expeditious conduct of proceedings or the outcome of the trial and for which an immediate resolution by the Appeals Chamber may materially advance the proceedings.

Trial Chambers of the ICTY have granted certification in relation to the various matters. For example, in *Prosecutor v. Halilovic* Decision on Motion for Reconsideration or Alternatively Certification, April 2, 2004, regarding when a trial chamber will exercise its authority to issue a subpoena. Certification was granted in *Prosecutor v. Galić*, Decision on Interlocutory Appeal Concerning Rule 92*bis*, June 7, 2002 regarding the admission of out of court statements for proof of facts. Certification was granted in *Prosecutor v. Hadžihasanović*, Decision on the Refreshment of a Witness's Memory and on a Motion for Certification to Appeal, December 19, 2003 regarding the use of a witness' prior statement to refresh memory.

Trial Chambers have not provided extensive reasons as to why, in the circumstances of the individual cases, the two criteria are met. In *Prosecutor v. Brdanin and Talic*, Decision to Grant Certification to Appeal the Trial Chamber's Decision on Motion to Set Aside Confidential Subpoena to give Evidence, June 19, 2002, the Trial Chamber certified that an interlocutory appeal was warranted from its previous decision to subpoena a journalist to give evidence. The Trial Chamber, in granting certification, indicated that the determination of whether there existed a journalist privilege against testifying met the criteria for certification.

As a result of the amendment of the Rules of Procedure and Evidence (May 8, 2002, IT/203), the previous rule permitting the granting of leave to appeal by application to a three member Bench of the Appeals Chamber no longer exists. The previous criteria under Rule 73 for leave to appeal required a showing of prejudice which could not be cured by the final disposition of the trial including post-trial judgment or that the issue to be appealed was of general importance to the proceedings of the Tribunal or in international law generally. The Chamber has not ruled on whether these criteria may be relevant to the present test for certification.

Though not classified as certification, Article 82(1)(d) of the ICC Statute permits a Trial Chamber to refer an appeal to the Appeals Chamber if the trial decision involves an issue that would significantly affect the fair and expeditious conduct of the proceedings or the outcome of the trial and for which an immediate resolution by the Appeals Chamber may materially advance the proceedings.

III. APPEALS POST-JUDGMENT

19–116   Article 14(5) of the International Covenant on Civil and Political
Rights, 1966 states "Everyone convicted of a crime shall have the right
to his conviction and sentence being reviewed by a higher tribunal
according to law." Article 81 of the ICC Statute and Articles 25 and 24
of the ICTY and ICTR Statutes respectively preserve this right by
providing for appeals by the Prosecutor or an accused person convicted
by a Trial Chamber on the basis of an error of fact or of law. Similarly
see section 40.1 of UNTAET Regulation 2000/30 and Article 40 of the
Statute of the Special Court of Sierra Leone.

The ICTY and ICTR Statutes permit appeals by the Prosecutor and
convicted person on errors of law and errors of fact (Articles 25, 24
respectively). The ICC permits appeals by the Prosecutor and convicted
person on the same errors, plus on procedural errors (Article 81).
Further in the ICC, a convicted person is granted a right to appeal not
granted to the Prosecution, which is to appeal on any other ground that
affects the fairness or reliability of the proceedings or decision (Art.
81(1)(b)(iv)). In the Special Court for Sierra Leone, the Prosecutor and
convicted person can appeal errors of law, errors of fact and procedural
errors (Art. 20, Rule 106).

An appeal is not an opportunity for the parties to reargue their cases.
The Appellate Chamber "does not operate as a second Trial Chamber.
The role of the Appeals Chamber is limited, pursuant to Article 25 of
the Statute, to correcting errors of law invalidating a decision, and
errors of fact which have occasioned a miscarriage of justice". (In the
ICTY see: *Prosecutor v. Furundžija*, Judgment, Appeals Chamber, para.
40. See also *Prosecutor v. Kvočka et al.*, Judgment, Appeals Chamber,
February 28, 2005, para.14, *Prosecutor v. Kordic*, Judgment, Appeals
Chamber, December 17, 2004, *Prosecutor v. Kupreškić*, Judgment, Appeals
Chamber, October 23, 2001, para. 22.) The general rule is that the
Appeals Chamber will not "entertain arguments that do not allege
legal errors invalidating the judgment, or factual errors occasioning a
miscarriage of justice, apart from the exceptional situation where a
party has raised a legal issue that is of general significance to the
Tribunal's jurisprudence" (see *Prosecutor v. Kupreškić*, Judgment, Appeals
Chamber, October 23, 2001, para. 22).

The Appeals Chamber has recognised that it has the power to
entertain grounds of appeal if the issue is of a matter of general
significance for the Tribunal's jurisprudence, even if such error does not
have a bearing on the verdict in terms of Article 25(1) of the Statute (in
the ICTY see *Prosecutor v. Tadić*, Judgment July 15, 1999; in the ICTR
see *Prosecutor v. Akayesu*, Judgment, June 1, 2001).

A. Errors of Law

19–117   Article 25(1)(a) of the ICTY Statute and Article 24(1)(a) of the
ICTR Statute allow the Prosecutor or a convicted person to appeal the
decision of a Trial Chamber on the ground of "an error on a question of
law invalidating the decision".

The Appeals Chamber is the final arbiter of the law of the Tribunal and as such must determine whether there has been an error of law (see *Prosecutor v. Kamuhanda*, Judgment, Appeals Chamber, September 19, 2005, para. 6; *Prosecutor v. Kvocka et al.*, Judgment, Appeals Chamber, paras 16–17; *Prosecutor v. Furundžija*, Judgment, July 21, 2000 para. 35).

It is not any error of law that will lead to a revision or reversal of a decision of the Trial Chamber. The appellant must demonstrate that the error renders the decision of the Trial Chamber invalid (*Prosecutor v. Semanza*, Judgment, Appeals Chamber, para. 7); *Prosecutor v. Furundžija*, Judgment, Appeals Chamber, para. 36).

In alleging an error of law on the part of a Trial Chamber, the party **19–118** must at least identify the alleged error and advance arguments in support of the contention, otherwise the argument should not be raised on appeal. For example, Mirjan Kupreškić (*Prosecutor v. Kupreškić*, Judgment, Appeals Chamber, October 23, 2001, paras 26–27) made submissions on appeal regarding the preconditions for crimes against humanity and the elements of the crime of persecution under Article 5(h) of the ICTY Statute. The *Kupreškić* Appeals Chamber found that he had merely reargued the same case that he had argued before the Trial Chamber and thus dismissed his arguments for failing to identify any legal error on the part of the Trial Chamber. (See also *Prosecutor v. Furundžija*, Judgment, Appeals Chamber, July 21, 2000, para. 35.)

When arguments are advanced on an alleged error of law by a Trial Chamber, but they do not support the contention, "the Appeals Chamber may step in and for other reasons find an error of law" (see *Prosecutor v. Furundžija*, Judgment, Appeals Chamber, July 21, 2000, para. 35).

Where the Appeals Chamber finds that there is an error of law in the trial judgment arising from the application of the wrong legal standard, it is open to the Appeals Chamber to apply the correct legal standard to the evidence in the trial record and determine whether it is itself convinced beyond reasonable doubt as to the factual finding challenged, as a result of the legal error (*Prosecutor v. Kvočka et al.*, Judgment, Appeals Chamber, February 28, 2005, para.17).

B. ERRORS OF FACT

In determining whether an error of fact would overturn a factual **19–119** finding of a Trial Chamber, the appellant must show an error on the part of the Trial Chamber and show that this error resulted in a miscarriage of justice (see *Prosecutor v. Kordic and Cerkez*, Judgment, Appeals Chamber, December 17, 2004, para. 19; *Prosecutor v. Kamuhanda*, Judgment, Appeals Chamber, September 19, 2005, para. 7).

Not each and every error of fact will cause the Appeals Chamber to overturn a Trial Chamber's decision, only those leading to a miscarriage of justice. This means that the appellant must establish that the error of fact was crucial to the verdict reached and thereby resulted in a "grossly unfair outcome in judicial proceedings, as when a defendant is convicted despite a lack of evidence on an essential element of the crime (see *Prosecutor v. Kvocka*, Judgment, Appeals Chamber, February 28, 2005, paras 18–20).

The Appeals Chamber must always be mindful of the fact that the Trial Chamber's task is to hear, assess and weigh the evidence presented at trial. The Trial Chamber thus has the advantage of observing the testimony of witnesses first-hand and is in a better position to assess the reliability and credibility of witnesses (see *Prosecutor v. Furundžija*, Judgment, Appeals Chamber, July 21, 2000, para. 37). The Appeals Chamber must give "a margin of deference to a finding of fact reached by a Trial Chamber" (see *Prosecutor v. Tadić*, Judgment, Appeals Chamber, July 15, 1999, para. 64, followed in *Prosecutor v. Furundžija*, Judgment, Appeals Chamber, para. 37 *Prosecutor v. Kupreškić*, Judgment, Appeals Chamber, October 23, 2001, para. 30, and *Prosecutor v. Kordić and Čerkez*, Judgment, Appeals Chamber, December 17, 2004, para. 19).

19–120 The presence of inconsistencies in the evidence does not in itself require a Trial Chamber to reject the evidence as unreliable (see *Prosecutor v. Delalic et al.*, Judgment, February 20, 2001, para. 485 and paras 496–498). Similarly, the *Kupreškić* Appeals Chamber, Judgment, October 23, 2001, para. 31, stated that "factors such as the passage of time between the events and the testimony of the witness, the possible influence of third persons, discrepancies, or the existence of stressful conditions at the time the events took place do not automatically exclude the Trial Chamber from relying on the evidence. However, the Trial Chamber should consider such factors as it assesses and weighs the evidence".

When considering an alleged error of fact in relation to circumstantial evidence, the Appeals Chamber of the ICTY has held that the conclusion reached must be the only reasonable conclusion available. If there is another conclusion which is also reasonably open from that evidence, and which is consistent with the innocence of the accused, the accused must be acquitted (see *Prosecutor v. Delalic et al.*, Judgment, February 20, 2001).

The standard of review in relation to alleged errors of fact is one of reasonableness (*Prosecutor v. Kvočka et al.*, Judgment, ICTY Appeals Chamber, February 28, 2005, para. 18). The threshold for the Appeals Chamber to overturn a Trial Chamber's finding of fact is "where the evidence relied on by the Trial Chamber could not have been accepted by any reasonable tribunal of fact or where the evaluation of evidence is wholly erroneous". In only these cases can the Appeals Chamber substitute its own finding for that of the Trial Chamber (*Prosecutor v. Kupreškić*, Judgment, Appeals Chamber, October 23, 2001, para. 30, following the approach taken in *Prosecutor v. Aleksovski*, Judgment, Appeals Chamber, March 24, 2000, para. 63).

The Appeals Chamber articulated a different standard when new evidence has been admitted on appeal. In cases where the Defence alleges an error of fact in the Trial Chamber's findings, and additional evidence has been admitted on the appeal which was not before the Trial Chamber, the Appeals Chamber of the ICTY will proceed in two steps. First, the Appeals Chamber will determine on the basis of the trial record alone whether no reasonable trier of fact could have reached the conclusion of guilt beyond a reasonable doubt. If the Appeals Chamber concludes that a reasonable trier of fact could have convicted on the basis of the trial record, then the Chamber will consider the additional evidence before it. The Appeals Chamber will then consider, based on the trial evidence and the additional evidence, whether it is itself convinced beyond reasonable doubt as to guilt (*Prosecutor v. Blasklic*, Judgment, Appeals Chamber, July 29, 2004).

C. ERRORS OF PROCEDURE

The jurisprudence of the ICC and the Special Court for Sierra Leone   **19–121**
has not yet provided a definitive explanation of what constitutes procedural errors, as distinct from an error of law or error of fact.

D. SENTENCING APPEALS

Article 81 of the ICC Statute, Articles 25 and 24 of the ICTY and   **19–122**
ICTR Statutes respectively, and section 40 of UNTAET Regulation 2000/30 also apply to appeals against sentences. In the case of the ICC, Article 81(2) provides that sentence may be appealed on the basis of "disproportion between the crime and the sentence", as well as on the grounds that the sentence entailed an error of law or fact or procedural error set out in Article 81(1) of the ICC Statute.

The Appeals Chamber of the ICTY has held that although the Statute is silent on the question of appeal from sentence, it was considered that such a right was implied and so the Rule 108(A) of the ICTY Rules explicitly provides for appeal from "judgment or sentence" (see *Prosecutor v. Delalic et al.*, Decision on Application for Leave to Appeal (Provisional Release) by Hazim Delić, November 22, 1996; *Prosecutor v. Tadić*, Judgment in Sentencing Appeals, January 26, 2000).

Trial Chambers exercise a significant amount of discretion in imposing sentence. This is "largely because of the over-riding obligation to individualise a penalty to fit the individual circumstances of the accused and the gravity of the crime. To achieve this goal, Trial Chambers are obliged to consider both aggravating and mitigating circumstances" (*Prosecutor v. Delalic et al.*, Judgment, Appeals Chamber, February 20, 2001, para. 717).

Considering the importance of individual facts and circumstances to sentencing, the Appeals Chamber, in *Prosecutor v. Delalic et al.*, Judgment, Appeals Chamber, February 20, 2001, para. 718, rejected as inappropriate, any attempt to set out factors which should be taken account by Trial Chambers in determining sentence.

General comparisons between a case and previous cases which have   **19–123**
been the subject of final determination in an effort to persuade the Appeals Chamber to either increase or decrease a sentence are of limited assistance (*Prosecutor v. Delalic et al.*, Judgment, Appeals Chamber, February 20, 2001, para. 719). Sentences of like individuals in like cases should be comparable, and therefore the underlying question is whether the particular offences, the circumstances in which they were

committed and the individuals concerned can truly be considered "like". While comparison of other sentences may be of assistance, such assistance is often limited (*Prosecutor v. Kvočka et al.*, Judgment, Appeals Chamber, February 28, 2005, para. 681).

The test to be applied in deciding whether a sentence imposed by a Trial Chamber should be revised was examined in *Prosecutor v. Delalic et al.*, Judgment, Appeals Chamber, February 20, 2001. The general rule is that the Appeals Chamber will not substitute its sentence for that of the Trial Chamber unless "it believes that the Trial Chamber has committed an error in exercising its discretion or has failed to follow applicable law": *Prosecutor v. Delalic et al.*, Judgment, Appeals Chamber, February 20, 2001, para. 725, quoting and endorsing *Serushago v. Prosecutor*, Judgment, Appeals Chamber, April 6, 2000; see also *Prosecutor v. Furundžija*, Judgment, Appeals Chamber, July 21, 2000, para. 239, and *Prosecutor v. Aleksovski*, Judgment, Appeals Chamber, March 24, 2000, para. 187). In *Prosecutor v. Delalic et al.*, Judgment, Appeals Chamber, February 20, 2001, para. 725, the Appeals Chamber stated that it would only intervene if "it finds the error 'discernable'. As long as a Trial Chamber does not venture outside its 'discretionary framework' in imposing sentence the Appeals Chamber will not intervene" (see also *Prosecutor v. Tadić*, Judgment, Appeals Chamber, January 26, 2000, paras 20–22; *Prosecutor v. Aleksovski*, Judgment, Appeals Chamber, March 24, 2000, para. 187).

Each Appellant or the Prosecutor must demonstrate how a Trial Chamber ventured outside its discretionary framework in imposing sentence to found an appeal on sentence. The practical application of this test can be seen in *Prosecutor v. Tadić*, Judgment, Appeals Chamber, January 26, 2000, para. 20, in which the Appeals Chamber held that:

> "Insofar as the Appellant argues that the sentence of 20 years was unfair because it was longer than the facts underlying the charges required, the Appeals Chamber can find *no error in the exercise of the Trial Chamber's discretion* in this regard. The sentence of 20 years is within the discretionary framework provided to the Trial Chambers by the Statute and the Appeals Chamber will not, therefore, quash the sentence and substitute its own sentence instead."

E. APPEALS' PROCEDURE

19–124   Rule 150 of the ICC of Procedure and Evidence provides that an appeal against a decision of conviction, acquittal under Article 74 or sentence under Article 76 or a reparation order under Article 75 of the ICC Statute must be filed with the Registrar not later than 30 days from the date the party filing the appeal is notified of the decision, sentence or reparation order. These time-limits may be extended upon good cause being shown (Rule 150(2)).

Similarly, Rule 108 of the Rules of Procedure and Evidence of the ICTY and ICTR respectively provide that a party who seeks to appeal a judgment must file a notice of appeal not more than 30 days from the date on which the judgment was pronounced. The Rule 108 notice must set out in specific detail the grounds of appeal sought to be relied upon.

Pursuant to Rule 108 of both the ICTY and ICTR Rules, the Appellant or the Prosecution must identify the order, decision or ruling challenged, with specific reference to the date of its filing, and/or the transcript page. In addition, the notice must indicate the substance of the alleged errors and the relief sought.

Rule 111 of the ICTY and ICTR Rules of Procedure and Evidence requires that the Appellant's brief setting out all the arguments and authorities be filed within 75 days of filing of the notice of appeal pursuant to Rule 108. The Respondent's brief of argument and authorities must be filed within 40 days of the filing of the Appellant's brief in accordance with ICTY and ICTR Rule 112. The Appellant may file a brief in reply within 15 days of the Respondent's brief: Rule 113 of the ICTY and ICTR Rules of Procedure and Evidence.

In the SCSL, Rule 108 requires that a party seeking to appeal from judgment or sentence must file a notice within 14 days of receipt of the full judgment and sentence. For other appeals, see Rule 108(B) and (C). An appellant must file his written submissions within 21 days of the notice of appeal (Rule 111); the responding party must file written submissions within 14 days of receipt of the filing of the appellant's submissions (Rule 112); an appellant may file submissions in reply within five days of the filing of the respondent's submissions (Rule 113).

In the case of the Panels for Serious Crimes in East Timor, section 40.2 of UNTAET Regulation 2000/30 provides that the notice of appeal must be filed with the court of first instance no more than 10 days after the appealed decision is released. If no notice is filed, the party is deemed to have waived his or her right to an appeal and the decision of first instance is deemed final.

F. ADMISSIBILITY OF NEW EVIDENCE

The Rules of Procedure and Evidence of the ICTR and ICTY (Rule 115) provide for the admission of additional evidence during an appeal, if certain requirements are met. The Rules of the Special Court for Sierra Leone (Rule 115) also permit the admission of additional evidence during appeal proceedings. Though the admission of additional evidence is not addressed in the ICC Statute or Rules, the Regulations of the Court (Regulation 62) establish a procedure which permits the presentation of additional evidence before the Appeals Chamber of the ICC. Section 41 of UNTAET Regulation 2000/30 (East Timor) provides that new evidence may be presented before the Court of Appeal.

Rule 115 of the ICTY and ICTR Rules of Procedure and Evidence governs the admissibility of new evidence, allowing a party to apply by motion to present additional evidence before the Appeals Chamber which was not available at trial. The Rule applies to material relevant to the guilt or innocence of an accused, rather than to matters such as the fairness of the trial (see *Prosecutor v. Delalic*, Order on Esad Landzo's Motion (1) to vary in part order on motion to preserve and provide evidence, (2) to be permitted to prepare and present further evidence, and (3) that the Appeals Chamber take judicial notice of certain facts

19–125

and on his second motion for expedited consideration of the above motion, October 4, 1999).

A Rule 115 motion must be served on the other party and filed with the Registrar not less than 75 days from the date of the judgment.

The threshold for admission of this evidence is that the evidence was not available at trial through the exercise of due diligence, is relevant and credible and could have been a decisive factor in reaching the decision at trial. The last factor has been interpreted to mean the additional evidence could show that the conviction was unsafe. If it meets these criteria, the evidence will be admitted and considered with all other material on the record. If the evidence was available at trial, the Chamber retains the authority to admit such evidence if its exclusion would lead to a miscarriage of justice (see *Prosecutor v. Krstic*, Reasons for the Decision on Applications for Admission of Additional Evidence on Appeal, Appeals Chamber, April 6, 2004).

In the *Prosecutor v. Tadić*, Decision on Appellant's Motion for the Extension of the Time-limit and Admission of Additional Evidence, October 15, 1998, Tadić sought to call more than eighty new witnesses as well as to adduce new documentary evidence on appeal. The Appeals Chamber examined whether the appropriate procedure was in fact review under Article 26 and Rule 119 of the ICTY Statute and Rules, rather than admission of additional evidence as part of "appellate proceedings" under Article 25 of the ICTY Statute and Rule 115. It found that Rule 115 was applicable because the appellant proposed to admit "additional evidence of facts put in issue at trial" (see *Prosecutor v. Tadić*, Decision on Appellant's Motion for the Extension of the Time-limit and Admission of Additional Evidence, October 15, 1998, para. 32).

In the ICC, Regulation 62 permits the Appeals Chamber either to initially rule on admissibility and then proceed to the appeal, or to postpone the decision on admissibility and decide the issue jointly with other issues raised in the appeal.

(1) The evidence was not available at trial

19–126   A party seeking to admit additional evidence must demonstrate that the additional evidence was not available to him at trial nor discoverable through the exercise of due diligence (see *Prosecutor v. Tadić*, Decision on Appellant's Motion for the Extension of the Time-limit and Admission of Additional Evidence, October 15, 1998, para. 36, *Prosecutor v. Kupreškić*, Judgment, Appeals Chamber, October 23, 2001, para. 50). Trial counsel are required to be reasonably diligent, which means that they must make "appropriate use of all mechanisms of protection and compulsion available under the Statute and the Rules of the International Tribunal to bring evidence on behalf of an accused before the Trial Chamber" (see *Prosecutor v. Tadić*, Decision on Appellant's Motion for the Extension of the Time-limit and Admission of Additional Evidence, October 15, 1998, para. 47). The *Tadić Appeals Chamber* recognised an exception to the requirement that the new evidence "was not available" in cases where gross negligence is shown to exist on the part of trial counsel (see *Prosecutor v. Tadić*, Decision on Appellant's

Motion for the Extension of the Time-limit and Admission of Additional Evidence, October 15, 1998, paras 48 and 50).

(2) Relevant and Credible

The Appeals Chamber in the *Kupreškić* Appeal Judgment has held   **19–127**
that "if the new evidence does not relate to findings material to the conviction or sentence, in the sense that those findings were crucial or instrumental to the conviction or sentence, then the new evidence is not capable of demonstrating that a miscarriage of justice had been occasioned, and thus will not be admitted". (*Prosecutor v. Kupreškić*, Judgment, Appeals Chamber, October 23, 2001, para. 62). The evidence must be relevant to a "material" issue. In general, evidence is only "relevant" if it is probative, that is, if it has a tendency to make the existence of a fact which is of consequence to the determination of the case more probable or less probable (see *Prosecutor v. Musema*, Judgment (Declaration of Judge Shahabuddeen), Appeals Chamber, November 11, 2001).

In the ICTY and ICTR, a two stage approach has generally been adopted in relation to credibility, At the first stage, new evidence may not be subject to any form of adversarial scrutiny, save for the Appeals Chamber's initial assessment as to whether it is, on its face, credible (see *Prosecutor v. Tadić*, Decision on Appellant's Motion for the Extension of the Time-Limit and Admission of Additional Evidence, Appeals Chamber, Octoer 15, 1998, paras 52, 53). The testing of the additional evidence takes place at a second stage, for example, through cross-examination or rebuttal evidence.

(3) Decisive Factor at Trial

The applicant must demonstrate that the additional evidence could   **19–128**
have been a decisive factor in the lower court's decision. Proposed additional evidence will be rejected if the evidence could not have made any difference to the outcome of the Trial Chamber's Judgment. Further, the applicant should specify clearly the impact the additional evidence could have upon the Trial Chamber's decision. If it fails to do so, it runs the risk of the evidence being rejected without detailed consideration (see *Prosecutor v. Krstic*, Reasons for the Decision on Applications for Admission of Additional Evidence on Appeal, Appeals Chamber, April 6, 2004 para. 11, *Prosecutor v. Kupreškić*, Judgment, Appeals Chamber, October 23, 2001, para. 69).

(4) Miscarriage of Justice

The Appeals Chamber in *Prosecutor v. Tadić*, Judgment, July 15, 1999,   **19–129**
para. 35, recognised that the principle of finality militates against additional evidence being introduced on appeal, except if such admission would best serve the interests of justice. The Appeals

Chamber went on to state that "the principle of finality must be balanced against the need to avoid a miscarriage of justice; when there could be a miscarriage the principle of finality will not operate to prevent the admission of additional evidence that was not available at trial, if that evidence would assist in the determination of guilt or innocence".

Therefore, even where evidence was available at trial or could have been discovered through the exercise of due diligence, it will be admitted if the appellant satisfies the higher threshold that the exclusion of the evidence would lead to a miscarriage of justice. This heightened standard seeks to ensure the finality of judgements and the maximum effort by counsel at trial to obtain and present relevant evidence. At the same time, this standard would not permit a factually erroneous conviction to stand (see *Prosecutor v. Krstic*, Reasons for the Decision on Applications for Admission of Additional Evidence on Appeal, Appeals Chamber, April 6, 2004, para. 12).

The need to avoid a miscarriage of justice motivated the introduction of additional material under Rule 115 in *Prosecutor v. Semanza*, Appeals Chamber, May 31, 2000, paras 41–45. Although the Appeals Chamber found that the Prosecution had failed to demonstrate that the evidence was unavailable at trial, the Appeals Chamber admitted the evidence on the basis that "if henceforth it refuses to admit certain items of evidence in the instant case a miscarriage of justice will result". In *Prosecutor v. Jelisic*, Decision on Request to Admit Additional Evidence, November 15, 2000, paras 40–41, the Appeals Chamber maintained "an inherent power to admit evidence even if it was available at trial, in cases in which its exclusion would lead to a miscarriage of justice" (see also *Prosecutor v. Kupreškić*, October 23, 2001, para. 58).

IV. REVIEWS

A. STANDARD FOR REVIEW PROCEEDINGS

19–130   Articles 26 and 25 of the ICTY and ICTR Statutes respectively provide for review of a decision to be brought by the Prosecutor within one year of the judgment or by the convicted person. In the ICTR and ICTY, a Request for Review may be brought where a new fact has been discovered which was not known at trial or appeal and could not have been discovered through the exercise of due diligence. If a majority of the judges hearing the Review agree that the new fact, if proved, could have been a decisive factor in reaching a decision, the Chamber shall review the judgement and pronounce a further judgment after hearing the parties.

Article 84 of the ICC Statute permits the revision of a final judgment of conviction or sentence on three bases. First, where the new evidence was not available at the time of trial, and such unavailability was not wholly or partially attributable to the party making application; and the new evidence is sufficiently important that had it been proved at trial it would have been likely to have resulted in a different verdict. Second, where it has been discovered has been newly discovered that decisive evidence, taken into account at trial and upon which the conviction depends, was false, forged or falsified. Third, one of the judges who participated in conviction or confirmation of the charges has committed, in that case, an act of serious misconduct or serious breach of duty of sufficient gravity to justify his or her removal (see also ICC Rules 159–161, ICC Regulations of the Court, Regulation 66).

The SCSL also permits review proceedings (see Rules of Procedure and Evidence 120, 121)

The first review of a decision under Rule 120 of the ICTR Rules of Procedure and Evidence was conducted in *Barayagwiza v. Prosecutor*, Decision on Prosecutor's Request for Review or Reconsideration, March 31, 2000, para. 41. The Appeals Chamber held that "it is clear from the Statute and the Rules that, in order for a Chamber to carry out a review, it must be satisfied that four criteria have been met. There must be a new fact; this new fact must not have been known by the moving party at the time of the original proceedings; the lack of discovery of the new fact must not have been through the lack of due diligence on the part of the moving party; and it must be shown that the new fact could have been a decisive factor in reaching the original decision". These criteria were subsequently applied by the Appeals Chamber of the ICTY in the cases of *Prosecutor v. Delić*, Decision on Motion for Review, April 25, 2002, p. 7; *Prosecutor v. Jelisic*, Decision on Motion for Review, May 2, 2002, p. 3; *Prosecutor v. Tadić*, Decision on Motion for Review, July 30, 2002, para. 20; *Prosecutor v. Josipovic*, Decision on Motion for Review, April 2, 2004.

A new fact is a fact which did not exist at the time of trial. In **19–131** *Prosecutor v. Tadić*, Decision on Appellant's Motion for the Extention of the Time-limit and Admission of Additional Evidence, October 15, 1998, the Appeals Chamber, para. 30, expanded on the notion of a "new fact" under Rule 119. The Appeals Chamber held that in the case of an applicant seeking to present a new fact under Rule 119, the applicant is not seeking to admit additional evidence of a fact that was considered at trial but a new fact. In other words, it is not the evidence which is new, it is the underlying fact which the evidence seeks to demonstrate that is new. See also *Barayagwiza v. Prosecutor*, Decision on Prosecutor's Request for Review or Reconsideration, March 31, 2000, para. 43, and also the Separate Opinion of Judge Shahabuddeen, para. 47.

The requirement of a "new fact" relates to new facts which were not known by the Chamber itself at the time of its original decision (see *Barayagwiza v. Prosecutor*, Decision, March 31, 2000, paras 52 and 61).

The *Barayagwiza v. Prosecutor*, Decision on Prosecutor's Request for Review or Reconsideration, March 31, 2000, para. 65, construed the Rule 120 requirement that "the additional fact could not have been discovered through the exercise of due diligence" to be directory rather than mandatory in nature. This provided the Appeals Chamber with flexibility in the face of a possible miscarriage of justice "and in the wholly exceptional circumstances" of that case. See also Separate Opinion of Judge Shahabuddeen, paras 48–54. Whenever a Chamber is presented with a new fact which is of such strength that it would affect the verdict, it is required to examine whether or not the new fact is a decisive factor, even though the second and third criteria under Rule 119 are not formally met. (See *Prosecutor v. Tadić*, Decision on Motion for Review, July 30, 2002, para. 27).

The Appeals Chamber in *Barayagwiza v. Prosecutor*, Decision on Prosecutor's Request for Review or Reconsideration, March 31, 2000, para. 49, emphasised that "only a final judgment may be reviewed pursuant to Article 25 of the Statute and to Rule 120". In that case the Appeals Chamber found the decision of November 3, 1999 (a prior decision of the Appeals Chamber), to belong to that category, "since it dismissed the indictment against the Appellant and terminated the proceedings".

In *Prosecutor v. Jelisic*, Decision on Motion for Review, May 2, 2002, the Appeals Chamber held that legal developments in the jurisprudence of the Tribunal were not evidentiary in nature, and cannot be deemed to constitute new facts within the meaning of Article 26 of the Statute of the ICTY. See also *Prosecutor v. Tadić*, Decision on Motion for Review, July 30, 2002, para. 41. Article 21 of the Statute of the Special Court of Sierra Leone also provides for Review proceedings. It is very likely that considerable weight will be given to the jurisprudence of the ICTY and ICTR on Review, in particular as Article 20 of the Statute of the Special Court of Sierra Leone directs that the Judges of the Appeals Chamber "shall be guided" by such jurisprudence.

B. REVIEW PROCEDURE

19–132   Rules 119 and 120 for both the ICTY and ICTR provide that the Defence, or within one year of the pronouncement of the final judgment, the Prosecutor, may make a motion to the original Chamber for review of the judgment. Only a final judgment is subject to review. (See *Prosecutor v. Tadić, Ordonnance du président portant affectation de juges à la chambre d'appel*, October 5, 2001, p. 2.) Indeed the finality of a decision is a prerequisite to the exercise review. (See *Prosecutor v. Semanza*, Decision on the Request to Reconsider the Decision of the Appeals Chamber of May 31, 2000, May 4, 2001, p. 2.) The Appeals Chamber in *Prosecutor v. Tadić*, Decision on Motion for Review, July 30, 2002, para. 24 explained that this is because the review is "an extraordinary way of appealing a decision, and its purpose is precisely that of permitting an accused or the Prosecution to have a case re-examined in the presence of extraordinary circumstances".

Rule 119 of ICTY Rules of Procedure and Evidence provides that if any of the Judges who originally constituted the Chamber are no longer Judges of the Tribunal, the President must appoint Judges in their place. Rule 119 of ICTR Rules of Procedure and Evidence provides for the constitution of a new Chamber failing the reconstitution of the original Chamber. In *Prosecutor v. Tadić*, Decision on Motion for Review, July 30, 2002, para. 22, the Appeals Chamber held that the proper forum for the filing of a request for review is the judicial body which rendered the final judgment. That body may either be the Trial Chamber (when the parties have not lodged an appeal) or an Appeals Chamber, when the judgment has been appealed. In the latter case the Appeals Chamber will determine, as it does pursuant to Rule 122 of the Rules when the judgment sought to be reviewed is under appeal, whether it can deal with the motion itself or whether it is necessary to refer the case to a reconstituted (to the extent possible) Trial Chamber, or, should that not be possible, to a new Trial Chamber. (Also see *Prosecutor v. Barayagwiza*, Decision on Prosecutor's Request for Review or Reconsideration, March 31, 2000, para. 49.) In the event that some, or all of the judges who composed the original Trial chamber or Appeals Chamber are no longer available, the Request for Review should still be filed with the appropriate Chamber—and not the President. Once this is done, the President will appoint the judges to deal with the Request for Review as is done in cases of interlocutory appeals and appeals on the merits. See *Prosecutor v. Tadić*, Decision on Motion for Review, July 30, 2002, para. 23.

Rules 120 and 121 for both the ICTY and ICTR provide that if the majority of Judges of the Chamber constituted agree that the new fact, if proved, could have been a decisive factor in reaching a decision, the Chamber shall review the judgment, and pronounce a further judgment after hearing the parties.

returable case to a reconsideration to the system possible: *Trial Quilmbah*,
ees should that not be possible, to a new *Trial Quilmbah*. Also see
*Popasuwu, Request for Decision on Prosecution Request for Review or
Reconsideration* (March 16, 2000 para 43). In the event that though
all of the judges who composed the original Trial Chamber of Appeals
Chamber are no longer available, the Request for Review should still be
filled with the appropriate Chamber and not the President. Once this
is done, the President will appoint the judges to deal with the Request
for Review as is done in cases of interlocutory appeals and appeals on
the merits. See *Popasuwu, Trial Decision on Motion for Review* (Feb.
29, 1995 para 2).

Rules 120 and 122, for both the ICTY and ICTR provide that if the
majority of judges of the Chamber, seas[h]tured agree that the new fact,
if proven, could have been a decisive factor in reaching a decision, the
Chamber shall review the judgment, and pronounce a further Judgment
after hearing the parties.

CHAPTER 20

LEGAL AID & DEFENCE COUNSEL MATTERS

1. INTRODUCTION

20–1   This chapter mainly focuses on the International Criminal Tribunal for the former Yugoslavia ("ICTY) but also includes some basic information about the International Criminal Tribunal for Rwanda ("ICTR"), the International Criminal Court ("ICC") and the special courts for East Timor and Sierra Leone.

A. STATUS AND ROLE OF DEFENCE PRACTITIONERS AT THE ICTY AND THE ICTR

20–2   The basic rights of suspects and accused persons, and the function and role of the defence at these two tribunals are detailed in their Statutes and in various rules of the Rules of Procedure and Evidence ("RPE"). It is appropriate to consider the texts of Article 21 of the ICTY Statute and Rules 44, 45, 46 and 74*bis* of the ICTY's RPE (IT/32/Rev.34). Article 20 of the ICTR Statute contains similar details as the provision in the Statute of the ICTY as do Rules 42, 44, 44*bis*, 44*quater*, 46 of the ICTR's RPE. The status of defence practitioners and the defence as a body of professionals did not receive much regulation and attention at the ad hoc Tribunals at the time of their establishment. For the ICTY, it was only until several years into its existence, that an association of defence lawyers was officially recognised by the Tribunal. This association has since played an increasingly important role. In addition, the Registry, through, amongst others, its Office of Legal Aid and Detention Matters ("OLAD"), provides administrative support services to the defence. At the ICTR, an association of defence attorneys is active but it does not have official status. Additionally, the ICTR's Registry equally contains a defence counsel unit, which provides support services, entitled Defence Counsel Support Services Management.

20–3   The basic status of the defence at ICTY is governed by Rules 44 to 46 of the RPE. The most important other guiding legal instruments are the Directive on Assignment of Defence Counsel (IT/73/Rev.10, see Appendix C9, "Directive"), which sets out the parameters of the Tribunal's legal-aid system, the Code of Professional Conduct for Defence Counsel Appearing before the Tribunal (IT/125/Rev. 1, Appendix C10, "Code of Conduct") providing for basic rules of ethics to be followed by counsel and the Rules Governing the Detention of Persons awaiting Trial or Appeal before the Tribunal or otherwise Detained on the Authority of the Tribunal (IT/38/Rev. 9, Appendix C16, "Rules of Detention"), setting out the basic rules for the detention regime. The Directive has gained such importance because approximately 90 per cent of the accused are and have been defended through counsel assigned to them under the Tribunal's legal-aid system. Only in a handful of cases, accused have not requested legal-aid, have been found to be fully non-indigent or have elected to represent themselves.[1] This is a consequence of the high costs associated with defending a case before an international tribunal such as the ICTY, due to their complexity and length and the Tribunal's international character. Other important, relevant legal instruments include the Headquarters Agreement between the United Nations and the Host State, The Netherlands (S/1994/848, see Appendix C23), the Directive on Allowances for Witnesses and Expert Witnesses (IT/200, Appendix C15) and a number of regulations further stipulating the Rules of Detention. At the ICTR, similar instruments have been established laying out the basic status of the defence: see, for instance, *inter alia*, the ICTR's Directive on assignment of Defence Counsel (Appendix D10), the Code of Professional Conduct (Appendix D9), the Guidelines on the remuneration of expert witnesses (Appendix D12) and the Rules of Detention (Appendix D14).

Based on its rules and regulations, the Registry of the ICTY has **20–4** played a major role in securing a status for defence counsel that enables them to assist clients properly before the Tribunal. In July 2002, the judges of the Tribunal adopted an amendment to Rule 44A of the RPE requiring counsel acting before the Tribunal to be members of an association of defence counsel. An association of counsel was established under Dutch law on September 14, 2002, and subsequently recognized by the Registrar on October 1, 2002. It is now the only relevant professional body for Defence Counsel appearing before the ICTY. The official name of this association became, not surprisingly, the Association of Defence Counsel practicing before the ICTY ("ADC"). In July 2004, by virtue of a further amendment to the relevant rules of the RPE and the Directive, all counsel are now required to be members *in good standing* of an association of counsel practicing before the Tribunal recognised by the Registrar.

In contrast to its official status, the role of the defence and defence **20–5** counsel at the ICTY has been very important from the beginning. The various changes in the legal-aid system of the Tribunal since 1995 as reflected in multiple changes in the Directive, the Code of Conduct and relevant rules of the RPE, as well as the late establishment and official recognition of the ADC, indicate that the founders of the Tribunal had underestimated the necessity to properly regulate the profession. By mid-2005, approximately 500 persons, mostly lawyers had worked for defendants before the ICTY. About 90 percent of all persons represented before the ICTY have been assigned counsel on the basis of legal-aid, and since 1994 the Tribunal has spent roughly US$185 million in fees and travel expenses for assigned defence counsel and their support staff. The defence has thus far achieved: five full acquittals, some

---

[1] At the time of writing of this chapter, of 80 accused, 11 have not requested legal-aid, 19 have been found fully or partially indigent, and two accused are representing themselves. The following accused have retained their own counsel without applying for the assignment under Rule 45-List: Dario Kordic, Tihomir Blaskic, Ivan Cermak, Mladen Markac, Ramush Haradinaj. Two accused are currently representing themselves before the Tribunal: Slobodan Milosevic and Vojislav Šešelj. On May 25, 2005, the accused, Momcilo Krajisnik, has expressed the wish to represent himself, but the Chamber has not granted this wish at this late stage of the proceeding.

serious reductions of sentences,[2] numerous acquittals of accused on individual counts, assisted in reaching fifteen plea agreements and helped the Tribunal clarify numerous issues of international criminal law and procedural law. In addition, since 2003, defence counsel have—especially through the ADC after its recognition in 2002—played an increasingly active role in shaping rules and regulations applicable at the ICTY relevant to the rights of the accused and the defence.

II. BASIC INFORMATION: LOCATION AND FACILITIES

A. ACCESS TO ICTY AND OTHER INTERNATIONAL TRIBUNALS

Location of ICTY

20–6   The ICTY is located in The Hague, the Netherlands, the seat of the Dutch government. The Tribunal's main building is located in a suburb of The Hague, between the centre of the city and the coastal town of Scheveningen. The main building houses the courtrooms, the Appeals and Trial Chambers, the judicial administration of the Registry, the prosecution and an area reserved for defence counsel. Other buildings house the financial, personnel, general administration and translation units of the Registry. A third building, the so-called "beach building" is located in Scheveningen and holds more prosecution units. A further wing in this building is reserved for defence counsel and the ADC. The Tribunal's main address is Churchillplein 1, 2517 JW The Hague, Netherlands, or P.O. Box 13888, 2501 EW The Hague, the Netherlands. The Tribunal can be reached by train to The Hague from Amsterdam Schiphol Airport, or by car on highways A4, A2 and A12. The Tribunal's main phone number is +31 (70) 512 5000, and the main fax number is +31 (70) 512 5345. The Tribunal's website can be found at: *www.un.org/icty/*. The Tribunal further maintains a number of field offices in the former Yugoslavia, including in Belgrade, Sarajevo, Pristina and Zagreb. These offices generally handle prosecution matters, and include representatives of the Tribunal's Outreach Programme, established to inform the populations of the former Yugoslavia about the work of the Tribunal. The Tribunal's detention facility is located at Pompstationsweg 32, 2500 DE Scheveningen, at a distance of approximately 2 km from the Tribunal's main building ("Detention Facility"). The main point of contact for defence counsel at the Tribunal is the Office of Legal Aid and Detention Matters ("OLAD") in the Registry, located on the ground floor of the main building. The office can be reached through the main telephone number. In addition, defence counsel can

---

[2] A striking example is the *Blaskic* case where a sentence of 45 years' imprisonment promulgated by the Trial Chamber was reduced by the Appeals Chamber to nine years: *Prosecutor v Blaskić*, Case No. IT-95-14-T, Judgment March 3, 2000 (Trial Chamber Judgment); *Prosecutor v Blaskic*, Case No. IT-95-14-T, Judgment, July 29, 2004 (Appeals Chamber Judgment).

contact the ADC by phone at +31 (70) 512 5418 or through their official website, which can be found at: at: *www.adcicty.org*.

Location of ICTR

The Court Chambers and the Registry of the ICTR are based in Arusha, at the International Conference Centre, Tanzania. Defence counsel and their teams have been provided with an area in the Registry to maintain offices. The Tribunal's telephone number is: +1 (212) 963 2850/+255 (27) 250 4369/72. The fax number is: +1 (212) 963 2848 9 and +255 (27) 250 4000/4373. The ICTR website is found at: www.ictr.org/. The Office of the Prosecutor of the ICTR is based in Kigali, Rwanda. The address is Amahoro Hotel, P.O. Box 749, Kigali, Rwanda, with the following telephone and fax numbers respectively: +1 (212) 963 9906, +1 (212) 963 4001.   **20–7**

Location of Special Panels for Serious Crimes in East Timor

The main telephone number for UNTAET and its successor mission UNMISET in Dili, East Timor is: +670 331 2210, and the fax number is: +670 332 2007. The website can be found at: *www.unmiset.org*.   **20–8**

Location of Special Court for Sierra Leone

The Special Court for Sierra Leone is currently under construction. The Registry and Prosecution section are currently based at the Bank of Sierra Leone, Kingtom Complex, Jomo Kenyatta Road New England, Freetown, Sierra Leone, telephone: (212) 963 9915, ext. 5160/5162/5163; +232 (22) 297 039 (SL line). The fax number is: (212) 963 9915, ext. 5161. The website can be found at: *www.sc-sl.org/*.   **20–9**

Location of the ICC

The ICC, like the ICTY, is located in The Hague at Maanweg, 174, 2516 AB, The Hague, Netherlands. The main telephone number of the ICC is: + 31 (0)70 515 8515, and the Court's website can be referred to at: *www.icc-cpi.int*.   **20–10**

Visa and Immigration Status of Defence Counsel and Provision of Immunity before the ICTY

With regard to visa and immigration matters, defence counsel and their team members do not have special privileges in the Netherlands in the same way that Tribunal staff members do, unless the Host State   **20–11** decides to grant special privileges. Thus, the procedure for obtaining visas for counsel and their support staff has been developed in close cooperation with the Ministries of Foreign Affairs and Justice of the Host State. The Registry informs the Host State that a person is a counsel, or other legal staff member of a defence team and that his or her presence in the Netherlands is required for representing an accused before the Tribunal. The principal purpose of assisting individuals to obtain a Dutch visa is to ensure that the rights of the accused represented by counsel are protected. It appears that a distinction between the status and privileges of counsel and UN staff members is justified, but only to a certain extent. Whereas prosecution attorneys perform the majority of their work at the seat of the Tribunal, defence counsel perform most of their Tribunal-related work in the pre-trial and appeals stages at the location of their practice. However, during trial, this changes, when attendance at hearings in The Hague is usually required at least three out of four weeks per month, with interruptions only during the summer and winter recesses. During the pre-trial and appeals stages, counsel are not required to reside permanently at the seat of the Tribunal.

20–12 Lead and co-counsel retained by a suspect or accused (Rule 44(A)), or assigned under the Directive by the Registry (Rule 45(A)), enjoy the rights to immunity accorded to them by Article XIX of the Headquarters Agreement. Article XIX provides the following:

Article XIX—Counsel

1. The counsel of a suspect or an accused who has been admitted as such by the Tribunal shall not be subjected by the host country to any measure which may affect the free and independent exercise of his or her functions under the Statute.
2. In particular, the counsel shall, when holding a certificate that he or she has been admitted as a counsel by the Tribunal, be accorded:
   (a) exemption from immigration restrictions;
   (b) inviolability of all documents relating to the exercise of his or her functions as a counsel of a suspect or accused;
   (c) immunity from criminal and civil jurisdiction in respect of words spoken or written and acts performed by them in their official capacity as counsel. Such immunity shall continue to be accorded to them after termination of their functions as counsel of a suspect or accused.
3. This Article shall be without prejudice to such disciplinary rules as may be applicable to the counsel.
4. The right and the duty to waive the immunity referred to in paragraph 2 above in any particular case where it can be waived without prejudice to the administration of justice by the Tribunal and the purpose for which it is granted, shall lie with the Secretary-General.

20–13 This provision asserts basic conditions for counsel to perform their functions as professionally as possible, without having to answer to legal actions which could be initiated by any person or group, much like under national jurisdictions. In reality, several counsel have felt obliged to appeal to the Registry for support. In several cases, the Registry has provided such support by invoking this article from the Headquarters Agreement in cases where counsel were sued under either national (Dutch) law or their domestic disciplinary system related to acts carried out in their capacity as counsel. While the practice varies slightly, counsel and legal team members who stay on the defence team for longer periods of time are usually provided with a Dutch foreign residence ID card by the Ministry of Foreign Affairs through the Tribunal, which they have to return upon termination of their assignment or representation. The card enables counsel to enter into, exit from and move freely in the Netherlands and, if required, travel within the Schengen-States for the purpose of carrying out defence-related work.

Further privileges are not applicable to counsel as they are not staff members of the Tribunal. In particular, they do not enjoy the privileges granted under the Convention on the Privileges and Immunities of the United Nations (see Article V, Sections 18(b)—(g) of the Headquarters Agreement, Article XV 1(b)—(g)). To date, counsel's immunity as elaborated under Article XIX (2)(c) of the Headquarters Agreement has never been waived by the Secretary General. Nevertheless, the possibility for such waivers cannot be excluded, for example, in situations in which the Tribunal would want to undertake or allow action on serious allegations of abuse of the legal-aid system or fee-splitting arrangements between assigned counsel and their clients.

20–14

Visa and Immigration Status of other Defence Team Members, and other Persons

Legal assistants, investigators and case managers do not fall under the Headquarters Agreement. Nevertheless, the Registry, in cooperation with the Dutch Ministry of Foreign Affairs, has established a similar working practice on the basis of which support staff are provided with a Schengen- or Benelux-visa upon request, when such request is supported by the Registry. The Registry will support such requests if and when it is found to be of benefit to the defence team to grant the support staff member access to: the Tribunal, their clients, witnesses resident in the Schengen-states, or important archives. The duration of the visa depends upon the functions to be exercised.

20–15

The same rules apply to legal consultants and defence experts, whether the expert is appointed by Chambers under Rule 74*bis* of the Rules or whether the expert is assigned upon request by lead counsel (see paragraphs 20–82 *et seq.*). Travel by legal consultants and experts to The Hague usually requires only a short single-entry visa for team meetings, consulting case files, or attending hearings.

20–16

Security Provisions and Restrictions

All three Tribunal buildings and the Detention Facility are high security areas as the political dimension of the Tribunal's judicial work requires a more active security policy than may be necessary in most domestic jurisdictions. The Registry Safety and Security Section, (phone number +31 (70) 512 5000), maintains a strict system of security governing access to all three buildings for judges, defence counsel, staff

20–17

members, journalists and visitors. To access the buildings, all visitors, including journalists, must present a valid picture identification document to security personnel at the Tribunal's entrance. Visitors including journalists are issued a visit permit or entrance ticket to the courtrooms. The security personnel will keep the ID during the visit and return it when the visitor leaves the building. The Tribunal has the right to undertake security checks on all persons who request access to the building. Due to security precautions, every person entering the Tribunal must pass through one or more metal detectors and have their bags and personal belongings x-rayed. The Tribunal security may conduct personal searches if necessary.

Security procedures at the Detention Unit for counsel wishing to visit their clients are even stricter. At the Unit, two levels of security have to be passed, the first one maintained by Dutch officials of the "Penitentiary Complex Scheveningen", and the second one by the Tribunal (see paragraphs 20–202 *et seq.*).

20–18   All counsel are provided with a personalized Tribunal picture ID card by OLAD as necessary. This card, which bears the photograph and name of the counsel and a stamp "defence", allows entry into the main building and will facilitate entry to the Detention Facility. The card is primarily issued for access purposes to the Tribunal's facilities in The Hague, and is not intended to be for identification purposes of defence staff in the field. Judges, members of the prosecution, members of the Registry and all other Tribunal staff members are issued a similar card. It is the policy of the Registry to issue such cards for limited periods of time to long-term consultants, case managers, legal assistants, investigators and to defence interns if their presence in the main building or at the Detention Facility is required.

Access to Client

20–19   Proper communications with counsel is a fundamental component of the right to a fair trial and therefore included in the Statute. Hence, Article 21 of the Statute provides in paragraph (b) the accused's right to "have adequate time and facilities for the preparation of his defence *and to communicate with counsel* of his own choosing." Jurisdictions throughout the world have also recognised the right of accused persons to have privileged communications with their counsel. The Tribunal has included this right in Rule 65 of the Rules of Detention. More detailed information on access to clients and the Rules of Detention is provided under paragraphs 20–202 *et seq.*

B. Facilities Accessible to Defence Counsel at the ICTY

(1) Registry Judicial Services Sections

20–20   The Registry provides a number of judicial and administrative services to the Chambers, defence counsel and the prosecution. The Registry may be best compared to a blend of court management/support and a ministry of justice. The Registry comprises a number of sections, all destined to facilitate the judicial process and other aspects of the Tribunal's mandate. The United Nations administration department also falls under the authority of the Registry. The Registry does not take part in the judicial process itself. Nevertheless, a number of judicial and quasi-judicial tasks have been assigned to the Registrar by Statute, the Rules and other basic legal instruments of the Tribunal. Tasks which have been permanently delegated to the Registry include the assignment of counsel, the supervision of the detention of accused and the management of the protection of victims and witnesses.

The judicial services sections fall under the authority and respon-   **20–21**
sibility of the Deputy Registrar and the Registrar in accordance with Rules 33 and 33*bis* of the RPE. The Chambers Legal Support Section, the Court Management Services Section, the Office for Legal Aid and Detention Matters, the United Nations Detention Unit, and the Victims and Witnesses Section, in the first instance, report to the Deputy Registrar. The Court Management Support Section and the Victims and Witnesses Section provide services to Chambers, the prosecution and the defence. Court Management plans and organizes all hearings, records all case documents and exhibits and distributes case documents to the Chambers and the parties. The Victims and Witnesses Section is responsible for the transfer of witnesses for proofing and/or testimony at hearings to The Hague for both the defence and the prosecution (including expert witnesses), as well as for the Tribunal's witness protection program. OLAD, as indicated above, assigns and remunerates counsel and their defence teams where accused do not have sufficient means to pay for their own counsel. It also makes a determination of the indigency status of accused and provides counsel and the defence teams with a variety of other services ranging from access to documents in Tribunal cases to travel arrangements. Of additional relevance to the defence are the Conference Language Services Section ("CLSS") and the Office of Documentation Management, sections which provide translation and interpretation services to Chambers, prosecution and defence, as well as various other sections falling under the responsibility of the United Nations Administration such as the IT Services Section.

(2) Courtroom Facilities

The Tribunal has three specially built high-tech courtrooms, courtroom   **20–22**
III on the second floor of the main building being the largest, and courtroom II on the first floor being the smallest. Courtroom I is located on the first floor of the main building, just through the lobby and up the rotunda stairwell. The set up of all courtrooms provide for respective benches for prosecution and defence, a separate bench for the accused, a bench for the judges, seated at a higher level than the other benches, a bench for the Registry and a seat for witnesses. The defence bench provides for a number of facilities for counsel:

(1) Computer monitors on which counsel can see the English transcript of the hearing in real time or maximum delay of about five seconds, any documents presented, or the shots of the courtroom cameras;

(2) Computer access to relevant software and internet;

(3) Earphones providing simultaneous interpretation in the court-room in the two working languages of the Tribunal, English and French, in Serbo-Croat (working title at the Tribunal is Bosnian/Croatian/Serbian or "BCS") and, if required, in Albanian or Macedonian;

(4) A microphone for all statements and pleadings; the functioning of the transcript and interpretation service is dependent on hearing participants using the microphone.

20–23 Furthermore, present in the courtroom are an overhead-projector and other presentation equipment, ready for use if required; a courtroom usher to receive documents or other material presented to the court, and a court officer of the Registry for judicial-administrative assistance to the court (see further paragraphs 20–170 *et seq.*). Counsel have no electronic means of communication with their client in the courtroom during hearings, but are allowed to receive and pass on written messages to them. In addition, when counsel ask for adjournment or to confer with client regarding points of fact or law arising in court, the Registry's court officer(s) will assist in making it possible for counsel to confer with the client in between sessions in one of the holding cells.

(3) Defence Counsel Room and other Defence Rooms at the ICTY

20–24 Bearing in mind that counsel are not able to perform all Tribunal related duties from their own offices, the Registry has reserved an area adjacent to courtroom I for defence counsel. The area consists of a corridor, two rooms and restrooms for defence counsel. The rooms contain office equipment including computers with internet access and access to the electronic judicial database, a fax machine, printers, a TV set which allows the viewing of all ongoing hearings with a 30 minute delay, and telephones for local and international calls. The facilities are provided to counsel free of charge, except for international phone and fax costs. The rooms can only be accessed by defence counsel and other defence team members, members of the ADC, authorised Registry staff members such as security personnel, members of OLAD and technicians who have to pass through the corridor to reach the audio-visual department of the Registry. The ADC has increasingly exerted a coordinating role in this area. By May 2005, the Registry had made available to the ADC and the defence teams a whole wing at the beach building consisting of eight rooms which are fully equipped with desks, computers, printers, etc. The ADC has installed its secretariat there and, under ADC coordination, teams in pre-trial and appeal are expected to use these premises. The Registry further issues a lockable cabinet to counsel for files, their robes and other items.

20–25 The defence rooms enable counsel to study (and sometimes store) files and documentation, to access the electronic judicial database at the Tribunal and to deliberate with their team members and prepare for conference with the client in between sessions. These rooms also allow counsel to rest briefly in between sessions or write a quick motion. In view of the fact that since 2004, six trials have been running continuously in parallel accounting for a large presence of defence counsel and support staff, the defence counsel rooms at the main building are no longer suitable. The Registry intends to free up another room at the main building for the purposes of intra-team meetings. Otherwise, counsel will have to use their own offices or the offices available at the beach building. Counsel can access both the facilities at the main building and those at the beach building 24 hours a day, seven days per week. Counsel can also introduce visitors to the buildings during office hours, be it under strict security provisions (which apply in the same manner to all Tribunal staff members). If counsel intend to meet with protected, high profile, or sensitive witnesses or witnesses subject to special conditions (*e.g.* detained persons temporarily released for interview purposes) at Tribunal premises, they will need to obtain official permission beforehand through the Registry (OLAD).

The Tribunal's canteen is open to all Tribunal staff and defence counsel and defence team members.

(4) Documentation Room

The Registry maintains a room in the main building where hardcopies **20–26** of public indictments and all decisions of the Trial Chambers and Appeals Chamber are available. The room provides no facilities for study of documents obtained. The room is accessible through OLAD, and maintained by the Public Information Service.

(5) Library

The Tribunal maintains a specialised library tailored to international **20–27** criminal law, international humanitarian law and other relevant law. As well, the library contains specialised materials related to the conflicts in the former Yugoslavia and Rwanda. The library was established in 1994 and has, since then, developed into a modern reference and loan library which provides a substantial number of internet and legal research services via computer. It includes access to the Tribunal's judicial database, *Westlaw* and *Lexis-Nexis*. The facilities are open to judges, Tribunal staff members and defence counsel from 9:00am to 5:30pm, Monday to Friday. In addition, the library maintained by the International Court of Justice at the Peace Palace offers excellent research facilities. This library contains comprehensive documentation in the field of international law and can be accessed after only a 15 minutes walk from the Tribunal. It is open on Monday from 1:00pm to 5:00pm, and from Tuesday to Friday, from 10:00am to 5:00pm. The Peace Palace can be reached by phone at: +31 (70) 302 4125.

(6) Electronic Facilities and Defence Related Software

While it is presumed that defence counsel have access to a number of **20–28** research tools from their offices, the Tribunal offers additional research features free of charge. One of the main focuses of interest of defence counsel is research into the jurisprudence of the ICTY and the ICTR, as these Tribunals are currently the most important reference courts for international criminal law, while in future, also decisions from the special courts for Sierra Leone and East Timor can expected to provide relevant jurisprudence. In June 2003, for the purpose of providing electronic access and search tools to the entire ICTY jurisprudence, including all official filings in a case (for instance, indictments, orders, motions, decisions, transcripts, evidence, judgments, etc.), a comprehensive judicial database ("JDB") was rolled-out to all parties and the support service organs of the Tribunal. This database is updated on a daily basis and it replaces its less efficient predecessors. The JDB is structured in such a way to provide extensive search parameters and comprehensive overview of the entire ICTY jurisprudence, as well as controlled access to general ("public") and confidential documents. Its general part is accessible to all Tribunal staff members, including but not limited to judges, prosecutors and Registry staff, and to defence counsel. The confidential part is accessible only to the relevant parties in the case and to authorised Tribunal staff members who need access for their daily work. At present, the JDB is available to defence counsel from the Tribunal's premises only. The defence teams can access it both through the defence network (available since June 2005), and the ICTY Library. Among other things, the defence network provides all defence counsel with secure ICTY email accounts both for in-house communication and remote web-based access. Furthermore, the defence network offers access to the ICTY Tribunet—the Tribunal's official Intranet portal containing various useful information and latest news. A faster Internet connection through the defence network also improves the search on the Electronic Disclosure Suite ("EDS")—a web-based feature provided to the defence counsel by the Office of the Prosecutor as part of their disclosure obligations (Rules 66–68 of the RPE). At the time of writing this Chapter, the Registry was in the final stages of a testing project for remote access to the Defence network, which contains a link to the JDB, to be put at the disposal of all defence counsel. Once finalised, this facility is expected to drastically improve defence counsel's search and defence preparation capabilities from their home offices.

20–29   At present, the Tribunal also offers web-access to the most important decisions, orders, as well as all the indictments and judgements through the ICTY official internet site: *www.un.org/icty/*. This website also provides the possibility to follow court hearings (with a 30 minute delay). These features are intended to service practitioners, scholars and other interested parties. As practitioners and scholars would profit from a widely accessible and searchable database on the law of the two ad-hoc tribunals, the idea to make the ICTY's judicial database accessible for the public at large has been under discussion. The Tribunal's IT department is in the process of exploring technical solutions and estimating options for the development of this project, bearing in mind the prerogative of preserving the integrity and confidentiality of data stored in the JDB while sharing the ICTY heritage.

20–30   Apart from its activities on broadening the access to the Tribunal's JDB, the Registry is in the process of developing an electronic filing system that will dispense with paper filing. For transcript preparation, the Tribunal uses LiveNote real-time transcription software, which some defence teams have put to use as well. In addition, some defence teams have made use of case-preparation database software, such as CaseMap (the software used by the Office of the Prosecutor for this purpose) to organize their cases, and evidence, linking all such material to the issues identified in the case. Some defence teams have also made use of electronic presentations in court, using PowerPoint or Sanction software (the latter being the software used by the Office of the Prosecutor for this purpose), either to illustrate their arguments or to actually display evidentiary material. In 2005, the Tribunal ran a case using an electronic court system (e-Court), which involved the submission of all evidentiary material in electronic form, and the use of such evidence in court electronically. This nearly paperless approach to trial proceedings is being evaluated for possible expansion and use to some or all future trials at the Tribunal.

(7) Public Information Service/Outreach Program

The Public Information Service and Outreach Program are located on **20–31** the ground floor of the Tribunal's main building. Both services essentially perform comparable tasks, however the Outreach Program, which was founded by the former President of the Tribunal, Gabrielle Kirk MacDonald and the former Registrar, Dorothee de Sampayo Garrido-Nijgh, is focused on providing information, including Tribunal documents in BCS to the residents, journalists, and legal professionals of the newly formed countries of the former Yugoslavia; mainly Bosnia and Herzegovina, Croatia and Serbia and Montenegro. That includes the provision of such information in the region itself. Therefore, the Outreach Program maintains offices in the capitals of these countries, and is an essential element for the achievement one of the Tribunal's core missions, which is to contribute to the restoration and maintenance of peace in the region (Security Council Resolution 827, adopted May 25, 1993, (S/RES/827)). This goal can only be achieved if the peoples of the countries of the former Yugoslavia are informed of and benefit from the Tribunal's operations.

The internet site of the Tribunal is maintained by the Public Information Service, and this service is also the main provider of information to the outside. The Public Information Service informs journalists during weekly press briefings held by the spokesman of the Tribunal in coordination with the spokeswoman of the Prosecutor. The Registrar has approved the ADC to provide its own press briefing following the Tribunal's weekly press conference.

(8) Check-in/Check Out Procedure

The Registry has developed a check-in and check-out procedure in **20–32** order to provide defence counsel with a number of items and services upon commencement and to bind them to the rules and regulations of the Tribunal. The same applies to other members of the defence team who are professionally active in The Hague. Every defence counsel and support staff member of his/her team must sign a set of documents, acknowledging receipt of items and services and an undertaking of confidentiality. The items and services include a Tribunal security approved ID card, a residence ID card for The Netherlands, a defence locker card and defence cabinet key, access to the defence network and an email address, a password for confidential access to the JDB and a password for electronic disclosure access. Upon departure, a similar procedure is to be followed, whereby all items and documents have to be returned to the Tribunal and services will be terminated.

III. THE TRIBUNAL'S LEGAL-AID SYSTEM

20-33   The right of an accused charged with a criminal offence to legal representation before a court of law is a well established principle. In view of the fact that the penalty in most criminal cases is the deprivation of liberty, and due to the sheer complexity of defending a criminal matter, the interests of justice require that accused have legal representation—whether indigent or otherwise, subject to the accused's own waiver or desire for self-representation. Numerous national and international sources of law pay homage to this fundamental principle of the administration of justice,[3] and the Tribunal is no exception. The Tribunal's legal-aid system encapsulates this right for those accused who do not have sufficient means to pay their own counsel (whether in whole or in part). The basic principles of the Tribunal's legal-aid system can be found in Article 21(4)(d) of the Statute of the Tribunal, and Rules 42, 44 and 45 of the RPE and its basic features are contained in the Directive.

The Tribunal's legal-aid system, developed since the establishment of the Tribunal in 1993, currently performs three major functions: (1) assessment of the financial means of the accused (or suspect) for the purpose of determining indigency, and the extent to which claimants are capable of funding their own defence, (2) assignment of counsel to the indigent accused and suspects, and (3) providing payment/ remuneration to the more than hundred assigned defence counsel and their defence teams working before the Tribunal.

20-34   When the Tribunal's legal-aid system was established and developed, a comprehensive review of domestic legal regimes of countries from both common and civil law legal traditions was conducted.[4] The review

---

[3] See Article 14(3)(d) of the *International Covenant on Civil and Political Rights*, G.A. res. 2200A (XXI), 21 U.N. GAOR Supp. (No. 16) at 52, U.N. Doc. A/6316 (1966), 999 U.N.T.S. 171, entered into force March 23, 1976 ("ICCPR"); Article 6(3)(C) of the European Convention on Human Rights, *Convention for the Protection of Human Rights and Fundamental Freedoms*, as amended by Protocol No. 11; the Sixth Amendment of the Constitution of the United States of America, declaring that: "(i)n all criminal prosecutions, the accused shall enjoy the right [...] to have the Assistance of Counsel for his defence"; the United States Supreme Court decision of *Gideon v Wainwright*, 372 U.S. 335 (1963), per Justice H. Black; *The Canadian Charter of Rights and Freedoms*, Enacted as Schedule B to the Canada Act 1982 (U.K.) 1982, c. 11, which came into force on April 17, 1982, s. 10(b): "Everyone has the right on arrest or detention [...] to retain and instruct counsel without delay and to be informed of that right"; Article 2 of the International Criminal Tribunal for Rwanda's *Directive on the Assignment of Defence Counsel* (January 9, 1996).

[4] The Tribunal (Registry) reviewed the legal-aid regimes of numerous countries, including, *inter alia*: Australia, Belgium, Canada, Czech Republic, Denmark, Finland, Germany, Greece, Iceland, Ireland, Italy, Netherlands, New Zealand, Singapore, South Africa, Spain, Sweden, the United Kingdom, and the United States of America.

also included a study of the European Court of Human Rights' legal-aid regime, although this Court has a different mandate.[5] The guiding principles upon which the legal-aid system of the Tribunal is based are the same as those upon which its domestic counterparts are based. As is the aim of all legal-aid regimes, the purpose of the Tribunal's legal-aid system is to provide a fair and open legal system where *every* accused (and suspect) is given access to competent legal representation, irrespective of his/her financial means. The designers of the system and those in charge of developing it took into account the international nature of the Tribunal, the magnitude and complexity of its cases, related costs and the nature of the conflict and the geographic distance to the region. They considered the very mandate of the Tribunal which includes the aim that it, through its judgments, contributes to the maintenance and rebuilding of peace in the region of the former Yugoslavia as well as to the development of international law. They also took into account the fact that in the majority of the domestic legal-aid schemes, including those of the former republics of the former Yugoslavia, there are no provisions for legal-aid for the defence of cases before international tribunals.[6] All of the above considerations combined have formed the basis for the Tribunal's legal-aid system, which can only be seen as *sui generis*.

Another argument played a role when the system was developed. **20–35** This Tribunal did not want to repeat the same mistake as the Nuremberg and Tokyo trials, in which the role of the defence and the fairness of trials were not at the forefront of the founders' minds.[7] As

---

[5] The European Court of Human Rights ("ECHR") scheme only provides legal-aid for work done after a case has been deemed admissible to the court. Therefore, preliminary stages of the complaint process have to be personally funded. Similar to the system of the ICTY, according to the ECHR rules on legal-aid, funding is only granted when the applicant lacks enough means to meet all or part of the legal costs incurred. Further, the applicant must complete a detailed form of declaration (of means), which will contain information on number of dependants, income, capital assets, and financial debts and liabilities of the accused. This declaration must be certified, as is the case with the procedure at the ICTY (Article 9 of the Directive).

[6] For instance, in the following States, legal-aid schemes do not provide funding for cases before international tribunals: Albania, Barbados, Belgium, Canada, Cyprus, Czech Republic, Denmark, Dominica, Fiji, France, Germany, Hungary, Ireland, Italy, Jamaica, Namibia Poland, Philippines, Slovakia, South Africa, St. Lucia, Sweden, Syria, Switzerland, Turkey and the United Kingdom. Therefore, the availability of legal-aid for use before international human rights tribunals is a rarity. Further, various conventions relating to the rights of accused are confined to domestic proceedings: see e.g. Articles 2 and 14 of the ICCPR. For a more recent case in point, see *Toala v New Zealand*, No. 675/1995, Decision of November 22, 2000 at para. 6.2, where the New Zealand court declared that the ICCPR applies only to domestic procedures and that there is no authority to compel and extend domestic legal-aid for use in international proceedings.

[7] The Nuremberg and Tokyo tribunals were criticised, *inter alia*, as to their standards of fairness and due process. Some commentators called these tribunals "victor's justice", the by-product of victorious nations who wanted to punish their enemies and who applied standards of justice entirely differently to enemy troops than to their own. See, *e.g.* W. Pfaff, "Judging War crimes", *Survival*, Vol. 42 No. 1 (2000), pp. 46–58(13); T. Maga, "Away from Tokyo: the Pacific Islands War Criminal Trials 1945–1949", *Journal of Pacific History*, Vol. 36 No. 1. (June 1, 2001), pp. 37–50(14); and v Perskin, "Beyond Victor's Justice? The Challenge of Prosecuting the Winners at the International Criminal Tribunal for the Former Yugoslavia & Rwanda", *Journal of Human Rights*, Vol. 4, No. 2, (April-June 2005), pp. 213–231(19).

commentators as well as practitioners including judges at the Tribunal have stated, the final record and achievement of this Tribunal will be measured by the quality and achievements of the defence and the fairness of its trials.[8] The mandate of the Tribunal can only be achieved if there is public confidence and support for its trials and judgments and this, in turn, can only be realized through a fair justice system where parties are, to the greatest possible extent equal, and the right of an accused to a proper defence is given practical meaning. More than ten years after the Tribunal's inception, the system has developed into what it is currently a relatively well balanced, relatively efficient system of legal-aid, which protects the basic right to legal assistance for indigent accused enshrined in Article 21 of the Statute by providing qualified counsel and the requisite funding, but at the same time sets clear limits on disbursement of funds and provides some minimum guarantees and rules to tackle potential abuse of the system, while fitting both principally and administratively into the United Nations system.

A. LEGAL FOUNDATIONS AND THE RIGHT TO FREE LEGAL ASSISTANCE

(1) Statute and Rules of Procedure and Evidence

20–36 The Statute mentions the right to "legal assistance" in one sentence of Article 21, paragraph 4(d). The formulation has been based on the texts of the ICCPR, the European Convention of Human Rights and the American Convention on Human Rights.[9] Article 21(4)(d) of the Statute, the Tribunal's mother provision for the rights of the accused, provides as follows:

> *Article 21*
> 4. In the determination of any charge against the accused pursuant to the present Statute, the accused shall be entitled to the following minimum guarantees, in full equality: [...]
> (d) to be tried in his presence, and to defend himself in person or *through legal assistance of his own choosing*; to be informed, if he does not have legal assistance, of this right; *and to have legal assistance assigned to him, in any case where the interests of justice so require, and without payment by him in any such case if he does not have sufficient means to pay for it* [. . .]

20–37   The basic text is clear: the Statute provides for the right to counsel of choice if an accused retains and remunerates counsel himself and for the right to free legal assistance if he does not have sufficient means to

---

[8] See, *e.g. Prosecutor v Milošević*, Case No. IT-01-50, AR73.4, Dissenting Opinion of the Appeals Chamber of Judge David Hunt on Admissibility of Evidence in Chief in the Form of Written Statements, October 21, 2003, *per* J.D. Hunt at para. 22: "This Tribunal will not be judged by the number of convictions which it enters, or by the speed with which it concludes the Completion Strategy which the Security Council has endorsed, but by the fairness of its trials."

[9] See Article 14(3)(d) of the ICCPR; Article 6(3)(c) of the ECHR; Article 8(2)(d) and (e) of the American Convention on Human Rights. See also Article 21(4)(d) of the Statute of the ICTR.

pay for it. This right to free legal assistance has been further developed in the Rules, Directive and jurisprudence of the Tribunal. It has been developed and clarified that it does not incur an unlimited right to be assigned counsel of choice. It has been developed and clarified that it involves the right to free legal assistance *insofar* as the accused does not have sufficient means. Rules 44–46 of the RPE are relevant. The RPE reiterate the reference in the Statute to the interests of justice. Rule 45(A) of the RPE establishes that the Registrar shall assign counsel to indigent accused "when the interests of justice so demand". This link with the interests of justice is not specific, but it gives the Registrar the explicit authority to take more factors into account than only the financial status of a suspect or accused when deciding upon the request for assignment of legal-aid counsel (for further details, see paragraphs 20–64 *et seq.*).

(2) Directive on the Assignment of Counsel

The Registrar, in accordance with his function as the representative of the Secretary-General of the United Nations issues the Directive (see Article 17 of the Statute, Rules 33 and 45(A) of the RPE, Article 4(A) of the Directive). The Directive sets out more specifically the legal-aid system of the Tribunal. It is further complemented by regulations and policies. The first version of the Directive was promulgated in 1994, since then, it has been amended ten times. Although some parts of the initial text are still included, the many changes reflect the experiences gained from practice at the ICTY. As to its legal status, the Directive is, as the title indicates, an (international) administrative instruction. Its provisions are directly based on Statute and RPE. The Registrar is responsible for preparing and promulgating the Directive but the document needs to be approved by the judges. It does not formally qualify as "law" at the international level, as it is neither a treaty or an international customary practice, nor a judicial decision or a general principle of law (although it contains elements of some). It also lacks an adoption process by a decision of States or State bodies and it is not an international law-interpreting or -creating act by the Tribunal. Nevertheless, as indicated the Directive cannot be promulgated without the approval of the permanent judges of the Tribunal. This increases its weight. In addition, the Directive is considered binding upon the Registrar and his staff. It is also considered binding upon the addressees: suspects and accused who request legal-aid and assigned counsel and their support staff. Therefore, in actual effect, the Directive is applied as if it was law and forms part of the body of law of this Tribunal.

20–38

The laws of the Tribunal do not explicitly provide for a judicial review of the Directive per se (abstract control of norms) by the judges upon request of accused, counsel or third parties. Nevertheless, the Directive does contain a number of individual provisions, which indicate the possibility for the review of decisions on certain aspects of the Tribunal's legal-aid system. The decisions made on the basis of the Directive concern suspects, accused, counsel and defence team members and they need to be based upon, and/or be in conformity with the

20–39

underlying legal instruments, the Tribunal's Statute, the RPE, and other relevant international law. Specific review authority has been placed upon the President, and in some provisions, on the Chamber.[10] It appears that the drafters of the Directive wanted the review system to reflect the Trial Chambers' duties with respect to monitoring the fairness of trials (under Articles 20 and 21 of the Statute), and the President's overall supervisory duties over the Registry's work (see Rule 19 of the RPE). This would imply that all assignment related matters which bear an effect on the fairness of the trial may be subject to judicial review by Chambers, while all other important administrative decisions issued by the Registrar under the Directive would be subject to review by the President. The current Directive does not always reflect this principled division of review functions clearly enough. The Registrar has in July 2005 proposed an amended Directive to the judges, which directly addresses this concern, amongst others. If accepted, these latest amendments would become the eleventh revision since the initial version was promulgated in 1994. Amendments to the Directive can be proposed by a Judge, the Registrar or the Advisory Panel, in accordance with Article 4(B) of the Directive. If the proposal submitted by the Registrar in July 2005 is accepted, then in the future, amendments may also be proposed by the ADC. The ADC has already advanced such a proposal for the first time in June 2005, regarding proposed amendments to the provisions concerning duty counsel.

(3) Registry Practice

20–40   Registry administrative practice is an important pillar in the system governing legal-aid. As in any national public administration, statutory rules are unable to regulate all possible situations in detail and, hence, need addition and elaboration in policies and practice. In the statutory hierarchy, the most important principles are regulated in the Statute and the RPE. The Tribunal's Directive broadens the detail of regulations by further developing the principles set out in the basic texts. In its Article 8 for example, the Directive develops in much more specificity the determination of indigence; and in its Article 22, the Directive lays down the justification for, as well as the standard for verification of the disbursement of legal-aid fees and expenses. Nevertheless, the daily practice of the Tribunal necessitates that the principles laid out in the Directive are further developed. While some policies remain unwritten and have simply evolved over time, the Registry has in recent years developed a number of written policies and practices for the sake of transparency and clarity, responding in part to increased challenges to its policies and practices originating from the ADC and Chambers, and acknowledging in part the need to modernise and make more efficient and transparent existing practice. In this development process, the Registry increasingly involved the ADC as much as possible and as a consequence, some policies bear the marks of long, sometimes painstaking negotiations between Registry and ADC.

---

[10] For review powers granted to the President, see: *e.g.* Articles 13(A), 14(D) and (F), 15(C), 18(C), 19(F) of the Directive; to Chambers, see: Articles 13(B) and 18(C) of the Directive.

The most relevant are the newly introduced lump-sum payment policies in pre-trial and trial proceedings (November 2004, amended April 2005), and the Registry policy for determining the extent to which an accused is able to remunerate counsel (issued in May 2004)—all widely acknowledged as strong improvements.

Both the Chambers and the President have acknowledged their **20–41** responsibilities for review of Registry decisions. Several Chambers have critically reviewed the Registrar's decisions on the extent to which an accused is able to remunerate counsel. Chambers decisions on this aspect of the legal-aid regime became so critical in the period 2003–2004 that the Registry was forced to revise its previous policy by which it determines the financial status of accused. The President, on several occasions, has had to review challenges to the Registry's decisions concerning assignment and remuneration of counsel, including consultation questions pursuant to Article 31 of the Directive.[11] The general standard for judicial review of the Registry's decisions has been laid down by the Appeals Chamber in the *Prosecutor v Kvočka et al.*,[12] providing as follows:

"Judicial review of an administrative decision by the Registrar [...] is concerned initially with the propriety of the procedure by which the Registrar reached the particular decision and the manner in which he reached it. The administrative decision will be quashed if the Registrar has failed to comply with the legal requirements of the Directive [...] The administrative decision will also be quashed if the Registrar has failed to act with procedural fairness towards the person affected by the decision, or if he has taken into account irrelevant material or failed to take into account relevant material, or if he has reached a conclusion which no sensible person who has properly applied his mind to the issue could have reached. There can be no interference with the margin of appreciation of the facts or the merits of that case to which the maker of such an administrative decision is entitled."[13]

[11] Article 31 of the Directive, allows the Registrar: "(i)n the event of disagreement on questions relating to calculation and payment of remuneration or to reimbursement of expenses [...]" to consult the President, and if necessary the Advisory Panel, and make a decision based on such consultation(s).

[12] Case No. IT-98–30/1A, Decision on Review of Registrar's Decision to Withdraw Legal Aid from Zoran Žigić, February 7, 2003 ("*Kvočka* Decision").

[13] *Kvočka* Decision, *ibid.* at para. 13. The general rule is that the Registrar has the primary responsibility in making decisions as to remuneration of counsel under the legal-aid system of the Tribunal. The Appeals Chamber has previously held that where the Directive expressly provides for a review of the Registrar's decision, the Trial Chamber cannot interfere in the Registrar's decision, except to stay the trial until that procedure has been completed. Conversely, where the Directive does not expressly provide for a review of the Registrar's decision, the Trial Chamber, pursuant to its statutory obligation to ensure the fairness of the trial, is competent to review the Registrar's decision in the light of its effect upon the fairness of the trial. If there is no effect on the fairness of the trial, the accused should be left to his remedy as provided under Article 31 of the Directive: see *Prosecutor v Milutinovic et al.*, Case No. IT-99–37-AR73.2, Decision on Interlocutory Appeal on Motion for Additional Funds, November 13, 2003 at paras 19–20. Moreover, absent explicit provisions in the Directive or the RPE, the Registry has held the view that a person aggrieved by its decision ought to be able to seek review of that decision by a higher authority. As the President of the Tribunal has inherent jurisdiction to supervise the activities of the Registrar (Rule 19(A) of the RPE), the Registry's interpretatation is that by operation of Rule 19(A) of the RPE, the President is empowered to review the Registrar's administrative decisions when the Directive or the RPE are silent on a right of review.

20–42   The status of the Registry's legal-aid practice (which includes its publicly pronounced policies) is that of any administrative practice within an international organisation. The practice is self-binding for the Registry, but also binds the addressees of the practice, defence counsel and their team members, and ultimately the persons receiving legal-aid. The Directive provides that decisions based upon the administrative practice of the Registry can be challenged in the situation of a concrete case by counsel or accused and checked against the higher ranking regulations, ultimately the Statute.[14]

B. Indigence and Partial Indigence

20–43   The Tribunal provides free legal assistance only to those suspects or accused who are unable to cover the costs of their defence, and then only to the extent that they are unable to do so (Article 6(A) of the Directive). An accused will need to provide evidence to sustain his claim that he has insufficient funds to remunerate counsel; the burden of proof on his indigency status lies with the accused (Article 8(A) of the Directive).[15] Until the year 2000, the Tribunal's legal-aid system provided for assignment of counsel and concomitant remuneration either in full or not at all. With the arrival over the years of higher ranking and wealthier accused, it became clear that a number of accused were in a position to contribute to the costs of their own defence. Moreover, the Tribunal received information that some accused had misinformed the Tribunal as to their indigency situation, and that some of the legal-aid funds were wrongfully spent (See discussion on "Fee-splitting" in paragraphs 20–92 to 20–107). In most national jurisdictions, legal-aid systems establish a financial threshold, below which, an applicant will qualify for full legal assistance paid for by the State. This "all or nothing" approach is unworkable in the context of the Tribunal, due to the unusually large costs associated with defending against war crimes charges. During a plenary session held on December 15, 2000, upon the initiative of the Registrar, the judges of the Tribunal approved an amendment to the Directive on Assignment of Defence Counsel (Revision 8) that allows the Registry to pay only a portion of the costs incurred by the representation of an accused, when the accused possesses the means to partially remunerate counsel. The Registry adopted a "sliding scale" system to ensure that those accused who have sufficient means, are only granted as much assistance as they cannot afford themselves. Since that time, two systems for determining the eligibility of an applicant for legal-aid have been developed and applied by the Registry.

[14] See, *e.g. Prosecutor v Mrksic et al.*, Case No. IT-95–13–1-PT, Decision of Trial Chamber II on Defence Request for Review of the Registrar's Decision on Partial Indigence of Mrksic, March 9, 2004.

[15] For recent jurisprudence confirming this burden of proof, see decision regarding Praljak, *Prosecutor v Prlic et al.*, Case No. IT-04–74-PT, Decision by the Deputy Registrar, June 17, 2005, . . . upheld by the Trial Chamber on September 21, 2005 in its "Decision on (Redacted) Request for Review of the Deputy Registrar's Decision dated (Redacted) 2005 Regarding the Accused's Request for Assignment of Counsel".

In the initially applied system, the Registry determined the total **20–44** asset and income-base of the applicant and then subjected that figure to a formula in order to produce a "contribution" that the applicant could reasonably be expected to make towards the costs of his defence. This system worked much like a tax system, with a sliding scale designed to ensure that the contribution to be made by the applicant to the costs of his defence was commensurate with his means. A number of accused, found by the Registry to be partially eligible for legal-aid, challenged this system by way of judicial review before the Chambers. In several cases, the Registry's system of assessing eligibility for legal-aid was upheld or endorsed by the Chamber reviewing the decision.[16] However, in late 2003 and early 2004, the Appeals Chamber quashed several Registry decisions and effectively instructed the Registry to re-examine its system.[17]

After extensive research and review of national jurisdictions, the **20–45** Registry developed a new system and introduced the "Registry Policy for Determining the Extent to which an Accused is able to Remunerate Counsel" on May 4, 2004 ("Indigency Assessment Policy"). The Indigency Assessment Policy abolishes the "tax scale" element of the previous system in favour of a simpler and transparent approach which may be interpreted as fairer. This new system seeks to ensure that: a) an accused is not forced to realise assets that constitute the necessities of life for the accused and his family, and b) accused who own assets of exceptional value or receive extraordinary incomes are required to contribute a reasonable amount to the costs of their defence. The system is designed in this way to target the wealthier accused. The Indigency Assessment Policy requires the Registrar to determine the so-called "disposable means" of the applicant and then to deduct the living expenses of the accused and his family from the disposable means; the remainder being the contribution that the accused is expected to make to the costs of his defence. In this way, the formula used to determine the extent to which the accused is able to remunerate counsel under the Indigency Assessment Policy is as follows:

$$DM - ELE = C$$

Where—
    DM represents the applicant's disposable means;
    ELE represents the estimated living expenses for the applicant, his spouse, his dependents and the persons with whom he habitually resides;
    C   represents the contribution to be made by the applicant to his defence.

In the above formula, the key element in the equation is, what assets and income should be included in the accused's disposable means. The

---

[16] See, *e.g. Prosecutor v Mrkšić et al.*, note 14 above.

[17] See, *e.g. Prosecutor v Krajišnik*, Case No. IT-00–39, Decision on the Defence's motion for an Order Setting Aside the Registrar's Decision Declaring Momčilo Krajišnik Partially Indigent for Legal Aid Purposes, January 20, 2004; *Prosecutor v Šainović*, Decision on Defence Request for Review of Registrar's Decision, February 19, 2003; *Prosecutor v Žigić*, Case No. IT-98–30/1-A, Decision on Review on the Registrar's Decision to Withdraw Legal Aid from Zoran Žigić, February 7, 2003.

Indigency Assessment Policy gives comprehensive guidelines in this regard. In general terms, the Indigency Assessment Policy excludes from an accused's disposable means the assets and income that the accused and his family could not reasonably be expected to sell or borrow to pay for the costs of his defence. In particular, the following are excluded from the disposable means of the accused:

a) the equity in the accused's principal family home to the extent that the principal family home is reasonably necessary for the accused, his spouse and the persons with whom he habitually resides;

b) the equity in furnishings contained in the principal family home;

c) the equity in the accused's principal family vehicle to the extent that the principal family vehicle is reasonably necessary for the accused, his spouse and persons with whom he habitually resides;

d) the equity in assets owned by the accused, his spouse and persons with whom he habitually resides that are not readily disposable;

e) the equity in tools of the trade owned by the accused, his spouse and persons with whom he habitually resides that are reasonably necessary to the livelihood of the applicant, his spouse, his dependents or the persons with whom he habitually resides;

f) government welfare payments;

g) earnings of the accused's child or children; and

h) alimony, separation or maintenance payments owed to the accused's spouse, his dependents or persons with whom he habitually resides.

20–46   With minor exceptions, the Registrar may include all other assets and income in the accused's disposable means, provided it is reasonable to do so in the circumstances. From the disposable means of the accused, his estimated living expenses and those of his family are deducted. The remaining amount is the sum that the Registry deems that the accused can reasonably be expected to contribute to the costs of his defence.

20–47   By July 2005, of all legal-aid claims processed since the inception of the partial indigency system, 21.84 per cent of accused were found partially indigent, 41.38 per cent, fully indigent, with 25.29 per cent claims pending. The remainder have not requested legal-aid. Partial indigency decisions have resulted in 19 accused being found able to contribute a total of approximately US†11.7 million to their defence costs.[18] The Registrar has recently denied legal-aid to one accused, due to that accused's lack of cooperation with the Registry's inquiry into his means.[19]

20–48   The system developed by the Tribunal has a negative side effect in cases where accused refuse to pay their contributions, as assessed by the Registry. Such refusals effectively result into a lower amount of

---

[18] See, *e.g. Prosecutor v Krajicnik*, Case No. IT-00–39-T, Decision of the Deputy Registrar [on assignment of counsel], February 3, 2004, where the accused was found partially indigent and able to contribute $9,589 US per month to the cost of his defence.

[19] *Prosecutor v Praljak*, in *Prosecutor v Prlić et al.*, Case No. IT-04–74-PT, Decision by the Deputy Registrar, June 17, 2005, see note 15 above.

funds available to defence counsel and his support staff for the preparation of the defence of the same accused. It could be argued that by refusing to make his contribution, the accused renounces his right to have a properly resourced defence counsel and accepts a lesser quality defence as a consequence of the lower level of resources available. Nevertheless, especially in cases where expected contributions of accused are high, it has been argued that the rights of an accused to a proper defence are affected by the system in place, as it is difficult for counsel to negotiate with clients the conditions of remuneration, when the client has been found partially indigent. The ADC has opined that the Tribunal has to take responsibility for the enforcement of its indigency decisions and, if necessary, initiate local court proceedings. The Registry, while rejecting to take such direct responsibility at this stage, is exploring various alternative possibilities for enforcement of partial indigency decisions. In this exercise, it will have to balance a variety of factors. Aside from the rights of accused persons to proper legal assistance, other factors need to be taken into account such as the appearance of justice and how the work of the Tribunal is received and perceived in the region. Especially victims groups have difficulty accepting that wealthy accused receive legal-aid funds to cover the cost of their defence before the Tribunal.

IV. QUALIFICATIONS REQUIRED FOR COUNSEL

A. Right to Practise: Qualification Requirements

In an international setting like the Tribunal's, clear qualification and experience requirements of defence counsel are essential to establish and maintain a high level of quality of defence work. While national criminal proceedings may be as complex and intellectually challenging for an attorney as those at the ICTY, international criminal proceedings before international tribunals add further challenges and perspectives unknown at the national level. Some elements which any jurist involved in international criminal proceedings before ICTY or ICTR should take into account include the following:

20-49

— the scope and complexity of the conflict covered by the Tribunal;
— the magnitude and complexity of the crimes of which persons are accused before the Tribunal;
— the uniqueness of the legal system established at the Tribunal, which can at best be described as a reasonably well working hybrid system with elements of both common law and civil law;
— the wide variety of nationalities present and practicing at the Tribunal interpreting that same system, ranging from lawyers from common law countries such as the USA, Great Britain and Australia, to lawyers from the civil law tradition, from the newly formed countries of the former Yugoslavia region itself as well as the European continent, all bringing their own legal educations, traditions, perspectives and experiences;

— the cultural, language and geographic aspects involved in cases at the Tribunal;

— the temporary nature and United Nations dependency of the Tribunal.

20–50 It must be noted that these elements influenced the establishment of counsel qualification criteria at the outset of the Tribunal's activities, but were then interpreted quite differently. Thus, it was assessed unwise to bind the Registry or the Tribunal to overly strict criteria when assigning or admitting counsel. The absence of strict criteria led to a situation where a wide variety of counsel appeared before the Tribunal bringing a similar wide variety of legal and professional ethical education and experience. While this accounted for an enrichment of the legal environment at the ICTY, there was a downside: some counsel did not meet the required criteria of ethics and competence which, in turn, was a factor in making the legal-aid system more vulnerable to abuse. While a number of measures were put in place over the years to address aspects of abuse (see paragraphs 20–106 and 20–107), qualification criteria remained unaltered. After repetitive criticisms and absent a development of initiatives from the still embryonic association of defence counsel, a working group of judges was established to address all matters related to the assignment of counsel including qualification requirements of counsel ("Working Group on Assignment" or "Working Group"), with the ultimate aim of securing the rights of the accused to a proper defence as guaranteed under Article 21 of the Statute.[20] The work of this Working Group led to the introduction of stricter qualifications criteria into the Rules and the Directive in 2004 (see paragraphs 20–64 *et seq.*).

20–51 In the Tribunal's legislative system, Rule 44 of the RPE establishes the basic requirements that counsel must meet so as to be able to perform defence work at the Tribunal. Rule 45 adds requirements which need to be fulfilled by all counsel who are willing to be assigned by the Registry to suspects or accused, who lack the means to remunerate counsel. Rule 46 establishes parameters under which a Chamber or judge can interfere with counsel's representation before the Tribunal if this amounts to misconduct. Rule 46 has not been used regularly in practice. The Registry is "the" organ of the Tribunal generally responsible for the verification of the requisite qualifications of counsel under both Rules 44 and 45. Pursuant to Rule 45(B), the Registry maintains a list of counsel who have declared themselves willing to act for indigent accused and who fulfil, in the Registry's assessment, the necessary requirements under the RPE and the Directive. This so-called Rule 45-list is an important instrument in securing proper qualifications of counsel. Since 2002, after the Registrar officially recognized the ADC, this professional body of defence counsel involved itself in assisting the Registrar's responsibilities in ensuring that suspects and accused are provided with competent legal representation in proceedings before the Tribunal. By July 2005, it can be said that a good level of coordination and cooperation between Registry and ADC on both admission as members to the ADC and the

---

[20] For an explanation on abuse of the legal-aid system and the Registry's response to it, see UNGA Report A/58/288 (August 12, 2003) at paras 11, 40, 42, 46.

Registry's management of the Rule 45-list of counsel has been achieved, setting the basis for jointly verifying qualification requirements and setting higher standards for counsel.

Power of Attorney

The Registry accepts as a power of attorney, a one-page document stating that a person authorises a lawyer to represent him or her in criminal proceedings before the ICTY, signed by the person to be represented. Thus far, one accused in detention has granted a limited power of attorney to deal with matters regarding his detention, as he did not accept the jurisdiction of the ICTY. This limited power of the attorney was accepted by the Registry, as both persons referred to in the power were attorneys in good standing with their respective professional bars and agreed to be bound by the Tribunal's Code of Conduct. In the Milosevic case, the accused is self-represented. To accommodate the practical needs the accused faces when preparing his own defence, the Registry has recognised three legal associates in the case, who have undertaken to be bound by the Tribunal's RPE and its Code of Conduct. The Registry has further awarded limited rights of privileged communication to them. Mr Milosevic has not filed a power of attorney for these associates. Even after the Trial Chamber assigned counsel to Mr Milosevic in September 2004,[21] these associates have remained in place and continue to assist the accused.

20–52

Admission to a Bar or Professorship in Law

The basic qualification requirement is set out by Rule 44(A) of the RPE and Article 14 of the Directive. In order to be allowed to practice as counsel before the Tribunal, applicants must submit documentation to the Registry showing either that they are admitted to the practice of law (the bar) in a State, or that they are university professors of law. In order to satisfy these requirements, the Registry requires applicants to produce a copy of their graduation certificates as lawyers. In a number of countries, non-lawyers can be admitted to the bar under certain conditions, and it appears justified to ask counsel for this information to be added to his or her file. In addition, lawyers should submit a certificate of professional qualification by a competent professional body. The admission to the bar is certified by a simple document issued by the bar. A small percentage of counsel acting before the Tribunal, were or are professors of international or criminal law and procedure. For law professors, the Registry requires applicants to submit documen-

20–53

---

[21] See *Prosecutor v Milosević*, Case No. IT-02–54-T, Order on the Modalities to be Followed by Court Assigned Counsel, September 3, 2004; *Prosecutor v Milosević*, Case No. IT-02–54-AR73.7, Decision on Interlocutory Appeal of the Trial Chamber's Decision on the Assignment of Defence Counsel, November 1, 2004. Although, the accused, Mr Milosević, has been assigned counsel, he is still *de facto* conducting his own defence.

tation on the subjects of their *venia legendi*, and on their status as tenured professors. Associate or assistant professors would require admission to the bar in order to practice before the ICTY.

Language Requirement

20–54   The former version of the RPE already included the requirement for assigned counsel to be proficient in one of the two working languages of the Tribunal. The general rule as entrenched in Rule 44(A)(ii) of the RPE dictates that counsel *must* possess written and oral proficiency in one of the two working languages of the Tribunal (being English and French) and that exceptions can only be granted in the interests of justice (Rule 44(A)(ii); see also Article 14(A)(ii) of the Directive). The Tribunal has taken it upon itself to assess and test the applicant to confirm that he or she is proficient in one of the two working languages of the Tribunal, when warranted in the circumstances. Since the reforms initiated by the Working Group on Assignment, the requirement to sufficiently master one of the working languages at the Tribunal has been sharpened. The Registry has enforced the language test more often to counsel who want to be included in the Rule 45-list. By July 2005, in total, eight lawyers had been required to undergo the Tribunal's language test, of whom, three did not pass. Three lawyers were required to take the test since the amendments came into affect in July 2004, one of whom failed the test.

20–55   Possibilities for an exception to the general language requirement have been included in the rules and practice of the Tribunal as of its inception and examples of exceptions granted are numerous. They were almost entirely granted to counsel from the region who speak the native language of accused and/or who have previously represented the accused in domestic proceedings and hence had already built a relationship of trust with the accused. In such cases, the Registry found that waiving the language requirement was warranted "in the interests of justice", which was and remains to this day the test to be applied when making an exception to the language requirements of the RPE. The interests of justice are assessed on a case-to-case basis, and viewed in light of the circumstances of the particular case.[22] Counsel who were not proficient in the Tribunal's working languages have been permitted to appear before the Tribunal in, for instance, the Blaskić, Cermak and Markac, Krstić, M. Radić, Simić *et al.* cases. However, since the revision of the Rule 45-list in the fall of 2004, the Registry has been very strict in its application of the language requirement, and only two counsel who do not speak one of the working languages of the Tribunal, but who are still assigned to cases, have remained on the Rule 45-list. The

---

[22] Jurisprudence of the Tribunal is further developing what the "interests of justice" test entails when making an exception to the language requirements of the RPE and the Directive. For recent cases on this issue, see: *Prosecutor v Miletić et al.*, Case No. IT-05–88-PT, Decision on Appointment of Co-counsel for Radivoje Miletić, September 28, 2005, issued confidentially, which confidentiality was later lifted by Order of the Trial Chamber of 30 September 2005; *Prosecutor v Mrksić et al.*, Case No. IT-95–13/1-PT, Decision on Appointment of Co-counsel for Mile Mrksic, October 7, 2005.

Registry maintains a separate list of counsel, who do not meet the language requirements, but otherwise meet the other qualification criteria, for potential assignments as co-counsel if the Registry finds it to be the interests of justice to grant such assignments. The list contains mostly counsel formerly assigned to cases at the ICTY, who have been re-admitted following an application of the new, stricter, selection requirements.

The amendments introduced by the Working Group on Assignment, establish a difference in the enforcement of the language requirement between counsel retained by non-indigent accused and counsel assigned to indigent accused. Rule 44(B) provides for a general exception to the language requirement for *any* counsel, whereas Rule 45(B)(i) refers to the Directive in which it is stated that exceptions may only be granted to the second counsel: the *co-counsel*.[23] Hence, in all cases of Tribunal-funded legal assistance, lead-counsel *must* be selected from those competent to address the court, both orally and in writing in one of the working languages of the Tribunal. Although the considerations of the Working Group on Assignment are not made public, the ratio behind this proviso appears to be that there must be a difference when counsel are assigned and remunerated from public funds. The scope of the right to free choice of counsel must also have been considered now that it has been firmly established in Tribunal jurisprudence that the free choice of counsel is a limited right when it concerns indigent accused.[24] Proficiency in English or French is a qualification not to be underestimated in its importance. An effective representation of an accused by counsel depends, to a great extent, on excellent communication skills both orally and in writing. While in the courtroom, simultaneous interpretation is available, much of the work of counsel has to be done in a working language of the court, *i.e.* all motions have to be submitted in English or French, negotiations with the prosecution will be conducted mostly in English, meetings with the Registry will be in French or English, even though consecutive interpretation is available for all this, smooth communications are hampered and prolonged by the use of translation or interpretation intermediaries.

20–56

The ADC has voiced criticism on this amendment of the RPE, maintaining that it is in the interest of accused and the protection of their rights that they be allowed to choose lead counsel from the region, irrespective of that counsel's language abilities. The ADC finds support for its claims that the Tribunal must respect the freedom of choice of counsel by an accused person—whether indigent or not—and bear all concomitant language and translation costs in Article 21 of the Statute (in particular, Article 21(4)(b), (d) and (f) of the Statute). Tribunal jurisprudence as indicated does not seem to support this interpretation so far.

20–57

---

[23] See Articles 14(C) and 16(C)(ii) of the Directive. Under Article 16(C)(ii) of the Directive, the *burden is upon lead counsel* to satisfy the Registry that the assignment of the proposed co-counsel is in the interests of justice

[24] See paragaphs 20–108 *et seq.*, where seminal cases on this issue are discussed. See, *e.g.* *Prosecutor v Blagojević et al.*, Case No. IT-02–60-AR73.4, Public and Redacted Reasons for Decision on Appeal by Vidoje Blagojević to Replace his Defence Team, November 7, 2003 ("*Blagojević* Appeals Decision").

Member in Good Standing of an Association of Counsel and Previous Criminal or Disciplinary Proceedings

20–58 Both the Tribunal's Statute and the REP were, until recently, silent on the question of whether counsel's admission to practice or a university professorship in law must be devoid of disciplinary proceedings or convictions. While the law and practice of the Tribunal for assigned counsel on this issue is diverse and specific, there was little practice for counsel who were not assigned. The vacuum was noted by the Working Group on Assignment when considering previous Tribunal jurisprudence.[25] Hence, the Working Group introduced new amendments attempting to fill this vacuum by establishing two new criteria: counsel must demonstrate that he is a member in good standing of an association of counsel practicing at the Tribunal and recognised by the Registrar and, in short, that he has not been found guilty in relevant criminal and disciplinary proceedings. (See Rule 44(iii), (iv) and (v); see also Article 14 (A) (v), (vi) and (ix) of the Directive.)

20–59 The requirement included in Rule 44(A)(iii) that counsel has to be a member in good standing of an association of defence counsel practicing at the Tribunal, has been included, in part, to give more responsibility for verifying status and reputation of counsel to the ADC. The very inclusion of this requirement and its wording raised the importance of the ADC as the only representative body for counsel at the ICTY: all counsel who want to practice at ICTY need to become a member. Rule 44(A) of the Directive provides that "counsel shall be considered qualified to represent a suspect or accused if the counsel satisfied the Registrar that he or she is: [...] (iii) a member in good standing of an association of counsel practicing at the Tribunal recognized by the Registrar".

20–60 It has been left to the ADC to develop conditions for its membership. The implementation of this provision has been developed by the Registry in close coordination with the ADC. The Registry, in considering applications for the Rule 45-list, first verifies the applicant's status with the ADC and proceeds only after it has received notification that the applicant is a member in good standing with the ADC. In its Constitution, the ADC has listed six conditions to become a full ADC member, which are directly taken from the requirements of Rule 44 of the RPE.[26] Regarding the term "in good standing", the ADC has exerted a rather narrow interpretation: (1) a member who has not been suspended; and (2) who has paid the annual membership fee.[27] Once accepted as a member in good standing of the ADC, the Registry applies a full verification of all criteria, taking note of the finding and checks performed by the ADC. In this way, a double verification process has been effected, which provides for a much stricter qualifications

---

[25] See, *e.g. Prosecutor v Tadić*, Appeals Chamber Decision, January 31, 2000; Judgement on Allegations of Misconduct against prior Counsel, Milan Vujin; the Registrar's decision, dated June 8, 2001, withdrawing Mr Vujin's name from the Rule 45-List.

[26] See Part III, Article 3(2)(a)-(f) of the ADC Constitution. The first ADC Constitution was adopted in 2002, and subsequently amended by the General Assembly in 2004 ("ADC Constitution").

[27] See ADC Constitution., Article 13(2).

verification process, always bearing in mind the ultimate aim of providing good quality defence to the accused indicted before this Tribunal.

The requirements in Rule 44(A)(iv) and (v) set the standard for criminal and disciplinary records. Previously this standard had already been included in the Directive as basic requirements for assigned counsel—now it applies to all counsel. Permission to practice as a defence counsel at the Tribunal requires a "clean slate", in other words, a demonstration of absence of convictions in relevant criminal and disciplinary proceedings. The Registry has experience with the omission of relevant information with at least one (assigned) counsel. This attorney appeared to have an impressive record of disciplinary proceedings, which, however, only came to light late after his assignment. The attorney in question did not find it necessary to inform the Tribunal of any of these proceedings until he could no longer avoid this when a conviction in a disciplinary proceeding resulted in the suspension of his right to practice in his home jurisdiction. By then, when he had to be withdrawn from the case, the attorney and his co-counsel had received a significant amount of the Tribunals' legal-aid funds to prepare the defence's case, and the case was scheduled for trial. Counsel's omission of information and his withdrawal, not only led to a significant waste of public funds, but also disturbed the scheduling of the case in order to make preparation time available for a new defence team.

20–61

The requirement to disclose previous criminal and disciplinary convictions are included in both the RPE and the Directive and cover both retained and assigned counsel. As to the disciplinary records, the similar wordings of Rule 44(A)(iv) of the RPE and Article 14(A)(v) of the Directive have several components. Article 14(A)(v) refers to *all* disciplinary proceedings before the Tribunal and national bar(s) of which the counsel is a member. The language of the Rule is unequivocal in that it is only concerned with *convictions* resulting from disciplinary proceedings against counsel. Therefore, proceedings which have ended with an acquittal of counsel or were otherwise abandoned are of no concern to the Registrar. The Article also gives the Registrar latitude to assess whether the offence for which a lawyer might have been convicted in such disciplinary processes will adversely affect the administration of justice, and make a determination if "under the circumstances, it would be disproportionate to exclude such counsel." The word "relevant" offers further discretion to the Registrar in considering the weight of the conviction and the link to ICTY work. In practice, the Registrar is likely to place less weight on, for example, an applicant's conviction for late payment of professional membership fees, while convictions for more serious violations of ethical rules of conduct (*e.g.* actions amounting to fraud, tampering with evidence, breaking solicitor-client privileges, interfering with witnesses) will be seen as *prima facie* reasons for rejecting retention of counsel or the applicant's request for admission to the list. As for criminal records, Article 14(A)(vi) was first introduced into the Directive with the ninth revision of the text in August 2002, and has since July 2004 been included in Rule 44. Again, the word "relevant" in the language of the Article indicates that only criminal convictions which could have an impact on the fitness of counsel to practice before the Tribunal will be

20–62

taken into account by the Registrar. What is of interest to the Registrar, are serious crimes which give information about the counsel's character and ethical standards—particularly the candour and integrity of counsel. Further to be weighed in this determination are the timing of the conviction and the severity of the penalty for the crime.

Previous Conduct of Counsel and Provision of Information on Qualifications

20–63   Apart from the requirement that counsel has not been found guilty in relevant criminal and disciplinary proceedings, two new, related rules were introduced with the 2004 amendments, providing further criteria covering previous professional conduct by counsel in Rules 44(vi) and (vii) of the RPE embedding Tribunal jurisprudence in the RPE. A counsel must not have engaged in conduct which is dishonest or discreditable for a member of his profession, prejudicial to the administration of justice or likely to diminish public confidence in the Tribunal or the administration of justice or bring the Tribunal in disrepute; in addition, counsel's information with respect to his qualifications must have been proper. These two provisions offer further discretion to both the Registry and Chambers to consider previous conduct of counsel and its effects on the Tribunal's work and reputation. The ultimate aim remains to guarantee that accused are provided with a proper, good quality defence in line with Article 21 of the Statute, and that the Tribunal's basic judicial function—to render justice through fair and expeditious trials—is not frustrated by counsel who do not possess the minimum qualifications of ethical conduct. As articulated in *Prosecutor v Duško Tadić* and *Prosecutor v Radomir Kovac et al.*, *per* Judge Hunt:

> "The Tribunal [. . .] possess an inherent jurisdiction, deriving from its judicial function, to ensure that its exercise of the jurisdiction which is expressly given to it by the Tribunal's Statute is not frustrated and that its basic judicial functions are safeguarded. As an international criminal court, the Tribunal therefore possesses the inherent power to deal with conduct, which interferes with its administration of justice. Such interference may be way of conduct which obstructs, prejudices or abuses the Tribunal's administration of justice. *I am satisfied that such an inherent power includes the power to refuse audience to counsel [. . .] who is not a fit and proper person to appear before the Tribunal.*[28–29]

[28–29] *Prosecutor v Tadić*, Case 94–1-A-R77, Judgement on Allegations of Misconduct against prior Counsel, Milan Vujin, January 31, 2000 (Appeals Chamber), paras 12–18; Case No. IT-96–23-PT&23/1, Separate Opinion on the Request by Radomir Kovać to allow Milan Vujin to Appear as Counsel Acting Without Payment by the Tribunal, March 24, 2000, at para. 8 (part in brackets only in separate opinion of Judge Hunt in the Kovać case).

B. Additional Qualification Requirements for Counsel Assigned by the Registrar

Working Group on Assignment of Counsel

In May 2003, the Working Group on Assignment of Counsel was **20–64** established on the initiative of the President, consisting of the Vice President along with a number of judges of the Tribunal and convened to set higher quality standards for defence counsel and a more rigorous vetting of candidates for inclusion into the Rule 45-list. After numerous discussions and meetings between the Registry and the Working Group, which produced and canvassed various options, a number of principles were unanimously agreed upon. The Working Group reported to the Plenary on December 11, 2003 with a series of proposals to amend the RPE and the Directive, which were eventually adopted at the following Plenary on July 28, 2004. The changes included amendments to *inter alia* Rules 44 and 45 of the RPE and Articles 14 and 15 of the Directive. In effect, requirements for admission to the Rule 45-list were amended to specifically guarantee a higher level of competence of counsel admitted to "the list" with the ultimate aim of ensuring that the interests of the accused, and on balance, the interests of justice are best served. After the changes were adopted, the following criteria, in addition to the mentioned criteria above, now apply to counsel who want to be assigned to cases before the Tribunal:

a) Established Competence

Counsel must now *"possess established competence"* in criminal law and/or **20–65** international criminal law/international human rights law (see Rule 45(B)(ii) of the RPE, and Article 14(A)(iii) of the Directive). This language sets a higher standard than its predecessor, which simply required that counsel possess *"reasonable experience"* in the above listed legal disciplines. This should ensure that counsel have requisite experience in fields of law relevant to the work of the Tribunal. Moreover, the current requirement places the onus on counsel who desire to be included in the list, to prove to the satisfaction of the Registrar that in fact they meet this "established competence" requirement, leaving some discretion to the Registrar to develop the requirement further.

b) Seven Years of Experience in Criminal Proceedings

The second major change introduced to Rule 45(B) is the requirement **20–66** that counsel *"possess at least seven years of relevant experience in criminal proceedings."* (see Rule 45 (B)(iii) of the RPE; Article 14(A)(iv) of the Directive). No such requirement was present before the July 2004 amendments. This new requirement is added to set a clear and minimum experience standard so as to ensure that counsel included in the list, has sufficient experience with court proceedings of the sort that is dealt with at the tribunal, criminal trials. It also brings the standards of counsel on the Rule 45-list closer in line with the requirements imposed by other international organizations. For instance, the International Criminal Tribunal for Rwanda requires counsel to have ten years of practical legal experience (see Rule 45(A) of the ICTR Rules of Procedure and Evidence).[30]

c) Member of Good Standing and Disciplinary Record

20–67   See paragraphs 20–49 *et seq.* Under the previous rules, only a certificate of good standing from the applicant's national bar/regulating professional body was sufficient.

d) Review of Applicants by a Panel

20–68   Under Article 15(B) of the Directive, the possibility has been introduced to have applicants referred to a panel for an interview in which their qualifications will be assessed. Such a panel will consist of judges, members of the Advisory Panel, and/or fully qualified counsel, in other words, will include peers, who will make a recommendation on the applicant's suitability. While the Registry had, at the time of writing this Chapter, not yet invoked the Article, plans to invoke this Article exist.

e) Language Requirements of Counsel and Limited Exceptions

20–69   One of the more controversial issues discussed and grappled with by the Working Group on Assignment was the language requirement for admission to the Rule 45-list, controversial because the working languages of the Tribunal are not the languages of the accused and quite a number of counsel from the region addressed by this Tribunal do not sufficiently master English or French. The outcome of the work of the Working Group on this point, as adopted in the Plenary of Judges, is described in paragraphs 20–49 *et seq.* (See also Rules 44(A)(ii) and 44(B) of the RPE, Articles 14(A)(ii), 14(C) and 16(C)(ii) of the Directive.)

f) Closed List

20–70   Discussions have been held about introducing a closed, fixed list to which no names could be added. Many voices within and without the tribunal felt that indigent accused should be prohibited the right to

---

[30] See also Article 22(1) of the *Rules of Evidence and Procedure* of the ICC, where it stated that defence counsel "shall have established competence in international or criminal law and procedure, as well as the necessary relevant experience."

request just any desired counsel *unless* that counsel is on a closed Rule 45-list, in order to avoid fee-splitting schemes. The Working Group on Assignment also addressed this though did not include it in the amendments. In reality, the Rule 45-list is not a closed list, and the process of application is continuous throughout the year: counsel can be added to the list at any time, after he or she has been found to fulfil the (stricter) qualification requirements.

g) Duty Counsel

For the purpose of initial appearances when the accused is first brought before the Tribunal, a system of "duty counsel" has been established. In addition to the Rule 45-list, the Registry maintains a list of experienced counsel, who are available on short notice to be appointed for purposes of the accused's initial appearances. Usually, the list will include counsel practicing in the Netherlands and neighbouring countries, as well as counsel on the Rule 45-list who are more regularly present in The Hague. The system of duty counsel serves a number of purposes. It assures that accused have the benefit of preliminary legal advice they require at the initial appearance before the judge; and eases the pressure on the accused to select counsel immediately, giving them extra time to make an informed decision as to their preferred choice of counsel from the Rule 45-list. Finally and not unimportantly, the availability of duty counsel has benefits for the Registry, as it enables it to make an intelligible decision on the ultimate assignment of counsel by giving it extra time to perform proper qualification and conflict of interest checks.

20–71

Admission to the Rule-45 List of the Registrar

The actual admission to the Rule 45-list is handled by the Registry's OLAD. To be considered for inclusion into the Rule 45-list, interested applicants are required to submit the following documents and information to the Registry:

20–72

(1) An updated and detailed curriculum vitae emphasizing practical experience in criminal and international law;

(2) A certificate of professional qualification issued by the competent professional body, including a certificate of good standing detailing any disciplinary records available on the respective applicant;

(3) A copy of the domestic code of professional conduct applicable to the applicant;

(4) Evidence that the applicant has not been found guilty in relevant criminal proceedings;

(5) A declaration showing the willingness to be included on the Rule 45-list to represent *any* indigent accused or a suspect (in accordance with Rule 45(B)(iv) of the RPE, and Article 14 (A)(viii) of the Directive);

     (6) The names and contact information of two referees who
         practice in the fields of criminal law, international human-
         itarian law, international human rights law or international
         criminal law, and who are in a position to advise the Registrar
         as to the applicant's professional competence in these fields;
     (7) A copy of the professional identity card;
     (8) A copy of the law degree;
     (9) A certificate of proficiency in English and/or French; and
    (10) Optionally, a short biographical information on the applicant
         (no more than 400 words) to be provided at a later date to the
         indigent accused or suspects in order to facilitate their choice
         of counsel, in the event the applicant is successful in his or her
         application to be admitted into the Rule 45-list.

20–73   The procedure for admission is done through written submissions by
interested applicants. If the Registrar is satisfied that the applicant
meets the criteria set out in Rules 44 and 45 of the RPE, then the
applicant is admitted and receives a written confirmation. The Registrar acts alone in this approval process.[31] As mentioned above, under
Article 15(B) of the Directive, the Registrar can refer an applicant to
be interviewed by a panel composed of judges, members of the Advisory
Panel and/or qualified counsel for a recommendation on admission to
the Rule 45-list.

20–74   The amendments introduced by the Working Group came into effect
on July 28, 2004. The Registry then applied a complete revision of the
list and instructed all interested counsel to re-apply for re-admission
(the deadline was set at October 1, 2004). Counsel who did not re-apply
by this stipulated date were simply not included in the new Rule 45-list.
The Registry wanted to ensure that both new applicants for admission
to the Rule 45 list and counsel who were already included in the list
under the previous admission criteria meet the new, stricter qualification requirements. As of the date of writing this article, the Rule 45-list
comprised of 85 counsel, 52 of which have been assigned to a case
before the Tribunal. In 2003, before the amendments introduced by the
Working Group on Assignment, there were more than 100 lawyers on
the list. The more stringent requirements expected of counsel have
shortened the list, rendering it an ensemble of lawyers who are more
qualified and ready to represent the interests of accused before the
Tribunal.

Current Function of the List and Perspectives

20–75   The Rule 45-list represents the general admission to practice at the
Tribunal. The Rule 45-list must represent a list of lawyers of generally
good quality and solid competence. Counsel admitted to the list have

---

[31] The Registry is charged with the responsibility of establishing and maintaining the Rule 45-
list. Moreover, the Registry is also the sole decision maker when it comes to assignment of
counsel: see *Prosecutor v Hadžihasanović et al.*, Case No. IT-01–47-PT, Decision on Prosecution's Motion for Review of the Decision of the Registrar to Assign Mr Rodney Dixon as Co-
Counsel to the Accused Kubura, March 26, 2002, at para. 55: where the Trial Chamber
pronounced the following at para. 55: "The Registrar of the International Tribunal *has the
primary responsibility in determining which counsel it may appoint or assign, in accordance with the
Rules, the Directive, and the Code of Conduct*."

now gone through a relatively intensive vetting process of their qualifications and, in principle, are expected to meet the high professional and ethical standards set by the RPE and the Directive. In particular, the requirement that counsel have at least seven years of relevant experience in criminal proceedings and the more stringent language requirement as described above, have contributed to improving the quality, cost and sustainable effect of legal work at the Tribunal.

The quality vetting process preceding admission to the Rule 45-list will remain an important quality control mechanism for the Tribunal. The list's function to provide guidance to accused arriving at the Tribunal in choosing good quality legal representation in the complex international criminal procedures that await them, justifies such quality vetting process. The 2004 amendments have been instrumental in fortifying the criteria for admission to the Rule 45-list. Other measures may contribute to ensure that the list is and remains a safe pool of competent defence counsel. Examples include timely Registry and Chamber action to address situations where evidence has surfaced casting doubt on counsels' qualifications, in particular their competence. In that sense, efforts to strengthen the power of the Registry to take counsel off the list (see Articles 14(A), (D) and (E) of the Directive) are welcome, be it only when concrete evidence has surfaced casting doubt on the competence of counsel or other admission criteria. Obviously, such Registry action must itself be objective and of quality and ultimately be able to stand judicial scrutiny. Furthermore, regular training requirements for counsel may assist and in actual fact, they are presently being developed by the ADC in cooperation and coordination with the Registry. Other initiatives to ensure that counsel on the list remain qualified, should be considered. A more active role of the ADC in this respect may be expected.

20–76

Willingness to Represent any Suspect or Accused

Under the current Rule 45-list regime, the applicant is required to provide a declaration demonstrating his/her willingness to represent *any* indigent accused or suspect. This is a further precondition of being admitted to the Rule 45-list in accordance with Rule 45(B)(iv) of the RPE, and Article 14(A)(viii) of the Directive. Such statement of willingness beforehand would solve the problem in instances where counsel would refuse to represent an accused.[32] It is worth mentioning

20–77

---

[32] In practice, this occurs seldomly. However, there have been cases in the past where an attorney has refused to represent other accused, rather showing an interest in representing specific accused before the Tribunal. In 1996 for instance, an attorney made it known that he was not interested in representing anyone other than three of the four co-accused in the case of the *Prosecutor v Delalic et al.*, Case No. IT-96-21-T. The Registrar in that case refused to add the name of the attorney to the Rule 45-list. More recently, some counsel have conditioned their willingness to be assigned on the willingness of accused who had already been found partially indigent to contribute to his defence costs. The Registry condones this provided counsel expedite the negotiation with accused and provide a timely and unequivocal answer.

that, in the past and present practice of the Tribunal, accused mostly opt to include a counsel from the same ethnic background in their defence team, the small number of exceptions, being in cases where counsel from Western Europe and North America were assigned.

Previous Professional Conduct of Counsel and Criminal Records of Counsel

20–78   See paragraphs 20–49 *et seq.* The Directive provides the renewed texts in Articles 14(A)(ii), (v) and (vi).

Article 28 of the Directive

20–79   Article 28 of the Directive provides an additional measure, which the Registry takes into account when defence counsel request the assignment of a specific person who stand in a non-arms length relationship to them (family and friends) as team members. Under Article 28, family members and friends of, *inter alia*, counsel are not eligible for assignment, but the Registrar may grant the assignment if it is in the interests of justice to do so. See paragraphs 20–82 *et seq.*

Statistics

20–80   At the time of writing this Chapter, almost 90 per cent of accused persons indicted before the Tribunal, lack sufficient means to (fully) remunerate their defence counsel. In all these cases, the Registry has assigned counsel from the list or has added counsel proposed by an accused to the list after the necessary qualification checks. In mid-2005, the Rule 45-list comprised 85 names of counsel following the revision of the Rule 45-list in the fall of 2004, 52 of which are assigned to cases. A number of requests for admission were pending and more expected. Counsel on the list or engaged in active representation or having represented accused originate from twenty countries being law professors, attorneys and legal practitioners from Austria, Australia, Belgium, Bosnia & Herzegovina, Canada, Croatia, Denmark, France, Germany, Italy, Macedonia, The Netherlands, New Zealand, Serbia & Montenegro, South Africa, Sweden, Switzerland, Turkey, United Kingdom and the United States of America.

20–81   Since its inception, the Tribunal has seen more than 130 defence attorneys working before it, in the capacity of either lead or co-counsel, plus a large number of defence legal assistants or investigators, some of whom are qualified as counsel.

State	No. of Counsel*	Having Represented More than One Client	On Rule 45-list & Assigned (July 2005)	Rule 45-list (Assigned & Unassigned)	Contempt Proceedings
Australia	2				
Austria				1	
Belgium				1	
Bosnia and Herzegovina	10	4	6	5	
Canada	1	1	1	1	1
Croatia	19	9	4	4	4
Denmark				1	
France	2	2	2	3	
Germany	3	1	2	6	
Italy				1	
Kosovo	2				
Macedonia	2		2	3	
Netherlands	2	1	1	4	1
New Zealand				1	
Serbia and Montenegro	43	16	15	18	
South Africa	1	1			
Switzerland	2		1	1	
Sweden	1				
Turkey	1				
United Kingdom	19	5	7	13	1
USA	21	9	9	20	
Total	**131**	**49**	**50**	**83**	**7**

* The number of counsel listed in this column reflects the approximate total number of *assigned* counsel (lead and co-counsel). While a great number of counsel working *pro bono* before the Tribunal have been included, the actual number is not known as, at the Tribunal's early stages, not all *pro bono* counsel have been properly assigned.

C. QUALIFICATION REQUIREMENTS AND MISSION PARAMETERS FOR OTHER DEFENCE TEAM MEMBERS

The strict requirements applied to defence counsel do not apply in the **20–82** same manner to members of a defence counsel's support staff. Early in the Tribunal's existence, it was recognised that for the rights of an accused to proper legal assistance, the assistance of counsel is not enough. Considering the magnitude and complexity of cases before the Tribunal, counsel requires assistance to adequately prepare a defence case. While privately hired teams classify their positions according to their needs, assigned counsel can request the Registry to assign support staff to assist him. The qualifications for support staff are verified by OLAD, usually through a detailed review of submitted CVs and supporting documentation. In addition, a conflict of interest check is performed by the Registry, the purpose of which is to verify whether assignment of that individual as a support staff member does not conflict with previous or present work assignments (whether or not the work relates to the Tribunal), and whether the requested staff is not him or herself the subject of investigations.

20–83   In July 2002, the Directive was amended to drastically limit the possibility to assign family members and close friends of counsel and accused to the defence team, see Article 28 of the Directive. At its core, the Article is meant to avoid a circumstance where the independence of the judgment of the person in question, whether it be an expert, team member or co-counsel, could be jeopardized due to the non-arms' length relationship that may exist between that person and the accused and/or counsel. This provision was included especially because of specific experiences with assignment of family members to accused. While different domestic jurisdictions allow for family members to be involved in the defence, there are several arguments in favour of a stricter approach at the Tribunal. First and foremost of all, there is the previous experience with abuse of the legal-aid system involving family members of the accused, which the Registry, in its role as the guardian of public funds cannot accept. Further, there is the necessity of professional performance of all defence staff as well as the Tribunal's mandate and reputation in the region. Obviously, the effect of assignment of publicly funded family and friends of counsel and accused as members of an accused's defence team has a bearing on the appearance of justice (see also paragraphs 20–106 and 20–107). The rule allows for exceptions if the Registry is satisfied that it is in the interests of justice to allow the assignment. The Registry has applied some flexibility with respect to existing friendship or family relations *with counsel* and has granted exceptions in the interests of justice. For instance, in a situation where lead-counsel is in desperate need of a competent co-counsel in order to advance the interest of the accused in a timely manner, he may be able to have a duly qualified counsel assigned who also happens to be a friend, so long as it can be shown that the personal relationship between the individuals concerned will in no way interfere or adversely affect the representation of the accused.

20–84   In order to assist defence counsel and ultimately, the accused, in preparing his defence, the Registry can assign the following categories of support staff: legal consultants, legal assistants, investigators, expert consultants/experts, case managers, translators and interpreters. It is necessary for the lead counsel to address the Registry (OLAD) with reasoned requests for their assignment and to add their detailed curriculae to such requests.

Legal Consultants and Legal Assistants

20–85   A legal consultant is assigned to provide advice on specific legal issues, which counsel considers are necessary to examine, to ensure a proper defence. Legal consultants are assigned for a specific and limited period

of time. Issues which may need consultation include *inter alia*: questions
of humanitarian law, military law, constitutional laws in the region, or
sentencing. The qualifications set out in Rules 44 and 45 of the RPE do
not apply to legal consultants, although they are required to be lawyers
or have a sound academic background in law. Legal consultant mandates tend to be limited compared to other team members as they are
intended to perform work which does not require a full-time commitment. Under the ceiling system of payment at the appeal stage, which
is being phased out but still applicable at the pre-trial and appeals
stages of proceedings, consultant hours are deducted from the allotment of hours provided to counsel at a rate of between US$180 to
US$110 per hour (see Appendix I to the Directive). Under the new
lump-sum policies, consultants are paid from the lump-sum based on an
amount agreed upon by lead counsel and the consultant. For an
explanation of the lump-sum and ceiling systems, see paragraphs 20–
151 *et seq.*

Legal assistants mainly concentrate on legal research, drafting and   **20–86**
providing legal advice to counsel. In practice, these positions are
fulfilled by junior lawyers or law students. The Registry performs the
conflict of interest check referred to above and limited checks into the
qualifications of legal assistants. The Registry has refused requests for
assignment of persons who were neither legally trained nor following
legal training and, in one case, the request for assignment of an under-
aged student as legal assistant. Under the ceiling system of payment,
they are paid on an hourly basis at a rate of €15 to €25 per hour,
depending upon years of relevant work experience (see Appendix I to
the Directive). Under the lump-sum policies, legal assistants are paid
from the lump-sum based on an amount agreed upon by lead counsel
and the legal assistant. In the calculation of the lump-sum, the amounts
included for support staff such as legal assistants, investigators, case
managers, etc. are based on the same hourly rate as under the ceiling
system, multiplied by 150 work hours per month.

Investigators

Defence investigators are responsible for, *inter alia*, contacting and   **20–87**
interviewing witnesses, finding and reviewing documentation, visiting
the crime scene, taking photographs of locations. This assistance is
usually mostly needed in the former Yugoslavia, and at times, at other
locations, for example to interview witnesses relocated after the conflict
or placed in other locations and positions in their governments or
international organisations. The qualifications required for an investigator vary. The persons who have been assigned in this capacity have
included journalists, attorneys, former policemen, and economists. The
Registry's practice is to accept a candidate if his qualification and
experience appears to permit him to successfully assist the defence as
an investigator, *i.e.* is relevant. If it appears that the applicant's
credentials are not relevant, such as when a defence team once
requested the assignment of a priest, then the applicant's candidacy
may be denied. Investigators, as other support staff, answer to lead
counsel and not to the accused, an element which is not always

appreciated by the accused detained at the Tribunal who are mostly former high ranking officials in powerful positions. The Registry has had several experiences where accused instruct the investigators directly, outside of the knowledge and/or control of the lead counsel. It is for that reason that the Registry is very restrictive in allowing visits to accused by investigators: these can only happen exceptionally, for legitimate reasons and are always to take place under the supervision of counsel (see further paragraphs 20–193 *et seq.*). Investigators are remunerated according to the same policies as legal assistants.

Experts/Expert Consultants

20–88   Defence counsel can request the assistance of expert consultants: experts assigned to either give verbal and written advice for a limited period of time in a specific area of expertise or to draft a written report to be entered into evidence for the defence. Experts may also be assigned to testify for the defence during trial. Experts and expert consultants are assigned to assist in areas in which counsel and other defence team members are not expected to be proficient. These may include, *inter alia*, military, medicine, statistics, history, ballistics, geography, etc. Assignment by the Registry is made upon consideration of a detailed CV and further documentation if required. In the majority of cases, the defence requests experts suitably qualified to provide the expertise required, although there are a small number of cases in which the expert may not in fact have sufficient qualifications, or may have experience which places him in a position of conflict of interest. In one case, for example, the defence requested the expertise of an engineer to consider the technical features of a concentration camp. His assignment was rejected when it was discovered that he had previously worked as a journalist, publishing opinion articles on detention facilities in Bosnia and Herzegovina between 1991 and 1995.

20–89   The Registry deals with experts/expert consultants and expert witnesses differently although, in practice, the nature of their work may overlap. Consultants are either considered in a similar way to legal consultants dealt with above, as part of the team for a limited period of time to provide expertise on specific legal points, or as expert consultants who are responsible for the production of expert reports to be submitted into evidence. Expert witnesses are considered differently. Expert consultants who provide specific advice for a limited period of time are regarded as part of the team and fall within the ceiling or lump-sum payment system. Expert/expert consultants who are retained to produce written evidence are granted allotments by OLAD over and above the standard allotments for defence teams, and they are paid at an hourly rate of between US†l80 to US†l110 per hour. Expert witnesses testifying in court will receive services and remuneration from the Registry's Victims and Witnesses Section.

Interpreters and Translators

20–90   Most defence teams hire translators and interpreters to assist the team in communications with the accused and to translate documentation from Serbo-Croat into English or vice versa. Language assistants must demonstrate a good knowledge of English and/or French, and that they are native speakers of Serbo-Croat or another language of the accused. Until recently, language support staff were paid at rates ranging from €15 to €25 per hour consistent with their experience. This led to some discrepancy, as translators who worked at a slower pace were rewarded over faster ones. As of spring 2005, translators who submit invoices under the ceilings system (still valid in some cases in pre-trial and at the Appeals level) are being paid per word and their payment is deducted from the defence allotment of hours by way of an equation. Interpreters under the ceiling system are paid at a fixed hourly rate. Under the lump-sum policies, translators and interpreters are paid from the lump-sum, based on an amount agreed upon with lead counsel. Both the lump-sum and the ceiling systems allow for separate allotments for client-counsel interpretation and translation.

Case Managers

A number of Defence teams operate with a case manager, like their counterpart trial teams from the Office of the Prosecutor. A case manager manages documentation flow, keeps track of material being translated as well as of Prosecution disclosure material and provides general organisational assistance to counsel and co-counsel. In some cases, the case manager performs a dual role, acting as a legal assistant, or translator/interpreter, as well. The Defence team member is entitled to remuneration for work performed for both duties. Case Managers are remunerated according to the same policies as legal assistants.

20–91

V. ASSIGNMENT OF COUNSEL

A. INITIAL ASSIGNMENT PROCEDURE: DUTY COUNSEL AND TEMPORARY ASSIGNMENT OF COUNSEL

Request by Accused

The right of the accused to receive legal assistance through counsel in a criminal proceeding is a well established principle. As explained above, this basic tenet of "access to justice" has been entrenched in the Tribunal's Statute, the RPE and the Directive.[33] The Directive embeds this right in a system for suspects and accused who lack sufficient means to remunerate counsel. Part III, Chapter 2 of the Directive sets out the procedure for assignment of counsel under the Tribunal in a

20–92

---

[33] See Article 21(4) of the Statute, Rules 44 and 45 of the RPE and Article 5 of the Directive and further paragraphs 20–33 *et seq.* above. For international and domestic sources, which guarantee the accused's right to legal representation, see note 3 above.

precise and unambiguous manner. The Registry, in implementing the Directive's provisions, seeks to ensure that the accused who are brought before the Tribunal are, swiftly and without delay, provided with adequate legal representation.

20–93   In conformity with the requirements of Article 21 of the Statute, the Registry has adopted a standard procedure for assignment of counsel. Customarily, shortly after an accused's arrival at The Hague and once in the custody of the Tribunal, ordinarily within twelve hours a representative of OLAD will approach and brief the accused on his rights, which will include the rights to assignment of counsel in absence of sufficient means. The representative of the Registry provides the accused with a "welcome package", which contains the following documents:

— Rules of Procedure and Evidence;
— Rules of Detention;
— United Nations Detention Unit Complaints Procedure (IT/96);
— United Nations Detention Unit Disciplinary Procedure (IT/97);
— United Nations Detention Unit Regulations Governing Visits and Communications (IT/98);
— United Nations Detention Unit House Rules (IT/99);
— Statute of the Tribunal;
— Rights of the Accused: Article 21 of the Statute, Rules 42, and 43 of the RPE;
— Copy of the Rule 45-list;
— Declaration of means.

20–94   All of the above listed documents are provided in the language of the accused. For those accused who request the assignment of counsel claiming legal-aid, two documents of this list are of particular relevance: (1) a copy of the most up to date Rule 45-list as well as a (2) "declaration of means" which has to be filled out, certified, and submitted by the accused at a later date, as soon as possible (Articles 7, 9 of the Directive).

1) The Rule 45-list

20–95   The copy of the Rule 45-list provided to the accused contains relevant and detailed information on the listed counsel that will be of value to the accused when choosing a lawyer to represent him or her before the Tribunal. For instance, the profiles contained in the document will provide information as to, *inter alia*, the counsel's legal education and experiences; the year of his or her admission to the bar and the country or countries of admission to practice; whether counsel is or has in the past represented accused before the Tribunal, as well as contact details. Accused can request further details on the background of counsel, and will be provided additional information if available.

2) Declaration of Means

20–96   The declaration of means is an important form that the Registry needs to have completed by the accused in order to determine his or her level of indigence and the extent to which the accused may be able to remunerate counsel. For that reason, the standard form provided by the Registry contains questions which are aimed at deciphering the financial situation of the accused.[34]

While for the actual request for the assignment of counsel there is no similar standard form, it is required for the accused to make such request in writing and to sign it in order for it to be received and accepted by the Registry. In most cases, such written requests are written in the native language of the accused (*e.g.* Bosnian/Croatian/Serbian, ("B/C/S")), which then are translated by the Registry. Requests will usually be passed through the detention facility management to the Registry for consideration.

20–97

Assignment of Duty Counsel and Temporary Assignment

Since July 2004, in accordance with Rules 45(C) and 62(B) of the RPE and Articles 14(B) and 16(F) of the Directive, the Tribunal has put in place a system where the Registry will assign duty counsel if it deems this appropriate and in the interests of justice. In the period between August 2004 and June 2005, 23 new accused arrived at the seat of The Hague. Hence, the new system has had abundant opportunity to be tested.[35] In 19 cases, duty counsel were assigned for the purposes of the "initial appearance"—out of those cases, nine delayed their plea until assignment of counsel other than duty counsel had been effected, while three others also delayed their plea, but decided to represent themselves at subsequent appearances. In *Prosecutor v Rasim Delic*, the notion of duty counsel versus counsel of choice was put to the test and litigated (see paragraphs 20–108 *et seq.*). Mostly, duty counsel were assigned in cases where the Registry identified potential conflicts of interest related to the counsel of preference from the accused, or in cases where accused had not yet made a choice from the Rule 45-list. As mentioned previously, for the purpose of assigning duty counsel, in accordance with Rule 45(C), the Registry retains a list of experienced counsel, who will be available on short notice to act as duty counsel for the limited purposes of the accused's initial appearances. The high number of cases, in which pleas were postponed by accused awaiting the temporary assignment of counsel, shows some discomfort with the system change. Following the lessons learned from the first experiences at the Tribunal, in June 2005, the Registry and the ADC have agreed on a

20–98

---

[34] The declaration of means, in essence, provides the Registry with vital information in order to determine whether the suspect or accused is unable to remunerate counsel. As Article 8(B) provides, in reaching such determination, account shall be taken of "[...] means of all kinds of which he [the accused] has direct or indirect enjoyment or freely disposes, including but not limited to direct income, bank accounts, real or personal property, pensions, and stocks, bonds, or other assets held, but excluding any family or social benefits to which he may be entitled. In assessing such means, account shall also be taken of the means of the spouse of a suspect or accused, as well as those of persons with whom he habitually resides, provided that it is reasonable to take such means into account": see Article 8(B) of the Directive.

[35] See, *e.g. Prosecutor v Miletić*, Case No. IT-04–80-I, Decision of the Deputy Registrar, March 2, 2005; *Prosecutor v Perišić*, Case No. IT-04–81-I, Decision of the Registrar, March 9, 2005; *Prosecutor v Brahimaj*, Case No. IT-04–84-PT, Decision of the Registrar, March 11, 2005.

joint proposal for an amendment to the RPE and the Directive, to more clearly define what the duties of a duty counsel entail and what they do not entail. At the time of writing the proposal is before the Rules Committee and included in the pending proposed amendments to the Directive.

20–99   Although the accused regularly solicit advice from the Registry on a choice of counsel, it has been the strict *modus operandi* of the Registry to exert restraint in rendering such advice in the interest of neutrality. The Registry, if so requested, informs an accused of the profiles of counsel on the Rule 45-list, which would meet his wishes, as well as provide information on which counsel are not available to be assigned due to their commitments to other cases being heard before the Tribunal. Counsel may be tempted but are strictly prohibited from soliciting from potential clients: see Article 30(ii) of the Code of Conduct where it is stated that counsel: "shall *not* solicit work from a prospective client, if: 1. the prospective client, his relatives or acquaintances have made known to counsel a desire not to be solicited by counsel; or 2. the solicitation involves behaviour such as fraud, undue influence, coercion, duress or harassment." Moreover, the Registry also forewarns the accused that their choice of counsel is subject to further inquiries by the Registry to ensure that no actual or potential conflict of interest exists between counsel and client (for discussion on conflicts of interest and choice of counsel, see paragraphs 20–108 *et seq.*).

20–100   Pursuant to Rule 45(A) of the RPE and Article 11 of the Directive, while examining the declaration of means submitted by an accused who has requested the assignment of counsel, the Registry may temporarily assign counsel, when it is in the interests of justice to do so. These provisions have been included to make sure the right to counsel under Article 21(4) (d) of the Statute are respected, while the determination of the indigency of the accused is being assessed. This initial assignment will be for a period of 120 days (Article 11(B) of the Directive), and may be extended. The assignment is temporary until the Registry has completed its financial assessment and rendered a decision on the eligibility for legal-aid and assignment of counsel under Article 11(A) of the Directive. The Registrar applies Article 11(B) consistently, and has in 95 per cent of the cases temporarily assigned counsel. The texts of Rule 45(A) of the RPE and Article 11(B) of the Directive link the right to assignment of counsel to the interests of justice, and appear to leave some discretion to the Registrar when deciding upon temporary assignments. The Registrar has relied on this narrow area of discretion only once so far and, hence, its interpretation has not been much developed in jurisprudence. The Registrar applied his discretion in a case where an accused had not been cooperative in having the Registrar assess his financial situation.[36] Other situations cannot be excluded. Nevertheless, it is apparent that the Registry will not easily make such a decision. A refusal to assign temporary counsel could be interpreted as a violation

---

[36] In the *Prlić et al.* case, the Registry decided to deny a request for assignment under Article 11(B) of the Directive arguing that the accused had obstructed the Registry's inquiries into his financial status and hence not met his burden of proof to show that he had insufficient means to retain and remunerate his own counsel, *Prosecutor v Praljak*, Case No. IT–04–74–PT, Decision of the Deputy Registrar, June 17, 2005. The Chamber upheld the Registrar's decision on September 21, 2005 (decision filed confidentially and *ex parte*, note 15 above.

of the right of the accused to be represented by counsel, if for instance, such refusal will preclude him from being assisted in preparations of a motion before Chambers to challenge the decision of the Registrar on the status of his indigency. Depending on other circumstances, it is conceivable that in such a case, the interests of justice would require that the assignment be granted and allowed to continue pending the Chambers' review of the Registrar's decision.[37]

Assignment of Counsel Away from the Seat of the Tribunal: Suspects

Article 17 of the Directive sets out the basic structure for assignment of counsel away from the Seat of the Tribunal or otherwise termed as "assignments to *suspects*". They usually take place in the region. Suspects have similar rights under the Statute as accused to the assignment of counsel in case of (partial) indigency. The article is mostly used in situations when a suspect requires the benefit of counsel in interviews with the Tribunal's Office of the Prosecutor—interviews which can last anywhere between a few hours to a number of days, and in rare cases up to several months. In one exceptional case, a longstanding witness before the Tribunal became a suspect and, hence, subject to a series of interviews conducted by the Office of the Prosecutor, which lasted approximately six months. The person has subsequently been indicted and is now awaiting trial. In the practice of the Registry when considering such assignments, emphasis is placed upon the fact that suspects require quick, non-bureaucratic assistance in the protection of their rights.

20–101

Consequently, the procedure for verification of the financial status of an accused and the qualifications of a counsel and his assignment is much accelerated. The Registry, as a matter of course, requires a written confirmation by the Office of the Prosecutor that a person is a "suspect" as defined by the RPE ("A person concerning whom the Prosecutor possesses reliable information which tends to show that the person may have committed a crime over which the Tribunal has jurisdiction": Rule 2) a copy of a professional identity card of the requested counsel, a declaration of means and request for assignment by the suspect. Normally, the Registry will make direct contact with the suspect to explain him his rights independently from the Prosecutor, unless there is immediate urgency. Once in possession of the indicated documents, the Registry will assign the counsel as requested.

20–102

Short-term Assignments

Short term assignments are considered in cases where a potential conflict of interest with counsel exists. Such assignments are usually granted for a limited period of time and with a clear mandate.

20–103

---

[37] Other circumstances to take into account are—factually—the timing of the request for legal-aid, the assessment of the financial status on the basis of existing information and evidence and—legally—the interpretation of the burden of proof under Article 8(A) of the Directive.

Temporary assignments were previously made in cases of potential conflicts of interest of requested counsel, when the duty counsel system had not yet been put into place. Otherwise and more recently, temporary assignments have been made in cases of conflicts between accused and his counsel, or between counsel within one defence team.[38]

Choice of the Accused

20–104 Article 21(4)(d) of the Statute of the Tribunal establishes that an accused has the right to defend himself through legal assistance of his own choosing. Other than by the conditions set by the RPE, the Code of Conduct and the Directive, no further limitations on this right are apparent under the Tribunal's legal regime. Nevertheless, as will be delineated below in paragraphs 20–108 *et seq.*, the Tribunal's jurisprudence has in fact quite substantially defined limits on the right of an indigent or partially indigent accused to choose counsel. This has, however, not always been so clear and the Registry has in its early years taken a very tolerant approach towards the choice of an accused.

Fee-splitting

20–105 A phenomenon called "fee-splitting" is a consequence of a number of factors which include the initial liberal approach of the Tribunal vis-à-vis the choice of counsel of indigent accused. Article 18 of the Code of Conduct defines and deals with this notion: "arrangements, including but not limited to financial arrangements, between assigned counsel and their clients, relatives and/or agents of their clients are prohibited by the Tribunal." The term describes situations in which an accused and his assigned counsel conspire to have counsel transfer a substantial sum of the monies he lawfully earns at the Tribunal to the accused or to persons close to the accused, such as family, friends or other counsel functioning as trustees. This practice is clearly unethical for counsel and is a clear violation of the Code of Conduct. If and when an accused is discovered to be receiving kickbacks through this plotted scheme, he or she will immediately be denied indigent status. It must be noted that this notion has only been developed and introduced into the Code of Conduct as of July 12, 2002, following repeated allegations of fee-splitting arrangements.[39]

---

[38] See *Prosecutor v Martić*, Case No. IT-95–11-PT, Decision of the Deputy Registrar where Counsel Mr Strahinja Kastratović was Temporarily Assigned Pending Further Clarification of the Potential Conflict of Interest, May 31, 2002; *Prosecutor v Blagojević et al.*, Case No. IT-02–60A (Trial Chamber) Order on the Appointment of Independent Counsel, May 9, 2003, and Decision of the Registrar, May 23, 2003, where independent counsel (Mr Jan Sjöcrona) was assigned to mediate in a conflict between counsel and accused, for the purpose of advising the accused of his rights in relation to assignment of counsel, and assisting him in preparing documentation if any, that may follow from their consultation on these issues; see also *Prosecutor v Sefer Halilović*, Case No. IT-01–48-PT, in which the Registrar assigned independent councel (Karim Khan) to mediate in a conflict between the two counsel and lead counsel and the client.

[39] The Code of Conduct for Defence Counsel Appearing before the International Tribunal has only been amended once since its inception on July 12, 2002 (IT/125 Rev. 1). The inclusion of provisions dealing with "fee-splitting" formed part of the 2002 amendments.

The view has been expressed that if counsel were strictly chosen by **20–106** the Registrar, or if counsel could be easily replaced, less of an incentive would exist for assigned counsel to implicate themselves in such fraudulent schemes. Thus far, the Tribunal has been witness to only a single confirmed case of "fee-splitting", where the accused had his legal-aid withdrawn by the Registrar based on tangible evidence that the accused had received substantial monies from his former counsel.[40] There are, however, additional cases where fee-splitting is suspected and a number of allegations as to fee-splitting have been made.[41] While investigations may still be pending, it is noticeable that not one case since the Zigic case has revealed enough evidence to formally institute the necessary actions against the accused and their counsel. As so often, there is a discrepancy between the amount of rumours and allegations and actual evidence. It may be assumed that in some cases the allegations are untrue whereas in others the allegations themselves are credible but cannot be sufficiently sustained for the Registry to initiate action.

It must be noted that the Tribunal's initial liberal attitude towards **20–107** the choice of counsel is only one of the causes of fee-splitting. Other factors must have influenced and caused the development of this phenomenon. The initial lack of strict qualification requirements for counsel, the initial absence of an active disciplinary regime for counsel and a more stringent Code of Conduct, as well as the absence of active monitoring bodies and mechanisms are all relevant factors. In this respect, it must be noted that several initiatives have been taken which, aside from improving different aspects of the Tribunal's legal-aid system, have had a positive impact on the suppression of this phenomenon. The introduction of the partial indigency system in the period 2000–2002, the revision of the Code of Conduct in 2002 introducing a disciplinary regime and prohibiting the phenomenon, the first disciplinary decisions of the Disciplinary Panel of the Tribunal and the official recognition of the ADC and its enhanced role in monitoring defence counsel performance, all assisted. Further, the sharpening of counsel's qualification requirements pursuant to the work of the Working Group, as previously mentioned, has assisted; the present state of the relevant Rules, Directive and Code of Conduct is much better than in previous years. Recently, in the period 2004–2005, the

---

[40] *Prosecutor v Žigić et al.*, Case No. IT-98–30/1-A, Decision of the Registrar Withdrawing the Assignment of Counsel to the Accused and to Discontinue the Provision of Legal Aid to the Accused, July 8, 2002. The decision of the Registrar was finally upheld by the Appeals Chamber on February 7, 2003: see *Prosecutor v Žigić et al.*, Case No. IT-98–30/1-A, Decision on Review of the Registrar's Decision to Withdraw Legal Aid from Zoran Žigić, February 7, 2003.

[41] For an example case where serious but non-specific allegations against an accused were made by his counsel, see *Prosecutor v Blagojević*, Case No. IT-02–60-T, Decision on Independent Counsel for Vidoje Blagojević's Motion to Instruct the Registrar to Appoint New Lead and Co-counsel, July 3, 2003, para. 47, where counsel's response to the independent counsel's motion, filed confidentially is referred to as saying that a person proposed by the accused as co-counsel, in counsel's view, was "unqualified to be co-counsel and may engage in practices or defence strategies which lead counsel did and would not support". The lifting of confidentiality of certain filings and motions and an assertion of having considered the relevant interests is dealt with by the Chamber in the introduction of the decision.

Registry has also tackled several cases in which financial irregularities were identified. It has addressed several counsel and initialled a small number of disciplinary complaints. If the present, increased level of cooperation and coordination between Registry and the ADC—which has installed its own disciplinary body in addition to the existing one at the Tribunal—persists, it is hoped that existing and past fee-splitting cases be brought to light and the phenomenon itself will diminish to eventually disappear.

B. RIGHT TO CHOICE OF COUNSEL AND CONFLICTS OF INTEREST

Right to Choice of Counsel: A Fundamental Right

20–108   Article 21(4) of the ICTY Statute reads:

> "In the determination of any charge against the accused pursuant to the present Statute, the accused shall *be entitled to the following minimum guarantees, in full equality*: [...]
> (b) to have adequate time and facilities for the preparation of his defence *and to communicate with counsel of his own choosing*; [...]
> (d) to be tried in his presence, and to defend himself in person or *through legal assistance of his own choosing; to be informed, if he does not have legal assistance, of this right; and to have legal assistance assigned to him, in any case where the interests of justice so require, and without payment by him in any such case if he does not have sufficient means to pay for it*."

20–109   The RPE and the Directive aim to implement and elaborate the rights granted by the Statute. Article 6 of the Directive and Article 45(A) of the RPE extend the right to legal representation to indigent or partially indigent accused. Rule 45(A) of the RPE states that "(w)henever the interests of justice so demand, counsel shall be assigned to suspects or accused who lack the means to remunerate such counsel [...]" and Article 6(A) of the Directive reiterates that "suspects or accused who lack the means to remunerate counsel shall be entitled to assignment of counsel paid for by the Tribunal". The question whether the right to legal representation also includes a right to have counsel of one's choosing assigned, and if so, whether this aspect of the right to legal representation applies unconditionally, has become subject of extensive litigation before the Tribunal. Through its jurisprudence, the Tribunal has adopted the view that the right of an indigent or partially indigent accused to legal representation does not entitle the accused to an automatic right to choose counsel, a view which reflects the view prevailing at other relevant international fora.

Limitations of the Accused's Right to Choose Counsel

A) The Right of an Indigent / Partially Indigent Accused

20–110   The Tribunal's Chambers have acknowledged that the primary responsibility for the assignment of counsel lies with the Registrar based upon his statutory power but have stressed their own statutory obligation to

ensure the fair and expeditious conduct of proceedings with full respect
for the rights of the accused. Therefore, they have found that the
Registrar's decisions on assignment are subject to judicial review in so
far as they may affect the fairness or integrity of the proceeding.[42]
Abundant jurisprudence on this point has developed within the Tribunal, expressing the unequivocal position that the ability of an accused
to choose his own counsel is *not* absolute and is limited when the
accused is the recipient of legal-aid [see above]. The right to free legal
assistance by counsel does not confer the right to choose one's counsel.

In the Trial Chamber decision in *Prosecutor v Blagojević et al.*, where
the accused had challenged the assignment of a co-counsel with whom
he did not agree, the Chamber formulated this position as follows,
reiterating an excerpt from a decision of the Appeals Chamber of the
ICTR in *Prosecutor v Akayesu*:

> "In principle, the right to free legal assistance of counsel does not confer
> the right to counsel of one's own choosing. The right to choose counsel
> applies only to those Accused who can financially bear the costs of counsel.
> [. . .]
> To be sure, in practice an indigent Accused may choose from among
> counsel included in the list and the Registrar generally takes into
> consideration the choice of the Accused. Nevertheless, in the opinion of
> the Appeals Chamber the Registrar is not necessarily bound by the wishes
> of an indigent Accused. He has wide discretion, which he exercises in the
> interest of justice."[43]

Later in the same case *Prosecutor v Blagojević et al.*, the Trial Chamber   **20–111**
again faced the question if the right to legal representation for indigent
accused also entails the right to counsel of one's own choosing, when
the accused requested replacement of both lead and co-counsel and his
entire defence team. The Chamber considered precedents at the
Tribunal and other relevant international tribunals and concluded:

> "In assessing whether assigned counsel for an accused should be with-
> drawn, it is for the person seeking withdrawal to satisfy the Registrar that
> he should exercise his discretion to withdraw such counsel 'in the interests
> of justice'. [. . .] The burden of proof is squarely on the person requesting
> the withdrawal of assigned counsel to demonstrate good cause [. . .]
> There is no absolute right for an indigent accused to choose his or her
> assigned counsel. This is a limited right, and it is within the Registrar's
> discretion to override the wishes of an accused if relevant and sufficient
> grounds exist for holding that this is necessary in the interests of
> justice."[44]

---

[42] See *Prosecutor v Hadžihasanović et al.*, Case No. IT-01–47-PT, note 31 above, para. 55; *Prosecutor v Knežević*, Case No. IT-95–4-PT, Decision on Accused's Request for Review of the Registrar's Decision as to Assignment of Counsel, September 6, 2002; *Prosecutor v Blagojević*, Case No. IT-02–60-PT, Decision on Oral Motion to Replace Co-counsel, December 9, 2002 ("*Blagojević* Trial Chamber Decision I"). The Appeals Chamber has confirmed this but clearly outlines the boundaries: "the only inherent power that a Trial Chamber has is to ensure that a trial of an accused is fait; it cannot appropriate for itself a power which is conferred elsewhere": *Prosecutor v Blagojević*, Case No. IT-02–60-AR73.4, Public and Redacted Reasons for Decision on Appeal by Vidoje Blagojević to Replace his Defence Team, November 7, 2003 ("*Blagojević* Appeals Chamber Decision") at para. 7.

[43] *Blagojević* Trial Chamber Decision I; *Prosecutor v Akayesu*, Case No. ICTR-96–4-A, June 1, 2001 at paras 61–62.

[44] *Prosecutor v Blagojević*, Case No. IT-02–60-T, Decision of the Trial Chamber on Independent Counsel for Vidoje Blagojević's Motion to Instruct the Registrar to Appoint New Lead and Co-counsel, July 3, 2003 ("*Blagojević* Trial Chamber Decision II") at para. 117.

20–112   The Appeals Chamber upheld the Trial Chamber's decisions in appeal.[45]

This finding is consistent with an overwhelming majority of jurisprudence at other international fora outside of the Tribunal, including the ICTR.[46] Therefore, all relevant subsequent decisions have confirmed that an indigent accused's right to choose counsel is a limited right and that the Registrar can infringe upon it, if he finds it to be in the interests of justice to do so. Hence, the jurisprudence of the Tribunal has laid the matter to rest. While the Registrar should endeavour to accommodate the expressed preference of an indigent accused for a specific counsel, he is not bound by the accused's choice but will make an assessment of the interests of justice in the circumstances.

20–113   As to how much weight the Registrar should place on the accused's preference(s), the Appeals Chamber confirmed the Trial Chamber's view in *Prosecutor v Blagojević*, as cited above: "the Registrar *may [...] override [an accused's] preference if it considers that it is in the interest of justice to do so*."[47] The Trial Chamber had previously identified a non-exhaustive list of relevant factors to be taken into account by the Registrar in assessing whether the requested withdrawal of counsel would be in the interests of justice: "fulfilment of professional obligations and responsibilities; satisfaction of qualification requirements [...]; the existence of a conflict of interest; engagement in any form of misconduct; and performing responsibilities with diligence, competence and loyalty towards the client."[48] As a matter of practice, the Registry does take an accused's preference into account and attempts to have the counsel of preference assigned in most cases, after having done the necessary inquiries to ensure that the counsel in question meets the necessary requirements of the RPE and the Directive. These inquiries include, as stressed by Trial and Appeals Chamber, the verification that no conflict of interests (or other impediments) exist or may arise from the assignment.

B) The Choice of Counsel and Conflicts of Interests

20–114   Article 14, and 14(D) in particular, of the Tribunal's Code of Conduct creates a strict prohibition on representing an accused where a conflict of interest might be triggered by such representation and/or the

---

[45] *Blagojević* Appeals Chamber Decision, see note 42 above.
[46] See *Prosecutor v Akayesu*, note 43 above; *Prosecutor v Kambanda*, Case No. ICTR-97–23 A, September 19, 2000; *Prosecutor v Ntakirtimana*, Case No. ICTR-96–10, June 11, 1997; *Croissant v Germany*, ECHR, No. 62/1991/314/385, September 25, 1992; *Aston Little v Jamaica*, communication No. 283/1988; *Wright & Harvey v Jamaica*, communication No. 459/1991, UN Doc. CCPR/C/55/D/459/1991 (1995); *Kenneth Teesdale v Trinidad and Tobago*, 677/1996; *F. v Swiss Confederation*, Application No. 12152/86, Decision of May 9, 1989. See also the President's Decision in *Prosecutor v Šljivančanin*, Case No. IT-95–13/1-PT, Decision on Assignment of Defence Counsel, August 20, 2003, at paras 19–20; and for a recent decision: *Prosecutor v Delić*, Case No. IT-04–83-PT, Decision of the Trial Chamber Dismissing the Motion of the Accused Seeking Review of the Registry Decision stating that Mr Bourgon Cannot be Assigned to Represent Rasim Delić, May 10, 2005.
[47] *Blagojević* Appeals Chamber Decision, para. 22.
[48] *Blagojević* Trial Chamber Decision II, para. 116.

interests of the accused could be adversely affected. Counsel who breach this rule are subject to strict disciplinary measures.[49] A lawyer's duty of loyalty to his client is a basic obligation of the counsel-client relationship. It is universally agreed that clients are entitled to counsel whose representation are not limited by obligations to other present or past relationships. Consequently, as a matter of principle, counsel should not impede their client relationships with conflicts of interests. Therefore, actual or potential conflicts of interest pose a justified limit to the accused's choice of counsel, as has been recognized in Tribunal jurisprudence. An accused's preferred choice of a lawyer who is unable to advance his interests effectively due to a conflict should therefore be rejected.

1) Basic test for conflict of interest

The jurisprudence of the Tribunal has defined the basic test for the Registry's and Trial Chamber's interference with the choice of counsel on the basis of conflict of interest. To arrive at the basic test, it had to be understood what exactly a conflict of interest entails. In an early decision in the *Prosecutor v Simić et al.*, the Trial Chamber stated: **20–115**

> "A conflict of interest between an attorney and a client arises in any situation where, by reason of certain circumstances, representation by such an attorney prejudices, or could prejudice, the interests of the client and the wider interests of justice."[50]

In the recent case *Prosecutor v Prlić et al.*, the Trial Chamber describes the potential consequences of a conflict of interest for the defence of the accused or conduct of the proceedings: **20–116**

> "The existence, or risk of conflict of interest may impact on the conduct of the trial. Counsel may be reluctant to pursue a line of defence, to adduce certain items in evidence, or to plead certain mitigating factors at the sentencing stage, in order to avoid prejudicing another client. He may thus be prevented from providing full and complete assistance to his client. There is also a risk that a conflict of interest arises in the course of trial, which may prompt counsel to withdraw [...], thereby causing delay in the proceedings, to the detriment of the accused."[51]

In *Prosecutor v Prlić et al.* and *Prosecutor v Mejakić et al.*,[52] the Chambers establish the basic test. Once it has identified an actual or potential conflict, it falls within Chamber's duties to "assess factors such as the **20–117**

---

[49] See, *e.g.* Code of Conduct, Articles 35, 37–50; see *Prosecutor v Prlić et al.*, Case No. IT-04–74-PT, Decision on Requests for Appointment of Counsel, July 30, 2004 ("*Prlić* Trial Chamber Decision"), para. 14.

[50] *Prosecutor v Simić et al.*, Case No.IT-95–9-PT, March 25, 1999, Decision on the Prosecution Motion to Resolve Conflict of Interest Regarding Attorney Borislav Pisarević.

[51] *Prlić* Trial Chamber Decision, para. 15.

[52] *Prlić* Trial Chamber Decision; *Prosecutor v Prlić et al*, Case No. IT-04–74-AR73.1, Decision on Appeal by Bruno Stojić Against Trial chamber's Decision on Request for Appointment of Counsel, November 24, 2004 ("*Prlić* Appeals Chamber Decision"); *Prosecutor v Mejakić et al.*, Case No. IT-02–65-AR73.1, Decision on Appeal by the Prosecution to Resolve Conflict of Interest Regarding Counsel Jovan Simić, October 6, 2004.

objective likelihood of conflict and the harm that could be caused to the accused and the proceedings [...]. [T]he Trial Chamber determines whether the *risks and damage that could be caused are such as to jeopardise the right of the accused to a fair and expeditious trial or proper administration of justice* and, if it finds that that is so, takes the appropriate measures to restore or protect the fairness of trial and the integrity of the proceeding."[53] This is the real test and the basis for the Chamber's or the Registry's interference, its adverse effect on the fairness of the trial (including an accused's rights) and the integrity of the proceedings. Further decisions of the Appeals and Trial Chambers of the Tribunal have provided guidance as to specific circumstances although it is noted that the jurisprudence is very diverse and in full development.

2) Responsibilities of counsel; verification by the Registry and Chambers *ab initio*

20–118   Under its present Article 14, the Code of Conduct prescribes a detailed regime for counsel's conduct in case of existing, arising or potential conflicts of interests. Counsel should in the first place refrain from representation in case of a conflict which disadvantages one client (Article 14(D)) and, in case one arises after assignment, he shall inform his clients fully and promptly of the conflict and take all steps to remove it (Article 14 (E) Code of Conduct). Both the Registry and Chambers have pointed out the responsibilities of counsel. In the *Prosecutor v Prlić et al.*, the Trial Chamber quite extensively elaborates on the duties of counsel, stemming both from his "duty of loyalty to a client" and the "duty to the Tribunal to act with independence in the interests of justice":

> "An accused should be prevented from choosing counsel who is unable to defend him to the best of his interests. Under Article 14 of the [Code of Conduct], a counsel must refrain from representing a client when such representation is, or may reasonably be expected to, affect, or be affected by, the representation of another of his current or former clients."[54]

20–119   The Trial Chamber in *Prlić et al.* first professes its restraint in view of counsel's own professional obligations and his more suitable position to assess the consequences of a conflict, immediately to proceed by stressing its own statutory obligations to protect the integrity of the proceedings.[55] In similar cases where conflicts related to *assigned* counsel, Chambers had acknowledged the Registrar's primary responsibility in matters related to the assignment of counsel but confirmed that where the Directive does not provide a specific procedure for the removal of counsel in case of a conflict of interest, Chambers can rely on its inherent power to review an assignment matter.[56] It is obvious, the Registrar and Chambers must act pursuant to their respective

---

[53] *Prlić* Trial Chamber Decision, para. 16.
[54] *ibid.*, paras 13–14.
[55] *ibid.*, paras 14–16.
[56] *Prosecutor v Mejakić et al.*, note 52 above, para. 7.

responsibilities: the Registrar's responsibility for the assignment of counsel in the interests of justice and the Trial Chambers' general statutory obligation under Articles 20 and 21 of the Statute and inherent duty to protect the integrity of proceedings. Hence, even in instances where the choice of the accused has been sanctioned by the Registrar or where the Registrar has not acted, the Chambers may intervene and, if needed, reassign or instruct the Registrar to reassign counsel.[57] Because of its possible damaging impact on the proceedings later, it is incumbent upon the Registrar and the Trial Chamber, in their respective roles, to assess the matter of actual or potential conflict of interests at the outset.

Jurisprudence has confirmed that conflicts of interest are to be avoided *ab initio*. As pronounced in *Prosecutor v Mejakić et al.*:   **20–120**

> "Replacement of lead counsel inevitably causes delays and disrupts the conduct of the proceedings. It could even cause irreparable prejudice to the accused, as it may be difficult for the new counsel to alter the defence strategy adopted by his predecessor and plead the case as he would have, had he represented the client from the beginning of the case. *Replacement of counsel during proceedings should be avoided to the extent possible and a Trial Chamber*, under its inherent powers to ensure a fair and expeditious trial and proper administration of justice, will generally not allow withdrawal of counsel in the course of the proceedings [...]".[58]

In *Prosecutor v Hadžihasanović et al.*, the Trial Chamber stated that: **20–121** "(t)he Chamber cannot wait until foreseeable harm is done to the proceedings. It is for the Chamber to prevent such foreseeable harm."[59]

The Registrar will not hesitate to bring an actual or potential conflict **20–122** to the attention of counsel and Chambers also in cases where counsel are retained under Rule 44 of the RPE, as it did recently in the case *Prosecutor v Prlić et al.* The case involves the joined indictments of six Croat and Bosnian Croat co-defendants transferred to the Tribunal on April 5, 2004. None of the accused at that time had applied for legal-aid. Upon examining the powers of attorneys provided by the accused, the Registrar arrived at the view that in three cases, a conflict of interest could arise and invited the lawyers involved to submit the matter for clarification to the Trial Chamber. The Trial Chamber confirmed the concerns of the Registry and found the potential conflict strong enough to bar one of the three lawyers from being assigned on the ground that he was also representing other defendants before the Tribunal on charges arising from "the same or similar factual situations" as those charged against the accused being represented in the case at issue: "the Trial Chamber finds that a conflict of interest is very likely to arise and that such likelihood will very likely prevent [counsel] from defending [accused] in the best of his interests."[60]

---

[57] *Prlić* Trial Chamber Decision, para. 16. The Appeals chamber concurred: *Prlić* Appeals Chamber Decision, para. 21; also in *Prosecutor v Mejakić et al.*, note 52 above, paras 14–15.
[58] *Prosecutor v Mejakić et al.*, note 52 above, para. 31.
[59] *Prosecutor v Hadžihasanović et al.*, note 31 above, para. 45.
[60] *Prlić* Trial Chamber Decision, paras 13–16, 29–32.

3) Situations of conflict: counsel of choice cannot be assigned

20–123   Hence, Tribunal jurisprudence confirms that where the Registrar or the Trial Chamber is of the view that a *de facto* conflict of interest or the potential of one arising in the future exists, it may be justified to limit the right of the accused to choose counsel, in order to protect the integrity of the proceedings. There are many instances where the impact of a conflict of interest on the integrity of the proceedings will bar counsel's assignment or require his withdrawal.

20–124   A clear instance occurs where counsel's multiple representation of accused and/or co-defendants prevents or may prevent him from employing a defence strategy which could have otherwise been used for the benefit of the accused. In the *Prosecutor v Mejakić et al.*, there was a high probability that at some point in the proceedings one of the two accused represented by counsel might be called as a witness in the other accused's trial. It was also certain that the Office of the Prosecutor intended to interview the accused prior to making the decision whether to call this accused as a witness, making it difficult for counsel to properly represent the interests of the accused separately. The Appeals Chamber decided that in the circumstances of the case, there was clearly a conflict of interest and that this could adversely influence "the defence strategy" that counsel would have otherwise been able to employ had he solely been representing one of the two accused.[61]

20–125   Similarly, the Trial Chamber in *Prosecutor v Prlić et al.* found that where two accused were charged with the same criminal acts and were allegedly linked by a relatively close superior-subordinate relationship at the relevant time, a conflict of interest is likely to arise, if not already existing. The Trial Chamber further finds that this will very likely prevent counsel from defending one of the accused's best interests which, were this to arise in the proceedings, would substantially impact the course of the proceedings, which is not in the interests of justice. The Appeals Chamber has upheld this.[62]

20–126   The problem being that the conflict will create the unwanted situation where defence counsel will be hesitant to invoke a defence for one accused out of fears that it may compromise the case of the other accused he represents. There is a real danger that defence counsel would engage in a balancing act of the interests of both accused, as opposed to vigorously defending each one of them. Counsel: "may not be able to diligently and promptly protect his clients' best interests as expected and required of counsel: to suggest compromise rather than to pursue, without any restriction, the interests of his clients, is in contradiction with the counsel's professional obligations."[63] Further, a consequence may be that the question of testimony in one's case becomes an issue. Although the defence may choose not to use one

---

[61] The Appeals Chamber overturned the Trial Chamber which had estimated that it had not been satisfied at that stage that the conflict of interest was likely to affect the integrity of the proceedings and stressed that the conflict of interest did exist at this stage of the proceeding and had to be resolved now, *Prosecutor v Mejaki*, note 52 above, paras 9–12, 15.

[62] *Prlić* Trial Chamber Decision, paras 29–31; *Prlić* Appeals Chamber Decision, para. 24.

[63] *Prlić* Trial Chamber Decision, para. 29.

defendant to testify against the other initially, the temptation might be there in the future to do so. Defence counsel is caught in a catch 22. If he does not explore this option to the full, he may forgo a potential strategic advantage for one accused by balancing the interests of both accused. Alternatively, the prosecution may call an accused to testify against the other in the future. The defence again will be put in a position where it may have to restrain the defence of one person so as to protect the other. Where several accused are charged with the same crimes, there is a real risk that such situations will materialise.

Lastly, the Trial Chamber in *Prosecutor v Hadžihasanović* declared that: "the appearance of a just procedure is as important as a just result for a fair trial."[64] Given the close "nexus" which may exist between the accused being defended by the same counsel, the appearance that a counsel who represents both accused would be tempted to balance their interests as opposed to advance their cause is to be avoided. The importance of the appearance of a just procedure, calls for separate representation in such cases irrespective of the accused's preferred choice of counsel.   **20–127**

The above instances are illustrative of the reluctance of Chambers and the Registrar to have the same counsel defend different accused who have been involved in similar crimes, during a similar time period and location. Article 16(E) of the Directive now explicitly prohibits counsel from representing two accused, where such representation might be prejudicial to the interests of the accused or cause a potential conflict of interest. In the above examples, at least two counsel were barred from representing specific clients.   **20–128**

Conversely, both the Registrar and Chambers have in a number of cases assessed that the conflict of interest either was remote or minimal and had no adverse effect on the rights of the accused or the fairness of trial or was unlikely to materialize in future. In the mentioned *Prlić et al.* case, the Trial Chamber accepted arguments of two of the three counsel. "While [...] a superior-subordinate relationship does exist [...], the apparent remoteness of one from the other in the alleged hierarchy ensures that the likelihood for potential conflict of interest between them is acceptably low."[65] The Chamber took into account that the counsel would act as co-counsel which, in its view, reduced the risk for disruption and delays of the proceeding if a withdrawal because of conflict at a later stage would materialize. The Chamber also assessed the thoroughness of the conflict check undertaken by counsel himself. (See further examples in paragraphs 20–132 to 20–135.)   **20–129**

4) Conflicts that may arise in the future (potential conflicts)

If the Registrar or the Trial Chamber concludes that a given situation does not constitute an existing but simply a risk that a conflict of interest will arise in the future, that may in and of itself be sufficient to bar the accused's choice of counsel, if the continued representation of the client by that counsel would cause a potential infringement upon   **20–130**

---

[64] *Prosecutor v Hadžihasanović*, note 31 above, para. 46.
[65] *Prlić* Trial Chamber Decision, paras 43–44; *Prlić* Appeals Chamber Decision, paras 24, 25.

the right of the accused to fair and expeditious proceedings. Both the Registrar and several Chambers have addressed such cases. As noted by the Trial Chamber in *Prosecutor v Prlić et al.*: "(t)here is also a risk that a conflict of interest arises in the course of a trial, which may prompt counsel to withdraw from a case, thereby causing a delay in proceedings, to the detriment of the accused", a view which was upheld by the Appeals Chamber.[66]

20–131   In the *Prosecutor v Delić et al.*, the Registrar initially informed the accused that his preferred choice of counsel could not be assigned due to a *potential* conflict of interest. To have assigned the counsel of choice who was at the same time assigned to an accused in a related case (*Hadžihasanović*) would have been asking counsel to embark on dual representation and to work in a situation where the defence of one of the accused could well be opposed to the defence of the other with respect to some of the crimes for which both accused were indicted. This necessitated the Registrar's interference because of a *prima facie* potential conflict of interest. Delić filed a motion before the Trial Chamber to review the Registrar's decision not to have his counsel of choice assigned as lead counsel. The motion was dismissed, as the Trial Chamber supported the Registrar's assessment that a conflict of interest might arise in the case as both accused are charged, in part, with the same crimes and are linked by a relatively close superior-subordinate relationship at the relevant time.[67] This potential conflict could, therefore, have the effect of damaging the integrity of the proceedings or delay the trial when the conflict revealed itself at a later stage and counsel would need to be replaced at that time.

5) Other examples; test of prejudice to accused and/or proceedings

20–132   Conflicts of interest could also arise in instances where former staff of the Tribunal have changed roles and transferred over to work as defence counsel. This scenario occurred with respect to two defence counsel, both in relation to the case of *Prosecutor v Hadžihasanović et al.* In that case , the Registry first had to determine if a counsel, who had served as a legal adviser for the Office of the Prosecutor for approximately three years, and a chef de cabinet for the President of the Tribunal, could be assigned as co-counsel for the accused, Enver Hadžihasanović. Relying on a series of factors (including but not limited to the fact that the counsel concerned had signed a detailed affidavit confirming he had no conflict of interest), the Registrar concluded that based on the information made available to it at the time, the prior involvement of the counsel concerned with the Office of the Prosecutor did not constitute a conflict of interest which could reasonably affect the interests of justice, and granted the assignment. However, the Registrar left open the possibility that the counsel concerned could be withdrawn, if it became apparent at a later stage that a conflict of interests existed or was triggered after the assignment.[68]

---

[66] *Prosecutor v Hadžihasanović*, note 31 above, para. 46.

[67] Case No. IT-04–83-PT, Decision on Motion Seeking Review of the Registry Decision stating that Mr Bourgon Cannot be Assigned to Represent Rasim Delić, May 10, 2005.

[68] *Prosecutor v Hadžihasanović et al.*, Case No. IT-01–47-PT, Decision of Registrar on the Assignment of Counsel, December 19, 2001.

A similar contentious assignment in the same case was in relation to **20–133**
counsel to be assigned as co-counsel for the accused Amir Kubura by
the Deputy Registrar. The prosecution in the case brought a motion
before the Trial Chamber to have the assignment reviewed based on
the grounds that prior to private legal practice, the counsel concerned
had been a legal advisor with the Office of the Prosecutor for over four
years and for that reason a conflict of interest existed which was bound
to improperly prejudice the outcome of the proceedings. The Registry
followed the procedure which it has established in such cases: first, to
consult the parties as to whether there may be a potential conflict of
interest before the assignment is approved; secondly, where a party
alleges a conflict of interest, to verify, on the basis of the materials
presented whether the alleged conflict would be likely to prejudice the
outcome of the proceedings, or result in an improper advantage or
disadvantage for one of the parties; and further, to review the materials
to see whether the alleged conflict could result in a potential disadvantage to the accused.[69–70]

Having followed the above procedure, the Registry was of the view **20–134**
that there was insufficient evidence to conclude that the assignment of
the counsel concerned would likely prejudice the outcome of the trial
improperly, cause an unfair advantage to the defence, or result in
material disadvantage to the Office of the Prosecutor. The Trial
Chamber's reasoning elucidates the issue of how to treat instances
where a conflict of interest might arise from the fact that former
employees of Office of the Prosecutor have moved to the defence. As
articulated by presiding Judge Schomburg:

> "On the specific question of how to assess possible conflicts of interests
> between former employees of the Prosecution now assigned to defend an
> accused before the Tribunal, [...] (t)he Chamber could *therefore only address
> this question by remaining as close as possible to the general, but fundamental, duty to
> ensure the integrity of proceedings. The Chamber has developed the test that a real
> possibility must be proved that there is a conflict of interest between the former and
> present assignment of counsel. The most obvious example of such a conflict would if the
> counsel, now representing the accused, had worked for the Prosecution on the very same
> case against this very accused. That has not been established (here). In all other
> possible cases, the Chamber must be careful in drawing conclusions too readily."*[71]

The Trial Chamber concluded that the prosecution did not demon- **20–135**
strate a link between the counsel's involvement with the Office of the
Prosecutor and the case against Mr Kubura and any consequent
prejudice to its outcome.[72] The Trial Chamber refused to disqualify the
counsel as co-counsel, since, although he had worked on a number of
cases which were to a certain extent factually related to the case of the
accused, there was a "lack of more concrete indicators of a real possible
conflict of interest".[73] From the examples above, it is clear that Registry

---

[69–70] *Prosecutor v Hadžihasanović*, Decision by the Registrar on the Assignment of Counsel,
   November 26, 2001.
[71] *Prosecutor v Hadžihasanović et al.*, Trial Chamber Decision, note 31 above, para. 56.
[72] *ibid.*, para. 54.
[73] *ibid.*

and/or Chamber will have to undertake a fact finding exercise before being able to make a determination in the circumstances of the case: every case has its own specifics.

6) Consent of accused

20–136   Article 14(E) of the Code of Conduct places a positive duty on counsel to inform their clients of a potential conflict of interest related to their representation, fully and promptly and either (i) take all steps to remove the conflict or (ii) obtain full and informed consent of all potentially affected clients, "unless such consent is likely to irreversibly prejudice the administration of justice." This last phrase may be interpreted to mean—in light of the Tribunal's jurisprudence—that in case the consent itself is expected to have an adverse affect on the proceedings of one or the other accused, counsel is expected to stop the representation forthwith.

20–137   The Tribunal's jurisprudence indeed has placed little weight on the accused's consent to have legal representation continue where conflicts of interest exist. In *Prosecutor v Mejakić et al.*, the Appeals Chamber ordered counsel withdrawn due to a conflict of interest despite the express consent of the client to be represented by his counsel of choice.74 Similarly, the Trial Chamber in *Prosecutor v Prlić et al.*, has further held that an accused's right to consent to the assignment of counsel in spite of the presence of a conflict of interest is not absolute, and *"cannot have the effect of validating the appointment if the Trial Chamber is convinced that the interests of justice dictates otherwise."*[75]

20–138   Therefore, the fact that the accused gave his/her consent to be represented by a counsel, who he or she knows might be in a conflict of interest does *not* prevent the Registrar or Chambers from finding that the conflict of interest will interfere with the proper representation of that accused, and outright reject the choice of counsel.

Conclusion

20–139   The preliminary decision as to selection and assignment of counsel to (partially) indigent accused is a matter that is delegated to the Registrar by virtue of Rule 45 and Article 14 of the Directive. The accused's right to legal representation does not afford an absolute right to an indigent accused to choose his or her counsel. The Registrar may and ought to take into account the accused's choice of counsel, but it is within the Registrar's discretion when there are sufficient grounds to override that preference in the *interests of justice*, amongst others and in particular in case of a conflict of interest. While the Code of Conduct lays particular responsibilities on counsel themselves with regard to verifying and acting in case of actual and potential conflicts of interest, the Registrar has the power and responsibility to do the same. In

[75] *Prlić* Trial Chamber Decision, para. 32.

particular, the Registrar must ensure that assigned counsel are free of conflicts of interest and he may not assign counsel who has an actual conflict of interest. In case of potential conflicts, the Registrar must ensure that both counsel and accused are well informed about them before the assignment and he has to deny the assignment when assessing that a potential conflict poses a serious threat to the integrity or fairness of the proceedings and the proper and expedient administration of justice. Various Chambers of the Tribunal have confirmed the powers of the Registrar, under the supervision of the Chambers. In any event, Chambers have both a legislative, and an inherent power and duty in their roles as guardians of the integrity and fairness of the proceedings before the Tribunal, to review and reverse if necessary, a decision of the Registrar concerning assignment of counsel when it is in the interest of the accused and the administration of justice to do so and they have not hesitated to reiterate and use these powers. The same power applies when an actual or potential of a conflict of interest has been brought to its attention by the Registry in Rule 44 cases, where the accused are not seeking legal-aid and have retained counsel.

C. WITHDRAWAL, SUSPENSION AND REPLACEMENT OF COUNSEL

(1) Withdrawal and Suspension

Article 19(A) of the Directive creates three situations where withdrawals can be effected—an accused may request the withdrawal of lead counsel; the lead counsel may request his own withdrawal and/or the withdrawal of co-counsel; and/or co-counsel may request his own withdrawal from the case. It is up to the Registrar to assess whether it is in the interests of justice to grant such requests. Under Article 19(C), the Registrar *must* withdraw an assignment if: 1) a Chamber refuses audience to a counsel under Rule 46(A) of the RPE; 2) counsel no longer satisfies the requirements of assignment under Article 14(A); or 3) if counsel has been found in contempt in accordance with Rule 77 of the RPE. **20–140**

As an interim measure, the Registrar is empowered under Article 19(B) of the Directive to suspend the assignment of counsel until disciplinary or contempt proceedings are completed. No such interim measures are possible in other cases which may lead to withdrawal, such as temporary refusal to grant audience by a Chamber, or where counsel no longer satisfies one of the assignment criteria. Prior to 2002, there was no provision to suspend a counsel from practice at the Tribunal, although the Registrar had used his discretionary power to suspend in instances where counsel had been charged with contempt. The Directive was amended in 2002 to include the present provision. **20–141**

A decision made pursuant to Article 19(A), or a suspension under Article 19(B) is reviewable upon motion to the President within two weeks from notification of the decision (Article 19(F) and 19(B)). A decision under Article 19(C) appears not to be reviewable. The drafters obviously had in mind that considering the seriousness of the situations assignment of counsel. However it is doubtful that the President's office **20–142** would not hear a request for review in such cases, as it is in line with Tribunal jurisprudence that an avenue for judicial review must be open to decisions by the Registrar, even when it is not explicitly included in the RPE and regulations.[76] Article 19(D) stipulates that in the event of a withdrawal or suspension, the Registrar must notify the bar association or professional association of counsel.

20–143   It is interesting to compare Article 19 with Article 14, paras (D) and (E) of the Directive, which authorise respectively oblige the Registrar to remove a name from the Rule 45-list. Article 14(E) appears to have the same purpose as Article 19(C), but differs in that it does not deal with situations of contempt but with disciplinary proceedings instead, and it does not include the situation under Rule 46(A)(i), where the court refuses audience to counsel. Equally it does not explicitly allow for a review mechanism. The respective purposes of the Articles need to be borne in mind; where Article 14 authorises or prescribes the Registry to admit and remove names to and from the Rule 45-list, in other words deals with the availability for assignment, Article 19 authorises or prescribes the Registry to act on individual assignments to cases. It is for that reason that a finding of contempt obliges the Registrar to act on the assignment, but gives him the discretion as to the position of that counsel on the list (Article 14 (D), 19 (C) (iii)). Similarly, it is provided that the Chamber needs to be consulted when the Registry wants to suspend the assignment of counsel as this would have a direct bearing on an ongoing case (Article 19(B)). It is not entirely clear why Article 19(C)(i) obliges the Registry to act and withdraw the assignment of counsel in the situation envisaged under Rule 46(A)(i), when audience is refused to counsel as this could include situations where counsel are excluded from a hearing as a one off occasion as a warning. The Registrar does not have a similar obligation in its maintenance of the Rule 45-list (Article 14(E)(i) obligates the Registrar to remove counsel from the list in the situation under Rule 46(A)(ii) only, when a Chamber has decided that the misconduct of counsel was such that he or she can no longer be eligible for assignment overall). Article 19(C)(i) of the Directive seems to limit possibilities for the Chamber to use this tool as a warning mechanism.

20–144   In practice, the Registry has withdrawn the assignment of counsel in many cases, but only in few cases such occurred pursuant to an action by the Trial or Appeals Chamber under Rule 46.[77] Chambers generally exercise restraint in publicly criticising counsel's performance for obvious reasons. Nevertheless, some Chambers have, in their decisions,

---

[76] See, *e.g. Prosecutor v Delić*, Case No. IT-04–83-PT, Decision of the President on Request for Review, June 8, 2005, where the President states: "[...] any administrative decision that impinges upon the rights of an accused at this Tribunal must be subject to a process of judicial review, even where the Registrar is of the view that he has acted in strict compliance with the Rules and relevant Practice Directions, and that the Rules and Practice Directions should be read accordingly. That is, even where the Registrar claims that he has acted in strict compliance with the law of this Tribunal, an accused still has a right to ensure that the Registrar's claim to have acted in compliance is correct."

[77] See, *e.g. Prosecutor v Kunrać et al.*, Case No. IT-96–23-PT, Decision of the Trial Chamber II on the Request of the Accused Radomir Kovać to Allow Mr Milan Vujin to Appear as Co-counsel Acting Pro Bono, March 14, 2000. In this latter case, the Trial Chamber denied Mr Vujin the right of audience in the case. The Chamber declared, to do otherwise, would be: "failing in its duty to protect the interests of the accused." (*ibid.*, para. 18.)

listed, the Registrar should have no choice but to withdraw the criticised conduct and performance of counsel and, if serious enough, the Registry is bound to act in such cases, yet always in consultation with a Chamber. Withdrawal from the Rule 45-list has occurred more often. The recent re-qualification process for the list has given the ADC and the Registry an opportunity to refuse admission to counsel who did not meet the higher standards introduced in July 2004. In addition, the Registry has invoked Article 14(E)(iii) to remove counsel from the list where Chambers had expressed heavy criticism on counsel's performance—touching upon counsel's competence—in its decisions. Suspensions have occurred often as a result of disciplinary proceedings having been initiated under the Code of Conduct. The most recent suspension arose in 2005. A Registry investigation uncovered evidence which suggested that counsel for the accused had engaged in misconduct and the Registrar filed a disciplinary complaint against the counsel before the Tribunal's Disciplinary Panel. In such cases, the Registrar will act pursuant to Article 19(B)(i) of the Directive and generally considers it appropriate to suspend a counsel's representation while the Disciplinary Panel reviews the complaint. Former counsel will normally be replaced although the Registry may order counsel to continue acting for a period of 30 days beyond his suspension in accordance with Article 20(B) of the Directive, to ensure an efficient transition.

(2) Replacement

Article 20 of the Directive provides that where there has been a withdrawal of counsel, the withdrawn counsel must continue to act until a replacement counsel is found. The Registry takes a restrictive approach as to replacement of counsel during proceedings, particularly as trial approaches or during trial. This cautious approach is required as replacements of counsel are disruptive to proceedings and tend to cause delays necessary to allow time for the newly-assigned counsel to become familiar with the case. The Registrar must be satisfied that the replacement is justifiable. Indeed, for that reason, in January 2000, the Directive was amended to require that a withdrawal of counsel (and hence replacement) must be in the interests of justice. These interests of justice can be manifold and can relate to potential delays in proceedings and respect for the rights of witnesses or other accused. Financial aspects can also play role in considering the interests of justice, as every replacement of counsel requires a new counsel to familiarise himself with the matter, which leads to extra costs and expenditure to the Tribunal's legal-aid budget. The Registry's duty to guard proper expenditure of public funds, obliges it to have a look at this aspect as well. Otherwise, the Registry's main concerns are that the replacement is necessary, that the transition from a previous counsel to new counsel will be smooth and, of course, that sufficient preparation time is set aside for new counsel. **20–145**

Replacement of counsel will be necessary where a conflict of interests has arisen and the assigned counsel can no longer represent an accused without having his loyalty divided. There are numerous examples. This was the case in the *Prosecutor v Mejakić et al.*, where the Registrar was **20–146** ordered by the Appeals Chamber to withdraw the assignment of Mr Simić, a counsel who was acting simultaneously for Mr Željko Mejakić and Mr Dragoljub Prcać (an accused in the case of the *Prosecutor v Kvoćka et al.*) from one of the two cases.[78] The Prosecution in *Mejakic et al.*, had been allowed to include Mr Prcać in its witness list, which, the Prosecution contended, created an immediate conflict of interest. The Appeals Chamber agreed finding that a withdrawal was warranted as there was a real risk that the counsel would have to withdraw later in the course of the trial because of the conflict of interest, at that time triggering a delay in the proceedings for a replacement counsel to be sought. The Registrar and Chambers endeavour to avoid delays in proceedings at all costs. In *Prosecutor v Jokić*, the co-counsel had requested withdrawal in the middle of trial on personal health grounds. To avoid delay, the Defence had proposed the assignment of a counsel who had previously been assigned to the case and who was sufficiently familiar with the case to take over without difficulty. The counsel requesting withdrawal also timed the request to coincide with "court recess", and was in satisfactory health to assist the replacement counsel with the transition. The case of *Prosecutor v Halilović* is notorious for its defence team changes: on the instigation of the accused, four lawyers were replaced before finally a defence team was in place to present the defence in trial. At the fifth request from the accused for withdrawal of lead counsel, the Registry decided not to grant it and got into a protracted mediation and litigation exercise involving the accused, co-counsel and temporarily assigned counsel, before it finally was ordered by the President to allow another counsel change.[79]

20–147   Usually, the Registrar invokes Article 20(B) of the Directive, which provides that "(i)n the interests of justice, the withdrawn counsel may continue to represent the suspect or the accused for a period of not exceeding 30 days after the date on which the replacement is assigned. During this period, the costs necessarily and reasonably incurred by both counsel shall be met by the Tribunal."

20–148   Articles 19 and 20 of the Directive were put to the test recently when an accused invoked his right to represent himself under Article 21(4)(d) and Rule 45(F) of the RPE in the middle of his trial. The Statute and the RPE appear to clearly give an accused the right to opt for self-representation, and Article 20(A) of the Directive appears in line with that principle. However, the right to self-representation is by no means absolute. The situation was rather unique in this case because of the timing when the accused invoked this right. The Chamber, at the end, used its discretion and denied the accused's application for self-representation, citing as reasons, *inter alia*, the late timing of the accused's request, which, if granted, had the potential to disrupt proceedings.[80] These Articles of the Directive did not provide sufficient

---

[78] *Prosecutor v Mejakić et al.*, note 52 above.

[79] *Prosecutor v Halilović*, Case No. IT-01–48-PT, Decision of the Registrar to Withdraw Mr Stefan Kirsch and to Assign Mr Peter Morrissey as lead counsel, August 10, 2004.

[80] *Prosecutor v Krajišnik*, Case No. IT-00–39-T, Reasons for Oral Decision Denying Mr Momčilo Krajišnik's Request to Proceed Unrepresented by Counsel, August 18, 2005. The accused's application was primarily denied due to the fact that the Chamber was not convinced that the accused's application was a genuine request for self-representation, given the history of

guidance in this case and appeared not to have been formulated with this kind of situation in mind.

Conclusion

In summary, the Tribunal's jurisprudence has confirmed the principle   **20–149**
that accused have an inherent right to legal representation, and to choose counsel to represent their interests before the Tribunal. The Tribunal's practice has been to assign counsel to an accused as soon as he has made a claim for assignment and submitted a declaration of means. If necessary in the interests of justice, duty counsel will be assigned for the initial appearance, and pending the verification of the indigency status, counsel for a period of 120 days, possibly extended. The Tribunal's jurisprudence has equally declared that, in the case of indigent accused, the right to choice of counsel is not absolute, and is a limited right. The jurisprudence has further acknowledged that it is the responsibility of both the Registry and Chambers to verify whether an actual or potential conflict of interest exists in the assignment of the accused's counsel of choice, and if so, to intervene with that choice. Other possible limitations to the choice of counsel by indigent accused involve situations where counsel do not meet the requisite qualification standards including the necessary language requirements, or possess disciplinary records; if substantial delays or disruption of proceedings would be triggered by following the accused's choice of counsel, as well as other problems that might adversely affect the administration of justice. In practice, the Registry endeavours to accommodate the accused's choice as much as possible but increasingly runs into situations where actual or potential conflicts of interest exist or will likely arise. As it stands, the decision of the ICTY Chamber in *Prosecutor v Hadžihasanović et al.*,[81] clearly spells out the opinion of the Tribunal's judiciary on who bears the ultimate responsibility for the selection and assignment of counsel to indigent accused, and the answer is une-quivocally: the Registrar.

As to withdrawal, suspension and replacement of counsel, the Dir-   **20–150**
ective gives the Registry guidance both as to situations pertaining to the Rule 45 of the RPE and to assignments in an ongoing case. Practice has varied substantially and especially when withdrawal requests occur in ongoing cases, the Registry has had to engage in balancing exercises between the rights of an accused to a proper defence, the prevention of unnecessary delays and disruptions of proceedings, and the previous and future expenditure of public funds. This difficult balancing act, has become more of a challenge in light of the fact that the United Nations

---

the case and the equivocal nature of the accused's wish to represent himself. The Chamber, however, noted that the request would have been denied in any event due to the timing of the request and its likely disruption on the proceedings.
[81] *Prosecutor v Hadžihasanović et al.*, note 31 above.

has announced that the ICTY must complete its mandate in the years 2008–2010.[82]

VI. PAYMENT SYSTEMS FOR ASSIGNED COUNSEL AND DEFENCE TEAMS

A. HISTORY AND DEVELOPMENT OF PAYMENT SYSTEMS

20–151 The system applied to payment of defence counsel fees has undergone many changes since the establishment of the Tribunal.[83] The original payment system introduced in 1995 was based on hourly rates which would cover both remuneration and office costs. There was no limit on hours of invoicing, but counsel had to submit detailed invoices explaining the work performed. Since it soon turned out that the costs of the system were much too high, several successive ceiling systems replaced the original system, setting monthly maximums of hours for both counsel and support staff. In 2001, a major reform took place introducing a newly amended ceiling system, which set hourly maximums per stage of proceeding, for the pre-trial and appeals stages. It further distinguished the cases per level of complexity, the highest level receiving a much higher number of billable hours than the lowest. At trial, monthly maximums were applied until an amended lump-sum system was adopted for the trial stage, a system which was approved by the judges in July 2002 and enacted in 2003. Following positive feedback from he ADC, individual defence counsel and relevant sections at the Tribunal itself on this lump-sum payment system, the Registry developed a similar lump-sum system for the pre-trial stage, the 2004 Pre-Trial Legal Aid Policy, in consultation with the ADC. This policy was finalised in the fall of 2004 and enacted in December 2004. Both the trial and pre-trial lump-sum systems have subsequently been updated.

20–152 Main considerations for all these system changes were originally the excessive costs to the legal-aid system, which in combination with the discovery of cases of abuse, led to concerns at the United Nations as to the expenditure of public funds. In addition, the Tribunal had to consider the effects of surfacing allegations on cases of "fee-splitting" and other abuses of the legal-aid system on its mandate and reputation in the region itself.[84] The General Assembly of the United Nations took

---

[82] Security Council Res. 1503, adopted by the Security Council at its 4817th meeting, August 28, 2003, para. 7: "The Security Council, Calls on the ICTY [...] to take all possible measures to complete investigations by the end of 2004, to complete all trial activities at first instance by the end of 2008, and to complete all work in 2010 (the Completion Strategy)."

[83] For a comprehensive description of the developments from the establishment of the Tribunal until 2003, see "Comprehensive report on the progress made by the ICTY in reforming its legal-aid system", Report of the Secretary-General, August 12, 2003 (A/58/288), and, for a more recent update, see "First performance report of the ICTY for the biennium 2004–2005", Report of the Secretary-General, November 2, 2004 (A/59/547).

[84] See discussion on "fee-splitting" schemes in paragraphs 20–106 and 20–107.

measures to monitor more closely the Tribunal's legal-aid system and demanded reforms which were subsequently explained in reports from the Secretary-General to the General Assembly. As explained, additional safeguards have been put in place over the years: qualification requirements of counsel have been sharpened; the payment systems have been tightened and maximum allotments put in place; the ADC has enhanced its role and involvement in both developing policies and monitoring counsel conduct; and the system of partial indigency was introduced and in turn, the Registry's investigative section has uncovered and addressed some cases of abuse. In part, as a consequence of all these measures, and in particular the stricter payment systems, during the period of 2003–2004, positions between the Registry on the one hand and defence counsel and their representative organisation, the ADC on the other, sharpened. Defence teams accused the Tribunal and the Registry of applying too strict and inflexible standards on issuing resources and of imposing an administratively burdensome system of invoicing. Conversely, the Registry reproached defence counsel's inefficiency in managing funds and inaction of the ADC in policing those members who did not abide by the ethical standards and abused the system. Substantial litigation ensued related to remuneration matters between defence teams and the Registry and increasingly consumed the time that the administration and the defence could have used otherwise. Hence, in this context, the introduction of the much more efficient and less administratively burdensome lump-sum systems was quite timely and welcomed.

B. PRESENT SYSTEMS

(1) Pre-trial and Appeal: Ceiling System

The *payment ceiling system* adopted in 2001 for the pre-trial and appeals stages still applies in some cases. The systems established payment by remuneration of a maximum (ceiling) allotment of out-of-court hours per stage. A standard maximum allotment of hours was based on an assessment of preparatory (pre-trial) and appellate (appeals) work, and attached to the level of complexity at which a case would be ranked, in consultation with the Chamber—the ultimate aim, being a more efficient use of the resources and a better balance between expenditure on complex and less complex cases. Three levels of complexity were identified: level 1 (difficult), 2 (very difficult) and 3 (leadership case). Defence teams were paid a sum related to the number of hours granted for pre-trial and appeal and, in addition, all hearing hours. The following table sets out this system:

20–153

Team member:	PRE-TRIAL CASE LEVEL AND ESTIMATED NECESSARY PREPARATION TIME:			TRIAL	APPEAL CASE LEVAL AND ESTIMATED NECESSARY PREPARATION TIME:		
	Case level 1: difficult **4 MONTHS**	Case level 2: very difficult **6 MONTHS**	Case level 3: leadership cases **8 MONTHS**		Case level 1: difficult **3 months**	Case level 2: very difficult **4 months**	Case level 3: leadership cases **6 MONTHS**
Lead Counsel + Co-Counsel	* 1,400 hours total * **plus** all hearing for one counsel	* 2,100 hours total * **plus** all hearing hours for one counsel	* 2,800 hours total * **plus** all hearing hours for one counsel	All hearing hours Average monthly prep time: 115 hours + all hearing hours— applicable to both counsel	● 1,050 hours **total** * **plus** all hearing hours for one counsel	* 1,400 hours **total** * **plus** all hearing hours for one counsel	* 2,100 hours **total** * **plus** all hearing hours for one counsel
Legal Assistants Or Investigators	* 2,000 hours **total**	* 3,000 hours **total**	* 4,000 hours **total**	Max. average monthly working hours for duration of trial: 150	* 450 hours **total**	* 600 hours **total**	* 900 hours **total**
Total hours:	3,400	5,100	6,800	N/A	1,500	2,000	3,000

20–154   The appeals resources are structured differently and more focused on counsel hours, as appeals usually relate to findings of errors of law or procedure in the judgement. In a number of cases, where the prosecution has continued disclosure of documents to the defence during the appeals stage, or the defence has attempted to receive permission to introduce additional evidence according to Rule 115 of the RPE, the Registry has felt obliged to increase the resources of respective defence teams. An initially small extra allotment can be extended if a Rule 115 motion is granted based on the test used in the *Kupreškić* appeal.[85]

Payment of Fees for Counsel and Support Staff

20–155   The general guiding principle in assessing the invoices submitted by defence teams is laid out in Article 22 of the Directive: the Registrar shall reimburse the costs of legal representation necessarily and reasonably incurred: the "reasonable and necessary" test. The hourly rates for defence counsel and support staff were established by the Registrar in 1995, and have not changed since then. Under the ceiling system, they still apply as such. The US dollar value has varied towards European currencies (more than 70 per cent of all defence counsel working at the Tribunal and more than 80 per cent on the Rule 45-list are from Europe). While the years 1998 to 2001, had made the payment

[85] See *Prosecutor v Kupreškić et al.*, Case No. IT-95–16-A, Decision of the Appeals Chamber on the Admission of Additional Evidence Following the Hearing of March 30, 2001, April 11, 2001, in which the Rule 115 motion of Mr Vlatko Kupreškić for the admission of additional evidence was granted.

rates particularly favourable for European counsel, after the introduction of the euro in 2002, fluctuations in the exchange rate between the
dollar and euro have worked at the expense of counsel, as calculations
are made in dollars. The rates are regulated in Annex I to the
Directive. Counsel rates are between US†l80 and US†l110, depending
on the relevant professional experience of counsel. The assessment of
the relevant experience of counsel is made by the Registry. Working as
a defence attorney, a judge, a prosecutor or in another relevant legal
capacity can qualify as relevant experience. The standard hourly rate
for co-counsel is at US†l80, irrespective of counsel's experience. This
rate is also applied to legal consultants. Support staff are paid under
the ceiling system at rates between € 15 and € 25, depending upon their
professional experience. Legal assistants, investigators, case managers
and others are considered support staff, as are interpreters and
translators working in The Hague. The hourly rates were established in
comparison to work rates in the former Yugoslavia at the time when
most support staff originated from the region. Interpreters and translators, resident or working in the territory of the former Yugoslavia are
remunerated at rates between €5 and €20, depending upon assignment
and experience. The introduction of the lump-sum systems has reduced
the relevance of the rate system for counsel to those pre-trial cases
remunerated under the ceiling system and cases in appeal.

(2) Trial Lump-Sum Payment System

The revised payment system for the trial stage adopted in July 2002,   **20–156**
enacted in 2003, and since then amended twice (in 2004 and 2005), has
a lump-sum nature. The system combines predetermined cost ceilings
with easier administrative procedures for invoicing and sets the
requirement for more extensive reporting at the end of the phase. It
renders the financing more transparent than previously, while putting
the onus of financial planning on defence counsel. It attaches a monthly
sum to the level of complexity and the estimated duration of the case.
Calculation of the lump-sum is based on remuneration of lead and co-
counsel on the basis of an amount determined in comparison to the
salaries of the prosecution's (senior) trial attorneys, to which an office
cost component of 40 per cent is added. A support staff component is
added based on the level of complexity, for remuneration of one, three
or five support staff members. The Registry will disburse 80 per cent of
the lump-sum on the basis of simple monthly *pro forma* invoices in which
lead counsel will indicate how he wants the sum to be distributed to
counsel and team members. The last 20 per cent will be disbursed upon
submission of a detailed end-of-stage report providing a description of
the work performed by the team and a breakdown per team member.
Lead counsel are free to request from the Registry to assign additional
or fewer support staff members than the calculation foresees, and
similarly, to disburse the lump-sum in a different manner than foreseen
by the calculation. Nevertheless, the Registry reserves the right to
address lead counsel if it identifies unjustifiable discrepancies, as well
as issues related to the management of the team. In 2004, the ADC has
issued a resolution to its members laying out its views on the remunera-

tion of support staff under the lump-sum system. Since the last trial remunerated under the ceiling system was completed in 2004 (*Brdanin*), all present cases in trial are now remunerated under the lump-sum system.

20–157   The following table provides an overview of the monthly allotments during trial. The first amount indicates the counsel component which is based on the gross salaries of a P5 Step VII staff member and a P4 Step VII staff member plus a component for office costs amounting to 40 per cent of the total. The second amount indicates the support staff component which is based on the average hourly rate for support staff as specified in the Directive (€20) times 150 hours per month, and one member for a level 1 case, three for a level 2 case, and five for a level 3 case.

Difficulty Level(s)	Monthly Allotment	Monthly allotment for interpretation and translation
1 (Difficult)	$30,495 + €3,000.00	€1000 maximum
2 (Very Difficult)	$30,495 + €9,000.00	€1000 maximum
3 (Extremely Difficult/Leadership)	$30,495 €€15,000.00	€1000 maximum

The "reasonable and necessary" standard for Tribunal expenses on legal representation continues to apply but is mostly considered to be integrated in the lump-sum system. For further details on the trial lump-sum payment system, the policy can be accessed on the website of the ICTY at the following address: *www.un.org/icty/legaldoc-e/index.htm*.

(3) Pre-Trial Lump-Sum Payment System

20–158   Following the positive feedback on the lump-sum payment system in trial, the Registry developed a pre-trial lump-sum system and finalised it in November 2004, after intensive consultations with the ADC. The new pre-trial payment policy aims to bring better control of expenditure and better projection of costs associated with defence fees while streamlining the billing process for both the defence and the Registry while improving transparency. It again attaches a total lump-sum to be disbursed in accordance with the level of complexity of the case and provides for three phases of the pre-trial stage: 1) the initial appearance phase; 2) the second phase in which the defence counsel will review the supporting material to the indictment and initial disclosure, as well as submit preliminary motions; and 3) the third phase in which the defence team prepares the case for trial. The introduction of a defence work plan to be supplemented through regular progress reports (every four months) brings an incentive to the defence to be efficient and allows the Registry to monitor expenditure while invoicing remains relatively simple. As in the trial lump-sum system, the last 20 per cent of the lump-sum will be disbursed upon submission of a detailed end-of-stage report.

20–159   The same calculations of counsel and support staff components of the team allotments as in the trial lump-sum system apply in the pre-trial. The following are the total amounts for fees available to teams in the pre-trial divided per stage. The amounts do not include DSA and Travel which are covered separately in accordance with the applicable Registry policies (see below):

Complexity	Phase One— Initial Appearance	Phase Two	Phase Three	Allotment for Interpretation and Translation	TOTAL
Level 1	£2,000	$48,369	$112,162	(€1,000 max. per month)	$162,531 (+ €. . .)
Level 2	£2,000	$48,369	$229,250	(€1,000 max. per month)	$279,619 (+ €. . .)
Level 3	£2,000	$48,369	$405,515	(€1000 max. per month)	$455,884 (+ €. . .)

Again, the "reasonable and necessary" standard for Tribunal expenses on legal representation continues to apply but is mostly considered to be integrated in the lump-sum system. For details on the payment system, the calculation and distribution per stage and other parameters set by the policy, the policy can be visited on the website of the ICTY: *www.un.org/icty/legaldoc/indexdef.htm*.

Under all systems, counsel can request an upgrade to the level of complexity in their case, following a change in the criteria determining the complexity. In addition, counsel can request additional allotments over and above the ceiling, or an adjustment to the lump-sum. While the Registry always assesses such requests on their merits and has in many cases granted extra allotments,[86] the high amount of requests for extra allotments and upgrades under the ceiling systems—even after large sums of money had been spent in individual cases—led the Registry to stand increasingly firm and challenge the teams on their management of legal-aid funds. In various cases, the Registrar's decisions in rejecting requests for additional resources have been upheld by Chambers.[87] The lump-sum systems are more generous and are generally better designed to deal with unexpected circumstances. As they are the result of a series of consultations with the ADC ending in agreement, their application is expected to lead to less friction between defence counsel and the Registry, resulting in a decline in litigious matters.

20–160

---

[86] In the period from 2002 to April 2005, the Registry granted extra allotments in almost 20 cases. In the majority of cases, the allotments were small and intended to meet unexpected circumstances that may arise in the case beyond the control of the defence, such as plea negotiations, amendments to indictments and unprecedented amounts of extra disclosure by the prosecution. In addition, it granted six requests for upgrades in level of complexity. The Registry has rejected a similar number of requests during the same period.

[87] See, *e.g. Prosecutor v Milutinović et al.*, Case No. IT-99–37-PT, (Public) Decision on *ex parte* Motion for Additional Funds Filed by the Defence of D. Odjanić, July 8, 2003: where the Trial Chamber denied the motion; *Prosecutor v Hadžihasanović et al.*, Case No. IT-01–47-PT, (Public) Decision of the Trial Chamber on an Urgent Motion for *Ex Parte* Oral Hearing on Allocation of Resources to the Defence and Consequences thereof for the Rights of the Accused to a Fair Trial, June 17, 2003: where the Chamber dismissed the request for *ex parte* hearing, dismissing the motion as inadmissible and denying the request for certification.

(4) Resources for Review

20–161 The resources allocated to requests for review under Rule 119 of the RPE are limited, depending on the request of counsel. Usually no more than 30 working hours for counsel and travel and subsistence expenses as required. There have been a number of unsuccessful review requests during the period of 2001 to 2005. If however, a pre-review Judge were to declare an application admissible, the Registry would most likely consider the authorisation of further resources, within reason.

(5) Resources for Suspects

20–162 The remuneration of counsel assigned to suspects under Article 17 of the Directive has evolved over time. Previously, the financial allocation to counsel was based on a lump-sum amount of between US†1250 and US†1500, for the entire interview. Further, remuneration for counsel's preparation time prior to the interview or legal advice given to the suspect, before or after the interview, was also limited to a maximum of approx. of US†12.000 or 10 hours allowable billings. Presently, the Registry reimburses counsel for the entire duration of the interview based on the hourly (fee) rate of counsel in accordance with Annex I of the Directive. In practical terms, the Registry first reviews the qualifications and work experience of counsel and determines the hourly rate of the counsel in question, applying Annex I of the Directive. The Registry then sends a letter to counsel providing this information and requesting that they submit a detailed invoice specifying the number of working hours and the nature of work employed by the legal representation of the suspect. The invoice has to be submitted to the Registry within 120 days of the date on which the work was performed in order for it to be accepted (Article 22 of the Directive). In light of the existence of cases where the Office of the Prosecutor interviews have taken several months to complete, there is no longer a limit on the number of pre- and post-interview time for which counsel can be remunerated. Of course, the standard to be applied is that of reasonableness and necessity. The Registry will therefore limit and/or reduce the amount reimbursed to counsel for fees claimed, when given the specific circumstances of the case (*i.e.* based on the length of the interview, the nature of the case, etc.), the claimed fees are deemed excessive and unreasonable. The Registry has indeed done so in one or two cases thus far. The same applies to claimed costs and expenses (*e.g.* travel costs to attend the interview) related to the legal representation of the suspect.

(6) Determination of Rates and Office Expenses of Counsel

20–163 When the legal-aid system of the Tribunal was established in 1994, the Registrar based its parameters on a number of assumptions, which are listed below:

> (1) Counsel are not staff members of the Tribunal, but independent practitioners;

(2) Counsel do not work on a contractual basis with the Tribunal, but under a public judicial-administrative act by the Registry assigning them;

(3) Counsel are liable for taxes in the countries where they are admitted to the bar or professors, and also reside;

(4) Counsel should have approximately the same gross income as their counterparts in the prosecution, a lead counsel as a Senior Trial Attorney, and a co-counsel, as a Trial Attorney;

(5) This gross income is supplemented by approximately another 45 per cent of this gross income for office expenses;

(6) For a senior lead counsel, the addition of the fees and the office expenses results in a sum of approximately US†120,000 for one month of full-time work, which is divided by 175 working hours. A maximum 175 working hours per month appears to be appropriate, as it adds up to 2,100 billable working hours per annum, a reasonable figure, and

(7) The hourly rate of counsel in their respective home countries is not relevant, as all counsel assigned before the Tribunal provide services of equal quality to their clients.

The above resulted in the hourly rates for counsel being determined **20–164** according to their professional experience. The office expense rate of 45 per cent was taken from a survey amongst attorneys, who in average, had to spend this percentage of their income for office expenses. The Registry took into account that counsel have to maintain their own offices while practising before the Tribunal and, when in trial, will have to set up basic office facilities in The Hague. It was considered reasonable to limit this percentage, after consultation with the same attorneys, to 40 per cent. The analysis and conclusion that it is justified to add a remuneration component for office costs, has been maintained until this day. Article 22(B) of the Directive provides guidance as to what can be considered office costs. Under the ceiling system, counsel invoicing for office cost expenses saw and see their invoices being cut. Under the new lump-sum systems, this expenditure is absorbed in the lump-sum. In addition to the disbursement for office cost, while staying in The Hague, counsel will receive a daily allowance, which is provided to cover their costs for accommodations and food.

(6) Travel and DSA

Travel expenses of counsel and experts are authorised by the Registry's **20–165** OLAD as necessary and reasonable. Also in this respect, the Registry is guided by the "reasonable and necessary" standard under Articles 22 and 26 of the Directive. The latter provision only allows travel to assigned counsel, not to defence team members or experts/expert consultants. The procedure for travel applications for counsel is rather informal. Counsel have to merely submit a travel authorisation request seven days prior to travel, which will then be approved or rejected by the Registry. The details of the travel are arranged by the Registry (contact information, Tel.: +31 (70) 512 5309). The request form is self-explanatory and can be found on the websites of the Tribunal and the ADC.

20–166   Article 27 of the Directive provides for reimbursement of Daily Subsistence Allowance ("DSA"), intended to cover hotel and other costs of counsel. Again, under the Directive, defence support staff members are not entitled to DSA. Its technicalities, the rates, the administrative procedures and the like are governed by the standard United Nations System for travel allowances. The rates are published afresh every month, the rate for The Hague is roughly US$350 per night, and for the former Yugoslavia, it varies to an average US$200 per night.

20–167   The Registry reserves the right to assess requests on a case-by-case basis at any time, applying the general principles of indispensability and efficiency mentioned above and tying travel and subsistence to the work to be performed. In travel and DSA matters, the Registry has denied a number of travel authorisation requests which have been upheld by the President and Chambers. Nevertheless, the Registry has acknowledged that, in certain circumstances, defence team members should be allowed and reimbursed for defence related travel, and at times, accompanying DSA. In particular, it has allowed exceptions to defence investigators' travel, while clear explanations and justifications by lead counsel and prior approval by the Registry are required for these exceptions to be made. The Registry, is at present, revising its Travel and DSA policy and has proposed amendments to the Directive. Until any new proposal is adopted, the present policy, in place and developed since 1998 applies. These parameters represent the standard authorisation of travel and DSA. Other requests are dealt with on a case-by-case basis upon good cause being shown by lead counsel:

Team member	Phase	Standard Authorisation	Remarks
Lead Counsel	Pre-trial	• One trip per month to The Hague plus a maximum of 6 nights subsistence in The Hague	Subsistence drops to 75 per cent after 60 nights in The Hague, not necessarily consecutive (Article 27 Directive)
		• Maximum 5 trips to the Former Yugoslavia, plus a maximum of 6 nights subsistence	
	Trial	• Travel as required to The Hague for hearings, plus subsistence	Same
	Appeal	• One trip per two months to The Hague, plus a maximum of 6 nights subsistence in The Hague • Travel to appeals hearings, plus subsistence as required	
Co-Counsel	Pre-trial	• As Lead Counsel, subject to necessity of presence of a second counsel for an activity (case level relevant)	Subsistence drops to 75 per cent after 60 nights in The Hague, not necessarily consecutive (Article 27) of the Directive
	Trial	• As Lead Counsel	Same

Team member	Phase	Standard Authorisation	Remarks
Co-Counsel	Appeal	• As Lead Counsel, subject to necessity of presence of a second counsel for an activity (case level relevant)	
Support Staff (including legal and other consultants assigned to the team)	Pre-trial	• For investigators – trips to or within the former Yugoslavia only (both travel and DSA) • For other support staff – trips to the former Yugoslavia, if justified; trips to The Hague or elsewhere to review files only available in The Hague or for missions where legal assistants act *in lieu* of counsel on exceptional basis (only travel; no DSA)	Subsistence drops to 75 per cent after 60 nights in The Hague, not necessarily consecutive (Article 27 Directive)
	Trial	• Two to four trips for support staff to The Hague, depending on the case level and the needs of the Defence (no DSA)	Same
	Appeal	• Trips to or in the Former Yugoslavia only. Exceptionally, a trip to The Hague or to Counsel' place of residence may be authorised (no DSA)	

For counsel, terminal expenses to connect to and from airports or train stations can also be claimed in accordance with UN regulations. All claims are to be submitted on a properly filled-out "F.10" standard claims form of the United Nations. The inclusion of tickets and boarding passes is important and omission can lead to denial of the claim, hotel bills are not required.

(7) Other Defence Expenses

The Directive permits the Registry to cover other expenses of the defence in accordance with the above-mentioned general principles of reasonableness and necessity. The Registry has on that basis approved exceptional costs for the production of evidence such as videotapes, maps, photographs and models of a landscape or town, as well as exceptional costs of shipment of materials necessitated due to defence team changes.

20–168

(8) Auditing

The auditing of invoices under the ceiling systems has contributed much to the cost efficiency of the legal-aid system and maintaining the reasonableness of expenditures, establishing the right balance between

20–169

meeting strict United Nations monitoring requirements on the expenditure of UN funds and the disbursement of necessary and reasonable means for the defence of suspects and accused. While substantial cuts of invoices have, at times, been made when counsel billed the Tribunal for unreasonable or unnecessary costs (*e.g.* time spent reading general books on the former Yugoslavia or even Yugoslav literature; office and other administrative costs; meetings and communications with OLAD; travel time), close monitoring of defence expenditure has allowed the Registry to grant extra funding when so required and when justifiable under the circumstances. The new lump-sum systems orient the close auditing at the beginning, at regular intervals (work plan and progress reports in pre-trial) and at the end of a stage with the submission of an end of stage report. Initial experiences thus far indicate that the Registry often needs to address counsel and request that they provide more details and be more precise in their end-of-stage reports, as well as in the submission of their work plans. At the same time, all sides acknowledge that the administrative burden has tremendously decreased. It is worth mentioning that many counsel at the Tribunal work long hours and want to engage in a vigorous and professional defence of their client(s) rather than being sidetracked to debates about the disbursement of defence funds. Nevertheless, accounting and monitoring standards for the expenditure of public funds need to remain in place. The relatively new lump-sum systems of the Tribunal appear to provide a strong improvement in all these respects.

VII. PRESENTING THE CASE IN THE COURTROOM

A. THE COURTROOM

(1) Languages

20–170   The working languages of the ICTY are English and French (Rule 3(A) of the RPE), however, a judge can authorise the use of another language by a special requested made by a party. This is the reason why in the courtroom, defence lawyers from the former Yugoslavia are authorised to speak in their own language even if they can speak one of the working languages of the Tribunal (Rule 3(D) of the RPE). The accused is obviously permitted to express himself in his own language. In reference to the RPE and the Statute, he must be able to follow the discussion in his own language or in one of the languages he understands (Article 21(4)(f) of the Statute, Rule 3 of the RPE). Regarding the Serbo-Croatian language, the Tribunal has decided to refer to it as B/C/S for reasons of political sensitivity. The Tribunal treats these three languages the same, and does not differentiate between them. For example, an accused of Croatian ethnic background is expected be able to understand statements interpreted by a Serbian interpreter. In practice, some accused have insisted on receiving interpretation and translation services in one of the three mentioned versions of Serbo-Croat.[88-89] Other languages of accused are Macedonian and Albanian.

When witnesses who use other languages are requested to testify, the **20–171** Tribunal provides interpretation from and to the relevant language. Interpretation can be consecutive or simultaneous. Interpretation in the courtroom is essential. The main rule for the interpreter is to follow the mind of the narrator. Therefore, it is important to speak clearly and slowly to ensure a good understanding of the discussion in all the different languages used in court.

(2) Courtroom Etiquette

In the courtroom, a robe must be worn by all prosecution, and defence **20–172** attorneys, as well as, Chambers and Registry members appearing before the judges, including the judges themselves. Judges wear red and black robes, while others wear the traditional barristers' black robes. The black robes are usually identical, but counsel can use a robe they wear in their home jurisdictions. Wigs are authorised for the lawyers who wear them in their home jurisdictions and wish to wear them at the Tribunal. All parties and the accused must be present in the courtroom before the judges' arrival. Some judges prefer to have the accused come in to the courtroom after them. Sometimes it is not required that robes be worn during the hearing, for example during status conferences. This is ultimately the decision of the Chamber or the judge, and they will indicate their preferences. When a party addresses the Chamber, he or she must rise. The same applies to the accused.

(3) Oral Presentation of Arguments

Parties may present arguments during pre-trial hearings, status con- **20–173** ferences, in trial and appeal hearings. The Chamber will set the topics and may choose to hear oral or written arguments at its discretion. At trial, the proceedings follow a pre-set structure: opening statements of the parties (Rules 84 and 84*bis* of the RPE) are followed by the presentation of evidence (Rule 85) and closing arguments (Rule 86), and the pronouncement of the judgement. In the Tribunal's system, the taking of direct evidence, such as hearing live witnesses, takes prece-dence over written procedure, more dominant in some civil law jurisdictions. As to the exchange of arguments, the parties usually submit their arguments in written motions. Most Chambers will want to hear a brief elaboration of the arguments in court, giving the judges an opportunity to ask for further details and elaborations.

[88-89] The accused, Kordić and Seselj have publicly insisted they receive language assistance in Croatian and Serbian respectively, which they consider to be their (only) mother tongues. Kordić claimed at his initial appearance that he could not understand the interpreters. Seselj has also insisted on receiving the translated filings in the Cyrillic script. The Registry has not accommodated these requests and they have faded over time (confirm-ing the Registry's understanding about the minimal and acceptable differences between the language versions).

(4) Transcripts

20–174   All hearings taking place at the Tribunal are recorded into transcripts in French and English. During a hearing, all the parties can have access to an immediate transcription of the debates in English on all available screens. This is the job of the court reporters in the courtrooms. At times, the transcripts need to be corrected. If one of the parties notices errors in the transcript, it should note them as soon as possible during or after the hearing, so that the request for correction is also recorded. Bearing in mind that corrections, can affect the answers given by the witnesses, it is important to mention and specify the different problems during the examination and cross-examination. Additionally, transcripts are subject to redaction when required to protect certain witnesses. If a party notices that confidential information has been mentioned publicly, the party must inform the Chamber or the court officer, who will in turn inform the presiding judge of the Chamber seised of the matter. The presiding judge can then sign an order of expurgation directly during the hearing. In all circumstances, the parties and the Chambers are provided the draft transcripts and may submit corrections within a few days before the transcript becomes official. Once reviewed by the Registry, the transcripts are posted on the internet. The same procedure applies to the closed sessions (Rule 81 of the RPE), although closed session transcripts are not published. During the hearings, judges and parties may follow the transcript recording live on their screens as they are created using the real time transcription software (live-note).

(5) The Court Officer and the Usher

20–175   In the courtroom, a court officer (or deputy) and a court usher will assist the parties with documents and provide general assistance to witnesses. In each case, the Registrar has designated a court officer as his representative to be the privileged interlocutor in the relation between the parties of the Tribunal, and as such, must attend all hearings. Court officers also ensure that the case-related documents are delivered on time. They take minutes of the hearing. In trial proceedings, they maintain the list of witnesses and exhibits and are responsible for a smooth running of the hearing, assisting the good administration of justice. They ensure the presence of the accused, interpreters and security guards at hearings and keep all parties informed of changes in the court calendar.

(6) Electronic Presentation of Evidence

20–176   There are different ways to submit evidence in hearings. Most pieces of evidence are written documents. The simplest way to present documents is by way of an overhead projector for the witnesses. As every party has a screen, they can view the document from their seats. If a party wishes to make use of a map, upon request, the map can be scanned beforehand for viewing in court. Such requests must be forwarded to the head of the audio-visual unit in advance of the hearing. It is also possible to request a snapshot of the document to be printed and presented as an exhibit. Finally, it is possible to present videotapes or audio exhibits. The party needs to indicate the extracts he has selected on the transmission. If available, parties should provide originals. Once introduced as exhibits, the introduced original or copy can not be modified. The exhibits are saved by the Registry (Rule 81(C) of the RPE). Parties must follow the chain of custody of the exhibit before they submit them, and if necessary, be able to elaborate on the exhibit. The developments in e-Court may change the system substantially (see paragraphs 20–20 *et seq.*).

(7) Records of the Trial

The "Case file" must be certified in view of possible appeal proceedings being initiated. The record is composed of the following: **20–177**
— the indictment(s) and its supporting material;
— all exhibits admitted into evidence;
— all transcripts and recordings of proceedings and hearings, public and confidential;
— all filings in the case by the parties, Registry and Chambers;
— all Trial Chamber decisions;
— files of interlocutory appeals proceedings, and
— the judgment.
The Registry maintains all these files and is responsible for delivering   **20–178**
certified copies to relevant parties or institutions, when required. Copies of each document filed with the Registry or presented in court are given to the parties. In case of a change in the defence team, it is their responsibility to ensure communication and transfer of documents back to the Tribunal or directly to replacement counsel (see Article 9(D) of the Code of Conduct; see also Article 20(B) of the Directive for counsel handover period).

B. FACT WITNESSES

(1) Defence Witnesses

As indicated, witnesses play a significant part in the criminal proceed-   **20–179**
ings before the ICTY, as their evidence is a crucial tool for both defence and prosecution. The principle of equality of arms permits the accused to find and examine witnesses on their behalf under the same conditions as prosecution witnesses. Under Rule 90 of the RPE, every witness has the obligation to give a truthful testimony, and the failure to tell the truth under a solemn declaration may result in a heavy fine and/or prison sentence of up to seven years (Rule 91(G) of the RPE). Under Rule 90(E) of the RPE, a witness may object to giving statements which are self-incriminating. When a witness is compelled by the Trial

Chamber to answer a question, such testimony may not be used as evidence in a possible prosecution against the witness for any offence other than false testimony. Under the RPE, children are also allowed to testify, as long as the Trial Chamber is satisfied that the child has the level of maturity which will allow him or her to give testimony and that he or she comprehends the importance of telling the truth. Additionally, any witness who has heard the testimony of another witness may not be disqualified from testifying solely on the basis of such knowledge.

(2) Communication between Witness and Counsel

20-180   Defence counsel may speak to defence witnesses at any time before the testimony. Once the testimony has commenced, such communication is no longer possible. Prosecution witnesses should not be approached directly, as ethical questions may arise. When defence counsel considers it in the interests of advancing the defence of his or her client to interview prosecution witnesses, he or she should approach the prosecution directly for permission to do so.

(3) Role of the Victims and Witnesses Section

20-181   The Victims and Witnesses Section ("VWS") is set up under the authority of the Registrar. In accordance with Rule 34 of the RPE, the mandate of VWS is to recommend protective measures for victims and witnesses, and to provide counselling and support, in particular, in cases of rape and sexual assault. The VWS may go as far as recommend inclusion of a witness in a witness protection programme. The section is impartial and provides equitable services to witnesses and victims required to appear in court by both parties (defence and the prosecution) and the Chambers. In order to carry out its mandate fully, VWS also makes travel, accommodation, financial and other logistical and administrative arrangements. The section further ensures that the safety and security needs of witnesses are adequately met; and maintains close contact with the trial teams on all aspects of their appearance before the Tribunal. VWS is divided into three units and has a field office located in Sarajevo. (1) The Protection Unit, which coordinates responses to the security requirements; (2) The Support Unit, which provides social and psychological counselling and a 24-hour assistance program to witnesses, and (3) The Operations Unit , which is responsible for logistical operations, payments and witness administration. The VWS Field Office is mainly responsible for preparing witnesses for travelling to The Hague, and providing them follow-up support and protection services in the region.

(4) Protection of Witnesses

20-182   A Chamber may order protection measures with respect to a witness at the request of either party, the VWS, the witness concerned or *proprio motu*. Protective measures vary from expunging identifying information from the Tribunal's public records, non-disclosure to the public of identifying information, giving testimony through image and/or voice altering devices or closed circuit television, assignment of pseudonyms to testimony given in closed session, or any combination of the above. In addition, the VWS employs various internal and external procedures to ensure safety, and protect the confidentiality of *all* victims and witnesses. To this end, the VWS operates with the highest levels of integrity, impartiality and confidentiality. Only the VWS staff will have access to the identity of the witnesses. No other part of the Tribunal's administration, or service providers engaged by the Tribunal to provide accommodation, medical or other services to the witnesses, have access to the identity of the witnesses.

(5) Testimony and Travel

The VWS makes all travel, immigration, accommodation and related **20–183** arrangements for the victims and witnesses required at the seat of the hearings—regardless of the location—and covers those expenses from the Tribunal's witness budget. The witnesses are covered by the Tribunal's medical, travel and third-party liability insurance while they hold "travel status". If required, the VWS will provide an escort to accompany the witness from his/her residence to The Hague. The witnesses are collected by VWS staff from the airport or other point(s) of entry into The Netherlands and taken to their accommodation, where they will be met by a witness assistant. A thorough briefing on the practicalities of their stay is given to the witnesses upon arrival. The VWS ensures that the witnesses are transported to the Tribunal, as requested by the party calling the witnesses to testimony. During their stay in The Hague, the VWS provides a 24-hour coverage service for any emergency.

(6) Tribunal Facilities for Witnesses

The Tribunal provides for witness waiting rooms, supplied with refresh- **20–184** ments, adjacent to the courtrooms.

C. EXPERTS AND EXPERT WITNESSES

Expert Qualifications and Assignment

Experts are called to testify or assigned to provide written expertise on **20–185** a specific area of fact or law because of their specific knowledge, skill, experience or training on a matter relevant to the case. Experts can be assigned, usually on an ad hoc basis either by the court pursuant to Rule 74*bis* of the RPE or by the Registry pursuant to a request by a defence team. For court appointed experts, the scope of the expertise to be provided is determined by the relevant Chamber, while the Registry handles the administrative details of the assignment. Defence experts are assigned by the Registry (OLAD) upon request of the lead counsel in the case. Lead counsel must first specify the purpose of the expertise, and the amount of time, in hours, that the expert will require to complete the mandate. Further, lead counsel must set out the credentials of the prospective expert. The Registrar will consider the request, and identify whether the request pertains to an 1) expert consultant, 2) an expert witness, or 3) an expert who will produce a written expertise. In case of the latter, the Registrar will determine a maximum on working hours for the assignment.

Payment for Experts

20–186   Court appointed experts are paid by the Registry in accordance with the scope of the assignment ordered by the Chamber. Travel and DSA may be reimbursed if necessary to fulfil the scope of the assignment. Court appointed experts must submit a detailed invoice to the Registry, specifying the number of hours worked and the nature of the work performed. For Registry assigned defence experts, those hired to produce written evidence or expertise, a total allotment of 150 hours per stage may be allocated to the defence team. Typically, counsel will request a number of hours from the total allotment to be released for a particular expert. In principle, travel related expenses will not be reimbursed unless necessary to fulfil the scope of the assignment. Defence experts are paid per hour over and above the allotment granted to the defence either under the lump-sum or ceiling systems. Working hours for court-appointed and defence experts are paid in accordance with the applicable rate as established by the Registry after an assessment of the expert's seniority. The standard hourly rates outlined in Annex I to the Directive apply (US$180 to US$110).

Payment for Expert Witnesses

20–187   For expert witnesses, who are to testify in court, the Victims and Witnesses Section makes the travel arrangements and covers the expenses from the Tribunal's budget. Travel is arranged on the basis of United Nations standards using an economy class round trip air ticket by the shortest route. The VWS will also arrange for a visa to enter the Netherlands, if required. Expert witnesses receive a Daily Subsistence Allowance to cover the costs of accommodation, meals, incidental expenses and local transportation. Advances can be made upon request. Expert witnesses may be entitled to terminal expenses for transport to and from the airport at UN rates. In addition, expert witnesses are paid an Attendance Allowance as compensation for wages, earnings and time lost as a result of testifying at the rate of US$1200 per day. The allowance is paid only for working days. Expert witnesses are required to be present at the seat at the day(s) of the hearings. The payment of expenses for expert witnesses is regulated by the Directive on

Allowances for Witnesses and Expert Witnesses ((IT/200), December 5, 2001).

Medical Experts

The Tribunal covers travel expenses for medical, psychological or any **20–188** other experts that need to meet with the accused at the United Nations Detention Unit, or in the location of his provisional release. Travel request are to be addressed to OLAD. Travel expenses are usually covered on the basis of economy class tickets. Ground transport to and from airports will be compensated up to US $30 per transfer. Travel by private motor vehicle is reimbursable in accordance with the UN rates, and is determined per kilometre travelled. A daily subsistence allowance is also provided to experts to cover the costs of accommodation, meals and incidentals occurred as a result of travelling.

D. Written Motions

(1) Format of Motions

According to the Practice Direction of the Length of Briefs and Motions **20–189** (IT/184/Rev.1), dated 5 March 2002, briefs and motions are to be submitted on A4 paper with a margin of at least 2.5 centimetres on all four sides. All filings are to be paginated, excluding the cover sheet. The typeface should be 12 points with 1.5 line spacing and the average page should contain fewer than 300 words. An appellant's appeals brief from a final judgment of a Trial Chamber will usually not exceed 100 pages or 30,000 words. A party's motion to seek leave to pursue an interlocutory appeal should not exceed 15 pages or 4,500 words. An appellant's interlocutory appeals brief should not exceed 30 pages or 9,000 words. Pre-trial briefs and trial briefs should not exceed 50 pages (or 15,000 words) or 200 pages (or 60,000 words), respectively. Furthermore, headings, footnotes and quotations shall be included in the above-mentioned word limits. An appendix will not contain legal or factual arguments, but rather references, source materials, items from the record, exhibits, and other relevant, non-argumentative materials. If a party believes that it may exceed the allotted page limitations, it has to obtain formal authorisation from a Chamber in advance.

(2) Filing with Registry Court Management

Until September 2002, the Tribunal made exclusive use of a hard copy **20–190** filing system. However, as of October 1, 2002, parties and Chambers are asked to submit an electronic version of the filing as well, in order to facilitate the maintenance of an electronic database, which provides quick access to all judicial documents. The guidelines are as follows:

(1) All documents to be filed together shall constitute and be sent as a single file;

(2) If more than one filing is submitted in the same case on the same date, such filings shall be submitted in the order in which they have to be filed, and

(3) Accepted document formats are Microsoft Word 97, 2000, XP, PDF 3.0, PDF 4.0 and Standard TIF format. In case of TIF format, resolution of the document scanned must be at least 300dpi.

(3) Time Limits

20–191 According to the RPE, preliminary motions under Rule 72 challenging jurisdiction, alleging defects in the form of the indictment; seeking the severance of counts joined in one indictment under Rule 49; separate trials under Rule 82(B) of the RPE, or raising objections based on the refusal of a request for assignment of counsel made under Rule 45(C), shall be in writing and be brought no later than 30 days after disclosure by the Prosecutor to the defence of all material and statements referred to in Rule 66(A)(i) of the RPE. Appeals under Rule 72 (B)(i) shall be filed within 15 days, and requests for certification under Rule 72(B)(ii) shall be filed within seven days of filing of the impugned decision (Rule 72(C)). If certification is granted, the appeal shall be filed within a further seven days. Moreover, the Chamber will often issue a time line order in which it specifies the number of days a party has to file a response. Similar timelines apply to appeals against Chamber decisions on other motions, as elaborated in Rule 73 of the RPE. Filing of other motions can be done at any time and it is up to the respective defence teams to decide, whether and when they want to respond to motions from the prosecution, although it will always be put in a position to reply or be heard by the Chamber. The Chamber will usually set further timelines.

20–192 Time limits are hence foreseen by the RPE or set by the Chamber. Usually, the Registrar does not agree to a filing after close of business unless, due to technical reasons (fax or email problems), a filing could not be communicated, or unless a Chamber is willing to extend a deadline.

VIII. THE CLIENT IN DETENTION

A. RULES AND PRACTICE

(1) Overview of Applicable Rules

20–193 The following body of rules and regulations provides the legal regime which covers the detention of accused persons and the operational parameters under which the Detention Unit is managed:

(1) Rules Governing the Detention of Persons awaiting Trial or Appeal before the Tribunal or otherwise Detained on the Authority of the Tribunal (IT/38/Rev.9) ("Rules of Detention");

(2) United Nations Detention Unit Regulations to Govern the Supervision of Visits to and Communications with Detainees (IT/98/Rev.3) ("Regulations");

(3) United Nations Detention Unit House Rules for Detainees (IT/99) ("House Rules");

(4) United Nations Regulations for the Establishment of a Complaints Procedure for Detainees, Issued by the Registrar in April 1995 (IT/96) ("Complaints Procedure);

(5) United Nations Detention Unit Regulations for the Establishment of a Disciplinary Procedure for Detainees, Issued by the Registrar in April 1995 (IT/97) ("Disciplinary Procedure");

(6) Appointment of Inspecting Authority for the Detention Unit;

(7) Agreement on Security and Order, signed on July 14, 1994.

(2) Housing

Detainees are housed in individual cells equipped with a bed, shower, toilet, washing basin, desk, bookshelf, chair, and window. A single cell measures approximately 10m2 altogether. The United Nations Detention Unit ("UNDU") comprises two separate wings, with two or three floors per wing. Each wing has recreational facilities including space for physical activity, indoors and outdoors. Detainees are as a standard provided with three meals a day, and the opportunity to observe religious needs. Medical care is available when necessary. Detainees are also able to purchase food in the (virtual) supermarket of the UNDU which they can prepare themselves in a fully equipped kitchen.

20–194

(3) Medical Services

The UNDU is attended by a resident medical officer, a Dutch general medical practitioner, who holds clinics twice a week at the facility and is otherwise available on call around the clock. In addition, a nurse is available at the UNDU every weekday. The UNDU also provides, through the medical officer, access to a dentist, and other specialist doctors as required. Furthermore, the detainees have access to a psychiatrist who is available regularly and is a native Serbo-Croat speaker. Additional psychological assistance is also available if necessary or requested. If detainees wish to consult a private doctor, they can do so, however, the costs will not be covered by the Tribunal. Further, any treatment or medication prescribed by a doctor other than the resident medical officer must be agreed upon and administered by the resident medical officer himself. Information related to the physical and mental health of the detainees is kept confidential by the Registrar and can only be consulted for medical reasons with the consent of the detainee, or by judicial order if the interests of justice so require.

20–195

(4) Privileged Communications with Counsel

The Rules of Detention provide for the right of a detainee to have privileged communications with counsel (Rule 65). See paragraphs 20–202 *et seq.*

20–196

(5) Communications with the Outside other than with Counsel

20–197 Rules 58–68 of the Rules of Detention cover the detainees' rights to communications. As far as visits are concerned, importantly, detainees may have regular access to the recognised spiritual representatives of their respective religions or beliefs at the detention facility. This can be arranged either individually or for group services. Further, detainees have privileged access to recognised consular representatives of their respective countries. In relation to social visits, priority is given to first degree (immediate) family members in order to stimulate the maintenance of family ties, which can erode during periods of detention. Visits from extended family and friends can be facilitated, but are only allowed after a more thorough scrutiny during which both the detainee and the potential visitor must request the visit and explain their relationship, identify the purpose of the visit, and where warranted, go through a security check. All visitors shall make written requests to the Registry for a visit at least 10 days prior to the visit, using the "Application for Permission to Visit a Detainee" form available at the Tribunal's website, and providing a copy of their passport and contact details. In accordance with standard detention and prison rules, to protect the integrity of proceedings, to maintain the security and good order at the UNDU, and respect the principle of presumption of innocence, the detainees' contact with the media is approached in a restrictive manner. In accordance with the Rules of Detention, the Registrar may refuse to grant a visit if there are reasons to believe that the purpose of the visit is to obtain information, which may be subsequently reported to the media (Rule 61(b) of the Rules of Detention). Further, detainees are not permitted in principle to use the communication facilities at the UNDU to contact the media without previous approval of the Commanding Officer and the Registrar. In those situations in which the facilities have been abused, measures have been taken accordingly.[90–91]

20–198 For others who wish to visit a detainee at the UNDU, especially former public figures, high level politicians or military, the standard procedure applies: a timely request for a visit and a detailed explanation of the relationship with the accused and the purpose of the visit are needed, as well as a timely request from the accused explaining the same. The Registry takes a restrictive approach in granting such requests, and when it does grant them, it may require visitors to sign an undertaking that they will not disclose any information gathered in the course of the visit. The Registry applies an even more restrictive approach to requests from non-governmental organisations and will usually reject them, unless they are considered to be extraordinarily beneficial for the well being of accused and no other more important visits are scheduled.

[90–91] See *Prosecutor v Milošević*, Case No. IT-02–54, Decisions of the Deputy Registrar, December 11, 2003; *Prosecutor v Šešelj*, Case No. IT-03–67-PT, Decision of the Registrar, December 11, 2003. Interestingly, in issuing these decisions, the Registrar also considered the effects of both accused's contacts with the media from within the UNDU, itself prohibited, in relation to their political positions and candidacy in elections, on the Tribunal's mandate in the region, which includes the restoration of peace.

Detainees have access to non-privileged telephones during cell opening times. Private calls have to be paid for by detainees through the purchase of telephone cards. In exceptional circumstances, for those detainees that lack financial means, the Registrar may agree that the Tribunal bears such expenses within reason. In accordance with the Rules of Detention, non-privileged telephone calls may be monitored to guarantee security and good order at the UNDU, and ensure the good administration of justice, but only following the issue of an order of the Registrar.

(6) Segregation

The possibility exists for detainees to be segregated from each other in accordance with the Rules of Detention, for reasons of witness protection and in order to prevent manipulation of cases by collusion, particularly by co-accused (see Rules 42–44 of the Rules of Detention).   **20–199**

(7) Disciplinary Measures

The Rules (Rules 40–41 of the Rules of Detention) and Regulations (Disciplinary Procedure, IT/97) provide for a relatively clear and simple disciplinary regime. Thus far, it has been quite rare for formal disciplinary measures to be required at the UNDU. The ability of the management and the staff to devote sufficient time to the detainees has resulted in the fact that such measures are seldom required, perhaps twice a year at most. When formal disciplinary measures are taken, they are in accordance with the applicable disciplinary procedure, and need to adhere to the principle of proportionality. The Registrar supervises the Commanding Officer and his staff at the UNDU to this effect. Measures taken in previous years were the withdrawal of certain privileges, oral and written warnings, confiscation of items and suspended punishments.   **20–200**

(8) Complaints

Detainees are entitled to submit complaints regarding their conditions of detention to the Registrar and the President in accordance with the Rules of Detention (Rules 80–84) and Regulations (Complaints Procedure, IT/96). Informal complaints can be made to the Commanding Officer, who is authorised to deal with them directly. The number of formal complaints has dropped significantly between 1998 and 2004. Since 1999, the unannounced inspections of the UNDU by the inspecting authority, the International Committee of the Red Cross ("ICRC"), have not resulted in any substantial modifications of the detention conditions. The ICRC was assigned as the inspecting authority of the UNDU by a treaty between the Tribunal and the ICRC. The ICRC regularly visits the UNDU facilities and inspects the conditions of detention of the detainees. It also interviews and receives the views of   **20–201** the detainees themselves on their conditions of detention, and provides a report of its findings with recommendations to the Registrar. This has led to minor adaptations in the detention system.

B. ACCESS TO CLIENT

20–202   Proper communication between counsel and their clients is regarded as a fundamental component of the right to a fair trial. While accused persons are not entitled to unlimited access to counsel either in person, by mail or by phone, Article 21(4)(b) of the Statute envisages the accused's right to "have adequate time and facilities for the preparation of his defence and to communicate with counsel." The Rules of Detention and the Regulations ensure that accused have adequate facilities and time to communicate with counsel at the UNDU. For communications at the Tribunal's main building during breaks in court hearings, the Statute would apply directly. The UNDU falls under the supervision of the Deputy Registrar and is therefore considered to provide direct service to the judicial procedure in addition to its role of managing the detention of accused. Its day-to-day operations are managed by a Commanding Officer. OLAD assists the Deputy Registrar and the Commanding Officer mainly with legal and strategic detention matters.

Access to the Detention Unit

20–203   Counsel must access the detention facility through the security ring of the Dutch Penitentiary Complex (PI Haaglanden Scheveningen: Penitentiary Complex). The UNDU is an autonomous unit built within the grounds of the Penitentiary Complex. At the entrance to the Penitentiary Complex, counsel are required to present a valid identification, such as a passport (see Regulation 37 of the Regulations). In practice, the presentation of a visit permit is not required if the identification is accepted. Counsel must make an appointment with the detention facility directly, in order to be admitted. Visiting time with clients may be scheduled by phone, fax or mail to the UNDU. If counsel has not scheduled an appointment in advance and thus the Penitentiary Complex staff does not have the counsel's name on a daily list, counsel will not be given access. Counsel will only be on the list if the UNDU has confirmed to the Penitentiary Complex, that counsel has scheduled an appointment, and is in possession of a valid visit permit. Counsel can visit their clients from 9:00am to 4:45pm from Monday to Friday. If a case is in trial, counsel may visit their clients upon advance request. Such visits may also be possible from Monday to Friday, between 6:00pm and 7:45pm, provided the case is in trial the following work day. The Registry does not permit counsel visits on Saturdays and Sunday mornings, as such times are reserved for visits of families and friends of detainees. No visits at all are permitted on Sunday afternoons.

20–204   All persons including counsel are subject to the security requirements of the UNDU and the Penitentiary Complex, such as personal searches of clothing and x-ray examination of possessions on entry

(Regulations 38 and 39). These measures may be repeated during entry as deemed required by the Commanding Officer or the Penitentiary Complex. Searches of counsel do not extend to the reading or copying of privileged documents or materials in the possession of counsel (Regulation 39(B) Detention Regulations). Detainees may refuse to see visitors (see Rule 62 of the Rules of Detention). While at first glance, this may seem like an improbable occurrence, there have in fact been quite a few instances where detainees refused to see their visitors.

Visit Permits

Counsel who has presented a valid power of attorney, originating from a suspect or accused, to the Registry or is assigned to a detainee by the Registry will automatically be issued a regular visit permit to visit his client (see Regulation 31(A) of the Regulations). The permits are usually issued for between one week and a year, depending upon the circumstances. The permits will not be issued in paper to counsel, instead they will be transmitted directly to the UNDU. Thus, despite Regulation 37 of the Regulations, the requirement to show a written permit is not applied in practice. OLAD is counsel's contact point for any questions regarding permits. Counsel may request visit permits for support staff members (legal consultants, legal assistants, investigators, or interpreters) in a case. These permits are usually issued on a one-time basis, as the Registry considers that the main points of contact for accused are their lead and co-counsel, and not support staff members.

20–205

Privileged Communications

Rule 65 of the Rules of Detention establishes that all communications of counsel with their clients including those during visits are privileged:

"(A) Each detainee shall be entitled to communicate fully and without restraint with his legal representative, with the assistance of an interpreter where necessary.

(B) All such communications shall be privileged, unless the Registrar has reasonable grounds to believe that the privilege is being abused in an attempt to:

i. arrange an escape;
ii. interfere with or intimidate witnesses;
iii. interfere with the administration of justice; or
iv. otherwise endanger the security and safety of the Detention Unit.

Prior to such communications being monitored, the detainee and his counsel shall be notified by the Registrar of the reasons for monitoring. The detainee may at any time request the President to reverse any decision made by the Registrar under this Rule.

(C) Unless such legal representative and interpreter have been provided by the Tribunal on the basis of the indigency of the detainee, all such communications shall be borne at the expense of the detainee.

D) All such visits shall be made by prior arrangement with the Commanding Officer as to the time and duration of the visit and shall be

20–206

subject to the same security controls as are imposed under Rule 61. The Commanding Officer shall not refuse a request for such a visit without reasonable grounds.

(E) Subject to Sub-Rule (B) of this Rule, interviews with legal representatives and interpreters shall be conducted in the sight but not within the hearing, either direct or indirect, of the staff of the Detention Unit."

20–207   The practice of the Registry is to view the privilege as extending to lead and co-counsel in the event they are assigned counsel, and to two nominated counsel for an accused whose defence is privately funded. Legal assistants and investigators are not granted privileged permits, but fall under the category of "others" in Rules 58 and 62 of the Rules of Detention. However, if they visit together with counsel, the entire visit will be privileged. It should be noted that counsel, whether in attendance or not, take full responsibility for the conduct of his support staff members.

20–208   When counsel wishes to visit a detainee other than his/her client, a written reasoned request must be submitted to the Registry, together with written consent from both detainees and from counsel of the other detainee whom counsel wishes to visit. Such requests would again fall under Rule 61 of the Rules of Detention; they are thus considered non-privileged visits.

20–209   Visits of a counsel who has not yet obtained a power of attorney or whose assignment has been requested by a detainee, may be permitted and may be granted privilege, exceptionally. Detainees who have an assigned counsel or private lawyer, may receive visits from other lawyers under Rule 65 of the Rules of Detention, only if they have been authorised by the detainee to represent him/her in legal proceedings other than those before the Tribunal.

20–210   All visits, including privileged visits, will be monitored visually to ensure the safety of both the visitor and accused and the good order of the UNDU. A non-privileged visit means that the Registrar, through the Commanding Officer, may monitor a visit live by having a staff member of the detention facility attend the visit, or may choose other measures of monitoring.

Telephone and Fax Communications

20–211   Detainees can call their registered counsel every day on a registered privileged phone line to the office of counsel. Such calls can be made by detainees from 7:30am to 12:00pm, from 1:00pm until 5:00pm, and from 6:00pm until lock-up. Up to twenty detainees on a floor of the UNDU share one "privileged" phone. In case of urgency, the Commanding Officer is authorised to consider granting justified exceptions from these time limitations. All of detainees' calls to counsel are paid by the Tribunal.

20–212   The Registry is very restrictive in response to requests for privileged communications to the home telephones of counsel, because it is of the view that professional ethics and in particular independence of counsel, demand that counsel assist their clients from their office, not as private persons from home. Privileged communications to mobile phones are not allowed at all due to the high risk that a mobile phone may be transferred temporarily or permanently to another person than counsel, which would constitute an abuse of the privilege.

Nevertheless, abuses occur and are sometimes discovered, even though it is difficult to obtain the information. In the Tribunal's life, several detainees have abused the privilege by calling the office of their counsel abroad, not for seeking legal advice, but for communicating with acquaintances, family members, etc. In all circumstances, sanctions were imposed on the particular detainee. **20–213**

As for visit permits, the telephone privilege is not considered to extend to consultants, legal assistants, investigators or other persons assisting the defence. Interpreters for the defence may be included if counsel and client do not speak the same language.

Counsel can call their clients at the UNDU during the times indicated above. As UNDU staff are neither in a position to verify that a caller is actually the counsel of a detainee, nor to trace the number the call is made from, calls of counsel are not put through, rather, the detainee is informed immediately that counsel has called and can then place a call to his counsel. This procedure may appear complicated, but ensures that detainees do not receive calls from unauthorised persons effectively and without major difficulties or costs for detainees or counsel. In view of the distance of the office of most counsel from The Hague, as a courtesy, the Registry has enabled detainees to receive, within reason, faxes from their counsel at the UNDU. On an exceptional basis, detainees will be allowed to have faxes sent from the UNDU to their counsel. This is at the discretion of the Commanding Officer and will only be done in situations where no other suitable means of communication is available. The usual path of facsimile communications is through OLAD. **20–214**

Detainees have no access to the internet. Likewise, detainees are not permitted to possess portable phones or any other receiving or transmitting equipment. **20–215**

Exchange of Documentation

Detainees may receive mail and parcels from counsel. While these are privileged, based on security considerations they will be x-rayed, and if from the x-ray it appears that a letter or parcel contains anything other than paper documents it will be opened and the non-paper contents monitored before being forwarded to the detainee or retained by the UNDU if considered contraband. If the Commanding Officer has reasonable grounds to believe that this facility is being abused in an attempt to arrange escape, interfere with or intimidate a witness, interfere with the administration of justice, or otherwise disturb the good order of the UNDU, the Commander may take appropriate steps to rectify this situation.[92] The delivery of counsel mail or parcels into the facility requires an extra 24 hours in addition to the normal post distribution time, as does the sending of mail from detainees to counsel. **20–216**

---

[92] See Rule 59 of the Rules of Detention, and Regulations 11 and 14 of the Regulations.

According to the Regulations, only lead and co-counsel may pass an item to a detainee during a visit (see Regulations 40 and 41). The practice of the Registry also to allow detainees to pass paper documents to counsel during meetings at the UNDU. As legal meetings are conducted in the sight, but out of the hearing of UNDU staff, the staff intervene if contraband items are passed on to the detainee.

20–217   As the legal privilege extends only to documents relevant for the criminal case of a detainee, counsel would abuse the confidentiality privilege if he or she were to import or export to or from a privileged meeting with a detainee, a non-privileged document, such as contract papers, a last will, business papers, letters to third parties or other documents. Documents other than those necessary for the criminal case are monitored by the Registry for the purposes of the safe and secure detention of the accused; for witness protection purposes, and to prevent interference with the administration of justice (see Regulation 8 of the Regulations).

20–218   Counsel are allowed to import and export evidence audio- and videotapes, as well as some forms of digital material to and from their clients subject to the internal regulations of the UNDU. Thus, as these items require a strict security-clearance, the UNDU must be informed in advance and they must be submitted at least 24 hours before a detainee can receive them. Detainees may request to make use of audio and video playback facilities in their cells. The UNDU is currently designing a policy for the import and export of electronic means such as diskettes.

Visiting Facilities for Counsel at the Detention Unit

20–219   The detention facility has 12 visiting rooms available for visits from counsel, family, consular representatives or others. These facilities are shared between all detainees and are therefore limited, although they compare extremely well to what would be available at a detention facility in a non-international context. The visiting rooms permit confidential conversations out of sight and hearing of other detainees meeting other visitors, but within the sight of the UNDU Staff.

20–220   A visiting room must be booked in advance. In case of overbooking, the first selection principle applied will be first-come-first-served, giving priority however to legal visits and first degree family members. The visiting rooms are equipped with desks and chairs, but not with computers or other office equipment. If counsel wishes to make use of his own laptop during a visit at the UNDU, it must be requested at the same time as the visit appointment. One of the visiting rooms is currently being used as an office for the preparation of the defence of the accused, Slobodan Milošević, who is representing himself before the Tribunal.

Communications Facilities during the Hearings and in Hearing Breaks

20–221   At the main building, counsel can communicate with their clients during hearings and breaks. During hearings, they are able to pass on messages written on paper to their clients, and to receive messages from their clients in the same way. Unless authorised by the Chamber, counsel may not approach their clients during hearings, who are sitting behind them on a separate bench. During hearing breaks, counsel can meet with their clients in one of the many holding cells in the same building as the courtroom, within the sight of the Tribunal's security staff. Counsel are not allowed to bring equipment other than paper, documents and pencils into these cells, so mobile phones or any other communications equipment are not permitted. The Registry has installed a telephone in one of these holding cells for self-represented accused. In line with the practices at the UNDU for accused who are represented by counsel, the accused has privileged telephone access to one or two lawyers.

IX. DEONTOLOGY

A. ETHICAL RULES FOR COUNSEL

(1) Relevance

Ethical matters have been an important issue within the practice of the ICTY. Defence Counsel appearing before the Tribunal are bound to comply with the Code of Conduct. Failure to do so will be taken extremely seriously by the Tribunal, and may bring grave consequences. This message was brought home, as it were, in the judgment on contempt involving Milan Vujin, former defence counsel of the accused Dusan Tadić. Counsel Vujin was, in short, found guilty of witness intimidation and influencing and putting forward statements to the court which were known to him to be false. The Appeals Chamber, after confirming the Tribunal's right to punish for contempt (see paragraph 20–64), proceeded to address the counsel's conduct in the case[93]:

20–222

> "It unfortunately happens that counsel occasionally do abuse such privileges or act dishonestly or improperly. Such cases usually involve conduct on the part of counsel which is intended, for whatever reason, to assist in winning the case for the client whom counsel represents. That is bad enough. In the present case, the Respondent's conduct has been *against* the interests of his client. That is even worse, particularly where the client is in custody and relies so heavily upon his counsel for assistance. The conduct of the Respondent in this case strikes at the very heart of the criminal justice system. [...]
>
> The contempt requires punishment which serves not only as retribution for what has been done but also as deterrence of others who may be tempted to act in the same way. Before determining what punishment should be imposed, however, it is necessary to consider what other consequences may flow from the finding by the Appeals Chamber that the Respondent is in contempt of the Tribunal, so that those consequences may be taken into account in that determination.

[93] *Prosecutor v Tadić*, Case 94-1-A-R77, Judgement on Allegations of Misconduct against Prior Counsel, Milan Vujin, January 31, 2000 (Appeals Chamber), paras 12–18, 132–150, 160; and paragraphs 20–49 *et seq.* above.

The Code (of Conduct) defines professional misconduct as including any violation of the Code and engaging in conduct which involves dishonesty, deceit or misrepresentation or which is prejudicial to the proper administration of justice before the Tribunal. Knowingly making an incorrect statement of a material fact to the Tribunal and offering evidence which counsel knows to be incorrect amount to violations of Article 13 of the Code. The Respondent has been guilty of professional misconduct in all the categories described.

In the opinion of the Appeals Chamber, the Registrar has power generally to strike the Respondent off the list of assigned counsel because of his serious professional misconduct as demonstrated by the Appeals Chamber's findings. A direction will therefore be given to the Registrar to consider striking the Respondent off the list and reporting his conduct as found by the Appeals Chamber to the professional body to which he belongs. [. . .]"

20–223   These quotations are instructive for the framework of ethical rules for counsel at the Tribunal, and for the motivation of the judges to take unethical conduct of defence counsel serious. The framework for ethical standards for counsel conduct has been further set by the 2004 amendments to the RPE and the Directive related to the qualification requirements for counsel to be admitted to the Rule 45-list (see paragraphs 20–49 *et seq.* and paragraphs 20–106 and 20–107). The prosecution counsel are bound by their own ethical code of conduct as laid out in Prosecutor's Regulation No. 2 (1999)—Standards of Professional Conduct for Prosecution Counsel, of September 14, 1999.

(2) Contempt of Court

20–224   When the RPE was first drafted, it did not contain a substantial rule on contempt, and merely contained three paragraphs on contempt in Rule 77, and in addition, misconduct of counsel was mentioned in Rule 46. Since then, the contempt regime has been developed by the judges into a fully fledged procedure in Rule 77 of the RPE, a rule now covering three pages. So far, there have been eleven contempt proceedings initiated in respect of counsel.[94] Some of the cases conducted resulted in sentences and judgments, some in withdrawal of the charges or acquittals, while others are still ongoing. The judgments set out in detail the legal concepts advanced by the respective Trial or Appeals Chambers.

20–225   Rule 46 has been employed a number of times by Chambers, albeit never to the extent that audience was refused to a counsel during an ongoing trial.

(3) Code of Conduct

20–226   The Tribunal's Code of Conduct was first promulgated by the Registrar in the summer of 1997. The Code of Conduct contained a number of standard obligations of counsel, but was nevertheless rather

---

[94] Examples of cases where counsel acting before the Tribunal were charged with contempt under Rule 77 of the RPE: *Prosecutor v Simić*, Case No. IT-95-9-AR77, Judgment in the Matter of Contempt Allegations Against an Accused and his Counsel, June 30, 2000, *Prosecutor v Aleksovski*, Case No. IT-95-14/1-AR77, Decision of the Trial Chamber Finding Mr Zlatko Aleksovski in Contempt, December 11, 1998; *Prosecutor v Tadić*, Case No. IT-94-1-A-AR77, Judgment on Allegations of Contempt Against Prior Counsel, Milan Vujin, January 21, 2000. See also *Prosecutor v Brdanin*, Case No. IT-99-36-R77.

sketchy in other areas, such as enforcement of disciplinary measures, conflicts of interest and the like. However, it has been referred to on a large number of occasions by the Chambers when taking decisions on motions.

The Code of Conduct has been amended substantially in July 2002, **20–227** now comprising of 50 Articles instead of only 23. The structure has been completely revised, and the amended Code of Conduct contains substantial changes. Some of these changes are as follows:

(1) The Code of Conduct refers not only to the duty of counsel to his client, but also to his or her obligations as an officer of the court (Articles 3, 10);

(2) The Article on conflicts of interests was further elaborated (Article 14);

(3) A prohibition of fee-splitting practices was added (Article 18);

(4) A provision on proper conduct towards court officials is now contained in the text (Article 27);

(5) The soliciting of clients is now expressly prohibited (Article 30);

(6) The responsibility of counsel for the defence team is established (Article 34);

(7) A disciplinary regime is added (Articles 37 *et seq.*).

The amendments were approved by the judges. The disciplinary **20–228** regime has by now been firmly established in the rules and practice of the Tribunal.

(4) ADC Disciplinary Council

The disciplinary regime of the ADC is governed by the Disciplinary **20–229** Council, which in turn is guided by Articles 15 to 19 of the ADC Constitution, which specify the duties of the Council. The Disciplinary Council is an independent organ of the ADC, charged with three clearly defined functions as set out in Article 16 of the ADC Constitution. The Disciplinary Council is responsible: (1) for monitoring of the conduct of the members of the ADC in their representation of the accused before the Tribunal; (2) adjudicating complaints expressed against the ADC members for alleged misconduct in accordance with Article 18 of the ADC constitution; and (3) providing advisory opinions on matters relating to the Code of Conduct, and the Directive, as well as the interpretation of the ADC Constitution, pursuant to Article 19 of the ADC Constitution. The Disciplinary Council consists of five full members elected by General Assembly for a term of one year. The Council acting upon a complaint may a) mediate between the parties to the disagreement; b) issue a formal warning to the respondent member for his conduct; c) refer the complaint to the Disciplinary Panel of the International Tribunal; and/or d) terminate membership. All decisions made by the Disciplinary Council are taken by majority vote, and are guided by their empowering constitution, the Statute, Rules, Code of Conduct, the Directive and the Detention Rules of the Tribunal (Article 15 of the ADC Constitution). While the procedure laid out is different and separate from that in the Code of Conduct and the latter takes precedence in the Tribunal system, it is expected that the ADC and the Registry will increase their cooperation in disciplinary matters in future and that they will find a way to merge or coordinate between the two separately existing systems.

(5) Misconduct

20–230   The amended Code of Conduct contains a full disciplinary regime in its Articles 37–50. A Disciplinary Panel has been established under Article 40 of the Code of Conduct, consisting of members of the ADC, the Advisory Panel and the Registry, and it is competent to deal with "all matters relating to counsel ethics". Mostly, it receives and decides upon complaints. It is empowered to issue findings and a number of sanctions ranging from admonishments to fines and suspensions or bans from practice at the Tribunal (Article 47). By mid-2005, four cases have been brought before the Disciplinary Panel; the disciplinary panel has rendered a decision in one case,[95] and the remaining three are currently pending before the Disciplinary Panel.

(6) Relation to National Ethical Rules

20–231   Defence counsel at the Tribunal have frequently raised the issue of conflicting obligations, and were adamant that it was difficult to adhere to ICTY ethical rules in cases of conflicts, because they would risk losing their licence to practice law. From a viewpoint of international law, this appears not to be convincing, although practice may be different. The Tribunal's Code of Conduct is international law created on the basis of a proper procedure and with a legitimate interest to secure proper judicial proceedings. It would be difficult to acknowledge how national codes of ethics created for national systems could claim applicability over a code created by the Tribunal as a consequence of its powers provided by the Statute. Consequently, in case of inconsistency with the national codes, the Tribunal's Code of Conduct has supremacy (see Article 4 of the Code of Conduct).

However, it seems a fair practical point that if national professional associations take action against counsel for an act or omission committed in executing functions for a defence before the Tribunal, then counsel should be supported by the Registry before his professional association. It also remains possible that the ADC (or another ICTY counsel association) plays a role in this.

(7) Responsibility of the Registrar

20–232   For better or worse, thus far, the Registrar has exercised a number of functions which would usually be exercised by a professional association. Under the provisions of the Code of Conduct, the Registrar plays a

---

[95] The one case related to fraud and abuse of the Tribunal's legal-aid funds. The Disciplinary Panel disciplined the counsel in 2004, ordering the payment of a fine and a two year suspension from practicing before the Tribunal.

role in the investigating complaints and allegations of counsel misconduct in spite of the existence of the ADC. It is submitted that the Registrar is a suitable organ for this in the specific setting of this Tribunal, as his office is an independent service provider to the court and has the status and resources to investigate such matters. The Registrar has assigned a number of times *amicus curiae* prosecutors or investigators to do the initial verification of allegations. In an ideal setting, such inquiries would be undertaken and performed by or on behalf of a counsel association.

X. PROFESSIONAL BODIES

A. Association for Defence Counsel at the ICTY ("ADC")

The ADC was established to ensure that defence counsel practicing **20–233** before the Tribunal adhere to the highest standards of professional conduct and to guarantee that the interests of defence counsel practicing before the Tribunal were collectively represented by a single body. The judges of the Tribunal formally acknowledged the ADC during their plenary session of July 2002. In addition, during the same plenary, the judges adopted an amendment to the RPE recounted above, Rule 44(A)(iii) which stipulates that: "(c)ounsel engaged by a suspect or an accused [...] shall be considered qualified to represent a suspect or accused if the counsel satisfies the Registrar that he or she [...] is a member in good standing of an association of counsel practicing at the Tribunal recognized by the Registrar." The requirement detailed in Rule 44(A)(iii) presupposes that the association of counsel will play an active role in ensuring the professional integrity of its membership. The ADC's Disciplinary Council ("Council"), is the organ responsible for governing the conduct of its membership. The responsibilities of the ADC Disciplinary Council have been listed in paragraph 20–229. Complaints against an ADC member for alleged misconduct may be brought by a full member of the ADC, persons accused by the Tribunal, and staff members of the Tribunal, whose rights or interests are affected by the alleged professional or ethical misconduct.

Although the relationship between the Registry and the ADC has at **20–234** times been contentious, over time, as a result of joint consultations on a number of projects—cooperative efforts that have allowed the ADC to shape various issues affecting defence counsel—the relationship has improved. Projects on which the Registry and the ADC have had joint consultations include the development of the pre-trial and trial lump-sum payment policies, the shaping of the role and responsibilities of duty counsel, a translation policy and proposals for amendments to the Directive. In addition, with a view to communicating on the multitude of issues that concern defence counsel acting before the Tribunal, the Registry and the ADC engage in regular meetings. It is anticipated that the ADC will continue to grow as an important partner of the Tribunal, and work in collaboration with it, so as to best serve the interests of their memberships, the accused and at the end, the administration of justice.

B. ADVISORY PANEL

20–235   The Advisory Panel was initially established for the purpose of assisting the Registrar to carry out his mandate to create and implement the legal-aid system, and, to serve as a consultative body with respect to counsel and legal-aid issues. Although in its early years, especially in the very beginning in 1995-1996, the Panel made a substantial contribution to the development of the Tribunal's rules and practices regarding legal-aid, over time, the Panel's involvement and relevance decreased. In 1999, the Panel convened to discuss increasing its involvement in a number of important issues, including the qualification requirements for counsel acting before the Tribunal, a disciplinary regime regulating the conduct of defence counsel, and possible conflicts between the Tribunal's Code of Conduct and national codes regulating the conduct of defence counsel practicing before the Tribunal. In early 2001, the Advisory Panel's structure was reorganised to include at least two counsel, who have practice experience before the Tribunal. Issues raised were finally addressed by the Tribunal during the judges' plenary session of July 2002, and proposals led to, *inter alia*, a newly amended Code of Conduct.

20–236   In 2004, the ADC requested both the Registry and the Advisory Panel itself to clarify the Panel's exact role and function and to streamline and make more transparent its procedures and working methods. The Panel has expressed its preference, that it occupy a general policymaking role, as opposed to being involved in individual cases. It has begun implementing this role by advising the Registry on the issue of enforcement of fees owed by partially indigent accused to their Tribunal assigned defence counsel. The Registry, in its most recent proposal for an amended Directive (submitted to the judges in July 2005), has endeavoured to encompass the Advisory Panel's more general role and has withdrawn provisions which involve the Panel in individual case related questions (see Article 31 of the current Directive). In addition, the newly proposed Directive, for the first time, delegates an advisory role, to the ADC.

20–237   President of the Panel has been the longstanding and respected President of the Dutch Bar, an institution which has provided major support to the Registry and defence counsel.

XI. THE INTERNATIONAL CRIMINAL COURT

20–238   The International Criminal Court ("ICC")[96] was established in 2002, by the coming into force of the Rome Statute of the International Criminal Court ("Rome Statute").[97] The ICC is charged with prosecut-

---

[96] For a full discussion on the ICC, see generally W. Schabas, *An Introduction to the International Criminal Court* (Cambridge, Cambridge University Press, 2001).

[97] The Rome Statute came into force on July 1, 2002 ("Rome Statute"). The Statute was formerly adopted by the U.N. Diplomatic Conference of Plenipotetiatics on the Establishment of an International Criminal Court on July 17, 1998, pmbl., U.N. Doc. A/CONF. 183/9 (1998), 37 I.L.M. 999. Almost all participating states voted in favour of its establishment, the exceptions being: the United States, Israel, People's Republic of China, Iraq, Qatar, Libya and Yemen.

ing individuals for genocide, crimes against humanity, and war crimes as defined in the Rome Statute. The official seat of the ICC is based in The Hague, the Netherlands, although the court may sit elsewhere whenever it considers it desirable, as provided in the Statute (Article 3(1), (3) of the Rome Statute). As of May 12, 2005, 99 countries are official States Parties to the Rome Statute.[98] The establishment of the ICC is a major accomplishment in the protection and advancement of the international rule of law and human rights, although much will depend on the implementation of the Rome Statute and the cooperation of states. The words of the Secretary-General of the United Nations reflect high expectations for the permanent court: "(n)o ruler, no State, no junta and no army anywhere can abuse human rights with impunity [...] and that those who violate those rights will be punished"[99] and brought to face justice before the world. The development of the ICC is a logical extension of the establishment and work of ad hoc tribunals.

Differences between ad hoc Tribunals and the ICC

There are several notable differences between the ad hoc Tribunals **20–239** of the former Yugoslavia and Rwanda, as compared to the ICC. First, the ICTY and ICTR were created by the UN Security Council pursuant to Chapter VII of the UN Charter, and granted clear and limited mandates to respond to specific crises. As such their jurisdictions are limited in time (*ratione temporis*) and in scope (*ratione loci*). Conversely, the ICC is a treaty-born "permanent" and independent international organization. Due to its enduring nature, the ICC does away with the initial delays and costs associated with creating ad hoc tribunals. The ICC also does not have retroactive jurisdiction and can only try crimes committed after its inception (July 2002).[100] Further, ad hoc tribunals need the assistance of the Security Council, the General Assembly, or other UN bodies for specific matters such as the appointment of judges, approval of the budget, the enforcement of their sentences and forcing unwilling states to cooperate. Conversely, the relationship of the ICC with the UN is limited to Security Council referrals under the Rome Statute and assistance from the UN for payment of any prosecutions under such referrals. On the other hand, the ICC is very much dependent on the cooperation of states, in investigations, referrals and in matters of jurisdiction. Hence, the court's success depends to an extent on future cooperation of the most powerful states in the world some of which have not supported its establishment.

---

[98] The 99 countries divide consist of the following regional make-up: African States: 27, Asian States: 12, Eastern Europe: 15, Latin America and the Caribbean: 20, Western Europe and other States: 25. See the official ICC website, *State Parties to the Rome Statute*, www.icc-cpi.int/asp/statesparties.html.

[99] See Address of the Secretary General of the UN to the opening plenary of the Preparatory Commission of the ICC, delivered on February 16, 1999.

[100] Rome Statute, Article 11(1) provides: "The Court has jurisdiction only with respect to crimes committed after the entry into force of this Statute."

20–240   The ICTR,[101] ICTY[102] and the ICC[103] are the same in that they only possess jurisdiction to try natural persons. They are different in the fact that the ICTY and ICTR have primary jurisdiction, which means that in cases of a jurisdictional clash between a domestic jurisdiction and the ICTY or ICTR, the ad hoc tribunals will have exclusive jurisdiction. The jurisdiction of the ICC, on the other hand, is based on the principle of "complementarity", which allows for international proceedings to co-exist, rather than pre-empt national mechanisms already in existence. Thus, unlike the ICTY or the ICTR, the ICC will not assert its primacy over the crimes in question, and will only act when countries themselves are "unable"[104] or "unwilling"[105] to investigate or prosecute persons accused of crimes within its jurisdiction.[106]

20–241   Finally, in contrast to the relative haste in which ad hoc tribunals are usually set up and the involvement of the highest United Nations levels acting pursuant to world wide outrage at atrocities in the respective regions, the ICC has been established through a more comprehensive process of negotiations and preparations over the span of four years. This reality has afforded the court the opportunity to prepare and address, *inter alia*, financial matters, issues relating to privileges and cooperation with other organisations, as well as prepare the development of an association of defence attorneys (a process which had not been completed by the time of going to print). The ICC has also been in a position to equip itself and benefit from a pool of judges, prosecutors, defence counsel and judicial and other administrators who are familiar with the issues faced by an international criminal court.[107]

Lessons Learned

20–242   The new practices and methods pertaining to criminal investigation and prosecution in the international arena that have been developed so far by both the ICTY and ICTR have been of use and, to an extent, employed in the drafting of the *Rules of Procedure and Evidence* of the ICC. Other areas exist in which the experience of the ICTY and ICTR may appear crucial for the effective functioning of the ICC—whether or not it is to learn from lesions or to copy procedures and methods. The existing regimes for witness protection and legal-aid of the two tribunals are examples which should be looked at and the lessons taken into account. State cooperation is another, which is likely to be a significant issue for the ICC. The ICC, as a treaty based court, without

---

[101] See Statute of the International Criminal Tribunal for Rwanda, Article 5.

[102] See Statute of the Tribunal, Article 6.

[103] See Rome Statute, Article 25(1).

[104] A country may be "unable", when its law enforcement and judicial system no longer functions.

[105] A country may be regarded as "unwilling" if there are indications that it does not investigate or prosecute a crime because it is shielding someone from responsibility from crimes that can be tried by the ICC.

[106] See Rome Statute, Article 17(1) which provides that a case will be inadmissible before the ICC on a number of grounds, all of which are guided by the "complementarity principle".

[107] A number of ICTY staff, at all levels, have made the transfer to the ICC.

the Chapter VII origins of the ad hoc Tribunals, will be more dependent, than the ICTY or ICTR, on the compliance of States with requests for cooperation. Accordingly, the experiences and case-law of the ad hoc Tribunals will be of great importance to the ICC.

The Rights of Suspects and Accused under the ICC

Borrowing much of the language from the legal documents of the ICTY and the ICTY, the Rome Statute protects the rights of suspects[108] and accused persons.[109] The Rome Statute strikes a balance between upholding protection for the victims and precluding any infringements on the rights of the accused. The ICC Statute includes primary assurance of the right to fair trial recognised in international law and standards so that a person accused of genocide, crimes against humanity and war crimes will have the guarantees enshrined in the notion of a public, fair and unbiased trial. With regard to the provisions that address the rights of the accused, the Rome Statute requires the prosecutor to scrutinise not only incriminating evidence, but also exonerating evidence, so that such evidence can be made available to the defence as well (Article 67). Furthermore, trials *in absentia* are not allowed, however, trials will continue without the presence of the accused in the courtroom if the latter is disorderly. In such a case, the accused will have the right to observe the trial and instruct counsel during the proceedings from outside the courtroom. Of interest is the creation of a position for counsel for victims and victim groups with a role in the proceedings, a development which is to be monitored closely as to its effects on proceedings, on the regions and the people residing in those regions which are addressed in the ICC cases. **20–243**

The notion of presumption of innocence with respect to the accused, as in the practice of the ICTY and ICTR, has been given a more prominent place at the ICC. Apart from the usual position that the prosecution bears the burden of proof throughout the trial (Article 66 of the Rome Statute), if an accused person pleads guilty, the ICC has the duty to disregard such plea if it is not absolutely sure that it was made in a voluntary manner, and after thorough consultation with defence counsel, or if there is an indication that the accused does not comprehend the nature and possible consequences of such declaration. The stipulations on protection on witnesses and evidence (Articles 68 and 69 respectively), which allow for special measures such as in-camera hearing and recorded testimony will be allowed as far as they do not undermine the rights of the accused. Furthermore, the Pre-Trial Chamber has a key function in assessing the prosecutor's power and guaranteeing that the rights of the accused are upheld. One example of this is when there is a unique situation in which there is only a single chance of collecting evidence or taking testimony, which might not be available at a later stage of the proceedings to the detriment of the accused. In such a case, the Prosecutor must inform the Trial Chamber. **20–244**

---

[108] See Rome Statute, Article 55 ("Rights of Persons during an investigation").
[109] See Rome Statute, Article 67 ("Rights of the Accused").

If the judges believe that there are necessary measures to protect the right of the accused, it may assign an expert or a judge to supervise the proceeding.

XII. REFERRALS TO THE REGION UNDER RULE 11BIS

20–245   While one of the more pressing jurisdictional aims at the Tribunal's establishment was to ensure its primacy over national courts (Article 9 of the Statute), it was from the outset envisaged that the smaller war crimes cases would be returned to the region. The Tribunal has been established to address the political and military leaders implicated in war crimes, not the lower ranking individuals. With the arrival of higher ranking accused over the years and the domestic processes of rebuilding the rule of law systems since the conflict, referrals back to the region of the former Yugoslavia have become more logical and feasible. It also appears a welcome and useful tool to release the pending workload of trials (especially increased since the more than twenty arrivals since November 2004), also in light of the announce-ment of the Completion Strategy by the United Nations Security Council. The prosecution has recently initialled a number of referral requests under Rule 11*bis*. Rule 11*bis* has been extensively developed since the original Rule and now provides an extensive procedure for the referral of indictments to another court. The specifically established Referral Bench has already referred several cases under Rule 11*bis* and, with the support of the Appeals Chamber, established initial jurispru-dence on the legal and factual standards applied.[110]

---

[110] *Prosecutor v Ademi and Norać*, IT-04–78-PT, Decision for Referral to the Authorities of the Republic of Croatia pursuant to Rule 11*bis*, September 14, 2005; *Prosecutor v Stanković*, Case No. IT-96–23/2, IT-96-23/2-AR11*bis*.1, Referral Bench's Decision on Referral of Case under Rule 11bis, partly confidential and *ex parte*, May 17, 2005, and Appeals Chamber Decision, September 1, 2005. [decision was public, its annexes confidential and *ex parte*]" *Prosecutor v Mejakić et al.*, IT-02–65-PT, Decision on Prosecutor's Motion for Referral of Case Pursuant to Rule 11*bis*, July 20, 2005; *Prosecutor v Janković*, IT-96–23/2, Decision on Referral of Case under Rule 11*bis*, July 22, 2005; *Prosecutor v Rašević and Todović*, Case No. 97–25/1-PT, Decision on referral of case under Rule 11*bis*, with confidential annexes I and II *Prosecutor v Milosević*, IT-98–29/1, Decision on Referral of Case pursuant to Rule 11*bis*, July 8, 2005.

APPENDIX A

INTERNATIONAL TREATIES

1019

AA. Charter of the Nuremberg International Military Tribunal

August 8, 1945

I. CONSTITUTION OF THE INTERNATIONAL MILITARY TRIBUNAL

ARTICLE 1

AA–001   In pursuance of the Agreement signed on the 8th day of August 1945 by the Government of the United States of America, the Provisional Government of the French Republic, the Government of the United Kingdom of Great Britain and Northern Ireland and the Government of the Union of Soviet Socialist Republics, there shall be established an International Military Tribunal (hereinafter called "the Tribunal") for the just and prompt trial and punishment of the major war criminals of the European Axis.

ARTICLE 2

AA–002   The Tribunal shall consist of four members, each with an alternate. One member and one alternate shall be appointed by each of the Signatories. The alternates shall, so far as they are able, be present at all sessions of the Tribunal. In case of illness of any member of the Tribunal or his incapacity for some other reason to fulfil his functions, his alternate shall take his place.

ARTICLE 3

AA–003   Neither the Tribunal, its members nor their alternates can be challenged by the prosecution, or by the Defendants or their Counsel. Each Signatory may replace its members of the Tribunal or his alternate for reasons of health or for other good reasons, except that no replacement may take place during a Trial, other than by an alternate.

ARTICLE 4

AA–004   (a) The presence of all four members of the Tribunal or the alternate for any absent member shall be necessary to constitute the quorum.

(b) The members of the Tribunal shall, before any trial begins, agree among themselves upon the selection from their number of a President, and the President shall hold office during the trial, or as may otherwise be agreed by a vote of not less than three members. The principle of rotation of presidency for successive trials is agreed. If, however, a session of the Tribunal takes place on the territory of one of the four Signatories, the representative of that signatory on the Tribunal shall preside.

(c) Save as aforesaid the Tribunal shall take decisions by a majority vote and in case the votes are evenly divided, the vote of the President shall be decisive: provided always that convictions and sentences shall only be imposed by affirmative votes of at least three members of the Tribunal.

ARTICLE 5

AA–005   In case of need and depending on the number of the matters to be tried, other Tribunals may be set up; and the establishment, functions, and procedure of each Tribunal shall be identical, and shall be governed by this Charter.

II. Jurisdiction and General Principles

Article 6

The Tribunal established by the Agreement referred to in Article 1 hereof for the trial **AA–006** and punishment of the major war criminals of the European Axis countries shall have the power to try and punish persons who, acting in the interests of the European Axis countries, whether as individuals or as members of organizations, committed any of the following crimes.

The following acts, or any of them, are crimes coming within the jurisdiction of the Tribunal for which there shall be individual responsibility:

    (a) Crimes Against Peace: namely, planning, preparation, initiation or waging of a war of aggression, or a war in violation of international treaties, agreements or assurances, or participation in a common plan or conspiracy for the accomplishment of any of the foregoing;

    (b) War Crimes: namely, violations of the laws or customs of war. Such violations shall include, but not be limited to, murder, ill-treatment or deportation to slave labor or for any other purpose of civilian population of or in occupied territory, murder or ill-treatment of prisoners of war or persons on the seas, killing of hostages, plunder of public or private property, wanton destruction of cities, towns or villages, or devastation not justified by military necessity;

    (c) Crimes Against Humanity: namely, murder, extermination, enslavement, deportation, and other inhumane acts committed against any civilian population, before or during the war; or persecutions on political, racial or religious grounds in execution of or in connection with any crime within the jurisdiction of the Tribunal, whether or not in violation of the domestic law of the country where perpetrated.

Leaders, organizers, instigators and accomplices participating in the formulation or execution of a common plan or conspiracy to commit any of the foregoing crimes are responsible for all acts performed by any persons in execution of such plan.

Article 7

The official position of defendants, whether as Heads of State or responsible officials **AA–007** in Government Departments, shall not be considered as freeing them from responsibility or mitigating punishment.

Article 8

The fact that the Defendant acted pursuant to order of his Government or of a **AA–008** superior shall not free him from responsibility, but may be considered in mitigation of punishment if the Tribunal determines that justice so requires.

Article 9

At the trial of any individual member of any group or organization the Tribunal may **AA–009** declare (in connection with any act of which the individual may be convicted) that the group or organization of which the individual was a member was a criminal organization.

After the receipt of the Indictment the Tribunal shall give such notice as it thinks fit that the prosecution intends to ask the Tribunal to make such declaration and any member of the organization will be entitled to apply to the Tribunal for leave to be heard by the Tribunal upon the question of the criminal character of the organization. The Tribunal shall have power to allow or reject the application.

If the application is allowed, the Tribunal may direct in what manner the applicants shall be represented and heard.

ARTICLE 10

AA–010   In cases where a group or organization is declared criminal by the Tribunal, the competent national authority of any Signatory shall have the right to bring individual to trial for membership therein before national, military or occupation courts. In any such case the criminal nature of the group or organization is considered proved and shall not be questioned.

ARTICLE 11

AA–011   Any person convicted by the Tribunal may be charged before a national, military or occupation court, referred to in Article 10 of this Charter, with a crime other than of membership in a criminal group or organization and such court may, after convicting him, impose upon him punishment independent of and additional to the punishment imposed by the Tribunal for participation in the criminal activities of such group or organization.

ARTICLE 12

AA–012   The Tribunal shall have the right to take proceedings against a person charged with crimes set out in Article 6 of this Charter in his absence, if he has not been found or if the Tribunal, for any reason, finds it necessary, in the interests of justice, to conduct the hearing in his absence.

ARTICLE 13

AA–013   The Tribunal shall draw up rules for its procedure. These rules shall not be inconsistent with the provisions of this Charter.

III. COMMITTEE FOR THE INVESTIGATION AND PROSECUTION OF MAJOR WAR CRIMINALS

ARTICLE 14

AA–014   Each Signatory shall appoint a Chief Prosecutor for the investigation of the charges against and the prosecution of major war criminals.
    The Chief Prosecutors shall act as a committee for the following purposes:
    (a) to agree upon a plan of the individual work of each of the Chief Prosecutors and his staff,
    (b) to settle the final designation of major war criminals to be tried by the Tribunal,
    (c) to approve the Indictment and the documents to be submitted therewith,
    (d) to lodge the Indictment and the accompany documents with the Tribunal,
    (e) to draw up and recommend to the Tribunal for its approval draft rules of procedure, contemplated by Article 13 of this Charter. The Tribunal shall have the power to accept, with or without amendments, or to reject, the rules so recommended.
    The Committee shall act in all the above matters by a majority vote and shall appoint a Chairman as may be convenient and in accordance with the principle of rotation: provided that if there is an equal division of vote concerning the designation of a Defendant to be tried by the Tribunal, or the crimes with which he shall be charged, that proposal will be adopted which was made by the party which proposed that the particular Defendant be tried, or the particular charges be preferred against him.

ARTICLE 15

AA–015   The Chief Prosecutors shall individually, and acting in collaboration with one another, also undertake the following duties:

(a) investigation, collection and production before or at the Trial of all necessary evidence,
(b) the preparation of the Indictment for approval by the Committee in accordance with paragraph
(c) of Article 14 hereof,
    (c) the preliminary examination of all necessary witnesses and of all Defendants,
(d) to act as prosecutor at the Trial,
(e) to appoint representatives to carry out such duties as may be assigned them,
(f) to undertake such other matters as may appear necessary to them for the purposes of the preparation for and conduct of the Trial.

It is understood that no witness or Defendant detained by the Signatory shall be taken out of the possession of that Signatory without its assent.

IV. Fair Trial for Defendants

Article 16

In order to ensure fair trial for the Defendants, the following procedure shall be followed:

AA–016

(a) The Indictment shall include full particulars specifying in detail the charges against the Defendants. A copy of the Indictment and of all the documents lodged with the Indictment, translated into a language which he understands, shall be furnished to the Defendant at reasonable time before the Trial.
(b) During any preliminary examination or trial of a Defendant he will have the right to give any explanation relevant to the charges made against him.
(c) A preliminary examination of a Defendant and his Trial shall be conducted in, or translated into, a language which the Defendant understands.
(d) A Defendant shall have the right to conduct his own defense before the Tribunal or to have the assistance of Counsel.
(e) A Defendant shall have the right through himself or through his Counsel to present evidence at the Trial in support of his defense, and to cross-examine any witness called by the Prosecution.

V. Powers of the Tribunal and Conduct of the Trial

Article 17

The Tribunal shall have the power

AA–017

(a) to summon witnesses to the Trial and to require their attendance and testimony and to put questions to them
(b) to interrogate any Defendant,
(c) to require the production of documents and other evidentiary material,
(d) to administer oaths to witnesses,
(e) to appoint officers for the carrying out of any task designated by the Tribunal including the power to have evidence taken on commission.

Article 18

The Tribunal shall

AA–018

(a) confine the Trial strictly to an expeditious hearing of the cases raised by the charges,
(b) take strict measures to prevent any action which will cause reasonable delay, and rule out irrelevant issues and statements of any kind whatsoever,
(c) deal summarily with any contumacy, imposing appropriate punishment, including exclusion of any Defendant or his Counsel from some or all further proceedings, but without prejudice to the determination of the charges.

ARTICLE 19

AA–019   The Tribunal shall not be bound by technical rules of evidence. It shall adopt and apply to the greatest possible extent expeditious and nontechnical procedure, and shall admit any evidence which it deems to be of probative value.

ARTICLE 20

AA–020   The Tribunal may require to be informed of the nature of any evidence before it is entered so that it may rule upon the relevance thereof.

ARTICLE 21

AA–021   The Tribunal shall not require proof of facts of common knowledge but shall take judicial notice thereof. It shall also take judicial notice of official governmental documents and reports of the United Nations, including the acts and documents of the committees set up in the various allied countries for the investigation of war crimes, and of records and findings of military or other Tribunals of any of the United Nations.

ARTICLE 22

AA–022   The permanent seat of the Tribunal shall be in Berlin. The first meetings of the members of the Tribunal and of the Chief Prosecutors shall be held at Berlin in a place to be designated by the Control Council for Germany. The first trial shall be held at Nuremberg, and any subsequent trials shall be held at such places as the Tribunal may decide.

ARTICLE 23

AA–023   One or more of the Chief Prosecutors may take part in the prosecution at each Trial. The function of any Chief Prosecutor may be discharged by him personally, or by any person or persons authorized by him.

The function of Counsel for a Defendant may be discharged at the Defendant's request by any Counsel professionally qualified to conduct cases before the Courts of his own country, or by any other person who may be specially authorized thereto by the Tribunal.

ARTICLE 24

AA–024   The proceedings at the Trial shall take the following course:
  (a) The Indictment shall be read in court.
  (b) The Tribunal shall ask each Defendant whether he pleads "guilty" or "not guilty."
  (c) The prosecution shall make an opening statement.
  (d) The Tribunal shall ask the prosecution and the defense what evidence (if any) they wish to submit to the Tribunal, and the Tribunal shall rule upon the admissibility of any such evidence.
  (e) The witnesses for the Prosecution shall be examined and after that the witnesses for the Defense. Thereafter such rebutting evidence as may be held by the Tribunal to be admissible shall be called by either the Prosecution or the Defense.
  (f) The Tribunal may put any question to any witness and to any defendant, at any time.
  (g) The Prosecution and the Defense shall interrogate and may cross-examine any witnesses and any Defendant who gives testimony.

(h) The Defense shall address the court.
(i) The Prosecution shall address the court.
(j) Each Defendant may make a statement to the Tribunal.
(k) The Tribunal shall deliver judgment and pronounce sentence.

ARTICLE 25

All official documents shall be produced, and all court proceedings conducted, in **AA–025**
English, French and Russian, and in the language of the Defendant. So much of the
record and of the proceedings may also be translated into the language of any country in
which the Tribunal is sitting, as the Tribunal is sitting, as the Tribunal considers
desirable in the interests of the justice and public opinion.

VI. Judgment and Sentence

ARTICLE 26

The judgment of the Tribunal as to the guilt or the innocence of any Defendant shall **AA–026**
give the reasons on which it is based, and shall be final and not subject to review.

ARTICLE 27

The Tribunal shall have the right to impose upon a Defendant, on conviction, death or **AA–027**
such other punishment as shall be determined by it to be just.

ARTICLE 28

In addition to any punishment imposed by it, the Tribunal shall have the right to **AA–028**
deprive the convicted person of any stolen property and order its delivery to the Control
Council for Germany.

ARTICLE 29

In case of guilt, sentences shall be carried out in accordance with the orders of the **AA–029**
Control Council for Germany, which may at any time reduce or otherwise alter the
sentences, but may not increase the severity thereof. If the Control Council for
Germany, after any Defendant has been convicted and sentenced, discovers fresh
evidence which, in its opinion, would found a fresh charge against him, the Council shall
report accordingly to the Committee established under Article 14 hereof, for such action
as they may consider proper, having regard to the interests of justice.

VII. Expenses

ARTICLE 30

The expenses of the Tribunal and of the Trials, shall be charged by the Signatories **AA–030**
against the funds allotted for maintenance of the Control Council of Germany.

A1. Geneva Convention for the Amelioration of the Condition of the Wounded and Sick in Armed Forces in the Field

Adopted on 12 August 1949 by the Diplomatic Conference for the Establishment of International Conventions for the Protection of Victims of War, held in Geneva from 21 April to 12 August, 1949

entry into force **21 October 1950**

A1–001   This document may be found at *http://www.icrc.org/ihl.nsf/FULL/365?OpenDocument*

A2. Geneva Convention for the Amelioration of the Condition of Wounded, Sick and Shipwrecked Members of Armed Forces at Sea

Adopted on 12 August 1949 by the Diplomatic Conference for the Establishment of International Conventions for the Protection of Victims of War, held in Geneva from 21 April to 12 August, 1949

entry into force **21 October 1950**

A2–001   This document may be found at *http://www.icrc.org/ihl.nsf/FULL/370?OpenDocument*

A3. Geneva Convention relative to the Treatment of Prisoners of War

Adopted on 12 August 1949 by the Diplomatic Conference for the Establishment of International Conventions for the Protection of Victims of War, held in Geneva from 21 April to 12 August, 1949

entry into force **21 October 1950**

PART I

GENERAL PROVISIONS

ARTICLE 1

A3–001   The High Contracting Parties undertake to respect and to ensure respect for the present Convention in all circumstances.

ARTICLE 2

A3–002   In addition to the provisions which shall be implemented in peace time, the present Convention shall apply to all cases of declared war or of any other armed conflict which may arise between two or more of the High Contracting Parties, even if the state of war is not recognized by one of them.

The Convention shall also apply to all cases of partial or total occupation of the territory of a High Contracting Party, even if the said occupation meets with no armed resistance.

Although one of the Powers in conflict may not be a party to the present Convention, the Powers who are parties thereto shall remain bound by it in their mutual relations. They shall furthermore be bound by the Convention in relation to the said Power, if the latter accepts and applies the provisions thereof.

ARTICLE 3

In the case of armed conflict not of an international character occurring in the territory of one of the High Contracting Parties, each party to the conflict shall be bound to apply, as a minimum, the following provisions: **A3–003**

1. Persons taking no active part in the hostilities, including members of armed forces who have laid down their arms and those placed hors de combat by sickness, wounds, detention, or any other cause, shall in all circumstances be treated humanely, without any adverse distinction founded on race, colour, religion or faith, sex, birth or wealth, or any other similar criteria.

To this end the following acts are and shall remain prohibited at any time and in any place whatsoever with respect to the above-mentioned persons:

(a) Violence to life and person, in particular murder of all kinds, mutilation, cruel treatment and torture;
(b) Taking of hostages;
(c) Outrages upon personal dignity, in particular, humiliating and degrading treatment;
(d) The passing of sentences and the carrying out of executions without previous judgment pronounced by a regularly constituted court affording all the judicial guarantees which are recognized as indispensable by civilized peoples.

2. The wounded and sick shall be collected and cared for.

An impartial humanitarian body, such as the International Committee of the Red Cross, may offer its services to the Parties to the conflict.

The Parties to the conflict should further endeavour to bring into force, by means of special agreements, all or part of the other provisions of the present Convention.

The application of the preceding provisions shall not affect the legal status of the Parties to the conflict.

ARTICLE 4

A. Prisoners of war, in the sense of the present Convention, are persons belonging to one of the following categories, who have fallen into the power of the enemy: **A3–004**

1. Members of the armed forces of a Party to the conflict as well as members of militias or volunteer corps forming part of such armed forces.

2. Members of other militias and members of other volunteer corps, including those of organized resistance movements, belonging to a Party to the conflict and operating in or outside their own territory, even if this territory is occupied, provided that such militias or volunteer corps, including such organized resistance movements, fulfil the following conditions:

(a) That of being commanded by a person responsible for his subordinates;
(b) That of having a fixed distinctive sign recognizable at a distance;
(c) That of carrying arms openly;
(d) That of conducting their operations in accordance with the laws and customs of war.

3. Members of regular armed forces who profess allegiance to a government or an authority not recognized by the Detaining Power.

4. Persons who accompany the armed forces without actually being members thereof, such as civilian members of military aircraft crews, war correspondents, supply contrac-

tors, members of labour units or of services responsible for the welfare of the armed forces, provided that they have received authorization from the armed forces which they accompany, who shall provide them for that purpose with an identity card similar to the annexed model.

5. Members of crews, including masters, pilots and apprentices, of the merchant marine and the crews of civil aircraft of the Parties to the conflict, who do not benefit by more favourable treatment under any other provisions of international law.

6. Inhabitants of a non-occupied territory, who on the approach of the enemy spontaneously take up arms to resist the invading forces, without having had time to form themselves into regular armed units, provided they carry arms openly and respect the laws and customs of war.

B.The following shall likewise be treated as prisoners of war under the present Convention:

1. Persons belonging, or having belonged, to the armed forces of the occupied country, if the occupying Power considers it necessary by reason of such allegiance to intern them, even though it has originally liberated them while hostilities were going on outside the territory it occupies, in particular where such persons have made an unsuccessful attempt to rejoin the armed forces to which they belong and which are engaged in combat, or where they fail to comply with a summons made to them with a view to internment.

2. The persons belonging to one of the categories enumerated in the present Article, who have been received by neutral or non-belligerent Powers on their territory and whom these Powers are required to intern under international law, without prejudice to any more favourable treatment which these Powers may choose to give and with the exception of Articles 8, 10, 15, 30, fifth paragraph, 58–67, 92, 126 and, where diplomatic relations exist between the Parties to the conflict and the neutral or non-belligerent Power concerned, those Articles concerning the Protecting Power. Where such diplomatic relations exist, the Parties to a conflict on whom these persons depend shall be allowed to perform towards them the functions of a Protecting Power as provided in the present Convention, without prejudice to the functions which these Parties normally exercise in conformity with diplomatic and consular usage and treaties.

C. This Article shall in no way affect the status of medical personnel and chaplains as provided for in Article 33 of the present Convention.

ARTICLE 5

A3–005 The present Convention shall apply to the persons referred to in Article 4 from the time they fall into the power of the enemy and until their final release and repatriation.

Should any doubt arise as to whether persons, having committed a belligerent act and having fallen into the hands of the enemy, belong to any of the categories enumerated in Article 4, such persons shall enjoy the protection of the present Convention until such time as their status has been determined by a competent tribunal.

ARTICLE 6

A3–006 In addition to the agreements expressly provided for in Articles 10, 23, 28, 33, 60, 65, 66, 67, 72, 73, 75, 109, 110, 118, 119, 122 and 132, the High Contracting Parties may conclude other special agreements for all matters concerning which they may deem it suitable to make separate provision. No special agreement shall adversely affect the situation of prisoners of war, as defined by the present Convention, nor restrict the rights which it confers upon them.

Prisoners of war shall continue to have the benefit of such agreements as long as the Convention is applicable to them, except where express provisions to the contrary are contained in the aforesaid or in subsequent agreements, or where more favourable measures have been taken with regard to them by one or other of the Parties to the conflict.

ARTICLE 7

Prisoners of war may in no circumstances renounce in part or in entirety the rights secured to them by the present Convention, and by the special agreements referred to in the foregoing Article, if such there be.   **A3–007**

ARTICLE 8

The present Convention shall be applied with the cooperation and under the scrutiny **A3–008** of the Protecting Powers whose duty it is to safeguard the interests of the Parties to the conflict. For this purpose, the Protecting Powers may appoint, apart from their diplomatic or consular staff, delegates from amongst their own nationals or the nationals of other neutral Powers. The said delegates shall be subject to the approval of the Power with which they are to carry out their duties.

The Parties to the conflict shall facilitate to the greatest extent possible the task of the representatives or delegates of the Protecting Powers.

The representatives or delegates of the Protecting Powers shall not in any case exceed their mission under the present Convention. They shall, in particular, take account of the imperative necessities of security of the State wherein they carry out their duties.

ARTICLE 9

The provisions of the present Convention constitute no obstacle to the humanitarian **A3–009** activities which the International Committee of the Red Cross or any other impartial humanitarian organization may, subject to the consent of the Parties to the conflict concerned, undertake for the protection of prisoners of war and for their relief.

ARTICLE 10

The High Contracting Parties may at any time agree to entrust to an organization **A3–010** which offers all guarantees of impartiality and efficacy the duties incumbent on the Protecting Powers by virtue of the present Convention.

When prisoners of war do not benefit or cease to benefit, no matter for what reason, by the activities of a Protecting Power or of an organization provided for in the first paragraph above, the Detaining Power shall request a neutral State, or such an organization, to undertake the functions performed under the present Convention by a Protecting Power designated by the Parties to a conflict.

If protection cannot be arranged accordingly, the Detaining Power shall request or shall accept, subject to the provisions of this Article, the offer of the services of a humanitarian organization, such as the International Committee of the Red Cross, to assume the humanitarian functions performed by Protecting Powers under the present Convention.

Any neutral Power or any organization invited by the Power concerned or offering itself for these purposes, shall be required to act with a sense of responsibility towards the Party to the conflict on which persons protected by the present Convention depend, and shall be required to furnish sufficient assurances that it is in a position to undertake the appropriate functions and to discharge them impartially.

No derogation from the preceding provisions shall be made by special agreements between Powers one of which is restricted, even temporarily, in its freedom to negotiate with the other Power or its allies by reason of military events, more particularly where the whole, or a substantial part, of the territory of the said Power is occupied.

Whenever in the present Convention mention is made of a Protecting Power, such mention applies to substitute organizations in the sense of the present Article.

ARTICLE 11

A3–011   In cases where they deem it advisable in the interest of protected persons, particularly in cases of disagreement between the Parties to the conflict as to the application or interpretation of the provisions of the present Convention, the Protecting Powers shall lend their good offices with a view to settling the disagreement.

For this purpose, each of the Protecting Powers may, either at the invitation of one Party or on its own initiative, propose to the Parties to the conflict a meeting of their representatives, and in particular of the authorities responsible for prisoners of war, possibly on neutral territory suitably chosen. The Parties to the conflict shall be bound to give effect to the proposals made to them for this purpose. The Protecting Powers may, if necessary, propose for approval by the Parties to the conflict a person belonging to a neutral Power, or delegated by the International Committee of the Red Cross, who shall be invited to take part in such a meeting.

PART II

GENERAL PROTECTION OF PRISONERS OF WAR

ARTICLE 12

A3–012   Prisoners of war are in the hands of the enemy Power, but not of the individuals or military units who have captured them. Irrespective of the individual responsibilities that may exist, the Detaining Power is responsible for the treatment given them.

Prisoners of war may only be transferred by the Detaining Power to a Power which is a party to the Convention and after the Detaining Power has satisfied itself of the willingness and ability of such transferee Power to apply the Convention. When prisoners of war are transferred under such circumstances, responsibility for the application of the Convention rests on the Power accepting them while they are in its custody.

Nevertheless if that Power fails to carry out the provisions of the Convention in any important respect, the Power by whom the prisoners of war were transferred shall, upon being notified by the Protecting Power, take effective measures to correct the situation or shall request the return of the prisoners of war. Such requests must be complied with.

ARTICLE 13

A3–013   Prisoners of war must at all times be humanely treated. Any unlawful act or omission by the Detaining Power causing death or seriously endangering the health of a prisoner of war in its custody is prohibited, and will be regarded as a serious breach of the present Convention. In particular, no prisoner of war may be subjected to physical mutilation or to medical or scientific experiments of any kind which are not justified by the medical, dental or hospital treatment of the prisoner concerned and carried out in his interest.

Likewise, prisoners of war must at all times be protected, particularly against acts of violence or intimidation and against insults and public curiosity.

Measures of reprisal against prisoners of war are prohibited.

ARTICLE 14

A3–014   Prisoners of war are entitled in all circumstances to respect for their persons and their honour. Women shall be treated with all the regard due to their sex and shall in all cases benefit by treatment as favourable as that granted to men. Prisoners of war shall retain the full civil capacity which they enjoyed at the time of their capture. The Detaining Power may not restrict the exercise, either within or without its own territory, of the rights such capacity confers except in so far as the captivity requires.

ARTICLE 15

The Power detaining prisoners of war shall be bound to provide free of charge for their maintenance and for the medical attention required by their state of health.

A3–015

ARTICLE 16

Taking into consideration the provisions of the present Convention relating to rank and sex, and subject to any privileged treatment which may be accorded to them by reason of their state of health, age or professional qualifications, all prisoners of war shall be treated alike by the Detaining Power, without any adverse distinction based on race, nationality, religious belief or political opinions, or any other distinction founded on similar criteria.

A3–016

PART III

CAPTIVITY

Section I

Beginning of Captivity

ARTICLE 17

Every prisoner of war, when questioned on the subject, is bound to give only his surname, first names and rank, date of birth, and army, regimental, personal or serial number, or failing this, equivalent information. If he wilfully infringes this rule, he may render himself liable to a restriction of the privileges accorded to his rank or status.

A3–017

Each Party to a conflict is required to furnish the persons under its jurisdiction who are liable to become prisoners of war, with an identity card showing the owner's surname, first names, rank, army, regimental, personal or serial number or equivalent information, and date of birth. The identity card may, furthermore, bear the signature or the fingerprints, or both, of the owner, and may bear, as well, any other information the Party to the conflict may wish to add concerning persons belonging to its armed forces. As far as possible the card shall measure 6.5 š 10 cm. and shall be issued in duplicate. The identity card shall be shown by the prisoner of war upon demand, but may in no case be taken away from him.

No physical or mental torture, nor any other form of coercion, may be inflicted on prisoners of war to secure from them information of any kind whatever. Prisoners of war who refuse to answer may not be threatened, insulted, or exposed to any unpleasant or disadvantageous treatment of any kind.

Prisoners of war who, owing to their physical or mental condition, are unable to state their identity, shall be handed over to the medical service. The identity of such prisoners shall be established by all possible means, subject to the provisions of the preceding paragraph.

The questioning of prisoners of war shall be carried out in a language which they understand.

ARTICLE 18

All effects and articles of personal use, except arms, horses, military equipment and military documents shall remain in the possession of prisoners of war, likewise their metal helmets and gas masks and like articles issued for personal protection. Effects and articles used for their clothing or feeding shall likewise remain in their possession, even if such effects and articles belong to their regulation military equipment.

A3–018

At no time should prisoners of war be without identity documents. The Detaining Power shall supply such documents to prisoners of war who possess none.

Badges of rank and nationality, decorations and articles having above all a personal or sentimental value may not be taken from prisoners of war.

Sums of money carried by prisoners of war may not be taken away from them except by order of an officer, and after the amount and particulars of the owner have been recorded in a special register and an itemized receipt has been given, legibly inscribed with the name, rank and unit of the person issuing the said receipt. Sums in the currency of the Detaining Power, or which are changed into such currency at the prisoner's request, shall be placed to the credit of the prisoner's account as provided in Article 64.

The Detaining Power may withdraw articles of value from prisoners of war only for reasons of security; when such articles are withdrawn, the procedure laid down for sums of money impounded shall apply.

Such objects, likewise the sums taken away in any currency other than that of the Detaining Power and the conversion of which has not been asked for by the owners, shall be kept in the custody of the Detaining Power and shall be returned in their initial shape to prisoners of war at the end of their captivity.

ARTICLE 19

A3–019   Prisoners of war shall be evacuated, as soon as possible after their capture, to camps situated in an area far enough from the combat zone for them to be out of danger.

Only those prisoners of war who, owing to wounds or sickness, would run greater risks by being evacuated than by remaining where they are, may be temporarily kept back in a danger zone.

Prisoners of war shall not be unnecessarily exposed to danger while awaiting evacuation from a fighting zone.

ARTICLE 20

A3–020   The evacuation of prisoners of war shall always be effected humanely and in conditions similar to those for the forces of the Detaining Power in their changes of station.

The Detaining Power shall supply prisoners of war who are being evacuated with sufficient food and potable water, and with the necessary clothing and medical attention. The Detaining Power shall take all suitable precautions to ensure their safety during evacuation, and shall establish as soon as possible a list of the prisoners of war who are evacuated.

If prisoners of war must, during evacuation, pass through transit camps, their stay in such camps shall be as brief as possible.

Section II

Internment of Prisoners of War

CHAPTER I

GENERAL OBSERVATIONS

ARTICLE 21

A3–021   The Detaining Power may subject prisoners of war to internment. It may impose on them the obligation of not leaving, beyond certain limits, the camp where they are interned, or if the said camp is fenced in, of not going outside its perimeter. Subject to the provisions of the present Convention relative to penal and disciplinary sanctions, prisoners of war may not be held in close confinement except where necessary to safeguard their health and then only during the continuation of the circumstances which make such confinement necessary.

Prisoners of war may be partially or wholly released on parole or promise, in so far as is allowed by the laws of the Power on which they depend. Such measures shall be taken particularly in cases where this may contribute to the improvement of their state of health. No prisoner of war shall be compelled to accept liberty on parole or promise.

Upon the outbreak of hostilities, each Party to the conflict shall notify the adverse Party of the laws and regulations allowing or forbidding its own nationals to accept liberty on parole or promise. Prisoners of war who are paroled or who have given their promise in conformity with the laws and regulations so notified, are bound on their personal honour scrupulously to fulfil, both towards the Power on which they depend and towards the Power which has captured them, the engagements of their paroles or promises. In such cases, the Power on which they depend is bound neither to require nor to accept from them any service incompatible with the parole or promise given.

ARTICLE 22

Prisoners of war may be interned only in premises located on land and affording every **A3–022**
guarantee of hygiene and healthfulness. Except in particular cases which are justified by the interest of the prisoners themselves, they shall not be interned in penitentiaries.

Prisoners of war interned in unhealthy areas, or where the climate is injurious for them, shall be removed as soon as possible to a more favourable climate.

The Detaining Power shall assemble prisoners of war in camps or camp compounds according to their nationality, language and customs, provided that such prisoners shall not be separated from prisoners of war belonging to the armed forces with which they were serving at the time of their capture, except with their consent.

ARTICLE 23

No prisoner of war may at any time be sent to or detained in areas where he may be **A3–023**
exposed to the fire of the combat zone, nor may his presence be used to render certain points or areas immune from military operations.

Prisoners of war shall have shelters against air bombardment and other hazards of war, to the same extent as the local civilian population. With the exception of those engaged in the protection of their quarters against the aforesaid hazards, they may enter such shelters as soon as possible after the giving of the alarm. Any other protective measure taken in favour of the population shall also apply to them.

Detaining Powers shall give the Powers concerned, through the intermediary of the Protecting Powers, all useful information regarding the geographical location of prisoner of war camps.

Whenever military considerations permit, prisoner of war camps shall be indicated in the day-time by the letters PW or PG, placed so as to be clearly visible from the air. The Powers concerned may, however, agree upon any other system of marking. Only prisoner of war camps shall be marked as such.

ARTICLE 24

Transit or screening camps of a permanent kind shall be fitted out under conditions **A3–024**
similar to those described in the present Section, and the prisoners therein shall have the same treatment as in other camps.

CHAPTER II

QUARTERS, FOOD AND CLOTHING OF PRISONERS OF WAR

ARTICLE 25

A3–025   Prisoners of war shall be quartered under conditions as favourable as those for the forces of the Detaining Power who are billeted in the same area. The said conditions shall make allowance for the habits and customs of the prisoners and shall in no case be prejudicial to their health.

The foregoing provisions shall apply in particular to the dormitories of prisoners of war as regards both total surface and minimum cubic space, and the general installations, bedding and blankets.

The premises provided for the use of prisoners of war individually or collectively, shall be entirely protected from dampness and adequately heated and lighted, in particular between dusk and lights out. All precautions must be taken against the danger of fire.

In any camps in which women prisoners of war, as well as men, are accommodated, separate dormitories shall be provided for them.

ARTICLE 26

A3–026   The basic daily food rations shall be sufficient in quantity, quality and variety to keep prisoners of war in good health and to prevent loss of weight or the development of nutritional deficiencies. Account shall also be taken of the habitual diet of the prisoners.

The Detaining Power shall supply prisoners of war who work with such additional rations as are necessary for the labour on which they are employed.

Sufficient drinking water shall be supplied to prisoners of war. The use of tobacco shall be permitted.

Prisoners of war shall, as far as possible, be associated with the preparation of their meals; they may be employed for that purpose in the kitchens. Furthermore, they shall be given the means of preparing, themselves, the additional food in their possession.

Adequate premises shall be provided for messing.

Collective disciplinary measures affecting food are prohibited.

ARTICLE 27

A3–027   Clothing, underwear and footwear shall be supplied to prisoners of war in sufficient quantities by the Detaining Power, which shall make allowance for the climate of the region where the prisoners are detained. Uniforms of enemy armed forces captured by the Detaining Power should, if suitable for the climate, be made available to clothe prisoners of war.

The regular replacement and repair of the above articles shall be assured by the Detaining Power. In addition, prisoners of war who work shall receive appropriate clothing, wherever the nature of the work demands.

ARTICLE 28

A3–028   Canteens shall be installed in all camps, where prisoners of war may procure foodstuffs, soap and tobacco and ordinary articles in daily use. The tariff shall never be in excess of local market prices. The profits made by camp canteens shall be used for the benefit of the prisoners; a special fund shall be created for this purpose. The prisoners' representative shall have the right to collaborate in the management of the canteen and of this fund.

When a camp is closed down, the credit balance of the special fund shall be handed to an international welfare organization, to be employed for the benefit of prisoners of war of the same nationality as those who have contributed to the fund. In case of a general repatriation, such profits shall be kept by the Detaining Power, subject to any agreement to the contrary between the Powers concerned.

Chapter III

HYGIENE AND MEDICAL ATTENTION

Article 29

The Detaining Power shall be bound to take all sanitary measures necessary to ensure the cleanliness and healthfulness of camps and to prevent epidemics.   **A3–029**

Prisoners of war shall have for their use, day and night, conveniences which conform to the rules of hygiene and are maintained in a constant state of cleanliness. In any camps in which women prisoners of war are accommodated, separate conveniences shall be provided for them.

Also, apart from the baths and showers with which the camps shall be furnished, prisoners of war shall be provided with sufficient water and soap for their personal toilet and for washing their personal laundry; the necessary installations, facilities and time shall be granted them for that purpose.

Article 30

Every camp shall have an adequate infirmary where prisoners of war may have the attention they require, as well as appropriate diet. Isolation wards shall, if necessary, be set aside for cases of contagious or mental disease.   **A3–030**

Prisoners of war suffering from serious disease, or whose condition necessitates special treatment, a surgical operation or hospital care, must be admitted to any military or civilian medical unit where such treatment can be given, even if their repatriation is contemplated in the near future. Special facilities shall be afforded for the care to be given to the disabled, in particular to the blind, and for their rehabilitation, pending repatriation.

Prisoners of war shall have the attention, preferably, of medical personnel of the Power on which they depend and, if possible, of their nationality.

Prisoners of war may not be prevented from presenting themselves to the medical authorities for examination. The detaining authorities shall, upon request, issue to every prisoner who has undergone treatment, an official certificate indicating the nature of his illness or injury, and the duration and kind of treatment received. A duplicate of this certificate shall be forwarded to the Central Prisoners of War Agency.

The costs of treatment, including those of any apparatus necessary for the mainte-nance of prisoners of war in good health, particularly dentures and other artificial appliances, and spectacles, shall be borne by the Detaining Power.

Article 31

Medical inspections of prisoners of war shall be held at least once a month. They shall include the checking and the recording of the weight of each prisoner of war. Their purpose shall be, in particular, to supervise the general state of health, nutrition and cleanliness of prisoners and to detect contagious diseases, especially tuberculosis, malaria and venereal disease. For this purpose the most efficient methods available shall be employed, e.g. periodic mass miniature radiography for the early detection of tuberculosis.   **A3–031**

Article 32

Prisoners of war who, though not attached to the medical service of their armed forces, are physicians, surgeons, dentists, nurses or medical orderlies, may be required by the Detaining Power to exercise their medical functions in the interests of prisoners of   **A3–032** war dependent on the same Power. In that case they shall continue to be prisoners of war, but shall receive the same treatment as corresponding medical personnel retained by the Detaining Power. They shall be exempted from any other work under Article 49.

CHAPTER IV

MEDICAL PERSONNEL AND CHAPLAINS RETAINED TO ASSIST PRISONERS OF WAR

ARTICLE 33

A3–033   Members of the medical personnel and chaplains while retained by the Detaining Power with a view to assisting prisoners of war, shall not be considered as prisoners of war. They shall, however, receive as a minimum the benefits and protection of the present Convention, and shall also be granted all facilities necessary to provide for the medical care of, and religious inistration to, prisoners of war.

They shall continue to exercise their medical and spiritual functions for the benefit of prisoners of war, preferably those belonging to the armed forces upon which they depend, within the scope of the military laws and regulations of the Detaining Power and under the control of its competent services, in accordance with their professional etiquette. They shall also benefit by the following facilities in the exercise of their medical or spiritual functions:

   (a) They shall be authorized to visit periodically prisoners of war situated in working detachments or in hospitals outside the camp. For this purpose, the Detaining Power shall place at their disposal the necessary means of transport.
   (b) The senior medical officer in each camp shall be responsible to the camp military authorities for everything connected with the activities of retained medical personnel. For this purpose, Parties to the conflict shall agree at the outbreak of hostilities on the subject of the corresponding ranks of the medical personnel, including that of societies mentioned in Article 26 of the Geneva Convention for the Amelioration of the Condition of the Wounded and Sick in Armed Forces in the Field of August 12, 1949. This senior medical officer, as well as chaplains, shall have the right to deal with the competent authorities of the camp on all questions relating to their duties. Such authorities shall afford them all necessary facilities for correspondence relating to these questions.
   (c) Although they shall be subject to the internal discipline of the camp in which they are retained, such personnel may not be compelled to carry out any work other than that concerned with their medical or religious duties.

During hostilities, the Parties to the conflict shall agree concerning the possible relief of retained personnel and shall settle the procedure to be followed.

None of the preceding provisions shall relieve the Detaining Power of its obligations with regard to prisoners of war from the medical or spiritual point of view.

CHAPTER V

RELIGIOUS, INTELLECTUAL AND PHYSICAL ACTIVITIES

ARTICLE 34

A3–034   Prisoners of war shall enjoy complete latitude in the exercise of their religious duties, including attendance at the service of their faith, on condition that they comply with the disciplinary routine prescribed by the military authorities.

Adequate premises shall be provided where religious services may be held.

Article 35

Chaplains who fall into the hands of the enemy Power and who remain or are retained **A3–035** with a view to assisting prisoners of war, shall be allowed to minister to them and to exercise freely their ministry amongst prisoners of war of the same religion, in accordance with their religious conscience. They shall be allocated among the various camps and labour detachments containing prisoners of war belonging to the same forces, speaking the same language or practising the same religion. They shall enjoy the necessary facilities, including the means of transport provided for in Article 33, for visiting the prisoners of war outside their camp. They shall be free to correspond, subject to censorship, on matters concerning their religious duties with the ecclesiastical authorities in the country of detention and with international religious organizations. Letters and cards which they may send for this purpose shall be in addition to the quota provided for in Article 71.

Article 36

Prisoners of war who are ministers of religion, without having officiated as chaplains **A3–036** to their own forces, shall be at liberty, whatever their denomination, to minister freely to the members of their community. For this purpose, they shall receive the same treatment as the chaplains retained by the Detaining Power. They shall not be obliged to do any other work.

Article 37

When prisoners of war have not the assistance of a retained chaplain or of a prisoner **A3–037** of war minister of their faith, a minister belonging to the prisoners' or a similar denomination, or in his absence a qualified layman, if such a course is feasible from a confessional point of view, shall be appointed, at the request of the prisoners concerned, to fill this office. This appointment, subject to the approval of the Detaining Power, shall take place with the agreement of the community of prisoners concerned and, wherever necessary, with the approval of the local religious authorities of the same faith. The person thus appointed shall comply with all regulations established by the Detaining Power in the interests of discipline and military security.

Article 38

While respecting the individual preferences of every prisoner, the Detaining Power **A3–038** shall encourage the practice of intellectual, educational, and recreational pursuits, sports and games amongst prisoners, and shall take the measures necessary to ensure the exercise thereof by providing them with adequate premises and necessary equipment.

Prisoners shall have opportunities for taking physical exercise, including sports and games, and for being out of doors. Sufficient open spaces shall be provided for this purpose in all camps.

Chapter VI

DISCIPLINE

Article 39

Every prisoner of war camp shall be put under the immediate authority of a **A3–039** responsible commissioned officer belonging to the regular armed forces of the Detaining Power. Such officer shall have in his possession a copy of the present Convention; he shall ensure that its provisions are known to the camp staff and the guard and shall be responsible, under the direction of his government, for its application.

Prisoners of war, with the exception of officers, must salute and show to all officers of the Detaining Power the external marks of respect provided for by the regulations applying in their own forces.

Officer prisoners of war are bound to salute only officers of a higher rank of the Detaining Power; they must, however, salute the camp commander regardless of his rank.

ARTICLE 40

A3–040   The wearing of badges of rank and nationality, as well as of decorations, shall be permitted.

ARTICLE 41

A3–041   In every camp the text of the present Convention and its Annexes and the contents of any special agreement provided for in Article 6, shall be posted, in the prisoners' own language, at places where all may read them. Copies shall be supplied, on request, to the prisoners who cannot have access to the copy which has been posted.

Regulations, orders, notices and publications of every kind relating to the conduct of prisoners of war shall be issued to them in a language which they understand. Such regulations, orders and publications shall be posted in the manner described above and copies shall be handed to the prisoners' representative. Every order and command addressed to prisoners of war individually must likewise be given in a language which they understand.

ARTICLE 42

A3–042   The use of weapons against prisoners of war, especially against those who are escaping or attempting to escape, shall constitute an extreme measure, which shall always be preceded by warnings appropriate to the circumstances.

CHAPTER VII

RANK OF PRISONERS OF WAR

ARTICLE 43

A3–043   Upon the outbreak of hostilities, the Parties to the conflict shall communicate to one another the titles and ranks of all the persons mentioned in Article 4 of the present Convention, in order to ensure equality of treatment between prisoners of equivalent rank. Titles and ranks which are subsequently created shall form the subject of similar communications.

The Detaining Power shall recognize promotions in rank which have been accorded to prisoners of war and which have been duly notified by the Power on which these prisoners depend.

ARTICLE 44

A3–044   Officers and prisoners of equivalent status shall be treated with the regard due to their rank and age.

In order to ensure service in officers' camps, other ranks of the same armed forces who, as far as possible, speak the same language, shall be assigned in sufficient numbers, account being taken of the rank of officers and prisoners of equivalent status. Such orderlies shall not be required to perform any other work.

Supervision of the mess by the officers themselves shall be facilitated in every way.

Article 45

Prisoners of war other than officers and prisoners of equivalent status shall be treated with the regard due to their rank and age.   **A3–045**

Supervision of the mess by the prisoners themselves shall be facilitated in every way.

Chapter VIII

TRANSFER OF PRISONERS OF WAR AFTER THEIR ARRIVAL IN CAMP

Article 46

The Detaining Power, when deciding upon the transfer of prisoners of war, shall take into account the interests of the prisoners themselves, more especially so as not to increase the difficulty of their repatriation.   **A3–046**

The transfer of prisoners of war shall always be effected humanely and in conditions not less favourable than those under which the forces of the Detaining Power are transferred. Account shall always be taken of the climatic conditions to which the prisoners of war are accustomed and the conditions of transfer shall in no case be prejudicial to their health.

The Detaining Power shall supply prisoners of war during transfer with sufficient food and drinking water to keep them in good health, likewise with the necessary clothing, shelter and medical attention. The Detaining Power shall take adequate precautions especially in case of transport by sea or by air, to ensure their safety during transfer, and shall draw up a complete list of all transferred prisoners before their departure.

Article 47

Sick or wounded prisoners of war shall not be transferred as long as their recovery may be endangered by the journey, unless their safety imperatively demands it.   **A3–047**

If the combat zone draws closer to a camp, the prisoners of war in the said camp shall not be transferred unless their transfer can be carried out in adequate conditions of safety, or if they are exposed to greater risks by remaining on the spot than by being transferred.

Article 48

In the event of transfer, prisoners of war shall be officially advised of their departure and of their new postal address. Such notifications shall be given in time for them to pack their luggage and inform their next of kin.   **A3–048**

They shall be allowed to take with them their personal effects, and the correspondence and parcels which have arrived for them. The weight of such baggage may be limited, if the conditions of transfer so require, to what each prisoner can reasonably carry, which shall in no case be more than twenty-five kilograms per head.

Mail and parcels addressed to their former camp shall be forwarded to them without delay. The camp commander shall take, in agreement with the prisoners' representative, any measures needed to ensure the transport of the prisoners' community property and of the luggage they are unable to take with them in consequence of restrictions imposed by virtue of the second paragraph of this Article.

The costs of transfers shall be borne by the Detaining Power.

Section III

Labour of Prisoners of War

ARTICLE 49

A3–049   The Detaining Power may utilize the labour of prisoners of war who are physically fit, taking into account their age, sex, rank and physical aptitude, and with a view particularly to maintaining them in a good state of physical and mental health.

Non-commissioned officers who are prisoners of war shall only be required to do supervisory work. Those not so required may ask for other suitable work which shall, so far as possible, be found for them.

If officers or persons of equivalent status ask for suitable work, it shall be found for them, so far as possible, but they may in no circumstances be compelled to work.

ARTICLE 50

A3–050   Besides work connected with camp administration, installation or maintenance, prisoners of war may be compelled to do only such work as is included in the following classes:

    (a) Agriculture;

    (b) Industries connected with the production or the extraction of raw materials, and manufacturing industries, with the exception of metallurgical, machinery and chemical industries; public works and building operations which have no military character or purpose;

    (c) Transport and handling of stores which are not military in character or purpose;

    (d) Commercial business, and arts and crafts;

    (e) Domestic service;

    (f) Public utility services having no military character or purpose.

Should the above provisions be infringed, prisoners of war shall be allowed to exercise their right of complaint, in conformity with Article 78.

ARTICLE 51

A3–051   Prisoners of war must be granted suitable working conditions, especially as regards accommodation, food, clothing and equipment; such conditions shall not be inferior to those enjoyed by nationals of the Detaining Power employed in similar work; account shall also be taken of climatic conditions.

The Detaining Power, in utilizing the labour of prisoners of war, shall ensure that in areas in which prisoners are employed, the national legislation concerning the protection of labour, and, more particularly, the regulations for the safety of workers, are duly applied.

Prisoners of war shall receive training and be provided with the means of protection suitable to the work they will have to do and similar to those accorded to the nationals of the Detaining Power. Subject to the provisions of Article 52, prisoners may be submitted to the normal risks run by these civilian workers.

Conditions of labour shall in no case be rendered more arduous by disciplinary measures.

ARTICLE 52

A3–052   Unless he be a volunteer, no prisoner of war may be employed on labour which is of an unhealthy or dangerous nature.

No prisoner of war shall be assigned to labour which would be looked upon as humiliating for a member of the Detaining Power's own forces.

The removal of mines or similar devices shall be considered as dangerous labour.

ARTICLE 53

The duration of the daily labour of prisoners of war, including the time of the journey to and fro, shall not be excessive, and must in no case exceed that permitted for civilian workers in the district, who are nationals of the Detaining Power and employed on the same work.

A3–053

Prisoners of war must be allowed, in the middle of the day's work, a rest of not less than one hour. This rest will be the same as that to which workers of the Detaining Power are entitled, if the latter is of longer duration. They shall be allowed in addition a rest of twenty-four consecutive hours every week, preferably on Sunday or the day of rest in their country of origin. Furthermore, every prisoner who has worked for one year shall be granted a rest of eight consecutive days, during which his working pay shall be paid him.

If methods of labour such as piece-work are employed, the length of the working period shall not be rendered excessive thereby.

ARTICLE 54

The working pay due to prisoners of war shall be fixed in accordance with the provisions of Article 62 of the present Convention.

A3–054

Prisoners of war who sustain accidents in connection with work, or who contract a disease in the course, or in consequence of their work, shall receive all the care their condition may require. The Detaining Power shall furthermore deliver to such prisoners of war a medical certificate enabling them to submit their claims to the Power on which they depend, and shall send a duplicate to the Central Prisoners of War Agency provided for in Article 123.

ARTICLE 55

The fitness of prisoners of war for work shall be periodically verified by medical examinations at least once a month. The examinations shall have particular regard to the nature of the work which prisoners of war are required to do.

A3–055

If any prisoner of war considers himself incapable of working, he shall be permitted to appear before the medical authorities of his camp. Physicians or surgeons may recommend that the prisoners who are, in their opinion, unfit for work, be exempted therefrom.

ARTICLE 56

The organization and administration of labour detachments shall be similar to those of prisoner of war camps.

A3–056

Every labour detachment shall remain under the control of and administratively part of a prisoner of war camp. The military authorities and the commander of the said camp shall be responsible, under the direction of their government, for the observance of the provisions of the present Convention in labour detachments.

The camp commander shall keep an up-to-date record of the labour detachments dependent on his camp, and shall communicate it to the delegates of the Protecting Power, of the International Committee of the Red Cross, or of other agencies giving relief to prisoners of war, who may visit the camp.

ARTICLE 57

The treatment of prisoners of war who work for private persons, even if the latter are responsible for guarding and protecting them, shall not be inferior to that which is provided for by the present Convention. The Detaining Power, the military authorities

A3–057

and the commander of the camp to which such prisoners belong shall be entirely responsible for the maintenance, care, treatment, and payment of the working pay of such prisoners of war.

Such prisoners of war shall have the right to remain in communication with the prisoners' representatives in the camps on which they depend.

Section IV

Financial Resources of Prisoners of War

ARTICLE 58

A3–058   Upon the outbreak of hostilities, and pending an arrangement on this matter with the Protecting Power, the Detaining Power may determine the maximum amount of money in cash or in any similar form, that prisoners may have in their possession. Any amount in excess, which was properly in their possession and which has been taken or withheld from them, shall be placed to their account, together with any monies deposited by them, and shall not be converted into any other currency without their consent.

If prisoners of war are permitted to purchase services or commodities outside the camp against payment in cash, such payments shall be made by the prisoner himself or by the camp administration who will charge them to the accounts of the prisoners concerned. The Detaining Power will establish the necessary rules in this respect.

ARTICLE 59

A3–059   Cash which was taken from prisoners of war, in accordance with Article 18, at the time of their capture, and which is in the currency of the Detaining Power, shall be placed to their separate accounts, in accordance with the provisions of Article 64 of the present Section.

The amounts, in the currency of the Detaining Power, due to the conversion of sums in other currencies that are taken from the prisoners of war at the same time, shall also be credited to their separate accounts.

ARTICLE 60

A3–060   The Detaining Power shall grant all prisoners of war a monthly advance of pay, the amount of which shall be fixed by conversion, into the currency of the said Power, of the following amounts:

Category I: Prisoners ranking below sergeant: eight Swiss francs.

Category II: Sergeants and other non-commissioned officers, or prisoners of equivalent rank: twelve Swiss francs.

Category III: Warrant officers and commissioned officers below the rank of major or prisoners of equivalent rank: fifty Swiss francs.

Category IV: Majors, lieutenant-colonels, colonels or prisoners of equivalent rank: sixty Swiss francs.

Category V: General officers or prisoners of equivalent rank: seventy-five Swiss francs.

However, the Parties to the conflict concerned may by special agreement modify the amount of advances of pay due to prisoners of the preceding categories.

Furthermore, if the amounts indicated in the first paragraph above would be unduly high compared with the pay of the Detaining Power's armed forces or would, for any reason, seriously embarrass the Detaining Power, then, pending the conclusion of a special agreement with the Power on which the prisoners depend to vary the amounts indicated above, the Detaining Power:

(a) Shall continue to credit the accounts of the prisoners with the amounts indicated in the first paragraph above;

(b) May temporarily limit the amount made available from these advances of pay to prisoners of war for their own use, to sums which are reasonable, but which, for Category I, shall never be inferior to the amount that the Detaining Power gives to the members of its own armed forces.

The reasons for any limitations will be given without delay to the Protecting Power.

Article 61

The Detaining Power shall accept for distribution as supplementary pay to prisoners of war sums which the Power on which the prisoners depend may forward to them, on condition that the sums to be paid shall be the same for each prisoner of the same category, shall be payable to all prisoners of that category depending on that Power, and shall be placed in their separate accounts, at the earliest opportunity, in accordance with the provisions of Article 64. Such supplementary pay shall not relieve the Detaining Power of any obligation under this Convention.

A3–061

Article 62

Prisoners of war shall be paid a fair working rate of pay by the detaining authorities direct. The rate shall be fixed by the said authorities, but shall at no time be less than one-fourth of one Swiss franc for a full working day. The Detaining Power shall inform prisoners of war, as well as the Power on which they depend, through the intermediary of the Protecting Power, of the rate of daily working pay that it has fixed.

A3–062

Working pay shall likewise be paid by the detaining authorities to prisoners of war permanently detailed to duties or to a skilled or semi-skilled occupation in connection with the administration, installation or maintenance of camps, and to the prisoners who are required to carry out spiritual or medical duties on behalf of their comrades.

The working pay of the prisoners' representative, of his advisers, if any, and of his assistants, shall be paid out of the fund maintained by canteen profits. The scale of this working pay shall be fixed by the prisoners' representative and approved by the camp commander. If there is no such fund, the detaining authorities shall pay these prisoners a fair working rate of pay.

Article 63

Prisoners of war shall be permitted to receive remittances of money addressed to them individually or collectively.

A3–063

Every prisoner of war shall have at his disposal the credit balance of his account as provided for in the following Article, within the limits fixed by the Detaining Power, which shall make such payments as are requested. Subject to financial or monetary restrictions which the Detaining Power regards as essential, prisoners of war may also have payments made abroad. In this case payments addressed by prisoners of war to dependants shall be given priority.

In any event, and subject to the consent of the Power on which they depend, prisoners may have payments made in their own country, as follows: the Detaining Power shall send to the aforesaid Power through the Protecting Power a notification giving all the necessary particulars concerning the prisoners of war, the beneficiaries of the payments, and the amount of the sums to be paid, expressed in the Detaining Power's currency. The said notification shall be signed by the prisoners and countersigned by the camp commander. The Detaining Power shall debit the prisoners' account by a corresponding amount; the sums thus debited shall be placed by it to the credit of the Power on which the prisoners depend.

To apply the foregoing provisions, the Detaining Power may usefully consult the Model Regulations in Annex V of the present Convention.

Article 64

The Detaining Power shall hold an account for each prisoner of war, showing at least the following:

A3–064

1. The amounts due to the prisoner or received by him as advances of pay, as working pay or derived from any other source; the sums in the currency of the Detaining Power which were taken from him; the sums taken from him and converted at his request into the currency of the said Power.

2. The payments made to the prisoner in cash, or in any other similar form; the payments made on his behalf and at his request; the sums transferred under Article 63, third paragraph.

ARTICLE 65

A3–065   Every item entered in the account of a prisoner of war shall be countersigned or initialled by him, or by the prisoners' representative acting on his behalf.

Prisoners of war shall at all times be afforded reasonable facilities for consulting and obtaining copies of their accounts, which may likewise be inspected by the representatives of the Protecting Powers at the time of visits to the camp.

When prisoners of war are transferred from one camp to another, their personal accounts will follow them. In case of transfer from one Detaining Power to another, the monies which are their property and are not in the currency of the Detaining Power will follow them. They shall be given certificates for any other monies standing to the credit of their accounts.

The Parties to the conflict concerned may agree to notify to each other at specific intervals through the Protecting Power, the amount of the accounts of the prisoners of war.

ARTICLE 66

A3–066   On the termination of captivity, through the release of a prisoner of war or his repatriation, the Detaining Power shall give him a statement, signed by an authorized officer of that Power, showing the credit balance then due to him. The Detaining Power shall also send through the Protecting Power to the government upon which the prisoner of war depends, lists giving all appropriate particulars of all prisoners of war whose captivity has been terminated by repatriation, release, escape, death or any other means, and showing the amount of their credit balances. Such lists shall be certified on each sheet by an authorized representative of the Detaining Power.

Any of the above provisions of this Article may be varied by mutual agreement between any two Parties to the conflict.

The Power on which the prisoner of war depends shall be responsible for settling with him any credit balance due to him from the Detaining Power on the termination of his captivity.

ARTICLE 67

A3–067   Advances of pay, issued to prisoners of war in conformity with Article 60, shall be considered as made on behalf of the Power on which they depend. Such advances of pay, as well as all payments made by the said Power under Article 63, third paragraph, and Article 68, shall form the subject of arrangements between the Powers concerned, at the close of hostilities.

ARTICLE 68

A3–068   Any claim by a prisoner of war for compensation in respect of any injury or other disability arising out of work shall be referred to the Power on which he depends, through the Protecting Power. In accordance with Article 54, the Detaining Power will, in all cases, provide the prisoner of war concerned with a statement showing the nature of the injury or disability, the circumstances in which it arose and particulars of medical or hospital treatment given for it. This statement will be signed by a responsible officer of the Detaining Power and the medical particulars certified by a medical officer.

Any claim by a prisoner of war for compensation in respect of personal effects, monies or valuables impounded by the Detaining Power under Article 18 and not forthcoming on his repatriation, or in respect of loss alleged to be due to the fault of the Detaining Power or any of its servants, shall likewise be referred to the Power on which he depends. Nevertheless, any such personal effects required for use by the prisoners of war whilst in captivity shall be replaced at the expense of the Detaining Power. The Detaining Power will, in all cases, provide the prisoner of war with a statement, signed by a responsible officer, showing all available information regarding the reasons why such effects, monies or valuables have not been restored to him. A copy of this statement will be forwarded to the Power on which he depends through the Central Prisoners of War Agency provided for in Article 123.

Section V

Relations of Prisoners of War with the Exterior

ARTICLE 69

Immediately upon prisoners of war falling into its power, the Detaining Power shall inform them and the Powers on which they depend, through the Protecting Power, of the measures taken to carry out the provisions of the present Section. They shall likewise inform the parties concerned of any subsequent modifications of such measures.

A3–069

ARTICLE 70

Immediately upon capture, or not more than one week after arrival at a camp, even if it is a transit camp, likewise in case of sickness or transfer to hospital or another camp, every prisoner of war shall be enabled to write direct to his family, on the one hand, and to the Central Prisoners of War Agency provided for in Article 123, on the other hand, a card similar, if possible, to the model annexed to the present Convention, informing his relatives of his capture, address and state of health. The said cards shall be forwarded as rapidly as possible and may not be delayed in any manner.

A3–070

ARTICLE 71

Prisoners of war shall be allowed to send and receive letters and cards. If the Detaining Power deems it necessary to limit the number of letters and cards sent by each prisoner of war, the said number shall not be less than two letters and four cards monthly, exclusive of the capture cards provided for in Article 70, and conforming as closely as possible to the models annexed to the present Convention. Further limitations may be imposed only if the Protecting Power is satisfied that it would be in the interests of the prisoners of war concerned to do so owing to difficulties of translation caused by the Detaining Power's inability to find sufficient qualified linguists to carry out the necessary censorship. If limitations must be placed on the correspondence addressed to prisoners of war, they may be ordered only by the Power on which the prisoners depend, possibly at the request of the Detaining Power. Such letters and cards must be conveyed by the most rapid method at the disposal of the Detaining Power; they may not be delayed or retained for disciplinary reasons.

A3–071

Prisoners of war who have been without news for a long period, or who are unable to receive news from their next of kin or to give them news by the ordinary postal route, as well as those who are at a great distance from their homes, shall be permitted to send telegrams, the fees being charged against the prisoners of war's accounts with the Detaining Power or paid in the currency at their disposal. They shall likewise benefit by this measure in cases of urgency.

As a general rule, the correspondence of prisoners of war shall be written in their native language. The Parties to the conflict may allow correspondence in other languages.

Sacks containing prisoner of war mail must be securely sealed and labelled so as clearly to indicate their contents, and must be addressed to offices of destination.

ARTICLE 72

A3–072   Prisoners of war shall be allowed to receive by post or by any other means individual parcels or collective shipments containing, in particular, foodstuffs, clothing, medical supplies and articles of a religious, educational or recreational character which may meet their needs, including books, devotional articles, scientific equipment, examination papers, musical instruments, sports outfits and materials allowing prisoners of war to pursue their studies or their cultural activities.

Such shipments shall in no way free the Detaining Power from the obligations imposed upon it by virtue of the present Convention.

The only limits which may be placed on these shipments shall be those proposed by the Protecting Power in the interest of the prisoners themselves, or by the International Committee of the Red Cross or any other organization giving assistance to the prisoners, in respect of their own shipments only, on account of exceptional strain on transport or communications.

The conditions for the sending of individual parcels and collective relief shall, if necessary, be the subject of special agreements between the Powers concerned, which may in no case delay the receipt by the prisoners of relief supplies. Books may not be included in parcels of clothing and foodstuffs. Medical supplies shall, as a rule, be sent in collective parcels.

ARTICLE 73

A3–073   In the absence of special agreements between the Powers concerned on the conditions for the receipt and distribution of collective relief shipments, the rules and regulations concerning collective shipments, which are annexed to the present Convention, shall be applied.

The special agreements referred to above shall in no case restrict the right of prisoners' representatives to take possession of collective relief shipments intended for prisoners of war, to proceed to their distribution or to dispose of them in the interest of the prisoners.

Nor shall such agreements restrict the right of representatives of the Protecting Power, the International Committee of the Red Cross or any other organization giving assistance to prisoners of war and responsible for the forwarding of collective shipments, to supervise their distribution to the recipients.

ARTICLE 74

A3–074   All relief shipments for prisoners of war shall be exempt from import, customs and other dues.

Correspondence, relief shipments and authorized remittances of money addressed to prisoners of war or despatched by them through the post office, either direct or through the Information Bureaux provided for in Article 122 and the Central Prisoners of War Agency provided for in Article 123, shall be exempt from any postal dues, both in the countries of origin and destination, and in intermediate countries.

If relief shipments intended for prisoners of war cannot be sent through the post office by reason of weight or for any other cause, the cost of transportation shall be borne by the Detaining Power in all the territories under its control. The other Powers party to the Convention shall bear the cost of transport in their respective territories.

In the absence of special agreements between the Parties concerned, the costs connected with transport of such shipments, other than costs covered by the above exemption, shall be charged to the senders.

The High Contracting Parties shall endeavour to reduce, so far as possible, the rates charged for telegrams sent by prisoners of war, or addressed to them.

ARTICLE 75

Should military operations prevent the Powers concerned from fulfilling their obliga- **A3–075** tion to assure the transport of the shipments referred to in Articles 70, 71, 72 and 77, the Protecting Powers concerned, the International Committee of the Red Cross or any other organization duly approved by the Parties to the conflict may undertake to ensure the conveyance of such shipments by suitable means (railway wagons, motor vehicles, vessels or aircraft, etc.). For this purpose, the High Contracting Parties shall endeavour to supply them with such transport and to allow its circulation, especially by granting the necessary safe-conducts.

Such transport may also be used to convey:

(a) Correspondence, lists and reports exchanged between the Central Information Agency referred to in Article 123 and the National Bureaux referred to in Article 122;

(b) Correspondence and reports relating to prisoners of war which the Protecting Powers, the International Committee of the Red Cross or any other body assisting the prisoners, exchange either with their own delegates or with the Parties to the conflict.

These provisions in no way detract from the right of any Party to the conflict to arrange other means of transport, if it should so prefer, nor preclude the granting of safe-conducts, under mutually agreed conditions, to such means of transport.

In the absence of special agreements, the costs occasioned by the use of such means of transport shall be borne proportionally by the Parties to the conflict whose nationals are benefited thereby.

ARTICLE 76

The censoring of correspondence addressed to prisoners of war or despatched by them **A3–076** shall be done as quickly as possible. Mail shall be censored only by the despatching State and the receiving State, and once only by each.

The examination of consignments intended for prisoners of war shall not be carried out under conditions that will expose the goods contained in them to deterioration; except in the case of written or printed matter, it shall be done in the presence of the addressee, or of a fellow-prisoner duly delegated by him. The delivery to prisoners of individual or collective consignments shall not be delayed under the pretext of difficulties of censorship.

Any prohibition of correspondence ordered by Parties to the conflict, either for military or political reasons, shall be only temporary and its duration shall be as short as possible.

ARTICLE 77

The Detaining Powers shall provide all facilities for the transmission, through the **A3–077** Protecting Power or the Central Prisoners of War Agency provided for in Article 123, of instruments, papers or documents intended for prisoners of war or despatched by them, especially powers of attorney and wills.

In all cases they shall facilitate the preparation and execution of such documents on behalf of prisoners of war; in particular, they shall allow them to consult a lawyer and shall take what measures are necessary for the authentication of their signatures.

Section VI

Relations between Prisoners of War and the Authorities

CHAPTER I

COMPLAINTS OF PRISONERS OF WAR RESPECTING THE CONDITIONS OF CAPTIVITY

ARTICLE 78

A3–078   Prisoners of war shall have the right to make known to the military authorities in whose power they are, their requests regarding the conditions of captivity to which they are subjected.

They shall also have the unrestricted right to apply to the representatives of the Protecting Powers either through their prisoners' representative or, if they consider it necessary, direct, in order to draw their attention to any points on which they may have complaints to make regarding their conditions of captivity.

These requests and complaints shall not be limited nor considered to be a part of the correspondence quota referred to in Article 71. They must be transmitted immediately. Even if they are recognized to be unfounded, they may not give rise to any punishment.

Prisoners' representatives may send periodic reports on the situation in the camps and the needs of the prisoners of war to the representatives of the Protecting Powers.

CHAPTER II

PRISONER OF WAR REPRESENTATIVES

ARTICLE 79

A3–079   In all places where there are prisoners of war, except in those where there are officers, the prisoners shall freely elect by secret ballot, every six months, and also in case of vacancies, prisoners' representatives entrusted with representing them before the military authorities, the Protecting Powers, the International Committee of the Red Cross and any other organization which may assist them. These prisoners' representatives shall be eligible for re-election.

In camps for officers and persons of equivalent status or in mixed camps, the senior officer among the prisoners of war shall be recognized as the camp prisoners' representative. In camps for officers, he shall be assisted by one or more advisers chosen by the officers; in mixed camps, his assistants shall be chosen from among the prisoners of war who are not officers and shall be elected by them.

Officer prisoners of war of the same nationality shall be stationed in labour camps for prisoners of war, for the purpose of carrying out the camp administration duties for which the prisoners of war are responsible. These officers may be elected as prisoners' representatives under the first paragraph of this Article. In such a case the assistants to the prisoners' representatives shall be chosen from among those prisoners of war who are not officers.

Every representative elected must be approved by the Detaining Power before he has the right to commence his duties. Where the Detaining Power refuses to approve a prisoner of war elected by his fellow prisoners of war, it must inform the Protecting Power of the reason for such refusal.

In all cases the prisoners' representative must have the same nationality, language and customs as the prisoners of war whom he represents. Thus, prisoners of war distributed in different sections of a camp, according to their nationality, language or customs, shall have for each section their own prisoners' representative, in accordance with the foregoing paragraphs.

Article 80

Prisoners' representatives shall further the physical, spiritual and intellectual well-being of prisoners of war.

In particular, where the prisoners decide to organize amongst themselves a system of mutual assistance, this organization will be within the province of the prisoners' representative, in addition to the special duties entrusted to him by other provisions of the present Convention.

Prisoners' representatives shall not be held responsible, simply by reason of their duties, for any offences committed by prisoners of war.

Article 81

Prisoners' representatives shall not be required to perform any other work, if the accomplishment of their duties is thereby made more difficult.

Prisoners' representatives may appoint from amongst the prisoners such assistants as they may require. All material facilities shall be granted them, particularly a certain freedom of movement necessary for the accomplishment of their duties (inspection of labour detachments, receipt of supplies, etc.).

Prisoners' representatives shall be permitted to visit premises where prisoners of war are detained, and every prisoner of war shall have the right to consult freely his prisoners' representative.

All facilities shall likewise be accorded to the prisoners' representatives for communication by post and telegraph with the detaining authorities, the Protecting Powers, the International Committee of the Red Cross and their delegates, the Mixed Medical Commissions and with the bodies which give assistance to prisoners of war. Prisoners' representatives of labour detachments shall enjoy the same facilities for communication with the prisoners' representatives of the principal camp. Such communications shall not be restricted, nor considered as forming a part of the quota mentioned in Article 71.

Prisoners' representatives who are transferred shall be allowed a reasonable time to acquaint their successors with current affairs.

In case of dismissal, the reasons therefor shall be communicated to the Protecting Power.

Chapter III

PENAL AND DISCIPLINARY SANCTIONS

I. GENERAL PROVISIONS

Article 82

A prisoner of war shall be subject to the laws, regulations and orders in force in the armed forces of the Detaining Power; the Detaining Power shall be justified in taking judicial or disciplinary measures in respect of any offence committed by a prisoner of war against such laws, regulations or orders. However, no proceedings or punishments contrary to the provisions of this Chapter shall be allowed.

If any law, regulation or order of the Detaining Power shall declare acts committed by a prisoner of war to be punishable, whereas the same acts would not be punishable if committed by a member of the forces of the Detaining Power, such acts shall entail disciplinary punishments only.

ARTICLE 83

A3–083   In deciding whether proceedings in respect of an offence alleged to have been committed by a prisoner of war shall be judicial or disciplinary, the Detaining Power shall ensure that the competent authorities exercise the greatest leniency and adopt, wherever possible, disciplinary rather than judicial measures.

ARTICLE 84

A3–084   A prisoner of war shall be tried only by a military court, unless the existing laws of the Detaining Power expressly permit the civil courts to try a member of the armed forces of the Detaining Power in respect of the particular offence alleged to have been committed by the prisoner of war.

In no circumstances whatever shall a prisoner of war be tried by a court of any kind which does not offer the essential guarantees of independence and impartiality as generally recognized, and, in particular, the procedure of which does not afford the accused the rights and means of defence provided for in Article 105.

ARTICLE 85

A3–085   Prisoners of war prosecuted under the laws of the Detaining Power for acts committed prior to capture shall retain, even if convicted, the benefits of the present Convention.

ARTICLE 86

A3–086   No prisoner of war may be punished more than once for the same act, or on the same charge.

ARTICLE 87

A3–087   Prisoners of war may not be sentenced by the military authorities and courts of the Detaining Power to any penalties except those provided for in respect of members of the armed forces of the said Power who have committed the same acts.

When fixing the penalty, the courts or authorities of the Detaining Power shall take into consideration, to the widest extent possible, the fact that the accused, not being a national of the Detaining Power, is not bound to it by any duty of allegiance, and that he is in its power as the result of circumstances independent of his own will. The said courts or authorities shall be at liberty to reduce the penalty provided for the violation of which the prisoner of war is accused, and shall therefore not be bound to apply the minimum penalty prescribed.

Collective punishment for individual acts, corporal punishments, imprisonment in premises without daylight and, in general, any form of torture or cruelty, are forbidden.

No prisoner of war may be deprived of his rank by the Detaining Power, or prevented from wearing his badges.

ARTICLE 88

A3–088   Officers, non-commissioned officers and men who are prisoners of war undergoing a disciplinary or judicial punishment, shall not be subjected to more severe treatment than that applied in respect of the same punishment to members of the armed forces of the Detaining Power of equivalent rank.

A woman prisoner of war shall not be awarded or sentenced to a punishment more severe, or treated whilst undergoing punishment more severely, than a woman member of the armed forces of the Detaining Power dealt with for a similar offence.

In no case may a woman prisoner of war be awarded or sentenced to a punishment more severe, or treated whilst undergoing punishment more severely, than a male member of the armed forces of the Detaining Power dealt with for a similar offence.

Prisoners of war who have served disciplinary or judicial sentences may not be treated differently from other prisoners of war.

II. DISCIPLINARY SANCTIONS

ARTICLE 89

The disciplinary punishments applicable to prisoners of war are the following: **A3–089**
1. A fine which shall not exceed 50 per cent of the advances of pay and working pay which the prisoner of war would otherwise receive under the provisions of Articles 60 and 62 during a period of not more than thirty days.
2. Discontinuance of privileges granted over and above the treatment provided for by the present Convention.
3. Fatigue duties not exceeding two hours daily.
4. Confinement.The punishment referred to under (3) shall not be applied to officers.In no case shall disciplinary punishments be inhuman, brutal or dangerous to the health of prisoners of war.

ARTICLE 90

The duration of any single punishment shall in no case exceed thirty days. Any period   **A3–090** of confinement awaiting the hearing of a disciplinary offence or the award of disciplinary punishment shall be deducted from an award pronounced against a prisoner of war.

The maximum of thirty days provided above may not be exceeded, even if the prisoner of war is answerable for several acts at the same time when he is awarded punishment, whether such acts are related or not.

The period between the pronouncing of an award of disciplinary punishment and its execution shall not exceed one month.

When a prisoner of war is awarded a further disciplinary punishment, a period of at least three days shall elapse between the execution of any two of the punishments, if the duration of one of these is ten days or more.

ARTICLE 91

The escape of a prisoner of war shall be deemed to have succeeded when: **A3–091**
1. He has joined the armed forces of the Power on which he depends, or those of an allied Power;
2. He has left the territory under the control of the Detaining Power, or of an ally of the said Power;
3. He has joined a ship flying the flag of the Power on which he depends, or of an allied Power, in the territorial waters of the Detaining Power, the said ship not being under the control of the last-named Power.

Prisoners of war who have made good their escape in the sense of this Article and who are recaptured, shall not be liable to any punishment in respect of their previous escape.

ARTICLE 92

A prisoner of war who attempts to escape and is recaptured before having made good   **A3–092** his escape in the sense of Article 91 shall be liable only to a disciplinary punishment in respect of this act, even if it is a repeated offence.

A prisoner of war who is recaptured shall be handed over without delay to the competent military authority.

Article 88, fourth paragraph, notwithstanding, prisoners of war punished as a result of an unsuccessful escape may be subjected to special surveillance. Such surveillance must not affect the state of their health, must be undergone in a prisoner of war camp, and must not entail the suppression of any of the safeguards granted them by the present Convention.

ARTICLE 93

A3–093   Escape or attempt to escape, even if it is a repeated offence, shall not be deemed an aggravating circumstance if the prisoner of war is subjected to trial by judicial proceedings in respect of an offence committed during his escape or attempt to escape.

In conformity with the principle stated in Article 83, offences committed by prisoners of war with the sole intention of facilitating their escape and which do not entail any violence against life or limb, such as offences against public property, theft without intention of self-enrichment, the drawing up or use of false papers, the wearing of civilian clothing, shall occasion disciplinary punishment only.

Prisoners of war who aid or abet an escape or an attempt to escape shall be liable on this count to disciplinary punishment only.

ARTICLE 94

A3–094   If an escaped prisoner of war is recaptured, the Power on which he depends shall be notified thereof in the manner defined in Article 122, provided notification of his escape has been made.

ARTICLE 95

A3–095   A prisoner of war accused of an offence against discipline shall not be kept in confinement pending the hearing unless a member of the armed forces of the Detaining Power would be so kept if he were accused of a similar offence, or if it is essential in the interests of camp order and discipline.

Any period spent by a prisoner of war in confinement awaiting the disposal of an offence against discipline shall be reduced to an absolute minimum and shall not exceed fourteen days.

The provisions of Articles 97 and 98 of this Chapter shall apply to prisoners of war who are in confinement awaiting the disposal of offences against discipline.

ARTICLE 96

A3–096   Acts which constitute offences against discipline shall be investigated immediately.

Without prejudice to the competence of courts and superior military authorities, disciplinary punishment may be ordered only by an officer having disciplinary powers in his capacity as camp commander, or by a responsible officer who replaces him or to whom he has delegated his disciplinary powers.

In no case may such powers be delegated to a prisoner of war or be exercised by a prisoner of war.

Before any disciplinary award is pronounced, the accused shall be given precise information regarding the offences of which he is accused, and given an opportunity of explaining his conduct and of defending himself. He shall be permitted, in particular, to call witnesses and to have recourse, if necessary, to the services of a qualified interpreter. The decision shall be announced to the accused prisoner of war and to the prisoners' representative.

A record of disciplinary punishments shall be maintained by the camp commander and shall be open to inspection by representatives of the Protecting Power.

ARTICLE 97

A3–097   Prisoners of war shall not in any case be transferred to penitentiary establishments (prisons, penitentiaries, convict prisons, etc.) to undergo disciplinary punishment therein.

All premises in which disciplinary punishments are undergone shall conform to the sanitary requirements set forth in Article 25. A prisoner of war undergoing punishment shall be enabled to keep himself in a state of cleanliness, in conformity with Article 29.

Officers and persons of equivalent status shall not be lodged in the same quarters as non-commissioned officers or men.

Women prisoners of war undergoing disciplinary punishment shall be confined in separate quarters from male prisoners of war and shall be under the immediate supervision of women.

ARTICLE 98

A prisoner of war undergoing confinement as a disciplinary punishment, shall continue **A3–098**
to enjoy the benefits of the provisions of this Convention except in so far as these are necessarily rendered inapplicable by the mere fact that he is confined. In no case may he be deprived of the benefits of the provisions of Articles 78 and 126.

A prisoner of war awarded disciplinary punishment may not be deprived of the prerogatives attached to his rank.

Prisoners of war awarded disciplinary punishment shall be allowed to exercise and to stay in the open air at least two hours daily.

They shall be allowed, on their request, to be present at the daily medical inspections. They shall receive the attention which their state of health requires and, if necessary, shall be removed to the camp infirmary or to a hospital.

They shall have permission to read and write, likewise to send and receive letters. Parcels and remittances of money, however, may be withheld from them until the completion of the punishment; they shall meanwhile be entrusted to the prisoners' representative, who will hand over to the infirmary the perishable goods contained in such parcels.

III. JUDICIAL PROCEEDINGS

ARTICLE 99

No prisoner of war may be tried or sentenced for an act which is not forbidden by the **A3–099**
law of the Detaining Power or by international law, in force at the time the said act was committed.

No moral or physical coercion may be exerted on a prisoner of war in order to induce him to admit himself guilty of the act of which he is accused.

No prisoner of war may be convicted without having had an opportunity to present his defence and the assistance of a qualified advocate or counsel.

ARTICLE 100

Prisoners of war and the Protecting Powers shall be informed as soon as possible of the **A3–100**
offences which are punishable by the death sentence under the laws of the Detaining Power.

Other offences shall not thereafter be made punishable by the death penalty without the concurrence of the Power upon which the prisoners of war depend.

The death sentence cannot be pronounced on a prisoner of war unless the attention of the court has, in accordance with Article 87, second paragraph, been particularly called to the fact that since the accused is not a national of the Detaining Power, he is not bound to it by any duty of allegiance, and that he is in its power as the result of circumstances independent of his own will.

ARTICLE 101

If the death penalty is pronounced on a prisoner of war, the sentence shall not be **A3–101**
executed before the expiration of a period of at least six months from the date when the Protecting Power receives, at an indicated address, the detailed communication provided for in Article 107.

ARTICLE 102

A3–102   A prisoner of war can be validly sentenced only if the sentence has been pronounced by the same courts according to the same procedure as in the case of members of the armed forces of the Detaining Power, and if, furthermore, the provisions of the present Chapter have been observed.

ARTICLE 103

A3–103   Judicial investigations relating to a prisoner of war shall be conducted as rapidly as circumstances permit and so that his trial shall take place as soon as possible. A prisoner of war shall not be confined while awaiting trial unless a member of the armed forces of the Detaining Power would be so confined if he were accused of a similar offence, or if it is essential to do so in the interests of national security. In no circumstances shall this confinement exceed three months.

Any period spent by a prisoner of war in confinement awaiting trial shall be deducted from any sentence of imprisonment passed upon him and taken into account in fixing any penalty.

The provisions of Articles 97 and 98 of this Chapter shall apply to a prisoner of war whilst in confinement awaiting trial.

ARTICLE 104

A3–104   In any case in which the Detaining Power has decided to institute judicial proceedings against a prisoner of war, it shall notify the Protecting Power as soon as possible and at least three weeks before the opening of the trial. This period of three weeks shall run as from the day on which such notification reaches the Protecting Power at the address previously indicated by the latter to the Detaining Power.

The said notification shall contain the following information:
1. Surname and first names of the prisoner of war, his rank, his army, regimental, personal or serial number, his date of birth, and his profession or trade, if any;
2. Place of internment or confinement;
3. Specification of the charge or charges on which the prisoner of war is to be arraigned, giving the legal provisions applicable;
4 . Designation of the court which will try the case, likewise the date and place fixed for the opening of the trial.

The same communication shall be made by the Detaining Power to the prisoners' representative.

If no evidence is submitted, at the opening of a trial, that the notification referred to above was received by the Protecting Power, by the prisoner of war and by the prisoners' representative concerned, at least three weeks before the opening of the trial, then the latter cannot take place and must be adjourned.

ARTICLE 105

A3–105   The prisoner of war shall be entitled to assistance by one of his prisoner comrades, to defence by a qualified advocate or counsel of his own choice, to the calling of witnesses and, if he deems necessary, to the services of a competent interpreter. He shall be advised of these rights by the Detaining Power in due time before the trial.

Failing a choice by the prisoner of war, the Protecting Power shall find him an advocate or counsel, and shall have at least one week at its disposal for the purpose. The Detaining Power shall deliver to the said Power, on request, a list of persons qualified to present the defence.

Failing a choice of an advocate or counsel by the prisoner of war or the Protecting Power, the Detaining Power shall appoint a competent advocate or counsel to conduct the defence.

The advocate or counsel conducting the defence on behalf of the prisoner of war shall have at his disposal a period of two weeks at least before the opening of the trial, as well as the necessary facilities to prepare the defence of the accused. He may, in particular, freely visit the accused and interview him in private. He may also confer with any witnesses for the defence, including prisoners of war. He shall have the benefit of these facilities until the term of appeal or petition has expired.

Particulars of the charge or charges on which the prisoner of war is to be arraigned, as well as the documents which are generally communicated to the accused by virtue of the laws in force in the armed forces of the Detaining Power, shall be communicated to the accused prisoner of war in a language which he understands, and in good time before the opening of the trial. The same communication in the same circumstances shall be made to the advocate or counsel conducting the defence on behalf of the prisoner of war.

The representatives of the Protecting Power shall be entitled to attend the trial of the case, unless, exceptionally, this is held in camera in the interest of State security. In such a case the Detaining Power shall advise the Protecting Power accordingly.

ARTICLE 106

Every prisoner of war shall have, in the same manner as the members of the armed **A3–106** forces of the Detaining Power, the right of appeal or petition from any sentence pronounced upon him, with a view to the quashing or revising of the sentence or the reopening of the trial. He shall be fully informed of his right to appeal or petition and of the time limit within which he may do so.

ARTICLE 107

Any judgment and sentence pronounced upon a prisoner of war shall be immediately **A3–107** reported to the Protecting Power in the form of a summary communication, which shall also indicate whether he has the right of appeal with a view to the quashing of the sentence or the reopening of the trial. This communication shall likewise be sent to the prisoners' representative concerned. It shall also be sent to the accused prisoner of war in a language he understands, if the sentence was not pronounced in his presence. The Detaining Power shall also immediately communicate to the Protecting Power the decision of the prisoner of war to use or to waive his right of appeal.

Furthermore, if a prisoner of war is finally convicted or if a sentence pronounced on a prisoner of war in the first instance is a death sentence, the Detaining Power shall as soon as possible address to the Protecting Power a detailed communication containing:
1. The precise wording of the finding and sentence;
2. A summarized report of any preliminary investigation and of the trial, emphasizing in particular the elements of the prosecution and the defence;
3. Notification, where applicable, of the establishment where the sentence will be served.

The communications provided for in the foregoing subparagraphs shall be sent to the Protecting Power at the address previously made known to the Detaining Power.

ARTICLE 108

Sentences pronounced on prisoners of war after a conviction has become duly **A3–108** enforceable, shall be served in the same establishments and under the same conditions as in the case of members of the armed forces of the Detaining Power. These conditions shall in all cases conform to the requirements of health and humanity.

A woman prisoner of war on whom such a sentence has been pronounced shall be confined in separate quarters and shall be under the supervision of women.

In any case, prisoners of war sentenced to a penalty depriving them of their liberty shall retain the benefit of the provisions of Articles 78 and 126 of the present Convention. Furthermore, they shall be entitled to receive and despatch correspondence, to receive at least one relief parcel monthly, to take regular exercise in the open air, to have the medical care required by their state of health, and the spiritual assistance they may desire. Penalties to which they may be subjected shall be in accordance with the provisions of Article 87, third paragraph.

PART IV

TERMINATION OF CAPTIVITY

Section I

Direct Repatriation and Accommodation in Neutral Countries

ARTICLE 109

A3–109   Subject to the provisions of the third paragraph of this Article, Parties to the conflict are bound to send back to their own country, regardless of number or rank, seriously wounded and seriously sick prisoners of war, after having cared for them until they are fit to travel, in accordance with the first paragraph of the following Article.

Throughout the duration of hostilities, Parties to the conflict shall endeavour, with the cooperation of the neutral Powers concerned, to make arrangements for the accommodation in neutral countries of the sick and wounded prisoners of war referred to in the second paragraph of the following Article. They may, in addition, conclude agreements with a view to the direct repatriation or internment in a neutral country of able-bodied prisoners of war who have undergone a long period of captivity.

No sick or injured prisoner of war who is eligible for repatriation under the first paragraph of this Article, may be repatriated against his will during hostilities.

ARTICLE 110

A3–110   The following shall be repatriated direct:
   1. Incurably wounded and sick whose mental or physical fitness seems to have been gravely diminished.
   2. Wounded and sick who, according to medical opinion, are not likely to recover within one year, whose condition requires treatment and whose mental or physical fitness seems to have been gravely diminished.
   3. Wounded and sick who have recovered, but whose mental or physical fitness seems to have been gravely and permanently diminished.

The following may be accommodated in a neutral country:
   1. Wounded and sick whose recovery may be expected within one year of the date of the wound or the beginning of the illness, if treatment in a neutral country might increase the prospects of a more certain and speedy recovery.
   2. Prisoners of war whose mental or physical health, according to medical opinion, is seriously threatened by continued captivity, but whose accommodation in a neutral country might remove such a threat.

The conditions which prisoners of war accommodated in a neutral country must fulfil in order to permit their repatriation shall be fixed, as shall likewise their status, by agreement between the Powers concerned. In general, prisoners of war who have been accommodated in a neutral country, and who belong to the following categories, should be repatriated:
   1. Those whose state of health has deteriorated so as to fulfil the conditions laid down for direct repatriation;
   2. Those whose mental or physical powers remain, even after treatment, considerably impaired.

If no special agreements are concluded between the Parties to the conflict concerned, to determine the cases of disablement or sickness entailing direct repatriation or accommodation in a neutral country, such cases shall be settled in accordance with the principles laid down in the Model Agreement concerning direct repatriation and accommodation in neutral countries of wounded and sick prisoners of war and in the Regulations concerning Mixed Medical Commissions annexed to the present Convention.

ARTICLE 111

The Detaining Power, the Power on which the prisoners of war depend, and a neutral Power agreed upon by these two Powers, shall endeavour to conclude agreements which will enable prisoners of war to be interned in the territory of the said neutral Power until the close of hostilities.

A3–111

ARTICLE 112

Upon the outbreak of hostilities, Mixed Medical Commissions shall be appointed to examine sick and wounded prisoners of war, and to make all appropriate decisions regarding them. The appointment, duties and functioning of these Commissions shall be in conformity with the provisions of the Regulations annexed to the present Convention.

However, prisoners of war who, in the opinion of the medical authorities of the Detaining Power, are manifestly seriously injured or seriously sick, may be repatriated without having to be examined by a Mixed Medical Commission.

A3–112

ARTICLE 113

Besides those who are designated by the medical authorities of the Detaining Power, wounded or sick prisoners of war belonging to the categories listed below shall be entitled to present themselves for examination by the Mixed Medical Commissions provided for in the foregoing Article:
1. Wounded and sick proposed by a physician or surgeon who is of the same nationality, or a national of a Party to the conflict allied with the Power on which the said prisoners depend, and who exercises his functions in the camp.
2. Wounded and sick proposed by their prisoners' representative.
3. Wounded and sick proposed by the Power on which they depend, or by an organization duly recognized by the said Power and giving assistance to the prisoners.

Prisoners of war who do not belong to one of the three foregoing categories may nevertheless present themselves for examination by Mixed Medical Commissions, but shall be examined only after those belonging to the said categories.

The physician or surgeon of the same nationality as the prisoners who present themselves for examination by the Mixed Medical Commission, likewise the prisoners' representative of the said prisoners, shall have permission to be present at the examination.

A3–113

ARTICLE 114

Prisoners of war who meet with accidents shall, unless the injury is self-inflicted, have the benefit of the provisions of this Convention as regards repatriation or accommodation in a neutral country.

A3–114

ARTICLE 115

No prisoner of war on whom a disciplinary punishment has been imposed and who is eligible for repatriation or for accommodation in a neutral country, may be kept back on the plea that he has not undergone his punishment.

A3–115

Prisoners of war detained in connection with a judicial prosecution or conviction and who are designated for repatriation or accommodation in a neutral country, may benefit by such measures before the end of the proceedings or the completion of the punishment, if the Detaining Power consents.

Parties to the conflict shall communicate to each other the names of those who will be detained until the end of the proceedings or the completion of the punishment.

ARTICLE 116

A3–116   The costs of repatriating prisoners of war or of transporting them to a neutral country shall be borne, from the frontiers of the Detaining Power, by the Power on which the said prisoners depend.

ARTICLE 117

A3–117   No repatriated person may be employed on active military service.

Section II

Release and Repatriation of Prisoners of War at the Close of Hostilities

ARTICLE 118

A3–118   Prisoners of war shall be released and repatriated without delay after the cessation of active hostilities.

In the absence of stipulations to the above effect in any agreement concluded between the Parties to the conflict with a view to the cessation of hostilities, or failing any such agreement, each of the Detaining Powers shall itself establish and execute without delay a plan of repatriation in conformity with the principle laid down in the foregoing paragraph.

In either case, the measures adopted shall be brought to the knowledge of the prisoners of war.

The costs of repatriation of prisoners of war shall in all cases be equitably apportioned between the Detaining Power and the Power on which the prisoners depend. This apportionment shall be carried out on the following basis:

(a) If the two Powers are contiguous, the Power on which the prisoners of war depend shall bear the costs of repatriation from the frontiers of the Detaining Power.

(b) If the two Powers are not contiguous, the Detaining Power shall bear the costs of transport of prisoners of war over its own territory as far as its frontier or its port of embarkation nearest to the territory of the Power on which the prisoners of war depend. The Parties concerned shall agree between themselves as to the equitable apportionment of the remaining costs of the repatriation. The conclusion of this agreement shall in no circumstances justify any delay in the repatriation of the prisoners of war.

ARTICLE 119

A3–119   Repatriation shall be effected in conditions similar to those laid down in Articles 46 to 48 inclusive of the present Convention for the transfer of prisoners of war, having regard to the provisions of Article 118 and to those of the following paragraphs.

On repatriation, any articles of value impounded from prisoners of war under Article 18, and any foreign currency which has not been converted into the currency of the

Detaining Power, shall be restored to them. Articles of value and foreign currency which, for any reason whatever, are not restored to prisoners of war on repatriation, shall be despatched to the Information Bureau set up under Article 122.

Prisoners of war shall be allowed to take with them their personal effects, and any correspondence and parcels which have arrived for them. The weight of such baggage may be limited, if the conditions of repatriation so require, to what each prisoner can reasonably carry. Each prisoner shall in all cases be authorized to carry at least twenty-five kilograms.

The other personal effects of the repatriated prisoner shall be left in the charge of the Detaining Power which shall have them forwarded to him as soon as it has concluded an agreement to this effect, regulating the conditions of transport and the payment of the costs involved, with the Power on which the prisoner depends.

Prisoners of war against whom criminal proceedings for an indictable offence are pending may be detained until the end of such proceedings, and, if necessary, until the completion of the punishment. The same shall apply to prisoners of war already convicted for an indictable offence.

Parties to the conflict shall communicate to each other the names of any prisoners of war who are detained until the end of the proceedings or until punishment has been completed.

By agreement between the Parties to the conflict, commissions shall be established for the purpose of searching for dispersed prisoners of war and of assuring their repatriation with the least possible delay.

Section III

Death of Prisoners of War

Article 120

Wills of prisoners of war shall be drawn up so as to satisfy the conditions of validity **A3–120** required by the legislation of their country of origin, which will take steps to inform the Detaining Power of its requirements in this respect. At the request of the prisoner of war and, in all cases, after death, the will shall be transmitted without delay to the Protecting Power; a certified copy shall be sent to the Central Agency.

Death certificates in the form annexed to the present Convention, or lists certified by a responsible officer, of all persons who die as prisoners of war shall be forwarded as rapidly as possible to the Prisoner of War Information Bureau established in accordance with Article 122. The death certificates or certified lists shall show particulars of identity as set out in the third paragraph of Article 17, and also the date and place of death, the cause of death, the date and place of burial and all particulars necessary to identify the graves.

The burial or cremation of a prisoner of war shall be preceded by a medical examination of the body with a view to confirming death and enabling a report to be made and, where necessary, establishing identity.

The detaining authorities shall ensure that prisoners of war who have died in captivity are honourably buried, if possible according to the rites of the religion to which they belonged, and that their graves are respected, suitably maintained and marked so as to be found at any time. Wherever possible, deceased prisoners of war who depended on the same Power shall be interred in the same place.

Deceased prisoners of war shall be buried in individual graves unless unavoidable circumstances require the use of collective graves. Bodies may be cremated only for imperative reasons of hygiene, on account of the religion of the deceased or in accordance with his express wish to this effect. In case of cremation, the fact shall be stated and the reasons given in the death certificate of the deceased.

In order that graves may always be found, all particulars of burials and graves shall be recorded with a Graves Registration Service established by the Detaining Power. Lists of graves and particulars of the prisoners of war interred in cemeteries and elsewhere shall be transmitted to the Power on which such prisoners of war depended. Responsibility for the care of these graves and for records of any subsequent moves of the bodies shall rest on the Power controlling the territory, if a Party to the present Convention. These provisions shall also apply to the ashes, which shall be kept by the Graves Registration Service until proper disposal thereof in accordance with the wishes of the home country.

ARTICLE 121

A3–121   Every death or serious injury of a prisoner of war caused or suspected to have been caused by a sentry, another prisoner of war, or any other person, as well as any death the cause of which is unknown, shall be immediately followed by an official enquiry by the Detaining Power.

A communication on this subject shall be sent immediately to the Protecting Power. Statements shall be taken from witnesses, especially from those who are prisoners of war, and a report including such statements shall be forwarded to the Protecting Power.

If the enquiry indicates the guilt of one or more persons, the Detaining Power shall take all measures for the prosecution of the person or persons responsible.

PART V

INFORMATION BUREAUX AND RELIEF SOCIETIES FOR PRISONERS OF WAR

ARTICLE 122

A3–122   Upon the outbreak of a conflict and in all cases of occupation, each of the Parties to the conflict shall institute an official Information Bureau for prisoners of war who are in its power. Neutral or non-belligerent Powers who may have received within their territory persons belonging to one of the categories referred to in Article 4, shall take the same action with respect to such persons. The Power concerned shall ensure that the Prisoners of War Information Bureau is provided with the necessary accommodation, equipment and staff to ensure its efficient working. It shall be at liberty to employ prisoners of war in such a Bureau under the conditions laid down in the Section of the present Convention dealing with work by prisoners of war.

Within the shortest possible period, each of the Parties to the conflict shall give its Bureau the information referred to in the fourth, fifth and sixth paragraphs of this Article regarding any enemy person belonging to one of the categories referred to in Article 4, who has fallen into its power. Neutral or non-belligerent Powers shall take the same action with regard to persons belonging to such categories whom they have received within their territory.

The Bureau shall immediately forward such information by the most rapid means to the Powers concerned, through the intermediary of the Protecting Powers and likewise of the Central Agency provided for in Article 123.

This information shall make it possible quickly to advise the next of kin concerned. Subject to the provisions of Article 17, the information shall include, in so far as available to the Information Bureau, in respect of each prisoner of war, his surname, first names, rank, army, regimental, personal or serial number, place and full date of birth, indication of the Power on which he depends, first name of the father and maiden name of the mother, name and address of the person to be informed and the address to which correspondence for the prisoner may be sent.

The Information Bureau shall receive from the various departments concerned information regarding transfers, releases, repatriations, escapes, admissions to hospital, and deaths, and shall transmit such information in the manner described in the third paragraph above.

Likewise, information regarding the state of health of prisoners of war who are seriously ill or seriously wounded shall be supplied regularly, every week if possible.

The Information Bureau shall also be responsible for replying to all enquiries sent to it concerning prisoners of war, including those who have died in captivity; it will make any enquiries necessary to obtain the information which is asked for if this is not in its possession.

All written communications made by the Bureau shall be authenticated by a signature or a seal.

The Information Bureau shall furthermore be charged with collecting all personal valuables, including sums in currencies other than that of the Detaining Power and documents of importance to the next of kin, left by prisoners of war who have been repatriated or released, or who have escaped or died, and shall forward the said valuables to the Powers concerned. Such articles shall be sent by the Bureau in sealed packets which shall be accompanied by statements giving clear and full particulars of the identity of the person to whom the articles belonged, and by a complete list of the contents of the parcel. Other personal effects of such prisoners of war shall be transmitted under arrangements agreed upon between the Parties to the conflict concerned.

ARTICLE 123

A Central Prisoners of War Information Agency shall be created in a neutral country. **A3–123** The International Committee of the Red Cross shall, if it deems necessary, propose to the Powers concerned the organization of such an Agency.

The function of the Agency shall be to collect all the information it may obtain through official or private channels respecting prisoners of war, and to transmit it as rapidly as possible to the country of origin of the prisoners of war or to the Power on which they depend. It shall receive from the Parties to the conflict all facilities for effecting such transmissions.

The High Contracting Parties, and in particular those whose nationals benefit by the services of the Central Agency, are requested to give the said Agency the financial aid it may require.

The foregoing provisions shall in no way be interpreted as restricting the humanitarian activities of the International Committee of the Red Cross, or of the relief Societies provided for in Article 125.

ARTICLE 124

The national Information Bureaux and the Central Information Agency shall enjoy **A3–124** free postage for mail, likewise all the exemptions provided for in Article 74, and further, so far as possible, exemption from telegraphic charges or, at least, greatly reduced rates.

ARTICLE 125

Subject to the measures which the Detaining Powers may consider essential to ensure **A3–125** their security or to meet any other reasonable need, the representatives of religious organizations, relief societies, or any other organization assisting prisoners of war, shall receive from the said Powers, for themselves and their duly accredited agents, all necessary facilities for visiting the prisoners, distributing relief supplies and material, from any source, intended for religious, educational or recreative purposes, and for assisting them in organizing their leisure time within the camps. Such societies or organizations may be constituted in the territory of the Detaining Power or in any other country, or they may have an international character.

The Detaining Power may limit the number of societies and organizations whose delegates are allowed to carry out their activities in its territory and under its supervision, on condition, however, that such limitation shall not hinder the effective operation of adequate relief to all prisoners of war.

The special position of the International Committee of the Red Cross in this field shall be recognized and respected at all times.

As soon as relief supplies or material intended for the above-mentioned purposes are handed over to prisoners of war, or very shortly afterwards, receipts for each consignment, signed by the prisoners' representative, shall be forwarded to the relief society or organization making the shipment. At the same time, receipts for these consignments shall be supplied by the administrative authorities responsible for guarding the prisoners.

PART VI

EXECUTION OF THE CONVENTION

Section I

General Provisions

ARTICLE 126

A3–126   Representatives or delegates of the Protecting Powers shall have permission to go to all places where prisoners of war may be, particularly to places of internment, imprisonment and labour, and shall have access to all premises occupied by prisoners of war; they shall also be allowed to go to the places of departure, passage and arrival of prisoners who are being transferred. They shall be able to interview the prisoners, and in particular the prisoners' representatives, without witnesses, either personally or through an interpreter.

Representatives and delegates of the Protecting Powers shall have full liberty to select the places they wish to visit. The duration and frequency of these visits shall not be restricted. Visits may not be prohibited except for reasons of imperative military necessity, and then only as an exceptional and temporary measure.

The Detaining Power and the Power on which the said prisoners of war depend may agree, if necessary, that compatriots of these prisoners of war be permitted to participate in the visits.

The delegates of the International Committee of the Red Cross shall enjoy the same prerogatives. The appointment of such delegates shall be submitted to the approval of the Power detaining the prisoners of war to be visited.

ARTICLE 127

A3–127   The High Contracting Parties undertake, in time of peace as in time of war, to disseminate the text of the present Convention as widely as possible in their respective countries, and, in particular, to include the study thereof in their programmes of military and, if possible, civil instruction, so that the principles thereof may become known to all their armed forces and to the entire population.

Any military or other authorities, who in time of war assume responsibilities in respect of prisoners of war, must possess the text of the Convention and be specially instructed as to its provisions.

ARTICLE 128

A3–128   The High Contracting Parties shall communicate to one another through the Swiss Federal Council and, during hostilities, through the Protecting Powers, the official translations of the present Convention, as well as the laws and regulations which they may adopt to ensure the application thereof.

Article 129

The High Contracting Parties undertake to enact any legislation necessary to provide effective penal sanctions for persons committing, or ordering to be committed, any of the grave breaches of the present Convention defined in the following Article.

Each High Contracting Party shall be under the obligation to search for persons alleged to have committed, or to have ordered to be committed, such grave breaches, and shall bring such persons, regardless of their nationality, before its own courts. It may also, if it prefers, and in accordance with the provisions of its own legislation, hand such persons over for trial to another High Contracting Party concerned, provided such High Contracting Party has made out a prima facie case.

Each High Contracting Party shall take measures necessary for the suppression of all acts contrary to the provisions of the present Convention other than the grave breaches defined in the following Article.

In all circumstances, the accused persons shall benefit by safeguards of proper trial and defence, which shall not be less favourable than those provided by Article 105 and those following of the present Convention.

A3–129

Article 130

Grave breaches to which the preceding Article relates shall be those involving any of the following acts, if committed against persons or property protected by the Convention: wilful killing, torture or inhuman treatment, including biological experiments, wilfully causing great suffering or serious injury to body or health, compelling a prisoner of war to serve in the forces of the hostile Power, or wilfully depriving a prisoner of war of the rights of fair and regular trial prescribed in this Convention.

A3–130

Article 131

No High Contracting Party shall be allowed to absolve itself or any other High Contracting Party of any liability incurred by itself or by another High Contracting Party in respect of breaches referred to in the preceding Article.

A3–131

Article 132

At the request of a Party to the conflict, an enquiry shall be instituted, in a manner to be decided between the interested Parties, concerning any alleged violation of the Convention.

If agreement has not been reached concerning the procedure for the enquiry, the Parties should agree on the choice of an umpire who will decide upon the procedure to be followed.

Once the violation has been established, the Parties to the conflict shall put an end to it and shall repress it with the least possible delay.

A3–132

Section 11

Final Provisions

Article 133

The present Convention is established in English and in French. Both texts are equally authentic. The Swiss Federal Council shall arrange for official translations of the Convention to be made in the Russian and Spanish languages.

A3–133

Article 134

The present Convention replaces the Convention of 27 July 1929, in relations between the High Contracting Parties.

A3–134

ARTICLE 135

A3–135   In the relations between the Powers which are bound by The Hague Convention respecting the Laws and Customs of War on Land, whether that of July 29, 1899, or that of October 18, 1907, and which are parties to the present Convention, this last Convention shall be complementary to Chapter II of the Regulations annexed to the above-mentioned Conventions of The Hague.

ARTICLE 136

A3–136   The present Convention, which bears the date of this day, is open to signature until February 12, 1950, in the name of the Powers represented at the Conference which opened at Geneva on April 21, 1949; furthermore, by Powers not represented at that Conference, but which are parties to the Convention of July 27, 1929.

ARTICLE 137

A3–137   The present Convention shall be ratified as soon as possible and the ratifications shall be deposited at Berne.

A record shall be drawn up of the deposit of each instrument of ratification and certified copies of this record shall be transmitted by the Swiss Federal Council to all the Powers in whose name the Convention has been signed, or whose accession has been notified.

ARTICLE 138

A3–138   The present Convention shall come into force six months after not less than two instruments of ratification have been deposited.

Thereafter, it shall come into force for each High Contracting Party six months after the deposit of the instrument of ratification.

ARTICLE 139

A3–139   From the date of its coming into force, it shall be open to any Power in whose name the present Convention has not been signed, to accede to this Convention.

ARTICLE 140

A3–140   Accessions shall be notified in writing to the Swiss Federal Council, and shall take effect six months after the date on which they are received.

The Swiss Federal Council shall communicate the accessions to all the Powers in whose name the Convention has been signed, or whose accession has been notified.

ARTICLE 141

A3–141   The situations provided for in Articles 2 and 3 shall give immediate effect to ratifications deposited and accessions notified by the Parties to the conflict before or after the beginning of hostilities or occupation. The Swiss Federal Council shall communicate by the quickest method any ratifications or accessions received from Parties to the conflict.

ARTICLE 142

A3–142   Each of the High Contracting Parties shall be at liberty to denounce the present Convention.

The denunciation shall be notified in writing to the Swiss Federal Council, which shall transmit it to the Governments of all the High Contracting Parties.

The denunciation shall take effect one year after the notification thereof has been made to the Swiss Federal Council. However, a denunciation of which notification has been made at a time when the denouncing Power is involved in a conflict shall not take effect until peace has been concluded, and until after operations connected with the release and repatriation of the persons protected by the present Convention have been terminated.

The denunciation shall have effect only in respect of the denouncing Power. It shall in no way impair the obligations which the Parties to the conflict shall remain bound to fulfil by virtue of the principles of the law of nations, as they result from the usages established among civilized peoples, from the laws of humanity and the dictates of the public conscience.

ARTICLE 143

A3–143

The Swiss Federal Council shall register the present Convention with the Secretariat of the United Nations. The Swiss Federal Council shall also inform the Secretariat of the United Nations of all ratifications, accessions and denunciations received by it with respect to the present Convention.

IN WITNESS WHEREOF the undersigned, having deposited their respective full powers, have signed the present Convention.

DONE at Geneva this twelfth day of August 1949, in the English and French languages. The original shall be deposited in the Archives of the Swiss Confederation. The Swiss Federal Council shall transmit certified copies thereof to each of the signatory and acceding States.

ANNEX I

A3–144

Model agreement concerning direct repatriation and accommodation in neutral countries of wounded and sick prisoners of war

(see Article 110)

I. PRINCIPLES FOR DIRECT REPATRIATION AND ACCOMMODATION IN NEUTRAL COUNTRIES

A. DIRECT REPATRIATION

A3–145

The following shall be repatriated direct:
1. All prisoners of war suffering from the following disabilities as the result of trauma: loss of limb, paralysis, articular or other disabilities, when this disability is at least the loss of a hand or a foot, or the equivalent of the loss of a hand or a foot.

   Without prejudice to a more generous interpretation, the following shall be considered as equivalent to the loss of a hand or a foot:
   (a) Loss of a hand or of all the fingers, or of the thumb and forefinger of one hand; loss of a foot, or of all the toes and metatarsals of one foot.
   (b) Ankylosis, loss of osseous tissue, cicatricial contracture preventing the functioning of one of the large articulations or of all the digital joints of one hand.
   (c) Pseudarthrosis of the long bones.
   (d) Deformities due to fracture or other injury which seriously interfere with function and weight-bearing power.
2. All wounded prisoners of war whose condition has become chronic, to the extent that prognosis appears to exclude recovery-in spite of treatment-within one year from the date of the injury, as. for example, in case of:

(a) Projectile in the heart. even if the Mixed Medical Commission should fail, at the time of their examination, to detect any serious disorders.

(b) Metallic splinter in the brain or the lungs, even if the Mixed Medical Commission cannot, at the time of examination, detect any local or general reaction.

(c) Osteomyelitis, when recovery cannot be foreseen in the course of the year following the injury, and which seems likely to result in ankylosis of a joint, or other impairments equivalent to the loss of a hand or a foot.

(d) Perforating and suppurating injury to the large joints.

(e) Injury to the skull, with loss or shifting of bony tissue.

(f) Injury or burning of the face with loss of tissue and functional lesions.

(g) Injury to the spinal cord.

(h) Lesion of the peripheral nerves, the sequelae of which are equivalent to the loss of a hand or foot, and the cure of which requires more than a year from the date of injury, for example: injury to the brachial or lumbosacral plexus, the median or sciatic nerves, likewise combined injury to the radial and cubital nerves or to the lateral popliteal nerve *(N. peroneus communes)* and medial popliteal nerve *(N. tibialis)*; etc. The separate injury of the 'radial (musculo-spiral), cubital. lateral or medial popliteal nerves shall not, however, warrant repatriation except in case of contractures or of serious neurotrophic disturbance.

(i) Injury to the urinary system, with incapacitating results.

3. All sick prisoners of war whose condition has become chronic to the extent that prognosis seems to exclude recovery-in spite of treatment-within one year from the inception of the disease, as, for example, in case of:

(a) Progressive tuberculosis of any organ which, according to medical prognosis, cannot be cured, or at least considerably improved, by treatment in a neutral country.

(b) Exudate pleurisy.

(c) Serious diseases of the respiratory organs of non-tubercular etiology, presumed incurable. for example: serious pulmonary emphysema, with or without bronchitis, chronic asthma:* chronic bronchitis* lasting more than one year in captivity; bronchiectasis,* etc.

(d) Serious chronic affections of the circulatory system, for example: valvular lesions and myocarditis* which have shown signs of circulatory failure during captivity, even though the Mixed Medical Commission cannot detect any such signs at the time of examination; affections of the pericardium and the vessels (Buerger's disease, aneurism of the large vessels); etc.

(e) Serious chronic affections of the digestive organs, for example: gastric or duodenal ulcer-, sequelae of gastric operations performed in captivity; chronic gastritis, enteritis or colitis, having lasted more than one year and seriously affecting the general condition: cirrhosis of the liver, chronic cholecystopathy;* etc.

(f) Serious chronic affections of the genito-urinary organs, for example: chronic diseases of the kidney with consequent disorders; nephrectomy because of a tubercular kidney; chronic pyelitis or chronic cystitis: hydronephrosis or pyonephrosis; chronic grave gynaecological conditions-, normal pregnancy, and obstetrical disorder, where it is impossible to accommodate in a neutral country; etc.

(g) Serious chronic diseases of the central and peripheral nervous system, for example: all obvious psychoses and psychoneuroses, such as serious hysteria, serious captivity psychoneurosis, etc., duly verified by a specialist;* any epilepsy duly verified by the camp physicians.' cerebral arteriosclerosis-chronic neuritis lasting more than one year. etc.

(h) Serious chronic disease of the neuro-vegetative system, with considerable diminution of mental or physical fitness. noticeable loss of weight and general asthenia.

    (i) Blindness of both eyes, or of one eye when the vision of the other is less than I in spite of the use of corrective glasses; diminution of visual acuity in cases where it is impossible to restore it by correction to an acuity of 1/2 in at least one eye;* other grave ocular affections, for example: glaucoma, iritis, choroiditis; trachoma, etc.

    (k) Auditive disorders, such as total unilateral deafness, if the other car does not discern the ordinary spoken word at a distance of one metre;* etc.

    (l) Serious affections of metabolism, for example: diabetes mellitus requiring insulin treatment; etc.

    (m) Serious disorders of the endocrine glands, for example: thyrotoxicosis; hypothyrosis; Addison's disease; Simmonds' cachexia; tetany; etc.

    (n) Grave and chronic disorders of the blood-forming organs.

    (o) Serious cases of chronic intoxication, for example: lead poisoning, mercury poisoing, morphinism. cocainism, alcoholism; gas or radiation poisoning; etc.

    (p) Chronic affections of locomotion, with obvious functional disorders, for example: arthritis deformans, primary and secondary progressive chronic polyarthritis; rheumatism with serious clinical symptoms; etc.

    (q) Serious chronic skin diseases. not amenable to treatment.

    (r) Any malignant growth.

    (s) Serious chronic infectious diseases, persisting for one year after their inception, for example: malaria with decided organic impairment, amoebic or bacillary dysentery with grave disorders; tertiary visceral syphilis resistant to treatment; leprosy; etc.

    (t) Serious avitaminosis or serious inanition.

B. ACCOMMODATION IN NEUTRAL COUNTRIES

The following shall be eligible for accommodation in a neutral country: **A3–146**

1. All wounded prisoners of war who are not likely to recover in captivity, but who might be cured or whose condition might be considerably improved by accommodation in a neutral country.

2. Prisoners of war suffering from any form of tuberculosis, of whatever organ, and whose treatment in a neutral country would be likely to lead to recovery or at least to considerable improvement, with the exception of primary tuberculosis cured before captivity.

3. Prisoners of war suffering from affections requiring treatment of the respiratory, circulatory, digestive, nervous, sensory, genito-urinary, cutaneous. locomotive organs, etc., if such treatment would clearly have better results in a neutral country than in captivity.

4. Prisoners of war who have undergone a nephrectomy in captivity for a nontubercular renal affection; cases of osteomyelitis, on the way to recovery or latent; diabetes mellitus not requiring insulin treatment; etc.

5. Prisoners of war suffering from war or captivity neuroses.
       Cases of captivity neurosis which are not cured after three months of accommodation in a neutral country, or which after that length of time are not clearly on the way to complete cure, shall be repatriated.

6. All prisoners of war suffering from chronic intoxication (gases, metals, alkaloids, etc.), for whom the prospects of cure in a neutral country are especially favourable.

7. All women prisoners of war who are pregnant or mothers with infants and small children.

---

* The decision of the Mixed Medical Commission shall be based to a great extent on the records kept by camp physicians and surgeons of the same nationality as the prisoners of war, or on an examination by medical specialists of the Detaining Power.

The following cases shall not be eligible for accommodation in a neutral country:
1. All duly verified chronic psychoses.
2. All organic or functional nervous affections considered to be incurable.
3. All contagious diseases during the period in which they are transmissible, with the exception of tuberculosis.

II. GENERAL OBSERVATIONS

A3–147   1. The conditions given shall, in a general way, be interpreted and applied in as broad a spirit as possible.

Neuropathic and psychopathic conditions caused by war or captivity, as well as cases of tuberculosis in all stages, shall above all benefit by such liberal interpretation. Prisoners of war Who have sustained several wounds, none of which, considered by itself, justifies repatriation, shall be examined in the same spirit, with due regard for the psychic traumatism due to the number of their wounds.

2. All unquestionable cases giving the right to direct repatriation (amputation, total blindness or deafness. open pulmonary tuberculosis, mental disorder. malignant growth, etc.)shall be examined and repatriated as soon as possible by the camp physicians or by military medical commissions appointed by the Detaining Power.

3. Injuries and diseases which existed before the war and which have not become worse. as well as war injuries which have not prevented subsequent military service, shall not entitle to direct repatriation.

4. The provisions of this Annex shall be interpreted and applied in a similar manner in all countries party to the conflict. The Powers and authorities concerned shall grant to Mixed Medical Commissions all the facilities necessary for the accomplishment of their task.

5. The examples quoted under (1) above represent only typical cases. Cases which do not correspond exactly to these provisions shall be judged in the spirit of the provisions of Article I 10 of the present Convention, and of the principles embodied in the present Agreement.

ANNEX II

REGULATIONS CONCERNING MIXED MEDICAL COMMISSIONS (SEE ARTICLE 112)

ARTICLE 1

A3–148   The Mixed Medical Commissions provided for in Article 112 of the Convention shall be composed of three members, two of whom shall belong to a neutral country. the third being appointed by the Detaining Power. One of the neutral members shall take the chair.

ARTICLE 2

A3–149   The two neutral members shall be appointed by the International Committee of the Red Cross, acting in agreement with the Protecting Power, at the request of the Detaining Power. They may be domiciled either in their country of origin, in any other neutral country, or in the territory of the Detaining Power.

ARTICLE 3

A3–150   The neutral members shall be approved by the Parties to the conflict concerned, who notify their approval to the International Committee of the Red Cross and to the Protecting Power. Upon such notification, the neutral members shall be considered as effectively appointed.

Article 4

Deputy members shall also be appointed in sufficient number to replace the regular **A3–151** members in case of need. They shall be appointed at the same time as the regular members or, at least, as soon as possible.

Article 5

If for any reason the International Committee of the Red Cross cannot arrange for the **A3–152** appointment of the neutral members, this shall be done by the Power protecting the interests of the prisoners of war to be examined.

Article 6

So far as possible, one of the two neutral members shall be a surgeon and the other a **A3–153** physician.

Article 7

The neutral members shall be entirely independent of the Parties to the conflict, **A3–154** which shall grant them all facilities in the accomplishment of their duties.

Article 8

By agreement with the Detaining Power, the International Committee of the Red **A3–155** Cross, when making the appointments provided for in Articles 2 and 4 of the present Regulations, shall settle the terms of service of the nominees.

Article 9

The Mixed Medical Commissions shall begin their work as soon as possible after the **A3–156** neutral members have been approved, and in any case within a period of three months from the date of such approval.

Article 10

The Mixed Medical Commissions shall examine all the prisoners designated in Article **A3–157** 113 of the Convention. They shall propose repatriation, rejection, or reference to a later examination. Their decisions shall be made by a majority vote.

Article 11

The decisions made by the Mixed Medical Commissions in each specific case shall be **A3–158** communicated, during the month following their visit, to the Detaining Power, the Protecting Power and the International Committee of the Red Cross. The Mixed Medical Commissions shall also inform each prisoner of war examined of the decision made, and shall issue to those whose repatriation has been proposed, certificates similar to the model appended to the present Convention.

Article 12

The Detaining Power shall be required to carry out the decisions of the Mixed Medical **A3–159** Commissions within three months of the time when it receives due notification of such decisions.

ARTICLE 13

A3–160 If there is no neutral physician in a country where the services of a Mixed Medical Commission seem to be required, and if it is for any reason impossible to appoint neutral doctors who are resident in another country, the Detaining Power, acting in agreement with the Protecting Power, shall set up a Medical Commission which shall undertake the same duties as a Mixed Medical Commission, subject to the provisions of Articles 1, 2, 3, 4, 5 and 8 of the Present Regulations.

ARTICLE 14

A3–161 Mixed Medical Commissions shall function permanently and shall visit each camp at intervals of not more than six months.

ANNEX III

REGULATIONS CONCERNING COLLECTIVE RELIEF (SEE ARTICLE 73)

ARTICLE 1

A3–162 Prisoners' representatives shall be allowed to distribute collective relief shipments for which they are sible, to all prisoners of war administered by their camp, including those who am in hospitals or in prisons or other penal establishments.

ARTICLE 2

A3–163 The distribution of collective relief shipments shall be effected in accordance with the instructions of the donors and with a plan drawn up by the prisoners' representatives. 'Me issue of medical stores shall. however, be made for preference in agreement with the senior medical officers, and the latter may. in hospitals and infirmaries, waive the said instructions, if the needs of their patients so demand. Within the limits thus defined, the distribution shall always be carried out equitably.

ARTICLE 3

A3–164 The said prisoners' representatives or their assistants shall be allowed to go to the points of arrival of relief supplies near their camps. so as to enable the prisoners' representatives or their assistants to verify the quality as well as the quantity of the goods received, and to make out detailed reports thereon for the donors.

ARTICLE 4

A3–165 Prisoners' representatives shall be given the facilities necessary for verifying whether the distribution of collective relief in all sub-divisions and annexes of their camps has been carried out in accordance with their instructions.

ARTICLE 5

A3–166 Prisoners' representatives shall be allowed to fill up, and cause to be filled up by the prisoners' representatives of labour detachments or by the senior medical officers of infirmaries and hospitals, forms or questionnaires intended for the donors, relating to collective relief supplies (distribution. requirements, quantities, etc.). Such forms and questionnaires, duly completed, shall be forwarded to the donors without delay.

ARTICLE 6

In order to secure the regular issue of collective relief to the prisoners of war in their camp. and to meet any needs that may arise from the arrival of new contingents of prisoners, prisoners' representatives shall be allowed to build up and maintain adequate reserve stocks of collective relief. For this purpose, they shall have suitable warehouses at their disposal; each warehouse shall be provided with two locks, the prisoners' representative holding the keys of one lock and the camp commander the keys of the other.

A3–167

ARTICLE 7

When collective consignments of clothing am available each prisoner of war shall retain in his possession at least one complete set of clothes. If a prisoner has more than one set of clothes, the prisoners' representative shall be permitted to withdraw excess clothing from those with the largest number of sets, or particular articles in excess of one, if this is necessary in order to supply prisoners who are less well provided. He shall not, however, withdraw second sets of underclothing, socks or footwear, unless this is the only means of providing for prisoners of war with none.

A3–168

ARTICLE 8

The High Contracting Parties, and the Detaining Powers in particular, shall author-ize, as far as possible and subject to the regulations governing the supply of the population, all purchases of goods made in their territories for the distribution of collective relief to prisoners of war. They shall similarly facilitate the transfer of funds and other financial measures of a technical or administrative nature taken for the purpose of making such purchases.

A3–169

ARTICLE 9

The foregoing provisions shall not constitute an obstacle to the right of prisoners of war to receive collective relief before their arrival in a camp or in the course of transfer, nor to the possibility of representatives of the Protecting Power, the International Committee of the Red Cross, or any other body giving assistance to prisoners which may be responsible for the forwarding of such supplies, ensuring the distribution thereof to the addressees by any other means that they may deem useful.

A3–170

ANNEX IV

A. IDENTITYCARD

(see Article 4)
[. . .]

A3–171

B. CAPTURE CARD

(see Article 70)
[. . .]

A3–172

C. CORRESPONDENCE CARD AND LETTER

A3–173   (see Article 71)

[. . .]

D. NOTIFICATION OF DEATH

A3–174   (see Article 120)

[. . .]

E. REPATRIATION CERTIFICATE

A3–175   (see Annex II, Article 11)

REPATRIATION CERTIFICATE
    Date:
    Camp:
    Hospital:
    Surname:
    First names:
    Date of birth:
    Rank:
    Army number:
    P. W. number:
    Injury-Disease:
    Decision of the Commission:

Chairman of the
Mixed Medical Commission:

A   = direct repatriation
B   = accommodation in a neutral country
NC   = re-examination by next Commission

ANNEX V

MODEL REGULATIONS CONCERNING PAYMENTS SENT BY PRISONERS TO THEIR OWN COUNTRY

A3–176   1. The notification referred to in the third paragraph of Article 63 will show:
       (a) Number as specified in Article 17, rank, surname and first names of the prisoner of war who is the payer;
       (b) The name and address of the payee in the country of origin;
       (c) The amount to be so paid in the currency of the country in which he is detained.
     2. The notification will be signed by the prisoner of war, or his witnessed mark made upon if it he cannot write, and shall be countersigned by the prisoners' representative.
     3. The camp commander will add to this notification a certiciate that the prisoner of war concerned has a credit balance of not less than the amount registered as payable.
     4. The notification may be made up in lists, each sheet of such lists witnessed by the prisoners' representative and certified by the camp commander.

A4. Geneva Convention relative to the Protection of Civilian Persons in Time of War Adopted on 12 August 1949 by the Diplomatic Conference for the Establishment of International Conventions for the Protection of Victims of War, held in Geneva from 21 April to 12 August, 1949

entry into force 21 October 1950

PART I

GENERAL PROVISIONS

ARTICLE 1

The High Contracting Parties undertake to respect and to ensure respect for the present Convention in all circumstances.   **A4–001**

ARTICLE 2

In addition to the provisions which shall be implemented in peacetime, the present   **A4–002** Convention shall apply to all cases of declared war or of any other armed conflict which may arise between two or more of the High Contracting Parties, even if the state of war is not recognized by one of them.

The Convention shall also apply to all cases of partial or total occupation of the territory of a High Contracting Party, even if the said occupation meets with no armed resistance.

Although one of the Powers in conflict may not be a party to the present Convention, the Powers who are parties thereto shall remain bound by it in their mutual relations. They shall furthermore be bound by the Convention in relation to the said Power, if the latter accepts and applies the provisions thereof.

ARTICLE 3

In the case of armed conflict not of an international character occurring in the   **A4–003** territory of one of the High Contracting Parties, each Party to the conflict shall be bound to apply, as a minimum, the following provisions:

1. Persons taking no active part in the hostilities, including members of armed forces who have laid down their arms and those placed hors de combat by sickness, wounds, detention, or any other cause, shall in all circumstances be treated humanely, without any adverse distinction founded on race, colour, religion or faith, sex, birth or wealth, or any other similar criteria.

   To this end, the following acts are and shall remain prohibited at any time and in any place whatsoever with respect to the above-mentioned persons:
   (a) Violence to life and person, in particular murder of all kinds, mutilation, cruel treatment and torture;
   (b) Taking of hostages;
   (c) Outrages upon personal dignity, in particular humiliating and degrading treatment;
   (d) The passing of sentences and the carrying out of executions without previous judgment pronounced by a regularly constituted court, affording all the judicial guarantees which are recognized as indispensable by civilized peoples.

1073

2. The wounded and sick shall be collected and cared for.

An impartial humanitarian body, such as the International Committee of the Red Cross, may offer its services to the Parties to the conflict.

The Parties to the conflict should further endeavour to bring into force, by means of special agreements, all or part of the other provisions of the present Convention.

The application of the preceding provisions shall not affect the legal status of the Parties to the conflict.

ARTICLE 4

A4–004   Persons protected by the Convention are those who, at a given moment and in any manner whatsoever, find themselves, in case of a conflict or occupation, in the hands of a Party to the conflict or Occupying Power of which they are not nationals.

Nationals of a State which is not bound by the Convention are not protected by it. Nationals of a neutral State who find themselves in the territory of a belligerent State, and nationals of a co-belligerent State, shall not be regarded as protected persons while the State of which they are nationals has normal diplomatic representation in the State in whose hands they are.

The provisions of Part II are, however, wider in application, as defined in Article 13.

Persons protected by the Geneva Convention for the Amelioration of the Condition of the Wounded and Sick in Armed Forces in the Field of August 12, 1949, or by the Geneva Convention for the Amelioration of the Condition of Wounded, Sick and Shipwrecked Members of Armed Forces at Sea of August 12, 1949, or by the Geneva Convention relative to the Treatment of Prisoners of War of August 12, 1949, shall not be considered as protected persons within the meaning of the present Convention.

ARTICLE 5

A4–005   Where, in the territory of a Party to the conflict, the latter is satisfied that an individual protected person is definitely suspected of or engaged in activities hostile to the security of the State, such individual person shall not be entitled to claim such rights and privileges under the present Convention as would, if exercised in the favour of such individual person, be prejudicial to the security of such State.

Where in occupied territory an individual protected person is detained as a spy or saboteur, or as a person under definite suspicion of activity hostile to the security of the Occupying Power, such person shall, in those cases where absolute military security so requires, be regarded as having forfeited rights of communication under the present Convention.

In each case, such persons shall nevertheless be treated with humanity, and in case of trial, shall not be deprived of the rights of fair and regular trial prescribed by the present Convention. They shall also be granted the full rights and privileges of a protected person under the present Convention at the earliest date consistent with the security of the State or Occupying Power, as the case may be.

ARTICLE 6

A4–006   The present Convention shall apply from the outset of any conflict or occupation mentioned in Article 2.

In the territory of Parties to the conflict, the application of the present Convention shall cease on the general close of military operations.

In the case of occupied territory, the application of the present Convention shall cease one year after the general close of military operations; however, the Occupying Power shall be bound, for the duration of the occupation, to the extent that such Power exercises the functions of government in such territory, by the provisions of the following Articles of the present Convention: I to 12, 27, 29 to 34, 47, 49, 51, 52, 53, 59, 61 to 77, and 143.

Protected persons whose release, repatriation or re-establishment may take place after such dates shall meanwhile continue to benefit by the present Convention. Article 7.

In addition to the agreements expressly provided for in Articles 11, 14, 15, 17, 36, 108, 109, 132, 133 and 149, the High Contracting Parties may conclude other special agreements for all matters concerning which they may deem it suitable to make separate provision. No special agreement shall adversely affect the situation of protected persons, as defined by the present Convention, nor restrict the rights which it confers upon them.

Protected persons shall continue to have the benefit of such agreements as long as the Convention is applicable to them, except where express provisions to the contrary are contained in the aforesaid or in subsequent agreements, or where more favourable measures have been taken with regard to them by one or other of the Parties to the conflict.

ARTICLE 8

Protected persons may in no circumstances renounce in part or in entirety the rights secured to them by the present Convention, and by the special agreements referred to in the foregoing Article, if such there be.

A4–007

ARTICLE 9

The present Convention shall be applied with the cooperation and under the scrutiny of the Protecting Powers whose duty it is to safeguard the interests of the Parties to the conflict. For this purpose, the Protecting Powers may appoint, apart from their diplomatic or consular staff, delegates from amongst their own nationals or the nationals of other neutral Powers. The said delegates shall be subject to the approval of the Power with which they are to carry out their duties.

A4–008

The Parties to the conflict shall facilitate to the greatest extent possible the task of the representatives or delegates of the Protecting Powers.

The representatives or delegates of the Protecting Powers shall not in any case exceed their mission under the present Convention. They shall, in particular, take account of the imperative necessities of security of the State wherein they carry out their duties.

ARTICLE 10

The provisions of the present Convention constitute no obstacle to the humanitarian activities which the International Committee of the Red Cross or any other impartial humanitarian organization may, subject to the consent of the Parties to the conflict concerned, undertake for the protection of civilian persons and for their relief.

A4–009

ARTICLE 11

The High Contracting Parties may at any time agree to entrust to an organization which offers all guarantees of impartiality and efficacy the duties incumbent on the Protecting Powers by virtue of the present Convention.

A4–010

When persons protected by the present Convention do not benefit or cease to benefit, no matter for what reason, by the activities of a Protecting Power or of an organization provided for in the first paragraph above, the Detaining Power shall request a neutral State, or such an organization, to undertake the functions performed under the present Convention by a Protecting Power designated by the Parties to a conflict.

If protection cannot be arranged accordingly, the Detaining Power shall request or shall accept, subject to the provisions of this Article, the offer of the services of a humanitarian organization, such as the International Committee of the Red Cross, to assume the humanitarian functions performed by Protecting Powers under the present Convention.

Any neutral Power, or any organization invited by the Power concerned or offering itself for these purposes, shall be required to act with a sense of responsibility towards the Party to the conflict on which persons protected by the present Convention depend, and shall be required to furnish sufficient assurances that it is in a position to undertake the appropriate functions and to discharge them impartially.

No derogation from the preceding provisions shall be made by special agreements between Powers one of which is restricted, even temporarily, in its freedom to negotiate with the other Power or its allies by reason of military events, more particularly where the whole, or a substantial part, of the territory of the said Power is occupied.

Whenever in the present Convention mention is made of a Protecting Power, such mention applies to substitute organizations in the sense of the present Article.

The provisions of this Article shall extend and be adapted to cases of nationals of a neutral State who are in occupied territory or who find themselves in the territory of a belligerent State with which the State of which they are nationals has not normal diplomatic representation.

ARTICLE 12

A4–011   In cases where they deem it advisable in the interest of protected persons, particularly in cases of disagreement between the Parties to the conflict as to the application or interpretation of the provisions of the present Convention, the Protecting Powers shall lend their good offices with a view to settling the disagreement. For this purpose, each of the Protecting Powers may, either at the invitation of one Party or on its own initiative, propose to the Parties to the conflict a meeting of their representatives, and in particular of the authorities responsible for protected person, possibly on neutral territory suitably chosen. The Parties to the conflict shall be bound to give effect to the proposals made to them for this purpose. The Protecting Powers may, if necessary, propose for approval by the Parties to the conflict, a person belonging to a neutral Power or delegated by the International Committee of the Red Cross who shall be invited to take part in such a meeting.

PART II

GENERAL PROTECTION OF POPULATIONS AGAINST CERTAIN CONSEQUENCES OF WAR

ARTICLE 13

A4–012   The provisions of Part II cover the whole of the populations of the countries in conflict, without any adverse distinction based, in particular, on race, nationality, religion or political opinion, and are intended to alleviate the sufferings caused by war.

ARTICLE 14

A4–013   In time of peace, the High Contracting Parties and, after the outbreak of hostilities, the Parties thereto, may establish in their own territory and, if the need arises, in occupied areas, hospital and safety zones and localities so organized as to protect from the effects of war, wounded, sick and aged persons, children under fifteen, expectant mothers and mothers of children under seven.

Upon the outbreak and during the course of hostilities, the Parties concerned may conclude agreements on mutual recognition of the zones and localities they have created. They may for this purpose implement the provisions of the Draft Agreement annexed to the present Convention, with such amendments as they may consider necessary.

The Protecting Powers and the International Committee of the Red Cross are invited to lend their good offices in order to facilitate the institution and recognition of these hospital and safety zones and localities.

ARTICLE 15

Any Party to the conflict may, either directly or through a neutral State or some **A4–014** humanitarian organization, propose to the adverse Party to establish, in the regions where fighting is taking place, neutralized zones intended to shelter from the effects of war the following persons, without distinction:
(a) Wounded and sick combatants or non-combatants;
(b) Civilian persons who take no part in hostilities, and who, while they reside in the zones, perform no work of a military character.
When the Parties concerned have agreed upon the geographical position, administration, food supply and supervision of the proposed neutralized zone, a written agreement shall be concluded and signed by the representatives of the Parties to the conflict. The agreement shall fix the beginning and the duration of the neutralization of the zone.

ARTICLE 16

The wounded and sick, as well as the infirm, and expectant mothers, shall be the **A4–015** object of particular protection and respect.
As far as military considerations allow, each Party to the conflict shall facilitate the steps taken to search for the killed and wounded, to assist the shipwrecked and other persons exposed to grave danger, and to protect them against pillage and ill-treatment.

ARTICLE 17

The Parties to the conflict shall endeavour to conclude local agreements for the **A4–016** removal from besieged or encircled areas, of wounded, sick, infirm, and aged persons, children and maternity cases, and for the passage of ministers of all religions, medical personnel and medical equipment on their way to such areas.

ARTICLE 18

Civilian hospitals organized to give care to the wounded and sick, the infirm and **A4–017** maternity cases, may in no circumstances be the object of attack, but shall at all times be respected and protected by the Parties to the conflict.
States which are Parties to a conflict shall provide all civilian hospitals with certificates showing that they are civilian hospitals and that the buildings which they occupy are not used for any purpose which would deprive these hospitals of protection in accordance with Article 19.
Civilian hospitals shall be marked by means of the emblem provided for in Article 38 of the Geneva Convention for the Amelioration of the Condition of the Wounded and Sick in Armed Forces in the Field of August 12, 1949, but only if so authorized by the State.
The Parties to the conflict shall, in so far as military considerations permit, take the necessary steps to make the distinctive emblems indicating civilian hospitals clearly visible to the enemy land, air and naval forces in order to obviate the possibility of any hostile action.
In view of the dangers to which hospitals may be exposed by being close to military objectives, it is recommended that such hospitals be situated as far as possible from such objectives.

ARTICLE 19

The protection to which civilian hospitals are entitled shall not cease unless they are **A4–018** used to commit, outside their humanitarian duties, acts harmful to the enemy. Protection may, however, cease only after due warning has been given, naming, in all appropriate cases, a reasonable time limit, and after such warning has remained unheeded.

The fact that sick or wounded members of the armed forces are nursed in these hospitals, or the presence of small arms and ammunition taken from such combatants which have not yet been handed to the proper service, shall not be considered to be acts harmful to the enemy.

ARTICLE 20

A4–019   Persons regularly and solely engaged in the operation and administration of civilian hospitals, including the personnel engaged in the search for, removal and transporting of and caring for wounded and sick civilians, the infirm and maternity cases, shall be respected and protected.

In occupied territory and in zones of military operations, the above personnel shall be recognizable by means of an identity card certifying their status, bearing the photograph of the holder and embossed with the stamp of the responsible authority, and also by means of a stamped, water-resistant armlet which they shall wear on the left arm while carrying out their duties. This armlet shall be issued by the State and shall bear the emblem provided for in Article 38 of the Geneva Convention for the Amelioration of the Condition of the Wounded and Sick in Armed Forces in the Field of August 12, 1949.

Other personnel who are engaged in the operation and administration of civilian hospitals shall be entitled to respect and protection and to wear the armlet, as provided in and under the conditions prescribed in this Article, while they are employed on such duties. The identity card shall state the duties on which they are employed.

The management of each hospital shall at all times hold at the disposal of the competent national or occupying authorities an up-to-date list of such personnel.

ARTICLE 21

A4–020   Convoys of vehicles or hospital trains on land or specially provided vessels on sea, conveying wounded and sick civilians, the infirm and maternity cases, shall be respected and protected in the same manner as the hospitals provided for in Article 18, and shall be marked, with the consent of the State, by the display of the distinctive emblem provided for in Article 38 of the Geneva Convention for the Amelioration of the Condition of the Wounded and Sick in Armed Forces in the Field of August 12, 1949.

ARTICLE 22

A4–021   Aircraft exclusively employed for the removal of wounded and sick civilians, the infirm and maternity cases, or for the transport of medical personnel and equipment, shall not be attacked, but shall be respected while flying at heights, times and on routes specifically agreed upon between all the Parties to the conflict concerned.

They may be marked with the distinctive emblem provided for in Article 38 of the Geneva Convention for the Amelioration of the Condition of the Wounded and Sick in Armed Forces in the Field of August 12, 1949.

Unless agreed otherwise, flights over enemy or enemy-occupied territory are prohibited.

Such aircraft shall obey every summons to land. In the event of a landing thus imposed, the aircraft with its occupants may continue its flight after examination, if any.

ARTICLE 23

A4–022   Each High Contracting Party shall allow the free passage of all consignments of medical and hospital stores and objects necessary for religious worship intended only for civilians of another High Contracting Party, even if the latter is its adversary. It shall likewise permit the free passage of all consignments of essential foodstuffs, clothing and tonics intended for children under fifteen, expectant mothers and maternity cases.

The obligation of a High Contracting Party to allow the free passage of the consignments indicated in the preceding paragraph is subject to the condition that this Party is satisfied that there are no serious reasons for fearing:

(a) That the consignments may be diverted from their destination;

(b) That the control may not be effective; or

(c) That a definite advantage may accrue to the military efforts or economy of the enemy through the substitution of the above-mentioned consignments for goods which would otherwise be provided or produced by the enemy or through the release of such material, services or facilities as would otherwise be required for the production of such goods.

The Power which allows the passage of the consignments indicated in the first paragraph of this Article may make such permission conditional on the distribution to the persons benefited there by being made under the local supervision of the Protecting Powers.

Such consignments shall be forwarded as rapidly as possible, and the Power which permits their free passage shall have the right to prescribe the technical arrangements under which such passage is allowed.

ARTICLE 24

A4–023

The Parties to the conflict shall take the necessary measures to ensure that children under fifteen, who are orphaned or are separated from their families as a result of the war, are not left to their own resources, and that their maintenance, the exercise of their religion and their education are facilitated in all circumstances. Their education shall, as far as possible, be entrusted to persons of a similar cultural tradition.

The Parties to the conflict shall facilitate the reception of such children in a neutral country for the duration of the conflict with the consent of the Protecting Power, if any, and under due safeguards for the observance of the principles stated in the first paragraph.

They shall, furthermore, endeavour to arrange for all children under twelve to be identified by the wearing of identity discs, or by some other means.

ARTICLE 25

A4–024

All persons in the territory of a Party to the conflict, or in a territory occupied by it, shall be enabled to give news of a strictly personal nature to members of their families, wherever they may be, and to receive news from them. This correspondence shall be forwarded speedily and without undue delay.

If, as a result of circumstances, it becomes difficult or impossible to exchange family correspondence by the ordinary post, the Parties to the conflict concerned shall apply to a neutral intermediary, such as the Central Agency provided for in Article 140, and shall decide in consultation with it how to ensure the fulfilment of their obligations under the best possible conditions, in particular with the cooperation of the National Red Cross (Red Crescent, Red Lion and Sun) Societies.

If the Parties to the conflict deem it necessary to restrict family correspondence, such restrictions shall be confined to the compulsory use of standard forms containing twenty-five freely chosen words, and to the limitation of the number of these forms despatched to one each month.

ARTICLE 26

A4–025

Each Party to the conflict shall facilitate enquiries made by members of families dispersed owing to the war, with the object of renewing contact with one another and of meeting, if possible. It shall encourage, in particular, the work of organizations engaged on this task provided they are acceptable to it and conform to its security regulations.

PART III

STATUS AND TREATMENT OF PROTECTED PERSONS

Section I

Provisions Common to the Territories of the Parties to the Conflict and to Occupied Territories

ARTICLE 27

A4–026   Protected persons are entitled, in all circumstances, to respect for their persons, their honour, their family rights, their religious convictions and practices, and their manners and customs. They shall at all times be humanely treated, and shall be protected especially against all acts of violence or threats thereof and against insults and public curiosity.

Women shall be especially protected against any attack on their honour, in particular against rape, enforced prostitution, or any form of indecent assault.

Without prejudice to the provisions relating to their state of health, age and sex, all protected persons shall be treated with the same consideration by the Party to the conflict in whose power they are, without any adverse distinction based, in particular, on race, religion or political opinion.

However, the Parties to the conflict may take such measures of control and security in regard to protected persons as may be necessary as a result of the war.

ARTICLE 28

A4–027   The presence of a protected person may not be used to render certain points or areas immune from military operations.

ARTICLE 29

A4–028   The Party to the conflict in whose hands protected persons may be is responsible for the treatment accorded to them by its agents, irrespective of any individual responsibility which may be incurred.

ARTICLE 30

A4–029   Protected persons shall have every facility for making application to the Protecting Powers, the International Committee of the Red Cross, the National Red Cross (Red Crescent, Red Lion and Sun) Society of the country where they may be, as well as to any organization that might assist them.

These several organizations shall be granted all facilities for that purpose by the authorities, within the bounds set by military or security considerations.

Apart from the visits of the delegates of the Protecting Powers and of the International Committee of the Red Cross, provided for by Article 143, the Detaining or Occupying Powers shall facilitate as much as possible visits to protected persons by the representatives of other organizations whose object is to give spiritual aid or material relief to such persons.

ARTICLE 31

A4–030   No physical or moral coercion shall be exercised against protected persons, in particular to obtain information from them or from third parties.

ARTICLE 32

A4–031

The High Contracting Parties specifically agree that each of them is prohibited from taking any measure of such a character as to cause the physical suffering or extermination of protected persons in their hands. This prohibition applies not only to murder, torture, corporal punishment, mutilation and medical or scientific experiments not necessitated by the medical treatment of a protected person but also to any other measures of brutality whether applied by civilian or military agents.

ARTICLE 33

A4–032

No protected person may be punished for an offence he or she has not personally committed. Collective penalties and likewise all measures of intimidation or of terrorism are prohibited.

Pillage is prohibited.

Reprisals against protected persons and their property are prohibited.

ARTICLE 34

A4–033

The taking of hostages is prohibited.

Section 11

Aliens in the Territory of a Party to the Conflict

ARTICLE 35

A4–034

All protected persons who may desire to leave the territory at the outset of, or during a conflict, shall be entitled to do so, unless their departure is contrary to the national interests of the State. The applications of such persons to leave shall be decided in accordance with regularly established procedures and the decision shall be taken as rapidly as possible. Those persons permitted to leave may provide themselves with the necessary funds for their journey and take with them a reasonable amount of their effects and articles of personal use.

If any such person is refused permission to leave the territory, he shall be entitled to have such refusal reconsidered as soon as possible by an appropriate court or administrative board designated by the Detaining Power for that purpose.

Upon request, representatives of the Protecting Power shall, unless reasons of security prevent it, or the persons concerned object, be furnished with the reasons for refusal of any request for permission to leave the territory and be given, as expeditiously as possible, the names of all persons who have been denied permission to leave.

ARTICLE 36

A4–035

Departures permitted under the foregoing Article shall be carried out in satisfactory conditions as regards safety, hygiene, sanitation and food. All costs in connection therewith, from the point of exit in the territory of the Detaining Power, shall be borne by the country of destination, or, in the case of accommodation in a neutral country, by the Power whose nationals are benefited. The practical details of such movements may, if necessary, be settled by special agreements between the Powers concerned.

The foregoing shall not prejudice such special agreements as may be concluded between Parties to the conflict concerning the exchange and repatriation of their nationals in enemy hands.

ARTICLE 37

A4–036

Protected persons who are confined pending proceedings or serving a sentence involving loss of liberty shall during their confinement be humanely treated.

As soon as they are released, they may ask to leave the territory in conformity with the foregoing Articles.

ARTICLE 38

A4–037   With the exception of special measures authorized by the present Convention, in particular by Articles 27 and 41 thereof, the situation of protected persons shall continue to be regulated, in principle, by the provisions concerning aliens in time of peace. In any case, the following rights shall be granted to them:

1. They shall be enabled to receive the individual or collective relief that may be sent to them.
2. They shall, if their state of health so requires, receive medical attention and hospital treatment to the same extent as the nationals of the State concerned.
3. They shall be allowed to practise their religion and to receive spiritual assistance from ministers of their faith.
4. If they reside in an area particularly exposed to the dangers of war, they shall be authorized to move from that area to the same extent as the nationals of the State concerned.
5. Children under fifteen years, pregnant women and mothers of children under seven years shall benefit by any preferential treatment to the same extent as the nationals of the State concerned.

ARTICLE 39

A4–038   Protected persons who, as a result of the war, have lost their gainful employment, shall be granted the opportunity to find paid employment. That opportunity shall, subject to security considerations and to the provisions of Article 40, be equal to that enjoyed by the nationals of the Power in whose territory they are.

Where a Party to the conflict applies to a protected person methods of control which result in his being unable to support himself, and especially if such a person is prevented for reasons of security from finding paid employment on reasonable conditions, the said Party shall ensure his support and that of his dependents.

Protected persons may in any case receive allowances from their home country, the Protecting Power, or the relief societies referred to in Article 30.

ARTICLE 40

A4–039   Protected persons may be compelled to work only to the same extent as nationals of the Party to the conflict in whose territory they are.

If protected persons are of enemy nationality, they may only be compelled to do work which is normally necessary to ensure the feeding, sheltering, clothing, transport and health of human beings and which is not directly related to the conduct of military operations.

In the cases mentioned in the two preceding paragraphs, protected persons compelled to work shall have the benefit of the same working conditions and of the same safeguards as national workers, in particular as regards wages, hours of labour, clothing and equipment, previous training and compensation for occupational accidents and diseases.

If the above provisions are infringed, protected persons shall be allowed to exercise their right of complaint in accordance with Article 30.

ARTICLE 41

A4–040   Should the Power in whose hands protected persons may be consider the measures of control mentioned in the present Convention to be inadequate, it may not have recourse to any other measure of control more severe than that of assigned residence or internment, in accordance with the provisions of Articles 42 and 43.

In applying the provisions of Article 39, second paragraph, to the cases of persons required to leave their usual places of residences by virtue of a decision placing them in assigned residence elsewhere. the Detaining Power shall be guided as closely as possible by the standards of welfare set forth in Part III, Section IV of this Convention.

ARTICLE 42

A4–041

The internment or placing in assigned residence of protected persons may be ordered only if the security of the Detaining Power makes it absolutely necessary.

If any person, acting through the representatives of the Protecting Power, voluntarily demands internment, and if his situation renders this step necessary, he shall be interned by the Power in whose hands he may be.

ARTICLE 43

A4–042

Any protected person who has been interned or placed in assigned residence shall be entitled to have such action reconsidered as soon as possible by an appropriate court or administrative board designated by the Detaining Power for that purpose. If the internment or placing in assigned residence is maintained, the court or administrative board shall periodically, and at least twice yearly, give consideration to his or her case, with a view to the favourable amendment of the initial decision, if circumstances permit.

Unless the protected persons concerned object, the Detaining Power shall, as rapidly as possible, give the Protecting Power the names of any protected persons who have been interned or subjected to assigned residence, or who have been released from internment or assigned residence. The decisions of the courts or boards mentioned in the first paragraph of the present Article shall also, subject to the same conditions, be notified as rapidly as possible to the Protecting Power.

ARTICLE 44

A4–043

In applying the measures of control mentioned in the present Convention, the Detaining Power shall not treat as enemy aliens exclusively on the basis of their nationality de jure of an enemy State, refugees who do not, in fact, enjoy the protection of any government.

ARTICLE 45

A4–044

Protected persons shall not be transferred to a Power which is not a party to the Convention.

This provision shall in no way constitute an obstacle to the repatriation of protected persons, or to their return to their country of residence after the cessation of hostilities.

Protected persons may be transferred by the Detaining Power only to a Power which is a party to the present Convention and after the Detaining Power has satisfied itself of the willingness and ability of such transferee Power to apply the present Convention. If protected persons are transferred under such circumstances, responsibility for the application of the present Convention rests on the Power accepting them, while they are in its custody. Nevertheless, if that Power fails to carry out the provisions of the present Convention in any important respect, the Power by which the protected persons were transferred shall, upon being so notified by the Protecting Power, take effective measures to correct the situation or shall request the return of the protected persons. Such request must be complied with.

In no circumstances shall a protected person be transferred to a country where he or she may have reason to fear persecution for his or her political opinions or religious beliefs.

The provisions of this Article do not constitute an obstacle to the extradition, in pursuance of extradition treaties concluded before the outbreak of hostilities, of protected persons accused of offences against ordinary criminal law.

ARTICLE 46

A4–045   In so far as they have not been previously withdrawn, restrictive measures taken regarding protected persons shall be cancelled as soon as possible after the close of hostilities.

Restrictive measures affecting their property shall be cancelled, in accordance with the law of the Detaining Power, as soon as possible after the close of hostilities.

Section 111

Occupied Territories

ARTICLE 47

A4–046   Protected persons who are in occupied territory shall not be deprived, in any case or in any manner whatsoever, of the benefits of the present Convention by any change introduced, as the result of the occupation of a territory, into the institutions or government of the said territory, nor by any agreement concluded between the authorities of the occupied territories and the Occupying Power, nor by any annexation by the latter of the whole or part of the occupied territory.

ARTICLE 48

A4–047   Protected persons who are not nationals of the Power whose territory is occupied may avail themselves of the right to leave the territory subject to the provisions of Article 35, and decisions thereon shall be taken according to the procedure which the Occupying Power shall establish in accordance with the said Article.

ARTICLE 49

A4–048   Individual or mass forcible transfers, as well as deportations of protected persons from occupied territory to the territory of the Occupying Power or to that of any other country, occupied or not, are prohibited, regardless of their motive.

Nevertheless, the Occupying Power may undertake total or partial evacuation of a given area if the security of the population or imperative military reasons so demand. Such evacuations may not involve the displacement of protected persons outside the bounds of the occupied territory except when for material reasons it is impossible to avoid such displacement. Persons thus evacuated shall be transferred back to their homes as soon as hostilities in the area in question have ceased.

The Occupying Power undertaking such transfers or evacuations shall ensure, to the greatest practicable extent, that proper accommodation is provided to receive the protected persons, that the removals are effected in satisfactory conditions of hygiene, health, safety and nutrition, and that members of the same family are not separated.

The Protecting Power shall be informed of any transfers and evacuations as soon as they have taken place.

The Occupying Power shall not detain protected persons in an area particularly exposed to the dangers of war unless the security of the population or imperative military reasons so demand.

The Occupying Power shall not deport or transfer parts of its own civilian population into the territory it occupies.

ARTICLE 50

A4–049   The Occupying Power shall, with the cooperation of the national and local authorities, facilitate the proper working of all institutions devoted to the care and education of children.

The Occupying Power shall take all necessary steps to facilitate the identification of children and the registration of their parentage. It may not, in any case, change their personal status, nor enlist them in formations or organizations subordinate to it.

Should the local institutions be inadequate for the purpose, the Occupying Power shall make arrangements for the maintenance and education, if possible by persons of their own nationality, language and religion, of children who are orphaned or separated from their parents as a result of the war and who cannot be adequately cared for by a near relative or friend.

A special section of the Bureau set up in accordance with Article 136 shall be responsible for taking all necessary steps to identify children whose identity is in doubt. Particulars of their parents or other near relatives should always be recorded if available.

The Occupying Power shall not hinder the application of any preferential measures in regard to food, medical care and protection against the effects of war, which may have been adopted prior to the occupation in favour of children under fifteen years, expectant mothers, and mothers of children under seven years.

ARTICLE 51

The Occupying Power may not compel protected persons to serve in its armed or auxiliary forces. No pressure or propaganda which aims at securing voluntary enlistment is permitted. **A4–050**

The Occupying Power may not compel protected persons to work unless they are over eighteen years of age, and then only on work which is necessary either for the needs of the army of occupation, or for the public utility services, or for the feeding, sheltering, clothing, transportation or health of the population of the occupied country. Protected persons may not be compelled to undertake any work which would involve them in the obligation of taking part in military operations. The Occupying Power may not compel protected persons to employ forcible means to ensure the security of the installations where they are performing compulsory labour.

The work shall be carried out only in the occupied territory where the persons whose services have been requisitioned are. Every such person shall, so far as possible, be kept in his usual place of employment. Workers shall be paid a fair wage and the work shall be proportionate to their physical and intellectual capacities. The legislation in force in the occupied country concerning working conditions, and safeguards as regards, in particular, such matters as wages, hours of work, equipment, preliminary training and compensation for occupational accidents and diseases, shall be applicable to the protected persons assigned to the work referred to in this Article.

In no case shall requisition of labour lead to a mobilization of workers in an organization of a military or semi-military character.

ARTICLE 52

No contract, agreement or regulation shall impair the right of any worker, whether voluntary or not and wherever he may be, to apply to the representatives of the Protecting Power in order to request the said Power's intervention. **A4–051**

All measures aiming at creating unemployment or at restricting the opportunities offered to workers in an occupied territory, in order to induce them to work for the Occupying Power, are prohibited.

ARTICLE 53

Any destruction by the Occupying Power of real or personal property belonging individually or collectively to private persons, or to the State, or to other public authorities, or to social or cooperative organizations, is prohibited, except where such destruction is rendered absolutely necessary by military operations. **A4–052**

ARTICLE 54

A4–053   The Occupying Power may not alter the status of public officials or judges in the occupied territories, or in any way apply sanctions to or take any measures of coercion or discrimination against them, should they abstain from fulfilling their functions for reasons of conscience.

This prohibition does not prejudice the application of the second paragraph of Article 51. It does not affect the right of the Occupying Power to remove public officials from their posts.

ARTICLE 55

A4–054   To the fullest extent of the means available to it the Occupying Power has the duty of ensuring the food and medical supplies of the population; it should, in particular, bring in the necessary foodstuffs, medical stores and other articles if the resources of the occupied territory are inadequate.

The Occupying Power may not requisition foodstuffs, articles or medical supplies available in the occupied territory, except for use by the occupation forces and administration personnel, and then only if the requirements of the civilian population have been taken into account. Subject to the provisions of other international Conventions, the Occupying Power shall make arrangements to ensure that fair value is paid for any requisitioned goods.

The Protecting Power shall, at any time, be at liberty to verify the state of the food and medical supplies in occupied territories, except where temporary restrictions are made necessary by imperative military requirements.

ARTICLE 56

A4–055   To the fullest extent of the means available to it, the Occupying Power has the duty of ensuring and maintaining, with the cooperation of national and local authorities, the medical and hospital establishments and services, public health and hygiene in the occupied territory, with particular reference to the adoption and application of the prophylactic and preventive measures necessary to combat the spread of contagious diseases and epidemics. Medical personnel of all categories shall be allowed to carry out their duties.

If new hospitals are set up in occupied territory and if the competent organs of the occupied State are not operating there, the occupying authorities shall, if necessary, grant them the recognition provided for in Article 18. In similar circumstances, the occupying authorities shall also grant recognition to hospital personnel and transport vehicles under the provisions of Articles 20 and 21.

In adopting measures of health and hygiene and in their implementation, the Occupying Power shall take into consideration the moral and ethical susceptibilities of the population of the occupied territory.

ARTICLE 57

A4–056   The Occupying Power may requisition civilian hospitals only temporarily and only in cases of urgent necessity for the care of military wounded and sick, and then on condition that suitable arrangements are made in due time for the care and treatment of the patients and for the needs of the civilian population for hospital accommodation.

The material and stores of civilian hospitals cannot be requisitioned so long as they are necessary for the needs of the civilian population.

ARTICLE 58

A4–057   The Occupying Power shall permit ministers of religion to give spiritual assistance to the members of their religious communities.

The Occupying Power shall also accept consignments of books and articles required for religious needs and shall facilitate their distribution in occupied territory.

ARTICLE 59

If the whole or part of the population of an occupied territory is inadequately supplied,   **A4–058**
the Occupying Power shall agree to relief schemes on behalf of the said population, and shall facilitate them by all the means at its disposal.

Such schemes, which may be undertaken either by States or by impartial human-itarian organizations such as the International Committee of the Red Cross, shall consist, in particular, of the provision of consignments of foodstuffs, medical supplies and clothing.

All Contracting Parties shall permit the free passage of these consignments and shall guarantee their protection.

A Power granting free passage to consignments on their way to territory occupied by an adverse Party to the conflict shall, however, have the right to search the consign-ments, to regulate their passage according to prescribed times and routes, and to be reasonably satisfied through the Protecting Power that these consignments are to be used for the relief of the needy population and are not to be used for the benefit of the Occupying Power.

ARTICLE 60

Relief consignments shall in no way relieve the Occupying Power of any of its   **A4–059**
responsibilities under Articles 55, 56 and 59. The Occupying Power shall in no way whatsoever divert relief consignments from the purpose for which they are intended, except in cases of urgent necessity, in the interests of the population of the occupied territory and with the consent of the Protecting Power.

ARTICLE 61

The distribution of the relief consignments referred to in the foregoing Articles shall   **A4–060**
be carried out with the cooperation and under the supervision of the Protecting Power. This duty may also be delegated, by agreement between the Occupying Power and the Protecting Power, to a neutral Power, to the International Committee of the Red Cross or to any other impartial humanitarian body.

Such consignments shall be exempt in occupied territory from all charges, taxes or customs duties unless these are necessary in the interests of the economy of the territory. The Occupying Power shall facilitate the rapid distribution of these consignments.

All Contracting Parties shall endeavour to permit the transit and transport, free of charge, of such relief consignments on their way to occupied territories.

ARTICLE 62

Subject to imperative reasons of security, protected persons in occupied territories   **A4–061**
shall be permitted to receive the individual relief consignments sent to them.

ARTICLE 63

Subject to temporary and exceptional measures imposed for urgent reasons of security   **A4–062**
by the Occupying Power:
    (a) Recognized National Red Cross (Red Crescent, Red Lion and Sun) Societies
        shall be able to pursue their activities in accordance with Red Cross principles,

as defined by the International Red Cross Conferences. Other relief societies shall be permitted to continue their humanitarian activities under similar conditions;

(b) The Occupying Power may not require any changes in the personnel or structure of these societies, which would prejudice the aforesaid activities.

The same principles shall apply to the activities and personnel of special organizations of a non-military character, which already exist or which may be established, for the purpose of ensuring the living conditions of the civilian population by the maintenance of the essential public utility services, by the distribution of relief and by the organization of rescues.

ARTICLE 64

A4–063   The penal laws of the occupied territory shall remain in force, with the exception that they may be repealed or suspended by the Occupying Power in cases where they constitute a threat to its security or an obstacle to the application of the present Convention. Subject to the latter consideration and to the necessity for ensuring the effective administration of justice, the tribunals of the occupied territory shall continue to function in respect of all offences covered by the said laws.

The Occupying Power may, however, subject the population of the occupied territory to provisions which are essential to enable the Occupying Power to fulfil its obligations under the present Convention, to maintain the orderly government of the territory, and to ensure the security of the Occupying Power, of the members and property of the occupying forces or administration, and likewise of the establishments and lines of communication used by them.

ARTICLE 65

A4–064   The penal provisions enacted by the Occupying Power shall not come into force before they have been published and brought to the knowledge of the inhabitants in their own language. The effect of these penal provisions shall not be retroactive.

ARTICLE 66

A4–065   In case of a breach of the penal provisions promulgated by it by virtue of the second paragraph of Article 64, the Occupying Power may hand over the accused to its properly constituted, non-political military courts, on condition that the said courts sit in the occupied country. Courts of appeal shall preferably sit in the occupied country.

ARTICLE 67

A4–066   The courts shall apply only those provisions of law which were applicable prior to the offence, and which are in accordance with general principles of law, in particular the principle that the penalty shall be proportioned to the offence. They shall take into consideration the fact that the accused is not a national of the Occupying Power.

ARTICLE 68

A4–067   Protected persons who commit an offence which is solely intended to harm the Occupying Power, but which does not constitute an attempt on the life or limb of members of the occupying forces or administration, nor a grave collective danger, nor seriously damage the property of the occupying forces or administration or the installations used by them, shall be liable to internment or simple imprisonment, provided the duration of such internment or imprisonment is proportionate to the offence committed. Furthermore, internment or imprisonment shall, for such offences, be the only measure adopted for depriving protected persons of liberty. The courts provided for under Article 66 of the present Convention may at their discretion convert a sentence of imprisonment to one of internment for the same period.

The penal provisions promulgated by the Occupying Power in accordance with Articles 64 and 65 may impose the death penalty on a protected person only in cases where the person is guilty of espionage, of serious acts of sabotage against the military installations of the Occupying Power or of intentional offences which have caused the death of one or more persons, provided that such offences were punishable by death under the law of the occupied territory in force before the occupation began.

The death penalty may not be pronounced against a protected person unless the attention of the court has been particularly called to the fact that, since the accused is not a national of the Occupying Power, he is not bound to it by any duty of allegiance.

In any case, the death penalty may not be pronounced against a protected person who was under eighteen years of age at the time of the offence.

ARTICLE 69

In all cases, the duration of the period during which a protected person accused of an offence is under arrest awaiting trial or punishment shall be deducted from any period of imprisonment awarded.   **A4–068**

ARTICLE 70

Protected persons shall not be arrested, prosecuted or convicted by the Occupying Power for acts committed or for opinions expressed before the occupation, or during a temporary interruption thereof, with the exception of breaches of the laws and customs of war.   **A4–069**

Nationals of the Occupying Power who, before the outbreak of hostilities, have sought refuge in the territory of the occupied State, shall not be arrested, prosecuted, convicted or deported from the occupied territory, except for offences committed after the outbreak of hostilities, or for offences under common law committed before the outbreak of hostilities which, according to the law of the occupied State, would have justified extradition in time of peace.

ARTICLE 71

No sentence shall be pronounced by the competent courts of the Occupying Power except after a regular trial.   **A4–070**

Accused persons who are prosecuted by the Occupying Power shall be promptly informed, in writing, in a language which they understand, of the particulars of the charges preferred against them, and shall be brought to trial as rapidly as possible. The Protecting Power shall be informed of all proceedings instituted by the Occupying Power against protected persons in respect of charges involving the death penalty or imprisonment for two years or more; it shall be enabled, at any time, to obtain information regarding the state of such proceedings. Furthermore, the Protecting Power shall be entitled, on request, to be furnished with all particulars of these and of any other proceedings instituted by the Occupying Power against protected persons.

The notification to the Protecting Power, as provided for in the second paragraph above, shall be sent immediately, and shall in any case reach the Protecting Power three weeks before the date of the first hearing. Unless, at the opening of the trial, evidence is submitted that the provisions of this Article are fully complied with, the trial shall not proceed. The notification shall include the following particulars:

(a) Description of the accused;

(b) Place of residence or detention;

(c) Specification of the charge or charges (with mention of the penal provisions under which it is brought);

(d) Designation of the court which will hear the case;

(e) Place and date of the first hearing.

ARTICLE 72

A4–071   Accused persons shall have the right to present evidence necessary to their defence and may, in particular, call witnesses. They shall have the right to be assisted by a qualified advocate or counsel of their own choice, who shall be able to visit them freely and shall enjoy the necessary facilities for preparing the defence.

Failing a choice by the accused, the Protecting Power may provide him with an advocate or counsel. When an accused person has to meet a serious charge and the Protecting Power is not functioning, the Occupying Power, subject to the consent of the accused, shall provide an advocate or counsel.

Accused persons shall, unless they freely waive such assistance, be aided by an interpreter, both during preliminary investigation and during the hearing in court. They shall have the right at any time to object to the interpreter and to ask for his replacement.

ARTICLE 73

A4–072   A convicted person shall have the right of appeal provided for by the laws applied by the court. He shall be fully informed of his right to appeal or petition and of the time limit within which he may do so.

The penal procedure provided in the present Section shall apply, as far as it is applicable, to appeals. Where the laws applied by the Court make no provision for appeals, the convicted person shall have the right to petition against the finding and sentence to the competent authority of the Occupying Power.

ARTICLE 74

A4–073   Representatives of the Protecting Power shall have the right to attend the trial of any protected person, unless the hearing has, as an exceptional measure, to be held in camera in the interests of the security of the Occupying Power, which shall then notify the Protecting Power. A notification in respect of the date and place of trial shall be sent to the Protecting Power.

Any judgment involving a sentence of death, or imprisonment for two years or more, shall be communicated, with the relevant grounds, as rapidly as possible to the Protecting Power. The notification shall contain a reference to the notification made under Article 71, and in the case of sentences of imprisonment, the name of the place where the sentence is to be served. A record of judgments other than those referred to above shall be kept by the court and shall be open to inspection by representatives of the Protecting Power. Any period allowed for appeal in the case of sentences involving the death penalty, or imprisonment for two years or more, shall not run until notification of judgment has been received by the Protecting Power.

ARTICLE 75

A4–074   In no case shall persons condemned to death be deprived of the right of petition for pardon or reprieve.

No death sentence shall be carried out before the expiration of a period of at least six months from the date of receipt by the Protecting Power of the notification of the final judgment confirming such death sentence, or of an order denying pardon or reprieve.

The six months period of suspension of the death sentence herein prescribed may be reduced in individual cases in circumstances of grave emergency involving an organized threat to the security of the Occupying Power or its forces, provided always that the

Protecting Power is notified of such reduction and is given reasonable time and opportunity to make representations to the competent occupying authorities in respect of such death sentences.

Article 76

Protected persons accused of offences shall be detained in the occupied country, and if **A4–075** convicted they shall serve their sentences therein. They shall, if possible, be separated from other detainees and shall enjoy conditions of food and hygiene which will be sufficient to keep them in good health, and which will be at least equal to those obtaining in prisons in the occupied country.

They shall receive the medical attention required by their state of health.

They shall also have the right to receive any spiritual assistance which they may require.

Women shall be confined in separate quarters and shall be under the direct supervision of women.

Proper regard shall be paid to the special treatment due to minors.

Protected persons who are detained shall have the right to be visited by delegates of the Protecting Power and of the International Committee of the Red Cross, in accordance with the provisions of Article 143.

Such persons shall have the right to receive at least one relief parcel monthly.

Article 77

Protected persons who have been accused of offences or convicted by the courts in **A4–076** occupied territory shall be handed over at the close of occupation, with the relevant records, to the authorities of the liberated territory.

Article 78

If the Occupying Power considers it necessary, for imperative reasons of security, to **A4–077** take safety measures concerning protected persons, it may, at the most, subject them to assigned residence or to internment.

Decisions regarding such assigned residence or internment shall be made according to a regular procedure to be prescribed by the Occupying Power in accordance with the provisions of the present Convention. This procedure shall include the right of appeal for the parties concerned. Appeals shall be decided with the least possible delay. In the event of the decision being upheld, it shall be subject to periodical review, if possible every six months, by a competent body set up by the said Power.

Protected persons made subject to assigned residence and thus required to leave their homes shall enjoy the full benefit of Article 39 of the present Convention.

Section IV

Regulations for the Treatment of Internees

Chapter I

GENERAL PROVISIONS

Article 79

The Parties to the conflict shall not intern protected persons, except in accordance **A4–078** with the provisions of Articles 41, 42, 43, 68 and 78.

ARTICLE 80

A4–079   Internees shall retain their full civil capacity and shall exercise such attendant rights as may be compatible with their status.

ARTICLE 81

A4–080   Parties to the conflict who intern protected persons shall be bound to provide free of charge for their maintenance, and to grant them also the medical attention required by their state of health.

No deduction from the allowances, salaries or credits due to the internees shall be made for the repayment of these costs.

The Detaining Power shall provide for the support of those dependent on the internees, if such dependants are without adequate means of support or are unable to earn a living.

ARTICLE 82

A4–081   The Detaining Power shall, as far as possible, accommodate the internees according to their nationality, language and customs. Internees who are nationals of the same country shall not be separated merely because they have different languages.

Throughout the duration of their internment, members of the same family, and in particular parents and children, shall be lodged together in the same place of internment, except when separation of a temporary nature is necessitated for reasons of employment or health or for the purposes of enforcement of the provisions of Chapter IX of the present Section. Internees may request that their children who are left at liberty without parental care shall be interned with them.

Wherever possible, interned members of the same family shall be housed in the same premises and given separate accommodation from other internees, together with facilities for leading a proper family life.

CHAPTER II

PLACES OF INTERNMENT

ARTICLE 83

A4–082   The Detaining Power shall not set up places of internment in areas particularly exposed to the dangers of war.

The Detaining Power shall give the enemy Powers, through the intermediary of the Protecting Powers, all useful information regarding the geographical location of places of internment.

Whenever military considerations permit, internment camps shall be indicated by the letters IC, placed so as to be clearly visible in the daytime from the air. The Powers concerned may, however, agree upon any other system of marking. No place other than an internment camp shall be marked as such.

ARTICLE 84

A4–083   Internees shall be accommodated and administered separately from prisoners of war and from persons deprived of liberty for any other reason.

ARTICLE 85

A4–084   The Detaining Power is bound to take all necessary and possible measures to ensure that protected persons shall, from the outset of their internment, be accommodated in buildings or quarters which afford every possible safeguard as regards hygiene and health, and provide efficient protection against the rigours of the climate and the effects of the war. In no case shall permanent places of internment be situated in unhealthy areas or in districts the climate of which is injurious to the internees. In all cases where the district, in which a protected person is temporarily interned , is in an unhealthy area or has a climate which is harmful to his health, he shall be removed to a more suitable place of internment as rapidly as circumstances permit.

The premises shall be fully protected from dampness, adequately heated and lighted, in particular between dusk and lights out. The sleeping quarters shall be sufficiently spacious and well ventilated, and the internees shall have suitable bedding and sufficient blankets, account being taken of the climate, and the age, sex, and state of health of the internees.

Internees shall have for their use, day and night, sanitary conveniences which conform to the rules of hygiene and are constantly maintained in a state of cleanliness. They shall be provided with sufficient water and soap for their daily personal toilet and for washing their personal laundry; installations and facilities necessary for this purpose shall be granted to them.

Showers or baths shall also be available. The necessary time shall be set aside for washing and for cleaning.

Whenever it is necessary, as an exceptional and temporary measure, to accommodate women internees who are not members of a family unit in the same place of internment as men, the provision of separate sleeping quarters and sanitary conveniences for the use of such women internees shall be obligatory.

ARTICLE 86

The Detaining Power shall place at the disposal of interned persons, of whatever denomination, premises suitable for the holding of their religious services.

A4–085

ARTICLE 87

Canteens shall be installed in every place of internment, except where other suitable facilities are available. Their purpose shall be to enable internees to make purchases, at prices not higher than local market prices, of foodstuffs and articles of everyday use, including soap and tobacco, such as would increase their personal well-being and comfort.

A4–086

Profits made by canteens shall be credited to a welfare fund to be set up for each place of internment, and administered for the benefit of the internees attached to such place of internment. The Internee Committee provided for in Article 102 shall have the right to check the management of the canteen and of the said fund.

When a place of internment is closed down, the balance of the welfare fund shall be transferred to the welfare fund of a place of internment for internees of the same nationality, or, if such a place does not exist, to a central welfare fund which shall be administered for the benefit of all internees remaining in the custody of the Detaining Power. In case of a general release, the said profits shall be kept by the Detaining Power, subject to any agreement to the contrary between the Powers concerned.

ARTICLE 88

In all places of internment exposed to air raids and other hazards of war, shelters adequate in number and structure to ensure the necessary protection shall be installed. In case of alarms, the internees shall be free to enter such shelters as quickly as possible, excepting those who remain for the protection of their quarters against the aforesaid hazards. Any protective measures taken in favour of the population shall also apply to them.

A4–087

All due precautions must be taken in places of internment against the danger of fire.

CHAPTER III

FOOD AND CLOTHING

ARTICLE 89

A4–088　　　Daily food rations for internees shall be sufficient in quantity, quality and variety to keep internees in a good state of health and prevent the development of nutritional deficiencies. Account shall also be taken of the customary diet of the internees.

Internees shall also be given the means by which they can prepare for themselves any additional food in their possession.

Sufficient drinking water shall be supplied to internees. The use of tobacco shall be permitted.

Internees who work shall receive additional rations in proportion to the kind of labour which they perform.

Expectant and nursing mothers and children under fifteen years of age shall be given additional food, in proportion to their physiological needs.

ARTICLE 90

A4–089　　　When taken into custody, internees shall be given all facilities to provide themselves with the necessary clothing, footwear and change of underwear, and later on, to procure further supplies if required. Should any internees not have sufficient clothing, account being taken of the climate, and be unable to procure any, it shall be provided free of charge to them by the Detaining Power.

The clothing supplied by the Detaining Power to internees and the outward markings placed on their own clothes shall not be ignominious nor expose them to ridicule.

Workers shall receive suitable working outfits, including protective clothing, whenever the nature of their work so requires.

CHAPTER IV

HYGIENE AND MEDICAL ATTENTION

ARTICLE 91

A4–090　　　Every place of internment shall have an adequate infirmary, under the direction of a qualified doctor, where internees may have the attention they require, as well as an appropriate diet. Isolation wards shall be set aside for cases of contagious or mental diseases.

Maternity cases and internees suffering from serious diseases, or whose condition requires special treatment, a surgical operation or hospital care, must be admitted to any institution where adequate treatment can be given and shall receive care not inferior to that provided for the general population.

Internees shall, for preference, have the attention of medical personnel of their own nationality.

Internees may not be prevented from presenting themselves to the medical authorities for examination. The medical authorities of the Detaining Power shall, upon request, issue to every internee who has undergone treatment an official certificate showing the nature of his illness or injury, and the duration and nature of the treatment given. A duplicate of this certificate shall be forwarded to the Central Agency provided for in Article 140.

Treatment, including the provision of any apparatus necessary for the maintenance of internees in good health, particularly dentures and other artificial appliances and spectacles, shall be free of charge to the internee.

ARTICLE 92

Medical inspections of internees shall be made at least once a month. Their purpose **A4–091** shall be, in particular, to supervise the general state of health, nutrition and cleanliness of internees, and to detect contagious diseases, especially tuberculosis, malaria, and venereal diseases. Such inspections shall include, in particular, the checking of weight of each internee and, at least once a year, radioscopic examination.

CHAPTER V

RELIGIOUS, INTELLECTUAL AND PHYSICAL ACTIVITIES

ARTICLE 93

Internees shall enjoy complete latitude in the exercise of their religious duties, **A4–092** including attendance at the services of their faith, on condition that they comply with the disciplinary routine prescribed by the detaining authorities.

Ministers of religion who are interned shall be allowed to minister freely to the members of their community. For this purpose, the Detaining Power shall ensure their equitable allocation amongst the various places of internment in which there are internees speaking the same language and be longing to the same religion. Should such ministers be too few in number, the Detaining Power shall provide them with the necessary facilities, including means of transport, for moving from one place to another, and they shall be authorized to visit any internees who are in hospital. Ministers of religion shall be at liberty to correspond on matters concerning their ministry with the religious authorities in the country of detention and, as far as possible, with the international religious organizations of their faith. Such correspondence shall not be considered as forming a part of the quota mentioned in Article 107. It shall, however, be subject to the provisions of Article 112.

When internees do not have at their disposal the assistance of ministers of their faith, or should these latter be too few in number, the local religious authorities of the same faith may appoint, in agreement with the Detaining Power, a minister of the internees' faith or, if such a course is feasible from a denominational point of view, a minister of similar religion or a qualified layman. The latter shall enjoy the facilities granted to the ministry he has assumed. Persons so appointed shall comply with all regulations laid down by the Detaining Power in the interests of discipline and security.

ARTICLE 94

The Detaining Power shall encourage intellectual, educational and recreational **A4–093** pursuits, sports and games amongst internees, whilst leaving them free to take part in them or not. It shall take all practicable measures to ensure the exercise thereof, in particular by providing suitable premises.

All possible facilities shall be granted to internees to continue their studies or to take up new subjects. The education of children and young people shall be ensured; they shall be allowed to attend schools either within the place of internment or outside.

Internees shall be given opportunities for physical exercise, sports and outdoor games. For this purpose, sufficient open spaces shall be set aside in all places of internment. Special playgrounds shall be reserved for children and young people.

ARTICLE 95

The Detaining Power shall not employ internees as workers, unless they so desire. **A4–094** Employment which, if undertaken under compulsion by a protected person not in internment, would involve a breach of Articles 40 or 51 of the present Convention, and employment on work which is of a degrading or humiliating character are in any case prohibited.

After a working period of six weeks, internees shall be free to give up work at any moment, subject to eight days' notice.

These provisions constitute no obstacle to the right of the Detaining Power to employ interned doctors, dentists and other medical personnel in their professional capacity on behalf of their fellow internees, or to employ internees for administrative and mainte-nance work in places of internment and to detail such persons for work in the kitchens or for other domestic tasks, or to require such persons to undertake duties connected with the protection of internees against aerial bombardment or other war risks. No internee may, however, be required to perform tasks for which he is, in the opinion of a medical officer, physically unsuited.

The Detaining Power shall take entire responsibility for all working conditions, for medical attention, for the payment of wages, and for ensuring that all employed internees receive compensation for occupational accidents and diseases. The standards prescribed for the said working conditions and for compensation shall be in accordance with the national laws and regulations, and with the existing practice; they shall in no case be inferior to those obtaining for work of the same nature in the same district. Wages for work done shall be determined on an equitable basis by special agreements between the internees, the Detaining Power, and, if the case arises, employers other than the Detaining Power, due regard being paid to the obligation of the Detaining Power to provide for free maintenance of internees and for the medical attention which their state of health may require. Internees permanently detailed for categories of work mentioned in the third paragraph of this Article shall be paid fair wages by the Detaining Power. The working conditions and the scale of compensation for occupational accidents and diseases to internees thus detailed shall not be inferior to those applicable to work of the same nature in the same district.

ARTICLE 96

A4–095 All labour detachments shall remain part of and dependent upon a place of internment. The competent authorities of the Detaining Power and the commandant of a place of internment shall be responsible for the observance in a labour detachment of the provisions of the present Convention. The commandant shall keep an up-to-date list of the labour detachments subordinate to him and shall communicate it to the delegates of the Protecting Power, of the International Committee of the Red Cross and of other humanitarian organizations who may visit the places of internment.

CHAPTER VI

PERSONAL PROPER AND FINANCIAL RESOURCES

ARTICLE 97

A4–096 Internees shall be permitted to retain articles of personal use. Monies, cheques, bonds, etc., and valuables in their possession may not be taken from them except in accordance with established procedure. Detailed receipts shall be given therefor.

The amounts shall be paid into the account of every internee as provided for in Article 98. Such amounts may not be converted into any other currency unless legislation in force in the territory in which the owner is interned so requires or the internee gives his consent.

Articles which have above all a personal or sentimental value may not be taken away.

A woman internee shall not be searched except by a woman.

On release or repatriation, internees shall be given all articles, monies or other valuables taken from them during internment and shall receive in currency the balance of any credit to their accounts kept in accordance with Article 98, with the exception of any articles or amounts withheld by the Detaining Power by virtue of its legislation in force. If the property of an internee is so withheld, the owner shall receive a detailed receipt.

Family or identity documents in the possession of internees may not be taken away without a receipt being given. At no time shall internees be left without identity documents. If they have none, they shall be issued with special documents drawn up by the detaining authorities, which will serve as their identity papers until the end of their internment.

Internees may keep on their persons a certain amount of money, in cash or in the shape of purchase coupons, to enable them to make purchases.

ARTICLE 98

A4–097

All internees shall receive regular allowances, sufficient to enable them to purchase goods and articles, such as tobacco, toilet requisites, etc. Such allowances may take the form of credits or purchase coupons.

Furthermore, internees may receive allowances from the Power to which they owe allegiance, the Protecting Powers, the organizations which may assist them, or their families, as well as the income on their property in accordance with the law of the Detaining Power. The amount of allowances granted by the Power to which they owe allegiance shall be the same for each category of internees (infirm, sick, pregnant women, etc.), but may not be allocated by that Power or distributed by the Detaining Power on the basis of discrimination between internees which are prohibited by Article 27 of the present Convention.

The Detaining Power shall open a regular account for every internee, to which shall be credited the allowances named in the present Article, the wages earned and the remittances received, together with such sums taken from him as may be available under the legislation in force in the territory in which he is interned. Internees shall be granted all facilities consistent with the legislation in force in such territory to make remittances to their families and to other dependants. They may draw from their accounts the amounts necessary for their personal expenses, within the limits fixed by the Detaining Power. They shall at all times be afforded reasonable facilities for consulting and obtaining copies of their accounts. A statement of accounts shall be furnished to the Protecting Power on request, and shall accompany the internee in case of transfer.

CHAPTER VII

ADMINISTRATION AND DISCIPLINE

ARTICLE 99

A4–098

Every place of internment shall be put under the authority of a responsible officer, chosen from the regular military forces or the regular civil administration of the Detaining Power. The officer in charge of the place of internment must have in his possession a copy of the present Convention in the official language, or one of the official languages, of his country and shall be responsible for its application. The staff in control of internees shall be instructed in the provisions of the present Convention and of the administrative measures adopted to ensure its application.

The text of the present Convention and the texts of special agreements concluded under the said Convention shall be posted inside the place of internment, in a language which the internees understand, or shall be in the possession of the Internee Committee.

Regulations, orders, notices and publications of every kind shall be communicated to the internees and posted inside the places of internment, in a language which they understand.

Every order and command addressed to internees individually must likewise be given in a language which they understand.

ARTICLE 100

A4–099   The disciplinary regime in places of internment shall be consistent with humanitarian principles, and shall in no circumstances include regulations imposing on internees any physical exertion dangerous to their health or involving physical or moral victimization. Identification by tattooing or imprinting signs or markings on the body is prohibited.

In particular, prolonged standing and roll-calls, punishment drill, military drill and manoeuvres, or the reduction of food rations, are prohibited.

ARTICLE 101

A4–100   Internees shall have the right to present to the authorities in whose power they are any petition with regard to the conditions of internment to which they are subjected.

They shall also have the right to apply without restriction through the Internee Committee or, if they consider it necessary, direct to the representatives of the Protecting Power, in order to indicate to them any points on which they may have complaints to make with regard to the conditions of internment.

Such petitions and complaints shall be transmitted forthwith and without alteration, and even if the latter are recognized to be unfounded, they may not occasion any punishment.

Periodic reports on the situation in places of internment and as to the needs of the internees may be sent by the Internee Committees to the representatives of the Protecting Powers.

ARTICLE 102

A4–101   In every place of internment, the internees shall freely elect by secret ballot every six months, the members of a Committee empowered to represent them before the Detaining and the Protecting Powers, the International Committee of the Red Cross and any other organization which may assist them. The members of the Committee shall be eligible for re-election.

Internees so elected shall enter upon their duties after their election has been approved by the detaining authorities. The reasons for any refusals or dismissals shall be communicated to the Protecting Powers concerned.

ARTICLE 103

A4–102   The Internee Committees shall further the physical, spiritual and intellectual well-being of the internees.

In case the internees decide, in particular, to organize a system of mutual assistance amongst themselves, this organization would be within the competence of the Committees in addition to the special duties entrusted to them under other provisions of the present Convention.

ARTICLE 104

A4–103   Members of Internee Committees shall not be required to perform any other work, if the accomplishment of their duties is rendered more difficult thereby.

Members of Internee Committees may appoint from amongst the internees such assistants as they may require. All material facilities shall be granted to them, particularly a certain freedom of movement necessary for the accomplishment of their duties (visits to labour detachments, receipt of supplies, etc.).

All facilities shall likewise be accorded to members of Internee Committees for communication by post and telegraph with the detaining authorities, the Protecting

Powers, the International Committee of the Red Cross and their delegates, and with the organizations which give assistance to internees. Committee members in labour detachments shall enjoy similar facilities for communication with their Internee Committee in the principal place of internment. Such communications shall not be limited, nor considered as forming a part of the quota mentioned in Article 107.

Members of Internee Committees who are transferred shall be allowed a reasonable time to acquaint their successors with current affairs.

Chapter VIII

RELATIONS WITH THE EXTERIOR

Article 105

Immediately upon interning protected persons, the Detaining Power shall inform them, the Power to which they owe allegiance and their Protecting Power of the measures taken for executing the provisions of the present Chapter. The Detaining Power shall likewise inform the Parties concerned of any subsequent modifications of such measures. **A4–104**

Article 106

As soon as he is interned, or at the latest not more than one week after his arrival in a place of internment, and likewise in cases of sickness or transfer to another place of internment or to a hospital, every internee shall be enabled to send direct to his family, on the one hand, and to the Central Agency provided for by Article 140, on the other, an internment card similar, if possible, to the model annexed to the present Convention, informing his relatives of his detention, address and state of health. The said cards shall be forwarded as rapidly as possible and may not be delayed in any way. **A4–105**

Article 107

Internees shall be allowed to send and receive letters and cards. If the Detaining Power deems it necessary to limit the number of letters and cards sent by each internee, the said number shall not be less than two letters and four cards monthly; these shall be drawn up so as to conform as closely as possible to the models annexed to the present Convention. If limitations must be placed on the correspondence addressed to internees, they may be ordered only by the Power to which such internees owe allegiance, possibly at the request of the Detaining Power. Such letters and cards must be conveyed with reasonable despatch; they may not be delayed or retained for disciplinary reasons. **A4–106**

Internees who have been a long time without news, or who find it impossible to receive news from their relatives, or to give them news by the ordinary postal route, as well as those who are at a considerable distance from their homes, shall be allowed to send telegrams, the charges being paid by them in the currency at their disposal. They shall likewise benefit by this provision in cases which are recognized to be urgent.

As a rule, internees' mail shall be written in their own language. The Parties to the conflict may authorize correspondence in other languages.

Article 108

Internees shall be allowed to receive, by post or by any other means, individual parcels or collective shipments containing in particular foodstuffs, clothing, medical supplies, as well as books and objects of a devotional, educational or recreational character which may meet their needs. Such shipments shall in no way free the Detaining Power from the obligations imposed upon it by virtue of the present Convention. **A4–107**

1099

Should military necessity require the quantity of such shipments to be limited, due notice thereof shall be given to the Protecting Power and to the International Committee of the Red Cross, or to any other organization giving assistance to the internees and responsible for the forwarding of such shipments.

The conditions for the sending of individual parcels and collective shipments shall, if necessary, be the subject of special agreements between the Powers concerned, which may in no case delay the receipt by the internees of relief supplies. Parcels of clothing and foodstuffs may not include books. Medical relief supplies shall, as a rule, be sent in collective parcels.

ARTICLE 109

A4–108   In the absence of special agreements between Parties to the conflict regarding the conditions for the receipt and distribution of collective relief shipments, the regulations concerning collective relief which are annexed to the present Convention shall be applied.

The special agreements provided for above shall in no case restrict the right of Internee Committees to take possession of collective relief shipments intended for internees, to undertake their distribution and to dispose of them in the interests of the recipients.

Nor shall such agreements restrict the right of representatives of the Protecting Powers, the International Committee of the Red Cross, or any other organization giving assistance to internees and responsible for the forwarding of collective shipments, to supervise their distribution to the recipients.

ARTICLE 110

A4–109   All relief shipments for internees shall be exempt from import, customs and other dues.

All matter sent by mail, including relief parcels sent by parcel post and remittances of money, addressed from other countries to internees or despatched by them through the post office, either direct or through the Information Bureaux provided for in Article 136 and the Central Information Agency provided for in Article 140, shall be exempt from all postal dues both in the countries of origin and destination and in intermediate countries. To this end. in particular, the exemption provided by the Universal Postal Convention of 1947 and by the agreements of the Universal Postal Union in favour of civilians of enemy nationality detained in camps or civilian prisons, shall be extended to the other interned persons protected by the present Convention. The countries not signatory to the above-mentioned agreements shall be bound to grant freedom from charges in the same circumstances.

The cost of transporting relief shipments which are intended for internees and which, by reason of their weight or any other cause, cannot be sent through the post office, shall be borne by the Detaining Power in all the territories under its control. Other Powers which are Parties to the present Convention shall bear the cost of transport in their respective territories.

Costs connected with the transport of such shipments, which are not covered by the above paragraphs, shall be charged to the senders.

The High Contracting Parties shall endeavour to reduce, so far as possible, the charges for telegrams sent by internees, or addressed to them.

ARTICLE 111

A4–110   Should military operations prevent the Powers concerned from fulfilling their obligation to ensure the conveyance of the mail and relief shipments provided for in Articles 106, 107, 108 and 113, the Protecting Powers concerned, the International Committee of the Red Cross or any other organization duly approved by the Parties to the conflict may undertake the conveyance of such shipments by suitable means (rail, motor vehicles, vessels or aircraft, etc.). For this purpose, the High Contracting Parties shall endeavour to supply them with such transport, and to allow its circulation, especially by granting the necessary safe-conducts.

Such transport may also be used to convey:

(a) Correspondence, lists and reports exchanged between the Central Information Agency referred to in Article 140 and the National Bureaux referred to in Article 136;

(b) Correspondence and reports relating to internees which the Protecting Powers, the International Committee of the Red Cross or any other organization assisting the internees exchange either with their own delegates or with the Parties to the conflict.

These provisions in no way detract from the right of any Party to the conflict to arrange other means of transport if it should so prefer, nor preclude the granting of safe-conducts, under mutually agreed conditions, to such means of transport.

The costs occasioned by the use of such means of transport shall be borne, in proportion to the importance of the shipments, by the Parties to the conflict whose nationals are benefited thereby.

ARTICLE 112

The censoring of correspondence addressed to internees or despatched by them shall be done as quickly as possible.   **A4–111**

The examination of consignments intended for internees shall not be carried out under conditions that will expose the goods contained in them to deterioration. It shall be done in the presence of the addressee, or of a fellow-internee duly delegated by him. The delivery to internees of individual or collective consignments shall not be delayed under the pretext of difficulties of censorship.

Any prohibition of correspondence ordered by the Parties to the conflict, either for military or political reasons, shall be only temporary and its duration shall be as short as possible.

ARTICLE 113

The Detaining Powers shall provide all reasonable facilities for the transmission, through the Protecting Power or the Central Agency provided for in Article 140, or as otherwise required, of wills, powers of attorney letters of authority, or any other documents intended for internees or despatched by them.   **A4–112**

In all cases the Detaining Power shall facilitate the execution and authentication in due legal form of such documents on behalf of internees, in particular by allowing them to consult a lawyer.

ARTICLE 114

The Detaining Power shall afford internees all facilities to enable them to manage their property, provided this is not incompatible with the conditions of internment and the law which is applicable. For this purpose, the said Power may give them permission to leave the place of internment in urgent cases and if circumstances allow.   **A4–113**

ARTICLE 115

In all cases where an internee is a party to proceedings in any court, the Detaining Power shall, if he so requests, cause the court to be informed of his detention and shall, within legal limits, ensure that all necessary steps are taken to prevent him from being in any way prejudiced, by reason of his internment, as regards the preparation and conduct of his case or as regards the execution of any judgment of the court.   **A4–114**

Article 116

A4–115   Every internee shall be allowed to receive visitors, especially near relatives, at regular intervals and as frequently as possible.

As far as is possible, internees shall be permitted to visit their homes in urgent cases, particularly in cases of death or serious illness of relatives.

Chapter IX

PENAL AND DISCIPLINARY SANCTIONS

Article 117

A4–116   Subject to the provisions of the present Chapter, the laws in force in the territory in which they are detained will continue to apply to internees who commit offences during internment.

If general laws, regulations or orders declare acts committed by internees to be punishable, whereas the same acts are not punishable when committed by persons who are not internees, such acts shall entail disciplinary punishments only.

No internee may be punished more than once for the same act, or on the same count.

Article 118

A4–117   The courts or authorities shall in passing sentence take as far as possible into account the fact that the defendant is not a national of the Detaining Power. They shall be free to reduce the penalty prescribed for the offence with which the internee is charged and shall not be obliged, to this end, to apply the minimum sentence prescribed.

Imprisonment in premises without daylight, and, in general, all forms of cruelty without exception are forbidden.

Internees who have served disciplinary or judicial sentences shall not be treated differently from other internees.

The duration of preventive detention undergone by an internee shall be deducted from any disciplinary or judicial penalty involving confinement to which he may be sentenced.

Internee Committees shall be informed of all judicial proceedings instituted against internees whom they represent, and of their result.

Article 119

A4–118   The disciplinary punishments applicable to internees shall be the following:
1. A fine which shall not exceed 50 per cent of the wages which the internee would otherwise receive under the provisions of Article 95 during a period of not more than thirty days.
2. Discontinuance of privileges granted over and above the treatment provided for by the present Convention.
3. Fatigue duties, not exceeding two hours daily, in connection with the maintenance of the place of internment.
4. Confinement.

In no case shall disciplinary penalties be inhuman, brutal or dangerous for the health of internees. Account shall be taken of the internee's age, sex and state of health.

The duration of any single punishment shall in no case exceed a maximum of thirty consecutive days, even if the internee is answerable for several breaches of discipline when his case is dealt with, whether such breaches are connected or not.

Article 120

A4–119   Internees who are recaptured after having escaped or when attempting to escape shall be liable only to disciplinary punishment in respect of this act, even if it is a repeated offence.

Article 118, paragraph 3, notwithstanding, internees punished as a result of escape or attempt to escape, may be subjected to special surveillance, on condition that such surveillance does not affect the state of their health, that it is exercised in a place of internment and that it does not entail the abolition of any of the safeguards granted by the present Convention.

Internees who aid and abet an escape, or attempt to escape, shall be liable on this count to disciplinary punishment only.

Article 121

Escape, or attempt to escape, even if it is a repeated offence, shall not be deemed an aggravating circumstance in cases where an internee is prosecuted for offences committed during his escape.

A4–120

The Parties to the conflict shall ensure that the competent authorities exercise leniency in deciding whether punishment inflicted for an offence shall be of a disciplinary or judicial nature, especially in respect of acts committed in connection with an escape, whether successful or not.

Article 122

Acts which constitute offences against discipline shall be investigated immediately. This rule shall be applied, in particular, in cases of escape or attempt to escape. Recaptured internees shall be handed over to the competent authorities as soon as possible.

A4–121

In case of offences against discipline, confinement awaiting trial shall be reduced to an absolute minimum for all internees, and shall not exceed fourteen days. Its duration shall in any case be deducted from any sentence of confinement.

The provisions of Articles 124 and 125 shall apply to internees who are in confinement awaiting trial for offences against discipline.

Article 123

Without prejudice to the competence of courts and higher authorities, disciplinary punishment may be ordered only by the commandant of the place of internment, or by a responsible officer or official who replaces him, or to whom he has delegated his disciplinary powers.

A4–122

Before any disciplinary punishment is awarded, the accused internee shall be given precise information regarding the offences of which he is accused, and given an opportunity of explaining his conduct and of defending himself. He shall be permitted, in particular, to call witnesses and to have recourse, if necessary, to the services of a qualified interpreter. The decision shall be announced in the presence of the accused and of a member of the Internee Committee.

The period elapsing between the time of award of a disciplinary punishment and its execution shall not exceed one month.

When an internee is awarded a further disciplinary punishment, a period of at least three days shall elapse between the execution of any two of the punishments, if the duration of one of these is ten days or more.

A record of disciplinary punishments shall be maintained by the commandant of the place of internment and shall be open to inspection by representatives of the Protecting Power.

Article 124

Internees shall not in any case be transferred to penitentiary establishments (prisons, penitentiaries, convict prisons, etc.) to undergo disciplinary punishment therein.

A4–123

The premises in which disciplinary punishments are undergone shall conform to sanitary requirements; they shall in particular be provided with adequate bedding. Internees undergoing punishment shall be enabled to keep themselves in a state of cleanliness.

Women internees undergoing disciplinary punishment shall be confined in separate quarters from male internees and shall be under the immediate supervision of women.

ARTICLE 125

A4–124   Internees awarded disciplinary punishment shall be allowed to exercise and to stay in the open air at least two hours daily.

They shall be allowed, if they so request, to be present at the daily medical inspections. They shall receive the attention which their state of health requires and, if necessary, shall be removed to the infirmary of the place of internment or to a hospital.

They shall have permission to read and write, likewise to send and receive letters. Parcels and remittances of money, however, may be withheld from them until the completion of their punishment; such consignments shall meanwhile be entrusted to the Internee Committee, who will hand over to the infirmary the perishable goods contained in the parcels.

No internee given a disciplinary punishment may be deprived of the benefit of the provisions of Articles 107 and 143 of the present Convention.

ARTICLE 126

A4–125   The provisions of Articles 71 to 76 inclusive shall apply, by analogy, to proceedings against internees who are in the national territory of the Detaining Power.

CHAPTER X

TRANSFERS OF INTERNEES

ARTICLE 127

A4–126   The transfer of internees shall always be effected humanely. As a general rule, it shall be carried out by rail or other means of transport, and under conditions at least equal to those obtaining for the forces of the Detaining Power in their changes of station. If, as an exceptional measure, such removals have to be effected on foot, they may not take place unless the internees are in a fit state of health, and may not in any case expose them to excessive fatigue.

The Detaining Power shall supply internees during transfer with drinking water and food sufficient in quantity, quality and variety to maintain them in good health, and also with the necessary clothing, adequate shelter and the necessary medical attention. The Detaining Power shall take all suitable precautions to ensure their safety during transfer, and shall establish before their departure a complete list of all internees transferred.

Sick, wounded or infirm internees and maternity cases shall not be transferred if the journey would be seriously detrimental to them, unless their safety imperatively so demands.

If the combat zone draws close to a place of internment, the internees in the said place shall not be transferred unless their removal can be carried out in adequate conditions of safety, or unless they are exposed to greater risks by remaining on the spot than by being transferred.

When making decisions regarding the transfer of internees, the Detaining Power shall take their interests into account and, in particular, shall not do anything to increase the difficulties of repatriating them or returning them to their own homes.

ARTICLE 128

In the event of transfer, internees shall be officially advised of their departure and of their new postal address. Such notification shall be given in time for them to pack their luggage and inform their next of kin.

A4–127

They shall be allowed to take with them their personal effects, and the correspondence and parcels which have arrived for them. The weight of such baggage may be limited if the conditions of transfer so require, but in no case to less than twenty-five kilograms per internee.

Mail and parcels addressed to their former place of internment shall be forwarded to them without delay.

The commandant of the place of internment shall take, in agreement with the Internee Committee, any measures needed to ensure the transport of the internees' community property and of the luggage the internees are unable to take with them in consequence of restrictions imposed by virtue of the second paragraph.

CHAPTER XI

DEATHS

ARTICLE 129

The wills of internees shall be received for safe-keeping by the responsible authorities; and in the event of the death of an internee his will shall be transmitted without delay to a person whom he has previously designated.

A4–128

Deaths of internees shall be certified in every case by a doctor, and a death certificate shall be made out, showing the causes of death and the conditions under which it occurred.

An official record of the death, duly registered, shall be drawn up in accordance with the procedure relating thereto in force in the territory where the place of internment is situated, and a duly certified copy of such record shall be transmitted without delay to the Protecting Power as well as to the Central Agency referred to in Article 140.

ARTICLE 130

The detaining authorities shall ensure that internees who die while interned are honourably buried, if possible according to the rites of the religion to which they belonged, and that their graves are respected, properly maintained, and marked in such a way that they can always be recognized.

A4–129

Deceased internees shall be buried in individual graves unless unavoidable circumstances require the use of collective graves. Bodies may be' cremated only for imperative reasons of hygiene, on account of the religion of the deceased or in accordance with his expressed wish to this effect. In case of cremation, the fact shall be stated and the reasons given in the death certificate of the deceased. The ashes shall be retained for safe-keeping by the detaining authorities and shall be transferred as soon as possible to the next of kin on their request.

As soon as circumstances permit, and not later than the close of hostilities, the Detaining Power shall forward lists of graves of deceased internees to the Powers on whom the deceased internees depended, through the Information Bureaux provided for in Article 136. Such lists shall include all particulars necessary for the identification of the deceased internees, as well as the exact location of their graves.

ARTICLE 131

Every death or serious injury of an internee, caused or suspected to have been caused by a sentry, another internee or any other person, as well as any death the cause of which is unknown, shall be immediately followed by an official enquiry by the Detaining Power.

A4–130

A communication on this subject shall be sent immediately to the Projecting Power. The evidence of any witnesses shall be taken, and a report including such evidence shall be prepared and forwarded to the said Protecting power.

If the enquiry indicates the guilt of one or more persons, the Detaining Power shall take all necessary steps to ensure the prosecution of the person or persons responsible.

CHAPTER XII

RELEASE, REPATRIATION AND ACCOMMODATION IN NEUTRAL COUNTRIES

ARTICLE 132

A4–131   Each interned person shall be released by the Detaining Power as soon as the reasons which necessitated his internment no longer exist.

The Parties to the conflict shall, moreover, endeavour during the course of hostilities, to conclude agreements for the release, the repatriation, the return to places of residence or the accommodation in a neutral country of certain classes of internees, in particular children, pregnant women and mothers with infants and young children, wounded and sick, and internees who have been detained for a long time.

ARTICLE 133

A4–132   Internment shall cease as soon as possible after the close of hostilities.

Internees, in the territory of a Party to the conflict, against whom penal proceedings are pending for offences not exclusively subject to disciplinary penalties, may be detained until the close of such proceedings and, if circumstances require, until the completion of the penalty. The same shall apply to internees who have been previously sentenced to a punishment depriving them of liberty.

By agreement between the Detaining Power and the Powers concerned, committees may be set up after the close of hostilities, or of the occupation of territories, to search for dispersed internees.

ARTICLE 134

A4–133   The High Contracting Parties shall endeavour, upon the close of hostilities or occupation, to ensure the return of all internees to their last place of residence, or to facilitate their repatriation.

ARTICLE 135

A4–134   The Detaining Power shall bear the expense of returning released internees to the places where they were residing when interned, or, if it took them into custody while they were in transit or on the high seas, the cost of completing their journey or of their return to their point of departure.

Where a Detaining Power refuses permission to reside in its territory to a released internee who previously had his permanent domicile therein, such Detaining Power shall pay the cost of the said internee's repatriation. If, however, the internee elects to return to his country on his own responsibility or in obedience to the Government of the Power to which he owes allegiance, the Detaining Power need not pay the expenses of his journey beyond the point of his departure from its territory. The Detaining Power need not pay the costs of repatriation of an internee who was interned at his own request.

If internees are transferred in accordance with Article 45, the transferring and receiving Powers shall agree on the portion of the above costs to be borne by each.

1106

The foregoing shall not prejudice such special agreements as may be concluded between Parties to the conflict concerning the exchange and repatriation of their nationals in enemy hands.

Section V

Information Bureaux and Central Agency

ARTICLE 136

Upon the outbreak of a conflict and in all cases of occupation, each of the Parties to the conflict shall establish an official Information Bureau responsible for receiving and transmitting information in respect of the protected persons who are in its power.   **A4–135**

Each of the Parties to the conflict shall, within the shortest possible period, give its Bureau information of any measure taken by it concerning any protected persons who are kept in custody for more than two weeks, who are subjected to assigned residence or who are interned. It shall, furthermore, require its various departments concerned with such matters to provide the aforesaid Bureau promptly with information concerning all changes pertaining to these protected persons, as, for example, transfers, release, repatriations, escapes, admittances to hospitals, births and deaths.

ARTICLE 137

Each national Bureau shall immediately forward information concerning protected persons by the most rapid means to the Powers of whom the aforesaid persons are nationals, or to Powers in whose territory they resided, through the intermediary of the Protecting Powers and likewise through the Central Agency provided for in Article 140. The Bureaux shall also reply to all enquiries which may be received regarding protected persons.   **A4–136**

Information Bureaux shall transmit information concerning a protected person unless its transmission might be detrimental to the person concerned or to his or her relatives. Even in such a case, the information may not be withheld from the Central Agency which, upon being notified of the circumstances, will take the necessary precautions indicated in Article 140.

All communications in writing made by any Bureau shall be authenticated by a signature or a seal.

ARTICLE 138

The information received by the national Bureau and transmitted by it shall be of such a character as to make it possible to identify the protected person exactly and to advise his next of kin quickly. The information in respect of each person shall include at least his surname, first names, place and date of birth, nationality, last residence and distinguishing characteristics, the first name of the father and the maiden name of the mother, the date, place and nature of the action taken with regard to the individual, the address at which correspondence may be sent to him and the name and address of the person to be informed.   **A4–137**

Likewise, information regarding the state of health of internees who are seriously ill or seriously wounded shall be supplied regularly and if possible every week.

ARTICLE 139

Each national Information Bureau shall, furthermore, be responsible for collecting all personal valuables left by protected persons mentioned in Article 136, in particular those who have been repatriated or released, or who have escaped or died; it shall forward the   **A4–138** said valuables to those concerned, either direct, or, if necessary, through the Central Agency. Such articles shall be sent by the Bureau in sealed packets which shall be accompanied by statements giving clear and full identity particulars of the person to whom the articles belonged, and by a complete list of the contents of the parcel. Detailed records shall be maintained of the receipt and despatch of all such valuables.

ARTICLE 140

A4–139   A Central Information Agency for protected persons, in particular for internees, shall be created in a neutral country. The International Committee of the Red Cross shall, if it deems necessary, propose to the Powers concerned the organization of such an Agency, which may be the same as that provided for in Article 123 of the Geneva Convention relative to the Treatment of Prisoners of War of August 12, 1949.

The function of the Agency shall be to collect all information of the type set forth in Article 136 which it may obtain through official or private channels and to transmit it as rapidly as possible to the countries of origin or of residence of the persons concerned, except in cases where such transmissions might be detrimental to the persons whom the said information concerns, or to their relatives. It shall receive from the Parties to the conflict all reasonable facilities for effecting such transmissions.

The High Contracting Parties, and in particular those whose nationals benefit by the services of the Central Agency, are requested to give the said Agency the financial aid it may require.

The foregoing provisions shall in no way be interpreted as restricting the humanitarian activities of the International Committee of the Red Cross and of the relief Societies described in Article 142.

ARTICLE 141

A4–140   The national Information Bureaux and the Central Information Agency shall enjoy free postage for all mail, likewise the exemptions provided for in Article 110, and further, so far as possible, exemption from telegraphic charges or, at least, greatly reduced rates.

PART IV

EXECUTION OF THE CONVENTION

Section I

General Provisions

ARTICLE 142

A4–141   Subject to the measures which the Detaining Powers may consider essential to ensure their security or to meet any other reasonable need, the representatives of religious organizations, relief societies, or any other organizations assisting the protected persons, shall receive from these Powers, for themselves or their duly accredited agents, all facilities for visiting the protected persons, for distributing relief supplies and material from any source, intended for educational, recreational or religious purposes , or for assisting them in organizing their leisure time within the places of internment. Such societies or organizations may be constituted in the territory of the Detaining Power, or in any other country, or they may have an international character.

The Detaining Power may limit the number of societies and organizations whose delegates are allowed to carry out their activities in its territory and under its supervision, on condition, however, that such limitation shall not hinder the supply of effective and adequate relief to all protected persons.

The special position of the International Committee of the Red Cross in this field shall be recognized and respected at all times.

ARTICLE 143

Representatives or delegates of the Protecting Powers shall have permission to go to all places where protected persons are, particularly to places of internment, detention and work.

They shall have access to all premises occupied by protected persons and shall be able to interview the latter without witnesses, personally or through an interpreter.

Such visits may not be prohibited except for reasons of imperative military necessity, and then only as an exceptional and temporary measure Their duration and frequency shall not be restricted.

Such representatives and delegates shall have full liberty to select the places they wish to visit. The Detaining or Occupying Power, the Protecting Power and when occasion arises the Power of origin of the persons to be visited, may agree that compatriots of the internees shall be permitted to participate in the visits.

The delegates of the International Committee of the Red Cross shall also enjoy the above prerogatives. The appointment of such delegates shall be submitted to the approval of the Power governing the territories where they will carry out their duties.

A4–142

ARTICLE 144

The High Contracting Parties undertake, in time of peace as in time of war, to disseminate the text of the present Convention as widely as possible in their respective countries, and, in particular, to include the study thereof in their programmes of military and, if possible, civil instruction, so that the principles thereof may become known to the entire population.

Any civilian, military, police or other authorities, who in time of war assume responsibilities in respect of protected persons, must possess the text of the Convention and be specially instructed as to its provisions.

A4–143

ARTICLE 145

The High Contracting Parties shall communicate to one another through the Swiss Federal Council and, during hostilities, through the Protecting Powers, the official translations of the present Convention, as well as the laws and regulations which they may adopt to ensure the application thereof.

A4–144

ARTICLE 146

The High Contracting Parties undertake to enact any legislation necessary to provide effective penal sanctions for persons committing, or ordering to be committed, any of the grave breaches of the present Convention defined in the following Article.

Each High Contracting Party shall be under the obligation to search for persons alleged to have committed, or to have ordered to be committed, such grave breaches, and shall bring such persons, regardless of their nationality, before its own courts. It may also, if it prefers, and in accordance with the provisions of its own legislation, hand such persons over for trial to another

High Contracting Party concerned, provided such High Contracting Party has made out a prima facie case.

Each High Contracting Party shall take measures necessary for the suppression of all acts contrary to the provisions of the present Convention other than the grave breaches defined in the following Article.

A4–145

In all circumstances, the accused persons shall benefit by safeguards of proper trial and defence, which shall not be less favourable than those provided by Article 105 and those following of the Geneva Convention relative to the Treatment of Prisoners of War of August 12, 1949.

ARTICLE 147

A4–146   Grave breaches to which the preceding Article relates shall be those involving any of the following acts, if committed against persons or property protected by the present Convention: wilful killing, torture or inhuman treatment, including biological experiments, wilfully causing great suffering or serious injury to body or health, unlawful deportation or transfer or unlawful confinement of a protected person, compelling a protected person to serve in the forces of a hostile Power, or wilfully depriving a protected person of the rights of fair and regular trial prescribed in the present Convention, taking of hostages and extensive destruction and appropriation of property, not justified by military necessity and carried out unlawfully and wantonly.

ARTICLE 148

A4–147   No High Contracting Party shall be allowed to absolve itself or any other High Contracting Party of any liability incurred by itself or by another High Contracting Party in respect of breaches referred to in the preceding Article.

ARTICLE 149

A4–148   At the request of a Party to the conflict, an enquiry shall be instituted, in a manner to be decided between the interested Parties, concerning any alleged violation of the Convention.

If agreement has not been reached concerning the procedure for the enquiry, the Parties should agree on the choice of an umpire who will decide upon the procedure to be followed.

Once the violation has been established, the Parties to the conflict shall put an end to it and shall repress it with the least possible delay.

Section 11

Final Provisions

ARTICLE 150

A4–149   The present Convention is established in English and in French. Both texts are equally authentic.

The Swiss Federal Council shall arrange for official translations of the Convention to be made in the Russian and Spanish languages.

ARTICLE 151

A4–150   The present Convention, which bears the date of this day, is open to signature until February 12, 1950, in the name of the Powers represented at the Conference which opened at Geneva on April 21, 1949.

ARTICLE 152

A4–151   The present Convention shall be ratified as soon as possible and the ratifications shall be deposited at Berne.

A record shall be drawn up of the deposit of each instrument of ratification and certified copies of this record shall be transmitted by the Swiss Federal Council to all the Powers in whose name the Convention has been signed, or whose accession has been notified.

ARTICLE 153

A4–152

The present Convention shall come into force six months after not less than two instruments of ratification have been deposited.

Thereafter, it shall come into force for each High Contracting Party six months after the deposit of the instrument of ratification.

ARTICLE 154

A4–153

In the relations between the Powers who are bound by The Hague Conventions respecting the Laws and Customs of War on Land, whether that of 29 July, 1899, or that of 18 October, 1907, and who are parties to the present Convention, this last Convention shall be supplementary to Sections II and III of the Regulations annexed to the above-mentioned Conventions of The Hague.

ARTICLE 155

A4–154

From the date of its coming into force, it shall be open to any Power in whose name the present Convention has not been signed, to accede to this Convention.

ARTICLE 156

A4–155

Accessions shall be notified in writing to the Swiss Federal Council, and shall take effect six months after the date on which they are received.

The Swiss Federal Council shall communicate the accessions to all the Powers in whose name the Convention has been signed, or whose accession has been notified.

ARTICLE 157

A4–156

The situations provided for in Articles 2 and 3 shall give immediate effect to ratifications deposited and accessions notified by the Parties to the conflict before or after the beginning of hostilities or occupation. The Swiss Federal Council shall communicate by the quickest method any ratifications or accessions received from Parties to the conflict.

ARTICLE 158

A4–157

Each of the High Contracting Parties shall be at liberty to denounce the present Convention.

The denunciation shall be notified in writing to the Swiss Federal Council, which shall transmit it to the Governments of all the High Contracting Parties.

The denunciation shall take effect one year after the notification thereof has been made to the Swiss Federal Council. However, a denunciation of which notification has been made at a time when the denouncing Power is involved in a conflict shall not take effect until peace has been concluded, and until after operations connected with the release, repatriation and re-establishment of the persons protected by the present Convention have been terminated.

The denunciation shall have effect only in respect of the denouncing Power. It shall in no way impair the obligations which the Parties to the conflict shall remain bound to fulfil by virtue of the principles of the law of nations, as they result from the usages established among civilized peoples, from the laws of humanity and the dictates of the public conscience.

ARTICLE 159

A4–158   The Swiss Federal Council shall register the present Convention with the Secretariat of the United Nations. The Swiss Federal Council shall also inform the Secretariat of the United Nations of all ratifications, accessions and denunciations received by it with respect to the present Convention.

IN WITNESS WHEREOF the undersigned, having deposited their respective full powers, have signed the present Convention.

DONE at Geneva this twelfth day of August 1949, in the English and French languages. The original shall be deposited in the Archives of the Swiss Confederation. The Swiss Federal Council shall transmit certified copies thereof to each of the signatory and acceding States.

ANNEX I

DRAFT AGREEMENT RELATING TO HOSPITAL AND SAFETY ZONES AND LOCALITIES

ARTICLE I

A4–159   Hospital and safety zones shall be strictly reserved for the persons mentioned in Article 23 of the Geneva Convention for the Amelioration of the Condition of the Wounded and Sick in Armed Forces in the Field of 12 August, 1949, and in Article 14 of the Geneva Convention relative to the Protection of Civilian Persons in Time of War of 12 August, 1949, and for the personnel entrusted with the organization and administration of these zones and localities and with the care of the persons therein assembled.

Nevertheless, persons whose permanent residence is within such zones shall have the right to stay there.

ARTICLE 2

A4–160   No persons residing, in whatever capacity, in a hospital and safety zone shall perform any work, either within or without the zone, directly connected with military operations or the production of war material.

ARTICLE 3

A4–161   The Power establishing a hospital and safety zone shall take all necessary measures to prohibit access to all persons who have no right of residence or entry therein.

ARTICLE 4

A4–162   Hospital and safety zones shall fulfil the following conditions:
  (a) They shall comprise only a small part of the territory governed by the Power which has established them.
  (b) They shall be thinly populated in relation to the possibilities of accommodation.
  (c) They shall be far removed and free from all military objectives, or large industrial or administrative establishments.
  (d) They shall not be situated in areas which, according to every probability, may become important for the conduct of the war.

ARTICLE 5

Hospital and safety zones shall be subject to the following obligations: **A4–163**
    (a) The lines of communication and means of transport which they possess shall not be used for the transport of military personnel or material, even in transit.
    (b) They shall in no case be defended by military means.

ARTICLE 6

Hospital and safety zones shall be marked by means of oblique red bands on a white   **A4–164**
ground, placed on the buildings and outer precincts.

Zones reserved exclusively for the wounded and sick may be marked by means of the Red Cross (Red Crescent, Red Lion and Sun) emblem on a white ground.

They may be similarly marked at night by means of appropriate illumination.

ARTICLE 7

The Powers shall communicate to all the High Contracting Parties in peacetime or on   **A4–165**
the outbreak of hostilities, a list of the hospital and safety zones in the territories governed by them. They shall also give notice of any new zones set up during hostilities.

As soon as the adverse Party has received the above-mentioned notification, the zone shall be regularly established.

If, however, the adverse Party considers that the conditions of the present agreement have not been fulfilled, it may refuse to recognize the zone by giving immediate notice thereof to the Party responsible for the said zone, or may make its recognition of such zone dependent upon the institution of the control provided for in Article 8.

ARTICLE 8

Any Power having recognized one or several hospital and safety zones instituted by the   **A4–166**
adverse Party shall be entitled to demand control by one or more Special Commissions. for the purpose of ascertaining if the zones fulfil the conditions and obligations stipulated in the present agreement.

For this purpose, members of the Special Commissions shall at all times have free access to the various zones and may even reside there permanently. They shall be given all facilities for their duties of inspection.

ARTICLE 9

Should the Special Commissions note any facts which they consider contrary to the   **A4–167**
stipulations of the present agreement, they shall at once draw the attention of the Power governing the said zone to these facts, and shall fix a time limit of five days within which the matter should be rectified. They shall duly notify the Power who has recognized the zone.

If, when the time limit has expired. the Power governing the zone has not complied with the warning, the adverse Party may declare that it is no longer bound by the present agreement in respect of the said zone.

ARTICLE 10

Any Power setting up one or more hospital and safety zones, and the adverse Parties   **A4–168**
to whom their existence has been notified, shall nominate or have nominated by the Protecting Powers or by other neutral Powers, persons eligible to be members of the Special Commissions mentioned in Articles 8 and 9.

ARTICLE 11

A4–169 In no circumstances may hospital and safety zones be the object of attack. They shall be protected and respected at all times by the Parties to the conflict.

ARTICLE 12

A4–170 In the case of occupation of a territory, the hospital and safety zones therein shall continue to be respected and utilized as such.

Their purpose may, however, be modified by the Occupying Power, on condition that all measures are taken to ensure the safety of the persons accommodated.

ARTICLE 13

A4–171 The present agreement shall also apply to localities which the Powers may utilize for the same purposes as hospital and safety zones.

ANNEX 11

DRAFT REGULATIONS CONCERNING COLLECTIVE RELIEF

ARTICLE I

A4–172 The Internee Committees shall be allowed to distribute collective relief shipments for which they are responsible. to all internees who are dependent for administration on the said Committee's place of internment, including those internees who are in hospitals, or in prisons or other penitentiary establishments.

ARTICLE 2

A4–173 The distribution of collective relief shipments shall be effected in accordance with the instructions of the donors and with a plan drawn up by the Internee Committees. The issue of medical stores shall, however, be made for preference in agreement with the senior medical officers, and the latter may, in hospitals and infirmaries, waive the said instructions, if the needs of their patients so demand. Within the limits thus defined, the distribution shall always be carried out equitably.

ARTICLE 3

A4–174 Members of Internee Committees shall be allowed to go to the railway stations or other points of arrival of relief supplies near their places of internment so as to enable them to verify the quantity as well as the quality of the goods received and to make out detailed reports thereon for the donors.

ARTICLE 4

A4–175 Internee Committees shall be given the facilities necessary for verifying whether the distribution of collective relief in all subdivisions and annexes of their places of internment has been carried out in accordance with their instructions.

ARTICLE 5

Internee Committees shall be allowed to complete, and to cause to be completed by members of the Internee Committees in labour detachments or by the senior medical officers of infirmaries and hospitals, forms or questionnaires intended for the donors, relating to collective relief supplies (distribution, requirements, quantities, etc.). Such forms and questionnaires, duly completed, shall be forwarded to the donors without delay.

A4–176

ARTICLE 6

In order to secure the regular distribution of collective relief supplies to the internees in their place of internment, and to meet any needs that may arise through the arrival of fresh parties of internees, the Internee Committees shall be allowed to create and maintain sufficient reserve stocks of collective relief. For this purpose, they shall have suitable warehouses at their disposal; each warehouse shall be provided with two locks, the Internee Committee holding the keys of one lock, and the commandant of the place of internment the keys of the other.

A4–177

ARTICLE 7

The High Contracting Parties, and the Detaining Powers in particular, shall, so far as is in any way possible and subject to the regulations governing the food supply of the population, authorize purchases of goods to be made in their territories for the distribution of collective relief to the internees. They shall likewise facilitate the transfer of funds and other financial measures of a technical or administrative nature taken for the purpose of making such purchases.

A4–178

ARTICLE 8

The foregoing provisions shall not constitute an obstacle to the right of internees to receive collective relief before their arrival in a place of internment or in the course of their transfer, nor to the possibility of representatives of the Protecting Power, or of the International Committee of the Red Cross or any other humanitarian organization giving assistance to internees and responsible for forwarding such supplies, ensuring the distribution thereof to the recipients by any other means they may deem suitable.

A4–179

A5. Protocol Additional to the Geneva Conventions of 12 August 1949, and relating to the Protection of Victims of International Armed Conflicts (Protocol 1)

Adopted on 8 June 1977 by the Diplomatic Conference on the Reaffirmation and Development of International Humanitarian Law applicable in Armed Conflicts

entry into force 7 December 1979, in accordance with Article 95

PREAMBLE

A5–001   The High Contracting Parties,

Proclaiming their earnest wish to see peace prevail among peoples,

Recalling that every State has the duty, in conformity with the Charter of the United Nations, to refrain in its international relations from the threat or use of force against the sovereignty, territorial integrity or political independence of any State, or in any other manner inconsistent with the purposes of the United Nations.

Believing it necessary nevertheless to reaffirm and develop the provisions protecting the victims of armed conflicts and to supplement measures intended to reinforce their application,

Expressing their conviction that nothing in this Protocol or in the Geneva Conventions of 12 August 1949 can be construed as legitimizing or authorizing any act of aggression or any other use of force inconsistent with the Charter of the United Nations,

Reaffirming further that the provisions of the Geneva Conventions of 12 August 1949 and of this Protocol must be fully applied in all circumstances to all persons who are protected by those instruments, without any adverse distinction based on the nature or origin of the armed conflict or on the causes espoused by or attributed to the Parties to the conflicts,

Have agreed on the following:

PART I

GENERAL PROVISIONS

ARTICLE 1.—GENERAL PRINCIPLES AND SCOPE OF APPLICATION

A5–002   1. The High Contracting Parties undertake to respect and to ensure respect for this Protocol in all circumstances.

2. In cases not covered by this Protocol or by other international agreements, civilians and combatants remain under the protection and authority of the principles of international law derived from established custom, from the principles of humanity and from the dictates of public conscience.

3. This Protocol, which supplements the Geneva Conventions of 12 August 1949 for the protection of war victims, shall apply in the situations referred to in Article 2 common to those Conventions.

4. The situations referred to in the preceding paragraph include armed conflicts in which peoples are fighting against colonial domination and alien occupation and against racist regimes in the exercise of their right of self-determination, as enshrined in the Charter of the United Nations and the Declaration on Principles of International Law concerning Friendly Relations and Co-operation among States in accordance with the Charter of the United Nations.

ARTICLE 2.—DEFINITIONS

For the purposes of this Protocol: **A5–003**

(a) "First Convention", "Second Convention", "Third Convention" and "Fourth Convention" mean, respectively, the Geneva Convention for the Amelioration of the Condition of the Wounded and Sick in Armed Forces in the Field of 12 August 1949; the Geneva Convention for the Amelioration of the Condition of Wounded, Sick and Shipwrecked Members of Armed Forces at Sea of 12 August 1949; the Geneva Convention relative to the Treatment of Prisoners of War of 12 August 1949; the Geneva Convention relative to the Protection of Civilian Persons in Time of War of 12 August 1949; "the Conventions" means the four Geneva Conventions of 12 August 1949; for the protection of war victims;

(b) "Rules of international law applicable in armed conflict" means the rules applicable in armed conflict set forth in international agreements to which the Parties to the conflict are Parties and the generally recognized principles and rules of international law which are applicable to armed conflict;

(c) "Protecting Power" means a neutral or other State not a Party to the conflict which has been designated by a Party to the conflict and accepted by the adverse Party and has agreed to carry out the functions assigned to a Protecting Power under the Conventions and this Protocol;

(d) "Substitute" means an organization acting in place of a Protecting Power in accordance with Article 5.

ARTICLE 3.—BEGINNING AND END OF APPLICATION

Without prejudice to the provisions which are applicable at all times: **A5–004**

(a) The Conventions and this Protocol shall apply from the beginning of any situation referred to in Article 1 of this Protocol;

(b) The application of the Conventions and of this Protocol shall cease, in the territory of Parties to the conflict, on the general close of military operations and, in the case of occupied territories, on the termination of the occupation, except, in either circumstance, for those persons whose final release, repatriation or re-establishment takes place thereafter. These persons shall continue to benefit from the relevant provisions of the Conventions and of this Protocol until their final release, repatriation or re-establishment.

ARTICLE 4.—LEGAL STATUS OF THE PARTIES TO THE CONFLICT

The application of the Conventions and of this Protocol, as well as the conclusion of   **A5–005**
the agreements provided for therein, shall not affect the legal status of the Parties to the conflict. Neither the occupation of a territory nor the application of the Conventions and this Protocol shall affect the legal status of the territory in question.

ARTICLE 5.—APPOINTMENT OF PROTECTING POWERS AND OF THEIR SUBSTITUTE

1. It is the duty of the Parties to a conflict from the beginning of that conflict to   **A5–006**
secure the supervision and implementation of the Conventions and of this Protocol by the application of the system of Protecting Powers, including inter alia the designation and acceptance of those Powers, in accordance with the following paragraphs. Protecting Powers shall have the duty of safeguarding the interests of the Parties to the conflict.

2. From the beginning of a situation referred to in Article each Party to the conflict shall without delay designate a Protecting Power for the purpose of applying the Conventions and this Protocol and shall, likewise without delay and for the same purpose, permit the activities of a Protecting Power which has been accepted by it as such after designation by the adverse Party.

3. If a Protecting Power has not been designated or accepted from the beginning of a situation referred to in Article 1, the International Committee of the Red Cross, without prejudice to the right of any other impartial humanitarian organization to do likewise, shall offer its good offices to the Parties to the conflict with a view to the designation without delay of a Protecting Power to which the Parties to the conflict consent. For that purpose it may, inter alia, ask each Party to provide it with a list of at least five States which that Party considers acceptable to act as Protecting Power on its behalf in relation to an adverse Party, and ask each adverse Party to provide a list of at least five States which it would accept as the Protecting Power of the first Party; these lists shall be communicated to the Committee within two weeks after the receipt of the request; it shall compare them and seek the agreement of any proposed State named on both lists.

4. If, despite the foregoing, there is no Protecting Power, the Parties to the conflict shall accept without delay an offer which may be made by the International Committee of the Red Cross or by any other organization which offers all guarantees of impartiality and efficacy, after due consultations with the said Parties and taking into account the result of these consultations, to act as a substitute. The functioning of such a substitute is subject to the consent of the Parties to the conflict; every effort shall be made by the Parties to the conflict to facilitate the operations of the substitute in the performance of its tasks under the Conventions and this Protocol.

5. In accordance with Article 4, the designation and acceptance of Protecting Powers for the purpose of applying the Conventions and this Protocol shall not affect the legal status of the Parties to the conflict or of any territory, including occupied territory.

6. The maintenance of diplomatic relations between Parties to the conflict or the entrusting of the protection of a Party's interests and those of its nationals to a third State in accordance with the rules of international law relating to diplomatic relations is no obstacle to the designation of Protecting Powers for the purpose of applying the Conventions and this Protocol.

7. Any subsequent mention in this Protocol of a Protecting Power includes also a substitute.

ARTICLE 6.—QUALIFIED PERSONS

A5–007　　1. The High Contracting Parties shall, also in peacetime, endeavour, with the assistance of the national Red Cross (Red Crescent, Red Lion and Sun) Societies, to train qualified personnel to facilitate the application of the Conventions and of this Protocol, and in particular the activities of the Protecting Powers.

2. The recruitment and training of such personnel are within domestic jurisdiction.

3. The International Committee of the Red Cross shall hold at the disposal of the High Contracting Parties the lists of persons so trained which the High Contracting Parties may have established and may have transmitted to it for that purpose.

4. The conditions governing the employment of such personnel outside the national territory shall, in each case, be the subject of special agreements between the Parties concerned.

ARTICLE 7.—MEETINGS

A5–008　　The depositary of this Protocol shall convene a meeting of the High Contracting Parties, at the request of one or more of the said Parties and upon the approval of the majority of the said Parties, to consider general problems concerning the application of the Conventions and of the Protocol.

PART II

WOUNDED, SICK AND SHIPWRECKED

Section I.—General Protection

ARTICLE 8.—TERMINOLOGY

A5–009　　For the purposes of this Protocol:

(a) "Wounded" and "sick" mean persons, whether military or civilian, who, because of trauma, disease or other physical or mental disorder or disability, are in need of medical assistance or care and who refrain from any act of hostility. These terms also cover maternity cases, new-born babies and other persons who may be in need of immediate medical assistance or care, such as the infirm or expectant mothers, and who refrain from any act of hostility;

(b) "Shipwrecked" means persons, whether military or civilian, who are in peril at sea or in other waters as a result of misfortune affecting them or the vessel or aircraft carrying them and who refrain from any act of hostility. These persons, provided that they continue to refrain from any act of hostility, shall continue to be considered shipwrecked during their rescue until they acquire another status under the Conventions or this Protocol;

(c) "Medical personnel" means those persons assigned, by a Party to the conflict, exclusively to the medical purposes enumerated under subparagraph (e) or to the administration of medical units or to the operation or administration of medical transports. Such assignments may be either permanent or temporary. The term includes:

   (i) Medical personnel of a Party to the conflict, whether military or civilian, including those described in the First and Second Conventions, and those assigned to civil defence organizations;

  (ii) Medical personnel of national Red Cross (Red Crescent, Red Lion and Sun) Societies and other national voluntary aid societies duly recognized and authorized by a Party to the conflict;

 (iii) Medical personnel of medical units or medical transports described in Article 9, paragraph 2;

(d) "Religious personnel" means military or civilian persons, such as chaplains, who are exclusively engaged in the work of their ministry and attached:

   (i) To the armed forces of a Party to the conflict;

  (ii) To medical units or medical transports of a Party to the conflict;

 (iii) To medical units or medical transports described in Article 9, paragraph 2; or

 (iv) To civil defence organizations of a Party to the conflict.

The attachment of religious personnel may be either permanent or temporary, and the relevant provisions mentioned under sub-paragraph (k) apply to them;

(e) "Medical units" means establishments and other units, whether military or civilian, organized for medical purposes, namely the search for, collection, transportation, diagnosis or treatment-including first-aid treatment-of the wounded, sick and shipwrecked, or for the prevention of disease. The term includes, for example, hospitals and other similar units, blood transfusion centres, preventive medicine centres and institutes, medical depots and the medical and pharmaceutical stores of such units. Medical units may be fixed or mobile, permanent or temporary;

(g) 'Medical transportation" means the conveyance by land, water or air of the wounded, sick, shipwrecked, medical personnel, religious personnel, medical equipment or medical supplies protected by the Conventions and by this Protocol;

(g) "Medical transports" means any means of transportation. whether military or civilian, permanent or temporary, as signed exclusively to medical transportation and under the control of a competent authority of a Party to the conflict;

(h) "Medical vehicles" means any medical transports by land;

(i) "Medical ships and craft" means any medical transports by water;

(j) "Medical aircraft" means any medical transports by air;

(k) "Permanent medical personnel", "permanent medical units" and "permanent medical transports" mean those assigned exclusively to medical purposes for an indeterminate period. "Temporary medical personnel", "temporary medical units" and "temporary medical transports" mean those devoted exclusively to medical purposes for limited periods during the whole of such periods. Unless otherwise specified, the terms "medical personnel", " medical units" and "medical transports" cover both permanent and temporary categories;

(l) "Distinctive emblem" means the distinctive emblem of the red cross, red crescent or red lion and sun on a white ground when used for the protection of medical units and transports, or medical and religious personnel, equipment or supplies;

(m) "Distinctive signal" means any signal or message specified for the identification exclusively of medical units or transports in Chapter III of Annex I to this Protocol.

ARTICLE 9.—FIELD OF APPLICATION

A5–010   1. This Part, the provisions of which are intended to ameliorate the condition of the wounded, sick and shipwrecked, shall apply to all those affected by a situation referred to in Article 1, without any adverse distinction founded on race, colour, sex, language, religion or belief, political or other opinion, national or social origin, wealth, birth or other status, or on any other similar criteria.

2. The relevant provisions of Articles 27 and 32 of the First Convention shall apply to permanent medical units and transports (other than hospital ships, to which Article 25 of the Second Convention applies) and their personnel made available to a Party to the conflict for humanitarian purposes:

(a) By a neutral or other State which is not a Party to that conflict;

(b) By a recognized and authorized aid society of such a State;

(c) By an impartial international humanitarian organization.

ARTICLE 10.—PROTECTION AND CARE

A5–011   1. All the wounded, sick and shipwrecked, to whichever Party they belong, shall be respected and protected.

2. In all circumstances they shall be treated humanely and shall receive, to the fullest extent practicable and with the least possible delay, the medical care and attention required by their condition. There shall be no distinction among them founded on any grounds other than medical ones.

ARTICLE 11.—PROTECTION OF PERSONS

A5–012   1. The physical or mental health and integrity of persons who are in the power of the adverse Party or who are interned, detained or otherwise deprived of liberty as a result of a situation referred to in Article I shall not be endangered by any unjustified act or omission. Accordingly, it is prohibited to subject the persons described in this Article to any medical procedure which is not indicated by the state of health of the person concerned and which is not consistent with generally accepted medical standards which would be applied under similar medical circumstances to persons who are nationals of the Party conducting the procedure and who are in no way deprived of liberty.

2. It is, in particular, prohibited to carry out on such persons, even with their consent:

(a) Physical mutilations;

(b) Medical or scientific experiments;

(c) Removal of tissue or organs for transplantation, except where these acts are justified in conformity with the conditions provided for in paragraph 1.

3. Exceptions to the prohibition in paragraph 2 (c) may be made only in the case of donations of blood for transfusion or of skin for grafting, provided that they are given voluntarily and without any coercion or inducement, and then only for therapeutic purposes, under conditions consistent with generally accepted medical standards and controls designed for the benefit of both the donor and the recipient.

4. Any wilful act or omission which seriously endangers the physical or mental health or integrity of any person who is in the power of a Party other than the one on which he depends and which either violates any of the prohibitions in paragraphs 1 and 2 or fails to comply with the requirements of paragraph 3 shall be a grave breach of this Protocol.

5. The persons described in paragraph I have the right to refuse any surgical operation. In case of refusal, medical personnel shall endeavour to obtain a written statement to that effect, signed or acknowledged by the patient.

6. Each Party to the conflict shall keep a medical record for every donation of blood for transfusion or skin for grafting by persons referred to in paragraph 1, if that donation is made under the responsibility of that Party. In addition, each Party to the conflict shall endeavour to keep a record of all medical procedures undertaken with respect to any person who is interned, detained or otherwise deprived of liberty as a result of a situation referred to in Article 1. These records shall be available at all times for inspection by the Protecting Power.

ARTICLE 12.—PROTECTION OF MEDICAL UNITS

1. Medical units shall be respected and protected at all times and shall not be the object of attack. **A5–013**

2. Paragraph I shall apply to civilian medical units, provided that they:
   (a) Belong to one of the Parties to the conflict;
   (b) Are recognized and authorized by the competent authority of one of the Parties to the conflict; or
   (c) Are authorized in conformity with Article 9, paragraph 2, of this Protocol or Article 27 of the First Convention.

3. The Parties to the conflict are invited to notify each other of the location of their fixed medical units. The absence of such notification shall not exempt any of the Parties from the obligation to comply with the provisions of paragraph 1.

4. Under no circumstances shall medical units be used in an attempt to shield military objectives from attack. Whenever possible, the Parties to the conflict shall ensure that medical units are so sated that attacks against military objectives do not imperil their safety.

ARTICLE 13.—DISCONTINUANCE OF PROTECTION OF CIVILIAN MEDICAL UNITS

1. The protection to which civilian medical units are entitled shall not cease unless they are used to commit, outside their humanitarian function, acts harmful to the enemy. Protection may, however, cease only after a warning has been given setting, whenever appropriate, a reasonable time-limit, and after such warning has remained unheeded. **A5–014**

2. The following shall not be considered as acts harmful to the enemy;
   (a) That the personnel of the unit are equipped with light individual weapons for their own defence or for that of the wounded and sick in their charge;
   (b) That the unit is guarded by a picket or by sentries or by an escort;
   (c) That small arms and ammunition taken from the wounded and sick, and not yet handed to the proper service, are found in the units;
   (d) That members of the armed forces or other combatants are in the unit for medical reasons.

ARTICLE 14.—LIMITATIONS ON REQUISITION OF CIVILIAN MEDICAL UNITS

1. The Occupying Power has the duty to ensure that the medical needs of the civilian population in occupied territory continue to be satisfied. **A5–015**

2. The Occupying Power shall not, therefore, requisition civilian medical units, their equipment, their matériel or the services of their personnel, so long as these resources are necessary for the provision of adequate medical services for the civilian population and for the continuing medical care of any wounded and sick already under treatment.

3. Provided that the general rule in paragraph 2 continues to be observed, the Occupying Power may requisition the said resources, subject to the following particular conditions:

(a) That the resources are necessary for the adequate and immediate medical treatment of the wounded and sick members of the armed forces of the Occupying Power or of prisoners of war;

(b) That the requisition continues only while such necessity exists; and

(c) That immediate arrangements are made to ensure that the medical needs of the civilian population, as well as those of any wounded and sick under treatment who are affected by the requisition, continue to be satisfied.

ARTICLE 15.—PROTECTION OF CIVILIAN MEDICAL AND RELIGIOUS PERSONNEL

A5–016   1. Civilian medical personnel shall be respected and protected.

2. If needed, all available help shall be afforded to civilian medical personnel in an area where civilian medical services are disrupted by reason of combat activity.

3. The Occupying Power shall afford civilian medical personnel in occupied territories every assistance to enable them to perform, to the best of their ability, their humanitarian functions. The Occupying Power may not require that, in the performance of those functions, such personnel shall give priority to the treatment of any person except on medical grounds. They shall not be compelled to carry out tasks which are not compatible with their humanitarian mission.

4. Civilian medical personnel shall have access to any place where their services are essential, subject to such supervisory and safety measures as the relevant Party to the conflict may deem necessary.

5. Civilian religious personnel shall be respected and protected. The provisions of the Conventions and of this Protocol concerning the protection and identification of medical personnel shall apply equally to such persons.

ARTICLE 16.—GENERAL PROTECTION OF MEDICAL DUTIES

A5–017   1. Under no circumstances shall any person be punished for carrying out medical activities compatible with medical ethics, regardless of the person benefiting therefrom.

2. Persons engaged in medical activities shall not be compelled to perform acts or to carry out work contrary to the rules of medical ethics or to other medical rules designed for the benefit of the wounded and sick or to the provisions of the Conventions or of this Protocol, or to refrain from performing acts or from carrying out work required by those rules and provisions.

3. No person engaged in medical activities shall be compelled to give to anyone belonging either to an adverse Party, or to his own Party except as required by the law of the latter Party, any information concerning the wounded and sick who are, or who have been, under his care, if such information would, in his opinion, prove harmful to the patients concerned or to their families. Regulations for the compulsory notification of communicable diseases shall, however, be respected.

ARTICLE 17.—ROLE OF THE CIVILIAN POPULATION AND OF AID SOCIETIES

A5–018   1. The civilian population shall respect the wounded, sick and shipwrecked, even if they belong to the adverse Party, and shall commit no act of violence against them. The civilian population and aid societies, such as national Red Cross (Red Crescent, Red Lion and Sun) Societies, shall be permitted, even on their own initiative, to collect and care for the wounded, sick and shipwrecked, even in invaded or occupied areas. No one shall be harmed, prosecuted, convicted or punished for such humanitarian acts.

2. The Parties to the conflict may appeal to the civilian population and the aid societies referred to in paragraph 1 to collect and care for the wounded, sick and shipwrecked, and to search for the dead and report their location; they shall grant both protection and the necessary facilities to those who respond to this appeal. If the adverse Party gains or regains control of the area, that Party also shall afford the same protection and facilities for so long as they are needed.

Article 18.—Identification

1. Each Party to the conflict shall endeavour to ensure that medical and religious **A5–019**
personnel and medical units and transports are identifiable.

2. Each Party to the conflict shall also endeavour to adopt and to implement methods
and procedures which will make it possible to recognize medical units and transports
which use the distinctive emblem and distinctive signals.

3. In occupied territory and in areas where fighting is taking place or is likely to take
place, civilian medical personnel and civilian religious personnel should be recognizable
by the distinctive emblem and an identity card certifying their status.

4. With the consent of the competent authority, medical units and transports shall be
marked by the distinctive emblem. The ships and craft referred to in Article 22 of this
Protocol shall be marked in accordance with the provisions of the Second Convention.

5. In addition to the distinctive emblem, a Party to the conflict may, as provided in
Chapter III of Annex I to this Protocol, authorize the use of distinctive signals to identify
medical units and transports. Exceptionally, in the special cases covered in that Chapter,
medical transports may use distinctive signals without displaying the distinctive emblem.

6. The application of the provisions of paragraphs 1 to 5 of this Article is governed by
Chapters I to m of Annex I to this Protocol. Signals designated in Chapter m of the
Annex for the exclusive use of medical units and transports shall not, except as provided
therein, be used for any purpose other than to identify the medical units and transports
specified in that Chapter.

7. This Article does not authorize any wider use of the distinctive emblem in
peacetime than is prescribed in Article 44 of the First Convention.

8. The provisions of the Conventions and of this Protocol relating to supervision of the
use of the distinctive emblem and to the prevention and repression of any misuse thereof
shall be applicable to distinctive signals.

Article 19.—Neutral and other States not Parties to the conflict

Neutral and other States not Parties to the conflict shall apply the relevant provisions **A5–020**
of this Protocol to persons protected by this Part who may be received or interned within
their territory, and to any dead of the Parties to that conflict whom they may find.

Article 20.—Prohibition of reprisals

Reprisals against the persons and objects protected by this Part are prohibited. **A5–021**

Section II.—Medical Transportation

Article 21.—Medical vehicles

Medical vehicles shall be respected and protected in the same way as mobile medical **A5–022**
units under the Conventions and this Protocol.

Article 22.—Hospitals ships and coastal rescue craft

1. The provisions of the Conventions relating to: **A5–023**
   (a) Vessels described in Articles 22, 24, 25 and 27 of the Second Convention,
   (b) Their lifeboats and small craft,
   (c) Their personnel and crews; and
   (d) The wounded, sick and shipwrecked on board, shall also apply where these
       vessels carry civilian wounded, sick and shipwrecked who do not belong to any of
       the categories mentioned in Article 13 of the Second Convention. Such civilians

shall not, however, be subject to surrender to any Party which is not their own, or to capture at sea. If they find themselves in the power of a Party to the conflict other than their own they shall be covered by the Fourth Convention and by this Protocol.

2. The protection provided by the Conventions to vessels described in Article 25 of the Second Convention shall extend to hospital ships made available for humanitarian purposes to a Party to the conflict:

    (a) By a neutral or other State which is not a Party to that conflict; or

    (b) By an impartial international humanitarian organization, provided that, in either case, the requirements set out in that Article are complied with.

3. Small craft described in Article 27 of the Second Convention shall be protected even if the notification envisaged by that Article has not been made. The Parties to the conflict are, nevertheless, invited to inform each other of any details of such craft which will facilitate their identification and recognition.

ARTICLE 23.—OTHER MEDICAL SHIPS AND CRAFT

A5–024

1. Medical ships and craft other than those referred to in Article 22 of this Protocol and Article 38 of the Second Convention shall, whether at sea or in other waters, be respected and protected in the same way as mobile medical units under the Conventions and this Protocol. Since this protection can only be effective if they can be identified and recognized as medical ships or craft, such vessels should be marked with the distinctive emblem and as far as possible comply with the second paragraph of Article 43 of the Second Convention.

2. The ships and craft referred to in paragraph I shall remain subject to the laws of war. Any warship on the surface able immediately to enforce its command may order them to stop, order them off, or make them take a certain course, and they shall obey every such command. Such ships and craft may not in any other way be diverted from their medical mission so long as they are needed for the wounded, sick and shipwrecked on board.

3. The protection provided in paragraph I shall cease only under the conditions set out in Articles 34 and 35 of the Second Convention. A clear refusal to obey a command given in accordance with paragraph 2 shall be an act harmful to the enemy under Article 34 of the Second Convention.

4. A Party to the conflict may notify any adverse Party as far in advance of sailing as possible of the name, description, expected time of sailing, course and estimated speed of the medical ship or craft, particularly in the case of ships of over 2,000 gross tons, and may provide any other information which would facilitate identification and recognition. The adverse Party shall acknowledge receipt of such information.

5. The provisions of Article 37 of the Second Convention shall apply to medical and religious personnel in such ships and craft.

6. The provisions of the Second Convention shall apply to the wounded, sick and shipwrecked belonging to the categories referred to in Article 13 of the Second Convention and in Article 44 of this Protocol who may be on board such medical ships and craft. Wounded, sick and shipwrecked civilians who do not belong to any of the categories mentioned in Article 13 of the Second Convention shall not be subject, at sea, either to surrender to any Party which is not their own; or to removal from such ships or craft; if they find themselves in the power of a Party to the conflict other than their own, they shall be covered by the Fourth Convention and by this Protocol.

ARTICLE 24.—PROTECTION OF MEDICAL AIRCRAFT

A5–025   Medical aircraft shall be respected and protected, subject to the provisions of this Part.

ARTICLE 25.—MEDICAL AIRCRAFT IN AREAS NOT CONTROLLED BY AN ADVERSE PARTY

A5–026   In and over land areas physically controlled by friendly forces, or in and over sea areas not physically controlled by an adverse Party, the respect and protection of medical aircraft of a Party to the conflict is not dependent on any agreement with an adverse

Party. For greater safety, however, a Party to the conflict operating its medical aircraft in these areas may notify the adverse Party, as provided in Article 29, in particular when such aircraft are making flights bringing them within range of surface-to-air weapons systems of the adverse Party.

ARTICLE 26.—MEDICAL AIRCRAFT IN CONTACT OR SIMILAR ZONES

1. In and over those parts of the contact zone which are physically controlled by **A5–027** friendly forces and in and over those areas the physical control of which is not clearly established, protection for medical aircraft can be fully effective only by prior agreement between the competent military authorities of the Parties to the conflict, as provided for in Article 29. Although, in the absence of such an agreement, medical aircraft operate at their own risk, they shall nevertheless be respected after they have been recognized as such.

2. "Contact zone" means any area on land where the forward elements of opposing forces are in contact with each other, especially where they are exposed to direct fire from the ground.

ARTICLE 27.—MEDICAL AIRCRAFT IN AREAS CONTROLLED BY AN ADVERSE PARTY

1. The medical aircraft of a Party to the conflict shall continue to be protected while **A5–028** flying over land or sea areas physically controlled by an adverse Patty, provided that prior agreement to such flights has been obtained from the competent authority of the adverse Party.

2. A medical aircraft which flies over an area physically controlled by an adverse Party without, or in deviation from the terms of, an agreement provided for in paragraph 1, either through navigational error or because of an emergency affecting the safety of the flight, shall make every effort to identify itself and to inform the adverse Party of the circumstances. As soon as such medical aircraft has been recognized by the adverse Party, that Party shall make all reasonable efforts to given the order to land or to alight on water, referred to in Article 30, paragraph 1, or to take other measures to safeguard its own interests, and, in either case, to allow the aircraft time for compliance, before resorting to an attack against the aircraft.

ARTICLE 28.—RESTRICTIONS ON OPERATIONS OF MEDICAL AIRCRAFT

1. The Parties to the conflict are prohibited from using their medical aircraft to **A5–029** attempt to acquire any military advantage over an adverse Party. The presence of medical aircraft shall not be used in an attempt to render military objectives immune from attack.

2. Medical aircraft shall not be used to collect or transmit intelligence data and shall not carry any equipment intended for such purposes. They are prohibited from carrying any persons or cargo not included within the definition in Article 8, subparagraph (t). The carrying on board of the personal effects of the occupants or of equipment intended solely to facilitate navigation, communication or identification shall not be considered as prohibited.

3. Medical aircraft shall not carry any armament except small arms and ammunition taken from the wounded, sick and shipwrecked on board and not yet handed to the proper service, and such light individual weapons as may be necessary to enable the medical personnel on board to defend themselves and the wounded, sick and shipwrecked in their charge.

4. While carrying out the flights referred to in Articles 26 and 27, medical aircraft shall not, except by prior agreement with the adverse Party, be used to search for the wounded, sick and shipwrecked

ARTICLE 29.—NOTIFICATIONS AND AGREEMENTS CONCERNING MEDICAL AIRCRAFT

A5–030 1. Notifications under Article 25, or requests for prior agreement under Articles 26, 27, 28 (paragraph 4), or 31 shall state the proposed number of medical aircraft, their flight plans and means of identification, and shall be understood to mean that every flight will be carried out in compliance with Article 28.

2. A Party which receives a notification given under Article 25 shall at once acknowledge receipt of such notification.

3. A Party which receives a request for prior agreement under Articles 26, 27, 28 (paragraph 4), or 31 shall, as rapidly as possible, notify the requesting Party:

(a) That the request is agreed to;

(b) That the request is denied; or

(c) Of reasonable alternative proposals to the request. It may also propose a prohibition or restriction of other flights in the area during the time involved. If the Party which submitted the request accepts the alternative proposals, it shall notify the other Party of such acceptance.

4. The Parties shall take the necessary measures to ensure that notifications and agreements can be made rapidly.

5. The Parties shall also take the necessary measures to disseminate rapidly the substance of any such notifications and agreements to the military units concerned and shall instruct those units regarding the means of identification that will be used by the medical aircraft in question.

ARTICLE 30.—LANDING AND INSPECTION OF MEDICAL AIRCRAFT

A5–031 1. Medical aircraft flying over areas which are physically controlled by an adverse Party, or over areas the physical control of which is not clearly established, may be ordered to land or to alight on water, as appropriate, to permit inspection in accordance with the following paragraphs. Medical aircraft shall obey any such order.

2. If such an aircraft lands or alights on water, whether ordered to do so or for other reasons, it may be subjected to inspection solely to determine the matters referred to in paragraphs 3 and 4. Any such inspection shall be commenced without delay and shall be conducted expeditiously. The inspecting Party shall not require the wounded and sick to be removed from the aircraft unless their removal is essential for the inspection. That Party shall in any event ensure that the condition of the wounded and sick is not adversely affected by the inspection or by the removal.

3. If the inspection discloses that the aircraft:

(a) Is a medical aircraft within the meaning of Article 8, subparagraph (i);

(b) Is not in violation of the conditions prescribed in Article 28; and

(c) Has not flown without or in breach of a prior agreement where such agreement is required; the aircraft and those of its occupants who belong to the adverse Party or to a neutral or other State not a Party to the conflict shall be authorized to continue the flight without delay.

4. If the inspection discloses that the aircraft:

(a) Is not a medical aircraft within the meaning of Article 8, subparagraph (j);

(b) Is in violation of the conditions prescribed in Article 28; or,

(c) Has flown without or in breach of a prior agreement where such agreement is required; the aircraft may be seized. Its occupants shall be treated in conformity with the relevant provisions of the Conventions and of this Protocol. Any aircraft seized which had been assigned as a permanent medical aircraft may be used thereafter only as a medical aircraft.

ARTICLE 31.—NEUTRAL OR OTHER STATES NOT PARTIES TO THE CONFLICT

A5–032 1. Except by prior agreement, medical aircraft shall not fly over or land in the territory of a neutral or other State not a Party to the conflict. However, with such an agreement, they shall be respected throughout their flight and also for the duration of any calls in the territory. Nevertheless they shall obey any summons to land or to alight on water, as appropriate.

2. Should a medical aircraft, in the absence of an agreement or in deviation from the terms of an agreement, fly over the territory of a neutral or other State not a Party to the conflict, either through navigational error or because of an emergency affecting the safety o the flight, it shall make every effort to give notice of the flight and to identify itself. As soon as such medical aircraft is recognized, that State shall make all reasonable efforts to give the order to land or to alight on water referred to in Article 30, paragraph 1, or to take other measures to safeguard its own interests, and in either case, to allow the aircraft time for compliance, before resorting to an attack against the aircraft.

3. If a medical aircraft, either by agreement or in the circumstances mentioned in paragraph 2, lands or alights on water in the territory of a neutral or other State not Party to the conflict, whether ordered to do so or for other reasons, the aircraft shall be subject to inspection for the purposes of determining whether it is in fact a medical aircraft. The inspection shall be commenced without delay and shall be conducted expeditiously. The inspecting Party shall not require the wounded and sick of the Party operating the aircraft to be removed from it unless their removal is essential for the inspection. The inspecting Party shall in any event ensure that the condition of the wounded and sick is not adversely affected by the inspection or the removal. If the inspection discloses that the aircraft is in fact a medical aircraft, the aircraft with its occupants, other than those who must be detained in accordance with the rules of international law applicable in armed conflict, shall be allowed to resume its flight, and reasonable facilities shall be given for the continuation of the flight. If the inspection discloses that the aircraft is not a medical aircraft, it shall be seized and the occupants treated in accordance with paragraph 4.

4. The wounded, sick and shipwrecked disembarked, otherwise than temporarily, from a medical aircraft with the consent of the local authorities in the territory of a neutral or other State not a Party to the conflict shall, unless agreed otherwise between that State and the Parties to the conflict, be detained by that Sate where so required by the rules of international law applicable in armed conflict, in such a manner that they cannot again take part in the hostilities. The cost of hospital treatment and internment shall be borne by the State to which those persons belong.

5. Neutral or other States not Parties to the conflict shall apply any conditions and restrictions on the passage of medical aircraft over, or on the landing of medical aircraft in, their territory equally to all Parties to the conflict.

Section.—Missing and Dead Persons

ARTICLE 32.—GENERAL PRINCIPLE

In the implementation of this Section, the activities of the High Contracting Parties, of the Parties to the conflict and of the international humanitarian organizations mentioned in the Conventions and in this Protocol shall be prompted mainly by the right of families to know the fate of their relatives.

A5–033

ARTICLE 33.—MISSING PERSONS

1. As soon as circumstances permit, and at the latest from the end of active hostilities, each Party to the conflict shall search for the persons who have been reported missing by an adverse Party. Such adverse Party shall transmit all relevant information concerning such persons in order to facilitate such searches.

A5–034

2. In order to facilitate the gathering of information pursuant to the preceding paragraph, each Party to the conflict shall, with respect to persons who would not receive more favourable consideration under the Conventions and this Protocol:

    (a) Record the information specified in Article 138 of the Fourth Convention in respect of such persons who have been detained, imprisoned or otherwise held in captivity for more than two weeks as a result of hostilities or occupation, or who have died during any period of detention;

(b) To the fullest extent possible, facilitate and, if need be, carry out the search for and the recording of information concerning such persons if they have died in other circumstances as a result of hostilities or occupation.

3. Information concerning persons reported missing pursuant to paragraph I and requests for such information shall be transmitted either directly or through the Protecting Power or the Central Tracing Agency of the International Committee of the Red Cross or national Red Cross (Red Crescent, Red Lion and Sun) Societies. Where the information is not transmitted through the International Committee of the Red Cross and its Central Tracing Agency, each Party to the conflict shall ensure that such information is also supplied to the Central Tracing Agency.

4. The Parties to the conflict shall endeavour to agree on arrangements for teams to search for, identify and recover the dead from battlefield areas, including arrangements, if appropriate, for such teams to be accompanied by personnel of the adverse Party while carrying out the missions in areas controlled by the adverse Party. Personnel of such teams shall be respected and protected while exclusively carrying out these duties.

ARTICLE 34.—REMAINS OF DECEASED

A5–035

1. The remains of persons who have died for reasons related to occupation or in detention resulting from occupation or hostilities and those of persons not nationals of the country in which they have died as a result of hostilities shall be respected, and the gravesites of all such persons shall be respected, maintained and marked as provided for in Article 130 of the Fourth Convention, where their remains or gravesites would not receive more favourable consideration under the Conventions and this Protocol.

2. As soon as circumstances and the relations between the adverse Parties permit, the High Contracting Parties in whose territories graves and, as the case may be, other locations of the remains of persons who have died as a result of hostilities or during occupation or in detention are situated, shall conclude agreements in order:

(a) To facilitate access to the gravesites by relatives of the deceased and by representatives of official graves registration services and to regulate the practical arrangements for such access;

(b) To protect and maintain such gravesites permanently;

(c) To facilitate the return of the remains of the deceased and of personal effects to the home country upon its request or, unless that country objects, upon the request of the next of kin.

3. In the absence of the agreements provided for in paragraph 2 (b) or (c) and if the home country of such deceased is not willing to arrange at its expense for the maintenance of such gravesites, the High Contracting Party in whose territory the gravesites are situated may offer to facilitate the return of the remains of the deceased to the home country. Where such an offer has not been accepted the High Contracting Party may, after the expiry of five years from the date of the offer and upon due notice to the home country, adopt the arrangements laid down in its own laws relating to cemeteries and graves.

4. A High Contracting Party in whose territory the gravesites referred to in this Article are situated shall be permitted to exhume the remains only:

(a) In accordance with paragraphs 2 (c) and 3; or

(b) Where exhumation is a matter of overriding public necessity, including cases of medical and investigative necessity, in which case the High Contracting Party shall at all times respect the remains, and shall give notice to the home country of its intention to exhume the remains together with details of the intended place of reinterment.

PART III

METHODS AND MEANS OF WARFARE

COMBATANT AND PRISONER-OF-WAR STATUS

Section I.—Methods and Means of Warfare

ARTICLE 35.—BASIC RULES

1. In any armed conflict, the right of the Parties to the conflict to choose methods or means of warfare is not unlimited. **A5–036**

2. It is prohibited to employ weapons, projectiles and material and methods of warfare of a nature to cause superfluous injury or unnecessary suffering.

3. It is prohibited to employ methods or means of warfare which are intended, or may be expected, to cause widespread, long-term and severe damage to the natural environment.

ARTICLE 36.—NEW WEAPONS

In the study, development, acquisition or adoption of a new weapon, means or method of warfare, a High Contracting Party is under an obligation to determine whether its employment would, in some or all circumstances, be prohibited by this Protocol or by any other rule of international law applicable to the High Contracting Party. **A5–037**

ARTICLE 37.—PROHIBITION OF PERFIDY

1. It is prohibited to kill, injure or capture an adversary by resort to perfidy. Acts inviting the confidence of an adversary to lead him to believe that he is entitled to, or is obliged to accord, protection under the rules of international law applicable in armed conflict, with intent to betray that confidence, shall constitute perfidy. The following acts are examples of perfidy: **A5–038**

   (a) The feigning of an intent to negotiate under a flag of truce or of a surrender;
   (b) The feigning of an incapacitation by wounds or sickness;
   (c) The feigning of civilian, non-combatant status; and
   (d) The feigning of protected status by the use of signs, emblems or uniforms of the United Nations or of neutral or other States not Parties to the conflict.

2. Ruses of war are not prohibited. Such ruses are acts which are intended to mislead an adversary or to induce him to act recklessly but which infringe no rule of international law applicable in armed conflict and which are not perfidious because they do not invite the confidence of an adversary with respect to protection under that law. The following are examples of such ruses: the use of camouflage, decoys, mock operations and misinformation.

ARTICLE 38.—RECOGNIZED EMBLEMS

1. It is prohibited to make improper use of the distinctive emblem of the red cross, red crescent or red lion and sun or of other emblems, signs or signals provided for by the Conventions or by this Protocol. It is also prohibited to misuse deliberately in an armed conflict other internationally recognized protective emblems, signs or signals, including the flag of truce, and the protective emblem of cultural property. **A5–039**

2. It is prohibited to make use of the distinctive emblem of the United Nations, except as authorized by that Organization.

ARTICLE 39.—EMBLEMS OF NATIONALITY

A5–040   1. It is prohibited to make use in an armed conflict of the flags or military emblems, insignia or uniforms of neutral or other States not Parties to the conflict.
2. It is prohibited to make use of the flags or military emblems, insignia or uniforms of adverse Parties while engaging in attacks or in order to shield, favour, protect or impede military operations.
3. Nothing in this Article or in Article 37, paragraph 1 (d), shall affect the existing generally recognized rules of international law applicable to espionage or to the use of flags in the conduct of armed conflict at sea.

ARTICLE 40.—QUARTER

A5–041   It is prohibited to order that there shall be no survivors, to threaten an adversary therewith or to conduct hostilities on this basis.

ARTICLE 41.—SAFEGUARD OF AN ENEMY HORS DE COMBAT

A5–042   1. A person who is recognized or who, in the circumstances, should be recognized to be hors de combat shall not be made the object of attack.
2. A person is hors de combat if:
(a) He is in the power of an adverse Party;
(b) He clearly expresses an intention to surrender; or
(c) He has been rendered unconscious or is otherwise incapacitated by wounds or sickness, and therefore is incapable of defending himself; provided that in any of these cases he abstains from any hostile act and does not attempt to escape.
3. When persons entitled to protection as prisons of war have fallen into the power of an adverse Party under unusual conditions of combat which prevent their evacuation as provided for in Part m, Section I, of the Third Convention, they shall be released and all feasible precautions shall be taken to ensure their safety.

ARTICLE 42.—OCCUPANTS OF AIRCRAFT

A5–043   1. No person parachuting from an aircraft in distress shall be made the object of attack during his descent.
2. Upon reaching the ground in territory controlled by an adverse Party, a person who has parachuted from an aircraft in distress shall be given an opportunity to surrender before being made the object of attack, unless it is apparent that he is engaging in a hostile act.
3. Airborne troops are not protected by this Article.

Section.—Combatant and Prisoner-of-War Status

ARTICLE 43.—ARMED FORCES

A5–044   1. The armed forces of a Party to a conflict consist of all organized armed forces, groups and units which are under a command responsible to that Party for the conduct of its subordinates, even if that Party is represented by a government or an authority not recognized by an adverse Party. Such armed forces shall be subject to an internal disciplinary system which, inter alia, shall enforce compliance with the rules of international law applicable in armed conflict.

2. Members of the armed forces of a Party to a conflict (other than medical personnel and chaplains covered by Article 33 of the Third Convention) are combatants, that is to say, they have the right to participate directly in hostilities.

3. Whenever a Party to a conflict incorporates a paramilitary or armed law enforcement agency into its armed forces it shall so notify the other Parties to the conflict.

Article 44.—Combatants and prisoners of war

1. Any combatant, as defined in Article 43, who falls into the power of an adverse Party shall be a prisoner of war.

A5–045

2. While all combatants are obliged to comply with the rules of international law applicable in armed conflict, violations of these rules shall not deprive a combatant of his right to be a combatant or, if he falls into the power of an adverse Party, of his right to be a prisoner of war, except as provided in paragraphs 3 and 4.

3. In order to promote the protection of the civilian population from the effects of hostilities, combatants are obliged to distinguish themselves from the civilian population while they are engaged in an attack or in a military operation preparatory to an attack. Recognizing, however, that there are situations in armed conflicts where, owing to the nature of the hostilities an armed combatant cannot so distinguish himself, he shall retain his status as a combatant, provided that, in such situations, he carries his arms openly:

(a) During each military engagement, and

(b) During such time as he is visible to the adversary while he is engaged in a military deployment preceding the launching of an attack in which he is to participate.

Acts which comply with the requirements of this paragraph shall not be considered as perfidious within the meaning of Article 37, paragraph 1 (c).

4. A combatant who falls into the power of an adverse Party while failing to meet the requirements set forth in the second sentence of paragraph 3 shall forfeit his right to be a prisoner of war, but he shall, nevertheless, be given protections equivalent in all respects to those accorded to prisoners of war by the Third Convention and by this Protocol. This protection includes protections equivalent to those accorded to prisoners of war by the Third Convention in the case where such a person is tried and punished for any offences he has committed.

5. Any combatant who falls into the power of an adverse Party while not engaged in an attack or in a military operation preparatory to an attack shall not forfeit his rights to be a combatant and a prisoner of war by virtue of his prior activities.

6. This Article is without prejudice to the right of any person to be a prisoner of war pursuant to Article 4 of the Third Convention.

7. This Article is not intended to change the generally accepted practice of States with respect to the wearing of the uniform by combatants assigned to the regular, uniformed armed units of a Party to the conflict.

8. In addition to the categories of persons mentioned in Article 13 of the First and Second Conventions, all members of the armed forces of a Party to the conflict, as defined in Article 43 of this Protocol, shall be entitled to protection under those Conventions if they are wounded or sick or, in the case of the Second Convention, shipwrecked at sea or in other waters.

Article 45.—Protection of persons who have taken part in hostilities

1. A person who takes part in hostilities and falls into the power of an adverse Party shall be presumed to be a prisoner of war, and therefore shall be protected by the Third Convention, if he claims the status of prisoner of war, or if he appears to be entitled to such status, or if the Party on which he depends claims such status on his behalf by notification to the detaining Power or to the Protecting Power. Should any doubt arise as

A5–046

to whether any such person is entitled to the status of prisoner of war, he shall continue to have such status and, therefore, to be protected by the Third Convention and this Protocol until such time as his status has been determined by a competent tribunal.

2. If a person who has fallen into the power of an adverse Party is not held as a prisoner of war and is to be tried by that Party for an offence arising out of the hostilities, he shall have the right to assert his entitlement to prisoner-of-war status before a judicial tribunal and to have that question adjudicated. Whenever possible under the applicable procedure, this adjudication shall occur before the trial for the offence. The representatives of the Protecting Power shall be entitled to attend the proceedings in which that question is adjudicated, unless, exceptionally, the proceedings are held in camera in the interest of State security. In such a case the detaining Power shall advise the Protecting Power accordingly.

3. Any person who has taken part in hostilities, who is not entitled to prisoner-of-war status and who does not benefit from more favourable treatment in accordance with the Fourth Convention shall have the right at all times to the protection of Article 75 of this Protocol. In occupied territory, an such person, unless he is held as a spy, shall also be entitled, notwithstanding Article 5 of the Fourth Convention, to his rights of communication under that Convention.

ARTICLE 46.—SPIES

A5–047   1. Notwithstanding any other provision of the Conventions or of this Protocol, any member of the armed forces of a Party to the conflict who falls into the power of an adverse Party while engaging in espionage shall not have the right to the status of prisoner of war and may be treated as a spy.

2. A member of the armed forces of a Party to the conflict who, on behalf of that Party and in territory controlled by an adverse Party, gathers or attempts to gather information shall not be considered as engaging in espionage if, while so acting, he is in the uniform of his armed forces.

3. A member of the armed forces of a Party to the conflict who is a resident of territory occupied by an adverse Party and who, on behalf of the Party on which he depends, gathers or attempts to gather information of military value within that territory shall not be considered as engaging in espionage unless he does so through an act of false pretences or deliberately in a clandestine manner. Moreover, such a resident shall not lose his right to the status of prisoner of war and may not be treated as a spy unless he is captured while engaging in espionage.

4. A member of the armed forces of a Patty to the conflict who is not a resident of territory occupied by an adverse Party and who has engaged in espionage in that territory shall not lose his right to the status of prisoner of war and may not be treated as a spy unless he is captured before he has rejoined the armed forces to which he belongs.

ARTICLE 47.—MERCENARIES

A5–048   1. A mercenary shall not have the right to be a combatant or a prisoner of war.

2. A mercenary is any person who:
    (a) Is specially recruited locally or abroad in order to fight in an armed conflict;
    (b) Does, in fact, take a direct part in the hostilities;
    (c) Is motivated to take part in the hostilities essentially by the desire for private gain and, in fact, is promised, by or on behalf of a Party to the conflict, material compensation substantially in excess of that promised or paid to combatants of similar ranks and functions in the armed forces of that Party;
    (d) Is neither a national of a Party to the conflict nor a resident of territory controlled by a Party to the conflict;
    (e) Is not a member of the armed forces of a Party to the conflict; and
    (f) Has not been sent by a State which is not a Party to the conflict on official duty as a member of its armed forces.

Part IV

CIVILIAN POPULATION

Section I.—General Protection against Effects of Hostilities

Chapter 1.—Basic Rule and Field of Application

Article 48.—Basic rule

In order to ensure respect for and protection of the civilian population and civilian **A5–049** objects, the Parties to the conflict shall at all times distinguish between the civilian population and combatants and between civilian objects and military objectives and accordingly shall direct their operations only against military objectives.

Article 49.—Definition of attacks and scope of application

1. "Attacks" means acts of violence against the adversary, whether in offence or in **A5–050** defence.

2. The provisions of this Protocol with respect to attacks apply to all attacks in whatever territory conducted, including the national territory belonging to a Party to the conflict but under the control of an adverse Party.

3. The provisions of this Section apply to any land, air or sea warfare which may affect the civilian population, individual civilians or civilian objects on land. They further apply to all attacks from the sea or from the air against objectives on land but do not otherwise affect the rules of international law applicable in armed conflict at sea or in the air.

4. The provisions of this Section are additional to the rules concerning humanitarian protection contained in the Fourth Convention, particularly in Part II thereof, and in other international agreements binding upon the High Contracting Parties, as well as to other rules of international law relating to the protection of civilians and civilian objects on land, at sea or in the air against the effects of hostilities.

Chapter 11.—Civilians and Civilian Population

Article 50.—Definition of civilians and civilian population

1. A civilian is any person who does not belong to one of the categories of persons **A5–051** referred to in Article 4 A (1), (2), (3) and (6) of the Third Convention and in Article 43 of this Protocol. In case of doubt whether a person is a civilian, that person shall be considered to be a civilian.

2. The civilian population comprises all persons who are civilians.

3. The presence within the civilian population of individuals who do not come within the definition of civilians does not deprive the population of its civilian character.

Article 51.—Protection of the civilian population

1. The civilian population and individual civilians shall enjoy general protection **A5–052** against dangers arising from military operations. To give effect to this protection, the following rules, which are additional to other applicable rules of international law, shall be observed in circumstances.

2. The civilian population as such, as well as individual civilians, shall not be the object of attack. Acts or threats of violence the primary purpose of which is to spread terror among the civilian population are prohibited.

3. Civilians shall enjoy the protection afforded by this Section, unless and for such time as they take a direct part in hostilities.

4. Indiscriminate attacks are prohibited. Indiscriminate attacks are:

(a) Those which are not directed at a specific military objective;

(b) Those which employ a method or means of combat which cannot be directed at a specific military objective; or

(c) Those which employ a method or means of combat the effects of which cannot be limited as required by this Protocol; and consequently, in each such case, are of a nature to strike military objectives and civilians or civilian objects without distinction.

5. Among others, the following types of attacks are to be considered as indiscriminate:

(a) An attack by bombardment by any methods or means which treats as a single military objective a number of clearly separated and distinct military objectives located in a city, town, village or other area containing a similar concentration of civilians or civilian objects; and

(b) An attack which may be expected to cause incidental loss of civilian life, injury to civilians, damage to civilian objects, or a combination thereof, which would be excessive in relation to the concrete and direct military advantage anticipated.

6. Attacks against the civilian population or civilians by way of reprisals are prohibited.

7. The presence or movements of the civilian population or individual civilians shall not be used to render certain points or areas immune from military operations, in particular in attempts to shield military objectives from attacks or to shield, favour or impede military operations. The Parties to the conflict shall not direct the movement of the civilian population or individual civilians in order to attempt to shield military objectives from attacks or to shield military operations.

8. Any violation of these prohibitions shall not release the Parties to the conflict from their legal obligations with respect to the civilian population and civilians, including the obligation to take the precautionary measures provided for in Article 57.

CHAPTER III.—CIVILIAN OBJECTS

ARTICLE 52.—GENERAL PROTECTION OF CIVILIAN OBJECTS

A5–053   1. Civilian objects shall not be the object of attack or of reprisals. Civilian objects are all objects which are not military objectives as defined in paragraph 2.

2. Attacks shall be limited strictly to military objectives. In so far as objects are concerned, military objectives are limited to those objects which by their nature, location, purpose or use make an effective contribution to military action and whose total or partial destruction, capture or neutralization, in the circumstances ruling at the time, offers a definite military of advantage.

3. In case of doubt whether an object which is normally dedicated to civilian purposes, such as a place of worship, a house or other dwelling or a school, is being used to make an effective contribution to military action, it shall be presumed not to be so used.

ARTICLE 53.—PROTECTION OF CULTURAL OBJECTS AND OF PLACES OF WORSHIP

A5–054   Without prejudice to the provisions of the Hague Convention for the Protection of Cultural Property in the Event of Armed Conflict of 14 May 1954, and of other relevant international instruments, it is prohibited:

(a) To commit any acts of hostility directed against the historic monuments, works of art or places of worship which constitute the cultural or spiritual heritage of peoples;

(b) To use such objects in support of the military effort;

(c) To make such objects the object of reprisals.

Article 54.—Protection of objects indispensable to the survival of the civilian population

1. Starvation of civilians as a method of warfare is prohibited.

2. It is prohibited to attack, destroy, remove or render useless objects indispensable to the survival of the civilian population, such as foodstuffs, agricultural areas for the production of foodstuffs, crops, livestock, drinking water installations and supplies and irrigation works, for the specific purpose of denying them for their sustenance value to the civilian population or to the adverse Party, whatever the motive, whether in order to starve out civilians, to cause them to move away, or for any other motive.

3. The prohibitions in paragraph 2 shall not apply to such of the objects covered by it as are used by an adverse Party:

    (a) As sustenance solely for the members of its armed forces; or

    (b) If not as sustenance, then in direct support of military action, provided, however, that in no event shall actions against these objects be taken which may be expected to leave the civilian population with such inadequate food or water as to cause its starvation or force its movement.

4. These objects shall not be made the object of reprisals.

5. In recognition of the vital requirements of any Party to the conflict in the defence of its national territory against invasion, derogation from the prohibitions contained in paragraph 2 may be made by a Party to the conflict within such territory under its own control where required by imperative military necessity.

A5–055

Article 55.—Protection of the natural environment

1. Care shall be taken in warfare to protect the natural environment against widespread, long-term and severe damage. This protection includes a prohibition of the use of methods or means of warfare which are intended or may be expected to cause such damage to the natural environment and thereby to prejudice the health or survival of the population.

2. Attacks against the natural environment by way of reprisals are prohibited.

A5–056

Article 56.—Protection of works and installations containing dangerous forces

1. Works or installations containing dangerous forces, namely dams, dykes and nuclear electrical generating stations, shall not be made the object of attack, even where these objects are military objectives, if such attack may cause the release of dangerous forces and consequent severe losses among the civilian population. Other military objectives located at or in the vicinity of these works or installations shall not be made the object of attack if such attack may cause the release of dangerous forces from the works or installations and consequent severe losses among the civilian population.

2. The special protection against attack provided by paragraph 1 shall cease:

    (a) For a dam or a dyke only if it is used for other than its normal function and in regular, significant and direct support of military operations and if such attack is the only feasible way to terminate such support;

    (b) For a nuclear electrical generating station only if it provides electric power in regular, significant and direct support of military operations and if such attack is the only feasible way to terminate such support;

    (c) For other military objectives located at or in the vicinity of these works or installations only if they are used in regular, significant and direct support of military operations and if such attack is the only feasible way to terminate such support.

3. In all cases, the civilian population and individual civilians shall remain entitled to all the protection accorded them by international law, including the protection of the

A5–057

precautionary measures provided for in Article 57. If the protection ceases and any of the works, installations or military objectives mentioned in paragraph I is attacked, all practical precautions shall be taken to avoid the release of the dangerous forces.

4. It is prohibited to make any of the works, installations or military objectives mentioned in paragraph 1 the object of reprisals.

5. The Parties to the conflict shall endeavour to avoid locating any military objectives in the vicinity of the works or installations mentioned in paragraph 1. Nevertheless, installations erected for the sole purpose of defending the protected works or installations from attack are permissible and shall not themselves be made the object of attack, provided that they are not used in hostilities except for defensive actions necessary to respond to attacks against the protected works or installations and that their armament is limited to weapons capable only of repelling hostile action against the protected works or installations.

6. The High Contracting Parties and the Parties to the conflict are urged to conclude further agreements among themselves to provide additional protection for objects containing dangerous forces.

7. In order to facilitate the identification of the objects protected by this article, the Parties to the conflict may mark them with a special sign consisting of a group of three bright orange circles placed on the same axis, as specified in Article 16 of Annex I to this Protocol. The absence of such marking in no way relieves any Party to the conflict of its obligations under this Article.

CHAPTER IV.—PRECAUTIONARY MEASURES

ARTICLE 57.—PRECAUTIONS IN ATTACK

A5–058   1. In the conduct of military operations, constant care shall be taken to spare the civilian population, civilians and civilian objects.

2. With respect to attacks, the following precautions shall be taken:
  (a) Those who plan or decide upon an attack shall:
    (i) Do everything feasible to verify that the objectives to be attacked are neither civilians nor civilian objects and are not subject to special protection but are military objectives within the meaning of paragraph 2 of Article 52 and that it is not prohibited by the provisions of this Protocol to attack them;
    (ii) Take all feasible precautions in the choice of means and methods of attack with a view to avoiding, and in any event to minimizing, incidental loss of civilian life, injury to civilians and damage to civilian objects;
    (iii) Refrain from deciding to launch any attack which may be expected to cause incidental loss of civilian life, injury to civilians, damage to civilian objects, or a combination thereof, which would be excessive in relation to the concrete and direct military advantage anticipated;
  (b) An attack shall be cancelled or suspended if it becomes apparent that the objective is not a military one or is subject to special protection or that the attack may be expected to cause incidental loss of civilian life, injury to civilians, damage to civilian objects, or a combination thereof, which would be excessive in relation to the concrete and direct military advantage anticipated;
  (c) Effective advance warning shall be given of attacks which may affect the civilian population, unless circumstances do not permit.

3. When a choice is possible between several military objectives for obtaining a similar military advantage, the objective to be selected shall be that the attack on which may be expected to cause the least danger to civilian lives and to civilian objects.

4. In the conduct of military operations at sea or in the air, each Party to the conflict shall, in conformity with its rights and duties under the rules of international law applicable in armed conflict, take all reasonable precautions to avoid losses of civilian lives and damage to civilian objects.

5. No provision of this Article may be construed as authorizing any attacks against the civilian population, civilians or civilian objects.

ARTICLE 58.—PRECAUTIONS AGAINST THE EFFECTS OF ATTACKS

The Parties to the conflict shall, to the maximum extent feasible: **A5–059**
- (a) Without prejudice to Article 49 of the Fourth Convention, endeavour to remove the civilian population, individual civilians and civilian objects under their control from the vicinity of military objectives;
- (b) Avoid locating military objectives within or near densely populated areas;
- (c) Take the other necessary precautions to protect the civilian population, individual civilians and civilian objects under their control against the dangers resulting from military operations.

CHAPTER V.—LOCALITIES AND ZONES UNDER SPECIAL PROTECTION

ARTICLE 59.—NON-DEFENDED LOCALITIES

1. It is prohibited for the parties to the conflict to attack, by any means whatsoever, **A5–060** non-defended localities.

2. The appropriate authorities of a Party to the conflict may declare as a non-defended locality any inhabited place near or in a zone where armed forces are in contact which is open for occupation by an adverse Party. Such a locality shall fulfil the following conditions:
- (a) All combatants, as well as mobile weapons and mobile military equipment must have been evacuated;
- (b) No hostile use shall be made of fixed military installations or establishments;
- (c) No acts of hostility shall be committed by the authorities or by the population; and
- (d) No activities in support of military operations shall be undertaken.

3. The presence, in this locality, of persons specially protected under the Conventions and this Protocol, and of police forces retained for the sole purpose of maintaining law and order, is not contrary to the conditions laid down in paragraph 2.

4. The declaration made under paragraph 2 shall be addressed to the adverse Party and shall define and describe, as precisely as possible, the limits of the non-defended locality. The Party to the conflict to which the declaration is addressed shall acknowledge its receipt and shall treat the locality as a non-defended locality unless the conditions laid down in paragraph 2 are not in fact fulfilled, in which event it shall immediately so inform the Party making the declaration. Even if the conditions laid down in paragraph 2 are not fulfilled, the locality shall continue to enjoy the protection provided by the other provisions of this Protocol and the other rules of international law applicable in armed conflict.

5. The Parties to the conflict may agree on the establishment of non- defended localities even if such localities do not fulfil the conditions laid down in paragraph 2. The agreement should define and describe, as precisely as possible, the limits of the non-defended locality; if necessary, it may lay down the methods of supervision.

6. The Party which is in control of a locality governed by such an agreement shall mark it, so far as possible, by such signs as may be agreed upon with the other Party, which shall be displayed where they are clearly visible, especially on its perimeter and limits and on highways.

7. A locality loses its status as a non-defended locality when it ceases to fulfil the conditions laid down in paragraph 2 or in the agreement referred to in paragraph 5. In such an eventuality, the locality shall continue to enjoy the protection provided by the other provisions of this Protocol and the other rules of international law applicable in armed conflict.

ARTICLE 60.—DEMILITARIZED ZONES

1. It is prohibited for the Parties to the conflict to extend their military operations to **A5–061** zones on which they have conferred by agreement the status of demilitarized zone, if such extension is contrary to the terms of this agreement.

1137

2. The agreement shall be an express agreement, may be concluded verbally or in writing, either directly or through a Protecting Power or any impartial humanitarian organization, and may consist of reciprocal and concordant declarations. The agreement may be concluded in peacetime, as well as after the outbreak of hostilities, and should define and describe, as precisely as possible, the limits of the demilitarized zone and, if necessary, lay down the methods of supervision.

3. The subject of such an agreement shall normally be any zone which fulfils the following conditions:

    (a) All combatants, as well as mobile weapons and mobile military equipment, must have been evacuated;

    (b) No hostile use shall be made of fixed military installations or establishments;

    (c) No acts of hostility shall be committed by the authorities or by the population; and

    (d) Any activity linked to the military effort must have ceased.

The Parties to the conflict shall agree upon the interpretation to be given to the condition laid down in sub-paragraph (d) and upon persons to be admitted to the demilitarized zone other than those mentioned in paragraph 4.

4. The presence, in this zone, of persons specially protected under the Conventions and this Protocol, and of police forces retained for the sole purpose of maintaining law and order, is not contrary to the conditions laid down in paragraph 3.

5. The Party which is in control of such a zone shall mark it, so far as possible, by such signs as may be agreed upon with the other Party, which shall be displayed where they are clearly visible, especially on its perimeter and limits and on highways.

6. If the fighting draws near to a demilitarized zone, and if the Parties to the conflict have so agreed, none of them may use the zone for purposes related to the conduct of military operations or unilaterally revoke its status.

7. If one of the Parties to the conflict commits a material breach of the provisions of paragraphs 3 or 6, the other Party shall be released from its obligations under the agreement conferring upon the zone the status of demilitarized zone. In such an eventuality, the zone loses its status but shall continue to enjoy the protection provided by the other provisions of this Protocol and the other rules of international law applicable in armed conflict.

Chapter VI.—Civil Defence

Article 61.—Definitions and scope

A5–062   For the purposes of this Protocol:

    (a) "Civil defence" means the performance of some or all of the undermentioned humanitarian tasks intended to protect the civilian population against the dangers, and to help it to recover from the immediate effects, of hostilities or disasters and also to provide the conditions necessary for its survival. These tasks are:

      (i) Warning; (ii) Evacuation;

     (iii) Management of shelters;

     (iv) Management of blackout measures;

      (v) Rescue;

     (vi) Medical services, including first aid, and religious assistance;

     (vii) Fire-fighting;

    (viii) Detection and marking of danger areas;

     (ix) Decontamination and similar protective measures;

      (x) Provision of emergency accommodation and supplies;

     (xi) Emergency assistance in the restoration and maintenance of order in distressed areas;

     (xii) Emergency repair of indispensable public utilities;

    (xiii) Emergency disposal of the dead;

    (xiv) Assistance in the preservation of objects essential for survival;

(xv) Complementary activities necessary to carry out any of the tasks mentioned above, including, but not limited to, planning and organization;

(b) "Civil defence organizations" means those establishments and other units which are organized or authorized by the competent authorities of a Party to the conflict to perform any of the tasks mentioned under subparagraph (a), and which are assigned and devoted exclusively to such tasks;

(c) "Personnel" of civil defence organizations means those persons assigned by a Party to the conflict exclusively to the performance of the tasks mentioned under sub-paragraph (a), including personnel assigned by the competent authority of that Party exclusively to the administration of these organizations;

(d) "Matériel" of civil defence organizations means equipment, supplies and transports used by these organizations for the performance of the tasks mentioned under sub-paragraph (a).

Article 62.—General protection

1. Civilian civil defence organizations and their personnel shall be respected and **A5–063** protected, subject to the provisions of this Protocol, particularly the provisions of this Section. They shall be entitled to perform their civil defence tasks except in case of imperative military necessity.

2. The provisions of paragraph 1 shall also apply to civilians who, although not members of civilian civil defence organizations, respond to an appeal from the competent authorities and perform civil defence tasks under their control.

3. Buildings and matériel used for civil defence purposes and shelters provided for the civilian population are covered by Article 52. Objects used for civil defence purposes may not be destroyed or diverted from their proper use except by the Party to which they belong.

Article 63.—Civil defence in occupied territories

1. In occupied territories, civilian civil defence organizations shall receive from the **A5–064** authorities the facilities necessary for the performance of their tasks. In no circumstances shall their personnel be compelled to perform activities which would interfere with the proper performance of these tasks. The Occupying Power shall not change the structure or personnel of such organizations in any way which might jeopardize the efficient performance of their mission. These organizations shall not be required to give priority to the nationals or interests of that Power.

2. The Occupying Power shall not compel, coerce or induce civilian civil defense organizations to perform their tasks in an manner prejudicial to the interests of the civilian population.

3. The Occupying Power may disarm civil defense personnel for reasons of security.

4. The Occupying Power shall neither divert from their proper use nor requisition buildings or matériel belonging to or used by civil defense organizations if such diversion or requisition would be harmful to the civilian population.

5. Provided that the general rule in paragraph 4 continues to be observed, the occupying Power may requisition or divert these resources, subject to the following particular conditions:

(a) That the buildings or matériel are necessary for other needs of the civilian population; and

(b) That the requisition or diversion continues only while such necessity exists.

6. The Occupying Power shall neither divert nor requisition shelters provided for the use of the civilian population or needed by such population.

Article 64.—Civilian civil defence organizations of neutral or other States not Parties to the conflict and international co-ordinating organizations

1. Articles 62, 63, 65 and 66 shall also apply to the personnel and matériel of civilian **A5–065** civil defence organizations of neutral or other States not Parties to the conflict which perform civil defense tasks mentioned in Article 61 in the territory of a Party to the

conflict, with the consent and under the control of that Party. Notification of such assistance shall be given as soon as possible to any adverse Party concerned. In no circumstances shall this activity be deemed to be an interference in the conflict. This activity should, however, be performed with due regard to the security interests of the Parties to the conflict concerned.

2. The Parties to the conflict receiving the assistance referred to in paragraph 1 and the High Contracting Parties granting it should facilitate international co-ordination of such civil defence actions when appropriate. In such cases the relevant international organizations are covered by the provisions of this Chapter.

3. In occupied territories, the Occupying Power may only exclude or restrict the activities of civilian civil defence organizations of neutral or other States not Parties to the conflict and of international co-ordinating organizations if it can ensure the adequate performance of civil defence tasks from its own resources or those of the occupied territory.

ARTICLE 65.—CESSATION OF PROTECTION

A5–066   1. The protection to which civilian civil defence organizations, their personnel, buildings, shelters and matériel are entitled shall not cease unless they commit or are used to commit, outside their proper tasks, acts harmful to the enemy. Protection may, however, cease only after a warning has been given setting, whenever appropriate, a reasonable time-limit, and after such warning has remained unheeded.

2. The following shall not be considered as acts harmful to the enemy:
   (a) That civil defence tasks are carried out under the direction or control of military authorities;
   (b) That civilian civil defence personnel co-operate with military personnel in the performance of civil defence tasks, or that some military personnel are attached to civilian civil defence organizations;
   (c) That the performance of civil defence tasks may incidentally benefit military victims, particularly those who are hors de combat.

3. It shall also not be considered as an act harmful to the enemy that civilian defence personnel bear light individual weapons for the purpose of maintaining order or for self-defence. However, in areas where land fighting it taking place or is likely to take place, the Parties to the conflict shall undertake the appropriate measures to limit these weapons to handguns, such as pistols or revolvers, in order to assist in distinguishing between civil defence personnel and combatants. Although civil defence personnel bear other light individual weapons in such areas, they shall nevertheless be respected and protected as soon as they have been recognized as such.

4. The formation of civilian civil defence organizations along military lines, and compulsory service in them, shall also not deprive them of the protection conferred by this Chapter.

ARTICLE 66.—IDENTIFICATION

A5–067   1. Each Party to the conflict shall endeavour to ensure that its civil defence organizations, their personnel, buildings and matériel, are identifiable while they are exclusively devoted to the performance of civil defence tasks. Shelters provided for the civilian population should be similarly identifiable.

2. Each Party to the conflict shall also endeavour to adopt and implement methods and procedures which will make it possible to recognize civilian shelters as well as civil defence personnel, buildings and matériel on which the international distinctive sign of civil defence is displayed.

3. In occupied territories and in areas where fighting is taking place or is likely to take place, civilian civil defence personnel should be recognizable by the international distinctive sign of civil defence and by an identity and certifying their status.

4. The international distinctive sign of civil defence is an equilateral blue triangle on an orange ground when used for the protection of civil defence organizations, their personnel, buildings and matériel and for civilian shelters.

5. In addition to the distinctive sign, Parties to the conflict may agree upon the use of distinctive signals for civil defence identification purposes.

6. The application of the provisions of paragraphs 1 to 4 is governed by Chapter V of Annex I to this Protocol.

7. In time of peace, the sign described in paragraph 4 may, with the consent of the competent national authorities, be used for civil defence identification purposes.

8. The High Contracting Parties and the Parties to the conflict shall take the measures necessary to supervise the display of the international distinctive sign of civil defence and to prevent and repress any misuse thereof.

9. The identification of civil defence medical and religious personnel, medical units and medical transports is also governed by Article 18.

ARTICLE 67.—MEMBERS OF THE ARMED FORCES AND MILITARY UNITS ASSIGNED TO CIVIL DEFENCE ORGANIZATIONS

1. Members of the armed forces and military units assigned to civil defence **A5–068** organizations shall be respected and protected, provided that:
   (a) Such personnel and such units are permanently assigned and exclusively devoted to the performance of any of the tasks mentioned in Article 61;
   (b) If so assigned, such personnel do not perform any other military duties during the conflict;
   (c) Such personnel are clearly distinguishable from the other members of the armed forces by prominently displaying the international distinctive sign of civil defence, which shall be as large as appropriate, and such personnel are provided with the identity card referred to in Chapter V of Annexe I to this Protocol certifying their status;
   (d) Such personnel and such units are equipped only with light individual weapons for the purpose of maintaining order or for self-defence. The provisions of Article 65, paragraph 3 shall also apply in this case;
   (e) Such personnel do not participate directly in hostilities, and do not commit, or are not used to commit, outside their civil defence tasks, acts harmful to the adverse Party;
   (f) Such personnel and such units perform their civil defence tasks only within the national territory of their Party.

The non-observance of the conditions stated in (e) above by any member of the armed forces who is bound by the conditions prescribed in (a) and (b) above is prohibited.

2. Military personnel serving within civil defence organizations shall, if they fall into the power of an adverse Party, be prisoners of war. In occupied territory they may, but only in the interest of the civilian population of that territory, be employed on civil defence tasks in so far as the need arises, provided however that, if such work is dangerous, they volunteer for such tasks.

3. The buildings and major items of equipment and transports of military units assigned to civil defence organizations shall be clearly marked with the international distinctive sign of civil defence. This distinctive sign shall be as large as appropriate.

4. The matériel and buildings of military units permanently assigned to civil defence organizations and exclusively devoted to the performance of civil defence tasks shall, if they fall into the hands of an adverse Party, remain subject to the laws of war. They may not be diverted from their civil defence purpose so long as they are required for the performance of civil defence tasks, except in case of imperative military necessity, unless previous arrangements have been made for adequate provision for the needs of the civilian population.

Section II.—Relief in Favour of the Civilian Population

ARTICLE 68.—FIELD OF APPLICATION

The provisions of this Section apply to the civilian population as defined in this **A5–069** Protocol and are supplementary to Articles 23, 55, 59, 60, 61 and 62 and other relevant provisions of the Fourth Convention.

ARTICLE 69.—BASIC NEEDS IN OCCUPIED TERRITORIES

A5–070   1. In addition to the duties specified in Article 55 of the Fourth Convention concerning food and medical supplies, the Occupying Power shall, to the fullest extent of the means available to it and without any adverse distinction, also ensure the provision of clothing, bedding, means of shelter, other supplies essential to the survival of the civilian population of the occupied territory and objects necessary for religious worship.

2. Relief actions for the benefit of the civilian population of occupied territories are governed by Articles 59, 60, 61, 62, 108, 109, 110 and 111 of the Fourth Convention, and by Article 71 of this Protocol, and shall be implemented without delay.

ARTICLE 70.—RELIEF ACTIONS

A5–071   1. If the civilian population of any territory under the control of a Party to the conflict, other than occupied territory, is not adequately provided with the supplies mentioned in Article 69, relief actions which are humanitarian and impartial in character and conducted without any adverse distinction shall be undertaken, subject to the agreement of the Parties concerned in such relief actions. Offers of such relief shall not be regarded as interference in the armed conflict or as unfriendly acts. In the distribution of relief consignments, priority shall be given to those persons, such as children, expectant mothers, maternity cases and nursing mothers, who, under the Fourth Convention or under this Protocol, are to be accorded privileged treatment or special protection.

2. The Parties to the conflict and each High Contracting Party shall allow and facilitate rapid and unimpeded passage of all relief consignments, equipment and personnel provided in accordance with this Section, even if such assistance is destined for the civilian population of the adverse Party.

3. The Parties to the conflict and each High Contracting Party which allow the passage of relief consignments, equipment and personnel in accordance with paragraph 2:

    (a) Shall have the right to prescribe the technical arrangements, including search, under which such passage is permitted;

    (b) May make such permission conditional on the distribution of this assistance being made under the local supervision of a Protecting Power;

    (c) Shall, in no way whatsoever, divert relief consignments from the purpose for which they are intended nor delay their forwarding, except in cases of urgent necessity in the interest of the civilian population concerned.

4. The Parties to the conflict shall protect relief consignments and facilitate their rapid distribution.

5. The Parties to the conflict and each High Contracting Party concerned shall encourage and facilitate effective international co-ordination of the relief actions referred to in paragraph 1.

ARTICLE 71.—PERSONNEL PARTICIPATING IN RELIEF ACTIONS

A5–072   1. Where necessary, relief personnel may form part of the assistance provided in any relief action, in particular for the transportation and distribution of relief consignments; the participation of such personnel shall be subject to the approval of the Party in whose territory they will carry out their duties.

2. Such personnel shall be respected and protected.

3. Each Party in receipt of relief consignments shall, to the fullest extent practicable, assist the relief personnel referred to in paragraph 1 in carrying out their relief mission. Only in case of imperative military necessity may the activities of the relief personnel be limited or their movements temporarily restricted.

4. Under no circumstances may relief personnel exceed the terms of their mission under this Protocol. In particular they shall take account of the security requirements of the Party in whose territory they are carrying out their duties. The mission of any of the personnel who do not respect these conditions may be terminated.

Section III.—Treatment of Persons in the Power of a Party to the Conflict

Chapter 1.—Field of Application and Protection of Persons and Objects

Article 72.—Field of application

The provisions of this Section are additional to the rules concerning humanitarian **A5–073** protection of civilians and civilian objects in the power of a Party to the conflict contained in the Fourth Convention, particularly Parts I and m thereof, as well as to other applicable rules of international law relating to the protection of fundamental human rights during international armed conflict.

Article 73.—Refugees and stateless persons

Persons who, before the beginning of hostilities, were considered as stateless persons **A5–074** or refugees under the relevant international instruments accepted by the Parties concerned or under the national legislation of the State of refuge or State of residence shall be protected persons within the meaning of Parts I and III of the Fourth Convention, in all circumstances and without any adverse distinction.

Article 74.—Reunion of dispersed families

The High Contracting Parties and the Parties to the conflict shall facilitate in every **A5–075** possible way the reunion of families dispersed as a result of armed conflicts and shall encourage in particular the work of the humanitarian organizations engaged in this task in accordance with the provisions of the Conventions and of this Protocol and in conformity with their respective security regulations.

Article 75.—Fundamental guarantees

1. In so far as they are affected by a situation referred to in Article 1 of this Protocol, **A5–076** persons who are in the power of a Party to the conflict and who do not benefit from more favourable treatment under the Conventions or under this Protocol shall be treated humanely in all circumstances and shall enjoy, as a minimum, the protection provided by this Article without any adverse distinction based upon race, colour, sex, language, religion or belief, political or other opinion, national or social origin, wealth, birth or other status, or on any other similar criteria. Each Party shall respect the person, honour, convictions and religious practices of all such persons.

2. The following acts are and shall remain prohibited at any time and in any place whatsoever, whether committed by civilian or by military agents:
  (a) Violence to the life, health, or physical or mental well-being of persons, in particular:
   (i) Murder;
   (ii) Torture of all kinds, whether physical or mental;
   (iii) Corporal punishment ; and
   (iv) Mutilation;
  (b) Outrages upon personal dignity, in particular humiliating and degrading treatment, enforced prostitution and any form of indecent assault;
  (c) The taking of hostages;
  (d) Collective punishments; and
  (e) Threats to commit any of the foregoing acts.

3. Any person arrested, detained or interned for actions related to the armed conflict shall be informed promptly, in a language he understands, of the reasons why these measures have been taken. Except in cases of arrest or detention for penal offences, such

persons shall be released with the minimum delay possible and in any event as soon as the circumstances justifying the arrest, detention or internment have ceased to exist.

4. No sentence may be passed and no penalty may be executed on a person found guilty of a penal offence related to the armed conflict except pursuant to a conviction pronounced by an impartial and regularly constituted court respecting the generally recognized principles of regular judicial procedure, which include the following:

    (a) The procedure shall provide for an accused to be informed without delay of the particulars of the offence alleged against him and shall afford the accused before and during his trial all necessary rights and means of defence;

    (b) No one shall be convicted of an offence except on the basis of individual penal responsibility;

    (c) No one shall be accused or convicted of a criminal offence on account of any act or omission which did not constitute a criminal offence under the national or international law to which he was subject at the time when it was committed; nor shall a heavier penalty be imposed than that which was applicable at the time when the criminal offence was committed; if, after the commission of the offence, provision is made by law for the imposition of a lighter penalty, the offender shall benefit thereby;

    (d) Anyone charged with an offence is presumed innocent until proved guilt according to law;

    (e) Anyone charged with an offence shall have the right to be tried in his presence;

    (f) No one shall be compelled to testify against himself or to confess guilt;

    (g) Anyone charged with an offence shall have the right to examine, or have examined, the witnesses against him and to obtain the attendance and examination of witnesses on his behalf under the same conditions as witnesses against him;

    (h) No one shall be prosecuted or punished by the same Party for an offence in respect of which a final judgement acquitting or convicting that person has been previously pronounced under the same law and judicial procedure;

    (i) Anyone prosecuted for an offence shall have the right to have the judgement pronounced publicly; and

    (j) A convicted person shall be advised on conviction of his judicial and other remedies and of the time-limits within which they may be exercised.

5. Women whose liberty has been restricted for reasons related to the armed conflict shall be held in quarters separated from men's quarters. They shall be under the immediate supervision of women. Nevertheless, in cases where families are detained or interned, they shall, whenever possible, be held in the same place and accommodated as family units.

6. Persons who are arrested, detained or interned for reasons related to the armed conflict shall enjoy the protection provided by this Article until their final release, repatriation or re-establishment, even after the end of the armed conflict.

7. In order to avoid any doubt concerning the prosecution and trial of persons accused of war crimes or crimes against humanity, the following principles shall apply:

    (a) Persons who are accused of such crimes should be submitted for the purpose of prosecution and trial in accordance with the applicable rules of international law; and

    (b) Any such persons who do not benefit from more favourable treatment under the Conventions or this Protocol shall be accorded the treatment provided by this Article, whether or not the crimes of which they are accused constitute grave breaches of the Conventions or of this Protocol.

8. No provision of this Article may be construed as limiting or infringing any other more favourable provision granting greater protection, under any applicable rules of international law, to persons covered by paragraph 1.

CHAPTER 11.—MEASURES IN FAVOUR OF WOMEN AND CHILDREN

ARTICLE 76.—PROTECTION OF WOMEN

A5–077   1. Women shall be the object of special respect and shall be protected in particular against rape, forced prostitution and any other form of indecent assault.

2. Pregnant women and mothers having dependent infants who are arrested, detained or interned for reasons related to the armed conflict, shall have their cases considered with the utmost priority.

3. To the maximum extent feasible, the Parties to the conflict shall endeavour to avoid the pronouncement of the death penalty on pregnant women or mothers having dependent infants, for an offence related to the armed conflict. The death penalty for such offences shall not be executed on such women.

ARTICLE 77.—PROTECTION OF CHILDREN

1. Children shall be the object of special respect and shall be protected against any **A5–078** form of indecent assault. The Parties to the conflict shall provide them with the care and aid they require, whether because of their age or for any other reason.

2. The Parties to the conflict shall take all feasible measures in order that children who have not attained the age of fifteen years do not take a direct part in hostilities and, in particular, they shall refrain from recruiting them into their armed forces. In recruiting among those persons who have attained the age of fifteen years but who have not attained the age of eighteen years, the Parties to the conflict shall endeavour to give priority to those who are oldest.

3. If, in exceptional cases, despite the provisions of paragraph 2, children who have not attained the age of fifteen years take a direct part in hostilities and fall into the power of an adverse Party, they shall continue to benefit from the special protection accorded by this Article, whether or not they are prisoners of war.

4. If arrested, detained or interned for reasons related to the armed conflict, children shall be held in quarters separate from the quarters of adults, except where families are accommodated as family units as provided in Article 75, paragraph 5.

5. The death penalty for an offence related to armed conflict shall not be executed on persons who had not attained the age of eighteen years at the time the offence was committed.

ARTICLE 78.—EVACUATION OF CHILDREN

1. No Party to the conflict shall arrange for the evacuation of children, other than its **A5–079** own nationals, to a foreign country except for a temporary evacuation where compelling reasons of the health or medical treatment of the children or, except in occupied territory, their safety, so require. Where the parents or legal guardians can be found, their written consent to such evacuation is required. If these persons cannot be found, the written consent to such evacuation of the persons who by law or custom are primarily responsible for the care of the children is required. Any such evacuation shall be supervised by the Protecting Power in agreement with the Parties concerned, namely, the Party arranging for the evacuation, the Party receiving the children and any Parties whose nationals are being evacuated. In each case, all Parties to the conflict shall take all feasible precautions to avoid endangering the evacuation.

2. Whenever an evacuation occurs pursuant to paragraph 1, each child's education, including his religious and moral education as his parents desire, shall be provided while he is away with the greatest possible continuity.

3. With a view to facilitating the return to their families and country of children evacuated pursuant to this Article, the authorities of the Party arranging for the evacuation and, as appropriate, the authorities of the receiving country shall establish for each child a card with photographs, which they shall send to the Central Tracing Agency of the International Committee of the Red Cross. Each card shall bear, whenever possible, and whenever it involves no risk of harm to the child, the following information:

    (a) Surname(s) of the child;

    (b) The child's first name(s);

    (c) The child's sex;

    (d) The place and date of birth (or, if that date is not known, the approximate age);

(e) The father's full name;

(f) The mother's full name and her maiden name;

(g) The child's next-of-kin;

(h) The child's nationality;

(i) The child's native language, and any other languages he speaks;

(j) The address of the child's family;

(k) Any identification number for the child;

(l) The child's state of health;

(m) The child's blood group;

(n) Any distinguishing features;

(o) The date on which and the place where the child was found;

(p) The date on which and the place from which the child left the country;

(q) The child's religion, if any;

(r) The child's present address in the receiving country;

(s) Should the child die before his return, the date, place and circumstances of death and place of interment.

CHAPTER III.—JOURNALISTS

ARTICLE 79.—MEASURES OF PROTECTION FOR JOURNALISTS

A5–080   1. Journalists engaged in dangerous professional missions in areas of armed conflict shall be considered as civilians within the meaning of Article 50, paragraph 1.

2. They shall be protected as such under the Conventions and this Protocol, provided that they take no action adversely affecting their status as civilians, and without prejudice to the right of war correspondents accredited to the armed forces to the status provided for in Article 4 A (4) of the Third Convention.

3. They may obtain an identity card similar to the model in Annex II of this Protocol. This card, which shall be issued by the government of the State of which the journalist is a national or in whose territory he resides or in which the news medium employing him is located, shall attest to his status as a journalist.

PART V EXECUTION OF THE CONVENTIONS AND OF THIS PROTOCOL

Section I.—General Provisions

ARTICLE 80.—MEASURES FOR EXECUTION

A5–081   1. The High Contracting Parties and the Parties to the conflict shall without delay take all necessary measures for the execution of their obligations under the Conventions and this Protocol.

2. The High Contracting Parties and the Parties to the conflict shall give orders and instructions to ensure observance of the Conventions and this Protocol, and shall supervise their execution.

ARTICLE 81.—ACTIVITIES OF THE RED CROSS AND OTHER HUMANITARIAN ORGANIZATIONS

A5–082   1. The Parties to the conflict shall grant to the International Committee of the Red Cross all facilities within their power so as to enable it to carry out the humanitarian functions assigned to it by the Conventions and this Protocol in order to ensure protection and assistance to the victims of conflicts; the International Committee of the Red Cross may also carry out any other humanitarian activities in favour of these victims, subject to the consent of the Parties to the conflict concerned.

2. The Parties to the conflict shall grant to their respective Red Cross (Red Crescent, Red Lion and Sun) organizations the facilities necessary for carrying out their humanitarian activities in favour of the victims of the conflict, in accordance with the provisions of the Conventions and this Protocol and the fundamental principles of the Red Cross as formulated by the International Conferences of the Red Cross.

3. The High Contracting Parties and the Parties to the conflict shall facilitate in every possible way the assistance which Red Cross (Red Crescent, Red Lion and Sun) organizations and the League of Red Cross Societies extend to the victims of conflicts in accordance with the provisions of the Conventions and this Protocol and with the fundamental principles of the Red Cross as formulated by the International Conferences of the Red Cross.

4. The High Contracting Parties and the Parties to the conflict shall, as far as possible, make facilities similar to those mentioned in paragraphs 2 and 3 available to the other humanitarian organizations referred to in the Conventions and this Protocol which are duly authorized by the respective Parties to the conflict and which perform their humanitarian activities in accordance with the provisions of the Conventions and this Protocol.

ARTICLE 82.—LEGAL ADVISERS IN ARMED FORCES

The High Contracting Parties at all times, and the Parties to the conflict in time of armed conflict, shall ensure that legal advisers are available, when necessary, to advise military commanders at the appropriate level on the application of the Conventions and this Protocol and on the appropriate instruction to be given to the armed forces on this subject.

A5–083

ARTICLE 83.—DISSEMINATION

1. The High Contracting Parties undertake, in time of peace as in time of armed conflict, to disseminate the Conventions and this Protocol as widely as possible in their respective countries and, in particular, to include the study thereof in their programmes of military instruction and to encourage the study thereof by the civilian population, so that those instruments may become known to the armed forces and to the civilian population.

2. Any military or civilian authorities who, in time of armed conflict, assume responsibilities in respect of the application of the Conventions and this Protocol shall be fully acquainted with the text thereof.

A5–084

ARTICLE 84.—RULES OF APPLICATION

The High Contracting Parties shall communicate to one another, as soon as possible, through the depositary and, as appropriate, through the Protecting Powers, their official translations of this Protocol, as well as the laws and regulations which they may adopt to ensure its application.

A5–085

Section II.—Repression of Breaches of the Conventions and of this Protocol

ARTICLE 85.—REPRESSION OF BREACHES OF THIS PROTOCOL

1. The provisions of the Conventions relating to the repression of breaches and grave breaches, supplemented by this Section, shall apply to the repression of breaches and grave breaches of this Protocol.

2. Acts described as grave breaches in the Conventions are grave breaches of this Protocol if committed against persons in the power of an adverse Party protected by Articles 44, 45 and 73 of this Protocol, or against the wounded, sick and shipwrecked of

A5–086

the adverse Party who are protected by this Protocol, or against those medical or religious personnel, medical units or medical transports which are under the control of the adverse Party and are protected by this Protocol.

3. In addition to the grave breaches defined in Article 11, the following acts shall be regarded as grave breaches of this Protocol, when committed wilfully, in violation of the relevant provisions of this Protocol, and causing death or serious injury to body or health:

(a) Making the civilian population or individual civilians the object of attack;

(b) Launching an indiscriminate attack affecting the civilian population or civilian objects in the knowledge that such attack will cause excessive loss of life, injury to civilians or damage to civilian objects, as defined in Article 57, paragraph 2 (a) (iii);

(c) Launching an attack against works or installations containing dangerous forces in the knowledge that such attack will cause excessive loss of life, injury to civilians or damage to civilian objects, as defined in Article 57, paragraph 2 (a) (iii);

(d) Making non-defended localities and demilitarized zones the object of attack;

(e) Making a person the object of attack in the knowledge that he is hors de combat;

(f) The perfidious use, in violation of Article 37, of the distinctive emblem of the red cross, red crescent or red lion and sun or of other protective signs recognized by the Conventions or this Protocol.

4. In addition to the grave breaches defined in the preceding paragraphs and in the Conventions, the following shall be regarded as grave breaches of this Protocol, when committed wilfully and in violation of the Conventions of the Protocol;

(a) The transfer by the Occupying Power of parts of its own civilian population into the territory it occupies, or the deportation or transfer of all or parts of the population of the occupied territory within or outside this territory, in violation of Article 49 of the Fourth Convention;

(b) Unjustifiable delay in the repatriation of prisoners of war or civilians;

(c) Practices of apartheid and other inhuman and degrading practices involving outrages upon personal dignity, based on racial discrimination;

(d) Making the clearly-recognized historic monuments, works of art or places of worship which constitute the cultural or spiritual heritage of peoples and to which special protection has been given by special arrangement, for example, within the framework of a competent international organization, the object of attack, causing as a result extensive destruction thereof, where there is no evidence of the violation by the adverse Party of Article 53, sub-paragraph (b), and when such historic monuments, works of art and places of worship are not located in the immediate proximity of military objectives:

(e) Depriving a person protected by the Conventions or referred to in paragraph 2 of this Article of the rights of fair and regular trial.

5. Without prejudice to the application of the Conventions and of this Protocol, grave breaches of these instruments shall be regarded as war crimes.

ARTICLE 86.—FAILURE TO ACT

A5–087　　1. The High Contracting Parties and the Parties to the conflict shall repress grave breaches, and take measures necessary to suppress all other breaches, of the Conventions or of this Protocol which result from a failure to act when under a duty to do so.

2. The fact that a breach of the Conventions or of this Protocol was committed by a subordinate does not absolve his superiors from penal or disciplinary responsibility, as the case may be, if they knew, or had information which should have enabled them to conclude in the circumstances at the time, that he was committing or was going to commit such a breach and if they did not take all feasible measures within their power to prevent or repress the breach.

Article 87.—Duty of Commanders

1. The High Contracting Parties and the Parties to the conflict shall require military **A5–088** commanders, with respect to members of the armed forces under their command and other persons under their control, to prevent and, where necessary, to suppress and to report to competent authorities breaches of the Conventions and of this Protocol.

2. In order to prevent and suppress breaches, High Contracting Parties and Parties to the conflict shall require that, commensurate with their level of responsibility, commanders ensure that members of the armed forces under their command are aware of their obligations under the Conventions and this Protocol.

3. The High Contracting Parties and Parties to the conflict shall require any commander who is aware that subordinates or other persons under his control are going to commit or have committed a breach of the Conventions or of this Protocol, to initiate such steps as are necessary to prevent such violations of the Conventions or this Protocol, and, where appropriate, to initiate disciplinary or penal action against violators thereof.

Article 88.—Mutual Assistance in Criminal Matters

1. The High Contracting Parties shall afford one another the greatest measure of **A5–089** assistance in connexion with criminal proceedings brought in respect of grave breaches of the Conventions or of this Protocol.

2. Subject to the rights and obligations established in the Conventions and in Article 85, paragraph 1, of this Protocol, and when circumstances permit, the High Contracting Parties shall co-operate in the matter of extradition. They shall give due consideration to the request of the State in whose territory the alleged offence has occurred.

3. The law of the High Contracting Party requested shall apply in all cases. The provisions of the preceding paragraphs shall not, however, affect the obligations arising from the provisions of any other treaty of a bilateral or multilateral nature which governs or will govern the whole or part of the subject of mutual assistance in criminal matters.

Article 89.—Co-operation

In situations of serious violations of the Conventions or of this Protocol, the High **A5–090** Contracting Parties undertake to act, jointly or individually, in co-operation with the United Nations and in conformity with the United Nations Charter.

Article 90.—International Fact-Finding Commission

1. (a) An International Fact-Finding Commission (hereinafter referred to as "the **A5–091** Commission") consisting of fifteen members of high moral standing and acknowledged impartiality shall be established.
   (b) When not less than twenty High Contracting Parties have agreed to accept the competence of the Commission pursuant to paragraph 2, the depositary shall then, and at intervals of five years thereafter, convene a meeting of representatives of those High Contracting Parties for the purpose of electing the members of the Commission. At the meeting, the representatives shall elect the members of the Commission by secret ballot from a list of person s to which each of those High Contracting Parties may nominate one person.
   (c) The members of the Commission shall serve in their personal capacity and shall hold office until the election of new members at the ensuing meeting.
   (d) At the election, the High Contracting Parties shall ensure that the persons to be elected to the Commission individually possess the qualifications required and that, in the Commission as a whole, equitable geographical representation is assured.

(e) In the case of a casual vacancy, the Commission itself shall fill the Z vacancy, having due regard to the provisions of the preceding sub paragraphs.

(f) the depositary shall make available to the Commission the necessary administrative facilities for the performance of its functions.

2. (a) The High Contracting Parties may at the time of signing, ratifying or acceding to the Protocol, or at any other subsequent time, declare that they recognize ipsofacto and without special agreement, in relation to any other High Contracting Party accepting the same obligation, the competence of the Commission to enquire into allegations by such other Party, as authorized by this Article.

(b) The declarations referred to above shall be deposited with the depositary, which shall transmit copies thereof to the High Contracting Parties.

(c) The Commission shall be competent to:

(i) Enquire into any facts alleged to be a grave breach as defined in the Conventions and this Protocol or other serious violation of the Conventions or of this Protocol;

(ii) Facilitate, through its good offices, the restoration of an attitude of respect for the Conventions and this Protocol.

(d) In other situations, the Commission shall institute an enquiry at the request of a Party to the conflict only with the consent of the other Party or Parties concerned.

(e) Subject to the foregoing provisions of this paragraph, the provisions of Article 52 of the First Convention, Article 53 of the Second Convention, Article 132 of the Third Convention and Article 149 of the Fourth Convention shall continue to apply to any alleged violation of the Conventions and shall extend to any alleged violation of this Protocol.

3. (a) Unless otherwise agreed by the Parties concerned, all enquiries shall be undertaken by a Chamber consisting of seven members appointed as follows:

(i) Five members of the Commission, not nationals of any Party to the conflict, appointed by the President of the Commission on the basis of equitable representation of the geographical areas, after consultation with the Parties to the conflict;

(ii) Two ad hoc members, not nationals of any Party to the conflict, one to be appointed by each side.

(b) Upon receipt of the request for an enquiry, the President of the Commission shall specify an appropriate time limit for setting up a Chamber. If any ad hoc member has not been appointed within the time limit, the President shall immediately appoint such additional member or members of the Commission as may be necessary to complete the membership of the Chamber.

4. (a) The Chamber set up under paragraph 3 to undertake an enquiry shall invite the Parties to the conflict to assist it and to present evidence. The Chamber may also seek such other evidence as it deems appropriate and may carry out an investigation of the situation in loco.

(b) All evidence shall be fully disclosed to the Parties, which shall have the right to comment on it to the Commission.

(c) Each Party shall have the right to challenge such evidence.

5. (a) The Commission shall submit to the Parties a report on the findings of fact of the Chamber, with such recommendations as it may deem appropriate.

(b) If the Chamber is unable to secure sufficient evidence for factual and impartial findings, the Commission shall state the reasons for that inability.

(c) The Commission shall not report its findings publicly, unless all the Parties to the conflict have requested the Commission to do so.

6. The Commission shall establish its own rules, including rules for the presidency of the Commission and the presidency of the Chamber. Those rules shall ensure that the functions of the President of the Commission are exercised at all times and that, in the case of an enquiry, they are exercised by a person who is not a national of a Party to the conflict.

7. The administrative expenses of the Commission shall be met by contributions from the High Contracting Parties which made declarations under paragraph 2, and by

voluntary contributions. The Party or Parties to the conflict requesting an enquiry shall advance the necessary funds for expenses incurred by a Chamber and shall be reimbursed by the Party or Parties against which the allegations are made to the extent of fifty per cent of the costs of the Chamber. Where there are counter-allegations before the Chamber each side shall advance fifty per cent of the necessary funds.

Article 91.—Responsibility

A Party to the conflict which violates the provisions of the Conventions or of this Protocol shall, if the case demands, be liable to pay compensation. It shall be responsible for all acts committed by persons forming part of its armed forces.

A5–092

Part VI FinaL Provisions

Article 92.—Signature

This Protocol shall be open for signature by the Parties to the Conventions six months after the signing of the Final Act and will remain open for a period of twelve months.

A5–093

Article 93.—Ratification

This Protocol shall be ratified as soon as possible. The instruments of ratification shall be deposited with the Swiss Federal Council, depositary of the Conventions.

A5–094

Article 94.—Accession

This Protocol shall be open for accession by any Party to the Conventions which has not signed it. The instruments of accession shall be deposited with the depositary.

A5–095

Article 95.—Entry into force

1. This Protocol shall enter into force six months after two instruments of ratification or accession have been deposited.
2. For each Party to the Conventions thereafter ratifying or acceding to this Protocol, it shall enter into force six months after the deposit by such Party of its instrument of ratification or accession.

A5–096

Article 96.—Treaty relations upon entry into force of this Protocol

1. When the Parties to the Conventions are also Parties to this Protocol, the Conventions shall apply as supplemented by this Protocol.
2. When one of the Parties to the conflict is not bound by this Protocol, the Parties to the Protocol shall remain bound by it in their mutual relations. They shall furthermore be bound by this Protocol in relation to each of the Parties which are not bound by it, if the latter accepts and applies the provisions thereof.
3. The authority representing a people engaged against a High Contracting Party in an armed conflict of the type referred to in Article 1, paragraph 4, may undertake to apply the Conventions and this Protocol in relation to that conflict by means of a unilateral declaration addressed to the depositary. Such declaration shall, upon its receipt by the depositary, have in relation to that conflict the following effects:
   (a) The Conventions and this Protocol are brought into force for the said authority as a Party to the conflict with immediate effect;

A5–097

(b) The said authority assumes the same rights and obligations as those which have been assumed by a High Contracting Party to the Conventions and this Protocol; and

(c) The Conventions and this Protocol are equally binding upon all Parties to the conflict.

ARTICLE 97.—AMENDMENT

A5–098   1. Any High Contracting Party may propose amendments to this Protocol. The text of any proposed amendment shall be communicated to the depositary, which shall decide, after consultation with all the High Contracting Parties and the International Committee of the Red Cross, whether a conference should be convened to consider the proposed amendment.

2. The depositary shall invite to that conference all the High Contracting Parties as well as the Parties to the Conventions, whether or not they are signatories of this Protocol.

ARTICLE 98.—REVISION OF ANNEX L

A5–099   1. Not later than four years after the entry into force of this Protocol and thereafter at intervals of not less than four years, the International Committee of the Red Cross shall consult the High Contracting Parties concerning Annex I to this Protocol and, if it considers it necessary, may propose a meeting of technical experts to review Annex I and to propose such amendments to it as may appear to be desirable. Unless, within six months of the communication of a proposal for such a meeting to the High Contracting Parties, one third of them object, the International Committee of the Red Cross shall convene the meeting, inviting also observers of appropriate international organizations. Such a meeting shall also be convened by the International Committee of the Red Cross at any time at the request of one third of the High Contracting Parties.

2. The depositary shall convene a conference of the High Contracting Parties and the Parties to the Conventions to consider amendments proposed by the meeting of technical experts if, after that meeting, the International Committee of the Red Cross or one third of the High Contracting Parties so request.

3. Amendments to Annex I may be adopted at such a conference by a two-thirds majority of the High Contracting Parties present and voting.

4. The depositary shall communicate any amendment so adopted to the High Contracting Parties and to the Parties to the Conventions. The amendment shall be considered to have been accepted at the end of a period of one year after it has been so communicated, unless within that period a declaration of non-acceptance of the amendment has been communicated to the depositary by not less than one third of the High Contracting Parties.

5. An amendment considered to have been accepted in accordance with paragraph 4 shall enter into force three months after its acceptance for all High Contracting Parties other than those which have made a declaration of non-acceptance in accordance with that paragraph. Any Party making such a declaration may at any time withdraw it and the amendment shall then enter into force for that Party three months thereafter.

6. The depositary shall notify the High Contracting Parties and the Parties to the Conventions of the entry into force of any amendment, of the Parties bound thereby, of the date of its entry into force in relation to each Party, of declarations of non-acceptance made in accordance with paragraph 4, and of withdrawals of such declarations.

ARTICLE 99.—DENUNCIATION

A5–100   1. In case a High Contracting Party should denounce this Protocol, the denunciation shall only take effect one year after receipt of the instrument of denunciation. If, however, on the expiry of that year the denouncing Party is engaged in one of the situations referred to in Article 1, the denunciation shall not take effect before the end of the armed conflict or occupation and not, in any case, before operations connected with the final release, repatriation or re-establishment of the persons protected by the Conventions or this Protocol have been terminated.

2. The denunciation shall be notified in writing to the depositary, which shall transmit it to all the High Contracting Parties.

3. The denunciation shall have effect only in respect of the denouncing Party.

4. Any denunciation under paragraph I shall not affect the obligations already incurred, by reason of the armed conflict, under this Protocol by such denouncing Party in respect of any act committed before this denunciation becomes effective.

ARTICLE 100.—NOTIFICATIONS

The depositary shall inform the High Contracting Parties as well as the Parties to the Conventions, whether or not they are signatories of this Protocol, of: **A5–101**
   (a) Signatures affixed to this Protocol and the deposit of instruments of ratification and accession under Articles 93 and 94;
   (b) The date of entry into force of this Protocol under Article 95;
   (c) Communications and declarations received under Articles 84, 90 and 97;
   (d) Declarations received under Article 96, paragraph 3, which shall be communicated by the quickest methods; and
   (e) Denunciations under Article 99.

ARTICLE 101.—REGISTRATION

1. After its entry into force, this Protocol shall be transmitted by the depositary to the Secretariat of the United Nations for registration and publication, in accordance with Article 102 of the Charter of the United Nations. **A5–102**

2. The depositary shall also inform the Secretariat of the United Nations of all ratifications, accessions and denunciations received by it with respect to this Protocol.

ARTICLE 102.—AUTHENTIC TEXTS

The original of this Protocol, of which the Arabic, Chinese, English, French, Russian and Spanish texts are equally authentic, shall be deposited with the depositary, which shall transmit certified true copies thereof to all the Parties to the Conventions. **A5–103**

ANNEX I

Regulations concerning identification

CHAPTER 1.—IDENTITY CARDS

ARTICLE I.—IDENTITY CARD FOR PERMANENT CIVILIAN MEDICAL AND RELIGIOUS PERSONNEL

1. The identity card for permanent civilian medical and religious personnel referred to in Article 18, paragraph 3, of the Protocol should: **A5–104**
   (a) Bear the distinctive emblem and be of such size that it can be carried in the pocket;
   (b) Be as durable as practicable;

(c) Be worded in the national or official language (and may in addition be worded in other languages);

(d) Mention the name, the date of birth (or, if that date is not available, the age at the time of issue) and the identity number, if any, of the holder,

(e) State in what capacity the holder is entitled to the protection of the Conventions and of the Protocol;

(f) Bear the photograph of the holder as well as his signature or this thumbprint, or both;

(g) Bear the stamp and signature of the competent authority;

(h) State the date of issue and date of expiry of the card.

2. The identity card shall be uniform throughout the territory of each High Contracting Party and, as far as possible, of the same type for all Parties to the conflict. The Parties to the conflict may be guided by the single-language model shown in Figure 1. At the outbreak of hostilities, they shall transmit to each other a specimen of the model they are using, if such model differs from that shown in Figure 1. The identity card shall be made out, if possible, in duplicate, one copy being kept by the issuing authority, which should maintain control of the cards which it has issued.

3. In no circumstances may permanent civilian medical and religious personnel be deprived of their identity cards. In the event of the loss of a card, they shall be entitled to obtain a duplicate copy.

ARTICLE 2.—IDENTITY CARD FOR TEMPORARY CIVILIAN MEDICAL AND RELIGIOUS PERSONNEL

A5–105　　1. The identity card for temporary civilian medical and religious personnel should, whenever possible, be similar to that provided for in Article I of these Regulations. The Parties to the conflict may be guided by the model shown in Figure 1.

2. When circumstances preclude the provision to temporary civilian medical and religious personnel of identity cards similar to those described in Article I of these Regulations, the said personnel may be provided with a certificate signed by the competent authority certifying that the person to whom it is issued is assigned to duty as temporary personnel and stating, if possible, the duration of such assignment and his right to wear the distinctive emblem. The certificate should mention the holder's name and date of birth (or if that date is not available, his age at the time when the certificate was issued), his function and identity number, if any. It shall bear his signature or his thumbprint, or both.

CHAPTER 11.—THE DISTINCTIVE EMBLEM

ARTICLE 3.—SHAPE AND NATURE

A5–106　　1. The distinctive emblem (red on a white ground) shall be as large as appropriate under the circumstances. For the shapes of the cross, the crescent or the lion and sun, the High Contracting Parties may be guided by the models shown in Figure 2.

2. At night or when visibility is reduced, the distinctive emblem may be lighted or illuminated; it may also be made of materials rendering it recognizable by technical means of detection.

ARTICLE 4.—USE

A5–107　　1. The distinctive emblem shall, whenever possible, be displayed on a flat surface or on flags visible from as many directions and from as far away as possible.

2. Subject to the instructions of the competent authority, medical and religious personnel carrying out their duties in the battle area shall, as far as possible, wear headgear and clothing bearing the distinctive emblem.

Chapter 111.—Distinctive Signals

Article 5.—Optional Use

1. Subject to the provisions of Article 6 of these Regulations, the signals specified in **A5–108** this Chapter for exclusive use by medical units and transports shall nol be used for any other purpose. The use of all signals referred to in this Chapter is optional.

2. Temporary medical aircraft which cannot, either for lack of time or because of their characteristics, be marked with the distinctive emblem, may use the distinctive signals authorized in this Chapter. The best method of effective identification and recognition of medical aircraft is, however, the use of a visual signal, either the distinctive emblem or the light signal specified in Article 6, or both, supplemented by the other signals referred to in Articles 7 and 8 of these Regulations.

Article 6.—Light signal

1. The light signal, consisting of a flashing blue light, is established for the use of **A5–109** medical aircraft to signal their identity. No other aircraft shall use this signal. The recommended blue colour is obtained by using, as trichromatic co-ordinates:

green boundary $y = 0.065 + 0.805x$

white boundary $y = 0.400 - x$

purple boundary $x = 0.133 + 0.600y$

The recommended flashing rate of the blue light is between sixty and one hundred flashes per minute.

2. Medical aircraft should be equipped with such lights as may be necessary to make the light signal visible in as many directions as possible.

3. In the absence of a special agreement between the Parties to the conflict reserving the use of flashing blue lights for the identification of medical vehicles and ships and craft, the use of such signals for other vehicles or ships is not prohibited.

Article 7.—Radio signal

1. The radio signal shall consist of a radiotelephonic or radiotelegraphic message **A5–110** preceded by a distinctive priority signal to be designated and approved by a World Administrative Radio Conference of the International Telecommunication Union. It shall be transmitted three times before the call sign of the medical transport involved. This message shall be transmitted in English at appropriate intervals on a frequency or frequencies specified pursuant to paragraph 3. The use of the priority signal shall be restricted exclusively to medical units and transports.

2. The radio message preceded by the distinctive priority signal mentioned in paragraph I shall convey the following data:

    (a) Call sign of the medical transport;

    (b) Position of the medical transport;

    (c) Number and type of medical transports;

    (d) Intended route;

    (e) Estimated time en route and of departure and arrival, as appropriate;

    (f) Any other information such as flight altitude, radio frequencies guarded, languages and secondary surveillance radar modes and codes.

3. In order to facilitate the communications referred to in paragraphs 1 and 2, as well as the communications referred to in Articles 22, 23, 25, 26, 27, 28, 29, 30 and 31 of the Protocol, the High Contracting Parties, the Parties to a conflict, or one of the Parties to a conflict, acting in agreement or alone, may designate, in accordance with the Table of Frequency Allocations in the Radio Regulations annexed to the International Telecommunication Convention, and publish selected national frequencies to be used by them for such communications. These frequencies shall be notified to the International Telecommunication Union in accordance with procedures to be approved by a World Administrative Radio Conference.

ARTICLE 8.—ELECTRONIC IDENTIFICATION

A5–111   1. The Secondary Surveillance Radar (SSR) system, as specified in Annex 10 to the Chicago Convention on International Civil Aviation of 7 December 1944, as amended from time to time, may be used to identify and to follow the course of medical aircraft. The SSR mode and code to be reserved for the exclusive use of medical aircraft shall be established by the High Contracting Parties, the Parties to a conflict, or one of the Parties to a conflict, acting in agreement or alone, in accordance with procedures to be recommended by the International Civil Aviation Organization.

2. Parties to a conflict may, by special agreement between them, establish for their use a similar electronic system for the identification of medical vehicles, and medical ships and craft.

CHAPTER IV.—COMMUNICATIONS

ARTICLE 9.—RADIOCOMMUNICATIONS

A5–112   The priority signal provided for in Article 7 of these Regulations may precede appropriate radiocommunications by medical units and transports in the application of the procedures carried out under Articles 22, 23, 25, 26, 27, 28, 29, 30 and 31 of the Protocol.

ARTICLE 10.—USE OF INTERNATIONAL CODES

A5–113   Medical units and transports may also use the codes and signals laid down by the International Telecommunication Union, the International Civil Aviation Organization and the Inter-Governmental Maritime Consultative Organization. These codes and signals shall be used in accordance with the standards, practices and procedures established by these Organizations.

ARTICLE 11.—OTHER MEANS OF COMMUNICATION

A5–114   When two-way radiocommunication is not possible, the signals provided for in the International Code of Signals adopted by the Inter-Governmental Maritime Consultative Organization or in the appropriate Annex to the Chicago Convention on International Civil Aviation of 7 December 1944, as amended from time to time, may be used.

ARTICLE 12.—FLIGHT PLANS

A5–115   The agreements and notifications relating to flight plans provided for in Article 29 of the Protocol shall as far as possible be formulated in accordance with procedures laid down by the International Civil Aviation Organization.

ARTICLE 13.—SIGNALS AND PROCEDURES FOR THE INTERCEPTION OF MEDICAL AIRCRAFT

A5–116   If an intercepting aircraft is used to verify the identity of a medical aircraft in flight or to require it to land in accordance with Articles 30 and 31 of the Protocol, the standard visual and radio interception procedures prescribed by Annex 2 to the Chicago Convention on International Civil Aviation of 7 December 1944, as amended from time to time, should be used by the intercepting and the medical aircraft.

Chapter V.—Civil Defence Article 14.—Identity card

1. The identity card of the civil defence personnel provided for in Article 66. paragraph 3, of the Protocol is governed by the relevant provisions of Article I of these Regulations.

2. The identity card for civil defence personnel may follow the model shown in Figure 3.

3. If civil defence personnel are permitted to carry light individual weapons, an entry to that effect should be made on the card mentioned.

Article 15.—International distinctive sign

1. The international distinctive sign of civil defence provided for in Article 66, paragraph 4, of the Protocol is an equilateral blue triangle on an orange ground. A model is shown in Figure 4:

2. It is recommended that:
   (a) If the blue triangle is on a flag or armlet or tabard. the ground to the triangle be the orange flag, armlet or tabard;
   (b) One of the angles of the triangle be pointed vertically upwards;
   (c) No angle of the triangle touch the edge of the orange ground.

3. The international distinctive sign shall be as large as appropriate under the circumstances. The distinctive sign shall, whenever possible, be displayed on flat surfaces or on flags visible from as many directions and from as far away as possible. Subject to the instructions of the competent authority, civil defence personnel shall, as far as possible, wear headgear and clothing bearing the international distinctive sign. At night or when visibility is reduced, the sign may be lighted or illuminated; it may also be made of materials rendering it recognizable by technical means of detection.

Chapter VI.—Works and Installations Containing Dangerous Forces

Article 16.—International special sign

1. The international special sign for works and installations containing dangerous forces, as provided for in Article 56, paragraph 7, of the Protocol. shall be a group of three bright orange circles of equal size, placed on the same axis, the distance between each circle being one radius, in accordance with Figure 5 illustrated below.

2. The sign shall be as large as appropriate under the circumstances. When displayed over an extended surface it may be repeated as often as appropriate under the circumstances. It shall, whenever possible, be displayed on flat surfaces or on flags so as to be visible from as many directions and from as far away as possible.

3. On a flag, the distance between the outer limits of the sign and the adjacent sides of the flag shall be one radius of a circle. The flag shall be rectangular and shall have a white ground.

4. At night or when visibility is reduced, the sign may be lighted or illuminated. It may also be made of materials rendering it recognizable by technical means of detection.

A6. Protocol Additional to the Geneva Conventions of 12 August 1949, and Relating to the Protection of Victims of Non-International Armed Conflicts (Protocol II)

Adopted on 8 June 1977 by the Diplomatic Conference on the Reaffirmation and Development of International Humanitarian Law applicable in Armed Conflicts

entry into force 7 December 1978, in accordance with Article 23

PREAMBLE

A6–001   The High Contracting Parties,

Recalling that the humanitarian principles enshrined in Article 3 common to the Geneva Conventions of 12 August 1949 constitute the foundation of respect for the human person in cases of armed conflict not of an international character,

Recalling furthermore that international instruments relating to human rights offer a basic protection to the human person,

Emphasizing the need to ensure a better protection for the victims of those armed conflicts,

Recalling that, in cases not covered by the law in force, the human person remains under the protection of the principles of humanity and the dictates of the public conscience,

Have agreed on the following:

PART I

SCOPE OF THIS PROTOCOL

ARTICLE 1.—MATERIAL FIELD OF APPLICATION

A6–002   1. This Protocol, which develops and supplements Article 3 common to the Geneva Conventions of 12 August 1949 without modifying its existing conditions of application, shall apply to all armed conflicts which are not covered by Article 1 of the Protocol Additional to the Geneva Conventions of 12 August 1949, and relating to the Protection of Victims of International Armed Conflicts (Protocol I) and which take place in the territory of a High Contracting Party between its armed forces and dissident armed forces or other organized armed groups which, under responsible command, exercise such control over a part of its territory as to enable them to carry out sustained and concerted military operations and to implement this Protocol.

2. This Protocol shall not apply to situations of internal disturbances and tensions, such as riots, isolated and sporadic acts of violence and other acts of a similar nature, as not being armed conflicts.

ARTICLE 2.—PERSONAL FIELD OF APPLICATION

A6–003   1. This Protocol shall be applied without any adverse distinction founded on race, colour, sex, language, religion or belief, political or other opinion, national or social origin, wealth, birth or other status, or on any other similar criteria (hereinafter referred to as "adverse distinction") to all persons affected by an armed conflict as defined in Article 1.

2. At the end of the armed conflict, all the persons who have been deprived of their liberty or whose liberty has been restricted for reasons related to such conflict, as well as

those deprived of their liberty or whose liberty is restricted after the conflict for the same reasons, shall enjoy the protection of Articles 5 and 6 until the end of such deprivation or restriction of liberty.

Article 3.—Non-intervention

1. Nothing in this Protocol shall be invoked for the purpose of affecting the **A6–004** sovereignty of a State or the responsibility of the government, by all legitimate means, to maintain or re-establish law and order in the State or to defend the national unity and territorial integrity of the State.

2. Nothing in this Protocol shall be invoked as a justification for intervening, directly or indirectly, for any reason whatever, in the armed conflict or in the internal or external affairs of the High Contracting Party in the territory of which that conflict occurs.

Part II

HUMANE TREATMENT

Article 4.—Fundamental guarantees

1. All persons who do not take a direct part or who have ceased to take part in **A6–005** hostilities, whether or not their liberty has been restricted, are entitled to respect for their person, honour and convictions and religious practices. They shall in all circumstances be treated humanely, without any adverse distinction. It is prohibited to order that there shall be no survivors.

2. Without prejudice to the generality of the foregoing, the following acts against the persons referred to in paragraph I are and shall remain prohibited at any time and in any place whatsoever:

    (a) Violence to the life, health and physical or mental well-being of persons, in particular murder as well as cruel treatment such as torture, mutilation or any form of corporal punishment;

    (b) Collective punishments;

    (c) Taking of hostages;

    (d) Acts of terrorism;

    (e) Outrages upon personal dignity, in particular humiliating and degrading treatment, rape, enforced prostitution and any form of indecent assault;

    (f) Slavery and the slave trade in all their forms;

    (g) Pillage;

    (h) Threats to commit any of the foregoing acts.

3. Children shall be provided with the care and aid they require, and in particular:

    (a) They shall receive an education, including religious and moral education, in keeping with the wishes of their parents, or in the absence of parents, of those responsible for their care;

    (b) All appropriate steps shall be taken to facilitate the reunion of families temporarily separated;

    (c) Children who have not attained the age of fifteen years shall neither be recruited in the armed forces or groups nor allowed to take part in hostilities;

    (d) The special protection provided by this Article to children who have not attained the age of fifteen years shall remain applicable to them if they take a direct part in hostilities despite the provisions of sub-paragraph (c) and are captured;

    (e) Measures shall be taken, if necessary, and whenever possible with the consent of their parents or persons who by law or custom are primarily responsible for their care, to remove children temporarily from the area in which hostilities are taking place to a safer area within the country and ensure that they are accompanied by persons responsible for their safety and well-being.

ARTICLE 5.—PERSONS WHOSE LIBERTY HAS BEEN RESTRICTED

A6–006   1. In addition to the provisions of Article 4, the following provisions shall be respected as a minimum with regard to persons deprived of their liberty for reasons related to the armed conflict, whether they are interned or detained:

    (a) The wounded and the sick shall be treated in accordance with Article 7;

    (b) The persons referred to in this paragraph shall, to the same extent as the local civilian population, be provided with food and drinking water and be afforded safeguards as regards health and hygiene and protection against the rigours of the climate and the dangers of the armed conflict;

    (c) They shall be allowed to receive individual or collective relief;

    (d) They shall be allowed to practise their religion and, if requested and appropriate, to receive spiritual assistance from persons, such as chaplains, performing religious functions;

    (e) They shall, if made to work, have the benefit of working conditions and safeguards similar to those enjoyed by the local civilian population.

2. Those who are responsible for the internment or detention of the persons referred to in paragraph I shall also, within the limits of their capabilities, respect the following provisions relating to such persons:

    (a) Except when men and women of a family are accommodated together, women shall be held in quarters separated from those of men and shall be under the immediate supervision of women;

    (b) They shall be allowed to send and receive letters and cards, the number of which may be limited by the competent authority if it deems necessary;

    (c) Places of internment and detention shall not be located close to the combat zone. The persons referred to in paragraph 1 shall be evacuated when the places where they are interned or detained become particularly exposed to danger arising out of the armed conflict, if their evacuation can be carried out under adequate conditions of safety;

    (d) They shall have the benefit of medical examinations;

    (e) Their physical or mental health and integrity shall not be endangered by an unjustified act or omission. Accordingly, it is prohibited to subject the persons described in this Article to any medical procedure which is not indicated by the state of health of the person concerned, and which is not consistent with the generally accepted medical standards applied to free persons under similar medical circumstances.

3. Persons who are not covered by paragraph I but whose liberty has been restricted in any way whatsoever for reasons related to the armed conflict shall be treated humanely in accordance with Article 4 and with paragraphs 1 (a), (c) and (d), and 2 (b) of this Article.

4. If it is decided to release persons deprived of their liberty, necessary measures to ensure their safety shall be taken by those so deciding.

ARTICLE 6.—PENAL PROSECUTIONS

A6–007   1. This Article applies to the prosecution and punishment of criminal offences related to the armed conflict.

2. No sentence shall be passed and no penalty shall be executed on a person found guilty of an offence except pursuant to a conviction pronounced by a court offering the essential guarantees of independence and impartiality. In particular:

    (a) The procedure shall provide for an accused to be informed without delay of the particulars of the offence alleged against him and shall afford the accused before and during his trial all necessary rights and means of defence;

    (b) No one shall be convicted of an offence except on the basis of individual penal responsibility;

    (c) No one shall be held guilty of any criminal offence on account of any act or omission which did not constitute a criminal offence, under the law, at the time when it was committed; nor shall a heavier penalty be imposed than that which was applicable at the time when the criminal offence was committed; if, after the commission of the offence, provision is made by law for the imposition of a lighter penalty, the offender shall benefit thereby;

(d) Anyone charged with an offence is presumed innocent until proved guilty according to law;

(e) Anyone charged with an offence shall have the right to be tried in his presence;

(f) No one shall be compelled to testify against himself or to confess guilt.

3. A convicted person shall be advised on conviction of his judicial and other remedies and of the time-limits within which they may be exercised.

4. The death penalty shall not be pronounced on persons who were under the age of eighteen years at the time of the offence and shall not be carried out on pregnant women or mothers of young children.

5. At the end of hostilities, the authorities in power shall endeavour to grant the broadest possible amnesty to persons who have participated in the armed conflict, or those deprived of their liberty for reasons related to the armed conflict, whether they are interned or detained.

Part III

WOUNDED, SICK AND SHIPWRECKED

Article 7.—Protection and care

1. All the wounded, sick and shipwrecked, whether or not they have taken part in the armed conflict, shall be respected and protected. **A6–008**

2. In all circumstances they shall be treated humanely and shall receive, to the fullest extent practicable and with the least possible delay, the medical care and attention required by their condition. There shall be no distinction among them founded on any grounds other than medical ones.

Article 8.—Search

Whenever circumstances permit, and particularly after an engagement, all possible measures shall be taken, without delay, to search for and collect the wounded, sick and shipwrecked, to protect them against pillage and ill- treatment, to ensure their adequate care, and to search for the dead, prevent their being despoiled, and decently dispose of them. **A6–009**

Article 9.—Protection of medical and religious personnel

1. Medical and religious personnel shall be respected and protected and shall be granted all available help for the performance of their duties. They shall not be compelled to carry out tasks which are not compatible with their humanitarian mission. **A6–010**

2. In the performance of their duties medical personnel may not be required to give priority to any person except on medical grounds.

Article 10.—General protection of medical duties

1. Under no circumstances shall any person be punished for having carried out medical activities compatible with medical ethics, regardless of the person benefiting therefrom. **A6–011**

2. Persons engaged in medical activities shall neither be compelled to perform acts or to carry out work contrary to, nor be compelled to refrain from acts required by, the

rules of medical ethics or other rules designed for the benefit of the wounded and sick, or this Protocol.

3. The professional obligations of persons engaged in medical activities regarding information which they may acquire concerning the wounded and sick under their care shall, subject to national law, be respected.

4. Subject to national law, no person engaged in medical activities may be penalized in any way for refusing or failing to give information concerning the wounded and sick who are, or who have been, under his care.

ARTICLE 11.—PROTECTION OF MEDICAL UNITS AND TRANSPORTS

A6–012   1. Medical units and transports shall be respected and protected at all times and shall not be the object of attack.

2. The protection to which medical units and transports are entitled shall not cease unless they are used to commit hostile acts, outside their humanitarian function. Protection may, however, cease only after a warning has been given setting, whenever appropriate, a reasonable time-limit, and after such warning has remained unheeded.

ARTICLE 12.—THE DISTINCTIVE EMBLEM

A6–013   Under the direction of the competent authority concerned, the distinctive emblem of the red cross, red crescent or red lion and sun on a white ground shall be displayed by medical and religious personnel and medical units, and on medical transports. It shall be respected in all circumstances. It shall not be used improperly.

PART IV

CIVILIAN POPULATION

ARTICLE 13.—PROTECTION OF THE CIVILIAN POPULATION

A6–014   1. The civilian population and individual civilians shall enjoy general protection against the dangers arising from military operations. To give effect to this protection, the following rules shall be observed in all circumstances.

2. The civilian population as such, as well as individual civilians, shall not be the object of attack. Acts or threats of violence the primary purpose of which is to spread terror among the civilian population are prohibited.

3. Civilians shall enjoy the protection afforded by this Part, unless and for such time as they take a direct part in hostilities.

ARTICLE 14.—PROTECTION OF OBJECTS INDISPENSABLE TO THE SURVIVAL OF THE CIVILIAN POPULATION

A6–015   Starvation of civilians as a method of combat is prohibited. It is therefore prohibited to attack, destroy, remove or render useless, for that purpose, objects indispensable to the survival of the civilian population, such as foodstuffs, agricultural areas for the production of foodstuffs, crops, livestock, drinking water installations and supplies and irrigation works.

ARTICLE 15.—PROTECTION OF WORKS AND INSTALLATIONS CONTAINING DANGEROUS FORCES

A6–016   Works or installations containing dangerous forces, namely dams, dykes and nuclear electrical generating stations, shall not be made the object of attack, even where these objects are military objectives, if such attack may cause the release of dangerous forces and consequent severe losses among the civilian population.

Article 16.—Protection of cultural objects and of places of worship

Without prejudice to the provisions of The Hague Convention for the Protection of **A6–017** Cultural Property in the Event of Armed Conflict of 14 May 1954, it is prohibited to commit any acts of hostility directed against historic monuments, works of art or places of worship which constitute the cultural or spiritual heritage of peoples, and to use them in support of the military effort.

Article 17.—Prohibition of forced movement of civilians

1. The displacement of the civilian population shall not be ordered for reasons related **A6–018** to the conflict unless the security of the civilians involved or imperative military reasons so demand. Should such displacements have to be carried out, all possible measures shall be taken in order that the civilian population may be received under satisfactory conditions of shelter, hygiene, health, safety and nutrition.
2. Civilians shall not be compelled to leave their own territory for reasons connected with the conflict.

Article 18.—Relief societies and relief actions

1. Relief societies located in the territory of the High Contracting Party, such as Red **A6–019** Cross (Red Crescent, Red Lion and Sun) organizations, may offer their services for the performance of their traditional functions in relation to the victims of the armed conflict. The civilian population may, even on its own initiative, offer to collect and care for the wounded, sick and shipwrecked.
2. If the civilian population is suffering undue hardship owing to a lack of the supplies essential for its survival, such as foodstuffs and medical supplies, relief actions for the civilian population which are of an exclusively humanitarian and impartial nature and which are conducted without any adverse distinction shall be undertaken subject to the consent of the High Contracting Party concerned.

Part V

FINAL PROVISIONS

Article 19.—Dissemination

This Protocol shall be disseminated as widely as possible. **A6–020**

Article 20.—Signature

This Protocol shall be open for signature by the Parties to the Conventions six months **A6–021** after the signing of the Final Act and will remain open for a period of twelve months.

Article 21.—Ratification

This Protocol shall be ratified as soon as possible. The instruments of ratification shall **A6–022** be deposited with the Swiss Federal Council, depositary of the Conventions.

Article 22.—Accession

This Protocol shall be open for accession by any Party to the Conventions which has **A6–023** not signed it. The instruments of accession shall be deposited with the depositary.

ARTICLE 23.—ENTRY INTO FORCE

A6–024   1. This Protocol shall enter into force six months after two instruments of ratification or accession have been deposited.

2. For each Party to the Conventions thereafter ratifying or acceding to this Protocol, it shall enter into force six months after the deposit by such Party of its instrument of ratification or accession.

ARTICLE 24.—AMENDMENT

A6–025   1. Any High Contracting Party may propose amendments to this Protocol. The text of any proposed amendment shall be communicated to the depositary which shall decide, after consultation with all the High Contracting Parties and the International Committee of the Red Cross, whether a conference should be convened to consider the proposed amendment.

2. The depositary shall invite to that conference all the High Contracting Parties as well as the Parties to the Conventions, whether or not they are signatories of this Protocol.

ARTICLE 25.—DENUNCIATION

A6–026   1. In case a High Contracting Party should denounce this Protocol, the denunciation shall only take effect six months after receipt of the instrument of denunciation. If, however, on the expiry of six months, the denouncing Party is engaged in the situation referred to in Article 1, the denunciation shall not take effect before the end of the armed conflict. Persons who have been deprived of liberty, or whose liberty has been restricted, for reasons related to the conflict shall nevertheless continue to benefit from the provisions of this Protocol until their final release.

2. The denunciation shall be notified in writing to the depositary, which shall transmit it to all the High Contracting Parties.

ARTICLE 26.—NOTIFICATIONS

A6–027   The depositary shall inform the High Contracting Parties as well as the Parties to the Conventions, whether or not they are signatories of this Protocol, of:

    (a) Signatures affixed to this Protocol and the deposit of instruments of ratification and accession under Articles 21 and 22;

    (b) The date of entry into force of this Protocol under Article 23; and

    (c) Communications and declarations received under Article 24.

ARTICLE 27.—REGISTRATION

A6–028   1. After its entry into force, this Protocol shall be transmitted by the depositary to the Secretariat of the United Nations for registration and publication, in accordance with Article 102 of the Charter of the United Nations.

2. The depositary shall also inform the Secretariat of the United Nations of all ratifications and accessions received by it with respect to this Protocol.

ARTICLE 28.—AUTHENTIC TEXTS

A6–029   The original of this Protocol, of which the Arabic, Chinese, English, French, Russian and Spanish texts are equally authentic shall be deposited with the depositary, which shall transmit certified true copies thereof to all the Parties to the Conventions.

A7. International Covenant on Civil and Political Rights

Adopted and opened for signature, ratification and accession by General Assembly resolution 2200A (XXI) of 16 December 1966

entry into force **23 March 1976, in accordance with Article 49**

This document may be found at *http://www.ohchr.org/english/law/pdf/ccpr.pdf*   **A7–001**

A8. Optional Protocol to the International Covenant on Civil and Political Rights

Adopted and opened for signature, ratification and accession by General Assembly resolution 2200A (XXI) of 16 December 1966

entry into force **23 March 1976, in accordance with Article 9**

This document may be found at *http://www.ohchr.org/english/law/pdf/ccpr-one.pdf*   **A8–001**

A9. Second Optional Protocol to the International Covenant on Civil and Political Rights, aiming at the abolition of the death penalty

Adopted and proclaimed by General Assembly resolution 44/128 of 15 December 1989

This document may be found at *http://www.ohchr.org/english/law/pdf/ccpr-death.pdf*   **A9–001**

A10. Convention on the Prevention and Punishment of the Crime of Genocide

Approved and proposed for signature and ratification or accession by General Assembly resolution 260 A (III) of 9 December 1948

entry into force **12 January 1951, in accordance with article XIII**

The Contracting Parties,   **A10–001**

Having considered the declaration made by the General Assembly of the United Nations in its resolution 96 (I) dated 11 December 1946 that genocide is a crime under international law, contrary to the spirit and aims of the United Nations and condemned by the civilized world,

Recognizing that at all periods of history genocide has inflicted great losses on humanity, and

Being convinced that, in order to liberate mankind from such an odious scourge, international co-operation is required,

Hereby agree as hereinafter provided:

ARTICLE 1

A10–002   The Contracting Parties confirm that genocide, whether committed in time of peace or in time of war, is a crime under international law which they undertake to prevent and to punish.

ARTICLE 2

A10–003   In the present Convention, genocide means any of the following acts committed with intent to destroy, in whole or in part, a national, ethnical, racial or religious group, as such:

(a) Killing members of the group;
(b) Causing serious bodily or mental harm to members of the group;
(c) Deliberately inflicting on the group conditions of life calculated to bring about its physical destruction in whole or in part;
(d) Imposing measures intended to prevent births within the group;
(e) Forcibly transferring children of the group to another group.

ARTICLE 3

A10–004   The following acts shall be punishable:

(a) Genocide;
(b) Conspiracy to commit genocide;
(c) Direct and public incitement to commit genocide;
(d) Attempt to commit genocide;
(e) Complicity in genocide.

ARTICLE 4

A10–005   Persons committing genocide or any of the other acts enumerated in article III shall be punished, whether they are constitutionally responsible rulers, public officials or private individuals.

ARTICLE 5

A10–006   The Contracting Parties undertake to enact, in accordance with their respective Constitutions, the necessary legislation to give effect to the provisions of the present Convention, and, in particular, to provide effective penalties for persons guilty of genocide or any of the other acts enumerated in article III.

ARTICLE 6

A10–007   Persons charged with genocide or any of the other acts enumerated in article III shall be tried by a competent tribunal of the State in the territory of which the act was committed, or by such international penal tribunal as may have jurisdiction with respect to those Contracting Parties which shall have accepted its jurisdiction.

ARTICLE 7

A10–008   Genocide and the other acts enumerated in article III shall not be considered as political crimes for the purpose of extradition.

The Contracting Parties pledge themselves in such cases to grant extradition in accordance with their laws and treaties in force.

ARTICLE 8

Any Contracting Party may call upon the competent organs of the United Nations to take such action under the Charter of the United Nations as they consider appropriate for the prevention and suppression of acts of genocide or any of the other acts enumerated in article III.

A10–009

ARTICLE 9

Disputes between the Contracting Parties relating to the interpretation, application or fulfilment of the present Convention, including those relating to the responsibility of a State for genocide or for any of the other acts enumerated in article III, shall be submitted to the International Court of Justice at the request of any of the parties to the dispute.

A10–010

ARTICLE 10

The present Convention, of which the Chinese, English, French, Russian and Spanish texts are equally authentic, shall bear the date of 9 December 1948.

A10–011

ARTICLE 11

The present Convention shall be open until 31 December 1949 for signature on behalf of any Member of the United Nations and of any nonmember State to which an invitation to sign has been addressed by the General Assembly.

The present Convention shall be ratified, and the instruments of ratification shall be deposited with the Secretary-General of the United Nations.

After 1 January 1950, the present Convention may be acceded to on behalf of any Member of the United Nations and of any non-member State which has received an invitation as aforesaid. Instruments of accession shall be deposited with the Secretary-General of the United Nations.

A10–012

ARTICLE 12

Any Contracting Party may at any time, by notification addressed to the Secretary-General of the United Nations, extend the application of the present Convention to all or any of the territories for the conduct of whose foreign relations that Contracting Party is responsible.

A10–013

ARTICLE 13

On the day when the first twenty instruments of ratification or accession have been deposited, the Secretary-General shall draw up a proces-verbal and transmit a copy thereof to each Member of the United Nations and to each of the non-member States contemplated in article 11.

The present Convention shall come into force on the ninetieth day following the date of deposit of the twentieth instrument of ratification or accession.

Any ratification or accession effected, subsequent to the latter date shall become effective on the ninetieth day following the deposit of the instrument of ratification or accession.

A10–014

ARTICLE 14

The present Convention shall remain in effect for a period of ten years as from the date of its coming into force.

A10–015

It shall thereafter remain in force for successive periods of five years for such Contracting Parties as have not denounced it at least six months before the expiration of the current period.

Denunciation shall be effected by a written notification addressed to the Secretary-General of the United Nations.

ARTICLE 15

A10–016   If, as a result of denunciations, the number of Parties to the present Convention should become less than sixteen, the Convention shall cease to be in force as from the date on which the last of these denunciations shall become effective.

ARTICLE 16

A10–017   A request for the revision of the present Convention may be made at any time by any Contracting Party by means of a notification in writing addressed to the Secretary-General.

The General Assembly shall decide upon the steps, if any, to be taken in respect of such request.

ARTICLE 17

A10–018   The Secretary-General of the United Nations shall notify all Members of the United Nations and the non-member States contemplated in article XI of the following:
- (a) Signatures, ratifications and accessions received in accordance with article 11;
- (b) Notifications received in accordance with article 12;
- (c) The date upon which the present Convention comes into force in accordance with article 13;
- (d) Denunciations received in accordance with article 14;
- (e) he abrogation of the Convention in accordance with article 15;
- (f) Notifications received in accordance with article 16.

ARTICLE 18

A10–019   The original of the present Convention shall be deposited in the archives of the United Nations.

A certified copy of the Convention shall be transmitted to each Member of the United Nations and to each of the non-member States contemplated in article XI.

ARTICLE 19

A10–020   The present Convention shall be registered by the Secretary-General of the United Nations on the date of its coming into force.

A11. Convention against Torture and Other Cruel, Inhuman or Degrading Treatment or Punishment

Adopted and opened for signature, ratification and accession by General Assembly resolution 39/46 of 10 December 1984

entry into force **26 June 1987, in accordance with article 27(1)**

A11–001   This document may be found at *http://www.ohchr.org/english/law/pdf/cat.pdf*

A12. Optional Protocol to the Convention against Torture and other Cruel, Inhuman or Degrading Treatment or Punishment

Adopted on 18 December 2002 at the fifty-seventh session of the General Assembly of the United Nations by resolution A/RES/57/199.

These documents may be found at *http://www.ohchr.org/english/law/cat-one.htm* and *http://untreaty.un.org/English/notpubl/iv—9bE.pdf*   **A12–001**

A13. Convention on the Non-Applicability of Statutory Limitations to War Crimes and Crimes Against Humanity

Adopted and opened for signature, ratification and accession by General Assembly resolution 2391 (XXIII) of 26 November 1968

Entry into force 11 November 1970, in accordance with article VIII

PREAMBLE

This document may be found at *http://www.ohchr.org/english/law/pdf/warcrimes.pdf*   **A13–001**

A14. Convention (IV) respecting the Laws and Customs of War on Land and its annex: Regulations concerning the Laws and Customs of War on Land. The Hague, 18 October 1907.

This document may be found at *http://www.icrc.org/ihl.nsf/FULL/195?OpenDocument*   **A14–001**

A15. Convention for the Protection of Cultural Property in the Event of Armed Conflict. The Hague, 14 May 1954.

This document may be found at *http://www.icrc.org/ihl.nsf/FULL/400?OpenDocument*   **A15–001**

A16. Protocol for the Protection of Cultural Property in the Event of Armed Conflict. The Hague, 14 May 1954.

This document may be found at *http://www.icrc.org/ihl.nsf/FULL/410?OpenDocument*   **A16–001**

A17. Second Protocol to the Hague Convention of 1954 for the Protection of Cultural Property in the Event of Armed Conflict The Hague, 26 March 1999

This document may be found at *http://www.icrc.org/ihl.nsf/FULL/590?OpenDocument*   **A17–001**

A18. Principles of international co-operation in the detection, arrest, extradition and punishment of persons guilty of war crimes and crimes against humanity

Adopted by General Assembly resolution 3074 (XXVIII) of 3 December 1973

A18–001   This document may be found at *http://www.unhchr.ch/html/menu3/b/p—extrad.htm*

A19. Convention for the Protection of Human Rights and Fundamental Freedoms, as amended by Protocol No. 11

A19–001   The text of the Convention had been amended according to the provisions of Protocol No. 3 (ETS No. 45), which entered into force on 21 September 1970, of Protocol No. 5 (ETS No. 55), which entered into force on 20 December 1971 and of Protocol No. 8 (ETS No. 118), which entered into force on 1 January 1990, and comprised also the text of Protocol No. 2 (ETS No. 44) which, in accordance with Article 5, paragraph 3 thereof, had been an integral part of the Convention since its entry into force on 21 September 1970. All provisions which had been amended or added by these Protocols are replaced by Protocol No. 11 (ETS No. 155), as from the date of its entry into force on 1 November 1998. As from that date, Protocol No. 9 (ETS No. 140), which entered into force on 1 October 1994, is repealed and Protocol No. 10 (ETS no. 146) has lost its purpose.

A19–002   The governments signatory hereto, being members of the Council of Europe,

Considering the Universal Declaration of Human Rights proclaimed by the General Assembly of the United Nations on 10th December 1948;

Considering that this Declaration aims at securing the universal and effective recognition and observance of the Rights therein declared;

Considering that the aim of the Council of Europe is the achievement of greater unity between its members and that one of the methods by which that aim is to be pursued is the maintenance and further realisation of human rights and fundamental freedoms;

Reaffirming their profound belief in those fundamental freedoms which are the foundation of justice and peace in the world and are best maintained on the one hand by an effective political democracy and on the other by a common understanding and observance of the human rights upon which they depend;

Being resolved, as the governments of European countries which are like-minded and have a common heritage of political traditions, ideals, freedom and the rule of law, to take the first steps for the collective enforcement of certain of the rights stated in the Universal Declaration,

Have agreed as follows:

ARTICLE 1[1]—OBLIGATION TO RESPECT HUMAN RIGHTS

A19–003   The High Contracting Parties shall secure to everyone within their jurisdiction the rights and freedoms defined in Section I of this Convention.

Section I[1]—Rights and freedoms

ARTICLE 2[1]—RIGHT TO LIFE

A19–004   1 Everyone's right to life shall be protected by law. No one shall be deprived of his life intentionally save in the execution of a sentence of a court following his conviction of a crime for which this penalty is provided by law.

---

[1] Heading added according to the provisions of Protocol No. 11 (ETS No. 155).

2 Deprivation of life shall not be regarded as inflicted in contravention of this article when it results from the use of force which is no more than absolutely necessary:

    a in defence of any person from unlawful violence;

    b in order to effect a lawful arrest or to prevent the escape of a person lawfully detained;

    c in action lawfully taken for the purpose of quelling a riot or insurrection.

ARTICLE 3[1]—PROHIBITION OF TORTURE

No one shall be subjected to torture or to inhuman or degrading treatment or punishment.

A19–005

ARTICLE 4[1]—PROHIBITION OF SLAVERY AND FORCED LABOUR

1 No one shall be held in slavery or servitude.

A19–006

2 No one shall be required to perform forced or compulsory labour.

3 For the purpose of this article the term "forced or compulsory labour" shall not include:

    a any work required to be done in the ordinary course of detention imposed according to the provisions of Article 5 of this Convention or during conditional release from such detention;

    b any service of a military character or, in case of conscientious objectors in countries where they are recognised, service exacted instead of compulsory military service;

    c any service exacted in case of an emergency or calamity threatening the life or well-being of the community;

    d any work or service which forms part of normal civic obligations.

ARTICLE 5[1]—RIGHT TO LIBERTY AND SECURITY

1 Everyone has the right to liberty and security of person. No one shall be deprived of his liberty save in the following cases and in accordance with a procedure prescribed by law:

A19–007

    a the lawful detention of a person after conviction by a competent court;

    b the lawful arrest or detention of a person for non- compliance with the lawful order of a court or in order to secure the fulfilment of any obligation prescribed by law;

    c the lawful arrest or detention of a person effected for the purpose of bringing him before the competent legal authority on reasonable suspicion of having committed an offence or when it is reasonably considered necessary to prevent his committing an offence or fleeing after having done so;

    d the detention of a minor by lawful order for the purpose of educational supervision or his lawful detention for the purpose of bringing him before the competent legal authority;

    e the lawful detention of persons for the prevention of the spreading of infectious diseases, of persons of unsound mind, alcoholics or drug addicts or vagrants;

    f the lawful arrest or detention of a person to prevent his effecting an unauthorised entry into the country or of a person against whom action is being taken with a view to deportation or extradition.

2 Everyone who is arrested shall be informed promptly, in a language which he understands, of the reasons for his arrest and of any charge against him.

3 Everyone arrested or detained in accordance with the provisions of paragraph 1.c of this article shall be brought promptly before a judge or other officer authorised by law to

---

[1] Heading added according to the provisions of Protocol No. 11 (ETS No. 155).

exercise judicial power and shall be entitled to trial within a reasonable time or to release pending trial. Release may be conditioned by guarantees to appear for trial.

4 Everyone who is deprived of his liberty by arrest or detention shall be entitled to take proceedings by which the lawfulness of his detention shall be decided speedily by a court and his release ordered if the detention is not lawful.

5 Everyone who has been the victim of arrest or detention in contravention of the provisions of this article shall have an enforceable right to compensation.

Article 6[1]—Right to a fair trial

A19–008   1 In the determination of his civil rights and obligations or of any criminal charge against him, everyone is entitled to a fair and public hearing within a reasonable time by an independent and impartial tribunal established by law. Judgment shall be pronounced publicly but the press and public may be excluded from all or part of the trial in the interests of morals, public order or national security in a democratic society, where the interests of juveniles or the protection of the private life of the parties so require, or to the extent strictly necessary in the opinion of the court in special circumstances where publicity would prejudice the interests of justice.

2 Everyone charged with a criminal offence shall be presumed innocent until proved guilty according to law.

3 Everyone charged with a criminal offence has the following minimum rights:

    a to be informed promptly, in a language which he understands and in detail, of the nature and cause of the accusation against him;

    b to have adequate time and facilities for the preparation of his defence;

    c to defend himself in person or through legal assistance of his own choosing or, if he has not sufficient means to pay for legal assistance, to be given it free when the interests of justice so require;

    d to examine or have examined witnesses against him and to obtain the attendance and examination of witnesses on his behalf under the same conditions as witnesses against him;

    e to have the free assistance of an interpreter if he cannot understand or speak the language used in court.

Article 7[1]—No punishment without law

A19–009   1 No one shall be held guilty of any criminal offence on account of any act or omission which did not constitute a criminal offence under national or international law at the time when it was committed. Nor shall a heavier penalty be imposed than the one that was applicable at the time the criminal offence was committed.

2 This article shall not prejudice the trial and punishment of any person for any act or omission which, at the time when it was committed, was criminal according to the general principles of law recognised by civilised nations.

Article 8[1]—Right to respect for private and family life

A19–010   1 Everyone has the right to respect for his private and family life, his home and his correspondence.

2 There shall be no interference by a public authority with the exercise of this right except such as is in accordance with the law and is necessary in a democratic society in the interests of national security, public safety or the economic well-being of the country, for the prevention of disorder or crime, for the protection of health or morals, or for the protection of the rights and freedoms of others.

---

[1] Heading added according to the provisions of Protocol No. 11 (ETS No. 155).

Article 9[1]—Freedom of thought, conscience and religion

1 Everyone has the right to freedom of thought, conscience and religion; this right **A19–011**
includes freedom to change his religion or belief and freedom, either alone or in
community with others and in public or private, to manifest his religion or belief, in
worship, teaching, practice and observance.
2 Freedom to manifest one's religion or beliefs shall be subject only to such
limitations as are prescribed by law and are necessary in a democratic society in the
interests of public safety, for the protection of public order, health or morals, or for the
protection of the rights and freedoms of others.

Article 10[1]—Freedom of expression

1 Everyone has the right to freedom of expression. This right shall include freedom to **A19–012**
hold opinions and to receive and impart information and ideas without interference by
public authority and regardless of frontiers. This article shall not prevent States from
requiring the licensing of broadcasting, television or cinema enterprises.
2 The exercise of these freedoms, since it carries with it duties and responsibilities,
may be subject to such formalities, conditions, restrictions or penalties as are prescribed
by law and are necessary in a democratic society, in the interests of national security,
territorial integrity or public safety, for the prevention of disorder or crime, for the
protection of health or morals, for the protection of the reputation or rights of others, for
preventing the disclosure of information received in confidence, or for maintaining the
authority and impartiality of the judiciary.

Article 11[1]—Freedom of assembly and association

1 Everyone has the right to freedom of peaceful assembly and to freedom of **A19–013**
association with others, including the right to form and to join trade unions for the
protection of his interests.
2 No restrictions shall be placed on the exercise of these rights other than such as are
prescribed by law and are necessary in a democratic society in the interests of national
security or public safety, for the prevention of disorder or crime, for the protection of
health or morals or for the protection of the rights and freedoms of others. This article
shall not prevent the imposition of lawful restrictions on the exercise of these rights by
members of the armed forces, of the police or of the administration of the State.

Article 12[1]—Right to marry

Men and women of marriageable age have the right to marry and to found a family, **A19–014**
according to the national laws governing the exercise of this right.

Article 13[1]—Right to an effective remedy

Everyone whose rights and freedoms as set forth in this Convention are violated shall **A19–015**
have an effective remedy before a national authority notwithstanding that the violation
has been committed by persons acting in an official capacity.

Article 14[1]—Prohibition of discrimination

The enjoyment of the rights and freedoms set forth in this Convention shall be **A19–016**
secured without discrimination on any ground such as sex, race, colour, language,
religion, political or other opinion, national or social origin, association with a national
minority, property, birth or other status.

[1] Heading added according to the provisions of Protocol No. 11 (ETS No. 155).

ARTICLE 15[1]—DEROGATION IN TIME OF EMERGENCY

A19–017   1 In time of war or other public emergency threatening the life of the nation any High Contracting Party may take measures derogating from its obligations under this Convention to the extent strictly required by the exigencies of the situation, provided that such measures are not inconsistent with its other obligations under international law.

2 No derogation from Article 2, except in respect of deaths resulting from lawful acts of war, or from Articles 3, 4 (paragraph 1) and 7 shall be made under this provision.

3 Any High Contracting Party availing itself of this right of derogation shall keep the Secretary General of the Council of Europe fully informed of the measures which it has taken and the reasons therefor. It shall also inform the Secretary General of the Council of Europe when such measures have ceased to operate and the provisions of the Convention are again being fully executed.

ARTICLE 16[1]—RESTRICTIONS ON POLITICAL ACTIVITY OF ALIENS

A19–018   Nothing in Articles 10, 11 and 14 shall be regarded as preventing the High Contracting Parties from imposing restrictions on the political activity of aliens.

ARTICLE 17[1]—PROHIBITION OF ABUSE OF RIGHTS

A19–019   Nothing in this Convention may be interpreted as implying for any State, group or person any right to engage in any activity or perform any act aimed at the destruction of any of the rights and freedoms set forth herein or at their limitation to a greater extent than is provided for in the Convention.

ARTICLE 18[1]—LIMITATION ON USE OF RESTRICTIONS ON RIGHTS

A19–020   The restrictions permitted under this Convention to the said rights and freedoms shall not be applied for any purpose other than those for which they have been prescribed.

Section II[2]—European Court of Human Rights

ARTICLE 19—ESTABLISHMENT OF THE COURT

A19–021   To ensure the observance of the engagements undertaken by the High Contracting Parties in the Convention and the Protocols thereto, there shall be set up a European Court of Human Rights, hereinafter referred to as "the Court". It shall function on a permanent basis.

ARTICLE 20—NUMBER OF JUDGES

A19–022   The Court shall consist of a number of judges equal to that of the High Contracting Parties.

ARTICLE 21—CRITERIA FOR OFFICE

A19–023   1 The judges shall be of high moral character and must either possess the qualifications required for appointment to high judicial office or be jurisconsults of recognised competence.

---

[1] Heading added according to the provisions of Protocol No. 11 (ETS No. 155).
[2] New Section II according to the provisions of Protocol No. 11 (ETS No. 155).

2 The judges shall sit on the Court in their individual capacity.

3 During their term of office the judges shall not engage in any activity which is incompatible with their independence, impartiality or with the demands of a full-time office; all questions arising from the application of this paragraph shall be decided by the Court.

Article 22—Election of judges

1 The judges shall be elected by the Parliamentary Assembly with respect to each High Contracting Party by a majority of votes cast from a list of three candidates nominated by the High Contracting Party.

A19–024

2 The same procedure shall be followed to complete the Court in the event of the accession of new High Contracting Parties and in filling casual vacancies.

Article 23—Terms of office

1 The judges shall be elected for a period of six years. They may be re-elected. However, the terms of office of one-half of the judges elected at the first election shall expire at the end of three years.

A19–025

2 The judges whose terms of office are to expire at the end of the initial period of three years shall be chosen by lot by the Secretary General of the Council of Europe immediately after their election.

3 In order to ensure that, as far as possible, the terms of office of one-half of the judges are renewed every three years, the Parliamentary Assembly may decide, before proceeding to any subsequent election, that the term or terms of office of one or more judges to be elected shall be for a period other than six years but not more than nine and not less than three years.

4 In cases where more than one term of office is involved and where the Parliamentary Assembly applies the preceding paragraph, the allocation of the terms of office shall be effected by a drawing of lots by the Secretary General of the Council of Europe immediately after the election.

5 A judge elected to replace a judge whose term of office has not expired shall hold office for the remainder of his predecessor's term.

6 The terms of office of judges shall expire when they reach the age of 70.

7 The judges shall hold office until replaced. They shall, however, continue to deal with such cases as they already have under consideration.

Article 24—Dismissal

No judge may be dismissed from his office unless the other judges decide by a majority of two-thirds that he has ceased to fulfil the required conditions.

A19–026

Article 25—Registry and legal secretaries

The Court shall have a registry, the functions and organisation of which shall be laid down in the rules of the Court. The Court shall be assisted by legal secretaries.

A19–027

Article 26—Plenary Court

The plenary Court shall

A19–028

    a elect its President and one or two Vice-Presidents for a period of three years; they may be re-elected;

    b set up Chambers, constituted for a fixed period of time;

    c elect the Presidents of the Chambers of the Court; they may be re-elected;

d adopt the rules of the Court, and

e elect the Registrar and one or more Deputy Registrars.

ARTICLE 27—COMMITTEES, CHAMBERS AND GRAND CHAMBER

A19–029

1 To consider cases brought before it, the Court shall sit in committees of three judges, in Chambers of seven judges and in a Grand Chamber of seventeen judges. The Court's Chambers shall set up committees for a fixed period of time.

2 There shall sit as an ex officio member of the Chamber and the Grand Chamber the judge elected in respect of the State Party concerned or, if there is none or if he is unable to sit, a person of its choice who shall sit in the capacity of judge.

3 The Grand Chamber shall also include the President of the Court, the Vice-Presidents, the Presidents of the Chambers and other judges chosen in accordance with the rules of the Court. When a case is referred to the Grand Chamber under Article 43, no judge from the Chamber which rendered the judgment shall sit in the Grand Chamber, with the exception of the President of the Chamber and the judge who sat in respect of the State Party concerned.

ARTICLE 28—DECLARATIONS OF INADMISSIBILITY BY COMMITTEES

A19–030

A committee may, by a unanimous vote, declare inadmissible or strike out of its list of cases an application submitted under Article 34 where such a decision can be taken without further examination. The decision shall be final.

ARTICLE 29—DECISIONS BY CHAMBERS ON ADMISSIBILITY AND MERITS

A19–031

1 If no decision is taken under Article 28, a Chamber shall decide on the admissibility and merits of individual applications submitted under Article 34.

2 A Chamber shall decide on the admissibility and merits of inter-State applications submitted under Article 33.

3 The decision on admissibility shall be taken separately unless the Court, in exceptional cases, decides otherwise.

ARTICLE 30—RELINQUISHMENT OF JURISDICTION TO THE GRAND CHAMBER

A19–032

Where a case pending before a Chamber raises a serious question affecting the interpretation of the Convention or the protocols thereto, or where the resolution of a question before the Chamber might have a result inconsistent with a judgment previously delivered by the Court, the Chamber may, at any time before it has rendered its judgment, relinquish jurisdiction in favour of the Grand Chamber, unless one of the parties to the case objects.

ARTICLE 31—POWERS OF THE GRAND CHAMBER

A19–033

The Grand Chamber shall

1   a determine applications submitted either under Article 33 or Article 34 when a Chamber has relinquished jurisdiction under Article 30 or when the case has been referred to it under Article 43; and

b consider requests for advisory opinions submitted under Article 47.

ARTICLE 32—JURISDICTION OF THE COURT

A19–034

1 The jurisdiction of the Court shall extend to all matters concerning the interpretation and application of the Convention and the protocols thereto which are referred to it as provided in Articles 33, 34 and 47.

2 In the event of dispute as to whether the Court has jurisdiction, the Court shall decide.

ARTICLE 33—INTER-STATE CASES

Any High Contracting Party may refer to the Court any alleged breach of the provisions of the Convention and the protocols thereto by another High Contracting Party.

A19–035

ARTICLE 34—INDIVIDUAL APPLICATIONS

The Court may receive applications from any person, non-governmental organisation or group of individuals claiming to be the victim of a violation by one of the High Contracting Parties of the rights set forth in the Convention or the protocols thereto. The High Contracting Parties undertake not to hinder in any way the effective exercise of this right.

A19–036

ARTICLE 35—ADMISSIBILITY CRITERIA

1 The Court may only deal with the matter after all domestic remedies have been exhausted, according to the generally recognised rules of international law, and within a period of six months from the date on which the final decision was taken.

A19–037

2 The Court shall not deal with any application submitted under Article 34 that

    a is anonymous; or

    b is substantially the same as a matter that has already been examined by the Court or has already been submitted to another procedure of international investigation or settlement and contains no relevant new information.

3 The Court shall declare inadmissible any individual application submitted under Article 34 which it considers incompatible with the provisions of the Convention or the protocols thereto, manifestly ill-founded, or an abuse of the right of application.

4 The Court shall reject any application which it considers inadmissible under this Article. It may do so at any stage of the proceedings.

ARTICLE 36—THIRD PARTY INTERVENTION

1 In all cases before a Chamber or the Grand Chamber, a High Contracting Party one of whose nationals is an applicant shall have the right to submit written comments and to take part in hearings.

A19–038

2 The President of the Court may, in the interest of the proper administration of justice, invite any High Contracting Party which is not a party to the proceedings or any person concerned who is not the applicant to submit written comments or take part in hearings.

ARTICLE 37—STRIKING OUT APPLICATIONS

1 The Court may at any stage of the proceedings decide to strike an application out of its list of cases where the circumstances lead to the conclusion that

A19–039

    a the applicant does not intend to pursue his application; or

    b the matter has been resolved; or

    c for any other reason established by the Court, it is no longer justified to continue the examination of the application.

However, the Court shall continue the examination of the application if respect for human rights as defined in the Convention and the protocols thereto so requires.

2 The Court may decide to restore an application to its list of cases if it considers that the circumstances justify such a course.

ARTICLE 38—EXAMINATION OF THE CASE AND FRIENDLY SETTLEMENT PROCEEDINGS

A19–040

1 If the Court declares the application admissible, it shall

    a pursue the examination of the case, together with the representatives of the parties, and if need be, undertake an investigation, for the effective conduct of which the States concerned shall furnish all necessary facilities;

    b place itself at the disposal of the parties concerned with a view to securing a friendly settlement of the matter on the basis of respect for human rights as defined in the Convention and the protocols thereto.

2 Proceedings conducted under paragraph 1.b shall be confidential.

ARTICLE 39—FINDING OF A FRIENDLY SETTLEMENT

A19–041

If a friendly settlement is effected, the Court shall strike the case out of its list by means of a decision which shall be confined to a brief statement of the facts and of the solution reached.

ARTICLE 40—PUBLIC HEARINGS AND ACCESS TO DOCUMENTS

A19–042

1 Hearings shall be in public unless the Court in exceptional circumstances decides otherwise.

2 Documents deposited with the Registrar shall be accessible to the public unless the President of the Court decides otherwise.

ARTICLE 41—JUST SATISFACTION

A19–043

If the Court finds that there has been a violation of the Convention or the protocols thereto, and if the internal law of the High Contracting Party concerned allows only partial reparation to be made, the Court shall, if necessary, afford just satisfaction to the injured party.

ARTICLE 42—JUDGMENTS OF CHAMBERS

A19–044

Judgments of Chambers shall become final in accordance with the provisions of Article 44, paragraph 2.

ARTICLE 43—REFERRAL TO THE GRAND CHAMBER

A19–045

1 Within a period of three months from the date of the judgment of the Chamber, any party to the case may, in exceptional cases, request that the case be referred to the Grand Chamber.

2 A panel of five judges of the Grand Chamber shall accept the request if the case raises a serious question affecting the interpretation or application of the Convention or the protocols thereto, or a serious issue of general importance.

3 If the panel accepts the request, the Grand Chamber shall decide the case by means of a judgment.

ARTICLE 44—FINAL JUDGMENTS

A19–046

1 The judgment of the Grand Chamber shall be final.

2 The judgment of a Chamber shall become final

    a when the parties declare that they will not request that the case be referred to the Grand Chamber; or b three months after the date of the judgment, if reference of the case to the Grand Chamber has not been requested; or

c when the panel of the Grand Chamber rejects the request to refer under Article 43.

3 The final judgment shall be published.

Article 45—Reasons for judgments and decisions

1 Reasons shall be given for judgments as well as for decisions declaring applications admissible or inadmissible.   **A19–047**

2 If a judgment does not represent, in whole or in part, the unanimous opinion of the judges, any judge shall be entitled to deliver a separate opinion.

Article 46—Binding force and execution of judgments

1 The High Contracting Parties undertake to abide by the final judgment of the Court in any case to which they are parties.   **A19–048**

2 The final judgment of the Court shall be transmitted to the Committee of Ministers, which shall supervise its execution.

Article 47—Advisory opinions

1 The Court may, at the request of the Committee of Ministers, give advisory opinions on legal questions concerning the interpretation of the Convention and the protocols thereto.   **A19–049**

2 Such opinions shall not deal with any question relating to the content or scope of the rights or freedoms defined in Section I of the Convention and the protocols thereto, or with any other question which the Court or the Committee of Ministers might have to consider in consequence of any such proceedings as could be instituted in accordance with the Convention.

3 Decisions of the Committee of Ministers to request an advisory opinion of the Court shall require a majority vote of the representatives entitled to sit on the Committee.

Article 48—Advisory jurisdiction of the Court

The Court shall decide whether a request for an advisory opinion submitted by the Committee of Ministers is within its competence as defined in Article 47.   **A19–050**

Article 49—Reasons for advisory opinions

1 Reasons shall be given for advisory opinions of the Court.   **A19–051**

2 If the advisory opinion does not represent, in whole or in part, the unanimous opinion of the judges, any judge shall be entitled to deliver a separate opinion.

3 Advisory opinions of the Court shall be communicated to the Committee of Ministers.

Article 50—Expenditure on the Court

The expenditure on the Court shall be borne by the Council of Europe.   **A19–052**

Article 51—Privileges and immunities of judges

The judges shall be entitled, during the exercise of their functions, to the privileges and immunities provided for in Article 40 of the Statute of the Council of Europe and in the agreements made thereunder.   **A19–053**

APPENDIX A

Section III[1,2]—Miscellaneous provisions

ARTICLE 52[1]—INQUIRIES BY THE SECRETARY GENERAL

A19–054   On receipt of a request from the Secretary General of the Council of Europe any High Contracting Party shall furnish an explanation of the manner in which its internal law ensures the effective implementation of any of the provisions of the Convention.

ARTICLE 53[1]—SAFEGUARD FOR EXISTING HUMAN RIGHTS

A19–055   Nothing in this Convention shall be construed as limiting or derogating from any of the human rights and fundamental freedoms which may be ensured under the laws of any High Contracting Party or under any other agreement to which it is a Party.

ARTICLE 54[1]—POWERS OF THE COMMITTEE OF MINISTERS

A19–056   Nothing in this Convention shall prejudice the powers conferred on the Committee of Ministers by the Statute of the Council of Europe.

ARTICLE 55[1]—EXCLUSION OF OTHER MEANS OF DISPUTE SETTLEMENT

A19–057   The High Contracting Parties agree that, except by special agreement, they will not avail themselves of treaties, conventions or declarations in force between them for the purpose of submitting, by way of petition, a dispute arising out of the interpretation or application of this Convention to a means of settlement other than those provided for in this Convention.

ARTICLE 56[1]—TERRITORIAL APPLICATION

A19–058   1[2] Any State may at the time of its ratification or at any time thereafter declare by notification addressed to the Secretary General of the Council of Europe that the present Convention shall, subject to paragraph 4 of this Article, extend to all or any of the territories for whose international relations it is responsible.

2 The Convention shall extend to the territory or territories named in the notification as from the thirtieth day after the receipt of this notification by the Secretary General of the Council of Europe.

3 The provisions of this Convention shall be applied in such territories with due regard, however, to local requirements.

4[3] Any State which has made a declaration in accordance with paragraph 1 of this article may at any time thereafter declare on behalf of one or more of the territories to which the declaration relates that it accepts the competence of the Court to receive applications from individuals, non-governmental organisations or groups of individuals as provided by Article 34 of the Convention.

ARTICLE 57[1]—RESERVATIONS

A19–059   1 Any State may, when signing this Convention or when depositing its instrument of ratification, make a reservation in respect of any particular provision of the Convention to the extent that any law then in force in its territory is not in conformity with the provision. Reservations of a general character shall not be permitted under this article.

---

[1] Heading added according to the provisions of Protocol No. 11 (ETS No. 155).
[2] The articles of this Section are renumbered according to the provisions of Protocol No. 11 (ETS No. 155).
[3] Text amended according to the provisions of Protocol No. 11 (ETS No. 155).

2 Any reservation made under this article shall contain a brief statement of the law concerned.

ARTICLE 58[1]—DENUNCIATION

1 A High Contracting Party may denounce the present Convention only after the expiry of five years from the date on which it became a party to it and after six months' notice contained in a notification addressed to the Secretary General of the Council of Europe, who shall inform the other High Contracting Parties.

2 Such a denunciation shall not have the effect of releasing the High Contracting Party concerned from its obligations under this Convention in respect of any act which, being capable of constituting a violation of such obligations, may have been performed by it before the date at which the denunciation became effective.

3 Any High Contracting Party which shall cease to be a member of the Council of Europe shall cease to be a Party to this Convention under the same conditions.

4[1] The Convention may be denounced in accordance with the provisions of the preceding paragraphs in respect of any territory to which it has been declared to extend under the terms of Article 56.

A19–060

ARTICLE 59[2]—SIGNATURE AND RATIFICATION

1 This Convention shall be open to the signature of the members of the Council of Europe. It shall be ratified. Ratifications shall be deposited with the Secretary General of the Council of Europe.

2 The present Convention shall come into force after the deposit of ten instruments of ratification.

3 As regards any signatory ratifying subsequently, the Convention shall come into force at the date of the deposit of its instrument of ratification.

4 The Secretary General of the Council of Europe shall notify all the members of the Council of Europe of the entry into force of the Convention, the names of the High Contracting Parties who have ratified it, and the deposit of all instruments of ratification which may be effected subsequently.

Done at Rome this 4th day of November 1950, in English and French, both texts being equally authentic, in a single copy which shall remain deposited in the archives of the Council of Europe. The Secretary General shall transmit certified copies to each of the signatories.

A19–061

PROTOCOL TO THE CONVENTION FOR THE PROTECTION OF HUMAN RIGHTS AND FUNDAMENTAL FREEDOMS

PARIS, 20.III.1952

The governments signatory hereto, being members of the Council of Europe,

Being resolved to take steps to ensure the collective enforcement of certain rights and freedoms other than those already included in Section I of the Convention for the Protection of Human Rights and Fundamental Freedoms signed at Rome on 4 November 1950 (hereinafter referred to as "the Convention"),

Have agreed as follows:

A19–062

ARTICLE 1—PROTECTION OF PROPERTY

Every natural or legal person is entitled to the peaceful enjoyment of his possessions. No one shall be deprived of his possessions except in the public interest and subject to the conditions provided for by law and by the general principles of international law.

A19–063

[1] Heading added according to the provisions of Protocol No. 11 (ETS No. 155).
[2] Text amended according to the provisions of Protocol No. 11 (ETS No. 155).

The preceding provisions shall not, however, in any way impair the right of a State to enforce such laws as it deems necessary to control the use of property in accordance with the general interest or to secure the payment of taxes or other contributions or penalties.

ARTICLE 2—RIGHT TO EDUCATION

A19–064   No person shall be denied the right to education. In the exercise of any functions which it assumes in relation to education and to teaching, the State shall respect the right of parents to ensure such education and teaching in conformity with their own religious and philosophical convictions.

ARTICLE 3—RIGHT TO FREE ELECTIONS

A19–065   The High Contracting Parties undertake to hold free elections at reasonable intervals by secret ballot, under conditions which will ensure the free expression of the opinion of the people in the choice of the legislature.

ARTICLE 4—TERRITORIAL APPLICATION

A19–066   Any High Contracting Party may at the time of signature or ratification or at any time thereafter communicate to the Secretary General of the Council of Europe a declaration stating the extent to which it undertakes that the provisions of the present Protocol shall apply to such of the territories for the international relations of which it is responsible as are named therein.

Any High Contracting Party which has communicated a declaration in virtue of the preceding paragraph may from time to time communicate a further declaration modifying the terms of any former declaration or terminating the application of the provisions of this Protocol in respect of any territory.

A declaration made in accordance with this article shall be deemed to have been made in accordance with paragraph 1 of Article 56 of the Convention.

ARTICLE 5—RELATIONSHIP TO THE CONVENTION

A19–067   As between the High Contracting Parties the provisions of Articles 1, 2, 3 and 4 of this Protocol shall be regarded as additional articles to the Convention and all the provisions of the Convention shall apply accordingly.

ARTICLE 6—SIGNATURE AND RATIFICATION

A19–068   This Protocol shall be open for signature by the members of the Council of Europe, who are the signatories of the Convention; it shall be ratified at the same time as or after the ratification of the Convention. It shall enter into force after the deposit of ten instruments of ratification. As regards any signatory ratifying subsequently, the Protocol shall enter into force at the date of the deposit of its instrument of ratification.

The instruments of ratification shall be deposited with the Secretary General of the Council of Europe, who will notify all members of the names of those who have ratified.

Done at Paris on the 20th day of March 1952, in English and French, both texts being equally authentic, in a single copy which shall remain deposited in the archives of the Council of Europe. The Secretary General shall transmit certified copies to each of the signatory governments.

PROTOCOL NO. 4 TO THE cONVENTION FOR THE PROTECTION OF HUMAN RIGHTS AND FUNDAMENTAL FREEDOMS SECURING CERTAIN RIGHTS AND FREEDOMS OTHER THAN THOSE ALREADY INCLUDED IN THE CONVENTION AND IN THE FIRST PROTOCOL THERETO

STRASBOURG, 16.IX.1963

The governments signatory hereto, being members of the Council of Europe,   **A19–069**
Being resolved to take steps to ensure the collective enforcement of certain rights and freedoms other than those already included in Section I of the Convention for the Protection of Human Rights and Fundamental Freedoms signed at Rome on 4th November 1950 (hereinafter referred to as the "Convention") and in Articles 1 to 3 of the First Protocol to the Convention, signed at Paris on 20th March 1952,
Have agreed as follows:

ARTICLE 1—PROHIBITION OF IMPRISONMENT FOR DEBT

No one shall be deprived of his liberty merely on the ground of inability to fulfil a   **A19–070**
contractual obligation.

ARTICLE 2—FREEDOM OF MOVEMENT

1 Everyone lawfully within the territory of a State shall, within that territory, have the   **A19–071**
right to liberty of movement and freedom to choose his residence.
2 Everyone shall be free to leave any country, including his own.
3 No restrictions shall be placed on the exercise of these rights other than such as are in accordance with law and are necessary in a democratic society in the interests of national security or public safety, for the maintenance of ordre public, for the prevention of crime, for the protection of health or morals, or for the protection of the rights and freedoms of others.
4 The rights set forth in paragraph 1 may also be subject, in particular areas, to restrictions imposed in accordance with law and justified by the public interest in a democratic society.

ARTICLE 3—PROHIBITION OF EXPULSION OF NATIONALS

1 No one shall be expelled, by means either of an individual or of a collective measure,   **A19–072**
from the territory of the State of which he is a national.
2 No one shall be deprived of the right to enter the territory of the state of which he is a national.

ARTICLE 4—PROHIBITION OF COLLECTIVE EXPULSION OF ALIENS

Collective expulsion of aliens is prohibited.   **A19–073**

ARTICLE 5—TERRITORIAL APPLICATION

1 Any High Contracting Party may, at the time of signature or ratification of this   **A19–074**
Protocol, or at any time thereafter, communicate to the Secretary General of the Council of Europe a declaration stating the extent to which it undertakes that the provisions of this Protocol shall apply to such of the territories for the international relations of which it is responsible as are named therein.

2 Any High Contracting Party which has communicated a declaration in virtue of the preceding paragraph may, from time to time, communicate a further declaration modifying the terms of any former declaration or terminating the application of the provisions of this Protocol in respect of any territory.

3 A declaration made in accordance with this article shall be deemed to have been made in accordance with paragraph 1 of Article 56 of the Convention.

4 The territory of any State to which this Protocol applies by virtue of ratification or acceptance by that State, and each territory to which this Protocol is applied by virtue of a declaration by that State under this article, shall be treated as separate territories for the purpose of the references in Articles 2 and 3 to the territory of a State.

5 Any State which has made a declaration in accordance with paragraph 1 or 2 of this Article may at any time thereafter declare on behalf of one or more of the territories to which the declaration relates that it accepts the competence of the Court to receive applications from individuals, non-governmental organisations or groups of individuals as provided in Article 34 of the Convention in respect of all or any of Articles 1 to 4 of this Protocol."

ARTICLE 6—RELATIONSHIP TO THE CONVENTION

A19–075   As between the High Contracting Parties the provisions of Articles 1 to 5 of this Protocol shall be regarded as additional Articles to the Convention, and all the provisions of the Convention shall apply accordingly.

ARTICLE 7—SIGNATURE AND RATIFICATION

A19–076   1 This Protocol shall be open for signature by the members of the Council of Europe who are the signatories of the Convention; it shall be ratified at the same time as or after the ratification of the Convention. It shall enter into force after the deposit of five instruments of ratification. As regards any signatory ratifying subsequently, the Protocol shall enter into force at the date of the deposit of its instrument of ratification.

2 The instruments of ratification shall be deposited with the Secretary General of the Council of Europe, who will notify all members of the names of those who have ratified.

In witness whereof the undersigned, being duly authorised thereto, have signed this Protocol.

Done at Strasbourg, this 16th day of September 1963, in English and in French, both texts being equally authoritative, in a single copy which shall remain deposited in the archives of the Council of Europe. The Secretary General shall transmit certified copies to each of the signatory states.

PROTOCOl NO. 6 TO THE CONVENTION FOR THE PROTECTION OF HUMAN RIGHTS AND FUNDAMENTAL FREEDOMS CONCERNING THE ABOLITION OF THE DEATH PENALTY

STRASBOURG, 28.IV.1983

A19–077   The member States of the Council of Europe, signatory to this Protocol to the Convention for the Protection of Human Rights and Fundamental Freedoms, signed at Rome on 4 November 1950 (hereinafter referred to as "the Convention"),

Considering that the evolution that has occurred in several member States of the Council of Europe expresses a general tendency in favour of abolition of the death penalty;

Have agreed as follows:

Article 1—Abolition of the death penalty

The death penalty shall be abolished. No-one shall be condemned to such penalty or executed.   **A19–078**

Article 2—Death penalty in time of war

A State may make provision in its law for the death penalty in respect of acts committed in time of war or of imminent threat of war; such penalty shall be applied only in the instances laid down in the law and in accordance with its provisions. The State shall communicate to the Secretary General of the Council of Europe the relevant provisions of that law.   **A19–079**

Article 3—Prohibition of derogations

No derogation from the provisions of this Protocol shall be made under Article 15 of the Convention.   **A19–080**

Article 4—Prohibition of reservations

No reservation may be made under Article 57 of the Convention in respect of the provisions of this Protocol.   **A19–081**

Article 5—Territorial application

1 Any State may at the time of signature or when depositing its instrument of ratification, acceptance or approval, specify the territory or territories to which this Protocol shall apply.   **A19–082**

2 Any State may at any later date, by a declaration addressed to the Secretary General of the Council of Europe, extend the application of this Protocol to any other territory specified in the declaration. In respect of such territory the Protocol shall enter into force on the first day of the month following the date of receipt of such declaration by the Secretary General.

3 Any declaration made under the two preceding paragraphs may, in respect of any territory specified in such declaration, be withdrawn by a notification addressed to the Secretary General. The withdrawal shall become effective on the first day of the month following the date of receipt of such notification by the Secretary General.

Article 6—Relationship to the Convention

As between the States Parties the provisions of Articles 1 and 5 of this Protocol shall be regarded as additional articles to the Convention and all the provisions of the Convention shall apply accordingly.   **A19–083**

Article 7—Signature and ratification

The Protocol shall be open for signature by the member States of the Council of Europe, signatories to the Convention. It shall be subject to ratification, acceptance or approval. A member State of the Council of Europe may not ratify, accept or approve this Protocol unless it has, simultaneously or previously, ratified the Convention. Instruments of ratification, acceptance or approval shall be deposited with the Secretary General of the Council of Europe.   **A19–084**

ARTICLE 8—ENTRY INTO FORCE

A19–085　1 This Protocol shall enter into force on the first day of the month following the date on which five member States of the Council of Europe have expressed their consent to be bound by the Protocol in accordance with the provisions of Article 7.

2 In respect of any member State which subsequently expresses its consent to be bound by it, the Protocol shall enter into force on the first day of the month following the date of the deposit of the instrument of ratification, acceptance or approval.

ARTICLE 9—DEPOSITARY FUNCTIONS

A19–086　The Secretary General of the Council of Europe shall notify the member States of the Council of:

    a any signature;

    b the deposit of any instrument of ratification, acceptance or approval;

    c any date of entry into force of this Protocol in accordance with articles 5 and 8;

    d any other act, notification or communication relating to this Protocol.

In witness whereof the undersigned, being duly authorised thereto, have signed this Protocol.

Done at Strasbourg, this 28th day of April 1983, in English and in French, both texts being equally authentic, in a single copy which shall be deposited in the archives of the Council of Europe. The Secretary General of the Council of Europe shall transmit certified copies to each member State of the Council of Europe.

PROTOCOL NO. 7 TO THE CONVENTION FOR THE PROTECTION OF HUMAN RIGHTS AND FUNDAMENTAL FREEDOMS

STRASBOURG, 22.XI.1984

A19–087　The member States of the Council of Europe signatory hereto,

Being resolved to take further steps to ensure the collective enforcement of certain rights and freedoms by means of the Convention for the Protection of Human Rights and Fundamental Freedoms signed at Rome on 4 November 1950 (hereinafter referred to as "the Convention"),

Have agreed as follows :

ARTICLE 1—PROCEDURAL SAFEGUARDS RELATING TO EXPULSION OF ALIENS

A19–088　1 An alien lawfully resident in the territory of a State shall not be expelled therefrom except in pursuance of a decision reached in accordance with law and shall be allowed:

    a to submit reasons against his expulsion,

    b to have his case reviewed, and

    c to be represented for these purposes before the competent authority or a person or persons designated by that authority.

2 An alien may be expelled before the exercise of his rights under paragraph 1.a, b and c of this Article, when such expulsion is necessary in the interests of public order or is grounded on reasons of national security.

ARTICLE 2—RIGHT OF APPEAL IN CRIMINAL MATTERS

A19–089　1 Everyone convicted of a criminal offence by a tribunal shall have the right to have his conviction or sentence reviewed by a higher tribunal. The exercise of this right, including the grounds on which it may be exercised, shall be governed by law.

2 This right may be subject to exceptions in regard to offences of a minor character, as prescribed by law, or in cases in which the person concerned was tried in the first instance by the highest tribunal or was convicted following an appeal against acquittal.

ARTICLE 3—COMPENSATION FOR WRONGFUL CONVICTION

When a person has by a final decision been convicted of a criminal offence and when **A19–090** subsequently his conviction has been reversed, or he has been pardoned, on the ground that a new or newly discovered fact shows conclusively that there has been a miscarriage of justice, the person who has suffered punishment as a result of such conviction shall be compensated according to the law or the practice of the State concerned, unless it is proved that the non-disclosure of the unknown fact in time is wholly or partly attributable to him.

ARTICLE 4—RIGHT NOT TO BE TRIED OR PUNISHED TWICE

1 No one shall be liable to be tried or punished again in criminal proceedings under **A19–091** the jurisdiction of the same State for an offence for which he has already been finally acquitted or convicted in accordance with the law and penal procedure of that State.

2 The provisions of the preceding paragraph shall not prevent the reopening of the case in accordance with the law and penal procedure of the State concerned, if there is evidence of new or newly discovered facts, or if there has been a fundamental defect in the previous proceedings, which could affect the outcome of the case.

3 No derogation from this Article shall be made under Article 15 of the Convention.

ARTICLE 5—EQUALITY BETWEEN SPOUSES

Spouses shall enjoy equality of rights and responsibilities of a private law character **A19–092** between them, and in their relations with their children, as to marriage, during marriage and in the event of its dissolution. This Article shall not prevent States from taking such measures as are necessary in the interests of the children.

ARTICLE 6—TERRITORIAL APPLICATION

1 Any State may at the time of signature or when depositing its instrument of **A19–093** ratification, acceptance or approval, specify the territory or territories to which the Protocol shall apply and state the extent to which it undertakes that the provisions of this Protocol shall apply to such territory or territories.

2 Any State may at any later date, by a declaration addressed to the Secretary General of the Council of Europe, extend the application of this Protocol to any other territory specified in the declaration. In respect of such territory the Protocol shall enter into force on the first day of the month following the expiration of a period of two months after the date of receipt by the Secretary General of such declaration.

3 Any declaration made under the two preceding paragraphs may, in respect of any territory specified in such declaration, be withdrawn or modified by a notification addressed to the Secretary General. The withdrawal or modification shall become effective on the first day of the month following the expiration of a period of two months after the date of receipt of such notification by the Secretary General.

4 A declaration made in accordance with this Article shall be deemed to have been made in accordance with paragraph 1 of Article 56 of the Convention.

5 The territory of any State to which this Protocol applies by virtue of ratification, acceptance or approval by that State, and each territory to which this Protocol is applied by virtue of a declaration by that State under this Article, may be treated as separate territories for the purpose of the reference in Article 1 to the territory of a State.

6 Any State which has made a declaration in accordance with paragraph 1 or 2 of this Article may at any time thereafter declare on behalf of one or more of the territories to

which the declaration relates that it accepts the competence of the Court to receive applications from individuals, non-governmental organisations or groups of individuals as provided in Article 34 of the Convention in respect of Articles 1 to 5 of this Protocol.

ARTICLE 7—RELATIONSHIP TO THE CONVENTION

A19–094   As between the States Parties, the provisions of Article 1 to 6 of this Protocol shall be regarded as additional Articles to the Convention, and all the provisions of the Convention shall apply accordingly.

ARTICLE 8—SIGNATURE AND RATIFICATION

A19–095   This Protocol shall be open for signature by member States of the Council of Europe which have signed the Convention. It is subject to ratification, acceptance or approval. A member State of the Council of Europe may not ratify, accept or approve this Protocol without previously or simultaneously ratifying the Convention. Instruments of ratification, acceptance or approval shall be deposited with the Secretary General of the Council of Europe.

ARTICLE 9—ENTRY INTO FORCE

A19–096   1 This Protocol shall enter into force on the first day of the month following the expiration of a period of two months after the date on which seven member States of the Council of Europe have expressed their consent to be bound by the Protocol in accordance with the provisions of Article 8.
2 In respect of any member State which subsequently expresses its consent to be bound by it, the Protocol shall enter into force on the first day of the month following the expiration of a period of two months after the date of the deposit of the instrument of ratification, acceptance or approval.

ARTICLE 10—DEPOSITARY FUNCTIONS

A19–097   The Secretary General of the Council of Europe shall notify all the member States of the Council of Europe of:
    a any signature;
    b the deposit of any instrument of ratification, acceptance or approval;
    c any date of entry into force of this Protocol in accordance with Articles 6 and 9;
    d any other act, notification or declaration relating to this Protocol.
In witness whereof the undersigned, being duly authorised thereto, have signed this Protocol.
Done at Strasbourg, this 22nd day of November 1984, in English and French, both texts being equally authentic, in a single copy which shall be deposited in the archives of the Council of Europe. The Secretary General of the Council of Europe shall transmit certified copies to each member State of the Council of Europe.

PROTOCOL NO. 12 TO THE CONVENTION FOR THE PROTECTION OF HUMAN RIGHTS AND FUNDAMENTAL FREEDOMS

ROME, 4.XI.2000

A19–098   The member States of the Council of Europe signatory hereto,
Having regard to the fundamental principle according to which all persons are equal before the law and are entitled to the equal protection of the law;

Being resolved to take further steps to promote the equality of all persons through the collective enforcement of a general prohibition of discrimination by means of the Convention for the Protection of Human Rights and Fundamental Freedoms signed at Rome on 4 November 1950 (hereinafter referred to as "the Convention");

Reaffirming that the principle of non-discrimination does not prevent States Parties from taking measures in order to promote full and effective equality, provided that there is an objective and reasonable justification for those measures,

Have agreed as follows:

ARTICLE 1—GENERAL PROHIBITION OF DISCRIMINATION

1 The enjoyment of any right set forth by law shall be secured without discrimination on any ground such as sex, race, colour, language, religion, political or other opinion, national or social origin, association with a national minority, property, birth or other status.   **A19–099**

2 No one shall be discriminated against by any public authority on any ground such as those mentioned in paragraph 1.

ARTICLE 2— TERRITORIAL APPLICATION

1 Any State may, at the time of signature or when depositing its instrument of ratification, acceptance or approval, specify the territory or territories to which this Protocol shall apply.   **A19–100**

2 Any State may at any later date, by a declaration addressed to the Secretary General of the Council of Europe, extend the application of this Protocol to any other territory specified in the declaration. In respect of such territory the Protocol shall enter into force on the first day of the month following the expiration of a period of three months after the date of receipt by the Secretary General of such declaration.

3 Any declaration made under the two preceding paragraphs may, in respect of any territory specified in such declaration, be withdrawn or modified by a notification addressed to the Secretary General of the Council of Europe. The withdrawal or modification shall become effective on the first day of the month following the expiration of a period of three months after the date of receipt of such notification by the Secretary General.

4 A declaration made in accordance with this article shall be deemed to have been made in accordance with paragraph 1 of Article 56 of the Convention.

5 Any State which has made a declaration in accordance with paragraph 1 or 2 of this article may at any time thereafter declare on behalf of one or more of the territories to which the declaration relates that it accepts the competence of the Court to receive applications from individuals, non-governmental organisations or groups of individuals as provided by Article 34 of the Convention in respect of Article 1 of this Protocol.

ARTICLE 3— RELATIONSHIP TO THE CONVENTION

As between the States Parties, the provisions of Articles 1 and 2 of this Protocol shall be regarded as additional articles to the Convention, and all the provisions of the Convention shall apply accordingly.   **A19–101**

ARTICLE 4—SIGNATURE AND RATIFICATION

This Protocol shall be open for signature by member States of the Council of Europe which have signed the Convention. It is subject to ratification, acceptance or approval. A member State of the Council of Europe may not ratify, accept or approve this Protocol without previously or simultaneously ratifying the Convention. Instruments of ratification, acceptance or approval shall be deposited with the Secretary General of the Council of Europe.   **A19–102**

ARTICLE 5—ENTRY INTO FORCE

A19–103   1 This Protocol shall enter into force on the first day of the month following the expiration of a period of three months after the date on which ten member States of the Council of Europe have expressed their consent to be bound by the Protocol in accordance with the provisions of Article 4.

2 In respect of any member State which subsequently expresses its consent to be bound by it, the Protocol shall enter into force on the first day of the month following the expiration of a period of three months after the date of the deposit of the instrument of ratification, acceptance or approval.

ARTICLE 6—DEPOSITARY FUNCTIONS

A19–104   The Secretary General of the Council of Europe shall notify all the member States of the Council of Europe of:

a any signature;

b the deposit of any instrument of ratification, acceptance or approval;

c any date of entry into force of this Protocol in accordance with Articles 2 and 5;

d any other act, notification or communication relating to this Protocol.

In witness whereof the undersigned, being duly authorised thereto, have signed this Protocol.

Done at Rome, this 4th day of November 2000, in English and in French, both texts being equally authentic, in a single copy which shall be deposited in the archives of the Council of Europe. The Secretary General of the Council of Europe shall transmit certified copies to each member State of the Council of Europe.

PROTOCOL NO. 13 TO THE CONVENTION FOR THE PROTECTION OF HUMAN RIGHTS AND FUNDAMENTAL FREEDOMS CONCERNING THE ABOLITION OF THE DEATH PENALTY IN ALL CIRCUMSTANCES

VILNIUS, 3.V.2002

A19–105   The member States of the Council of Europe signatory hereto,

Convinced that everyone's right to life is a basic value in a democratic society and that the abolition of the death penalty is essential for the protection of this right and for the full recognition of the inherent dignity of all human beings;

Wishing to strengthen the protection of the right to life guaranteed by the Convention for the Protection of Human Rights and Fundamental Freedoms signed at Rome on 4 November 1950 (hereinafter referred to as "the Convention");

Noting that Protocol No. 6 to the Convention, concerning the Abolition of the Death Penalty, signed at Strasbourg on 28 April 1983, does not exclude the death penalty in respect of acts committed in time of war or of imminent threat of war;

Being resolved to take the final step in order to abolish the death penalty in all circumstances,

Have agreed as follows:

ARTICLE 1—ABOLITION OF THE DEATH PENALTY

A19–106   The death penalty shall be abolished. No one shall be condemned to such penalty or executed.

ARTICLE 2—PROHIBITIONS OF DEROGATIONS

A19–107   No derogation from the provisions of this Protocol shall be made under Article 15 of the Convention.

ARTICLE 3—PROHIBITIONS OF RESERVATIONS

No reservation may be made under Article 57 of the Convention in respect of the **A19–108** provisions of this Protocol.

ARTICLE 4—TERRITORIAL APPLICATION

1 Any state may, at the time of signature or when depositing its instrument of **A19–109** ratification, acceptance or approval, specify the territory or territories to which this Protocol shall apply.

2 Any state may at any later date, by a declaration addressed to the Secretary General of the Council of Europe, extend the application of this Protocol to any other territory specified in the declaration. In respect of such territory the Protocol shall enter into force on the first day of the month following the expiration of a period of three months after the date of receipt by the Secretary General of such declaration.

3 Any declaration made under the two preceding paragraphs may, in respect of any territory specified in such declaration, be withdrawn or modified by a notification addressed to the Secretary General. The withdrawal or modification shall become effective on the first day of the month following the expiration of a period of three months after the date of receipt of such notification by the Secretary General.

ARTICLE 5—RELATIONSHIP TO THE CONVENTION

As between the states Parties the provisions of Articles 1 to 4 of this Protocol shall be **A19–110** regarded as additional articles to the Convention, and all the provisions of the Convention shall apply accordingly.

ARTICLE 6—SIGNATURE AND RATIFICATION

This Protocol shall be open for signature by member states of the Council of Europe **A19–111** which have signed the Convention. It is subject to ratification, acceptance or approval. A member state of the Council of Europe may not ratify, accept or approve this Protocol without previously or simultaneously ratifying the Convention. Instruments of ratification, acceptance or approval shall be deposited with the Secretary General of the Council of Europe.

ARTICLE 7—ENTRY INTO FORCE

1 This Protocol shall enter into force on the first day of the month following the **A19–112** expiration of a period of three months after the date on which ten member states of the Council of Europe have expressed their consent to be bound by the Protocol in accordance with the provisions of Article 6.

2 In respect of any member state which subsequently expresses its consent to be bound by it, the Protocol shall enter into force on the first day of the month following the expiration of a period of three months after the date of the deposit of the instrument of ratification, acceptance or approval.

ARTICLE 8—DEPOSITARY FUNCTIONS

The Secretary General of the Council of Europe shall notify all the member states of **A19–113** the Council of Europe of:

a any signature;

b the deposit of any instrument of ratification, acceptance or approval;

c any date of entry into force of this Protocol in accordance with Articles 4 and 7;

d any other act, notification or communication relating to this Protocol;

In witness whereof the undersigned, being duly authorised thereto, have signed this Protocol.

Done at Vilnius, this 3rd day of May 2002, in English and in French, both texts being equally authentic, in a single copy which shall be deposited in the archives of the Council of Europe. The Secretary General of the Council of Europe shall transmit certified copies to each member state of the Council of Europe.

APPENDIX B

ICC

B1. Rome Statute of the International Criminal Court*

[* Text of the Rome Statute circulated as document A/CONF.183/9 of 17 July 1998 and corrected by procœ0s-verbaux of 10 November 1998, 12 July 1999, 30 November 1999, 8 May 2000, 17 January 2001 and 16 January 2002. The Statute entered into force on 1 July 2002.]

PREAMBLE

The States Parties to this Statute,

B1–001

Conscious that all peoples are united by common bonds, their cultures pieced together in a shared heritage, and concerned that this delicate mosaic may be shattered at any time,

Mindful that during this century millions of children, women and men have been victims of unimaginable atrocities that deeply shock the conscience of humanity,

Recognizing that such grave crimes threaten the peace, security and well-being of the world,

Affirming that the most serious crimes of concern to the international community as a whole must not go unpunished and that their effective prosecution must be ensured by taking measures at the national level and by enhancing international cooperation,

Determined to put an end to impunity for the perpetrators of these crimes and thus to contribute to the prevention of such crimes,

Recalling that it is the duty of every State to exercise its criminal jurisdiction over those responsible for international crimes,

Reaffirming the Purposes and Principles of the Charter of the United Nations, and in particular that all States shall refrain from the threat or use of force against the territorial integrity or political independence of any State, or in any other manner inconsistent with the Purposes of the United Nations,

Emphasizing in this connection that nothing in this Statute shall be taken as authorizing any State Party to intervene in an armed conflict or in the internal affairs of any State,

Determined to these ends and for the sake of present and future generations, to establish an independent permanent International Criminal Court in relationship with the United Nations system, with jurisdiction over the most serious crimes of concern to the international community as a whole,

Emphasizing that the International Criminal Court established under this Statute shall be complementary to national criminal jurisdictions,

Resolved to guarantee lasting respect for and the enforcement of international justice,

Have agreed as follows:

PART 1. ESTABLISHMENT OF THE COURT

ARTICLE 1

THE COURT

B1–002   An International Criminal Court ("the Court") is hereby established. It shall be a permanent institution and shall have the power to exercise its jurisdiction over persons for the most serious crimes of international concern, as referred to in this Statute, and shall be complementary to national criminal jurisdictions. The jurisdiction and functioning of the Court shall be governed by the provisions of this Statute.

ARTICLE 2

RELATIONSHIP OF THE COURT WITH THE UNITED NATIONS

B1–003   The Court shall be brought into relationship with the United Nations through an agreement to be approved by the Assembly of States Parties to this Statute and thereafter concluded by the President of the Court on its behalf.

ARTICLE 3

SEAT OF THE COURT

B1–004   1. The seat of the Court shall be established at The Hague in the Netherlands ("the host State").

2. The Court shall enter into a headquarters agreement with the host State, to be approved by the Assembly of States Parties and thereafter concluded by the President of the Court on its behalf.

3. The Court may sit elsewhere, whenever it considers it desirable, as provided in this Statute.

ARTICLE 4

LEGAL STATUS AND POWERS OF THE COURT

1. The Court shall have international legal personality. It shall also have such legal capacity as may be necessary for the exercise of its functions and the fulfilment of its purposes. **B1–005**
2. The Court may exercise its functions and powers, as provided in this Statute, on the territory of any State Party and, by special agreement, on the territory of any other State.

PART 2. JURISDICTION, ADMISSIBILITY AND APPLICABLE LAW

ARTICLE 5

CRIMES WITHIN THE JURISDICTION OF THE COURT

1. The jurisdiction of the Court shall be limited to the most serious crimes of concern to the international community as a whole. The Court has jurisdiction in accordance with this Statute with respect to the following crimes: **B1–006**
    (a) The crime of genocide;
    (b) Crimes against humanity;
    (c) War crimes;
    (d) The crime of aggression.
2. The Court shall exercise jurisdiction over the crime of aggression once a provision is adopted in accordance with articles 121 and 123 defining the crime and setting out the conditions under which the Court shall exercise jurisdiction with respect to this crime. Such a provision shall be consistent with the relevant provisions of the Charter of the United Nations.

ARTICLE 6

GENOCIDE

For the purpose of this Statute, "genocide" means any of the following acts committed with intent to destroy, in whole or in part, a national, ethnical, racial or religious group, as such: **B1–007**
    (a) Killing members of the group;
    (b) Causing serious bodily or mental harm to members of the group;
    (c) Deliberately inflicting on the group conditions of life calculated to bring about its physical destruction in whole or in part;
    (d) Imposing measures intended to prevent births within the group;
    (e) Forcibly transferring children of the group to another group.

ARTICLE 7

CRIMES AGAINST HUMANITY

1. For the purpose of this Statute, "crime against humanity" means any of the following acts when committed as part of a widespread or systematic attack directed against any civilian population, with knowledge of the attack: **B1–008**
    (a) Murder;
    (b) Extermination;

    (c) Enslavement;

    (d) Deportation or forcible transfer of population;

    (e) Imprisonment or other severe deprivation of physical liberty in violation of fundamental rules of international law;

    (f) Torture;

    (g) Rape, sexual slavery, enforced prostitution, forced pregnancy, enforced sterilization, or any other form of sexual violence of comparable gravity;

    (h) Persecution against any identifiable group or collectivity on political, racial, national, ethnic, cultural, religious, gender as defined in paragraph 3, or other grounds that are universally recognized as impermissible under international law, in connection with any act referred to in this paragraph or any crime within the jurisdiction of the Court;

    (i) Enforced disappearance of persons;

    (j) The crime of apartheid;

    (k) Other inhumane acts of a similar character intentionally causing great suffering, or serious injury to body or to mental or physical health.

2. For the purpose of paragraph 1:

    (a) "Attack directed against any civilian population" means a course of conduct involving the multiple commission of acts referred to in paragraph 1 against any civilian population, pursuant to or in furtherance of a State or organizational policy to commit such attack;

    (b) "Extermination" includes the intentional infliction of conditions of life, *inter alia* the deprivation of access to food and medicine, calculated to bring about the destruction of part of a population;

    (c) "Enslavement" means the exercise of any or all of the powers attaching to the right of ownership over a person and includes the exercise of such power in the course of trafficking in persons, in particular women and children;

    (d) "Deportation or forcible transfer of population" means forced displacement of the persons concerned by expulsion or other coercive acts from the area in which they are lawfully present, without grounds permitted under international law;

    (e) "Torture" means the intentional infliction of severe pain or suffering, whether physical or mental, upon a person in the custody or under the control of the accused; except that torture shall not include pain or suffering arising only from, inherent in or incidental to, lawful sanctions;

    (f) "Forced pregnancy" means the unlawful confinement of a woman forcibly made pregnant, with the intent of affecting the ethnic composition of any population or carrying out other grave violations of international law. This definition shall not in any way be interpreted as affecting national laws relating to pregnancy;

    (g) "Persecution" means the intentional and severe deprivation of fundamental rights contrary to international law by reason of the identity of the group or collectivity;

    (h) "The crime of apartheid" means inhumane acts of a character similar to those referred to in paragraph 1, committed in the context of an institutionalized regime of systematic oppression and domination by one racial group over any other racial group or groups and committed with the intention of maintaining that regime;

    (i) "Enforced disappearance of persons" means the arrest, detention or abduction of persons by, or with the authorization, support or acquiescence of, a State or a political organization, followed by a refusal to acknowledge that deprivation of freedom or to give information on the fate or whereabouts of those persons, with the intention of removing them from the protection of the law for a prolonged period of time.

3. For the purpose of this Statute, it is understood that the term "gender" refers to the two sexes, male and female, within the context of society. The term "gender" does not indicate any meaning different from the above.

ARTICLE 8

WAR CRIMES

1. The Court shall have jurisdiction in respect of war crimes in particular when **B1–009**
committed as part of a plan or policy or as part of a large-scale commission of such
crimes.

2. For the purpose of this Statute, "war crimes" means:

(a) Grave breaches of the Geneva Conventions of 12 August 1949, namely, any of
the following acts against persons or property protected under the provisions of
the relevant Geneva Convention:

(i) Wilful killing;
(ii) Torture or inhuman treatment, including biological experiments;
(iii) Wilfully causing great suffering, or serious injury to body or health;
(iv) Extensive destruction and appropriation of property, not justified by
military necessity and carried out unlawfully and wantonly;
(v) Compelling a prisoner of war or other protected person to serve in the
forces of a hostile Power;
(vi) Wilfully depriving a prisoner of war or other protected person of the
rights of fair and regular trial;
(vii) Unlawful deportation or transfer or unlawful confinement;
(viii) Taking of hostages.

(b) Other serious violations of the laws and customs applicable in international
armed conflict, within the established framework of international law, namely,
any of the following acts:

(i) Intentionally directing attacks against the civilian population as such or
against individual civilians not taking direct part in hostilities;
(ii) Intentionally directing attacks against civilian objects, that is, objects
which are not military objectives;
(iii) Intentionally directing attacks against personnel, installations, material,
units or vehicles involved in a humanitarian assistance or peacekeeping
mission in accordance with the Charter of the United Nations, as long as
they are entitled to the protection given to civilians or civilian objects
under the international law of armed conflict;
(iv) Intentionally launching an attack in the knowledge that such attack will
cause incidental loss of life or injury to civilians or damage to civilian
objects or widespread, long-term and severe damage to the natural
environment which would be clearly excessive in relation to the concrete
and direct overall military advantage anticipated;
(v) Attacking or bombarding, by whatever means, towns, villages, dwellings
or buildings which are undefended and which are not military objectives;
(vi) Killing or wounding a combatant who, having laid down his arms or
having no longer means of defence, has surrendered at discretion;
(vii) Making improper use of a flag of truce, of the flag or of the military
insignia and uniform of the enemy or of the United Nations, as well as of
the distinctive emblems of the Geneva Conventions, resulting in death or
serious personal injury;
(viii) The transfer, directly or indirectly, by the Occupying Power of parts of its
own civilian population into the territory it occupies, or the deportation
or transfer of all or parts of the population of the occupied territory
within or outside this territory;
(ix) Intentionally directing attacks against buildings dedicated to religion,
education, art, science or charitable purposes, historic monuments,
hospitals and places where the sick and wounded are collected, provided
they are not military objectives;
(x) Subjecting persons who are in the power of an adverse party to physical
mutilation or to medical or scientific experiments of any kind which are

neither justified by the medical, dental or hospital treatment of the person concerned nor carried out in his or her interest, and which cause death to or seriously endanger the health of such person or persons;

(xi) Killing or wounding treacherously individuals belonging to the hostile nation or army;

(xii) Declaring that no quarter will be given;

(xiii) Destroying or seizing the enemy's property unless such destruction or seizure be imperatively demanded by the necessities of war;

(xiv) Declaring abolished, suspended or inadmissible in a court of law the rights and actions of the nationals of the hostile party;

(xv) Compelling the nationals of the hostile party to take part in the operations of war directed against their own country, even if they were in the belligerent's service before the commencement of the war;

(xvi) Pillaging a town or place, even when taken by assault;

(xvii) Employing poison or poisoned weapons;

(xviii) Employing asphyxiating, poisonous or other gases, and all analogous liquids, materials or devices;

(xix) Employing bullets which expand or flatten easily in the human body, such as bullets with a hard envelope which does not entirely cover the core or is pierced with incisions;

(xx) Employing weapons, projectiles and material and methods of warfare which are of a nature to cause superfluous injury or unnecessary suffering or which are inherently indiscriminate in violation of the international law of armed conflict, provided that such weapons, projectiles and material and methods of warfare are the subject of a comprehensive prohibition and are included in an annex to this Statute, by an amendment in accordance with the relevant provisions set forth in articles 121 and 123;

(xxi) Committing outrages upon personal dignity, in particular humiliating and degrading treatment;

(xxii) Committing rape, sexual slavery, enforced prostitution, forced pregnancy, as defined in article 7, paragraph 2 (f), enforced sterilization, or any other form of sexual violence also constituting a grave breach of the Geneva Conventions;

(xxiii) Utilizing the presence of a civilian or other protected person to render certain points, areas or military forces immune from military operations;

(xxiv) Intentionally directing attacks against buildings, material, medical units and transport, and personnel using the distinctive emblems of the Geneva Conventions in conformity with international law;

(xxv) Intentionally using starvation of civilians as a method of warfare by depriving them of objects indispensable to their survival, including wilfully impeding relief supplies as provided for under the Geneva Conventions;

(xxvi) Conscripting or enlisting children under the age of fifteen years into the national armed forces or using them to participate actively in hostilities.

(c) In the case of an armed conflict not of an international character, serious violations of article 3 common to the four Geneva Conventions of 12 August 1949, namely, any of the following acts committed against persons taking no active part in the hostilities, including members of armed forces who have laid down their arms and those placed *hors de combat* by sickness, wounds, detention or any other cause:

(i) Violence to life and person, in particular murder of all kinds, mutilation, cruel treatment and torture;

(ii) Committing outrages upon personal dignity, in particular humiliating and degrading treatment;

(iii) Taking of hostages;

(iv) The passing of sentences and the carrying out of executions without previous judgement pronounced by a regularly constituted court, affording all judicial guarantees which are generally recognized as indispensable.

(d) Paragraph 2 (c) applies to armed conflicts not of an international character and thus does not apply to situations of internal disturbances and tensions, such as riots, isolated and sporadic acts of violence or other acts of a similar nature.

(e) Other serious violations of the laws and customs applicable in armed conflicts not of an international character, within the established framework of international law, namely, any of the following acts:

(i) Intentionally directing attacks against the civilian population as such or against individual civilians not taking direct part in hostilities;

(ii) Intentionally directing attacks against buildings, material, medical units and transport, and personnel using the distinctive emblems of the Geneva Conventions in conformity with international law;

(iii) Intentionally directing attacks against personnel, installations, material, units or vehicles involved in a humanitarian assistance or peacekeeping mission in accordance with the Charter of the United Nations, as long as they are entitled to the protection given to civilians or civilian objects under the international law of armed conflict;

(iv) Intentionally directing attacks against buildings dedicated to religion, education, art, science or charitable purposes, historic monuments, hospitals and places where the sick and wounded are collected, provided they are not military objectives;

(v) Pillaging a town or place, even when taken by assault;

(vi) Committing rape, sexual slavery, enforced prostitution, forced pregnancy, as defined in article 7, paragraph 2 (f), enforced sterilization, and any other form of sexual violence also constituting a serious violation of article 3 common to the four Geneva Conventions;

(vii) Conscripting or enlisting children under the age of fifteen years into armed forces or groups or using them to participate actively in hostilities;

(viii) Ordering the displacement of the civilian population for reasons related to the conflict, unless the security of the civilians involved or imperative military reasons so demand;

(ix) Killing or wounding treacherously a combatant adversary;

(x) Declaring that no quarter will be given;

(xi) Subjecting persons who are in the power of another party to the conflict to physical mutilation or to medical or scientific experiments of any kind which are neither justified by the medical, dental or hospital treatment of the person concerned nor carried out in his or her interest, and which cause death to or seriously endanger the health of such person or persons;

(xii) Destroying or seizing the property of an adversary unless such destruction or seizure be imperatively demanded by the necessities of the conflict;

(f) Paragraph 2 (e) applies to armed conflicts not of an international character and thus does not apply to situations of internal disturbances and tensions, such as riots, isolated and sporadic acts of violence or other acts of a similar nature. It applies to armed conflicts that take place in the territory of a State when there is protracted armed conflict between governmental authorities and organized armed groups or between such groups.

3. Nothing in paragraph 2 (c) and (e) shall affect the responsibility of a Government to maintain or re-establish law and order in the State or to defend the unity and territorial integrity of the State, by all legitimate means.

Article 9

ELEMENTS OF CRIMES

1. Elements of Crimes shall assist the Court in the interpretation and application of articles 6, 7 and 8. They shall be adopted by a two-thirds majority of the members of the Assembly of States Parties.

B1–010

2. Amendments to the Elements of Crimes may be proposed by:

    (a) Any State Party;
    (b) The judges acting by an absolute majority;
    (c) The Prosecutor.

Such amendments shall be adopted by a two-thirds majority of the members of the Assembly of States Parties.

3. The Elements of Crimes and amendments thereto shall be consistent with this Statute.

ARTICLE 10

B1–011   Nothing in this Part shall be interpreted as limiting or prejudicing in any way existing or developing rules of international law for purposes other than this Statute.

ARTICLE 11

JURISDICTION RATIONE TEMPORIS

B1–012   1. The Court has jurisdiction only with respect to crimes committed after the entry into force of this Statute.

2. If a State becomes a Party to this Statute after its entry into force, the Court may exercise its jurisdiction only with respect to crimes committed after the entry into force of this Statute for that State, unless that State has made a declaration under article 12, paragraph 3.

ARTICLE 12

PRECONDITIONS TO THE EXERCISE OF JURISDICTION

B1–013   1. A State which becomes a Party to this Statute thereby accepts the jurisdiction of the Court with respect to the crimes referred to in article 5.

2. In the case of article 13, paragraph (a) or (c), the Court may exercise its jurisdiction if one or more of the following States are Parties to this Statute or have accepted the jurisdiction of the Court in accordance with paragraph 3:
    (a) The State on the territory of which the conduct in question occurred or, if the crime was committed on board a vessel or aircraft, the State of registration of that vessel or aircraft;
    (b) The State of which the person accused of the crime is a national.

3. If the acceptance of a State which is not a Party to this Statute is required under paragraph 2, that State may, by declaration lodged with the Registrar, accept the exercise of jurisdiction by the Court with respect to the crime in question. The accepting State shall cooperate with the Court without any delay or exception in accordance with Part 9.

ARTICLE 13

EXERCISE OF JURISDICTION

B1–014   The Court may exercise its jurisdiction with respect to a crime referred to in article 5 in accordance with the provisions of this Statute if:
    (a) A situation in which one or more of such crimes appears to have been committed is referred to the Prosecutor by a State Party in accordance with article 14;
    (b) A situation in which one or more of such crimes appears to have been committed is referred to the Prosecutor by the Security Council acting under Chapter VII of the Charter of the United Nations; or

(c) The Prosecutor has initiated an investigation in respect of such a crime in accordance with article 15.

Article 14

REFERRAL OF A SITUATION BY A STATE PARTY

1. A State Party may refer to the Prosecutor a situation in which one or more crimes **B1–015** within the jurisdiction of the Court appear to have been committed requesting the Prosecutor to investigate the situation for the purpose of determining whether one or more specific persons should be charged with the commission of such crimes.

2. As far as possible, a referral shall specify the relevant circumstances and be accompanied by such supporting documentation as is available to the State referring the situation.

Article 15

PROSECUTOR

1. The Prosecutor may initiate investigations proprio motu on the basis of information **B1–016** on crimes within the jurisdiction of the Court.

2. The Prosecutor shall analyse the seriousness of the information received. For this purpose, he or she may seek additional information from States, organs of the United Nations, intergovernmental or non-governmental organizations, or other reliable sources that he or she deems appropriate, and may receive written or oral testimony at the seat of the Court.

3. If the Prosecutor concludes that there is a reasonable basis to proceed with an investigation, he or she shall submit to the Pre-Trial Chamber a request for authorization of an investigation, together with any supporting material collected. Victims may make representations to the Pre-Trial Chamber, in accordance with the Rules of Procedure and Evidence.

4. If the Pre-Trial Chamber, upon examination of the request and the supporting material, considers that there is a reasonable basis to proceed with an investigation, and that the case appears to fall within the jurisdiction of the Court, it shall authorize the commencement of the investigation, without prejudice to subsequent determinations by the Court with regard to the jurisdiction and admissibility of a case.

5. The refusal of the Pre-Trial Chamber to authorize the investigation shall not preclude the presentation of a subsequent request by the Prosecutor based on new facts or evidence regarding the same situation.

6. If, after the preliminary examination referred to in paragraphs 1 and 2, the Prosecutor concludes that the information provided does not constitute a reasonable basis for an investigation, he or she shall inform those who provided the information. This shall not preclude the Prosecutor from considering further information submitted to him or her regarding the same situation in the light of new facts or evidence.

Article 16

DEFERRAL OF INVESTIGATION OR PROSECUTION

No investigation or prosecution may be commenced or proceeded with under this **B1–017** Statute for a period of 12 months after the Security Council, in a resolution adopted under Chapter VII of the Charter of the United Nations, has requested the Court to that effect; that request may be renewed by the Council under the same conditions.

ARTICLE 17

ISSUES OF ADMISSIBILITY

B1–018   1. Having regard to paragraph 10 of the Preamble and article 1, the Court shall determine that a case is inadmissible where:

(a) The case is being investigated or prosecuted by a State which has jurisdiction over it, unless the State is unwilling or unable genuinely to carry out the investigation or prosecution;

(b) The case has been investigated by a State which has jurisdiction over it and the State has decided not to prosecute the person concerned, unless the decision resulted from the unwillingness or inability of the State genuinely to prosecute;

(c) The person concerned has already been tried for conduct which is the subject of the complaint, and a trial by the Court is not permitted under article 20, paragraph 3;

(d) The case is not of sufficient gravity to justify further action by the Court.

2. In order to determine unwillingness in a particular case, the Court shall consider, having regard to the principles of due process recognized by international law, whether one or more of the following exist, as applicable:

(a) The proceedings were or are being undertaken or the national decision was made for the purpose of shielding the person concerned from criminal responsibility for crimes within the jurisdiction of the Court referred to in article 5;

(b) There has been an unjustified delay in the proceedings which in the circumstances is inconsistent with an intent to bring the person concerned to justice;

(c) The proceedings were not or are not being conducted independently or impartially, and they were or are being conducted in a manner which, in the circumstances, is inconsistent with an intent to bring the person concerned to justice.

3. In order to determine inability in a particular case, the Court shall consider whether, due to a total or substantial collapse or unavailability of its national judicial system, the State is unable to obtain the accused or the necessary evidence and testimony or otherwise unable to carry out its proceedings.

ARTICLE 18

PRELIMINARY RULINGS REGARDING ADMISSIBILITY

B1–019   1. When a situation has been referred to the Court pursuant to article 13 (a) and the Prosecutor has determined that there would be a reasonable basis to commence an investigation, or the Prosecutor initiates an investigation pursuant to articles 13 (c) and 15, the Prosecutor shall notify all States Parties and those States which, taking into account the information available, would normally exercise jurisdiction over the crimes concerned. The Prosecutor may notify such States on a confidential basis and, where the Prosecutor believes it necessary to protect persons, prevent destruction of evidence or prevent the absconding of persons, may limit the scope of the information provided to States.

2. Within one month of receipt of that notification, a State may inform the Court that it is investigating or has investigated its nationals or others within its jurisdiction with respect to criminal acts which may constitute crimes referred to in article 5 and which relate to the information provided in the notification to States. At the request of that State, the Prosecutor shall defer to the State's investigation of those persons unless the Pre-Trial Chamber, on the application of the Prosecutor, decides to authorize the investigation.

3. The Prosecutor's deferral to a State's investigation shall be open to review by the Prosecutor six months after the date of deferral or at any time when there has been a

significant change of circumstances based on the State's unwillingness or inability genuinely to carry out the investigation.

4. The State concerned or the Prosecutor may appeal to the Appeals Chamber against a ruling of the Pre-Trial Chamber, in accordance with article 82. The appeal may be heard on an expedited basis.

5. When the Prosecutor has deferred an investigation in accordance with paragraph 2, the Prosecutor may request that the State concerned periodically inform the Prosecutor of the progress of its investigations and any subsequent prosecutions. States Parties shall respond to such requests without undue delay.

6. Pending a ruling by the Pre-Trial Chamber, or at any time when the Prosecutor has deferred an investigation under this article, the Prosecutor may, on an exceptional basis, seek authority from the Pre-Trial Chamber to pursue necessary investigative steps for the purpose of preserving evidence where there is a unique opportunity to obtain important evidence or there is a significant risk that such evidence may not be subsequently available.

7. A State which has challenged a ruling of the Pre-Trial Chamber under this article may challenge the admissibility of a case under article 19 on the grounds of additional significant facts or significant change of circumstances.

ARTICLE 19

CHALLENGES TO THE JURISDICTION OF THE COURT OR THE ADMISSIBILITY OF A CASE

1. The Court shall satisfy itself that it has jurisdiction in any case brought before it. **B1–020** The Court may, on its own motion, determine the admissibility of a case in accordance with article 17.

2. Challenges to the admissibility of a case on the grounds referred to in article 17 or challenges to the jurisdiction of the Court may be made by:

    (a) An accused or a person for whom a warrant of arrest or a summons to appear has been issued under article 58;

    (b) A State which has jurisdiction over a case, on the ground that it is investigating or prosecuting the case or has investigated or prosecuted; or

    (c) A State from which acceptance of jurisdiction is required under article 12.

3. The Prosecutor may seek a ruling from the Court regarding a question of jurisdiction or admissibility. In proceedings with respect to jurisdiction or admissibility, those who have referred the situation under article 13, as well as victims, may also submit observations to the Court.

4. The admissibility of a case or the jurisdiction of the Court may be challenged only once by any person or State referred to in paragraph 2. The challenge shall take place prior to or at the commencement of the trial. In exceptional circumstances, the Court may grant leave for a challenge to be brought more than once or at a time later than the commencement of the trial. Challenges to the admissibility of a case, at the commencement of a trial, or subsequently with the leave of the Court, may be based only on article 17, paragraph 1 (c).

5. A State referred to in paragraph 2 (b) and (c) shall make a challenge at the earliest opportunity.

6. Prior to the confirmation of the charges, challenges to the admissibility of a case or challenges to the jurisdiction of the Court shall be referred to the Pre-Trial Chamber. After confirmation of the charges, they shall be referred to the Trial Chamber. Decisions with respect to jurisdiction or admissibility may be appealed to the Appeals Chamber in accordance with article 82.

7. If a challenge is made by a State referred to in paragraph 2 (b) or (c), the Prosecutor shall suspend the investigation until such time as the Court makes a determination in accordance with article 17.

8. Pending a ruling by the Court, the Prosecutor may seek authority from the Court:

(a) To pursue necessary investigative steps of the kind referred to in article 18, paragraph 6;

(b) To take a statement or testimony from a witness or complete the collection and examination of evidence which had begun prior to the making of the challenge; and

(c) In cooperation with the relevant States, to prevent the absconding of persons in respect of whom the Prosecutor has already requested a warrant of arrest under article 58.

9. The making of a challenge shall not affect the validity of any act performed by the Prosecutor or any order or warrant issued by the Court prior to the making of the challenge.

10. If the Court has decided that a case is inadmissible under article 17, the Prosecutor may submit a request for a review of the decision when he or she is fully satisfied that new facts have arisen which negate the basis on which the case had previously been found inadmissible under article 17.

11. If the Prosecutor, having regard to the matters referred to in article 17, defers an investigation, the Prosecutor may request that the relevant State make available to the Prosecutor information on the proceedings. That information shall, at the request of the State concerned, be confidential. If the Prosecutor thereafter decides to proceed with an investigation, he or she shall notify the State to which deferral of the proceedings has taken place.

ARTICLE 20

NE BIS IN IDEM

B1–021   1. Except as provided in this Statute, no person shall be tried before the Court with respect to conduct which formed the basis of crimes for which the person has been convicted or acquitted by the Court.

2. No person shall be tried by another court for a crime referred to in article 5 for which that person has already been convicted or acquitted by the Court.

3. No person who has been tried by another court for conduct also proscribed under article 6, 7 or 8 shall be tried by the Court with respect to the same conduct unless the proceedings in the other court:

(a) Were for the purpose of shielding the person concerned from criminal responsibility for crimes within the jurisdiction of the Court; or

(b) Otherwise were not conducted independently or impartially in accordance with the norms of due process recognized by international law and were conducted in a manner which, in the circumstances, was inconsistent with an intent to bring the person concerned to justice.

ARTICLE 21

APPLICABLE LAW

B1–022   1. The Court shall apply:

(a) In the first place, this Statute, Elements of Crimes and its Rules of Procedure and Evidence;

(b) In the second place, where appropriate, applicable treaties and the principles and rules of international law, including the established principles of the international law of armed conflict;

(c) Failing that, general principles of law derived by the Court from national laws of legal systems of the world including, as appropriate, the national laws of States that would normally exercise jurisdiction over the crime, provided that those principles are not inconsistent with this Statute and with international law and internationally recognized norms and standards.

2. The Court may apply principles and rules of law as interpreted in its previous decisions.

3. The application and interpretation of law pursuant to this article must be consistent with internationally recognized human rights, and be without any adverse distinction founded on grounds such as gender as defined in article 7, paragraph 3, age, race, colour, language, religion or belief, political or other opinion, national, ethnic or social origin, wealth, birth or other status.

PART 3. GENERAL PRINCIPLES OF CRIMINAL LAW

ARTICLE 22

NULLUM CRIMEN SINE LEGE

1. A person shall not be criminally responsible under this Statute unless the conduct in question constitutes, at the time it takes place, a crime within the jurisdiction of the Court.

B1–023

2. The definition of a crime shall be strictly construed and shall not be extended by analogy. In case of ambiguity, the definition shall be interpreted in favour of the person being investigated, prosecuted or convicted.

3. This article shall not affect the characterization of any conduct as criminal under international law independently of this Statute.

ARTICLE 23

NULLA POENA SINE LEGE

A person convicted by the Court may be punished only in accordance with this Statute.

B1–024

ARTICLE 24

NON-RETROACTIVITY RATIONE PERSONAE

1. No person shall be criminally responsible under this Statute for conduct prior to the entry into force of the Statute.

B1–025

2. In the event of a change in the law applicable to a given case prior to a final judgement, the law more favourable to the person being investigated, prosecuted or convicted shall apply.

ARTICLE 25

INDIVIDUAL CRIMINAL RESPONSIBILITY

1. The Court shall have jurisdiction over natural persons pursuant to this Statute.

B1–026

2. A person who commits a crime within the jurisdiction of the Court shall be individually responsible and liable for punishment in accordance with this Statute.

3. In accordance with this Statute, a person shall be criminally responsible and liable for punishment for a crime within the jurisdiction of the Court if that person:

   (a) Commits such a crime, whether as an individual, jointly with another or through another person, regardless of whether that other person is criminally responsible;

   (b) Orders, solicits or induces the commission of such a crime which in fact occurs or is attempted;

1205

　(c) For the purpose of facilitating the commission of such a crime, aids, abets or otherwise assists in its commission or its attempted commission, including providing the means for its commission;

　(d) In any other way contributes to the commission or attempted commission of such a crime by a group of persons acting with a common purpose. Such contribution shall be intentional and shall either:

　　(i) Be made with the aim of furthering the criminal activity or criminal purpose of the group, where such activity or purpose involves the commission of a crime within the jurisdiction of the Court; or

　　(ii) Be made in the knowledge of the intention of the group to commit the crime;

　(e) In respect of the crime of genocide, directly and publicly incites others to commit genocide;

　(f) Attempts to commit such a crime by taking action that commences its execution by means of a substantial step, but the crime does not occur because of circumstances independent of the person's intentions. However, a person who abandons the effort to commit the crime or otherwise prevents the completion of the crime shall not be liable for punishment under this Statute for the attempt to commit that crime if that person completely and voluntarily gave up the criminal purpose.

　4. No provision in this Statute relating to individual criminal responsibility shall affect the responsibility of States under international law.

ARTICLE 26

EXCLUSION OF JURISDICTION OVER PERSONS UNDER EIGHTEEN

B1–027　　The Court shall have no jurisdiction over any person who was under the age of 18 at the time of the alleged commission of a crime.

ARTICLE 27

IRRELEVANCE OF OFFICIAL CAPACITY

B1–028　　1. This Statute shall apply equally to all persons without any distinction based on official capacity. In particular, official capacity as a Head of State or Government, a member of a Government or parliament, an elected representative or a government official shall in no case exempt a person from criminal responsibility under this Statute, nor shall it, in and of itself, constitute a ground for reduction of sentence.

　2. Immunities or special procedural rules which may attach to the official capacity of a person, whether under national or international law, shall not bar the Court from exercising its jurisdiction over such a person.

ARTICLE 28

RESPONSIBILITY OF COMMANDERS AND OTHER SUPERIORS

B1–029　　In addition to other grounds of criminal responsibility under this Statute for crimes within the jurisdiction of the Court:

　(a) A military commander or person effectively acting as a military commander shall be criminally responsible for crimes within the jurisdiction of the Court committed by forces under his or her effective command and control, or effective authority and control as the case may be, as a result of his or her failure to exercise control properly over such forces, where:

    (i) That military commander or person either knew or, owing to the circumstances at the time, should have known that the forces were committing or about to commit such crimes; and

    (ii) That military commander or person failed to take all necessary and reasonable measures within his or her power to prevent or repress their commission or to submit the matter to the competent authorities for investigation and prosecution.

(b) With respect to superior and subordinate relationships not described in paragraph (a), a superior shall be criminally responsible for crimes within the jurisdiction of the Court committed by subordinates under his or her effective authority and control, as a result of his or her failure to exercise control properly over such subordinates, where:

    (i) The superior either knew, or consciously disregarded information which clearly indicated, that the subordinates were committing or about to commit such crimes;

    (ii) The crimes concerned activities that were within the effective responsibility and control of the superior; and

    (iii) The superior failed to take all necessary and reasonable measures within his or her power to prevent or repress their commission or to submit the matter to the competent authorities for investigation and prosecution.

ARTICLE 29

NON-APPLICABILITY OF STATUTE OF LIMITATIONS

The crimes within the jurisdiction of the Court shall not be subject to any statute of limitations.

B1–030

ARTICLE 30

MENTAL ELEMENT

1. Unless otherwise provided, a person shall be criminally responsible and liable for punishment for a crime within the jurisdiction of the Court only if the material elements are committed with intent and knowledge.

B1–031

2. For the purposes of this article, a person has intent where:

    (a) In relation to conduct, that person means to engage in the conduct;

    (b) In relation to a consequence, that person means to cause that consequence or is aware that it will occur in the ordinary course of events.

3. For the purposes of this article, "knowledge" means awareness that a circumstance exists or a consequence will occur in the ordinary course of events. "Know" and "knowingly" shall be construed accordingly.

ARTICLE 31

GROUNDS FOR EXCLUDING CRIMINAL RESPONSIBILITY

1. In addition to other grounds for excluding criminal responsibility provided for in this Statute, a person shall not be criminally responsible if, at the time of that person's conduct:

B1–032

    (a) The person suffers from a mental disease or defect that destroys that person's capacity to appreciate the unlawfulness or nature of his or her conduct, or capacity to control his or her conduct to conform to the requirements of law;

(b) The person is in a state of intoxication that destroys that person's capacity to appreciate the unlawfulness or nature of his or her conduct, or capacity to control his or her conduct to conform to the requirements of law, unless the person has become voluntarily intoxicated under such circumstances that the person knew, or disregarded the risk, that, as a result of the intoxication, he or she was likely to engage in conduct constituting a crime within the jurisdiction of the Court;

(c) The person acts reasonably to defend himself or herself or another person or, in the case of war crimes, property which is essential for the survival of the person or another person or property which is essential for accomplishing a military mission, against an imminent and unlawful use of force in a manner proportionate to the degree of danger to the person or the other person or property protected. The fact that the person was involved in a defensive operation conducted by forces shall not in itself constitute a ground for excluding criminal responsibility under this subparagraph;

(d) The conduct which is alleged to constitute a crime within the jurisdiction of the Court has been caused by duress resulting from a threat of imminent death or of continuing or imminent serious bodily harm against that person or another person, and the person acts necessarily and reasonably to avoid this threat, provided that the person does not intend to cause a greater harm than the one sought to be avoided. Such a threat may either be:

　(i) Made by other persons; or

　(ii) Constituted by other circumstances beyond that person's control.

2. The Court shall determine the applicability of the grounds for excluding criminal responsibility provided for in this Statute to the case before it.

3. At trial, the Court may consider a ground for excluding criminal responsibility other than those referred to in paragraph 1 where such a ground is derived from applicable law as set forth in article 21. The procedures relating to the consideration of such a ground shall be provided for in the Rules of Procedure and Evidence.

ARTICLE 32

MISTAKE OF FACT OR MISTAKE OF LAW

B1–033　　1. A mistake of fact shall be a ground for excluding criminal responsibility only if it negates the mental element required by the crime.

2. A mistake of law as to whether a particular type of conduct is a crime within the jurisdiction of the Court shall not be a ground for excluding criminal responsibility. A mistake of law may, however, be a ground for excluding criminal responsibility if it negates the mental element required by such a crime, or as provided for in article 33.

ARTICLE 33

SUPERIOR ORDERS AND PRESCRIPTION OF LAW

B1–034　　1. The fact that a crime within the jurisdiction of the Court has been committed by a person pursuant to an order of a Government or of a superior, whether military or civilian, shall not relieve that person of criminal responsibility unless:

(a) The person was under a legal obligation to obey orders of the Government or the superior in question;

(b) The person did not know that the order was unlawful; and

(c) The order was not manifestly unlawful.

2. For the purposes of this article, orders to commit genocide or crimes against humanity are manifestly unlawful.

PART 4. COMPOSITION AND ADMINISTRATION OF THE COURT

ARTICLE 34

ORGANS OF THE COURT

The Court shall be composed of the following organs: **B1–035**
  (a) The Presidency;
  (b) An Appeals Division, a Trial Division and a Pre-Trial Division;
  (c) The Office of the Prosecutor;
  (d) The Registry.

ARTICLE 35

SERVICE OF JUDGES

1. All judges shall be elected as full-time members of the Court and shall be available   **B1–036**
to serve on that basis from the commencement of their terms of office.

2. The judges composing the Presidency shall serve on a full-time basis as soon as they
are elected.

3. The Presidency may, on the basis of the workload of the Court and in consultation
with its members, decide from time to time to what extent the remaining judges shall be
required to serve on a full-time basis. Any such arrangement shall be without prejudice
to the provisions of article 40.

4. The financial arrangements for judges not required to serve on a full-time basis
shall be made in accordance with article 49.

ARTICLE 36

QUALIFICATIONS, NOMINATION AND ELECTION OF JUDGES

1. Subject to the provisions of paragraph 2, there shall be 18 judges of the Court.   **B1–037**

2. (a) The Presidency, acting on behalf of the Court, may propose an increase in the
       number of judges specified in paragraph 1, indicating the reasons why this is
       considered necessary and appropriate. The Registrar shall promptly circulate
       any such proposal to all States Parties.

   (b) Any such proposal shall then be considered at a meeting of the Assembly of
       States Parties to be convened in accordance with article 112. The proposal shall
       be considered adopted if approved at the meeting by a vote of two thirds of the
       members of the Assembly of States Parties and shall enter into force at such
       time as decided by the Assembly of States Parties.

   (c) (i) Once a proposal for an increase in the number of judges has been adopted
            under subparagraph (b), the election of the additional judges shall take
            place at the next session of the Assembly of States Parties in accordance
            with paragraphs 3 to 8, and article 37, paragraph 2;

       (ii) Once a proposal for an increase in the number of judges has been adopted
            and brought into effect under subparagraphs (b) and (c) (i), it shall be
            open to the Presidency at any time thereafter, if the workload of the Court
            justifies it, to propose a reduction in the number of judges, provided that
            the number of judges shall not be reduced below that specified in
            paragraph 1. The proposal shall be dealt with in accordance with the
            procedure laid down in subparagraphs (a) and (b). In the event that the
            proposal is adopted, the number of judges shall be progressively decreased

as the terms of office of serving judges expire, until the necessary number has been reached.

3. (a) The judges shall be chosen from among persons of high moral character, impartiality and integrity who possess the qualifications required in their respective States for appointment to the highest judicial offices.

   (b) Every candidate for election to the Court shall:

      (i) Have established competence in criminal law and procedure, and the necessary relevant experience, whether as judge, prosecutor, advocate or in other similar capacity, in criminal proceedings; or

      (ii) Have established competence in relevant areas of international law such as international humanitarian law and the law of human rights, and extensive experience in a professional legal capacity which is of relevance to the judicial work of the Court;

   (c) Every candidate for election to the Court shall have an excellent knowledge of and be fluent in at least one of the working languages of the Court.

4. (a) Nominations of candidates for election to the Court may be made by any State Party to this Statute, and shall be made either:

      (i) By the procedure for the nomination of candidates for appointment to the highest judicial offices in the State in question; or

      (ii) By the procedure provided for the nomination of candidates for the International Court of Justice in the Statute of that Court.

Nominations shall be accompanied by a statement in the necessary detail specifying how the candidate fulfils the requirements of paragraph 3.

   (b) Each State Party may put forward one candidate for any given election who need not necessarily be a national of that State Party but shall in any case be a national of a State Party.

   (c) The Assembly of States Parties may decide to establish, if appropriate, an Advisory Committee on nominations. In that event, the Committee's composition and mandate shall be established by the Assembly of States Parties.

5. For the purposes of the election, there shall be two lists of candidates:

List A containing the names of candidates with the qualifications specified in paragraph 3 (b) (i); and

List B containing the names of candidates with the qualifications specified in paragraph 3 (b) (ii).

A candidate with sufficient qualifications for both lists may choose on which list to appear. At the first election to the Court, at least nine judges shall be elected from list A and at least five judges from list B. Subsequent elections shall be so organized as to maintain the equivalent proportion on the Court of judges qualified on the two lists.

6. (a) The judges shall be elected by secret ballot at a meeting of the Assembly of States Parties convened for that purpose under article 112. Subject to paragraph 7, the persons elected to the Court shall be the 18 candidates who obtain the highest number of votes and a two-thirds majority of the States Parties present and voting.

   (b) In the event that a sufficient number of judges is not elected on the first ballot, successive ballots shall be held in accordance with the procedures laid down in subparagraph (a) until the remaining places have been filled.

7. No two judges may be nationals of the same State. A person who, for the purposes of membership of the Court, could be regarded as a national of more than one State shall be deemed to be a national of the State in which that person ordinarily exercises civil and political rights.

8. (a) The States Parties shall, in the selection of judges, take into account the need, within the membership of the Court, for:

      (i) The representation of the principal legal systems of the world;

      (ii) Equitable geographical representation; and

      (iii) A fair representation of female and male judges.

   (b) States Parties shall also take into account the need to include judges with legal expertise on specific issues, including, but not limited to, violence against women or children.

9. (a) Subject to subparagraph (b), judges shall hold office for a term of nine years and, subject to subparagraph (c) and to article 37, paragraph 2, shall not be eligible for re-election.

   (b) At the first election, one third of the judges elected shall be selected by lot to serve for a term of three years; one third of the judges elected shall be selected by lot to serve for a term of six years; and the remainder shall serve for a term of nine years.

   (c) A judge who is selected to serve for a term of three years under subparagraph (b) shall be eligible for re-election for a full term.

10. Notwithstanding paragraph 9, a judge assigned to a Trial or Appeals Chamber in accordance with article 39 shall continue in office to complete any trial or appeal the hearing of which has already commenced before that Chamber.

Article 37

JUDICIAL VACANCIES

1. In the event of a vacancy, an election shall be held in accordance with article 36 to fill the vacancy. **B1–038**

2. A judge elected to fill a vacancy shall serve for the remainder of the predecessor's term and, if that period is three years or less, shall be eligible for re-election for a full term under article 36.

Article 38

THE PRESIDENCY

1. The President and the First and Second Vice-Presidents shall be elected by an absolute majority of the judges. They shall each serve for a term of three years or until the end of their respective terms of office as judges, whichever expires earlier. They shall be eligible for re-election once. **B1–039**

2. The First Vice-President shall act in place of the President in the event that the President is unavailable or disqualified. The Second Vice-President shall act in place of the President in the event that both the President and the First Vice-President are unavailable or disqualified.

3. The President, together with the First and Second Vice-Presidents, shall constitute the Presidency, which shall be responsible for:

   (a) The proper administration of the Court, with the exception of the Office of the Prosecutor; and

   (b) The other functions conferred upon it in accordance with this Statute.

4. In discharging its responsibility under paragraph 3 (a), the Presidency shall coordinate with and seek the concurrence of the Prosecutor on all matters of mutual concern.

Article 39

CHAMBERS

1. As soon as possible after the election of the judges, the Court shall organize itself into the divisions specified in article 34, paragraph (b). The Appeals Division shall be composed of the President and four other judges, the Trial Division of not less than six judges and the Pre-Trial Division of not less than six judges. The assignment of judges to divisions shall be based on the nature of the functions to be performed by each division and the qualifications and experience of the judges elected to the Court, in such a way **B1–040**

that each division shall contain an appropriate combination of expertise in criminal law and procedure and in international law. The Trial and Pre-Trial Divisions shall be composed predominantly of judges with criminal trial experience.

    2. (a) The judicial functions of the Court shall be carried out in each division by Chambers.

      (b) (i) The Appeals Chamber shall be composed of all the judges of the Appeals Division;

          (ii) The functions of the Trial Chamber shall be carried out by three judges of the Trial Division;

          (iii) The functions of the Pre-Trial Chamber shall be carried out either by three judges of the Pre-Trial Division or by a single judge of that division in accordance with this Statute and the Rules of Procedure and Evidence;

      (c) Nothing in this paragraph shall preclude the simultaneous constitution of more than one Trial Chamber or Pre-Trial Chamber when the efficient management of the Court's workload so requires.

    3. (a) Judges assigned to the Trial and Pre-Trial Divisions shall serve in those divisions for a period of three years, and thereafter until the completion of any case the hearing of which has already commenced in the division concerned.

      (b) Judges assigned to the Appeals Division shall serve in that division for their entire term of office.

    4. Judges assigned to the Appeals Division shall serve only in that division. Nothing in this article shall, however, preclude the temporary attachment of judges from the Trial Division to the Pre-Trial Division or vice versa, if the Presidency considers that the efficient management of the Court's workload so requires, provided that under no circumstances shall a judge who has participated in the pre-trial phase of a case be eligible to sit on the Trial Chamber hearing that case.

ARTICLE 40

INDEPENDENCE OF THE JUDGES

B1–041   1. The judges shall be independent in the performance of their functions.

    2. Judges shall not engage in any activity which is likely to interfere with their judicial functions or to affect confidence in their independence.

    3. Judges required to serve on a full-time basis at the seat of the Court shall not engage in any other occupation of a professional nature.

    4. Any question regarding the application of paragraphs 2 and 3 shall be decided by an absolute majority of the judges. Where any such question concerns an individual judge, that judge shall not take part in the decision.

ARTICLE 41

EXCUSING AND DISQUALIFICATION OF JUDGES

B1–042   1. The Presidency may, at the request of a judge, excuse that judge from the exercise of a function under this Statute, in accordance with the Rules of Procedure and Evidence.

    2. (a) A judge shall not participate in any case in which his or her impartiality might reasonably be doubted on any ground. A judge shall be disqualified from a case in accordance with this paragraph if, *inter alia*, that judge has previously been involved in any capacity in that case before the Court or in a related criminal case at the national level involving the person being investigated or prosecuted. A judge shall also be disqualified on such other grounds as may be provided for in the Rules of Procedure and Evidence.

      (b) The Prosecutor or the person being investigated or prosecuted may request the disqualification of a judge under this paragraph.

(c) Any question as to the disqualification of a judge shall be decided by an absolute majority of the judges. The challenged judge shall be entitled to present his or her comments on the matter, but shall not take part in the decision.

Article 42

THE OFFICE OF THE PROSECUTOR

1. The Office of the Prosecutor shall act independently as a separate organ of the Court. It shall be responsible for receiving referrals and any substantiated information on crimes within the jurisdiction of the Court, for examining them and for conducting investigations and prosecutions before the Court. A member of the Office shall not seek or act on instructions from any external source. **B1–043**

2. The Office shall be headed by the Prosecutor. The Prosecutor shall have full authority over the management and administration of the Office, including the staff, facilities and other resources thereof. The Prosecutor shall be assisted by one or more Deputy Prosecutors, who shall be entitled to carry out any of the acts required of the Prosecutor under this Statute. The Prosecutor and the Deputy Prosecutors shall be of different nationalities. They shall serve on a full-time basis.

3. The Prosecutor and the Deputy Prosecutors shall be persons of high moral character, be highly competent in and have extensive practical experience in the prosecution or trial of criminal cases. They shall have an excellent knowledge of and be fluent in at least one of the working languages of the Court.

4. The Prosecutor shall be elected by secret ballot by an absolute majority of the members of the Assembly of States Parties. The Deputy Prosecutors shall be elected in the same way from a list of candidates provided by the Prosecutor. The Prosecutor shall nominate three candidates for each position of Deputy Prosecutor to be filled. Unless a shorter term is decided upon at the time of their election, the Prosecutor and the Deputy Prosecutors shall hold office for a term of nine years and shall not be eligible for re-election.

5. Neither the Prosecutor nor a Deputy Prosecutor shall engage in any activity which is likely to interfere with his or her prosecutorial functions or to affect confidence in his or her independence. They shall not engage in any other occupation of a professional nature.

6. The Presidency may excuse the Prosecutor or a Deputy Prosecutor, at his or her request, from acting in a particular case.

7. Neither the Prosecutor nor a Deputy Prosecutor shall participate in any matter in which their impartiality might reasonably be doubted on any ground. They shall be disqualified from a case in accordance with this paragraph if, *inter alia*, they have previously been involved in any capacity in that case before the Court or in a related criminal case at the national level involving the person being investigated or prosecuted.

8. Any question as to the disqualification of the Prosecutor or a Deputy Prosecutor shall be decided by the Appeals Chamber.

(a) The person being investigated or prosecuted may at any time request the disqualification of the Prosecutor or a Deputy Prosecutor on the grounds set out in this article;

(b) The Prosecutor or the Deputy Prosecutor, as appropriate, shall be entitled to present his or her comments on the matter;

9. The Prosecutor shall appoint advisers with legal expertise on specific issues, including, but not limited to, sexual and gender violence and violence against children.

Article 43

THE REGISTRY

1. The Registry shall be responsible for the non-judicial aspects of the administration and servicing of the Court, without prejudice to the functions and powers of the Prosecutor in accordance with article 42. **B1–044**

2. The Registry shall be headed by the Registrar, who shall be the principal administrative officer of the Court. The Registrar shall exercise his or her functions under the authority of the President of the Court.

3. The Registrar and the Deputy Registrar shall be persons of high moral character, be highly competent and have an excellent knowledge of and be fluent in at least one of the working languages of the Court.

4. The judges shall elect the Registrar by an absolute majority by secret ballot, taking into account any recommendation by the Assembly of States Parties. If the need arises and upon the recommendation of the Registrar, the judges shall elect, in the same manner, a Deputy Registrar.

5. The Registrar shall hold office for a term of five years, shall be eligible for re-election once and shall serve on a full-time basis. The Deputy Registrar shall hold office for a term of five years or such shorter term as may be decided upon by an absolute majority of the judges, and may be elected on the basis that the Deputy Registrar shall be called upon to serve as required.

6. The Registrar shall set up a Victims and Witnesses Unit within the Registry. This Unit shall provide, in consultation with the Office of the Prosecutor, protective measures and security arrangements, counselling and other appropriate assistance for witnesses, victims who appear before the Court, and others who are at risk on account of testimony given by such witnesses. The Unit shall include staff with expertise in trauma, including trauma related to crimes of sexual violence.

ARTICLE 44

STAFF

B1–045   1. The Prosecutor and the Registrar shall appoint such qualified staff as may be required to their respective offices. In the case of the Prosecutor, this shall include the appointment of investigators.

2. In the employment of staff, the Prosecutor and the Registrar shall ensure the highest standards of efficiency, competency and integrity, and shall have regard, *mutatis mutandis*, to the criteria set forth in article 36, paragraph 8.

3. The Registrar, with the agreement of the Presidency and the Prosecutor, shall propose Staff Regulations which include the terms and conditions upon which the staff of the Court shall be appointed, remunerated and dismissed. The Staff Regulations shall be approved by the Assembly of States Parties.

4. The Court may, in exceptional circumstances, employ the expertise of gratis personnel offered by States Parties, intergovernmental organizations or non-governmental organizations to assist with the work of any of the organs of the Court. The Prosecutor may accept any such offer on behalf of the Office of the Prosecutor. Such gratis personnel shall be employed in accordance with guidelines to be established by the Assembly of States Parties.

ARTICLE 45

SOLEMN UNDERTAKING

B1–046   Before taking up their respective duties under this Statute, the judges, the Prosecutor, the Deputy Prosecutors, the Registrar and the Deputy Registrar shall each make a solemn undertaking in open court to exercise his or her respective functions impartially and conscientiously.

Article 46

REMOVAL FROM OFFICE

1. A judge, the Prosecutor, a Deputy Prosecutor, the Registrar or the Deputy Registrar shall be removed from office if a decision to this effect is made in accordance with paragraph 2, in cases where that person: **B1–047**
    (a) Is found to have committed serious misconduct or a serious breach of his or her duties under this Statute, as provided for in the Rules of Procedure and Evidence; or
    (b) Is unable to exercise the functions required by this Statute.
2. A decision as to the removal from office of a judge, the Prosecutor or a Deputy Prosecutor under paragraph 1 shall be made by the Assembly of States Parties, by secret ballot:
    (a) In the case of a judge, by a two-thirds majority of the States Parties upon a recommendation adopted by a two-thirds majority of the other judges;
    (b) In the case of the Prosecutor, by an absolute majority of the States Parties;
    (c) In the case of a Deputy Prosecutor, by an absolute majority of the States Parties upon the recommendation of the Prosecutor.
3. A decision as to the removal from office of the Registrar or Deputy Registrar shall be made by an absolute majority of the judges.
4. A judge, Prosecutor, Deputy Prosecutor, Registrar or Deputy Registrar whose conduct or ability to exercise the functions of the office as required by this Statute is challenged under this article shall have full opportunity to present and receive evidence and to make submissions in accordance with the Rules of Procedure and Evidence. The person in question shall not otherwise participate in the consideration of the matter.

Article 47

DISCIPLINARY MEASURES

A judge, Prosecutor, Deputy Prosecutor, Registrar or Deputy Registrar who has committed misconduct of a less serious nature than that set out in article 46, paragraph 1, shall be subject to disciplinary measures, in accordance with the Rules of Procedure and Evidence. **B1–048**

Article 48

PRIVILEGES AND IMMUNITIES

1. The Court shall enjoy in the territory of each State Party such privileges and immunities as are necessary for the fulfilment of its purposes. **B1–049**
2. The judges, the Prosecutor, the Deputy Prosecutors and the Registrar shall, when engaged on or with respect to the business of the Court, enjoy the same privileges and immunities as are accorded to heads of diplomatic missions and shall, after the expiry of their terms of office, continue to be accorded immunity from legal process of every kind in respect of words spoken or written and acts performed by them in their official capacity.
3. The Deputy Registrar, the staff of the Office of the Prosecutor and the staff of the Registry shall enjoy the privileges and immunities and facilities necessary for the performance of their functions, in accordance with the agreement on the privileges and immunities of the Court.
4. Counsel, experts, witnesses or any other person required to be present at the seat of the Court shall be accorded such treatment as is necessary for the proper functioning

of the Court, in accordance with the agreement on the privileges and immunities of the Court.

5. The privileges and immunities of:

  (a) A judge or the Prosecutor may be waived by an absolute majority of the judges;
  (b) The Registrar may be waived by the Presidency;
  (c) The Deputy Prosecutors and staff of the Office of the Prosecutor may be waived by the Prosecutor;
  (d) The Deputy Registrar and staff of the Registry may be waived by the Registrar.

ARTICLE 49

SALARIES, ALLOWANCES AND EXPENSES

B1–050   The judges, the Prosecutor, the Deputy Prosecutors, the Registrar and the Deputy Registrar shall receive such salaries, allowances and expenses as may be decided upon by the Assembly of States Parties. These salaries and allowances shall not be reduced during their terms of office.

ARTICLE 50

OFFICIAL AND WORKING LANGUAGES

B1–051   1. The official languages of the Court shall be Arabic, Chinese, English, French, Russian and Spanish. The judgements of the Court, as well as other decisions resolving fundamental issues before the Court, shall be published in the official languages. The Presidency shall, in accordance with the criteria established by the Rules of Procedure and Evidence, determine which decisions may be considered as resolving fundamental issues for the purposes of this paragraph.

2. The working languages of the Court shall be English and French. The Rules of Procedure and Evidence shall determine the cases in which other official languages may be used as working languages.

3. At the request of any party to a proceeding or a State allowed to intervene in a proceeding, the Court shall authorize a language other than English or French to be used by such a party or State, provided that the Court considers such authorization to be adequately justified.

ARTICLE 51

RULES OF PROCEDURE AND EVIDENCE

B1–052   1. The Rules of Procedure and Evidence shall enter into force upon adoption by a two-thirds majority of the members of the Assembly of States Parties.

2. Amendments to the Rules of Procedure and Evidence may be proposed by:

  (a) Any State Party;
  (b) The judges acting by an absolute majority; or
  (c) The Prosecutor.

Such amendments shall enter into force upon adoption by a two-thirds majority of the members of the Assembly of States Parties.

3. After the adoption of the Rules of Procedure and Evidence, in urgent cases where the Rules do not provide for a specific situation before the Court, the judges may, by a two-thirds majority, draw up provisional Rules to be applied until adopted, amended or rejected at the next ordinary or special session of the Assembly of States Parties.

4. The Rules of Procedure and Evidence, amendments thereto and any provisional Rule shall be consistent with this Statute. Amendments to the Rules of Procedure and

Evidence as well as provisional Rules shall not be applied retroactively to the detriment of the person who is being investigated or prosecuted or who has been convicted.

5. In the event of conflict between the Statute and the Rules of Procedure and Evidence, the Statute shall prevail.

ARTICLE 52

REGULATIONS OF THE COURT

B1–053

1. The judges shall, in accordance with this Statute and the Rules of Procedure and Evidence, adopt, by an absolute majority, the Regulations of the Court necessary for its routine functioning.

2. The Prosecutor and the Registrar shall be consulted in the elaboration of the Regulations and any amendments thereto.

3. The Regulations and any amendments thereto shall take effect upon adoption unless otherwise decided by the judges. Immediately upon adoption, they shall be circulated to States Parties for comments. If within six months there are no objections from a majority of States Parties, they shall remain in force.

PART 5. INVESTIGATION AND PROSECUTION

ARTICLE 53

INITIATION OF AN INVESTIGATION

B1–054

1. The Prosecutor shall, having evaluated the information made available to him or her, initiate an investigation unless he or she determines that there is no reasonable basis to proceed under this Statute. In deciding whether to initiate an investigation, the Prosecutor shall consider whether:

    (a) The information available to the Prosecutor provides a reasonable basis to believe that a crime within the jurisdiction of the Court has been or is being committed;

    (b) The case is or would be admissible under article 17; and

    (c) Taking into account the gravity of the crime and the interests of victims, there are nonetheless substantial reasons to believe that an investigation would not serve the interests of justice.

If the Prosecutor determines that there is no reasonable basis to proceed and his or her determination is based solely on subparagraph (c) above, he or she shall inform the Pre-Trial Chamber.

2. If, upon investigation, the Prosecutor concludes that there is not a sufficient basis for a prosecution because:

    (a) There is not a sufficient legal or factual basis to seek a warrant or summons under article 58;

    (b) The case is inadmissible under article 17; or

    (c) A prosecution is not in the interests of justice, taking into account all the circumstances, including the gravity of the crime, the interests of victims and the age or infirmity of the alleged perpetrator, and his or her role in the alleged crime;

the Prosecutor shall inform the Pre-Trial Chamber and the State making a referral under article 14 or the Security Council in a case under article 13, paragraph (b), of his or her conclusion and the reasons for the conclusion.

3. (a) At the request of the State making a referral under article 14 or the Security Council under article 13, paragraph (b), the Pre-Trial Chamber may review a decision of the Prosecutor under paragraph 1 or 2 not to proceed and may request the Prosecutor to reconsider that decision.

(b) In addition, the Pre-Trial Chamber may, on its own initiative, review a decision of the Prosecutor not to proceed if it is based solely on paragraph 1 (c) or 2 (c). In such a case, the decision of the Prosecutor shall be effective only if confirmed by the Pre-Trial Chamber.

4. The Prosecutor may, at any time, reconsider a decision whether to initiate an investigation or prosecution based on new facts or information.

ARTICLE 54

DUTIES AND POWERS OF THE PROSECUTOR WITH RESPECT TO INVESTIGATIONS

B1–055   1. The Prosecutor shall:
(a) In order to establish the truth, extend the investigation to cover all facts and evidence relevant to an assessment of whether there is criminal responsibility under this Statute, and, in doing so, investigate incriminating and exonerating circumstances equally;
(b) Take appropriate measures to ensure the effective investigation and prosecution of crimes within the jurisdiction of the Court, and in doing so, respect the interests and personal circumstances of victims and witnesses, including age, gender as defined in article 7, paragraph 3, and health, and take into account the nature of the crime, in particular where it involves sexual violence, gender violence or violence against children; and
(c) Fully respect the rights of persons arising under this Statute.

2. The Prosecutor may conduct investigations on the territory of a State:
(a) In accordance with the provisions of Part 9; or
(b) As authorized by the Pre-Trial Chamber under article 57, paragraph 3 (d).

3. The Prosecutor may:
(a) Collect and examine evidence;
(b) Request the presence of and question persons being investigated, victims and witnesses;
(c) Seek the cooperation of any State or intergovernmental organization or arrangement in accordance with its respective competence and/or mandate;
(d) Enter into such arrangements or agreements, not inconsistent with this Statute, as may be necessary to facilitate the cooperation of a State, intergovernmental organization or person;
(e) Agree not to disclose, at any stage of the proceedings, documents or information that the Prosecutor obtains on the condition of confidentiality and solely for the purpose of generating new evidence, unless the provider of the information consents; and
(f) Take necessary measures, or request that necessary measures be taken, to ensure the confidentiality of information, the protection of any person or the preservation of evidence.

ARTICLE 55

RIGHTS OF PERSONS DURING AN INVESTIGATION

B1–056   1. In respect of an investigation under this Statute, a person:
(a) Shall not be compelled to incriminate himself or herself or to confess guilt;
(b) Shall not be subjected to any form of coercion, duress or threat, to torture or to any other form of cruel, inhuman or degrading treatment or punishment;
(c) Shall, if questioned in a language other than a language the person fully understands and speaks, have, free of any cost, the assistance of a competent interpreter and such translations as are necessary to meet the requirements of fairness; and

(d) Shall not be subjected to arbitrary arrest or detention, and shall not be deprived of his or her liberty except on such grounds and in accordance with such procedures as are established in this Statute.

2. Where there are grounds to believe that a person has committed a crime within the jurisdiction of the Court and that person is about to be questioned either by the Prosecutor, or by national authorities pursuant to a request made under Part 9, that person shall also have the following rights of which he or she shall be informed prior to being questioned:

(a) To be informed, prior to being questioned, that there are grounds to believe that he or she has committed a crime within the jurisdiction of the Court;

(b) To remain silent, without such silence being a consideration in the determination of guilt or innocence;

(c) To have legal assistance of the person's choosing, or, if the person does not have legal assistance, to have legal assistance assigned to him or her, in any case where the interests of justice so require, and without payment by the person in any such case if the person does not have sufficient means to pay for it; and

(d) To be questioned in the presence of counsel unless the person has voluntarily waived his or her right to counsel.

Article 56

ROLE OF THE PRE-TRIAL CHAMBER IN RELATION TO A UNIQUE INVESTIGATIVE OPPORTUNITY

1. (a) Where the Prosecutor considers an investigation to present a unique opportunity to take testimony or a statement from a witness or to examine, collect or test evidence, which may not be available subsequently for the purposes of a trial, the Prosecutor shall so inform the Pre-Trial Chamber. **B1–057**

(b) In that case, the Pre-Trial Chamber may, upon request of the Prosecutor, take such measures as may be necessary to ensure the efficiency and integrity of the proceedings and, in particular, to protect the rights of the defence.

(c) Unless the Pre-Trial Chamber orders otherwise, the Prosecutor shall provide the relevant information to the person who has been arrested or appeared in response to a summons in connection with the investigation referred to in subparagraph (a), in order that he or she may be heard on the matter.

2. The measures referred to in paragraph 1 (b) may include:

(a) Making recommendations or orders regarding procedures to be followed;

(b) Directing that a record be made of the proceedings;

(c) Appointing an expert to assist;

(d) Authorizing counsel for a person who has been arrested, or appeared before the Court in response to a summons, to participate, or where there has not yet been such an arrest or appearance or counsel has not been designated, appointing another counsel to attend and represent the interests of the defence;

(e) Naming one of its members or, if necessary, another available judge of the Pre-Trial or Trial Division to observe and make recommendations or orders regarding the collection and preservation of evidence and the questioning of persons;

(f) Taking such other action as may be necessary to collect or preserve evidence.

3. (a) Where the Prosecutor has not sought measures pursuant to this article but the Pre-Trial Chamber considers that such measures are required to preserve evidence that it deems would be essential for the defence at trial, it shall consult with the Prosecutor as to whether there is good reason for the Prosecutor's failure to request the measures. If upon consultation, the Pre-Trial Chamber concludes that the Prosecutor's failure to request such measures is unjustified, the Pre-Trial Chamber may take such measures on its own initiative.

(b) A decision of the Pre-Trial Chamber to act on its own initiative under this paragraph may be appealed by the Prosecutor. The appeal shall be heard on an expedited basis.

4. The admissibility of evidence preserved or collected for trial pursuant to this article, or the record thereof, shall be governed at trial by article 69, and given such weight as determined by the Trial Chamber.

ARTICLE 57

FUNCTIONS AND POWERS OF THE PRE-TRIAL CHAMBER

B1–058   1. Unless otherwise provided in this Statute, the Pre-Trial Chamber shall exercise its functions in accordance with the provisions of this article.

2. (a) Orders or rulings of the Pre-Trial Chamber issued under articles 15, 18, 19, 54, paragraph 2, 61, paragraph 7, and 72 must be concurred in by a majority of its judges.

(b) In all other cases, a single judge of the Pre-Trial Chamber may exercise the functions provided for in this Statute, unless otherwise provided for in the Rules of Procedure and Evidence or by a majority of the Pre-Trial Chamber.

3. In addition to its other functions under this Statute, the Pre-Trial Chamber may:

(a) At the request of the Prosecutor, issue such orders and warrants as may be required for the purposes of an investigation;

(b) Upon the request of a person who has been arrested or has appeared pursuant to a summons under article 58, issue such orders, including measures such as those described in article 56, or seek such cooperation pursuant to Part 9 as may be necessary to assist the person in the preparation of his or her defence;

(c) Where necessary, provide for the protection and privacy of victims and witnesses, the preservation of evidence, the protection of persons who have been arrested or appeared in response to a summons, and the protection of national security information;

(d) Authorize the Prosecutor to take specific investigative steps within the territory of a State Party without having secured the cooperation of that State under Part 9 if, whenever possible having regard to the views of the State concerned, the Pre-Trial Chamber has determined in that case that the State is clearly unable to execute a request for cooperation due to the unavailability of any authority or any component of its judicial system competent to execute the request for cooperation under Part 9.

(e) Where a warrant of arrest or a summons has been issued under article 58, and having due regard to the strength of the evidence and the rights of the parties concerned, as provided for in this Statute and the Rules of Procedure and Evidence, seek the cooperation of States pursuant to article 93, paragraph 1 (k), to take protective measures for the purpose of forfeiture, in particular for the ultimate benefit of victims.

ARTICLE 58

ISSUANCE BY THE PRE-TRIAL CHAMBER OF A WARRANT OF ARREST OR A SUMMONS TO APPEAR

B1–059   1. At any time after the initiation of an investigation, the Pre-Trial Chamber shall, on the application of the Prosecutor, issue a warrant of arrest of a person if, having examined the application and the evidence or other information submitted by the Prosecutor, it is satisfied that:

(a) There are reasonable grounds to believe that the person has committed a crime within the jurisdiction of the Court; and

  (b) The arrest of the person appears necessary:
    (i) To ensure the person's appearance at trial,
    (ii) To ensure that the person does not obstruct or endanger the investigation or the court proceedings, or
    (iii) Where applicable, to prevent the person from continuing with the commission of that crime or a related crime which is within the jurisdiction of the Court and which arises out of the same circumstances.
2. The application of the Prosecutor shall contain:
  (a) The name of the person and any other relevant identifying information;
  (b) A specific reference to the crimes within the jurisdiction of the Court which the person is alleged to have committed;
  (c) A concise statement of the facts which are alleged to constitute those crimes;
  (d) A summary of the evidence and any other information which establish reasonable grounds to believe that the person committed those crimes; and
  (e) The reason why the Prosecutor believes that the arrest of the person is necessary.
3. The warrant of arrest shall contain:
  (a) The name of the person and any other relevant identifying information;
  (b) A specific reference to the crimes within the jurisdiction of the Court for which the person's arrest is sought; and
  (c) A concise statement of the facts which are alleged to constitute those crimes.
4. The warrant of arrest shall remain in effect until otherwise ordered by the Court.
5. On the basis of the warrant of arrest, the Court may request the provisional arrest or the arrest and surrender of the person under Part 9.
6. The Prosecutor may request the Pre-Trial Chamber to amend the warrant of arrest by modifying or adding to the crimes specified therein. The Pre-Trial Chamber shall so amend the warrant if it is satisfied that there are reasonable grounds to believe that the person committed the modified or additional crimes.
7. As an alternative to seeking a warrant of arrest, the Prosecutor may submit an application requesting that the Pre-Trial Chamber issue a summons for the person to appear. If the Pre-Trial Chamber is satisfied that there are reasonable grounds to believe that the person committed the crime alleged and that a summons is sufficient to ensure the person's appearance, it shall issue the summons, with or without conditions restricting liberty (other than detention) if provided for by national law, for the person to appear. The summons shall contain:
  (a) The name of the person and any other relevant identifying information;
  (b) The specified date on which the person is to appear;
  (c) A specific reference to the crimes within the jurisdiction of the Court which the person is alleged to have committed; and
  (d) A concise statement of the facts which are alleged to constitute the crime.
The summons shall be served on the person.

ARTICLE 59

ARREST PROCEEDINGS IN THE CUSTODIAL STATE

1. A State Party which has received a request for provisional arrest or for arrest and **B1–060** surrender shall immediately take steps to arrest the person in question in accordance with its laws and the provisions of Part 9.
2. A person arrested shall be brought promptly before the competent judicial authority in the custodial State which shall determine, in accordance with the law of that State, that:
  (a) The warrant applies to that person;
  (b) The person has been arrested in accordance with the proper process; and
  (c) The person's rights have been respected.
3. The person arrested shall have the right to apply to the competent authority in the custodial State for interim release pending surrender.

4. In reaching a decision on any such application, the competent authority in the custodial State shall consider whether, given the gravity of the alleged crimes, there are urgent and exceptional circumstances to justify interim release and whether necessary safeguards exist to ensure that the custodial State can fulfil its duty to surrender the person to the Court. It shall not be open to the competent authority of the custodial State to consider whether the warrant of arrest was properly issued in accordance with article 58, paragraph 1 (a) and (b).

5. The Pre-Trial Chamber shall be notified of any request for interim release and shall make recommendations to the competent authority in the custodial State. The competent authority in the custodial State shall give full consideration to such recommendations, including any recommendations on measures to prevent the escape of the person, before rendering its decision.

6. If the person is granted interim release, the Pre-Trial Chamber may request periodic reports on the status of the interim release.

7. Once ordered to be surrendered by the custodial State, the person shall be delivered to the Court as soon as possible.

ARTICLE 60

INITIAL PROCEEDINGS BEFORE THE COURT

B1–061   1. Upon the surrender of the person to the Court, or the person's appearance before the Court voluntarily or pursuant to a summons, the Pre-Trial Chamber shall satisfy itself that the person has been informed of the crimes which he or she is alleged to have committed, and of his or her rights under this Statute, including the right to apply for interim release pending trial.

2. A person subject to a warrant of arrest may apply for interim release pending trial. If the Pre-Trial Chamber is satisfied that the conditions set forth in article 58, paragraph 1, are met, the person shall continue to be detained. If it is not so satisfied, the Pre-Trial Chamber shall release the person, with or without conditions.

3. The Pre-Trial Chamber shall periodically review its ruling on the release or detention of the person, and may do so at any time on the request of the Prosecutor or the person. Upon such review, it may modify its ruling as to detention, release or conditions of release, if it is satisfied that changed circumstances so require.

4. The Pre-Trial Chamber shall ensure that a person is not detained for an unreasonable period prior to trial due to inexcusable delay by the Prosecutor. If such delay occurs, the Court shall consider releasing the person, with or without conditions.

5. If necessary, the Pre-Trial Chamber may issue a warrant of arrest to secure the presence of a person who has been released.

ARTICLE 61

CONFIRMATION OF THE CHARGES BEFORE TRIAL

B1–062   1. Subject to the provisions of paragraph 2, within a reasonable time after the person's surrender or voluntary appearance before the Court, the Pre-Trial Chamber shall hold a hearing to confirm the charges on which the Prosecutor intends to seek trial. The hearing shall be held in the presence of the Prosecutor and the person charged, as well as his or her counsel.

2. The Pre-Trial Chamber may, upon request of the Prosecutor or on its own motion, hold a hearing in the absence of the person charged to confirm the charges on which the Prosecutor intends to seek trial when the person has:

(a) Waived his or her right to be present; or

(b) Fled or cannot be found and all reasonable steps have been taken to secure his or her appearance before the Court and to inform the person of the charges and that a hearing to confirm those charges will be held.

In that case, the person shall be represented by counsel where the Pre-Trial Chamber determines that it is in the interests of justice.

3. Within a reasonable time before the hearing, the person shall:

(a) Be provided with a copy of the document containing the charges on which the Prosecutor intends to bring the person to trial; and

(b) Be informed of the evidence on which the Prosecutor intends to rely at the hearing.

The Pre-Trial Chamber may issue orders regarding the disclosure of information for the purposes of the hearing.

4. Before the hearing, the Prosecutor may continue the investigation and may amend or withdraw any charges. The person shall be given reasonable notice before the hearing of any amendment to or withdrawal of charges. In case of a withdrawal of charges, the Prosecutor shall notify the Pre-Trial Chamber of the reasons for the withdrawal.

5. At the hearing, the Prosecutor shall support each charge with sufficient evidence to establish substantial grounds to believe that the person committed the crime charged. The Prosecutor may rely on documentary or summary evidence and need not call the witnesses expected to testify at the trial.

6. At the hearing, the person may:

(a) Object to the charges;

(b) Challenge the evidence presented by the Prosecutor; and

(c) Present evidence.

7. The Pre-Trial Chamber shall, on the basis of the hearing, determine whether there is sufficient evidence to establish substantial grounds to believe that the person committed each of the crimes charged. Based on its determination, the Pre-Trial Chamber shall:

(a) Confirm those charges in relation to which it has determined that there is sufficient evidence, and commit the person to a Trial Chamber for trial on the charges as confirmed;

(b) Decline to confirm those charges in relation to which it has determined that there is insufficient evidence;

(c) Adjourn the hearing and request the Prosecutor to consider:

(i) Providing further evidence or conducting further investigation with respect to a particular charge; or

(ii) Amending a charge because the evidence submitted appears to establish a different crime within the jurisdiction of the Court.

8. Where the Pre-Trial Chamber declines to confirm a charge, the Prosecutor shall not be precluded from subsequently requesting its confirmation if the request is supported by additional evidence.

9. After the charges are confirmed and before the trial has begun, the Prosecutor may, with the permission of the Pre-Trial Chamber and after notice to the accused, amend the charges. If the Prosecutor seeks to add additional charges or to substitute more serious charges, a hearing under this article to confirm those charges must be held. After commencement of the trial, the Prosecutor may, with the permission of the Trial Chamber, withdraw the charges.

10. Any warrant previously issued shall cease to have effect with respect to any charges which have not been confirmed by the Pre-Trial Chamber or which have been withdrawn by the Prosecutor.

11. Once the charges have been confirmed in accordance with this article, the Presidency shall constitute a Trial Chamber which, subject to paragraph 9 and to article 64, paragraph 4, shall be responsible for the conduct of subsequent proceedings and may exercise any function of the Pre-Trial Chamber that is relevant and capable of application in those proceedings.

Part 6. The Trial

Article 62

PLACE OF TRIAL

Unless otherwise decided, the place of the trial shall be the seat of the Court. **B1–063**

ARTICLE 63

TRIAL IN THE PRESENCE OF THE ACCUSED

B1–064   1. The accused shall be present during the trial.

2. If the accused, being present before the Court, continues to disrupt the trial, the Trial Chamber may remove the accused and shall make provision for him or her to observe the trial and instruct counsel from outside the courtroom, through the use of communications technology, if required. Such measures shall be taken only in exceptional circumstances after other reasonable alternatives have proved inadequate, and only for such duration as is strictly required.

ARTICLE 64

FUNCTIONS AND POWERS OF THE TRIAL CHAMBER

B1–065   1. The functions and powers of the Trial Chamber set out in this article shall be exercised in accordance with this Statute and the Rules of Procedure and Evidence.

2. The Trial Chamber shall ensure that a trial is fair and expeditious and is conducted with full respect for the rights of the accused and due regard for the protection of victims and witnesses.

3. Upon assignment of a case for trial in accordance with this Statute, the Trial Chamber assigned to deal with the case shall:

(a) Confer with the parties and adopt such procedures as are necessary to facilitate the fair and expeditious conduct of the proceedings;

(b) Determine the language or languages to be used at trial; and

(c) Subject to any other relevant provisions of this Statute, provide for disclosure of documents or information not previously disclosed, sufficiently in advance of the commencement of the trial to enable adequate preparation for trial.

4. The Trial Chamber may, if necessary for its effective and fair functioning, refer preliminary issues to the Pre-Trial Chamber or, if necessary, to another available judge of the Pre-Trial Division.

5. Upon notice to the parties, the Trial Chamber may, as appropriate, direct that there be joinder or severance in respect of charges against more than one accused.

6. In performing its functions prior to trial or during the course of a trial, the Trial Chamber may, as necessary:

(a) Exercise any functions of the Pre-Trial Chamber referred to in article 61, paragraph 11;

(b) Require the attendance and testimony of witnesses and production of documents and other evidence by obtaining, if necessary, the assistance of States as provided in this Statute;

(c) Provide for the protection of confidential information;

(d) Order the production of evidence in addition to that already collected prior to the trial or presented during the trial by the parties;

(e) Provide for the protection of the accused, witnesses and victims; and

(f) Rule on any other relevant matters.

7. The trial shall be held in public. The Trial Chamber may, however, determine that special circumstances require that certain proceedings be in closed session for the purposes set forth in article 68, or to protect confidential or sensitive information to be given in evidence.

8. (a) At the commencement of the trial, the Trial Chamber shall have read to the accused the charges previously confirmed by the Pre-Trial Chamber. The Trial Chamber shall satisfy itself that the accused understands the nature of the charges. It shall afford him or her the opportunity to make an admission of guilt in accordance with article 65 or to plead not guilty.

(b) At the trial, the presiding judge may give directions for the conduct of proceedings, including to ensure that they are conducted in a fair and impartial manner. Subject to any directions of the presiding judge, the parties may submit evidence in accordance with the provisions of this Statute.

9. The Trial Chamber shall have, *inter alia*, the power on application of a party or on its own motion to:
  (a) Rule on the admissibility or relevance of evidence; and
  (b) Take all necessary steps to maintain order in the course of a hearing.

10. The Trial Chamber shall ensure that a complete record of the trial, which accurately reflects the proceedings, is made and that it is maintained and preserved by the Registrar.

ARTICLE 65

PROCEEDINGS ON AN ADMISSION OF GUILT

1. Where the accused makes an admission of guilt pursuant to article 64, paragraph 8 **B1–066** (a), the Trial Chamber shall determine whether:
  (a) The accused understands the nature and consequences of the admission of guilt;
  (b) The admission is voluntarily made by the accused after sufficient consultation with defence counsel; and
  (c) The admission of guilt is supported by the facts of the case that are contained in:
    (i) The charges brought by the Prosecutor and admitted by the accused;
    (ii) Any materials presented by the Prosecutor which supplement the charges and which the accused accepts; and
    (iii) Any other evidence, such as the testimony of witnesses, presented by the Prosecutor or the accused.

2. Where the Trial Chamber is satisfied that the matters referred to in paragraph 1 are established, it shall consider the admission of guilt, together with any additional evidence presented, as establishing all the essential facts that are required to prove the crime to which the admission of guilt relates, and may convict the accused of that crime.

3. Where the Trial Chamber is not satisfied that the matters referred to in paragraph 1 are established, it shall consider the admission of guilt as not having been made, in which case it shall order that the trial be continued under the ordinary trial procedures provided by this Statute and may remit the case to another Trial Chamber.

4. Where the Trial Chamber is of the opinion that a more complete presentation of the facts of the case is required in the interests of justice, in particular the interests of the victims, the Trial Chamber may:
  (a) Request the Prosecutor to present additional evidence, including the testimony of witnesses; or
  (b) Order that the trial be continued under the ordinary trial procedures provided by this Statute, in which case it shall consider the admission of guilt as not having been made and may remit the case to another Trial Chamber.

5. Any discussions between the Prosecutor and the defence regarding modification of the charges, the admission of guilt or the penalty to be imposed shall not be binding on the Court.

ARTICLE 66

PRESUMPTION OF INNOCENCE

1. Everyone shall be presumed innocent until proved guilty before the Court in **B1–067** accordance with the applicable law.

2. The onus is on the Prosecutor to prove the guilt of the accused.

3. In order to convict the accused, the Court must be convinced of the guilt of the accused beyond reasonable doubt.

ARTICLE 67

RIGHTS OF THE ACCUSED

B1–068   1. In the determination of any charge, the accused shall be entitled to a public hearing, having regard to the provisions of this Statute, to a fair hearing conducted impartially, and to the following minimum guarantees, in full equality:

(a) To be informed promptly and in detail of the nature, cause and content of the charge, in a language which the accused fully understands and speaks;

(b) To have adequate time and facilities for the preparation of the defence and to communicate freely with counsel of the accused's choosing in confidence;

(c) To be tried without undue delay;

(d) Subject to article 63, paragraph 2, to be present at the trial, to conduct the defence in person or through legal assistance of the accused's choosing, to be informed, if the accused does not have legal assistance, of this right and to have legal assistance assigned by the Court in any case where the interests of justice so require, and without payment if the accused lacks sufficient means to pay for it;

(e) To examine, or have examined, the witnesses against him or her and to obtain the attendance and examination of witnesses on his or her behalf under the same conditions as witnesses against him or her. The accused shall also be entitled to raise defences and to present other evidence admissible under this Statute;

(f) To have, free of any cost, the assistance of a competent interpreter and such translations as are necessary to meet the requirements of fairness, if any of the proceedings of or documents presented to the Court are not in a language which the accused fully understands and speaks;

(g) Not to be compelled to testify or to confess guilt and to remain silent, without such silence being a consideration in the determination of guilt or innocence;

(h) To make an unsworn oral or written statement in his or her defence; and

(i) Not to have imposed on him or her any reversal of the burden of proof or any onus of rebuttal.

2. In addition to any other disclosure provided for in this Statute, the Prosecutor shall, as soon as practicable, disclose to the defence evidence in the Prosecutor's possession or control which he or she believes shows or tends to show the innocence of the accused, or to mitigate the guilt of the accused, or which may affect the credibility of prosecution evidence. In case of doubt as to the application of this paragraph, the Court shall decide.

ARTICLE 68

PROTECTION OF THE VICTIMS AND WITNESSES AND THEIR PARTICIPATION IN THE PROCEEDINGS

B1–069   1. The Court shall take appropriate measures to protect the safety, physical and psychological well-being, dignity and privacy of victims and witnesses. In so doing, the Court shall have regard to all relevant factors, including age, gender as defined in article 7, paragraph 3, and health, and the nature of the crime, in particular, but not limited to, where the crime involves sexual or gender violence or violence against children. The Prosecutor shall take such measures particularly during the investigation and prosecution of such crimes. These measures shall not be prejudicial to or inconsistent with the rights of the accused and a fair and impartial trial.

2. As an exception to the principle of public hearings provided for in article 67, the Chambers of the Court may, to protect victims and witnesses or an accused, conduct any part of the proceedings in camera or allow the presentation of evidence by electronic or other special means. In particular, such measures shall be implemented in the case of a

victim of sexual violence or a child who is a victim or a witness, unless otherwise ordered by the Court, having regard to all the circumstances, particularly the views of the victim or witness.

3. Where the personal interests of the victims are affected, the Court shall permit their views and concerns to be presented and considered at stages of the proceedings determined to be appropriate by the Court and in a manner which is not prejudicial to or inconsistent with the rights of the accused and a fair and impartial trial. Such views and concerns may be presented by the legal representatives of the victims where the Court considers it appropriate, in accordance with the Rules of Procedure and Evidence.

4. The Victims and Witnesses Unit may advise the Prosecutor and the Court on appropriate protective measures, security arrangements, counselling and assistance as referred to in article 43, paragraph 6.

5. Where the disclosure of evidence or information pursuant to this Statute may lead to the grave endangerment of the security of a witness or his or her family, the Prosecutor may, for the purposes of any proceedings conducted prior to the commencement of the trial, withhold such evidence or information and instead submit a summary thereof. Such measures shall be exercised in a manner which is not prejudicial to or inconsistent with the rights of the accused and a fair and impartial trial.

6. A State may make an application for necessary measures to be taken in respect of the protection of its servants or agents and the protection of confidential or sensitive information.

ARTICLE 69

EVIDENCE

1. Before testifying, each witness shall, in accordance with the Rules of Procedure and Evidence, give an undertaking as to the truthfulness of the evidence to be given by that witness. **B1–070**

2. The testimony of a witness at trial shall be given in person, except to the extent provided by the measures set forth in article 68 or in the Rules of Procedure and Evidence. The Court may also permit the giving of *viva voce* (oral) or recorded testimony of a witness by means of video or audio technology, as well as the introduction of documents or written transcripts, subject to this Statute and in accordance with the Rules of Procedure and Evidence. These measures shall not be prejudicial to or inconsistent with the rights of the accused.

3. The parties may submit evidence relevant to the case, in accordance with article 64. The Court shall have the authority to request the submission of all evidence that it considers necessary for the determination of the truth.

4. The Court may rule on the relevance or admissibility of any evidence, taking into account, *inter alia*, the probative value of the evidence and any prejudice that such evidence may cause to a fair trial or to a fair evaluation of the testimony of a witness, in accordance with the Rules of Procedure and Evidence.

5. The Court shall respect and observe privileges on confidentiality as provided for in the Rules of Procedure and Evidence.

6. The Court shall not require proof of facts of common knowledge but may take judicial notice of them.

7. Evidence obtained by means of a violation of this Statute or internationally recognized human rights shall not be admissible if:

(a) The violation casts substantial doubt on the reliability of the evidence; or

(b) The admission of the evidence would be antithetical to and would seriously damage the integrity of the proceedings.

8. When deciding on the relevance or admissibility of evidence collected by a State, the Court shall not rule on the application of the State's national law.

ARTICLE 70

OFFENCES AGAINST THE ADMINISTRATION OF JUSTICE

B1–071   1. The Court shall have jurisdiction over the following offences against its administration of justice when committed intentionally:
   (a) Giving false testimony when under an obligation pursuant to article 69, paragraph 1, to tell the truth;
   (b) Presenting evidence that the party knows is false or forged;
   (c) Corruptly influencing a witness, obstructing or interfering with the attendance or testimony of a witness, retaliating against a witness for giving testimony or destroying, tampering with or interfering with the collection of evidence;
   (d) Impeding, intimidating or corruptly influencing an official of the Court for the purpose of forcing or persuading the official not to perform, or to perform improperly, his or her duties;
   (e) Retaliating against an official of the Court on account of duties performed by that or another official;
   (f) Soliciting or accepting a bribe as an official of the Court in connection with his or her official duties.
   2. The principles and procedures governing the Court's exercise of jurisdiction over offences under this article shall be those provided for in the Rules of Procedure and Evidence. The conditions for providing international cooperation to the Court with respect to its proceedings under this article shall be governed by the domestic laws of the requested State.
   3. In the event of conviction, the Court may impose a term of imprisonment not exceeding five years, or a fine in accordance with the Rules of Procedure and Evidence, or both.
   4. (a) Each State Party shall extend its criminal laws penalizing offences against the integrity of its own investigative or judicial process to offences against the administration of justice referred to in this article, committed on its territory, or by one of its nationals;
   (b) Upon request by the Court, whenever it deems it proper, the State Party shall submit the case to its competent authorities for the purpose of prosecution. Those authorities shall treat such cases with diligence and devote sufficient resources to enable them to be conducted effectively.

ARTICLE 71

SANCTIONS FOR MISCONDUCT BEFORE THE COURT

B1–072   1. The Court may sanction persons present before it who commit misconduct, including disruption of its proceedings or deliberate refusal to comply with its directions, by administrative measures other than imprisonment, such as temporary or permanent removal from the courtroom, a fine or other similar measures provided for in the Rules of Procedure and Evidence.
   2. The procedures governing the imposition of the measures set forth in paragraph 1 shall be those provided for in the Rules of Procedure and Evidence.

ARTICLE 72

PROTECTION OF NATIONAL SECURITY INFORMATION

B1–073   1. This article applies in any case where the disclosure of the information or documents of a State would, in the opinion of that State, prejudice its national security interests. Such cases include those falling within the scope of article 56, paragraphs 2 and 3, article 61, paragraph 3, article 64, paragraph 3, article 67, paragraph 2, article 68, paragraph 6, article 87, paragraph 6 and article 93, as well as cases arising at any other stage of the proceedings where such disclosure may be at issue.

2. This article shall also apply when a person who has been requested to give information or evidence has refused to do so or has referred the matter to the State on the ground that disclosure would prejudice the national security interests of a State and the State concerned confirms that it is of the opinion that disclosure would prejudice its national security interests.

3. Nothing in this article shall prejudice the requirements of confidentiality applicable under article 54, paragraph 3 (e) and (f), or the application of article 73.

4. If a State learns that information or documents of the State are being, or are likely to be, disclosed at any stage of the proceedings, and it is of the opinion that disclosure would prejudice its national security interests, that State shall have the right to intervene in order to obtain resolution of the issue in accordance with this article.

5. If, in the opinion of a State, disclosure of information would prejudice its national security interests, all reasonable steps will be taken by the State, acting in conjunction with the Prosecutor, the defence or the Pre-Trial Chamber or Trial Chamber, as the case may be, to seek to resolve the matter by cooperative means. Such steps may include:

(a) Modification or clarification of the request;

(b) A determination by the Court regarding the relevance of the information or evidence sought, or a determination as to whether the evidence, though relevant, could be or has been obtained from a source other than the requested State;

(c) Obtaining the information or evidence from a different source or in a different form; or

(d) Agreement on conditions under which the assistance could be provided including, among other things, providing summaries or redactions, limitations on disclosure, use of *in camera* or *ex parte* proceedings, or other protective measures permissible under the Statute and the Rules of Procedure and Evidence.

6. Once all reasonable steps have been taken to resolve the matter through cooperative means, and if the State considers that there are no means or conditions under which the information or documents could be provided or disclosed without prejudice to its national security interests, it shall so notify the Prosecutor or the Court of the specific reasons for its decision, unless a specific description of the reasons would itself necessarily result in such prejudice to the State's national security interests.

7. Thereafter, if the Court determines that the evidence is relevant and necessary for the establishment of the guilt or innocence of the accused, the Court may undertake the following actions:

(a) Where disclosure of the information or document is sought pursuant to a request for cooperation under Part 9 or the circumstances described in paragraph 2, and the State has invoked the ground for refusal referred to in article 93, paragraph 4:

(i) The Court may, before making any conclusion referred to in subparagraph 7 (a) (ii), request further consultations for the purpose of considering the State's representations, which may include, as appropriate, hearings *in camera* and *ex parte*;

(ii) If the Court concludes that, by invoking the ground for refusal under article 93, paragraph 4, in the circumstances of the case, the requested State is not acting in accordance with its obligations under this Statute, the Court may refer the matter in accordance with article 87, paragraph 7, specifying the reasons for its conclusion; and

(iii) The Court may make such inference in the trial of the accused as to the existence or non-existence of a fact, as may be appropriate in the circumstances; or

(b) In all other circumstances:

(i) Order disclosure; or

(ii) To the extent it does not order disclosure, make such inference in the trial of the accused as to the existence or non-existence of a fact, as may be appropriate in the circumstances.

ARTICLE 73

THIRD-PARTY INFORMATION OR DOCUMENTS

B1–074   If a State Party is requested by the Court to provide a document or information in its custody, possession or control, which was disclosed to it in confidence by a State, intergovernmental organization or international organization, it shall seek the consent of the originator to disclose that document or information. If the originator is a State Party, it shall either consent to disclosure of the information or document or undertake to resolve the issue of disclosure with the Court, subject to the provisions of article 72. If the originator is not a State Party and refuses to consent to disclosure, the requested State shall inform the Court that it is unable to provide the document or information because of a pre-existing obligation of confidentiality to the originator.

ARTICLE 74

REQUIREMENTS FOR THE DECISION

B1–075   1. All the judges of the Trial Chamber shall be present at each stage of the trial and throughout their deliberations. The Presidency may, on a case-by-case basis, designate, as available, one or more alternate judges to be present at each stage of the trial and to replace a member of the Trial Chamber if that member is unable to continue attending.

2. The Trial Chamber's decision shall be based on its evaluation of the evidence and the entire proceedings. The decision shall not exceed the facts and circumstances described in the charges and any amendments to the charges. The Court may base its decision only on evidence submitted and discussed before it at the trial.

3. The judges shall attempt to achieve unanimity in their decision, failing which the decision shall be taken by a majority of the judges.

4. The deliberations of the Trial Chamber shall remain secret.

5. The decision shall be in writing and shall contain a full and reasoned statement of the Trial Chamber's findings on the evidence and conclusions. The Trial Chamber shall issue one decision. When there is no unanimity, the Trial Chamber's decision shall contain the views of the majority and the minority. The decision or a summary thereof shall be delivered in open court.

ARTICLE 75

REPARATIONS TO VICTIMS

B1–076   1. The Court shall establish principles relating to reparations to, or in respect of, victims, including restitution, compensation and rehabilitation. On this basis, in its decision the Court may, either upon request or on its own motion in exceptional circumstances, determine the scope and extent of any damage, loss and injury to, or in respect of, victims and will state the principles on which it is acting.

2. The Court may make an order directly against a convicted person specifying appropriate reparations to, or in respect of, victims, including restitution, compensation and rehabilitation.

Where appropriate, the Court may order that the award for reparations be made through the Trust Fund provided for in article 79.

3. Before making an order under this article, the Court may invite and shall take account of representations from or on behalf of the convicted person, victims, other interested persons or interested States.

4. In exercising its power under this article, the Court may, after a person is convicted of a crime within the jurisdiction of the Court, determine whether, in order to give effect

to an order which it may make under this article, it is necessary to seek measures under article 93, paragraph 1.

5. A State Party shall give effect to a decision under this article as if the provisions of article 109 were applicable to this article.

6. Nothing in this article shall be interpreted as prejudicing the rights of victims under national or international law.

Article 76

SENTENCING

1. In the event of a conviction, the Trial Chamber shall consider the appropriate sentence to be imposed and shall take into account the evidence presented and submissions made during the trial that are relevant to the sentence. **B1–077**

2. Except where article 65 applies and before the completion of the trial, the Trial Chamber may on its own motion and shall, at the request of the Prosecutor or the accused, hold a further hearing to hear any additional evidence or submissions relevant to the sentence, in accordance with the Rules of Procedure and Evidence.

3. Where paragraph 2 applies, any representations under article 75 shall be heard during the further hearing referred to in paragraph 2 and, if necessary, during any additional hearing.

4. The sentence shall be pronounced in public and, wherever possible, in the presence of the accused.

Part 7. Penalties

Article 77

APPLICABLE PENALTIES

1. Subject to article 110, the Court may impose one of the following penalties on a person convicted of a crime referred to in article 5 of this Statute: **B1–078**
    (a) Imprisonment for a specified number of years, which may not exceed a maximum of 30 years; or
    (b) A term of life imprisonment when justified by the extreme gravity of the crime and the individual circumstances of the convicted person.

2. In addition to imprisonment, the Court may order:
    (a) A fine under the criteria provided for in the Rules of Procedure and Evidence;
    (b) A forfeiture of proceeds, property and assets derived directly or indirectly from that crime, without prejudice to the rights of bona fide third parties.

Article 78

DETERMINATION OF THE SENTENCE

1. In determining the sentence, the Court shall, in accordance with the Rules of Procedure and Evidence, take into account such factors as the gravity of the crime and the individual circumstances of the convicted person. **B1–079**

2. In imposing a sentence of imprisonment, the Court shall deduct the time, if any, previously spent in detention in accordance with an order of the Court. The Court may deduct any time otherwise spent in detention in connection with conduct underlying the crime.

3. When a person has been convicted of more than one crime, the Court shall pronounce a sentence for each crime and a joint sentence specifying the total period of

imprisonment. This period shall be no less than the highest individual sentence pronounced and shall not exceed 30 years imprisonment or a sentence of life imprisonment in conformity with article 77, paragraph 1 (b).

ARTICLE 79

TRUST FUND

B1–080   1. A Trust Fund shall be established by decision of the Assembly of States Parties for the benefit of victims of crimes within the jurisdiction of the Court, and of the families of such victims.

2. The Court may order money and other property collected through fines or forfeiture to be transferred, by order of the Court, to the Trust Fund.

3. The Trust Fund shall be managed according to criteria to be determined by the Assembly of States Parties.

ARTICLE 80

NON-PREJUDICE TO NATIONAL APPLICATION OF PENALTIES AND NATIONAL LAWS

B1–081   Nothing in this Part affects the application by States of penalties prescribed by their national law, nor the law of States which do not provide for penalties prescribed in this Part.

PART 8. APPEAL AND REVISION

ARTICLE 81

APPEAL AGAINST DECISION OF ACQUITTAL OR CONVICTION OR AGAINST SENTENCE

B1–082   1. A decision under article 74 may be appealed in accordance with the Rules of Procedure and Evidence as follows:
  (a) The Prosecutor may make an appeal on any of the following grounds:
   (i) Procedural error,
   (ii) Error of fact, or
   (iii) Error of law;
  (b) The convicted person, or the Prosecutor on that person's behalf, may make an appeal on any of the following grounds:
   (i) Procedural error,
   (ii) Error of fact,
   (iii) Error of law, or
   (iv) Any other ground that affects the fairness or reliability of the proceedings or decision.
2. (a) A sentence may be appealed, in accordance with the Rules of Procedure and Evidence, by the Prosecutor or the convicted person on the ground of disproportion between the crime and the sentence;
  (b) If on an appeal against sentence the Court considers that there are grounds on which the conviction might be set aside, wholly or in part, it may invite the Prosecutor and the convicted person to submit grounds under article 81, paragraph 1 (a) or (b), and may render a decision on conviction in accordance with article 83;

(c) The same procedure applies when the Court, on an appeal against conviction only, considers that there are grounds to reduce the sentence under paragraph 2 (a).

3. (a) Unless the Trial Chamber orders otherwise, a convicted person shall remain in custody pending an appeal;

(b) When a convicted person's time in custody exceeds the sentence of imprisonment imposed, that person shall be released, except that if the Prosecutor is also appealing, the release may be subject to the conditions under subparagraph (c) below;

(c) In case of an acquittal, the accused shall be released immediately, subject to the following:

(i) Under exceptional circumstances, and having regard, *inter alia*, to the concrete risk of flight, the seriousness of the offence charged and the probability of success on appeal, the Trial Chamber, at the request of the Prosecutor, may maintain the detention of the person pending appeal;

(ii) A decision by the Trial Chamber under subparagraph (c) (i) may be appealed in accordance with the Rules of Procedure and Evidence.

4. Subject to the provisions of paragraph 3 (a) and (b), execution of the decision or sentence shall be suspended during the period allowed for appeal and for the duration of the appeal proceedings.

ARTICLE 82

APPEAL AGAINST OTHER DECISIONS

1. Either party may appeal any of the following decisions in accordance with the Rules **B1–083**
of Procedure and Evidence:

(a) A decision with respect to jurisdiction or admissibility;

(b) A decision granting or denying release of the person being investigated or prosecuted;

(c) A decision of the Pre-Trial Chamber to act on its own initiative under article 56, paragraph 3;

(d) A decision that involves an issue that would significantly affect the fair and expeditious conduct of the proceedings or the outcome of the trial, and for which, in the opinion of the Pre-Trial or Trial Chamber, an immediate resolution by the Appeals Chamber may materially advance the proceedings.

2. A decision of the Pre-Trial Chamber under article 57, paragraph 3 (d), may be appealed against by the State concerned or by the Prosecutor, with the leave of the Pre-Trial Chamber. The appeal shall be heard on an expedited basis.

3. An appeal shall not of itself have suspensive effect unless the Appeals Chamber so orders, upon request, in accordance with the Rules of Procedure and Evidence.

4. A legal representative of the victims, the convicted person or a bona fide owner of property adversely affected by an order under article 75 may appeal against the order for reparations, as provided in the Rules of Procedure and Evidence.

ARTICLE 83

PROCEEDINGS ON APPEAL

1. For the purposes of proceedings under article 81 and this article, the Appeals **B1–084**
Chamber shall have all the powers of the Trial Chamber.

2. If the Appeals Chamber finds that the proceedings appealed from were unfair in a way that affected the reliability of the decision or sentence, or that the decision or sentence appealed from was materially affected by error of fact or law or procedural error, it may:

(a) Reverse or amend the decision or sentence; or
(b) Order a new trial before a different Trial Chamber.

For these purposes, the Appeals Chamber may remand a factual issue to the original Trial Chamber for it to determine the issue and to report back accordingly, or may itself call evidence to determine the issue. When the decision or sentence has been appealed only by the person convicted, or the Prosecutor on that person's behalf, it cannot be amended to his or her detriment.

3. If in an appeal against sentence the Appeals Chamber finds that the sentence is disproportionate to the crime, it may vary the sentence in accordance with Part 7.

4. The judgement of the Appeals Chamber shall be taken by a majority of the judges and shall be delivered in open court. The judgement shall state the reasons on which it is based. When there is no unanimity, the judgement of the Appeals Chamber shall contain the views of the majority and the minority, but a judge may deliver a separate or dissenting opinion on a question of law.

5. The Appeals Chamber may deliver its judgement in the absence of the person acquitted or convicted.

ARTICLE 84

REVISION OF CONVICTION OR SENTENCE

B1–085   1. The convicted person or, after death, spouses, children, parents or one person alive at the time of the accused's death who has been given express written instructions from the accused to bring such a claim, or the Prosecutor on the person's behalf, may apply to the Appeals Chamber to revise the final judgement of conviction or sentence on the grounds that:

(a) New evidence has been discovered that:
  (i) Was not available at the time of trial, and such unavailability was not wholly or partially attributable to the party making application; and
  (ii) Is sufficiently important that had it been proved at trial it would have been likely to have resulted in a different verdict;
(b) It has been newly discovered that decisive evidence, taken into account at trial and upon which the conviction depends, was false, forged or falsified;
(c) One or more of the judges who participated in conviction or confirmation of the charges has committed, in that case, an act of serious misconduct or serious breach of duty of sufficient gravity to justify the removal of that judge or those judges from office under article 46.

2. The Appeals Chamber shall reject the application if it considers it to be unfounded. If it determines that the application is meritorious, it may, as appropriate:

(a) Reconvene the original Trial Chamber;
(b) Constitute a new Trial Chamber; or
(c) Retain jurisdiction over the matter,

with a view to, after hearing the parties in the manner set forth in the Rules of Procedure and Evidence, arriving at a determination on whether the judgement should be revised.

ARTICLE 85

COMPENSATION TO AN ARRESTED OR CONVICTED PERSON

B1–086   1. Anyone who has been the victim of unlawful arrest or detention shall have an enforceable right to compensation.

2. When a person has by a final decision been convicted of a criminal offence, and when subsequently his or her conviction has been reversed on the ground that a new or

newly discovered fact shows conclusively that there has been a miscarriage of justice, the person who has suffered punishment as a result of such conviction shall be compensated according to law, unless it is proved that the non-disclosure of the unknown fact in time is wholly or partly attributable to him or her.

3. In exceptional circumstances, where the Court finds conclusive facts showing that there has been a grave and manifest miscarriage of justice, it may in its discretion award compensation, according to the criteria provided in the Rules of Procedure and Evidence, to a person who has been released from detention following a final decision of acquittal or a termination of the proceedings for that reason.

PART 9. INTERNATIONAL COOPERATION AND JUDICIAL ASSISTANCE

ARTICLE 86

GENERAL OBLIGATION TO COOPERATE

States Parties shall, in accordance with the provisions of this Statute, cooperate fully **B1–087** with the Court in its investigation and prosecution of crimes within the jurisdiction of the Court.

ARTICLE 87

REQUESTS FOR COOPERATION: GENERAL PROVISIONS

1. (a) The Court shall have the authority to make requests to States Parties for **B1–088** cooperation. The requests shall be transmitted through the diplomatic channel or any other appropriate channel as may be designated by each State Party upon ratification, acceptance, approval or accession.

Subsequent changes to the designation shall be made by each State Party in accordance with the Rules of Procedure and Evidence.

(b) When appropriate, without prejudice to the provisions of subparagraph (a), requests may also be transmitted through the International Criminal Police Organization or any appropriate regional organization.

2. Requests for cooperation and any documents supporting the request shall either be in or be accompanied by a translation into an official language of the requested State or one of the working languages of the Court, in accordance with the choice made by that State upon ratification, acceptance, approval or accession.

Subsequent changes to this choice shall be made in accordance with the Rules of Procedure and Evidence.

3. The requested State shall keep confidential a request for cooperation and any documents supporting the request, except to the extent that the disclosure is necessary for execution of the request.

4. In relation to any request for assistance presented under this Part, the Court may take such measures, including measures related to the protection of information, as may be necessary to ensure the safety or physical or psychological well-being of any victims, potential witnesses and their families. The Court may request that any information that is made available under this Part shall be provided and handled in a manner that protects the safety and physical or psychological well-being of any victims, potential witnesses and their families.

5. (a) The Court may invite any State not party to this Statute to provide assistance under this Part on the basis of an ad hoc arrangement, an agreement with such State or any other appropriate basis.

(b) Where a State not party to this Statute, which has entered into an ad hoc arrangement or an agreement with the Court, fails to cooperate with requests pursuant to any such arrangement or agreement, the Court may so inform the

Assembly of States Parties or, where the Security Council referred the matter to the Court, the Security Council.

6. The Court may ask any intergovernmental organization to provide information or documents. The Court may also ask for other forms of cooperation and assistance which may be agreed upon with such an organization and which are in accordance with its competence or mandate.

7. Where a State Party fails to comply with a request to cooperate by the Court contrary to the provisions of this Statute, thereby preventing the Court from exercising its functions and powers under this Statute, the Court may make a finding to that effect and refer the matter to the Assembly of States Parties or, where the Security Council referred the matter to the Court, to the Security Council.

ARTICLE 88

AVAILABILITY OF PROCEDURES UNDER NATIONAL LAW

B1–089   States Parties shall ensure that there are procedures available under their national law for all of the forms of cooperation which are specified under this Part.

ARTICLE 89

SURRENDER OF PERSONS TO THE COURT

B1–090   1. The Court may transmit a request for the arrest and surrender of a person, together with the material supporting the request outlined in article 91, to any State on the territory of which that person may be found and shall request the cooperation of that State in the arrest and surrender of such a person. States Parties shall, in accordance with the provisions of this Part and the procedure under their national law, comply with requests for arrest and surrender.

2. Where the person sought for surrender brings a challenge before a national court on the basis of the principle of *ne bis in idem* as provided in article 20, the requested State shall immediately consult with the Court to determine if there has been a relevant ruling on admissibility. If the case is admissible, the requested State shall proceed with the execution of the request. If an admissibility ruling is pending, the requested State may postpone the execution of the request for surrender of the person until the Court makes a determination on admissibility.

3. (a) A State Party shall authorize, in accordance with its national procedural law, transportation through its territory of a person being surrendered to the Court by another State, except where transit through that State would impede or delay the surrender.

   (b) A request by the Court for transit shall be transmitted in accordance with article 87. The request for transit shall contain:

      (i) A description of the person being transported;

      (ii) A brief statement of the facts of the case and their legal characterization; and

      (iii) The warrant for arrest and surrender;

   (c) A person being transported shall be detained in custody during the period of transit;

   (d) No authorization is required if the person is transported by air and no landing is scheduled on the territory of the transit State;

   (e) If an unscheduled landing occurs on the territory of the transit State, that State may require a request for transit from the Court as provided for in subparagraph (b). The transit State shall detain the person being transported until the request for transit is received and the transit is effected, provided that detention for purposes of this subparagraph may not be extended beyond 96 hours from the unscheduled landing unless the request is received within that time.

4. If the person sought is being proceeded against or is serving a sentence in the requested State for a crime different from that for which surrender to the Court is sought, the requested State, after making its decision to grant the request, shall consult with the Court.

ARTICLE 90

COMPETING REQUESTS

B1–091

1. A State Party which receives a request from the Court for the surrender of a person under article 89 shall, if it also receives a request from any other State for the extradition of the same person for the same conduct which forms the basis of the crime for which the Court seeks the person's surrender, notify the Court and the requesting State of that fact.

2. Where the requesting State is a State Party, the requested State shall give priority to the request from the Court if:

   (a) The Court has, pursuant to article 18 or 19, made a determination that the case in respect of which surrender is sought is admissible and that determination takes into account the investigation or prosecution conducted by the requesting State in respect of its request for extradition; or

   (b) The Court makes the determination described in subparagraph (a) pursuant to the requested State's notification under paragraph 1.

3. Where a determination under paragraph 2 (a) has not been made, the requested State may, at its discretion, pending the determination of the Court under paragraph 2 (b), proceed to deal with the request for extradition from the requesting State but shall not extradite the person until the Court has determined that the case is inadmissible. The Court's determination shall be made on an expedited basis.

4. If the requesting State is a State not Party to this Statute the requested State, if it is not under an international obligation to extradite the person to the requesting State, shall give priority to the request for surrender from the Court, if the Court has determined that the case is admissible.

5. Where a case under paragraph 4 has not been determined to be admissible by the Curt, the requested State may, at its discretion, proceed to deal with the request for extradition from the requesting State.

6. In cases where paragraph 4 applies except that the requested State is under an existing international obligation to extradite the person to the requesting State not Party to this Statute, the requested State shall determine whether to surrender the person to the Court or extradite the person to the requesting State. In making its decision, the requested State shall consider all the relevant factors, including but not limited to:

   (a) The respective dates of the requests;

   (b) The interests of the requesting State including, where relevant, whether the crime was committed in its territory and the nationality of the victims and of the person sought; and

   (c) The possibility of subsequent surrender between the Court and the requesting State.

7. Where a State Party which receives a request from the Court for the surrender of a person also receives a request from any State for the extradition of the same person for conduct other than that which constitutes the crime for which the Court seeks the person's surrender:

   (a) The requested State shall, if it is not under an existing international obligation to extradite the person to the requesting State, give priority to the request from the Court;

   (b) The requested State shall, if it is under an existing international obligation to extradite the person to the requesting State, determine whether to surrender the person to the Court or to extradite the person to the requesting State. In making its decision, the requested State shall consider all the relevant factors, including but not limited to those set out in paragraph 6, but shall give special consideration to the relative nature and gravity of the conduct in question.

8. Where pursuant to a notification under this article, the Court has determined a case to be inadmissible, and subsequently extradition to the requesting State is refused, the requested State shall notify the Court of this decision.

ARTICLE 91

CONTENTS OF REQUEST FOR ARREST AND SURRENDER

B1–092   1. A request for arrest and surrender shall be made in writing. In urgent cases, a request may be made by any medium capable of delivering a written record, provided that the request shall be confirmed through the channel provided for in article 87, paragraph 1 (a).

2. In the case of a request for the arrest and surrender of a person for whom a warrant of arrest has been issued by the Pre-Trial Chamber under article 58, the request shall contain or be supported by:

(a) Information describing the person sought, sufficient to identify the person, and information as to that person's probable location;

(b) A copy of the warrant of arrest; and

(c) Such documents, statements or information as may be necessary to meet the requirements for the surrender process in the requested State, except that those requirements should not be more burdensome than those applicable to requests for extradition pursuant to treaties or arrangements between the requested State and other States and should, if possible, be less burdensome, taking into account the distinct nature of the Court.

3. In the case of a request for the arrest and surrender of a person already convicted, the request shall contain or be supported by:

(a) A copy of any warrant of arrest for that person;

(b) A copy of the judgement of conviction;

(c) Information to demonstrate that the person sought is the one referred to in the judgement of conviction; and

(d) If the person sought has been sentenced, a copy of the sentence imposed and, in the case of a sentence for imprisonment, a statement of any time already served and the time remaining to be served.

4. Upon the request of the Court, a State Party shall consult with the Court, either generally or with respect to a specific matter, regarding any requirements under its national law that may apply under paragraph 2 (c). During the consultations, the State Party shall advise the Court of the specific requirements of its national law.

ARTICLE 92

PROVISIONAL ARREST

B1–093   1. In urgent cases, the Court may request the provisional arrest of the person sought, pending presentation of the request for surrender and the documents supporting the request as specified in article 91.

2. The request for provisional arrest shall be made by any medium capable of delivering a written record and shall contain:

(a) Information describing the person sought, sufficient to identify the person, and information as to that person's probable location;

(b) A concise statement of the crimes for which the person's arrest is sought and of the facts which are alleged to constitute those crimes, including, where possible, the date and location of the crime;

(c) A statement of the existence of a warrant of arrest or a judgement of conviction against the person sought; and

(d) A statement that a request for surrender of the person sought will follow.

3. A person who is provisionally arrested may be released from custody if the requested State has not received the request for surrender and the documents supporting the request as specified in article 91 within the time limits specified in the Rules of Procedure and Evidence. However, the person may consent to surrender before the expiration of this period if permitted by the law of the requested State. In such a case, the requested State shall proceed to surrender the person to the Court as soon as possible.

4. The fact that the person sought has been released from custody pursuant to paragraph 3 shall not prejudice the subsequent arrest and surrender of that person if the request for surrender and the documents supporting the request are delivered at a later date.

ARTICLE 93

OTHER FORMS OF COOPERATION

1. States Parties shall, in accordance with the provisions of this Part and under procedures of national law, comply with requests by the Court to provide the following assistance in relation to investigations or prosecutions:

B1–094

(a) The identification and whereabouts of persons or the location of items;

(b) The taking of evidence, including testimony under oath, and the production of evidence, including expert opinions and reports necessary to the Court;

(c) The questioning of any person being investigated or prosecuted;

(d) The service of documents, including judicial documents;

(e) Facilitating the voluntary appearance of persons as witnesses or experts before the Court;

(f) The temporary transfer of persons as provided in paragraph 7;

(g) The examination of places or sites, including the exhumation and examination of grave sites;

(h) The execution of searches and seizures;

(i) The provision of records and documents, including official records and documents;

(j) The protection of victims and witnesses and the preservation of evidence;

(k) The identification, tracing and freezing or seizure of proceeds, property and assets and instrumentalities of crimes for the purpose of eventual forfeiture, without prejudice to the rights of bona fide third parties; and

(l) Any other type of assistance which is not prohibited by the law of the requested State, with a view to facilitating the investigation and prosecution of crimes within the jurisdiction of the Court.

2. The Court shall have the authority to provide an assurance to a witness or an expert appearing before the Court that he or she will not be prosecuted, detained or subjected to any restriction of personal freedom by the Court in respect of any act or omission that preceded the departure of that person from the requested State.

3. Where execution of a particular measure of assistance detailed in a request presented under paragraph 1, is prohibited in the requested State on the basis of an existing fundamental legal principle of general application, the requested State shall promptly consult with the Court to try to resolve the matter. In the consultations, consideration should be given to whether the assistance can be rendered in another manner or subject to conditions. If after consultations the matter cannot be resolved, the Court shall modify the request as necessary.

4. In accordance with article 72, a State Party may deny a request for assistance, in whole or in part, only if the request concerns the production of any documents or disclosure of evidence which relates to its national security.

5. Before denying a request for assistance under paragraph 1 (l), the requested State shall consider whether the assistance can be provided subject to specified conditions, or

whether the assistance can be provided at a later date or in an alternative manner, provided that if the Court or the Prosecutor accepts the assistance subject to conditions, the Court or the Prosecutor shall abide by them.

6. If a request for assistance is denied, the requested State Party shall promptly inform the Court or the Prosecutor of the reasons for such denial.

7. (a) The Court may request the temporary transfer of a person in custody for purposes of identification or for obtaining testimony or other assistance. The person may be transferred if the following conditions are fulfilled:

     (i) The person freely gives his or her informed consent to the transfer; and

     (ii) The requested State agrees to the transfer, subject to such conditions as that State and the Court may agree.

  (b) The person being transferred shall remain in custody. When the purposes of the transfer have been fulfilled, the Court shall return the person without delay to the requested State.

8. (a) The Court shall ensure the confidentiality of documents and information, except as required for the investigation and proceedings described in the request.

  (b) The requested State may, when necessary, transmit documents or information to the Prosecutor on a confidential basis. The Prosecutor may then use them solely for the purpose of generating new evidence.

  (c) The requested State may, on its own motion or at the request of the Prosecutor, subsequently consent to the disclosure of such documents or information. They may then be used as evidence pursuant to the provisions of Parts 5 and 6 and in accordance with the Rules of Procedure and Evidence.

9. (a) (i) In the event that a State Party receives competing requests, other than for surrender or extradition, from the Court and from another State pursuant to an international obligation, the State Party shall endeavour, in consultation with the Court and the other State, to meet both requests, if necessary by postponing or attaching conditions to one or the other request.

    (ii) Failing that, competing requests shall be resolved in accordance with the principles established in article 90.

  (b) Where, however, the request from the Court concerns information, property or persons which are subject to the control of a third State or an international organization by virtue of an international agreement, the requested States shall so inform the Court and the Court shall direct its request to the third State or international organization.

10. (a) The Court may, upon request, cooperate with and provide assistance to a State Party conducting an investigation into or trial in respect of conduct which constitutes a crime within the jurisdiction of the Court or which constitutes a serious crime under the national law of the requesting State.

  (b) (i) The assistance provided under subparagraph (a) shall include, *inter alia*:

     a. The transmission of statements, documents or other types of evidence obtained in the course of an investigation or a trial conducted by the Court; and

     b. The questioning of any person detained by order of the Court;

    (ii) In the case of assistance under subparagraph (b) (i) a:

     a. If the documents or other types of evidence have been obtained with the assistance of a State, such transmission shall require the consent of that State;

     b. If the statements, documents or other types of evidence have been provided by a witness or expert, such transmission shall be subject to the provisions of article 68.

  (c) The Court may, under the conditions set out in this paragraph, grant a request for assistance under this paragraph from a State which is not a Party to this Statute.

Article 94

POSTPONEMENT OF EXECUTION OF A REQUEST IN RESPECT OF ONGOING INVESTIGATION OR PROSECUTION

1. If the immediate execution of a request would interfere with an ongoing investigation or prosecution of a case different from that to which the request relates, the requested State may postpone the execution of the request for a period of time agreed upon with the Court. However, the postponement shall be no longer than is necessary to complete the relevant investigation or prosecution in the requested State. Before making a decision to postpone, the requested State should consider whether the assistance may be immediately provided subject to certain conditions.   **B1–095**

2. If a decision to postpone is taken pursuant to paragraph 1, the Prosecutor may, however, seek measures to preserve evidence, pursuant to article 93, paragraph 1 (j).

Article 95

POSTPONEMENT OF EXECUTION OF A REQUEST IN RESPECT OF AN ADMISSIBILITY CHALLENGE

Where there is an admissibility challenge under consideration by the Court pursuant to article 18 or 19, the requested State may postpone the execution of a request under this Part pending a determination by the Court, unless the Court has specifically ordered that the Prosecutor may pursue the collection of such evidence pursuant to article 18 or 19.   **B1–096**

Article 96

CONTENTS OF REQUEST FOR OTHER FORMS OF ASSISTANCE UNDER ARTICLE 93

1. A request for other forms of assistance referred to in article 93 shall be made in writing. In urgent cases, a request may be made by any medium capable of delivering a written record, provided that the request shall be confirmed through the channel provided for in article 87, paragraph 1 (a).   **B1–097**

2. The request shall, as applicable, contain or be supported by the following:
   (a) A concise statement of the purpose of the request and the assistance sought, including the legal basis and the grounds for the request;
   (b) As much detailed information as possible about the location or identification of any person or place that must be found or identified in order for the assistance sought to be provided;
   (c) A concise statement of the essential facts underlying the request;
   (d) The reasons for and details of any procedure or requirement to be followed;
   (e) Such information as may be required under the law of the requested State in order to execute the request; and
   (f) Any other information relevant in order for the assistance sought to be provided.

3. Upon the request of the Court, a State Party shall consult with the Court, either generally or with respect to a specific matter, regarding any requirements under its national law that may apply under paragraph 2 (e). During the consultations, the State Party shall advise the Court of the specific requirements of its national law.

4. The provisions of this article shall, where applicable, also apply in respect of a request for assistance made to the Court.

CONSULTATIONS

B1–098   Where a State Party receives a request under this Part in relation to which it identifies problems which may impede or prevent the execution of the request, that State shall consult with the Court without delay in order to resolve the matter. Such problems may include, *inter alia*:
>   (a) Insufficient information to execute the request;
>   (b) In the case of a request for surrender, the fact that despite best efforts, the person sought cannot be located or that the investigation conducted has determined that the person in the requested State is clearly not the person named in the warrant; or
>   (c) The fact that execution of the request in its current form would require the requested State to breach a pre-existing treaty obligation undertaken with respect to another State.

COOPERATION WITH RESPECT TO WAIVER OF IMMUNITY AND CONSENT TO SURRENDER

B1–099   1. The Court may not proceed with a request for surrender or assistance which would require the requested State to act inconsistently with its obligations under international law with respect to the State or diplomatic immunity of a person or property of a third State, unless the Court can first obtain the cooperation of that third State for the waiver of the immunity.

2. The Court may not proceed with a request for surrender which would require the requested State to act inconsistently with its obligations under international agreements pursuant to which the consent of a sending State is required to surrender a person of that State to the Court, unless the Court can first obtain the cooperation of the sending State for the giving of consent for the surrender.

EXECUTION OF REQUESTS UNDER ARTICLES 93 AND 96

B1–100   1. Requests for assistance shall be executed in accordance with the relevant procedure under the law of the requested State and, unless prohibited by such law, in the manner specified in the request, including following any procedure outlined therein or permitting persons specified in the request to be present at and assist in the execution process.

2. In the case of an urgent request, the documents or evidence produced in response shall, at the request of the Court, be sent urgently.

3. Replies from the requested State shall be transmitted in their original language and form.

4. Without prejudice to other articles in this Part, where it is necessary for the successful execution of a request which can be executed without any compulsory measures, including specifically the interview of or taking evidence from a person on a voluntary basis, including doing so without the presence of the authorities of the requested State Party if it is essential for the request to be executed, and the examination without modification of a public site or other public place, the Prosecutor may execute such request directly on the territory of a State as follows:
>   (a) When the State Party requested is a State on the territory of which the crime is alleged to have been committed, and there has been a determination of

admissibility pursuant to article 18 or 19, the Prosecutor may directly execute such request following all possible consultations with the requested State Party;
  (b) In other cases, the Prosecutor may execute such request following consultations with the requested State Party and subject to any reasonable conditions or concerns raised by that State Party. Where the requested State Party identifies problems with the execution of a request pursuant to this subparagraph it shall, without delay, consult with the Court to resolve the matter.
  5. Provisions allowing a person heard or examined by the Court under article 72 to invoke restrictions designed to prevent disclosure of confidential information connected with national security shall also apply to the execution of requests for assistance under this article.

ARTICLE 100

COSTS

1. The ordinary costs for execution of requests in the territory of the requested State **B1–101** shall be borne by that State, except for the following, which shall be borne by the Court:
  (a) Costs associated with the travel and security of witnesses and experts or the transfer under article 93 of persons in custody;
  (b) Costs of translation, interpretation and transcription;
  (c) Travel and subsistence costs of the judges, the Prosecutor, the Deputy Prosecutors, the Registrar, the Deputy Registrar and staff of any organ of the Court;
  (d) Costs of any expert opinion or report requested by the Court;
  (e) Costs associated with the transport of a person being surrendered to the Court by a custodial State; and
  (f) Following consultations, any extraordinary costs that may result from the execution of a request.
2. The provisions of paragraph 1 shall, as appropriate, apply to requests from States Parties to the Court. In that case, the Court shall bear the ordinary costs of execution.

ARTICLE 101

RULE OF SPECIALITY

1. A person surrendered to the Court under this Statute shall not be proceeded **B1–102** against, punished or detained for any conduct committed prior to surrender, other than the conduct or course of conduct which forms the basis of the crimes for which that person has been surrendered.
2. The Court may request a waiver of the requirements of paragraph 1 from the State which surrendered the person to the Court and, if necessary, the Court shall provide additional information in accordance with article 91. States Parties shall have the authority to provide a waiver to the Court and should endeavour to do so.

ARTICLE 102

USE OF TERMS

For the purposes of this Statute: **B1–103**
  (a) "surrender" means the delivering up of a person by a State to the Court, pursuant to this Statute.
  (b) "extradition" means the delivering up of a person by one State to another as provided by treaty, convention or national legislation.

PART 10. ENFORCEMENT

ARTICLE 103

ROLE OF STATES IN ENFORCEMENT OF SENTENCES OF IMPRISONMENT

B1–104   1. (a) A sentence of imprisonment shall be served in a State designated by the Court from a list of States which have indicated to the Court their willingness to accept sentenced persons.

(b) At the time of declaring its willingness to accept sentenced persons, a State may attach conditions to its acceptance as agreed by the Court and in accordance with this Part.

(c) A State designated in a particular case shall promptly inform the Court whether it accepts the Court's designation.

2. (a) The State of enforcement shall notify the Court of any circumstances, including the exercise of any conditions agreed under paragraph 1, which could materially affect the terms or extent of the imprisonment. The Court shall be given at least 45 days' notice of any such known or foreseeable circumstances. During this period, the State of enforcement shall take no action that might prejudice its obligations under article 110.

(b) Where the Court cannot agree to the circumstances referred to in subparagraph (a), it shall notify the State of enforcement and proceed in accordance with article 104, paragraph 1.

3. In exercising its discretion to make a designation under paragraph 1, the Court shall take into account the following:

(a) The principle that States Parties should share the responsibility for enforcing sentences of imprisonment, in accordance with principles of equitable distribution, as provided in the Rules of Procedure and Evidence;

(b) The application of widely accepted international treaty standards governing the treatment of prisoners;

(c) The views of the sentenced person;

(d) The nationality of the sentenced person;

(e) Such other factors regarding the circumstances of the crime or the person sentenced, or the effective enforcement of the sentence, as may be appropriate in designating the State of enforcement.

4. If no State is designated under paragraph 1, the sentence of imprisonment shall be served in a prison facility made available by the host State, in accordance with the conditions set out in the headquarters agreement referred to in article 3, paragraph 2. In such a case, the costs arising out of the enforcement of a sentence of imprisonment shall be borne by the Court.

ARTICLE 104

CHANGE IN DESIGNATION OF STATE OF ENFORCEMENT

B1–105   1. The Court may, at any time, decide to transfer a sentenced person to a prison of another State.

2. A sentenced person may, at any time, apply to the Court to be transferred from the State of enforcement.

ARTICLE 105

ENFORCEMENT OF THE SENTENCE

B1–106   1. Subject to conditions which a State may have specified in accordance with article 103, paragraph 1 (b), the sentence of imprisonment shall be binding on the States Parties, which shall in no case modify it.

2. The Court alone shall have the right to decide any application for appeal and revision. The State of enforcement shall not impede the making of any such application by a sentenced person.

ARTICLE 106

SUPERVISION OF ENFORCEMENT OF SENTENCES AND CONDITIONS OF IMPRISONMENT

B1–107

1. The enforcement of a sentence of imprisonment shall be subject to the supervision of the Court and shall be consistent with widely accepted international treaty standards governing treatment of prisoners.
2. The conditions of imprisonment shall be governed by the law of the State of enforcement and shall be consistent with widely accepted international treaty standards governing treatment of prisoners; in no case shall such conditions be more or less favourable than those available to prisoners convicted of similar offences in the State of enforcement.
3. Communications between a sentenced person and the Court shall be unimpeded and confidential.

ARTICLE 107

TRANSFER OF THE PERSON UPON COMPLETION OF SENTENCE

B1–108

1. Following completion of the sentence, a person who is not a national of the State of enforcement may, in accordance with the law of the State of enforcement, be transferred to a State which is obliged to receive him or her, or to another State which agrees to receive him or her, taking into account any wishes of the person to be transferred to that State, unless the State of enforcement authorizes the person to remain in its territory.
2. If no State bears the costs arising out of transferring the person to another State pursuant to paragraph 1, such costs shall be borne by the Court.
3. Subject to the provisions of article 108, the State of enforcement may also, in accordance with its national law, extradite or otherwise surrender the person to a State which has requested the extradition or surrender of the person for purposes of trial or enforcement of a sentence.

ARTICLE 108

LIMITATION ON THE PROSECUTION OR PUNISHMENT OF OTHER OFFENCES

B1–109

1. A sentenced person in the custody of the State of enforcement shall not be subject to prosecution or punishment or to extradition to a third State for any conduct engaged in prior to that person's delivery to the State of enforcement, unless such prosecution, punishment or extradition has been approved by the Court at the request of the State of enforcement.
2. The Court shall decide the matter after having heard the views of the sentenced person.
3. Paragraph 1 shall cease to apply if the sentenced person remains voluntarily for more than 30 days in the territory of the State of enforcement after having served the full sentence imposed by the Court, or returns to the territory of that State after having left it.

ARTICLE 109

ENFORCEMENT OF FINES AND FORFEITURE MEASURES

B1–110   1. States Parties shall give effect to fines or forfeitures ordered by the Court under Part 7, without prejudice to the rights of bona fide third parties, and in accordance with the procedure of their national law.

2. If a State Party is unable to give effect to an order for forfeiture, it shall take measures to recover the value of the proceeds, property or assets ordered by the Court to be forfeited, without prejudice to the rights of bona fide third parties.

3. Property, or the proceeds of the sale of real property or, where appropriate, the sale of other property, which is obtained by a State Party as a result of its enforcement of a judgement of the Court shall be transferred to the Court.

ARTICLE 110

REVIEW BY THE COURT CONCERNING REDUCTION OF SENTENCE

B1–111   1. The State of enforcement shall not release the person before expiry of the sentence pronounced by the Court.

2. The Court alone shall have the right to decide any reduction of sentence, and shall rule on the matter after having heard the person.

3. When the person has served two thirds of the sentence, or 25 years in the case of life imprisonment, the Court shall review the sentence to determine whether it should be reduced. Such a review shall not be conducted before that time.

4. In its review under paragraph 3, the Court may reduce the sentence if it finds that one or more of the following factors are present:

(a) The early and continuing willingness of the person to cooperate with the Court in its investigations and prosecutions;

(b) The voluntary assistance of the person in enabling the enforcement of the judgements and orders of the Court in other cases, and in particular providing assistance in locating assets subject to orders of fine, forfeiture or reparation which may be used for the benefit of victims; or

(c) Other factors establishing a clear and significant change of circumstances sufficient to justify the reduction of sentence, as provided in the Rules of Procedure and Evidence.

5. If the Court determines in its initial review under paragraph 3 that it is not appropriate to reduce the sentence, it shall thereafter review the question of reduction of sentence at such intervals and applying such criteria as provided for in the Rules of Procedure and Evidence.

ARTICLE 111

ESCAPE

B1–112   If a convicted person escapes from custody and flees the State of enforcement, that State may, after consultation with the Court, request the person's surrender from the State in which the person is located pursuant to existing bilateral or multilateral arrangements, or may request that the Court seek the person's surrender, in accordance with Part 9. It may direct that the person be delivered to the State in which he or she was serving the sentence or to another State designated by the Court.

Part 11. Assembly of States Parties

Article 112

ASSEMBLY OF STATES PARTIES

1. An Assembly of States Parties to this Statute is hereby established. Each State Party shall have one representative in the Assembly who may be accompanied by alternates and advisers. Other States which have signed this Statute or the Final Act may be observers in the Assembly.

2. The Assembly shall:
   (a) Consider and adopt, as appropriate, recommendations of the Preparatory Commission;
   (b) Provide management oversight to the Presidency, the Prosecutor and the Registrar regarding the administration of the Court;
   (c) Consider the reports and activities of the Bureau established under paragraph 3 and take appropriate action in regard thereto;
   (d) Consider and decide the budget for the Court;
   (e) Decide whether to alter, in accordance with article 36, the number of judges;
   (f) Consider pursuant to article 87, paragraphs 5 and 7, any question relating to non-cooperation;
   (g) Perform any other function consistent with this Statute or the Rules of Procedure and Evidence.

3. (a) The Assembly shall have a Bureau consisting of a President, two Vice-Presidents and 18 members elected by the Assembly for three-year terms.
   (b) The Bureau shall have a representative character, taking into account, in particular, equitable geographical distribution and the adequate representation of the principal legal systems of the world.
   (c) The Bureau shall meet as often as necessary, but at least once a year. It shall assist the Assembly in the discharge of its responsibilities.

4. The Assembly may establish such subsidiary bodies as may be necessary, including an independent oversight mechanism for inspection, evaluation and investigation of the Court, in order to enhance its efficiency and economy.

5. The President of the Court, the Prosecutor and the Registrar or their representatives may participate, as appropriate, in meetings of the Assembly and of the Bureau.

6. The Assembly shall meet at the seat of the Court or at the Headquarters of the United Nations once a year and, when circumstances so require, hold special sessions. Except as otherwise specified in this Statute, special sessions shall be convened by the Bureau on its own initiative or at the request of one third of the States Parties.

7. Each State Party shall have one vote. Every effort shall be made to reach decisions by consensus in the Assembly and in the Bureau. If consensus cannot be reached, except as otherwise provided in the Statute:
   (a) Decisions on matters of substance must be approved by a two-thirds majority of those present and voting provided that an absolute majority of States Parties constitutes the quorum for voting;
   (b) Decisions on matters of procedure shall be taken by a simple majority of States Parties present and voting.

8. A State Party which is in arrears in the payment of its financial contributions towards the costs of the Court shall have no vote in the Assembly and in the Bureau if the amount of its arrears equals or exceeds the amount of the contributions due from it for the preceding two full years. The Assembly may, nevertheless, permit such a State Party to vote in the Assembly and in the Bureau if it is satisfied that the failure to pay is due to conditions beyond the control of the State Party.

9. The Assembly shall adopt its own rules of procedure.

10. The official and working languages of the Assembly shall be those of the General Assembly of the United Nations.

PART 12. FINANCING

ARTICLE 113

FINANCIAL REGULATIONS

B1–114   Except as otherwise specifically provided, all financial matters related to the Court and the meetings of the Assembly of States Parties, including its Bureau and subsidiary bodies, shall be governed by this Statute and the Financial Regulations and Rules adopted by the Assembly of States Parties.

ARTICLE 114

PAYMENT OF EXPENSES

B1–115   Expenses of the Court and the Assembly of States Parties, including its Bureau and subsidiary bodies, shall be paid from the funds of the Court.

ARTICLE 115

FUNDS OF THE COURT AND OF THE ASSEMBLY OF STATES PARTIES

B1–116   The expenses of the Court and the Assembly of States Parties, including its Bureau and subsidiary bodies, as provided for in the budget decided by the Assembly of States Parties, shall be provided by the following sources:
(a) Assessed contributions made by States Parties;
(b) Funds provided by the United Nations, subject to the approval of the General Assembly, in particular in relation to the expenses incurred due to referrals by the Security Council.

ARTICLE 116

VOLUNTARY CONTRIBUTIONS

B1–117   Without prejudice to article 115, the Court may receive and utilize, as additional funds, voluntary contributions from Governments, international organizations, individuals, corporations and other entities, in accordance with relevant criteria adopted by the Assembly of States Parties.

ARTICLE 117

ASSESSMENT OF CONTRIBUTIONS

B1–118   The contributions of States Parties shall be assessed in accordance with an agreed scale of assessment, based on the scale adopted by the United Nations for its regular budget and adjusted in accordance with the principles on which that scale is based.

ARTICLE 118

ANNUAL AUDIT

The records, books and accounts of the Court, including its annual financial statements, shall be audited annually by an independent auditor.

B1–119

PART 13. FINAL CLAUSES

ARTICLE 119

SETTLEMENT OF DISPUTES

1. Any dispute concerning the judicial functions of the Court shall be settled by the decision of the Court.

B1–120

2. Any other dispute between two or more States Parties relating to the interpretation or application of this Statute which is not settled through negotiations within three months of their commencement shall be referred to the Assembly of States Parties. The Assembly may itself seek to settle the dispute or may make recommendations on further means of settlement of the dispute, including referral to the International Court of Justice in conformity with the Statute of that Court.

ARTICLE 120

RESERVATION

No reservations may be made to this Statute.

B1–121

ARTICLE 121

AMENDMENTS

1. After the expiry of seven years from the entry into force of this Statute, any State Party may propose amendments thereto. The text of any proposed amendment shall be submitted to the Secretary-General of the United Nations, who shall promptly circulate it to all States Parties.

B1–122

2. No sooner than three months from the date of notification, the Assembly of States Parties, at its next meeting, shall, by a majority of those present and voting, decide whether to take up the proposal. The Assembly may deal with the proposal directly or convene a Review Conference if the issue involved so warrants.

3. The adoption of an amendment at a meeting of the Assembly of States Parties or at a Review Conference on which consensus cannot be reached shall require a two-thirds majority of States Parties.

4. Except as provided in paragraph 5, an amendment shall enter into force for all States Parties one year after instruments of ratification or acceptance have been deposited with the Secretary-General of the United Nations by seven-eighths of them.

5. Any amendment to articles 5, 6, 7 and 8 of this Statute shall enter into force for those States Parties which have accepted the amendment one year after the deposit of their instruments of ratification or acceptance. In respect of a State Party which has not accepted the amendment, the Court shall not exercise its jurisdiction regarding a crime covered by the amendment when committed by that State Party's nationals or on its territory.

6. If an amendment has been accepted by seven-eighths of States Parties in accordance with paragraph 4, any State Party which has not accepted the amendment

may withdraw from this Statute with immediate effect, notwithstanding article 127, paragraph 1, but subject to article 127, paragraph 2, by giving notice no later than one year after the entry into force of such amendment.

7. The Secretary-General of the United Nations shall circulate to all States Parties any amendment adopted at a meeting of the Assembly of States Parties or at a Review Conference.

ARTICLE 122

AMENDMENTS TO PROVISIONS OF AN INSTITUTIONAL NATURE

B1–123   1. Amendments to provisions of this Statute which are of an exclusively institutional nature, namely, article 35, article 36, paragraphs 8 and 9, article 37, article 38, article 39, paragraphs 1 (first two sentences), 2 and 4, article 42, paragraphs 4 to 9, article 43, paragraphs 2 and 3, and articles 44, 46, 47 and 49, may be proposed at any time, notwithstanding article 121, paragraph 1, by any State Party. The text of any proposed amendment shall be submitted to the Secretary-General of the United Nations or such other person designated by the Assembly of States Parties who shall promptly circulate it to all States Parties and to others participating in the Assembly.

2. Amendments under this article on which consensus cannot be reached shall be adopted by the Assembly of States Parties or by a Review Conference, by a two-thirds majority of States Parties. Such amendments shall enter into force for all States Parties six months after their adoption by the Assembly or, as the case may be, by the Conference.

ARTICLE 123

REVIEW OF THE STATUTE

B1–124   1. Seven years after the entry into force of this Statute the Secretary-General of the United Nations shall convene a Review Conference to consider any amendments to this Statute. Such review may include, but is not limited to, the list of crimes contained in article 5. The Conference shall be open to those participating in the Assembly of States Parties and on the same conditions.

2. At any time thereafter, at the request of a State Party and for the purposes set out in paragraph 1, the Secretary-General of the United Nations shall, upon approval by a majority of States Parties, convene a Review Conference.

3. The provisions of article 121, paragraphs 3 to 7, shall apply to the adoption and entry into force of any amendment to the Statute considered at a Review Conference.

ARTICLE 124

TRANSITIONAL PROVISION

B1–125   Notwithstanding article 12, paragraphs 1 and 2, a State, on becoming a party to this Statute, may declare that, for a period of seven years after the entry into force of this Statute for the State concerned, it does not accept the jurisdiction of the Court with respect to the category of crimes referred to in article 8 when a crime is alleged to have been committed by its nationals or on its territory. A declaration under this article may be withdrawn at any time. The provisions of this article shall be reviewed at the Review Conference convened in accordance with article 123, paragraph 1.

ARTICLE 125

SIGNATURE, RATIFICATION, ACCEPTANCE, APPROVAL OR ACCESSION

1. This Statute shall be open for signature by all States in Rome, at the headquarters **B1–126** of the Food and Agriculture Organization of the United Nations, on 17 July 1998. Thereafter, it shall remain open for signature in Rome at the Ministry of Foreign Affairs of Italy until 17 October 1998. After that date, the Statute shall remain open for signature in New York, at United Nations Headquarters, until 31 December 2000.

2. This Statute is subject to ratification, acceptance or approval by signatory States. Instruments of ratification, acceptance or approval shall be deposited with the Secretary-General of the United Nations.

3. This Statute shall be open to accession by all States. Instruments of accession shall be deposited with the Secretary-General of the United Nations.

ARTICLE 126

ENTRY INTO FORCE

1. This Statute shall enter into force on the first day of the month after the 60th day **B1–127** following the date of the deposit of the 60th instrument of ratification, acceptance, approval or accession with the Secretary-General of the United Nations.

2. For each State ratifying, accepting, approving or acceding to this Statute after the deposit of the 60th instrument of ratification, acceptance, approval or accession, the Statute shall enter into force on the first day of the month after the 60th day following the deposit by such State of its instrument of ratification, acceptance, approval or accession.

ARTICLE 127

WITHDRAWAL

1. A State Party may, by written notification addressed to the Secretary-General of the **B1–128** United Nations, withdraw from this Statute. The withdrawal shall take effect one year after the date of receipt of the notification, unless the notification specifies a later date.

2. A State shall not be discharged, by reason of its withdrawal, from the obligations arising from this Statute while it was a Party to the Statute, including any financial obligations which may have accrued. Its withdrawal shall not affect any cooperation with the Court in connection with criminal investigations and proceedings in relation to which the withdrawing State had a duty to cooperate and which were commenced prior to the date on which the withdrawal became effective, nor shall it prejudice in any way the continued consideration of any matter which was already under consideration by the Court prior to the date on which the withdrawal became effective.

ARTICLE 128

AUTHENTIC TEXTS

The original of this Statute, of which the Arabic, Chinese, English, French, Russian **B1–129** and Spanish texts are equally authentic, shall be deposited with the Secretary-General of the United Nations, who shall send certified copies thereof to all States.

IN WITNESS WHEREOF, the undersigned, being duly authorized thereto by their respective Governments, have signed this Statute.

DONE at Rome, this 17th day of July 1998.

B2. Rules of Procedure and Evidence

B2–001   **Explanatory note**: The Rules of Procedure and Evidence are an instrument for the application of the Rome Statute of the International Criminal Court, to which they are subordinate in all cases. In elaborating the Rules of Procedure and Evidence, care has been taken to avoid rephrasing and, to the extent possible, repeating the provisions of the Statute. Direct references to the Statute have been included in the Rules, where appropriate, in order to emphasize the relationship between the Rules and the Rome Statute, as provided for in article 51, in particular, paragraphs 4 and 5.

In all cases, the Rules of Procedure and Evidence should be read in conjunction with and subject to the provisions of the Statute.

The Rules of Procedure and Evidence of the International Criminal Court do not affect the procedural rules for any national court or legal system for the purpose of national proceedings.

Contents

CHAPTER 1

GENERAL PROVISIONS

RULE 1

USE OF TERMS

In the present document: **B2–002**
  – "article" refers to articles of the Rome Statute;
  – "Chamber" refers to a Chamber of the Court;
  – "Part" refers to the Parts of the Rome Statute;
  – "Presiding Judge" refers to the Presiding Judge of a Chamber;
  – "the President" refers to the President of the Court;
  – "the Regulations" refers to the Regulations of the Court;
  – "the Rules" refers to the Rules of Procedure and Evidence.

RULE 2

AUTHENTIC TEXTS

B2–003   The Rules have been adopted in the official languages of the Court established by article 50, paragraph 1. All texts are equally authentic.

RULE 3

AMENDMENTS

B2–004   1. Amendments to the rules that are proposed in accordance with article 51, paragraph 2, shall be forwarded to the President of the Bureau of the Assembly of States Parties.

2. The President of the Bureau of the Assembly of States Parties shall ensure that all proposed amendments are translated into the official languages of the Court and are transmitted to the States Parties.

3. The procedure described in sub-rules 1 and 2 shall also apply to the provisional rules referred to in article 51, paragraph 3.

CHAPTER 2

COMPOSITION AND ADMINISTRATION OF THE COURT

Section I

General provisions relating to the composition and administration of the Court

RULE 4

PLENARY SESSIONS

B2–005   1. The judges shall meet in plenary session not later than two months after their election. At that first session, after having made their solemn undertaking, in conformity with rule 5, the judges shall:

(a) Elect the President and Vice-Presidents;

(b) Assign judges to divisions.

2. The judges shall meet subsequently in plenary session at least once a year to exercise their functions under the Statute, the Rules and the Regulations and, if necessary, in special plenary sessions convened by the President on his or her own motion or at the request of one half of the judges.

3. The quorum for each plenary session shall be two-thirds of the judges.

4. Unless otherwise provided in the Statute or the Rules, the decisions of the plenary sessions shall be taken by the majority of the judges present. In the event of an equality of votes, the President, or the judge acting in the place of the President, shall have a casting vote.

5. The Regulations shall be adopted as soon as possible in plenary sessions.

RULE 5

SOLEMN UNDERTAKING UNDER ARTICLE 45

B2–006   1. As provided in article 45, before exercising their functions under the Statute, the following solemn undertakings shall be made:

(a) In the case of a judge:

"I solemnly undertake that I will perform my duties and exercise my powers as a judge of the International Criminal Court honourably, faithfully, impartially and conscientiously, and that I will respect the confidentiality of investigations and prosecutions and the secrecy of deliberations.";

(b) In the case of the Prosecutor, a Deputy Prosecutor, the Registrar and the Deputy Registrar of the Court:

"I solemnly undertake that I will perform my duties and exercise my powers as (title) of the International Criminal Court honourably, faithfully, impartially and conscientiously, and that I will respect the confidentiality of investigations and prosecutions."

2. The undertaking, signed by the person making it and witnessed by the President or a Vice-President of the Bureau of the Assembly of States Parties, shall be filed with the Registry and kept in the records of the Court.

RULE 6

SOLEMN UNDERTAKING BY THE STAFF OF THE OFFICE OF THE PROSECUTOR, THE REGISTRY, INTERPRETERS AND TRANSLATORS

1. Upon commencing employment, every staff member of the Office of the Prosecutor **B2–007** and the Registry shall make the following undertaking:

"I solemnly undertake that I will perform my duties and exercise my powers as (title) of the International Criminal Court honourably, faithfully, impartially and conscientiously, and that I will respect the confidentiality of investigations and prosecutions.";

The undertaking, signed by the person making it and witnessed, as appropriate, by the Prosecutor, the Deputy Prosecutor, the Registrar or the Deputy Registrar, shall be filed with the Registry and kept in the records of the Court.

2. Before performing any duties, an interpreter or a translator shall make the following undertaking:

"I solemnly declare that I will perform my duties faithfully, impartially and with full respect for the duty of confidentiality.";

The undertaking, signed by the person making it and witnessed by the President of the Court or his or her representative, shall be filed with the Registry and kept in the records of the Court.

RULE 7

SINGLE JUDGE UNDER ARTICLE 39, PARAGRAPH 2 (B) (III)

1. Whenever the Pre-Trial Chamber designates a judge as a single judge in **B2–008** accordance with article 39, paragraph 2 (b) (iii), it shall do so on the basis of objective pre-established criteria.

2. The designated judge shall make the appropriate decisions on those questions on which decision by the full Chamber is not expressly provided for in the Statute or the Rules.

3. The Pre-Trial Chamber, on its own motion or, if appropriate, at the request of a party, may decide that the functions of the single judge be exercised by the full Chamber.

RULE 8

CODE OF PROFESSIONAL CONDUCT

B2–009   1. The Presidency, on the basis of a proposal made by the Registrar, shall draw up a draft Code of Professional Conduct for counsel, after having consulted the Prosecutor. In the preparation of the proposal, the Registrar shall conduct the consultations in accordance with rule 20, sub-rule 3.

2. The draft Code shall then be transmitted to the Assembly of States Parties, for the purpose of adoption, according to article 112, paragraph 7.

3. The Code shall contain procedures for its amendment.

Section II

The Office of the Prosecutor

RULE 9

OPERATION OF THE OFFICE OF THE PROSECUTOR

B2–010   In discharging his or her responsibility for the management and administration of the Office of the Prosecutor, the Prosecutor shall put in place regulations to govern the operation of the Office. In preparing or amending these regulations, the Prosecutor shall consult with the Registrar on any matters that may affect the operation of the Registry.

RULE 10

RETENTION OF INFORMATION AND EVIDENCE

B2–011   The Prosecutor shall be responsible for the retention, storage and security of information and physical evidence obtained in the course of the investigations by his or her Office.

RULE 11

DELEGATION OF THE PROSECUTOR'S FUNCTIONS

B2–012   Except for the inherent powers of the Prosecutor set forth in the Statute, *inter alia*, those described in articles 15 and 53, the Prosecutor or a Deputy Prosecutor may authorize staff members of the Office of the Prosecutor, other than those referred to in article 44, paragraph 4, to represent him or her in the exercise of his or her functions.

Section III

The Registry

Subsection 1

General provisions relating to the Registry

RULE 12

QUALIFICATIONS AND ELECTION OF THE REGISTRAR AND THE DEPUTY REGISTRAR

B2–013   1. As soon as it is elected, the Presidency shall establish a list of candidates who satisfy the criteria laid down in article 43, paragraph 3, and shall transmit the list to the Assembly of States Parties with a request for any recommendations.

2. Upon receipt of any recommendations from the Assembly of States Parties, the President shall, without delay, transmit the list together with the recommendations to the plenary session.

3. As provided for in article 43, paragraph 4, the Court, meeting in plenary session, shall, as soon as possible, elect the Registrar by an absolute majority, taking into account any recommendations by the Assembly of States Parties. In the event that no candidate obtains an absolute majority on the first ballot, successive ballots shall be held until one candidate obtains an absolute majority.

4. If the need for a Deputy Registrar arises, the Registrar may make a recommendation to the President to that effect. The President shall convene a plenary session to decide on the matter. If the Court, meeting in plenary session, decides by an absolute majority that a Deputy Registrar is to be elected, the Registrar shall submit a list of candidates to the Court.

5. The Deputy Registrar shall be elected by the Court, meeting in plenary session, in the same manner as the Registrar.

Rule 13

FUNCTIONS OF THE REGISTRAR

1. Without prejudice to the authority of the Office of the Prosecutor under the Statute   **B2–014**
to receive, obtain and provide information and to establish channels of communication
for this purpose, the Registrar shall serve as the channel of communication of the Court.

2. The Registrar shall also be responsible for the internal security of the Court in consultation with the Presidency and the Prosecutor, as well as the host State.

Rule 14

OPERATION OF THE REGISTRY

1. In discharging his or her responsibility for the organization and management of the   **B2–015**
Registry, the Registrar shall put in place regulations to govern the operation of the
Registry. In preparing or amending these regulations, the Registrar shall consult with
the Prosecutor on any matters which may affect the operation of the Office of the
Prosecutor. The regulations shall be approved by the Presidency.

2. The regulations shall provide for defence counsel to have access to appropriate and reasonable administrative assistance from the Registry.

Rule 15

RECORDS

1. The Registrar shall keep a database containing all the particulars of each case   **B2–016**
brought before the Court, subject to any order of a judge or Chamber providing for the
non-disclosure of any document or information, and to the protection of sensitive
personal data. Information on the database shall be available to the public in the
working languages of the Court.

2. The Registrar shall also maintain the other records of the Court.

Subsection 2

Victims and Witnesses Unit

Rule 16

RESPONSIBILITIES OF THE REGISTRAR RELATING TO VICTIMS AND WITNESSES

1. In relation to victims, the Registrar shall be responsible for the performance of the   **B2–017**
following functions in accordance with the Statute and these Rules:

(a) Providing notice or notification to victims or their legal representatives;

(b) Assisting them in obtaining legal advice and organizing their legal representation, and providing their legal representatives with adequate support, assistance and information, including such facilities as may be necessary for the direct performance of their duty, for the purpose of protecting their rights during all stages of the proceedings in accordance with rules 89 to 91;

(c) Assisting them in participating in the different phases of the proceedings in accordance with rules 89 to 91;

(d) Taking gender-sensitive measures to facilitate the participation of victims of sexual violence at all stages of the proceedings.

2. In relation to victims, witnesses and others who are at risk on account of testimony given by such witnesses, the Registrar shall be responsible for the performance of the following functions in accordance with the Statute and these Rules:

(a) Informing them of their rights under the Statute and the Rules, and of the existence, functions and availability of the Victims and Witnesses Unit;

(b) Ensuring that they are aware, in a timely manner, of the relevant decisions of the Court that may have an impact on their interests, subject to provisions on confidentiality.

3. For the fulfilment of his or her functions, the Registrar may keep a special register for victims who have expressed their intention to participate in relation to a specific case.

4. Agreements on relocation and provision of support services on the territory of a State of traumatized or threatened victims, witnesses and others who are at risk on account of testimony given by such witnesses may be negotiated with the States by the Registrar on behalf of the Court. Such agreements may remain confidential.

RULE 17

FUNCTIONS OF THE UNIT

B2–018   1. The Victims and Witnesses Unit shall exercise its functions in accordance with article 43, paragraph 6.

2. The Victims and Witnesses Unit shall, *inter alia*, perform the following functions, in accordance with the Statute and the Rules, and in consultation with the Chamber, the Prosecutor and the defence, as appropriate:

(a) With respect to all witnesses, victims who appear before the Court, and others who are at risk on account of testimony given by such witnesses, in accordance with their particular needs and circumstances:

(i) Providing them with adequate protective and security measures and formulating long- and short-term plans for their protection;

(ii) Recommending to the organs of the Court the adoption of protection measures and also advising relevant States of such measures;

(iii) Assisting them in obtaining medical, psychological and other appropriate assistance;

(iv) Making available to the Court and the parties training in issues of trauma, sexual violence, security and confidentiality;

(v) Recommending, in consultation with the Office of the Prosecutor, the elaboration of a code of conduct, emphasizing the vital nature of security and confidentiality for investigators of the Court and of the defence and all intergovernmental and non-governmental organizations acting at the request of the Court, as appropriate;

(vi) Cooperating with States, where necessary, in providing any of the measures stipulated in this rule;

(b) With respect to witnesses:

(i) Advising them where to obtain legal advice for the purpose of protecting their rights, in particular in relation to their testimony;

(ii) Assisting them when they are called to testify before the Court;

(iii) Taking gender-sensitive measures to facilitate the testimony of victims of sexual violence at all stages of the proceedings.

3. In performing its functions, the Unit shall give due regard to the particular needs of children, elderly persons and persons with disabilities. In order to facilitate the participation and protection of children as witnesses, the Unit may assign, as appropriate, and with the agreement of the parents or the legal guardian, a child-support person to assist a child through all stages of the proceedings.

RULE 18

RESPONSIBILITIES OF THE UNIT

For the efficient and effective performance of its work, the Victims and Witnesses **B2–019** Unit shall:
   (a) Ensure that the staff in the Unit maintain confidentiality at all times;
   (b) While recognizing the specific interests of the Office of the Prosecutor, the defence and the witnesses, respect the interests of the witness, including, where necessary, by maintaining an appropriate separation of the services provided to the prosecution and defence witnesses, and act impartially when cooperating with all parties and in accordance with the rulings and decisions of the Chambers;
   (c) Have administrative and technical assistance available for witnesses, victims who appear before the Court, and others who are at risk on account of testimony given by such witnesses, during all stages of the proceedings and thereafter, as reasonably appropriate;
   (d) Ensure training of its staff with respect to victims' and witnesses' security, integrity and dignity, including matters related to gender and cultural sensitivity;
   (e) Where appropriate, cooperate with intergovernmental and non-governmental organizations.

RULE 19

EXPERTISE IN THE UNIT

In addition to the staff mentioned in article 43, paragraph 6, and subject to article 44, **B2–020** the Victims and Witnesses Unit may include, as appropriate, persons with expertise, *inter alia*, in the following areas:
   (a) Witness protection and security;
   (b) Legal and administrative matters, including areas of humanitarian and criminal law;
   (c) Logistics administration;
   (d) Psychology in criminal proceedings;
   (e) Gender and cultural diversity;
   (f) Children, in particular traumatized children;
   (g) Elderly persons, in particular in connection with armed conflict and exile trauma;
   (h) Persons with disabilities;
   (i) Social work and counselling;
   (j) Health care;
   (k) Interpretation and translation.

Subsection 3

Counsel for the defence

RULE 20

RESPONSIBILITIES OF THE REGISTRAR RELATING TO THE RIGHTS OF THE DEFENCE

B2–021   1. In accordance with article 43, paragraph 1, the Registrar shall organize the staff of the Registry in a manner that promotes the rights of the defence, consistent with the principle of fair trial as defined in the Statute. For that purpose, the Registrar shall, *inter alia*:

(a) Facilitate the protection of confidentiality, as defined in article 67, paragraph 1 (b);
(b) Provide support, assistance, and information to all defence counsel appearing before the Court and, as appropriate, support for professional investigators necessary for the efficient and effective conduct of the defence;
(c) Assist arrested persons, persons to whom article 55, paragraph 2, applies and the accused in obtaining legal advice and the assistance of legal counsel;
(d) Advise the Prosecutor and the Chambers, as necessary, on relevant defence-related issues;
(e) Provide the defence with such facilities as may be necessary for the direct performance of the duty of the defence;
(f) Facilitate the dissemination of information and case law of the Court to defence counsel and, as appropriate, cooperate with national defence and bar associations or any independent representative body of counsel and legal associations referred to in sub-rule 3 to promote the specialization and training of lawyers in the law of the Statute and the Rules.

2. The Registrar shall carry out the functions stipulated in sub-rule 1, including the financial administration of the Registry, in such a manner as to ensure the professional independence of defence counsel.

3. For purposes such as the management of legal assistance in accordance with rule 21 and the development of a Code of Professional Conduct in accordance with rule 8, the Registrar shall consult, as appropriate, with any independent representative body of counsel or legal associations, including any such body the establishment of which may be facilitated by the Assembly of States Parties.

RULE 21

ASSIGNMENT OF LEGAL ASSISTANCE

B2–022   1. Subject to article 55, paragraph 2 (c), and article 67, paragraph 1 (d), criteria and procedures for assignment of legal assistance shall be established in the Regulations, based on a proposal by the Registrar, following consultations with any independent representative body of counsel or legal associations, as referred to in rule 20, sub-rule 3.

2. The Registrar shall create and maintain a list of counsel who meet the criteria set forth in rule 22 and the Regulations. The person shall freely choose his or her counsel from this list or other counsel who meets the required criteria and is willing to be included in the list.

3. A person may seek from the Presidency a review of a decision to refuse a request for assignment of counsel. The decision of the Presidency shall be final. If a request is refused, a further request may be made by a person to the Registrar, upon showing a change in circumstances.

4. A person choosing to represent himself or herself shall so notify the Registrar in writing at the first opportunity.

5. Where a person claims to have insufficient means to pay for legal assistance and this is subsequently found not to be so, the Chamber dealing with the case at that time may make an order of contribution to recover the cost of providing counsel.

Rule 22

APPOINTMENT AND QUALIFICATIONS OF COUNSEL FOR THE DEFENCE

B2–023

1. A counsel for the defence shall have established competence in international or criminal law and procedure, as well as the necessary relevant experience, whether as judge, prosecutor, advocate or in other similar capacity, in criminal proceedings. A counsel for the defence shall have an excellent knowledge of and be fluent in at least one of the working languages of the Court. Counsel for the defence may be assisted by other persons, including professors of law, with relevant expertise.

2. Counsel for the defence engaged by a person exercising his or her right under the Statute to retain legal counsel of his or her choosing shall file a power of attorney with the Registrar at the earliest opportunity.

3. In the performance of their duties, Counsel for the defence shall be subject to the Statute, the Rules, the Regulations, the Code of Professional Conduct for Counsel adopted in accordance with rule 8 and any other document adopted by the Court that may be relevant to the performance of their duties.

Section IV

Situations that may affect the functioning of the Court

Subsection 1

Removal from office and disciplinary measures

Rule 23

GENERAL PRINCIPLE

B2–024

A judge, the Prosecutor, a Deputy Prosecutor, the Registrar and a Deputy Registrar shall be removed from office or shall be subject to disciplinary measures in such cases and with such guarantees as are established in the Statute and the Rules.

Rule 24

DEFINITION OF SERIOUS MISCONDUCT AND SERIOUS BREACH OF DUTY

B2–025

1. For the purposes of article 46, paragraph 1 (a), "serious misconduct" shall be constituted by conduct that:

(a) If it occurs in the course of official duties, is incompatible with official functions, and causes or is likely to cause serious harm to the proper administration of justice before the Court or the proper internal functioning of the Court, such as:

(i) Disclosing facts or information that he or she has acquired in the course of his or her duties or on a matter which is *sub judice*, where such disclosure is seriously prejudicial to the judicial proceedings or to any person;

1265

(ii) Concealing information or circumstances of a nature sufficiently serious to have precluded him or her from holding office;

(iii) Abuse of judicial office in order to obtain unwarranted favourable treatment from any authorities, officials or professionals; or

(b) If it occurs outside the course of official duties, is of a grave nature that causes or is likely to cause serious harm to the standing of the Court.

2. For the purposes of article 46, paragraph 1 (a), a "serious breach of duty" occurs where a person has been grossly negligent in the performance of his or her duties or has knowingly acted in contravention of those duties. This may include, *inter alia*, situations where the person:

(a) Fails to comply with the duty to request to be excused, knowing that there are grounds for doing so;

(b) Repeatedly causes unwarranted delay in the initiation, prosecution or trial of cases, or in the exercise of judicial powers.

RULE 25

DEFINITION OF MISCONDUCT OF A LESS SERIOUS NATURE

B2–026   1. For the purposes of article 47, "misconduct of a less serious nature" shall be constituted by conduct that:

(a) If it occurs in the course of official duties, causes or is likely to cause harm to the proper administration of justice before the Court or the proper internal functioning of the Court, such as:

(i) Interfering in the exercise of the functions of a person referred to in article 47;

(ii) Repeatedly failing to comply with or ignoring requests made by the Presiding Judge or by the Presidency in the exercise of their lawful authority;

(iii) Failing to enforce the disciplinary measures to which the Registrar or a Deputy Registrar and other officers of the Court are subject when a judge knows or should know of a serious breach of duty on their part; or

(b) If it occurs outside the course of official duties, causes or is likely to cause harm to the standing of the Court.

2. Nothing in this rule precludes the possibility of the conduct set out in sub-rule 1 (a) constituting "serious misconduct" or "serious breach of duty" for the purposes of article 46, paragraph 1 (a).

RULE 26

RECEIPT OF COMPLAINTS

B2–027   1. For the purposes of article 46, paragraph 1, and article 47, any complaint concerning any conduct defined under rules 24 and 25 shall include the grounds on which it is based, the identity of the complainant and, if available, any relevant evidence. The complaint shall remain confidential.

2. All complaints shall be transmitted to the Presidency, which may also initiate proceedings on its own motion, and which shall, pursuant to the Regulations, set aside anonymous or manifestly unfounded complaints and transmit the other complaints to the competent organ. The Presidency shall be assisted in this task by one or more judges, appointed on the basis of automatic rotation, in accordance with the Regulations.

RULE 27

COMMON PROVISIONS ON THE RIGHTS OF THE DEFENCE

B2–028   1. In any case in which removal from office under article 46 or disciplinary measures under article 47 is under consideration, the person concerned shall be so informed in a written statement.

2. The person concerned shall be afforded full opportunity to present and receive evidence, to make written submissions and to supply answers to any questions put to him or her.

3. The person may be represented by counsel during the process established under this rule.

RULE 28

SUSPENSION FROM DUTY

Where an allegation against a person who is the subject of a complaint is of a **B2–029** sufficiently serious nature, the person may be suspended from duty pending the final decision of the competent organ.

RULE 29

PROCEDURE IN THE EVENT OF A REQUEST FOR REMOVAL FROM OFFICE

1. In the case of a judge, the Registrar or a Deputy Registrar, the question of removal **B2–030** from office shall be put to a vote at a plenary session.

2. The Presidency shall advise the President of the Bureau of the Assembly of States Parties in writing of any recommendation adopted in the case of a judge, and any decision adopted in the case of the Registrar or a Deputy Registrar.

3. The Prosecutor shall advise the President of the Bureau of the Assembly of States Parties in writing of any recommendation he or she makes in the case of a Deputy Prosecutor.

4. Where the conduct is found not to amount to serious misconduct or a serious breach of duty, it may be decided in accordance with article 47 that the person concerned has engaged in misconduct of a less serious nature and a disciplinary measure imposed.

RULE 30

PROCEDURE IN THE EVENT OF A REQUEST FOR DISCIPLINARY MEASURES

1. In the case of a judge, the Registrar or a Deputy Registrar, any decision to impose a **B2–031** disciplinary measure shall be taken by the Presidency.

2. In the case of the Prosecutor, any decision to impose a disciplinary measure shall be taken by an absolute majority of the Bureau of the Assembly of States Parties.

3. In the case of a Deputy Prosecutor:
   (a) Any decision to give a reprimand shall be taken by the Prosecutor;
   (b) Any decision to impose a pecuniary sanction shall be taken by an absolute majority of the Bureau of the Assembly of States Parties upon the recommendation of the Prosecutor.

4. Reprimands shall be recorded in writing and shall be transmitted to the President of the Bureau of the Assembly of States Parties.

RULE 31

REMOVAL FROM OFFICE

Once removal from office has been pronounced, it shall take effect immediately. The **B2–032** person concerned shall cease to form part of the Court, including for unfinished cases in which he or she was taking part.

RULE 32

DISCIPLINARY MEASURES

B2–033   The disciplinary measures that may be imposed are:
(a) A reprimand; or
(b) A pecuniary sanction that may not exceed six months of the salary paid by the Court to the person concerned.

Subsection 2

Excusing, disqualification, death and resignation

RULE 33

EXCUSING OF A JUDGE, THE PROSECUTOR OR A DEPUTY PROSECUTOR

B2–034   1. A judge, the Prosecutor or a Deputy Prosecutor seeking to be excused from his or her functions shall make a request in writing to the Presidency, setting out the grounds upon which he or she should be excused.
2. The Presidency shall treat the request as confidential and shall not make public the reasons for its decision without the consent of the person concerned.

RULE 34

DISQUALIFICATION OF A JUDGE, THE PROSECUTOR OR A DEPUTY PROSECUTOR

B2–035   1. In addition to the grounds set out in article 41, paragraph 2, and article 42, paragraph 7, the grounds for disqualification of a judge, the Prosecutor or a Deputy Prosecutor shall include, *inter alia*, the following:
(a) Personal interest in the case, including a spousal, parental or other close family, personal or professional relationship, or a subordinate relationship, with any of the parties;
(b) Involvement, in his or her private capacity, in any legal proceedings initiated prior to his or her involvement in the case, or initiated by him or her subsequently, in which the person being investigated or prosecuted was or is an opposing party;
(c) Performance of functions, prior to taking office, during which he or she could be expected to have formed an opinion on the case in question, on the parties or on their legal representatives that, objectively, could adversely affect the required impartiality of the person concerned;
(d) Expression of opinions, through the communications media, in writing or in public actions, that, objectively, could adversely affect the required impartiality of the person concerned.
2. Subject to the provisions set out in article 41, paragraph 2, and article 42, paragraph 8, a request for disqualification shall be made in writing as soon as there is knowledge of the grounds on which it is based. The request shall state the grounds and attach any relevant evidence, and shall be transmitted to the person concerned, who shall be entitled to present written submissions.
3. Any question relating to the disqualification of the Prosecutor or a Deputy Prosecutor shall be decided by a majority of the judges of the Appeals Chamber.

Rule 35

DUTY OF A JUDGE, THE PROSECUTOR OR A DEPUTY PROSECUTOR TO REQUEST TO BE EXCUSED

Where a judge, the Prosecutor or a Deputy Prosecutor has reason to believe that a **B2–036** ground for disqualification exists in relation to him or her, he or she shall make a request to be excused and shall not wait for a request for disqualification to be made in accordance with article 41, paragraph 2, or article 42, paragraph 7, and rule 34. The request shall be made and the Presidency shall deal with it in accordance with rule 33.

Rule 36

DEATH OF A JUDGE, THE PROSECUTOR, A DEPUTY PROSECUTOR, THE REGISTRAR OR A DEPUTY REGISTRAR

The Presidency shall inform, in writing, the President of the Bureau of the Assembly **B2–037** of States Parties of the death of a judge, the Prosecutor, a Deputy Prosecutor, the Registrar or a Deputy Registrar.

Rule 37

RESIGNATION OF A JUDGE, THE PROSECUTOR, A DEPUTY PROSECUTOR, THE REGISTRAR OR A DEPUTY REGISTRAR

1. A judge, the Prosecutor, a Deputy Prosecutor, the Registrar or a Deputy Registrar **B2–038** shall communicate to the Presidency, in writing, his or her decision to resign. The Presidency shall inform, in writing, the President of the Bureau of the Assembly of States Parties.

2. A judge, the Prosecutor, a Deputy Prosecutor, the Registrar or a Deputy Registrar shall endeavour to give notice of the date on which his or her resignation will take effect at least six months in advance. Before the resignation of a judge takes effect, he or she shall make every effort to discharge his or her outstanding responsibilities.

Subsection 3

Replacements and alternate judges

Rule 38

REPLACEMENTS

1. A judge may be replaced for objective and justified reasons, *inter alia*:   **B2–039**
   (a) Resignation;
   (b) Accepted excuse;
   (c) Disqualification;
   (d) Removal from office;
   (e) Death.

2. Replacement shall take place in accordance with the pre-established procedure in the Statute, the Rules and the Regulations.

RULE 39

ALTERNATE JUDGES

B2–040   Where an alternate judge has been assigned by the Presidency to a Trial Chamber pursuant to article 74, paragraph 1, he or she shall sit through all proceedings and deliberations of the case, but may not take any part therein and shall not exercise any of the functions of the members of the Trial Chamber hearing the case, unless and until he or she is required to replace a member of the Trial Chamber if that member is unable to continue attending. Alternate judges shall be designated in accordance with a procedure pre-established by the Court.

Section V

Publication, languages and translation

RULE 40

PUBLICATION OF DECISIONS IN OFFICIAL LANGUAGES OF THE COURT

B2–041   1. For the purposes of article 50, paragraph 1, the following decisions shall be considered as resolving fundamental issues:
   (a) All decisions of the Appeals Division;
   (b) All decisions of the Court on its jurisdiction or on the admissibility of a case pursuant to articles 17, 18, 19 and 20;
   (c) All decisions of a Trial Chamber on guilt or innocence, sentencing and reparations to victims pursuant to articles 74, 75 and 76;
   (d) All decisions of a Pre-Trial Chamber pursuant to article 57, paragraph 3 (d).
   2. Decisions on confirmation of charges under article 61, paragraph 7, and on offences against the administration of justice under article 70, paragraph 3, shall be published in all the official languages of the Court when the Presidency determines that they resolve fundamental issues.
   3. The Presidency may decide to publish other decisions in all the official languages when such decisions concern major issues relating to the interpretation or the implementation of the Statute or concern a major issue of general interest.

RULE 41

WORKING LANGUAGES OF THE COURT

B2–042   1. For the purposes of article 50, paragraph 2, the Presidency shall authorize the use of an official language of the Court as a working language when:
   (a) That language is understood and spoken by the majority of those involved in a case before the Court and any of the participants in the proceedings so requests; or
   (b) The Prosecutor and the defence so request.
   2. The Presidency may authorize the use of an official language of the Court as a working language if it considers that it would facilitate the efficiency of the proceedings.

RULE 42

TRANSLATION AND INTERPRETATION SERVICES

B2–043   The Court shall arrange for the translation and interpretation services necessary to ensure the implementation of its obligations under the Statute and the Rules.

RULE 43

PROCEDURE APPLICABLE TO THE PUBLICATION OF DOCUMENTS OF THE COURT

The Court shall ensure that all documents subject to publication in accordance with the Statute and the Rules respect the duty to protect the confidentiality of the proceedings and the security of victims and witnesses.

B2–044

CHAPTER 3

JURISDICTION AND ADMISSIBILITY

Section I

Declarations and referrals relating to articles 11, 12, 13 and 14

RULE 44

DECLARATION PROVIDED FOR IN ARTICLE 12, PARAGRAPH 3

1. The Registrar, at the request of the Prosecutor, may inquire of a State that is not a Party to the Statute or that has become a Party to the Statute after its entry into force, on a confidential basis, whether it intends to make the declaration provided for in article 12, paragraph 3.

B2–045

2. When a State lodges, or declares to the Registrar its intent to lodge, a declaration with the Registrar pursuant to article 12, paragraph 3, or when the Registrar acts pursuant to sub-rule 1, the Registrar shall inform the State concerned that the declaration under article 12, paragraph 3, has as a consequence the acceptance of jurisdiction with respect to the crimes referred to in article 5 of relevance to the situation and the provisions of Part 9, and any rules there under concerning States Parties, shall apply.

RULE 45

REFERRAL OF A SITUATION TO THE PROSECUTOR

A referral of a situation to the Prosecutor shall be in writing.

B2–046

Section II

Initiation of investigations under article 15

RULE 46

INFORMATION PROVIDED TO THE PROSECUTOR UNDER ARTICLE 15, PARAGRAPHS 1 AND 2

Where information is submitted under article 15, paragraph 1, or where oral or written testimony is received pursuant to article 15, paragraph 2, at the seat of the Court, the Prosecutor shall protect the confidentiality of such information and testimony or take any other necessary measures, pursuant to his or her duties under the Statute.

B2–047

Rule 47

TESTIMONY UNDER ARTICLE 15, PARAGRAPH 2

B2–048   1. The provisions of rules 111 and 112 shall apply, *mutatis mutandis*, to testimony received by the Prosecutor pursuant to article 15, paragraph 2.

2. When the Prosecutor considers that there is a serious risk that it might not be possible for the testimony to be taken subsequently, he or she may request the Pre-Trial Chamber to take such measures as may be necessary to ensure the efficiency and integrity of the proceedings and, in particular, to appoint a counsel or a judge from the Pre-Trial Chamber to be present during the taking of the testimony in order to protect the rights of the defence. If the testimony is subsequently presented in the proceedings, its admissibility shall be governed by article 69, paragraph 4, and given such weight as determined by the relevant Chamber.

Rule 48

DETERMINATION OF REASONABLE BASIS TO PROCEED WITH AN INVESTIGATION UNDER ARTICLE 15, PARAGRAPH 3

B2–049   In determining whether there is a reasonable basis to proceed with an investigation under article 15, paragraph 3, the Prosecutor shall consider the factors set out in article 53, paragraph 1 (a) to (c).

Rule 49

DECISION AND NOTICE UNDER ARTICLE 15, PARAGRAPH 6

B2–050   1. Where a decision under article 15, paragraph 6, is taken, the Prosecutor shall promptly ensure that notice is provided, including reasons for his or her decision, in a manner that prevents any danger to the safety, well-being and privacy of those who provided information to him or her under article 15, paragraphs 1 and 2, or the integrity of investigations or proceedings.

2. The notice shall also advise of the possibility of submitting further information regarding the same situation in the light of new facts and evidence.

Rule 50

PROCEDURE FOR AUTHORIZATION BY THE PRE-TRIAL CHAMBER OF THE COMMENCEMENT OF THE INVESTIGATION

B2–051   1. When the Prosecutor intends to seek authorization from the Pre-Trial Chamber to initiate an investigation pursuant to article 15, paragraph 3, the Prosecutor shall inform victims, known to him or her or to the Victims and Witnesses Unit, or their legal representatives, unless the Prosecutor decides that doing so would pose a danger to the integrity of the investigation or the life or well-being of victims and witnesses. The Prosecutor may also give notice by general means in order to reach groups of victims if he or she determines in the particular circumstances of the case that such notice could not pose a danger to the integrity and effective conduct of the investigation or to the security and well-being of victims and witnesses. In performing these functions, the Prosecutor may seek the assistance of the Victims and Witnesses Unit as appropriate.

2. A request for authorization by the Prosecutor shall be in writing.

3. Following information given in accordance with sub-rule 1, victims may make representations in writing to the Pre-Trial Chamber within such time limit as set forth in the Regulations.

4. The Pre-Trial Chamber, in deciding on the procedure to be followed, may request additional information from the Prosecutor and from any of the victims who have made representations, and, if it considers it appropriate, may hold a hearing.

5. The Pre-Trial Chamber shall issue its decision, including its reasons, as to whether to authorize the commencement of the investigation in accordance with article 15, paragraph 4, with respect to all or any part of the request by the Prosecutor. The Chamber shall give notice of the decision to victims who have made representations.

6. The above procedure shall also apply to a new request to the Pre-Trial Chamber pursuant to article 15, paragraph 5.

Section III

Challenges and preliminary rulings under articles 17, 18 and 19

RULE 51

INFORMATION PROVIDED UNDER ARTICLE 17

In considering the matters referred to in article 17, paragraph 2, and in the context of **B2–052** the circumstances of the case, the Court may consider, *inter alia*, information that the State referred to in article 17, paragraph 1, may choose to bring to the attention of the Court showing that its courts meet internationally recognized norms and standards for the independent and impartial prosecution of similar conduct, or that the State has confirmed in writing to the Prosecutor that the case is being investigated or prosecuted.

RULE 52

NOTIFICATION PROVIDED FOR IN ARTICLE 18, PARAGRAPH 1

1. Subject to the limitations provided for in article 18, paragraph 1, the notification **B2–053** shall contain information about the acts that may constitute crimes referred to in article 5, relevant for the purposes of article 18, paragraph 2.

2. A State may request additional information from the Prosecutor to assist it in the application of article 18, paragraph 2. Such a request shall not affect the one-month time limit provided for in article 18, paragraph 2, and shall be responded to by the Prosecutor on an expedited basis.

RULE 53

DEFERRAL PROVIDED FOR IN ARTICLE 18, PARAGRAPH 2

When a State requests a deferral pursuant to article 18, paragraph 2, that State shall **B2–054** make this request in writing and provide information concerning its investigation, taking into account article 18, paragraph 2. The Prosecutor may request additional information from that State.

RULE 54

APPLICATION BY THE PROSECUTOR UNDER ARTICLE 18, PARAGRAPH 2

1. An application submitted by the Prosecutor to the Pre-Trial Chamber in accord- **B2–055** ance with article 18, paragraph 2, shall be in writing and shall contain the basis for the application. The information provided by the State under rule 53 shall be communicated by the Prosecutor to the Pre-Trial Chamber.

2. The Prosecutor shall inform that State in writing when he or she makes an application to the Pre-Trial Chamber under article 18, paragraph 2, and shall include in the notice a summary of the basis of the application.

RULE 55

PROCEEDINGS CONCERNING ARTICLE 18, PARAGRAPH 2

B2–056   1. The Pre-Trial Chamber shall decide on the procedure to be followed and may take appropriate measures for the proper conduct of the proceedings. It may hold a hearing.

2. The Pre-Trial Chamber shall examine the Prosecutor's application and any observations submitted by a State that requested a deferral in accordance with article 18, paragraph 2, and shall consider the factors in article 17 in deciding whether to authorize an investigation.

3. The decision and the basis for the decision of the Pre-Trial Chamber shall be communicated as soon as possible to the Prosecutor and to the State that requested a deferral of an investigation.

RULE 56

APPLICATION BY THE PROSECUTOR FOLLOWING REVIEW UNDER ARTICLE 18, PARAGRAPH 3

B2–057   1. Following a review by the Prosecutor as set forth in article 18, paragraph 3, the Prosecutor may apply to the Pre-Trial Chamber for authorization in accordance with article 18, paragraph 2. The application to the Pre-Trial Chamber shall be in writing and shall contain the basis for the application.

2. Any further information provided by the State under article 18, paragraph 5, shall be communicated by the Prosecutor to the Pre-Trial Chamber.

3. The proceedings shall be conducted in accordance with rules 54, sub-rule 2, and 55.

RULE 57

PROVISIONAL MEASURES UNDER ARTICLE 18, PARAGRAPH 6

B2–058   An application to the Pre-Trial Chamber by the Prosecutor in the circumstances provided for in article 18, paragraph 6, shall be considered ex parte and in camera. The Pre-Trial Chamber shall rule on the application on an expedited basis.

RULE 58

PROCEEDINGS UNDER ARTICLE 19

B2–059   1. A request or application made under article 19 shall be in writing and contain the basis for it.

2. When a Chamber receives a request or application raising a challenge or question concerning its jurisdiction or the admissibility of a case in accordance with article 19, paragraph 2 or 3, or is acting on its own motion as provided for in article 19, paragraph 1, it shall decide on the procedure to be followed and may take appropriate measures for the proper conduct of the proceedings. It may hold a hearing. It may join the challenge or question to a confirmation or a trial proceeding as long as this does not cause undue delay, and in this circumstance shall hear and decide on the challenge or question first.

3. The Court shall transmit a request or application received under sub-rule 2 to the Prosecutor and to the person referred to in article 19, paragraph 2, who has been surrendered to the Court or who has appeared voluntarily or pursuant to a summons, and shall allow them to submit written observations to the request or application within a period of time determined by the Chamber.

4. The Court shall rule on any challenge or question of jurisdiction first and then on any challenge or question of admissibility.

RULE 59

PARTICIPATION IN PROCEEDINGS UNDER ARTICLE 19, PARAGRAPH 3

1. For the purpose of article 19, paragraph 3, the Registrar shall inform the following **B2-060** of any question or challenge of jurisdiction or admissibility which has arisen pursuant to article 19, paragraphs 1, 2 and 3:
   (a) Those who have referred a situation pursuant to article 13;
   (b) The victims who have already communicated with the Court in relation to that case or their legal representatives.

2. The Registrar shall provide those referred to in sub-rule 1, in a manner consistent with the duty of the Court regarding the confidentiality of information, the protection of any person and the preservation of evidence, with a summary of the grounds on which the jurisdiction of the Court or the admissibility of the case has been challenged.

3. Those receiving the information, as provided for in sub-rule 1, may make representation in writing to the competent Chamber within such time limit as it considers appropriate.

RULE 60

COMPETENT ORGAN TO RECEIVE CHALLENGES

If a challenge to the jurisdiction of the Court or to the admissibility of a case is made **B2-061** after a confirmation of the charges but before the constitution or designation of the Trial Chamber, it shall be addressed to the Presidency, which shall refer it to the Trial Chamber as soon as the latter is constituted or designated in accordance with rule 130.

RULE 61

PROVISIONAL MEASURES UNDER ARTICLE 19, PARAGRAPH 8

When the Prosecutor makes application to the competent Chamber in the circum- **B2-062** stances provided for in article 19, paragraph 8, rule 57 shall apply.

RULE 62

PROCEEDINGS UNDER ARTICLE 19, PARAGRAPH 10

1. If the Prosecutor makes a request under article 19, paragraph 10, he or she shall **B2-063** make the request to the Chamber that made the latest ruling on admissibility. The provisions of rules 58, 59 and 61 shall be applicable.

2. The State or States whose challenge to admissibility under article 19, paragraph 2, provoked the decision of inadmissibility provided for in article 19, paragraph 10, shall be

notified of the request of the Prosecutor and shall be given a time limit within which to make representations.

CHAPTER 4

PROVISIONS RELATING TO VARIOUS STAGES OF THE PROCEEDINGS

Section I

Evidence

RULE 63

GENERAL PROVISIONS RELATING TO EVIDENCE

B2–064   1. The rules of evidence set forth in this chapter, together with article 69, shall apply in proceedings before all Chambers.

2. A Chamber shall have the authority, in accordance with the discretion described in article 64, paragraph 9, to assess freely all evidence submitted in order to determine its relevance or admissibility in accordance with article 69.

3. A Chamber shall rule on an application of a party or on its own motion, made under article 64, subparagraph 9 (a), concerning admissibility when it is based on the grounds set out in article 69, paragraph 7.

4. Without prejudice to article 66, paragraph 3, a Chamber shall not impose a legal requirement that corroboration is required in order to prove any crime within the jurisdiction of the Court, in particular, crimes of sexual violence.

5. The Chambers shall not apply national laws governing evidence, other than in accordance with article 21.

RULE 64

PROCEDURE RELATING TO THE RELEVANCE OR ADMISSIBILITY OF EVIDENCE

B2–065   1. An issue relating to relevance or admissibility must be raised at the time when the evidence is submitted to a Chamber. Exceptionally, when those issues were not known at the time when the evidence was submitted, it may be raised immediately after the issue has become known. The Chamber may request that the issue be raised in writing. The written motion shall be communicated by the Court to all those who participate in the proceedings, unless otherwise decided by the Court.

2. A Chamber shall give reasons for any rulings it makes on evidentiary matters. These reasons shall be placed in the record of the proceedings if they have not already been incorporated into the record during the course of the proceedings in accordance with article 64, paragraph 10, and rule 137, sub-rule 1.

3. Evidence ruled irrelevant or inadmissible shall not be considered by the Chamber.

RULE 65

COMPELLABILITY OF WITNESSES

B2–066   1. A witness who appears before the Court is compellable by the Court to provide testimony, unless otherwise provided for in the Statute and the Rules, in particular rules 73, 74 and 75.

2. Rule 171 applies to a witness appearing before the Court who is compellable to provide testimony under sub-rule 1.

Rule 66

SOLEMN UNDERTAKING

B2–067

1. Except as described in sub-rule 2, every witness shall, in accordance with article 69, paragraph 1, make the following solemn undertaking before testifying:
"I solemnly declare that I will speak the truth, the whole truth and nothing but the truth."
2. A person under the age of 18 or a person whose judgement has been impaired and who, in the opinion of the Chamber, does not understand the nature of a solemn undertaking may be allowed to testify without this solemn undertaking if the Chamber considers that the person is able to describe matters of which he or she has knowledge and that the person understands the meaning of the duty to speak the truth.
3. Before testifying, the witness shall be informed of the offence defined in article 70, paragraph 1 (a).

Rule 67

LIVE TESTIMONY BY MEANS OF AUDIO OR VIDEO-LINK TECHNOLOGY

B2–068

1. In accordance with article 69, paragraph 2, a Chamber may allow a witness to give viva voce (oral) testimony before the Chamber by means of audio or video technology, provided that such technology permits the witness to be examined by the Prosecutor, the defence, and by the Chamber itself, at the time that the witness so testifies.
2. The examination of a witness under this rule shall be conducted in accordance with the relevant rules of this chapter.
3. The Chamber, with the assistance of the Registry, shall ensure that the venue chosen for the conduct of the audio or video-link testimony is conducive to the giving of truthful and open testimony and to the safety, physical and psychological well-being, dignity and privacy of the witness.

Rule 68

PRIOR RECORDED TESTIMONY

B2–069

When the Pre-Trial Chamber has not taken measures under article 56, the Trial Chamber may, in accordance with article 69, paragraph 2, allow the introduction of previously recorded audio or video testimony of a witness, or the transcript or other documented evidence of such testimony, provided that:
(a) If the witness who gave the previously recorded testimony is not present before the Trial Chamber, both the Prosecutor and the defence had the opportunity to examine the witness during the recording; or
(b) If the witness who gave the previously recorded testimony is present before the Trial Chamber, he or she does not object to the submission of the previously recorded testimony and the Prosecutor, the defence and the Chamber have the opportunity to examine the witness during the proceedings.

Rule 69

AGREEMENTS AS TO EVIDENCE

B2–070

The Prosecutor and the defence may agree that an alleged fact, which is contained in the charges, the contents of a document, the expected testimony of a witness or other evidence is not contested and, accordingly, a Chamber may consider such alleged fact as being proven, unless the Chamber is of the opinion that a more complete presentation of the alleged facts is required in the interests of justice, in particular the interests of the victims.

RULE 70

PRINCIPLES OF EVIDENCE IN CASES OF SEXUAL VIOLENCE

B2–071   In cases of sexual violence, the Court shall be guided by and, where appropriate, apply the following principles:
   (a) Consent cannot be inferred by reason of any words or conduct of a victim where force, threat of force, coercion or taking advantage of a coercive environment undermined the victim's ability to give voluntary and genuine consent;
   (b) Consent cannot be inferred by reason of any words or conduct of a victim where the victim is incapable of giving genuine consent;
   (c) Consent cannot be inferred by reason of the silence of, or lack of resistance by, a victim to the alleged sexual violence;
   (d) Credibility, character or predisposition to sexual availability of a victim or witness cannot be inferred by reason of the sexual nature of the prior or subsequent conduct of a victim or witness.

RULE 71

EVIDENCE OF OTHER SEXUAL CONDUCT

B2–072   In the light of the definition and nature of the crimes within the jurisdiction of the Court, and subject to article 69, paragraph 4, a Chamber shall not admit evidence of the prior or subsequent sexual conduct of a victim or witness.

RULE 72

IN CAMERA PROCEDURE TO CONSIDER RELEVANCE OR ADMISSIBILITY OF EVIDENCE

B2–073   1. Where there is an intention to introduce or elicit, including by means of the questioning of a victim or witness, evidence that the victim consented to an alleged crime of sexual violence, or evidence of the words, conduct, silence or lack of resistance of a victim or witness as referred to in principles (a) through (d) of rule 70, notification shall be provided to the Court which shall describe the substance of the evidence intended to be introduced or elicited and the relevance of the evidence to the issues in the case.
   2. In deciding whether the evidence referred to in sub-rule 1 is relevant or admissible, a Chamber shall hear in camera the views of the Prosecutor, the defence, the witness and the victim or his or her legal representative, if any, and shall take into account whether that evidence has a sufficient degree of probative value to an issue in the case and the prejudice that such evidence may cause, in accordance with article 69, paragraph 4. For this purpose, the Chamber shall have regard to article 21, paragraph 3, and articles 67 and 68, and shall be guided by principles (a) to (d) of rule 70, especially with respect to the proposed questioning of a victim.
   3. Where the Chamber determines that the evidence referred to in sub-rule 2 is admissible in the proceedings, the Chamber shall state on the record the specific purpose for which the evidence is admissible. In evaluating the evidence during the proceedings, the Chamber shall apply principles (a) to (d) of rule 70.

RULE 73

PRIVILEGED COMMUNICATIONS AND INFORMATION

B2–074   1. Without prejudice to article 67, paragraph 1 (b), communications made in the context of the professional relationship between a person and his or her legal counsel shall be regarded as privileged, and consequently not subject to disclosure, unless:

(a) The person consents in writing to such disclosure; or

(b) The person voluntarily disclosed the content of the communication to a third party, and that third party then gives evidence of that disclosure.

2. Having regard to rule 63, sub-rule 5, communications made in the context of a class of professional or other confidential relationships shall be regarded as privileged, and consequently not subject to disclosure, under the same terms as in sub-rules 1 (a) and 1 (b) if a Chamber decides in respect of that class that:

(a) Communications occurring within that class of relationship are made in the course of a confidential relationship producing a reasonable expectation of privacy and non-disclosure;

(b) Confidentiality is essential to the nature and type of relationship between the person and the confidant; and

(c) Recognition of the privilege would further the objectives of the Statute and the Rules.

3. In making a decision under sub-rule 2, the Court shall give particular regard to recognizing as privileged those communications made in the context of the professional relationship between a person and his or her medical doctor, psychiatrist, psychologist or counsellor, in particular those related to or involving victims, or between a person and a member of a religious clergy; and in the latter case, the Court shall recognize as privileged those communications made in the context of a sacred confession where it is an integral part of the practice of that religion.

4. The Court shall regard as privileged, and consequently not subject to disclosure, including by way of testimony of any present or past official or employee of the International Committee of the Red Cross (ICRC), any information, documents or other evidence which it came into the possession of in the course, or as a consequence, of the performance by ICRC of its functions under the Statutes of the International Red Cross and Red Crescent Movement, unless:

(a) After consultations undertaken pursuant to sub-rule 6, ICRC does not object in writing to such disclosure, or otherwise has waived this privilege; or

(b) Such information, documents or other evidence is contained in public statements and documents of ICRC.

5. Nothing in sub-rule 4 shall affect the admissibility of the same evidence obtained from a source other than ICRC and its officials or employees when such evidence has also been acquired by this source independently of ICRC and its officials or employees.

6. If the Court determines that ICRC information, documents or other evidence are of great importance for a particular case, consultations shall be held between the Court and ICRC in order to seek to resolve the matter by cooperative means, bearing in mind the circumstances of the case, the relevance of the evidence sought, whether the evidence could be obtained from a source other than ICRC, the interests of justice and of victims, and the performance of the Court's and ICRC's functions.

RULE 74

SELF-INCRIMINATION BY A WITNESS

1. Unless a witness has been notified pursuant to rule 190, the Chamber shall notify a witness of the provisions of this rule before his or her testimony.   **B2–075**

2. Where the Court determines that an assurance with respect to self-incrimination should be provided to a particular witness, it shall provide the assurances under sub-rule 3, paragraph (c), before the witness attends, directly or pursuant to a request under article 93, paragraph (1) (e).

3.

(a) A witness may object to making any statement that might tend to incriminate him or her.

(b) Where the witness has attended after receiving an assurance under sub-rule 2, the Court may require the witness to answer the question or questions.

(c) In the case of other witnesses, the Chamber may require the witness to answer the question or questions, after assuring the witness that the evidence provided in response to the questions:

      (i) Will be kept confidential and will not be disclosed to the public or any State; and

      (ii) Will not be used either directly or indirectly against that person in any subsequent prosecution by the Court, except under articles 70 and 71.

4. Before giving such an assurance, the Chamber shall seek the views of the Prosecutor, ex parte, to determine if the assurance should be given to this particular witness.

5. In determining whether to require the witness to answer, the Chamber shall consider:

    (a) The importance of the anticipated evidence;

    (b) Whether the witness would be providing unique evidence;

    (c) The nature of the possible incrimination, if known; and

    (d) The sufficiency of the protections for the witness, in the particular circumstances.

6. If the Chamber determines that it would not be appropriate to provide an assurance to this witness, it shall not require the witness to answer the question. If the Chamber determines not to require the witness to answer, it may still continue the questioning of the witness on other matters.

7. In order to give effect to the assurance, the Chamber shall:

    (a) Order that the evidence of the witness be given in camera;

    (b) Order that the identity of the witness and the content of the evidence given shall not be disclosed, in any manner, and provide that the breach of any such order will be subject to sanction under article 71;

    (c) Specifically advise the Prosecutor, the accused, the defence counsel, the legal representative of the victim and any Court staff present of the consequences of a breach of the order under subparagraph (b);

    (d) Order the sealing of any record of the proceedings; and

    (e) Use protective measures with respect to any decision of the Court to ensure that the identity of the witness and the content of the evidence given are not disclosed.

8. Where the Prosecutor is aware that the testimony of any witness may raise issues with respect to self-incrimination, he or she shall request an in camera hearing and advise the Chamber of this, in advance of the testimony of the witness. The Chamber may impose the measures outlined in sub-rule 7 for all or a part of the testimony of that witness.

9. The accused, the defence counsel or the witness may advise the Prosecutor or the Chamber that the testimony of a witness will raise issues of self-incrimination before the witness testifies and the Chamber may take the measures outlined in sub-rule 7.

10. If an issue of self-incrimination arises in the course of the proceedings, the Chamber shall suspend the taking of the testimony and provide the witness with an opportunity to obtain legal advice if he or she so requests for the purpose of the application of the rule.

RULE 75

INCRIMINATION BY FAMILY MEMBERS

B2–076   1. A witness appearing before the Court, who is a spouse, child or parent of an accused person, shall not be required by a Chamber to make any statement that might tend to incriminate that accused person. However, the witness may choose to make such a statement.

2. In evaluating the testimony of a witness, a Chamber may take into account that the witness, referred to in sub-rule 1, objected to reply to a question which was intended to contradict a previous statement made by the witness, or the witness was selective in choosing which questions to answer.

Section II

Disclosure

Rule 76

PRE-TRIAL DISCLOSURE RELATING TO PROSECUTION WITNESSES

1. The Prosecutor shall provide the defence with the names of witnesses whom the Prosecutor intends to call to testify and copies of any prior statements made by those witnesses. This shall be done sufficiently in advance to enable the adequate preparation of the defence.

2. The Prosecutor shall subsequently advise the defence of the names of any additional prosecution witnesses and provide copies of their statements when the decision is made to call those witnesses.

3. The statements of prosecution witnesses shall be made available in original and in a language which the accused fully understands and speaks.

4. This rule is subject to the protection and privacy of victims and witnesses and the protection of confidential information as provided for in the Statute and rules 81 and 82.

B2–077

Rule 77

INSPECTION OF MATERIAL IN POSSESSION OR CONTROL OF THE PROSECUTOR

The Prosecutor shall, subject to the restrictions on disclosure as provided for in the Statute and in rules 81 and 82, permit the defence to inspect any books, documents, photographs and other tangible objects in the possession or control of the Prosecutor, which are material to the preparation of the defence or are intended for use by the Prosecutor as evidence for the purposes of the confirmation hearing or at trial, as the case may be, or were obtained from or belonged to the person.

B2–078

Rule 78

INSPECTION OF MATERIAL IN POSSESSION OR CONTROL OF THE DEFENCE

The defence shall permit the Prosecutor to inspect any books, documents, photographs and other tangible objects in the possession or control of the defence, which are intended for use by the defence as evidence for the purposes of the confirmation hearing or at trial.

B2–079

Rule 79

DISCLOSURE BY THE DEFENCE

1. The defence shall notify the Prosecutor of its intent to:
   (a) Raise the existence of an alibi, in which case the notification shall specify the place or places at which the accused claims to have been present at the time of the alleged crime and the names of witnesses and any other evidence upon which the accused intends to rely to establish the alibi; or

B2–080

(b) Raise a ground for excluding criminal responsibility provided for in article 31, paragraph 1, in which case the notification shall specify the names of witnesses and any other evidence upon which the accused intends to rely to establish the ground.

2. With due regard to time limits set forth in other rules, notification under sub-rule 1 shall be given sufficiently in advance to enable the Prosecutor to prepare adequately and to respond. The Chamber dealing with the matter may grant the Prosecutor an adjournment to address the issue raised by the defence.

3. Failure of the defence to provide notice under this rule shall not limit its right to raise matters dealt with in sub-rule 1 and to present evidence.

4. This rule does not prevent a Chamber from ordering disclosure of any other evidence.

RULE 80

PROCEDURES FOR RAISING A GROUND FOR EXCLUDING CRIMINAL RESPONSIBILITY UNDER ARTICLE 31, PARAGRAPH 3

B2–081   1. The defence shall give notice to both the Trial Chamber and the Prosecutor if it intends to raise a ground for excluding criminal responsibility under article 31, paragraph 3. This shall be done sufficiently in advance of the commencement of the trial to enable the Prosecutor to prepare adequately for trial.

2. Following notice given under sub-rule 1, the Trial Chamber shall hear both the Prosecutor and the defence before deciding whether the defence can raise a ground for excluding criminal responsibility.

3. If the defence is permitted to raise the ground, the Trial Chamber may grant the Prosecutor an adjournment to address that ground.

RULE 81

RESTRICTIONS ON DISCLOSURE

B2–082   1. Reports, memoranda or other internal documents prepared by a party, its assistants or representatives in connection with the investigation or preparation of the case are not subject to disclosure.

2. Where material or information is in the possession or control of the Prosecutor which must be disclosed in accordance with the Statute, but disclosure may prejudice further or ongoing investigations, the Prosecutor may apply to the Chamber dealing with the matter for a ruling as to whether the material or information must be disclosed to the defence. The matter shall be heard on an ex parte basis by the Chamber. However, the Prosecutor may not introduce such material or information into evidence during the confirmation hearing or the trial without adequate prior disclosure to the accused.

3. Where steps have been taken to ensure the confidentiality of information, in accordance with articles 54, 57, 64, 72 and 93, and, in accordance with article 68, to protect the safety of witnesses and victims and members of their families, such information shall not be disclosed, except in accordance with those articles. When the disclosure of such information may create a risk to the safety of the witness, the Court shall take measures to inform the witness in advance.

4. The Chamber dealing with the matter shall, on its own motion or at the request of the Prosecutor, the accused or any State, take the necessary steps to ensure the confidentiality of information, in accordance with articles 54, 72 and 93, and, in accordance with article 68, to protect the safety of witnesses and victims and members of their families, including by authorizing the non-disclosure of their identity prior to the commencement of the trial.

5. Where material or information is in the possession or control of the Prosecutor which is withheld under article 68, paragraph 5, such material and information may not be subsequently introduced into evidence during the confirmation hearing or the trial without adequate prior disclosure to the accused.

6. Where material or information is in the possession or control of the defence which is subject to disclosure, it may be withheld in circumstances similar to those which would allow the Prosecutor to rely on article 68, paragraph 5, and a summary thereof submitted instead. Such material and information may not be subsequently introduced into evidence during the confirmation hearing or the trial without adequate prior disclosure to the Prosecutor.

RULE 82

RESTRICTIONS ON DISCLOSURE OF MATERIAL AND INFORMATION PROTECTED UNDER ARTICLE 54, PARAGRAPH 3 (E)

1. Where material or information is in the possession or control of the Prosecutor **B2–083** which is protected under article 54, paragraph 3 (e), the Prosecutor may not subsequently introduce such material or information into evidence without the prior consent of the provider of the material or information and adequate prior disclosure to the accused.

2. If the Prosecutor introduces material or information protected under article 54, paragraph 3 (e), into evidence, a Chamber may not order the production of additional evidence received from the provider of the initial material or information, nor may a Chamber for the purpose of obtaining such additional evidence itself summon the provider or a representative of the provider as a witness or order their attendance.

3. If the Prosecutor calls a witness to introduce in evidence any material or information which has been protected under article 54, paragraph 3 (e), a Chamber may not compel that witness to answer any question relating to the material or information or its origin, if the witness declines to answer on grounds of confidentiality.

4. The right of the accused to challenge evidence which has been protected under article 54, paragraph 3 (e), shall remain unaffected subject only to the limitations contained in sub-rules 2 and 3.

5. A Chamber dealing with the matter may order, upon application by the defence, that, in the interests of justice, material or information in the possession of the accused, which has been provided to the accused under the same conditions as set forth in article 54, paragraph 3 (e), and which is to be introduced into evidence, shall be subject *mutatis mutandis* to sub-rules 1, 2 and 3.

RULE 83

RULING ON EXCULPATORY EVIDENCE UNDER ARTICLE 67, PARAGRAPH 2

The Prosecutor may request as soon as practicable a hearing on an ex parte basis **B2–084** before the Chamber dealing with the matter for the purpose of obtaining a ruling under article 67, paragraph 2.

RULE 84

DISCLOSURE AND ADDITIONAL EVIDENCE FOR TRIAL

In order to enable the parties to prepare for trial and to facilitate the fair and **B2–085** expeditious conduct of the proceedings, the Trial Chamber shall, in accordance with article 64, paragraphs 3 (c) and 6 (d), and article 67, paragraph (2), and subject to article 68, paragraph 5, make any necessary orders for the disclosure of documents or information not previously disclosed and for the production of additional evidence. To avoid delay and to ensure that the trial commences on the set date, any such orders shall include strict time limits which shall be kept under review by the Trial Chamber.

Section III

Victims and witnesses

Subsection 1

Definition and general principle relating to victims

RULE 85

DEFINITION OF VICTIMS

B2–086   For the purposes of the Statute and the Rules of Procedure and Evidence:
  (a) "Victims" means natural persons who have suffered harm as a result of the commission of any crime within the jurisdiction of the Court;
  (b) Victims may include organizations or institutions that have sustained direct harm to any of their property which is dedicated to religion, education, art or science or charitable purposes, and to their historic monuments, hospitals and other places and objects for humanitarian purposes.

RULE 86

GENERAL PRINCIPLE

B2–087   A Chamber in making any direction or order, and other organs of the Court in performing their functions under the Statute or the Rules, shall take into account the needs of all victims and witnesses in accordance with article 68, in particular, children, elderly persons, persons with disabilities and victims of sexual or gender violence.

Subsection 2

Protection of victims and witnesses

RULE 87

PROTECTIVE MEASURES

B2–088   1. Upon the motion of the Prosecutor or the defence or upon the request of a witness or a victim or his or her legal representative, if any, or on its own motion, and after having consulted with the Victims and Witnesses Unit, as appropriate, a Chamber may order measures to protect a victim, a witness or another person at risk on account of testimony given by a witness pursuant to article 68, paragraphs 1 and 2. The Chamber shall seek to obtain, whenever possible, the consent of the person in respect of whom the protective measure is sought prior to ordering the protective measure.
  2. A motion or request under sub-rule 1 shall be governed by rule 134, provided that:
    (a) Such a motion or request shall not be submitted ex parte;
    (b) A request by a witness or by a victim or his or her legal representative, if any, shall be served on both the Prosecutor and the defence, each of whom shall have the opportunity to respond;

(c) A motion or request affecting a particular witness or a particular victim shall be served on that witness or victim or his or her legal representative, if any, in addition to the other party, each of whom shall have the opportunity to respond;

(d) When the Chamber proceeds on its own motion, notice and opportunity to respond shall be given to the Prosecutor and the defence, and to any witness or any victim or his or her legal representative, if any, who would be affected by such protective measure; and

(e) A motion or request may be filed under seal, and, if so filed, shall remain sealed until otherwise ordered by a Chamber. Responses to motions or requests filed under seal shall also be filed under seal.

3. A Chamber may, on a motion or request under sub-rule 1, hold a hearing, which shall be conducted in camera, to determine whether to order measures to prevent the release to the public or press and information agencies, of the identity or the location of a victim, a witness or other person at risk on account of testimony given by a witness by ordering, *inter alia*:

(a) That the name of the victim, witness or other person at risk on account of testimony given by a witness or any information which could lead to his or her identification, be expunged from the public records of the Chamber;

(b) That the Prosecutor, the defence or any other participant in the proceedings be prohibited from disclosing such information to a third party;

(c) That testimony be presented by electronic or other special means, including the use of technical means enabling the alteration of pictures or voice, the use of audio-visual technology, in particular videoconferencing and closed-circuit television, and the exclusive use of the sound media;

(d) That a pseudonym be used for a victim, a witness or other person at risk on account of testimony given by a witness; or

(e) That a Chamber conduct part of its proceedings in camera.

RULE 88

SPECIAL MEASURES

1. Upon the motion of the Prosecutor or the defence, or upon the request of a witness or a victim or his or her legal representative, if any, or on its own motion, and after having consulted with the Victims and Witnesses Unit, as appropriate, a Chamber may, taking into account the views of the victim or witness, order special measures such as, but not limited to, measures to facilitate the testimony of a traumatized victim or witness, a child, an elderly person or a victim of sexual violence, pursuant to article 68, paragraphs 1 and 2. The Chamber shall seek to obtain, whenever possible, the consent of the person in respect of whom the special measure is sought prior to ordering that measure.

B2–089

2. A Chamber may hold a hearing on a motion or a request under sub-rule 1, if necessary in camera or ex parte, to determine whether to order any such special measure, including but not limited to an order that a counsel, a legal representative, a psychologist or a family member be permitted to attend during the testimony of the victim or the witness.

3. For *inter partes* motions or requests filed under this rule, the provisions of rule 87, sub-rules 2 (b) to (d), shall apply *mutatis mutandis*.

4. A motion or request filed under this rule may be filed under seal, and if so filed shall remain sealed until otherwise ordered by a Chamber. Any responses to *inter partes* motions or requests filed under seal shall also be filed under seal.

5. Taking into consideration that violations of the privacy of a witness or victim may create risk to his or her security, a Chamber shall be vigilant in controlling the manner of questioning a witness or victim so as to avoid any harassment or intimidation, paying particular attention to attacks on victims of crimes of sexual violence.

Participation of victims in the proceedings

RULE 89

APPLICATION FOR PARTICIPATION OF VICTIMS IN THE PROCEEDINGS

B2–090　　1. In order to present their views and concerns, victims shall make written application to the Registrar, who shall transmit the application to the relevant Chamber. Subject to the provisions of the Statute, in particular article 68, paragraph 1, the Registrar shall provide a copy of the application to the Prosecutor and the defence, who shall be entitled to reply within a time limit to be set by the Chamber. Subject to the provisions of sub-rule 2, the Chamber shall then specify the proceedings and manner in which participation is considered appropriate, which may include making opening and closing statements.

2. The Chamber, on its own initiative or on the application of the Prosecutor or the defence, may reject the application if it considers that the person is not a victim or that the criteria set forth in article 68, paragraph 3, are not otherwise fulfilled. A victim whose application has been rejected may file a new application later in the proceedings.

3. An application referred to in this rule may also be made by a person acting with the consent of the victim, or a person acting on behalf of a victim, in the case of a victim who is a child or, when necessary, a victim who is disabled.

4. Where there are a number of applications, the Chamber may consider the applications in such a manner as to ensure the effectiveness of the proceedings and may issue one decision.

RULE 90

LEGAL REPRESENTATIVES OF VICTIMS

B2–091　　1. A victim shall be free to choose a legal representative.

2. Where there are a number of victims, the Chamber may, for the purposes of ensuring the effectiveness of the proceedings, request the victims or particular groups of victims, if necessary with the assistance of the Registry, to choose a common legal representative or representatives. In facilitating the coordination of victim representation, the Registry may provide assistance, *inter alia*, by referring the victims to a list of counsel, maintained by the Registry, or suggesting one or more common legal representatives.

3. If the victims are unable to choose a common legal representative or representatives within a time limit that the Chamber may decide, the Chamber may request the Registrar to choose one or more common legal representatives.

4. The Chamber and the Registry shall take all reasonable steps to ensure that in the selection of common legal representatives, the distinct interests of the victims, particularly as provided in article 68, paragraph 1, are represented and that any conflict of interest is avoided.

5. A victim or group of victims who lack the necessary means to pay for a common legal representative chosen by the Court may receive assistance from the Registry, including, as appropriate, financial assistance.

6. A legal representative of a victim or victims shall have the qualifications set forth in rule 22, sub-rule 1.

RULE 91

PARTICIPATION OF LEGAL REPRESENTATIVES IN THE PROCEEDINGS

1. A Chamber may modify a previous ruling under rule 89.

B2–092

2. A legal representative of a victim shall be entitled to attend and participate in the proceedings in accordance with the terms of the ruling of the Chamber and any modification thereof given under rules 89 and 90. This shall include participation in hearings unless, in the circumstances of the case, the Chamber concerned is of the view that the representative's intervention should be confined to written observations or submissions. The Prosecutor and the defence shall be allowed to reply to any oral or written observation by the legal representative for victims.

3. (a) When a legal representative attends and participates in accordance with this rule, and wishes to question a witness, including questioning under rules 67 and 68, an expert or the accused, the legal representative must make application to the Chamber. The Chamber may require the legal representative to provide a written note of the questions and in that case the questions shall be communicated to the Prosecutor and, if appropriate, the defence, who shall be allowed to make observations within a time limit set by the Chamber.

(b) The Chamber shall then issue a ruling on the request, taking into account the stage of the proceedings, the rights of the accused, the interests of witnesses, the need for a fair, impartial and expeditious trial and in order to give effect to article 68, paragraph 3. The ruling may include directions on the manner and order of the questions and the production of documents in accordance with the powers of the Chamber under article 64. The Chamber may, if it considers it appropriate, put the question to the witness, expert or accused on behalf of the victim's legal representative.

4. For a hearing limited to reparations under article 75, the restrictions on questioning by the legal representative set forth in sub-rule 2 shall not apply. In that case, the legal representative may, with the permission of the Chamber concerned, question witnesses, experts and the person concerned.

RULE 92

NOTIFICATION TO VICTIMS AND THEIR LEGAL REPRESENTATIVES

1. This rule on notification to victims and their legal representatives shall apply to all proceedings before the Court, except in proceedings provided for in Part 2.

B2–093

2. In order to allow victims to apply for participation in the proceedings in accordance with rule 89, the Court shall notify victims concerning the decision of the Prosecutor not to initiate an investigation or not to prosecute pursuant to article 53. Such a notification shall be given to victims or their legal representatives who have already participated in the proceedings or, as far as possible, to those who have communicated with the Court in respect of the situation or case in question. The Chamber may order the measures outlined in sub-rule 8 if it considers it appropriate in the particular circumstances.

3. In order to allow victims to apply for participation in the proceedings in accordance with rule 89, the Court shall notify victims regarding its decision to hold a hearing to confirm charges pursuant to article 61. Such a notification shall be given to victims or their legal representatives who have already participated in the proceedings or, as far as possible, to those who have communicated with the Court in respect of the case in question.

4. When a notification for participation as provided for in sub-rules 2 and 3 has been given, any subsequent notification as referred to in sub-rules 5 and 6 shall only be

1287

provided to victims or their legal representatives who may participate in the proceedings in accordance with a ruling of the Chamber pursuant to rule 89 and any modification thereof.

5. In a manner consistent with the ruling made under rules 89 to 91, victims or their legal representatives participating in proceedings shall, in respect of those proceedings, be notified by the Registrar in a timely manner of:

    (a) Proceedings before the Court, including the date of hearings and any postponements thereof, and the date of delivery of the decision;

    (b) Requests, submissions, motions and other documents relating to such requests, submissions or motions.

6. Where victims or their legal representatives have participated in a certain stage of the proceedings, the Registrar shall notify them as soon as possible of the decisions of the Court in those proceedings.

7. Notifications as referred to in sub-rules 5 and 6 shall be in writing or, where written notification is not possible, in any other form as appropriate. The Registry shall keep a record of all notifications. Where necessary, the Registrar may seek the cooperation of States Parties in accordance with article 93, paragraph 1 (d) and (l).

8. For notification as referred to in sub-rule 3 and otherwise at the request of a Chamber, the Registrar shall take necessary measures to give adequate publicity to the proceedings. In doing so, the Registrar may seek, in accordance with Part 9, the cooperation of relevant States Parties, and seek the assistance of intergovernmental organizations.

RULE 93

VIEWS OF VICTIMS OR THEIR LEGAL REPRESENTATIVES

B2–094   A Chamber may seek the views of victims or their legal representatives participating pursuant to rules 89 to 91 on any issue, *inter alia*, in relation to issues referred to in rules 107, 109, 125, 128, 136, 139 and 191. In addition, a Chamber may seek the views of other victims, as appropriate.

Subsection 4

Reparations to victims

RULE 94

PROCEDURE UPON REQUEST

B2–095   1. A victim's request for reparations under article 75 shall be made in writing and filed with the Registrar. It shall contain the following particulars:

    (a) The identity and address of the claimant;

    (b) A description of the injury, loss or harm;

    (c) The location and date of the incident and, to the extent possible, the identity of the person or persons the victim believes to be responsible for the injury, loss or harm;

    (d) Where restitution of assets, property or other tangible items is sought, a description of them;

    (e) Claims for compensation;

    (f) Claims for rehabilitation and other forms of remedy;

    (g) To the extent possible, any relevant supporting documentation, including names and addresses of witnesses.

2. At commencement of the trial and subject to any protective measures, the Court shall ask the Registrar to provide notification of the request to the person or persons

named in the request or identified in the charges and, to the extent possible, to any interested persons or any interested States. Those notified shall file with the Registry any representation made under article 75, paragraph 3.

Rule 95

PROCEDURE ON THE MOTION OF THE COURT

1. In cases where the Court intends to proceed on its own motion pursuant to article 75, paragraph 1, it shall ask the Registrar to provide notification of its intention to the person or persons against whom the Court is considering making a determination, and, to the extent possible, to victims, interested persons and interested States. Those notified shall file with the Registry any representation made under article 75, paragraph 3.   **B2–096**

2. If, as a result of notification under sub-rule 1:
    (a) A victim makes a request for reparations, that request will be determined as if it had been brought under rule 94;
    (b) A victim requests that the Court does not make an order for reparations, the Court shall not proceed to make an individual order in respect of that victim.

Rule 96

PUBLICATION OF REPARATION PROCEEDINGS

1. Without prejudice to any other rules on notification of proceedings, the Registrar shall, insofar as practicable, notify the victims or their legal representatives and the person or persons concerned. The Registrar shall also, having regard to any information provided by the Prosecutor, take all the necessary measures to give adequate publicity of the reparation proceedings before the Court, to the extent possible, to other victims, interested persons and interested States.   **B2–097**

2. In taking the measures described in sub-rule 1, the Court may seek, in accordance with Part 9, the cooperation of relevant States Parties, and seek the assistance of intergovernmental organizations in order to give publicity, as widely as possible and by all possible means, to the reparation proceedings before the Court.

Rule 97

ASSESSMENT OF REPARATIONS

1. Taking into account the scope and extent of any damage, loss or injury, the Court may award reparations on an individualized basis or, where it deems it appropriate, on a collective basis or both.   **B2–098**

2. At the request of victims or their legal representatives, or at the request of the convicted person, or on its own motion, the Court may appoint appropriate experts to assist it in determining the scope, extent of any damage, loss and injury to, or in respect of victims and to suggest various options concerning the appropriate types and modalities of reparations. The Court shall invite, as appropriate, victims or their legal representatives, the convicted person as well as interested persons and interested States to make observations on the reports of the experts.

3. In all cases, the Court shall respect the rights of victims and the convicted person.

Rule 98

TRUST FUND

1. Individual awards for reparations shall be made directly against a convicted person.   **B2–099**

2. The Court may order that an award for reparations against a convicted person be deposited with the Trust Fund where at the time of making the order it is impossible or impracticable to make individual awards directly to each victim. The award for reparations thus deposited in the Trust Fund shall be separated from other resources of the Trust Fund and shall be forwarded to each victim as soon as possible.

3. The Court may order that an award for reparations against a convicted person be made through the Trust Fund where the number of the victims and the scope, forms and modalities of reparations makes a collective award more appropriate.

4. Following consultations with interested States and the Trust Fund, the Court may order that an award for reparations be made through the Trust Fund to an intergovernmental, international or national organization approved by the Trust Fund.

5. Other resources of the Trust Fund may be used for the benefit of victims subject to the provisions of article 79.

RULE 99

COOPERATION AND PROTECTIVE MEASURES FOR THE PURPOSE OF FORFEITURE UNDER ARTICLES 57, PARAGRAPH 3 (E), AND 75, PARAGRAPH 4

B2–100   1. The Pre-Trial Chamber, pursuant to article 57, paragraph 3 (e), or the Trial Chamber, pursuant to article 75, paragraph 4, may, on its own motion or on the application of the Prosecutor or at the request of the victims or their legal representatives who have made a request for reparations or who have given a written undertaking to do so, determine whether measures should be requested.

2. Notice is not required unless the Court determines, in the particular circumstances of the case, that notification could not jeopardize the effectiveness of the measures requested. In the latter case, the Registrar shall provide notification of the proceedings to the person against whom a request is made and so far as is possible to any interested persons or interested States.

3. If an order is made without prior notification, the relevant Chamber shall request the Registrar, as soon as is consistent with the effectiveness of the measures requested, to notify those against whom a request is made and, to the extent possible, to any interested persons or any interested States and invite them to make observations as to whether the order should be revoked or otherwise modified.

4. The Court may make orders as to the timing and conduct of any proceedings necessary to determine these issues.

Section IV

Miscellaneous provisions

RULE 100

PLACE OF THE PROCEEDINGS

B2–101   1. In a particular case, where the Court considers that it would be in the interests of justice, it may decide to sit in a State other than the host State.

2. An application or recommendation changing the place where the Court sits may be filed at any time after the initiation of an investigation, either by the Prosecutor, the defence or by a majority of the judges of the Court. Such an application or recommendation shall be addressed to the Presidency. It shall be made in writing and specify in which State the Court would sit. The Presidency shall satisfy itself of the views of the relevant Chamber.

3. The Presidency shall consult the State where the Court intends to sit. If that State agrees that the Court can sit in that State, then the decision to sit in a State other than the host State shall be taken by the judges, in plenary session, by a two-thirds majority.

Rule 101

TIME LIMITS

1. In making any order setting time limits regarding the conduct of any proceedings, the Court shall have regard to the need to facilitate fair and expeditious proceedings, bearing in mind in particular the rights of the defence and the victims.   **B2–102**

2. Taking into account the rights of the accused, in particular under article 67, paragraph (1) (c), all those participating in the proceedings to whom any order is directed shall endeavour to act as expeditiously as possible, within the time limit ordered by the Court.

Rule 102

COMMUNICATIONS OTHER THAN IN WRITING

Where a person is unable, due to a disability or illiteracy, to make a written request, application, observation or other communication to the Court, the person may make such request, application, observation or communication in audio, video or other electronic form.   **B2–103**

Rule 103

AMICUS CURIAE AND OTHER FORMS OF SUBMISSION

1. At any stage of the proceedings, a Chamber may, if it considers it desirable for the proper determination of the case, invite or grant leave to a State, organization or person to submit, in writing or orally, any observation on any issue that the Chamber deems appropriate.   **B2–104**

2. The Prosecutor and the defence shall have the opportunity to respond to the observations submitted under sub-rule 1.

3. A written observation submitted under sub-rule 1 shall be filed with the Registrar, who shall provide copies to the Prosecutor and the defence. The Chamber shall determine what time limits shall apply to the filing of such observations.

Chapter 5

INVESTIGATION AND PROSECUTION

Section I

Decision of the Prosecutor regarding the initiation of an investigation under article 53, paragraphs 1 and 2

Rule 104

EVALUATION OF INFORMATION BY THE PROSECUTOR

1. In acting pursuant to article 53, paragraph 1, the Prosecutor shall, in evaluating the information made available to him or her, analyse the seriousness of the information received.   **B2–105**

2. For the purposes of sub-rule 1, the Prosecutor may seek additional information from States, organs of the United Nations, intergovernmental and non-governmental organizations, or other reliable sources that he or she deems appropriate, and may receive written or oral testimony at the seat of the Court. The procedure set out in rule 47 shall apply to the receiving of such testimony.

RULE 105

NOTIFICATION OF A DECISION BY THE PROSECUTOR NOT TO INITIATE AN INVESTIGATION

B2–106   1. When the Prosecutor decides not to initiate an investigation under article 53, paragraph 1, he or she shall promptly inform in writing the State or States that referred a situation under article 14, or the Security Council in respect of a situation covered by article 13, paragraph (b).

2. When the Prosecutor decides not to submit to the Pre-Trial Chamber a request for authorization of an investigation, rule 49 shall apply.

3. The notification referred to in sub-rule 1 shall contain the conclusion of the Prosecutor and, having regard to article 68, paragraph 1, the reasons for the conclusion.

4. In case the Prosecutor decides not to investigate solely on the basis of article 53, paragraph 1 (c), he or she shall inform in writing the Pre-Trial Chamber promptly after making that decision.

5. The notification shall contain the conclusion of the Prosecutor and the reasons for the conclusion.

RULE 106

NOTIFICATION OF A DECISION BY THE PROSECUTOR NOT TO PROSECUTE

B2–107   1. When the Prosecutor decides that there is not a sufficient basis for prosecution under article 53, paragraph 2, he or she shall promptly inform in writing the Pre-Trial Chamber, together with the State or States that referred a situation under article 14, or the Security Council in respect of a situation covered by article 13, paragraph (b).

2. The notifications referred to in sub-rule 1 shall contain the conclusion of the Prosecutor and, having regard to article 68, paragraph 1, the reasons for the conclusion.

Section II

Procedure under article 53, paragraph 3

RULE 107

REQUEST FOR REVIEW UNDER ARTICLE 53, PARAGRAPH 3 (A)

B2–108   1. A request under article 53, paragraph 3, for a review of a decision by the Prosecutor not to initiate an investigation or not to prosecute shall be made in writing, and be supported with reasons, within 90 days following the notification given under rule 105 or 106.

2. The Pre-Trial Chamber may request the Prosecutor to transmit the information or documents in his or her possession, or summaries thereof, that the Chamber considers necessary for the conduct of the review.

3. The Pre-Trial Chamber shall take such measures as are necessary under articles 54, 72 and 93 to protect the information and documents referred to in sub-rule 2 and, under article 68, paragraph 5, to protect the safety of witnesses and victims and members of their families.

4. When a State or the Security Council makes a request referred to in sub-rule 1, the Pre-Trial Chamber may seek further observations from them.

5. Where an issue of jurisdiction or admissibility of the case is raised, rule 59 shall apply.

RULE 108

DECISION OF THE PRE-TRIAL CHAMBER UNDER ARTICLE 53, PARAGRAPH 3 (A)

1. A decision of the Pre-Trial Chamber under article 53, paragraph 3 (a), must be concurred in by a majority of its judges and shall contain reasons. It shall be communicated to all those who participated in the review.   **B2–109**

2. Where the Pre-Trial Chamber requests the Prosecutor to review, in whole or in part, his or her decision not to initiate an investigation or not to prosecute, the Prosecutor shall reconsider that decision as soon as possible.

3. Once the Prosecutor has taken a final decision, he or she shall notify the Pre-Trial Chamber in writing. This notification shall contain the conclusion of the Prosecutor and the reasons for the conclusion. It shall be communicated to all those who participated in the review.

RULE 109

REVIEW BY THE PRE-TRIAL CHAMBER UNDER ARTICLE 53, PARAGRAPH 3 (B)

1. Within 180 days following a notification given under rule 105 or 106, the Pre-Trial Chamber may on its own initiative decide to review a decision of the Prosecutor taken solely under article 53, paragraph 1 (c) or 2 (c). The Pre-Trial Chamber shall inform the Prosecutor of its intention to review his or her decision and shall establish a time limit within which the Prosecutor may submit observations and other material.   **B2–110**

2. In cases where a request has been submitted to the Pre-Trial Chamber by a State or by the Security Council, they shall also be informed and may submit observations in accordance with rule 107.

RULE 110

DECISION BY THE PRE-TRIAL CHAMBER UNDER ARTICLE 53, PARAGRAPH 3 (B)

1. A decision by the Pre-Trial Chamber to confirm or not to confirm a decision taken by the Prosecutor solely under article 53, paragraph 1 (c) or 2 (c), must be concurred in by a majority of its judges and shall contain reasons. It shall be communicated to all those who participated in the review.   **B2–111**

2. When the Pre-Trial Chamber does not confirm the decision by the Prosecutor referred to in sub-rule 1, he or she shall proceed with the investigation or prosecution.

Section III

COLLECTION OF EVIDENCE

RULE 111

RECORD OF QUESTIONING IN GENERAL

B2–112   1. A record shall be made of formal statements made by any person who is questioned in connection with an investigation or with proceedings. The record shall be signed by the person who records and conducts the questioning and by the person who is questioned and his or her counsel, if present, and, where applicable, the Prosecutor or the judge who is present. The record shall note the date, time and place of, and all persons present during the questioning. It shall also be noted when someone has not signed the record as well as the reasons therefor.

2. When the Prosecutor or national authorities question a person, due regard shall be given to article 55. When a person is informed of his or her rights under article 55, paragraph 2, the fact that this information has been provided shall be noted in the record.

RULE 112

RECORDING OF QUESTIONING IN PARTICULAR CASES

B2–113   1. Whenever the Prosecutor questions a person to whom article 55, paragraph 2, applies, or for whom a warrant of arrest or a summons to appear has been issued under article 58, paragraph 7, the questioning shall be audio- or video-recorded, in accordance with the following procedure:

    (a) The person questioned shall be informed, in a language he or she fully understands and speaks, that the questioning is to be audio- or video-recorded, and that the person concerned may object if he or she so wishes. The fact that this information has been provided and the response given by the person concerned shall be noted in the record. The person may, before replying, speak in private with his or her counsel, if present. If the person questioned refuses to be audio- or video-recorded, the procedure in rule 111 shall be followed;

    (b) A waiver of the right to be questioned in the presence of counsel shall be recorded in writing and, if possible, be audio- or video-recorded;

    (c) In the event of an interruption in the course of questioning, the fact and the time of the interruption shall be recorded before the audio- or video-recording ends as well as the time of resumption of the questioning;

    (d) At the conclusion of the questioning, the person questioned shall be offered the opportunity to clarify anything he or she has said and to add anything he or she may wish. The time of conclusion of the questioning shall be noted;

    (e) The tape shall be transcribed as soon as practicable after the conclusion of the questioning and a copy of the transcript supplied to the person questioned together with a copy of the recorded tape or, if multiple recording apparatus was used, one of the original recorded tapes;

    (f) The original tape or one of the original tapes shall be sealed in the presence of the person questioned and his or her counsel, if present, under the signature of the Prosecutor and the person questioned and the counsel, if present.

2. The Prosecutor shall make every reasonable effort to record the questioning in accordance with sub-rule 1. As an exception, a person may be questioned without the questioning being audio- or video-recorded where the circumstances prevent such recording taking place. In this case, the reasons for not recording the questioning shall be stated in writing and the procedure in rule 111 shall be followed.

3. When, pursuant to sub-rule 1 (a) or 2, the questioning is not audio- or video-recorded, the person questioned shall be provided with a copy of his or her statement.

4. The Prosecutor may choose to follow the procedure in this rule when questioning other persons than those mentioned in sub-rule 1, in particular where the use of such procedures could assist in reducing any subsequent traumatization of a victim of sexual or gender violence, a child or a person with disabilities in providing their evidence. The Prosecutor may make an application to the relevant Chamber.

5. The Pre-Trial Chamber may, in pursuance of article 56, paragraph 2, order that the procedure in this rule be applied to the questioning of any person.

RULE 113

COLLECTION OF INFORMATION REGARDING THE STATE OF HEALTH OF THE PERSON CONCERNED

1. The Pre-Trial Chamber may, on its own initiative or at the request of the **B2–114** Prosecutor, the person concerned or his or her counsel, order that a person having the rights in article 55, paragraph 2, be given a medical, psychological or psychiatric examination. In making its determination, the Pre-Trial Chamber shall consider the nature and purpose of the examination and whether the person consents to the examination.

2. The Pre-Trial Chamber shall appoint one or more experts from the list of experts approved by the Registrar, or an expert approved by the Pre-Trial Chamber at the request of a party.

RULE 114

UNIQUE INVESTIGATIVE OPPORTUNITY UNDER ARTICLE 56

1. Upon being advised by the Prosecutor in accordance with article 56, paragraph 1 **B2–115** (a), the Pre-Trial Chamber shall hold consultations without delay with the Prosecutor and, subject to the provisions of article 56, paragraph 1 (c), with the person who has been arrested or who has appeared before the Court pursuant to summons and his or her counsel, in order to determine the measures to be taken and the modalities of their implementation, which may include measures to ensure that the right to communicate under article 67, paragraph 1 (b), is protected.

2. A decision of the Pre-Trial Chamber to take measures pursuant to article 56, paragraph 3, must be concurred in by a majority of its judges after consultations with the Prosecutor. During the consultations, the Prosecutor may advise the Pre-Trial Chamber that intended measures could jeopardize the proper conduct of the investigation.

RULE 115

COLLECTION OF EVIDENCE IN THE TERRITORY OF A STATE PARTY UNDER ARTICLE 57, PARAGRAPH 3 (D)

1. Where the Prosecutor considers that article 57, paragraph 3 (d), applies, the **B2–116** Prosecutor may submit a written request to the Pre-Trial Chamber for authorization to take certain measures in the territory of the State Party in question. After a submission of such a request, the Pre-Trial Chamber shall, whenever possible, inform and invite views from the State Party concerned.

2. In arriving at its determination as to whether the request is well founded, the Pre-Trial Chamber shall take into account any views expressed by the State Party concerned.

The Pre-Trial Chamber may, on its own initiative or at the request of the Prosecutor or the State Party concerned, decide to hold a hearing.

3. An authorization under article 57, paragraph 3 (d), shall be issued in the form of an order and shall state the reasons, based on the criteria set forth in that paragraph. The order may specify procedures to be followed in carrying out such collection of evidence.

RULE 116

COLLECTION OF EVIDENCE AT THE REQUEST OF THE DEFENCE UNDER ARTICLE 57, PARAGRAPH 3 (B)

B2–117   1. The Pre-Trial Chamber shall issue an order or seek cooperation under article 57, paragraph 3 (b), where it is satisfied:

(a) That such an order would facilitate the collection of evidence that may be material to the proper determination of the issues being adjudicated, or to the proper preparation of the person's defence; and

(b) In a case of cooperation under Part 9, that sufficient information to comply with article 96, paragraph 2, has been provided.

2. Before taking a decision whether to issue an order or seek cooperation under article 57, paragraph 3 (b), the Pre-Trial Chamber may seek the views of the Prosecutor.

Section IV

Procedures in respect of restriction and deprivation of liberty

RULE 117

DETENTION IN THE CUSTODIAL STATE

B2–118   1. The Court shall take measures to ensure that it is informed of the arrest of a person in response to a request made by the Court under article 89 or 92. Once so informed, the Court shall ensure that the person receives a copy of the arrest warrant issued by the Pre-Trial Chamber under article 58 and any relevant provisions of the Statute. The documents shall be made available in a language that the person fully understands and speaks.

2. At any time after arrest, the person may make a request to the Pre-Trial Chamber for the appointment of counsel to assist with proceedings before the Court and the Pre-Trial Chamber shall take a decision on such request.

3. A challenge as to whether the warrant of arrest was properly issued in accordance with article 58, paragraph 1 (a) and (b), shall be made in writing to the Pre-Trial Chamber. The application shall set out the basis for the challenge. After having obtained the views of the Prosecutor, the Pre-Trial Chamber shall decide on the application without delay.

4. When the competent authority of the custodial State notifies the Pre-Trial Chamber that a request for release has been made by the person arrested, in accordance with article 59, paragraph 5, the Pre-Trial Chamber shall provide its recommendations within any time limit set by the custodial State.

5. When the Pre-Trial Chamber is informed that the person has been granted interim release by the competent authority of the custodial State, the Pre-Trial Chamber shall inform the custodial State how and when it would like to receive periodic reports on the status of the interim release.

Rule 118

PRE-TRIAL DETENTION AT THE SEAT OF THE COURT

1. If the person surrendered to the Court makes an initial request for interim release **B2–119** pending trial, either upon first appearance in accordance with rule 121 or subsequently, the Pre-Trial Chamber shall decide upon the request without delay, after seeking the views of the Prosecutor.

2. The Pre-Trial Chamber shall review its ruling on the release or detention of a person in accordance with article 60, paragraph 3, at least every 120 days and may do so at any time on the request of the person or the Prosecutor.

3. After the first appearance, a request for interim release must be made in writing. The Prosecutor shall be given notice of such a request. The Pre-Trial Chamber shall decide after having received observations in writing of the Prosecutor and the detained person. The Pre-Trial Chamber may decide to hold a hearing, at the request of the Prosecutor or the detained person or on its own initiative. A hearing must be held at least once every year.

Rule 119

CONDITIONAL RELEASE

1. The Pre-Trial Chamber may set one or more conditions restricting liberty, **B2–120** including the following:

   (a) The person must not travel beyond territorial limits set by the Pre-Trial Chamber without the explicit agreement of the Chamber;

   (b) The person must not go to certain places or associate with certain persons as specified by the Pre-Trial Chamber;

   (c) The person must not contact directly or indirectly victims or witnesses;

   (d) The person must not engage in certain professional activities;

   (e) The person must reside at a particular address as specified by the Pre-Trial Chamber;

   (f) The person must respond when summoned by an authority or qualified person designated by the Pre-Trial Chamber;

   (g) The person must post bond or provide real or personal security or surety, for which the amount and the schedule and mode of payment shall be determined by the Pre-Trial Chamber;

   (h) The person must supply the Registrar with all identity documents, particularly his or her passport.

2. At the request of the person concerned or the Prosecutor or on its own initiative, the Pre-Trial Chamber may at any time decide to amend the conditions set pursuant to sub-rule 1.

3. Before imposing or amending any conditions restricting liberty, the Pre-Trial Chamber shall seek the views of the Prosecutor, the person concerned, any relevant State and victims that have communicated with the Court in that case and whom the Chamber considers could be at risk as a result of a release or conditions imposed.

4. If the Pre-Trial Chamber is convinced that the person concerned has failed to comply with one or more of the obligations imposed, it may, on such basis, at the request of the Prosecutor or on its own initiative, issue a warrant of arrest in respect of the person.

5. When the Pre-Trial Chamber issues a summons to appear pursuant to article 58, paragraph 7, and intends to set conditions restricting liberty, it shall ascertain the relevant provisions of the national law of the State receiving the summons. In a manner that is in keeping with the national law of the State receiving the summons, the Pre-Trial Chamber shall proceed in accordance with sub-rules 1, 2 and 3. If the Pre-Trial Chamber receives information that the person concerned has failed to comply with conditions imposed, it shall proceed in accordance with sub-rule 4.

RULE 120

INSTRUMENTS OF RESTRAINT

B2–121   Personal instruments of restraint shall not be used except as a precaution against escape, for the protection of the person in the custody of the Court and others or for other security reasons, and shall be removed when the person appears before a Chamber.

Section V

Proceedings with regard to the confirmation of charges under article 61

RULE 121

PROCEEDINGS BEFORE THE CONFIRMATION HEARING

B2–122   1. A person subject to a warrant of arrest or a summons to appear under article 58 shall appear before the Pre-Trial Chamber, in the presence of the Prosecutor, promptly upon arriving at the Court. Subject to the provisions of articles 60 and 61, the person shall enjoy the rights set forth in article 67. At this first appearance, the Pre-Trial Chamber shall set the date on which it intends to hold a hearing to confirm the charges. It shall ensure that this date, and any postponements under sub-rule 7, are made public.

2. In accordance with article 61, paragraph 3, the Pre-Trial Chamber shall take the necessary decisions regarding disclosure between the Prosecutor and the person in respect of whom a warrant of arrest or a summons to appear has been issued. During disclosure:

(a) The person concerned may be assisted or represented by the counsel of his or her choice or by a counsel assigned to him or her;

(b) The Pre-Trial Chamber shall hold status conferences to ensure that disclosure takes place under satisfactory conditions. For each case, a judge of the Pre-Trial Chamber shall be appointed to organize such status conferences, on his or her own motion, or at the request of the Prosecutor or the person;

(c) All evidence disclosed between the Prosecutor and the person for the purposes of the confirmation hearing shall be communicated to the Pre-Trial Chamber.

3. The Prosecutor shall provide to the Pre-Trial Chamber and the person, no later than 30 days before the date of the confirmation hearing, a detailed description of the charges together with a list of the evidence which he or she intends to present at the hearing.

4. Where the Prosecutor intends to amend the charges pursuant to article 61, paragraph 4, he or she shall notify the Pre-Trial Chamber and the person no later than 15 days before the date of the hearing of the amended charges together with a list of evidence that the Prosecutor intends to bring in support of those charges at the hearing.

5. Where the Prosecutor intends to present new evidence at the hearing, he or she shall provide the Pre-Trial Chamber and the person with a list of that evidence no later than 15 days before the date of the hearing.

6. If the person intends to present evidence under article 61, paragraph 6, he or she shall provide a list of that evidence to the Pre-Trial Chamber no later than 15 days before the date of the hearing. The Pre-Trial Chamber shall transmit the list to the Prosecutor without delay. The person shall provide a list of evidence that he or she intends to present in response to any amended charges or a new list of evidence provided by the Prosecutor.

7. The Prosecutor or the person may ask the Pre-Trial Chamber to postpone the date of the confirmation hearing. The Pre-Trial Chamber may also, on its own motion, decide to postpone the hearing.

8. The Pre-Trial Chamber shall not take into consideration charges and evidence presented after the time limit, or any extension thereof, has expired.

9. The Prosecutor and the person may lodge written submissions with the Pre-Trial Chamber, on points of fact and on law, including grounds for excluding criminal responsibility set forth in article 31, paragraph 1, no later than three days before the date of the hearing. A copy of these submissions shall be transmitted immediately to the Prosecutor or the person, as the case may be.

10. The Registry shall create and maintain a full and accurate record of all proceedings before the Pre-Trial Chamber, including all documents transmitted to the Chamber pursuant to this rule. Subject to any restrictions concerning confidentiality and the protection of national security information, the record may be consulted by the Prosecutor, the person and victims or their legal representatives participating in the proceedings pursuant to rules 89 to 91.

RULE 122

PROCEEDINGS AT THE CONFIRMATION HEARING IN THE PRESENCE OF THE PERSON CHARGED

1. The Presiding Judge of the Pre-Trial Chamber shall ask the officer of the Registry **B2-123** assisting the Chamber to read out the charges as presented by the Prosecutor. The Presiding Judge shall determine how the hearing is to be conducted and, in particular, may establish the order and the conditions under which he or she intends the evidence contained in the record of the proceedings to be presented.

2. If a question or challenge concerning jurisdiction or admissibility arises, rule 58 applies.

3. Before hearing the matter on the merits, the Presiding Judge of the Pre-Trial Chamber shall ask the Prosecutor and the person whether they intend to raise objections or make observations concerning an issue related to the proper conduct of the proceedings prior to the confirmation hearing.

4. At no subsequent point may the objections and observations made under sub-rule 3 be raised or made again in the confirmation or trial proceedings.

5. If objections or observations referred to in sub-rule 3 are presented, the Presiding Judge of the Pre-Trial Chamber shall invite those referred to in sub-rule 3 to present their arguments, in the order which he or she shall establish. The person shall have the right to reply.

6. If the objections raised or observations made are those referred to in sub-rule 3, the Pre-Trial Chamber shall decide whether to join the issue raised with the examination of the charges and the evidence, or to separate them, in which case it shall adjourn the confirmation hearing and render a decision on the issues raised.

7. During the hearing on the merits, the Prosecutor and the person shall present their arguments in accordance with article 61, paragraphs 5 and 6.

8. The Pre-Trial Chamber shall permit the Prosecutor and the person, in that order, to make final observations.

9. Subject to the provisions of article 61, article 69 shall apply *mutatis mutandis* at the confirmation hearing.

RULE 123

MEASURES TO ENSURE THE PRESENCE OF THE PERSON CONCERNED AT THE CONFIRMATION HEARING

1. When a warrant of arrest or summons to appear in accordance with article 58, **B2-124** paragraph 7, has been issued for a person by the Pre-Trial Chamber and the person is arrested or served with the summons, the Pre-Trial Chamber shall ensure that the person is notified of the provisions of article 61, paragraph 2.

2. The Pre-Trial Chamber may hold consultations with the Prosecutor, at the request of the latter or on its own initiative, in order to determine whether there is cause to hold a hearing on confirmation of charges under the conditions set forth in article 61, paragraph 2 (b). When the person concerned has a counsel known to the Court, the consultations shall be held in the presence of the counsel unless the Pre-Trial Chamber decides otherwise.

3. The Pre-Trial Chamber shall ensure that a warrant of arrest for the person concerned has been issued and, if the warrant of arrest has not been executed within a reasonable period of time after the issuance of the warrant, that all reasonable measures have been taken to locate and arrest the person.

RULE 124

WAIVER OF THE RIGHT TO BE PRESENT AT THE CONFIRMATION HEARING

B2–125   1. If the person concerned is available to the Court but wishes to waive the right to be present at the hearing on confirmation of charges, he or she shall submit a written request to the Pre-Trial Chamber, which may then hold consultations with the Prosecutor and the person concerned, assisted or represented by his or her counsel.

2. A confirmation hearing pursuant to article 61, paragraph 2 (a), shall only be held when the Pre-Trial Chamber is satisfied that the person concerned understands the right to be present at the hearing and the consequences of waiving this right.

3. The Pre-Trial Chamber may authorize and make provision for the person to observe the hearing from outside the courtroom through the use of communications technology, if required.

4. The waiving of the right to be present at the hearing does not prevent the Pre-Trial Chamber from receiving written observations on issues before the Chamber from the person concerned.

RULE 125

DECISION TO HOLD THE CONFIRMATION HEARING IN THE ABSENCE OF THE PERSON CONCERNED

B2–126   1. After holding consultations under rules 123 and 124, the Pre-Trial Chamber shall decide whether there is cause to hold a hearing on confirmation of charges in the absence of the person concerned, and in that case, whether the person may be represented by counsel. The Pre-Trial Chamber shall, when appropriate, set a date for the hearing and make the date public.

2. The decision of the Pre-Trial Chamber shall be notified to the Prosecutor and, if possible, to the person concerned or his or her counsel.

3. If the Pre-Trial Chamber decides not to hold a hearing on confirmation of charges in the absence of the person concerned, and the person is not available to the Court, the confirmation of charges may not take place until the person is available to the Court. The Pre-Trial Chamber may review its decision at any time, at the request of the Prosecutor or on its own initiative.

4. If the Pre-Trial Chamber decides not to hold a hearing on confirmation of charges in the absence of the person concerned, and the person is available to the Court, it shall order the person to appear.

RULE 126

CONFIRMATION HEARING IN THE ABSENCE OF THE PERSON CONCERNED

B2–127   1. The provisions of rules 121 and 122 shall apply *mutatis mutandis* to the preparation for and holding of a hearing on confirmation of charges in the absence of the person concerned.

2. If the Pre-Trial Chamber has determined that the person concerned shall be represented by counsel, the counsel shall have the opportunity to exercise the rights of that person.

3. When the person who has fled is subsequently arrested and the Court has confirmed the charges upon which the Prosecutor intends to pursue the trial, the person charged shall be committed to the Trial Chamber established under article 61, paragraph 11. The person charged may request in writing that the Trial Chamber refer issues to the Pre-Trial Chamber that are necessary for the Chamber's effective and fair functioning in accordance with article 64, paragraph 4.

Section VI

Closure of the pre-trial phase

RULE 127

PROCEDURE IN THE EVENT OF DIFFERENT DECISIONS ON MULTIPLE CHARGES

If the Pre-Trial Chamber is ready to confirm some of the charges but adjourns the hearing on other charges under article 61, paragraph 7 (c), it may decide that the committal of the person concerned to the Trial Chamber on the charges that it is ready to confirm shall be deferred pending the continuation of the hearing. The Pre-Trial Chamber may then establish a time limit within which the Prosecutor may proceed in accordance with article 61, paragraph 7 (c) (i) or (ii).

B2–128

RULE 128

AMENDMENT OF THE CHARGES

1. If the Prosecutor seeks to amend charges already confirmed before the trial has begun, in accordance with article 61, the Prosecutor shall make a written request to the Pre-Trial Chamber, and that Chamber shall so notify the accused.

2. Before deciding whether to authorize the amendment, the Pre-Trial Chamber may request the accused and the Prosecutor to submit written observations on certain issues of fact or law.

3. If the Pre-Trial Chamber determines that the amendments proposed by the Prosecutor constitute additional or more serious charges, it shall proceed, as appropriate, in accordance with rules 121 and 122 or rules 123 to 126.

B2–129

RULE 129

NOTIFICATION OF THE DECISION ON THE CONFIRMATION OF CHARGES

The decision of the Pre-Trial Chamber on the confirmation of charges and the committal of the accused to the Trial Chamber shall be notified, if possible, to the Prosecutor, the person concerned and his or her counsel. Such decision and the record of the proceedings of the Pre-Trial Chamber shall be transmitted to the Presidency.

B2–130

RULE 130

CONSTITUTION OF THE TRIAL CHAMBER

When the Presidency constitutes a Trial Chamber and refers the case to it, the Presidency shall transmit the decision of the Pre-Trial Chamber and the record of the proceedings to the Trial Chamber. The Presidency may also refer the case to a previously constituted Trial Chamber.

B2–131

CHAPTER 6

TRIAL PROCEDURE

RULE 131

RECORD OF THE PROCEEDINGS TRANSMITTED BY THE PRE-TRIAL CHAMBER

B2–132   1. The Registrar shall maintain the record of the proceedings transmitted by the Pre-Trial Chamber, pursuant to rule 121, sub-rule 10.

2. Subject to any restrictions concerning confidentiality and the protection of national security information, the record may be consulted by the Prosecutor, the defence, the representatives of States when they participate in the proceedings, and the victims or their legal representatives participating in the proceedings pursuant to rules 89 to 91.

RULE 132

STATUS CONFERENCES

B2–133   1. Promptly after it is constituted, the Trial Chamber shall hold a status conference in order to set the date of the trial. The Trial Chamber, on its own motion, or at the request of the Prosecutor or the defence, may postpone the date of the trial. The Trial Chamber shall notify the trial date to all those participating in the proceedings. The Trial Chamber shall ensure that this date and any postponements are made public.

2. In order to facilitate the fair and expeditious conduct of the proceedings, the Trial Chamber may confer with the parties by holding status conferences as necessary.

RULE 133

MOTIONS CHALLENGING ADMISSIBILITY OR JURISDICTION

B2–134   Challenges to the jurisdiction of the Court or the admissibility of the case at the commencement of the trial, or subsequently with the leave of the Court, shall be dealt with by the Presiding Judge and the Trial Chamber in accordance with rule 58.

RULE 134

MOTIONS RELATING TO THE TRIAL PROCEEDINGS

B2–135   1. Prior to the commencement of the trial, the Trial Chamber on its own motion, or at the request of the Prosecutor or the defence, may rule on any issue concerning the conduct of the proceedings. Any request from the Prosecutor or the defence shall be in writing and, unless the request is for an ex parte procedure, served on the other party. For all requests other than those submitted for an ex parte procedure, the other party shall have the opportunity to file a response.

2. At the commencement of the trial, the Trial Chamber shall ask the Prosecutor and the defence whether they have any objections or observations concerning the conduct of the proceedings which have arisen since the confirmation hearings. Such objections or observations may not be raised or made again on a subsequent occasion in the trial proceedings, without leave of the Trial Chamber in this proceeding.

3. After the commencement of the trial, the Trial Chamber, on its own motion, or at the request of the Prosecutor or the defence, may rule on issues that arise during the course of the trial.

Rule 135

MEDICAL EXAMINATION OF THE ACCUSED

B2–136

1. The Trial Chamber may, for the purpose of discharging its obligations under article 64, paragraph 8 (a), or for any other reasons, or at the request of a party, order a medical, psychiatric or psychological examination of the accused, under the conditions set forth in rule 113.

2. The Trial Chamber shall place its reasons for any such order on the record.

3. The Trial Chamber shall appoint one or more experts from the list of experts approved by the Registrar, or an expert approved by the Trial Chamber at the request of a party.

4. Where the Trial Chamber is satisfied that the accused is unfit to stand trial, it shall order that the trial be adjourned. The Trial Chamber may, on its own motion or at the request of the prosecution or the defence, review the case of the accused. In any event, the case shall be reviewed every 120 days unless there are reasons to do otherwise. If necessary, the Trial Chamber may order further examinations of the accused. When the Trial Chamber is satisfied that the accused has become fit to stand trial, it shall proceed in accordance with rule 132.

Rule 136

JOINT AND SEPARATE TRIALS

B2–137

1. Persons accused jointly shall be tried together unless the Trial Chamber, on its own motion or at the request of the Prosecutor or the defence, orders that separate trials are necessary, in order to avoid serious prejudice to the accused, to protect the interests of justice or because a person jointly accused has made an admission of guilt and can be proceeded against in accordance with article 65, paragraph 2.

2. In joint trials, each accused shall be accorded the same rights as if such accused were being tried separately.

Rule 137

RECORD OF THE TRIAL PROCEEDINGS

B2–138

1. In accordance with article 64, paragraph 10, the Registrar shall take measures to make, and preserve, a full and accurate record of all proceedings, including transcripts, audio- and video-recordings and other means of capturing sound or image.

2. A Trial Chamber may order the disclosure of all or part of the record of closed proceedings when the reasons for ordering its non-disclosure no longer exist.

3. The Trial Chamber may authorize persons other than the Registrar to take photographs, audio- and video-recordings and other means of capturing the sound or image of the trial.

Rule 138

CUSTODY OF EVIDENCE

B2–139

The Registrar shall retain and preserve, as necessary, all the evidence and other materials offered during the hearing, subject to any order of the Trial Chamber.

RULE 139

DECISION ON ADMISSION OF GUILT

B2–140   1. After having proceeded in accordance with article 65, paragraph 1, the Trial Chamber, in order to decide whether to proceed in accordance with article 65, paragraph 4, may invite the views of the Prosecutor and the defence.

2. The Trial Chamber shall then make its decision on the admission of guilt and shall give reasons for this decision, which shall be placed on the record.

RULE 140

DIRECTIONS FOR THE CONDUCT OF THE PROCEEDINGS AND TESTIMONY

B2–141   1. If the Presiding Judge does not give directions under article 64, paragraph 8, the Prosecutor and the defence shall agree on the order and manner in which the evidence shall be submitted to the Trial Chamber. If no agreement can be reached, the Presiding Judge shall issue directions.

2. In all cases, subject to article 64, paragraphs 8 (b) and 9, article 69, paragraph 4, and rule 88, sub-rule 5, a witness may be questioned as follows:

  (a) A party that submits evidence in accordance with article 69, paragraph 3, by way of a witness, has the right to question that witness;

  (b) The prosecution and the defence have the right to question that witness about relevant matters related to the witness's testimony and its reliability, the credibility of the witness and other relevant matters;

  (c) The Trial Chamber has the right to question a witness before or after a witness is questioned by a participant referred to in sub-rules 2 (a) or (b);

  (d) The defence shall have the right to be the last to examine a witness.

3. Unless otherwise ordered by the Trial Chamber, a witness other than an expert, or an investigator if he or she has not yet testified, shall not be present when the testimony of another witness is given. However, a witness who has heard the testimony of another witness shall not for that reason alone be disqualified from testifying. When a witness testifies after hearing the testimony of others, this fact shall be noted in the record and considered by the Trial Chamber when evaluating the evidence.

RULE 141

CLOSURE OF EVIDENCE AND CLOSING STATEMENTS

B2–142   1. The Presiding Judge shall declare when the submission of evidence is closed.

2. The Presiding Judge shall invite the Prosecutor and the defence to make their closing statements. The defence shall always have the opportunity to speak last.

RULE 142

DELIBERATIONS

B2–143   1. After the closing statements, the Trial Chamber shall retire to deliberate, in camera. The Trial Chamber shall inform all those who participated in the proceedings of the date on which the Trial Chamber will pronounce its decision. The pronouncement shall be made within a reasonable period of time after the Trial Chamber has retired to deliberate.

2. When there is more than one charge, the Trial Chamber shall decide separately on each charge. When there is more than one accused, the Trial Chamber shall decide separately on the charges against each accused.

Rule 143

ADDITIONAL HEARINGS ON MATTERS RELATED TO SENTENCE OR REPARATIONS

Pursuant to article 76, paragraphs 2 and 3, for the purpose of holding a further **B2–144** hearing on matters related to sentence and, if applicable, reparations, the Presiding Judge shall set the date of the further hearing. This hearing can be postponed, in exceptional circumstances, by the Trial Chamber, on its own motion or at the request of the Prosecutor, the defence or the legal representatives of the victims participating in the proceedings pursuant to rules 89 to 91 and, in respect of reparations hearings, those victims who have made a request under rule 94.

Rule 144

DELIVERY OF THE DECISIONS OF THE TRIAL CHAMBER

1. Decisions of the Trial Chamber concerning admissibility of a case, the jurisdiction **B2–145** of the Court, criminal responsibility of the accused, sentence and reparations shall be pronounced in public and, wherever possible, in the presence of the accused, the Prosecutor, the victims or the legal representatives of the victims participating in the proceedings pursuant to rules 89 to 91, and the representatives of the States which have participated in the proceedings.
2. Copies of all the above-mentioned decisions shall be provided as soon as possible to:
   (a) All those who participated in the proceedings, in a working language of the Court;
   (b) The accused, in a language he or she fully understands or speaks, if necessary to meet the requirements of fairness under article 67, paragraph 1 (f).

Chapter 7

PENALTIES

Rule 145

DETERMINATION OF SENTENCE

1. In its determination of the sentence pursuant to article 78, paragraph 1, the Court **B2–146** shall:
   (a) Bear in mind that the totality of any sentence of imprisonment and fine, as the case may be, imposed under article 77 must reflect the culpability of the convicted person;
   (b) Balance all the relevant factors, including any mitigating and aggravating factors and consider the circumstances both of the convicted person and of the crime;
   (c) In addition to the factors mentioned in article 78, paragraph 1, give consideration, *inter alia*, to the extent of the damage caused, in particular the harm caused to the victims and their families, the nature of the unlawful behaviour and the means employed to execute the crime; the degree of participation of

the convicted person; the degree of intent; the circumstances of manner, time and location; and the age, education, social and economic condition of the convicted person.

2. In addition to the factors mentioned above, the Court shall take into account, as appropriate:

(a) Mitigating circumstances such as:

(i) The circumstances falling short of constituting grounds for exclusion of criminal responsibility, such as substantially diminished mental capacity or duress;

(ii) The convicted person's conduct after the act, including any efforts by the person to compensate the victims and any cooperation with the Court;

(b) As aggravating circumstances:

(i) Any relevant prior criminal convictions for crimes under the jurisdiction of the Court or of a similar nature;

(ii) Abuse of power or official capacity;

(iii) Commission of the crime where the victim is particularly defenceless;

(iv) Commission of the crime with particular cruelty or where there were multiple victims;

(v) Commission of the crime for any motive involving discrimination on any of the grounds referred to in article 21, paragraph 3;

(vi) Other circumstances which, although not enumerated above, by virtue of their nature are similar to those mentioned.

3. Life imprisonment may be imposed when justified by the extreme gravity of the crime and the individual circumstances of the convicted person, as evidenced by the existence of one or more aggravating circumstances.

RULE 146

IMPOSITION OF FINES UNDER ARTICLE 77

B2–147   1. In determining whether to order a fine under article 77, paragraph 2 (a), and in fixing the amount of the fine, the Court shall determine whether imprisonment is a sufficient penalty. The Court shall give due consideration to the financial capacity of the convicted person, including any orders for forfeiture in accordance with article 77, paragraph 2 (b), and, as appropriate, any orders for reparation in accordance with article 75. The Court shall take into account, in addition to the factors referred to in rule 145, whether and to what degree the crime was motivated by personal financial gain.

2. A fine imposed under article 77, paragraph 2 (a), shall be set at an appropriate level. To this end, the Court shall, in addition to the factors referred to above, in particular take into consideration the damage and injuries caused as well as the proportionate gains derived from the crime by the perpetrator. Under no circumstances may the total amount exceed 75 per cent of the value of the convicted person's identifiable assets, liquid or realizable, and property, after deduction of an appropriate amount that would satisfy the financial needs of the convicted person and his or her dependants.

3. In imposing a fine, the Court shall allow the convicted person a reasonable period in which to pay the fine. The Court may provide for payment of a lump sum or by way of instalments during that period.

4. In imposing a fine, the Court may, as an option, calculate it according to a system of daily fines. In such cases, the minimum duration shall be 30 days and the maximum duration five years. The Court shall decide the total amount in accordance with sub-rules 1 and 2. It shall determine the amount of daily payment in the light of the individual circumstances of the convicted person, including the financial needs of his or her dependants.

5. If the convicted person does not pay the fine imposed in accordance with the conditions set above, appropriate measures may be taken by the Court pursuant to rules 217 to 222 and in accordance with article 109. Where, in cases of continued wilful non-

payment, the Presidency, on its own motion or at the request of the Prosecutor, is satisfied that all available enforcement measures have been exhausted, it may as a last resort extend the term of imprisonment for a period not to exceed a quarter of such term or five years, whichever is less. In the determination of such period of extension, the Presidency shall take into account the amount of the fine, imposed and paid. Any such extension shall not apply in the case of life imprisonment. The extension may not lead to a total period of imprisonment in excess of 30 years.

6. In order to determine whether to order an extension and the period involved, the Presidency shall sit in camera for the purpose of obtaining the views of the sentenced person and the Prosecutor. The sentenced person shall have the right to be assisted by counsel.

7. In imposing a fine, the Court shall warn the convicted person that failure to pay the fine in accordance with the conditions set out above may result in an extension of the period of imprisonment as described in this rule.

RULE 147

ORDERS OF FORFEITURE

1. In accordance with article 76, paragraphs 2 and 3, and rules 63, sub-rule 1, and 143, at any hearing to consider an order of forfeiture, Chamber shall hear evidence as to the identification and location of specific proceeds, property or assets which have been derived directly or indirectly from the crime. **B2–148**

2. If before or during the hearing, a Chamber becomes aware of any bona fide third party who appears to have an interest in relevant proceeds, property or assets, it shall give notice to that third party.

3. The Prosecutor, the convicted person and any bona fide third party with an interest in the relevant proceeds, property or assets may submit evidence relevant to the issue.

4. After considering any evidence submitted, a Chamber may issue an order of forfeiture in relation to specific proceeds, property or assets if it is satisfied that these have been derived directly or indirectly from the crime.

RULE 148

ORDERS TO TRANSFER FINES OR FORFEITURES TO THE TRUST FUND

Before making an order pursuant to article 79, paragraph 2, a Chamber may request the representatives of the Fund to submit written or oral observations to it. **B2–149**

CHAPTER 8

APPEAL AND REVISION

Section I

General provisions

RULE 149

RULES GOVERNING PROCEEDINGS IN THE APPEALS CHAMBER

Parts 5 and 6 and rules governing proceedings and the submission of evidence in the Pre-Trial and Trial Chambers shall apply *mutatis mutandis* to proceedings in the Appeals Chamber. **B2–150**

Section II

Appeals against convictions, acquittals, sentences and reparation orders

RULE 150

APPEAL

B2–151   1. Subject to sub-rule 2, an appeal against a decision of conviction or acquittal under article 74, a sentence under article 76 or a reparation order under article 75 may be filed not later than 30 days from the date on which the party filing the appeal is notified of the decision, the sentence or the reparation order.

2. The Appeals Chamber may extend the time limit set out in sub-rule 1, for good cause, upon the application of the party seeking to file the appeal.

3. The appeal shall be filed with the Registrar.

4. If an appeal is not filed as set out in sub-rules 1 to 3, the decision, the sentence or the reparation order of the Trial Chamber shall become final.

RULE 151

PROCEDURE FOR THE APPEAL

B2–152   1. Upon the filing of an appeal under rule 150, the Registrar shall transmit the trial record to the Appeals Chamber.

2. The Registrar shall notify all parties who participated in the proceedings before the Trial Chamber that an appeal has been filed.

RULE 152

DISCONTINUANCE OF THE APPEAL

B2–153   1. Any party who has filed an appeal may discontinue the appeal at any time before judgement has been delivered. In such case, the party shall file with the Registrar a written notice of discontinuance of appeal. The Registrar shall inform the other parties that such a notice has been filed.

2. If the Prosecutor has filed an appeal on behalf of a convicted person in accordance with article 81, paragraph 1 (b), before filing any notice of discontinuance, the Prosecutor shall inform the convicted person that he or she intends to discontinue the appeal in order to give him or her the opportunity to continue the appeal proceedings.

RULE 153

JUDGEMENT ON APPEALS AGAINST REPARATION ORDERS

B2–154   1. The Appeals Chamber may confirm, reverse or amend a reparation order made under article 75.

2. The judgement of the Appeals Chamber shall be delivered in accordance with article 83, paragraphs 4 and 5.

Section III

Appeals against other decisions

RULE 154

APPEALS THAT DO NOT REQUIRE THE LEAVE OF THE COURT

B2–155   1. An appeal may be filed under article 81, paragraph 3 (c) (ii), or article 82, paragraph 1 (a) or (b), not later than five days from the date upon which the party filing the appeal is notified of the decision.

2. An appeal may be filed under article 82, paragraph 1 (c), not later than two days from the date upon which the party filing the appeal is notified of the decision.

3. Rule 150, sub-rules 3 and 4, shall apply to appeals filed under sub-rules 1 and 2 of this rule.

Rule 155

APPEALS THAT REQUIRE LEAVE OF THE COURT

1. When a party wishes to appeal a decision under article 82, paragraph 1 (d), or **B2–156** article 82, paragraph 2, that party shall, within five days of being notified of that decision, make a written application to the Chamber that gave the decision, setting out the reasons for the request for leave to appeal.

2. The Chamber shall render a decision and shall notify all parties who participated in the proceedings that gave rise to the decision referred to in sub-rule 1.

Rule 156

PROCEDURE FOR THE APPEAL

1. As soon as an appeal has been filed under rule 154 or as soon as leave to appeal has **B2–157** been granted under rule 155, the Registrar shall transmit to the Appeals Chamber the record of the proceedings of the Chamber that made the decision that is the subject of the appeal.

2. The Registrar shall give notice of the appeal to all parties who participated in the proceedings before the Chamber that gave the decision that is the subject of the appeal, unless they have already been notified by the Chamber under rule 155, sub-rule 2.

3. The appeal proceedings shall be in writing unless the Appeals Chamber decides to convene a hearing.

4. The appeal shall be heard as expeditiously as possible.

5. When filing the appeal, the party appealing may request that the appeal have suspensive effect in accordance with article 82, paragraph 3.

Rule 157

DISCONTINUANCE OF THE APPEAL

Any party who has filed an appeal under rule 154 or who has obtained the leave of a **B2–158** Chamber to appeal a decision under rule 155 may discontinue the appeal at any time before judgement has been delivered. In such case, the party shall file with the Registrar a written notice of discontinuance of appeal. The Registrar shall inform the other parties that such a notice has been filed.

Rule 158

JUDGEMENT ON THE APPEAL

1. An Appeals Chamber which considers an appeal referred to in this section may **B2–159** confirm, reverse or amend the decision appealed.

2. The judgement of the Appeals Chamber shall be delivered in accordance with article 83, paragraph 4.

Section IV

Revision of conviction or sentence

RULE 159

APPLICATION FOR REVISION

B2–160   1. An application for revision provided for in article 84, paragraph 1, shall be in writing and shall set out the grounds on which the revision is sought. It shall as far as possible be accompanied by supporting material.

2. The determination on whether the application is meritorious shall be taken by a majority of the judges of the Appeals Chamber and shall be supported by reasons in writing.

3. Notification of the decision shall be sent to the applicant and, as far as possible, to all the parties who participated in the proceedings related to the initial decision.

RULE 160

TRANSFER FOR THE PURPOSE OF REVISION

B2–161   1. For the conduct of the hearing provided for in rule 161, the relevant Chamber shall issue its order sufficiently in advance to enable the transfer of the sentenced person to the seat of the Court, as appropriate.

2. The determination of the Court shall be communicated without delay to the State of enforcement.

3. The provisions of rule 206, sub-rule 3, shall be applicable.

RULE 161

DETERMINATION ON REVISION

B2–162   1. On a date which it shall determine and shall communicate to the applicant and to all those having received notification under rule 159, sub-rule 3, the relevant Chamber shall hold a hearing to determine whether the conviction or sentence should be revised.

2. For the conduct of the hearing, the relevant Chamber shall exercise, *mutatis mutandis*, all the powers of the Trial Chamber pursuant to Part 6 and the rules governing proceedings and the submission of evidence in the Pre-Trial and Trial Chambers.

3. The determination on revision shall be governed by the applicable provisions of article 83, paragraph 4.

CHAPTER 9

OFFENCES AND MISCONDUCT AGAINST THE COURT

Section I

Offences against the administration of justice under article 70

RULE 162

EXERCISE OF JURISDICTION

B2–163   1. Before deciding whether to exercise jurisdiction, the Court may consult with States Parties that may have jurisdiction over the offence.

2. In making a decision whether or not to exercise jurisdiction, the Court may consider, in particular:

(a) The availability and effectiveness of prosecution in a State Party;
(b) The seriousness of an offence;
(c) The possible joinder of charges under article 70 with charges under articles 5 to 8;
(d) The need to expedite proceedings;
(e) Links with an ongoing investigation or a trial before the Court; and
(f) Evidentiary considerations.

3. The Court shall give favourable consideration to a request from the host State for a waiver of the power of the Court to exercise jurisdiction in cases where the host State considers such a waiver to be of particular importance.

4. If the Court decides not to exercise its jurisdiction, it may request a State Party to exercise jurisdiction pursuant to article 70, paragraph 4.

Rule 163

APPLICATION OF THE STATUTE AND THE RULES

1. Unless otherwise provided in sub-rules 2 and 3, rule 162 and rules 164 to 169, the Statute and the Rules shall apply *mutatis mutandis* to the Court's investigation, prosecution and punishment of offences defined in article 70.

B2–164

2. The provisions of Part 2, and any rules thereunder, shall not apply, with the exception of article 21.

3. The provisions of Part 10, and any rules thereunder, shall not apply, with the exception of articles 103, 107, 109 and 111.

Rule 164

PERIODS OF LIMITATION

1. If the Court exercises jurisdiction in accordance with rule 162, it shall apply the periods of limitation set forth in this rule.

B2–165

2. Offences defined in article 70 shall be subject to a period of limitation of five years from the date on which the offence was committed, provided that during this period no investigation or prosecution has been initiated. The period of limitation shall be interrupted if an investigation or prosecution has been initiated during this period, either before the Court or by a State Party with jurisdiction over the case pursuant to article 70, paragraph 4 (a).

3. Enforcement of sanctions imposed with respect to offences defined in article 70 shall be subject to a period of limitation of 10 years from the date on which the sanction has become final. The period of limitation shall be interrupted with the detention of the convicted person or while the person concerned is outside the territory of the States Parties.

Rule 165

INVESTIGATION, PROSECUTION AND TRIAL

1. The Prosecutor may initiate and conduct investigations with respect to the offences defined in article 70 on his or her own initiative, on the basis of information communicated by a Chamber or any reliable source.

B2–166

2. Articles 53 and 59, and any rules thereunder, shall not apply.

3. For purposes of article 61, the Pre-Trial Chamber may make any of the determinations set forth in that article on the basis of written submissions, without a hearing, unless the interests of justice otherwise require.

4. A Trial Chamber may, as appropriate and taking into account the rights of the defence, direct that there be joinder of charges under article 70 with charges under articles 5 to 8.

RULE 166

SANCTIONS UNDER ARTICLE 70

B2–167   1. If the Court imposes sanctions with respect to article 70, this rule shall apply.

2. Article 77, and any rules thereunder, shall not apply, with the exception of an order of forfeiture under article 77, paragraph 2 (b), which may be ordered in addition to imprisonment or a fine or both.

3. Each offence may be separately fined and those fines may be cumulative. Under no circumstances may the total amount exceed 50 per cent of the value of the convicted person's identifiable assets, liquid or realizable, and property, after deduction of an appropriate amount that would satisfy the financial needs of the convicted person and his or her dependants.

4. In imposing a fine the Court shall allow the convicted person a reasonable period in which to pay the fine. The Court may provide for payment of a lump sum or by way of instalments during that period.

5. If the convicted person does not pay a fine imposed in accordance with the conditions set forth in sub-rule 4, appropriate measures may be taken by the Court pursuant to rules 217 to 222 and in accordance with article 109. Where, in cases of continued wilful non-payment, the Court, on its own motion or at the request of the Prosecutor, is satisfied that all available enforcement measures have been exhausted, it may as a last resort impose a term of imprisonment in accordance with article 70, paragraph 3. In the determination of such term of imprisonment, the Court shall take into account the amount of fine paid.

RULE 167

INTERNATIONAL COOPERATION AND JUDICIAL ASSISTANCE

B2–168   1. With regard to offences under article 70, the Court may request a State to provide any form of international cooperation or judicial assistance corresponding to those forms set forth in Part 9. In any such request, the Court shall indicate that the basis for the request is an investigation or prosecution of offences under article 70.

2. The conditions for providing international cooperation or judicial assistance to the Court with respect to offences under article 70 shall be those set forth in article 70, paragraph 2.

RULE 168

NE BIS IN IDEM

B2–169   In respect of offences under article 70, no person shall be tried before the Court with respect to conduct which formed the basis of an offence for which the person has already been convicted or acquitted by the Court or another court.

RULE 169

IMMEDIATE ARREST

B2–170   In the case of an alleged offence under article 70 committed in the presence of a Chamber, the Prosecutor may orally request that Chamber to order the immediate arrest of the person concerned.

Section II

Misconduct before the Court under article 71

RULE 170

DISRUPTION OF PROCEEDINGS

Having regard to article 63, paragraph 2, the Presiding Judge of the Chamber dealing **B2–171**
with the matter may, after giving a warning:
  (a) Order a person disrupting the proceedings of the Court to leave or be removed
    from the courtroom; or,
  (b) In case of repeated misconduct, order the interdiction of that person from
    attending the proceedings.

RULE 171

REFUSAL TO COMPLY WITH A DIRECTION BY THE COURT

1. When the misconduct consists of deliberate refusal to comply with an oral or **B2–172**
written direction by the Court, not covered by rule 170, and that direction is
accompanied by a warning of sanctions in case of breach, the Presiding Judge of the
Chamber dealing with the matter may order the interdiction of that person from the
proceedings for a period not exceeding 30 days or, if the misconduct is of a more serious
nature, impose a fine.

2. If the person committing misconduct as described in sub-rule 1 is an official of the
Court, or a defence counsel, or a legal representative of victims, the Presiding Judge of
the Chamber dealing with the matter may also order the interdiction of that person
from exercising his or her functions before the Court for a period not exceeding 30 days.

3. If the Presiding Judge in cases under sub-rules 1 and 2 considers that a longer
period of interdiction is appropriate, the Presiding Judge shall refer the matter to the
Presidency, which may hold a hearing to determine whether to order a longer or
permanent period of interdiction.

4. A fine imposed under sub-rule 1 shall not exceed 2,000 euros, or the equivalent
amount in any currency, provided that in cases of continuing misconduct, a new fine may
be imposed on each day that the misconduct continues, and such fines shall be
cumulative.

5. The person concerned shall be given an opportunity to be heard before a sanction
for misconduct, as described in this rule, is imposed.

RULE 172

CONDUCT COVERED BY BOTH ARTICLES 70 AND 71

If conduct covered by article 71 also constitutes one of the offences defined in article **B2–173**
70, the Court shall proceed in accordance with article 70 and rules 162 to 169.

CHAPTER 10

COMPENSATION TO AN ARRESTED OR CONVICTED PERSON

RULE 173

REQUEST FOR COMPENSATION

1. Anyone seeking compensation on any of the grounds indicated in article 85 shall **B2–174**
submit a request, in writing, to the Presidency, which shall designate a Chamber
composed of three judges to consider the request. These judges shall not have

participated in any earlier judgement of the Court regarding the person making the request.

2. The request for compensation shall be submitted not later than six months from the date the person making the request was notified of the decision of the Court concerning:

    (a) The unlawfulness of the arrest or detention under article 85, paragraph 1;

    (b) The reversal of the conviction under article 85, paragraph 2;

    (c) The existence of a grave and manifest miscarriage of justice under article 85, paragraph 3.

3. The request shall contain the grounds and the amount of compensation requested.

4. The person requesting compensation shall be entitled to legal assistance.

RULE 174

PROCEDURE FOR SEEKING COMPENSATION

B2–175   1. A request for compensation and any other written observation by the person filing the request shall be transmitted to the Prosecutor, who shall have an opportunity to respond in writing. Any observations by the Prosecutor shall be notified to the person filing the request.

2. The Chamber designated under rule 173, sub-rule 1, may either hold a hearing or determine the matter on the basis of the request and any written observations by the Prosecutor and the person filing the request. A hearing shall be held if the Prosecutor or the person seeking compensation so requests.

3. The decision shall be taken by the majority of the judges. The decision shall be notified to the Prosecutor and to the person filing the request.

RULE 175

AMOUNT OF COMPENSATION

B2–176   In establishing the amount of any compensation in conformity with article 85, paragraph 3, the Chamber designated under rule 173, sub-rule 1, shall take into consideration the consequences of the grave and manifest miscarriage of justice on the personal, family, social and professional situation of the person filing the request.

CHAPTER 11

INTERNATIONAL COOPERATION AND JUDICIAL ASSISTANCE

Section I

Requests for cooperation under article 87

RULE 176

ORGANS OF THE COURT RESPONSIBLE FOR THE TRANSMISSION AND RECEIPT OF ANY COMMUNICATIONS RELATING TO INTERNATIONAL COOPERATION AND JUDICIAL ASSISTANCE

B2–177   1. Upon and subsequent to the establishment of the Court, the Registrar shall obtain from the Secretary-General of the United Nations any communication made by States pursuant to article 87, paragraphs 1 (a) and 2.

2. The Registrar shall transmit the requests for cooperation made by the Chambers and shall receive the responses, information and documents from requested States. The Office of the Prosecutor shall transmit the requests for cooperation made by the Prosecutor and shall receive the responses, information and documents from requested States.

3. The Registrar shall be the recipient of any communication from States concerning subsequent changes in the designation of the national channels charged with receiving requests for cooperation, as well as of any change in the language in which requests for cooperation should be made, and shall, upon request, make such information available to States Parties as may be appropriate.

4. The provisions of sub-rule 2 are applicable *mutatis mutandis* where the Court requests information, documents or other forms of cooperation and assistance from an intergovernmental organization.

5. The Registrar shall transmit any communications referred to in sub-rules 1 and 3 and rule 177, sub-rule 2, as appropriate, to the Presidency or the Office of the Prosecutor, or both.

Rule 177

CHANNELS OF COMMUNICATION

1. Communications concerning the national authority charged with receiving requests for cooperation made upon ratification, acceptance, approval or accession shall provide all relevant information about such authorities. **B2–178**

2. When an intergovernmental organization is asked to assist the Court under article 87, paragraph 6, the Registrar shall, when necessary, ascertain its designated channel of communication and obtain all relevant information relating thereto.

Rule 178

LANGUAGE CHOSEN BY STATES PARTIES UNDER ARTICLE 87, PARAGRAPH 2

1. When a requested State Party has more than one official language, it may indicate upon ratification, acceptance, approval or accession that requests for cooperation and any supporting documents can be drafted in any one of its official languages. **B2–179**

2. When the requested State Party has not chosen a language for communication with the Court upon ratification, acceptance, accession or approval, the request for cooperation shall either be in or be accompanied by a translation into one of the working languages of the Court pursuant to article 87, paragraph 2.

Rule 179

LANGUAGE OF REQUESTS DIRECTED TO STATES NOT PARTY TO THE STATUTE

When a State not party to the Statute has agreed to provide assistance to the Court under article 87, paragraph 5, and has not made a choice of language for such requests, the requests for cooperation shall either be in or be accompanied by a translation into one of the working languages of the Court. **B2–180**

Rule 180

CHANGES IN THE CHANNELS OF COMMUNICATION OR THE LANGUAGES OF REQUESTS FOR COOPERATION

1. Changes concerning the channel of communication or the language a State has chosen under article 87, paragraph 2, shall be communicated in writing to the Registrar at the earliest opportunity. **B2–181**

2. Such changes shall take effect in respect of requests for cooperation made by the Court at a time agreed between the Court and the State or, in the absence of such an agreement, 45 days after the Court has received the communication and, in all cases, without prejudice to current requests or requests in progress.

Section II

Surrender, transit and competing requests under articles 89 and 90

RULE 181

CHALLENGE TO ADMISSIBILITY OF A CASE BEFORE A NATIONAL COURT

B2–182 When a situation described in article 89, paragraph 2, arises, and without prejudice to the provisions of article 19 and of rules 58 to 62 on procedures applicable to challenges to the jurisdiction of the Court or the admissibility of a case, the Chamber dealing with the case, if the admissibility ruling is still pending, shall take steps to obtain from the requested State all the relevant information about the *nebis in idem* challenge brought by the person.

RULE 182

REQUEST FOR TRANSIT UNDER ARTICLE 89, PARAGRAPH 3 (E)

B2–183 1. In situations described in article 89, paragraph 3 (e), the Court may transmit the request for transit by any medium capable of delivering a written record.

2. When the time limit provided for in article 89, paragraph 3 (e), has expired and the person concerned has been released, such a release is without prejudice to a subsequent arrest of the person in accordance with the provisions of article 89 or article 92.

RULE 183

POSSIBLE TEMPORARY SURRENDER

B2–184 Following the consultations referred to in article 89, paragraph 4, the requested State may temporarily surrender the person sought in accordance with conditions determined between the requested State and the Court. In such case the person shall be kept in custody during his or her presence before the Court and shall be transferred to the requested State once his or her presence before the Court is no longer required, at the latest when the proceedings have been completed.

RULE 184

ARRANGEMENTS FOR SURRENDER

B2–185 1. The requested State shall immediately inform the Registrar when the person sought by the Court is available for surrender.

2. The person shall be surrendered to the Court by the date and in the manner agreed upon between the authorities of the requested State and the Registrar.

3. If circumstances prevent the surrender of the person by the date agreed, the authorities of the requested State and the Registrar shall agree upon a new date and manner by which the person shall be surrendered.

4. The Registrar shall maintain contact with the authorities of the host State in relation to the arrangements for the surrender of the person to the Court.

Rule 185

RELEASE OF A PERSON FROM THE CUSTODY OF THE COURT OTHER THAN UPON

COMPLETION OF SENTENCE

1. Subject to sub-rule 2, where a person surrendered to the Court is released from the **B2–186** custody of the Court because the Court does not have jurisdiction, the case is inadmissible under article 17, paragraph 1 (b), (c) or (d), the charges have not been confirmed under article 61, the person has been acquitted at trial or on appeal, or for any other reason, the Court shall, as soon as possible, make such arrangements as it considers appropriate for the transfer of the person, taking into account the views of the person, to a State which is obliged to receive him or her, to another State which agrees to receive him or her, or to a State which has requested his or her extradition with the consent of the original surrendering State. In this case, the host State shall facilitate the transfer in accordance with the agreement referred to in article 3, paragraph 2, and the related arrangements.

2. Where the Court has determined that the case is inadmissible under article 17, paragraph 1 (a), the Court shall make arrangements, as appropriate, for the transfer of the person to a State whose investigation or prosecution has formed the basis of the successful challenge to admissibility, unless the State that originally surrendered the person requests his or her return.

Rule 186

COMPETING REQUESTS IN THE CONTEXT OF A CHALLENGE TO THE ADMISSIBILITY OF THE CASE

In situations described in article 90, paragraph 8, the requested State shall provide the **B2–187** notification of its decision to the Prosecutor in order to enable him or her to act in accordance with article 19, paragraph 10.

Section III

Documents for arrest and surrender under articles 91 and 92

Rule 187

TRANSLATION OF DOCUMENTS ACCOMPANYING REQUEST FOR SURRENDER

For the purposes of article 67, paragraph 1 (a), and in accordance with rule 117, sub- **B2–188** rule 1, the request under article 91 shall be accompanied, as appropriate, by a translation of the warrant of arrest or of the judgement of conviction and by a translation of the text of any relevant provisions of the Statute, in a language that the person fully understands and speaks.

RULE 188

TIME LIMIT FOR SUBMISSION OF DOCUMENTS AFTER PROVISIONAL ARREST

B2–189   For the purposes of article 92, paragraph 3, the time limit for receipt by the requested State of the request for surrender and the documents supporting the request shall be 60 days from the date of the provisional arrest.

RULE 189

TRANSMISSION OF DOCUMENTS SUPPORTING THE REQUEST

B2–190   When a person has consented to surrender in accordance with the provisions of article 92, paragraph 3, and the requested State proceeds to surrender the person to the Court, the Court shall not be required to provide the documents described in article 91 unless the requested State indicates otherwise.

Section IV

Cooperation under article 93

RULE 190

INSTRUCTION ON SELF-INCRIMINATION ACCOMPANYING REQUEST FOR WITNESS

B2–191   When making a request under article 93, paragraph 1 (e), with respect to a witness, the Court shall annex an instruction, concerning rule 74 relating to self-incrimination, to be provided to the witness in question, in a language that the person fully understands and speaks.

RULE 191

ASSURANCE PROVIDED BY THE COURT UNDER ARTICLE 93, PARAGRAPH 2

B2–192   The Chamber dealing with the case, on its own motion or at the request of the Prosecutor, defence or witness or expert concerned, may decide, after taking into account the views of the Prosecutor and the witness or expert concerned, to provide the assurance described in article 93, paragraph 2.

RULE 192

TRANSFER OF A PERSON IN CUSTODY

B2–193   1. Transfer of a person in custody to the Court in accordance with article 93, paragraph 7, shall be arranged by the national authorities concerned in liaison with the Registrar and the authorities of the host State.

2. The Registrar shall ensure the proper conduct of the transfer, including the supervision of the person while in the custody of the Court.

3. The person in custody before the Court shall have the right to raise matters concerning the conditions of his or her detention with the relevant Chamber.

4. In accordance with article 93, paragraph 7 (b), when the purposes of the transfer have been fulfilled, the Registrar shall arrange for the return of the person in custody to the requested State.

Rule 193

TEMPORARY TRANSFER OF THE PERSON FROM THE STATE OF ENFORCEMENT

1. The Chamber that is considering the case may order the temporary transfer from **B2–194** the State of enforcement to the seat of the Court of any person sentenced by the Court whose testimony or other assistance is necessary to the Court. The provisions of article 93, paragraph 7, shall not apply.

2. The Registrar shall ensure the proper conduct of the transfer, in liaison with the authorities of the State of enforcement and the authorities of the host State. When the purposes of the transfer have been fulfilled, the Court shall return the sentenced person to the State of enforcement.

3. The person shall be kept in custody during his or her presence before the Court. The entire period of detention spent at the seat of the Court shall be deducted from the sentence remaining to be served.

Rule 194

COOPERATION REQUESTED FROM THE COURT

1. In accordance with article 93, paragraph 10, and consistent with article 96, mutatis **B2–195** mutandis, a State may transmit to the Court a request for cooperation or assistance to the Court, either in or accompanied by a translation into one of the working languages of the Court.

2. Requests described in sub-rule 1 are to be sent to the Registrar, which shall transmit them, as appropriate, either to the Prosecutor or to the Chamber concerned.

3. If protective measures within the meaning of article 68 have been adopted, the Prosecutor or Chamber, as appropriate, shall consider the views of the Chamber which ordered the measures as well as those of the relevant victim or witness, before deciding on the request.

4. If the request relates to documents or evidence as described in article 93, paragraph 10 (b) (ii), the Prosecutor or Chamber, as appropriate, shall obtain the written consent of the relevant State before proceeding with the request.

5. When the Court decides to grant the request for cooperation or assistance from a State, the request shall be executed, insofar as possible, following any procedure outlined therein by the requesting State and permitting persons specified in the request to be present.

Section V

Cooperation under article 98

Rule 195

PROVISION OF INFORMATION

1. When a requested State notifies the Court that a request for surrender or **B2–196** assistance raises a problem of execution in respect of article 98, the requested State shall provide any information relevant to assist the Court in the application of article 98. Any

concerned third State or sending State may provide additional information to assist the Court.

2. The Court may not proceed with a request for the surrender of a person without the consent of a sending State if, under article 98, paragraph 2, such a request would be inconsistent with obligations under an international agreement pursuant to which the consent of a sending State is required prior to the surrender of a person of that State to the Court.

Section VI

Rule of speciality under article 101

RULE 196

PROVISION OF VIEWS ON ARTICLE 101, PARAGRAPH 1

B2–197   A person surrendered to the Court may provide views on a perceived violation of the provisions of article 101, paragraph 1.

RULE 197

EXTENSION OF THE SURRENDER

B2–198   When the Court has requested a waiver of the requirements of article 101, paragraph 1, the requested State may ask the Court to obtain and provide the views of the person surrendered to the Court.

CHAPTER 12

ENFORCEMENT

Section I

Role of States in enforcement of sentences of imprisonment and change in designation of State of enforcement under articles 103 and 104

RULE 198

COMMUNICATIONS BETWEEN THE COURT AND STATES

B2–199   Unless the context otherwise requires, article 87 and rules 176 to 180 shall apply, as appropriate, to communications between the Court and a State on matters relating to enforcement of sentences.

RULE 199

ORGAN RESPONSIBLE UNDER PART 10

B2–200   Unless provided otherwise in the Rules, the functions of the Court under Part 10 shall be exercised by the Presidency.

RULE 200

LIST OF STATES OF ENFORCEMENT

1. A list of States that have indicated their willingness to accept sentenced persons **B2–201**
shall be established and maintained by the Registrar.

2. The Presidency shall not include a State on the list provided for in article 103,
paragraph 1 (a), if it does not agree with the conditions that such a State attaches to its
acceptance. The Presidency may request any additional information from that State
prior to taking a decision.

3. A State that has attached conditions of acceptance may at any time withdraw such
conditions. Any amendments or additions to such conditions shall be subject to
confirmation by the Presidency.

4. A State may at any time inform the Registrar of its withdrawal from the list. Such
withdrawal shall not affect the enforcement of the sentences in respect of persons that
the State has already accepted.

5. The Court may enter bilateral arrangements with States with a view to establishing
a framework for the acceptance of prisoners sentenced by the Court. Such arrangements
shall be consistent with the Statute.

RULE 201

PRINCIPLES OF EQUITABLE DISTRIBUTION

Principles of equitable distribution for purposes of article 103, paragraph 3, shall **B2–202**
include:
  (a) The principle of equitable geographical distribution;
  (b) The need to afford each State on the list an opportunity to receive sentenced
      persons;
  (c) The number of sentenced persons already received by that State and other
      States of enforcement;
  (d) Any other relevant factors.

RULE 202

TIMING OF DELIVERY OF THE SENTENCED PERSON TO
THE STATE OF ENFORCEMENT

The delivery of a sentenced person from the Court to the designated State of **B2–203**
enforcement shall not take place unless the decision on the conviction and the decision
on the sentence have become final.

RULE 203

VIEWS OF THE SENTENCED PERSON

1. The Presidency shall give notice in writing to the sentenced person that it is **B2–204**
addressing the designation of a State of enforcement. The sentenced person shall, within
such time limit as the Presidency shall prescribe, submit in writing his or her views on
the question to the Presidency.

2. The Presidency may allow the sentenced person to make oral presentations.

3. The Presidency shall allow the sentenced person:
  (a) To be assisted, as appropriate, by a competent interpreter and to benefit from
      any translation necessary for the presentation of his or her views;

(b) To be granted adequate time and facilities necessary to prepare for the presentation of his or her views.

RULE 204

INFORMATION RELATING TO DESIGNATION

B2–205   When the Presidency notifies the designated State of its decision, it shall also transmit the following information and documents:
  (a) The name, nationality, date and place of birth of the sentenced person;
  (b) A copy of the final judgement of conviction and of the sentence imposed;
  (c) The length and commencement date of the sentence and the time remaining to be served;
  (d) After having heard the views of the sentenced person, any necessary information concerning the state of his or her health, including any medical treatment that he or she is receiving.

RULE 205

REJECTION OF DESIGNATION IN A PARTICULAR CASE

B2–206   Where a State in a particular case rejects the designation by the Presidency, the Presidency may designate another State.

RULE 206

DELIVERY OF THE SENTENCED PERSON TO THE STATE OF ENFORCEMENT

B2–207   1. The Registrar shall inform the Prosecutor and the sentenced person of the State designated to enforce the sentence.
   2. The sentenced person shall be delivered to the State of enforcement as soon as possible after the designated State of enforcement accepts.
   3. The Registrar shall ensure the proper conduct of the delivery of the person in consultation with the authorities of the State of enforcement and the host State.

RULE 207

TRANSIT

B2–208   1. No authorization is required if the sentenced person is transported by air and no landing is scheduled on the territory of the transit State. If an unscheduled landing occurs on the territory of the transit State, that State shall, to the extent possible under the procedure of national law, detain the sentenced person in custody until a request for transit as provided in sub-rule 2 or a request under article 89, paragraph 1, or article 92 is received.
   2. To the extent possible under the procedure of national law, a State Party shall authorize the transit of a sentenced person through its territory and the provisions of article 89, paragraph 3 (b) and (c), and articles 105 and 108 and any rules relating thereto shall, as appropriate, apply. A copy of the final judgement of conviction and of the sentence imposed shall be attached to such request for transit.

RULE 208

COSTS

B2–209   1. The ordinary costs for the enforcement of the sentence in the territory of the State of enforcement shall be borne by that State.

2. Other costs, including those for the transport of the sentenced person and those referred to in article 100, paragraph 1 (c), (d) and (e), shall be borne by the Court.

Rule 209

CHANGE IN DESIGNATION OF STATE OF ENFORCEMENT

1. The Presidency, acting on its own motion or at the request of the sentenced person **B2–210** or the Prosecutor, may at any time act in accordance with article 104, paragraph 1.

2. The request of the sentenced person or of the Prosecutor shall be made in writing and shall set out the grounds upon which the transfer is sought.

Rule 210

PROCEDURE FOR CHANGE IN THE DESIGNATION OF A STATE OF ENFORCEMENT

1. Before deciding to change the designation of a State of enforcement, the Presidency **B2–211** may:

  (a) Request views from the State of enforcement;
  (b) Consider written or oral presentations of the sentenced person and the Prosecutor;
  (c) Consider written or oral expert opinion concerning, *inter alia*, the sentenced person;
  (d) Obtain any other relevant information from any reliable sources.

2. The provisions of rule 203, sub-rule 3, shall apply, as appropriate.

3. If the Presidency refuses to change the designation of the State of enforcement, it shall, as soon as possible, inform the sentenced person, the Prosecutor and the Registrar of its decision and of the reasons therefor. It shall also inform the State of enforcement.

Section II

Enforcement, supervision and transfer under articles 105, 106 and 107

Rule 211

SUPERVISION OF ENFORCEMENT OF SENTENCES AND CONDITIONS OF IMPRISONMENT

1. In order to supervise the enforcement of sentences of imprisonment, the **B2–212** Presidency:

  (a) Shall, in consultation with the State of enforcement, ensure that in establishing appropriate arrangements for the exercise by any sentenced person of his or her right to communicate with the Court about the conditions of imprisonment, the provisions of article 106, paragraph 3, shall be respected;
  (b) May, when necessary, request any information, report or expert opinion from the State of enforcement or from any reliable sources;
  (c) May, where appropriate, delegate a judge of the Court or a member of the staff of the Court who will be responsible, after notifying the State of enforcement, for meeting the sentenced person and hearing his or her views, without the presence of national authorities;
  (d) May, where appropriate, give the State of enforcement an opportunity to comment on the views expressed by the sentenced person under sub-rule 1 (c).

2. When a sentenced person is eligible for a prison programme or benefit available under the domestic law of the State of enforcement which may entail some activity outside the prison facility, the State of enforcement shall communicate that fact to the Presidency, together with any relevant information or observation, to enable the Court to exercise its supervisory function.

RULE 212

INFORMATION ON LOCATION OF THE PERSON FOR ENFORCEMENT OF FINES, FORFEITURES OR REPARATION MEASURES

B2–213   For the purpose of enforcement of fines and forfeiture measures and of reparation measures ordered by the Court, the Presidency may, at any time or at least 30 days before the scheduled completion of the sentence served by the sentenced person, request the State of enforcement to transmit to it the relevant information concerning the intention of that State to authorize the person to remain in its territory or the location where it intends to transfer the person.

RULE 213

PROCEDURE FOR ARTICLE 107, PARAGRAPH 3

B2–214   With respect to article 107, paragraph 3, the procedure set out in rules 214 and 215 shall apply, as appropriate.

Section III

Limitation on the prosecution or punishment of other offences under article 108

RULE 214

REQUEST TO PROSECUTE OR ENFORCE A SENTENCE FOR PRIOR CONDUCT

B2–215   1. For the application of article 108, when the State of enforcement wishes to prosecute or enforce a sentence against the sentenced person for any conduct engaged in prior to that person's transfer, it shall notify its intention to the Presidency and transmit to it the following documents:
  (a) A statement of the facts of the case and their legal characterization;
  (b) A copy of any applicable legal provisions, including those concerning the statute of limitation and the applicable penalties;
  (c) A copy of any sentence, warrant of arrest or other document having the same force, or of any other legal writ which the State intends to enforce;
  (d) A protocol containing views of the sentenced person obtained after the person has been informed sufficiently about the proceedings.
2. In the event of a request for extradition made by another State, the State of enforcement shall transmit the entire request to the Presidency with a protocol containing the views of the sentenced person obtained after informing the person sufficiently about the extradition request.
3. The Presidency may in all cases request any document or additional information from the State of enforcement or the State requesting extradition.
4. If the person was surrendered to the Court by a State other than the State of enforcement or the State seeking extradition, the Presidency shall consult with the State that surrendered the person and take into account any views expressed by that State.

5. Any information or documents transmitted to the Presidency under sub-rules 1 to 4 shall be transmitted to the Prosecutor, who may comment.

6. The Presidency may decide to conduct a hearing.

Rule 215

DECISION ON REQUEST TO PROSECUTE OR ENFORCE A SENTENCE

1. The Presidency shall make a determination as soon as possible. This determination shall be notified to all those who have participated in the proceedings.

B2–216

2. If the request submitted under sub-rules 1 or 2 of rule 214 concerns the enforcement of a sentence, the sentenced person may serve that sentence in the State designated by the Court to enforce the sentence pronounced by it or be extradited to a third State only after having served the full sentence pronounced by the Court, subject to the provisions of article 110.

3. The Presidency may authorize the temporary extradition of the sentenced person to a third State for prosecution only if it has obtained assurances which it deems to be sufficient that the sentenced person will be kept in custody in the third State and transferred back to the State responsible for enforcement of the sentence pronounced by the Court, after the prosecution.

Rule 216

INFORMATION ON ENFORCEMENT

The Presidency shall request the State of enforcement to inform it of any important event concerning the sentenced person, and of any prosecution of that person for events subsequent to his or her transfer.

B2–217

Section IV

Enforcement of fines, forfeiture measures and reparation orders

Rule 217

COOPERATION AND MEASURES FOR ENFORCEMENT OF FINES, FORFEITURE OR REPARATION ORDERS

For the enforcement of fines, forfeiture or reparation orders, the Presidency shall, as appropriate, seek cooperation and measures for enforcement in accordance with Part 9, as well as transmit copies of relevant orders to any State with which the sentenced person appears to have direct connection by reason of either nationality, domicile or habitual residence or by virtue of the location of the sentenced person's assets and property or with which the victim has such connection. The Presidency shall, as appropriate, inform the State of any third-party claims or of the fact that no claim was presented by a person who received notification of any proceedings conducted pursuant to article 75.

B2–218

Rule 218

ORDERS FOR FORFEITURE AND REPARATIONS

1. In order to enable States to give effect to an order for forfeiture, the order shall specify:

B2–219

1325

(a) The identity of the person against whom the order has been issued;

(b) The proceeds, property and assets that have been ordered by the Court to be forfeited; and

(c) That if the State Party is unable to give effect to the order for forfeiture in relation to the specified proceeds, property or assets, it shall take measures to recover the value of the same.

2. In the request for cooperation and measures for enforcement, the Court shall also provide available information as to the location of the proceeds, property and assets that are covered by the order for forfeiture.

3. In order to enable States to give effect to an order for reparations, the order shall specify:

(a) The identity of the person against whom the order has been issued;

(b) In respect of reparations of a financial nature, the identity of the victims to whom individual reparations have been granted, and, where the award for reparations shall be deposited with the Trust Fund, the particulars of the Trust Fund for the deposit of the award; and

(c) The scope and nature of the reparations ordered by the Court, including, where applicable, the property and assets for which restitution has been ordered.

4. Where the Court awards reparations on an individual basis, a copy of the reparation order shall be transmitted to the victim concerned.

RULE 219

NON-MODIFICATION OF ORDERS FOR REPARATION

B2–220   The Presidency shall, when transmitting copies of orders for reparations to States Parties under rule 217, inform them that, in giving effect to an order for reparations, the national authorities shall not modify the reparations specified by the Court, the scope or the extent of any damage, loss or injury determined by the Court or the principles stated in the order, and shall facilitate the enforcement of such order.

RULE 220

NON-MODIFICATION OF JUDGEMENTS IN WHICH FINES WERE IMPOSED

B2–221   When transmitting copies of judgements in which fines were imposed to States Parties for the purpose of enforcement in accordance with article 109 and rule 217, the Presidency shall inform them that in enforcing the fines imposed, national authorities shall not modify them.

RULE 221

DECISION ON DISPOSITION OR ALLOCATION OF PROPERTY OR ASSETS

B2–222   1. The Presidency shall, after having consulted, as appropriate, with the Prosecutor, the sentenced person, the victims or their legal representatives, the national authorities of the State of enforcement or any relevant third party, or representatives of the Trust Fund provided for in article 79, decide on all matters related to the disposition or allocation of property or assets realized through enforcement of an order of the Court.

2. In all cases, when the Presidency decides on the disposition or allocation of property or assets belonging to the sentenced person, it shall give priority to the enforcement of measures concerning reparations to victims.

Rule 222

ASSISTANCE FOR SERVICE OR ANY OTHER MEASURE

B2–223

The Presidency shall assist the State in the enforcement of fines, forfeiture or reparation orders, as requested, with the service of any relevant notification on the sentenced person or any other relevant persons, or the carrying out of any other measures necessary for the enforcement of the order under the procedure of the national law of the enforcement State.

Section V

Review concerning reduction of sentence under article 110

Rule 223

CRITERIA FOR REVIEW CONCERNING REDUCTION OF SENTENCE

B2–224

In reviewing the question of reduction of sentence pursuant to article 110, paragraphs 3 and 5, the three judges of the Appeals Chamber shall take into account the criteria listed in article 110, paragraph 4 (a) and (b), and the following criteria:

    (a) The conduct of the sentenced person while in detention, which shows a genuine dissociation from his or her crime;

    (b) The prospect of the resocialization and successful resettlement of the sentenced person;

    (c) Whether the early release of the sentenced person would give rise to significant social instability;

    (d) Any significant action taken by the sentenced person for the benefit of the victims as well as any impact on the victims and their families as a result of the early release;

    (e) Individual circumstances of the sentenced person, including a worsening state of physical or mental health or advanced age.

Rule 224

PROCEDURE FOR REVIEW CONCERNING REDUCTION OF SENTENCE

B2–225

1. For the application of article 110, paragraph 3, three judges of the Appeals Chamber appointed by that Chamber shall conduct a hearing, unless they decide otherwise in a particular case, for exceptional reasons. The hearing shall be conducted with the sentenced person, who may be assisted by his or her counsel, with interpretation, as may be required. Those three judges shall invite the Prosecutor, the State of enforcement of any penalty under article 77 or any reparation order pursuant to article 75 and, to the extent possible, the victims or their legal representatives who participated in the proceedings, to participate in the hearing or to submit written observations. Under exceptional circumstances, this hearing may be conducted by way of a videoconference or in the State of enforcement by a judge delegated by the Appeals Chamber.

2. The same three judges shall communicate the decision and the reasons for it to all those who participated in the review proceedings as soon as possible.

3. For the application of article 110, paragraph 5, three judges of the Appeals Chamber appointed by that Chamber shall review the question of reduction of sentence

every three years, unless it establishes a shorter interval in its decision taken pursuant to article 110, paragraph 3. In case of a significant change in circumstances, those three judges may permit the sentenced person to apply for a review within the three-year period or such shorter period as may have been set by the three judges.

4. For any review under article 110, paragraph 5, three judges of the Appeals Chamber appointed by that Chamber shall invite written representations from the sentenced person or his or her counsel, the Prosecutor, the State of enforcement of any penalty under article 77 and any reparation order pursuant to article 75 and, to the extent possible, the victims or their legal representatives who participated in the proceedings. The three judges may also decide to hold a hearing.

5. The decision and the reasons for it shall be communicated to all those who participated in the review proceedings as soon as possible.

Section VI

Escape

RULE 225

MEASURES UNDER ARTICLE 111 IN THE EVENT OF ESCAPE

B2–226   1. If the sentenced person has escaped, the State of enforcement shall, as soon as possible, advise the Registrar by any medium capable of delivering a written record. The Presidency shall then proceed in accordance with Part 9.

2. However, if the State in which the sentenced person is located agrees to surrender him or her to the State of enforcement, pursuant to either international agreements or its national legislation, the State of enforcement shall so advise the Registrar in writing. The person shall be surrendered to the State of enforcement as soon as possible, if necessary in consultation with the Registrar, who shall provide all necessary assistance, including, if necessary, the presentation of requests for transit to the States concerned, in accordance with rule 207. The costs associated with the surrender of the sentenced person shall be borne by the Court if no State assumes responsibility for them.

3. If the sentenced person is surrendered to the Court pursuant to Part 9, the Court shall transfer him or her to the State of enforcement. Nevertheless, the Presidency may, acting on its own motion or at the request of the Prosecutor or of the initial State of enforcement and in accordance with article 103 and rules 203 to 206, designate another State, including the State to the territory of which the sentenced person has fled.

4. In all cases, the entire period of detention in the territory of the State in which the sentenced person was in custody after his or her escape and, where sub-rule 3 is applicable, the period of detention at the seat of the Court following the surrender of the sentenced person from the State in which he or she was located shall be deducted from the sentence remaining to be served.

B3. Elements of Crimes

Explanatory note: The structure of the elements of the crimes of genocide, crimes **B3–001** against humanity and war crimes follows the structure of the corresponding provisions of articles 6, 7 and 8 of the Rome Statute. Some paragraphs of those articles of the Rome Statute list multiple crimes. In those instances, the elements of crimes appear in separate paragraphs which correspond to each of those crimes to facilitate the identification of the respective elements.

CONTENTS

8(2)(b)(ii)	War crime of attacking civilian objects
8(2)(b)(iii)	War crime of attacking personnel or objects involved in a humanitarian assistance or peacekeeping mission
8(2)(b)(iv)	War crime of excessive incidental death, injury, or damage
8(2)(b)(v)	War crime of attacking undefended places
8(2)(b)(vi)	War crime of killing or wounding a person *hors de combat*
(2)(b)(vii)–1	War crime of improper use of a flag of truce
8(2)(b)(vii)–2	War crime of improper use of a flag, insignia or uniform of the hostile party
8(2)(b)(vii)–3	War crime of improper use of a flag, insignia or uniform of the United Nations
8(2)(b)(vii)–4	War crime of improper use of the distinctive emblems of the Geneva Conventions
8(2)(b)(viii)	The transfer, directly or indirectly, by the Occupying Power of parts of its own civilian population into the territory it occupies, or the deportation or transfer of all or parts of the population of the occupied territory within or outside this territory
8(2)(b)(ix)	War crime of attacking protected objects
8(2)(b)(x)–1	War crime of mutilation
8(2)(b)(x)–2	War crime of medical or scientific experiments
8(2)(b)(xi)	War crime of treacherously killing or wounding
8(2)(b)(xii)	War crime of denying quarter
8(2)(b)(xiii)	War crime of destroying or seizing the enemy's property
8(2)(b)(xiv)	War crime of depriving the nationals of the hostile power of rights or actions
8(2)(b)(xv)	War crime of compelling participation in military operations
8(2)(b)(xvi)	War crime of pillaging
8(2)(b)(xvii)	War crime of employing poison or poisoned weapons
8(2)(b)(xviii)	War crime of employing prohibited gases, liquids, materials or devices
8(2)(b)(xix)	War crime of employing prohibited bullets
8(2)(b)(xx)	War crime of employing weapons, projectiles or materials or methods of warfare listed in the Annex to the Statute
8(2)(b)(xxi)	War crime of outrages upon personal dignity
8(2)(b)(xxii)–1	War crime of rape
8(2)(b)(xxii)–2	War crime of sexual slavery
8(2)(b)(xxii)–3	War crime of enforced prostitution
8(2)(b)(xxii)–4	War crime of forced pregnancy
8(2)(b)(xxii)–5	War crime of enforced sterilization
8(2)(b)(xxii)–6	War crime of sexual violence
8(2)(b)(xxiii)	War crime of using protected persons as shields
8(2)(b)(xxiv)	War crime of attacking objects or persons using the distinctive emblems of the Geneva Conventions
8(2)(b)(xxv)	War crime of starvation as a method of warfare
8(2)(b)(xxvi)	War crime of using, conscripting or enlisting children

Article 8 (2) (c)

8(2)(c)(i)–1	War crime of murder
8(2)(c)(i)–2	War crime of mutilation
8(2)(c)(i)–3	War crime of cruel treatment
8(2)(c)(i)–4	War crime of torture
8(2)(c)(ii)	War crime of outrages upon personal dignity
8(2)(c)(iii)	War crime of taking hostages
8(2)(c)(iv)	War crime of sentencing or execution without due process

Article 8 (2) (e)

8(2)(e)(i)	War crime of attacking civilians
8(2)(e)(ii)	War crime of attacking objects or persons using the distinctive emblems of the Geneva Conventions
8(2)(e)(iii)	War crime of attacking personnel or objects involved in a humanitarian assistance or peacekeeping mission

8(2)(e)(iv)	War crime of attacking protected objects
8(2)(e)(v)	War crime of pillaging
8(2)(e)(vi)–1	War crime of rape
8(2)(e)(vi)–2	War crime of sexual slavery
8(2)(e)(vi)–3	War crime of enforced prostitution
8(2)(e)(vi)–4	War crime of forced pregnancy
8(2)(e)(vi)–5	War crime of enforced sterilization
8(2)(e)(vi)–6	War crime of sexual violence
8(2)(e)(vii)	War crime of using, conscripting and enlisting children
8(2)(e)(viii)	War crime of displacing civilians
8(2)(e)(ix)	War crime of treacherously killing or wounding
8(2)(e)(x)	War crime of denying quarter
8(2)(e)(xi)–1	War crime of mutilation
8(2)(e)(xi)–2	War crime of medical or scientific experiments
8(2)(e)(xii)	War crime of destroying or seizing the enemy's property

GENERAL INTRODUCTION

1. Pursuant to article 9, the following Elements of Crimes shall assist the Court in the interpretation and application of articles 6, 7 and 8, consistent with the Statute. The provisions of the Statute, including article 21 and the general principles set out in Part 3, are applicable to the Elements of Crimes.

B3–002

2. As stated in article 30, unless otherwise provided, a person shall be criminally responsible and liable for punishment for a crime within the jurisdiction of the Court only if the material elements are committed with intent and knowledge. Where no reference is made in the Elements of Crimes to a mental element for any particular conduct, consequence or circumstance listed, it is understood that the relevant mental element, i.e., intent, knowledge or both, set out in article 30 applies. Exceptions to the article 30 standard, based on the Statute, including applicable law under its relevant provisions, are indicated below.

3. Existence of intent and knowledge can be inferred from relevant facts and circumstances.

4. With respect to mental elements associated with elements involving value judgement, such as those using the terms "inhumane" or "severe", it is not necessary that the perpetrator personally completed a particular value judgement, unless otherwise indicated.

5. Grounds for excluding criminal responsibility or the absence thereof are generally not specified in the elements of crimes listed under each crime.[1]

6. The requirement of "unlawfulness" found in the Statute or in other parts of international law, in particular international humanitarian law, is generally not specified in the elements of crimes.

7. The elements of crimes are generally structured in accordance with the following principles:
  - As the elements of crimes focus on the conduct, consequences and circumstances associated with each crime, they are generally listed in that order;
  - When required, a particular mental element is listed after the affected conduct, consequence or circumstance;
  - Contextual circumstances are listed last.

8. As used in the Elements of Crimes, the term "perpetrator" is neutral as to guilt or innocence. The elements, including the appropriate mental elements, apply, *mutatis mutandis*, to all those whose criminal responsibility may fall under articles 25 and 28 of the Statute.

---

[1] This paragraph is without prejudice to the obligation of the Prosecutor under article 54, paragraph 1, of the Statute.

9. A particular conduct may constitute one or more crimes.
10. The use of short titles for the crimes has no legal effect.

ARTICLE 6

GENOCIDE

INTRODUCTION

B3–003   With respect to the last element listed for each crime:
    – The term "in the context of" would include the initial acts in an emerging pattern;
    – The term "manifest" is an objective qualification;
    – Notwithstanding the normal requirement for a mental element provided for in article 30, and recognizing that knowledge of the circumstances will usually be addressed in proving genocidal intent, the appropriate requirement, if any, for a mental element regarding this circumstance will need to be decided by the Court on a case-by-case basis.

ARTICLE 6 (A)

GENOCIDE BY KILLING

ELEMENTS

B3–004   1. The perpetrator killed[2] one or more persons.
2. Such person or persons belonged to a particular national, ethnical, racial or religious group.
3. The perpetrator intended to destroy, in whole or in part, that national, ethnical, racial or religious group, as such.
4. The conduct took place in the context of a manifest pattern of similar conduct directed against that group or was conduct that could itself effect such destruction.

ARTICLE 6 (B)

GENOCIDE BY CAUSING SERIOUS BODILY OR MENTAL HARM

ELEMENTS

B3–005   1. The perpetrator caused serious bodily or mental harm to one or more persons.[3]
2. Such person or persons belonged to a particular national, ethnical, racial or religious group.
3. The perpetrator intended to destroy, in whole or in part, that national, ethnical, racial or religious group, as such.
4. The conduct took place in the context of a manifest pattern of similar conduct directed against that group or was conduct that could itself effect such destruction.

---

[2] The term "killed" is interchangeable with the term "caused death".
[3] This conduct may include, but is not necessarily restricted to, acts of torture, rape, sexual violence or inhuman or degrading treatment.

ARTICLE 6 (C)

GENOCIDE BY DELIBERATELY INFLICTING CONDITIONS OF LIFE CALCULATED TO BRING ABOUT PHYSICAL DESTRUCTION

ELEMENTS

1. The perpetrator inflicted certain conditions of life upon one or more persons.

B3–006

2. Such person or persons belonged to a particular national, ethnical, racial or religious group.

3. The perpetrator intended to destroy, in whole or in part, that national, ethnical, racial or religious group, as such.

4. The conditions of life were calculated to bring about the physical destruction of that group, in whole or in part.[4]

5. The conduct took place in the context of a manifest pattern of similar conduct directed against that group or was conduct that could itself effect such destruction.

ARTICLE 6 (D)

GENOCIDE BY IMPOSING MEASURES INTENDED TO PREVENT BIRTHS

ELEMENTS

1. The perpetrator imposed certain measures upon one or more persons.

B3–007

2. Such person or persons belonged to a particular national, ethnical, racial or religious group.

3. The perpetrator intended to destroy, in whole or in part, that national, ethnical, racial or religious group, as such.

4. The measures imposed were intended to prevent births within that group.

5. The conduct took place in the context of a manifest pattern of similar conduct directed against that group or was conduct that could itself effect such destruction.

ARTICLE 6 (E)

GENOCIDE BY FORCIBLY TRANSFERRING CHILDREN

ELEMENTS

1. The perpetrator forcibly transferred one or more persons.[5]

B3–008

2. Such person or persons belonged to a particular national, ethnical, racial or religious group.

3. The perpetrator intended to destroy, in whole or in part, that national, ethnical, racial or religious group, as such.

---

[4] The term "conditions of life" may include, but is not necessarily restricted to, deliberate deprivation of resources indispensable for survival, such as food or medical services, or systematic expulsion from homes.

[5] The term "forcibly" is not restricted to physical force, but may include threat of force or coercion, such as that caused by fear of violence, duress, detention, psychological oppression or abuse of power, against such person or persons or another person, or by taking advantage of a coercive environment.

4. The transfer was from that group to another group.

5. The person or persons were under the age of 18 years.

6. The perpetrator knew, or should have known, that the person or persons were under the age of 18 years.

7. The conduct took place in the context of a manifest pattern of similar conduct directed against that group or was conduct that could itself effect such destruction.

ARTICLE 7

CRIMES AGAINST HUMANITY

INTRODUCTION

B3–009   1. Since article 7 pertains to international criminal law, its provisions, consistent with article 22, must be strictly construed, taking into account that crimes against humanity as defined in article 7 are among the most serious crimes of concern to the international community as a whole, warrant and entail individual criminal responsibility, and require conduct which is impermissible under generally applicable international law, as recognized by the principal legal systems of the world.

2. The last two elements for each crime against humanity describe the context in which the conduct must take place. These elements clarify the requisite participation in and knowledge of a widespread or systematic attack against a civilian population. However, the last element should not be interpreted as requiring proof that the perpetrator had knowledge of all characteristics of the attack or the precise details of the plan or policy of the State or organization. In the case of an emerging widespread or systematic attack against a civilian population, the intent clause of the last element indicates that this mental element is satisfied if the perpetrator intended to further such an attack.

3. "Attack directed against a civilian population" in these context elements is understood to mean a course of conduct involving the multiple commission of acts referred to in article 7, paragraph 1, of the Statute against any civilian population, pursuant to or in furtherance of a State or organizational policy to commit such attack. The acts need not constitute a military attack. It is understood that "policy to commit such attack" requires that the State or organization actively promote or encourage such an attack against a civilian population.[6]

ARTICLE 7 (1) (A)

CRIME AGAINST HUMANITY OF MURDER

ELEMENTS

B3–010   1. The perpetrator killed[7] one or more persons.

2. The conduct was committed as part of a widespread or systematic attack directed against a civilian population.

3. The perpetrator knew that the conduct was part of or intended the conduct to be part of a widespread or systematic attack against a civilian population.

---

[6] A policy which has a civilian population as the object of the attack would be implemented by State or organizational action. Such a policy may, in exceptional circumstances, be implemented by a deliberate failure to take action, which is consciously aimed at encouraging such attack. The existence of such a policy cannot be inferred solely from the absence of governmental or organizational action.

[7] The term "killed" is interchangeable with the term "caused death". This footnote applies to all elements which use either of these concepts.

Article 7 (1) (b)

CRIME AGAINST HUMANITY OF EXTERMINATION

ELEMENTS

1. The perpetrator killed[8] one or more persons, including by inflicting conditions of life calculated to bring about the destruction of part of a population.[9]

2. The conduct constituted, or took place as part of,[10] a mass killing of members of a civilian population.

3. The conduct was committed as part of a widespread or systematic attack directed against a civilian population.

4. The perpetrator knew that the conduct was part of or intended the conduct to be part of a widespread or systematic attack directed against a civilian population.

B3–011

Article 7 (1) (c)

CRIME AGAINST HUMANITY OF ENSLAVEMENT

ELEMENTS

1. The perpetrator exercised any or all of the powers attaching to the right of ownership over one or more persons, such as by purchasing, selling, lending or bartering such a person or persons, or by imposing on them a similar deprivation of liberty.[11]

2. The conduct was committed as part of a widespread or systematic attack directed against a civilian population.

3. The perpetrator knew that the conduct was part of or intended the conduct to be part of a widespread or systematic attack directed against a civilian population.

B3–012

Article 7 (1) (d)

CRIME AGAINST HUMANITY OF DEPORTATION OR FORCIBLE TRANSFER OF POPULATION

ELEMENTS

1. The perpetrator deported or forcibly[12] transferred,[13] without grounds permitted under international law, one or more persons to another State or location, by expulsion or other coercive acts.

B3–013

---

[8] The conduct could be committed by different methods of killing, either directly or indirectly.

[9] The infliction of such conditions could include the deprivation of access to food and medicine.

[10] The term "as part of" would include the initial conduct in a mass killing.

[11] It is understood that such deprivation of liberty may, in some circumstances, include exacting forced labour or otherwise reducing a person to a servile status as defined in the Supplementary Convention on the Abolition of Slavery, the Slave Trade, and Institutions and Practices Similar to Slavery of 1956. It is also understood that the conduct described in this element includes trafficking in persons, in particular women and children.

[12] The term "forcibly" is not restricted to physical force, but may include threat of force or coercion, such as that caused by fear of violence, duress, detention, psychological oppression or abuse of power against such person or persons or another person, or by taking advantage of a coercive environment.

[13] "Deported or forcibly transferred" is interchangeable with "forcibly displaced".

2. Such person or persons were lawfully present in the area from which they were so deported or transferred.

3. The perpetrator was aware of the factual circumstances that established the lawfulness of such presence.

4. The conduct was committed as part of a widespread or systematic attack directed against a civilian population.

5. The perpetrator knew that the conduct was part of or intended the conduct to be part of a widespread or systematic attack directed against a civilian population.

ARTICLE 7 (1) (E)

CRIME AGAINST HUMANITY OF IMPRISONMENT OR OTHER SEVERE DEPRIVATION OF PHYSICAL LIBERTY

ELEMENTS

B3–014   1. The perpetrator imprisoned one or more persons or otherwise severely deprived one or more persons of physical liberty.

2. The gravity of the conduct was such that it was in violation of fundamental rules of international law.

3. The perpetrator was aware of the factual circumstances that established the gravity of the conduct.

4. The conduct was committed as part of a widespread or systematic attack directed against a civilian population.

5. The perpetrator knew that the conduct was part of or intended the conduct to be part of a widespread or systematic attack directed against a civilian population.

ARTICLE 7 (1) (F)

CRIME AGAINST HUMANITY OF TORTURE[14]

ELEMENTS

B3–015   1. The perpetrator inflicted severe physical or mental pain or suffering upon one or more persons.

2. Such person or persons were in the custody or under the control of the perpetrator.

3. Such pain or suffering did not arise only from, and was not inherent in or incidental to, lawful sanctions.

4. The conduct was committed as part of a widespread or systematic attack directed against a civilian population.

5. The perpetrator knew that the conduct was part of or intended the conduct to be part of a widespread or systematic attack directed against a civilian population.

ARTICLE 7 (1) (G)–1

CRIME AGAINST HUMANITY OF RAPE

ELEMENTS

B3–016   1. The perpetrator invaded[15] the body of a person by conduct resulting in penetration, however slight, of any part of the body of the victim or of the perpetrator with a sexual organ, or of the anal or genital opening of the victim with any object or any other part of the body.

[14] It is understood that no specific purpose need be proved for this crime.
[15] The concept of "invasion" is intended to be broad enough to be gender-neutral.

2. The invasion was committed by force, or by threat of force or coercion, such as that caused by fear of violence, duress, detention, psychological oppression or abuse of power, against such person or another person, or by taking advantage of a coercive environment, or the invasion was committed against a person incapable of giving genuine consent.[16]

3. The conduct was committed as part of a widespread or systematic attack directed against a civilian population.

4. The perpetrator knew that the conduct was part of or intended the conduct to be part of a widespread or systematic attack directed against a civilian population.

ARTICLE 7 (1) (G)–2

CRIME AGAINST HUMANITY OF SEXUAL SLAVERY[17]

ELEMENTS

1. The perpetrator exercised any or all of the powers attaching to the right of ownership over one or more persons, such as by purchasing, selling, lending or bartering such a person or persons, or by imposing on them a similar deprivation of liberty.[18] **B3–017**

2. The perpetrator caused such person or persons to engage in one or more acts of a sexual nature.

3. The conduct was committed as part of a widespread or systematic attack directed against a civilian population.

4. The perpetrator knew that the conduct was part of or intended the conduct to be part of a widespread or systematic attack directed against a civilian population.

ARTICLE 7 (1) (G)–3

CRIME AGAINST HUMANITY OF ENFORCED PROSTITUTION

ELEMENTS

1. The perpetrator caused one or more persons to engage in one or more acts of a sexual nature by force, or by threat of force or coercion, such as that caused by fear of violence, duress, detention, psychological oppression or abuse of power, against such person or persons or another person, or by taking advantage of a coercive environment or such person's or persons' incapacity to give genuine consent. **B3–018**

2. The perpetrator or another person obtained or expected to obtain pecuniary or other advantage in exchange for or in connection with the acts of a sexual nature.

3. The conduct was committed as part of a widespread or systematic attack directed against a civilian population.

4. The perpetrator knew that the conduct was part of or intended the conduct to be part of a widespread or systematic attack directed against a civilian population.

---

[16] It is understood that a person may be incapable of giving genuine consent if affected by natural, induced or age-related incapacity. This footnote also applies to the corresponding elements of article 7 (1) (g)–3, 5 and 6.

[17] Given the complex nature of this crime, it is recognized that its commission could involve more than one perpetrator as a part of a common criminal purpose.

[18] It is understood that such deprivation of liberty may, in some circumstances, include exacting forced labour or otherwise reducing a person to a servile status as defined in the Supplementary Convention on the Abolition of Slavery, the Slave Trade, and Institutions and Practices Similar to Slavery of 1956. It is also understood that the conduct described in this element includes trafficking in persons, in particular women and children.

ARTICLE 7 (1) (G)–4

CRIME AGAINST HUMANITY OF FORCED PREGNANCY

ELEMENTS

B3–019   1. The perpetrator confined one or more women forcibly made pregnant, with the intent of affecting the ethnic composition of any population or carrying out other grave violations of international law.

2. The conduct was committed as part of a widespread or systematic attack directed against a civilian population.

3. The perpetrator knew that the conduct was part of or intended the conduct to be part of a widespread or systematic attack directed against a civilian population.

ARTICLE 7 (1) (G)–5

CRIME AGAINST HUMANITY OF ENFORCED STERILIZATION

ELEMENTS

B3–020   1. The perpetrator deprived one or more persons of biological reproductive capacity.[19]

2. The conduct was neither justified by the medical or hospital treatment of the person or persons concerned nor carried out with their genuine consent.[20]

3. The conduct was committed as part of a widespread or systematic attack directed against a civilian population.

4. The perpetrator knew that the conduct was part of or intended the conduct to be part of a widespread or systematic attack directed against a civilian population.

ARTICLE 7 (1) (G)–6

CRIME AGAINST HUMANITY OF SEXUAL VIOLENCE

ELEMENTS

B3–021   1. The perpetrator committed an act of a sexual nature against one or more persons or caused such person or persons to engage in an act of a sexual nature by force, or by threat of force or coercion, such as that caused by fear of violence, duress, detention, psychological oppression or abuse of power, against such person or persons or another person, or by taking advantage of a coercive environment or such person's or persons' incapacity to give genuine consent.

2. Such conduct was of a gravity comparable to the other offences in article 7, paragraph 1 (g), of the Statute.

3. The perpetrator was aware of the factual circumstances that established the gravity of the conduct.

4. The conduct was committed as part of a widespread or systematic attack directed against a civilian population.

---

[19] The deprivation is not intended to include birth-control measures which have a non-permanent effect in practice.

[20] It is understood that "genuine consent" does not include consent obtained through deception.

5. The perpetrator knew that the conduct was part of or intended the conduct to be part of a widespread or systematic attack directed against a civilian population.

ARTICLE 7 (1) (H)

CRIME AGAINST HUMANITY OF PERSECUTION

ELEMENTS

1. The perpetrator severely deprived, contrary to international law,[21] one or more persons of fundamental rights.
2. The perpetrator targeted such person or persons by reason of the identity of a group or collectivity or targeted the group or collectivity as such.
3. Such targeting was based on political, racial, national, ethnic, cultural, religious, gender as defined in article 7, paragraph 3, of the Statute, or other grounds that are universally recognized as impermissible under international law.
4. The conduct was committed in connection with any act referred to in article 7, paragraph 1, of the Statute or any crime within the jurisdiction of the Court.[22]
5. The conduct was committed as part of a widespread or systematic attack directed against a civilian population.
6. The perpetrator knew that the conduct was part of or intended the conduct to be part of a widespread or systematic attack directed against a civilian population.

B3–022

ARTICLE 7 (1) (I)

CRIME AGAINST HUMANITY OF ENFORCED DISAPPEARANCE OF PERSONS[23, 24]

ELEMENTS

1. The perpetrator:
   (a) Arrested, detained[25, 26] or abducted one or more persons; or
   (b) Refused to acknowledge the arrest, detention or abduction, or to give information on the fate or whereabouts of such person or persons.
2. (a) Such arrest, detention or abduction was followed or accompanied by a refusal to acknowledge that deprivation of freedom or to give information on the fate or whereabouts of such person or persons; or
   (b) Such refusal was preceded or accompanied by that deprivation of freedom.
3. The perpetrator was aware that[27]:

B3–023

---

[21] This requirement is without prejudice to paragraph 6 of the General Introduction to the Elements of Crimes.
[22] It is understood that no additional mental element is necessary for this element other than that inherent in element 6.
[23] Given the complex nature of this crime, it is recognized that its commission will normally involve more than one perpetrator as a part of a common criminal purpose.
[24] This crime falls under the jurisdiction of the Court only if the attack referred to in elements 7 and 8 occurs after the entry into force of the Statute.
[25] The word "detained" would include a perpetrator who maintained an existing detention.
[26] It is understood that under certain circumstances an arrest or detention may have been lawful.
[27] This element, inserted because of the complexity of this crime, is without prejudice to the General Introduction to the Elements of Crimes.

(a) Such arrest, detention or abduction would be followed in the ordinary course of events by a refusal to acknowledge that deprivation of freedom or to give information on the fate or whereabouts of such person or persons[28]; or

(b) Such refusal was preceded or accompanied by that deprivation of freedom.

4. Such arrest, detention or abduction was carried out by, or with the authorization, support or acquiescence of, a State or a political organization.

5. Such refusal to acknowledge that deprivation of freedom or to give information on the fate or whereabouts of such person or persons was carried out by, or with the authorization or support of, such State or political organization.

6. The perpetrator intended to remove such person or persons from the protection of the law for a prolonged period of time.

7. The conduct was committed as part of a widespread or systematic attack directed against a civilian population.

8. The perpetrator knew that the conduct was part of or intended the conduct to be part of a widespread or systematic attack directed against a civilian population.

ARTICLE 7 (1) (J)

CRIME AGAINST HUMANITY OF APARTHEID

ELEMENTS

B3–024

1. The perpetrator committed an inhumane act against one or more persons.

2. Such act was an act referred to in article 7, paragraph 1, of the Statute, or was an act of a character similar to any of those acts.[29]

3. The perpetrator was aware of the factual circumstances that established the character of the act.

4. The conduct was committed in the context of an institutionalized regime of systematic oppression and domination by one racial group over any other racial group or groups.

5. The perpetrator intended to maintain such regime by that conduct.

6. The conduct was committed as part of a widespread or systematic attack directed against a civilian population.

7. The perpetrator knew that the conduct was part of or intended the conduct to be part of a widespread or systematic attack directed against a civilian population.

ARTICLE 7 (1) (K)

CRIME AGAINST HUMANITY OF OTHER INHUMANE ACTS

ELEMENTS

B3–025

1. The perpetrator inflicted great suffering, or serious injury to body or to mental or physical health, by means of an inhumane act.

2. Such act was of a character similar to any other act referred to in article 7, paragraph 1, of the Statute.[30]

3. The perpetrator was aware of the factual circumstances that established the character of the act.

---

[28] It is understood that, in the case of a perpetrator who maintained an existing detention, this element would be satisfied if the perpetrator was aware that such a refusal had already taken place.

[29] It is understood that "character" refers to the nature and gravity of the act.

[30] It is understood that "character" refers to the nature and gravity of the act.

4. The conduct was committed as part of a widespread or systematic attack directed against a civilian population.

5. The perpetrator knew that the conduct was part of or intended the conduct to be part of a widespread or systematic attack directed against a civilian population.

ARTICLE 8

WAR CRIMES

INTRODUCTION

B3–026

The elements for war crimes under article 8, paragraph 2 (c) and (e), are subject to the limitations addressed in article 8, paragraph 2 (d) and (f), which are not elements of crimes.

The elements for war crimes under article 8, paragraph 2, of the Statute shall be interpreted within the established framework of the international law of armed conflict including, as appropriate, the international law of armed conflict applicable to armed conflict at sea.

With respect to the last two elements listed for each crime:

- There is no requirement for a legal evaluation by the perpetrator as to the existence of an armed conflict or its character as international or non-international;
- In that context there is no requirement for awareness by the perpetrator of the facts that established the character of the conflict as international or non-international;
- There is only a requirement for the awareness of the factual circumstances that established the existence of an armed conflict that is implicit in the terms "took place in the context of and was associated with".

ARTICLE 8 (2) (A)

ARTICLE 8 (2) (A) (I)

WAR CRIME OF WILFUL KILLING

ELEMENTS

1. The perpetrator killed one or more persons.[31]

B3–027

2. Such person or persons were protected under one or more of the Geneva Conventions of 1949.

3. The perpetrator was aware of the factual circumstances that established that protected status.[32, 33]

4. The conduct took place in the context of and was associated with an international armed conflict.[34]

---

[31] The term "killed" is interchangeable with the term "caused death". This footnote applies to all elements which use either of these concepts.

[32] This mental element recognizes the interplay between articles 30 and 32. This footnote also applies to the corresponding element in each crime under article 8 (2) (a), and to the element in other crimes in article 8 (2) concerning the awareness of factual circumstances that establish the status of persons or property protected under the relevant international law of armed conflict.

[33] With respect to nationality, it is understood that the perpetrator needs only to know that the victim belonged to an adverse party to the conflict. This footnote also applies to the corresponding element in each crime under article 8 (2) (a).

[34] The term "international armed conflict" includes military occupation. This footnote also applies to the corresponding element in each crime under article 8 (2) (a).

5. The perpetrator was aware of factual circumstances that established the existence of an armed conflict.

ARTICLE 8 (2) (A) (II)–1

WAR CRIME OF TORTURE

ELEMENTS[35]

B3–028   1. The perpetrator inflicted severe physical or mental pain or suffering upon one or more persons.

2. The perpetrator inflicted the pain or suffering for such purposes as: obtaining information or a confession, punishment, intimidation or coercion or for any reason based on discrimination of any kind.

3. Such person or persons were protected under one or more of the Geneva Conventions of 1949.

4. The perpetrator was aware of the factual circumstances that established that protected status.

5. The conduct took place in the context of and was associated with an international armed conflict.

6. The perpetrator was aware of factual circumstances that established the existence of an armed conflict.

ARTICLE 8 (2) (A) (II)–2

WAR CRIME OF INHUMAN TREATMENT

ELEMENTS

B3–029   1. The perpetrator inflicted severe physical or mental pain or suffering upon one or more persons.

2. Such person or persons were protected under one or more of the Geneva Conventions of 1949.

3. The perpetrator was aware of the factual circumstances that established that protected status.

4. The conduct took place in the context of and was associated with an international armed conflict.

5. The perpetrator was aware of factual circumstances that established the existence of an armed conflict.

ARTICLE 8 (2) (A) (II)–3

WAR CRIME OF BIOLOGICAL EXPERIMENTS

ELEMENTS

B3–030   1. The perpetrator subjected one or more persons to a particular biological experiment.

---

[35] As element 3 requires that all victims must be "protected persons" under one or more of the Geneva Conventions of 1949, these elements do not include the custody or control requirement found in the elements of article 7 (1) (e).

2. The experiment seriously endangered the physical or mental health or integrity of such person or persons.

3. The intent of the experiment was non-therapeutic and it was neither justified by medical reasons nor carried out in such person's or persons' interest.

4. Such person or persons were protected under one or more of the Geneva Conventions of 1949.

5. The perpetrator was aware of the factual circumstances that established that protected status.

6. The conduct took place in the context of and was associated with an international armed conflict.

7. The perpetrator was aware of factual circumstances that established the existence of an armed conflict.

ARTICLE 8 (2) (A) (III)

WAR CRIME OF WILFULLY CAUSING GREAT SUFFERING

ELEMENTS

1. The perpetrator caused great physical or mental pain or suffering to, or serious injury to body or health of, one or more persons.   **B3–031**

2. Such person or persons were protected under one or more of the Geneva Conventions of 1949.

3. The perpetrator was aware of the factual circumstances that established that protected status.

4. The conduct took place in the context of and was associated with an international armed conflict.

5. The perpetrator was aware of factual circumstances that established the existence of an armed conflict.

ARTICLE 8 (2) (A) (IV)

WAR CRIME OF DESTRUCTION AND APPROPRIATION OF PROPERTY

ELEMENTS

1. The perpetrator destroyed or appropriated certain property.   **B3–032**

2. The destruction or appropriation was not justified by military necessity.

3. The destruction or appropriation was extensive and carried out wantonly.

4. Such property was protected under one or more of the Geneva Conventions of 1949.

5. The perpetrator was aware of the factual circumstances that established that protected status.

6. The conduct took place in the context of and was associated with an international armed conflict.

7. The perpetrator was aware of factual circumstances that established the existence of an armed conflict.

ARTICLE 8 (2) (A) (V)

WAR CRIME OF COMPELLING SERVICE IN HOSTILE FORCES

ELEMENTS

1. The perpetrator coerced one or more persons, by act or threat, to take part in military operations against that person's own country or forces or otherwise serve in the forces of a hostile power.   **B3–033**

2. Such person or persons were protected under one or more of the Geneva Conventions of 1949.

3. The perpetrator was aware of the factual circumstances that established that protected status.

4. The conduct took place in the context of and was associated with an international armed conflict.

5. The perpetrator was aware of factual circumstances that established the existence of an armed conflict.

ARTICLE 8 (2) (A) (VI)

WAR CRIME OF DENYING A FAIR TRIAL

ELEMENTS

B3–034   1. The perpetrator deprived one or more persons of a fair and regular trial by denying judicial guarantees as defined, in particular, in the third and the fourth Geneva Conventions of 1949.

2. Such person or persons were protected under one or more of the Geneva Conventions of 1949.

3. The perpetrator was aware of the factual circumstances that established that protected status.

4. The conduct took place in the context of and was associated with an international armed conflict.

5. The perpetrator was aware of factual circumstances that established the existence of an armed conflict.

ARTICLE 8 (2) (A) (VII)–1

WAR CRIME OF UNLAWFUL DEPORTATION AND TRANSFER

ELEMENTS

B3–035   1. The perpetrator deported or transferred one or more persons to another State or to another location.

2. Such person or persons were protected under one or more of the Geneva Conventions of 1949.

3. The perpetrator was aware of the factual circumstances that established that protected status.

4. The conduct took place in the context of and was associated with an international armed conflict.

5. The perpetrator was aware of factual circumstances that established the existence of an armed conflict.

ARTICLE 8 (2) (A) (VII)–2

WAR CRIME OF UNLAWFUL CONFINEMENT

ELEMENTS

B3–036   1. The perpetrator confined or continued to confine one or more persons to a certain location.

2. Such person or persons were protected under one or more of the Geneva Conventions of 1949.

3. The perpetrator was aware of the factual circumstances that established that protected status.

4. The conduct took place in the context of and was associated with an international armed conflict.

5. The perpetrator was aware of factual circumstances that established the existence of an armed conflict.

ARTICLE 8 (2) (A) (VIII)

WAR CRIME OF TAKING HOSTAGES

ELEMENTS

1. The perpetrator seized, detained or otherwise held hostage one or more persons.   **B3–037**

2. The perpetrator threatened to kill, injure or continue to detain such person or persons.

3. The perpetrator intended to compel a State, an international organization, a natural or legal person or a group of persons to act or refrain from acting as an explicit or implicit condition for the safety or the release of such person or persons.

4. Such person or persons were protected under one or more of the Geneva Conventions of 1949.

5. The perpetrator was aware of the factual circumstances that established that protected status.

6. The conduct took place in the context of and was associated with an international armed conflict.

7. The perpetrator was aware of factual circumstances that established the existence of an armed conflict.

ARTICLE 8 (2) (B)

ARTICLE 8 (2) (B) (I)

WAR CRIME OF ATTACKING CIVILIANS

ELEMENTS

1. The perpetrator directed an attack.   **B3–038**

2. The object of the attack was a civilian population as such or individual civilians not taking direct part in hostilities.

3. The perpetrator intended the civilian population as such or individual civilians not taking direct part in hostilities to be the object of the attack.

4. The conduct took place in the context of and was associated with an international armed conflict.

5. The perpetrator was aware of factual circumstances that established the existence of an armed conflict.

ARTICLE 8 (2) (B) (II)

WAR CRIME OF ATTACKING CIVILIAN OBJECTS

ELEMENTS

1. The perpetrator directed an attack.   **B3–039**

2. The object of the attack was civilian objects, that is, objects which are not military objectives.

3. The perpetrator intended such civilian objects to be the object of the attack.

4. The conduct took place in the context of and was associated with an international armed conflict.

5. The perpetrator was aware of factual circumstances that established the existence of an armed conflict.

ARTICLE 8 (2) (B) (III)

WAR CRIME OF ATTACKING PERSONNEL OR OBJECTS INVOLVED IN A HUMANITARIAN ASSISTANCE OR PEACEKEEPING MISSION

ELEMENTS

B3–040　　1. The perpetrator directed an attack.

2. The object of the attack was personnel, installations, material, units or vehicles involved in a humanitarian assistance or peacekeeping mission in accordance with the Charter of the United Nations.

3. The perpetrator intended such personnel, installations, material, units or vehicles so involved to be the object of the attack.

4. Such personnel, installations, material, units or vehicles were entitled to that protection given to civilians or civilian objects under the international law of armed conflict.

5. The perpetrator was aware of the factual circumstances that established that protection.

6. The conduct took place in the context of and was associated with an international armed conflict.

7. The perpetrator was aware of factual circumstances that established the existence of an armed conflict.

ARTICLE 8 (2) (B) (IV)

WAR CRIME OF EXCESSIVE INCIDENTAL DEATH, INJURY, OR DAMAGE

ELEMENTS

B3–041　　1. The perpetrator launched an attack.

2. The attack was such that it would cause incidental death or injury to civilians or damage to civilian objects or widespread, long-term and severe damage to the natural environment and that such death, injury or damage would be of such an extent as to be clearly excessive in relation to the concrete and direct overall military advantage anticipated.[36]

---

[36] The expression "concrete and direct overall military advantage" refers to a military advantage that is foreseeable by the perpetrator at the relevant time. Such advantage may or may not be temporally or geographically related to the object of the attack. The fact that this crime admits the possibility of lawful incidental injury and collateral damage does not in any way justify any violation of the law applicable in armed conflict. It does not address justifications for war or other rules related to jus ad bellum. It reflects the proportionality requirement inherent in determining the legality of any military activity undertaken in the context of an armed conflict.

3. The perpetrator knew that the attack would cause incidental death or injury to civilians or damage to civilian objects or widespread, long-term and severe damage to the natural environment and that such death, injury or damage would be of such an extent as to be clearly excessive in relation to the concrete and direct overall military advantage anticipated.[37]

4. The conduct took place in the context of and was associated with an international armed conflict.

5. The perpetrator was aware of factual circumstances that established the existence of an armed conflict.

ARTICLE 8 (2) (B) (V)

WAR CRIME OF ATTACKING UNDEFENDED PLACES[38]

ELEMENTS

1. The perpetrator attacked one or more towns, villages, dwellings or buildings.   **B3–042**
2. Such towns, villages, dwellings or buildings were open for unresisted occupation.
3. Such towns, villages, dwellings or buildings did not constitute military objectives.
4. The conduct took place in the context of and was associated with an international armed conflict.
5. The perpetrator was aware of factual circumstances that established the existence of an armed conflict.

ARTICLE 8 (2) (B) (VI)

WAR CRIME OF KILLING OR WOUNDING A PERSON *HORS DE COMBAT*

ELEMENTS

1. The perpetrator killed or injured one or more persons.   **B3–043**
2. Such person or persons were *hors de combat*.
3. The perpetrator was aware of the factual circumstances that established this status.
4. The conduct took place in the context of and was associated with an international armed conflict.
5. The perpetrator was aware of factual circumstances that established the existence of an armed conflict.

ARTICLE 8 (2) (B) (VII)–1

WAR CRIME OF IMPROPER USE OF A FLAG OF TRUCE

ELEMENTS

1. The perpetrator used a flag of truce.   **B3–044**

---

[37] As opposed to the general rule set forth in paragraph 4 of the General Introduction, this knowledge element requires that the perpetrator make the value judgement as described therein. An evaluation of that value judgement must be based on the requisite information available to the perpetrator at the time.

[38] The presence in the locality of persons specially protected under the Geneva Conventions of 1949 or of police forces retained for the sole purpose of maintaining law and order does not by itself render the locality a military objective.

2. The perpetrator made such use in order to feign an intention to negotiate when there was no such intention on the part of the perpetrator.

3. The perpetrator knew or should have known of the prohibited nature of such use.[39]

4. The conduct resulted in death or serious personal injury.

5. The perpetrator knew that the conduct could result in death or serious personal injury.

6. The conduct took place in the context of and was associated with an international armed conflict.

7. The perpetrator was aware of factual circumstances that established the existence of an armed conflict.

ARTICLE 8 (2) (B) (VII)–2

WAR CRIME OF IMPROPER USE OF A FLAG, INSIGNIA OR UNIFORM OF THE HOSTILE PARTY

ELEMENTS

B3–045   1. The perpetrator used a flag, insignia or uniform of the hostile party.

2. The perpetrator made such use in a manner prohibited under the international law of armed conflict while engaged in an attack.

3. The perpetrator knew or should have known of the prohibited nature of such use.[40]

4. The conduct resulted in death or serious personal injury.

5. The perpetrator knew that the conduct could result in death or serious personal injury.

6. The conduct took place in the context of and was associated with an international armed conflict.

7. The perpetrator was aware of factual circumstances that established the existence of an armed conflict.

ARTICLE 8 (2) (B) (VII)–3

WAR CRIME OF IMPROPER USE OF A FLAG, INSIGNIA OR UNIFORM OF THE UNITED NATIONS

ELEMENTS

B3–046   1. The perpetrator used a flag, insignia or uniform of the United Nations.

2. The perpetrator made such use in a manner prohibited under the international law of armed conflict.

3. The perpetrator knew of the prohibited nature of such use.[41]

4. The conduct resulted in death or serious personal injury.

5. The perpetrator knew that the conduct could result in death or serious personal injury.

---

[39] This mental element recognizes the interplay between article 30 and article 32. The term "prohibited nature" denotes illegality.

[40] This mental element recognizes the interplay between article 30 and article 32. The term "prohibited nature" denotes illegality.

[41] This mental element recognizes the interplay between article 30 and article 32. The "should have known" test required in the other offences found in article 8 (2) (b) (vii) is not applicable here because of the variable and regulatory nature of the relevant prohibitions.

6. The conduct took place in the context of and was associated with an international armed conflict.

7. The perpetrator was aware of factual circumstances that established the existence of an armed conflict.

ARTICLE 8 (2) (B) (VII)–4

WAR CRIME OF IMPROPER USE OF THE DISTINCTIVE EMBLEMS OF THE GENEVA CONVENTIONS

ELEMENTS

1. The perpetrator used the distinctive emblems of the Geneva Conventions.

B3–047

2. The perpetrator made such use for combatant purposes[42] in a manner prohibited under the international law of armed conflict.

3. The perpetrator knew or should have known of the prohibited nature of such use.[43]

4. The conduct resulted in death or serious personal injury.

5. The perpetrator knew that the conduct could result in death or serious personal injury.

6. The conduct took place in the context of and was associated with an international armed conflict.

7. The perpetrator was aware of factual circumstances that established the existence of an armed conflict.

ARTICLE 8 (2) (B) (VIII)

THE TRANSFER, DIRECTLY OR INDIRECTLY, BY THE OCCUPYING POWER OF PARTS OF ITS OWN CIVILIAN POPULATION INTO THE TERRITORY IT OCCUPIED, OR THE DEPORTATION OR TRANSFER OF ALL OR PARTS OF THE POPULATION OF THE OCCUPIED TERRITORY WITHIN OR OUTSIDE THIS TERRITORY

ELEMENTS

1. The perpetrator:

B3–048

(a) Transferred, [44] directly or indirectly, parts of its own population into the territory it occupies; or

(b) Deported or transferred all or parts of the population of the occupied territory within or outside this territory.

2. The conduct took place in the context of and was associated with an international armed conflict.

3. The perpetrator was aware of factual circumstances that established the existence of an armed conflict.

[42] "Combatant purposes" in these circumstances means purposes directly related to hostilities and not including medical, religious or similar activities.

[43] This mental element recognizes the interplay between article 30 and article 32. The term "prohibited nature" denotes illegality.

[44] The term "transfer" needs to be interpreted in accordance with the relevant provisions of international humanitarian law.

ARTICLE 8 (2) (B) (IX)

WAR CRIME OF ATTACKING PROTECTED OBJECTS[45]

ELEMENTS

B3–049
1. The perpetrator directed an attack.
2. The object of the attack was one or more buildings dedicated to religion, education, art, science or charitable purposes, historic monuments, hospitals or places where the sick and wounded are collected, which were not military objectives.
3. The perpetrator intended such building or buildings dedicated to religion, education, art, science or charitable purposes, historic monuments, hospitals or places where the sick and wounded are collected, which were not military objectives, to be the object of the attack.
4. The conduct took place in the context of and was associated with an international armed conflict.
5. The perpetrator was aware of factual circumstances that established the existence of an armed conflict.

ARTICLE 8 (2) (B) (X)–1

WAR CRIME OF MUTILATION

ELEMENTS

B3–050
1. The perpetrator subjected one or more persons to mutilation, in particular by permanently disfiguring the person or persons, or by permanently disabling or removing an organ or appendage.
2. The conduct caused death or seriously endangered the physical or mental health of such person or persons.
3. The conduct was neither justified by the medical, dental or hospital treatment of the person or persons concerned nor carried out in such person's or persons' interest.[46]
4. Such person or persons were in the power of an adverse party.
5. The conduct took place in the context of and was associated with an international armed conflict.
6. The perpetrator was aware of factual circumstances that established the existence of an armed conflict.

ARTICLE 8 (2) (B) (X)–2

WAR CRIME OF MEDICAL OR SCIENTIFIC EXPERIMENTS

ELEMENTS

B3–051
1. The perpetrator subjected one or more persons to a medical or scientific experiment.

[45] The presence in the locality of persons specially protected under the Geneva Conventions of 1949 or of police forces retained for the sole purpose of maintaining law and order does not by itself render the locality a military objective.

[46] Consent is not a defence to this crime. The crime prohibits any medical procedure which is not indicated by the state of health of the person concerned and which is not consistent with generally accepted medical standards which would be applied under similar medical circumstances to persons who are nationals of the party conducting the procedure and who are in no way deprived of liberty. This footnote also applies to the same element for article 8 (2) (b) (x)–2.

2. The experiment caused death or seriously endangered the physical or mental health or integrity of such person or persons.

3. The conduct was neither justified by the medical, dental or hospital treatment of such person or persons concerned nor carried out in such person's or persons' interest.

4. Such person or persons were in the power of an adverse party.

5. The conduct took place in the context of and was associated with an international armed conflict.

6. The perpetrator was aware of factual circumstances that established the existence of an armed conflict.

Article 8 (2) (b) (xi)

WAR CRIME OF TREACHEROUSLY KILLING OR WOUNDING

ELEMENTS

1. The perpetrator invited the confidence or belief of one or more persons that they were entitled to, or were obliged to accord, protection under rules of international law applicable in armed conflict.   **B3–052**

2. The perpetrator intended to betray that confidence or belief.

3. The perpetrator killed or injured such person or persons.

4. The perpetrator made use of that confidence or belief in killing or injuring such person or persons.

5. Such person or persons belonged to an adverse party.

6. The conduct took place in the context of and was associated with an international armed conflict.

7. The perpetrator was aware of factual circumstances that established the existence of an armed conflict.

Article 8 (2) (b) (xii)

WAR CRIME OF DENYING QUARTER

ELEMENTS

1. The perpetrator declared or ordered that there shall be no survivors.   **B3–053**

2. Such declaration or order was given in order to threaten an adversary or to conduct hostilities on the basis that there shall be no survivors.

3. The perpetrator was in a position of effective command or control over the subordinate forces to which the declaration or order was directed.

4. The conduct took place in the context of and was associated with an international armed conflict.

5. The perpetrator was aware of factual circumstances that established the existence of an armed conflict.

Article 8 (2) (b) (xiii)

WAR CRIME OF DESTROYING OR SEIZING THE ENEMY'S PROPERTY

ELEMENTS

1. The perpetrator destroyed or seized certain property.   **B3–054**

2. Such property was property of a hostile party.

3. Such property was protected from that destruction or seizure under the international law of armed conflict.

4. The perpetrator was aware of the factual circumstances that established the status of the property.

5. The destruction or seizure was not justified by military necessity.

6. The conduct took place in the context of and was associated with an international armed conflict.

7. The perpetrator was aware of factual circumstances that established the existence of an armed conflict.

ARTICLE 8 (2) (B) (XIV)

WAR CRIME OF DEPRIVING THE NATIONALS OF THE HOSTILE POWER OF RIGHTS OR ACTIONS

ELEMENTS

B3–055   1. The perpetrator effected the abolition, suspension or termination of admissibility in a court of law of certain rights or actions.

2. The abolition, suspension or termination was directed at the nationals of a hostile party.

3. The perpetrator intended the abolition, suspension or termination to be directed at the nationals of a hostile party.

4. The conduct took place in the context of and was associated with an international armed conflict.

5. The perpetrator was aware of factual circumstances that established the existence of an armed conflict.

ARTICLE 8 (2) (B) (XV)

WAR CRIME OF COMPELLING PARTICIPATION IN MILITARY OPERATIONS

ELEMENTS

B3–056   1. The perpetrator coerced one or more persons by act or threat to take part in military operations against that person's own country or forces.

2. Such person or persons were nationals of a hostile party.

3. The conduct took place in the context of and was associated with an international armed conflict.

4. The perpetrator was aware of factual circumstances that established the existence of an armed conflict.

ARTICLE 8 (2) (B) (XVI)

WAR CRIME OF PILLAGING

ELEMENTS

B3–057   1. The perpetrator appropriated certain property.

2. The perpetrator intended to deprive the owner of the property and to appropriate it for private or personal use.[47]

---

[47] As indicated by the use of the term "private or personal use", appropriations justified by military necessity cannot constitute the crime of pillaging.

3. The appropriation was without the consent of the owner.

4. The conduct took place in the context of and was associated with an international armed conflict.

5. The perpetrator was aware of factual circumstances that established the existence of an armed conflict.

ARTICLE 8 (2) (B) (XVII)

WAR CRIME OF EMPLOYING POISON OR POISONED WEAPONS

ELEMENTS

1. The perpetrator employed a substance or a weapon that releases a substance as a **B3–058** result of its employment.

2. The substance was such that it causes death or serious damage to health in the ordinary course of events, through its toxic properties.

3. The conduct took place in the context of and was associated with an international armed conflict.

4. The perpetrator was aware of factual circumstances that established the existence of an armed conflict.

ARTICLE 8 (2) (B) (XVIII)

WAR CRIME OF EMPLOYING PROHIBITED GASES, LIQUIDS, MATERIALS OR DEVICES

ELEMENTS

1. The perpetrator employed a gas or other analogous substance or device.   **B3–059**

2. The gas, substance or device was such that it causes death or serious damage to health in the ordinary course of events, through its asphyxiating or toxic properties.[48]

3. The conduct took place in the context of and was associated with an international armed conflict.

4. The perpetrator was aware of factual circumstances that established the existence of an armed conflict.

ARTICLE 8 (2) (B) (XIX)

WAR CRIME OF EMPLOYING PROHIBITED BULLETS

ELEMENTS

1. The perpetrator employed certain bullets.   **B3–060**

2. The bullets were such that their use violates the international law of armed conflict because they expand or flatten easily in the human body.

3. The perpetrator was aware that the nature of the bullets was such that their employment would uselessly aggravate suffering or the wounding effect.

---

[48] Nothing in this element shall be interpreted as limiting or prejudicing in any way existing or developing rules of international law with respect to the development, production, stockpiling and use of chemical weapons.

4. The conduct took place in the context of and was associated with an international armed conflict.

5. The perpetrator was aware of factual circumstances that established the existence of an armed conflict.

Article 8 (2) (b) (xx)

WAR CRIME OF EMPLOYING WEAPONS, PROJECTILES OR MATERIALS OR METHODS OF WARFARE LISTED IN THE ANNEX TO THE STATUTE

ELEMENTS

B3–061   *[Elements will have to be drafted once weapons, projectiles or material or methods of warfare have been included in an annex to the Statute.]*

Article 8 (2) (b) (xxi)

WAR CRIME OF OUTRAGES UPON PERSONAL DIGNITY

ELEMENTS

B3–062   1. The perpetrator humiliated, degraded or otherwise violated the dignity of one or more persons.[49]

2. The severity of the humiliation, degradation or other violation was of such degree as to be generally recognized as an outrage upon personal dignity.

3. The conduct took place in the context of and was associated with an international armed conflict.

4. The perpetrator was aware of factual circumstances that established the existence of an armed conflict.

Article 8 (2) (b) (xxii)–1

WAR CRIME OF RAPE

ELEMENTS

B3–063   1. The perpetrator invaded[50] the body of a person by conduct resulting in penetration, however slight, of any part of the body of the victim or of the perpetrator with a sexual organ, or of the anal or genital opening of the victim with any object or any other part of the body.

2. The invasion was committed by force, or by threat of force or coercion, such as that caused by fear of violence, duress, detention, psychological oppression or abuse of power, against such person or another person, or by taking advantage of a coercive environment, or the invasion was committed against a person incapable of giving genuine consent.[51]

---

[49] For this crime, "persons" can include dead persons. It is understood that the victim need not personally be aware of the existence of the humiliation or degradation or other violation. This element takes into account relevant aspects of the cultural background of the victim.

[50] The concept of "invasion" is intended to be broad enough to be gender-neutral.

[51] It is understood that a person may be incapable of giving genuine consent if affected by natural, induced or age-related incapacity. This footnote also applies to the corresponding elements of article 8 (2) (b) (xxii)–3, 5 and 6.

3. The conduct took place in the context of and was associated with an international armed conflict.

4. The perpetrator was aware of factual circumstances that established the existence of an armed conflict.

Article 8 (2) (b) (xxii)–2

WAR CRIME OF SEXUAL SLAVERY[52]
ELEMENTS

1. The perpetrator exercised any or all of the powers attaching to the right of ownership over one or more persons, such as by purchasing, selling, lending or bartering such a person or persons, or by imposing on them a similar deprivation of liberty.[53]   **B3–064**

2. The perpetrator caused such person or persons to engage in one or more acts of a sexual nature.

3. The conduct took place in the context of and was associated with an international armed conflict.

4. The perpetrator was aware of factual circumstances that established the existence of an armed conflict.

Article 8 (2) (b) (xxii)–3

WAR CRIME OF ENFORCED PROSTITUTION

ELEMENTS

1. The perpetrator caused one or more persons to engage in one or more acts of a sexual nature by force, or by threat of force or coercion, such as that caused by fear of violence, duress, detention, psychological oppression or abuse of power, against such person or persons or another person, or by taking advantage of a coercive environment or such person's or persons' incapacity to give genuine consent.   **B3–065**

2. The perpetrator or another person obtained or expected to obtain pecuniary or other advantage in exchange for or in connection with the acts of a sexual nature.

3. The conduct took place in the context of and was associated with an international armed conflict.

4. The perpetrator was aware of factual circumstances that established the existence of an armed conflict.

Article 8 (2) (b) (xxii)–4

WAR CRIME OF FORCED PREGNANCY

ELEMENTS

1. The perpetrator confined one or more women forcibly made pregnant, with the intent of affecting the ethnic composition of any population or carrying out other grave violations of international law.   **B3–066**

---

[52] Given the complex nature of this crime, it is recognized that its commission could involve more than one perpetrator as a part of a common criminal purpose.

[53] It is understood that such deprivation of liberty may, in some circumstances, include exacting forced labour or otherwise reducing a person to servile status as defined in the Supplementary Convention on the Abolition of Slavery, the Slave Trade, and Institutions and Practices Similar to Slavery of 1956. It is also understood that the conduct described in this element includes trafficking in persons, in particular women and children.

1355

2. The conduct took place in the context of and was associated with an international armed conflict.

3. The perpetrator was aware of factual circumstances that established the existence of an armed conflict.

ARTICLE 8 (2) (B) (XXII)–5

WAR CRIME OF ENFORCED STERILIZATION

ELEMENTS

B3–067　　1. The perpetrator deprived one or more persons of biological reproductive capacity.[54]

2. The conduct was neither justified by the medical or hospital treatment of the person or persons concerned nor carried out with their genuine consent.[55]

3. The conduct took place in the context of and was associated with an international armed conflict.

4. The perpetrator was aware of factual circumstances that established the existence of an armed conflict.

ARTICLE 8 (2) (B) (XXII)–6

WAR CRIME OF SEXUAL VIOLENCE

ELEMENTS

B3–068　　1. The perpetrator committed an act of a sexual nature against one or more persons or caused such person or persons to engage in an act of a sexual nature by force, or by threat of force or coercion, such as that caused by fear of violence, duress, detention, psychological oppression or abuse of power, against such person or persons or another person, or by taking advantage of a coercive environment or such person's or persons' incapacity to give genuine consent.

2. The conduct was of a gravity comparable to that of a grave breach of the Geneva Conventions.

3. The perpetrator was aware of the factual circumstances that established the gravity of the conduct.

4. The conduct took place in the context of and was associated with an international armed conflict.

5. The perpetrator was aware of factual circumstances that established the existence of an armed conflict.

ARTICLE 8 (2) (B) (XXIII)

WAR CRIME OF USING PROTECTED PERSONS AS SHIELDS

ELEMENTS

B3–069　　1. The perpetrator moved or otherwise took advantage of the location of one or more civilians or other persons protected under the international law of armed conflict.

---

[54] The deprivation is not intended to include birth-control measures which have a non-permanent effect in practice.

[55] It is understood that "genuine consent" does not include consent obtained through deception.

2. The perpetrator intended to shield a military objective from attack or shield, favour or impede military operations.

3. The conduct took place in the context of and was associated with an international armed conflict.

4. The perpetrator was aware of factual circumstances that established the existence of an armed conflict.

ARTICLE 8 (2) (B) (XXIV)

WAR CRIME OF ATTACKING OBJECTS OR PERSONS USING THE DISTINCTIVE EMBLEMS OF THE GENEVA CONVENTIONS

ELEMENTS

1. The perpetrator attacked one or more persons, buildings, medical units or transports or other objects using, in conformity with international law, a distinctive emblem or other method of identification indicating protection under the Geneva Conventions. **B3–070**

2. The perpetrator intended such persons, buildings, units or transports or other objects so using such identification to be the object of the attack.

3. The conduct took place in the context of and was associated with an international armed conflict.

4. The perpetrator was aware of factual circumstances that established the existence of an armed conflict.

ARTICLE 8 (2) (B) (XXV)

WAR CRIME OF STARVATION AS A METHOD OF WARFARE

ELEMENTS

1. The perpetrator deprived civilians of objects indispensable to their survival. **B3–071**

2. The perpetrator intended to starve civilians as a method of warfare.

3. The conduct took place in the context of and was associated with an international armed conflict.

4. The perpetrator was aware of factual circumstances that established the existence of an armed conflict.

ARTICLE 8 (2) (B) (XXVI)

WAR CRIME OF USING, CONSCRIPTING OR ENLISTING CHILDREN

ELEMENTS

1. The perpetrator conscripted or enlisted one or more persons into the national armed forces or used one or more persons to participate actively in hostilities. **B3–072**

2. Such person or persons were under the age of 15 years.

3. The perpetrator knew or should have known that such person or persons were under the age of 15 years.

4. The conduct took place in the context of and was associated with an international armed conflict.

5. The perpetrator was aware of factual circumstances that established the existence of an armed conflict.

ARTICLE 8 (2) (C)

ARTICLE 8 (2) (C) (I)–1

WAR CRIME OF MURDER

ELEMENTS

B3–073
1. The perpetrator killed one or more persons.
2. Such person or persons were either *hors de combat*, or were civilians, medical personnel, or religious personnel[56] taking no active part in the hostilities.
3. The perpetrator was aware of the factual circumstances that established this status.
4. The conduct took place in the context of and was associated with an armed conflict not of an international character.
5. The perpetrator was aware of factual circumstances that established the existence of an armed conflict.

ARTICLE 8 (2) (C) (I)–2

WAR CRIME OF MUTILATION

ELEMENTS

B3–074
1. The perpetrator subjected one or more persons to mutilation, in particular by permanently disfiguring the person or persons, or by permanently disabling or removing an organ or appendage.
2. The conduct was neither justified by the medical, dental or hospital treatment of the person or persons concerned nor carried out in such person's or persons' interests.
3. Such person or persons were either *hors de combat*, or were civilians, medical personnel or religious personnel taking no active part in the hostilities.
4. The perpetrator was aware of the factual circumstances that established this status.
5. The conduct took place in the context of and was associated with an armed conflict not of an international character.
6. The perpetrator was aware of factual circumstances that established the existence of an armed conflict.

ARTICLE 8 (2) (C) (I)–3

WAR CRIME OF CRUEL TREATMENT

ELEMENTS

B3–075
1. The perpetrator inflicted severe physical or mental pain or suffering upon one or more persons.
2. Such person or persons were either *hors de combat*, or were civilians, medical personnel, or religious personnel taking no active part in the hostilities.

---

[56] The term "religious personnel" includes those non-confessional non-combatant military personnel carrying out a similar function.

3. The perpetrator was aware of the factual circumstances that established this status.

4. The conduct took place in the context of and was associated with an armed conflict not of an international character.

5. The perpetrator was aware of factual circumstances that established the existence of an armed conflict.

ARTICLE 8 (2) (C) (I)–4

WAR CRIME OF TORTURE

ELEMENTS

1. The perpetrator inflicted severe physical or mental pain or suffering upon one or more persons.

2. The perpetrator inflicted the pain or suffering for such purposes as: obtaining information or a confession, punishment, intimidation or coercion or for any reason based on discrimination of any kind.

3. Such person or persons were either *hors de combat*, or were civilians, medical personnel or religious personnel taking no active part in the hostilities.

4. The perpetrator was aware of the factual circumstances that established this status.

5. The conduct took place in the context of and was associated with an armed conflict not of an international character.

6. The perpetrator was aware of factual circumstances that established the existence of an armed conflict.

B3–076

ARTICLE 8 (2) (C) (II)

WAR CRIME OF OUTRAGES UPON PERSONAL DIGNITY

ELEMENTS

1. The perpetrator humiliated, degraded or otherwise violated the dignity of one or more persons.[57]

2. The severity of the humiliation, degradation or other violation was of such degree as to be generally recognized as an outrage upon personal dignity.

3. Such person or persons were either *hors de combat*, or were civilians, medical personnel or religious personnel taking no active part in the hostilities.

4. The perpetrator was aware of the factual circumstances that established this status.

5. The conduct took place in the context of and was associated with an armed conflict not of an international character.

6. The perpetrator was aware of factual circumstances that established the existence of an armed conflict.

B3–077

ARTICLE 8 (2) (C) (III)

WAR CRIME OF TAKING HOSTAGES

ELEMENTS

1. The perpetrator seized, detained or otherwise held hostage one or more persons.

B3–078

---

[57] For this crime, "persons" can include dead persons. It is understood that the victim need not personally be aware of the existence of the humiliation or degradation or other violation. This element takes into account relevant aspects of the cultural background of the victim.

2. The perpetrator threatened to kill, injure or continue to detain such person or persons.

3. The perpetrator intended to compel a State, an international organization, a natural or legal person or a group of persons to act or refrain from acting as an explicit or implicit condition for the safety or the release of such person or persons.

4. Such person or persons were either *hors de combat*, or were civilians, medical personnel or religious personnel taking no active part in the hostilities.

5. The perpetrator was aware of the factual circumstances that established this status.

6. The conduct took place in the context of and was associated with an armed conflict not of an international character.

7. The perpetrator was aware of factual circumstances that established the existence of an armed conflict.

ARTICLE 8 (2) (C) (IV)

WAR CRIME OF SENTENCING OR EXECUTION WITHOUT DUE PROCESS

ELEMENTS

B3–079   1. The perpetrator passed sentence or executed one or more persons.[58]

2. Such person or persons were either *hors de combat*, or were civilians, medical personnel or religious personnel taking no active part in the hostilities.

3. The perpetrator was aware of the factual circumstances that established this status.

4. There was no previous judgement pronounced by a court, or the court that rendered judgement was not "regularly constituted", that is, it did not afford the essential guarantees of independence and impartiality, or the court that rendered judgement did not afford all other judicial guarantees generally recognized as indispensable under international law.[59]

5. The perpetrator was aware of the absence of a previous judgement or of the denial of relevant guarantees and the fact that they are essential or indispensable to a fair trial.

6. The conduct took place in the context of and was associated with an armed conflict not of an international character.

7. The perpetrator was aware of factual circumstances that established the existence of an armed conflict.

ARTICLE 8 (2) (E)

ARTICLE 8 (2) (E) (I)

WAR CRIME OF ATTACKING CIVILIANS

ELEMENTS

B3–080   1. The perpetrator directed an attack.

2. The object of the attack was a civilian population as such or individual civilians not taking direct part in hostilities.

---

[58] The elements laid down in these documents do not address the different forms of individual criminal responsibility, as enunciated in articles 25 and 28 of the Statute.

[59] With respect to elements 4 and 5, the Court should consider whether, in the light of all relevant circumstances, the cumulative effect of factors with respect to guarantees deprived the person or persons of a fair trial.

3. The perpetrator intended the civilian population as such or individual civilians not taking direct part in hostilities to be the object of the attack.

4. The conduct took place in the context of and was associated with an armed conflict not of an international character.

5. The perpetrator was aware of factual circumstances that established the existence of an armed conflict.

ARTICLE 8 (2) (E) (II)

WAR CRIME OF ATTACKING OBJECTS OR PERSONS USING THE DISTINCTIVE EMBLEMS OF THE GENEVA CONVENTIONS

ELEMENTS

1. The perpetrator attacked one or more persons, buildings, medical units or transports or other objects using, in conformity with international law, a distinctive emblem or other method of identification indicating protection under the Geneva Conventions.

B3–081

2. The perpetrator intended such persons, buildings, units or transports or other objects so using such identification to be the object of the attack.

3. The conduct took place in the context of and was associated with an armed conflict not of an international character.

4. The perpetrator was aware of factual circumstances that established the existence of an armed conflict.

ARTICLE 8 (2) (E) (III)

WAR CRIME OF ATTACKING PERSONNEL OR OBJECTS INVOLVED IN A HUMANITARIAN ASSISTANCE OR PEACEKEEPING MISSION

ELEMENTS

1. The perpetrator directed an attack.

B3–082

2. The object of the attack was personnel, installations, material, units or vehicles involved in a humanitarian assistance or peacekeeping mission in accordance with the Charter of the United Nations.

3. The perpetrator intended such personnel, installations, material, units or vehicles so involved to be the object of the attack.

4. Such personnel, installations, material, units or vehicles were entitled to that protection given to civilians or civilian objects under the international law of armed conflict.

5. The perpetrator was aware of the factual circumstances that established that protection.

6. The conduct took place in the context of and was associated with an armed conflict not of an international character.

7. The perpetrator was aware of factual circumstances that established the existence of an armed conflict.

ARTICLE 8 (2) (E) (IV)

WAR CRIME OF ATTACKING PROTECTED OBJECTS[60]
ELEMENTS

B3–083   1. The perpetrator directed an attack.

2. The object of the attack was one or more buildings dedicated to religion, education, art, science or charitable purposes, historic monuments, hospitals or places where the sick and wounded are collected, which were not military objectives.

3. The perpetrator intended such building or buildings dedicated to religion, education, art, science or charitable purposes, historic monuments, hospitals or places where the sick and wounded are collected, which were not military objectives, to be the object of the attack.

4. The conduct took place in the context of and was associated with an armed conflict not of an international character.

5. The perpetrator was aware of factual circumstances that established the existence of an armed conflict.

ARTICLE 8 (2) (E) (V)

WAR CRIME OF PILLAGING

ELEMENTS

B3–084   1. The perpetrator appropriated certain property.

2. The perpetrator intended to deprive the owner of the property and to appropriate it for private or personal use.[61]

3. The appropriation was without the consent of the owner.

4. The conduct took place in the context of and was associated with an armed conflict not of an international character.

5. The perpetrator was aware of factual circumstances that established the existence of an armed conflict.

ARTICLE 8 (2) (E) (VI)–1

WAR CRIME OF RAPE

ELEMENTS

B3–085   1. The perpetrator invaded[62] the body of a person by conduct resulting in penetration, however slight, of any part of the body of the victim or of the perpetrator with a sexual organ, or of the anal or genital opening of the victim with any object or any other part of the body.

2. The invasion was committed by force, or by threat of force or coercion, such as that caused by fear of violence, duress, detention, psychological oppression or abuse of power, against such person or another person, or by taking advantage of a coercive environ-

---

[60] The presence in the locality of persons specially protected under the Geneva Conventions of 1949 or of police forces retained for the sole purpose of maintaining law and order does not by itself render the locality a military objective.

[61] As indicated by the use of the term "private or personal use", appropriations justified by military necessity cannot constitute the crime of pillaging.

[62] The concept of "invasion" is intended to be broad enough to be gender-neutral.

ment, or the invasion was committed against a person incapable of giving genuine consent.[63]

3. The conduct took place in the context of and was associated with an armed conflict not of an international character.

4. The perpetrator was aware of factual circumstances that established the existence of an armed conflict.

ARTICLE 8 (2) (E) (VI)–2

WAR CRIME OF SEXUAL SLAVERY[64]
ELEMENTS

1. The perpetrator exercised any or all of the powers attaching to the right of **B3–086** ownership over one or more persons, such as by purchasing, selling, lending or bartering such a person or persons, or by imposing on them a similar deprivation of liberty.[65]

2. The perpetrator caused such person or persons to engage in one or more acts of a sexual nature.

3. The conduct took place in the context of and was associated with an armed conflict not of an international character.

4. The perpetrator was aware of factual circumstances that established the existence of an armed conflict.

ARTICLE 8 (2) (E) (VI)–3

WAR CRIME OF ENFORCED PROSTITUTION

ELEMENTS

1. The perpetrator caused one or more persons to engage in one or more acts of a **B3–087** sexual nature by force, or by threat of force or coercion, such as that caused by fear of violence, duress, detention, psychological oppression or abuse of power, against such person or persons or another person, or by taking advantage of a coercive environment or such person's or persons' incapacity to give genuine consent.

2. The perpetrator or another person obtained or expected to obtain pecuniary or other advantage in exchange for or in connection with the acts of a sexual nature.

3. The conduct took place in the context of and was associated with an armed conflict not of an international character.

4. The perpetrator was aware of factual circumstances that established the existence of an armed conflict.

ARTICLE 8 (2) (E) (VI)–4

WAR CRIME OF FORCED PREGNANCY

ELEMENTS

1. The perpetrator confined one or more women forcibly made pregnant, with the **B3–088** intent of affecting the ethnic composition of any population or carrying out other grave violations of international law.

---

[63] It is understood that a person may be incapable of giving genuine consent if affected by natural, induced or age-related incapacity. This footnote also applies to the corresponding elements in article 8 (2) (e) (vi)–3, 5 and 6.

[64] Given the complex nature of this crime, it is recognized that its commission could involve more than one perpetrator as a part of a common criminal purpose.

[65] It is understood that such deprivation of liberty may, in some circumstances, include exacting forced labour or otherwise reducing a person to servile status as defined in the Supplementary Convention on the Abolition of Slavery, the Slave Trade, and Institutions and Practices Similar to Slavery of 1956. It is also understood that the conduct described in this element includes trafficking in persons, in particular women and children.

2. The conduct took place in the context of and was associated with an armed conflict not of an international character.

3. The perpetrator was aware of factual circumstances that established the existence of an armed conflict.

ARTICLE 8 (2) (E) (VI)–5

WAR CRIME OF ENFORCED STERILIZATION

ELEMENTS

B3–089 1. The perpetrator deprived one or more persons of biological reproductive capacity.[66]

2. The conduct was neither justified by the medical or hospital treatment of the person or persons concerned nor carried out with their genuine consent.[67]

3. The conduct took place in the context of and was associated with an armed conflict not of an international character.

4. The perpetrator was aware of factual circumstances that established the existence of an armed conflict.

ARTICLE 8 (2) (E) (VI)–6

WAR CRIME OF SEXUAL VIOLENCE

ELEMENTS

B3–090 1. The perpetrator committed an act of a sexual nature against one or more persons or caused such person or persons to engage in an act of a sexual nature by force, or by threat of force or coercion, such as that caused by fear of violence, duress, detention, psychological oppression or abuse of power, against such person or persons or another person, or by taking advantage of a coercive environment or such person's or persons' incapacity to give genuine consent.

2. The conduct was of a gravity comparable to that of a serious violation of article 3 common to the four Geneva Conventions.

3. The perpetrator was aware of the factual circumstances that established the gravity of the conduct.

4. The conduct took place in the context of and was associated with an armed conflict not of an international character.

5. The perpetrator was aware of factual circumstances that established the existence of an armed conflict.

ARTICLE 8 (2) (E) (VII)

WAR CRIME OF USING, CONSCRIPTING AND ENLISTING CHILDREN

ELEMENTS

B3–091 1. The perpetrator conscripted or enlisted one or more persons into an armed force or group or used one or more persons to participate actively in hostilities.

[66] The deprivation is not intended to include birth-control measures which have a non-permanent effect in practice.
[67] It is understood that "genuine consent" does not include consent obtained through deception.

2. Such person or persons were under the age of 15 years.
3. The perpetrator knew or should have known that such person or persons were under the age of 15 years.
4. The conduct took place in the context of and was associated with an armed conflict not of an international character.
5. The perpetrator was aware of factual circumstances that established the existence of an armed conflict.

ARTICLE 8 (2) (E) (VIII)

WAR CRIME OF DISPLACING CIVILIANS

ELEMENTS

1. The perpetrator ordered a displacement of a civilian population. **B3-092**
2. Such order was not justified by the security of the civilians involved or by military necessity.
3. The perpetrator was in a position to effect such displacement by giving such order.
4. The conduct took place in the context of and was associated with an armed conflict not of an international character.
5. The perpetrator was aware of factual circumstances that established the existence of an armed conflict.

ARTICLE 8 (2) (E) (IX)

WAR CRIME OF TREACHEROUSLY KILLING OR WOUNDING

ELEMENTS

1. The perpetrator invited the confidence or belief of one or more combatant **B3-093** adversaries that they were entitled to, or were obliged to accord, protection under rules of international law applicable in armed conflict.
2. The perpetrator intended to betray that confidence or belief.
3. The perpetrator killed or injured such person or persons.
4. The perpetrator made use of that confidence or belief in killing or injuring such person or persons.
5. Such person or persons belonged to an adverse party.
6. The conduct took place in the context of and was associated with an armed conflict not of an international character.
7. The perpetrator was aware of factual circumstances that established the existence of an armed conflict.

ARTICLE 8 (2) (E) (X)

WAR CRIME OF DENYING QUARTER

ELEMENTS

1. The perpetrator declared or ordered that there shall be no survivors. **B3-094**
2. Such declaration or order was given in order to threaten an adversary or to conduct hostilities on the basis that there shall be no survivors.

3. The perpetrator was in a position of effective command or control over the subordinate forces to which the declaration or order was directed.

4. The conduct took place in the context of and was associated with an armed conflict not of an international character.

5. The perpetrator was aware of factual circumstances that established the existence of an armed conflict.

ARTICLE 8 (2) (E) (XI)–1

WAR CRIME OF MUTILATION

ELEMENTS

B3–095   1. The perpetrator subjected one or more persons to mutilation, in particular by permanently disfiguring the person or persons, or by permanently disabling or removing an organ or appendage.

2. The conduct caused death or seriously endangered the physical or mental health of such person or persons.

3. The conduct was neither justified by the medical, dental or hospital treatment of the person or persons concerned nor carried out in such person's or persons' interest.[68]

4. Such person or persons were in the power of another party to the conflict.

5. The conduct took place in the context of and was associated with an armed conflict not of an international character.

6. The perpetrator was aware of factual circumstances that established the existence of an armed conflict.

ARTICLE 8 (2) (E) (XI)–2

WAR CRIME OF MEDICAL OR SCIENTIFIC EXPERIMENTS

ELEMENTS

B3–096   1. The perpetrator subjected one or more persons to a medical or scientific experiment.

2. The experiment caused the death or seriously endangered the physical or mental health or integrity of such person or persons.

3. The conduct was neither justified by the medical, dental or hospital treatment of such person or persons concerned nor carried out in such person's or persons' interest.

4. Such person or persons were in the power of another party to the conflict.

5. The conduct took place in the context of and was associated with an armed conflict not of an international character.

6. The perpetrator was aware of factual circumstances that established the existence of an armed conflict.

---

[68] Consent is not a defence to this crime. The crime prohibits any medical procedure which is not indicated by the state of health of the person concerned and which is not consistent with generally accepted medical standards which would be applied under similar medical circumstances to persons who are nationals of the party conducting the procedure and who are in no way deprived of liberty. This footnote also applies to the similar element in article 8 (2) (e) (xi)–2.

ARTICLE 8 (2) (E) (XII)

WAR CRIME OF DESTROYING OR SEIZING THE ENEMY'S PROPERTY

ELEMENTS

1. The perpetrator destroyed or seized certain property. **B3–097**
2. Such property was property of an adversary.
3. Such property was protected from that destruction or seizure under the international law of armed conflict.
4. The perpetrator was aware of the factual circumstances that established the status of the property.
5. The destruction or seizure was not required by military necessity.
6. The conduct took place in the context of and was associated with an armed conflict not of an international character.
7. The perpetrator was aware of factual circumstances that established the existence of an armed conflict.

B4. List of State Ratifications of the ICC

This document may be found at *http://www.icc-cpi.int/asp/statesparties.html* **B4–001**

[Next document is numbered B6.]

B6. Proposal for a draft Code of Professional Conduct for Counsel before the International Criminal Court

This document may be found at *http://www.icc-cpi.int/library/asp/ICC-ASP-3-11-Rev1-English.pdf* **B6–001**

B7. Financial Regulations and Rules

This document may be found at *http://www.icc-cpi.int/library/about/officialjournal/Financial_Regulations_and_Rules_120704-EN.pdf*

B8. Agreement on the Privileges and Immunities of the International Criminal Court

This document may be found at *http://www.un.org/law/icc/asp/1stsession/report/english/part_ii_e_e.pdf*

B9. Regulations of the Court ICC–BD/01–01–04

TABLE OF CONTENTS

CHAPTER 4

COUNSEL ISSUES AND LEGAL ASSISTANCE

CHAPTER 5

VICTIMS PARTICIPATION AND REPARATIONS

CHAPTER 1

GENERAL PROVISIONS

REGULATION 1

ADOPTION OF THESE REGULATIONS

1. These Regulations have been adopted pursuant to article 52 and shall be read **B9–001**
subject to the Statute and the Rules.

2. These Regulations have been adopted in English and French. Translations in the official languages of the Court are equally authentic.

REGULATION 2

USE OF TERMS

B9–002   1. In these Regulations:
- "article" refers to an article of the Statute;
- "Assembly" refers to the Assembly of States Parties to the Statute;
- "Chamber" refers to a Chamber of the Court;
- "Chief Custody Officer" refers to the officer appointed by the Court as the head of the staff of the detention centre;
- "counsel" refers to a defence counsel and a legal representative of a victim;
- "Court" refers to the International Criminal Court;
- "Deputy Prosecutor" refers to a Deputy Prosecutor of the Court;
- "Deputy Registrar" refers to the Deputy Registrar of the Court;
- "detained person" refers to any person detained in a detention centre;
- "detention centre" refers to any prison facility other than the prison facility described in article 103, paragraph 4, maintained by the Court or maintained by other authorities and made available to the Court;
- "Division" refers to a Division of the Court;
- "Elements of Crimes" refers to the Elements of Crimes as described in article 9;
- "host State" refers to the Netherlands;
- "judge" refers to a judge of the Court;
- "list of counsel" refers to the list of counsel as described in rule 21, sub-rule 2;
- "Office of the Prosecutor" refers to the organ of the Court as described in article 34;
- "plenary session" refers to a plenary session of the judges as described in rule 4;
- "Presidency" refers to the organ of the Court as described in article 34 comprised of the President and the First and Second Vice-Presidents of the Court;
- "President" refers to the President of the Court;
- "Presiding Judge" refers to the Presiding Judge of a Chamber;
- "Prosecutor" refers to the Prosecutor of the Court;
- "Registrar" refers to the Registrar of the Court;
- "Registry" refers to the organ of the Court as described in article 34;
- "regulation" refers to a regulation of these Regulations;
- "Regulations" refers to the Regulations of the Court as adopted pursuant to article 52;
- "rule" refers to a rule of the Rules, including provisional rules drawn up under article 51, paragraph 3;
- "Rules" refers to the Rules of Procedure and Evidence;
- State Party" refers to a State Party to the Statute;
- "Statute" refers to the Rome Statute of the Court.

2. In these Regulations the singular shall include the plural and vice versa.

REGULATION 3

COORDINATION COUNCIL

B9–003   1. There shall be a Coordination Council comprised of the President on behalf of the Presidency, the Prosecutor and the Registrar.

2. The Coordination Council shall meet at least once a month and on any other occasion at the request of one of its members in order to discuss and coordinate on, where necessary, the administrative activities of the organs of the Court.

REGULATION 4

ADVISORY COMMITTEE ON LEGAL TEXTS

1. There shall be an Advisory Committee on Legal Texts comprised of: **B9–004**
   (a) Three judges, one from each Division, elected from amongst the members of the Division, who shall be members of the Advisory Committee for a period of three years;
   (b) One representative from the Office of the Prosecutor;
   (c) One representative from the Registry; and
   (d) One representative of counsel included in the list of counsel.

2. The Advisory Committee shall elect a judge as chairperson for a period of three years who shall be eligible for re-election once. The Advisory Committee shall meet at least twice a year and at any time at the request of the Presidency.

3. The Chairperson of the Advisory Committee may, as appropriate, invite other interested groups or persons to present their views if considered relevant for the work of the Advisory Committee. The Chairperson may also seek the advice of experts.

4. The Advisory Committee shall consider and report on proposals for amendments to the Rules, Elements of Crimes and these Regulations. Subject to sub-regulation 5, it shall submit a written report in both working languages of the Court setting out its recommendations on such proposals to a plenary session. A copy thereof shall be provided to the Prosecutor and the Registrar. The Advisory Committee shall also consider and report on any matter referred to it by the Presidency.

5. When a proposal for an amendment to the Rules or to the Elements of Crimes is presented by the Prosecutor, the Advisory Committee shall transmit its report to the Prosecutor.

6. The Presidency may, as appropriate, designate one person, who may be assisted by others, to provide administrative and legal support to the Advisory Committee.

7. The Advisory Committee shall adopt its own rules of procedure.

REGULATION 5

AMENDMENTS TO THE RULES AND ELEMENTS OF CRIMES

1. Any proposal for amendments to the Rules pursuant to article 51 or to the **B9–005**
Elements of Crimes pursuant to article 9 shall be submitted by a judge to the Advisory Committee on Legal Texts. The Prosecutor may submit proposals to the Advisory Committee on Legal Texts. All proposals, together with any explanatory material, shall be presented in writing in both working languages of the Court.

2. In urgent cases, where the Rules do not provide for a specific situation before the Court, the Presidency, on its own motion or at the request of a judge or the Prosecutor, may submit proposals for provisional rules under article 51, paragraph 3, directly to the judges for their consideration in a plenary session.

REGULATION 6

AMENDMENTS TO THESE REGULATIONS

1. Any proposal for amendments to these Regulations shall be accompanied by **B9–006**
explanatory material, and those documents shall be presented in writing to the Advisory Committee on Legal Texts in both working languages of the Court.

2. In urgent cases, the Presidency, on its own motion or at the request of a judge, the Prosecutor or the Registrar, may submit proposals for amendments to these Regulations directly to the judges for their consideration in a plenary session.

1375

3. Amendments to these Regulations shall not be applied retroactively to the detriment of the person to whom article 55, paragraph 2, or article 58 applies, the accused, convicted or acquitted person.

REGULATION 7

PUBLICATION IN THE OFFICIAL JOURNAL

B9–007   1. An Official Journal of the Court shall be created and shall contain the following texts and amendments thereto:
  (a) The Statute;
  (b) The Rules;
  (c) The Elements of Crimes;
  (d) These Regulations;
  (e) The Regulations of the Office of the Prosecutor;
  (f) The Regulations of the Registry;
  (g) The Code of Professional Conduct for counsel;
  (h) The Code of Judicial Ethics;
  (i) The Staff Regulations;
  (j) The Financial Regulations and Rules;
  (k) The Agreement on the Privileges and Immunities of the International Criminal Court;
  (l) The Relationship Agreement between the Court and the United Nations;
  (m) The Headquarters Agreement with the host State;
  (n) Any other material as decided by the Presidency in consultation with the Prosecutor and/or the Registrar.
  2. The Official Journal shall indicate the date when the text or any amendment thereto came into force.

REGULATION 8

WEBSITE OF THE COURT

B9–008   The following materials shall be published on the website of the Court:
  (a) The Official Journal of the Court referred to in regulation 7;
  (b) The calendar of the Court;
  (c) Decisions and orders of the Court and other particulars of each case brought before the Court as described in rule 15;
  (d) Any other material as decided by the Presidency, the Prosecutor or the Registrar.

CHAPTER 2

COMPOSITION AND ADMINISTRATION OF THE COURT

REGULATION 9

TERM OF OFFICE

B9–009   1. The term of office of judges shall commence on the eleventh of March following the date of their election.
  2. The term of office of a judge elected to replace a judge whose term of office has not expired shall commence on the date of his or her election and shall continue for the remainder of the term of his or her predecessor.

REGULATION 10

PRECEDENCE

1. In the exercise of their judicial functions, the judges, irrespective of age, date of election or length of service, are of equal status.

2. The President, the First Vice-President and the Second Vice-President, while holding these offices, shall take precedence over all other judges.

3. Judges shall take precedence according to the date of the commencement of their respective terms of office.

4. Judges whose terms of office begin on the same date shall take precedence according to seniority of age.

5. A judge who is re-elected in accordance with article 36, paragraph 9 (c), or article 37, paragraph 2, shall retain his or her precedence.

B9–010

REGULATION 11

THE PRESIDENCY

1. The members of the Presidency shall attempt to achieve unanimity in any decision taken in carrying out their responsibilities under article 38, paragraph 3, failing which any such decision shall be taken by majority.

2. In the event that a member of the Presidency is unavailable or disqualified, his or her responsibilities as a member of the Presidency shall be carried out by the next available judge having precedence in accordance with regulation 10.

3. In exceptional circumstances such as in an emergency, where there is a need for the Presidency to act and where it is not possible for all three members of the Presidency to act together, the members of the Presidency who are immediately available may take the action required.

4. In the event that the President, the First Vice-President and the Second Vice-President are unavailable or disqualified, the functions of the President shall be carried out by the next available judge having precedence in accordance with regulation 10.

B9–011

REGULATION 12

SERVICE WITHIN THE APPEALS CHAMBER

In the event that a member of the Appeals Chamber is disqualified, or unavailable for a substantial reason, the Presidency shall, in the interests of the administration of justice, attach to the Appeals Chamber on a temporary basis a judge from either the Trial or Pre-Trial Division, subject to article 39, paragraph 1. Under no circumstances shall a judge who has participated in the pre-trial or trial phase of a case be eligible to sit on the Appeals Chamber hearing that case; nor shall a judge who has participated in the appeal phase of a case be eligible to sit on the pre-trial or trial phase of that case.

B9–012

REGULATION 13

PRESIDING JUDGES

1. The judges of the Appeals Chamber shall decide on a Presiding Judge for each appeal.

2. The judges of each Trial Chamber and of each Pre-Trial Chamber shall elect from amongst their members a Presiding Judge who shall carry out the functions conferred upon him or her by the Statute, Rules or otherwise.

B9–013

REGULATION 14

PRESIDENT OF THE DIVISION

B9–014   The judges of each Division shall elect a President of the Division from amongst their members to oversee the administration of the Division. The President of the Division shall carry out this function for a period of one year.

REGULATION 15

REPLACEMENTS

B9–015   1. The Presidency shall be responsible for the replacement of a judge pursuant to rule 38 and in accordance with article 39 and shall also take into account, to the extent possible, gender and equitable geographical representation.
2. Without prejudice to the criteria listed in sub-regulation 1, replacement within the Appeals Chamber shall take place in accordance with regulation 12.

REGULATION 16

ALTERNATE JUDGES

B9–016   Subject to the provisions of article 39 and pursuant to article 74, paragraph 1, alternate judges may be designated by the Presidency, on a case-by-case basis, first taking into account the availability of judges from the Trial Division and thereafter from the Pre-Trial Division.

REGULATION 17

DUTY JUDGE

B9–017   1. The Presidency shall establish a duty roster of judges of the Pre-Trial Division. Each judge shall be on duty for a period of 14 days.
2. The duty judge shall be responsible for dealing with requests or applications:
    (a) Where the request or application is submitted outside normal Registry hours, if the duty judge is satisfied that it is urgent; or
    (b) Where the request or application is submitted during normal Registry hours and the Pre-Trial Chamber or Chamber referred to in regulation 46, sub-regulation 3, is unavailable, provided that the duty judge is satisfied that the matter is urgent and that it is appropriate for him or her to deal with it.
3. The duty roster of judges of the Pre-Trial Division shall be maintained by the Presidency and made available to the Registry.

REGULATION 18

DUTY LEGAL OFFICERS OF THE CHAMBERS

B9–018   1. The Presidency shall establish a duty roster of legal officers of the Chambers. Each legal officer shall be on duty for a period of 14 days.
2. The duty legal officer of the Chambers shall be responsible for assisting the duty judge.
3. The duty roster of legal officers of the Chambers shall be maintained by the Presidency and made available to the Registry.

REGULATION 19

DUTY OFFICERS OF THE REGISTRY

The Registrar shall establish a duty roster of officers of the Registry. Each officer shall be on duty for the period specified in the Regulations of the Registry.

B9–019

CHAPTER 3

PROCEEDINGS BEFORE THE COURT

Section 1

Provisions relating to all stages of the proceedings

Subsection 1

General provisions

REGULATION 20

PUBLIC HEARINGS

1. All hearings shall be held in public, unless otherwise provided in the Statute, Rules, these Regulations or ordered by the Chamber.

B9–020

2. When a Chamber orders that certain hearings be held in closed session, the Chamber shall make public the reasons for such an order.

3. A Chamber may order the disclosure of all or part of the record of closed proceedings when the reasons for ordering its non-disclosure no longer exist.

REGULATION 21

BROADCASTING, RELEASE OF TRANSCRIPTS AND RECORDINGS

1. The publicity of hearings may extend beyond the courtroom and may be through broadcasting by the Registry or release of transcripts or recordings, unless otherwise ordered by the Chamber.

B9–021

2. In order to protect sensitive information, broadcasts of audio- and video-recordings of all hearings shall, unless otherwise ordered by the Chamber, be delayed by at least 30 minutes.

3. Witnesses and participants shall be informed that the public hearings of the Chamber are broadcast in accordance with this regulation. Any objection raised shall be ruled on by the Chamber in accordance with sub-regulations 4 and 5.

4. Any objection to the release of transcripts or recordings, or requests that certain testimony be excluded from broadcast, shall be made as soon as possible and, in any event, no later than at the commencement of the session at which the witness or participant is to appear.

5. The Chamber may decide to prohibit the broadcasting of any hearing of an objection until that objection has been ruled on.

6. The Chamber may order the termination of the broadcast of a hearing at any time.

7. All documentary evidence and other evidence introduced by a participant during a public hearing shall be available for broadcast, unless otherwise ordered by the Chamber.

8. At the request of a participant or the Registry, or *proprio motu*, and when possible within the time set out in sub-regulation 2, the Chamber may, in the interests of justice, order that any information likely to present a risk to the security or safety of victims, witnesses or other persons, or likely to be prejudicial to national security interests, shall not be published in any broadcast, audio- or video-recording or transcript of a public hearing.

9. The audio- and video-record of hearings shall be made available to the participants and the public in accordance with the procedures set out in the Regulations of the Registry, unless otherwise ordered by the Chamber.

REGULATION 22

DEFINITION OF DOCUMENTS

B9–022   The term "document" shall include any motion, application, request, response, reply, observation, representation and any other submission in a form capable of delivering a written record to the Court.

REGULATION 23

CONTENT OF DOCUMENTS

B9–023   1. Unless otherwise provided in the Statute, Rules, these Regulations or ordered by the Chamber, any document filed with the Court shall, as far as practicable, state:
  (a) The identity of the person filing the document;
  (b) The situation or case number, the name of the person to whom article 55, paragraph 2, or article 58 applies, the accused, convicted or acquitted person, the name of counsel or representative, if any, and the Chamber to which the matter has been assigned;
  (c) A brief summary of the reason for filing the document which is not a response or reply and the relief sought, if any;
  (d) All relevant legal and factual issues, including details of the articles, rules, regulations or other applicable law relied upon.

2. All standard forms and templates for use during the proceedings before the Court shall be approved by the Presidency. The Presidency may refer any matter relating to the standard forms and templates to the Advisory Committee on Legal Texts for its consideration.

3. Subject to any order of the Chamber, a participant shall file, with each document, copies of any authorities relied upon or, if appropriate, internet links. Participants are not required to file copies of decisions or orders of the Court. Authorities shall be provided in an authorised version together with a translation in at least one of the working languages of the Court if the original is not in one of those languages.

REGULATION 24

RESPONSES AND REPLIES

B9–024   1. The Prosecutor and the defence may file a response to any document filed by any participant in the case in accordance with the Statute, Rules, these Regulations and any order of the Chamber.

2. Victims or their legal representatives may file a response to any document when they are permitted to participate in the proceedings in accordance with article 68, paragraph 3, and rule 89, sub-rule 1, subject to any order of the Chamber.

3. States participating in the proceedings may file a response to any document, subject to any order of the Chamber.

4. A response referred to in sub-regulations 1 to 3 may not be filed to any document which is itself a response or reply.

5. Participants may only reply to a response with the leave of the Chamber, unless otherwise provided in these Regulations.

REGULATION 25

COMMUNICATIONS OTHER THAN IN WRITING

A person making a communication to the Court under rule 102 shall indicate at the start of the communication: **B9–025**
  (a) His or her identity;
  (b) The situation or case number, if known;
  (c) The Chamber seized of the matter, if known;
  (d) The name of the person to whom article 55, paragraph 2, or article 58 applies, the accused, convicted or acquitted person, if known;
  (e) The purpose of the communication;
  (f) When referring to a specific event, to the extent possible, the location, date and individuals involved.

REGULATION 26

ELECTRONIC MANAGEMENT

1. The Court shall establish a reliable, secure, efficient electronic system which supports its daily judicial and operational management and its proceedings.   **B9–026**

2. The Registry shall be responsible for the implementation of the system described in sub-regulation 1, taking into account the specific requirements of the judicial activity of the Court, including the need to ensure authenticity, accuracy, confidentiality and preservation of judicial records and material.

3. Documents, decisions and orders shall, whenever possible, be submitted in electronic version for registration by the Registry. The electronic version of filings shall be authoritative.

4. In proceedings before the Court, evidence other than live testimony shall be presented in electronic form whenever possible. The original form of such evidence shall be authoritative.

REGULATION 27

TRANSCRIPTS

1. Real time transcripts of hearings shall be provided in at least one of the working languages of the Court to the extent technically possible. Transcripts of proceedings other than hearings may be provided upon request.   **B9–027**

2. The transcripts constitute an integral part of the record of the proceedings. The electronic version of transcripts shall be authoritative.

REGULATION 28

QUESTIONS BY A CHAMBER

1. A Chamber may order the participants to clarify or to provide additional details on any document within a time limit specified by the Chamber.   **B9–028**

2. A Chamber may order the participants to address specific issues in their written or oral submissions within a time limit specified by the Chamber.

3. These provisions are without prejudice to the inherent powers of the Chamber.

Regulation 29

NON-COMPLIANCE WITH THESE REGULATIONS AND WITH ORDERS OF A CHAMBER

B9–029   1. In the event of non-compliance by a participant with the provisions of any regulation, or with an order of a Chamber made thereunder, the Chamber may issue any order that is deemed necessary in the interests of justice.

2. This provision is without prejudice to the inherent powers of the Chamber.

Regulation 30

STATUS CONFERENCES

B9–030   A Chamber may hold status conferences by way of hearings, including by way of audio- or video-link technology or by way of written submissions. The Chamber may require use of standard forms at a status conference as appropriate. Such standard forms shall be approved in accordance with regulation 23, sub-regulation 2.

Subsection 2

Distribution of documents

Regulation 31

NOTIFICATION

B9–031   1. Subject to the Statute, Rules, these Regulations or any order of a Chamber, all participants in the relevant proceedings shall be notified of any document registered by the Registry or any decision or order, unless, with regard to a document, the participant submitting that document requests otherwise. All participants shall provide to the Registry an electronic, facsimile or postal contact address for notification of documents, preferably in The Hague.

2. Unless otherwise provided in the Statute, Rules, these Regulations or ordered by the Chamber, a participant is deemed notified, informed of or to have had communicated to him or her, a document, decision or order on the day it is effectively sent from the Court by the Registry. Such date shall be written on the notification form to be appended to all copies of the document, decision or order, as relevant. If the document, decision or order is not received, a participant may raise the issue and, as appropriate, may ask for a variation of the time limit in accordance with regulation 35. The Registrar shall retain and, if required, produce proof that the document, decision or order was effectively sent.

3. The relevant person shall be notified by way of personal service of the following documents:

(a) Warrants of arrest;

(b) Summonses to appear;

(c) Documents containing the charges; and

(d) Such other documents, decisions or orders ordered by the Chamber to be notified by way of personal service.

4. Notification by way of personal service may be proved in the following manner:

    (a) By confirmation in writing on the prescribed form by the person serving the document that notification by way of personal service has been effected; and

    (b) By a signed acknowledgement of notification by way of personal service on the prescribed form by the relevant person.

Where the relevant person declines or is unable to sign an acknowledgement of notification by way of personal service, the confirmation in (a) above shall be proof of such notification.

5. In respect of oral decisions or orders, notification shall be deemed effective on the day the decision or order is rendered orally by the Chamber unless:

    (a) A participant was not present or represented when the decision or order was pronounced, in which case that participant shall be notified of the oral decision or order in accordance with sub-regulation 2; or

    (b) The Chamber has indicated that a written decision or order will follow, in which case participants shall be notified of the written decision or order in accordance with sub-regulation 2.

REGULATION 32

RECIPIENTS OF DOCUMENTS, DECISIONS AND ORDERS NOTIFIED BY THE COURT

1. A State shall be deemed notified when the official representative designated for **B9–032** proceedings before the Court has been notified of a document, decision or order. If a State does not designate such a representative, the State shall be deemed notified of the document, decision or order when it has been notified through the channel designated by that State in accordance with article 87.

2. Intergovernmental organisations and other organisations and institutions shall be deemed notified when the designated representative identified by the Registrar or the appropriate channel referred to in rule 177 has been notified of a document, decision or order.

3. A participant represented by counsel shall be deemed notified when his or her counsel has been notified of a document, decision or order at the electronic, facsimile or postal address which that counsel has indicated to the Registry in accordance with regulation 31, sub-regulation 1, unless otherwise provided in the Statute, Rules, these Regulations or ordered by the Chamber.

4. A person who is not represented by counsel shall be deemed notified when that person or the person, organisation or institution designated by that person has been notified of a document, decision or order.

5. The Prosecutor shall be deemed notified when the Office of the Prosecutor has been notified of a document, decision or order, unless it is explicitly specified that the Prosecutor shall be notified of the document, decision or order in person.

Subsection 3

Time and page limits

REGULATION 33

CALCULATION OF TIME LIMITS

1. The calculation of time for the purposes of any proceedings before the Court shall **B9–033** be made as follows:

    (a) Days shall be understood as calendar days. When the last day of a time period falls upon a Saturday, a Sunday or an official holiday of the Court, the next working day of the Court shall be considered the last day;

(b) Days shall only be understood as "full days", the day of notification of a document or the day of filing of a response or a reply by a participant to that document not being taken into consideration for the calculation of the time period available to file a document.

2. Documents shall be filed with the Registry between 9am and 4pm The Hague time or the time of such other place as designated by the Registrar.

REGULATION 34

TIME LIMITS FOR DOCUMENTS FILED WITH THE COURT

B9–034   Unless otherwise provided in the Statute, Rules or these Regulations, or unless otherwise ordered:

(a) A Chamber may fix time limits for the submission of the initial document to be filed by a participant;

(b) A response referred to in regulation 24 shall be filed within 21 days of notification in accordance with regulation 31 of the document to which the participant is responding;

(c) Subject to leave being granted by a Chamber in accordance with regulation 24, sub-regulation 5, a reply shall be filed within ten days of notification in accordance with regulation 31 of the response.

REGULATION 35

VARIATION OF TIME LIMITS

B9–035   1. Applications to extend or reduce any time limit as prescribed in these Regulations or as ordered by the Chamber shall be made in writing or orally to the Chamber seized of the matter setting out the grounds on which the variation is sought.

2. The Chamber may extend or reduce a time limit if good cause is shown and, where appropriate, after having given the participants an opportunity to be heard. After the lapse of a time limit, an extension of time may only be granted if the participant seeking the extension can demonstrate that he or she was unable to file the application within the time limit for reasons outside his or her control.

REGULATION 36

FORMAT OF DOCUMENTS AND CALCULATION OF PAGE LIMITS

B9–036   1. Headings, footnotes and quotations shall be counted in calculating the page limits.

2. The following shall not be counted in calculating the page limits:

(a) Any *addendum* containing *verbatim* quotations of the Statute, Rules or these Regulations;

(b) Any appendix containing references, authorities, copies from the record, exhibits and other relevant, non-argumentative material. An appendix shall not contain submissions.

3. Before the Registry notifies in accordance with regulation 31, sub-regulation 1, the participant shall, within the applicable time limit, file an index for approval by the Registrar that shall include relevant internet links and the proposed length of the appendix. If necessary, the participant may seek a ruling on the contents of an appendix from the Chamber. Any appendix shall be filed immediately upon approval of the index by the Registrar or following the ruling of the Chamber.

4. All documents shall be submitted on A4 format. Margins shall be at least 2.5 centimetres on all four sides. All documents that are filed shall be paginated, including

the cover sheet. The typeface of all documents shall be 12 point with 1.5 line spacing for the text and 10 point with single spacing for footnotes. An average page shall not exceed 300 words.

REGULATION 37

PAGE LIMITS FOR DOCUMENTS FILED WITH THE REGISTRY

1. A document filed with the Registry shall not exceed 20 pages, unless otherwise provided in the Statute, Rules, these Regulations or ordered by the Chamber. **B9–037**

2. The Chamber may, at the request of a participant, extend the page limit in exceptional circumstances.

REGULATION 38

SPECIFIC PAGE LIMITS

1. Unless otherwise ordered by the Chamber, the page limit shall not exceed 100 pages for the following documents and responses thereto, if any: **B9–038**

    (a) A request under article 57, paragraph 3 (d), and rule 115, sub-rule 1, and the views submitted by the State Party as referred to in those provisions;

    (b) The application of the Prosecutor for authorisation of the investigation under article 18, paragraph 2;

    (c) Challenges to the admissibility or jurisdiction of the Court under article 19, paragraph 2;

    (d) Requests by the State Party or the Security Council under article 53, paragraph 3 (a), to the Pre-Trial Chamber to reconsider a decision of the Prosecutor under article 53, paragraphs 1 and 2;

    (e) The request for authorisation of an investigation under article 15, paragraph 3, and rule 50, sub-rule 2;

    (f) Representations under article 75.

2. Unless otherwise ordered by the Chamber, the page limit shall not exceed 50 pages for the following documents and responses thereto, if any:

    (a) Representations made by victims to the Pre-Trial Chamber under article 15, paragraph 3, and rule 50, sub-rule 3;

    (b) Requests by the Prosecutor for a ruling regarding questions of jurisdiction or admissibility under article 19, paragraph 3;

    (c) Requests by the Prosecutor to the Pre-Trial Chamber under article 18, paragraph 6, or article 19, paragraph 8;

    (d) A document of the Prosecutor under article 56, paragraph 1 (a), containing the information that a unique investigative opportunity has arisen;

    (e) A request by any participant to the Pre-Trial Chamber to take specific measures or to issue orders and warrants or to seek State cooperation;

    (f) A request under rule 173 for compensation.

Subsection 4

Translation and Interpretation

REGULATION 39

LANGUAGE REQUIREMENTS

1. All documents and materials filed with the Registry shall be in English or French, unless otherwise provided in the Statute, Rules, these Regulations or authorised by the Chamber or the Presidency. If the original document or material is not in one of these languages, a participant shall attach a translation thereof. **B9–039**

2. Sub-regulation 1 shall not apply to victims who are not represented and do not have a sufficient knowledge of a working language of the Court or any other language authorised by the Chamber or the Presidency.

3. When a Chamber, in accordance with article 50, paragraph 3, and following consultation with the Registrar, authorises use by a participant of a language other than English or French, the expenses for interpretation and translation shall be borne by the Court.

REGULATION 40

LANGUAGE SERVICES OF THE REGISTRY

B9–040   1. The Registrar shall ensure that the decisions and texts envisaged in article 50, paragraph 1, and in rule 40, are translated into all the official languages of the Court. In addition, the Registrar shall ensure translation of those texts referred to in regulation 7, which the Presidency decides should be translated into all the official languages of the Court.

2. The Registrar shall ensure that interpretation services are provided in all proceedings:

    (a) For English and French and any other official language used as a working language in accordance with rule 41;

    (b) For the language of the person to whom article 58 applies, the accused, convicted or acquitted person if he or she does not fully understand or speak any of the working languages;

    (c) For the other language, if any, authorised by the Chamber pursuant to article 50, paragraph 3, subject to regulation 39, sub-regulation 3.

3. The Registrar shall ensure translation into the other working language(s) of all decisions or orders taken by Chambers during proceedings.

4. The Registrar shall ensure translation and interpretation for the cases listed in regulation 39, sub-regulation 2.

5. The Registrar shall, if necessary, ensure translation into the language chosen by the requested State of requests under Part 9 of the Statute transmitted by the Registrar in accordance with article 87, paragraph 2, and rule 176, sub-rule 2.

6. The Registrar shall ensure translation into the language of the person to whom article 55, paragraph 2, or article 58 applies, the accused, convicted or acquitted person, if he or she does not fully understand or speak any of the working languages, of all decisions or orders in his or her case. Counsel shall be responsible for informing that person of the other documents in his or her case.

Subsection 5

Protective measures

REGULATION 41

VICTIMS AND WITNESSES UNIT

B9–041   The Victims and Witnesses Unit may, pursuant to article 68, paragraph 4, draw any matter to the attention of a Chamber where protective or special measures under rules 87 and 88 require consideration.

REGULATION 42

APPLICATION AND VARIATION OF PROTECTIVE MEASURES

B9–042   1. Protective measures once ordered in any proceedings in respect of a victim or witness shall continue to have full force and effect in relation to any other proceedings before the Court and shall continue after proceedings have been concluded, subject to revision by a Chamber.

2. When the Prosecutor discharges disclosure obligations in subsequent proceedings, he or she shall respect the protective measures as previously ordered by a Chamber and shall inform the defence to whom the disclosure is being made of the nature of these protective measures.

3. Any application to vary a protective measure shall first be made to the Chamber which issued the order. If that Chamber is no longer seized of the proceedings in which the protective measure was ordered, application may be made to the Chamber before which a variation of the protective measure is being requested. That Chamber shall obtain all relevant information from the proceedings in which the protective measure was first ordered.

4. Before making a determination under sub-regulation 3, the Chamber shall seek to obtain, whenever possible, the consent of the person in respect of whom the application to rescind, vary or augment protective measures has been made.

Subsection 6

Evidence

REGULATION 43

TESTIMONY OF WITNESSES

Subject to the Statute and the Rules, the Presiding Judge, in consultation with the **B9–043** other members of the Chamber, shall determine the mode and order of questioning witnesses and presenting evidence so as to:

(a) Make the questioning of witnesses and the presentation of evidence fair and effective for the determination of the truth;

(b) Avoid delays and ensure the effective use of time.

REGULATION 44

EXPERTS

1. The Registrar shall create and maintain a list of experts accessible at all times to **B9–044** all organs of the Court and to all participants. Experts shall be included on such a list following an appropriate indication of expertise in the relevant field. A person may seek review by the Presidency of a negative decision of the Registrar.

2. The Chamber may direct the joint instruction of an expert by the participants.

3. On receipt of the report prepared by an expert jointly instructed, a participant may apply to the Chamber for leave to instruct a further expert.

4. The Chamber may *proprio motu* instruct an expert.

5. The Chamber may issue any order as to the subject of an expert report, the number of experts to be instructed, the mode of their instruction, the manner in which their evidence is to be presented and the time limits for the preparation and notification of their report.

Section 2

Pre-trial

REGULATION 45

INFORMATION PROVIDED BY THE PROSECUTOR

The Prosecutor shall inform the Presidency in writing as soon as a situation has been **B9–045** referred to the Prosecutor by a State Party under article 14 or by the Security Council under article 13, sub-paragraph (b); and shall provide the Presidency with any other information that may facilitate the timely assignment of a situation to a Pre-Trial Chamber, including, in particular, the intention of the Prosecutor to submit a request under article 15, paragraph 3.

REGULATION 46

PRE-TRIAL CHAMBER

B9–046   1. The Presidency shall constitute permanent Pre-Trial Chambers with fixed compositions.

2. The Presidency shall assign a situation to a Pre-Trial Chamber as soon as the Prosecutor has informed the Presidency in accordance with regulation 45. The Pre-Trial Chamber shall be responsible for any matter, request or information arising out of the situation assigned to it, save that, at the request of a Presiding Judge of a Pre-Trial Chamber, the President of the Pre-Trial Division may decide to assign a matter, request or information arising out of that situation to another Pre-Trial Chamber in the interests of the administration of justice.

3. Any matter, request or information not arising out of a situation assigned to a Pre-Trial Chamber in accordance with sub-regulation 2, shall be directed by the President of the Pre-Trial Division to a Pre-Trial Chamber according to a roster established by the President of that Division.

REGULATION 47

SINGLE JUDGE

B9–047   1. The designation of a single judge in accordance with article 39, paragraph 2 (b) (iii), and rule 7 shall be based on criteria agreed upon by the Pre-Trial Chamber, including seniority of age and criminal trial experience. Other criteria may include consideration of the issues involved and the circumstances of the proceedings before the Chamber, as well as the distribution of work within the Chamber and the proper management and efficiency in the handling of cases.

2. The single judge designated by the Pre-Trial Chamber shall, as far as possible, act for the duration of a case. The Pre-Trial Chamber may designate more than one single judge when the efficient management of the workload of the Chamber so requires.

REGULATION 48

INFORMATION NECESSARY FOR THE PRE-TRIAL CHAMBER

B9–048   1. The Pre-Trial Chamber may request the Prosecutor to provide specific or additional information or documents in his or her possession, or summaries thereof, that the Pre-Trial Chamber considers necessary in order to exercise the functions and responsibilities set forth in article 53, paragraph 3 (b), article 56, paragraph 3 (a), and article 57, paragraph 3 (c).

2. The Pre-Trial Chamber shall take such measures as are necessary under articles 54, 72 and 93 to protect the information and documents referred to in sub-regulation 1 and under article 68, paragraph 5, to protect the safety of witnesses and victims and members of their families.

3. Nothing in this regulation shall prejudice the requirements of confidentiality applicable under article 54, paragraph 3 (e) and (f).

REGULATION 49

THE REQUEST FOR AUTHORISATION

B9–049   1. A request by the Prosecutor to a Pre-Trial Chamber for authorisation of an investigation pursuant to article 15, paragraph 3, shall be in writing and shall contain:

(a) A reference to the crimes which the Prosecutor believes have been or are being committed and a statement of the facts being alleged to provide the reasonable basis to believe that those crimes have been or are being committed;

(b) A declaration of the Prosecutor with reasons that the listed crimes fall within the jurisdiction of the Court.

2. The statement of the facts referred to in sub-regulation 1 (a) shall indicate, as a minimum:

(a) The places of the alleged commission of the crimes, e.g. country, town, as precisely as possible;

(b) The time or time period of the alleged commission of the crimes; and

(c) The persons involved, if identified, or a description of the persons or groups of persons involved.

3. The appendix to the request shall include, if possible:

(a) The chronology of relevant events;

(b) Maps showing relevant information, including the location of the alleged crimes; and

(c) An explanatory glossary of relevant names of persons, locations and institutions.

REGULATION 50

SPECIFIC TIME LIMITS

1. The time limit for victims to make representations under article 15, paragraph 3, and rule 50, sub-rule 3, shall be 30 days following information given in accordance with rule 50, sub-rule 1.   **B9–050**

2. The time limit for a State Party to express its views on a request by the Prosecutor for authorisation to take certain measures within its territory in accordance with rule 115, sub-rule 2, shall be ten days from notification.

REGULATION 51

DECISION ON INTERIM RELEASE

For the purposes of a decision on interim release, the Pre-Trial Chamber shall seek observations from the host State and from the State to which the person seeks to be released.   **B9–051**

REGULATION 52

DOCUMENT CONTAINING THE CHARGES

The document containing the charges referred to in article 61 shall include: **B9–052**

(a) The full name of the person and any other relevant identifying information;

(b) A statement of the facts, including the time and place of the alleged crimes, which provides a sufficient legal and factual basis to bring the person or persons to trial, including relevant facts for the exercise of jurisdiction by the Court;

(c) A legal characterisation of the facts to accord both with the crimes under articles 6, 7 or 8 and the precise form of participation under articles 25 and 28.

REGULATION 53

DECISION OF THE PRE-TRIAL CHAMBER FOLLOWING THE CONFIRMATION HEARING

The written decision of the Pre-Trial Chamber setting out its findings on each of the charges shall be delivered within 60 days from the date the confirmation hearing ends.   **B9–053**

Section 3

Trial

REGULATION 54

STATUS CONFERENCES BEFORE THE TRIAL CHAMBER

B9–054   At a status conference, the Trial Chamber may, in accordance with the Statute and the Rules, issue any order in the interests of justice for the purposes of the proceedings on, *inter alia*, the following issues:

(a) The length and content of legal arguments and the opening and closing statements;

(b) A summary of the evidence the participants intend to rely on;

(c) The length of the evidence to be relied on;

(d) The length of questioning of the witnesses;

(e) The number and identity (including any pseudonym) of the witnesses to be called;

(f) The production and disclosure of the statements of the witnesses on which the participants propose to rely;

(g) The number of documents as referred to in article 69, paragraph 2, or exhibits to be introduced together with their length and size;

(h) The issues the participants propose to raise during the trial;

(i) The extent to which a participant can rely on recorded evidence, including the transcripts and the audio- and video-record of evidence previously given;

(j) The presentation of evidence in summary form;

(k) The extent to which evidence is to be given by an audio- or video-link;

(l) The disclosure of evidence;

(m) The joint or separate instruction by the participants of expert witnesses;

(n) Evidence to be introduced under rule 69 as regards agreed facts;

(o) The conditions under which victims shall participate in the proceedings;

(p) The defences, if any, to be advanced by the accused.

REGULATION 55

AUTHORITY OF THE CHAMBER TO MODIFY THE LEGAL CHARACTERISATION OF FACTS

B9–055   1. In its decision under article 74, the Chamber may change the legal characterisation of facts to accord with the crimes under articles 6, 7 or 8, or to accord with the form of participation of the accused under articles 25 and 28, without exceeding the facts and circumstances described in the charges and any amendments to the charges.

2. If, at any time during the trial, it appears to the Chamber that the legal characterisation of facts may be subject to change, the Chamber shall give notice to the participants of such a possibility and having heard the evidence, shall, at an appropriate stage of the proceedings, give the participants the opportunity to make oral or written submissions. The Chamber may suspend the hearing to ensure that the participants have adequate time and facilities for effective preparation or, if necessary, it may order a hearing to consider all matters relevant to the proposed change.

3. For the purposes of sub-regulation 2, the Chamber shall, in particular, ensure that the accused shall:

(a) Have adequate time and facilities for the effective preparation of his or her defence in accordance with article 67, paragraph 1 (b); and

(b) If necessary, be given the opportunity to examine again, or have examined again, a previous witness, to call a new witness or to present other evidence admissible under the Statute in accordance with article 67, paragraph 1 (e).

REGULATION 56

EVIDENCE UNDER ARTICLE 75

The Trial Chamber may hear the witnesses and examine the evidence for the **B9–056** purposes of a decision on reparations in accordance with article 75, paragraph 2, at the same time as for the purposes of trial.

Section 4

Appeal and revision

Subsection 1

Appeal

REGULATION 57

APPEAL

For the purposes of rule 150, the appellant shall file a notice of appeal which shall **B9–057** state:
(a) The name and number of the case;
(b) The date of the decision of conviction or acquittal, sentence or reparation order appealed against;
(c) Whether the appeal is directed against the whole decision or part thereof;
(d) The relief sought.

REGULATION 58

DOCUMENT IN SUPPORT OF THE APPEAL

1. Having filed an appeal in accordance with regulation 57, the appellant shall file a **B9–058** document in support of the appeal within 90 days of notification of the relevant decision.
2. The document in support of the appeal shall contain the grounds of appeal. Each ground of appeal shall be divided into two parts:
(a) The ground of appeal;
(b) The legal and/or factual reasons in support of the ground of appeal.
3. The legal and/or factual reasons referred to in sub-regulation 2 (b) shall be set out in separate paragraphs. Reference shall be made to the relevant part of the record or any other document or source of information as regards any factual issue. Each legal reason shall be set out together with reference to any relevant article, rule, regulation or other applicable law, and any authority cited in support thereof. Where applicable, the finding or ruling challenged in the decision shall be identified, with specific reference to the page and paragraph number.
4. Grounds of appeal may be advanced cumulatively or in the alternative.
5. The document in support of the appeal shall not exceed 100 pages.

REGULATION 59

RESPONSE

1. A participant may file a response within 60 days of notification of the document in **B9–059** support of the appeal described in regulation 58 as follows:

(a) Each ground of appeal shall be answered separately, stating whether it is opposed, in whole or in part, together with the grounds put forward in support thereof; it shall also be stated whether the relief sought is opposed, in whole or in part, together with the grounds of opposition in support thereto;

(b) When facts are relied on that are not already set out in the appeal or the document in support of the appeal, reference shall be made to the relevant part of the record or any other document or source of information;

(c) Each legal reason relied on in support of the response shall be set out together with reference to any relevant article, rule, regulation or other applicable law, and any authority cited in support thereof.

2. The response shall not exceed 100 pages. To the extent possible, it shall be set out and numbered in the same order as in the document described in regulation 58.

REGULATION 60

REPLY

B9–060   1. Whenever the Appeals Chamber considers it necessary in the interests of justice, it may order the appellant to file a reply within such time as it may specify in its order.

2. Any reply filed in accordance with sub-regulation 1 shall not exceed 50 pages. To the extent possible, it shall be set out and numbered in the same order as in the documents described in regulations 58 and 59.

REGULATION 61

VARIATION OF GROUNDS OF APPEAL PRESENTED BEFORE THE APPEALS CHAMBER

B9–061   1. An application for variation of grounds of appeal shall state the name and number of the case and shall specify the variation sought and the reasons in support thereof.

2. The application for variation shall be filed as soon as the reasons warranting it become known.

3. Participants may file a response within seven days of notification of the application for variation.

4. The response shall state the name and number of the case and shall specify the legal or factual reasons advanced by way of opposition.

5. If the variation is granted, the Appeals Chamber shall specify both the time limit within which the appellant shall file the document setting out the grounds of appeal as varied and the page limit for that document. Regulation 58, sub-regulations 2 and 3, shall apply *mutatis mutandis*.

6. Any response to the document described in sub-regulation 5 shall be filed within the time limit specified by the Appeals Chamber. The Appeals Chamber may also fix a page limit for the response and otherwise regulation 59 shall apply *mutatis mutandis*.

7. Regulation 60 shall apply *mutatis mutandis* with regard to any reply to the response filed in accordance with sub-regulation 6.

REGULATION 62

ADDITIONAL EVIDENCE PRESENTED BEFORE THE APPEALS CHAMBER

B9–062   1. A participant seeking to present additional evidence shall file an application setting out:

(a) The evidence to be presented;

(b) The ground of appeal to which the evidence relates and the reasons, if relevant, why the evidence was not adduced before the Trial Chamber.

2. The Appeals Chamber may:

(a) Decide to first rule on the admissibility of the additional evidence, in which case it shall direct the participant affected by the application filed under sub-regulation 1 to address the issue of admissibility of the evidence in his or her response, and to adduce any evidence in response only after a decision on the admissibility of that evidence has been issued by the Appeals Chamber; or

(b) Decide to rule on the admissibility of the additional evidence jointly with the other issues raised in the appeal, in which case it shall direct the participant affected by the application filed under sub-regulation 1 to both file a response setting out arguments on that application and to adduce any evidence in response.

3. The responses described in sub-regulation 2 shall be filed within a time limit specified by the Appeals Chamber and shall be set out and numbered, to the extent possible, in the same order as in the application to present evidence.

4. If several defendants are participants in the appeal, the evidence admitted on behalf of any of them shall, where relevant, be considered in respect of all of them.

REGULATION 63

CONSOLIDATED APPEALS UNDER RULE 150

1. Unless otherwise ordered by the Appeals Chamber, in a case of more than one appeal under rule 150:   **B9–063**

(a) When the Prosecutor appeals, he or she shall file one consolidated document in support of all appeals in accordance with regulation 58;

(b) When more than one convicted person files a document in support of the appeal, the Prosecutor shall file a consolidated response in accordance with regulation 59.

2. Regulation 60 shall apply *mutatis mutandis* and any reply filed by the Prosecutor shall be by way of a consolidated reply.

3. For a consolidated document in support of more than one appeal and a consolidated response, as described in sub-regulation 1, the page limit shall be 100 pages plus a further 40 pages for each additional convicted or acquitted person. The page limit for any consolidated reply as described in sub-regulation 2 shall be 50 pages plus a further 20 pages for each additional convicted or acquitted person.

4. The time limit for filing a consolidated response by the Prosecutor shall run from notification of the last document filed in support of the appeal by a convicted person in a given case.

REGULATION 64

APPEALS UNDER RULE 154

1. An appeal filed under rule 154 shall state: **B9–064**

(a) The name and number of the case or situation;

(b) The title and date of the decision being appealed;

(c) The specific provision of the Statute pursuant to which the appeal is filed;

(d) The relief sought.

2. Subject to sub-regulations 5 and 6, the appellant shall file a document in support of the appeal, with reference to the appeal, within 21 days of notification of the relevant decision. The document in support of the appeal shall set out the grounds of appeal and shall contain the legal and/or factual reasons in support of each ground of appeal. Each reason shall be set out in separate paragraphs. Reference shall be made to the relevant

part of the record or any other document or source of information as regards any factual issue. Each legal reason shall be set out together with reference to any relevant article, rule, regulation or other applicable law, and any authority cited in support thereof. The document in support of the appeal shall, where applicable, identify the finding or ruling challenged in the decision, with specific reference to the page and paragraph number.

3. Grounds of appeal may be advanced cumulatively or in the alternative.

4. Subject to sub-regulations 5 and 6, a participant may file a response within 21 days of notification of the document in support of the appeal as follows:

(a) Each ground of appeal shall be answered separately, stating whether it is opposed, in whole or in part, together with the grounds put forward in support thereof; it shall also be stated whether the relief sought is opposed, in whole or in part, together with the grounds of opposition in support thereto;

(b) The legal and/or factual reasons in support.

5. For appeals filed under article 82, paragraph 1 (b), the document in support of the appeal shall be filed by the appellant within seven days of notification of the relevant decision. The response shall be filed within five days of notification of the document in support of the appeal.

6. For appeals filed under article 82, paragraph 1 (c), the document in support of the appeal shall be filed by the appellant within four days of notification of the relevant decision. The response shall be filed within two days of notification of the document in support of the appeal.

REGULATION 65

APPEALS UNDER RULE 155

B9–065   1. An application for leave to appeal under rule 155 shall state the name and number of the case or situation and shall specify the legal and/or factual reasons in support thereof. If the facts relied upon in support are not apparent from the record of the proceedings, they shall, as far as possible, be substantiated by a solemn affirmation by a person having knowledge of the facts stated therein.

2. An application for leave to appeal under article 82, paragraph 1 (d), shall specify the reasons warranting immediate resolution by the Appeals Chamber of the matter at issue.

3. Participants may file a response within three days of notification of the application described in sub-regulation 1, unless the Pre-Trial or Trial Chamber concerned orders an immediate hearing of the application. In the latter case, the participants shall be afforded an opportunity to be heard orally.

4. When leave to appeal is granted, the appellant shall file, within ten days of notification of the decision granting leave to appeal, a document in support of the appeal in accordance with regulation 64, sub-regulation 2. Such document shall also contain the precise title and date of filing of the decision granting leave to appeal.

5. Participants may file a response within ten days of notification of the document in support of the appeal. Regulation 64, sub-regulation 4, shall apply *mutatis mutandis*.

Subsection 2

Revision

REGULATION 66

PROCEDURE LEADING TO THE DETERMINATION ON REVISION

B9–066   1. An application for revision under article 84, paragraph 1, and rule 159 shall state the name and number of the original case. An application under article 84, paragraph 1 (a), shall set out the new facts or evidence, unknown or unavailable at the time of trial, and shall indicate the effect that the production of such facts or evidence at the trial might have had upon the decision of the Court. Other applications shall set out the reasons in accordance with article 84, paragraph 1 (b) or (c). The facts relied upon in any application for revision shall, as far as possible, be supported by a solemn affirmation by a person having knowledge of the facts. The application shall not exceed 100 pages.

2. As far as possible, the application for revision shall be notified to the participants in the original proceedings and to any other person having a direct interest in the revision proceedings. Such participants and persons may file a response within 40 days of notification of that application.

3. The response described in sub-regulation 2 shall contain the name and number of the case and shall set out the legal and/or factual reasons advanced in support thereof. Facts tending to deny or contradict the existence of the facts upon which the application is founded shall be outlined in the response and shall be supported by a solemn affirmation by a person having knowledge of such facts. The response shall not exceed 100 pages.

4. Whenever the Appeals Chamber considers it necessary in the interests of justice, it may order the appellant to file a reply within such time as it may specify in its order.

CHAPTER 4

COUNSEL ISSUES AND LEGAL ASSISTANCE

Section 1

List of counsel and duty counsel

REGULATION 67

CRITERIA TO BE MET BY COUNSEL

1. The necessary relevant experience for counsel as described in rule 22 shall be at **B9–067** least ten years.

2. Counsel should not have been convicted of a serious criminal or disciplinary offence considered to be incompatible with the nature of the office of counsel before the Court.

REGULATION 68

ASSISTANTS TO COUNSEL

Persons assisting counsel as described in rule 22, sub-rule 1, may include persons who **B9–068** can assist counsel in the presentation of the case before a Chamber. The criteria to be met by these persons shall be determined in the Regulations of the Registry.

REGULATION 69

PROOF AND CONTROL OF CRITERIA TO BE MET BY COUNSEL

1. A person seeking to be included in the list of counsel shall complete the forms **B9–069** provided by the Registrar for this purpose.

2. A person referred to in sub-regulation 1 shall also provide:

(a) A detailed *curriculum vitae*;

(b) A certificate issued by each Bar association the person is registered with, and/or each relevant controlling administrative authority confirming his or her qualifications, the right to practise and the existence, if any, of disciplinary sanctions or ongoing disciplinary proceedings; and

(c) A certificate issued by the relevant authority of each State of which the person is a national or where the person is domiciled stating the existence, if any, of criminal convictions.

3. A person referred to in sub-regulation 1 or counsel already included in the list of counsel shall immediately inform the Registrar of any changes to the information he or she has provided that are more than *de minimis*, including the initiation of any criminal or disciplinary proceedings against the person.

4. The Registrar may at any stage take steps to verify the information provided by any person referred to in sub-regulation 1 and by counsel already included in the list of counsel.

REGULATION 70

INCLUSION IN THE LIST OF COUNSEL

B9–070   1. On receipt of an application by a person seeking to be included in the list of counsel, the Registrar shall establish whether the person has provided the information required under regulation 69. Thereafter, the Registrar shall acknowledge receipt of the application and, where relevant, direct the person to submit additional information.

2. The decision as to whether a person shall be included in the list of counsel shall be notified to that person. If the application is refused, the Registrar shall provide reasons and information on how to apply for review of that decision in accordance with regulation 72.

REGULATION 71

REMOVAL AND SUSPENSION FROM THE LIST OF COUNSEL

B9–071   1. The Registrar shall remove a counsel from the list of counsel where he or she:

(a) No longer meets the criteria required for inclusion in the list of counsel;

(b) Has been permanently banned from practising before the Court as a result of disciplinary proceedings held in accordance with the Code of Professional Conduct for counsel;

(c) Has been found guilty of an offence against the administration of justice as described in article 70, paragraph 1; or

(d) Has been permanently interdicted from exercising his or her functions before the Court in accordance with rule 171, sub-rule 3.

2. The Registrar shall suspend a counsel from the list of counsel where he or she has been:

(a) Temporarily suspended in a disciplinary proceeding according to the Code of Professional Conduct for counsel; or

(b) Temporarily interdicted from exercising his or her functions before the Court for a period exceeding 30 days in accordance with rule 171, sub-rule 3.

3. The Registrar shall notify the relevant counsel of his or her decision under sub-regulations 1 or 2. The Registrar shall provide reasons and information on how to apply for review of that decision in accordance with regulation 72.

REGULATION 72

REVIEW OF DECISIONS OF THE REGISTRAR

B9–072   1. Application may be made to the Presidency for review of:

(a) A decision under regulation 70, sub-regulation 2, refusing to include a person in the list of counsel;

(b) A decision under regulation 71, sub-regulation 1, removing counsel from the list of counsel; or

(c) A decision under regulation 71, sub-regulation 2, suspending counsel from the list of counsel.

2. Applications as described in sub-regulation 1 shall be set out in accordance with regulation 23 and be filed within 15 days of notification of the relevant decision of the Registrar.

3. The Registrar may file a response within 15 days of notification of the application as referred to in sub-regulations 1 and 2.

4. The Presidency may ask the Registrar to provide any additional information necessary to decide on the application. The decision of the Presidency shall be final.

REGULATION 73

DUTY COUNSEL

1. The Registrar shall establish and maintain a roster of counsel included in the list of counsel who are available at any time to represent any person before the Court or to represent the interests of the defence.   **B9–073**

2. If any person requires urgent legal assistance and has not yet secured legal assistance, or where his or her counsel is unavailable, the Registrar may appoint duty counsel, taking into account the wishes of the person, and the geographical proximity of, and the languages spoken by, the counsel.

Section 2

Defence through counsel

REGULATION 74

DEFENCE THROUGH COUNSEL

1. Defence counsel shall act in proceedings before the Court either when chosen by the person entitled to legal assistance in accordance with rule 21, sub-rule 2, or when the Chamber has appointed counsel in accordance with the Statute, Rules or these Regulations.   **B9–074**

2. When represented by defence counsel, the person entitled to legal assistance shall, subject to article 67, paragraph 1 (h), act before the Court through his or her counsel, unless otherwise authorised by the Chamber.

REGULATION 75

CHOICE OF DEFENCE COUNSEL

1. If the person entitled to legal assistance chooses a counsel included in the list of counsel, the Registrar shall contact that counsel. If the counsel is willing and ready to represent the person, the Registrar shall facilitate the issuance of a power of attorney for this counsel by the person.   **B9–075**

2. If the person entitled to legal assistance chooses a counsel not on the list of counsel who is willing and ready to represent him or her and to be included in the list, the Registrar shall decide on the eligibility of that counsel in accordance with regulation 70

and, upon inclusion in the list, shall facilitate the issuance of a power of attorney. Until the filing of a power of attorney, the person entitled to legal assistance may be represented by duty counsel in accordance with regulation 73.

REGULATION 76

APPOINTMENT OF DEFENCE COUNSEL BY A CHAMBER

B9–076   1. A Chamber, following consultation with the Registrar, may appoint counsel in the circumstances specified in the Statute and the Rules or where the interests of justice so require.

2. Where the Chamber decides to appoint counsel in accordance with sub-regulation 1, and where the counsel considered for appointment is not included in the list of counsel, the Registrar shall first decide on the eligibility of that counsel to be included in the list in accordance with regulation 70. The Chamber may also appoint counsel from the Office of Public Counsel for the defence.

REGULATION 77

OFFICE OF PUBLIC COUNSEL FOR THE DEFENCE

B9–077   1. The Registrar shall establish and develop an Office of Public Counsel for the defence for the purpose of providing assistance as described in sub-regulations 4 and 5.

2. The Office of Public Counsel for the defence shall fall within the remit of the Registry solely for administrative purposes and otherwise shall function as a wholly independent office. Counsel and assistants within the Office shall act independently.

3. The Office of Public Counsel for the defence may include a counsel who meets the criteria set out in rule 22 and regulation 67. The Office shall include assistants as referred to in regulation 68.

4. The tasks of the Office of Public Counsel for the defence shall include representing and protecting the rights of the defence during the initial stages of the investigation, in particular for the application of article 56, paragraph 2 (d), and rule 47, sub-rule 2.

5. The Office of Public Counsel for the defence shall also provide support and assistance to defence counsel and to the person entitled to legal assistance, including, where appropriate:

    (a) Legal research and advice; and

    (b) Appearing before a Chamber in respect of specific issues.

REGULATION 78

WITHDRAWAL OF DEFENCE COUNSEL

B9–078   Prior to withdrawal from a case, defence counsel shall seek the leave of the Chamber.

Section 3

Legal representatives of victims

REGULATION 79

DECISION OF THE CHAMBER CONCERNING LEGAL REPRESENTATIVES OF VICTIMS

B9–079   1. The decision of the Chamber to request the victims or particular groups of victims to choose a common legal representative or representatives may be made in conjunction with the decision on the application of the victim or victims to participate in the proceedings.

2. When choosing a common legal representative for victims in accordance with rule 90, sub-rule 3, consideration should be given to the views of the victims, and the need to respect local traditions and to assist specific groups of victims.

3. Victims may request the relevant Chamber to review the Registrar's choice of a common legal representative under rule 90, sub-rule 3, within 30 days of notification of the Registrar's decision.

REGULATION 80

APPOINTMENT OF LEGAL REPRESENTATIVES OF VICTIMS BY A CHAMBER

1. A Chamber, following consultation with the Registrar, may appoint a legal representative of victims where the interests of justice so require.   **B9–080**

2. The Chamber may appoint counsel from the Office of Public Counsel for victims.

REGULATION 81

OFFICE OF PUBLIC COUNSEL FOR VICTIMS

1. The Registrar shall establish and develop an Office of Public Counsel for victims for the purpose of providing assistance as described in sub-regulation 4.   **B9–081**

2. The Office of Public Counsel for victims shall fall within the remit of the Registry solely for administrative purposes and otherwise shall function as a wholly independent office. Counsel and assistants within the Office shall act independently.

3. The Office of Public Counsel for victims may include a counsel who meets the criteria set out in rule 22 and regulation 67. The Office shall include assistants as referred to in regulation 68.

4. The Office of Public Counsel for victims shall provide support and assistance to the legal representative for victims and to victims, including, where appropriate:

(a) Legal research and advice; and

(b) Appearing before a Chamber in respect of specific issues.

REGULATION 82

WITHDRAWAL OF LEGAL REPRESENTATIVES OF VICTIMS

Prior to withdrawal from a case, legal representatives of victims shall seek the leave of the Chamber.   **B9–082**

Section 4

Legal assistance paid by the Court

REGULATION 83

GENERAL SCOPE OF LEGAL ASSISTANCE PAID BY THE COURT

1. Legal assistance paid by the Court shall cover all costs reasonably necessary as determined by the Registrar for an effective and efficient defence, including the remuneration of counsel, his or her assistants as referred to in regulation 68 and staff,   **B9–083**

expenditure in relation to the gathering of evidence, administrative costs, translation and interpretation costs, travel costs and daily subsistence allowances.

2. The scope of legal assistance paid by the Court regarding victims shall be determined by the Registrar in consultation with the Chamber, where appropriate.

3. A person receiving legal assistance paid by the Court may apply to the Registrar for additional means which may be granted depending on the nature of the case.

4. Decisions by the Registrar on the scope of legal assistance paid by the Court as defined in this regulation may be reviewed by the relevant Chamber on application by the person receiving legal assistance.

REGULATION 84

DETERMINATION OF MEANS

B9–084   1. Where a person applies for legal assistance to be paid by the Court, the Registrar shall determine the applicant's means and whether he or she shall be provided with full or partial payment of legal assistance.

2. The means of the applicant shall include means of all kinds in respect of which the applicant has direct or indirect enjoyment or power freely to dispose, including, but not limited to, direct income, bank accounts, real or personal property, pensions, stocks, bonds or other assets held, but excluding any family or social benefits to which he or she may be entitled. In assessing such means, account shall also be taken of any transfers of property by the applicant which the Registrar considers relevant, and of the apparent lifestyle of the applicant. The Registrar shall allow for expenses claimed by the applicant provided they are reasonable and necessary.

REGULATION 85

DECISIONS ON PAYMENT OF LEGAL ASSISTANCE

B9–085   1. In accordance with the procedure set out in the Regulations of the Registry, the Registrar shall decide within one month of the submission of an application or, within one month of expiry of a time limit set in accordance with the Regulations of the Registry, whether legal assistance should be paid by the Court. The decision shall be notified to the applicant together with the reasons for the decision and instructions on how to apply for review. The Registrar may, in appropriate circumstances, make a provisional decision to grant payment of legal assistance.

2. The Registrar shall reconsider his or her decision on payment of legal assistance if the financial situation of the person receiving such legal assistance is found to be different than indicated in the application, or if the financial situation of the person has changed since the application was submitted. Any revised decision shall be notified to the person together with the reasons for the decision and instructions on how to apply for review.

3. Persons as referred to in sub-regulations 1 and 2 may seek review of the decisions described in those provisions by the Presidency within 15 days of notification of the relevant decision. The decision of the Presidency shall be final.

4. Subject to rule 21, sub-rule 5, where legal assistance has been paid by the Court and it is subsequently established that the information provided to the Registrar on the applicant's means was inaccurate, the Registrar may seek an order from the Presidency for recovery of the funds paid from the person who received legal assistance paid by the Court. The Registrar may seek the assistance of the relevant States Parties to enforce that order.

CHAPTER 5

VICTIMS PARTICIPATION AND REPARATIONS

REGULATION 86

PARTICIPATION OF VICTIMS IN THE PROCEEDINGS UNDER RULE 89

B9–086

1. For the purposes of rule 89 and subject to rule 102 a victim shall make a written application to the Registrar who shall develop standard forms for that purpose which shall be approved in accordance with regulation 23, sub-regulation 2. These standard forms shall, to the extent possible, be made available to victims, groups of victims, or intergovernmental and non-governmental organizations, which may assist in their dissemination, as widely as possible. These standard forms shall, to the extent possible, be used by victims.

2. The standard forms or other applications described in sub-regulation 1 shall contain, to the extent possible, the following information:

(a) The identity and address of the victim, or the address to which the victim requests all communications to be sent; in case the application is presented by someone other than the victim in accordance with rule 89, sub-rule 3, the identity and address of that person, or the address to which that person requests all communications to be sent;

(b) If the application is presented in accordance with rule 89, sub-rule 3, evidence of the consent of the victim or evidence on the situation of the victim, being a child or a disabled person, shall be presented together with the application, either in writing or in accordance with rule 102;

(c) A description of the harm suffered resulting from the commission of any crime within the jurisdiction of the Court, or, in case of a victim being an organization or institution, a description of any direct harm as described in rule 85 (b);

(d) A description of the incident, including its location and date and, to the extent possible, the identity of the person or persons the victim believes to be responsible for the harm as described in rule 85;

(e) Any relevant supporting documentation, including names and addresses of witnesses;

(f) Information as to why the personal interests of the victim are affected;

(g) Information on the stage of the proceedings in which the victim wishes to participate, and, if applicable, on the relief sought;

(h) Information on the extent of legal representation, if any, which is envisaged by the victim, including the names and addresses of potential legal representatives, and information on the victim's or victims' financial means to pay for a legal representative.

3. Victims applying for participation in the trial and/or appeal proceedings shall, to the extent possible, make their application to the Registrar before the start of the stage of the proceedings in which they want to participate.

4. The Registrar may request further information from victims or those presenting an application in accordance with rule 89, sub-rule 3, in order to ensure that such application contains, to the extent possible, the information referred to in sub-regulation 2, before transmission to a Chamber. The Registrar may also seek additional information from States, the Prosecutor and intergovernmental or non-governmental organizations.

5. The Registrar shall present all applications described in this regulation to the Chamber together with a report thereon. The Registrar shall endeavour to present one report for a group of victims, taking into consideration the distinct interests of the victims.

6. Subject to any order of the Chamber, the Registrar may also submit one report on a number of applications received in accordance with sub-regulation 1 to the Chamber

seized of the case or situation in order to assist that Chamber in issuing only one decision on a number of applications in accordance with rule 89, sub-rule 4. Reports covering all applications received in a certain time period may be presented on a periodic basis.

7. Before deciding on an application, the Chamber may request, if necessary with the assistance of the Registrar, additional information from, *inter alia*, States, the Prosecutor, the victims or those acting on their behalf or with their consent. If information is received from States or the Prosecutor, the Chamber shall provide the relevant victim or victims with an opportunity to respond.

8. A decision taken by a Chamber under rule 89 shall apply throughout the proceedings in the same case, subject to the powers of the relevant Chamber in accordance with rule 91, sub-rule 1.

9. There shall be a specialised unit dealing with victims' participation and reparations under the authority of the Registrar. This unit shall be responsible for assisting victims and groups of victims.

REGULATION 87

INFORMATION TO VICTIMS

B9–087   1. The Prosecutor shall notify the Pre-Trial Chamber as to information provided pursuant to rule 50, sub-rule 1, including the date the information was provided.

2. The Prosecutor shall inform the Registry of his or her decision not to initiate an investigation or not to prosecute pursuant to article 53, paragraphs 1 and 2, respectively, and shall provide all relevant information for notification by the Registry to victims in accordance with rule 92, sub-rule 2.

REGULATION 88

REQUESTS FOR REPARATIONS IN ACCORDANCE WITH RULE 94

B9–088   1. For the application of rule 94, the Registrar shall develop a standard form for victims to present their requests for reparations and shall make it available to victims, groups of victims, or intergovernmental and non-governmental organizations which may assist in its dissemination, as widely as possible. This standard form shall be approved in accordance with regulation 23, sub-regulation 2, and shall, to the extent possible, be used by victims.

2. The Registrar shall seek all necessary additional information from a victim in order to complete his or her request in accordance with rule 94, sub-rule 1, and shall assist victims in completing such a request. The request shall then be registered and stored electronically in order to be notified by the unit described in regulation 86, sub-regulation 9, in accordance with rule 94, sub-rule 2.

CHAPTER 6

DETENTION MATTERS

Section 1

General provisions

REGULATION 89

SCOPE OF THIS CHAPTER

B9–089   The detention of persons detained by the Court under the Statute shall be governed by the provisions of this chapter.

Regulation 90

MANAGEMENT OF THE DETENTION CENTRE

1. Subject to the Statute, Rules and these Regulations, the Registrar shall have overall **B9–090** responsibility for all aspects of management of the detention centre, including security and order, and shall make all decisions relating thereto.

2. The day-to-day fulfilment of the functions described in sub-regulation 1 shall be delegated to the Chief Custody Officer. The Chief Custody Officer may, as appropriate, delegate specific functions to other persons.

Regulation 91

TREATMENT OF DETAINED PERSONS

1. All detained persons shall be treated with humanity and with respect for the **B9–091** inherent dignity of the human person.

2. There shall be no discrimination of detained persons on grounds of gender, age, race, colour, language, religion or belief, political or other opinion, national, ethnic or social origin, wealth, birth or other status. Measures applied under these Regulations and the Regulations of the Registry to protect the rights and special status of particular categories of detained persons shall not be deemed to be discriminatory.

Regulation 92

CONFIDENTIALITY OF THE DETENTION RECORD

1. The detention record of each detained person shall be confidential. **B9–092**

2. The detention record shall be made accessible to the detained person, his or her counsel and persons authorised by the Registrar, save as regards such information as the Chief Custody Officer, in consultation with the Registrar, determines should be withheld in the interests of the proper management of the detention centre.

3. A Chamber may, *proprio motu* or at the request of any interested person, order that the detention record or part thereof be withheld or disclosed.

4. The detained person shall be informed of any request for access to his or her detention record and shall be given the opportunity to be heard or to submit his or her views. In exceptional circumstances such as in an emergency, an order may be made prior to the detained person being informed of the request. In such a case, the detained person shall, as soon as practicable, be informed and shall be given the opportunity to be heard or to submit his or her views.

Regulation 93

INFORMATION ON ARRIVAL AT THE DETENTION CENTRE

1. When a detained person arrives at the detention centre, he or she shall be provided **B9–093** with a copy of these Regulations and the Regulations of the Registry relevant to detention matters in a language which he or she fully understands and speaks.

2. To the extent that relevant written material as described in sub-regulation 1 is not immediately available, and pending the provision of a translation of those documents which shall be provided in a language that the detained person fully understands and speaks, the detained person shall have the assistance of an interpreter.

Regulation 94

INSPECTIONS OF THE DETENTION CENTRE

1. The Presidency may, at any time, appoint a judge of the Court to inspect the **B9–094** detention centre and to report on the conditions of detention and the administration of the detention centre.

2. There shall be regular and unannounced inspections by an independent inspecting authority appointed by the Presidency. This authority shall be responsible for examining the manner in which detained persons are being held and treated.

3. Following an inspection carried out in accordance with sub-regulation 2, the inspecting authority shall provide a confidential report to the Presidency and the Registrar setting out its findings and any recommendations.

4. Upon receipt of the report referred to in sub-regulation 3, the Registrar shall take such action as he or she considers appropriate in consultation, where necessary, with the relevant authorities which have made the detention centre available to the Court. If the Registrar does not agree with the recommendations made by the inspecting authority, he or she shall submit a report to the Presidency setting out his or her reasons.

5. The Presidency may make any direction, decision or order that it considers appropriate.

REGULATION 95

DISCIPLINE

B9–095   1. Discipline and order shall be maintained by the Chief Custody Officer in the interests of safe custody and good administration of the detention centre.

2. Details of the disciplinary procedure for detained persons shall be set out in the Regulations of the Registry. This procedure shall provide a detained person with the right to be heard on the subject of any offence alleged to have been committed, and shall include a right for the detained person to address the Presidency.

REGULATION 96

SUSPENSION OF REGULATIONS ON DETENTION

B9–096   1. In the event of a serious disturbance or other emergency occurring within the detention centre, the Chief Custody Officer may take such action as is immediately necessary to ensure the safety of detained persons and staff of the detention centre, or the security of the detention centre.

2. Any action taken by the Chief Custody Officer under sub-regulation 1 shall be reported immediately to the Registrar, who may, with the approval of the Presidency, temporarily suspend the operation of all or part of these Regulations or the Regulations of the Registry relevant to detention matters to the extent necessary to restore the security and good order of the detention centre.

Section 2

Rights of a detained person and conditions of detention

REGULATION 97

COMMUNICATION WITH DEFENCE COUNSEL

B9–097   1. A detained person shall be informed of his or her right to communicate fully, where necessary with the assistance of an interpreter, with his or her defence counsel or assistants to his or her defence counsel as referred to in regulation 68.

2. All communication between a detained person and his or her defence counsel or assistants to his or her defence counsel as referred to in regulation 68 and interpreters shall be conducted within the sight but not the hearing, either direct or indirect, of the staff of the detention centre.

REGULATION 98

DIPLOMATIC AND CONSULAR ASSISTANCE

1. A detained person shall be informed of his or her right to communicate with and to **B9–098**
receive visits from:
  (a) A diplomatic and/or consular representative from the State of which the person
      is a national accredited to the State in which the detention centre is situated or
      the authority which has made the detention centre available to the Court; or
  (b) Where the State of which the person is a national has no diplomatic or consular
      representation in the State in which the detention centre is situated, a
      diplomatic and/or consular representative of the State which takes charge of the
      interests of the State of which the person is a national; or
  (c) In case of refugees or stateless persons, a representative of a national or
      international authority whose task it is to represent the interests of such
      persons.
2. All communication between a detained person and the persons described in sub-
regulation 1 (a), (b) or (c), and interpreters shall be conducted within the sight but not
the hearing, either direct or indirect, of the staff of the detention centre.

REGULATION 99

GENERAL ENTITLEMENTS OF DETAINED PERSONS

1. Every detained person shall be entitled, *inter alia*, to the following: **B9–099**
  (a) To participate in a work programme;
  (b) To keep in his or her possession authorised clothing and personal items for his
      or her use;
  (c) To procure reading and writing materials and other items for the purposes of
      recreation and education;
  (d) To keep himself or herself regularly informed of the news by way of newspapers,
      periodicals and other publications, radio and television broadcasts;
  (e) To the use of a common space equipped with reading and writing materials, a
      television, radio and computer, which shall be provided for the general use of all
      detained persons;
  (f) To a period of exercise in the open air of at least one hour per day;
  (g) To engage in sporting activities;
  (h) To receive correspondence, mail and packages;
  (i) To communicate by letter or telephone with his or her family and other persons.
2. The relevant details for the application of sub-regulation 1 shall be set out in the
Regulations of the Registry, including any restrictions necessary in the interests of the
administration of justice or for the maintenance of the security and good order of the
detention centre.

REGULATION 100

VISITS

1. A detained person shall be entitled to receive visits.   **B9–100**
2. A detained person must be informed of the identity of each visitor and may refuse
to see any visitor.
3. The relevant conditions for visits as well as restrictions and supervision that may be
necessary in the interests of the administration of justice or for the maintenance of the
security and good order of the detention centre shall be set out in the Regulations of the
Registry.

Regulation 101

RESTRICTIONS TO ACCESS TO NEWS AND CONTACT

B9–101   1. A Chamber seized of the case may, at the request of the Prosecutor, order that access to the news be restricted, if it is considered necessary in the interests of the administration of justice, in particular, if unrestricted access could prejudice the outcome of the proceedings against that detained person or the outcome of any other investigation.

2. The Prosecutor may request the Chamber seized of the case to prohibit, regulate or set conditions for contact between a detained person and any other person, with the exception of counsel, if the Prosecutor has reasonable grounds to believe that such contact:

(a) Is for the purposes of attempting to arrange the escape of a detained person from the detention centre;

(b) Could prejudice or otherwise affect the outcome of the proceedings against a detained person, or any other investigation;

(c) Could be harmful to a detained person or any other person;

(d) Could be used by a detained person to breach an order for non-disclosure made by a judge;

(e) Is against the interests of public safety; or

(f) Is a threat to the protection of the rights and freedom of any person.

3. The detained person shall be informed of the Prosecutor's request and shall be given the opportunity to be heard or to submit his or her views. In exceptional circumstances such as in an emergency, an order may be made prior to the detained person being informed of the request. In such a case, the detained person shall, as soon as practicable, be informed and shall be given the opportunity to be heard or to submit his or her views.

Regulation 102

SPIRITUAL WELFARE

B9–102   1. A detained person shall be entitled to practise his or her religion or belief.

2. A detained person shall, on arrival at the detention centre or at any time thereafter, be entitled, in accordance with the Regulations of the Registry, to establish contact with a minister or spiritual adviser available in the State in which the detention centre is situated.

Regulation 103

HEALTH AND SAFETY OF DETAINED PERSONS

B9–103   1. Arrangements shall be made by the Registrar to protect the health and the safety of detained persons.

2. Arrangements shall be made by the Registrar in order to meet the needs of detained persons with disabilities.

3. Medical services, including dental care, shall be made available for detained persons.

4. A qualified medical officer with experience in psychiatry shall be available to attend the detention centre. A nurse shall be present at the detention centre at all times. A detained person may be visited by and consult with a doctor of his or her own choice, subject to the relevant details and restrictions set out in the Regulations of the Registry.

5. A detained person who requires specialist treatment shall, as far as possible, be treated within the detention centre. Should hospitalization be necessary, the detained

person shall be transferred to a hospital without delay. The Registrar shall ensure the continuous detention of the person both at the place of treatment and when in transit.

6. Arrangements shall be made by the Registrar for the detention of mentally ill persons and for those who suffer from serious psychiatric conditions. By order of the Chamber, a detained person who is determined to be mentally ill or who suffers from a serious psychiatric condition may be transferred to a specialised institution for appropriate treatment.

6. In the event of death or serious illness or injury of a detained person, the Presidency may order an inquiry into the circumstances.

REGULATION 104

ARRANGEMENTS FOR THE CARE OF INFANTS

1. Arrangements shall be made by the Registrar for a detained person to give birth in   **B9–104**
a hospital outside the detention centre. Special accommodation shall be provided for all necessary pre-natal and post-natal care and treatment.

2. Where the Registrar, following consultation with the Chief Custody Officer, authorises an infant to remain or to stay within the detention centre, arrangements shall be made for a nursery staffed with qualified personnel for the care of such an infant.

REGULATION 105

ACCOMMODATION

1. Men and women shall be detained in separate areas within the detention centre.   **B9–105**

2. Persons convicted and in respect of whom final sentence has been passed shall, whenever possible, be accommodated separately from detained persons awaiting trial or appeal.

3. A detained person shall occupy a cell unit by himself or herself except in exceptional circumstances or in cases where the Chief Custody Officer, with the approval of the Registrar, considers that it is necessary to share accommodation.

REGULATION 106

COMPLAINTS

1. A detained person shall have the right to file a complaint against any administra-   **B9–106**
tive decision or order or with regard to any other matter concerning his or her detention.

2. The complaints procedure shall be set out in the Regulations of the Registry and shall include a right for the detained person to address the Presidency.

CHAPTER 7

COOPERATION AND ENFORCEMENT

Section 1

Cooperation

REGULATION 107

ARRANGEMENTS AND AGREEMENTS ON COOPERATION

1. All agreements with any State not party to the Statute or any intergovernmental   **B9–107**
organization, setting out a general framework for cooperation on matters within the competency of more than one organ of the Court, shall be negotiated under the

authority of the President who shall seek recommendations from the Advisory Committee on Legal Texts. Such agreements shall be concluded by the President on behalf of the Court. The existence of an agreement concluded in accordance with this sub-regulation does not preclude the Prosecutor from entering into those agreements referred to in article 54, paragraph 3 (d).

2. Each organ of the Court shall inform the Presidency of any arrangement or agreement on cooperation, not being one setting out a general framework for cooperation as referred to in sub-regulation 1, that the organ intends to negotiate, unless such information is inappropriate for reasons of confidentiality. Subject to article 54, paragraph 3 (d), and to reasons of confidentiality, such arrangements and agreements shall be concluded by the President or by delegation by the relevant organ under whose authority the arrangement or agreement has been negotiated.

REGULATION 108

RULING REGARDING THE LEGALITY OF A REQUEST FOR COOPERATION

B9–108   1. In case of a dispute regarding the legality of a request for cooperation under article 93, a requested State may apply for a ruling from the competent Chamber.

2. A ruling under sub-regulation 1 may be sought only after a declaration has been made by the requesting body that consultations have been exhausted and within 15 days following such declaration. In case of requests under article 99, paragraph 4, and should no further consultations be possible, the requested State may seek a ruling within 15 days from the day on which the requested State is informed of or became aware of the direct execution.

3. An application under sub-regulation 1 shall not of itself have suspensive effect, unless the Chamber so orders.

4. The Chamber may hear from participants to the proceedings on the matter.

5. If the Chamber rejects the application referred to in sub-regulation 1, the Chamber may grant the requested State additional time within which it shall execute the request or the Chamber shall lift any suspension of direct execution.

REGULATION 109

FAILURE TO COMPLY WITH A REQUEST FOR COOPERATION

B9–109   1. An application for a finding under article 87, paragraph 7, may be made to the competent Chamber by the requesting body either where no application has been made under regulation 108, following the lapse of the time limit referred to in sub-regulation 2 of that provision, or where an application has been made, following a ruling by the Chamber under sub-regulation 5 of that provision and, if applicable, following the lapse of the time limit referred to therein.

2. When a Chamber has made a request for cooperation, proceedings under article 87, paragraph 7, may be initiated by that Chamber. Sub-regulation 1 shall apply *mutatis mutandis*.

3. Before making a finding in accordance with article 87, paragraph 7, the Chamber shall hear from the requested State.

4. Where a finding under article 87, paragraph 7, has been made, the President shall refer the matter to the Assembly or the Security Council in accordance with that provision and, as regards the Security Council, in accordance with the agreement to be concluded under article 2.

REGULATION 110

COOPERATION FOR THE PURPOSES OF NOTIFICATION BY WAY OF PERSONAL SERVICE

For the purposes of notification by way of personal service as described in regulation 31, sub-regulation 4, the requesting body shall, where necessary, make a request for cooperation to the relevant State under articles 93, paragraph 1 (d), and 99, paragraph 1.   **B9–110**

REGULATION 111

INFORMATION ABOUT ADMISSIBILITY RULING

When transmitting a request for the arrest and surrender of a person in accordance with article 89, paragraph 1, the Registrar shall enclose a copy of any relevant admissibility ruling of the Court.   **B9–111**

REGULATION 112

VIEWS OF THE SURRENDERING STATE IN OR AFTER ADMISSIBILITY PROCEEDINGS

At any time before making a decision on a challenge to admissibility based on the grounds set out in article 17, paragraph 1 (a), the Chamber shall hear from the State which originally surrendered the person as to whether that State objects to the transfer of the person to the State which brought the challenge to admissibility.   **B9–112**

Section 2

Enforcement

REGULATION 113

ENFORCEMENT UNIT WITHIN THE PRESIDENCY

1. The Presidency shall establish an enforcement unit within the Presidency to assist it in the exercise of its functions under Part 10 of the Statute, in particular: **B9–113**

   (a) The supervision of enforcement of sentences and conditions of imprisonment; and

   (b) The enforcement of fines, forfeiture orders and reparation orders.

2. The record for each sentenced person shall be maintained by the Registrar in accordance with rule 15.

REGULATION 114

BILATERAL ARRANGEMENTS UNDER RULE 200, SUB-RULE 5

Bilateral arrangements as described in rule 200, sub-rule 5, shall be negotiated under the authority of the Presidency and thereafter concluded with the relevant State by the President.   **B9–114**

REGULATION 115

EXERCISE OF FUNCTIONS UNDER RULE 214, SUB-RULE 4

B9–115   In the exercise of its functions under rule 214, sub-rule 4, the Presidency shall have due regard to the principles of international law on re-extradition.

REGULATION 116

ENFORCEMENT OF FINES, FORFEITURE ORDERS AND REPARATION ORDERS

B9–116   1. For the purposes of enforcement of fines, forfeiture orders and reparation orders, the Presidency, with the assistance of the Registry as appropriate, shall make the arrangements necessary in order to, *inter alia*:
   (a) Receive payment of fines as described in article 77, paragraph 2 (a);
   (b) Receive, as described in article 109, paragraph 3, property or the proceeds of the sale of real property or, where appropriate, the sale of other property;
   (c) Account for interest gained on money received under (a) and (b) above;
   (d) Ensure the transfer of money to the Trust Fund or to victims, as appropriate.
   2. Following the transfer to or deposit in the Trust Fund of property or assets realized through enforcement of an order of the Court, the Presidency shall, subject to article 75, paragraph 2, and rule 98, decide on their disposition or allocation in accordance with rule 221.

REGULATION 117

ONGOING MONITORING OF FINANCIAL SITUATION OF THE SENTENCED PERSON

B9–117   The Presidency shall, if necessary, and with the assistance of the Registrar as appropriate, monitor the financial situation of the sentenced person on an ongoing basis, even following completion of a sentence of imprisonment, in order to enforce fines, forfeiture orders or reparation orders, and may, *inter alia*:
   (a) Request relevant information, expert opinions or reports, where necessary by way of a request for cooperation, and, if appropriate, on a periodic basis;
   (b) Contact, where appropriate in the manner described in rule 211, paragraph 1 (c), the sentenced person and his or her counsel in order to inquire into the financial situation of the sentenced person;
   (c) Ask for observations from the Prosecutor, victims and legal representatives of victims.

REGULATION 118

PROCEDURE UNDER RULE 146, SUB-RULE 5

B9–118   1. In making its decision on the extension of the term of imprisonment in accordance with rule 146, sub-rules 5 and 6, the Presidency may ask for observations from States in which attempts to enforce fines did not succeed and shall ask for observations from the State in which the sentence of imprisonment is being served.
   2. Where the term of imprisonment has been extended under rule 146, sub-rule 5, and the sentenced person subsequently pays the fine or a portion thereof, the Presidency shall revoke or in case of partial payment reduce the extension previously ordered.

CHAPTER 8

REMOVAL FROM OFFICE AND DISCIPLINARY MEASURES

REGULATION 119

RECEIPT AND ADMINISTRATION OF COMPLAINTS

1. All complaints against a judge, the Prosecutor, a Deputy Prosecutor, the Registrar **B9–119** or the Deputy Registrar concerning conduct defined under rules 24 and 25 shall be submitted directly to the Presidency, which shall notify the person against whom the complaint has been directed of that complaint.

2. The Presidency shall make all necessary arrangements for administrative assistance when dealing with a complaint.

REGULATION 120

PROCEDURE UNDER RULE 26, SUB-RULE 2

1. The Presidency shall be assisted by three judges, appointed on the basis of **B9–120** automatic rotation following the English alphabet of the surnames of all judges not comprising the Presidency or the judge being complained against, in order to determine whether a complaint is anonymous or manifestly unfounded.

2. The judges appointed in accordance with sub-regulation 1 shall, where necessary, seek additional comments from either the person being complained against or the complainant and shall make a recommendation to the Presidency on whether such complaint is admissible or should be set aside in accordance with rule 26, sub-rule 2. The appointed judges shall also make a recommendation as to whether the complaint against a judge, the Registrar or Deputy Registrar relates to conduct which falls manifestly outside the scope of rule 24.

3. The Presidency shall decide whether to accept any recommendation described in sub-regulation 2.

4. If a complaint relates to a member of the Presidency, he or she shall not carry out any function as a member of the Presidency with regard to the complaint and his or her functions in that respect shall be exercised by the next available judge having precedence in accordance with regulation 10.

REGULATION 121

DECISION UNDER RULE 26, SUB-RULE 2, AND TRANSMISSION OF COMPLAINT TO THE COMPETENT ORGAN

1. In case the Presidency decides that a complaint against a judge, the Registrar or **B9–121** Deputy Registrar is not anonymous or manifestly unfounded, it shall transmit the complaint to a plenary session, unless the Presidency determines that the conduct complained of falls manifestly outside the scope of rule 24, in which case the matter shall be considered by the Presidency in accordance with article 47, rule 30, sub-rule 1 and regulation 122.

2. In case the Presidency decides that a complaint against the Prosecutor or a Deputy Prosecutor is not anonymous or manifestly unfounded, it shall:

(a) With regard to the Prosecutor, transmit the complaint to the Bureau of the Assembly;

(b) With regard to the Deputy Prosecutor, transmit the complaint to the Prosecutor.

REGULATION 122

PROCEDURE BEFORE THE PRESIDENCY ON DISCIPLINARY MEASURES FOR A JUDGE, THE REGISTRAR OR THE DEPUTY REGISTRAR

B9–122   1. When it is determined in accordance with regulation 121, sub-regulation 1, that a complaint should be considered by the Presidency, that complaint shall be dealt with in accordance with rule 27.

2. If the Presidency decides to impose disciplinary measures, the judge, Registrar or Deputy Registrar concerned may file an appeal against that decision to a plenary session within 30 days of notification of the decision.

REGULATION 123

PROCEDURE FOR REMOVAL FROM OFFICE OF A JUDGE, THE REGISTRAR OR THE DEPUTY REGISTRAR

B9–123   1. The judges appointed under regulation 120, sub-regulation 1, shall conduct the proceedings under article 46, paragraph 4, and rule 27 and shall report thereon to a plenary session.

2. The procedure to be followed prior to the adoption of any recommendation concerning a judge under article 46, paragraph 2, and rule 29, sub-rule 1, is without prejudice to any additional procedure to be followed by the Assembly under article 46, paragraph 4, and rule 27.

REGULATION 124

SUSPENSION FROM DUTY

B9–124   1. For the purposes of rule 28, a judge, the Prosecutor, a Deputy Prosecutor, the Registrar or the Deputy Registrar may be suspended from duty following the decision of the Presidency under rule 26, sub-rule 2, by the organ competent to make a decision under article 46, paragraphs 2 and 3.

2. Suspension from duty shall not affect salary and allowances.

REGULATION 125

INITIATION OF PROCEEDINGS BY THE PRESIDENCY

B9–125   In cases where the Presidency initiates proceedings on its own motion, the preliminary assessment of whether complaints are anonymous or manifestly unfounded under rule 26, sub-rule 2, shall not be required and regulations 121 to 124 shall apply *mutatis mutandis*.

Chapter 9

ADOPTION OF THE CODE OF JUDICIAL ETHICS

Regulation 126

ADOPTION OF THE CODE OF JUDICIAL ETHICS

1. The Presidency shall draw up a Code of Judicial Ethics, after having consulted the judges.

B9–126

2. The draft Code shall then be transmitted to the judges meeting in plenary session for the purpose of adoption by the majority of the judges.

B10. Amendments to the Regulations of the Court 7–9 March 2005

B10–001   By decision of the Judges of the Court at the 6th Plenary Session, the following provisions of the Regulations of the Court are amended:

Regulation 29, Sub-regulation 1: Non-compliance with these Regulations and with Orders of a Chamber

French only

B10–002   1. Lorsqu'un participant n'observe pas les dispositions du Règlement **ou ne respecte pas** une ordonnance rendue par une chambre en vertu dudit Règlement, cette dernière peut rendre toute ordonnance qui se révèle nécessaire dans l'intérêt de la justice.

Regulation 66, Sub-regulation 1: Procedure Leading to the Determination on Revision

French only

B10–003   1. Toute requête en révision présentée en vertu du paragraphe 1er de l'article 84 ainsi que de la règle 159 indique l'intitulé et le numéro de la procédure originale. Une requête présentée en vertu de l'alinéa a) du paragraphe 1er de l'article 84 énonce les nouveaux faits ou éléments de preuve, qui n'étaient **ni** connus ni disponibles au moment du procès, et indique l'effet que la présentation de tels faits ou éléments de preuve auraient pu avoir sur la décision de la Cour. Les autres requêtes exposent les raisons visées aux alinéas b) et c) du paragraphe 1er de l'article 84. Dans toute requête en révision, les faits invoqués s'accompagnent, dans la mesure du possible, d'un engagement solennel de la part de la personne qui a connaissance desdits faits. La demande n'excède pas cent pages.

Regulation 92, Sub-regulation 3: Confidentiality of the Detention Record

French only

B10–004   3. La chambre peut, de sa propre initiative ou à la demande de toute personne intéressée, **ordonner** ou interdire la communication de tout ou partie du dossier de détention.

Regulation 95, Sub-regulation 2: Discipline

French only

B10–005   2. **Les détails de** la procédure disciplinaire applicable à la personne détenue **sont exposés dans le Règlement du Greffe**. Ladite procédure donne à cette dernière le droit d'être entendue au sujet de toute infraction qui aurait été commise ainsi que le droit de former un recours auprès de la Présidence.

Regulation 103, Sub-regulation 6: Health and Safety of Detained Persons

French only

B10–006   6. Le Greffier prend les dispositions nécessaires pour toute personne détenue souffrant d'aliénation mentale ou atteinte de graves troubles psychiatriques. Par ordonnance de la chambre, toute personne détenue reconnue comme souffrant d'aliénation mentale ou atteinte de graves troubles psychiatriques peut être transférée dans un établissement spécialisé afin d'y recevoir les soins adéquats.

The above-mentioned regulations are amended pursuant to article 52 of the Statute.

Pursuant to article 52, paragraph 3, of the Statute the amendments take effect on 9 March 2005 and shall remain in force if there are no objections from a majority of States within six months from 18 May 2005, date of the circulation to States Parties.

The text as amended is also published on the website of the Court at the address *www.icc-cpi.int*.

B11. Staff regulations for the International Criminal Court

This document may be found at *http://www.icc-cpi.int/library/about/officialjournal/Staff_ Regulations_120704-EN.pdf*   **B11–001**

B12. Final Act of the United Nations Diplomatic Conference of Plenipotentiaries on the Establishment of an International Criminal Court

This document may be found at *http://www.un.org/law/icc/statute/finalfra.htm*   **B12–001**

B13. Code of Judicial Ethics

ICC–BD/02–01–05

This document may be found at *http://www.icc-cpi.int/library/about/officialjournal/ICC-BD02-01-05_En.pdf*   **B13–001**

B14. Negotiated Relationship Agreement between the International Criminal Court and the United Nations

This document may be found at *http://www.icc-cpi.int/library/asp/ICC-ASP-3-Res1_ English.pdf*   **B14–001**

B15. Resolutions adopted by the Assembly of States Parties

RESOLUTION ICC–ASP/3/RES.1

Adopted at the 3rd plenary meeting, on 7 September 2004, by consensus   **B15–001**

This document may be found at *http://www.icc-cpi.int/library/asp/ICC-ASP-3-25-III_ English.pdf*

APPENDIX C

ICTY

Security Council Resolution 808 (1993)

Adopted by the Secutiry Council at its 3175th meeting, on 22 February 1993

C1–001   *The Security Council,*

Reaffirming its resolution 713 (1991) of 25 September 1991 and all subsequent relevant resolutions,

Recalling paragraph 10 of its resolution 764 (1992) of 13 July 1992, in which it reaffirmed that all parties are bound to comply with the obligations under international humanitarian law and in particular the Geneva Conventions of 12 August 1949, and that persons who commit or order the commission of grave breaches of the Conventions are individually responsible in respect of such breaches,

Recalling also its resolution 771 (1992) of 13 August 1992, in which, *inter alia*, it demanded that all parties and others concerned in the former Yugoslavia, and all military forces in Bosnia and Herzegovina, immediately cease and desist from all breaches of international humanitarian law,

Recalling further its resolution 780 (1992) of 6 October 1992, in which it requested the Secretary-General to establish, as a matter of urgency, an impartial Commission of Experts to examine and analyse the information submitted pursuant to resolutions 771 (1992) and 780 (1992), together with such further information as the Commission of Experts may obtain, with a view to providing the Secretary-General with its conclusions on the evidence of grave breaches of the Geneva Conventions and other violations of international humanitarian law committed in the territory of the former Yugoslavia,

Having considered the interim report of the Commission of Experts established by resolution 780 (1992) (S/25274), in which the Commission observed that a decision to establish an ad hoc international tribunal in relation to events in the territory of the former Yugoslavia would be consistent with the direction of its work,

Expressing once again its grave alarm at continuing reports of widespread violations of international humanitarian law occurring within the territory of the former Yugoslavia, including reports of mass killings and the continuance of the practice of "ethnic cleansing",

Determining that this situation constitutes a threat to international peace and security,

Determined to put an end to such crimes and to take effective measures to bring to justice the persons who are responsible for them,

Convinced that in the particular circumstances of the former Yugoslavia the establishment of an international tribunal would enable this aim to be achieved and would contribute to the restoration and maintenance of peace,

Noting in this regard the recommendation by the Co-Chairmen of the Steering Committee in the International Conference on the Former Yugoslavia for the establishment of such a tribunal (S/25221),

Noting also with grave concern the "report of the European Community investigative mission into the treatment of Muslim women in the former Yugoslavia" (S/25240, Annex 1),

Noting further the report of the committee of jurists submitted by France (S/25266), the report of the commission of jurists submitted by Italy (S/25300), and the report transmitted by the Permanent Representatives of Sweden on behalf of the Chairman-in-Office of the Conference on Security and Cooperation in Europe (CSCE) (S/25307),

1. *Decides* that an international tribunal shall be established for the prosecution of persons responsible for serious violations of international humanitarian law committed in the territory of the former Yugoslavia since 1991;

2. *Requests* the Secretary-General to submit for consideration by the Council at the earliest possible date, and if possible no later than 60 days after the adoption of the present resolution, a report on all the aspects of this matter, including specific proposals and where appropriate options for the effective and expeditious implementation of the decision contained in paragraph 1 above, taking into account suggestions put forward in this regard by Member States;

3. *Decides* to remain actively seized of the matter.

**C2. Report of the Secretary-General Pursuant to Paragraph 2 of
Security Council Resolution 808 (1993) Presented 3 May 1993
(S/25704)**

CONTENTS

INTRODUCTION

C2–001   1. By paragraph 1 of resolution 808 (1993) of 22 February 1993, the Security Council decided "that an international tribunal shall be established for the prosecution of persons responsible for serious violations of international humanitarian law committed in the territory of the former Yugoslavia since 1991".

2. By paragraph 2 of the resolution, the Secretary-General was requested "to submit for consideration by the Council at the earliest possible date, and if possible no later than 60 days after the adoption of the present resolution, a report on all aspects of this matter, including specific proposals and where appropriate options for the effective and

expeditious implementation of the decision [to establish an international tribunal], taking into account suggestions put forward in this regard by Member States."

3. The present report is presented pursuant to that request.[1]

A

4. Resolution 808 (1993) represents a further step taken by the Security Council in a series of resolutions concerning serious violations of international humanitarian law occurring in the territory of the former Yugoslavia.

C2–002

5. In resolution 764 (1992) of 13 July 1992, the Security Council reaffirmed that all parties to the conflict are bound to comply with their obligations under international humanitarian law and in particular the Geneva Conventions of 12 August 1949, and that persons who commit or order the commission of grave breaches of the Conventions are individually responsible in respect of such breaches.

6. In resolution 771 (1992) of 13 August 1992, the Security Council expressed grave alarm at continuing reports of widespread violations of international humanitarian law occurring within the territory of the former Yugoslavia and especially in Bosnia and Herzegovina, including reports of mass forcible expulsion and deportation of civilians, imprisonment and abuse of civilians in detention centres, deliberate attacks on non-combatants, hospitals and ambulances, impeding the delivery of food and medical supplies to the civilian population, and wanton devastation and destruction of property. The Council strongly condemned any violations of international humanitarian law, including those involved in the practice of "ethnic cleansing", and demanded that all parties to the conflict in the former Yugoslavia cease and desist from all breaches of international humanitarian law. It called upon States and international humanitarian organizations to collate substantiated information relating to the violations of human-itarian law, including grave breaches of the Geneva Conventions, being committed in the territory of the former Yugoslavia and to make this information available to the Council. Furthermore, the Council decided, acting under Chapter VII of the Charter of the United Nations, that all parties and others concerned in the former Yugoslavia, and all military forces in Bosnia and Herzegovina, should comply with the provisions of that resolution, failing which the Council would need to take further measures under the Charter.

7. In resolution 780 (1992) of 6 October 1992, the Security Council requested the Secretary-General to establish an impartial Commission of Experts to examine and analyse the information as requested by resolution 771 (1992), together with such further information as the Commission may obtain through its own investigations or efforts, of other persons or bodies pursuant to resolution 771 (1992), with a view to providing the Secretary-General with its conclusions on the evidence of grave breaches of the Geneva Conventions and other violations of international humanitarian law com-mitted in the territory of the former Yugoslavia.

8. On 14 October 1992 the Secretary-General submitted a report to the Security Council pursuant to paragraph 3 of resolution 780 (1992) in which he outlined his decision to establish a five-member Commission of Experts (S/24657). On 26 October 1992, the Secretary-General announced the appointment of the Chairman and members of the Commission of Experts.

9. By a letter dated 9 February 1993, the Secretary-General submitted to the President of the Security Council an interim report of the Commission of Experts (S/25274), which concluded that grave breaches and other violations of international humanitarian law had been committed in the territory of the former Yugoslavia, including wilful killing, "ethnic cleansing", mass killings, torture, rape, pillage and destruction of civilian property, destruction of cultural and religious property and

---

[1] On 19 April 1993, the Secretary-General addressed a letter to the President of the Security Council informing him that the report would be made available to the Security Council no later than 6 May 1993.

arbitrary arrests. In its report, the Commission noted that should the Security Council or another competent organ of the United Nations decide to establish an ad hoc international tribunal, such a decision would be consistent with the direction of its work.

10. It was against this background that the Security Council considered and adopted resolution 808 (1993). After recalling the provisions of resolutions 764 (1992), 771 (1992) and 780 (1992) and, taking into consideration the interim report of the Commission of Experts, the Security Council expressed once again its grave alarm at continuing reports of widespread violations of international humanitarian law occurring within the territory of the former Yugoslavia, including reports of mass killings and the continuation of the practice of "ethnic cleansing". The Council determined that this situation constituted a threat to international peace and security, and stated that it was determined to put an end to such crimes and to take effective measures to bring to justice the persons who are responsible for them. The Security Council stated its conviction that in the particular circumstances of the former Yugoslavia the establishment of an international tribunal would enable this aim to be achieved and would contribute to the restoration and maintenance of peace.

11. The Secretary-General wishes to recall that in resolution 820 (1993) of 17 April 1993, the Security Council condemned once again all violations of international humanitarian law, including in particular, the practice of "ethnic cleansing" and the massive, organized and systematic detention and rape of women, and reaffirmed that those who commit or have committed or order or have ordered the commission of such acts will be held individually responsible in respect of such acts.

B

C2–003   12. The Security Council's decision in resolution 808 (1993) to establish an international tribunal is circumscribed in scope and purpose: the prosecution of persons responsible for serious violations of international humanitarian law committed in the territory of the former Yugoslavia since 1991. The decision does not relate to the establishment of an international criminal jurisdiction in general nor to the creation of an international criminal court of a permanent nature, issues which are and remain under active consideration by the International Law Commission and the General Assembly.

C

C2–004   13. In accordance with the request of the Security Council, the Secretary-General has taken into account in the preparation of the present report the suggestions put forward by Member States, in particular those reflected in the following Security Council documents submitted by Member States and noted by the Council in its resolution 808 (1993): the report of the committee of jurists submitted by France (S/25266), the report of the commission of jurists submitted by Italy (S/25300), and the report submitted by the Permanent Representative of Sweden on behalf of the Chairman-in-Office of the Conference on Security and Cooperation in Europe (CSCE) (S/25307). The Secretary-General has also sought the views of the Commission of Experts established pursuant to Security Council resolution 780 (1992) and has made use of the information gathered by that Commission. In addition, the Secretary-General has taken into account suggestions or comments put forward formally or informally by the following Member States since the adoption of resolution 808 (1993): Australia, Austria, Belgium, Brazil, Canada, Chile, China, Denmark, Egypt*, Germany, Iran (Islamic Republic of)*, Ireland, Italy, Malaysia*, Mexico, Netherlands, New Zealand, Pakistan*, Portugal, Russian Federation, Saudi Arabia*, Senegal*, Slovenia, Spain, Sweden, Turkey*, United Kingdom of Great Britain and Northern Ireland, United States of America and Yugoslavia. He has also received suggestions or comments from a non-member State (Switzerland).

---

* On behalf of the members of the Organization of the Islamic Conference (OIC) and as members of the Contact Group of OIC on Bosnia and Herzegovina.

14. The Secretary-General has also received comments from the International Committee of the Red Cross (ICRC), the International Criminal Police Organization and from the following non-governmental organizations: Amnesty International, Association Internationale des Jeunes Avocats, Ethnic Minorities Barristers' Association, Fáedáeration internationale des femmes des carrières juridiques, Jacob Blaustein Institution for the Advancement of Human Rights, Lawyers Committee for Human Rights, National Alliance of Women's Organisations (NAWO), and Parliamentarians for Global Action. Observations have also been received from international meetings and individual experts in relevant fields.

15. The Secretary-General wishes to place on record his appreciation for the interest shown by all the Governments, organizations and individuals who have offered valuable suggestions and comments.

D

16. In the main body of the report which follows, the Secretary-General first examines **C2–005** the legal basis for the establishment of the International Tribunal foreseen in resolution 808 (1993). The Secretary-General then sets out in detail the competence of the International Tribunal as regards the law it will apply, the persons to whom the law will be applied, including considerations as to the principle of individual criminal responsibility, its territorial and temporal reach and the relation of its work to that of national courts. In succeeding chapters, the Secretary-General sets out detailed views on the organization of the international tribunal, the investigation and pre-trial proceedings, trial and post-trial proceedings, and cooperation and judicial assistance. A concluding chapter deals with a number of general and organizational issues such as privileges and immunities, the seat of the international tribunal, working languages and financial arrangements.

17. In response to the Security Council's request to include in the report specific proposals, the Secretary-General has decided to incorporate into the report specific language for inclusion in a statute of the International Tribunal. The formulations are based upon provisions found in existing international instruments, particularly with regard to competence *ratione materiae* of the International Tribunal. Suggestions and comments, including suggested draft articles, received from States, organizations and individuals as noted in paragraphs 13 and 14 above, also formed the basis upon which the Secretary-General prepared the statute. Texts prepared in the past by United Nations or other bodies for the establishment of international criminal courts were consulted by the Secretary-General, including texts prepared by the United Nations Committee on International Criminal Jurisdiction,[2] the International Law Commission, and the International Law Association. Proposals regarding individual articles are, therefore, made throughout the body of the report; the full text of the statute of the International Tribunal is contained in the annex to the present report.

I. THE LEGAL BASIS FOR THE ESTABLISHMENT OF THE INTERNATIONAL TRIBUNAL

18. Security Council resolution 808 (1993) states that an international tribunal shall **C2–006** be established for the prosecution of persons responsible for serious violations of international humanitarian law committed in the territory of the former Yugoslavia since 1991. It does not, however, indicate how such an international tribunal is to be established or on what legal basis.

19. The approach which, in the normal course of events, would be followed in establishing an international tribunal would be the conclusion of a treaty by which the States parties would establish a tribunal and approve its statute. This treaty would be

---

[2] The 1953 Committee on International Criminal Jurisdiction was established by General Assembly resolution 687 (VII) of 5 December 1952.

drawn up and adopted by an appropriate international body (e.g., the General Assembly or a specially convened conference), following which it would be opened for signature and ratification. Such an approach would have the advantage of allowing for a detailed examination and elaboration of all the issues pertaining to the establishment of the international tribunal. It also would allow the States participating in the negotiation and conclusion of the treaty fully to exercise their sovereign will, in particular whether they wish to become parties to the treaty or not.

20. As has been pointed out in many of the comments received, the treaty approach incurs the disadvantage of requiring considerable time to establish an instrument and then to achieve the required number of ratifications for entry into force. Even then, there could be no guarantee that ratifications will be received from those States which should be parties to the treaty if it is to be truly effective.

21. A number of suggestions have been put forward to the effect that the General Assembly, as the most representative organ of the United Nations, should have a role in the establishment of the international tribunal in addition to its role in the administrative and budgetary aspects of the question. The involvement of the General Assembly in the drafting or the review of the statute of the International Tribunal would not be reconcilable with the urgency expressed by the Security Council in resolution 808 (1993). The Secretary-General believes that there are other ways of involving the authority and prestige of the General Assembly in the establishment of the International Tribunal.

22. In the light of the disadvantages of the treaty approach in this particular case and of the need indicated in resolution 808 (1993) for an effective and expeditious implementation of the decision to establish an international tribunal, the Secretary-General believes that the International Tribunal should be established by a decision of the Security Council on the basis of Chapter VII of the Charter of the United Nations. Such a decision would constitute a measure to maintain or restore international peace and security, following the requisite determination of the existence of a threat to the peace, breach of the peace or act of aggression.

23. This approach would have the advantage of being expeditious and of being immediately effective as all States would be under a binding obligation to take whatever action is required to carry out a decision taken as an enforcement measure under Chapter VII.

24. In the particular case of the former Yugoslavia, the Secretary-General believes that the establishment of the International Tribunal by means of a Chapter VII decision would be legally justified, both in terms of the object and purpose of the decision, as indicated in the preceding paragraphs, and of past Security Council practice.

25. As indicated in paragraph 10 above, the Security Council has already determined that the situation posed by continuing reports of widespread violations of international humanitarian law occurring in the former Yugoslavia constitutes a threat to international peace and security. The Council has also decided under Chapter VII of the Charter that all parties and others concerned in the former Yugoslavia, and all military forces in Bosnia and Herzegovina, shall comply with the provisions of resolution 771 (1992), failing which it would need to take further measures under the Charter. Furthermore, the Council has repeatedly reaffirmed that all parties in the former Yugoslavia are bound to comply with the obligations under international humanitarian law and in particular the Geneva Conventions of 12 August 1949, and that persons who commit or order the commission of grave breaches of the Conventions are individually responsible in respect of such breaches.

26. Finally, the Security Council stated in resolution 808 (1993) that it was convinced that in the particular circumstances of the former Yugoslavia, the establishment of an international tribunal would bring about the achievement of the aim of putting an end to such crimes and of taking effective measures to bring to justice the persons responsible for them, and would contribute to the restoration and maintenance of peace.

27. The Security Council has on various occasions adopted decisions under Chapter VII aimed at restoring and maintaining international peace and security, which have involved the establishment of subsidiary organs for a variety of purposes. Reference may be made in this regard to Security Council resolution 687 (1991) and subsequent resolutions relating to the situation between Iraq and Kuwait.

28. In this particular case, the Security Council would be establishing, as an enforcement measure under Chapter VII, a subsidiary organ within the terms of Article 29 of the Charter, but one of a judicial nature. This organ would, of course, have to perform its functions independently of political considerations; it would not be subject to the authority or control of the Security Council with regard to the performance of its judicial functions. As an enforcement measure under Chapter VII, however, the life span of the international tribunal would be linked to the restoration and maintenance of international peace and security in the territory of the former Yugoslavia, and Security Council decisions related thereto.

29. It should be pointed out that, in assigning to the International Tribunal the task of prosecuting persons responsible for serious violations of international humanitarian law, the Security Council would not be creating or purporting to "legislate" that law. Rather, the International Tribunal would have the task of applying existing international humanitarian law.

30. On the basis of the foregoing considerations, the Secretary-General proposes that the Security Council, acting under Chapter VII of the Charter, establish the International Tribunal. The resolution so adopted would have annexed to it a statute the opening passage of which would read as follows:

Having been established by the Security Council acting under Chapter VII of the Charter of the United Nations, the International Tribunal for the Prosecution of Persons Responsible for Serious Violations of International Humanitarian Law Committed in the Territory of the Former Yugoslavia since 1991 (hereinafter referred to as "the International Tribunal") shall function in accordance with the provisions of the present Statute.

II. COMPETENCE OF THE INTERNATIONAL TRIBUNAL

31. The competence of the International Tribunal derives from the mandate set out in paragraph 1 of resolution 808 (1993). This part of the report will examine and make proposals regarding these fundamental elements of its competence: *ratione materiae* (subject-matter jurisdiction), *ratione personae* (personal jurisdiction), *ratione loci* (territorial jurisdiction) and *ratione temporis* (temporal jurisdiction), as well as the question of the concurrent jurisdiction of the International Tribunal and national courts. **C2–007**

32. The statute should begin with a general article on the competence of the International Tribunal which would read as follows:

ARTICLE 1

COMPETENCE OF THE INTERNATIONAL TRIBUNAL

The International Tribunal shall have the power to prosecute persons responsible for serious violations of international humanitarian law committed in the territory of the former Yugoslavia since 1991 in accordance with the provisions of the present Statute. **C2–008**

A. Competence ratione materiae (subject-matter jurisdiction)

33. According to paragraph 1 of resolution 808 (1993), the international tribunal shall prosecute persons responsible for serious violations of international humanitarian law committed in the territory of the former Yugoslavia since 1991. This body of law exists in the form of both conventional law and customary law. While there is international customary law which is not laid down in conventions, some of the major conventional humanitarian law has become part of customary international law. **C2–009**

34. In the view of the Secretary-General, the application of the principle nullum crimen sine lege requires that the international tribunal should apply rules of international humanitarian law which are beyond any doubt part of customary law so that the

problem of adherence of some but not all States to specific conventions does not arise. This would appear to be particularly important in the context of an international tribunal prosecuting persons responsible for serious violations of international humanitarian law.

35. The part of conventional international humanitarian law which has beyond doubt become part of international customary law is the law applicable in armed conflict as embodied in: the Geneva Conventions of 12 August 1949 for the Protection of War Victims[3]; the Hague Convention (IV) Respecting the Laws and Customs of War on Land and the Regulations annexed thereto of 18 October 1907[4]; the Convention on the Prevention and Punishment of the Crime of Genocide of 9 December 1948[5]; and the Charter of the International Military Tribunal of 8 August 1945.[6]

36. Suggestions have been made that the international tribunal should apply domestic law in so far as it incorporates customary international humanitarian law. While international humanitarian law as outlined above provides a sufficient basis for subject-matter jurisdiction, there is one related issue which would require reference to domestic practice, namely, penalties (see para. 111).

Grave breaches of the 1949 Geneva Conventions

C2–010 37. The Geneva Conventions constitute rules of international humanitarian law and provide the core of the customary law applicable in international armed conflicts. These Conventions regulate the conduct of war from the humanitarian perspective by protecting certain categories of persons: namely, wounded and sick members of armed forces in the field; wounded, sick and shipwrecked members of armed forces at sea; prisoners of war, and civilians in time of war.

38. Each Convention contains a provision listing the particularly serious violations that qualify as "grave breaches" or war crimes. Persons committing or ordering grave breaches are subject to trial and punishment. The lists of grave breaches contained in the Geneva Conventions are reproduced in the article which follows.

39. The Security Council has reaffirmed on several occasions that persons who commit or order the commission of grave breaches of the 1949 Geneva Conventions in the territory of the former Yugoslavia are individually responsible for such breaches as serious violations of international humanitarian law.

40. The corresponding article of the statute would read:

ARTICLE 2

GRAVE BREACHES OF THE GENEVA CONVENTIONS OF 1949

C2–011 The International Tribunal shall have the power to prosecute persons committing or ordering to be committed grave breaches of the Geneva Conventions of 12 August 1949, namely the following acts against persons or property protected under the provisions of the relevant Geneva Convention:

[3] Convention for the Amelioration of the Condition of the Wounded and Sick in Armed Forces in the Field of 12 August 1949, Convention for the Amelioration of the Condition of the Wounded, Sick and Shipwrecked Members of Armed Forces at Sea of 12 August 1949, Convention relative to the Treatment of Prisoners of War of 12 August 1949, Convention relative to the Protection of Civilian Persons in Time of War of 12 August 1949 (United Nations, *Treaty Series*, vol. 75, No. 970–973).
[4] Carnegie Endowment for International Peace, *The Hague Conventions and Declarations of 1899 and 1907* (New York, Oxford University Press, 1915), p. 100.
[5] United Nations, Treaty Series, vol. 78, No. 1021.
[6] The Agreement for the Prosecution and Punishment of the Major War Criminals of the European Axis, signed at London on 8 August 1945 (United Nations, *Treaty Series*, vol. 82, No. 251); see also Judgement of the International Military Tribunal for the Prosecution and Punishment of the Major War Criminals of the European Axis (United States Government Printing Office, *Nazi Conspiracy and Aggression, Opinion and Judgement*) and General Assembly resolution 95 (I) of 11 December 1946 on the Affirmation of the Principles of International Law Recognized by the Charter of the Nuremberg Tribunal.

(a) wilful killing;
(b) torture or inhuman treatment, including biological experiments;
(c) wilfully causing great suffering or serious injury to body or health;
(d) extensive destruction and appropriation of property, not justified by military necessity and carried out unlawfully and wantonly;
(e) compelling a prisoner of war or a civilian to serve in the forces of a hostile power;
(f) wilfully depriving a prisoner of war or a civilian of the rights of fair and regular trial;
(g) unlawful deportation or transfer or unlawful confinement of a civilian;
(h) taking civilians as hostages.

Violations of the laws or customs of war

41. The 1907 Hague Convention (IV) Respecting the Laws and Customs of War on Land and the Regulations annexed thereto comprise a second important area of conventional humanitarian international law which has become part of the body of international customary law.   **C2–012**

42. The NÝrnberg Tribunal recognized that many of the provisions contained in the Hague Regulations, although innovative at the time of their adoption were, by 1939, recognized by all civilized nations and were regarded as being declaratory of the laws and customs of war. The NÝrnberg Tribunal also recognized that war crimes defined in article 6(b) of the NÝrnberg Charter were already recognized as war crimes under international law, and covered in the Hague Regulations, for which guilty individuals were punishable.

43. The Hague Regulations cover aspects of international humanitarian law which are also covered by the 1949 Geneva Conventions. However, the Hague Regulations also recognize that the right of belligerents to conduct warfare is not unlimited and that resort to certain methods of waging war is prohibited under the rules of land warfare.

44. These rules of customary law, as interpreted and applied by the NúYrnberg Tribunal, provide the basis for the corresponding article of the statute which would read as follows:

ARTICLE 3

VIOLATIONS OF THE LAWS OR CUSTOMS OF WAR

The International Tribunal shall have the power to prosecute persons violating the laws or customs of war. Such violations shall include, but not be limited to: **C2–013**

(a) employment of poisonous weapons or other weapons calculated to cause unnecessary suffering;
(b) wanton destruction of cities, towns or villages, or devastation not justified by military necessity;
(c) attack, or bombardment, by whatever means, of undefended towns, villages, dwellings, or buildings;
(d) seizure of, destruction or wilful damage done to institutions dedicated to religion, charity and education, the arts and sciences, historic monuments and works of art and science;
(e) plunder of public or private property.

Genocide

45. The 1948 Convention on the Prevention and Punishment of the Crime of Genocide confirms that genocide, whether committed in time of peace or in time of war, is a crime under international law for which individuals shall be tried and punished. The Convention is today considered part of international customary law as evidenced by the   **C2–014**

International Court of Justice in its Advisory Opinion on Reservations to the Convention on the Prevention and Punishment of the Crime of Genocide, 1951.[7]

46. The relevant provisions of the Genocide Convention are reproduced in the corresponding article of the statute, which would read as follows:

ARTICLE 4

GENOCIDE

C2–015   1. The International Tribunal shall have the power to prosecute persons committing genocide as defined in paragraph 2 of this article or of committing any of the other acts enumerated in paragraph 3 of this article.

2. Genocide means any of the following acts committed with intent to destroy, in whole or in part, a national, ethnical, racial or religious group, as such:

(a) killing members of the group;
(b) causing serious bodily or mental harm to members of the group;
(c) deliberately inflicting on the group conditions of life calculated to bring about its physical destruction in whole or in part;
(d) imposing measures intended to prevent births within the group;
(e) forcibly transferring children of the group to another group.

3. The following acts shall be punishable:

(a) genocide;
(b) conspiracy to commit genocide;
(c) direct and public incitement to commit genocide;
(d) attempt to commit genocide;
(e) complicity in genocide.

Crimes against humanity

C2–016   47. Crimes against humanity were first recognized in the Charter and Judgement of the Núurnberg Tribunal, as well as in Law No. 10 of the Control Council for Germany.[8] Crimes against humanity are aimed at any civilian population and are prohibited regardless of whether they are committed in an armed conflict, international or internal in character.[9]

48. Crimes against humanity refer to inhumane acts of a very serious nature, such as wilful killing, torture or rape, committed as part of a widespread or systematic attack against any civilian population on national, political, ethnic, racial or religious grounds. In the conflict in the territory of the former Yugoslavia, such inhumane acts have taken the form of so-called "ethnic cleansing" and widespread and systematic rape and other forms of sexual assault, including enforced prostitution.

49. The corresponding article of the statute would read as follows:

---

[7] Reservations to the Convention on the Prevention and Punishment of the Crime of Genocide: Advisory Opinion of 28 May 1951, International Court of Justice Reports, 1951, p. 23.

[8] *Official Gazette of the Control Council for Germany, No. 3, p. 22, Military Government Gazette, Germany, British Zone of Control, No. 5, p. 46, Journal Officiel du Commandement en Chef Franlcais en Allemagne, No. 12 of 11 January 1946.*

[9] In this context, it is to be noted that the International Court of Justice has recognized that the prohibitions contained in common article 3 of the 1949 Geneva Conventions are based on "elementary considerations of humanity" and cannot be breached in an armed conflict, regardless of whether it is international or internal in character. *Case concerning Military and Paramilitary Activities in and against Nicaragua (Nicaragua v. United States of America), Judgement of 27 June 1986: I.C.J. Reports 1986, p. 114.*

ARTICLE 5

CRIMES AGAINST HUMANITY

The International Tribunal shall have the power to prosecute persons responsible for the following crimes when committed in armed conflict, whether international or internal in character, and directed against any civilian population: **C2–017**
  (a) murder;
  (b) extermination;
  (c) enslavement;
  (d) deportation;
  (e) imprisonment;
  (f) torture;
  (g) rape;
  (h) persecutions on political, racial and religious grounds;
  (i) other inhumane acts.

B. Competence ratione personae (personal jurisdiction) and individual criminal responsibility

50. By paragraph 1 of resolution 808 (1993), the Security Council decided that the International Tribunal shall be established for the prosecution of persons responsible for serious violations of international humanitarian law committed in the territory of the former Yugoslavia since 1991. In the light of the complex of resolutions leading up to resolution 808 (1993) (see paras. 5–7 above), the ordinary meaning of the term "persons responsible for serious violations of international humanitarian law" would be natural persons to the exclusion of juridical persons. **C2–018**

51. The question arises, however, whether a juridical person, such as an association or organization, may be considered criminal as such and thus its members, for that reason alone, be made subject to the jurisdiction of the International Tribunal. The Secretary-General believes that this concept should not be retained in regard to the International Tribunal. The criminal acts set out in this statute are carried out by natural persons; such persons would be subject to the jurisdiction of the International Tribunal irrespective of membership in groups.

52. The corresponding article of the statute would read:

ARTICLE 6

PERSONAL JURISDICTION

The International Tribunal shall have jurisdiction over natural persons pursuant to the provisions of the present Statute. **C2–019**

Individual criminal responsibility

53. An important element in relation to the competence *ratione personae* (personal jurisdiction) of the International Tribunal is the principle of individual criminal responsibility. As noted above, the Security Council has reaffirmed in a number of resolutions that persons committing serious violations of international humanitarian law in the former Yugoslavia are individually responsible for such violations. **C2–020**

54. The Secretary-General believes that all persons who participate in the planning, preparation or execution of serious violations of international humanitarian law in the former Yugoslavia contribute to the commission of the violation and are, therefore, individually responsible.

55. Virtually all of the written comments received by the Secretary-General have suggested that the statute of the International Tribunal should contain provisions with

regard to the individual criminal responsibility of heads of State, government officials and persons acting in an official capacity. These suggestions draw upon the precedents following the Second World War. The Statute should, therefore, contain provisions which specify that a plea of head of State immunity or that an act was committed in the official capacity of the accused will not constitute a defence, nor will it mitigate punishment.

56. A person in a position of superior authority should, therefore, be held individually responsible for giving the unlawful order to commit a crime under the present statute. But he should also be held responsible for failure to prevent a crime or to deter the unlawful behaviour of his subordinates. This imputed responsibility or criminal negligence is engaged if the person in superior authority knew or had reason to know that his subordinates were about to commit or had committed crimes and yet failed to take the necessary and reasonable steps to prevent or repress the commission of such crimes or to punish those who had committed them.

57. Acting upon an order of a Government or a superior cannot relieve the perpetrator of the crime of his criminal responsibility and should not be a defence. Obedience to superior orders may, however, be considered a mitigating factor, should the International Tribunal determine that justice so requires. For example, the International Tribunal may consider the factor of superior orders in connection with other defences such as coercion or lack of moral choice.

58. The International Tribunal itself will have to decide on various personal defences which may relieve a person of individual criminal responsibility, such as minimum age or mental incapacity, drawing upon general principles of law recognized by all nations.

59. The corresponding article of the statute would read:

ARTICLE 7

INDIVIDUAL CRIMINAL RESPONSIBILITY

C2–021   1. A person who planned, instigated, ordered, committed or otherwise aided and abetted in the planning, preparation or execution of a crime referred to in articles 2 to 5 of the present Statute, shall be individually responsible for the crime.

2. The official position of any accused person, whether as Head of State or Government or as a responsible Government official, shall not relieve such person of criminal responsibility nor mitigate punishment.

3. The fact that any of the acts referred to in articles 2 to 5 of the present Statute was committed by a subordinate does not relieve his superior of criminal responsibility if he knew or had reason to know that the subordinate was about to commit such acts or had done so and the superior failed to take the necessary and reasonable measures to prevent such acts or to punish the perpetrators thereof.

4. The fact that an accused person acted pursuant to an order of a Government or of a superior shall not relieve him of criminal responsibility, but may be considered in mitigation of punishment if the International Tribunal determines that justice so requires.

C. Competence ratione loci (territorial jurisdiction) and ratione temporis (temporal jurisdiction)

C2–022   60. Pursuant to paragraph 1 of resolution 808 (1993), the territorial and temporal jurisdiction of the International Tribunal extends to serious violations of international humanitarian law to the extent that they have been "committed in the territory of the former Yugoslavia since 1991".

61. As far as the territorial jurisdiction of the International Tribunal is concerned, the territory of the former Yugoslavia means the territory of the former Socialist Federal Republic of Yugoslavia, including its land surface, airspace and territorial waters.

62. With regard to temporal jurisdiction, Security Council resolution 808 (1993) extends the jurisdiction of the International Tribunal to violations committed "since

1991". The Secretary-General understands this to mean anytime on or after 1 January 1991. This is a neutral date which is not tied to any specific event and is clearly intended to convey the notion that no judgement as to the international or internal character of the conflict is being exercised.

63. The corresponding article of the statute would read:

ARTICLE 8

TERRITORIAL AND TEMPORAL JURISDICTION

The territorial jurisdiction of the International Tribunal shall extend to the territory of the former Socialist Federal Republic of Yugoslavia, including its land surface, airspace and territorial waters. The temporal jurisdiction of the International Tribunal shall extend to a period beginning on 1 January 1991. **C2–023**

D. Concurrent jurisdiction and the principle of non-bis-in-idem

64. In establishing an international tribunal for the prosecution of persons responsible for serious violations committed in the territory of the former Yugoslavia since 1991, it was not the intention of the Security Council to preclude or prevent the exercise of jurisdiction by national courts with respect to such acts. Indeed national courts should be encouraged to exercise their jurisdiction in accordance with their relevant national laws and procedures. **C2–024**

65. It follows therefore that there is concurrent jurisdiction of the International Tribunal and national courts. This concurrent jurisdiction, however, should be subject to the primacy of the International Tribunal. At any stage of the procedure, the International Tribunal may formally request the national courts to defer to the competence of the International Tribunal. The details of how the primacy will be asserted shall be set out in the rules of procedure and evidence of the International Tribunal.

66. According to the principle of *non-bis-in-idem*, a person shall not be tried twice for the same crime. In the present context, given the primacy of the International Tribunal, the principle of *non-bis-in-idem* would preclude subsequent trial before a national court. However, the principle of *non-bis-in idem* should not preclude a subsequent trial before the International Tribunal in the following two circumstances:

(a) the characterization of the act by the national court did not correspond to its characterization under the statute; or

(b) conditions of impartiality, independence or effective means of adjudication were not guaranteed in the proceedings before the national courts.

67. Should the International Tribunal decide to assume jurisdiction over a person who has already been convicted by a national court, it should take into consideration the extent to which any penalty imposed by the national court has already been served.

68. The corresponding articles of the statute would read:

ARTICLE 9

CONCURRENT JURISDICTION

1. The International Tribunal and national courts shall have concurrent jurisdiction to prosecute persons for serious violations of international humanitarian law committed in the territory of the former Yugoslavia since 1 January 1991. **C2–025**

2. The International Tribunal shall have primacy over national courts. At any stage of the procedure, the International Tribunal may formally request national courts to defer to the competence of the International Tribunal in accordance with the present Statute and the Rules of Procedure and Evidence of the International Tribunal.

ARTICLE 10

NON-BIS-IN-IDEM

C2–026   1. No person shall be tried before a national court for acts constituting serious violations of international humanitarian law under the present Statute, for which he or she has already been tried by the International Tribunal.

2. A person who has been tried by a national court for acts constituting serious violations of international humanitarian law may be subsequently tried by the International Tribunal only if:

(a) the act for which he or she was tried was characterized as an ordinary crime; or

(b) the national court proceedings were not impartial or independent, were designed to shield the accused from international criminal responsibility, or the case was not diligently prosecuted.

3. In considering the penalty to be imposed on a person convicted of a crime under the present Statute, the International Tribunal shall take into account the extent to which any penalty imposed by a national court on the same person for the same act has already been served.

III. THE ORGANIZATION OF THE INTERNATIONAL TRIBUNAL

C2–027   69. The organization of the International Tribunal should reflect the functions to be performed by it. Since the International Tribunal is established for the prosecution of persons responsible for serious violations of international humanitarian law committed in the territory of the former Yugoslavia, this presupposes an international tribunal composed of a judicial organ, a prosecutorial organ and a secretariat. It would be the function of the prosecutorial organ to investigate cases, prepare indictments and prosecute persons responsible for committing the violations referred to above. The judicial organ would hear the cases presented to its Trial Chambers, and consider appeals from the Trial Chambers in its Appeals Chamber. A secretariat or Registry would be required to service both the prosecutorial and judicial organs.

70. The International Tribunal should therefore consist of the following organs: the Chambers, comprising two Trial Chambers and one Appeals Chamber; a Prosecutor; and a Registry.

71. The corresponding article of the statute would read as follows:

ARTICLE 11

ORGANIZATION OF THE INTERNATIONAL TRIBUNAL

C2–028   The International Tribunal shall consist of the following organs:

(a) the Chambers, comprising two Trial Chambers and an Appeals Chamber;

(b) the Prosecutor; and

(c) a Registry, servicing both the Chambers and the Prosecutor.

A. The Chambers

1. Composition of the Chambers

C2–029   72. The Chambers should be composed of 11 independent judges, no 2 of whom may be nationals of the same State. Three judges would serve in each of the two Trial Chambers and five judges would serve in the Appeals Chamber.

73. The corresponding article of the statute would read as follows:

ARTICLE 12

COMPOSITION OF THE CHAMBERS

C2–030   The Chambers shall be composed of eleven independent judges, no two of whom may be nationals of the same State, who shall serve as follows:

(a) three judges shall serve in each of the Trial Chambers;
(b) five judges shall serve in the Appeals Chamber.

2. Qualifications and election of judges

74. The judges of the International Tribunal should be persons of high moral character, impartiality and integrity who possess the qualifications required in their respective countries for appointment to the highest judicial offices. Impartiality in this context includes impartiality with respect to the acts falling within the competence of the International Tribunal. In the overall composition of the Chambers, due account should be taken of the experience of the judges in criminal law, international law, including international humanitarian law and human rights law.

C2–031

75. The judges should be elected by the General Assembly from a list submitted by the Security Council. The Secretary-General would invite nominations for judges from States Members of the United Nations as well as non-member States maintaining permanent observer missions at United Nations Headquarters. Within 60 days of the date of the invitation of the Secretary-General, each State would nominate up to two candidates meeting the qualifications mentioned in paragraph 74 above, who must not be of the same nationality. The Secretary-General would forward the nominations received to the Security Council. The Security Council would, as speedily as possible, establish from the nominations transmitted by the Secretary-General, a list of not less than 22 and not more than 33 candidates, taking due account of the adequate representation of the principal legal systems of the world. The President of the Security Council would then transmit the list to the General Assembly. From that list, the General Assembly would proceed as speedily as possible to elect the 11 judges of the International Tribunal. The candidates declared elected shall be those who have received an absolute majority of the votes of the States Members of the United Nations and of the States maintaining permanent observer missions at United Nations Headquarters. Should two candidates of the same nationality obtain the required majority vote, the one who received the higher number of votes shall be considered elected.

76. The judges shall be elected for a term of four years. The terms and conditions of service shall be those of the Judges of the International Court of Justice. They shall be eligible for re-election.

77. In the event of a vacancy occurring in the Chambers, the Secretary-General, after consultation with the Presidents of the Security Council and the General Assembly, would appoint a person meeting the qualifications of paragraph 74 above, for the remainder of the term of office concerned.

78. The corresponding article of the statute would read as follows:

ARTICLE 13

QUALIFICATIONS AND ELECTION OF JUDGES

1. The judges shall be persons of high moral character, impartiality and integrity who possess the qualifications required in their respective countries for appointment to the highest judicial offices. In the overall composition of the Chambers due account shall be taken of the experience of the judges in criminal law, international law, including international humanitarian law and human rights law.

C2–032

2. The judges of the International Tribunal shall be elected by the General Assembly from a list submitted by the Security Council, in the following manner:
   (a) the Secretary-General shall invite nominations for judges of the International Tribunal from States Members of the United Nations and non-member States maintaining permanent observer missions at United Nations Headquarters;
   (b) within sixty days of the date of the invitation of the Secretary-General, each State may nominate up to two candidates meeting the qualifications set out in paragraph 1 above, no two of whom shall be of the same nationality;

(c) the Secretary-General shall forward the nominations received to the Security Council. From the nominations received the Security Council shall establish a list of not less than twenty-two and not more than thirty-three candidates, taking due account of the adequate representation of the principal legal systems of the world;

(d) the President of the Security Council shall transmit the list of candidates to the President of the General Assembly. From that list the General Assembly shall elect the eleven judges of the International Tribunal. The candidates who receive an absolute majority of the votes of States Members of the United Nations and of the non-member States maintaining permanent observer missions at United Nations Headquarters, shall be declared elected. Should two candidates of the same nationality obtain the required majority vote, the one who received the higher number of votes shall be considered elected.

3. In the event of a vacancy in the Chambers, after consultation with the Presidents of the Security Council and of the General Assembly, the Secretary-General shall appoint a person meeting the qualifications of paragraph 1 above, for the remainder of the term of office concerned.

4. The judges shall be elected for a term of four years. The terms and conditions of service shall be those of the Judges of the International Court of justice. They shall be eligible for re-election.

3. Officers and members of the Chambers

C2–033   79. The judges would elect a President of the International Tribunal from among their members who would be a member of the Appeals Chamber and would preside over the appellate proceedings.

80. Following consultation with the members of the Chambers, the President would assign the judges to the Appeals Chamber and to the Trial Chambers. Each judge would serve only in the chamber to which he or she was assigned.

81. The members of each Trial Chamber should elect a presiding judge who would conduct all of the proceedings before the Trial Chamber as a whole.

82. The corresponding article of the statute would read as follows:

ARTICLE 14

OFFICERS AND MEMBERS OF THE CHAMBERS

C2–034   1. The judges of the International Tribunal shall elect a President.

2. The President of the International Tribunal shall be a member of the Appeals Chamber and shall preside over its proceedings.

3. After consultation with the judges of the International Tribunal, the President shall assign the judges to the Appeals Chamber and to the Trial Chambers. A judge shall serve only in the Chamber to which he or she was assigned.

4. The judges of each Trial Chamber shall elect a Presiding Judge, who shall conduct all of the proceedings of the Trial Chamber as a whole.

4. Rules of procedure and evidence

C2–035   83. The judges of the International Tribunal as a whole should draft and adopt the rules of procedure and evidence of the International Tribunal governing the pre-trial phase of the proceedings, the conduct of trials and appeals, the admission of evidence, the protection of victims and witnesses and other appropriate matters.

84. The corresponding article of the statute would read as follows:

ARTICLE 15

RULES OF PROCEDURE AND EVIDENCE

The judges of the International Tribunal shall adopt rules of procedure and evidence for the conduct of the pre-trial phase of the proceedings, trials and appeals, the admission of evidence, the protection of victims and witnesses and other appropriate matters.

B. The Prosecutor

85. Responsibility for the conduct of all investigations and prosecutions of persons responsible for serious violations of international humanitarian law committed in the territory of the former Yugoslavia since 1 January 1991 should be entrusted to an independent Prosecutor. The Prosecutor should act independently as a separate organ of the International Tribunal. He or she shall not seek or receive instructions from any Government or from any other source. **C2–036**

86. The Prosecutor should be appointed by the Security Council, upon nomination by the Secretary-General. He or she should possess the highest level of professional competence and have extensive experience in the conduct of investigations and prosecutions of criminal cases. The Prosecutor should be appointed for a four-year term of office and be eligible for reappointment. The terms and conditions of service of the Prosecutor shall be those of an Under-Secretary-General of the United Nations.

87. The Prosecutor would be assisted by such other staff as may be required to perform effectively and efficiently the functions entrusted to him or her. Such staff would be appointed by the Secretary-General on the recommendation of the Prosecutor. The Office of the Prosecutor should be composed of an investigation unit and a prosecution unit.

88. Staff appointed to the Office of the Prosecutor should meet rigorous criteria of professional experience and competence in their field. Persons should be sought who have had relevant experience in their own countries as investigators, prosecutors, criminal lawyers, law enforcement personnel or medical experts. Given the nature of the crimes committed and the sensitivities of victims of rape and sexual assault, due consideration should be given in the appointment of staff to the employment of qualified women.

89. The corresponding article of the statute would read as follows:

ARTICLE 16

THE PROSECUTOR

1. The Prosecutor shall be responsible for the investigation and prosecution of persons responsible for serious violations of international humanitarian law committed in the territory of the former Yugoslavia since 1 January 1991. **C2–037**

2. The Prosecutor shall act independently as a separate organ of the International Tribunal. He or she shall not seek or receive instructions from any Government or from any other source.

3. The Office of the Prosecutor shall be composed of a Prosecutor and such other qualified staff as may be required.

4. The Prosecutor shall be appointed by the Security Council on nomination by the Secretary-General. He or she shall be of high moral character and possess the highest level of competence and experience in the conduct of investigations and prosecutions of criminal cases. The Prosecutor shall serve for a four-year term and be eligible for reappointment. The terms and conditions of service of the Prosecutor shall be those of an Under-Secretary-General of the United Nations.

C. *The Registry*

C2–038   90. As indicated in paragraph 69 above, a Registry would be responsible for the servicing of the International Tribunal. The Registry would be headed by a Registrar, whose responsibilities shall include but should not be limited to the following:

    (a) public information and external relations;

    (b) preparation of minutes of meetings;

    (c) conference-service facilities;

    (d) printing and publication of all documents;

    (e) all administrative work, budgetary and personnel matters; and

    (f) serving as the channel of communications to and from the International Tribunal.

91. The Registrar should be appointed by the Secretary-General after consultation with the President of the International Tribunal. He or she would be appointed to serve for a four-year term and be eligible for reappointment. The terms and conditions of service of the Registrar shall be those of an Assistant Secretary-General of the United Nations.

92. The corresponding article of the statute would read as follows:

ARTICLE 17

THE REGISTRY

C2–039   1. The Registry shall be responsible for the administration and servicing of the International Tribunal.

2. The Registry shall consist of a Registrar and such other staff as may be required.

3. The Registrar shall be appointed by the Secretary-General athosefter consultation with the President of the International Tribunal. He or she shall serve for a four-year term and be eligible for reappointment. The terms and conditions of service of the Registrar shall be of an Assistant Secretary-General of the United Nations.

4. The staff of the Registry shall be appointed by the Secretary-General on the recommendation of the Registrar.

IV. INVESTIGATION AND PRE-TRIAL PROCEEDINGS

C2–040   93. The Prosecutor would initiate investigations ex officio, or on the basis of information obtained from any source, particularly from Governments or United Nations organs, intergovernmental and non-governmental organizations. The Prosecutor would assess the information received or obtained and decide whether there is a sufficient basis to proceed.

94. In conducting his investigations, the Prosecutor should have the power to question suspects, victims and witnesses, to collect evidence and to conduct on-site investigations. In carrying out these tasks, the Prosecutor may, as appropriate, seek the assistance of the State authorities concerned.

95. Upon the completion of the investigation, if the Prosecutor has determined that a prima facie case exists for prosecution, he would prepare an indictment containing a concise statement of the facts and the crimes with which the accused is charged under the statute. The indictment would be transmitted to a judge of a Trial Chamber, who would review it and decide whether to confirm or to dismiss the indictment.

96. If the investigation includes questioning of the suspect, then he should have the right to be assisted by counsel of his own choice, including the right to have legal assistance assigned to him without payment by him in any such case if he does not have sufficient means to pay for it. He shall also be entitled to the necessary translation into and from a language he speaks and understands.

97. Upon confirmation of the indictment, the judge would, at the request of the Prosecutor, issue such orders and warrants for the arrest, detention, surrender and transfer of persons, or any other orders as may be necessary for the conduct of the trial.

98. The corresponding articles of the statute would read as follows:

Article 18

INVESTIGATION AND PREPARATION OF INDICTMENT

1. The Prosecutor shall initiate investigations ex officio or on the basis of information obtained from any source, particularly from Governments, United Nations organs, intergovernmental and non-governmental organizations. The Prosecutor shall assess the information received or obtained and decide whether there is sufficient basis to proceed.

2. The Prosecutor shall have the power to question suspects, victims and witnesses, to collect evidence and to conduct on-site investigations. In carrying out these tasks the Prosecutor may, as appropriate, seek the assistance of the State authorities concerned.

3. If questioned, the suspect shall be entitled to be assisted by counsel of his own choice, including the right to have legal assistance assigned to him without payment by him in any such case if he does not have sufficient means to pay for it, as well as to necessary translation into and from a language he speaks and understands.

4. Upon a determination that a prima facie case exists, the Prosecutor shall prepare an indictment containing a concise statement of the facts and the crime or crimes with which the accused is charged under the Statute. The indictment shall be transmitted to a judge of the Trial Chamber.

C2–041

Article 19

REVIEW OF THE INDICTMENT

1. The judge of the Trial Chamber to whom the indictment has been transmitted shall review it. If satisfied that a prima facie case has been established by the Prosecutor, he shall confirm the indictment. If not so satisfied, the indictment shall be dismissed.

2. Upon confirmation of an indictment, the judge may, at the request of the Prosecutor, issue such orders and warrants for the arrest, detention, surrender or transfer of persons, and any other orders as may be required for the conduct of the trial.

C2–042

V. Trial and Post-Trial Proceedings

A. Commencement and conduct of trial proceedings

99. The Trial Chambers should ensure that a trial is fair and expeditious and that proceedings are conducted in accordance with the rules of procedure and evidence and with full respect for the rights of the accused. The Trial Chamber should also provide appropriate protection for victims and witnesses during the proceedings.

100. A person against whom an indictment has been confirmed would, pursuant to an order or a warrant of the International Tribunal, be informed of the contents of the indictment and taken into custody.

101. A trial should not commence until the accused is physically present before the International Tribunal. There is a widespread perception that trials in absentia should not be provided for in the statute as this would not be consistent with article 14 of the International Covenant on Civil and Political Rights,[10] which provides that the accused shall be entitled to be tried in his presence.

C2–043

[10] United Nations, *Treaty Series*, vol. 999, No. 14668, p. 171 and vol. 1057, p. 407 (proces-verbal of rectification of authentic Spanish text).

102. The person against whom an indictment has been confirmed would be transferred to the seat of the International Tribunal and brought before a Trial Chamber without undue delay and formally charged. The Trial Chamber would read the indictment, satisfy itself that the rights of the accused are respected, confirm that the accused understands the indictment, and instruct the accused to enter a plea. After the plea has been entered, the Trial Chamber would set the date for trial.

103. The hearings should be held in public unless the Trial Chamber decides otherwise in accordance with its rules of procedure and evidence.

104. After hearing the submissions of the parties and examining the witnesses and evidence presented to it, the Trial Chamber would close the hearing and retire for private deliberations.

105. The corresponding article of the statute would read:

ARTICLE 20

COMMENCEMENT AND CONDUCT OF TRIAL PROCEEDINGS

C2–044

1. The Trial Chambers shall ensure that a trial is fair and expeditious and that proceedings are conducted in accordance with the rules of procedure and evidence, with full respect for the rights of the accused and due regard for the protection of victims and witnesses.

2. A person against whom an indictment has been confirmed shall, pursuant to an order or an arrest warrant of the International Tribunal, be taken into custody, immediately informed of the charges against him and transferred to the International Tribunal.

3. The Trial Chamber shall read the indictment, satisfy itself that the rights of the accused are respected, confirm that the accused understands the indictment, and instruct the accused to enter a plea. The Trial Chamber shall then set the date for trial.

4. The hearings shall be public unless the Trial Chamber decides to close the proceedings in accordance with its rules of procedure and evidence.

B. Rights of the accused

C2–045

106. It is axiomatic that the International Tribunal must fully respect internationally recognized standards regarding the rights of the accused at all stages of its proceedings. In the view of the Secretary-General, such internationally recognized standards are, in particular, contained in article 14 of the International Covenant on Civil and Political Rights.

107. The corresponding article of the statute would read as follows:

ARTICLE 21

RIGHTS OF THE ACCUSED

C2–046

1. All persons shall be equal before the International Tribunal.

2. In the determination of charges against him, the accused shall be entitled to a fair and public hearing, subject to article 22 of the Statute.

3. The accused shall be presumed innocent until proved guilty according to the provisions of the present Statute.

4. In the determination of any charge against the accused pursuant to the present Statute, the accused shall be entitled to the following minimum guarantees, in full equality:

   (a) to be informed promptly and in detail in a language which he understands of the nature and cause of the charge against him;

    (b) to have adequate time and facilities for the preparation of his defence and to communicate with counsel of his own choosing;

    (c) to be tried without undue delay;

    (d) to be tried in his presence, and to defend himself in person or through legal assistance of his own choosing; to be informed, if he does not have legal assistance, of this right; and to have legal assistance assigned to him, in any case where the interests of justice so require, and without payment by him in any such case if he does not have sufficient means to pay for it;

    (e) the attendance and examination of witnesses on his behalf under the same conditions as witnesses against him.

    (f) to have the free assistance of an interpreter if he cannot understand or speak the language used in the International Tribunal;

    (g) not to be compelled to testify against himself or to confess guilt.

C. Protection of victims and witnesses

108. In the light of the particular nature of the crimes committed in the former Yugoslavia, it will be necessary for the International Tribunal to ensure the protection of victims and witnesses. Necessary protection measures should therefore be provided in the rules of procedure and evidence for victims and witnesses, especially in cases of rape or sexual assault. Such measures should include, but should not be limited to the conduct of *in camera* proceedings, and the protection of the victim's identity.   **C2–047**

109. The corresponding article of the statute would read as follows:

ARTICLE 22

PROTECTION OF VICTIMS AND WITNESSES

The International Tribunal shall provide in its rules of procedure and evidence for the protection of victims and witnesses. Such protection measures shall include, but shall not be limited to, the conduct of *in camera* proceedings and the protection of the victim's identity.   **C2–048**

D. Judgement and penalties

110. The Trial Chambers would have the power to pronounce judgements and impose sentences and penalties on persons convicted of serious violations of international humanitarian law. A judgement would be rendered by a majority of the judges of the Chamber and delivered in public. It should be written and accompanied by a reasoned opinion. Separate or dissenting opinions should be permitted.   **C2–049**

111. The penalty to be imposed on a convicted person would be limited to imprisonment. In determining the term of imprisonment, the Trial Chambers should have recourse to the general practice of prison sentences applicable in the courts of the former Yugoslavia.

112. The International Tribunal should not be empowered to impose the death penalty.

113. In imposing sentences, the Trial Chambers should take into account such factors as the gravity of the offence and the individual circumstances of the convicted person.

114. In addition to imprisonment, property and proceeds acquired by criminal conduct should be confiscated and returned to their rightful owners. This would include the return of property wrongfully acquired by means of duress. In this connection the Secretary-General recalls that in resolution 779 (1992) of 6 October 1992, the Security Council endorsed the principle that all statements or commitments made under duress, particularly those relating to land and property, are wholly null and void.

115. The corresponding articles of the statute would read as follows:

ARTICLE 23

JUDGEMENT

C2–050   1. The Trial Chambers shall pronounce judgements and impose sentences and penalties on persons convicted of serious violations of international humanitarian law.

2. The judgement shall be rendered by a majority of the judges of the Trial Chamber, and shall be delivered by the Trial Chamber in public. It shall be accompanied by a reasoned opinion in writing, to which separate or dissenting opinions may be appended.

ARTICLE 24

PENALTIES

C2–051   1. The penalty imposed by the Trial Chamber shall be limited to imprisonment. In determining the terms of imprisonment, the Trial Chambers shall have recourse to the general practice regarding prison sentences in the courts of the former Yugoslavia.

2. In imposing the sentences, the Trial Chambers should take into account such factors as the gravity of the offence and the individual circumstances of the convicted person.

3. In addition to imprisonment, the Trial Chambers may order the return of any property and proceeds acquired by criminal conduct, including by means of duress, to their rightful owners.

E. Appellate and review proceedings

C2–052   116. The Secretary-General is of the view that the right of appeal should be provided for under the Statute. Such a right is a fundamental element of individual civil and political rights and has, *inter alia*, been incorporated in the International Covenant on Civil and Political Rights. For this reason, the Secretary-General has proposed that there should be an Appeals Chamber.

117. The right of appeal should be exercisable on two grounds: an error on a question of law invalidating the decision or, an error of fact which has occasioned a miscarriage of justice. The Prosecutor should also be entitled to initiate appeal proceedings on the same grounds.

118. The judgement of the Appeals Chamber affirming, reversing or revising the judgement of the Trial Chamber would be final. It would be delivered by the Appeals Chamber in public and be accompanied by a reasoned opinion to which separate or dissenting opinions may be appended.

119. Where a new fact has come to light which was not known at the time of the proceedings before the Trial Chambers or the Appeals Chamber, and which could have been a decisive factor in reaching the decision, the convicted person or the Prosecutor should be authorized to submit to the International Tribunal an application for review of the judgement.

120. The corresponding articles of the statute would read as follows:

ARTICLE 25

APPELLATE PROCEEDINGS

C2–053   1. The Appeals Chamber shall hear appeals from persons convicted by the Trial Chambers or from the Prosecutor on the following grounds:

    (a) an error on a question of law invalidating the decision; or

    (b) an error of fact which has occasioned a miscarriage of justice.

2. The Appeals Chamber may affirm, reverse or revise the decisions taken by the Trial Chambers.

ARTICLE 26

REVIEW PROCEEDINGS

Where a new fact has been discovered which was not known at the time of the proceedings before the Trial Chambers or the Appeals Chamber and which could have been a decisive factor in reaching the decision, the convicted person or the Prosecutor may submit to the International Tribunal an application for review of the judgement.

C2–054

F. Enforcement of sentences

121. The Secretary-General is of the view that, given the nature of the crimes in question and the international character of the tribunal, the enforcement of sentences should take place outside the territory of the former Yugoslavia. States should be encouraged to declare their readiness to carry out the enforcement of prison sentences in accordance with their domestic laws and procedures, under the supervision of the International Tribunal.

C2–055

122. The Security Council would make appropriate arrangements to obtain from States an indication of their willingness to accept convicted persons. This information would be communicated to the Registrar, who would prepare a list of States in which the enforcement of sentences would be carried out.

123. The accused would be eligible for pardon or commutation of sentence in accordance with the laws of the State in which sentence is served. In such an event, the State concerned would notify the International Tribunal, which would decide the matter in accordance with the interests of justice and the general principles of law.

124. The corresponding article of the statute would read as follows:

ARTICLE 27

ENFORCEMENT OF SENTENCES

Imprisonment shall be served in a State designated by the International Tribunal from a list of States which have indicated to the Security Council their willingness to accept convicted persons. Such imprisonment shall be in accordance with the applicable law of the State concerned, subject to the supervision of the International Tribunal.

C2–056

ARTICLE 28

PARDON OR COMMUTATION OF SENTENCES

If, pursuant to the applicable law of the State in which the convicted person is imprisoned, he or she is eligible for pardon or commutation of sentence, the State concerned shall notify the International Tribunal accordingly. The President of the International Tribunal, in consultation with the judges, shall decide the matter on the basis of the interests of justice and the general principles of law.

C2–057

VI. COOPERATION AND JUDICIAL ASSISTANCE

125. As pointed out in paragraph 23 above, the establishment of the International Tribunal on the basis of a Chapter VII decision creates a binding obligation on all States to take whatever steps are required to implement the decision. In practical terms, this

C2–058

means that all States would be under an obligation to cooperate with the International Tribunal and to assist it in all stages of the proceedings to ensure compliance with requests for assistance in the gathering of evidence, hearing of witnesses, suspects and experts, identification and location of persons and the service of documents. Effect shall also be given to orders issued by the Trial Chambers, such as warrants of arrest, search warrants, warrants for surrender or transfer of persons, and any other orders necessary for the conduct of the trial.

126. In this connection, an order by a Trial Chamber for the surrender or transfer of persons to the custody of the International Tribunal shall be considered to be the application of an enforcement measure under Chapter VII of the Charter of the United Nations.

127. The corresponding article of the statute would read as follows:

ARTICLE 29

COOPERATION AND JUDICIAL ASSISTANCE

C2–059 1. States shall cooperate with the International Tribunal in the investigation and prosecution of persons accused of committing serious violations of international humanitarian law.

2. States shall comply without undue delay with any request for assistance or an order issued by a Trial Chamber, including, but not limited to:

  (a) the identification and location of persons;
  (b) the taking of testimony and the production of evidence;
  (c) the service of documents;
  (d) the arrest or detention of persons;
  (e) the surrender or the transfer of the accused to the International Tribunal.

VII. GENERAL PROVISIONS

A. The status, privileges and immunities of the International Tribunal

C2–060 128. the Convention on the Privileges and Immunities of the United Nations of 13 February 1946 would apply to the International Tribunal, the judges, the Prosecutor and his staff, and the Registrar and his staff. The judges, the Prosecutor, and the Registrar would be granted the privileges and immunities, exemptions and facilities accorded to diplomatic envoys in accordance with international law. The staff of the Prosecutor and the Registrar would enjoy the privileges and immunities of officials of the United Nations within the meaning of articles V and VII of the Convention.

129. Other persons, including the accused, required at the seat of the International Tribunal would be accorded such treatment as is necessary for the proper functioning of the International Tribunal.

130. The corresponding article of the statute would read:

ARTICLE 30

THE STATUS, PRIVILEGES AND IMMUNITIES OF THE INTERNATIONAL TRIBUNAL

C2–061 1. The Convention on the Privileges and Immunities of the United Nations of 13 February 1946 shall apply to the International Tribunal, the judges, the Prosecutor and his staff, and the Registrar and his staff.

2. The judges, the Prosecutor and the Registrar shall enjoy the privileges and immunities, exemptions and facilities accorded to diplomatic envoys, in accordance with international law.

3. The staff of the Prosecutor and of the Registrar shall enjoy the privileges and immunities accorded to officials of the United Nations under articles V and VII of the Convention referred to in paragraph 1 of this article.

4. Other persons, including the accused, required at the seat of the International Tribunal shall be accorded such treatment as is necessary for the proper functioning of the International Tribunal.

B. Seat of the International Tribunal

131. While it will be for the Security Council to determine the location of the seat of the International Tribunal, in the view of the Secretary-General, there are a number of elementary considerations of justice and fairness, as well as administrative efficiency and economy which should be taken into account. As a matter of justice and fairness, it would not be appropriate for the International Tribunal to have its seat in the territory of the former Yugoslavia or in any State neighbouring upon the former Yugoslavia. For reasons of administrative efficiency and economy, it would be desirable to establish the seat of the International Tribunal at a European location in which the United Nations already has an important presence. The two locations which fulfil these requirements are Geneva and The Hague. Provided that the necessary arrangements can be made with the host country, the Secretary-General believes that the seat of the International Tribunal should be at The Hague.   **C2–062**

132. The corresponding article of the statute would read:

ARTICLE 31

SEAT OF THE INTERNATIONAL TRIBUNAL

The International Tribunal shall have its seat at The Hague.   **C2–063**

C. Financial arrangements

133. The expenses of the International Tribunal should be borne by the regular budget of the United Nations in accordance with Article 17 of the Charter of the United Nations.   **C2–064**

134. The corresponding article of the statute would read:

ARTICLE 32

EXPENSES OF THE INTERNATIONAL TRIBUNAL

The expenses of the International Tribunal shall be borne by the regular budget of the United Nations in accordance with Article 17 of the Charter of the United Nations.   **C2–065**

D. Working languages

135. The working languages of the Tribunal should be English and French.   **C2–066**

136. The corresponding article of the statute would read as follows:

ARTICLE 33

WORKING LANGUAGES

The working languages of the International Tribunal shall be English and French. **C2–067**

E. Annual report

C2–068   137. The International Tribunal should submit an annual report on its activities to the Security Council and the General Assembly.

138. The corresponding article of the statute would read:

Article 34

ANNUAL REPORT

C2–069   The President of the International Tribunal shall submit an annual report of the International Tribunal to the Security Council and to the General Assembly.

C3. Resolution 827 (1993)

(ADOPTED 25 MAY 1993)
(S/RES/827 (1993))

The Security Council,

C3–001

Reaffirming its resolution 713 (1991) of 25 September 1991 and all subsequent relevant resolutions,

Having considered the report of the Secretary-General (S/25704 and Add.1) pursuant to paragraph 2 of resolution 808 (1993),

Expressing once again its grave alarm at continuing reports of widespread and flagrant violations of international humanitarian law occurring within the territory of the former Yugoslavia, and especially in the Republic of Bosnia and Herzegovina, including reports of mass killings, massive, organized and systematic detention and rape of women, and the continuance of the practice of "ethnic cleansing", including for the acquisition and the holding of territory,

Determining that this situation continues to constitute a threat to international peace and security,

Determined to put an end to such crimes and to take effective measures to bring to justice the persons who are responsible for them,

Convinced that in the particular circumstances of the former Yugoslavia the establishment as an ad hoc measure by the Council of an international tribunal and the prosecution of persons responsible for serious violations of international humanitarian law would enable this aim to be achieved and would contribute to the restoration and maintenance of peace,

Believing that the establishment of an international tribunal and the prosecution of persons responsible for the above-mentioned violations of international humanitarian law will contribute to ensuring that such violations are halted and effectively redressed,

Noting in this regard the recommendation by the Co-Chairmen of the Steering Committee of the International Conference on the Former Yugoslavia for the establishment of such a tribunal (S/25221),

Reaffirming in this regard its decision in resolution 808 (1993) that an international tribunal shall be established for the prosecution of persons responsible for serious violations of international humanitarian law committed in the territory of the former Yugoslavia since 1991,

Considering that, pending the appointment of the Prosecutor of the International Tribunal, the Commission of Experts established pursuant to resolution 780 (1992) should continue on an urgent basis the collection of information relating to evidence of grave breaches of the Geneva Conventions and other violations of international humanitarian law as proposed in its interim report (S/25274),

Acting under Chapter VII of the Charter of the United Nations,

C3–002

1. *Approves* the report of the Secretary-General;

2. *Decides* hereby to establish an international tribunal for the sole purpose of prosecuting persons responsible for serious violations of international humanitarian law committed in the territory of the former Yugoslavia between 1 January 1991 and a date to be determined by the Security Council upon the restoration of peace and to this end to adopt the Statute of the International Tribunal annexed to the above-mentioned report;

3. *Requests* the Secretary-General to submit to the judges of the International Tribunal, upon their election, any suggestions received from States for the rules of procedure and evidence called for in Article 15 of the Statute of the International Tribunal;

4. *Decides* that all States shall cooperate fully with the International Tribunal and its organs in accordance with the present resolution and the Statute of the International Tribunal and that consequently all States shall take any measures necessary under their domestic law to implement the provisions of the present resolution and the Statute,

including the obligation of States to comply with requests for assistance or orders issued by a Trial Chamber under Article 29 of the Statute;

5. *Urges* States and intergovernmental and non-governmental organizations to contribute funds, equipment and services to the International Tribunal, including the offer of expert personnel;

6. *Decides* that the determination of the seat of the International Tribunal is subject to the conclusion of appropriate arrangements between the United Nations and the Netherlands acceptable to the Council, and that the International Tribunal may sit elsewhere when it considers it necessary for the efficient exercise of its functions;

7. *Decides* also that the work of the International Tribunal shall be carried out without prejudice to the right of the victims to seek, through appropriate means, compensation for damages incurred as a result of violations of international humanitarian law;

8. *Requests* the Secretary-General to implement urgently the present resolution and in particular to make practical arrangements for the effective functioning of the International Tribunal at the earliest time and to report periodically to the Council;

9. *Decides* to remain actively seized of the matter.

C4. Statute of the International Criminal Tribunal for the Former Yugoslavia

(Adopted 25 May 1993 by resolution 827)
(As amended 13 May 1998 by resolution 1166)
(As amended 30 November 2000 by resolution 1329)
(As amended 17 May 2002 by resolution 1411)
(As amended 14 August 2002 by resolution 1431)
(As amended 19 May 2003 by resolution 1481)

Having been established by the Security Council acting under Chapter VII of the **C4–001** Charter of the United Nations, the International Tribunal for the Prosecution of Persons Responsible for Serious Violations of International Humanitarian Law Committed in the Territory of the Former Yugoslavia since 1991 (hereinafter referred to as "the International Tribunal") shall function in accordance with the provisions of the present Statute.

ARTICLE 1

COMPETENCE OF THE INTERNATIONAL TRIBUNAL

The International Tribunal shall have the power to prosecute persons responsible for **C4–002** serious violations of international humanitarian law committed in the territory of the former Yugoslavia since 1991 in accordance with the provisions of the present Statute.

ARTICLE 2

GRAVE BREACHES OF THE GENEVA CONVENTIONS OF 1949

The International Tribunal shall have the power to prosecute persons committing or **C4–003** ordering to be committed grave breaches of the Geneva Conventions of 12 August 1949, namely the following acts against persons or property protected under the provisions of the relevant Geneva Convention:
(a) wilful killing;
(b) torture or inhuman treatment, including biological experiments;
(c) wilfully causing great suffering or serious injury to body or health;
(d) extensive destruction and appropriation of property, not justified by military necessity and carried out unlawfully and wantonly;
(e) compelling a prisoner of war or a civilian to serve in the forces of a hostile power;
(f) wilfully depriving a prisoner of war or a civilian of the rights of fair and regular trial;
(g) unlawful deportation or transfer or unlawful confinement of a civilian;
(h) taking civilians as hostages.

ARTICLE 3

VIOLATIONS OF THE LAWS OR CUSTOMS OF WAR

The International Tribunal shall have the power to prosecute persons violating the **C4–004** laws or customs of war. Such violations shall include, but not be limited to:

1447

(a) employment of poisonous weapons or other weapons calculated to cause unnecessary suffering;

(b) wanton destruction of cities, towns or villages, or devastation not justified by military necessity;

(c) attack, or bombardment, by whatever means, of undefended towns, villages, dwellings, or buildings;

(d) seizure of, destruction or wilful damage done to institutions dedicated to religion, charity and education, the arts and sciences, historic monuments and works of art and science;

(e) plunder of public or private property.

ARTICLE 4

GENOCIDE

C4–005   1. The International Tribunal shall have the power to prosecute persons committing genocide as defined in paragraph 2 of this article or of committing any of the other acts enumerated in paragraph 3 of this article.

2. Genocide means any of the following acts committed with intent to destroy, in whole or in part, a national, ethnical, racial or religious group, as such:

(a) killing members of the group;

(b) causing serious bodily or mental harm to members of the group;

(c) deliberately inflicting on the group conditions of life calculated to bring about its physical destruction in whole or in part;

(d) imposing measures intended to prevent births within the group;

(e) forcibly transferring children of the group to another group.

3. The following acts shall be punishable:

(a) genocide;

(b) conspiracy to commit genocide;

(c) direct and public incitement to commit genocide;

(d) attempt to commit genocide;

(e) complicity in genocide.

ARTICLE 5

CRIMES AGAINST HUMANITY

C4–006   The International Tribunal shall have the power to prosecute persons responsible for the following crimes when committed in armed conflict, whether international or internal in character, and directed against any civilian population:

(a) murder;

(b) extermination;

(c) enslavement;

(d) deportation;

(e) imprisonment;

(f) torture;

(g) rape;

(h) persecutions on political, racial and religious grounds;

(i) other inhumane acts.

ARTICLE 6

PERSONAL JURISDICTION

C4–007   The International Tribunal shall have jurisdiction over natural persons pursuant to the provisions of the present Statute.

ARTICLE 7

INDIVIDUAL CRIMINAL RESPONSIBILITY

1. A person who planned, instigated, ordered, committed or otherwise aided and **C4–008**
abetted in the planning, preparation or execution of a crime referred to in articles 2 to 5
of the present Statute, shall be individually responsible for the crime.

2. The official position of any accused person, whether as Head of State or Government or as a responsible Government official, shall not relieve such person of criminal
responsibility nor mitigate punishment.

3. The fact that any of the acts referred to in articles 2 to 5 of the present Statute was
committed by a subordinate does not relieve his superior of criminal responsibility if he
knew or had reason to know that the subordinate was about to commit such acts or had
done so and the superior failed to take the necessary and reasonable measures to
prevent such acts or to punish the perpetrators thereof.

4. The fact that an accused person acted pursuant to an order of a Government or of a
superior shall not relieve him of criminal responsibility, but may be considered in
mitigation of punishment if the International Tribunal determines that justice so
requires.

ARTICLE 8

TERRITORIAL AND TEMPORAL JURISDICTION

The territorial jurisdiction of the International Tribunal shall extend to the territory **C4–009**
of the former Socialist Federal Republic of Yugoslavia, including its land surface,
airspace and territorial waters. The temporal jurisdiction of the International Tribunal
shall extend to a period beginning on 1 January 1991.

ARTICLE 9

CONCURRENT JURISDICTION

1. The International Tribunal and national courts shall have concurrent jurisdiction **C4–010**
to prosecute persons for serious violations of international humanitarian law committed
in the territory of the former Yugoslavia since 1 January 1991.

2. The International Tribunal shall have primacy over national courts. At any stage of
the procedure, the International Tribunal may formally request national courts to defer
to the competence of the International Tribunal in accordance with the present Statute
and the Rules of Procedure and Evidence of the International Tribunal.

ARTICLE 10

NON-BIS-IN-IDEM

1. No person shall be tried before a national court for acts constituting serious **C4–011**
violations of international humanitarian law under the present Statute, for which he or
she has already been tried by the International Tribunal.

2. A person who has been tried by a national court for acts constituting serious
violations of international humanitarian law may be subsequently tried by the International Tribunal only if:

    (a) the act for which he or she was tried was characterized as an ordinary crime; or

    (b) the national court proceedings were not impartial or independent, were
        designed to shield the accused from international criminal responsibility, or the
        case was not diligently prosecuted.

3. In considering the penalty to be imposed on a person convicted of a crime under the present Statute, the International Tribunal shall take into account the extent to which any penalty imposed by a national court on the same person for the same act has already been served.

ARTICLE 11

ORGANIZATION OF THE INTERNATIONAL TRIBUNAL

C4–012   The International Tribunal shall consist of the following organs:
(a) the Chambers, comprising three Trial Chambers and an Appeals Chamber;
(b) the Prosecutor; and
(c) a Registry, servicing both the Chambers and the Prosecutor.

ARTICLE 12

COMPOSITION OF THE CHAMBERS

C4–013   1. The Chambers shall be composed of sixteen permanent independent judges, no two of whom may be nationals of the same State, and a maximum at any one time of nine *ad litem* independent judges appointed in accordance with article 13 ter, paragraph 2, of the Statute, no two of whom may be nationals of the same State.
2. Three permanent judges and a maximum at any one time of six *ad litem* judges shall be members of each Trial Chamber. Each Trial Chamber to which *ad litem* judges are assigned may be divided into sections of three judges each, composed of both permanent and *ad litem* judges. A section of a Trial Chamber shall have the same powers and responsibilities as a Trial Chamber under the Statute and shall render judgement in accordance with the same rules.
3. Seven of the permanent judges shall be members of the Appeals Chamber. The Appeals Chamber shall, for each appeal, be composed of five of its members.
4. A person who for the purposes of membership of the Chambers of the International Tribunal could be regarded as a national of more than one State shall be deemed to be a national of the State in which that person ordinarily exercises civil and political rights.

ARTICLE 13

QUALIFICATIONS OF JUDGES

C4–014   The permanent and *ad litem* judges shall be persons of high moral character, impartiality and integrity who possess the qualifications required in their respective countries for appointment to the highest judicial offices. In the overall composition of the Chambers and sections of the Trial Chambers, due account shall be taken of the experience of the judges in criminal law, international law, including international humanitarian law and human rights law.

ARTICLE 13*bis*

ELECTION OF PERMANENT JUDGES

C4–015   1. Fourteen of the permanent judges of the International Tribunal shall be elected by the General Assembly from a list submitted by the Security Council, in the following manner:
(a) The Secretary-General shall invite nominations for judges of the International Tribunal from States Members of the United Nations and non-member States maintaining permanent observer missions at United Nations Headquarters;

(b) Within sixty days of the date of the invitation of the Secretary-General, each State may nominate up to two candidates meeting the qualifications set out in article 13 of the Statute, no two of whom shall be of the same nationality and neither of whom shall be of the same nationality as any judge who is a member of the Appeals Chamber and who was elected or appointed a permanent judge of the International Criminal Tribunal for the Prosecution of Persons Responsible for Genocide and Other Serious Violations of International Humanitarian Law Committed in the Territory of Rwanda and Rwandan Citizens Responsible for Genocide and Other Such Violations Committed in the Territory of Neighbouring States, between 1 January 1994 and 31 December 1994 (hereinafter referred to as "The International Tribunal for Rwanda") in accordance with article 12*bis* of the Statute of that Tribunal;

(c) The Secretary-General shall forward the nominations received to the Security Council. From the nominations received the Security Council shall establish a list of not less than twenty-eight and not more than forty-two candidates, taking due account of the adequate representation of the principal legal systems of the world;

(d) The President of the Security Council shall transmit the list of candidates to the President of the General Assembly. From that list the General Assembly shall elect fourteen permanent judges of the International Tribunal. The candidates who receive an absolute majority of the votes of the States Members of the United Nations and of the non-member States maintaining permanent observer missions at United Nations Headquarters, shall be declared elected. Should two candidates of the same nationality obtain the required majority vote, the one who received the higher number of votes shall be considered elected.

2. In the event of a vacancy in the Chambers amongst the permanent judges elected or appointed in accordance with this article, after consultation with the Presidents of the Security Council and of the General Assembly, the Secretary-General shall appoint a person meeting the qualifications of article 13 of the Statute, for the remainder of the term of office concerned.

3. The permanent judges elected in accordance with this article shall be elected for a term of four years. The terms and conditions of service shall be those of the judges of the International Court of Justice. They shall be eligible for re-election.

ARTICLE 13*ter*

ELECTION AND APPOINTMENT OF *AD LITEM* JUDGES

1. The *ad litem* judges of the International Tribunal shall be elected by the General Assembly from a list submitted by the Security Council, in the following manner:

C4–016

(a) The Secretary-General shall invite nominations for *ad litem* judges of the International Tribunal from States Members of the United Nations and non-member States maintaining permanent observer missions at United Nations Headquarters.

(b) Within sixty days of the date of the invitation of the Secretary-General, each State may nominate up to four candidates meeting the qualifications set out in article 13 of the Statute, taking into account the importance of a fair representation of female and male candidates.

(c) The Secretary-General shall forward the nominations received to the Security Council. From the nominations received the Security Council shall establish a list of not less than fifty-four candidates, taking due account of the adequate representation of the principal legal systems of the world and bearing in mind the importance of equitable geographical distribution.

(d) The President of the Security Council shall transmit the list of candidates to the President of the General Assembly. From that list the General Assembly shall elect the twenty-seven *ad litem* judges of the International Tribunal. The candidates who receive an absolute majority of the votes of the States Members of the United Nations and of the non-member States maintaining permanent observer missions at United Nations Headquarters shall be declared elected.

(e) The *ad litem* judges shall be elected for a term of four years. They shall not be eligible for re-election.

2. During their term, ad litem judges will be appointed by the Secretary-General, upon request of the President of the International Tribunal, to serve in the Trial Chambers for one or more trials, for a cumulative period of up to, but not including, three years. When requesting the appointment of any particular *ad litem* judge, the President of the International Tribunal shall bear in mind the criteria set out in article 13 of the Statute regarding the composition of the Chambers and sections of the Trial Chambers, the considerations set out in paragraphs 1 (b) and (c) above and the number of votes the *ad litem* judge received in the General Assembly.

ARTICLE 13*quarter*

STATUS OF *AD LITEM* JUDGES

C4–017   1. During the period in which they are appointed to serve in the International Tribunal, *ad litem* judges shall:

(a) Benefit from the same terms and conditions of service mutatis mutandis as the permanent judges of the International Tribunal;

(b) Enjoy, subject to paragraph 2 below, the same powers as the permanent judges of the International Tribunal;

(c) Enjoy the privileges and immunities, exemptions and facilities of a judge of the International Tribunal;

(d) Enjoy the power to adjudicate in pre-trial proceedings in cases other than those that they have been appointed to try.

2. During the period in which they are appointed to serve in the International Tribunal, *ad litem* judges shall not:

(a) Be eligible for election as, or to vote in the election of, the President of the Tribunal or the Presiding Judge of a Trial Chamber pursuant to article 14 of the Statute;

(b) Have power:

(i) To adopt rules of procedure and evidence pursuant to article 15 of the Statute. They shall, however, be consulted before the adoption of those rules;

(ii) To review an indictment pursuant to article 19 of the Statute;

(iii) To consult with the President in relation to the assignment of judges pursuant to article 14 of the Statute or in relation to a pardon or commutation of sentence pursuant to article 28 of the Statute.

ARTICLE 14

OFFICERS AND MEMBERS OF THE CHAMBERS

C4–018   1. The permanent judges of the International Tribunal shall elect a President from amongst their number.

2. The President of the International Tribunal shall be a member of the Appeals Chamber and shall preside over its proceedings.

3. After consultation with the permanent judges of the International Tribunal, the President shall assign four of the permanent judges elected or appointed in accordance with Article 13*bis* of the Statute to the Appeals Chamber and nine to the Trial Chambers.

4. Two of the permanent judges of the International Tribunal for Rwanda elected or appointed in accordance with article 12*bis* of the Statute of that Tribunal shall be

assigned by the President of that Tribunal, in consultation with the President of the International Tribunal, to be members of the Appeals Chamber and permanent judges of the International Tribunal.

5. After consultation with the permanent judges of the International Tribunal, the President shall assign such *ad litem* judges as may from time to time be appointed to serve in the International Tribunal to the Trial Chambers.

6. A judge shall serve only in the Chamber to which he or she was assigned.

7. The permanent judges of each Trial Chamber shall elect a Presiding Judge from amongst their number, who shall oversee the work of the Trial Chamber as a whole.

ARTICLE 15

RULES OF PROCEDURE AND EVIDENCE

The judges of the International Tribunal shall adopt rules of procedure and evidence for the conduct of the pre-trial phase of the proceedings, trials and appeals, the admission of evidence, the protection of victims and witnesses and other appropriate matters.

C4-019

ARTICLE 16

THE PROSECUTOR

1. The Prosecutor shall be responsible for the investigation and prosecution of persons responsible for serious violations of international humanitarian law committed in the territory of the former Yugoslavia since 1 January 1991.

C4-020

2. The Prosecutor shall act independently as a separate organ of the International Tribunal. He or she shall not seek or receive instructions from any Government or from any other source.

3. The Office of the Prosecutor shall be composed of a Prosecutor and such other qualified staff as maybe required.

4. The Prosecutor shall be appointed by the Security Council on nomination by the Secretary-General. He or she shall be of high moral character and possess the highest level of competence and experience in the conduct of investigations and prosecutions of criminal cases. The Prosecutor shall serve for a four-year term and be eligible for reappointment. The terms and conditions of service of the Prosecutor shall be those of an Under-Secretary-General of the United Nations.

5. The staff of the Office of the Prosecutor shall be appointed by the Secretary-General on the recommendation of the Prosecutor.

ARTICLE 17

THE REGISTRY

1. The Registry shall be responsible for the administration and servicing of the International Tribunal.

C4-021

2. The Registry shall consist of a Registrar and such other staff as may be required.

3. The Registrar shall be appointed by the Secretary-General after consultation with the President of the International Tribunal. He or she shall serve for a four-year term and be eligible for reappointment. The terms and conditions of service of the Registrar shall be those of an Assistant Secretary-General of the United Nations.

4. The staff of the Registry shall be appointed by the Secretary-General on the recommendation of the Registrar.

ARTICLE 18

INVESTIGATION AND PREPARATION OF INDICTMENT

C4–022   1. The Prosecutor shall initiate investigations *ex-officio* or on the basis of information obtained from any source, particularly from Governments, United Nations organs, intergovernmental and non-governmental organisations. The Prosecutor shall assess the information received or obtained and decide whether there is sufficient basis to proceed.

2. The Prosecutor shall have the power to question suspects, victims and witnesses, to collect evidence and to conduct on-site investigations. In carrying out these tasks, the Prosecutor may, as appropriate, seek the assistance of the State authorities concerned.

3. If questioned, the suspect shall be entitled to be assisted by counsel of his own choice, including the right to have legal assistance assigned to him without payment by him in any such case if he does not have sufficient means to pay for it, as well as to necessary translation into and from a language he speaks and understands.

4. Upon a determination that a *prima facie* case exists, the Prosecutor shall prepare an indictmentcontaining a concise statement of the facts and the crime or crimes with which the accused is charged under the Statute. The indictment shall be transmitted to a judge of the Trial Chamber.

ARTICLE 19

REVIEW OF THE INDICTMENT

C4–023   1. The judge of the Trial Chamber to whom the indictment has been transmitted shall review it. If satisfied that a *prima facie* case has been established by the Prosecutor, he shall confirm the indictment. If not so satisfied, the indictment shall be dismissed.

2. Upon confirmation of an indictment, the judge may, at the request of the Prosecutor, issue such orders and warrants for the arrest, detention, surrender or transfer of persons, and any other orders as maybe required for the conduct of the trial.

ARTICLE 20

COMMENCEMENT AND CONDUCT OF TRIAL PROCEEDINGS

C4–024   1. The Trial Chambers shall ensure that a trial is fair and expeditious and that proceedings are conducted in accordance with the rules of procedure and evidence, with full respect for the rights of the accused and due regard for the protection of victims and witnesses.

2. A person against whom an indictment has been confirmed shall, pursuant to an order or an arrest warrant of the International Tribunal, be taken into custody, immediately informed of the charges against him and transferred to the International Tribunal.

3. The Trial Chamber shall read the indictment, satisfy itself that the rights of the accused are respected, confirm that the accused understands the indictment, and instruct the accused to enter a plea. The Trial Chamber shall then set the date for trial.

4. The hearings shall be public unless the Trial Chamber decides to close the proceedings in accordance with its rules of procedure and evidence.

ARTICLE 21

RIGHTS OF THE ACCUSED

C4–025   1. All persons shall be equal before the International Tribunal.

2. In the determination of charges against him, the accused shall be entitled to a fair and public hearing, subject to article 22 of the Statute.

3. The accused shall be presumed innocent until proved guilty according to the provisions of the present Statute.

4. In the determination of any charge against the accused pursuant to the present Statute, the accused shall be entitled to the following minimum guarantees, in full equality:

    (a) to be informed promptly and in detail in a language which he understands of the nature and cause of the charge against him;

    (b) to have adequate time and facilities for the preparation of his defence and to communicate with counsel of his own choosing;

    (c) to be tried without undue delay;

    (d) to be tried in his presence, and to defend himself in person or through legal assistance of his own choosing; to be informed, if he does not have legal assistance, of this right; and to have legal assistance assigned to him, in any case where the interests of justice so require, and without payment by him in any such case if he does not have sufficient means to pay for it;

    (e) to examine, or have examined, the witnesses against him and to obtain the attendance and examination of witnesses on his behalf under the same conditions as witnesses against him;

    (f) to have the free assistance of an interpreter if he cannot understand or speak the language used in the International Tribunal;

    (g) not to be compelled to testify against himself or to confess guilt.

ARTICLE 22

PROTECTION OF VICTIMS AND WITNESSES

C4–026

The International Tribunal shall provide in its rules of procedure and evidence for the protection of victims and witnesses. Such protection measures shall include, but shall not be limited to, the conduct of in camera proceedings and the protection of the victim's identity.

ARTICLE 23

JUDGEMENT

C4–027

1. The Trial Chambers shall pronounce judgements and impose sentences and penalties on persons convicted of serious violations of international humanitarian law.

2. The judgement shall be rendered by a majority of the judges of the Trial Chamber, and shall be delivered by the Trial Chamber in public. It shall be accompanied by a reasoned opinion in writing, to which separate or dissenting opinions may be appended.

ARTICLE 24

PENALTIES

C4–028

1. The penalty imposed by the Trial Chamber shall be limited to imprisonment. In determining the terms of imprisonment, the Trial Chambers shall have recourse to the general practice regarding prison sentences in the courts of the former Yugoslavia.

2. In imposing the sentences, the Trial Chambers should take into account such factors as the gravity of the offence and the individual circumstances of the convicted person.

3. In addition to imprisonment, the Trial Chambers may order the return of any property and proceeds acquired by criminal conduct, including by means of duress, to their rightful owners.

Article 25

APPELLATE PROCEEDINGS

C4–029   1. The Appeals Chamber shall hear appeals from persons convicted by the Trial Chambers or from the Prosecutor on the following grounds:

(a) an error on a question of law invalidating the decision; or

(b) an error of fact which has occasioned a miscarriage of justice.

2. The Appeals Chamber may affirm, reverse or revise the decisions taken by the Trial Chambers.

Article 26

REVIEW PROCEEDINGS

C4–030   Where a new fact has been discovered which was not known at the time of the proceedings before the Trial Chambers or the Appeals Chamber and which could have been a decisive factor in reaching the decision, the convicted person or the Prosecutor may submit to the International Tribunal an application for review of the judgement.

Article 27

ENFORCEMENT OF SENTENCES

C4–031   Imprisonment shall be served in a State designated by the International Tribunal from a list of States which have indicated to the Security Council their willingness to accept convicted persons. Such imprisonment shall be in accordance with the applicable law of the State concerned, subject to the supervision of the International Tribunal.

Article 28

PARDON OR COMMUTATION OF SENTENCES

C4–032   If, pursuant to the applicable law of the State in which the convicted person is imprisoned, he or she is eligible for pardon or commutation of sentence, the State concerned shall notify the International Tribunal accordingly. The President of the International Tribunal, in consultation with the judges, shall decide the matter on the basis of the interests of justice and the general principles of law.

Article 29

CO-OPERATION AND JUDICIAL ASSISTANCE

C4–033   1. States shall co-operate with the International Tribunal in the investigation and prosecution of persons accused of committing serious violations of international humanitarian law.

2. States shall comply without undue delay with any request for assistance or an order issued by a Trial Chamber, including, but not limited to:

(a) the identification and location of persons;

(b) the taking of testimony and the production of evidence;

(c) the service of documents;

(d) the arrest or detention of persons;

(e) the surrender or the transfer of the accused to the International Tribunal.

ARTICLE 30

THE STATUS, PRIVILEGES AND IMMUNITIES OF THE INTERNATIONAL TRIBUNAL

1. The Convention on the Privileges and Immunities of the United Nations of 13 **C4–034** February 1946 shall apply to the International Tribunal, the judges, the Prosecutor and his staff, and the Registrar and his staff.

2. The judges, the Prosecutor and the Registrar shall enjoy the privileges and immunities, exemptions and facilities accorded to diplomatic envoys, in accordance with international law.

3. The staff of the Prosecutor and of the Registrar shall enjoy the privileges and immunities accorded to officials of the United Nations under articles V and VII of the Convention referred to in paragraph 1 of this article.

4. Other persons, including the accused, required at the seat of the International Tribunal shall be accorded such treatment as is necessary for the proper functioning of the International Tribunal.

ARTICLE 31

SEAT OF THE INTERNATIONAL TRIBUNAL

The International Tribunal shall have its seat at The Hague.   **C4–035**

ARTICLE 32

EXPENSES OF THE INTERNATIONAL TRIBUNAL

The expenses of the International Tribunal shall be borne by the regular budget of the **C4–036** United Nations in accordance with Article 17 of the Charter of the United Nations.

ARTICLE 33

WORKING LANGUAGES

The working languages of the International Tribunal shall be English and French.   **C4–037**

ARTICLE 34

ANNUAL REPORT

The President of the International Tribunal shall submit an annual report of the **C4–038** International Tribunal to the Security Council and to the General Assembly.

[*NEXT PARAGRAPH IS C4–041.*]

Resolution 1166 (1998)

ADOPTED BY THE SECURITY COUNCIL AT ITS 3878TH MEETING, ON 13 MAY 1998

C4–041   *The Security Council,*

Reaffirming its resolution 827 (1993) of 25 May 1993,

Remaining convinced that the prosecution of persons responsible for serious violations of international humanitarian law committed in the territory of the former Yugoslavia contributes to the restoration and maintenance of peace in the former Yugoslavia,

Having considered the letter from the Secretary-General to the President of the Security Council dated 5 May 1998 (S/1998/376),

Convinced of the need to increase the number of judges and Trial Chambers, in order to enable the International Tribunal for the Prosecution of Persons Responsible for Serious Violations of International Humanitarian Law Committed in the Territory of the Former Yugoslavia since 1991 ("the International Tribunal") to try without delay the large number of accused awaiting trial,

Noting the significant progress being made in improving the procedures of the International Tribunal, and convinced of the need for its organs to continue their efforts to further such progress,

Acting under Chapter VII of the Charter of the United Nations,

1. *Decides* to establish a third Trial Chamber of the International Tribunal, and to this end decides to amend articles 11, 12 and 13 of the Statute of the International Tribunal and to replace those articles with the provisions set out in the annex to this resolution;

2. *Decides* that three additional judges shall be elected as soon as possible to serve in the additional Trial Chamber, and decides also, without prejudice to article 13.4 of the Statute of the International Tribunal, that once elected they shall serve until the date of the expiry of the terms of office of the existing judges, and that for the purpose of that election the Security Council shall, notwithstanding article 13.2 (c)of the Statute, establish a list from the nominations received of not less than six and not more than nine candidates;

3. *Urges* all States to cooperate fully with the International Tribunal and its organs in accordance with their obligations under resolution 827 (1993) and the Statute of the International Tribunal and welcomes the cooperation already extended to the Tribunal in the fulfilment of its mandate;

4. *Requests* the Secretary-General to make practical arrangements for the elections mentioned in paragraph 2 above and for enhancing the effective functioning of the International Tribunal, including the timely provision of personnel and facilities, in particular for the third Trial Chamber and related offices of the Prosecutor, and *further requests* him to keep the Security Council closely informed of progress in this regard;

5. *Decides* to remain actively seized of the matter.

Annex

Article 11

ORGANIZATION OF THE INTERNATIONAL TRIBUNAL

C4–042   The International Tribunal shall consist of the following organs:

(a) the Chambers, comprising three Trial Chambers and an Appeals Chamber;

(b) the Prosecutor; and

(c) a Registry, servicing both the Chambers and the Prosecutor.

Article 12

COMPOSITION OF THE CHAMBERS

The Chambers shall be composed of fourteen independent judges, no two of whom may be nationals of the same State, who shall serve as follows:

    (a) three judges shall serve in each of the Trial Chambers; and

    (b) five judges shall serve in the Appeals Chamber.

C4–043

Article 13

QUALIFICATIONS AND ELECTION OF JUDGES

1. The judges shall be persons of high moral character, impartiality and integrity who possess the qualifications required in their respective countries for appointment to the highest judicial offices. In the overall composition of the Chambers due account shall be taken of the experience of the judges in criminal law, international law, including international humanitarian law and human rights law.

2. The judges of the International Tribunal shall be elected by the General Assembly from a list submitted by the Security Council, in the following manner:

    (a) The Secretary-General shall invite nominations for judges of the International Tribunal from States Members of the United Nations and non-member States maintaining permanent observer missions at United Nations Headquarters.

    (b) Within sixty days of the date of the invitation of the Secretary-General, each State may nominate up to two candidates meeting the qualifications set out in paragraph 1 above, no two of whom shall be of the same nationality.

    (c) The Secretary-General shall forward the nominations received to the Security Council. From the nominations received the Security Council shall establish a list of not less than twenty-eight and not more than forty-two candidates, taking due account of the adequate representation of the principal legal systems of the world.

    (d) The President of the Security Council shall transmit the list of candidates to the President of the General Assembly. From that list the General Assembly shall elect the fourteen Judges of the International Tribunal. The candidates who receive an absolute majority of the votes of the States Members of the United Nations and of the non-member States maintaining permanent observer missions at United Nations Headquarters, shall be declared elected. Should two candidates of the same nationality obtain the required majority vote, the one who received the higher number of votes shall be considered elected.

3. In the event of a vacancy in the Chambers, after consultation with the Presidents of the Security Council and of the General Assembly, the Secretary-General shall appoint a person meeting the qualifications of paragraph 1 above, for the remainder of the term of office concerned.

4. The judges shall be elected for a term of four years. The terms and conditions of service shall be those of the judges of the International Court of Justice. They shall be eligible for re-election.

C4–044

Resolution 1329 (2000)

ADOPTED BY THE SECURITY COUNCIL AT ITS 4240TH MEETING, ON 30 NOVEMBER 2000

The Security Council,

C4–045

Reaffirming its resolutions 827 (1993) of 25 May 1993 and 955 (1994) of 8 November 1994,

Remaining convinced that the prosecution of persons responsible for serious violations of international humanitarian law committed in the territory of the former Yugoslavia contributes to the restoration and maintenance of peace in the former Yugoslavia,

Remaining convinced also that in the particular circumstances of Rwanda the prosecution of persons responsible for genocide and other serious violations of international humanitarian law contributes to the process of national reconciliation and to the restoration and maintenance of peace in Rwanda and in the region,

Having considered the letter from the Secretary-General to the President of the Security Council dated 7 September 2000 (S/2000/865) and the annexed letters from the President of the International Tribunal for the Former Yugoslavia addressed to the Secretary-General dated 12 May 2000 and from the President of the International Tribunal for Rwanda dated 14 June 2000,

Convinced of the need to establish a pool of *ad litem* judges in the International Tribunal for the Former Yugoslavia and to increase the number of judges in the Appeals Chambers of the International Tribunals in order to enable the International Tribunals to expedite the conclusion of their work at the earliest possible date,

Noting the significant progress being made in improving the procedures of the International Tribunals, and convinced of the need for their organs to continue their efforts to further such progress,

Taking note of the position expressed by the International Tribunals that civilian, military and paramilitary leaders should be tried before them in preference to minor actors,

Recalling that the International Tribunals and national courts have concurrent jurisdiction to prosecute persons for serious violations of international humanitarian law, and noting that the Rules of Procedure and Evidence of the International Tribunal for the Former Yugoslavia provide that a Trial Chamber may decide to suspend an indictment to allow for a national court to deal with a particular case,

Taking note with appreciation of the efforts of the judges of the International Tribunal for the Former Yugoslavia, as reflected in annex I to the letter from the Secretary-General of 7 September 2000, to allow competent organs of the United Nations to begin to form a relatively exact idea of the length of the mandate of the Tribunal,

Acting under Chapter VII of the Charter of the United Nations,

1. *Decides* to establish a pool of *ad litem* judges in the International Tribunal for the Former Yugoslavia and to enlarge the membership of the Appeals Chambers of the International Tribunal for the Former Yugoslavia and the International Tribunal for Rwanda, and to this end *decides* to amend articles 12, 13 and 14 of the Statute of the International Tribunal for the Former Yugoslavia and to replace those articles with the provisions set out in annex I to this resolution and *decides also* to amend articles 11, 12 and 13 of the Statute of the International Tribunal for Rwanda and to replace those articles with the provisions set out in annex II to this resolution;

2. *Decides* that two additional judges shall be elected as soon as possible as judges of the International Tribunal for Rwanda and *decides also*, without prejudice to Article 12, paragraph 4, of the Statute of that Tribunal, that, once elected, they shall serve until the date of the expiry of the terms of office of the existing judges, and that for the purpose of that election the Security Council shall, notwithstanding Article 12, paragraph 2 (c) of the Statute, establish a list from the nominations received of not less than four and not more than six candidates;

3. *Decides* that, once two judges have been elected in accordance with paragraph 2 above and have taken up office, the President of the International Tribunal for Rwanda shall, in accordance with Article 13, paragraph 3, of the Statute of the International Tribunal for Rwanda and Article 14, paragraph 4, of the Statute of the International Tribunal for the Former Yugoslavia, take the necessary steps as soon as is practicable to assign two of the judges elected or appointed in accordance with Article 12 of the Statute of the International Tribunal for Rwanda to be members of the Appeals Chambers of the International Tribunals;

4. *Requests* the Secretary-General to make practical arrangements for the elections mentioned in paragraph 2 above, for the election as soon as possible of twenty-seven *ad litem* judges in accordance with Article 13 ter of the Statute of the International Tribunal for the Former Yugoslavia, and for the timely provision to the International Tribunal for the Former Yugoslavia and the International Tribunal for Rwanda of personnel and facilities, in particular, for the *ad litem* judges and the Appeals Chambers and related offices of the Prosecutor, and *further requests* him to keep the Security Council closely informed of progress in this regard;

5. *Urges* all States to cooperate fully with the International Tribunals and their organs in accordance with their obligations under resolutions 827 (1993) and 955 (1994) and the Statutes of the International Tribunals, and *welcomes* the cooperation already extended to the Tribunals in the fulfilment of their mandates;

6. *Requests* the Secretary-General to submit to the Security Council, as soon as possible, a report containing an assessment and proposals regarding the date ending the temporal jurisdiction of the International Tribunal for the Former Yugoslavia;

7. Decides to remain actively seized of the matter.

ANNEX I

ARTICLE 12

COMPOSITION OF THE CHAMBERS

1. The Chambers shall be composed of *sixteen* **permanent** independent judges, no two   **C4–046**
of whom may be nationals of the same State, **and a maximum at any one time of nine**
***ad litem* independent judges appointed in accordance with article 13*ter*, paragraph**
2, of the Statute, no two of whom may be nationals of the same State.

**2. Three permanent judges and a maximum at any one time of six *ad litem*
judges shall be members of each Trial Chamber. Each Trial Chamber to which *ad
litem* judges are assigned may be divided into sections of three judges each,
composed of both permanent and *ad litem* judges. A section of a Trial Chamber
shall have the same powers and responsibilities as a Trial Chamber under the
Statute and shall render judgement in accordance with the same rules.**

3. *Seven of the permanent judges shall be members of the Appeals Chamber. The Appeals Chamber shall, for each appeal, be composed of five of its members.*

ARTICLE 13

QUALIFICATIONS OF JUDGES

The **permanent** and ***ad litem*** judges shall be persons of high moral character,   **C4–047**
impartiality and integrity who possess the qualifications required in their respective
countries for appointment to the highest judicial offices. In the overall composition of
the Chambers and sections of the Trial Chambers, due account shall be taken of the
experience of the judges in criminal law, international law, including international
humanitarian law and human rights law.

ARTICLE 13*bis*

ELECTION OF PERMANENT JUDGES

1. *Fourteen of* the **permanent** judges of the International Tribunal shall be elected by   **C4–048**
the General Assembly from a list submitted by the Security Council, in the following
manner:

(a) The Secretary-General shall invite nominations for judges of the International Tribunal from States Members of the United Nations and non-member States maintaining permanent observer missions at United Nations Headquarters.

(b) Within sixty days of the date of the invitation of the Secretary-General, each State may nominate up to two candidates meeting the qualifications set out in article 13 of the Statute, no two of whom shall be of the same nationality *and neither of whom shall be of the same nationality as any judge who is a member of the Appeals Chamber and who was elected or appointed a judge of the International Criminal Tribunal for the Prosecution of Persons Responsible for Genocide and Other Serious Violations of International Humanitarian Law Committed in the Territory of Rwanda and Rwandan Citizens Responsible for Genocide and Other Such Violations Committed in the Territory of Neighbouring States, between 1 January 1994 and 31 December 1994 (hereinafter referred to as "The International Tribunal for Rwanda") in accordance with article 12 bis of the Statute of that Tribunal.*

(c) The Secretary-General shall forward the nominations received to the Security Council. From the nominations received the Security Council shall establish a list of not less than twenty-eight and not more than forty-two candidates, taking due account of the adequate representation of the principal legal systems of the world.

(d) The President of the Security Council shall transmit the list of candidates to the President of the General Assembly. From that list the General Assembly shall elect fourteen permanent judges of the International Tribunal. The candidates who receive an absolute majority of the votes of the States Members of the United Nations and of the non-member States maintaining permanent observer missions at United Nations Headquarters, shall be declared elected. Should two candidates of the same nationality obtain the required majority vote, the one who received the higher number of votes shall be considered elected.

2. In the event of a vacancy in the Chambers **amongst the permanent judges** *elected or appointed in accordance with this article*, after consultation with the Presidents of the Security Council and of the General Assembly, the Secretary-General shall appoint a person meeting the qualifications of article 13 of the Statute, for the remainder of the term of office concerned.

3. The **permanent** judges *elected in accordance with this article* shall be elected for a term of four years. The terms and conditions of service shall be those of the judges of the International Court of Justice. They shall be eligible for re-election.

ARTICLE 13*ter*

ELECTION AND APPOINTMENT OF *AD LITEM* JUDGES

C4–049   1. The *ad litem* judges of the International Tribunal shall be elected by the General Assembly from a list submitted by the Security Council, in the following manner:

(a) The Secretary-General shall invite nominations for *ad litem* judges of the International Tribunal from States Members of the United Nations and non-member States maintaining permanent observer missions at United Nations Headquarters.

(b) Within sixty days of the date of the invitation of the Secretary-General, each State may nominate up to four candidates meeting the qualifications set out in article 13 of the Statute, taking into account the importance of a fair representation of female and male candidates.

(c) The Secretary-General shall forward the nominations received to the Security Council. From the nominations received the Security Council shall establish a list of not less than fifty-four candidates, taking due account of the adequate representation of the principal legal systems of the world and bearing in mind the importance of equitable geographical distribution.

(d) The President of the Security Council shall transmit the list of candidates to the President of the General Assembly. From that list the General Assembly shall elect the twenty-seven *ad litem* judges of the International Tribunal. The candidates who receive an absolute majority of the votes of the States Members of the United Nations and of the non-member States maintaining permanent observer missions at United Nations Headquarters shall be declared elected.

(e) The *ad litem* judges shall be elected for a term of four years. They shall not be eligible for re-election.

2. During their term, *ad litem* judges will be appointed by the Secretary-General, upon request of the President of the International Tribunal, to serve in the Trial Chambers for one or more trials, for a cumulative period of up to, but not including, three years. When requesting the appointment of any particular *ad litem* judge, the President of the International Tribunal shall bear in mind the criteria set out in article 13 of the Statute regarding the composition of the Chambers and sections of the Trial Chambers, the considerations set out in paragraphs 1 (b) and (c) above and the number of votes the *ad litem* judge received in the General Assembly.

Article 13*quater*

STATUS OF *AD LITEM* JUDGES

1. During the period in which they are appointed to serve in the International Tribunal, *ad litem* judges shall: **C4–050**

(a) benefit from the same terms and conditions of service mutatis mutandis as the permanent judges of the International Tribunal;

(b) enjoy, subject to paragraph 2 below, the same powers as the permanent judges of the International Tribunal;

(c) enjoy the privilegeand immunities, exemptions and facilities of a judge of the International Tribunal.

2. During the period in which they are appointed to serve in the International Tribunal, *ad litem* judges shall not:

(a) be eligible for election as, or to vote in the election of, the President of the Tribunal or the Presiding Judge of a Trial Chamber pursuant to article 14 of the Statute;

(b) have power:

(i) to adopt rules of procedure and evidence pursuant to article 15 of the Statute. They shall, however, be consulted before the adoption of those rules;

(ii) to review an indictment pursuant to article 19 of the Statute;

(iii) to consult with the President in relation to the assignment of judges pursuant to article 14 of the Statute or in relation to a pardon or commutation of sentence pursuant to article 28 of the Statute;

(iv) to adjudicate in pre-trial proceedings.

Article 14

OFFICERS AND MEMBERS OF THE CHAMBERS

1. The *permanent* judges of the International Tribunal shall elect a President *from amongst their number*. **C4–051**

2. The President of the International Tribunal shall be a member of the Appeals Chamber and shall preside over its proceedings.

3. After consultation with the *permanent* judges of the International Tribunal, the President shall assign *four of the permanent judges elected or appointed in accordance with Article 13 bis of the Statute* to the Appeals Chamber and *nine* to the Trial Chambers.

4. *Two of the permanent judges of the International Tribunal for Rwanda elected or appointed in accordance with article 12 bis of the Statute of that Tribunal shall be assigned by the President of that*

Tribunal, in consultation with the President of the International Tribunal, to be members of the Appeals Chamber and permanent judges of the International Tribunal.

5. *After consultation with the permanent judges of the International Tribunal, the President shall assign such* ad litem *judges as may from time to time be appointed to serve in the International Tribunal to the Trial Chambers.*

6. A judge shall serve only in the Chamber to which he or she was assigned.

7. The *permanent* judges of each Trial Chamber shall elect a Presiding Judge *from amongst their number*, who shall *oversee the work* of the Trial Chamber as a whole.

ANNEX II

ARTICLE 11

COMPOSITION OF THE CHAMBERS

C4–052   The Chambers shall be composed of *sixteen* independent judges, no two of whom may be nationals of the same State, who shall serve as follows:

  (a) three judges shall serve in each of the Trial Chambers;
  (b) *seven judges shall be members of* the Appeals Chamber. *The Appeals Chamber shall, for each appeal, be composed of five of its members.*

ARTICLE 12

QUALIFICATION AND ELECTION OF JUDGES

C4–053   1. The judges shall be persons of high moral character, impartiality and integrity who possess the qualifications required in their respective countries for appointment to the highest judicial offices. In the overall composition of the Chambers due account shall be taken of the experience of the judges in criminal law, international law, including international humanitarian law and human rights law.

2. *Eleven of* the judges of the International Tribunal for Rwanda shall be elected by the General Assembly from a list submitted by the Security Council, in the following manner:

  (a) The Secretary-General shall invite nominations for judges from States Members of the United Nations and non-member States maintaining permanent observer missions at United Nations Headquarters.
  (b) Within *sixty* days of the date of the invitation of the Secretary-General, each State may nominate up to two candidates meeting the qualifications set out in paragraph 1 above, no two of whom shall be of the same nationality and neither of whom shall be of the same nationality as any judge *who is a member of* the Appeals Chamber *and who was elected or appointed a permanent judge of the International Tribunal for the Prosecution of Persons Responsible for Serious Violations of International Humanitarian Law Committed in the Territory of the former Yugoslavia since 1991 (hereinafter referred to as "the International Tribunal for the Former Yugoslavia") in accordance with article 13 bis of the Statute of that Tribunal.*
  (c) The Secretary-General shall forward the nominations received to the Security Council. From the nominations received the Security Council shall establish a list of not less than *twenty-two* and not more than *thirty-three* candidates, taking due account of the adequate representation on the International Tribunal for Rwanda of the principal legal systems of the world.
  (d) The President of the Security Council shall transmit the list of candidates to the President of the General Assembly. From that list the General Assembly shall elect *eleven* judges of the International Tribunal for Rwanda. The candidates who receive an absolute majority of the votes of the States Members of the United Nations and of the non-member States maintaining permanent observer

1464

missions at United Nations Headquarters, shall be declared elected. Should two candidates of the same nationality obtain the required majority vote, the one who received the higher number of votes shall be considered elected.

3. In the event of a vacancy in the Chambers *amongst the judges elected or appointed in accordance with this article*, after consultation with the Presidents of the Security Council and of the General Assembly, the Secretary-General shall appoint a person meeting the qualifications of paragraph 1 above, for the remainder of the term of office concerned.

4. The judges *elected in accordance with this article* shall be elected for a term of four years. The terms and conditions of service shall be those of the judges of the International Tribunal for the Former Yugoslavia. They shall be eligible for re-election.

ARTICLE 13

OFFICERS AND MEMBERS OF THE CHAMBERS

1. The judges of the International Tribunal for Rwanda shall elect a President.

2. *The President of the International Tribunal for Rwanda shall be a member of one of its Trial Chambers.*

3. After consultation with the judges of the International Tribunal for Rwanda, the President shall assign *two of the judges elected or appointed in accordance with Article 12 of the present Statute to be members of the Appeals Chamber of the International Tribunal for the Former Yugoslavia and eight to* the Trial Chambers *of the International Tribunal for Rwanda*. A judge shall serve only in the Chamber to which he or she was assigned.

4. *The members of the Appeals Chamber of the International Tribunal for the Former Yugoslavia shall also serve as the members of the Appeals Chamber of the International Tribunal for Rwanda.*

5. The judges of each Trial Chamber shall elect a Presiding Judge, who shall conduct all of the proceedings of that Trial Chamber as a whole.

C4–054

RESOLUTION 1411 (2002)

ADOPTED BY THE SECURITY COUNCIL AT ITS 4535TH MEETING, ON 17 MAY 2002

The Security Council,

Reaffirming its resolutions 827 (1993) of 25 May 1993, 955 (1994) of 8 November 1994, 1165 (1998) of 30 April 1998, 1166 (1998) of 13 May 1998 and 1329 (2000) of 30 November 2000,

Recognizing that persons who are nominated for, or who are elected or appointed as, judges of the International Tribunal for the Former Yugoslavia or of the International Tribunal for Rwanda may bear the nationalities of two or more States,

Being aware that at least one such person has already been elected a judge of one of the International Tribunals,

Considering that, for the purposes of membership of the Chambers of the International Tribunals, such persons should be regarded as bearing solely the nationality of the State in which they ordinarily exercise civil and political rights,

Acting under Chapter VII of the Charter of the United Nations,

1. *Decides* to amend article 12 of the Statute of the International Tribunal for the former Yugoslavia and to replace that article with the provisions set out in annex I to this resolution;

2. *Decides also* to amend article 11 of the Statute of the International Tribunal for Rwanda and to replace that article with the provisions set out in annex II to this resolution;

3. *Decides* to remain actively seized of the matter.

C4–055

ANNEX I

ARTICLE 12

COMPOSITION OF THE CHAMBERS

C4–056   1. The Chambers shall be composed of sixteen permanent independent judges, no two of whom may be nationals of the same State, and a maximum at any one time of nine *ad litem* independent judges appointed in accordance with article 13*ter*, paragraph 2, of the Statute, no two of whom may be nationals of the same State.

2. Three permanent judges and a maximum at any one time of six *ad litem* judges shall be members of each Trial Chamber. Each Trial Chamber to which *ad litem* judges are assigned may be divided into sections of three judges each, composed of both permanent and *ad litem* judges. A section of a Trial Chamber shall have the same powers and responsibilities as a Trial Chamber under the Statute and shall render judgement in accordance with the same rules.

3. Seven of the permanent judges shall be members of the Appeals Chamber. The Appeals Chamber shall, for each appeal, be composed of five of its members.

4. **A person who for the purposes of membership of the Chambers of the International Tribunal could be regarded as a national of more than one State shall be deemed to be a national of the State in which that person ordinarily exercises civil and political rights.**

ANNEX II

ARTICLE 11

COMPOSITION OF THE CHAMBERS

C4–057   1. The Chambers shall be composed of sixteen independent judges, no two of whom may be nationals of the same State, who shall serve as follows:

(a) three judges shall serve in each of the Trial Chambers;

(b) seven judges shall be members of the Appeals Chamber. The Appeals Chamber shall, for each appeal, be composed of five of its members.

2. **A person who for the purposes of membership of the Chambers of the International Tribunal for Rwanda could be regarded as a national of more than one State shall be deemed to be a national of the State in which that person ordinarily exercises civil and political rights.**

RESOLUTION 1431 (2002)

ADOPTED BY THE SECURITY COUNCIL AT ITS 4601ST MEETING, ON 14 AUGUST 2002

C4–058   *The Security Council,*

Reaffirming its resolutions 827 (1993) of 25 May 1993, 955 (1994) of 8 November 1994, 1165 (1998) of 30 April 1998, 1166 (1998) of 13 May 1998 and 1329 (2000) of 30 November 2000,

Reaffirming its resolutions 827 (1993) of 25 May 1993, 955 (1994) of 8 November 1994, 1165 (1998) of 30 April 1998, 1166 (1998) of 13 May 1998, 1329 (2000) of 30 November 2000 and 1411 (2002) of 17 May 2002,

Having considered the letter from the Secretary-General to the President of the Security Council dated 14 September 2001 (S/2001/764) and the annexed letter from the President of the International Tribunal for Rwanda addressed to the Secretary-General dated 9 July 2001,

Having considered also the letter from the Secretary-General to the President of the Security Council dated 4 March 2002 (S/2002/241) and the annexed letter from the President of the International Tribunal for Rwanda addressed to the Secretary-General dated 6 February 2002,

Convinced of the need to establish a pool of *ad litem* judges in the International Tribunal for Rwanda in order to enable the International Tribunal for Rwanda to expedite the conclusion of its work at the earliest possible date and determined to follow closely the progress of the operation of the International Tribunal for Rwanda,

Acting under Chapter VII of the Charter of the United Nations,

1. *Decides* to establish a pool of *ad litem* judges in the International Tribunal for Rwanda, and to this end *decides* to amend articles 11, 12 and 13 of the Statute of the International Tribunal for Rwanda and to replace those articles with the provisions set out in annex I to this resolution and *decides also* to amend articles 13 bis and 14 of the Statute of the International Tribunal for the Former Yugoslavia and to replace those articles with the provisions set out in annex II to this resolution;

2. *Requests* the Secretary-General to make practical arrangements for the election as soon as possible of eighteen *ad litem* judges in accordance with Article 12 ter of the Statute of the International Tribunal for Rwanda and for the timely provision to the International Tribunal for Rwanda of personnel and facilities, in particular, for the *ad litem* judges and related offices of the Prosecutor, and *further requests* him to keep the Security Council closely informed of progress in this regard;

3. *Urges* all States to cooperate fully with the International Tribunal for Rwanda and its organs in accordance with their obligations under resolution 955 (1994) and the Statute of the International Tribunal for Rwanda;

4. *Decides* to remain actively seized of the matter.

ANNEX I

ARTICLE 11

COMPOSITION OF THE CHAMBERS

C4–059

1. The Chambers shall be composed of sixteen permanent independent judges, no two of whom may be nationals of the same State, and a maximum at any one time of four *ad litem* independent judges appointed in accordance with article 12*ter*, paragraph 2, of the present Statute, no two of whom may be nationals of the same State.

2. Three permanent judges and a maximum at any one time of four *ad litem* judges shall be members of each Trial Chamber. Each Trial Chamber to which *ad litem* judges are assigned may be divided into sections of three judges each, composed of both permanent and *ad litem* judges. A section of a Trial Chamber shall have the same powers and responsibilities as a Trial Chamber under the present Statute and shall render judgement in accordance with the same rules.

3. Seven of the permanent judges shall be members of the Appeals Chamber. The Appeals Chamber shall, for each appeal, be composed of five of its members.

4. A person who for the purposes of membership of the Chambers of the International Tribunal for Rwanda could be regarded as a national of more than one State shall be deemed to be a national of the State in which that person ordinarily exercises civil and political rights.

ARTICLE 12

QUALIFICATIONS OF JUDGES

C4–060

The permanent and *ad litem* judges shall be persons of high moral character, impartiality and integrity who possess the qualifications required in their respective countries for appointment to the highest judicial offices. In the overall composition of the Chambers and sections of the Trial Chambers, due account shall be taken of the experience of the judges in criminal law, international law, including international humanitarian law and human rights law.

ARTICLE 12*bis*

ELECTION OF PERMANENT JUDGES

C4–061   1. Eleven of the permanent judges of the International Tribunal for Rwanda shall be elected by the General Assembly from a list submitted by the Security Council, in the following manner:

(a) The Secretary-General shall invite nominations for permanent judges of the International Tribunal for Rwanda from States Members of the United Nations and non-member States maintaining permanent observer missions at United Nations Headquarters;

(b) Within sixty days of the date of the invitation of the Secretary-General, each State may nominate up to two candidates meeting the qualifications set out in article 12 of the present Statute, no two of whom shall be of the same nationality and neither of whom shall be of the same nationality as any judge who is a member of the Appeals Chamber and who was elected or appointed a permanent judge of the International Tribunal for the Prosecution of Persons Responsible for Serious Violations of International Humanitarian Law Committed in the Territory of the former Yugoslavia since 1991 (hereinafter referred to as "the International Tribunal for the Former Yugoslavia") in accordance with article 13*bis* of the Statute of that Tribunal;

(c) The Secretary-General shall forward the nominations received to the Security Council. From the nominations received the Security Council shall establish a list of not less than twenty-two and not more than thirty-three candidates, taking due account of the adequate representation on the International Tribunal for Rwanda of the principal legal systems of the world;

(d) The President of the Security Council shall transmit the list of candidates to the President of the General Assembly. From that list the General Assembly shall elect eleven permanent judges of the International Tribunal for Rwanda. The candidates who receive an absolute majority of the votes of the States Members of the United Nations and of the non-member States maintaining permanent observer missions at United Nations Headquarters, shall be declared elected. Should two candidates of the same nationality obtain the required majority vote, the one who received the higher number of votes shall be considered elected.

2. In the event of a vacancy in the Chambers amongst the permanent judges elected or appointed in accordance with this article, after consultation with the Presidents of the Security Council and of the General Assembly, the Secretary-General shall appoint a person meeting the qualifications of article 12 of the present Statute, for the remainder of the term of office concerned.

3. The permanent judges elected in accordance with this article shall be elected for a term of four years. The terms and conditions of service shall be those of the permanent judges of the International Tribunal for the Former Yugoslavia. They shall be eligible for re-election.

ARTICLE 12*ter*

ELECTION AND APPOINTMENT OF *AD LITEM* JUDGES

C4–062   1. The *ad litem* judges of the International Tribunal for Rwanda shall be elected by the General Assembly from a list submitted by the Security Council, in the following manner:

(a) The Secretary-General shall invite nominations for *ad litem* judges of the International Tribunal for Rwanda from States Members of the United Nations and non-member States maintaining permanent observer missions at United Nations Headquarters;
(b) Within sixty days of the date of the invitation of the Secretary-General, each State may nominate up to four candidates meeting the qualifications set out in article 12 of the present Statute, taking into account the importance of a fair representation of female and male candidates;
(c) The Secretary-General shall forward the nominations received to the Security Council. From the nominations received the Security Council shall establish a list of not less than thirty-six candidates, taking due account of the adequate representation of the principal legal systems of the world and bearing in mind the importance of equitable geographical distribution;
(d) The President of the Security Council shall transmit the list of candidates to the President of the General Assembly. From that list the General Assembly shall elect the eighteen *ad litem* judges of the International Tribunal for Rwanda. The candidates who receive an absolute majority of the votes of the States Members of the United Nations and of the non-member States maintaining permanent observer missions at United Nations Headquarters shall be declared elected;
(e) The *ad litem* judges shall be elected for a term of four years. They shall not be eligible for re-election.

2. During their term, *ad litem* judges will be appointed by the Secretary-General, upon request of the President of the International Tribunal for Rwanda, to serve in the Trial Chambers for one or more trials, for a cumulative period of up to, but not including, three years. When requesting the appointment of any particular *ad litem* judge, the President of the International Tribunal for Rwanda shall bear in mind the criteria set out in article 12 of the present Statute regarding the composition of the Chambers and sections of the Trial Chambers, the considerations set out in paragraphs 1 (b) and (c) above and the number of votes the *ad litem* judge received in the General Assembly.

ARTICLE 12*quarter*

STATUS OF *AD LITEM* JUDGES

1. During the period in which they are appointed to serve in the International **C4–063**
Tribunal for Rwanda, *ad litem* judges shall:
(a) Benefit from the same terms and conditions of service mutatis mutandis as the permanent judges of the International Tribunal for Rwanda;
(b) Enjoy, subject to paragraph 2 below, the same powers as the permanent judges of the International Tribunal for Rwanda;
(c) Enjoy the privileges and immunities, exemptions and facilities of a judge of the International Tribunal for Rwanda.

2. During the period in which they are appointed to serve in the International Tribunal for Rwanda, *ad litem* judges shall not:
(a) Be eligible for election as, or to vote in the election of, the President of the International Tribunal for Rwanda or the Presiding Judge of a Trial Chamber pursuant to article 13 of the present Statute;
(b) Have power:
  (i) To adopt rules of procedure and evidence pursuant to article 14 of the present Statute. They shall, however, be consulted before the adoption of those rules;
  (ii) To review an indictment pursuant to Article 18 of the present Statute;
  (iii) To consult with the President of the International Tribunal for Rwanda in relation to the assignment of judges pursuant to article 13 of the present Statute or in relation to a pardon or commutation of sentence pursuant to article 27 of the present Statute;
  (iv) To adjudicate in pre-trial proceedings.

ARTICLE 13

OFFICERS AND MEMBERS OF THE CHAMBERS

C4–064   1. The permanent judges of the International Tribunal for Rwanda shall elect a President from amongst their number.

2. The President of the International Tribunal for Rwanda shall be a member of one of its Trial Chambers.

3. After consultation with the permanent judges of the International Tribunal for Rwanda, the President shall assign two of the permanent judges elected or appointed in accordance with Article 12*bis* of the present Statute to be members of the Appeals Chamber of the International Tribunal for the Former Yugoslavia and eight to the Trial Chambers of the International Tribunal for Rwanda.

4. The members of the Appeals Chamber of the International Tribunal for the Former Yugoslavia shall also serve as the members of the Appeals Chamber of the International Tribunal for Rwanda.

5. After consultation with the permanent judges of the International Tribunal for Rwanda, the President shall assign such *ad litem* judges as may from time to time be appointed to serve in the International Tribunal for Rwanda to the Trial Chambers.

6. A judge shall serve only in the Chamber to which he or she was assigned.

7. The permanent judges of each Trial Chamber shall elect a Presiding Judge from amongst their number, who shall oversee the work of that Trial Chamber as a whole.

INTERNATIONAL TRIBUNAL FOR THE FORMER YUGOSLAVIA

ANNEX II

ARTICLE 13*bis*

ELECTION OF PERMANENT JUDGES

C4–065   1. Fourteen of the permanent judges of the International Tribunal shall be elected by the General Assembly from a list submitted by the Security Council, in the following manner:

(a) The Secretary-General shall invite nominations for judges of the International Tribunal from States Members of the United Nations and non-member States maintaining permanent observer missions at United Nations Headquarters;

(b) Within sixty days of the date of the invitation of the Secretary-General, each State may nominate up to two candidates meeting the qualifications set out in article 13 of the Statute, no two of whom shall be of the same nationality and neither of whom shall be of the same nationality as any judge who is a member of the Appeals Chamber and who was elected or appointed a permanent judge of the International Criminal Tribunal for the Prosecution of Persons Responsible for Genocide and Other Serious Violations of International Humanitarian Law Committed in the Territory of Rwanda and Rwandan Citizens Responsible for Genocide and Other Such Violations Committed in the Territory of Neighbouring States, between 1 January 1994 and 31 December 1994 (hereinafter referred to as "The International Tribunal for Rwanda") in accordance with article 12*bis* of the Statute of that Tribunal;

(c) The Secretary-General shall forward the nominations received to the Security Council. From the nominations received the Security Council shall establish a list of not less than twenty-eight and not more than forty-two candidates, taking due account of the adequate representation of the principal legal systems of the world;

(d) The President of the Security Council shall transmit the list of candidates to the President of the General Assembly. From that list the General Assembly shall elect fourteen permanent judges of the International Tribunal. The candidates who receive an absolute majority of the votes of the States Members of the United Nations and of the non-member States maintaining permanent observer missions at United Nations Headquarters, shall be declared elected. Should two candidates of the same nationality obtain the required majority vote, the one who received the higher number of votes shall be considered elected.

2. In the event of a vacancy in the Chambers amongst the permanent judges elected or appointed in accordance with this article, after consultation with the Presidents of the Security Council and of the General Assembly, the Secretary-General shall appoint a person meeting the qualifications of article 13 of the Statute, for the remainder of the term of office concerned.

3. The permanent judges elected in accordance with this article shall be elected for a term of four years. The terms and conditions of service shall be those of the judges of the International Court of Justice. They shall be eligible for re-election.

ARTICLE 14

OFFICERS AND MEMBERS OF THE CHAMBERS

1. The permanent judges of the International Tribunal shall elect a President from amongst their number. **C4–066**

2. The President of the International Tribunal shall be a member of the Appeals Chamber and shall preside over its proceedings.

3. After consultation with the permanent judges of the International Tribunal, the President shall assign four of the permanent judges elected or appointed in accordance with Article 13*bis* of the Statute to the Appeals Chamber and nine to the Trial Chambers.

4. Two of the permanent judges of the International Tribunal for Rwanda elected or appointed in accordance with article 12*bis* of the Statute of that Tribunal shall be assigned by the President of that Tribunal, in consultation with the President of the International Tribunal, to be members of the Appeals Chamber and permanent judges of the International Tribunal.

5. After consultation with the permanent judges of the International Tribunal, the President shall assign such *ad litem* judges as may from time to time be appointed to serve in the International Tribunal to the Trial Chambers.

6. A judge shall serve only in the Chamber to which he or she was assigned.

7. The permanent judges of each Trial Chamber shall elect a Presiding Judge from amongst their number, who shall oversee the work of the Trial Chamber as a whole.

RESOLUTION 1481 (2003)

ADOPTED BY THE SECURITY COUNCIL AT ITS 4759TH MEETING, ON 19 MAY 2003

The Security Council, **C4–067**

Reaffirming its resolutions 827 (1993) of 25 May 1993, 1166 (1998) of 13 May 1998, 1329 (2000) of 30 November 2000, 1411 (2002) of 17 May 2002 and 1431 (2002) of 14 August 2002,

Having considered the letter from the Secretary-General to the President of the Security Council dated 18 March 2002 (S/2002/304) and the annexed letter from the President of the International Tribunal for the Former Yugoslavia addressed to the Secretary-General dated 12 March 2002,

Having considered also the letter from the Secretary-General to the President of the Security Council dated 7 May 2003 (S/2003/530) and the annexed letter from the

President of the International Tribunal for the Former Yugoslavia addressed to the President of the Security Council dated 1 May 2003,

Convinced of the advisability of enhancing the powers of *ad litem* judges in the International Tribunal for the Former Yugoslavia so that, during the period of their appointment to a trial, they might also adjudicate in pre-trial proceedings in other cases, should the need arise and should they be in a position to do so,

Acting under Chapter VII of the Charter of the United Nations,

1. *Decides* to amend article 13 *quarter* of the Statute of the International Tribunal for the Former Yugoslavia and to replace that article with the provisions set out in the annex to this resolution;

2. *Decides* to remain seized of the matter.

ANNEX

ARTICLE 13*quarter*

STATUS OF *AD LITEM* JUDGES

C4–068   1. During the period in which they are appointed to serve in the International Tribunal, *ad litem* judges shall:

    (a) Benefit from the same terms and conditions of service mutatis mutandis as the permanent judges of the International Tribunal;

    (b) Enjoy, subject to paragraph 2 below, the same powers as the permanent judges of the International Tribunal;

    (c) Enjoy the privileges and immunities, exemptions and facilities of a judge of the International Tribunal;

    (d) **Enjoy the power to adjudicate in pre-trial proceedings in cases other than those that they have been appointed to try**.

2. During the period in which they are appointed to serve in the International Tribunal, *ad litem* judges shall not:

    (a) Be eligible for election as, or to vote in the election of, the President of the Tribunal or the Presiding Judge of a Trial Chamber pursuant to article 14 of the Statute;

    (b) Have power:

        (i) To adopt rules of procedure and evidence pursuant to article 15 of the Statute. They shall, however, be consulted before the adoption of those rules;

        (ii) To review an indictment pursuant to article 19 of the Statute;

        (iii) To consult with the President in relation to the assignment of judges pursuant to article 14 of the Statute or in relation to a pardon or commutation of sentence pursuant to article 28 of the Statute.

RESOLUTION 1503 (2003)

ADOPTED BY THE SECURITY COUNCIL AT ITS 4817TH MEETING, ON 28 AUGUST 2003

C4–069   *The Security Council*,

Recalling its resolutions 827 (1993) of 25 May 1993, 955 (1994) of 8 November 1994, 978 (1995) of 27 February 1995, 1165 (1998) of 30 April 1998, 1166 (1998) of 13 May 1998, 1329 (2000) of 30 November 2000, 1411 (2002) of 17 May 2002, 1431 (2002) of 14 August 2002, and 1481 (2003) of 19 May 2003,

Noting the letter from the Secretary-General to the President of the Security Council dated 28 July 2003 (S/2003/766),

Commending the important work of the International Criminal Tribunal for the Former Yugoslavia (ICTY) and the International Criminal Tribunal for Rwanda (ICTR) in contributing to lasting peace and security in the former Yugoslavia and Rwanda and the progress made since their inception,

Noting that an essential prerequisite to achieving the objectives of the ICTY and ICTR Completion Strategies is full cooperation by all States, especially in apprehending all remaining at-large persons indicted by the ICTY and the ICTR,

Welcoming steps taken by States in the Balkans and the Great Lakes region of Africa to improve cooperation and apprehend at-large persons indicted by the ICTY and ICTR, but noting with concern that certain States are still not offering full cooperation,

Urging Member States to consider imposing measures against individuals and groups or organizations assisting indictees at large to continue to evade justice, including measures designed to restrict the travel and freeze the assets of such individuals, groups, or organizations,

Recalling and reaffirming in the strongest terms the statement of 23 July 2002 made by the President of the Security Council (S/PRST/2002/21), which endorsed the ICTY's strategy for completing investigations by the end of 2004, all trial activities at first instance by the end of 2008, and all of its work in 2010 (ICTY Completion Strategy) (S/2002/678), by concentrating on the prosecution and trial of the most senior leaders suspected of being most responsible for crimes within the ICTY's jurisdiction and transferring cases involving those who may not bear this level of responsibility to competent national jurisdictions, as appropriate, as well as the strengthening of the capacity of such jurisdictions,

Urging the ICTR to formalize a detailed strategy, modelled on the ICTY Completion Strategy, to transfer cases involving intermediate- and lower-rank accused to competent national jurisdictions, as appropriate, including Rwanda, in order to allow the ICTR to achieve its objective of completing investigations by the end of 2004, all trial activities at first instance by the end of 2008, and all of its work in 2010 (ICTR Completion Strategy),

Noting that the above-mentioned Completion Strategies in no way alter the obligation of Rwanda and the countries of the former Yugoslavia to investigate those accused whose cases would not be tried by the ICTR or ICTY and take appropriate action with respect to indictment and prosecution, while bearing in mind the primacy of the ICTY and ICTR over national courts,

Noting that the strengthening of national judicial systems is crucially important to the rule of law in general and to the implementation of the ICTY and ICTR Completion Strategies in particular,

Noting that an essential prerequisite to achieving the objectives of the ICTY Completion Strategy is the expeditious establishment under the auspices of the High Representative and early functioning of a special chamber within the State Court of Bosnia and Herzegovina (the "War Crimes Chamber") and the subsequent referral by the ICTY of cases of lower-or intermediate-rank accused to the Chamber,

Convinced that the ICTY and the ICTR can most efficiently and expeditiously meet their respective responsibilities if each has its own Prosecutor,

Acting under Chapter VII of the Charter of the United Nations,

1. *Calls* on the international community to assist national jurisdictions, as part of the completion strategy, in improving their capacity to prosecute cases transferred from the ICTY and the ICTR and encourages the ICTY and ICTR Presidents, Prosecutors, and Registrars to develop and improve their outreach programmes;

2. *Calls* on all States, especially Serbia and Montenegro, Croatia, and Bosnia and Herzegovina, and on the Republika Srpska within Bosnia and Herzegovina, to intensify cooperation with and render all necessary assistance to the ICTY, particularly to bring Radovan Karadzic and Ratko Mladic, as well as Ante Gotovina and all other indictees to the ICTY and calls on these and all other at-large indictees of the ICTY to surrender to the ICTY;

3. *Calls* on all States, especially Rwanda, Kenya, the Democratic Republic of the Congo, and the Republic of the Congo, to intensify cooperation with and render all necessary assistance to the ICTR, including on investigations of the Rwandan Patriotic Army and efforts to bring Felicien Kabuga and all other such indictees to the ICTR and calls on this and all other at-large indictees of the ICTR to surrender to the ICTR;

4. *Calls* on all States to cooperate with the International Criminal Police Organization (ICPO-Interpol) in apprehending and transferring persons indicted by the ICTY and the ICTR;

5. *Calls* on the donor community to support the work of the High Representative to Bosnia and Herzegovina in creating a special chamber, within the State Court of Bosnia and Herzegovina, to adjudicate allegations of serious violations of international humanitarian law;

6. *Requests* the Presidents of the ICTY and the ICTR and their Prosecutors, in their annual reports to the Council, to explain their plans to implement the ICTY and ICTR Completion Strategies;

7. *Calls* on the ICTY and the ICTR to take all possible measures to complete investigations by the end of 2004, to complete all trial activities at first instance by the end of 2008, and to complete all work in 2010 (the Completion Strategies);

8. *Decides* to amend Article 15 of the Statute of the International Tribunal for Rwanda and to replace that Article with the provision set out in Annex I to this resolution, and requests the Secretary-General to nominate a person to be the Prosecutor of the ICTR;

9. *Welcomes* the intention expressed by the Secretary-General in his letter dated 28 July 2003, to submit to the Security Council the name of Mrs. Carla Del Ponte as nominee for Prosecutor for the ICTY;

10. *Decides* to remain actively seized of the matter.

ANNEX I

ARTICLE 15

THE PROSECUTOR

C4–070   1. The Prosecutor shall be responsible for the investigation and prosecution of persons responsible for serious violations of international humanitarian law committed in the territory of Rwanda and Rwandan citizens responsible for such violations committed in the territory of neighbouring States, between 1 January 1994 and 31 December 1994.

2. The Prosecutor shall act independently as a separate organ of the International Tribunal for Rwanda. He or she shall not seek or receive instructions from any government or from any other source.

3. The Office of the Prosecutor shall be composed of a Prosecutor and such other qualified staff as may be required.

4. The Prosecutor shall be appointed by the Security Council on nomination by the Secretary-General. He or she shall be of high moral character and possess the highest level of competence and experience in the conduct of investigations and prosecutions of criminal cases. The Prosecutor shall serve for a four-year term and be eligible for reappointment. The terms and conditions of service of the Prosecutor shall be those of an Under-Secretary-General of the United Nations.

5. The staff of the Office of the Prosecutor shall be appointed by the Secretary-General on the recommendation of the Prosecutor.

RESOLUTION 1504 (2003)

ADOPTED BY THE SECURITY COUNCIL AT ITS 4819TH MEETING, ON 4 SEPTEMBER 2003

C4–071   *The Security Council,*

Recalling its resolution 1503 (2003) of 28 August 2003,

Noting that by that resolution the Council created a new position of Prosecutor for the International Tribunal for Rwanda,

Noting that by its resolution 1503 (2003) the Council welcomed the intention of the Secretary-General to submit to the Council the name of Mrs. Carla Del Ponte as nominee for Prosecutor for the International Tribunal for the Former Yugoslavia,

Having regard to Article 16(4) of the Statute of the International Tribunal for the Former Yugoslavia,

Having considered the nomination by the Secretary-General of Mrs. Carla Del Ponte as Prosecutor of the International Tribunal for the Former Yugoslavia,

Appoints Mrs. Carla Del Ponte as Prosecutor of the International Tribunal for the Former Yugoslavia with effect from 15 September 2003 for a four-year term.

RESOLUTION 1534 (2004)

ADOPTED BY THE SECURITY COUNCIL AT ITS 4935TH MEETING, ON 26 MARCH 2004

The Security Council,   **C4–072**

Recalling its resolutions 827 (1993) of 25 May 1993, 955 (1994) of 8 November 1994, 978 (1995) of 27 February 1995, 1165 (1998) of 30 April 1998, 1166 (1998) of 13 May 1998, 1329 (2000) of 30 November 2000, 1411 (2002) of 17 May 2002, 1431 (2002) of 14 August 2002, and 1481 (2003) of 19 May 2003,

Recalling and reaffirming in the strongest terms the statement of 23 July 2002 made by the President of the Security Council (S/PRST/2002/21) endorsing the ICTY's completion strategy and its resolution 1503 (2003) of 28 August 2003,

Recalling that resolution 1503 (2003) called on the International Criminal Tribunal for the Former Yugoslavia (ICTY) and the International Criminal Tribunal for Rwanda (ICTR) to take all possible measures to complete investigations by the end of 2004, to complete all trial activities at first instance by the end of 2008, and to complete all work in 2010 (the Completion Strategies), and requested the Presidents and Prosecutors of the ICTY and ICTR, in their annual reports to the Council, to explain their plans to implement the Completion Strategies,

Welcoming the presentations made by the ICTY and ICTR Presidents and Prosecutors to the Security Council on 9 October 2003,

Commending the important work of both Tribunals in contributing to lasting peace and security and national reconciliation and the progress made since their inception, commending them on their efforts so far to give effect to the Completion Strategies and calling on them to ensure effective and efficient use of their budgets, with accountability,

Reiterating its support for the ICTY and ICTR Prosecutors in their continuing efforts to bring at large indictees before the ICTY and the ICTR,

Noting with concern the problems highlighted in the presentations to the Security Council on 9 October 2003 in securing adequate regional cooperation,

Also noting with concern indications in the presentations made on 9 October, that it might not be possible to implement the Completion Strategies set out in resolution 1503 (2003),

Acting under Chapter VII of the Charter of the United Nations,

1. *Reaffirms* the necessity of trial of persons indicted by the ICTY and reiterates its call on all States, especially Serbia and Montenegro, Croatia and Bosnia and Herzegovina, and on the Republika Srpska within Bosnia and Herzegovina, to intensify cooperation with and render all necessary assistance to the ICTY, particularly to bring Radovan Karadzic and Ratko Mladic, as well as Ante Gotovina and all other indictees to the ICTY and calls on all at-large indictees of the ICTY to surrender to the ICTY;

2. *Reaffirms* the necessity of trial of persons indicted by the ICTR and reiterates its call on all States, especially Rwanda, Kenya, the Democratic Republic of the Congo and the Republic of the Congo to intensify cooperation with and render all necessary assistance to the ICTR, including on investigations of the Rwandan Patriotic Army and efforts to bring Felicien Kabuga and all other such indictees to the ICTR and calls on all at-large indictees of the ICTR to surrender to the ICTR;

3. *Emphasizes* the importance of fully implementing the Completion Strategies, as set out in paragraph 7 of resolution 1503 (2003), that calls on the ICTY and ICTR to take all possible measures to complete investigations by the end of 2004, to complete all trial activities at first instance by the end of 2008 and to complete all work in 2010, and urges each Tribunal to plan and act accordingly;

4. *Calls* on the ICTY and ICTR Prosecutors to review the case load of the ICTY and ICTR respectively in particular with a view to determining which cases should be proceeded with and which should be transferred to competent national jurisdictions, as well as the measures which will need to be taken to meet the Completion Strategies referred to in resolution 1503 (2003) and urges them to carry out this review as soon as possible and to include a progress report in the assessments to be provided to the Council under paragraph 6 of this resolution;

5. *Calls* on each Tribunal, in reviewing and confirming any new indictments, to ensure that any such indictments concentrate on the most senior leaders suspected of being most responsible for crimes within the jurisdiction of the relevant Tribunal as set out in resolution 1503 (2003);

6. *Requests* each Tribunal to provide to the Council, by 31 May 2004 and every six months thereafter, assessments by its President and Prosecutor, setting out in detail the progress made towards implementation of the Completion Strategy of the Tribunal, explaining what measures have been taken to implement the Completion Strategy and what measures remain to be taken, including the transfer of cases involving intermediate and lower rank accused to competent national jurisdictions; and expresses the intention of the Council to meet with the President and Prosecutor of each Tribunal to discuss these assessments;

7. *Declares* the Council's determination to review the situation, and in the light of the assessments received under the foregoing paragraph to ensure that the time frames set out in the Completion Strategies and endorsed by resolution 1503 (2003) can be met;

8. *Commends* those States which have concluded agreements for the enforcement of sentences of persons convicted by the ICTY or the ICTR or have otherwise accepted such convicted persons to serve their sentences in their respective territories; encourages other States in a position to do so to act likewise; and invites the ICTY and the ICTR to continue and intensify their efforts to conclude further agreements for the enforcement of sentences or to obtain the cooperation of other States in this regard;

9. *Recalls* that the strengthening of competent national judicial systems is crucially important to the rule of law in general and to the implementation of the ICTY and ICTR Completion Strategies in particular;

10. *Welcomes* in particular the efforts of the Office of the High Representative, ICTY, and the donor community to create a war crimes chamber in Sarajevo; encourages all parties to continue efforts to establish the chamber expeditiously; and encourages the donor community to provide sufficient financial support to ensure the success of domestic prosecutions in Bosnia and Herzegovina and in the region;

11. *Decides* to remain actively seized of the matter.

C5. Statements by the President of the Security Council

JULY 23, 2002

At the 4582nd meeting of the Security Council, held on 23 July 2002, in connection **C5–001** with the Council's consideration of the item entitled "International Tribunal for the Prosecution of Persons Responsible for Serious Violations of International Humanitarian Law Committed in the Territory of the Former Yugoslavia since 1991", the President of the Security Council made the following statement on behalf of the Council.

"The Security Council welcomes the report on the judicial status of the International Criminal Tribunal for the Former Yugoslavia and the prospects for referring certain cases to national courts (S/2002/678) submitted by the President of the Tribunal on 10 June 2002.

"The Council recognizes, as it has done on other occasions (for example in its resolution 1329 (2000) of 30 November 2000), that the ICTY should concentrate its work on the prosecution and trial of the civilian, military and paramilitary leaders suspected of being responsible for serious violations of international humanitarian law committed in the territory of the former Yugoslavia since 1991, rather than on minor actors.

"The Security Council therefore endorses the report's broad strategy for the transfer of cases involving intermediary and lower-level accused to competent national jurisdictions as likely to be in practice the best way of allowing the ICTY to achieve its current objective of completing all trial activities at first instance by 2008. The Council invites States and relevant international and regional organizations to contribute as appropriate to the strengthening of national judicial systems of the States of the former Yugoslavia in order to facilitate the implementation of this policy.

"The Security Council takes note of the recommendations of the ICTY with regard to the creation, as proposed by the High Representative to Bosnia and Herzegovina, of a specific Chamber, within the State Court of Bosnia and Herzegovina, to deal with serious violations of international humanitarian law. The Security Council is ready to look constructively and positively at this matter when more details of the proposed arrangements are available. The Council also takes note of the intention of the ICTY to amend its Rules of Procedure and Evidence in order to facilitate the referral of cases to competent national jurisdictions.

"The Security Council will remain seized of this matter."

MAY 8, 1996

At the 3663rd meeting of the Security Council, held on 8 May 1996 in connection with **C5–002** the Council's consideration of the item entitled "International Tribunal for the Prosecution of Persons Responsible for Serious Violations of International Humanitarian Law Committed in the Territory of the Former Yugoslavia", the President of the Security Council made the following statement on behalf of the Council:

"The Security Council expresses its profound concern at recent instances of failure to cooperate with the International Tribunal established pursuant to resolution 827 (1993) of 25 May 1993, and in particular the failure of cooperation by the Federal Republic of Yugoslavia described in the letter of 24 April 1996 from the President of the Tribunal to the President of the Council (S/1996/319).

"The Security Council recalls its decision in resolution 827 (1993) that all States shall cooperate fully with the International Tribunal and its organs in accordance with that resolution and the Statute of the Tribunal and that consequently all States shall take any measures necessary under their domestic law to implement the provisions of the resolution and the Statute, including the obligation of States to comply with requests for assistance or orders issued by Trial Chamber under Article 29 of the Statute. The Council underlines the importance of these obligations, as well as the obligations undertaken by the parties to the General Framework Agreement for Peace in Bosnia and Herzegovina and the annexes thereto (the Peace Agreement, S/1995/999, annex) to cooperate fully with the International Tribunal.

"The Security Council deplores the failure to date of the Federal Republic of Yugoslavia to execute the arrest warrants issued by the Tribunal against the three individuals referred to in the letter of 24 April 1996, and calls for the execution of those arrest warrants without delay.

"The Security Council calls upon all States and others concerned to comply fully with their obligations with respect to cooperation with the Tribunal, and in particular their obligation to execute arrest warrants transmitted to them by the Tribunal. It recalls the provisions of its resolution 1022 (1995) of 22 November 1995 which notes *inter alia* that compliance with the requests and orders of the Tribunal constitutes an essential aspect of implementing the Peace Agreement. The Council calls upon all States which have not already done so to make provision in their domestic law enabling them to comply fully with their obligations with respect to cooperation with the Tribunal.

"The Security Council will remain seized of the matter."

OCTOBER 27, 2003

C5–003   At the 4849th meeting of the Security Council, held on 27 October 2003, in connection with the Council's consideration of the item entitled "International Criminal Tribunal for the Prosecution of Persons Responsible for Genocide and Other Serious Violations of International Humanitarian Law Committed in the Territory of Rwanda and Rwandan Citizens Responsible for Genocide and Other Such Violations Committed in the Territory of Neighbouring States between 1 January and 31 December 1994", the President of the Security Council made the following statement on behalf of the Council:

"The Security Council notes the invitation of the General Assembly contained in operative paragraph 7 of its resolution 57/289 of 20 December 2002 that it address uncertainties regarding the power of the International Tribunal for Rwanda under its Statute to finance the upgrading of prison accommodation in which persons convicted by the Tribunal are to serve their sentences.

"The Security Council confirms that it is within the lawful powers of the International Tribunal for Rwanda under its Statute to fund the renovation and refurbishment of prison facilities in States that have concluded agreements with the United Nations for the carrying out of prison sentences of the Tribunal. Such funds shall be used to bring up to international minimum standards the prison accommodation to be occupied or used pursuant to those agreements.

"The Security Council will remain seized of this matter."

AUGUST 4, 2004

C5–004   At the 5016th meeting of the Security Council, held on 4 August 2004, in connection with the Council's consideration of the item entitled "International Tribunal for the Prosecution of Persons Responsible for Serious Violations of International Humanitarian Law Committed in the Territory of the Former Yugoslavia since 1991; International Criminal Tribunal for the Prosecution of Persons Responsible for Genocide and Other Serious Violations of International Humanitarian Law Committed in the Territory of Rwanda and Rwandan Citizens Responsible for Genocide and Other Such Violations Committed in the Territory of Neighbouring States, between 1 January 1994 and 31 December 1994", the President of the Security Council made the following statement on behalf of the Council:

"The Security Council takes note of the letter dated 21 May 2004 from the President of the International Tribunal for the Prosecution of Persons Responsible for Serious Violations of International Humanitarian Law Committed in the Territory of the Former Yugoslavia since 1991 (ICTY) addressed to the President of the Security Council (S/2004/420).

"The Security Council also takes note of the letter dated 30 April 2004 from the President of the International Criminal Tribunal for the Prosecution of Persons Responsible for Genocide and Other Serious Violations of International Humanitarian Law Committed in the Territory of Rwanda and Rwandan Citizens Responsible for Genocide and Other Such Violations Committed in the Territory of Neighbouring States between 1 January and 31 December 1994 (ICTR) addressed to the President of the Security Council (S/2004/341).

"The Security Council thanks the Presidents and Prosecutors of the ICTY and ICTR for these assessments requested by its resolution 1534 (2004), as supplemented by their oral reports at the 4999th meeting of the Security Council on 29 June 2004.

"The Security Council reaffirms its support for the ICTY and the ICTR and welcomes the efforts of both Tribunals to carry out their Completion Strategies. The Council strongly encourages the Tribunals to undertake every effort to ensure that they remain on track to meet the target dates of the Completion Strategies.

"The Security Council stresses that the full cooperation of all States with the Tribunals is not only a mandatory obligation of all States under its resolutions 827 (1993) and 955 (1994) and the Statutes of the Tribunals, but also is an essential element in realizing the Completion Strategies. In this regard the Council takes careful note of the assessments presented with respect to the level of cooperation by the authorities of Serbia and Montenegro and the Republika Srpska within Bosnia and Herzegovina with the ICTY. We welcome as well the commitments made by the new government in Serbia regarding cooperation with the ICTY. The Council takes note of developments in Croatian and Rwandan cooperation with the ICTY and ICTR respectively.

"The Security Council reiterates its call on all States, especially Serbia and Montenegro, Croatia, Bosnia and Herzegovina, and on the Republika Srpska within Bosnia and Herzegovina, to intensify cooperation with and render all necessary assistance to the ICTY, particularly to bring Radovan Karadzic and Ratko Mladic, as well as Ante Gotovina and all other such indictees to the ICTY.

"The Security Council reiterates its call on all States, especially Rwanda, Kenya, the Democratic Republic of the Congo, and the Republic of the Congo, to intensify cooperation with and render all necessary assistance to the ICTR, including on investigations of the Rwandan Patriotic Army and efforts to bring Felicien Kabuga and all other such indictees to the ICTR.

"The Security Council notes with concern that the shortfall in financial contributions from Member States is having a disruptive effect on the work of the Tribunals and urges Member States to fulfil their commitments in a timely manner.

"The Security Council emphasizes the importance of the referral of cases involving lower and intermediate rank accused to competent national jurisdictions in achieving the Completion Strategies, and recalls the provisions of its resolutions 1503 (2003) and 1534 (2004), including the call for assistance to ensure the success of this effort.

"The Security Council also notes the concerns expressed by the President of the ICTY on the effect the expiry of the terms of Permanent Judges may have on case management and takes note of the letter of 15 July 2004 from the Acting Legal Counsel bringing forward an invitation to Member States to submit nominations for Permanent Judges of the International Tribunal for the Former Yugoslavia before 13 September 2004.

"The Security Council encourages further dialogue between the Tribunals and its Working Group on matters of mutual concern.

"The Security Council will remain seized of the matter."

C6. Rules of Procedure and Evidence

(Adopted On 11 February 1994)
(As Amended 5 May 1994)
(As Further Amended 4 October 1994)
(As Revised 30 January 1995)
(As Amended 3 May 1995)
(As Further Amended 15 June 1995)
(As Amended 6 October 1995)
(As Further Amended 18 January 1996)
(As Amended 23 April 1996)
(As Amended 25 June and 5 July 1996)
(As Amended 3 December 1996)
(As Further Amended 25 July 1997)
(As Revised 12 November 1997)
(As Amended 10 July 1998)
(As Amended 4 December 1998)
(As Amended 25 February 1999)
(As Amended 2 July 1999)
(As Amended 17 November 1999)
(As Amended 14 July 2000)
(As Amended 1 and 13 December 2000)
(As Amended 12 April 2001)
(As Amended 12 July 2001)
(As Amended 13 December 2001)
(Incorporating IT/32/Rev. 22/Corr.1)
(As Amended 23 April 2002)
(As Amended 12 July 2002)
(As Amended 10 October 2002)
(As Amended 12 December 2002)
(As Amended 24 June 2003)
(As Amended 17 July 2003)
(As Amended 12 December 2003)
(As Amended 6 April 2004)
(As Amended 10 June 2004)
(As Amended 28 July 2004)
(As Amended 8 December 2004)
(As Amended 11 February 2005)
(As Amended 11 March 2005)
(As Amended 21 July 2005)

IT/32/Rev. 36

Contents

PART ONE GENERAL PROVISIONS

PART EIGHT REVIEW PROCEEDINGS

Rule 119 Request for Review
Rule 120 Preliminary Examination
Rule 121 Appeals
Rule 122 Return of Case to Trial Chamber

PART NINE PARDON AND COMMUTATION OF SENTENCE

Rule 123 Notification by States
Rule 124 Determination by the President
Rule 125 General Standards for Granting Pardon or Commutation

PART TEN TIME

Rule 126 General Provisions
Rule 126*bis* Time for Filing Responses to Motions
Rule 127 Variation of Time-limits

Part One

GENERAL PROVISIONS

Rule 1

ENTRY INTO FORCE

(Adopted 11 Feb 1994)

These Rules of Procedure and Evidence, adopted pursuant to Article 15 of the Statute **C6–001**
of the Tribunal, shall come into force on 14 March 1994.

Rule 2

DEFINITIONS

(Adopted 11 Feb 1994)

A. In the Rules, unless the context otherwise requires, the following terms shall mean:

Rules: The Rules of Procedure and Evidence in force;
(Amended 25 July 1997)

Statute: The Statute of the Tribunal adopted by Security Council resolution 827 of 25 May 1993;

Tribunal: The International Tribunal for the Prosecution of Persons Responsible for Serious Violations of International Humanitarian Law Committed in the Territory of the Former Yugoslavia since 1991, established by Security Council resolution 827 of 25 May 1993.

* * *

Accused: A person against whom one or more counts in an indictment have been **C6–002**
confirmed in accordance with Rule 47; (Amended 25 July 1997)

1485

Ad litem Judge: A Judge appointed pursuant to Article 13*ter* of the Statute; (Amended 12 Apr 2001)

Arrest: The act of taking a suspect or an accused into custody pursuant to a warrant of arrest or under Rule 40;
(Amended 25 July 1997)

Bureau: A body composed of the President, the Vice-President and the Presiding Judges of the Trial Chambers;

Defence: The accused, and/or the accused's counsel;
(Amended 17 Nov 1999)

Investigation: All activities undertaken by the Prosecutor under the Statute and the Rules for the collection of information and evidence, whether before or after an indictment is confirmed; (Amended 25 July 1997)

Parties: The Prosecutor and the Defence; (Amended 17 Nov 1999)

Permanent Judge: A Judge elected or appointed pursuant to Article 13*bis* of the Statute; (Amended 12 Apr 2001)

President: The President of the Tribunal;

Prosecutor: The Prosecutor appointed pursuant to Article 16 of the Statute;

Regulations: The provisions framed by the Prosecutor pursuant to Rule 37 (A) for the purpose of directing the functions of the Office of the Prosecutor; (Revised 30 Jan 1995, revised 12 Nov 1997)

State:
    (i) A State Member or non-Member of the United Nations;
    (ii) an entity recognised by the constitution of Bosnia and Herzegovina, namely, the Federation of Bosnia and Herzegovina and the Republic Srpska; or
    (iii) a self-proclaimed entity de facto exercising governmental functions, whether recognised as a State or not;
(Revised 30 Jan 1995, amended 12 Dec 2002)

Suspect: A person concerning whom the Prosecutor possesses reliable information which tends to show that the person may have committed a crime over which the Tribunal has jurisdiction; (Revised 30 Jan 1995, revised 12 Nov 1997)

Transaction: A number of acts or omissions whether occurring as one event or a number of events, at the same or different locations and being part of a common scheme, strategy or plan;

Victim: A person against whom a crime over which the Tribunal has jurisdiction has allegedly been committed.

B. In the Rules, the masculine shall include the feminine and the singular the plural, and vice-versa.

RULE 3

LANGUAGES

(Adopted 11 Feb 1994)

C6–003   (A) The working languages of the Tribunal shall be English and French.

(B) An accused shall have the right to use his or her own language. (Revised 12 Nov 1997)

(C) Other persons appearing before the Tribunal, other than as counsel, who do not have sufficient knowledge of either of the two working languages, may use their own language. (Revised 30 Jan 1995, revised 12 Nov 1997)

(D) Counsel for an accused may apply to the Presiding Judge of a Chamber for leave to use a language other than the two working ones or the language of the accused. If such leave is granted, the expenses of interpretation and translation shall be borne by the Tribunal to the extent, if any, determined by the President, taking into account the rights of the defence and the interests of justice.

(E) The Registrar shall make any necessary arrangements for interpretation and translation into and from the working languages.

(F) If:
  (i) a party is required to take any action within a specified time after the filing or service of a document by another party; and
  (ii) pursuant to the Rules, that document is filed in a language other than one of the working languages of the Tribunal,

time shall not run until the party required to take action has received from the Registrar a translation of the document into one of the working languages of the Tribunal. (Amended 25 July 1997)

RULE 4

MEETINGS AWAY FROM THE SEAT OF THE TRIBUNAL

(Adopted 11 Feb 1994)

A Chamber may exercise its functions at a place other than the seat of the Tribunal, if **C6–004** so authorised by the President in the interests of justice.

RULE 5

NON-COMPLIANCE WITH RULES

(Adopted 11 Feb 1994, revised 30 Jan 1995)

(A) Where an objection on the ground of non-compliance with the Rules or Regu- **C6–005** lations is raised by a party at the earliest opportunity, the Trial Chamber shall grant relief if it finds that the alleged non-compliance is proved and that it has caused material prejudice to that party. (Revised 12 Nov 1997)

(B) Where such an objection is raised otherwise than at the earliest opportunity, the Trial Chamber may in its discretion grant relief if it finds that the alleged non-compliance is proved and that it has caused material prejudice to the objecting party. (Revised 12 Nov 1997)

(C) The relief granted by a Trial Chamber under this Rule shall be such remedy as the Trial Chamber considers appropriate to ensure consistency with the fundamental principles of fairness. (Revised 12 Nov 1997)

RULE 6

AMENDMENT OF THE RULES

(Adopted 11 Feb 1994)

(A) Proposals for amendment of the Rules may be made by a Judge, the Prosecutor or **C6–006** the Registrar and shall be adopted if agreed to by not less than ten permanent Judges at a plenary meeting of the Tribunal convened with notice of the proposal addressed to all Judges. (Amended 4 Dec 1998, amended 12 Apr 2001)

(B) An amendment to the Rules may be otherwise adopted, provided it is unanimously approved by the permanent Judges. (Amended 12 Apr 2001)

(C) Proposals for amendment of the Rules may otherwise be made in accordance with the Practice Direction issued by the President. (Amended 4 Dec 1998)

(D) An amendment shall enter into force seven days after the date of issue of an official Tribunal document containing the amendment, but shall not operate to prejudice the rights of the accused or of a convicted or acquitted person in any pending case. (Amended 4 Dec 1998, amended 1 Dec 2000 and 13 Dec 2000)

RULE 7

AUTHENTIC TEXTS

(Adopted 11 Feb 1994)

C6–007   The English and French texts of the Rules shall be equally authentic. In case of discrepancy, the version which is more consonant with the spirit of the Statute and the Rules shall prevail.

PART TWO

PRIMACY OF THE TRIBUNAL

RULE 7*bis*

NON-COMPLIANCE WITH OBLIGATIONS

(Adopted 25 July 1997)

C6–008   (A) In addition to cases to which Rule 11, Rule 13, Rule 59 or Rule 61 applies, where a Trial Chamber or a permanent Judge is satisfied that a State has failed to comply with an obligation under Article 29 of the Statute which relates to any proceedings before that Chamber or Judge, the Chamber or Judge may advise the President, who shall report the matter to the Security Council. (Amended 12 Apr 2001)

(B) If the Prosecutor satisfies the President that a State has failed to comply with an obligation under Article 29 of the Statute in respect of a request by the Prosecutor under Rule 8, Rule 39 or Rule 40, the President shall notify the Security Council thereof.

RULE 8

REQUEST FOR INFORMATION

(Adopted 11 Feb 1994, revised 30 Jan 1995, revised 12 Nov 1997)

C6–009   Where it appears to the Prosecutor that a crime within the jurisdiction of the Tribunal is or has been the subject of investigations or criminal proceedings instituted in the courts of any State, the Prosecutor may request the State to forward all relevant information in that respect, and the State shall transmit such information to the Prosecutor forthwith in accordance with Article 29 of the Statute.

RULE 9

PROSECUTOR'S REQUEST FOR DEFERRAL

(Adopted 11 Feb 1994)

C6–010   Where it appears to the Prosecutor that in any such investigations or criminal proceedings instituted in the courts of any State:

(i) the act being investigated or which is the subject of those proceedings is characterized as an ordinary crime;

(ii) there is a lack of impartiality or independence, or the investigations or proceedings are designed to shield the accused from international criminal responsibility, or the case is not diligently prosecuted; or

(iii) what is in issue is closely related to, or otherwise involves, significant factual or legal questions which may have implications for investigations or prosecutions before the Tribunal,

the Prosecutor may propose to the Trial Chamber designated by the President that a formal request be made that such court defer to the competence of the Tribunal. (Revised 30 Jan 1995)

RULE 10

FORMAL REQUEST FOR DEFERRAL

(Adopted 11 Feb 1994)

(A) If it appears to the Trial Chamber seised of a proposal for deferral that, on any of the grounds specified in Rule 9, deferral is appropriate, the Trial Chamber may issue a formal request to the State concerned that its court defer to the competence of the Tribunal. (Revised 30 Jan 1995) **C6–011**

(B) A request for deferral shall include a request that the results of the investigation and a copy of the court's records and the judgement, if already delivered, be forwarded to the Tribunal.

(C) Where deferral to the Tribunal has been requested by a Trial Chamber, any subsequent trial shall be held before another Trial Chamber. (Amended 3 May 1995, amended 17 Nov 1999)

RULE 11

NON-COMPLIANCE WITH A REQUEST FOR DEFERRAL

(Adopted 11 Feb 1994, amended 25 July 1997)

If, within sixty days after a request for deferral has been notified by the Registrar to the State under whose jurisdiction the investigations or criminal proceedings have been instituted, the State fails to file a response which satisfies the Trial Chamber that the State has taken or is taking adequate steps to comply with the request, the Trial Chamber may request the President to report the matter to the Security Council. **C6–012**

RULE 11*bis*

REFERRAL OF THE INDICTMENT TO ANOTHER COURT

(Adopted 12 Nov 1997, revised 30 Sept 2002)

(A) After an indictment has been confirmed and prior to the commencement of trial, irrespective of whether or not the accused is in the custody of the Tribunal, the President may appoint a bench of three Permanent Judges selected from the Trial Chambers (hereinafter referred to as the "Referral Bench"), which solely and exclusively shall determine whether the case should be referred to the authorities of a State: **C6–013**

(i) in whose territory the crime was committed; or

(ii) in which the accused was arrested; or

(Amended 10 June 2004)

(iii) having jurisdiction and being willing and adequately prepared to accept such a case,

    (Amended 10 June 2004)

so that those authorities should forthwith refer the case to the appropriate court for trial within that State. (Revised 30 Sept 2002, amended 11 Feb 2005)

(B) The Referral Bench may order such referral proprio motu or at the request of the Prosecutor, after having given to the Prosecutor and, where applicable, the accused, the opportunity to be heard and after being satisfied that the accused will receive a fair trial and that the death penalty will not be imposed or carried out. (Revised 30 Sept 2002, amended 10 June 2004, amended 11 Feb 2005)

(C) In determining whether to refer the case in accordance with paragraph (A), the Referral Bench shall, in accordance with Security Council resolution 1534 (2004) , consider the gravity of the crimes charged and the level of responsibility of the accused. (Revised 30 Sept 2002, amended 28 July 2004, amended 11 Feb 2005)

(D) Where an order is issued pursuant to this Rule:

  (i) the accused, if in the custody of the Tribunal, shall be handed over to the authorities of the State concerned;

 (ii) the Referral Bench may order that protective measures for certain witnesses or victims remain in force;

    (Amended 11 Feb 2005)

(iii) the Prosecutor shall provide to the authorities of the State concerned all of the information relating to the case which the Prosecutor considers appropriate and, in particular, the material supporting the indictment;

(iv) the Prosecutor may send observers to monitor the proceedings in the national courts on her behalf. (Revised 30 Sept 2002)

(E) The Referral Bench may issue a warrant for the arrest of the accused, which shall specify the State to which he is to be transferred to trial. (Revised 30 Sept 2002, amended 11 Feb 2005)

(F) At any time after an order has been issued pursuant to this Rule and before the accused is found guilty or acquitted by a national court, the Referral Bench may, at the request of the Prosecutor and upon having given to the State authorities concerned the opportunity to be heard, revoke the order and make a formal request for deferral within the terms of Rule 10. (Revised 30 Sept 2002, amended 11 Feb 2005)

(G) Where an order issued pursuant to this Rule is revoked by the Referral Bench, it may make a formal request to the State concerned to transfer the accused to the seat of the Tribunal and the State shall accede to such a request without delay in keeping with Article 29 of the Statute. The Referral Bench or a Judge may also issue a warrant for the arrest of the accused. (Revised 30 Sept 2002, amended 11 Feb 2005)

(H) A Referral Bench shall have the powers of, and insofar as applicable shall follow the procedures laid down for, a Trial Chamber under the Rules. (Amended 11 Feb 2005)

(I) An appeal by the accused or the Prosecutor shall lie as of right from a decision of the Referral Bench whether or not to refer a case. Notice of appeal shall be filed within fifteen days of the decision unless the accused was not present or represented when the decision was pronounced, in which case the time-limit shall run from the date on which the accused is notified of the decision. (Amended 11 Feb 2005)

RULE 12

DETERMINATIONS OF COURTS OF ANY STATE

(Adopted 11 Feb 1994, revised 30 Jan 1995, amended 10 July 1998)

C6–014　Subject to Article 10, paragraph 2, of the Statute, determinations of courts of any State are not binding on the Tribunal.

RULE 13

NON BIS IN IDEM

(Adopted 11 Feb 1994, revised 30 Jan 1995)

When the President receives reliable information to show that criminal proceedings **C6–015**
have been instituted against a person before a court of any State for a crime for which
that person has already been tried by the Tribunal, a Trial Chamber shall, following
mutatis mutandis the procedure provided in Rule 10, issue a reasoned order requesting
that court permanently to discontinue its proceedings. If that court fails to do so, the
President may report the matter to the Security Council.

PART THREE

ORGANIZATION OF THE TRIBUNAL

Section 1: The Judges

RULE 14

SOLEMN DECLARATION

(Adopted 11 Feb 1994)

(A) Before taking up duties each Judge shall make the following solemn declaration: **C6–016**
"I solemnly declare that I will perform my duties and exercise my powers as a Judge
of the International Tribunal for the Prosecution of Persons Responsible for Serious
Violations of International Humanitarian Law Committed in the Territory of the
Former Yugoslavia since 1991 honourably, faithfully, impartially and conscientiously". (Revised 12 Nov 1997)
(B) The declaration shall be signed by the Judge and witnessed by, or by a
representative of, the Secretary-General of the United Nations. The declaration shall be
kept in the records of the Tribunal. (Revised 12 Nov 1997)
(C) A Judge whose service continues without interruption after expiry of a previous
period of service shall not make a new declaration. (Revised 12 Nov 1997)

RULE 15

DISQUALIFICATION OF JUDGES

(Adopted 11 Feb 1994, amended 15 June 1995, amended 25 June 1996 and 5 July 1996, amended 25 July 1997, amended 17 Nov 1999)

(A) A Judge may not sit on a trial or appeal in any case in which the Judge has a
personal interest or concerning which the Judge has or has had any association which
might affect his or her impartiality. The Judge shall in any such circumstance withdraw,
and the President shall assign another Judge to the case.

(B) (i) Any party may apply to the Presiding Judge of a Chamber for the disqualification and withdrawal of a Judge of that Chamber from a trial or appeal upon the above grounds. The Presiding Judge shall confer with the Judge in question and report to the President. (Revised 30 Jan 1995)

(ii) Following the report of the Presiding Judge, the President shall, if necessary, appoint a panel of three Judges drawn from other Chambers to report to him its decision on the merits of the application. If the decision is to uphold the application, the President shall assign another Judge to sit in the place of the Judge in question.

(iii) The decision of the panel of three Judges shall not be subject to interlocutory appeal.

(iv) If the Judge in question is the President, the responsibility of the President in accordance with this paragraph shall be assumed by the Vice-President or, if he or she is not able to act in the application, by the permanent Judge most senior in precedence who is able to act. (Amended 21 July 2005)

(C) The Judge of the Trial Chamber who reviews an indictment against an accused, pursuant to Article 19 of the Statute and Rules 47 or 61, shall not be disqualified for sitting as a member of the Trial Chamber for the trial of that accused. Such a Judge shall also not be disqualified for sitting as a member of the Appeals Chamber to hear any appeal in that case. (Amended 6 Oct 1995, amended 2 July 1999, amended 17 Nov 1999, amended 1 Dec 2000 and 13 Dec 2000, amended 12 Dec 2002, amended 21 July 2005)

(D) (i) No Judge shall sit on any appeal in a case in which that Judge sat as a member of the Trial Chamber. (Amended 10 July 1998, amended 4 Dec 1998, amended 1 Dec 2000 and 13 Dec 2000, amended 12 Dec 2002, amended 21 July 2005)

(ii) No Judge shall sit on any State Request for Review pursuant to Rule 108*bis* in a matter in which that Judge sat as a member of the Trial Chamber whose decision is to be reviewed. (Amended 10 July 1998)

RULE 15*bis*

ABSENCE OF A JUDGE

(Adopted 17 Nov 1999)

C6–017　　(A) If

(i) a Judge is, for illness or other urgent personal reasons, or for reasons of authorised Tribunal business, unable to continue sitting in a part-heard case for a period which is likely to be of short duration, and

(Amended 1 Dec 2000 and 13 Dec 2000)

(ii) the remaining Judges of the Chamber are satisfied that it is in the interests of justice to do so, (Amended 12 Dec 2002)

those remaining Judges of the Chamber may order that the hearing of the case continue in the absence of that Judge for a period of not more than five working days.

(B) If

(i) a Judge is, for illness or urgent personal reasons, or for reasons of authorised Tribunal business, unable to continue sitting in a part-heard case for a period which is likely to be of short duration, and

(Amended 1 Dec 2000 and 13 Dec 2000)

(ii) the remaining Judges of the Chamber are not satisfied that it is in the interests of justice to order that the hearing of the case continue in the absence of that Judge, then

(a) those remaining Judges of the Chamber may nevertheless conduct those matters which they are satisfied it is in the interests of justice that they be disposed of notwithstanding the absence of that Judge, and

(b) the Presiding Judge may adjourn the proceedings.

(C) If, by reason of death, illness, resignation from the Tribunal, or non-reelection, a Judge is, for any reason, unable to continue sitting in a part-heard case for a period which is likely to be longer than of a short duration, the Presiding Judge shall report to the President who may assign another Judge to the case and order either a rehearing or continuation of the proceedings from that point. However, after the opening statements provided for in Rule 84, or the beginning of the presentation of evidence pursuant to Rule 85, the continuation of the proceedings can only be ordered with the consent of the accused, except as provided for in paragraph (D). (Amended 12 Dec 2002)

(D) If, in the circumstances mentioned in the last sentence of paragraph (C), the accused withholds his consent, the remaining Judges may nonetheless decide to continue the proceedings before a Trial Chamber with a substitute Judge if, taking all the circumstances into account, they determine unanimously that doing so would serve the interests of justice. This decision is subject to appeal directly to a full bench of the Appeals Chamber by either party. If no appeal is taken or the Appeals Chamber affirms the decision of the Trial Chamber, the President shall assign to the existing bench a Judge, who, however, can join the bench only after he or she has certified that he or she has familiarised himself or herself with the record of the proceedings. Only one substitution under this paragraph may be made. (Amended 12 Dec 2002)

(E) Appeals under paragraph (D) shall be filled within seven days of filing of the impugned decision. When such decision is rendered orally, this time-limit shall run from the date of the oral decision, unless

    (i) the party challenging the decision was not present or represented when the decision was pronounced, in which case the time-limit shall run from the date on which the challenging party is notified of the oral decision; or

    (ii) the Trial Chamber has indicated that a written decision will follow, in which case, the time-limit shall run from filing of the written decision.

(Amended 12 Dec 2002)

(F) In case of illness or an unfilled vacancy or in any other similar circumstances, the President may, if satisfied that it is in the interests of justice to do so, authorise a Chamber to conduct routine matters, such as the delivery of decisions, in the absence of one or more of its members.

RULE 16

RESIGNATION

(Adopted 11 Feb 1994)

A Judge who decides to resign shall communicate the resignation in writing to the **C6–018** President who shall transmit it to the Secretary-General of the United Nations.

RULE 17

PRECEDENCE

(Adopted 11 Feb 1994)

(A) All Judges are equal in the exercise of their judicial functions, regardless of dates **C6–019** of election, appointment, age or period of service.

(B) The Presiding Judges of the Trial Chambers shall take precedence according to age after the President and the Vice-President.

(C) Permanent Judges elected or appointed on different dates shall take precedence according to the dates of their election or appointment; Judges elected or appointed on the same date shall take precedence according to age. (Amended 12 Apr 2001)

(D) In case of re-election, the total period of service as a Judge of the Tribunal shall be taken into account.

(E) *Ad litem* Judges shall take precedence after the permanent Judges according to the dates of their appointment. *Ad litem* Judges appointed on the same date shall take precedence according to age. (Amended 12 Apr 2001)

Section 2: The Presidency

RULE 18

ELECTION OF THE PRESIDENT

(Adopted 11 Feb 1994)

C6–020   (A) The President shall be elected for a term of two years, or such shorter term as shall coincide with the duration of his or her term of office as a Judge. The President may be re-elected once. (Revised 12 Nov 1997)

(B) If the President ceases to be a member of the Tribunal or resigns from office before the expiration of his or her term, the permanent Judges shall elect from among their number a successor for the remainder of the term. (Revised 12 Nov 1997, amended 12 Apr 2001)

(C) The President shall be elected by a majority of the votes of the permanent Judges composing the Tribunal. If no Judge obtains such a majority, the second ballot shall be limited to the two Judges who obtained the greatest number of votes on the first ballot. In the case of equality of votes on the second ballot, the Judge who takes precedence in accordance with Rule 17 shall be declared elected. (Amended 12 Apr 2001)

RULE 19

FUNCTIONS OF THE PRESIDENT

(Adopted 11 Feb 1994)

C6–021   (A) The President shall preside at all plenary meetings of the Tribunal. The President shall coordinate the work of the Chambers and supervise the activities of the Registry as well as exercise all the other functions conferred on the President by the Statute and the Rules. (Revised 12 Nov 1997)

(B) The President may from time to time, and in consultation with the Bureau, the Registrar and the Prosecutor, issue Practice Directions, consistent with the Statute and the Rules, addressing detailed aspects of the conduct of proceedings before the Tribunal. (Revised 12 Nov 1997)

RULE 20

THE VICE-PRESIDENT

(Adopted 11 Feb 1994)

C6–022   (a) The Vice-President shall be elected for a term of two years, or such shorter term as shall coincide with the duration of his or her term of office as a permanent Judge. The Vice President may be re-elected once. (Revised 12 Nov 1997, amended 12 Apr 2001)

(B) The Vice-President may sit as a member of a Trial Chamber or of the Appeals Chamber.

(C) Rules 18 (B) and (C) shall apply *mutatis mutandis* to the Vice-President. (Amended 1 Dec 2000 and 13 Dec 2000)

RULE 21

FUNCTIONS OF THE VICE-PRESIDENT

(Adopted 11 Feb 1994, revised 12 Nov 1997, amended 1 Dec 2000 and 13 Dec 2000)

Subject to Rule 22 (B), the Vice-President shall exercise the functions of the President in case of the latter's absence or inability to act.

C6–023

RULE 22

Replacements

(Adopted 11 Feb 1994)

(A) If neither the President nor the Vice-President remains in office or is able to carry out the functions of the President, these shall be assumed by the senior permanent Judge, determined in accordance with Rule 17 (C). (Amended 12 Apr 2001, amended 12 July 2001)

C6–024

(B) If the President is unable to exercise the functions of Presiding Judge of the Appeals Chamber, that Chamber shall elect a Presiding Judge from among its number. (Revised 12 Nov 1997)

(C) The President and the Vice-President, if still permanent Judges, shall continue to discharge their functions after the expiration of their terms until the election of the President and the Vice-President has taken place. (Amended 12 July 2001)

Section 3 : Internal Functioning of the Tribunal

RULE 23

THE BUREAU

(Adopted 11 Feb 1994)

(A) The Bureau shall be composed of the President, the Vice-President and the Presiding Judges of the Trial Chambers.

C6–025

(B) The President shall consult the other members of the Bureau on all major questions relating to the functioning of the Tribunal.

(C) The President may consult with the *ad litem* Judges on matters to be discussed in the Bureau and may invite a representative of the *ad litem* Judges to attend Bureau meetings. (Amended 12 Apr 2001)

(D) A Judge may draw the attention of any member of the Bureau to issues that the Judge considers ought to be discussed by the Bureau or submitted to a plenary meeting of the Tribunal.

(E) If any member of the Bureau is unable to carry out any of the functions of the Bureau, these shall be assumed by the senior available Judge determined in accordance with Rule 17. (Amended 25 Feb 1999)

RULE 23*bis*

THE COORDINATION COUNCIL

(Adopted 1 Dec 2000 and 13 Dec 2000)

C6–026   (A) The Coordination Council shall be composed of the President, the Prosecutor and the Registrar.

(B) In order to achieve the mission of the Tribunal, as defined in the Statute, the Coordination Council ensures, having due regard for the responsibilities and the independence of any member, the coordination of the activities of the three organs of the Tribunal.

(C) The Coordination Council shall meet once a month at the initiative of the President. A member may at any time request that additional meetings be held. The President shall chair the meetings.

(D) The Vice-President, the Deputy Prosecutor and the Deputy Registrar may *ex officio* represent respectively, the President, the Prosecutor and the Registrar.

RULE 23*ter*

THE MANAGEMENT COMMITTEE

(Adopted 1 Dec 2000 and 13 Dec 2000)

C6–027   (A) The Management Committee shall be composed of the President, the Vice-President, a Judge elected by the Judges in plenary session for a one year renewable mandate, the Registrar, the Deputy Registrar and the Chief of Administration.

(B) The Management Committee shall assist the President with respect to the functions set forth in Rules 19 and 33, concerning in particular, all Registry activities relating to the administrative and judicial support provided to the Chambers and to the Judges. To this end, the Management Committee shall coordinate the preparation and implementation of the budget of the Tribunal with the exception of budgetary lines specific to the activities of the Office of the Prosecutor.

(C) The Management Committee shall meet twice a month at the initiative of the President. Two members may at any time request that additional meetings be held. The President shall chair the meetings.

(D) In the performance of its functions, the Management Committee may call on the services of one or several advisers or experts.

RULE 24

PLENARY MEETINGS OF THE TRIBUNAL

(Adopted 11 Feb 1994)

C6–028   Subject to the restrictions on the voting rights of ad litem Judges set out in Article 13 quater of the Statute, the Judges shall meet in plenary to:
      (i) elect the President and Vice-President;
      (ii) adopt and amend the Rules;
      (iii) adopt the Annual Report provided for in Article 34 of the Statute;
      (iv) decide upon matters relating to the internal functioning of the Chambers and
        the Tribunal;

    (v) determine or supervise the conditions of detention;
    (vi) exercise any other functions provided for in the Statute or in the Rules.
(Amended 12 Apr 2001)

Rule 25

DATES OF PLENARY SESSIONS

(Adopted 11 Feb 1994)

(A) The dates of the plenary sessions of the Tribunal shall normally be agreed upon in July of each year for the following calendar year.

(B) Other plenary meetings shall be convened by the President if so requested by at least nine permanent Judges, and may be convened whenever the exercise of the President's functions under the Statute or the Rules so requires. (Revised 12 Nov 1997, amended 4 Dec 1998, amended 12 Apr 2001)

C6–029

Rule 26

QUORUM AND VOTE

(Adopted 11 Feb 1994)

(A) The quorum for each plenary meeting of the Tribunal shall be ten permanent Judges. (Amended 4 Dec 1998, amended 12 Apr 2001)

(B) Subject to Rules 6 (A), (B) and 18 (C), the decisions of the plenary meetings of the Tribunal shall be taken by the majority of the Judges present. In the event of an equality of votes, the President or the Judge acting in the place of the President shall have a casting vote. (Amended 12 Apr 2001)

C6–030

Section 4: The Chambers

Rule 27

ROTATION

(Adopted 11 Feb 1994)

(A) Permanent Judges shall rotate on a regular basis between the Trial Chambers and the Appeals Chamber. Rotation shall take into account the efficient disposal of cases. (Amended 12 Apr 2001)

(B) The Judges shall take their places in their new Chamber as soon as the President thinks it convenient, having regard to the disposal of part-heard cases.

(C) The President may at any time temporarily assign a member of a Trial Chamber or of the Appeals Chamber to another Chamber.

C6–031

RULE 28

REVIEWING AND DUTY JUDGES

(Adopted 11 Feb 1994, revised 30 Jan 1995, amended 23 Apr 1996, revised 12 Nov 1997)

C6–032   (A) On receipt of an indictment for review from the Prosecutor, the Registrar shall consult with the President. The President shall refer the matter to the Bureau which shall determine whether the indictment, prima facie, concentrates on one or more of the most senior leaders suspected of being most responsible for crimes within the jurisdiction of the Tribunal. If the Bureau determines that the indictment meets this standard, the President shall designate one of the permanent Trial Chamber Judges for the review under Rule 47. If the Bureau determines that the indictment does not meet this standard, the President shall return the indictment to the Registrar to communicate this finding to the Prosecutor. (Amended 17 Nov 1999, amended 12 Apr 2001, amended 6 Apr 2004)

(B) The President, in consultation with the Judges, shall maintain a roster designating one permanent Judge as duty Judge for the assigned period of seven days. The duty Judge shall be available at all times, including out of normal Registry hours, for dealing with applications pursuant to paragraphs (C) and (D) but may refuse to deal with any application out of normal Registry hours if not satisfied as to its urgency. The roster of duty Judges shall be published by the Registrar. (Revised 12 Nov 1997, amended 17 Nov 1999, amended 12 Apr 2001)

(C) All applications in a case not otherwise assigned to a Chamber, other than the review of indictments, shall be transmitted to the duty Judge. Where accused are jointly indicted, a submission relating only to an accused who is not in the custody of the Tribunal, other than an application to amend or withdraw part of the indictment pursuant to Rule 50 or Rule 51, shall be transmitted to the duty Judge, notwithstanding that the case has already been assigned to a Chamber in respect of some or all of the co-accused of that accused. The duty Judge shall act pursuant to Rule 54 in dealing with applications under this Rule. (Amended 17 Nov 1999, amended 21 Dec 2001)

(D) Where a case has already been assigned to a Trial Chamber:
    (i) where the application is made out of normal Registry hours, the application shall be dealt with by the duty Judge if satisfied as to its urgency;
    (ii) where the application is made within the normal Registry hours and the Trial Chamber is unavailable, it shall be dealt with by the duty Judge if satisfied as to its urgency or that it is otherwise appropriate to do so in the absence of the Trial Chamber.

In such case, the Registry shall serve a copy of all orders or decisions issued by the duty Judge in connection therewith on the Chamber to which the matter is assigned. (Amended 17 Nov 1999, amended 21 Dec 2001)

(E) During periods of court recess, regardless of the Chamber to which he or she is assigned, in addition to applications made pursuant to paragraph (D) above, the duty Judge may:
    (i) take decisions on provisional detention pursuant to Rule 40*bis*;
    (ii) conduct the initial appearance of an accused pursuant to Rule 62.

The Registry shall serve a copy of all orders or decisions issued by the duty Judge in connection therewith on the Chamber to which the matter is assigned. (Amended 14 July 2000, amended 21 Dec 2001)

(F) The provisions of this Rule shall apply *mutatis mutandis* to applications before the Appeals Chamber. (Amended 21 Dec 2001)

RULE 29

DELIBERATIONS

(Adopted 11 Feb 1994)

The deliberations of the Chambers shall take place in private and remain secret. **C6–033**

Section 5: The Registry

RULE 30

APPOINTMENT OF THE REGISTRAR

(Adopted 11 Feb 1994, amended 10 July 1998, amended 12 Apr 2001)

The President shall seek the opinion of the permanent Judges on the candidates for the post of Registrar, before consulting with the Secretary-General of the United Nations pursuant to Article 17, paragraph 3, of the Statute. **C6–034**

RULE 31

APPOINTMENT OF THE DEPUTY REGISTRAR AND REGISTRY STAFF

(Adopted 11 Feb 1994)

The Registrar, after consultation with the Bureau, shall make recommendations to the Secretary-General of the United Nations for the appointment of the Deputy Registrar and other Registry staff. **C6–035**

RULE 32

SOLEMN DECLARATION

(Adopted 11 Feb 1994)

(A) Before taking up duties, the Registrar shall make the following declaration before the President: **C6–036**

"I solemnly declare that I will perform the duties incumbent upon me as Registrar of the International Tribunal for the Prosecution of Persons Responsible for Serious Violations of International Humanitarian Law Committed in the Territory of the Former Yugoslavia since 1991 in all loyalty, discretion and good conscience and that I will faithfully observe all the provisions of the Statute and the Rules of Procedure and Evidence of the Tribunal". (Revised 12 Nov 1997)

(B) Before taking up duties, the Deputy Registrar shall make a similar declaration before the President. (Revised 12 Nov 1997)

(C) Every staff member of the Registry shall make a similar declaration before the Registrar.

RULE 33

FUNCTIONS OF THE REGISTRAR

(Adopted 11 Feb 1994)

C6–037   (A) The Registrar shall assist the Chambers, the plenary meetings of the Tribunal, the Judges and the Prosecutor in the performance of their functions. Under the authority of the President, the Registrar shall be responsible for the administration and servicing of the Tribunal and shall serve as its channel of communication. (Revised 12 Nov 1997)

(B) The Registrar, in the execution of his or her functions, may make oral and written representations to the President or Chambers on any issue arising in the context of a specific case which affects or may affect the discharge of such functions, including that of implementing judicial decisions, with notice to the parties where necessary. (Amended 17 Nov 1999, amended 1 Dec 2000 and 13 Dec 2000)

(C) The Registrar shall report regularly on his or her activities to the Judges meeting in plenary and to the Prosecutor. (Amended 1 Dec 2000 and 13 Dec 2000)

RULE 33*bis*

FUNCTIONS OF THE DEPUTY REGISTRAR

(Adopted 1 Dec 2000 and 13 Dec 2000)

C6–038   (A) The Deputy Registrar shall exercise the functions of the Registrar in the event of the latter's absence from duty or inability to act or upon the Registrar's delegation.

(B) The Deputy Registrar, in consultation with the President, shall in particular:

  (i) direct and administer the Chambers Legal Support Section; in particular, in conjunction with the administrative services of the Registry, the Deputy Registrar shall oversee the assignment of appropriate resources to the Chambers with a view to enabling them to accomplish their mission;

  (ii) take all appropriate measures so that the decisions rendered by the Chambers and Judges are executed, especially sentences and penalties;

  (iii) make recommendations regarding the missions of the Registry which affect the judicial activity of the Tribunal.

RULE 34

VICTIMS AND WITNESSES SECTION

(Adopted 11 Feb 1994)

C6–039   (A) There shall be set up under the authority of the Registrar a Victims and Witnesses Section consisting of qualified staff to:

  (i) recommend protective measures for victims and witnesses in accordance with Article 22 of the Statute; and

  (ii) provide counselling and support for them, in particular in cases of rape and sexual assault.

(Amended 2 July 1999)

(B) Due consideration shall be given, in the appointment of staff, to the employment of qualified women.

Rule 35

MINUTES

(Adopted 11 Feb 1994, revised 12 Nov 1997)

Except where a full record is made under Rule 81, the Registrar, or Registry staff designated by the Registrar, shall take minutes of the plenary meetings of the Tribunal and of the sittings of the Chambers, other than private deliberations.   **C6–040**

Rule 36

RECORD BOOK

(Adopted 11 Feb 1994, revised 30 Jan 1995, revised 12 Nov 1997)

The Registrar shall keep a Record Book which shall list, subject to any Practice Direction under Rule 19 or any order of a Judge or Chamber providing for the non-disclosure of any document or information, all the particulars of each case brought before the Tribunal. The Record Book shall be open to the public.   **C6–041**

Section 6: The Prosecutor

Rule 37

FUNCTIONS OF THE PROSECUTOR

(Adopted 11 Feb 1994)

(A) The Prosecutor shall perform all the functions provided by the Statute in accordance with the Rules and such Regulations, consistent with the Statute and the Rules, as may be framed by the Prosecutor. Any alleged inconsistency in the Regulations shall be brought to the attention of the Bureau to whose opinion the Prosecutor shall defer. (Revised 30 Jan 1995, revised 12 Nov 1997)   **C6–042**

(B) The Prosecutor's powers and duties under the Rules may be exercised by staff members of the Office of the Prosecutor authorised by the Prosecutor, or by any person acting under the Prosecutor's direction. (Amended 25 July 1997, revised 12 Nov 1997)

Rule 38

DEPUTY PROSECUTOR

(Adopted 11 Feb 1994)

(A) The Prosecutor shall make recommendations to the Secretary-General of the United Nations for the appointment of a Deputy Prosecutor. (Revised 12 Nov 1997)   **C6–043**

(B) The Deputy Prosecutor shall exercise the functions of the Prosecutor in the event of the latter's absence from duty or inability to act or upon the Prosecutor's express instructions. (Amended 25 July 1997, revised 12 Nov 1997)

PART FOUR

INVESTIGATIONS AND RIGHTS OF SUSPECTS

Section 1: Investigations

RULE 39

CONDUCT OF INVESTIGATIONS

(Adopted 11 Feb 1994)

C6–044   In the conduct of an investigation, the Prosecutor may:
  (i) summon and question suspects, victims and witnesses and record their statements, collect evidence and conduct on-site investigations;
  (ii) undertake such other matters as may appear necessary for completing the investigation and the preparation and conduct of the prosecution at the trial, including the taking of special measures to provide for the safety of potential witnesses and informants;
(Revised 30 Jan 1995)
  (iii) seek, to that end, the assistance of any State authority concerned, as well as of any relevant international body including the International Criminal Police Organization (INTERPOL); and
  (iv) request such orders as may be necessary from a Trial Chamber or a Judge.

RULE 40

PROVISIONAL MEASURES

(Adopted 11 Feb 1994)

C6–045   In case of urgency, the Prosecutor may request any State:
  (i) to arrest a suspect or an accused provisionally;
  (Amended 4 Dec 1998)
  (ii) to seise physical evidence;
  (iii) to take all necessary measures to prevent the escape of a suspect or an accused, injury to or intimidation of a victim or witness, or the destruction of evidence.
  The State concerned shall comply forthwith, in accordance with Article 29 of the Statute.
(Revised 30 Jan 1995)

RULE 40*bis*

TRANSFER AND PROVISIONAL DETENTION OF SUSPECTS

(Adopted 23 Apr 1996)

C6–046   (A) In the conduct of an investigation, the Prosecutor may transmit to the Registrar, for an order by a Judge assigned pursuant to Rule 28, a request for the transfer to and provisional detention of a suspect in the premises of the detention unit of the Tribunal. This request shall indicate the grounds upon which the request is made and, unless the Prosecutor wishes only to question the suspect, shall include a provisional charge and a summary of the material upon which the Prosecutor relies.

(B) The Judge shall order the transfer and provisional detention of the suspect if the following conditions are met:

    (i) the Prosecutor has requested a State to arrest the suspect provisionally, in accordance with Rule 40, or the suspect is otherwise detained by State authorities;

    (ii) after hearing the Prosecutor, the Judge considers that there is a reliable and consistent body of material which tends to show that the suspect may have committed a crime over which the Tribunal has jurisdiction; and

    (iii) the Judge considers provisional detention to be a necessary measure to prevent the escape of the suspect, injury to or intimidation of a victim or witness or the destruction of evidence, or to be otherwise necessary for the conduct of the investigation.

(C) The order for the transfer and provisional detention of the suspect shall be signed by the Judge and bear the seal of the Tribunal. The order shall set forth the basis of the application made by the Prosecutor under paragraph (A), including the provisional charge, and shall state the Judge's grounds for making the order, having regard to paragraph (B). The order shall also specify the initial time-limit for the provisional detention of the suspect, and be accompanied by a statement of the rights of a suspect, as specified in this Rule and in Rules 42 and 43. (Amended 12 Apr 2001)

(D) The provisional detention of a suspect shall be ordered for a period not exceeding thirty days from the date of the transfer of the suspect to the seat of the Tribunal. At the end of that period, at the Prosecutor's request, the Judge who made the order, or another permanent Judge of the same Trial Chamber, may decide, subsequent to an *inter partes* hearing of the Prosecutor and the suspect assisted by counsel, to extend the detention for a period not exceeding thirty days, if warranted by the needs of the investigation. At the end of that extension, at the Prosecutor's request, the Judge who made the order, or another permanent Judge of the same Trial Chamber, may decide, subsequent to an *inter partes* hearing of the Prosecutor and the suspect assisted by counsel, to extend the detention for a further period not exceeding thirty days, if warranted by special circumstances. The total period of detention shall in no case exceed ninety days, at the end of which, in the event the indictment has not been confirmed and an arrest warrant signed, the suspect shall be released or, if appropriate, be delivered to the authorities of the requested State. (Amended 25 July 1997, revised 12 Nov 1997, amended 1 Dec 2000 and 13 Dec 2000, amended 12 Apr 2001)

(E) The provisions in Rules 55 (B) to 59*bis* shall apply *mutatis mutandis* to the execution of the transfer order and the provisional detention order relative to a suspect.

(F) After being transferred to the seat of the Tribunal, the suspect, assisted by counsel, shall be brought, without delay, before the Judge who made the order, or another permanent Judge of the same Trial Chamber, who shall ensure that the rights of the suspect are respected. (Revised 12 Nov 1997, amended 12 Apr 2001)

(G) During detention, the Prosecutor and the suspect or the suspect's counsel may submit to the Trial Chamber of which the Judge who made the order is a member, all applications relative to the propriety of provisional detention or to the suspect's release. (Revised 12 Nov 1997)

(H) Without prejudice to paragraph (D), the Rules relating to the detention on remand of accused persons shall apply *mutatis mutandis* to the provisional detention of persons under this Rule. (Amended 1 Dec 2000 and 13 Dec 2000)

Rule 41

RETENTION OF INFORMATION

(Adopted 11 Feb 1994, revised 12 Nov 1997, amended 1 Dec 2000 and 13 Dec 2000)

Subject to Rule 81, the Prosecutor shall be responsible for the retention, storage and security of information and physical material obtained in the course of the Prosecutor's investigations until formally tendered into evidence.

C6–047

Rule 42

RIGHTS OF SUSPECTS DURING INVESTIGATION

(Adopted 11 Feb 1994)

C6–048 (A) A suspect who is to be questioned by the Prosecutor shall have the following rights, of which the Prosecutor shall inform the suspect prior to questioning, in a language the suspect understands:

    (i) the right to be assisted by counsel of the suspect's choice or to be assigned legal assistance without payment if the suspect does not have sufficient means to pay for it; (Revised 30 Jan 1995)

    (ii) the right to have the free assistance of an interpreter if the suspect cannot understand or speak the language to be used for questioning; and (Revised 30 Jan 1995)

    (iii) the right to remain silent, and to be cautioned that any statement the suspect makes shall be recorded and may be used in evidence. (Revised 30 Jan 1995)

(Revised 12 Nov 1997, amended 21 July 2005)

(B) Questioning of a suspect shall not proceed without the presence of counsel unless the suspect has voluntarily waived the right to counsel. In case of waiver, if the suspect subsequently expresses a desire to have counsel, questioning shall thereupon cease, and shall only resume when the suspect has obtained or has been assigned counsel. (Revised 12 Nov 1997)

Rule 43

RECORDING QUESTIONING OF SUSPECTS

(Adopted 11 Feb 1994)

C6–049 Whenever the Prosecutor questions a suspect, the questioning shall be audio-recorded or video-recorded, in accordance with the following procedure:

    (i) the suspect shall be informed in a language the suspect understands that the questioning is being audio-recorded or video-recorded;
    (Amended 6 Oct 1995, revised 12 Nov 1997, amended 21 July 2005)

    (ii) in the event of a break in the course of the questioning, the fact and the time of the break shall be recorded before audio-recording or video-recording ends and the time of resumption of the questioning shall also be recorded;
    (Amended 6 Oct 1995)

    (iii) at the conclusion of the questioning the suspect shall be offered the opportunity to clarify anything the suspect has said, and to add anything the suspect may wish, and the time of conclusion shall be recorded;
    (Revised 12 Nov 1997)

    (iv) a copy of the recorded tape will be supplied to the suspect or, if multiple recording apparatus was used, one of the original recorded tapes;
    (Revised 30 Jan 1995, amended 12 Dec 2002)

    (v) after a copy has been made, if necessary, of the recorded tape, the original recorded tape or one of the original tapes shall be sealed in the presence of the suspect under the signature of the Prosecutor and the suspect; and
    (Amended 12 Dec 2002)

    (vi) the tape shall be transcribed if the suspect becomes an accused.
    (Amended 12 Dec 2002)
    (Amended 6 Oct 1995)

Section 2: Of Counsel

Rule 44

APPOINTMENT, QUALIFICATIONS AND DUTIES OF COUNSEL

(Adopted 11 Feb 1994, amended 25 July 1997)

(A) Counsel engaged by a suspect or an accused shall file a power of attorney with the Registrar at the earliest opportunity. Subject to any determination by a Chamber pursuant to Rule 46 or 77, a counsel shall be considered qualified to represent a suspect or accused if the counsel satisfies the Registrar that he or she:

C6–050

   (i) is admitted to the practice of law in a State, or is a university professor of law;

   (ii) has written and oral proficiency in one of the two working languages of the Tribunal, unless the Registrar deems it in the interests of justice to waive this requirement, as provided for in paragraph (B);

   (iii) is a member in good standing of an association of counsel practicing at the Tribunal recognised by the Registrar;

   (iv) has not been found guilty or otherwise disciplined in relevant disciplinary proceedings against him in a national or international forum, including proceedings pursuant to the Code of Professional Conduct for Defence Counsel Appearing Before the International Tribunal, unless the Registrar deems that, in the circumstances, it would be disproportionate to exclude such counsel;

   (v) has not been found guilty in relevant criminal proceedings;

   (vi) has not engaged in conduct whether in pursuit of his or her profession or otherwise which is dishonest or otherwise discreditable to a counsel, prejudicial to the administration of justice, or likely to diminish public confidence in the International Tribunal or the administration of justice, or otherwise bring the International Tribunal into disrepute; and

   (vii) has not provided false or misleading information in relation to his or her qualifications and fitness to practice or failed to provide relevant information. (Revised 12 Nov 1997, amended 1 Dec 2000 and 13 Dec 2000, amended 14 July 2000, amended 13 Dec 2001, amended 12 July 2002, amended 28 July 2004)

B) At the request of the suspect or accused and where the interests of justice so demand, the Registrar may admit a counsel who does not speak either of the two working languages of the Tribunal but who speaks the native language of the suspect or accused. The Registrar may impose such conditions as deemed appropriate, including the requirement that the counsel or accused undertake to meet all translations and interpretation costs not usually met by the Tribunal, and counsel undertakes not to request any extensions of time as a result of the fact that he does not speak one of the working languages. A suspect or accused may seek the President's review of the Registrar's decision. (Amended 14 July 2000, amended 28 July 2004)

(C) In the performance of their duties counsel shall be subject to the relevant provisions of the Statute, the Rules, the Rules of Detention and any other rules or regulations adopted by the Tribunal, the Host Country Agreement, the Code of Professional Conduct for Defence Counsel Appearing Before the International Tribunal and the codes of practice and ethics governing their profession and, if applicable, the Directive on the Assignment of Defence Counsel adopted by the Registrar and approved by the permanent Judges. (Amended 25 July 1997, amended 1 Dec 2000 and 13 Dec 2000, amended 13 Dec 2001, amended 28 July 2004)

(D) An Advisory Panel shall be established to assist the President and the Registrar in all matters relating to defence counsel. The Panel members shall be selected from representatives of professional associations and from counsel who have appeared before the Tribunal. They shall have recognised professional legal experience. The composition of the Advisory Panel shall be representative of the different legal systems. A Directive of the Registrar shall set out the structure and areas of responsibility of the Advisory Panel. (Amended 14 July 2000)

Rule 45

ASSIGNMENT OF COUNSEL

(Adopted 11 Feb 1994, revised 30 Jan 1995, revised 12 Nov 1997)

C6–051　　(A) Whenever the interests of justice so demand, counsel shall be assigned to suspects or accused who lack the means to remunerate such counsel. Such assignments shall be treated in accordance with the procedure established in a Directive set out by the Registrar and approved by the permanent Judges. (Amended 14 July 2000, amended 12 Apr 2001)

(B) For this purpose, the Registrar shall maintain a list of counsel who:

　(i) fulfil all the requirements of Rule 44, although the language requirement of Rule 44 (A)(ii) may be waived by the Registrar as provided for in the Directive;

　(ii) possess established competence in criminal law and/or international criminal law/international humanitarian law/international human rights law;

　(iii) possess at least seven years of relevant experience, whether as a judge, prosecutor, attorney or in some other capacity, in criminal proceedings; and

　(iv) have indicated their availability and willingness to be assigned by the Tribunal to any person detained under the authority of the Tribunal lacking the means to remunerate counsel, under the terms set out in the Directive.

(Amended 25 June 1996 and 5 July 1996, amended 14 July 2000, amended 28 July 2004)

(C) The Registrar shall maintain a separate list of counsel who, in addition to fulfilling the qualification requirements set out in paragraph (B), are readily available as "duty counsel" for assignment to an accused for the purposes of the initial appearance, in accordance with Rule 62. (Amended 10 July 1998, amended 14 July 2000, amended 28 July 2004)

(D) The Registrar shall, in consultation with the permanent Judges, establish the criteria for the payment of fees to assigned counsel. (Amended 12 Apr 2001, amended 12 Dec 2002)

(E) Where a person is assigned counsel and is subsequently found not to be lacking the means to remunerate counsel, the Chamber may, on application by the Registrar, make an order of contribution to recover the cost of providing counsel. (Revised 30 Jan 1995, amended 14 July 2000, amended 28 July 2004)

(F) A suspect or an accused electing to conduct his or her own defence shall so notify the Registrar in writing at the first opportunity. (Revised 30 Jan 1995, revised 12 Nov 1997)

Rule 45*bis*

DETAINED PERSONS

(Adopted 25 June 1996 and 5 July 1996)

C6–052　　Rules 44 and 45 shall apply to any person detained under the authority of the Tribunal.

Rule 46

MISCONDUCT OF COUNSEL

(Adopted 11 Feb 1994, amended 13 Dec 2001)

C6–053　　(A) If a Judge or a Chamber finds that the conduct of a counsel is offensive, abusive or otherwise obstructs the proper conduct of the proceedings, or that a counsel is negligent or otherwise fails to meet the standard of professional competence and ethics in the performance of his duties, the Chamber may, after giving counsel due warning:

(i) refuse audience to that counsel; and/or
(ii) determine, after giving counsel an opportunity to be heard, that counsel is no longer eligible to represent a suspect or an accused before the Tribunal pursuant to Rule 44 and 45.
(Revised 12 Nov 1997, amended 13 Dec 2001, amended 28 July 2004)

(B) A Judge or a Chamber may also, with the approval of the President, communicate any misconduct of counsel to the professional body regulating the conduct of counsel in the counsel's State of admission or, if a university professor of law and not otherwise admitted to the profession, to the governing body of that counsel's University. (Revised 12 Nov 1997, amended 28 July 2004)

(C) Under the supervision of the President, the Registrar shall publish and oversee the implementation of a Code of Professional Conduct for defence counsel. (Amended 14 July 2000)

PART FIVE

PRE-TRIAL PROCEEDINGS

Section 1: Indictments

RULE 47

SUBMISSION OF INDICTMENT BY THE PROSECUTOR

(Adopted 11 Feb 1994, amended 25 July 1997)

(A) An indictment, submitted in accordance with the following procedure, shall be reviewed by a Judge designated in accordance with Rule 28 for this purpose. (Amended 25 July 1997)

C6–054

(B) The Prosecutor, if satisfied in the course of an investigation that there is sufficient evidence to provide reasonable grounds for believing that a suspect has committed a crime within the jurisdiction of the Tribunal, shall prepare and forward to the Registrar an indictment for confirmation by a Judge, together with supporting material. (Revised 12 Nov 1997)

(C) The indictment shall set forth the name and particulars of the suspect, and a concise statement of the facts of the case and of the crime with which the suspect is charged.

(D) The Registrar shall forward the indictment and accompanying material to the designated Judge, who will inform the Prosecutor of the date fixed for review of the indictment. (Revised 30 Jan 1995, amended 25 July 1997)

(E) The reviewing Judge shall examine each of the counts in the indictment, and any supporting materials the Prosecutor may provide, to determine, applying the standard set forth in Article 19, paragraph 1, of the Statute, whether a case exists against the suspect. (Amended 25 July 1997)

(F) The reviewing Judge may:
(i) request the Prosecutor to present additional material in support of any or all counts;
(Amended 10 July 1998, amended 2 July 1999)
(ii) confirm each count;
(iii) dismiss each count; or
(iv) adjourn the review so as to give the Prosecutor the opportunity to modify the indictment.
(Amended 25 July 1997)

(G) The indictment as confirmed by the Judge shall be retained by the Registrar, who shall prepare certified copies bearing the seal of the Tribunal. If the accused does not understand either of the official languages of the Tribunal and if the language understood is known to the Registrar, a translation of the indictment in that language shall also be prepared, and shall be included as part of each certified copy of the indictment. (Revised 12 Nov 1997)

    (H) Upon confirmation of any or all counts in the indictment,

      (i) the Judge may issue an arrest warrant, in accordance with Rule 55 (A), and any orders as provided in Article 19 of the Statute, and

        (Amended 1 Dec 2000 and 13 Dec 2000)

      (ii) the suspect shall have the status of an accused.

        (Amended 25 July 1997)

    (I) The dismissal of a count in an indictment shall not preclude the Prosecutor from subsequently bringing an amended indictment based on the acts underlying that count if supported by additional evidence. (Amended 25 July 1997)

RULE 48

JOINDER OF ACCUSED

(Adopted 11 Feb 1994)

C6–055   Persons accused of the same or different crimes committed in the course of the same transaction may be jointly charged and tried.

RULE 49

JOINDER OF CRIMES

(Adopted 11 Feb 1994)

C6–056   Two or more crimes may be joined in one indictment if the series of acts committed together form the same transaction, and the said crimes were committed by the same accused.

RULE 50

AMENDMENT OF INDICTMENT

(Adopted 11 Feb 1994)

C6–057   (A) (i) The Prosecutor may amend an indictment:

        (a) at any time before its confirmation, without leave;

          (Amended 17 Nov 1999, amended 14 July 2000)

        (b) between its confirmation and the assignment of the case to a Trial Chamber, with the leave of the Judge who confirmed the indictment, or a Judge assigned by the President; and

          (Amended 10 July 1998, amended 17 Nov 1999, amended 14 July 2000)

        (c) after the assignment of the case to a Trial Chamber, with the leave of that Trial Chamber or a Judge of that Chamber, after having heard the parties.

          (Amended 17 Nov 1999, amended 14 July 2000)

      (ii) Independently of any other factors relevant to the exercise of the discretion, leave to amend an indictment shall not be granted unless the Trial Chamber or Judge is satisfied there is evidence which satisfies the standard set forth in

Article 19, paragraph 1, of the Statute to support the proposed amendment. (Amended 10 July 1998, amended 17 Nov 1999, amended 14 July 2000, amended 28 July 2004)
- (iii) Further confirmation is not required where an indictment is amended by leave. (Amended 28 July 2004)
- (iv) Rule 47 (G) and Rule 53*bis* apply mutatis mutandis to the amended indictment. (Amended 18 Jan 1996, amended 3 Dec 1996, revised 12 Nov 1997, amended 10 July 1998)

(B) If the amended indictment includes new charges and the accused has already appeared before a Trial Chamber in accordance with Rule 62, a further appearance shall be held as soon as practicable to enable the accused to enter a plea on the new charges. (Amended 18 Jan 1996)

(C) The accused shall have a further period of thirty days in which to file preliminary motions pursuant to Rule 72 in respect of the new charges and, where necessary, the date for trial may be postponed to ensure adequate time for the preparation of the defence. (Amended 18 Jan 1996, revised 12 Nov 1997, amended 10 July 1998)

RULE 51

WITHDRAWAL OF INDICTMENT

(Adopted 11 Feb 1994)

(A) The Prosecutor may withdraw an indictment:　　　　　　　　　　　　　　**C6–058**
- (i) at any time before its confirmation, without leave; (Amended 12 Dec 2002)
- (ii) between its confirmation and the assignment of the case to a Trial Chamber, with the leave of the Judge who confirmed the indictment, or a Judge assigned by the President; and (Amended 12 Dec 2002)
- (iii) after the assignment of the case to a Trial Chamber, by motion before that Trial Chamber pursuant to Rule 73. (Amended 12 Dec 2002)
(Amended 3 Dec 1996, revised 12 Nov 1997)

(B) The withdrawal of the indictment shall be promptly notified to the suspect or the accused and to the counsel of the suspect or accused. (Revised 12 Nov 1997)

RULE 52

PUBLIC CHARACTER OF INDICTMENT

(Adopted 11 Feb 1994)

Subject to Rule 53, upon confirmation by a Judge of a Trial Chamber, the indictment　**C6–059**
shall be made public.

RULE 53

NON-DISCLOSURE

(Adopted 11 Feb 1994)

(A) In exceptional circumstances, a Judge or a Trial Chamber may, in the interests of　**C6–060**
justice, order the non-disclosure to the public of any documents or information until further order. (Amended 25 June 1996 and 5 July 1996)

(B) When confirming an indictment the Judge may, in consultation with the Prosecutor, order that there be no public disclosure of the indictment until it is served on the accused, or, in the case of joint accused, on all the accused.

(C) A Judge or Trial Chamber may, in consultation with the Prosecutor, also order that there be no disclosure of an indictment, or part thereof, or of all or any part of any particular document or information, if satisfied that the making of such an order is required to give effect to a provision of the Rules, to protect confidential information obtained by the Prosecutor, or is otherwise in the interests of justice. (Revised 30 Jan 1995)

(D) Notwithstanding paragraphs (A), (B) and (C), the Prosecutor may disclose an indictment or part thereof to the authorities of a State or an appropriate authority or international body where the Prosecutor deems it necessary to prevent an opportunity for securing the possible arrest of an accused from being lost. (Amended 4 Dec 1998, amended 12 Apr 2001)

RULE 53*bis*

SERVICE OF INDICTMENT

(Adopted 12 Nov 1997)

C6–061 (A) Service of the indictment shall be effected personally on the accused at the time the accused is taken into custody or as soon as reasonably practicable thereafter.

(B) Personal service of an indictment on the accused is effected by giving the accused a copy of the indictment certified in accordance with Rule 47 (G).

Section 2: Orders & Warrants

RULE 54

GENERAL RULE

(Adopted 11 Feb 1994, revised 30 Jan 1995, amended 6 Oct 1995)

C6–062 At the request of either party or *proprio motu*, a Judge or a Trial Chamber may issue such orders, summonses, subpoenas, warrants and transfer orders as may be necessary for the purposes of an investigation or for the preparation or conduct of the trial.

RULE 54*bis*

ORDERS DIRECTED TO STATES FOR THE PRODUCTION OF DOCUMENTS

(Adopted 17 Nov 1999)

C6–063 (A) A party requesting an order under Rule 54 that a State produce documents or information shall apply in writing to the relevant Judge or Trial Chamber and shall:
(i) identify as far as possible the documents or information to which the application relates;
(ii) indicate how they are relevant to any matter in issue before the Judge or Trial Chamber and necessary for a fair determination of that matter; and
(iii) explain the steps that have been taken by the applicant to secure the State's assistance.

(B) The Judge or Trial Chamber may reject an application under paragraph (A) *in limine* if satisfied that:

(i) the documents or information are not relevant to any matter in issue in the proceedings before them or are not necessary for a fair determination of any such matter; or

(ii) no reasonable steps have been taken by the applicant to obtain the documents or information from the State.
(Amended 12 Apr 2001)

(C) (i) A decision by a Judge or a Trial Chamber under paragraph (B) or (E) shall be subject to:

(a) review under Rule 108*bis*; or

(b) appeal (Amended 21 July 2005).

(ii) An appeal under paragraph (i) shall be filed within seven days of filing of the impugned decision. Where such decision is rendered orally, this time-limit shall run from the date of the oral decision, unless

(a) the party challenging the decision was not present or represented when the decision was pronounced, in which case the time-limit shall run from the date on which the challenging party is notified of the oral decision; or

(b) the Trial Chamber has indicated that a written decision will follow, in which case, the time-limit shall run from filing of the written decision. (Amended 21 July 2005), (Amended 12 Apr 2001, amended 13 Dec 2001, amended 12 Dec 2002)

(D) (i) Except in cases where a decision has been taken pursuant to paragraph (B) or paragraph (E), the State concerned shall be given notice of the application, and not less than fifteen days' notice of the hearing of the application, at which the State shall have an opportunity to be heard. (Amended 12 Apr 2001)

(ii) Except in cases where the Judge or Trial Chamber determines otherwise, only the party making the application and the State concerned shall have the right to be heard. (Amended 13 Dec 2001)

(E) If, having regard to all circumstances, the Judge or Trial Chamber has good reasons for so doing, the Judge or Trial Chamber may make an order to which this Rule applies without giving the State concerned notice or the opportunity to be heard under paragraph (D), and the following provisions shall apply to such an order:

(i) the order shall be served on the State concerned;

(ii) subject to paragraph (iv), the order shall not have effect until fifteen days after such service;

(iii) a State may, within fifteen days of service of the order, apply by notice to the Judge or Trial Chamber to have the order set aside, on the grounds that disclosure would prejudice national security interests. Paragraph (F) shall apply to such a notice as it does to a notice of objection;
(Amended 12 Apr 2001);

(iv) where notice is given under paragraph (iii), the order shall thereupon be stayed until the decision on the application;

(v) paragraphs (F) and (G) shall apply to the determination of an application made pursuant to paragraph (iii) as they do to the determination of an application of which notice is given pursuant to paragraph (D);
(Amended 12 Apr 2001);

(vi) the State and the party who applied for the order shall, subject to any special measures made pursuant to a request under paragraphs (F) or (G), have an opportunity to be heard at the hearing of an application made pursuant to paragraph (E)(iii) of this Rule.
(Amended 12 Apr 2001)
(Amended 12 Apr 2001)

(F) The State, if it raises an objection pursuant to paragraph (D), on the grounds that disclosure would prejudice its national security interests, shall file a notice of objection not less than five days before the date fixed for the hearing, specifying the grounds of objection. In its notice of objection the State:

(i) shall identify, as far as possible, the basis upon which it claims that its national security interests will be prejudiced; and

(ii) may request the Judge or Trial Chamber to direct that appropriate protective measures be made for the hearing of the objection, including in particular:

    (a) hearing the objection in camera and *ex parte*;
    (b) allowing documents to be submitted in redacted form, accompanied by an affidavit signed by a senior State official explaining the reasons for the redaction;
    (c) ordering that no transcripts be made of the hearing and that documents not further required by the Tribunal be returned directly to the State without being filed with the Registry or otherwise retained.
    (Amended 12 Apr 2001)

(G) With regard to the procedure under paragraph (F) above, the Judge or Trial Chamber may order the following protective measures for the hearing of the objection:
    (i) the designation of a single Judge from a Chamber to examine the documents or hear submissions; and/or
    (ii) that the State be allowed to provide its own interpreters for the hearing and its own translations of sensitive documents.
    (Amended 12 Apr 2001)

(H) Rejection of an application made under this Rule shall not preclude a subsequent application by the requesting party in respect of the same documents or information if new circumstances arise.

(I) An order under this Rule may provide for the documents or information in question to be produced by the State under appropriate arrangements to protect its interests, which may include those arrangements specified in paragraphs (F)(ii) or (G). (Amended 12 Apr 2001)

RULE 55

EXECUTION OF ARREST WARRANTS

(Adopted 11 Feb 1994)

C6–064   (A) A warrant of arrest shall be signed by a permanent Judge. It shall include an order for the prompt transfer of the accused to the Tribunal upon the arrest of the accused. (Revised 12 Nov 1997, amended 12 Apr 2001)

(B) The original warrant shall be retained by the Registrar, who shall prepare certified copies bearing the seal of the Tribunal. (Revised 12 Nov 1997)

(C) Each certified copy shall be accompanied by a copy of the indictment certified in accordance with Rule 47 (G) and a statement of the rights of the accused set forth in Article 21 of the Statute, and in Rules 42 and 43 *mutatis mutandis*. If the accused does not understand either of the official languages of the Tribunal and if the language understood by the accused is known to the Registrar, each certified copy of the warrant of arrest shall also be accompanied by a translation of the statement of the rights of the accused in that language. (Revised 12 Nov 1997)

(D) Subject to any order of a Judge or Chamber, the Registrar may transmit a certified copy of a warrant of arrest to the person or authorities to which it is addressed, including the national authorities of a State in whose territory or under whose jurisdiction the accused resides, or was last known to be, or is believed by the Registrar to be likely to be found. (Revised 30 Jan 1995, amended 18 Jan 1996, amended 25 July 1997, revised 12 Nov 1997)

(E) The Registrar shall instruct the person or authorities to which a warrant is transmitted that at the time of arrest the indictment and the statement of the rights of the accused be read to the accused in a language that he or she understands and that the accused be cautioned in that language that the accused has the right to remain silent, and that any statement he or she makes shall be recorded and may be used in evidence. (Revised 30 Jan 1995, amended 18 Jan 1996, amended 25 July 1997, revised 12 Nov 1997)

(F) Notwithstanding paragraph (E), if at the time of arrest the accused is served with, or with a translation of, the indictment and the statement of rights of the accused in a language that the accused understands and is able to read, these need not be read to the accused at the time of arrest. (Revised 12 Nov 1997, amended 12 Apr 2001)

(G) When an arrest warrant issued by the Tribunal is executed by the authorities of a State, or an appropriate authority or international body, a member of the Office of the Prosecutor may be present as from the time of the arrest. (Revised 12 Nov 1997)

RULE 56

COOPERATION OF STATES

(Adopted 11 Feb 1994, amended 18 Jan 1996)

The State to which a warrant of arrest or a transfer order for a witness is transmitted **C6–065** shall act promptly and with all due diligence to ensure proper and effective execution thereof, in accordance with Article 29 of the Statute.

RULE 57

PROCEDURE AFTER ARREST

(Adopted 11 Feb 1994, revised 30 Jan 1995, revised 12 Nov 1997)

Upon arrest, the accused shall be detained by the State concerned which shall **C6–066** promptly notify the Registrar. The transfer of the accused to the seat of the Tribunal shall be arranged between the State authorities concerned, the authorities of the host country and the Registrar.

RULE 58

NATIONAL EXTRADITION PROVISIONS

(Adopted 11 Feb 1994, amended 6 Oct 1995)

The obligations laid down in Article 29 of the Statute shall prevail over any legal **C6–067** impediment to the surrender or transfer of the accused or of a witness to the Tribunal which may exist under the national law or extradition treaties of the State concerned.

RULE 59

FAILURE TO EXECUTE A WARRANT OR TRANSFER ORDER

(Adopted 11 Feb 1994, amended 18 Jan 1996)

(A) Where the State to which a warrant of arrest or transfer order has been **C6–068** transmitted has been unable to execute the warrant, it shall report forthwith its inability to the Registrar, and the reasons therefor.

(B) If, within a reasonable time after the warrant of arrest or transfer order has been transmitted to the State, no report is made on action taken, this shall be deemed a failure to execute the warrant of arrest or transfer order and the Tribunal, through the President, may notify the Security Council accordingly.

RULE 59*bis*

TRANSMISSION OF ARREST WARRANTS

(Adopted 18 Jan 1996)

C6–069　　(A) Notwithstanding Rules 55 to 59, on the order of a permanent Judge, the Registrar shall transmit to an appropriate authority or international body or the Prosecutor a copy of a warrant for the arrest of an accused, on such terms as the Judge may determine, together with an order for the prompt transfer of the accused to the Tribunal in the event that the accused be taken into custody by that authority or international body or the Prosecutor. (Amended 25 June 1996 and 5 July 1996, revised 12 Nov 1997, amended 12 Apr 2001)

(B) At the time of being taken into custody an accused shall be informed immediately, in a language the accused understands, of the charges against him or her and of the fact that he or she is being transferred to the Tribunal. Upon such transfer, the indictment and a statement of the rights of the accused shall be read to the accused and the accused shall be cautioned in such a language.(Revised 12 Nov 1997)

(C) Notwithstanding paragraph (B), the indictment and statement of rights of the accused need not be read to the accused if the accused is served with these, or with a translation of these, in a language the accused understands and is able to read. (Revised 12 Nov 1997, amended 12 Apr 2001)

RULE 60

ADVERTISEMENT OF INDICTMENT

(Adopted 11 Feb 1994, amended 25 July 1997, revised 12 Nov 1997)

C6–070　　At the request of the Prosecutor, a form of advertisement shall be transmitted by the Registrar to the national authorities of any State or States, for publication in newspapers or for broadcast via radio and television, notifying publicly the existence of an indictment and calling upon the accused to surrender to the Tribunal and inviting any person with information as to the whereabouts of the accused to communicate that information to the Tribunal.

RULE 61

PROCEDURE IN CASE OF FAILURE TO EXECUTE A WARRANT

(Adopted 11 Feb 1994)

C6–071　　(A) If, within a reasonable time, a warrant of arrest has not been executed, and personal service of the indictment has consequently not been effected, the Judge who confirmed the indictment shall invite the Prosecutor to report on the measures taken. When the Judge is satisfied that:

　　(i) the Registrar and the Prosecutor have taken all reasonable steps to secure the arrest of the accused, including recourse to the appropriate authorities of the State in whose territory or under whose jurisdiction and control the person to be served resides or was last known to them to be; and

(Amended 18 Jan 1996, revised 12 Nov 1997)

(ii) if the whereabouts of the accused are unknown, the Prosecutor and the Registrar have taken all reasonable steps to ascertain those whereabouts, including by seeking publication of advertisements pursuant to Rule 60,
(Amended 18 Jan 1996, revised 12 Nov 1997, amended 4 Dec 1998)

the Judge shall order that the indictment be submitted by the Prosecutor to the Trial Chamber of which the Judge is a member. (Amended 3 May 1995, amended 18 Jan 1996, revised 12 Nov 1997, amended 4 Dec 1998)

(B) Upon obtaining such an order the Prosecutor shall submit the indictment to the Trial Chamber in open court, together with all the evidence that was before the Judge who initially confirmed the indictment. The Prosecutor may also call before the Trial Chamber and examine any witness whose statement has been submitted to the confirming Judge. In addition, the Trial Chamber may request the Prosecutor to call any other witness whose statement has been submitted to the confirming Judge. (Revised 30 Jan 1995, amended 25 July 1997)

(C) If the Trial Chamber is satisfied on that evidence, together with such additional evidence as the Prosecutor may tender, that there are reasonable grounds for believing that the accused has committed all or any of the crimes charged in the indictment, it shall so determine. The Trial Chamber shall have the relevant parts of the indictment read out by the Prosecutor together with an account of the efforts to effect service referred to in paragraph (A) above. (Amended 12 Apr 2001)

(D) The Trial Chamber shall also issue an international arrest warrant in respect of the accused which shall be transmitted to all States. Upon request by the Prosecutor or *proprio motu*, after having heard the Prosecutor, the Trial Chamber may order a State or States to adopt provisional measures to freeze the assets of the accused, without prejudice to the rights of third parties. (Amended 23 Apr 1996)

(E) If the Prosecutor satisfies the Trial Chamber that the failure to effect personal service was due in whole or in part to a failure or refusal of a State to cooperate with the Tribunal in accordance with Article 29 of the Statute, the Trial Chamber shall so certify. After consulting the Presiding Judges of the Chambers, the President shall notify the Security Council thereof in such manner as the President thinks fit. (Amended 18 Jan 1996)

Section 3: Preliminary Proceedings

Rule 62

INITIAL APPEARANCE OF ACCUSED

(Adopted 11 Feb 1994)

(A) Upon transfer of an accused to the seat of the Tribunal, the President shall forthwith assign the case to a Trial Chamber. The accused shall be brought before that Trial Chamber or a Judge thereof without delay, and shall be formally charged. The Trial Chamber or the Judge shall:

§C6–072

(i) satisfy itself, himself or herself that the right of the accused to counsel is respected;
(Amended 17 Nov 1999)

(ii) read or have the indictment read to the accused in a language the accused understands, and satisfy itself, himself or herself that the accused understands the indictment;
(Revised 12 Nov 1997, amended 17 Nov 1999, amended 24 June 2003)

(iii) inform the accused that, within thirty days of the initial appearance, he or she will be called upon to enter a plea of guilty or not guilty on each count but that, should the accused so request, he or she may immediately enter a plea of guilty or not guilty on one or more count;
(Amended 4 Dec 1998)

      (iv) if the accused fails to enter a plea at the initial or any further appearance, enter a plea of not guilty on the accused's behalf;
        (Amended 15 June 1995, revised 12 Nov 1997, amended 4 Dec 1998)
      (v) in case of a plea of not guilty, instruct the Registrar to set a date for trial;
        (Revised 30 Jan 1995)
      (vi) in case of a plea of guilty:
        (a) if before the Trial Chamber, act in accordance with Rule 62*bis*, or
          (Amended 17 Nov 1999)
        (b) if before a Judge, refer the plea to the Trial Chamber so that it may act in accordance with Rule 62*bis*;
          (Amended 17 Nov 1999)
          (Revised 30 Jan 1995, revised 12 Nov 1997)
      (vii) instruct the Registrar to set such other dates as appropriate.
        (Revised 30 Jan 1995)
        (Revised 12 Nov 1997, amended 17 Nov 1999, amended 12 Apr 2001, amended 17 July 2003)
  (B) Where the interests of justice so require, the Registrar may assign a duty counsel as within Rule 45 (C) to represent the accused at the initial appearance. Such assignments shall be treated in accordance with the relevant provisions of the Directive referred to in Rule 45 (A). (Amended 28 July 2004)

RULE 62*bis*

GUILTY PLEAS

(Adopted 12 Nov 1997)

C6–073   If an accused pleads guilty in accordance with Rule 62 (vi), or requests to change his or her plea to guilty and the Trial Chamber is satisfied that:
      (i) the guilty plea has been made voluntarily;
      (ii) the guilty plea is informed;
        (Amended 17 Nov 1999)
      (iii) the guilty plea is not equivocal; and
      (iv) there is a sufficient factual basis for the crime and the accused's participation in it, either on the basis of independent indicia or on lack of any material disagreement between the parties about the facts of the case,
the Trial Chamber may enter a finding of guilt and instruct the Registrar to set a date for the sentencing hearing. (Amended 10 July 1998, amended 4 Dec 1998)

RULE 62*ter*

PLEA AGREEMENT PROCEDURE

(Adopted 13 Dec 2001)

C6–074   (A) The Prosecutor and the defence may agree that, upon the accused entering a plea of guilty to the indictment or to one or more counts of the indictment, the Prosecutor shall do one or more of the following before the Trial Chamber:
      (i) apply to amend the indictment accordingly;
      (ii) submit that a specific sentence or sentencing range is appropriate;
      (iii) not oppose a request by the accused for a particular sentence or sentencing range.
  (B) The Trial Chamber shall not be bound by any agreement specified in paragraph (A).

(C) If a plea agreement has been reached by the parties, the Trial Chamber shall require the disclosure of the agreement in open session or, on a showing of good cause, in closed session, at the time the accused pleads guilty in accordance with Rule 62 (vi), or requests to change his or her plea to guilty.

Rule 63

QUESTIONING OF ACCUSED

(Adopted 11 Feb 1994, amended 3 Dec 1996)

(A) Questioning by the Prosecutor of an accused, including after the initial **C6–075** appearance, shall not proceed without the presence of counsel unless the accused has voluntarily and expressly agreed to proceed without counsel present. If the accused subsequently expresses a desire to have counsel, questioning shall thereupon cease, and shall only resume when the accused's counsel is present.

(B) The questioning, including any waiver of the right to counsel, shall be audio-recorded or video-recorded in accordance with the procedure provided for in Rule 43. The Prosecutor shall at the beginning of the questioning caution the accused in accordance with Rule 42 (A)(iii).

Rule 64

DETENTION ON REMAND

(Adopted 11 Feb 1994, amended 25 July 1997, revised 12 Nov 1997)

Upon being transferred to the seat of the Tribunal, the accused shall be detained in **C6–076** facilities provided by the host country, or by another country. In exceptional circumstances, the accused may be held in facilities outside of the host country. The President may, on the application of a party, request modification of the conditions of detention of an accused.

Rule 65

PROVISIONAL RELEASE

(Adopted 11 Feb 1994)

(A) Once detained, an accused may not be released except upon an order of a **C6–077** Chamber. (Amended 14 July 2000)

(B) Release may be ordered by a Trial Chamber only after giving the host country and the State to which the accused seeks to be released the opportunity to be heard and only if it is satisfied that the accused will appear for trial and, if released, will not pose a danger to any victim, witness or other person. (Revised 30 Jan 1995, amended 17 Nov 1999, amended 13 Dec 2001)

(C) The Trial Chamber may impose such conditions upon the release of the accused as it may determine appropriate, including the execution of a bail bond and the observance of such conditions as are necessary to ensure the presence of the accused for trial and the protection of others. (Revised 12 Nov 1997)

(D) Any decision rendered under this Rule by a Trial Chamber shall be subject to appeal. Subject to paragraph (F) below, an appeal shall be filed within seven days of filing of the impugned decision. Where such decision is rendered orally, the application shall be filed within seven days of the oral decision, unless

> (i) the party challenging the decision was not present or represented when the decision was pronounced, in which case the time-limit shall run from the date on which the challenging party is notified of the oral decision; or
> (Amended 10 July 1998)
> (ii) the Trial Chamber has indicated that a written decision will follow, in which case, the time-limit shall run from filing of the written decision.
> (Amended 10 July 1998)

(Amended 25 July 1997, revised 12 Nov 1997, amended 10 July 1998, amended 17 Nov 1999, amended 14 July 2000, amended 1 Dec 2000 and 13 Dec 2000, amended 21 July 2005)

(E) The Prosecutor may apply for a stay of a decision by the Trial Chamber to release an accused on the basis that the Prosecutor intends to appeal the decision, and shall make such an application at the time of filing his or her response to the initial application for provisional release by the accused. (Amended 17 Nov 1999)

(F) Where the Trial Chamber grants a stay of its decision to release an accused, the Prosecutor shall file his or her appeal not later than one day from the rendering of that decision. (Amended 17 Nov 1999)

(G) Where the Trial Chamber orders a stay of its decision to release the accused pending an appeal by the Prosecutor, the accused shall not be released until either:

> (i) the time-limit for the filing of an appeal by the Prosecutor has expired, and no such application is filed; (Amended 21 July 2005)
> (ii) the Appeals Chamber dismisses the appeal; or
> (iii) the Appeals Chamber otherwise orders. (Amended 21 July 2005)
> (Amended 17 Nov 1999, amended 21 July 2005)

(H) If necessary, the Trial Chamber may issue a warrant of arrest to secure the presence of an accused who has been released or is for any other reason at liberty. The provisions of Section 2 of Part Five shall apply *mutatis mutandis*. (Amended 25 July 1997)

(I) Without prejudice to the provisions of Rule 107, the Appeals Chamber may grant provisional release to convicted persons pending an appeal or for a fixed period if it is satisfied that:

> (i) the appellant, if released, will either appear at the hearing of the appeal or will surrender into detention at the conclusion of the fixed period, as the case may be;
> (ii) the appellant, if released, will not pose a danger to any victim, witness or other person, and
> (iii) special circumstances exist warranting such release.

The provisions of paragraphs (C) and (H) shall apply *mutatis mutandis*. (Amended 14 July 2000, amended 1 Dec 2000 and 13 Dec 2000)

RULE 65*bis*

STATUS CONFERENCES

(Adopted 25 July 1997)

C6–078   (A) A Trial Chamber or a Trial Chamber Judge shall convene a status conference within one hundred and twenty days of the initial appearance of the accused and thereafter within one hundred and twenty days after the last status conference:

> (i) to organize exchanges between the parties so as to ensure expeditious preparation for trial;
> (ii) to review the status of his or her case and to allow the accused the opportunity to raise issues in relation thereto, including the mental and physical condition of the accused.
> (Amended 4 Dec 1998, amended 17 Nov 1999, amended 12 Apr 2001, amended 17 July 2003)

(B) The Appeals Chamber or an Appeals Chamber Judge shall convene a status conference, within one hundred and twenty days of the filing of a notice of appeal and thereafter within one hundred and twenty days after the last status conference, to allow any person in custody pending appeal the opportunity to raise issues in relation thereto, including the mental and physical condition of that person. (Amended 17 Nov 1999)

(C) With the written consent of the accused, given after receiving advice from his counsel, a status conference under this Rule may be conducted

(i) in his presence, but with his counsel participating either via tele-conference or video-conference; or

(ii) in Chambers in his absence, but with his participation via tele-conference if he so wishes and/or participation of his counsel via tele-conference or video-conference.

(Amended 12 Dec 2002)

RULE 65*ter*

PRE-TRIAL JUDGE

(Adopted 10 July 1998, amended 17 Nov 1999)

(A) The Presiding Judge of the Trial Chamber shall, no later than seven days after   **C6–079**
the initial appearance of the accused, designate from among its members a Judge responsible for the pre-trial proceedings (hereinafter "pre-trial Judge"). (Amended 17 Nov 1999, amended 12 Apr 2001, amended 17 July 2003)

(B) The pre-trial Judge shall, under the authority and supervision of the Trial Chamber seised of the case, coordinate communication between the parties during the pre-trial phase. The pre-trial Judge shall ensure that the proceedings are not unduly delayed and shall take any measure necessary to prepare the case for a fair and expeditious trial.

(C) The pre-trial Judge shall be entrusted with all of the pre-trial functions set forth in Rule 66, Rule 67, Rule 73*bis* and Rule 73*ter*, and with all or part of the functions set forth in Rule 73. (Amended 17 Nov 1999, amended 12 Apr 2001, amended 12 Dec 2003)

(D) (i) The pre-trial Judge may be assisted in the performance of his or her duties by one of the Senior Legal Officers assigned to Chambers.

(ii) The pre-trial Judge shall establish a work plan indicating, in general terms, the obligations that the parties are required to meet pursuant to this Rule and the dates by which these obligations must be fulfilled.

(iii) Acting under the supervision of the pre-trial Judge, the Senior Legal Officer shall oversee the implementation of the work plan and shall keep the pre-trial Judge informed of the progress of the discussions between and with the parties and, in particular, of any potential difficulty. He or she shall present the pre-trial Judge with reports as appropriate and shall communicate to the parties, without delay, any observations and decisions made by the pre-trial Judge.

(iv) The pre-trial Judge shall order the parties to meet to discuss issues related to the preparation of the case, in particular, so that the Prosecutor can meet his or her obligations pursuant to paragraphs (E) (i) to (iii) of this Rule and for the defence to meet its obligations pursuant to paragraph (G) of this Rule and of Rule 73*ter*.

(v) Such meetings are held *inter partes* or, at his or her request, with the Senior Legal Officer and one or more of the parties. The Senior Legal Officer ensures that the obligations set out in paragraphs (E) (i) to (iii) of this Rule and, at the appropriate time, that the obligations in paragraph (G) and Rule 73*ter*, are satisfied in accordance with the work plan set by the pre-trial Judge.

(vi) The presence of the accused is not necessary for meetings convened by the Senior Legal Officer.

   (vii) The Senior Legal Officer may be assisted by a representative of the Registry in the performance of his or her duties pursuant to this Rule and may require a transcript to be made.
      (Amended 12 Apr 2001)

(E) Once any existing preliminary motions filed within the time-limit provided by Rule 72 are disposed of, the pre-trial Judge shall order the Prosecutor, upon the report of the Senior Legal Officer, and within a time-limit set by the pre-trial Judge and not less than six weeks before the Pre-Trial Conference required by Rule 73*bis*, to file the following:

   (i) the final version of the Prosecutor's pre-trial brief including, for each count, a summary of the evidence which the Prosecutor intends to bring regarding the commission of the alleged crime and the form of responsibility incurred by the accused; this brief shall include any admissions by the parties and a statement of matters which are not in dispute; as well as a statement of contested matters of fact and law;
      (Amended 12 Apr 2001)

   (ii) the list of witnesses the Prosecutor intends to call with:
      (a) the name or pseudonym of each witness;
      (b) a summary of the facts on which each witness will testify;
      (c) the points in the indictment as to which each witness will testify, including specific references to counts and relevant paragraphs in the indictment;
         (Amended 12 Apr 2001)
      (d) the total number of witnesses and the number of witnesses who will testify against each accused and on each count;
         (Amended 12 Apr 2001)
      (e) an indication of whether the witness will testify in person or pursuant to Rule 92*bis* by way of written statement or use of a transcript of testimony from other proceedings before the Tribunal; and
         (Amended 12 Apr 2001)
      (f) the estimated length of time required for each witness and the total time estimated for presentation of the Prosecutor's case.
         (Amended 12 Apr 2001)

   (iii) the list of exhibits the Prosecutor intends to offer stating where possible whether the defence has any objection as to authenticity. The Prosecutor shall serve on the defence copies of the exhibits so listed.
      (Amended 12 Apr 2001, amended 13 Dec 2001)
      (Amended 17 Nov 1999, amended 12 Apr 2001, amended 12 July 2001)

(F) After the submission by the Prosecutor of the items mentioned in paragraph (E), the pre-trial Judge shall order the defence, within a time-limit set by the pre-trial Judge, and not later than three weeks before the Pre-Trial Conference, to file a pre-trial brief addressing the factual and legal issues, and including a written statement setting out:

   (i) in general terms, the nature of the accused's defence;
   (ii) the matters with which the accused takes issue in the Prosecutor's pre-trial brief; and
   (iii) in the case of each such matter, the reason why the accused takes issue with it.
      (Amended 17 Nov 1999, amended 12 Apr 2001)

(G) After the close of the Prosecutor's case and before the commencement of the defence case, the pre-trial Judge shall order the defence to file the following:

   (i) a list of witnesses the defence intends to call with:
      (a) the name or pseudonym of each witness;
      (b) a summary of the facts on which each witness will testify;
      (c) the points in the indictment as to which each witness will testify;
         (Amended 12 Apr 2001)
      (d) the total number of witnesses and the number of witnesses who will testify for each accused and on each count;
         (Amended 12 Apr 2001)

        (e) an indication of whether the witness will testify in person or pursuant to Rule 92*bis* by way of written statement or use of a transcript of testimony from other proceedings before the Tribunal; and
        (Amended 12 Apr 2001)
        (f) the estimated length of time required for each witness and the total time estimated for presentation of the defence case; and
        (Amended 12 Apr 2001)
     (ii) a list of exhibits the defence intends to offer in its case, stating where possible whether the Prosecutor has any objection as to authenticity. The defence shall serve on the Prosecutor copies of the exhibits so listed.
     (Amended 13 Dec 2001)
     (Amended 17 Nov 1999)

(H) The pre-trial Judge shall record the points of agreement and disagreement on matters of law and fact. In this connection, he or she may order the parties to file written submissions with either the pre-trial Judge or the Trial Chamber. (Amended 17 Nov 1999)

(I) In order to perform his or her functions, the pre-trial Judge may *proprio motu*, where appropriate, hear the parties without the accused being present. The pre-trial Judge may hear the parties in his or her private room, in which case minutes of the meeting shall be taken by a representative of the Registry. (Amended 17 Nov 1999, amended 12 Apr 2001)

(J) The pre-trial Judge shall keep the Trial Chamber regularly informed, particularly where issues are in dispute and may refer such disputes to the Trial Chamber.

(K) The pre-trial Judge may set a time for the making of pre-trial motions and, if required, any hearing thereon. A motion made before trial shall be determined before trial unless the Judge, for good cause, orders that it be deferred for determination at trial. Failure by a party to raise objections or to make requests which can be made prior to trial at the time set by the Judge shall constitute waiver thereof, but the Judge for cause may grant relief from the waiver. (Amended 12 Apr 2001)

(L)(i) After the filings by the Prosecutor pursuant to paragraph (E), the pre-trial Judge shall submit to the Trial Chamber a complete file consisting of all the filings of the parties, transcripts of status conferences and minutes of meetings held in the performance of his or her functions pursuant to this Rule.
     (ii) The pre-trial Judge shall submit a second file to the Trial Chamber after the defence filings pursuant to paragraph (G).
     (Amended 17 Nov 1999, amended 12 Apr 2001)

(M) The Trial Chamber may *proprio motu* exercise any of the functions of the pre-trial Judge. (Amended 17 Nov 1999)

(N) Upon a report of the pre-trial Judge, the Trial Chamber shall decide, should the case arise, on sanctions to be imposed on a party which fails to perform its obligations pursuant to the present Rule. Such sanctions may include the exclusion of testimonial or documentary evidence. (Amended 12 Apr 2001)

Section 4: Production of Evidence

Rule 66

DISCLOSURE BY THE PROSECUTOR

(Adopted 11 Feb 1994)

(A) Subject to the provisions of Rules 53 and 69, the Prosecutor shall make available **C6–080** to the defence in a language which the accused understands
     (i) within thirty days of the initial appearance of the accused, copies of the supporting material which accompanied the indictment when confirmation was

sought as well as all prior statements obtained by the Prosecutor from the accused; and
(Revised 12 Nov 1997)

(ii) within the time-limit prescribed by the Trial Chamber or by the pre-trial Judge appointed pursuant to Rule 65*ter*, copies of the statements of all witnesses whom the Prosecutor intends to call to testify at trial, and copies of all written statements taken in accordance with Rule 92*bis*; copies of the statements of additional prosecution witnesses shall be made available to the defence when a decision is made to call those witnesses.
(Revised 12 Nov 1997, amended 10 July 1998, amended 17 Nov 1999, amended 1 Dec 2000 and 13 Dec 2000)
(Revised 30 Jan 1995, amended 3 Dec 1996, revised 12 Nov 1997, amended 10 July 1998)

(B) The Prosecutor shall, on request, permit the defence to inspect any books, documents, photographs and tangible objects in the Prosecutor's custody or control, which are material to the preparation of the defence, or are intended for use by the Prosecutor as evidence at trial or were obtained from or belonged to the accused.

(C) Where information is in the possession of the Prosecutor, the disclosure of which may prejudice further or ongoing investigations, or for any other reasons may be contrary to the public interest or affect the security interests of any State, the Prosecutor may apply to the Trial Chamber sitting in camera to be relieved from an obligation under the Rules to disclose that information. When making such application the Prosecutor shall provide the Trial Chamber (but only the Trial Chamber) with the information that is sought to be kept confidential. (Revised 30 Jan 1995, amended 10 July 1998, amended 17 Nov 1999)

RULE 67

ADDITIONAL DISCLOSURE

(Adopted 11 Feb 1994, amended 12 Dec 2003)

C6–081   (A) Within the time-limit prescribed by the Trial Chamber or by the pre-trial Judge appointed pursuant to Rule 65*ter*:

(i) the defence shall notify the Prosecutor of its intent to offer:

    (a) the defence of alibi; in which case the notification shall specify the place or places at which the accused claims to have been present at the time of the alleged crime and the names and addresses of witnesses and any other evidence upon which the accused intends to rely to establish the alibi;

    (b) any special defence, including that of diminished or lack of mental responsibility; in which case the notification shall specify the names and addresses of witnesses and any other evidence upon which the accused intends to rely to establish the special defence; and

(ii) the Prosecutor shall notify the defence of the names of the witnesses that the Prosecutor intends to call in rebuttal of any defence plea of which the Prosecutor has received notice in accordance with paragraph (i) above.
(Revised 12 Nov 1997, amended 12 Apr 2001)
(Amended 12 Dec 2003)

(B) Failure of the defence to provide notice under this Rule shall not limit the right of the accused to testify on the above defences.

(C) If either party discovers additional evidence or material which should have been disclosed earlier pursuant to the Rules, that party shall immediately disclose that evidence or material to the other party and the Trial Chamber. (Amended 13 Dec 2001)

RULE 68

DISCLOSURE OF EXCULPATORY AND OTHER RELEVANT MATERIAL

(Adopted 11 Feb 1994, revised 30 Jan 1995, amended 12 July 2001, amended 12 Dec 2003, amended 28 July 2004)

Subject to the provisions of Rule 70, **C6–082**

    (i) the Prosecutor shall, as soon as practicable, disclose to the Defence any material which in the actual knowledge of the Prosecutor may suggest the innocence or mitigate the guilt of the accused or affect the credibility of Prosecution evidence.

    (ii) without prejudice to paragraph (i), the Prosecutor shall make available to the defence, in electronic form, collections of relevant material held by the Prosecutor, together with appropriate computer software with which the defence can search such collections electronically.

    (iii) the Prosecutor shall take reasonable steps, if confidential information is provided to the Prosecutor by a person or entity under Rule 70 (B) and contains material referred to in paragraph (i) above, to obtain the consent of the provider to disclosure of that material, or the fact of its existence, to the accused.

    (iv) the Prosecutor shall apply to the Chamber sitting in camera to be relieved from an obligation under paragraph (i) to disclose information in the possession of the Prosecutor, if its disclosure may prejudice further or ongoing investigations, or for any other reason may be contrary to the public interest or affect the security interests of any State, and when making such application, the Prosecutor shall provide the Trial Chamber (but only the Trial Chamber) with the information that is sought to be kept confidential.

    (v) notwithstanding the completion of the trial and any subsequent appeal, the Prosecutor shall disclose to the other party any material referred to in paragraph (i) above.

RULE 68*bis*

FAILURE TO COMPLY WITH DISCLOSURE OBLIGATIONS

(Adopted 13 Dec 2001)

The pre-trial Judge or the Trial Chamber may decide *proprio motu*, or at the request of **C6–083** either party, on sanctions to be imposed on a party which fails to perform its disclosure obligations pursuant to the Rules.

RULE 69

PROTECTION OF VICTIMS AND WITNESSES

(Adopted 11 Feb 1994)

(A) In exceptional circumstances, the Prosecutor may apply to a Judge or Trial **C6–084** Chamber to order the non-disclosure of the identity of a victim or witness who may be in danger or at risk until such person is brought under the protection of the Tribunal. (Amended 13 Dec 2001)

(B) In the determination of protective measures for victims and witnesses, the Judge or Trial Chamber may consult the Victims and Witnesses Section. (Amended 15 June 1995, amended 2 July 1999, amended 13 Dec 2001)

(C) Subject to Rule 75, the identity of the victim or witness shall be disclosed in sufficient time prior to the trial to allow adequate time for preparation of the defence.

RULE 70

MATTERS NOT SUBJECT TO DISCLOSURE

(Adopted 11 Feb 1994)

C6–085

(A) Notwithstanding the provisions of Rules 66 and 67, reports, memoranda, or other internal documents prepared by a party, its assistants or representatives in connection with the investigation or preparation of the case, are not subject to disclosure or notification under those Rules.

(B) If the Prosecutor is in possession of information which has been provided to the Prosecutor on a confidential basis and which has been used solely for the purpose of generating new evidence, that initial information and its origin shall not be disclosed by the Prosecutor without the consent of the person or entity providing the initial information and shall in any event not be given in evidence without prior disclosure to the accused. (Amended 4 Oct 1994, revised 30 Jan 1995, revised 12 Nov 1997)

(C) If, after obtaining the consent of the person or entity providing information under this Rule, the Prosecutor elects to present as evidence any testimony, document or other material so provided, the Trial Chamber, notwithstanding Rule 98, may not order either party to produce additional evidence received from the person or entity providing the initial information, nor may the Trial Chamber for the purpose of obtaining such additional evidence itself summon that person or a representative of that entity as a witness or order their attendance. A Trial Chamber may not use its power to order the attendance of witnesses or to require production of documents in order to compel the production of such additional evidence. (Amended 6 Oct 1995, amended 25 July 1997)

(D) If the Prosecutor calls a witness to introduce in evidence any information provided under this Rule, the Trial Chamber may not compel that witness to answer any question relating to the information or its origin, if the witness declines to answer on grounds of confidentiality. (Amended 6 Oct 1995, amended 25 July 1997)

(E) The right of the accused to challenge the evidence presented by the Prosecution shall remain unaffected subject only to the limitations contained in paragraphs (C) and (D). (Amended 6 Oct 1995, amended 12 Apr 2001)

(F) The Trial Chamber may order upon an application by the accused or defence counsel that, in the interests of justice, the provisions of this Rule shall apply *mutatis mutandis* to specific information in the possession of the accused. (Amended 25 July 1997)

(G) Nothing in paragraph (C) or (D) above shall affect a Trial Chamber's power under Rule 89 (D) to exclude evidence if its probative value is substantially outweighed by the need to ensure a fair trial. (Amended 6 Oct 1995, amended 12 Apr 2001)

Section 5: Depositions

RULE 71

DEPOSITIONS

(Adopted 11 Feb 1994, amended 10 July 1998)

C6–086

(A) Where it is in the interests of justice to do so, a Trial Chamber may order, *proprio motu* or at the request of a party, that a deposition be taken for use at trial, whether or not the person whose deposition is sought is able physically to appear before the

Tribunal to give evidence. The Trial Chamber shall appoint a Presiding Officer for that purpose. (Amended 17 Nov 1999)

(B) The motion for the taking of a deposition shall indicate the name and where-abouts of the person whose deposition is sought, the date and place at which the deposition is to be taken, a statement of the matters on which the person is to be examined, and of the circumstances justifying the taking of the deposition. (Amended 17 Nov 1999)

(C) If the motion is granted, the party at whose request the deposition is to be taken shall give reasonable notice to the other party, who shall have the right to attend the taking of the deposition and cross-examine the person whose deposition is being taken.

(D) Deposition evidence may be taken either at or away from the seat of the Tribunal, and it may also be given by means of a video-conference. (Amended 17 Nov 1999)

(E) The Presiding Officer shall ensure that the deposition is taken in accordance with the Rules and that a record is made of the deposition, including cross-examination and objections raised by either party for decision by the Trial Chamber. The Presiding Officer shall transmit the record to the Trial Chamber.

Rule 71*bis*

TESTIMONY BY VIDEO-CONFERENCE LINK

(Adopted 17 Nov 1999)

At the request of either party, a Trial Chamber may, in the interests of justice, order **C6–087** that testimony be received via video-conference link.

Section 6: Motions

Rule 72

PRELIMINARY MOTIONS

(Adopted 11 Feb 1994, amended 10 July 1998, amended 4 Dec 1998, amended 21 July 2005)

(A) Preliminary motions, being motions which **C6–088**
  (i) challenge jurisdiction;
  (ii) allege defects in the form of the indictment;
  (iii) seek the severance of counts joined in one indictment under Rule 49 or seek separate trials under Rule 82 (B); or
  (iv) raise objections based on the refusal of a request for assignment of counsel made under Rule 45 (C)
shall be in writing and be brought not later than thirty days after disclosure by the Prosecutor to the defence of all material and statements referred to in Rule 66 (A)(i) and shall be disposed of not later than sixty days after they were filed and before the commencement of the opening statements provided for in Rule 84.(Revised 12 Nov 1997)

(B) Decisions on preliminary motions are without interlocutory appeal save
  (i) in the case of motions challenging jurisdiction;
  (Amended 25 June 1996 and 5 July 1996, amended 23 Apr 2002);
  (ii) in other cases where certification has been granted by the Trial Chamber, which may grant such certification if the decision involves an issue that would significantly affect the fair and expeditious conduct of the proceedings or the outcome of the trial, and for which, in the opinion of the Trial Chamber, an immediate resolution by the Appeals Chamber may materially advance the proceedings.

(Amended 25 June 1996 and 5 July 1996, amended 25 July 1997, revised 12 Nov 1997, amended 23 Apr 2002)

(Revised 30 Jan 1995, revised 12 Nov 1997)

(C) Appeals under paragraph (B)(i) shall be filed within fifteen days and requests for certification under paragraph (B)(ii) shall be filed within seven days of filing of the impugned decision. Where such decision is rendered orally, this time-limit shall run from the date of the oral decision, unless

    (i) the party challenging the decision was not present or represented when the decision was pronounced, in which case the time-limit shall run from the date on which the challenging party is notified of the oral decision; or

    (ii) the Trial Chamber has indicated that a written decision will follow, in which case, the time-limit shall run from filing of the written decision.

If certification is given, a party shall appeal to the Appeals Chamber within seven days of the filing of the decision to certify.(Revised 12 Nov 1997, amended 10 July 1998, amended 17 Nov 1999, amended 1 Dec 2000 and 13 Dec 2000, amended 23 Apr 2002)

(D) For the purpose of paragraphs (A)(i) and (B)(i), a motion challenging jurisdiction refers exclusively to a motion which challenges an indictment on the ground that it does not relate to:

    (i) any of the persons indicated in Articles 1, 6, 7 and 9 of the Statute;

    (ii) the territories indicated in Articles 1, 8 and 9 of the Statute;

    (iii) the period indicated in Articles 1, 8 and 9 of the Statute;

    (iv) any of the violations indicated in Articles 2, 3, 4, 5 and 7 of the Statute.

(Amended 1 Dec 2000 and 13 Dec 2000)

RULE 73

OTHER MOTIONS

(Adopted 11 Feb 1994, revised 12 Nov 1997, amended 12 Apr 2001, amended 13 Dec 2001, amended 23 Apr 2002)

C6–089

(A) After a case is assigned to a Trial Chamber, either party may at any time move before the Chamber by way of motion, not being a preliminary motion, for appropriate ruling or relief. Such motions may be written or oral, at the discretion of the Trial Chamber. (Revised 12 Nov 1997)

(B) Decisions on all motions are without interlocutory appeal save with certification by the Trial Chamber, which may grant such certification if the decision involves an issue that would significantly affect the fair and expeditious conduct of the proceedings or the outcome of the trial, and for which, in the opinion of the Trial Chamber, an immediate resolution by the Appeals Chamber may materially advance the proceedings. (Amended 12 Apr 2001, amended 23 Apr 2002)

(C) Requests for certification shall be filed within seven days of the filing of the impugned decision. Where such decision is rendered orally, this time-limit shall run from the date of the oral decision, unless

    (i) the party challenging the decision was not present or represented when the decision was pronounced, in which case the time-limit shall run from the date on which the challenging party is notified of the oral decision; or

    (ii) the Trial Chamber has indicated that a written decision will follow, in which case the time-limit shall run from filing of the written decision.

If certification is given, a party shall appeal to the Appeals Chamber within seven days of the filing of the decision to certify.(Revised 12 Nov 1997, amended 10 July 1998, amended 12 Apr 2001, amended 23 Apr 2002)

(D) Irrespective of any sanctions which may be imposed under Rule 46 (A), when a Chamber finds that a motion is frivolous or is an abuse of process, the Registrar shall withhold payment of fees associated with the production of that motion and/ or costs thereof. (Amended 8 Dec 2004)

Section 7: Conferences

RULE 73*bis*

PRE-TRIAL CONFERENCE

(Adopted 10 July 1998, amended 17 Nov 1999, amended 17 July 2003)

(A) Prior to the commencement of the trial, the Trial Chamber shall hold a Pre-Trial **C6–090**
Conference.

(B) In the light of the file submitted to the Trial Chamber by the pre-trial Judge pursuant to Rule 65*ter* (L)(i), the Trial Chamber may call upon the Prosecutor to shorten the estimated length of the examination-in-chief for some witnesses. (Amended 17 Nov 1999, amended 12 Apr 2001)

(C) In the light of the file submitted to the Trial Chamber by the pre-trial Judge pursuant to Rule 65*ter* (L)(i), the Trial Chamber, after having heard the Prosecutor, shall determine

    (i) the number of witnesses the Prosecutor may call; and

    (ii) the time available to the Prosecutor for presenting evidence.

    (Amended 17 Nov 1999, amended 12 Apr 2001, amended 17 July 2003)

(D) After having heard the Prosecutor, the Trial Chamber may fix a number of crime sites or incidents comprised in one or more of the charges in respect of which evidence may be presented by the Prosecutor which, having regard to all the relevant circumstances, including the crimes charged in the indictment, their classification and nature, the places where they are alleged to have been committed, their scale and the victims of the crimes, are reasonably representative of the crimes charged. (Amended 17 July 2003)

(E) After commencement of the trial, the Prosecutor may file a motion to vary the decision as to the number of crime sites or incidents in respect of which evidence may be presented or the number of witnesses that are to be called or for additional time to present evidence and the Trial Chamber may grant the Prosecutor's request if satisfied that this is in the interests of justice. (Amended 17 Nov 1999, amended 12 Apr 2001, amended 17 July 2003)

RULE 73*ter*

PRE-DEFENCE CONFERENCE

(Adopted 10 July 1998, amended 17 Nov 1999)

(A) Prior to the commencement by the defence of its case the Trial Chamber may **C6–091**
hold a Conference.

(B) In the light of the file submitted to the Trial Chamber by the pre-trial Judge pursuant to Rule 65*ter* (L)(ii), the Trial Chamber may call upon the defence to shorten the estimated length of the examination-in-chief for some witnesses. (Amended 17 Nov 1999, amended 12 Apr 2001)

(C) In the light of the file submitted to the Trial Chamber by the pre-trial Judge pursuant to Rule 65*ter* (L)(ii), the Trial Chamber, after having heard the defence, shall set the number of witnesses the defence may call. (Amended 17 Nov 1999, amended 12 Apr 2001)

(D) After commencement of the defence case, the defence may, if it considers it to be in the interests of justice, file a motion to reinstate the list of witnesses or to vary the decision as to which witnesses are to be called. (Amended 12 Apr 2001)

(E) After having heard the defence, the Trial Chamber shall determine the time available to the defence for presenting evidence. (Amended 12 Apr 2001)

(F) During a trial, the Trial Chamber may grant a defence request for additional time to present evidence if this is in the interests of justice. (Amended 12 Apr 2001)

PART SIX

PROCEEDINGS BEFORE TRIAL CHAMBERS

Section 1: General Provisions

RULE 74

AMICUS CURIAE

(Adopted 11 Feb 1994)

C6–092   A Chamber may, if it considers it desirable for the proper determination of the case, invite or grant leave to a State, organization or person to appear before it and make submissions on any issue specified by the Chamber.

RULE 74*bis*

MEDICAL EXAMINATION OF THE ACCUSED

(Adopted 10 July 1998, amended 12 Apr 2001)

C6–093   A Trial Chamber may, *proprio motu* or at the request of a party, order a medical, psychiatric or psychological examination of the accused. In such a case, unless the Trial Chamber otherwise orders, the Registrar shall entrust this task to one or several experts whose names appear on a list previously drawn up by the Registry and approved by the Bureau.

RULE 75

MEASURES FOR THE PROTECTION OF VICTIMS AND WITNESSES

(Adopted 11 Feb 1994)

C6–094   (A) A Judge or a Chamber may, *proprio motu* or at the request of either party, or of the victim or witness concerned, or of the Victims and Witnesses Section, order appropriate measures for the privacy and protection of victims and witnesses, provided that the measures are consistent with the rights of the accused. (Amended 15 June 1995, amended 2 July 1999)

(B) A Chamber may hold an in camera proceeding to determine whether to order:

(i) measures to prevent disclosure to the public or the media of the identity or whereabouts of a witness or a victim, or of persons related to or associated with a victim or witness by such means as:

(Revised 12 Nov 1997):

(a) expunging names and identifying information from the Tribunal's public records;

(b) non-disclosure to the public of any records identifying the victim;

    (c) giving of testimony through image- or voice- altering devices or closed circuit television; and

    (d) assignment of a pseudonym;

  (ii) closed sessions, in accordance with Rule 79;

  (iii) appropriate measures to facilitate the testimony of vulnerable victims and witnesses, such as one-way closed circuit television.

(Revised 30 Jan 1995)

(C) The Victims and Witnesses Section shall ensure that the witness has been informed before giving evidence that his or her testimony and his or her identity may be disclosed at a later date in another case, pursuant to Rule 75 (F). (Amended 12 Dec 2002)

(D) A Chamber shall, whenever necessary, control the manner of questioning to avoid any harassment or intimidation.

(E) When making an order under paragraph (A) above, a Judge or Chamber shall wherever appropriate state in the order whether the transcript of those proceedings relating to the evidence of the witness to whom the measures relate shall be made available for use in other proceedings before the Tribunal. (Amended 12 July 2002)

(F) Once protective measures have been ordered in respect of a victim or witness in any proceedings before the Tribunal (the "first proceedings"), such protective measures:

  (i) shall continue to have effect *mutatis mutandis* in any other proceedings before the Tribunal (the "second proceedings") unless and until they are rescinded, varied or augmented in accordance with the procedure set out in this Rule; but

  (ii) shall not prevent the Prosecutor from discharging any disclosure obligation under the Rules in the second proceedings, provided that the Prosecutor notifies the Defence to whom the disclosure is being made of the nature of the protective measures ordered in the first proceedings.

    (Amended 17 Nov 1999, amended 1 Dec 2000 and 13 Dec 2000, amended 13 Dec 2001, amended 12 July 2002)

(G) A party to the second proceedings seeking to rescind, vary or augment protective measures ordered in the first proceedings must apply:

  (i) to any Chamber, however constituted, remaining seised of the first proceedings; or

  (ii) if no Chamber remains seised of the first proceedings, to the Chamber seised of the second proceedings.

    (Amended 12 July 2002)

(H) Before determining an application under paragraph (G)(ii) above, the Chamber seised of the second proceedings shall obtain all relevant information from the first proceedings, and shall consult with any Judge who ordered the protective measures in the first proceedings, if that Judge remains a Judge of the Tribunal. (Amended 12 July 2002, amended 12 Dec 2002)

(I) An application to a Chamber to rescind, vary or augment protective measures in respect of a victim or witness may be dealt with either by the Chamber or by a Judge of that Chamber, and any reference in this Rule to "a Chamber" shall include a reference to "a Judge of that Chamber". (Amended 12 July 2002)

RULE 76

SOLEMN DECLARATION BY INTERPRETERS AND TRANSLATORS

(Adopted 11 Feb 1994)

Before performing any duties, an interpreter or a translator shall solemnly declare to **C6–095** do so faithfully, independently, impartially and with full respect for the duty of confidentiality.

Rule 77

CONTEMPT OF THE TRIBUNAL

(Adopted 11 Feb 1994, revised 30 Jan 1995, amended 25 July 1997, revised 12 Nov 1997, amended 13 Dec 2001)

C6–096   (A) The Tribunal in the exercise of its inherent power may hold in contempt those who knowingly and wilfully interfere with its administration of justice, including any person who

  (i) being a witness before a Chamber, contumaciously refuses or fails to answer a question;

  (ii) discloses information relating to those proceedings in knowing violation of an order of a Chamber; (Amended 4 Dec 1998)

  (iii) without just excuse fails to comply with an order to attend before or produce documents before a Chamber;

  (iv) threatens, intimidates, causes any injury or offers a bribe to, or otherwise interferes with, a witness who is giving, has given, or is about to give evidence in proceedings before a Chamber, or a potential witness; or
  (Amended 4 Dec 1998, amended 13 Dec 2001)

  (v) threatens, intimidates, offers a bribe to, or otherwise seeks to coerce any other person, with the intention of preventing that other person from complying with an obligation under an order of a Judge or Chamber.
  (Amended 4 Dec 1998, amended 13 Dec 2001)
  (Amended 10 July 1998, revised 12 Nov 1997, amended 13 Dec 2001)

  (B) Any incitement or attempt to commit any of the acts punishable under paragraph (A) is punishable as contempt of the Tribunal with the same penalties. (Amended 4 Dec 1998, amended 13 Dec 2001)

  (C) When a Chamber has reason to believe that a person may be in contempt of the Tribunal, it may:

  (i) direct the Prosecutor to investigate the matter with a view to the preparation and submission of an indictment for contempt;

  (ii) where the Prosecutor, in the view of the Chamber, has a conflict of interest with respect to the relevant conduct, direct the Registrar to appoint an *amicus curiae* to investigate the matter and report back to the Chamber as to whether there are sufficient grounds for instigating contempt proceedings; or

  (iii) initiate proceedings itself.
  (Revised 12 Nov 1997, amended 10 July 1998, amended 4 Dec 1998, amended 13 Dec 2001)

  (D) If the Chamber considers that there are sufficient grounds to proceed against a person for contempt, the Chamber may:

  (i) in circumstances described in paragraph (C)(i), direct the Prosecutor to prosecute the matter; or

  (ii) in circumstances described in paragraph (C)(ii) or (iii), issue an order in lieu of an indictment and either direct *amicus curiae* to prosecute the matter or prosecute the matter itself.
  (Amended 13 Dec 2001)

  (E) The rules of procedure and evidence in Parts Four to Eight shall apply *mutatis mutandis* to proceedings under this Rule. (Amended 13 Dec 2001)

  (F) Any person indicted for or charged with contempt shall, if that person satisfies the criteria for determination of indigence established by the Registrar, be assigned counsel in accordance with Rule 45. (Revised 12 Nov 1997, amended 13 Dec 2001)

  (G) The maximum penalty that may be imposed on a person found to be in contempt of the Tribunal shall be a term of imprisonment not exceeding seven years, or a fine not exceeding 100,000 Euros, or both. (Amended 4 Dec 1998, amended 1 Dec 2000 and 13 Dec 2000, amended 13 Dec 2001)

(H) Payment of a fine shall be made to the Registrar to be held in a separate account.

(I) If a counsel is found guilty of contempt of the Tribunal pursuant to this Rule, the Chamber making such finding may also determine that counsel is no longer eligible to represent a suspect or accused before the Tribunal or that such conduct amounts to misconduct of counsel pursuant to Rule 46, or both. (Amended 13 Dec 2001)

(J) Any decision rendered by a Trial Chamber under this Rule shall be subject to appeal. Notice of appeal shall be filed within fifteen days of filing of the impugned decision. Where such decision is rendered orally, the notice shall be filed within fifteen days of the oral decision, unless

    (i) the party challenging the decision was not present or represented when the decision was pronounced, in which case the time-limit shall run from the date on which the challenging party is notified of the oral decision; or

    (ii) the Trial Chamber has indicated that a written decision will follow, in which case the time-limit shall run from filing of the written decision.
    (Revised 12 Nov 1997, amended 10 July 1998, amended 4 Dec 1998, amended 1 Dec 2000 and 13 Dec 2000)

(K) In the case of decisions under this Rule by the Appeals Chamber sitting as a Chamber of first instance, an appeal may be submitted in writing to the President within fifteen days of the filing of the impugned decision. Such appeal shall be decided by five different Judges as assigned by the President. Where the impugned decision is rendered orally, the appeal shall be filed within fifteen days of the oral decision, unless

    (i) the party challenging the decision was not present or represented when the decision was pronounced, in which case the time-limit shall run from the date on which the challenging party is notified of the oral decision; or

    (ii) the Appeals Chamber has indicated that a written decision will follow, in which case the time-limit shall run from filing of the written decision.
    (Amended 12 July 2002)

Rule 77*bis*

PAYMENT OF FINES

(Adopted 2 July 1999)

(A) In imposing a fine under Rule 77 or Rule 91, a Chamber shall specify the time for its payment. (Amended 13 Dec 2001)   **C6–097**

(B) Where a fine imposed under Rule 77 or Rule 91 is not paid within the time specified, the Chamber imposing the fine may issue an order requiring the person on whom the fine is imposed to appear before, or to respond in writing to, the Tribunal to explain why the fine has not been paid. (Amended 13 Dec 2001)

(C) After affording the person on whom the fine is imposed an opportunity to be heard, the Chamber may make a decision that appropriate measures be taken, including:

    (i) extending the time for payment of the fine;

    (ii) requiring the payment of the fine to be made in instalments;

    (iii) in consultation with the Registrar, requiring that the moneys owed be deducted from any outstanding fees owing to the person by the Tribunal where the person is a counsel retained by the Tribunal pursuant to the Directive on the Assignment of Defence Counsel;
    (Amended 17 Nov 1999)

    (iv) converting the whole or part of the fine to a term of imprisonment not exceeding twelve months.
    (Amended 17 Nov 1999, amended 13 Dec 2001)

(D) In addition to a decision under paragraph (C), the Chamber may find the person in contempt of the Tribunal and impose a new penalty applying Rule 77 (G), if that person was able to pay the fine within the specified time and has wilfully failed to do so.

This penalty for contempt of the Tribunal shall be additional to the original fine imposed. (Amended 12 Apr 2001, amended 13 Dec 2001)

(E) The Chamber may, if necessary, issue an arrest warrant to secure the person's presence where he or she fails to appear before or respond in writing pursuant to an order under paragraph (B). A State or authority to whom such a warrant is addressed, in accordance with Article 29 of the Statute, shall act promptly and with all due diligence to ensure proper and effective execution thereof. Where an arrest warrant is issued under this Sub-rule, the provisions of Rules 45, 57, 58, 59, 59*bis*, and 60 shall apply *mutatis mutandis*. Following the transfer of the person concerned to the Tribunal, the provisions of Rules 64, 65 and 99 shall apply *mutatis mutandis*.(Amended 12 Apr 2001, amended 13 Dec 2001)

(F) Where under this Rule a penalty of imprisonment is imposed, or a fine is converted to a term of imprisonment, the provisions of Rules 102, 103 and 104 and Part Nine shall apply *mutatis mutandis*.

(G) Any finding of contempt or penalty imposed under this Rule shall be subject to appeal as allowed for in Rule 77 (J).

RULE 78

OPEN SESSIONS

(Adopted 11 Feb 1994)

C6–098   All proceedings before a Trial Chamber, other than deliberations of the Chamber, shall be held in public, unless otherwise provided.

RULE 79

CLOSED SESSIONS

(Adopted 11 Feb 1994)

C6–099   (A) The Trial Chamber may order that the press and the public be excluded from all or part of the proceedings for reasons of:
    (i) public order or morality;
    (ii) safety, security or non-disclosure of the identity of a victim or witness as provided in Rule 75; or
    (iii) the protection of the interests of justice.
(B) The Trial Chamber shall make public the reasons for its order.

RULE 80

CONTROL OF PROCEEDINGS

(Adopted 11 Feb 1994)

C6–100   (A) The Trial Chamber may exclude a person from the courtroom in order to protect the right of the accused to a fair and public trial, or to maintain the dignity and decorum of the proceedings.

(B) The Trial Chamber may order the removal of an accused from the courtroom and continue the proceedings in the absence of the accused if the accused has persisted in disruptive conduct following a warning that such conduct may warrant the removal of the accused from the courtroom.

Rule 81

RECORDS OF PROCEEDINGS AND EVIDENCE

(Adopted 11 Feb 1994)

(A) The Registrar shall cause to be made and preserve a full and accurate record of **C6–101** all proceedings, including audio recordings, transcripts and, when deemed necessary by the Trial Chamber, video recordings.

(B) The Trial Chamber, after giving due consideration to any matters relating to witness protection, may order the disclosure of all or part of the record of closed proceedings when the reasons for ordering its non-disclosure no longer exist. (Amended 1 Dec 2000 and 13 Dec 2000)

(C) The Registrar shall retain and preserve all physical evidence offered during the proceedings subject to any Practice Direction or any order which a Chamber may at any time make with respect to the control or disposition of physical evidence offered during proceedings before that Chamber. (Amended 25 July 1997)

(D) Photography, video-recording or audio-recording of the trial, otherwise than by the Registrar, may be authorised at the discretion of the Trial Chamber.

Section 2: Case Presentation

Rule 82

JOINT AND SEPARATE TRIALS

(Adopted 11 Feb 1994)

(A) In joint trials, each accused shall be accorded the same rights as if such accused **C6–102** were being tried separately. (Revised 12 Nov 1997)

(B) The Trial Chamber may order that persons accused jointly under Rule 48 be tried separately if it considers it necessary in order to avoid a conflict of interests that might cause serious prejudice to an accused, or to protect the interests of justice.

Rule 83

INSTRUMENTS OF RESTRAINT

(Adopted 11 Feb 1994, amended 4 Dec 1998)

Instruments of restraint, such as handcuffs, shall be used only on the order of the **C6–103** Registrar as a precaution against escape during transfer or in order to prevent an accused from self-injury, injury to others or to prevent serious damage to property. Instruments of restraint shall be removed when the accused appears before a Chamber or a Judge.

Rule 84

OPENING STATEMENTS

(Adopted 11 Feb 1994, revised 12 Nov 1997)

Before presentation of evidence by the Prosecutor, each party may make an opening **C6–104** statement. The defence may, however, elect to make its statement after the conclusion of the Prosecutor's presentation of evidence and before the presentation of evidence for the defence.

Rule 84*bis*

STATEMENT OF THE ACCUSED

(Adopted 2 July 1999)

C6–105   (A) After the opening statements of the parties or, if the defence elects to defer its opening statement pursuant to Rule 84, after the opening statement of the Prosecutor, if any, the accused may, if he or she so wishes, and the Trial Chamber so decides, make a statement under the control of the Trial Chamber. The accused shall not be compelled to make a solemn declaration and shall not be examined about the content of the statement.

(B) The Trial Chamber shall decide on the probative value, if any, of the statement.

Rule 85

PRESENTATION OF EVIDENCE

(Adopted 11 Feb 1994)

C6–106   (A) Each party is entitled to call witnesses and present evidence. Unless otherwise directed by the Trial Chamber in the interests of justice, evidence at the trial shall be presented in the following sequence:

(i) evidence for the prosecution;
(ii) evidence for the defence;
(iii) prosecution evidence in rebuttal;
(iv) defence evidence in rejoinder;
(v) evidence ordered by the Trial Chamber pursuant to Rule 98; and
(Amended 10 July 1998)
(vi) any relevant information that may assist the Trial Chamber in determining an appropriate sentence if the accused is found guilty on one or more of the charges in the indictment.
(Amended 10 July 1998)

(B) Examination-in-chief, cross-examination and re-examination shall be allowed in each case. It shall be for the party calling a witness to examine such witness in chief, but a Judge may at any stage put any question to the witness.

(C) If the accused so desires, the accused may appear as a witness in his or her own defence.

Rule 86

CLOSING ARGUMENTS

(Adopted 11 Feb 1994, revised 12 Nov 1997)

C6–107   (A) After the presentation of all the evidence, the Prosecutor may present a closing argument; whether or not the Prosecutor does so, the defence may make a closing argument. The Prosecutor may present a rebuttal argument to which the defence may present a rejoinder. (Amended 10 July 1998)

(B) Not later than five days prior to presenting a closing argument, a party shall file a final trial brief. (Amended 10 July 1998, amended 1 Dec 2000 and 13 Dec 2000)

(C) The parties shall also address matters of sentencing in closing arguments. (Amended 10 July 1998)

RULE 87

DELIBERATIONS

(Adopted 11 Feb 1994)

(A) When both parties have completed their presentation of the case, the Presiding **C6–108** Judge shall declare the hearing closed, and the Trial Chamber shall deliberate in private. A finding of guilt may be reached only when a majority of the Trial Chamber is satisfied that guilt has been proved beyond reasonable doubt.

(B) The Trial Chamber shall vote separately on each charge contained in the indictment. If two or more accused are tried together under Rule 48, separate findings shall be made as to each accused.

(C) If the Trial Chamber finds the accused guilty on one or more of the charges contained in the indictment, it shall impose a sentence in respect of each finding of guilt and indicate whether such sentences shall be served consecutively or concurrently, unless it decides to exercise its power to impose a single sentence reflecting the totality of the criminal conduct of the accused. (Amended 10 July 1998, amended 1 Dec 2000 and 13 Dec 2000)

RULE 88

[DELETED]

(Adopted 11 Feb 1994, revised 30 Jan 1995, revised 12 Nov 1997, deleted 10 July 1998) **C6–109**

RULE 88*bis*

[DELETED]

(Adopted 12 Nov 1997, deleted 10 July 1998) **C6–110**

Section 3: Rules of Evidence

RULE 89

GENERAL PROVISIONS

(Adopted 11 Feb 1994)

(A) A Chamber shall apply the rules of evidence set forth in this Section, and shall **C6–111** not be bound by national rules of evidence. (Amended 1 Dec 2000 and 13 Dec 2000)

(B) In cases not otherwise provided for in this Section, a Chamber shall apply rules of evidence which will best favour a fair determination of the matter before it and are consonant with the spirit of the Statute and the general principles of law.

(C) A Chamber may admit any relevant evidence which it deems to have probative value.

(D) A Chamber may exclude evidence if its probative value is substantially outweighed by the need to ensure a fair trial.

(E) A Chamber may request verification of the authenticity of evidence obtained out of court.

(F) A Chamber may receive the evidence of a witness orally or, where the interests of justice allow, in written form. (Amended 1 Dec 2000 and 13 Dec 2000)

Rule 90

TESTIMONY OF WITNESSES

(Adopted 11 Feb 1994, revised 30 Jan 1995, amended 25 July 1997, amended 17 Nov 1999, amended 1 Dec 2000 and 13 Dec 2000)

C6–112   (A) Every witness shall, before giving evidence, make the following solemn declaration: "I solemnly declare that I will speak the truth, the whole truth and nothing but the truth".

(B) A child who, in the opinion of the Chamber, does not understand the nature of a solemn declaration, may be permitted to testify without that formality, if the Chamber is of the opinion that the child is sufficiently mature to be able to report the facts of which the child had knowledge and understands the duty to tell the truth. A judgement, however, cannot be based on such testimony alone. (Revised 30 Jan 1995)

(C) A witness, other than an expert, who has not yet testified shall not be present when the testimony of another witness is given. However, a witness who has heard the testimony of another witness shall not for that reason alone be disqualified from testifying.

(D) Notwithstanding paragraph (C), upon order of the Chamber, an investigator in charge of a party's investigation shall not be precluded from being called as a witness on the ground that he or she has been present in the courtroom during the proceedings. (Amended 25 July 1997, amended 1 Dec 2000 and 13 Dec 2000)

(E) A witness may object to making any statement which might tend to incriminate the witness. The Chamber may, however, compel the witness to answer the question. Testimony compelled in this way shall not be used as evidence in a subsequent prosecution against the witness for any offence other than false testimony. (Revised 30 Jan 1995, amended 1 Dec 2000 and 13 Dec 2000)

(F) The Trial Chamber shall exercise control over the mode and order of interrogating witnesses and presenting evidence so as to
> (i) make the interrogation and presentation effective for the ascertainment of the truth; and
> (ii) avoid needless consumption of time.
> (Amended 10 July 1998)

(G) The Trial Chamber may refuse to hear a witness whose name does not appear on the list of witnesses compiled pursuant to Rules 73*bis* (C) and 73*ter* (C). (Amended 12 Apr 2001)
> (H)(i) Cross-examination shall be limited to the subject-matter of the evidence-in-chief and matters affecting the credibility of the witness and, where the witness is able to give evidence relevant to the case for the cross-examining party, to the subject-matter of that case.
> (ii) In the cross-examination of a witness who is able to give evidence relevant to the case for the cross-examining party, counsel shall put to that witness the nature of the case of the party for whom that counsel appears which is in contradiction of the evidence given by the witness.
> (iii) The Trial Chamber may, in the exercise of its discretion, permit enquiry into additional matters.
> (Amended 10 July 1998, amended 17 Nov 1999)

Rule 90*bis*

TRANSFER OF A DETAINED WITNESS

(Adopted 6 Oct 1995)

C6–113   (A) Any detained person whose personal appearance as a witness has been requested by the Tribunal shall be transferred temporarily to the detention unit of the Tribunal, conditional on the person's return within the period decided by the Tribunal.

(B) The transfer order shall be issued by a permanent Judge or Trial Chamber only after prior verification that the following conditions have been met:

    (i) the presence of the detained witness is not required for any criminal proceedings in progress in the territory of the requested State during the period the witness is required by the Tribunal;

    (ii) transfer of the witness does not extend the period of detention as foreseen by the requested State.

    (Amended 12 Apr 2001)

(C) The Registrar shall transmit the order of transfer to the national authorities of the State on whose territory, or under whose jurisdiction or control, the witness is detained. Transfer shall be arranged by the national authorities concerned in liaison with the host country and the Registrar. (Revised 12 Nov 1997)

(D) The Registrar shall ensure the proper conduct of the transfer, including the supervision of the witness in the detention unit of the Tribunal; the Registrar shall remain abreast of any changes which might occur regarding the conditions of detention provided for by the requested State and which may possibly affect the length of the detention of the witness in the detention unit and, as promptly as possible, shall inform the relevant Judge or Chamber.(Revised 12 Nov 1997)

(E) On expiration of the period decided by the Tribunal for the temporary transfer, the detained witness shall be remanded to the authorities of the requested State, unless the State, within that period, has transmitted an order of release of the witness, which shall take effect immediately.

(F) If, by the end of the period decided by the Tribunal, the presence of the detained witness continues to be necessary, a permanent Judge or Chamber may extend the period on the same conditions as stated in paragraph (B). (Amended 12 Apr 2001)

Rule 91

FALSE TESTIMONY UNDER SOLEMN DECLARATION

(Adopted 11 Feb 1994)

(A) A Chamber, *proprio motu* or at the request of a party, may warn a witness of the duty to tell the truth and the consequences that may result from a failure to do so. (Amended 25 July 1997)   **C6–114**

(B) If a Chamber has strong grounds for believing that a witness has knowingly and wilfully given false testimony, it may:

    (i) direct the Prosecutor to investigate the matter with a view to the preparation and submission of an indictment for false testimony; or

    (Amended 13 Dec 2001)

    (ii) where the Prosecutor, in the view of the Chamber, has a conflict of interest with respect to the relevant conduct, direct the Registrar to appoint an *amicus curiae* to investigate the matter and report back to the Chamber as to whether there are sufficient grounds for instigating proceedings for false testimony.

    (Amended 13 Dec 2001)

(C) If the Chamber considers that there are sufficient grounds to proceed against a person for giving false testimony, the Chamber may:

    (i) in circumstances described in paragraph (B)(i), direct the Prosecutor to prosecute the matter; or

    (ii) in circumstances described in paragraph (B)(ii), issue an order in lieu of an indictment and direct amicus curiae to prosecute the matter.

    (Amended 13 Dec 2001)

(D) The rules of procedure and evidence in Parts Four to Eight shall apply *mutatis mutandis* to proceedings under this Rule.

(E) Any person indicted for or charged with false testimony shall, if that person satisfies the criteria for determination of indigence established by the Registrar, be assigned counsel in accordance with Rule 45. (Amended 13 Dec 2001)

(F) No Judge who sat as a member of the Trial Chamber before which the witness appeared shall sit for the trial of the witness for false testimony.

(G) The maximum penalty for false testimony under solemn declaration shall be a fine of 100,000 Euros or a term of imprisonment of seven years, or both. The payment of any fine imposed shall be paid to the Registrar to be held in the account referred to in Rule 77 (H). (Amended 18 Jan 1996, amended 25 July 1997, revised 12 Nov 1997, amended 4 Dec 1998, amended 1 Dec 2000 and 13 Dec 2000, amended 13 Dec 2001)

(H) Paragraphs (B) to (G) apply *mutatis mutandis* to a person who knowingly and willingly makes a false statement in a written statement taken in accordance with Rule 92*bis* which the person knows or has reason to know may be used as evidence in proceedings before the Tribunal. (Amended 17 Nov 1999, amended 1 Dec 2000 and 13 Dec 2000, amended 13 Dec 2001)

(I) Any decision rendered by a Trial Chamber under this Rule shall be subject to appeal. Notice of appeal shall be filed within fifteen days of filing of the impugned decision. Where such decision is rendered orally, the notice shall be filed within fifteen days of the oral decision, unless

> (i) the party challenging the decision was not present or represented when the decision was pronounced, in which case the time-limit shall run from the date on which the challenging party is notified of the oral decision; or
> (ii) the Trial Chamber has indicated that a written decision will follow, in which case the time-limit shall run from filing of the written decision.

(Amended 1 Dec 2000 and 13 Dec 2000)

RULE 92

CONFESSIONS

(Adopted 11 Feb 1994)

C6–115   A confession by the accused given during questioning by the Prosecutor shall, provided the requirements of Rule 63 were strictly complied with, be presumed to have been free and voluntary unless the contrary is proved.

RULE 92*bis*

PROOF OF FACTS OTHER THAN BY ORAL EVIDENCE

(Adopted 1 Dec 2000 and 13 Dec 2000)

C6–116   (A) A Trial Chamber may admit, in whole or in part, the evidence of a witness in the form of a written statement in lieu of oral testimony which goes to proof of a matter other than the acts and conduct of the accused as charged in the indictment.

> (i) Factors in favour of admitting evidence in the form of a written statement include but are not limited to circumstances in which the evidence in question:
>> (a) is of a cumulative nature, in that other witnesses will give or have given oral testimony of similar facts;
>> (b) relates to relevant historical, political or military background;
>> (c) consists of a general or statistical analysis of the ethnic composition of the population in the places to which the indictment relates;
>> (d) concerns the impact of crimes upon victims;
>> (e) relates to issues of the character of the accused; or
>> (f) relates to factors to be taken into account in determining sentence.
> (ii) Factors against admitting evidence in the form of a written statement include whether:

(a) there is an overriding public interest in the evidence in question being presented orally;

(b) a party objecting can demonstrate that its nature and source renders it unreliable, or that its prejudicial effect outweighs its probative value; or

(c) there are any other factors which make it appropriate for the witness to attend for cross-examination.

(B) A written statement under this Rule shall be admissible if it attaches a declaration by the person making the written statement that the contents of the statement are true and correct to the best of that person's knowledge and belief and

(i) the declaration is witnessed by:

(a) a person authorised to witness such a declaration in accordance with the law and procedure of a State; or

(b) a Presiding Officer appointed by the Registrar of the Tribunal for that purpose; and

(ii) the person witnessing the declaration verifies in writing:

(a) that the person making the statement is the person identified in the said statement;

(b) that the person making the statement stated that the contents of the written statement are, to the best of that person's knowledge and belief, true and correct;

(c) that the person making the statement was informed that if the content of the written statement is not true then he or she may be subject to proceedings for giving false testimony; and

(d) the date and place of the declaration.

The declaration shall be attached to the written statement presented to the Trial Chamber.

(C) A written statement not in the form prescribed by paragraph (B) may nevertheless be admissible if made by a person who has subsequently died, or by a person who can no longer with reasonable diligence be traced, or by a person who is by reason of bodily or mental condition unable to testify orally, if the Trial Chamber:

(i) is so satisfied on a balance of probabilities; and

(ii) finds from the circumstances in which the statement was made and recorded that there are satisfactory indicia of its reliability.

(D) A Chamber may admit a transcript of evidence given by a witness in proceedings before the Tribunal which goes to proof of a matter other than the acts and conduct of the accused.

(E) Subject to Rule 127 or any order to the contrary, a party seeking to adduce a written statement or transcript shall give fourteen days notice to the opposing party, who may within seven days object. The Trial Chamber shall decide, after hearing the parties, whether to admit the statement or transcript in whole or in part and whether to require the witness to appear for cross-examination.

RULE 93

EVIDENCE OF CONSISTENT PATTERN OF CONDUCT

(Adopted 11 Feb 1994)

(A) Evidence of a consistent pattern of conduct relevant to serious violations of **C6–117** international humanitarian law under the Statute may be admissible in the interests of justice. (Amended 18 Jan 1996)

(B) Acts tending to show such a pattern of conduct shall be disclosed by the Prosecutor to the defence pursuant to Rule 66. (Revised 30 Jan 1995)

RULE 94

JUDICIAL NOTICE

(Adopted 11 Feb 1994)

C6–118   (A) A Trial Chamber shall not require proof of facts of common knowledge but shall take judicial notice thereof.

(B) At the request of a party or proprio motu, a Trial Chamber, after hearing the parties, may decide to take judicial notice of adjudicated facts or documentary evidence from other proceedings of the Tribunal relating to matters at issue in the current proceedings. (Amended 10 July 1998)

RULE 94*bis*

TESTIMONY OF EXPERT WITNESSES

(Adopted 10 July 1998)

C6–119   (A) The full statement of any expert witness to be called by a party shall be disclosed within the time-limit prescribed by the Trial Chamber or by the pre-trial Judge. (Amended 14 July 2000, amended 1 Dec 2000 and 13 Dec 2000, amended 13 Dec 2001)

(B) Within thirty days of disclosure of the statement of the expert witness, or such other time prescribed by the Trial Chamber or pre-trial Judge, the opposing party shall file a notice indicating whether:

    (i) it accepts the expert witness statement; or

    (ii) it wishes to cross-examine the expert witness; and

    (iii) it challenges the qualifications of the witness as an expert or the relevance of all or parts of the report and, if so, which parts

        (Amended 12 Dec 2002)

        (Amended 13 Dec 2001)

(C) If the opposing party accepts the statement of the expert witness, the statement may be admitted into evidence by the Trial Chamber without calling the witness to testify in person.

RULE 94*ter*

[DELETED]

C6–120   (Adopted 4 Dec 1998, amended 17 Nov 1999, deleted 1 Dec 2000 and 13 Dec 2000)

RULE 95

EXCLUSION OF CERTAIN EVIDENCE

(Adopted 11 Feb 1994, revised 30 Jan 1995, revised 12 Nov 1997)

C6–121   No evidence shall be admissible if obtained by methods which cast substantial doubt on its reliability or if its admission is antithetical to, and would seriously damage, the integrity of the proceedings.

RULE 96

EVIDENCE IN CASES OF SEXUAL ASSAULT

(Adopted 11 Feb 1994)

C6–122   In cases of sexual assault:

    (i) no corroboration of the victim's testimony shall be required;
    (ii) consent shall not be allowed as a defence if the victim
        (a) has been subjected to or threatened with or has had reason to fear violence, duress, detention or psychological oppression, or
        (b) reasonably believed that if the victim did not submit, another might be so subjected, threatened or put in fear;
        (Amended 3 May 1995)
    (iii) before evidence of the victim's consent is admitted, the accused shall satisfy the Trial Chamber in camera that the evidence is relevant and credible;
    (Revised 30 Jan 1995)
    (iv) prior sexual conduct of the victim shall not be admitted in evidence.

RULE 97

LAWYER-CLIENT PRIVILEGE

(Adopted 11 Feb 1994)

All communications between lawyer and client shall be regarded as privileged, and **C6–123** consequently not subject to disclosure at trial, unless:
    (i) the client consents to such disclosure; or
    (ii) the client has voluntarily disclosed the content of the communication to a third party, and that third party then gives evidence of that disclosure.

RULE 98

POWER OF CHAMBERS TO ORDER PRODUCTION OF ADDITIONAL EVIDENCE

(Adopted 11 Feb 1994, amended 25 July 1997)

A Trial Chamber may order either party to produce additional evidence. It may *proprio* **C6–124** *motu* summon witnesses and order their attendance.

Section 4: Judgement

RULE 98*bis*

JUDGEMENT OF ACQUITTAL

(Adopted 10 July 1998, amended 17 Nov 1999, amended 8 Dec 2004)

At the close of the Prosecutor's case, the Trial Chamber shall, by oral decision and **C6–125** after hearing the oral submissions of the parties, enter a judgement of acquittal on any count if there is no evidence capable of supporting a conviction.

RULE 98*ter*

JUDGEMENT

(Adopted 10 July 1998)

(A) The judgement shall be pronounced in public, on a date of which notice shall have **C6–126** been given to the parties and counsel and at which they shall be entitled to be present, subject to the provisions of Rule 102 (B). (Amended 10 July 1998, amended 12 Apr 2001)

(B) If the Trial Chamber finds the accused guilty of a crime and concludes from the evidence that unlawful taking of property by the accused was associated with it, it shall make a specific finding to that effect in its judgement. The Trial Chamber may order restitution as provided in Rule 105.

(C) The judgement shall be rendered by a majority of the Judges. It shall be accompanied or followed as soon as possible by a reasoned opinion in writing, to which separate or dissenting opinions may be appended.

(D) A copy of the judgement and of the Judges' opinions in a language which the accused understands shall as soon as possible be served on the accused if in custody. Copies thereof in that language and in the language in which they were delivered shall also as soon as possible be provided to counsel for the accused.

RULE 99

STATUS OF THE ACQUITTED PERSON

(Adopted 11 Feb 1994, revised 12 Nov 1997)

C6–127   (A) Subject to paragraph (B), in the case of an acquittal or the upholding of a challenge to jurisdiction, the accused shall be released immediately. (Amended 12 Apr 2001)

(B) If, at the time the judgement is pronounced, the Prosecutor advises the Trial Chamber in open court of the Prosecutor's intention to file notice of appeal pursuant to Rule 108, the Trial Chamber may, on application in that behalf by the Prosecutor and upon hearing the parties, in its discretion, issue an order for the continued detention of the accused, pending the determination of the appeal. (Amended 10 July 1998)

Section 5: Sentencing and Penalties

RULE 100

SENTENCING PROCEDURE ON A GUILTY PLEA

(Adopted 11 Feb 1994, amended 10 July 1998)

C6–128   (A) If the Trial Chamber convicts the accused on a guilty plea, the Prosecutor and the defence may submit any relevant information that may assist the Trial Chamber in determining an appropriate sentence. (Amended 25 June 1996 and 5 July 1996)

(B) The sentence shall be pronounced in a judgement in public and in the presence of the convicted person, subject to Rule 102 (B).

RULE 101

PENALTIES

(Adopted 11 Feb 1994, amended 10 July 1998, amended 1 Dec 2000 and 13 Dec 2000)

C6–129   (A) A convicted person may be sentenced to imprisonment for a term up to and including the remainder of the convicted person's life. (Revised 12 Nov 1997)

(B) In determining the sentence, the Trial Chamber shall take into account the factors mentioned in Article 24, paragraph 2, of the Statute, as well as such factors as:

(i) any aggravating circumstances;

(ii) any mitigating circumstances including the substantial cooperation with the Prosecutor by the convicted person before or after conviction;

(iii) the general practice regarding prison sentences in the courts of the former Yugoslavia;

(iv) the extent to which any penalty imposed by a court of any State on the convicted person for the same act has already been served, as referred to in Article 10, paragraph 3, of the Statute.
(Revised 30 Jan 1995, amended 10 July 1998)
(Amended 10 July 1998)

(C) Credit shall be given to the convicted person for the period, if any, during which the convicted person was detained in custody pending surrender to the Tribunal or pending trial or appeal. (Revised 30 Jan 1995)

RULE 102

STATUS OF THE CONVICTED PERSON

(Adopted 11 Feb 1994)

(A) The sentence shall begin to run from the day it is pronounced. However, as soon **C6–130** as notice of appeal is given, the enforcement of the judgement shall thereupon be stayed until the decision on the appeal has been delivered, the convicted person meanwhile remaining in detention, as provided in Rule 64. (Amended 10 July 1998)

(B) If, by a previous decision of the Trial Chamber, the convicted person has been released, or is for any other reason at liberty, and is not present when the judgement is pronounced, the Trial Chamber shall issue a warrant for the convicted person's arrest. On arrest, the convicted person shall be notified of the conviction and sentence, and the procedure provided in Rule 103 shall be followed. (Revised 12 Nov 1997)

RULE 103

PLACE OF IMPRISONMENT

(Adopted 11 Feb 1994)

(A) Imprisonment shall be served in a State designated by the President of the **C6–131** Tribunal from a list of States which have indicated their willingness to accept convicted persons. (Amended 10 July 1998)

(B) Transfer of the convicted person to that State shall be effected as soon as possible after the time-limit for appeal has elapsed.

(C) Pending the finalisation of arrangements for his or her transfer to the State where his or her sentence will be served, the convicted person shall remain in the custody of the Tribunal. (Amended 4 Dec 1998)

RULE 104

SUPERVISION OF IMPRISONMENT

(Adopted 11 Feb 1994)

All sentences of imprisonment shall be supervised by the Tribunal or a body **C6–132** designated by it.

RULE 105

RESTITUTION OF PROPERTY

(Adopted 11 Feb 1994)

C6–133   (A) After a judgement of conviction containing a specific finding as provided in Rule 98*ter* (B), the Trial Chamber shall, at the request of the Prosecutor, or may, *proprio motu*, hold a special hearing to determine the matter of the restitution of the property or the proceeds thereof, and may in the meantime order such provisional measures for the preservation and protection of the property or proceeds as it considers appropriate. (Amended 25 July 1997, amended 10 July 1998, amended 12 Apr 2001)

    (B) The determination may extend to such property or its proceeds, even in the hands of third parties not otherwise connected with the crime of which the convicted person has been found guilty.

    (C) Such third parties shall be summoned before the Trial Chamber and be given an opportunity to justify their claim to the property or its proceeds.

    (D) Should the Trial Chamber be able to determine the rightful owner on the balance of probabilities, it shall order the restitution either of the property or the proceeds or make such other order as it may deem appropriate. (Revised 30 Jan 1995)

    (E) Should the Trial Chamber not be able to determine ownership, it shall notify the competent national authorities and request them so to determine.

    (F) Upon notice from the national authorities that an affirmative determination has been made, the Trial Chamber shall order the restitution either of the property or the proceeds or make such other order as it may deem appropriate. (Revised 30 Jan 1995)

    (G) The Registrar shall transmit to the competent national authorities any summonses, orders and requests issued by a Trial Chamber pursuant to paragraphs (C), (D), (E) and (F). (Revised 30 Jan 1995, amended 12 Apr 2001)

RULE 106

COMPENSATION TO VICTIMS

(Adopted 11 Feb 1994)

C6–134   (A) The Registrar shall transmit to the competent authorities of the States concerned the judgement finding the accused guilty of a crime which has caused injury to a victim.

    (B) Pursuant to the relevant national legislation, a victim or persons claiming through the victim may bring an action in a national court or other competent body to obtain compensation. (Revised 12 Nov 1997)

    (C) For the purposes of a claim made under paragraph (B) the judgement of the Tribunal shall be final and binding as to the criminal responsibility of the convicted person for such injury. (Amended 12 Apr 2001)

PART SEVEN

APPELLATE PROCEEDINGS

RULE 107

GENERAL PROVISION

(Adopted 11 Feb 1994)

C6–135   The rules of procedure and evidence that govern proceedings in the Trial Chambers shall apply *mutatis mutandis* to proceedings in the Appeals Chamber.

Rule 108

NOTICE OF APPEAL

(Adopted 11 Feb 1994, revised 30 Jan 1995, amended 25 July 1997, revised 12 Nov 1997, amended 10 July 1998, amended 2 July 1999, amended 17 Nov 1999, amended 13 Dec 2001)

A party seeking to appeal a judgement shall, not more than thirty days from the date **C6–136** on which the judgement was pronounced, file a notice of appeal, setting forth the grounds. The Appellant should also identify the order, decision or ruling challenged with specific reference to the date of its filing, and/or the transcript page, and indicate the substance of the alleged errors and the relief sought. The Appeals Chamber may, on good cause being shown by motion, authorise a variation of the grounds of appeal.

Rule 108*bis*

STATE REQUEST FOR REVIEW

(Adopted 25 July 1997)

(A) A State directly affected by an interlocutory decision of a Trial Chamber may, **C6–137** within fifteen days from the date of the decision, file a request for review of the decision by the Appeals Chamber if that decision concerns issues of general importance relating to the powers of the Tribunal. (Amended 2 July 1999)

(B) The party upon whose motion the Trial Chamber issued the impugned decision shall be heard by the Appeals Chamber. The other party may be heard if the Appeals Chamber considers that the interests of justice so require. (Amended 17 Nov 1999)

(C) The Appeals Chamber may at any stage suspend the execution of the impugned decision. (Amended 17 Nov 1999)

(D) Rule 116*bis* shall apply *mutatis mutandis*.

Rule 109

RECORD ON APPEAL

(Adopted 11 Feb 1994, revised 12 Nov 1997, amended 1 Dec 2000 and 13 Dec 2000)

The record on appeal shall consist of the trial record, as certified by the Registrar. **C6–138**

Rule 110

COPIES OF RECORD

(Adopted 11 Feb 1994)

The Registrar shall make a sufficient number of copies of the record on appeal for the **C6–139** use of the Judges of the Appeals Chamber and of the parties.

Rule 111

APPELLANT'S BRIEF

(Adopted 11 Feb 1994, revised 12 Nov 1997, amended 10 July 1998, amended 17 Nov 1999, amended 13 Dec 2001)

An Appellant's brief setting out all the arguments and authorities shall be filed within **C6–140** seventy-five days of filing of the notice of appeal pursuant to Rule 108.

RULE 112

RESPONDENT'S BRIEF

(Adopted 11 Feb 1994, amended 17 Nov 1999, amended 13 Dec 2001)

C6–141   A Respondent's brief of argument and authorities shall be filed within forty days of the filing of the Appellant's brief.

RULE 113

BRIEF IN REPLY

(Adopted 11 Feb 1994)

C6–142   An Appellant may file a brief in reply within fifteen days after the filing of the Respondent's brief.

RULE 114

DATE OF HEARING

(Adopted 11 Feb 1994)

C6–143   After the expiry of the time-limits for filing the briefs provided for in Rules 111, 112 and 113, the Appeals Chamber shall set the date for the hearing and the Registrar shall notify the parties.

RULE 115

ADDITIONAL EVIDENCE

(Adopted 11 Feb 1994, amended 12 July 2002)

C6–144   (A) A party may apply by motion to present additional evidence before the Appeals Chamber. Such motion shall clearly identify with precision the specific finding of fact made by the Trial Chamber to which the additional evidence is directed, and must be served on the other party and filed with the Registrar not later than seventy-five days from the date of the judgement, unless good cause is shown for further delay. Rebuttal material may be presented by any party affected by the motion. (Amended 30 Sept 2002)

(B) If the Appeals Chamber finds that the additional evidence was not available at trial and is relevant and credible, it will determine if it could have been a decisive factor in reaching the decision at trial. If it could have been such a factor, the Appeals Chamber will consider the additional evidence and any rebuttal material along with that already on the record to arrive at a final judgement in accordance with Rule 117.

(C) The Appeals Chamber may decide the motion prior to the appeal, or at the time of the hearing on appeal. It may decide the motion with or without an oral hearing.

(D) If several defendants are parties to the appeal, the additional evidence admitted on behalf of any one of them will be considered with respect to all of them, where relevant.

Rule 116

[DELETED]

(Adopted 11 Feb 1994, deleted 12 Nov 1997)

Rule 116*bis*

EXPEDITED APPEALS PROCEDURE

(Adopted 30 Jan 1995, amended 17 Nov 1999, amended 1 Dec 2000 and 13 Dec 2000)

(A) An appeal under Rule 72 or Rule 73 or appeal from a decision rendered under Rule 54*bis*, Rule 65, Rule 77 or Rule 91 shall be heard expeditiously on the basis of the original record of the Trial Chamber. Appeals may be determined entirely on the basis of written briefs. (Revised 12 Nov 1997, amended 17 Nov 1999, amended 14 July 2000, amended 1 Dec 2000 and 13 Dec 2000, amended 13 Dec 2001)

(B) Rules 109 to 114 shall not apply to such appeals.

(C) The Presiding Judge, after consulting the members of the Appeals Chamber, may decide not to apply Rule 117 (D). (Amended 25 July 1997, amended 17 Nov 1999, amended 1 Dec 2000 and 13 Dec 2000)

Rule 117

JUDGEMENT ON APPEAL

(Adopted 11 Feb 1994)

(A) The Appeals Chamber shall pronounce judgement on the basis of the record on appeal together with such additional evidence as has been presented to it.

(B) The judgement shall be rendered by a majority of the Judges. It shall be accompanied or followed as soon as possible by a reasoned opinion in writing, to which separate or dissenting opinions may be appended. (Revised 30 Jan 1995)

(C) In appropriate circumstances the Appeals Chamber may order that the accused be retried according to law. (Revised 30 Jan 1995)

(D) The judgement shall be pronounced in public, on a date of which notice shall have been given to the parties and counsel and at which they shall be entitled to be present. (Revised 30 Jan 1995)

Rule 118

STATUS OF THE ACCUSED FOLLOWING APPEAL

(Adopted 11 Feb 1994)

(A) A sentence pronounced by the Appeals Chamber shall be enforced immediately.

(B) Where the accused is not present when the judgement is due to be delivered, either as having been acquitted on all charges or as a result of an order issued pursuant to Rule 65, or for any other reason, the Appeals Chamber may deliver its judgement in the absence of the accused and shall, unless it pronounces an acquittal, order the arrest or surrender of the accused to the Tribunal. (Revised 12 Nov 1997)

PART EIGHT

REVIEW PROCEEDINGS

RULE 119

REQUEST FOR REVIEW

(Adopted 11 Feb 1994)

C6–149   (A) Where a new fact has been discovered which was not known to the moving party at the time of the proceedings before a Trial Chamber or the Appeals Chamber, and could not have been discovered through the exercise of due diligence, the defence or, within one year after the final judgement has been pronounced, the Prosecutor, may make a motion to that Chamber for review of the judgement. If, at the time of the request for review, any of the Judges who constituted the original Chamber are no longer Judges of the Tribunal, the President shall appoint a Judge or Judges in their place. (Amended 12 July 2001)

(B) Any brief in response to a request for review shall be filed within forty days of the filing of the request. (Amended 12 July 2002)

(C) Any brief in reply shall be filed within fifteen days after the filing of the response. (Amended 12 July 2002)

RULE 120

PRELIMINARY EXAMINATION

(Adopted 11 Feb 1994, amended 12 July 2001)

C6–150   If a majority of Judges of the Chamber constituted pursuant to Rule 119 agree that the new fact, if proved, could have been a decisive factor in reaching a decision, the Chamber shall review the judgement, and pronounce a further judgement after hearing the parties.

RULE 121

APPEALS

(Adopted 11 Feb 1994)

C6–151   The judgement of a Trial Chamber on review may be appealed in accordance with the provisions of Part Seven.

RULE 122

RETURN OF CASE TO TRIAL CHAMBER

(Adopted 11 Feb 1994)

C6–152   If the judgement to be reviewed is under appeal at the time the motion for review is filed, the Appeals Chamber may return the case to the Trial Chamber for disposition of the motion.

Part Nine

PARDON AND COMMUTATION OF SENTENCE

Rule 123

NOTIFICATION BY STATES

(Adopted 11 Feb 1994, amended 5 May 1994, revised 12 Nov 1997)

If, according to the law of the State of imprisonment, a convicted person is eligible for **C6–153** pardon or commutation of sentence, the State shall, in accordance with Article 28 of the Statute, notify the Tribunal of such eligibility.

Rule 124

DETERMINATION BY THE PRESIDENT

(Adopted 11 Feb 1994, amended 12 Apr 2001, amended 11 Feb 2005)

The President shall, upon such notice, determine, in consultation with the members of **C6–154** the Bureau and any permanent Judges of the sentencing Chamber who remain Judges of the Tribunal, whether pardon or commutation is appropriate.

Rule 125

GENERAL STANDARDS FOR GRANTING PARDON OR COMMUTATION

(Adopted 11 Feb 1994)

In determining whether pardon or commutation is appropriate, the President shall **C6–155** take into account, *inter alia*, the gravity of the crime or crimes for which the prisoner was convicted, the treatment of similarly-situated prisoners, the prisoner's demonstration of rehabilitation, as well as any substantial cooperation of the prisoner with the Prosecutor.

Part Ten

TIME

Rule 126

GENERAL PROVISIONS

(Adopted 12 Nov 1997, amended 13 Dec 2001)

(A) Where the time prescribed by or under these Rules for the doing of any act is to **C6–156** run as from the occurrence of an event, that time shall begin to run as from the date of the event.

(B) Should the last day of a time prescribed by a Rule or directed by a Chamber fall upon a day when the Registry of the Tribunal does not accept documents for filing it shall be considered as falling on the first day thereafter when the Registry does accept documents for filing. (Amended 12 July 2002)

RULE 126*BIS*

TIME FOR FILING RESPONSES TO MOTIONS

(Adopted 13 Dec 2001)

C6–157 Unless otherwise ordered by a Chamber either generally or in the particular case, a response, if any, to a motion filed by a party shall be filed within fourteen days of the filing of the motion. A reply to the response, if any, shall be filed within seven days of the filing of the response, with the leave of the relevant Chamber.

RULE 127

VARIATION OF TIME-LIMITS

(Adopted 12 Nov 1997)

C6–158 (A) Save as provided by paragraph (C), a Trial Chamber may, on good cause being shown by motion,
   (i) enlarge or reduce any time prescribed by or under these Rules;
   (ii) recognize as validly done any act done after the expiration of a time so prescribed on such terms, if any, as is thought just and whether or not that time has already expired.
   (Amended 1 Dec 2000 and 13 Dec 2000)
   (B) In relation to any step falling to be taken in connection with an appeal the Appeals Chamber may exercise the like power as is conferred by paragraph (A) and in like manner and subject to the same conditions as are therein set out. (Amended 1 Dec 2000 and 13 Dec 2000, amended 21 July 2005)
   (C) This Rule shall not apply to the times prescribed in Rules 40*bis* and 90*bis*.

C7. Amendment to the Rules of Procedure and Evidence

By unanimous decision of the permanent Judges, pursuant to Rule 6(B) of the Rules of **C7–001** Procedure and Evidence ("Rules"), Rule 28 is amended.

Pursuant to Rule 6(D), this amendment shall enter into force seven days after the date of issue of this official document, i.e., on **18 March 2005**.

The full text of the amended Rule is set out in the Annex to this document, in which the substantive amendment has been highlighted.

Carmel Agius
Judge
Chair of the Rules Committee
Dated this eleventh day of March 2005
At The Hague
The Netherlands

ANNEX

RULE 28

REVIEWING AND DUTY JUDGES

(A) On receipt of an indictment for review from the Prosecutor, the Registrar shall **C7–002** consult with the President. The President shall refer the matter to the Bureau which shall determine whether the indictment, prima facie, concentrates on one or more of the most senior leaders suspected of being most responsible for crimes within the jurisdiction of the Tribunal. If the Bureau determines that the indictment meets this standard, the President shall designate one of the permanent Trial Chamber Judges for the review under Rule 47. If the Bureau determines that the indictment does not meet this standard, the President shall return the indictment to the Registrar to communicate this finding to the Prosecutor.

(B) The President, in consultation with the Judges, shall maintain a roster designating one Judge as duty Judge for the assigned period of seven days. The duty Judge shall be available at all times, including out of normal Registry hours, for dealing with applications pursuant to paragraphs (C) and (D) but may refuse to deal with any application out of normal Registry hours if not satisfied as to its urgency. The roster of duty Judges shall be published by the Registrar.

(C) All applications in a case not otherwise assigned to a Chamber, other than the review of indictments, shall be transmitted to the duty Judge. Where accused are jointly indicted, a submission relating only to an accused who is not in the custody of the Tribunal, other than an application to amend or withdraw part of the indictment pursuant to Rule 50 or Rule 51, shall be transmitted to the duty Judge, notwithstanding that the case has already been assigned to a Chamber in respect of some or all of the co-accused of that accused. The duty Judge shall act pursuant to Rule 54 in dealing with applications under this Rule.

(D) Where a case has already been assigned to a Trial Chamber:
   (i) where the application is made out of normal Registry hours, the application shall be dealt with by the duty Judge if satisfied as to its urgency;
   (ii) where the application is made within the normal Registry hours and the Trial Chamber is unavailable, it shall be dealt with by the duty Judge if satisfied as to its urgency or that it is otherwise appropriate to do so in the absence of the Trial Chamber.
In such case, the Registry shall serve a copy of all orders or decisions issued by the duty Judge in connection therewith on the Chamber to which the matter is assigned.

(E) During periods of court recess, regardless of the Chamber to which he or she is assigned, in addition to applications made pursuant to paragraph (D) above, the duty Judge may:

(i) take decisions on provisional detention pursuant to Rule 40*bis*;

(ii) conduct the initial appearance of an accused pursuant to Rule 62.

The Registry shall serve a copy of all orders or decisions issued by the duty Judge in connection therewith on the Chamber to which the matter is assigned.

(F) The provisions of this Rule shall apply *mutatis mutandis* to applications before the Appeals Chamber.

C8. Practice Direction on Procedure for the Proposal, Consideration of and Publication of Amendments to the Rules of Procedure and Evidence of the International Tribunal (As amended)

INTRODUCTION

In accordance with Rule 19 (B) of the Rules of Procedure and Evidence of the **C8–001** International Tribunal ("the Rules"), pursuant to Rule 6 of the Rules, I issue this Practice Direction in order to establish a procedure for the proposal, consideration of and publication of amendments to the Rules:

THE RULES COMMITTEE

1. (a) The Rules Committee shall consider all proposals for amendment of the Rules **C8–002** forwarded to it by the President, a Judge of the International Tribunal or other body. The Committee shall submit a report setting out the proposals and recommendations to the Plenary for action, or to the permanent Judges of the International Tribunal for adoption under Rule 6 (C).

(b) The report of the Rules Committee shall be circulated to all Judges at least one week prior to the plenary session at which it is to be discussed. *Ad litem* Judges of the Tribunal may submit written comments on the report to the Chair of the Rules Committee not less than two working days before the start of the plenary session and may participate in the debate on the amendments in the plenary session.

2. The Rules Committee shall be made up of a minimum of three permanent Judges of the International Tribunal and a non-voting representative, each, of the Registry, Office of the Prosecutor and Defence Counsel. The Committee Secretariat shall consist of, at a minimum, a Senior Legal Officer and Associate Legal Officer of the Chambers Legal Support Section of the International Tribunal.

THE PLENARY'S CONSIDERATION OF AMENDMENT OF THE RULES

3. The Plenary shall consider proposals for amendment to the Rules at the final **C8–003** meeting of the Plenary in each calendar year, subject to paragraph 6 below.

SUBMISSION OF PROPOSALS

4. All proposals directed to the President or the Rules Committee are to be submitted **C8–004** in both working languages of the International Tribunal not less than two months prior to the sitting of the Plenary at which proposed amendments of the Rules are to be considered.

5. Proposals received within that two-month period may in exceptional circumstances be considered by the Rules Committee and presented to the Plenary for consideration.

6. This Practice Direction shall not prevent the consideration of proposals for amendment of the Rules at other Plenary meetings in cases of urgency or exceptional circumstances.

OTHER AMENDMENTS

7. An amendment to the Rules may be otherwise adopted, provided it is unanimously **C8–005** approved by the permanent Judges.

ENTRY INTO FORCE OF AMENDMENT TO THE RULES

C8–006   8. Upon agreement by the Plenary of amendment to the Rules, the Rules Committee will, as soon as practicable, issue an official document of the International Tribunal ("official document") setting out the amendments in both working languages of the International Tribunal. No commentary or explanation will accompany the amendments.

9. The amendments will enter into force seven days after the date of issue of the official document referred to in paragraph 8 above. A fully amended text of the Rules will be issued as soon as possible thereafter.

PUBLICISING AMENDMENTS TO THE RULES

C8–007   10. In accordance with Chambers practice, the official document containing the amendments to the Rules shall be distributed on the day of issue to all Judges, the Registry, Office of the Prosecutor, Defence Counsel Unit, Press Office and Library, and shall be submitted for publication in the next edition of the Bulletin of the International Tribunal.

(signed)
Claude Jorda
President

C9. Directive on Assignment of Defence Counsel
(Directive No. 1/94)

(As amended 30 January 1995)
(As amended 25 June 1996)
(As amended 1 August 1997)
(As revised 17 November 1997)
(As amended 10 July 1998)
(As amended 19 July 1999)
(As amended 15 December 2000)
(As amended 12 July 2002)
(As amended 28 July 2004)

(IT/73/REV. 10)

TABLE OF CONTENTS

I–PREAMBLE

C9–001　　The Registrar of the Tribunal,
CONSIDERING the Statute of the Tribunal as adopted by the Security Council under resolution 827 (1993) of 25 May 1993, as subsequently amended, and in particular Articles 18 and 21 thereof;
CONSIDERING the Rules of Procedure and Evidence as adopted by the Tribunal on 11 February 1994, as subsequently amended, and in particular Rules 42, 45 and 55 thereof;
CONSIDERING the host country agreement between the United Nations and the Kingdom of the Netherlands concerning the seat of the Tribunal signed at New York on 29 July 1994, and in particular Articles XIX and XX thereof;
CONSIDERING the Directive on the Assignment of Defence Counsel as adopted by the Tribunal on 28 July 1994, as subsequently amended, and as last amended on 12 July 2002;
HEREBY PROMULGATES Revision ten of the Directive on Assignment of Defence Counsel, as attached.

Hans Holthuis
Registrar

Dated this fourth day of August 2004
At The Hague
The Netherlands

ISSUES REVISION 10 OF THE DIRECTIVE ON THE ASSIGNMENT OF DEFENCE COUNSEL AS FOLLOWS:

II–GENERAL PROVISIONS

ARTICLE 1

ENTRY INTO FORCE

C9–002　　This Directive establishes the conditions and arrangements for assignment of counsel and shall enter into force on the first day of August nineteen hundred and ninety four (1 August 1994).

ARTICLE 2

DEFINITIONS

C9–003　　Under this Directive, the following terms shall mean:

Accused: a person against whom one or more counts in an indictment have been confirmed in accordance with Rule 47 of the Rules of Procedure and Evidence;

Code of Conduct: the Code of Professional Conduct for Defence Counsel Appearing Before the International Tribunal as promulgated by the Registrar on 12 June 1997 as latest amended;

Counsel: a person eligible to be assigned pursuant to Rules 44, 45 and 45*bis* of the Rules;

Directive: Directive No. 1/94 on the Assignment of Defence Counsel as latest amended;

President: the President of the Tribunal;

Prosecutor the Prosecutor appointed pursuant to Article 16 of the Statute;

Registrar: the Registrar of the Tribunal;

Rules: the Rules of Procedure and Evidence adopted by the Tribunal on 11 February 1994, and as subsequently amended;

Stage of procedure: each of the stages of procedure laid down by the Rules in which the suspect or the accused may be involved (investigation, indictment, proceedings in the Trial Chamber, appeal, review).

Statute: the Statute of the Tribunal adopted by the Security Council under Resolution 827 (1993) of 25 May 1993, as subsequently amended;

Suspect: a person concerning whom the Prosecutor possesses reliable information which tends to show that the person may have committed a crime over which the Tribunal has jurisdiction;

Tribunal: the International Tribunal for the Prosecution of Persons Responsible for Serious Violations of International Humanitarian Law Committed in the Territory of the Former Yugoslavia since 1991.

In this Directive, the masculine shall include the feminine and the singular the plural, and vice versa. All references in this Directive to suspects or accused shall also be understood to apply to any persons detained on the authority of the Tribunal.

ARTICLE 3

AUTHENTIC TEXTS

The English and French texts of the Directive shall be equally authentic. In case of **C9–004** discrepancy, the version which is more consonant with the spirit of the Statute, Rules and the Directive shall prevail.

ARTICLE 4

AMENDMENT OF THE DIRECTIVE

A. Proposals for amendment of the Directive may be made by a Judge, the Registrar **C9–005** or the Advisory Panel. Amendments shall be promulgated by the Registrar in accordance with Rule 45 of the Rules.

B. Without prejudice to the rights of the accused in any pending case, an amendment of the Directive shall enter into force seven days after the day of issue of an official Tribunal document containing the amendment.

III–RIGHT TO HAVE COUNSEL ASSIGNED

Chapter 1 : Basic principles

ARTICLE 5

RIGHT TO COUNSEL

Without prejudice to the right of an accused to conduct his own defence: **C9–006**

     i. a suspect who is to be questioned by the Prosecutor during an investigation;

     ii. an accused upon whom personal service of the indictment has been effected; and

     iii. any person detained on the authority of the Tribunal, including any person detained in accordance with Rule 90*bis*;

shall have the right to be assisted by counsel.

ARTICLE 6

RIGHT TO ASSIGNED COUNSEL

C9–007   A. Suspects or accused who lack the means to remunerate counsel shall be entitled to assignment of counsel paid for by the Tribunal.

B. A suspect or accused lacks the means to remunerate counsel if he does not dispose of means, which would allow him to remunerate counsel at the rates provided for by this Directive. For the purposes of Section III of this Directive, the remuneration of counsel also includes counsel's expenses.

C. For suspects or accused who dispose of means to partially remunerate counsel, the Tribunal shall pay that portion, which the suspect or accused does not have sufficient means to pay for.

Chapter 2 : Procedure for assignment of counsel

ARTICLE 7

REQUEST FOR ASSIGNMENT OF COUNSEL

C9–008   A. Subject to the provisions of Article 17, a suspect or accused who wishes to be assigned counsel shall make a request to the Registrar of the Tribunal on the form provided by the Registry. A request shall be lodged with the Registry, or transmitted to it, by the suspect or accused himself or by a person authorised by him to do so on his behalf.

B. For the purposes of Article 8, a suspect or accused requesting the assignment of counsel is required to make a declaration of his means on the form provided by the Registry.

C. To ensure that the provisions of Article 8 are met, a suspect or accused must update his declaration of means at any time a change relevant to his declaration of means occurs.

ARTICLE 8

DETERMINATION OF THE MEANS OF SUSPECTS AND ACCUSED

C9–009   A. A suspect or accused who requests the assignment of counsel must produce evidence that he is unable to remunerate counsel.

B. In order to determine whether the suspect or accused is unable to remunerate counsel, there shall be taken into account means of all kinds of which he has direct or indirect enjoyment or freely disposes, including but not limited to direct income, bank accounts, real or personal property, pensions, and stocks, bonds, or other assets held, but excluding any family or social benefits to which he may be entitled. In assessing such means, account shall also be taken of the means of the spouse of a suspect or accused, as well as those of persons with whom he habitually resides, provided that it is reasonable to take such means into account.

C. Account may also be taken of the apparent lifestyle of a suspect or accused, and of his enjoyment of any property, movable or immovable, and whether or not he derives income from it.

ARTICLE 9

CERTIFICATION OF THE DECLARATION OF MEANS

A declaration must, so far as possible, be certified by an appropriate authority, either that of the place where the suspect or accused resides or is found or that of any other place considered appropriate in the circumstances which it shall be for the Registrar to assess.

C9–010

ARTICLE 10

INFORMATION

A. For the purpose of establishing whether the suspect or accused satisfies the requisite conditions for assignment of counsel, the Registrar may inquire into his means, request the gathering of any information, hear the suspect or accused, consider any representation, or request the production of any documents likely to verify the request.

C9–011

B. In executing this stipulation and even after counsel has been assigned, the Registrar shall be authorised to request any relevant information at any time from any person who appears to be able to supply relevant information.

Chapter 3 : The decision

ARTICLE 11

DECISION BY THE REGISTRAR

A. After examining the declaration of means laid down in Article 7 (B) and (C) and relevant information obtained pursuant to Article 10, the Registrar shall determine how far the suspect or accused lacks means to remunerate counsel, and shall decide, providing reasons for his decision:

C9–012

   i. without prejudice to Article 18, to assign counsel and choose for this purpose a name from the list drawn up in accordance with Rule 45 (B) of the Rules and Article 14; or,
   ii. without prejudice to Article 18, that the suspect or accused disposes of means to partially remunerate counsel in which case the decision shall indicate which costs shall be borne by the Tribunal; or
   iii. not to grant the request for assignment of counsel.

B. To ensure that the right to counsel is not affected while the Registrar examines the declaration of means laid down in Article 7 (B) and (C) and the information obtained pursuant to Article 10 the Registrar may temporarily assign counsel to a suspect or an accused for a period not exceeding 120 days.

C. If a suspect or an accused, either
   i. requests an assignment of counsel but does not comply with the requirements set out above within a reasonable time; or
   ii. fails to obtain or to request assignment of counsel; or
   iii. fails to elect in writing that he intends to conduct his own defence;
the Registrar may nevertheless, in the interests of justice, assign him counsel from the list, and in accordance with Rule 45 (B) of the Rules, and without prejudice to Article 18.

ARTICLE 12

NOTIFICATION OF THE DECISION

The Registrar shall notify the suspect or accused of his decision, and shall also notify the counsel so assigned and his professional or governing body of his decision.

C9–013

Chapter 4 : Remedy

ARTICLE 13

REMEDY AGAINST THE REGISTRAR'S DECISION

C9–014   A. The suspect whose request for assignment of counsel has been denied may, within fifteen days of the date of notification to him, seek the President's review of the decision of the Registrar. The President may either confirm the Registrar's decision or decide that a counsel should be assigned.

B. The accused whose request for assignment of counsel has been denied, may, within two weeks of the date of notification to him, make a motion to the Chamber before which he is due to appear for immediate review of the Registrar's decision. The Chamber may

    i. confirm the Registrar's decision; or

    ii. rule that the suspect or accused has means to partially remunerate counsel, in which case it shall refer the matter again to the Registrar for determination of which parts shall be borne by the Tribunal; or

    iii. rule that a counsel should be assigned.

IV–PREREQUISITIES FOR ASSIGNMENT AS COUNSEL

ARTICLE 14

QUALIFICATIONS AND STANDING OF COUNSEL

C9–015   A. Any person may be assigned as counsel to an accused if the Registrar is satisfied that he is admitted to the list of counsel envisaged in Rule 45 (B) of the Rules. A person is eligible for admission to the list if:

    i. he is admitted to the practice of law in a State, or is a university professor of law;

    ii. he has written and oral proficiency in one of the two working languages of the Tribunal;

    iii. he possesses established competence in criminal law and/or international criminal law/international humanitarian law/ international human rights law;

    iv. he possesses at least seven years of relevant experience, whether as a judge, prosecutor, attorney or in some other capacity, in criminal proceedings;

    v. he has not been found guilty or otherwise disciplined in relevant disciplinary proceedings against him in a national or international forum, including proceedings pursuant to the Code of Professional Conduct for Defence Counsel Appearing Before the International Tribunal, unless the Registrar deems that, in the circumstances, it would be disproportionate to exclude such counsel;

    vi. he has not been found guilty in relevant criminal proceedings;

    vii. he has not engaged in conduct whether in pursuit of his profession or otherwise which is dishonest or otherwise discreditable to a counsel, prejudicial to the administration of justice, or likely to diminish public confidence in the International Tribunal or the administration of justice, or otherwise bring the International Tribunal into disrepute;

    viii. he has indicated his availability to be assigned as counsel by the Registrar to represent any indigent suspect or accused under the terms of this Directive; and

    ix. he is a member in good standing of an association of counsel practising at the Tribunal.

B. Any person may be assigned as duty counsel to an accused for the purposes of the initial appearance if the Registrar is satisfied that he is admitted to the list of counsel envisaged in Rule 45 (C) of the Rules. A person is eligible for admission to that list if:

     i. he fulfils all requirements of Article 14(A); and

     ii. he has informed the Registrar that he is readily available for assignment to an accused for the purposes of the initial appearance in accordance with Rule 62 of the Rules.

C. A person who does not have written and oral proficiency in either of the two working languages of the Tribunal but who speaks a language spoken in the territory over which the Tribunal has jurisdiction, and who fulfils all other requirements set out in Article 14 (A), may be admitted to the list envisaged in Rule 45 (B) of the Rules, if the Registrar deems it justified. Such person can be assigned only as co-counsel in accordance with Article 16 (C).

D. The Registrar may, after giving counsel a warning and an opportunity to respond, remove the name of counsel from the lists referred to in Rules 45 (B) and (C) of the Rules:

     i. upon a decision by a Chamber under Rule 46 (A)(i) of the Rules; or

     ii. where counsel has been found to be in contempt pursuant to Rule 77 of the Rules, in consultation with the Chamber;

     iii. where counsel has provided false information in relation to his or her qualification to be admitted to the list, or has failed to provide relevant information;

     iv. where counsel has been found guilty of a disciplinary offense under the Code of Conduct, in accordance with the relevant provision of the Code, in consultation with the Chamber.

Counsel may seek review of the Registrar's decision before the President within fourteen days of having been notified of that decision.

E. The Registrar shall remove the name of counsel from the lists referred to in Rules 45 (B) and (C) of the Rules:

     i. upon a decision by a Chamber under Rule 46 (A)(ii);

     ii. upon a final decision of the Disciplinary Panel or Disciplinary Board that counsel is banned from practicing before the Tribunal, in accordance with Article 47 (C)(vi) of the Code of Professional Conduct;

     iii. where counsel no longer satisfies the requirements of Article 14 (A).

F. The Registrar may refuse a request for assignment of a counsel where a procedure pursuant to Rule 77 of the Rules, or, in accordance with Article 45 of the Code of Conduct, if a disciplinary procedure under Part Three of the Code of Professional Conduct has been initiated against that counsel. Counsel may seek review of the Registrar's decision before the President within fourteen days of having been notified of that decision.

G. Counsel admitted to the lists referred to in Rules 45 (B) and (C) of the Rules shall:

     i. confirm his continued availability to be assigned to indigent suspects or accused every two years from the date of their admission to the list; and

     ii. immediately advise the Registrar if he is no longer available to represent an accused or suspect for an extended period, being more than 6 months.

If counsel fails to confirm his availability, the Registrar may, after giving notice to counsel, remove his name from the list.

Article 15

PROFESSIONAL CERTIFICATION

A. An applicant for admission to the lists envisaged in Rules 45 (B) and (C) of the Rules shall supply the Registrar with: **C9–016**

     ii. for applicants whose native language is not English or French, a certificate from a language institute or other evidence of proficiency in English or French; the Registrar may also require such applicants to demonstrate their language ability by means of a language proficiency test;

     iii. a certificate of professional qualification issued by the competent professional or governing body, including a certificate of current practice and good standing;

iv. the names and addresses of two referees, who practise in the fields of criminal law, international humanitarian law, international human rights law or international criminal law, and who are in a position to advise the Registrar as to the professional competence of the applicants in these fields;

v. and such other documentation the Registrar deems necessary.

B. The Registrar may refer an applicant for admission to lists referred to in Rules 45 (B) and (C) of the Rules to a panel composed of judges, members of the Advisory Panel, and/or fully qualified counsel to interview the applicant and make a recommendation on his application.

C. An applicant who was denied admission to the list may seek review of the Registrar's decision before the President within fourteen days of receiving notification of this decision.

V—SCOPE OF ASSIGNMENT

ARTICLE 16

BASIC PRINCIPLES

C9–017   F. A suspect or accused shall be entitled to have one counsel assigned to him, and that counsel shall handle all stages of the procedure and all matters arising out of the conduct of the suspect's or accused's defence, including where two or more crimes are joined in one indictment, except where a second counsel has been assigned to the defence in accordance with Article 16 (C).

G. Where persons accused of the same or different crimes are jointly charged or tried, each accused shall be entitled to request assignment of separate counsel.

C. (i) In the interests of justice and at the request of the person assigned as counsel, the Registrar may, in accordance with Article 14 above, assign other counsel to the defence. The counsel first assigned shall be called the lead counsel.

(ii) At the request of lead counsel and where the interests of justice so require, the Registrar may assign a co-counsel who does not speak either of the two working languages of the Tribunal but who speaks the native language of the accused. The Registrar may impose such conditions as deemed appropriate.

(iii) At the request of lead counsel, the Registrar may assign other persons such as legal assistants, consultants, investigators and interpreters, as required, to provide support to counsel.

D. Lead counsel is responsible for all aspects of the defence, including selecting and supervising co-counsel and other members of the defence team. Under the authority of lead counsel, co-counsel may deal with all stages of the procedure and all matters arising out of the representation of the accused or of the conduct of his defence. Lead counsel shall sign all documents submitted to the Tribunal unless he authorises co-counsel, in writing, to sign on his behalf.

E. No counsel shall be assigned to more than one suspect or accused at a time, unless:

viii. Each accused has received independent legal advice from the Registrar and both have consented in writing;

ix. The assignment would neither cause prejudice to the defence of either accused, nor a potential conflict of interest.

F. Counsel assigned pursuant to Rule 62 shall represent the accused for the purposes of his initial appearance only, unless the Registrar deems it appropriate that the representation continue until such time a permanent counsel is assigned by the Tribunal or retained by the accused.

ARTICLE 17

ASSIGNMENT OF COUNSEL AWAY FROM THE SEAT OF THE TRIBUNAL

C9–018   A. Away from the seat of the Tribunal, and in a case of urgency, a suspect who, during the investigation, requests assignment of counsel, may indicate the name of counsel if he knows one who may be assigned in accordance with the provisions of this Directive.

B. Where the suspect fails to indicate a name, the Prosecutor, or a person authorised by him or acting under his direction, may contact the local Bar Association and obtain the name of counsel who may be assigned in accordance with the provisions of this Directive.

C. In the situations envisaged in paragraphs (A) and (B), the procedure for assignment of counsel as set out in this Directive shall apply *mutatis mutandis* but shall be accelerated where necessary.

VI–SUSPENSION AND WITHDRAWAL OF ASSIGNMENT

ARTICLE 18

ABILITY OF SUSPECTS OR ACCUSED TO REMUNERATE COUNSEL

J. Assignment of counsel or partial remuneration of counsel and/or payment of counsel's expenses may be withdrawn by the Registrar if: **C9–019**
  xi. after his decision, the suspect or accused comes into means which, had they been available at the time the request in Article 7 was made, would have caused the Registrar not to grant the request;
  xii. information is obtained which establishes that the suspect or accused has sufficient means to allow him to pay for the cost of his defence.
B. The Registrar's decision shall be reasoned and notified to the suspect or accused and to the counsel assigned, and shall take effect from the date of receipt of the notification.

C. The provisions of Article 13 shall apply *mutatis mutandis* where a suspect or accused seeks a review of the Registrar's decision.

ARTICLE 19

SUSPENSION AND WITHDRAWAL OF COUNSEL

A. In the interests of justice, the Registrar may: **C9–020**
  xiii. at the request of the accused, or his counsel, withdraw the assignment of counsel;
  xiv. at the request of lead counsel withdraw the assignment of co-counsel.
B. The Registrar may suspend the assignment of counsel for a reasonable and limited time in consultation with the Chamber:
  xv. if a disciplinary procedure under Part Three of the Code of Professional Conduct has been initiated against that counsel; or
  xvi. if contempt proceedings have been initiated against that counsel.
The counsel may seek the President's review within two weeks from the notification of the decision to counsel.
C. The Registrar shall withdraw the assignment of counsel:
  xvii. upon the decision by a Chamber to refuse audience to assigned counsel for misconduct under Rule 46 (A);
  xviii. where counsel no-longer satisfies the requirements of Article 14 (A); or
  xix. where counsel has been found to be in contempt pursuant to Rule 77 of the Rules.
C. In such cases the withdrawal or suspension shall be notified to the accused, to the counsel concerned and to his professional or governing body.

E. The Registrar shall immediately assign a new counsel to the suspect or accused.

F. Where a request for withdrawal, made pursuant to paragraph A, has been denied the person making the request may seek the President's review of the decision of the Registrar within two weeks from the notification of the decision to him.

ARTICLE 20

REPLACEMENT OF COUNSEL

C9–021   A. Where the assignment of counsel is withdrawn by the Registrar or where the services of assigned counsel are discontinued, the counsel assigned may not withdraw from acting until either a replacement counsel has been provided by the Tribunal or by the suspect or accused, or the suspect or accused has declared his intention in writing to conduct his own defence.

B. In the interests of justice, the withdrawn counsel may continue to represent the suspect or the accused for a period of not exceeding 30 days after the date on which the replacement is assigned. During this period, the costs necessarily and reasonably incurred by both counsel shall be met by the Tribunal.

ARTICLE 21

PAYMENT *PRO RATA TEMPORIS*

C9–022   When, during engagement, an assigned counsel is replaced in the same capacity by another assigned counsel for whatever reason, the remuneration shall be paid to each of them *pro rata temporis*.

VII–COSTS OF REPRESENTATION

ARTICLE 22

RESPONSIBILITY FOR REMUNERATION AND EXPENSES

C9–023   A. Where counsel has been assigned, the costs of legal representation of the suspect or accused necessarily and reasonably incurred shall be met by the Tribunal subject to the budgetary provisions, rules and regulations, and practice set by the United Nations. All costs are subject to prior authorization by the Registrar. If authorization was not obtained, the Registrar may refuse to meet costs. The Registrar establishes maximum allotments for each defence at the beginning of every stage of the procedure taking into account his estimate of the duration of the phase. In the event that a stage of the procedure is substantially longer or shorter than estimated, the Registrar may adapt the allotment. In the event of disagreement on the maximum allotment, the Registrar shall make a decision, after consulting the Chamber and, if necessary, the Advisory Panel.

B. Such costs to be met by the Tribunal shall include all remuneration due to counsel in accordance with Article 23. They shall also include expenses resulting from the assignment of legal and investigative assistance, expenses relating to the production of evidence for the defence, to the ascertainment of facts, expenses relating to temporary consultancy on specific questions, expert opinion paid at the rates established in Annex I, and accommodation and transportation of witnesses. They shall include travel expenses, travel taxes and similar duties. General office costs are included in the remuneration for counsel. This embraces in any case, but not exclusively costs for phone and mail or express mail, photocopies, books and journals, lease of office space, purchase of office equipment, office supplies and secretarial support.

C. The Registrar shall reimburse the sums claimed by assigned counsel for the remuneration and expenses as provided in paragraphs (A) and (B) above on receipt of a statement of expenses made out using the format provided by the Registry, which must be presented within 120 days from the last day of the month during which work was performed or an expense was incurred and be approved by the Registrar. Counsel may request monthly payment of equal parts of the maximum allotment established by the

Registrar under paragraph (A) above. The statement shall in any case be submitted in an electronic version.

ARTICLE 23

REMUNERATION PAID TO ASSIGNED COUNSEL

A. Without prejudice to Article 6 (C), assigned counsel are paid fees calculated on the basis of a fixed hourly rate applied to the number of hours of reasonable and necessary work at each stage of the proceedings or, where applicable, a lump sum calculated according to the work that is reasonable and necessary for the preparation and/or presentation of the defence.   **C9–024**

B. The applicable rates shall be set by the Registrar and approved by the Judges.

C. Without prejudice to Article 6 (C), assigned counsel who receives remuneration from the Tribunal shall not accept remuneration for the assignment from any other source.

ARTICLE 24

FIXED RATE

T. In addition to the fees envisaged in Article 23 (A), a fixed rate of two thousand United States Dollars shall be paid to any newly-assigned counsel for his initial consultations with the accused and in order to become familiar with the case.   **C9–025**

U. For counsel assigned pursuant to Rule 62 (B) of the Rules, this fixed rate shall include the initial appearance of the accused.

ARTICLE 25

FEES

The fixed hourly rate for fees envisaged in Article 23 (A) (ii) shall be assessed by the Registrar on the basis of the seniority and experience of counsel, according to Annex I. This rate includes general office costs.   **C9–026**

ARTICLE 26

TRAVEL EXPENSES

A. Travel expenses shall be reimbursed for an assigned counsel who does not usually reside in the territory of the host country or in the country where the particular stage of the procedure is being conducted, on the basis of one economy class standard fixed-date round trip air ticket by the shortest route or within limits laid down by and subject to prior authorization of the Registrar, on presentation of a statement of travel expenses using the form provided by the Registry, accompanied by the original counterfoil of the ticket and the ticket stubs.   **C9–027**

B. Travel expenses shall be reimbursed to assigned counsel residing in the territory of the host country but not in the town where he is serving, on the basis of either first class public transportation tickets or fixed rates as established by the United Nations Schedule of Rates of Reimbursement for Travel by Private Motor Vehicle applicable to different groups of Countries and Territories, per kilometre travelled on the outward and return journeys by the shortest route, on presentation of a statement of travel expenses using the form provided by the Registry.

C. Counsel shall submit all travel requests to the Registry at least one week before their scheduled travel, unless they can demonstrate that circumstances beyond their control prevent them from complying with this requirement. The Registry reserves the right to deduct cancellation fees, arising from changes in travel arrangement, from counsel's remuneration in cases where changes are not sufficiently related to his professional obligations as assigned counsel.

Article 27

DAILY ALLOWANCES

C9–028   A. Counsel shall be entitled to a daily allowance calculated on the basis of fixed rates as established by the United Nations Schedule of Daily Subsistence Allowance Rates applied to the number of days of work. Counsel is not entitled to subsistence allowance while staying at his place of residence.

B. The rate for daily allowance shall be calculated on the basis of the current daily subsistence allowance rates applicable in the country where he is acting as an assigned counsel.

C. In accordance with the regulations in force at the United Nations, the applicable rate shall be lowered by twenty-five percent when counsel has spent more than 60 days in total from the date of his assignment in the country where he is acting as an assigned counsel.

Article 28

FAMILY MEMBERS AND FRIENDS OF SUSPECTS, ACCUSED AND COUNSEL

C9–029   Members of the family or close friends of suspects, accused and counsel are not eligible for an assignment under the Directive as counsel, expert, legal assistant, investigator, translator or interpreter unless an assignment is in the interests of justice.

Article 29

PROVISIONAL PAYMENT

C9–030   In exceptional circumstances and with the authorisation of the Registrar, a provisional payment of the daily allowance set out in Article 27 above or expenses of counsel may be made on presentation by counsel of a provisional statement using the forms provided by the Registry whether applicable covering the corresponding period or the expenses.

Article 30

RESPONSIBILITY FOR PAYMENTS

C9–031   A. All sums payable to assigned counsel under the provisions of this Directive shall be paid by the Financial Officer of the Registry.

B. The statement of remuneration and the statement of travel or other expenses, envisaged under Articles 23, 26, and 27, must receive the prior approval of the Registrar.

Article 31

SETTLEMENT OF DISPUTES

C9–032   In the event of disagreement on questions relating to calculation and payment of remuneration or to reimbursement of expenses, the Registrar shall make a decision, after consulting the President and, if necessary, the Advisory Panel.

VIII–Advisory Panel

Article 32

ADVISORY PANEL

A. An Advisory Panel shall be set up consisting of two members chosen by the President by ballot from the list referred to in Article 14 and who have appeared before the Tribunal, two members proposed by the International Bar Association, two members proposed by the Union Internationale des Avocats, and the President of the Nederlandse Orde van Advokaten or his representative. Each member of the Advisory Panel must have a minimum of 10 years legal experience.

C9–033

B. The President of the Advisory Panel will be the President of the Nederlandse Orde van Advokaten or his representative. The membership of the Advisory Panel shall come up for appointment every two years on the anniversary date of the entry into force of this Directive.

C. The Advisory Panel may be consulted as and when necessary by the Registrar or the President on matters relating to assignment of counsel.

D. The Advisory Panel may also of its own initiative refer to the Registrar, or to the Registrar and the President, any matter relating to the assignment of counsel.

Annex I:

Fixed gross hourly rate for Counsel in US $
(general office costs are included in this sum)

Lead Counsel / Counsel

C9–034

20 years' professional experience or more 110 US$
15–19 years' professional experience 100 US$
10–14 years' professional experience 90 US$
0–9 years' professional experience 80 US$

Co-counsel
Fixed rate of 80 US$

**Fixed gross hourly rate for allotments to
Legal Assistants and Investigators in Euros (€)
(general office costs are included in this sum)**

10 years' professional experience or more € 25
5–9 years' professional experience € 20
0–4 years' professional experience € 15

C.10 Code of Professional Conduct for Counsel Appearing before the International Tribunal
(As amended on 12 July 2002)
(IT/125 REV. 1)

TABLE OF CONTENTS

PART THREE DISCIPLINARY REGIME

PREAMBLE

The Registrar of the Tribunal,   **C10–001**
Considering the Statute of the Tribunal adopted by Security Council under Resolution
827 of 25 May 1993, as subsequently amended, and in particular Article 21 thereof;
Considering the Rules of Procedure and Evidence ("Rules") adopted by the Tribunal
on 11 February 1994, as subsequently amended, and in particular Rules 44 to 46, 77 and
91 thereof;
Considering the Directive on Assignment of Defence Counsel (IT/73) adopted on 1
August 1994, as subsequently amended;
Considering that counsel shall adhere to a Code of Professional Conduct in the
performance of their duties;
Considering that counsel appearing before the Tribunal come from various jurisdic-
tions, and that the interests of justice require all counsel to adhere to the same Code of
Professional Conduct;
Considering that this first revision of the Code of Professional Conduct for Defence
Counsel Appearing Before the International Tribunal is adopted in accordance with
Article 6 of the Code;
Pursuant to Rules 44 to 46 of the Rules;
**ISSUES REVISION 1 OF THE CODE OF PROFESSIONAL CONDUCT FOR
COUNSEL APPEARING BEFORE THE INTERNATIONAL TRIBUNAL AS
FOLLOWS:**

PART ONE

GENERAL PROVISIONS

ARTICLE 1

DEFINITIONS

(A) In this Code, unless the context otherwise requires, the following terms shall   **C10–002**
mean:
Code: The Code of Professional Conduct for Counsel Appearing Before the Inter-
national Tribunal in force;
Directive: The Directive on Assignment of Defence Counsel (IT/73) adopted on 1
August 1994, as subsequently amended;
Rules: The Rules of Procedure and Evidence of the Tribunal adopted on 11 February
1994, as subsequently amended;

Statute: The Statute of the Tribunal adopted by Security Council resolution 827 of 25 May 1993, as subsequently amended;

Tribunal: The International Tribunal for the Prosecution of Persons Responsible for Serious Violations of International Humanitarian Law Committed in the Territory of the Former Yugoslavia since 1991, established by Security Council resolution 827 of 25 May 1993.

* * *

Advisory Panel: Body established to assist the President and the Registrar in all matters relating to defence counsel under Rule 44 (D) of the Rules;

Association of Counsel: An association recognised by the Registrar in accordance with Rule 44 of the Rules;

Client: An accused, suspect, detainee, witness or other person who has engaged counsel or has been assigned counsel by the Registry;

Counsel: Any person who is or has been engaged by a client and has filed a power of attorney with the Registrar; who is or has been assigned by the Registrar to represent a client; or who is in communication with a prospective client;

Firm: Persons belonging to a private firm, a legal department of an organisation or a legal services organisation;

Parties: The Prosecution and the Defence;

Team: Counsel, co-counsel, legal and non-legal associates and other persons who perform services for counsel for the purpose of representing a client before the Tribunal.

(B) Any term not defined in this Code has the same meaning given to it by the Statute or by the Rules.

(C) General provisions of this Code should not be read or applied in a restrictive way by reason of any particular or illustrative provisions.

(D) In this Code, the masculine shall include the feminine and the singular the plural, and vice versa.

ARTICLE 2

ENTRY INTO FORCE

C10–003   This Code shall enter into force on 12 June 1997.

ARTICLE 3

BASIC PRINCIPLES

C10–004   This Code is based, in particular, on the fundamental principles that:
  i. clients have the right to legal assistance of their own choosing;
  ii. as legal practitioners, counsel shall maintain high standards of professional conduct;
  iii. the role of counsel as advocates in the administration of justice requires them to act honestly, independently, fairly, skilfully, diligently, efficiently and courageously;
  iv. counsel have a duty of loyalty to their clients consistent with their duty to the Tribunal to act with independence in the administration of justice;
  v. counsel shall take all necessary steps to ensure that their actions do not bring proceedings before the Tribunal into disrepute; and
  vi. counsel may be subject to disciplinary proceedings and should be informed of the circumstances under which such proceedings may take place and his rights and obligations in those proceedings.

[THE NEXT PARAGRAPH IS C10–006]

ARTICLE 4

CONFLICTS

If there is any inconsistency between this Code and any other codes of practice and **C10–006** ethics governing counsel, the terms of this Code prevail in respect of counsel's conduct before the Tribunal.

ARTICLE 5

AUTHENTIC TEXTS

The English and French texts of this Code shall be equally authentic. In case of discrepancy, the version that is more consonant with the spirit of the Statute, the Rules, the Directive and this Code shall prevail.

ARTICLE 6

AMENDMENT

A. Under the supervision of the President, amendments shall be promulgated by the **C10–007** Registrar after consultation with the permanent Judges, the Association of Counsel and the Advisory Panel.

B. An amendment shall enter into force seven days after the date of issue of an official Tribunal document containing the amendment, but shall not operate to prejudice the rights of counsel or clients in any pending case.

PART TWO

OBLIGATIONS OF COUNSEL

ARTICLE 7

PURPOSE

The purpose of this Part is to provide for standards of conduct for counsel in the **C10–008** interests of the fair and proper administration of justice.

Section 1: Obligations of Counsel to Clients

ARTICLE 8

SCOPE OF REPRESENTATION

A. Counsel shall advise and represent a client until counsel's representation is **C10–009** terminated by the client or withdrawn by the Registrar.

B. When representing a client, counsel shall:
  i. abide by the client's decisions concerning the objectives of representation;
  ii. consult with the client about the means by which those objectives are to be pursued, but is not bound by the client's decision; and
  iii. seek or accept only those instructions which emanate from the client and which are not given as the result of an inducement from any person, organisation or State.

C. Counsel shall not advise or assist a client to engage in conduct which counsel knows is criminal or fraudulent, in breach of the Statute, the Rules, this Code or any other applicable law and, where counsel has been assigned to the client, the Directive. However, counsel may discuss the legal consequences of any proposed course of conduct with a client and may advise or assist a client in good faith to determine the validity, scope or meaning of the applicable law.

ARTICLE 9

DECLINING, TERMINATING OR WITHDRAWING REPRESENTATION

C10–010   A. Counsel shall not represent a client if:
  i. representation will result in conduct which is criminal, fraudulent or a violation of the Statute, the Rules, this Code or any other applicable law;
  ii. counsel's physical or mental condition materially impairs counsel's ability to represent the client; or
  iii. counsel's representation is terminated by the client or withdrawn by the Registrar.
  B. Counsel may terminate or request, if applicable subject to the provisions of the Directive, withdrawal of his representation of a client if such termination or withdrawal can be accomplished without material adverse effect on the interests of the client, or if:
  i. the client has used counsel's services to perpetrate a crime or fraud, or persists in a course of action involving counsel's services that counsel reasonably believes is criminal or fraudulent;
  ii. the client insists upon pursuing an objective that counsel considers repugnant or imprudent;
  iii. the client fails to substantially fulfil an obligation to counsel regarding counsel's services and has been given reasonable warning that counsel will terminate or request withdrawal of his representation unless the obligation is fulfilled; or
  iv. other good cause for termination or withdrawal exists.
  C. Subject to leave from the Chamber, if representation by counsel is to be terminated or withdrawn, counsel shall not do so until a replacement counsel is engaged by the client or assigned by the Registrar, or the client has notified the Registrar in writing of his intention to conduct his own defence.
  D. Upon termination or withdrawal of representation, counsel shall take steps to the extent reasonably practicable to protect the client's interests, such as giving sufficient notice to the client, surrendering papers and property to which the client or the Tribunal is entitled and refunding any advance payment of fee that has not been earned.

ARTICLE 10

COMPETENCE, INTEGRITY AND INDEPENDENCE

C10–011   In the course of providing representation to a client, counsel shall:
  i. act with competence, skill, care, honesty and loyalty;
  ii. exercise independent professional judgement and render open and honest advice;
  iii. never be influenced in the matter of his representation;
  iv. preserve their own integrity and that of the legal profession as a whole;
  v. never permit their independence, integrity and standards to be compromised by external pressures.

ARTICLE 11

DILIGENCE

C10–012   Counsel shall represent a client diligently and promptly in order to protect the client's best interests. Unless the representation is terminated or withdrawn, counsel shall carry through to conclusion all matters undertaken for a client within the scope of his legal representation.

ARTICLE 12

COMMUNICATION

Counsel shall keep a client informed about the status of a matter before the Tribunal **C10–013** in which the client is an interested party and must promptly comply with all reasonable requests for information.

ARTICLE 13

CONFIDENTIALITY

A. Whether or not counsel continues to represent a client, counsel shall preserve the **C10–014** confidentiality of the client's affairs and shall not reveal to any other person, other than to members of his team who need such information for the performance of their duties, information which has been entrusted to him in confidence or use such information to the client's detriment or to his own or another client's advantage.

B. Notwithstanding paragraph (A), counsel may reveal information which has been entrusted to him in confidence under the following circumstances:

   i. when the client has been fully consulted and knowingly consents;
   ii. when the client has voluntarily disclosed the content of the communication to a third party, and that third party then gives evidence of that disclosure; or
   iii. when essential to establish a claim or defence on behalf of counsel in a controversy between counsel and the client, to establish a defence to a criminal or disciplinary charge or other claim formally instituted against counsel based upon conduct in which the client was involved, or to respond to allegations in any proceeding concerning counsel's representation of the client; or

C. to prevent an act which counsel reasonably believes:

   i. is, or may be, criminal within the territory in which it may occur or under the Statute or the Rules; and
   ii. may result in death or substantial bodily harm to any person unless the information is disclosed.

ARTICLE 14

CONFLICT OF INTEREST

A. Counsel owes a duty of loyalty to a client. Counsel also has a duty to the Tribunal **C10–015** to act with independence in the interests of justice and shall put those interests before his own interests or those of any other person, organisation or State.

B. Counsel shall exercise all care to ensure that no conflict of interest arises.

C. Counsel shall not represent a client in connection with a matter in which counsel participated personally and substantially as an official or staff member of the Tribunal or in any other capacity, unless the Registrar determines, after consultation with the parties and taking account the views of the Chamber, that there is no real possibility shown that a conflict between the former and present assignment exists.

D. Counsel or his firm shall not represent a client with respect to a matter if:

   i. such representation will be, or may reasonably be expected to be, adversely affected by representation of another client;
   ii. representation of another client will be, or may reasonably be expected to be, adversely affected by such representation;
   iii. the matter is the same or substantially related to another matter in which counsel or his firm had formerly represented another client ("former client"), and the interests of the client are materially adverse to the interests of the former client; or

iv. counsel's professional judgement on behalf of the client will be, or may reasonably be expected to be, adversely affected by:
    1. counsel's responsibilities to, or interests in, a third party; or
    2. to counsel's own financial, business, property or personal interests.

E. Where a conflict of interest does arise, counsel shall:
  i. promptly and fully inform each potentially affected present and former client of the nature and extent of the conflict; and
  ii. either:
    1. take all steps necessary to remove the conflict; or
    2. obtain the full and informed consent of all potentially affected present and former clients to continue the representation unless such consent is likely to irreversibly prejudice the administration of justice.

ARTICLE 15

SEXUAL RELATIONS WITH CLIENTS

C10–016   Counsel shall not:
  i. require or demand sexual relations with a client as a condition of professional representation;
  ii. employ coercion, intimidation or undue influence in sexual relations with a client; or
  iii. represent or continue to represent a client with whom counsel has or had sexual relations if such sexual relations may reasonably be expected to result in violations of this Code.

ARTICLE 16

CLIENT UNDER A DISABILITY

C10–017   When a client's ability to make adequately considered decisions in connection with his representation is affected because of a mental disability, his status as a minor or any other reason, counsel shall:
  i. inform the Judge or Chamber hearing the matter, if any, of the client's mental disability or status as a minor; and
  ii. take such steps as are necessary to ensure the adequate legal representation of that client.

ARTICLE 17

CONSULTATIONS WITH CLIENTS ON PROVISIONAL RELEASE OR AT LIBERTY

C10–018   A. Counsel shall not consult with a client on provisional release or at liberty at the client's place of residence.

B. Notwithstanding paragraph (A), counsel may exceptionally consult with a client at his residence if illness, physical disability or other constraints restrict the client's mobility and preferably in the presence of an independent person.

ARTICLE 18

FEE-SPLITTING

C10–019   A. Fee-splitting arrangements, including but not limited to financial arrangements, between assigned counsel and their clients, relatives and/or agents of their clients are prohibited by the Tribunal.

B. Where assigned counsel are being requested, induced or encouraged by their clients to enter into fee-splitting arrangements, they shall advise their clients on the prohibition of such practice and shall report the incident to the Registrar forthwith.

C. Counsel shall inform the Registrar of any alleged fee-splitting arrangement by any member of his or any other defence team.

D. Following receipt of information regarding possible fee-splitting arrangements between assigned counsel and their clients, the Registrar shall investigate such information in order to determine whether it is substantiated.

E. Where assigned counsel is found to have engaged in a practice of fee-splitting or to have entered into a fee-splitting arrangement with his client, the Registrar shall consider taking action in accordance with the Directive.

F. Where the Registrar has granted leave, counsel may provide their clients with equipment and materials necessary for the preparation of their defence.

ARTICLE 19

FEES AND COMPENSATION

A. Counsel, other than counsel assigned by the Registrar, shall provide to a client, in writing and before counsel is engaged to represent a client, a statement of costs of representation, including: **C10–020**

    i. the basis for calculating the costs;

    ii. the billing arrangements;

    iii. and the client's right to receive a bill of costs.

B. Counsel, other than counsel assigned by the Registrar, shall not accept compensation for representing a client from a source other than that client unless:

    i. that client consents in writing after being fully informed by counsel of the source and any other information relevant to the interests of the client; and

    ii. there is no interference with counsel's independence of professional judgement nor with the client-counsel relationship.

C. Counsel, if assigned by the Registrar, shall not accept compensation for representing a client except as provided for under the Directive.

Section 2: Conduct before the Tribunal

ARTICLE 20

RULES OF THE TRIBUNAL

Counsel shall at all times comply with the Statute, the Rules, this Code or any other applicable law including such rulings as to conduct and procedure as may be issued by the Tribunal in its proceedings. Counsel shall at all times have due regard to the fair conduct of proceedings. **C10–021**

ARTICLE 21

DISCRIMINATORY CONDUCT

Counsel shall not engage directly or indirectly in discriminatory conduct in relation to any other person because of race, colour, ethnic or national origin, nationality, citizenship, sex, sexual orientation, marital status, disability, religion or political persuasion. **C10–022**

ARTICLE 22

COMMUNICATIONS WITH THE CHAMBERS

C10–023　　Unless permitted by the Rules, this Code or the Judge or Chamber hearing the matter, counsel shall not:
- i. make contact with a Judge or Chamber in relation to the merits of a particular case, except within the proper context of the proceedings in the case; or
- ii. submit exhibits, notes or documents to a Judge or Chamber without transmitting them through the Registry, except in an emergency or when at the same time transmitted to the Registry.

ARTICLE 23

CANDOUR TOWARD THE TRIBUNAL

C10–024　　A. Counsel shall be personally responsible toward the Tribunal for the conduct and presentation of a client's case.

B. Counsel shall not knowingly:
- i. make an incorrect statement of material fact or law to the Tribunal; or
- ii. offer evidence which counsel knows to be incorrect.

A. Notwithstanding paragraph (B)(i), counsel will not have made an incorrect statement of material fact or law to another party to the proceedings or to the Tribunal simply by failing to correct an error on any matter stated to counsel or to the Tribunal during proceedings.

B. Counsel shall take all necessary steps to correct an incorrect statement of material fact or law by counsel in proceedings before the Tribunal as soon as possible after counsel becomes aware that the statement was incorrect.

C. Counsel may refuse to offer evidence if counsel makes a reasoned determination that the material in question is irrelevant or lacks probative value.

ARTICLE 24

INTEGRITY OF EVIDENCE

C10–025　　Counsel shall at all times maintain the integrity of evidence, whether in written, oral or any other form, which is or may be submitted to the Tribunal.

ARTICLE 25

MERITORIOUS PROCEEDINGS AND CLAIMS

C10–026　　Counsel shall not bring or defend a proceeding or action unless there is a basis for doing so that is not frivolous. It shall not be considered frivolous for counsel to defend a proceeding so as to require that every element of the case be established.

ARTICLE 26

COUNSEL AS WITNESS

C10–027　　Counsel shall not act as an advocate in a proceeding in which counsel is likely to be a necessary witness except where:

i. the testimony relates to an uncontested issue;
ii. the testimony relates to the nature and value of legal services rendered in the case; or
iii. substantial hardship would be caused to the client if that counsel does not so act.

Section 3: Obligations of Counsel to Others

ARTICLE 27

PERSONS FACILITATING OR PARTICIPATING IN THE PROCEEDINGS

A. Counsel shall demonstrate respect, integrity and courtesy for officials and staff members of the Tribunal and for all persons who facilitate and participate in the proceedings. **C10–028**

B. Counsel shall not seek to influence or communicate with a Judge, official, or staff member of the Tribunal by means prohibited by the Statute, the Rules, this Code or any other applicable law.

C. Counsel shall recognise the representatives of the parties as professional colleagues and shall act fairly, honestly and courteously towards them.

D. Counsel shall not communicate with the client of another counsel without the authorisation of that client's counsel unless permitted under the Rules, this Code or any other applicable law.

ARTICLE 28

VICTIMS AND WITNESSES

A. Counsel shall not use any means that have no substantial purpose other than to embarrass, delay or burden victims and witnesses, or use coercive or other methods of obtaining evidence that violate the Statute, the Rules or this Code. **C10–029**

B. Counsel shall not make any payments in monies or assets to witnesses or potential witnesses for the purpose of unduly influencing or inducing such witnesses or potential witnesses.

ARTICLE 29

UNREPRESENTED PERSONS

A. Counsel communicating, on behalf of a client, with a person who is not represented by counsel ("unrepresented person"), shall not: **C10–030**
   i. knowingly mislead the unrepresented person, to the prejudice of that person, concerning the identity and interests of counsel's client;
   ii. coerce, harass or threaten the unrepresented person or his relatives;
   iii. state or imply that counsel is disinterested;
   iv. make other statements prohibited by applicable law;
   v. fail to disclose information required by applicable law; or
   vi. give advice to the unrepresented person, except to retain counsel and in relation to matters specified under paragraph (B), if the interests of that person are or may reasonably be expected to be in conflict with the interests of his client.

B. Whether or not a conflict exists or may exist with the interests of counsel's client, counsel shall inform the unrepresented person of:
   i. the role counsel plays in the matter;

ii. the person's right to counsel under the Rules; and
iii. the nature of legal representation in general.

ARTICLE 30

PROSPECTIVE CLIENTS

C10–031   Counsel shall not:
i. contact a prospective client, his relatives or acquaintances directly or indirectly;
ii. solicit work from a prospective client, if:
 1. the prospective client, his relatives or acquaintances have made known to counsel a desire not to be solicited by counsel; or
 2. the solicitation involves behaviour such as fraud, undue influence, coercion, duress or harassment; or
iii. make false, misleading or deceptive communications to a prospective client, his relatives or acquaintances about the counsel or another counsel's services.

ARTICLE 31

REFERRAL FEES

C10–032   A. Counsel shall not demand or accept from another counsel or any other person a fee, commission or any other compensation for referring or recommending the counsel to a client.
B. Counsel shall not pay any person a fee, commission or any other compensation as a consideration for referring a client to the counsel.

Section 4: Supervisory and Subordinate Conduct

ARTICLE 32

RESPONSIBILITIES OF SUPERVISORY COUNSEL

C10–033   A. Counsel having direct supervisory authority over another counsel in his team shall make reasonable efforts to ensure that the other counsel adheres to this Code.
B. Counsel shall be responsible for another counsel's violation of this Code if:
i. counsel orders, or with knowledge of the specific conduct, approves the conduct involved; or
ii. counsel has direct supervisory authority over the other counsel, and knew or had reason to know of the conduct at a time when its consequences can be avoided or mitigated but fails to take reasonable remedial action.

ARTICLE 33

RESPONSIBILITIES OF SUBORDINATE COUNSEL

C10–034   A. Counsel is bound by this Code notwithstanding that counsel acted at the direction of another counsel.
B. Counsel reasonably acting in accordance with a supervisory counsel's reasonable resolution of an arguable question of professional duty shall not be considered to have violated this Article.

ARTICLE 34

RESPONSIBILITY FOR OTHER TEAM MEMBERS

C10–035

A. Counsel having direct supervisory authority over other members of his team shall make reasonable efforts to ensure that such members' conduct is compatible with the professional obligations of counsel.

B. Counsel shall be responsible for the conduct of other members of his team who provide services for counsel that would be a violation of this Code if engaged by counsel if:

   i. counsel orders or, with knowledge of the specific conduct, approves the conduct involved; or

   ii. counsel has direct supervisory authority over the team member, and knows of the conduct at a time when its consequences can be avoided or mitigated but fails to take reasonable remedial action.

Section 5: Maintenance of the Integrity of the Profession

ARTICLE 35

MISCONDUCT

C10–036

It shall be professional misconduct for counsel, *inter alia*, to:

   i. violate or attempt to violate the Statute, the Rules, this Code or any other applicable law, or to knowingly assist or induce another person to do so, or to do so through the acts of another person;

   ii. commit a criminal act which reflects adversely on counsel's honesty, trustworthiness or fitness as counsel;

   iii. engage in conduct involving dishonesty, fraud, deceit or misrepresentation;

   iv. engage in conduct which is prejudicial to the proper administration of justice before the Tribunal; or

   v. provide inaccurate information or fail to disclose information regarding counsel's qualifications to practice before the Tribunal as set out in the Rules and, where counsel has been assigned to a client, the Directive.

ARTICLE 36

REPORTING MISCONDUCT

C10–037

In accordance with the disciplinary regime set out in Part Three of this Code, counsel shall inform the Disciplinary Panel if counsel knows that another counsel has breached this Code or has otherwise engaged in professional misconduct.

PART THREE

DISCIPLINARY REGIME

ARTICLE 37

PURPOSE

C10–038

The purposes of this Part are:

    a. to protect clients and other individuals, and particularly witnesses from counsel who have not discharged, will not discharge or are unlikely to discharge their professional responsibilities and to provide every person the right to submit a complaint about the conduct of counsel;

    b. to ensure compliance by individual counsel with the necessary standards of professionalism, competence, diligence and honesty and to maintain at a significantly high level the ethics and practice of the legal system operated by the Tribunal; and

    c. to guarantee that procedural fairness is applied to any disciplinary proceedings taken against counsel.

ARTICLE 38

INHERENT POWERS OF THE TRIBUNAL

C10–039   This Part shall not affect the inherent powers of the Tribunal to deal with conduct which interferes with the administration of justice under the Statute, the Rules or any other applicable law.

ARTICLE 39

FILINGS, DECISIONS AND ORDERS

C10–040   Unless otherwise provided in this disciplinary regime, all filings, decisions and orders in relation to the disciplinary regime shall be submitted in confidence to, or transmitted by, the Registry in a working language of the Tribunal. The Registry shall maintain all records for the purposes of this disciplinary regime.

ARTICLE 40

DISCIPLINARY PANEL

C10–041   A. A Disciplinary Panel shall deal with all matters relating to counsel ethics. The Panel shall consist of:

    i. a member of the Association of Counsel to be appointed in accordance with the Association's statute;

    ii. a member of the Advisory Panel having practised at the Tribunal to be appointed by the President of the Advisory Panel;

    iii. the Registrar of the Tribunal, or a senior Registry legal official designated by him.

B. The members of the Panel shall select at its first meeting a counsel chairperson from amongst its members. The chairperson shall be appointed for a term of two years.

C. Except as otherwise provided by this Code, the Panel may determine its own procedure for the filing of briefs and presentation of argument.

D. Complaints concerning the conduct of a counsel or a member of his team relating to matters before the Tribunal and specified in Article 35 shall be submitted to the Chairperson of the Panel in accordance with Article 39. Where the Panel itself has reasonable grounds to suspect that counsel or a member of his team has engaged in such conduct, it may commence, *proprio motu*, an investigation into the matter.

ARTICLE 41

SUBMISSION OF COMPLAINTS

C10–042   1. Complaints may be submitted by a client, a party to proceedings before the Tribunal, or any other person, organisation or State whose rights or interests could be substantially affected by an alleged misconduct.

2. The complaint, which shall be in writing and submitted in accordance with Article 39, shall identify the complainant and the counsel against whom the complaint is made, and describe in sufficient detail the alleged misconduct of the counsel.

3. The complaint shall be submitted within twelve months after the alleged misconduct is brought to the attention of the complainant or within twelve months after the complainant should have reasonably known about the existence or occurrence of the alleged misconduct. The Disciplinary Panel may pursue complaints after these deadlines if the matter is of general importance for the Tribunal or in the interests of justice in a pending case.

ARTICLE 42

SUMMARY DISMISSAL OF COMPLAINTS

In consultation with the Duty Judge of the Tribunal, the Disciplinary Panel may dismiss a complaint if it is vexatious, misconceived, frivolous, lacking in substance or out of time.

C10–043

ARTICLE 43

WITHDRAWAL OF COMPLAINTS

A. By notice in writing served on the Chairperson of the Disciplinary Panel, a complaint may be withdrawn by the complainant in writing. The withdrawal of a complaint does not impact upon the Panel's competencies under Article 40 (D) to investigate the matter raised in the complaint.

C10–044

B. The withdrawal of the complaint does not prevent a further complaint being made under this Part by the same or any other complainant, with respect to the subject matter of the withdrawn complaint; or action being taken on any other complaint made with respect to that matter.

ARTICLE 44

INVESTIGATION OF ALLEGED MISCONDUCT

A. The Disciplinary Panel shall conduct, as soon as possible, an investigation into the alleged misconduct specified in Article 35, provided that a complaint is not summarily dismissed.

C10–045

B. In the investigation of the conduct, the Panel:
  i. shall send particulars of the conduct to the respective counsel or team member ("respondent") in a language he understands, and invite him to submit a written explanation in response to the complaint;
  ii. may order, by notice served in writing, the respondent to:
    1. produce, at any time and place specified in the notice, any books, documents, papers, accounts or records that are in his possession or under his control and that relate to the subject-matter of the complaint; or
    2. otherwise assist in, or co-operate with, the investigation of the complaint in a specified manner.

C. The Disciplinary Panel may inspect any book, document, paper, account or record produced in accordance with paragraph (B)(ii)(1) and may retain it for such period as it deems necessary for the purposes of the investigation. For the purpose of investigating an alleged misconduct of counsel involving allegations of fee-sharing, the Panel may request the Registrar to provide information on his related inquiries into the financial status of an accused, if any.

D. Any respondent who, without reasonable justification or excuse, refuses or fails to comply with any order or requirement of the Disciplinary Panel under this Article may be fined by the Disciplinary Panel with a penalty of up to 10.000 €.

Article 45

INTERIM SUSPENSION FROM PRACTICE

C10–046   A. At any time after a complaint against a respondent has been filed or the Disciplinary Panel has commenced an investigation *propriu motu*, if there are reasonable grounds to conclude that the alleged misconduct is likely to cause immediate and irreparable harm to the interests of justice, a party to the proceedings, a witness, the respondent's client or any other prospective client, the Panel may, without prior notice to the respondent, issue a reasoned order that the respondent be suspended from practising before the Tribunal until the charge has been heard and disposed of.

B. If counsel is representing a suspect or accused while the Disciplinary Panel considers an order for suspension, the Panel must obtain approval from the Presiding Judge of the Chamber in front of which counsel appears before issuing an order.

C. The respondent, or his client, may at any time apply to the President of the Tribunal for the revocation of the order. The President of the Tribunal shall review such application within seven days after it has been received and may grant or refuse the application as he deems fit.

Article 46

CHARGES AGAINST COUNSEL AND INSTITUTION OF PROCEEDINGS AND HEARINGS

C10–047   A. The Disciplinary Panel shall inquire into each particularised allegation, and if there are reasonable grounds that the counsel has committed misconduct, formulate charges against counsel.

B. The Disciplinary Panel may order, if it is in the interests of justice, the joinder of:
     i. more than one charge against the same respondent; or
     ii. a charge against one or more respondents if all the charges are founded on the same, or closely related, acts or omissions.

C. During the course of the inquiry, the respondent shall be provided the opportunity to file a reply to the allegation in the charge in accordance with the rules of the Disciplinary Panel.

D. If there are any material issues of fact raised in the pleadings or if the respondent requests the opportunity to be heard in mitigation, the Disciplinary Panel shall hold a hearing in public at the seat of the Tribunal unless it decides, *proprio motu* or upon application by the respondent, to exclude the public.

E. During the hearing the respondent shall have the right to be represented by counsel, to examine evidence submitted by the complainant or gathered by the Disciplinary Panel, cross-examine witnesses and to present evidence. The complainant, if any, shall be permitted to address the Disciplinary Panel concerning the respondent's alleged misconduct and its effect on him.

F. The Disciplinary Panel may admit any evidence which is relevant or which has probative value, whether oral or written, whether direct or hearsay and whether or not the same would be admissible in a court of law.

G. Every witness appearing before the Disciplinary Panel shall, before giving evidence, make the solemn declaration as set out in the Rules. The provisions of the Rules relating to false testimony under solemn declaration shall apply, *mutatis mutandis*, to witnesses appearing before the Disciplinary Panel.

ARTICLE 47

FINDINGS AND SANCTIONS

A. The findings of the Disciplinary Panel on each charge shall be rendered, in **C10–048** consultation with the Duty Judge of the Tribunal, by the majority of its members and shall be accompanied by a reasoned opinion in writing, to which separate or dissenting opinions may be appended.

B. The Disciplinary Panel may conclude its proceedings without a finding of misconduct, or dismiss any charge. The Panel may suspend or dismiss a complaint, before, during or after the investigation of the complaint, if it is in the interests of justice to do so or it fails to find reasonable grounds to conclude that the respondent committed the alleged misconduct.

C. A respondent against whom a charge of professional misconduct has been found proved beyond a reasonable doubt may be sentenced by the Disciplinary Panel to be, either alternatively or cumulatively:

    i. admonished by the Disciplinary Panel; given advice by the Disciplinary Panel as to his future conduct;

    ii. publicly reprimanded by the Disciplinary Panel;

    iii. ordered to pay a fine of up to 50,000 ů to the Tribunal;

    iv. suspended from practising before the Tribunal for an appropriate fixed period of time not exceeding two years;

    v. banned from practising before the Tribunal.

D. In determining the sentence imposed, the Disciplinary Panel must take into account any mitigating factors it considers relevant, including, *inter alia*, the fact that the respondent was acting pursuant to a provision of another code of practice and ethics which governs his conduct and that provision is inconsistent with this Code. A sentence must be proportionate in view of the misconduct.

E. The decision of the Disciplinary Panel shall be notified in writing to the complainant, if any, and to the respondent in a language the respondent understands.

F. A copy of the decision shall be communicated to the Association of Counsel as well as the professional body regulating the conduct of the respondent in his State of admission, or to the governing body of the university where counsel is a law professor.

G. The Registry shall take such action as may be required to enforce the sentence.

ARTICLE 48

APPEAL TO THE DISCIPLINARY BOARD

A. In cases where one or more charges of professional misconduct have been proved, **C10–049** the respondent may file an appeal with a Disciplinary Board within fourteen days of notification of the decision of the Disciplinary Panel.

B. In cases where the Disciplinary Panel has decided that a charge has not been proved, the Registrar may file an appeal with the Disciplinary Board within fourteen days of notification of the decision to the respondent.

C. The Disciplinary Board shall consist of:

    i. three Judges to be appointed by the President of the Tribunal;

    ii. two members of the Association of Counsel, to be appointed for a two year period, and in accordance with the Association's statute. No member of the Disciplinary Panel shall be a member of the Disciplinary Board at the same time.

D. No Judge who sat as a member of the Chamber before which the respondent appeared shall be eligible to sit as a member of the Disciplinary Board on the hearing or determination of any charge against the respondent for professional misconduct.

E. The members of the Disciplinary Board shall, at its first meeting, select a chairperson from amongst their number.

1583

F. Except as otherwise provided by this Code, the Disciplinary Board may determine its own procedure for the filing of briefs and presentation of argument. During its review, however, the Disciplinary Board shall not receive or consider any evidence that was not presented to the Disciplinary Panel, unless it considers that the interests of justice so require.

G. Any respondent who, without reasonable justification or excuse, refuses or fails to comply with any order or requirement of the Disciplinary Board under this Article may be fined by the Board with a penalty of up to 10.000 €.

H. The Disciplinary Board may confirm, reverse or modify the decision on appeal.

I. In any case in which the respondent has given notice of appeal to the Disciplinary Board, the actions set out in Article 47 paragraph (G) shall be deferred until the appeal has been disposed of by the Disciplinary Board with or without a hearing. The Board may at any time after it was seized order a measure in accordance with Article 45 (A). Article 45 (B) does not apply.

J. The decision of the Disciplinary Board is final, and shall in particular not be subject to any remedy before the President or a Chamber of the Tribunal.

ARTICLE 49

COSTS

C10–050   A. If a respondent is sentenced by the Disciplinary Panel, and an appeal is not filed, or by the Disciplinary Board, the respondent shall bear the costs of the procedure. These costs consist of necessary and reasonable travel costs of the Panel or Board members in accordance with the Tribunal's practice for travel of defence counsel, if any, and an office expenses lump sum of up to 1000 € to be determined by the Disciplinary Panel or Board.

B. If a proceeding or complaint is dismissed by the Disciplinary Panel, and an appeal is not filed, or by the Disciplinary Board, the Tribunal bears the costs of the proceedings, unless the Panel or Board decides, on the basis of reasonable cause, that the respondent should bear up to fifty percent of the costs.

C. All costs shall be paid to the Registrar.

ARTICLE 50

NON BIS IN IDEM

C10–051   Once a proceeding or complaint has been finally adjudicated by the Disciplinary Board and an appeal has not been filed to the Disciplinary Board within fourteen days of notification, or by the Disciplinary Panel, no further action shall be taken by the Disciplinary Panel or Disciplinary Board against the respondent with respect to the subject matter of the proceeding or complaint.

C11. The Code of Ethics for Interpreters and Translators Employed by the International Criminal Tribunal for the Former Yugoslavia

(IT/144)

DECISION

THE REGISTRAR   C11–001

CONSIDERING Rule 76 of the Rules of Procedure and Evidence ("the Rules") which confers on the Registrar the responsibility for ensuring that interpreters and translators perform their duties faithfully, independently, impartially and with full respect for the duty of confidentiality;

CONSIDERING that being subject to a Code of Ethics is an integral attribute of being an interpreter and translator employed in a judicial environment;

CONSIDERING that interpreters and translators employed by the International Tribunal are hired under different terms and conditions and, as part of their functions, undertake various tasks within the three constituent parts of the International Tribunal;

CONSIDERING that a draft Code of Ethics, prepared by the Registrar, has been circulated to the Judges and Prosecutor of the International Tribunal and that they have voiced no objections to its promulgation;

TAKING NOTE of the comments of the Judges and the Prosecutor on the said draft;

PURSUANT TO Rule 76 of the Rules;

HEREBY PROMULGATES the Code of Ethics for Interpreters and Translators Employed by the International Criminal Tribunal for the former Yugoslavia, attached as Annex 1;

DONE in English and French, the English text being authoritative.
Dorothee de Sampayo Garrido-Nijgh
Registrar

Dated this fifth day of March 1999
At The Hague
The Netherlands

ANNEX 1

THE CODE OF ETHICS OF INTERPRETERS AND TRANSLATORS EMPLOYED BY THE INTERNATIONAL CRIMINAL TRIBUNAL FOR THE FORMER YUGOSLAVIA

PREAMBLE

This Code is promulgated in the belief that: C11–002

1. As employees of the Tribunal, interpreters and translators shall maintain high standards of professional conduct;

2. The functions performed by interpreters and translators require them to act faithfully, independently, impartially and with full respect for the duty of confidentiality.

3. Since the duties and responsibilities that they have towards the Tribunal continue after the expiration or termination of their employment, interpreters and translators may be held accountable for any breach thereto, including, but not limited to, referral to their respective national or international professional association. It is therefore necessary that such persons be aware of these duties and responsibilities.

To these ends, this Code and its Articles of conduct have been formulated.

ARTICLE 1

DEFINITIONS

C11–003   1. In this Code, unless a different interpretation is required by the provisions of the Code or the context in which they appear, the following terms shall mean:

"CLSS" the Conference and Language Services Section of the Tribunal.

"Interpreters" persons employed by the Tribunal under:

(a) a fixed-term contract who interpret in simultaneous mode the proceedings held in the Tribunal's courtrooms;

(b) a short-term contract or a Special Services Agreement during field-assignments outside the Tribunal headquarters in The Hague or outside the Tribunal courtrooms;

(c) a short-term contract who reinforce the Tribunal's interpretation teams and interpret in simultaneous mode the proceedings held in the Tribunal's courtrooms.

"Translators" persons employed by the Tribunal under:

(a) a fixed-term contract who translate in writing the documents referred to CLSS;

(b) a short-term contract who translate in writing, at home, documents meant to be used by the Tribunal.

"Tribunal" the International Tribunal for the Prosecution of Persons Responsible for Serious Violations of International Humanitarian Law Committed in the Territory of the Former Yugoslavia since 1991, established by Security Council Resolution 827 of 25 May 1993.

2. This Code must be read and applied so as to most effectively attain the objectives and uphold the values expressed in the Preamble.

3. General provisions of this Code should not be read or applied in a restrictive way by reason of any particular or illustrative provision.

4. The singular includes the plural and vice versa.

ARTICLE 2

ENTRY INTO FORCE

C11–004   This Code shall enter into force on the twenty-sixth day of February 1999.

ARTICLE 3

GENERAL PURPOSE AND APPLICATION

C11–005   1. The general purpose of this Code is to provide for standards of conduct on the part of interpreters and translators that all persons employed by the Tribunal in such a capacity are bound to respect.

2. This code applies to interpreters and translators as defined in Article 1(1) of this Code.

3. In addition to this Code, as staff members of the Tribunal, interpreters and translators shall be bound by the provisions of the United Nations Staff Rules and Regulations, and the administration instructions thereto.

PROFESSIONAL CONDUCT

ARTICLE 4

STANDARDS OF CONDUCT

C11–006   1. Interpreters and translators shall behave in a courteous, polite and dignified manner at all times.

2. Interpreters shall at all times maintain a professional attitude in dealings with Judges, court officers, witnesses, lawyers and other persons inside the courtroom. Interpreters should strive for professional detachment at all times.

ARTICLE 5

PROFESSIONAL INTEGRITY AND DIGNITY

C11–007

1. Interpreters and translators shall not allow any personal or other interest to interfere with the discharge of their duties.

2. Interpreters and translators shall not, in the performance of their duties, solicit or accept any gratuities or other consideration, benefit or advantage of any kind.

3. Interpreters and translators shall not exercise power or influence over their listeners or readers.

4. Interpreters and translators shall maintain their integrity and independence at all times.

ARTICLE 6

RELIABILITY

C11–008

1. Interpreters and translators shall adhere to appointment times and deadlines, or otherwise advise their supervisor accordingly so that the necessary action may be taken.

2. Interpreters, when working in the courtrooms, shall inform the Judges of any doubt arising from a possible lexical lacuna in the source or target language.

GENERAL OBLIGATIONS OF INTERPRETERS AND TRANSLATORS TOWARDS THE TRIBUNAL

ARTICLE 7

CONFIDENTIALITY

1. General Obligations

C11–009

(a) Interpreters and translators shall exercise the utmost discretion in all matters relating to their functions and should not communicate at any time to the media or to any institution, person, governmental or non-governmental organisation or other authority external to the Tribunal any information that has not been made public and which has become known to them in the course of their duties.

(b) Interpreters and translators shall not communicate any information that has been entrusted to them in confidence, that has become known to them by reason of their functions, or that they otherwise know to be confidential to any person within the Tribunal other than to those persons who need to have such information for the performance of their duties or with the authorisation of their supervisor.

(c) Translated documents remain the property of the Tribunal at all times and shall not be shown or released by interpreters or translators to third persons without the express permission of their supervisor or by order of the Tribunal.

(d) Interpreters and translators shall not discuss the facts of any case pending before the Tribunal, except as regards matters of a professional nature within the CLSS.

      (e) Interpreters and translators shall not derive any personal profit or advantage from any confidential information that they may have acquired during the performance of their duties.

2. Information Sharing

C11–010   Where team work is required, and with their supervisor's permission, it may be necessary for interpreters or translators to brief other interpreters or translators from the team involved in the assignment. In such circumstances, the ethical obligation for confidentiality extends to all members of the team.

3. Lawyer-Client Privilege

C11–011   Information gained by interpreters and translators from consultations or communications between suspects or accused and their legal representatives is protected under the rule of legal professional privilege, and must not be disclosed to any other person without the express consent of the suspect or accused concerned and his or her counsel.

4. Continuation of Obligations

C11–012   The duty of professional secrecy continues after the expiration or termination of the interpreter's or translator's employment with the Tribunal.

ARTICLE 8

IMPARTIALITY

C11–013   1. Interpreters and translators are bound to the strictest impartiality in the discharge of their duties.

    2. Interpreters and translators shall not give legal advice to any person, whether solicited or not, nor refer suspects or accused to specific defence counsel.

    3. Interpreters and translators shall frankly disclose to their supervisor any actual or apparent conflict of interest that may arise during the performance of their duties.

PROFICIENCY

ARTICLE 9

COMPETENCE

1. Level of Expertise

C11–014   (a) Interpreters and translators shall only accept assignments that they are competent to perform.

      (b) During the course of an assignment, if it becomes apparent to interpreters and translators that expertise beyond their technical or language competence is required, they shall offer to withdraw from the assignment.

      (c) It is the responsibility of interpreters and translators to ensure that the conditions under which they operate facilitate communication. In the event that an external element—including technical hindrances such as poor quality sound and illegible photocopies—interferes with the accuracy or the completeness of their interpretation or translation, they shall inform their listeners or readers promptly.

2. Preparation

Interpreters and translators shall ascertain beforehand what may be expected of them during impending assignments, and undertake the necessary preparations. **C11–015**

ARTICLE 10

ACCURACY

1. Truth and completeness

(a) Interpreters and translators shall convey with the greatest fidelity and accuracy, and with complete neutrality, the wording used by the persons they interpret or translate. **C11–016**

(b) Interpreters shall convey the whole message, including vulgar or derogatory remarks, insults and any non-verbal clue, such as the tone of voice and emotions of the speaker, which might facilitate the understanding of their listeners.

(c) Interpreters and translators shall not embellish, omit or edit anything from their assigned work.

(d) If patent mistakes or untruths are spoken or written, interpreters and translators shall convey these accurately as presented.

2. Uncertainties in Transmission and Comprehension

(a) Interpreters and translators shall acknowledge and rectify promptly any mistake in their interpretation or translation. **C11–017**

(b) If anything is unclear, interpreters and translators shall ask for repetition, rephrasing or explanation.

3. Clear Transmission

Interpreters shall ensure, where practicable, that speech is clearly heard and understood by their audience. **C11–018**

DUTIES TOWARDS THE PROFESSION

ARTICLE 11

PROFESSIONAL DEVELOPMENT

1. Upgrading

Interpreters and translators shall maintain and continually improve their interpreting and translating skills, and increase their knowledge of court proceedings and technical vocabulary that might be encountered during the performance of their duties. **C11–019**

2. Professional solidarity

(a) It is incumbent on interpreters and translators to support and encourage the professional development of their colleagues. **C11–020**

(b) Interpreters and translators should provide their colleagues, whenever possible, with any specialised knowledge they acquire which may be useful to the exercise of their duties.

C12. Practice Direction on Formal Requirements for Appeals from Judgement

(IT/201)

7 MARCH 2002

I. INTRODUCTION

C12–001   In accordance with Rule 19(B) of the Rules of Procedure and Evidence of the International Tribunal for the Prosecution of Persons Responsible for Serious Violations of International Humanitarian Law Committed in the Territory of the Former Yugoslavia since 1991 ("Rules" and "International Tribunal", respectively) and having consulted with the Bureau, the Registrar, the Prosecutor and the Appeals Chamber, I issue this Practice Direction in order to establish the formal requirements for appeals from judgement ("Practice Direction") before the International Tribunal:

II. FORMAL REQUIREMENTS

The Appellant's Notice of Appeal

C12–002   1. A party seeking to appeal from a judgement of a Trial Chamber ("Appellant") shall file, in accordance with the Statute of the International Criminal Tribunal for the Former Yugoslavia ("Statute"), in particular Article 25 of the Statute, and the Rules, a Notice of Appeal containing, in the following order:
   (a) the date of the judgement;
   (b) the specific provision of the Rules pursuant to which the Notice of Appeal is filed;
   (c) the grounds of appeal, clearly specifying in respect of each ground of appeal:
       (i) any alleged error on a question of law invalidating the decision, and/or
       (ii) any alleged error of fact which has occasioned a miscarriage of justice;
       (iii) an identification of the finding or ruling challenged in the judgement, with specific reference to the page number and paragraph number;
       (iv) an identification of any other order, decision or ruling challenged, with specific reference to the date of its filing, and/or transcript page;
       (v) the precise relief sought;
   (d) if relevant, the overall relief sought.

Variation of the Grounds of Appeal

C12–003   2. Any party applying to vary the grounds of appeal must do so by way of motion in accordance with the Rules, setting out:
   (a) the specific Rule under which the variation is sought; and
   (b) the arguments in support of the request to vary the grounds of appeal as required by that Rule.
   3. If leave is granted to vary the grounds of appeal then the varied grounds of appeal shall comply with the requirements of this Practice Direction *mutatis mutandis*.

The Appellant's Brief

C12–004   4. After having filed a Notice of Appeal, the Appellant shall file, in accordance with the Statute and the Rules, an Appellant's Brief containing, in the following order:
   (a) an introduction with a concise summary of the relevant procedural history including the date of the judgement as well as the case number and date of any interlocutory filing or decision relevant to the appeal;

(b) the arguments in support of each ground of appeal, including, but not limited to;

    (i) legal arguments, giving clear and precise references to relevant provisions of the Statute, the Rules, the jurisprudence of the International Tribunal or other legal authorities relied upon;

    (ii) factual arguments and, if applicable, arguments in support of any objections as to whether a fact has been sufficiently proven or not, with precise reference to any relevant exhibit, transcript page, decision or paragraph number in the judgement;

    (iii) arguments in support of the submitted causal link between any alleged error on a question of law invalidating the decision and/or any alleged error of fact which has occasioned a miscarriage of justice;

    (iv) the precise relief sought;

(c) the arguments in support of any overall relief sought.

The grounds of appeal and the arguments must be set out and numbered in the same order as in the Appellant's Notice of Appeal, unless otherwise varied with leave of the Appeals Chamber.

The Respondent's Brief

5. The opposite party ("Respondent") shall file, in accordance with the Statute and the Rules, a Respondent's Brief, containing for each ground of appeal, in the following order: **C12–005**

(a) a statement on whether or not the relief sought by the Appellant is opposed;

(b) a statement on whether or not the ground of appeal is opposed;

(c) arguments in support of these statements, containing:

    (i) legal arguments, including clear and precise references to the relevant provisions of the Statute, the Rules, the jurisprudence of the International Tribunal or other legal authorities relied upon;

    (ii) factual arguments including, if applicable, the arguments in support of the assertion that a fact has been sufficiently proven or not, with precise reference to any relevant exhibit, transcript page, decision or paragraph number in the judgement;

    (iii) arguments pertaining to the submitted causal link between any alleged error on a question of law invalidating the decision and/or any alleged error of fact which has occasioned a miscarriage of justice.

The statements and the arguments must be set out and numbered in the same order as in the Appellant's Brief and shall be limited to arguments made in response to that brief. However, if an Appellant relies on a particular ground to reverse an acquittal, the Respondent may support the acquittal on additional grounds.

The Appellant's Brief in Reply

6. An Appellant may file, in accordance with the Statute and the Rules, an Appellant's Brief in Reply, limited to arguments in reply to the Respondent's Brief, set out and numbered in the same order as in previous briefs. **C12–006**

The Book of Authorities

7. A Book of Authorities must be attached to the Appellant's Brief and the Respondent's Brief, in accordance with the Rules, containing a separate compilation setting out clearly all authorities relied upon. **C12–007**

8. The Book of Authorities shall include a table of contents describing each document and exhibit including the date and reference.

9. Authorities of the International Tribunal and the International Criminal Tribunal for Rwanda (together "International Tribunals") need not be provided. All other authorities shall be provided in an authorised version of the authority in question,

complete with an English or French translation, if the original is not in one of the languages of the International Tribunals.

10. A party may object to a translation by filing a motion no later than fifteen days from the filing of the Book of Authorities containing the translation challenged.

Additional Evidence

C12–008   11. Any party applying to present additional evidence shall do so by way of motion filed, in accordance with the Statute and the Rules, such motion containing, in the following order:

(a) a precise list of the evidence the party is seeking to have presented;
(b) an identification of each ground of appeal to which the evidence relates and, where applicable, a request to submit any additional grounds of appeal based on such evidence;
(c) arguments in relation to the requirement of non-availability at trial;
(d) arguments in relation to the requirement that the admission of the evidence is in the interests of justice;

The relevant documents and exhibits, where applicable, shall be translated into one of the languages of the International Tribunal.

12. If a party is authorised to present additional evidence then the requirements of this Practice Direction apply *mutatis mutandis*.

III. GENERAL REQUIREMENTS

C12–009   13. Where filings of the parties refer to passages in a judgement, decision, transcripts, exhibits or other authorities, they shall indicate precisely the date, exhibit number, page number and paragraph number of the text or exhibit referred to.

14. Any abbreviations or designations used by the parties in their filings shall be uniform throughout. Pages and paragraphs shall be numbered consecutively from the beginning to the end.

15. Any time limits prescribed under this Practice Direction shall run from, but shall not include, the day upon which the relevant document is filed. Should the last day of a time prescribed fall upon a non-working day of the International Tribunal it shall be considered as falling on the first working day thereafter.

16. The provisions of this Practice Direction are without prejudice to any such orders or decisions that may be made by a designated Pre-Appeal Judge or the Appeals Chamber. In particular a Pre-Appeal Judge or the Appeals Chamber may vary any time limit or recognise, as validly done any act done after the expiration of a time limit prescribed in this Practice Direction.

IV. NON-COMPLIANCE WITH THE REQUIREMENTS

C12–010   17. Where a party fails to comply with the requirements laid down in this Practice Direction, or where the wording of a filing is unclear or ambiguous, a designated Pre-Appeal Judge or the Appeals Chamber may, within its discretion, decide upon an appropriate sanction, which can include an order for clarification or re-filing. The Appeals Chamber may also reject a filing or dismiss submissions therein.

_____Signed_____
Claude Jorda
President

C13. Practice Direction on the Length of Briefs and Motions

(IT/184/REV. 2)

16 SEPTEMBER 2005

INTRODUCTION

In accordance with the Rules of Procedure and Evidence of the International Tribunal ("the Rules"), I issue this Practice Direction in order to establish a limit on the length of written briefs and motions at trial and on appeal. **C13–001**

(A) Paper size and format

Briefs and motions will be submitted on A4 paper. Margins will be at least 2.5 centimetres on all four sides. All filings will be paginated, excluding the cover sheet. **C13–002**

(B) Typeface

The typeface will be 12 point with 1.5 line spacing. An average page should contain fewer than 300 words. **C13–003**

(C) Length

1. Appeals from judgement

(a) The brief of an appellant on appeal from a final judgement of a Trial Chamber will not exceed 30,000 words (12,000 where the appeal is restricted to sentencing): **C13–004**
  (i) provided that, where the Prosecutor, as appellant, files a separate brief in respect of each appellee or a consolidated brief, the total number of words filed shall not exceed 30,000 words in respect of one appellee and a further 10,000 in respect of each additional appellee;
  (ii) and provided that the time-limit for filing such a consolidated brief shall run from the filing date of the last notice of appeal.
(b) The response of an appellee on an appeal from a final judgement of a Trial Chamber will not exceed 30,000 words (12,000 where the appeal is restricted to sentencing), subject to the proviso in (a) (i) applying mutatis mutandis to any brief in response filed by the Prosecutor, and provided that, the time-limit for filing a consolidated brief in response shall run from the filing date of the last appellant's brief.
(c) The reply brief of an appellant in an appeal from a final judgement of a Trial Chamber will not exceed 9,000 words (3,000 where the appeal is restricted to sentencing):
  (i) provided that, where the Prosecutor files a reply brief in respect of more than one appellee, either by filing a separate brief in respect of each appellee or a consolidated brief, the total number of pages shall not exceed 9,000 words in respect of one appellee and a further 3,000 in respect of each additional appellee;
  (ii) and provided that the time-limit for filing such a consolidated reply brief shall run from the filing date of the last appellee's response.

2. Interlocutory appeals

(1) The brief of an appellant in an interlocutory appeal will not exceed 9,000 words. **C13–005**

(2) The brief of an appellee in an interlocutory appeal will not exceed 9,000 words.

(3) The reply brief of an appellant in an interlocutory appeal will not exceed 3,000 words.

3. *Pre-trial briefs*

C13–006   The pre-trial briefs will not exceed 15,000 words.

4. *Final trial briefs*

C13–007   The final trial briefs will not exceed 60,000 words.

5. *Other motions, replies, and responses*

C13–008   Motions, responses and replies before a Chamber will not exceed 3,000 words. Where related to Rule 115 additional evidence, motions and responses shall not exceed 9,000 words, while replies shall not exceed 3,000 words. Where related to Rule 115 rebuttal material, motions and replies shall not exceed 3,000 words.

6. *Materials excluded from page and word limits*

C13–009   Headings, footnotes and quotations count towards the above word limitations. Any addendum containing verbatim quotations of the International Tribunal's Statute or Rules does not count towards the page limit. Any appendix or book of authorities does not count towards the page limit. An appendix or book of authorities will not contain legal or factual arguments, but rather references, source materials, items from the record, exhibits, and other relevant, non-argumentative material. An appendix will be of reasonable length, which is normally three times the page limit for that class of motion or brief (e.g., for a brief that is limited to 30 pages by the above practice direction, the appendix should be limited to 90 pages), although it is understood that the length of appendices will naturally vary more than the length of briefs.

7. *Variation from page limits*

C13–010   A party must seek authorization in advance from the Chamber to exceed the word limits in this Practice Direction and must provide an explanation of the exceptional circumstances that necessitate the oversized filing. Upon filing by a party of a motion for an extension of time or word limit, the pre-appeal Judge may dispose of the motion without hearing the other party, unless he/she considers that there is a risk that the other party may be prejudiced.

8. *Reporting the word count*

Parties shall conduct a word count of any document they file which is subject to the length limitations set forth in this Practice Direction and shall include this information in the form "Word count: _____" at the end of the document, before the signature line.

Theodor Meron
President

C14. Practice Direction on Procedure for the Filing of Written Submissions in Appeal Proceedings before the International Tribunal

(IT/155/REV. 3)

16 SEPTEMBER 2005

I. INTRODUCTION

In accordance with Sub-rule 19(B) of the Rules of Procedure and Evidence of the International Tribunal for the Prosecution of Persons Responsible for Serious Violations of International Humanitarian Law Committed in the Territory of the Former Yugoslavia since 1991 ("Rules" and "International Tribunal" respectively) and having consulted with the Bureau, the Registrar, the Prosecutor and the Appeals Chamber, I issue this revised Practice Direction in order to establish a procedure for the filing of written submissions in appeal proceedings before the International Tribunal:

C14–001

II. APPEALS FROM DECISIONS WHERE INTERLOCUTORY APPEAL LIES AS OF RIGHT

1. A party wishing to appeal from a decision of a Trial Chamber ("appellant) where an interlocutory appeal lies as of right shall file, in accordance with the Rules, an interlocutory appeal containing:

C14–002

    (a) the precise title and date of filing of the appealed decision;
    (b) a summary of the proceedings before the Trial Chamber relating to the appealed decision including an identification of all relevant documents in the proceedings before the Trial Chamber, clearly stating the title and date of filing of each document or the page number of a transcript;
    (c) the specific provision of the Rules pursuant to which the appeal is filed;
    (d) a concise statement as to why it is contended that the provision relied upon is applicable to the appeal;
    (e) the grounds on which the appeal is made;
    (f) the relief sought.

2. The opposite party shall file a response within ten days of the filing of the interlocutory appeal. Such a response shall clearly state whether or not the interlocutory appeal is opposed and the grounds therefor. It shall further set out any objection to the applicability of the provision of the Rules relied upon by the appellant as the basis for the appeal.

3. The appellant may file a reply within four days of the filing of the response. The Appeals Chamber may thereafter decide the appeal without further submissions from the parties.

III. APPEALS FROM RULE 11*bis*, RULE 77 AND RULE 91 DECISIONS

4. A party wishing to appeal from a decision of a Trial Chamber ("appellant") pursuant to Rule 11*bis*, Rule 77 or Rule 91 shall file notice of appeal within 15 days of the decision unless the accused was not present or represented when the decision was pronounced, in which case the time-limit shall run from the date on which the accused is notified of the decision;

C14–003

5. An appellant must file the appeal brief within 15 days after filing the notice of appeal. In accordance with the Rules, the appeal shall contain:

    (a) the precise title and date of filing of the appealed decision;

    (b) a summary of the proceedings before the Trial Chamber relating to the appealed decision including an identification of all relevant documents in the proceedings before the Trial Chamber, clearly stating the title and date of filing of each document or the page number of a transcript;

    (c) the grounds on which the appeal is made;

    (d) the relief sought.

6. The opposite party shall file a response within ten days of the filing of the appeal brief.

7. The appellant may file a reply within four days of the filing of the response. The Appeals Chamber may thereafter decide the appeal without further submissions from the parties.

8. Paragraph (C)(2) of the Practice Direction on the Length of Briefs and Motions (IT/184/Rev. 2, 14 September 2005) applies to filings under this provision.

IV. APPEALS FROM DECISIONS WHERE CERTIFICATION HAS BEEN GRANTED BY A TRIAL CHAMBER

C14–004   9. Where certification has been granted by a Trial Chamber, a party shall within seven days of the filing of the decision to certify file an interlocutory appeal containing:

    (a) the precise title and date of filing of the appealed decision and of the decision of the Trial Chamber granting certification;

    (b) a summary of the proceedings before the Trial Chamber relating to the appealed decision;

    (c) the specific provision of the Rules pursuant to which the appeal is filed;

    (d) the grounds on which the appeal is made;

    (e) the relief sought.

10. The opposite party shall file a response within ten days of the filing of the interlocutory appeal. This response shall clearly state whether or not the interlocutory appeal is opposed and the grounds therefor.

11. The appellant may file a reply within four days of the filing of the response. The Appeals Chamber may thereafter decide the appeal without further submissions from the parties.

V. MOTIONS DURING APPEALS FROM JUDGEMENT

C14–005   12. Where an appeal has been filed from a judgement, a party wishing to move the Appeals Chamber for a specific ruling or relief ("moving party") shall file, in accordance with the Rules, a motion containing:

    (a) the precise ruling or relief sought;

    (b) the specific provision of the Rules under which the ruling or relief is sought;

    (c) the grounds on which the ruling or relief is sought.

13. The opposite party shall file a response within ten days of the filing of the motion or, in the event of a motion pursuant to Rule 115, within 30 days of the motion. This response shall clearly state whether or not the motion is opposed and the grounds therefor.

14. The moving party may file a reply within four days of the filing of the response, or, in the event of a motion pursuant to Rule 115, within 14 days of the response.

15. Where filings are related to a Rule 115 motion, parties are permitted to file supplemental briefs on the impact of the additional evidence within 15 days of the expiry of the time-limit for the filing of rebuttal material, if no such material is filed, or, if rebuttal material is filed, within 15 days of the decision on the admissibility of that material.

VI. CALCULATION OF TIME

C14–006   16. The time-limits prescribed under this Practice Direction shall run from, but shall not include, the day upon which the relevant document is filed. Should the last day of a time prescribed fall upon a non-working day of the International Tribunal it shall be considered as falling on the first working day thereafter.

VII. GENERAL REQUIREMENTS FOR THE WRITTEN SUBMISSIONS

17. Where filings of the parties refer to passages in a judgement, decision, transcripts, exhibits or other authorities, they shall indicate precisely the date, exhibit number, page number and paragraph number of the text or exhibit referred to. **C14–007**

18. Any abbreviations or designations used by the parties in their filings shall be uniform throughout. Pages and paragraphs shall be numbered consecutively from the beginning to the end.

VIII. VARIATION OF PROCEDURE

19. The provisions of this Practice Direction are without prejudice to any such orders or decisions that may be made by the Appeals Chamber or a Pre-Appeal Judge. In particular, the Appeals Chamber or Pre-Appeal Judge may vary any time-limit prescribed under this Practice Direction or recognise as validly done any act done after the expiration of a time-limit so prescribed. The Appeals Chamber may at its discretion entertain oral motions brought in the course of appeals against Judgement. **C14–008**

IX. NON-COMPLIANCE WITH THIS PRACTICE DIRECTION

20. Where a party fails to comply with the requirements laid down in this Practice Direction, or where the wording of a filing is unclear or ambiguous, the Appeals Chamber may, within its discretion, decide upon an appropriate sanction, which can include an order for clarification or re-filing. The Appeals Chamber may also reject a filing or dismiss submissions therein. **C14–009**

Signed

———————————
Theodor Meron
President

C15. Directive on Allowances for Witnesses and Expert Witnesses

(ADOPTED 5 DECEMBER 2001)

(IT/200)

TABLE OF CONTENTS

I—PREAMBLE

C15–001   The Registrar of the Tribunal,
Considering the Statute of the Tribunal as adopted by the Security Council under resolution 827 (1993) of 25 May 1993, as subsequently amended, and in particular Articles 20, 21 and 22 thereof;
Considering the Rules of Procedure and Evidence as adopted by the Tribunal on 11 February 1994, as subsequently amended, and in particular Rules 34, 54, 69, 71, 71*bis*, 75, 89, 90, 90*bis*, 92*bis* and 98 thereof;
Considering the Agreement between the United Nations and the Kingdom of the Netherlands Concerning the Headquarters of the Tribunal signed at New York on 29 July 1994, and in particular Articles XVIII thereof;
Considering the Declaration of Basic Principles of Justice for Victims of Crime and Abuse of Power adopted by the General Assembly by Resolution 40/34 of 29 November 1985, and in particular Paragraph 6 thereof;

ISSUES THE DIRECTIVE ON ALLOWANCES FOR WITNESSES AND EXPERT WITNESSES AS FOLLOWS;

II—General Provisions

Article 1

ENTRY INTO FORCE

This Directive establishes the provision of allowances for witnesses and expert witnesses and shall enter into force on the 1st day of January two thousand and two (01 January 2002). **C15–002**

Article 2

DEFINITIONS

(A) Under this Directive, the following terms shall mean: **C15–003**
Chambers: The Chambers of the Tribunal referred to in Article 11 of the Statute;
Directive: Directive on Allowances for Witnesses and Expert Witnesses (IT/200);
Expert Witness: A person who provides or is due to provide expert testimony before the Chambers as a result of being called by the parties in accordance with Rule 94*bis* of the Rules; or as a result of being summoned by the Chambers in accordance with Rule 54 or 98 of the Rules;
Parties: The Prosecutor and the Defence;
President: The President of the Tribunal referred to in Article 14 of the Statute;
Prosecutor: the Prosecutor appointed pursuant to Article 16 of the Statute;
Registrar: the Registrar of the Tribunal appointed pursuant to Article 17 of the Statute;
Rule 92*bis* witness: a person who, under Rule 92*bis* of the Rules, gives a declaration witnessed by a person authorised to witness such a declaration in accordance with the law and procedure of a State, or a Presiding Officer appointed by the Registrar of the Tribunal;
Rules: the Rules of Procedure and Evidence adopted by the Tribunal on 11 February 1994, as subsequently amended;
Statute: the Statute of the Tribunal adopted by the Security Council under Resolution 827 (1993) of 25 May 1993, as subsequently amended;
Victims and Witnesses Section: the Victims and Witnesses Section referred to in Rule 34 of the Rules;
Witness: a person who provides or is due to provide testimony before the Chambers as a result of being called by the parties; summoned by the Chambers under Rule 54 or 98 of the Rules; or ordered by the Chambers to give testimony by deposition under Rule 71 of the Rules or video-conference link under Rule 71*bis* of the Rules;
Tribunal: the International Tribunal for the Prosecution of Persons Responsible for Serious Violations of International Humanitarian Law Committed in the Territory of the Former Yugoslavia since 1991.
(B) In the Directive, the masculine shall include the feminine and the singular the plural, and vice versa.
(C) The Directive does not apply to witnesses who are awaiting relocation.

Article 3

AUTHENTIC TEXTS

The English and French texts of the Directive shall be equally authentic. In case of a discrepancy, the version which is more consonant with the spirit of the Statute, Rules and the Directive shall prevail. **C15–004**

ARTICLE 4

AMENDMENT OF THE DIRECTIVE

C15–005   (A) Proposals for amendment of the Directive may be made by a Judge, the Parties or the Registrar. Amendments shall be decided upon and promulgated by the Registrar.

(B) Without prejudice to the rights of witnesses in any pending case, an amendment of the Directive shall enter into force seven days after the day of issue of an official Tribunal document containing the amendment.

ARTICLE 5

RESPONSIBILITY FOR PAYMENT OF ALLOWANCES

C15–006   The costs of allowances necessarily and reasonably incurred by witnesses and expert witnesses as a result of testifying before the Chambers shall be met by the Tribunal as set out in the Directive, subject to the budgetary provisions, rules and regulations, and practice set by the United Nations.

ARTICLE 6

DELEGATION OF AUTHORITY

C15–007   The Registrar may delegate any of his authority under the provisions of the Directive to the Chief of the Victims and Witnesses Section.

III—WITNESSES

ARTICLE 7

ATTENDANCE ALLOWANCE

C15–008   (A) The Tribunal shall provide witnesses with an attendance allowance as compensation for wages, earnings and time lost as a result of testifying. Witnesses shall not be required to submit a request or any supporting documentation in order to receive the attendance allowance.

(B) The attendance allowance shall be calculated by multiplying: (i) the daily minimum wage rate applicable for United Nations personnel in the country in which the witness is residing at the time he testifies by (ii) the number of days the witness testifies, including days spent on journeys in connection with testifying. A part of a day used in connection with testifying will be considered a full day for the purpose of calculating the attendance allowance.

(C) The daily minimum wage rate envisioned in paragraph (B) (i) shall be determined by dividing: (i) the annual salary of United Nations personnel at the General Services 1, Step 1 level in the country in which the witness is residing at the time he testifies by (ii) the number of days per year, as set out in the Annex. For witnesses residing in countries in which there are no United Nations personnel present, the daily minimum wage rate for witnesses residing in the Netherlands will be used. The Annex will be updated regularly as the Registrar deems necessary, but at least on an annual basis.

ARTICLE 8

EXTRAORDINARY LOSSES

C15–009   (A) A witness who will suffer or who has suffered undue hardship as a result of testifying may request the compensation of extraordinary losses. Such requests may be submitted before or after a witness testifies, but in all cases must be accompanied by supporting documentation.

(B) The Registrar shall examine all requests for the compensation of extraordinary losses made in accordance with paragraph (A). In determining whether to grant compensation of extraordinary losses, the Registrar shall examine any supplementary information provided by the witness, the Victims and Witnesses Section, or the parties and consider such factors as:

    (i) the amount of the extraordinary losses claimed;

    (ii) the sufficiency of the supporting documentation submitted with the request;

    (iii) the existence of a direct link between the witness's giving of testimony and the extraordinary losses; and

    (iv) the undue hardship which would be suffered if the witness were not compensated for the extraordinary losses.

(C) All decisions of the Registrar under this Article are final and are not subject to review.

(D) All decisions of the Registrar under this Article will be communicated to the witness in a timely manner.

Article 9

TRAVEL

(A) The Tribunal shall provide and arrange transportation necessary for witnesses to travel to and from the location where they testify, including arrangements and costs for any travel documents which may be required.   **C15–010**

(B) Travel shall be based on:

    (i) an economy class round trip air ticket by the shortest route or within limits laid down by or subject to prior authorisation of the Registrar;

    (ii) first class public transportation tickets by the shortest route or within limits laid down by and subject to prior authorisation of the Registrar; or

    (iii) fixed rates as established by the United Nations Schedule of Rates of Reimbursement for Travel by Private Motor Vehicle applicable to different groups of Countries and Territories, per kilometre travelled on the outward and return journeys by the shortest route, on presentation of a statement of travel expenses using the form provided by the Registry.

Article 10

ACCOMMODATION

The Tribunal shall provide and arrange overnight accommodation for witnesses when required at the location where witnesses testify, and during travel to and from such location, provided they do not receive a daily subsistence allowance under Article 13 of this Directive.   **C15–011**

Article 11

MEALS

(A) The Tribunal shall provide and arrange meals for witnesses who require overnight accommodation, provided they do not receive a daily subsistence allowance under Article 13.   **C15–012**

(B) Witnesses who do not require overnight accommodation shall be entitled to a meal allowance.

(C) The meal allowance envisioned in paragraph (B) shall be twenty percent of the daily subsistence allowance determined in accordance with Article 13. In the case of witnesses testifying in the Netherlands, the meal allowance will be a fixed rate of forty Euros. This fixed rate will be updated regularly as the Registrar deems necessary, but at least on an annual basis.

ARTICLE 12

INCIDENTAL ALLOWANCE

C15–013   (A) The Tribunal shall provide an incidental allowance for reasonable personal expenses to witnesses who require overnight accommodation, provided they do not receive a daily subsistence allowance under Article 13.

(B) The incidental allowance envisioned in paragraph (A) shall be calculated by multiplying (i) fifteen percent of the daily subsistence allowance determined in accordance with Article 13 by (ii) the number of nights of accommodation required at the location where the witness testifies, and during travel to and from such location. In the case of witnesses testifying in the Netherlands, the daily incidental allowance will be a fixed rate of thirty Euros. This allowance will be updated regularly as the Registrar deems necessary, but at least on an annual basis.

ARTICLE 13

DAILY SUBSISTENCE ALLOWANCE

C15–014   (A) The Registrar may provide witnesses who require overnight accommodation a daily subsistence allowance in lieu of providing accommodation under Article 10, meals under Article 11 and an incidental allowance under Article 12. Witnesses who do not require overnight accommodation shall not be entitled to a daily subsistence allowance.

(B) In determining whether to provide a witness with a daily subsistence allowance, the Registrar shall consider such factors as:

   (i) the protection and support needs of the witness;
   (ii) the capability of the witness to be self-sufficient; and
   (iii) the profession and/or official position of the witness.

(C) The daily subsistence allowance shall be calculated by multiplying: (i) a fixed rate based on the United Nations Schedule of Daily Subsistence Allowance applicable in the country where the witness testifies by (ii) the number of nights of accommodation required at the location where the witness testifies, and during travel to and from such location.

ARTICLE 14

CHILDCARE

C15–015   (A) A witness who requires childcare or other forms of care for his dependants in order to testify may request reimbursement of childcare expenses. Such requests shall be submitted before a witness testifies before the Chambers.

(B) The Registrar shall examine all requests for the reimbursement of childcare expenses made in accordance with paragraph (A). In determining whether to grant reimbursement, the Registrar shall examine any supplementary information provided by the witness, the Victims and Witnesses Section or the parties and consider such factors as:

      (i) the existence of a direct link between a witness's giving of testimony before the Chambers and the availability of childcare;
      (ii) the availability of alternative childcare arrangements; and
      (iii) the reasonableness and appropriateness of the expenses claimed.

(C) All decisions of the Registrar under this Article are final and are not subject to review.

(D) All decisions of the Registrar under this Article will be communicated to the witness in a timely manner.

ARTICLE 15

ACCOMPANYING DEPENDANTS AND SUPPORT PERSONS

C15–016

(A) Dependants and support persons who are authorised by the Registrar to accompany witnesses to and from the location where they testify shall not be entitled to the attendance allowance under Article 7.

(B) Dependants and support persons who are authorised by the Registrar to accompany witnesses to and from the location where they testify are entitled to the provision of extraordinary losses, travel, accommodation, meals, incidental allowance, daily subsistence allowance and childcare under Articles 8, 9, 10, 11, 12, 13 and 14 respectively.

ARTICLE 16

RULE 92*BIS* WITNESSES

C15–017

(A) Rule 92*bis* witnesses who are not required to travel to and from the locations where they are making their declarations shall not be entitled to any allowances.

(B) Rule 92*bis* witnesses who are required to travel to and from the location where they are making their declarations are entitled to the provision of extraordinary losses, travel, accommodation, meals, incidental allowance, daily subsistence allowance and childcare under Articles 8, 9, 10, 11, 12, 13 and 14 respectively.

IV—EXPERT WITNESSES

ARTICLE 17

ATTENDANCE ALLOWANCE

C15–018

(A) The Tribunal shall provide expert witnesses with an attendance allowance as compensation for wages, earnings and time lost as a result of testifying. Expert witnesses shall not be required to submit a request or any supporting documentation in order to receive the attendance allowance.

(B) The attendance allowance shall be calculated by multiplying: (i) the daily attendance allowance by (ii) the number of days the expert witness testifies, including days spent on journeys in connection with testifying. A part of a day used in connection with testifying will be considered a full day for the purpose of calculating the attendance allowance.

(C) The daily attendance allowance envisioned in paragraph (B) (i) is a fixed rate of two hundred United States Dollars, regardless of the country in which the expert witness is residing at the time he testifies. This allowance will be updated regularly as the Registrar deems necessary, but at least on an annual basis.

ARTICLE 18

TRAVEL

C15–019

(A) The Tribunal shall provide and arrange transportation necessary for expert witnesses to travel to and from the location where they testify, including arrangements and costs for any travel documents which may be required.

(B) Travel shall be based on:
  (i) an economy class round trip air ticket by the shortest route or within limits laid down by or subject to prior authorisation of the Registrar;
  (ii) first class public transportation tickets by the shortest route or within limits laid down by and subject to prior authorisation of the Registrar; or
  (iii) fixed rates as established by the United Nations Schedule of Rates of Reimbursement for Travel by Private Motor Vehicle applicable to different groups of Countries and Territories, per kilometre travelled on the outward and return journeys by the shortest route, on presentation of a statement of travel expenses using the form provided by the Registry.

ARTICLE 19

DAILY SUBSISTENCE ALLOWANCE

C15–020   (A) The Tribunal shall provide expert witnesses with a daily subsistence allowance to cover the costs of accommodation, meals and incidentals incurred as a result of testifying.
(B) The daily subsistence allowance shall be calculated by multiplying: (i) a fixed rate based on the United Nations Schedule of Daily Subsistence Allowance Rates applicable in the country in which the expert witness testifies by (ii) the number of nights of accommodation required at the location where the expert witness testifies, and during travel to and from such location.

ANNEX

UNITED NATIONS GS 1 STEP 1 DAILY RATES FOR SELECTED STATES

(AS OF DECEMBER 2001)

C15–021

State	Daily Rate in USD	Daily Rate in Euros
Bosnia and Herzegovina	22.84	25.35
Croatia	24.25	26.92
Federal Republic of Yugoslavia	23.16	25.71
Germany	45.25	50.23
Netherlands	45.25	50.23
United Kingdom	47.71	52.96
United States	61.18	67.91

C16. Rules Governing the Detention of Persons Awaiting Trial or Appeal before the Tribunal or otherwise Detained on the Authority of the Tribunal

("RULES OF DETENTION")
(ADOPTED ON 5 MAY 1994)
(AS AMENDED ON 16 MARCH 1995)
(AS REVISED ON 14 JULY 1995)
(AS AMENDED ON 3 DECEMBER 1996)
(AS AMENDED ON 25 JULY 1997)
(AS AMENDED ON 17 NOVEMBER 1997)
(AS AMENDED ON 29 NOVEMBER 1999)

(IT/38/REV.8)

CONTENTS

PREAMBLE

The purpose of these Rules of Detention is to govern the administration of the **C16–001** detention unit for detainees awaiting trial or appeal at the Tribunal or any other person detained on the authority of the Tribunal and to ensure the continued application and protection of their individual rights while in detention. The primary principles on which these Rules of Detention rest reflect the overriding requirements of humanity, respect for human dignity and the presumption of innocence.

In particular, these Rules of Detention are intended to regulate, in general terms, the rights and obligations of detainees at all stages from reception to release, and to provide the basic criteria for management of the detention unit.

DEFINITIONS

C16–002   (i) In these Rules of Detention the following terms shall mean:
Bureau:
the body comprised of the President, the Vice-President and the Presiding Judges of the Trial Chambers established pursuant to Rule 23 of the Rules of Procedure and Evidence;
Commanding Officer:
the official of the United Nations appointed as the head of the staff responsible for the administration of the detention unit;
Detainee:
any person detained awaiting trial or appeal before the Tribunal, or being held pending transfer to another institution, and any other person detained on the authority of the Tribunal;
Detention unit:
the unit for detainees erected within the grounds of the host prison;
General Director:
the head of the host prison appointed by the authorities of the Host State;
Host prison:
the penitentiary complex maintained by the authorities of the Host State and located at*;
Host State:
the Kingdom of the Netherlands;
Medical officer:
the medical officer for the time being appointed by agreement between the Registrar and the General Director of the host prison;
Prosecutor:
the Prosecutor appointed pursuant to Article 18 of the Statute of the Tribunal adopted by Security Council resolution 827 of 25 May 1993, or any person authorized by him or acting under his direction;
Registrar:
the Registrar of the Tribunal appointed pursuant to Article 17(3) of the Statute of the Tribunal, or any person authorized by him or acting under his direction;
Rules of Procedure and Evidence:
the Rules of Procedure and Evidence of the Tribunal as adopted on 11 February 1994 as subsequently amended;
Staff of the detention unit:
the staff employed by the United Nations to run the detention unit;
Tribunal:
the International Tribunal for the Prosecution of Persons Responsible for Serious Violations of International Humanitarian Law Committed in the Territory of the Former Yugoslavia since 1991, established by Security Council resolution 827 of 25 May 1993.

(ii) In these Rules of Detention, the masculine shall include the feminine and the singular the plural and vice-versa.

(iii) These Rules of Detention shall enter into force as of 1 August 1994.

---

* References to the location of the Host Prison and the Detention Unit have been deleted for security reasons.

BASIC PRINCIPLES

RULE 1

These Rules of Detention are to be applied in conjunction with the relevant provisions of the Headquarters Agreement entered into between the Host State and the United Nations and, in particular, the Annex on matters relating to security and order.   **C16–003**

RULE 2

The United Nations shall retain the ultimate responsibility and liability for all aspects of detention pursuant to these Rules of Detention. All detainees shall be subject to the sole jurisdiction of the Tribunal at all times that they are so detained, even though physically absent from the detention unit, until final release or transfer to another institution. Subject to the overriding jurisdiction of the Tribunal, the Commanding Officer shall have sole responsibility for all aspects of the day-to-day management of the detention unit, including security and order, and may make all decisions relating thereto, except where otherwise provided in these Rules of Detention.   **C16–004**

RULE 3

These Rules of Detention shall be applied impartially. There shall be no discrimination on grounds of race, colour, sex, language, religion, political or other opinion, national, ethnic or social origin, property, birth, economic or other status.   **C16–005**

RULE 4

A detainee is entitled to observe the religious beliefs and moral precepts of the group to which he belongs and that right shall be respected at all times.   **C16–006**

RULE 5

All detainees, other than those who have been convicted by the Tribunal, are presumed to be innocent until found guilty and are to be treated as such at all times.   **C16–007**

RULE 6

(A) The Bureau may, at any time, appoint a Judge or the Registrar of the Tribunal to inspect the detention unit and to report to the Tribunal on the general conditions of implementation of these Rules of Detention or of any particular aspect thereof with a view to ensuring that the detention unit is administered in accordance with the Rules of Detention.   **C16–008**

(B) There shall be regular and unannounced inspections by inspectors whose duty it is to examine the manner in which detainees are treated. The Bureau shall act upon all such reports as it sees fit, in consultation with the relevant authorities of the Host State where necessary.

RULE 7

These Rules of Detention and any regulations made hereunder shall be made readily available to the staff of the detention unit in the working languages of the Tribunal and that of the Host State.   **C16–009**

RULE 8

These Rules of Detention and any regulations made hereunder shall be made readily available to each detainee in those languages and in the language of the detainee.   **C16–010**

MANAGEMENT OF THE DETENTION UNIT

RECEPTION

RULE 9

C16–011   No person shall be received in the detention unit without a warrant of arrest or an order for detention duly issued by a Judge or a Chamber of the Tribunal.

RULE 10

C16–012   A. Upon being received in the detention unit, the Commanding Officer shall obtain the photograph and fingerprints of each detainee and any other information necessary to maintain the security and good order of the detention unit.

(B) A complete, secure and current record shall be kept concerning each detainee received. It shall include:

    (i) information concerning the identity of the detainee and his next of kin, and other information obtained pursuant to Sub-Rule 10(A);

    (ii) the date of issue of the indictment against the detainee and of the warrant of arrest;

    (iii) the date and time of admission;

    (iv) the name of counsel, if known;

    (v) the date, time and reason for all absences from the detention unit, whether to attend at the Tribunal, for medical or other approved reasons, or on final release or transfer to another institution.

RULE 11

C16–013   All information concerning detainees shall be treated as confidential and made accessible only to the detainee, his counsel and persons authorized by the Registrar. The detainee shall be informed of this fact upon his arrival at the detention unit.

RULE 12

C16–014   (A) As soon as practicable after admission, each detainee shall be provided with information concerning legal, diplomatic and consular representation available to him.

(B) The detainee shall be given the opportunity at this time to notify, within reason, his family, his counsel, the appropriate diplomatic or consular representative and, at the discretion of the Commanding Officer, any other person, of his whereabouts, at the expense of the Tribunal. The detainee shall be asked at this time to name a person or authority to be notified of special events affecting him.

RULE 13

C16–015   (A) On arrival at the detention unit, the Commanding Officer shall order that a detainee's body and clothes be searched for articles that may constitute a danger to:

    (i) the security and proper running of the detention unit, or

    (ii) the detainee, any other detainee or any member of the staff of the detention unit.

(B) Such items shall be removed.

RULE 14

C16–016   (A) An inventory, which shall be signed by the detainee, shall be made of all money, valuables, clothing and other effects belonging to a detainee which, under these Rules of Detention or the rules of the host prison, he is not permitted to retain.

(B) All items which a detainee is not permitted to retain shall be placed in safe custody or, at the request and expense of the detainee, sent to an address provided by him.

(C) If the items are retained within the detention unit, all reasonable steps shall be taken by the staff of the detention unit to keep them in good condition.

D. If it is found necessary to destroy an item, this shall be recorded and the detainee informed accordingly.

RULE 15

Each detainee shall be examined by the medical officer or his deputy on the day of admission and thereafter as necessary, with a view particularly to the discovery of physical or mental illness and the taking of all necessary measures for medical treatment and the segregation of detainees suspected of infectious or contagious conditions.

C16–017

ACCOMMODATION

RULE 16

Each detainee shall occupy a cell unit by himself except in exceptional circumstances or in cases where the Commanding Officer, with the approval of the Registrar, considers that there are advantages in sharing accommodation.

C16–018

RULE 17

Each detainee shall be provided with a separate bed and with appropriate bedding which shall be kept in good order and changed on a regular basis so as to ensure its cleanliness.

C16–019

RULE 18

The detention unit shall, at all times, meet all requirements of health and hygiene, due regard being paid to climatic conditions, lighting, heating and ventilation.

C16–020

RULE 19

Each detainee shall be permitted unrestricted access to the sanitary, hygiene and drinking water arrangements in his cell unit.

C16–021

RULE 20

All parts of the detention unit shall be properly maintained and kept clean at all times. In particular, each detainee shall be expected to keep his cell unit clean and tidy at all times.

C16–022

PERSONAL HYGIENE

RULE 21

Detainees shall be required to keep themselves clean, and shall be provided with such toilet articles as are necessary for health and cleanliness.

C16–023

RULE 22

C16–024   Facilities shall be provided by the host prison for the proper care of the hair and beard, and male detainees shall be enabled to shave regularly.

CLOTHING

RULE 23

C16–025   (A) Detainees may wear their own civilian clothing if, in the opinion of the Commanding Officer, it is clean and suitable.

(B) A detainee who lacks financial means, as determined by the Regitsrar, shall be provided with suitable and sufficient civilian clothing at the cost of the Tribunal.

RULE 24

C16–026   All clothing shall be clean and kept in proper condition. Underclothing shall be changed and washed as often as necessary for the maintenance of hygiene, in accordance with the regime of the host prison.

FOOD

RULE 25

C16–027   The host prison shall provide each detainee at the normal hours with food which is suitably prepared and presented, and which satisfies in quality and quantity the standards of dietetics and modern hygiene and takes into account the age, health, religious and, as far as possible, cultural requirements of the detainee.

PHYSICAL EXERCISE AND SPORT

RULE 26

C16–028   (A) Each detainee shall be allowed at least one hour of walking or other suitable exercise in the open air daily, if the weather permits.

(B) Where possible, arrangements may be made with the General Director for use by detainees of indoor and outdoor sporting facilities outside the detention unit but within the host prison.

RULE 27

C16–029   A properly organized programme of physical education, sport and other recreational activities shall be arranged by the Commanding Officer to ensure physical fitness, adequate exercise and recreational opportunities.

RULE 28

C16–030   A. The Commanding Officer, acting on the advice of the medical officer, shall ensure that any detainee who participates in such a programme is physically fit to do so.

(B) Special arrangements shall be made, under medical direction, for remedial or therapeutic treatment for any detainee who is unable to participate in the regular programme.

MEDICAL SERVICES

Rule 29

(A) The medical services of the host prison, including psychiatric and dental care, shall be fully available to detainees, subject to any practical arrangements made with the General Director.

(B) A person capable of providing first-aid shall be present at the detention unit at all times.

C16–031

Rule 30

(A) Detainees may be visited by, and consult with, a doctor or dentist of their choice at their own expense. All such visits shall be made by prior arrangement with the Commanding Officer as to the time and duration of the visit and shall be subject to the same security controls as are imposed under Rule 63.

(B) The Commanding Officer shall not refuse a request for such a visit without reasonable grounds.

C. Any treatment or medication recommended by such a doctor or dentist shall be administered solely by the medical officer or his deputy. The medical officer may, in his sole discretion, refuse to administer any such treatment or medication.

Rule 31

Detainees who require specialist or in-patient treatment shall be treated within the host prison to the fullest extent possible or transferred to a civil hospital.

C16–032

Rule 32

(A) The Registrar shall be informed immediately upon the death or serious illness or injury of a detainee. The Registrar shall immediately inform the spouse or nearest relative of the detainee and shall, in any event, inform any other person previously designated by the detainee.

(B) In the event of the death of a detainee, an inquest will be conducted in accordance with the legal requirements of the Host State.

C. The President may order an inquiry into the circumstances surrounding the death or serious injury of any detainee.

C16–033

Rule 33

The medical officer shall have the care of the physical and mental health of the detainees and shall see, on a daily basis or more often if necessary, all sick detainees, all who complain of illness and any detainee to whom his attention is specially directed.

C16–034

Rule 34

(A) The medical officer shall report to the Commanding Officer whenever he considers that the physical or mental health of a detainee has been or will be adversely affected by any condition of his detention.

(B) The Commanding Officer shall immediately submit the report to the Registrar who, after consultation with the President, shall take all necessary action.

C16–035

Rule 35

A competent authority appointed by the Tribunal pursuant to Rule 6 shall regularly inspect the detention unit and advise the Commanding Officer and the Registrar upon:

C16–036

(i) the quantity, quality, preparation and serving of food;
(ii) the hygiene and cleanliness of the detention unit and of the detainees;
(iii) the sanitation, heating, lighting and ventilation of the detention unit;
(iv) the suitability and cleanliness of the detainees' clothing and bedding.

RULE 36

C16–037 The Registrar shall, if he concurs with the recommendations made, take immediate steps to give effect to those recommendations; if he does not concur with them, he shall immediately submit both a personal report and a copy of the recommendations to the Tribunal.

RULE 36BIS

C16–038 (A) The Commanding Officer of the Detention Unit may decide upon the search of a detainee's cell if he suspects that the cell contains an item which constitutes a threat to the security or good order of the detention unit or the host prison, or the health and safety of any person therein. Any such items found in the cell of the detainee shall be confiscated pursuant to Rule 78.

(B) Following a search of a detainee's cell the Commanding Officer shall inform the detainee in writing that his cell was searched and shall specify any items that were confiscated. A copy of this letter shall be forwarded to the Registrar and to the President.

RULE 36TER

C16–039 (A) In exceptional circumstances, in order to protect the health or the safety of the detainee, the Registrar, with the approval of the President, may order that the cell of the detainee be monitored by video surveillance equipment for a period not exceeding thirty days.

(B) Renewals which shall not exceed a period of thirty days shall be reported to the President.

(C) The detainee shall be notified of the Registrar's decision within twenty-four hours, and may at any time request the President to reverse any such decision by the Registrar.

DISCIPLINE

RULE 37

C16–040 Discipline and order shall be maintained by the staff of the detention unit in the interests of safe custody and the well-ordered running of the detention unit.

RULE 38

C16–041 The Commanding Officer, in consultation with the Registrar, shall issue regulations:
(i) defining conduct constituting a disciplinary offence;
(ii) regulating the type of punishment that can be imposed;
(iii) specifying the authority that can impose such punishment;
(iv) providing for a right of appeal to the President.

RULE 39

C16–042 The disciplinary regulations shall provide a detainee with the right to be heard on the subject of any offence which he is alleged to have committed.

SEGREGATION

RULE 40

The Registrar, acting on the request of the Prosecutor, or on his own initiative, and **C16–043** after seeking medical advice, may order that a detainee be segregated from all or some of the other detainees so as to avoid any potential conflict within the detention unit, or danger to the detainee in question.

RULE 41

(A) At any time, the Commanding Officer may order that a detainee be segregated **C16–044** from some or all of the other detainees for
    (i) the preservation of security and good order in the detention unit; or,
    (ii) the protection of the detainee in question.
(B) The Commanding Officer shall report all incidents of segregation to the medical officer who shall confirm the physical and mental fitness of the detainee for such segregation.
(C) Segregation shall not to be used as a disciplinary measure.

RULE 42

(A) A detainee may ask to be segregated from all or some of the other detainees. **C16–045**
(B) Upon receipt of such a request, the Commanding Officer shall consult the medical officer to determine whether such segregation is medically acceptable. A request for segregation will be granted unless, in the opinion of the medical officer, such segregation would be injurious to the mental or physical health of the detainee.

RULE 43

The Commanding Officer shall review all cases of individual segregation of detainees **C16–046** at least once a week and report to the Registrar thereon.

RULE 44

(A) The Commanding Officer may organize the use of communal areas of the **C16–047** detention unit so as to segregate certain groups of detainees from others in the interests of the safety of the detainees and the proper conduct and operation of the detention unit.
(B) If such segregation is put into practice, care shall be taken to ensure that all such groupings are treated on an equal basis, having regard to the number of detainees falling within each group.
(C) All such segregations must be reported to the Tribunal, which may vary the nature, basis or conditions of such segregation.

ISOLATION UNIT

RULE 45

(A) A detainee may be confined to the isolation unit only in the following **C16–048** circumstances:
    (i) by order of the Registrar, acting in consultation with the President; such an order may be based upon a request from any interested person, including the Prosecutor;

    (ii) by order of the Commanding Officer in order to prevent the detainee from inflicting injury on other detainees or to preserve the security and good order of the detention unit;

    (iii) as a punishment pursuant to Rule 38.

  (B) A record shall be kept of all events concerning a detainee confined to the isolation unit.

RULE 46

C16–049   (A) All cases of use of the isolation unit shall be reported to the medical officer who shall confirm the physical and mental fitness of the detainee for such isolation.

  (B) A detainee who has been confined to the isolation unit shall be visited by the medical officer or his deputy as often as the medical officer deems necessary.

RULE 47

C16–050   A detainee who has been confined to the isolation unit may at any time request a visit from the medical officer, such visit to be made as soon as possible and, in any event, within twenty-four hours of the request.

RULE 48

C16–051   (A) All cases of use of the isolation unit shall be reported to the Registrar immediately, who shall report the matter to the President.

  (B) The President may order the release of a detainee from the isolation unit at any time.

RULE 49

C16–052   In principle, no detainee may be kept in the isolation unit for more than seven consecutive days. If further isolation is necessary, the Commanding Officer shall report the matter to the Registrar before the end of the seven-day period and the medical officer shall confirm the physical and mental fitness of the detainee to continue such isolation for a further period not to exceed seven days. Each and every extension of use of the isolation unit shall be subject to the same procedure.

INSTRUMENTS OF RESTRAINT AND THE USE OF FORCE

RULE 50

C16–053   (A) Instruments of restraint, such as handcuffs, shall only be used in the following exceptional circumstances:

    (i) as a precaution against escape during transfer from the detention unit to any other place, including access to the premises of the host prison for any reason;

    (ii) on medical grounds by direction and under the supervision of the medical officer;

    (iii) to prevent a detainee from self-injury, injury to others or to prevent serious damage to property.

  (B) In all incidents involving the use of instruments of restraint, the Commanding Officer shall consult the medical officer and report to the Registrar, who may report the matter to the President.

RULE 51

C16–054   Instruments of restraint shall be removed at the earliest possible opportunity.

Rule 52

If the use of any instrument of restraint is required under Rule 50, the restrained detainee shall be kept under constant and adequate supervision.

C16–055

Rule 53

(A) The staff of the detention unit shall not use force against a detainee except:
  (i) in self-defence; or,
  (ii) in cases of:
    (a) attempted escape; or
    (b) active or passive resistance to an order based upon these Rules of Detention or any regulations issued hereunder.
(B) Staff who have recourse to force must use no more than is strictly necessary and must report the incident immediately to the Commanding Officer, who shall provide a report on the matter to the Registrar.

C16–056

Rule 54

(A) A detainee against whom force has been used shall have the right to be examined immediately and treated, if necessary, by the medical officer. The medical examination shall be conducted in private and in the absence of any non-medical staff.
(B) The results of the examination, including any relevant statement by the detainee and the medical officer's opinion, shall be formally recorded and made available to:
  (i) the detainee, in a language accessible to him;
    (ii) the Commanding Officer;
    (iii) the Registrar;
    (iv) the President; and,
  (v) the Prosecutor.

C16–057

Rule 55

A record shall be kept of every instance of the use of force against a detainee.

C16–058

DISTURBANCES

Rule 56

(A) If, in the opinion of the Commanding Officer, a situation exists or is developing which threatens the security and good order of the detention unit, the Commanding Officer shall contact the General Director who will request the immediate assistance of the authorities of the Host State to maintain control within the detention unit.
(B) All such requests shall be reported to the Registrar and the President immediately.

C16–059

SUSPENSION OF THE RULES OF DETENTION

Rule 57

(A) If there is serious danger of disturbances occurring within the detention unit or the host prison, the Commanding Officer or the General Director, as appropriate, may temporarily suspend the operation of all or part of these Rules of Detention for a maximum of two days.

C16–060

(B) Any such suspension must be reported to the Registrar immediately, who shall in turn report the matter to the President.

(C) Thereupon, the President, acting in consultation with the Bureau, shall consult with the relevant authorities of the Host State and take such action in connection therewith as may be seen fit at the time.

INFORMATION TO DETAINEES

Rule 58

C16–061   In addition to the copies of these Rules of Detention and any regulations to be provided to each detainee pursuant to Rule 8, each detainee shall on admission be provided with written information in the working languages of the Tribunal or in his own language concerning:

    (i) the rights and treatment of detainees;
    (ii) the disciplinary requirements of the detention unit;
    (iii) the authorized methods of seeking information and making complaints; and,
    (iv) all other matters necessary to enable him to understand both his rights and obligations and to adapt himself to the routine of the detention unit.

Rule 59

C16–062   At any time at which there is a detainee in the detention unit who speaks and understands neither of the working languages of the Tribunal nor that spoken by any of the staff of the detention unit, arrangements shall be made for an interpreter to be available on reasonable notice and, in any event, in cases of emergency, to permit the detainee to communicate freely with the staff and administration of the detention unit.

RIGHTS OF DETAINEES

COMMUNICATIONS AND VISITS

Rule 60

C16–063   (A) Subject to the provisions of Rule 66, detainees shall be entitled, under such conditions of supervision and time-restraints as the Commanding Officer deems necessary, to communicate with their families and other persons with whom it is in their legitimate interest to correspond by letter and by telephone at their own expense.

(B) In the case of a detainee who lacks financial means, the Registrar may agree that the Tribunal will bear such expenses within reason.

Rule 61

C16–064   (A) All correspondence and mail, including packages, shall be inspected for explosives or other irregular material.

(B) The Commanding Officer, in consultation with the Registrar, shall lay down conditions as to the inspection of correspondence, mail and packages in the interests of maintaining order in the detention unit and to obviate the danger of escape.

Rule 62

C16–065   A detainee shall be informed at once of the death or serious illness of any near relative.

RULE 63

(A) Detainees shall be entitled to receive visits from family, friends and others, subject only to the provisions of Rule 66 and to such restrictions and supervision as the Commanding Officer, in consultation with the Registrar, may impose. Such restrictions and supervision must be necessary in the interests of the administration of justice or the security and good order of the host prison and the detention unit.

C16–066

(B) The Registrar may refuse to allow a person to visit a detainee if he has reason to believe that the purpose of the visit is to obtain information which may be subsequently reported in the media.

(C) All visitors must comply with the separate requirements of the visiting regime of the host prison. These restrictions may include personal searches of clothing and X-ray examination of possessions on entry to either or both of the detention unit and the host prison.

D. Any person, including defence counsel for a detainee or a diplomatic or consular representative accredited to the Host State, who refuses to comply with such requirements, whether of the detention unit or of the host prison, may be refused access.

RULE 64

A detainee must be informed of the identity of each visitor and may refuse to see any visitor other than a representative of the Prosecutor.

C16–067

RULE 65

Detainees shall be allowed to communicate with and receive visits from the diplomatic and consular representative accredited to the Host State of the State to which they belong or, in the case of detainees who are without diplomatic or consular representation in the Host State and refugees or stateless persons, with the diplomatic representative accredited to the Host State of the State which takes charge of their interests or of a national or international authority whose task it is to serve the interests of such persons.

C16–068

RULE 66

(A) The Prosecutor may request the Registrar or, in cases of emergency, the Commanding Officer, to prohibit, regulate or set conditions for contact between a detainee and any other person if the Prosecutor has reasonable grounds for believing that such contact:

C16–069

  (i) is for the purposes of attempting to arrange the escape of the detainee from the detention unit;
 (ii) could prejudice or otherwise affect the outcome of:
    (a) the proceedings against the detainee; or,
    (b) any other investigation;
(iii) could be harmful to the detainee or any other person; or,
 (iv) could be used by the detainee to breach an order for non-disclosure made by a Judge or a Chamber pursuant to Rule 53 or Rule 75 of the Rules of Procedure and Evidence.

(B) If the request is made to the Commanding Officer on grounds of urgency, the Prosecutor shall immediately inform the Registrar of the request, together with the reasons therefor. The detainee shall immediately be informed of the fact of any such request.

(C) A detainee may at any time request the President to deny or reverse a request for prohibition of contact made by the Prosecutor under this rule.

LEGAL ASSISTANCE

RULE 67

(A) Each detainee shall be entitled to communicate fully and without restraint with his defence counsel, with the assistance of an interpreter where necessary. All such correspondence and communications shall be privileged.

C16–070

(B) Unless such counsel and interpreter have been provided by the Tribunal on the basis of the indigency of the detainee, all such communications shall be at the expense of the detainee.

(C) All visits shall be made by prior arrangement with the Commanding Officer as to the time and duration of the visit and shall be subject to the same security controls as are imposed under Rule 63. The Commanding Officer shall not refuse a request for such a visit without reasonable grounds.

(D) Interviews with legal counsel and interpreters shall be conducted in the sight but not within the hearing, either direct or indirect, of the staff of the detention unit.

SPIRITUAL WELFARE

RULE 68

C16–071   Every detainee shall be entitled to indicate, on arrival at the detention unit or thereafter, whether he wishes to establish contact with any of the ministers or spiritual advisers of the host prison.

RULE 69

C16–072   (A) A qualified representative of each religion or system of beliefs held by any detainee shall be appointed and approved by the Bureau.

(B) Such representative shall be permitted to hold regular services and activities within the detention unit and to pay pastoral visits to any detainee of his religion, subject to the same considerations of the security and good order of the detention unit and of the host prison as apply to other visits.

RULE 70

C16–073   (A) Access to a representative of any religion shall not be refused to any detainee, subject only to the same restrictions and conditions provided for in Rule 63.

(B) A detainee may refuse to see any such religious representative.

RULE 71

C16–074   (A) So far as is practicable, every detainee shall be allowed to satisfy the needs of his religious, spiritual and moral life by attending services or meetings held in the detention unit and having in his possession any necessary books or literature.

(B) By arrangement with the General Director, a detainee may, on request, be permitted to visit any religious facility within the grounds of the host prison.

WORK PROGRAMME

RULE 72

C16–075   The Commanding Officer, after consultation with the General Director, and as far as is practicable, shall institute a work programme to be performed by detainees either in the individual cell units or in the communal areas of the detention unit.

RULE 73

C16–076   (A) Detainees shall be offered the opportunity to enrol in such work programme but shall not be required to work.

(B) A detainee who chooses to work shall be paid for his work at rates to be established by the Commanding Officer in consultation with the Registrar and may use part of his earnings to purchase articles for his own use pursuant to Rule 82. The balance of any monies earned shall be held to his account in accordance with Rule 14.

RECREATIONAL ACTIVITIES

Rule 74

Detainees shall be allowed to procure at their own expense books, newspapers, reading and writing materials and other means of occupation as are compatible with the interests of the administration of justice and the security and good order of the detention unit and of the host prison.

C16–077

Rule 75

(A) In particular, detainees shall be entitled to keep themselves regularly informed of the news by reading newspapers, periodicals and other publications and by radio and television broadcasts, all necessary equipment to be provided at their own expense.

(B) The Commanding Officer may refuse the installation of any such equipment which he considers to be a potential risk to the safety and good order of the detention unit or to any of the detainees.

C16–078

Rule 76

(A) If, in the opinion of the Prosecutor, the interests of justice would not be served by allowing a particular detainee unrestricted access to the news, or that such unrestricted access could prejudice the outcome of the proceedings against the detainee or of any other investigation, the Prosecutor may request the Registrar, or in cases of urgency, the Commanding Officer to restrict such access.

(B) If the request is made to the Commanding Officer on grounds of urgency, the Prosecutor shall immediately inform the Registrar of the request, together with the reasons therefor. The detainee shall immediately be informed of the fact of any such request.

(C) A detainee may at any time request the President to deny or reverse such a request for restriction of access.

C16–079

Rule 77

By arrangement with the General Director, detainees may use the library and such vocational or other facilities of the host prison as may be made available.

C16–080

PERSONAL POSSESSIONS OF DETAINEES

Rule 78

(A) A detainee may keep in his possession all clothing and personal items for his own use or consumption unless, in the opinion of the Commanding Officer or the General Director, such items constitute a threat to the security or good order of the detention unit or the host prison, or to the health or safety of any person therein.

(B) All items so removed shall be retained by the staff of the detention unit as provided for in Rule 14.

C16–081

Rule 79

(A) Any item received from outside, including any item introduced by any visitor to a detainee, shall be subject to separate security controls by both the detention unit and the host prison and may be transported through the host prison to the detention unit by staff of either the detention unit or of the host prison.

C16–082

(B) The Commanding Officer or the General Director may refuse to receive any item intended for consumption by detainees.

Rule 80

C16–083   As far as practicable, any item received for a detainee from outside shall be treated as provided for in Rule 14 unless intended and permitted under these Rules of Detention and the rules of the host prison for use during imprisonment.

Rule 81

C16–084   (A) The possession and use of any medication shall be subject to the control and supervision of the medical officer.

(B) Detainees may possess cigarettes and smoke them at such times and places as the Commanding Officer permits.

(C) The possession or consumption of alcohol is not permitted.

Rule 82

C16–085   (A) Each detainee shall be authorized to spend his own money to purchase items of a personal nature from the store operated by the host prison.

(B) In the case of a detainee who lacks financial means, the Registrar may authorize the purchase of such items, within reason, for the account of the Tribunal.

(C) Detainees shall have the right to purchase such items within seven days of arrival and at least once a week thereafter.

Rule 83

C16–086   On release of the detainee from the detention unit, or transfer to another institution, all articles and money retained within the detention unit shall be returned to the detainee except in so far as he has been authorized to spend money or send such property out of the detention unit, or it has been found necessary on hygienic grounds to destroy any article of clothing. The detainee shall sign a receipt for the articles and money returned to him.

COMPLAINTS

Rule 84

C16–087   Each detainee may make a complaint to the Commanding Officer or his representative at any time.

Rule 85

C16–088   A detainee, if not satisfied with the response from the Commanding Officer, has the right to make a written complaint, without censorship, to the Registrar, who shall forward it to the President.

Rule 86

C16–089   Each detainee may freely communicate with the competent inspecting authority. During an inspection of the detention unit, the detainee shall have the opportunity to talk to the inspector out of the sight and hearing of the staff of the detention unit.

Rule 87

The right of complaint shall include confidential access to the relevant authority pursuant to Rule 85.   **C16–090**

Rule 88

Every complaint made to the Registrar shall be acknowledged within twenty-four hours. Each complaint shall be dealt with promptly and replied to without delay and, in any event, no later than two weeks of receipt.   **C16–091**

Removal and Transport of Detainees

Rule 89

When detainees are being removed to or from the detention unit, they shall be exposed to public view as little as possible and all proper safeguards shall be adopted to protect them from insult, injury, curiosity and publicity in any form.   **C16–092**

Rule 90

Detainees shall at all times be transported in vehicles with adequate ventilation and light and in such a way as will not subject them to unnecessary physical hardship or indignity.   **C16–093**

Rule 91

The transport of detainees through the host prison shall be conducted jointly by personnel of the detention unit and of the host prison.   **C16–094**

Amendment of the Rules of Detention

Rule 92

(A) Proposals for amendment of the Rules of Detention may be made by a Judge, the Prosecutor or the Registrar and shall be adopted if agreed to by not less than nine Judges at a plenary meeting of the Tribunal convened with notice of the proposal addressed to all Judges.   **C16–095**

(B) An amendment to the Rules of Detention may be otherwise adopted, provided it is unanimously approved by the Judges.

(C) An amendment shall enter into force seven days after the date of issue of an official Tribunal document containing the amendment.

C17. House Rules for Detainees
(IT/99)
ISSUED BY THE REGISTRAR IN
APRIL 1995
AMENDED JUNE 1995

HOUSE RULES

C17–001   You are now in the United Nations detention unit for persons awaiting trial or appeal before the International Criminal Tribunal for the Former Yugoslavia.

While you are in this detention unit, you are subject to a number of rules and regulations which have been passed by the Tribunal, including the Rules of Procedure and Evidence, the Rules of Detention and various Regulations relating to disciplinary and complaints procedures and the arrangements for visits and communications with people outside the detention unit, including your lawyer. In addition, there are certain facilities which are provided by the host prison in which the detention unit is situated ("the host prison"), which are subject to separate control. This pamphlet contains the basic information you need to know about these matters and the general running of the detention unit. You will also be given copies of the Rules of Detention and all applicable Regulations in a language you read and understand. If you are unable to read, all of these documents will be read to you in a language you understand.

LEGAL ASSISTANCE

C17–002   You are entitled to engage the lawyer of your choice to assist you with the proceedings before the Tribunal. He should send a copy of his power of attorney to the Registrar as soon as possible if he has not already done so. If you do not have sufficient funds to engage your own lawyer, the Tribunal may assign a lawyer to you and will pay the fees for that lawyer. If you need such assistance, you may ask the Commanding Officer of the detention unit to provide you with the necessary application forms. An interpreter is available to assist you in completing the forms.

You may write freely to your lawyer as often as you want and receive mail from him without it being opened or inspected. Telephone calls to your lawyer are not monitored or recorded. The Tribunal may assist with the cost of calls if you do not have sufficient funds.

Your lawyer may visit you at any time between 9 a.m. and 5 p.m. Outside these hours visits are by special arrangement only. These visits are not recorded although they may be observed by members of the staff of the detention unit. Your lawyer may pass written materials and documents to you at meetings.

DIPLOMATIC OR CONSULAR ASSISTANCE

C17–003   You are entitled to communicate with, and receive visits from, the diplomatic or consular official representing your nation. A list of representatives in the Netherlands is available in the detention unit. You may ask for your diplomatic representative to be informed of your admission to the United Nations detention unit and this will be done without delay.

INTERPRETATION FACILITIES

C17–004   Members of the staff of the detention unit speak a wide variety of languages. If you do not understand any of the languages spoken, or if that member of staff is not present at the time, you may at any time request an interpreter to assist you with any matter relating to the detention unit. The interpreter will be contacted by telephone or brought to the prison unit as quickly as possible. If you are unable to communicate with the staff of the detention unit on any matter, simply point to this paragraph and they will know to fetch an interpreter. You may also request an interpreter to assist you in meetings with your lawyer.

DISCIPLINE

Detainees shall obey all orders and instructions given by the staff of the detention unit. Disciplinary procedures are set down by regulation and you should familiarize yourself with this. A copy of the disciplinary procedure is available in your cell unit.

C17–005

MEDICAL SERVICES

You may request medical attention from the medical officer of the host prison at any time. In addition, your own personal doctor or dentist may visit you, at your own expense, by prior arrangement with the Commanding Officer. Your doctor will be subject to the standard search and security procedures for entry to the detention unit. All medicines prescribed by your own doctor or which you had in your possession on admission to the detention unit will be administered by the medical officer of the host prison or a member of his staff. The medical officer of the host prison may, at any time, in consultation with the Commanding Officer, refuse to administer any such medicine. You may file a formal complaint against such decision.

C17–006

FOOD

You will be provided with two cold meals and one hot meal per day. You may request a specific diet on admission on religious or health grounds. Additional facilities for hot and cold drinks and snacks are also available.

C17–007

CLOTHING AND PERSONAL POSSESSIONS

While in the detention unit you may wear your own civilian clothing if, in the opinion of the Commanding Officer, it is both clean and suitable. Civilian clothing may also be provided by the detention unit when needed.

You may keep with you in the detention unit personal items that are not a threat to the safety and good order of the detention unit. All such items will be returned to you immediately on completion of the reception procedures. Any items which are removed will be stored by the detention unit. You will be asked to sign a list of all such items, which will be restored to you on release or final transfer from the detention unit. Similar procedures apply in respect of items sent to you from outside. The Commanding Officer may confiscate any prohibited item enclosed.

In addition, you may purchase small items for your own use once a week from the prison store, using your own funds. If you do not have sufficient funds, you may ask the Commanding Officer to apply to the Registrar for funds for this purpose.

C17–008

PERSONAL HYGIENE

Each cell unit has its own shower and lavatory area. You are expected to keep yourself and your clothing and surroundings clean and tidy at all times and you will be provided with the necessary materials to do so. Clothing shall be changed at regular intervals and more often if needed and laundry facilities are available. A barber will visit the detention unit at regular intervals.

C17–009

FRESH AIR AND EXERCISE

The detention unit has its own open-air exercise yard. At the discretion of the Commanding Officer, groups of up to four detainees may be permitted to use the exercise yard at the same time for recreational purposes. Each detainee is entitled to at least one hour per day in the exercise yard.

C17–010

The detention unit also has limited facilities for indoor exercise which can be used under the supervision of the staff of the detention unit, as permitted by the Commanding Officer. The Commanding Officer may refuse access to these facilities for security reasons or for improper use or destruction of the equipment.

RECREATIONAL ACTIVITIES

C17–011   Subject to any restriction imposed at the request of the Tribunal's Prosecutor, you may purchase, at your own expense, and retain in your cell unit, books, newspapers and other reading and writing materials in such quantities as the Commanding Officer may permit. With the express permission of the Commanding Officer you may also have the materials and equipment necessary for any hobby which is compatible with the security and good order of the detention unit. In addition, books may be borrowed on a weekly basis from the library of the host prison.

Television sets and radios may be rented with the express permission of the Commanding Officer, who will also be responsible for setting the rate.

MAIL AND TELEPHONE CALLS

C17–012   Subject to any individual restrictions that may be imposed at the request of the Tribunal Prosecutor, you may receive and send letters and correspondence while in the detention unit. Other than letters to and from your lawyer and save other official bodies, your mail will be opened and inspected by the Registrar of the Tribunal.

You may make telephone calls at your own expense at any time from 9 a.m. to 5 p.m. on working days. If you have no funds, you may make a request to the Commanding Officer to make telephone calls at the Tribunal's expense. Permission to make such calls will only be granted after the Commanding Officer has confirmed with the Registrar that these costs may be incurred on your behalf. Telephone calls will not usually be monitored or recorded. Additional restrictions may be imposed if there is reason to believe that you may be abusing this freedom.

VISITS

C17–013   Subject to any individual restrictions that may be imposed at the request of the Tribunal Prosecutor, you may receive visits from family, friends or others during the visiting hours set by the Commanding Officer. Details of these hours are available from the Registry of the Tribunal.

You may refuse to see any visitor other than a representative from the Tribunal Prosecutor or an official inspector appointed by the Tribunal. All visitors must apply to the Registrar of the Tribunal for permission to visit. Visits will be supervised by staff of the detention unit but conversations will not usually be listened to or recorded. Additional restrictions may be imposed if there is reason to believe that you may be abusing this freedom.

SPIRITUAL WELFARE

C17–014   You may ask to receive a visit from the local representative of your religion approved by the Tribunal. In addition, you may retain in your possession any necessary books or literature you may have which relate to your religious, spiritual and moral welfare. You may make a request to the Commanding Officer to attend a service or meeting to be held in the detention unit. In addition, you may request permission to visit a religious facility within the grounds of the host prison and this will be arranged if possible.

COMPLAINTS

C17–015   A formal complaints procedure has been established and a copy of the complaints procedure is available in your cell unit. All complaints or requests should be made initially to the Commanding Officer who will deal with them promptly if they are justified and within his authority to resolve. A formal complaint may also be made to the Registrar of the Tribunal at any time, provided that not more than two weeks have elapsed since the incident complained of. All such complaints must be acknowledged within twenty-four hours of receipt and must be dealt within two weeks of receipt.

C18. Regulations to Govern the Supervision of Visits to and Communications with Detainees

(Issued by the registrar in April 1995)
(As amended June 1995)
(As amended January 1997)
(As amended September 1997)
(As amended November 1997)
(As amended July 1999)

(IT/98/Rev. 3)

PREAMBLE

C18–001　　Issued by the Registrar of the Tribunal and the Commanding Officer pursuant to Rules 61 and 63 of the Rules Governing the Detention of Persons Awaiting Trial or Appeal before the Tribunal or otherwise Detained on the Authority of the Tribunal ("Rules of Detention").

These Regulations are subject to the provisions of the Rules of Detention of the Tribunal and, where applicable, to its Rules of Procedure and Evidence. In particular , the rights of a detainee in respect of visits or communications are subject to any order prohibiting contact between the detainee and any other person made pursuant to Rule 66 of the Rules of Detention.

MAIL

REGULATION 1

C18–002　　A detainee has the right to send and receive mail to or from any person, subject to the following Regulations.

REGULATION 2

C18–003　　All mail entering or leaving the detention unit shall be inspected for explosives or irregular material by using X-ray and metal and explosives detectors.

REGULATION 3

C18–004　　Incoming mail will be inspected both on delivery to the host prison and to the United Nations detention unit.

REGULATION 4

C18–005　　(A) The Commanding Officer may confiscate any item which, in his opinion, constitutes a threat to:

(i) the security or good order of the detention unit or the host prison; or,

(ii) the health or safety of any person therein.

(B) Any such item confiscated by the Commanding Officer shall be retained or disposed of in accordance with Rule 14 of the Rules of Detention.

REGULATION 5

C18–006　　(A) Materials for outgoing mail, including postage, shall be for the cost of the detainee or, in the case of a detainee who lacks financial means as determined by the Registrar, shall be provided upon confirmation from the Registrar that such costs shall be borne by the Tribunal.

(B) The Registrar may impose reasonable limits on the amount and weight of correspondence sent by any detainee who lacks financial means as determined by the Registrar.

(C) A detainee who lacks financial means as determined by the Registrar may at any time request the President to vary any such restrictions imposed by the Registrar.

REGULATION 6

All incoming and outgoing mail shall be subject to review by the Registrar, other than items addressed to or sent by:

    (i) counsel for the detainee;

    (ii) the Tribunal;

    (iii) the Inspecting Authority; or,

    (iv) the diplomatic or consular representative accredited to the Host State of the State to which the detainee belongs or which takes charge of his interests.

C18–007

REGULATION 7

(A) The Commanding Officer shall forward to the Registrar all incoming and outgoing mail to or from a detainee, other than that addressed to or from:

    (i) counsel for the detainee;

    (ii) the Tribunal;

    (iii) the Inspecting Authority; or,

    (iv) the diplomatic or consular representative accredited to the Host State of the State to which the detainee belongs or which takes charge of his interests.

(B) A log of all such mail shall be kept by the Commanding Officer, with details of the name of the detainee, the name of the sender (if known) or of the addressee and the date on which it was sent to the Registrar.

(C) A copy of each entry shall be given to the detainee in a language he understands.

C18–008

REGULATION 8

(A) The Registrar, or a person authorised by him, shall, within twenty-four hours of receipt, open and read, or have read, each item of mail.

(B) Items of opened mail shall be delivered to the detainee or posted to the addressee immediately thereafter and the detainee informed accordingly unless the item:

    (i) is in breach of:

        (a) the Rules of Detention;

        (b) these Regulations; or,

        (c) an Order of the Tribunal;

    (ii) gives reasonable grounds to the Registrar, or a person authorised by him, to believe that the detainee may be attempting to:

        (a) arrange escape;

        (b) interfere with or intimidate a witness;

        (c) interfere with the administration of justice; or,

        (d) otherwise disturb the security and good order of the detention unit.

C18–009

REGULATION 9

(A) If the Registrar, or a person authorised by him, finds there to have been a breach of the Rules of Detention, these Regulations or an Order of the Tribunal, an offending item of:

    (i) outgoing mail shall be returned to the detainee together with a note from the Registrar, in a language the detainee understands, giving the reasons for refusal to post the offending item;

C18–010

  (ii) incoming mail shall, in the sole discretion of the Registrar, either be returned
    to the sender or retained by the Registrar and the detainee shall be informed
    accordingly.

 (B) Detainees shall be given the opportunity to rewrite items of outgoing mail
omitting the offending part.

 (C) A copy shall be kept by the Registrar of all offending items and any offending
enclosure may be confiscated.

 (D) The Registrar may also notify the Prosecutor, the Commanding Officer and, if
deemed necessary, the Dutch authorities of the breach and of the nature of the offending
item.

REGULATION 10

C18–011 A detainee may at any time request the President to reverse any decision by the
Registrar taken under Regulation 9(A).

REGULATION 11

C18–012 (A) Correspondence addressed to or from counsel for the detainee shall not be
interfered with in any manner unless the Commanding Officer or the Registrar has
reasonable grounds for believing that this facility is being abused in an attempt to:

  (i) arrange escape;
  (ii) interfere with or intimidate a witness;
  (iii) interfere with the administration of justice; or,
  (iv) otherwise disturb the good order of the detention unit.

 (B) In any such case, the Commanding Officer shall immediately forward the item in
question to the Registrar, unopened, and shall enter details of the interception in the log
referred to above and notify the detainee accordingly.

 (C) The Registrar shall contact the counsel to whom the item is addressed or by
whom it was sent and request counsel to open the item in his presence.

 (D) Counsel may be required to explain to the Registrar, in one of the working
languages of the Tribunal, the nature of the item and to hand over any offending item or
enclosure.

REGULATION 12

C18–013 (A) Any item which is copied or confiscated under Regulation 9(C) shall be retained
by the Registrar.

 (B) Such items shall not be handed over to the Prosecutor as evidence of contempt of
the Tribunal pursuant to Rule 77(C) of the Rules of Procedure and Evidence without
prior notice and disclosure to counsel for the detainee.

REGULATION 13

 A detainee whose mail has been intercepted or confiscated may make a formal
complaint in accordance with the Complaints Procedure.

REGULATION 14

C18–014 (A) A detainee may receive parcels which will also be inspected in accordance with these
Regulations.

 (B) Limits may be imposed by the Registrar as to the quantity and weight of parcels
received.

 (C) Parcels containing items that, in the sole discretion of the Commanding Officer ,
pose a threat to the safety and good order of the detention unit shall be confiscated and

their contents retained or disposed of in accordance with Rule 14 of the Rules of Detention and the detainee informed accordingly.

TELEPHONE CALLS

REGULATION 15

The Commanding Officer may, in consultation with the Registrar, place such restrictions upon the time that a detainee may spend on any one telephone call as are reasonable for the good order of the detention unit. **C18–015**

REGULATION 16

(A) All incoming calls for a detainee shall be received by the Commanding Officer or a member of the staff of the detention unit. Details of the call, including the name and contact telephone number of the caller and the time and date of the call shall be noted by the Commanding Officer or member of staff and passed to the detainee. **C18–016**

(B) The Commanding Officer may, at his sole discretion, permit a detainee to receive an incoming call in an emergency.

REGULATION 17

(A) Outgoing calls may be made by a detainee, on request to the Commanding Officer , at any time from 9 a.m. to 5 p.m. on working days, subject to the reasonable demands of the daily schedule of the detention unit. **C18–017**

(B) In exceptional circumstances, the Commanding Officer, at his sole discretion , may permit a detainee to make calls outside these times, unless the calls of the detainee are being monitored by order of the Registrar made in accordance with Regulation 21.

REGULATION 18

(A) Outgoing calls shall be for the expense of the detainee or, in the case of a detainee who lacks financial means as determined by the Registrar, upon confirmation from the Registrar that such costs shall be borne by the Tribunal. **C18–018**

(B) The Registrar may impose reasonable limits on the number and duration of calls made by any detainee who lacks financial means as determined by the Registrar.

(C) A detainee who lacks financial means as determined by the Registrar may at any time request the President to vary any such restrictions imposed by the Registrar.

REGULATION 19

If the Commanding Officer believes that he has reasonable grounds for intervention , he may immediately terminate a call and advise the detainee of his reasons for so doing. The Commanding Officer shall also report the matter to the Registrar. **C18–019**

REGULATION 20

Telephone conversations will not be recorded or monitored unless: **C18–020**
(A) the Commanding Officer or the Registrar has reasonable grounds for believing that the detainee may be attempting to:
   (i) arrange escape;
   (ii) interfere with or intimidate a witness;
   (iii) interfere with the administration of justice; or,

(iv) otherwise disturb the maintenance of good order in the detention unit;

(B) an Order for non-disclosure has been made by a Judge or a Chamber pursuant to Rule 53 and Rule 75 of the Rules of Procedure and Evidence;

(C) specifically requested by the Prosecutor following the disclosure to the defence of the names of witnesses pursuant to Rule 67 of the Rules of Procedure and Evidence.

REGULATION 21

C18–021   (A) If one of the situations listed in Regulation 20 arises, the Registrar may order all telephone calls to and from that detainee, other than with counsel and diplomatic representatives, to be recorded or monitored for a period not exceeding thirty days.

(B) Renewals of the period, which shall not exceed thirty days, shall be reported to the President.

(C) The detainee and his counsel shall be notified of the Registrar's decision within twenty-four hours.

REGULATION 22

C18–022   The detainee may at any time request the President to reverse any decision of the Registrar taken under Regulation 21.

REGULATION 23

C18–023   (A) A log of all recorded or monitored calls shall be kept by the Commanding Officer , with details of the name of the detainee, the number called, the name of the other party if known, the reason for recording or monitoring and the date on which the Registrar made the relevant order.

(B) A copy of each entry shall be given to the detainee in a language he understands.

REGULATION 24

C18–024   Details of all recorded or monitored calls shall be forwarded to the Registrar within twenty-four hours, who shall make a determination whether to listen to, or have transcribed and read, each individual recorded call.

REGULATION 25

C18–025   If, having reviewed a call, the Registrar determines that there has been no breach of the Rules of Detention, these Regulations or an Order of the Tribunal and the call does not provide any other reason for further action, the tape recording of the call shall be erased within forty-eight hours.

REGULATION 26

C18–026   (A) If the Registrar finds there to have been a breach of the Rules of Detention , these Regulations or an Order of the Tribunal, the offending call will be transcribed by the Registry and, where necessary, translated into one of the working languages of the Tribunal.

(B) The Registrar may notify the Prosecutor, the Commanding Officer and, if deemed necessary, the Dutch authorities of the nature of the breach.

REGULATION 27

C18–027   (A) Any offending call which is transcribed shall be retained by the Registrar.

(B) Such transcriptions shall not be handed over to the Prosecutor as evidence of contempt of the Tribunal pursuant to Rule 77(C) of the Rules of Procedure and Evidence without prior notice and disclosure to counsel for the detainee.

REGULATION 28

A detainee whose calls have been monitored may make a formal complaint in accordance with the Complaints Procedure. **C18–028**

VISITS

REGULATION 29

The Commanding Officer shall, in consultation with the Registrar, fix the daily **C18–029** visiting hours for all visitors, taking into account the reasonable demands of the daily schedule of the detention unit and the facilities and staff available.

REGULATION 30

(A) Subject to the regulations below, counsel may make arrangements by telephone **C18–030** with the Commanding Officer to visit a detainee from Monday through Friday from 9 a.m. to 5 p.m.

(B) A detainee may request a visit from his counsel outside these hours or at the weekend. Such a request shall be granted at the sole discretion of the Commanding Officer.

REGULATION 31

(A) The Registrar shall automatically issue defence counsel with a written regular **C18–031** permit as soon as such counsel is entered on the record or assigned by the Tribunal.

(B) The Registrar may issue permits to counsel for one-time visits prior to the initial appearance of the detainee based on a written request from the detainee, identifying the counsel in question.

REGULATION 32

All visitors, other than counsel or a representative of the Tribunal, shall first apply to **C18–032** the Registrar for permission to visit a named detainee.

Other than in exceptional circumstances, permission shall be applied for in writing in one of the working languages of the Tribunal, not later than ten working days prior to the day a visit is requested.

REGULATION 33

(A) Permission shall be granted for such visits unless the Registrar or the Command- **C18–033** ing Officer has reasonable grounds for believing that the detainee may be attempting to:
  (i) arrange escape;
  (ii) interfere with or intimidate a witness;
  (iii) interfere with the administration of justice; or,
  (iv) otherwise disturb the maintenance of good order in the detention unit.

(B) Permission may be denied if the Registrar has reason to believe that the purpose of the visit is to obtain information which may be subsequently reported in the media.

(C) Where permission has been granted, the Registrar shall issue the visitor with a written permit for a one-time visit. At his discretion, the Registrar may issue a visitor with a written permit for regular visits.

(D) The Commanding Officer shall be given a copy of all permits issued.

REGULATION 34

C18–034   Both the detainee and the visitor shall be notified in writing, by the Registrar, of any request for permission to visit which is denied, giving reasons for such refusal.

REGULATION 35

C18–035   The detainee may request the President to reverse any decision of the Registrar taken under paragraphs A and B of Regulation 33.

REGULATION 36

C18–036   The detainee must be informed of the identity of each visitor and may refuse to see any visitor other than a representative of the Prosecutor.

REGULATION 37

C18–037   The written permission of the Registrar, together with some official identification bearing a current photograph, must be produced by all visitors in order to gain access to the premises of the host prison and of the detention unit.

REGULATION 38

C18–038   All persons, including counsel and diplomatic representatives, are subject to the security requirements of the host prison, including personal searches of clothing and X-ray examination of possessions on entry, pursuant to the Agreement on Security and Order.

REGULATION 39

C18–039   (A) All persons, including counsel and diplomatic representatives, are also subject to personal searches of clothing, X-ray examination of possessions and other security measures as determined by the Commanding Officer, on entry to the United Nations detention unit.

(B) Searches of counsel shall not extend to reading or copying documents brought to the detention unit by counsel.

REGULATION 40

C18–040   (A) No visitor, other than counsel, may pass any item to a detainee during a visit.

(B) Any items intended for a detainee must be handed to the staff of the detention unit on entry and shall be dealt with as provided for in Rules 79 and 80 of the Rules of Detention.

REGULATION 41

C18–041   (A) Counsel may pass documents to and from a detainee during a visit. Any quantity of documents which is too large to be physically passed over by counsel to the detainee at the visiting facility shall be handed to the Commanding Officer who shall pass them unopened and unread to the detainee.

(B) All documents passed to and from a detainee in this manner shall be treated as mail for the purposes of these regulations and, in particular, Regulation 11 concerning incoming mail shall apply.

REGULATION 42

(A) If the Commanding Officer believes that he has reasonable grounds for intervention , or that these Regulations are being breached in any way, he may immediately terminate the visit and advise the detainee and the visitor of his reasons for so doing. **C18–042**

(B) The visitor may be required to leave the detention unit and the Commanding Officer shall report the matter to the Registrar.

(C) This provision applies equally to visits by counsel.

REGULATION 43

(A) All visits shall be conducted within the sight of the staff of the detention unit, save in exceptional circumstances and at the discretion of the Commanding Officer in consultation with the Registrar. **C18–043**

(B) Discussions between the detainee and the visitor shall not be recorded unless:
  (i) the Commanding Officer has reasonable grounds for believing that the detainee may be attempting to:
    (a) arrange escape;
    (b) interfere with or intimidate a witness;
    (c) interfere with the administration of justice; or,
    (d) otherwise disturb the maintenance of good order in the detention unit;
  (ii) an Order for non-disclosure has been made by a Judge or a Chamber pursuant to Rule 53 or Rule 75 of the Rules of Procedure and Evidence.
  (iii) specifically requested by the Prosecutor following the disclosure to the defence of the names of witnesses pursuant to Rule 67 of the Rules of Procedure and Evidence.

REGULATION 44

(A) If one of the situations listed in Regulation 43(B) arises, the Registrar may , at the request of the Commanding Officer or otherwise, order that all visits to that detainee, other than by counsel and diplomatic representatives, be recorded for a period not exceeding seven days. **C18–044**

(B) Renewal of the period, which shall not exceed seven days, shall be reported to the President.

(C) The detainee and his counsel shall be notified of the request and of the Registrar's decision within twenty-four hours.

REGULATION 45

The detainee may at any time request the President to reverse any decision of the Registrar taken under Regulation 44. **C18–045**

REGULATION 46

(A) A log of all recorded visits shall be kept by the Commanding Officer, with details of the name of the detainee, the name and address of the visitor, the reason for recording the visit and the date on which the Registrar made the relevant order. **C18–046**

(B) A copy of each entry shall be given to the detainee in a language he understands.

REGULATION 47

Details of all recorded visits shall be forwarded to the Registrar within twenty -four hours, who shall make a determination whether to listen to, or have transcribed and read, each individual recorded visit. **C18–047**

REGULATION 48

C18–048   If, having reviewed a recorded visit, the Registrar determines that there has been no breach of the Rules of Detention, these Regulations or an order of the Tribunal and the recorded visit does not provide any other reason for further action, the tape recording of the recorded visit shall be erased within forty-eight hours.

REGULATION 49

C18–049   (A) If the Registrar finds there to have been a breach of the Rules of Detention , these Regulations or an Order of the Tribunal, the offending conversation will be transcribed by the Registry and, where necessary, translated into one of the working languages of the Tribunal.

(B) The Registrar may notify the Prosecutor, the Commanding Officer and, if deemed necessary, the Dutch authorities of the nature of the breach.

REGULATION 50

C18–050   (A) Any conversation which is transcribed under Regulation 49 shall be retained by the Registrar.

(B) Such transcriptions shall not be handed over to the Prosecutor as evidence of contempt of the Tribunal pursuant to Rule 77(C) of the Rules of Procedure and Evidence without prior notice and disclosure to counsel for the defence.

REGULATION 51

C18–051   A detainee whose visits have been recorded by order of the Registrar may make a formal complaint in accordance with the Complaints Procedure.

C19. Regulations for the Establishment of a Complaints Procedure for Detainees

Issued by the registrar in April 1995

(IT/96)

REGULATIONS FOR THE ESTABLISHMENT OF A COMPLAINTS PROCEDURE FOR DETAINEES

Issued by the Registrar pursuant to Rules 84—88 of the Rules Governing the Detention of Persons Awaiting Trial or Appeal before the Tribunal or otherwise Detained on the Authority of the Tribunal ("Rules of Detention").

C19–001

COMPLAINTS PROCEDURE

1. A detainee may make an oral or written complaint or request concerning the conditions of his detention direct to the Commanding Officer or his representative at any time. A daily log shall be kept of all such complaints and of the action taken in respect thereof.

C19–002

2. If, in the opinion of the Commanding Officer, the complaint is justified and it is within the power of the Commanding Officer to rectify the matter complained of, the Commanding Officer shall advise the detainee accordingly and shall take action to rectify the matter as soon as practicable.

3. If, in the opinion of the Commanding Officer, the complaint is justified but the power to rectify it does not lie with the Commanding Officer or the Commanding Officer does not believe the complaint is justified, the Commanding Officer shall advise the detainee accordingly. The detainee may then make a formal complaint to the Registrar in accordance with these Regulations.

4. A detainee may make a formal complaint concerning the conditions of his detention, including an alleged breach of the Rules of Detention or of any Regulations adopted thereunder, to the Registrar at any time, whether or not such complaint has already been raised with the Commanding Officer, provided that not more than two weeks have elapsed since the incident complained of. The complaint shall not be read or censored by the staff of the prison unit and shall be passed to the Registrar without delay.

5. Counsel for the detainee may assist the detainee in connection with any formal complaint.

6. The Registrar shall acknowledge receipt of all formal complaints within twenty-four hours of receipt.

7. The Registrar shall examine the substance of the complaint and determine whether it should be dealt with by the Registrar, being a complaint about an administrative matter or a matter of general concern, or whether it relates to an alleged breach of the rights of the individual detainee, in which case it shall be referred to the President for consideration. The Registrar shall, in any event, forward a copy of each and every complaint to the President. The Registrar shall advise the detainee of his decision and shall inform the detainee of the time-frame, being not more than two weeks, in which he may expect determination of the complaint. If the detainee is not satisfied with the Registrar's classification of the matter, he may, within one week of receipt of the Registrar's determination, request the Registrar to put the matter to the President for a final decision as to who should handle the complaint.

8. The Registrar or the President shall investigate the complaint promptly and efficiently and shall seek the views of all relevant persons or bodies, including the Commanding Officer. The detainee shall be permitted to communicate freely and without censorship on the matter with the Registrar during this period and the Registrar shall, where appropriate, pass all such communications to the President without delay.

9. The Registrar shall respond to the complaint on his own behalf or on behalf of the President within one week of receipt where possible and, in any event, not more than two weeks from receipt. If the complaint is justified, action to rectify it shall be taken within that two-week period if possible and the detainee advised accordingly. If the complaint is justified but will take longer than two weeks to rectify, the Registrar shall notify both the detainee and the President and shall keep them informed, on a weekly basis, of the action that is being taken.

10. If the complaint is found to be justified and is capable of rectification, the Registrar shall implement such rectification as soon as practicable. Rectification may include cancellation, reversal or revision of a previous decision relating to the conditions of detention of the detainee. If the complaint is found to be justified but is not susceptible to practical rectification, the Registrar may, in consultation with the President, take whatever action he sees fit and is empowered to exercise.

11. If the Registrar or the President finds the complaint to be unfounded, the Registrar shall notify the detainee in writing, giving reasons for rejection of the complaint.

12. Rejection of a complaint by the Registrar or the President does not bar the detainee from raising such complaint again. In such cases, the Registrar, in consultation with the President, may reject the complaint without further enquiry if it reveals no additional matters not already considered.

13. In addition to the above, a detainee may, at any time during an inspection of the detention unit by inspectors appointed by the Tribunal, raise a complaint concerning the conditions of his detention with the inspectors and shall be entitled to talk with such inspectors out of the sight and hearing of the staff of the detention unit.

C20. Regulations for the Establishment of a Disciplinary Procedure for Detainees

Issued by the registrar in April 1995

(IT 97)

REGULATIONS FOR THE ESTABLISHMENT OF A DISCIPLINARY PROCEDURE FOR DETAINEES

Issued by the Commanding Officer and the Registrar pursuant to Rules 38–39 of the Rules Governing the Detention of Persons Awaiting Trial or Appeal before the Tribunal or otherwise Detained on the Authority of the Tribunal ("Rules of Detention").   **C20–001**

DISCIPLINARY PROCEDURES

These Regulations are subject to the provisions of the Rules of Detention of the Tribunal and, where applicable, its Rules of Procedure and Evidence.   **C20–002**

1. No detainee may be punished except in accordance with these Regulations and never twice for the same act.

2. The following conduct shall constitute a disciplinary offence:

failure to obey an order or instruction given by a member of the staff of the detention unit;

verbal abuse directed against a member of the staff of the detention unit, another detainee or any lawful visitor to the detention unit;

violent behaviour or aggression towards a member of the staff of the detention unit, another detainee or any lawful visitor to the detention unit;

possession of any illegal object or substance;

repeated misconduct after a warning has been given pursuant to paragraph 7 of these Regulations.

3. If a detainee refuses to obey any order or instruction given by a member of the staff of the detention unit, the Commanding Officer shall be called immediately and, in accordance with these Regulations, shall determine whether the detainee is justified in refusing to obey such order or instruction. The Commanding Officer's determination may be formally challenged by way of the complaints procedure.

4. All instances of misconduct shall be reported to the Commanding Officer immediately and a record shall be kept of the time and full details of the offence.

5. The member of staff who has witnessed or been involved in the alleged incident may impose temporary punishment, such as restriction to the detainee's cell or removal of the offending item, until the Commanding Officer or the senior officer on duty can be summoned, such period not to exceed one hour during daytime or eight hours at night. The Commanding Officer or senior officer on duty may continue, vary or revoke any such temporary punishment pending completion of examination of the incident pursuant to Regulation 6 of these Regulations, provided however, that the period of such temporary punishment shall not exceed twelve hours in total.

6. The Commanding Officer shall conduct a thorough examination of the incident before imposing any punishment other than a temporary punishment pursuant to Regulation 5 of these Regulations. As part of such examination, the alleged incident of misconduct shall be explained to the detainee by the Commanding Officer, through an interpreter if necessary, and the detainee shall be given the opportunity to explain his behaviour.

7. The Commanding Officer may impose any of the following punishments, or all or any combination thereof, as he thinks fit:

confiscation of an offending item;

removal or reduction of privileges or use of personal possessions, e.g., television, radio, books, for a period not exceeding one week;

oral or written warning;

written notice of suspended punishment to come into effect immediately upon a further breach of these regulations within a period of not more than two weeks from the date of the initial offence;

monetary fine, to be paid from the detainee's personal funds;

confinement in isolation, subject to the express provisions of Rules 45–49 of the Rules of Detention.

8. Each punishment shall be recorded and explained to the detainee in a language he understands. A written copy of the punishment and the reasons therefor shall be given to the detainee in one of the working languages of the Tribunal forthwith; if he does not understand the language in which the statement of punishment is written, a translation into a language he understands shall be provided to the detainee as soon as possible and, in any event, not later than twelve hours after the imposition of the punishment.

9. A detainee may appeal to the President of the Tribunal both against the determination of a disciplinary offence and against the punishment imposed. The detainee must advise the Commanding Officer of his wish to appeal within twenty-four hours of the incident or of the punishment being imposed, whichever is later. Such notice may be given orally and the Commanding Officer shall record the request and notify the Registrar immediately. The Registrar shall forward details of the appeal to the President within twenty-four hours. The appeal proceedings may be conducted orally or in writing, as the President may determine.

10. Counsel for the detainee may assist the detainee in connection with any such appeal.

11. Any punishment imposed by the Commanding Officer shall continue in full force and effect pending appeal.

12. The President shall notify the detainee of the outcome of the appeal in writing, in a language he understands, within three days of receipt by him. The President may order the restoration of confiscated articles or privileges, repayment of any fine imposed, cancellation of any warning or suspended sentence or immediate release from isolation. The President may take any other action he sees fit in the circumstances.

C21. Practice Direction on the Procedure for the International Tribunal's Designation of the State in which a Convicted person is to Serve his/her Sentence of Imprisonment

9 July 1998

INTRODUCTION

1. In accordance with Rule 19(B) of the Rules of Procedure and Evidence, pursuant to Article 27 of the Statute and Rule 103(A) of the Rules of Procedure and Evidence, considering Article 2 paragraph 1 of the Model Agreement on the Enforcement of Sentences and having consulted with the Bureau, the Registrar and the Prosecutor, I issue this Practice Direction in order to establish an internal procedure for the International Tribunal's designation of the State in which a convicted person is to serve his/her sentence of imprisonment: **C21–001**

PROCEDURE

2. After the sentence of the convicted person has become final, the Registrar of the International Tribunal shall make a preliminary inquiry of the States that, pursuant to Article 27 of the Statute, have declared their willingness to accept convicted persons and have signed an agreement with the International Tribunal to that effect. The Registrar will ask the Governments concerned to give, before a certain date, a preliminary indication on their preparedness to carry out the sentence of the convicted person. The Registrar shall provide the following documents with the inquiry: **C21–002**
   a) a certified copy of the judgement;
   b) a statement indicating how much of the sentence has already been served, including information on pre-trial detention;
   c) any other documents of relevance.
3. On the basis of the Governments' indications on their willingness to accept the convicted person, the Registrar shall prepare a confidential memorandum for the President of the International Tribunal. This memorandum will enumerate the States in which the sentence of the convicted person can be carried out and shall contain information concerning:
   a) the convicted person's marital status, his/her dependants and other family relations, their usual place of residence and, when appropriate, the financial resources they have available to visit the convicted person;
   b) whether the convicted person is expected to serve as a witness in further proceedings of the International Tribunal;
   c) whether the convicted person is expected to be relocated as a witness and, in such case, which States have entered into relocation agreements with the International Tribunal;
   d) when appropriate, any medical or psychological reports on the convicted person;
   e) linguistic skills of the convicted person;
   f) if possible, general conditions of imprisonment and rules governing security and liberty in the State concerned;
   g) any other considerations related to the case.
4. The President of the International Tribunal will, on basis of the submitted information and on any other inquiries he/she chooses to make, determine the State in which imprisonment is to be served. Particular consideration shall be given to the proximity to the convicted person's relations. Before deciding the matter, the President may consult with the Sentencing Chamber or with its Presiding Judge. The President may, furthermore, request the opinion of the convicted person and/or of the International Tribunal's Office of the Prosecutor.
5. The President shall transmit the decision to the Registrar. The President may decide that the designation of the State shall not be made public.

REQUEST TO THE DESIGNATED STATE

C21–003   6. The Registrar shall, in accordance with the relevant provisions of the agreement on the enforcement of sentences between the International Tribunal and the State that has been determined by the President, request the Government of that State to enforce the sentence of the convicted person. The request shall be signed by both the Registrar and the President.

NOTIFICATION OF THE ADOPTED DECISION

C21–004   7. If the requested Government, after the request has been decided upon in accordance with national law, accepts the International Tribunal's request to receive the convicted person, the Registrar will notify the President and, when appropriate, the Sentencing Chamber or its Presiding Judge accordingly. The Registrar will furthermore inform the convicted person of the State that has been designated, the contents of the agreement on the enforcement of sentences between the International Tribunal and the State concerned, and on any other issues of relevance for the matter.

REFERRAL TO THE PRESIDENT

C21–005   8. If the requested Government, after the request has been decided upon in accordance with national law, rejects the International Tribunal's request to enforce the sentence of the convicted person, the Registrar shall refer the issue back to the President, who will designate another State in accordance with paragraph 4 of this Practice Direction.

Gabrielle Kirk McDonald
President

C22. Proposed Terms and Conditions of Service of the *ad litem* Judges of the International Criminal Tribunal for the Former Yugoslavia

Please find below a brief summary of the report of the Advisory Committee on Administrative and Budgetary Questions of the General Assembly of the United Nations (UN Doc. A/55/806) setting out the terms and conditions of the *ad litem* judges of the International Criminal Tribunal for the former Yugoslavia (hereinafter the International Tribunal).   **C22–001**

In reading the terms and conditions, it should be noted that, to date, the report only contains *recommendations*, which are still subject to approval by the General Assembly of the United Nations.

Ad litem judges will be elected for a term of four years and will not be eligible for re-election. They will take up office by appointment of the Secretary-General, upon request of the President of the International Tribunal, to serve in the Trial Chambers for one or more trials for a cumulative period of less than three years.

While the *ad litem* judges have the same status and general terms and conditions as those applicable to the permanent judges of the International Criminal Tribunal for the former Yugoslavia, the International Criminal Tribunal for Rwanda and the International Court of Justice, some modifications of the conditions have been necessary, in view of the temporary nature of service and the different length in terms of the *ad litem* judges.

Thus, the Advisory Committee proposes the following conditions to be applicable to the service of the *ad litem* judges:

SALARY:

The *ad litem* judges shall receive an annual salary of US$ 160,000.00.   **C22–002**

OFFICIAL STATUS:

The *ad litem* judges will have the status of Under-Secretary-General of the United   **C22–003**
Nations.

TRAVEL AND SUBSISTENCE REGULATIONS:

The *ad litem* judges shall enjoy the same facilities for the travel and daily subsistence   **C22–004**
allowance as the permanent judges of the International Tribunal, including business class travel.

RELOCATION ALLOWANCE:

By virtue of the limitation of their length of appointment and the fact that *ad litem*   **C22–005**
judges are not required to reside at the seat of the International Tribunal, the Advisory Committee proposes that the *ad litem* judges would not be eligible for payment of a relocation allowance.

EDUCATION ALLOWANCE AND LUMP-SUM SURVIVOR BENEFIT:

Uncertainty as to the length of appointment and the probability of breaks in service,   **C22–006**
indicates to the Advisory Committee that there would be no need for education allowance or lump-sum survivor benefit for the *ad litem* judges.

PENSION:

C22–007   The limitation of service to a cumulative period of less than three years, leads the Advisory Committee to conclude that the *ad litem* judges may not be eligible for the same pension benefits as are applicable to the permanent judges. It is therefore anticipated that *ad litem* judges may wish to seek pension benefits from their nominating governments.

DISABILITY:

C22–008   The Committee recommends that disability payments to *ad litem* judges be limited to injury or illness attributable to service with the International Tribunal, in accordance with the Rules and Regulations of the United Nations.

HOME LEAVE:

C22–009   As is the case with the permanent judges, the *ad litem* judges are entitled to a return journey every second calendar year from the seat of the Tribunal to his or her home at the time of appointment.

PRIVILEGES AND IMMUNITIES:

C22–010   The *ad litem* judges will be accorded privileged status in the Netherlands and shall enjoy full diplomatic immunity within the scope of Article XIV of the UN-ICTY Headquarters Agreement. As such, the *ad litem* judges will be entitled to the same privileges, immunities and facilities as is accorded to the permanent judges, i.e. exemption from the payment of income tax on their salary and emoluments, exemption from the payment of VAT on goods, as well as enjoying the possibility of purchasing personal vehicles tax free.

C23. Headquarter Agreement
(S/1994/848)

AGREEMENT BETWEEN THE UNITED NATIONS AND THE KINGDOM OF THE NETHERLANDS CONCERNING THE HEADQUARTERS OF THE INTERNATIONAL TRIBUNAL FOR THE PROSECUTION OF PERSONS RESPONSIBLE FOR SERIOUS VIOLATIONS OF INTERNATIONAL HUMANITARIAN LAW COMMITTED IN THE TERRITORY OF THE FORMER YUGOSLAVIA SINCE 1991

C23–001   This document may be found at *http://www.un.org/icty/legaldoc-e/basic/statut/S1994_848-849.htm*

C24. Practice Direction on the Procedure for the Determination of Applications for Pardon, Commutation of Sentence and early Release of Persons Convicted by the International Tribunal

INTRODUCTION

In accordance with Rule 19 (B) of the Rules of Procedure and Evidence of the **C24–001** International Tribunal ("the Rules"), and pursuant to Article 28 of the Statute and Rules 123 through 125 of the Rules and having consulted with the Bureau, the Prosecutor and the Registrar, I issue this Practice Direction in order to establish an internal procedure for the determination of applications for pardon, commutation of sentence and early release of persons convicted by the International Tribunal:

NOTIFICATION OF ELIGIBILITY

1. Upon a convicted person becoming eligible for pardon, commutation of sentence or **C24–002** early release under the law of the State in which the convicted person is serving his or her sentence ("the enforcing State"), the enforcing State shall, in accordance with its agreement with the International Tribunal on the enforcement of sentences ("the Agreement") and, where practicable, at least forty-five (45) days prior to the date of eligibility, notify the International Tribunal accordingly.

DUTIES OF THE REGISTRAR

2. After receiving such notification, the Registry shall: **C24–003**
   a. inform the convicted person that he or she may be eligible for pardon, commutation of sentence or early release and advise him or her of the steps that will be taken;
   b. request reports and observations from the relevant authorities in the enforcing State as to the behaviour of the convicted person during his or her period of incarceration and the general conditions under which he or she was imprisoned, and request from such authorities any psychiatric or psychological evaluations prepared on the mental condition of the convicted person during the period of incarceration;
   c. request the Prosecutor to submit a detailed report of any co-operation that the convicted person has provided to the Office of the Prosecutor and the significance thereof; and
   d. obtain any other information that the President considers relevant.
3. After receiving the required information, which should be submitted in one of the two working languages of the International Tribunal within fourteen (14) days where possible, the Registry shall forward a copy of the said information to the President, as well as to the convicted person.

PARTICIPATION OF THE CONVICTED PERSON

4. The convicted person shall be given ten (10) days to examine the information, **C24–004** following which the President shall hear him or her either through written submissions or, alternatively, by video- or telephone-link.

THE CONSULTATION PROCESS

5. The President shall forward to the members of the Bureau as well as the **C24–005** sentencing Chamber a copy of the information received from the enforcing State and the Office of the Prosecutor, the President's comments regarding the convicted person's

demonstration of rehabilitation and any other information he or she considers relevant. The Judges concerned shall be given a specified period of time to survey the material provided, following which appropriate consultation shall be undertaken.

CONFIDENTIALITY OF INFORMATION

C24–006　　6. All information received by the President pursuant to paragraphs 2 through 5 above shall be considered confidential.

THE DECISION

C24–007　　7. Having regard to the criteria specified in Rule 125, the provisions of which are annexed hereto, and any other information that he or she considers relevant, and after taking into account the views of the members of the Bureau and the sentencing Chamber, the President shall determine whether pardon, commutation of sentence or early release is to be granted. The decision of the President, shall be rendered at least seven (7) days prior to the date of eligibility. Unless the President decides otherwise, the decision shall be made public.

8. In cases involving applications for early release, in the event that the President decides that early release is inappropriate the decision shall specify the date on which the convicted person will next become eligible for consideration for early release, unless specified by the domestic law of the enforcing State.

9. The decision of the President shall be final and is thus not subject to appeal.

THE EXECUTION OF THE DECISION

C24–008　　10. The Registry shall transmit the decision immediately to the relevant authorities of the enforcing State, who shall, in accordance with the Agreement, execute the terms of the decision promptly. A copy of the decision shall also be forwarded to the convicted person and other interested parties.

11. Where appropriate, at the direction of the President, the Registry shall inform persons who testified before the International Tribunal during the trial of the convicted person of his or her release, the destination he or she will travel to upon release, and any other information that the President considers relevant.

Gabrielle Kirk McDonald
President

ANNEX I

RULE 125

GENERAL STANDARDS FOR GRANTING PARDON OR COMMUTATION

C24–009　　In determining whether pardon or commutation is appropriate, the President shall take into account, inter alia, the gravity of the crime or crimes for which the prisoner was convicted, the treatment of similarly-situated prisoners, the prisoner's demonstration of rehabilitation, as well as any substantial cooperation of the prisoner with the Prosecutor.

C25. Constitution

Association of Defence Counsel Practising before the International Tribunal for the Prosecution of Persons Responsible for Serious Violations of International Humanitarian Law Committed in the Territory of the Former Yugoslavia since 1991

PREAMBLE

Defence Counsels practising before the International Criminal Tribunal for the Former Yugoslavia, **C25–001**

ASSEMBLED in The Hague on 23 October 2004 on the occasion of the 3rd General Assembly of the Association of Defence Counsel Practising Before the International Tribunal;

CONSIDERING the amendments to the Rules of Procedure and Evidence adopted by the Judges during their 27th Plenary Session held in July 2002;

RECALLING the creation in October 2002 of the Association of Defence Counsel Practising Before the International Tribunal;

NOTING the official recognition of the Association of Defence Counsel Practising Before the International Tribunal in December 2002;

MINDFUL of the obligation and the necessity of ensuring fair trials before the International Tribunal;

CONVINCED of the importance of the essential role played by Defence Counsels in ensuring fair trials and respect for the rights of persons accused in accordance with internationally recognized standards; and

RECOGNIZING that the Association of Defence Counsel Practising Before the International Tribunal is a partner, along with the organs of the International Tribunal, in promoting the fairness of the proceedings and the accomplishment of the mission of the International Tribunal pursuant to United Nations Security Council Resolution 827 (1993);

HAVE ADOPTED the following modified Constitution.

PART I

GENERAL PROVISIONS

ARTICLE I–NAME AND SEAT

1. The name of the Association shall be the "Association of Defence Counsel **C25–002** Practising Before the International Tribunal for the Prosecution of Persons Responsible for Serious Violations of International Humanitarian Law Committed in the Territory of the former Yugoslavia since 1991".

2. The short name for the Association is "ADC-ICTY".

3. The seat of the ADC-ICTY is established at The Hague in the Netherlands.

ARTICLE 2–OBJECTIVES

The objectives of the ADC-ICTY are: **C25–003**

1. To support the function, efficiency and independence of Defence Counsel practising before the International Tribunal for the Prosecution of Persons Responsible for Serious Violations of International Humanitarian Law Committed in the Territory of the former Yugoslavia since 1991 ("International Tribunal");

2. To promote and ensure the proficiency and competence of Defence Counsel Practising Before the International Tribunal in the fields of advocacy, substantive

international criminal law and information technology systems relevant to the representation of persons accused before the International Tribunal;

3. To offer advice to the President, the Chambers and the Registrar of the International Tribunal in relation to the right of the accused to a fair trial and the Rules of Procedure and Evidence as well as Regulations, Practice Directives and Policies related to the work of Defence Counsel, such as *inter alia*, the Directive on the Assignment of Counsel, the Code of Professional Conduct for Counsel Appearing Before the International Tribunal and the applicable Legal Aid Policies; and

4. To oversee the performance and professional conduct of Defence Counsel, in so far as it is relevant to their duties, responsibilities and obligations pursuant to the Statute, the Rules of Procedure and Evidence, the Code of Professional Conduct for Counsel Appearing Before the International Tribunal, the Directive on the Assignment of Defence Counsel, and the Detention Rules and Regulations of the International Tribunal.

PART II

MEMBERSHIP

ARTICLE 3–QUALIFICATIONS

C25–004   1. The membership of the ADC-ICTY is comprised of Full Members and Associate Members.

2. Any person who fulfils the following requirements is eligible to be a Full member:
   a. Being admitted to the practice of law in a state, or being a university professor of law;
   b. Possessing established competence in criminal and/or international criminal law / international humanitarian law / international human rights law;
   c. Possessing at least seven years of relevant experience, whether as a judge, prosecutor, attorney or in some other capacity, in criminal proceedings;
   d. Having written and oral proficiency in one of the two working languages of the Tribunal or having obtained a waiver pursuant to Rule 44 B of the Rules of Procedure and Evidence.
   e. Not having been found guilty or otherwise been disciplined in relevant disciplinary proceedings where being admitted to the practice of law or a university professor of law;
   f. Not having been found guilty in relevant criminal proceedings.

3. Only Full Members are eligible to act as counsel to represent persons accused before the international Tribunal. The requirement at paragraph 2c may be waived for a counsel retained by a person accused.

4. Any person who supports the objectives of the ADC-ICTY is eligible to be an Associate Member.

5. Any person who does not fulfil the requirements in paragraph 2, but who, as of 28 July 2004, was assigned to a case as Lead Counsel or Co-counsel, is eligible to be a Full Member of the ADC-ICTY for the period of their assignment to that case.

ARTICLE 4–MEMBERSHIP COMMITTEE & ADMISSION

C25–005   1. The Membership Committee is comprised of five Full Members. Members of the Membership Committee are elected by the General Assembly by majority vote. Membership Committee members are elected for a term of one year and may be re-elected for a second and third term. No Membership Committee member may serve more than three terms. Members of the Executive Committee are not eligible to serve on the Membership Committee.

2. The Membership Committee reviews, and approves or denies membership applications on the basis of the criteria found in Article 3. An applicant is admitted if three members of the Membership Committee support the application.

3. The Membership Committee may adopt internal procedures to govern the procedure for admission.

4. A person whose membership application as a Full member is denied is promptly notified of such decision in writing and offered to join the ADC-ICTY as an Associate Member. The decision of the Membership Committee may be appealed before the Executive Committee within 30 days of reception of the notice.

Article 5–Fees

1. The membership year runs from the 1 January until 31 December inclusive.

C25–006

2. All members of the ADC-ICTY must pay an annual membership fee. The annual membership fee is determined by the General Assembly on the recommendation of the Executive Committee. The annual membership fee must be paid in one instalment, either within 30 days of the beginning of the membership year or, for new members, within 30 days of approval of membership, on the basis of the number of months remaining in the current membership year.

3. In addition, Full members assigned as counsel to a case before the International Tribunal pay an additional monthly fee during the Pre-trial, Trial and Appeals phases of the proceedings. The monthly fee for each phase is determined by the General Assembly on the recommendation of the Executive Committee. Membership fees may be paid in one lump sum or in monthly instalments but no later than 30 days following the end of each respective month.

Article 6–Termination of Membership

1. Membership ceases upon:

C25–007

   a. the death of the member;

   b. the resignation of the member, which becomes effective upon receipt by the ADC-ICTY of the member's written resignation;

   c. the discontinuation of membership, following a decision by the Membership committee if:

      i. a member no longer satisfies the requirements for membership as outlined in the Constitution of the ADC-ICTY; or

      ii. a member no longer consistently fulfils his or her obligations towards the ADC-ICTY; or

      iii. the ADC-ICTY cannot reasonably be expected to allow the membership to continue;

   d. the discontinuation of membership by the Disciplinary Council, which may only be decided upon when a member persistently acts contrary to the articles, regulations and resolutions of the ADC-ICTY, or where the conduct adversely affects the ADC-ICTY in an unreasonable manner.

2. The membership will end at the earliest date allowed following the day on which notice was given.

3. A member whose membership is discontinued will be promptly notified in writing of the resolution and the reason(s) for which membership is being discontinued or not renewed. The member may file an appeal to the Executive Committee within 30 days of the receipt of the notice of the resolution. Pending the resolution of the appeal, the member shall be suspended from membership privileges. The suspended member, however, shall have the right to make representations before the Executive Committee.

4. The Disciplinary Council or Membership Committee may only adopt a resolution to discontinue membership if the reasons for doing so are grave and for members who are currently assigned or appointed to cases, after consulting with the Registrar, considering that discontinuation implies that the member no longer satisfies the requirements of Rule 44 of the Rules of Evidence and Procedure of the International Tribunal and therefore may no longer practise before the International Tribunal.

PART III

EXECUTIVE COMMITTEE

ARTICLE 7–COMPOSITION

C25–008 1. The Executive Committee is composed of the President and four Vice-Presidents.

2. The members of the Executive Committee are elected by the General Assembly from a list of nominees. All members of the ADC-ICTY may nominate a Full Member for election. A Full Member is officially nominated to run for election when nominated/supported by five members. The list of nominees shall be submitted to all members no later than five days before the election. In exceptional circumstances, nominations can be made during the General Assembly prior to the election.

3. The members of the Executive Committee are elected for a term of one year and are eligible to be re-elected for two additional terms.

4. One of the members of the Executive Committee is elected as President of the ADC-ICTY by the members of the Executive Committee. The election of the President is held immediately following the election of the Executive Committee.

5. The membership of the Executive Committee shall reflect the legal traditions of the common law and civil law systems and the geographical distribution of the members.

ARTICLE 8–DUTIES OF THE EXECUTIVE COMMITTEE

C25–009 1. The Executive Committee is responsible to the General Assembly for the day-to-day operations and management of the ADC-ICTY, subject to the limitations set out in the Constitution.

2. The day-to-day operations and management of the ADC-ICTY includes *inter alia*: maintaining an updated list of members, servicing members in accordance with the present Constitution, keeping records of all activities, managing the financial assets of the ADC-ICTY, taking all necessary measures to achieve the objectives of the ADC-ICTY, organizing and managing the rooms and equipment made available to Defence Counsel, maintaining effective liaison with the Office of Legal Aid and Detention Matters (OLAD), maintaining the website of the ADC-ICTY, convening General Assemblies and representing the ADC-ICTY as detailed in paragraph 3.

3. Representation of the ADC-ICTY refers to the representation of all members as a collective body before (1) the organs of the International Tribunal (Chambers, Office of the Prosecutor and Registry), (2) International organizations, (3) Non-Governmental Organizations, (4) Persons accused before the International Tribunal, (5) the media, (6) the public and (7) any other agency whether public or private, for the purposes of achieving the objectives of the ADC-ICTY.

4. The Executive Committee appoints one of its members or any other Full Member to the Disciplinary Panel established pursuant to Article 40 of the Code of Professional Conduct for Counsel Appearing Before the International Tribunal and two of its members or any other Full Members to the Disciplinary Board established pursuant to Article 48 of the Code of Professional Conduct for Counsel Appearing Before the International Tribunal. Members of the Executive Committee shall be appointed to the Disciplinary Panel and to the Disciplinary Board for the duration of their term of office as members of the Executive Committee of the ADC-ICTY.

5. The Executive Committee may create special *ad hoc* committees in addition to the membership committee, training committee and disciplinary council, for the purpose of assisting it in the accomplishment of its duties.

6. One of the Vice Presidents is assigned by the President to take minutes of Executive Committee meetings. The minutes are confirmed by the President and posted on the members-only section of the ADC-ICTY website

7. The Executive Committee may adopt internal directives or procedures as necessary for its functioning and for the day-to-day operations and management of the ADC-ICTY.

Such internal directives or procedures must be consistent with the present Constitution, the Statute, the Rules of Procedure and Evidence, Practice directives, and Orders of the International Tribunal,

8. The Executive Committee may secure the services of a full time employee to act as Head of Office of the ADC-ICTY. The ADC-ICTY Head of Office reports to the President and is responsible to the Executive Committee for the accomplishment of his duties. The terms and conditions of service of the ADC-ICTY Head of Office are determined by the Executive Committee subject to the adoption of the budget by the General Assembly. The Executive Committee may also secure the services of one or more part-time employees as necessary subject to the same conditions.

9. The express consent of three members of the Executive Committee is required to legally bind the ADC-ICTY towards third parties.

10. The Executive Committee is authorized to enter into agreements to purchase, alienate or encumber registered goods or services not exceeding 40,000 euros.

Article 9–Termination of Membership of the Executive Committee

1. Membership in the Executive Committee ends if: **C25–010**
   a. The member ceases to be a Full member of the ADC-ICTY;
   b. The member resigns from the Executive Committee; or
   c. The member is dismissed by the General Assembly.

2. The General Assembly may, on the recommendation of the Executive Committee or *proprio motu*, dismiss a member of the Executive Committee for cause, by an absolute majority of the votes cast, including a minimum of 25 full members. The General Assembly may also suspend a member of the Executive Committee for a period not exceeding 90 days. If the suspension is not followed within three months by a resolution to dismiss the member, the suspension shall be deemed to have lapsed.

3. A member of the Executive Committee may request to temporarily withdraw from the Executive Committee for a period not exceeding 45 days. If at this time he has not requested to be reinstated as a member of the Executive Committee, the member will be deemed to have resigned.

4. The Executive Committee may, after giving the member an opportunity to be heard, suspend a member of the Executive Committee for a period not exceeding 45 days by unanimous vote of the four other members of the Executive Committee. The object of such suspension must be to refer the matter to the General Assembly for consideration. If no action has been taken by the General Assembly after 45 days, the suspension shall be deemed to have lapsed.

5. Without prejudice to paragraphs 2, 3 and 4, if the membership of the Executive Committee falls below five members, the committee remains lawfully constituted. The Executive Committee shall however convene a meeting of the General Assembly to proceed with the election of a new member of the Executive Committee within a maximum of 45 days.

Article 10–Finances

1. The financial year of the ADC-ICTY runs from the first day of January up to and **C25–011** including the thirty-first day of December.

2. On behalf of the Executive Committee, the Vice President (Finance) is responsible for keeping detailed and complete financial records and accounts of the ADC-ICTY. The full financial records are disclosed to the members on an annual basis and made public in accordance with the applicable laws of the Netherlands.

3. The Vice President (Finance) is responsible for preparing the end of year financial report of the ADC-ICTY, including a statement of revenues and expenditures as well as a balance sheet, no later than 30 January of the new financial year.

4. The end of year financial report of the ADC-ICTY is approved by the Executive Committee for onwards submission to the Internal Auditors of the ADC-ICTY. The end

of year financial report is communicated to all members no later than 28 February of the new financial year along with the report of the Internal Auditors, including a recommendation that it be adopted or if necessary that further measures be implemented before its adoption.

5. Two full members of the ADC-ICTY are appointed by the General Assembly to act as Internal Auditors. Internal Auditors are elected on the basis of their knowledge of accounting and experience in accounting and financial management. They are appointed for a term of one year and may be re-appointed for a maximum of two additional terms. Internal Auditors may not be members of the Disciplinary Council or any permanent committee of the ADC-ICTY.

6. The role of Internal Auditors is to verify the financial records and accounting practices of the Executive Committee of the ADC-ICTY, both during and at the end of the financial year. The Internal Auditors, may at any time, request access to all the financial records of the ADC-ICTY.

7. The Executive Committee shall keep the financial records referred to in paragraphs 2 and 3 for a period of five years.

Part IV

GENERAL ASSEMBLY

Article 11–General Assembly

C25–012　　1. The General Assembly consists of all the members of the ADC-ICTY.

2. All the powers of the ADC-ICTY that have not been entrusted to the Executive Committee by the laws of the Netherlands or by the present Constitution are vested in the General Assembly.

3. The General Assembly shall hold an Annual meeting during the last three months of the financial year. The following topics must be discussed at the Annual meeting of the General Assembly:

 a. the annual report of the Executive Committee;

 b. the annual report of the Membership Committee;

 c. the annual report of the Training Committee;

 d. the annual report of the Disciplinary Council;

 e. the annual report on the activities of any *ad hoc* committees created by the Executive Committee;

 f. the election of members to the Executive Committee, Disciplinary Council, Membership Committee and Training Committee;

 g. the report of the Vice President (Finance) on the current financial situation of the ADC-ICTY as well as on the expected financial results for the current year;

 h. the report of the Internal Auditors;

 i. the appointment of the Internal Auditors;

 j. the proposed plan of activities for the upcoming financial year;

 k. the proposed budget for the upcoming financial year; and

 l. any other proposals by the Executive Committee or by any other member.

4. Additional meetings of the General Assembly may be convened by the Executive Committee as necessary.

5. A special General Assembly Meeting may also be held at the request of one-tenth of the Full Members. A request for a special General Assembly Meeting shall be made in writing. Upon reception of a valid request, the Executive Committee shall convene a special General Assembly Meeting within 30 days.

6. The convening of General Assembly meetings shall be in writing, not less than twenty-one days from the date of the meeting. The convocation shall list the subjects to be discussed. All members may also submit issues by communicating the issue in writing, by facsimile transmission or by electronic mail to the Executive Committee at least three working days prior to the date of the meeting.

7. All members in Good Standing of the ADC-ICTY may attend meetings of the General Assembly.

8. The General Assembly may adopt regulations that are neither contrary to the law of the Netherlands, the Constitution, the Statute, the Rules of Procedure and Evidence, Practice directives, and Orders of the International Tribunal,

9. Without prejudice to Article 22 paragraph 1, the *quorum* of the General Assembly is one-fifth of the Full Members present in person or by proxy. The quorum is confirmed before a General Assembly Meeting is called to order. If the quorum is not obtained, a new General Assembly Meeting shall be convened.

ARTICLE 12–CHAIR AND MINUTES

1. General Assembly Meetings are chaired by the President of the ADC-ICTY. If the President is absent, one of the other members of the Executive Committee acts as Chair. Where a Chair cannot be designated in this manner, the General Assembly shall designate the Chair.

C25–013

2. One of the Vice Presidents or the Head of Office is assigned by the President to keep minutes of the proceedings of each meeting of the General Assembly. The minutes are confirmed by the Chair and posted on the members-only section of the ADC-ICTY website.

ARTICLE 13–VOTING RIGHT

1. Each member in Good Standing of the ADC-ICTY is entitled to vote.

C25–014

2. A member of the ADC-ICTY in Good Standing refers to a members who has not been suspended and has paid the annual membership fee; and if applicable the monthly dues

3. Votes shall be cast by personal attendance. A member who is unable to vote in person may vote by proxy. Proxies must be in writing. A member may represent up to five members by proxy.

4. Abstentions shall not be counted as a vote.

ARTICLE 14–PROCEDURE FOR ELECTIONS AND RESOLUTIONS

1. Resolutions of the General Assembly and elections of members to one of the Committees and the Disciplinary Council are adopted by absolute majority, unless specified otherwise in the Constitution.

C25–015

2. In addition to the subjects in the agenda circulated to the members prior to the opening session of the General Assembly Meeting, a member of the ADC-ICTY may submit proposals for resolutions relevant to the objectives of the ADC-ICTY. Proposed resolutions must be submitted in writing to the Executive Committee not less than two days before the opening of the General Assembly Meeting. A resolution submitted after this deadline may only be considered by the General Assembly if the Executive Committee grants a waiver of the time limitation.

3. A copy of proposed resolutions is provided to all members of the ADC-ICTY before the General Assembly. Copies of proposed resolutions received less than two days before the opening may be distributed at the General Assembly.

4. The Executive Committee shall report its recommendations on each resolution to the General Assembly. The members shall be given a reasonable opportunity to be heard on proposed resolutions submitted.

5. All matters shall be voted by a show of hands, except for the election of members to the officers of the ADC-ICTY.

6. The adoption of a resolution by the General Assembly is pronounced by the Chair. This pronouncement is determinative.

7. The election of the officers of the ADC-ICTY (President and Vice Presidents) and of the members of the Disciplinary Council, Membership Committee and Training Committee are done by secret ballot.

8. The General Assembly first proceeds with the appointment of a member to preside over the elections (Elections chair). The Elections Chair may not be nominated for a position.

9. The Elections Chair may be assisted by persons who are not members to examine and count the ballots.

10. The Elections Chair examines the proxies received and confirms the quorum for the elections.

11. Election to any position requires an absolute majority of the votes.

12. The Elections Chair holds as many ballots as are necessary, proceeding in the following order until members have been elected to each position: Executive committee (5), Disciplinary Council (5), Membership Committee (5) and Training Committee (3).

PART V

DISCIPLINARY COUNCIL

ARTICLE 15—COMPOSITION

C25–016   1. The Disciplinary Council is comprised of five Full Members elected by the General Assembly for a term of one year. Members may be re-elected for a maximum of one additional term. Members of the Council may not be a member of any permanent committee of the ADC-ICTY. One of the five members of the Disciplinary Council shall be designated as chair by the other members. All decisions of the Disciplinary Council shall taken by majority vote.

2. Decisions by the Disciplinary Council shall be governed by the present Constitution, the Statute, the Rules of Procedure and Evidence, the Code of Professional Conduct for Counsel Appearing Before the International Tribunal, the Directive on the Assignment of Defence Counsel, and the Detention Rules and Regulations of the International Tribunal. It shall also take into consideration the codes of practice governing the legal profession in the home jurisdiction of members.

3. The Disciplinary Council shall determine its own procedure, which must be approved by the Executive Committee. The Executive Committee shall ensure that all members of the ADC-ICTY are duly informed of this procedure.

ARTICLE 16—DUTIES

C25–017   1. The Disciplinary Council is an independent organ of the ADC-ICTY, responsible to the General Assembly for the following tasks:

   a. To monitor the conduct of members of the ADC-ICTY in the representation of a suspect or accused;
   b. To adjudicate on complaints received against members of the ADC-ICTY for alleged misconduct;
   c. To provide advisory opinions on matters relating to the Code of Professional Conduct for Counsel Appearing Before the International Tribunal, the Directive on the Assignment of Counsel and the interpretation of the present Constitution.

ARTICLE 17—MONITORING

C25–018   1. The Disciplinary Council does not engage in active monitoring.

2. Where, however, the Disciplinary Council receives reliable information which gives it reason to believe that a Full member of the ADC-ICTY has allegedly engaged in conduct contrary to, or in violation of the present Constitution, the Statute, the Rules of Procedure and Evidence, the Code of Professional Conduct for Counsel Appearing Before the International Tribunal, the Directive on the Assignment of Defence Counsel,

and the Detention Rules and Regulations of the International Tribunal, it may decide to wait until a complaint is filed or inform the member of the alleged misconduct with a view to allowing the member to review his or her conduct. This information will be treated confidentially and will not be communicated to any other person.

ARTICLE 18–DJUDICATING ON COMPLAINTS

1. Complaints on alleged misconduct of Full Members may be filed before the **C25–019**
Disciplinary Council by:
    a. Any Full member of the ADC-ICTY;
    b. Persons accused by the International Tribunal; and
    c. Staff members of the International Tribunal who consider their rights or interests are affected by the alleged professional or ethical misconduct.
2. Complaints must be submitted in writing, identifying the alleged misconduct.
3. Upon receiving a complaint, the Disciplinary Council shall, on the basis of the complaint, decide whether there are sufficient grounds to proceed on the complaint.
4. In the event the Disciplinary Council decides not to proceed on the complaint it shall inform the complainant of the reasons for doing so and of the possibility and procedure for the complainant to address the matter with the Disciplinary Panel of the International Tribunal.
5. In the event the Disciplinary Council decides to proceed on the basis of the complaint, it shall inform the respondent member of the complaint and request his consent for the matter to be adjudicated by the Disciplinary Council without prejudice to the jurisdiction of the International Tribunal, in particular the Disciplinary Panel and Disciplinary Board. Should the respondent not consent, the Disciplinary Council shall refer the complaint to the Disciplinary Panel of the International Tribunal.
6. Upon consent being provided, the Disciplinary Council shall provide the respondent member with the opportunity to be heard in relation to the complaint.
7. The Disciplinary Council shall review the substance of the complaint as well as the submissions of the complainant and of the respondent member in light of the applicable regulations. Where necessary, the Disciplinary Council may seek to obtain further information from third parties on a confidential basis.
8. Having reviewed all available information, the Disciplinary Council may:
    a. Mediate between the parties to the complaint; or
    b. Issue a formal warning to the respondent member for his conduct; or
    c. Refer the complaint to the Disciplinary Panel of the International Tribunal; or
    d. Terminate membership of that member in accordance with Article 6 paragraph 1(d).
9. The Disciplinary Council shall inform the respondent member and the complainant of its decision within 21 days of receipt of the complaint. It shall also inform the Executive Committee of its decision.
10. Following a decision pursuant to paragraph 8(b) and 8(d), the respondent member may appeal the decision before the Executive Committee of the ADC-ICTY. The appeal must be filed in writing within 7 days of receipt of the decision by the Disciplinary Council.
11. All information acquired and decisions are confidential.

ARTICLE 19–ADVISORY OPINIONS.

1. Members may requests the Disciplinary Council to provide advisory opinions on the **C25–020**
Code of Professional Conduct for Counsel Appearing Before the Tribunal, the Directive on the Assignment of Counsel and the interpretation of the present Constitution.

PART VI

TRAINING COMMITTEE

ARTICLE 20–COMPOSITION

C25–021   The Training Committee is comprised of three members elected by the General Assembly for a term of one year, of which at least two must be Full members. Members may be re-elected for additional terms. One of the three members of the Training Committee shall be designated as chair by the other members. The chair of the Training Committee reports to the Executive Committee.

ARTICLE 21–DUTIES

C25–022   The Training Committee is responsible for the design and implementation of advocacy training and training on substantive international criminal law for all members of the ADC-ICTY, whether assigned to a case or not. They are also responsible for assisting the Executive Committee in obtaining funding to make such training possible.

PART VI

FINAL PROVISIONS

ARTICLE 22–AMENDMENTS

C25–023   1. Amendments to the present Constitution come into force for all members of the ADC-ICTY when two-thirds of the Full Members are present, in person or by proxy, in a General Assembly Meeting and have voted in favour of adoption.
     2. A General Assembly Meeting for the purpose of reviewing the Constitution of the ADC-ICTY may be held at a date to be fixed by the Executive Committee.
     3. A copy of the recommended amendments to the present Constitution is submitted to the Executive Committee not less than twenty-one days before the convening of the General Assembly Meeting. The proposed amendments are made available to all members.
     4. If a General Assembly Meeting does not have the quorum of two-thirds of the Full Members, in person or by proxy, then a second meeting shall be held within four weeks of the time of the original meeting and the same resolution with the proposed amendments shall be placed on the agenda. The proposed resolution shall then be adopted when a majority of the Full Members are present, in person or by proxy, in the second General Assembly Meeting and have voted in favour of adoption.
     5. Amendments adopted by the General Assembly shall be deemed effective only after a notarial instrument has been drawn up thereof. Each member of the Executive Committee shall be authorized to execute the instrument.

ARTICLE 23–DISSOLUTION

C25–024   1. The General Assembly may dissolve the ADC-ICTY by way of a resolution.
     2. The provisions in paragraphs 1, 2, 3 and 4 of Article 5 shall apply accordingly.
     3. The balance of the funds remaining after liquidation shall be divided among those who were members at the time when the resolution to dissolve was adopted. Each of them shall receive an equal share. However, the resolution to dissolve may also specify another destination for the remaining balance.

C26. Comprehensive Report on the Progress made by the International Criminal Tribunal for the Former Yugoslavia in reforming its Legal Aid System

These documents may be found at *http://daccess-ods.un.org/TMP/7052217.html* and *http://* **C26–001** *www.un.org/ga/58/documentation/list2.html*

C27. Resolution 1503 (2003)

Adopted by the Security Council at its 4817th Meeting, on 28 August 2003

This document may be found at *http://www.ictr.org/ENGLISH/Resolutions/s-res-1503e.pdf* **C27–001**

C28. Resolution 1534 (2004)

Adopted by the Security Council at its 4935th Meeting, on 26 March 2004

This document may be found at *http://www.ictr.org/ENGLISH/Resolutions/s-res-1534e.pdf* **C28–001**

C29. Practice Direction on Procedure for the Implementation of Rule 92*bis*(B) of the Rules of Procedure and Evidence

(The Presiding Officer)

(IT/192)

C29–001 Rule 92*bis* sets out the procedure for the admission into evidence of written statements in lieu of oral testimony. In order for such statements to be admissible, paragraph B of the rule requires:

a. a declaration by the person making the written statement that the contents of the statement are true and correct to the best of that person's knowledge and belief;

b. such declaration to be attached to the written statement; and

c. witnessed by a person authorized to do so in accordance with the law and procedure of a State or by a Presiding Officer appointed by the Registrar of the Tribunal for that purpose; and

d. that the person witnessing the declaration draws up a certificate pursuant to Rule 92*bis*(B)(ii).

In the case of the appointment of a Presiding Officer pursuant to Rule 92bis(B)(i)(b), the following procedure shall apply:

1. The party seeking to have one or more written statements admitted as evidence (hereinafter "the requesting party") shall submit a request to the Registrar to appoint a Presiding Officer.

2. The requesting party shall inform the Registrar of the following:
   ○ The number of written statements the party wants to have admitted.
   ○ the dates and places where the procedure pursuant to Rule 92*bis*B might be implemented.
   ○ The personal data of the persons making the written statements (hereinafter 'witnesses'); i.e.
      first and last name.
      date and place of birth.
      place of residence.
      identity card number or passport number.

3. The requesting party shall inform the Victims and Witnesses Section of the names and whereabouts of the witnesses.The Victims and Witnesses Section shall provide any necessary support and relevant informationfor the witnesses.

4. Without prejudice to the orders or decisions of a Chamber, the Registrar shall submit recommendations to the requesting party regarding the implementation of the procedure, taking into account the resources of the Tribunal and the availability of the alternative to appointing a Presiding Officer.

5. If appropriate, the Registrar shall designate a Presiding Officer for the purposes of Rule 92*bis*(B). The Presiding Officer may be the Registrar, the Deputy Registrar, or any other person duly mandated to this end.

6. The designated Presiding Officer shall make all necessary arrangements for the efficient implementation of the procedure pursuant to article 92*bis*(B) which shall include a requirement that a representative of the requesting party attend.

7. The designated Presiding Officer shall inform the witnessof his/her name and position. In this connection, the Presiding Officer shall provide the witness with a copy of the decision, by which the Registrar appointed the Presiding Officer, in a language the witness understands.

8. The Presiding Officer shall examine the identifying document of the witness (passport or identity card) in order to verify that the witness is the person identified in the written statement.

9. The Presiding Officer shall verify that the statement is provided to the witness in a language he/she understands.

10. The Presiding Officer may not make corrections, amendments or additions to the witness's statement. If the witness disagrees with the contents of the statement, or wishes to amend it or add to it, it will be the task of the representative of the requesting party to obtain a complete and final version of the statement. The Presiding Officer may not be involved in any way in the process of correction, amendment or modification of the statement.

11. The Presiding Officer shall inform the witness that he/she may be subject to prosecution for giving false testimony, if the contents of the written statement are not true to the best of his/her knowledge and belief; in this connection the Presiding Officer shall provide the witness with the text of Rule 91 of the Tribunal's Rules of Procedure and Evidence in a language which the witness understands.

12. The Presiding Officer shall witness the signing of a written declaration (see Annex I) by the witness stating, in a language which the witness understands, that the contents of the statement are true and correct to the best of his/her knowledge and belief and that the witness is aware that he/she may be subject to prosecution for giving false testimony if the contents are not so true and correct.

13. The Presiding Officer shall certify the date and place of the above mentioned declaration and sign it.

14. The Presiding Officer shall number and certify each page of the witness's statement by means of a UN stamp and shall keep a copy of the certified statement and of the witness's declaration.

15. The Presiding Officer shall record the persons present during the making of the declaration and, in the case of the presence of persons other than the representative of the party and the interpreter, shall record the specific reason for their being allowed by the Presiding Officer to be present.

16. The Presiding Officer shall draw up a written declaration certifying the events enumerated in Rule 92*bis*(B)(ii) (see Annex II).

THE REGISTRAR

ANNEX I

DECLARATION BY PERSON MAKING A WRITTEN STATEMENT PURSUANT TO RULE 92*bis*(B)

I, (*witness's first and last name, date and place of birth, identity card no. or passport no.*), hereby confirm, in the presence of the Presiding Officer (*Presiding Officer's first and last name*), that the contents of the written statement(s) I made on (*date of the statement(s)*) and which is (are) now attached to this declaration, are true and correct to the best of my knowledge and belief.

C29–002

I have also been provided with a copy of Rule 91 of the Tribunal's Rules of Procedure and Evidence in a language which I understand and I understand that I may be subject to prosecution for giving false testimony if the contents of my written statement(s) are not so true and correct.

Done this (date)

At (place)

Witness's signature

Presiding Officer's signature

Annex II

ATTESTATION BY THE PRESIDING OFFICER PURSUANT TO RULE 92*bis*(B)

C29–003   I, (Presiding Officer's first and last name) Presiding Officer appointed by the Registrar of the International Criminal Tribunal for the Former Yugoslavia on (*date*) pursuant to Rule 92*bis*(B) of the Rules of Procedure and Evidence, with the assistance of a certified interpreter, certify:

- that on (*date of the witness's declaration*) in (*specific place where the witness's declaration is taken*), the following person appeared:
- witness's first and last name
- date and place of birth
- identity card no . . . (or passport no . . .)
- habitual residence
- that in the attached statement dated (*date of the statement*) and certified by the undersigned on (*date of the Presiding Officer's certification of the statement*) the said (*witness's first and last name*) is identified as his (her) author.
- that (*witness's first and last name*) was provided with a version of the said statement in a language that he (she) understands.
- that (*witness's first and last name*) was informed, in a language that he (she) understands, by the Presiding Officer that if the contents of the written statement are not true to the best of his (her) knowledge and belief then he or she may be subject to proceeding for giving false testimony.
- that (*witness's first and last name*) was provided with a text of Rule 91 of the Rule of Procedure and Evidence, in a language he (she) understands.
- that witness's first and last name) declared that the content of his (her) written statement are true and correct to the best of his (her) knowledge and belief.
- that no pressure was brought to bear on the witness and that he (she) voluntarily signed the attached declaration dated (*date of the declaration*).
- that the following persons were present during the said declaration:
  (*in the case of the presence of persons other than the representative of the party and the interpreter, the specific reasons for allowing the presence of the concerned persons shall be specified*).

Done this (date)

At (place)

Signature of the Presiding Officer

C30. Practice Direction on Procedure for the Investigation and Prosecution of Contempt before the International Tribunal

I. INTRODUCTION

In accordance with Sub-rule 19(B) of the Rules of Procedure and Evidence of the **C30–001** International Tribunal for the Prosecution of Persons Responsible for Serious Violations of International Humanitarian Law Committed in the Territory of the Former Yugoslavia since 1991 ("Rules" and "International Tribunal" respectively) and having consulted with the Bureau, the Registrar, the Prosecutor and the Appeals Chamber, I issue this Practice Direction in order to establish a procedure for the investigation and prosecution of contempt before the International Tribunal:

II. GENERAL

1. Part III of this practice direction applies to instances where the Prosecutor is **C30–002** directed or an *amicus curiae* is appointed to investigate an allegation of contempt pursuant to Rule 77(C) (i) or (ii) of the Rules, respectively.

2. Part IV of this practice direction applies to instances where the Prosecutor or an *amicus curiae* appointed to prosecute an allegation of contempt pursuant to Rule 77(D) (i) or (ii) of the Rules, respectively

3. Reference to "Respondent(s)" shall mean the person(s) against whom the allegation of contempt is made.

III. INVESTIGATION

4. A request to a Chamber to investigate an allegation of contempt must be made **C30–003** prior to the commencement of the investigation.

5. The request for an investigation shall be made *ex parte* and confidentially before the Chamber in which the contempt allegedly occurred.

6. The application to investigate must be by written motion and supported by a statement setting out all available information, including *inter alia*:

   (i) The facts and/or evidence relied upon on which the investigation is being sought and must identify separately and numerically, each alleged act(s) (or series of acts) to be investigated; and

   (ii) The name, description and the address of the Respondent (if known) or such available information relevant to the identity of the person(s) behind the alleged act(s) (or series of acts).

Upon submission, an amendment to the application may be made with leave of the Chamber but not otherwise.

7. Upon a Chamber having considered the application for investigation and having reason to believe that a person (other than the Prosecutor) may be in contempt of the Tribunal, the Chamber will in the first instance direct the Prosecutor to investigate the contempt allegation unless the Prosecutor makes a showing of a conflict of interest with respect to the relevant conduct of the alleged contempt. The Prosecutor shall make the showing by way of a statement supported by the facts giving rise to a conflict of interest, and shall be submitted to the Chamber *ex parte* and confidentially.

8. Where the Chamber *proprio motu* or upon a showing by the Prosecutor pursuant to paragraph 7 above is of the view that the Prosecutor has a conflict of interest, the Chamber may issue an order directing the Registrar to appoint an *amicus curiae* to investigate the matter and report back and make recommendations to the Chamber. The Chamber's order shall be confidential and *ex parte* and shall set out *inter alia*:

   (i) the incident to be investigated;

   (ii) the documents and filings, including confidential material which the Registry of the International Tribunal and/or the Prosecutor shall make available to the *Amicus Curiae* Investigator for the purposes of the investigation;

(iii) investigative instructions (if any) including instructions concerning the summoning and questioning of witnesses, recording their statements and collecting evidence and such other matters as may be necessary for the conduct and completion of the investigation;

(iv) the due date for the *Amicus Curiae* Investigator to report back to the Chamber.

9. Upon the Registrar having identified the *Amicus Curiae* Investigator to be appointed, the Registrar shall first consult the Chamber as to the suitability of the candidate and require a solemn declaration and undertaking in the form set out in Annex I to this Practice Direction, to be made by the *Amicus Curiae* Investigator. The Registrar shall thereafter issue a confidential & *ex parte* order appointing the *Amicus Curiae* Investigator and transmit the order to the *Amicus Curiae* Investigator together with the following:

(i) the application together with the supporting documents mentioned in paragraph 6 above; and

(ii) the order mentioned in paragraph 8 above and such other material as instructed by the Chamber in paragraph 8(ii) above.

10. A request for clarification or further instructions as a result of the order in paragraph 8 above may be made by the Registrar through a confidential and *ex parte* application to the Chamber that issued the order. The appointed *Amicus Curiae* Investigator may petition the Chamber for this purpose but shall be restricted to seeking clarification and/or further instructions concerning the matters contained in paragraph 8(i)–(iv) above or related matters.

11. If during the course of investigations ordered by the Chamber in paragraph 8 above, the Registrar becomes aware of any reason which may prejudice or affect the conduct of the investigations, the Registrar shall immediately notify the Chamber that issued the said order and upon consultation with that Chamber, take remedial action including terminating and/or appointing a new or additional *Amicus Curiae* Investigator.

12. The completed report of the *Amicus Curiae* Investigator shall be confidentially submitted to the Registrar within the time limit prescribed in the order of the Chamber in paragraph 8 (or such other time as prescribed by that Chamber) for onward transmission to that Chamber.

IV. PROSECUTION

C30–004   13. Upon completion of the investigation of an alleged contempt of the International Tribunal pursuant to Rule 77 (C)(i) or (ii) of the Rules, and where sufficient grounds have been determined by a Chamber in order to proceed against a person for contempt, the Chamber in which the contempt allegedly occurred shall adjudicate the matter unless there are exceptional circumstances such as cases in which the impartiality of a Chamber may be called into question, warranting the assignment of the case to another Chamber.

14. In accordance with Rule 77(D) of the Rules, where the Prosecutor investigated the contempt allegation pursuant to Rule 77(C)(i), the adjudicating Chamber will direct the Prosecutor to prosecute the alleged contempt. Where an *Amicus Curiae* Investigator was appointed to investigate the allegation pursuant to Rule 77(C)(ii), the adjudicating Chamber may direct *amicus curiae* to prosecute the matter.

15. Where the adjudicating Chamber decides to issue an order in lieu of an indictment and directs an *amicus curiae* to prosecute the matter, such order shall be public unless otherwise determined by the adjudicating Chamber, shall be served without delay on the Respondent and shall:

(i) detail the charges against the Respondent and set a date for the Respondent to be called upon to appear before the adjudicating Chamber to enter a plea with respect to the charges of contempt of the Tribunal;

(ii) direct the Registrar to appoint, on behalf of the adjudicating Chamber, an impartial party as the *Amicus Curiae* Prosecutor to prosecute the charges detailed by the adjudicating Chamber;

(iii) set out the documents and filings including confidential material which the adjudicating Chamber considers necessary, at this stage, for the preparation of the case and which the Registry of the International Tribunal and/or the Prosecutor shall make available to the *Amicus Curiae* Prosecutor;

(iv) set out the terms of reference for the *Amicus Curiae* Prosecutor; and

(v) set out any other case management instructions.

16. Prior to the date as set out in paragraph 15(i) above, the Registrar shall, pursuant to the directive stated in paragraph 15(ii) above, identify the *Amicus Curiae* Prosecutor to be appointed and shall first require a solemn declaration and undertaking, to be made by the *Amicus Curiae* Prosecutor, in the from set out in Annex II to this Practice Direction. The Registrar shall thereafter issue an order appointing the *Amicus Curiae* Prosecutor and transmit such order to the *Amicus Curiae* Prosecutor together with the following:

(i) the order of the adjudicating Chamber mentioned in paragraph 15 above; and

(ii) such other material as instructed by the adjudicating Chamber in paragraph 15(iii) above.

17. The Registrar may, if so required, request for clarification or further instructions as a result of the order in paragraph 15 above, from the adjudicating Chamber.

18. In contempt proceedings before the adjudicating Chamber where an *Amicus Curiae* Prosecutor is directed to prosecute pursuant paragraph 15 above, unless otherwise determined by the adjudicating Chamber, the Prosecutor and defence of the accused person(s) ("Defence") in the proceedings where the contempt allegedly occurred, shall have the liberty to appear at any hearing of the contempt proceedings as concerned parties. All confidential filings by the *Amicus Curiae* Prosecutor or the Respondent in the contempt proceedings shall not be disclosed to the Prosecutor and the Defence except by order of the adjudicating Chamber *proprio motu* or upon the request of the Prosecutor or Defence and after hearing the *Amicus Curiae* Prosecutor and/or the Respondent.

19. In the case of contempt proceedings before the International Tribunal, the Registrar shall ensure that the Registry of the International Tribunal:

(i) provides the Respondent with assistance reasonably required in matters relating to the Respondent's defence, such matters being those normally provided by the Registry of the International Tribunal to accused persons but taking into account that the Respondent's position is that of an accused person for contempt before the International Tribunal and subject to rules, regulations, instructions or directives applicable to such assistance, including assignment of counsel pursuant to Rule 45 of the Rules in the case of indigence, obtaining travel visas for the Netherlands if necessary and securing access to the premises of the International Tribunal;

(ii) provides the *Amicus Curiae* Investigator and/or *Amicus Curiae* Prosecutor with assistance, subject to rules, regulations, instructions or directives applicable to such assistance, as is reasonably necessary for the conduct and completion of the investigative task and prosecution respectively, but without prejudice to the functions and mandate of the Registry of the International Tribunal, including the management of all matters relating to the assignment to investigate or the prosecution, travel necessary for the investigation or prosecution and daily subsistence for such travel, travel visas for the Netherlands if necessary and securing access to the premises of the International Tribunal;

The Registrar shall be at liberty to request for clarification and directions from the Chamber ordering the investigation or the adjudicating Chamber with respect to the matters aforesaid.

20. Pursuant to Rule 77(E) of the Rules, the adjudicating Chamber may, subject to the rights of the Respondent as an accused person before the International Tribunal, reduce any time prescribed by or under the Rules having regard to the complexity of issues raised in the contempt proceedings.

Theodor Meron
President

ANNEX I

CONFIDENTIAL AND *EX PARTE*

C30–005   **In the matter of** [describe the order of the Chamber directing the Registrar to appoint an *Amicus Curiae* Investigator pursuant paragraph [8] of the Practice Direction IT/xx] (the "Chamber" and "Order" respectively) and [briefly describe the task to be investigated] (the "Investigation").

I, the undersigned, in anticipation of an appointment as *Amicus Curiae* Investigator pursuant to the Order, hereby solemnly declare and undertake as follows:

(A) I am not in a position of conflict or potential conflict with regards to the Investigation and declare that there are no circumstances whatsoever, past or present including information in my possession or previous employment that would impact on my impartiality or ability to perform the Investigation and conscientiously believe this to be true in every particular.

(B) I shall perform the duties incumbent upon me in all loyalty, discretion and good conscience and I will faithfully observe all rules, regulations, instructions or directives applicable to my assignment.

(C) I shall respect the impartiality and independence of the Investigation and shall not seek nor accept instructions regarding my functions from any institution, person or other authority other than the Chamber or Registrar of the International Tribunal or his designated representative.

(D) Save for that which is required for the Investigation and the terms set out in the Order, I shall not communicate, at any time, without the authorisation of the Registrar or his designated representative, to any institution, person or other authority other than the Chamber or Registrar of the International Tribunal or his designated representative, any information which has become known to me by reason of my function, or use any such information in any other way. These obligations do not lapse upon termination of the Investigation.

ANNEX II

C30–006   **In the matter of** [describe the order of the Chamber directing the Registrar to appoint an *Amicus Curiae* Prosecutor pursuant paragraph [15] of the Practice Direction IT/xx] (the "Chamber" and "Order" respectively) and [briefly describe the task to be prosecuted] (the "Proceedings").

I, the undersigned, in anticipation of an appointment as *Amicus Curiae* Prosecutor pursuant to the Order, hereby solemnly declare and undertake as follows:

(A) I am not in a position of conflict or potential conflict with regards to the Proceedings and declare that there are no circumstances whatsoever, past or present including information in my possession or previous employment that would impact on my impartiality or ability to prosecute in the Proceedings and conscientiously believe this to be true in every particular.

(B) I shall perform the duties incumbent upon me in all loyalty, discretion and good conscience and I will faithfully observe all rules, regulations, instructions or directives applicable to my assignment.

(C) I shall respect the impartiality and independence of role of *Amicus Curiae* Prosecutor in the Proceedings and shall not seek nor accept instructions regarding my functions from any institution, person or other authority other than the authority of the Chamber in connection with the adjudication of the Proceedings.

C31. Practice Direction on the Procedure for Amending Regulations Issued by the Registrar

INTRODUCTION

1. In accordance with Rule 19(B) of the Rules of Procedure and Evidence of the **C31–001** International Tribunal ("the Rules"), pursuant to Rule 6 of the Rules, I issue this Practice Direction in order to establish a procedure for the amending the regulations issued by the Registrar.

2. This Practice Direction will regulate the procedure for amendment of regulations issued by the Registrar, including but not limited to the Directive on Assignment of Defence Counsel. Directive on the Registry Judicial Department Court Management and Support Services, House Rules for Detainees, Regulations to Govern the Supervision of Visits to and Communications with Detainees, Regulations for the Establishment of a Complaints Procedure for Detainees, Regulations for the Establishment of a Disciplinary Procedure, Code of Professional Conduct for Defence Counsel Appearing before the Tribunal, Code of Ethics for Interpreters and Translators employed by the International Criminal Tribunal for the Former Yugoslavia.

SUBMISSION OF PROPOSALS

3. The Judges, the Prosecutor, and the Registry may submit proposals for amend- **C31–002** ments. Proposals shall be submitted in both working languages of the Tribunal and be addressed to the Deputy Registrar.

4. The Deputy Registrar shall, in consultation with the relevant Sections of the Registry, submit a report to the Registrar setting out the proposals.

CONSULTATIONS

5. Before adopting an amendment the Registrar shall consult or seek the approval of **C31–003** the President or the Judges, as appropriate in accordance with the rules and regulations.

ADOPTION

6. The Registrar shall adopt an amendment by a decision, setting out the amendment **C31–004** in both working languages of the Tribunal, which shall be issued as an IT-document.

DISTRIBUTION AND ENTRY IN FORCE

7. The amendment shall be registered and then distributed to all Judges, the **C31–005** Prosecutor, the Registrar and the United Nations Office of Legal Affairs in New York.

8. The amendment shall enter into force seven days after the date of issue referred to in paragraph 6, above, unless otherwise indicated in the amendment.

9. An amended text of the entire document shall be issued.

C32. Defence Counsel—Pre-Trial Legal Aid Policy

C32–001   This policy shall be the authoritative version of the modified payment scheme for pre-trial (the "2004 Pre-Trial Payment Scheme"), as previously amended on 1 November 2004. In case of any inconsistency between this policy and any previous information disseminated, this policy shall prevail.

The policy will apply to all new cases in which legal aid is granted as of 1 December 2004.

The revised amounts included in this amended version will apply retroactively as of 1 January 2005 to all cases in pre-trial to which this Pre-Trial Legal Aid Policy applies.

TABLE OF CONTENTS

DEFENCE COUNSEL PAYMENT SCHEME FOR THE PRE-TRIAL STAGE

A. INTRODUCTION

C32–002   1. The Pre-Trial Legal Aid Policy is based on a lump sum payment system designed to give Lead Counsel maximum flexibility in the use of resources and to allow Lead Counsel to use the lump sum to hire members of the Defence team as he/she sees fit. The Registrar must, however, approve all members of the Defence team to ensure there is no conflict of interest or other ethical concerns.

2. This Pre-Trial Legal Aid Policy follows a scheme attaching payment to a one of three complexity values in each case: (1) difficult, (2) very difficult, (3) extremely difficult/leadership. Payment to counsel is made accordingly in lump sums attached to the level of complexity. The lump sum is distributed in monthly stipends; monthly stipends do not represent a monthly allotment of hours. The pre-trial stage consists of

three phases: Phase One—the Initial Appearance Phase, Phase Two—the Phase in which preliminary motions and a work plan are submitted—and Phase Three—the trial preparation *per se*.

3. All aspects of representation except for necessary travel and DSA are to be covered by the lump sum. These include, but are not limited to:

- lead counsel fees
- co-counsel fees
- interpretation and translation costs (see par. 4)
- legal assistant fees
- investigator fees
- office costs
- administrative expenses
- consultant fees.

4. Included in the lump sum are all interpretation costs and costs of translation of documents other than those documents to be adduced as evidence which should be translated by the ICTY's translation services (CLSS), in accordance with the Registrar's interpretation and translation policies. Further, not included are interpretation and translation costs incurred pursuant to Article 21(4) under a), b) and f) of the Statute. The Defence team may invoice separately for those costs, up to a maximum of €1000 per month.

5. The Pre-Trial Lump Sums are as follows:

Complexity	Phase One– Initial appearance	Phase Two	Phase Three	Allotment for interpretation and translation[1]	TOTAL
Level 1	$2,000	$48,369	$112,162	(€1,000 max. per month)	$ 162,531 (+ € ..)[2]
Level 2	$2,000	$48,369	$229,250	(€1,000 max. per month)	$ 279,619 (+ € ..)[3]
Level 3	$2,000	$48,369	$405,515	(€1,000 max. per month)	$ 455,884 (+ € ..)[4]

B. PHASE ONE—INITIAL APPEARANCE

6. Counsel will be assigned to represent an accused for his or her initial appearance . This phase begins with the assignment of counsel and ends one day following the entrance of a plea by the accused.

C32–003

7. Counsel will be paid a standard lump sum of US$2,000 for the initial appearance in addition to a maximum of 10 days DSA during this phase.

---

[1] See supra paras. 3 and 4.
[2] The amount does not include DSA and Travel which are to be covered separately in accordance with the applicable Registry policies.
[3] Id.
[4] Id.

Invoicing and Payment

C32–004   8. Payment of the standard lump sum to assigned counsel will be made upon submission of a *pro forma* invoice which must be submitted within 60 days following the end of the phase. The *pro forma* invoice is signed by counsel. Payment will then be made, in principle within one month of submission of a valid and accurate invoice, directly into the accounts of the respective Defence team members who have been officially assigned by the Registrar.

Adjustment of the Standard Lump Sum

C32–005   9. The standard lump sum for Phase One will only be adjusted in the event of compelling factual and legal circumstances or developments in the course of the initial appearance which lead to a substantial increase in the work necessary during Phase One. A request for an adjustment of the standard lump sum must be submitted to the Registrar in writing within 30 days following the end of the phase and be substantiated by a detailed invoice of hourly activities.

C. PHASE TWO

C32–006   10. In the event that counsel assigned for the initial appearance continues to represent his/her client beyond the plea, Phase Two will commence the day following the date on which a plea is entered either by or on behalf of the accused. Where a new counsel is assigned following the plea, Phase Two will begin on the day of assignment. Phase Two concludes 90 days from its commencement or upon submission of the Work Plan (see paras 17–21 below) whichever is later. The lump sum for this phase is not contingent on the complexity of the case.

11. The work to be performed by assigned counsel during this phase includes:
    I. The review of the Indictment Supporting Material;
    II. The review of material disclosed by the Prosecution pursuant to Rules 66 and 68 (until day 60 following the initial appearance of the Accused);
    III. The filing of any preliminary motions as well as the filing of replies to any Prosecution responses; and
    IV. The preparation of a Work Plan for the Defence (see paras. 17–21).

Calculation of the Lump Sum

C32–007   12. The Registrar calculates the Phase Two lump sum on the basis that it requires preparation by one Lead Counsel working three-quarters of all working hours and one support staff working full time. The lump sum is calculated based partly on the monthly salary of a P5 Step VII senior trial attorney (as in the 2004 Defense Counsel Payment Scheme for the Trial Stage), to which an office cost component (40%) has been added , and partly on the monthly salary for support staff, based on a pay rate of 20 Euros per hour at 150 hours per month, in accordance with Annex 1 of the Directive on Assignment of Counsel.

13. The Phase Two Pre-Trial Lump Sum is as follows:

1 counsel* + 40% office costs:	$12,523
1 support staff*:	$ 3,600
Total per month:	$16,123
Total three months:	**$48,369**

*Calculated at 75% of the gross-P5 Step VII salary as of January 2005[5] for counsel and 100% of €3000 for support staff at September 2004 exchange rate.

[5] The UN salary scale has most recently been amended in January 2005.

The composition of the Phase Two Lump Sum described in this paragraph does not prevent counsel from requesting the assignment of a second counsel for Phase Two nor for the whole duration of the phase or any other given part thereof. Such an assignment shall not, however, result in an increase of the lump sum received by the defence team in Phase Two.

Invoicing and Payment

14. The Phase Two lump sum may be paid in three equal monthly stipends of **C32–008** US$16,123. The first two will be paid upon submission by counsel of a pro forma invoice at the end of each month. The last monthly stipend will be paid upon submission of both a *pro forma* invoice and counsel's Work Plan for Phase Three of the pre-trial stage (see paras 17–21).

15. The *pro forma* invoice is signed by the Lead Counsel, advising the Registrar how to distribute the stipend between the respective Defence team members. Payments will then be made in principle within one month of submission of a valid and accurate invoice, directly into the accounts of the respective Defence team members who have been officially assigned by the Registrar.

Adjustment of the standard lump sum

16. The standard lump sum for Phase Two may only be adjusted in the event of **C32–009** compelling factual and legal circumstances or developments in the course of Phase Two which lead to a substantial increase in the work necessary during Phase Two. A request for an adjustment of the standard lump sum must be submitted to the Registrar in writing within 30 days following the end of the phase and be substantiated by a detailed invoice of hourly activities.

D. FROM PHASE TWO TO PHASE THREE

Drafting the Work Plan

17. The Lead Counsel is required to submit a Work Plan by the end of Phase Two. **C32–010** The plan shall include, *inter alia*:
- Members of the Defence team assigned or to be assigned to work on the preparation of the case for the defence and their capacity;
- The projected distribution of work among Defence team members;
- The location of the Defence team offices and material (documents);
- A time-line for completion of pre-trial Phase Three;
- Significant actions to be undertaken (including planned motions, number of witness statements to be taken, documents to be gathered and studied, etc.);
- A Defence investigation plan including the number and location of sites to be visited (in general terms) and the estimated time to be spent at each location, specifying where possible the concrete tasks to be undertaken (e.g. to obtain documents, visit the crime scene, identify, interview and prepare (potential) defence witnesses, identify, interview and prepare (potential) expert witnesses etc.);
- The estimated number and names/pseudonyms of Prosecution witnesses to be interviewed and their location;
- The estimated number and names/pseudonyms of Defence witnesses to be interviewed and prepared and their location;
- The work required or estimated to be required to review and analyse the material disclosed by the Prosecutor pursuant to Rules 66 and 68 of the Rules of Procedure and Evidence;
- A travel plan for counsel and support staff;[6] and

---

[6] Remuneration of Travel and DSA will be in accordance with the applicable Registry practice and policies.

- The estimated number of Rule 65*ter* conferences, status conferences, meetings with the Prosecution, working sessions with the Accused, working sessions with the Defence team of a co-accused if applicable, etc.

18. The Work Plan is solely a judicial management document. Its purpose is to provide the Registrar with objective information related to the planning and preparation of the case for the Defence. It also aims at allowing the Registrar to monitor the preparation of the case for the Defence while at the same time providing a reference for the allocation of resources to Defence teams under paras. 22 and 35–40. As such , the Work Plan will be considered in conjunction with the Progress Reports (see para 34).

19. The Work Plan is a confidential work-product of the Defence team and will be kept confidential within the Registry.[7] Under no circumstances will it or any of its contents be shared with the Office of the Prosecutor (OTP).

20. It is the Lead Counsel's responsibility to prepare a reasonable and meaningful Work Plan without disclosing information subject to the Counsel-Client privilege.

21. The Registrar shall consider the Work Plan within 30 days of its submission. It must be accepted by the Registrar before any invoice for Phase Three is paid.

Assessing the Complexity Level

C32–011   22. At the time the Work Plan is submitted, the Defence team shall present the Registrar with a reasoned submission relating to the assignment of a complexity level for the case. Following the Defence team's submission, the Registrar will make a determination as to the complexity of the pre-trial stage—Level 1 (difficult), Level 2 (very difficult), or Level 3 (extremely difficult/leadership)—after consulting with the Chamber seized of the case and with the Defence team. The complexity level will be based on, but not limited to, the following factors, which should be reflected in the Work Plan:
- the position of the accused within the political/military hierarchy
- the number and nature of counts in the indictment
- whether the case raises any novel issues
- whether the case involves multiple municipalities (geographical scope)
- the complexity of legal and factual arguments involved
- the number and type of witnesses and documents involved.

E. PHASE THREE

C32–012   23. Phase Three will commence the day after the conclusion of Phase Two and will terminate with the commencement of trial.

Calculation of the Lump Sum

C32–013   24. The Registrar calculates the lump sum for Phase Three of the pre-trial stage based on the complexity of the case as determined by the Registrar, *i.e.* the amount of work reasonably required for the phase rather than on its duration. The lump sum is based partly on the monthly salary of a P5 Step VII senior trial attorney and partly on the monthly salary of a P4 Step VII trial attorney. In addition, the Registrar factors in support staff fees (see paras. 26–28) and "office costs" which have been set at 40% of counsel fees. All figures are based on United Nations pay scale figures for January 2005.[8]

---

[7] Access to the Work Plan will be limited to staff of the Registry's Office of Legal Aid and Detention Matters and the Deputy Registrar and Registrar. In case one of these persons finds it necessary to grant access to additional members of the Registry, this can be allowed only after consultation with the Lead Counsel of the Defence team in question and on the authority of the Head of OLAD, the Deputy Registrar or the Registrar.
[8] The UN salary scale has most recently been amended in January 2005.

25. Phase Three Pre-trial lump sums are the following:

Complexity	Lump Sum
Level 1 (Difficult)	US$112,162
Level 2 (Very Difficult)	US$229,250
Level 3 (Extremely Difficult/Leadership)	US$405,515

26. The lump sum for a Level 1 Phase Three case is calculated on the basis that it requires preparation by one counsel and two support staff[9] working full time for a period of three and a quarter months over and above the Phase Two period to prepare such a case for trial. Funding is provided for a co- counsel to join the team for the last two and a half months of the phase.

27. The lump sum for a Level 2 Phase Three case is calculated on the basis that it requires preparation by one counsel and three support staff[10] working full time for a period of six and one-third months over and above the Phase Two period to prepare such a case for trial. Funding is provided for a co-counsel to join the team for the last four months of the phase.

28. The lump sum for a Level 3 Phase Three case is calculated on the basis that it requires preparation by one counsel and five support staff [11] working full time for a period of nine and a half months over and above the Phase Two period to prepare such a case for trial. Funding is provided for a co-counsel to join the team for the last five and a half months of the phase.

29. The Breakdown of the calculation of the lump sum in Phase Three is set forth below . The members of each Defence team and their rates of pay are estimated as to what is deemed reasonable for calculating the lump sum, but should in no way be considered prescriptive. The Lead Counsel has complete flexibility in how to compose and compensate her/his team:

---

[9] This portion of the lump sum is based on a component of two support staff working 150 hours in a month at an hourly pay rate of €20 in accordance with Annex 1 of the Directive on Assignment of Defence Counsel.

[10] This portion of the lump sum is based on a component of three support staff working 150 hours in a month at an hourly pay rate of €20 in accordance with Annex 1 of the Directive on Assignment of Defence Counsel.

[11] This portion of the lump sum is based on a component of five support staff working 150 hours in a month at an hourly pay rate of €20 in accordance with Annex 1 of the Directive on Assignment of Defence Counsel.

Level	Defence Team Members	Monthly pay estimates per member	Total per month	Amount of work in months[12]	Total Pre-trial Phase Three lump sum
1	Lead counsel	P5 + 40% = **$16,698**	**$23,898**	3.25	$77,669 +
	Two support staff	$3,600 × 2 = **$ 7,200**		($77,669)	$34,493 =
	Co-counsel	P4 + 40% = **$13,797**	**$13,797**	2.5 ($34,493)	**$112,162**
2	Lead counsel	P5 + 40% = **$16,698**	**$27,498**	6.33	$174,062 +
	Three support staff	$3,600 × 3 = **$10,800**		($174,062)	$55,188 =
	Co-counsel	P4 + 40% = **$13,797**	**$13,797**	4 ($55,188)	**$229,250**
3	Lead counsel	P5 + 40% = **$16,698**	**$34,698**	9.5	$329,631 +
	Five support staff	$3,600 × 5 = **$18,000**		($329,631)	$75,884 =
	Co-counsel	P4 + 40% = **$13,797**	**$13,797**	5.5 ($75,884)	**$405,515**

Invoicing and Payment

C32–014 30. Counsel will submit monthly *pro forma* invoices beginning at the end of the first month of the phase. Payment will be made upon submission of the invoice in monthly stipends and will commence only after the Work Plan, submitted by counsel at the end of Phase Two, is accepted by the Registrar.

31. Eighty percent (80%) of the Phase Three lump sum will be paid in monthly stipends while the remaining twenty percent (20%) will be paid after acceptance by the Registrar of the Defence team's End-of-Stage Report (see paras. 41–46) which is unrelated to the matters dealt with in paras. 35–40. The stipend for this phase is calculated by dividing 80% of the lump sum by the estimated number of months in the phase as estimated by the Registrar after consulting Defence Counsel, OTP and Chambers. Absent a clear estimate of the duration of Phase Three the figures below will be applied for the purpose of distributing the lump sum:
Level 1: 12 Months
Level 2: 15 Months
Level 3: 18 Months

32. The *pro forma* invoice is signed by the Lead Counsel, advising the Registrar how to distribute the stipend between the respective Defence team members. Payments will then be made, in principle within one month of submission of a valid and accurate invoice, directly into the accounts of the respective Defence team members who have been officially assigned by the Registrar.

33. The monthly pro-forma invoices need not detail the work performed. However, Lead Counsel must keep a record of the hours and work performed by the Defence team as the Lead Counsel is required to submit progress reports every four months during Phase Three (see para. 34) and a detailed End-of-Stage report at the end of Phase Three (see paras. 41–46).

Progress Reports

C32–015 34. At the end of every four months within Phase Three the Defence team will submit a Progress Report with its *pro forma* invoice. The Progress Report must summarise the work performed by the Defence team including the progress made based on the items

---

[12] The amount of work in months has been based on an agreement between the Association of Defence Counsel and the Registry regarding the total figures, reason for the amounts to be curbed in order to match the total figures agreed upon.

included in the Work Plan. On its own initiative or on request of the Lead Counsel, the Registrar may organise a meeting to discuss a progress report.

Upgrade in the Level of Complexity

35. A Defence team working on a case determined to be of level 1 or 2 may submit a request for a change in the complexity level. Such a request must be submitted in writing and include a description of a change in the criteria specified in paragraph 22 and the manner in which that change affects the preparation of the defence case.   **C32–016**

36. In the event that a request for an upgrade in the complexity level of a case is granted, any additional funds provided pursuant to the upgrade will be disbursed in accordance with paragraph 31.

Adjustment of the Lump Sum

37. The Registrar may increase the lump sum (while maintaining the level of complexity) if the Lead Counsel demonstrates unforeseeable circumstances beyond the control of the Defence, which substantially impact upon the preparation reasonably required by the Defence team. The extended duration of the phase does not itself justify additional allotments; the relevant consideration is the amount of work reasonably required.   **C32–017**

38. In deciding upon a request for an increase of the lump sum based on unforeseeable circumstances, the Registrar shall request and take into account information from the Pre-Trial Judge on the nature of the circumstances and their impact on the preparation of the case for the Defence. Information requested will include whether the circumstances can be attributed fully or in part to the manner in which the Prosecution or the Defence conducted their pre-trial preparation, including their planning and organization.

39. In addition, in specific circumstances such as an accused entering a guilty plea or the withdrawal of counts in the indictment, the Registrar will consider *proprio motu* whether it is necessary to adjust the lump sum.[13] In such circumstances, the lump sum may be decreased only after consultation with the Lead Counsel and with the consent of the Chamber seized of the case.

40. If additional work is required because of the replacement of the Lead Counsel as approved by the Registrar, the newly appointed counsel should not be penalized for this reason. Such issues will be addressed on a case-by-case basis.

End-of-Stage Report

41. At the end of Phase Three of the pre-trial stage, the Defence team is entitled to receive the portion of the lump sum that was withheld. This will be paid upon acceptance by the Registrar of the Defence team's End-of-Stage Report. The Lead Counsel must submit the End-of-Stage Report within 60 days of the commencement of the trial.   **C32–018**

42. The End-of-Stage Report must contain a formal accounting of hours covering the pre -trial stage as well as details on the type of work performed by each team member during this period. More specifically, the End-of-Stage Report shall include the following information:

    a. For each month, the name of each member of the Defence team and their respective assignment/tasks for the particular month;

    b. For each month, the number of hours worked per assignment/task and a detailed description of the work performed by each member of the Defence team;

---

[13] In the case of a guilty plea early in the process, it may be inappropriate to pay the full lump sum allocated for the pre-trial stage as it may generate a significant windfall for the Defence counsel whose client pleads guilty.

    c. For the total phase, a recapitulation of the total number of hours worked by each member of the Defence team and by category of work; and

    d. For the entire pre-trial stage, a recapitulation of the work performed and its output[14] with sufficient specificity to allow the Registrar to verify that the work was performed. The Report will include information such as the number and names/pseudonyms of witnesses met and interviewed, amount of research done, filings prepared and filings submitted, and documents reviewed including disclosure and the number of pages of such documents.

43. In the review of the End-of-Stage Report, the Registrar shall verify that:

    a. All information requested in paragraph 42 is included;

    b. The work performed by each Defence team member is sufficiently described to establish that it was accomplished for the purpose of preparing the case for trial;

    c. The work reported by all members of the Defence team member was actually performed , and justifies the payment of the Pre-Trial Lump Sum; and;

    d. All legal aid funds were paid to authorized individuals (members of the team or other persons duly assigned by the Registrar), as requested by Lead Counsel.

44. The Registrar may request the Lead Counsel to provide additional information highlighting specific concerns and questions to be addressed before deciding on the amount to be paid.

45. Based on the End-of-Stage Report and any additional information received from Lead Counsel, the Registrar shall disburse the remainder of the Phase Three lump sum, unless he has reason to believe that irregularities in the work or conduct of the Defence team may have taken place. In such a case, the Registrar shall either: a) consult with the Pre-Trial Judge seized of the case and/or the Association of Defence Counsel practising before the Tribunal; or b) refer the matter to the Disciplinary Panel or the Pre-Trial Judge seized of the case. Only after such consultation or referral and after having given Lead Counsel an opportunity to respond, may the Registrar decide to suspend payment of all or part of the end of phase payment. The Registrar may also, if instructed by the Pre-Trial Judge or a Chamber, deduct any fees associated with the production of a motion which has been declared frivolous or an abuse of process, in accordance with the Rules of Procedure and Evidence

46. Should the Lead Counsel disagree with the Registrar's decision not to pay all or part of the Phase Three lump sum or with the amount to be disbursed, Lead Counsel may request a review of the Registrar's decision in accordance with the procedure set forth in Article 31 of the Directive on the Assignment of Defence Counsel.

Progress Meetings

C32–019   47. At any time during Phase Three of the pre-trial stage the Lead Counsel or his representative may be invited to attend a meeting to discuss the progress made in the preparation of the Defence case.

F. FINAL PROVISIONS

C32–020   48. The Registrar may, at any time during the proceedings, request information and perform checks into the work performed by any or all members of the Defence team. Defence Counsel shall, for this purpose, retain all Defence files for a period of, at least , five years after the end of the proceedings.

---

[14] The output of the work performed will in no way be judged upon the success or failure of the Defence team's performance.

C33. Defence Counsel—Trial Legal Aid Policy

This policy shall be the authoritative version of the modified payment scheme for trial **C33–001** (the "2003 Trial Payment Scheme"), as previously amended on 1 November 2004. In case of any inconsistency between this policy or amendment made and any previous information disseminated, this policy shall prevail.

The policy will apply to all new cases in which legal aid is granted as of 1 December 2004.

The revised amounts included in this amended version will apply retroactively as of 1 January 2005 to all cases in trial to which this Trial Legal Aid Policy applies.

TABLE OF CONTENTS

DEFENCE COUNSEL PAYMENT SCHEME FOR THE TRIAL STAGE

AMENDED AS OF 1 APRIL 2005

A. DETERMINATION OF THE LUMP SUM

1. The lump sum allotment shall be determined by the Registrar after consulting with **C33–002** the Trial Chamber and the parties by evaluating both: (1) the estimated duration of the stage (see Section C infra), and (2) the complexity of the stage (see Section D infra).

2. Such factors may be difficult to assess in advance, particularly for large cases. To make the forecasting more manageable, and the forecasts more realistic, the trial stage will be divided into different phases: (a) the Prosecution phase, and (b) the Defence phase. In the event that either of these phases is predicted to last longer than 12 months, it may be sub-divided into two separate phases. Separate lump sums will then be calculated and allocated for each different phase of the trial at the time each phase of the trial is set to begin. In the event that the whole trial stage is expected to last less than 12 months, it will constitute one phase for the purpose of this policy.

B. DISTRIBUTION OF THE LUMP SUM

3. This payment scheme has a lump sum nature. In contrast to the previous system **C33–003** (the "2001 system") in which Defence Counsel were allocated a maximum allotment of hours, payment of the lump sum is linked to the completion of a phase of the proceedings, and is not contingent on the number of hours actually worked per month or the actual duration of the phase.

4. From an analysis of various domestic lump sum or costing systems in other countries, it appears that the standard practice is to disburse the lump sum at the completion of the case. However, ICTY proceedings can be lengthy and the Registrar

does not believe that it would be appropriate to require Defence Counsel to work for long periods without any payment. Accordingly, the Defence team will receive an up-front payment, a monthly stipend paid automatically for each month of the phase, and a final end-of-phase distribution. This up-front payment and the monthly stipend are effectively an advance payment of the lump sum in instalments and do not represent any allotment of hours. Thus, irrespective of whether the court is in recess or sitting every available day, the Defence team will be paid the stipend. The stipend will continue to be paid each month for the duration of the estimated phase. At the completion of the phase, upon submission of a more detailed accounting of the work done throughout the phase as well as details on the type of work performed by the team members, the Defence team will be paid the lump sum in full, minus the amount of the lump sum which has been advanced to the Defence team in the form of the up-front payment and the monthly stipends.

I. Up-front initial distribution

C33–004   5. The Registrar recognises that at the commencement of the Prosecution phase, the Defence team may incur several costs associated with relocation and the establishment of their office in The Hague. The Registrar will therefore issue 10% of the lump sum at the commencement of the Prosecution phase on the day that the trial proceedings begin, to facilitate any extraordinary expenses that might be incurred.

II. Distribution of Monthly Stipend

C33–005   6. As stated above, the monthly stipend is a distribution of the lump sum in instalments and does not represent a monthly allotment of hours. The stipend is calculated by dividing the lump sum by the estimated number of months, and multiplying this amount by 70%.

7. Defence Counsel will be required to submit a monthly statement, a pro forma invoice[1] signed by the Lead Counsel, advising the Registrar how to distribute the stipend between the respective Defence team members. Payments will then, in principle, be made within one month of submission of a valid and acceptable invoice, directly into the accounts of the respective Defence team members who have been officially assigned by the Registrar. Only at the end of the phase will they be required to account for the hours and work performed in the course of that phase, with a detailed statement presented to the Registrar (see below).

8. In the event that the actual duration exceeds the estimated duration, the Defence team will continue to receive the office costs component of their allotment (40% of the Counsel and Co-Counsel allotment) each month, which is not deducted from the lump sum. As of January 2004, this amounts to $12,198.00 per month.

III. End of Phase Payment

C33–006   9. At the end of the respective phase, the Defence team is entitled to receive that part of the lump sum that was withheld, which equates to the Lump Sum less the 10% initial payment less any amounts paid out in monthly stipends. If the actual duration is the same as the estimated duration, then the end of phase payment will equate to 20% of the Lump Sum: 10% up-front + 70% in monthly stipends + 20% end-of-phase = 100%.

10. This sum will be paid within one month following the acceptance by the Registrar of the End of Phase Report, which must be submitted by the Lead Counsel within 60 days of the end of the respective trial phase as per paragraphs 16–18.

IV. End of Phase Report

C33–007   11. The End of Phase Report must contain a formal accounting of hours covering the Phase as well as details on the type of work performed by each team member during this period. More specifically, the End of Phase Report shall include the following information:

---

[1] UN accounting rules will require an invoice, a requirement which can be met with a pro forma invoice—a form requiring dates and signature—for processing.

a. For each month, the name of each member of the Defence team and their respective assignment/tasks for the particular month;

b. For each month, the number of hours worked with a detailed description of the work performed by each member of the Defence team;

c. For the total phase, a recapitulation of the total number of hours worked by each member of the Defence team and by category of work; and

d. For the entire trial phase, a recapitulation of the work performed and its output[2] with sufficient specificity to allow the Registrar to verify that the work was performed. The Report will include information such as the number and names/pseudonyms of witnesses met and interviewed, amount of research done, filings prepared and filings submitted, and documents reviewed including disclosure and the number of pages of such documents.

12. In the review of the End of Phase Report, the Registrar shall verify if :

a. All information requested in paragraph 11 is included;

b. The work performed by each Defence team member is sufficiently described to establish that it was accomplished for the purpose of presenting the case for the Defence at trial;

c. The work reported by all members of the Defence team member was actually performed and justifies the payment of the Trial Lump Sum; and

d. All legal aid funds were paid to authorized individuals (members of the team or other persons duly assigned by the Registrar), as requested by Lead Counsel.

13. The Registrar may request the Lead Counsel to provide additional information highlighting specific concerns and questions to be addressed before deciding on the amount to be paid.

14. Based on the End of Phase Report and any additional information received from Lead Counsel, the Registrar shall disburse the remainder of the lumpsum, unless he has reason to believe that irregularities in the work or conduct of the Defence team may have taken place. In such a case, the Registrar shall either: a) consult with the Chamber seized of the case and/or the Association of Defence Counsel practising before the Tribunal, or b) refer the matter to the Disciplinary Panel or the Chamber seized of the case. Only after such consultation or referral and after having given Lead Counsel an opportunity to respond, may the Registrar decide to suspend payment of all or part of the End of Phase Payment. The Registrar may also, if instructed by a Chamber, deduct any fees associated with the production of a motion which the Chamber has declared frivolous or an abuse of process, in accordance with the Rules of Procedure and Evidence.

15. Should the Lead Counsel disagree with the Registrar's decision not to pay all or part of the End of Phase payment or with the amount to be disbursed, Lead Counsel may request a review of the Registrar's decision in accordance with the procedure set forth in Article 31 of the Directive on the Assignment of Defence Counsel.

C. ASSESSMENT OF THE DURATION OF A PHASE

C33–008

16. As the Trial Chamber is ultimately responsible for controlling the proceedings, the estimated duration of the Prosecution phase will be based on the time allocated for the presentation of the Prosecution case, as set by the Trial Chamber at the Pre-Trial Conference in accordance with Rule 73*bis*(C), and the anticipated time it will take to issue the Rule 98bis ruling after the Prosecution phase.

17. Similarly, for the Defence phase, the duration will be based on the time allocated by the Trial Chamber for the presentation of the Defence case (Rule 73*ter*(E)). For the purpose of this payment policy, the Defence phase shall end with the presentation of the Defence's closing arguments.

18. In the event that the Trial Chamber, proprio motu or at the request of the parties, has modified the duration of either the Prosecution or Defence Phase before its

---

[2] The output of the work performed will in no way be judged upon the success or failure of the Defence Team's performance.

completion, the Registrar will decide to adjust the lump sum, unless the Registrar finds, after consulting the Trial Chamber, that the increase or decrease in time does not result in an increase or decrease of work.

D. ASSESSMENT OF THE COMPLEXITY OF A CASE

C33–009　　19. The complexity of a phase will be determined by the Registrar after consulting with representatives of the Chamber, the Prosecution, and Defence at a meeting taking place no later than 5 days after the last Rule 65*ter* conference for the Prosecution phase, and no later than 5 days after the issuance of the Rule 98*bis* decision for the Defence phase, and will be based on, inter alia, the following factors:
- the position of the accused within the political/military hierarchy;
- the number and nature of counts in the indictment;
- whether the case raises any novel issues;
- whether the case involves multiple municipalities (geographical scope of case);
- the complexity of legal and factual arguments involved; and
- the number and type of witnesses and documents involved.

20. The complexity of a case is not necessarily correlated with the estimated duration of a case. It is possible to have a case in which the Trial Chamber permits many witnesses to testify because there are multiple defendants, which is nonetheless neither factually nor legally complex, since the accused may be lowly ranked and there may be few counts in each respective indictment.

21. It is possible that a case may be ranked differently during the different phases, or from the pre-trial stage to the trial stage, since the ranking reflects the complexity of legal and factual issues raised during a particular stage or phase, and not during the case in general. Accordingly, the Registrar will issue separate determinations of the complexity for the Prosecution and Defence phases respectively.

22. In view of the fact that the Chamber seized of the case is familiar with the aforementioned criteria, and is thus in the best position to render an objective determination of the complexity of the phase, the Registrar will give due consideration to the Chamber's recommendation of the complexity of the case. The Registrar shall therefore invite comments from the Presiding Judge sitting in the trial and, for the Prosecution phase, the Pre-Trial Judge.

23. On the basis of the above factors, the Registrar will rank the cases as being either Level 1 (difficult), Level 2 (very difficult), or Level 3 (extremely difficult/leadership).

E. CALCULATION OF THE LUMP SUM

C33–010　　24. The lump sum for each case is calculated by multiplying the following allotments by the estimated number of months of the duration of the case. These allotments are calculated on the basis of three components:
- a. the gross salary of a P5 Step VII staff member plus a component for office costs amounting to 40% of the total [a total of $16, 698 using UN salary scale as of January 1, 2005[3]] (for Lead Counsel);
- b. the gross salary of a P4 Step VII staff member plus a component for office costs amounting to 40% of the total [a total of $13, 797 under the January 2005 scale] (for Co-Counsel); and
- c. a support staff component which varies according to the complexity of the case (as set out in the table below) (for one (level 1), three (level 2) or five (level 3) support staff members).

---

[3] The UN salary scale has most recently been amended in January 2005.

Support Staff Allotment per Level (A)

Difficulty	Support Allotment
1 (Difficult)	€3,000.00
2 (Very Difficult)	€9,000.00
3 (Extremely Difficult / Leadership)	€15,000.00

25. The monthly allotment in total (Lead Counsel, Co-Counsel and support staff) is thus as follows:[4]

Difficulty	Monthly Allotment	Monthly allotment for inter-pretation and translation
1 (Difficult)	$30, 495 + €3,000.00	€1000 maximum
2 (Very Difficult)	$30, 495 + €9,000.00	€1000 maximum
3 (Extremely Difficult / Leadership)	$30, 495 + €15,000.00	€1000 maximum

26. All aspects of representation except for necessary travel and DSA are to be covered by the lump sum. These include, but are not limited to:
   o lead counsel fees
   o co-counsel fees
   o legal assistant fees
   o investigator fees
   o interpretation and translation costs (see par. 27)
   o office costs
   o administrative expenses
   o consultant fees.

27. Included in the lumpsum are all interpretation costs and costs of translation of documents other than those documents to be adduced as evidence which should be translated by the International Tribunal's translation services (CLSS), in accordance with the Registry's interpretation and translation policies. Not included are further interpretation and translation costs incurred pursuant to Article 21 (4) a), b) and f) of the Statute. Defence teams may invoice separately for those costs, up to a maximum of €1000 per month.

28. In view of the fact that duration is likely to differ between cases of different complexities, the ultimate difference will not necessarily be fully reflected by the above allotments. For example, the lump sum that would be allocated for a level 2 phase which is predicted to last 10 months would be ($30,495 + €9,000.00) × 10). At the exchange rates current as of January 2005, this adds up to $427,070, the lump sum for the 10–month phase.

---

[4] Please be aware that the amendment of 16 April 2004, whereby the support staff component of the lump sum was increased by 1,000 Euros in each level to cover the cost of interpretation/translation between client and counsel, is no longer in force. As agreed during Registry-ADC consultations in August 2004, interpretation/translation between client and counsel is treated differently in the present document (see paras 26 and 27 main text). The support staff component is based on the average hourly rate for support staff as specified in the Directive (€20) times 150 hours per month and one member for a level 1 case, three for a level 2 case and five for a level 3 case.

F. END OF PHASE ADJUSTMENT

C33–011   29. The total lump sum for the Prosecution or Defence phases may be modified if:
   a. The phase lasts longer than the duration initially determined by the Trial Chamber; or
   b. The trial lasts shorter than the duration initially determined by the Trial Chamber.

30. In the event that the Chamber seized of the case has granted additional time for the presentation of either the Prosecution or the Defence cases, based on specific circumstances which have arisen in the course of the phase, the Lead Counsel may request an increase in the Lump Sum in writing, explaining the reasons why the phase lasted longer and including a detailed report highlighting the additional work performed by all members of the Defence team as a consequence of the specific circumstances.

31. In determining whether an increase of the lump sum is warranted, the Registrar shall:
   a. Verify that the information contained in the request fulfils the criteria stipulated in paragraph 12;
   b. Acquire information from the Trial Chamber whether the granting of additional time for the presentation of either the Prosecution or Defence case has impacted upon the work reasonably required by the defence. The Trial Chamber will be requested to provide its view whether the extended duration of the phase can be attributed, fully or in part, to the manner in which the Prosecution or Defence conducted their respective cases, including their planning and organization;
   c. Consider whether the work conducted by the Defence as a result of the longer duration of the phase was directly relevant and necessary to the preparation and presentation of the case;
   d. If deemed necessary, convene an official meeting with Defence Counsel to discuss the above matters.

32. Should the phase last shorter than initially determined (paragraph 28(b)), the Registrar may decrease the Lump Sum for the Phase in accordance with its actual duration. In determining whether such a decrease is warranted the Registrar shall:
   a. Verify that the criteria stipulated in Paragraph 12 are fulfilled;
   b. Acquire information from the Trial Chamber with regard to the reasons for the decreased duration of the Phase; and
   c. Request the Lead Counsel to provide information on the work performed during the Phase by each member of the Defence team and make representations as to the decrease of the Lump sum.

33. If additional work is required because of the replacement of Counsel as approved by the Registrar, the newly appointed Counsel should not normally be penalized for this reason. Such issues will be addressed on a case-by-case basis.

G. FINAL PROVISIONS

34. The Registrar may, at any time during the proceedings, request information and perform checks into the work performed by any and all members of the Defence team. Defence Counsel shall, for this purpose, retain all Defence files for a period of, at least, five years after the end of the proceedings

C34. Agreement on Security and Order

(Signed 14 July 1994)

This document may be found at *http://www.un.org/icty/legaldoc-e/basic/detention/agree.htm* **C34–001**

C35. Appointment of Inspecting Authority for the Detention Unit

This document may be found at *http://www.un.org/icty/legaldoc-e/basic/detention/appoint.htm*

C36. Agreements on the Enforcement of Sentences

These documents may be found at *http://www.un.org/icty/legaldoc-e/basic/cooperation/* **C36–001**
agreegarde.htm
http://www.un.org/icty/legaldoc-e/basic/cooperation/sent-austria-e.htm
http://www.un.org/icty/legaldoc-e/basic/cooperation/sent-denmark-e.htm
http://www.un.org/icty/legaldoc-e/basic/cooperation/sent-finland-e.htm
http://www.un.org/icty/legaldoc-e/basic/cooperation/sent-france-e.htm
http://www.un.org/icty/legaldoc-e/basic/cooperation/sent-italy-e.htm
http://www.un.org/icty/legaldoc-e/basic/cooperation/sent-norway-e.htm
http://www.un.org/icty/legaldoc-e/basic/cooperation/sent-spain-e.htm and
http://www.un.org/icty/legaldoc-e/basic/cooperation/sent-sweden-e.htm

C37. Legislation Implementing the ICTY Statute

These documents may be found at *http://www.un.org/icty/legaldoc-e/basic/cooperation/leg-* **C37–001**
australia-e.htm
http://www.un.org/icty/legaldoc-e/basic/cooperation/leg-austria-e.htm
http://www.un.org/icty/legaldoc-e/basic/cooperation/leg-belgium-e.htm
http://www.un.org/icty/legaldoc-e/basic/cooperation/leg-bosniaherz-e.htm
http://www.un.org/icty/legaldoc-e/basic/cooperation/leg-croatia-e.htm
http://www.un.org/icty/legaldoc-e/basic/cooperation/leg-denmark-e.htm
http://www.un.org/icty/legaldoc-e/basic/cooperation/leg-finland-e.htm
http://www.un.org/icty/legaldoc-e/basic/cooperation/leg-france-e.htm
http://www.un.org/icty/legaldoc-e/basic/cooperation/leg-germany-e.htm
http://www.un.org/icty/legaldoc-e/basic/cooperation/leg-grece-e.htm
http://www.un.org/icty/legaldoc-e/basic/cooperation/leg-hungary-e.htm
http://www.un.org/icty/legaldoc-e/basic/cooperation/leg-italy-e.htm
http://www.un.org/icty/legaldoc-e/basic/cooperation/leg-netherlands-e.htm
http://www.un.org/icty/legaldoc-e/basic/cooperation/leg-newzealand-e.htm
http://www.un.org/icty/legaldoc-e/basic/cooperation/leg-norway-e.htm
http://www.un.org/icty/legaldoc-e/basic/cooperation/leg-roumanie-e.htm
http://www.un.org/icty/legaldoc-e/basic/cooperation/leg-spain-e.htm
http://www.un.org/icty/legaldoc-e/basic/cooperation/leg-sweden-e.htm
http://www.un.org/icty/legaldoc-e/basic/cooperation/leg-switzer-e.htm
http://www.un.org/icty/legaldoc-e/basic/cooperation/leg-uk-e.htm and
http://www.un.org/icty/legaldoc-e/basic/cooperation/leg-usa-e.htm

C38. Resolution 1504 (2003)

ADOPTED BY THE SECURITY COUNCIL AT ITS 4819TH MEETING, ON 4 SEPTEMBER 2003

C38–001   This document may be found at *http://www.unmikonline.org/misc/N0348774.pdf*

APPENDIX D

ICTR

D1. Resolution 955 (1994) Adopted by the Security Council at its 3453rd meeting, on 8 November 1994

D1–001   *The Security Council,*

Reaffirming all its previous resolutions on the situation in Rwanda,

Having considered the reports of the Secretary-General pursuant to paragraph 3 of resolution 935 (1994) of 1 July 1994 (S/1994/879 and S/1994/906),and *having taken note* of the reports of the Special Rapporteur for Rwanda of the United Nations Commission on Human Rights (S/1994/1157, annex I and annex II),

Expressing appreciation for the work of the Commission of Experts established pursuant to resolution 935 (1994), in particular its preliminary report on violations of international humanitarian law in Rwanda transmitted by the Secretary-General's letter of 1 October 1994 (S/1994/1125),

Expressing once again its grave concern at the reports indicating that genocide and other systematic, widespread and flagrant violations of international humanitarian law have been committed in Rwanda,

Determining that this situation continues to constitute a threat to international peace and security,

Determined to put an end to such crimes and to take effective measures to bring to justice the persons who are responsible for them,

Convinced that in the particular circumstances of Rwanda, the prosecution of persons responsible for serious violations of international humanitarian law would enable this aim to be achieved and would contribute to the process of national reconciliation and to the restoration and maintenance of peace,

Believing that the establishment of an international tribunal for the prosecution of persons responsible for genocide and the other above-mentioned violations of international humanitarian law will contribute to ensuring that such violations are halted and effectively redressed,

Stressing also the need for international cooperation to strengthen the courts and judicial system of Rwanda, having regard in particular to the necessity for those courts to deal with large numbers of suspects,

Considering that the Commission of Experts established pursuant to resolution 935 (1994) should continue on an urgent basis the collection of information relating to evidence of grave violations of international humanitarian law committed in the territory of Rwanda and should submit its final report to the Secretary-General by 30 November 1994,

Acting under Chapter VII of the Charter of the United Nations,

1. *Decides* hereby, having received the request of the Government of Rwanda (S/1994/1115), to establish an international tribunal for the sole purpose of prosecuting persons responsible for genocide and other serious violations of international humanitarian law committed in the territory of Rwanda and Rwandan citizens responsible for genocide and other such violations committed in the territory of neighbouring States, between 1 January 1994 and31 December 1994 and to this end to adopt the Statute of the International Criminal Tribunal for Rwanda annexed hereto;

2. *Decides* that all States shall cooperate fully with the International Tribunal and its organs in accordance with the present resolution and the Statute of the International Tribunal and that consequently all States shall take any measures necessary under their domestic law to implement the provisions of the present resolution and the Statute, including the obligation of States to comply with requests for assistance or orders issued by a Trial Chamber under Article 28 of the Statute, and *requests* States to keep the Secretary-General informed of such measures;

3. *Considers* that the Government of Rwanda should be notified prior to the taking of decisions under articles 26 and 27 of the Statute;

4. *Urges* States and intergovernmental and non-governmental organizations to contribute funds, equipment and services to the International Tribunal, including the offer of expert personnel;

---

* Reissued for technical reasons.

5. *Requests* the Secretary-General to implement this resolution urgently and in particular to make practical arrangements for the effective functioning of the International Tribunal, including recommendations to the Council as to possible locations for the seat of the International Tribunal at the earliest time and to report periodically to the Council;

6. *Decides* that the seat of the International Tribunal shall be determined by the Council having regard to considerations of justice and fairness as well as administrative efficiency, including access to witnesses, and economy, and subject to the conclusion of appropriate arrangements between the United Nations and the State of the seat, acceptable to the Council, having regard to the fact that the International Tribunal may meet away from its seat when it considers it necessary for the efficient exercise of its functions; and *decides* that an office will be established and proceedings will be conducted in Rwanda, where feasible and appropriate, subject to the conclusion of similar appropriate arrangements;

7. *Decides* to consider increasing the number of judges and Trial Chambers of the International Tribunal if it becomes necessary;

8. *Decides* to remain actively seized of the matter.

ANNEX

STATUTE OF THE INTERNATIONAL TRIBUNAL FOR RWANDA

Having been established by the Security Council acting under Chapter VII of the **D1-002** Charter of the United Nations, the International Criminal Tribunal for the Prosecution of Persons Responsible for Genocide and Other Serious Violations of International Humanitarian Law Committed in the Territory of Rwanda and Rwandan citizens responsible for genocide and other such violations committed in the territory of neighbouring States, between 1 January 1994 and 31 December 1994(hereinafter referred to as "the International Tribunal for Rwanda") shall function in accordance with the provisions of the present Statute.

ARTICLE 1

COMPETENCE OF THE INTERNATIONAL TRIBUNAL FOR RWANDA

The International Tribunal for Rwanda shall have the power to prosecute persons **D1-003** responsible for serious violations of international humanitarian law committed in the territory of Rwanda and Rwandan citizens responsible for such violations committed in the territory of neighbouring States, between1 January 1994 and 31 December 1994, in accordance with the provisions of the present Statute.

ARTICLE 2

GENOCIDE

1. The International Tribunal for Rwanda shall have the power to prosecute persons **D1-004** committing genocide as defined in paragraph 2 of this article or of committing any of the other acts enumerated in paragraph 3 of this article.

2. Genocide means any of the following acts committed with intent to destroy, in whole or in part, a national, ethnical, racial or religious group, as such:
   (a) Killing members of the group;
   (b) Causing serious bodily or mental harm to members of the group;

(c) Deliberately inflicting on the group conditions of life calculated to bring about its physical destruction in whole or in part;
(d) Imposing measures intended to prevent births within the group;
(e) Forcibly transferring children of the group to another group.

3. The following acts shall be punishable:
(a) Genocide;
(b) Conspiracy to commit genocide;
(c) Direct and public incitement to commit genocide;
(d) Attempt to commit genocide;
(e) Complicity in genocide.

ARTICLE 3

CRIMES AGAINST HUMANITY

D1–005   The International Tribunal for Rwanda shall have the power to prosecute persons responsible for the following crimes when committed as part of a widespread or systematic attack against any civilian population on national, political, ethnic, racial or religious grounds:
(a) Murder;
(b) Extermination;
(c) Enslavement;
(d) Deportation;
(e) Imprisonment;
(f) Torture;
(g) Rape;
(h) Persecutions on political, racial and religious grounds;
(i) Other inhumane acts.

ARTICLE 4

VIOLATIONS OF ARTICLE 3 COMMON TO THE GENEVA CONVENTIONS AND OF ADDITIONAL PROTOCOL II

D1–006   The International Tribunal for Rwanda shall have the power to prosecute persons committing or ordering to be committed serious violations of Article 3 common to the Geneva Conventions of 12 August 1949 for the Protection of War Victims, and of Additional Protocol II thereto of 8 June 1977. These violations shall include, but shall not be limited to:
(a) Violence to life, health and physical or mental well-being of persons, in particular murder as well as cruel treatment such as torture, mutilation or any form of corporal punishment;
(b) Collective punishments;
(c) Taking of hostages;
(d) Acts of terrorism;
(e) Outrages upon personal dignity, in particular humiliating and degrading treatment, rape, enforced prostitution and any form of indecent assault;
(f) Pillage;
(g) The passing of sentences and the carrying out of executions without previous judgement pronounced by a regularly constituted court, affording all the judicial guarantees which are recognized as indispensable by civilized peoples;
(h) Threats to commit any of the foregoing acts.

ARTICLE 5

PERSONAL JURISDICTION

D1–007   The International Tribunal for Rwanda shall have jurisdiction over natural persons pursuant to the provisions of the present Statute.

Article 6

INDIVIDUAL CRIMINAL RESPONSIBILITY

1. A person who planned, instigated, ordered, committed or otherwise aided and abetted in the planning, preparation or execution of a crime referred to in articles 2 to 4 of the present Statute, shall be individually responsible for the crime.

D1–008

2. The official position of any accused person, whether as Head of State or Government or as a responsible Government official, shall not relieve such person of criminal responsibility nor mitigate punishment.

3. The fact that any of the acts referred to in articles 2 to 4 of the present Statute was committed by a subordinate does not relieve his or her superior of criminal responsibility if he or she knew or had reason to know that the subordinate was about to commit such acts or had done so and the superior failed to take the necessary and reasonable measures to prevent such acts or to punish the perpetrators thereof.

4. The fact that an accused person acted pursuant to an order of a Government or of a superior shall not relieve him or her of criminal responsibility, but may be considered in mitigation of punishment if the International Tribunal for Rwanda determines that justice so requires.

Article 7

TERRITORIAL AND TEMPORAL JURISDICTION

The territorial jurisdiction of the International Tribunal for Rwanda shall extend to the territory of Rwanda including its land surface and airspace as well as to the territory of neighbouring States in respect of serious violations of international humanitarian law committed by Rwandan citizens. The temporal jurisdiction of the International Tribunal for Rwanda shall extend to a period beginning on 1 January 1994 and ending on 31 December 1994.

D1–009

Article 8

CONCURRENT JURISDICTION

1. The International Tribunal for Rwanda and national courts shall have concurrent jurisdiction to prosecute persons for serious violations of international humanitarian law committed in the territory of Rwanda and Rwandan citizens for such violations committed in the territory of neighbouring States, between 1 January 1994 and 31 December 1994.

D1–010

2. The International Tribunal for Rwanda shall have primacy over the national courts of all States. At any stage of the procedure, the International Tribunal for Rwanda may formally request national courts to defer to its competence in accordance with the present Statute and the Rules of Procedure and Evidence of the International Tribunal for Rwanda.

Article 9

NON BIS IN IDEM

1. No person shall be tried before a national court for acts constituting serious violations of international humanitarian law under the present Statute, for which he or she has already been tried by the International Tribunal for Rwanda.

D1–011

2. A person who has been tried by a national court for acts constituting serious violations of international humanitarian law may be subsequently tried by the International Tribunal for Rwanda only if:

    (a) The act for which he or she was tried was characterized as an ordinary crime; or

    (b) The national court proceedings were not impartial or independent, were designed to shield the accused from international criminal responsibility, or the case was not diligently prosecuted.

3. In considering the penalty to be imposed on a person convicted of a crime under the present Statute, the International Tribunal for Rwanda shall take into account the extent to which any penalty imposed by a national court on the same person for the same act has already been served.

ARTICLE 10

ORGANIZATION OF THE INTERNATIONAL TRIBUNAL FOR RWANDA

D1–012　The International Tribunal for Rwanda shall consist of the following organs:

    (a) The Chambers, comprising two Trial Chambers and an Appeals Chamber;

    (b) The Prosecutor; and

    (c) A Registry.

ARTICLE 11

COMPOSITION OF THE CHAMBERS

D1–013　The Chambers shall be composed of eleven independent judges, no two of whom may be nationals of the same State, who shall serve as follows:

    (a) Three judges shall serve in each of the Trial Chambers;

    (b) Five judges shall serve in the Appeals Chamber.

ARTICLE 12

QUALIFICATION AND ELECTION OF JUDGES

D1–014　1. The judges shall be persons of high moral character, impartiality and integrity who possess the qualifications required in their respective countries for appointment to the highest judicial offices. In the overall composition of the Chambers due account shall be taken of the experience of the judges in criminal law, international law, including international humanitarian law and human rights law.

2. The members of the Appeals Chamber of the International Tribunal for the Prosecution of Persons Responsible for Serious Violations of International Humanitarian Law Committed in the Territory of the Former Yugoslavia since 1991(hereinafter referred to as "the International Tribunal for the Former Yugoslavia") shall also serve as the members of the Appeals Chamber of the International Tribunal for Rwanda.

3. The judges of the Trial Chambers of the International Tribunal for Rwanda shall be elected by the General Assembly from a list submitted by the Security Council, in the following manner:

    (a) The Secretary-General shall invite nominations for judges of the Trial Chambers from States Members of the United Nations and non-member States maintaining permanent observer missions at United Nations Headquarters;

    (b) Within thirty days of the date of the invitation of the Secretary-General, each State may nominate up to two candidates meeting the qualifications set out in paragraph 1 above, no two of whom shall be of the same nationality and neither of whom shall be of the same nationality as any judge on the Appeals Chamber;

(c) The Secretary-General shall forward the nominations received to the Security Council. From the nominations received the Security Council shall establish a list of not less than twelve and not more than eighteen candidates, taking due account of adequate representation on the International Tribunal for Rwanda of the principal legal systems of the world;

(d) The President of the Security Council shall transmit the list of candidates to the President of the General Assembly. From that list the General Assembly shall elect the six judges of the Trial Chambers. The candidates who receive an absolute majority of the votes of the States Members of the United Nations and of the non-Member States maintaining permanent observer missions at United Nations Headquarters, shall be declared elected. Should two candidates of the same nationality obtain the required majority vote, the one who received the higher number of votes shall be considered elected.

4. In the event of a vacancy in the Trial Chambers, after consultation with the Presidents of the Security Council and of the General Assembly, the Secretary-General shall appoint a person meeting the qualifications of paragraph 1 above, for the remainder of the term of office concerned.

5. The judges of the Trial Chambers shall be elected for a term of four years. The terms and conditions of service shall be those of the judges of the International Tribunal for the Former Yugoslavia. They shall be eligible for re-election.

ARTICLE 13

OFFICERS AND MEMBERS OF THE CHAMBERS

1. The judges of the International Tribunal for Rwanda shall elect a President. **D1–015**
2. After consultation with the judges of the International Tribunal for Rwanda, the President shall assign the judges to the Trial Chambers. A judge shall serve only in the Chamber to which he or she was assigned.
3. The judges of each Trial Chamber shall elect a Presiding Judge, who shall conduct all of the proceedings of that Trial Chamber as a whole.

ARTICLE 14

RULES OF PROCEDURE AND EVIDENCE

The judges of the International Tribunal for Rwanda shall adopt, for the purpose of **D1–016** proceedings before the International Tribunal for Rwanda, the rules of procedure and evidence for the conduct of the pre-trial phase of the proceedings, trials and appeals, the admission of evidence, the protection of victims and witnesses and other appropriate matters of the International Tribunal for the Former Yugoslavia with such changes as they deem necessary.

ARTICLE 15

THE PROSECUTOR

1. The Prosecutor shall be responsible for the investigation and prosecution of persons **D1–017** responsible for serious violations of international humanitarian law committed in the territory of Rwanda and Rwandan citizens responsible for such violations committed in the territory of neighbouring States, between 1 January 1994 and 31 December 1994.

2. The Prosecutor shall act independently as a separate organ of the International Tribunal for Rwanda. He or she shall not seek or receive instructions from any Government or from any other source.

3. The Prosecutor of the International Tribunal for the Former Yugoslavia shall also serve as the Prosecutor of the International Tribunal for Rwanda. He or she shall have additional staff, including an additional Deputy Prosecutor, to assist with prosecutions before the International Tribunal for Rwanda. Such staff shall be appointed by the Secretary-General on the recommendation of the Prosecutor.

ARTICLE 16

THE REGISTRY

D1–018   1. The Registry shall be responsible for the administration and servicing of the International Tribunal for Rwanda.

2. The Registry shall consist of a Registrar and such other staff as maybe required.

3. The Registrar shall be appointed by the Secretary-General after consultation with the President of the International Tribunal for Rwanda. He or she shall serve for a four-year term and be eligible for reappointment. The terms and conditions of service of the Registrar shall be those of an Assistant Secretary-General of the United Nations.

4. The staff of the Registry shall be appointed by the Secretary-General on the recommendation of the Registrar.

ARTICLE 17

INVESTIGATION AND PREPARATION OF INDICTMENT

D1–019   1. The Prosecutor shall initiate investigations ex-officio or on the basis of information obtained from any source, particularly from Governments, United Nations organs, intergovernmental and non-governmental organizations. The Prosecutor shall assess the information received or obtained and decide whether there is sufficient basis to proceed.

2. The Prosecutor shall have the power to question suspects, victims and witnesses, to collect evidence and to conduct on-site investigations. In carrying out these tasks, the Prosecutor may, as appropriate, seek the assistance of the State authorities concerned.

3. If questioned, the suspect shall be entitled to be assisted by counsel of his or her own choice, including the right to have legal assistance assigned to the suspect without payment by him or her in any such case if he or she does not have sufficient means to pay for it, as well as to necessary translation into and from a language he or she speaks and understands.

4. Upon a determination that a prima facie case exists, the Prosecutor shall prepare an indictment containing a concise statement of the facts and the crime or crimes with which the accused is charged under the Statute. The indictment shall be transmitted to a judge of the Trial Chamber.

ARTICLE 18

REVIEW OF THE INDICTMENT

D1–020   1. The judge of the Trial Chamber to whom the indictment has been transmitted shall review it. If satisfied that a prima facie case has been established by the Prosecutor, he or she shall confirm the indictment. If not so satisfied, the indictment shall be dismissed.

2. Upon confirmation of an indictment, the judge may, at the request of the Prosecutor, issue such orders and warrants for the arrest, detention, surrender or transfer of persons, and any other orders as may be required for the conduct of the trial.

ARTICLE 19

COMMENCEMENT AND CONDUCT OF TRIAL PROCEEDINGS

1. The Trial Chambers shall ensure that a trial is fair and expeditious and that **D1–021** proceedings are conducted in accordance with the rules of procedure and evidence, with full respect for the rights of the accused and due regard for the protection of victims and witnesses.

2. A person against whom an indictment has been confirmed shall, pursuant to an order or an arrest warrant of the International Tribunal for Rwanda, betaken into custody, immediately informed of the charges against him or her and transferred to the International Tribunal for Rwanda.

3. The Trial Chamber shall read the indictment, satisfy itself that the rights of the accused are respected, confirm that the accused understands the indictment, and instruct the accused to enter a plea. The Trial Chamber shall then set the date for trial.

4. The hearings shall be public unless the Trial Chamber decides to close the proceedings in accordance with its rules of procedure and evidence.

ARTICLE 20

RIGHTS OF THE ACCUSED

1. All persons shall be equal before the International Tribunal for Rwanda. **D1–022**

2. In the determination of charges against him or her, the accused shall be entitled to a fair and public hearing, subject to article 21 of the Statute.

3. The accused shall be presumed innocent until proved guilty according to the provisions of the present Statute.

4. In the determination of any charge against the accused pursuant to the present Statute, the accused shall be entitled to the following minimum guarantees, in full equality:
   (a) To be informed promptly and in detail in a language which he or she understands of the nature and cause of the charge against him or her;
   (b) To have adequate time and facilities for the preparation of his or her defence and to communicate with counsel of his or her own choosing;
   (c) To be tried without undue delay;
   (d) To be tried in his or her presence, and to defend himself or herself in person or through legal assistance of his or her own choosing; to be informed, if he or she does not have legal assistance, of this right; and to have legal assistance assigned to him or her, in any case where the interests of justice so require, and without payment by him or her in any such case if he or she does not have sufficient means to pay for it;
   (e) To examine, or have examined, the witnesses against him or her and to obtain the attendance and examination of witnesses on his or her behalf under the same conditions as witnesses against him or her;
   (f) To have the free assistance of an interpreter if he or she cannot understand or speak the language used in the International Tribunal for Rwanda;
   (g) Not to be compelled to testify against himself or herself or to confess guilt.

ARTICLE 21

PROTECTION OF VICTIMS AND WITNESSES

The International Tribunal for Rwanda shall provide in its rules of procedure and **D1–023** evidence for the protection of victims and witnesses. Such protection measures shall include, but shall not be limited to, the conduct of in camera proceedings and the protection of the victim's identity.

Article 22

JUDGEMENT

D1–024   1. The Trial Chambers shall pronounce judgements and impose sentences and penalties on persons convicted of serious violations of international humanitarian law.

2. The judgement shall be rendered by a majority of the judges of the Trial Chamber, and shall be delivered by the Trial Chamber in public. It shall be accompanied by a reasoned opinion in writing, to which separate or dissenting opinions may be appended.

Article 23

PENALTIES

D1–025   1. The penalty imposed by the Trial Chamber shall be limited to imprisonment. In determining the terms of imprisonment, the Trial Chambers shall have recourse to the general practice regarding prison sentences in the courts of Rwanda.

2. In imposing the sentences, the Trial Chambers should take into account such factors as the gravity of the offence and the individual circumstances of the convicted person.

3. In addition to imprisonment, the Trial Chambers may order the return of any property and proceeds acquired by criminal conduct, including by means of duress, to their rightful owners.

Article 24

APPELLATE PROCEEDINGS

D1–026   1. The Appeals Chamber shall hear appeals from persons convicted by the Trial Chambers or from the Prosecutor on the following grounds:

(a) An error on a question of law invalidating the decision; or

(b) An error of fact which has occasioned a miscarriage of justice.

2. The Appeals Chamber may affirm, reverse or revise the decisions taken by the Trial Chambers.

Article 25

REVIEW PROCEEDINGS

D1–027   Where a new fact has been discovered which was not known at the time of the proceedings before the Trial Chambers or the Appeals Chamber and which could have been a decisive factor in reaching the decision, the convicted person or the Prosecutor may submit to the International Tribunal for Rwanda an application for review of the judgement.

Article 26

ENFORCEMENT OF SENTENCES

D1–028   Imprisonment shall be served in Rwanda or any of the States on a list of States which have indicated to the Security Council their willingness to accept convicted persons, as designated by the International Tribunal for Rwanda. Such imprisonment shall be in accordance with the applicable law of the State concerned, subject to the supervision of the International Tribunal for Rwanda.

ARTICLE 27

PARDON OR COMMUTATION OF SENTENCES

If, pursuant to the applicable law of the State in which the convicted person is imprisoned, he or she is eligible for pardon or commutation of sentence, the State concerned shall notify the International Tribunal for Rwanda accordingly. There shall only be pardon or commutation of sentence if the President of the International Tribunal for Rwanda, in consultation with the judges, so decides on the basis of the interests of justice and the general principles of law.

D1–029

ARTICLE 28

COOPERATION AND JUDICIAL ASSISTANCE

1. States shall cooperate with the International Tribunal for Rwanda in the investigation and prosecution of persons accused of committing serious violations of international humanitarian law.

2. States shall comply without undue delay with any request for assistance or an order issued by a Trial Chamber, including, but not limited to:
   (a) The identification and location of persons;
   (b) The taking of testimony and the production of evidence;
   (c) The service of documents;
   (d) The arrest or detention of persons;
   (e) The surrender or the transfer of the accused to the International Tribunal for Rwanda.

D1–030

ARTICLE 29

THE STATUS, PRIVILEGES AND IMMUNITIES OF THE INTERNATIONAL TRIBUNAL FOR RWANDA

1. The Convention on the Privileges and Immunities of the United Nations of 13 February 1946 shall apply to the International Tribunal for Rwanda, the judges, the Prosecutor and his or her staff, and the Registrar and his or her staff.

2. The judges, the Prosecutor and the Registrar shall enjoy the privileges and immunities, exemptions and facilities accorded to diplomatic envoys, in accordance with international law.

3. The staff of the Prosecutor and of the Registrar shall enjoy the privileges and immunities accorded to officials of the United Nations under articles V and VII of the Convention referred to in paragraph 1 of this article.

4. Other persons, including the accused, required at the seat or meeting place of the International Tribunal for Rwanda shall be accorded such treatment as is necessary for the proper functioning of the International Tribunal for Rwanda.

D1–031

ARTICLE 30

EXPENSES OF THE INTERNATIONAL TRIBUNAL FOR RWANDA

The expenses of the International Tribunal for Rwanda shall be expenses of the Organization in accordance with Article 17 of the Charter of the United Nations.

D1–032

ARTICLE 31

WORKING LANGUAGES

D1–033   The working languages of the International Tribunal shall be English and French.

ARTICLE 32

ANNUAL REPORT

D1–034   The President of the International Tribunal for Rwanda shall submit an annual report of the International Tribunal for Rwanda to the Security Council and to the General Assembly.

D2. Report of the Secretary-General Pursuant to Paragraph 5 of Security Council Resolution 955 (1994)

I. Introduction

1. Resolution 955 (1994) of 8 November 1994, by which the Security Council **D2–001** established an international tribunal for the sole purpose of prosecuting persons responsible for genocide and other serious violations of international humanitarian law committed in the territory of Rwanda and Rwandese citizens responsible for genocide and other such violations committed in the territory of neighbouring States, represented the culmination of a series of resolutions in which the Council had condemned the systematic and widespread violations of international humanitarian law in Rwanda and, in particular, the mass killing of tens of thousands of civilians with impunity.

2. In resolution 918 (1994) of 17 May 1994, the Secretary-General was requested to present a report on the investigation of serious violations of international humanitarian law committed in Rwanda. In my report to the Council of 31 May 1994 (S/1994/640), I noted that massacres and killings had continued in a systematic manner throughout Rwanda and that only a proper investigation could establish the facts in order to determine responsibility.

3. By resolution 935 (1994) of 1 July 1994, the Secretary-General was requested to establish an impartial commission of experts. In its interim report (S/1994/1125), the Commission submitted its preliminary conclusions on serious breaches of international humanitarian law and acts of genocide committed in Rwanda, and recommended that the individuals responsible for those acts be brought to justice before an independent and impartial international criminal tribunal. In its final report (S/1994/1405), the Commission concluded that there existed overwhelming evidence to prove that acts of genocide against the Tutsi ethnic group had been committed by Hutu elements in a concerted, planned, systematic and methodical way, in violation of article II of the Convention on the Prevention and Punishment of the Crime of Genocide, 1948[1] (hereinafter "the Genocide Convention"); that crimes against humanity and serious violations of international humanitarian law were committed by individuals on both sides of the conflict, but there was no evidence to suggest that acts committed by Tutsi elements were perpetrated with an intent to destroy the Hutu ethnic group as such, within the meaning of the Genocide Convention.

4. The present report is submitted pursuant to paragraph 5 of resolution955 (1994), by which the Security Council requested the Secretary-General to implement the resolution urgently and to make practical arrangements for the effective functioning of the Tribunal, including recommendations to the Council as to possible locations for the seat of the Tribunal, and to report periodically to the Council.

5. While the Council has been periodically informed of the implementation of resolution 955 (1994), through letters from the Secretary-General, oral briefings and recently through the progress report on the United Nations Assistance Mission for Rwanda (UNAMIR) (S/1995/107, paras. 19–22), this is the first time that the Secretary-General is submitting a formal report on the Tribunal. Accordingly, I have decided that it would be useful to provide the Council with a comprehensive report. The first section analyses the legal basis for the establishment of the International Tribunal for Rwanda (hereinafter also referred to as "the Rwanda Tribunal") and its legal status. The second contains a succinct review of the main provisions of the statute of the Rwanda Tribunal where they differ from the provisions of the statute of the International Tribunal for the Prosecution of Persons Responsible for Serious Violations of International Humanitarian Law Committed in the Territory of the Former Yugoslavia (hereinafter "the Yugoslav Tribunal") (see S/25704). The third section of the report outlines the two-stage approach

---

[1] General Assembly resolution 260 (A) (III).

to the establishment of the Rwanda Tribunal and the practical arrangements made thus far for its functioning. Finally, in the fourth section of the report, the Secretary-General examines the various options for the location of the seat of the Tribunal in the light of the criteria set out in paragraph 6 of resolution955 (1994) and makes his recommendation for the location of the seat of the Tribunal.

II. LEGAL BASIS FOR THE ESTABLISHMENT OF THE INTERNATIONAL TRIBUNAL FOR RWANDA

D2–002   6. Having determined on two previous occasions that the situation in Rwanda constituted a threat to peace and security in the region,[2] the Council, in its resolution 955 (1994), determined that the situation in Rwanda continued to constitute a threat to international peace and security and, accordingly, decided to establish the International Tribunal for Rwanda under Chapter VII of the Charter of the United Nations. The establishment of the International Tribunal under Chapter VII, notwithstanding the request received from the Government of Rwanda,[3] was necessary to ensure not only the cooperation of Rwanda throughout the life-span of the Tribunal, but the cooperation of all States in whose territory persons alleged to have committed serious violations of international humanitarian law and acts of genocide in Rwanda might be situated. A Tribunal based on a Chapter VII resolution was also necessary to ensure a speedy and expeditious method of establishing the Tribunal.

7. Unlike the establishment of the Yugoslav Tribunal, which was done in a two-stage process of two Security Council resolutions (resolutions 808 (1993) and827 (1993)), the Security Council decided that, in drawing upon the experience gained in the Yugoslav Tribunal, a one-step process and a single resolution would suffice to establish the International Tribunal for Rwanda.

8. The International Tribunal for Rwanda is a subsidiary organ of the Security Council within the meaning of Article 29 of the Charter. As such, it is dependent in administrative and financial matters on various United Nations organs; as a judicial body, however, it is independent of any one particular State or group of States, including its parent body, the Security Council.

9. The establishment of the Rwanda Tribunal at a time when the Yugoslav Tribunal was already in existence, dictated a similar legal approach to the establishment of the Tribunal. It also mandated that certain organizational and institutional links be established between the two Tribunals to ensure a unity of legal approach, as well as economy and efficiency of resources. The statute of the Rwanda Tribunal, which was an adaptation of the statute of the Yugoslav Tribunal to the circumstances of Rwanda, was drafted by the original sponsors of Security Council resolution 955 (1994) and discussed among members of the Council. Rwanda, as a member of the Security Council at the time that resolution 955 (1994) was adopted, thus participated fully in the deliberations on the statute and the negotiations leading to the adoption of the resolution.

---

[2] In resolution 918 (1994), the Council decided to impose sanctions against Rwanda and, in resolution 929 (1994), it authorized a temporary humanitarian operation under the command and control of a Member State("Operation Turquoise").

[3] In its letter to the Secretary-General of 6 August 1994, the Government of Rwanda stated that an international tribunal, along the lines of the Yugoslav Tribunal, would help to promote peace and reconciliation among the parties and remove destabilizing elements from Rwanda and neighbouring States. The Government undertook to prevent summary executions and to hold in custody persons alleged to have committed acts of genocide pending prosecution by the International Tribunal. In addition, in a statement dated 28 September 1994 on the question of refugees and security in Rwanda (S/1994/1115, annex), the Government of Rwanda called for the setting up, as soon as possible, of an international tribunal to try persons alleged to have committed genocide.

III. Main Provisions of the Statute of The International Tribunal for Rwanda

A. COMPETENCE OF THE INTERNATIONAL TRIBUNAL

10. The competence of the International Tribunal for Rwanda is circumscribed in time, place and subject-matter jurisdiction. Article 1 of the statute provides that the International Tribunal shall have the power to prosecute persons responsible for serious violations of international humanitarian law committed in the territory of Rwanda and Rwandese citizens responsible for such violations committed in the territory of neighbouring States, between 1 January 1994 and 31 December 1994. The crimes in respect of which the Tribunal is competent are set out in articles 2 to 4 of the statute.

D2–003

1. Subject-matter jurisdiction

11. Given the nature of the conflict as non-international in character, the Council has incorporated within the subject-matter jurisdiction of the Tribunal violations of international humanitarian law which may either be committed in both international and internal armed conflicts, such as the crime of genocide[4] and crimes against humanity,[5] or may be committed only in internal armed conflict, such as violations of article 3 common to the four Geneva Conventions,[6] as more fully elaborated in article 4 of Additional Protocol II.[7]

D2–004

12. In that latter respect, the Security Council has elected to take a more expansive approach to the choice of the applicable law than the one underlying the statute of the Yugoslav Tribunal, and included within the subject-matter jurisdiction of the Rwanda Tribunal international instruments regardless of whether they were considered part of customary international law or whether they have customarily entailed the individual criminal responsibility of the perpetrator of the crime. Article 4 of the statute, accordingly, includes violations of Additional Protocol II, which, as a whole, has not yet been universally recognized as part of customary international law, and for the first time criminalizes common article 3 of the four Geneva Conventions.[8]

2. Territorial and temporal jurisdiction

13. The territorial jurisdiction of the International Tribunal extends beyond the territory of Rwanda to that of neighbouring States, in respect of serious violations of international humanitarian law committed by Rwandese citizens. In extending the

D2–005

---

[4] Genocide, according to article I of the Genocide Convention, is a crime under international law whether committed in time of peace or in time of war.

[5] Crimes against humanity were described in article 5 of the statute of the Yugoslav Tribunal as those enumerated in the article, "when committed in armed conflict, whether international or internal in character". Article 3 of the Rwanda statute makes no reference to the temporal scope of the crime; there is, therefore, no reason to limit its application in that respect.

[6] Convention for the Amelioration of the Condition of the Wounded and Sick in Armed Forces in the Field, of 12 August 1949, Convention for the Amelioration of the Condition of the Wounded, Sick and Shipwrecked Members of Armed Forces at Sea, of 12 August 1949, Convention relative to the Treatment of Prisoners-of-War of 12 August 1949, Convention relative to the Protection of Civilian Persons in Time of War, of 12 August 1949 (United Nations, *Treaty Series*, vol. 75, No. 970–973).

[7] Protocol Additional to the Geneva Conventions of 12 August 1949 and relating to the Protection of Victims of Non-International Armed Conflicts(Protocol II) of 8 June 1977, (United Nations, Treaty Series, vol. 1125, No. 17513).

[8] Although the question of whether common article 3 entails the individual responsibility of the perpetrator of the crime is still debatable, some of the crimes included therein, when committed against the civilian population, also constitute crimes against humanity and as such are customarily recognized as entailing the criminal responsibility of the individual.

territorial jurisdiction of the Tribunal beyond the territorial bounds of Rwanda, the Council envisaged mainly the refugee camps in Zaire and other neighbouring countries in which serious violations of international humanitarian law are alleged to have been committed in connection with the conflict in Rwanda.

14. The temporal jurisdiction of the Tribunal is limited to one year, beginning on 1 January 1994 and ending on 31 December 1994. Although the crash of the aircraft carrying the Presidents of Rwanda and Burundi on 6 April 1994 is considered to be the event that triggered the civil war and the acts of genocide that followed, the Council decided that the temporal jurisdiction of the Tribunal would commence on 1 January 1994, in order to capture the planning stage of the crimes.

B. ORGANIZATION AND STRUCTURE OF THE INTERNATIONAL TRIBUNAL

D2–006   15. The International Tribunal for Rwanda consists of three organs:
  (a) The chambers, comprising two trial chambers and an appeals chamber; each Trial Chamber is composed of three judges and the Appeals Chamber is composed of five;
  (b) A Prosecutor; and
  (c) A Registry.

16. Under article 12, paragraph 2, of the statute, the members of the Appeals Chamber of the International Tribunal for the Former Yugoslavia shall also serve as the members of the Appeals Chamber of the International Tribunal for Rwanda. In providing for a common Appeals Chamber for the two Tribunals, the Council was aware of the fact that, if no restrictions are put on the nationalities of nominees for judges, there could be a situation where more than one judge of the Rwanda Tribunal will have the same nationality. In order to prevent such an eventuality, article 12, paragraph 3 (b), of the Rwanda statute provides in its relevant part that:

". . . each State may nominate up to two candidates meeting the qualifications set out in paragraph 1 above, no two of whom shall be of the same nationality and neither of whom shall be of the same nationality as any judge of the Appeals Chamber".

17. Article 15, paragraph 3 of the Statute of the Rwanda Tribunal provides that the Prosecutor of the International Tribunal for the Former Yugoslavia shall also serve as the Prosecutor of the International Tribunal for Rwanda, with such additional staff, including an additional Deputy Prosecutor, to assist with prosecutions before the International Tribunal for Rwanda. The statute thus envisages commonality not only in the person of the Prosecutor, but also in the staff of the Prosecutor's Office.

C. OTHER STATUTORY PROVISIONS

D2–007   18. Article 14 of the statute of the Rwanda Tribunal provides that the judges of the International Tribunal shall adopt the rules of procedure and evidence for the conduct of the pretrial phase of the proceedings, trials and appeals, the admission of evidence, the protection of victims and witnesses and other appropriate matters of the International Tribunal for the Former Yugoslavia, with such changes as they deem necessary. It was thus the intention of the Council that, although the rules of procedure and evidence of the Yugoslav Tribunal should not be made expressly applicable to the Rwanda Tribunal, they should nevertheless serve as a model from which deviations will be made when the particular circumstances of Rwanda so warrant.

19. Imprisonment shall, according to article 26 of the statute, be served in Rwanda, or in any of the States on a list of States that have indicated to the Security Council their willingness to accept convicted persons. Unlike the former Yugoslavia, Rwanda is not excluded from the list of States where prison sentences pronounced by the International Tribunal for Rwanda may be served.

20. Article 30 of the statute provides that the expenses of the Tribunal shall be the expenses of the Organization in accordance with Article 17 of the Charter. In clearly

distinguishing between the competence of the Security Council to establish the International Tribunal and the budgetary authority of the General Assembly to decide on its financing, the Security Council did not pronounce itself on the mode of financing, i.e., regular budget or a special account.

III. Practical Implementation of Security Council Resolution 955 (1994)

21. The urgent need to start up the operation of the International Tribunal for **D2–008** Rwanda immediately necessitated a phased approach to the establishment of the Tribunal in accordance with the chronological order of the legal process, from the stage of the investigation and the preparation of indictments to the conduct of trial proceedings. A phased approach also facilitated more accurate estimates of the full financial requirements of the Tribunal over time and as information became gradually available.

22. I, therefore, approved a plan for the establishment of the Tribunal in two phases. The first phase envisaged the establishment of an investigative/prosecutorial unit, the appointment of the Deputy Prosecutor and a core unit of investigators, prosecutors and interpreters, the retention of office premises for the Investigative/prosecutorial Unit, the establishment of an Administrative unit and a secretariat, and the preparation of a request for initial funding. In the second phase, judges will be elected, practical arrangements for the establishment of the seat will be put in place, the staffing will be completed and the Tribunal, as a whole, will be fully operational.

A. FIRST PHASE OF THE OPERATION OF THE INTERNATIONAL TRIBUNAL

23. The first phase of the operation of the International Tribunal for Rwanda began **D2–009** with the establishment of the Investigative/prosecutorial Unit in Kigali. The main functions of the Unit are to establish the Prosecutor's Office and recruit staff, gather documents and information from Governments, intergovernmental and non-governmental organizations, transfer all information collected from the Commission of Experts established pursuant to Security Council resolution 935 (1994) and the Special Investigative Unit established by the High Commissioner for Human Rights, develop the investigative strategy and field operational procedures and initiate the process of investigations and the preparation of indictments.

24. With a view to utilizing, to the extent possible, existing human and financial resources and drawing upon the experience already gained by the Prosecutor and the High Commissioner for Human Rights in the investigations of serious violations of international humanitarian law, it was decided that the core Investigative Unit would consist of investigators of the Prosecutor's Office of the International Tribunal for the Former Yugoslavia and of the Special Investigative Unit established by the High Commissioner for Human Rights.

25. In accordance with article 15, paragraph 3, of the statute of the Rwanda Tribunal, I appointed Mr. Honoráe Rakotomanana (Madagascar) as the Deputy Prosecutor. Mr. Rakotomanana has already initiated the operation of the Unit in Kigali and is engaged in staffing his Office.

26. Temporary office space for the initial phase of the operation of the Investigative/Prosecutorial Unit has been identified in the UNICEF Building in Kigali, where the core investigative Unit is currently located. Office premises in the UNAMIR compound have also been identified as a possible permanent location for the Unit.

27. Security for the Investigative/Prosecutorial Unit, its premises and investigators while on mission, will be provided by UNAMIR in accordance with Security Council resolution 965 (1994).

28. A small Administrative Unit has been established, initially within the Office of Legal Affairs, to support the start-up operations of the Prosecutor's Office in Rwanda. The Administrative Unit, which forms the core registry, is presently handling all

administrative, financial and personnel matters pertaining to the commencement of the operation of the Tribunal.

29. A trust fund to assist in the activities of the International Tribunal for Rwanda was established by the Secretary-General pursuant to Security Council resolution 955 (1994), and a letter inviting States, intergovernmental and non-governmental organizations to contribute funds, equipment and services to the International Tribunal, including the offer of expert personnel, was sent out on 9 January 1995. Contributions to the Trust Fund have already been received from several States, including a pledge to donate equipment in the equivalent amount of $1 million.

30. Pending the preparation of a full budgetary submission to the General Assembly of the estimated financial requirements of the International Tribunal for Rwanda for the biennium 1994-1995, a request has been submitted to the Advisory Committee on Administrative and Budgetary Questions (ACABQ) for the initial funding of the first phase of the operation, i.e., 1 January-31 March 1995. The estimated requirements, based on the anticipated activities to be carried out during that period are in the amount of $3,951,200. They include recruitment of the core investigative and administrative staff, retention of office premises, procurement and establishment of computer and communications systems, administrative costs, costs of transfer of materials between Rwanda, Geneva and The Hague in connection with the Commission of Experts and travel costs on official business between these locations and within Rwanda.

31. Pending consideration of the request by ACABQ, resources have been made available from the Trust Fund to permit initial recruitment and travel of staff from the Yugoslav Tribunal to Rwanda. In addition, the Secretary-General has authorized expenditures up to a maximum of $191,600 for the period 15 January to14 February 1995.

B. SECOND PHASE OF THE OPERATION OF THE INTERNATIONAL TRIBUNAL

D2–010 32. Once the Security Council has made a determination as to the seat of the Tribunal, the process of electing judges will commence. With a common Appeals Chamber composed of five judges already in place, only six trial judges will have to be elected. Since the judges have to adopt rules of procedure and evidence, it is essential that they are elected as soon as possible. At the same time it is important that the judges take office shortly before the commencement of trial proceedings to avoid the financial implications entailed in their taking office too early. I therefore envisage a special session of the judges to be convened for the sole purpose of adopting the rules of procedure and evidence.

33. Upon the determination of the seat, negotiations will be undertaken by the Office of Legal Affairs with the host country to conclude a headquarters agreement and a lease agreement for the premises of the Tribunal.

34. During the second stage of the operation of the Tribunal, the process of the staffing of the Prosecutor's Office and the Registry will be completed and the Tribunal, as a whole, will be fully operational.

IV. LOCATION OF THE SEAT OF THE INTERNATIONAL TRIBUNAL FOR RWANDA

A. GUIDELINES FOR THE DETERMINATION OF THE SEAT

D2–011 35. By paragraph 6 of its resolution 955 (1994), the Security Council decided that the seat of the International Tribunal would be determined by the Council, having regard to considerations of justice and fairness as well as administrative efficiency, including access to witnesses, and economy and subject to the conclusion of appropriate arrangements between the United Nations and the State of the seat acceptable to the Council, having regard to the fact that the International Tribunal may meet away from its seat when it considers it necessary for the efficient exercise of its functions. The Council further more decided that an office will be established and proceedings will be conducted in Rwanda, where feasible and appropriate, subject to the conclusion of similar appropriate arrangements.

36. In examining the question of the seat for the purpose of paragraph 6 of Security Council resolution 955 (1994), a flexible approach was adopted. Although normally, the seat of a tribunal would indicate the place where all its organs are located, in the present case the "seat" of the International Tribunal for Rwanda is interpreted to mean the place where trial proceedings are held and trial chambers are located. With a common Appeals Chamber and a common Prosecutor already located in The Hague and the Investigative/Prosecutorial Unit already established in Kigali, the operations of the Rwanda Tribunal, ranging from investigation, preparation of indictments and trial proceedings, both in the Trial Chambers and in the Appeals Chamber, will most probably be carried out in three different locations. It may be noted, however, that, although the various organs of the International Tribunal, wherever located, form part of the Tribunal, a determination of the seat is required by paragraph 6 of resolution955 (1994) only in respect of the location of trial proceedings.

37. In examining the possible locations for the seat of the Tribunal in the light of the criteria set out in paragraph 6 of resolution 955 (1994), the Secretary-General has been guided by the preference expressed for Rwanda as the location of the seat if feasible and appropriate, or for any other location meeting the criteria set out in the resolution, including, in particular," access to witnesses". A preference for an "African seat" was thus indicated by the Security Council. Based on this preference the Secretary-General decided that a technical mission to identify suitable premises for the seat of the International Tribunal would visit Rwanda and two of its neighbouring countries, Kenya and the United Republic of Tanzania.

B. VARIOUS OPTIONS FOR THE LOCATION OF THE SEAT

1. Technical mission report

38. A technical mission headed by the Chief, Administrative and Operations Section, Buildings Management Service of the United Nations Secretariat, visited Rwanda, Kenya and the United Republic of Tanzania during the second half of December 1994. In surveying available premises for the seat of the Tribunal in all three locations, the mission concluded that:

D2–012

(a) There is a severe shortage of premises in Kigali that could accommodate the needs of the Tribunal properly and provide adequate security. Most buildings suffered heavy damage as a result of the war and extensive and costly repairs would be needed to make them operational again;

(b) Nairobi, as a possible location for the seat of the Tribunal, has the advantage of having the necessary infrastructure, support facilities and communication systems and, more importantly, it has a large United Nations presence. Government officials initially indicated that they would be willing to assist in identifying suitable premises if requested to do so by their Government;

(c) Unlike Nairobi, Arusha lacks adequate infrastructure, and a great number of support facilities would have to be imported. The Government of the United Republic of Tanzania, however, indicated its willingness to support the International Tribunal and assist in its accommodation in Arusha. In that connection a concrete offer was made for the Tribunal to use the premises of the Arusha International Conference Centre for its seat. The mission concluded that, with the necessary construction work, the Centre, which is a self-contained complex equipped with a developed communication system and other facilities, could constitute suitable premises for the seat of the Tribunal.

39. Following the submission of the technical report, a formal request was addressed by the Legal Counsel to the Kenyan Mission to the United Nations to assist in identifying suitable premises for the seat of the Tribunal. In response, the Permanent Representative of Kenya informed the Legal Counsel that, after careful consideration of

the various aspects relating to the location of the Tribunal, the Kenyan Government decided that it would not be in a position to provide a seat for the Tribunal.

40. The question of the seat was also raised in a meeting between the Director and Deputy to the Under-Secretary-General, Office of the Legal Counsel, and the Permanent Representative of Rwanda to the United Nations. The Rwandan Ambassador reiterated his Government's position that the seat of the Tribunal should be located in Kigali for the moral and educational value that its presence there would have for the local population. In a spirit of compromise and cooperation, however, he indicated that his Government would raise no objection to the seat of the Tribunal being established in a location easily accessible to Rwanda in a neighbouring State.

2. Criteria for determination of the seat

D2–013   41. Against this background the Secretary-General has undertaken an examination of the criteria set out in paragraph 6 of resolution 955 (1994) in respect of two countries: Rwanda and the United Republic of Tanzania.

"Justice and fairness"

D2–014   42. In the view of the Secretary-General, the criterion of "justice and fairness" in the context of selecting a location for the seat means the conduct of trial proceedings in an environment that would ensure justice and fairness to both victims and accused. Although the international character of the Rwanda Tribunal is a guarantee of the just and fair conduct of the legal process, it is nevertheless necessary to ensure not only the reality but also the appearance of complete impartiality and objectivity in the prosecution of persons responsible for crimes committed by both sides to the conflict. Justice and fairness, therefore, require that trial proceedings be held in a neutral territory.

43. In this connection, the Secretary-General notes that, in the atmosphere now prevailing in Rwanda, there are serious security risks in bringing into the country leaders of the previous regime alleged to have committed acts of genocide to stand trial before the International Tribunal.

"Administrative efficiency and economy"

D2–015   44. On the basis of the technical report, the choice of Kigali as the seat of the Tribunal, even if premises were available, would have entailed extensive and costly repairs to make them operational again. Arusha, on the other hand, has the advantage of having readily available premises, which may be offered either rent-free, or at a very low rate. Furthermore, the proximity of Arusha to victims, witnesses and potential accused persons situated in Rwanda and neighbouring States, and its accessibility by air to and from all of these locations, will considerably reduce the travel costs that would be otherwise entailed in the choice of a more distant location.

3. Recommendation for the seat

D2–016   45. On the basis of the foregoing and given the positions of the Governments of Rwanda, Kenya and the United Republic of Tanzania and having, in addition, examined the considerations of justice and fairness as well as administrative efficiency, including access to witnesses, and economy, as mandated by paragraph 6 of Security Council resolution 955 (1994), it is my conclusion that the choice of Rwanda as the location of the seat would not be feasible or appropriate and that Arusha, the United Republic of Tanzania, should be selected as the seat of the Tribunal. I, therefore, recommend to the Security Council that, subject to appropriate arrangements between the United Nations and the Government of the United Republic of Tanzania acceptable to the Council, Arusha be determined as the seat of the International Tribunal for Rwanda.

D3. Statute of the International Tribunal

As amended

CONTENTS

STATUTE OF THE INTERNATIONAL CRIMINAL TRIBUNAL FOR RWANDA

RESOLUTION 1165 (1998) ADOPTED BY THE SECURITY COUNCIL AT ITS 3877TH MEETING, ON 30 APRIL 1998

D3–001   *The Security Council,*

Reaffirming its resolution 955 (1994) of 8 November 1994,

Recalling its decision in that resolution to consider increasing the number of judges and Trial Chambers of the International Tribunal for Rwanda if it becomes necessary,

Remaining convinced that in the particular circumstances of Rwanda, the prosecution of persons responsible for serious violations of international humanitarian law will contribute to the process of national reconciliation and to the restoration and maintenance of peace in Rwanda and in the region,

Stressing the need for international cooperation to strengthen the Courts and Judicial System of Rwanda, having regard in particular to the necessity for those Courts to deal with a large number of accused awaiting trial,

Having considered the letter of the President of the International Tribunal for Rwanda, transmitted by identical letters from the Secretary-General to the Presidents of the Security Council and the General Assembly dated 15 October 1997 (S/1997/812),

Convinced of the need to increase the number of judges and Trial Chambers, in order to enable the International Tribunal for Rwanda to try without delay the large number of accused awaiting trial,

Noting the progress being made in improving the efficient functioning of the International Tribunal for Rwanda, and convinced of the need for its organs to continue their efforts to further such progress,

Acting under Chapter VII of the Charter of the United Nations,

1. *Decides* to establish a third Trial Chamber of the International Tribunal for Rwanda, and to this end *decides* to amend Articles 10, 11 and 12 of the Statute of the Tribunal and to replace those Articles with the provisions set out in the annex to this resolution;

2. *Decides* that the elections for the judges of the three Trial Chambers shall be held together, for a term of office to expire on 24 May 2003;

3. *Decides* that, as an exceptional measure to enable the third Trial Chamber to begin to function at the earliest possible date and without prejudice to Article 12, paragraph 5, of the Statute of the International Tribunal for Rwanda, three newly elected judges, designated by the Secretary-General in consultation with the President of the International Tribunal, shall commence their term of office as soon as possible following the elections;

4. *Urges* all States to cooperate fully with the International Tribunal for Rwanda and its organs in accordance with resolution 955 (1994), and *welcomes* the cooperation already extended to the International Tribunal in the fulfilment of its mandate;

5. *Urges also* the organs of the International Tribunal for Rwanda actively to continue their efforts to increase further the efficiency of the work of the International Tribunal in their respective area and in this connection *further calls upon* them to consider how their procedures and methods of work could be enhanced, taking into account relevant recommendations in this regard;

6. *Requests* the Secretary-General to make practical arrangements for the elections mentioned in paragraph 2 above and for enhancing the effective functioning of the International Tribunal for Rwanda, including the timely provision of personnel and facilities, in particular for the third Trial Chamber and related offices of the Prosecutor, and further requests him to keep the Security Council closely informed of progress in this regard;

7. *Decides* to remain actively seized of the matter.

[*NEXT PARAGRAPH IS D3–003*]

RESOLUTION 1329 (2000) ADOPTED BY THE SECURITY COUNCIL AT ITS 4240TH MEETING, ON 30 NOVEMBER 2000

The Security Council,

Reaffirming its resolutions 827 (1993) of 25 May 1993 and 995 (1994) of 8 November 1994,

Remaining convinced that the prosecution of persons responsible for serious violations of international humanitarian law committed in the territory of the former Yugoslavia contributes to the restoration and maintenance of peace in the former Yugoslavia,

Remaining convinced also that in the particular circumstances of Rwanda the prosecution of persons responsible for genocide and other serious violations of international humanitarian law contributes to the process of national reconciliation and to the restoration and maintenance of peace in Rwanda and in the region,

Having considered the letter from the Secretary-General to the President of the Security Council dated 7 September 2000 (S/2000/865) and the annexed letters from the President of the International Tribunal for the Former Yugoslavia addressed to the Secretary-General dated 12 May 2000 and from the President of the International Tribunal for Rwanda dated 14 June 2000,

Convinced of the need to establish a pool of *ad litem* judges in the International Tribunal for the Former Yugoslavia and to increase the number of judges in the Appeals Chambers of the International Tribunals in order to enable the International Tribunals to expedite the conclusion of their work at the earliest possible date,

Noting the significant progress being made in improving the procedures of the International Tribunals, and convinced of the need for their organs to continue their efforts to further such progress,

Taking note of the position expressed by the International Tribunals that civilian, military and paramilitary leaders should be tried before them in preference to minor actors,

Recalling that the International Tribunals and national courts have concurrent jurisdiction to prosecute persons for serious violations of international humanitarian law, and noting that the Rules of Procedure and Evidence of the International Tribunal for the Former Yugoslavia provide that a Trial Chamber ma y decide to suspend an indictment to allow for a national court to deal with a particular case,

Taking note with appreciation of the efforts of the judges of the International Tribunal for the Former Yugoslavia, as reflected in annex I to the letter from the Secretary-General of 7 September 2000, to allow competent organs of the United Nations to begin to form a relatively exact idea of the length of the mandate of the Tribunal,

Acting under Chapter VII of the Charter of the United Nations,

1. *Decides* to establish a pool of *ad litem* judges in the International Tribunal for the Former Yugoslavia and to enlarge the membership of the Appeals Chambers of the International Tribunal for the Former Yugoslavia and the International Tribunal for Rwanda, and to this end decides to amend articles 12, 13 and 14 of the Statute of the International Tribunal for the Former Yugoslavia and to replace those articles with the provisions set out in annex I to this resolution and decides also to amend articles 11, 12 and 13 of the Statute of the International Tribunal for Rwanda and to replace those articles with the provisions set out in annex II to this resolution;

2. *Decides* that two additional judges shall be elected as soon as possible as judges of the International Tribunal for Rwanda and decides also, without prejudice to Article 12, paragraph 4, of the Statut e of that Tribunal, that, once elected, they shall serve until the date of the expiry of the terms of office of the existing judges, and that for the purpose of that election the Security Council shall, notwithstanding Article 12, paragraph 2 (c) of the Statute, establish a list from the nominations received of not less than four and not more than six candidates;

3. *Decides* that, once two judges have been elected in accordance with paragraph 2 above and have taken up office, the President of the International Tribunal for Rwanda shall, in accordance with Article 13, paragraph 3, of the Statute of the International Tribunal for Rwanda and Article 14, paragraph 4, of the Statute of the International

Tribunal for the Former Yugoslavia, take the necessary steps as soon as is practicable to assign two of the judges elected or appointed in accordance with Article 12 of the Statute of the International Tribunal for Rwanda to be members of the Appeals Chambers of the International Tribunals;

4. *Requests* the Secretary-General to make practical arrangements for the elections mentioned in paragraph 2 above, for the election as soon as possible of twenty-seven *ad litem* judges in accordance with Article 13*ter* of the Statute of the International Tribunal for the Former Yugoslavia, and for the timely provision to the International Tribunal for the Former Yugoslavia and the International Tribunal for Rwanda of personnel and facilities, in particular, for the *ad litem* judges and the Appeals Chambers and related offices of the Prosecutor, and further requests him to keep the Security Council closely informed of progress in this regard;

5. *Urges* all States to cooperate fully with the International Tribunals and their organs in accordance with their obligations under resolutions 827 (1993) and 955 (1994) and the Statutes of the International Tribunals, and welcomes the cooperation already extended to the Tribunals in the fulfilment of their mandates;

6. *Requests* the Secretary-General to submit to the Security Council, as soon as possible, a report containing an assessment and proposals regarding the date ending the temporal jurisdiction of the International Tribunal for the Former Yugoslavia;

7. *Decides* to remain actively seized of the matter.

RESOLUTION 1411 (2002) ADOPTED BY THE SECURITY COUNCIL AT ITS 4535TH MEETING, ON 17 MAY 2002

D3–004   *The Security Council*,

Reaffirming its resolutions 827 (1993) of 25 May 1993, 955 (1994) of 8 November 1994, 1165 (1998) of 30 April 1998, 1166 (1998) of 13 May 1998 and 1329 (2000) of 30 November 2000,

Recognizing that persons who are nominated for, or who are elected or appointed as, judges of the International Tribunal for the Former Yugoslavia or of the International Tribunal for Rwanda may bear the nationalities of two or more States,

Being aware that at least one such person has already been elected a judge of one of the International Tribunals,

Considering that, for the purposes of membership of the Chambers of the International Tribunals, such persons should be regarded as bearing solely the nationality of the State in which they ordinarily exercise civil and political rights,

Acting under Chapter VII of the Charter of the United Nations,

1. *Decides* to amend article 12 of the Statute of the International Tribunal for the Former Yugoslavia and to replace that article with the provisions set out in annex I to this resolution;

2. *Decides* also to amend article 11 of the Statute of the International Tribunal for Rwanda and to replace that article with the provisions set out in annex II to this resolution;

3. *Decides* to remain actively seized of the matter.

[NEXT PARAGRAPH IS D3–006]

RESOLUTION 1503 (2003) ADOPTED BY THE SECURITY COUNCIL AT ITS 4817TH MEETING, ON 28 AUGUST 2003

D3–006   *The Security Council*,

Recalling its resolutions 827 (1993) of 25 May 1993, 955 (1994) of 8 November 1994, 978 (1995) of 27 February 1995, 1165 (1998) of 30 April 1998,1166 (1998) of 13 May

1998, 1329 (2000) of 30 November 2000, 1411 (2002) of 17 May 2002, 1431 (2002) of 14 August 2002, and 1481 (2003) of 19 May 2003,

Noting the letter from the Secretary-General to the President of the Security Council dated 28 July 2003 (S/2003/766),

Commending the important work of the International Criminal Tribunal for the Former Yugoslavia (ICTY) and the International Criminal Tribunal for Rwanda (ICTR) in contributing to lasting peace and security in the former Yugoslavia and Rwanda and the progress made since their inception,

Noting that an essential prerequisite to achieving the objectives of the ICTY and ICTR Completion Strategies is full cooperation by all States, especially in apprehending all remaining at-large persons indicted by the ICTY and the ICTR,

Welcoming steps taken by States in the Balkans and the Great Lakes region of Africa to improve cooperation and apprehend at-large persons indicted by the ICTY and ICTR, but noting with concern that certain States are still not offering full cooperation,

Urging Member States to consider imposing measures against individuals and groups or organizations assisting indictees at large to continue to evade justice, including measures designed to restrict the travel and freeze the assets of such individuals, groups, or organizations,

Recalling and reaffirming in the strongest terms the statement of 23 July 2002 made by the President of the Security Council (S/PRST/2002/21), which endorsed the ICTY's strategy for completing investigations by the end of 2004, all trial activities at first instance by the end of 2008, and all of its work in 2010 (ICTY Completion Strategy) (S/2002/678), by concentrating on the prosecution and trial of the most senior leaders suspected of being most responsible for crimes within the ICTY's jurisdiction and transferring cases involving those who may not bear this level of responsibility to competent national jurisdictions, as appropriate, as well as the strengthening of the capacity of such jurisdictions,

Urging the ICTR to formalize a detailed strategy, modelled on the ICTY Completion Strategy, to transfer cases involving intermediate- and lower-rank accused to competent national jurisdictions, as appropriate, including Rwanda, in order to allow the ICTR to achieve its objective of completing investigations by the end of 2004, all trial activities at first instance by the end of 2008, and all of its work in 2010 (ICTR Completion Strategy),

Noting that the above-mentioned Completion Strategies in no way alter the obligation of Rwanda and the countries of the former Yugoslavia to investigate those accused whose cases would not be tried by the ICTR or ICTY and take appropriate action with respect to indictment and prosecution, while bearing in mind the primacy of the ICTY and ICTR over national courts,

Noting that the strengthening of national judicial systems is crucially important to the rule of law in general and to the implementation of the ICTY and ICTR Completion Strategies in particular,

Noting that an essential prerequisite to achieving the objectives of the ICTY Completion Strategy is the expeditious establishment under the auspices of the High Representative and early functioning of a special chamber within the State Court of Bosnia and Herzegovina (the "War Crimes Chamber") and the subsequent referral by the ICTY of cases of lower- or intermediate-rank accused to the Chamber,

Convinced that the ICTY and the ICTR can most efficiently and expeditiously meet their respective responsibilities if each has its own Prosecutor,

Acting under Chapter VII of the Charter of the United Nations,

1. *Calls* on the international community to assist national jurisdictions, as part of the completion strategy, in improving their capacity to prosecute cases transferred from the ICTY and the ICTR and encourages the ICTY and ICTR Presidents, Prosecutors, and Registrars to develop and improve their outreach programmes;

2. *Calls* on all States, especially Serbia and Montenegro, Croatia, and Bosnia and Herzegovina, and on the Republika Srpska within Bosnia and Herzegovina, to intensify cooperation with and render all necessary assistance to the ICTY, particularly to bring Radovan Karadzic and Ratko Mladic, as well as Ante Gotovina and all other indictees to the ICTY and calls on these and all other at-large indictees of the ICTY to surrender to the ICTY;

3. *Calls* on all States, especially Rwanda, Kenya, the Democratic Republic of the Congo, and the Republic of the Congo, to intensify cooperation with and render all necessary assistance to the ICTR, including on investigations of the Rwandan Patriotic Army and efforts to bring Felicien Kabuga and all other such indictees to the ICTR and calls on this and all other at-large indictees of the ICTR to surrender to the ICTR;

4. *Calls* on all States to cooperate with the International Criminal Police Organization (ICPO-Interpol) in apprehending and transferring persons indicted bythe ICTY and the ICTR;

5. *Calls* on the donor community to support the work of the High Representative to Bosnia and Herzegovina in creating a special chamber, within the State Court of Bosnia and Herzegovina, to adjudicate allegations of serious violations of international humanitarian law;

6. *Requests* the Presidents of the ICTY and the ICTR and their Prosecutors, in their annual reports to the Council, to explain their plans to implement the ICTY and ICTR Completion Strategies;

7. *Calls* on the ICTY and the ICTR to take all possible measures to complete investigations by the end of 2004, to complete all trial activities at first instance by the end of 2008, and to complete all work in 2010 (the Completion Strategies);

8. *Decides* to amend Article 15 of the Statute of the International Tribunal for Rwanda and to replace that Article with the provision set out in Annex I to this resolution, and requests the Secretary-General to nominate a person to be the Prosecutor of the ICTR;

9. *Welcomes* the intention expressed by the Secretary-General in his letter dated 28 July 2003, to submit to the Security Council the name of Mrs. Carla Del Ponte as nominee for Prosecutor for the ICTY;

10. *Decides* to remain actively seized of the matter.

ANNEX I

ARTICLE 15

THE PROSECUTOR

D3–007　　1. The Prosecutor shall be responsible for the investigation and prosecution of persons responsible for serious violations of international humanitarian law committed in the territory of Rwanda and Rwandan citizens responsible for such violations committed in the territory of neighbouring States, between 1 January 1994 and 31 December 1994.

2. The Prosecutor shall act independently as a separate organ of the International Tribunal for Rwanda. He or she shall not seek or receive instructions from any government or from any other source.

3. The Office of the Prosecutor shall be composed of a Prosecutor and suchother qualified staff as may be required.

4. The Prosecutor shall be appointed by the Security Council on nomination by the Secretary-General. He or she shall be of high moral character and possess the highest level of competence and experience in the conduct of investigations and prosecutions of criminal cases. The Prosecutor shall serve for a four-year term and be eligible for reappointment. The terms and conditions of service of the Prosecutorshall be those of an Under-Secretary-General of the United Nations.

5. The staff of the Office of the Prosecutor shall be appointed by the Secretary-General on the recommendation of the Prosecutor.

[NEXT PARAGRAPH IS D3–011]

RESOLUTION 1534 (2004) ADOPTED BY THE SECURITY COUNCIL AT ITS 4935TH MEETING, ON 26 MARCH 2004

D3–011　　*The Security Council,*

Recalling its resolutions 827 (1993) of 25 May 1993, 955 (1994) of 8 November 1994, 978 (1995) of 27 February 1995, 1165 (1998) of 30 April 1998, 1166 (1998) of 13 May 1998, 1329 (2000) of 30 November 2000, 1411 (2002) of 17 May 2002, 1431 (2002) of 14 August 2002, and 1481 (2003) of 19 May 2003,

Recalling and *reaffirming* in the strongest terms the statement of 23 July 2002 made by the President of the Security Council (S/PRST/2002/21) endorsing the ICTY's completion strategy and its resolution 1503 (2003) of 28 August 2003,

Recalling that resolution 1503 (2003) called on the International Criminal Tribunal for the Former Yugoslavia (ICTY) and the International Criminal Tribunal for Rwanda (ICTR) to take all possible measures to complete investigations by the end of 2004, to complete all trial activities at first instance by the end of 2008, and to complete all work in 2010 (the Completion Strategies), and requested the Presidents and Prosecutors of the ICTY and ICTR, in their annual reports to the Council, to explain their plans to implement the Completion Strategies,

Welcoming the presentations made by the ICTY and ICTR Presidents and Prosecutors to the Security Council on 9 October 2003,

Commending the important work of both Tribunals in contributing to lasting peace and security and national reconciliation and the progress made since their inception, commending them on their efforts so far to give effect to the Completion Strategies and calling on them to ensure effective and efficient use of their budgets, with accountability,

Reiterating its support for the ICTY and ICTR Prosecutors in their continuing efforts to bring at large indictees before the ICTY and the ICTR,

Noting with concern the problems highlighted in the presentations to the Security Council on 9 October 2003 in securing adequate regional cooperation,

Also noting with concern indications in the presentations made on 9 October, that it might not be possible to implement the Completion Strategies set out in resolution 1503 (2003),

Acting under Chapter VII of the Charter of the United Nations,

1. *Reaffirms* the necessity of trial of persons indicted by the ICTY and reiterates its call on all States, especially Serbia and Montenegro, Croatia and Bosnia and Herzegovina, and on the Republika Srpska within Bosnia and Herzegovina, to intensify cooperation with and render all necessary assistance to the ICTY, particularly to bring Radovan Karadzic and Ratko Mladic, as well as Ante Gotovina and all other indictees to the ICTY and calls on all at-large indictees of the ICTY to surrender to the ICTY;

2. *Reaffirms* the necessity of trial of persons indicted by the ICTR and reiterates its call on all States, especially Rwanda, Kenya, the Democratic Republic of the Congo and the Republic of the Congo to intensify cooperation with and render all necessary assistance to the ICTR, including on investigations of the Rwandan Patriotic Army and efforts to bring Felicien Kabuga and all other such indictees to the ICTR and calls on all at-large indictees of the ICTR to surrender to the ICTR;

3. *Emphasizes* the importance of fully implementing the Completion Strategies, as set out in paragraph 7 of resolution 1503 (2003), that calls on the ICTY and ICTR to take all possible measures to complete investigations by the end of 2004, to complete all trial activities at first instance by the end of 2008 and to complete all work in 2010, and urges each Tribunal to plan and act accordingly;

4. *Calls* on the ICTY and ICTR Prosecutors to review the case load of the ICTY and ICTR respectively in particular with a view to determining which cases should be proceeded with and which should be transferred to competent national jurisdictions, as well as the measures which will need to be taken to meet the Completion Strategies referred to in resolution 1503 (2003) and urges them to carry out this review as soon as possible and to include a progress report in the assessments to be provided to the Council under paragraph 6 of this resolution;

5. *Calls on* each Tribunal, in reviewing and confirming any new indictments, to ensure that any such indictments concentrate on the most senior leaders suspected of being most responsible for crimes within the jurisdiction of the relevant Tribunal as set out in resolution 1503 (2003);

6. *Requests* each Tribunal to provide to the Council, by 31 May 2004 and every six months thereafter, assessments by its President and Prosecutor, setting out in detail the

progress made towards implementation of the Completion Strategy of the Tribunal, explaining what measures have been taken to implement the Completion Strategy and what measures remain to be taken, including the transfer of cases involving intermediate and lower rank accused to competent national jurisdictions; and expresses the intention of the Council to meet with the President and Prosecutor of each Tribunal to discuss these assessments;

7. *Declares* the Council's determination to review the situation, and in the light of the assessments received under the foregoing paragraph to ensure that the time frames set out in the Completion Strategies and endorsed by resolution 1503 (2003) can be met;

8. *Commends* those States which have concluded agreements for the enforcement of sentences of persons convicted by the ICTY or the ICTR or have otherwise accepted such convicted persons to serve their sentences in their respective territories; encourages other States in a position to do so to act likewise; and invites the ICTY and the ICTR to continue and intensify their efforts to conclude further agreements for the enforcement of sentences or to obtain the cooperation of other States in this regard;

9. *Recalls* that the strengthening of competent national judicial systems is crucially important to the rule of law in general and to the implementation of the ICTY and ICTR Completion Strategies in particular;

10. *We comes* in particular the efforts of the Office of the High Representative, ICTY, and the donor community to create a war crimes chamber in Sarajevo; encourages all parties to continue efforts to establish the chamber expeditiously; and encourages the donor community to provide sufficient financial support to ensure the success of domestic prosecutions in Bosnia and Herzegovina and in the region;

11. *Decides* to remain actively seized of the matter.

STATUTE OF THE INTERNATIONAL TRIBUNAL FOR RWANDA

D3–012   As amended by the Security Council acting under Chapter VII of the Charter of the United Nations, the International Criminal Tribunal for the Prosecution of Persons Responsible for Genocide and Other Serious Violations of International Humanitarian Law Committed in the Territory of Rwanda and Rwandan Citizens responsible for genocide and other such violations committed in the territory of neighbouring States, between 1 January 1994 and 31 December 1994 (hereinafter referred to as "The International Tribunal for Rwanda") shall function in accordance with the provisions of the present Statute.

ARTICLE 1: COMPETENCE OF THE INTERNATIONAL TRIBUNAL FOR RWANDA

D3–013   The International Tribunal for Rwanda shall have the power to prosecute persons responsible for serious violations of international humanitarian law committed in the territory of Rwanda and Rwandan citizens responsible for such violations committed in the territory of neighbouring States between 1 January 1994 and 31 December 1994, in accordance with the provisions of the present Statute.

ARTICLE 2: GENOCIDE

D3–014   1. The International Tribunal for Rwanda shall have the power to prosecute persons committing genocide as defined in paragraph 2 of this Article or of committing any of the other acts enumerated in paragraph 3 of this Article.

2. Genocide means any of the following acts committed with intent to destroy, in whole or in part, a national, ethnical, racial or religious group, as such:

    (a) Killing members of the group;

    (b) Causing serious bodily or mental harm to members of the group;

    (c) Deliberately inflicting on the group conditions of life calculated to bring about its physical destruction in whole or in part;

(d) Imposing measures intended to prevent births within the group;
(e) Forcibly transferring children of the group to another group.
3. The following acts shall be punishable:
(a) Genocide;
(b) Conspiracy to commit genocide;
(c) Direct and public incitement to commit genocide;
(d) Attempt to commit genocide;
(e) Complicity in genocide.

ARTICLE 3: CRIMES AGAINST HUMANITY

The International Tribunal for Rwanda shall have the power to prosecute persons responsible for the following crimes when committed as part of a widespread or systematic attack against any civilian population on national, political, ethnic, racial or religious grounds:
(a) Murder;
(b) Extermination;
(c) Enslavement;
(d) Deportation;
(e) Imprisonment;
(f) Torture;
(g) Rape;
(h) Persecutions on political, racial and religious grounds;
(i) Other inhumane acts.

D3–015

ARTICLE 4: VIOLATIONS OF ARTICLE 3 COMMON TO THE GENEVA CONVENTIONS AND OF ADDITIONAL PROTOCOL II

The International Tribunal for Rwanda shall have the power to prosecute persons committing or ordering to be committed serious violations of Article 3 common to the Geneva Conventions of 12 August 1949 for the Protection of War Victims, and of Additional Protocol II thereto of 8 June 1977. These violations shall include, but shall not be limited to:
(a) Violence to life, health and physical or mental well-being of persons, in particular murder as well as cruel treatment such as torture, mutilation or any form of corporal punishment;
(b) Collective punishments;
(c) Taking of hostages;
(d) Acts of terrorism;
(e) Outrages upon personal dignity, in particular humiliating and degrading treatment, rape, enforced prostitution and any form of indecent assault;
(f) Pillage;
(g) The passing of sentences and the carrying out of executions without previous judgement pronounced by a regularly constituted court, affording all the judicial guarantees which are recognized as indispensable by civilised peoples;
(h) Threats to commit any of the foregoing acts.

D3–016

ARTICLE 5: PERSONAL JURISDICTION

The International Tribunal for Rwanda shall have jurisdiction over natural persons pursuant to the provisions of the present Statute.

D3–017

ARTICLE 6: INDIVIDUAL CRIMINAL RESPONSIBILITY

1. A person who planned, instigated, ordered, committed or otherwise aided and abetted in the planning, preparation or execution of a crime referred to in Articles 2 to 4 of the present Statute, shall be individually responsible for the crime.

D3–018

2. The official position of any accused person, whether as Head of state or government or as a responsible government official, shall not relieve such person of criminal responsibility nor mitigate punishment.

3. The fact that any of the acts referred to in Articles 2 to 4 of the present Statute was committed by a subordinate does not relieve his or her superior of criminal responsibility if he or she knew or had reason to know that the subordinate was about to commit such acts or had done so and the superior failed to take the necessary and reasonable measures to prevent such acts or to punish the perpetrators thereof.

4. The fact that an accused person acted pursuant to an order of a government or of a superior shall not relieve him or her of criminal responsibility, but may be considered in mitigation of punishment if the International Tribunal for Rwanda determines that justice so requires.

ARTICLE 7: TERRITORIAL AND TEMPORAL JURISDICTION

D3–019   The territorial jurisdiction of the International Tribunal for Rwanda shall extend to the territory of Rwanda including its land surface and airspace as well as to the territory of neighbouring States in respect of serious violations of international humanitarian law committed by Rwandan citizens. The temporal jurisdiction of the International Tribunal for Rwanda shall extend to a period beginning on 1 January 1994 and ending on 31 December 1994.

ARTICLE 8: CONCURRENT JURISDICTION

D3–020   1. The International Tribunal for Rwanda and national courts shall have concurrent jurisdiction to prosecute persons for serious violations of international humanitarian law committed in the territory of Rwanda and Rwandan citizens for such violations committed in the territory of the neighbouring States, between 1 January 1994 and 31 December 1994.

2. The International Tribunal for Rwanda shall have the primacy over the national courts of all States. At any stage of the procedure, the International Tribunal for Rwanda may formally request national courts to defer to its competence in accordance with the present Statute and the Rules of Procedure and Evidence of the International Tribunal for Rwanda.

ARTICLE 9: *NON BIS IN IDEM*

D3–021   1. No person shall be tried before a national court for acts constituting serious violations of international humanitarian law under the present Statute, for which he or she has already been tried by the International Tribunal for Rwanda.

2. A person who has been tried before a national court for acts constituting serious violations of international humanitarian law may be subsequently tried by the International Tribunal for Rwanda only if:

(a) The act for which he or she was tried was characterised as an ordinary crime; or

(b) The national court proceedings were not impartial or independent, were designed to shield the accused from international criminal responsibility, or the case was not diligently prosecuted.

3. In considering the penalty to be imposed on a person convicted of a crime under the present Statute, the International Tribunal for Rwanda shall take into account the extent to which any penalty imposed by a national court on the same person for the same act has already been served.

ARTICLE 10: ORGANISATION OF THE INTERNATIONAL TRIBUNAL FOR RWANDA

D3–022   The International Tribunal for Rwanda shall consist of the following organs:

(a) The Chambers, comprising three Trial Chambers and an Appeals Chamber;
(b) The Prosecutor;
(c) A Registry.

ARTICLE 11: COMPOSITION OF THE CHAMBERS

1. The Chambers shall be composed of sixteen permanent independent judges, no two **D3–023**
of whom may be nationals of the same State, and a maximum at any one time of nine *ad
litem* independent judges appointed in accordance with article 12 *ter*, paragraph 2, of the
present Statute, no two of whom may be nationals of the same State.
2. Three permanent judges and a maximum at any one time of six *ad litem* judges
shall be members of each Trial Chamber. Each Trial Chamber to which *ad litem* judges
are assigned may be divided into sections of three judges each, composed of both
permanent and *ad litem* judges. A section of a Trial Chamber shall have the same powers
and responsibilities as a Trial Chamber under the present Statute and shall render
judgement in accordance with the same rules.
3. Seven of the permanent judges shall be members of the Appeals Chamber. The
Appeals Chamber shall, for each appeal, be composed of five of its members.
4. A person who for the purposes of membership of the Chambers of the International
Tribunal for Rwanda could be regarded as a national of more than one State shall be
deemed to be a national of the State in which that person ordinarily exercises civil and
political rights.

ARTICLE 12: QUALIFICATION AND ELECTION OF JUDGES

The permanent and *ad litem* judges shall be persons of high moral character, **D3–024**
impartiality and integrity who possess the qualifications required in their respective
countries for appointment to the highest judicial offices. In the overall composition of
the Chambers and sections of the Trial Chambers, due account shall be taken of the
experience of the judges in criminal law, international law, including international
humanitarian law and human rights law.

ARTICLE 12*bis*: ELECTION OF PERMANENT JUDGES

1. Eleven of the permanent judges of the International Tribunal for Rwanda shall be **D3–025**
elected by the General Assembly from a list submitted by the Security Council, in the
following manner:
(a) The Secretary-General shall invite nominations for permanent judges of the
   International Tribunal for Rwanda from States Members of the United Nations
   and non-member States maintaining permanent observer missions at United
   Nations Headquarters;
(b) Within sixty days of the date of the invitation of the Secretary-General, each
   State may nominate up to two candidates meeting the qualifications set out in
   article 12 of the present Statute, no two of whom shall be of the same
   nationality and neither of whom shall be of the same nationality as any judge
   who is a member of the Appeals Chamber and who was elected or appointed a
   permanent judge of the International Tribunal for the Prosecution of Persons
   Responsible for Serious Violations of International Humanitarian Law Committed in the Territory of the Former Yugoslavia since 1991 (hereinafter
   referred to as 'the International Tribunal for the Former Yugoslavia') in
   accordance with article 13 *bis* of the Statute of that Tribunal;
(c) The Secretary-General shall forward the nominations received to the Security
   Council. From the nominations received the Security Council shall establish a
   list of not less than twenty-two and not more than thirty-three candidates,
   taking due account of the adequate representation on the International
   Tribunal for Rwanda of the principal legal systems of the world;

(d) The President of the Security Council shall transmit the list of candidates to the President of the General Assembly. From that list the General Assembly shall elect eleven permanent judges of the International Tribunal for Rwanda. The candidates who receive an absolute majority of the votes of the States Members of the United Nations and of the non-member States maintaining permanent observer missions at United Nations Headquarters, shall be declared elected. Should two candidates of the same nationality obtain the required majority vote, the one who received the higher number of votes shall be considered elected.

2. In the event of a vacancy in the Chambers amongst the permanent judges elected or appointed in accordance with this article, after consultation with the Presidents of the Security Council and of the General Assembly, the Secretary-General shall appoint a person meeting the qualifications of article 12 of the present Statute, for the remainder of the term of office concerned.

3. The permanent judges elected in accordance with this article shall be elected for a term of four years. The terms and conditions of service shall be those of the permanent judges of the International Tribunal for the Former Yugoslavia. They shall be eligible for re-election.

ARTICLE 12*ter*: ELECTION AND APPOINTMENT OF *AD LITEM* JUDGES

D3–026 1. The *ad litem* judges of the International Tribunal for Rwanda shall be elected by the General Assembly from a list submitted by the Security Council, in the following manner:

(a) The Secretary-General shall invite nominations for *ad litem* judges of the International Tribunal for Rwanda from States Members of the United Nations and non-member States maintaining permanent observer missions at United Nations Headquarters;

(b) Within sixty days of the date of the invitation of the Secretary-General, each State may nominate up to four candidates meeting the qualifications set out in article 12 of the present Statute, taking into account the importance of a fair representation of female and male candidates;

(c) The Secretary-General shall forward the nominations received to the Security Council. From the nominations received the Security Council shall establish a list of not less than thirty-six candidates, taking due account of the adequate representation of the principal legal systems of the world and bearing in mind the importance of equitable geographical distribution;

(d) The President of the Security Council shall transmit the list of candidates to the President of the General Assembly. From that list the General Assembly shall elect the eighteen *ad litem* judges of the International Tribunal for Rwanda. The candidates who receive an absolute majority of the votes of the States Members of the United Nations and of the non-member States maintaining permanent observer missions at United Nations Headquarters shall be declared elected;

(e) The *ad litem* judges shall be elected for a term of four years. They shall not be eligible for re-election.

2. During their term, *ad litem* judges will be appointed by the Secretary-General, upon request of the President of the International Tribunal for Rwanda, to serve in the Trial Chambers for one or more trials, for a cumulative period of up to, but not including, three years. When requesting the appointment of any particular *ad litem* judge, the President of the International Tribunal for Rwanda shall bear in mind the criteria set out in article 12 of the present Statute regarding the composition of the Chambers and sections of the Trial Chambers, the considerations set out in paragraphs 1 (b) and (c) above and the number of votes the *ad litem* judge received in the General Assembly.

ARTICLE 12*quarter*: STATUS OF *AD LITEM* JUDGES

D3–027 1. During the period in which they are appointed to serve in the International Tribunal for Rwanda, *ad litem* judges shall:

(a) Benefit from the same terms and conditions of service *mutatis mutandis* as the permanent judges of the International Tribunal for Rwanda;

(b) Enjoy, subject to paragraph 2 below, the same powers as the permanent judges of the International Tribunal for Rwanda;

(c) Enjoy the privileges and immunities, exemptions and facilities of a judge of the International Tribunal for Rwanda;

(d) Enjoy the power to adjudicate in pre-trial proceedings in cases other than those that they have been appointed to try.

2. During the period in which they are appointed to serve in the International Tribunal for Rwanda, *ad litem* judges shall not:

(a) Be eligible for election as, or to vote in the election of, the President of the International Tribunal for Rwanda or the Presiding Judge of a Trial Chamber pursuant to article 13 of the present Statute;

(b) Have power:

    (i) To adopt rules of procedure and evidence pursuant to article 14 of the present Statute. They shall, however, be consulted before the adoption of those rules;

    (ii) To review an indictment pursuant to article 18 of the present Statute;

    (iii) To consult with the President of the International Tribunal for Rwanda in relation to the assignment of judges pursuant to article 13 of the present Statute or in relation to a pardon or commutation of sentence pursuant to article 27 of the present Statute.

ARTICLE 13: OFFICERS AND MEMBERS OF THE CHAMBERS

D3–028

1. The permanent judges of the International Tribunal for Rwanda shall elect a President from amongst their number.

2. The President of the International Tribunal for Rwanda shall be a member of one of its Trial Chambers.

3. After consultation with the permanent judges of the International Tribunal for Rwanda, the President shall assign two of the permanent judges elected or appointed in accordance with article 12*bis* of the present Statute to be members of the Appeals Chamber of the International Tribunal for the Former Yugoslavia and eight to the Trial Chambers of the International Tribunal for Rwanda.

4. The members of the Appeals Chamber of the International Tribunal for the Former Yugoslavia shall also serve as the members of the Appeals Chamber of the International Tribunal for Rwanda.

5. After consultation with the permanent judges of the International Tribunal for Rwanda, the President shall assign such *ad litem* judges as may from time to time be appointed to serve in the International Tribunal for Rwanda to the Trial Chambers.

6. A judge shall serve only in the Chamber to which he or she was assigned.

7. The permanent judges of each Trial Chamber shall elect a Presiding Judge from amongst their number, who shall oversee the work of that Trial Chamber as a whole.

ARTICLE 14: RULES OF PROCEDURE AND EVIDENCE

D3–029

The Judges of the International Tribunal for Rwanda shall adopt, for the purpose of proceedings before the International Tribunal for Rwanda, the Rules of Procedure and Evidence for the conduct of the pre-trial phase of the proceedings, trials and appeals, the admission of evidence, the protection of victims and witnesses and other appropriate matters of the International Tribunal for the former Yugoslavia with such changes as they deem necessary.

ARTICLE 15: THE PROSECUTOR

D3–030

1. The Prosecutor shall be responsible for the investigation and prosecution of persons responsible for serious violations of international humanitarian law committed in the territory of Rwanda and Rwandan citizens responsible for such violations committed in the territory of neighbouring States, between 1 January 1994 and 31 December 1994.

2. The Prosecutor shall act independently as a separate organ of the International Tribunal for Rwanda. He or she shall not seek or receive instructions from any government or from any other source.

3. The Office of the Prosecutor shall be composed of a Prosecutor and such other qualified staff as may be required.

4. The Prosecutor shall be appointed by the Security Council on nomination by the Secretary-General. He or she shall be of high moral character and possess the highest level of competence and experience in the conduct of investigations and prosecutions of criminal cases. The Prosecutor shall serve for a four-year term and be eligible for reappointment. The terms and conditions of service of the Prosecutor shall be those of an Under-Secretary-General of the United Nations.

5. The staff of the Office of the Prosecutor shall be appointed by the Secretary-General on the recommendation of the Prosecutor.

ARTICLE 16: THE REGISTRY

D3–031   1. The Registry shall be responsible for the administration and servicing of the International Tribunal for Rwanda.

2. The Registry shall consist of a Registrar and such other staff as may be required.

3. The Registrar shall be appointed by the Secretary-General after consultation with the President of the International Tribunal for Rwanda. He or she shall serve for a four-year term and be eligible for re-appointment. The terms and conditions of service of the Registrar shall be those of an Assistant Secretary-General of the United Nations.

4. The Staff of the Registry shall be appointed by the Secretary-General on the recommendation of the Registrar.

ARTICLE 17: INVESTIGATION AND PREPARATION OF INDICTMENT

D3–032   1. The Prosecutor shall initiate investigations ex-officio or on the basis of information obtained from any source, particularly from governments, United Nations organs, intergovernmental and non-governmental organizations. The Prosecutor shall assess the information received or obtained and decide whether there is sufficient basis to proceed.

2. The Prosecutor shall have the power to question suspects, victims and witnesses, to collect evidence and to conduct on-site investigations. In carrying out these tasks, the Prosecutor may, as appropriate, seek the assistance of the State authorities concerned.

3. If questioned, the suspect shall be entitled to be assisted by Counsel of his or her own choice, including the right to have legal assistance assigned to the suspect without payment by him or her in any such case if he or she does not have sufficient means to pay for it, as well as necessary translation into and from a language he or she speaks and understands.

4. Upon a determination that a *prima facie* case exists, the Prosecutor shall prepare an indictment containing a concise statement of the facts and the crime or crimes with which the accused is charged under the Statute. The indictment shall be transmitted to a judge of the Trial Chamber.

ARTICLE 18: REVIEW OF THE INDICTMENT

D3–033   1. The judge of the Trial Chamber to whom the indictment has been transmitted shall review it. If satisfied that a *prima facie* case has been established by the Prosecutor, he or she shall confirm the indictment. If not so satisfied, the indictment shall be dismissed.

2. Upon confirmation of an indictment, the judge may, at the request of the Prosecutor, issue such orders and warrants for the arrest, detention, surrender or transfer of persons, and any other orders as may be required for the conduct of the trial.

ARTICLE 19: COMMENCEMENT AND CONDUCT OF TRIAL PROCEEDINGS

D3–034   1. The Trial Chambers shall ensure that a trial is fair and expeditious and that proceedings are conducted in accordance with the Rules of Procedure and Evidence, with full respect for the rights of the accused and due regard for the protection of victims and witnesses.

2. A person against whom an indictment has been confirmed shall, pursuant to an order or an arrest warrant of the International Tribunal for Rwanda, be taken into custody, immediately informed of the charges against him or her and transferred to the International Tribunal for Rwanda.

3. The Trial Chamber shall read the indictment, satisfy itself that the rights of the accused are respected, confirm that the accused understands the indictment, and instruct the accused to enter a plea. The Trial Chamber shall then set the date for trial.

4. The hearings shall be public unless the Trial Chamber decides to close the proceedings in accordance with its Rules of Procedure and Evidence.

ARTICLE 20: RIGHTS OF THE ACCUSED

1. All persons shall be equal before the International Tribunal for Rwanda. **D3–035**

2. In the determination of charges against him or her, the accused shall be entitled to a fair and public hearing, subject to Article 21 of the Statute.

3. The accused shall be presumed innocent until proven guilty according to the provisions of the present Statute.

4. In the determination of any charge against the accused pursuant to the present Statute, the accused shall be entitled to the following minimum guarantees, in full equality:

    (a) To be informed promptly and in detail in a language which he or she understands of the nature and cause of the charge against him or her;

    (b) To have adequate time and facilities for the preparation of his or her defence and to communicate with counsel of his or her own choosing;

    (c) To be tried without undue delay;

    (d) To be tried in his or her presence, and to defend himself or herself in person or through legal assistance of his or her own choosing; to be informed, if he or she does not have legal assistance, of this right; and to have legal assistance assigned to him or her, in any case where the interest of justice so require, and without payment by him or her in any such case if he or she does not have sufficient means to pay for it;

    (e) To examine, or have examined, the witnesses against him or her and to obtain the attendance and examination of witnesses on his or her behalf under the same conditions as witnesses against him or her;

    (f) To have the free assistance of an interpreter if he or she cannot understand or speak the language used in the International Tribunal for Rwanda;

    (g) Not to be compelled to testify against himself or herself or to confess guilt.

ARTICLE 21: PROTECTION OF VICTIMS AND WITNESSES

The International Tribunal for Rwanda shall provide in its Rules of Procedure and **D3–036** Evidence for the protection of victims and witnesses. Such protection measures shall include, but shall not be limited to, the conduct of in camera proceedings and the protection of the victim's identity.

ARTICLE 22: JUDGEMENT

1. The Trial Chambers shall pronounce judgements and impose sentences and **D3–037** penalties on persons convicted of serious violations of international humanitarian law.

2. The judgement shall be rendered by a majority of the judges of the Trial Chamber, and shall be delivered by the Trial Chamber in public. It shall be accompanied by a reasoned opinion in writing, to which separate or dissenting opinions may be appended.

ARTICLE 23: PENALTIES

1. The penalty imposed by the Trial Chamber shall be limited to imprisonment. In **D3–038** determining the terms of imprisonment, the Trial Chambers shall have recourse to the general practice regarding prison sentences in the courts of Rwanda.

2. In imposing the sentences, the Trial Chambers should take into account such factors as the gravity of the offence and the individual circumstances of the convicted person.

3. In addition to imprisonment, the Trial Chambers may order the return of any property and proceeds acquired by criminal conduct, including by means of duress, to their rightful owners.

ARTICLE 24: APPELLATE PROCEEDINGS

D3–039   1. The Appeals Chamber shall hear appeals from persons convicted by the Trial Chambers or from the Prosecutor on the following grounds:

(a) An error on a question of law invalidating the decision; or

(b) An error of fact which has occasioned a miscarriage of justice.

2. The Appeals Chamber may affirm, reverse or revise the decisions taken by the Trial Chambers.

ARTICLE 25: REVIEW PROCEEDINGS

D3–040   Where a new fact has been discovered which was not known at the time of the proceedings before the Trial Chambers or the Appeals Chamber and which could have been a decisive factor in reaching the decision, the convicted person or the Prosecutor may submit to the International Tribunal for Rwanda an application for review of the judgement.

ARTICLE 26: ENFORCEMENT OF SENTENCES

D3–041   Imprisonment shall be served in Rwanda or any of the States on a list of States which have indicated to the Security Council their willingness to accept convicted persons, as designated by the International Tribunal for Rwanda. Such imprisonment shall be in accordance with the applicable law of the State concerned, subject to the supervision of the International Tribunal for Rwanda.

ARTICLE 27: PARDON OR COMMUTATION OF SENTENCES

D3–042   If, pursuant to the applicable law of the State in which the convicted person is imprisoned, he or she is eligible for pardon or commutation of sentence, the State concerned shall notify the International Tribunal for Rwanda accordingly. There shall only be pardon or commutation of sentence if the President of the International Tribunal for Rwanda, in consultation with the judges, so decides on the basis of the interests of justice and the general principles of law.

ARTICLE 28: COOPERATION AND JUDICIAL ASSISTANCE

D3–043   1. States shall cooperate with the International Tribunal for Rwanda in the investigation and prosecution of persons accused of committing serious violations of international humanitarian law.

2. States shall comply without undue delay with any request for assistance or an order issued by a Trial Chamber, including but not limited to:

(a) The identification and location of persons;

(b) The taking of testimony and the production of evidence;

(c) The service of documents;

(d) The arrest or detention of persons;

(e) The surrender or the transfer of the accused to the International Tribunal for Rwanda.

ARTICLE 29: THE STATUS, PRIVILEGES AND IMMUNITIES OF THE INTERNATIONAL TRIBUNAL FOR RWANDA

1. The Convention on the Privileges and Immunities of the United Nations of 13 **D3–044** February 1946 shall apply to the International Tribunal for Rwanda, the judges, the Prosecutor and his or her staff, and the Registrar and his or her staff.

2. The judges, the Prosecutor and the Registrar shall enjoy the privileges and immunities, exemptions and facilities accorded to diplomatic envoys, in accordance with international law.

3. The staff of the Prosecutor and of the Registrar shall enjoy the privileges and immunities accorded to officials of the United Nations under Articles V and VII of the Convention referred to in paragraph 1 of this article.

4. Other persons, including the accused, required at the seat or meeting place of the International Tribunal for Rwanda shall be accorded such treatment as is necessary for the proper functioning of the International Tribunal for Rwanda.

ARTICLE 30: EXPENSES OF THE INTERNATIONAL TRIBUNAL FOR RWANDA

The expenses of the International Tribunal for Rwanda shall be expenses of the **D3–045** Organisation in accordance with Article 17 of the Charter of the United Nations.

ARTICLE 31: WORKING LANGUAGES

The working languages of the International Tribunal for Rwanda shall be English and **D3–046** French.

ARTICLE 32: ANNUAL REPORT

The President of the International Tribunal for Rwanda shall submit an annual report **D3–047** of the International Tribunal for Rwanda to the Security Council and to the General Assembly.

D4. Resolution 1431 (2002) Adopted by the Security Council at its 4601st meeting, on 14 August 2002

D4–001   *The Security Council,*

Reaffirming its resolutions 827 (1993) of 25 May 1993, 955 (1994) of 8 November 1994, 1165 (1998) of 30 April 1998, 1166 (1998) of 13 May 1998, 1329 (2000) of 30 November 2000 and 1411 (2002) of 17 May 2002,

Having considered the letter from the Secretary-General to the President of the Security Council dated 14 September 2001 (S/2001/764) and the annexed letter from the President of the International Tribunal for Rwanda addressed to the Secretary-General dated 9 July 2001,

Having considered also the letter from the Secretary-General to the President of the Security Council dated 4 March 2002 (S/2002/241) and the annexed letter from the President of the International Tribunal for Rwanda addressed to the Secretary-General dated 6 February 2002,

Convinced of the need to establish a pool of ad litem judges in the International Tribunal for Rwanda in order to enable the International Tribunal for Rwanda to expedite the conclusion of its work at the earliest possible date and determined to follow closely the progress of the operation of the International Tribunal for Rwanda,

Acting under Chapter VII of the Charter of the United Nations,

1. *Decides* to establish a pool of ad litem judges in the International Tribunal for Rwanda, and to this end *decides* to amend articles 11, 12 and 13 of the Statute of the International Tribunal for Rwanda and to replace those articles with the provisions set out in annex I to this resolution and *decides also* to amend articles 13*bis* and 14 of the Statute of the International Tribunal for the Former Yugoslavia and to replace those articles with the provisions set out in annex II to this resolution;

2. *Requests* the Secretary-General to make practical arrangements for the election as soon as possible of eighteen ad litem judges in accordance with Article 12 ter of the Statute of the International Tribunal for Rwanda and for the timely provision to the International Tribunal for Rwanda of personnel and facilities, in particular, for the ad litem judges and related offices of the Prosecutor, and *further requests* him to keep the Security Council closely informed of progress in this regard;

3. *Urges* all States to cooperate fully with the International Tribunal for Rwanda and its organs in accordance with their obligations under resolution 955 (1994) and the Statute of the International Tribunal for Rwanda;

4. *Decides* to remain actively seized of the matter.

INTERNATIONAL TRIBUNAL FOR RWANDA

Annex I

Article 11

COMPOSITION OF THE CHAMBERS

D4–002   1. The Chambers shall be composed of sixteen permanent independent judges, no two of whom may be nationals of the same State, and a maximum at any one time of four ad litem independent judges appointed in accordance with article 12 ter, paragraph 2, of the present Statute, no two of whom may be nationals of the same State.

2. Three permanent judges and a maximum at any one time of four *ad litem* judges shall be members of each Trial Chamber. Each Trial Chamber to which *ad litem* judges are assigned may be divided into sections of three judges each, composed of both permanent and ad litem judges. A section of a Trial Chamber shall have the same powers and responsibilities as a Trial Chamber under the present Statute and shall render judgement in accordance with the same rules.

3. Seven of the permanent judges shall be members of the Appeals Chamber. The Appeals Chamber shall, for each appeal, be composed of five of its members.

4. A person who for the purposes of membership of the Chambers of the International Tribunal for Rwanda could be regarded as a national of more than one State shall be deemed to be a national of the State in which that person ordinarily exercises civil and political rights.

ARTICLE 12

QUALIFICATIONS OF JUDGES

The permanent and *ad litem* judges shall be persons of high moral character, **D4–003** impartiality and integrity who possess the qualifications required in their respective countries for appointment to the highest judicial offices. In the overall composition of the Chambers and sections of the Trial Chambers, due account shall be taken of the experience of the judges in criminal law, international law, including international humanitarian law and human rights law.

ARTICLE 12*bis*

ELECTION OF PERMANENT JUDGES

1. Eleven of the permanent judges of the International Tribunal for Rwanda shall be **D4–004** elected by the General Assembly from a list submitted by the Security Council, in the following manner:

    (a) The Secretary-General shall invite nominations for permanent judges of the International Tribunal for Rwanda from States Members of the United Nations and non-member States maintaining permanent observer missions at United Nations Headquarters;

    (b) Within sixty days of the date of the invitation of the Secretary-General, each State may nominate up to two candidates meeting the qualifications set out in article 12 of the present Statute, no two of whom shall be of the same nationality and neither of whom shall be of the same nationality as any judge who is a member of the Appeals Chamber and who was elected or appointed a permanent judge of the International Tribunal for the Prosecution of Persons Responsible for Serious Violations of International Humanitarian Law Committed in the Territory of the former Yugoslavia since 1991 (hereinafter referred to as "the International Tribunal for the Former Yugoslavia") in accordance with article 13*bis* of the Statute of that Tribunal;

    (c) The Secretary-General shall forward the nominations received to the Security Council. From the nominations received the Security Council shall establish a list of not less than twenty-two and not more than thirty-three candidates, taking due account of the adequate representation on the International Tribunal for Rwanda of the principal legal systems of the world;

    (d) The President of the Security Council shall transmit the list of candidates to the President of the General Assembly. From that list the General Assembly shall elect eleven permanent judges of the International Tribunal for Rwanda. The candidates who receive an absolute majority of the votes of the States Members of the United Nations and of the non-member States maintaining permanent observer missions at United Nations Headquarters, shall be declared elected. Should two candidates of the same nationality obtain the required majority vote, the one who received the higher number of votes shall be considered elected.

2. In the event of a vacancy in the Chambers amongst the permanent judges elected or appointed in accordance with this article, after consultation with the Presidents of the

Security Council and of the General Assembly, the Secretary-General shall appoint a person meeting the qualifications of article 12 of the present Statute, for the remainder of the term of office concerned.

3. The permanent judges elected in accordance with this article shall be elected for a term of four years. The terms and conditions of service shall be those of the permanent judges of the International Tribunal for the Former Yugoslavia. They shall be eligible for re-election.

ARTICLE 12*ter*

ELECTION AND APPOINTMENT OF AD LITEM JUDGES

D4–005   1. The ad litem judges of the International Tribunal for Rwanda shall be elected by the General Assembly from a list submitted by the Security Council, in the following manner:

(a) The Secretary-General shall invite nominations for ad litem judges of the International Tribunal for Rwanda from States Members of the United Nations and non-member States maintaining permanent observer missions at United Nations Headquarters;

(b) Within sixty days of the date of the invitation of the Secretary-General, each State may nominate up to four candidates meeting the qualifications set out in article 12 of the present Statute, taking into account the importance of a fair representation of female and male candidates;

(c) The Secretary-General shall forward the nominations received to the Security Council. From the nominations received the Security Council shall establish a list of not less than thirty-six candidates, taking due account of the adequate representation of the principal legal systems of the world and bearing in mind the importance of equitable geographical distribution;

(d) The President of the Security Council shall transmit the list of candidates to the President of the General Assembly. From that list the General Assembly shall elect the eighteen ad litem judges of the International Tribunal for Rwanda. The candidates who receive an absolute majority of the votes of the States Members of the United Nations and of the non-member States maintaining permanent observer missions at United Nations Headquarters shall be declared elected;

(e) The *ad litem* judges shall be elected for a term of four years. They shall not be eligible for re-election.

2. During their term, ad litem judges will be appointed by the Secretary-General, upon request of the President of the International Tribunal for Rwanda, to serve in the Trial Chambers for one or more trials, for a cumulative period of up to, but not including, three years. When requesting the appointment of any particular ad litem judge, the President of the International Tribunal for Rwanda shall bear in mind the criteria set out in article 12 of the present Statute regarding the composition of the Chambers and sections of the Trial Chambers, the considerations set out in paragraphs 1 (b) and (c) above and the number of votes the *ad litem* judge received in the General Assembly.

ARTICLE 12*quater*

STATUS OF *AD LITEM* JUDGES

D4–006   1. During the period in which they are appointed to serve in the International Tribunal for Rwanda, ad litem judges shall:

(a) Benefit from the same terms and conditions of service mutatis mutandis as the permanent judges of the International Tribunal for Rwanda;

(b) Enjoy, subject to paragraph 2 below, the same powers as the permanent judges of the International Tribunal for Rwanda;

(c) Enjoy the privileges and immunities, exemptions and facilities of a judge of the International Tribunal for Rwanda.

2. During the period in which they are appointed to serve in the International Tribunal for Rwanda, ad litem judges shall not:

(a) Be eligible for election as, or to vote in the election of, the President of the International Tribunal for Rwanda or the Presiding Judge of a Trial Chamber pursuant to article 13 of the present Statute;

(b) Have power:

(i) To adopt rules of procedure and evidence pursuant to article 14 of the present Statute. They shall, however, be consulted before the adoption of those rules;

(ii) To review an indictment pursuant to Article 18 of the present Statute;

(iii) To consult with the President of the International Tribunal for Rwanda in relation to the assignment of judges pursuant to article 13 of the present Statute or in relation to a pardon or commutation of sentence pursuant to article 27 of the present Statute;

(iv) To adjudicate in pre-trial proceedings.

ARTICLE 13

OFFICERS AND MEMBERS OF THE CHAMBERS

1. The permanent judges of the International Tribunal for Rwanda shall elect a **D4–007** President from amongst their number.

2. The President of the International Tribunal for Rwanda shall be a member of one of its Trial Chambers.

3. After consultation with the permanent judges of the International Tribunal for Rwanda, the President shall assign two of the permanent judges elected or appointed in accordance with Article 12 bis of the present Statute to be members of the Appeals Chamber of the International Tribunal for the Former Yugoslavia and eight to the Trial Chambers of the International Tribunal for Rwanda.

4. The members of the Appeals Chamber of the International Tribunal for the Former Yugoslavia shall also serve as the members of the Appeals Chamber of the International Tribunal for Rwanda.

5. After consultation with the permanent judges of the International Tribunal for Rwanda, the President shall assign such ad litem judges as may from time to time be appointed to serve in the International Tribunal for Rwanda to the Trial Chambers.

6. A judge shall serve only in the Chamber to which he or she was assigned.

7. The permanent judges of each Trial Chamber shall elect a Presiding Judge from amongst their number, who shall oversee the work of that Trial Chamber as a whole.

INTERNATIONAL TRIBUNAL FOR THE FORMER YUGOSLAVIA

ANNEX II

ARTICLE 13*bis*

ELECTION OF PERMANENT JUDGES

1. Fourteen of the permanent judges of the International Tribunal shall be elected by **D4–008** the General Assembly from a list submitted by the Security Council, in the following manner:

(a) The Secretary-General shall invite nominations for judges of the International Tribunal from States Members of the United Nations and non-member States maintaining permanent observer missions at United Nations Headquarters;

(b) Within sixty days of the date of the invitation of the Secretary-General, each State may nominate up to two candidates meeting the qualifications set out in article 13 of the Statute, no two of whom shall be of the same nationality and neither of whom shall be of the same nationality as any judge who is a member of the Appeals Chamber and who was elected or appointed a permanent judge of the International Criminal Tribunal for the Prosecution of Persons Responsible for Genocide and Other Serious Violations of International Humanitarian Law Committed in the Territory of Rwanda and Rwandan Citizens Responsible for Genocide and Other Such Violations Committed in the Territory of Neighbouring States, between 1 January 1994 and 31 December 1994 (hereinafter referred to as "The International Tribunal for Rwanda") in accordance with article 12 bis of the Statute of that Tribunal;

(c) The Secretary-General shall forward the nominations received to the Security Council. From the nominations received the Security Council shall establish a list of not less than twenty-eight and not more than forty-two candidates, taking due account of the adequate representation of the principal legal systems of the world;

(d) The President of the Security Council shall transmit the list of candidates to the President of the General Assembly. From that list the General Assembly shall elect fourteen permanent judges of the International Tribunal. The candidates who receive an absolute majority of the votes of the States Members of the United Nations and of the non-member States maintaining permanent observer missions at United Nations Headquarters, shall be declared elected. Should two candidates of the same nationality obtain the required majority vote, the one who received the higher number of votes shall be considered elected.

2. In the event of a vacancy in the Chambers amongst the permanent judges elected or appointed in accordance with this article, after consultation with the Presidents of the Security Council and of the General Assembly, the Secretary-General shall appoint a person meeting the qualifications of article 13 of the Statute, for the remainder of the term of office concerned.

3. The permanent judges elected in accordance with this article shall be elected for a term of four years. The terms and conditions of service shall be those of the judges of the International Court of Justice. They shall be eligible for re-election.

ARTICLE 14

OFFICERS AND MEMBERS OF THE CHAMBERS

D4–009　　1. The permanent judges of the International Tribunal shall elect a President from amongst their number.

2. The President of the International Tribunal shall be a member of the Appeals Chamber and shall preside over its proceedings.

3. After consultation with the permanent judges of the International Tribunal, the President shall assign four of the permanent judges elected or appointed in accordance with Article 13 bis of the Statute to the Appeals Chamber and nine to the Trial Chambers.

4. Two of the permanent judges of the International Tribunal for Rwanda elected or appointed in accordance with article 12 bis of the Statute of that Tribunal shall be assigned by the President of that Tribunal, in consultation with the President of the International Tribunal, to be members of the Appeals Chamber and permanent judges of the International Tribunal.

5. After consultation with the permanent judges of the International Tribunal, the President shall assign such ad litem judges as may from time to time be appointed to serve in the International Tribunal to the Trial Chambers.

6. A judge shall serve only in the Chamber to which he or she was assigned.

7. The permanent judges of each Trial Chamber shall elect a Presiding Judge from amongst their number, who shall oversee the work of the Trial Chamber as a whole.

D5. Resolution 1512 (2003) Adopted by the Security Council at its 4849th meeting, on 27 October 2003

D5–001   *The Security Council,*

Reaffirming its resolutions 955 (1994) of 8 November 1994, 1165 (1998) of 30 April 1998, 1329 (2000) of 30 November 2000, 1411 (2002) of 17 May 2002, 1431 (2002) of 14 August 2002 and 1503 (2003) of 28 August 2003,

Having considered the letter from the Secretary-General to the President of the Security Council dated 12 September 2003 (S/2003/879) and the annexed letter from the President of the International Tribunal for Rwanda addressed to the Secretary-General dated 8 September 2003,

Having considered also the letter from the Secretary-General to the President of the Security Council dated 3 October 2003 (S/2003/946) and the annexed letter from the President of the International Tribunal for Rwanda addressed to the Secretary-General dated 29 September 2003,

Convinced of the advisability of enhancing the powers of *ad litem* judges in the International Tribunal for Rwanda so that, during the period of their appointment to a trial, they might also adjudicate in pre-trial proceedings in other cases, should the need arise and should they be in a position to do so,

Convinced also of the advisability of increasing the number of *ad litem* judges that may be appointed at any one time to serve in the Trial Chambers of the International Tribunal for Rwanda so that the Tribunal might be better placed to complete all trial activities at first instance by the end of 2008, as envisaged in its Completion Strategy,

Acting under Chapter VII of the Charter of the United Nations,

1. *Decides* to amend articles 11 and 12 quater of the Statute of the International Tribunal for Rwanda and to replace those articles with the provisions set out in the annex to this resolution;

2. *Decides* to remain actively seized of the matter.

ANNEX

ARTICLE 11

COMPOSITION OF THE CHAMBERS

D5–002   1. The Chambers shall be composed of sixteen permanent independent judges, no two of whom may be nationals of the same State, and a maximum at any one time of **nine** *ad litem* independent judges appointed in accordance with article 12*ter*, paragraph 2, of the present Statute, no two of whom may be nationals of the same State.

2. Three permanent judges and a maximum at any one time of **six** *ad litem* judges shall be members of each Trial Chamber. Each Trial Chamber to which *ad litem* judges are assigned may be divided into sections of three judges each, composed of both permanent and *ad litem* judges. A section of a Trial Chamber shall have the same powers and responsibilities as a Trial Chamber under the present Statute and shall render judgement in accordance with the same rules.

3. Seven of the permanent judges shall be members of the Appeals Chamber. The Appeals Chamber shall, for each appeal, be composed of five of its members.

4. A person who for the purposes of membership of the Chambers of the International Tribunal for Rwanda could be regarded as a national of more than one State shall be deemed to be a national of the State in which that person ordinarily exercises civil and political rights.

ARTICLE 12 QUARTER

STATUS OF *AD LITEM* JUDGES

D5–003   1. During the period in which they are appointed to serve in the International Tribunal for Rwanda, *ad litem* judges shall:

(a) Benefit from the same terms and conditions of service mutatis mutandis as the permanent judges of the International Tribunal for Rwanda;

(b) Enjoy, subject to paragraph 2 below, the same powers as the permanent judges of the International Tribunal for Rwanda;

(c) Enjoy the privileges and immunities, exemptions and facilities of a judge of the International Tribunal for Rwanda;

(d) Enjoy the power to adjudicate in pre-trial proceedings in cases other than those that they have been appointed to try.

2. During the period in which they are appointed to serve in the International Tribunal for Rwanda, *ad litem* judges shall not:

(a) Be eligible for election as, or to vote in the election of, the President of the International Tribunal for Rwanda or the Presiding Judge of a Trial Chamber pursuant to article 13 of the present Statute;

(b) Have power:

    (i) To adopt rules of procedure and evidence pursuant to article 14 of the present Statute. They shall, however, be consulted before the adoption of those rules;

    (ii) To review an indictment pursuant to article 18 of the present Statute;

    (iii) To consult with the President of the International Tribunal for Rwanda in relation to the assignment of judges pursuant to article 13 of the present Statute or in relation to a pardon or commutation of sentence pursuant to article 27 of the present Statute.

D6. Rules of Procedure and Evidence

Adopted on 29 June 1995; as amended on

12 January	1996
15 May	1996
4 July	1996
5 June	1997
8 June	1998
1 July	1999
21 February	2000
26 June	2000
3 November	2000
31 May	2001
6 July	2002
27 May	2003
15 May	2004
7 June	2005

TABLE OF CONTENTS

Section 2: Case Presentation

Section 3: Rules of Evidence

Section 4: Sentencing Procedure

Part Seven APPELLATE PROCEEDINGS

PART ONE

GENERAL PROVISIONS

RULE 1: ENTRY INTO FORCE

D6–001   These Rules of Procedure and Evidence, adopted pursuant to Article 14 of the Statute of the Tribunal, shall come into force on 29 June 1995.

RULE 2: DEFINITIONS

D6–002   (A) In the Rules, unless the context otherwise requires, the following terms shall mean:

Rules:	The Rules referred to in Rule 1;
Statute:	The Statute of the Tribunal adopted by Security Council resolution 955 of 8 November 1994;
Tribunal:	The International Criminal Tribunal for the Prosecution of Persons Responsible for Genocide and other Serious Violations of International Humanitarian Law Committed in the Territory of Rwanda and Rwandan citizens responsible for Genocide and other such violations committed in the territory of neighbouring States, between 1 January 1994 and 31 December 1994, established by Security Council Resolution 955 of 8 November 1994;
Accused:	A person against whom one or more counts in an indictment have been confirmed in accordance with Rule 47;
Ad litem Judge:	A Judge appointed pursuant to Article 12*ter* of the Statute;
Arrest:	The act of apprehending and taking a suspect or an accused into custody pursuant to a warrant of arrest or under Rule 40;
Bureau:	A body composed of the President, the Vice-President and the Presiding Judges of the Trial Chambers;
Investigation:	All activities undertaken by the Prosecutor under the Statute and the Rules for the collection of information and evidence, whether before or after confirmation of an indictment;
Transaction:	A number of acts or omissions whether occurring as one event or a number of events, at the same or different locations and being part of a common scheme, strategy or plan;
Party:	The Prosecutor or the accused;
Permanent Judge:	A Judge elected or appointed pursuant to Article 12*bis* of the Statute;

President:	The President of the Tribunal;
Prosecutor:	The Prosecutor designated pursuant to Article 15 of the Statute;
Regulations:	The provisions framed by the Prosecutor pursuant to Rule 37 (A) for the purpose of directing the functions of the Office of the Prosecutor;
Suspect:	A person concerning whom the Prosecutor possesses reliable information which tends to show that he may have committed a crime over which the Tribunal has jurisdiction;
Victim:	A person against whom a crime over which the Tribunal has jurisdiction has allegedly been committed.

(B) In the Rules, the masculine shall include the feminine and the singular the plural, and vice-versa.

Rule 3: Languages

(A) The working languages of the Tribunal shall be English and French. **D6–003**

(B) The accused or suspect shall have the right to use his own language.

(C) Counsel for the accused may apply to a Judge or a Chamber for leave to use a language other than the two working ones or the language of the accused. If such leave is granted, the expenses of interpretation and translation shall be borne by the Tribunal to the extent, if any, determined by the President, taking into account the rights of the Defence and the interests of justice.

(D) Any other person appearing before the Tribunal, who does not have sufficient knowledge of either of the two working languages, may use his own language.

(E) The Registrar shall make any necessary arrangements for interpretation and translation of the working languages.

Rule 4: Sittings Away from the Seat of the Tribunal

A Chamber or a Judge may exercise their functions away from the Seat of the **D6–004**
Tribunal, if so authorized by the President in the interests of justice.

Rule 5: Non-Compliance with Rules

(A) Where an objection on the ground of non-compliance with the Rules or Regu- **D6–005**
lations is raised by a party at the earliest opportunity, the Trial Chamber shall grant relief, if it finds that the alleged non-compliance is proved and that it has caused material prejudice to that party.

(B) Where such an objection is raised otherwise than at the earliest opportunity, the Trial Chamber may in its discretion grant relief, if it finds that the alleged non-compliance is proved and that it has caused material prejudice to the objecting party.

(C) The relief granted by a Trial Chamber under this Rule shall be such remedy as the Trial Chamber considers appropriate to ensure consistency with fundamental principles of fairness.

Rule 6: Amendment of the Rules

(A) Proposals for amendment of the Rules may be made by a Judge, the Prosecutor or **D6–006**
the Registrar and shall be adopted, if agreed to by not less than ten Judges at a Plenary Meeting of the Tribunal convened with notice of the proposal addressed to all Judges.

(B) An amendment of the Rules may be adopted otherwise than as stipulated in Sub-Rule (A) above, provided it is approved unanimously by any appropriate means either done in writing or confirmed in writing.

(C) An amendment shall enter into force immediately, but shall not operate to prejudice the rights of the accused in any pending case.

RULE 7: AUTHENTIC TEXTS

D6–007　　The English and French texts of the Rules shall be equally authentic. In case of discrepancy, the version which is more consonant with the spirit of the Statute and the Rules shall prevail.

RULE 7*bis*: NON COMPLIANCE WITH OBLIGATIONS

D6–008　　(A) Except in cases to which Rules 11, 13, 59 or 61 applies, where a Trial Chamber or a Judge is satisfied that a State has failed to comply with an obligation under Article 28 of the Statute relating to any proceedings before that Chamber or Judge, the Chamber or Judge may request the President to report the matter to the Security Council.

(B) If the Prosecutor satisfies the President that a State has failed to comply with an obligation under Article 28 of the Statute in respect of a request by the Prosecutor under Rules 8 or 40, the President shall notify the Security Council thereof.

RULE 7*ter*: TIME LIMITS

D6–009　　(A) Unless otherwise ordered by the Chambers or otherwise provided by the Rules, where the time prescribed by or under the Rules for the doing of any act shall run as from the occurrence of an event, that time shall run from the date on which notice of the occurrence of the event has been received in the normal course of transmission by counsel for the accused or the Prosecutor as the case may be.

(B) Where a time limit is expressed in days, only ordinary calendar days shall be counted. Weekdays, Saturdays, Sundays and public holidays shall be counted as days. However, should the time limit expire on a Saturday, Sunday or public holiday, the time limit shall automatically be extended to the subsequent working day.

PART TWO

PRIMACY OF THE TRIBUNAL

RULE 8: REQUEST FOR INFORMATION

D6–010　　Where it appears to the Prosecutor that a crime within the jurisdiction of the Tribunal is or has been the subject of investigations or criminal proceedings instituted in the courts of any State, he may request the State to forward to him all relevant information in that respect, and the State shall transmit to him such information forthwith in accordance with Article 28 of the Statute.

RULE 9: PROSECUTOR'S APPLICATION FOR DEFERRAL

D6–011　　Where it appears to the Prosecutor that crimes which are the subject of investigations or criminal proceedings instituted in the courts of any State:

(i) Are the subject of an investigation by the Prosecutor;
(ii) Should be the subject of an investigation by the Prosecutor considering, *inter alia*:
　　(a) The seriousness of the offences;
　　(b) The status of the accused at the time of the alleged offences;
　　(c) The general importance of the legal questions involved in the case;
(iii) Are the subject of an indictment in the Tribunal,

the Prosecutor may apply to the Trial Chamber designated by the President to issue a formal request that such court defer to the competence of the Tribunal.

Rule 10: Formal Request for Deferral

(A) If it appears to the Trial Chamber seized of a request by the Prosecutor under **D6–012**
Rule 9 that paragraphs (i), (ii) or (iii) of Rule 9 are satisfied, the Trial Chamber shall
issue a formal request to the State concerned that the Court defer to the competence of
the Tribunal.

(B) A request for deferral shall include a request that the results of the investigation
and a copy of the court's records and the judgement, if already delivered, be forwarded
to the Tribunal.

(C) The State to which the formal request for deferral is addressed shall comply
without undue delay in accordance with Article 28 of the Statute.

Rule 11: Non-Compliance with a Formal Request for Deferral

If, within sixty days after a request for deferral has been notified by the Registrar to **D6–013**
the State under whose jurisdiction the investigations or criminal proceedings have been
instituted, the State fails to file a response which satisfies the Trial Chamber that the
State has taken or is taking adequate steps to comply with the request, the Trial
Chamber may invite the President to report the matter to the Security Council.

Rule 11*bis*: Referral of the Indictment to another Court

(A) If an indictment has been confirmed, whether or not the accused is in the custody **D6–014**
of the Tribunal, the President may designate a Trial Chamber which shall determine
whether the case should be referred to the authorities of a State:

  (i) in whose territory the crime was committed; or
  (ii) in which the accused was arrested; or
  (iii) having jurisdiction and being willing and adequately prepared to accept such
      a case, so that those authorities should forthwith refer the case to the
      appropriate court for trial within that State.

(B) The Trial Chamber may order such referral *proprio motu* or at the request of the
Prosecutor, after having given to the Prosecutor and, where the accused is in the custody
of the Tribunal, the accused, the opportunity to be heard.

(C) In determining whether to refer the case in accordance with paragraph (A), the
Trial Chamber shall satisfy itself that the accused will receive a fair trial in the courts of
the State concerned and that the death penalty will not be imposed or carried out.

(D) Where an order is issued pursuant to this Rule:

  (i) the accused, if in the custody of the Tribunal, shall be handed over to the
      authorities of the State concerned;
  (ii) the Trial Chamber may order that protective measures for certain witnesses or
      victims remain in force;
  (iii) the Prosecutor shall provide to the authorities of the State concerned all of the
      information relating to the case which the Prosecutor considers appropriate
      and, in particular, the material supporting the indictment;
  (iv) the Prosecutor may send observers to monitor the proceedings in the courts of
      the State concerned on his behalf.

(E) The Trial Chamber may issue a warrant for the arrest of the accused, which shall
specify the State to which he is to be transferred for trial.

(F) At any time after an order has been issued pursuant to this Rule and before the
accused is found guilty or acquitted by a court in the State concerned, the Trial
Chamber may, at the request of the Prosecutor and upon having given to the authorities
of the State concerned the opportunity to be heard, revoke the order and make a formal
request for deferral within the terms of Rule 10.

(G) Where an order issued pursuant to this Rule is revoked by the Trial Chamber, it
may make a formal request to the State concerned to transfer the accused to the seat of
the Tribunal, and the State shall accede to such a request without delay in keeping with

Article 28 of the Statute. The Trial Chamber or a Judge may also issue a warrant for the arrest of the accused.

(H) An appeal by the accused or the Prosecutor shall lie as of right from a decision of the Trial Chamber whether or not to refer a case. Notice of appeal shall be filed within fifteen days of the decision unless the accused was not present or represented when the decision was pronounced, in which case the time-limit shall run from the date on which the accused is notified of the decision.

RULE 12: DETERMINATIONS OF COURTS OF ANY STATE

D6–015   Subject to Article 9 (2) of the Statute, determinations of courts of any State are not binding on the Tribunal.

RULE 13: *NON BIS IN IDEM*

D6–016   When the President receives reliable information to show that criminal proceedings have been instituted against a person before a court of any State for acts constituting serious violations of international humanitarian law under the Statute for which that person has already been tried by the Tribunal, a Trial Chamber shall, following *mutatis mutandis* the procedure provided in Rule 10, issue a reasoned order requesting that court permanently to discontinue its proceedings. If that court fails to do so, the President may report the matter to the Security Council.

PART III

ORGANIZATION OF THE TRIBUNAL

Section 1: The Judges

RULE 14: SOLEMN DECLARATION

D6–017   (A) Before taking up his duties each Judge shall make the following solemn declaration:

"I solemnly declare that I will perform my duties and exercise my powers as a Judge of the International Criminal Tribunal for the Prosecution of Persons Responsible for Genocide and other Serious Violations of International Humanitarian Law Committed in the Territory of Rwanda and Rwandan citizens responsible for Genocide and other such violations committed in the territory of neighbouring States, between 1 January 1994 and 31 December 1994, honourably, faithfully, impartially and conscientiously."

(B) The text of the declaration, signed by the Judge and witnessed by the Secretary-General of the United Nations or his representative, shall be kept in the records of the Tribunal.

RULE 14*bis*

D6–018   The members of the Tribunal shall continue to discharge their duties until their places have been filled.

RULE 15: DISQUALIFICATION OF JUDGES

D6–019   (A) A Judge may not sit in any case in which he has a personal interest or concerning which he has or has had any association which might affect his impartiality. He shall in any such circumstance withdraw from that case. Where the Judge withdraws from the

Trial Chamber, the President shall assign another Trial Chamber Judge to sit in his place. Where a Judge withdraws from the Appeals Chamber, the Presiding Judge of that Chamber shall assign another Judge to sit in his place.

(B) Any party may apply to the Presiding Judge of a Chamber for the disqualification of a Judge of that Chamber from a case upon the above grounds. After the Presiding Judge has conferred with the Judge in question, the Bureau, if necessary, shall determine the matter. If the Bureau upholds the application, the President shall assign another Judge to sit in place of the disqualified Judge.

(C) The Judge who reviews an indictment against an accused, pursuant to Article 18 of the Statute and Rule 47 or 61, shall not be disqualified from sitting as a member of a Trial Chamber for the trial of that accused.

(D) No member of the Appeals Chamber shall hear any appeal in a case in which another Judge of the same nationality sat as a member of the Trial Chamber.

RULE 15*bis*: ABSENCE OF A JUDGE

(A) If   **D6–020**
   (i) a Judge is, for illness or other urgent personal reasons, or for reasons of authorised Tribunal business, unable to continue sitting in a part-heard case for a period which is likely to be of short duration, and
   (ii) the remaining Judges of the Chamber are satisfied that it is in the interests of justice to do so,
those remaining Judges of the Chamber may order that the hearing of the case continue in the absence of that Judge for a period of not more than five working days.

(B) If
   (i) a Judge is, for illness or urgent personal reasons, or for reasons of authorised Tribunal business, unable to continue sitting in a part-heard case for a period which is likely to be of short duration, and
   (ii) the remaining Judges of the Chamber are not satisfied that it is in the interests of justice to order that the hearing of the case continue in the absence of that Judge, then
     (a) those remaining Judges of the Chamber may nevertheless conduct those matters which they are satisfied it is in the interests of justice that they be disposed of notwithstanding the absence of that Judge, and
     (b) the Presiding Judge may adjourn the proceedings.

(C) If, by reason of death, illness, resignation from the Tribunal, non-reelection, non-extension of term of office or for any other reason, a Judge is unable to continue sitting in a part-heard case for a period which is likely to be longer than of a short duration, the Presiding Judge shall report to the President who may assign another Judge to the case and order either a rehearing or continuation of the proceedings from that point. However, after the opening statements provided for in Rule 84, or the beginning of the presentation of evidence pursuant to Rule 85, the continuation of the proceedings can only be ordered with the consent of the accused, except as provided for in paragraph (D).

(D) If, in the circumstances mentioned in the last sentence of paragraph (C), the accused withholds his consent, the remaining Judges may nonetheless decide to continue the proceedings before a Trial Chamber with a substitute Judge if, taking all the circumstances into account, they determine unanimously that doing so would serve the interests of justice. This decision is subject to appeal directly to a full bench of the Appeals Chamber by either party. If no appeal is taken or the Appeals Chamber affirms the decision of the Trial Chamber, the President shall assign to the existing bench a Judge, who, however, can join the bench only after he or she has certified that he or she has familiarised himself or herself with the record of the proceedings. Only one substitution under this paragraph may be made.

(E) Appeals under paragraph (D) shall be filed within seven days of filing of the impugned decision. When such decision is rendered orally, this time-limit shall run from the date of the oral decision, unless

(i) the party challenging the decision was not present or represented when the decision was pronounced, in which case the time-limit shall run from the date on which the challenging party is notified of the oral decision; or

(ii) the Trial Chamber has indicated that a written decision will follow, in which case, the time-limit shall run from filing of the written decision.

(F) In case of illness or an unfilled vacancy or in any other similar circumstances, the President may, if satisfied that it is in the interests of justice to do so, authorise a Chamber to conduct routine matters, such as the delivery of decisions, in the absence of one or more of its members.

Rule 16: Resignation

D6–021   A Judge who decides to resign shall give notice of his resignation in writing to the President, who shall transmit it to the Secretary-General of the United Nations.

Rule 17: Precedence

D6–022   (A) All Judges are equal in the exercise of their judicial functions, regardless of dates of election, appointment, age or period of service.

(B) The Presiding Judges of the Chambers shall take precedence according to the dates of their election or appointment as judges, after the President and the Vice-President. Presiding Judges elected or appointed on the same date shall take precedence according to age.

(C) Judges elected or appointed on different dates shall take precedence according to the dates of their election or appointment; Judges elected or appointed on the same date shall take precedence according to age.

(D) In case of re-election, the total period of service as a Judge of the Tribunal shall be taken into account.

Section 2: The Presidency

Rule 18: Election of the President

D6–023   (A) The President shall be elected for a term of two years, or such shorter term as shall coincide with the duration of his term of office as a Judge. The President may be re-elected once.

(B) If the President ceases to be a member of the Tribunal or resigns his office before the expiration of his term, the Judges shall elect from among their number a successor for the remainder of the term.

(C) The President shall be elected by a majority of the votes of the Judges of the Tribunal. If no Judge obtains such a majority, the second ballot shall be limited to the two Judges who obtained the greatest number of votes on the first ballot. In the case of equality of votes on the second ballot, the Judge who takes precedence in accordance with Rule 17 shall be declared elected.

Rule 19: Functions of the President

D6–024   (A) The President shall preside at all plenary meetings of the Tribunal, co-ordinate the work of the Chambers and supervise the activities of the Registry as well as exercise all the other functions conferred on him by the Statute and the Rules.

(B) The President may, in consultation with the Bureau, the Registrar and the Prosecutor, issue Practice Directions, consistent with the Statute and the Rules, addressing detailed aspects of the conduct of proceedings before the Tribunal.

Rule 20: The Vice-President

(A) The Vice-President shall be elected for a term of two years, or such shorter term **D6–025** as shall coincide with the duration of his term of office as a Judge. The Vice-President may be re- elected once.

(B) Rules 18 (B) and (C) shall apply *mutatis mutandis* to the Vice-President.

Rule 21: Functions of the Vice-President

The Vice-President shall exercise the functions of the President in case the latter is **D6–026** absent or is unable to act.

Rule 22: Replacements

If neither the President nor the Vice-President can carry out the functions of the **D6–027** Presidency, this shall be assumed by the senior Judge of the Trial Chambers, determined in accordance with Rule 17.

Section 3: Internal Functioning of the Tribunal

Rule 23: The Bureau

(A) The Bureau shall be composed of the President, the Vice-President and the **D6–028** Presiding Judges of the Trial Chambers.

(B) The President shall consult the other members of the Bureau on all major questions relating to the functioning of the Tribunal.

(C) A Judge may draw the attention of any member of the Bureau to issues that in his opinion ought to be discussed by the Bureau or submitted to a Plenary Meeting of the Tribunal.

Rule 23*bis*: The Coordination Council

(A) The Coordination Council shall be composed of the President, the Prosecutor and **D6–029** the Registrar.

(B) In order to achieve the mission of the Tribunal, as defined in the Statute, the Coordination Council ensures the coordination of the activities of the three organs of the Tribunal.

(C) The Coordination Council shall meet once a month at the initiative of the President. A member may at any time request that additional meetings be held. The President shall chair the meetings.

(D) The Vice-President, the Deputy Prosecutor and the Deputy Registrar may *ex officio* represent respectively, the President, the Prosecutor and the Registrar.

Rule 23*ter*: The Management Committee

(A) The Management Committee shall be composed of the President, the Vice- **D6–030** President, a Judge elected by the Judges in plenary session for a one year renewable mandate, the Registrar, the Deputy Registrar and the Chief of Administration.

(B) The Management Committee shall assist the President with respect to the functions set forth in Rules 19 and 33, concerning in particular, all Registry activities relating to the administrative and judicial support provided to the Chambers and to the Judges. To this end, the Management Committee shall coordinate the preparation and implementation of the budget of the Tribunal with the exception of budgetary lines specific to the activities of the Office of the Prosecutor.

(C) The Management Committee shall meet once a month at the initiative of the President. Two members may at any time request that additional meetings be held. The President shall chair the meetings.

(D) In the performance of its functions, the Management Committee may call on the services of one or several advisers or experts.

RULE 24: PLENARY MEETINGS OF THE TRIBUNAL

D6–031 The Judges shall meet in plenary to:
  (i) Elect the President and Vice-President;
  (ii) Adopt and amend the Rules;
  (iii) Adopt the Annual Report provided for in Article 32 of the Statute;
  (iv) Decide upon matters relating to the internal functioning of the Chambers and the Tribunal;
  (v) Determine or supervise the conditions of detention;
  (vi) Exercise any other functions provided for in the Statute or in the Rules.

RULE 25: DATES OF PLENARY MEETINGS

D6–032 (A) The dates of the scheduled Plenary Meetings of the Tribunal shall normally be agreed upon in July of each year for the following calendar year.

(B) Other Plenary Meetings shall be convened by the President if so requested by at least eight Judges, and may be convened whenever the exercise of his functions under the Statute or the Rules so requires.

RULE 26: QUORUM AND VOTE

D6–033 (A) The quorum for each Plenary Meeting of the Tribunal shall be ten Judges.

(B) Subject to Rule 6 (A) and (B) and Rule 18 (C), the decisions of the Plenary Meeting of the Tribunal shall be taken by the majority of the Judges present. In the event of an equality of votes, the President or the Judge who acts in his place shall have a casting vote.

Section 4: The Chambers

RULE 27: ROTATION OF THE JUDGES

D6–034 (A) Judges shall rotate on a regular basis between the Trial Chambers. Rotation shall take into account the efficient disposal of cases.

(B) The Judges shall take their places in their assigned Chamber as soon as the President thinks it convenient, having regard to the disposal of pending cases.

(C) The President may at any time temporarily assign a member of one Trial Chamber to another Trial Chamber.

RULE 28: DUTY JUDGES

D6–035 Every six months and after consultation with the Judges, the President shall, designate for each month of the next six months one Judge from each Trial Chamber to whom indictments, warrants, and other submissions not pertaining to a case already assigned to a Chamber, shall be transmitted for review. The duty roster shall be published by the Registrar. However, in exceptional circumstances, a Judge on duty may request another Judge of the same Chamber to replace him, after having informed the President and the Registrar.

Rule 29: Deliberations

The deliberations of the Chambers shall take place in private and remain secret.   **D6–036**

Section 5: The Registrar

Rule 30: Appointment of the Registrar

The President shall seek the opinion of the Judges on the candidates for the post of **D6–037** Registrar, before consulting with the Secretary-General of the United Nations pursuant to Article 16 (3) of the Statute.

Rule 31: Appointment of the Deputy Registrar and Registry Staff

The Registrar, after consultation with the President, shall make his recommendations **D6–038** to the Secretary-General of the United Nations for the appointment of the Deputy Registrar and other Registry staff.

Rule 32: Solemn Declaration

(A) Before taking up his duties, the Registrar shall make the following declaration **D6–039** before the President:

"I solemnly declare that I will perform the duties incumbent upon me as Registrar of the International Criminal Tribunal for the Prosecution of Persons Responsible for Genocide and other Serious Violations of International Humanitarian Law Committed in the Territory of Rwanda and Rwandan citizens responsible for Genocide and other such violations committed in the territory of neighbouring States, between 1 January 1994 and 31 December 1994, in all loyalty, discretion and good conscience and that I will faithfully observe all the provisions of the Statute and the Rules of Procedure and Evidence of the Tribunal."

(B) Before taking up his duties, the Deputy Registrar shall make a similar declaration before the President.

(C) Every staff member of the Registry shall make a similar declaration before the Registrar.

Rule 33: Functions of the Registrar

(A) The Registrar shall assist the Chambers, the Plenary Meetings of the Tribunal, **D6–040** the Judges and the Prosecutor in the performance of their functions. Under the authority of the President, he shall be responsible for the administration and servicing of the Tribunal and shall serve as its channel of communication.

(B) The Registrar, in the execution of his functions, may make oral or written representations to Chambers on any issue arising in the context of a specific case which affects or may affect the discharge of such functions, including that of implementing judicial decisions, with notice to the parties where necessary.

(C) The Registrar may, in consultation with the President of the Tribunal and the Presiding Judge of the Appeals Chamber, as the case may be, issue Practice Directions addressing particular aspects of the practice and procedure in the Registry of the Tribunal and in respect of other matters within the powers of the Registrar.

Rule 34: Victims and Witnesses Support Unit

(A) There shall be set up under the authority of the Registrar a Victims and **D6–041** Witnesses Support Unit consisting of qualified staff to:

(i) Recommend the adoption of protective measures for victims and witnesses in accordance with Article 21 of the Statute;

(ii) Ensure that they receive relevant support, including physical and psychological rehabilitation, especially counselling in cases of rape and sexual assault; and

(iii) Develop short term and long term plans for the protection of witnesses who have testified before the Tribunal and who fear a threat to their life, property or family.

(B) A gender sensitive approach to victims and witnesses protective and support measures should be adopted and due consideration given, in the appointment of staff within this Unit, to the employment of qualified women.

RULE 35: MINUTES

D6–042   Except where a full record is made under Rule 81, the Registrar, or Registry staff designated by him, shall take minutes of the Plenary Meetings of the Tribunal and of the sittings of the Chambers or a Judge, other than private deliberations.

RULE 36: RECORD BOOK

D6–043   The Registrar shall keep a Record Book which shall list, subject to Rule 53, all the particulars of each case brought before the Tribunal. The Record Book shall be open to the public.

Section 6: The Prosecutor

RULE 37: FUNCTIONS OF THE PROSECUTOR

D6–044   (A) The Prosecutor shall perform all the functions provided by the Statute in accordance with the Rules and such Regulations, consistent with the Statute and the Rules, as may be framed by him. Any alleged inconsistency in the Regulations shall be brought to the attention of the Bureau to whose opinion the Prosecutor shall defer.

(B) The Prosecutor's powers under Parts Four to Eight of the Rules may be exercised by staff members of the Office of the Prosecutor authorized by him, or by any person acting under his direction.

RULE 38: DEPUTY PROSECUTOR

D6–045   (A) The Prosecutor shall make his recommendations to the Secretary-General of the United Nations for the appointment of a Deputy Prosecutor.

(B) The Deputy Prosecutor shall exercise the functions of the Prosecutor in the event of his absence or inability to act or upon the Prosecutor's express instructions.

PART FOUR

INVESTIGATIONS AND RIGHTS OF SUSPECTS

Section 1: Investigations

RULE 39: CONDUCT OF INVESTIGATIONS

D6–046   In the conduct of an investigation, the Prosecutor may:

(i) Summon and question suspects, interview victims and witnesses and record their statements, collect evidence and conduct on-site investigations;

(ii) Take all measures deemed necessary for the purpose of the investigation and to support the prosecution at trial, including the taking of special measures to provide for the safety of potential witnesses and informants;

(iii) Seek, to that end, the assistance of any State authority concerned, as well as of any relevant international body including the International Criminal Police Organization (INTERPOL); and

(iv) Request such orders as may be necessary from a Trial Chamber or a Judge.

Rule 40: Provisional Measures

(A) In case of urgency, the Prosecutor may request any State: **D6–047**

(i) To arrest a suspect and place him in custody;

(ii) To seize all physical evidence;

(iii) To take all necessary measures to prevent the escape of a suspect or an accused, injury to or intimidation of a victim or witness, or the destruction of evidence.

The State concerned shall comply forthwith, in accordance with Article 28 of the Statute.

(B) Upon showing that a major impediment does not allow the State to keep the suspect in custody or to take all necessary measures to prevent his escape, the Prosecutor may apply to a Judge designated by the President for an order to transfer the suspect to the seat of the Tribunal or to such other place as the Bureau may decide, and to detain him provisionally. After consultation with the Prosecutor and the Registrar, the transfer shall be arranged between the State authorities concerned, the authorities of the host Country of the Tribunal and the Registrar.

(C) In the cases referred to in paragraph B, the suspect shall, from the moment of his transfer, enjoy all the rights provided for in Rule 42, and may apply for review to a Trial Chamber of the Tribunal. The Chamber, after hearing the Prosecutor, shall rule upon the application.

(D) The suspect shall be released if (i) the Chamber so rules; or (ii) the Prosecutor fails to issue an indictment within twenty days of the transfer.

Rule 40*bis*: Transfer and Provisional Detention of Suspects

(A) In the conduct of an investigation, the Prosecutor may transmit to the Registrar, **D6–048** for an order by a Judge assigned pursuant to Rule 28, a request for the transfer to and provisional detention of a suspect in the premises of the detention unit of the Tribunal. This request shall indicate the grounds upon which the request is made and, unless the Prosecutor wishes only to question the suspect, shall include a provisional charge and a summary of the material upon which the Prosecutor relies.

(B) The Judge shall order the transfer and provisional detention of the suspect if the following conditions are met:

(i) The Prosecutor has requested a State to arrest the suspect and to place him in custody, in accordance with Rule 40, or the suspect is otherwise detained by a State;

(ii) After hearing the Prosecutor, the Judge considers that there is a reliable and consistent body of material which tends to show that the suspect may have committed a crime over which the Tribunal has jurisdiction; and

(iii) The Judge considers provisional detention to be a necessary measure to prevent the escape of the suspect, physical or mental injury to or intimidation of a victim or witness or the destruction of evidence, or to be otherwise necessary for the conduct of the investigation.

(C) The provisional detention of the suspect may be ordered for a period not exceeding 30 days from the day after the transfer of the suspect to the detention unit of the Tribunal.

(D) The order for the transfer and provisional detention of the suspect shall be signed by the Judge and bear the seal of the Tribunal. The order shall set forth the basis of the request made by the Prosecutor under Sub-Rule (A), including the provisional charge, and shall state the Judge's grounds for making the order, having regard to Sub-Rule (B). The order shall also specify the initial time limit for the provisional detention of the suspect, and be accompanied by a statement of the rights of a suspect, as specified in this Rule and in Rules 42 and 43.

(E) As soon as possible, copies of the order and of the request by the Prosecutor are served upon the suspect and his counsel by the Registrar.

(F) At the Prosecutor's request indicating the grounds upon which it is made and if warranted by the needs of the investigation, the Judge who made the initial order, or another Judge of the same Trial Chamber, may decide, subsequent to an *inter partes* hearing and before the end of the period of detention, to extend the provisional detention for a period not exceeding 30 days.

(G) At the Prosecutors request indicating the grounds upon which it is made and if warranted by special circumstances, the Judge who made the initial order, or another Judge of the same Trial Chamber, may decide, subsequent to an *inter partes* hearing and before the end of the period of detention, to extend the detention for a further period not exceeding 30 days.

(H) The total period of provisional detention shall in no case exceed 90 days after the day of transfer of the suspect to the Tribunal, at the end of which, in the event the indictment has not been confirmed and an arrest warrant signed, the suspect shall be released or, if appropriate, be delivered to the authorities of the State to which the request was initially made.

(I) The provisions in Rules 55(B) to 59 shall apply *mutatis mutandis* to the execution of the order for the transfer and provisional detention of the suspect.

(J) After his transfer to the seat of the Tribunal, the suspect, assisted by his counsel, shall be brought, without delay, before the Judge who made the initial order, or another Judge of the same Trial Chamber, who shall ensure that his rights are respected.

(K) During detention, the Prosecutor, the suspect or his counsel may submit to the Trial Chamber of which the Judge who made the initial order is a member, all applications relative to the propriety of provisional detention or to the suspect's release.

(L) Without prejudice to Sub-Rules (C) to (H), the Rules relating to the detention on remand of accused persons shall apply *mutatis mutandis* to the provisional detention of persons under this Rule.

RULE 41: PRESERVATION OF INFORMATION

D6–049   (A) The Prosecutor shall be responsible for the preservation, storage and security of information and physical evidence obtained in the course of his investigations.

(B) The Prosecutor shall draw up an inventory of all materials seized from the accused, including documents, books, papers, and other objects, and shall serve a copy thereof on the accused. Materials that are of no evidentiary value shall be returned without delay to the accused.

RULE 42: RIGHTS OF SUSPECTS DURING INVESTIGATION

D6–050   (A) A suspect who is to be questioned by the Prosecutor shall have the following rights, of which he shall be informed by the Prosecutor prior to questioning, in a language he speaks and understands:
   (i) The right to be assisted by counsel of his choice or to have legal assistance assigned to him without payment if he does not have sufficient means to pay for it;
   (ii) The right to have the free assistance of an interpreter if he cannot understand or speak the language to be used for questioning; and
   (iii) The right to remain silent, and to be cautioned that any statement he makes shall be recorded and may be used in evidence.

(B) Questioning of a suspect shall not proceed without the presence of counsel unless the suspect has voluntarily waived his right to counsel. In case of waiver, if the suspect subsequently expresses a desire to have counsel, questioning shall thereupon cease, and shall only resume when the suspect has obtained or has been assigned counsel.

Rule 43: Recording Questioning of Suspects

Whenever the Prosecutor questions a suspect, the questioning shall be audio-recorded **D6–051** or video-recorded, in accordance with the following procedure:
  (i) The suspect shall be informed in a language he speaks and understands that the questioning is being audio-recorded or video-recorded;
  (ii) In the event of a break in the course of the questioning, the fact and the time of the break shall be recorded before audio-recording or video-recording ends and the time of resumption of the questioning shall also be recorded;
  (iii) At the conclusion of the questioning the suspect shall be offered the opportunity to clarify anything he has said, and to add anything he may wish, and the time of conclusion shall be recorded;
  (iv) The content of the recording shall then be transcribed as soon as practicable after the conclusion of questioning and a copy of the transcript supplied to the suspect, together with a copy of the recording or, if multiple recording apparatus was used, one of the original recorded tapes; and
  (v) After a copy has been made, if necessary, of the recorded tape for purposes of transcription, the original recorded tape or one of the original tapes shall be sealed in the presence of the suspect under the signature of the Prosecutor and the suspect.

Section 2: Of Counsel

Rule 44: Appointment and Qualifications of Counsel

(A) Counsel engaged by a suspect or an accused shall file his power of attorney with **D6–052** the Registrar at the earliest opportunity. Subject to verification by the Registrar, a counsel shall be considered qualified to represent a suspect or accused, provided that he is admitted to the practice of law in a State, or is a University professor of law.

(B) In the performance of their duties counsel shall be subject to the relevant provisions of the Statute, the Rules, the Rules of Detention and any other rules or regulations adopted by the Tribunal, the Host Country Agreement, the Code of Conduct and the codes of practice and ethics governing their profession and, if applicable, the Directive on the Assignment of Defence Counsel.

Rule 44bis: Duty Counsel

(A) A list of duty counsel who speak one or both working languages of the Tribunal **D6–053** and have indicated their willingness to be assigned pursuant to this Rule shall be kept by the Registrar.

(B) Duty counsel shall fulfill the requirements of Rule 44, and shall be situated within reasonable proximity to the Detention Facility and the Seat of the Tribunal.

(C) The Registrar shall at all times ensure that duty counsel will be available to attend the Detention Facility in the event of being summoned.

(D) If an accused, or suspect transferred under Rule 40 bis, is unrepresented at any time after being transferred to the Tribunal, the Registrar shall as soon as practicable summon duty counsel to represent the accused or suspect until counsel is engaged by the accused or suspect, or assigned under Rule 45.

(E) In providing initial legal advice and assistance to a suspect transferred under Rule 40 bis, duty counsel shall advise the suspect of his or her rights including the rights referred to in Rule 55 (A).

RULE 45: ASSIGNMENT OF COUNSEL

D6–054　　(A) A list of counsel who speak one or both of the working languages of the Tribunal, meet the requirements of Rule 44, have at least 10 years' relevant experience, and have indicated their willingness to be assigned by the Tribunal to indigent suspects or accused, shall be kept by the Registrar.

(B) The criteria for determination of indigence shall be established by the Registrar and approved by the Judges.

(C) In assigning counsel to an indigent suspect or accused, the following procedure shall be observed:

　(i) A request for assignment of counsel shall be made to the Registrar;

　(ii) The Registrar shall enquire into the financial means of the suspect or accused and determine whether the criteria of indigence are met;

　(iii) If he decides that the criteria are met, he shall assign counsel from the list; if he decides to the contrary, he shall inform the suspect or accused that the request is refused.

(D) If a request is refused, a further reasoned request may be made by the suspect or the accused to the Registrar upon showing a change in circumstances.

(E) The Registrar shall, in consultation with the Judges, establish the criteria for the payment of fees to assigned counsel.

(F) If a suspect or an accused elects to conduct his own defence, he shall so notify the Registrar in writing at the first opportunity.

(G) Where an alleged indigent person is subsequently found not to be indigent, the Chamber may make an order of contribution to recover the cost of providing counsel.

(H) Under exceptional circumstances, at the request of the suspect or accused or his counsel, the Chamber may instruct the Registrar to replace an assigned counsel, upon good cause being shown and after having been satisfied that the request is not designed to delay the proceedings.

(I) It is understood that Counsel will represent the accused and conduct the case to finality. Failure to do so, absent just cause approved by the Chamber, may result in forfeiture of fees in whole or in part. In such circumstances the Chamber may make an order accordingly. Counsel shall only be permitted to withdraw from the case to which he has been assigned in the most exceptional circumstances.

RULE 45*bis*: DETAINED PERSONS

D6–055　　Rules 44 and 45 shall apply to any person detained under the authority of the Tribunal.

RULE 45*ter*: AVAILABILITY OF COUNSEL

D6–056　　(A) Counsel and Co-Counsel, whether assigned by the Registrar or appointed by the client for the purposes of proceedings before the Tribunal, shall furnish the Registrar, upon date of such assignment or appointment, a written undertaking that he will appear before the Tribunal within a reasonable time as specified by the Registrar.

(B) Failure by Counsel or Co-Counsel to appear before the Tribunal, as undertaken, shall be a ground for withdrawal by the Registrar of the assignment of such Counsel or Co-Counsel or the refusal of audience by the Tribunal or the imposition of any other sanctions by the Chamber concerned.

RULE 45*quarter*: ASSIGNMENT OF COUNSEL IN THE INTERESTS OF JUSTICE

D6–057　　The Trial Chamber may, if it decides that it is in the interests of justice, instruct the Registrar to assign a counsel to represent the interests of the accused.

Rule 46: Misconduct of Counsel

(A) A Chamber may, after a warning, impose sanctions against a counsel if, in its **D6–058**
opinion, his conduct remains offensive or abusive, obstructs the proceedings, or is
otherwise contrary to the interests of justice. This provision is applicable *mutatis mutandis*
to Counsel for the prosecution.

(B) A Judge or a Chamber may also, with the approval of the President, communicate
any misconduct of counsel to the professional body regulating the conduct of counsel in
his State of admission or, if a professor and not otherwise admitted to the profession, to
the governing body of his University.

(C) If a counsel assigned pursuant to Rule 45 is sanctioned in accordance with Sub-
Rule A) by being refused audience, the Chamber shall instruct the Registrar to replace
the counsel.

(D) The Registrar may set up a Code of Professional Conduct enunciating the
principles of professional ethics to be observed by counsel appearing before the Tribunal,
subject to adoption by the Plenary Meeting. Amendments to the Code shall be made in
consultation with representatives of the Prosecutor and Defence counsel, and subject to
adoption by the Plenary Meeting. If the Registrar has strong grounds for believing that
Counsel has committed a serious violation of the Code of Professional Conduct so
adopted, he may report the matter to the President or the Bureau for appropriate action
under this rule.

PART FIVE

PRE-TRIAL PROCEEDINGS

Section 1: Indictments

Rule 47: Submission of Indictment by the Prosecutor

(A) An indictment, submitted in accordance with the following procedure, shall be **D6–059**
reviewed by a Judge designated in accordance with Rule 28 for this purpose.

(B) The Prosecutor, if satisfied in the course of an investigation that there is sufficient
evidence to provide reasonable grounds for believing that a suspect has committed a
crime within the jurisdiction of the Tribunal, shall prepare and forward to the Registrar
an indictment for confirmation by a Judge, together with supporting material.

(C) The indictment shall set forth the name and particulars of the suspect, and a
concise statement of the facts of the case and of the crime with which the suspect is
charged.

(D) The Registrar shall forward the indictment and accompanying material to the
designated Judge, who will inform the Prosecutor of the scheduled date for review of the
indictment.

(E) The reviewing Judge shall examine each of the counts in the indictment, and any
supporting materials the Prosecutor may provide, to determine, applying the standard
set forth in Article 18 of the Statute, whether a case exists against the suspect.

(F) The reviewing Judge may:
  (i) Request the Prosecutor to present additional material in support of any or all
      counts, or to take any further measures which appear appropriate;
  (ii) Confirm each count;
  (iii) Dismiss each count; or
  (iv) Adjourn the review so as to give the Prosecutor the opportunity to modify the
      indictment.

(G) The indictment as confirmed by the Judge shall be retained by the Registrar, who
shall prepare certified copies bearing the seal of the Tribunal. If the accused does not
understand either of the official languages of the Tribunal and if the language

understood is known to the Registrar, a translation of the indictment in that language shall also be prepared, and a copy of the translation attached to each certified copy of the indictment.

(H) Upon confirmation of any or all counts in the indictment:
- (i) The Judge may issue an arrest warrant, in accordance with Sub-Rule 55 (A), and any orders as provided in Article 19 of the Statute; and
- (ii) The suspect shall have the status of an accused.

(I) The dismissal of a count in an indictment shall not preclude the Prosecutor from subsequently bringing an amended indictment based on the acts underlying that count if supported by additional evidence.

RULE 48: JOINDER OF ACCUSED

D6–060   Persons accused of the same or different crimes committed in the course of the same transaction may be jointly charged and tried.

RULE 48*bis*: JOINDER OF TRIALS

D6–061   Persons who are separately indicted, accused of the same or different crimes committed in the course of the same transaction, may be tried together, with leave granted by a Trial Chamber pursuant to Rule 73.

RULE 49: JOINDER OF CRIMES

D6–062   Two or more crimes may be joined in one indictment if the series of acts committed together form the same transaction, and the said crimes were committed by the same accused.

RULE 50: AMENDMENT OF INDICTMENT

D6–063   (A)(i) The Prosecutor may amend an indictment, without prior leave, at any time before its confirmation, but thereafter, until the initial appearance of the accused before a Trial Chamber pursuant to Rule 62, only with leave of the Judge who confirmed it but, in exceptional circumstances, by leave of a Judge assigned by the President. At or after such initial appearance, an amendment of an indictment may only be made by leave granted by that Trial Chamber pursuant to Rule 73. If leave to amend is granted, Rule 47 (G) and Rule 53 *bis* apply *mutatis mutandis* to the amended indictment.

(ii) In deciding whether to grant leave to amend the indictment, the Trial Chamber or, where applicable, a Judge shall, *mutatis mutandis*, follow the procedures and apply the standards set out in Sub-Rules 47(E) and (F) in addition to considering any other relevant factors.

(B) If the amended indictment includes new charges and the accused has already appeared before a Trial Chamber in accordance with Rule 62, a further appearance shall be held as soon as practicable to enable the accused to enter a plea on the new charges.

(C) The accused shall have a further period of thirty days in which to file preliminary motions pursuant to Rule 72 in respect of the new charges and, where necessary, the date for trial may be postponed to ensure adequate time for the preparation of the defence.

RULE 51: WITHDRAWAL OF INDICTMENT

D6–064   (A) The Prosecutor may withdraw an indictment, without prior leave, at any time before its confirmation, but thereafter, until the initial appearance of the accused before a Trial Chamber pursuant to Rule 62, only with leave of the Judge who confirmed it but, in exceptional circumstances, by leave of a Judge assigned by the President. At or after such initial appearance an indictment may only be withdrawn by leave granted by a Trial Chamber pursuant to Rule 73.

(B) The withdrawal of the indictment shall be promptly notified to the suspect or the accused and to the counsel of the suspect or accused.

Rule 52: Public Character of Indictment

Subject to Rule 53, upon confirmation by a Judge of a Trial Chamber, the indictment shall be made public. **D6–065**

Rule 53: Non-Disclosure

(A) In exceptional circumstances, a Judge or a Trial Chamber may, in the interests of justice, order the non-disclosure to the public of any documents or information until further order. **D6–066**

(B) When confirming an indictment the Judge may, in consultation with the Prosecutor, order that there be no public disclosure of the indictment until it is served on the accused, or, in the case of joint accused, on all the accused.

(C) A Judge or Trial Chamber may, in consultation with the Prosecutor, also order that there be no disclosure of an indictment, or part thereof, or of all or any part of any particular document or information, if satisfied that the making of such an order is required to give effect to a provision of the Rules, to protect confidential information obtained by the Prosecutor, or is otherwise in the interests of justice.

(D) Notwithstanding sub-rules (A), (B) and (C), the Prosecutor may disclose an indictment or part thereof to the authorities of a State or an appropriate authority or international body where the Prosecutor deems it necessary to secure the possible arrest of an accused.

Rule 53*bis*: Service of Indictment

(A) Service of the indictment shall be effected personally on the accused at the time the accused is taken into the custody of the Tribunal or as soon as possible thereafter. **D6–067**

(B) Personal service of an indictment on the accused is effected by giving the accused a copy of the indictment certified in accordance with Rule 47 (G).

Section 2: Orders and Warrants

Rule 54: General Provision

At the request of either party or *proprio motu*, a Judge or a Trial Chamber may issue such orders, summonses, subpoenas, warrants and transfer orders as may be necessary for the purposes of an investigation or for the preparation or conduct of the trial. **D6–068**

Rule 55: Execution of Arrest Warrants

(A) A warrant of arrest shall be signed by a Judge and shall bear the seal of the Tribunal. It shall be accompanied by a copy of the indictment, and a statement of the rights of the accused. These rights include those set forth in Article 20 of the Statute, and in Rules 42 and 43 *mutatis mutandis*, together with the right of the accused to remain silent, and to be cautioned that any statement he makes shall be recorded and may be used in evidence. **D6–069**

(B) The Registrar shall transmit to the national authorities of the State in whose territory or under whose jurisdiction or control the accused resides, or was last known to be, three sets of certified copies of:

    (i) The warrant for arrest of the accused and an order for his surrender to the Tribunal;

    (ii) The confirmed indictment;

    (iii) A statement of the rights of the accused; and if necessary a translation thereof in a language understood by the accused.

(C) The Registrar shall instruct the said authorities to:

    (i) Cause the arrest of the accused and his transfer to the Tribunal;

    (ii) Serve a set of the aforementioned documents upon the accused;

    (iii) Cause the documents to be read to the accused in a language understood by him and to caution him as to his rights in that language; and

    (iv) Return one set of the documents together with proof of service, to the Tribunal.

(D) When an arrest warrant issued by the Tribunal is executed, a member of the Prosecutor's Office may be present as from the time of arrest.

RULE 55*bis*: WARRANT OF ARREST TO ALL STATES

D6–070   (A) Upon the request of the Prosecutor, and if satisfied that to do so would facilitate the arrest of an accused who may move from State to State, or whose whereabouts are unknown, a Judge may without having recourse to the procedures set out in Rule 61, and subject to sub-rule (B), address a warrant of arrest to all States.

(B) The Registrar shall transmit such a warrant to the national authorities of such States as may be indicated by the Prosecutor.

RULE 56: COOPERATION OF STATES

D6–071   The State to which a warrant of arrest or a transfer order for a witness is transmitted shall act promptly and with all due diligence to ensure proper and effective execution thereof, in accordance with Article 28 of the Statute.

RULE 57: PROCEDURE AFTER ARREST

D6–072   Upon the arrest of the accused, the State concerned shall detain him, and shall promptly notify the Registrar. The transfer of the accused to the seat of the Tribunal, or to such other place as the Bureau may decide, after consultation with the Prosecutor and the Registrar, shall be arranged by the State authorities concerned, in liaison with the authorities of the host country and the Registrar.

RULE 58: NATIONAL EXTRADITION PROVISIONS

D6–073   The obligations laid down in Article 28 of the Statute shall prevail over any legal impediment to the surrender or transfer of the accused or of a witness to the Tribunal which may exist under the national law or extradition treaties of the State concerned.

RULE 59: FAILURE TO EXECUTE A WARRANT OF ARREST OR TRANSFER ORDER

D6–074   (A) Where the State to which a warrant of arrest or transfer order has been transmitted has been unable to execute the warrant of arrest or transfer order, it shall report forthwith its inability to the Registrar, and the reasons therefore.

(B) If, within a reasonable time after the warrant of arrest or transfer order has been transmitted to the State, no report is made on action taken, this shall be deemed a failure to execute the warrant of arrest or transfer order and the Tribunal, through the President, may notify the Security Council accordingly.

RULE 60: PUBLICATION OF INDICTMENT

At the request of the Prosecutor, a form of advertisement shall be transmitted by the **D6–075**
Registrar to the national authorities of any State or States, for publication in newspapers
or for broadcast via radio, transmission via Internet or television, notifying publicly the
existence of an indictment and calling upon the accused to surrender to the Tribunal
and inviting any person with information as to the whereabouts of the accused to
communicate that information to the Tribunal.

RULE 61: PROCEDURE IN CASE OF FAILURE TO EXECUTE A WARRANT OF ARREST

(A) If, within a reasonable time, a warrant of arrest has not been executed, and **D6–076**
personal service of the indictment has consequently not been effected, the Judge who
confirmed the indictment shall invite the Prosecutor to report on the measures taken.
When the Judge is satisfied that:
  (i) The Registrar and the Prosecutor have taken all reasonable steps to secure the
      arrest of the accused, including recourse to the appropriate authorities of the
      State in whose territory or under whose jurisdiction and control the accused to
      be served resides or was last known to be; and
  (ii) If the whereabouts of the accused are unknown, the Prosecutor and the
      Registrar have taken all reasonable steps to ascertain those whereabouts,
      including by seeking publication of advertisement pursuant to Rule 60,
the Judge shall order that the indictment be submitted by the Prosecutor to his Trial
Chamber.

(B) Upon obtaining such an order the Prosecutor shall submit the indictment to the
Trial Chamber in open court, together with all the evidence that was before the Judge
who initially confirmed the indictment and any other evidence submitted to him after
confirmation of the indictment. The Prosecutor may also call before the Trial Chamber
and examine any witness whose statement has been submitted to the confirming Judge.

(C) If the Trial Chamber is satisfied on that evidence, together with such additional
evidence as the Prosecutor may tender, that there are reasonable grounds for believing
that the accused has committed all or any of the crimes charged in the indictment, it
shall so determine. The Trial Chamber shall have the relevant parts of the indictment
read out by the Prosecutor together with an account of the efforts to effect service
referred to in Sub- Rule (A) above.

(D) The Trial Chamber shall also issue an international arrest warrant in respect of
the accused which shall be transmitted to all States. Upon request by the Prosecutor or
proprio motu, after having heard the Prosecutor, the Trial Chamber may order a State or
States to adopt provisional measures to freeze the assets of the accused, without
prejudice to the rights of third parties.

(E) If, during the hearing, the Prosecutor satisfies the Trial Chamber that the failure
to effect personal service of the indictment was due in whole or in part to a failure or
refusal of a State to co-operate with the Tribunal in accordance with Article 28 of the
Statute, the Trial Chamber shall so certify. After consulting the Presiding Judges of the
Chambers, the President shall notify the Security Council thereof in such manner as he
thinks fit.

RULE 62: INITIAL APPEARANCE OF ACCUSED AND PLEA

(A) Upon his transfer to the Tribunal, the accused shall be brought before a Trial **D6–077**
Chamber or a Judge thereof without delay, and shall be formally charged. The Trial
Chamber or the Judge shall:
  (i) Satisfy itself or himself that the right of the accused to counsel is respected;
  (ii) Read or have the indictment read to the accused in a language he understands,
      and satisfy itself or himself that the accused understands the indictment;

(iii) Call upon the accused to enter a plea of guilty or not guilty on each count; should the accused fail to do so, enter a plea of not guilty on his behalf;
(iv) In case of a plea of not guilty, instruct the Registrar to set a date for trial;
(v) In case of a plea of guilty:
    (a) if before a Judge, refer the plea to the Trial Chamber so that it may act in accordance with Rule 62 (B); or
    (b) if before a Trial Chamber, act in accordance with Rule 62 (B);
(B) If an accused pleads guilty in accordance with Rule 62 (A)(v), or requests to change his plea to guilty, the Trial Chamber shall satisfy itself that the guilty plea:
    (i) is made freely and voluntarily;
    (ii) is an informed plea;
    (iii) is unequivocal; and
    (iv) is based on sufficient facts for the crime and accused's participation in it, either on the basis of objective indicia or of lack of any material disagreement between the parties about the facts of the case.

Thereafter the Trial Chamber may enter a finding of guilt and instruct the Registrar to set a date for the sentencing hearing.

RULE 62*bis*: PLEA AGREEMENT PROCEDURE

D6–078   (A) The Prosecutor and the Defence may agree that, upon the accused entering a plea of guilty to the indictment or to one or more counts of the indictment, the Prosecutor shall do one or more of the following before the Trial Chamber:
    (i) apply to amend the indictment accordingly;
    (ii) submit that a specific sentence or sentencing range is appropriate;
    (iii) not oppose a request by the accused for a particular sentence or sentencing range.
    (B) The Trial Chamber shall not be bound by any agreement specified in paragraph (A).
    (C) If a plea agreement has been reached by the parties, the Trial Chamber shall require the disclosure of the agreement in open session or, on a showing of good cause, in closed session, at the time the accused pleads guilty in accordance with Rule 62 (A) (v), or requests to change his or her plea to guilty.

RULE 63: QUESTIONING OF THE ACCUSED

D6–079   (A) Questioning by the Prosecutor of an accused, including after the initial appearance, shall not proceed without the presence of counsel unless the accused has voluntarily and expressly agreed to proceed without counsel present. If the accused subsequently expresses a desire to have counsel, questioning shall thereupon cease, and shall only resume when the accused's counsel is present.
    (B) The questioning, including any waiver of the right to counsel, shall be audio-recorded or video-recorded in accordance with the procedure provided for in Rule 43. The Prosecutor shall at the beginning of the questioning caution the accused in accordance with Rule 42 (A)(iii).

RULE 64: DETENTION ON REMAND

D6–080   Upon his transfer to the Tribunal, the accused shall be detained in facilities provided by the host country or by another country. The President may, on the application of a party, request modification of the conditions of detention of an accused.

RULE 65: PROVISIONAL RELEASE

D6–081   (A) Once detained, an accused may not be provisionally released except upon an order of a Trial Chamber.

(B) Provisional release may be ordered by a Trial Chamber only after giving the host country and the country to which the accused seeks to be released the opportunity to be heard, and only if it is satisfied that the accused will appear for trial and, if released, will not pose a danger to any victim, witness or other person.

(C) The Trial Chamber may impose such conditions upon the provisional release of the accused as it may determine appropriate, including the execution of a bail bond and the observance of such conditions as are necessary to ensure the presence of the accused at trial and the protection of others.

(D) Any decision rendered under this Rule shall be subject to appeal in cases where leave is granted by a bench of three Judges of the Appeals Chamber, upon good cause being shown. Subject to paragraph (F) below, applications for leave to appeal shall be filed within seven days of filing of the impugned decision. Where such decision is rendered orally, the application shall be filed within seven days of the oral decision unless:

(i) the party challenging the decision was not present or represented when the decision was pronounced, in which case the time-limit shall run from the date on which the challenging party is notified of the oral decision; or

(ii) the Trial Chamber has indicated that a written decision will follow, in which case, the time-limit shall run from filing of the written decision.

(E) The Prosecutor may apply for a stay of a decision by the Trial Chamber to release an accused on the basis that the Prosecutor intends to appeal the decision, and shall make such an application at the time of filing his or her response to the initial application for provisional release by the accused.

(F) Where the Trial Chamber grants a stay of its decision to release an accused, the Prosecutor shall file his or her appeal not later than one day from the rendering of that decision.

(G) Where the Trial Chamber orders a stay of its decision to release the accused pending an appeal by the Prosecutor, the accused shall not be released until either:

(i) the time-limit for the filing of an application for leave to appeal by the Prosecutor has expired, and no such application is filed;

(ii) a bench of three Judges of the Appeals Chamber rejects the application for leave to appeal;

(iii) the Appeals Chamber dismisses the appeal; or

(iv) a bench of three Judges of the Appeals Chamber or the Appeals Chamber otherwise orders.

(H) If necessary, the Trial Chamber may issue a warrant of arrest to secure the presence of an accused who has been provisionally released or is for any other reason at large. The provisions of Section 2 of Part Five shall apply *mutatis mutandis*.

(I) Without prejudice to the provisions of Rule 107, the Appeals Chamber may grant provisional release to convicted persons pending an appeal or for a fixed period if it is satisfied that:

(i) the appellant, if released, will either appear at the hearing of the appeal or will surrender into detention at the conclusion of the fixed period, as the case may be;

(ii) the appellant, if released, will not pose a danger to any victim, witness or other person, and

(iii) special circumstances exist warranting such release.

The provisions of paragraphs (C) and (H) shall apply *mutatis mutandis*.

Rule 65*bis*: Status Conferences

(A) A status conference may be convened by a Trial Chamber or a Judge thereof. Its **D6–082** purpose is to organise exchanges between the parties so as to ensure expeditious trial proceedings.

(B) The Appeals Chamber or an Appeals Chamber Judge may convene a status conference.

(C) A status conference held pursuant to paragraph (B) of this Rule may be conducted with the participation of counsel via tele-conference or video-conference.

Section 3: Production of Evidence

RULE 66: DISCLOSURE OF MATERIALS BY THE PROSECUTOR

D6–083   Subject to the provisions of Rules 53 and 69;
(A) The Prosecutor shall disclose to the Defence:
   i) Within 30 days of the initial appearance of the accused copies of the supporting material which accompanied the indictment when confirmation was sought as well as all prior statements obtained by the Prosecutor from the accused, and
   ii) No later than 60 days before the date set for trial, copies of the statements of all witnesses whom the Prosecutor intends to call to testify at trial; upon good cause shown a Trial Chamber may order that copies of the statements of additional prosecution witnesses be made available to the defence within a prescribed time.
(B) At the request of the defence, the Prosecutor shall, subject to Sub-Rule (C), permit the defence to inspect any books, documents, photographs and tangible objects in his custody or control, which are material to the preparation of the defence, or are intended for use by the Prosecutor as evidence at trial or were obtained from or belonged to the accused.
(C) Where information or materials are in the possession of the Prosecutor, the disclosure of which may prejudice further or ongoing investigations, or for any other reasons may be contrary to the public interest or affect the security interests of any State, the Prosecutor may apply to the Trial Chamber sitting *in camera* to be relieved from the obligation to disclose pursuant to Sub-Rule (A) and (B). When making such an application the Prosecutor shall provide the Trial Chamber, and only the Trial Chamber, with the information or materials that are sought to be kept confidential.

RULE 67: RECIPROCAL DISCLOSURE OF EVIDENCE

D6–084   Subject to the provisions of Rules 53 and 69:
(A) As early as reasonably practicable and in any event prior to the commencement of the trial:
   (i) The Prosecutor shall notify the defence of the names of the witnesses that he intends to call to establish the guilt of the accused and in rebuttal of any defence plea of which the Prosecutor has received notice in accordance with Sub-Rule (ii) below;
   (ii) The defence shall notify the Prosecutor of its intent to enter:
      (a) The defence of alibi; in which case the notification shall specify the place or places at which the accused claims to have been present at the time of the alleged crime and the names and addresses of witnesses and any other evidence upon which the accused intends to rely to establish the alibi;
      (b) Any special defence, including that of diminished or lack of mental responsibility; in which case the notification shall specify the names and addresses of witnesses and any other evidence upon which the accused intends to rely to establish the special defence.
(B) Failure of the defence to provide such notice under this Rule shall not limit the right of the accused to rely on the above defences.
(C) If the defence makes a request pursuant to Rule 66 (B), the Prosecutor shall in turn be entitled to inspect any books, documents, photographs and tangible objects, which are within the custody or control of the defence and which it intends to use as evidence at the trial.
(D) If either party discovers additional evidence or information or materials which should have been produced earlier pursuant to the Rules, that party shall promptly notify the other party and the Trial Chamber of the existence of the additional evidence or information or materials.

Rule 68: Disclosure of Exculpatory and Other Relevant Material

(A) The Prosecutor shall, as soon as practicable, disclose to the Defence any material, **D6–085** which in the actual knowledge of the Prosecutor may suggest the innocence or mitigate the guilt of the accused or affect the credibility of Prosecution evidence.

(B) Where possible, and with the agreement of the Defence, and without prejudice to paragraph (A), the Prosecutor shall make available to the Defence, in electronic form, collections of relevant material held by the Prosecutor, together with appropriate computer software with which the defence can search such collections electronically.

(C) The Prosecutor shall take reasonable steps, if confidential information is provided to the Prosecutor by a person or entity under Rule 70(B) and contains material referred to in paragraph (A) above, to obtain the consent of the provider to disclosure of that material, or the fact of its existence, to the accused.

(D) The Prosecutor shall apply to the Chamber sitting *in camera* to be relieved from an obligation under the Rules to disclose information in the possession of the Prosecutor, if its disclosure may prejudice further or ongoing investigations, or for any other reason may be contrary to the public interest or affect the security interests of any State, and when making such application, the Prosecutor shall provide the Trial Chamber (but only the Trial Chamber) with the information that is sought to be kept confidential.

(E) Notwithstanding the completion of the trial and any subsequent appeal, the Prosecutor shall disclose to the other party any material referred to in paragraph (A) above.

Rule 69: Protection of Victims and Witnesses

(A) In exceptional circumstances, either of the parties may apply to a Trial Chamber **D6–086** to order the non-disclosure of the identity of a victim or witness who may be in danger or at risk, until the Chamber decides otherwise.

(B) In the determination of protective measures for victims and witnesses, the Trial Chamber may consult the Victims and Witness Support Unit.

(C) Subject to Rule 75, the identity of the victim or witness shall be disclosed within such time as determined by Trial Chamber to allow adequate time for preparation of the prosecution and the defence.

Rule 70: Matters Not Subject to Disclosure

(A) Notwithstanding the provisions of Rules 66 and 67, reports, memoranda, or other **D6–087** internal documents prepared by a party, its assistants or representatives in connection with the investigation or preparation of the case, are not subject to disclosure or notification under the aforementioned provisions.

(B) If the Prosecutor is in possession of information which has been provided to him on a confidential basis and which has been used solely for the purpose of generating new evidence, that initial information and its origin shall not be disclosed by the Prosecutor without the consent of the person or entity providing the initial information and shall in any event not be given in evidence without prior disclosure to the accused.

(C) If, after obtaining the consent of the person or entity providing information under this Rule, the Prosecutor elects to present as evidence any testimony, document or other material so provided, the Trial Chamber, notwithstanding Rule 98, may not order either party to produce additional evidence received from the person or entity providing the initial information, nor may the Trial Chamber for the purpose of obtaining such additional evidence itself summon that person or a representative of that entity as a witness or order their attendance.

(D) If the Prosecutor calls as a witness the person providing or a representative of the entity providing information under this Rule, the Trial Chamber may not compel the witness to answer any question the witness declines to answer on grounds of confidentiality.

(E) The right of the accused to challenge the evidence presented by the Prosecution shall remain unaffected subject only to limitations contained in Sub-Rules (C) and (D).

(F) Nothing in Sub-Rule (C) or (D) above shall affect a Trial Chamber's power under Rule 89 (C) to exclude evidence if its probative value is substantially outweighed by the need to ensure a fair trial.

Section 4: Depositions

RULE 71: DEPOSITIONS

D6–088   (A) At the request of either party, a Trial Chamber may, in exceptional circumstances and in the interests of justice, order that a deposition be taken for use at trial, and appoint, for that purpose, a Presiding Officer.

(B) The motion for the taking of a deposition shall be in writing and shall indicate the name and whereabouts of the witness whose deposition is sought, the date and place at which the deposition is to be taken, a statement of the matters on which the person is to be examined, and of the exceptional circumstances justifying the taking of the deposition.

(C) If the motion is granted, the party at whose request the deposition is to be taken shall give reasonable notice to the other party, who shall have the right to attend the taking of the deposition and cross-examine the witness.

(D) The deposition may also be given by means of a video-conference.

(E) The Presiding Officer shall ensure that the deposition is taken in accordance with the Rules and that a record is made of the deposition, including cross-examination and objections raised by either party for decision by the Trial Chamber. He shall transmit the record to the Trial Chamber.

Section 5: Preliminary Motions

RULE 72: PRELIMINARY MOTIONS

D6–089   (A) Preliminary motions, being motions which:
(i) challenge jurisdiction;
(ii) allege defects in the form of the indictment;
(iii) seek the severance of counts joined in one indictment under Rule 49 or seek separate trials under Rule 82 (B); or
(iv) raise objections based on the refusal of a request for assignment of counsel made under Rule 45 (C)

shall be in writing and be brought not later than thirty days after disclosure by the Prosecutor to the Defence of all material and statements referred to in Rule 66(A)(i) and shall be disposed of not later than sixty days after they were filed and before the commencement of the opening statements provided for in Rule 84. The Trial Chamber may rule on such motions based solely on the briefs of the parties, unless it is decided to hear the motion in open Court.

(B) Decisions on preliminary motions are without interlocutory appeal, save:
(i) in the case of motions challenging jurisdiction, where an appeal by either party lies as of right;
(ii) in other cases where certification has been granted by the Trial Chamber, which may grant such certification if the decision involves an issue that would significantly affect the fair and expeditious conduct of the proceedings or the outcome of the trial, and for which, in the opinion of the Trial Chamber, an immediate resolution by the Appeals Chamber may materially advance the proceedings.

(C) Appeals under paragraph (B)(i) shall be filed within fifteen days and requests for certification under paragraph (B)(ii) shall be filed within seven days of filing of the impugned decision. Where such decision is rendered orally, this time-limit shall run from the date of the oral decision, unless

    (i) the party challenging the decision was not present or represented when the decision was pronounced, in which case the time-limit shall run from the date on which the challenging party is notified of the oral decision; or

    (ii) the Trial Chamber has indicated that a written decision will follow, in which case, the time-limit shall run from filing of the written decision.

If certification is given, a party shall appeal to the Appeals Chamber within seven days of the filing of the decision to certify.

(D) For purposes of paragraphs (A)(i) and (B)(i), a motion challenging jurisdiction refers exclusively to a motion which challenges an indictment on the ground that it does not relate to:

    (i) any of the persons indicated in Articles 1, 5, 6 and 8 of the Statute;

    (ii) the territories indicated in Articles 1, 7 and 8 of the Statute;

    (iii) the period indicated in Articles 1, 7, and 8 of the Statute; or

    (iv) any of the violations indicated in Articles 2, 3, 4 and 6 of the Statute.

(E) An appeal brought under paragraph (B)(i) may not be proceeded with if a bench of three Judges of the Appeals Chamber, assigned by the presiding Judge of the Appeals Chamber, decides that the appeal is not capable of satisfying the requirements of paragraph (D), in which case the appeal shall be dismissed.

(F) Objections to the form of the indictment, including an amended indictment, shall be raised by a party in one motion only, unless otherwise allowed by a Trial Chamber.

(G) Failure to comply with the time limits prescribed in this Rule shall constitute a waiver of the rights. The Trial Chamber may, however, grant relief from the waiver upon showing good cause.

PART SIX

PROCEEDINGS BEFORE TRIAL CHAMBERS

Section 1: General Provisions

RULE 73: MOTIONS

(A) Subject to Rule 72, either party may move before a Trial Chamber for appropriate ruling or relief after the initial appearance of the accused. The Trial Chamber, or a Judge designated by the Chamber from among its members, may rule on such motions based solely on the briefs of the parties, unless it is decided to hear the motion in open Court. **D6–090**

(B) Decisions rendered on such motions are without interlocutory appeal save with certification by the Trial Chamber, which may grant such certification if the decision involves an issue that would significantly affect the fair and expeditious conduct of the proceedings or the outcome of the trial, and for which, in the opinion of the Trial Chamber, an immediate resolution by the Appeals Chamber may materially advance the proceedings.

(C) Requests for certification shall be filed within seven days of the filing of the impugned decision. Where such decision is rendered orally, this time-limit shall run from the date of the oral decision, unless

    (i) the party challenging the decision was not present or represented when the decision was pronounced, in which case the time-limit shall run from the date on which the challenging party is notified of the oral decision; or

    (ii) the Trial Chamber has indicated that a written decision will follow, in which case the time-limit shall run from filing of the written decision.

If certification is granted, a party shall appeal to the Appeals Chamber within seven days of the filing of the decision to certify.

(D) Where a date has been set for the hearing of a motion, including a preliminary motion, any additional motions to be heard on that date and any supporting material to the motions must be filed at least ten days before the hearing of the motion. Failure to observe this Rule will mean that the later motion will not be considered on the hearing date, nor will any adjournment of the original motion be granted on the basis of subsequent motions filed, save in exceptional circumstances.

(E) A responding party shall, thereafter, file any reply within five days from the date on which Counsel received the motion.

(F) In addition to the sanctions envisaged by Rule 46, a Chamber may impose sanctions against Counsel if Counsel brings a motion, including a preliminary motion, that, in the opinion of the Chamber, is frivolous or is an abuse of process. Such sanctions may include non-payment, in whole or in part, of fees associated with the motion and/or costs thereof.

(G) Notwithstanding the time limits in Rule 72(A), the time limit in the present Rule applies.

RULE 73*bis*: PRE-TRIAL CONFERENCE

D6–091   (A) The Trial Chamber shall hold a Pre-Trial Conference prior to the commencement of the trial.

(B) At the Pre-Trial Conference the Trial Chamber or a Judge, designated from among its members, may order the Prosecutor, within a time limit set by the Trial Chamber or the said Judge, and before the date set for trial, to file the following:

   (i) A pre-trial brief addressing the factual and legal issues;
   (ii) Admissions by the parties and a statement of other matters not in dispute;
   (iii) A statement of contested matters of fact and law;
   (iv) A list of witnesses the Prosecutor intends to call with:
      (a) The name or pseudonym of each witness;
      (b) A summary of the facts on which each witness will testify;
      (c) The points in the indictment on which each witness will testify; and
      (d) The estimated length of time required for each witness;
   (v) A list of exhibits the Prosecutor intends to offer stating, where possible, whether or not the defence has any objection as to authenticity.

The Trial Chamber or the Judge may order the Prosecutor to provide the Trial Chamber with copies of written statements of each witness whom the Prosecutor intends to call to testify.

(C) The Trial Chamber or the designated Judge may order the Prosecutor to shorten the examination-in-chief of some witnesses.

(D) The Trial Chamber or the designated Judge may order the Prosecutor to reduce the number of witnesses, if it considers that an excessive number of witnesses are being called to prove the same facts.

(E) After commencement of Trial, the Prosecutor, if he considers it to be in the interests of justice, may move the Trial Chamber for leave to reinstate the list of witnesses or to vary his decision as to which witnesses are to be called.

(F) At the Pre-Trial Conference, the Trial Chamber or the designated Judge may order the defence to file a statement of admitted facts and law and a pre-trial brief addressing the factual and legal issues, not later than seven days prior to the date set for trial.

RULE 73*ter*: PRE-DEFENCE CONFERENCE

D6–092   (A) The Trial Chamber may hold a Conference prior to the commencement by the Defence of its case.

(B) At that Conference, the Trial Chamber or a Judge, designated from among its members, may order that the Defence, before the commencement of its case but after the close of the case for the prosecution, file the following:

   (i) Admissions by the parties and a statement of other matters which are not in dispute;
   (ii) A statement of contested matters of fact and law;

(iii) A list of witnesses the Defence intends to call with:
    (a) The name or pseudonym of each witness;
    (b) A summary of the facts on which each witness will testify;
    (c) The points in the indictment as to which each witness will testify; and
    (d) The estimated length of time required for each witness;
 (iv) A list of exhibits the Defence intends to offer in its case, stating where possible whether or not the Prosecutor has any objection as to authenticity.

The Trial Chamber or the Judge may order the Defence to provide the Trial Chamber and the Prosecutor with copies of the written statements of each witness whom the Defence intends to call to testify.

(C) The Trial Chamber or the designated Judge may order the Defence to shorten the estimated length of the examination-in-chief for some witnesses.

(D) The Trial Chamber or the designated Judge may order the Defence to reduce the number of witnesses, if it considers that an excessive number of witnesses are being called to prove the same facts.

(E) After commencement of the Defence case, the Defence, if it considers it to be in the interests of justice, may move the Trial Chamber for leave to reinstate the list of witnesses or to vary its decision as to which witnesses are to be called.

RULE 74: *AMICUS CURIAE*

A Chamber may, if it considers it desirable for the proper determination of the case, invite or grant leave to any State, organization or person to appear before it and make submissions on any issue specified by the Chamber.

D6–093

RULE 74*bis*: MEDICAL EXAMINATION OF THE ACCUSED

A Trial Chamber may, *proprio motu* or at the request of a party, order a medical, including psychiatric examination or a psychological examination of the accused. In such case, the Registrar shall entrust this task to one or several experts whose names appear on a list previously drawn up by the Registry and approved by the Bureau.

D6–094

RULE 75: MEASURES FOR THE PROTECTION OF VICTIMS AND WITNESSES

(A) A Judge or a Chamber may, *proprio motu* or at the request of either party, or of the victim or witness concerned, or of the Victims and Witnesses Section, order appropriate measures for the privacy and protection of victims and witnesses, provided that the measures are consistent with the rights of the accused.

D6–095

(B) A Chamber may hold an in camera proceeding to determine whether to order notably:
 (i) measures to prevent disclosure to the public or the media of the identity or whereabouts of a victim or a witness, or of persons related to or associated with a victim or witness by such means as:
    (a) expunging names and identifying information from the Tribunal's public records;
    (b) non-disclosure to the public of any records identifying the victim;
    (c) giving of testimony through image- or voice-altering devices or closed circuit television; and
    (d) assignment of a pseudonym;
 (ii) Closed sessions, in accordance with Rule 79;
 (iii) Appropriate measures to facilitate the testimony of vulnerable victims and witnesses, such as one-way closed circuit television.

(C) The Victims and Witnesses Section shall ensure that the witness has been informed before giving evidence by the party calling that witness that his testimony and his identity may be disclosed at a later date in another case, pursuant to Rule 75 (F).

(D) A Chamber shall control the manner of questioning to avoid any harassment or intimidation.

(E) When making an order under paragraph (A) above, a Judge or a Chamber shall wherever appropriate state in the order whether the transcript of those proceedings relating to the evidence of the witness to whom the measures relate shall be made available for use in other proceedings before the Tribunal.

(F) Once protective measures have been ordered in respect of a victim or witness in any proceedings before the Tribunal (the "first proceedings"), such protective measures:

(i) shall continue to have effect *mutatis mutandis* in any other proceedings before the Tribunal (the "second proceedings") unless and until they are rescinded, varied or augmented in accordance with the procedure set out in this Rule; but

(ii) shall not prevent the Prosecutor from discharging any disclosure obligation under the Rules in the second proceedings, provided that the Prosecutor notifies the Defence to whom the disclosure is being made of the nature of the protective measures ordered in the first proceedings.

(G) A party to the second proceedings seeking to rescind, vary or augment protective measures ordered in the first proceedings must apply:

(i) to any Chamber, however constituted, remaining seised of the first proceedings; or

(ii) if no Chamber remains seised of the first proceedings, to the Chamber seised of the second proceedings.

(H) Before determining an application under paragraph (G)(ii) above, the Chamber seised of the second proceedings shall obtain all relevant information from the first proceedings, and shall consult with any Judge who ordered the protective measures in the first proceedings, if that Judge remains a Judge of the Tribunal.

(I) An application to a Chamber to rescind, vary or augment protective measures in respect of a victim or witness may be dealt with either by the Chamber or by a Judge of that Chamber, and any reference in this Rule to "a Chamber" shall include a reference to "a Judge of that Chamber".

RULE 76: SOLEMN DECLARATION BY INTERPRETERS AND TRANSLATORS

D6–096   Before performing any duties, an interpreter or a translator shall solemnly declare to do so faithfully, independently, impartially and with full respect for the duty of confidentiality.

RULE 77: CONTEMPT OF THE TRIBUNAL

D6–097   (A) The Tribunal in the exercise of its inherent power may hold in contempt those who knowingly and wilfully interfere with its administration of justice, including any person who

(i) being a witness before a Chamber, contumaciously refuses or fails to answer a question;

(ii) discloses information relating to those proceedings in knowing violation of an order of a Chamber;

(iii) without just excuse fails to comply with an order to attend before or produce documents before a Chamber;

(iv) threatens, intimidates, causes any injury or offers a bribe to, or otherwise interferes with, a witness who is giving, has given, or is about to give evidence in proceedings before a Chamber, or a potential witness; or

(v) threatens, intimidates, offers a bribe to, or otherwise seeks to coerce any other person, with the intention of preventing that other person from complying with an obligation under an order of a Judge or Chamber.

(B) Any incitement or attempt to commit any of the acts punishable under paragraph (A) is punishable as contempt of the Tribunal with the same penalties.

(C) When a Chamber has reason to believe that a person may be in contempt of the Tribunal, it may:

(i) direct the Prosecutor to investigate the matter with a view to the preparation and submission of an indictment for contempt;

(ii) where the Prosecutor, in the view of the Chamber, has a conflict of interest with respect to the relevant conduct, direct the Registrar to appoint an *amicus curiae* to investigate the matter and report back to the Chamber as to whether there are sufficient grounds for instigating contempt proceedings; or

(iii) initiate proceedings itself.

(D) If the Chamber considers that there are sufficient grounds to proceed against a person for contempt, the Chamber may:

(i) in circumstances described in paragraph (C) (i), direct the Prosecutor to prosecute the matter; or

(ii) in circumstances described in paragraph (C) (ii) or (iii), issue an order in lieu of an indictment and either direct *amicus curiae* to prosecute the matter or prosecute the matter itself.

(E) The Rules of Procedure and Evidence in Parts Four to Eight shall apply *mutatis mutandis* to proceedings under this Rule.

(F) Any person indicted for or charged with contempt shall, if that person satisfies the criteria for determination of indigence established by the Registrar, be assigned counsel in accordance with Rule 45.

(G) The maximum penalty that may be imposed on a person found to be in contempt of the Tribunal shall be a term of imprisonment not exceeding five years, or a fine not exceeding USD10,000, or both.

(H) Payment of a fine shall be made to the Registrar to be held in a separate account.

(I) If a counsel is found guilty of contempt of the Tribunal pursuant to this Rule, the Chamber making such finding may also determine that counsel is no longer eligible to represent a suspect or accused before the Tribunal or that such conduct amounts to misconduct of counsel pursuant to Rule 46, or both.

(J) Any decision rendered by a Trial Chamber under this Rule shall be subject to appeal. Notice of appeal shall be filed within fifteen days of filing of the impugned decision. Where such decision is rendered orally, the notice shall be filed within fifteen days of the oral decision, unless

(i) the party challenging the decision was not present or represented when the decision was pronounced, in which case the time-limit shall run from the date on which the challenging party is notified of the oral decision; or

(ii) the Trial Chamber has indicated that a written decision will follow, in which case the time-limit shall run from filing of the written decision.

(K) In the case of decisions under this Rule by the Appeals Chamber sitting as a Chamber of first instance, an appeal may be submitted in writing to the President within fifteen days of the filing of the impugned decision. Such appeal shall be decided by five different Judges as assigned by the President. Where the impugned decision is rendered orally, the appeal shall be filed within fifteen days of the oral decision, unless

(i) the party challenging the decision was not present or represented when the decision was pronounced, in which case the time-limit shall run from the date on which the challenging party is notified of the oral decision; or

(ii) the Appeals Chamber has indicated that a written decision will follow, in which case the time-limit shall run from filing of the written decision.

RULE 78: OPEN SESSIONS

All proceedings before a Trial Chamber, other than deliberations of the Chamber, **D6–098** shall be held in public, unless otherwise provided.

RULE 79: CLOSED SESSIONS

(A) The Trial Chamber may order that the press and the public be excluded from all **D6–099** or part of the proceedings for reasons of:

(i) Public order or morality;

(ii) Safety, security or non-disclosure of the identity of a victim or witness as provided in Rule 75; or

(iii) The protection of the interests of justice.

(B) The Trial Chamber shall make public the reasons for its order.

RULE 80: CONTROL OF PROCEEDINGS

D6–100   (A) The Trial Chamber may exclude a person from the proceedings in order to protect the right of the accused to a fair and public trial, or to maintain the dignity and decorum of the proceedings.

(B) The Trial Chamber may order the removal of an accused from the proceedings and continue the proceedings in his absence if he has persisted in disruptive conduct following a warning that he may be removed.

RULE 81: RECORDS OF PROCEEDINGS AND PRESERVATION OF EVIDENCE

D6–101   (A) The Registrar shall cause to be made and preserve a full and accurate record of all proceedings, including audio recordings, transcripts and, when deemed necessary by the Trial Chamber, video recordings.

(B) The Trial Chamber may order the disclosure of all or part of the record of closed proceedings when the reasons for ordering the non disclosure no longer exist.

(C) The Registrar shall retain and preserve all physical evidence offered during the proceedings.

(D) Photography, video-recording or audio-recording of the trial, otherwise than by the Registry, may be authorised at the discretion of the Trial Chamber.

Section 2: Case Presentation

RULE 82: JOINT AND SEPARATE TRIALS

D6–102   (A) In joint trials, each accused shall be accorded the same rights as if he were being tried separately.

(B) The Trial Chamber may order that persons accused jointly under Rule 48 be tried separately if it considers it necessary in order to avoid a conflict of interests that might cause serious prejudice to an accused, or to protect the interests of justice.

RULE 82*bis*: TRIAL IN THE ABSENCE OF ACCUSED

D6–103   If an accused refuses to appear before the Trial Chamber for trial, the Chamber may order that the trial proceed in the absence of the accused for so long as his refusal persists, provided that the Trial Chamber is satisfied that:

(i) the accused has made his initial appearance under Rule 62;

(ii) the Registrar has duly notified the accused that he is required to be present for trial;

(iii) the interests of the accused are represented by counsel.

RULE 83: INSTRUMENTS OF RESTRAINT

D6–104   Instruments of restraint, such as handcuffs, shall not be used except as a precaution against escape during transfer or for security reasons, and shall be removed when the accused appears before a Chamber.

Rule 84: Opening Statements

Before presentation of evidence by the Prosecutor, each party may make an opening **D6–105** statement. The defence may however elect to make its statement after the Prosecutor has concluded presentation of evidence and before the presentation of evidence for the defence.

Rule 85: Presentation of Evidence

(A) Each party is entitled to call witnesses and present evidence. Unless otherwise **D6–106** directed by the Trial Chamber in the interests of justice, evidence at the trial shall be presented in the following sequence:
  (i) Evidence for the prosecution;
  (ii) Evidence for the defence;
  (iii) Prosecution evidence in rebuttal;
  (iv) Defence evidence in rejoinder;
  (v) Evidence ordered by the Trial Chamber pursuant to Rule 98.
  (vi) Any relevant information that may assist the Trial Chamber in determining an appropriate sentence, if the accused is found guilty on one or more of the charges in the indictment.
(B) Examination-in-chief, cross-examination and re-examination shall be allowed in each case. It shall be for the party calling a witness to examine him in chief, but a Judge may at any stage put any question to the witness.
(C) The accused may, if he so desires, appear as a witness in his own defence.

Rule 86: Closing Arguments

(A) After the presentation of all the evidence, the Prosecutor may present a closing **D6–107** argument. Whether or not the Prosecutor does so, the defence may make a closing argument. The Prosecutor may present a rebuttal argument to which the defence may present a rejoinder.
(B) A party shall file a final trial brief with the Trial Chamber not later than five days prior to the day set for the presentation of that party's closing argument.
(C) The parties shall also address matters of sentencing in closing arguments.

Rule 87: Deliberations

(A) After presentation of closing arguments, the Presiding Judge shall declare the **D6–108** hearing closed, and the Trial Chamber shall deliberate in private. A finding of guilty may be reached only when a majority of the Trial Chamber is satisfied that guilt has been proved beyond reasonable doubt.
(B) The Trial Chamber shall vote separately on each count contained in the indictment. If two or more accused are tried together under Rule 48, separate findings shall be made as to each accused.
(C) If the Trial Chamber finds the accused guilty on one or more of the counts contained in the indictment, it shall also determine the penalty to be imposed in respect of each of the counts.

Rule 88: Judgement

(A) The judgement shall be pronounced in public, on a date of which notice shall have **D6–109** been given to the parties and counsel and at which they shall be entitled to be present.
(B) If the Trial Chamber finds the accused guilty of a crime and concludes from the evidence that unlawful taking of property by the accused was associated with it, it shall

make a specific finding to that effect in its judgement. The Trial Chamber may order restitution as provided in Rule 105.

(C) The judgement shall be rendered by a majority of the Judges. It shall be accompanied or followed as soon as possible by a reasoned opinion in writing. Separate or dissenting opinions may be appended.

Section 3: Rules of Evidence

RULE 89: GENERAL PROVISIONS

D6–110   (A) The rules of evidence set forth in this Section shall govern the proceedings before the Chambers. The Chambers shall not be bound by national rules of evidence.

(B) In cases not otherwise provided for in this Section, a Chamber shall apply rules of evidence which will best favour a fair determination of the matter before it and are consonant with the spirit of the Statute and the general principles of law.

(C) A Chamber may admit any relevant evidence which it deems to have probative value.

(D) A Chamber may request verification of the authenticity of evidence obtained out of court.

RULE 90: TESTIMONY OF WITNESSES

D6–111   (A) Witnesses shall, in principle, be heard directly by the Chambers unless a Chamber has ordered that the witness be heard by means of a deposition as provided for in Rule 71.

(B) Every witness shall, before giving evidence, make the following solemn declaration:

> "I solemnly declare that I will speak the truth, the whole truth and nothing but the truth."

(C) A child who, in the opinion of the Chamber, does not understand the nature of a solemn declaration, may be permitted to testify without that formality, if the Chamber is of the opinion that the child is sufficiently mature to be able to report the facts of which the child had knowledge and understands the duty to tell the truth. A judgement, however, cannot be based on such testimony alone.

(D) A witness, other than an expert, who has not yet testified shall not be present when the testimony of another witness is given. However, a witness who has heard the testimony of another witness shall not for that reason alone be disqualified from testifying.

(E) A witness may refuse to make any statement which might tend to incriminate him. The Chamber may, however, compel the witness to answer the question. Testimony compelled in this way shall not be used as evidence in a subsequent prosecution against the witness for any offence other than perjury.

(F) The Trial Chamber shall exercise control over the mode and order of interrogating witnesses and presenting evidence so as to:

   (i) Make the interrogation and presentation effective for the ascertainment of the truth; and

   (ii) Avoid needless consumption of time.

(G)(i) Cross-examination shall be limited to the subject-matter of the evidence-in-chief and matters affecting the credibility of the witness and, where the witness is able to give evidence relevant to the case for the cross-examining party, to the subject-matter of the case.

   (ii) In the cross-examination of a witness who is able to give evidence relevant to the case for the cross-examining party, counsel shall put to that witness the nature of the case of the party for whom that counsel appears which is in contradiction of the evidence given by the witness.

   (iii) The Trial Chamber may, in the exercise of its discretion, permit enquiry into additional matters.

RULE 90*bis*: TRANSFER OF A DETAINED WITNESS

(A) Any detained person whose personal appearance as a witness has been requested **D6–112** by the Tribunal shall be transferred temporarily to the Detention Unit of the Tribunal, conditional on his return within the period decided by the Tribunal.

(B) The transfer order shall be issued by a Judge or Trial Chamber only after prior verification that the following conditions have been met:

    (i) The presence of the detained witness is not required for any criminal proceedings in progress in the territory of the requested State during the period the witness is required by the Tribunal;

    (ii) Transfer of the witness does not extend the period of his detention as foreseen by the requested State;

(C) The Registry shall transmit the order of transfer to the national authorities of the State on whose territory, or under whose jurisdiction or control, the witness is detained. Transfer shall be arranged by the national authorities concerned in liaison with the host country and the Registrar.

(D) The Registry shall ensure the proper conduct of the transfer, including the supervision of the witness in the Detention Unit of the Tribunal; it shall remain abreast of any changes which might occur regarding the conditions of detention provided for by the requested State and which may possibly affect the length of the detention of the witness in the Detention Unit and, as promptly as possible, shall inform the relevant Judge or Chamber.

(E) On expiration of the period decided by the Tribunal for the temporary transfer, the detained witness shall be remanded to the authorities of the requested State, unless the State, within that period, has transmitted an order of release of the witness, which shall take effect immediately.

(F) If, by the end of the period decided by the Tribunal, the presence of the detained witness continues to be necessary, a Judge or a Chamber may extend the period, on the same conditions stated in the Sub-Rule (B).

RULE 91: FALSE TESTIMONY UNDER SOLEMN DECLARATION

(A) A Chamber, *proprio motu* or at the request of a party, may warn a witness of the **D6–113** duty to tell the truth and the consequences that may result from a failure to do so.

(B) If a Chamber has strong grounds for believing that a witness has knowingly and wilfully given false testimony, it may:

    (i) direct the Prosecutor to investigate the matter with a view to the preparation and submission of an indictment for false testimony; or

    (ii) where the Prosecutor, in the view of the Chamber, has a conflict of interest with respect to the relevant conduct, direct the Registrar to appoint an *amicus curiae* to investigate the matter and report back to the Chamber as to whether there are sufficient grounds for instigating proceedings for false testimony.

(C) If the Chamber considers that there are sufficient grounds to proceed against a person for giving false testimony, the Chamber may:

    (i) in circumstances described in paragraph (B) (i), direct the Prosecutor to prosecute the matter; or

    (ii) in circumstances described in paragraph (B) (ii), issue an order in lieu of an indictment and direct *amicus curiae* to prosecute the matter.

(D) The Rules of Procedure and Evidence in Parts Four to Eight shall apply *mutatis mutandis* to proceedings under this Rule.

(E) Any person indicted for or charged with false testimony shall, if that person satisfies the criteria for determination of indigence established by the Registrar, be assigned counsel in accordance with Rule 45.

(F) No Judge who sat as a member of the Trial Chamber before which the witness appeared shall sit for the trial of the witness for false testimony.

(G) The maximum penalty for false testimony under solemn declaration shall be a fine of USD10,000 or a term of imprisonment of five years, or both. The payment of any fine imposed shall be paid to the Registrar to be held in the account referred to in Rule 77 (H).

(H) Paragraphs (B) to (G) apply *mutatis mutandis* to a person who knowingly and willingly makes a false statement in a written statement taken in accordance with Rule 92 *bis* which the person knows or has reason to know may be used as evidence in proceedings before the Tribunal.

(I) Any decision rendered by a Trial Chamber under this Rule shall be subject to appeal. Notice of appeal shall be filed within fifteen days of filing of the impugned decision. Where such decision is rendered orally, the notice shall be filed within fifteen days of the oral decision, unless

  (i) the party challenging the decision was not present or represented when the decision was pronounced, in which case the time-limit shall run from the date on which the challenging party is notified of the oral decision; or

  (ii) the Trial Chamber has indicated that a written decision will follow, in which case the time-limit shall run from filing of the written decision.

RULE 92: CONFESSIONS

D6–114   A confession by the accused given during questioning by the Prosecutor shall, provided the requirements of Rule 63 were strictly complied with, be presumed to have been free and voluntary unless the contrary is proved.

RULE 92*bis*: PROOF OF FACTS OTHER THAN BY ORAL EVIDENCE

D6–115   (A) A Trial Chamber may admit, in whole or in part, the evidence of a witness in the form of a written statement in lieu of oral testimony which goes to proof of a matter other than the acts and conduct of the accused as charged in the indictment.

  (i) Factors in favour of admitting evidence in the form of a written statement include, but are not limited to, circumstances in which the evidence in question:

    (a) is of a cumulative nature, in that other witnesses will give or have given oral testimony of similar facts;

    (b) relates to relevant historical, political or military background;

    (c) consists of a general or statistical analysis of the ethnic composition of the population in the places to which the indictment relates;

    (d) concerns the impact of crimes upon victims;

    (e) relates to issues of the character of the accused; or

    (f) relates to factors to be taken into account in determining sentence.

  (ii) Factors against admitting evidence in the form of a written statement include whether:

    (a) there is an overriding public interest in the evidence in question being presented orally;

    (b) a party objecting can demonstrate that its nature and source renders it unreliable, or that its prejudicial effect outweighs its probative value; or

    (c) there are any other factors which make it appropriate for the witness to attend for cross-examination.

(B) A written statement under this Rule shall be admissible if it attaches a declaration by the person making the written statement that the contents of the statement are true and correct to the best of that person's knowledge and belief and

  (i) the declaration is witnessed by:

    (a) a person authorised to witness such a declaration in accordance with the law and procedure of a State; or

    (b) a Presiding Officer appointed by the Registrar of the Tribunal for that purpose; and

  (ii) the person witnessing the declaration verifies in writing:

    (a) that the person making the statement is the person identified in the said statement;

    (b) that the person making the statement stated that the contents of the written statement are, to the best of that person's knowledge and belief, true and correct;

    (c) that the person making the statement was informed that if the content of the written statement is not true then he or she may be subject to proceedings for giving false testimony; and

    (d) the date and place of the declaration.

The declaration shall be attached to the written statement presented to the Trial Chamber.

(C) A written statement not in the form prescribed by paragraph (B) may nevertheless be admissible if made by a person who has subsequently died, or by a person who can no longer with reasonable diligence be traced, or by a person who is by reason of bodily or mental condition unable to testify orally, if the Trial Chamber:

    (i) is so satisfied on a balance of probabilities; and

    (ii) finds from the circumstances in which the statement was made and recorded that there are satisfactory *indicia* of its reliability.

(D) A Chamber may admit a transcript of evidence given by a witness in proceedings before the Tribunal which goes to proof of a matter other than the acts and conduct of the accused.

(E) Subject to any order of the Trial Chamber to the contrary, a party seeking to adduce a written statement or transcript shall give fourteen days notice to the opposing party, who may within seven days object. The Trial Chamber shall decide, after hearing the parties, whether to admit the statement or transcript in whole or in part and whether to require the witness to appear for cross-examination.

Rule 93: Evidence of Consistent Pattern of Conduct

(A) Evidence of a consistent pattern of conduct relevant to serious violations of international humanitarian law under the Statute may be admissible in the interests of justice. **D6–116**

(B) Acts tending to show such a pattern of conduct shall be disclosed by the Prosecutor to the defence pursuant to Rule 66.

Rule 94: Judicial Notice

(A) A Trial Chamber shall not require proof of facts of common knowledge but shall take judicial notice thereof. **D6–117**

(B) At the request of a party or *proprio motu*, a Trial Chamber, after hearing the parties, may decide to take judicial notice of adjudicated facts or documentary evidence from other proceedings of the Tribunal relating to the matter at issue in the current proceedings.

Rule 94*bis*: Testimony of Expert Witnesses

(A) Notwithstanding the provisions of Rule 66 (A) (ii), Rule 73 *bis* (B) (iv) (b) and Rule 73 *ter* (B) (iii) (b) of the present Rules, the full statement of any expert witness called by a party shall be disclosed to the opposing party as early as possible and shall be filed with the Trial Chamber not less than twenty-one days prior to the date on which the expert is expected to testify. **D6–118**

(B) Within fourteen days of filing of the statement of the expert witness, the opposing party shall file a notice to the Trial Chamber indicating whether:

    (i) It accepts or does not accept the witness's qualification as an expert;

    (ii) It accepts the expert witness statement; or

    (iii) It wishes to cross-examine the expert witness.

(C) If the opposing party accepts the statement of the expert witness, the statement may be admitted into evidence by the Trial Chamber without calling the witness to testify in person.

RULE 95: EXCLUSION OF EVIDENCE ON THE GROUNDS OF THE MEANS BY WHICH IT WAS OBTAINED

D6–119 No evidence shall be admissible if obtained by methods which cast substantial doubt on its reliability or if its admission is antithetical to, and would seriously damage, the integrity of the proceedings.

RULE 96: RULES OF EVIDENCE IN CASES OF SEXUAL ASSAULT

D6–120 In cases of sexual assault:
 (i) Notwithstanding Rule 90 (C), no corroboration of the victim's testimony shall be required;
 (ii) Consent shall not be allowed as a defence if the victim:
  (a) Has been subjected to or threatened with or has had reason to fear violence, duress, detention or psychological oppression; or
  (b) Reasonably believed that if the victim did not submit, another might be so subjected, threatened or put in fear;
 (iii) Before evidence of the victim's consent is admitted, the accused shall satisfy the Trial Chamber *in camera* that the evidence is relevant and credible;
 (iv) Prior sexual conduct of the victim shall not be admitted in evidence or as defence.

RULE 97: LAWYER-CLIENT PRIVILEGE

D6–121 (A) All communications between lawyer and client shall be regarded as privileged, and consequently disclosure cannot be ordered, unless:
 (i) The client consents to such disclosure; or
 (ii) The client has voluntarily disclosed the content of the communication to a third party, and that third party then gives evidence of that disclosure.
 (B) Nothing in this rule shall be interpreted as permitting the use of confidentiality between Counsel and Client to conceal the participation of Counsel in illegal practices such as fee- splitting with client.

RULE 98: POWER OF CHAMBERS TO ORDER PRODUCTION OF ADDITIONAL EVIDENCE

D6–122 A Trial Chamber may *proprio motu* order either party to produce additional evidence. It may itself summon witnesses and order their attendance.

RULE 98*bis*: MOTION FOR JUDGEMENT OF ACQUITTAL

D6–123 If after the close of the case for the prosecution, the Trial Chamber finds that the evidence is insufficient to sustain a conviction on one or more counts charged in the indictment, the Trial Chamber, on motion of an accused filed within seven days after the close of the Prosecutor's case-in-chief, unless the Chamber orders otherwise, or *proprio motu*, shall order the entry of judgement of acquittal in respect of those counts.

Section 4: Sentencing Procedure

RULE 99: STATUS OF THE ACQUITTED PERSON

D6–124 (A) In case of acquittal, the accused shall be released immediately.
 (B) If, at the time the judgement is pronounced, the Prosecutor advises the Trial Chamber in open court of his intention to file notice of appeal pursuant to Rule 108, the

Trial Chamber may, at the request of the Prosecutor, issue a warrant for the arrest and further detention of the accused to take effect immediately.

Rule 100: Sentencing Procedure on a Guilty Plea

(A) If the Trial Chamber convicts the accused on a guilty plea, the Prosecutor and the **D6–125** defence may submit any relevant information that may assist the Trial Chamber in determining an appropriate sentence.

(B) The sentence shall be pronounced in a judgement in public and in the presence of the convicted person, subject to Sub-Rule 102 (B).

Rule 101: Penalties

(A) A person convicted by the Tribunal may be sentenced to imprisonment for a fixed **D6–126** term or the remainder of his life.

(B) In determining the sentence, the Trial Chamber shall take into account the factors mentioned in Article 23 (2) of the Statute, as well as such factors as:

   (i) Any aggravating circumstances;

  (ii) Any mitigating circumstances including the substantial cooperation with the Prosecutor by the convicted person before or after conviction;

 (iii) The general practice regarding prison sentences in the courts of Rwanda;

 (iv) the extent to which any penalty imposed by a court of any State on the convicted person for the same act has already been served, as referred to in Article 9 (3) of the Statute.

(C) The Trial Chamber shall indicate whether multiple sentences shall be served consecutively or concurrently.

(D) Credit shall be given to the convicted person for the period, if any, during which the convicted person was detained in custody pending his surrender to the Tribunal or pending trial or appeal.

Rule 102: Status of the Convicted Person

(A) Subject to the Trial Chamber's directions in terms of Rule 101, the sentence shall **D6–127** begin to run from the day it is pronounced under Rule 100 (B). However, as soon as notice of appeal is given, the enforcement of the judgement shall thereupon be stayed until the decision on the appeal has been delivered, the convicted person meanwhile remaining in detention, as provided in Rule 64.

(B) If, by a previous decision of the Trial Chamber, the convicted person has been provisionally released, or is for any other reason at liberty, and he is not present when the judgement is pronounced, the Trial Chamber shall issue a warrant for his arrest. On arrest, he shall be notified of the conviction and sentence, and the procedure provided in Rule 103 shall be followed.

Rule 103: Place of Imprisonment

(A) Imprisonment shall be served in Rwanda or any State designated by the Tribunal **D6–128** from a list of States which have indicated their willingness to accept convicted persons for the serving of sentences. Prior to a decision on the place of imprisonment, the Chamber shall notify the Government of Rwanda.

(B) Transfer of the convicted person to that State shall be effected as soon as possible after the time limit for appeal has elapsed.

Rule 104: Supervision of Imprisonment

All sentences of imprisonment shall be served under the supervision of the Tribunal or **D6–129** a body designated by it.

RULE 105: RESTITUTION OF PROPERTY

D6–130 (A) After a judgement of conviction containing a specific finding as provided in Rule 88 (B), the Trial Chamber shall, at the request of the Prosecutor, or may, at its own initiative, hold a special hearing to determine the matter of the restitution of the property or the proceeds thereof, and may in the meantime order such provisional measures for the preservation and protection of the property or proceeds as it considers appropriate.

(B) The determination may extend to such property or its proceeds, even in the hands of third parties not otherwise connected with the crime of which the convicted person has been found guilty.

(C) Such third parties shall be summoned before the Trial Chamber and be given an opportunity to justify their claim to the property or its proceeds.

(D) Should the Trial Chamber be able to determine the rightful owner on the balance of probabilities, it shall order the restitution either of the property or the proceeds or make such other order as it may deem appropriate.

(E) Should the Trial Chamber not be able to determine ownership, it shall notify the competent national authorities and request them so to determine.

(F) Upon notice from the national authorities that an affirmative determination has been made, the Trial Chamber shall order the restitution either of the property or the proceeds or make such other order as it may deem appropriate.

(G) The Registrar shall transmit to the competent national authorities any summonses, orders and requests issued by a Trial Chamber pursuant to Sub-Rules (C), (D), (E) and (F).

RULE 106: COMPENSATION TO VICTIMS

D6–131 (A) The Registrar shall transmit to the competent authorities of the States concerned the judgement finding the accused guilty of a crime which has caused injury to a victim.

(B) Pursuant to the relevant national legislation, a victim or persons claiming through him may bring an action in a national court or other competent body to obtain compensation.

(C) For the purposes of a claim made under Sub-Rule (B) the judgement of the Tribunal shall be final and binding as to the criminal responsibility of the convicted person for such injury.

PART SEVEN

APPELLATE PROCEEDINGS

RULE 107: GENERAL PROVISION

D6–132 The rules of procedure and evidence that govern proceedings in the Trial Chambers shall apply *mutatis mutandis* to proceedings in the Appeals Chamber.

RULE 107*bis*: PRACTICE DIRECTIONS FOR THE APPEALS CHAMBER

D6–133 The Presiding Judge of the Appeals Chamber may issue Practice Directions, in consultation with the President of the Tribunal, addressing detailed aspects of the conduct of proceedings before the Appeals Chamber.

RULE 108: NOTICE OF APPEAL

A party seeking to appeal a judgement or sentence shall, not more than thirty days from the date on which the judgement or the sentence was pronounced, file a notice of appeal, setting forth the grounds. The Appellant should also identify the order, decision or ruling challenged with specific reference to the date of its filing, and/or the transcript page, and indicate the substance of the alleged errors and the relief sought. The Appeals Chamber may, on good cause being shown by motion, authorise a variation of the grounds of appeal.

RULE 108*bis*: PRE-APPEAL JUDGE

(A) The Presiding Judge of the Appeals Chamber may designate from among its members a Judge responsible for the pre-hearing proceedings (the "Pre-Appeal Judge"). **D6–134**

(B) The Pre-Appeal Judge shall ensure that the proceedings are not unduly delayed and shall take any measures related to procedural matters, including the issuing of decisions, orders and directions with a view to preparing the case for a fair and expeditious hearing.

(C) The Pre-Appeal Judge shall record the points of agreement and disagreement between the parties on matters of law and fact. In this connection, he or she may order the parties to file further written submissions with the Pre-Appeal Judge or the Appeals Chamber.

(D) In order to perform his or her functions, the Pre-Appeal Judge may *proprio motu*, where appropriate; hear the parties without the convicted or acquitted person being present. The Pre-Appeal Judge may hear the parties in his or her office, in which case minutes of the meeting shall be taken by a representative of the Registry.

(E) A motion made in the course of the proceedings shall be determined before the hearing unless the Pre-Appeal Judge, for good cause, orders that it be deferred for determination by the Appeals Chamber. Failure by a party to raise objections or to make requests which can be made prior to the hearing shall constitute waiver thereof, but the Pre-Appeal Judge for good cause may grant relief from the waiver.

(F) The Pre-Appeal Judge shall keep the Appeals Chamber regularly informed, particularly where issues are in dispute and may refer such disputes to the Appeals Chamber.

(G) Upon a report of the Pre-Appeal Judge, the Appeals Chamber shall decide, should the case arise, on appropriate sanctions to be imposed on a party which fails to perform its obligations pursuant to the present Section of the Rules.

(H) The Appeals Chamber may *proprio motu* exercise any of the functions of the Pre-Appeal Judge.

RULE 109: RECORD ON APPEAL

(A) The record on appeal shall consist of the trial record, as certified by the Registrar. **D6–135**

(B) A certified true copy of the record on appeal shall be promptly transmitted to the Appeals Unit of the Appeals Chamber of the International Criminal Tribunal for Rwanda, located in The Hague.

RULE 110: LIST OF CERTIFIED DOCUMENTS TO THE PARTIES

The Registrar shall make available to the parties the list of documents constituting the record on appeal as certified by him and shall provide them with any of these documents on demand. **D6–136**

RULE 111: APPELLANT'S BRIEF

An Appellant's brief setting out all the arguments and authorities shall be filed within seventy-five days of filing of the notice of appeal pursuant to Rule 108. **D6–137**

RULE 112: RESPONDENT'S BRIEF

D6–138   A Respondent's brief of argument and authorities shall be filed within forty days of the filing of the Appellant's brief.

RULE 113: BRIEF IN REPLY

D6–139   An Appellant may file a brief in reply within fifteen days after the filing of the Respondent's brief.

RULE 114: DATE OF HEARING

D6–140   After the expiry of the time-limits for filing the briefs provided for in Rules 111, 112 and 113, the Appeals Chamber shall set the date for the hearing and the Registrar shall notify the parties.

RULE 115: ADDITIONAL EVIDENCE

D6–141   (A) A party may apply by motion to present additional evidence before the Appeals Chamber. Such motion shall clearly identify with precision the specific finding of fact made by the Trial Chamber to which the additional evidence is directed, and must be served on the other party and filed with the Registrar not later than seventy-five days from the date of the judgement, unless good cause is shown for further delay. Rebuttal material may be presented by any party affected by the motion.

(B) If the Appeals Chamber finds that the additional evidence was not available at trial and is relevant and credible, it will determine if it could have been a decisive factor in reaching the decision at trial. If it could have been such a factor, the Appeals Chamber will consider the additional evidence and any rebuttal material along with that already on the record to arrive at a final judgement in accordance with Rule 118.

(C) The Appeals Chamber may decide the motion prior to the appeal, or at the time of the hearing on appeal. It may decide the motion with or without an oral hearing.

(D) If several defendants are parties to the appeal, the additional evidence admitted on behalf of any one of them will be considered with respect to all of them, where relevant.

RULE 116: EXTENSION OF TIME LIMITS

D6–142   (A) The Appeals Chamber may grant a motion to extend a time limit upon a showing of good cause.

(B) Where the ability of the accused to make full answer and Defence depends on the availability of a decision in an official language other than that in which it was originally issued, that circumstance shall be taken into account as a good cause under the present Rule.

RULE 117: EXPEDITED APPEALS PROCEDURE

D6–143   (A) An appeal under Rule 65, Rule 72 (D), Rule 77 or Rule 91 shall be heard expeditiously on the basis of the original record of the Trial Chamber. Appeals may be determined entirely on the basis of written briefs.

(B) Rules 109 to 114 shall not apply to such appeals.

(C) The Presiding Judge, after consulting the members of the Appeals Chamber, may decide not to apply Rule 118 (D).

Rule 117*bis*: Parties' Books

(A) In every appeal before the Appeals Chamber, the Appellant and the Respondent **D6–144** shall each prepare and file an Appeal Book respectively to be entitled "APPELLANT'S APPEAL BOOK" and "RESPONDENT'S APPEAL BOOK", in consecutively numbered pages or tabs arranged in the following order:

    (i) a table of contents describing each document, including each exhibit, by its nature, date, and where applicable, number, with an indication of the page or tab where the document will be found in the Appeal Book, and

    (ii) a legible copy of the pages of or excerpts from every document in the case to which the party actually refers in the party's briefs or intends to refer in the party's oral arguments.

(B) In every appeal before the Appeals Chamber, the Appellant and the Respondent shall each prepare and file a Book of Authorities respectively to be entitled "APPELLANT'S BOOK OF AUTHORITIES" and "RESPONDENT'S BOOK OF AUTHORITIES", in consecutively numbered pages or tabs arranged in the following order:

    (i) a table of contents describing each document, including each exhibit, by its nature, date, and where applicable, number, with an indication of the page or tab where the document will be found in the Appeal Book, and

    (ii) a legible copy of the pages of or excerpts from every reference material, including case law, statutory and regulatory provisions, from international and national sources, to which the party actually refers in the party's briefs or intends to refer in the party's oral arguments.

(C) Unless otherwise ordered in any particular case by the Appeals Chamber *proprio motu* or upon a motion by a party, each party shall file sufficient copies of his Appeal Book and of his Book of Authorities at the Registry of the place where the Appeals Chamber is to hold its hearing, four weeks before the date set for the said hearing. The Registry shall advise the parties of the number of copies required.

(D) Failure to file the books prescribed above shall not bar the Appeals Chamber from rendering a judgement, a decision or an order as it sees fit in the appeal.

Rule 117*ter*: Filing of the Appeal Documents

The notice of Appeal under Rule 108 and, where necessary, the briefs earmarked **D6–145** under Rules 111, 112, 113, 115 and 117 shall be filed, by the parties, either with the Registry or with an officer of the Registry specifically designated by the Registrar at the Appeals Unit of the Appeals Chamber of the International Criminal Tribunal for Rwanda, located in The Hague. Two similar records shall be kept: one at the Registry of the Tribunal and the other in The Hague. Depending on the place of filing, each record shall consist of the original documents or certified true copies thereof.

Rule 118: Judgement on Appeal

(A) The Appeals Chamber shall pronounce judgement on the basis of the record on **D6–146** appeal and on any additional evidence as has been presented to it.

(B) The judgement shall be rendered by a majority of the Judges. It shall be accompanied or followed as soon as possible by a reasoned opinion in writing, to which separate or dissenting opinions may be appended.

(C) In appropriate circumstances the Appeals Chamber may order that the accused be re tried before the Trial Chamber.

(D) The judgement shall be pronounced in public, on a date of which notice shall have been given to the parties and counsel and at which they shall be entitled to be present.

(E) The written judgement shall be filed and registered with the Registry or with an officer of the Registry specifically designated by the Registrar at the Appeals Unit of the Appeals Chamber of the International Criminal Tribunal for Rwanda, located in The Hague.

Rule 119: Status of the Accused Following Judgement on Appeal

D6–147   (A) A sentence pronounced by the Appeals Chamber shall be enforced immediately.

(B) Where the accused is not present when the judgement is due to be delivered, either as having been acquitted on all charges or as a result of an order issued pursuant to Rule 65, or for any other reason, the Appeals Chamber may deliver its judgement in the absence of the accused and shall, unless it pronounces his acquittal, order his arrest or surrender to the Tribunal.

Part Eight

REVIEW PROCEEDINGS

Rule 120: Request for Review

D6–148   (A) Where a new fact has been discovered which was not known to the moving party at the time of the proceedings before a Trial Chamber or the Appeals Chamber and could not have been discovered through the exercise of due diligence, the Defence or, within one year after the final judgement has been pronounced, the Prosecutor, may make a motion to that Chamber for review of the judgement. If, at the time of the request for review, any of the Judges who constituted the original Chamber are no longer Judges of the Tribunal, the President shall appoint a Judge or Judges in their place.

(B) Any brief in response to a request for review shall be filed within forty days of the filing of the request.

(C) Any brief in reply shall be filed within fifteen days after the filing of the response.

Rule 121: Preliminary Examination

D6–149   If the Chamber constituted pursuant to Rule 120 agrees that the new fact, if it had been proven, could have been a decisive factor in reaching a decision, the Chamber shall review the judgement, and pronounce a further judgement after hearing the parties.

Rule 122: Appeals

D6–150   The judgement of a Trial Chamber on review may be appealed in accordance with the provisions of Part Seven.

Rule 123: Return of the Case to the Trial Chamber

D6–151   If the judgement to be reviewed is under appeal at the time the motion for review is filed, the Appeals Chamber may return the case to the Trial Chamber for disposition of the motion.

Part Nine

PARDON AND COMMUTATION OF SENTENCE

Rule 124: Notification by States

D6–152   If, according to the law of a State in which a convicted person is imprisoned, he is eligible for pardon or commutation of sentence, the State shall, in accordance with Article 27 of the Statute, notify the Tribunal of such eligibility.

Rule 125: Determination by the President

The President shall, upon such notice, determine, in consultation with the Judges and after notification to the Government of Rwanda, whether pardon or commutation is appropriate.

Rule 126: General Standards for Granting Pardon or Commutation

In determining whether pardon or commutation is appropriate, the President shall take into account, *inter alia*, the gravity of the crime or crimes for which the prisoner was convicted, the treatment of similarly-situated prisoners, the prisoner's demonstration of rehabilitation, as well as any substantial cooperation of the prisoner with the Prosecutor.

D7. Prosecutor's Regulation No. 1 (1999) as amended on 21 October 1999 International Criminal Tribunal for Rwanda (ICTR)

CONCERNING

THE PROCEDURE TO BE ADOPTED FOLLOWING A REQUEST BY A NATIONAL AUTHORITY TO TAKE EVIDENCE FROM A PERSON *INTER ALIA* IN THE CUSTODY OF THE INTERNATIONAL CRIMINAL TRIBUNAL FOR RWANDA

D7–001   I, CARLA DEL PONTE, Prosecutor of the International Criminal Tribunal for Rwanda,

NOTING that the national authorities of a State may on occasion request the assistance of the Tribunal to take evidence for the purposes of national proceedings from a person who are *inter alia* in the custody of the Tribunal;

CONSIDERING that the Rules of Procedure and Evidence of the Tribunal make no provision for the procedure to be adopted in that event, but that the questioning of suspects and the collection of evidence are functions provided to the Prosecutor by the Statute of the Tribunal;

MAKE THIS REGULATION in the following terms:

1. A request by the authorities of a State for assistance to question or take evidence from a person *inter alia* in the custody of the Tribunal ("a detainee") shall be transmitted to the Prosecutor.

2. Requests should be in writing and should contain:

(a) details of the authority making the request;

(b) the name of the detainee to whom the request relates;

(c) details of the purpose of the request and a summary of the reason for it;

(d) a description of the offences or suspected offences charged or likely to be charged or under investigation;

(e) any relevant dates, such as the date of the trial at which the evidence is required, or any cause for special urgency;

(f) details of any rules on privilege which a witness or suspect may be entitled to claim, and any caution which should if possible be given under the law of the requesting State;

(g) a description of the evidence sought, and a list of any specific questions to be asked;

(h) whether it is desired that any persons from the requesting State should be present during the taking of the evidence, and whether the request is for such persons to be permitted to participate in the questioning.

3. The prosecutor will consider each request on its own merits, and will endeavour to assist the national authorities to the extent possible without prejudicing the Prosecutor's own investigations or the preparation or prosecution of any case before the International Tribunal. Wherever possible, before finally concluding that a request cannot be executed (either wholly or in part) the Prosecutor will consult the requesting State to discuss any possibilities for overcoming the difficulties preventing execution.

4. The Prosecutor shall inform the detainee and his/her defence counsel that the request has been made. In doing so the Prosecutor shall inform the detainee that he or she:

(i) may seek legal advice before deciding to provide evidence, and may have counsel present during any questioning;

(ii) shall have counsel present during any questioning after his or her initial appearance;

(iii) will have the services of an interpreter during questioning, and that questioning will be audio or video recorded; and

(iv) may decline to answer any question and that any statement may be used to subsequent proceedings before the ICTR, as well as the proceedings or investigations for which the questioning has been requested by the national authorities.

5. The Prosecutor shall set up a date for the interview and transmit the decision to accede to the request to the Registrar with a request that arrangements be made by the Registrar for the questioning of the detainee.

6. At the discretion of the Prosecutor, a representative of the requesting State may conduct questioning of the detainee. The Prosecutor shall attend questioning and may participate as she sees fit.

7. The Prosecutor shall retain the audio recording or video recording of the evidence obtained, and shall provide a copy of the requesting State.

(signed)

Carla Del Ponte

Prosecutor

Dated this twenty first day of October 1999

The Hague

D8. Practical Information for Counsel
13th September 2000

This document, prepared by the **Lawyers and Detention Facilities Management Section (LDFMS)**, contains pertinent information and administrative forms for Defence Counsel who are representing persons suspect of and/or charged with crimes falling under the jurisdiction of the International Criminal Tribunal for Rwanda (ICTR).

1 LAW OF THE TRIBUNAL

1.1 Judicial Documents.
  1.1.1 The Statute of the Tribunal.
  1.1.2 The Rules of Procedure and Evidence.
  1.1.3 The Directive on the Assignment of Defence Counsel.
  1.1.4 The Code of Professional Conduct for Defence Counsel.
  1.1.5 The Rules Covering the Detention of Persons Awaiting Trial or Appeal Before the Tribunal or Otherwise Detained on the Authority of the Tribunal.
  1.1.6 The Directive of the Registry on court management.
    1.1.6.1 The Judicial and Legal Services Division.
      1.1.6.1.1 The Court Management Section.
      1.16.1.2 The General Legal Services section
      1.16.1.3 The Chambers Support Section.
      1.16.1.4 The Lawyers and Detention Facilities Management Section.
      1.16.1.5 Visits
      1.16.1.6 The Witness and Victim Support Section for Prosecution Witnesses
      1.16.1.7 The Witness and Victim Support Section for Defence Witnesses

2 DEFENCE TEAM COMPOSITION FOR INDIGENT DETAINEES

2.1 Counsel.
  2.1.1 General Rules.
  2.1.2 Lead Counsel.
    2.1.2.1 Remuneration of Lead Counsel.
  2.1.3 Co-Counsel.
    2.1.3.1 Remuneration of Co-Counsel.
  2.1.4 Duty Counsel.
    2.1.4.1 Remuneration of Duty Counsel.
  2.1.5 Assistants, Investigators and Expert Witnesses.
    2.1.5.1 Assistants and Investigators.
    2.1.5.2 Expert Witnesses.
  2.1.6 Payment of fees and reimbursements to ICTR.

3 PRACTICAL INFORMATION REGARDING FACILITIES AT THE ICTR

3.1 Office Space for Counsel, equipment and other.
  3.1.1 Offices.
  3.1.2 Furniture.
  3.1.3 Equipment.
  3.1.4 Pin Codes (Telephone Access Code).
  3.1.5 ID Cards.
  3.1.6 "TRIM".
  3.1.7 Library.
  3.1.8 Pigeonholes (Locked Mailboxes).

3.1.9 Wardrobes (Standing Closets).
3.1.10 Web Site.
3.1.11 Forms.
3.1.12 Office Hours of the Registry in Arusha.
3.1.13 Registry Stamp.
3.1.14 Copy of Correspondence.
3.1.15 Working languages.
3.1.16 Association of Defence Attorneys ("ADAD").
3.2 Transportation and Travel.
3.2.1 Travel Requests.
3.2.2 Transportation to and from the Tribunal.
3.2.3 Shuttle to the Detention Facilities.
3.2.4 Round Trip Transportation (Airport-Tribunal-Airport).
3.2.5 Travel to Tanzania.
3.2.6 Travel via Nairobi.
3.2.7 Travel to Rwanda.
3.2.8 Flight Reservations, Hotel Bookings, and Other Travel Arrangements.
3.2.9 Mission Letters.
3.2.10 Annexes

1 LAW OF THE TRIBUNAL

1.1 JUDICIAL DOCUMENTS

1.1.1 The Statute of the Tribunal

The Statute is an annex to Resolution 955 (1994) of the Security Council of the United Nations, adopted on 8 November 1994, pursuant to Chapter VII of the Charter of the United Nations. **D8–001**

1.1.2 The Rules of Procedure and Evidence

In the performance of their duties, Defence Counsel shall be subject to the relevant provisions of The **Rules of Procedure and Evidence** ("**the Rules**"). **D8–002**

1.1.3 The Directive on the Assignment of Defence Counsel

The **Directive on the assignment of Defence Counsel** ("**the Directive**") was adopted by the Judges of the Tribunal on 9 January 1996. **D8–003**
The **Lawyers and Detention Facilities Management Section is responsible for the application of the** Directive.

1.1.4 The Code of Professional Conduct for Defence Counsel

In the exercise of their duties, Defence Counsel shall be subject to **The Code of Professional Conduct for Defence Counsel** ("**the Code of Conduct**"), as well as to the national codes of practice and ethics governing their profession. **D8–004**

1.1.5 The Rules Covering the Detention of Persons Awaiting Trial or Appeal Before the Tribunal or Otherwise Detained on the Authority of the Tribunal

In accordance with **The Rules covering the detention of persons awaiting trial or appeal before the Tribunal or otherwise detained on the authority of the Tribunal** ("**the Rules of Detention**"), the Commanding Officer of the Detention Unit **D8–005** shall have sole responsibility for all aspects of the daily management of the Detention Unit, including security and order, any make all decisions relating thereto, except where otherwise provided in these **Rules**. Any requests or inquiries concerning visitation, security, or living conditions of a detainee shall be made directly to the Commanding Officer.

1.1.6 The Directive of the Registry on court management

D8–006   The Registrar, the Deputy Registrar, the Judicial and Legal Services Division, and the Registry staff serve the Registry to assist the Judges, the Chambers, the Prosecutor and the Defence Counsel in the Performance of their duties. The Registry is responsible for the administration of the Tribunal and serves as its channel of communication.

1.1.6.1 The Judicial and Legal Services Division

D8–007   The Judicial and Legal Services Division is divided into five Sections as follows:

1.1.6.1.1 The Court Management Section

D8–008   The Court Management Section organizes the judicial proceedings of the Chambers. The Section also maintains the Judicial Archives of the Tribunal and has custody of the seals and stamps. It is also responsible for the distribution of documents and the preparation of minutes and records. Defence Counsel shall contact this Section, inter *alia,* in regard to all matters related to the judicial calendar, judicial documents and courtroom etiquette.

1.1.6.1.2 The General Legal Services Section

D8–009   The General Legal Services Sectionserves as an in-house legal counsel and provides advice to the Registrar and management of the Tribunal on legal matters pertaining to agreements between the Tribunal and host Governments and on international legal matters arising from relations between the Tribunal and third countries or international organizations, with regard to arrest and surrender of suspects or accused; and to assume responsibility for the substantive preparation of the plenary sessions of the judges and for the subsequent implementation of those decisions falling within the Registry's mandate. The section provides legal advisory services on contractual agreements, including commercial agreements between the Tribunal and third parties, on cases of litigation between the Tribunal and third parties or claims brought against the Tribunal by host countries or third parties, and on internal challenges to decisions taken by management. It also serves the various administrative bodies, such as the Grievance Committee and disciplinary bodies.

    The Section is also in charge of writing legal briefs and opinions on judicial matters that have an impact on the Registry's operations as per rule 33 (B) adopted by the last plenary of judges.

1.1.6.1.3 The Chambers Support Section

D8–010   This Section provides assistance to the Chambers in legal research and drafting of decisions, judgments, opinions and orders. The Section is also responsible for ensuring that translations of the decisions, Judgments and Orders issued by the Chambers are correct and in proper form before they are filed with the Court Management Section

1.1.6.1.4 The Lawyers and Detention Facilities Management Section

D8–011   The Section serves as the channel of communication between the Tribunal and the Defence Counsel and is responsible for processing all matters related to (i) assignment of counsel; (ii) the composition of a defence team (assistants, investigators); (iii)

payment of fees and reimbursement of expenses; (iv) travel requests; etc. The Section also supervises the Detention Unit (UNDF) on legal and administrative matters.

1.1.6.1.5 Visits

Please note that hours of visitation at the LDFMS for both the Defence teams and the **D8–012** public at large are as follows:

Monday to Thursday:
8:30 a.m. to 10:00 a.m. and 4:00 p.m. to 5:00 p.m.
Friday:
8:30 a.m. to 9:30 a.m.

Defence Counsel with scheduled appointments will be allowed to visit the LDFMS staff outside of the above-established visiting hours.

Visiting hours at the UNDF:

Monday through Thursday	0900–1700h
Friday	0900–1330h
Saturday	0900–1230h (prior notice required)
Sunday and public holidays	No visits authorised

All visits between Defence Counsels and client will take place during the above hours in order that routine of the Detention Facility can be maintained. However, Defence Counsels wishing to meet their clients during non-visiting hours, may request permission in advance from the Commanding Officer (providing a valid reason is given) or with written permission from the Registrar, President or per order of the tribunal. Due to the fact that the number of Defence Counsels wishing to visit the UNDF is increasing and that there is only limited space, an appointment schedule will be devised to accommodate the visits of Defence Counsels. The Commanding Officer of the UNDF retains the right to refuse a meeting on the grounds that there is insufficient space available.

1.1.6.1.6 The Witness and Victim Support Section for Prosecution Witnesses

This Section is responsible for protecting victims and prosecution witnesses who have **D8–013** testified before the Tribunal. Such protective measures shall encompass, but shall not be limited to, in camera proceedings, protection of victims' and witnesses' identities, and relevant support, including physical re-education and psychological rehabilitation.

1.1.6.1.7 The Witness and Victim Support Section for Defence Witnesses

This Section is responsible for protecting victims and defence witnesses who have **D8–014** testified before the Tribunal. Such protective measures shall encompass, but shall not be limited to, in camera proceedings, protection of victims' and witnesses' identities, and relevant support, including physical re-education and psychological rehabilitation.

2. Defence Team Composition for Indigent Detainees

2.1 COUNSEL

2.1.1 General Rules

On behalf of the Registrar, the LDFMS retains a list of counsel who are likely to be **D8–015** assigned and who:

- Speak one or both of the working languages of the Tribunal (namely French or English).
- Are admitted to practice law in a State, or are professors of law at university or similar institution.

- Have at least 10 years' relevant experience, and
- Have indicated their willingness to be assigned by the Tribunal to indigent suspects or accused.

Counsel shall fill in the **Form IL2** and attach all documents required by the said form.

Within the territory of Tanzania, Defence Counsel is not subject to any measures that may affect the free and independent exercise of their professional contract with the International Criminal Tribunal for Rwanda. Accordingly, all documents relating to the exercise of Counsel's functions are inviolable. Counsel shall be accorded immunity from prosecution on the basis of words spoken or written or acts performed in their official capacity as Counsel, both during and after the termination of their duties as counsel before the Tribunal. The same protection shall be afforded to Defence Counsel who has been privately employed by a suspect or an accused called before the Tribunal.

2.1.2 Lead Counsel

D8–016   All suspects or accused called before the Tribunal have the right to legal assistance assigned to him or her in any case where the interest of justice so require if he or she does not have sufficient means to pay for legal representation. The Registrar will assign counsel upon request of the suspect or the accused. Assigned Counsel shall furnish the Court Management Section, upon date of such assignment, a written undertaking that he will appear before the Tribunal within a reasonable time as specified by the Registrar.

2.1.2.1 Remuneration of Lead Counsel

D8–017   Remuneration of counsel is calculated on an hourly basis rate as follows:

Up to 9 years of experience	US $ 80 per hour
From 10 to 14 years of experience	US $ 90 per hour
From 15 to 19 years of experience	US $ 100 per hour
More than 20 years of experience	US $ 110 per hour

Counsel will receive the fixed sum of U.S. $2,000.00 at the conclusion of each stage of the procedure: pre-trial, trial, pre-sentencing hearing, appeal, and review.

Assigned Counsel who, because of defence work on behalf of clients awaiting trial before the ICTR, must remain outside of their established place of residence for more than fourteen days are entitled to payment of a daily subsistence allowance ("DSA").

For further information, please refer to the "**Guidelines for the Remuneration of Counsel Appearing before the ICTR**" establish on 1st September 1998.

2.1.3 Co-Counsel

D8–018   Whenever appropriate and at the request of the assigned Counsel, the Registrar may, appoint a co-Counsel to assist the assigned Counsel. The first Counsel shall thereafter be designated Lead Counsel. Assignment of co-Counsel, if appropriate, will be made about 60 days prior to the commencement of the trial. This designation will be effective for the duration of the trial and has to be renewed on an express as well as motivated request of the Lead Counsel. To initiate the request lead counsel shall fill out the "**Request of Co-counsel form**" and attach all required documents specified in said form. Co-Counsel shall furnish the Court Management Section, upon date of such assignment, a written undertaking that he will appear within a reasonable time before the Tribunal as specified by the Registrar. He shall fulfill the requirements of Rule 44 of **The Rules**.

2.1.3.1 Remuneration of Co-Counsel

D8–019   A uniform hourly rate of US$80 has been established for all Co-Counsel, irrespective of legal experience. All policies concerning remuneration of Lead Counsel shall also apply to co-Counsel.

2.1.4 Duty Counsel

The Registrar, as soon as practicable, shall assign Duty Counsel to represent an accused or a suspect, having no legal Counsel, who has been transferred to the Detention Facility of the Tribunal. Duty Counsel shall be available until such time as the subject suspect or accused has engaged permanent Counsel. Duty Counsel shall furnish a written undertaking to the Court Management Section of the Tribunal, upon date of such assignment, that he or she will appear to represent the interests of the subject suspect or accused before the Tribunal within reasonable time specified by the Registrar.

D8–020

2.1.4.1 Remuneration of Duty Counsel

A fixed rate of payment has been established for Duty Counsel. All policies concerning remuneration of Lead Counsel shall also apply to Duty Counsel

D8–021

2.1.5 Assistants, Investigators and Expert Witnesses

2.1.5.1 Assistants and Investigators

Counsel must follow the appropriate administrative procedure authorized by the Registry to recruit an assistant or an investigator:
- First, fill out the required form for recruitment of an assistant or an investigator;
- Second, verify that you have specified the assignment for the recruit and the duration of the assignment;
- Third, file the complete administrative work with the Registry;
- Fourth, ascertain that the request has been authorised by the Registry.

D8–022

The remuneration for an assistant or an investigator is a flat hourly rate of U.S.$ twenty-five (25), with a maximum monthly payment not to exceed one hundred (100) hours. The duration of the original contract may not exceed three (3) months for an investigator or six months for an assistant. Counsel may apply to the Registry for an extension of the contract of an assistant and/or an investigator. The Lead Counsel shall introduce all requests concerning team members.

The Registry may authorize a maximum of three provisional staff for each Defence team (two investigators and one assistant or two assistants and one investigator), in addition to the Lead Counsel and, if any, the co-Counsel.

2.1.5.2 Expert Witnesses

For information regarding expert witnesses, please contact the Witness and Victim Support Section for Defence.

D8–023

2.1.6 Payment of fees and reimbursements to ICTR

- Please note that the ICTR makes payment in the form of cheques issued in U.S. dollars drawn on the Chase Manhattan Bank in New York or on the Stanbic Bank in Arusha, Tanzania. Counsel may receive payment by credit transfer to a designated bank of choice in any country in the world. Counsel may also open a bank account in Arusha, Tanzania, to which account the ICTR will transfer payment. Please note that, pursuant to Article 17 of the Financial Rules of the United Nations, Counsel are responsible for all expenses which they incur.
- After the review of the statement of remuneration of the defence team, the Lawyers and Detention Facilities Section shall provide the defence team with a provisional revised statement in order to allow them, shall it happen, to lodge a claim after the Finance Section has completed payment .
- Claims shall be lodged within 12 months after the initial request for payment has been submitted.

D8–024

1781

3. PRACTICAL INFORMATION REGARDING FACILITIES AT THE ICTR

3.1 OFFICE SPACE FOR COUNSEL, EQUIPMENT, ETC.

3.1.1 Offices

D8–025   Seven offices (S435,436,437,438) have been reserved for Defence Counsel use only. Four offices are located on the 4th floor of the "Serengeti" Wing across the corridor from the offices of the LDFMS. Three offices are located on the 2nd and 4th floors of the Kilimanjaro Wing behind the courtrooms. Counsels are requested to return the key to the Security Desk, located at the principal entry/exit of the Tribunal every day before leaving.

3.1.2 Furniture

D8–026   The offices reserved for Defence Counsel are fully furnished.

3.1.3 Equipment

D8–027   Computers, fax machines, telephone lines, photocopy machine, furniture, ink for printer, software, etc. are provided free of charge for the exclusive benefit of counsel. Counsel may also use the photocopy machine of **LDFMS** and any other photocopy or fax machines in the ICTR. The Tribunal's photocopying service, located on the mezzanine, is also available to Defence Counsel.

3.1.4 Pin Codes (Telephone Access Code)

D8–028   All the members of the Defence Counsel team will be issued a pin code on request. The code permits a user to make local or international telephone calls from any telephone in the ICTR. The Tribunal will bill the user for all calls registered under his or her code.

3.1.5 ID Cards

D8–029   Like other staff members, Defence Counsel will be issued with ID cards, to allow them to freely circulate within the Tribunal. ID photos, to be used with the cards, will be taken on the premises of the Tribunal.

3.1.6 "TRIM"

D8–030   "TRIM" software allows electronic access to any public documents related to suspects or accused which have been entered into a data base Counsel may retrieve and print relevant information.

3.1.7 Library

D8–031   Counsel may consult the reference text and use the "Lexis-Nexis" and "West Law "data base systems in the ICTR Library, located on the first floor of the Tribunal. All library reference services are provided free of charge.

3.1.8 Pigeonholes (Locked Mailboxes)

D8–032   Counsel may use the pigeonholes (mailboxes), located near the Defence Counsel offices in Serengeti Wing.

3.1.9 Wardrobes (Standing Closets)

There are several wardrobes in the Defence offices located behind the courtrooms in the Kilimanjaro Wing of the Tribunal. Counsels are responsible for the safety of all items stored therein. The Tribunal takes no responsibility whatsoever for any loss or damage occasioned. Counsel may obtain a key from LDFMS for a wardrobe where he or she may lock up files, robes, or personal effects. Counsel must kindly return the key to LDFMS before leaving Arusha.

D8–033

3.1.10 eb Site

Counsels are invited to access the ICTR web site: http://www.ictr.org

D8–034

3.1.11 Forms

Several administrative forms are provided by LDFMS to facilitate Counsel's work in transmitting information to the Registry. All the forms shall be typed when submitted to the Registry.

D8–035

3.1.12 Office Hours of the Registry in Arusha

Monday to Thursday
8:30 a.m. to 5:30 p.m.
Friday
8:30 a.m. to 2:00 p.m.
In the event of an emergency, please call the Security officer on duty for any assistance at (255–57) 4207 or (1–212) 963 2850

D8–036

3.1.13 Registry Stamp

The Registry will receive, record, and then forward to LDFMS all appropriately addressed correspondence.

D8–037

3.1.14 Copy of Correspondence

In the interest of efficient communication between Defence Counsel and the Tribunal, the Registry requires that:
- All correspondence from Counsel be typewritten;
- All correspondence from Counsel be addressed directly to the Section concerned;
- All requests be made on the appropriate request forms;
- And all request filled in on said forms be typewritten.

The Registry will not respond to any handwritten communication, in exception to provisions 1–4 above, unless submitting Counsel provides proper medical or official certification to explain why he or she is unable to adhere to Registrar's policy.

D8–038

3.1.15 Working languages

- Counsel bears the responsibility for rectifying difficulties in communication between Counsel and his/her client in one of the languages of the Tribunal.
- If the accused lacks sufficient knowledge of one of the official languages of the Tribunal and thus prefers to use Kinyarwanda as the working language, the Tribunal will assume responsibility for the translation and the interpretation.
- The Tribunal will also be responsible for the interpretation if the accused does not understand or does not speak the language used at the hearing.

D8–039

3.1.16 Association of Defence Attorneys ("ADAD")

D8–040   ADAD, a newly formed organisation of Defence Attorneys, provides a support system for Defence Counsel. The Registry supports all initiatives to facilitate the work of assigned counsel.

3.2 TRANSPORTATION AND TRAVEL

3.2.1 Travel Requests

D8–041   Counsel must obtain written authorisation from the Registrar prior to any official travel. The Registry has established the following travel guidelines to assist Counsel:

1) File the proper administrative form ina timely manner with the Registry;
2) File the official request in due time to allow for the Registry to examine the request.
3) Counsel is responsible for obtaining up-to-date information from knowledgeable national government authority regarding visas and other formalities required for travel to Tanzania.

3.2.2 Transportation to and from the Tribunal

D8–042   The Tribunal offers round-trip shuttle bus service (residence-Tribunal-residence) for all staff in the morning and in the evening free of charge. Once you have arrived in Arusha, please inform the Transport Section of the location of your residence and obtain the current shuttle schedule.

3.2.3 Shuttle to the Detention Facilities

D8–043   Shuttle Service to the United Nations Detention Facility ("UNDF"). Counsel may use the Shuttle Service to the UNDF and back to the Tribunal, free of charge, as follows:

From Monday to Friday

D8–044

Departure from the Tribunal	Departure from UNDF
0930 hrs	1000 hrs
1100 hrs	1130 hrs
1230 hrs	1300 hrs
1400 hrs	1430 hrs
1530 hrs	1600 hrs
1630 hrs	1715 hrs

Saturdays and Sunday

D8–045   Counsel should confirm both the transportation and the detention facility schedules to ascertain that he or she will have sufficient time to visit a detainee at the UNDF. It is possible for Counsel to arrange for visitation on a non-week day with special advance written authorisation from the Commanding Officer. For example, if Counsel wishes to go to UNDF on Saturday morning, he or she must request transport through LDFMSbefore noon on Friday preceding the day of the intended visit.

3.2.4 Round Trip Transportation (Airport-Tribunal-Airport)

D8–046   Shuttle bus service from the Kilimanjaro or the Arusha airport to the Tribunal or from the Tribunal to the Arusha or Kilimanjaro airport is available free of charge for Counsel who officially request this service at least twelve working hours in advance.

3.2.5 Travel to Tanzania

A valid passport and current visa are required to visit Tanzania. It is the responsibility **D8–047**
of Counsel to procure their visas from the Tanzanian Embassy in their countries before
departure. While it is possible at present to be issued a visa at an airport in Tanzania
after landing, it is not certain how long this practice will continue. Therefore Counsel is
cautioned to make timely application for a visa and to address all requests for current
travel information to the appropriate Tanzanian authorities.

Vaccination for yellow fever is required for visitors to Tanzania. Consult your doctor
regarding other recommended vaccinations.

3.2.6 Travel via Nairobi

Counsel travelling via Nairobi will be responsible for their transportation to the **D8–048**
Tribunal. Only under exceptional circumstances will transportation be provided to
Counsel arriving or departing from Nairobi. Counsel is cautioned to make timely
application for required visas and vaccinations.

3.2.7 Travel to Rwanda

It is the Registry's policy that Defence Counsel travelling to Rwanda on behalf of their **D8–049**
clients must file travels requests no less than one month in advance of the intended
mission. He must also submit a detailed programme of his mission in Rwanda.

3.2.8 Flight Reservations, Hotel Bookings, and Other Travel Arrangements

Counsel shall be responsible for their flight reservations, hotel bookings, and travel **D8–050**
plans.

3.2.9 Mission Letters

Upon request, LDFMS will provide Counsel with mission letters to facilitate their **D8–051**
work in different countries throughout the world. The LDFMS is not authorized to
deliver other certificates.

3.2.10 Annexes

1. Guidelines for the Remuneration of Counsel appearing before the ICTR; **D8–052**
2. Work schedule form;
3. Request of DSA advance form;
4. Request of payment of fees and reimbursement;
5. Request for assistant, investigator form;
6. Composition of defence team's form;
7. Request of co-counsel form (v.4);
8. Standards Acronyms.

D9. Code of Professional Conduct for Defence Counsel

DECISION

D9–001   **THE REGISTRAR,**
CONSIDERING the Statute of the Tribunal as adopted by the Security Council under Resolution 955 (1994) of 8 November 1994 and in particular Articles 14 thereof,
CONSIDERING Rules 44 to 46 of the Rules of Procedure of Evidence (the Rules) concerning Counsel, which confer on the Registrar the responsibility for ensuring that only Counsel who are qualified to do so appear before the Tribunal,
CONSIDERING that being subject to a professional Code of Conduct is an essential attribute of being qualified as Counsel,
CONSIDERING that Counsel appearing before the Tribunal come from jurisdictions from all over the world, and that it is in the interests of the Tribunal that they all be subject to the same Code of Conduct,
CONSIDERING that a Draft Code of Conduct has been circulated to the Judges of the Tribunal and that they have voiced no objections to its promulgation,
CONSIDERING that the Plenary Session of the Judges of the ICTR adopted a Code of Conduct for Counsels on 4 June 1998,
CONSIDERING that the same Draft Code of Conduct has been submitted to the Advisory Panel established under Article 29 of the Directive on the Assignment of Defence Counsel of the International Criminal Tribunal for Rwanda, and that the members of the Advisory Panel have voiced no objections to its promulgation,
TAKING NOTE of the Advisory Panel's comments on the Draft Code of Conduct,
PURSUANT TO Rules 44 to 46 of the Rules,
HEREBY PROMULGATES this Code of Conduct, annexed.
DONE in English and French.

Agwu U. Okali
Registrar

Dated this 8 day of June 1998
At Arusha
Tanzania

ANNEX

CODE OF PROFESSIONAL CONDUCT FOR DEFENCE COUNSEL

INTRODUCTION

D9–002   This Code is made in the belief that:
1. As legal practitioners, Counsel must maintain high standards of professional conduct;
2. The role of Counsel as specialist advocates in the administration of justice requires them to act honestly, fairly, skilfully, diligently and courageously;
3. Counsel have an overriding duty to defend their client's interests, to the extent that they can do so without acting dishonestly or by improperly prejudicing the administration of justice;
4. Counsel may be subject to disciplinary proceedings under Rule 46 of the Rules of Procedure and Evidence of the Trib unal. It is therefore necessary that Counsel be aware of their rights and obligations toward the Tribunal;
To these ends, this Code and its Articles of conduct have been formulated.

PART I: PRELIMINARY

ARTICLE 1

DEFINITIONS

(1) In this Code, unless a different interpretation is required by the provisions of the **D9–003** Code or the context in which they appear, the following terms shall mean:

Client: An accused, suspect, detainee, witness or other person who has engaged Counsel for his legal representation before the Tribunal;

Counsel: Any person who has satisfied the Registrar that he is admitted to the practice of law in a State, or is a University professor of law, and
(a) Has filed his or her power of attorney with the Registrar; or
(b) Has been assigned under the Rules to a suspect, accused, detainee, witness or other person.
Any reference to Counsel includes a reference to any Co-counsel jointly and to each of them severally.

Directive: The directive entitled "Directive on Assignment of Defence Counsel", as amended (No. 1/96 (ICTR/2/L.2);

Rules: The Rules of Procedure and Evidence of the Tribunal adopted on 5 July 1995, as amended;

Statute: The Statute of the Tribunal adopted by Security Council Resolution 955 of 8 November 1994;

Tribunal: The International Criminal Tribunal for the Prosecution of Persons Responsible for Genocide and Other Serious Violations of International Humanitarian Law Committed in the Territory of Rwanda and Rwandan Citizens Responsible for Genocide and other such violations committed in the territory of neighbouring States, between 1January1994 and 31 December 1994, established by Security Council Resolution 955 of 8 November 1994.

(2) In the event of any inconsistency between this Code and the Directive, the terms and provisions of the Directive prevail.

(3) Any term not defined in this Code has the same meaning given to it by the Statute or by the Rules.

(4) While Counsel is bound by this Code, it is not, and should not be read as if it were a complete or detailed Code of Conduct for Counsel. Other standards and requirements may be imposed on the conduct of Counsel by virtue of the Tribunal's inherent jurisdiction and the code of conduct of any national body to which Counsel belongs.

(5) This Code must be read and applied so as to most effectively attain the objects and uphold the values expressed in the Preamble.

(6) General provisions of this Code should not be read or applied in a restrictive way by reason of any particular or illustrative provisions.

(7) The singular includes the plural and vice versa.

ARTICLE 2

ENTRY INTO FORCE

This Code enters into force on 4 June 1998.   **D9–004**

ARTICLE 3

GENERAL PURPOSE AND APPLICATION

(1) The general purpose of this Code is to provide for standards of conduct on the **D9–005**

part of Counsel which are appropriate in the interests of the fair and proper administration of justice.

(2) This Code applies to Counsel as defined in Article 1(1) of this Code.

PART II: GENERAL OBLIGATIONS OF COUNSEL TO CLIENTS

ARTICLE 4

SCOPE AND TERMINATION OF REPRESENTATION

D9–006 (1) Counsel must advise and represent their client until the client duly terminates Counsel's position, or Counsel is otherwise withdrawn with the consent of the Tribunal.

(2) When representing a client, Counsel must:

(a) Abide by a client's decisions concerning the objectives of representation if not inconsistent with Counsels ethical duties; and

(b) Consult with the client about the means by which those objectives are to be pursued.

(3) Counsel must not advise or assist a client to engage in conduct which Counsel knows is in breach of the Statute, the Rules or this Code and, where Counsel has been assigned to the client, the Directive.

ARTICLE 5

COMPETENCE AND INDEPENDENCE

D9–007 In providing representation to a client, Counsel must:

(a) Act with competence, dignity, skill, care, honesty and loyalty;

(b) Exercise independent professional judgement and render open and honest advice;

(c) Never be influenced by improper or patently dishonest behaviour on the part of a client;

(d) Preserve their own integrity and that of the legal profession as a whole;

(e) Never permit their independence, integrity and standards to be compromised by external pressures.

ARTICLE 5*BIS*

FEE SPLITTING

D9–008 (1) Fee-splitting arrangements, including but not limited to financial arrangements, between Counsel and their clients, relatives and/or agent of their clients are not permitted by the Tribunal.

(2) Where Counsel are being requested, induced or encouraged by their clients to enter into fee splitting arrangements they shall advice their clients on the unlawfulness of such practice shall report the incident to the Registrar forthwith.

(3) Counsel shall inform the Registrar of any alleged fee splitting arrangement by any member of Defence team.

(4) Following receipt of information regarding possible fee splitting arrangements between Counsel and their clients, the Registrar shall investigate such information in order to determine whether it is substantiated.

(5) Where Counsel is found to have engaged in a practice of fee splitting or to have entered into a fee splitting arrangement with his client, the Registrar shall take action in accordance with Article 19(A)(iii) of the Directive on assignment of Defence Counsel.

(6) In exceptional circumstances, and only where the Registrar has granted leave, Counsel may provide their clients with equipment and materials necessary for the preparation of their defence.

ARTICLE 6

DILIGENCE

Counsel must represent a client diligently in order to protect the client's best interests. Unless the representation is terminated, Counsel must carry through to conclusion all matters undertaken for a client within the scope of his legal representation.

D9–009

ARTICLE 7

COMMUNICATION

Counsel must keep a client informed about the status of a matter before the Tribunal in which the client is an interested party and must promptly comply with all reasonable requests for information.

D9–010

ARTICLE 8

CONFIDENTIALITY

(1) Whether or not the relation of Counsel and client continues, Counsel must preserve the confidentiality of his client's affairs and, subject to sub-article (2), must not reveal to any other person, other than to any assistants who need to know it for the performance of their duties, information which has been entrusted to him in confidence or use such information to his client's detriment or to his own or another client's advantage.

D9–011

(2) Notwithstanding sub-article (1), and subject to Article 19 ("Conflicts"), Counsel may reveal information which has been entrusted to him in confidence in any one of the following circumstances:

(a) When the client has been fully consulted and knowingly consents; or

(b) When the client has voluntarily disclosed the content of the communication to a third party, and that third party then gives evidence of that disclosure; or

(c) When essential to establish a defence to a criminal or disciplinary charge or civil claim formally instituted against Counsel; or

(d) To prevent an act which Counsel reasonably believes:

(i) Is, or may be, criminal within the territory in which it may occur or under the Statute or the Rules; and

(ii) May result in death or substantial bodily harm to any person unless the information is disclosed.

(3) For the purposes of this Article, Counsel includes employees or associates of Counsel and all others whose services are used by Counsel.

ARTICLE 9

CONFLICT OF INTEREST

(1) Counsel owes a duty of loyalty to his or her client. Counsel must at all times act in the best interests of the client and must put those interests before their own interests or those of any other person.

D9–012

(2) In the course of representing a client, Counsel must exercise all care to ensure that no conflict of interest arises.

(3) Without limiting the generality of sub-articles (1) and (2), Counsel must not represent a client with respect to a matter if:

(a) Such representation will be or is likely to be adversely affected by representation of another client;

(b) Representation of another client will be or is likely to be adversely affected by such representation;

(c) The Counsels professional judgement on behalf of the client will be, or may reasonably be expected to be, adversely affected by:

(i) The Counsels responsibilities to, or interests in, a third party; or

(ii) The Counsels own financial, business, property or personal interests; or

(iii) The matter is the same or substantially related to another matter in which Counsel had formerly represented another client (the former client); and the interests of the client are materially adverse to the interests of the former client, unless the former client consents after consultation.

(4) Counsel must not accept compensation for representing a client from a source other than that client or, if assigned by the Tribunal, from a source other than the Tribunal, unless:

(a) That client consents after consultation; and

(b) There is no interference thereby with the Counsels independence of professional judgement nor with the client-Counsel relationship.

(5) Where a conflict of interest does arise, Counsel must:

(a) Promptly and fully inform each potentially affected client of the nature and extent of the conflict; and

(b) Either:

(i) Take all steps necessary to remove the conflict; or

(ii) Obtain the full and informed consent of all potentially affected clients to continue the representation, so long as Counsel is able to fulfil all other obligations under this Code.

ARTICLE 10

CLIENT UNDER A DISABILITY

D9–013   When a client's ability to make adequately considered decisions in connection with their representation is impaired because of minority, mental disability or any other reason, Counsel must:

(a) Inform the Judge or Chamber of the Tribunal hearing the matter, if any, of the disability;

(b) Take such steps as are necessary to ensure the adequate legal representation of that client; and

(c) As far as reasonably possible maintain a normal Counsel-client relationship with the client.

ARTICLE 11

ACCOUNTING FOR TIME

D9–014   Counsel should account in good faith for the time spent working on a case and maintain and preserve detailed records of time spent. Counsel is under a duty to set his bills and fees with moderation.

PART III: CONDUCT BEFORE THE TRIBUNAL

ARTICLE 12

RULES OF THE TRIBUNAL

D9–015   (1) Counsel must at all times comply with the Rules and such rulings as to conduct and procedure as may be applied by the Tribunal in its proceedings. Counsel must at all times have due regard to the fair conduct of proceedings.

(2) Counsel must not, unless permitted by the Rules or this Code or the Judge or Chamber hearing the matter:
  (a) Make contact with a Judge or Chamber of the Tribunal without first or concurrently informing Counsel acting for any other party to the proceedings;
  (b) Submit exhibits, notes or documents to the Judge without communicating them first or concurrently to Counsel acting for any other party to the proceedings.

ARTICLE 13

CANDOUR TOWARD THE TRIBUNAL

D9–016

(1) Counsel is personally responsible for the conduct and presentation of their Client's case, and must exercise personal judgement upon the substance and purpose of statements made and questions asked.

(2) Counsel must not knowingly:
  (a) Make an incorrect statement of material fact to the Tribunal; or
  (b) Offer evidence which the Counsel knows to be incorrect.

(3) Despite sub-article (2) (a), Counsel will not have made an incorrect statement to another party to the proceedings or to the Tribunal simply by failing to correct an error on any matter stated to Counsel or to the Tribunal during proceedings.

(4) Counsel must take all necessary steps to correct an incorrect statement made by Counsel in proceedings before the Tribunal as soon as possible after Counsel becomes aware that the statement was incorrect.

ARTICLE 14

INTEGRITY OF EVIDENCE

D9–017

(1) Counsel must at all times maintain the integrity of evidence, whether in written, oral or any other form, which is or may be submitted to the Tribunal.

(2) If Counsel's representation of a client terminates for any reason, Counsel shall return evidence and other materials, which have come into his possession as a result of the said representation, to his former client, to the latter's Counsel, or under seal to the Registrar for onward transmission to the said client or Counsel, as appropriate.

ARTICLE 15

IMPARTIALITY OF THE TRIBUNAL

D9–018

(1) Counsel must take all necessary steps to ensure that their actions do not bring proceedings before the Tribunal into disrepute.

(2) Counsel must not seek to influence a Judge or other official of the Tribunal by means prohibited by the Statute, the Rules or this Code.

ARTICLE 16

COUNSEL AS WITNESS

D9–019

Counsel must not act as advocate in a trial in which the Counsel is likely to be a necessary witness except where the testimony relates to an uncontested issue or where substantial hardship would be caused to the client if that Counsel does not so act.

PART IV: DUTY OF COUNSEL TO OTHERS

ARTICLE 17

FAIRNESS AND COURTESY

D9–020

(1) Counsel must act fairly, honestly and courteously towards all persons with whom they have professional contact, namely other Counsel, their clients, Judges, members of the Office of the Prosecutor and Registry staff. Counsel shall recognize all other Counsel

appearing or acting in relation to proceedings before the Tribunal as professional colleagues.

(2) Counsel must not communicate with the client of another Counsel except through or with the permission of that client's Counsel.

ARTICLE 18

DEALING WITH UNREPRESENTED PERSONS

D9–021   (1) If, on behalf of a client, Counsel is dealing with a person who is not represented by Counsel, Counsel:

   (a) Must not give advice to this unrepresented person if the interests of the person are, or have a reasonable possibility of being, in conflict with the interests of the Counsel's client; but

   (b) May advise the unrepresented person to secure legal representation.

(2) Counsel must inform the unrepresented person of the role Counsel plays in the matter, the persons right to Counsel under the Rules, and the nature of legal representation in general.

This information must be given whether or not a conflict exists or may exist with the interests of Counsel's client.

PART V: MAINTENANCE OF THE INTEGRITY OF THE PROFESSION

ARTICLE 19

CONFLICTS

D9–022   If there is any inconsistency between this Code and any other code which Counsel is bound to honour, the terms of this Code prevail in respect of Counsel's conduct before the Tribunal.

ARTICLE 20

MISCONDUCT

D9–023   It is professional misconduct for Counsel, *inter alia*, to:

   (a) Violate or attempt to violate this Code or to knowingly assist or induce another person to do so, or to do so through the acts of another person;

   (b) Commit a reprehensible act which reflects adversely on Counsel's honesty, trustworthiness or fitness as Counsel;

   (c) Engage in conduct involving dishonesty, fraud, deceit or misrepresentation;

   (d) Engage in conduct which is prejudicial to the proper administration of justice before the Tribunal; or

   (e) Attempt to influence an officer of the Tribunal in an improper manner.

ARTICLE 21

REPORTING MISCONDUCT

D9–024   (1) If:

   (a) Counsel knows that another Counsel has breached this Code or has otherwise engaged in professional misconduct; and

   (b) That violation or conduct raises a substantial question as to the other Counsel's honesty, trustworthiness or fitness as Counsel.

Counsel may inform the Judge or Chamber of the Tribunal before which Counsel is appearing.

(2) The Registrar may also communicate any misconduct of Counsel to the professional body regulating the conduct of Counsel in his State of admission or, if a Professor and not otherwise admitted to the profession, to the governing body of his University.

ARTICLE 22. ENFORCEMENT

Counsel must abide by and voluntarily submit to any enforcement and disciplinary procedures as may be established by the Tribunal in accordance with the Rules.   **D9–025**

ARTICLE 23

AMENDMENT

This Code may be amended by the Registrar, after consultation with the Judges.   **D9–026**

D10. Directive on the Assignment of Defence Counsel

Document prepared by the Registrar and approved by the Tribunal on 9 January 1996 as amended 6 June 1997, 8 June 1998, 1 July 1999, 27 May 2003 and 15 May 2004

TABLE OF CONTENTS

AMENDMENT OF THE DIRECTIVE

Article 32: Amendment of the Directive

(DIRECTIVE NO. 1/96)

PREAMBLE

The Registrar of the International Criminal Tribunal for Rwanda,

Considering the Statute of the Tribunal as adopted by the Security Council under Resolution 955 (1994) of 8 November 1994 and in particular Articles 17 and 20 thereof,

Considering also the Rules of Procedure and Evidence as adopted pursuant to Article 14 of the Statute of the Tribunal on 29 June 1995, and in particular Rules 42, 45 and 55 thereof,

Bearing in mind the Rules Covering the Detention of Persons Awaiting Trial or Appear Before the Tribunal or Otherwise Detained on the Authority of the Tribunal as adopted by the Tribunal on 9 January 1996, and in particular Rule 67 thereof, and

Bearing in mind also the host country agreement between the United Nations and the United Republic of Tanzania, signed at New York on 31 August 1995, and in particular Article XX thereof,

Issues this Directive, laying down the conditions and arrangements for the assignment of Defence Counsel as approved by the Tribunal at its Second Plenary Session on 9 January 1996, as amended on 6 June 1997, 8 June 1998, 1 July 1999, 27 May 2003 and 15 May 2004.

D10–001

GENERAL PROVISIONS

ARTICLE 1: USE OF TERMS

(A) For the purposes of this Directive:

D10–002

President:	Means the President of the Tribunal;
Registrar:	Means the Registrar of the Tribunal;
Rules:	Means the Rules of Procedure and Evidence adopted by the Tribunal on 29 June 1995, as amended;
Rules of Detention:	Means the Rules Covering the Detention of Persons Awaiting Trial or Appeal the Tribunal or Otherwise Detained on the Authority of the Tribunal adopted by the Tribunal on 9 January 1996;
Statute:	Means the Statute of the Tribunal adopted by the Security Council under Resolution 955 (1994) of 8 November 1994;
Tribunal:	Means the International Criminal Tribunal for the Prosecution of Persons Responsible for Genocide and other Serious Violations of International Humanitarian Law Committed in the Territory of Rwanda and Rwandan citizens responsible for genocide and other violations committed in the territory of neighbouring States, between 1 January 1994 and 31 December 1994;
Stage of Procedure:	Means the following stages of procedure: Pre-Trial, Trial, Sentencing Hearing, Appeal and Review.

(B) The masculine shall include the feminine and the singular the plural, and vice-versa.

ARTICLE 2: RIGHT TO COUNSEL

(A) Without prejudice to the right of an accused to conduct his own Defence, a suspect who is to be questioned by the Prosecutor during an investigation and an accused upon whom personal service of the indictment has been effected shall have the right to be assisted by Counsel provided that he has not expressly waived his right to Counsel.

D10–003

(B) Any person detained on the authority of the Tribunal, including any person detained in accordance with Rule 90 *bis*, also has the right to be assisted by Counsel provided that the person has not expressly waived his right to Counsel.

(C) All references in this Directive to suspects or accused shall also be understood to apply to any persons detained on the authority of the Tribunal.

ARTICLE 3: PERSON TO WHOM COUNSEL IS ASSIGNED

D10–004   If he has insufficient means, the suspect during an investigation or the accused being prosecuted before the Tribunal may be assigned Counsel free of charge on the following terms and conditions.

ARTICLE 4: INDIGENCE

D10–005   A person shall be considered to be fully or partially indigent if he does not have sufficient means to engage Counsel of his choice and to have himself legally represented or assisted by Counsel of his choice.

PROCEDURE FOR THE ASSIGNMENT OF COUNSEL

ARTICLE 5: REQUEST FOR ASSIGNMENT OF COUNSEL

D10–006   Subject to the provisions of Article 21, a suspect or accused who wishes to be assigned Counsel shall make a request to the Registrar of the Tribunal by means of the appropriate form established by the Registrar, with the approval of the Bureau. A request shall be lodged with the Registry, or transmitted to it, by the suspect or accused himself or by a person authorised by him to do so on his behalf.

ARTICLE 6: APPLICANT'S FINANCIAL SITUATION

D10–007   (A) A suspect or accused who requests the assignment of Counsel, must fulfil the requirement of indigence as defined in Article 4.

(B) In order to determine whether the suspect or accused is indigent, there shall be taken into account means of all kinds of which he has direct or indirect enjoyment or freely disposes, excluding any family or social benefits to which he may be entitled. In assessing such means, account shall also be taken of the means of the spouse of a suspect or accused, as well as those of persons with whom he habitually resides.

(C) Account shall also be taken of the apparent lifestyle of a suspect or accused, and of his enjoyment of any property, movable or immovable, and whether or not he derives income from it.

ARTICLE 7: DECLARATION OF MEANS

D10–008   For the purposes of Article 6, the Registrar shall invite a suspect or accused requesting the assignment of Counsel to make a declaration of his means on the appropriate form established by the Registrar, with the approval of the Bureau.

ARTICLE 8: CERTIFICATION OF THE DECLARATION OF MEANS

D10–009   A declaration must, so far as possible, be certified by an appropriate authority located either in the place where the suspect or accused resides or is found, or any other place considered appropriate in the circumstances to be determined by the Registrar. If the declaration is not certified within a reasonable period of time, the Registrar may assign Counsel without prejudice to Articles 9 and 18.

Article 9: Information

(A) For the purpose of establishing whether the suspect or accused satisfies the **D10–010** requisite conditions for assignment of Counsel, the Registrar may request the gathering of any information, hear the suspect or accused, consider any representation, or request the production of any documents likely to support the request.

(B) When communicated confidentially, such information or its source shall not be subject to disclosure or notification to the Parties but shall be made available by the Registrar to a Judge or a Trial Chamber *in camera* upon a request from the Judge or the Chamber, as the interests of Justice may require.

Article 10: Decision by the Registrar

(A) After examining the declaration of means laid down in Article 7 and relevant **D10–011** information obtained pursuant to Article 9, the Registrar shall determine if the suspect or accused is indigent or not, and shall decide:

    (i) Without prejudice to Article 18, either to assign Counsel and choose for this purpose a name from the list drawn up in accordance with Article 13; or

    (ii) Not to grant the request for assignment of Counsel, in which case the decision shall be accompanied by a written explanation giving reasons therefor.

(B) To ensure that the right to Counsel is not affected while the Registrar examines the declaration of means laid down in Article 7 and the information obtained pursuant to Article 9, the Registrar may temporarily assign Counsel to a suspect or accused for a period not exceeding 30 days.

Article 10*bis*: Assignment of Counsel in the Interests of Justice

If a suspect or accused, **D10–012**

    (i) Either requests an assignment of Counsel but does not comply with the requirement set out above within a reasonable time; or

    (ii) Fails to obtain or to request assignment of Counsel, or to elect in writing that he intends to conduct his own defence,

the Registrar may nevertheless assign him Counsel in the interests of justice in accordance with Rule 45(E) of the Rules and without prejudice to Article 18.

Article 11: Notification of the Decision

(A) The Registrar shall notify the suspect or accused of his decision. **D10–013**

(B) The Registrar shall also notify the assigned Counsel and Counsel's professional or governing body of his decision.

Article 12: Remedy Against a Decision Not to Assign Counsel

(A) The suspect whose request for assignment of Counsel has been denied may seek **D10–014** the President's review of the decision of the Registrar. The President may either confirm the Registrar's decision or decide that a Counsel should be assigned.

(B) The accused whose request for assignment of Counsel for his initial appearance has been denied, may make a motion to the Trial Chamber before which he is due to appear for immediate review of the Registrar's decision. The Trial Chamber may either confirm the Registrar's decision or decide that a Counsel should be assigned.

(C) After the initial appearance of the accused, an objection to the denial of his request for the assignment of Counsel shall take the form of a preliminary motion by him before the Trial Chamber not later than 60 days after his first appearance and, in any event, before the hearing on the merits.

STATUS OF ASSIGNED COUNSEL

ARTICLE 13: PRE-REQUISITES FOR ASSIGNMENT OF COUNSEL

D10–015   Any person may be assigned as Counsel if the Registrar is satisfied that he fulfils the following pre-requisites:

    (i) He is admitted to practice law in a State, or is a professor of law at a university or similar academic institution and has at least 10 years' relevant experience;

    (ii) He speaks one of the working languages of the Tribunal, namely French or English;

    (iii) He agrees to be assigned as Counsel by the Tribunal to represent a suspect or accused;

    (iv) His name has been included in the list envisaged in Rule 45(A) of the Rules; and

    (v) He undertakes to appear before the Tribunal within a reasonable time, as specified by the Registrar.

ARTICLE 14: PROFESSIONAL CERTIFICATION

D10–016   In support of the pre-requisites provided for in Article 13(i), the Registrar shall be supplied with certification of professional qualifications issued by the competent professional or governing body for that Counsel and such other documentation as the Registrar deems necessary.

ARTICLE 15: SCOPE OF THE ASSIGNMENT

D10–017   (A) A suspect or accused shall only be entitled to have one Counsel assigned to him and that Counsel shall deal with all stages of procedure and all matters arising out of the representation of the suspect or accused or of the conduct of his Defence. No Counsel shall be assigned to more than one suspect or accused.

(B) Where persons accused of the same or different counts are jointly charged or tried, each accused shall be entitled to request assignment of separate Counsel.

(C) Whenever appropriate and at the request of the assigned Counsel, the Registrar may, pursuant to Article 13 above, appoint a co-Counsel to assist the assigned Counsel. The first Counsel shall thereafter be designated lead Counsel.

(D) The lead Counsel may request the Chamber to authorize the withdrawal of the assignment of the co-Counsel.

(E) Under the authority of Lead Counsel, who has primary responsibility for the Defence, co-Counsel may deal with all stages of the procedure and all matters arising out of the representation of the accused or of the conduct of his Defence. Lead Counsel shall sign all the documents submitted to the Tribunal unless he authorizes co-Counsel, in writing, to sign on his behalf.

(F) Any reference to Counsel in this Directive shall apply to both the lead Counsel and the co-Counsel.

(G) The co-Counsel shall be remunerated according to Article 22 of this Directive.

ARTICLE 16: APPLICABLE LAW

D10–018   In the performance of their duties assigned Counsel shall be subject to the relevant provisions of the Statute, of the Rules, of the Rules of Detention, of any other rules or regulations adopted by the Tribunal, of the Host Country Agreement, of this Directive, of the Code of Conduct and of the codes of practice and ethics governing the profession.

ARTICLE 17: RESPONSIBILITY FOR COSTS AND EXPENSES

D10–019   (A) Where Counsel has been assigned, the costs and expenses of legal representation of the suspect or accused necessarily and reasonably incurred shall be met by the Tribunal, subject to availability of funds and applicable United Nations rules and regulations and the procedures established by the Registrar with the approval of the Bureau.

(B) Such costs and expenses to be met by the Tribunal shall include costs relating to investigative and procedural steps, measures taken for the production of evidence to assist or support the Defence, expenses for ascertainment of facts, consultancy and expert opinion, transportation and accommodation of witnesses, postal charges, registration fees, taxes or similar duties, and all remuneration due to Counsel in accordance with Articles 22 and 27.

(C) When Counsel has not been assigned, and if Counsel so requests, the Registrar, subject to reservations of paragraph (A), may determine that all or part of the costs and expenses of legal representation of the suspect or accused necessarily and reasonably incurred shall be covered by the Tribunal to the extent that such expenses cannot be borne by the suspect or the accused because of his financial situation.

(D) The Registry shall reimburse the sums claimed by assigned Counsel for the expenses, as provided in paragraph (A) and (B) above, upon receipt of a statement of expenses made out on the appropriate form established by the Registrar with the approval of the Bureau.

(E) The Registrar may however authorize, under exceptional circumstances, direct payment by the Tribunal of some of the costs and expenses referred to in paragraph (B) above, subject to the Counsel providing, at the end of the specific mission for which such direct payment has been requested, originals of receipts for the expenses under consideration.

ARTICLE 18: WITHDRAWAL OF ASSIGNMENT WHEN THE SUSPECT OR ACCUSED IS NO LONGER INDIGENT

(A) Assignment of Counsel may be withdrawn by the Registrar if, after his decision, **D10–020** the suspect or accused comes into means which, if available at the time the request in Article 5 was made, would have caused the Registrar not to grant the request.

(B) Assignment of Counsel may be withdrawn if information obtained according to Article 9 establishes that the suspect or accus ed has sufficient means to allow him to pay for the cost of his Defence.

(C) The decision to withdraw the assignment shall be accompanied by a written explanation giving reasons for such decision and the suspect or accused and the assigned Counsel shall be so notified. Such withdrawal shall take effect from the date of receipt of the notification.

(D) After the notification of the withdrawal of the assignment of Counsel, all the costs and expenses incurred by the representation of the suspect or accused shall cease to be met by the Tribunal.

(E) The provisions of Article 12 shall apply *mutatis mutandis* where there is dissatisfaction with the decision withdrawing the assignment of Counsel.

ARTICLE 19: WITHDRAWAL OF ASSIGNMENT IN OTHER SITUATIONS

(A) The Registrar may: **D10–021**
   (i) In exceptional circumstances, at the request of the accused, or his Counsel, withdraw the assignment of Counsel;
   (ii) In exceptional circumstances, at the request of Lead Counsel withdraw the assignment of co-Counsel;
   (iii) In the case of a serious violation of the Code of Conduct, withdraw the assignment of Counsel or co-Counsel.
(B) The Registrar shall withdraw the assignment of Counsel:
   (i) Upon the decision by a Chamber to refuse audience to assigned Counsel for misconduct under Rule 46 (A) of the Rules;
   (ii) Where Counsel no longer satisfies the requirements of Article 13 (i) of this Directive.

    (iii) Where Counsel or co-Counsel fails to observe the undertaking made by him pursuant to Rule 45*ter*.

    (C) The accused, the Counsel concerned and his respective professional or governing body shall be notified of the withdrawal.

    (D) The Registrar shall immediately assign a new Counsel to the suspect or accused, and where appropriate, a co-Counsel.

    (E) Where a request for withdrawal, made pursuant to paragraph (A), has been denied, the person making the request may seek the President's review of the decision of the Registrar.

ARTICLE 20: REPLACEMENT

D10–022   (A) Where the assignment of Counsel is withdrawn by the Registrar or where the services of assigned Counsel are discontinued, the Counsel assigned may not withdraw from acting until either a replacement Counsel has been provided by the Tribunal or by the suspect or accused, or the suspect or accused has declared his intention in writing to conduct his own defence.

    (B) Where the assignment of Counsel is withdrawn by the Registrar or where the services of assigned Counsel are discontinued, the Counsel must deliver within fifteen days of withdrawal all the original documents in the file to the Counsel who succeeds him, or otherwise, to his client.

    (C) In the case of the withdrawal of the assignment of a co-Counsel, such delivery of documents shall be made to the Counsel within seven days.

    (D) Failure by Counsel to comply with the requirement of this article may result in withholding counsel's fees, notification to the professional body regulating the conduct of counsel in his place of admission and, if he is a professor and not otherwise admitted to the profession, to the governing body of his University.

    (E)(i) If Counsel is not available, co-Counsel shall assume responsibility of carrying on the proceedings.

      (ii) If there is no co-Counsel, the Registrar may appoint one, in consultation with Counsel.

ARTICLE 21: ASSIGNMENT OF COUNSEL AWAY FROM THE SEAT OF THE TRIBUNAL

D10–023   (A) Away from the seat of the Tribunal, and in a case of urgency, a suspect who, during the investigation, requests assignment of Counsel, may indicate the name of Counsel if he knows one who may be assigned in accordance with the provisions of this Directive.

    (B) Where the suspect fails to indicate a name, and none of the Counsel on the list maintained by the Registrar resides in the area or the country in question, the Registrar or a person authorized by him or acting under his direction, may contact the local Bar Association and obtain the name of Counsel who may be assigned in accordance with the provisions of this Directive.

    (C) In the situations envisaged in paragraphs (A) and (B), the procedure for assignment of Counsel as set out in this Directive shall apply *mutatis mutandis* but shall be accelerated where necessary.

REMUNERATION AND TRAVEL EXPENSES

ARTICLE 22: REMUNERATION PAID TO ASSIGNED COUNSEL

D10–024   (A) The remuneration paid to assigned Counsel for any one case and at any one stage of the procedure shall include:

      (i) A fixed rate,
          (ii) Fees calculated on the basis of a fixed hourly rate determined by the Registrar based on the Counsel's seniority and experience in accordance with the table of rates published by the Registrar after consultation with the Bureau. This rate includes the charges related to general costs;
       (ii) A daily subsistence allowance based on the United Nations Schedule of Daily Subsistence Allowance Rates in force at the time when work was done.[1]

(B) Assigned Counsel who receives remuneration from the Tribunal, shall not be entitled to receive remuneration from any other source with respect to the same assignment.

(C) The Registrar, with the concurrence of the President, may establish an alternative scheme of payment based on a fixed fee ("lump sum") system consisting of a maximum allotment of moneys for each Defence Team in respect of each stage of the procedure taking into account the Registrar's estimate of the duration of the stage and the apparent complexity of the case. In the event that a stage of the procedure is of substantially longer or shorter duration than estimated, the Registrar may adapt the allotment, whether by increasing or decreasing it. In the event of disagreement on the quantum of the maximum allotment, the Registrar shall make a decision, after consulting the Chamber and, if he deems it expedient to do so, the Advisory Panel.

(D) Claims for remuneration and reimbursement of expenses under this Article shall be submitted to the Registrar no later than ninety days from the last day of the calendar month during which the work was performed or the expense was incurred. Any such claim that is submitted later shall not be paid, unless the Registrar is persuaded that extenuating circumstances of an exceptional nature existed so as to justify such late submission.

ARTICLE 23: FIXED RATE

The fixed rate envisaged in Article 22 (A) (i) shall be determined by the Registrar in consultation with the local Bar[2] and is payable at the conclusion of each stage of procedure as set out in paragraph (A) of Article 1 of the Directive.

D10–025

ARTICLE 24: STATEMENT OF REMUNERATION

(A) Subject to the provisions of Article 25, payment of the fees envisaged in Article 22 (A) shall be made at the conclusion of the relevant stage of procedure, or, as appropriate, at the conclusion of a minimum period of one month, on presentation by Counsel of a detailed statement using the appropriate form established by the Registrar, with the approval of the Bureau and any other documentation required by the Registrar.

D10–026

(B) The statement shall indicate, *inter alia*, the name of the suspect or the accused, the registration number in the Record Book, the stage of the procedure at which assigned Counsel was involved, and a statement of the fees. To support the statement of fees, the Counsel shall provide as much information as possible, including the nature of the services rendered; and, as appropriate, the relation between these and the case pending before the Tribunal.

ARTICLE 25: PROVISIONAL PAYMENT

(A) When the engagement of assigned Counsel outside his place of residence lasts more than two weeks, a provisional payment of the daily subsistence allowance, set out in Article 22(A)(iii) above may be made.

D10–027

---

[1] According to current United Nations regulations, the applicable rate will be lowered by 20% at the end of an initial period of 60 days; and by 40% at the end of a period of 120 days.
[2] The rate is set at US$ 2000 since September 1998.

(B) The Registrar authorizes the provisional payment on the basis of the provisional engagement program submitted by the assigned Counsel and approved by the Registrar. At the conclusion of the specific mission for which such provisional payment was made, the Counsel shall provide the Registrar, for regularisation purposes, with the originals of the supporting documents showing that he has actually fulfilled his assignment.

ARTICLE 26: PAYMENT *PRO RATA TEMPORIS*

D10–028   When, during engagement, an assigned Counsel is replaced in the same capacity by another assigned Counsel for whatever reason, the remuneration shall be paid to each of them *pro rata temporis.*

ARTICLE 27: TRAVEL EXPENSES

D10–029   (A) Travel expenses shall be reimbursed for an assigned Counsel who does not usually reside in the territory of the host country or in the country where the particular stage of the procedure is being conducted, on the basis of one economy class round trip air ticket by the shortest route or within limits laid down by the Registrar, on presentation of a statement of travel expenses using the appropriate form established by the Registrar, with the approval of the Bureau, accompanied by the original counterfoil of the ticket, as well as the original of the invoice and any receipt including receipt showing payment by credit card.

(B) Travel expenses shall be reimbursed to assigned Counsel residing in the territory of the country but not in the town where he is serving, on the basis of either first class public transportation tickets or fixed rates as established by the United Nations Schedule of Rates of Reimbursement for Travel by Private Motor Vehicle applicable to different groups of Countries and Territories, per kilometre traveled on the outward and return journeys by the shortest route, on presentation of a statement of travel expenses using the appropriate form established by the Registrar, with the approval of the Bureau.

(C) Notwithstanding paragraphs (A) and (B), the Registrar shall assess, after consulting the President and depending on the circumstances of the case, whether the Tribunal, in the interests of justice and in order to ensure the full exercise of Defence rights, is required to meet other travel expenses of assigned Counsel.

(D) Travel expenses, and daily subsistence allowance payable under Article 25 of the present Directive, shall only be reimbursed when prior authorization for travel by assigned Counsel has been sought by assigned Counsel and authorized by the Registrar.

ARTICLE 28: APPROVAL OF REMUNERATION AND EXPENSES

D10–030   (A) All sums payable to assigned Counsel under the provisions of this Directive shall be paid by the Registry.

(B) The statement of expenses, the statement of remuneration (be it provisional or final) and the statement of travel expenses envisaged under Articles 17, 24, 25 and 27, must receive the prior approval of the Registrar.

ADVISORY PANEL

ARTICLE 29: ADVISORY PANEL

D10–031   (A) An Advisory Panel shall be set up consisting of two members chosen by the President by ballot from the list referred to in Rule 45, two members proposed by the International Bar Association, two members proposed by the Union Internationale des Avocats, and the President of the Tanganyika Law Society or his representative.

(B) The President of the Advisory Panel will be the President of the Tanganyika Law Society or his representative. The membership of the Advisory Panel shall come up for appointment every two years on the anniversary date of the entry into force of this Directive.

(C) The Advisory Panel may be consulted as and when necessary by the Registrar or the President on matters relating to assignment of Counsel.

(D) The Advisory Panel may also of its own initiative refer to the Registrar any matter relating to the assignment of Counsel.

Article 30: Settlement of Disputes

In the event of disagreement on questions relating to the calculation and payment of remuneration, or to the reimbursement of expenses, the Registrar shall make a decision after consulting the President and, if necessary, the Advisory Panel, on an equitable basis. The Registrar may also consult the President and, if necessary, the Advisory Panel, and make a decision under this Article, if it appears to the Registrar that a Counsel has been submitting inflated claims for remuneration or claims for expenses which are unnecessary or unreasonable.

D10–032

FACILITIES

Article 31: Provision of Facilities

(a) Assigned Counsel who do not have professional facilities close to the seat of the Tribuna l shall, subject to availability of space and resources, be provided with reasonable facilities and equipment such as photocopiers, computer equipment, various types of office equipment, and telephone lines.

(b) At the seat of the Tribunal, assigned Counsel may use the libraries and the documentation centre used by the Judges of the Tribunal.

D10–033

AMENDMENT OF THE DIRECTIVE

Article 32: Amendment of the Directive

(a) Any article of the Directive may be amended during a plenary meeting at the request of a Judge, the Prosecutor or the Registrar if agreed to by not less than ten Judges.

(b) An Amendment of the Directive may be otherwise adopted, provided it has been circulated to all the Judges, and has received the approval of at least ten Judges. Amendments proposed under this paragraph shall also be circulated to the Prosecutor and the Registrar.

(c) The amendments shall enter into force upon adoption, but without prejudice to the rights of the accused in any pending case.

D10–034

D11. Directive for the Registry of the International Criminal Tribunal for Rwanda

JUDICIAL AND LEGAL SERVICES DIVISION
Court Management Section

(As amended on 1 July 1999, 21 February 2000 and 31 May 2001)

TABLE OF CONTENTS

PREAMBLE

D11–001   The Registrar of the Tribunal,
CONSIDERING the Statute of the Tribunal as adopted by the Security Council under resolution 955 (1994) of 8 November 1994, and in particular Article 16 thereof,
CONSIDERING the Rules of Procedure and Evidence as adopted by the Tribunal on 29 June 1995 and further amended, and in particular Part 3, Section 5 thereof,
CONSIDERING the approval of this Directive by the Judges of the Tribunal on 8 June 1998,
HEREBY ISSUES the Directive for the Judicial and Legal Services Division, Court Management Section.

SECTION I: INTRODUCTION

ARTICLE 1: ENTRY INTO FORCE

D11–002   The Directive shall enter into force on 8 June 1998.

ARTICLE 2: AMENDMENTS

D11–003   The Registrar may amend the Directive in consultation with the Judges and the Office of the Prosecutor. These amendments shall not come into force until adopted by the Judges at the Plenary Meeting.

ARTICLE 3: DEFINITIONS

D11–004   In the Directive the masculine shall include the feminine and the singular the plural, and vice-versa. The following terms shall mean:

Statute: The Statute of the Tribunal adopted by Security Council resolution 955 of 8 November 1994.

Tribunal: The International Tribunal for the Prosecution of Persons Responsible for Genocide and other Serious Violations of International Humanitarian Law Committed in the Territory of Rwanda and Rwandan citizens responsible for genocide and other violations committed in the territory of neighbouring States, between 1 January 1994 and 31 December 1994, established by Security Council resolution 955 of 8 November 1994.

Rules: The Rules of Procedure and Evidence, adopted pursuant to Article 14 of the Statute of the Tribunal, adopted on 29 June 1995 and further amended on 12 January 1996, 15 May 1996, 4 July 1996, 5 June 1997 and 8 June 1998.

Bureau: A body composed of the President, the Vice-President and the more senior Presiding Judge of the Trial Chambers. When the more senior of the Presiding Judges of the Trial Chamber is also either the President or Vice-President, the Presiding Judge of the other Trial Chamber sits as a member of the Bureau.

Chamber(s):   The Trial Chamber and/or the Appeals Chamber of the Tribunal.

Appeals Chamber: The Appeals Chamber of the ICTR, or the Judges thereof located at the Hague.

Prosecutor: The Prosecutor appointed pursuant to Article 15 of the Statute.

Party: The Prosecutor and the Accused.

Registrar: The Registrar appointed pursuant to Article 16 (3) of the Statute.

Registry: An organ of the Tribunal, responsible for the administration and servicing of the Tribunal pursuant to Article 16 of the Statute.

SECTION II: THE REGISTRY

ARTICLE 4: COMPOSITION AND ORGANIZATION OF THE REGISTRY

1. The Registry shall be composed of the Registrar, the Deputy Registrar and such **D11–005** other staff as may be required for the efficient discharge of its functions in accordance with Article 16 of the Statute.

2. The Registry consists of two divisions—the Judicial and Legal Services Division and the Division of Administration—and the Office of the Registrar, comprising the Immediate Office of the Registrar and the Press and Public Affairs Unit.

3. The Judicial and Legal Services Division is divided into four sections: Court Management Section, General Legal Services and Chambers Support Section, Lawyers and Detention Facilities Management Section, and Witnesses and Victims Support Section.

4. The Registrar shall assist the Chambers, the Plenary meetings of the Tribunal, the Judges and the Prosecutor in the performance of their functions. Under the authority of the President, he shall be responsible for the administration and servicing of the Tribunal. He is head of the Registry.

ARTICLE 5: THE REGISTRAR

1. The Registrar shall discharge his functions in accordance with Article 16 of the **D11–006** Statute and Rule 33 of the Rules.

2. The Registrar may delegate any of his tasks to his staff, either orally or in writing, implicitly or explicitly, but he remains ultimately responsible for them.

ARTICLE 6: DEPUTY REGISTRAR

1. The Deputy Registrar shall assist the Registrar, act as Registrar in his temporary **D11–007** absence and, in the event of the office becoming vacant, exercise the functions of Registrar until the office has been filled.

2. The Deputy Registrar has primary responsibility, under the authority of the Registrar, for the Judicial and Legal Services Division of the Registry. He is assisted by the Heads of the four Sections of the Judicial and Legal Services Division and other Registry staff.

ARTICLE 7: DUTIES OF REGISTRY STAFF

1. The Registrar, the Deputy Registrar, all Staff and all persons assisting the Registry **D11–008** shall refrain from any action which might reflect adversely on the Tribunal and shall not seek nor receive instructions from anyone external to the Tribunal.

2. Before commencing their duties, the Registrar, the Deputy Registrar and all Registry Staff shall make a Solemn Declaration in the form provided by Rule 32 of the Rules. They are also under a duty of confidentiality not to reveal any non-public information which they have access to in the course of the work performed on behalf of the Tribunal.

3. Registry Staff are responsible for reporting diligently to the Registrar or the Deputy Registrar.

SECTION III: THE JUDICIAL AND LEGAL SERVICES DIVISION

ARTICLE 8: THE JUDICIAL AND LEGAL SERVICES DIVISION

1. The Deputy Registrar acts as the Head of the Judicial and Legal Services Division, **D11–009** under the supervision of the Registrar.

2. The Judicial and Legal Services Division is, in general, responsible for administering and providing assistance to the Chambers, the Office of the Prosecutor and Defence Counsel in the performance of their functions.

3. The Judicial and Legal Services Division comprises four sections, the particular responsibilities of which are as follows:

(A) Court Management Section, headed by a Senior Legal Officer. The responsibilities of this Section is the subject of the present Directive, and in particular Article 9 thereof.

(B) General Legal Services and Chambers Support Section, headed by a Section Chief. This Section is responsible for providing legal, drafting and administrative support to the Judges.

(C) Lawyers and Detention Facilities Management Section, headed by a Section Chief. This Section serves as the channel of communication between the Tribunal and Counsel for the accused, and supervises and coordinates the assignment of Defence Counsel in accordance with the Directive on the Assignment of Defence Counsel. The Section also supervises the administration of the Tribunal's Detention Unit, including visits to detainees and the rules and regulations governing detention.

(D) Witnesses and Victims Support Section, headed by a Section Chief. This Section is responsible for protecting victims and witnesses in accordance with the rôle conferred upon it by the Statute and the Rules, in particular Article 21 of the Statute and Rules 34, 69 and 75 of the Rules.

SECTION IV: THE COURT MANAGEMENT SECTION

ARTICLE 9: THE COURT MANAGEMENT SECTION

D11–010   The functions of the Court Management Section of the Judicial and Legal Services Division are as follows:

(i) To maintain the Judicial Archives of the Tribunal, as described in Article 10 below;

(ii) To have custody of the seals and stamps;

(iii) To organize the proceedings of the Chambers, including arrangements for the distribution of documents to Judges, Legal Officers, the Parties and the Press and Public Affairs Unit, the provision of technical assistance and the preparation of minutes and records, pursuant to Rule 35 of the Rules;

(iv) To file and distribute, on an expeditious basis, judgements, orders, requests, pleadings, and other official documents of the Tribunal to Judges, the supporting Legal Staff, the Parties and the Press and Public Affairs Unit;

(v) To ensure that non-confidential information in the custody of the Section is publicly available;

(vi) To maintain the Record Book, pursuant to Rule 36 of the Rules, and a "Summary of Judicial Activities Sheet".

SECTION V: FUNCTIONS OF THE COURT MANAGEMENT SECTION

PART ONE: JUDICIAL ARCHIVES

ARTICLE 10: JUDICIAL ARCHIVES

D11–011   1. The Court Management Section is responsible for maintaining the Judicial Archives of the Tribunal.

2. The Judicial Archives shall contain:

(a) Case files, maintained in accordance with Article 13 below;

(b) Correspondence files;

(c) The Record Book, including the "Summary of Judicial Activities Sheet" ("the Summary Sheet") (cf. Articles 18 and 19 of the present Directive);

(d) Audio and video cassettes, diskettes, microfiches and photographs including negatives.

3. The Judicial Archives shall not include correspondence directly addressed to a Judge or to the Prosecutor of the Tribunal, unless they transmit such correspondence to the Court Management Section.

4. All documents in the Judicial Archives shall be kept securely locked when not in use by Court Management Section staff. No file or original of any document contained in the archives may be consulted without first obtaining permission from a designated member of the Court Management Section, nor removed from the Judicial Archives except for the purposes of making a photocopy, again only with the prior permission of a designated member of the Court Management Section. If a photocopy is made, the original must be returned to the Judicial Archives immediately afterwards.

PART TWO: FILING, REPRODUCTION AND DISTRIBUTION OF DOCUMENTS

ARTICLE 11: GENERAL FUNCTIONS

The Court Management Section is responsible for the expeditious management, filing, reproduction, and distribution of the documents of the Tribunal to Judges, the Parties and the Press and Public Affairs Unit, including:

D11–012

(a) Official documents, as defined in Article 12;
(b) Minutes, transcripts and recordings of sessions of the Tribunal;
(c) Any other document required for proceedings.

ARTICLE 12: OFFICIAL DOCUMENTS OF THE TRIBUNAL

1. The official documents of the Tribunal are:

D11–013

(a) Original documents, namely documents which are integral to the Tribunal's proceedings and are issued by the Tribunal:
　(i) Original documents issued by the Chambers bearing the signature of a Judge or Judges, and the Seal of the Tribunal, e.g. Decisions, Orders and Judgements;
　(ii) Original documents issued by the Office of the Prosecutor bearing the signature of the Prosecutor, or his delegate, and the stamp of the Office of the Prosecutor;
　(iii) Original documents issued by the Court Management Section bearing the signature of the Registrar, or his delegate, and the stamp of the Tribunal;
　(iv) All documents concerning cases before the Tribunal which are sent to the Tribunal by the Parties or by an *amicus curiae* and filed with the Court Management Section; and
　(v) Translation of the original documents duly certified by the Language and Conference Services Section of the Tribunal.
(b) Copies of original documents as described in (a) and (b) which have been certified in accordance with the procedure set down in Article 21 of the present Directive.

2. The Court Management Section shall ensure that every original document issued by the Tribunal conforms to the above requirements.

ARTICLE 12*bis:* SUBMISSION OF DOCUMENTS BY THE PARTIES

The parties may file a document with the Court Management Section in both English and French under arrangements agreed with the Registrar. It is the responsibility of the Registry to ensure that a document filed in only one language shall be translated.

D11–014

ARTICLE 13: CASE FILES

1. Case files shall contain all documents pertaining to each case brought before a Judge or Chamber.

D11–015

2. In the case of an original document issued in one single copy but relevant to two or more files, a certified copy of the original document shall be inserted in the relevant file(s).

3. Each document shall be numbered in chronological order, and filed in accordance with the Instructions for the Court Management Section.

4. The title and the reference number of each document inserted in a folder must be noted in the Indexes (public or confidential) of the relevant case file.

5. Documents in more than one language shall be filed in accordance with the Instructions for the Court Management Section.

6. When a document is filed with the Court Management Section, the Section shall make the appropriate arrangements for its translation into the working languages of the Tribunal.

7. The Court Management Section shall ensure that an electronic copy of a document is filed simultaneously with the filing of the document. It shall request the person filing the document to provide electronic copy if he has not already done so. The electronic copy shall then be transmitted to the person responsible for the Tribunal's Website for the purposes of review and loading onto the homepage.

8. If possible, the Court Management Section will establish a copy set for each case file which shall be stored away from the Tribunal's facilities and shall be certified in accordance with the procedure set down in Article 21 of the present Directive.

ARTICLE 14: PRINCIPLES GOVERNING MANAGEMENT OF CONFIDENTIAL DOCUMENTS

D11–016   1. Documents which are confidential in whole or in part, or which include words or phrases which should not be disclosed to the public, shall be filed and classified in accordance with the procedure described in Article 13 herein. These documents shall remain a part of the relevant case file, but they shall be placed in a sealed envelope or distinct folder that is inaccessible to the public.

2. A certificate and/or an expurgated version shall replace the original documents in the *public* case file.

3. The practical mechanisms relating to the establishment of confidential folders shall be laid down by the Registrar in the Instructions for the Court Management Section.

ARTICLE 15: CASE FILE INDEXES

D11–017   1. Each case file shall have an index listing all the documents filed in that case. Documents which contain confidential information but whose existence is not confidential may be listed in the public index, provided the listing does not divulge any confidential information and provided that the confidential information does not appear in the case-file. Documents the *existence* of which is confidential must *only* be listed in confidential indexes.

2. The indexes shall be inserted at the beginning of each folder of each case file. All of the non-confidential indexes shall be collected together in a "Compilation of Indexes".

PART THREE: CORRESPONDENCE

ARTICLE 16: CORRESPONDENCE

D11–018   Official correspondence of the Court Management Section shall be signed by the Registrar, or by the Deputy-Registrar or Court Management Section officials, in so far as the Registrar may delegate to them his signature for this purpose.

ARTICLE 17: FILING OF CORRESPONDENCE AND RELATED DOCUMENTS

D11–019   1. The Court Management Section shall file official correspondence addressed to or received by the Court Management Section in the case-file, in accordance with Article 13 of the present Directive. A separate correspondence file may be maintained, if necessary, for any case.

2. The Court Management Section shall file, following the same principles, all documents sent by the Section and their annexes noting the name of the addressee and in due course stapling, where available, the proof of receipt to the document or its copy.

PART FOUR: RECORD BOOK AND SUMMARY SHEET

ARTICLE 18: RECORD BOOK

1. The Record Book shall be open to the public and otherwise maintained in accordance with Rule 36 of the Rules. It shall be in diary format, with one page for each day. Non-confidential particulars of each case and each document filed in the case file, including orders, decisions and judgements, shall be noted in the Record Book on their day of filing.   **D11–020**

2. The Record Book is a permanent record of the Tribunal and shall not be destroyed. It shall be maintained in the archives.

ARTICLE 19: SUMMARY SHEET

1. The Summary Sheet shall contain the essential information relating to all cases which are before a Judge or Chamber of the Tribunal, and the dates of the various stages so far reached in those cases, excluding those subject to an order for non disclosure.   **D11–021**

2. The Summary Sheet, which shall be an integral part of the Record Book, is principally intended to facilitate the location of documents in the case file, to provide a quick reference for basic information concerning the case, and to provide a basis for compiling information or statistics for the preparation of annual and budgetary reports.

PART FIVE: MANAGEMENT OF AUDIO-VISUAL, ELECTRONIC, MICRO-FICHE AND PHOTOGRAPHIC MATERIALS

ARTICLE 20: MANAGEMENT OF AUDIO-VISUAL, ELECTRONIC, MICROFICHE AND PHOTOGRAPHIC MATERIALS

1. The original of each audio or video cassette, each diskette, each microfiche and each photograph filed with or produced by the Court Management Section must be properly indexed chronologically. All such materials shall appear on separate lists. The materials shall remain under the control of the Court Management Section.   **D11–022**

2. In order to preserve the audio-visual archives, taking into account the physical deterioration of tapes, the Court Management Section shall make timely reproductions of the tapes and keep them separately.

3. If possible, a spare copy of all audio and video archives should also be made and stored away from the Tribunal's facilities.

4. The practical mechanisms implementing this Article shall be laid down by the Registrar in the Instructions for the Court Management Section.

PART SIX: CERTIFIED COPIES

ARTICLE 21: CERTIFIED COPIES

1. Certified copies of original documents issued by the Tribunal must bear the stamp of the Tribunal and the signature or initials in blue ink of the Registrar or his delegate. Copies certified in this manner shall be regarded as exact and unaltered reproduction of the original.   **D11–023**

2. To certify documents, the Registrar may also make use of certificates under conditions to be established in the Instructions for the Court Management Section.

Thus, documents covered by a certificate signed by the Registrar or his delegate will also be considered certified copies.

PART SEVEN: COURT MANAGEMENT SECTION CHARGES

ARTICLE 22: COURT MANAGEMENT SECTION CHARGES

D11–024   1. Fees may be imposed upon Court Management Section acts or services which involve cost to the Registry; in particular, certifying copies of judgements, orders, minutes, transcripts, official documents, or extracts from the Record Book and making copies of non-confidential audio-visual materials.

2. The charges referred to in this Article shall be determined by decision of the Registrar.

3. Upon written request to the Registrar, all of the above-mentioned services may be provided after payment of Court Management Section charges, and subject to technical feasibility.

4. Court Management Section charges shall not be imposed on Non-Profit Organizations, Academic Institutions, or any member of either of these, or on a State.

PART EIGHT: CASE OPENING AND ASSIGNMENT OF CASES

ARTICLE 23: CASE OPENING

D11–025   1. The Court Management Section shall open a new case file upon receipt of:
  (a) An application for deferral under Rule 9 of the Rules; or
  (b) An indictment under Rule 47 of the Rules;
  (c) An application for the Transfer and Provisional Detention of a Suspect under Rule 40*bis*.

2. Upon receipt of any other application which does not relate to a pre-existing case, the documents relating to that motion shall be filed in a "Miscellaneous" file.

3. Only one case file shall be opened for each case. Where two or more accused are joined in one indictment, only one case number shall be assigned and one case file maintained. In case of separate trials, however, the Registrar may disjoin the initial case file and assign new case numbers. A case file may be placed in several folders, whether public or confidential, which folders shall be numbered sequentially.

4. The following symbols shall be used in assigning a Case Number (e.g. ICTR-95–14R61):

ICTR   = International Criminal Tribunal for Rwanda
95   = year of indictment, i.e. 1995
14   = sequential number of case, i.e. the 14th case to come before the Tribunal
A   = Appeal (followed by Rule, if necessary, e.g. AR108 = Appeal of Rule 108)
T   = Trial
PT   = Pre-Trial
I   = Indictment
R61   = Rule 61 hearings
D   = Deferral hearings (Rule 10)
DP   = Rule 40*bis* proceedings (*détention provisoire*).

ARTICLE 24: ASSIGNMENT OF CASES

D11–026   1. The Registrar shall assign each new case to a Judge or a Chamber according to the instructions of the President, which are contained in a roster, established in accordance with Rule 28, a copy of which shall be filed in the case file.

2. The Court Management Section shall record the assignment of a case to a Judge or a Chamber in the Record Book.

3. The Court Management Section shall, at the request of the President, make the necessary arrangements for the reassignment of a case.

PART NINE: PROVISION OF DOCUMENTS

ARTICLE 25: GENERAL PRINCIPLES

1. All documents which the Parties wish to serve on a Judge or Chamber must be first **D11–027** submitted to the Court Management Section, which shall be responsible for the distribution of certified copies of the documents to Judges, the Parties and the Press and Public Affairs Unit.

2. All written motions applying for an order from a Judge or Chamber should be accompanied by a draft order, bearing the word "DRAFT" thereon.

ARTICLE 26: JUDICIAL FORMS

The judicial forms used by the Tribunal shall be in a standard format issued by the **D11–028** Court Management Section. They are available for consultation by the parties.

ARTICLE 27: RECEIVING DOCUMENTS

1. Documents may be delivered to the Court Management Section by hand, by fax or **D11–029** by post. The relevant Court Management form is to be used in order to address documents to the Legal Officer providing support to the Trial Chamber to which the case has been assigned. Documents delivered to the General Registry of the Tribunal shall be considered misdelivered and the Party so filing the document shall be responsible for any delay in the transmission of the document from the General Registry to the Court Management Section.

2. *Format of Motions and other processes.* The Court Management Section shall ensure that Motions and other processes which are filed are in proper form. In particular, when counsel files a Motion before a Judge or Chamber, Counsel must in all cases provide the court with the following documents:

(i) A Notice of Motion, appropriately entitled, informing the reader of the type and nature of the process;
(ii) A Memorial or Brief of Argument;
(iii) A supporting affidavit or Declaration. Note that a party who wishes the Chamber to make any determination on a question of fact in dispute should not make unsworn assertions of fact orally before the Chamber, but should, in his or her Motion, state contentious facts under oath, in an affidavit, affirmation or other solemn declaration;
(iv) A Book of Authority, in a standard format;
(v) A draft Order, in a standard format;
(vi) A Backing Sheet (Back Cover), in a standard format.

Motions and other processes not conforming to these requirements may be returned to the filing Party without filing and with instructions as to how to remedy the deficient filing, in accordance with Article 31 of the present Directive.

3. The Court Management Section shall file all documents submitted in a case following the provisions laid down in Article 13 of the present Directive.

4. The date of filing is the date that the document was received by the Court Management Section. The Court Management Section shall date-stamp the document legibly with the date of its receipt, subject to the provisions of Articles 28 to 31 of the present Directive. This date-stamp shall be endorsed with the signature of the Court Management Section staff member who received the document.

ARTICLE 28: FILING BY FACSIMILE TRANSMISSION

1. The Court Management Section shall process documents sent by facsimile trans- **D11–030** mission in accordance with the provisions laid down in Article 27.

2. Parties who send documents by facsimile must also deliver the signed original document within a reasonable period.

ARTICLE 29: AFTER-HOURS FILING

D11–031   1. After-hours filing refers to the filing of documents on weekends or public holidays or outside of the following hours local time: 9 a.m. to 5.30 p.m., Monday through Thursday and 9 a.m. to 2 p.m. on Friday, or on weekends or public holidays.

2. A party anticipating a late filing must notify the Court Management Section during business hours to request permission and instructions for after-hours filing.

ARTICLE 30: URGENT MEASURES

D11–032   1. A party filing a document which requires urgent measures to be taken shall bring the urgent nature of the document to the attention of the Court Management Section, with an accompanying note bearing the word "URGENT" in red capital letters.

2. The Court Management Section should then process the document in accordance with Article 37 of the present Directive, and in any event on an expedited basis, as provided for in the Instructions for the Court Management Section, and forward a certified copy to the appropriate Judge or Chamber immediately.

ARTICLE 31: DEFICIENT FILING

D11–033   1. The Court Management Section is responsible for verifying compliance with the formal requirements laid down in Articles 27 to 30 of the present Directive.

2. The Court Management Section shall inform the party who submitted a formal defective document of the deficiency and requesting that it be corrected.

3. A party who presents a defective document may correct the deficiency by letter or facsimile.

PART TEN: PUBLIC ACCESS TO THE JUDICIAL ARCHIVES

ARTICLE 32: PRINCIPLE OF PUBLICITY

D11–034   In conformity with the principle of publicity of the work of the Tribunal, the Court Management Section shall provide public access to documents. This access shall be free and complete with two reservations: the provisions of Article 22, concerning Court Management Section charges, and Article 33, concerning public access to the Judicial Archives of the Tribunal, of the present Directive.

ARTICLE 33: PUBLIC ACCESS TO THE JUDICIAL ARCHIVES

D11–035   1. Subject to paragraphs 3 (b) and 5 below, disclosure of the following to the public is unrestricted:
   (a) Orders, decisions or judgements of a Judge or a Chamber, from the moment they are issued or as specified in the order, decision or judgement itself;
   (b) Requests for deferral by the Prosecutor, as provided for in Rule 9 of the Rules, from the moment that the Trial Chamber has been notified and the Court Management Section has ensured their transmission to the State concerned;
   (c) Non-confidential motions filed by the parties, from the moment they are filed;
   (d) Notices of appeal, as soon as they have been distributed by the Court Management Section to the Appeals Chamber and the parties;
   (e) Transcripts and recordings of public hearings;
   (f) Minutes of proceedings taken in accordance with Article 44 of the present Directive.

2. The following are to be disclosed subject to Rules 53, 75, 79 and 81 of the Rules:
   (a) Indictments, upon confirmation;
   (b) Confirmations of indictments as soon as they are signed by a Judge;
   (c) Warrants of arrest once they have been issued;
   (d) Materials concerning the arrest and transfer of an accused;
   (e) Preliminary motions and the requests by the parties (including texts and attachments);
   (f) Any evidence disclosed during the hearing as soon as such evidence has been declared admissible by the Trial Chamber in open court;
   (g) Minutes, transcripts and recordings of *in camera* proceedings;
   (h) *Amicus curiae* briefs, as soon as they have been submitted to the parties and to a Judge or a Chamber, unless the Judge or Chamber has decided otherwise in the ruling authorizing the submission of the brief.
3. The following are strictly confidential:
   (a) Materials or documents relating to hearings held pursuant to Rule 75 (B) of the Rules unless or until otherwise ordered by the Chamber;
   (b) Materials or documents subject to an order for non-disclosure in accordance with Rule 53 of the Rules, which documents or materials shall not be disclosed absent a further ruling by the appropriate Judge or Chamber;
   (c) Supporting materials to the indictment in accordance with Rule 47 of the Rules, which shall not be made public at the time the indictment is publicly disclosed nor at the time the materials are made available to the accused, unless or until otherwise ordered by the Chamber;
   (d) All written witness statements used in conjunction with hearings pursuant to Rule 61 of the Rules even if such document is relied upon by the Trial Chamber in making its decision, absent further order.
4. Parties submitting documents which they do not wish to have disclosed, in whole or in part, shall bring to the attention of the Court Management Section the confidential nature of these documents by stamping or writing the word "CONFIDENTIAL" in red ink on the cover page of the documents.
5. Notwithstanding the above provisions, if the Registrar believes that a particular document should not be publicly disclosed, he may delay public access to the document and, within 48 hours of the filing of the document with the Court Management Section, bring the matter to the attention of the appropriate Judge or Chamber for decision pursuant to Rule 53 (A) of the Rules.

PART ELEVEN: SCHEDULING JUDICIAL ACTIVITIES

ARTICLE 34: CALENDAR

1. The Court Management Section is responsible for keeping a daily calendar of the scheduled hearings of the Tribunal to be used in scheduling other hearings, to provide notice and to ensure the efficient administration of justice. **D11–036**

2. The calendar shall be notified to the Judges and relevant Parties in a timely manner, and if no objection is received to the calendar within forty-eight hours of such notification, it shall become mandatory. A copy of the calendar of the scheduled hearings shall be posted in public view in the Tribunal. This calendar should provide the case name and number, the Judge or the Chamber, the date and time of the proceeding and whether it is a public or closed proceeding.

ARTICLE 35: SCHEDULING

1. The Registrar, Deputy Registrar or their delegate shall, in consultation with the appropriate Judge or Chamber, schedule the date and time of hearings before the Tribunal for each case, taking into account the requirements of justice and notably the right of an accused to be tried without undue delay. Judicial vacations shall be scheduled in accordance with official United Nations holidays . **D11–037**

2. In scheduling hearings, precedence shall be given to urgent and extremely urgent motions, to the initial appearance of the accused, to motions for provisional release, transfer or detention of a suspect, accused or detained witness, to arrest warrants, and to motions for protective orders for victims or witnesses.

3. The Registrar, Deputy Registrar or their delegate shall inform the President and the Presiding Judge of scheduled hearings in a timely manner.

ARTICLE 36: ADJOURNMENT

D11–038
1. Either party requesting an adjournment must do so by filing a written motion accompanied by a draft order to postpone the scheduled hearing.

2. Parties who agree to the adjournment of a scheduled hearing must nevertheless appear at that hearing unless an order for adjournment has been signed by the appropriate Judge or Chamber prior to the scheduled hearing.

3. Such order for adjournment shall be forwarded without undue delay by the Court Management Section to the Parties.

ARTICLE 37: MOTIONS PRACTICE

D11–039
1. The Court Management Section will allocate two half-days every week (which at present are Monday and Friday afternoons) for the hearing of Motions. These days shall hereinafter be referred to as "motion days".

2. *Ordinary Motions Practice.* When the Party filing a Motion does not move for a prompt hearing or for an immediate decision or emergency relief, the following procedure shall be followed. The Court Management Section shall bring the motion and request for hearing to the attention of the Judge or Chamber assigned to the case, which will decide whether to grant a hearing, and if so, will instruct the Court Management Section to schedule such a hearing. The Judge or Chamber may postpone taking such a decision until all the relevant pleadings, including a brief from the opposing party and reply from the moving party, if allowed, have been filed.

3. Any party may move for a prompt hearing if an immediate decision or emergency relief from the court is desired. The Party should indicate whether the Motion is "Urgent" or "Extremely Urgent", in accordance with Article 30 of the present Directive.

4. *Urgent Motions.* An urgent Motion shall be set down for hearing no later than the first motion day after it is filed, provided that there is sufficient time between the date of filing and the first motion day to allow the Parties to make the appropriate arrangements to attend the hearing.

5. *Extremely Urgent Motions.* In the case of motions which are marked "Extremely Urgent", the Court Management Section, upon receiving such a Motion, shall immediately bring it to the attention of the appropriate Judge or Chamber. In the event that the appropriate Judge or Chamber is not available, any other, available Judge or Chamber shall be seized of the Motion. Extremely Urgent Motions shall be set down for hearing no more than three days from the date of filing and in any event as soon as possible. If necessary, the Court Management Section, under the direction of a Judge or Chamber, shall arrange telephone conference facilities for the Parties to be heard without delay by the Judge or Chamber.

6. Parties shall be cautioned against the unwarranted use of the "Urgent" and "Extremely Urgent" designations.

7. Whenever a hearing is granted, the Court Management Section shall immediately issue a written notice to the Judges, Parties and Press and Public Affairs Unit of the date and time of the hearing and, in case of urgency, shall despatch such notice by facsimile and notify the Parties by telephone.

8. *Pending Motions.* A list of pending motions in each case shall be maintained by the Court Management Section. The Court Management Section shall bring pending motions to the attention of the Judges and relevant Parties—and, where the Motions are public, to the Press and Public Affairs Unit—in a timely manner, and, in any event, at least on a weekly basis.

ARTICLE 38: STATUS CONFERENCE

1. At the initial appearance of an accused or at any time before trial, the Trial **D11–040**
Chamber, upon request of a party *or proprio motu,* may order a status conference to
consider any matter that will promote a fair and expeditious trial.
2. The Court Management Section shall be responsible for the preparation of status
conferences and, whenever necessary, shall cause minutes to be made of the conference
for the approval of the Presiding Judge. The provisions of Article 35 of the present
Directive shall apply to the schedule adopted at the status conference.

ARTICLE 39: FAILURE TO COMPLY WITH AN ORDER

The Court Management Section shall bring to the attention of the Judges of the Trial **D11–041**
or Appeals Chamber assigned to the case the failure to comply with an order by the
deadline set by the Tribunal as soon as it becomes aware of such failure.

PART TWELVE: HEARINGS

ARTICLE 40: MANAGEMENT OF HEARINGS

The Court Management Section is responsible for making all necessary arrangements **D11–042**
for hearings and conferences, either public or *in camera,* and for providing the services
required during the hearings and conferences, including court reporter services.

ARTICLE 41: COURTROOM OFFICER

1. The Courtroom Officer represents the Registrar at hearings and is assisted by **D11–043**
Courtroom Assistants. In the absence of a Courtroom Officer, or non-appointment
thereof, his functions may be performed by such other staff as may be designated by the
Registrar, Deputy Registrar or Head of the Court Management Section.
2. Under the authority of the Deputy Registrar, the Courtroom Officer is responsible
for the functions entrusted to the Court Management Section with respect to hearings,
in particular the efficient administration thereof.

ARTICLE 42: MANAGEMENT OF PLEADINGS FILED IN THE COURTROOM

1. The Courtroom Officer is responsible for receiving documents filed in the court- **D11–044**
room during the proceeding.
2. The Courtroom Officer is responsible for ensuring that all documents received are
filed in the appropriate folder after the conclusion of each day's proceedings, and
distributed to the Chamber, Parties and Press and Public Affairs Unit, as necessary.

ARTICLE 43: EXHIBITS

1. Objects only become exhibits after they have been admitted into evidence by the **D11–045**
Trial or Appeals Chamber.
2. Prosecution and Defence shall be informed that, once admitted, the exhibits are in
the custody of the Courtroom Officer or his Assistants, and under the authority of the
Trial or Appeals Chamber, and that they may not be removed or tampered with in any
way.
3. The admission of exhibits should be recorded in the minutes of the proceedings.
4. The Court Management Section shall keep an inventory of all exhibits stored in the
Archives.

ARTICLE 44: MINUTES OF PROCEEDINGS

D11–046　　Where necessary, the Courtroom Officer is responsible for preparing, for the approval of the Presiding Judge, minutes of the proceedings to provide a record in summary form of the significant events that occur during a proceeding, including, but not limited to:
　　　　(a) Deadlines imposed by the Trial or Appeals Chamber;
　　　　(b) The Trial or Appeals Chamber's rulings on particular motions and other matters.

PART THIRTEEN: APPEAL

ARTICLE 45: APPEALS OFFICER

D11–047　　1. The Appeals Officer represents the Registrar at hearings of appeal matters.
　　　　2. Under the authority of the Deputy Registrar, the Appeals Officer is responsible for the functions entrusted to the Court Management Section with respect to hearing of Appeals.
　　　　3. The Appeals Officer is responsible for verifying compliance with the official requirements concerning appeals as laid down in this Directive.
　　　　4. The Appeals Officer is responsible for the expeditious management, filing, reproduction and distribution of all appeal documents.

ARTICLE 46: TIME LIMIT FOR NOTICE OF APPEAL

D11–048　　1. Unless otherwise ordered by the Chambers or otherwise provided by the Rules, where the time prescribed by or under the Rules for the doing of any act is to run as from the occurrence of an event, that time shall begin to run as from the date on which notice of the occurrence of the event would have been received in the normal course of transmission by Counsel for the accused or the Prosecutor as the case may be.
　　　　2. Where a time limit is expressed in days, only whole days shall be counted. Weekdays, Saturdays, Sundays and public holidays shall be counted as days. However, should the time limit for appeal expire on a Saturday, Sunday or public holiday, the time limit shall automatically be extended to the subsequent working day.
　　　　3. If the time for filing a notice of appeal has expired, and a notice of appeal is received by the Court Management Section, the notice of appeal shall be accepted for filing. The Court Management Section shall notify Counsel for the Appellant of the untimely receipt of the notice of appeal and inform the Appeals Chamber.

PART FOURTEEN: HEARINGS OTHER THAN AT THE SEAT AND VIDEO-CONFERENCES

ARTICLE 47: HEARINGS OTHER THAN AT THE SEAT

D11–049　　The Registrar will make the necessary arrangements whenever the Tribunal is to sit at a place other than its seat.

ARTICLE 48: VIDEO-CONFERENCES

D11–050　　The Registrar will make the necessary arrangements whenever it is ordered that a witness be heard by means of a video conference, pursuant to Rules 71 and 96 of the Rules.

SECTION VI: RELATIONSHIPS TO THE CHAMBERS

ARTICLE 49: RELATIONSHIP OF THE REGISTRY TO THE CHAMBERS

1. Pursuant to Article 16 of the Statute of the Tribunal, the Registry is responsible for **D11–051** the administration and servicing of the Tribunal. Pursuant to Rule 33 of the Rules, the Registrar assists the Chambers, the plenary meetings of the Tribunal, the Judges and the Prosecutor in the performance of their functions. Under the authority of the President, the Registrar is responsible for the administration and servicing of the Tribunal and serves as its channel of communication.

2. To ensure smooth coordination between the Registry and the Chambers, the Registrar shall regularly schedule meetings with the Judges to share ideas and concerns and to work out means for enhanced cooperation and improved efficiency in the workings of the Tribunal.

ARTICLE 50: RELATIONSHIP OF THE JUDICIAL AND LEGAL SERVICES DIVISION TO THE CHAMBERS

The Judicial and Legal Services Division of the Registry assists the Chambers, and the **D11–052** Parties, in four areas: Court Management, Defence Counsel and Detention Facility, Victims and Witnesses and General Legal Services and Chambers Support. The Court Management Section has the specific responsibility towards the Chambers of providing the necessary support and infrastructure for the conduct of trials and the filing and dissemination of Court documents.

ARTICLE 51: RESPECTIVE ROLES AND RESPONSIBILITIES OF THE COURT MANAGEMENT SECTION AND THE GENERAL LEGAL SERVICES AND CHAMBERS SUPPORT SECTION

1. The Court Management Section assists the Chambers in the management of **D11–053** hearings, in the sealing, filing and distribution of documents to Judges, the Parties and the Press and Public Affairs Unit, and in the other tasks set out in the present Directive. The Court Management Section may also be called upon to assist the Chambers by 3providing drafts of Orders and Warrants, particularly those of a routine nature, as the Judges see fit. Warrants requested by the Office of the Prosecutor should, however, be prepared by the Office of the Prosecutor, in accordance with Article 25 (2) of the present Directive.

2. *Translation*. The Court Management Section shall be responsible for requesting translation of documents into the working languages of the Tribunal in accordance with Article 13 (6) of the present Directive. The General Legal Services and Chambers Support Section shall be responsible for ensuring that translations of decisions, judgements and orders issued by the Chambers are correct and in proper form before they are filed with the Court Management Section.

3. The General Legal Services and Chambers Support Section is responsible for providing assistance to the Chambers in legal research and drafting of decisions, judgements, opinions and orders. The Section is headed by a Section Chief who is responsible for assisting the Chambers in the manner described, for ensuring that decisions, judgements, opinions and orders are in proper form and duly signed, and for organizing the work of the Legal Officers assigned to the Chambers. It shall be for the Judges to decide whether they wish the Senior Coordinator or Legal Officers to be present and to assist in their deliberations.

4. The administration of the General Legal Services and Chambers Support Section is not the subject of the present Directive, but may be addressed by a separate Directive on that Section or by internal guidelines issued by the Chambers.

SECTION VII: INTER-SECTIONAL MANAGEMENT OF THE TRIBUNAL'S WEBSITE

ARTICLE 52: INTER-SECTIONAL MANAGEMENT OF THE TRIBUNAL'S WEBSITE

D11–054

1. The Tribunal shall maintain a Website, namely a homepage on the internet which shall feature the Tribunal's basic texts, decisions, judgements, orders, indictments, bulletins, Press releases and other materials.

2. The Website shall be managed by an inter-sectional "ICTR Internet Task Force", under the authority of the Registrar.

3. Pursuant to Article 13 (7) of the present Directive, the Court Management Section shall ensure that electronic copy of a document is filed simultaneously with the filing of the document. The electronic copy shall then be transmitted to the person responsible for the Tribunal's Website for the purposes of review and loading onto the homepage.

D12. Guidelines on the Remuneration of Expert Witnesses Appearing Before the International Criminal Tribunal for Rwanda

TABLE OF CONTENTS

PART ONE:

DEFINITION OF TERMS USED

ARTICLE 1

DEFINITIONS

(a) **Expert witness**: anyone with specific and relevant information on and/or knowledge of the matter brought before the Tribunal. Such specific information or knowledge which qualifies an individual to appear as an expert witness may have been acquired through training or actual studies, special aptitudes, experience or some reputation in the field or through any other means considered by the party calling the witness to give testimony as being necessary and sufficient to qualify him as an expert witness;

(b) **Registrar**: The Registrar of the Tribunal;

(c) **The Party calling the witness**: The Prosecutor, a defence counsel or a Trial Chamber of the Tribunal who or which calls an expert to testify before the Tribunal or who or which requests an expert to carry out a study or a special assignment on his, or her or its behalf;

(d) **Tribunal**: The International Criminal Tribunal for the prosecution of persons responsible fro genocide and other serious violations of international humanitarian law committed in the territory of Rwanda and Rwandan citizens responsible for genocide and other such violations committed in the territory of neighbouring States between 1 January 1994 and 31 December 1994;

(e) **Stage of the Proceeding**: Each of the stages laid down by the Rules of Procedure and Evidence adopted by the Tribunal, stages during which the suspect or accused may be involved (investigations and proceedings before the Trial Chamber).

D12–001

ARTICLE 2

ACCREDITATION OF EXPERT WITNESS

D12–002   Obviously, it is the right of the Trial Chamber to allow the witness to make deposition as an expert on special issues referred to it or to hear the witness' testimony and, where necessary, to assess its value. However, the conditions defined under the United Nations Financial and Accounting Rules and Procedures require the submission of the expert witness' references as well as evidence of his expertise to the Registrar to back up any request for payment of his fees or reimbursement of expenses incurred by him.

ARTICLE 3

DOCUMENTARY EVIDENCE OF THE WITNESS'S EXPERTISE

D12–003   The witness shall provide the following documents attesting to his special knowledge, competence, experience, training or education:
— a statement made under oath by the witness
— a statement made under oath by the party calling the witness references such as:
— concise information on his studies, training, skills and competence, experience professional reputation, etc.,
— data on grade, seniority and remuneration in the profession in question

PART TWO:

REMUNERATION OF THE EXPERT WITNESS

ARTICLE 4

REMUNERATION OF THE EXPERT WITNESS

D12–004   The fees paid to an expert witness for any one case and at any stage of the proceedings shall include:
(a) fees calculated on the basis of a fixed daily rate determined by the Registrar who, in so doing, will take into consideration the nature of the expertise, the witness' experience in the area concerned, his university qualifications, professional reputation and seniority. In accordance with the table of fees shown in Annex 1 of the Guidelines, this rate shall comprise office overhead expenses;
(b) a daily subsistence allowance equivalent to United Nations rates applicable during the period of appearance of the expert witness before the Tribunal and until the completion of his testimony;
Any expert witness who has received payment from the Tribunal shall not be authorised to receive payment from any other source for the same services.

ARTICLE 5

PERIOD OF REMUNERATION

D12–005   (a) The payment to be made to an expert witness shall be limited to the period of his tay in Arusha for the purpose of testifying before the Tribunal. It shall be calculated on the basis of the fixed rate provided for in Article 4(a). After its determination by the

Registrar, it shall be due at the end of the period of appearance of the expert witness before the Tribunal;

(b) The payment referred to in 5 (a) above shall, in addition to the daily subsistence allowance provided for in article 4(b), be due for the period of the said stay at the seat of the Tribunal.

ARTICLE 6

REMUNERATION FOR A SPECIAL SERVICES CONTRACT

(a) In the event where preparatory work requiring research which does not fall within the area of specialisation of the expert witness and/or which goes beyond the investigation resources of the party calling the witness is deemed necessary and relevant to the trial, the Registrar, shall at the request of the calling parties, negotiate the contract to recruit the expert witness who shall in this case receive a lump-sum fee calculated on the basis of the conditions applied by the Untied Nations for short-term contracts;

D12–006

(b) In this case, the daily subsistence allowance provided for in article 4(b) and applicable to the place where the field research is taking place (Rwanda and its neighbouring countries, including the seat of the Tribunal) shall be paid to the expert witness, subject to the prior approval of the athorization to carry out the said research work. The daily subsistence allowance shall in this case be an integral part of the short-term contract;

(c) Similarly, the travel expenses provided for in Article 9 shall be borne by theTribunal, subject to the prior approval of the Registrar, as in the preceding case.

ARTICLE 7

REQUEST FOR PAYMENT

(a) Fees shall be payable upon completion of testimony before the Triubnal, as stipulated in Article 5, or upon the completion of a s specific task assigned to the expert witness by the party calling the witness and subject to submission by the witness of a final mission report in the event where, as provided for in Article 6, he is not called to appear before the Tribunal. In both cases, however, the witness shall, through the party that called him submit to the Registrar for approval a detailed request for payment certified by the said party;

D12–007

(b) The statement of fees due shall, in particular, comprise the name of the expert witness, that of the calling the witness, the reference number of the case, as entered in the Court Register, the date of recruitment of the expert witness, the date and duration of his appearance before the Tribunal, the number of days spent on preparatory work, the stage of the proceeding at which the expert witness was involved and a breakdown of his fees. In support of his request for payment, the expert witness shall provide as much information as possible, especially information on his services and, where necessary, documentary evidence of his specialized knowledge, as provided for in Article 3 above.

ARTICLE 8

DAILY SUBSISTENCE ALLOWANCE ADVANCES

(a) On his arrival at the seat of the Tribunal (Arusha) to testify before the Tribunal, the expert witness shall, provisionally, receive a daily subsistence allowance advance calculated on the basis of an estimate of the duration of his stay at the seat of the Tribunal;

D12–008

(b) The Registrar shall, on the basis of a provisional programme of engagement drawn up in accordance with the duration of stay of the expert witness in Arusha, which programme shall be submitted by the calling party and approved by the Registrar, authorize the payment of a daily subsistence allowance advance. At the end of the period of stay for which a daily subsistence allowance advance was approved, the expert witness shall, through the calling party, submit to the Registrar, for the purpose of regularization, a written statement made under oath by the afore said party to certify that the expert witness has, indeed, accomplished the task assigned to him.

ARTICLE 9

TRAVEL EXPENSES

D12–009　　　(a) In order to facilitate the processing of travel authorization requests and the booking of hotel rooms for expert witnesses, such requests shall be submitted to the Registrar at least ten working days prior to the actual date of travel to the seat of the Tribunal in Arusha;

(b) Once a travel authorization has been approved, the Travel Service of the Tribunal shall be directed to prepare a travel authorization and to ensure the issue of an economy class return air ticket by the most direct route or a ticket whose cost shall not exceed the ceiling determined by the Registrar;

(c) The booking of a hotel room shall be done by the Witnesses and Victims Support Unit in the name of the expert witness and for the entire period of his stay, Pursuant to the provisions of Article 8(b) above, the corresponding amount of his daily subsistence allowance shall, on his arrival, be paid to him at the Cashier's office in Arusha;

(d) Subject to the Registrar's prior authorization to travel, travel expenses paid personally by the expert witness whose habitual place of residence is outside the country hosting the seat of the Tribunal, shall be refunded to him, pursuant to Article 9(b) above and on the basis of the itinerary and dates approved by the Registrar. To this end, the expert witness shall submit a statement of expenditure certified by the calling party. Ticket stubs and the original of the bill and/or any receipt confirming the purchase of a ticket, including supporting documents for all payments made by credit card, shall be attached to the statement of expenditure;

(e) Upon the presentation of a statement of travel expenses incurred, expenses regarding the transportation of the expert witness from his place of residence to the airport of departure to the host country of the Tribunal shall be refunded to him, if he lives in his country of origin or in the country where he is working. Such refund shall be based on either the cost of a first class public transport ticket or on the rates established in the United Nations scale for the refund of expenses for travelling by private vehicle, applicable to various groups of countries and territories. The refund shall also be based on the return journey mileage by the most direct route. Any request for a refund of travel expenses by any other means of surface transport shall be subject to the same treatment as in the above-mentioned cases;

(f) Notwithstanding the provisions of paragraphs (d) and (e), the Registrar, after consulting with the Advisory Panel (Article 11), may decide, in the interest of fairness and taking into account the resources available that the Tribunal bear, depending on the case, other travel expenses claimed by the expert witness.

ARTICLE 10

APPROVAL OF REMUNERATION OF EXPENSES

D12–010　　　(a) All amounts owed to an expert witness pursuant to the provisions of these Guidelines shall be paid to him by the Tribunal.

(b) The statement of payments (whether partial or full) as well as the statement of refundable travel expenses must receive the prior approval of the Registrar.

PART THREE:

APPEALS OR ARBITRATION

ARTICLE 11

ADVISORY PANEL

In the event of a dispute between the Tribunal and the expert witness regarding the **D12–011** Guidelines, for example, where an expert witness is exceptionally well qualified or where it is difficult to evaluate him according to established criteria and to determine the rate of the fee to be paid to him, or if there is any other problem concerning payment, an advisory panel assigned to the registrar shall promptly examine the issue, determine, if need be, the amount of fee to be paid and make a recommendation to this effect to the Registrar. The advisory panel shall comprise the following:
— a representative of the Office of the Registrar;
— a representative of the Witnesses and Victims Support Unit;
— a representative of the Finance and Budget Section; and
— a representative of the party calling the witness (Trial Chamber, Defence Counsel, or Office of the Prosecutor, as the case may be).

ARTICLE 12

SETTLEMENT OF DISPUTES

In case of a dispute between the Tribunal and the expert witness regarding the **D12–012** Guidelines, the Registrar shall, after consultation with the Advisory Panel provided for in Article 11 above, determine the issue on an equitable basis.

ARTICLE 13

AMENDMENT AND CIRCULATION OF THE GUIDELINES

(a) The Guidelines defining the conditions of remuneration applicable to expert **D12–013** witnesses shall be circulated to all the calling parties.

(b) Any article of the Guidelines may be amended by the Registrar after consultation, if need be, with the Advisory Panel. Any such amendment shall also be circulated to all the parties concerned.

(c) Without prejudice to the rights of the expert witness, amendments shall enter into force upon their adoption.

ANNEX I

TABLE OF FEES

The fixed rate provided for in Article 4(a) shall be determined by the Registrar **D12–014** according to the table below. It shall be calculated on the basis of the average of gross annual salaries corresponding to the salary scale drawn up by the International Civil Service Commission (ICSC) and applicable to staff members of all United Nations agencies and staff of other organisations. The daily rate shall be rounded off to the nearest multiple of fifty U.S. dollars.

ICSC post classification	Expert's seniority in the profession	Daily rate
D–2	25 years and more	US$ 450
D–1	21–25 years	US$ 400
P–5	16–20 years	US$ 350
P–4	10–15 years	US$ 300
P–3	4–9 years	US$ 250
P–2	1–3 years	US$ 200

The last year in the seniority bracket should be a complete year.

D13. Circular

For the attention of Defence Counsel and Senior Trial Attorneys of the Office of the Prosecutor

SUBJECT: INTERPRETATION NOTE ON CERTAIN PROVISIONS OF THE *GUIDELINES ON THE REMUNERATION OF EXPERT WITNESSES APPEARING BEFORE THE INTERNATIONAL CRIMINAL TRIBUNAL FOR RWANDA.*

Further to the adoption by the Registry of the above-mentioned Guidelines, a copy of **D13–001** which was sent to you by letter of 10 December 1997, we would request you to kindly take not of the following explanations aimed at enabling you to better understand the provisions of the Guidelines:

It emerges, in fact, from the above-mentioned document that expert witnesses called by the parties shall be remunerated according to the nature of the work required:

Testimony only before the Tribunal (cf. Article 5 relating to the Period of Remuneration:

(a) the payment to be made to an expert witness shall be limited to the period of his stay in Arusha for the purpose of testifying before the Tribunal. . . .; (b) The payment referred to in 5(a) above shall, in addition to the daily subsistence allowance provided for in Article 4(b), be due for the period of the said stay at the seat of the Tribunal): or

Preparatory work towards the appearance before the Tribunal (cf. Article 6 on the Remuneration of a Special Services Contract:"*(a) in the event where preparatory work requiring research which does not fall within the area of specialization of the expert and/or which goes beyond the investigation resources of the party calling the witness is deemed necessary and relevant to the trial, the Registrar shall at the request of the calling parties negotiate the contract to recruit the expert witness who shall in this case receive a lump-sum fee calculated on the basis of the conditions applied by the United Nations for short-term contracts; (b) In this case, the daily subsistence allowance provided for in Article 4(b) and applicable to the place where the field research is taking place (Rwanda and its neighboring countries, including the seat of the Tribunal) shall be paid to the expert witness, subject to the prior approval of and authorization to carry out the said research work. The daily subsistence allowance shall in this case be an integral part of the short-term contract: (c) Similarly, the travel expenses provided for in Article 9 shall be borne by the Tribunal, subject to the prior approval of the Registrar, as in the preceding case.*

It is also important to note that no provision in the Guidelines obliges the parties to choose one or the other form of expert assistance, or sets a ceiling on the remuneration of any of these services. Apart from the remuneration for the period of stay of the expert witness in Arusha for the purpose of testifying before the Tribunal (Article 5), the expert witness shall also be entitled to remuneration for any relevant preparatory work done under a special services contract concluded between the expert witness and the Tribunal, subject to prior approval by the Registrar in accordance with the conditions set forth in Article 7 of the Guidelines.

Further, Article 7 (b) provides that: *The statement of fees due shall, in particular comprise the name of the expert witness, that of the party calling the witness, the reference number of the case, as entered in the Court Register, the date of recruitment of the expert witness, the date and duration of his appearance before the Tribunal, the number of days spent on preparatory work, the stage of the proceeding at which the expert witness was involved and a breakdown of his fees. In support of his request for payment, the expert witness shall provide as much information as possible, especially information on his services and, where necessary, documentary evidence of his specialized knowledge, as provided for in Article 3 above.*

It is clearly seen that the above-mentioned Article also lays down the administrative procedure to be followed, based on United Nations Rule of administrative and financial management, for payment of fees due to the expert witnesses. This Article complements the provisions of Article 7 (a) which states: *A Fees shall be payable upon completion of testimony before the Tribunal, as stipulated in Article 5, or upon the completion of a specific task assigned to the expert witness by the party calling the witness and subject to submission by the witness of a final mission report in the event where, as provided for in Article 6, he is not called to appear before the Tribunal. In both cases, however, the witness shall through the party that called him, submit to the Registrar for approval a detailed request for payment.*

To sum up:

1. The Guidelines recognize that right of the expert witness to payment for all preparatory work carried out prior to and fro the testimony before the Tribunal, in addition to the daily subsistence allowance paid for the period of stay in Arusha for the purposes of his/her hearing.

2. A fixed daily rate for the expert witness shall be determined according to the Table of Fees (cf. Annex 1 of the Guidelines) corresponding to the Salary Scale established by the International Civil Service Commission for staff of all United Nations agencies and other organizations. There is no hourly rate for the expert witnesses nor ceiling on the number of hours to be remunerated as is the case for lawyers, legal assistants and investigators.

3. Any request for the services of an expert witness shall be submitted for the Registrar's prior approval according to the following procedure:

X The party seeking to engage an expert witness for a short-term contract shall submit a written request to the Registrar for approval.

This request must be accompanied by the documents indicated in Article 3 of the Guidelines, including the curriculum vitae of the expert witness, a sworn statement by him/her attesting to his/her competence and his/her availability to carry out the work required by the calling party; a sworn statement by the calling party informing the Registrar of the choice of the expert and certifying that an offer has been made for the required service; a brief description of the tasks to be performed by the expert witness; period within which the expert witness must accomplish the tasks; the number of days required for preparatory work; the date of submission of the report(s) to the calling party; the approximate date of the expert's appearance before the Tribunal in Arusha to testify; the approximate duration of his/her stay in Arusha; an indication of the fees quoted by the expert witness for the period of his/her testimony in Arusha and all other information relating to his/her travel(s) to accomplish his/her mission.

X After approval by the Registrar, the file shall be sent to the Personnel Section and other competent services of the Tribunal for processing.

Where preparatory work is required prior to the expert witness? testimony, the Personnel Section of the Tribunal shall determine the fixed daily rates to be paid to the expert witness following the assessment his/her curriculum vitae and other qualifications, and thereafter draw up a special services contract for him/her. This contract shall be countersigned by the expert witness, the Chief of Administration of the Tribunal and the party calling the expert witness.

X The procedure to be followed for the payment of fees is described in Articles 7 (b) and 10 and that for advances on the daily subsistence allowance in Article 8.

X The Travel Unit of the Tribunal shall be responsible for organizing the travel(s) of the expert witness under the conditions laid down in Article 9 of the Guidelines.

We are counting on your full cooperation and understanding to ensure strict compliance with the procedure laid down in the Guidelines.

The Witnesses and Victims Support Section of the Tribunal's Registry is at your disposal to provide any further clarifications you may require on all the points in the Guidelines.

(Signed for the Registrar)
Roland K. Amoussounga
OIC of the Witnessess and
Victims Support Section

D14. Rules Covering the Detention of Persons Awaiting Trial or Appeal Before the Tribunal or Otherwise Detained on the Authority of the Tribunal

TABLE OF CONTENTS

Spiritual Welfare

Work Programme

Recreational Activities

Personal Possessions of Detainees

Complaints

REMOVAL AND TRANSPORT OF DETAINEES

AMENDMENT

ACCESSIBILITY

PROVISIONAL APPLICATION

ENTRY INTO FORCE

PREAMBLE

The Plenary session of the Judges of the International Criminal Tribunal for Rwanda **D14–001**
Recognizing the need for rules governing the administration of the detention unit for detainees awaiting trial or appeal at the Tribunal or any other person detained on the authority of the Tribunal and to ensure the continued application and protection of their individual rights while in detention,

Mindful of the need to ensure respect for human rights and fundamental freedoms particularly the presumption of innocence,
Sitting this 5 June 1998,
Hereby adopts these Rules of Detention.

Short Title: Rules of Detention

USE OF TERMS

Rule 1

D14–002 For the purposes of these rules:

(a) **Bureau**	Means the body comprised of the President, Vice-President and the Presiding Judges of the Trial Chambers established pursuant to Rule 23 of the Rules of Procedure and Evidence;
Commanding Officer	Means the official of the United Nations appointed as head of the staff responsible for the administration of the Detention Unit;
Detainee	Means any person detained awaiting trial or appeal before the Tribunal, or being held pending transfer to another institution, and any other person detained on the authority of the Tribunal;
Detention Unit	Means the unit for detainees erected within the grounds of the host prison;
General Director	Means the head of the host prison appointed by the authorities of the Host State;
Host Prison	Means the penitentiary complex maintained by the authorities of the Host State and located at Arusha;
Host State	Means the United Republic of Tanzania;
Medical Officer	Means the medical officer for the time being appointed by agreement between the Registrar and the General Director of the host prison;
Prosecutor	Means the Prosecutor appointed pursuant to Article 17 (3) of the Statute of the Tribunal adopted by the Security Council Resolution 955(1994) of 8 November 1994 as amended by Resolution 1165(1998) of 30 April 1998, or any person authorized by him or acting under his direction;
Registrar	Means the Registrar of the Tribunal appointed pursuant to Article 16 (3) of the Statute of the Tribunal, or any person authorized by him or acting under his direction;
Rules of Procedure and Evidence	Means the Rules of Procedure and Evidence of the Tribunal as adopted on 29 June 1995 as amended latest on 15 May 2004;
Staff of the Detention Unit	Means the staff employed by the United Nations to operate the Detention Unit;
Tribunal	Means the International Criminal Tribunal for the Prosecution of Persons Responsible for Genocide and other Serious Violations of International Humanitarian Law Committed in the Territory of Rwanda and Rwandan Citizens Responsible for Genocide and other Violations Committed in the Territory of Neighbouring States between 1 January 1994 and 31 December 1994.

(B) The masculine shall include the feminine and the singular the plural, and vice-versa.

BASIC PROVISIONS

Rule 2

D14–003 (A) These Rules are to be applied in conjunction with the relevant provisions of the Headquarters Agreement entered into between the Host State and the United Nations and in particular, the Annex on matters relating to security and order.

(B) They shall be applied impartially without discrimination on grounds of race, colour, sex, language, religion, political or other opinion, national, ethnic or social origin, property, birth, economic or other status.

RULE 3

D14–004

The United Nations shall retain ultimate responsibility for all aspects of detention pursuant to these Rules. All detainees shall be subject to the sole jurisdiction of the Tribunal at all times they are so detained, even though physically absent from the Detention Unit, until final release or transfer to another institution. Subject to the overriding jurisdiction of the Tribunal, the Commanding Officer shall have sole responsibility for all aspects of the daily management of the Detention Unit, including security and order, and may make all decisions relating thereto, except where otherwise provided in these Rules.

RULE 4

D14–005

Subject to peace and order, a detainee is entitled to observe the religious beliefs and moral precepts of the group to which he belongs.

RULE 5

D14–006

All detainees, other than those who have been convicted by the Tribunal, are presumed to be innocent until found guilty and are to be treated as such at all times.

RULE 6

D14–007

The Bureau may, at any time, appoint a Judge or the Registrar of the Tribunal to inspect the detention unit and to report to the Tribunal on the general conditions of implementation of these Rules or of any particular aspect thereof with a view to ensuring that the Detention Unit is administered in accordance with the Rules. In addition, there shall be regular and unannounced inspections by inspectors whose duty is to examine the manner in which detainees are treated. The Bureau shall act upon all such reports as it sees fit, in consultation with the relevant authorities of the Host State where necessary.

MANAGEMENT OF THE DETENTION UNIT

RECEPTION

RULE 7

D14–008

No person shall be received in the Detention Unit without a valid commitment order duly issued by a Judge or a Chamber of the Tribunal.

RULE 8

D14–009

A complete, secure and current record shall be kept concerning each detainee received. It shall include:
  a. Information concerning the identity of the detainee and his next of kin;
  b. The date of issue of the indictment against the detainee and of the warrant of arrest;

c. The date and time of admission;
d. The name of Counsel, if known;
e. The date, time and reason for all absences from the Detention Unit, whether to attend at the Tribunal, for medical or other approved reasons, or on final release or transfer to another institution.

RULE 9

D14–010   All information concerning detainees shall be treated as confidential and made accessible only to the detainee, his Counsel and persons authorized by the Registrar. The detainee shall be informed of this fact upon his arrival at the Detentio n Unit.

RULE 10

D14–011   As soon as practicable after admission, each detainee shall be provided with information concerning legal, diplomatic and consular representation available to him. The detainee shall be given the opportunity at this time to notify, within reason, his family, his Counsel, the appropriate diplomatic or consular representative and, at the discretion of the Commanding Officer, any other person, of his whereabouts, at the expense of the Tribunal. The detainee shall be asked at this time to name a person or authority to be notified of special events affecting him.

RULE 11

D14–012   On arrival at the Detention Unit, the Commanding Officer shall order that a detainee's body and clothes may be searched for articles that may constitute a danger to the security and proper running of the Detention Unit, or which may constitute a danger to the detainee, any other detainee, or any member of the staff of the Detention Unit and shall remove any such items.

RULE 12

D14–013   An inventory shall be taken and recorded of all money, valuables, and other effects belonging to a detainee which, under these Rules or the rules of the host, he is not permitted to retain. The record of inventory shall be signed by the detainee. All such items shall be placed in safe custody or at the request and expense of the detainee, sent to an address provided by him. If the items are retained with the Detention Unit, all reasonable steps shall be taken by the staff of the Detention Unit to keep them in good order. If it is found necessary to destroy an item, this shall be recorded and the detainee informed.

RULE 13

D14–014   Each detainee shall be examined by the medical officer or his deputy on the day of admission and thereafter as necessary, for the purpose of establishing the physical and mental condition of the detainee and to take all necessary measures for medical treatment and the segregation of those detainees suspected of infectious or contagious conditions.

ACCOMMODATION

RULE 14

D14–015   Each detainee shall occupy a cell unit by himself except in exceptional circumstances or in cases where the Commanding Officer, with the approval of the Registrar, considers that there are advantages to the sharing of accommodations.

Rule 15

Each detainee shall be provided with a separate bed and with appropriate bedding **D14–016** which shall be kept in good order and changed on a regular basis so as to ensure its cleanliness.

Rule 16

The Detention Unit shall, at all times, meet all requirements of health and hygiene, **D14–017** with due regard being paid to climatic conditions, lighting, heating and ventilation.

Rule 17

Each detainee shall be permitted unrestricted access to the sanitary, hygiene and **D14–018** drinking water arrangements in his cell unit.

Rule 18

All parts of the Detention Unit shall be properly maintained and kept clean at all **D14–019** times. In particular, each detainee shall be expected to keep his cell unit clean and tidy at all times.

PERSONAL HYGIENE

Rule 19

Detainees shall be required to keep themselves clean and shall be provided with such **D14–020** toilet articles as are necessary for health and cleanliness.

Rule 20

Facilities shall be provided for the proper care of personal hygiene. **D14–021**

CLOTHING

Rule 21

Detainees may wear their own civilian clothing if, in the opinion of the Commanding **D14–022** Officer, it is clean and suitable. An indigent detainee shall be provided with suitable and sufficient civilian clothing at the cost of the Tribunal.

Rule 22

All clothing shall be kept clean and in proper condition. Underclothing shall be **D14–023** changed and washed as often as necessary for the maintenance of hygiene, in accordance with the regime of the host prison.

FOOD

Rule 23

Each detainee shall at the normal hours receive food which is suitably prepared and **D14–024** presented, and which satisfies in quality and quantity the standards of dietetics and modern hygiene and takes into account the age, health, religious and, as far as possible, cultural requirements of the detainee.

PHYSICAL EXERCISE AND SPORT AND RECREATIONAL OPPORTUNITIES

Rule 24

D14–025   Each detainee shall be allowed at least one hour of walking or other suitable exercise in the open air daily, if the weather permits. Where possible, arrangements may be made with the General Director for use by detainees of indoor and outdoor sporting facilities outside the Detention Unit but within the host prison.

Rule 25

D14–026   A properly organized programme of physical education, sport and other recreational activities shall be arranged by the Commanding Officer to ensure physical fitness, adequate exercise and recreational opportunities.

Rule 26

D14–027   The Commanding Officer, acting on the advice of the medical officer, shall ensure that any detainee who participates in such programme is physically fit to do so. Special arrangements shall be made, under medical direction, for remedial or therapeutic treatment for any detainee who is unable to participate in the regular programme.

MEDICAL SERVICES

Rule 27

D14–028   Medical services shall be available to detainees to the extent practically possible and subject to any arrangements made with the General Director. A person capable of providing first aid shall be present in the Detention Unit at all times.

Rule 28

D14–029   Detainees may be visited by and consult with a doctor or dentist of their choice at their own expense. All such visits shall be made by prior arrangement with the Commanding Officer as to the time and duration of the visit and shall be subject to the same security controls as are imposed under Rule 61. The Commanding Officer shall not refuse a request for such a visit without reasonable grounds. Any treatment or medication recommended by such a doctor or dentist shall be administered solely by the medical officer or his deputy. The medical officer may, at his sole discretion, refuse to administer any such treatment or medication.

Rule 29

D14–030   Detainees who require specialist or in-patient treatment shall be treated within the host prison to the fullest extent possible or transferred to a civil hospital.

Rule 30

D14–031   The Registrar shall be informed immediately upon the serious illness, injury or death of the detainee. The Registrar shall immediately inform the spouse or nearest relative of the detainee and shall, in any event, inform any other person previously designated by the detainee. In the event of the death of a detainee, an inquest will be conducted in accordance with the legal requirements of the Host State. The President may also order an inquiry into the circumstances surrounding the death or serious injury of any detainee.

Rule 31

The medical officer shall be responsible for the care of the physical and mental health of the detainees and shall see, on a daily basis or more often if necessary, all sick detainees, all who complain of illness and any detainee to whom his attention is specially directed.   **D14–032**

Rule 32

The medical officer shall report to the Commanding Officer whenever he considers that the physical or mental health of a detainee has been or will be adversely affected by any condition of his detention. The Commanding Officer shall immediately submit the report to the Registrar who, after consultation with the President, shall take all necessary action.   **D14–033**

Rule 33

A competent authority appointed by the Tribunal pursuant to Rule 6 shall regularly inspect the Detention Unit and advise the Commanding Officer and the Registrar upon: **D14–034**
    a. The quantity, quality, preparation and serving of food;
    b. The hygiene and cleanliness of the Detention Unit and of the detainees;
    c. The sanitation, heating, light and ventilation of the Detention Unit;
    d. The suitability and cleanliness of the detainees' clothing and bedding.

Rule 34

The Registrar shall, if he concurs with the recommendation made, take immediate steps to give effect to those recommendations; if he does not concur with them, he shall immediately submit both a personal report and a copy of the recommendations to the President.   **D14–035**

DISCIPLINE

Rule 35

Discipline and order shall be maintained by the staff of the Detention Unit in the interests of safe custody and the well-ordered running of the Detention Unit.   **D14–036**

Rule 36

The Commanding Officer, in consultation with the Registrar, shall issue regulations: **D14–037**
    a. Defining conduct constituting a disciplinary offence;
    b. Regulating the type of punishment that can be imposed;
    c. Specifying the authority that can impose such punishment;
    d. Providing for a right of appeal to the President.

Rule 37

The disciplinary regulations shall provide a detainee with the right to be heard on the subject of any offence which he is alleged to have committed.   **D14–038**

SEGREGATION

RULE 38

D14–039   The Registrar, acting on the request of the Prosecutor, or on his own initiative, and after seeking medical advice, may order that a detainee be segregated from all or some of the other detainees so as to avoid any potential conflict within the Detention Unit or danger to the detainee in question.

RULE 39

D14–040   At any time, the Commanding Officer may also order that a detainee be segregated from some or all of the other detainees for the preservation of security and good order in the Detention Unit or for the protection of the detainee in question. The Commanding Officer shall report all incidents of segregation to the medical officer who shall confirm the physical and mental fitness of the detainee for such segregation. Segregation is not to be used as a disciplinary measure.

RULE 40

D14–041   In case a detainee asks to be segregated from all or some of the other detainees, upon receipt of such a request, the Commanding Officer shall consult the medical officer to determine whether such segregation is medically acceptable. A request for segregation may be granted unless, in the opinion of the medical officer, such segregation would be injurious to the mental or physical health of the detainee.

RULE 41

D14–042   The Commanding Officer shall review all cases of individual segregation of all detainees at least once a week and report to the Registrar thereon.

RULE 42

D14–043   The Commanding Officer may organize the use of communal areas of the Detention Unit so as to segregate certain groups of detainees from others in the interests of the safety of the detainees and the proper conduct and operation of the Detention Unit. If such segregation is put into practice, care shall be taken to ensure that all such groupings are treated on an equal basis, having regard to the number of detainees falling within each group. All such segregation must be reported to the Tribunal which may vary the nature, basis, or conditions of such segregation.

ISOLATION UNIT

RULE 43

D14–044   A detainee may be confined to the isolation unit only in the following circumstances:
    a. By order of the Registrar, acting in consultation with the President; such an order may be based upon a request from any interested person, including the Prosecutor;
    b. By order of the Commanding Officer in order to prevent the detainee from inflicting injury on any other detainees or to preserve the security and good order of the Detention Unit;
    c. As a punishment pursuant to Rule 36.

A record shall be kept of all events concerning a detainee assigned to the isolation unit.

Rule 44

All cases of the use of the isolation unit shall be reported to the medical officer who shall confirm the physical and mental fitness of the detainee for such isolation. A detainee who has been confined to the isolation unit shall be visited by the medical officer or his deputy as often as the medical officer deems necessary.

D14–045

Rule 45

In case a detainee who has been confined to the isolation unit requests a visit from a medical officer, such a visit is to be made as soon as possible and, in any event, within twenty-four hours of the request.

D14–046

Rule 46

All cases of use of the isolation unit shall be reported immediately to the Registrar who shall report the matter to the President. The President may order the release of a detainee from the isolation unit at any time.

D14–047

Rule 47

In principle, no detainee may be kept in the isolation unit for more than seven consecutive days. If further isolation is necessary, the Commanding Officer shall report the matter to the Registrar before the end of the seven-day period and the medical officer shall confirm the physical and mental fitness of the detainee to continue such isolation for a further period not to exceed seven days. Each and every extension of use of the isolation unit shall be subject to the same procedure.

D14–048

FUNDAMENTALS OF RESTRAINT AND THE USE OF FORCE

Rule 48

Instruments of restraint, such as handcuffs, shall only be used in the following exceptional circumstances:
  a. As a precaution against escape during transfer from the Detention Unit to any other place, including access to the premises of the host prison for any reason;
  b. On medical grounds by direction and under the supervision of the medical officer;
  c. To prevent a detainee from self-injury, injury to others or to prevent serious damage to property.
In all accidents involving the use of instruments of restraint, the Commanding Officer shall consult the medical officer and report to the Registrar, who may report the matter to the President.

D14–049

Rule 49

Instruments of restraint shall be removed at the earliest possible opportunity.

D14–050

Rule 50

If the use of any instrument of restraint is required under Rule 48, the restrained detainee shall be kept under constant and adequate supervision.

D14–051

RULE 51

D14–052   The staff of the Detention Unit shall not use force against a detainee except in self-defense or in cases of attempted escape or active or passive resistance to an order based upon these Rules or any regulations issued pursuant thereto. Staff who have recourse to force must use no more than is strictly necessary and must report the incident immediately to the Commanding Officer, who shall provide a report on the matter to the Registrar.

RULE 52

D14–053   A detainee against whom force has been used shall have the right to be examined immediately and treated, if necessary, by the medical officer. The medical examination shall be conducted in private and in the absence of any non-medical staff. The results of the examination, including any relevant statement by the detainee and the medical officer's opinion shall be recorded and made available to the detainee in a language accessible to him, to the Commanding Officer, to the Registrar, to the President, and to the Prosecutor.

RULE 53

D14–054   A record shall be kept of any instance of the use of force against a detainee.

DISTURBANCES

RULE 54

D14–055   If, in the opinion of the Commanding Officer, a situation exists or is developing which threatens the security and good order of the Detention Unit, the Commanding Officer shall contact the General Director who will request the immediate assistance of the authorities of the Host State to maintain control within the Detention Unit. All such requests must be reported to the Registrar and the President.

SUSPENSION OF THE RULES OF DETENTION

RULE 55

D14–056   If there is serious danger of disturbances occurring within the Detention Unit or the host prison, the Commanding Officer or the General Director, as appropriate, may temporarily suspend the operation of all or part of these Rules for a maximum of two days. Any such suspension must be reported immediately to the Registrar. Thereupon, the President, acting in consultation with the Bureau, shall consult with the relevant authorities of the Host State and take such action in connection therewith as may be seen fit at the time.

INFORMATION TO DETAINEES

RULE 56

D14–057   In addition to the copies of these Rules and any regulations to be provided to each detainee pursuant to Rule 91, each detainee shall on admission be provided with written information in the working languages of the Tribunal or in his own language concerning the rights and treatment of detainees, the disciplinary requirements of the Detention Unit, the authorized methods of seeking information and making complaints, and all matters necessary to enable him to understand both his rights and obligations and to adapt himself to the routine of the Detention Unit.

RULE 57

At any time at which there is a detainee in the Detention Unit who speaks and understands neither of the working languages of the Tribunal nor that spoken by any of the staff of the Detention Unit, arrangements shall be made for an interpreter to be available on reasonable notice and, in any event, in cases of emergency, to permit the detainee to communicate freely with the staff and administration of the Detention Unit.   **D14–058**

RIGHT OF DETAINESS

CONTACT WITH THE OUTSIDE WORLD

RULE 58

Subject to the provisions of Rule 64, detainees shall be entitled, under such conditions of supervision and time constraints as the Commanding Officer deems necessary, to communicate with their families and other persons with whom it is in their legitimate interest to correspond by letter and by telephone at their own expense. In the case of an indigent detainee, the Registrar may agree that the Tribunal will bear such expenses within reason.   **D14–059**

RULE 59

All correspondence and mail, including packages, shall be inspected for explosives or other restricted materials. The Commanding Officer, in consultation with the Registrar, shall lay down conditions as to the inspection of correspondence, mail and packages in the interests of maintaining order in the Detention Unit and to obviate the danger of escape.   **D14–060**

RULE 60

A detainee shall be informed at once of the available information on the death or serious illness of any near relative.   **D14–061**

RULE 61

(i) Detainees shall be allowed, subject to Rule 64, to receive visits from their family and friends at regular intervals under such restrictions and supervision as the Commanding Officer, in consultation with the Registrar, may deem necessary.   **D14–062**
(ii) All visitors must comply with the separate requirements of the visiting regime of the host prison. These restrictions may include personal searches of clothing and X-ray examination of possessions on entry to either or both of the Detention Unit and the host prison. Any person, including Defence Counsel for a detainee or a diplomatic or consular representative accredited to the Host State, who refuses to comply with such requirements, whether of the Detention Unit or of the host prison, may be refused access.

RULE 62

A detainee must be informed of the identity of each visitor and may refuse to see any visitor other than a representative of the Prosecutor.   **D14–063**

Rule 63

D14–064   Detainees shall be allowed to communicate with and receive visits from the diplomatic and consular representative of the State to which they belong accredited to the Host State or, in the case of detainees who are without diplomatic or consular representation in the Host State and refugees or stateless persons, with the diplomatic representative accredited to the Host State of the State which takes charge of their interests or of a national or international authority whose task it is to serve the interests of such persons.

Rule 64

D14–065   The Prosecutor may request the Registrar or, in cases of emergency, the Commanding Officer, to prohibit, regulate or set conditions for contact between a detainee and any other person if the Prosecutor has reasonable grounds for believing that such contact is for the purposes of attempting to arrange the escape of the detainee from the Detention Unit, or could prejudice or otherwise affect the outcome of the proceedings against the detainee, or of any other investigation, or that such contact could be harmful to the detainee or any other person or may be used by the detainee to breach an order for non-disclosure made by a Judge or a Chamber pursuant to Rule 53 or Rule 75 of the Rules of Procedure and Evidence. If the request is made to the Commanding Officer on grounds of urgency, the Prosecutor shall immediately inform the Registrar of the request, together with the reasons therefor. The detainee shall immediately be informed of the fact of any such request. A detainee may, at any time, request the President to deny or reverse such a request for prohibition of contact.

LEGAL ASSISTANCE

Rule 65

D14–066   Each detainee shall be entitled to communicate fully and without restraint with his Defence Counsel, with the assistance of an interpreter where necessary. Unless such Counsel and interpreter have been provided by the Tribunal on the basis of the indigence of the detainee, all such communications shall be at the expense of the detainee. All such correspondence and communications shall be privileged. All visits shall be made by prior arrangement with the Commanding Officer as to the time and duration of the visit and shall be subject to the same security controls as are imposed under Rule 61. The Commanding Officer shall not refuse a request for such a visit without reasonable grounds. Interviews with legal Counsel and interpreters shall be conducted in the sight but not within the hearing, either direct or indirect, of the staff of the Detention Unit.

SPIRITUAL WELFARE

Rule 66

D14–067   Every detainee shall be entitled to indicate, on arrival at the Detention Unit or thereafter, whether he wishes to establish contact with any of the ministers or spiritual advisers of the host prison.

Rule 67

D14–068   A qualified representative of each religion or system of beliefs held by any detainee shall be appointed and approved by the Bureau. Such representative shall be permitted to hold regular services and activities within the Detention Unit and to pay pastoral visits to any detainee of his religion, subject to the same considerations of the security and good order of the Detention Unit and of the host prison as apply to other visits.

RULE 68

Access to a representative of any religion shall not be refused to any detainee, subject only to the same restrictions and conditions provided for in Rule 61. A detainee may refuse to see any such religious representative.

D14–069

RULE 69

So far as is practicable, every detainee shall be allowed to satisfy the needs of his religious, spiritual and moral life by attending services or meetings held in the Detention Unit and having in his possession any necessary books or literature. By arrangement with the General Director, a detainee may, on request, be permitted to visit any religious facility within the grounds of the host prison.

D14–070

WORK PROGRAMME

RULE 70

The Commanding Officer, after consultation with the General Director, and as far as is practicable, shall institute a work programme to be performed by detainees either in the individual cell units or in the communal areas of the Detention Unit.

D14–071

RULE 71

Detainees shall be offered the opportunity to enrol in such work programme but shall not be required to work. A detainee who chooses to work shall be paid for his work at rates to be established by the Commanding Officer in consultation with the Registrar and may use part of his earnings to purchase articles for his own use pursuant to Rule 80. The balance of any monies earned shall be held to his account in accordance with Rule 12.

D14–072

RECREATIONAL ACTIVITIES

RULE 72

Detainees shall be allowed to procure at their own expense books, newspapers, reading and writing materials and other means of occupation as are compatible with the interests of the administration of justice and the security and good order of the Detention Unit and of the host prison.

D14–073

RULE 73

In particular, detainees shall be entitled to keep themselves regularly informed of the news by reading newspapers, periodicals, and other publications and by radio and television broadcasts, all necessary equipment to be provided at their own expense. The Commanding Officer may refuse the installation of any such equipment which he considers to be a potential risk to the safety and good order of the Detention Unit or to any of the detainees.

D14–074

RULE 74

If, in the opinion of the Prosecutor, the interests of justice would not be served by allowing a particular detainee unrestricted access to the news, or that such unrestricted access could prejudice the outcome of the proceedings against the detainee or of any

D14–075

other investigation, the Prosecutor may request the Registrar, or in cases of urgency, the Commanding Officer to restrict such access. If the request is made to the Commanding Officer on grounds of urgency, the Prosecutor shall immediately inform the Registrar of the request, together with the reasons therefor. The detainee shall immediately be informed of the fact of any such request. A detainee may at any time request the President to deny or reverse such a request for restriction of access.

RULE 75

D14–076   By arrangement with the General Director, detainees may use the library and such vocational or other facilities of the host prison as may be made available.

PERSONAL POSSESSIONS OF DETAINEES

RULE 76

D14–077   A detainee may keep in his possession all clothing and personal items for his own use or consumption unless, in the opinion of the Commanding Officer or the General Director, such items constitute a threat to the security or good order of the Detention Unit or the host prison, or to the health or safety of any person therein. All items so removed shall be retained by the staff of the Detention Unit as provided for in Rule 12.

RULE 77

D14–078   Any item received from outside, including any item introduced by any visitor to a detainee, shall be subject to separate security controls by both the Detention Unit and the host prison, and may be transported through the host prison to the Detention Unit by staff of either the Detention Unit or of the host prison. The General Director may refuse access to the host prison of any item intended for consumption by detainees.

RULE 78

D14–079   As far as is practicable, any item received for a detainee from outside shall be treated as provided for in Rule 12 unless intended and permitted under these Rules and the rules of the host prison for use during imprisonment.

RULE 79

D14–080   The possession and use of any medication shall be subject to the control and supervision of the medical officer. Detainees may possess cigarettes and smoke them at such times and places as the Commanding Officer permits. The possession or consumption of alcohol is not permitted.

RULE 80

D14–081   Each detainee shall be authorized to spend his own money to purchase items of a personal nature from the store operated by the host prison, if any. In the case of an indigent detainee, the Registrar may authorize the purchase of such items, within reason, for the account of the Tribunal. Detainees shall have the right to purchase such items within seven days of arrival and at least once a week thereafter.

RULE 81

D14–082   On release of the detainee from the Detention Unit, or transfer to another institution, all articles and money retained within the Detention Unit shall be returned to the detainee except in so far as he has been authorized to spend money or send property out of the Detention Unit, or it has been found necessary on hygienic grounds to destroy any article of clothing. The detainee shall sign a receipt for the articles and money returned to him.

COMPLAINTS

Rule 82

Each detainee may make a complaint to the Commanding Officer or his representative at any time.

D14–083

Rule 83

A detainee, if not satisfied with the response from the Commanding Officer, has the right to make a written complaint, without censorship, to the Registrar, who shall forward it to the President.

D14–084

Rule 84

Each detainee may freely communicate with the competent inspecting authority. During an inspection of the Detention Unit, the detainee shall have the opportunity to talk to the inspector out of the sight and hearing of the staff of the Detention Unit.

D14–085

Rule 85

The right of complaint shall include confidential access to the relevant authority pursuant to Rule 83.

D14–086

Rule 86

Every complaint made to the Registrar shall be acknowledged within seventy-two hours. Each complaint shall be dealt with promptly and replied within a reasonable period of time.

D14–087

REMOVAL AND TRANSPORT OF DETAINEES

Rule 87

When detainees are being removed to or from the Detention Unit, they shall be exposed to public view as little as possible and all proper safeguards shall be adopted to protect them from insult, injury, curiosity and publicity in any form.

D14–088

Rule 88

Detainees shall at all times be transported in vehicles with adequate ventilation and light and in such a way as will not subject them to unnecessary physical hardship or indignity.

D14–089

Rule 89

The transport of detainees through the host prison shall be conducted jointly by personnel of the Detention Unit and of the host prison.

D14–090

AMENDMENT

RULE 90

D14–091   Proposals for amendment of the Rules may be made by a Judge, the Prosecutor or the Registrar and shall be adopted if agreed to by not less than ten Judges at a plenary meeting of the Tribunal convened with notice of the proposal addressed to all Judges. An amendment to the Rules may be otherwise adopted, provided it is unanimously approved by the Judges. Any such amendment shall enter into force immediately unless the Tribunal decides otherwise.

ACCESSIBILITY

RULE 91

D14–092   These Rules and any regulations issued pursuant thereto shall be made readily available to the staff of the Detention Unit and to each detainee in the working languages of the Tribunal, and in the official languages of the Host State and, as appropriate, of the detainees.

PROVISIONAL APPLICATION

RULE 92

D14–093   These Rules, as well as any amendments thereto, may apply provisionally with the written assent of the judges pending their formal adoption by the Tribunal at a plenary meeting.

ENTRY INTO FORCE

RULE 93

D14–094   These Rules, having been adopted by the Tribunal at the Second Plenary Session on 9 January 1996, shall enter into force on a date to be certified by the President.

D15. Resolution 1503 (2003)

ADOPTED BY THE SECURITY COUNCIL AT ITS 4817TH MEETING, ON 28 AUGUST 2003

This document may be found at *http://www.ictr.org/ENGLISH/Resolutions/s-res-1503e.pdf*   **D15–001**

D16. Resolution 1534 (2004)

ADOPTED BY THE SECURITY COUNCIL AT ITS 4935TH MEETING, ON 26 MARCH 2004

This document may be found at *http://www.ictr.org/ENGLISH/Resolutions/s-res-1534e.pdf*   **D16–001**

D17. Practice Direction on Formal Requirements for Appeals from Judgement

I. INTRODUCTION

D17–001   In accordance with Rule 107*bis* of the Rules of Procedure and Evidence of the International Criminal Tribunal for the Prosecution of Persons Responsible for Genocide and Other Serious Violation of International Humanitarian Law Committed in the Territory of Rwanda and Rwandan Citizens responsible for genocide and other such violations committed in the territory of neighbouring Stated between 1 January 1994 and 31 December 1994 ("the Rules" and "the Tribunal"), and having consulted with the President of the Tribunal, I issue this Practice Direction in order to establish the formal requirements for appeals from judgement ("Practice Direction") before the International Tribunal:

II. FORMAL REQUIREMENTS

THE APPELLANT'S NOTICE OF APPEAL

D17–002   1. A party seeking to appeal from a judgement of a Trial Chamber ("Appellant") shall file, in accordance with the Statute of the Tribunal ("the Statute"), in particular Article 24 of the Statute, and the Rules, a Notice of Appeal containing, in the following order:
- (a) the date of the judgement;
- (b) the specific provision of the Rules pursuant to which the Notice of Appeal is filed;
- (c) the grounds of appeal, clearly specifying in respect of each ground of appeal:
  - (i) any alleged error on a question of law invalidating the decision, and/or
  - (ii) any alleged error of fact which has occasioned a miscarriage of justice;
  - (iii) an identification of the finding or ruling challenged in the judgement, with specific reference to the page number and paragraph number;
  - (iv) an identification of any other order, decision or ruling challenged, with specific reference to the date of its filing, and/or transcript page;
  - (v) the precise relief sought;
- (d) if relevant, the overall relief sought.

VARIATION OF THE GROUNDS OF APPEAL

D17–003   2. Any party applying to vary the grounds of appeal must do so by way of motion in accordance with the Rules, setting out:
- (a) the specific Rule under which the variation is sought; and
- (b) the arguments in support of the request to vary the grounds of appeal as required by that Rule.

    3. If leave is granted to vary the grounds of appeal then the varied grounds of appeal shall comply with the requirements of this Practice Direction *mutatis mutandis*.

THE APPELLANT'S BRIEF

D17–004   4. After having filed a Notice of Appeal, the Appellant shall file, in accordance with the Statute and the Rules, an Appellant's Brief containing, in the following order:
- (a) an introduction with a concise summary of the relevant procedural history including the date of the judgement as well as the case number and date of any interlocutory filing or decision relevant to the appeal;
- (b) the arguments in support of each ground of appeal, including, but not limited to;

  (i) legal arguments, giving clear and precise references to relevant provisions of the Statute, the Rules, the jurisprudence of the Tribunal or other legal authorities relied upon;
  (ii) factual arguments and, if applicable, arguments in support of any objections as to whether a fact has been sufficiently proven or not, with precise reference to any relevant exhibit, transcript page, decision or paragraph number in the judgement;
  (iii) arguments in support of the submitted causal link between any alleged error on a question of law invalidating the decision and/or any alleged error of fact which has occasioned a miscarriage of justice;
  (iv) the precise relief sought;
 (c) the arguments in support of any overall relief sought.

The grounds of appeal and the arguments must be set out and numbered in the same order as in the Appellant's Notice of Appeal, unless otherwise varied with leave of the Appeals Chamber.

THE RESPONDENT'S BRIEF

5. The opposite party ("Respondent") shall file, in accordance with the Statute and the Rules, a Respondent's Brief, containing for each ground of appeal, in the following order: **D17–005**
 (a) a statement on whether or not the relief sought by the Appellant is opposed;
 (b) a statement on whether or not the ground of appeal is opposed;
 (c) arguments in support of these statements, containing:
  (i) legal arguments, including clear and precise references to the relevant provisions of the Statute, the Rules, the jurisprudence of the Tribunal or other legal authorities relied upon;
  (ii) factual arguments including, if applicable, the arguments in support of the assertion that a fact has been sufficiently proven or not, with precise reference to any relevant exhibit, transcript page, decision or paragraph number in the judgement;
  (iii) arguments pertaining to the submitted causal link between any alleged error on a question of law invalidating the decision and/or any alleged error of fact which has occasioned a miscarriage of justice.

The statements and the arguments must be set out and numbered in the same order as in the Appellant's Brief and shall be limited to arguments made in response to that brief. However, if an Appellant relies on a particular ground to reverse an acquittal, the Respondent may support the acquittal on additional grounds.

THE APPELLANT'S BRIEF IN REPLY

6. An Appellant may file, in accordance with the Statute and the Rules, an Appellant's Brief in Reply, limited to arguments in reply to the Respondent's Brief, set out and numbered in the same order as in previous briefs. **D17–006**

ADDITIONAL EVIDENCE

7. Any party applying to present additional evidence shall do so by way of motion filed, in accordance with the Statute and the Rules, such motion containing, in the following order: **D17–007**
 (a) a precise list of the evidence the party is seeking to have presented;
 (b) an identification of each ground of appeal to which the evidence relates and, where applicable, a request to submit any additional grounds of appeal based on such evidence;
 (c) arguments in relation to the requirement of non-availability at trial;
 (d) arguments in relation to the requirement that the admission of the evidence is in the interests of justice;

The relevant documents and exhibits, where applicable, shall be translated into one of the languages of the Tribunal.

8. If a party is authorised to present additional evidence then the requirements of this Practice Direction apply *mutatis mutandis.*

III. GENERAL REQUIREMENTS

D17–008 9. Where filings of the parties refer to passages in a judgement, decision, transcripts, exhibits or other authorities, they shall indicate precisely the date, exhibit number, page number and paragraph number of the text or exhibit referred to.

10. Any abbreviations or designations used by the parties in their filings shall be uniform throughout. Pages and paragraphs shall be numbered consecutively from the beginning to the end.

11. Any time limits prescribed under this Practice Direction shall run from, but shall not include, the day upon which the relevant document is filed. Should the last day of a time prescribed fall upon a non-working day of the Tribunal it shall be considered as falling on the first working day thereafter.

12. The provisions of this Practice Direction are without prejudice to any such orders or decisions that may be made by a Pre-Appeal Judge or the Appeals Chamber. In particular a Pre-Appeal Judge or the Appeals Chamber may vary any time limit or recognise, as validly done any act done after the expiration of a time limit prescribed in this Practice Direction.

IV. NON-COMPLIANCE WITH THE REQUIREMENTS

D17–009 13. Where a party fails to comply with the requirements laid down in this Practice Direction, or where the wording of a filing is unclear or ambiguous, a Pre-Appeal Judge or the Appeals Chamber may, within its discretion, decide upon an appropriate sanction, which can include an order for clarification or re-filing. The Appeals Chamber may also reject a filing or dismiss submissions therein.

Claude Jorda
Presiding Judge of the Appeals Chamber

Done this 16th day of September 2002
At The Hague,
The Netherlands.

[Seal of the Tribunal]

D18. Practice Direction on Procedure for the Filing of written submissions in Appeal Proceedings before the Tribunal

I. Introduction

In accordance with Rule 107*bis* of the Rules of Procedure and Evidence of the **D18–001**
International Criminal Tribunal for the Prosecution of Persons Responsible for Genocide
and Other Serious Violation of International Humanitarian Law Committed in the
Territory of Rwanda and Rwandan Citizens responsible for genocide and other such
violations committed in the territory of neighbouring States between 1 January 1994 and
31 December 1994 ("the Tribunal"), and having consulted with the President of the
Tribunal, I issue this revised Practice Direction in order to establish a procedure for the
filing of written submissions in appeal proceedings before the International Tribunal:

Part II or Part III of this Practice Direction shall apply *mutatis mutandis* to any appeal
from a decision of a Trial Chamber (that is to say other than appeals from post final
judgement).

II. Appeals from decisions where appeal lies as of right

1. A party wishing to appeal from a decision of a Trial Chamber ("Appellant") where **D18–002**
an appeal lies as of right shall file, in accordance with the Rules, an appeal containing:
    (a) the precise title and date of filing of the appealed decision;
    (b) a summary of the proceedings before the Trial Chamber relating to the
    appealed decision including an identification of all relevant documents in the
    proceedings before the Trial Chamber, clearly stating the title and date of filing
    of each document or the page number of a transcript;
    (c) the specific provision of the Rules pursuant to which the appeal is filed;
    (d) a concise statement as to why it is contended that the provision relied upon is
    applicable to the appeal;
    (e) the grounds on which the appeal is made;
    (f) the relief sought.
2. The opposite party shall file a response within ten days of the filing of the appeal.
Such a response shall clearly state whether or not the appeal is opposed and the grounds
therefore. It shall further set out any objection to the applicability of the provision of the
Rules relied upon by the Appellant as the basis for the appeal.
3. The Appellant may file a reply within four days of the filing of the response. The
Appeals Chamber may thereafter decide the appeal without further submissions from
the parties.

III. Appeals from decisions where appeal lies only with the leave of a bench of three Judges of the appeals chamber

4. A party wishing to appeal from a decision of a Trial Chamber which may be **D18–003**
appealed only with the leave of a bench of three Judges of the Appeals Chamber shall
file, in accordance with the Rules, an application for leave to appeal containing:
    (a) the precise title and date of filing of the decision sought to be appealed;
    (b) a summary of the proceedings before the Trial Chamber relating to the decision
    sought to be appealed including an identification of all relevant documents in
    the proceedings before the Trial Chamber, clearly stating the title and date of
    filing of each document or the page number of a transcript;
    (c) the specific provision of the Rules under which leave to appeal is sought;
    (d) a concise statement as to why it is contended that the applicable criteria for the
    granting of leave to appeal under the provision relied upon have been met.
5. The opposite party shall file a response within ten days of the filing of the
application for leave to appeal. Such a response shall clearly state whether or not the

application for leave to appeal is opposed and the grounds therefore. It shall further indicate any objection to the applicability of the provision of the Rules relied upon by the Appellant as the basis for the application for leave to appeal.

6. The Appellant may file a reply within four days of the filing of the response. The bench of three Judges of the Appeals Chamber may thereafter decide the application for leave to appeal without further submissions from the parties.

7. Where leave to appeal is granted, the Appellant shall within ten days of the filing of the decision of the bench of three Judges of the Appeals Chamber file an appeal containing:

    (a) the precise title and date of filing of the appealed decision and the decision by a bench of three Judges of the Appeals Chamber granting leave to appeal;

    (b) a summary of the proceedings before the Trial Chamber relating to the appealed decision;

    (c) the specific provision of the Rules pursuant to which the appeal is filed;

    (d) the grounds on which the appeal is made;

    (e) the relief sought.

8. The opposite party shall file a response within ten days of the filing of the appeal. This response shall clearly state whether or not the appeal is opposed and the grounds therefore.

9. The Appellant may file a reply within four days of the filing of the response. The Appeals Chamber may thereafter decide the appeal without further submissions from the parties.

IV. MOTIONS DURING APPEALS FROM JUDGEMENT

D18–004   10. Where an appeal has been filed from a judgement, a party wishing to move the Appeals Chamber for a specific ruling or relief ("moving party") shall file, in accordance with the Rules, a motion containing:

    (a) the precise ruling or relief sought;

    (b) the specific provision of the Rules under which the ruling or relief is sought;

    (c) the grounds on which the ruling or relief is sought.

The motion shall comply with article 25(2) of the Directive for the Registry of the Tribunal: Judicial and Legal Services Division, which entered into force on 8 June 1998.

11. The opposite party shall file a response within ten days of the filing of the motion. This response shall clearly state whether or not the motion is opposed and the grounds therefore.

12. The moving party may file a reply within four days of the filing of the response. The Appeals Chamber or the Pre-Appeal Judge may thereafter decide the motion without further submissions from the parties.

V. CALCULATION OF TIME

D18–005   13. The time-limits prescribed under this Practice Direction shall run from, but shall not include, the day upon which the relevant document is filed. Should the last day of a time prescribed fall upon a non-working day of the Tribunal it shall be considered as falling on the first working day thereafter.

VI. GENERAL REQUIREMENTS FOR THE WRITTEN SUBMISSIONS

D18–006   14. Where filings of the parties refer to passages in a judgement, decision, transcripts, exhibits or other authorities, they shall indicate precisely the date, exhibit number, page number and paragraph number of the text or exhibit referred to.

15. Any abbreviations or designations used by the parties in their filings shall be uniform throughout. Pages and paragraphs shall be numbered consecutively from the beginning to the end.

VII. VARIATION OF PROCEDURE

D18–007   16. The provisions of this Practice Direction are without prejudice to any such orders or decisions that may be made by the Appeals Chamber, a bench of three Judges of the Appeals Chamber or a Pre-Appeal Judge. In particular, the Appeals Chamber, a bench of three Judges of the Appeals Chamber or a Pre-Appeal Judge may vary any time-limit prescribed under this Practice Direction or recognise as validly done any act done after the expiration of a time-limit so prescribed. The Appeals Chamber may at its discretion entertain oral motions brought in the course of appeals against judgement.

17. Notwithstanding the pleading sequence provided for above, the Appeals Chamber or a bench of three Judges of the Appeals Chamber may, in accordance with existing practice, dismiss an interlocutory appeal if it is of the opinion that the appeal does not on its face fall within the category of admissible interlocutory appeals.

18. Notwithstanding the pleading sequence provided for above, a motion for an extension of time may, in accordance with existing practice, be disposed of without giving the other party the opportunity to respond to the motion if, on the face of the motion, the Appeals Chamber or a bench of three Judges of the Appeals Chamber or the Pre-Appeal Judge is of the opinion that no prejudice would be caused to the other party.

VIII. Non-compliance with this Practice Direction

19. Where a party fails to comply with the requirements laid down in this Practice Direction, or where the wording of a filing is unclear or ambiguous, the Appeals Chamber, a bench of three Judges of the Appeals Chamber or a Pre-Appeal Judge may, within its discretion, decide upon an appropriate sanction, which can include an order for clarification or re-filing. The Appeals Chamber may also reject a filing or dismiss submissions therein.

D18–008

Claude Jorda
Presiding Judge of the Appeals Chamber

Done this 16th day of September 2002
At The Hague,
The Netherlands.

[Seal of the Tribunal]

D19. Practice direction on the length of briefs and motions on appeal

I. I<small>NTRODUCTION</small>

D19–001   In accordance with Rule *107bis* of the Rules of Procedure and Evidence of the International Criminal Tribunal for the Prosecution of Persons Responsible for Genocide and Other Serious Violation of International Humanitarian Law Committed in the Territory of Rwanda and Rwandan Citizens responsible for genocide and other such violations committed in the territory of neighbouring States between 1 January 1994 and 31 December 1994 ("the Rules" and "the Tribunal"), and having consulted with the President of the Tribunal, I issue this revised Practice Direction in order to establish a limit on the length of written briefs and motions on appeal:

(A) PAPER SIZE AND FORMAT

D19–002   Briefs and motions will be submitted on A4 paper. Margins will be at least 2.5 centimetres on all four sides. All filings will be paginated, excluding the cover sheet.

(B) TYPEFACE

D19–003   The typeface will be 12 points with 1.5 line spacing. An average page should contain fewer than 300 words.

(C) LENGTH

1. Merits appeals

D19–004   (a) The brief of an appellant on appeal from a final judgement of a Trial Chamber will not exceed 100 pages or 30,000 words, whichever is greater:

    (i) provided that, where the Prosecutor, as appellant, files a separate brief in respect of each appellee or a consolidated brief, the total number of pages filed shall not exceed 100 or 30,000 words, whichever is the greater, in respect of one appellee and a further 35 pages or 10,000 words, whichever is the greater, in respect of each additional appellee;

    (ii) and provided that the time-limit for filing such a consolidated brief shall run from the filing date of the last notice of appeal.

(b) The response of an appellee on an appeal from a final judgement of a Trial Chamber will not exceed 100 pages or 30,000 words, whichever is greater, subject to the proviso in (a) (i) applying *mutatis mutandis* to any brief in response filed by the Prosecutor, and provided that, the time- limit for filing a consolidated brief in response shall run from the filing date of the last appellant's brief.

(c) The reply brief of an appellant in an appeal from a final judgement of a Trial Chamber will not exceed 30 pages or 9,000 words, whichever is greater:

    (i) provided that, where the Prosecutor files a reply brief in respect of more than one appellee, either by filing a separate brief in respect of each appellee or a consolidated brief, the total number of pages shall not exceed 30 pages or 9,000 words, whichever is the greater, in respect of one appellee and a further 10 pages or 3,000 words, whichever is the greater, in respect of each additional appellee; and

    (ii) and provided that the time-limit for filing such a consolidated reply brief shall run from the filing date of the last appellee's response.

2. Interlocutory appeals

(a) Appeal where appeal lies as of right

D19–005   (1) The motion of a party wishing to appeal where appeal lies as of right will not exceed 15 pages or 4,500 words, whichever is greater.

(2) The response to a motion for appeal will not exceed 15 pages or 4,500 words, whichever is greater.

(3) The reply to such a response will not exceed 7 pages or 2,100 words, whichever is greater.

(b) Leave to appeal

(1) The motion of a party seeking leave to pursue an appeal with leave of a bench of three Judges of the Appeals Chamber will not exceed 15 pages or 4,500 words, whichever is greater. **D19–006**

(2) The response to a motion for leave to appeal will not exceed 15 pages or 4,500 words, whichever is greater.

(3) The reply to such a response will not exceed 7 pages or 2,100 words, whichever is greater.

(c) Appeal where leave to appeal is granted

(1) The appeal of a party where leave to appeal is granted will not exceed 15 pages or 4,500 words, whichever is greater. **D19–007**

(2) The response to an appeal where leave to appeal is granted will not exceed 15 pages or 4,500 words, whichever is greater.

(3) The reply to such a response will not exceed 7 pages or 2,100 words, whichever is greater.

(d) Merits of interlocutor)' appeal where leave to file briefs is granted or ordered proprio motu

(1) The brief of an appellant in an interlocutory appeal will not exceed 30 pages or 9,000 words, whichever is greater. **D19–008**

(2) The brief of an appellee in an interlocutory appeal will not exceed 30 pages or 9,000 words, whichever is greater.

(3) The reply brief of an appellant in an interlocutory appeal will not exceed 10 pages or 3,000 words, whichever is greater.

3. Other motions, responses and replies

Motions, responses and replies thereto before the Appeals Chamber will not exceed 10 pages or 3,000 words, whichever is greater. **D19–009**

4. Materials excluded from page and word limits

Headings, footnotes and quotations count towards the above word and page limitations. Any addendum containing verbatim quotations of the Tribunal's Statute or Rules does not count towards the page limit. Any appendix or book of authorities does not count towards the page limit. An appendix or book of authorities will not contain legal or factual arguments, but rather references, source materials, items from the record, exhibits, and other relevant, non-argumentative material. An appendix will be of reasonable length, which is normally three times the page limit for that class of motion or brief (e.g., for a brief that is limited to 30 pages by the above practice direction, the appendix should be limited to 90 pages), although it is understood that the length of appendices will naturally vary more than the length of briefs. **D19–010**

5. Variation from page limits

A party must seek authorisation in advance from the Appeals Chamber, a bench of three Judges of the Appeals Chamber or the Pre-Appeal Judge to exceed the page limits in this Practice Direction and must provide an explanation of the exceptional circumstances that necessitate the oversized filing. **D19–011**

6. Motions on variation from page limits

D19–012   A motion to exceed the page limits in this Practice Direction may, in accordance with existing practice, be disposed of without giving the other party the opportunity to respond to the motion if, on the face of the motion, the Appeals Chamber, a bench of three Judges of the Appeals Chamber or the Pre-Appeal Judge is of the opinion that no prejudice would be caused to the other party.

_____

Claude Jorda
Presiding Judge of the Appeals Chamber

Done this 16th day of September 2002
At The Hague,
The Netherlands.

[Seal of the Tribunal]

D20. Agreements on enforcement of sentences: Benin, France, Italy, Mali, Swaziland, Sweden

These documents may be found at *http://www.ictr.org/ENGLISH/agreements/benin.pdf* **D20–001**
http://www.ictr.org/ENGLISH/agreements/france.pdf
http://www.ictr.org/ENGLISH/agreements/italy.pdf
http://www.ictr.org/ENGLISH/agreements/mali.pdf
http://www.ictr.org/ENGLISH/agreements/swaziland.pdf and
http://www.ictr.org/ENGLISH/agreements/sweden.pdf

D21. Resolution 977 (1995) Adopted by the Security Council at its 3502nd meeting, on 22 February 1995

This document may be found at *http://www.ictr.org/ENGLISH/Resolutions/scr977e.htm* **D21–001**

D22. Resolution 978 (1995) Adopted by the Security Council at its 3504th meeting on 27 February 1995

This document may be found at *http://www.ictr.org/ENGLISH/Resolutions/978e.htm* **D22–001**

D23. Resolution 1165 (1998) Adopted by the Security Council at its 3877th meeting on 30 April 1998

This document may be found at *http://www.ictr.org/ENGLISH/Resolutions/1165e.htm* **D23–001**

D24. Resolution 1166 (1998) Adopted by the Security Council at its 3878th meeting on 13 May 1998

This document may be found at *http://www.ictr.org/ENGLISH/Resolutions/* **D24–001**
scr1166(1998)e.pdf

D25. Resolution 1329 (2000) Adopted by the Security Council at its 4240th meeting, on 30 November 2000

This document may be found at *http://www.ictr.org/ENGLISH/Resolutions/1329e.htm* **D25–001**

D26. Resolution 1411 (2002) Adopted by the Security Council at its 4535th meeting, on 17 May 2002

This document may be found at *http://www.ictr.org/ENGLISH/Resolutions/scr411e.pdf* **D26–001**

D27. Resolution 1505 (2003) Adopted by the Security Council at its 4819th meeting, on 4 September 2003

D27–001   These documents may be found at *http://daccess-ods.un.org/TMP/9355174.html* and *http:// www.un.org/Docs/sc/unsc—resolutions03.html*

D28. Report of the International Criminal Tribunal for the Prosecution of Persons Responsible for genocide and other serious violations of International Humanitarian Law committed in the territory of Rwanda and Rwandan citizens responsible for genocide and other such violations committed in the territory of neighbouring States Between 1 January and 31 December 1994

D28–001   This document may be found at *http://www.ictr.org/ENGLISH/annualreports/ a51/9625167e.htm#appendix*

APPENDIX E

BOSNIA AND HERZEGOVINA

Source materials for Bosnia and Herzegovina may be found on the websites below:

Document	Website
Criminal Code of Bosnia and Herzegovina	http://www.ohr.int/ohr-dept/legal/oth-legist/doc/ criminal-code-of-bih.doc
Criminal Procedure Code of Bosnia and Herzegovina	http://www.ohr.int/ohr-dept/legal/oth-legist/doc/ criminal-procedure-code-of-bih.doc
Criminal Code of the Federation of Bosnia and Herzegovina	http://www.ohr.int/ohr-dept/legal/oth-legist/doc/ fbih-criminal-code-new.doc
Criminal Procedure Code of the Federation of Bosnia and Herzegovina	http://www.ohr.int/ohr-dept/legal/oth-legist/doc/ fbih-criminal-procedure-code.doc
Law on Court of Bosnia and Herzegovina	http://www.ohr.int/ohr-dept/legal/oth-legist/doc/ LAW-ON-THE-COURT-OF-BiH.doc
Law on Amendments to the Law on Court of Bosnia and Herzegovina	http://www.ohr.int/ohr-dept/legal/oth-legist/doc/ LAW-ON-AMENDMENTS-TO-THE-LAW-ON-COURT-OF-BiH.doc
Law on the High Judicial and Prosecutorial Council of Bosnia and Herzegovina	http://www.ohr.int/ohr-dept/legal/oth-legist/doc/ LAW-ON-HIGH-JUDICIAL-AND-PROSECUTORIAL-COUNCIL-OF-BH.doc
Law on Attorneys' Profession of the Federation of Bosnia and Herzegovina	http://www.ohr.int/ohr-dept/legal/oth-legist/doc/ law-on-the-attorneys'-profession-of-fbih.doc
Law on the Attorneys' Profession of the Republika Srpska	http://www.ohr.int/ohr-dept/legal/oth-legist/doc/ LAW-ON-THE-ATTORNEYS-PROFESSION-OF-THE-RS.doc
Law on the Centre for Judicial and Prosecutorial Training of the Federation of Bosnia and Herzegovina	http://www.ohr.int/ohr-dept/legal/oth-legist/doc/ LAW-ON-THE-CENTRE-FOR-JUDICIAL-AND-PROSECUTORIAL-TRAINING-FBH.doc
Rules of Procedure of the High Judicial and Prosecutorial Council	http://www.hjpc.ba/intro/?cid=1790,1,1
Constitution of Bosnia and Herzegovina	http://www.ohr.int/dpa/default.asp?content_ id=372

1859

Constitution of the Federation of Bosnia and Herzegovina	http://www.ohr.int/ohr-dept/legal/oth-legist/doc/fbih-constitution.doc
Constitution of Republika Srpska	http://www.ohr.int/ohr-dept/legal/oth-legist/doc/rs-constitution.doc
Constituent Peoples' Decision of the BiH Constitutional Court	http://www.ohr.int/ohr-dept/legal/const/default.asp?content_id=5853
Agreement on the Implementation of the Constituent Peoples' Decision of the Constitutional Court of Bosnia and Herzegovina	http://www.ohr.int/ohr-dept/legal/const/default.asp?content_id=7273
Statute of the Brcko District of Bosnia and Herzegovina	http://www.ohr.int/ohr-dept/legal/const/doc/brcko-statute.doc
Correction of the Statute of the Brcko District of Bosnia and Herzegovina, as published in the Official Gazette of Bosnia and Herzegovina 9/00	http://www.ohr.int/ohr-dept/legal/const/doc/correction-of-the-brcko-statute.doc

APPENDIX F

CAMBODIA

Source materials for Cambodia may be found on the websites below:

Document	Website
Law on the Establishment of the Extraordinary Chambers, with inclusion of amendments as promulgated on 27 October 2004, NS/RKM/1004/006.	http://www.cambodia.gov.kh/krt/pdfs/KR%20Law%20as%20amended%2027%20Oct%202004%20Eng.pdf
Decision of the Cambodia Constitutional Council, August 2001	http://www.cambodia.gov.kh/krt/pdfs/Constitutional%20Council%20Decision%20August%202001.pdf
Decision of the Cambodia Constitutional Council, February 2001	http://www.cambodia.gov.kh/krt/pdfs/Const%20Council%20Res%20on%20KR%20Law%2012%20Feb%202001.pdf
History of the Negotiations on the Khmer Rouge Tribunal between the United Nations and Cambodia, February 2002	http://www.embassy.org/cambodia/press/historyTHEnegotiation.pdf
Report of the Secretary-General on Khmer Rouge Trials, March 2003, A/57/769	http://daccess-ods.un.org/TMP/2500896.html http://www.un.org/ga/57/document2.htm#751
General Assembly Resolution on the Khmer Rouge Trials, May 2003, A/RES/57/228	http://daccess-ods.un.org/TMP/5753524.html http://www.un.org/Depts/dhl/resguide/r57.htm
General Assembly Resolution on the Situation of Human Rights in Cambodia, March 2004, A/RES/58/191	http://daccess-ods.un.org/TMP/3954175.html http://www.un.org/Depts/dhl/resguide/r58.htm
Agreement between the United Nations and the Royal Government of Cambodia Concerning the Prosecution under Cambodian Law of Crimes Committed during the Period of Democratic Kampuchea, June 2003	http://www.cambodia.gov.kh/krt/english/image%20doc.htm http://www.cambodia.gov.kh/krt/pdfs/Agreement%20between%20UN%20and%20RGC.pdf

Instrument of Ratification on the Agreement between the United Nations and the Royal Government of Cambodia Concerning the Prosecution under Cambodian Law of Crimes Committed during the Period of Democratic Kampuchea, 19 October 2004.	http://www.cambodia.gov.kh/krt/pdfs/Instrument%20of%20Ratification%20of%20Agreement.pdf
Kram promulgating the Law Approving the Agreement between the United Nations and the Royal Government of Cambodia Concerning the Prosecution under Cambodian Law of Crimes Committed during the Period of Democratic Kampuchea, 19 October 2004	http://www.cambodia.gov.kh/krt/pdfs/Kram%20promulgating%20Agreement%2019%20October%202004-En.pdf
Decision to Establish the Task Force for Cooperation with Foreign Legal Experts for the Preparation of the Proceedings for the Trial of Khmer Rouge Criminals	http://www.cambodia.gov.kh/krt/pdfs/Decision%20to%20est%20Task%20Force.pdf
2001 Circular Concerning Preservation of Remains of the Victims of the Genocide Committed During the Regime of Democratic Kampuchea (1975-1978), and Preparation of Anlong Veng to Become a Region for Historical Tourism	http://www.cambodia.gov.kh/krt/pdfs/Circular%20on%20remains.pdf
1999 Constitutional Council Decision on the Law on Temporary Detention	http://www.cambodia.gov.kh/krt/pdfs/1999-Constitunal%20Council%20Decision%20on%20Law%20of%20Temporary%20Detention.pdf
1999 Law on Temporary Detention (CS-RKM-0899-09)	http://www.cambodia.gov.kh/krt/pdfs/Temporary%20Detention%20Period%20Law%20(CS-RKM-0899-09).pdf
1996 Pardon for Ieng Sary	http://www.cambodia.gov.kh/krt/pdfs/pardon%20for%20ieng%20sary.pdf
1994 Law on the Outlawing of the "Democratic Kampuchea" Group	http://www.cambodia.gov.kh/krt/pdfs/Law%20to%20Outlaw%20DK%20Group%201994.pdf
List of Indictments and Detention Orders	http://www.cambodia.gov.kh/krt/english/indictments.htm

APPENDIX G

EAST TIMOR

Source materials for East Timor may be found on the websites below:

Document	Internet Address
United Nations Security Council Resolution No. 1272, S/Res/1272 (1999), 25 October 1999	http://daccess-ods.un.org/TMP/9782269.html http://www.un.org/peace/etimor/docs/UntaetDrs.htm
Regulation 2000/15 on the establishment of Panels with Exclusive Jurisdiction over Serious Criminal Offences, UNTAET/REG/2000/15. 6 June 2005	http://www.un.org/peace/etimor/untaetR/Reg0015E.pdf
Regulation 2000/11 on the Organization of Courts in East Timor, UNTAET/REG/2000/11, March 6, 2000	http://www.un.org/peace/etimor/untaetR/Reg11.pdf AMENDED AND REPLACED BY UNTAET/Reg/2001/25 ANNEX I.
Regulation 2000/14 Amending Regulation 2000/11, UNTAET/Reg/2000/14, 10 May 2000	http://www.un.org/peace/etimor/untaetR/Reg0014E.pdf AMENDED AND REPLACED BY UNTAET/Reg/2001/25 ANNEX I.
Regulation 2001/18 Amending Regulation 2000/11, UNTAET/Reg/2001/18, 21 July 2001	http://www.un.org/peace/etimor/untaetR/2001-18.pdf AMENDED AND REPLACED BY UNTAET/Reg/2001/25 ANNEX I.
Regulation 2000/30 on Transitional Rules of Criminal Procedure, UNTAET/REG/2000/30, 25 September 2000 Amended by UNTAET/Reg/2001/25, September 14, 2001	http://www.un.org/peace/etimor/untaetR/reg200030.pdf AMENDED AND REPLACED BY UNTAET/Reg/2001/25 ANNEX II.

Regulation 2001/25 On the Amendment of UNTAET Regulation No.2000/11 on the Organization of Courts in East Timor and UNTAET Regulation No.2000/30 on the Transitional Rules of Criminal Procedure, UNTAET/ Reg/2001/25 September 14, 2001	http://www.un.org/peace/etimor/untaetR/ 2001-25.pdf
Policy on Justice and Return Procedures in East Timor, March 23, 2002	http://www.un.org/peace/etimor/DB/ procedures.pdf
United Nations Security Council Resolution 1410, S/Res/1410 (2002), May 17, 2002	http://daccess-ods.un.org/TMP/3515677.html http://www.un.org/Docs/scres/2002/sc2002.htm
Regulation No. 1999/1 on the Authority of the Transitional Administration in East Timor, UNTAET/REG/1999/1, 27 November 1999	http://www.un.org/peace/etimor/untaetR/ etreg1.htm
Regulation No. 1999/3 on the Establishment of a Transitional Judicial Service Commission, UNTAET/ REG/1999/3, 3 December 1999	http://www.un.org/peace/etimor/untaetR/ etreg3.htm AMENDED AND REPLACED BY UNTAET/ Reg/2001/26 ANNEX I.
Memorandum of Understanding between the Republic of Indonesia and the UNTAET Regarding Cooperation in Legal, Judicial and Human Rights Related Matters, April 6, 2000	http://www.moj.gov-rdtl.org/tlaw/Other-Docs/mou-id-untaet.htm
Regulation No. 2000/16 on the Organization of the Public Prosecution Service in East Timor, UNTAET/ REG/2000/16, 6 June 2000	http://www.un.org/peace/etimor/untaetR/ Reg0016E.pdf AMENDED AND REPLACED BY UNTAET/ Reg/2001/26 ANNEX II.
Regulation No. 2001/10 on the Establishment of a Commission for Reception, Truth and Reconciliation in East Timor, UNTAET/ REG/2001/10, 13 July 2001	http://www.un.org/peace/etimor/untaetR/ Reg10e.pdf
Regulation No. 2001/12 on the Establishment of a Code of Military Discipline for the Defence Force of East Timor, UNTAET/REG/2001/12, 20 July 2001	http://www.un.org/peace/etimor/ untaetR/2001-12.pdf

Regulation No. 2001/22 on the Establishment of the East Timor Police Service, UNTAET/REG/2001/22, 10 August 2001	http://www.un.org/peace/etimor/untaet R/2001-22.pdf
Regulation No. 2001/23 on the Establishment of a Prison System in East Timor, UNTAET/REG/2001/23, 28 August 2001	http://www.un.org/peace/etimor/ untaetR/2001-23.pdf Amended by Regulation No. 2001/27
Regulation No. 2001/24 on the Establishment of a Legal Aid Service in East Timor, UNTAET/REG/2001/24, 5 September 2001	http://www.un.org/peace/etimor/untaet R/2001-24.pdf
Regulation 2001/26 on the Amendment of UNTAET Regulation No. 1999/3 on the Establishment of a Transitional Judicial Service Commission and on the Amendment of UNTAET Regulation No. 2000/16 on the Organization of the Public Prosecution Service in East Timor, UNTAET/ REG/2001/26, 14 September 2001	http://www.un.org/peace/etimor/untaet R/2001-26.pdf
Regulation 2001/27 on the Amendment of UNTAET Regulation No.2001/23 on the Establishment of a Prison Service in East Timor, UNTAET/REG/2001/27, 19 September 2001	http://www.un.org/peace/etimor/untaet R/2001-27.pdf

APPENDIX H

IRAQ

Source materials for Iraq may be found on the websites below:

Document	Website
Coalition Provisional Authority Order Number 48: Delegation of Authority Regarding an Iraqi Special Tribunal and the Statute of the Iraqi Special Tribunal, December 2003	http://cpa-iraq.org/regulations/20031210_CPAORD_48_IST_and_Appendix_A.pdf
Unofficial English Translation of the Revised Iraqi Special Tribunal Statute, August 2005	http://www.law.case.edu/saddamtrial/content.asp?id=2 http://www.law.case.edu/saddamtrial/documents/IST_statute_unofficialenglish.pdf
Iraqi High Criminal Court Rules of Proceedings and Evidence Gathering, August 2005	http://www.law.case.edu/saddamtrial/documents/IST_rules_procedure_evidence.pdf
Iraqi Penal Code of 1969 with amendments	http://www.iraqispecialtribunal.org/en/docs/IraqiPenalCodeof1969.doc http://www.law.case.edu/saddamtrial/documents/Iraqi_Penal_Code_1969.pdf
The Law of the Public Prosecutor	http://www.iraqispecialtribunal.org/en/docs/The%20law%20of%20the%20Public%20Prosecutors.doc
Law on Criminal Proceedings with amendments	http://www.iraqispecialtribunal.org/en/laws/LawOnCriminalProceedings.htm http://www.law.case.edu/saddamtrial/documents/Iraqi_Criminal_Procedure_Code.pdf
Iraqi Special Tribunal Elements of the Crimes	http://www.law.case.edu/saddamtrial/documents/IST_Elements.pdf

APPENDIX I

KOSOVO

Source materials for Kosovo may be found on the websites below:

Document	Website
Constitutional Framework for Provisional Self-Government in Kosovo, UNMIK/REG/2001/9–15 May 2001	http://www.unmikonline.org/constframework.htm
Kosovo Judicial and Prosecutorial Council Code of Ethics and Professional Conduct for Judges, July 31, 2001	http://www.pict-pcti.org/courts/pdf/kosovo/CodeJudges.pdf
Kosovo Judicial and Prosecutorial Council Code of Ethics and Conduct for Lay-Judges, July 31, 2001	http://www.pict-pcti.org/courts/pdf/kosovo/CodeLayjudges.pdf
Kosovo Judicial and Prosecutorial Council Code of Ethics and Professional Conduct for Prosecutors, July 31, 2001	http://www.pict-pcti.org/courts/pdf/kosovo/CodeProsecutors.pdf
Regulation No. 1999/1 On the Authority of the Interim Administration in Kosovo, UNMIK/REG/1999/1, July 25, 1999	http://www.unmikonline.org/regulations/1999/re99_01.pdf
Amended by UNMIK/REG/1999/25, December 12 , 1999, and by UNMIK/REG/2000/54, September 27, 2000	Amendments: http://www.unmikonline.org/regulations/1999/re99_25.pdf http://www.unmikonline.org/regulations/2000/reg54-00.htm
Regulation No. 1999/5 On the Establishment of an Ad Hoc Court of Final Appeal and an Ad Hoc Office of the Public Prosecutor, UNMIK/REG/1999/5, September 4, 1999	http://www.unmikonline.org/regulations/1999/re99_05.pdf

Regulation No. 1999/6 On Recommendations for the Structure and Administration of the Judiciary and Prosecution Service, UNMIK/REG/1999/6, September 7, 1999	http://www.unmikonline.org/regulations/1999/re99_06.pdf
Regulation No. 1999/7 On Appointment and Removal from Office of Judges and Prosecutors, UNMIK/REG/1999/7, September 7, 1999	http://www.unmikonline.org/regulations/1999/re99_07.pdf
Amended by UNMIK/REG/2000/57, October 6, 2000	Amendment: http://www.unmikonline.org/regulations/2000/reg57-00.htm
Regulation No. 1999/18 On the Appointment and Removal from Office of Lay Judges, UNMIK/REG/1999/18, November 10, 1999	http://www.unmikonline.org/regulations/1999/re99_18.pdf
Regulation No. 1999/24 On the Law Applicable in Kosovo, UNMIK/REG/1999/24, December 12, 1999	http://www.unmikonline.org/regulations/1999/re1999_24.htm
Amended by UNMIK/REG/2000/59, October 27, 2000	Amendment: http://www.unmikonline.org/regulations/2000/reg59-00.htm
Regulation No. 1999/25, Amending UNMIK Regulation No. 1999/1 on the Authority of the Interim Administration in Kosovo, UNMIK/REG/1999/25 December 12, 1999	http://www.unmikonline.org/regulations/1999/re99_25.pdf
Amended by UNMIK/REG/2000/54, September 27, 2000	Amendment: http://www.unmikonline.org/regulations/2000/reg54-00.htm
Regulation No. 2000/4 On the Prohibition against Inciting to National, Racial, Religious or Ethnic Hatred, Discord or Intolerance, UNMIK/REG/2000/4, February 1, 2000	http://www.unmikonline.org/regulations/2000/re2000_04.htm

Regulation No. 2000/6 On the Appointment and Removal from Office of International Judges and International Prosecutors, UNMIK/ REG/2000/6, 15, February 2000	http://www.unmikonline.org/regulations/2000/ re2000_06.htm
Amended by UNMIK/ REG/2000/34, May 27, 2000, and by UNMIK/REG/2001/2, January 12, 2001	Amendments: http://www.unmikonline.org/regulations/2000/ re2000_34.htm http://www.unmikonline.org/regulations/2001/ reg02-01.html
Regulation No. 2000/14 On the Extension of Custody of Persons Held Pending the Petition for Extradition UNMIK/REG/2000/14, March 18, 2000	http://www.unmikonline.org/regulations/2000/ re2000_14.htm
Regulation No. 2000/15 On the Establishment of the Administrative Department of Justice, UNMIK/REG/2000/15, March 21, 2000	http://www.unmikonline.org/regulations/2000/ re2000_15.htm
Regulation No. 2000/17 On the Admissibility of Certain Witness Statements in Preliminary Investigations, UNMIK/REG/2000/17, March 23, 2000	http://www.unmikonline.org/regulations/2000/ re2000_17.htm
Regulation No. 2000/28 On the Victim Recovery and Identification Commission, UNMIK/REG/2000/28, May 11, 2000	http://www.unmikonline.org/regulations/2000/ re2000_28.htm
Regulation No. 2000/30, On Stamps and Headings of Official Documents of Courts, Prosecutors' Offices and Penal Establishments, UNMIK/ REG/2000/30, May 20, 2000	http://www.unmikonline.org/regulations/2000/ re2000_30.htm
Regulation No. 2000/34, Amending UNMIK Regulation No. 2000/6 on the Appointment and Removal from Office of International Judges and International Prosecutors, UNMIK/ REG/2000/34, May 27, 2000	http://www.unmikonline.org/regulations/2000/ re2000_34.htm
Amended by UNMIK/ REG/2001/2, January 12, 2001	Amendment: http://www.unmikonline.org/regulations/2001/ reg02-01.html

Regulation No. 2000/46 On the Use of Language in Court Proceedings in which an International Judge of International Prosecutor Participates, UNMIK/REG/2000/46, August 15, 2000	http://www.unmikonline.org/regulations/2000/re2000_46.htm
Regulation No. 2000/54, Amending UNMIK Regulation No. 1999/1, As Amended on the Authority of the Interim Administration in Kosovo, UNMIK/REG/2000/54, September 27, 2000	http://www.unmikonline.org/regulations/2000/re2000_54.htm
Regulation No. 2000/57, Amending UNMIK Regulation No. 1999/7 on Appointment and Removal from Office of judges and Prosecutors, UNMIK/REG/2000/57, October 6, 2000	http://www.unmikonline.org/regulations/2000/re2000_57.htm
Regulation No. 2000/64, On Assignment of International Judges/Prosecutors and/or Change of Venue, UNMIK/REG/2000/64, December 15, 2000	http://www.unmikonline.org/regulations/2000/re2000_64.htm
Amended by UNMIK/REG/2001/34, December 15, 2001; by UNMIK/REG/2002/20, December 14, 2002; by UNMIK/REG/2003/36, December 14, 2003; and by UNMIK/REG/2004/54, December 15, 2004	Amendments: http://www.unmikonline.org/regulations/2001/RE%202001-34.pdf http://www.unmikonline.org/regulations/2002/RE2002_20.pdf http://www.unmikonline.org/regulations/2003/RE2003_36.pdf http://www.unmikonline.org/regulations/2004/re2004_54.pdf
Regulation No. 2000/59, Amending UNMIK Regulation No. 1999/24 on the Law Applicable in Kosovo, UNMIK/REG/2000/59, October 27, 2000	http://www.unmikonline.org/regulations/2000/re2000_59.htm
Regulation No. 2001/1 On the Prohibition of Trials in Absentia for Serious Violations of International Humanitarian Law, UNMIK/REG/2001/1, January 12, 2001	http://www.unmikonline.org/regulations/2001/reg01-01.html

Regulation No. 2001/2, Amending UNMIK Regulation No. 2000/6, as Amended on the Appointment and Removal from Office of International Judges and International Prosecutors, NMIK/REG/2001/2, January 12, 2001	http://www.unmikonline.org/regulations/2001/reg02-01.html
Regulation No. 2001/8 On the Establishment of the Kosovo Judicial and Prosecutorial Council, UNMIK/REG/2001/8, April 6, 2001	http://www.unmikonline.org/regulations/2001/reg08-01.html
Regulation No. 2001/12, On the Prohibition of Terrorism and Related Offences, UNMIK/REG/2001/12, June 14, 2001	http://www.unmikonline.org/regulations/2001/reg12-01.pdf
Regulation No. 2001/18 On the Establishment of a Detention Review Commission for Extra-Judicial Detentions Based on Executive Orders, UNMIK/REG/2001/18, August 25, 2001	http://www.unmikonline.org/regulations/2001/reg18-01.pdf
Regulation No. 2001/20 On the Protection of Injured Parties and Witnesses in Criminal Proceedings, UNMIK/REG/2001/20, September 19, 2001 Amended by UNMIK/REG/2002/1, January 24, 2002	http://www.unmikonline.org/regulations/2001/reg20-01.pdf Amendment: http://www.unmikonline.org/regulations/2002/RE2002_01.pdf
Regulation No. 2001/21 on Co-operative Witnesses, UNMIK/REG/2001/21, September 19, 2001 Amended by UNMIK/REG/2002/2, January 24, 2002	http://www.unmikonline.org/regulations/2001/reg21-01.pdf Amendment: http://www.unmikonline.org/regulations/2002/RE2002_02.pdf
Regulation No. 2001/22 On Measures Against Organized Crime, NMIK/REG/2001/22, September 20, 2001	http://www.unmikonline.org/regulations/2001/reg22-01.pdf
Regulation No. 2001/28 On the Rights of Persons Arrested by Law Enforcement Authorities, UNMIK/REG/2001/28, October 11, 2001	http://www.unmikonline.org/regulations/2001/reg28-01.pdf

Regulation No. 2001/34, Amending UNMIK Regulation No. 2000/64 on Assignment of International Judges/ Prosecutors and/or Change of Venue, UNMIK/REG/2001/34 December 15, 2001	http://www.unmikonline.org/regulations/2001/ RE%202001-34.pdf
Amended by UNMIK/ REG/2002/20, December 14, 2002; by UNMIK/ REG/2003/36, December 14, 2003; and by UNMIK/ REG/2004/54, December 15, 2004	Amendments: http://www.unmikonline.org/regulations/2002/ RE2002_20.pdf http://www.unmikonline.org/regulations/2003/ RE2003_36.pdf http://www.unmikonline.org/regulations/2004/ re2004_54.pdf
Regulation No. 2002/1, Amending UNMIK Regulation NO. 2001/20 on the Protection of Injured Parties and Witnesses in Criminal Proceedings, UNMIK/ REG/2002/1, January 24, 2002	http://www.unmikonline.org/regulations/2002/ RE2002_01.pdf
Regulation No. 2002/2, Amending UNMIK Regulation No. 2001/21 on Co-operative Witnesses, UNMIK/ REG/2002/2, January 24, 2002	http://www.unmikonline.org/regulations/2002/ RE2002_02.pdf
Regulation No. 2002/7 On the Use in Criminal Proceedings of Written Records of Interviews Conducted by Law Enforcement Authorities, UNMIK/REG/2002/7, March 28, 2002	http://www.unmikonline.org/regulations/2002/ RE2002_07.pdf
Regulation No. 2002/20, Amending UNMIK Regulation No. 2000/64, as amended, on Assignment of International Judges/Prosecutors and/or Change of Venue, UNMIK/ REG/2002/20, December 14, 2002 Amended by UNMIK/ REG/2003/36, December 14, 2003; and by UNMIK/ REG/2004/54, December 15, 2004	http://www.unmikonline.org/regulations/2002/ RE2002_20.pdf Amendments: http://www.unmikonline.org/regulations/2003/ RE2003_36.pdf http://www.unmikonline.org/regulations/2004/ re2004_54.pdf
Regulation No. 2003/1 Amending the Applicable Law on Criminal Offences Involving Sexual Violence, UNMIK/REG/2003/1, January 6, 2003	http://www.unmikonline.org/regulations/2003/ RE2003_01.pdf

Provisional Criminal Code of Kosovo, UNMIK/ REG/2003/25, re-issued July 6, 2003	http://www.unmikonline.org/regulations/2003/ RE2003-25.pdf http://www.unmikonline.org/regulations/2003/ RE2003_25_criminal_code.pdf
Amended by UNMIK/ REG/2004/19, June 16, 2004	Amendment: http://www.unmikonline.org/regulations/2004/ re2004_19.pdf
Provisional Criminal Procedure Code of Kosovo, UNMIK/REG/2003/26, re-issued July 6, 2003	http://www.unmikonline.org/regulations/2003/ RE2003-26.pdf http://www.unmikonline.org/regulations/2003/ RE2003_26_PCPC.pdf
Regulation No. 2003/34 Amending the Applicable Law on Procedures for the Transfer of Residents of Kosovo to Foreign Jurisdictions, UNMIK/ REG/2003/34, November 14, 2003	http://www.unmikonline.org/regulations/2003/ RE2003_34.pdf
Regulation No. 2003/36, Amending UNMIK Regulation No. 2000/64, as amended, on Assignment of International Judges/Prosecutors and/or Change of Venue, UNMIK/ REG/2003/36, December 14, 2003	http://www.unmikonline.org/regulations/2003/ RE2003_36.pdf
Amended by UNMIK/ REG/2004/54, December 15, 2004	Amendment: http://www.unmikonline.org/regulations/2004/ re2004_54.pdf
Regulation No. 2004/2 On the Deterrence of Money Laundering and Related Criminal Offences, UNMIK/ REG/2004/2, February 5, 2004	http://www.unmikonline.org/regulations/2004/ RE2004_02.pdf
Amended by UNMIK/ REG/2004/10, April 29, 2004, and by UNMIK/REG/2005/9, February 23, 2005, and by UNMIK/REG/2005/42 August 30, 2005	Amendments: http://www.unmikonline.org/regulations/2004/ RE2004_10.pdf http://www.unmikonline.org/regulations/2005/ RE2005_09.pdf http://www.unmikonline.org/regulations/2005/ RE2005_42.pdf
Regulation No. 2004/8, On the Juvenile Justice Code of Kosovo, UNMIK/REG/2004/8, April 20, 2004 (with cover sheet)	http://www.unmikonline.org/regulations/2004/ RE2004_08%20(cover).pdf http://www.unmikonline.org/regulations/2004/ RE2004_08%20JJC.pdf

Regulation No. 2004/10, Amending UNMIK Regulation No. 2004/2 on the Deterrence of Money Laundering and Related Criminal Offences, UNMIK/REG/2004/10, April 29, 2004	http://www.unmikonline.org/regulations/2004/RE2004_10.pdf
Amended by UNMIK/REG/2005/9, February 23, 2005, and by UNMIK/REG/2005/42 August 30, 2005	Amendments: http://www.unmikonline.org/regulations/2005/RE2005_09.pdf http://www.unmikonline.org/regulations/2005/RE2005_42.pdf
Regulation No. 2004/19, Amending the Provisional Criminal Code of Kosovo, UNMIK/REG/2004/19, June 16, 2004	http://www.unmikonline.org/regulations/2004/re2004_19.pdf
Regulation No. 2004/34 On Criminal Proceedings Involving Perpetrators with a Mental Disorder, UNMIK/REG/2004/34, August 24, 2004	http://www.unmikonline.org/regulations/2004/re2004_34.pdf
Law on Execution of Penal Sanctions, UNMIK/REG/2004/46	http://www.unmikonline.org/regulations/2004/re2004_46_law.pdf http://www.unmikonline.org/regulations/2004/re2004_46.pdf
Regulation No. 2004/54, Amending UNMIK Regulation No. 2000/64, as amended, on Assignment of International Judges/Prosecutors and/or Change of Venue, UNMIK/REG/2004/54, December 15, 2004	http://www.unmikonline.org/regulations/2004/re2004_54.pdf
Regulation No. 2005/9, Amending UNMIK Regulation No. 2004/2, as amended, on the Deterrence of Money Laundering and Related Criminal Offences, UNMIK/REG/2005/9, February 23, 2005	http://www.unmikonline.org/regulations/2005/RE2005_09.pdf
Amended by UNMIK/REG/2005/42 August 30, 2005	Amendment: http://www.unmikonline.org/regulations/2005/RE2005_42.pdf

Regulation No. 2005/42, Amending UNMIK Regulation No. 2004/2, as amended, on the Deterrence of Money Laundering and Related Criminal Offences, UNMIK/REG/2005/42 August 30, 2005	http://www.unmikonline.org/regulations/2005/RE2005_42.pdf

Regulation No. 2005/42 Amending UNMIK Regulation No. 2004/2, as amended, on the Deterrence of Money Laundering and Related Criminal Offences, UNMIK (Blue Book) August 30, 2005.	http://www.unmikonline.org/regulations/2005/ RE2005_42.pdf

APPENDIX J

SIERRA LEONE

Source materials for Sierra Leone may be found on the websites below:

Document	Website
Security Council Resolution 1315 (2000), 14 August 2000	http://daccess-ods.un.org/TMP/2894027.html http://www.un.org/Docs/scres/2000/sc2000.htm
Report of the Secretary General to the Security Council on the establishment of a Special Court for Sierra Leone, UN doc. S2000/915, 4 October 2000	http://daccess-ods.un.org/TMP/3932331.html http://www.un.org/Docs/sc/reports/2000/sgrep00.htm
Agreement between the United Nations and the Government of Sierra Leone on the Establishment of Special Court of Sierra Leone, annexed to the Report of the Secretary-General, UN doc. S2000/915, October 4, 2000, as amended by agreement between the United Nations and Sierra Leone, 16 January 2002	http://www.sc-sl.org/scsl-agreement.html
Statute of the Special Court of Sierra Leone, annexed to the Report of the Secretary-General, UN doc. S2000/915, 4 October 2000, as amended by agreement between the United Nations and the Government of Sierra Leone, 16 January 2002	http://www.sc-sl.org/scsl-statute.html
The Special Court Agreement, 2002, Ratification Act, 2002, Supplement to the Sierra Leone Gazette Vol. CXXX, No. 11, March 7, 2002, Implementing legislation passed 19 March 2002, Presidential assent received 29 March 2002, amended 15 July 2002	http://www.sc-sl.org/specialcourtact2002.pdf

The Special Court Agreement (2002) (Ratification) (Amendment) Act, 2002	http://www.sc-sl.org/Documents/ specialcourtratificationact2002.pdf
Composition of Special Court for Sierra Leone http:// www.sc-sl.org/chambers.html	
Headquarters Agreement Between the Republic of Sierra Leone and the Special Court for Sierra Leone, 21 October 2003	http://www.sc-sl.org/headquartersagreement.pdf
Cooperation Agreement Between Interpol and the Special Court of Sierra Leone, 3 November 2003	http://www.sc-sl.org/interpolagreement.pdf
Rules Governing the Detention of Persons Awaiting Trial or Appeal before the Special Court for Sierra Leone or Otherwise Detained on the Authority of the Special Court for Sierra Leone ("Rules of Detention"), adopted 7 March 2003, last amended 14 May 2005	http://www.sc-sl.org/rulesofdetention.pdf
Rules of Procedure and Evidence, last amended 14 May 2005	http://www.sc-sl.org/ rulesofprocedureandevidence.pdf
Code of Ethics for Interpreters and Translators Employed by the Special Court for Sierra Leone, adopted on 25 May 2004	http://www.sc-sl.org/interpreters-codeofethics.html
Directive on the Assignment of Counsel, entered into force 3 October 2003	http://www.sc-sl.org/assignmentofcounsel.html
Practice Direction on Disclosure by the Prosecutor Pursuant to Rule 66 of the Rules of Procedure and Evidence of the Special Court for Sierra Leone, adopted 23 February 2004	http://www.sc-sl.org/disclosurebyprosecutor.pdf
Practice Direction on Filing *Amicus Curiae* Applications Pursuant to Rule 74 of the Rules of Procedure and Evidence of the Special Court for Sierra Leone, adopted 20 October 2004	http://www.sc-sl.org/Documents/SCSL-04-16-PT-112.pdf

Practice Direction on Filing Documents Before the Special Court for Sierra Leone, adopted 27 February 2003, amended 10 June 2005	http://www.sc-sl.org/Documents/practicedirectiononfiling.pdf
Practice Direction on Filing Documents Under Rule 72 of the Rules of Procedure and Evidence Before the Appeals Chamber of the Special Court for Sierra Leone, entered into force 22 September 2003	http://www.sc-sl.org/filingdocuments-rule72.html
Practice Direction on the procedure following a request by a State, the Truth and Reconciliation Commission, or other legitimate authority to take a statement from a person in the custody of the Special Court for Sierra Leone, adopted 9 September 2003, amended 4 October 2003	http://www.sc-sl.org/practicedirection-090903.html
Practice Direction for Certain Appeals before the Special Court, 30 September 2004	http://www.sc-sl.org/practicedirectionforappeals-093004.pdf
Malicious Damage Act (Sierra Leone)	http://www.sc-sl.org/maliciousdamageact.pdf
Sierra Leone Constitution, 1991	http://www.sc-sl.org/sierraleoneconstitution.pdf
Prevention of Cruelty to Children (Sierra Leone)	http://www.sc-sl.org/preventionofcrueltytochildren.html
The Criminal Procedure Act, 1965 Sierra Leone (as amended)	http://www.sc-sl.org/criminalprocedureact.html
Truth and Reconciliation Commission Act 2000	http://www.sc-sl.org/truthandreconciliationact2000.pdf
Code of Professional Conduct for Counsel with the Right of Audience before the Special Court for Sierra Leone, adopted on 14 May 2005	http://www.sc-sl.org/Documents/defencecodeofconduct.pdf
Completion Strategy, 18 May 2005	http://www.sc-sl.org/Documents/completionstrategy.pdf

APPENDIX K

TERRORISM AND RELATED OFFENCES

Source materials dealing with terrorism and related offences may be found on the websites below:

Document	Website
Convention on Offences and Certain Other Acts Committed on Board Aircraft, signed at Tokyo on 14 September 1963	http://untreaty.un.org/English/Terrorism/ Conv1.pdf
Convention for the Suppression of Unlawful Seizure of Aircraft, signed at the Hague on 16 December 1970	http://untreaty.un.org/English/Terrorism/ Conv2.pdf
OAS Convention to Prevent and Punish Acts of Terrorism Taking the Form of Crimes against Persons and Related Extortion that are of International Significance concluded at Washington, D.C. on 2 February 1971	http://untreaty.un.org/English/Terrorism/ Conv16.pdf
Convention for the Suppression of Unlawful Acts against the Safety of Civil Aviation, signed at Montreal on 23 September 1971	http://untreaty.un.org/English/Terrorism/ Conv3.pdf
Convention on the Prevention and Punishment of Crimes against Internationally Protected Persons, including Diplomatic Agents, adopted by the General Assembly of the United Nations on 14 December 1973	http://untreaty.un.org/English/Terrorism/ Conv4.pdf
European Convention on the Suppression of Terrorism, concluded at Strasbourg on 27 January 1977	http://untreaty.un.org/English/Terrorism/ Conv15.pdf

Protocol Amending the European Convention on the Suppression of Terrorism, May 15, 2003 Not yet in force.	http://conventions.coe.int/Treaty/EN/CadreListeTraites.htm
International Convention against the Taking of Hostages, adopted by the General Assembly of the United Nations on 17 December 1979	http://untreaty.un.org/English/Terrorism/Conv5.pdf
Convention on the Physical Protection of Nuclear Material, signed at Vienna on 3 March 1980	http://untreaty.un.org/English/Terrorism/Conv6.pdf
SAARC Regional Convention on Suppression of Terrorism, signed at Katmandu on 4 November 1987	http://untreaty.un.org/English/Terrorism/Conv18.pdf
Additional Protocol to the SAARC Regional Convention on Suppression of Terrorism	http://www.saarc-sec.org/data/summit12/additionalprotocolterrorism.pdf
Protocol of the Suppression of Unlawful Acts of Violence at Airports Serving International Civil Aviation, supplementary to the Convention for the Suppression of Unlawful Acts against the Safety of Civil Aviation, signed at Montreal on 24 February 1988	http://untreaty.un.org/English/Terrorism/Conv7.pdf
Convention for the Suppression of Unlawful Acts against the Safety of Maritime Navigation, done at Rome on 10 March 1988	http://untreaty.un.org/English/Terrorism/Conv8.pdf A diplomatic Conference to adopt amendments to the Convention for the Suppression of Unlawful Acts against the Safety of Maritime Navigation, 1988, and its Protocol of 1988 related to Fixed Platforms located on the Continental Shelf will be held in October 2005. See http://www.imo.org/home.asp.
Protocol for the Suppression of Unlawful Acts Against the Safety of Fixed Platforms Located on the Continental Shelf	http://untreaty.un.org/English/Terrorism/Conv9.pdf
Convention on the Marking of Plastic Explosives for the Purpose of Detection, signed at Montreal on 1 March 1991	http://untreaty.un.org/English/Terrorism/Conv10.pdf

Arab Convention on the Suppression of Terrorism, signed at a meeting held at the General Secretariat of the League of Arab States in Cairo on 22 April 1998	http://www.al-bab.com/arab/docs/league/terrorism98.htm
International Convention for the Suppression of Terrorist Bombings, adopted by the General Assembly of the United Nations on 15 December 1997, UN Resolution 52/164	http://untreaty.un.org/English/Terrorism/Conv11.pdf
Convention on the Organization of the Islamic Conference on Combating International Terrorism, adopted at Ouagadougou on 1 July 1999, Annex to Resolution No: 59/26-P	http://www.oic-un.org/26icfm/c.html
International Convention for the Suppression of the Financing of Terrorism, adopted by the General Assembly of the United Nations on 9 December 1999	http://untreaty.un.org/English/Terrorism/Conv12.pdf
United States Department of Defense Military Order on the Rules and Procedures governing Trials before Military Commissions, issued on March 21, 2002	http://www.defenselink.mil/news/Mar2002/d20020321ord.pdf
United States Department of Defense Military Commission Order on the Procedures for Trials by Military Commissions of Certain Non-United States Citizens in the War Against Terrorism, August 31,2005	http://www.defenselink.mil/news/Sep2005/d20050902order.pdf
Organization of African Unity Convention on the Prevention and Combating of Terrorism, adopted July 14, 1999	http://untreaty.un.org/English/Terrorism/oau—e.pdf
Treaty on Cooperation among the States Members of the Commonwealth of Independent States in Combating Terrorism, June 4, 1999	http://untreaty.un.org/English/Terrorism/csi—e.pdf

United Nations Security Council Resolution S/RES/1373, September 28, 2001	http://www.un.org/terrorism/sc.htm

APPENDIX L

EXTRADITION AND MUTUAL ASSISTANCE

Source materials dealing with extradition and mutual assistance may be found on the websites below:

Document	Website
UN Model Treaty on Extradition, 14 December 1990, A/RES/45/116	http://www.un.org/documents/ga/res/45/a45r116.htm http://www.unodc.org/pdf/model_treaty_extradition.pdf
United Nations General Assembly Resolution A/RES/52/88, International Cooperation in Criminal Matters, February 4, 1998	http://www.unodc.org/pdf/model_treaty_extradition.pdf
European Convention on Extradition, 13 December 1957	http://conventions.coe.int/treaty/en/Treaties/Html/024.htm
Additional Protocol to European Convention on Extradition, 15 October 1975	http://conventions.coe.int/treaty/en/Treaties/Html/086.htm
Second Additional Protocol to European Convention on Extradition, 17 March 1978	http://conventions.coe.int/treaty/en/Treaties/Html/098.htm
UN Model Treaty on Mutual Assistance in Criminal Matters, 14 December 1990, United Nations A/RES/45/117, subsequently amended by General Assembly Resolution 53/112	http://www.unodc.org/pdf/model_treaty_mutual_assistance_criminal_matters.pdf
United Nations General Assembly Resolution A/RES/53/112, Mutual Assistance and International Cooperation in Criminal Matters, January 20, 1999	http://www.unodc.org/pdf/model_treaty_mutual_assistance_criminal_matters.pdf

Optional Protocol to the UN Model Treaty on Mutual Assistance in Criminal Matters concerning the Proceeds of Crime (1990)	http://www.un.org/documents/ga/res/45/a45r117.htm
European Convention on Mutual Assistance in Criminal Matters, April 20, 1959	http://conventions.coe.int/treaty/en/Treaties/Html/030.htm
Additional Protocol to European Convention on Mutual Assistance in Criminal Matters, March 17, 1978	http://conventions.coe.int/treaty/en/Treaties/Html/099.htm
Second Additional Protocol to European Convention on Mutual Assistance in Criminal Matters, 19 September 2001	http://conventions.coe.int/treaty/en/Treaties/Html/182.htm
UN Model Treaty on the Transfer of Proceedings in Criminal Matters (1990)	http://www.unhchr.ch/html/menu3/b/51.htm
Constitution of Interpol (1956) (last amendments in 1999)	http://www.interpol.int/Public/ICPO/LegalMaterials/constitution/constitutionGenReg/constitution.asp
Europol Convention, 18 July 1995, SN 3549/95	http://www.europol.eu.int/index.asp?page=legalconv
Council act of 28 November 2002 drawing up a Protocol amending the Convention on the establishment of a European Police Office (Europol Convention) and the Protocol on the privileges and immunities of Europol, the members of its organs, the deputy directors and the employees of Europol [Official Journal C 312 of 16.12.2002].	http://europa.eu.int/scadplus/leg/en/lvb/l14005b.htm
United Nations Convention against Illicit Traffic in Narcotic Drugs and Psychotropic Substances (1988)	http://www.unodc.org/pdf/convention_1988_en.pdf
List of United Nations Crime and Drug Conventions	http://www.unodc.org/unodc/en/drug_and_crime_conventions.html

APPENDIX M

LOCKERBIE TRIAL AND APPEAL

Source materials dealing with the Lockerbie trial and appeal may be found on the websites below:

Document	Website
Questions of Interpretation and Application of the 1971 Montreal Convention Arising from the Aerial Incident at Lockerbie (Libyan Arab Jamahiriya v. United Kingdom), Judgment, Orders and Pleadings of the International Court of Justice	http://www.icj-cij.org/icjwww/idocket/iluk/iluk2frame.htm
Questions of Interpretation and Application of the 1971 Montreal Convention Arising from the Aerial Incident at Lockerbie (Libyan Arab Jamahiriya v. United States of America), Judgment, Orders and Pleadings of the International Court of Justice	http://www.icj-cij.org/icjwww/idocket/ilus/ilusframe.htm
Her Majesty's Advocate v. Abdelbaset Ali Mohmed al Megrahi and Al Amin Khalifa Fhimah, Case Number 1475/99, High Court of Justiciary at Camp Zeist, Trial Judgment, 31 January 2001.	http://www.scotcourts.gov.uk/library/lockerbie/docs/lockerbiejudgement.pdf
Appeal against Conviction of Abdelbaset Ali Mohmed Al Megrahi against Her Majesty's Advocate, Appeal Number C104/01, Appeal Court, High Court of the Justiciary, Appeal Judgment, 14 March 2002.	http://www.scotcourts.gov.uk/library/lockerbie/docs/lockerbieappealjudgement.pdf
A Aust 'Lockerbie: The Other Case' (2000) 49 ICLQ 278.	http://iclq.oxfordjournals.org/
F Beveridge 'The Lockerbie Cases' (1999) 48 ICLQ 658.	http://iclq.oxfordjournals.org/

MP Scharf 'The Lockerbie Trial Verdict' ASIL Insights February 2001.	http://www.asil.org/insights/insigh61.htm

APPENDIX N

SAMPLE INDICTMENTS AND CHARGES

Source materials for sample indictments and charges may be found on the websites below:

Document	Website
Indictment of *Prosecutor v. Milošević* (Kosovo and Bosnia), ICTY, IT-99-37-PT Kosovo: Second Amended Indictment, 29 October 2001 Bosnia: Amended Indictment, 21 April 2004	http://www.un.org/icty/indictment/english/mil-2ai011029e.htm http://www.un.org/icty/indictment/english/mil-ai040421-e.htm
Indictment of *Prosecutor v. Galić*, ICTY, IT-98-29-I	http://www.un.org/icty/indictment/english/gal-ii990326e.htm
Indictment of *Prosecutor v. Kordić and Čerkez*, ICTY, IT-95-14	http://www.un.org/icty/indictment/english/kor-1ai980930e.htm
Indictment of *Prosecutor v. Delalić et al.*, ICTY, IT-96-21	http://www.un.org/icty/indictment/english/cel-ii960321e.htm
Indictment of *Prosecutor v. Kambanda*, ICTR, ICTR-97-23-DP	http://www.ictr.org
Indictment of *Prosecutor v. Marques et al.*, East Timor	http://jsmp.minihub.org/courtmonitoring/Documents%20SPSC/SPSC%202000/09-2000%20Joni%20Marques%20et%20al/09-2000%20Joni%20Mar-ques%20et%20al%20Indictment.pdf
RUF Indictment (in two parts), Sierra Leone.	http://www.sc-sl.org/Documents/SCSL-04-15-PT-122-6181-6191.pdf http://www.sc-sl.org/Documents/SCSL-04-15-PT-12-6192-6202.pdf
AFRC Indictment, Sierra Leone	http://www.sc-sl.org/Documents/SCSL-04-16-PT-147.pdf
CDF Indictment, Sierra Leone	http://www.sc-sl.org/Documents/SCSL-04-14-PT-003.pdf

Order to Forward Case for Investigation (Mok and Duch, 2nd Indictment), Cambodia	http://www.cambodia.gov.kh/krt/pdfs/ Mok%20&%20Duch%202nd%20indictment.pdf

INDEX

[In this Index all the references are to paragraph number.
and the following abbreviations or acronyms have been used throughout:

ICC   International Criminal Court
ICT   International Criminal Tribunals
ICTR   International Criminal Tribunal for Rwanda
ICTY   International Criminal Tribunal for Yugoslavia

Cambodia (Extraordinary Chambers)—*cont.*
premises, 3–121
privileges and immunities
Counsel, 3–128
judges, 3–107, 3–126
personnel, 3–127
prosecutors, 3–116
security, safety and protection, 3–131
sentencing
Law on Establishment, 3–110
UN Agreement, 3–120
UN Agreement, 3–112—3–135
victim protection, 3–130
war crimes, and
crimes against humanity, 11–10
generally, 11–11
genocide, 11–10
grave breaches of Geneva
Conventions, 11–10
witnesses
generally, 3–129
protection, 3–130
withdrawal of cooperation, 3–135
working languages
Law on Establishment, 3–111.1
UN Agreement, 3–133

Case law
principles of interpretation, and,
5–35—5–36

Case management
cross-examination 8–73
East Timor, 8–68
ICC
Code of Ethics, 8–60
Regulations, 8–58—8–59
Rules, 8–56—8–57
Statute, 8–54—8–55
ICTR, 8–65—8–67
ICTY, 8–61—8–64
pre-trial conferences, and,
7–168—7–168.1
Sierra Leone, 8–69—8–71
variation of prosecution witness list,
8–72

Case presentation
absence of accused
East Timor, 8–24
ICC, 8–17—8–18
ICTR, 8–21—8–23
ICTY, 8–19—8–20
Sierra Leone, 8–25—8–26
trial *in absentia*, 8–27

Case presentation—*cont.*
burden of proof
defence, on, 8–33
East Timor, 8–31
ICC, 8–28
ICTR, 8–30
ICTY, 8–29
other, 8–34
prosecution, on, 8–32
Sierra Leone, 8–30
case file, 20–177
closing speeches
East Timor, 8–92
ICC, 8–89
ICTR, 8–91
ICTY, 8–90
Sierra Leone, 8–93
control of proceedings
cross-examination 8–73
East Timor, 8–68
ICC Code of Ethics, 8–60
ICC Regulations, 8–58—8–59
ICC Rules, 8–56—8–57
ICC Statute, 8–54—8–55
ICTR, 8–65—8–67
ICTY, 8–61—8–64
Sierra Leone, 8–69—8–71
variation of prosecution witness list,
8–72
Court Officer, 20–175
courtroom etiquette, 20–172
cross-examination 8–73
electronic presentation of evidence,
20–176
evidence, and
East Timor, 8–46
fresh evidence, 8–52
generally, 8–48
ICC Rules, 8–43—8–44
ICC Statute, 8–42
ICTR, 8–45
ICTY, 8–45
judicial control, 8–53
prosecution, for, 8–49
rebuttal, in, 8–50
rejoinder, in, 8–51
Sierra Leone, 8–47
expert witnesses
assignments, 20–185
payment, 20–186—20–188
qualifications, 20–185
fresh evidence, 8–52

Murder—*cont.*
  ICTY
    crimes against humanity, 12–3
    genocide, 13–2
    war crimes, 11–3
  Iraq
    crimes against humanity, 12–8
    genocide, 13–7
    war crimes, 11–8
  laws and customs of war, 11–147
  Sierra Leone
    crimes against humanity, 12–6
    genocide, 13–5
    war crimes, 11–8
  violation of customs and laws of war,
    11–147
  war crimes
    Cambodia, 11–11
    East Timor, 11–6
    elements of crime, 11–19
    generally, 11–108—11–108
    ICC, 11–1
    ICTR, 11–5
    ICTY, 11–3
    Iraq, 11–12
    Sierra Leone, 11–8
Mutilation
  crimes against humanity, and, 12–57
  violation of customs and laws of war,
    and, 11–147
  war crimes, and, 11–42, 11–66, 11–87
Mutual assistance
  main international treaties, etc., 15–56
  overview, 15–57

Narcotic Drugs, Convention on (1961)
  generally, 15–23—15–24
National groups
  genocide, and, 13–28
National security
  see **State security**
Nationality
  protected persons' status, and,
    11–98—11–100
Natural and foreseeable consequences
  see **Foreseeability**
Ne bis in idem
  see **Double jeopardy**
Necessity
  duress, and, 17–57—17–61
  East Timor, 17–20
  generally, 17–67
  ICC, 17–7

Necessity—*cont.*
  violation of customs and laws of war,
    and, 11–138
**New York Convention on Protection of
  Crimes Against Internationally
  Protected Persons 1973**
  generally, 15–5
No case to answer
  East Timor, 8–85—8–86
  ICC, 8–80—8–81
  ICTR, 8–84
  ICTY, 8–82—8–83
  Sierra Leone, 8–87
  test to be applied, 8–88
No punishment without law
  nulla poena sine lege
    East Timor, 17–19
    generally, 17–40
    ICC, 17–3
  nullum crimem sine lege
    East Timor, 17–18
    generally 17–36—17–39
    ICC, 17–2
Nomination of judges
  ICC, 3–11
**Non-applicability of statute of
  limitations**
  ICC, 17–6
Non bis in idem
  see **Double jeopardy**
**Nuclear Material, Convention on
  Protection of (1980)**
  generally, 15–10
  summary of provisions, 15–49
Nulla poena sine lege
  see **No punishment without law**
Nullum crimem sine lege
  see **No punishment without law**
**Nuremberg International Military
  Tribunal**
  Charter, AA–001
  crimes of aggression, and, 14–7—14–8
  historical background, 2–2

Object of instruments
  generally, 5–22
  introduction, 5–21
Office expenses
  see **Expenses**
Office of the Prosecutor
  and see **Prosecutor**
  ICC
    generally, 3–7
    operation, 3–22
  ICTR, 3–68
  ICTY, 3–67

1978

Witness protection—*cont.*
measures —*cont.*
  ICC, 8–121—8–123
  ICTR, 8–131—8–132
  ICTY, 8–126—8–128
participation of in proceedings
  East Timor, 8–158
  ICC, 8–152—8–156
  ICTR, 8–157
  ICTY, 8–157
  Sierra Leone, 8–157
pre trial measures
  disclosure in other cases, 8–147
  ex parte hearings, 8–144
  exceptional circumstances,
    8–142—8–143
  generally, 8–141
  non-disclosure to public, 8–146
  reasonable time before trial for
    disclosure of identity, 8–145
  Sierra Leone, 8–138—8–139
  test, 8–150
scheme, 8–131
trial, during, 8–148—8–149
Witness statements
acts of accused, 9–37
conduct of accused, 9–37
cross-examination, 9–38
cumulative nature, 9–39
deceased persons, of, 9–40
general principles, 9–35—9–36
procedural requirements, 9–41
Witness summonses
ICT, and
  generally, 4–39
  introduction, 4–31
  need, 4–32
  power to issue, 4–6—4–7
Witnesses
ICTY
  accommodation arrangements,
    20–183
  communications with counsel,
    20–180
  generally, 20–179
  protection, 20–181—20–182
  travel arrangements, 20–183
  tribunal facilities, 20–184

Witnesses—*cont.*
participation in proceedings of
  East Timor, 8–158
  ICC, 8–152—8–156
  ICTR, 8–157
  ICTY, 8–157
  Sierra Leone, 8–157
protection of
  and see **Witness protection**
  Cambodia, 3–130
  generally, 8–119—8–135
  ICTY, 20–181—20–182
testimony
  Cambodia, 3–129
  East Timor, 8–68, 9–22
  ICC, 8–59
  ICTR, 8–67, 9–19
  ICTY, 8–64, 9–15
  Sierra Leone, 8–71
Working languages
Cambodia
  Law on Establishment, 3–111.1
  UN Agreement, 3–133
East Timor, 3–93.18
ICC, 3–21
ICTR, 3–50
ICTY, 3–50
Sierra Leone, 3–99.1
Wounded soldiers
laws of war, and, 2–25—2–27
Wounding persons hors de combat
war crimes, and, 11–35
Writ of habeas corpus
see **Habeas corpus**
Written motions
see **Motions**
Written submissions
ICTY, C14–001

Yugoslavia
and see **ICT Yugoslavia**
historical background, 2–1
structure, 3–49—3–77